SOMATOFORM DISORDERS
Somatization Disorder
Conversion Disorder
Hypochondriasis Body Dysmorphic Disorder
Pain Disorder

FACTITIOUS DISORDERS
Factitious Disorder

DISSOCIATIVE DISORDERS
Dissociative Amnesia
Dissociative Fugue
Dissociative Identity Disorder (Multiple Personality Disorder)
Depersonalization Disorder

SEXUAL AND GENDER IDENTITY DISORDERS
Sexual Dysfunctions
Sexual Desire Disorders: Hypoactive Sexual Desire Disorder; Sexual Aversion Disorder / Sexual Arousal Disorders: Female Sexual Arousal Disorder; Male Erectile Disorder / Orgasmic Disorders: Female Orgasmic Disorder (Inhibited Female Orgasm); Male Orgasmic Disorder (Inhibited Male Orgasm); Premature Ejaculation / Sexual Pain Disorders: Dyspareunia; Vaginismus / Sexual Dysfunction Due to a General Medical Condition / Substance-induced Sexual Dysfunction
Paraphilias
Exhibitionism / Fetishism / Frotteurism / Pedophilia / Sexual Masochism / Sexual Sadism / Voyeurism / Transvestic Fetishism
Gender Identity Disorders
Gender Identity Disorder: in Children; in Adolescents or Adults (Transsexualism)

EATING DISORDERS
Anorexia Nervosa
Bulimia Nervosa

SLEEP DISORDERS
Primary Sleep Disorders
Dyssomnias: Primary Insomnia; Primary Hypersomnia; Narcolepsy; Breathing-related Sleep Disorder; Circadian Rhythm Sleep Disorder (Sleep-Wake Schedule Disorder) / Parasomnias; Nightmare Disorder (Dream Anxiety Disorder); Sleep Terror Disorder; Sleepwalking Disorder / Sleep Disorders Related to Another Mental Disorder
Sleep Disorder Due to a General Medical Condition
Substance-induced Sleep Disorder

IMPULSE CONTROL DISORDERS NOT ELSEWHERE CLASSIFIED
Intermittent Explosive Disorder
Kleptomania
Pyromania
Pathological Gambling
Trichotillomania

ADJUSTMENT DISORDERS
Adjustment Disorder
With Anxiety / with Depressed Mood / with Disturbance of Conduct / with Mixed Disturbance of Emotions and Conduct / with Mixed Anxiety and Depressed Mood

AXIS II

Mental Retardation
Mild Mental Retardation / Moderate Mental Retardation / Severe Mental Retardation / Profound Mental Retardation

PERSONALITY DISORDERS
Paranoid Personality Disorder
Schizoid Personality Disorder
Schizotypal Personality Disorder
Antisocial Personality Disorder
Borderline Personality Disorder
Histrionic Personality Disorder
Narcissistic Personality Disorder
Avoidant Personality Disorder
Dependent Personality Disorder
Obsessive-Compulsive Personality Disorder

OTHER CONDITIONS THAT MAY BE A FOCUS OF CLINICAL ATTENTION
Psychological Factors Affecting Medical Condition
Medication-induced Movement Disorders
Relational Problems
Relational Problem Related to a Mental Disorder or General Medical Condition / Parent-Child Relational Problem / Partner Relational Problem / Sibling Relational Problem
Problems Related to Abuse or Neglect
Physical Abuse of Child / Sexual Abuse of Child / Neglect of Child / Physical Abuse of Adult / Sexual Abuse of Adult
Additional Conditions That May Be a Focus of Clincal Attention
Bereavement / Borderline Intellectual Functioning / Academic Problem / Occupational Problem / Child or Adolescent Antisocial Behavior / Adult Antisocial Behavior / Malingering / Phase of Life Problem / Noncompliance with Treatment / Identity Problem / Religious or Spiritual Problem / Acculturation Problem / Age-related Cognitive Decline

fourth canadian edition

abnormal psychology

GERALD C. DAVISON
University of Southern California

KIRK R. BLANKSTEIN
University of Toronto (Emeritus)

GORDON L. FLETT
York University

JOHN M. NEALE
State University of New York at Stony Brook

John Wiley & Sons Canada, Ltd.

Library and Archives Canada Cataloguing in Publication

Abnormal psychology / Gerald C. Davison ... [et al.] -- 4th Canadian ed.

Has supplement: Study guide to accompany Abnormal psychology, fourth Canadian edition.
ISBN 978-0-470-16103-6

1. Psychology, Pathological--Textbooks. I. Davison, Gerald C II. Title.
RC454.D39 2010   616.89   C2010-905209-9

Production Credits
Publisher: Veronica Visentin
Acquisitions Editor: Rodney Burke
Editorial Manager: Karen Staudinger
Developmental Editor: Andrea Grzybowski
Vice President, Publishing Services: Karen Bryan
Creative Director: Ian Koo
Marketing Manager: Patty Maher
New Media Editor: Channade Fenandoe
Cover Design: Ian Koo
Interior Layout & Design: Adrian So
Typesetting: Prepare

Printing & Binding: R.R. Donnelly-Willard
Cover Image: Pegi Nicol MacLeod, Canadian 1904–1949, Tenements 1945, Watercolour on woven paper 74.5 x 57.3 cm. National Gallery of Canada, Ottawa photo © National Gallery of Canada
Printed and bound in United States of America

14 13 12 11 10 RRD 5 4 3 2 1

John Wiley & Sons Canada, Ltd.
6045 Freemont Blvd.
Mississauga, Ontario L5R 4J3
Visit our website at: www.wiley.ca

Dedicated to

Mary, Karen, Andrea, Brett, P. P., M. E. J., and Diesel
(K.R.B.)

Kathy, Hayley, and Alison
(G.F.)

ABOUT THE AUTHORS

GERALD C. DAVISON earned his B.A in social relations from Harvard and his Ph.D. in psychology from Stanford. He is currently Dean of the University of Southern California (USC) Davis School of Gerontology and Executive Director of the Andrus Gerontology Center. He is a Fellow of the American Psychological Association (APA), a Charter Fellow of the Association for Psychological Science, and a member of the Gerontological Society of America. In 2006–2007, he was President of the Society of Clinical Psychology (Division 12 of the American Psychological Association).

Among his awards and honours are an outstanding achievement award from the American Psychological Association's Board of Social and Ethical Responsibility, the USC Associates Award for Excellence in Teaching, the Outstanding Educator Award, and the Lifetime Achievement Award of the Association for Behavioral and Cognitive Therapies.

Among his more than 150 publications, his book *Clinical Behavior Therapy*, co-authored in 1976 with Marvin Goldfried and reissued in expanded form in 1994, is one of two publications that have been recognized as Citation Classics by the Social Sciences Citation Index. His publications emphasize experimental and philosophical analyses of psychopathology, assessment, and therapeutic change. His current research focuses on the relationships between cognition and a variety of behavioural and emotional problems via his articulated thoughts in simulated situations think-aloud paradigm.

KIRK R. BLANKSTEIN is Professor Emeritus of Psychology at the University of Toronto Mississauga (UTM). He received his Honours B.A. from McMaster University and M.A. and Ph.D. in Clinical Psychology from the University of Waterloo. He completed his clinical internship at Duke University Medical Center in 1970 following a period as a Research Associate at the Institute of Psychiatry in London, England. One of his passions has been teaching undergraduate students and training future psychologists. He began his teaching career as an Introductory

Psychology instructor and although he has taught over twenty different undergraduate and graduate courses, he was primarily responsible for the abnormal psychology part of the program, including Introduction to Abnormal Psychology, separate courses on adult disorders and disorders of children, and a fourth-year special topics in abnormal psychology course. Cross-appointed to the Forensic Science Program, he taught students about psychopaths and serial killers. Professor Blankstein enjoyed enlivening his lectures with tongue-in-cheek references to himself and his family, using their names in association with illustrative cases and examples, and in test questions and assignments. Students quickly determined that the famous, infamous, Mr., Mrs., Dr., Prof., etc. Motley or Barkley was actually one of his beloved Miniature Schnauzers—Motley or Barkley Blankstein! He subsequently "broke in" a new special teaching assistant, a Cockapoo named Professor Diesel.

Professor Blankstein is a past recipient of the UTM Teaching Excellence Award. In 2003 he was recognized as an "Exceptional Teacher" in celebration of "175 Years of Great Teaching" at the University of Toronto. In 2007, he received the inaugural Leadership in Faculty Teaching Award from the Government of Ontario awarded to "faculty who influence, motivate and inspire students and demonstrate leadership in teaching methods for the diverse student body." A crux of his teaching involved students in research from the beginning of their exposure to Psychology. He developed a program that enabled first-year students to critique and get involved in current psychological research. He also initiated, developed, and coordinated the formal undergraduate Psychology Thesis Research course (which celebrated its 33rd year in 2010), wherein senior undergraduates have an opportunity to do high-level original research. He personally collaborated with undergraduates to produce over 60 of his many publications, often including the students as first authors. Many of his students have gone on to distinguished careers as professional psychologists, physicians, social workers, lawyers, criminologists, one High Commissioner, and an Ontario Court Judge.

Professor Blankstein's research focuses on the psychological problems of young people, especially anxiety, depression, somatic distress, and poor academic performance. He has conducted research in diverse areas, including early work on the applications of biofeedback, and the assessment and treatment of test anxiety. A major focus of current research is on factors (such as stress, coping, and social support) that mediate and moderate the link between cognitive-personality vulnerability factors (such as self-critical perfectionism) and negative adaptational outcomes. He recently developed two new measures of the key maladaptive aspects of perfectionism that are employed in treatment studies with anxiety and mood disorder clients (e.g., *International Journal of Cognitive Therapy*, 2011). Besides his many journal articles and invited chapters, Professor Blankstein co-edited a series of volumes on communication and affect. He serves as a regular reviewer for numerous professional journals.

In 2005, Professor Blankstein received the prestigious Northrop Frye Award in recognition of his contributions to the integration of teaching and research. The award recognizes faculty who have set "... themselves apart through innovation in teaching and commitment to conveying the excitement and importance of research to undergraduate and graduate students." After 39 years at UTM, Professor Blankstein retired in June, 2009 to devote more time to family and friends, including his wife, children, grandchildren, and Diesel. He and his family are avid cottagers who also travel extensively. He has won numerous photographic awards for his nature and landscape photography. Professor Blankstein still writes most days and continues to publish book chapters and scientific papers. He maintains regular contact with many of his former students and continues to advise current students.

GORDON L. FLETT is a Professor of Psychology at York University in Toronto. He has served as Director of Undergraduate Studies in the Department of Psychology at York University, and he received the Outstanding Teaching Award from the Faculty of Arts at York University in 1993 and again in 1997. Dr. Flett has taught courses in abnormal psychology, introduction to personality, and personality theory and behavioural disorders at the undergraduate level, as well as courses in personality theory and research and in the self-concept at the graduate level. He received his B.Sc., M.A., and Ph.D. from the University of Toronto, and he began his appointment at York University in 1987.

In 1996, Dr. Flett was recognized by the American Psychological Society as one of the top 25 scholars in psychology, based on the number of publications over a five-year period. In 1999, he received the Dean's Award for Outstanding Research from the Faculty of Arts at York University. In 2004, Dr. Flett was awarded a Tier I Canada Research Chair in Personality and Health and in 2007, he was nominated and made a Fellow of the Association for Psychological Science in recognition of his "distinguished contributions to psychological science."

His research interests include the role of personality factors in depression, as well as the continuity of depression, and the interpersonal aspects of anxiety. One current research focus is the role of personality factors in postpartum adjustment among new mothers and fathers. He also investigates depression and suicide in various age groups, including adolescents and the elderly.

Dr. Flett is perhaps most recognized for his seminal contributions to research and theory on the role of perfectionism in psychopathology. His collaborative work with Dr. Paul Hewitt (University of British Columbia) has helped establish that perfectionism is multidimensional with salient interpersonal components that contribute to personal and interpersonal maladjustment. Their work on perfectionism has received international attention and has been the subject of numerous media stories, including coverage on CTV, CNN, and the BBC.

Dr. Flett has published over 150 journal articles and chapters as well as collaborating on the first academic book on perfectionism, published in 2002. In 2007, he authored the book Personality Theory and Research: An International Perspective, which is also published by Wiley Canada. His work with Dr. Hewitt on perfectionism has led to the creation of the Multidimensional Perfectionism Scale, the Child-Adolescent Perfectionism Scale, the Perfectionism Cognitions Inventory, and the Perfectionistic Self-Presentation Scale. Dr. Flett is also the co-creator of the newly developed Endler Multidimensional Anxiety Scales (EMAS)—Social Anxiety Scales. He has also worked extensively with Dr. Marnin Heisel on the development of the Geriatric Suicide Ideation Scale and related research. Dr. Flett has also served as guest editor on three special issues on perfectionism for the Journal of Rational- Emotive and Cognitive-Behaviour Therapy.

In addition to his academic interests, Dr. Flett has been involved actively in the school system. Dr. Flett served for many years as the chair of the school council at Middlebury Public School in Mississauga, Ontario, and he was the spokesperson for the Parents of Peel, an advocacy group for parents interested in improving and protecting public education. In 1999, his civic contributions were acknowledged when Dr. Flett was awarded the City of Mississauga Certificate of Recognition for "Outstanding Commitment to the Community." Dr. Flett was honoured with the Community and Leadership Award from Toastmasters International in May 2006.

JOHN M. NEALE is Professor Emeritus of Psychology at the State University of New York at Stony Brook, where he regularly taught the undergraduate course in abnormal psychology. He received his B.A. from the University of Toronto and his M.A. and Ph.D. from Vanderbilt University. His internship in clinical psychology was as a Fellow in Medical Psychology at the Langley Porter Neuropsychiatric Institute. In 1975 he was a Visiting Fellow at the Institute of Psychiatry, London, England. In 1974 he won the American Psychological Association's Early Career Award for his research on cognitive processes in schizophrenia. In 1991 he won a Distinguished Scientist Award from the American Psychological Association's Society for a Science of Clinical Psychology. He has been on the editorial boards of several journals and has been Associate Editor of the Journal of Abnormal Psychology. Besides his numerous articles in professional journals, he has published books on the effects of televised violence on children, research methodology, schizophrenia, case studies in abnormal psychology, and psychological influences on health. Schizophrenia was a major focus of his research, and he also conducted research on the influence of stress on health.

Davison and Neale's classic text *Abnormal Psychology* introduced the field of abnormal psychology to over one million readers over several decades. Kirk Blankstein and Gordon Flett responded to calls for a text with a greater focus on Canadian issues by adapting this classic work. The publication in 2002 of the first edition of Davison, Neale, Blankstein, & Flett, *Abnormal Psychology*, Canadian Edition meant that Canadian students could now benefit from the structure and principles of the classic text but within the context of extensive Canadian content that highlighted the unique aspects of the people of Canada. The publication of this new volume, the fourth edition, reflects efforts undertaken over the past decade to continually improve this book by representing key new developments in the field and in Canadian society. This blend of the Davison and Neale approach with material pertinent to Canadians has met with critical acclaim and has been widely appreciated by instructors and their students. We feel that the end result is a text that is very pertinent and highly engaging for today's student.

GOALS OF THE BOOK

Our main goals in writing *Abnormal Psychology*, Fourth Canadian Edition, were to continue to build upon the strengths of a classic text and present abnormal psychology from a unique Canadian perspective with a contemporary emphasis. Acknowledged strengths are as follows:

A SCIENTIFIC, CLINICAL APPROACH The study of abnormal psychology is a science and this edition, like its predecessors, retains a strong commitment to the scientific approach and Davison and Neale's emphasis on encouraging readers to think critically and consider the merits of various viewpoints. Tough choices have to be made when selecting from among the vast literature and these choices are guided by the need to accurately represent the field and continue to a fair and comprehensive presentation of the various conceptualizations in contemporary psychopathology.

PARADIGMS AS AN ORGANIZING PRINCIPLE One of the reasons we have used the Davison text over many years and sought to use it as a base for our Canadian text is that it has always been consistent with our orientation toward abnormal psychology and with our teaching philosophy. A recurrent theme in the book is the importance of major points of view or, to use Kuhn's (1962) phrase, "paradigms." Our experience in teaching undergraduates has made us very much aware of the importance of making explicit the unspoken assumptions underlying any quest for knowledge. In our handling of the paradigms, we have tried to make their premises clear. Long

after specific facts are forgotten, the student should retain a grasp of the basic problems in the field of psychopathology and understand that the answers one arrives at are constrained by the questions one poses and the methods employed to ask those questions. Throughout the book we discuss four major paradigms: psychoanalytic, learning (behavioural), cognitive, and biological (neuroscientific).

AN AUTHORITATIVE, CONTEMPORARY APPROACH *Abnormal Psychology, Fourth Canadian Edition* furthers its reputation as one of the most current, authoritative overviews of the theories and research in psychopathology and intervention. It maintains the widely praised scientific clinical approach that blends the clinical and empirical/experimental, as the authors examine each disorder from multiple perspectives. The field of abnormal psychology is evolving and expanding at a phenomenal rate. Additions and modification to this text are significant and not merely cosmetic. Why? Because it is vitally important to incorporate a wide range of new findings in this edition to ensure that this text is an accurate source of contemporary developments. This is perhaps best exemplified by the changes outlined in the draft version of the fifth edition of the *Diagnostic and Statistical Manual of Mental Disorders* (DSM-5), which appeared just recently in 2010. Several sections of this book were modified to incorporate these changes. More generally, however, three primary questions continue to guide our writing: What causes psychopathology? Which treatments are most effective in preventing or reducing psychological suffering? And what are the key implications for Canadian society and Canada's mental health system? We tried to not only present theories and research in psychopathology and intervention, but also to convey some of the intellectual excitement that is associated with the search for answers to some of life's most puzzling questions.

NEW TO THIS EDITION

Preparation for the new edition starts as soon as the previous edition is published. It begins with an exhaustive evaluation of the contents of the previous edition by several reviewers, including current users of the text. We have been responsive to their insightful feedback while remaining consistent with the sage approach and framework used historically by Davison and Neale. Typically, suggestions focus on incorporating new research developments and modifying how much focus is placed on various theoretical orientations. For instance, reviewers suggested placing less emphasis on the classical psychoanalytic orientation and instead placing greater emphasis on the cognitive-behavioural orientation and the biological/physiological orientation. The book is also assessed on an ongoing basis to ensure that we retain a high level of readability and continue to highlight the relevance of the material by incorporating case studies and case vignettes of interest to our readers. Key additions and changes to the book are outlined below.

CONTEMPORARY FOCUS

As a reflection of the important new developments, over 900 new references have been integrated throughout the text, with the vast majority of these references published between 2007 and 2010. New material was added only if it represented important new research or key themes. Consistent with the approach used in the third edition, we retained the joint emphasis on incorporating new research conducted in Canada, but also incorporated key new international references so that students would have a contemporary representation of the current state of the field.

Historically, with each revision of this text, three or more chapters are selected and extensive changes and updates are made. In this fourth edition, comprehensive updates were incorporated in Chapter 9, "Psychophysiological Disorders and Health Psychology;" in Chapter 15, "Disorders of Childhood;" and in Chapter 17, "Psychotherapy."

CONTENT REVISION

Content areas have been considerably strengthened. For example, beginning with the second edition, the biological perspective was updated and expanded; this trend has continued and is clearly reflected in the fourth edition. It is vital that any book purporting to be representative has increased coverage of advances in neuroscience and genetic research but it is also important to consider these developments within broad conceptual frameworks such as the biopsychosocial model that is outlined later in the book.

More material on neuroscience and genetic factors has been added to this edition than was added in previous editions. We will provide some illustrative examples. Additional material begins in Chapter 2 with a feature on the neuroscience of ADHD. Chapter 4 contains new examples of biological assessment and the role of neuroscience. Chapter 8 focuses on data on hippocampal volume in depression, while Chapter 12 updates the findings on schizophrenia and Chapter 12 highlights neurocognitive deficits and cannabis use. An intriguing new aspect is covered in the discussion in Chapter 18 of "neurolaw" and the use of neuroscientific data in legal proceedings. Several chapters include new updates on genetic research, including genetic factors in phobic and panic disorder (Chapter 6), the role of anomalous genes in the development of depression (Chapter 8), the heritability of addiction and the gene-environment interaction (Chapter 12), genetic factors in psychopathy (Chapter 13), as well as genetic factors in a host of disorders experienced by children and adolescents (Chapter 15). A central aim in revising the content was to provide expanded descriptions of several "hot topics." We further explored those

topics already included in the previous edition, but also added emerging issues, including some issues specific to Canada. These issues include controversial issues reflected in the draft of *DSM-5* as well as the continuing fate of harm reduction efforts to treat addiction in Vancouver and the evidence in support of harm reduction. *Key* emerging themes of growing significance and new developments discussed at length in this edition include mental health literacy initiatives in Canada (Chapter 1); increasing use of individualized case formulations (Chapter 4); ethical and legal obligations for people receiving placebo controls (Chapter 5); gatekeeper training and suicide prevention (Chapter 8); the status of cognitive-behaviour therapy and the treatment of schizophrenia as well as updates on the role of early invention for first episode patients with psychosis (Chapter 11); the mental illness treatment crisis among children and youth in Canada (Chapter 15);the "rising tide" of the prevalence of Alzheimer's disease in Canada and around the world (Chapter 16); whether some therapies can be considered harmful (Chapter 17); and mental health, mental illness, and homelessness in Canada (Chapter 18).

FOCUS ON DISCOVERY

Several new Focus on Discovery boxes have been added to the fourth edition, as well as significant updates to existing boxes. Significant additions include:

- Focus on Discovery 1.2 –The Way of the Future: Integration and Collaborative Care
- Focus on Discovery 2.2–The Neuroscience of ADHD
- Focus on Discovery 5.2–Selective Reporting of Antidepressant Trials?
- Focus On Discovery 8.2–Stress Generation and Depression
- Focus On Discovery 9.1–Chronic Obstructive Pulmonary Disease
- Focus On Discovery 9.3–Health Status of Students
- Focus on Discovery 10.1–Eating Disorders and Intentional Self-Harm

CANADIAN PERSPECTIVES

- Updated Canadian Perspectives 3.1 on pathological gambling in Canada
- Updated Canadian Perspectives 8.1 on the epidemiology of mood disorders in Canada
- Updated Canadian Perspectives box 11.1, "The New CAMH: A Model for Canada and the World"
- Updated Canadian Perspectives 16.1 to reflect new developments emerging from the Canadian Study of Health and Aging and the Canadian Longitudinal Study of Aging

CANADIAN CONTRIBUTIONS

- Updated Canadian Contributions 9.2 on Norman Endler and the interaction model of anxiety, stress, and coping

- Updated Canadian Contributions 15.2 on Richard Tremblay and the GRIP Research Unit
- Updated Canadian Contributions 16.1, "Charles Morin and the Treatment of Insomnia in Older Adults"

CANADIAN CLINIC FOCUS

- The Canadian Clinic Focus boxes, which begin in Chapter 6, Anxiety Disorders, have been revised and updated. New material has been added, including a new feature in Canadian Clinic Focus 12. 1, "Recovery and Relapse: Starting From Zero All The Time"

SUPPLEMENTARY MATERIALS

- CBC videos have been compiled and updated to accompany *Abnormal Psychology, Fourth Canadian Edition.*
- *The Handbook of Selected DSM-IV-TR Criteria* will be packaged at no additional cost with every Abnormal Psychology, Fourth Canadian Edition textbook. This handy guide lists 30 selected *DSM-IV-TR* criteria to some of the disorders mentioned in the text. Further, there are two case studies at the end of the booklet that help show the reader how the DSM criteria are used in real-life situations.
- The Test Bank, Instructor's Manual, PowerPoint slides, and Study Guide have also been thoroughly revised.

ORGANIZATION OF THE TEXT

In Part 1 (Chapters 1–5), we place the field in historical context, present the concept of paradigms in science, describe the major paradigms in psychopathology and intervention, discuss the role of cultural factors in a Canadian setting, introduce our readers to Canada's mental health care system, review the fourth edition of the *Diagnostic and Statistical Manual of Mental Disorders (DSM-IV)* and pending changes in *DSM-5*, provide an overview of major approaches and techniques in clinical assessment, and then describe the major research methods of the field.

Specific disorders and their treatment are discussed in Parts 2 and 3 (Chapters 6–16). Chapter 16 on aging provides comprehensive coverage of this important topic from a uniquely Canadian perspective. Note that a change was made in the order of the chapters. Mood disorders is now covered in Chapter 8 and Chapter 9 is now "Psychophysiological Disorders and Health Psychology." This change was made in order to more meaningfully discuss the role of mood disorders in health problems in Chapter 9.

The final section, Part 4, consists of Chapters 17 and 18. Chapter 17 discusses process and outcome research on treatment and controversial issues surrounding the therapy enterprise. Chapter 17 was re-written, in part, to highlight the nonspecific factors (e.g., client motives and beliefs) that influence and impact on the effectiveness of treatment. In Chapter 18, legal and ethical issues are discussed and extensive Canadian content is provided. This closing chapter is devoted to an in-depth study of the complex interplay between scientific findings and theories, on the one hand, and the role of ethics and the law.

Throughout this book we have included considerable material on cultural factors in the study of psychopathology and intervention, as well as discussion of the different ways abnormal behaviour is conceptualized in cultures other than our own. For instance, we examine in-depth the ways that *DSM-IV* sensitizes clinicians and researchers to the role of culture in shaping abnormal behaviour, as well as the ways psychological abnormality is manifested in different parts of the world. However, a unique feature of this Canadian adaptation is our focus on how cultural factors are reflected in our Canadian setting, and we address content and issues that are uniquely Canadian. For example, we present a portrait of Canada as a multicultural country (including French Canadians, Canada's Aboriginal peoples, and those whose first language is neither English nor French), and discuss the social policy and mental health implications of our cultural diversity. We also summarize the origins of mental health problems among Canada's Aboriginal peoples and discuss the issue of a possible bias in the assessment of intelligence in Aboriginal children. Consistent with this focus on Native Canadians, we also examine the high rates of suicide and inhalant abuse among Aboriginal children. Other examples of the role of the Canadian cultural mosaic can be found throughout the book. For example, in Chapter 4 on assessment, we address issues related to Canadian standardization and validation of psychological tests, including tests for use with French-speaking Canadians.

FEATURES OF THIS BOOK

In addition to the content and organization, a variety of pedagogical features support the approach of this text. These features were introduced in the first edition and are designed to make it easier for students to master and enjoy the material.

CANADIAN FOCUS BOXES

There are three types of text boxes that focus solely on placing the material in a Canadian context and on highlighting past and current practices in the treatment of abnormal psychology in Canada and the research contributions Canadians have made in the field. They are: Canadian Perspectives, Canadian Clinic Focus, and Canadian Contributions. The Canadian Clinic Focus boxes examine specific clinics in various regions of Canada and clinical intervention issues.

FOCUS ON DISCOVERY BOXES

There are many in-depth discussions of selected topics encased in Focus on Discovery boxes throughout the book. This feature allows us to involve the reader in topics that are sometimes very specialized, in a way that does not detract from the flow of the regular text. Sometimes a Focus box expands on a point in the text; sometimes it deals with an entirely separate but relevant issue, often a controversial one; often it presents material of particular interest to the Canadian student. Reading these boxes with care will deepen understanding of the subject matter.

CHAPTER-OPENING CASES

In addition to the case of J. Brett Barkley introduced at the beginning of Chapter 1 and discussed at various points in Part 1 of the text, the syndrome chapters (6 through 16) open with extended case illustrations. These accounts provide a clinical context for the theories and research that occupy most of our attention in the chapters and help make vivid the real-life implications of the empirical work of psychopathologists and clinicians. New chapter-opening cases have been included in Chapters 8 and 9 to reflect more contemporary themes.

IN-TEXT CASES

As indicated above, many new case examples and case vignettes have been added throughout the chapters to further illustrate key concepts. Several of the chapter-opening and in-text cases are actual Canadian cases, and existing case vignettes have been updated. These new cases begin in Chapter 2 with the horrible abusiveness of Joseph Fritzl and in Chapter 5, the case study of Possum, the Canadian medical technician with zoophilia. Detailed case studies have been added to illustrate anxiety disorders (Chapter 6: Case study of woman from Winnipeg with post-traumatic stress disorder despite having no amygdala; Case study of Nicholas John Arnold in British Columbia, who sued after developing post-traumatic stress disorder), eating disorders (Chapter 10: Natalie, case illustration of intentional self-harm; Claudia Tianne Chan from British Columbia and her experience with an eating disorder), and personality disorders (Chapter 13: the classic case of the psychopath who cited Robert Hare as a reference source). Our review of case studies from previous editions was decidedly biased toward retaining descriptions and depictions of Canadians who have suffered from adjustment difficulties. Students have often reported that they have been impacted by uniquely Canadian cases. This is particularly evident in Chapter 6, which begins with an account of the PTSD experiences of Sergeant Bob Bilodeau and later includes the story of Margot Paul, who suffered from panic disorder with agoraphobia. Additional cases are found throughout the book, including a detailed account of the development of obsessive-compulsive disorder in Howie Mandel. The book concludes in Chapter 18 with a flurry of new additions, including a profile of Oak Ridge serial killer Peter Woodcock, the case of Ahmed v. Stafaniu and its relevance to the issue of the duty to warn, and last but not least, the patient who thought he was a ninja.

CHAPTER SUMMARIES

A summary appears at the end of each chapter. We suggest that the student read it before beginning the chapter itself in order to get a good sense of what lies ahead. Rereading the summary after completing the chapter itself will enhance the student's understanding and provide an immediate sense of what has been learned in just one reading of the chapter. These summaries are presented in bulleted format to enhance student retention.

KEY TERMS

When an important term is introduced, it is boldfaced and defined or discussed immediately. Most such terms appear again later in the book, in which case they will not be highlighted in this way. All of these terms are listed after each chapter summary as key terms. The page number on which the term is defined appears in this list.

DSM-IV-TR TABLE

The endpapers of the book contain a summary of the current psychiatric nomenclature found in the fourth edition of the *Diagnostic and Statistical Manual of Mental Disorders*, known as *DSM-IV-TR*. This provides a handy guide to where particular disorders appear in the "official" taxonomy or classification. We make considerable use of *DSM-IV* and the draft of *DSM-5*, though in a selective and sometimes critical vein. Sometimes we find it more effective to discuss theory and research on a particular problem in a way that is different from DSM's conceptualization.

REFERENCES

As noted above, our commitment to current and forward-looking scholarship is reflected in the inclusion of hundreds of new references among the more than 4,000 references, with about one half of them published since the first edition. We have also included many important Canadian references; those published since 2000 are highlighted in the list of References with the authors' names appearing in bold.

ACKNOWLEDGMENTS

It is a pleasure to acknowledge the contributions of a number of colleagues who helped with their valuable comments and feedback in the writing of four Canadian editions. We would like to acknowledge a number of our colleagues whose thoughtful comments and expert feedback helped us in writing the fourth Canadian edition. They are:

John Conklin —Camosun College
Richard Day—McMaster University
Christopher Earls —University of Montreal
Joel Goldberg—York University
Sandy Jun —Grant McEwan College
Rex Kline—Concordia University
Nancy Kocovski—Wilfrid Laurier University
Dawn McBride—University of Lethbridge
Stephen Porter—Dalhousie University
Uzma Rehman—University of Waterloo
Alan Scoboria—University of Windsor

Many thanks to the staff at John Wiley and Sons Canada, Ltd. for their ongoing enthusiastic support of this project. Members of the very impressive "team" at Wiley we would like to thank include Karen Staudinger, Editorial Manager, who has shown her continuing faith in this project over the years. We extend a special thank you to our Acquisitions Editor, Rodney Burke, for overseeing this edition of the text and providing helpful and timely advice. We also thank Andrea Grzybowski, our Developmental Editor, for her remarkable efforts on the project and her exceptional patience. We also offer our gratitude to Patty Maher, Marketing Manager; and of course all the sales representatives who brought the text to you. The amazing editorial contributions of Laurel Hyatt, Alison Arnot, Belle Wong, and Jamie Whittla (copyediting, proofreading indexing, and photo research) are very much appreciated as is the assistance with the references provided by Laura Hwee, Cynthia Lessard, and Lynda Jess. Special thanks to John Conklin (Camosun College) for compiling the Study Guide, Instructor's Manual, and Student Quizzes, and Réjeanne Dupuis at Mt. Royal University for providing the PowerPoint slides and the Test Bank.

We would also like to offer our sincere gratitude to the authors who graciously provided us with preprints that described their research; this was a great help to us as we wrote the manuscript. These people are too numerous to name, but you know who you are! We would also like to thank a number of scholars who provided us with valuable assistance and advice, including Lynne Angus, Jacques Barber, Abby Goldstein, Marnin Heisel, Paul Hewitt, Stanley Messer, Patricia Pliner, Zindel Segal, and Mary Lou Smith. A special thank you is extended to the Honourable Mr. Justice Richard Schneider for his contributions over the years to Chapter 18. Most importantly, we must thank our respective families for their endless support and encouragement throughout the writing of every edition of this text. We are very fortunate, plain and simple. Thank you Karen and Kathy, for your patience, affection, and understanding, and for reminding us that there is much more to life than writing books. Finally, as was the case with previous editions, suggestions and comments from users of this book are appreciated. We have striven to produce an error-free text, but just as no one is perfect, error-free books are rare despite the extensive checks undertaken. Accordingly, please let us know so that corrections can be made to subsequent printings.

Kirk Blankstein
Gordon Flett

September 2010

BRIEF TABLE OF CONTENTS

CONTENTS

CHAPTER 14

CHAPTER 15

CHAPTER 16

CANADIAN PERSPECTIVES, CANADIAN CLINIC FOCUS, CANADIAN CONTRIBUTIONS, AND FOCUS ON DISCOVERY BOXES

INTRODUCTION: DEFINITIONAL AND HISTORICAL CONSIDERATIONS, AND CANADA'S MENTAL HEALTH SYSTEM

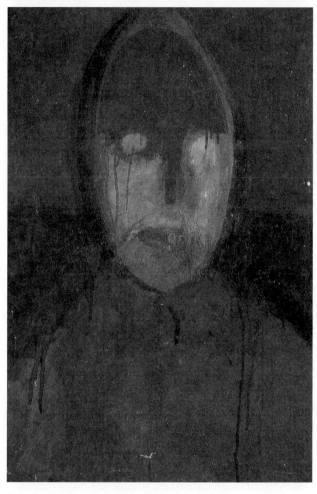

Greg Curnoe, Canadian 1936–1992, *Self*, 1960, Oil on untempered hardboard, 91.0 × 60.8 cm, Art Gallery of Ontario, Toronto. Gift of the Bick Family, 2001. © Estate of Greg Curnoe/SODRAC (2007)

"We are all born mad. Some remain so."
—Samuel Beckett, *Waiting for Godot*, II

"There can be no question though that where the insane are concerned the public are not only indifferent, but terror stricken and very often heartless."
—C. K. Clarke, Canada's first professor of psychiatry (Greenland, 1996)

"Progressive destigmatization of mental illness may be reflected by public funding for care, research, and education which is proportionate to the prevalence and the morbidity engendered by mental illnesses—a day we are nowhere near. This change will require a concerted partnership between the profession and the public—to reduce fear and ignorance, and to promote hope, compassion, and understanding."
—Paul E. Garfinkel, president and CEO, and David S. Goldbloom, physician-in-chief, of the Centre for Addiction and Mental Health, Toronto (2000, pp. 164–5)

"An investment in community outreach programs that support individuals to live productive, meaningful, and connected lives is an essential, cost-effective alternative to hospital-based care."
—The Human Face of Mental Health and Mental Illness in Canada 2006 (p. 50)

WHAT IS ABNORMAL BEHAVIOUR?

HISTORY OF PSYCHOPATHOLOGY

CANADA'S MENTAL HEALTH CARE SYSTEM

SUMMARY

BRETT'S CHILDHOOD Slumping in a comfortable leather chair, J. Brett Barkley (not his real name), a 35-year-old police officer, looked sceptically at his therapist as he struggled to relate a series of problems. His recent inability to maintain an erection when making love to his wife was the immediate reason for his seeking therapy, but Brett recounted a host of other difficulties, some dating from his childhood but most originating during the previous several years.

Brett did not have a happy childhood. His mother died suddenly when he was only 6, and for the next 10 years he lived either with his father or with a maternal aunt. His father drank heavily and the man's moods were extremely variable; he had even been hospitalized with a diagnosis of manic-depressive psychosis. His father's income was so irregular that he seldom paid bills on time and could only afford to live in run-down neighbourhoods. At times Brett's father was totally incapable of caring for himself, let alone for his son. Brett would then spend weeks with his aunt in a nearby suburb.

Despite these apparent handicaps, Brett completed high school, qualified for a student loan, and entered the university near his home. He was able to support himself by waiting tables at a small restaurant. His psychological problems began to concern him at this time. He often became profoundly depressed for no apparent reason, and these bouts of sadness were sometimes followed by periods of manic elation. He was greatly troubled by his lack of control over these mood swings, for he had observed this same pattern in his alcoholic father. He also felt an acute self-consciousness with people who he felt had authority over him—his boss, his professors, and even some of his classmates. Brett was especially sensitive about his clothes, which were old and worn compared with those of his peers.

Brett first saw his future wife on the opening day of classes in his third year. When the slender young woman moved to her seat with grace and self-assurance, his were not the only eyes that followed her. Brett spent the rest of that semester watching her from afar. Then one day, as they and the other students were leaving class, they bumped into each other quite by accident, and her warmth and charm emboldened him to ask her to join him for some coffee. When she said yes, he almost wished she had not.

Amazingly enough, as he saw it, they fell in love and were married before the end of his senior year. Brett could never quite believe that his charming wife really cared for him. As the years wore on, his doubts about himself and about her feelings toward him continued to grow.

He had hoped to enter law school—both his grades and his scores on the law-school boards made these plans a possibility—but decided instead to enter the police academy. As he later told

his therapist, he had doubts about his intellectual abilities and felt increasing uneasiness in situations in which he felt himself being evaluated. Seminars had become unbearable for him in his last year in university, and he had hopes that the badge and uniform of a police officer would give him the instant respect that he seemed incapable of earning on his own.

To help him get through the academy, his wife quit university after her third year, despite Brett's pleas, and sought a secretarial job. He felt she was far brighter than he and saw no reason why she should sacrifice her potential to help him make his way in life. But he recognized the fiscal realities and grudgingly accepted her financial support.

The police academy proved to be even more stressful than university. Brett's mood swings, though less frequent, still troubled him. And like his father, now confined to a mental hospital, Brett drank to ease his psychological pain. He felt that his instructors had considered him a fool when he had difficulty speaking up in front of the class, but he made it through the rigours of the academy and was assigned to foot patrol in one of the wealthier sections of the city.

Several years later, he found himself in even greater turmoil. Now 32 years old, with a fairly secure job that paid reasonably well, he began to think about starting a family. His wife wanted this as well, and it was at this time that his problems with erectile dysfunction began. He thought at first it was the alcohol—he was drinking at least six ounces of rye most nights—but soon he wondered whether he was actually avoiding the responsibility of having a child. Later he began to doubt that his wife found him attractive and desirable. The more understanding and patient she was about his sometimes frantic efforts to consummate sex with her, the less manly he felt. The problems in bed spread to other areas of their lives. The less often they made love, the more suspicious he was of his wife, for she had become even more beautiful and vibrant as she entered her 30s. She had also been promoted to the position of administrative assistant at the law firm where she worked and she would mention long, martini-filled lunches with her boss.

The impetus for contacting the therapist was an ugly argument with his wife one evening when she came home late from work. Brett had been agitated for several days, nightly consuming almost a bottle of rye to combat his fear that he was losing control. Already very drunk by the time his wife walked in the door on that final evening, he attacked her both verbally and physically about her alleged infidelity. In her own anger and fear, she questioned his masculinity in striking a woman and taunted him about their unsatisfying lovemaking. Brett stormed out, spent the night at a local bar, and the next day pulled himself together enough to seek professional help.

Every day of our lives we try to understand other people. Acquiring insight into what we consider normal, expected behaviour is difficult. Understanding human behaviour that is beyond the normal range, such as the behaviour of the police officer just described, is even more difficult.

This book deals with abnormality as it applies to psychological disorders, including their description, causes, and treatment. As you will see, we know with certainty much less about our field than we would like. As we approach the study of **psychopathology**, the field concerned with the nature and development of abnormal behaviour, thoughts, and feelings, we do well to keep in mind that the subject offers few hard and fast answers.

Another challenge we face in studying abnormal psychology is the need to remain objective. Our subject matter is personal and it is powerfully affecting, making objectivity difficult but no less necessary. The disturbing effects of abnormal behaviour intrude on our own lives. Who has not experienced irrational thoughts, fantasies, and feelings? Who has not felt profound sadness that is more extreme than circumstances can explain? Most of you will have known someone whose behaviour was upsetting and impossible to fathom, and realize how frustrating and frightening it is to try to help a person suffering psychological difficulties.

This feeling of familiarity with the subject matter adds to its intrinsic fascination—undergraduate courses in abnormal psychology are among the most popular in psychology departments and indeed in the entire university or college curriculum. But it has one distinct disadvantage. All of us bring to our study preconceived notions of what the subject matter is. We have developed certain ways of thinking and talking about behaviour, certain words and concepts that somehow seem to fit.

As scientists, we have to grapple with the difference between what we may feel is the appropriate way to talk about human behaviour and experience and what may be a more productive way of defining it in order to study and learn about it. The concepts and labels we use in the scientific study of abnormal behaviour must be free of the subjective feelings of appropriateness ordinarily attached to certain human phenomena. As you read this book and try to understand the mental disorders it discusses, you may be asked to adopt frames of reference different from those to which you are accustomed.

The case study at the beginning of this chapter is open to a wide range of interpretations. No doubt you have some ideas about how J. Brett Barkley's problems developed, what his primary difficulties are, and perhaps even how you might try to help him. We know of no greater intellectual or emotional challenge than deciding both how to conceptualize the life of a person with psychological problems and how best to treat him or her. In subsequent chapters, we will refer again to the case of J. Brett Barkley to illustrate how clinicians from different theoretical orientations might describe him and try to help him.

Now we will turn to a discussion of what we mean by the term "abnormal behaviour." Then we will look briefly at how our view of abnormality has evolved through history to the more scientific perspectives of today. We will next discuss current attitudes toward people with psychological problems and introduce you to the system of mental health care in Canada.

WHAT IS ABNORMAL BEHAVIOUR?

One of the more difficult challenges facing those in the field of abnormal psychology is how to define abnormal behaviour. Several characteristics have been proposed as components. No single one is adequate, although each has merit and captures some part of what might be a full definition. Consequently, abnormality is usually determined by the presence of several characteristics at one time. Our best definition of **abnormal behaviour** includes such characteristics as statistical infrequency, violation of norms, personal distress, disability or dysfunction, and unexpectedness.

STATISTICAL INFREQUENCY

One aspect of abnormal behaviour is that it is *infrequent* in the general population. For example, alternating episodes of depression and mania such as those J. Brett Barkley experienced occur in only about 1% of the population. The **normal curve**, or bell-shaped curve, places the majority of people in the middle as far as any particular characteristic is concerned; very few people fall at either extreme. An assertion that a person is normal implies that he or she does not deviate much from the average in a particular trait or behaviour pattern.

Statistical infrequency is used explicitly in diagnosing mental retardation. Figure 1.1 shows the normal distribution of intelligence quotient (IQ) measures in the population. Though a number of criteria are used to diagnose mental retardation, low intelligence is a principal one. When an individual's IQ is below 70, his or her intellectual functioning is considered sufficiently subnormal to be designated as mental retardation. Although some infrequent behaviours or characteristics of people do strike us as abnormal, in some instances,

FIGURE 1.1 The distribution of intelligence among adults, illustrating a normal, or bell-shaped, curve.

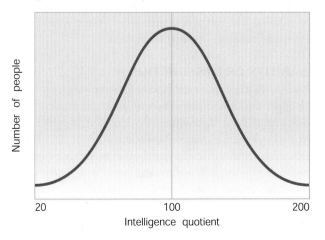

the relationship breaks down. Having great athletic ability is infrequent, but few would regard it as part of the field of abnormal psychology. Only certain infrequent behaviours, such as experiencing hallucinations or deep depression, fall into the domain considered in this book. Unfortunately, the statistical component gives us little guidance in determining which infrequent behaviours psychopathologists should study.

VIOLATION OF NORMS

Another characteristic to consider is whether the behaviour *violates social norms* or threatens or makes anxious those observing it. J. Brett Barkley's verbal and physical attacks on his wife illustrate this criterion. This characteristic also rings true, at least partially. The anti-social behaviour of the psychopath fits the definition of abnormal, as do the obsessive-compulsive person's complex rituals and the psychotic persons's conversation with imaginary voices. Violation of norms explicitly makes abnormality a relative concept; various forms of unusual behaviour can be tolerated, depending on the prevailing cultural norms. Yet violation of norms is at once too broad and too narrow. Criminals and prostitutes, for example, violate social norms but are not usually studied within the domain of abnormal psychology, and the highly anxious person, who is generally regarded as a central character in the field of abnormal psychology, typically does not violate social norms and would not be bothersome to many lay observers.

In addition, cultural diversity can affect how people view social norms. What is the norm in one culture may be abnormal in another. This subtle issue is addressed throughout the book (see especially chapters 2 and 4).

PERSONAL DISTRESS

Another characteristic is *personal suffering*; that is, behaviour is abnormal if it creates great distress and torment in the person experiencing it. J. Brett Barkley's self-consciousness and distress about being evaluated illustrate this criterion. Personal distress clearly fits many of the forms of abnormality considered in this book—people experiencing anxiety disorders and depression truly suffer greatly—but some disorders do not necessarily involve distress. The psychopath, for example, treats others cold-heartedly and may continually violate the law without experiencing any guilt, remorse, or anxiety whatsoever. And not all forms of distress—for example, hunger or the pain of childbirth—belong to the field.

DISABILITY OR DYSFUNCTION

Disability—that is, impairment in some important area of life (e.g., work or personal relationships) because of an abnormality—can also be a component of abnormal behaviour. The disruption of J. Brett Barkley's marital relationship fits this criterion. Substance-use disorders are also defined in part by the social or occupational disability (e.g., poor work performance, serious arguments with one's spouse) created by substance abuse and addiction. Similarly, a phobia can produce both distress and disability; for example, a severe fear of flying may prevent someone from taking a job

Although abnormal behaviour is infrequent, so, too, is great athletic talent, such as that of the proud members of the Canadian women's hockey team. Team Canada has won gold in the past three winter Olympics, winning at the 2002, 2006 and 2010 games. Therefore, infrequency is not a sufficient definition of abnormal behaviour. CP Image Archive/Jonathan Hayward.

promotion. Like suffering, disability applies to some, but not all, disorders. Transvestism (cross-dressing for sexual pleasure), for example, which is currently diagnosed as a mental disorder if it distresses the person, is not necessarily a disability. Most transvestites are married, lead conventional lives, and usually cross-dress in private. Other characteristics that might in some circumstances be considered disabilities—such as being short if you want to be a professional basketball player—do not fall within the domain of abnormal psychology. We do not have a rule that tells us which disabilities belong and which do not.

Abnormal behaviour frequently produces disability or dysfunction, but some diagnoses, such as transvestism, are not clearly disabilities. Stockbyte/Ryan McVay.

UNEXPECTEDNESS

We have just described how not all distress or disability falls into the domain of abnormal psychology. Distress and disability are considered abnormal when they are *unexpected* responses to environmental stressors (Wakefield, 1992). For example, an anxiety disorder is diagnosed when the anxiety is unexpected and out of proportion to the situation, as when a person who is well off worries constantly about his or her financial situation. Hunger, on the other hand, is an expected response to not eating and thus would be excluded as a state of distress that is relevant to abnormal behaviour. J. Brett Barkley was experiencing some life stress, but many people do so without developing psychological problems.

We have considered here several key characteristics of a definition of abnormal behaviour. Again, none by itself yields a fully satisfactory definition, but together they offer a useful framework for beginning to define abnormality. In this volume we will study a list of human problems that are currently considered abnormal. The disorders on the list will undoubtedly change with time, for the field is continually evolving, and it is not possible to offer a simple definition of abnormality that captures it in its entirety. The characteristics presented constitute a partial definition, but they do not equally apply to every diagnosis. The American Psychiatric Association's specific definition is summarized in Chapter 3.

Focus on Discovery 1.1 describes the education and training of professionals who study and treat mental disorders. Goering, Wasylenki, and Durbin (2000) estimated that approximately 3,600 practising psychiatrists, about 13,000 psychologists and psychological associates, and about 11,000 nurses specialize in the mental health area in Canada. Thousands of social workers also work in the mental health field. Non-medical practitioners usually work within hospital or agency settings on a salary or in private practice. Public health plan reimbursement of fees-for-service is limited to medical doctors. In fact, according to Goering et al. (2000), "The major proportion of primary mental health care in Canada is delivered by general practitioners (GPs)" (p. 350). Psychiatrists (who are medical doctors) have a great deal of clinical autonomy. The majority are self-employed professionals whose clinical income is usually based on billing their provincial health plan. As noted by Latimer (2005), "Psychiatrists are essentially free to choose the patient population they wish to care for, and how" (p. 566).

FOCUS ON DISCOVERY 1.1
THE MENTAL HEALTH PROFESSIONS

The training of **clinicians**, the various professionals authorized to provide psychological services, takes different forms. Here, we discuss several types of clinicians, the training they receive, and a few related issues.

To be a **clinical psychologist** typically requires a Ph.D. or Psy.D. degree, which entails four to seven years of graduate study. However, in Canada, professional regulation of the psychology profession is within the jurisdiction of the provinces and territories and, depending upon regulatory statutes, a psychologist may have either a doctoral- or a master's-level degree (Hunsley & Johnston, 2000). In some jurisdictions the title "psychologist" is reserved for doctoral-level registrants, whereas master's-level registrants are referred to as "psychological associates." Specific curriculum requirements vary across jurisdictions. Gauthier (2002) concluded that there was effectively no consensus among the provinces on the minimal academic requirements, the required length of supervised practice, and the timing of such practice (i.e., before or after the degree is achieved).

The 1995 Agreement on Internal Trade (AIT) stipulated that a framework for mobility had to be developed so that the credentials of professional psychologists from one part of Canada would be recognized in other parts of Canada. A Mutual Recognition Agreement was signed in June 2001. According to Gauthier (2002), this requires a person to obtain five core competencies in order to become a registered psychologist: (1) interpersonal relationships; (2) assessment and evaluation (including diagnosis); (3) intervention and consultation; (4) research; and (5) ethics and standards.

Training for a Ph.D. in clinical psychology requires a heavy emphasis on laboratory work, research design, statistics, and the empirically based study of human and animal behaviour. The Ph.D. is basically a research degree, and candidates are required to research and write a dissertation on a specialized topic. But candidates in clinical psychology learn skills in two additional areas, which distinguishes them from other Ph.D. candidates in psychology. First, they learn techniques of **assessment** and **diagnosis** of mental disorders. Second, they learn how to practise **psychotherapy**, a primarily verbal means of helping troubled individuals change their thoughts, feelings, and behaviour to reduce distress and to achieve greater life satisfaction. Students take courses in which they master specific techniques under close professional supervision; then, during an intensive internship or post-doctoral training, they gradually assume increasing responsibility for the care of clients.

Other clinical graduate programs are more focused on practice. These programs offer the relatively new degree of Psy.D. (doctor of psychology). The curriculum is similar to that required of Ph.D. students, with less emphasis on research and more on clinical training. The Ph.D. approach is based on a scientist-practitioner model, while the Psy.D. approach is based on a scholar-practitioner model. The Canadian Psychological Association (CPA) Psy.D. Task Force (1998) described a scholar-practitioner as a "flexible, socially responsible, thinking practitioner who derives his/her skills from core knowledge in scientific psychology. This comprehensively trained professional is capable of performing in a number of roles, and would not be trained simply to be a technician in specific areas" (p. 13). As of 2007 there were two Psy.D. programs in Canada, at the Université du Québec and Université Laval, both offered in French. Memorial University initiated an English-language Psy.D. program that began in the fall of 2009. According to the CPA, psychologists are Canada's single largest group of licensed and specialized mental health care providers. Further, psychologists are the primary researchers and providers of evidence-based psychological treatments.

A **psychiatrist** holds an MD degree and has had postgraduate training, called a residency, in which he or she has received supervision in the practice of diagnosis and psychotherapy. By virtue of the medical degree, and in contrast with psychologists, psychiatrists can also continue functioning as physicians—giving physical examinations, diagnosing medical problems, and the like. Most often, however, the primary aspect of medical practice in which psychiatrists engage is prescribing **psychoactive drugs**, chemical compounds that can influence how people feel and think. Nonetheless, a recent study (Hadjipavlou & Ogrodniczuk, 2007), concluded that current psychiatry residents in Canada have a strong interest in psychotherapy training.

A **psychoanalyst** has received specialized training at a psychoanalytic institute. The program usually involves several years of clinical training as well as the in-depth psychoanalysis of the trainee. Although Sigmund Freud held that psychoanalysts do not need medical training, until recently most psychoanalytic institutes required of their graduates an MD and a psychiatric residency. It can take up to 10 years of graduate work to become a psychoanalyst. However, fewer and fewer people now attend psychoanalytic institutes and become accredited analysts.

A **social worker** obtains an M.S.W. (master of social work) degree. Programs for **counselling psychologists** are somewhat similar to graduate training in clinical psychology but usually have less emphasis on research and the more severe forms of psychopathology. A **psychiatric nurse** specializes in the mental health field.

Analyses of the results of the National Population Health Survey (NPHS; Statistics Canada, 1995) indicated that approximately 2.15% of respondents had consulted with a psychologist one or more times in the preceding 12 months (Hunsley, Lee, & Aubry, 1999)—equivalent to almost 515,000 people in the Canadian population aged 12 and older. Hunsley and colleagues concluded, however, that psychological services are vastly underused. They also determined that psychological services are more available in urban areas than in rural areas and that psychiatrists tend to practise in major urban centres. Thus, many areas of Canada are underserved by two important mental health professions.

There has been a lively and sometimes acrimonious debate concerning the merits of allowing clinical psychologists with suitable training to prescribe psychoactive drugs (see Westra, Eastwood, Bouffard, & Gerritsen, 2006). Predictably, such a move is opposed by psychiatrists for it would represent a clear invasion of their professional turf. It is also opposed by many psychologists, who view it as an ill-advised dilution of the behavioural science focus of psychology. Profits, reducing costs, increasing treatment efficacy, and improving access to treatment are issues, but so is the question of whether a non-MD can learn enough about biochemistry and physiology to monitor the effects of drugs and protect clients from adverse side effects and drug interactions. This debate will undoubtedly continue for some time before any resolution is reached.

HISTORY OF PSYCHOPATHOLOGY

"Those who cannot remember the past are condemned to repeat it."

—George Santayana, *The Life of Reason*

The search for the causes of deviant behaviour has gone on for a long time. Before the age of scientific inquiry, all good and bad manifestations of power beyond the control of humankind—eclipses, earthquakes, storms, fire, serious and disabling diseases, the passing of the seasons—were regarded as supernatural. Behaviour seemingly outside individual control was subject to similar interpretation. Many early philosophers, theologians, and physicians who studied the troubled mind believed that deviancy reflected the displeasure of the gods or possession by demons.

EARLY DEMONOLOGY

The doctrine that an evil being, such as the devil, may dwell within a person and control his or her mind and body is called **demonology**. Examples of demonological thinking are found in the records of the early Chinese, Egyptians, Babylonians, and Greeks. Among the Hebrews, deviancy was attributed to possession of the person by bad spirits, after God in his wrath had withdrawn protection. Christ is reported to have cured a man with an unclean spirit by casting out the devils from within him and hurling them onto a herd of swine (Mark 5:8–13).

Following from the belief that abnormal behaviour was caused by possession, its treatment often involved **exorcism**, the casting out of evil spirits by ritualistic chanting or torture. Exorcism typically took the form of elaborate rites of prayer, noisemaking, forcing the afflicted to drink terrible-tasting brews, and on occasion more extreme measures, such as flogging and starvation, to render the body uninhabitable to devils.

Trepanning of skulls (the making of a surgical opening in a living skull by some instrument) by Stone Age or neolithic cave dwellers was quite widespread. One popular theory is that it was a way of treating conditions such as epilepsy, headaches, and psychological disorders attributed to demons within the cranium. It was presumed that the individual would return to a normal state by creating an opening through which evil spirits could escape. Trepanning was presumably introduced into the Americas from Siberia.

Although the practice was most common in Peru and Bolivia, three Aboriginal specimens have been found in Canada, all on the Pacific coast in British Columbia. One skull is that of a young male believed to be of high rank, since he received a "copper burial" (his forehead and chest were covered by thin sheets of copper). The openings were located in the same area in all three specimens, the upper central occipital; the operations were performed using the same techniques and instruments; and in two cases the person survived long enough for healing to occur (Kidd, 1946). Despite the extensive focus in Aboriginal cultures on possession by spirits, the widely accepted interpretation of the historical data has been disputed. Kidd (1946) suggested that the trepannings "were done to relieve pressure resulting from depressed fractures caused by war clubs" (p. 515).

SOMATOGENESIS

In the fifth century B.C., Hippocrates (ca. 460–377 B.C.), often regarded as the father of modern medicine, separated medicine from religion, magic, and superstition. He rejected the prevailing Greek belief that the gods sent serious physical diseases and mental disturbances as punishment and insisted instead that such illnesses had natural causes and hence should be treated like other, more common maladies, such as colds and constipation. Hippocrates regarded the brain as the organ of consciousness, of intellectual life and emotion; thus, he thought that deviant thinking and behaviour were indications of some kind of brain pathology. Hippocrates is often considered one of the very earliest proponents of **somatogenesis**—the notion that something wrong with the soma, or physical body, disturbs thought and action. **Psychogenesis**, in contrast, is the belief that a disturbance has psychological origins.

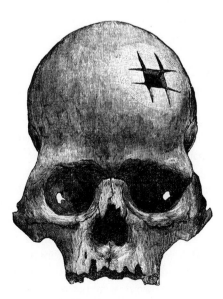

Was trepanning by the Aboriginals of British Columbia performed to allow evil spirits to escape the body? The Auger Photo Archive.

Hippocrates classified mental disorders into three categories: mania, melancholia, and phrenitis (or brain fever). Through his teachings, the phenomena of abnormal behaviour became more clearly the province of physicians than of priests. The treatments Hippocrates suggested were quite different from exorcistic tortures. For melancholia he prescribed tranquillity, sobriety, care in choosing food and drink, and abstinence from sexual activity. Such a regimen was assumed to have a healthful effect on the brain and the body. Because Hippocrates believed in natural rather than supernatural causes, he depended on his own keen observations and made a valuable contribution as a clinician. He also left behind remarkably detailed records describing many of the symptoms now recognized in epilepsy, alcoholic delusion, stroke, and paranoia.

Hippocrates's physiology was rather crude, however, for he conceived of normal brain functioning, and therefore of mental health, as dependent on a delicate balance among four humours, or fluids, of the body, namely, blood, black bile, yellow bile, and phlegm. An imbalance produced disorders. If a person was sluggish and dull, for example, the body supposedly contained a preponderance of phlegm. A preponderance of black bile was the explanation for melancholia; too much yellow bile explained irritability and anxiousness; and too much blood, changeable temperament.

Hippocrates's humoral physiology did not withstand later scientific scrutiny. However, his basic premise—that human behaviour is markedly affected by bodily structures or substances and that abnormal behaviour is produced by some kind of physical imbalance or even damage—did foreshadow aspects of contemporary thought. In the next seven centuries, Hippocrates's naturalistic approach to disorder was generally accepted by other Greeks as well as by the Romans, who adopted the medicine of the Greeks after their city became the seat of power in the ancient European world.

THE DARK AGES AND DEMONOLOGY

Historians have often suggested that the death of Galen (130–200 A.D.), the second-century Greek who is regarded as the last major physician of the classical era, marked the beginning of the Dark Ages for Western European medicine and for the treatment and investigation of abnormal behaviour. Over several centuries of decay, Greek and Roman civilization ceased to exist. The churches gained in influence, and the papacy was declared independent of the state. Christian monasteries, through their missionary and educational work, replaced physicians as healers and as authorities on mental disorder. The monks cared for and nursed the sick. A few monasteries were repositories for the classic Greek medical manuscripts, even though the monks may not have made use of the knowledge within these works. When monks cared for the mentally disordered, they prayed over them and touched them with relics or they concocted fantastic potions for them to drink in the waning phase of the moon. The families of the deranged might take them to shrines. Many of the mentally ill roamed the countryside, becoming more and more disturbed.

The Greek physician Hippocrates held a somatogenic view of abnormal behaviour, considering psychopathology a disease of the brain. © Jeremy Horner/CORBIS.

Illumination from a 15th-century manuscript showing Christ exorcising a demon from a possessed youth. The Granger Collection.

THE PERSECUTION OF WITCHES During the thirteenth and the following few centuries, a populace that was already suffering from social unrest and recurrent famines and plagues again turned to demonology to explain these disasters. People in Europe became obsessed with the devil. Witchcraft, viewed as instigated by Satan, was seen as a heresy and a denial of God. Faced with inexplicable and frightening occurrences, people tended to seize on whatever explanation was available. The times conspired to heap enormous blame on those regarded as witches, and these unfortunates were persecuted with great zeal.

In 1484 Pope Innocent VIII exhorted the clergy of Europe to leave no stone unturned in the search for witches. He sent two Dominican monks to northern Germany as inquisitors. Two years later they issued a comprehensive and explicit manual, *Malleus Maleficarum* ("the witches' hammer"), to guide the witch hunts. This legal and theological document came to be regarded by Catholics and Protestants alike as a textbook on witchcraft. Those accused of witchcraft were to be tortured if they did not confess; those convicted and penitent were to be imprisoned for life; and those convicted and unrepentant were to be handed over to the law for execution. The manual specified that a person's loss of reason was a symptom of demonic possession and that burning was the usual method of driving out the supposed demon. Although records of the period are not reliable, it is thought that over the next several centuries, hundreds of thousands of women, men, and children were accused, tortured, and put to death.

WITCHCRAFT AND MENTAL ILLNESS The prevailing interpretation for some time in the later Middle Ages was that the mentally ill were generally considered witches (Zilboorg & Henry, 1941). In their confessions the accused sometimes reported having had intercourse with the devil and having flown to sabbats, the secret meetings of their cults. These reports have been interpreted by some writers as delusions or hallucinations and thus are taken to indicate that some of the so-called witches were psychotic. More detailed examination of this historical period, however, indicates that many of the accused were not mentally ill. Careful analyses of the witch hunts reveal that many more sane than insane people were tried. The delusion-like confessions were typically obtained during brutal torture; words were put on the tongues of the tortured by their accusers and by the beliefs of the times. Indeed, in England, where torture was not allowed, the con-

In the dunking test, if the woman did not drown, she was thought to be in league with the devil, the ultimate no-win situation. © Bettman/CORBIS.

A tour of St. Mary of Bethlehem (Bedlam) provides amusement for two upper-class women in Hogarth's 18th-century painting. © CORBIS.

fessions did not usually contain descriptions indicative of delusions or hallucinations (Schoeneman, 1977).

Other information, moreover, indicates that witchcraft was not the primary interpretation of mental illness. From the thirteenth century on, as the cities of Europe grew larger, hospitals began to come under secular jurisdiction. Municipal authorities, gaining in power, tended to supplement or take over some of the activities of the church, one of these being the care of the ill. The foundation deed for the Holy Trinity Hospital in Salisbury, England, dating from the mid-fourteenth century, specified the purposes of the hospital, among them that the "mad are kept safe until they are restored of reason." English laws during this period allowed both the dangerously insane and the incompetent to be confined in a hospital. Notably, the people who were confined were not described as being possessed (Allderidge, 1979).

Beginning in the thirteenth century, "lunacy" trials to determine a person's sanity were held in England. The trials were conducted under the Crown's right to protect the mentally impaired, and a judgement of insanity allowed the Crown to become guardian of the lunatic's estate (Neugebauer, 1979). The defendant's orientation, memory, intellect, daily life, and habits were at issue in the trial. Strange behaviour was typically linked to physical illness or injury or to some emotional shock. In all the cases that Neugebauer examined, only one referred to demonological possession. The preponderance of evidence thus indicates that this explanation of mental disturbance was not as dominant during the Middle Ages as was once thought.

DEVELOPMENT OF ASYLUMS

Until the end of the Crusades in the fifteenth century, there were very few mental hospitals in Europe, although there were thousands of hospitals for lepers. In the twelfth century, England and Scotland had 220 leprosy hospitals for a population of 1.5 million. After the principal Crusades had been waged, leprosy gradually disappeared from Europe, probably because with the end of the wars came a break with the eastern sources of the infection. With leprosy no longer of such great social concern, attention seems to have turned to the mad.

Confinement of the mentally ill began in earnest in the fifteenth and sixteenth centuries. Leprosariums were converted to **asylums**, refuges established for the confinement and care of the mentally ill. Many of these asylums took in a mixed lot of disturbed people and beggars. Beggars were regarded as a great social problem at the time; in sixteenth-century Paris the population of fewer than 100,000 included 30,000 beggars (Foucault, 1965). These asylums had no specific regimen for their inmates other than to get them to work, but during the same period, hospitals geared more specifically for the confinement of the mentally ill also emerged.

BETHLEHEM AND OTHER EARLY ASYLUMS The Priory of St. Mary of Bethlehem was founded in 1243. In 1547 Henry VIII handed it over to the City of London, thereafter to be a hospital devoted solely to the confinement of the mentally ill. The conditions in Bethlehem were deplorable. Over the years the word **bedlam**, a contraction and popular name for this hospital, became a descriptive term for a place or scene of wild uproar and confusion. Bethlehem eventually became one of London's great tourist attractions, by the eighteenth century rivalling both Westminster Abbey and the Tower of London. Even as late as the nineteenth century, viewing the violent patients and their antics was considered entertainment, and tickets of admission to Bedlam were sold. Similarly, in the Lunatics' Tower constructed in Vienna in 1784, patients were confined in the spaces between inner square rooms and the outer walls, where they could be viewed by passersby.

It should not be assumed that the inclusion of abnormal behaviour within the domain of hospitals and medicine necessarily led to more humane and effective treatment. Medical treatments were often crude and painful. Benjamin Rush (1745–1813), who began practising medicine in Philadelphia in 1769, is considered the father of American psychiatry. He believed that mental disorder was caused by an excess of blood in the brain. Consequently, his favoured treatment was to draw great quantities of blood (Farina, 1976)! Further, he believed that many "lunatics" could be cured by being frightened. A New England doctor of the nineteenth century implemented this prescription in an ingenious manner: "On his premises stood a tank of water, into which a patient, packed into a coffin-like box pierced with holes, was lowered. He was kept under water until the bubbles of air ceased to rise, after which he was taken out, rubbed, and revived—if he had not already passed beyond reviving!" (Deutsch, 1949, p. 82).

MORAL TREATMENT Philippe Pinel (1745–1826) is considered a primary figure in the movement for humanitarian treatment of the mentally ill in asylums. In 1793, while the French Revolution raged, he was put in charge of a large asylum in Paris known as La Bicêtre. It has long been asserted that Pinel removed the chains of the people imprisoned there, although Pinel subsequently adopted the practice. It appears that it was a former patient orderly, Jean-Baptiste Pussin, who first removed the chains (Weiner, 1994). Pinel also began to treat the patients as sick human beings rather than as beasts. Many who had been completely unmanageable became calm and much easier to handle. They strolled through the hospital and grounds with no inclination to create disturbances or harm anyone. Light and airy rooms replaced dungeons. Some patients who had been incarcerated for years were eventually discharged.

Pinel also believed that the patients in his care were essentially normal people who should be approached with compassion and understanding and treated with dignity as individual human beings. He surmised that if their reason had left them because of severe personal and social problems, it might be restored to them through comforting counsel and purposeful activity. However, for all the good Pinel did for people with mental illness, he was not a complete paragon of enlightenment and egalitarianism. The more humanitarian treatment he reserved for the upper classes; patients of the lower classes were still subjected to terror and coercion as a means of control.

In the wake of Pinel's revolutionary work in La Bicêtre, the hospitals established in Europe and the United States were for a time relatively small and privately supported. A prominent merchant and Quaker, William Tuke (1732–1822), shocked by the conditions at York Asylum in England, proposed to the Society of Friends that it found its own institution. In 1796 the York Retreat was established on a country estate, providing mentally ill people with a quiet and religious atmosphere in which to live, work, and rest. Patients discussed their difficulties with attendants, worked in the garden, and took walks through the countryside.

In the United States the Friends' Asylum, founded in 1817 in Pennsylvania, and the Hartford Retreat, established in 1824 in Connecticut, were patterned after the York Retreat. Other U.S. hospitals were influenced by the sympathetic and attentive treatment provided by Pinel and Tuke. In accordance with this approach, which became known as **moral treatment**, patients had close contact with the attendants, who talked and read to them and encouraged them to engage in purposeful activity; residents led as normal lives as possible and in general took responsibility for themselves within the constraints of their disorders. According to Charland (2007), Pinel believed that a central aspect of moral treatment was re-

Pinel's freeing of the patients at La Bicêtre is often considered to mark the beginning of more humanitarian treatment of people with mental illness. Historical Picture Services/Stock Montage.

storing a patient's sense of self-esteem by letting her or him demonstrate self-restraint.

Despite the emphasis on moral treatment in the early nineteenth century, drugs were also used frequently in mental hospitals. Two findings emerged from a review of detailed case records of the York Retreat from 1880 to 1884 (Renvoise & Beveridge, 1989). First, drugs were the most common treatment and included alcohol, cannabis, opium, and chloral hydrate (knockout drops). Second, the outcomes were not very favourable; fewer than one third of the patients were discharged as improved or recovered.

Moral treatment was abandoned in the latter part of the nineteenth century. Ironically, the efforts of Dorothea Dix (1802–77), a crusader for improved conditions for people with mental illness, helped effect this change. Dix, a Boston schoolteacher, taught a Sunday-school class at the local prison and was shocked at the deplorable conditions in which the inmates lived. Her interest spread to the conditions of patients in private mental hospitals and to the mentally ill people of the time who had nowhere to go for treatment. Dix campaigned vigorously to improve the lot of people with mental illness; she personally helped see that 32 state hospitals were built to take in the many patients whom the private ones could not accommodate. Unfortunately, state hospital staff members were unable to provide the individual attention that was a hallmark of moral treatment (Bockhoven, 1963). Moreover, the hospitals came to be administered by physicians who were interested in the biological aspects of illness and in the physical, rather than the psychological, well-being of mental patients. The money that once paid the salaries of personal attendants now paid for equipment and laboratories. Nonetheless, on March 2, 2009, as part of National Women's History Month and its 100th anniversary celebration, Mental Health America honoured the significant contributions of Dorothea Dix to the field.

For a limited time, there were attempts to apply moral treatment in certain regions of Canada, but these were undermined by the political and economic decisions of those in power. LaJeunesse (2002) documented how attempts at moral treatment in Alberta in the early twentieth century were undercut by

In the 19th century, Dorothea Dix was a tireless social reformer who lobbied for improvement of the deplorable treatment of mentally ill people. © CORBIS.

Premier Arthur Sifton's decision to focus on larger institutions, where patients were crowded into buildings with inadequate space. Dr. Henry Hunt Stabb made heroic efforts to institute moral treatment and non-restraint at the Lunatic Asylum in St. John's, Newfoundland (see O'Brien, 1989). He presided at this site until his death in 1892, but his efforts were hindered by inadequate financial resources and more patients than the hospital could reasonably accommodate. Also, beginning in the late 1870s, the hospital often played a custodial role, as Stabb was made to take in low-functioning patients deemed untreatable.

ASYLUMS IN CANADA

"This, you must remember, that patients here within,
Are here, because we all were born into a world of sin ....
Now come inside the building, and enter into the halls,
You will see many patients, whose sorrows for pity calls.
But pay no attention, to what might be said of you,
Some of them had fine intellects 'fore trouble their minds o'erthrew ...."

–Graeme L., 1907, patient at the Toronto Hospital for the Insane (Rheaume, 2000)

A network of asylums was eventually established in Canada. The history of the development of this network is a history of the institutionalization of people with serious psychological disorders. However, as pointed out by Sussman (1998), the process "began with humane intentions as part of a progressive and reformist movement, which attempted to overcome neglect and suffering in the community, jails, penitentiaries, almshouses, poorhouses, and hospitals" (p. 260). Dorothea Dix described poignant and shameful examples of this neglectful community care and human suffering in her eloquent

1850 memorial prayer to the Nova Scotia Legislative Assembly (see Canadian Perspectives 1.1).

Around this time, J. F. Lehman (1840) wrote the first textbook published in Canada with a focus on the care and control of mentally ill people. In contrast to the compassionate, humane views of reformers such as Dorothea Dix and Henry Hunt Stabb, Lehman recommended stringent discipline and harsh treatments, including flogging. Although his views failed to stimulate much popular or medical support, as we will see, many strategies employed in Canada during the twentieth century were just as harsh and a few were much more severe and had tragic consequences.

Sussman (1998) argued that the development of services for the mentally ill in Canada and British North America was largely ad hoc, with little cross-fertilization of ideas from province to province. During the 1840s through to the 1880s, when most of the formal asylums were first established, all of the jurisdictions could be characterized as having a need to develop separate facilities with better conditions for the mentally ill. As noted by Sussman (1998), "This segregated form of care, the psychiatric institution known as the asylum, was the very beginning of state provisions for mentally ill people in a vast and sparsely populated country" (p. 261).

The earliest precursor to the nineteenth-century asylums was the Hôtel-Dieu, established in Quebec City in 1714 by the Duchess d'Aiguillon, niece of Cardinal Richelieu, the effective ruler of New France. The facility cared for indigents and crippled people in addition to "idiots." Similar "hospitals" were built in other parts of Quebec, using a contracting-out system whereby the King of France paid religious orders of the French Roman Catholic Church to care for the mentally ill. However, following the 1763 Treaty of Paris, the English assumed power over the area and, although the contracting-out practice and the influence of the Catholic Church continued, "the British influence on care practices, daily asylum management, and funding moderated the differences between Quebec and the rest of Canada" (Sussman, 1998, p. 261). The reform movement was led primarily by pioneers from Great Britain (e.g., the Tukes) who influenced the design and construction of asylums.

Table 1.1 presents a summary of the first asylums in Canada and British North America, built during the institution-building period prior to the First World War. Alberta was the last province to open an asylum for the insane, which meant that mentally ill people no longer had to be transported from Alberta to Manitoba by the Royal North West Mounted Police. Typically, asylum superintendents were British-trained physicians who modelled the asylums after British forms of structure, treatment, and administration, although Bartlett (2000), in a comparative analysis of structures in Ontario and England, concluded that they functioned differently and reflected very different norms of social governance.

In Upper Canada, power rested with the asylum doctor. A few years before Confederation, the Annual Report of the Board of Inspectors of Asylums, Prisons, &c., for the Year 1864 (1865, p. iii) included a memorandum "on the necessity

CANADIAN PERSPECTIVES 1.1

DOROTHEA DIX AND THE DEVELOPMENT OF THE ASYLUMS IN CANADA: LIGHT INTO THE DARKNESS?

"One lost mind whose star is quenched
Has lessons for mankind."
    —Dorothea Dix, 1850 (Hurd, 1916, Volume I, p. 492)

Dorothea Dix visited "the Canadas" in 1843 and 1844, discovered appalling conditions suffered by the "insane" incarcerated in the Toronto jail and the Quebec Lunatic Asylum (Hurd, 1916, Volume I).

On January 21, 1850, Dix presented a compelling "memorial prayer" on behalf of the mentally ill to the Nova Scotia legislature and requested construction of a public mental hospital. She stated that "[t]hroughout the province, in short, I found cases incurable through long neglect, doomed to a life-long burden to themselves through suffering, and a life-long charge either upon their friends or the public for care and maintenance" (Hurd, 1916, Volume I, p. 485). Dix also discussed moral treatment and the consequences of failure to obtain help at an early point. Her emphasis on early detection and treatment over 150 years ago is consistent with current views (e.g., see the discussion of early risk detection and intervention for schizophrenia in Chapter 11). Dix appealed to the members to consider what it was like to be mentally ill in Canada:

In imagination, for a short hour, place yourselves in their stead; enter the horrid, noisome cell, invest yourselves with the foul, tattered garments which scantily serve the purposes of decent protection; cast yourselves upon the loathsome pile of filthy straw; find companionship in your own cries and groans, . . . then, if self-possession is not overwhelmed under the imaginary miseries of what are the actual distresses of the insane, return to the consciousness of your sound intellectual health, and answer if you will longer refuse or delay to make adequate appropriations for the establishment of a provincial hospital for those who are deprived of reason, and thereby of all that gladdens life or makes existence a blessing. (Hurd, 1916, Volume I, p. 493)

The Halifax Poor House being rebuilt in 1899 following a fire in 1882. J. M. Margeson. Photo courtesy of Nova Scotia Archives and Records Management.

This appears to be Dorothea Dix's only *public* appeal to a Canadian province. She did take an active role in selecting the site for the Nova Scotia hospital and helped Henry Hunt Stabb raise funds for the St. John's, Newfoundland asylum (see O'Brien, 1989).

Thinking Critically

1. Imagine yourself back in 1850 Nova Scotia. You're suffering with a major psychiatric disorder such as schizophrenia, living under conditions similar to those described by Dorothea Dix. What would it be like for you? What could realistically be done to help you?
2. Given the establishment of a public "asylum," what model of care would you propose? How should the "inmates" be "treated"?
3. Assuming that people in the community treated you with humanity and compassion, cared for and supported you, do you think that it would be possible for you to live among them?

of providing additional accommodation for lunatics in Upper and Lower Canada." The inspectors gave a glowing report on behalf of the medical superintendent of the Provincial Lunatic Asylum in Toronto, the principal asylum in Upper Canada. However, the superintendent reported that both the Chief Asylum and the University Branch (a smaller asylum near the University of Toronto) were "dangerously overcrowded" and lamented the fact that this overcrowding was responsible for a striking increase in the death list (composed mostly of females) and for the impaired general health of the inmates. Further, the majority of the patients remaining in the Chief Asylum at the end of the year were "the noisy, the unruly, and the violent." Most of the women inmates were sent to the University Branch. Dr. Workman, the medical superintendent, argued that "under a system of management which will,

from an inability to give prompt admission to every new case of insanity, convert every case into incurable, death will become the sole creator of vacancies" (p. 11). The average cost of caring for each patient to the province in 1864 was $152.88! Over the years since the asylum was opened in 1841, the superintendent calculated the discharge rate to be 52%. Almost 20% of the inmates died while in the institution, a large number due to "general paresis of the insane" and to a condition called "phthisis."

We currently hear much about the possibility that Canada is developing a two-tier medical system in which the wealthy will have more opportunity for, and quick access to, superior quality care (e.g., Adams & Laghi, 2000). Such a system had the force of law in the era of institution building, at least in Upper Canada (present-day Ontario). In 1853 the legislature

TABLE 1.1
ASYLUMS IN CANADA AND BRITISH NORTH AMERICA BUILT DURING THE INSTITUTION-BUILDING ERA

Jurisdiction	Name and place	Date
Alberta	Insane Asylum, Ponoka	1911
British Columbia	Public Hospital for the Insane, New Westminster (moved from smaller building in Victoria, opened 1872)	1878
	British Columbia Mental Hospital, Coquitlam	1913
Manitoba	Selkirk Asylum, Selkirk	1886
	Home for Incurables, Portage la Prairie	1890
	Brandon Asylum, Brandon	1891
New Brunswick	Provincial Hospital, Saint John (temporary pioneer Canadian institution in converted cholera hospital)	1835
	Provincial Lunatic Asylum	1848
Nova Scotia	Nova Scotia Hospital for Insane, Halifax	1857
Ontario	The Provincial Lunatic Asylum, Toronto (Old York Jail made into a temporary asylum in 1841; renamed the Asylum for Insane in 1871)	1850
	Kingston Asylum (Rockwood), Kingston	1856
	London Asylum, London	1859
	Orillia Asylum for Idiots, Orillia	1861
	Hamilton Asylum, Hamilton	1876
	Mimico Branch Asylum, Mimico	1890
	Hospital for Insane, Brockville	1894
	Cobourg Asylum, Cobourg	1902
	Penetanguishene Asylum, Penetanguishene	1904
	Whitby Hospital, Whitby	1914
Prince Edward Island	The Prince Edward Island Hospital for the Insane	1877
Quebec	Quebec Lunatic Asylum (Beauport), Beauport	1845
	L'Hospice St. Jean de Dieu (Longue Point)	1856
	Provincial Lunatic Asylum, St. Jean	1861
	L'Hospice St. Julien, St. Ferdinand d'Halifax	1873
	St. Benedict Joseph Asylum, near City of Montreal	1885
	L'Hospice Ste Anne, Baie St. Paul	1890
	Protestant Hospital for the Insane (Verdun), Verdun	1890
Saskatchewan	The Saskatchewan Provincial Hospital, Battleford	1914
Newfoundland (Crown colony)	Asylum for the Insane, St. John's	1855
Yukon	Taken to New Westminster by Royal North West Mounted Police	
Northwest Territories	Taken to asylums in Alberta and Saskatchewan	

Source: Hurd (1916), Volume IV.

passed the *Private Lunatic Asylums Act* to accommodate the wealthy in alternatives to the public asylums. The inspectors' report of 1885 noted that "as regards the insane persons of the wealthy class, it is manifest that our public Asylums ... cannot afford such persons the partial seclusion and special personal attention which they desire and are prepared to pay for" (cited in Warsh, 1989, p. 9). As a consequence of the preferential legislation, the Homewood Retreat, a profit-oriented, independent, private asylum, was established in 1883 at Guelph, Ontario. Dr. Lett, the first medical superintendent, believed in the humane care of patients. Despite his resistance to the "cult of curability" ascribed to by practitioners of moral therapy, he encouraged his staff to employ the principles of moral therapy

in order to provide symptomatic relief to his wealthy charges (Warsh, 1989).

The history of the development of institutions for the mentally disordered in Canada can be characterized in terms of two distinctive trends: (1) with the advent of the asylums, provisions for the mentally ill were separate from provisions for the physically ill, indigents, and criminals; and (2) the process was segregated from the wider community—"The institution and the community were two separate and distinct solitudes" (Sussman, 1998, p. 262).

Canadian Perspectives 1.2 examines mental institutions in Canada in the latter part of the twentieth century and the beginning of the new millennium.

CANADIAN PERSPECTIVES 1.2
THE MENTAL HOSPITAL IN CANADA: THE TWENTIETH CENTURY AND INTO THE NEW MILLENNIUM

Despite the humane motives that stimulated the institution-building period in Canada, the results during much of the twentieth century were not very positive, especially from a patient's perspective. Provincial mental hospitals became extremely overcrowded, and in too many instances individual treatment was unavailable with the exception of some radical treatments (e.g., lobotomy) and whatever psychoactive drugs were available in different eras. Drugs became the central means of treatment, especially after the introduction of the antipsychotic phenothiazines in the 1950s. As Sussman (1998) noted, "Eventually, institutionalization in Canada became a synonym for an inhumane response to mentally ill people, often because of a scarcity of resources" (p. 262).

In the 1970s, concerns about the restrictive nature of confinement in a mental hospital led to the deinstitutionalization of a large number of mental hospital patients. The goal in Canada was to shift care from psychiatric hospitals into the community. As Wasylenki, Goering, and MacNaughton (1994) reported, the result of this changed philosophy was a drop in the bed capacity of Canadian mental hospitals from almost 50,000 beds to about 15,000 beds between 1960 and 1976. At the same time, beds in general hospital psychiatric units increased from fewer than 1,000 to almost 6,000. Budget cuts in the 1980s and 1990s caused the trend of deinstitutionalization to continue. However, the enthusiasm for deinstitutionalization has been tempered by the fact that many discharged people lead lives of poverty in the community, with a significant number included among the homeless and the prison population. Although the official position of all provincial and territorial governments is an increased focus on community support systems, community mental health programs were allocated only about 3% of provincial mental health budgets as recently as 1990. Most of the money still goes to the hospitals via global budgets and to physicians via fee-for-service (e.g., Goering, Wasylenki, & Durbin, 2000).

But the problems of chronic patients, many of whom cannot easily be deinstitutionalized, have yet to be handled adequately. Mental hospitals are run as part of our national universal health insurance program—medicare. Although administered by the provincial and territorial governments, medicare is regulated and in part financed by the federal government. In contrast to the United States, which pays for services mainly for the elderly and disabled, in Canada medicare pays basic medical and hospital costs for all Canadians. As noted by Goering et al. (2000), "The federal government sets standards in order to maintain common values and elements within distinct province-sponsored health insurance plans, which are responsible for delivery of services and regulation of services and professionals" (p. 345). Although the situation in Canada has been considerably better than in the United States, treatment of chronic patients in our provincial mental institutions can still be considered primarily custodial in nature. Patients are kept in a protected environment, but receive little individual psychosocial treatment; their

The Asylum for Insane in Toronto, Ontario (circa 1871), notorious for its nickname, associated with the devil: "999 Queen." Archives of the Centre for Addiction and Mental Health.

existence is monotonous and sedentary for the most part. Despite their staggering costs and significant improvements in physical amenities and patient care, some of our **provincial psychiatric hospitals** remain old, grim, and somewhat removed from major metropolitan centres. Nonetheless, they are far superior to the vast majority of "state" mental hospitals in the United States.

A somewhat specialized mental hospital, sometimes called a prison or forensic hospital, is reserved for people who have been arrested and judged unable to stand trial and for those who have been acquitted of a crime because they are "not criminally responsible on account of mental disorder." Although these patients have not been sent to prison, their lives are controlled by guards and tight security. Treatment of some kind is supposed to take place during their incarceration. In Canada there are three maximum-security forensic hospitals, in Ontario, Quebec, and British Columbia. Also, in Ontario, forensic services are provided through the operation of small, medium-security regional forensic units based in the provincial psychiatric hospitals (e.g., METFORS—Metropolitan Toronto Forensic Service).

Even in the best hospitals, patients usually have precious little contact with psychiatrists or clinical psychologists, a situation confirmed (at least in the United States) by the careful observations of Gordon Paul and his co-workers (e.g., Paul & Menditto, 1992). Most patients had no contact with staff for 80 to 90% of their waking hours and the clinical staff spent less than one quarter of their working time in contact with patients. Except for the most severely disturbed, patients do have access to the various facilities of a hospital (e.g., swimming pool, gymnasium). Most hospitals require patients to attend group therapy—here, a general term indicating only that at least two patients attempt to relate to each other and to a group leader in a room for a specific period. Some patients have a few sessions alone with a professional therapist. For the most part, however, traditional hospital treatment over the past 50 years has been oriented toward dispensing drugs rather than toward offering psychotherapy. The institutional setting itself is used as a way to provide supportive care, to try to ensure that patients take their medication, and to protect and look after patients whose conditions make it impossible for them to care for themselves or render them an unreasonable burden or threat to others. One nagging problem is that an institutionalized mindset is difficult to reverse once people have resided in mental hospitals for more than a year. Some people become so accustomed to the protected environment that the prospect of leaving is as frightening to them as the prospect of entering a mental hospital is to those who have never lived in one.

In Canada the current emphasis is on psychiatric-hospital bed reduction and closure. According to Goering et al. (2000), the total bed complement in provincial psychiatric hospitals had been reduced to 11,000 beds in the remaining 41 hospitals. Most provinces plan further bed reductions. For example, in Ontario, the Health Services Restructuring Commission recommended closing half the remaining 10 provincial psychiatric hospitals. The commission set a target of 35 beds per 100,000 population for mental health services by 2003. Further, only 14 of the 35 beds should be used for longer-term care. Wasylenki et al. (2000) suggested that these beds could be reduced to as few as 7 per 100,000 people, contingent on the availability of specialized outreach and alternative residential settings.

·The role of provincial psychiatric hospitals in the new millennium will be "tertiary"; that is, they will "provide specialized treatment and rehabilitation services for individuals whose needs for care are too complex to be managed in the community" (Goering et al., 2000, p. 349). As provincial governments move to develop portable and community-based tertiary care and "delink" delivery from particular settings (Goering et al., 2000), the provincial psychiatric hospitals will play a minimal role. Nonetheless, according to a report by the Canadian Institute for Health Information (CIHI, 2006), Canadians who left hospital with a mental illness diagnosis in 2003–04 had stayed over 6.6 million days. The majority (57.8%) were days spent in psychiatric hospitals, where the length of stay for most patients (72.8%) was between one month and one year (an average of 148.5 days vs. 16.9 days for general hospitals). Stays in dedicated psychiatric hospitals are now shorter but still average more than 100 days (CIHI, 2008). Although hospitalization can be an option for treatment of moderate levels of mental illness (Dewa, Rochefort, Rogers, & Goering, 2003), it is usually the most severe cases that require hospitalization. The CIHI (2006) analyses revealed that schizophrenia, psychotic, and mood disorders made up over half of the 192,562 departures from both psychiatric hospitals and general hospitals in 2003–04.

On March 31, 2009, Ontario officially closed its institutions for the mentally disabled (retarded) after the last residents left the Huronia Regional Centre in Orillia (Crawford, 2009, March 31). The province had announced its intention to shut down all such centres in 1987 and since then over 6,000 residents have returned to communities. At one point in the early 1960s there were over 7,000 people in 16 institutions, many of them children. Other provinces are scaling down similar institutions. Newfoundland and Labrador and British Columbia had already closed their institutions.

In 2008, the Psychiatric Patient Advocate Office in Ontario celebrated 25 years of progress in mental health advocacy and rights protection. However, an ongoing concern is the need to balance the rights of mentally ill individuals with the rights of the community to be protected from them if they are a danger. Across Canada, stakeholders have been debating the value of **community treatment orders** (CTOs), a legal tool issued by a medical practitioner that establishes the conditions under which a mentally ill person may live in the community, including compliance with treatment (O'Reilly, 2004). The consequence for a patient of failing to follow the CTO is being returned to a psychiatric facility for assessment. We examine this emotionally charged, contentious issue in detail in Chapter 18.

One thing is certain. The "asylums" as we have known them over the past 150 years will no doubt all but disappear in the twenty-first century. Indeed, the Centre for Addiction and Mental Health (CAMH) in Toronto has embarked on a 12-year project to integrate the mentally ill into society that is intended to serve as a model for Canada and the world (see Chapter 11).

Thinking Critically

1. The "new" CAMH will refer to people with psychological problems or psychiatric disorders—historically and traditionally called "patients"—as "clients." This term has also been used commonly in the past by many practising psychologists, particularly by those who adopt a less biological, medically oriented approach (see Chapter 2). The authors of this textbook also prefer the term client and will use it throughout the remainder of the book whenever appropriate. Do you agree with this decision? Why, or why not?

2. How should chronic patients (now referred to as clents) be managed and treated so that their dignity is respected but society is protected? Think about this issue in the context of plans to close the majority of the remaining mental hospitals.

3. In 1988 the federal government published *Mental Health for Canadians: Striking a Balance* (Government of Canada, 1988). It claimed that closure of psychiatric hospitals was not offset by "strengthening community resources" and that psychiatric patients (clients) "face a life of deprivation, danger and neglect." Is there still a huge gap between deinstitutionalization, outpatient care, and community care? Does society have a responsibility for the treatment of the vulnerable mentally ill?

4. If there is a major gap, how would you close it? Is a major restructuring of our Canadian mental health system necessary and justified? Design a comprehensive and integrated system that would be responsive and accessible to all Canadians. Would CTOs be a part of your system?

THE BEGINNING OF CONTEMPORARY THOUGHT

Recall that in the West the death of Galen and the decline of Greco-Roman civilization temporarily ended inquiries into the nature of both physical and mental illness. Not until the late Middle Ages did any new facts begin to appear, discovered thanks to an emerging empirical approach to medical science that gathered knowledge by direct observation. One development that fostered progress was the discovery by the Flemish anatomist and physician Vesalius (1514–64) that Galen's presentation of human anatomy was incorrect. Galen had presumed that human physiology mirrored that of the apes he studied. It took more than a thousand years for autopsy studies of humans—not allowed during Galen's time—to begin to prove that he was wrong. Further progress came from the efforts of the English physician Thomas Sydenham (1624–89). He was particularly successful in advocating an empirical approach to classification and diagnosis, one that subsequently influenced those interested in mental disorders.

AN EARLY SYSTEM OF CLASSIFICATION One of those impressed by Sydenham's approach was the German physician Wilhelm Griesinger, who insisted that any diagnosis of mental disorder specify a biological cause—a clear return to the somatogenic views first espoused by Hippocrates. A textbook of psychiatry, written by Griesinger's well-known follower Emil Kraepelin (1856–1926) and first published in 1883, furnished a classification system in order to establish the biological nature of mental illnesses.

Kraepelin discerned among mental disorders a tendency for a certain group of symptoms, called a **syndrome**, to appear together regularly enough to be regarded as having an underlying physical cause, much as a particular medical disease and its syndrome may be attributed to a biological dysfunction. He regarded each mental illness as distinct from all others, having its own genesis, symptoms, course, and outcome. Even though cures had not been worked out, at least the course of the disease could be predicted.

Kraepelin proposed two major groups of severe mental diseases: dementia praecox, an early term for schizophrenia, and manic-depressive psychosis (now called bipolar disorder). He postulated a chemical imbalance as the cause of schizophrenia and an irregularity in metabolism as the explanation of manic-depressive psychosis. Kraepelin's scheme for classifying these and other mental illnesses became the basis for the present diagnostic categories, described in Chapter 3.

GENERAL PARESIS AND SYPHILIS Although the workings of the nervous system were understood somewhat by the mid-1800s, not enough was known to reveal all the expected abnormalities in structure that might underlie various mental disorders. Degenerative changes in the brain cells associated with senile and presenile psychoses and some structural pathologies that accompany mental retardation were identified, however. Perhaps the most striking medical success was the discovery of the full nature and origin of syphilis, a venereal disease that had been recognized for several centuries.

The story of this discovery provides a wonderful picture of the empirical approach, the basis for contemporary science. Since 1798 it was known that a number of mental patients manifested a syndrome characterized by a steady deterioration of both physical and mental abilities and that these patients suffered multiple impairments, including delusions of grandeur and progressive paralysis. Soon after these symptoms were recognized, it was observed that these patients never recovered. In 1825 this deterioration in mental and physical health was designated a disease, **general paresis**. Although it was established in 1857 that some patients with paresis had earlier had syphilis, there were many competing theories for the origin of paresis. For example, in attempting to account for the high rate of the disorder among sailors, some supposed that seawater might be the cause. And Griesinger, in trying to explain the higher incidence among men, speculated that liquor, tobacco, and coffee might be implicated.

In the 1860s and 1870s, Louis Pasteur established the **germ theory of disease**, which set forth the view that disease is caused by infection of the body by minute organisms. This theory laid the groundwork for demonstrating the relation between syphilis and general paresis. In 1897, after Richard von Krafft-Ebing inoculated paretic patients with matter from syphilitic sores, the patients did not develop syphilis, since they had been infected earlier. Finally, in 1905, the specific micro-organism that causes syphilis was discovered. A causal link had been established between infection, destruction of certain areas of the brain, and a form of psychopathology. If one type of psychopathology had a biological cause, so could others. Somatogenesis gained credibility, and the search for more biological causes was off and running.

PSYCHOGENESIS The search for somatogenic causes dominated the field of abnormal psychology until well into the twentieth century, no doubt partly because of the stunning discoveries made about general paresis. But in the late eighteenth and throughout the nineteenth century, some investigators considered mental illnesses to have an entirely different origin. Various psychogenic points of view, which attributed mental disorders to psychological malfunctions, were fashionable in France and Austria.

Mesmer and Charcot Many people in Western Europe were at that time subject to hysterical states; they suffered from physical incapacities, such as blindness or paralysis, for which no physical cause could be found. Franz Anton Mesmer (1734–1815), an Austrian physician practising in Vienna and Paris in the late eighteenth century, believed that hysterical disorders were caused by a particular distribution of a universal magnetic fluid in the body. Moreover, he felt that one person could influence the fluid of another to bring about a change in the other's behaviour. Mesmer conducted meetings cloaked in

Mesmer's procedure for transmitting animal magnetism was generally considered a form of hypnosis. Jean-Loup Charmet/Photo Researchers, Inc.

mystery and mysticism at which afflicted patients sat around a covered *baquet*, or tub. Iron rods protruded through the cover of the baquet from bottles underneath that contained various chemicals. Mesmer would enter a room, take various rods from the tub, and touch afflicted parts of his patients' bodies. The rods were believed to transmit animal magnetism and adjust the distribution of the universal magnetic fluid, thereby removing the hysterical disorder. Whatever we may think of what seems today to be a questionable theoretical explanation and procedure, Mesmer apparently helped many people overcome their hysterical problems.

You may wonder about our discussing Mesmer's work under the rubric of psychogenic causes, since Mesmer regarded hysterical disorders as strictly physical. Because of the setting in which Mesmer worked with his patients, however, he is generally considered one of the earlier practitioners of modern-day hypnosis. The word "mesmerize" is an older term

The French psychiatrist Jean Charcot lectures on hysteria in this famous painting. Charcot was an important figure in reviving interest in psychogenesis. © Bettman/CORBIS.

for "hypnotize." (The phenomenon itself, however, was known to the ancients of probably every culture and was part of the sorcery and magic of conjurers, fakirs, and faith healers.)

Although Mesmer was regarded as a quack by his contemporaries, the study of hypnosis gradually became respectable. A great Parisian neurologist, Jean Martin Charcot (1825–93), also studied hysterical states, including anesthesia (loss of sensation), paralysis, blindness, deafness, convulsive attacks, and gaps in memory. Charcot initially espoused a somatogenic point of view. One day, however, some of his enterprising students hypnotized a normal woman and prompted her to display certain hysterical symptoms. Charcot was deceived into believing that she was an actual hysterical patient. When the students showed him how readily they could remove the woman's symptoms by waking her, Charcot changed his mind about hysteria and became interested in non-physiological interpretations of these very puzzling phenomena.

Breuer and the cathartic method At about this time, in Vienna, a physician named Josef Breuer (1842–1925) treated a young woman who had become bedridden with a number of hysterical symptoms. Her legs and right arm and side were paralyzed, her sight and hearing were impaired, and she often had difficulty speaking. She also sometimes went into a dreamlike state, or "absence," during which she mumbled to herself, seemingly preoccupied with troubling thoughts. During one treatment session, Breuer hypnotized Anna O. and repeated some of her mumbled words. He succeeded in getting her to talk more freely—ultimately, with considerable emotion—about some very upsetting past events. Frequently, on awakening from these hypnotic sessions, she felt much better. With Anna O. and other hysterical patients, Breuer found that the relief and cure of symptoms seemed to last longer if, under hypnosis, they were able to recall the precipitating event for the symptom and if their original emotion was expressed. The experience of reliving an earlier emotional catastrophe and releasing the emotional tension caused by suppressed thoughts about the event was called *catharsis*. Breuer's method became known as the **cathartic method**. In 1895 one of his colleagues joined him in the publication of *Studies in Hysteria*, a book considered a milestone in abnormal psychology. In the next chapter we examine the thinking of Breuer's collaborator, Sigmund Freud.

Many people go about the study of abnormal psychology without considering the nature of the perspective, conceptual framework, or paradigm (see Chapter 2) they have adopted. The choice of a paradigm, however, has important consequences for the way in which abnormal behaviour is defined, investigated, and treated. Canadian Perspectives 1.3 examines, from a historical perspective, some of the treatment strategies that developed as a result of adopting a particular paradigm, and leads us to consider the lesson of history. It raises ethical issues and concerns that we will address in detail in Chapter 18.

CANADIAN PERSPECTIVES 1.3
THE LESSON OF HISTORY: A VIEW FROM THE TWENTY-FIRST CENTURY

"CIA brainwash settlement 'a flea': Spy agency escaped lightly in lawsuit, Winnipegger says"
—The Canadian Press, October 6, 1988

"Brainwash 'guinea pig' seeks more damages: Canadian victim of CIA experiment in late 1950s tries to launch class-action suit against Ottawa"
—The Canadian Press, January 8, 2007

These Canadian Press reports describe the settlement of a lawsuit resulting from what is probably the greatest abuse of psychiatric power in Canadian history. Similar abuses occurred in the United States and elsewhere during the same era and, tragically, are common in some parts of the world even today. However, before proceeding to tell the CIA story, we should point out that a majority of psychiatric patients in Canada were treated with decency and humanity within the constraints of scientific knowledge and accepted clinical practice at the time.

Dr. Ewen Cameron, a world-renowned Montreal psychiatrist, was head of the Allan Memorial Institute at McGill University in the 1950s and early 1960s. At one point, he was president of the Quebec, Canadian, American, and World Psychiatric Associations. In 1955 he initiated a nine-year series of experiments on unsuspecting psychiatric patients, apparently in a misguided attempt to discover breakthrough treatments or a "cure" for mental illness. None of his patients or their families was asked for consent, nor informed that the patients were being administered experimental treatments that were beyond the limits of acceptable treatments for the era. Dr. Cameron's quest led to a bizarre theory of "beneficial brainwashing" that had tragic consequences for hundreds of Canadians, some of whom had only relatively mild problems, such as leg pain or fatigue, when they first came to the institute. Many years later, it was determined that his shocking mind-control experiments were funded secretly by the U.S. Central Intelligence Agency (through a front called the Society for the Investigation of Human Ecology) and the federal government of Canada. The CIA believed that these brainwashing strategies might be used on "enemies" during the Cold War (Gillmor, 1987).

What did Dr. Cameron—and his staff—do that was of such great interest to the CIA? He administered massive doses of hallucinogenic drugs, such as LSD. He administered intensive, repeated courses of electroconvulsive therapy (ECT), or "shock treatment," often three times each day, while patients were kept in a drug-induced coma for as long as three months. He also administered so-called psychic driving, in which subliminal messages, such as "You killed your mother," were repeated over and over while the patient was in the drug-induced state (Collins, 1988). The alleged purpose of these "treatments" was to "wipe away" the troubled past of his patients. It succeeded. Linda Macdonald, who initiated a lawsuit against the federal government, claimed that the experiments erased her memory for the first 26 years of her life. She received over 100 electroshock treatments and was kept in a drug-induced sleep for 86 days. Theoretically, Dr. Cameron would bestow a "new," healthy personality on her. Ms. Macdonald claimed, however, that there was no subsequent care directed at the psychological difficulties that brought her to the institute in the first place, or for the effects of Dr. Cameron's experiments on her. Victims claimed that they suffered permanent damage. Those still alive (several committed suicide) remain in psychiatric hospitals or attempt to live in the community but require extensive support.

The role of the CIA was not discovered until 1977. In 1988 the U.S. government settled out of court for a total of $750,000 with a group of nine former patients who had initiated a lawsuit in 1980. At the time, Val Orlikow, one of the former patients and the wife of a then Winnipeg Member of Parliament, stated that with the settlement, the CIA had merely "flicked a flea off the sleeve of their jacket" (The Canadian Press, 1988). She told CBC's investigative news program *the fifth estate* that Dr. Cameron had let her down. "It was an awful thing to realize, when I found this out, that the man whom I had thought cared about what happened to me didn't give a damn. I was a fly, just a fly." Her husband later told *The New York Times* that Val was left emotionally disabled, and even though she was very bright, she was no longer able to read after her three years of treatment (see Tousley, 2009).

In 1992 the Canadian government finally agreed to a settlement of up to $100,000 per person. Neither the CIA nor the Canadian government apologized to the surviving patients who lost their identities and their dignity, or to the families of approximately 150 former patients who died. In 1998, following an exposé on *the fifth estate*, CBC Television aired a miniseries dramatizing the work of Dr. Cameron and the occurrences in his "Sleep Room." In early 2007 another victim sought approval to launch a class-action lawsuit against the federal government of Canada. She and more than 250 others had been denied compensation by the government because they had not suffered "total depatterning" and were not rendered to a child-like state (The Canadian Press, 2007).

Several radical approaches for the treatment of serious mental disorders were introduced during the twentieth century. At the time, they were considered to be breakthrough developments within mainstream medicine, but many are now considered just as controversial, just as inappropriate, and, in the view of some professionals and many psychiatric consumers, just as damaging as Dr. Cameron's depatterning techniques. We can include here the various shock treatments, starting with metrazol shock treatment, progressing to insulin coma treatment, and culminating with Cerletti and Bini's (1938) introduction of electroconvulsive therapy or ECT (which became a component of Dr. Cameron's experimental approach). The latter is still used today, albeit in a very different and safer form (see the discussion of modern ECT in Chapter 8). Nonetheless, it remains a controversial intervention.

Not without controversy today is the issue of lobotomy or psychosurgery (discussed in Chapter 11). In this surgical procedure, the tracts connecting the frontal lobes to lower centres of the brain are destroyed. Egas Moniz of Lisbon introduced prefrontal lobotomy into psychiatry in 1935 on the strength of hearing at a medical conference about the experimental use of the procedure on two cats. Twenty years later, he was awarded the Nobel Prize for Physiology and Medicine for his use of the procedure in the treatment of schizophrenia. Psychosurgery was used and abused in Canada into the 1970s, when legislation and a general acknowledgement within the mental health professions of its ineffectiveness with, and harmful effects on, psychiatric patients led to its demise. The first lobotomies in Canada were performed in Ontario in 1944 on 19 female patients from various mental hospitals (Simmons, 1987). Simmons (1987) demonstrated that psychosurgery was used in Ontario for several reasons, including out of curiosity, to observe the consequences to patients.

Did patients or their families give informed consent as the law required? According to Simmons (1987), "given the superintendent's belief that lack of consent should not prevent them from giving treatment, it is probable that legal niceties did not constitute a major obstacle to the lobotomy program" (p. 544). Initially, media reports of a high success rate actually led to public pressure to increase the frequency of psychosurgical procedures! Simmons (1987) concluded, however, that the public's belief that psychiatrists abused their authority was responsible for the subsequent imposition of restrictions on psychosurgical operations. Three operations conducted in 1981 were the last lobotomies performed in Ontario (Simmons, 1987). Lobotomies were effectively banned in all public psychiatric hospitals.

What is the lesson of history with respect to society's "treatment" of the mentally ill? The examples presented here, together with examples from the more distant past and knowledge of circumstances surrounding events, suggest the following:

1. Periods in which people exhibiting psychologically disordered behaviour were persecuted and treated cruelly (e.g., witch hunts, bloodletting, asylums) have often alternated with periods of humanitarian reform and care for suffering people (e.g., Hippocrates's humanitarian treatments, Pinel's reform of the asylums).
2. Cycles of persecution, neglect, and humanitarianism in the treatment of the mentally ill have occurred irrespective of the helping agency, whether religious, medical, or psychological.
3. Just as we now look back with revulsion on what were once accepted treatments (e.g., bloodletting), future generations may regard some of our more recent and current practices as cruel and inhumane (e.g., lobotomy, earlier versions of ECT).
4. Recent reforms may easily be reversed (as they have been throughout history) during adverse economic, political, and social conditions.

Thinking Critically

1. Are you aware of any "treatment" of people with psychological disorders that illustrates the wisdom of paying attention to Santayana's famous dictum? Is continued progress in Canada inevitable? What economic, political, and social circumstances could potentially contribute to a lack of progress?
2. What steps would you take to ensure that tragic incidents, such as the "treatments" employed by Dr. Cameron, never occur again in Canada?
3. Do you think that lobotomy was ever justified? (After you think critically about this issue, refer to the discussion of ethical dilemmas of research and therapy in Chapter 18.)

CURRENT ATTITUDES TOWARD PEOPLE WITH PSYCHOLOGICAL DISORDERS

"Changing attitudes to mental illness continues to be our biggest challenge. Discrimination, ignorance and fear remain the enemies that we have to conquer."
—Bill Gaudette, National President, Canadian Mental Health Association, May 2001

"In some ways, mental illness is the final frontier of socially acceptable discrimination."
—Brian Day, past president of the Canadian Medical Association, August 2008

Many Canadians are suspicious of people with psychological disorders. Their concerns have been reinforced by incidents involving threats, violence, and other examples of frightening behaviour on the part of seriously mentally ill people, many of whom had refused to take or were no longer taking their prescribed medications. We will likely never forget the media reports of the tragic, horrific, brutal case of 40-year-old Vince Li, who stabbed, beheaded, and mutilated the body of a young passenger he didn't even know on a bus in Manitoba in 2008. At Li's trial, it was revealed that he told a psychiatrist that he was commanded by God to kill the young man because he was a force of evil:

Suddenly the sunshine came in the bus and the voice said, 'Quick. Hurry up. Kill him and then you'll be safe.' It was so quick, such an angry voice, and I had to do what it said. I was told that if I didn't listen to the voice, I would die immediately. (Puxley, 2009, March 6, p. A2)

The judge, with the agreement of both the Crown and the defence, declared Li not criminally responsible due to mental illness. Psychiatrists testified that Li was suffering from **schizophrenia**. As we will see, cases such as this one, and numerous others that you can probably recall, are actually extremely rare. Unfortunately, they can leave an indelible impression on people and impact negatively on our attitudes toward people with mental health issues or psychological problems.

Consistent with other minority groups in Canada, people with psychological disorders often face negative **stereotyping** and **stigmatization**. For example, according to the Centre for Addiction and Mental Health in Toronto (CAMH, 2000), the social stigma surrounding depression is the primary reason why only one third of the estimated three million people in Canada who suffer from depression seek help. According to a report on the 2002 Mental Health and Well-being Survey (Government of Canada, 2006), over 50% of Canadians who suffered from mood, anxiety, or substance dependence disorders in the previous year felt embarrassed about their problems and reported facing discrimination. A recent Canadian study (Bahm & Forchuk, 2009) found that people with both a psychiatric and a physical disability faced more perceived stigma and discrimination than those with a psychiatric disability alone.

A much publicized example of the issue of stereotyping and stigmatizing of the mentally ill was the 2000 movie starring Canadian actor Jim Carrey entitled *Me, Myself & Irene*. The character played by Mr. Carrey develops a "split personality" and fights against himself. A coalition of Canadian health organizations and advocacy groups, including the Canadian Mental Health Association, wanted disclaimers attached to the film, arguing it reinforces negative stereotypes of people suffering from psychiatric disorders, in particular the schizophrenias. Carrey's character is misidentified as having schizophrenia rather than **dissociative identity disorder** (see chapters 7 and 11).

Mental illness can occur regardless of fame, fortune, or power, and there are many examples of well-known Canadians, or their loved ones, who have experienced a diagnosable psychological disorder (see Nunes & Simmie, 2002). Canadian Contributions 1.1 identifies some of these celebrities, all of whom have acknowledged their adjustment problems despite the possible stigma associated with admitting a mental health problem.

THE PUBLIC PERCEPTION Many common misconceptions or myths of mental illness can be dispelled. For example, as noted above, it is a common belief that people with psychological disorders are unstable and dangerous. We will revisit this issue in subsequent chapters but at this point we can state that recent research does not provide confirmation of this widespread idea although there is a small but significant relation between schizophrenia and violent acts (see Taylor, 2008, for review). A recent major American epidemiological study (Elbogen & Johnson, 2009) found that the incidence of violence was higher for people with severe mental illness; however, the effect was significant only for those with co-occurring substance abuse or dependence. The majority of

mentally ill people never perpetrate violent acts; in fact, they are more likely to be victims (Taylor, 2008).

Another insidious myth is the belief that people with psychological disorders can never be "cured" and can never contribute meaningfully to society again. As you read the research findings presented in this text, you will readily conclude that such a belief is a major misconception. Further, you will no doubt be able to cite examples of people who, though never "cured" of their psychological problems, nevertheless went on to make significant contributions to humanity. One such individual was Clarence Hincks. He suffered from serious, chronic psychological problems but was able to devote his life to helping the mentally ill and to trying to change the public's attitudes toward them. Hincks was a founder and long-term medical director of the **Canadian Mental Health Association** (CMHA). See Canadian Perspectives 1.4 for further information about Hincks, the CMHA, and the issue of misconceptions about the mentally ill.

A survey released for the 50th anniversary of Mental Health Week in Canada, in May 2001 (CMHA, 2001), found that the majority of Canadians believe that maintaining mental health is "very important" (95% of women and 88% of men). However, relative to a 1997 survey, fewer Canadians were willing to tell their bosses (only 42%) or friends (only 50%) if they were receiving help for depression. Women were more willing to admit to receiving treatment than men.

A recent national Ipsos Reid online survey, commissioned by the Canadian Medical Association, was released on August 18, 2008 (see Kirkey, 2008) and shows the extent of current negative attitudes and discrimination. The following were some of the findings:

- Almost 50% of Canadians (46%) believe "we call some things mental illness because it gives some people an excuse for poor behaviour and personal failings."
- About 50% indicated they would avoid socializing with (42%) or marrying (55%) someone who is mentally ill.
- Twenty-seven percent are afraid to even be around someone with a serious mental illness.
- About 50% would decline to tell friends or co-workers about a family member suffering from a mental illness (but 72% would share a cancer diagnosis).
- Most wouldn't hire a doctor, a lawyer, a financial adviser, someone to care for or teach their child, or even a landscaper who has a mental illness!

Dr. David Goldbloom, vice-chairman of the Mental Health Commission of Canada, summarized the message from this survey about Canadians' attitudes toward mental illness: "They're not going to talk about it. They're not going to disclose. And they're not going to disclose as long as there is a culture of shame, secrecy and stigma" (Kirkey, 2008, p. A1). However, on the bright side, 72% of survey respondents agreed that funding to treat mental illness should be comparable to funding for physical illnesses such as cancer (see Zon, 2009).

CANADIAN CONTRIBUTIONS 1.1
THE ADVOCACY OF WELL-KNOWN CANADIANS WITH MENTAL HEALTH PROBLEMS

A growing number of Canadian celebrities have been open about their history of mental health problems and they have advocated for more treatment resources and greater awareness of the impact that mental illness has on our citizens. One example is Margot Kidder, the actress from Yellowknife who is famous for her role as Superman's girlfriend in the Superman movies starring the late Christopher Reeve. Kidder's problems with bipolar disorder led to her temporary retention in a psychiatric facility. She has campaigned against the drug treatments she received.

Another celebrity from the same era is Margaret Trudeau, who married Prime Minister Pierre Trudeau in 1971 when she was only 22 years old. Margaret Trudeau has been open about her long history of battles with bipolar depression, including her symptoms while being the prime minister's wife. In 2006, she recalled, "It was never talked about in those days, and barely recognized, no matter what sector of society you lived in. And so, in the public eye and under public scrutiny, I tried to manage as best I could" (Berthiame, 2006, p. A6).

Margaret Trudeau is the mother-in-law of another well-known Canadian with a history of mental health problems. Sophie Gregoire, wife of Justin Trudeau, admitted her history with an eating disorder in 2006. Gregoire has worked extensively in recent years on behalf of the Montreal-based BACA Eating Disorders Clinic.

Canadian entertainers have been particularly open about the mental health challenges they have faced. Perhaps the most well-known is Howie Mandel, star of the hit television show *Deal or No Deal*. Mandel suffers from obsessive-compulsive disorder and it is his fear of contamination that makes him uneasy about shaking the hands of contestants on the show (and he shaves his head so that germs will not get in his hair!).

Mary Walsh (formerly of *This Hour Has 22 Minutes* and co-star in several films) is another celebrity with a history of mental health issues. Walsh had a difficult upbringing in St. John's, Newfoundland. She took her first drink at the age of 13 and eventually developed alcohol abuse. In 2005, she was given the Centre for Addiction and Mental Health *Courage to Come Back Award*.

Walsh's recovery was assisted by her membership in Alcoholics Anonymous (see Chapter 12).

Singer Alanis Morissette revealed her battles with anorexia and bulimia in 2005. She acknowledged that as a teenage prodigy, she struggled with the symptoms when she was between the ages of 14 and 18, and much of it was due to the need to meet high expectations. She stated, "The pressure was hardcore. For four to six months at a time, I would barely eat, so I constantly felt dizzy. I lived on a lot of Melba toast, carrots and black coffee" (*The Vancouver Sun*, 2005, p. C3). Morissette has fought against the unrealistic body image pressures prescribed for females.

Other Canadians in the music industry have similarly revealed their difficulties. Singer Amy Sky acknowledged at a fundraiser for the Mood Disorders Association of Ontario that she suffered from debilitating postpartum depression. How bad was it? Sky revealed in a television interview that "I just didn't feel like myself. And my brain was disintegrating and not functioning. I couldn't think in a linear manner. I couldn't do anything. I couldn't drive. I was completely exhausted, I had anxiety attacks and hallucinations. It was just like a bad dream" (CTV Television, 2006, June 1).

More recently, Canadian rocker Matthew Good revealed in Vancouver that he has struggled with anxiety and depression for years and he dealt with it by becoming a seemingly tireless worker. Good was eventually hospitalized after ingesting 50 Ativan pills. He has since recovered after receiving treatment (Patch, 2009, D4).

Some scholars have suggested that the professional performers who are vulnerable often experience psychological distress because of the heightened self-consciousness and self-focused attention that comes from being in the public spotlight. Given the potential stigma associated with admitting a mental health problem, it is particularly impressive when these celebrities acknowledge their issues and instead shine that same spotlight on the significant psychological disorders that afflict people in Canada and around the world. Congratulations to all of them!

ANTI-STIGMA CAMPAIGNS Over the past decade there have been numerous widely publicized campaigns in Canada and throughout the world to try to destigmatize mental illness. Michael Wilson, a prominent former federal minister of finance, lost a young son, who suffered from depression, to suicide. Wilson became a tireless crusader to help reduce the stigma associated with depression. Wilson encourages people to seek help for themselves or for loved ones and friends. He served as chair of a multi-year campaign launched by CAMH and various partners to remove barriers that impede people from seeking treatment for mental health and addiction problems. The reduction of the stigma of schizophrenia

(see Chapter 11) is the focus of a worldwide campaign by the World Psychiatric Association. Although the results of an anti-stigma initiative in Alberta suggest that citizens have a higher level of acceptance of people with schizophrenia and more knowledge about the condition than expected (see Thompson et al., 2002), 40% of the general public continued to endorse the belief that people with schizophrenia have the potential to be dangerous. Subsequent to their 2001 survey, the CMHA launched a national public awareness initiative designed to force Canadians to question their attitudes about who becomes mentally ill and to combat the shame associated with having a psychiatric disorder (see CMHA, 2003).

A preventive intervention (see Stuart, 2006a) aimed at reducing stigma in high school students involved a video-based active learning program (The Schizophrenia Society of Canada's Reaching Out program) that chronicled the challenges of actual people with schizophrenia. Exposure to the program resulted in increased knowledge of schizophrenia and its treatment and less social distancing (and presumably less stigma). Female students showed greater gains in understanding than males. Although it is not known whether a lasting improvement in knowledge resulted, this study illustrates the potential of such programs with young people. Indeed, programs that send speakers to talk in public about mental health have been used worldwide and effectively improve knowledge and attitudes of students toward the mentally ill (see Sartorius & Schultze, 2005). The term **mental health literacy** has been created to refer to the accurate knowledge that a person develops about mental illness and its causes and treatment.

Media images of mental illness with a focus on dangerousness, criminality, and unpredictability, and that model negative reactions to people with psychological problems such as fear, rejection, and ridicule, can inhibit help-seeking behaviours, medication adherence, and recovery (see Stuart, 2006b). However, "The media have produced some of the most sensitive, educational and award-winning material on mental illness and the mentally ill" (Stuart, 2006b, p. 99). Thus, the media can play a strong role as allies in anti-stigma activities and can challenge prejudice and discrimination, project positive human-interest stories that promote understanding and compassion, and encourage help-seeking and self-esteem in the mentally ill. A recent example is a landmark, award-winning series published in June 2008 by *The Globe and Mail* (called "Breakdown: Canada's Mental Health Crisis"). The series ended with a 12-point plan (Picard, 2008) that outlines specific goals to reduce the impact of mental disorders on individuals, families, and the community, to prevent mental illness and promote mental health and wellness (see Chapter 18).

Do you believe that the Canadian public's perception of people with psychological problems has become more positive and supportive in the past 10 years? Unfortunately, educational efforts have not been particularly successful at minimizing social rejection. However, we must continue to work toward changing the "culture of shame, secrecy and stigma." Attitudes only change when they are challenged! It is our hope and expectation that you will treat all people, including those with psychiatric disorders, whether real or imagined, with decency and dignity. We further hope that many of our students will take an active role in advocating for, or helping, people with psychological problems.

CANADIAN PERSPECTIVES 1.4
CLARENCE M. HINCKS AND THE CANADIAN MENTAL HEALTH ASSOCIATION

"$20,000 Secured for Institute: Canadian National Committee for Mental Hygiene Started in Mrs. Dunlap's Home"

—*The Globe and Mail*, January 26, 1918

Thus began the Canadian National Committee for Mental Hygiene (CNCMH), precursor to the CMHA. Clarence Meredith Hincks (1885–1964), a co-founder, devoted his life to crusading on behalf of the mentally ill. Born in St. Mary's, Ontario,

he graduated in medicine from the University of Toronto and became involved in working with school children who, in the pejorative jargon of the era, were often labelled "feeble-minded" or "idiots." Hincks, however, had a less pessimistic view of them, thanks to his own experiences. As a university student, he had experienced a bout of what we now refer to as major depression; he recovered (although he would experience further episodes) and was imbued with a sense of optimism about the impermanence and treatability of mental illness. He became familiar with the similar experiences and work of the American Clifford W. Beers (*A Mind That Found Itself*, 1908), a founder of the mental hygiene movement in the United States (and a national committee now known as Mental Health America), and was inspired to do something similar in Canada. The purposes and objectives of the CNCMH were fivefold: (1) psychiatric examination and care of war recruits and returning soldiers suffering from "shell shock"; (2) post-war psychiatric screening of immigrants; (3) adequate facilities for diagnosis and treatment of "mental disease"; (4) adequate care of the "mentally deficient"; and (5) prevention.

Hincks toured mental institutions in Manitoba with C. K. Clarke, dean of medicine and professor of psychiatry at the University of Toronto. They found overcrowding, people who should not have been patients, and appalling custodial care. A description of one of the most astonishing cases is contained in an excerpt from Hincks's unpublished autobiography (in Griffin, 1989):

> At the end of a long dark ward a cupboard was found containing a naked woman with deathly pale skin. There was no furniture, no bed, not even a mattress. The woman had a small piece of shawl which she placed over her eyes when the door was opened. Apparently she was unaccustomed to the light. When the Superintendent was asked how long this woman had been left in the cupboard, he replied, "two years." Hincks asked how often she had been permitted out during that period. "Once, and then only for ten minutes in a cage. She was restless, so we returned her to the cupboard." (pp. 20–1)

The Government of Manitoba implemented many recommendations. Over the next 10 years, other provinces requested similar inspections. Numerous horror stories came to light. Roland (1990) noted:

> ... In the asylum at Saint John, New Brunswick, a certain group of patients on the upper floor were put to bed in coffin like boxes with hay in the bottom and slats on the top. All boxes except two were locked at night, the two being occupied by patients who had been designated "trustees," with the responsibility of dealing with noisy patients. This they accomplished by urinating through the slats on the patients' faces. In Edmonton, Alberta, a novel method of caring for low-grade, mentally defective children was observed. At bedtime, the children were rolled in long strips of cotton with their arms and legs bound, and piled on a shelf. (p. 55)

Hincks and the CNCMH conducted surveys of schoolchildren that resulted in the establishment of over 150 special classes for retarded children. He served as medical director of the CNCMH from 1924 and for CMHA until his retirement in 1952, and helped organize the International Committee for Mental Hygiene, which eventually became the consultative mental health agency for the World Health Organization. In 1962 he announced courageously that he suffered from manic depression (bipolar disorder) in an attempt to dispel public fears and myths about mental illness.

In 1950 the committee changed its name to the Canadian Mental Health Association. Each year, CMHA helps consumers, their families, and friends, through direct service to more than 100,000 Canadians via the efforts of over 10,000 volunteers and staff in locally run organizations and 135 branches throughout Canada. Programs include assistance with employment, housing, and early psychosis intervention for youth; peer support and recreation services; stress-reduction workshops; and community education campaigns. Advocacy, research, and information services are important parts of their mandate to promote the mental health of all Canadians.

From the perspective of history, we cannot regard all of the efforts of C. M. Hincks in a positive light. For example, he played a substantial role in getting the Alberta legislature to pass the *Sexual Sterilization Act* in 1928 (see Chapter 15) allowing the sterilization of "mental defectives." In 1946, he wrote a brief article for *Maclean's* magazine titled "Sterilize the Unfit." His views reflected his belief that "mental defectiveness" has a substantial genetic component and reflects hereditary weakness.

Sources: CMHA website, www.cmha.ca; Dowbiggin (1997); Griffin (1989); Roland (1990).

Thinking Critically

1. How could a tireless crusader on behalf of the downtrodden and psychologically disturbed support a eugenics movement that was so wrong and is so reviled today?
2. Are some segments or groups of people within contemporary Canadian society (e.g., women) more compassionate and supportive of the mentally ill than others? Are some more prone to believe various "myths" of mental illness? How would you test your hypotheses?
3. Can you recognize attitudes and behaviours that support the stigma of mental illness? Assume that you encounter a media report that could contribute to public misunderstanding about mental disorders. What could you do about it?

CANADA'S MENTAL HEALTH CARE SYSTEM

In Canadian Perspectives 1.2 we introduced you to medicare and to our mental health care system in the context of the mental hospital. We continue that discussion with a focus on additional aspects of, and issues involving, our health care system and the mental health of Canadians, and take a look into the future, especially in view of the 2002 publication of the Romanow Report on the future of Canada's health care system and the Senate Committee on Social Affairs, Science and Technology Final Report on Mental Health, Mental Illness and Addiction in Canada—*Out of the Shadows at Last*, released in May 2006.

Every society or culture has its own ideas and expectations with regard to health care practices, including mental health. A cultural difference between Canada and many other countries, including the United States, concerns the value placed on a health care system that is readily available to everyone. At least in this area, we value self-sacrifice and sharing of responsibility for the good of our country. In Canada, mental health services are tied closely to the health care system. Thus, we can place the mental health of Canadians within the context of health in general. Of course, we in Canada are much better off than tens of millions of people in the developing world where, according to the World Health Organization (WHO, 2008, October 9), more than 75% of people suffering from mental disorders receive no treatment or care. In the majority of these countries, less than 2% of limited health funds are spent on mental health.

According to Bowman (2000), Canadians are better off than Americans across virtually all major health indicators (e.g., infant mortality rate, life expectancy, years free of disability, five-year survival rates for cancer and heart disease). Some research suggests that in Canada there is a lower prevalence of psychiatric disorders and less use of illicit drugs. Further, health indicators are less strongly associated with income inequalities in Canada than in the United States. Kessler et al. (1997) concluded that the "match" between psychiatric needs and outpatient services is better in Canada than in the United States. Thus, while a smaller percentage of Canadians receive mental health services (8%), their needs are significant and are directly met (Bowman, 2000); conversely, while more people (13.3%) in the United States receive mental health services, their disorders are less severe—a reflection of the lack of access for the poor (primarily minorities).

MEDICARE

Why is the health of Canadians better than the health of Americans? There is one critical national difference. In Canada, taxes are employed for universal health care, including care for people with psychological disorders. The Canadian **medicare** system has been in effect since 1970. The *Canada Health Act*, the last major piece of legislation in this area (Ritchie & Edwards, 1998), was passed in 1984 and is the legislative cornerstone of our national health care system (Health Canada, 2005). Whereas in the United States health care is rationed by individual income (40% of families have no health insurance), in Canada it is rationed by medical judgements and the level of funding to the system (Bowman, 2000). Poorer Canadians actually make greater use of the system than richer Canadians!

Governments in Canada are currently involved in a massive restructuring of the health care system, including mental health care, and concerns have been expressed about the possibility of a "two-tier" system where higher-income Canadians would have access to private care. Nevertheless, according to Ritchie and Edwards (1998),

> Canadians remain strongly committed to the five core principles on which Medicare is based (accessibility, comprehensiveness, portability, public administration, universality) but are increasingly open-minded about the possibility of changing health service delivery mechanisms in view of economic and other realities, provided that the core principles are respected. (p. 387)

Canadians value medicare not only because it is needed but also because it brings Canadians together as a national community. In March 2009 physicians chose a strong advocate of publicly funded health care as president-elect of the Canadian Medical Association, a departure from the last two leaders, who advocated a stronger role for private medicine that could create a two-tier system.

MENTAL HEALTH OF CANADIANS: FIRST VIEW

WHAT FACTORS ARE ASSOCIATED WITH MENTAL HEALTH IN CANADA? We can get a first indication from a national study. Stephens, Dulberg, and Joubert (1999) analyzed data from the National Population Health Survey (NPHS), a comprehensive study of people living in Canada's 10 provinces (excluding the territories). They reported that:

- Current stress, social support, life events, education, and childhood trauma were strongly and independently associated with multiple indicators of both positive (e.g., self-esteem, mastery, and happiness) and negative (e.g., level of distress, cognitive impairment) **mental health status**.
- The amount of current stress was the strongest correlate of mental health status, since it was consistently positively associated with all positive indicators (e.g., mastery) and negatively associated with all negative measures (e.g., distress).
- Second only to current stress in importance, social support was similarly associated with a majority of the indicators.
- The number of childhood traumas was strongly associated with several negative indicators, including depression.
- The amount of formal education was strongly related to positive indicators of mental health.

Stephens et al. (1999) concluded that mental health is relatively poor among young people but tends to improve with age. This association runs counter to some older studies. The authors pointed out, however, that the social and economic circumstances for older people have improved markedly in Canada, whereas the lot of young people has declined. Sex differences existed on a number of measures. Women, for example, were more likely to be depressed, whereas men were more likely to report a higher sense of mastery. Nonetheless, Stephens et al. concluded that past studies might have given an impression that sex differences are more widespread than they actually are. Throughout the book, we will address these issues and many others as we describe the current status of Canadians' mental health.

WHAT IS THE EXTENT OF MENTAL HEALTH PROBLEMS IN THE PEOPLE OF CANADA? A more in-depth examination of the extent of psychological disorders is presented in Chapter 3's Canadian Perspectives 3.2 and in the context of discussions of specific disorders. However, to anticipate this discussion, a large community study (Ontario Ministry of Health, 1994) found that about 20% of people in Ontario have one or more mental disorders (during a one-year period). Further, many of these people have difficulty performing their main activity (e.g., their job); have difficulty conducting the typical activities of daily living; and have troubled relationships, marital problems, and difficulties relating to children. They are dissatisfied with life, income, main activity, leisure activity, and housing. It was concluded that about 2% of Ontarians can be considered severely mentally ill. A majority of these people (72%) fall in the age range from 25 to 44 years old and are separated, divorced, or widowed. Similar results were found in a national survey of mental illness in Canada (Gravel & Beland, 2005).

REGIONAL DIFFERENCES Does the mental health of the population differ from one region of Canada to another? Do the provinces and territories differ from one another in terms of mental health? These questions are difficult to answer. There are, of course, some obvious differences in certain parts of Canada. In Chapter 2, for example, we will discuss the high level of mental health problems among some of Canada's Aboriginal people. However, Stephens et al. (1999) did not find any major independent association between mental health and a respondent's province of residence. There are, however, a few consistent differences. One of these is the good mental health in both Newfoundland and Labrador and Prince Edward Island. People in these two provinces reported the most happiness and the least distress. Quebec is noteworthy because it reported very high levels of self-esteem and mastery but the least happiness and most distress. It will be important for future research to determine the reasons for these unusual findings and whether or not they still exist today. Unfortunately, possible differences between francophones and anglophones were not reported. We should not take this study as the final word on the extent of regional differences in mental health. It is difficult to determine the pervasiveness of psychological problems among people in remote areas.

TREATMENT AND PREVENTION

How do the Canadian medicare system and other initiatives affect the treatment and prevention of psychological disorders in Canada? The current focus on the restructuring of the health care system has major implications for service delivery. Further, there are clearly practical constraints associated with being a small population in a geographically large country (Hunsley & Johnston, 2000), which can lead to underserving and/or insufficient support of people's needs, especially in rural and remote areas (e.g., Goering et al., 2000). There is a need to place greater emphasis on community psychology and prevention. On a positive note, in 9 of the 10 provinces, much of the health care decision-making has devolved to local authorities to contain costs and improve the integration of services (Lomas, Woods, & Veenstra, 1997). Although provincial and territorial health ministries are primarily responsible for mental health matters, other ministries play a significant role. For example, in Ontario, in addition to the Ministry of Health and Long-Term Care, 13 other ministries have some involvement with mental health. As Romanow and Marchildon (2004) have noted, less than half of health care in Canada is the hospital and physician services that we refer to as medicare.

DEINSTITUTIONALIZATION AND OTHER CHALLENGES TO SERVICE DELIVERY As stated previously, there is an emphasis in Canada on psychiatric bed reduction and closure. The consequences of **deinstitutionalization** are multiple and include homelessness and a lack of supported housing, the jailing of the mentally ill, the failure to achieve an ideal of community-focused care for people with mental disorders, a lack of home care, insufficient intensive case management, too few community-based crisis response systems, concerns about community treatment orders, and so forth. Although deinstitutionalization was a well-intended attempt to reintegrate the mentally ill with the rest of Canadian society and to prevent involuntary hospitalization and treatment, to this point many professionals and "psychiatric survivors" or "consumers" would consider it a failure. We will revisit some of these issues in Chapter 18.

There are now approximately 370 general-hospital psychiatric units in Canada, providing about 10,000 inpatient beds with provincially mandated services that include inpatient care, outpatient care, daycare, emergency care, and consultation (Goering et al., 2000). However, the preferred mental health service model is one that emphasizes intensive local community supports and services, along with the general-hospital psychiatric units and regional tertiary care centres (the provincial psychiatric hospitals or their replacements). Sealy and Whitehead (2004) determined that if psychiatric and general hospitals were combined, the number of days of inpatient psychiatric care per 1,000 population declined more than 40% between 1985–86 and 1998–99, from 486 to 286. Further, the 2006 CIHI report determined that over a 10-year period ending in 2003–04, there was a decline in hospital separations and inpatient episodes. It was hypothesized that the reasons could include a reduced number of available beds or increased use of community services. For 2003–04 the average length of stay (collapsed across general and psychiatric hospitals) was 35 days, a 47% decrease from 1994–95. On the other hand, the CIHI (2006) reported that 37% of patients discharged from a general hospital with a mental illness diagnosis were readmitted within a year. These readmissions were highest among people diagnosed with personality disorders, schizophrenic and psychotic disorders, and those with a co-occurring substance-related disorder.

The most recent CIHI (2008) analysis reported that psychiatric patients are being discharged earlier:

- The average length of stay for those admitted to general hospitals dropped by more than half in the five years ending in 2006, to 16 days from 36 days.
- Patients in Manitoba and New Brunswick reported the longest average general hospital stays (24) but Nunavut had the shortest (3 days).
- Overall, there were almost 171,000 admissions to general hospitals and 2.8 million days stayed in 2005–06.
- The majority of admissions were men between the ages of 25 to 44, and more than half were diagnosed with more than one psychiatric disorder.

• Mood disorders (e.g., depression and bipolar disorder) were the most common psychiatric disorders leading to hospital treatment followed by schizophrenia, substance abuse, dementia, anxiety, and personality disorders. The exceptions were in the Northwest Territories and Yukon Territory, where substance abuse more commonly led to hospitalization.

The shorter general hospital stays were hypothesized to be due to the pressure to free up hospital beds, which frequently results in people being discharged prematurely. As noted by Dr. Patrick White, President of the Canadian Psychiatric Association, "there's continuous pressure to get patients admitted, treated and out" (Tam, 2008).

Treatment of psychological problems in the North and other remote areas is usually carried out at a community level or people are "exported" to major centres, often a long way away. Hospitalization is not as common as it is in urban areas, except for serious conditions, such as psychosis or high risk of suicide. Nonetheless, there are innovative programs. For example, in 1999 Yukon's Whitehorse General Hospital launched an innovative native "healing" building (CMAJ, 1999) as an addition to a very successful Aboriginal healing program. Aboriginal people account for approximately half the admissions of all types at the 49-bed hospital. The program is staffed by First Nations professionals, many of whom are fluent in one or more of the seven Aboriginal languages spoken in the Yukon. This program should serve as a template for similar programs in the North. It is consistent with the recommendation of Kirmayer et al. (2000) that community development and local control of the health care system be extended to Canada's Aboriginal people in order to (1) make services responsive to the needs of Aboriginal people and (2) promote the sense of individual and collective efficacy and pride that contributes to positive mental health. Conventional programs, such as those that help people with substance abuse, are also needed in many regions (e.g., Kirmayer et al., 2000). "Telemental" health applications (Internet- and telephone-based interventions and video conferencing approaches) are possibly helpful (see Hailey, Roine, & Ohinmaa, 2008) and could be especially helpful when used to serve rural and remote communities with limited access to professional services (see Chapter 17).

Our universal health care system will face many challenges in the future. For example, much is said in the media and popular books about the consequences to the system of an aging baby boom population. Meeting the mental health needs of elderly people will require multidisciplinary teams to provide community outreach, in-home assessment and treatment, caregiver support, and so forth (CAG, 2000a). We will discuss community-based care of the elderly in Chapter 16. In addition to destigmatization and compassion, people with the most serious mental disorders (e.g., schizophrenia and bipolar disorder) will also need comprehensive, integrated, coordinated, and multidisciplinary services and support (e.g., Latimer, 2005). People with cognitive disabilities (e.g., mental

retardation) live longer than previously but some are prone to develop Alzheimer's-like dementia and will require expanded or additional home services (CAG, 2000b). As noted by Goering et al. (2000), until quite recently, provision of mental health services was fragmented, lacked mechanisms to coordinate or integrate services, and was not accountable.

Garfinkel and Goldbloom (2000) predicted that there will be enhanced home care (see the discussion of the Romanow Report on p. 30) and the further development of innovative models for service delivery, both within and outside institutions. Just as there is currently an emphasis on evidence-based treatment, there is also a focus on **best practice models** of service delivery (e.g., Health Canada, 1998). Goering et al. (2000) provided two examples, the first ensuring that newer antipsychotic and other medications are available to those who can benefit from them (see Chapter 11) and the second ensuring that new and effective rehabilitation approaches, such as community treatment teams (see chapters 11 and 18), are widely available. However, as Grol (2008) observed, "While our knowledge about effective (mental health) care is growing fast, transfer of this knowledge to practice and use in day-to-day patient care is often failing" (p. 275).

Another challenge is how best to use pharmacotherapy, a widely used treatment in Canada. For people with severe and chronic disorders (e.g., schizophrenia and bipolar disorder), it is a necessary but not sufficient component of interventions. However, best practices are not always followed. Depression is a good case in point since it affects so many Canadians (about 5% annually). Effective antidepressant treatment can have numerous positive effects (e.g., symptom remission and improved interpersonal and occupational or academic functioning). Unfortunately, inappropriate antidepressant prescription is relatively common. Sewitch et al. (2007) examined patients in Quebec newly diagnosed with major depression and concluded that only 8% were treated appropriately (21% received benzodiazepines [anti-anxiety drugs] rather than antidepressants) and most patients were undertreated. Newman and Schopflocher (2008) expressed concern about whether the increase in the volume of antidepressant prescriptions in the elderly in Canada conforms to national practice guidelines. Smith et al. (2008) compared the type and rate of benzodiazepine prescribing in those aged 65 years and older (who are particularly susceptible to side effects) in Nova Scotia and Australia. Although there have been explicit guidelines on the inappropriateness of benzodiazepines in older people since 1991, use was more than twice as high in Nova Scotia. The authors concluded that physicians need to be more aware of the level and burden of benzodiazepine use in older people, and the use of guidelines to improve prescribing.

Although the trend is toward regionalization of administration of provincial care, a review of community-based care for those with severe mental illness (Latimer, 2005) concluded that key evidence-based practices (e.g., assertive community treatment, supportive employment, and integrated treatment for concurrent disorders) are relatively unavailable in most of

Canada. Existing community-based care is provided primarily by a wide variety of non-profit community mental health programs. Most programs receive funding from provincial governments, often in association with private donations, frequently channelled by the United Way. Latimer (2005) noted that there are over 400 community mental health programs and over 120 addiction programs in Quebec. Ontario has over 300 community mental health and addiction programs. However, he also noted that a majority of these organizations are small and rarely have annual budgets over $1 million. These programs offer a variety of services, including case management, vocational rehabilitation, supervised housing, crisis intervention, family support, self-help, and so forth. Only a few are multi-service agencies.

Currently, there is an emphasis on the development of consumer/survivor-run services and there are approximately 60 such projects in Ontario. For example, there are approximately 11 consumer-run businesses that employ a total of about 600 psychiatric survivors. In Quebec, the government promotes the participation of consumers in planning processes at the local, regional, and provincial levels (see Latimer, 2005).

Latimer (2005) argued that if evidence-based practices are to be implemented with any real success, they require integration of people from different agencies within the same clinical team and specialized support. He concluded, "An evolutionary approach of gradually introducing integrated, evidence-based programs, supported by centralized technical assistance and support services, may provide the most feasible strategy for improving the system" (p. 571).

According to Goering et al. (2000), over a five-year period, use of mental health services (offered by psychiatrists and general practitioners) in British Columbia and Ontario increased faster than use of services for other health problems. Such increased demands have possibly contributed to the problem of wait times. A 2008 report by The Fraser Institute (*Waiting Your Turn: Hospital Waiting Lists in Canada*) noted that the national median wait time for those seeking psychiatric treatment (i.e., the time to begin a treatment program after being referred by a general practitioner to a psychiatric specialist) in 2008 was 18.6 weeks—nearly 170% longer than what specialists believe is appropriate. More specific findings included the following:

- The shortest wait times were in Manitoba, British Columbia, and Ontario (15.8, 16.3, and 17 weeks, respectively).
- The longest wait times were in Prince Edward Island, Newfoundland and Labrador, and Alberta (54, 33.3, and 29.8 weeks, respectively).
- The time spent waiting for treatment after an appointment with a specialist was longer than the wait to see a specialist after GP referral.
- The median wait time to see a psychiatrist on an urgent basis was 1.8 weeks, whereas on an elective basis it was 7.9 weeks.
- Among specific treatments surveyed, patients waited longest to enter a housing program (21.3 weeks), whereas wait times were shortest for pharmacotherapy (4.2 weeks).

Report co-author Nadeem Esmail commented that, "Long wait times for access to medical care are a reality for patients in need of mental health services . . . We need a wholesale re-examination of Canada's overall health care system, one that is not founded in a belief that waiting for health care is a necessary evil Canadians must endure" (Fraser Institute, 2008, October 29).

DELIVERY OF PSYCHOTHERAPY

"The best practice will continue to be based on the best science."

—Alan E. Kazdin on evidence-based treatment and practice (2008, p. 157)

Restructuring health care services has implications for people treated with psychotherapy or a combination of psychological and biological interventions. Evaluation of the effectiveness of psychotherapy has become a significant issue because of the increasing demands placed on psychotherapists by both the universal health care system and third-party insurance companies (Hunsley & Johnston, 2000). Psychotherapists are being asked to restrict themselves to the most effective and efficient treatments. Professional organizations are becoming involved as well. For example, the Section on Clinical Psychology of the Canadian Psychological Association (CPA) has been spearheading efforts to reach consensus on which treatments are supported by enough controlled data to be regarded as an **evidence-based treatment** or psychological practice (Hunsley, Dobson, Johnston, & Mikail, 1999; also see Epp & Dobson, 2010; Hunsley, 2007).

Since time-limited psychotherapy is available as an alternative to classic psychodynamic treatment, which sometimes requires many years, provincial governments concerned about cost-effectiveness are limiting or attempting to limit the use of classical analysis and other forms of long-term psychotherapy within the medicare system. Medication-based treatments benefit from the major marketing efforts of huge pharmaceutical companies. In contrast, evidence-based psychological and psychosocial interventions rarely reach the average client in a timely fashion and when they do, research on the quality of care for various disorders sometimes shows gaps between treatments shown to be efficacious in clinical research trials and the care provided people with these problems "in the real world," leading Unutzer (2008) to question if "this tremendous activity in clinical research is having an impact on the millions of patients living with depression and anxiety disorders or if this important work is 'getting lost in translation'" (p.726). Waller (2009) recently outlined common errors in clinical practice that can impede cognitive-behavioural therapy (CBT; see Chapter 2), arguably the evidence-based psychotherapeutic treatment of choice for many disorders. Waller described the common phenomenon of "therapist drift" away from using evidenced-based therapies that can occur in the real world—typically a shift from "doing therapies" to "talking therapies." Nonetheless, Hunsley and Lee (2007) examined 35 "effectiveness" studies on a variety of disorders and concluded that improvement rates as a result of CBT were comparable in actual clinical practice to the improvement rates or outcomes ("efficacy") obtained in randomized, tightly controlled clinical trials within an experimental setting. The issues are complex. As noted by Kazdin (2008), "Researchers and clinicians alike see dangers in prescriptive and inflexible treatments" (p. 146). In fact, most psychological treatments are implemented in a flexible way (see Murphy et al., 2009). We will revisit these issues in Chapter 17.

HELP-SEEKING AND PERCEIVED NEED FOR HELP As we will see in the next chapter, some people from minority groups have difficulty asking for help for psychological problems. What is the situation for the Canadian population in general? The Ontario Health Survey (*Mental Health Supplement*) determined that 7.8% of respondents used mental health services in the past year (Lin, Goering, Offord, Campbell, & Boyle, 1996). About half of those seeking help had a concurrent psychiatric diagnosis. The vast majority sought help from outpatient service providers. Over 75% of those with a diagnosed disorder (see Chapter 3) in the past year did not seek help; however, 27.1% of those who sought help did not qualify for a diagnosis. Lin et al. (1996) concluded that there is a mismatch between people's needs and the care received. Although the strongest predictor of help-seeking was psychiatric diagnosis, help-seeking was also associated with marital disruption and poverty.

Another study confirms that professional services are underused. The Women's Health Study conducted in Ontario found that only about 5 out of 10 women with at least one lifetime psychiatric disorder sought mental health services (Frise et al., 2002). The presence of three or more disorders—called "comorbid" if they exist simultaneously—was associated with increased likelihood of seeking help, but it was still the case that 35% of women with three or more disorders did not seek help.

This problem of underuse may be underestimated because women are actually more willing to seek help than men. An analysis of data from the *Mental Health Supplement* to the Ontario Health Survey confirmed the existence of gender differences in the use of outpatient mental health services for mood disorders, anxiety disorders, substance-use disorders, and anti-social behaviours (Rhodes, Goering, To, & Williams, 2002). Moreover, these gender differences remain evident after controlling for differences in type of mental disorder and associated differences in social and economic factors. Vasiliadis et al. (2009) reported that men are less likely to consult with a family physician and other resources (although not with a psychiatrist). They concluded that promotional campaigns in seeking mental health care need to be aimed toward men.

Sareen et al. (2005) observed that the issue of who needs treatment and whether people are under-serviced can be examined according to the extent to which people perceive that they need treatment (even though it excludes people who need treatment but lack self-awareness and do not realize they need treatment). Sareen et al. (2005) analyzed data from the Canadian Community Health Survey (CCHS, Cycle 1.2; see Chapter 3) and found that the past year prevalence of seeking help was 8.7%, with another 2.9% indicating a need for help with emotional symptoms but not actually seeking help. Perceived need was identified as a crucial variable because even after controlling for other factors, perceived need for treatment but not receiving treatment was associated with higher levels of distress, disability, and suicide ideation. Sareen et al. noted that if actual diagnoses are combined with perceived need, an estimated one in five Canadians require mental health services. In other analyses of the CCHS data set, it was determined that 21.6% of people who were clinically depressed, anxious, or dependent on drugs in the preceding 12 months indicated a desire for help for their mental health problems but they could not obtain help (see Government of Canada, 2006).

Bergeron et al. (2005) examined a subsample of young Canadians (aged 15 to 24 years) from the CCHS data set who were identified as having a mood disorder, an anxiety disorder, or a substance-related disorder in the 12 months preceding the survey in order to identify determinants of service use. They concluded that there is a particular need for interventions to encourage service use in young men, young persons living with their parents or unrelated others, and young people diagnosed with an anxiety or a substance-related disorder (relative to those with a mood disorder).

Although completed suicide is the second leading cause of death for young Canadians (see Cheung & Dewa, 2007), many depressed and suicidal adolescents and young adults do not receive mental health services. Cheung and Dewa (2007) used data from the CCHS to identify young people, aged 15 to 24 years, who screened positive for depression and suicidality in the past 12 months. The findings are disturbing. In Canada, almost 50% of adolescents and young adults with depression and suicidality do not access any mental health services. The major clinical implications are obvious: there is a need to increase service use in depressed and suicidal young people.

There seems to be widespread socio-economic disparities in accessing the system. Steele, Glazier, and Lin (2006) made the point that simply providing a system that theoretically provides universal and equitable coverage is not enough. Their study conducted in Toronto found that people with high socio-economic status (SES), relative to people living in the lowest SES neighbourhoods, were 1.6 times more likely to use psychiatric services (even though poverty contributes to a greater prevalence of mental disorder). Also, of those who did receive care, people with high SES, relative to those with low SES, had significantly more claims for psychiatric problems. Steele, Dewa, and Lee (2007) examined the association between education and income levels and various barriers to mental health care in Canadians with an anxiety or mood disorder in the past 12 months (CCHS 1.2 data set). People with a high school diploma or higher income were least likely to report acceptability barriers to care. The authors concluded that there is a need to develop outreach programs that target low-income, working individuals who have not completed high school.

A recent Quebec study (Preville et al., 2008) provided information about the prevalence of specific psychiatric disorders in the elderly. Although 12.7% of respondents met criteria for a diagnosis of depression, mania, anxiety disorders, or benzodiazepine dependency during the preceding 12 months (see Chapter 3), only 39% of these individuals reported having used health services for their psychological distress. A majority of those who consulted health services (85%) visited a general practitioner.

A national study in the United States (Wang et al., 2005) determined that the vast majority of people with "lifetime" disorders (see Chapter 5) eventually make treatment contact; however, this is more likely for mood disorders relative to anxiety, impulse control, or substance disorders. Delays ranged from 6 to 8 years for mood disorders and 9 to 23 years for anxiety disorders.

COMMUNITY PSYCHOLOGY AND PREVENTION Much of our discussion of therapy and interventions has focused on situations in which professionals make themselves available to clients in offices, clinics, or hospitals. This type of service delivery, long referred to as "the waiting mode" (Rappaport & Chinsky, 1974), is characteristic of traditional therapy, whether inpatient or outpatient. **Community psychology** (see Chapter 17), in contrast, operates in "the seeking mode." Rather than waiting for people to initiate contact, community psychologists seek out problems, or even potential problems. They often focus on **prevention**, in contrast to the more usual situation of trying to reduce the severity or duration of an existing problem. We must focus on preventive measures if we are ever going to solve the problem of mental illness in Canada. In particular, there is a need for programs that promote the psychological, social, and physical well-being of all people in Canada.

Although we have had some success, we have a long way to go. For example, despite a proclamation by governments in Canada that child poverty would be eliminated by the year 2000, it actually increased (Denton, 2000). Nonetheless, there are ongoing programs that promise to fulfil prevention goals in the future. Here is one example. In 1995 the federal government established Aboriginal Head Start to help the development and school readiness of Aboriginal children by meeting their psychological, emotional, social, health, and nutritional needs. The initiative is intended to "encourage the development of locally controlled projects in First Nations communities that strive to instil a sense of pride, a desire to learn, provide parenting skills, foster emotional and social development, increase confidence, and improve family

relationships" (Health Canada, 1998, p. 1). The program was expanded in 1998, with approximately $25 million annual funding to continue indefinitely beyond 2002.

We will examine prevention and community psychology programs throughout this book. These programs often focus on attempting to reduce "risk" factors and to facilitate the development of "protective" factors (see Chapter 2). Examples of these programs include

- efforts to prevent educational deficits and associated social and economic disadvantages
- eating-disorder prevention programs
- programs for the early detection and prevention of schizophrenia
- school-based prevention and early intervention programs for anxiety
- school-based programs for the prevention of cigarette smoking
- the establishment of suicide prevention centres with telephone hotlines that desperate people can use to survive a suicidal crisis
- a parent and child training program for francophones in Montreal to prevent early onset of delinquent behaviour

Many of the prevention programs in Canada focus on children (see Prilleltensky & Nelson, 2000). According to Nelson, Lavoie, and Mitchell (2007), Quebec led the way in progressive prevention policies, including its $7 per day childcare program, and in developing an infrastructure for community-based prevention programs. Further, while numerous programs focus on interventions that reduce the incidence of disorder, governments in Canada, led by the federal government (see Government of Canada, 2006), are increasingly focusing on *mental health promotion*; that is, they are focusing on enhanced functioning, well-being, and optimal functioning. (For a discussion of the distinctions between prevention and promotion and Canadian guidelines and proposals, see Epp [1988], *Mental Health for Canadians: Striking a Balance*.) Unfortunately, widespread prevention and promotion programs are simply not possible in Canada with the current resources available. Nonetheless, the contributions of community psychologists are numerous and varied, especially in Quebec, which has made a greater commitment to promotion and prevention in health care and social policies relative to other provinces (see Nelson et al., 2007).

COST OF MENTAL HEALTH PROBLEMS

"A newly coined term, 'presenteeism,' describes those who currently work but are depressed and non-productive."

–Patrick J. White, President of the Canadian Psychiatric Association, February 2008

What is the cost of mental health problems in Canada? The cost in misery and human suffering among both the people who experience psychological problems and those they touch—their family, friends, and even strangers—is incalculable. An Ontario Ministry of Health study (1994) reported that disability costs to society, which often go unrecognized owing to the stigma attached to symptoms of mental disorders and their treatment, include (1) personal misery, (2) disruption of family life, (3) lower quality of life, and (4) loss of productivity. Regarding the last point, in Ontario the monthly total number of work days lost by people with mental disorders was estimated at more than 1.8 million in 1990. A recent study (Ormel et al., 2008) reported on the administration of epidemiological surveys in 15 countries through the World Health Organization Mental Health Survey initiative. It was found that respondents in both high-income and low- and middle-income countries attributed higher disability to mental disorders than to commonly occurring physical disorders. Further, this higher disability was limited to disability in social and personal role functioning. Productive role functioning was generally comparable for mental and physical disorders. Despite higher disability, mental disorders were generally under-treated in all countries.

The financial burden in terms of direct costs (e.g., charges to medicare) and indirect costs (e.g., loss of productivity) is staggering. Of course, hospital treatment is much more expensive than other forms of direct mental health care, such as outpatient or community treatment, and continues to account for the largest component of direct costs (Stephens & Joubert, 2001). A 2002 Health Canada report used 1998 data and concluded that direct costs for mental disorders (including hospital, drug, and physician care) exceeded $4.7 billion and indirect costs (disability and premature mortality) were $3.2 billion. However, these costs do not take into account lost productivity, third-party insurance costs, and the costs of services of other professionals not covered by health insurance.

Jacobs and his colleagues (2008) measured total direct public and private expenditures on mental health and addictions in each province in 2003–04 and reported that total spending was $6.6 billion. The majority of the spending ($5.5 billion) was from public sources primarily for hospitals, followed by community mental health expenses, and then physicians and pharmaceuticals. The national average was $172 per person. The per capita amount was lowest in Saskatchewan and highest in British Columbia. There were numerous omissions from the analysis (e.g., hospital outpatient services, forensic and prison services, federal government services). The authors concluded that total mental health care spending in Canada is only about 5% of the total health care spending—a rate that is below most comparable developed countries (e.g., Australia and the United Kingdom).

Estimates of direct costs only dramatically underestimate the extent of the problem. Gnam et al. (2006) examined the costs of mental disorders and alcohol, tobacco, and illicit drug abuse in Ontario in 2000. Overall, they pegged the cost at $33.9 billion, with lost productivity alone accounting for $28.7 billion. In terms of specific disorders, the cost of mood disorders, anxiety disorders, and minor depression was estimated at approximately $20.1 billion. The abuse of alcohol, tobacco, and illicit drugs cost almost $12 billion. Recently, Lim et al. (2008) reported on a new population-based measure of the economic burden of mental illness in Canada that incorporated the use of medical resources and long-term (unemployment) and short-term (absenteeism) productivity losses due to long-term and short-term disability, and reductions in health-related quality of life, for the diagnosed and undiagnosed population with mental illness. The analysis was based on the population-based 2003 Canadian Community Health Survey (CCHS, Cycle 2.1). The economic burden—the difference in dollar measures between the populations with and without mental illness—was $51 billion in 2003. The undiagnosed population accounted for more than a quarter of the total burden, including about 30% of the direct medical cost.

The estimated economic burden of serious mental illness in Canada is substantial. Missing from tabulations is the cost to family members who, in addition to a tremendous emotional burden, bear much of the financial burden. Consider other excluded costs (e.g., incarceration and homelessness) and it's not unreasonable to assume that the cost of mental illness exceeds $1,000 per year for every man, woman, and child in Canada. The situation begs an answer to an urgent question: How can we ensure that care for Canadians with psychological disorders is both cost-efficient and effective? We must also ask ourselves: How much we should invest in finding and disseminating better treatments in order to reduce these costs, and how much should we invest in the prevention of disorders in the first place?

THE FUTURE

"Medicare is sustainable if we want it to be."

—Roy Romanow, Ottawa, November 28, 2002

"Our recommendation to create a Canadian Mental Health Commission will focus national attention on this long-neglected area. The strong support shown by the provinces and territories will ensure its success in facilitating a national approach to end the long-standing fragmentation of services, and reducing the stigma and discrimination faced by persons living with mental illness."

—Senator Wilbert Keon, Ottawa, May 9, 2006

THE ROMANOW REPORT The Government of Canada established the Commission on the Future of Health Care in Canada in April 2001 and appointed the former premier of Saskatchewan, Roy Romanow, as commissioner. The mandate was to engage Canadians in a national dialogue and to assess options for a long-term, sustainable, universally accessible, publicly funded health care system. Although the commission intended to examine mental health issues, various stakeholders formed an alliance (the Canadian Alliance on Mental Illness and Mental Health or CAMIMH) to address

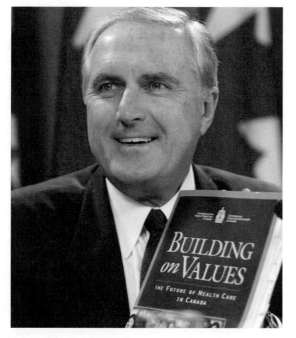

Health care commissioner Roy Romanow recommended crucial changes to Canada's system. The Canadian Press/Fred Chartrand.

what they saw as two key policy weaknesses in the mental health area in Canada (see Canadian Psychiatric Association, 2002): (1) a fragmented constituency, and (2) the lack of a comprehensive national plan. CAMIMH is an alliance of five national organizations representing major consumer, family, community, and medical constituencies: the Canadian Mental Health Association, the Mood Disorders Association of Canada, the Schizophrenia Society of Canada, the National Network of Mental Health, and the Canadian Psychiatric Association. The accord reached meant that for the first time these diverse interests could speak in a unified way about policies in Canada that affect the mentally ill. Among other things, the organization called for a national, coordinated action plan on mental illness and mental health. Other stakeholders in the mental health field, such as the Canadian Psychological Association, as well as private citizens, made presentations and submissions to Mr. Romanow at public hearings as he criss-crossed the country.

Mr. Romanow released his final report on November 28, 2002 (Romanow, 2002). A comprehensive template for the development of health care in Canada, it reaffirmed and expanded upon the five principles of the *Canada Health Act*. It also proposed sweeping changes to medicare and made 47 specific recommendations. Perhaps the central element of the report was the proposal to expand medicare coverage beyond just physicians and hospitals. We focus here on the mental health implications. Calling mental health the "orphan child of medicare," Mr. Romanow recommended that it be made a priority within the system. Of particular relevance, he recommended broadening medicare to include a limited number of home care services and, eventually, some drug treatments and a national drug agency.

The report's proposed expansion of the *Canada Health Act* would specifically include home care coverage for mental health case management and intervention services (over $500 million of new funding) as part of a $1-billion home care transfer. Mr. Romanow also proposed the establishment of a new program to provide direct support to informal caregivers (e.g., family and friends) to allow them to be away from work to provide necessary home care assistance at critical times. Although he stopped short of full pharmacare, he recommended a $1-billion "catastrophic drug transfer" to cover 50% of the cost of drug insurance plans in excess of $1,500 per person a year, a strategy that would improve access to necessary medications for people with severe, chronic psychiatric disorders such as schizophrenia and bipolar disorder. The report also called for an improvement in services to rural and remote communities, including Aboriginal communities. Consistent with our previous discussion of best practice models and evidence-based treatment, the report stated that the principle of **accountability** must be added to the *Canada Health Act*.

Numerous mental health professional and advocacy groups (e.g., CAMIMH) endorsed these and other key recommendations and urged the minister of health to include them in any proposed implementation plans, in order to offer hope to people with serious mental illnesses (see CPA, 2002a). Further, the proposed transformation strategies (such as for primary care and services to remote areas) were presumed to offer a chance to improve integration of primary care and mental health reforms. However, Mr. Romanow subsequently expressed frustration because his recommendations had not been implemented (Romanow, 2006; Walkom, 2003).

THE SENATE COMMITTEE FINAL REPORT On May 9, 2006, the Senate Committee on Social Affairs, Science and Technology released its final report relating to mental health, mental illness, and addiction in Canada. Michael Kirby was chair and Wilbert Keon deputy chair of the three-year study that culminated in the most comprehensive report on mental health in Canada ever completed. The committee held public hearings in every province and territory, offered two on-line questionnaires, received briefs (including from CMHA, CAMIMH, and CPA), conducted literature searches, and explored international innovations before preparing the report *Out of the Shadows at Last: Transforming Mental Health, Mental Illness and Addiction Services in Canada*, also known as the Kirby Report (Government of Canada, 2006). In a subsequent interview, Mr. Kirby stated:

> We managed to ignore the issue of mental health for a very long time. If you look at the services on the ground, they are hugely fragmented. There is no cohesive, patient-oriented system. Mental health has not been at the top of the political agenda. The overwhelming reason for that is the stigma of mental health, which is the reason it has never had the kind of public support that other health issues, such as cancer,

Michael Kirby chaired the Senate study that resulted in a 2006 comprehensive report on mental health in Canada. After retiring from the Senate, he was subsequently appointed chair of the Mental Health Commission of Canada. Most recently, he was promoted to officer of the Order of Canada, which recognizes a lifetime of achievement and merit of a high degree, especially in service to Canada or to humanity at large. The Canadian Press/Sean Kilpatrick.

have had. The second reason is that services for the mentally ill do not fall under a single department—some aspects address health, others relate to housing or training. (CMAJ, 2006, p. 39)

The Senate committee put forward 118 specific recommendations for transforming Canada's mental health system. Two recommendations were key—the creation of a Canadian mental health commission and the Mental Health Transition Fund (MHTF):

1. Canadian mental health commission: The commission would pave the way for a national action plan. It would complement work being done by people and existing structures at all government levels and be designed according to two key principles: an independent not-for-profit organization at arm's length from governments and extant stakeholder organizations, and one with a central focus on those living with mental illness and their families. The committee recommended that the commission be composed of 19 members (one third from governments and two thirds without any government connection), independent of narrowly focused interest groups.

   The mission of the commission would be to
   • act as facilitator, enabler, and supporter of a national approach to mental health issues
   • be a catalyst for reform of mental health policies and improvements in service delivery

• educate all Canadians about mental health and increase mental health literacy
• diminish the stigma and discrimination faced by mentally ill Canadians and their families

   The commission was agreed to by all the provinces and territories, except Quebec (for constitutional reasons).

2. Mental Health Transition Fund (MHTF): The MHTF is intended to be in place for 10 years. The purpose is to allow the federal government to make a time-limited investment to cover transition costs and to speed the process of developing a community-based system of mental health service delivery. The provinces and territories would decide how to allocate the funds. The mental health commission would administer the fund.

   There would be two main fund components:
   • A Mental Health Housing Initiative to provide for the development of new affordable housing units and rent supplements for people living with mental illness to rent accommodation at market rates ($224 million a year for 10 years). The report estimated that 140,000 Canadians do not have adequate housing as a consequence of deinstitutionalization. (The 2006 Federal Budget set aside about $800 million for affordable housing for all Canadians, in cooperation with the provinces.)
   • A Basket of Community Services that will assist the provinces and territories to provide a range of supports and services in the community for people living with mental illness ($215 million per year).

Annual costs for implementing all of the committee's recommendations would total $536 million. In order to fund the investments and initiatives, the committee recommended that the Government of Canada raise the excise tax on alcohol by a nickel for a standard drink. Committee members expressed optimism that the federal government would act quickly on its key recommendations. Canada is the only G8 country that does not have a national mental health strategy.

On August 31, 2007, Prime Minister Stephen Harper formally announced the selection of the board of directors for the newly created Mental Health Commission of Canada, "the cornerstone" of the government's strategy to address mental health issues in Canada. Michael Kirby was appointed chair. In its 2007 Budget, the government had committed $55 million over five years toward the commission. In a one-year status report (Howlett, August 23, 2008), the commission president reported on the establishment of eight advisory committees with specialists from all over Canada dealing with specific target areas: child and youth, mental health; and the law; seniors; workforce; First Nations; Inuit and Metis; family caregivers; service "systems;" and science. In comments about the promise and challenge of the commission in *Canadian Psychiatry Aujourd'hui* (2007), Mr. Kirby stated:

...we must build a mental health system that places people living with mental illness at its centre, allowing them to choose those services and supports they need to help them recover. These services must be oriented toward helping people live meaningful and productive lives in their own communities, and must be integrated to provide a seamless continuum of care across the lifespan.

In the spring of 2009 the commission released its draft vision for a national mental health strategy—*Toward Recovery and Well-Being*, including eight major goals for a transformed system (see Bacic, 2009). As of January, 2010, the government had not made a decision about supporting the proposal for a Mental Health Transition Fund.

THE FUTURE ROLE OF PSYCHOLOGY What will be psychology's role in a restructured Canadian mental health system? Back in 1998, Ritchie and Edwards anticipated that the upcoming changes would provide a tailor-made opportunity for psychologists "whose knowledge and skills are well suited for the planning, implementation, and evaluation of action-oriented programs with targeted outcomes" (p. 387). Hunsley and colleagues (Hunsley, Dobson et al.,1999; Hunsley & Lee, 2007) cited evidence that psychological interventions are effective in treating a wide range of disorders and are cost-effective for the health care system.

Although the Canadian Psychological Association endorsed many of the Romanow Report recommendations (CPA, 2002b) in a *Psychology Specific Analysis* (also see Romanow & Marchildon, 2003), it eschewed the "physical medicine vision" and expressed disappointment that psychology's "vision was not embraced or even referenced" (p. 4). For example, the report did not mention psychological services not covered by medicare plans, nor did it discuss ways of linking these services to the public system. Further, the report did not address research on the efficacy of medication combined with psychological interventions or findings about the superiority of psychological treatments. With respect to the report's emphasis on strengthening the role of prevention, the CPA observed that the "physical health focus is disappointing considering the well-documented role of psychology in prevention, the plethora of health issues involving psychological factors and the central role of mental health and mental illness" (p. 11). On a positive note, the CPA saw the possibility of the meaningful involvement of psychology in the proposed Centres for Health Innovation because of the research skills and knowledge base of psychology. In a rejoinder to three formal responses to their 2003 paper published in *Canadian Psychology*, Romanow and Marchildon (2004) argued that "if psychologists are able to become a part of the primary-care teams of the future, they will be able to provide an array of prevention, diagnostic, and curative services currently not available to many Canadians because of cost" (p. 240). The cost savings could range as high as 80% of currently dominant treatments, including medication. CPA named Mr. Romanow its Honorary President for 2004–05 (see Romanow, 2006).

CPA's response to the Senate Committee Final Report was somewhat predictable and consistent with the reaction to the Romanow Report. It concluded that the consensus document could lead to improved mental health in Canada. The discussions about income support for the mentally ill; the call for the federal government to address mental health issues in its areas of responsibility (e.g., Aboriginals, the criminal justice system, armed forces, the civil service); the mental health needs of immigrants; and the lengthy treatment of issues facing First Nations, Metis, and Inuit people were cited as particular strengths. However, concern was expressed about a perceived pervasive bias toward serious and persistent mental illness, the publicly funded system, and the physician-centred system. CPA also eschewed the omission of school psychologists from school-based mental health programs; the failure to examine health psychology in depth; and the failure to include in-depth discussion of promotion, prevention, and resilience. There was also a worry that the commission could be over-represented by one or two professions to the exclusion of psychology.

It is unlikely that psychologists will be invited to participate directly in medicare in the future, and the CPA appraisal of the Kirby Report concludes that there is a "limitation of the field of possibilities for psychology" (CPA, 2002b, p. 8). However, when thinking about the costs of psychological disorders, we should remind ourselves of the other side of the equation. As Hunsley, Lee, and Aubrey (1999) concluded over a decade ago, "It is essential that policy-makers recognize the long-term costs of failing to invest in psychological services" (p. 237). Integration of mental health services into primary health care and collaborative care teams represent the way of the future (see Focus on Discovery 1.2).

MENTAL HEALTH LITERACY In July 2008, the Canadian Alliance on Mental Illness and Mental Health presented its report on Mental Health Literacy in Canada. Funded by Health Canada, the report is the culmination of approximately four years of research, planning, and consultation across Canada. Among the findings of the first phase of the national mental healt literacy survey:

- Canadians are optimistic about the prospect of recovery from common mental health problems.

FOCUS ON DISCOVERY 1.2
THE WAY OF THE FUTURE: INTEGRATION AND COLLABORATIVE CARE

The WHO and World Organization of Family Doctors (WON-CA) are advocating for the integration of mental health services into primary health care as a viable, cost-effective way of ensuring that people receive needed mental health care (see Bacic, February 2009). Presumably, offering a full package of primary health care-led services over a 10-year period would require an investment of $0.30 (U.S.) per capita per year in lower middle-income countries and only $0.20 in low-income countries. However, as we have noted, even in a high-income country such as Canada, with a higher investment in mental health relative to low-income countries, low socio-economic status can be a barrier to mental health service use.

In a comprehensive review, Franx et al. (2008) concluded that there is a positive impact of multidisciplinary teams and integrated care changes on outcomes for people with severe mental disorders, relative to conventional services. The improved quality of care has positive effects on symptom severity, functioning, employment, and housing. Similarly, Smolders et al. (2008) reviewed the relevant literature related to improving care for anxiety patients and concluded that collaborative care models that involve combinations of clinician and patient education, enhanced support from specialist psychiatric services, and monitoring of drug concordance can be clinically effective.

In Canada, psychologists can play an important role via involvement in new, comprehensive approaches to community-based care that require interdisciplinary skills and integrated teams that provide a full range of health and other services (including psychological services) to people with mental disorders. In 2006, the University of Western Ontario received a grant under Health Canada's initiative that seeks to "change the way we educate health providers so Canadians will have better and faster access to the health-care provider they need when they need it, ultimately boosting the satisfaction of both patients and health-care providers" (Health Canada, n.d.). The overall goal of Creating Interprofessional Collaborative Teams for Comprehensive Mental Health Services was to facilitate collaboration among professionals in both education and practice settings (i.e., community agencies that offer student placement). The 22-month project relied on the involvement of numerous partners from academia (e.g., medicine and psychiatry, clinical psychology, nursing, social work, and occupational and physical therapy) and the community (e.g., community agencies that provide mental health and homelessness services, including a psychiatric consumer-run peer support self-help organization). The findings indicated that students are interested in interprofessional collaboration and valued the collaborative learning experiences leading to a number of recommendations and recognition that "meaningful, substantial change in educational and practices settings and in people's beliefs and practices takes significant time" (Forchuk & Vingilis, 2008, p. 8). Nonetheless, psychology can play an important role in the change process that will undoubtedly take many years but could lead to the effective implementation of evidence into mental health practice (see Grol, 2008).

- Most Canadians see mental health as a medical problem (66% recommend medical intervention for schizophrenia, 61% for depression, and 46% for anxiety).
- Many Canadians are cautious about the use of psychiatric medications (e.g., while 60% believe that antidepressants can be helpful, 51% agree that they can be harmful).
- Canadians prefer a holistic treatment approach but are largely unaware of the range of available treatment options.
- About 90% of Canadians believe that anyone can suffer from a mental disorder.
- Common mental problems, such as anxiety or depression, are viewed as more likely caused by psychosocial factors whereas mental illnesses such as schizophrenia are viewed as more serious and more likely caused by biomedical factors.
- Canadians might not seek help even if available because of shame and stigma, especially for serious mental health problems.

You can take the mental health literacy survey yourself at www.camimh.ca/mental_health_literacy.html.

There is room for improvement in our mental health literacy. A next step will be the development of an Integrated National Strategy since enhanced mental health literacy can confer numerous benefits, including prevention, early recognition and intervention, and reduction of stigma.

SUMMARY

- The study of psychopathology is a search for why people behave, think, and feel in unexpected, sometimes bizarre, and typically self-defeating ways. Much less is known than we would like.
- This book will focus on the ways in which psychopathologists have been trying to determine the causes of abnormal behaviour and what they know about preventing and alleviating it.
- Several characteristics are considered in evaluating whether a behaviour is abnormal: statistical infrequency, violation of societal norms, personal distress, disability or dysfunction, and unexpectedness. Each characteristic tells us something about what can be considered abnormal, but none by itself provides a fully satisfactory definition. It is impossible to offer a simple definition that captures abnormality in its entirety.
- The field of abnormal psychology has its origins in ancient demonology and crude medical theorizing. Since the beginning of scientific inquiry into abnormal behaviour, two major points of view have vied for attention: the somatogenic, which assumes that every mental aberration is caused by a physical malfunction; and the psychogenic, which assumes that the person's body is intact and that difficulties are to be explained in psychological terms.
- The somatogenic viewpoint originated in the writings of Hippocrates. After the fall of Greco-Roman civilization, it became less prominent, but then re-emerged in the eighteenth and nineteenth centuries through the writings of such people as Kraepelin.
- The psychogenic viewpoint is akin to early demonology. Its more modern version emerged in the nineteenth century from the work of Charcot and the seminal writings of Breuer and Freud.
- We examined a number of issues and events that are of historical and current relevance to students in a Canadian setting or to students who are particularly interested in developments in Canada. For example, we described the role of Dorothea Dix and the confluence of factors that led to the development of the first asylums and that ushered in the institution-building era in Canada. Despite humane motives, the long-term results were not very positive, as we learned from our discussion of provincial psychiatric hospitals in the latter part of the twentieth century. In Canada the current emphasis is on psychiatric hospital bed reduction and closure.
- Public perception of the mentally ill can be negative at times. If people's attitudes are currently more favourable than in the past, it is in part due to the efforts of Clarence Hincks and the Canadian Mental Health Association.
- The mental health system in Canada is closely tied to medicare, the universal health care system. The system will face many challenges in the future. There is a need for an increased focus on and funding for community-based interventions and prevention programs.
- The report from the Commission on the Future of Health Care in Canada (the Romanow Report) recommended that mental health be made a priority within the system. Specific recommendations included broadening medicare to include a limited number of home care services and some drug treatments.
- The Senate Committee Final Report (the Kirby Report) relating to mental health, mental illness, and addiction made 118 recommendations, including establishing a Canadian mental health commission to focus national attention on mental illness, and a proposal to fund the development of a community-based system of mental health service delivery.

KEY TERMS

abnormal behaviour (p. 3)
accountability (p. 31)
assessment (p. 5)
asylums (p. 9)
bedlam (p. 9)
best practice model (p. 26)
Canadian Mental Health Association (p. 20)
cathartic method (p. 17)
clinical psychologist (p. 5)
clinician (p. 5)
community psychology (p. 29)
community treatment order (p. 15)
counselling psychologist (p. 6)
deinstitutionalization (p. 25)

demonology (p. 6)
diagnosis (p. 5)
dissociative identity disorder (p. 20)
evidence-based treatment (p. 27)
exorcism (p. 6)
general paresis (p. 16)
germ theory (of disease) (p. 16)
medicare (p. 24)
mental health literacy (p. 22)
mental health status (p. 24)
moral treatment (p. 10)
normal curve (p. 3)
prevention (p. 29)
provincial psychiatric hospital (p. 14)

psychiatric nurse (p. 6)
Psychiatrist (p. 6)
psychoactive drugs (p. 6)
Psychoanalyst (p. 6)
psychogenesis (p. 7)
psychopathology (p. 3)
psychotherapy (p. 5)
schizophrenia (p. 19)
social worker (p. 6)
somatogenesis (p. 7)
stereotyping (p. 20)
stigmatization (p. 20)
syndrome (p. 16)
trepanning (p. 6)

REFLECTIONS: PAST, PRESENT, AND FUTURE

- In your opinion, based on your reading and thinking about the material presented in this first chapter, what is the meaning or significance of each of the quotations presented at the beginning of the chapter? Do you agree with the theme of each quotation?

- Think about the material presented in this chapter and develop your own comprehensive definition of abnormal psychology. When you have finished the exercise, turn to Chapter 3 and think about the definition accepted by the American (and Canadian) Psychiatric Association in the current version of the *Diagnostic and Statistical Manual of Mental Disorders* or *DSM-IV-TR* (American Psychiatric Association, 2000).

- Think of someone you have heard about (or possibly someone you know) who appears to suffer from a psychological disorder or to behave abnormally at times. How would you conceptualize that person's disorder or behaviour in terms of the somatogenic and psychogenic hypotheses? We will examine modern scientific perspectives in the next chapter. You should know that current views typically integrate several perspectives or paradigms.

- Is mental health the "orphan child" of medicare? Would you and your family and friends be willing to pay an extra nickel a drink to help cover most of the cost of the Senate Committee's proposed Mental Health Transition Fund?

- How should we try to help the person who has a psychological disorder or problem? Are you in favour of biological interventions, psychological treatments, self-help, or social change? Do our views about the causes of psychological disorders affect our beliefs in how they should be treated?

2 CURRENT PARADIGMS AND THE ROLE OF CULTURAL FACTORS

Tom Thomson, *The West Wind*, 1917, oil on canvas, 120.7 × 137.2 cm, Art Gallery of Ontario, Toronto. Gift of the Canadian Club of Toronto, 1926. ©2007 AGO

"Luke, you're going to find that many of the truths we cling to depend greatly on our own point of view."
—Ben (Obi-Wan) Kenobi, Return of the Jedi (1983)

"We are too much accustomed to attribute to a single cause that which is the product of several, and the majority of our controversies come from that."
—Baron Justus von Liebig (1803–73)

"Culture is the whole complex of relationships, knowledge, languages, social institutions, beliefs, values, and ethical rules that bind people together and give a collective and its individual members a sense of who they are and where they belong."
—Royal Commission on Aboriginal Peoples
(1996, p. 25)

The subject of Chapter 1 was the nature of abnormality—its history and how it has been defined by characteristics such as personal distress and the violation of norms. We ended the chapter with a summary of current issues related to Canada's mental health system. In this chapter, we consider current paradigms of abnormal behaviour and treatment. A paradigm is a set of basic assumptions, a general perspective, that defines how to conceptualize and study a subject, how to gather and interpret relevant data, even how to think about a particular subject. Our discussion of paradigms lays the groundwork for the examination of the major categories of disorders and intervention. Following our discussion of paradigms, we will examine the role of cultural factors in psychopathology from a Canadian perspective.

THE ROLE OF PARADIGMS

Science is bound by the limitations imposed on scientific inquiry by the current state of knowledge. It is also bound by whether the scientist can remain objective when trying to understand and study abnormal behaviour. Unfortunately, science is not a completely objective and certain enterprise. Rather, as suggested by philosopher of science Thomas Kuhn (1962), subjective factors as well as limitations in our perspective on the universe enter into the conduct of scientific inquiry.

Central to any application of scientific principles, in Kuhn's view, is the notion of **paradigm**, the conceptual framework or approach within which the scientist works. A paradigm is a set of basic assumptions that outline the particular universe of scientific inquiry. It has profound implications for how scientists operate, for "[people] whose research is based on shared paradigms are committed to the same rules and standards for scientific practice" (Kuhn, 1962, p. 11). Paradigms specify what problems scientists will investigate and how they will go about the investigation. Paradigms are an intrinsic part of a science, serving the vital function of indicating the rules to be followed.

A paradigm injects inevitable biases into the definition and collection of data and may also affect the interpretation of facts. In other words, the meaning or import given to data may depend to a considerable extent on a paradigm. In this chapter, we will describe the major paradigms of abnormal psychology and provide an idea of how they operate. We first present four major types of paradigms: biological, cognitive-behavioural, psychoanalytic, and humanistic-existential. The psychodynamic and humanistic-existential paradigms have become less influential over the years, but have some modern applications and themes that continue to have a significant impact.

Our discussion of each paradigm will conclude with an evaluation section. These sections will focus on the paradigm itself and, briefly, on treatment. Treatments will be evaluated in greater detail in the chapters dealing with specific disorders as well as in Chapter 17.

Current thinking about abnormal behaviour tends to be multi-faceted, and contemporary views of abnormal behaviour and its treatment tend to integrate several paradigms.

Accordingly, later in this chapter we will describe two highly influential paradigms—the diathesis–stress and biopsychosocial—that provide the basis for an integrative approach.

THE BIOLOGICAL PARADIGM

"Biology will not replace psychology within our explanatory systems. Rather we will slowly clarify, through progress in neuroscience, how the brain implements psychological functions. That iterative process will deepen our understanding of both biological and psychological processes."

—Kenneth S. Kendler, Explanatory Models for Psychiatric Illness (2008, p. 700).

The **biological paradigm** of abnormal behaviour is a continuation of the somatogenic hypothesis. This broad perspective holds that mental disorders are caused by aberrant biological processes. This paradigm has often been referred to as the **medical model** or **disease model**.

The study of abnormal behaviour is linked historically to medicine. Early and contemporary workers have used the model of physical illness as the basis for understanding deviant behaviour. Within the field of abnormal behaviour, the terminology of medicine is pervasive. As we described earlier, when Louis Pasteur discovered the relationship between bacteria and disease and soon thereafter postulated viruses, the germ theory of disease provided a new explanation for pathology. External symptoms were assumed to be produced through infection of the body by minute organisms and viruses. For a time, the germ theory was the paradigm of medicine, but it soon became apparent that this theory could not account for all diseases. Heart disease is one example. Many factors—genetic makeup, smoking, obesity, life stress, and perhaps even a person's personality—are causes of heart disease. Medical illnesses can differ widely from one another in their causes. However, they all share one characteristic: in all of them, some biological process is disrupted or not functioning normally. That is why we call this the biological paradigm.

The biological paradigm was the dominant paradigm in Canada and elsewhere from the late 1800s until at least the middle of the twentieth century. An extreme example of its influence is Hall's (1900) use of gynecological procedures to treat "insanity" in women from British Columbia. He maintained that "insanity exists when the Ego is dominated and controlled by the influence from a diseased periphery nerve tract or center ... the removal of a small part of the physical disease might result in the restoration of the balance of power to such an organism and diminish if not remove the abnormal psychic phenomena" (Hall, 1900, p. 3). Removal of ovarian cysts or the entire ovaries was employed as treatment for melancholia, mania, and delusions. In one such example, "Mrs. D" was reported to have delusions that her husband was trying to poison her, and she would frequently wander away from home. Her behaviour was attributed to a cyst "the size of a walnut," and both her ovaries were removed as the form of treatment.

CONTEMPORARY APPROACHES TO THE BIOLOGICAL PARADIGM

More sophisticated approaches are used today, of course, and there is now an extensive literature on biological factors relevant to psychopathology. Heredity probably predisposes a person to have an increased risk of developing schizophrenia (see Chapter 11), depression may result from chemical imbalances within the brain (Chapter 8), anxiety disorders may stem from a defect within the autonomic nervous system that causes a person to be too easily aroused (Chapter 6), and dementia can be traced to impairments in structures of the brain (Chapter 16). In each case, the psychopathology is viewed as caused by the disturbance of some biological process. Those working with the biological paradigm assume that answers to puzzles of psychopathology will be found within the body. In this section, we will look at three areas of research within this paradigm in which the data are particularly interesting: behaviour genetics, molecular genetics, and biochemistry.

BEHAVIOUR GENETICS When the ovum, the female reproductive cell, is joined by the male's spermatozoon, a zygote, or fertilized egg, is produced. It has 46 chromosomes, the number characteristic of a human being. Each chromosome is made up of thousands of **genes**, the carriers of the genetic information (DNA) passed from parents to child.

Behaviour genetics is the study of individual differences in behaviour that are attributable in part to differences in genetic makeup. The total genetic makeup of an individual, consisting of inherited genes, is referred to as the genotype. An individual's **genotype** is his or her unobservable genetic constitution; in contrast, an individual's **phenotype** is the totality of his or her observable, behavioural characteristics, such as level of anxiety. The genotype is fixed at birth, but it should not be viewed as a static entity. Genes controlling various features of development switch off and on at specific times to control aspects of physical development.

The phenotype changes over time and is viewed as the product of an interaction between the genotype and the environment. For example, an individual may be born with the capacity for high intellectual achievement, but whether he or she develops this genetically given potential depends on such environmental factors as upbringing and education. Hence, any measure of intelligence is best viewed as an index of the phenotype.

It is critical to recognize that various clinical syndromes are disorders of the phenotype, not of the genotype. Thus, it is not correct to speak of the direct inheritance of schizophrenia or anxiety disorders; at most, only the genotypes for these disorders can be inherited. Whether these genotypes will eventually engender the phenotypic behaviour disorder will depend on environment and experience. A predisposition, also known as a *diathesis*, may be inherited, but not the disorder itself.

The study of behaviour genetics has relied on four basic methods to uncover whether a predisposition for psychopathology is inherited: comparison of members of a family,

Behaviour genetics studies the degree to which characteristics such as physical resemblance or psychopathology are shared by family members because of shared genes. The University of British Columbia twin study led by Kerry Jang (shown here) and John Livesley is a long-term investigation of the contribution of shared genes to personality factors and behavioural disorders. Courtesy of Kerry Jang.

comparison of pairs of twins, the investigation of adoptees, and linkage analysis. The **family method** can be used to study a genetic predisposition among members of a family because the average number of genes shared by two blood relatives is known. Children receive a random sample of half their genes from one parent and half from the other; therefore, on average, siblings as well as parents and their children are identical in 50% of their genetic background. People who share 50% of their genes with a given individual are called *first-degree relatives* of that person. Relatives not as closely related share fewer genes. Nephews and nieces share 25% of the genetic makeup of an uncle and are called *second-degree relatives*. If a predisposition for a mental disorder can be inherited, a study of the family should reveal a relationship between the number of shared genes and the prevalence of the disorder in relatives.

The starting point in such investigations is the collection of a sample of individuals who bear the diagnosis in question. These people are referred to as **index cases**, or **probands**. Then, relatives are studied to determine the frequency with which the same diagnosis might be applied to them. If a genetic predisposition to the disorder being studied is present, first-degree relatives of the index cases should have the disorder at a rate higher than that found in the general population. For example, about 10% of the first-degree relatives of index cases with schizophrenia can be diagnosed as having schizophrenia, compared with about 1% of the general population.

In the **twin method**, both **monozygotic (MZ) twins** and **dizygotic (DZ) twins** are compared. MZ, or identical, twins develop from a single fertilized egg and are genetically the same. DZ, or fraternal, pairs develop from separate eggs and are on average only 50% alike genetically, no more alike than any other two siblings. MZ twins are always the same sex, but DZ twins can be either the same or the opposite sex. Twin studies begin with diagnosed cases and then search for the presence of the disorder in the other twin. When the twins are similar diagnostically, they are said to be concordant. To the extent that a predisposition for a mental disorder can be inherited, **concordance** for the disorder should be greater in genetically identical MZ pairs than in DZ pairs. When the MZ concordance rate is higher than the DZ rate, the characteristic being studied is said to be heritable. We will see in later chapters that the concordance for many forms of psychopathology is higher in MZ twins than in DZ twins.

Although the methodology of the family and twin studies is clear, the data they yield are not always easy to interpret. Let us assume that children of parents with panic disorder (see Chapter 6) are themselves more likely than average to have panic disorder. Does this mean that a predisposition for this anxiety disorder is genetically transmitted? Not necessarily. The greater number of children with panic disorder could reflect the child-rearing practices of the panic disorder parents, as well as the children's imitation of adult behaviour. In other words, the data show that panic disorder runs in families, but that a genetic predisposition is not necessarily involved.

The ability to offer a genetic interpretation of data from twin studies hinges on what is called the *equal environment assumption*. The equal environment assumption is that the environmental factors that are partial causes of concordance are equally influential for MZ pairs and DZ pairs. This does not mean that the environments of MZ and DZ twins are equal in all respects. The assumption of equality applies only to factors that are plausible environmental causes of psychopathology. The equal environment assumption would assert that MZ pairs and DZ pairs have equivalent numbers of stressful life experiences. In general, the equal environment assumption seems to be reasonable, although it is clearly in need of further study (Kendler, 1993).

Other factors can also complicate the results of twin research. In a study of post-traumatic stress disorder (an anxiety disorder discussed in Chapter 6) in community residents, Stein et al. (2002) identified three factors as biasing heritability estimates: violation of the equal environments assumption, the sex of the participant, and his or her age when the assessment took place. When they controlled statistically for the effects of age and sex differences, they found that genetic and non-shared environmental factors contributed to symptoms of post-traumatic stress disorder. Analyses of the role of these factors in a person's exposure to traumatic events revealed that only environmental factors contributed to exposure to events involving non-assaultive traumas (e.g., motor vehicle accidents, natural disasters), but both genetic and environmental factors contributed to exposure to assaultive traumas (e.g., sexual assaults). Thus, genetic factors may determine, in part, the extent to which a person is likely to experience post-traumatic stress after an assaultive trauma. This study is illuminating because it is the first to examine this issue in a non-military sample and the first to include women. Unfortunately, it is limited because the researchers had to rely on self-report measures of trauma.

Researchers using the **adoptees method** study children with abnormal disorders who were adopted and reared apart from their parents. Though infrequent, this situation has the benefit of eliminating the effects of being raised by disordered parents. If a high frequency of panic disorder were found in children reared apart from parents who also had panic disorder, we would have support for the theory that a genetic predisposition figures in the disorder. (The study of MZ twins reared apart would also be valuable, but this situation occurs so rarely that there is virtually no research using this method to study psychopathology. Research involving separated twins does, however, exist in the study of the inheritance of personality traits, as we will see in Chapter 13.)

MOLECULAR GENETICS Molecular genetics is a highly advanced approach that goes beyond mere attempts to show whether a disorder has a genetic component; it tries to specify the particular gene or genes involved and the precise functions of these genes.

Each cell consists of 46 chromosomes (23 pairs) with thousands of genes per chromosome. The chromosomes are our genetic material and one of each pair comes from a person's mother and his or her father. The term "allele" refers to any one of several DNA codings that occupy the same position or location on a chromosome. A person's genotype is his or her set of alleles.

The term "genetic polymorphism" refers to variability among members of the species. It involves differences in the DNA sequence that can manifest in very different forms among members in the same habitat. It entails mutations in a chromosome that can be induced or naturally occurring.

For many years, genetic discoveries involving humans have primarily been the product of extensive lines of research conducted initially with animals. Discoveries are made in animal research, and then, where feasible, the generalizability and applicability to humans has been evaluated. For instance, it was discovered in 2004 with research on male meadow voles that manipulating a gene, the vasopressin receptor, by locating it in the reward centre of the brain had the effect of making an amorous, promiscuous vole into a monogamous vole (Lim et al., 2004). It is possible that a similar process determines whether humans refrain from having more than one partner. Another focus of current animal research involves attempts to identify specific genes that contribute to longevity. Is living a longer life, at least in part, determined genetically?

Linkage analysis is a method in molecular genetics that is used to study people. Researchers using this method typically study families in which a disorder is heavily concentrated. They collect diagnostic information and blood samples from affected individuals and their relatives and use the blood samples to study the inheritance pattern of characteristics whose genetics are fully understood, referred to as *genetic markers*. Eye colour, for example, is known to be controlled by a gene in a specific location on a specific chromosome. If the occurrence of a form of psychopathology among relatives goes along with the occurrence of another characteristic whose genetics are known (the genetic marker), it is concluded that the gene predisposing individuals to the psychopathology is on the same chromosome and in a similar location on that chromosome (i.e., it is linked) as the gene controlling the other characteristic. An illustration of linkage analysis is research conducted in Toronto that has established an association between obsessive-compulsive disorder (OCD) and the gamma-aminobutyric acid (GABA) type B receptor 1 (GABBR1) gene (Zai et al., 2005). We will see several additional examples of linkage analysis in subsequent chapters, especially when we discuss mood disorders (Chapter 8) and schizophrenia (Chapter 11). However, it should be noted that replicable support for candidate genes is not always or even usually found (see Crow, 2007; Hamilton, 2008). The greatest success of the method thus far has been in identifying specific genes on several chromosomes that are extremely important in Alzheimer's disease (see Chapter 16). However, other exciting findings are continuing to emerge. For instance, a study of genetic linkage in adolescents and young adults indicated that a locus on chromosome 9 is associated with enhanced risk for externalizing psychopathology (i.e., aggression and conduct disorder) (see Stallings et al., 2005).

Note that researchers in this area often hypothesize *gene–environment interactions*. This is the notion that a disorder or related symptoms are the joint product of a genetic vulnerability and specific environmental experiences or conditions. According to Moffitt, Caspi, and Rutter (2006), when such interactions were found in the past, they were viewed as rare and atypical, but these authors make a strong argument that such interactions are much more common and important (both theoretically and practically) than previously imagined. The possibility of gene–environment interactions is becoming a predominant theme in depression literature, as illustrated by a recent study by Hayden and colleagues at the University of Western Ontario (Hayden et al., 2008). This study posits a link among the serotonin transporter promoter (5-HTTLPR) genotype, the development of cognitive vulnerabilities, stressful events, and depression.

A focus on gene–environment interactions is important in qualifying the perceived influence of genetic factors. One concern is that an exclusive focus on genetic factors promotes the notion that illness and mental illness are predetermined. A recent Canadian survey indicated that three out of five respondents believed that genetic factors pose a moderate risk or high risk for health problems, including depression (Etchegary, Lemyre, Wilson, & Krewski, 2009). Nevertheless, it was still concluded that most Canadians do not hold overly deterministic views of the causes of illness and this is encouraging because believing that "biology is destiny" could limit the extent to which people try to modify lifestyle and environmental factors that contribute to health and mental health problems.

NEUROSCIENCE AND BIOCHEMISTRY IN THE NERVOUS SYSTEM *Neuroscience* is the study of the brain and the nervous system. Neuroscience can come in numerous forms, including cognitive neuroscience, molecular neuroscience, and cellular neuroscience. The nervous system is composed of billions of neurons. Although neurons differ in some respects, each **neuron** has four major parts: (1) the cell body; (2) several dendrites (the short and thick extensions); (3) one or more axons of varying lengths (usually only one long and thin axon extending a considerable distance from the cell body); and (4) terminal buttons on the many end branches of the axon (Figure 2.1). When a

FIGURE 2.1 The neuron, the basic unit of the nervous system

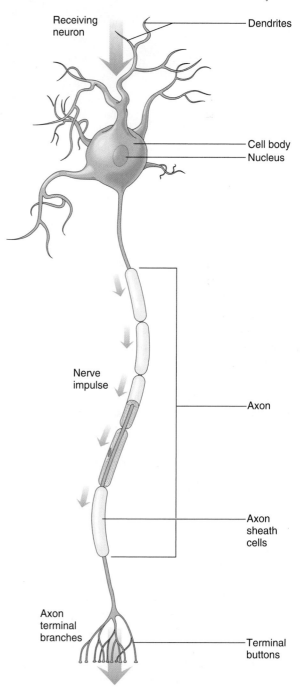

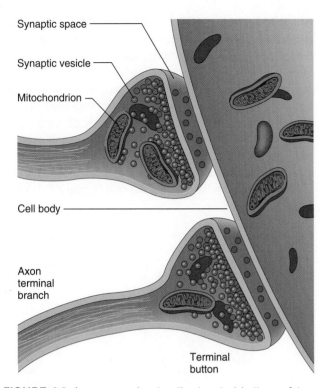

Synaptic space

Synaptic vesicle

Mitochondrion

Cell body

Axon
terminal
branch

Terminal
button

FIGURE 2.2 A synapse, showing the terminal buttons of two axon branches in close contact with a very small portion of the cell body of another neuron

neuron is appropriately stimulated at its cell body or through its dendrites, a **nerve impulse**, which is a change in the electric potential of the cell, travels down the axon to the terminal endings. Between the terminal endings of the sending axon and the cell membrane of the receiving neuron, there is a small gap, called the **synapse** (see Figure 2.2).

For a nerve impulse to pass from one neuron to another and for communication to occur, the impulse must have a way of bridging the synaptic gap. The terminal buttons of each axon contain synaptic vesicles, small structures that are filled with **neurotransmitters**, chemical substances that allow a nerve impulse to cross the synapse. Nerve impulses cause the synaptic vesicles to release molecules of their transmitter substances, and these molecules flood the synapse and diffuse toward the receiving, or postsynaptic, neuron. The cell membrane of the postsynaptic cell contains proteins, called receptor sites, that are configured so that specific neurotransmitters can fit into them. When a neurotransmitter fits into a receptor site, a message can be sent to the postsynaptic cell. What actually happens to the postsynaptic neuron depends on its integrating thousands of similar messages. Sometimes these messages are excitatory, leading to the creation of a nerve impulse in the postsynaptic cell; at other times, the messages can be inhibitory, making the postsynaptic cell less likely to fire.

Once a presynaptic neuron (the sending neuron) has released its neurotransmitter, the last step is for the synapse to be returned to its normal state. Not all of the released neurotransmitter has found its way to postsynaptic receptors.

Some of what remains in the synapse is broken down by enzymes, and some is pumped back into the presynaptic cell through a process called **reuptake**.

Several key neurotransmitters have been implicated in psychopathology. Norepinephrine, a neurotransmitter of the peripheral **sympathetic nervous system**, is involved in producing states of high arousal and thus may be involved in anxiety disorders. Both serotonin and dopamine are neurotransmitters in the brain. Serotonin may be involved in depression, and dopamine in schizophrenia. Another important brain transmitter is GABA, which inhibits some nerve impulses and may be involved in anxiety disorders.

Maturational changes influence neurotransmitter levels. For instance, the onset of puberty in adolescents results in a decrease in serotonin and a decrease in dopamine activity in certain cortical areas. These changes and increases in the secretion of gonadal hormones as the brain continues to develop throughout adolescence have been implicated as contributing to increased risk for psychopathology during adolescence (Walker, 2002).

Some of the theories linking neurotransmitters to psychopathology have proposed that a given disorder is caused by either too much or too little of a particular transmitter (e.g., mania results from too much norepinephrine, and anxiety disorders from too little GABA). Neurotransmitters are synthesized in the neuron through a series of metabolic steps, beginning with an amino acid. Each reaction along the way to producing an actual transmitter is catalyzed by an enzyme, speeding up the metabolic process. Too much or too little of a particular transmitter could result from an error in these metabolic pathways. Similar disturbances in the amounts of specific transmitters could result from alterations in the usual processes by which transmitters are deactivated after being released into the synapse. For example, a failure to pump leftover neurotransmitter molecules back into the presynaptic cell (reuptake) would leave excess transmitter molecules in the synapse. Then, when a new nerve impulse caused further neurotransmitter substances to be released into the synapse, the postsynaptic neuron would, in a sense, get a double dose of neurotransmitter, making it more likely for a new nerve impulse to be created.

Finally, contemporary research has focused to a large extent on the possibility that the receptors are at fault in some psychopathologies. If the receptors on the postsynaptic neuron were too numerous or too easily excited, the result would be akin to having too much transmitter released. There would simply be more sites available with which the neurotransmitter could interact, increasing the chances that the postsynaptic neuron would be stimulated. The delusions and hallucinations of schizophrenia may result from an overabundance of dopamine receptors.

For many years, researchers and clinicians have attempted to observe directly or make inferences about the functioning of the brain and other parts of the nervous system in their efforts to understand both normal and abnormal psychological functioning. See Focus on Discovery 2.1 for a description of the structure and function of the human brain. We will discuss aspects of the autonomic nervous system and the neuroendocrine system in subsequent chapters. These systems are both important in the study of emotional behaviour and psychopathology.

Focus on Discovery 2.2 extends this discussion of brain functioning and illustrates the relevance of neuroscience in abnormal behaviour by examining recent research in attention deficit hyperactivity disorder (ADHD). This disorder is the most commonly diagnosed behavioural disorder in childhood and is described in more detail in Chapter 15.

FOCUS ON DISCOVERY 2.1
STRUCTURE AND FUNCTION OF THE HUMAN BRAIN

Inside the skull, the brain is enveloped within three layers of non-neural tissue, membranes referred to as **meninges**. Viewed from the top, the brain is divided by a midline fissure into two mirror-image **cerebral hemispheres**, together constituting most of the cerebrum. The cerebrum is the "thinking" centre of the brain, which includes the cortex and subcortical structures such as the basal ganglia and limbic system. The major connection between the two hemispheres is a band of nerve fibres called the **corpus callosum**. Figure 2.3 shows the surface of one of the cerebral hemispheres. The upper, side, and some of the lower surfaces of the hemispheres form the **cerebral cortex**. The cortex consists of six layers of tightly packed neuron cell bodies with many short, unsheathed interconnecting processes. These neurons, estimated to number 10 to 15 billion, make up a thin outer covering, the so-called grey matter of the brain. The cortex is vastly convoluted; the ridges are called **gyri**, and the depressions between them **sulci**, or fissures. Deep fissures divide the cerebral hemispheres into several distinct areas called lobes. The **frontal lobe** lies in front of the central sul-

cus; the **parietal lobe** is behind it and above the lateral sulcus; the **temporal lobe** is located below the lateral sulcus; and the **occipital lobe** lies behind the parietal and temporal lobes. Different functions tend to be localized in particular areas of the lobes: vision in the occipital; discrimination of sounds in the temporal; reasoning and other higher mental processes, as well as the regulation of fine voluntary movement, in the frontal; initiation of movements of the skeletal musculature in a band in front of the central sulcus; and receipt of sensations of touch, pressure, pain, temperature, and body position from skin, muscles, tendons, and joints in a band behind the central sulcus.

The two hemispheres of the brain have different functions. The left hemisphere, which generally controls the right half of the body because of the crossing over of motor and sensory fibres, is responsible for speech and, according to some neuropsychologists, for analytical thinking in right-handed people and in a fair number of left-handed people as well. The right hemisphere controls the left side of the body, discerns spatial relations and patterns, and is involved in emotion and intuition. But analytical thinking cannot be located exclusively in the left hemisphere, or intuitive and even creative thinking exclusively in the right; the two hemispheres communicate with each other constantly via the corpus callosum. Localization of apparently different modes of thought is probably not as clear-cut as some people would believe.

If the brain is sliced in half, separating the two cerebral hemispheres (see Figure 2.4), additional important features can be seen. The grey matter of the cerebral cortex does not extend throughout the interior of the brain. Much of the interior is **white matter**, made up of large tracts or bundles of myelinated (sheathed) fibres that connect cell bodies in the cortex with those in the spinal cord and other centres lower in the brain. These centres are pockets of grey matter, referred to as **nuclei**. The nuclei serve both as way stations, connecting tracts from the cortex with other ascending and descending tracts, and as integrating motor and sensory control centres. Some cortical cells project their long fibres or axons to motor neurons in the spinal cord, but others project them only as far as these clusters of interconnecting neuron cell bodies. Four masses are deep within each hemisphere, called collectively the *basal ganglia*. Also deep within the brain are cavities called **ventricles**; these are continuous with the central canal of the spinal cord and are filled with cerebrospinal fluid.

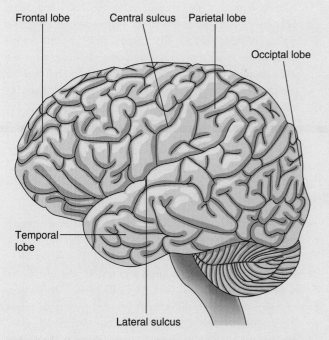

Frontal lobe   Central sulcus   Parietal lobe

Occipital lobe

Temporal lobe

Lateral sulcus

FIGURE 2.3 Surface of the left cerebral hemisphere, indicating the lobes and the two principal fissures of the cortex

Figure 2.4 depicts four important functional areas or structures:

1. The **diencephalon**, connected in the front with the hemispheres and behind with the midbrain, contains the **thalamus** and the **hypothalamus**, both consisting of groups of nuclei. The thalamus is a relay station for all sensory pathways except the olfactory. The nuclei making up the thalamus receive nearly all the impulses arriving from the different sensory areas of the body and then pass them on to the cerebrum, where they are interpreted as conscious sensations. The hypothalamus is the highest centre of integration for many visceral processes, regulating metabolism, temperature, perspiration, blood pressure, sleeping, and appetite.

2. The **midbrain** is a mass of nerve-fibre tracts connecting the cerebral cortex with the pons, the medulla oblongata, the cerebellum, and the spinal cord.

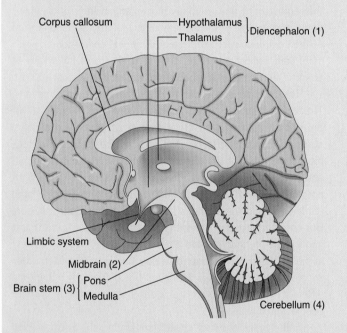

FIGURE 2.4 Slice of brain through the medial plane, showing the internal structures

3. The **brain stem** comprises the pons and the medulla oblongata and functions primarily as a neural relay station. The **pons** contains tracts that connect the cerebellum with the spinal cord and with motor areas of the cerebrum. The **medulla oblongata** serves as the main line of traffic for tracts ascending from the spinal cord and descending from the higher centres of the brain. At the bottom of the medulla, many of the motor fibres cross to the opposite side. The medulla also contains nuclei that maintain the regular life rhythms of the heartbeat, of the rising and falling diaphragm, and of the constricting and dilating blood vessels. In the core of the brain stem is the **reticular formation**, sometimes called the *reticular activating system* because of the important role it plays in arousal and alertness. The tracts of the pons and medulla send in fibres to connect with the profusely interconnected cells of the reticular formation, which in turn sends fibres to the cortex, the basal ganglia, the hypothalamus, the septal area, and the cerebellum.

4. The **cerebellum**, like the cerebrum, consists primarily of two deeply convoluted hemispheres with an exterior cortex of grey matter and an interior of white tracts. The cerebellum receives sensory information from the inner ear and from muscles, tendons, and joints. The information received and integrated relates to balance, posture, equilibrium, and to the smooth coordination of the body when in motion.

5. A fifth important part of the brain, the **limbic system**, comprises structures that are continuous with one another in the lower cerebrum and that developed earlier than the mammalian cerebral cortex. The limbic system controls the visceral and physical expressions of emotion—quickened heartbeat and respiration, trembling, sweating, and alterations in facial expressions—as well as appetite and other primary drives, namely, hunger, thirst, mating, defence, attack, and flight. Important structures in the limbic system are the cingulate gyrus, stretching about the corpus callosum; the septal area, which is anterior to the thalamus; the long, tube-like hippocampus, which stretches from the septal area into the temporal lobe; and the amygdala (one of the basal ganglia), which is embedded in the tip of the temporal lobe.

FOCUS ON DISCOVERY 2.2
THE NEUROSCIENCE OF ATTENTION DEFICIT HYPERACTIVITY DISORDER (ADHD)

At present, theory and research on the neuroscience of ADHD is one of the most exciting areas of inquiry in the field of the neuroscience of abnormal behaviour. In a recent review, Poissant, Emond, and Joyal (2008) concluded that there is extensive evidence implicating fronto striatal circuitry in ADHD (i.e., the lateral prefrontal cortex, the dorsal anterior cingulated cortex, and the caudate nucleus). According to the authors, other research highlights the potential significance of pervasive reductions in volume throughout the cerebrum and cerebellum. One intriguing study receiving

widespread interest found that ADHD clients experience delays in cortical maturation, as reflected by attaining peak levels of cortical thickness at an older age (Shaw et al., 2007). The sequence of development was the same for those with and without ADHD, but it was delayed by up to five years in ADHD clients. The delay in cortical maturation was most evident in the lateral prefrontal cortex, which is the region responsible for working memory and attention.

Related research on the cognitive neuroscience of attention has focused on the role of the dopaminergic and the noradrenergic neurotransmitter systems (Vaidya & Stollstorff, 2008). The dopaminergic hypothesis is that ADHD is due to a dopamine deficit believed to be genetic in origin.

Rosemary Tannock from the Hospital for Sick Children in Toronto is one of the leading Canadian researchers in this field. Tannock and her colleagues have been particularly critical of the lack of theoretical models of the causes of ADHD in the neuroscience field (see Coghill, Nigg, Rothenberger, Sonuga-Barke, & Tannock, 2005). In one of the most widely cited papers, Castellanos and Tannock (2002) suggested that three particular features of ADHD are particularly amenable to collaborative neuroscientific investigation: (1) a specific abnormality in reward-related circuitry that leads to shortened delay gradients; (2) deficits in temporal processing that result in high intrasubject intertrial variability; and (3) deficits in working memory. Tannock is in the process of creating a network of Canadian researchers focusing on the neuroscientific aspects of inattention.

BIOLOGICAL APPROACHES TO TREATMENT

An important implication of the biological paradigm is that prevention or treatment of mental disorders should be possible by altering bodily functioning. Certainly, if a deficiency in a particular biochemical substance is found to underlie or contribute to some problem, it makes sense to attempt to correct the imbalance by providing appropriate doses of the deficient chemical. In such cases, a clear connection exists between the cause of a disorder (a biological defect) and its treatment (a biological intervention).

Most biological interventions in common use, however, have not been derived from knowledge of what causes a given disorder. Nonetheless, the use of psychoactive drugs has been increasing. In 1985, psychoactive drugs were prescribed in the United States at about 33 million physician visits, and in 1994, at almost 46 million (Pincus et al., 1998). Tranquilizers such as Valium can be effective in reducing the tension associated with some anxiety disorders, perhaps by stimulating GABA neurons to inhibit other neural systems that create the physical symptoms of anxiety. Antidepressants (such as Prozac), now the most widely prescribed psychoactive drugs, increase neural transmission in neurons that use serotonin as a neurotransmitter by inhibiting the reuptake of serotonin. Antipsychotic drugs such as Clozaril, used in the treatment of schizophrenia, reduce the activity of neurons that use dopamine as a neurotransmitter by blocking their receptors. Stimulants such as Ritalin are often employed in treating children with attention deficit hyperactivity disorder. Stimulants increase the levels of several neurotransmitters that help children pay attention.

Given the specificity and complexity of drug interventions, including issues related to side effects and risks, we will discuss psychoactive drugs in greater detail in the context of our discussions of specific disorders. Drugs are an important component of any interventions for mental disorders. Indeed, for some disorders they are a necessary, even critical, intervention, such as for the schizophrenias and bipolar disorder. In contrast to psychological interventions that require some time to achieve effects, drugs can act efficiently and often provide symptomatic improvement relatively quickly. As an example, selective serotonin reuptake inhibitors (SSRIs) are frequently described as having a delayed onset. However, Mathews, Taylor, Freemantle, Geddes, and Bhagwagar (2006) incorporated data from 28 randomized controlled trials (RCTs) and concluded that treatment of depression with SSRIs rather than a placebo is associated with clinical improvement of symptoms by the end of the first week of use. They further concluded that improvement continues at a decreasing rate for at least six weeks.

Contemporary approaches to biological assessment are discussed in detail in Chapter 4. These approaches involve attempts to make inferences about the functioning of the nervous system (e.g., neuropsychological assessment) or to "see" the actual structure and functioning of the brain and other parts of the nervous system (e.g., magnetic resonance imaging (MRI)). For example, neuroimaging studies have become an increasingly important area of psychiatric research over the past 30 years and have advanced our understanding of the pathophysiology and treatment of disorders such as obsessive-compulsive disorder (OCD) (Friedlander & Desrocher, 2006), schizophrenia and bipolar disorder (McIntosh et al., 2008; Zipursky, Meyer, & Verhoeff, 2007), and depression and dementia (Zipursky et al., 2007). For example, Zipursky (2007) noted that due to findings from brain-imaging research, antipsychotic medications can now be prescribed at a fraction of the dosages considered standard just 10 years ago. Further, neuroimaging research is beginning to show the involvement of prefrontal and limbic regions in the perception and modulation of psychological stress (see Dedovic, D'Aguiar, & Pruessner, 2009) and to identify differences that might have significance related to the difference in vulnerability to psychological disorders in women and men (van Stegeren, 2009). Pine and Freedman (2009), in an editorial on recent MRI research involving children, commented that "MRI provides heretofore unseen opportunities to observe the living, functioning, thinking child's brain in action" and noted that it portends "unique, transformative changes in child psychiatry" (p. 4). The general public in Canada has become more aware of the potential usefulness of neuroimaging as a result of Daniel Levitin's book *This Is Your Brain on Music*. Levitin is a cognitive neuroscientist at McGill University in Montreal whose work is providing novel information on the functioning of the auditory cortex. Neuroimaging has not yet had a major impact on the diagnosis of psychiatric disorders (see Chapter 3).

It should be noted that a clinical scientist can believe in a biological basis for a mental problem yet recommend psychological intervention. Contemporary workers realize that non-biological interventions can have beneficial effects. For example, preventing a person from performing a compulsive ritual is an effective behavioural treatment for OCD that also has measureable effects on brain activity. Linden (2006) reviewed functional neuroimaging studies on the effects of psychotherapy. He found that studies of the effects of cognitive-behavioural therapy (CBT), described in a subsequent section, on OCD showed decreased metabolism in the right caudate nucleus, whereas CBT for phobia resulted in decreased activity in limbic and paralimbic areas. He noted that these effects are similar to those observed after successful treatment with SSRIs and concluded that it suggests "commonalities in the biological mechanisms of psycho- and pharmacotherapy" (p. 528). In contrast, in depression he noted both decreases and increases in prefrontal metabolism following psychological treatment and differences relative to drug treatment. Although the effects weren't clear-cut, they suggest the possibility of different mechanisms for the effects of the different types of intervention. Linden (2006) concluded that functional imaging could ultimately prove useful to monitor treatment effects and facilitate choice of intervention.

EVALUATING THE BIOLOGICAL PARADIGM

Over the past several decades, biological researchers have made great progress in elucidating brain-behaviour relationships and the role of specific genetic factors. Biologically based research on both causes and treatment of psychopathology is proceeding rapidly. Although we view these developments in a positive light, we also want to caution against reductionism. **Reductionism** refers to the view that whatever is being studied can and should be reduced to its most basic elements or constituents. In the case of mental disorders, the position proposes reducing complex mental and emotional responses to simple biology. Using this logic, the argument could be taken even further to propose that biology be reduced to atomic physics. In its extreme form, reductionism asserts that psychology, psychiatry, and psychopathology will ultimately be nothing more than biology. Indeed, back in 1989 a well-known psychiatrist and proponent of this view wrote an article entitled "Biological psychiatry: Is there any other kind?"

Although reductionism is an influential viewpoint among biological psychiatrists, in philosophical circles, it has been severely criticized. Once basic elements, such as individual nerve cells, are organized into more complex structures or systems, such as neural pathways or circuits, the properties of these systems cannot be deduced from the properties of the constituents. The whole is often greater than the sum of its parts. As for the field of abnormal psychology, problems such as delusional beliefs and dysfunctional attitudes may well be impossible to explain biologically, even with a detailed understanding of the behaviour of individual neurons (Turkheimer, 1998). Further, nervous system dysfunction is not always due to biological causes. It can be a result of psychological or social factors. Note too that psychological interventions can be as effective as drug treatment and produce changes in the functioning of our brains (e.g., Baxter et

al., 2000). In a recent review, Ian Gold (2009), the Canada Research Chair in philosophy and psychiatry at McGill University, examined the doctrine of reductionism in psychiatry and concluded that "there is little reason to think that any significant portion of psychiatric theory will be reduced to neuroscience or genetics" (p. 506). In a companion review, Joel Paris (2009), also from McGill's psychiatry department concluded that the applied neuroscience model is most appropriate to severe mental disorders, that psychiatric disorders cannot be reduced to abnormalities in neuronal or molecular activity, and that psychological problems need to be understood at multiple levels. As noted previously by Bennett and Hacker (2003) in the *Philosophical Foundations of Neuroscience*, psychology will not be reduced or eliminated by neuroscience! Nonetheless, insights from neuroscience promise to improve psychological treatments. For example, in his review of the mechanisms of exposure therapy Richard McNally concluded that, "psychological treatments for anxiety disorders have reached a plateau, and further advancements may arise from neighbouring disciplines such as neuroscience" (McNally, 2007, p.757).

We now consider psychological paradigms. The cognitive-behavioural paradigm is highly influential today and is regarded as a generally effective, evidence-based approach. We provide an overview of the **behavioural** (sometimes referred to as the **learning**) **paradigm** and cognitive (sometimes referred to separately as the cognitive paradigm) approaches that were eventually combined or integrated into the cognitive-behavioural paradigm. Our discussion of paradigms concludes with other psychological paradigms (i.e., the psychodynamic and humanistic-existential), which have less influence today than in the past, but still provide us with some important insights, principles, and treatment approaches. All of these approaches emphasize the role of social factors, including socio-cultural considerations and internal psychological processes. The role of early experience is central to both biological and psychological paradigms. Ultimately, our challenge will be to integrate the different biological and psychosocial approaches or viewpoints into a comprehensive, theoretically consistent, integrative paradigm.

THE COGNITIVE-BEHAVIOURAL PARADIGM

"Cognitive-behavioural therapy (CBT) has a wide-ranging empirical base, supporting its place as the evidence-based treatment of choice for the majority of psychological disorders."

—Waller, 2009, p. 119.

Contemporary versions of cognitive-behavioural therapy are primarily cognitive in their emphasis, but key principles from a behavioural or learning perspective have been incorporated as well.

THE BEHAVIOURAL PERSPECTIVE

Psychologists operating primarily from a behavioural perspective view abnormal behaviour as responses learned in the same ways other human behaviour is learned.

THE RISE OF BEHAVIOURISM John B. Watson (1878–1958) is a key figure in the rise of behaviourism. As a response to the focus on **introspection** favoured by many others in the field of human psychology, in 1913, Watson promoted a focus on behaviourism by extrapolating from the work of psychologists who were investigating learning in animals. Because of his efforts, the dominant focus of psychology switched from thinking to learning. **Behaviourism** can be defined as an approach that focuses on observable behaviour rather than on consciousness. Three types of learning have attracted the research efforts of psychologists.

Classical conditioning One type of learning, **classical conditioning**, was discovered by the Russian physiologist and Nobel laureate Ivan Pavlov (1849–1936) at the turn of the century. In Pavlov's studies of the digestive system, a dog was given meat powder to make it salivate. Before long, Pavlov's laboratory assistants became aware that the dog began salivating when it saw the person who fed it. As the experiment continued, the dog began to salivate even earlier, when it heard the footsteps of its feeder. Intrigued by these findings, Pavlov decided to study the dog's reactions systematically. In the first of many experiments, a bell was rung behind the dog, and then the meat powder was placed in its mouth. After this procedure had been repeated a number of times, the dog began salivating as soon as it heard the bell.

In this experiment, because the meat powder automatically elicits salivation with no prior learning, the powder is termed an **unconditioned stimulus** (UCS) and the response to it, salivation, an **unconditioned response** (UCR). When the offering of meat powder is preceded several times by the ringing of a bell, a neutral stimulus, the sound of the bell alone (the **conditioned stimulus**, CS) is able to elicit

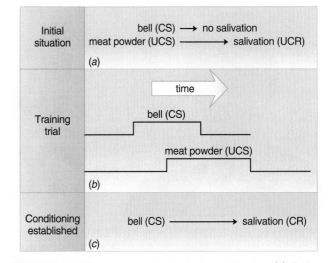

FIGURE 2.5 The process of classical conditioning. (a) Before learning, the meat powder (UCS) elicits salivation (UCR), but the bell (CS) does not. (b) A training or learning trial consists of presentations of the CS, followed closely by the UCS. (c) Classical conditioning has been accomplished when the previously neutral bell elicits salivation (CR)

the salivary response (the **conditioned response**, CR) (see Figure 2.5). The CR usually differs somewhat from the UCR (Rescorla, 1988), but these subtleties are beyond the needs of this book. As the number of paired presentations of the bell and the meat powder increases, the number of salivations elicited by the bell alone increases. **Extinction** refers to what happens to the CR when the repeated soundings of the bell are later not followed by meat powder; fewer and fewer salivations are elicited, and the CR gradually disappears.

A famous experiment, conducted by John Watson and Rosalie Rayner (1920), discovered that classical conditioning could instill pathological fear. They introduced a white rat to an 11-month-old boy, Little Albert, who indicated no fear of the animal. Whenever the boy reached for the rat, the experimenter made a loud noise (the UCS) by striking a steel bar behind Albert's head, causing him great fright (the UCR). After five such experiences, Albert became very frightened (the CR) by the sight of the white rat, even when the steel bar was not struck. The fear initially associated with the loud noise had come to be elicited by the previously neutral stimulus, the white rat (now the CS). This study suggests the possible association between classical conditioning and the development of certain emotional disorders, including phobias. Contemporary research in abnormal psychology has continued to implicate classical conditioning in the development of anxiety disorders (see Mineka & Oehlberg, 2008). The role of classical conditioning may be more pervasive than realized; indeed, a recent study conducted in Toronto indicated that the abnormal tendency of people with schizophrenia to make context-inappropriate associations may be an example of classical conditioning gone awry as strong associations are made to seemingly neutral stimuli (Jensen et al., 2008).

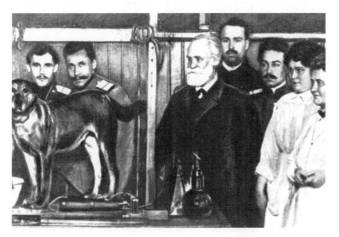

Ivan P. Pavlov, Russian physiologist and Nobel laureate, was responsible for extensive research and theory in classical conditioning. Culver Pictures Inc.

B. F. Skinner was responsible for the study of operant behaviour and the extension of this approach to education, psychotherapy, and society as a whole. John Wiley & Sons photo by Kathy Bendo.

Aggressive responses in children are often rewarded, which makes such behaviour more likely to occur in the future. © Image Source/CORBIS.

Operant conditioning Over 60 years ago, B. F. Skinner (1904–1990) introduced **operant conditioning**, so named because it applied to behaviour that operates on the environment. He reformulated the **law of effect** by shifting the focus from the linking of stimuli and responses (S-R connections) to the relationships between responses and their consequences or contingencies. This subtle distinction reflects Skinner's contention that stimuli do not so much get connected to responses as they become the occasions for responses to occur, if in the past they have been reinforced. Skinner introduced the concept of **discriminative stimulus** to refer to external events that in effect tell an organism that if it performs a certain behaviour, a certain consequence will follow.

Skinner distinguished two types of reinforcement that influence behaviour. **Positive reinforcement** refers to the strengthening of a tendency to respond by virtue of the presentation of a pleasant event, called a *positive reinforcer*. For example, a water-deprived pigeon will tend to repeat behaviours (operants) that are followed by the availability of water. **Negative reinforcement** also strengthens a response, but it does so via the removal of an aversive event, such as the cessation of electric shock. Skinner called such consequences *negative reinforcers*. Extrapolating his work with pigeons to human behaviour, Skinner argued that freedom of choice is a myth and that all behaviour is determined by the reinforcers provided by the environment.

Operant conditioning can produce abnormal behaviour. Consider a key feature of conduct disorder, a high frequency of aggressive behaviour (see Chapter 15). Aggression is often rewarded, as when one child hits another to get a toy (getting the toy is the reinforcer).

Modelling In real life, learning often goes on even in the absence of reinforcers. We all learn by watching and imitating others, a process called vicarious learning or **modelling**. Experimental work by Albert Bandura and others (see Canadian Contributions 2.1) has demonstrated that witnessing someone perform certain activities can increase or decrease diverse kinds of behaviour. Albert Bandura and Menlove (1968) used a modelling treatment to reduce fear of dogs in children. After witnessing a fearless model engage in various activities with a dog, initially fearful children became more willing to approach and handle a dog. Modelling may explain the acquisition of abnormal behaviour (see Askew & Field, 2008, for a review of the underlying mechanisms). Children of parents with phobias or substance-abuse problems may acquire similar behaviour patterns, in part through modelling.

CANADIAN CONTRIBUTIONS 2.1
ALBERT BANDURA: THE WORLD'S GREATEST LIVING PSYCHOLOGIST?

According to Haggbloom et al. (2002), Albert Bandura is the world's greatest living psychologist—fourth in the twentieth century in terms of his impact (behind Skinner, Piaget, and Freud). Born in Mundare, Alberta, in 1925, he obtained his early education in a one-room schoolhouse in this northern Alberta farming community. According to Bandura's (2007) autobiographical statement, his father worked laying railroad tracks for the trans-Canada rail line after immigrating from Poland, while his mother worked in the general store in town. As a student, Bandura received his B.A. degree in 1949 from the University of British Columbia and his Ph.D. from the University of Iowa in 1952. He joined the faculty at Stanford University in 1953, where he remains to this day. Albert Bandura has received many awards for his scientific contributions. He has served as president of the American Psychological Association and honorary president of the Canadian Psychological Association.

Albert Bandura developed social learning and cognitive self-regulation theories that influenced the development of both learning and cognitive paradigms. Courtesy Albert Bandura.

Bandura's work is based on the premise that it is important to be able to study clinical phenomena in experimental situations. His initial work focused on social learning theory and on the idea that much of what we learn is through the process of imitation.

Other people provide us with a range of behaviours that can be imitated. His initial observations were published in books co-authored with his first graduate student, Canadian Richard Walters (Bandura & Walters, 1959, 1963). Their classic 1963 book, *Social Learning and Personality Development*, was critical of the psychodynamic approach and offered an empirically based alternative.

In many respects, research on social learning theory is synonymous with the famous Bobo doll study conducted by Bandura, Ross, and Ross (1961). In this study, children who witnessed an adult being aggressive with a plastic Bobo doll were observed imitating this aggression while playing with other children. Bandura and associates conducted several other classic studies designed to test how situational factors contributed to observational learning (e.g., witnessing a model who is rewarded for aggression). These variations led Bandura to conclude that there are four key processes in observational learning: (1) attention (noticing the model's behaviour); (2) retention (remembering the model's behaviour); (3) reproduction (personally exhibiting the behaviour); and (4) motivation (repeating imitated behaviours if they received positive consequences).

Bandura's more recent work is a cognitive self-regulation theory known as social cognitive theory that focuses on the concept of human agency and **self-efficacy**, an individual's perceived sense of being capable (see Bandura, 1986, 2001). Self-regulation is a multi-stage process that involves self-observation, self-judgement by comparing personal achievements and behaviours with standards and goals, and self-response in the form of self-reinforcement and praise or self-punishment and criticism. In a wide variety of contexts, self-control therapies have been applied that focus on improving an individual's sense of personal efficacy in order to lessen distress and promote adaptive behaviours.

Bandura's (2006) recent work examines human agency from an expanded perspective that incorporates various forms of efficacy, which supplement individual differences in personal efficacy. Fostering a sense of group efficacy and collective efficacy (i.e., the power of the people as a whole) has the potential to create enormous social change for the betterment of societies. Interested readers are encouraged to review the possible developments that Bandura links with group and collective agency.

Bandura's focus on both social learning and self-regulation underscores the close interplay between external forces (models in our environment to be imitated) and internal forces (personal beliefs about the self) in adaptive and maladaptive behaviours. The focus on personal, group, and collective agency promotes the view that we are key players who can act proactively to determine the factors and influences in our lives.

BEHAVIOURAL THERAPY A new way of treating psychopathology, called **behaviour therapy**, emerged in the 1950s. In its initial form, this therapy applied procedures based on classical and operant conditioning to alter clinical problems. Sometimes the term **behaviour modification** is used as well, particularly by therapists who employ operant conditioning as a means of treatment. Behaviour therapy is an attempt to change abnormal behaviour, thoughts, and feelings by applying in a clinical context the methods used and the discoveries made by experimental psychologists in their study of both normal and abnormal behaviour.

It is helpful to distinguish three theoretical approaches in behaviour therapy: in addition to the role of modelling, discussed above, there are counterconditioning and exposure, as well as the application of operant conditioning. Cognitive behaviour therapy is often considered a fourth aspect of behaviour therapy, but we will discuss it separately in the section on the cognitive approach because of its focus on thought processes.

Counterconditioning and exposure

"Embodying the principle of exposure, today's treatments affirm that the conquest of our fears requires confrontation with the things we fear the most."
–Richard J. McNally, 2007, p. 750.

Because behavioural approaches assume that behaviour is the result of learning, treatment often involves relearning a new, more adaptive response. **Counterconditioning** is relearning achieved by eliciting a new response in the presence of a particular stimulus. A response (R_1) to a given stimulus (S) can be eliminated by eliciting a new response (R_2) in the presence of that stimulus, as diagrammed in Figure 2.6. For example, in an early and now famous demonstration, Mary Cover Jones successfully treated a young boy's fear of rabbits by feeding him in the presence of a rabbit. The animal was at first kept several feet away and then gradually moved closer on successive occasions. In this way, the fear (R_1) produced by the rabbit (S) was replaced by the stronger positive feelings evoked by eating (R_2).

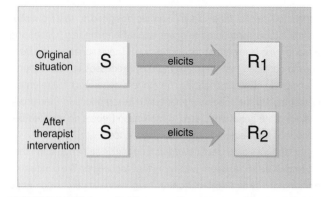

FIGURE 2.6 Schematic diagram of counterconditioning, whereby an original response (R$_1$) to a given stimulus (S) is eliminated by evoking a new response (R$_2$) to the same stimulus

Joseph Wolpe, one of the pioneers in behaviour therapy, is known particularly for systematic desensitization, a widely applied behavioural technique. Courtesy Public Relations Department, Temple University—Health Sciences Center.

The counterconditioning principle is behind an important behaviour therapy technique, **systematic desensitization**, developed by Joseph Wolpe (1958). A person who suffers from anxiety works with the therapist to compile a list of feared situations, starting with those that arouse minimal anxiety and progressing to the most frightening. The person is also taught to relax deeply. Step by step, while relaxed, the person imagines the graded series of anxiety-provoking situations. The relaxation tends to inhibit any anxiety that might otherwise be elicited by the imagined scenes. The fearful person becomes able to tolerate increasingly more difficult imagined situations as he or she climbs the hierarchy over a number of therapy sessions. Wolpe hypothesized that counterconditioning underlies the efficacy of desensitization; a state or response antagonistic to anxiety is substituted for anxiety as the person is exposed gradually to stronger and stronger doses of what he or she fears. Some experiments (e.g., Davison, 1968b) suggest Wolpe's hypothesis, but other explanations are possible. Most contemporary theorists believe that exposure per se to what the person fears is important. Relaxation is then considered merely a useful way to encourage a frightened individual to confront what he or she fears (Wilson & Davison, 1971). This technique is useful in reducing a wide variety of fears. Indeed, the treatment of anxiety disorders with exposure-based therapies has been a major success story in clinical psychology (see McNally, 2007). However, in a recent review of the cognitive processes in exposure therapy, Hofmann (2008) concluded that exposure therapy is "a form of cognitive intervention that specifically changes the expectancy of harm" (p. 1999).

Another type of counterconditioning, **aversive conditioning**, also played an important historical role in the development of behaviour therapy. In aversive conditioning, a stimulus attractive to the client is paired with an unpleasant event, such as a drug that produces nausea, in the hope of endowing it with negative properties. For example, a problem drinker who wishes to stop drinking might be asked to smell alcohol while he or she is being made nauseous by a drug. Aversive techniques have been employed to reduce smoking, drug use, and socially inappropriate desires, such as those of pedophiles.

Operant conditioning as an intervention Several behavioural procedures derive from operant conditioning. Much of this work has been done with children. Making positive reinforcers contingent on behaviour is used to increase the frequency of desirable behaviour. For example, a socially withdrawn child could be reinforced for playing with others. Problems treated with this method include autism, learning disabilities, mental retardation, bedwetting, aggression, hyperactivity, tantrums, and social withdrawal. The main premise is that the same learning conditions and processes that created maladaptive behaviour can also be used to change maladaptive behaviour (i.e., unlearning the behaviour).

BRIEF CASE EXAMPLE: DRESSING FOR SUCCESS?
The client was a 47-year-old woman from Saskatchewan with chronic schizophrenia. She had been hospitalized for nine years. One of her main symptoms was that she always wore excessive amounts of clothing. How excessive? When she first appeared at the hospital, it was reported that her clothes included:

> ... several sweaters, shawls, dresses, undergarments and stockings. The clothing also included sheets and towels wrapped around her body, and a turban-like head-dress made up of several towels. In addition, the patient carried two to three cups in one hand while holding a bundle of miscellaneous clothing, and a large purse in the other. (Ayllon, 1963, p. 58).

The average weight of her clothing at the beginning of treatment was 11 kilograms!

A behaviour intervention resulted in dramatic reductions in the amount of clothing worn by the client. Food reinforcement was used. The client was weighed prior to meals. If she did not meet the weight criterion set for her, the nurse told the client, "Sorry, you weigh too much. You'll have to weigh less." Failure to comply meant missing the meal (i.e., not obtaining the reinforcement). As indicated, the intervention was quite successful. The client went eventually from 11 kilograms to 1.5 kilograms of clothing.

This example also serves as an illustration of the behavioural concept of **successive approximations**. Initially, the client was allowed access to the meal room if she removed 1 kilogram of clothing. Once this goal was achieved (along with no longer bringing her own cups), the criterion was made more stringent on successive trials until the goal of 1.5 kilograms of clothing was achieved.

Time-out is an operant procedure wherein the consequence for misbehaviour is removal to an environment with no positive reinforcers. The Palma Collection/PhotoDisc/Getty Images.

THE COGNITIVE PERSPECTIVE

"The mind is its own place, and in itself
Can make a Heav'n of Hell, a Hell of Heav'n."
—John Milton, Paradise Lost

Cognition is a term that groups together the mental processes of perceiving, recognizing, conceiving, judging, and reasoning. The **cognitive paradigm** focuses on how people (and animals as well) structure their experiences, how they make sense of them, and how they relate their current experiences to past ones that have been stored in memory.

THE BASICS OF COGNITIVE THEORY At any given moment, we are bombarded by far more stimuli than we can possibly respond to. How do we filter this overwhelming input, put it into words or images, form hypotheses, and arrive at a perception of

what is out there? Cognitive psychologists consider the learning process much more complex than the passive formation of new stimulus–response associations. Cognitive psychologists regard the learner as an active interpreter of a situation, with the learner's past knowledge imposing a perceptual funnel on the experience. The learner fits new information into an organized network of already accumulated knowledge, often referred to as a **schema**, or cognitive set (Neisser, 1976). New information may fit the schema, but if it does not, the learner reorganizes the schema to fit the information or construes the information in such a way as to fit the schema. The cognitive approach may remind you of our earlier discussions of paradigms; scientific paradigms are similar in function to a cognitive schema, for they act as filters to our experience of the world.

Currently, cognitive explanations are quite predominant and appear more and more often in the search for the causes of abnormality and for new methods of intervention. A widely held view of depression, for example, places the blame on a particular cognitive set, namely, the individual's overriding sense of hopelessness. Many people who are depressed believe that they have no important effect on their surroundings regardless of what they do. Their destiny seems to them to be out of their hands, and they expect their future to be negative. If depression does develop from a sense of hopelessness, this fact could have implications for how clinicians treat the disorder. Cognitive theorizing will be included in discussions of most of the disorders described in this book.

BECK'S COGNITIVE THERAPY

". . .the model of automatic cognitive misprocessing that now guides the widespread clinical practice of cognitive therapy for depression is based on a brain dysfunction that can be demonstrated by physiological brain imaging. The goal of 100 years ago is now a reality that provides a scientific basis for our most widely practiced psychotherapy for depression."
—Robert Freedman, Editor, *American Journal of Psychiatry*, commenting on Beck's linking of negative cognitive bias and recent brain imaging findings (2008, p. 1512)

The psychiatrist Aaron Beck developed a cognitive therapy (CT) for depression based on the idea that a depressed mood is caused by distortions in the way people perceive life experiences (Beck, 1976; Salkovskis, 1996). For example, a depressed person may focus exclusively on negative happenings and ignore positive ones, or interpret positive experiences in a negative manner. This is illustrated by revelations made in her autobiography by Canadian prima ballerina Karen Kain (see Kain, 1994). Kain admitted having experienced severe depression and had this to say about occasions when her performance did not meet her own exacting standards:

Sometimes my lacklustre performance would be evident, and the applause would be muted, merely polite. But at other times—and these were even worse for a perfectionist like me—people would give me a warm reception, perhaps even stand and applaud, when I knew I'd been dreadful, and I would interpret their enthusiasm as proof positive that I'd never been any good. I had always danced badly, and somehow nobody had ever noticed. (Kain, 1994, p. 158)

Beck's therapy (examined in detail in Chapter 8) tries to persuade clients to change their opinions of themselves and the way in which they interpret life events. When a depressed person expresses feelings that nothing ever goes right, for example, the therapist offers counter-examples, pointing out how the client has overlooked favourable happenings. The general goal of Beck's therapy is to provide clients with experiences, both inside and outside the consulting room, that will alter their negative schemas and dysfunctional beliefs and attitudes.

The role of cognitive factors is clearly evident in the following case study of Thomas, an elderly man suffering jointly from depression and a medical condition.

Thomas was a 68-year-old married man, diagnosed with Parkinson's disease four years previously. As a consequence of his disease he had become uncertain and fearful of others' reactions to him in professional and social situations and he had increasingly avoided such situations. This had profoundly affected his self-concept; he was experiencing many features of depression.

A cognitive formulation of Thomas' presenting problems suggested that at a core level, central to his sense of self, Thomas had assimilated the belief that his acceptability as a person was conditional on being respected and regarded as competent in all domains and at all times. His career as a carpenter and his retirement interests involved fine motor skills that had been essentially lost through the progression of his Parkinson's disease…

Thomas attended 16 therapy meetings over eight months. Initially meetings were weekly, but later meetings were biweekly and then monthly. The steps in cognitive therapy were:
(1) education about social anxiety, depression, and the cognitive model to normalize Thomas' experience, (2) diary keeping of thoughts, feelings and behaviour across a range of upsetting situations to help Thomas further understand his beliefs and their role in his psychological difficulties,
(3) reducing avoidance of feared situations in graded homework assignments and, (4) testing and challenging hypothesized conditional and core beliefs. (Kuyken & Beck, 2007, pp. 27–28)

Because this approach focused on the role of dysfunctional thoughts and beliefs, the main emphasis of therapy is replacing these thoughts with more adaptive thoughts. Thus, Beck dismissed the old psychoanalytic theory (see p. 56) that depression is self-directed hostility. He replaced it with a model of negative cognitive bias—an automatic misprocessing of information. In a seminal 2008 paper entitled, "The evolution of the cognitive model of depression and its neurobiological correlates," Beck (2008) linked his cognitive constructs to current brain imaging studies that demonstrate overreaction of the amygdala to negative stimuli.

RATIONAL-EMOTIVE BEHAVIOUR THERAPY Albert Ellis was another leading cognitive therapist. His principal thesis was that sustained emotional reactions are caused by internal sentences that people repeat to themselves, and these self-statements reflect sometimes unspoken assumptions—**irrational beliefs**—about what is necessary to lead a meaningful life. In Ellis's rational-emotive therapy (RET), subsequently renamed **rational-emotive behaviour therapy (REBT)** (Ellis, 1995; Dryden, David, & Ellis, 2010), the aim is to eliminate self-defeating beliefs through a rational examination of them. Anxious persons, for example, may create their own problems by making unrealistic demands on themselves or others, such as "I must win the love of everyone." Or a depressed person may say several times a day, "What a worthless jerk I am." Ellis proposes that people interpret what is happening around them, that sometimes these interpretations can cause emotional turmoil, and that a therapist's attention should be focused on these beliefs rather than on historical causes or, indeed, on overt behaviour (Ellis, 1962).

Ellis used to list a number of irrational beliefs that people can harbour. One very common notion was that they must be thoroughly competent in everything they do. Ellis suggested that many people actually believe this untenable assumption and evaluate every event within this context. Thus, if a person makes an error, it becomes a catastrophe because it violates the deeply held conviction that he or she must be perfect (Ellis, 2002). It sometimes comes as a shock to clients to realize that they actually believe such strictures and have thus run their lives in a way that makes it is virtually impossible to live comfortably or productively.

More recently, Ellis (2002) shifted from a cataloguing of specific beliefs to the more general concept of demandingness—the "musts" or "shoulds" that people impose on themselves and others. Thus, instead of wanting something to be a certain way, feeling disappointed when it is not, and then engaging in behaviour that might bring about the desired

Aaron Beck developed a cognitive theory of depression and a cognitive therapy for the biases of depressed people. Photo courtesy Aaron T. Beck, M.D.

outcome, the person demands that it be so. This unrealistic, unproductive demand is hypothesized to create severe emotional distress and behavioural dysfunction.

Clinical implementation of REBT After becoming familiar with the client's problems, the therapist presents the basic theory of rational-emotive behaviour therapy so that the client can understand and accept it. The following transcript is from a session with a young man who had inordinate fears about speaking in front of groups. The therapist guides the client to view his inferiority complex in terms of the unreasonable things he may be telling himself. The therapist's thoughts during the interview are indicated in italics within square brackets.

Client: My primary difficulty is that I become very uptight when I have to speak in front of a group of people. I guess it's just my own inferiority complex.

Therapist: [*I don't want to get sidetracked at this point by talking about that conceptualization of his problem. I'll just try to finesse it and make a smooth transition to something else.*] I don't know if I would call it an inferiority complex, but I do believe that people can, in a sense, bring on their own upset and anxiety in certain kinds of situations. When you're in a particular situation, your anxiety is often not the result of the situation itself, but rather the way in which you interpret the situation—what you tell yourself about the situation. For example, look at this pen. Does this pen make you nervous?

Client: No.

Therapist: Why not?

Client: It's just an object. It's just a pen.

Therapist: It can't hurt you?

Client: No …

Therapist: It's really not the object that creates emotional upset in people, but rather what you think about the object. [*Hopefully, this Socratic-like dialogue will eventually bring him to the conclusion that self-statements can mediate emotional arousal.*] Now this holds true for … situations where emotional upset is caused by what a person tells himself about the situation. Take, for example, two people who are about to attend the same social gathering. Both of them may know exactly the same number of people at the party, but one person can be optimistic and relaxed about the situation, whereas the other one can be worried about how he will appear, and consequently be very anxious. [*I'll try to get him to verbalize the basic assumption that attitude or perception is most important here.*] So, when these two people walk into the place where the party is given, are their emotional reactions at all associated with the physical arrangements at the party?

Client: No, obviously not.

Therapist: What determines their reactions, then?

Client: They obviously have different attitudes toward the party.

Therapist: Exactly, and their attitudes—the ways in which they approach the situation—greatly influence their emotional reactions. (Goldfried & Davison, 1994, pp. 163–165)

Having persuaded the client that his or her emotional problems will benefit from rational examination, the therapist proceeds to teach the person to substitute for irrational self-statements an internal dialogue meant to ease the emotional turmoil. Therapists who implement Ellis's ideas differ greatly on how they persuade clients to change their self-talk. Some therapists, like Ellis himself, argue with clients, cajoling and teasing them, sometimes in very blunt language. Others, believing that social influence should be more subtle and that individuals should participate more in changing themselves, encourage clients to discuss their own irrational thinking and then gently lead them to discover more rational ways of regarding the world (Goldfried & Davison, 1994).

Once a client verbalizes a different belief or self-statement during a therapy session, it must be made part of everyday thinking. Ellis and his followers provide clients with homework assignments designed to help them experiment with the new self-talk and to experience the positive consequences of viewing life in less catastrophic ways. Ellis emphasizes the importance of getting the client to behave differently, both to test out new beliefs and to learn to cope with life's disappointments. This is how this approach becomes both cognitive and behavioural. In practice, Beck's cognitive therapy also employs behavioural strategies and is now considered to be a leading CBT approach.

COGNITIVE BEHAVIOUR THERAPY Classical behavioural therapies emphasize the direct manipulation of overt behaviour and occasionally of covert behaviour, with thoughts and feelings being construed as internal behaviours (referred to as mediational learning). They pay relatively little attention to direct alteration of the thinking and reasoning processes of the client. Theorists such as Bandura were influential in promoting the notion that external events are also represented and reflected internally by cognitions, and when focusing on a particular person, it is important to consider the interplay of behaviours and cognitions. **Cognitive behaviour therapy (CBT)** does incorporate theory and research on cognitive and behavioural processes and represents a blend of cognitive and learning principles. Cognitive behaviour therapists pay attention to private events—thoughts, perceptions, judgements, self-statements, and even tacit (unconscious) assumptions—and have studied and manipulated these processes in their attempts to understand and modify overt and covert disturbed behaviour. **Cognitive restructuring** is a general term for changing a pattern of thought that is presumed to be causing a disturbed emotion or behaviour. This restructuring is implemented in several ways by CBT therapists.

Meichenbaum's cognitive-behaviour modification Donald Meichenbaum is a leading cognitive behaviour therapist. In contrast to Beck and Ellis, who came from psychoanalytic backgrounds, Meichenbaum was trained first in the principles of behaviour modification. Nonetheless, his approach, originally referred to as cognitive-behaviour modification, also addresses issues that are typically focused on by psychodynamically oriented clinicians (see Canadian Contributions 2.2). In recent years, Meichenbaum has shifted in a "constructivist" direction (see Neimeyer & Raskin, 2001), emphasizing the narrative organization of experience (e.g., Meichenbaum, 1995; Meichenbaum & Fitzpatrick, 1995; also see chapters 6 and 17). The term *constructivist* is used "to encompass the broad panoply of perspectives that emphasize those processes by which meaning is constructed by human beings in personal, interpersonal, and social contexts" (Neimeyer & Raskin, 2001, p. 423). Meichenbaum's approach is more integrative than that of Beck and Ellis. He addresses issues related to psychotherapy practice that will be explored in Chapter 17.

CANADIAN CONTRIBUTIONS 2.2
DONALD MEICHENBAUM: EVOLUTION OF A LIFESPAN COGNITIVE BEHAVIOURAL ECOLOGICAL APPROACH

Donald Meichenbaum, a Canadian clinical psychologist, is a pioneer in bridging the gap between the various therapeutic approaches. Meichenbaum developed a set of psychotherapeutic procedures that he now calls cognitive behavioural therapy. Two illustrative procedures are **self-instructional training** and **stress-inoculation training**.

In self-instructional training (Meichenbaum, 1977), the therapist helps the client prepare to make specific coping statements when confronted with difficult situations. In stress-inoculation training (Meichenbaum, 1977, 1992), Meichenbaum developed a multi-component coping-skills approach that incorporates self-instructional training and has proven to be a very effective therapeutic strategy. The approach emphasizes systematic acquisition of coping skills through learning to cope with small but manageable amounts of stress. This strategy is assumed to facilitate the maintenance of treatment gains and generalization to other stressful situations. The rationale is credible: people who learn to cope with relatively mild levels of stress can be "inoculated" against uncontrollable levels. This stress inoculation training can be conducted with individuals, families, or groups (Meichenbaum, 2009).

These cognitive behaviour procedures were employed initially with impulsive individuals who experienced self-control problems, such as children, adolescents, and adults who had problems with anger control (e.g., Meichenbaum & Novaco, 1977); schizophrenics who had attentional control problems (Meichenbaum, 1969); and people with pain management problems (e.g., Turk & Meichenbaum, 1987). In all of these cases, the therapy involved educating clients (and family members) about their disabilities and teaching them how to "think before they act." Clients were taught, by means of direct instruction, modelling rehearsal, and feedback, how to "notice, catch, interrupt, plan, monitor, and self-reinforce" their behaviour. In a problem-solving fashion, clients were taught a behavioural routine consisting of "goal, plan, do, check."

But Meichenbaum's cognitive behaviour approach did not stop there. Therapists and clients worked collaboratively to consider what factors might get in the way of clients using such coping skills. Sometimes, the barriers reflected the client's beliefs (e.g., lack of self-confidence, perfectionistic standards) or lack of motivation

Donald Meichenbaum developed an integrative, collaborative, constructivist brand of CBT that includes strategies such as self-instructional training and stress-inoculation training, a focus on "barriers" to treatment, and the use of personal narratives. Courtesy Donald Meichenbaum.

(e.g., a "paralysis of will"). Sometimes the barriers were interpersonal in nature (e.g., lack of reinforcement, family members undermining improvement). The cognitive behaviour therapist and the clients worked on ways to anticipate and address these potential barriers. The psychodynamic features found their way into cognitive behaviour treatment because sometimes the "barriers" to improvement come from early childhood/adolescent experiences. It is not merely the harsh developmental history experienced by many clients (e.g., about 50% of psychiatric clients have historical victimization), but also what clients tell themselves and others—the "stories" they construct about what they experienced—that influence their current adjustment and future outlook (a **constructivist-narrative approach**). Cognitive behaviour therapists who adopt Meichenbaum's approach help clients understand the narratives they create and learn ways to alter how they appraise events and their abilities to handle stressful events. Although he recognizes that various cognitive approaches are viable, Meichenbaum has indicated that when trying to help someone, he is more inclined to focus on developing new life narratives rather than removing negative automatic thoughts and cognitive distortions (see David, 2005). Meichenbaum's (1994) comprehensive constructivist-narrative approach to the treatment of people with post-traumatic stress disorder (PTSD) is described in detail in Chapter 6.

Along with other cognitive therapists, such as Albert Ellis and Aaron Beck, Don Meichenbaum has contributed significantly to the development of an integrative and empirically validated treatment approach. He is regarded as one of the 10 most influential psychotherapists of the twentieth century. Meichenbaum is distinguished professor emeritus at the University of Waterloo and research director of the Melissa Institute for Violence Prevention and Treatment of Victims of Violence in Miami, Florida. He is also a member of the American Psychological Association Task Force on

Fostering Resilience in Response to Terrorism. Keep his current work in mind when you are reading the subsequent section in this chapter on the biopsychosocial model. Meichenbaum describes his current approach to the treatment and prevention of violence as multi-faceted and a "lifespan cognitive-behavioural ecological approach." This approach teaches emotion self-regulatory skills with stress inoculation procedures; promotes client strengths (individual, social, or systemic); and assesses and deals with individual, social, and familial barriers. It is the ecological component that reflects psychosocial factors.

THE COGNITIVE-BEHAVIOUR INTEGRATED APPROACH

Carter, Forys, and Oswald (2008) conducted a recent review of the cognitive-behavioural paradigm. They made the astute observation that cognitive-behavioural models when applied to various disorders differ in terms of how much emphasis is placed on cognitive versus behavioural factors. However, they observed that all of these models are based on the basic premise that the person is influenced as much and perhaps more by his or her perception of events versus the objective features of these events.

Figure 2.7 is a proposed cognitive-behavioural model of panic disorder (Carter et al., 2008). Panic disorder is described in more detail in Chapter 6. It is clearly shown in Figure 2.7 that catastrophic cognitions (e.g., "I'm going to die") are at the root of this disorder, but clear behavioural manifestations play a role in the form of escape and avoidance behaviours as panic mounts. Feedback arrows suggest that cognitions influence behaviours but these avoidance and escape behaviours also further contribute to the ongoing experience of catastrophic cognitions.

EVALUATING THE COGNITIVE-BEHAVIOURAL PARADIGM

While the learning explanation of abnormal behaviour has led to many treatment innovations, the fact that a treatment

based on learning principles is effective in changing behaviour does not mean that the behaviour was itself learned in a similar way. For example, while the mood of depressed people may be elevated by rewards for increased activity, this cannot be considered evidence that the depression was initially produced by an absence of rewards. How does a person's observation of a model lead to changes in his or her overt behaviour? As mentioned in Canadian Contributions 2.1, Bandura and Walters (1963) asserted that an observer could somehow learn new behaviour by watching others. However, in order for imitation to occur, cognitive processes must become engaged, including the ability to remember later on what had happened. Findings of research on social learning led some behavioural researchers and clinicians to include cognitive variables in their analyses of psychopathology and therapy. However, some criticisms of the cognitive component of the cognitive-behavioural paradigm should also be noted. The concepts on which it is based (e.g., schema) are abstract and not always well defined. Furthermore, cognitive explanations of psychopathology do not always explain much. That a depressed person has a negative schema tells us that the person thinks gloomy thoughts. However, such a pattern of thinking is actually part of the diagnosis of depression. What is distinctive in the cognitive perspective is that the thoughts are given causal status; they are regarded as causing the other features of the disorder, such as sadness. Left unanswered is the question of where the negative schema came from in the first place. Cognitive explanations of psychopathology tend to focus more on current determinants of a disorder and less on its historical antecedents.

Is the cognitive point of view basically different and separate from the learning perspective? Much of what we have just considered suggests that it is. The growing field of CBT gives us pause, however, because its researchers study the complex interplay of beliefs, expectations, perceptions, and attitudes on the one hand, and overt behaviour on the other. For example, as a leading advocate of changing behaviour through cognitive means, Bandura (1977) uses his concept of self-efficacy (see Canadian Contributions 2.1) to

FIGURE 2.7 Cognitive-Behavioural Model (Carter et al., 2008.) Reprinted with permission of John Wiley & Sons, Inc.

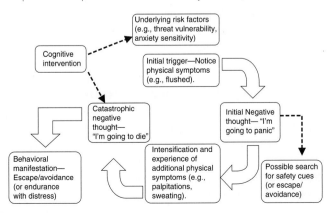

argue that different therapies produce improvement by increasing people's belief that they can achieve desired goals. At the same time, though, he argues that changing behaviour through behavioural techniques is the most powerful way to enhance self-efficacy. Therapists such as Ellis, in contrast, emphasize direct alteration of cognitions (through argument, persuasion, Socratic dialogue, and the like) to bring about improvements in emotion and behaviour. Complicating matters further, Ellis places importance on homework assignments that require clients to behave in ways they have been unable to previously because of negative thoughts. Ellis renamed his therapy "rational-emotive behaviour therapy" to highlight the importance of overt behaviour. Thus, CBT therapists work at both the cognitive and behavioural levels, and most of those who use cognitive concepts and try to change beliefs with verbal means also use behavioural procedures to alter behaviour directly, hence our integration of the behavioural (learning) and cognitive perspectives.

This issue is reflected in the terminology used to refer to people such as Beck and Ellis. Are they cognitive therapists or cognitive behaviour therapists? For the most part we will use the latter term because it denotes both that the therapist regards cognitions as major determinants of emotion and behaviour and that he or she maintains the focus on overt behaviour that has always characterized behaviour therapy. Nonetheless, Beck, even though he assigns many behavioural tasks as part of his therapy, is usually referred to as the founder of cognitive therapy (CT); Ellis's rational-emotive therapy (RET) was once considered separate from behaviour therapy.

However, the issue is not just a matter of terminology. A recent placebo-controlled comparison study (Dimidjian et al., 2006) found behavioural activation (a treatment condition that uses the basic behavioural components of CT with an increased focus on avoidance behaviours in the context of a behavioural rationale) to be as effective as antidepressants and superior to CT in the treatment of depressed adults. In a follow-up study, Coffman, Martell, Dimidjian, Gallop, and Hollon (2007) examined a subset of the clients who exhibited a pattern of extreme nonresponse to CT in their own reports. They concluded that "there might be a subset of patients who see themselves as doing better with sustained attention to behavior change in time-limited treatment" (Coffman et al., 2007, p. 531). Beck himself (e.g., Beck et al., 1979; DeRubeis, Webb, Tang, & Beck, 2010) recommended that therapists use more behavioural strategies with severely depressed people. This suggestion may be especially true with people with a combination of severe depression, great functional impairment, and interpersonal and family problems and challenging life circumstances (see Coffman et al., 2007). The reasons for this finding and related issues will be explored in detail in Chapter 17. In a recent review of component studies, Longmore and Worrell (2007) asked, "Do we need to challenge thoughts in CBT?" They concluded that "there is little empirical support for the role of cognitive change as causal in the symptomatic improvements achieved in CBT" (p. 173). Similarly, Waller

(2009) noted that some clinicians "drift" from implementing the full range of tasks that are vital to effective CBT, especially behavioural change. As noted in Chapter 1, he claims that this therapist drift is a common phenomenon that typically involves a shift from "doing therapies" to "talking therapies."

Suffice to say at this point that both cognitive and behavioural factors can be important foci of intervention. For example, in a randomized controlled trial of people with major depression, Keith Dobson from the University of Calgary and his colleagues (Dobson et al., 2008) reported that clients previously exposed to CT were significantly less likely to relapse following the termination of treatment than clients withdrawn from medication. The authors further concluded that both cognitive therapy and behavioural activation are less expensive and more enduring (observed at a two-year follow-up) alternatives to medication in the treatment of depression.

The cognitive-behavioural approach has had a vital impact on psychiatry and clinical psychology and evidence continues to accumulate for the efficacy and effectiveness of CBT to reduce clinical symptoms and improve quality of life for people with a variety of psychological disorders and clinical problems in addition to depression, such as anxiety, eating disorders, autism, and schizophrenia (e.g., Butler, Chapman, Forman, & Beck, 2006). Nonetheless, some authorities (e.g., Ost, 2008; Waller, 2009) caution against the premature adoption of so-called "third wave" CBT therapies (e.g., acceptance and commitment therapy, dialectical behaviour therapy, mindfulness training, schema therapy) that lack a clear evidence base (see Chapter 17).

We now turn to a discussion of the psychoanalytic paradigm followed by the humanistic-existential paradigms. While the classic psychoanalytic paradigm has diminished in its influence, some approaches reflecting this paradigm are growing in impact (e.g., interpersonal therapy). Also, as the psychoanalytic approach reminds us, it is important not to lose sight of the potential influence that early life experiences can have on subsequent manifestations of abnormal behaviour.

THE PSYCHOANALYTIC PARADIGM

The central assumption of the **psychoanalytic** or **psychodynamic paradigm**, originally developed by Sigmund Freud (1856–1939), is that psychopathology results from unconscious conflicts in the individual. We will look at the significant impact of Freud in the development of this paradigm, but we will also examine the ways in which the focus of this paradigm has shifted.

CLASSICAL PSYCHOANALYTIC THEORY

Classical psychoanalytic theory refers to the original views of Freud. His theories encompassed both the structure of the mind itself and the development and dynamics of personality.

STRUCTURE OF THE MIND Freud divided the mind, or the psyche, into three principal parts: id, ego, and superego. These are metaphors for specific functions or energies. According to operates on the **reality principle** as it mediates between the demands of reality and the immediate gratification desired by the id.

The final part of the psyche to emerge is the **super-ego**, which operates roughly as the conscience and develops throughout childhood. Freud believed that the superego developed from the ego much as the ego developed from the id. As children discover that many of their impulses, such as biting or bedwetting, are not acceptable to their parents, they begin to incorporate, or introject, parental values as their own to enjoy parental approval and avoid disapproval.

The behaviour of the human being, as conceptualized by Freud, is thus a complex interplay of these three parts of the psyche. The interplay of these forces is referred to as the **psychodynamics** of the personality.

The id's instincts as well as many of the superego's activities are not known to the conscious mind. While the ego is primarily conscious and is involved in thinking and planning, it, too, has important unconscious aspects (the defence mechanisms) that protect it from anxiety. Freud considered most of the important determinants of behaviour to be unconscious.

NEUROTIC ANXIETY When one's life is in jeopardy, one feels **objective (realistic) anxiety**—the ego's reaction, according to Freud, to danger in the external world. The person whose personality has not developed fully, perhaps because he or she is fixated at one or another stage, may experience **neurotic anxiety**, a feeling of fear that is not connected to reality or to any real threat. **Moral anxiety** arises when the impulses of the superego punish an individual for not meeting expectations and thereby satisfying the principle that drives the superego—namely, the perfection principle.

Sigmund Freud was the founder of the psychoanalytic paradigm, both proposing a theory of the causes of mental disorder and devising a new method of therapy. National Library of Medicine/Photo Researchers, Inc.

Freud, the **id** is present at birth and is the part of the mind that accounts for all the energy needed to run the psyche. It comprises the basic urges for food, water, elimination, warmth, affection, and sex. Trained as a neurologist, Freud saw the source of all the id's energy as biological. Only later, as the infant develops, is this energy, which Freud called **libido**, converted into psychic energy, all of it **unconscious**, below the level of awareness.

The id seeks immediate gratification and operates according to the **pleasure principle**. When the id is not satisfied, tension is produced, and the id strives to eliminate this tension. For example, the infant feels hunger, an aversive drive, and is impelled to move about, sucking, to reduce the tension. Another means of obtaining gratification is **primary process thinking**, generating images—in essence, fantasies—of what is desired. The infant who wants the mother's milk imagines sucking at the mother's breast and thereby obtains some short-term satisfaction.

The ego is the next aspect of the psyche to develop. Unlike the id, the **ego** is primarily conscious and begins to develop from the id during the second six months of life. Its task is to deal with reality. Through its planning and decision-making functions, called **secondary process thinking**, the ego realizes that operating on the pleasure principle at all times is not the most effective way of maintaining life. The ego thus

In classical psychoanalytic theory, too much or too little gratification during one of the psychosexual stages is hypothesized to lead to regression to this stage during stress. © Jennie Woodcock: Reflections Photolibrary/CORBIS.

DEFENCE MECHANISMS: COPING WITH ANXIETY

According to Freud and elaborated by his daughter Anna (A. Freud, 1966), the discomfort experienced by the anxious ego can be reduced in several ways. Objective anxiety, rooted in reality, can often be handled by removing or avoiding the danger in the external world or by dealing with it in a rational way. Neurotic anxiety can be handled by means of a defence mechanism. A **defence mechanism** is a strategy, unconsciously used, to protect the ego from anxiety. Perhaps the most important is **repression**, which pushes unacceptable impulses and thoughts into the unconscious. By remaining repressed, these infantile memories and desires cannot be corrected by adult experience and therefore retain their original intensity and immaturity. **Denial**, another important defence mechanism, entails disavowing a traumatic experience, such as being raped, and pushing it into the unconscious. **Projection** attributes to external agents characteristics or desires that an individual possesses but cannot accept in his or her conscious awareness. For example, a woman who unconsciously is averse to regarding herself as angry at others may instead see others as angry with her. Other defence mechanisms are **displacement**, redirecting emotional responses from a perhaps dangerous object to a substitute (e.g., yelling at one's spouse instead of at one's boss); **reaction formation**, converting one feeling (e.g., hate) into its opposite (in this case, love); **regression**, retreating to the behavioural patterns of an earlier age; **rationalization**, inventing a reason for an unreasonable action or attitude; and **sublimation**, converting sexual or aggressive impulses into socially valued behaviours, especially creative activity.

All these defence mechanisms allow the ego to discharge some id energy while not facing frankly the true nature of the motivation. Because defence mechanisms are more readily observed than other symptoms of a disordered personality, they often make people aware of their troubled natures and provide the impetus for consulting a therapist. It should be noted that contemporary psychoanalytic theorists consider some use of defence mechanisms to be adaptive and healthy. A period of denial after the death of a loved one, for example, can help in adjusting to the loss. For the most part, however, defence mechanisms are maladaptive.

PSYCHOANALYTIC THERAPY

Since Freud's time, the body of psychoanalytic thinking has changed in important ways, but all treatments purporting to be psychoanalytic have some basic tenets in common. (See Focus on Discovery 2.3 for a discussion about psychotherapy.) Classical psychoanalysis is based on Freud's second theory of neurotic anxiety, that neurotic anxiety is the reaction of the ego when a previously punished and repressed id impulse presses for expression. When the unconscious part of the ego encounters a situation that reminds it of a repressed conflict from childhood—one usually having to do with sexual or aggressive impulses—it is overcome by debilitating tension. Psychoanalytic therapy is an insight therapy. It attempts to remove the earlier repression and help the client face the childhood conflict, gain insight into it, and resolve it in the light of adult reality. The repression, occurring so long ago, has prevented the ego from growing in an adult fashion; the lifting of the repression is supposed to enable this relearning to take place.

FOCUS ON DISCOVERY 2.3
WHAT IS PSYCHOTHERAPY?

Shorn of its theoretical complexities, any **psychotherapy** is a social interaction in which a trained professional tries to help another person, the client or patient, behave and feel differently. The therapist follows procedures that are to a greater or lesser extent prescribed by a certain theory or school of thought. The basic assumption is that particular kinds of verbal and non-verbal exchanges in a trusting relationship can achieve goals, such as reducing anxiety and eliminating self-defeating or dangerous behaviour.

Basic as this definition may seem, there is little general agreement about what really constitutes psychotherapy. A person's next-door neighbour might utter the same words of comfort as a clinical psychologist, but should we regard this as psychotherapy? In what way is psychotherapy different from such non-professional reassurance? Is the distinction made on the straightforward basis of whether the dispenser of reassurance has a particular academic degree? Does it relate to whether the giver of information has a theory that dictates what he or she says? These are difficult questions.

Generally, people who seek or are sent for professional help have first tried non-professional avenues to feeling better. They have confided in friends or a spouse, perhaps spoken to the family doctor or a member of the clergy, and maybe tried several of the many self-help books and programs that are so popular. For most people in psychological distress, one or more of these options provide enough relief, and they seek no further help. But for others, these attempts fall short. These are the people who go to mental health clinics, university counselling centres, and the private offices of independent practitioners.

London (1986) categorized psychotherapies as **insight therapies** or **action (behavioural) therapies**. Insight therapies, such as psychoanalysis, assume that behaviour, emotions, and thoughts become disordered because people do not understand what motivates them, especially when their needs and drives conflict. Insight therapies try to help people discover why they behave, feel, and think as they do. The premise is that greater awareness of motivations will yield greater control over and subsequent improvement in thought, emotion, and behaviour. However, more recent findings imply that attaining insight is not necessarily the sole or prime factor in determining the therapeutic effect of dynamic psychotherapy (e.g., Messer & Abbass, 2010; see Chapter 17).

Of course, insight is not exclusive to the insight therapies. The action, or behavioural, therapies bring insight to the individual as well, and the newer cognitive therapies can be seen as a blend of insight and behavioural therapies. It is a matter of emphasis, of focus. In the behavioural therapies, the focus is on changing behaviour; insight is often a peripheral benefit. In the insight therapies, the focus is less on changing people's behaviour directly than on enhancing their understanding of their motives, fears, and conflicts. To facilitate such insights, therapists of different theoretical persuasions employ a variety of techniques. There are scores of theories and psychotherapies, each with its enthusiastic supporters. We present in this chapter a detailed description of the more prominent theories and methods of intervention. We hope to provide you with the means to evaluate critically new therapies that arise or, at the very least, to know what questions to ask in order to evaluate them effectively.

Analysts employ a number of techniques in their efforts to lift repressions. Perhaps the best known is **free association**. The client reclines on a couch, facing away from the analyst, and is encouraged to give free rein to his or her thoughts, verbalizing whatever comes to mind without the censoring done in everyday life. It is assumed that the client can learn this skill, gradually overcoming defences built up over many years, but there often arise blocks to free association. The client may suddenly become silent or change the topic. These **resistances** are noted by the analyst as they are assumed to signal a sensitive, or ego-threatening, area. These sensitive areas are precisely what the analyst will want to probe further.

Dream analysis is another analytic technique. Psychoanalytic theory holds that, in sleep, ego defences are relaxed, allowing normally repressed material to enter the sleeper's consciousness. Since this material is extremely threatening, it is rarely allowed into consciousness in its actual form; rather, the repressed material is disguised and dreams take on heavily symbolic content (referred to as the **latent content** of the dream). For example, a woman who fears sexual advances from men may dream of being attacked by warriors with spears; the spears are considered phallic symbols, substituting for an explicit sexual advance.

Another key component of psychoanalytic therapy is **transference**. Here, the client's responses to the analyst are not in keeping with the analyst–client relationship but seem instead to reflect relationships with important people in the client's past. For example, a client may feel that the analyst is bored by what he or she is saying (as a parent might have seemed) and, as a result, might struggle to be entertaining (as he or she had done in the past to gain parental attention). Analysts encourage the development of transference by intentionally remaining shadowy figures, sitting behind their clients and divulging little of their personal lives or feelings during a session. Through careful observation of these transferred attitudes, analysts can gain insight into the childhood origin of repressed conflicts. It is precisely when analysts notice transference developing that they begin to hope that an important repressed conflict is getting closer to the surface.

Countertransference refers to the analyst's feelings toward the client. Analysts must be aware of their own feelings so that they can see the client clearly. Thus, psychoanalysis of the analyst-in-training is typically part of their training.

As previously repressed material begins to appear in therapy, **interpretation** comes into play. The analyst points out to the client the meaning of certain behaviours. Defence mechanisms, the ego's unconscious tools for warding off anxiety, are a principal focus of interpretation. For instance, a man might change the subject whenever anything touches on closeness during the course of a session. The analyst will at some point interpret the client's behaviour, pointing out its defensive nature in the hope of stimulating the client to acknowledge that he has trouble with intimacy.

MODIFICATIONS IN PSYCHOANALYTIC THERAPY As happens with all paradigms, psychoanalytic therapy has evolved substantially over time. One innovation was to apply it to groups of people rather than only to individuals. Some therapists focus on the psychodynamics of individuals in the group, using typical techniques, such as free association, interpretation, and dream analysis (Wolf & Kutash, 1990). Others conceive of the group itself as having a collective set of psychodynamics, manifested by such things as group transference to the therapist. Within psychoanalytic circles, there has been controversy about the value of a group approach. The key issue is whether the group format dilutes the transference to the therapist and thus makes the therapy ineffective.

Other current analytic therapies include ego analysis, brief psychodynamic therapy, and interpersonal psychodynamic therapy.

Ego analysis After Freud's death, a group of practitioners, generally referred to as ego analysts, introduced important modifications to psychoanalytic therapy. Their approach is sometimes described as psychodynamic rather than psychoanalytic. The major figures in this loosely formed movement include Karen Horney, Anna Freud, Erik Erikson, David Rapaport, and Heinz Hartmann. Although Freud did not ignore people's interactions with the environment, he essentially believed that they are driven by intrapsychic urges. Those who subscribe to **ego analysis** place greater emphasis on a person's ability to control the environment and to select the time and the means for satisfying instinctual drives, contending that the individual is as much ego as id. In addition, they focus more on the person's current living conditions than did Freud.

Ego analysts believe in a set of ego functions that are primarily conscious, capable of controlling both id instincts and the external environment, and that, significantly, do not depend on the id for their energy. They assume that these ego functions and capabilities are present at birth and develop through experience.

Brief psychodynamic therapy Freud originally conceived of psychoanalysis as a relatively short-term process. He thought that the analyst should focus on specific problems, make it clear to the client that therapy would not exceed a certain number of sessions, and structure sessions in a directive fashion. Freud thus envisioned a more active and briefer psychoanalysis than what eventually developed.

Doidge and associates investigated the nature of psychodynamic therapy in an Ontario survey (see Doidge, 1999; Doidge, Simon, Gillies, & Ruskin, 1994). They found that 59% of those receiving psychoanalysis were women and that the mean number of current diagnoses was four. On average, each client had one diagnosable personality disorder. Overall, 82% of the clients had tried other forms of therapy, including drug treatment. Most clients had received psychoanalytic treatment for many years. A follow-up study found that the average length of time in treatment was 4.8 years (see Doidge et al., 2002).

Time-limited psychotherapy is available as an alternative to the many years sometimes required for classic psychodynamic treatment. The early pioneers in time-limited psychotherapy, called **brief therapy**, were the psychoanalysts Ferenczi (1952) and Alexander and French (1946). This shorter form was developed to meet the expectations of the many clients who prefer therapy to be fairly short term and targeted to specific problems in their everyday lives.

The growth of brief therapy also evolved from the need to respond to psychological emergencies (Koss & Shiang, 1994). Cases of shell shock during the Second World War led to Grinker and Spiegel's (1945) classic short-term analytic treatment of what is now called post-traumatic stress disorder. A related contribution came from Lindemann's (1944) crisis intervention with the survivors of Boston's famous Cocoanut Grove nightclub fire in 1942.

Insurance companies and government health plans have played a role in shortening the duration of treatment by encouraging therapists to adapt their ideas to brief therapy. They have become increasingly reluctant to cover more than a limited number of psychotherapy sessions in a given calendar year and have set limits on reimbursement amounts.

All these factors, combined with the growing acceptability of psychotherapy in the population at large, have set the stage for a stronger focus on time-limited psychodynamic therapy. Brief therapies share several common elements (Koss & Shiang, 1994):

- Assessment tends to be rapid and early.
- It is made clear right away that therapy will be limited and that improvement is expected within a small number of sessions (from 6 to 25).

Over 400 lives were lost in the fire at the Cocoanut Grove nightclub in 1942. The crisis intervention work that followed influenced the development of brief psychodynamic therapy. Bettman/CORBIS.

- Goals are concrete and focused on improving the client's worst symptoms, helping the client understand what is going in his or her life, and enabling the client to cope better in the future.
- Interpretations are directed more toward present life circumstances and client behaviour than on the historical significance of feelings.
- Development of transference is not encouraged.
- There is a general understanding that psychotherapy does not cure, but that it can help individuals learn to deal better with life's inevitable stressors.

Contemporary psychoanalytic thought Lerner (2008) has provided a contemporary assessment of psychoanalysis and current psychodynamic perspectives. He concluded that "... psychoanalysis since Freud has undergone enormous revisions and transformations that have altered many fundamental aspects of Freud's original ideas. Profound shifts in the psychoanalytic understanding of female sexuality, infant and child development, and severe psychopathology are crucial examples of the psychoanalytic landscape" (Lerner, 2008, p. 129). Lerner identified five conceptual approaches that are predominant in contemporary psychoanalytic thought: (1) modern structural theory; (2) self-psychology; (3) object relations theory; (4) interpersonal-relational; and (5) attachment theory. We now discuss interpersonal therapy as an illustration of how this conceptual approach has been incorporated into contemporary forms of treatment.

Interpersonal therapy Interpersonal therapy is a contemporary variation of brief psychodynamic therapy that has grown in popularity and impact. This approach emphasizes the interactions between a client and his or her social environment. The American psychiatrist Harry Stack Sullivan pioneered the interpersonal approach. Other key figures, including attachment theorist John Bowlby, and recent versions of interpersonal therapy incorporate a more extensive focus on attachment needs (for a historical overview, see Weissman, 2006). According to Sullivan, our needs are interpersonal in that whether they are met depends on the complementary needs of other people. A key turning point for the infant is when he or she realizes that survival depends on the mother's co-operation in satisfying the infant's basic needs. Sometimes called a neo-Freudian, Sullivan held that a client's basic difficulty is a misperception of reality stemming from disorganization in the interpersonal relationships of childhood, primarily the relationship between child and parents. He conceived of the analyst as a "participant observer" in the therapy process (not as a blank screen for transference), arguing that the therapist, like the scientist, is a part of the process that he or she is studying—an analyst does not see clients without at the same time affecting them. While interpersonal therapy focuses on past relationships, an important goal is to examine these past influences in terms of how they impact on and contribute to current relationships.

Particularly prominent is the **interpersonal therapy (IPT)** of Klerman and Weissman (Klerman et al., 1984). The IPT therapist concentrates on the client's current interpersonal difficulties and discusses with the client better ways of relating to others. Although IPT incorporates some psychodynamic ideas, it is distinct in several ways from traditional forms of psychoanalysis. *Mastering Depression: The Patient's Guide to Therapy* contains the following section in the description of IPT:

> The IPT therapist will not: 1) Interpret your dreams;
> 2) Have treatment go on indefinitely; 3) Delve into your early childhood; 4) Encourage you to free associate; 5) Make you feel very dependent on the treatment or the therapist. (Weissman, 1995, pp. 11–12)

IPT's techniques combine empathic listening with suggestions for behavioural changes, as well as how to implement them. The IPT therapist might explore with the client the complexities of present-day problems, with an emphasis on the client's relationships with others. The therapist might then encourage the client to make specific behavioural changes, sometimes facilitating these shifts by having the client practise new behaviours in the consulting room (**role-playing**).

According to Weissman (2006), IPT has been used successfully in many cultures and it is equally effective for clients of diverse backgrounds. Weissman has observed that it is somewhat remarkable that only minor adaptations are needed when modifying IPT for use in various cultures.

The potential benefits of IPT have been demonstrated in many studies. IPT is used most commonly to treat depression. For instance, a study led by Queen's University researcher Kate Harkness (Harkness et al., 2002) found that the usual link between stressful events and bouts of depression is weakened considerably among women who received IPT and then two years of maintenance IPT. IPT has been applied to various forms of depression, including postpartum depression and depression in the elderly. It was also used as a potential treatment for heart patients recovering from cardiac difficulties, but was not found to be particularly effective relative to other interventions (Lespérance et al., 2007). This finding is somewhat surprising given that interpersonal hostility is a key factor that seems to put people at risk for heart disease and poorer recoveries (see Chida & Steptoe, 2009).

EVALUATING THE PSYCHOANALYTIC PARADIGM

Perhaps no investigator of human behaviour has been so honoured and so criticized as Freud. Freud was vilified when he proposed his theory of infantile sexuality (i.e., the notion that infants and children are motivated by sexual drives). In turn-of-the-century Vienna, sexuality was rarely discussed. One criticism levelled against Freud's theory applies to other psychoanalytic theories as well: theories based on anecdotal evidence gathered during therapy sessions are not grounded in objectivity and therefore are not scientific. Unlike those who work within the biological paradigm or within the learning and cognitive paradigms (which entail conducting formal research on the causes and treatments of abnormal behaviour), Freud believed that the information obtained from therapy sessions was enough to validate his theory and demonstrate the effectiveness of the therapy. His clients, however, were not merely a small sample. They were also atypical, being largely affluent, educated, and Viennese. In Chapter 5, we will discuss the severe limitations of such data.

It is also important to keep in mind that psychodynamic concepts, such as id, ego, and the unconscious, though meant to be used as metaphors to describe psychic functions, sometimes were described as though they had an existence of their own, with the power to act and think. Freud (1937) spoke of their attempts to ensure their own survival and the attempts of the id and superego to overthrow the ego.

Even with these substantial criticisms, however, Freud's contribution to the field of abnormal psychology remains enormous. His ongoing influence is most evident in the following three commonly held assumptions:

1. *Childhood experiences help shape adult personality.* Contemporary clinicians and researchers still view childhood experiences as crucial, and this is largely due to Freud's influence. Indeed, recent longitudinal research demonstrates that childhood predictors of psychopathology can be manifested 40 years later (see Pine, 2007).
2. *There are unconscious influences on behaviour.* Research shows that people can be unaware of the causes of their behaviour. While unconscious factors and processes may influence us, it is doubtful that the unconscious is a repository of id instincts.
3. *People use defence mechanisms to control anxiety or stress.* There is a great deal of research on coping with stress (see Chapter 9), and defence mechanisms are included in an

appendix of the *DSM-IV-TR* (the catalogue of mental disorders published by the American Psychiatric Association and reviewed in the next chapter).

Although there are many legitimate concerns about the validity and usefulness of Freud's work, it is impossible to acquire a good grasp of the field of abnormal psychology without some familiarity with his writings. Further, as noted by Tryon (2008), "the psychodynamic model of psychopathology . . . continues to be widely taught and to broadly inform clinical practice" (p. 963). In addition, although certain aspects of psychoanalytic theory are vague or abstract and difficult to test, research on psychoanalytic interventions seems to attest to their effectiveness. Saskia de Maat and colleagues (de Maat, de Jonghe, Schoevers, & Dekker, 2009) conducted a systematic review of 27 studies dealing with the effectiveness of long-term psychoanalytic therapy published since 1970. They concluded that psychotherapy resulted in high mean overall success rates (64% at termination; 55% at follow-up). A meta-analysis (see Chapter 5) of 17 studies on the effectiveness of short-term psychodynamic therapy showed that it yielded significant improvements that were maintained at follow-up and were comparable in magnitude to the gains achieved through other forms of treatment (Leichsenring, Rabung, & Leibing, 2004). A follow-up investigation of 23 treatment studies found once again that short-term psychodynamic therapy led to significant improvements relative to control conditions and it yielded comparable benefits relative to other forms of therapy, including CBT (Leichsenring & Leibing, 2007). However, of the included studies that used adequate methodology, only three psychodynamic studies and five CBT studies used a stringent randomized, controlled clinical trials procedure (Oldham, 2007; see Chapter 5). Recently, Milrod et al. (2007) demonstrated the efficacy of a manualized, panic-focused psychodynamic psychotherapy (relative to applied relaxation training) for panic disorder in a randomized controlled clinical trial (RCT). In another RCT, Hoglend et al. (2008) found that transference interpretations are particularly important for people with long-standing, more severe interpersonal problems. Leichsenring and Rabung (2008) conducted a meta-analysis of 11 RCTs and 12 observational studies of long-term psychodynamic psychotherapy (LTPP), i.e., therapy lasting for at least a year or 50 sessions. Relative to shorter forms of psychotherapy, LTPP showed significantly higher outcomes in overall effectiveness, target problems, and personality functioning. Further, with respect to overall effectiveness, the authors concluded that, "after treatment with LTPP patients with complex mental disorders on average were better off than 96% of the patients in the comparison groups" (p. 1551). Leichsenring and Rabung noted the need for research to address the outcome of LTPP in specific psychiatric disorders.

THE HUMANISTIC-EXISTENTIAL PARADIGMS

Humanistic and existential therapies, like psychoanalytic therapies, are insight-focused, based on the assumption that disordered behaviour results from a lack of insight, and can best be treated by increasing the individual's awareness of motivations and needs. There are, however, useful contrasts between psychoanalysis and its offshoots on the one hand and humanistic and existential approaches on the other. The psychoanalytic paradigm assumes that human nature, the id, is something in need of restraint; that effective socialization requires the ego to mediate between the environment and the basically anti-social, at best asocial, impulses stemming from biological urges. Humanistic and existential paradigms place greater emphasis on the person's freedom of choice, regarding free will as the person's most important characteristic. Yet, free will is a double-edged sword, for it can bring not only fulfillment and pleasure, but also acute pain and suffering. Its exercise, therefore, requires special courage. Not everyone can meet this challenge. Those who cannot are regarded as candidates for client-centred and existential therapies. Humanistic and existential paradigms, also referred to as experiential or phenomenological, seldom focus on how psychological problems develop. Their main influence is on intervention, and so our discussion deals primarily with therapy.

CARL ROGERS'S CLIENT-CENTRED THERAPY

Carl Rogers was an American psychologist of enormous influence whose theorizing about psychotherapy grew slowly out of years of intensive clinical experience. After teaching at the university level in the 1940s and 1950s, he helped organize the Center for Studies of the Person in La Jolla, California. How influential is Rogers? A recent survey was conducted of 2,400 North American psychotherapists and Rogers was identified as the most influential psychotherapist figure (Cook, Biyanova, & Coyne, 2009). Beck and Ellis finished second and sixth, respectively.

Rogers's **client-centred therapy** (also referred to as person-centred therapy) is based on several assumptions about human nature and the way we can try to understand it (Rogers, 1951, 1961):

- People can be understood only from the vantage point of their own perceptions and feelings; that is, from their phenomenological world. We must look at the way they experience events because this is the major determinant of behaviour and makes each person unique.
- Healthy people are aware of their behaviour. In this sense, Rogers's system is similar to psychoanalysis and ego analysis, for it emphasizes the desirability of being aware of motives. People with a high level of self-awareness and a sense of personal agency are said to be thoughtful, and this is a primary goal of counselling (Rennie, 1998).
- Healthy people are innately good and effective. They become ineffective and disturbed only when faulty learning intervenes.
- Healthy people are purposive and goal-directed. They do not respond passively to the influence of their environment or to their inner drives. They are self-directed.

Carl Rogers, a humanistic therapist, proposed that the key ingredient in therapy is the attitude and style of the therapist rather than specific techniques. © Roger Ressmeyer/CORBIS.

- Therapists should not attempt to manipulate events for the individual. Rather, they should create conditions that will facilitate independent decision-making by the client. When people are not concerned with the evaluations, demands, and preferences of others, their lives are guided by an innate tendency toward **self-actualization**.

This emphasis on self-actualization and maximizing potential and the belief that people are innately good are in keeping with the current movement toward *positive psychology*. Positive psychology promotes a focus on attributes and personal characteristics (e.g., resilience, optimism, hope) that emphasizes "wellness" and being able to function, as opposed to psychology's seeming preoccupation with negative outcomes and dysfunction. Thus, rather than focusing on vulnerability factors, positive psychology focuses on protective factors.

ROGERS'S THERAPEUTIC INTERVENTION Consistent with his view of human nature, Rogers avoided imposing goals on the client during therapy. The client is to take the lead and direct the course of the conversation and the session. The therapist's job is to create the conditions that, during the session, help the client return to his or her basic nature and judge which course of life is intrinsically gratifying. Because of his positive view of people, Rogers assumed that their decisions would not only make them happy with themselves but also turn them into good, civilized people. The road to these good decisions is not easy, however.

According to Rogers and other humanistic and existential therapists, people must take responsibility for themselves, even when they are troubled. It is often difficult for a therapist to refrain from giving advice, from taking charge of a client's life, especially when the client appears incapable of making decisions. But Rogerians hold steadfastly to the rule that a person's innate capacity for growth and self-direction will assert itself if the therapeutic atmosphere is warm, attentive, and receptive, and especially if the therapist accepts the person for whom he or she is, providing what he called **unconditional positive regard**.

Other people set what Rogers called "conditions of worth" (e.g., "I will love you if ..."). In contrast, unconditional positive regard is reflected by the client-centred therapist valuing clients as they are, whatever their behaviour. People have value merely for being people, and the therapist must care deeply for and respect a client for the simple reason that he or she is another human being engaged in the struggle of growing and being alive.

Although client-centred therapy is not technique-oriented, one strategy is central to this approach: empathy. Because empathy is so important in Rogerian therapy and in all other kinds of therapy (not to mention ordinary social intercourse), let us examine it more closely.

Empathy It is useful to distinguish the following two types of empathy (Egan, 1975):

- *Primary empathy* refers to the therapist's understanding, accepting, and communicating to the client what the client is thinking or feeling. The therapist conveys primary empathy by restating the client's thoughts and feelings, pretty much in the client's own words.
- *Advanced empathy* entails an inference by the therapist of the thoughts and feelings that lie behind what the client is saying, and of which the client may only be dimly, if at all, aware. Advanced empathy essentially involves an interpretation by the therapist of the meaning of what the client is thinking and feeling.

At the primary empathic level, the therapist accepts the client's view, understands it, and communicates to the client that it is appreciated. At the advanced or interpretive level, however, the therapist offers something new, a perspective that he or she hopes is better, more productive, and that implies new modes of action. Advanced empathizing builds on the information provided over a number of sessions in which the therapist concentrates on making primary-level empathic statements.

The client-centred therapist, operating within a phenomenological philosophy, must have as the goal the movement of a client from his or her present phenomenological world to another one—hence the importance of the advanced-empathy stage. Since people's emotions and actions are determined by how they construe themselves and their surroundings—by their phenomenology—those who are dysfunctional or otherwise dissatisfied with their present mode of living are in need of a new phenomenology. From the very outset then, client-centred therapy—and all other phenomenological therapies—concentrates on clients adopting frameworks different from those they had upon beginning treatment. Merely reflecting back to clients their current phenomenology cannot in itself bring therapeutic change. A new phenomenology must be acquired.

In our view, advanced empathy represents theory building on the part of the therapist. After considering over a number of sessions what the client has been saying and how he or she has been saying it, the therapist generates a hypothesis about what may be the true source of distress hidden from the client.

Exposure to an empathetic therapist can have a powerful, positive effect, as shown in studies conducted by Coons and associates with clients diagnosed with schizophrenia from Ontario psychiatric hospitals (see Coons, 1967; Coons & Peacock, 1970). Participation in groups led by an empathetic therapist led to substantial improvements in personality and intellectual functioning, improvements greater than those from insight-based psychotherapy.

EXISTENTIAL THERAPY

Humanism and existentialism have much in common, but the humanistic work of North Americans, such as Rogers, can be contrasted with the more European existential approach that derives from the writings of philosophers (e.g., Sartre and Kierkegaard) and psychiatrists (e.g., Binswanger and Frankl).

The existential and humanist points of view both emphasize personal growth. Yet, there are important distinctions between the two. Humanism stresses the goodness of human nature. It holds that if unfettered by groundless fears and societal restrictions, human beings will develop normally, even exceptionally. Existentialism is gloomier. Although it embraces free will and responsibility, it stresses the anxiety that is inevitable in making important choices, the existential choices on which existence depends, such as staying or not staying with a spouse, with a job, or even with this world. Avoiding choices may protect people from anxiety, but it also deprives them of living a life with meaning and is at the core of psychopathology.

THE GOALS OF EXISTENTIAL THERAPY Therapists operating within an existential framework encourage clients to confront their anxieties concerning choices about how they will live, what they will value, and how they will relate to others. They support their clients in examining what is really meaningful in life. Sometimes a choice will occasion extreme discomfort. Life is not easy for those who would be true to themselves.

At some point during therapy, the client must begin to behave differently, toward both the therapist and the outside world, to change his or her own existential condition. Hence, although the existential view is highly subjective, it entails relating to others in an open, spontaneous, and loving manner. Yet, paradoxically, each of us is essentially alone. We came into the world alone, and we must create our own existence in the world alone.

In the existential view, people create their existence anew at each moment. The potential for disorder as well as for growth is ever-present. Individuals must be encouraged to accept responsibility for their own existence and to realize that, within certain limits, they can redefine themselves at any moment and behave and feel differently within their own social environment.

The existential writers are vague about what therapeutic techniques will help the client grow. A reliance on technique may even be seen as an objectifying process in which the therapist acts on the client as though he or she were a thing to be manipulated (Prochaska, 1984). The existential approach is best understood as a general attitude taken by certain therapists toward human nature rather than as a set of therapeutic techniques.

EVALUATING THE HUMANISTIC AND EXISTENTIAL PARADIGMS

Rogers and the existential therapists focus on the client's phenomenology, but how can the therapist ever know that he or she is truly understanding a client's world as it appears to the client? The validity of the inferences made by therapists about the client's phenomenology is an important and unsolved issue. That people are innately good and, if faulty learning does not interfere, will make choices that are personally fulfilling is also an assumption that can be questioned. Other social philosophers (e.g., Thomas Hobbes) have taken a decidedly less optimistic view of human nature.

Rogers should be credited with originating the field of psychotherapy research. He insisted that therapy outcomes be empirically evaluated, and he pioneered the use of tape recordings so that therapists' behaviour could be related to therapeutic outcomes. The major prediction of Rogerian therapy, of course, is that therapists' empathy should relate to outcomes. The findings are inconsistent (Greenberg, Elliott, & Lietaer, 1994). However, it probably makes sense to continue to emphasize empathy in the training of therapists, as this quality is likely to make it easier for clients to reveal highly personal and sometimes unpleasant facts about themselves.

CONSEQUENCES OF ADOPTING A PARADIGM

The student who adopts a particular paradigm necessarily makes a prior decision concerning what kinds of data will be collected and how they will be interpreted. Thus, he or she may very well ignore possibilities and overlook other information in advancing what seems to be the most probable explanation. A behaviourist is prone to attribute the high prevalence of schizophrenia in lower-class groups to the paucity of social rewards that these people received, based on the assumption that normal development requires a certain amount of reinforcement patterning. A biologically oriented theorist will be quick to remind the behaviourist of the many deprived people who do not become schizophrenic. The behaviourist will undoubtedly counter with the argument that those who do not become schizophrenic had different reinforcement histories. The biologically oriented theorist will reply that such post hoc statements can always be made.

DIFFERENT PERSPECTIVES ON A CLINICAL PROBLEM: J. BRETT BARKLEY

To provide a concrete example of how it is possible to conceptualize a clinical case using different paradigms, we now reconsider the case of officer J. Brett Barkley with which this book began. If you hold a biological point of view, you are attentive to the similarity between the man's alternately manic and depressed states and the cyclical mood swings of his father. You are probably aware of research (see Chapter 8) that suggests a genetic factor in mood disorders. You do not discount environmental contributions to Brett's problems, but you hypothesize that some inherited, probably biochemical, defect predisposes him to break down under stress.

If you have a behavioural or cognitive behaviour perspective, you may focus on Brett's self-consciousness at university, which seems related to the fact that, compared with his fellow students, he grew up with few advantages. Economic insecurity and hardship may have made him unduly sensitive to criticism and rejection. Moreover, he regards his wife as warm and charming, pointing to his own perceived lack of social skills. Alcohol has been his escape from such tensions, but heavy drinking, coupled with persistent doubt about his own worth as a human being, has interfered with sexual functioning, worsening an already deteriorating marital relationship and further undermining his confidence. As a behaviour therapist, you may employ systematic desensitization. You teach Brett to relax deeply as he imagines a hierarchy of situations in which he is being evaluated by others. Or you may decide on rational-emotive behaviour therapy to convince Brett that he need not obtain universal approval for every undertaking. Or, you may choose **behaviour rehearsal** to teach him how to function effectively in social situations. You might follow more than one of these strategies.

A psychoanalytic viewpoint emphasizes that events in early childhood are of great importance in later patterns of adjustment. Thus, you hypothesize that Brett is still grieving for his mother and has blamed his father for her early death. Anger at the father has been repressed, but Brett has not been able to regard him as a competent, worthwhile adult or to identify with him.

DIFFERENT PERSPECTIVES ON A CLINICAL PROBLEM: CATHY— A CASE OF TRICHOTILLOMANIA

The disorders described in subsequent sections of the book can usually be interpreted from the perspective of several paradigms. For instance, consider the following case excerpt of a Canadian university student with trichotillomania (TTM), an impulse control disorder involving chronic hair pulling, discussed further in Chapter 5.

> She wanted to work on her problem of hair pulling because it made her both depressed and angry. The problem kept her from being able to study and perform in school because, according to her, she could spend a mean of 4 hours pulling her hair in a 7-hour study period. Cathy had already been in therapy with psychoanalytic treatment for almost 2 years . . . without any effect on the severity and frequency of her pulling behavior. She also had been treated with medication (Prozac) for 5 months, which according to her made her problem worse because "she was feeling so happy she didn't

care if she was pulling at all anymore" . . . She complained of pulling her own hair, every day, up to a maximum of 100 hairs on the worst days. She also had two other habit disorders— biting her cheeks and nail biting—that she considered less disruptive. She experienced tension prior to pulling and was most at risk to pull during academic performances. Ideas about failing preoccupied her . . . Cathy believed her TTM had started when she was 12 years old, after her parents' divorce. At the time, her grades in school were falling and consequently, she felt very anxious about failing her school year. (Pelissier & O'Connor, 2004, p. 59–60).

How can Cathy's behaviour be interpreted? A behavioural theorist would focus on the reinforcement of the relief of tension provided by the chronic hair pulling. A psychoanalytic theorist would focus on the interpersonal dynamics and early life experiences. The trichotillomania could be attributed to a sense of anxiety reflecting the unconscious interplay of the id and the superego, with this conflict distracting the ego from the conscious need to study and do well in school. Finally, if viewed from a cognitive perspective, which was the main perspective adopted by the authors, the theorist would focus on irrational fears about failure. As it turned out, Cathy suffered from extreme levels of perfectionism and concern over mistakes, and this became a central focus of treatment.

ECLECTICISM IN PSYCHOTHERAPY: PRACTICE MAKES IMPERFECT

A word is needed about paradigms and the activities of therapists. The treatment approaches, as described so far, may appear to be separate, non-overlapping schools of therapy. You may have the impression that a behaviour therapist would never listen to a client's report of a dream, nor would a psychoanalyst be caught dead prescribing **assertion training** to a client. Such suppositions could not be further from the truth. Many therapists subscribe to **eclecticism**, employing ideas and therapeutic techniques from a variety of schools (Hunsley & Lefebvre, 1990). A trend toward integrating psychotherapies has culminated in a combined approach known as *prescriptive eclectic therapy* (see Norcross & Beutler, 2000) and a survey of therapists treating eating disorder clients suggests that an eclectic approach may be the norm rather than the exception (von Ranson & Robinson, 2006). This survey of clinicians in Calgary found that eclectic therapy was the main approach employed by half of the clinicians. CBT was the second most popular option and was used by one third of the clinicians. Those who engage in eclectic therapy prefer the term "integrative" rather than "eclectic," and the most common integration is cognitive therapy (Norcross, Karpiak, & Lister, 2005; also see Fruzzetti & Erikson, 2010; Harwood, Beutler, & Charvat, 2010; and Martin & Young, 2010).

Therapists often behave in ways not entirely consistent with the theories they hold. For years, practising behaviour therapists have been listening empathically to clients, trying to make out their perspectives on events, on the assumption that this understanding would help them plan a better program for changing troublesome behaviour. Behavioural theories do not prescribe such a procedure, but on the basis of clinical experience, and perhaps through their own humanity, behaviour therapists have realized that empathic listening helps them establish rapport, determine what is really bothering the client, and plan a sensible therapy program. Freud himself is said to have been more directive and to have done far more to change immediate behaviour than would be concluded from his writings alone.

Treatment is a complex and ultimately highly individual process, and these are weighty issues. In Chapter 17, we will return to these and other issues and give them the attention they deserve. You should be aware of this complexity at the beginning, however, to better appreciate the intricacies and realities of psychotherapy.

DIATHESIS–STRESS AND BIOPSYCHOSOCIAL: INTEGRATIVE PARADIGMS

"Rather than adopting a single explanatory perspective, as is often advocated in traditional theories of science, etiological models for psychiatric disorders need to be pluralistic or multilevel. . . . A range of compelling evidence indicates that these disorders involve causal processes that act within and outside of the individual, and that involve processes best understood from biological, psychological, and sociocultural perspectives."

—Kenneth S. Kendler, Explanatory Models for Psychiatric Illness (2008, p. 695).

Clearly, abnormal behaviour is much too diverse to be explained or treated adequately by any one of the current paradigms. It is probably advantageous that psychologists do not agree on which paradigm is the best. We know far too little to make hard-and-fast decisions on the exclusive superiority of any one paradigm. The best approach is often to assume multiple causation. A particular disorder is likely to be quite complex and develop through an interaction of factors. Two integrative paradigms are now explored.

THE DIATHESIS–STRESS PARADIGM

A paradigm more general than the ones discussed so far, called the **diathesis–stress paradigm**, links biological, psychological, and environmental factors. It is not limited to one particular school of thought, such as learning, cognitive, or psychodynamic, but focuses on the interaction between a predisposition toward disease—the diathesis—and environmental, or life, disturbances—the stress. Diathesis refers most precisely to a constitutional predisposition toward illness, but the term may be extended to any characteristic or set of characteristics that increases a person's chance of developing a disorder.

In the realm of biology, a number of disorders appear to have a genetically transmitted diathesis; that is, having a close relative with the disorder increases a person's risk for the dis-

Life stress, such as being overwhelmed at work or living in a war zone, is an important component of the diathesis–stress paradigm.
© Images.com/Corbis.

order since there is a sharing of genetic endowment to some degree. Although the precise nature of these genetic diatheses is currently unknown (e.g., we don't know exactly what is inherited that increases susceptibility to schizophrenia), it is clear that a genetic predisposition is an important component of many psychopathologies. Other biological diatheses include oxygen deprivation at birth, poor nutrition, a maternal viral infection, or maternal smoking during pregnancy. Each of these conditions may lead to changes in the brain that predispose toward psychopathology.

In the psychological realm, a diathesis for depression may be the cognitive set already mentioned: the chronic feeling of hopelessness sometimes found in depressed people. Or, taking a psychodynamic view, it may be an extreme sense of dependency on others, perhaps because of frustrations during one of the psychosexual stages. Another psychological diathesis is the ability to be easily hypnotized, which may be a diathesis for dissociative identity disorder (formerly called multiple personality disorder).

These psychological diatheses can arise for a variety of reasons. Some, such as hypnotizability, are personality characteristics that are, in part, genetically determined. Others, such as a sense of hopelessness, may result from adverse life experiences. The diathesis–stress paradigm is integrative because it draws on all these diverse sources of information about the causes of diatheses.

Possessing the diathesis for a disorder increases a person's risk of developing it but does not guarantee that the disorder will develop. It is the stress part of diathesis–stress that accounts for how a diathesis may be translated into an actual disorder. In this context, stress generally refers to some noxious or unpleasant environmental stimulus that triggers psychopathology. Psychological stressors include both major traumatic events (e.g., losing one's job, divorce, death of a spouse) and more mundane happenings (e.g., being stuck in traffic). The diathesis–stress model goes beyond the major paradigms we have already discussed by including these environmental events.

The key point of the diathesis–stress model is that both diathesis and stress are necessary in the development of disorders (see Figure 2.8). Some people, for example, inherit a biological predisposition that places them at high risk for schizophrenia (see Chapter 11); given a certain amount of stress, they stand a good chance of developing schizophrenia. Other people, at low genetic risk, are not likely to develop schizophrenia, regardless of how difficult their lives are.

In a recent study, Keller and colleagues (Keller, Neale, & Kendler, 2007) reported that different types of life events are linked to specific patterns of depressive symptoms, suggesting that even if a person carries a genetic diathesis for depression, the clinical manifestations of that diathesis might be strongly influenced by specific types of life experiences. A further implication is that the development of new drug treatments for depression should possibly consider not only the underlying genetic and molecular neurobiology of the disorder, but also the ways in which that neurobiology might be differentially shaped by stressful life events.

Another feature of the diathesis–stress paradigm is that psychopathology is unlikely to result from any single factor. As seen in our earlier discussion of gene–environment interactions, a genetically transmitted diathesis may be necessary for some disorders, but it is embedded in a network of other factors that also play a part, for example, genetically transmitted diatheses for other personality characteristics, childhood experiences that shape personality, the development of behavioural competencies and coping strategies, stressors encountered in adulthood, and cultural influences.

THE BIOPSYCHOSOCIAL PARADIGM

Some clinical scientists describe an integrative paradigm that is quite similar to and overlaps with the diathesis–stress perspective: the **biopsychosocial paradigm**. Biological, psychological, and social factors are conceptualized as different levels of analysis or subsystems within the paradigm (Engel, 1980). Like the diathesis–stress paradigm, the biopsychosocial paradigm is not limited to a particular school of thought. Figure 2.9 illustrates the biopsychosocial paradigm. The figure incorporates an array of the possible causal factors, including some of those described in connection with the discussion of the diathesis–stress paradigm. The key point about the biopsychosocial paradigm is that explanations for the causes of disorders typically involve complex interactions among many biological, psychological, and socio-environmental and socio-cultural factors. The actual variables and the degree of influence of the variables from the different domains typically differ from disorder to disorder. Thus, similar to the diathesis–stress paradigm, the biopsychosocial paradigm is integrative because it accepts the interplay of many factors and draws on diverse sources of information about the causes of psychological disorders.

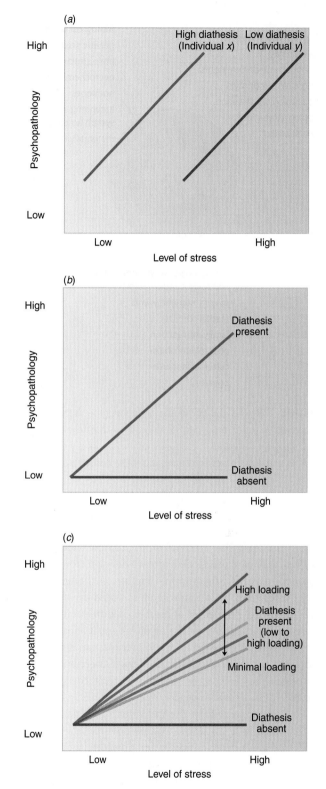

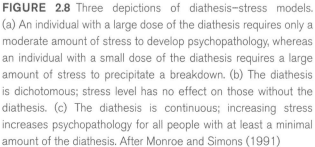

FIGURE 2.8 Three depictions of diathesis–stress models. (a) An individual with a large dose of the diathesis requires only a moderate amount of stress to develop psychopathology, whereas an individual with a small dose of the diathesis requires a large amount of stress to precipitate a breakdown. (b) The diathesis is dichotomous; stress level has no effect on those without the diathesis. (c) The diathesis is continuous; increasing stress increases psychopathology for all people with at least a minimal amount of the diathesis. After Monroe and Simons (1991)

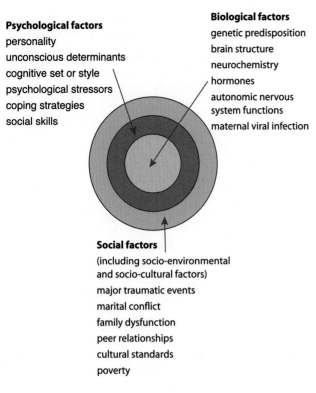

Psychological factors
personality
unconscious determinants
cognitive set or style
psychological stressors
coping strategies
social skills

Biological factors
genetic predisposition
brain structure
neurochemistry
hormones
autonomic nervous
system functions
maternal viral infection

Social factors
(including socio-environmental
and socio-cultural factors)
major traumatic events
marital conflict
family dysfunction
peer relationships
cultural standards
poverty

FIGURE 2.9 The biopsychosocial paradigm. Although disturbances in each area can contribute to the development of psychological disorders, the causes cannot be neatly divided and there is usually interaction among the three domains of influence

Many scholarly articles and research papers are based on the diathesis–stress and biopsychosocial paradigms (e.g., Kendler, 2008), a reflection of the now widely accepted view that psychological disorders develop from complex interactions involving multiple factors. Although both of these integrative paradigms tend to focus on the factors that interact to put people at greater **risk** of—or make them more vulnerable to—developing disorders, it should also be recognized that certain factors, if present, can help protect individuals from developing disorders. Protection from risk factors, or the ability to bounce back in the face of adversity, is referred to as **resilience** (Smith & Prior, 1995). Protective factors can occur within the individual (e.g., perseverance and courage in a child who suffers poverty; the ability to think and act independently in an adolescent whose parent is diagnosed with a psychiatric disorder) but can also reside in the environment (e.g., a close relationship with one parent; support from a caring teacher) (see Government of Canada, 2006; Phares, 2003, for a more complete discussion of protective factors and resiliency.) Tables 2.1 and 2.2 summarize risk factors and protective factors that potentially influence the development of mental health problems and mental disorders in people. These tables, adapted from the recent report *The Human Face of Mental Health and Mental Illness in Canada 2006* (Government of Canada, 2006), illustrate the complexity and variety of both risk and protective

factors that can be considered from a diathesis–stress or biopsychosocial perspective. For example, homelessness is listed as a situational risk factor for mental disorders, but not all homeless people develop mental disorders (an issue revisited in Chapter 18). What individual factors can protect against the development of mental (and physical) health problems in the homeless? While low self-esteem is listed as a risk factor in Table 2.2, high self-esteem can play a protective role. This effect was illustrated in a recent study conducted by Sean Kidd from McMaster University and Golan Shahar from Yale University (Kidd & Shahar, 2008) who examined the protective role of self-esteem in homeless youths in Toronto and New York City. Among various factors, high self-esteem emerged as the key protective factor. It predicted lower levels of loneliness, feeling trapped, and suicidal ideation. Thus, the self-concept plays an important role in determining risk and resilience in this extremely high-risk population, many of whom come from abusive and chaotic family backgrounds.

The occurrence of many risk factors is specific to particular stages of the lifespan, particularly childhood. Contemporary biopsychosocial models of psychopathology in children are described in Chapter 15. These models typically incorporate a developmental psychopathology focus (see Cicchetti, 1984); i.e., a general framework for understanding disordered behaviour in relation to normal development.

Maltreatment or abuse is a powerful risk factor: a history of maltreatment in childhood is acknowledged as a consistent and strong predictor of subsequent emotional difficulties. According to the World Health Organization (2004), tens of millions of children are abused and neglected each year, and 20% of females and 10% of males are victims of childhood sexual abuse. Canadian data suggest that levels of maltreatment may be on the rise! The 2003 Canadian Incidence Study of Reported Child Abuse and Neglect led by Nico Trocmé found that in the nine provinces surveyed (all but Quebec), there was a 125% increase over five years, with 9.64 substantiated cases per thousand children in 1998 versus 21.71 in 2003 (see Trocmé et al., 2005).

A horrific case of physical, emotional, and sexual abuse drew revulsion worldwide in 2008 when a woman, then 42 years old, escaped from a squalid, rat-infested cellar built beneath the family's home near Vienna, Austria. Her father had locked her in the dungeon when she was 18. Over the next 24 years, he raped her more than 3,000 times, fathered her seven children, and let one die in captivity as a newborn (Oleksyn & Kole, 2009).

On March 19, 2009, Josef Fritzl, 73, pleaded guilty to homicide, enslavement, rape, incest, forced imprisonment, and coercion. He was sentenced to life in a secure psychiatric ward. One can hardly imagine the terrible psychological consequences to his daughter Elizabeth, who was described by prosecutors as a "broken" woman, and her six surviving children, three of whom had never seen daylight until the crime was exposed. She and the children, who ranged in age from 6 to 20, spent months recovering in a psychiatric clinic.

TABLE 2.1

RISK FACTORS POTENTIALLY INFLUENCING THE DEVELOPMENT OF MENTAL HEALTH PROBLEMS AND MENTAL DISORDERS IN INDIVIDUALS

Individual Factors	Family/Social Factors	School Context	Life Events and Situations	Community and Cultural Factors
• Prenatal brain damage • Prematurity • Birth injury • Low birth weight, birth complications • Physical and intellectual disability • Poor health in infancy • Insecure attachment in infant/child • Low intelligence • Difficult temperament • Chronic illness • Poor social skills • Low self-esteem • Alienation • Impulsivity	• Having a teenage mother • Having a single parent • Absence of father in childhood • Large family size • Anti-social role models (in childhood) • Family violence and disharmony • Marital discord in parents • Poor supervision and monitoring of child • Low parental involvement in child's activities • Neglect in childhood • Long-term parent unemployment • Criminality in parent • Parent substance misuse • Parent mental disorder • Harsh or inconsistent discipline style • Social isolation • Experiencing rejection	• Lack of warmth and affection • Bullying • Peer rejection • Poor attachment to school • Inadequate behaviour management • Deviant peer group • School failure	• Physical, sexual, and emotional abuse • School transitions • Divorce and family breakup • Death of family member • Physical illness/impairment • Unemployment, homelessness • Incarceration • Poverty/economic insecurity • Job insecurity • Unsatisfactory workplace relationships • Workplace accident/injury • Caring for someone with an illness/disability • Living in nursing home or aged care hostel • War or natural disasters	• Socio-economic disadvantage • Social or cultural discrimination • Isolation • Neighbourhood violence and crime • Population density and housing conditions • Lack of support services including transport, shopping, recreational facilities

*Many of these factors are specific to particular stages of the lifespan, particularly childhood; others have an impact across the lifespan; for example, socio-economic disadvantage.

Source: Australia 2005.

We will explore this important risk factor and its often tragic consequences in greater detail in Chapter 5, Canadian Perspectives 5.1, and examine it in relation to other psychosocial risk and protective factors, since maltreatment often operates as part of a complex set of psychosocial factors (e.g., family disruption and poverty; Bagley & Mallick, 2000). However, despite our focus on psychosocial factors, note that a biological vulnerability also seems to play a role in influencing the impact of maltreatment. Some people show remarkable resilience and overcome a history of maltreatment, while others do not. A provocative study of maltreatment and subsequent aggression found that maltreated children with a genotype conferring high levels of monoamine oxidase A (MAO-A) were substantially less likely to display anti-social behaviour

Josef Fritzl locked his daughter in a dungeon for 24 years and subjected her to continuous physical, emotional, and sexual abuse. (AP Photo/Robert Jaeger, Pool, File)

TABLE 2.2

PROTECTIVE FACTORS POTENTIALLY INFLUENCING THE DEVELOPMENT OF MENTAL HEALTH PROBLEMS AND MENTAL DISORDERS IN INDIVIDUALS

Individual Factors	Family/Social Factors	School Context	Life Events and Situations	Community and Cultural Factors
• Easy temperament • Adequate nutrition • Attachment to family • Above-average intelligence • School achievement • Problem-solving skills • Internal locus of control • Social competence • Social skills • Good coping style • Optimism • Moral beliefs • Values • Positive self-related cognitions	• Supportive caring parents • Family harmony • Secure and stable family • Small family size • More than two years between siblings • Responsibility within the family (for child or adult) • Supportive relationship with other adult (for a child or adult) • Strong family norms and morality	• Sense of belonging • Positive school climate • Prosocial peer group • Required responsibility and helpfulness • Opportunities for some success and recognition of achievement • School norms against violence	• Involvement with significant other person (partner/mentor) • Availability of opportunities at critical turning points or major life transitions • Economic security • Good physical health	• Sense of connectedness • Attachment to and networks within the community • Participation in church or other community group • Strong cultural identity and ethnic pride • Access to support services • Community/cultural norms against violence

*Many of these factors are specific to particular stages of the lifespan, particularly childhood; others have an impact across the lifespan; for example, economic security.

Source: Australia 2005.

---

as adults (Caspi et al., 2002). This is a classic example of a gene–environment interaction. This finding was qualified by the results of a newer study that found that lifetime levels of maltreatment and conduct disorder were associated robustly but there was no evidence of a gene–environment interaction (Young et al., 2006). That is, there was no support for the hypothesis that polymorphism in the gene encoding MAO-A confers risk for conduct disorder. Additional research is needed to examine this possibility.

Some factors, such as socio-economic disadvantage, can occur and have an impact across the lifespan. However, as you will see in the following section, the link to psychological disorders is complex. Even our relatively brief discussion highlights the complex interplay of factors in the biopsychosocial model.

AN EXAMPLE: SOCIO-ECONOMIC STATUS AND POVERTY It is generally accepted that extreme poverty and low socio-economic status (SES) confer risk for increased rates of mental illness. This is a tricky issue to some extent because profound mental illness can limit socio-economic opportunities, so it is important, wherever possible, to examine the role of SES in longitudinal research that can establish that low socio-economic status preceded the onset of mental health problems. Further, socio-economic status might be closely related to relevant "third variables" (see Chapter 5), including job status, education, perceived stress, neighbourhood violence

and crime, social support, physical health, marital and family functioning, parental psychopathology, and so forth.

Recent Canadian data do support a link between SES and mental health. The Canadian Community Mental Health Survey's Mental Health and Well-being Cycle documented an apparent steady decline in mental health as a function of lower levels of household income (see Government of Canada, 2006). This effect is illustrated in Figure 2.10.

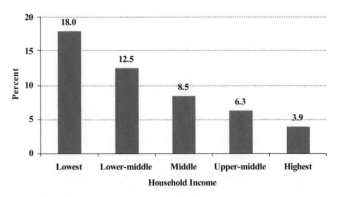

FIGURE 2.10 Mental health perceived as fair or poor among adults aged 15+ years, by household income, Canada, 2002
Source: Adapted from Statistics Canada, Canadian Community Health Survey, Mental Health and Well-being Public Use Microdata FIle 82M0021CB, Cycle 1.2

While money is needed to cover basic life necessities and this serves as a protective factor, it should not be assumed that being rich is a surefire route to happiness. A classic, comparative study of very wealthy people on the Forbes 500 list found that relative to other people, the very wealthy had slightly higher levels of well-being, and none of these billionaires and millionaires identified money as a major source of happiness (Diener, Horowitz, & Emmons, 1985). At the global level, Diener and Seligman (2004) reported that economic output had risen sharply in recent years, with no corresponding increase in average levels of well-being; instead, there have been large increases in depression and distrust. They concluded that income is a relatively minor predictor of well-being relative to strong predictors (i.e., social relationships and work enjoyment). Even though many students lack money and will be paying off student loans for many years to come, when it comes to determining what constitutes "the good life," students place great importance on being happy and finding meaning in life, while money is relatively unimportant (see King & Napa, 1998).

While money can't buy happiness, some money is essential because basic needs must be met. We can only hope that campaigns to end poverty throughout the world will someday be successful. In Canada, in 1989, politicians in the House of Commons pledged to eradicate child poverty by the year 2000. This goal is still not close to being achieved, and this is underscored by a 2006 report that almost one out of every six (almost 1.2 million) children in Canada live in poverty; one in four Aboriginal children live in poverty (see Campaign 2000, 2006). Indeed, Canada still lacks a national, comprehensive strategy to end poverty, although specific plans have been proposed (National Council of Welfare, 2007). Quebec passed anti-poverty legislation in 2002 and has since cut child poverty in half (see Monsebraaten & Talaga, 2009). On May 6, 2009, Ontario passed legislation that commits the province to become a leading jurisdiction in the battle against poverty. The Poverty Reduction Act was hailed by advocates as "historic." More than 350 groups pushed the government to adopt the goal of cutting child poverty by 25% in five years. The act requires successive governments to draft poverty-fighting strategies with specific goals every five years and to report annually to the legislature on progress. All parties supported the legislation.

How might SES combine with other factors in the biopsychosocial model? Essex et al. (2006) confirmed in longitudinal research that children with higher SES have less severe internalizing and externalizing mental health symptoms. Different etiologic pathways were identified for those with low vs. high SES backgrounds. The key factor for those with low SES was chronic maternal stress during the child's infancy. The key factor for those from a high SES background was a parental history of depression along with a family history of psychopathology. For all children, an absence of social and academic impairment during the transition to school was a mediator or buffer of possible mental health problems.

One last study highlights the interplay between genetic and psychosocial factors. This study inquired as to why some children show amazing resilience in the face of profound socio-economic deprivation. It was found that SES deprivation was mitigated by maternal warmth, being engaged in stimulating activities, and having a sociable, outgoing temperament (Kim-Cohen, Moffitt, Caspi, & Taylor, 2004). Temperament is determined, at least in part, by genetic factors that we inherit.

An important caveat about SES is that many of the effects are actually due to living in an impoverished neighbourhood. The negative impact of being poor is amplified when the person lives in a poor neighbourhood, which is defined as poor-quality housing, few available resources, and unsafe conditions (Cutrona, Wallace, & Wesner, 2006). Cutrona et al. (2006) focused on how a poor neighbourhood escalates levels of depression. They identified three specific processes associated with poor neighbourhoods that increase depression: (1) increased daily stress; (2) greater vulnerability to negative events; and (3) disrupted social ties (i.e., less chance to develop positive affiliations). The message is clear: not only do people need a certain level of money, they also need to live in a better location.

Throughout this book, you will discover elaborate explanations of disorders in which numerous variables, both risk and protective, including some of the additional factors summarized in tables 2.1 and 2.2, work together to bring about maladaptive or adaptive outcomes. We now focus on another critical factor.

CULTURAL CONSIDERATIONS

Despite our increasing understanding of biological and psychological factors in the nature and treatment of mental illness, and consistent with our discussion of the biopsychosocial paradigm, social circumstances are ignored only at great risk. We will now visit the important issue of **cultural diversity**, especially as it pertains to Canada. Cultural diversity is important to highly heterogeneous countries such as Canada, since most of our discussion of psychopathology is presented within the context and constraints of Western European society.

J. BRETT BARKLEY: A QUESTION OF CULTURE?

Return once again to the case of J. Brett Barkley. We should consider his cultural, ethnic, or racial background and whether his background contributes to an understanding of his problems. For example, what if Brett was French Canadian, the therapist was English Canadian, and neither was fluent in the other's language? Would Brett have more rapport with a French-Canadian clinician?

What if Brett was of Asian descent? Brett realized that he needed help with his emotional problems after he abused his wife, but if he was Asian, would he feel uncomfortable about seeking professional help because of the "loss of face" involved?

What if he was an Aboriginal Canadian who has never fully accepted the values of the majority culture in Canada? Would he be guarded and less talkative with a white therapist and more open and spontaneous with an Aboriginal clinician?

Judgements about what is acceptable or normal vary considerably from culture to culture. Will it be more difficult for the therapist to understand what Brett is thinking and feeling if he comes from a cultural background very different from the therapist's? Will the therapist see more or perhaps less pathology in Brett's behaviour if he comes from another culture? These are legitimate questions. Unfortunately, we do not have clear answers to all of them.

Studies of the influences of culture on psychopathology have proliferated in recent years. A caveat: our discussion runs the risk of stereotyping because we are going to review generalizations that experts make about groups of people from different cultures. People from minority groups are, however, individuals who can differ as much from each other as their cultural or racial group differs from another cultural or racial group (cf. Weizmann, Weiner, Wiesenthal, & Ziegler, 1991). It is critical to keep this point in mind as cultural differences are discussed in this and subsequent chapters. Nonetheless, a consideration of group characteristics is important and is part of a specialty called *minority mental health* (see Sue & Sue, 2003). The major paradigms have on occasion been revised to assist clinicians in their work with people from different cultural backgrounds. For example, cultural differences in internal dialogue and beliefs about adaptive coping have been incorporated into cognitive-behavioural paradigms (e.g., Ivey, Ivey, & Simek-Morgan, 1997). Theories of **multicultural counselling and therapy** (e.g., Sue & Sue,

2003) attempt to incorporate these revisions into an integrated perspective. Recently, Hwang, Myers, Abe-Kim, and Ting (2008) developed an integrative, conceptual paradigm for understanding how culture influences different mental health domains (prevalence, etiology, phenomenology, diagnostic and assessment issues, coping styles and help-seeking pathways, and treatment and intervention issues). The Cultural Influences on Mental Health model is an important framework for understanding the complexities of interrelationships among the different domains of mental health.

While our focus in this section is on cultural, ethnic, and racial factors related to people suffering from psychological disorders in Canada, relatively little controlled research has been conducted in Canada. Therefore, we sometimes must extrapolate from relevant research conducted in the United States. Unfortunately, a majority of investigations with American minorities fail to provide information relevant to the assessment and treatment of people in Canada (Bowman, 2000).

Canada is a pluralistic society that has a policy of multiculturalism (Esses & Gardner, 1996). If clinicians in Canada are to do more than pay lip service to cultural considerations, it is important that they understand the cultural fabric of the country. Canadian Perspectives 2.1 summarizes multiculturalism in Canada and compares and contrasts cultural diversity in Canada with that in the United States.

CANADIAN PERSPECTIVES 2.1
CANADA: COLLECTIVE PORTRAIT OF A MULTICULTURAL COUNTRY

"French-speaking Canadians and foreign-born immigrants represent the largest and most culturally significant minority groups in Canada. Visible groups consisting of African-Americans and Hispanics represent the largest and most significant minorities in the United States. Further, Canada's largest minority represents a far larger portion (24%) of the population than does the Black minority group (13%) in the U.S."

—Bowman (2000, p. 237)

About one in six people in Canada are immigrants who were born outside the country (Government of Canada, 2006). According to Queen's University researcher John Berry (1999), **acculturation** (where a dominant group values both diversity and equity) rather than **assimilation** (where a dominant group strives for cultural uniformity for everyone) better represents current Canadian goals of tolerance, diversity, and equity. Thus, a Canadian "cultural mosaic" model of preserving minority cultures contrasts with the American "melting pot" policy of assimilation. Acculturation can be a difficult task as it requires maintaining ethnic heritage while learning a new predominant culture (Wintre, Sugar, Yaffe, & Costin [2000]).

What is the nature of cultural diversity in Canada? Bowman (2000) reviewed the differences between Canada and the United States in terms of well-being, social policy, and the nature of diversity within each country. She used several grouping variables

for diversity (described below). As noted in the quotation, the most dominant minorities in Canada are defined by first language and foreign birth. Much of our discussion focuses on differences between Canada and the United States, in part because the published research in psychology is dominated by American influences, including powerful associations such as the American Psychological Association and the American Psychiatric Association. Although there are many similarities, differences between the two countries abound.

Language as a Grouping Variable for Diversity
Linguistic minorities represent a far more important issue in Canada than in the United States. Canada is a bilingual country with both English and French as official languages and the largest minority group (now roughly 22% of the population) has French as its mother tongue. There is a significant francophone community outside of Quebec. There are more people who speak French at home in Canada than people who speak a non-English language at home in the United States (14%). Blacks form the largest minority group in the United States at 13%. In contrast to the socio-economic disadvantage of Blacks in the United States, French Canadians typically earn more than people of British ethnicity (Lian & Mathews, 1999). Also, Canada has a greater proportion of first generation immigrants (many of whom enter the country unable to speak English or French) than the United States.

The impact of first language is particularly striking in Canadian cities (Bowman, 2000). For example, in Richmond, B.C. (adjoining Vancouver), almost half of the elementary and high school students speak neither English nor French as their first language. Their first language is primarily Chinese. In Toronto, almost 40% of residents speak neither English nor French as their mother tongue. In fact, telephone translation is offered in 148 languages for people who contact the city government (Purvis, 1999). In a study of more than 1,000 first-year, unmarried students at York University, the participants reported 69 primary languages or combinations of languages spoken at home (Wintre et al., 2000). The most frequently spoken languages were English, Cantonese, Italian, and Greek.

Foreign Birth as a Grouping Variable for Diversity

Consistent with the fact that, among Western nations, Canada is the least culturally homogeneous (25% homogeneity relative to 50% in the United States, for example), the students participating in the Wintre et al. (2000) study revealed 94 countries of origin and identification with 203 cultural or ethnic groups. According to Bowman (2000), 57% of Canadian immigrants come from Asia (compared with only 17% in the United States). The next largest group comes from Europe, especially the United Kingdom.

Canada has entered a period of declining births and rising immigration that will further transform the Canadian mosaic. Further, the pattern of immigration has changed. In 1990, 14% of immigrants came from Hong Kong and 39% came from other Asian countries. By 2000, only 0.5% came from Hong Kong and people from other Asian countries accounted for 61% of all immigrants (Frank, 2001). They ranged across East Asia (mainland China, Singapore, Vietnam, and Japan), Southeast Asia (the Philippines), South Asia (Pakistan, India, and Sri Lanka), and West Asia. Immigrants from Europe had declined from 24% to 19%. In 2000, the next largest groups came from Africa (8%) and Central and South America (7.5%).

Visible Racial Differences as a Grouping Variable for Diversity

Minorities can be grouped on the basis of visible differences associated with geographic ancestry (Bowman, 2000). A race-based

During the Second World War, 22,000 Japanese Canadians were interned in camps such as this one. Public Archives of Canada.

During and following the Second World War, Japanese Canadians were resettled in other parts of Canada. Despite the fact that they were Canadian citizens, they were required to carry identity cards. Kirk Blankstein.

system is typically used in the United States to group minorities: Blacks, Hispanics, Asians, and Natives. Blacks comprise the largest visible minority group, and most members of visible minorities speak English and are not foreign-born. However, only 2% of the population in Canada is of African origin, and these individuals are far more culturally heterogeneous than Blacks in the United States.

In contrast to the United States, where a majority of the Asian population have come from a narrow range of countries and have belonged to American society for more than a generation, the majority of Canada's Asian population came in recent years from a wide array of cultures and languages (Bowman, 2000).

Although differences abound, a subset of people in both countries share an unfortunate past. Canadians and Americans of Japanese heritage living along the Pacific coast were interned or imprisoned in camps similar to concentration camps for several years during the Second World War, without any evidence that they posed a security threat. A majority of the 22,000 Japanese Canadians who were forcibly interned were born in Canada. They lost virtually everything they owned. Most were eventually resettled in the interior of Canada and forced to carry identity cards for several years after the end of the war. Thousands were repatriated to war-ravaged Japan. In 1988, the Government of Canada apologized to Japanese Canadians on behalf of the people of Canada. No doubt some of the survivors still show the emotional scars of their treatment. More subtle but nonetheless hurtful discrimination is found in everyday occurrences in more recent times, not only toward the Japanese but toward other visible minorities, as well.

Canada and the United States also differed with respect to relations between First Nations/Aboriginal peoples and European migrants (see Bowman, 2000). In early French Canada, the fur traders worked with and married Aboriginals and developed mutually advantageous policies and treaties in advance of migration that led to peaceful coexistence. There was little open conflict in Canada, but in the United States, rapid and extensive agricultural settlement led to massive theft of treaty lands and decades of Plains Indian wars, resulting in decimation of the Aboriginal people. Thus, in contrast to the situation in the United States, Aboriginal people in Canada survived at a relatively high rate, their population rising from 220,000 when the Europeans arrived to approximately 800,000 today (Bowman, 2000). Sadly, the history of Canada's Aboriginal people since the beginning of colonization is a history of suppression and oppression (see Canadian Perspectives 2.2).

Thinking Critically

1. Does the cultural mosaic model practised in Canada place more stress on new immigrants? What practical suggestions do you have that could reduce or minimize the stress?
2. Imagine that you were a Japanese Canadian living with your family in British Columbia at the time of the December 7,

1941, attack on Pearl Harbor. As Toyo Takata wrote in *Nikkei Legacy* (1983), a nightmare that was to last many years began very quickly and unexpectedly: Mary Nagata, a University of British Columbia student, was preparing for an exam when two Mounties appeared at the door seeking her businessman father. As they escorted him out, one officer scooped up her study notes, which were never returned. What do you think it was like for people like Mary Nagata over the next several years of internment? What were the probable psychological and physical consequences of being put in an internment camp? As you read about disorders such as post-traumatic stress disorder (Chapter 6), psychophysiological disorders (Chapter 9), and mood disorders (Chapter 8), speculate about symptoms that some of the Japanese Canadians probably experienced. What factors, if any, would have protected them from the development of symptoms or disorders?

MENTAL HEALTH IMPLICATIONS OF CULTURAL DIVERSITY IN CANADA

Our analysis of cultural diversity in Canada has implications for clinical practice. Mental health practitioners, including psychologists, need to be aware of Canada's unique cultural diversity. Clinicians must respect the dignity and worth of each individual, regardless of cultural background. Should members of minority groups be recruited into the mental health professions? Greater availability of clinicians from different cultures would possibly better meet the needs of clients with values different from those of the majority culture.

PSYCHIATRIC PROBLEMS IN MINORITY GROUPS

The issue of whether psychiatric problems are more or less frequent in minority groups, relative to other groups, is complex because the answer depends on which minority group is being investigated. Do French Canadians differ from Anglo

Canadians in the extent of their mental health problems? Probably they do not, at least not in any major way. Romano, Tremblay, Vitaro, Zoccolillo, and Pagani (2001) assessed a community sample of French-speaking 14- to 17-year-olds in Quebec and noted that the prevalence of psychiatric disorders fell within the range reported in research with English-speaking children.

Although Aboriginal people constitute only 4% of the Canadian population, studies report proportionally higher levels of mental health problems in many Canadian Aboriginal communities. We will examine the problem of suicide among young Native people in Chapter 8 (Canadian Perspectives 8.3) and highlight other issues throughout this book. Canadian Perspectives 2.2 provides an overview of these problems and discusses historical and current social factors that can contribute to psychological distress and disorder in Aboriginal people, at both the individual and community levels.

CANADIAN PERSPECTIVES 2.2
ORIGINS OF MENTAL HEALTH PROBLEMS AMONG CANADA'S ABORIGINAL PEOPLE

"The last time Marcia Martel saw her mother at home, it was late summer and she was a chubby little Indian kid of 4. She doesn't remember much because she was crying and clutching the tall grass as strange people pulled her away."
—from *Nation of Lost Souls*, Diebel, March 16, 2009, p. A1.

"Mr. Speaker, I stand before you today to offer an apology to former students of Indian residential schools. The treatment of children in Indian residential schools is a sad chapter in our history. . . . The government now recognizes that the consequences of the Indian residential schools policy were profoundly negative and that this policy has had a lasting and damaging impact on aboriginal culture, heritage and language."
—from the text of Prime Minister Stephen Harper's statement of apology, June 11, 2008.

"The Holy Father expressed his sorrow at the anguish caused by the deplorable conduct of some members of the church and he offered his sympathy and prayerful solidarity."
—from the Vatican statement on the occasion of Pope Benedict's offer of sorrow to Aboriginal Canadians who were physically and sexually abused at church-run residential schools, Winfield, April 30, 2009.

Laurence Kirmayer and his colleagues (Kirmayer, Brass, & Tait, 2000) reviewed research on the mental health of the First Nations, Inuit, and Métis of Canada. Depression, drug abuse, suicide, low self-esteem, symptoms of post-traumatic stress, and violence are widespread problems in many communities, especially among children and youth. Drug abuse frequently leads to child abuse, including child sexual abuse, an issue that also needs to be considered when there is family conflict. Kirmayer et al. (2000) attribute these mental health problems to cultural discontinuity and oppression, noting that Aboriginal Canadians have experienced institutional discrimination for more than 300 years. In many cases, they have been forbidden to speak their own language, prohibited from engaging in religious and cultural practices, driven from the land they had inhabited for hundreds of years, and forced onto reserves in undesirable locations without regard for the special sanctity that land has for them. In one disastrous "experiment," Inuit people were relocated to the Far North to protect Canadian sovereignty (Tester & Kulchyski, 1994). Poverty and economic marginalization are endemic in many Aboriginal communities. Disproportionately high rates of obesity, diabetes, and other physical diseases are also a problem.

The federal and provincial governments systematically sought the cultural assimilation of Aboriginal children through forced attendance at residential schools, followed by out-of-community adoption by non-Aboriginal families (Kirmayer et al., 2000). The residential schools were a 100-year failed experiment (e.g., Miller, 1996). Between 1879 and 1973, more than 100,000 Aboriginal children were taken from their families and sent to church-run and government-administered boarding schools mandated to educate the children. Aboriginal parents were considered to be incapable of educating their children and passing on "proper" European values. Only recently has the extent of the physical, emotional, and sexual abuse that occurred in many of the schools been documented and acknowledged (e.g., Royal Commission on Aboriginal Peoples, 1996). The last federally run residential school closed in Saskatchewan in 1996. Kirmayer et al. (2000) noted:

> Beyond the impact on individuals of abrupt separation from their families, multiple losses, deprivation, and brutality, the residential school system denied Aboriginal communities the basic human right to transmit their traditions and maintain their cultural identity. (p. 608)

Thousands of Aboriginal people have been involved in lawsuits against the federal government and the Anglican, United, and Roman Catholic churches for the abuses they suffered. On December 15, 2006, an historic settlement was reached in favour of the abused former students. It's estimated that over 80,000 people in total are entitled to benefits at an estimated cost to the federal government of $2 billion in restitution (Canadian Press, 2006). Implementation of the Indian Residential Schools Settlement Agreement began on September 19, 2007. On June 1, 2008, the government formed the Truth and Reconciliation Commission as part of the court-approved agreement (negotiated between legal counsel for former students, legal counsel for the churches, the Government of Canada, the Assembly of First Nations, and other Aboriginal organizations). The truth and reconciliation approach is a form of "restorative justice" that, in contrast to the customary adversarial or retributive justice, focuses on healing relationships between offenders, victims, and the community in which an offence takes place. In 2009, another class-action lawsuit was filed against the Attorney General of Canada over the treatment of

Fort Resolution, N.W.T, Bishop Breynat and Aboriginal pupils of the Roman Catholic Mission. National Archives of Canada.

thousands of Aboriginal children from 1965 to 1985 (see Diebel, 2009). Marcia Martel was one of those children.

When the provinces took over responsibility for health, welfare, and educational services in the 1960s, child and welfare services focused on "child neglect," and social workers chose adoption and long-term foster care for many Aboriginal children. By the end of the 1960s, between 30 and 40% of children who were legal wards of the provinces were Aboriginal children (Kirmayer et al., 2000). In 1959 the rate had been only 1%!

Kirmayer et al. (2000) believe that it was short-sighted policies such as these (and many others) that produced the "collective trauma, loss, and grief" that, in conjunction with poverty and the sense of deprivation created by "the values of consumer capitalism," led to the high rates of physical health problems and psychiatric disorders found in many Aboriginal communities (p. 609). Conflicts about identification can be severe. Young Aboriginal people in particular can be torn between traditional values and those of the more privileged majority culture, and this in part may underlie the high rates of psychological and social problems among Aboriginal young people. For many of them, there is little hope of wage-earning jobs, and the pursuit of higher education is fraught with obstacles. Is it any wonder that so many Aboriginal youth have no clear sense of identity or life direction?

Aboriginal communities do differ, of course, in their political structure, religious activities, and social and psychological problems. Some communities have experienced cultural revitalization and political empowerment. The Cree of James Bay, for example, are particularly politically active. In 1975 they won significant rights and major concessions (including monetary compensation; land-claims settlement; provisions for environmental and traditional activity protection; and some control over health, social, and education services) from the Government of Quebec in return for allowing hydroelectric development on traditional lands. In 1984, local self-government of Cree communities was legislated with the Cree-Naskapi (of Quebec) Act.

Within communities, potential protective factors (as well as risk factors) may be associated with levels of psychological distress in individuals. In one study of the Cree of James Bay, Kirmayer and his colleagues (Kirmayer, Boothroyd, Tanner,

Adelson, & Robinson, 2000) found that having a good relationship with other people in the community and "spending more time in the bush" predicted less distress. The Cree are noted for the degree to which extended families go to the bush to hunt and trap. Why should living in the bush be related to reduced distress?

> A large part of bush life involves contact with nature, spiritual relations with animals, consumption of valued foods and participation in other traditional activities. Increased time in the bush may confer mental health benefits by increasing family solidarity and social support, reinforcing cultural identity, improving physical health with nutritious bush foods and exercise, or providing respite from the pressures of settlement life. (Kirmayer et al., 2000, p. 48)

The Cree suicide rate is not any higher than the rate among non-Aboriginal Canadians.

Just as there are community success stories, we can cite many examples at the individual level where Aboriginal people have risen above the circumstances we have outlined. Paul Okalik is one success story. His story is eloquently told in *Maclean's* magazine.

> At 17, Okalik went through an all-too-common rite of passage for troubled Inuit teenagers: he was thrown in jail. Okalik was drinking heavily, got kicked out of school, and then was caught trying to break into a post office to steal liquor. The three-month sentence he was given might have marked the start of a dissolute life. (Geddes, 2001, p.16)

In 1999, at the age of 34, Paul Okalik became premier of Canada's newest territory in the central and eastern Arctic—Nunavut, Canada's first public government with a majority of Aboriginal lawmakers. Nunavut celebrated its tenth birthday on April 1, 2009. Sadly, although "Nunavut has been heavily marketed by the federal government around the world as a unique and progressive Canadian way to accommodate an aboriginal people" (Amagoalik, 2009, p. A23), it has continuing socio-economic problems, including

Paul Okalik, who "wrestled personal demons to the ground" (Geddes, 2001, p. 17), became the first premier of the Territory of Nunavut. The Canadian Press/Jonathan Hayward.

overcrowded housing, a tuberculosis epidemic, high unemployment, and only a 25% high school graduation rate.

Thinking Critically

1. The survey used by Kirmayer et al. (2000) did not assess traditional pursuits other than time in the bush. Do you think that pursuits such as healing practices or dream interpretation could promote mental health among Aboriginal people?

2. How can you account for Paul Okalik's success at such a young age? Did he experience fewer risk factors than his peers, or did certain protective factors make it possible for him to take the harder path to success? Speculate about possible risk and protective factors.

3. Would you agree that solutions to mental health problems among Canada's Aboriginal people require societal and economic strategies, in addition to psychological interventions?

Some cultural and religious groups receive attention not for elevated rates of mental disorder, but for atypically low rates of mental disorder. The Hutterites in Manitoba, who live in isolated, religious communities that are relatively free from outside influences, have remarkably low levels of mental illness. This German-speaking, Anabaptist sect emigrated in the 1870s from central Europe to Manitoba. Research conducted in 1953 (Eaton & Weil, 1953) found that they had the lowest lifetime prevalence of schizophrenia (1.1 per 1,000) of any group studied thus far in North America. A reanalysis of the original data (Torrey, 1995) and another study (Nimgaonkar et al., 2000) confirmed this finding. Genetic and lifestyle factors probably play a role in contributing to these low rates.

Research on the mental health of immigrants to Canada has found additional evidence for what is known as the **healthy immigrant effect**, and this has been attributed in part to pre-screening processes that limit entry to potential immigrants with health problems (Government of Canada, 2006). A Statistics Canada report indicated that immigrants had comparatively lower rates of depression and alcohol dependence than Canadian-born members of the population (Ali, 2002), unrelated to language proficiency in English or French, employment status, or sense of belonging. Secondary analyses found that Asian immigrants had the lowest rates of depression, while African immigrants had the lowest rates of alcohol dependence. The healthy immigrant effect was stronger among recent arrivals than among those who had been living in Canada for some time. Subsequently, Tiwari and Wang (2006) used Canadian Community Mental Health (CCHS) data to estimate and compare the lifetime and 12-month prevalence of mood disorders, anxiety disorders, and substance dependence in white, Chinese, and other Asian populations in Canada. The prevalence of mental disorders among Chinese people was lower than in white respondents and resembled the rate of mental disorders in China. Other Asian participants were less likely than white people to have had any mood or anxiety disorder in their lifetime. However, the Chinese had poorer self-rated mental health than the white and other Asian respondents.

In a recent study, Rousseau, Hassan, Measham, and Lashley (2008) investigated the prevalence of behavioural problems among Filipino-Canadian and Caribbean-Canadian youth in Montreal, either immigrants themselves (first generation) or born in Canada to immigrant parents (second generation). In both the Filipino and Caribbean groups, mothers typically migrate alone to work in the Canadian domestic workers program and then sponsor their children and spouses to join them several years later. Concerns have been raised about a possible link between the experience of family separations and the development of conduct problems in adolescents. Consistent with the healthy immigrant effect, relative to a sample of white, French-speaking, Canadian-born teenagers in the same school environment, Caribbean-Canadian and Filipino-Canadian youth and their parents did not report more externalizing symptoms. However, high levels of perceived racism and low collective self-esteem predicted problem behaviours in these adolescents. The authors concluded that the discrimination encountered by the youth in Canada is more important than the prior family separation in predicting future behavioural problems.

Reitmanova and Gustafson (2009) conducted a qualitative study of the mental health needs of visible minority immigrants to St. John's, Newfoundland, considered a small urban centre. They examined facilitators and barriers to maintaining mental health. Numerous factors interacted in dynamic ways as stressors of immigrant mental health, including lack of family and social support, unemployment and low socio-economic status, inhospitable social and physical environments (e.g., racial and ethnic inequality and discrimination), lack of freedom to practise religious beliefs and cultural traditions, limited autonomy of some immigrant women, inadequate coping skills, and delayed use of mental health services and obstacles to accessing them (see next section). Reitmanova and Gustafson (2009) offered 18 recommendations directed toward decision-makers in government, health agencies, and social services. A major recommendation was that mental health authorities and policy makers recognize immigrants as a unique population that should qualify for special services:

> These mental health services may adopt the guidelines proposed by the American Psychological Association which suggest developing multicultural and multilingual services, educating and training of mental health providers in multicultural sensitivity, and providing culturally and linguistically sensitive information about mental illness, mental health promotion programs and healthcare services. (p. 53)

HELP-SEEKING AMONG MINORITY GROUPS Despite the accessibility of Canada's universal health care system, some minority groups consistently underuse mainstream mental health services. The Greater Vancouver Mental Health Service Society (Peters, 1988) conducted a survey that determined that use by South Asian and Chinese Canadians was significantly lower than that of English Canadians. Roberts and Crockford (1997) reported that far fewer Asian Canadians were admitted to an adolescent inpatient unit in Calgary than would be expected on the basis of demographics. In analyses of CCHS 1.1 data, Tiwari and Wang (2008) determined the use of mental health services by ethnic minority groups. During the previous year, white people were more likely to have used mental health services than Chinese, South Asian, and South East Asian immigrants. Further, even among those who had experienced a major depressive episode, white respondents were more likely to have used mental health services than Chinese immigrants. In general, Asian groups tend to show a greater tendency than whites to be ashamed of emotional suffering, to be relatively unassertive, and to experience greater reluctance to seek out professional help. Asians in Canada tend to rely on members of their families and various informal sources of support when they experience psychological difficulties (e.g., Naidoo, 1992), despite the fact that in some centres there are well-established mental health services for the large Asian communities. These include Vancouver's Cross Cultural Mental Health Services (Ganesan & Janze, 2005) and Toronto's Hong Fook Mental Health Association (Lo & Chung, 2005).

Li and Browne (2000) conducted in-depth personal interviews with Asian Canadians (Chinese, Indian, and Filipino) in a northern community in B.C. What did the Asian Canadians perceive as insurmountable barriers to accessing and using mental health services? The two most serious difficulties were: (1) poor English-language ability, especially among the Chinese and Indian respondents; and (2) a culturally determined interpretation of psychological disorders that decreased the likelihood of their seeking help (e.g., family problems remain inside the house). Participants tended to describe psychological problems as somatic illnesses, presumably an acceptable interpretation, since physical illnesses, in comparison to mental disorders, are considered to be treatable, curable, and no cause for shame. Li and Browne (2000) cite the following quote by an Indian participant to illustrate the sense of shame attached to psychological problems: "If my neighbour knows that my husband has a mental health problem, he will not let his daughter marry my son" (p. 153). Additional barriers included a lack of knowledge about how to access mental health services and racial discrimination. Length of stay in Canada was unrelated to the number of perceived barriers. Are the barriers perceived to be the same by all immigrant groups? Li and Browne (2000) indicated that Filipino participants reported fewer difficulties in accessing mental health services. Perhaps there is less stigmatization or shame attached to seeking help for psychological problems among Filipinos.

Kirmayer et al. (2007) interviewed immigrants in Montreal who were born in the Caribbean, Vietnam, or the Philippines in order to assess their health care use for somatic symptoms, psychological distress, and recent life events. Although overall rates of use of medical services were similar in immigrants and non-immigrants, rates of use of both medical and specialty mental health services for psychological distress were significantly lower among immigrants. Vietnamese and Filipino immigrants were one-third as likely as the Canadian-born to use mental health services, even though we have universal health insurance. Kirmayer et al. (2007) concluded that, "Ensuring access to care and appropriate use of mental health services will require identifying and addressing social and cultural barriers to care specific to immigrant groups" (p. 295). In a related study, Whitley, Kirmayer, and Groleau (2006) conducted in-depth interviews with West Indian immigrants to Montreal and identified significant factors that explained their reluctance to use mental health services: (1) a perceived overwillingness of doctors to rely on medications; (2) a perceived dismissive attitude from physicians in previous encounters; and (3) a belief in the curative power of non-medical interventions (e.g., God).

Li and Browne (2000) recommended that mental health agencies attempt to increase public awareness about how to access services, particularly among ethnic groups that experience language and cultural barriers. Since Asian participants perceived that health care providers were unfamiliar with their cultures, Li and Browne (2000) also recommended increased cultural awareness and sensitivity training for health care providers and an expanded range of culturally based mental health services for Asian Canadians. There is clearly a need for more bilingual and bicultural mental health professionals in different sectors of the Canadian mental health system. Because Asian Canadians tend to look to their families for assistance, it is important for mental health workers to respect and make use of their clients' informal support networks (Roberts & Crockford, 1997).

DIAGNOSIS AND ASSESSMENT OF PSYCHIATRIC DISORDERS Cultural diversity has implications for the diagnosis (see Chapter 3) and assessment (see Chapter 4) of psychological disorders. A widely used manual of mental disorders (see American Psychiatric Association, 2000), attempts to enhance clinicians' sensitivity to cultural and ethnic variations in psychopathology in several ways (see Focus on Discovery 3.2). In one example, the manual asserts the importance of differentiating separation anxiety disorder, a problem seen in children (see Chapter 15), from the high value placed on strong interdependence among family members by some cultures. In terms of clinical assessment, it is problematic that clinicians often have to interact with clients who have difficulty conversing in one of the official languages of Canada. Imagine a distressed Portuguese-speaking mother having to take her 10-year-old daughter along to act as the interpreter when she talks to her therapist about her profound depression and suicidal thoughts! Further, few major standardized clinical tests have norms for Canada or norms for its major minority groups, including French Canadians.

PSYCHOLOGICAL INTERVENTION Bowman (2000) is critical of the quality and fragmented nature of information about minority-specific treatments. Indeed, few studies of empirically validated treatments with minorities are specific even to United States minority groups (Doyle, 1998). Bowman is especially critical of specialized approaches proposed for small Canadian minorities, such as Aboriginals, since they are "typically based on impressionistic anecdotes published in obscure journals" (p. 240). Although it is important to consider that it is often the minority groups themselves that propose the minority-specific treatments, Bowman believes it "unlikely that any major literature will develop for group-specific valid treatments for Canadian minorities" because minorities in Canada are so differentiated and their nature is continually changing (p. 240).

Nonetheless, professional organizations share our belief that clinicians should be sensitive to cultural issues. In its Code of Ethics, the Canadian Psychological Association (2000) acknowledges the need for psychologists to be sensitive to the needs and experiences of people from various cultures. Psychologists are given the responsibility to make themselves aware of and be sensitive to possible cultural differences in rights and responsibilities. If possible, in the delivery of services, assistance should be provided by "persons relevant to the culture or belief systems of those served" (p. 18).

With due regard for individual differences, such as the degree to which the person is assimilated into the majority culture, some generalizations can be made that pertain to interventions. We close this section by providing several examples.

It is generally assumed that clients do better with therapists who are similar to them in cultural and ethnic background. Therapists of similar background, perhaps even of the same gender, will better know the life circumstance of those in need and, most important, will be more acceptable to them. In psychoanalytic terms, similarity between client and therapist may strengthen the therapeutic alliance, one of the most important ingredients in any psychotherapy (Elvins & Green, 2008; Messer & Wolitzky, 2009; see Chapter 17). Although extensive research on modelling provides some justification for these assumptions, it has not been demonstrated that better outcomes are achieved when client and therapist are similar in race or ethnicity (Beutler, Machado, & Neufeldt, 1994). The jury is out on this question. Although there is some evidence from American studies that people who choose to retain their distinct cultural identities not only prefer ethnically similar therapists but also do better in therapy (e.g., Sue, 1998), Merali (1999) concluded that "similarity in values or cognitive match may be a better criterion for equating counsellors and clients than matching based on cultural background" (p. 30). Bowman (2000) agrees that an ability to identify a culture's key values (e.g., individualism/collectivism, tradition/change, empirical/spiritual explanations) is important in a country as culturally diverse as Canada in order to respond appropriately. For example, a value placed on co-operativeness rather than competitiveness could be misinterpreted by a culturally unaware therapist as lack of motivation.

Under some circumstances, the "linguistic divide" between client and therapist may be so great that it is very difficult to employ biological interventions and virtually impossible to practise traditional forms of psychotherapy. One of us knew a Japanese lady who came to Canada as a young woman. Although she remained in Canada for the rest of her life, raised 12 children, and lived to be over 100 years old, she never learned to speak English! This lady would have needed someone fluent in Japanese or an interpreter. In some cultures, the use of an interpreter can create a risk—the interpreter may minimize the client's problems to save face (Marcos, 1979). Nonetheless, the use of professional interpreters needs to become universal across Canada in order to facilitate proper assessments (see Kirmayer, 2007).

Let us return to the distressed Portuguese mother who does not speak English. Toronto has a large Portuguese community and many of its members do not speak English very well, despite having lived in Canada for decades. Since the community has not integrated well in terms of language, it has been difficult for many Portuguese Canadians to take advantage of mainstream mental health services (Murray, 2000). However, Portuguese Mental Health and Addiction Services—a program attached to Toronto Western Hospital University Health Network—provides language- and culture-specific services to Portuguese clients. The program sees about 1,000 people each year (Murray, 2000). Specialized programs are a possible solution to language barriers when the cultural group is large and professionals from that group are available.

We can extrapolate from a review by Sue and Sue (2003) and apply some of their wisdom to the treatment of Asian Canadians. They advise therapists to be sensitive to the personal losses that many Asian refugees have suffered, especially in light of the great importance that family connections have for them. To put it another way, therapists should appreciate the role of post-traumatic stress in Asian Canadians who have come to Canada as refugees. Therapists should also be aware of Asian Canadians' tendency to "somaticize"—to experience and to talk about stress in physical terms, such as headaches and fatigue, rather than in psychological terms, which Asian Canadians associate with being crazy or inferior. Their values are also different from the Western values of the majority culture in Canada. For example—and allowing for considerable individual variation—Asians respect structure and formality in interpersonal relationships, whereas a Western therapist is likely to favour informality and a less authoritarian attitude. Respect for authority may take the form of agreeing readily to what the therapist does and proposes—and perhaps, rather than discussing differences openly, just not showing up for the next session. The acceptability of psychotherapy as a way to handle stress is likely to be much lower among Asian Canadians, who probably tend to see emotional distress as something to be handled on one's own and through willpower. Asian Canadians may also consider some areas off-limits for discussion (e.g., the nature of the marital relationship, especially sex). Further, as Peter Waxer of York University reported, the therapist may have to be more directive and active than he or she otherwise might be, given the preference of many Asians for a directive, structured approach over a reflective one (Waxer, 1990).

Unique non-Western psychotherapies developed in different parts of the world are generally not practised in the West, including Canada. For example, Morita therapy, practised in some Asian countries, "involves cultivating acceptance through a structured corrective experience, including isolation, guided reflection, and behavioral prescriptions in a protective environment" (Fung & Lo, 2007, p. 3). However, the boundaries between these culture-influenced non-Western therapies and the common psychotherapies practised in Western parts of the world have become blurred in recent years. For example, many Western therapies, either implicitly or explicitly, incorporate Eastern practices or philosophies, particularly evident in the "third wave psychotherapies," such as dialectical behavioural therapy, mindfulness-based cognitive therapy, and acceptance commitment therapy (see Chapter 17). These newer therapies share in common the use of acceptance and mindfulness as part of the therapy process—concepts consonant with Zen-Buddhism (Fung & Lo, 2007; also see Fruzzetti & Erikson, 2010). Fung and Lo and others at the University of Toronto have been working on initiatives to enhance the cultural competence of the next generation of psychiatrists.

Very little controlled research has been conducted on Aboriginal Canadians in therapy. Kirmayer et al. (2000) lament the fact that mental health services in urban areas have rarely been adapted to the needs of Aboriginal clients, resulting in low rates of use among those communities. They also point out that some of the features of Aboriginal communities make it difficult to deliver conventional treatment and prevention programs, and that government policies lead to insufficient support for treatment programs. We need to be especially sensitive to cultural differences and needs involving Aboriginal children. Because these children are often looked after in the households of various relatives, the pattern of a child or young adult moving among different households is not necessarily a sign of trouble. The importance of family may make it advisable to conduct treatment in the home with family members present and an integral part of the intervention. According to Kirmayer et al. (2000), many forms of traditional healing and traditional practices, such as the sweat lodge, are undergoing a renaissance. Indeed, some culturally embedded healing practices may share some common "healing" elements with typical Western psychotherapies (Fung & Lo, 2007). Kirmayer et al. (2000) see some hope for the future: "A new generation of practitioners is emerging—people able to combine local knowledge about health and healing with the most useful aspects of psychiatry and psychology" (p. 613). We will discuss an example of this approach in Canadian Perspectives 12.2.

Racial differences are not insurmountable barriers to understanding between counsellor and client (Beutler et al., 1994). Therapists with considerable empathy are perceived as more helpful by clients, regardless of the racial mix. However, therapists need to know that many minority groups in Canada have encountered prejudice and racism, and some must wrestle with their anger and rage at a sometimes insensitive majority culture. While remaining sensitive to possible social oppression, therapists should still seek to foster feelings of empowerment among minority clients.

Finally, La Roche (2008) noted that advocates of services to culturally diverse groups consistent with their own cultural characteristics and advocates of empirically supported or evidence-based psychotherapy could be "on the road to a collision" (p. 333). As noted by Hwang et al. (2008), ethnic minorities have for the most part been left out of initiatives to establish, define, and validate empirically supported treatments. Thus, practitioners have just three options: (1) implement an "as-is approach" to disseminating evidence-based treatments to culturally different ethnic groups; (2) adapt evidence-based treatments to be more culturally congruent; or (3) develop new culture-specific, evidence-based treatments for each ethnic group. La Roche (2008) proposed general recommendations on how to bridge the gap between empirically supported and culturally sensitive interventions, and Hwang (2006) developed a systematic framework to help facilitate adaptation of psychotherapy for use with ethnic minorities. Recently, Pantalone, Iwamasa, and Martell (2010) detailed how CBT can be used with a variety of diverse populations. They noted that CBT and multicultural therapy are compatible despite the fact that diverse individuals are underrepresented in the CBT literature, and concluded that, "The more knowledgeable, flexible, and open a therapist is to a culturally informed idiographic assessment and case conceptualization, the more likely he or she is to build a strong relationship with a client and achieve a successful outcome" (p. 462).

Practitioners and policy makers in Canada can learn from the successes (and failures) in other jurisdictions. For example, Fernando (2005) noted that successful multicultural services in the United Kingdom typically employ a number of "good practices," including

- the use of multicultural multidisciplinary teams
- specific cultural sensitivity and anti-racist practice trainings
- anti-oppressive practices in establishing collaborative ties with communities and helping clients deal with racism
- increasing the number of ethnic minority staff and improving the educational pipeline
- linking psychological support to housing
- providing advocacy to help clients deal with services
- integrating cultural spirituality and alternative treatments to psychotherapeutic services
- culturally adapting psychotherapy for clientele

SUMMARY

- Scientific inquiry is a special way in which human beings acquire knowledge about their world. People may see only what they are prepared to see, and certain phenomena may go undetected because scientists can discover only the things about which they already have some general idea. One is better able to keep track of subjective influences by making explicit one's paradigm, or scientific perspective.
- Several major paradigms, or points of view, are current in the study of psychopathology and therapy. The biological paradigm assumes that psychopathology is caused by an organic defect. Two biological factors relevant to psychopathology are genetics and neurochemistry. Biological therapies attempt to rectify the specific biological defects underlying disorders or to alleviate symptoms of disorders, often using drugs to do so.
- At present, the most influential psychological paradigm is the cognitive-behavioural paradigm, which is a blend of the cognitive and behavioural approaches. Behavioural, or learning, paradigms suggest that aberrant behaviour has developed through classical conditioning, operant conditioning, or modelling. Investigators who believe that abnormal behaviour may have been learned examine all situations affecting behaviour and define concepts carefully. Behaviour therapists try to apply learning principles to bring about change in overt behaviour, thought, and emotion. Less attention is paid to the historical causes of abnormal behaviour than to what maintains it, such as the reward and punishment contingencies that encourage problematic response patterns.
- More recently, cognitive theorists have argued that certain schemas and irrational interpretations are major factors in abnormality. Theorists such as Ellis focus on irrational beliefs while Beck focuses on negative thoughts and dysfunctional attitudes about the self, other people, and the future.
- Another paradigm derives from the work of Sigmund Freud. The psychoanalytic, or psychodynamic, point of view directs our attention to repressions and other unconscious processes traceable to early-childhood conflicts that have set in motion certain psychodynamics. Whereas present-day ego analysts, who are part of this tradition, place greater emphasis on conscious ego functions, the psychoanalytic paradigm has generally searched the unconscious and early life of the client for the causes of abnormality. Therapeutic interventions based on psychoanalytic theory usually attempt to lift repressions so that the client can examine the infantile and unfounded nature of his or her fears.
- Humanistic and existential therapies are insight-oriented, like psychoanalysis, and regard freedom to choose and personal responsibility as key human characteristics. Rogers's client-centred therapy entails complete acceptance of and empathy for the client, restating the client's thoughts and feelings and sometimes offering new perspectives on the

client's problem. The existential therapies emphasize personal growth and the need to confront the anxieties that attend the choices we have to make in life.

- Because each of these paradigms seems to have something to offer to our understanding of mental disorders, there has been a movement to develop more integrative paradigms. The diathesis–stress paradigm assumes that people are predisposed to react adversely to environmental stressors. The diathesis may be biological, as appears to be the case in schizophrenia, or psychological, such as the chronic sense of hopelessness that seems to contribute to depression. Diatheses may be caused by early-childhood experiences, genetically determined personality traits, or socio-cultural influences. Similarly, the biopsychosocial paradigm presumes that disorders are a function of multifactorial interactions involving biological, psychological, and social variables.
- The most important implication of paradigms is that they determine where and how investigators look for answers. Paradigms necessarily limit perceptions of the world, for investigators will interpret data differently according to their points of view. In our opinion, it is fortunate that workers are not all operating within the same paradigm, for at this point too little is known about psychopathology and its treatment to settle on any one of them.

- Paralleling the current interest in integrative paradigms, most clinicians are eclectic in their approach to intervention, employing techniques that are outside their paradigm but that seem useful in dealing with the complexities of human psychological problems.
- Studies of the influences of culture on psychopathology have proliferated in recent years. The cultural and racial backgrounds of clients present a variety of challenges. Particular issues in Canada surround the assessment and treatment of French Canadians, Aboriginal Canadians, Asian Canadians, and foreign-born Canadians whose first language is not English or French, including the kinds of problems these groups may have and the kinds of sensitivities clinicians should possess to deal respectfully and effectively with people from minority groups.
- Revisions are sometimes made to the major paradigms to assist clinicians in their work with people from different cultural backgrounds. However, it is critical to keep in mind that there are typically more differences within cultural groups than there are between them. Remembering this important point can help avoid the dangers of stereotyping members of a culture.

KEY TERMS

acculturation (p. 72)

action (behavioural) therapies (p. 58)

adoptees method (p. 40)

assertion training (p. 65)

assimilation (p. 72)

aversive conditioning (p. 50)

behavioural (or learning) model (p. 46)

behaviour genetics (p. 39)

behaviour modification (p. 49)

behaviour rehearsal (p. 65)

behaviour therapy (p. 49)

behaviourism (p. 47)

biological paradigm (p. 38)

biopsychosocial paradigm (p. 67)

brain stem (p. 44)

brief therapy (p. 60)

cerebellum (p. 44)

cerebral cortex (p. 43)

cerebral hemispheres (p. 43)

classical conditioning (p. 47)

client-centred therapy (p. 62)

cognition (p. 51)

cognitive behaviour therapy (CBT) (p. 53)

cognitive paradigm (p. 51)

cognitive restructuring (p. 53)

concordance (p. 40)

conditioned response (p. 47)

conditioned stimulus (p. 47)

constructivist-narrative approach (p. 54)

corpus callosum (p. 43)

counterconditioning (p. 49)

countertransference (p. 59)

cultural diversity (p. 71)

defence mechanism (p. 58)

denial (p. 58)

diathesis–stress paradigm (p. 66)

diencephalon (p. 44)

discriminative stimulus (p. 48)

disease model (p. 38)

displacement (p. 58)

dizygotic (DZ) twins (p. 39)

dream analysis (p. 59)

eclecticism (p. 65)

ego (p. 57)

ego analysis (p. 59)

extinction (p. 47)

family method (p. 39)

free association (p. 59)

frontal lobe (p. 43)

genes (p. 39)

genotype (p. 39)

gyri (p. 43)

healthy immigrant effect (p. 76)

humanistic and existential therapies (p. 62)

hypothalamus (p. 44)

id (p. 57)

index cases (probands) (p. 39)

insight therapies (p. 58)

interpersonal therapy (IPT) (p. 61)

interpretation (p. 59)

introspection (p. 47)

irrational beliefs (p. 52)

latent content (p. 59)

law of effect (p. 48)

libido (p. 57)

limbic system (p. 44)

linkage analysis (p. 40)

medical model (p. 38)

medulla oblongata (p. 44)

meninges (p. 43)

midbrain (p. 44)

modelling (p. 48)

monozygotic (MZ) twins (p. 39)

moral anxiety (p. 57)

multicultural counselling and
   therapy (p. 72)

negative reinforcement (p. 48)

nerve impulse (p. 42)

neuron (p. 41)

neurotic anxiety (p. 57)

neurotransmitters (p. 42)

nuclei (p. 43)

objective (realistic) anxiety (p. 57)

occipital lobe (p. 43)

operant conditioning (p. 48)

paradigm (p. 38)

parietal lobe (p. 43)

phenotype (p. 39)

pleasure principle (p. 57)

pons (p. 44)

positive reinforcement (p. 48)

primary process thinking (p. 57)

projection (p. 58)

psychoanalytic (psychodynamic)
   paradigm (p. 56)

psychodynamics (p. 57)

psychotherapy (p. 58)

rational-emotive behaviour therapy
   (REBT) (p. 52)

rationalization (p. 58)

reaction formation (p. 58)

reality principle (p. 57)

reductionism (p. 46)

regression (p. 58)

repression (p. 58)

resilience (p. 68)

resistances (p. 59)

reticular formation (p. 44)

reuptake (p. 42)

risk (p. 68)

role-playing (p. 61)

schema (p. 51)

secondary process thinking (p. 57)

self-actualization (p. 63)

self-efficacy (p. 49)

self-instructional training (p. 54)

stress-inoculation training (p. 54)

sublimation (p. 58)

successive approximations (p. 51)

sulci (p. 43)

superego (p. 57)

sympathetic nervous system (p. 42)

synapse (p. 42)

systematic desensitization (p. 50)

temporal lobe (p. 43)

thalamus (p. 44)

transference (p. 59)

twin method (p. 39)

unconditional positive regard
   (p. 63)

unconditioned response (p. 47)

unconditioned stimulus (p. 47)

unconscious (p. 57)

ventricles (p. 43)

white matter (p. 43)

REFLECTIONS: PAST, PRESENT, AND FUTURE

- Recall the quote by von Liebig at the outset of this chapter. A "single cause" approach has been abandoned by most clinicians and psychopathologists, who now believe that psychological disorders arise from multiple causes. Assume that you are asked to name 10 major causes or risk factors for a mental disorder. Based on your understanding of the different paradigms, which factors would you nominate?

- Our integrative paradigms focus on the interaction between a predisposition toward disease (the diathesis) and environmental, or life, disturbances (the stress), and the interaction among biological, psychological, and social factors. How would you incorporate your 10 causes into a diathesis–stress perspective or the biopsychosocial paradigm? Using a diagram, illustrate your application of the biopsychosocial paradigm to J. Brett Barkley.

- Why and how do some people succumb to biopsychosocial risk factors while others react in adaptive ways, sometimes in the face of overwhelming adversity? We need to better understand the complexities of protective factors (resiliency) and the mechanisms underlying the consequences of such factors. Do various resiliency factors interact to produce protection from diatheses or multiple risk factors? What are the mechanisms or underlying processes that provide protection? Are there critical times in a person's life (e.g., childhood) when resiliency factors can play a vital role in the development of psychological outcomes?

- Do you agree with Bowman's assessment about the likelihood of developing minority-specific treatments in Canada? How would you develop and evaluate a specialized treatment program for depression or substance abuse among the Innu of Labrador (see Chapters 8 and 12)? Do you think it will ever be possible to develop valid treatments that are specific to other minority groups in Canada, such as Asian Canadians? What factors would need to be incorporated into the treatments described in this chapter?

CLASSIFICATION AND DIAGNOSIS

Marian Scott, *Tenants*, 1939–40, oil on board, 63.6 × 42 cm, Art Gallery of Ontario, Toronto. Gift from the J.S. McLean Collection, by Canada Packers Inc., 1990 © 2007 AGO

"It is more important to cure people than to make diagnoses."
   —**August Bier (1861–1949)**

"Clinical diagnosis is at a crossroads and it currently is unclear which path it will take as we move through the twenty-first century."
   —**Watson and Clark on *DSM-5* (2006, p. 210)**

"Classifications are fictions imposed on a complex world to understand it and manage it. . . . They must be useful to both researchers and clinicians."
   —**Mataix-Cols, Pertusa, and Leckman (2007, p. 1313)**

"We accept categories. Psychiatry cannot break with the medical tradition of categorical classification. Use of categories does not mean that dimensions cannot be used within a category."
   —**Maser and colleagues (2009, p. 24)**

A BRIEF HISTORY OF CLASSIFICATION

THE CURRENT DIAGNOSTIC SYSTEM OF THE AMERICAN PSYCHIATRIC ASSOCIATION (*DSM-IV* AND *DSM-IV-TR*)

ISSUES IN THE CLASSIFICATION OF ABNORMAL BEHAVIOUR

DSM-5 AND BEYOND: DIAGNOSIS IS AT A CROSSROADS

SUMMARY

Diagnosis is a critical aspect of the field of abnormal psychology. It is essential for professionals to be able to communicate accurately with one another about the types of cases they are treating or studying. Furthermore, a disorder must be classified correctly before its causes or best treatments can be found. For example, if one research group has found a successful treatment for depression but has defined the treatment in an unconventional manner, the finding is not likely to be replicated by another group of investigators. Only in recent decades, however, has diagnosis been accorded the attention it deserves.

To beginning students of abnormal psychology, diagnosis can seem tedious because it sometimes relies on fine distinctions. For example, anxiety in social situations—being extremely tense around others—is a symptom of both schizotypal and avoidant personality disorders. In a person with schizotypal personality disorder, however, the anxiety does not decrease as the individual becomes more familiar with people, whereas in a person with avoidant personality disorder, exposure does tend to reduce social anxiety. This fine distinction could certainly be viewed as hairsplitting, but, as we will discuss, the decisive factor is whether the distinction is useful in differentiating the two diagnoses.

In this chapter we focus on the official diagnostic system widely employed by mental health professionals, the *Diagnostic and Statistical Manual of Mental Disorders (DSM)*, now in its fourth edition, commonly referred to as *DSM-IV* (1994) or *DSM-IV-TR* (2000). The *DSM* is published by the American Psychiatric Association and has an interesting history.

A BRIEF HISTORY OF CLASSIFICATION

By the end of the nineteenth century, medicine had progressed far beyond its practice during the Middle Ages, when bloodletting was at least part of the treatment of virtually all physical problems. Gradually, people recognized that different illnesses required different treatments. Diagnostic procedures were improved, diseases classified, and applicable remedies administered. Impressed by the successes that new diagnostic procedures had achieved in the field of medicine, investigators of abnormal behaviour also sought to develop classification schemes. Advances in other sciences, such as botany and chemistry, had followed the development of classification systems, reinforcing hope that similar efforts in the field of abnormal behaviour might bring progress. Unfortunately, progress in classifying mental disorders was not to be easily gained.

EARLY EFFORTS AT CLASSIFICATION

During the nineteenth and early twentieth centuries, there was great inconsistency in the classification of abnormal behaviour. By the end of the nineteenth century, the diversity of classifications was recognized as a serious problem that impeded communication among people in the field, and several attempts were made to produce a system of classification that would be widely adopted. In the United Kingdom in 1882, for example, the Statistical Committee of the Royal

Medico-Psychological Association produced a classification scheme; however, even though it was revised several times, it was never adopted by the association's members. In Paris in 1889, the Congress of Mental Science adopted a single classification system, but it was never widely used. In the United States, the Association of Medical Superintendents of American Institutions for the Insane, a forerunner of the American Psychiatric Association, adopted a somewhat revised version of the British system in 1886. Then, in 1913, this group accepted a new classification scheme that incorporated some of Emil Kraepelin's ideas. Again, consistency was lacking. The New York State Commission on Lunacy, for example, insisted on retaining its own system (Kendell, 1975).

DEVELOPMENT OF THE WHO AND *DSM* SYSTEMS

More recent efforts at achieving uniformity of classification have not been totally successful either. In 1939, the World Health Organization (WHO) added mental disorders to the *International List of Causes of Death*. In 1948, the list was expanded to become the *International Statistical Classification of Diseases, Injuries, and Causes of Death (ICD)*, a comprehensive listing of all diseases, including a classification of abnormal behaviour. Although this nomenclature was unanimously adopted at a WHO conference, the mental disorders section was not widely accepted. Even though American psychiatrists had played a prominent role in the WHO effort, the American Psychiatric Association published its own *Diagnostic and Statistical Manual (DSM)* in 1952.

In 1969, the WHO published a new classification system that was more widely accepted. A second version of the American Psychiatric Association's *DSM*, *DSM-II* (1968), was similar to the WHO system, and, in the United Kingdom, a glossary of definitions was produced to accompany it (General Register Office, 1968). But true consensus still eluded the field. The WHO classifications were simply a listing of diagnostic categories; the actual behaviour or symptoms that were the bases for the diagnoses were not specified. *DSM-II* and the British *Glossary of Mental Disorders* provided some of this crucial information but did not specify the same symptoms for a given disorder. Thus, actual diagnostic practices still varied widely. In 1980, the American Psychiatric Association published an extensively revised diagnostic manual (*DSM-III*); a somewhat revised version, *DSM-III-R*, appeared in 1987.

In 1988, the American Psychiatric Association appointed a task force, chaired by psychiatrist Allen Frances, to begin work on *DSM-IV*. Working groups that included many psychologists were established to review sections of *DSM-III-R*, prepare literature reviews, analyze previously collected data, and collect new data if needed. An important change in the process for this edition was the adoption of a conservative approach to making changes in the diagnostic criteria—the reasons for changes in diagnoses would be explicitly stated and clearly supported by data. In previous versions, the reasons for diagnostic changes had not always been explicit. More than two dozen Canadian psychologists and psychiatrists sat on the *DSM-IV* committees or participated in consultations with them. *DSM-IV* is used throughout the United States and Canada and is becoming widely accepted around much of the world.

DSM-IV was published in 1994 and the American Psychiatric Association subsequently completed a "text revision" (*DSM-IV-TR*; American Psychiatric Association, 2000). The revised version contains very few substantive changes to the different diagnostic categories and criteria, although some sections were rewritten to enhance clarity and incorporate recent research findings related to issues such as the prevalence, course, and etiology of disorders. Canadian psychologist Paula Caplan (e.g., 1995) has been outspoken in her criticism of current and past versions of the *DSM*, especially of the fact that many people with divergent viewpoints are not given the opportunity to participate in the decision-making process. Among those who are critical of the *DSM*, one group asserts that classification per se is irrelevant to the field of abnormal behaviour, and a second group finds specific deficiencies in the manner in which diagnoses are made in the *DSM*.

It is important to note at the outset that the *DSM* is, indeed, controversial. To many clinical scientists and practitioners, it is not "the book of truth" about psychological problems, nor is it universally embraced by psychiatrists, psychologists, and others in the field. It was developed originally by physicians who applied a medical model to the diagnosis of presumed psychiatric illnesses and assumed that categorical diagnoses correspond to actual underlying disease entities with specific symptoms, treatments, and prognoses. Some question whether the majority of *DSM* categories correspond to real, underlying entities; they argue that the categories refer to hypothetical constructs that may or may not exist in reality. Thus, most psychiatric diagnoses are not identical to medical diagnoses where the basic cause is frequently known and the presence of the disease can usually be objectively determined (for example, by a blood or urine test).

In this chapter we present the major *DSM-IV-TR* categories in summary. We then evaluate classification in general and the *DSM* in particular. In the next chapter we consider the assessment procedures that provide the data on which diagnostic decisions are based.

THE CURRENT DIAGNOSTIC SYSTEM OF THE AMERICAN PSYCHIATRIC ASSOCIATION (*DSM-IV* AND *DSM-IV-TR*)

DEFINITION OF MENTAL DISORDER

How does the *DSM* define the subject matter of this text? Recognizing that the term **"mental disorder"** is problematic and that "no definition adequately specifies precise boundaries for the concept," *DSM-IV-TR* provides the following definition:

A clinically significant behavioral or psychological syndrome or pattern that occurs in an individual and that is associated with present distress (e.g., a painful symptom) or disability (i.e., impairment in one or more important areas of functioning) or with a significantly increased risk of suffering death, pain, disability, or an important loss of freedom. (American Psychiatric Association, 2000, p. xxxi)

A number of conditions are excluded from consideration:

In addition, this syndrome or pattern must not be merely an expectable and culturally sanctioned response to a particular event, for example, the death of a loved one. Whatever its original cause, it must currently be considered a manifestation of a behavioral, psychological, or biological dysfunction in the individual. (American Psychiatric Association, 2000, p. xxxi)

FIVE DIMENSIONS OF CLASSIFICATION

Several major innovations distinguish the third edition and subsequent versions of the *DSM*. Perhaps the most sweeping change is the use of **multiaxial classification**, whereby each individual is rated on five separate dimensions, or axes. In this section we briefly discuss these five axes and then describe the major diagnostic categories. The five axes are

- *Axis I*. All diagnostic categories except personality disorders and mental retardation
- *Axis II*. Personality disorders and mental retardation
- *Axis III*. General medical conditions
- *Axis IV*. Psychosocial and environmental problems
- *Axis V*. Current level of functioning

The multiaxial system, by requiring judgements on each of the five axes, forces the diagnostician to consider a broad range of information.

Axis I includes all diagnostic categories except personality disorders and mental retardation, which make up Axis II. Thus, axes I and II compose the classification of abnormal behaviour. A detailed presentation of axes I and II appears inside the front cover of this book. Axes I and II are separated to ensure that the presence of long-term disturbances is not overlooked. Most people consult a mental health professional for an Axis I condition, such as depression or an anxiety disorder, but prior to the onset of their Axis I condition, they may have had an Axis II condition, such as dependent personality disorder. The separation of axes I and II is meant to encourage clinicians to be attentive to this possibility. The presence of an Axis II disorder along with an Axis I disorder generally means that the person's problems will be more difficult to treat.

Although the remaining three axes are not needed to make the actual diagnosis, their inclusion in the *DSM* indicates that factors other than a person's symptoms should be considered in an assessment so that the person's overall life situation can be better understood. On Axis III the clinician indicates any general medical conditions believed to be relevant to the mental disorder in question. For example, the existence of a heart condition in a person who has also been diagnosed with depression would have important implications for treatment; some antidepressant drugs could worsen the heart condition. Axis III conditions may be quite common. A Toronto study found that more than half of the inpatients had an identifiable medical condition and that having an infectious disease was associated with disruptive behaviour (Boggild, Heisel, & Links, 2004).

Axis IV codes psychosocial and environmental problems that the person has been experiencing and that may be contributing to the disorder. These include occupational problems, economic problems, interpersonal difficulties with family members, and a variety of problems in other life areas that may influence psychological functioning. Finally, on Axis V, the clinician indicates the person's current level of adaptive functioning. Life areas considered are social relationships, occupational functioning, and use of leisure time. Ratings of current functioning are supposed to give information about the need for treatment. See the inside back cover for a detailed description of the Global Assessment of Functioning (GAF) Scale and a summary of the other axes.

DIAGNOSTIC CATEGORIES

In this section we provide a brief description of the major diagnostic categories of axes I and II. Before presenting the diagnoses, we should note that, for many of them, the *DSM* indicates that the disorder may be due to a medical condition or substance abuse. For example, depression resulting from an endocrine gland dysfunction would be included in the depression section of the *DSM* but listed as caused by a medical problem. Clinicians must therefore be sensitive not only to the symptoms of their clients, but also to the possible medical causes of their clients' conditions. It should also be noted that beginning with *DSM-III*, there has been a dramatic expansion of the number of diagnostic categories. Eating disorders, some anxiety disorders (for example, post-traumatic stress disorder), several personality disorders (for example, schizotypal personality disorder), and many of the disorders of childhood were all added in *DSM-III* or subsequent editions.

DISORDERS USUALLY FIRST DIAGNOSED IN INFANCY, CHILDHOOD, OR ADOLESCENCE Within this broadranging category are the intellectual, emotional, and physical disorders that usually begin in infancy, childhood, or adolescence.

- The child with *separation anxiety disorder* has excessive anxiety about being away from home or parents.
- Children with *conduct disorder* repeatedly violate social norms and rules.
- Individuals with *attention deficit hyperactivity disorder* have difficulty sustaining attention and are unable to control their activity when the situation calls for it.
- Individuals with *mental retardation* (listed on Axis II) show subnormal intellectual functioning and deficits in adaptive functioning.

- The *pervasive developmental disorders* include autistic disorder, a severe condition in which the individual has problems in acquiring communication skills and deficits in relating to other people.
- *Learning disorders* refer to delays in the acquisition of speech, reading, arithmetic, and writing skills.

These disorders are discussed in Chapter 15.

SUBSTANCE-RELATED DISORDERS A *substance-related disorder* is diagnosed when the ingestion of some substance—alcohol, opiates, cocaine, amphetamines, and so on—has changed behaviour enough to impair social or occupational functioning. The individual may become unable to control or discontinue ingestion of the substance and may develop withdrawal symptoms if he or she stops using it. These substances may also cause or contribute to the development of other Axis I disorders, such as mood or anxiety disorders. These disorders are examined in Chapter 12.

SCHIZOPHRENIA For individuals with schizophrenia, contact with reality is faulty. Their language and communication are disordered, and they may shift from one subject to another in ways that make them difficult to understand. They commonly experience delusions, such as believing that thoughts that are not their own have been placed in their heads. In addition, they are sometimes plagued by hallucinations, commonly hearing voices that come from outside themselves. Their emotions are blunted, flattened, or inappropriate, and their social relationships and ability to work show marked deterioration. This serious mental disorder is discussed in Chapter 11.

MOOD DISORDERS As the name implies, these diagnoses are applied to people whose moods are extremely high or low.

- In *major depressive disorder*, the person is deeply sad and discouraged and is also likely to lose weight and energy and to have suicidal thoughts and feelings of self-reproach.
- The person with *mania* may be described as exceedingly euphoric, irritable, more active than usual, distractible, and possessed of unrealistically high self-esteem.
- *Bipolar disorder* is diagnosed if the person experiences episodes of mania or of both mania and depression.

The mood disorders are surveyed in Chapter 8.

ANXIETY DISORDERS Anxiety disorders have some form of irrational or overblown fear as the central disturbance.

- Individuals with a *phobia* fear an object or situation so intensely that they must avoid it, even though they know that their fear is unwarranted and unreasonable and disrupts their lives.
- In *panic disorder*, the person is subject to sudden but brief attacks of intense apprehension, so upsetting that he or

Constant checking, for example, to see if doors are locked, is a common compulsion in obsessive-compulsive disorder. SUPERSTOCK.

she is likely to tremble and shake, feel dizzy, and have trouble breathing. Panic disorder may be accompanied by *agoraphobia* when the person is also fearful of leaving familiar surroundings.

- In people diagnosed with *generalized anxiety disorder*, fear and apprehension are pervasive, persistent, and uncontrollable. They worry constantly, feel generally on edge, and are easily tired.
- A person with *obsessive-compulsive disorder* is subject to persistent obsessions or compulsions. An obsession is a recurrent thought, idea, or image that uncontrollably dominates a person's consciousness. A compulsion is an urge to perform a stereotyped act, with the usually impossible purpose of warding off an impending feared situation. Attempts to resist a compulsion create so much tension that the individual usually yields to it.
- Experiencing anxiety and emotional numbness in the aftermath of a very traumatic event is called *post-traumatic stress disorder*. Individuals have painful, intrusive recollections by day and bad dreams at night. They find it difficult to concentrate and feel detached from others and from ongoing affairs.
- *Acute stress disorder* is similar to post-traumatic stress disorder, but the symptoms do not last as long.

The anxiety disorders are reviewed in Chapter 6.

SOMATOFORM DISORDERS The physical symptoms of somatoform disorders have no known physiological cause but seem to serve a psychological purpose.

- People with *somatization disorder* have a long history of multiple physical complaints for which they have taken medicine or consulted doctors.
- People with *conversion disorder* report the loss of motor or sensory function, such as a paralysis, an anaesthesia (loss of sensation), or blindness.
- Individuals with *pain disorder* suffer from severe and prolonged pain.

- *Hypochondriasis* is the misinterpretation of minor physical sensations as serious illness.
- People with body *dysmorphic disorder* are preoccupied with an imagined defect in their appearance.

These disorders are covered in Chapter 7.

DISSOCIATIVE DISORDERS Psychological dissociation is a sudden alteration in consciousness that affects memory and identity.

- People with *dissociative amnesia* may forget their entire past or lose their memory for a particular time period.
- With *dissociative fugue* the individual suddenly and unexpectedly travels to a new locale, starts a new life, and cannot remember his or her previous identity.
- The person with *dissociative identity disorder* (formerly called multiple personality disorder) possesses two or more distinct personalities, each complex and dominant one at a time.
- *Depersonalization disorder* is a severe and disruptive feeling of self-estrangement or unreality.

These rare disorders are studied in Chapter 7.

SEXUAL AND GENDER IDENTITY DISORDERS The sexual disorders section of *DSM-IV-TR* lists three principal subcategories:

- In the *paraphilias*, the sources of sexual gratification—as in exhibitionism, voyeurism, sadism, and masochism—are unconventional.
- People with *sexual dysfunctions* are unable to complete the usual sexual response cycle. Inability to maintain an erection, premature ejaculation, and inhibition of orgasm are examples of their problems.
- People with *gender identity disorder* feel extreme discomfort with their anatomical sex and identify themselves as members of the opposite sex.

These disorders are studied in Chapter 14.

SLEEP DISORDERS Two major subcategories of sleep disorders are distinguished in *DSM-IV-TR*:

- In the *dyssomnias*, sleep is disturbed in amount (e.g., the person is not able to maintain sleep or sleeps too much), quality (the person does not feel rested after sleep), or timing (e.g., the person experiences inability to sleep during conventional sleep times).
- In the *parasomnias*, an unusual event occurs during sleep (e.g., nightmares, sleepwalking).

These disorders are discussed in Chapter 16.

EATING DISORDERS Eating disorders fall into two major categories:

- In *anorexia nervosa*, the person avoids eating and becomes emaciated, usually because of an intense fear of becoming fat.
- In *bulimia nervosa*, frequent episodes of binge eating are coupled with compensatory activities such as self-induced vomiting and heavy use of laxatives.

These disorders are discussed in Chapter 10.

FACTITIOUS DISORDER A diagnosis of *factitious disorder* is applied to people who intentionally produce or complain of physical or psychological symptoms, apparently because of a psychological need to assume the role of a sick person. This disorder is discussed in Chapter 7.

ADJUSTMENT DISORDERS An *adjustment disorder* involves the development of emotional or behavioural symptoms following the occurrence of a major life stressor. However, the symptoms that ensue do not meet diagnostic criteria for any other Axis I diagnosis. A person can have an adjustment disorder with a depressed mood or an anxious mood, but the depression/anxiety is not significant enough to warrant a diagnosis of anxiety or depression. Scholars of adjustment disorders note that these disorders remind us of the role of life stress and other contextual factors (see Baumeister, Maercker, & Casey, 2009).

IMPULSE-CONTROL DISORDERS *Impulse-control disorders* include a number of conditions in which the person's behaviour is inappropriate and seemingly out of control.

- In *intermittent explosive disorder*, the person has episodes of violent behaviour that result in destruction of property or injury to another person.
- In *kleptomania*, the person steals repeatedly, but not for the monetary value or use of the object.

Pathological gambling is an example of an impulse-control disorder in which the person's behaviour is out of control. John Howard.

- In *pyromania*, the person purposefully sets fires and derives pleasure from doing so.
- In *pathological gambling*, the person is preoccupied with gambling, is unable to stop, and gambles as a way to escape from problems.
- *Trichotillomania* is diagnosed when the person cannot resist the urge to pluck out his or her hair, often resulting in significant hair loss.

These disorders are discussed further in Chapter 5.

PERSONALITY DISORDERS Personality disorders are defined as enduring, inflexible, and maladaptive patterns of behaviour and inner experience. They are listed on Axis II of the *DSM*.

- In *schizoid personality disorder*, the person is aloof, has few friends, and is indifferent to praise and criticism.
- The individual with a *narcissistic personality disorder* has an overblown sense of self-importance, fantasizes about great successes, requires constant attention, and is likely to exploit others.
- *Anti-social personality disorder* surfaces as conduct disorder before the person reaches age 15 and is manifested in truancy, running away from home, delinquency, and general belligerence. In adulthood, the person is indifferent about holding a job, being a responsible partner or parent, planning for the future or even for tomorrow, and staying on the right side of the law. People with anti-social personality disorder—also called psychopathy—do not feel guilt or shame for transgressing social mores.

Chapter 13 covers the personality disorders.

OTHER CONDITIONS THAT MAY BE A FOCUS OF CLINICAL ATTENTION This all-encompassing category is composed of conditions that are not regarded as mental disorders per se but still may be a focus of attention or treatment. This category seems to exist so that anyone entering the mental health system can be categorized, even in the absence of a formally designated mental disorder.

If an individual's medical illness appears to be caused in part or exacerbated by a psychological condition, the diagnosis is *psychological factors affecting physical condition*. Referred to previously as a psychophysiological or psychosomatic disorder, this condition is reviewed in detail in Chapter 9. Among the other diagnoses in this category are the following:

- academic problem (e.g., underachievement)
- anti-social behaviour (e.g., in professional thieves)
- malingering (faking physical or psychological symptoms to achieve a goal, such as avoiding work)
- relational problem (e.g., poor relationship with sibling or spouse)

- occupational problem (e.g., dissatisfaction with work)
- physical or sexual abuse
- bereavement
- noncompliance with treatment (e.g., refusing medication)
- religious or spiritual problem (e.g., questioning one's faith)
- phase-of-life problem (difficulties created by a life transition, such as beginning school)

In this context, it is interesting to recall our discussion of the difficulties of defining mental disorder. Should these life difficulties really be included in a listing of mental disorders? Are mental health professionals qualified, for example, to "treat" religious doubt? Many of these conditions will not be covered in this book, although malingering is discussed in Chapter 7; therapy for couples problems in Chapter 17; and physical and sexual abuse in chapters 5, 7, and 14.

CANADIAN PERSPECTIVES 3.1
PATHOLOGICAL GAMBLING IN CANADA

There have been many highly publicized cases of people with severe gambling problems. Well-known is the story of Brian Malony, whose life was displayed in the 2003 movie *Owning Mahowny* (with the character of Dan Mahowny, a pseudonym for Malony, played by actor Philip Seymour Hoffman). Malony, a compulsive gambler, embezzled more than $10 million from the CIBC during an 18-month gambling spree. In Canada, gambling problems have increased, in part, because several provinces have adopted liberal attitudes toward legalized gambling. In the *fifth estate* documentary *You Bet Your Life* televised in 2004, experts opined that governments themselves have become addicted to the revenue generated by gambling. There are now more than 100 casinos in Canada. By 2000, gambling revenue from government-run casinos, lotteries, and video lottery terminals (VLTs) exceeded $9 billion (McLaurin & McLaurin, 2003). The amount of gambling is actually much higher due to on-line gambling (which is illegal in Canada). The Kahnawake Mohawk reserve outside Montreal is the third-largest source of Internet gambling in the world. Three quarters of Canadians 15 years old and over spent money on gambling activities in 2002 (see Government of Canada, 2006). Average spending by those 18 years and older was $483 per person—greater than a threefold increase from the $130 spent in 1992. Are there dangers from the "marriage" between government and gambling? Researchers argue that there are many (CMAJ, 2008).

The essential feature of **pathological gambling** is "persistent and recurrent maladaptive gambling behavior ... that disrupts personal, family or vocational pursuits" (American Psychiatric Association, 1994, p. 615). It is characterized by loss of control over gambling that leads to negative consequences such as deception about the extent of gambling involvement, "chasing" losses, theft, and relationship and job loss. The diagnosis involves meeting at least 5 of 10 criteria. Problem gambling is often operationalized as fulfilling 3 or 4 criteria.

Gambling Facts
- A nationally representative survey (Canadian Community Health Survey or CCHS) reported a current 12-month prevalence of gambling problems of 2.0%, with an additional 2 to 4% considered "at risk." The highest rates emerged in areas with high concentrations of VLTs combined with permanent casinos (see Cox, Yu, Afifi, & Ladouceur, 2005).

- The opening of a casino affects gambling activities. After the opening of the first major Canadian casino in Winnipeg in 1993, adults who were interviewed reported a lifetime prevalence rate of 2.6% for "probable pathological gambling" and a further 3.0% met criteria for problem gambling (Cox, Kwong, Michaud, & Enns, 2000). Respondents from the Hull and Quebec City areas were assessed both before and a year after the 1996 opening of the Casino de Hull. The "experimental" group exposed to the casino reported an increase in the negative consequences of gambling (e.g., money lost gambling) (Jacques, Ladouceur, & Ferland, 2000).
- The chances of experiencing gambling-related harm increase the more often one gambles and the more money one spends on gambling. The optimal limits for low-risk participation include gambling no more than two to three times per month, and spending no more than $501 to $1,000 per year, and no more than 1% of gross family income on gambling activities. (Currie et al., 2006).
- On-line problem gamblers, relative to social gamblers, are more likely to spend more time gambling per session; to gamble alone, from school, or with a cell phone; to gamble with more money; to wager on-line while consuming alcohol or illicit drugs; and to lose more money gambling online (McBride & Derevensky, 2009).

Who Is Most Likely to Have a Gambling Problem?
- Gambling has a negative impact on vulnerable or marginalized groups and special populations, including youth, women, older adults, Aboriginal people, other ethnocultural groups, people who rely on community assistance, and people with substance-use and mental disorders. Problem gamblers are more likely to be male, single, under the age of 30, and to have begun gambling by age 18 (see Korn, 2000 for review; Lepage, Ladouceur, & Jacques, 2000).
- Irrational gambling cognitions (e.g., the "gambler's fallacy"—a belief that they are more likely to win after a series of losses) are related to risky gambling practices and moderate the relationship between risky gambling practices (e.g., heavy alcohol consumption) and gambling intensity (percent of income spent on gambling). Thus, people engaging in risky

practices spent less of their income on gambling when they had fewer gambling cognitions relative to those with more cognitions (Miller & Currie, 2008).

Gambling in Children, Adolescents, and Young Adults

- Youth are clearly at greater risk for gambling problems than adults. In analyses of the CCHS, Huang and Boyer (2007) reported a current 12-month prevalence of moderate risk or problem gambling for youth aged 15 to 24 years of 2.2% (3.3% in males and 1.1% in females). Regional prevalence was highest in Ontario (2.75%) and lowest in British Columbia (1.4%). A recent Norwegian study (Molde et al., 2009), reporting similar prevalence rates, revealed that depression, alcohol use, and dissociation were related to problem gambling.
- Abby Goldstein from York University (2009) examined correlates of past year gambling measures in youths aged 14 to 18 who presented to an inner-city emergency department. Gambling correlates included being male, African American, out of school, working for pay, alcohol and marijuana use, severe general violence, severe dating violence, and carrying a weapon.
- What about gambling in students? A study of University of Lethbridge students found that 7.5% of them were problem or pathological gamblers. There was an especially high level among Asian students (41%) (see Williams et al., 2006). Gupta, Derevensky, and Ellenbogen (2006) found that adolescent gamblers had higher levels of disinhibition, boredom susceptibility, cheerfulness and excitability, and low conformity and self-discipline. For these adolescents, gambling is largely a form of sensation seeking.
- Prevalence rates of adolescent involvement in gambling are rising. Among students in grades 7, 9, 10, and 12 in the Atlantic provinces, 8.2% and 6.4% met a "broad definition" of at-risk and problem gambling, respectively. Lying about one's age or using fake identification was identified as an independent risk factor (Poulin, 2000). A sample of Quebec high school students was divided into three linguistic groupings. An "allophone" group (an expanding subset of the Quebec population who have a strong cultural heritage other than French and English) had the highest proportion of youth who gambled on a weekly basis and reported gambling problems, followed by anglophone and then francophone groups. Acculturation difficulties were related to gambling problems (Ellenbogen, Gupta, & Derevensky, 2007).

Consequences of Gambling

- There is a high cost of gambling to families "in terms of dysfunctional relationships, violence and abuse, financial pressure, and disruption of growth and development of children" (Korn, 2000, p. 63). Experts say social costs also include depression and social isolation (CMAJ, 2008).

- Male and female adolescent severe problem gamblers have similar prevalence rates of depression, substance use, and weekly gambling (Ellenbogen, Derevensky, & Gupta, 2007).
- Pathological gambling is linked in the CCHS with attempted suicide (Newman & Thompson, 2007); however, it's not possible to say whether the association represents a causal relation. Sadly, there are many documented cases of suicides among people with extreme gambling problems. This is reflected in the title of the CBC documentary *You Bet Your Life*.
- On a positive note, a review by LaPlante et al. (2008) concluded that gambling problems are not always progressive and enduring, contrary to conventional and professional wisdom.

Can Pathological Gamblers Be Helped?

Robert Ladouceur and his colleagues from the Université Laval demonstrated the efficacy of cognitive-behavioural treatments in both adults and adolescents (e.g., Ladouceur et al., 2001). In a comparison of those who had completed treatment with those who had not, Leblond, Ladouceur, and Blaszczynski (2003) found no group differences in depression, anxiety, problem-solving skills, and alcohol use; however, those who did not complete treatment were significantly higher in impulsivity. Is "controlled" gambling (as opposed to abstinence) a viable goal for pathological gamblers? Although they were unable to predict who would benefit from control rather than abstinence, Ladouceur, Lachance, and Fournier (2009) demonstrated that a cognitive-behavioural treatment aimed at controlled gambling can be effective with many pathological gamblers. Based on the premise that few problem gamblers are willing to attend formal treatment, researchers at the University of Calgary (e.g., Hodgins, Currie, el-Guebaly, & Peden, 2004) developed an approach that incorporates information about self-change strategies into a brief self-help workbook together with brief motivational telephone support. They reported that more than 35% of participants abstained from gambling after two years.

In 1993, provincial governments began to fund services for pathological and problem gamblers. Clinics and treatment programs have opened across Canada, some of which focus on vulnerable, high-risk groups. However, only a small percentage of people experiencing problems related to gambling are seeking help from specialized treatment programs. One study found that fewer than one fifth of youth who met criteria for pathological gambling classified themselves as having a serious problem (Hardoon, Derevensky, & Gupta, 2003), which is unfortunate, as the vast majority may thus never seek help for their problem. In 2009, an Ontario a man who lost hundreds of thousands of dollars, two homes to foreclosure, and his job, and became anxious and depressed, sued the Ontario Lottery and Gaming Corporation for $3.5 billion (Wallace, 2009, April 8). He claimed the province's voluntary "self-exclusion program" failed to prevent him and others from gambling. The program allows problem gamblers to authorize casino and racetrack staff to use "best efforts" to bar or remove the gamblers if caught inside.

Because many problem gamblers do not seek treatment, it is vitally important to develop innovative approaches to prevention. Dickson, Derevensky, and Gupta (2002) of the International Centre for Youth Gambling Problems and High-Risk Behaviors (a McGill University Research Centre) outlined one such approach: a general risk-taking model that acknowledges common risk factors across various addictions. The Centre has developed prevention tools for elementary, high school, and college-age students, including brochures, self-evaluation screening cards, and a Centre-produced docudrama video entitled Clean Break. The Centre also has developed two interactive computer games, The Amazing Château for elementary school children, and Hooked City for high school students, which were distributed to all Quebec schools in November 2004. As of fall 2008, the Centre featured a new prevention game, Know Limits (Dés Joués in French), for teens in high schools and treatment or rehabilitation centres. The prevention tools are being used in North America, Europe, Southeast Asia, Australia, and New Zealand. (See www.youthgambling.com.)

To focus on the at-risk 18–24 demographic, the Responsible Gaming Council, with input from colleges and universities, developed Know the Score (KTS)—an interactive problem gambling awareness program that aims to engage students in a fun and informative way. KTS dispels common myths about winning and losing, shares signs of problem gambling, makes students aware of local sources of help for gambling-related problems, and suggests ways to minimize risks. Since the program was piloted in 2002, it has been delivered more than 350 times on 97 campuses in Ontario, British Columbia, Manitoba, Newfoundland and Labrador, New Brunswick, Nova Scotia, Prince Edward Island, and New York State. (See www.knowthescore.ca.)

Korn (2000) outlined recommendations for ways to strengthen Canadian health and social policy related to gambling, including the need to (1) "ensure that there is a responsible balance between encouraging gambling as entertainment and protecting the public from gambling-related harm," and to (2) "adopt harm-reduction strategies directed toward minimizing the adverse health, social and economic consequences of gambling behaviour for individuals, families and communities" (p. 63). Recently, Currie et al. (2008) demonstrated that "a population-based approach to planning strategies to prevent harm at the level of the individual gambler may be feasible" (p. 333).

Thinking Critically

1. Should governments in Canada be in the business of promoting gambling for profit? What is their responsibility to address the consequences of legalized, for-government-profit gambling? How do you balance this with personal responsibility for behavioural choices? Is it "fair" for pathological gamblers, once they have recognized that they have an addiction, to transfer responsibility for the consequences onto a third party?

2. In his harm-reduction recommendation, Korn (2000) included strategies such as healthy-gambling guidelines, early identification of gambling problems, and inclusion of moderation and abstinence goals. Design a prevention and treatment program for a vulnerable, high-risk population.

3. Should parents be concerned about the possibility of their children becoming involved in on-line "cybercasinos"?

4. How would you know if Know the Score works?

DELIRIUM, DEMENTIA, AMNESTIC, AND OTHER COGNITIVE DISORDERS This category covers disorders in which cognition is seriously disturbed.

- *Delirium* is a clouding of consciousness, wandering attention, and an incoherent stream of thought. It may be caused by several medical conditions, such as malnutrition, as well as by substance abuse.

- *Dementia*, a deterioration of mental capacities, especially memory, is associated with Alzheimer's disease, stroke, and several other medical conditions, as well as with substance abuse.

- *Amnestic syndrome* is an impairment in memory when there is no delirium or dementia.

Delirium and dementia are discussed in detail in Chapter 16 because they are often associated with aging. Amnestic syndrome is considered in Chapter 12 because it is often linked to alcohol abuse.

DIAGNOSIS OF J. BRETT BARKLEY Now that we have briefly described the *DSM's* diagnostic categories and axes, we return to the case of J. Brett Barkley with which the book began. Table 3.1 shows how Brett's diagnosis would look. On Axis I, he is diagnosed with alcohol dependence, a condition that has also created a problem with sexual arousal. His current problems with his marriage are noted, as is his prior history of bipolar disorder. In addition, Brett is diagnosed on Axis II as having avoidant personality disorder. His feelings of inferiority, his self-consciousness when around others, and his avoidance of activities because of fear of criticism are the basis of this diagnosis. He has no general medical condition relevant to his problems, so he has no diagnosis on Axis III. His problems with his marriage are noted on Axis IV, and his current level of functioning is assessed at 55 on the GAF scale (indicating a moderate level of impairment). Though alcohol may be Brett's most immediate problem, the multiaxial diagnosis gives clinicians a fairly full picture of the set of interrelated problems that will need to be addressed in treatment.

TABLE 3.1
DSM-IV MULTIAXIAL DIAGNOSIS OF J. BRETT BARKLEY

Axis I	Alcohol dependence Alcohol-induced sexual problem, with impaired arousal Bipolar I disorder, most recent episode Manic, in full remission Partner relational problem
Axis II	Avoidant personality disorder
Axis III	None
Axis IV	Problem with primary support group
Axis V	GAF = 55

PREVALENCE OF DSM DISORDERS

It is of interest to know how many people have the different disorders. Briefly, **epidemiology** is the study of the frequency and distribution of a disorder in a population. In epidemiological research, data are gathered about the rates of a disorder and its possible correlates in a large sample or population. One focus of epidemiology is to determine the proportion of a population that has a disorder at a given time. This determination is known as **prevalence**. For example, "12-month prevalence" refers to the proportion of a sample that had experienced a disorder in the year preceding an interview. **Lifetime prevalence** is the proportion of the sample that had ever experienced the disorder up to the time of the interview. Canadian Perspectives 3.1 provides information about the prevalence of pathological gambling in Canada. In Canadian Perspectives 3.2, we take a look at the first comprehensive, national epidemiological study conducted in Canada. In Chapter 5, we will discuss epidemiology as a research method. At appropriate points in this book, we will summarize the results of numerous other epidemiological studies conducted in Canadian settings. These studies often have a specific focus, such as the epidemiology of the *DSM* anxiety disorders (see Chapter 6).

National studies conducted in the United States provide useful information about lifetime prevalence. The largest epidemiologic investigation ever conducted in the United States—the Epidemiologic Catchment Area (ECA) Study (Robins & Regier, 1991)—reported an overall lifetime prevalence rate of 32%. The National Comorbidity Survey (NCS; Kessler et al., 1994) also included Axis II disorders and reported the one-year prevalence of any disorder to be 29.5% and the comparable lifetime prevalence to be a whopping 48%. The National Comorbidity Survey—Replication (NCS-R; Kessler, Berglund, et al., 2005; Kessler & Wang, 2008) yielded lifetime prevalence estimates as follows: any anxiety disorder, 28.8%; mood disorders, 20.8%; impulse-control disorders, 24.8%; substance use disorders, 14.6%; and, any disorder, 46.4%. In other words, almost half the population will have a diagnosable mental disorder at some time. If these estimates are accurate and the focus is on lifetime prevalence, it can be concluded that abnormality is almost the norm. Kessler, Berglund, et al. (2005) also reported that half of all lifetime cases start by age 14 and three quarters by age 24. Median age of onset was earlier for anxiety (11 years) and impulse-control (11 years) disorders relative to substance abuse (20 years) and mood (30 years) disorders.

Comorbidity, or co-occurrence of different disorders, has been called "the premier challenge facing mental health professionals" (Kendall & Clarkin, 1992, p. 833). It can be a major problem because it makes treatment planning more difficult, affects treatment compliance, and complicates the coordination of the delivery of services (Nathan & Langenbucher, 1999). A major criticism of the evidence-based treatment literature is that it usually excludes cases with co-occurring conditions despite the fact that high rates of comorbidity are common in clinical samples (e.g., Westen, Novotny, & Thompson-Brenner, 2004). The rate of comorbidity was very high in the original NCS—79% of people with one disorder also had another *DSM* disorder (Kessler et al., 1994). In analyses of 12-month prevalence, comorbidity, and severity of disorders in the NCS-R, Kessler, Chiu, Demler, Merikangas, and Walters (2005) reported that "serious" cases (22.3% of all cases) are concentrated among cases with high comorbidity. Why is comorbidity so high? Perhaps factors involved in the development of one disorder, such as stress, also affect the development of other disorders.

CANADIAN PERSPECTIVES 3.2
HOW PREVALENT ARE PSYCHOLOGICAL DISORDERS IN CANADA?

"Conservatively, we estimate that 7.5 million Canadians suffer from depression, anxiety, substance abuse or another mental health disorder."
—Phil Upshall, National Executive Director of the Mood Disorders Society of Canada, and chair of Mental Illness Awareness Week (*Canadian Psychiatry Aujourd'hui*, October 2008)

The Canadian Community Health Survey (CCHS) (Cycle 1.2) *Mental Health and Well-being Survey*
A relatively comprehensive and carefully designed epidemiological study was conducted in Ontario in 1990 and 1991 as part of the Ontario Health Survey, *Mental Health Supplement* (Ontario Ministry of Health, 1994). Surprisingly, this was the first province-wide study in which respondents were chosen to be representative of

the entire population. Almost 1 in 5 (19%) of Ontarians aged 15 to 64 years had one or more of the assessed mental disorders (one-year prevalence rate). Further, 5% of males and 4% of females could be diagnosed with two or more disorders. However, the CCHS 1.2 is the first comprehensive Canadian *national* study to use a full current version of the Composite International Diagnostic Interview (developed by the WHO). For this reason and because of the large sample size (N = 36,984 community dwelling respondents), the CCHS 1.2 provides the best currently available description of selected disorders in Canada (see Gravel & Beland, 2005, for a description). Conducted by Statistics Canada in 2002, the survey collected information on the prevalence of five mental disorders (within the 12 months prior to the interview): major depression, mania, panic disorder, social phobia, and agoraphobia, as well as alcohol and illicit drug dependence, eating attitude problems, and problem gambling or moderate risk for problem gambling. The target population was household residents aged 15 and older throughout Canada (excluding the three territories, Native reserves, the armed forces, and people living in institutions and in some remote areas).

Preliminary results were reported by Statistics Canada in September 2003; however, the publication process is ongoing. We will examine further details of current findings in our discussions of specific disorders in subsequent chapters. Here, we note some major findings (see Government of Canada, 2006):

- 1 out of every 10 Canadians aged 15 and over (about 2.7 million people) reported *symptoms* consistent with a mood or anxiety disorder, or alcohol or illicit drug dependence during the previous 12 months.
- 1 in 20 met criteria for either major depression or bipolar disorder.
- 1 in 20 met criteria for panic disorder, agoraphobia, or social phobia.
- 1 in 30 met criteria for substance dependence (alcohol or illicit drug use).

- 1 in 50 met criteria for moderate risk of problem gambling.
- Women were 1.5 times more likely than men to meet criteria for a mood or anxiety disorder; men were 2.6 times more likely than women to meet criteria for substance dependence.
- Eating attitude problems and agoraphobia were 6 times and 5 times more common among women than men, respectively.
- Two thirds (68.8%) of young people 15–24 with a mood or anxiety disorder reported that their symptoms started prior to age 15.
- About half (47.9%) of people 45–64 and one third (34.1%) of seniors stated that their disorder began prior to age 25.
- Mood and anxiety disorders also developed during each life stage.

Only 32% of those who suffered from any of the surveyed problems had seen or talked to a health care professional in the preceding year. In Chapter 1 we noted that comorbidity plays a role in help-seeking. In an Alberta study, Bland, Newman, and Orn (1997a) reported that the **help-seeking** rate for those with one disorder was only 20.3% whereas the rate for those with more than one diagnosis was 42.8%.

Thinking Critically

1. There are significant differences in prevalence rates for specific psychological disorders between Canadian men and women. What biological, psychological, and social factors could account for these differences? In the *Mental Health Supplement* study, people aged 15 to 24 were oversampled. Why?
2. The WHO Consortium (2000) concluded that lifetime prevalence rates have increased in certain groups. However, the increase was less for the anxiety disorders than for both mood and substance use disorders. What do you think will happen to prevalence rates in Canada and around the world in the future? Is the prevalence of specific disorders likely to increase? Why? What are the implications?

ISSUES IN THE CLASSIFICATION OF ABNORMAL BEHAVIOUR

Our review of the major diagnostic categories of abnormal behaviour was brief because the diagnoses will be examined in more detail throughout this text. On the basis of this overview, however, we will examine here the usefulness of the current diagnostic system.

GENERAL CRITICISMS OF CLASSIFICATION

Some critics of classification argue that to classify someone as depressed or anxious results in a loss of information about that person, thereby reducing some of the uniqueness of the individual being studied. In evaluating this claim, recall our earlier discussions of paradigms and their effect on how we glean information about our world. It appears to be in the nature of humankind to categorize whenever we perceive and

think about anything. Those who argue against classification per se are overlooking the inevitability of classification and categorization in human thought.

In classification, some information must inevitably be lost. What matters is whether the information lost is relevant, and relevance depends on the purposes of the classification system. Any classification is designed to group together objects sharing a common property and to ignore differences in the objects that are not relevant to the purposes at hand. If our intention is merely to count odd and even rolls of a die, it is irrelevant whether a die comes up one, three, or five, or two, four, or six. In judging abnormal behaviour, however, we cannot so easily decide what is wheat and what is chaff, for the relevant and irrelevant dimensions of abnormal behaviour are uncertain. Thus, when we do classify, we may be grouping people together on rather trivial bases while ignoring their extremely important differences.

In some epidemiological research, interviewers go to homes in a community, conducting interviews to determine the rates of different disorders. Ken Cavanagh/ Photo Researchers, Inc.

In Chapter 1, we discussed issues related to attitudes toward people with psychological disorders. We must revisit the topic in the current context to reinforce the fact that classification can have negative effects on a person. Consider how your life might be changed after being diagnosed as having schizophrenia. You might become guarded and suspicious lest someone recognize your disorder. Or you might be chronically on edge, fearing the onset of another episode. The fact that you are a "former mental patient" could have a stigmatizing effect. Friends and loved ones might treat you differently, and you might have difficulty obtaining employment. There is little doubt that diagnosis can have such negative consequences. The general public holds a relatively negative view of "mental patients," especially those diagnosed with one of the psychotic disorders, and clients and their families believe that such stigmatizing effects are common. We must recognize and be on guard against the possible social stigma of a diagnosis.

THE VALUE OF CLASSIFICATION AND DIAGNOSES

The various types of abnormal behaviour differ from one another in many ways, and thus classifying them is essential, for these differences may constitute keys to the causes and treatments of various deviant behaviours. For example, mental retardation is sometimes caused by phenylketonuria. A deficiency in the metabolism of the protein phenylalanine results in the release of incomplete metabolites that injure the brain. A diet drastically reduced in phenylalanine prevents some of

this injury. However, had we taken 1,000 people with mental retardation and placed them all on the phenylalanine-free diet, the response would have been insignificant and the diet would have been discarded as a treatment. It was first necessary to recognize a subtype of mental retardation, phenylketonuria, and then subject the value of a phenylalanine-free diet to investigation in this specific population.

Forming categories furthers knowledge, for once a category is formed, additional information may be ascertained about it. Even though the category is only an asserted, and not a proven entity, it may still be heuristically useful in that it facilitates the acquisition of new information. Only after a diagnostic category has been formed can we study people who fit its definition in the hope of uncovering factors responsible for the development of their problems and of devising treatments that may help them. For example, bipolar disorder was once not typically distinguished from depression. If this distinction had not been made, it is unlikely that lithium would have been recognized as an effective treatment for bipolar disorder.

SPECIFIC CRITICISMS OF CLASSIFICATION

In addition to general criticisms of psychiatric classification, more specific criticisms are commonly made. The principal ones concern whether discrete diagnostic categories are justifiable and whether the diagnostic categories are reliable and valid. These criticisms were frequently levelled at *DSM-I* and *DSM-II*. At the close of this section, we will see how subsequent editions of the *DSM* have come to grips with them.

DISCRETE ENTITY VERSUS CONTINUUM The *DSM* represents a **categorical classification**, a yes–no approach to classification. Does the client have schizophrenia or not? It may be argued that this type of classification, because it postulates discrete (separate) diagnostic entities, does not allow continuity between normal and abnormal behaviour to be taken into consideration. Those who advance the continuity argument hold that abnormal and normal behaviours differ only in intensity or degree, not in kind; therefore, discrete diagnostic categories foster a false impression of discontinuity.

In contrast, in **dimensional classification**, the entities or objects being classified must be ranked on a quantitative dimension (e.g., a 1-to-10 scale of anxiety, where 1 represents minimal and 10 extreme). Classification would be accomplished by assessing clients on the relevant dimensions and perhaps plotting the location of the client in a system of coordinates defined by his or her score on each dimension. (See Figure 3.1 for an illustration of the difference between dimensional and categorical classification.) A dimensional system can subsume a categorical system by specifying a cutting point, or threshold, on one of the quantitative dimensions. This capability is a potential advantage of the dimensional approach.

A dimensional approach also allows for the possibility that certain individuals may experience a number of troubling symptoms of a disorder but not meet the number of symp-

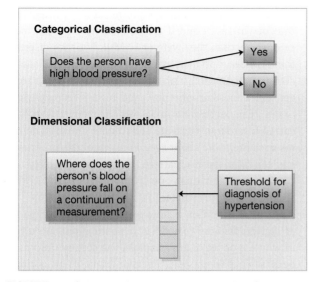

FIGURE 3.1 Categorical versus dimensional classification

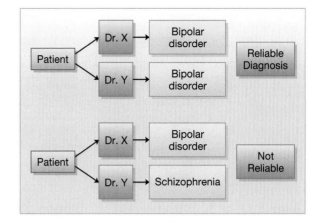

FIGURE 3.2 Inter-rater reliability

toms required for an actual diagnosis. Contemporary research on disorders such as depression shows that there is substantial evidence for continuity and that people who experience symptoms of depression but do not meet the criteria for a diagnosis nevertheless experience significant levels of distress and impairment and appear to warrant treatment (see Flett, Vredenburg, & Krames, 1997; Maser et al., 2009).

Clearly, a dimensional system can be applied to most of the symptoms that constitute the diagnoses of the *DSM*. Anxiety, depression, and the many personality traits that are included in the personality disorders are found in different people to varying degrees and thus do not seem to fit well with the *DSM* categorical model.

The choice between a categorical and a dimensional system of classification, however, is not as simple as it might seem initially. Consider hypertension (high blood pressure), a topic discussed at length in Chapter 9. Blood-pressure measurements form a continuum, which clearly fits a dimensional approach; yet researchers have found it useful to categorize certain people as having high blood pressure in order to research the causes and possible treatments for the condition. A similar situation could exist for the *DSM* categories. Even though anxiety clearly exists in differing degrees in different people and thus is a dimensional variable, it could prove useful to create a diagnostic category for those people whose anxiety is extreme. There is a certain inevitable arbitrariness to such a categorization (where exactly should the cutoff be?), but it could be fruitful nonetheless. We will return to this issue in Focus on Discovery 3.3 and in our discussion of personality disorders in Chapter 13.

RELIABILITY: THE CORNERSTONE OF A DIAGNOSTIC SYSTEM

The extent to which a classification system, or a test or measurement of any kind, produces the same scientific observation each time it is applied is the measure of its **reliability**. An example of an unreliable measure would be a flexible, elastic-like

ruler whose length changed every time it was used. This flawed ruler would yield different values for the height of the same object every time the object was measured. In contrast, a reliable measure, such as a standard wooden ruler, produces consistent results.

Inter-rater reliability refers to the extent to which two judges agree about an event. For example, suppose you wanted to know whether a child suspected of having attention deficit hyperactivity disorder did indeed have difficulty paying attention and staying seated in the classroom. You could decide to observe the child during a day at school. To determine whether the observational data were reliable, you would want to have at least two people watch the child and make independent judgements about the level of attention and activity. The extent to which the raters agreed would be an index of inter-rater reliability. (See Figure 3.2 for an illustration.)

Reliability is a primary criterion for judging any classification system. For a classification system to be useful, those applying it must be able to agree on what is and what is not an instance of a particular category. A person diagnosed as having an anxiety disorder by one clinician should be given the same diagnosis by another clinician, as well. After all, if someone is not diagnosed correctly, he or she may not receive the best treatment available. Prior to *DSM-III*, diagnostic reliability was not acceptable, mainly because the criteria for making a diagnosis were not presented clearly and methods of assessing a client's symptoms were not standardized (Ward et al., 1962).

The two components of reliability—agreeing on who is a member of a class and who is not—are termed *sensitivity* and *specificity*. Sensitivity refers to agreement regarding the presence of a specific diagnosis; specificity refers to agreement concerning the absence of a diagnosis. As we will see, reliability for most current diagnostic categories is relatively good.

HOW VALID ARE DIAGNOSTIC CATEGORIES?

Validity is a complex topic. We will describe the several types of validity in Chapter 4, but here we will focus on the type of validity that is most important for diagnosis—**construct**

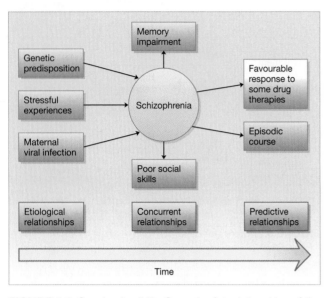

FIGURE 3.3 Construct validity. Some lawful relationships of the construct of schizophrenia

validity. As noted previously, the diagnoses of the *DSM* are referred to as hypothetical constructs because they are inferred, not proven, entities. A diagnosis of schizophrenia, for instance, does not have the same status as a diagnosis of diabetes. In the case of diabetes, we know the symptoms, the biological malfunction that produces them, and some of the causes. For schizophrenia, we have a proposed set of symptoms but only very tentative information regarding mechanisms that may produce the symptoms.

Construct validity is determined by evaluating the extent to which accurate statements and predictions can be made about a category once it has been formed. In other words, to what extent does the construct enter into a network of lawful relationships? Some of these relationships may be about possible causes of the disorder; for example, a genetic predisposition or a biochemical imbalance. Others could be about characteristics of the disorder that are not symptoms but that occur frequently in association with it; for example, poor social skills in people with schizophrenia. Other relationships could refer to predictions about the course of the disorder or the probable response to particular treatments. The greater the number and strength of relationships into which a diagnosis enters, the greater the construct validity (see Figure 3.3).

We have organized this book around the major *DSM* diagnostic categories because we believe that they possess construct validity. Certain categories have greater validity than others, however, and we will discuss these differences in the chapters on each of the major diagnostic categories.

THE *DSM* AND CRITICISMS OF DIAGNOSIS

Beginning with *DSM-III*, an effort was made to create more reliable and valid diagnostic categories. Major improvements include the following:

1. The characteristics and symptoms of each diagnostic category in axes I and II are now described much more extensively than they were in *DSM-II*. For each disorder, there is a description of essential features, then of associated features, such as laboratory findings (e.g., enlarged ventricles in schizophrenia), and results from physical exams (e.g., electrolyte imbalances in people who have eating disorders). Next are statements drawn from the research literature about age of onset, course, prevalence and sex ratio, familial pattern, and differential diagnosis (i.e., how to distinguish one diagnosis from another that is symptomatically similar to it).

2. Much more attention is now paid to how the symptoms of a given disorder may differ depending on the culture in which it appears. For example, the core symptoms of both schizophrenia (e.g., delusions and hallucinations) and depression (e.g., depressed mood and loss of interest or pleasure in activities) are similar cross-culturally (Draguns, 1989), but other symptoms of depression can differ around the world. For example, guilt is a frequent symptom of depression in Western society but an infrequent symptom in Japan and Iran. (Focus on Discovery 3.2 describes efforts by the *DSM* to be more sensitive to the effects of culture and explores cultural factors from an assessment perspective).

3. Specific *diagnostic criteria*—the symptoms and other facts that must be present to justify the diagnosis—are spelled out more precisely, and the clinical symptoms that constitute a diagnosis are defined in a glossary. Table 3.2 compares the descriptions of a manic episode given in *DSM-II* with the diagnostic criteria given in *DSM-IV-TR*. The bases for making diagnoses are decidedly more detailed and concrete in *DSM-IV-TR*.

The improved explicitness of the *DSM* criteria has reduced the descriptive inadequacies that were the major source of diagnostic unreliability and thus has led to improved reliability. Another factor in improved reliability is the use of standardized, reliably scored interviews for collecting the information needed for a diagnosis. (We will describe such interviews in the next chapter.) Results of an extensive evaluation of the reliability of *DSM-III-R* (Williams et al., 1992) determined that the reliabilities vary but are acceptable for most of the major categories. The study used a statistic called "kappa," which measures the proportion of agreement over and above what would be expected by chance. Generally, kappas over .70 are considered good. The kappas ranged between .47 and .86 for the selected diagnoses. The relatively low figures for anxiety disorders (.47 for social phobia and .58 for panic disorder) were higher in other studies that used an assessment interview specifically tailored for them (DiNardo et al., 1993). The reliabilities of *DSM-IV* diagnoses are comparable (e.g., Zanarini et al., 2000). Nonetheless, there is clearly room for improvement since the reliability of some specific diagnoses is well below expectations and acceptable standards.

TABLE 3.2
DESCRIPTION OF MANIC DISORDER IN *DSM-II* VS. *DSM-IV-TR*

DSM-II (1968, p. 36)

Manic-depressive illness, manic type. This disorder consists exclusively of manic episodes. These episodes are characterized by excessive elation, irritability, talkativeness, flight of ideas, and accelerated speech and motor activity. Brief periods of depression sometimes occur, but they are never true depressive episodes.

DSM-IV-TR (2000, p. 362)

Diagnostic Criteria for a Manic Episode

1. A distinct period of abnormally and persistently elevated, expansive, or irritable mood, lasting at least one week (or any duration if hospitalization is necessary).
2. During the period of mood disturbance, three (or more) of the following symptoms have persisted (four if the mood is only irritable) and have been present to a significant degree:
    1. inflated self-esteem or grandiosity
    2. decreased need for sleep (e.g., feels rested after only three hours of sleep)
    3. more talkative than usual or pressure to keep talking
    4. flight of ideas or subjective experience that thoughts are racing
    5. distractibility (i.e., attention too easily drawn to unimportant or irrelevant external stimuli)
    6. increase in goal-directed activity (either socially, at work or school, or sexually) or psychomotor agitation
    7. excessive involvement in pleasurable activities that have a high potential for painful consequences (e.g., engaging in unrestrained buying sprees, sexual indiscretions, or foolish business investments)
3. The symptoms do not meet criteria for a Mixed Episode.
4. The mood disturbance is sufficiently severe to cause marked impairment in occupational functioning or in usual social activities or relationships with others, or to necessitate hospitalization to prevent harm to self or others, or there are psychotic features.
5. The symptoms are not due to the direct physiological effects of a substance (e.g., a drug of abuse, a medication, or other treatment) or a general medical condition (e.g., hyperthyroidism).

Source: DSM-IV-TR material reprinted with permission from the *DSM-IV-TR*, American Psychiatric Association, 2000.

Thus far we have described the *DSM* in positive terms. The attainment of adequate diagnostic reliability is a considerable achievement, but a number of problems remain.

1. The discrete entity versus continuum issue, discussed earlier, has not been satisfactorily resolved.
2. It is unclear whether the rules for making diagnostic decisions are ideal. Examining Table 3.2, we see that for people to be diagnosed as suffering from mania, they must have three symptoms from a list of seven, or four if their mood is irritable. But why require three symptoms rather than two or five? Just as there is a degree of arbitrariness about the point at which a person is diagnosed as having high blood pressure, so is there an element of arbitrariness to the *DSM's* diagnostic rules.
3. The reliability of axes I and II may not always be as high in everyday practice as it is in formal research studies, for diagnosticians may not adhere as precisely to the criteria as do those whose work is being scrutinized.
4. Although the improved reliability of the *DSM* may lead to more validity, there is no guarantee that it will. The diagnoses made according to the *DSM* criteria may not reveal anything useful about the clients.
5. Subjective factors still play a role in evaluations made according to *DSM-IV-TR*. Consider again the criteria for manic syndrome. What exactly does it mean to say that

the elevated mood must be abnormally and persistently elevated? Or, what level of involvement in pleasurable activities with high potential for painful consequences is excessive? As another example, on Axis V the clinician must judge the client's level of current functioning. The clinician determines the client's level of adaptive functioning and how his or her behaviour compares with that of an average person. Such a judgement sets the stage for the insertion of cultural biases as well as the clinician's own personal ideas of what the average person should be doing at a given stage of life and in particular circumstances.
6. Not all of the *DSM* classification changes seem positive. Should a problem such as difficulty in learning arithmetic or reading be considered a psychiatric disorder? By expanding its coverage, the *DSM* seems to have made too many childhood problems into psychiatric disorders, without good justification for doing so.

In sum, although the *DSM* continues to improve, it is far from perfect. Throughout this book, as we present the literature on various disorders, we will have further opportunities to describe both the strengths and the weaknesses of *DSM-IV-TR* and to consider how it may deal with some of the problems that still exist. What is most heartening about the *DSM* is that its attempts to be explicit about the rules for diagnosis make it easier to detect problems in the diagnostic system.

FOCUS ON DISCOVERY 3.1
ETHNIC AND CULTURAL CONSIDERATIONS IN *DSM-IV-TR*

The following clinical vignette taken from Kirmayer, Rousseau, Jarvis, and Guzder (2003) illustrates the need for a complex and sensitive approach to diagnosis and clinical assessment that recognizes differences in cultural backgrounds.

CASE

A 16-year-old girl from Haiti presents with disorganized schizophrenia, which began around age 14. Her family has not been compliant with treatment and this has led to several hospitalizations of the patient in a dehydrated state. During the third hospitalization, the clinical team decide to explore the family's interpretation of the illness. A grand-aunt insists on sending the girl to Haiti for a traditional diagnosis. The traditional healer indicates that the problem is due to an ancestor's spirit in the mother's family and that for this reason it will be a prolonged illness. This explanation helps to restore cohesion in the extended family by rallying people around the patient, and her family receives much support. The traditional interpretation and treatment has broken the family's sense of shame and isolation and promoted an alliance with the medical team and the acceptance of antipsychotic medication (Kirmayer et al., 2003, p. 25).

Previous editions of the *DSM* were criticized for their lack of attention to cultural and ethnic variations in psychopathology. *DSM-IV-TR* attempts to enhance its cultural sensitivity in three ways: (1) by including in the main body of the manual a discussion of cultural and ethnic factors for each disorder; (2) by providing in the appendix a general framework for evaluating the role of culture and ethnicity; and (3) by describing culture-bound syndromes in an appendix.

The core symptoms of depression appear to be similar cross-culturally. However, guilt is less frequent in Japan than in Western cultures.
© Bloomimage/CORBIS.

Among the cultural issues of which clinicians need to be aware are language differences between the therapist and the client and the way in which the client's culture talks about emotional distress. Many cultures, for example, describe grief or anxiety in physical terms—"I am sick in my heart" or "My heart is heavy"—rather than in psychological terms. Individuals also vary in the degree to which they identify with their cultural or ethnic group. Some value assimilation into the majority culture, whereas others wish to maintain close ties to their ethnic background. In general, clinicians are advised to be constantly mindful of how culture and ethnicity influence diagnosis and treatment, a topic discussed in the next chapter.

The *DSM* also describes 25 "locality-specific patterns of aberrant behaviour and troubling experience that may or may not be linked to a particular *DSM-IV* diagnostic category" (*DSM-IV-TR*, 2000, p. 898). The following are some examples that may occur in clinical practices in North America.

- *amok*—a dissociative episode in which there is a period of brooding followed by a violent and sometimes homicidal outburst. The episode tends to be triggered by an insult and is found primarily among men. Persecutory delusions are often present, as well. The term is Malaysian and is defined by the dictionary as a murderous frenzy. You have probably encountered the phrase "run amok."

- *brain fag*—originally used in West Africa, this term refers to a condition reported by high school and university students in response to academic pressures. Symptoms include fatigue, tightness in the head and neck, and blurring of vision. This syndrome resembles certain anxiety, depressive, and somatoform disorders.

- *koro*—reported in south and east Asia, an episode of intense anxiety about the possibility that the penis or nipples will recede into the body, possibly leading to death.

Kirmayer, Rousseau, and Santhanam (2003) suggested that one viable approach is to work in multidisciplinary teams that are culturally diverse and reflective of the client population. This strategy could involve working closely with interpreters and "culture brokers" who would assist with the clarification of the cultural context.

Although *DSM-IV* introduced an "Outline for Cultural Formulation" designed to guide treatment planning from a perspective sensitive to differences in ethnocultural backgrounds and context, in practice, this outline has had little impact; 57% of consultants working at the McGill Cultural Consultation Service in Montreal indicated that they had little or no familiarity with it. Upon using it, however, 61% found it to be very useful or extremely useful in organizing their assessments and consultation reports (Kirmayer et al., 2008).

DSM-5 AND BEYOND: DIAGNOSIS IS AT A CROSSROADS

"In all, [DSM-5] is a combination of suspense, mystery and prepublication controversy that many publishers would die for. The psychiatric association knows it has a corner on the market and a blockbuster series."

—Benedict Carey, *The New York Times*, December 18, 2008

"The APA is committed to developing a manual that is both based on the best science available and useful to clinicians and researchers."

—David Kupfer, M.D., Chair of the *DSM-5* Task Force, February 10, 2010

Planning for the **DSM-5** began in 1999 with collaboration between the American Psychiatric Association and the U.S. National Institute of Mental Health (NIMH) designed to stimulate research to address key issues in psychiatric nosology (the classification of disorders). A major objective is to initiate a renewed focus on the validity of diagnosis. Another objective is to eliminate disparities between the *DSM* and the WHO's ICD (whose version 11 is slated for publication around 2014). The resulting publications are intended to serve as resources for the *DSM* task force and disorder-specific work groups. The *DSM-5* task force was announced in July 2007. It has 27 members and is chaired by David Kupfer with Daniel A. Regier as co-chair. The 120 members of the 13 work groups charged with reviewing scientific advances and research-based information to develop the fifth edition manual were announced on May 1, 2008. According to a statement from the American Psychiatric Association, "Individual work groups may propose revisions to existing disorder criteria, inclusion of new disorders, removal of existing disorders, or no changes to a disorder or its criteria." The composition of the work groups has not been without controversy. For example, Dr. Kenneth J. Zucker, from Ontario's Centre for Addiction and Mental Health, was named chair of the Sexual and Gender Identity Disorders Work Group. Soon after the announcement, transgender advocates circulated on-line petitions objecting to the appointment because they consider his work to be "demeaning" since he uses "reparative therapy to cure gender-variant children" and were critical about alleged "secrecy" related to nondisclosure agreements signed by working group members. The American Psychiatric Association responded to the criticism and the Board of Trustees voted to create a task force to review the scientific and clinical literature on gender identity disorder treatment.

In a recent paper, Watson and Clark (2006) reviewed the widespread dissatisfaction with the existing system and noted further that the *DSM* is (1) atheoretical, (2) cumbersome to use, and (3) plagued by problems of comorbidity and heterogeneity. They reflected on the pressure to replace the descriptive approach with a system that models basic underlying causes (e.g., genetic diatheses, trait vulnerabilities) but concluded that "it is uncertain to what extent etiological considerations will play a key role in reshaping the *DSM* in the foreseeable future" (Watson & Clark, 2006, p. 210). Although succeeding revisions have included more and more diagnostic categories, subtypes, and specifiers in order to allow finer discriminations, the nosology has become cumbersome and confusing. Even First (2005), a major architect and editor of *DSM-IV*, appears to acknowledge that clinicians use it by ignoring the complexity. Although the empirical co-occurrence of different disorders (i.e., comorbidity) is the norm in *DSM-IV* (Widiger & Samuel, 2005), Watson and Clark (2006) consider this to be problematic only "if diagnostic entities are intended to reflect discrete, independent disorders, whereas it has the positive effect of illuminating important phenomena across disorders" (p. 211). Finally, the heterogeneity within many *DSM* disorders (see Watson, 2003) can possibly reduce power and obscure findings from various studies (e.g., neuroimaging) (see Mataix-Cols, do Rosario-Campos, & Leckman, 2005).

Watson and Clark (2006) concluded that "we currently lack a compelling approach that could be implemented readily to replace the current *DSM* system" (p. 210). Nonetheless, they explored two potential alternatives:

1. *Reorganizing the diagnostic classes.* Watson (2005) had proposed a hierarchical system. Instead of grouping disorders into diagnostic classes (e.g., anxiety disorders) based on "shared phenomenological features" (American Psychiatric Association, 2000, p. 10), the system would be based on "empirically based classes that reflect the actual real-world similarities between disorders (e.g., comorbidity, shared treatment response)" (Watson & Clark, 2006, p. 211). For example, generalized anxiety disorder and unipolar mood disorders would be placed within the same diagnostic class.
2. *Implementation of fully dimensional schemes.* Livesley (2005) summarized support for a dimensional scheme for the Axis II personality disorders based on higher order dimensions (e.g., neuroticism-emotional stability), which can be decomposed into several specific dimensions. Watson and Clark (2006) suggested that a fully dimensional taxonomy could be developed but conclude that *DSM-5* will probably not include a dimensional model for Axis I disorders.

What can we expect in the future? Watson and Clark (2006) suggested two possibilities:

1. *A hybrid system?* Axis II could be transformed into a dimensional scheme, but Axis I would remain categorical (Widiger & Samuel, 2005).
2. *Multiple systems?* There could be different systems for different purposes. First (2005) has indicated that

clinical utility will be vitally important in the development of *DSM-5*; however, a second system might prove more useful for psychopathology researchers.

Watson and Clark (2006) concluded that "a temporary dual system merits serious consideration as we move toward *DSM-5* and beyond" (p. 214). Maser and colleagues (2009) also recommend a "paradigm shift" toward a mixed categorical-dimensional system for *DSM-5*. However, in contrast to Watson and Clark, Maser et al. recommended the use of broad categories with added dimensions because it "enriches patient characterization and conforms to the way patients think" (p. 25). They proposed that the new system would reduce comorbidity, allow symptom weighting, eliminate "Not otherwise specified" categories, and provide new directions to biological researchers. There would, of course, be drawbacks, including the necessity to retrain clinicians and possibly reinterpret data under the old model. In a recent commentary on the conceptual development of *DSM-5*, the chairpersons and coordinators of the revision process (Regier, Narrow, Kuhl, & Kupfer, 2009) stated:

> The single most important precondition for moving forward to improve the clinical and scientific utility of DSM-5 will be the incorporation of simple dimensional measures for assessing syndromes within broad diagnostic categories and supraordinate dimensions that cross current diagnostic boundaries. Thus, we have decided that one, if not the major difference between DSM-IV and DSM-5 will be the more prominent use of dimensional measures in DSM-5 (p. 649).

Many of the possible and proposed changes have been reported and debated in recent years, and continue to be debated. The *American Journal of Psychiatry* has been publishing brief editorials on issues that should be considered in the formulation of the fifth edition.

TASK FORCE AND WORK GROUP DRAFT PROPOSALS

In a news release on February 10, 2010, the American Psychiatric Association posted the proposed draft disorders and draft diagnostic criteria for *DSM-5* (see www.dsm5.org). These draft disorders and criteria represent content changes under consideration that were available for public review and written comment until April 20, 2010. It was noted that the criteria would be reviewed and refined over the subsequent two years, during which the association would conduct three phases of field trials in order to test some of the proposed diagnostic criteria "in real-world clinical settings." New diagnostic categories were proposed, other categories were eliminated or subsumed under other new or old categories, and categories were proposed for future consideration. Some of these proposed changes are listed in Focus on Discovery 3.2. In addition, the work groups had under review a long list of conditions proposed by outside sources, including Internet addiction, parental alienation disorder, apathy syndrome, complicated grief disorder, male to eunuch gender identity disorder, and fetal alcohol syndrome.

A subgroup charged with examining the utility of Axis III recommended that *DSM-5* collapse axes I, II, and III into one axis. This axis would contain all psychiatric and general medical diagnoses and bring *DSM-5* into greater harmony with the single-axis approach used in the World Health Organization's *International Classification of Diseases*. Changes to axes IV and V were also being considered.

As important as the proposed changes to the diagnostic categories and criteria are, the American Psychiatric Association also formally proposed to add "dimensional assessments" to diagnostic evaluations. These dimensions would allow clinicians to evaluate the severity of symptoms and to take into account so-called "cross-cutting symptoms" that exist across several different diagnoses in order to refine diagnostic assessment and treatment planning. Examples of dimensions are anxiety, suicide assessment, and substance abuse severity dimensions. This proposal is consistent with a shift toward a mixed categorical-dimensional system. The proposed dimensional assessments would be tested during the field trials for both feasibility and acceptability.

A gender and cross-cultural study group used several methods and sources of input to determine if diagnostic criteria had to be revised in order to be sensitive to the different ways in which gender, race, and culture can affect the expression of symptoms. For example, the study group recommended changes to the diagnostic criteria for panic disorder based on different cultural expressions among some Asian cultures (see Lewis-Fernandez, 2010).

Although not included in the drafts proposed on February 10, 2010, the diagnostic spectra study group considered the possibility of there being larger groupings of the primary mental disorders within the classification—a more parsimonious "meta-structure" based on shared risk (e.g., genetic and specific environmental) and clinical (e.g., comorbidity and treatment response) factors. In a series of papers published in late 2009 in *Psychological Medicine*, the study group identified possible clusters and their internal coherence using external validating criteria (see Andrews et al., 2009). As noted by Andrews and colleagues, the approach "is a step away from a classification based on symptom picture alone" (p. 197). The final clusters identified were emotional, externalizing, psychosis, neurodevelopmental, and neurocognitive. A large, residual group of disorders (e.g., eating disorders, dissociative disorders, sexual disorders) did not "fit" into one of the five identified clusters. It remains to be determined whether this identification of clusters is useful.

It is not known which, if any, of the many proposals will actually be adopted. These and other ideas and issues for *DSM-5* will be discussed at appropriate points throughout this book. The work groups are expected to propose final revisions in 2012 and release the final, approved *DSM-5* in May 2013 (a revision of the May 2012 original timeline).

FOCUS ON DISCOVERY 3.2
DSM-5 TASK FORCE DRAFT REVISIONS—CATEGORIES AND SPECIFIC DISORDERS

> "... DSM-5 is still very much a work in progress—and these proposed revisions are by no means final."
>
> —Alan Schatzberg, M.D., President of the American Psychiatric Association, February 10, 2010

The following are some of the proposals for revisions to categories and specific disorders in the *DSM-5*:

• Creation of a new category of "behavioural addictions." Gambling would be the sole disorder in the category.

• OCD will be included under a grouping of "anxiety and obsessive-compulsive spectrum disorders."

• "Hoarding disorder" will be included either in the main manual or in an "appendix for further research."

• Body dysmorphic disorder will be reclassified from somatoform disorders to "anxiety and obsessive-compulsive spectrum disorders."

• "Hair-pulling disorder" (trichotillomania) will be reclassified from impulse control disorders not elsewhere classified to "anxiety and obsessive-compulsive spectrum disorders."

• Somatoform disorders, psychological factors affecting medical condition, and factitious disorders will be combined into one group entitled "somatic symptom disorders." The common feature of these disorders is the central place in the clinical presentation of physical symptoms and/or concern about medical illness.

• All of the somatoform disorders will be subsumed into a new disorder: "complex somatic symptom disorder," with optional specifiers (e.g., high health anxiety [previously, hypochondriasis]).

• Adjustment disorders will be included in a grouping of "trauma and stress-related disorders."

• "Mixed anxiety depression" is in an appendix of *DSM-IV* and is in the *ICD-10*. It will be formally included in *DSM-5*.

• Repeated self-injury co-occurs with a variety of diagnoses. "Non-suicidal self injury" will formally be included as a mood disorder.

• Consideration of the possibility that "premenstrual dysphoric disorder," a controversial disorder listed in an appendix in *DSM-IV*, might classify as a separate and distinct disorder from mood disorders or a specifier for mood disorders.

• New recognition of "binge eating" as an eating disorder defined as at least one binge a week for three months accompanied by severe guilt and plunges in mood.

• Replace the current categories of substance abuse and dependence with a new category—"addiction-related disorders." The category would include substance use disorders with each drug identified in its own specific category. Elimination of the category of dependence is intended to help differentiate between the compulsive drug-seeking addiction behaviour and normal tolerance and withdrawal that can be experienced when using certain prescribed medications.

• "Paraphilic coercive disorder" will be a distinct syndrome, separate from sexual sadism. For a minority of males—those with paraphilic coercive disorder— salient coercion cues lead to heightened arousal. Coercive sexual fantasy is commonly reported by or observed in rapists. This proposal is likely to be very controversial, as it was when it was first proposed in *DSM-III*, since many women fear that rapists' coercive acts could be "excused" because they are due to a mental disorder.

• "Hypersexual disorder" will be a new sexual disorder diagnostic category. It is in part when "a great deal of time is consumed by sexual fantasies and urges; and in planning for and engaging in sexual behavior." In the pop vernacular this disorder has been known as sex addiction. It's alleged that pro golfer Tiger Woods received treatment for it in 2010 following disclosure of his marital infidelity.

• The diagnostic term "mental retardation" will be changed to "intellectual disability" to align the criteria with terminology used by other disciplines.

• A single diagnostic category, "autism spectrum disorders," will incorporate the current diagnoses of autistic disorder, Asperger's disorder, childhood disintegrative disorder, and pervasive developmental disorder, not otherwise specified.

• A new category, "temper dysregulation with dysphoria," will help clinicians differentiate children with these symptoms from those with bipolar disorder or ODD.

• A significant reformulation of the approach to the assessment and diagnosis of personality psychopathology, including the proposal of a revised general category of personality disorder, and the provision for clinicians to rate dimensions of personality traits, a limited set of personality types, and the overall severity of personality dysfunction.

• Passive-aggressive (negativistic) and depressive personality disorders, two disorders considered as possible new syndromes in *DSM-IV*, will be represented and diagnosed by a combination of core impairment in personality functioning and specific pathological personality traits (rather than as specific types).

• Consideration of a new "risk syndromes" category. It would provide information to help clinicians identify earlier stages of disorders such as psychosis and dementia.

• In view of their minimal utility and diagnostic stability, the classic subtypes of schizophrenia (paranoid, catatonic, disorganized, undifferentiated, and residual), will be eliminated. Instead, dimensions will be used.

- The delirium, dementia, amnestic, and other cognitive disorders will be divided into three broad syndromes: "delirium," "major neurocognitive disorder," and "minor neurocognitive disorder."

- "Skin picking disorder" will be included, probably in an appendix for further research.

- "Olfactory reference syndrome" will be included, probably in an appendix for further research. What is this disorder? It's a preoccupation with the belief that one emits a foul or offensive body odour, which is not perceived by others!

FOCUS ON DISCOVERY 3.3
"INTERNET ADDICTION DISORDER": FAD OR SCOURGE DISORDER OF THE TWENTY-FIRST CENTURY?

"If you are playing these games you can easily move into another world. Our world becomes more and more foreign. . . . . Addiction sets in when one feels responsible for what happens in the online world."

> —Louise Nadeau, psychologist at the Université de Montréal and director of an addiction institute (Kuitenbrouwer, 2008)

". . . he could put on a new identity like a new suit of clothes, becoming someone who walked on water, healed others, and cast lightning bolts, in stark contrast to his daily experience of himself as inadequate."

> —Allison et al. (2006, p. 384) on the Internet and role-playing fantasy games

On November 5, 2008, following a three-week search, the body of 15-year-old Brandon Crisp was found deep in the bush by hunters, just north of Barrie, Ontario. Brandon died from injuries consistent with a fall from a tree. Foul play was not involved.

While hundreds of volunteers and police had searched on the ground, in cyberspace the police had probed the virtual world of on-line gaming. Brandon disappeared on Thanksgiving after getting into an argument with his parents over his "obsession" with the on-line video game "Call of Duty 4: Modern Warfare" in which several players in different places, possibly all around the world, fight wars alongside a squadron of others with whom they communicate over the Internet using headphones and speakers. Brandon's parents confiscated his gaming console because his on-line gaming was affecting adversely both his school work and his social life. In response, Brandon ran away from home, with tragic consequences. His death was so widely felt on the Internet that there were at least 42 Facebook groups dedicated to Brandon, including a "virtual vigil" group where members could light a "candle" in his memory.

The Internet can be a boon to many. College students are heavy users when compared with the general population and report that the Internet can be used as a tool to support and enhance their academic pursuits (Douglas et al., 2008). Further, its networking capabilities can be socially enabling. However, there has been increasing criticism that it can be just as socially isolating. The term "Internet addiction disorder" (IAD), sometimes referred to as cyber disorder, Internet overuse, problematic computer use, or pathological computer use or video game playing, typically refers to excessive and out-of-control use that interferes with daily living (academic, occupational, social, financial, and physical functional impairment).

In 1995, physician Ivan Goldberg proposed IAD as a disorder using *DSM-IV* pathological gambling as his model—in a satirical hoax! Subsequently, Kimberly Young, also using pathological gambling as her model, in 1998 published the results of a serious investigation of (1) the existence of Internet addiction, and (2) the extent of problems caused by potential misuse. She compared 396 "dependent" Internet users with 100 "nondependent" users and found significant behavioural (e.g., difficulty controlling usage) and functional (e.g., severity of problems) differences between the two groups. Although there were methodological shortcomings to her study, Young "kick-started a new era of academic enquiry" (Griffiths, 2008, p. 244). IAD has been researched extensively over the past decade or more and its classification as a psychological disorder has been and continues to be debated—sometimes heatedly (see Douglas et al., 2008).

Should IAD be included as a disorder in *DSM-5*? Jerald Block (2008) has made the case for inclusion of IAD. He described the diagnosis as a "compulsive-impulsive spectrum disorder that involves on-line and/or offline computer usage" (p. 306). In addition to excessive gaming, he includes sexual preoccupation and email/text messaging subtypes in this common disorder. (Internet gambling is already subsumed under *DSM-IV*, pathological gambling.) According to Block, the variants share four components:

- excessive use (associated with loss of the sense of time)
- withdrawal symptoms (e.g., anger, tension, feeling "blue") when access is denied)
- tolerance (including need for better equipment, more software, or more hours of use)
- negative repercussions (e.g., fatigue, arguments, lying, poor achievement, social isolation)

Block (2008) noted that diagnosis is complicated by the fact that about 86% of IAD cases have another *DSM* diagnosis and that in the United States (and presumably in Canada), people generally present for only the comorbid condition(s) and that, "unless the therapist is specifically looking for Internet addiction, it is unlikely to be detected" (p. 306).

In Asia, therapists are trained to screen for IAD. Why? Because the problem is more visible there! Much of the activity occurs publicly in Internet cafes, whereas in Western countries it is private and usually engaged in at home. Nonetheless, a study of Internet addiction among Norwegian adults (Bakken et al., 2008) reported the highest prevalence among young males (among those 16–29 years, 4.1% were addicted and 19.0% were at risk; among those 30–39 years, the rates were 3.3% and 10.7%, respectively). Male gender, young age, university-level education, and an unsatisfactory financial situation were positively associated with problematic Internet use. In a meta-synthesis of qualitative research over a decade, Douglas et al. (2008) concluded, "the Internet provides an entertaining and interactive environment where those susceptible to its allure can find escape by coping with negative emotions such as loneliness, isolation and boredom, release stress, discharge anger and frustration, and feel a sense of belonging and recognition. . . . The Internet addict tends to neglect almost everything in their lives in an effort to satisfy their desire of being online" (p. 304).

Extensive recent research has been conducted in South Korea and China, where IAD is viewed as a serious public health issue. Note the following, adapted from Block (2008):

- In South Korea, approximately 210,000 children (2.1% of those aged 6–19) are diagnosed with IAD and are said to require treatment.
- About 80% of those needing treatment may require psychotropic medication and as many as 24% require hospitalization.
- Since high school students spend about 23 hours each week gaming (on average), another 1.2 million children are believed to be at risk for addiction.
- Increasing numbers are dropping out of school or work to spend more time on computers.

- More than 1,000 counsellors were trained in the treatment of IAD, almost 200 hospitals and treatment centres were enlisted, and prevention measures were introduced into schools (as of 2007).
- According to one Chinese authority, 13.7% of Chinese adolescent Internet users meet IAD criteria—some 10 million teens.
- Current Chinese laws reportedly restrict computer game use to three hours daily.

"Facts" like these suggest that researchers and clinicians such as Young, Block, and others might be correct to lobby for the recognition of Internet abuse as a distinct clinical disorder for *DSM-5*. Indeed, others have proposed a litany of serious consequences of IAD, including family conflict, marital discord, academic failure, job loss, excessive financial debt, fatigue and sleep problems, poor eating and exercise patterns, depression, anxiety, low self-esteem, attention deficit problems, lack of social skills, social withdrawal, and even murder (although there does not appear to be any scientific evidence for a hypothesized link between violent video game exposure and school shooting incidents).

Nonetheless, others argue that IAD is neither an addiction nor a specific disorder. Indeed, various organizations, including the American Medical Association, recommended against including IAD as a formal diagnosis in the revised *DSM*. Is it a true addiction or simply symptomatic of existing disorders? It is difficult to determine causality. Indeed, Internet abuse may be symptomatic of other disorders. Was Brandon's "obsession" with on-line gaming truly an addiction or just a consequence or manifestation of loneliness, social anxiety, dysphoria, parental conflict, or some other psychological difficulty? Some insights may be obtained from the CBC's *the fifth estate* segment about Brandon's case that aired on March 6, 2009 (see www.cbc.ca/fifth/2008-2009/top_gun/).

What is your own position on this issue? Do you think IAD should be included as a new clinical disorder in *DSM-5*? Whatever you decide, it appears clear that children like Brandon could be at risk and could benefit from or require professional care. Unfortunately, there is still a need to develop effective treatment protocols. There is currently no evidence base from which guidelines can be developed.

In fact, Internet addiction was considered for the proposed "behavioral addictions" diagnostic category of the *DSM-5*. However, work group members concluded that there was insufficient research evidence for a new disorder but recommended that it be included in the *DSM-5* appendix with a goal of encouraging further research.

Sources: Bakken et al. (2008); Block (2008); Douglas et al. (2008); Ferguson (2008); Griffiths (2008); Kuitenbrouwer (2008); Young (1998).

SUMMARY

- Diagnosis is a critical aspect of the field of abnormal psychology. Having an agreed-upon system of classification makes it possible for clinicians to communicate effectively with one another and facilitates the search for causes and treatments for the various disorders.

- The recent editions of the *Diagnostic and Statistical Manual of Mental Disorders*, published by the American Psychiatric Association, reflect the continuing efforts by mental health professionals to classify the various psychopathologies.

- A novel feature of the *DSM* is its multiaxial organization; every time a diagnosis is made, the clinician must describe the client's condition according to each of five axes, or dimensions. Axes I and II make up the mental disorders per se, Axis III lists any physical disorders believed to have bearing on the mental disorder in question, Axis IV is used to indicate the psychosocial and environmental problems that the person has been experiencing, and Axis V rates the person's current level of adaptive functioning.

- A multiaxial diagnosis is believed to provide a more multidimensional and useful description of the client's mental disorder.

- Several general and specific issues must be considered in evaluating the classification of abnormality. An important one is whether the categorical approach of the *DSM*, as opposed to a dimensional classification system, is best for the field.

- Because recent versions of the *DSM* are far more concrete and descriptive than was *DSM-II*, diagnoses based on these versions are more reliable; that is, independent diagnosticians are now more likely to agree on the diagnosis they make of a particular case.

- Construct validity—how well the diagnosis relates to other aspects of the disorder, such as prognosis and response to treatment—remains more of an open question. In chapters dealing with specific disorders, we will see that validity varies with the diagnostic category being considered.

KEY TERMS

categorical classification (p. 94)	**DSM-IV** (p. 84)	**lifetime prevalence** (p. 92)
comorbidity (p. 92)	**DSM-IV-TR** (p. 84)	**mental disorder** (p. 85)
construct validity (p. 95)	**DSM-5** (p. 99)	**multiaxial classification** (p. 85)
Diagnostic and Statistical Manual of	**epidemiology** (p. 92)	**pathological gambling** (p. 89)
Mental Disorders (DSM) (p. 84)	**help-seeking** (p. 93)	**prevalence** (p. 92)
dimensional classification (p. 94)	**inter-rater reliability** (p. 95)	**reliability** (p. 95)

REFLECTIONS: PAST, PRESENT, AND FUTURE

- How does the current *DSM* definition of mental disorder (and the exclusion criteria) compare and contrast with our discussion of definitional considerations in Chapter 1? How does the *DSM* definition compare with your own implicit or explicit definition?

- What is your own position on issues of classification and diagnosis of psychological disorders? Is the *DSM-IV-TR* really a major improvement over past versions? Does it lead to more effective and efficient treatment? How would you refine and improve upon it?

- In reaction to critics of the participation process in the development of the *DSM*, Sadler (2004) proposed that final decisions be based on a democratic voting process. Would you agree? Could a scientifically valid decision be "politically incorrect" and thereby voted against?

- *DSM-IV-TR* is more culturally sensitive than previous versions. However, do you think that an axis that specifies the influence of cultural factors on a person's clinical condition should be included in future revisions to the *DSM*? Do you think the *DSM* should include an axis that lists an individual's strengths?

- Do you think psychiatric nosology is ready for a "paradigm shift" in *DSM-5*? What other changes would you "vote" on for the new manual?

- In the next chapter, we will examine clinical assessment procedures. Sometimes assessment is used to facilitate decisions about diagnosis or differential diagnosis. What other assessment questions would you propose? Are answers to these questions necessary for the development of comprehensive, multifaceted treatment or intervention plans?

CLINICAL ASSESSMENT PROCEDURES

J. W. G. Macdonald, Canadian 1897–1960, *Indian Church, Friendly Cove* (recto); *Departing Day* (verso), 1935, Oil on wood panel, 37.9 × 30.5 cm, Art Gallery of Ontario, Toronto. Purchased with assistance from Wintario, 1979 © Mrs. Fiona Davenport.

"The one thing psychologists can count on is that their subjects will talk, if only to themselves; and not infrequently whether relevant or irrelevant, the things people say to themselves determine the rest of the things they do."
—I. E. Farber, *The Things People Say to Themselves*

"Every man has reminiscences which he would not tell to everyone, but only to his friends. He has other matters in his mind which he would not reveal even to his friends, but only to himself, and that in secret. But there are other things which a man is afraid to tell even to himself, and every decent man has a number of such things stored away in his mind."
—Fyodor Dostoevsky, *Notes from Underground*

"Case formulation is the link that ties together the clinical assessment and intervention phases of therapy and, as such, is an integral part of the therapy process."
— Jose and Goldfried, 2008, p. 212

This book began with an account of a police officer, J. Brett Barkley, who had bipolar disorder as well as drinking and marital problems, and the preceding chapter included a diagnosis of his condition. Yet a *DSM* diagnosis is only a starting point. Many other questions remain to be answered. Why does J. Brett Barkley behave as he does? Do his mood swings and violent outbursts constitute a true disorder? Why does he doubt his wife's love for him? What can be done to resolve his marital conflicts? Is his difficulty maintaining an erection caused by physical or psychological factors or both? Has he performed up to his intellectual potential in school and in his career? What type of treatment would be helpful to him? What obstacles might interfere with treatment? Can his marriage be saved? Should it be saved? These are the types of questions that mental health professionals address before therapy begins and as it unfolds. A clinical assessment helps them find answers.

All clinical assessment procedures are more or less formal ways of finding out what is wrong with a person, what may have caused a problem or problems, and what steps may be taken to improve the individual's condition. Some of these procedures are also used to evaluate the effects of therapeutic interventions.

In this chapter, we describe and discuss the most widely used psychological and biological assessment techniques. We also discuss a sometimes neglected aspect of assessment: the role of cultural diversity and clinician bias. The numerous linguistic minorities in Canada make this an especially important issue. We begin our discussion with two concepts that play a key role in assessment: reliability and validity.

RELIABILITY AND VALIDITY IN ASSESSMENT

The concepts of reliability and validity are extremely complex. There are several kinds of each, and an entire subfield of psychology—psychometrics—exists primarily for their study. We provide here a general overview that supplements our brief discussion in Chapter 3.

RELIABILITY

In the most general sense, reliability refers to consistency of measurement. There are several types of reliability, some of which we discuss here.

- **Inter-rater reliability**, discussed in the preceding chapter, refers to the degree to which two independent observers or judges agree. To take an example from baseball, the third-base umpire may or may not agree with the home-plate umpire as to whether a line drive down the left-field line is fair or foul.
- **Test-retest reliability** measures the extent to which people being observed twice or taking the same test twice, perhaps several weeks or months apart, score in generally the same way. This kind of reliability makes sense only when the theory assumes that people will

Reliability is an essential property of all assessment procedures. One means of determining reliability is to find out whether different judges agree, as happens when a court decides a case. © POOL/FRED CHARTRAND/Reuters/Corbis.

not change appreciably between testings on the variable being measured; a prime example of a situation in which this type of reliability makes sense is in evaluating intelligence tests.

- Sometimes psychologists use two forms of a test rather than giving the same test twice, perhaps when there is concern that people will remember their answers from the first test and aim merely to be consistent. This approach enables the tester to determine **alternate-form reliability**, the extent to which scores on the two forms of the test are consistent.
- Finally, **internal consistency reliability** assesses whether the items on a test are related to one another. For example, with an anxiety questionnaire containing 20 items we would expect the items to be interrelated, or to correlate with one another, if they truly tap anxiety. A person who reports a dry mouth in a threatening situation would be expected to report increases in muscle tension, as well.

In each of these types of reliability, a correlation—a measure of how closely two variables are related—is calculated between raters or sets of items. The higher the correlation, the better the reliability.

VALIDITY

Validity is generally related to whether a measure fulfills its intended purpose. For example, if a questionnaire is intended to measure a person's hostility, does it in fact do so? Before we describe several types of validity, it is important to note that validity is related to reliability: unreliable measures will not have good validity. Because an unreliable measure does not yield consistent results (recall our example about trying to measure with a ruler whose length is constantly changing), an unreliable measure will not relate very strongly to other measures. For example, an unreliable measure of coping is not likely to relate well to how a person adjusts to a stressful life experience.

Content validity refers to whether a measure adequately samples the domain of interest. For example, later in this chapter we will describe an interview that is often used to make an Axis I diagnosis. It has excellent content validity because it contains questions about all the symptoms that are involved in Axis I diagnoses. As another example, refer to a measure of life stress that will be considered in more detail in Chapter 9. It consists of a list of 43 life experiences. Respondents indicate which of these experiences—for example, losing one's job—they have had in some time period, such as the past year. Content validity is less certain here. After looking over the experiences in Table 9.2, you will likely think of stressors that are not on the list (e.g., the serious illness of someone close to you).

Criterion validity is evaluated by determining whether a measure is associated in an expected way with some other measure (the criterion). Sometimes these relationships may be concurrent (both variables are measured at the same point in time, and the resulting validity is sometimes referred to as *concurrent validity*). For example, we will describe later a measure of the distorted thoughts believed to play an important role in depression. Criterion validity for this test could be established by showing that the test is actually related to depression; that is, depressed people score higher on the test than do non-depressed people. Alternatively, criterion validity can be assessed by evaluating the measure's ability to predict some other variable that is measured in the future; this kind of criterion validity is often referred to as *predictive validity*. For example, IQ tests were originally developed to predict future school performance. Similarly, a measure of distorted thinking could be used to predict the development of episodes of depression in the future.

Construct validity, discussed in Chapter 3, is relevant when we want to interpret a test as a measure of some characteristic or construct that is not simply defined (Cronbach & Meehl, 1955). A construct is an inferred attribute, such as anxiousness or distorted cognition, that a test is trying to measure. Consider an anxiety-proneness questionnaire as an example. The construct validity question is whether the variation we observe between people on a self-report test of anxiety proneness is really due to individual differences in anxiety proneness. Just because we call our test a measure of anxiety proneness and the items seem to be about the tendency to become anxious ("I find that I become anxious in many situations"), it is not certain that the test is a valid measure of anxiety proneness. People's responses to a questionnaire are determined by more variables than simply the construct being measured. For example, people vary in their willingness to admit to undesirable characteristics such as anxiety proneness; thus, scores on the questionnaire will be partly determined by this characteristic as well as by anxiety proneness itself.

Construct validity is evaluated by looking at a wide variety of data from multiple sources. For example, people diagnosed as having an anxiety disorder and people without such a diagnosis could be compared on their scores on the self-report measure of anxiety proneness. The self-report measure would achieve some construct validity if the people with anxiety disorders scored higher than a control group. Similarly, the self-report measure could be related to other measures thought to suggest anxiety, such as observations of fidgeting, trembling, or excessive sweating. When the self-report measure is associated with the observational one, its construct validity is increased. Studies may also examine change on the self-report measure. For example, if the measure has construct validity, we would expect scores of clients with anxiety disorders to become lower after a course of a therapy that is effective in reducing anxiety.

More broadly, the question of construct validity is related to a particular theory of anxiety proneness. For example, we might hypothesize that a proneness to anxiety is caused by certain childhood experiences. We could then obtain further evidence for the construct validity of our questionnaire by showing that it relates to these childhood experiences. At the same time, we would have also gathered support for our theory of anxiety proneness. Thus, construct validation is an important part of the process of theory testing.

PSYCHOLOGICAL ASSESSMENT

Psychological assessment techniques are designed to determine cognitive, emotional, personality, and behavioural factors in psychopathological functioning. We will see that beyond the basic interview, which is used in various guises almost universally, many of the assessment techniques stem from the paradigms presented in Chapter 2. We discuss here clinical interviews, psychological tests (many of which are psychodynamic in nature), and behavioural and cognitive assessment techniques.

CLINICAL INTERVIEWS

Most of us have probably been interviewed at one time or another, although the conversation may have been so informal that we did not regard it as an interview. To the layperson, the word "interview" connotes a formal, highly structured conversation, but we find it useful to construe the term as any interpersonal encounter, conversational in style, in which one person, the interviewer, uses language as the principal means of finding out about another person, the interviewee. Thus, a pollster who asks a college student which party he or she will vote for in an upcoming election is interviewing with the restricted goal of learning which party the student prefers. A clinical psychologist who asks a client about the circumstances of his or her most recent hospitalization is similarly conducting an interview.

CHARACTERISTICS OF CLINICAL INTERVIEWS One way in which a **clinical interview** is perhaps different from a casual conversation or a poll is the attention the interviewer pays to how the respondent answers—or does not answer—questions. For example, if a client is recounting marital conflicts, the clinician will generally be attentive to any emotion accompanying the comments. If the person does not seem upset about a

difficult situation, the answers will probably be understood differently than they would be if the person were crying or agitated while relating the story.

The paradigm within which an interviewer operates influences the type of information sought, how it is obtained, and how it is interpreted. A psychoanalytically trained clinician can be expected to inquire about the person's childhood. He or she is also likely to remain sceptical of verbal reports because the analytic paradigm holds that the most significant aspects of a disturbed or normal person's developmental history are repressed into the unconscious. Of course, how the data are interpreted is influenced by the paradigm. The behaviourally oriented clinician is likely to focus on current environmental conditions that can be related to changes in the person's behaviour; for example, the circumstances under which the person becomes anxious. Thus, the clinical interview varies with the paradigm adopted by the interviewer. Like scientists, clinical interviewers in some measure find only the information for which they are looking.

Great skill is necessary to carry out good clinical interviews, for they are usually conducted with people who are under considerable stress. Clinicians, regardless of their theoretical orientation, recognize the importance of establishing rapport with the client. The interviewer must obtain the trust of the person; it is naive to assume that a client will easily reveal information to another, even to an authority figure with the title "Doctor." Even a client who sincerely, perhaps desperately, wants to recount intensely personal problems to a professional may not be able to do so without assistance. Psychodynamic clinicians assume that people entering therapy usually are not even aware of what is truly bothering them. Behavioural clinicians, although they concentrate more on what can be observed, also appreciate the difficulties people have in sorting out the factors responsible for their distress.

Most clinicians empathize with their clients in an effort to draw them out, to encourage them to elaborate on their concerns, and to examine different facets of a problem. Humanistic therapists employ specific empathy techniques to accomplish these goals. A simple summary statement of what the client has been saying can help sustain the momentum of talk about painful and possibly embarrassing events and feelings, and an accepting attitude toward personal disclosures dispels the fear that revealing "secrets of the heart" (London, 1964) to another human being will have disastrous consequences.

The interview can be a source of considerable information to the clinician. Its importance in abnormal psychology and psychiatry is unquestionable. Whether the information gleaned can always be depended on is not so clear, however. Clinicians often tend to overlook situational factors of the interview that may exert strong influences on what the client says or does. Consider for a moment how a teenager is likely to respond to the question, "How often have you used illegal drugs?" when it is asked by a young, informally dressed psychologist as opposed to a 60-year-old psychologist in a business suit.

Interviews vary in the degree to which they are structured. In practice, most clinicians operate from only the vaguest outlines. Exactly *how* information is collected is left largely up to the particular interviewer and depends, too, on the responsiveness and responses of the interviewee. Through years of clinical experience and both teaching and learning from students and colleagues, each clinician develops ways of asking questions with which he or she is comfortable and that seem to draw out the information that will be of maximum benefit to the client. Thus, to the extent that an interview is unstructured, the interviewer must rely on intuition and general experience. As a consequence, reliability for initial clinical interviews is probably low; that is, two interviewers may well reach different conclusions about the same client. And because the overwhelming majority of clinical interviews are conducted within confidential relationships, it has not been possible to establish either their reliability or their validity through systematic research.

We need to look at the broader picture here to avoid a judgement that may be too harsh. Both reliability and validity may indeed be low for a single clinical interview that is conducted in an unstructured fashion. But clinicians usually do more than one interview with a given client, and hence a self-corrective process is probably at work. The clinician may regard as valid what a client said in the first interview, but then at the sixth recognize it to have been incorrect or only partially correct.

STRUCTURED INTERVIEWS At times, mental health professionals need to collect standardized information, particularly for making diagnostic judgements based on the *DSM*. Investigators have developed structured interviews, such as the Structured Clinical Interview Diagnosis (SCID) for Axis I of *DSM-IV* (Spitzer, Gibbon, & Williams, 1996), which assists researchers and clinicians in making diagnostic decisions. A **structured interview** is one in which the questions are set out in a prescribed fashion for the interviewer.

The SCID is a branching interview; that is, the client's response to one question determines the next question that is asked. It also contains detailed instructions to the interviewer concerning when and how to probe in detail and when to go on to questions bearing on another diagnosis. Most symptoms are rated on a three-point scale of severity, with instructions in the interview schedule for directly translating the symptom ratings into diagnoses. The initial questions pertaining to obsessive-compulsive disorder (OCD; discussed in Chapter 6) are presented in Figure 4.1. The interviewer begins by asking about obsessions. If the responses elicit a rating of 1 (absent), the interviewer turns to questions about compulsions. If the client's responses again elicit a rating of 1, the interviewer is instructed to proceed to questions for post-traumatic stress disorder. On the other hand, if positive responses (a rating of 2 or 3) are elicited about obsessive-compulsive disorder, the interviewer continues with further questions about that problem. The use of structured interviews is a major factor in the improvement of diagnostic reliability (described in Chapter 3).

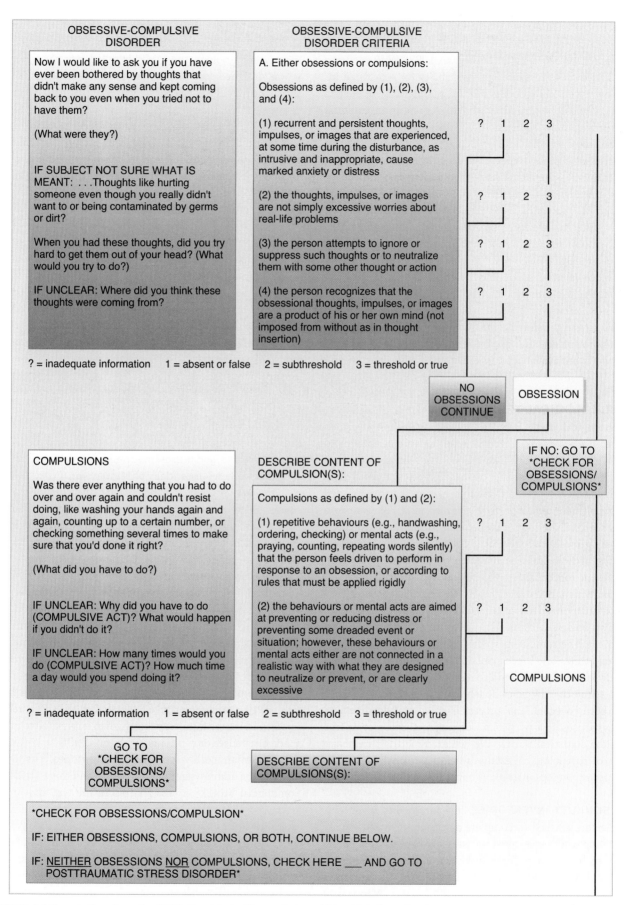

FIGURE 4.1 Sample item from the SCID. Reprinted with permission of New York State Psychiatric Institute Biometrics Research Division. Copyright © 1996 by the Board of Trustees of the Leland Stanford Junior University. Reprinted with permission of Stanford University Press.

Structured interviews have also been developed for diagnosing personality disorders and more specific disorders, such as the anxiety disorders (DiNardo et al., 1993). With adequate training of clinicians, inter-rater reliability for structured interviews is generally good (Blanchard & Brown, 1998). Rogers (2003) argued that structured clinical interviews are essential in order to improve the validity of diagnoses. On the basis of available data, including evidence that more than half of the cases of depression in primary settings are not detected, he concluded, "The diagnosis of mental disorders in primary health settings is clearly a hit-or-miss proposition" (Rogers, 2003, p. 220). Rogers then analyzed which clinical interview is best suited to actual use in particular assessment situations depending on the primary goal of the assessor. He recommended the SCID for the clinician who is pressed for time and wishes to evaluate the possible existence of selected Axis I disorders. To cite another example, the International Personality Disorder Examination has been translated into 10 languages and, as a result, is suited for use across different cultures. The main point made by Rogers is that many structured clinical interviews are available and should have high clinical utility across assessment situations.

PSYCHOLOGICAL TESTS

Psychological tests are standardized procedures designed to measure a person's performance on a particular task or to assess his or her personality, or thoughts, feelings, and behaviour. If the results of a diagnostic interview are inconclusive, psychological tests can provide information that can be used in a supplementary way to arrive at a diagnosis. For example, a client with schizophrenia may be very guarded during an interview and choose not to reveal information regarding delusional beliefs. Psychological tests may alert the clinician to the possible presence of schizophrenia. These tests also yield important information in their own right, such as personality characteristics or situational determinants of a person's problems.

Psychological tests further structure the process of assessment. The same test is administered to many people at different times, and the responses are analyzed to indicate how certain kinds of people tend to respond. Statistical norms for the test can thereby be established as soon as sufficient data have been collected. This process is called **standardization**. The responses of a particular person can then be compared with the statistical norms. We will examine the three basic types of psychological tests: self-report personality inventories, projective personality tests, and tests of intelligence.

PERSONALITY INVENTORIES In a **personality inventory**, the person is asked to complete a self-report questionnaire indicating whether statements assessing habitual tendencies apply to him or her. The best-known and most frequently used and researched psychological test in the United States (see Butcher, Nezami, & Exner, 1998) is the **Minnesota Multiphasic Personality Inventory (MMPI)**. The MMPI was developed in the early 1940s by Hathaway and McKinley

(1943) and revised in 1989 as the MMPI-2 (Butcher et al., 1989). Intended to serve as an inexpensive means of detecting psychopathology, the MMPI is called *multiphasic* because it was designed to detect a number of psychological problems. The MMPI has been widely used to screen large groups of people for whom clinical interviews are not feasible.

In developing the test, the investigators relied on factual information. First, many clinicians provided statements that they considered indicative of various mental problems. Second, these items were rated as self-descriptive or not by clients already diagnosed as having particular disorders and by a large group of individuals considered normal. Items that "discriminated" among the clients were retained; that is, items were selected if clients in one clinical group responded to them more often in a certain way than did those in other groups.

With additional refinements, sets of these items were established as scales for determining whether a respondent should be diagnosed in a particular way. If an individual answered a large number of the items in a scale in the same way as had a certain diagnostic group, his or her behaviour was expected to resemble that of the particular diagnostic group. The 10 scales are described in Table 4.1.

The MMPI-2 (Butcher et al., 1989) has several noteworthy changes designed to improve its validity and acceptability. The original sample of 60 years ago lacked representation of racial minorities, including African Americans and Native Americans; its standardization sample was restricted to white men and women—essentially to Minnesotans.

The new version was standardized using a sample that was much larger and more representative of 1980 U.S. census figures. Several items containing allusions to sexual adjustment, bowel and bladder functions, and excessive religiosity were removed because they were judged in some testing contexts to be needlessly intrusive and objectionable. Sexist wording was eliminated, along with outmoded idioms. Several new scales deal with substance abuse, Type A behaviour, and marital problems.

Aside from these differences, MMPI-2 is quite similar to the original, having the same format, yielding the same scale scores and profiles, and providing continuity with the vast literature already existing on the original MMPI. Items similar to those on the various scales are presented in Table 4.1. The extensive research literature shows that the MMPI is reliable and has adequate criterion validity when it is related to ratings made by spouses or clinicians (Graham, 1990).

Like many other personality inventories, the MMPI can now be administered by computer, and there are several commercial MMPI services that score the test and provide narratives about the respondent. Of course, the validity and usefulness of the printouts are only as good as the program, which in turn is only as good as the competency and experience of the psychologist who wrote it. Figure 4.2 shows a hypothetical profile. Such profiles can be used in conjunction with a therapist's evaluation to help diagnose a client, assess personality functioning and coping style, and identify likely obstacles to treatment.

TABLE 4.1
TYPICAL CLINICAL INTERPRETATIONS OF ITEMS SIMILAR TO THOSE ON THE MMPI-2

Scale	Sample Item	Interpretation
? (cannot say)	This is merely the number of reading items left unanswered or marked both true and false.	A high score indicates evasiveness, difficulties, or other problems that could invalidate the results of the test. A very high score could also suggest severe depression or obsessional tendencies.
L (Lie)	I approve of every person I meet. (True)	Person is trying to look good, to present self as someone with an ideal personality.
F (Infrequency)	Everything tastes sweet. (True)	Person is trying to look abnormal, perhaps to ensure getting special attention from the clinician.
K (Correction)	Things couldn't be going any better for me. (True)	Person is guarded, defensive in taking test, wishes to avoid appearing incompetent or poorly adjusted.
1. Hs (Hypochondriasis)	I am seldom aware of tingling feelings in my body. (False)	Person is overly sensitive to and concerned about bodily sensations as signs of possible physical illness.
2. D (Depression)	Life usually feels worth while to me. (False)	Person is discouraged, pessimistic, sad, self-deprecating, feeling inadequate.
3. Hy (Hysteria)	My muscles often twitch for no apparent reason. (True)	Person has somatic complaints unlikely to be due to physical problems; also tends to be demanding and histrionic.
4. Pd (Psychopathy)	I don't care about what people think of me. (True)	Person expresses little concern for social mores; is irresponsible; has only superficial relationships.
5. Mf (Masculinity-femininity)	I like taking care of plants and flowers. (True, female)	Person shows non-traditional gender characteristics, e.g., men with high scores tend to be artistic and sensitive; women with high scores tend to be rebellious and assertive.
6. Pa (Paranoia)	If they were not afraid of being caught, most people would lie and cheat. (True)	Person tends to misinterpret the motives of others; is suspicious and jealous, vengeful, and brooding.
7. Pt (Psychasthenia)	I am not as competent as most other people I know. (True)	Person is overanxious, full of self-doubts, moralistic, and generally obsessive-compulsive.
8. Sc (Schizophrenia)	I sometimes smell things others don't sense. (True)	Person has bizarre sensory experiences and beliefs; is socially seclusive.
9. Ma (Hypomania)	Sometimes I have a strong impulse to do something that others will find appalling. (True)	Person has overly ambitious aspirations and can be hyperactive, impatient, and irritable.
10. Si (Social introversion)	Rather than spend time alone, I prefer to be around other people. (False)	Person is very modest and shy, preferring solitary activities.

Note: The first four scales assess the validity of the test; the numbered scales are the clinical or content scales.
Source: Hathaway and McKinley (1943); revised by Butcher et al. (1989). Minnesota Multiphasic Personality Inventory-2 (MMPI-2). Copyright © 1989, 1998, 2001 University of Minnesota Press. Reproduced with permission of the exclusive publisher NCS Pearson, Inc. All rights reserved. "Minnesota Multiphasic Personality Inventory" and "MMPI" are trademarks of the University of Minnesota, Minneapolis, MN.

We may well wonder whether answers that would designate a person as normal might not be easy to fake. A superficial knowledge of contemporary abnormal psychology, for example, would alert even a seriously disturbed person that in order to be regarded as normal, he or she must not admit to worrying a great deal about germs on doorknobs. There is evidence that these tests *can* be "psyched out." In most testing circumstances, however, people do not want to falsify their responses, because they *want* to be helped.

Moreover, as shown in Table 4.1, the test designers have included as part of the MMPI several so-called validity scales designed to detect deliberately faked responses. In one of these, the lie scale, a series of statements sets a trap for the person who is trying to look too good. An item on the lie scale might be, "I read the newspaper editorials every night." The assumption is that few people would be able to endorse such a statement honestly. Individuals who endorse a large number of the statements

in the lie scale might well be attempting to present themselves in a particularly good light. Their scores on other scales are generally viewed with more than the usual scepticism. Being aware of these validity scales, however, does allow people to effectively fake a normal profile (Baer & Sekirnjak, 1997).

PROJECTIVE PERSONALITY TESTS A **projective test** is a psychological assessment device in which a set of standard stimuli—inkblots or drawings—ambiguous enough to allow variation in responses is presented to the individual. The assumption is that because the stimulus materials are unstructured, the client's responses will be determined primarily by unconscious processes and will reveal his or her true attitudes, motivations, and modes of behaviour. This notion is referred to as the **projective hypothesis.** If a client reports seeing eyes in an ambiguous inkblot, for example, the projective hypothesis might be that the client tends toward paranoia.

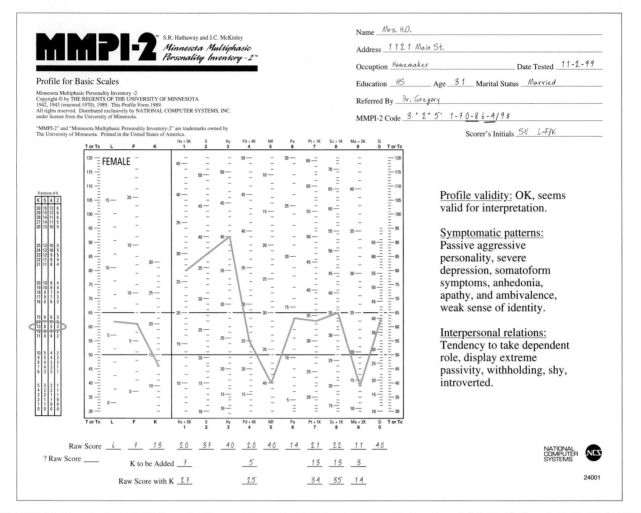

FIGURE 4.2 Hypothetical MMPI-2 profile. Source: Minnesota Multiphasic Personality Inventory-2 (MMPI-2). Copyright © 1989, 1998, 2001 University of Minnesota Press. Reproduced with permission of the exclusive publisher NCS Pearson, Inc. All rights reserved. "Minnesota Multiphasic Personality Inventory" and "MMPI" are trademarks of the University of Minnesota, Minneapolis, MN.

The **Rorschach Inkblot Test** is perhaps the best-known projective technique. In the Rorschach test, a person is shown 10 inkblots, one at a time, and asked to tell what figures or objects he or she sees in each of them. Half the inkblots are in black, white, and shades of grey, two also have red splotches, and three are in pastel colours.

The **Thematic Apperception Test (TAT)** is another well-known projective test. In this test, a person is shown a series of black-and-white pictures one by one and asked to tell a story related to each. For example, a client seeing a picture of a pre-pubescent girl looking at fashionably attired mannequins in a store window may tell a story that contains angry references to the girl's parents. The clinician may, through the projective hypothesis, infer that the client harbours resentment toward his or her parents.

As you might guess, projective techniques are derived from the psychoanalytic paradigm. The use of projective tests assumes that the respondent would be either unable or unwilling to express his or her true feelings if asked directly. Psychoanalytically oriented clinicians often favour such tests, a tendency consistent with the psychoanalytic assumption that people protect themselves from unpleasant thoughts and

feelings by repressing them into the unconscious. Thus, the real purposes of a test are best left unclear so as to bypass the defence mechanism of repression and get to the basic causes of distress.

Our discussion of projective tests has focused on how they were conceptualized and used originally—as a stimulus to fantasy that was assumed to bypass ego defences. The content of the person's responses was viewed as *symbolic* of internal dynamics; for example, a man might be judged to have homosexual interests on the basis of his seeing buttocks in the Rorschach inkblots (Chapman & Chapman, 1969).

Other uses of the Rorschach test, however, concentrate more on the *form* of the person's responses. The test is considered more as a perceptual-cognitive task, and the person's responses are viewed as a sample of how he or she perceptually and cognitively organizes real-life situations (Exner, 1986). Erdberg and Exner (1984), for example, concluded from the research literature that respondents who see a great deal of human movement in the Rorschach inkblots (e.g., "The man is running to catch a plane") tend to use inner resources when coping with their needs, whereas those whose Rorschach responses involve colour ("The red spot is a kidney") are more likely to seek

During a ride in the country with his two children, Hermann Rorschach (1884–1922), a Swiss psychiatrist, noticed that what they saw in the clouds reflected their personalities. From this observation came the famous inkblot test.

interaction with the environment. Rorschach suggested this approach in his original manual, *Psychodiagnostics: A Diagnostic Test Based on Perception* (1921), but he died only eight months after publishing his 10 inkblots and his immediate followers devised other methods of interpreting the test.

Though many, perhaps most, clinical practitioners still rely on the projective hypothesis in analyzing Rorschach responses, academic researchers have been paying a good deal of attention to Exner's work. Regarding its reliability and validity, this work has enthusiastic supporters, as well as harsh critics (e.g., Garb, Wood, Lilienfeld, & Nezworski, 2005). Attempting to make a blanket statement about the validity of the Exner system for scoring the Rorschach is perhaps not the right approach, for the system may have more validity in some cases than in others. It appears, for instance, to have considerable validity in identifying people with schizophrenia or at risk of developing schizophrenia (Viglione, 1999). The utility of the Rorschach in this case can most likely be attributed to the fact that a person's responses on the test are highly related to the communication disturbances that are an important symptom of schizophrenia. However, as argued by Hunsley and Bailey (2001), even in this case it is possible that the information provided by the Rorschach could have been obtained more simply and directly through, for example, an interview.

The Roberts Apperception Test for Children (Roberts, 1982) illustrates how the use of projective tests has evolved to provide more standardized, objectively scored assessment tools.

In this test, much as in the Thematic Apperception Test, pictures of children and families are presented to the child, who tells a story about each one. Whereas many scoring approaches to the TAT are impressionistic and non-standardized, the Roberts test provides objective criteria for scoring, along with normative data to determine whether the child's pattern of responses is abnormal. Unique to this test are the scales that provide information about a child's coping skills. For example, the response "The boy asked his mother for help with his homework, and she helped him get started on his story" would be scored for both "Reliance on Others" and "Support from Others."

Critics of projective testing have been and remain particularly concerned about its use as part of assessment and testimony in the courtroom. For example, Wood, Nezworski, Lilienfeld, and Garb (2009) stated that the Rorschach, TAT, and other projective tests are used in a substantial number of legal cases and about one third of forensic psychologists indicate that they continue to use these measures. The authors suggested that these measures continue to be used because they "overpathologize" the respondent, suggesting that they are psychologically sick or dangerous in a way that might fit the agendas of certain lawyers. That is, a parent seeking custody of a child may be portrayed as psychologically unfit, or a dismissed employee who is seeking damages for wrongful dismissal will be asked to take the Rorschach and then be deemed to be unreliable and delusional. Another common use is to establish post-traumatic stress dysfunction in personal injury cases. Thus, these measures are often used regardless of concerns about their reliability and validity. However, others have argued that validity concerns have been overstated and evidence of the validity of such measures has been ignored (e.g., Woike & McAdams, 2001). Meyer's (2004) review of meta-analytic findings led him to conclude that the Rorschach and TAT have "reasonable evidence" supporting their reliability and validity and they are "not noticeably deficient" (p. 231) relative to other commonly used assessment procedures. Allen and Dana (2004) concluded that the current claims about the usefulness of the Rorschach across cultural groups has been overstated in part because there is a need for improved normative data. They concluded that cultural processes are central to responses on the Rorschach but have not received adequate empirical examination.

How often are projective tests used? It is suggested that such methods remain popular (see Garb et al., 2005), even though a survey of British psychiatrists found that they spent only 1% of their time conducting assessments with projective measures, while more objective measures accounted for 20% of their time and structured interviews accounted for 69% of their time (Bekhit, Thomas, Lalonde, & Jolley, 2002). However, a recent study of school psychologists in the United States found that projective techniques continue to be used across grades for various educational purposes, including determining eligibility for certain programs and indicating intervention needs (Hojnoski, Morrison, Brown, & Matthews, 2006). School psychologists in this survey characterized projective measures as "moderately useful."

INTELLIGENCE TESTS Alfred Binet, a French psychologist, originally constructed mental tests to help the Parisian school board predict which children were in need of special schooling. Intelligence testing has since developed into one of the largest psychological industries. An **intelligence test**, often referred as an IQ (intelligence quotient) test, is a standardized means of assessing a person's current mental ability. Individually administered tests, such as the Wechsler Adult Intelligence Scale (WAIS), the Wechsler Intelligence Scale for Children (WISC), and the Stanford-Binet, are all based on the assumption that a detailed sample of an individual's current intellectual functioning can predict how well he or she will perform in school. Intelligence tests are also used

- in conjunction with achievement tests, to diagnose learning disabilities and to identify areas of strengths and weaknesses for academic planning;
- to help determine whether a person is mentally retarded;
- to identify intellectually gifted children so that appropriate instruction can be provided to them in school; and
- as part of neuropsychological evaluations, for example, the periodic testing of a person believed to be suffering from a degenerative dementia so that deterioration of mental ability can be followed over time.

IQ tests tap several functions asserted to constitute intelligence, including language skills, abstract thinking, non-verbal reasoning, visual-spatial skills, attention and concentration, and speed of processing. Scores on most IQ tests are standardized so that 100 is the mean and 15 or 16 is the standard deviation (a measure of how scores are dispersed above and below the average). Approximately 65% of the population receives scores between 85 and 115. Those with a score below 70 are two standard deviations below the mean of the population and are considered to have "significant subaverage general intellectual functioning." Those with scores above 130 (two standard deviations above the mean) are considered "intellectually gifted." Approximately 2.5% of the population falls at each of these extremes. In Chapter 15, we discuss people whose IQ falls at the low end of the distribution.

IQ tests are highly reliable (e.g., Carnivez & Watkins, 1998) and have good criterion validity. For example, they distinguish between individuals who are intellectually gifted and individuals with mental retardation and between people with different occupations or levels of educational attainment (Reynolds et al., 1997). They also predict later educational attainment and occupational success (e.g., Barody, 1985).

Regarding construct validity, it is important to keep in mind that IQ tests measure only what psychologists consider to be intelligence. The tasks and items on IQ tests were, after all, invented by psychologists. In addition, factors other than what we think of as pure intelligence play an important role in how people will do in school—factors such as family and personal circumstances, motivation to do well, and the difficulty of the curriculum. Though the correlations between IQ scores

The French psychologist Alfred Binet developed the first IQ test to predict how well children would do in school. Courtesy Archives of the History of American Psychology/The University of Akron.

and school performance are statistically significant, IQ tests explain only a small part of the differences in people's school performance; much more is unexplained by IQ test scores than is explained.

Interest has also focused on "emotional intelligence," reflected in such abilities as delaying gratification and being sensitive to the needs of others (Goleman, 1995). This aspect of human functioning may be as important to future success as the strictly intellectual achievements measured by traditional IQ tests. Emotional intelligence may also be an important protective factor in terms of levels of adjustment. High levels of emotional intelligence are associated negatively with alexithymia (see Saklofske, Austin, & Minski, 2003), a condition of reduced emotional awareness that is a risk factor for a variety of adjustment problems. Moreover, high levels of emotional intelligence are associated with greater levels of subjective well-being and reduced proneness to depression (Saklofske et al., 2003).

BEHAVIOURAL AND COGNITIVE ASSESSMENT AND CASE FORMULATION

Traditional assessment concentrates on measuring underlying personality structures and traits, such as obsessiveness, paranoia, coldness, aggressiveness, and so on. In addition to a focus on specific cognitive and behavioural assessment instruments, cognitive-behavioural clinicians develop a specific case formulation for each client. A case formulation is "a provisional map of a person's presenting problems that describes the territory of the problems and explains the processes that caused and maintain the problem" (Bieling & Kuyken, 2003, p. 53). It includes a clinician's inferences about underlying processes that can be tested as hypotheses. It is used as the basis for planning interventions and evolves over time as further information is discovered.

Classically, behaviourally oriented clinicians often use a system that involves the assessment of four sets of variables, sometimes referred to by the acronym SORC (Kanfer & Phillips, 1970).

- *S* stands for stimuli, the environmental situations that precede the problem. For instance, the clinician will try to ascertain which situations tend to elicit anxiety.
- *O* stands for organismic, referring to both physiological and psychological factors assumed to be operating "under the skin." Perhaps the client's fatigue is caused in part by excessive use of alcohol or by a cognitive tendency toward self-deprecation manifested in such statements as "I never do anything right, so what's the point in trying?"
- *R* refers to overt responses. These probably receive the most attention from behavioural clinicians, who must determine what behaviour is problematic, as well as the behaviour's frequency, intensity, and form. For example, a client might say that he or she is forgetful and procrastinates. Does the person mean that he or she does not return phone calls, arrives late for appointments, or both?
- Finally, *C* refers to consequent variables, events that appear to be reinforcing or punishing the behaviour in question. When the client avoids a feared situation, does his or her spouse offer sympathy and excuses, thereby unwittingly keeping the person from facing up to his or her fears?

A behaviourally oriented clinician attempts to specify SORC factors for a particular client. As might be expected, *O* variables are underplayed by Skinnerians, who focus more on observable stimuli and responses, and *C* variables receive less attention from cognitively oriented therapists than do *O* variables because these therapists' perspective does not typically emphasize reinforcement.

Several alternative approaches to individual **cognitive-behavioural case formulation** have been described by cognitive and cognitive-behavioural therapists (e.g., Boschen & Oei, 2008; Jose & Goldfried, 2008; Meichenbaum, 1994; Persons & Davidson, 2001, 2010). These approaches place considerably more emphasis on cognitive events such as people's distorted

thinking patterns, negative self-instructions, irrational automatic thoughts and beliefs, and schemas. Complex psychological problems can present a challenge for clinicians from the perspective of assigning diagnoses, assessing and conceptualizing the problems, identifying obstacles to treatment, and developing an appropriate and effective treatment plan. McCabe and Antony (2004) described one such complex case: a 60-year-old retired teacher who presented with a wide range of health anxiety symptoms. Different cognitive-behavioural perspectives on conceptualization and treatment were provided by experts in the area. The strategies were similar to those used by Jacqueline Persons and her colleagues, which are summarized in Focus on Discovery 4.1. Recently, Boschen and Oei (2008) presented a cognitve-behavioural case formulation framework for anxiety disorders. In this framework, etiological and maintaining factors are summarized in a simple visual framework. According to the authors, the approach is especially useful with "novel presentations for which no manualized treatment exists" (Boschen & Oei, 2008, p. 811). Further, Moscovitch (2009) reported on a new model to facilitate individualized case conceptualization of social phobia. Haynes, Mumma, and Pinson (2009) reviewed the conceptual and psychometric foundations of individualized behavioural assessment and provided a step-by-step guide for the development and evaluation of an idiographic assessment instrument.

According to Boschen and Oei (2008), "There exists a strong general consensus among practising clinicians from all therapeutic schools that CF (case formulation) is an essential step to providing effective, purposive treatment, particularly for complex presentations" (p. 811). In this vein, Campbell and Rohrbaugh (2006) developed a guide for mental health professionals from a broader perspective—the integrative biopsychological formulation. With respect to the psychological component, themes are analyzed from a psychodynamic as well as from cognitive and behavioural perspectives. Jose and Goldfried (2008) also described a "transtheoretical" approach that is not specific to only a cognitive-behavioural case formulation. The Causal Analysis and Synthesis of Events (CASE) system is a comprehensive, systematic, but flexible and "theoretically neutral" method intended to be useful when dealing with both intrapersonal and interpersonal clinical problems. It is expected to be helpful in training therapists and to facilitate dialogue between therapists of different theoretical orientations.

FOCUS ON DISCOVERY 4.1
COGNITIVE-BEHAVIOURAL CASE FORMULATION

"Persons . . . tells us quite correctly that the best way to administer empirically supported treatments in clinical settings is to modify them based on the needs of the individual client."

–Heimberg, 2009, p. 136

Jacqueline Persons and her colleagues (e.g., Persons & Davidson, 2001, 2010; Persons, 2005; Persons & Tompkins, 2007) have described an approach that formulates an individualized cognitive-behavioural "theory" about a particular case with a view to helping a therapist develop an effective and efficient plan for treatment. The formulation is, of course, based on a general cognitive-behavioural theory (e.g., Beck's cognitive theory of psychological disorders). A key purpose of the formulation is to explain how a client's problems relate to one another in order to help the therapist select treatment "targets," since it is usually appropriate to first focus on issues that seem to play a causal role in other problems (e.g., depression causes marital problems, which contribute to behaviour problems in a child).

Different formulations imply different intervention strategies. Persons and Davidson (2001) described the case of a person complaining of severe fatigue. Two formulations appeared possible: abuse of sleep medication or negative thinking in reaction to a stressor. Either one of them could explain the fatigue, and each would lead to different treatments. As Persons and Davidson (2001) noted, "All formulations are considered hypotheses, and the therapist is constantly revising and sharpening the formulations as the therapy proceeds" (p. 89).

Persons and Davidson (2001) use the case of "Judy," a 35-year-old single woman who lived alone and worked as a teacher, to illustrate the five components of their approach: problem list, diagnosis, working hypothesis, strengths and assets, and treatment plan.

PROBLEM LIST

A problem list includes difficulties the client is having in various domains: psychological, interpersonal, occupational, medical, financial, housing, legal, and leisure. A comprehensive list helps ensure that significant problems are not missed and facilitates the search for themes and speculation about causal relations. Psychological problems, in particular, are described in terms of cognitive, behavioural, and mood components (consistent with Beck's cognitive theory). Judy's problem list included the following: depressed, dissatisfied, passive; disorganized, unfocused, and unproductive; job dissatisfaction; social isolation; no relationship; and unassertive.

DIAGNOSIS

Although a psychiatric diagnosis is not a required part of cognitive-behavioural case formulations, Persons and Davidson include it because a diagnosis can lead to initial hypotheses about how to formulate the case and provide information about possible interventions. Judy received an Axis I diagnosis of *DSM-IV* dysthymic disorder (i.e., persistent and chronic depression that is milder in intensity than the depression in major depressive disorders). Although there was no Axis II or III diagnosis or information, Judy was described as socially isolated and as having occupational problems on Axis IV. Her GAF score on Axis V was 60, indicating some mild symptoms or difficulties in social or occupational functioning.

WORKING HYPOTHESIS

The working hypothesis is the "heart" of Persons and Davidson's formulation. The mini-theory of the case develops through adaptation of a general theory and describes relations among the problems. For example, according to Beck's theory, stressful events activate schemas (core beliefs) to produce problems and symptoms.

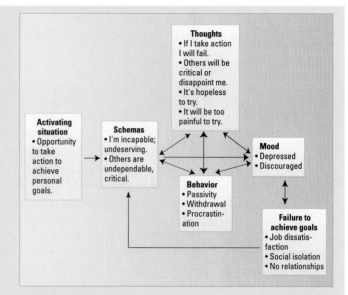

FIGURE 4.3 The working hypothesis for the client "Judy." From Persons and Davidson, Cognitive-behavioural case formulation, *Handbook of cognitive-behavioral therapies*, 2001. Reprinted with permission of the Guilford Press.

Therefore, the working hypothesis would describe the hypotheses about the negative schemas (e.g., beliefs about self, others, the world, and the future) that appear to cause the problems—external precipitants (e.g., a poor work evaluation) or activating situations (e.g., attending meetings with the boss) that activate internal structures (schemas)—and the origins or historical incidents or circumstances that contributed to the development of the schemas or functional relationships among the problems. In a summary of the working hypothesis, the clinician "tells a story" that describes the relations among the components of the working hypothesis and integrates them with the problems on the list. Persons and Davidson (2001) summarized Judy's working hypothesis as follows:

> When she was faced with taking actions to further her goals, her schemata that she was incapable and damaged were activated. She had learned from her mother's passive behaviours and from her father's abusive ones that she was damaged and incapable of taking action. When these schemata were activated, she became passive and inactive, with the result that she did not achieve her goals and felt dissatisfied and discouraged. This pattern occurred repeatedly in both work and social situations, and led to the difficulties she experienced in both those settings. (p. 97)

Figure 4.3 illustrates this "working hypothesis" for Judy in the form of a flow chart.

STRENGTHS AND ASSETS

Information about strengths and assets (e.g., social skills, sense of humour, financial resources, social support, stable lifestyle) can help the therapist to develop the working hypothesis, enhance the treatment plan, and determine realistic treatment goals. Judy had several strengths and assets, including a stable lifestyle, intelligence, excellent social skills, and a strong support network.

TREATMENT PLAN

According to Persons and Davidson, the treatment plan is based directly on the cognitive-behavioural case formulation and has six components: goals, modality, frequency, initial interventions, adjunct therapies, and obstacles. The "goals" and "obstacles" components are especially crucial. Judy's treatment plan had six goals, including reducing dysphoria and procrastination, improving her ability to prioritize and organize, finding a more satisfying job, spending more time with friends, beginning to date in order to find a partner, and being more assertive. Obstacles to treatment included her procrastination, unassertiveness, and belief that she cannot be successful.

The possible clinical uses of the case formulation are multiple. In Judy's case, Persons and Davidson noted that it helped clarify treatment goals, helped the therapist to maintain a "clear focus" and address multiple problems, facilitated the client's taking an active and collaborative role, and assisted the therapist to cope with negative emotional reactions to working with the client. Of course, if the treatment plan based on the case formulation does not work, it is probably necessary to revise the formulation and the treatment plan.

Do you believe that individual cognitive-behavioural therapy (CBT) is appropriate in Judy's case, and if so, how often should she meet with her therapist? What initial interventions would you propose? Under what circumstances would you employ adjunct treatments, such as pharmacotherapy?

Persons and Bertagnolli (1999) assessed whether clinicians could correctly identify clients' overt problems and underlying schemas. Clinicians offered CBT formulations after listening to initial interviews with depressed women. Clinicians identified 67% of clients' problems. When schema ratings were averaged over five judges, inter-rater reliability was good; however, single judges showed poor inter-rater reliability. The later finding indicates that the identification of underlying schemas is not an easy task. Indeed, in their own evaluation of the evidence base, Bieling and Kuyken (2003) concluded that the evidence for the reliability of the cognitive case formulation method is modest and there is a need for research to examine the validity of case formulations and to determine their impact on treatment outcome. Eells et al. (2005) reported that case formulation quality did not vary as a function of therapist orientation; however, it did vary as a function of expertise. Persons and her colleagues (Persons, Roberts, Zalecki, & Brechwald, 2006) reported on a case formulation-driven individual CBT approach to the treatment of anxious depressed clients seen in a private practice setting. The clients showed changes in anxiety and depression that were comparable to changes reported in trials of empirically supported therapies for single anxiety and mood disorders. The authors concluded that the findings "support the proposal that anxious depressed patients who have multiple comorbidities and require multiple therapies can benefit from empirically supported treatments guided by a case formulation and weekly outcome monitoring" (p. 1041). Recently, Mumma and Fluck (2009) developed a clinician-friendly approach to the intraindividual empirical testing of a cognitive-behavioural case formulation. Unfortunately, few studies have compared clinical outcomes from manualized and case formulation-based treatment approaches under controlled conditions (see Boschen & Oei, 2008). It is vital for future research programs to determine if the promise of the case formulation approach can be fulfilled.

The information necessary for a behavioural or cognitive assessment and case formulation is gathered by several methods, including direct observation of behaviour in real life as well as in contrived settings, interviews and self-report measures, and various other methods of cognitive assessment (Blankstein & Segal, 2001; Dunkley, Blankstein, & Segal, 2010).

DIRECT OBSERVATION OF BEHAVIOUR It is not surprising that behaviour therapists have paid considerable attention to careful observation of overt behaviour in a variety of settings, but it should not be assumed that they simply go out and *observe*. Like other scientists, they try to fit events into a framework consistent with their points of view. The following excerpt from a case report by Gerald Patterson and his colleagues (1969), describing an interaction between a boy named Kevin and his mother, father, and sister Freida, serves as the first part of an example.

Kevin goes up to father's chair and stands alongside it. Father puts his arms around Kevin's shoulders. Kevin says to mother as Freida looks at Kevin, "Can I go out and play after supper?" Mother does not reply. Kevin raises his voice and repeats the question. Mother says, "You don't have to yell; I can hear you." Father says, "How many times have I told you not to yell at your mother?" Kevin scratches a bruise on his arm while mother tells Freida to get started on the dishes, which Freida does. Kevin continues to rub and scratch his arm while mother and daughter are working at the kitchen sink. (p. 21)

This informal description could probably be provided by any observer. But in formal **behavioural observation**, the observer divides the uninterrupted sequence of behaviour into various parts and applies terms that make sense within a learning framework.

Kevin begins the exchange by asking a routine question in a normal tone of voice. This ordinary behaviour, however, is not reinforced by the mother's attention; for she does not reply. Because she does not reply, the normal behaviour of Kevin ceases and he yells his question. The mother expresses disapproval—punishing her son—by telling him that he does not have to yell. And this punishment is supported by the father's reminding Kevin that he should not yell at his mother. (Patterson et al., 1969, p. 21)

Behavioural assessment often involves direct observation of behaviour, as in this case, where the observer is behind a one-way mirror. Spencer Grant / Photo Researchers, Inc.

This behavioural rendition acknowledges the consequences of ignoring a child's question. At some point, the behaviour therapist will undoubtedly advise the parents to attend to Kevin's requests when expressed in an ordinary tone of voice, lest he begin yelling. This example indicates an important aspect of behavioural assessment—its link to *intervention* (O'Brien & Hayes, 1995). The behavioural clinician's way of conceptualizing a situation typically implies a way to try to change it.

It is difficult to observe most behaviour as it actually takes place, and little control can be exercised over where and when it may occur. For this reason, many therapists contrive artificial situations in their consulting rooms or in a laboratory so that they can observe how a client or a family acts under certain conditions. For example, Barkley (1981) had a mother and her hyperactive child spend time together in a laboratory living room, complete with sofas and television set. The mother was given a list of tasks for the child to complete, such as picking up toys or doing arithmetic problems. Observers behind a one-way mirror watched the proceedings and reliably coded the child's reactions to the mother's efforts to control, as well as the mother's reactions to the child's compliant or non-compliant responses. These behavioural assessment procedures yielded data that could be used to measure the effects of treatment.

Most of the research of the kind just described was conducted within an operant framework, employing no inferential concepts. But observational techniques can also be applied within a framework that makes use of mediators. Gordon Paul (1966) was interested in assessing the anxiety of public speakers. He decided to count the frequency of behaviours indicative of this emotional state. One of his principal measures was the Timed Behavioural Checklist for Performance Anxiety. Participants were asked to deliver a speech before a group. Some members of the group had been trained to reliably rate the participant's behaviour every 30 seconds and to record the presence or absence of 20 specific behaviours.

By summing the scores, Paul arrived at a behavioural index of anxiety. This study provides one example of how observations of overt behaviour have been used to infer the presence of an internal state.

Who is best at predicting an emotional state, especially when a child is involved? DiBartolo and Grills (2006) examined the validity of child, parent, and teacher reports of social anxiety in children in predicting a child's responses to a social evaluative task. Children, parents, and teachers each completed a measure of social anxiety and a measure that asked them to predict the child's anxiety during a behavioural approach task whereby the child had to read aloud in front of a video camera. The results indicated that there was poor agreement across respondents. Consistent with other studies, children predicted their own anxious feelings and behaviour during the task better than parents and teachers. At the very least, such findings suggest that it is important to use multiple informants, including the children themselves, when attempting to predict children's real-life behaviour.

SELF-OBSERVATION In Paul's study, people other than the public speaker made the observations. For many years, behaviour therapists and researchers have also asked individuals to observe their own behaviour and to keep track of various categories of response. This approach is called **self-monitoring.** Self-monitoring has been used to collect a wide variety of data of interest to both clinicians and researchers, including moods, stressful experiences, coping behaviours, and thoughts (Stone et al., 1998).

Self-observation has also been referred to as **ecological momentary assessment**, or **EMA** (Stone & Shiffman, 1994). EMA involves the collection of data in real time as opposed to the more usual methods of having people reflect back over some time period and report on recently experienced thoughts, moods, or stressors. The methods for implementing EMA range from having people complete diaries at specified times during the day (perhaps signalled by a wristwatch that beeps at those times) to supplying them with handheld computers that not only signal when reports are to be made but also allow them to enter their responses directly into the computer (see Shiffman, Stone, & Huffard, 2008). Shiffman et al. (2008) concluded that "EMA holds unique promise to advance the science and practice of clinical psychology by shedding light on the dynamics of behavior in real-world settings" (p. 1).

The main reason for using EMA is that the retrospective recall of moods, thoughts, or experiences may be inaccurate. Consider, for example, how difficult it would be for you to recall accurately the exact thoughts you had when you encountered a stressor. Memory researchers have shown not only that simple forgetting leads to inaccurate retrospective recall, but also that recalled information can be biased. For example, a report of a person's mood for a whole day is overly influenced by moods the person has experienced most recently (Strongman & Russell, 1986).

Given these problems in retrospective recall, some theories in the field of abnormal psychology almost demand the use of EMA. For example, current theories of both anxiety disorders and depression propose that emotional reactions to a stressor are determined by thoughts that the stressor elicits. It is unlikely, however, that these thoughts can be recalled accurately in retrospect. Consider also a prominent theory in the health psychology field that proposes that a person's response to a stressor depends on his or her appraising or evaluating it, attempting to cope with it, and then reappraising it (Lazarus & Folkman, 1984). It isn't at all likely that this process could be captured by retrospective recall.

EMA may also be useful in clinical settings, revealing information that traditional assessment procedures might miss. For example, Hurlburt (1997) describes a case of a man with severe attacks of anxiety. In clinical interviews, the client reported that his life was going very well, that he loved his wife and children, and that his work was both financially and personally rewarding. No cause of the anxiety attacks could be discerned. The man was asked to record his thoughts as he went about his daily routine. Surprisingly, about a third of his thoughts concerned annoyance with his children (e.g., "He left the record player on again").

> Once the high frequency of annoyance thoughts was pointed out to him, he … accepted that he was in fact often annoyed with his children. However, he believed that anger at his children was sinful and felt unfit as a father for having such thoughts and feelings … [He] entered into brief therapy that

Self-monitoring generally leads to increases in desirable behaviours and decreases in undesirable ones. A personal digital assistant can help people record their moods and thoughts at a given time as part of EMA.
© James Leynse/Corbis.

> focused on the normality of being annoyed by one's children and on the important distinction between being annoyed and acting out aggressively. Almost immediately, his anxiety attacks disappeared. (Hurlburt, 1997, p. 944)

Although some research indicates that self-monitoring or EMA can provide accurate measurement of such behaviour, considerable research indicates that behaviour may be altered by the very fact that it is being self-monitored; that is, the self-consciousness required for self-monitoring affects the behaviour (Haynes & Horn, 1982). The phenomenon of behaviour changing because it is being observed is called **reactivity**. In general, desirable behaviour, such as engaging in social conversation, often increases in frequency when self-monitored, whereas behaviour the person wishes to reduce, such as cigarette smoking, diminishes.

INTERVIEWS AND SELF-REPORT INVENTORIES For all their interest in direct observation of behaviour, behavioural clinicians still rely very heavily on the interview to assess the needs of their clients (Sarwer & Sayers, 1998). Within a trusting relationship, the behaviour therapist's job is to determine, by skillful questioning and careful observation of the client's emotional reactions during the interview, the factors that help the therapist conceptualize the client's problem.

Behaviour therapists also make use of self-report inventories. Some of these questionnaires are similar to the personality tests we have already described. But others have a greater situational focus than traditional questionnaires. McFall and Lillesand (1971), for example, employed a Conflict Resolution Inventory containing 35 items that focused on the respondent's ability to refuse unreasonable requests. Each item described a specific situation in which a person was asked for something unreasonable. For example, "You are in the thick of studying for exams when a person you know slightly comes into your room and says, 'I'm tired of studying. Mind if I come in and take a break for a while?'" Students were asked to indicate the likelihood that they would refuse such a request and how comfortable they would be in doing so. Concurrent validity for this self-report inventory was established by showing that it correlated with a variety of direct observational data on social skills (Frisch & Higgins, 1986). This and similar inventories can be used by clinicians and have helped cognitive-behavioural researchers measure the outcome of clinical interventions, as well.

The most widely employed cognitive assessment methods are also self-report questionnaires that tap a wide range of cognitions, such as fear of negative evaluation, a tendency to think irrationally, and a tendency to make negative inferences about life experiences. "When someone criticizes you in class, what thoughts go through your mind?" is a question a client might be asked in an interview or on a paper-and-pencil inventory.

The self-report measures employed by cognitive-behavioural clinicians must be reliable and valid. Sometimes influential measures are developed consistent with a salient theoretical approach but are not subjected to rigorous psychometric evaluation in a timely fashion or the relevant findings are unpublished. A recent example is the Cognitive Style Questionnaire (CSQ), a measure of the cognitive vulnerability factor featured in the hopelessness theory of depression discussed in Chapter 8. Abramson and Metalsky created the CSQ in 1982 and it has been used in over 30 published studies. However, despite widespread use, detailed information about its psychometric and validity properties had not been published until Abramson, Metalsky, and colleagues (Haeffel et al., 2008) described the development of the CSQ and reviewed reliability and validity evidence. They concluded that the CSQ is a reliable measure of cognitive vulnerability with a high degree of construct validity, at least in college samples.

New cognitive-behavioural self-report measures are regularly constructed and they must be subjected to psychometric evaluation. For example, Carleton, Collimore, and Asmundson (2007) from the University of Regina reported on the construct validity of a brief measure of the fear of negative evaluation (BFNE-II), a characteristic of social anxiety disorders. Similarly, Carleton, Norton, and Asmundson (2007) developed a brief Intolerance of Uncertainty Scale (IUS) to assess anxious and avoidance components of the tendency to consider the possibility of a negative event occurring to be unacceptable, irrespective of the probability of occurrence. Intolerance of uncertainty is a key component of worry.

SPECIALIZED APPROACHES TO COGNITIVE ASSESSMENT

When clients are asked about their thoughts in interviews and self-report inventories, they have to reflect backward in time and provide a retrospective and rather general report of their thoughts in certain situations. We have already seen how such retrospective reporting can provide inaccurate information.

As with all kinds of assessment, a key feature of contemporary approaches in cognitive assessment is that the development of methods is determined by theory as well as by the purposes of the assessment (Blankstein & Segal, 2001; Dunkley et al., 2010). For example, much research on depression is concerned with cognition—the things people consciously and sometimes unconsciously tell themselves as well as the underlying assumptions or attitudes that can be inferred from their behaviour and verbal reports. One cognitive theory (Beck, 1967), which we will examine in greater detail in Chapter 8, holds that depression is caused primarily by negative ideas people have about themselves, their world, and their future. People may believe, for instance, that they are not worth much and that things are never going to get better.

These pessimistic attitudes, or schemas, bias the way in which depressed people interpret events. So great is this bias that a misstep that might be taken in stride by a non-depressed person, such as forgetting to mail a birthday card, is construed by a depressed individual as compelling evidence of his or her ineptitude and worthlessness. Researchers employing cognitive assessment set themselves the task of trying to

identify these different kinds of cognitions. They obtain their ideas both from clinical reports of practitioners who have first-hand experience with depressed clients and from controlled research that adheres to the methodological principles discussed in the next chapter.

One assessment device used in this context is the Dysfunctional Attitude Scale (DAS). The DAS contains items such as "People will probably think less of me if I make a mistake" (Weissman & Beck, 1978). Supporting the theory of construct validity, researchers have shown that they can differentiate between depressed and non-depressed people on the basis of their scores on this scale and that scores decrease (i.e., improve) after interventions that relieve depression. Furthermore, the DAS relates to other aspects of cognition in ways consistent with Beck's theory. For example, it correlates with an instrument called the Cognitive Bias Questionnaire (Krantz & Hammen, 1979), which measures the ways in which depressed clients distort information. An accumulating body of data is helping to establish both the validity and the reliability of these instruments (Blankstein & Segal, 2001; Dunkley et al., 2010).

Since people's responses to inventories and to questions asked by interviewers about their thoughts in past situations may differ from what they would report had they been able to do so in the immediate circumstance, researchers have developed ways to enable people to tap into their immediate, ongoing thought processes when confronted with particular circumstances. Can we show, for example, that a socially anxious person does in fact, as Ellis would predict, view criticism from others as catastrophic, whereas someone who is not socially insecure does not?

The Articulated Thoughts in Simulated Situations (ATSS) method of Davison and his associates (Davison, Robins, & Johnson, 1983) is one way to assess immediate thoughts in specific situations. Zanov and Davison (2009) examined over 25 years of the paradigm's usage and concluded that "the ATSS paradigm is useful in assessing complex cognitions in a variety of investigator-controlled situations." In this procedure, a person pretends that he or she is a participant in a situation, such as listening to a teaching assistant criticize a term paper. Presented on audio tape, the scene pauses every 10 or 15 seconds. During the ensuing 30 seconds of silence, the participant talks aloud about whatever is going through his or her mind in reaction to the words just heard.

Participants readily become involved in the pretend situations, regarding them as credible and realistic. Furthermore, the participants' responses can be reliably coded (Zanov & Davison, 2009). Research using this approach indicates that socially anxious therapy clients articulate thoughts of greater irrationality (e.g., "Oh God, I wish I were dead; I'm so embarrassed") than do non-anxious members of control groups (Bates, Campbell, & Burgess, 1990). Other research with this method shows that aggressive adolescents, relative to non-aggressive adolescents, express more anger and aggressive intent when assessed via the ATSS and these articulated

Cognitive assessment focuses on the person's perception of a situation, since the same event can be perceived differently by different people or at different times. For example, moving could be regarded as very stressful or seen in a positive light. David Sacks.

thoughts are correlated significantly with scores on a trait anger measure (DiLiberto, Katz, Beauchamp, & Howells, 2002). The use of the ATSS was studied recently in an experiment to compare the responses of participants high vs. low in aggressiveness in a simulated interpersonal conflict situation vs. a neutral situation (Eckhardt & Crane, 2008). Participants either consumed an alcoholic drink or a placebo beverage. The main finding is displayed in Figure 4.4. No group differences were found in the neutral condition. However, intoxicated participants high in dispositional aggressiveness had substantially more aggressive verbalizations when assessed with the ATSS method. Note the absence of this tendency when a non-alcoholic placebo was ingested.

Other cognitive assessment methods have also proved useful (cf. Blankstein & Segal, 2001; Dunkley et al., 2010). In **thought listing**, for example, the person writes down his or her thoughts prior to or following an event of interest, such as entering a room to talk to a stranger, as a way to determine the cognitive components of social anxiety (Cacioppo, von Hippel, & Ernst, 1997). Open-ended techniques, such as the ATSS and thought listing, may be preferable when investigators know relatively little about the participant and want to get general ideas about the cognitive terrain. For example, thought-listing studies conducted at the University of Toronto demonstrate that among test-anxious students, there is a preponderance of negative thoughts about the "self" and a relative absence of positive thoughts about the self (e.g., Blankstein, Flett, Boase, & Toner, 1990). This focus on negative, self-referential thinking deflects attention from the task at hand and eats away at the motivation to succeed. The procedures and instructions for administering the thought-listing procedure and for coding the data

must be considered carefully and the rated thoughts must be evaluated by independent, trained raters or judges in order to make valid inferences about the meaning of the listed thoughts and to determine the reliability of assessment (e.g., Blankstein & Flett, 1990).

Videotape reconstruction (e.g., Meichenbaum & Butler, 1980) is an interesting strategy for assessing people's thoughts and feelings. The procedure involves videotaping an individual while he or she is engaged in some task or an actual or role-played problematic situation. The person then watches the videotape while attempting to *reconstruct* his or her thoughts and feelings at the time as accurately as possible. It is, of course, difficult to determine with certainty the degree to which people are actually reconstructing or are simply constructing the flow of thoughts and feelings as they observe themselves on videotape.

More focused techniques, such as questionnaires, may be better—and are certainly more easily scored—when investigators have more prior knowledge about the cognitions of interest. Dunkley et al. (2010) reviewed structured endorsement and unstructured production approaches to thought assessment and summarized the advantages and limitations of the different methods. So far, the various cognitive assessment techniques often correlate poorly with one another, presenting an important challenge to researchers and clinicians alike. This challenge can be especially difficult when it comes to cognitive assessment of children (e.g., Lodge, Tripp, & Harte, 2000). Furthermore, some cognitive constructs, including automatic thoughts, schemas, and dysfunctional beliefs, have proved difficult to measure accurately (Blankstein & Segal, 2001). One implication, of course, is that we can have more confidence in the results of our assessments if several different strategies are employed.

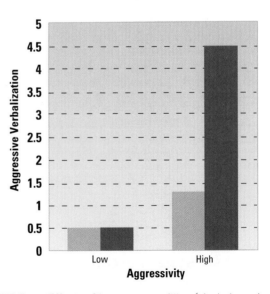

FIGURE 4.4 Effects of beverage condition (alcohol vs. placebo) and aggressivity (high vs. low) on frequency of ATSS anger scenario aggressive verbalizations. ATSS, articulated thoughts in simulated situations. Reproduced with permission of Wiley-Liss, Inc. a subsidiary of John Wiley & Sons Inc.

Nonetheless, according to Blankstein and Segal (2001), the trend toward diversification is a healthy development within cognitive assessment that provides "a more enriched and vital armamentarium of assessment tools for the study of the relationship among cognition, emotion, and behavior" (p. 73). At the same time, it is important to achieve integration within cognitive assessment and with other approaches, including neurobiological perspectives.

FAMILY ASSESSMENT

Much of the focus in abnormal psychology is on the problems of individuals. However, it is important to recognize that many forms of dysfunction have their developmental origins in problematic family interactions. Even if abnormal behaviour is not due, at least in part, to family characteristics, family factors can play a significant role in the persistence of abnormal behaviour. Thus, it is important to assess current or previous types and levels of **family functioning** before implementing various forms of treatment, including family therapy.

The possible role of the family in the development of abnormal behaviour is central to classical psychoanalytic theories, to more recent object-relations theories (e.g., Kernberg, 1985) that focus on an infant's attachment to the mother figure, to social learning theory with its emphasis on the role of imitation of powerful parent figures (e.g., Bandura & Walters, 1963), and interpersonal theories (e.g., Sullivan, 1953) that regard people as products of their social interactions. Contemporary views of the role of the family in psychopathology are generally based on a family systems perspective (e.g., Minuchin et al., 1975) that holds that behaviours produced in the family environment reflect the various components that are present in the family setting, including the characteristics of each family member and the various interactions between family members. The therapist must focus on the entire family system rather than on a particular individual, and abnormal functioning in an individual is a reflection of a broader problem involving family dysfunction. The family is dynamic and changing rather than static, so it is important to measure ongoing changes in the family and not focus exclusively on the past. Another important principle involves the concept of *equifinality* (see von Bertalanffy, 1968), the notion that the same goal or endpoint can result from many different starting points and different processes. For example, two people can

have the same symptoms of depression, but they can reach this point through very different background factors and different interpersonal processes.

There is a tendency for clinicians and researchers to rely heavily on self-report measures of the family environment and family functioning, and these measures provide little insight into the family as an interacting system of various components. One such measure is the Family Environment Scale (FES) developed by Moos and colleagues (Moos & Moos, 1986) to assess three main themes: (1) the family relationship, (2) personal growth, and (3) system maintenance. In a Canadian study, the FES was used to examine the link between perceived childhood family environment and levels of alcohol misuse and personality disorder as an adult (Jang, Vernon, & Livesley, 2000). The FES was designed to measure the actual family environment (either now or in the past), and perceptions of the ideal family environment and the family environment that the respondent feels ought to exist. Although it is generally regarded as a valid and reliable instrument, some researchers have questioned the validity of certain subscales in specific clinical populations (see Sanford, Bingham, & Zucker, 1999).

The Family Adaptation and Cohesion Evaluation Scale—Third Edition (FACES-III; Olson, Portner, & Lavee, 1985) stems from a circumplex model of family functioning. The two dimensions of Olson's circumplex model are a family's degree of cohesion (i.e., closeness) and degree of adaptability (i.e., ability to adjust by appropriate changes to roles and rules in the family). Both of these dimensions have four levels (enmeshed, connected, separated, and disengaged), with moderate levels reflecting appropriate family adjustment and the extremes reflecting maladjustment. A parent who is smothering and overcontrolling would contribute to a family situation of enmeshment, while a parent who is neglectful would contribute to a situation of disengagement. The two dimensions distinguish functional vs. dysfunctional families (see Rodick, Henggeler, & Hanson, 1986).

Two of the more widely used measures of family functioning were developed in Canada. See Canadian Perspectives 4.1.

Other commonly used measures focus directly on the role of parental factors in family adjustment. The Parental Bonding Inventory (PBI; Parker, Tupling, & Brown, 1979) can be completed for both the mother and the father. The two subscales assess the level of care or parental warmth, and the

---

CANADIAN PERSPECTIVES 4.1

FAMILY ASSESSMENT IN CANADA: THE MCMASTER FAMILY ASSESSMENT DEVICE AND THE FAMILY ASSESSMENT MEASURE-III

One of the earliest models of family functioning was developed in Canada by Nathan Epstein and Jack Santa-Barbera. The McMaster Family Assessment Device (MFAD; Epstein, Baldwin, & Bishop, 1983) is a 60-item self-report measure that assesses family functioning in terms of problem solving, communication, roles, affective responsiveness, affective involvement, and behaviour control.

The MFAD is useful as a general measure of perceived family adjustment, as shown in a study by Hewitt, Flett, and

Mikail (1995), who reported that chronic pain clients reported lower overall levels of family adjustment if their spouse was overly demanding and wanted them to be perfect. Ballash et al. (2007) used the MFAD, along with measures of anxiety control and anxiety, to determine whether control acts as a moderator or mediator between perceived family environment and anxiety in young adults. A perceived sense of lack of control mediated the relation between aspects of family functioning (e.g., overinvolvement, communication patterns, and behavioural control) and anxiety. More recently, Georgiades et al. (2008) conducted a multilevel analysis of whole family functioning using the MFAD. The data came from over 26,000 family members involved in the Ontario Health Survey. Although there was some agreement, overall there were large discrepancies in perceived family functioning across respondents (i.e., parents, dependents, and other household residents) when rating the same family, and there was substantial variability across families in the amount of the discrepancy, with some being very much in agreement and others not in agreement. Thus, whole family assessment should be assessed via reports from multiple respondents rather than a single informant. Interestingly, and consistent with our discussion in Chapter 2, this study also showed that higher family functioning was reported by those from higher socio-economic status families.

The process model of family functioning described by Skinner, Steinhauer, and Sitarenios (2000) is an improvement on the McMaster model because it includes a more explicit focus on the dynamic interactions of family functioning. It includes the link between interpersonal aspects of family functioning and the intrapsychic needs of individual family members and is currently assessed by the Family Assessment Measure-III (FAM-III). The FAM-III has seven main subscales that assess task accomplishment, role performance, communication, affective expression, involvement, control, and values/norms. It has two important advantages, relative to the McMaster measure: (1) the

FAM-III can be administered to tap three different levels of functioning, including the functioning of the entire family, certain dyadic relationships, and the individual's sense of his or her own level of functioning in the family context; and (2) the FAM-III includes social desirability and defensiveness subscales that can be used to determine the validity of self-reports.

Although concerns have been raised about the length of time it would take to administer the FAM-III if it were used to assess the family, relationships, and the self, ongoing research has demonstrated its usefulness. For example, research on eating-disorder clients from Toronto (Woodside, Carter, & Blackmore, 2004) confirmed the role of familial factors in the development of and recovery from eating disorders (explored in more detail in Chapter 10). In another study conducted in Toronto, family members of clients with brain injuries completed the FAM-III (Gan & Schuller, 2002). They reported greater family distress across all FAM-III subscales, relative to existing norms for the instrument. A follow-up study showed that poorer family functioning was associated with the stress experienced by the caregivers of those with brain injuries, and poorer family functioning was reported if the client with a head injury was female (Gan, Campbell, Gemeinhardt, & McFadden, 2006).

Thinking Critically

1. Do you believe that most psychological disorders are caused in part by dysfunction in the family or are at least exacerbated by such dysfunction?

2. Is it actual family dysfunction or the individual's *perception* of dysfunction in the family system that is most predictive of individual psychological dysfunction?

3. Do you think that it is generally appropriate and necessary to focus on the family system as a central component of case formulation and treatment planning?

level of controlling parental behaviours. Research with the PBI has identified a condition known as *affectionless control* (i.e., an overcontrolling parent who lacks warmth and caring). A link between affectionless control and suicidal tendencies has been confirmed in several studies (e.g., Adams et al., 1994). The *Egna Minnen Betraffande Uppfostran* ("Memories of My Childhood") or EMBU is another widely used self-report measure developed to assess memories of parental rearing styles (Perris, Jacobsson, Lindstrom, Von Knorring, & Perris, 1980). It assesses several components of perceived parenting behaviour, including emotional warmth, rejection, and overprotection. Extensive research has confirmed a link between EMBU maladaptive parenting styles and psychological disorders (e.g., Perris, Arrindell, & Eisemann, 1994). A nagging concern with measures such as the PBI and the EMBU is the possibility that negative ratings of parents are, at least

in part, a reflection of a mood bias; that is, dysphoric individuals will perceive their parents in a more negative way than non-depressed individuals. The concern points to the primary limitation of these measures: they measure subjective appraisals of parental characteristics and may not assess actual parental characteristics.

Behavioural assessment in the family context is a more objective approach that can provide richer sources of data that are less subject to cognitive biases. However, these behavioural assessments have other limitations, including the problem of reactivity—the extent to which family members alter their usual ways of interacting when they know that they are being observed and evaluated. Reactivity is regarded as a significant problem, but this is not always the case (e.g., Jacob, Tennenbaum, Seilhammer, Bargiel, & Sharon, 1994). A segment of the CBC television show *the fifth*

TABLE 4.2
MAJOR PSYCHOLOGICAL ASSESSMENT METHODS

Interviews	Clinical interviews	Conversational technique in which the clinician attempts to learn about the client's problems. Content of the interview varies depending on the paradigm of the interviewer.
	Structured interviews	Questions to be asked are spelled out in detail in a booklet; most often used for gathering information to make a diagnosis.
Psychological tests	Personality tests	Self-report questionnaires, used to assess either a broad range of characteristics, as in the MMPI, or a single characteristic, such as dysfunctional attitudes. Behaviourally oriented questionnaires tend to have a situational focus.
	Projective personality tests	Ambiguous stimuli, such as inkblots (Rorschach test), are presented and responses are thought to be determined by unconscious processes.
	Tests of family functioning	Self-report questionnaires used to assess perceptions of family environment and functioning or parental characteristics.
	Tests of cognition	Endorsement (self-report) and production (e.g., thought and listing) assessments of cognitive products, processes, and structures.
	Intelligence tests	Assessments of current mental functioning. Used to predict school performance and diagnose mental retardation.
Direct observation		Used by behavioural clinicians to identify SORC factors. Also used to assess cognition, as in the Articulated Thoughts in Simulated Situations technique.
Self-observation		Individuals monitor and keep records of their own behaviour; also referred to as ecological momentary assessment.

estate that aired in April 1994 (titled "The Trouble with Evan") illustrated that reactivity may not be a concern in the evaluation of some families. This show caused a national uproar because it depicted the emotional abuse of an 11-year-old boy named Evan who had engaged in anti-social behaviours, including stealing, lying, and putting paint in his teacher's coffee cup. The emotional abuse depicted in the show resulted in Evan and his 7-year-old sister being removed by the Children's Aid Society and placed in a foster home. One of the most remarkable aspects of this program is that the abuse occurred despite the fact that family patterns were being videotaped for broadcast to a national television audience, and over the 10-week period, the parents themselves were quite cooperative, often loading new tapes into the recording equipment. Thus, reactivity may not happen in all instances, especially when automatic family interaction patterns are involved. Another problem with behavioural assessment in a family context is that, ultimately, researchers must code behavioural data into meaningful units of analysis, and different researchers may use different coding schemes, thereby making it difficult to compare findings across studies.

Problems notwithstanding, some important findings have emerged from the use of behavioural measures to study the role of the family in psychopathology. For example, Gottman and associates (e.g., Waltz, Babcock, Jacobsen, & Gottman, 2000), using both behavioural and physiological measures to assess interactions between spouse abusers and their wives, found two types of abusers: (1) a distressed group characterized by high levels of arousal and likely to restrict their violence to the family context (i.e., domestically violent batterers); and (2) a psychopathic group with exceptionally low levels of arousal who have general anti-social tendencies that operate inside and outside the family context (i.e., generally violent batterers). Psychopathy is described in detail in Chapter 13.

The psychological assessments we have described are summarized in Table 4.2.

BIOLOGICAL ASSESSMENT

Recall from chapters 2 and 3 that some people interested in psychopathology have assumed, quite reasonably, that some malfunctions of the psyche are likely to be due to or at least reflected in malfunctions of the soma. We turn now to contemporary work in biological assessment.

BRAIN IMAGING: "SEEING" THE BRAIN

Because many behavioural problems can be brought on by brain abnormalities, neurological tests, such as checking the reflexes, examining the retina for any indication of blood-vessel damage, and evaluating motor coordination and perception, have been used for many years to diagnose brain dysfunction. More recently, devices have become available that allow clinicians and researchers a much more direct look at both the structure and functioning of the brain.

Computerized axial tomography, the **CT scan**, helps to assess structural brain abnormalities (and is able to image other parts of the body for medical purposes). A moving beam of X-rays passes into a horizontal cross-section of the client's brain, scanning it through 360 degrees; the moving X-ray detector on the other side measures the amount of radioactivity that penetrates, thus detecting subtle differences in tissue density. A computer uses the information to construct a two-dimensional, detailed image of the cross-section, giving it optimal contrasts. Then the client's head is moved, and the machine scans another cross-section of the brain. The resulting images can show the enlargement of ventricles, which signals degeneration of tissue and the locations of tumours and blood clots. Indeed, CT scans were used in a study in London, Ontario, to confirm that clients with a first episode of schizophrenia had a mild degree of enlargement of ventricles and cortical sulci (Malla et al., 2002). Single photon emission computerized tomography (SPECT) allows assessment of cerebral blood flow and is used increasingly in neuropsychiatry.

Newer computer-based devices for seeing the living brain include **magnetic resonance imaging**, also known as **MRI**, which is superior to the CT scan because it produces pictures of higher quality and does not rely on even the small amount of radiation required by a CT scan. In MRI, the person is placed inside a large, circular magnet, which causes the hydrogen atoms in the body to move. When the magnetic force is turned off, the atoms return to their original positions and thereby produce an electromagnetic signal. These signals are then read by the computer and translated into pictures of brain tissue. The implications of this technique are enormous. For example, it has allowed physicians to locate and remove delicate brain tumours that would have been considered inoperable without such sophisticated methods of viewing brain structures.

More recently, a modification, called **functional magnetic resonance imaging (fMRI)**, has been developed that allows researchers to take MRI pictures so quickly that metabolic changes can be measured, providing a picture of the brain at work rather than of its structure alone. It enables investigators to map cognitive, affective, and experiential processes onto brain substrates. Using this technique, one study found that there was less activation in the frontal lobes of clients with schizophrenia than in the frontal lobes of people with normal-functioning brains as they performed a cognitive task (Yurgelun-Todd et al., 1996).

A case study from Montreal illustrates the types of information that can emerge from fMRI assessments (Bentaleb, Beauregard, Liddle, & Stip, 2002). This research focused on a woman with schizophrenia who experienced auditory hallucinations that went away when she listened to loud external speech. She had learned to stop her hallucinations by turning up the volume of her radio or television. Comparisons using fMRI were made between her brain activity during the hallucinations and while listening to external speech, and these results were compared with the results for a matched control participant. The researchers found that auditory verbal hallucinations were linked with increased metabolic activity in the left primary auditory cortex and the right middle temporal gyrus. Overall, this case study clarified the mechanisms involved in auditory hallucinations by showing that they

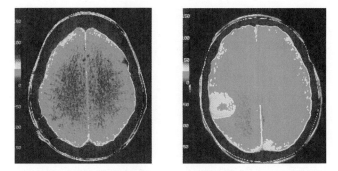

These two CT scans show a horizontal slice through the brain. The one on the left is normal; the one on the right has a tumour on the left side. Dan McCoy/Rainbow Images.

stem jointly from aberrant activation of the auditory cortex and the misinterpreted inner speech of the client with schizophrenia. Previous theorists did not consider the possibility that both factors might simultaneously play a role in auditory hallucinations.

Another study conducted in British Columbia used fMRI procedures to compare eight criminal psychopaths and eight criminals without psychopathy (Kiehl et al., 2001). The main focus was on affective processing while completing a memory task. The researchers were able to obtain evidence consistent with the view that "criminal psychopathy is associated with abnormalities in the function of structures in the limbic system and frontal cortex while engaged in processing of affective stimuli" (Kiehl et al., 2001, p. 682).

Since the fMRI can be used to determine where in the brain activity occurs during cognitive tasks, it may prove useful in determining the mechanisms related to changes that occur during cognitive-behavioural therapy. For example, Schwartz (1998) reported fMRI data indicating that obsessive-compulsive disorder (OCD) appears to be characterized by abnormal activation in the orbital-frontal complex and that cognitive-behavioural treatment produced changes in left orbital-frontal activation, but only in treatment responders. Thus treatment may influence directly the parts of the brain affected by the disorder.

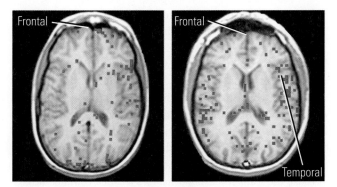

Functional magnetic resonance images (fMRI) of a client diagnosed with schizophrenia (right) and a healthy individual (left). The red squares represent activation of the brain during a verbal task compared with the baseline. The client shows less frontal and more temporal activation. (Yurgelun-Todd et al., 1996) Courtesy D. Yurgelun-Todd, McLean Hospital.

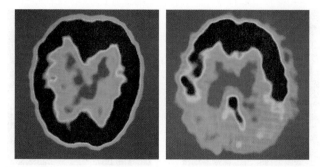

The PET scan on the left shows a normal brain; the one on the right shows the brain of a client with Alzheimer's disease. Dan McCoy/Rainbow Images.

Positron emission tomography, the **PET scan,** a more expensive and invasive procedure, allows measurement of brain function. A substance used by the brain is labelled with a short-lived radioactive isotope and injected into the bloodstream. The radioactive molecules of the substance emit a particle called a positron, which quickly collides with an electron. A pair of high-energy light particles shoot out from the skull in opposite directions and are detected by the scanner. The computer analyzes millions of such recordings and converts them into a picture of the functioning brain. The images are in colour; fuzzy spots of lighter and warmer colours are areas in which metabolic rates for the substance are higher.

Visual images of the working brain can indicate sites of epileptic seizures, brain cancers, strokes, and trauma from head injuries, as well as the distribution of psychoactive drugs in the brain. The PET scanner is also being used to study possible abnormal biological processes that underlie disorders, such as the failure of the frontal cortex of clients with schizophrenia to become activated while they attempt to perform a cognitive task. PET images are often overlaid on averaged MRI images to allow for the articulation of both function and structure.

CLINICAL UTILITY OF BIOLOGICAL ASSESSMENT MEASURES OF BRAIN STRUCTURE AND FUNCTION An important question is "What evidence is there that sophisticated biological assessment measures actually contribute meaningfully to the assessment, clinical management, and treatment of individual clients?" Do they make a real difference, and, if so, in what ways? Fortunately, evidence of the usefulness of these measures is accumulating. Velakoulis and Lloyd (1998) described the utility of SPECT scanning in clients with neuropsychiatric disorders involving early onset dementia. SPECT scanning confirmed the presence of abnormalities in 88% of the 56 clients tested; the authors noted that while in no cases were the SPECT scanning assessments the sole piece of evidence used to make diagnoses, they played a vital role in establishing the diagnosis. SPECT scans had to be interpreted within the context of other information because the scans reveal abnormalities that are common across various neurological conditions (i.e., they are non-specific).

Perhaps the ultimate test of the clinical utility of these measures is the extent to which the information gleaned actually changes diagnoses and makes them more accurate. One recent

study compared the conclusions reached about clinical decisions by two physicians who were either provided or not provided CT scan data (see Condefer, Haworth, & Wilcock, 2004). The clients were being assessed for memory disorders and dementia. The study showed that the CT scan data had an influence on diagnosis and treatment planning in 10 to 15% of the cases.

The clinical utility of biological assessment measures was clearly illustrated in a study by Hentschel et al. (2005) that was conducted with clients referred to a university clinic because of memory difficulties. This study showed that magnetic resonance imaging (MRI) along with the final comprehensive clinical diagnosis of neuropsychology status led to a change in the diagnosis of over one quarter of the clients assessed. The initial diagnoses and final diagnoses are shown in Figure 4.5. This figure illustrates the changes in diagnostic status for those who were thought initially to have no dementia, neurodegenerative dementia, or vascular dementia. If you are interested in learning more about these age-related disorders, you can find additional information in Chapter 16.

In another recent study, McIntosh et al. (2008) examined brain activation patterns in people with schizophrenia or psychotic bipolar disorder and normal controls using a sentence completion task as an experimental probe. They found that people diagnosed with schizophrenia demonstrated decreased activation of the dorsal prefrontal cortex. Those with bipolar disorder showed decreased anterior insula activation. Although the findings could be confounded due to the effects of different medications, they are consistent with the possibility of diagnosis-specific brain abnormalities. David A. Lewis (2008), an editor of the *American Journal of Psychiatry*, cited this study as "an example of the types of experimental designs that can generate the empirical data required for a rational revision of diagnostic categories and criteria in psychiatry" (p. 11512). It remains to be determined whether such findings will be useful at the level of the individual client.

Martin Paulus (2008) conducted a review to address the question of whether neuroimaging can contribute to the diagnosis and treatment of anxiety disorders. He concluded that fMRI has potential as a clinical tool, "but neuroimaging groups will need to better develop its specificity and sensitivity so that fMRI results can be meaningful for an individual patient not just for groups of individuals" (Paulus, 2008, p. 348). Similarly, Serene, Ashtari, Szeszko, and Kumra (2007) reviewed MRI studies of four childhood psychiatric disorders: attention deficit hyperactivity disorder (ADHD), major depressive disorder, bipolar disorder, and schizophrenia. The results revealed abnormalities in the developmental trajectories seen in healthy children, thereby potentially increasing our understanding of the pathophysiology of childhood psychiatric disorders. For example, frontostriatal abnormalities are reported consistently in ADHD, possibly a reflection of abnormalities in the development of cognitive control. However, Serene et al. (2007) concluded that "routine neuroimaging for children with severe emotional disturbances is not indicated for diagnostic purposes" (p. 135). On the other hand, the authors noted that a better

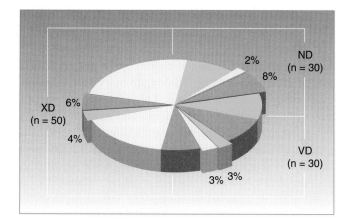

FIGURE 4.5 Changes in the diagnostic groups due to information from MRI and neuropsychology in a sample of clients investigated for cognitive disturbances in a memory clinic (n=100). The location in the diagram indicates the final comprehensive clinical diagnosis (XD=no dementia, ND=neurodegenerative dementia, VD=vascular dementia); the colour indicates the initial clinical diagnosis (beige: XD; green: ND; grey: VD). The sectors within each of the final diagnostic groups represent the changes from the initial diagnostic groups. The overall frequency of change in diagnosis (26%) is significantly different from chance level (CI: 0.260.09).
Source: Hentschel et al. (2005).

understanding of the neurobiology of such childhood disorders can possibly lead to the development of new therapies and predictors of treatment response.

NEUROCHEMICAL ASSESSMENT

It might seem that assessing the amount of a particular neurotransmitter or the quantity of its receptors in the brain would be straightforward. But it is not. Only recently has PET scanning allowed an assessment of receptors in a living brain. Most of the research on neurochemical theories of psychopathology—of increasing importance in recent years—has relied on indirect assessments.

In post-mortem studies, the brains of deceased clients are removed and the amount of specific neurotransmitters in particular brain areas can then be directly measured. Different brain areas can be infused with substances that bind to receptors, and the amount of binding can then be quantified; more binding indicates more receptors. In Chapter 11, we will discuss how this method has been used to study the dopamine theory of schizophrenia.

Another common method of neurochemical assessment involves analyzing the *metabolites* of neurotransmitters that have been broken down by enzymes. A metabolite, typically an acid, is produced when a neurotransmitter is deactivated. For example, the major metabolite of dopamine is homovanillic acid; of serotonin, 5-hydroxyindoleacetic acid. The metabolites can be detected in urine, blood, and cerebrospinal fluid (the fluid in the spinal column and in the brain's ventricles). A high level

of a particular metabolite indicates a high level of the transmitter, and a low level indicates a low level of the transmitter. We will see in Chapter 8 that people with depression have low levels of the main metabolite of serotonin—a fact that has played an important role in the serotonin theory of depression.

Imaging and neurochemical techniques provide startling pictures of and insights into internal organs and permit the gathering of information about living tissue, including the brain. Results, however, are not strong enough for these methods to be used in diagnosing psychopathology. Clinicians and researchers in many disciplines are currently using these techniques both to discover previously undetectable tumours and other brain problems and to conduct inquiries into the neural and chemical bases of thought, emotion, and behaviour.

NEUROPSYCHOLOGICAL ASSESSMENT

"With such a wide array of eminent researchers and institutions, human neuropsychology in Canada should continue to thrive well into the foreseeable future, and Canadian investigators can be expected to remain respected leaders in this scientific endeavour."
—Hayman-Abello, Hayman-Abello, and Rourke, 2003, p. 120, on human neuropsychology in Canada

The past decade has witnessed many advances in neuropsychological assessment. What exactly is neuropsychological assessment? It is important at this point to note a distinction between neurologists and neuropsychologists, even though both specialists are concerned with the study of the central nervous system. A **neurologist** is a physician who specializes in medical diseases that affect the nervous system, such as muscular dystrophy, cerebral palsy, or Alzheimer's disease. A **neuropsychologist** is a psychologist who studies how dysfunctions of the brain affect the way we think, feel, and behave. A neuropsychologist is trained as a psychologist—and as such is interested in thought, emotion, and behaviour—but one with a focus on how abnormalities of the brain affect behaviour in deleterious ways. Both kinds of specialists contribute much to each other as they work in different ways, often collaboratively, to learn how the nervous system functions and how to ameliorate problems caused by disease or injury to the brain.

The goals of neuropsychological testing were summarized by Seidman and Bruder (2003) as follows:

1. to measure as reliably, validly, and completely as possible the behavioural correlates of brain functions
2. to identify the characteristic profile associated with a neurobehavioural syndrome (differential diagnosis)
3. to establish possible localization, lateralization, and etiology of a brain lesion
4. to determine whether neuropsychological deficits are present (i.e., cognitive, perceptual, or motor) regardless of diagnosis
5. to describe neuropsychological strengths, weaknesses, and strategy of problem solving

6. to assess the patient's feelings about his or her syndrome
7. to provide treatment recommendations (i.e., to client, family, school)

Source: Adapted with permission from Seidman and Bruder (2003)

One might reasonably assume that neurologists and physicians, with the help of such procedures and technological devices as PET, CT, and MRI scans, can observe the brain and its functions more or less directly and thus assess all brain abnormalities. Many brain abnormalities and injuries, however, involve alterations in structure so subtle or slight in extent that they have thus far eluded direct physical examination.

Neuropsychologists have developed tests to assess behavioural disturbances caused by brain dysfunctions. The literature on these tests is extensive, and as with most areas of psychology, so, too, is disagreement about them. The weight of the evidence does indicate that psychological tests have some validity in the assessment of brain damage, however, and they are often used in conjunction with the brain-scanning techniques just described. They are accordingly called **neuropsychological tests**. All are based on the idea that different psychological functions (e.g., motor speed, memory, language) are localized in different areas of the brain. Thus, finding a deficit on a particular test can provide clues about where in the brain some damage may exist.

One neuropsychological test is Reitan's modification of a battery or group of tests previously developed by Halstead. The concept of using a battery of tests, each tapping a different function, is critical, for only by studying a person's pattern of performance can an investigator adequately judge whether the person is brain damaged and where the damage is located. The following are four of the tests included in the Halstead-Reitan battery.

1. *Tactile Performance Test—Time*. While blindfolded, the client tries to fit variously shaped blocks into spaces of a form board, first using the preferred hand, then the other, and finally both.
2. *Tactile Performance Test—Memory*. After completing the timed test, the participant is asked to draw the form board from memory, showing the blocks in their proper location. Both this and the timed test are sensitive to damage in the right parietal lobe.
3. *Category Test*. The client, seeing an image on a screen that suggests one of the numbers from one to four, presses a button to show which number he or she thinks it is. A bell indicates that the choice is correct, a buzzer that it is incorrect. The client must keep track of these images and signals in order to figure out the rules for making the correct choices. This test measures problem solving, in particular the ability to abstract a principle from a non-verbal array of events. Impaired performance on this test is the best overall indicator of brain damage.
4. *Speech Sounds Perception Test*. Participants listen to a series of nonsense words, each comprising two consonants with a long "e" sound in the middle. They then select the "word" they heard from a set of alternatives. This test measures left-hemisphere function, especially temporal and parietal areas.

Extensive research has demonstrated that the battery is valid for detecting brain damage resulting from a variety of conditions, such as tumours, stroke, and head injury. Furthermore, this battery of tests can play an important role in making difficult diagnostic decisions, helping the clinician discriminate, for example, between dementia due to depression and dementia due to a degenerative brain disease (Reed & Reed, 1997).

The Luria-Nebraska battery (Golden, Hammeke, & Purisch, 1978), based on the work of the Russian psychologist Aleksandr Luria (1902–77), is also in widespread use (Moses & Purisch, 1997). A battery of 269 items makes up 11 sections to determine basic and complex motor skills, rhythm and pitch abilities, tactile and kinesthetic skills, verbal and spatial skills, receptive speech ability, expressive speech ability, writing skills, reading skills, arithmetic skills, memory, and intellectual processes. The pattern of scores on these sections, as well as on the 32 items found to be the most discriminating and indicative of overall impairment, helps reveal damage to the frontal, temporal, sensorimotor, or parietal-occipital area of the right or left hemisphere.

The Luria-Nebraska battery can be administered in two and a half hours, and can be scored in a highly reliable manner (e.g., Kashden & Franzen, 1996). Criterion validity has been established by findings such as a correct classification rate of over 86% when used with a sample of neurological clients and control groups (Moses et al., 1992). The Luria-Nebraska is also believed to pick up effects of brain damage that are not (yet) detectable by neurological examination; such deficits are in the cognitive domain rather than in the motor or sensory domains on which neurological assessments focus (e.g., assessing reflexes). A particular advantage of the Luria-Nebraska tests is that one can control for educational level so that a less-educated person will not receive a lower score solely because of limited educational experience (Brickman

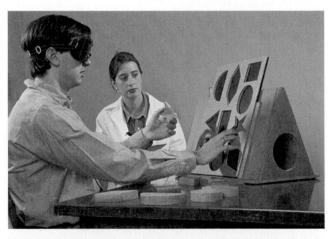

Neuropsychological tests assess various performance deficits in the hope of detecting a specific area of brain malfunction. Shown here is the Tactile Performance Test. Richard T. Nowitz/Photo Researchers, Inc.

et al., 1984). Finally, a version for children ages 8 to 12 has been found useful in diagnosing brain damage and in evaluating the educational strengths and weaknesses of children (Sweet et al., 1986).

Canadian research in human neuropsychology has a long legacy of eminent contributions, starting with the publication of Donald Hebb's *Organization of Behaviour* (1949), which described a theory of biological psychology that emphasized the role of behaviour. Canadian research in the various subspecialties of neuropsychology is in the vanguard of the field (e.g., Costa, 1996; Fuerst & Rourke, 1995; Hayman-Abello, Hayman-Abello, & Rourke, 2003). Indeed, Fuerst and Rourke (1995) noted that, "In proportion to respective populations, Canada harbours more eminent researchers in the field than any other country, including the United States" (p. 12). Much of this current Canadian research is in the area of neuropsychological assessment. For example, Donald T. Stuss, director of the Rotman Research Institute of the Baycrest Centre of Geriatric Care in Toronto, conducts neurobehavioural research with a focus on memory and frontal-lobe functions and on forms of dementia, including patterns of neuropsychological functioning in people with Alzheimer's disease. In one interesting early series of studies, he and his colleagues assessed the long-term residual effects of prefrontal leucotomies on neuropsychological functions (e.g., Stuss & Benson, 1983). Claude Braun from the Université du Québec à Montréal has investigated the sensitivity of neuropsychological tests to impairments from diffuse brain damage and the possible role of cortical damage or dysfunction in psychiatric disorders, including anorexia nervosa, mood disorders, and anti-social personality disorder (see Hayman-Abello et al., 2003). The contributions of Byron P. Rourke and his colleagues from the University of Windsor include extensive work on the development of non-verbal methods for the neuropsychological assessment of children and adults with learning disabilities, research on subtypes of psychosocial functioning in children with learning disabilities, and work on subgroups of people with Alzheimer's disease (see Hayman-Abello et al., 2003). Recently, Rourke (2008) discussed the implications of brain-behaviour relationships in humans and asked whether forms of psychosocial functioning are predictable from neuropsychological analysis in the individual case. He concluded that they often are.

> We have demonstrated that patterns of neuropsychological assets and deficits (involving auditory-perceptual, visual-perceptual, somatosensory, motor, psychomotor, and linguistic skills) are consistently related to particular forms and levels of severity of psychosocial functioning in children with LD (learning disabilities). (Rourke, 2008, p. 38).

In the late 1980s, the federal department Health and Welfare Canada allocated significant funding for a comprehensive, longitudinal study of the effects of dementia on Canadian society. This major research project involved the participation of over 10,000 Canadians at centres across Canada (Canadian

Byron P. Rourke, an eminent neuropsychologist at the University of Windsor, has conducted groundbreaking research on the neuropsychological assessment of people with learning disabilities. Photo courtesy Byron P. Rourke.

Study of Health and Aging Working Group, 1994a; Costa, 1996) and is referred to as the Canadian Study of Health and Aging (CSHA). The study is described in some detail in Canadian Perspectives 16.1. The full neuropsychological test battery administered to many of the participants was developed by a team of Canadian neuropsychologists charged with the task of producing a comprehensive neuropsychological battery that could be administered in approximately one hour. Details of the test battery and neuropsychological investigation are described by Holly Tuokko, from the University of Victoria, and her colleagues (Tuokko, Kristjansson, & Miller, 1995) and by Steenhuis and Ostbye (1995). According to Costa (1996), the CSHA is the largest epidemiological study of dementia to include a formal neuropsychological assessment.

At the University of Toronto, Konstantine Zakzanis and his colleagues (Zakzanis, Leach, & Kaplan, 1999) put together a compendium of neuropsychological profiles in which test sensitivities were compiled for several dementia (see Chapter 16) and neuropsychiatric disorders. The profiles were designed to help clinicians and researchers select neuropsychological tests on the basis of sensitivities of the tests to specific syndromes (as opposed to choosing tests on the basis of clinical lore, availability, history of use, and so forth). The work by Zakzanis et al. (1999) and other Canadian neuroscientists promises to place the selection and use of neuropsychological tests on firmer scientific ground.

PSYCHOPHYSIOLOGICAL ASSESSMENT

Psychophysiology is concerned with the bodily changes that accompany psychological events or that are associated with a person's psychological characteristics. Experimenters have used measures such as heart rate, tension in the muscles, blood flow in various parts of the body, and brain waves to study the physiological changes that occur when people are afraid, depressed, asleep, imagining, solving problems, and so on. The assessments we describe here are not sensitive enough to be used for diagnosis; they can, however, provide important information. For example, in using exposure to treat a client with an anxiety disorder, it would be useful to know the extent to which the client shows physiological arousal when exposed to the stimuli that create anxiety. Clients who show higher levels of physiological arousal may be experiencing higher levels of fear, which predict more benefit from the therapy (e.g., Foa et al., 1995).

The activities of the autonomic nervous system are frequently assessed by electrical and chemical measurements in attempt to understand the nature of emotion. One important measure is heart rate. Each heartbeat generates spreading changes in electrical potential, which can be recorded by an electrocardiograph, or on a suitably tuned polygraph, and graphically depicted in an **electrocardiogram**. Electrodes are usually placed on the chest and lead to an instrument for measuring electric currents. The deflections of this instrument may be seen as waves on a computer screen, or a pen recorder may register the waves on a continuously moving roll of graph paper. Both types of recordings are called electrocardiograms.

A second measure of autonomic nervous system activity is **electrodermal responding**, or skin conductance. Anxiety, fear, anger, and other emotions increase activity in the sympathetic nervous system, which then boosts sweat-gland activity. Increased sweat-gland activity increases the electrical conductance of the skin. Conductance is typically measured by determining the current that flows through the skin when a known small voltage derived from an external source is passed between two electrodes on the hand. This current shows a pronounced increase after activation of the sweat glands. Since the sweat glands are activated by the sympathetic nervous system, increased sweat-gland activity indicates sympathetic autonomic excitation and is often taken as a measure of emotional arousal. These measures are used widely in research in psychopathology.

Advances in technology allow researchers to track changes in physiological processes such as blood pressure in vivo, as people go about their normal business. Participants wear a portable device that automatically records blood pressure many times during the day. By combining these measures with self-reports recorded by the participants in specially designed diaries, researchers have been able to study how people's changing moods affect blood pressure—data of great interest to psychologically oriented researchers in hypertension (Kamarck et al., 1998; see Chapter 9).

Brain activity can be measured by an **electroencephalogram**, or **EEG**. Electrodes placed on the scalp record electrical activity in the underlying brain area. Abnormal patterns of electrical activity can indicate epilepsy or can help in locating brain lesions or tumours.

As with the brain-imaging techniques reviewed earlier, a more complete picture of a human being is obtained when physiological functioning is assessed while the person is engaging in some form of behaviour or cognitive activity. If experimenters are interested in the psychophysiological responses of clients with OCD, for example, they would likely study the clients while presenting stimuli, such as dirt, that would elicit the problematic behaviours.

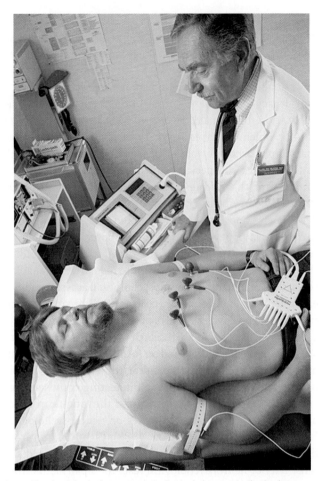

In psychophysiological assessment, physical changes in the body are measured. The electrocardiograph is one such assessment. Doug Plummer/Photo Researchers, Inc.

The biological assessment methods we have described are summarized in Table 4.3 and discussed in Canadian Perspectives 4.2.

A CAUTIONARY NOTE

Inasmuch as psychophysiology employs highly sophisticated electronic machinery and many psychologists aspire to be as scientific as possible, psychologists sometimes believe uncritically in these apparently objective assessment devices without appreciating their real limitations and complications. Many of the measurements do not differentiate clearly among emotional states. Skin conductance, for example, increases not only with anxiety but also with other emotions—among them, happiness.

There is also no one-to-one relationship between a score on a given neuropsychological test or a finding on a PET or CT scan on the one hand and psychological dysfunction on the other. This is especially so with chronic brain damage known or suspected to have been present for some years before the assessment is conducted. The reasons for these sometimes loose relationships have to do with such factors as how the person has, over time, reacted to and coped with the losses brought about by the brain damage. And, in turn, the success of efforts to cope has to do with the social environment in which the individual has lived.

TABLE 4.3
BIOLOGICAL ASSESSMENT METHODS

Brain imaging	CT and MRI scans reveal the structure of the brain. PET and fMRI are used to study brain function.
Neurochemical assessment	Includes post-mortem analysis of neurotransmitters and receptors, assays of metabolites of neurotransmitters, and PET scans of receptors.
Neuropsychological assessment	Behavioural tests such as the Halstead-Reitan and Luria-Nebraska assess abilities such as motor speed, memory, and spatial ability. Deficits on particular tests help localize an area of brain dysfunction.
Psychophysiological assessment	Includes measures of electrical activity in the autonomic nervous system, such as skin conductance, or in the central nervous system, such as the EEG and event-related potentials (ERPs).

CANADIAN PERSPECTIVES 4.2
COGNITIVE EVENT-RELATED POTENTIALS IN NEUROPSYCHOLOGICAL ASSESSMENT

"The stabbing victim listened helplessly as doctors told his family nothing could be done for him. They were wrong, but he had no way of letting them know."

—McIlroy (2001)

A vexing problem in clinical assessment is how to assess levels of intellectual functioning and related processes in clients who have experienced a trauma (e.g., a stroke) that has had an impact on their cognitive abilities and capacities. Many standard assessment devices, in order to be useful, require that the client have at least some communication ability and/or the ability to respond behaviourally. What can a clinician do when a person appears to lack the necessary communication abilities, but the clinician still must make some determination of neuropsychological functioning?

One innovative solution is outlined in a recent series of neuropsychological studies conducted by John Connolly and Ryan D'Arcy at Dalhousie University in Halifax (see Connolly, Marchard, Major, & D'Arcy, 2006). Their research is based on the use of cognitive event-related brain potentials. Cognitive **event-related potentials (ERPs)** are specific brain wave voltage potentials that can be evoked by standardized neuropsychological tests modified for computer presentation. Research has demonstrated that ERPs are sensitive to aspects of language, attention, and memory. Different ERP components reflect different cognitive processes. Connolly and his colleagues (2000) summarized their work this way: "Our working hypothesis is that regardless of the ability to execute the behavioural activity, the engaging of specific cognitive functions should lead to different ERP patterns" (p. 100).

The initial case that facilitated subsequent research on cognitive ERPs occurred in 1994. Connolly was asked to help evaluate the cognitive status of a 22-year-old man who was "unable to talk, gesture, or communicate in any way" (McIlroy, 2001, F1) after suffering brain damage as a result of being stabbed in the skull with a foot-long knife. The physicians were about to give up and write off the man's case as "hopeless." Connolly hooked the man up to a modified EEG machine and then presented him with nonsense sentences such as "The pizza was too hot to sing." Cognitively intact clients react to such sentences with a distinct electrical signal in the brain (i.e., ERPs). Much to everyone's surprise, including Connolly's, the young man showed the same ERP that intact people show when presented with such sentences. This technique revealed that the man's cognitive functioning was still "in there" and he would respond positively to rehabilitation efforts. He was able to walk out alone after more than four months of extensive treatment. He will never be able to speak but he was functioning quite well with his reading ability intact.

Connolly, D'Arcy, and associates argued that the use of cognitive ERPs in assessment offers a number of advantages in addition to addressing the problem inherent in evaluating clients who lack communication ability. Cognitive ERPs provide important information about the cognitive strategies used by an individual, for example, and the results can be clearly interpreted without ambiguity. Most importantly, these researchers have shown that it is possible to assess cognitive ERPs by creating and modifying computerized versions of standardized tests, such as the Token Test, the WISC-III and WAIS-R NI vocabulary subtests, the Wechsler Intelligence Scale for Children III, and the Peabody Picture Vocabulary Test—Revised (e.g., Connolly et al., 2006). Recent work with digit span performance tasks has shown that their distinct cognitive ERPs are related in meaningful and predictable ways to working memory (e.g., Marchand, Lefebvre, & Connolly, 2006). Thus, ERP tests can provide insights into a client's capacity to use working memory.

Gaetz (2002) noted that cognitive ERPs are particularly useful when brain damage is diffuse rather than focal, since other techniques, such as CT scans and MRI imaging, focus on identifying deficits in localized, precise areas and are less able to detect more widespread damage. Gaetz (2002) suggested that cognitive ERPs are high in clinical utility because "they are practical, easily administered, cost effective and brief procedures" that can often be completed within 30 minutes (p. 1665).

Connolly, Mate-Kole, and Joyce (1999) reported a case study of a young man with aphasia that serves as a vivid illustration of the usefulness and significance of cognitive ERPs in clinical assessment. Connolly (2000) described the outcome of this case in the following manner:

> Confined to a wheelchair, aphasic, and with no apparent ability to engage in goal-directed behavior, the young man was judged to have lost all intellectual function and to be a poor candidate for rehabilitation. Just prior to being discharged, he was assessed using cognitive ERPs in a congruous/incongruous sentence paradigm and found to respond normally to speech stimuli. He was admitted into a rehabilitation program on the basis of these results. About four months later he was discharged having responded well to rehabilitation efforts of the hospital staff. Such a result demonstrates unequivocally what can be achieved with cognitive ERPs just as it validates the basic cognitive ERP research upon which the paradigm was based. (p. 101)

The potential of cognitive ERPs is clearly evident from this case study and related research investigations, even though this specific research is still in its early phases. In addition to the clinical applicability of this work, it also facilitates—through analysis of ERP component patterns assessed within the context of a particular test—understanding about how people perform particular neuropsychological tasks (D'Arcy, Connolly, & Crocker, 1999).

Although the focus of Connolly and D'Arcy's work has been on the assessment of mental functions following neurological insult, it has been suggested by Ingram and Siegle (2001) that physiological measurement, such as the ERP, can "be incorporated during therapy sessions to gauge aspects of cognition during techniques such as role plays and thought challenges" (p. 121).

Thinking Critically

1. The Canadian government has been increasing demands for universities to collaborate with business and industry and questioning the relevance or contribution of some areas of psychological research to the needs of taxpayers (e.g., health issues). Do you consider research such as that conducted by Connolly, D'Arcy, and their colleagues to be "relevant"?

2. Do you think that cognitive ERP research has the potential for significant "impact capability" in areas relevant to abnormal psychology during the next quarter century?

3. How likely is it that approaches that combine findings from the different assessment areas and approaches described in this chapter will lay a foundation for and contribute to the development of effective rehabilitative and therapeutic interventions?

How understanding have parents been, for example, or how well has the school system met the individual's special educational needs? Therefore, in addition to taking into account the imperfect nature of the biological assessment instruments themselves and our incomplete understanding of how the brain actually functions, researchers must consider these experiential factors that operate over time to contribute to the clinical picture.

A final caution is reflected in the simple yet often unappreciated fact that in attempting to understand the neurocognitive consequences of any brain-injuring event, we must understand the abilities that the client has brought to that event (Boll, 1985). This straightforward truth brings to mind the story of the man who, recovering from an accident that has broken all the fingers in both hands, earnestly asks the surgeon whether he will be able to play the piano when his wounds heal. "Yes, I'm sure you will," says the doctor reassuringly. "That's wonderful," exclaims the man, "I've always wanted to be able to play the piano."

Canadian Perspectives 4.2 summarizes an ongoing program of research undertaken by Connolly and his colleagues that shows how the complexities involved in clinical assessment may require an equally complex approach, one that combines various aspects of abnormal, cognitive, and physiological psychology.

CULTURAL DIVERSITY AND CLINICAL ASSESSMENT

The accuracy and validity of a clinical assessment may depend upon a clinician's skill and ability to take into account the cultural context in which a client's psychological difficulties occur. At the same time, as stated in Chapter 2, it is important for the clinician to avoid stereotyping members of a culture. We should also note that the reliability and validity of various forms of psychological assessment have been questioned on the grounds that their content and scoring procedures reflect the culture of white European North Americans and so do not accurately assess people from other cultures. In this section we discuss problems of cultural bias in assessment and what can be done about them.

CULTURAL BIAS IN ASSESSMENT

The issue of **cultural bias** in assessment is not simple, nor is it clear that such biases make the assessment instruments useless. Some studies of bias in testing conducted in the United States have demonstrated that mainstream procedures, such as the Wechsler Intelligence Scale for Children—Revised, have equivalent predictive validity for minority and non-minority children (Sattler, 1992); IQ tests predict academic achievement equally well for both groups. Similarly, MMPI profiles relate equally well to clinician ratings among African Americans and Caucasians (McNulty et al., 1997). Nonetheless, some research studies suggest that there may be significant problems in using standardized intelligence testing with Native American and Canadian clients, especially children. Canadian Perspectives 4.3 addresses this issue.

Cultural biases work in different ways—they may cause clinicians to over- or underestimate psychological problems in members of other cultures (Lopez, 1996). As noted in Canadian Perspectives 4.3, Aboriginal children may be overrepresented in special-education classes, which may be a result of subtle or

Assessment must take the person's cultural background into account. For example, believing in possession by spirits is common in some cultures and thus should not always be taken to mean that the believer is psychotic. Jacques Jangoux/Photo Researchers, Inc.

Cultural differences can lead to different results on an IQ or aptitude test. For example, Aboriginal Canadian children may lack interest in the individualistic, competitive nature of IQ tests because of the cooperative, group-oriented values instilled by their culture. Health Canada.

not so subtle biases in the tests used to determine such placement. Yet consider the example of an Asian Canadian man who is very emotionally withdrawn. Should the clinician consider that lower levels of emotional expressiveness in men are viewed more positively in Asian cultures than in Euro–North American culture? A clinician who too quickly attributes the behaviour to a cultural difference rather than to a psychological disorder risks overlooking an emotional disorder that he or she would likely diagnose if the client were a white male. Again, the effect of cultural bias in clinical assessment works both ways.

How do such biases come about? As noted in Chapter 2, cultural differences in Canada are many, and they may affect assessment in various ways. Differences in language, religious and spiritual beliefs, illness beliefs, attitudes about family and relationships, cultural views of competition, and the alienation or timidity of members of visible minority cultures when being assessed by clinicians of the Euro–North American culture—all these factors and more can play a role. For example, Native North Americans, taught by their culture to cooperate with others, are less likely to warm to the task of taking an aptitude test, which is by nature highly individualistic and competitive (O'Conner, 1989). Non–English-speaking people being assessed by English-speaking clinicians may be poorly served by translators (Sabin, 1975). Clinicians who encounter clients claiming to be surrounded by or possessed by spirits might view this belief as a sign of schizophrenia. Yet in Inuit culture such a belief often occurs in distressed people, perhaps as a culture-bound defence mechanism and/or attempt at problem solving (e.g., Seltzer, 1983). Therefore, believing in spirit intrusion should probably not be taken as a sign of schizophrenia in an Inuit person. As noted in Chapter 2, language is a much more important diversity issue in Canada than in the United States.

Although it is important to be aware that cultural differences have the potential to bias clinical assessment, it is not clear that attempting to include cultural differences in one's assessment work necessarily contributes to a helpful diagnosis (e.g., Lopez & Hernandez, 1986). Assume that a clinician attaches less

psychopathological significance to the hallucinations of an Asian Canadian woman because the clinician believes that hallucinations are more prevalent among Asian Canadians. This clinician would be minimizing the seriousness of the woman's problems by attributing them to a *perceived* subcultural norm. As a result, the clinician might not consider a diagnosis of schizophrenia, a decision that may not be in the woman's best interest.

Cultural biases can affect not only *who* is diagnosed, but also *how* the person is diagnosed. American studies have reported that clinicians were more likely to diagnose a client as having schizophrenia if the case summary referred to the person as African American than if it described the person as white (Blake, 1973); that African American clients were overdiagnosed as having schizophrenia and underdiagnosed as having a mood disorder (Simon et al., 1973); and that, based on identical symptoms, lower-class African American clients were more likely to be diagnosed as alcoholic than were white, middle-class clients (Luepnitz, Randolph, & Gutsch, 1982).

Cultural differences cannot be avoided. And the cultural biases that can creep into clinical assessment do not necessarily yield to efforts to compensate for them. There is no simple answer. *DSM-IV-TR's* inclusion of cultural factors in the discussion of every category of disorder may well sensitize clinicians to the issue, a necessary first step (Lopez & Guarnaccia, 2000). When practitioners were surveyed a number of years ago, they overwhelmingly reported taking culture into account in their clinical work (Lopez, 1994), so it appears that the problem, if not the solution, is clearly in focus.

STRATEGIES FOR AVOIDING CULTURAL BIAS IN ASSESSMENT

Clinicians can—and do—use various methods to minimize the negative effects of cultural biases when assessing clients. Sattler (1982) makes some helpful suggestions that can guide clinicians in the selection and interpretation of tests and other

CANADIAN PERSPECTIVES 4.3
IQ TESTING AND ABORIGINAL CANADIANS

"Apparently, many well-meaning but misinformed members of our profession are using intelligence testing in a completely inappropriate and even harmful manner. The clients involved may not have the power or may not believe they have the power to do anything about it. With such a power imbalance, it is all the more important that counsellors be absolutely scrupulous about the ethics of testing."

–Wes G. Darrow of the Canadian International Development Agency, on the use of intelligence testing with Aboriginal Canadians (1986, p. 98)

Is bias in assessment present when the norms of the majority population are applied to culturally different minority group children and adults? More specifically, are there problems in the assessment of intelligence using standardized IQ tests with culturally different Canadian Aboriginal people?

This possibility was addressed in a study by Wilgosh, Mulcahy, and Watters (1986) for a sample of Canadian Inuit children whose WISC-R scores, using the original norms, would fall below a scaled score of 70 (see the section on mental retardation in Chapter 15). Past studies with Aboriginal Canadian children had typically reported below average verbal scores and average or above average performance scores for the WISC (e.g., St. John, Krichev, & Bauman, 1976) and the WISC-R (e.g., Seyfort, Spreen, & Lahmer, 1980). Seyfort et al. (1980) identified an apparent lack of internal consistency for many of the WISC-R subtests for their Aboriginal sample. They suggested that the children had difficulty understanding numerous items and/or that many WISC-R items tapped different abilities and skills in the Aboriginal sample relative to the majority population. The participants in the Wilgosh et al. (1986) Inuit Norming Study were a randomly selected representative sample of girls and boys between the ages of 7 years 0 months and 14 years 11 months from the Kitikmeot and Keewatin districts of the Northwest Territories. The full WISC-R was administered by skilled psychometrists with special training related to the assessment of northern Aboriginal children. The children were assessed individually, and an effort was made to optimize the testing conditions. Five items in the information subtest, one in the similarities subtest, and one in the comprehension subtest were modified to reflect Canadian content. In addition, one similarities item and two arithmetic items were reworded to facilitate understanding.

What did Wilgosh et al. (1986) find? Over three quarters of the children (77%) attained a verbal IQ scaled score less than 70, but only 5.7% of them had a performance scaled score less than 70. The respective percentage for full scale IQ was about 32. What do these results imply? Approximately 75% of Inuit children in the norming group would be classified as "retarded" *on the basis of their verbal IQ scores alone*. If the group had reflected the theoretical normal curve and the Wechsler normative group, the proportion would actually have approximated only 2.2% (Wilgosh et al., 1986). The authors concluded that, "using the Wechsler Verbal and Full Scale norms for the WISC-R would result in misclassification of great numbers of Inuit children" (Wilgosh et al.,

1986, p. 273). Further, a major factor resulting in the misclassification was presumed to be verbal comprehension of the English language, the second language for all of the Inuit children. The information and vocabulary subtests accounted for the majority of unanswered or incorrectly answered items.

Wilgosh et al. (1986) noted that "in actual educational programming for the Inuit children ... sole reliance is certainly not placed on the WISC-R scores" (p. 275). Nonetheless, Darou (1992) argued that many Aboriginal children are, in fact, streamed into special education programs on the basis of their IQ test results and that some Aboriginal administrative bodies perceive intelligence testing to be "just another tool of white domination" (p. 97). He believes that IQ tests are biased both *against* and *for* Aboriginals in unusual and complicated ways, as illustrated in this anecdote about Zachary, a hunter from a remote area near James Bay who was administered the Kohs Blocks subtest:

The test involves showing the subject a square drawing on a small card. The subject recreates the design with four or nine red and white cubes. The subject is assigned certain points depending upon how quickly he or she completes the task. This test has the highest validity of all the WISC sub-tests. When Zachary did it, he appeared to be in no hurry, he placed the blocks by an "S" pattern instead of by rows as most people do (the "S" saving two arm movements), and at the end he would frame the blocks with his fingers for a few seconds, and sometimes adjust the blocks a little. He did the test so fast that he went off-scale on all seven examples. The test goes off scale at an I.Q. equivalent of 180. (Darou, 1992, p. 97)

In discussions afterwards, Zachary explained that he believed the test was biased in his favour. He pointed out that, when he was young, his family ate or starved depending on his ability to recognize patterns. Despite anecdotes such as these, the weight of the available evidence indicates that Aboriginal people often perform poorly on standardized tests of intelligence, especially on measures developed to assess verbal intelligence, in comparison with the original normative group.

Thinking Critically

1. Do you think that "renorming" a test such as the WISC-R to a higher or locally determined standard of performance would be a solution to the problem of bias in testing? Under what circumstances would a comparison with national norms be considered relevant and appropriate? As Wilgosh et al. (1986) noted:

Whereas renorming of tests developed for use with the majority culture is useful in assessing the academic and intellectual performance of minority children, such tests do not assess social adaptability to the minority culture and adaptability to movement within the larger cultural context, and may mask differences in educational opportunity that render these children "retarded" in the broader cultural context. (p. 275)

2. Is it possible that the low-scaled scores for verbal intelligence of the Inuit children, relative to the normative data, reflect not a test bias, but differences in educational opportunities that have resulted in "real" differences in educational achievement?

3. Do you think that the findings reported by Wilgosh et al. (1986) are unique to the Inuit or do you think that they could apply to any minority group in Canada that has English as a second language, especially if that group lives in an isolated cultural and educational context?

4. What do you think should be the "culturally meaningful educational priorities" (Wilgosh et al., 1986, p. 275) for Aboriginal children in Canada? Should increased emphasis on comprehension of the English language be a high priority in the local cultural context? Or, as appeared to be the case with Zachary, should the focus be on adaptability within their own culture?

assessment data. First, clinicians should make efforts to learn about the culture of the person being assessed. This knowledge might come from reading, consultation with colleagues, and direct discussion with the client. Second, it is essential for clinicians to determine the client's preferred language and to consider testing in more than one language. The latter point is especially critical in Canada, given the importance of language as a grouping variable for diversity (Bowman, 2000). Recall that telephone translation is offered in 148 languages by the City of Toronto (Purvis, 1999)!

LANGUAGE AND BIAS The issue of testing in another language is both complex and difficult—especially if the clinician wants to adapt to the client's language standardized tests that were developed in a different language (typically English in North America). This can be problematic even when the clinician is fluent in the client's language. We have already pointed out that language can be a problem in the assessment of intelligence in Aboriginal children. Since language is important in every culture, if language is involved in any psychological test, then an accurate translation is required. Butcher et al. (1999) summarized generally accepted, sophisticated, and rigorous test translation and adaptation methods, including the following:

- careful translation of items by multiple translators;
- use of informants to verify both the linguistic and social appropriateness of items;
- integration of different translations of items into an experimental version;
- "back-translation" of items with re-translation of problem items followed by further back-translation until the desired form of items is achieved; and
- pretesting of the experimental version on a bilingual sample.

It is then vital for the test adapter to demonstrate that the test's validity (content, factorial, and predictive) is maintained in the target culture through rigorous research methodologies. You can readily see that appropriate test translation and validation is a difficult, time-consuming, and expensive process.

Although some widely used standardized tests have been translated into numerous languages and carefully validated in those languages, other tests (such as the many specialized inventories and measures developed for cognitive and behavioural assessment) are still in the adaptation process or are currently available in English only. Even when a test is available in the client's language, its use could be problematic if it had been validated on a different cultural group. For example, Bowman (2000) noted that psychologists in Quebec typically use French-language versions of the Wechsler individual intelligence tests that do not have any Canadian norms. Although Douglas Jackson from the University of Western Ontario has developed a group test with both English-Canadian and French-Canadian norms—the Multidimensional Aptitude Battery (Jackson, 1984, 1998)—there does not appear to be a good standardized test with norms for all the minority groups in Canada.

The MMPI-2 has been extensively adapted for international use and translated into numerous languages, including French. Clinicians in Canada, therefore, have a validated French-language version of the MMPI-2 and access to norms based on the U.S. standardization sample or the nationally derived norms for France (which are very close to the American norms). Since Canada is a bilingual country with a significant francophone community both inside and outside of Quebec, it is essential for clinicians to have access to tests written and validated in both French and English. Unfortunately, psychologists working with francophones generally use the major American tests translated into French. Typically, contemporary Canadian standardization has not been completed. Although Jackson has also developed Canadian tests for the assessment of psychopathology (Jackson, 1988, 1997) and the dimensions of personality disorders (Jackson & Livesley, 1999), according to Bowman (2000), "These tests are less frequently used in Canadian clinical work or reported in research than are related American instruments" (p. 239).

In Chapter 6, we will examine anxiety disorders. At this point, consider that there is a multitude of cognitive-behavioural measures that have been developed in the English language to assess these disorders and constructs hypothesized to be associated with them (e.g., dysfunctional attitudes). All of these measures should be translated into French (especially Canadian French) and validated for clinical and research use with the millions of people in Canada whose first language is French. Some progress has been made. For example, for the assessment of panic disorder, researchers from the Université du Québec à Montréal produced validated francophone versions of the Mobility Inventory for Agoraphobia (Stephenson, Marchand, & Lavallee, 1997), the Agoraphobic Cognitions Questionnaire, and the Body Sensations Questionnaire (Stephenson, Marchand, & Lavallee, 1998, 1999). Radomsky and associates (2006) from Concordia University in Montreal reported on the psychometric properties of French and English versions of the Claustrophobia Questionnaire.

Deniz Fikretoglu and colleagues (2006) validated a French Canadian version of a measure of deployment risk and resilience factors (see Chapter 2) in Canadian veterans. They found that the factors assessed by the Deployment Risk and Resilience Inventory predicted a host of problems in physical and psychological functioning during and soon after deployment in operational missions.

Real Labelle and his colleagues (Labelle, Lachance, & Morval, 1996), also from the Université du Québec, validated a French Canadian version of the Reasons for Living Inventory, which is often used in clinical and research work on depression and suicide risk (see Chapter 8). Bourque and Beaudette (1982) previously developed a French version of the widely used Beck Depression Inventory that has been shown to have adequate internal consistency and validity. More recently, Favrod and colleagues (2008) demonstrated that the French translation of the Beck Cognitive Insight Scale (a quick self-assessment of cognitive insight) has acceptable psychometric properties and cross-cultural validity for its use with outpatients diagnosed with schizophrenia or schizoaffective disorders. These are but a few examples of the literally hundreds of cognitive-behavioural assessment instruments available in the English language, most of which are not validated for use with French Canadians.

There are, of course, other good examples of tests that have been translated and validated for use with French Canadians. As one example, recall our introduction to the Canadian Study of Health and Aging project. The sampling technique made it possible to test a representative sample of all Canadians, and participants could choose to respond in either English or French. The developers of the test battery, particularly the francophone neuropsychologists, were cognizant of the difference between literal test translation and the development of culturally equivalent tests and had to develop reliable and valid French versions of all of the tests that were part of the battery (Tuokko et al., 1995). Recent work has focused on whether the English and French versions of the neuropsychological battery have measurement equivalence (see Tuokko et al., 2009). Assessments with French-speaking and English-speaking respondents found only partial equivalence for the verbal ability factor but other latent variables (e.g., long-term retrieval and visuospatial speed) were equivalent. Thus, the authors supported the generality of the battery and its use across various groups.

Can we assume that a test in English developed for one culture or country (e.g., the United States) is appropriate for another English-speaking culture or country (e.g., Canada)? Perhaps not!

A case in point is the information subtest of the revised version of the Wechsler Adult Intelligence Scale (WAIS-R). Many of the questions are problematic for Canadian clients because of the culturally specific American content (e.g., Boer & Pugh, 1988; Pugh & Boer, 1989). As many as 10 of the 29 items lack face validity for non-Americans and could be judged as unfair and inappropriate by Canadian respondents. Further, some of the culturally specific questions could be disproportionately difficult for Canadians. For example, a question about "Senators" could be significantly more difficult for Canadian respondents than for Americans because Americans should be expected to be more familiar with this component of the political system in the United States. A common but makeshift solution on the part of many Canadian psychologists has been to substitute what they perceive to be more culturally appropriate questions. Pugh and Boer (1989) addressed these issues and determined that empirical assessments of level of difficulty for Canadians differed significantly from the American normative sample for most of the items that lack face validity. They also determined that 9 of 10 Canadian face-valid substitutes reflected more accurately the difficulty level of the original standardization data. Thus, use of the original information subtest could inappropriately *lower* the individual IQs of Canadian clients. Nonetheless, Don Saklofske from the University of Saskatchewan and his colleagues (e.g., Saklofske & Hildebrand, 1999) have been involved in efforts to "renorm" the Wechsler tests of intelligence downward, since Canadian raw score means actually appear to be *higher* than the equivalent scores in the United States. Although certain items may lack validity and norms need to be adjusted, Saklofske and associates have also shown that the actual factor structure (or major dimensions or components) of the third edition of the WAIS was comparable to the factor model of the American standardization sample when the WAIS was administered to a representative Canadian sample of adults (Saklofske, Hildebrand, & Gorsuch, 2000). More recently, Bowden, Lange, Weiss, and Saklofske (2008) examined the invariance of a "measurement model" (a description of the numerical and theoretical relation between "observed" scores and the corresponding "latent" variables or constructs) underlying WAIS third edition scores in the U.S. and Canadian standardization samples. The model satisfied the assumption of invariance across the two samples. Further, subtest scores were similarly reliable in both samples. Interestingly, slightly higher latent variable means were reported in the Canadian normative sample. Overall, however, the cultural relevance of content and population-specific norms remain key issues.

CANADIAN PSYCHOLOGICAL TESTS Is there really a need for specifically Canadian psychological tests? Although the issue is controversial, according to Bowman (2000), the evidence that cognitive abilities, personality, or emotional condition is structured differently in different cultures is sparse. With the exception of intelligence tests, Bowman asserts that the need for Canadian tests is still an open empirical question. Assessment procedures can, of course, be modified to ensure that the person truly understands the requirements of the task. It is important for clinicians in Canada to be aware of the cultural diversity of our country and the implications of such diversity for understanding the clients seen in their clinical practice. For example, suppose that a First Nations Canadian child performed poorly on a test measuring psychomotor speed. The examiner's hunch is that the child did not understand the importance of working quickly and was overconcerned with accuracy instead. The test could be administered again after a more thorough explanation of the importance of working quickly without worrying about mistakes. If the child's performance improves, the examiner has gained an important understanding of him or her and has avoided diagnosing psychomotor-speed deficits when the child's test-taking strategy was more at issue.

When the examiner and client have different ethnic backgrounds, the examiner may need to make an extra effort to establish a rapport that will result in the person's best performance. For example, when testing a shy, Filipino elementary school student, one of the authors was unable to obtain a verbal response to test questions. However, the boy's mother was able to provide the clinician with an audio tape of the boy talking in an animated and articulate manner to his father, leading to a judgement that the test results did not represent a valid assessment of the child's language skills. When testing was repeated in the child's own home with his mother present, advanced verbal abilities were observed.

As Lopez (1994) pointed out, however, "the distance between cultural responsiveness and cultural stereotyping can be short" (p. 123). To minimize such problems, clinicians are encouraged to be particularly tentative in drawing conclusions about minority clients. Rather, they are advised to make *hypotheses* about the influence of culture on a particular client, entertain alternative hypotheses, and then test those hypotheses.

In a case from our files, a young man was suspected of having schizophrenia. One prominent symptom he reported was hearing voices. However, he claimed that he heard voices only while meditating and that within his (Buddhist) culture this experience was not uncommon. To test this hypothesis, the examiner (with the permission of the client) contacted the family's religious leader. The Buddhist priest indicated that the symptom reported by this young man was very unusual, and it turned out that the religious community to which he belonged was quite concerned about his increasingly bizarre behaviour. Thus, the hypothesis that his symptom should be attributed to cultural factors was refuted, and an error of failing to detect psychopathology was avoided.

Whenever practical, it is preferable that the professional responsible for a client's assessment (and treatment) come from a similar cultural and ethnic background, speak the same language, and be sensitive to and understand the values, life experiences, and issues facing the client.

SUMMARY

- Clinicians rely on several modes of assessment in trying to find out how best to describe a client, search for the reasons a person is troubled, and design effective preventive or remedial treatments.
- Regardless of how unstructured an assessment method may appear, it inevitably reflects the paradigm of the investigator.
- However clinicians and researchers go about gathering assessment information, they must be concerned with both reliability and validity, the former referring to whether measurement is consistent and replicable, the latter to whether our assessments are tapping into what we want to be measuring. The many assessment procedures described in this chapter vary greatly in their reliability and validity.
- The two main approaches to assessment are psychological and biological. Psychological assessments include clinical interviews, structured or relatively unstructured conversations in which the clinician probes the client for information about his or her problems; psychological tests, which range from the presentation of ambiguous stimuli, as in the Rorschach Inkblot Test to empirically derived self-report questionnaires, such as

the Minnesota Multiphasic Personality Inventory; and intelligence tests, which evaluate a person's intellectual ability and predict how well he or she will do in future academic situations.
- In behavioural and cognitive assessment, information is often gathered on four sets of factors (SORC): situational determinants, organismic variables, responses, and the consequences of behaviour. An alternative approach formulates an individualized cognitive-behavioural theory about a case with a view to helping the therapist develop a plan for treatment. Whereas traditional assessment seeks to understand people in terms of general traits or personality structure, behavioural and cognitive assessment is concerned more with how people act, feel, and think in particular situations. Specificity is the hallmark of cognitive and behavioural assessment, the assumption being that assessing psychological variables such as anxiety or distorted cognitions as they occur in specific situations will yield more useful information about people.
- Behavioural and cognitive assessment approaches include direct observation of behaviour either in natural surroundings or in contrived settings; interviews and self-report measures that are situational in their focus; and

specialized, think-aloud cognitive assessment procedures that attempt to uncover beliefs, attitudes, and thinking patterns thought to be important in theories of psychopathology and therapy. Family assessment focuses on types and levels of family functioning.

- Biological assessments include sophisticated, computer-controlled imaging techniques, such as CT scans, that allow us to actually see various structures of the living brain; neurochemical assays that allow inferences about levels of neurotransmitters; neuropsychological tests, such as the Halstead-Reitan, that base inferences of brain defects on variations in responses to psychological tests; and psychophysiological measurements, such as heart rate, skin conductance, and event-related potentials.

- Cultural factors play a role in clinical assessment. Minority clients may react differently than majority clients to assessment techniques developed on the basis of research with majority populations. Clinicians can have biases when evaluating minority clients, which can lead to minimizing or overdiagnosing a client's psychopathology. The numerous linguistic minorities represent a significant diversity issue in Canada, one that has important implications for clinical assessment. Cultural differences and clinician bias are significant for scientific, practical, and ethical reasons.

KEY TERMS

alternate-form reliability (p. 106)
behavioural observation (p. 117)
clinical interview (p. 107)
cognitive-behavioural case formulation (p. 115)
construct validity (p. 107)
content validity (p. 107)
criterion validity (p. 107)
CT scan (p. 124)
cultural bias (p. 132)
ecological momentary assessment (EMA) (p. 118)
electrocardiogram (p. 130)
electrodermal responding (p. 130)
electroencephalogram (EEG) (p. 130)
event-related potentials (ERPs) (p. 131)

family functioning (p. 122)
functional magnetic resonance imaging (fMRI) (p. 125)
intelligence test (p. 114)
internal consistency reliability (p. 106)
inter-rater reliability (p. 106)
magnetic resonance imaging (MRI) (p. 125)
Minnesota Multiphasic Personality Inventory (MMPI) (p. 110)
neurologist (p. 127)
neuropsychological tests (p. 128)
neuropsychologist (p. 127)
personality inventory (p. 110)
PET scan (p. 126)
projective hypothesis (p. 111)

projective test (p. 111)
psychological tests (p. 110)
psychophysiology (p. 129)
reactivity (of behaviour) (p. 119)
Rorschach Inkblot Test (p. 112)
self-monitoring (p. 118)
standardization (p. 110)
structured interview (p. 108)
test-retest reliability (p. 106)
Thematic Apperception Test (TAT) (p. 112)
thought listing (p. 121)
videotape reconstruction (p. 121)

REFLECTIONS: PAST, PRESENT, AND FUTURE

- In Chapter 2, we examined contemporary paradigms of abnormal psychology, summarized the consequences of adopting a particular paradigm, and introduced integrative paradigms. Assume that you are a practising clinical psychologist. Will your approach to clinical assessment and the assessment procedures that you choose be influenced by the conceptual framework that you prefer? Will your choice of assessment strategies be influenced by the nature of the specific psychological disorders presented by your clients? Return to this question once you have studied all of the disorders described in this book.

- We described two different systems to guide cognitive-behavioural assessment: the traditional behavioural SORC

and the more recent case formulation approaches that place a greater emphasis on cognitive factors. Which of these approaches seems most relevant to you, and why? Do you think that there is any value to integrating the two approaches? What form would such integration take?

- Persons and Davidson (2001) described the case of "Judy." Among other problems, Judy was depressed. Based on the case formulation applied to Judy and your understanding of cognitive-behavioural treatment strategies, and in particular the treatment of depression as described in Chapter 8, summarize the specific interventions you would employ in Judy's case. Develop a comprehensive treatment plan.

RESEARCH METHODS IN THE STUDY OF ABNORMAL BEHAVIOUR

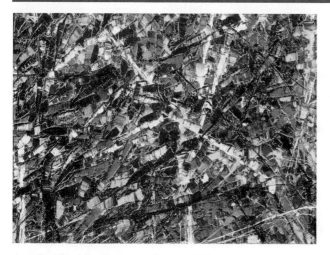

Jean-Paul Riopelle, *Coups sur Coups*, 1953 oil on canvas, 73.0 × 100.3 cm; Art Gallery of Ontario, Toronto. Gift from J. S. McLean, Canadian Fund, 1954. © 2007 AGO

"The great tragedy of science—the slaying of a beautiful hypothesis by an ugly fact."
  —T. H. Huxley, *Biogenesis and Abiognesis*

"It ain't so much the things we don't know that get us in trouble. It's the things we know that just ain't so."
  —Artemus Ward

"… it is clinical research which has dramatically altered the course of illness and of clinical care by taking us from ice wraps to lithium, from insulin shock to olanzepine, and from psychoanalytic regression to cognitive-behavioural therapy. This research has been meaningful at basic, clinical, and health-systems levels."
  —Paul E. Garfinkel, president and CEO, and David S. Goldbloom, physician-in-chief, the Centre for Addiction and Mental Health, Toronto (2000, p. 163)

SCIENCE AND SCIENTIFIC METHODS

THE RESEARCH METHODS OF ABNORMAL PSYCHOLOGY

SUMMARY

Given the different ways of conceptualizing and treating abnormal behaviour and the problems in its classification and assessment, it follows that there is also less than total agreement about how abnormal behaviour ought to be studied and what the facts of the field are. Yet it is precisely because facts about mental disorders are hard to come by that it is important to pursue them using the scientific research methods that are applied in contemporary psychopathology. This chapter discusses these methods and provides a sense of the strengths and limitations of each.

SCIENCE AND SCIENTIFIC METHODS

Science is the pursuit of systematized knowledge through observation. Thus, the term, which comes from the Latin *scire*, "to know," refers both to a method (the systematic acquisition and evaluation of information) and to a goal (the development of general theories that explain the information). It is always important for scientific observations and explanations to be testable (open to systematic probes) and reliable (replicable).

TESTABILITY AND REPLICABILITY

A scientific approach requires first that propositions and ideas be stated in a clear and precise way. Only then can scientific claims be exposed to systematic probes and tests, any one of which could negate the scientist's expectations about what will be found. Statements, theories, and assertions, regardless of how plausible they may seem, must be testable in the public arena and subject to disproof. It is not enough to assert, for example, that traumatic experiences during childhood may cause psychological maladjustment in adulthood. Such a hypothesis must be amenable to systematic testing that could show it to be false. Closely related to testability is the requirement that each observation that contributes to a scientific body of knowledge be replicable or reliable. Whatever is observed must be replicable; that is, it must occur under prescribed circumstances not once, but repeatedly. If the event cannot be reproduced, scientists become wary of the legitimacy of the original observation.

THE ROLE OF THEORY

> "In sum, a theory is corroborated to the extent that we have subjected it to risky tests; the more dangerous the tests it has survived, the better corroborated it is."
> —Kenneth N. Levy, 2008, p. 558

A **theory** is a set of propositions meant to explain a class of phenomena. A primary goal of science is to advance theories to account for data, often by proposing cause–effect relationships. The results of empirical research allow the adequacy of theories to be evaluated. Theories themselves can also play an important role in guiding research by suggesting that certain additional data be collected. More specifically, a theory permits the generation of **hypotheses**—expectations about what should occur if a theory is true—to be tested in research. For example, suppose you want to test a classical-conditioning theory of phobias. As a researcher, you begin by developing a specific hypothesis based on the theory. For example, if the classical-conditioning theory is valid, people with phobias should be more likely than those in the general population to have had traumatic experiences with the situations they fear, such as flying. By collecting data on the frequency of traumatic experiences with phobic stimuli among people with phobias and comparing this information with corresponding data from people without phobias, you could determine whether your hypothesis was confirmed, thus supporting the theory, or disconfirmed, thus invalidating the theory.

The generation of a theory is perhaps the most challenging part of the scientific enterprise. It is sometimes asserted that a scientist formulates a theory simply by considering data that have been previously collected and then deciding, in a rather straightforward fashion, that a given way of thinking about the data is the most economical and useful. Although some theory-building follows this course, not all does. Aspects too seldom mentioned are the *creativity* of the act and the *excitement* of finding a novel way to conceptualize things. A theory sometimes seems to leap from the scientist's head in a wonderful moment of insight. New ideas suddenly occur, and connections previously overlooked are suddenly grasped. What formerly seemed obscure or meaningless makes a new kind of sense within the framework of the new theory.

Theories are *constructions* put together by scientists. In formulating a theory, scientists must often make use of theoretical concepts: unobservable states or processes that are inferred from observable data. Repression is a theoretical concept. Theoretical concepts are inferred from observable data. For example, an analyst might infer the presence of a repressed conflict from a client's continual avoidance of discussing his or her relationship with authority figures.

Several advantages can be gained by using theoretical terms. For example, in abnormal psychology, we may want to bridge temporal gaps with theoretical concepts. If a child has had a particularly frightening experience and his or her behaviour changes for a lengthy period of time, we need to explain how the earlier event exerted an influence over subsequent behaviour. The unobservable and inferred concept of *acquired fear* has been very helpful in this regard. Theoretical concepts can also summarize already observed relationships. We may observe that whether people are taking an examination, are expecting a momentary electric shock, or are arguing with a companion, they all have sweaty palms, trembling hands, and a fast heartbeat. If we ask them how they feel, they all report that they are tense. The relationships can be depicted as shown in Figure 5.1a. We could also say that all the situations have made these individuals anxious

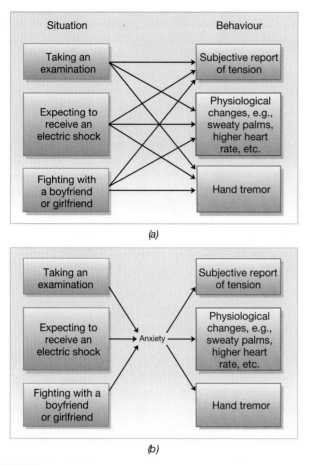

FIGURE 5.1 An illustration of the advantages of using anxiety as a theoretical concept. The arrows in (b) are fewer and more readily understood. After Miller (1959)

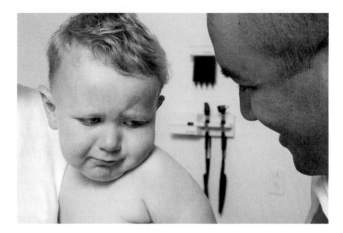

A theoretical concept, such as acquired fear, is useful in accounting for the fact that some earlier experience can have an effect on current behaviour. Blend Images/cpimages.com.

and that anxiety has in turn caused the reported tension, the sweaty palms, the faster heartbeat, and the trembling hands. Figure 5.1b shows anxiety as a theoretical concept explaining what has been observed. The first figure, which shows the relationships between the situations and the behaviour, is much more complex than the second, in which the theoretical concept of anxiety becomes a mediator of the relationships.

What criteria are applied in judging the legitimacy of a theoretical concept? One earlier school of thought, called *operationism*, proposed that each concept take as its meaning a single observable and measurable operation. In this way, each theoretical concept would be *nothing more* than one particular measurable event. For example, anxiety might be identified as nothing more than scoring above 50 on a particular anxiety questionnaire. It soon became clear that this approach deprived theoretical concepts of their greatest advantage. If each theoretical concept is operationalized in only one way, its generality is lost. If the theoretical concept of learning, for instance, is identified as a single operation or effect that can

be measured, such as how often a rat presses a bar, other behaviour, such as a child's performing arithmetic problems or a college student's studying this book, cannot also be called learning, and attempts to relate the different phenomena to one another might be discouraged.

The early operationist point of view quickly gave way to the more flexible position that a theoretical concept can be defined by sets of operations or effects. The concept can thus be linked to several different measurements, each of which taps a different facet of the concept. For example, in Figure 5.1b, a subjective report of tension, physiological changes, and hand trembling form a set of operations defining anxiety. Theoretical concepts are better defined by sets of operations than by a single operation.

THE RESEARCH METHODS OF ABNORMAL PSYCHOLOGY

All empirical research entails the collection of observable data. Sometimes research remains at a purely descriptive level, but often researchers observe several events and try to determine how they are associated or related. In the field of abnormal psychology, there is a large descriptive literature concerning the typical symptoms of people who have been diagnosed as having particular disorders. These symptoms can then be related to other characteristics, such as gender or social class. For example, eating disorders are more common in women than in men. But science demands more than descriptions of relationships. We often want to understand the causes of the relationships we have observed. For example, we want to know why eating disorders are found more often in women than in men. (Discussed more fully in Chapter 10, the answer may lie in social pressures for women to be thin.) In this section, we describe the most commonly used research methods in the study of abnormal behaviour. The methods vary in the extent to which they allow researchers to infer causal relationships.

THE CASE STUDY

The most familiar and time-honoured method of observing others is to study them one at a time and record detailed information about them. As we did in Chapter 1 with J. Brett Barkley, clinicians prepare a **case study** by collecting historical and biographical information on a single individual, often including experiences during therapy sessions. A comprehensive case study would cover family history and background, medical history, educational background, jobs held, marital history, and details concerning development, adjustment, personality, life course, and current situation. Important to bear in mind, though, is the role of the clinician's paradigm in determining the kinds of information actually collected and reported in a case study. To take but one example, case studies of psychoanalytically oriented clinicians contain more information about the client's early childhood and conflicts with parents than do reports made by behaviourally oriented practitioners.

Case studies from practising clinicians may lack the degree of control and objectivity of research using other methods, but these descriptive accounts have played an important role in the study of abnormal behaviour.

PROVIDING DETAILED DESCRIPTION Because it deals with a single individual, the case study can include much more detail than is typically included with other research methods. In a famous case history of multiple personality reported in 1954, psychiatrists Thigpen and Cleckley described a client, known as Eve White, who assumed at various times three very distinct personalities. Their description of the case required an entire book, *The Three Faces of Eve*. The following brief summary emphasizes the moments in which new personalities emerged and what the separate selves knew of one another.

Chris Sizemore was the subject of the famous "three faces of Eve" case. She subsequently claimed to have had 21 separate personalities. Gerald Martineau/The Washington Post/Getty Images.

Eve White had been seen in psychotherapy for several months because she was experiencing severe headaches accompanied by blackouts. Her therapist (Dr. Thigpen) described her as a retiring and gently conventional figure. One day during the course of an interview, however, she changed abruptly and in a surprising way.

> As if seized by sudden pain, she put both hands to her head. After a tense moment of silence, both hands dropped. There was a quick, reckless smile, and, in a bright voice that sparkled, she said, "Hi there, Doc!" The demure and constrained posture of Eve White had melted into buoyant repose. ... This new and apparently carefree girl spoke casually of Eve White and her problems, always using she or her in every reference, always respecting the strict bounds of a separate identity ... When asked her name, she immediately replied, "Oh, I'm Eve Black." (Thigpen & Cleckley, 1954, p. 137)

After this rather startling revelation, Eve was observed over a period of 14 months in a series of interviews that ran to almost 100 hours. A very important part of Eve White's therapy was to help her learn about Eve Black, her other, infectiously exuberant self, who added seductive and expensive clothing to her wardrobe and lived unremembered episodes of her life. During this period, a third personality, Jane, emerged while Eve White was recollecting an early incident in which she had been painfully scalded by water from a wash pot.

Jane, who from then on knew all that happened to the two Eves, although they did not share knowledge of her existence, was "far more mature, more vivid, more boldly capable, and more interesting than Eve White" (Thigpen & Cleckley, 1954, p. 137). Jane developed a deep and revering affection for the first Eve, who was considered somewhat a ninny by Eve Black. Jane knew nothing of Eve White's earlier life except what she learned through Eve's memories.

Some 11 months later, in a calamitous session with all three personalities present at different times, Eve Black emerged and reminisced for a moment about the many good times she had had in the past but then remarked that she did not seem to have real fun anymore. She began to sob, the only time Dr. Thigpen had seen her in tears. She told him that she wanted him to have her red dress to remember her by. All expression left her face and her eyes closed. Eve White opened them. When Jane was summoned a few minutes later, she soon realized that there was no longer any Eve Black or White and she began to experience a terrifying lost event. "No, no! ... Oh no, Mother ...I can't ...Don't make me do it," she cried. Jane, who earlier had known nothing of Eve's childhood, was five years old and at her grandmother's funeral. Her mother was holding her high off the floor and above the coffin and saying that she must touch her grandmother's face. As she felt her hand leave the clammy cheek, the young woman screamed so piercingly that Dr. Cleckley, Dr. Thigpen's associate, came running from his office across the hall.

The two physicians were not certain who confronted them. In the searing intensity of the remembered moment, a new personality had been welded. Their transformed client did not at first feel herself as apart and as sharply distinct a person as had the two Eves and Jane, although she knew a great deal about all of them. When her initial bewilderment lessened, she tended to identify herself with Jane. But the identification was not sure or complete, and she mourned the absence of the two Eves as though they were lost sisters. This new person decided to call herself Mrs. Evelyn White.

The case of Eve White, Eve Black, Jane, and eventually Evelyn constitutes a valuable classic in the literature because it is one of only a few detailed accounts of a rare phenomenon, multiple personality, now known as *dissociative identity disorder*, a controversial disorder discussed in Chapter 7. In addition to illustrating the disorder itself, the original report of Thigpen and Cleckley provides valuable details about the interview procedures they followed and how the treatment progressed in this specific case.

However, the validity of the information gathered in a case study is sometimes questionable. Indeed, the real Eve, a woman named Chris Sizemore, wrote a book that challenged Thigpen and Cleckley's account of her case (Sizemore & Pittillo, 1977). She claimed that, following her period of therapy with them, her personality continued to fragment. In all, 21 separate and distinct strangers inhabited her body at one time or another. And, contrary to Thigpen and Cleckley's report, Sizemore maintains that nine of the personalities existed before Eve Black ever appeared. One set of personalities—they usually came in threes—would weaken and fade, to be replaced by others. Eventually, her personality changes were so constant and numerous that she might become her three persons in rapid switches resembling the flipping of television channels. The debilitating round-robin of transformations and the fierce battle for dominance among her selves filled her entire day. After resolving what she hoped was her last trio, by realizing finally that her alternate personalities were true aspects of herself rather than strangers from without, Chris Sizemore decided to reveal her story as a means of coping with past ordeals. In a recent BBC interview (the "Hard Talk" program's March 25, 2009 episode) Sizemore stated that she is now a well person who has not experienced any symptoms over the last 30 years.

Another example illustrates the value of combining a series of cases of an unusual phenomenon using a sophisticated and reliable data analytic strategy. We previously mentioned trichotillomania, one of the *DSM-IV-TR* impulse control disorders. The irresistible urge to pull out one's hair is an understudied, poorly understood, but chronic condition that affects predominantly adolescent girls and women. Recent research (e.g., Lewin et al., 2009) suggests that symptoms of depression and anxiety may be pervasive among youth with trichotillomania and likely impact functional impairment. In an attempt to identify the concerns of compulsive hair pullers, Casati, Toner, and Yu (2000), from the Centre for Addiction and Mental Health in Toronto, conducted focus interviews with seven women who met the diagnostic criteria for trichotillomania. The transcripts were analyzed using a procedure called the *constant comparative method*, which consists of the identification of relevant units of information (unitizing), placing the units into categories that emerge from the data (categorizing), and providing organizational themes for the information (identifying themes). Casati et al. (2000) identified 10 major themes in the subjective experiences of the women with compulsive hair pulling. Six themes related to negative emotions (embarrassment/shame, isolation, fear and guilt, anger/frustration, humiliation/pain, and body image). The following case illustrates the humiliation associated with trichotillomania:

> Ms. A.: " … I remember once sitting in class and I overheard someone behind me whispering to their friend that I had a bald spot. I remember being humiliated and thinking that next time I would sit at the back of the class. And that's exactly what I did for the rest of the year. I sat in desks that were located at the back of the classroom." (Casati et al., 2000, p. 347)

Three themes related to the issue of control (lack of control, self-disclosure, and lack of information from the medical community), and the last theme related to triggers or precipitants of the compulsive hair-pulling (which varied considerably from woman to woman). Why is this study informative? The cases investigated by Casati et al. (2000) identified themes in the subjective experiences of compulsive hair pullers that practitioners should address when assessing and treating women with trichotillomania.

THE CASE STUDY AS EVIDENCE Case histories are especially useful when they negate an assumed universal relationship or law. Consider, for example, the proposition that episodes of depression are always preceded by an increase in life stress. Finding even a single case in which this is not true would negate the theory or at least force it to be changed to assert that only some episodes of depression are triggered by stress.

The case study fares less well as evidence in support of a particular theory or proposition. Case studies do not provide the means for ruling out alternative hypotheses. To illustrate this problem, let us consider a clinician who has developed a new treatment for depression, tries it out on a client, and observes that the depression lifts after 10 weeks of therapy. Although it would be tempting to conclude that the therapy worked, such a conclusion cannot legitimately be drawn because any of several other factors could also have produced the change. A stressful situation in the client's life may have resolved itself, or perhaps episodes of depression are naturally time-limited. Thus, several plausible rival hypotheses could account for the clinical improvement. The data yielded by the case study do not allow us to determine the true cause of the change.

GENERATING HYPOTHESES The case study plays a unique and important role in generating hypotheses. Through exposure to the life histories of a great number of clients, clinicians gain experience in understanding and interpreting them. Eventually, they may notice similarities of circumstances and outcomes and formulate important hypotheses that could not have been uncovered in a more controlled investigation. For example, in his clinical work with disturbed children, Kanner (1943) noticed that some children showed a similar constellation of symptoms, including failure to develop language and extreme isolation from other people. He proposed a new diagnosis—infantile autism—which was subsequently confirmed by larger-scale research (see Chapter 15).

Some case studies are so unique that it seems impossible to generalize to other individuals, including other people with the same disorder. A fascinating Canadian example is a case study of preferential bestiality (zoophilia) reported by Earls and Lalumiere (2002). A 54-year-old white male was serving a five-year prison sentence for cruelty to animals— a cruelty that had been exhibited in sexual activity with horses. He reported that his sexual attraction to animals developed while he grew up on a farm. The most distinguishing aspect of this case is reflected in the following excerpt:

> He also reported that his involvement with horses was not limited to sexual acts, but also included a strong emotional component. In his most recent offense, he inserted his arm to its full length into the vagina of a mare and punctured its vaginal wall. The horse subsequently died. The subject reported that the mare had shown interest in a stallion, and he had killed the mare as a result of jealousy.
> (Earls & Lalumiere, 2002, p. 86)

Case studies such as these are primarily informative in terms of the specific and unique manifestations of a disorder. However, when similar case studies begin to surface, it may result in the authors getting new insights into the nature of the phenomenon being considered. In this instance, Earls and Lalumiere (2009) have recently reported another extreme case of zoophilia. The new case of a 47-year-old man named "Possum" is fascinating in and of itself as it recounts his passion for horses. Equally important though is the authors' revised conclusion that zoophilia may not be as rare as first believed. In their earlier paper, the authors characterized zoophilia as

being extremely rare, but they have since modified this view. This modified conclusion was based, in part, on the many responses they received from the public about other cases of zoophilia when the media reported their original case study (see Earls & Lalumiere, 2009). This sequence of events illustrates the potential information value of case study accounts.

To sum up, the case study is an excellent way of examining the behaviour of a single individual in great detail and of generating hypotheses that can later be evaluated by controlled research. It is useful in clinical settings, where the focus is on just one person. But when general, universal laws are sought to explain phenomena, the case study is of limited use. A case study may not reveal principles characteristic of people in general and is unable to provide satisfactory evidence concerning cause–effect relationships.

EPIDEMIOLOGICAL RESEARCH

As described in Chapter 3, **epidemiology** is the study of the frequency and distribution of a disorder in a population. In epidemiological research, data are gathered about the rates of a disorder and its possible correlates in a large sample or population. This information can then be used to give a general picture of a disorder, how many people it affects, whether it is more common in men than in women, and whether its occurrence also varies according to social and cultural factors.

Epidemiological research focuses on determining three features of a disorder:

1. **prevalence**—the proportion of a population that has the disorder at a given point or period of time
2. **incidence**—the number of new cases of the disorder that occur in some period, usually a year
3. **risk factors**—conditions or variables that, if present, increase the likelihood of developing the disorder

Knowing the prevalence and incidence rates of various mental disorders and the risk factors associated with these disorders is important for planning health care facilities and services and for allocating provincial and federal grants for the study of disorders. Canadian Perspectives 5.1 presents additional information on how epidemiological and related research can be used to clarify the relationship between risk factors and mental disorder.

CANADIAN PERSPECTIVES 5.1
EARLY RISK FACTORS AND PSYCHOLOGICAL DISORDERS IN A CANADIAN SETTING: THE ROLE OF ABUSE

The 1990 Ontario *Mental Health Supplement* study (Offord et al., 1996; Ontario Ministry of Health, 1994) examined the relation between selected risk factors and mental disorders in people living in the community. Risk factors included the experience of severe physical or sexual abuse as a child, a history of paren-

tal mental disorder, and failure to graduate from high school. The relation between selected socio-demographic features (unemployment, public assistance, and low income) and mental disorders was also assessed. People with a disorder ("disordered group") were compared with those without a disorder ("healthy

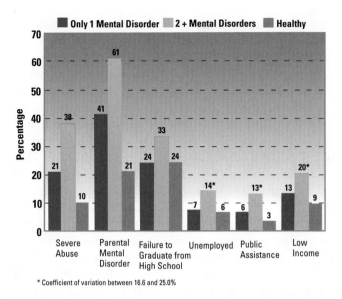

FIGURE 5.2 Early risk factors and associated socio-demographic features for people age 15 to 64 with one or with two or more mental disorders. Ontario Health Survey, 1990, *Mental Health Supplement*

group"). Figure 5.2 provides information on two groups with mental disorders: those with only one disorder and those with two or more disorders. Clearly, those with two or more disorders are especially disadvantaged, relative to both the healthy group and the single-disorder group, on all of the theorized risk and socio-demographic factors.

Parental mental disorder and **severe abuse** are the strongest risk factors from among all of the variables examined. For example, 61% of participants with two or more disorders and 41% of those with one disorder reported that their parents had a mental disorder, whereas only 21% of the healthy group reported evidence of mental disorder in a parent. These results are consistent with the findings related to "parental psychopathologies" and "familial aggregation" from the U.S. National Comorbidity Study (Kendler, Davis, & Kessler, 1997; Kessler, Davis, & Kendler, 1997). A long history of research findings supports an association between mental disorder in parents and psychological problems in their offspring. Evidence for the link between abuse, especially child sexual abuse (CSA), and mental disorders is relatively more recent. We will assess the link between child abuse and *specific* disorders in more detail in subsequent chapters. Issues related to intervention and prevention of CSA are also discussed in Chapter 14, and elder abuse in Canada is covered in Chapter 16.

The Ontario epidemiological study found that 38% of people with two or more disorders reported experiencing severe sexual or physical abuse as a child and that the comparable figures for the one-disorder and healthy groups were 21% and 10%, respectively. Sexual abuse ranged from repeated indecent exposure to being sexually attacked, while physical abuse included being pushed, grabbed, shoved, and physically attacked. Further analyses by Harriet MacMillan et al. (1997) of McMaster University found that 13% of women and 4% of men in the general population had been sexually abused

during childhood or adolescence. This history of abuse confers increased likelihood of lifetime psychopathology in various forms, an association that is stronger for women than men (MacMillan et al., 2001). According to the Government of Canada (2006) report summary, in excess of 30% of First Nations and Inuit adults probably experienced CSA. Among Ontario's First Nations communities, 14% of boys and 28% of girls in the current generation of youth (12–17 years old) reported some form of sexual abuse. These are much higher rates than for non-Aboriginal children.

Results similar to the Ontario study were reported by Kessler, Davis, and Kendler (1997), who found that interpersonal traumas (being molested, raped, mugged, or kidnapped; being physically attacked; suffering parental aggression) were the most consistent predictors of disorders after parental psychopathologies. A more recent analysis of the U.S. National Comorbidty Survey (Shevlin, Dorahy, & Adamson, 2007) determined that childhood physical abuse (after depression was controlled) increased the probability of a classification of psychosis and found a significant cumulative relation between trauma and psychosis, with the number of trauma types experienced increasing psychosis likelihood. Further, being raped had higher predictive value for psychosis in male participants.

In follow-up analyses of women in the Ontario study, McHolm, MacMillan, and Jamieson (2003) reported that childhood abuse is associated with increased suicide ideation among women with major depressive disorder. Subsequently, Tonmyr, Jamieson, Mery, and MacMillan (2005) reported that both CSA and physical abuse were important correlates of disability (limitations or restrictions in work or school performance or everyday activities) due to mental health problems. Among the approximately 3% of women with a disability, about 50% had been abused while growing up. In other analyses of these same women, respondents who reported abuse were two to four times more likely to report running away from home before age 16 years (Andres-Lemay, Jamieson, & MacMillan, 2005). The most significant additional correlate of running away was parental psychiatric disorder. There was a significant association between runaway behaviour and lifetime prevalence of psychiatric disorder.

Some cases of abuse are so appalling and disturbing as to defy credibility. Can these cases, even though rare, really happen in contemporary Canadian society? A high-profile case in the village of Blackstock, Ontario, that came to light in June 2001 was described by police officers as the worst case of child abuse they had ever seen. The parents of two teenaged boys, 14 and 15 years old, were charged with forcible confinement, assault, assault with a weapon, aggravated assault, and failing to provide the necessities of life. The mother was also charged with administering a noxious substance. Police alleged that the boys were locked in separate covered cribs for long periods over the preceding 10 years. They were apparently forced to wear diapers, physically punished, and denied sufficient food. Can you imagine the possible long-term psychological consequences of abuse such as this? Although the parents were initially given a sentence of only nine months, the Ontario Court of Appeal sentenced the mother and father to five and four years, respectively, in federal penitentiaries (Tyler, 2004).

What role should governments and individuals play in protecting children from abuse? Canada has had child protection legislation since 1893 (Walters, 1995). Since 1980, the provinces and territories have enacted "duty-to-report" legislation in order to further protect those children whose safety and needs are at risk. Thus, it is now mandatory to report children who need "protection" using a "best interests of the child" test. In the case of the two teens described above, a local child welfare agency reported the suspicion of abuse to the police. One major incentive behind Canada's duty-to-report legislation is to reduce the long-term negative consequences of abuse and neglect. Organizers of Capital Health's Child and Adolescent Protection Centre, an Edmonton program for investigating alleged child abuse, reported that they saw 50% more children than expected during the first year of operation (CMAJ, 2000). More than half of the 450 cases involved allegations of CSA and 236 cases involved children younger than five years old!

According to the 2003 Canadian Incidence Study of Reported Child Abuse and Neglect (Trocmé et al., 2005), the proportion of on-reserve First Nation children who have been investigated for alleged maltreatment is significantly higher than is the case for other Canadian children, and the most important reason why First Nation children come to the attention of child welfare personnel is parental physical neglect (due to poverty, poor housing, and addictions). According to Blackstock (2003) there are more Aboriginal children living in out-of-home care than there ever were during the era of residential schools. Wien, Blackstock, Loxley, and Trocmé (2007) claim that First Nation child welfare agencies can be better than provincial agencies "in finding ways to care for children in need within their own communities, and in providing services that are culturally appropriate" if given the flexibility and necessary resources (pp. 12–13).

People deplore sexual, physical, and emotional abuse and neglect of children and adults. But what about the use of "spanking" as punishment for naughty children? Spanking is a hotly debated issue (whether or not it should ever occur, under what circumstances, at what age, etc.) among both mental health professionals and the Canadian public. MacMillan and her colleagues (MacMillan et al., 1999) examined the link between retrospective reports of slapping and spanking and lifetime prevalence of four categories of psychiatric disorder using data from the *Mental Health Supplement* survey and concluded that there is a strong association between frequency of slapping and spanking and a lifetime prevalence of anxiety disorder, abuse of alcohol, and externalizing (or under-controlled) disorders, such as conduct disorder. The association with major depression was not significant. The authors included respondents who reported being spanked or slapped "often" or "sometimes," but only from among those *without* a history of physical or sexual abuse during childhood in order to remove the confounding effects of abusive experiences with spanking. (Spanking was not included as a criterion for physical abuse.)

While the findings appeared to support a link between spanking in childhood and the prevalence of mental disorders, certain shortcomings and limitations must be acknowledged. Similar limitations are found in many, if not most, epidemiological studies. As noted by MacMillan et al. (1999), the measure of spanking experience was taken retrospectively and there was no opportunity for objective, independent corroboration. Furthermore, people's inability or limited ability to recall experiences that occur before the age of five may have led to an *underestimation* of the prevalence of spanking, although it is also possible, given the self-report methodology, that some respondents were unwilling to disclose painful and embarrassing memories. It is also possible that some recollections of spanking and slapping (and of physical and sexual abuse) were recovered memories (see Chapter 7; also discussed in Chapter 18). Finally, the cross-sectional nature of the research precludes making definitive statements about cause–effect relationships.

In summary, the results of the major epidemiological study conducted in Ontario and other recent Canadian and international studies suggest that severe physical and sexual abuse and even spanking and slapping are risk factors for the onset and/or persistence of adult psychiatric disorders. The authors of the initial Ontario report (Ontario Ministry of Health, 1994) acknowledged that it is unclear how mistreatment in childhood leads to adult mental disorder but argued that research into the issue deserves government priority and that "there is an urgent need for effective programs both to prevent child abuse and to minimize its harmful after-effects" (p. 15). However, analyses of data from the National Comorbidity Survey indicate that caution is needed in interpreting the findings of single-adversity, single-disorder studies. Kessler, Davis, and Kendler (1997) reported a strong *clustering* among reported childhood adversities and lifetime comorbidity of *DSM-III-R* disorders. Thus, it is possible that *specific* adversities that occur in childhood do not result in specific disorders found in adulthood.

Although the strengths of Ontario's *Mental Health Supplement* study include a rigorous methodology, sophisticated sampling techniques, and a relatively large sample of respondents, the study has several limitations. For example, results from people over 64 years were excluded because prevalence rates were too low for meaningful analyses. Further, the sample did not include anyone living in an institution, homeless people, and Aboriginal people living on reserves. Schizophrenia and related psychoses were not reported because few people were identified with these conditions. Surprisingly, despite interest in eating disorders, anorexia nervosa was excluded "because of a mistake in the questionnaire" (Ontario Ministry of Health, 1994, p. 5).

Thinking Critically

1. Not everyone who experiences severe CSA develops a mental disorder. What other factors can play a role in determining how abuse affects a child? Is severe child abuse a necessary or sufficient condition for adult psychological disorders? Why or why not? What other risk or protective variables increase or decrease the likelihood that an abused child will develop a psychological disorder?

2. Based on your understanding of the cultural and contextual factors surrounding CSA in Canada's Aboriginal population,

how would you attempt to reduce the prevalence of abuse? Design a multifaceted intervention program. Should Native healing and spiritual activities play a role?

3. A history of childhood maltreatment is associated with a greater likelihood of dropping out of college or university. For example, Duncan (2000) found that only 35% of students with a history of multiple forms of abuse were still enrolled in the fourth year of their programs. What steps could be taken to improve the retention rates for students with a history of abuse?

4. Debate about whether or not slapping and spanking should be part of the spectrum of experiences that we classify as physical abuse has been divisive in Canada. Section 43 of the *Criminal Code* has permitted spanking of children provided that the force does not exceed what is "reasonable"

under the circumstances. On January 30, 2004, the Supreme Court, in a six–three decision (Canadian Foundation for Children, Youth and the Law v. Canada, 2004), ruled that parents, their stand-in caretakers, and teachers may use reasonable force if it is for "educative or corrective purposes"; however, the law does not protect or excuse "outbursts of violence against a child motivated by anger or animated by frustration." Infants under two and teenagers should never be spanked. What force is reasonable? The Court concluded that corporal punishment must involve only "minor corrective force of a transitory and trifling nature." What is your own position on this emotional issue? Would you ever consider it appropriate to "spank" your own child? Can we conclude that spanking *causes* psychological problems?

Clearly, knowledge about risk factors can give clues to the causes of disorders. For example, the Ontario study revealed that depression is about twice as common in women as in men. Thus, gender is a risk factor for depression. In Chapter 8, we will see that knowledge of this risk factor has led to a theory of depression that suggests that it is due to a particular style of coping with stress that is more common in women than in men. Thus, the results of epidemiological research may provide hypotheses that can be more thoroughly investigated using other research methods.

THE CORRELATIONAL METHOD

A great deal of research in psychopathology relies on the **correlational method**. This method establishes whether there is a relationship between or among two or more variables. It is often employed in epidemiological research, as well as in other studies. In correlational research, the variables being studied are measured as they exist in nature. This feature distinguishes the method from experimental research, in which variables are actually manipulated and controlled by the researcher. To understand this difference, consider that the possible role of stress in a disorder such as hypertension can be addressed with either a correlational or an experimental design. In a correlational study, we would measure stress levels by having people fill out a questionnaire or by interviewing them about their recent stressful experiences. Stress would then be correlated with blood pressure measurements collected from these same people. In an experimental study, in contrast, the experimenter would create or manipulate stress in the laboratory; for example, while their blood pressure was being monitored, some participants might be asked to give a speech to an audience about the aspect of their personal appearance they find least appealing (see Figure 5.3).

Correlational studies, then, address questions of the form "Are variable X and variable Y associated in some way so that they vary together (co-relate)?" For example, a national study

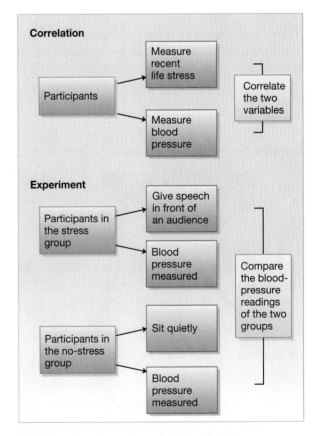

FIGURE 5.3 Correlational vs. experimental studies

of Canadian preschoolers showed that behavioural problems were higher among children from less affluent neighbourhoods (Kohen, Brooks-Gunn, Leventhal, & Hertzman, 2002).

MEASURING CORRELATION The first step in determining a correlation is to obtain pairs of observations of the variables in question, such as height and weight, for each member of a group of participants. Once such pairs of measurements are obtained, the strength of the relationship between the two sets of observations can be calculated to determine the **correlation coefficient**, denoted by the symbol r. This statistic may take any value between −1.00 and +1.00, and it measures both the magnitude and the direction of a relationship. The higher the absolute value of r, the larger or stronger the relationship between the two variables. An r of either +1.00 or −1.00 indicates the highest possible, or perfect, relationship, whereas an r of 0.00 indicates that the variables are unrelated. If the sign of r is positive, the two variables are said to be *positively related*; in other words, as the values for variable X increase, those for variable Y also tend to increase. For example, assume that the correlation between height and weight is +.88. This correlation would indicate a very strong positive relationship: as height increases, so does weight. Conversely, when the sign of r is negative, variables are said to be *negatively related*; as scores on one variable increase, those for the other tend to decrease. For example, the number of hours spent watching television is negatively correlated with grade point average.

Plotting a relationship graphically often helps make it clearer. Figure 5.4 presents what are called scatter diagrams of positive and negative correlations, as well as unrelated variables. In the diagrams, each point corresponds to two values determined for a given person, the value of variable X and that of variable Y. In perfect relationships, all the points fall on a straight line; if we know the value of only one of the variables for an individual, we can state with certainty the value of the other variable. Similarly, when the correlation is relatively large, there is only a small degree of scatter about the line of perfect correlation. The values tend to scatter increasingly and become dispersed as the correlations become lower. When the correlation reaches 0.00, knowledge of a person's score on one variable tells us nothing about his or her score on the other.

STATISTICAL SIGNIFICANCE Thus far we have established that the magnitude of a correlation coefficient tells us the strength of a relationship between two variables. But scientists demand a more rigorous evaluation of the importance of correlations and use the concept of statistical significance for this purpose. Essentially, **statistical significance** refers to the likelihood that the results of an investigation are due to chance. A statistically significant correlation is one that is not likely to have occurred by chance.

Traditionally, in psychological research, a correlation is considered statistically significant if the likelihood or probability that it is a chance finding is 5 or less in 100. This level of significance is called the .05 level, commonly written as $p = .05$ (the p stands for probability). In general, as

FIGURE 5.4 Scatter diagrams showing various degrees of correlational relationships

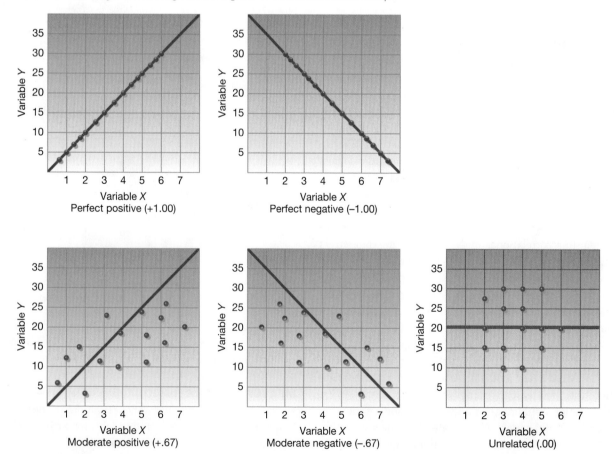

the size of the correlation coefficient increases, the result is more and more likely to be statistically significant. For example, a correlation of .80 is more likely to be significant than a correlation of .40. Whether a correlation attains statistical significance also depends on the number of observations made. The greater the number of observations, the smaller r (the correlation) needs to be to reach statistical significance. For example, a correlation of $r = .30$ is statistically significant when the number of observations is large—say, 300—but it would not be significant if only 20 observations were made. Thus, if the alcohol consumption of 10 depressed and 10 non-depressed men was studied and the correlation between depression and drinking was found to be .32, the correlation would not be statistically significant. However, the same correlation would be significant if two groups of 150 men were studied.

APPLICATIONS TO PSYCHOPATHOLOGY The correlational method is widely used in the field of abnormal psychology. Whenever we compare people given one diagnosis with those given another or with people without a psychological diagnosis, the study is correlational. For example, people with and people without an anxiety disorder may be compared on their physiological reactivity with a stressor administered in the laboratory.

When the correlational method is used in research on psychopathology, one of the variables is typically diagnosis; for example, whether the participant is diagnosed as having an anxiety disorder or not. To calculate a correlation between this variable and another one, diagnosis is quantified so that having an anxiety disorder is designated by a score of 1 and not having a disorder by a score of 2. (It does not matter what numbers are actually used.) The diagnosis variable can then be correlated with another variable, such as the amount of stress that has been recently experienced. An illustration of the data from such a study is presented in Table 5.1.

Often such investigations are not recognized as correlational, perhaps because participants come to a laboratory for testing. But the logic of such studies is correlational; the correlation between two variables—having an anxiety disorder or not and scores on the measure of recent life stress—is what is being examined. Variables such as having an anxiety disorder or not are called **classificatory variables.** The anxiety disorders were already present and were simply measured by the researcher. Other examples of classificatory variables are age, sex, social class, and body build. These variables are naturally occurring patterns and are not manipulated by the researcher, an important requirement for the experimental method discussed later. Thus, most research on the causes of psychopathology is correlational.

As an example, a recent U.S. study (Powers, Ressler, & Bradley, 2009) examined relations between reported childhood maltreatment, depression in adulthood, and perceived social support from family and friends. Childhood emotional abuse and neglect were shown to be more

TABLE 5.1 **DATA FOR A CORRELATIONAL STUDY**		
Participant Number	Diagnosis	Stress Score
1	1	65
2	1	72
3	2	40
4	1	86
5	2	72
6	2	21
7	1	65
8	2	40
9	1	37
10	2	28

Note: Diagnosis—having an anxiety disorder or not (with having an anxiety disorder designated as 1 and not having an anxiety disorder as 2)—is correlated with an assessment of recent life stress on a 0–100 scale. Higher scores indicate greater recent stress. As in previous examples, to make the point clearly, we present a smaller sample of cases than would be used in an actual research study. Notice that diagnosis is associated with recent life stress. Clients with an anxiety disorder tend to have higher stress scores than people without an anxiety disorder.

predictive of depression than sexual or physical abuse. Further, perceived friendship support appeared to protect (or "buffer") women against adult depression despite childhood maltreatment. In another 2009 study, MacMillan and her colleagues examined cortisol responses to a standard psychosocial stressor in a group of female youths exposed to childhood maltreatment, relative to a control group. While youth in the control group showed a typical increase in cortisol in reaction to the stressor, maltreated youth showed an attenuated response interpreted as support for hypothalamic-pituitary–adrenal axis dysregulation among maltreated youth that may play a role in their vulnerability to physical and psychological problems.

PROBLEMS OF CAUSALITY The correlational method, although often employed in abnormal psychology, has a critical drawback: it does not allow determination of cause–effect relationships. A sizeable correlation between two variables tells us only that they are related or tend to co-vary with each other, but we do not really know which is cause and which is effect or if either variable is actually the cause of the other.

The directionality problem When two variables are correlated, how can we tell which is the cause and which is the effect? For example, a correlation has been found between the diagnosis of schizophrenia and social class: lower-class people are more frequently diagnosed as having schizophrenia than are middle- and upper-class people. One possible explanation is that the stresses of living in the lowest social class cause an increase in the prevalence of schizophrenia. But a second and perhaps equally plausible hypothesis has been advanced. It may be that the disorganized behaviour patterns of individuals with schizophrenia cause them to perform poorly in their educational and occupational endeavours and thus to become impoverished. The **directionality problem**, as it is sometimes called, is present in many correlational research designs, hence the often-cited dictum, "Correlation does not imply causation."

Although correlation does not imply causation, determining whether two variables correlate may serve to disconfirm certain causal hypotheses; that is, causation does imply correlation. For example, if an investigator asserts that cigarette smoking causes lung cancer, he or she is implying that lung cancer and smoking will be correlated. Studies of these two variables must show this positive correlation or the theory will be disconfirmed.

One way of overcoming the directionality problem is based on the idea that causes must precede effects. According to this idea, studies investigating the hypothesized causes of psychopathology would use a prospective, longitudinal design in which the hypothesized causes are studied before a disorder has developed. In this way, the hypothesized causes could be measured before the effect. The most desirable way of collecting information about the development of schizophrenia, for example, would be to select a large sample of babies and follow them, measuring certain hypothesized causes, for the 20 to 45 years that are the period of risk for the onset of schizophrenia. But such a method would be prohibitively expensive, for only about 1 individual in 100 eventually develops schizophrenia. The yield of data from such a simple longitudinal study would be small indeed.

The **high-risk method** overcomes this problem. With this approach, only individuals with greater than average risk of developing schizophrenia in adulthood would be selected for study. Most current research using this methodology studies individuals who have a parent diagnosed with schizophrenia (having a parent with schizophrenia increases a person's risk for developing schizophrenia). The high-risk method is also used to study several other disorders, and we will examine these findings in subsequent chapters.

We can illustrate the longitudinal approach with a recent example in the area of maltreatment and depression. Prospective studies in this area are few. However, Liu, Alloy, Abramson, Iacoviella, and Whitehouse (2009) examined whether experiences of current emotional maltreatment predicted the development of new episodes of depression in vulnerable young adults followed prospectively for 2.5 years. Greater overall emotional maltreatment predicted shorter time to onset of new major and minor depression, and episodes of the subtype of hopelessness depression (see Chapter 8). Further, current emotional maltreatment from peers and from authority figures separately predicted shorter time to development of new hopelessness depression episodes.

The third-variable problem Another difficulty in interpreting correlational findings is called the **third-variable problem**; that is, the correlation may have been produced by a third, unforeseen factor. In the following example, an obvious third variable is identified.

> One regularly finds a high positive correlation between the number of churches in a city and the number of crimes committed in that city. That is, the more churches a city has, the more crimes are committed in it. Does this mean that religion fosters crime, or does it mean that crime fosters religion? It means neither. The relationship is due to a particular third variable—population. The higher the population of a particular community, the greater … the number of churches and … the frequency of criminal activity. (Neale & Liebert, 1980, p. 109)

Another example is the aforementioned study of Canadian preschoolers (see Kohen et al., 2002). Low neighbourhood income may be associated with child behaviour problems because of a third variable: children may be imitating frustrated parents who more frequently engage in behavioural dyscontrol.

Unfortunately, the psychopathologist is forced to make heavy use of the correlational method because diagnosis, a classificatory variable, is best suited to this strategy. But the relationships discovered between diagnosis and other variables are then clouded by the third-variable and directionality problems. Searching for the causes of the various psychopathologies will continue to be a challenging enterprise.

THE EXPERIMENT

The factors causing the associations and relationships revealed by correlational research cannot be determined with absolute certainty. The **experiment** is generally considered the most powerful tool for determining causal relationships between events. It involves the random assignment of participants to the different conditions being investigated, the manipulation of an independent variable, and the measurement of a dependent variable. In the field of psychopathology, the experiment is most often used to evaluate the effects of therapies.

As an introduction to the basic components of experimental research, let us consider here the major aspects of the design and results of a study of how expressing emotions about past traumatic events is related to health (Pennebaker, Kiecolt-Glaser, & Glaser, 1988). In this experiment, 50 undergraduates participated in a six-week study, one part of which required them to come to a laboratory for four consecutive days. On each of the four days, half the students wrote a short essay about a past traumatic event. They were instructed as follows:

> During each of the four writing days, I want you to write about the most traumatic and upsetting experiences of your entire life. You can write on different topics each day or on the same topic for all four days. The important thing is that you write about your deepest thoughts and feelings.

Ideally, whatever you write about should deal with an event or experience that you have not talked with others about in detail. (Pennebaker et al., 1988)

The remaining students also came to the laboratory each day, but they wrote essays describing such things as their daily activities, a recent social event, the shoes they were wearing, and their plans for the rest of the day.

Information about how often the participating undergraduates used the university health centre was obtained for the 15-week period before the study began and for the 6 weeks after it had begun. These data are shown in Figure 5.5. Members of the two groups had visited the health centre about equally prior to the experiment. After writing the essays, however, the number of visits declined for students who wrote about traumas and increased for the remaining students. (This increase may have been due to seasonal variation in rates of visits to the health centre, for the second measure of number of visits was taken in February, just before mid-term exams.) From these data the investigators concluded that expressing emotions has a beneficial effect on physical health.

BASIC FEATURES OF EXPERIMENTAL DESIGN The foregoing example illustrates many of the basic features of an experiment.

1. The researcher typically begins with an **experimental hypothesis**; that is, what he or she assumes will happen when a particular variable is manipulated. Pennebaker and his colleagues hypothesized that expressing emotion about a past event would improve health.
2. The investigator chooses an **independent variable** that can be manipulated; that is, some factor that will be under the experimenter's control. In the case of the Pennebaker study, some students wrote about past traumatic events and others about mundane happenings.
3. Participants are assigned to the two conditions by **random assignment** so that each participant has an equal chance of being in each condition.
4. The researcher arranges for the measurement of a **dependent variable**, something that is expected to depend on or vary with manipulations of the independent variable. The dependent variable in this study was the number of visits to the health centre.
5. When differences between groups are found to be a function of variations in the independent variable, the researcher is said to have produced an **experimental effect**.

An experiment led by Martin Zack from the Centre for Addiction and Mental Health involved manipulating mood by exposing University of Toronto introductory psychology students to either negative words, positive words, or neutral words (Zack et al., 2006). This experiment examined the effects of mood state on beer drinking. Thus, mood state was the independent variable and amount of beer drunk was the dependent variable. As expected, exposure to a negative mood state, relative to a positive or neutral mood state, resulted in drinking more beer. Long-suffering fans of the Toronto Maple Leafs may want to reflect on this finding!

To evaluate the importance of an experimental effect, as with correlations, researchers determine their statistical significance. To illustrate, consider a hypothetical study of the effectiveness of cognitive therapy in reducing depression among 20 depressed clients. In brief, the independent variable is cognitive therapy vs. no treatment; 10 clients are randomly assigned to receive cognitive therapy and 10 are randomly assigned to a no-treatment control group. The dependent variable is scores on a standardized measure of the severity of depression, assessed after 12 weeks of treatment or no treatment; higher scores reflect more severe depression.

Data for each of the clients in each group are presented in Table 5.2. Note that the average scores of the two groups differ considerably (8.3 for the cognitive-therapy group and 21.8 for the no-treatment group). This difference between groups, also called *between-group variance*, is the experimental effect; it has been caused by the independent variable. Note also from the table that the scores of individual participants within each group vary considerably; this is called *within-group variance*. Within the cognitive-therapy group, for example, most participants have low scores, but participant number 7 has a high score (18). Cognitive therapy did not seem to be of much help to this individual, but we don't know why. Similarly, most people in the no-treatment group have high scores, but participant number 17 has a low score (6). The cause of this within-group variability is unknown.

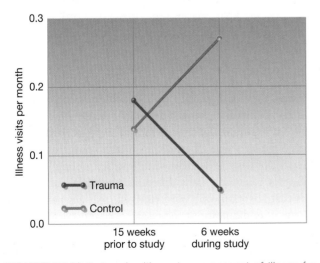

FIGURE 5.5 Visits to a health centre on account of illness for the periods before and during the experiment. From Pennebaker et al. (1988)

TABLE 5.2

RESULTS OF A HYPOTHETICAL STUDY COMPARING COGNITIVE THERAPY WITH NO TREATMENT FOR DEPRESSION

	Cognitive Therapy		No Treatment
Participant 1	8	Participant 11	22
Participant 2	6	Participant 12	14
Participant 3	12	Participant 13	26
Participant 4	4	Participant 14	28
Participant 5	3	Participant 15	19
Participant 6	6	Participant 16	27
Participant 7	18	Participant 17	6
Participant 8	14	Participant 18	32
Participant 9	7	Participant 19	21
Participant 10	5	Participant 20	23
Group Average	8.3		21.8

Note: Scores for each participant after treatment are shown.

Statistical significance is tested by dividing the between-group variance (the difference between the average scores of the two groups—in this example 21.8 − 8.3 = 13.5) by a measure of the within-group variance. When the average difference between the two groups is large relative to the within-group variance, the result is more likely to be statistically significant. From the results of this hypothetical experiment, we would conclude that cognitive therapy is more effective in decreasing depression than no treatment at all.

INTERNAL VALIDITY An important feature of any experimental design is the inclusion of at least one **control group** that does not receive the experimental treatment (the independent variable). A control group is necessary for comparative purposes if the effects in an experiment are to be attributed to the manipulation of the independent variable. In the Pennebaker study, the control group wrote about mundane happenings. In the cognitive-therapy example, the control group received no treatment. The data from a control group provide a standard against which the effects of an independent variable (in this case, expressing emotion or cognitive therapy) can be compared.

To illustrate this point with another example, consider a study of the effectiveness of a particular therapy in modifying some form of abnormal behaviour. An experiment conducted in Quebec examined the efficacy of cognitive-behavioural therapy in the treatment of generalized anxiety disorder (see Chapter 6). Laberge, Dugas, and Ladouceur (2000) found that the treatment was successful in reducing dysfunctional beliefs about worry. If there had been no control group, then it would not have been an experiment. However, the study did include a group of people with generalized anxiety disorder who were assigned randomly to a waiting list and had not yet received the therapeutic treatment. These individuals represented an effective comparison group because they were presumably similar in every respect to those who experienced the experimental treatment. If there had been no control group against which to compare the improvement, valid conclusions could not have been drawn. The reduction in dysfunctional beliefs from the beginning of the treatment to the end could have been brought about by several factors in addition to or instead of the treatment employed, such as the passage of time.

Variables such as the passage of time are often called **confounds.** Their effects are intermixed with those of the independent variable, and like the third variables in correlational studies, they make the results difficult or impossible to interpret. These confounds, as well as others, are widespread in research on the effects of psychotherapy, as is documented throughout this book. Studies in which the effect obtained cannot be attributed with confidence to the independent variable are called *internally invalid* studies. In contrast, research has **internal validity** when the effect can be confidently attributed to the manipulation of the independent variable.

In the study by Laberge et al. (2000), internal validity was improved by the inclusion of a control group. The changes in anxiety experienced by these control participants constituted a standard against which the effects of the independent variable could be assessed. If a change in anxiety is brought about by particular environmental events, quite beyond any therapeutic intervention, the experimental group receiving the treatment and the control group receiving no treatment are likely to be affected equally. On the other hand, if after six months the anxiety level of the treated group has lessened more than that of the untreated control group, we can be relatively confident that this difference is attributable to the treatment.

The inclusion of a control group does not always ensure internal validity, however. Consider yet another study of therapy: the treatment of two hospital wards of psychiatric clients. An investigator may decide to select one ward to receive an experimental treatment and another ward to be a control group. When the researcher later compares the frequencies of deviant behaviour in these two groups, he or she will want to attribute any differences between them to the fact that clients in one ward received treatment and those in the other did not. But the researcher cannot legitimately draw this inference, for there is a competing hypothesis that cannot be disproved. Even before treatment, the clients who happened to receive therapy might have had a lower level of deviant behaviour than the clients who became the control group. The principle of experimental design that was disregarded in this defective study is that of *random assignment*. This principle would be at work in a two-group experiment if a coin were tossed for each participant. If the coin turns up heads, the participant is assigned to one group; if tails, he or she is assigned to the other. This procedure minimizes the likelihood that differences between the groups after treatment will reflect pre-treatment differences in the samples rather than true experimental effects.

Furthermore, using both a control group and random assignment handles the type of confounds we described in our earlier example of treatment for high anxiety. When groups are formed by random assignment, confounds such as the resolution of a stressful life situation are equally likely to occur in both the treated group and the control group. There is no reason to believe that life stress would be resolved more often in one group than the other. Random assignment was employed in the experiments described earlier.

THE PLACEBO EFFECT Research on the effects of therapy—psychological or biological—should consider the **placebo effect**. This term refers to an improvement in a physical or psychological condition that is attributable to a client's expectations of help rather than to any specific active ingredient in a treatment. J. D. Frank (1978) related placebo effects to faith healing in prescientific or nonscientific societies. For centuries, suffering human beings have made pilgrimages to sanctified places and ingested sometimes foul-smelling concoctions in the belief that these efforts would improve their condition. Sometimes they did.

Many people dismiss placebo reactions as not real or as "second best" to the benefits of actual treatments. After all, if a person has a tension headache, what possible benefit can he or she hope to get from a pill that is totally devoid of chemical action or direct physiological effect? However, the placebo effect is commonly found and universally accepted in drug research. Indeed, the authors of a recent meta-analysis (see Focus on Discovery 5.1) of short-term placebo-controlled studies of newer antidepressants submitted to the U.S. Food and Drug Administration (FDA; Kirsch et al., 2008) concluded that "there seems little evidence to support the prescription of antidepressant medication to any but the most severely depressed patients unless alternative treatments have failed to provide benefit" (p. 0260). Although there may be problems with this conclusion (see Mathew & Charney, 2009), this research illustrates the importance of investigations that use a double-blind, placebo-controlled, randomized controlled trial (RCT) design, considered the "gold standard" in research to determine the efficacy of a given treatment. Similarly, Bridge and colleagues (2009) conducted a meta-analysis of "second generation" antidepressant trials conducted since 1995 involving children and adolescents with major depression. They reported that the average response to placebo was 48%, but the mean response to active medication was only

Young male Hindu pilgrims, known as Kanwarias, bathing in the Ganges River in India and collecting its sacred water to bring back to Hindu temples in their hometowns. The effects of religious pilgrimages like this one may be placebo effects. AP Photo/Rajesh Kumar Singh.

59%. We will examine the issue of the efficacy of antidepressants in greater detail in Focus on Discovery 5.1 and 5.2 and in chapters 8 and 15.

It is not a simple matter to extend the findings of research on chemical placebos directly to research on psychological placebos. In psychotherapy, the mere expectation of being helped can be an active ingredient. Why? If the theory adopted by the therapist holds that positive expectancy of improvement is an active ingredient, then improvement arising from the expectancy would by definition not be considered a placebo effect. Lambert, Shapiro, and Bergin (1986) argued that "placebo factors" should be replaced with the concept of "common factors" in the study of the effects of psychotherapy. They defined common factors as "those factors that are common to most therapies (such as expectation for improvement, persuasion, warmth and attention, understanding, encouragement, etc.)" (Lambert, Shapiro, & Bergin, 1986, p. 163). We will examine this issue in greater detail in Chapter 17.

Because of the importance of the placebo effect, researchers studying the effects of psychotherapy often use what are called **placebo control groups**. Clients in such groups typically have regular contact with a therapist and receive support and encouragement, but they do not receive what is regarded as the active ingredient in the kind of therapy under study (e.g., gradual exposure to a feared situation in a behavioural treatment of a phobia).

When the placebo control group design is used, clients are randomly assigned to either the treatment or the placebo group; to reduce the possibility of bias, neither the researchers nor the clients are allowed to know to which group any specific individual is assigned. Because neither the researchers nor the clients are aware of who has been placed in the treatment and placebo control groups, the design is referred to as a **double-blind procedure**. (Placebo control and double-blind procedures are, of course, also used in medication trials, as noted previously.)

Research in psychotherapy reveals that clients in placebo control groups generally improve more than clients in no-treatment groups—though often not as much as clients in treatment groups (Lambert et al., 1986). Most psychotherapies, because they offer support and encouragement, may share a common factor that contributes to improvement. The issue of common factors is important in the movement toward psychotherapy integration, a topic also examined in Chapter 17.

The place of placebo control groups in psychotherapy research is an often-debated and complex topic. A study that compares a particular therapy with no treatment at all and finds that therapy brings about more improvement does suggest that being treated is better than not being treated. This is not a trivial finding. But a given therapy usually tries to create improvement in a particular way—by removing the person's defences, by facilitating the individual's way to self-actualization, by extinguishing fears, and so forth. To determine whether these processes are at work and are effective, a study needs a control group of clients who are instilled with expectancies of help and who believe that something worthwhile and beneficial is being done for them. Indeed, Wampold, Minami, Tierney, Baskin, and Bhati (2005) claim that properly designed psychological placebos are as effective as accepted psychotherapies.

But using a placebo control group involves several problems. First, it raises ethical issues, for effective treatment is being withheld from some clients who might be harmed without treatment (e.g., suicidal individuals). Second, a double-blind placebo control group study is difficult to implement. Medications used in treating psychopathology typically produce side effects that are not produced by placebos. Therefore, both researchers and clients may come to know who is getting the active treatment and who is getting the placebo. Finally, informed consent is an issue. Potential participants in research must be informed about the details of the study in which they are being asked to participate. In a placebo control group study, participants must be told that they have some chance of being assigned to the placebo group. What does this knowledge do to the possibility of experiencing a placebo effect?

Problems such as these have led some researchers (e.g., Rothman & Michels, 1994) and organizations to suggest that placebo control groups in psychotherapy and drug treatment trials should be abandoned under most circumstances. Instead of comparing a group receiving a new treatment with a placebo control group, researchers could compare the group with one receiving the currently accepted standard treatment in the field. This approach is now frequently used. But what if there is no standard accepted treatment? Despite increased pressure against the use of placebo controls, others argue persuasively that they are a critical component of treatment trials (e.g., Charney et al., 2002). In a recent "In Debate" section of the *Canadian Journal of Psychiatry* on the

ethics of placebo-controlled clinical trials, Kathleen C. Glass, the Director of the Biomedical Ethics Unit at McGill University, concluded:

> Clinical and scientific arguments for the use of placebo controls, when there is established effective therapy, are unconvincing and conflict with recognized ethical and legal obligations. Further, physicians who are investigators cannot waive their obligations toward clients who participate in clinical trials. Participating in trials should never require the practice of substandard medicine or disadvantage clients. (Glass, 2008, p. 429)

EXTERNAL VALIDITY External validity is the extent to which results can be generalized beyond the immediate study. If investigators have demonstrated that a particular treatment helps a group of clients, they will undoubtedly want to conclude that this treatment will be effective in ministering to other clients, at other times, and in other places.

Determining the external validity of the results of a psychological experiment is difficult. Merely knowing that one is a participant in an experiment can alter behaviour, and thus the results produced in the laboratory might not automatically be produced in the natural environment. Furthermore, in the many instances where results are obtained from investigations with laboratory animals, such as rats, generalizations to human beings are risky indeed, since there are enormous differences between *Homo sapiens* and *Rattus norvegicus*. Researchers must be alert to the extent to which they claim generalization for findings, for there is no entirely adequate way of dealing with the questions of external validity. The best that can be done is to perform similar studies in new settings with new participants so that the limitations, or the generality, of a finding can be determined. This issue will be revisited in Chapter 17.

ANALOGUE EXPERIMENTS The experimental method is judged to be the most telling way to determine cause–effect relationships. The efficacy of treatments for psychopathology is usually evaluated by the experimental method, which has proved a powerful tool for determining whether a therapy reduces suffering. As mentioned earlier, however, this method has been little used by those seeking the causes of abnormal behaviour. Why?

Suppose that a researcher has hypothesized that a child's emotionally charged, overdependent relationship with his or her mother causes generalized anxiety disorder. An experimental test of this hypothesis would require assigning infants randomly to either of two groups of mothers. The mothers in one group would undergo an extensive training program to ensure that they would be able to create a highly emotional atmosphere and foster overdependence in children. The mothers in the second group would be trained not to create such a relationship with the children under their care. The researcher would wait until the participants in each group reached adulthood and then determine how many of them had developed generalized anxiety disorder.

Obviously, such an experimental design contains insurmountable practical problems. But practical issues are hardly the principal ones that must concern us. Consider the ethics of such an experiment. Would the potential scientific gain of proving that an overdependent relationship with a person's mother brings on generalized anxiety disorder outweigh the suffering that would be imposed on some of the participants? In almost any person's view, it would not. (Ethical issues are considered in detail in Chapter 18.)

In an effort to take advantage of the benefits of the experimental method, researchers seeking the causes of abnormal behaviour have sometimes used a format known as an **analogue experiment**. Investigators attempt to bring a related phenomenon—that is, an analogue—into the laboratory for more intensive study. Because a true experiment is now being conducted, results can be obtained that may be interpreted in cause–effect terms. However, the problem of external validity may be accentuated because the actual phenomenon of interest is not being studied.

In one type of analogue study, behaviour is rendered temporarily abnormal through experimental manipulations. For example, lactate infusion can elicit a panic attack, hypnotic suggestion can produce blindness similar to that seen in conversion disorder, and threats to self-esteem can increase anxiety and depression. If pathology can be experimentally induced by any one of these manipulations, the same process existing in the natural environment might well be a cause of the disorder.

The key to interpreting such studies lies in the validity of the independent variable as a reflection of some experience one might actually have in real life and of the dependent variable as an analogue of a clinical problem. Is a stressor encountered in the laboratory fundamentally similar to one that occurs in the natural environment? Are transient increases in anxiety or depression reasonable analogues of their clinical counterparts? Results of such experiments must be interpreted with great caution and generalized with care, although they can provide valuable information about the origins of psychopathology.

In another type of analogue study, participants are selected because they are considered similar to clients who have certain diagnoses. A large amount of research, for example, has been conducted with university students selected for study because they scored high on questionnaire measures of anxiety or depression. Are these somewhat anxious or depressed students, who do not have a clinical disorder, adequate analogues for those with an anxiety disorder or major depression?

Some animal experiments are analogue in nature. They become analogue data when we draw implications from them and apply them to other domains, such as anxiety in human

Harlow's famous analogue research examined the effects of early separation from the mother on infant monkeys. Even a cloth surrogate mother helps prevent the subsequent emotional distress and depression that would result from isolation. Martin Rogers/Woodfin Camp & Associates.

beings. For example, research on avoidance learning in rats was influential in the formulation of theories of anxiety in humans. We are arguing by analogy when we attempt to relate fear reactions of rats to anxiety in people.

We do not agree with those who regard analogue research as totally and intrinsically worthless for the study of abnormal behaviour. For example, although human beings and other mammals differ on many important dimensions, it does not follow that principles of behaviour derived from animal research are necessarily irrelevant to human behaviour. For example, Krishnan, Berton, & Nestler (2008) argued that animal models are essential to study developmental mechanisms for psychiatric disorders and to develop novel therapy approaches. They developed a mouse model of "resilience" to stress that employs a "chronic social defeat paradigm" in which social defeat (the stress response) is accomplished by forcing a mouse to enter a space "territorialized" by a larger, more aggressive mouse. Defeated mice were segregated into those that showed clear deficits in social interaction ("susceptible") and those that did not ("unsusceptible" or resilient). Krishnan et al. discovered that only susceptible mice showed mouse analogues of human depression (e.g., weight loss) and various unique differences in brain structure and function confirmed in postmortem depressed humans (i.e., elevations of brain-derived neurotrophic factor in the nucleus accumbens). It is important to consider analogue findings in concert with findings derived from other methods.

SINGLE-SUBJECT EXPERIMENTAL RESEARCH

We have been discussing experimental research as it is conducted on groups of participants, but experiments do not always have to be conducted on groups. In **single-subject experimental designs**, participants are studied one at a time and experience a manipulated variable. The strategy appears to violate many principles of research design. There is no control group to act as a check on a single subject. Moreover, generalization is difficult because the findings may relate to a unique aspect of the one individual whose behaviour has been explored. Hence, the study of a single individual would appear unlikely to yield any findings that could possess the slightest degree of internal or external validity. Nevertheless, the experimental study of a single subject can be an effective research technique for certain purposes.

A case study reported by Hendricks and Thompson (2005) serves as an example. They illustrated the integration of both cognitive-behavioural therapy (CBT) and interpersonal therapy (IPT) for the treatment of bulimia nervosa complicated by depression and alcohol abuse. Their approach was based on the case formulation method introduced in Chapter 4.

Rebecca, a 25-year-old Hispanic female, referred herself for treatment of eating difficulties and depressed mood. At intake, she was 6 ft tall and weighed 150 lb (body mass index [BMI] = 20.3). She reported binging and inducing vomiting approximately once per week, and dated the onset of this behavior at 3 months before coming to therapy. She recalled that she had never had any concerns about her physical appearance until the time of her first romantic relationship at age 21. Apparently, her first boyfriend criticized her 175-lb (BMI = 23.7) physique and pressured her to lose weight, substantially affecting the way she viewed her body. At the end of this relationship, Rebecca felt disgusted with her appearance and decided that the only way to ensure success in her future relationships was to lose weight. An additional precipitating factor for her eating disturbance appeared to be graduation from college at age 22. Feeling that she had little control over the direction of her life, Rebecca restricted her eating behavior in an attempt to "have control over something" in her life. At one point, her body weight dropped to 135 lb (BMI = 18.3). Alarmed at her behavior, Rebecca moved to her hometown to be closer to her family and friends. She slightly increased her food intake and gradually gained weight, however, she remained unhappy and was determined to restrict her diet and modify her appearance. According to her report, Rebecca began to binge and vomit as a way to cope with her depression. To further manage her negative affect,

she began drinking to intoxication two to three times per week. These binge drinking episodes often coincided with her episodes of binging/purging. (Hendricks & Thompson, 2005, pp. 171–172) Reprinted with permission of John Wiley & Sons, Inc.

Specific CBT and IPT strategies were selected and implemented by Hendricks and Thompson based on the conceptualization of the specific factors pertinent to Rebecca's difficulties. Figure 5.6 summarizes treatment outcomes for behavioural measures recorded throughout the treatment and follow-up: Stage 1 focused on reduction of restrictive eating behaviour and binge drinking through specific CBT techniques; Stage 2 focused on negative thoughts regarding shape and body appearance using other CBT techniques; Stage 3 additionally employed CBT relapse prevention strategies; Stage 4 employed IPT since Rebecca continued to purge in response to interpersonal crises. Rebecca was no longer experiencing clinically significant symptoms of bulimia, alcohol abuse, or depression at the end of treatment (12 months) or follow-up (18 months post-treatment onset).

Hendricks and Thompson (2005) concluded that CBT is possibly more effective in the elimination of binge eating and binge drinking, whereas IPT may be more effective in reducing purging. Not shown in Figure 5.6 is the reduction in depression, which is possibly due to either or both interventions. According to the authors, the findings have important implications because the results support (1) the possible effectiveness of the case formulation approach relative to a standard, manualized treatment; (2) the integration of CBT and IPT for the treatment of bulimia; and (3) theories that ascribe a critical

FIGURE 5.6 Self-reported incidence of binge eating (pink bars), vomiting (blue bars), and binge drinking (green bars). Stage 1=0–1 months; Stage 2=1–2 months; Stage 3=2–5 months; Stage 4=5–18 months

Source: "An Integration of Cognitive-Behavioural Therapy and Interpersonal Psychotherapy for Bulimia Nervosa: A Case Study Using the Case Formulation Method," by P. S. Hendricks and J. K. Thompson, 2005, *International Journal of Eating Disorders*, 37, pp. 171–174. Reprinted with permission of John Wiley & Sons, Inc.

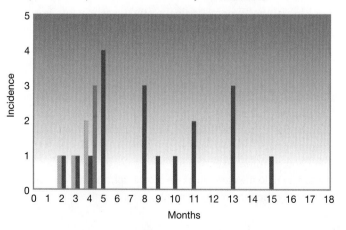

role for interpersonal difficulties in the "core eating disorder pathology" (Hendricks & Thompson, 2005, p. 174).

In another form of single-case design, usually referred to as a **reversal design or ABAB** design, some aspect of the participant's behaviour is carefully measured in a specific sequence: (1) during an initial time period, the baseline (A); (2) during a period when a treatment is introduced (B); (3) during a reinstatement of the conditions that prevailed in the baseline period (A); and (4) finally, during a reintroduction of the experimental manipulation (B). If behaviour in the experimental period is different from that in the baseline period, reverses when the experimentally manipulated conditions are reversed, and re-reverses when the treatment is again introduced, there is little doubt that the manipulation, rather than chance or uncontrolled factors, has produced the change. The reversal technique cannot always be employed, however, for a participant's initial state may not be recoverable. Treatment aims to produce enduring change—the goal of all therapeutic interventions. Further, reinstating the client's original condition would generally be considered unethical. The ABAB design is most appropriate when it is assumed that the effects of manipulations are temporary. Sometimes an AB time series design is informative. For example, Wragg and Whitehead (2004) investigated CBT with a 15-year-old girl with first episode psychosis. After a baseline assessment (A) she received a 16-week CBT intervention for psychosis (B). Previous work had not focused on CBT for adolescents with psychosis. Although there were improvements in symptoms of psychosis, anxiety, and depression, the results were inconclusive for other measures, including self-esteem and an integrative recovery style (related to relapse). The authors hypothesized that the girl's negative self-evaluations were responsible for the negative results and concluded that a further series of single case studies should be conducted to target negative person evaluations before initiating a randomized control trial.

The fact that a treatment works for a single subject does not necessarily imply that it will be universally effective. If the search for more widely applicable treatment is a major focus, the single-subject design may help investigators decide whether large-scale research with groups is warranted. Hendricks and Thompson (2005) suggested that future research should explore the efficacy of integrative CBT-IPT treatments with large samples of people with bulimia nervosa. This strategy was actually used successfully by Robert Ladouceur and his colleagues at Université Laval in Quebec City in the development of their cognitive-behavioural treatment of pathological gamblers (see Chapter 3). Bujold, Ladouceur, Sylvain, and Boisvert (1994) employed a single-subject design to test a treatment program that had four components: cognitive correction of erroneous perceptions about gambling, problem-solving training, social skills training, and relapse prevention. Following the combined treatment, participants no longer met the criteria for pathological gambling and the

positive outcome was maintained at a nine-month follow-up. This success led to evaluation of the efficacy of the treatment package in a controlled group study (see the next section on mixed designs). Sylvain et al. (1997) reported significant changes in the treatment group, relative to a wait-list control group, on various outcome measures. The therapeutic gains were maintained at 6- and 12-month follow-ups.

However, wouldn't it be useful to know more precisely what the active components of the program are? Ladouceur and his associates hypothesized that the key factor in the development and maintenance of pathological gambling is the erroneous perceptions that gamblers have. According to their theory (Ladouceur & Walker, 1998), the core cognitive error relates to the gambler's misconception about randomness. Gamblers develop a set of false beliefs, thinking that they can control events governed by chance. They develop superstitious behaviours that they believe can increase the likelihood of winning (e.g., wearing a lucky tie while gambling). But, in fact, the "house" ultimately wins in all legalized forms of gambling! Ladouceur et al. (1998), therefore, evaluated the efficacy of an exclusively cognitive intervention to correct the pathological gambler's dysfunctional schema. Five pathological gamblers were treated in a single-subject multiple-baseline design. The treatment was successful for four of the participants, suggesting that a cognitive intervention that focuses on the gambler's misconception about the notion of randomness holds promise as a treatment for pathological gambling. Of course, the fact that the treatment was unsuccessful with one participant is an indication that other factors must also be considered.

MIXED DESIGNS

Experimental and correlational research techniques can be combined in what is called a **mixed design**. Participants from two or more discrete and typically non-overlapping populations are assigned to each experimental condition. The two different types of populations—for example, clients with either schizophrenia or a phobia—constitute a classificatory variable; that is, the variables of schizophrenia and phobia were neither manipulated nor created by the investigator, and they can only be correlated with the manipulated conditions, which are true experimental variables.

As an example of how a mixed design is applied, consider an investigation of the effectiveness of three types of therapy (the experimental variable) on clients divided into two groups on the basis of the severity of their illnesses (the classificatory or correlational variable). The question is whether the effectiveness of the treatments varies with the severity of illness. The hypothetical outcome of such a study is presented in Figure 5.7. Figure 5.7a illustrates the unfortunate conclusions that would be drawn were the clients not divided into those with severe and those with less severe illnesses. When all clients are grouped together, treatment 3 produces the greatest amount of improvement. Therefore, if no information about differential characteristics of the clients is available, treatment 3 would be

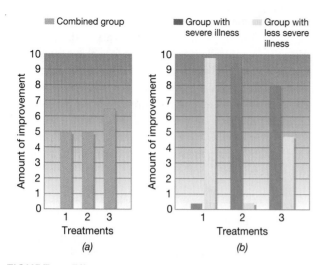

FIGURE 5.7 Effects of three treatments on clients whose symptoms vary in degree of severity. (*a*) When the severity of the illness is not known and the clients are grouped together, treatment number 3 appears to be the best. (*b*) The same data as in (*a*) are reanalyzed, dividing clients by severity. Now treatment 3 is no longer best for any clients

preferred. When the severity of the clients' difficulties is considered, however, treatment 3 is no longer the therapy of choice for any of the clients. Rather, as seen in Figure 5.7b, treatment 1 would be selected for those with less severe illness and treatment 2 for clients with more severe illness. Thus, a mixed design can identify which treatment applies best to which group of clients.

In interpreting the results of mixed designs, we must always be aware of the fact that one of the variables (severity of illness in our example) is not manipulated but is instead a classificatory or correlational variable. Therefore, the problems in interpreting correlations, especially the possible operation of third variables, arise in interpreting the results of mixed designs, as well.

Although not strictly a mixed design, the previously cited study by Bridge et al. (2009) focused on placebo response and they concluded that lower baseline depression severity and younger age are associated with higher placebo response. The strongest predictor of the placebo response was the number of study sites. Bridge et al. suggested that the methodology of clinical trials can be improved by carefully recruiting from fewer sites children and adolescents with moderate to severe depression. In an editorial comment, Emslie (2009) stated that, "including only moderately to severely depressed youths will increase the probability of identifying a signal of whether a particular compound has antidepressant properties in the pediatric age group by decreasing the number of subjects who respond to placebo" (p. 2).

A summary of the major research methods of abnormal psychology, and their strengths and weaknesses, appears in Table 5.3. You have probably concluded that there is no perfect method that will easily reveal the secrets of psychopathology and therapy. You are correct! Scientific knowledge is based on integrating or synthesizing a body of evidence yielded by investigations conducted with varying methodologies, not on merely considering individual studies one at a time.

TABLE 5.3
RESEARCH METHODS IN ABNORMAL PSYCHOLOGY

Method	Description	Evaluation
Case study	Collection of detailed historical and biographical information on a single individual	Excellent source of hypotheses but cannot determine causal relationships because cannot rule out alternative hypotheses
Epidemiology	Study of the frequency and distribution of a disorder in a population; determines incidence, prevalence, and risk factors	Knowledge of risk factors provides clues regarding causes of disorders
Correlation	Study of the relationship between two or more variables; variables are measured as they exist in nature	Cannot determine causality because of the directionality and third-variable problems; used extensively in research on the causes of psycho pathology because diagnosis is a correlational or classificatory variable
Experiment with groups of participants	Includes a manipulated independent variable, a dependent variable, at least one control group, and random assignment	Most powerful method for determining causal relationships; used mainly in studies of the effectiveness of therapies
Experiment with single subjects	Includes a manipulated variable and contrasts behaviour during the time the manipulation is occurring with behaviour during a period when the manipulation is not occurring (as in the ABAB design)	Can demonstrate causal relationships, although generalization can be a problem
Mixed design	Includes both an experimental (manipulated) variable and a classificatory (correlational) variable	Can demonstrate that an experimental condition (e.g., a type of therapy) has different effects depending on the variable (e.g., severity of illness)

How does a researcher or clinician go about drawing conclusions from a series of published or otherwise available investigations? A simple strategy is to read individual studies, mull them over, and decide what they mean overall. The disadvantage with this approach is that the researcher's biases and subjective impressions can play a significant role in determining what conclusion is drawn. It is fairly common for two scientists to read the same studies and reach very different conclusions. Is there a solution to this problem? Focus on Discovery 5.1 discusses how scientists synthesize information using a method called *meta-analysis*.

A clinician must have a very clear understanding of the evidence, both positive and negative, to adequately inform clients and caregivers. The primary source of such information comes from published articles in peer-reviewed scientific journals. But what if important evidence isn't published or otherwise readily available to clinicians? What if the "evidence" changes as a function of the publication process? Focus on Discovery 5.2 summarizes a controversial study on the selective publication of antidepressant trials and the influence on apparent efficacy.

FOCUS ON DISCOVERY 5.1
META-ANALYSIS: THE EFFECTS OF PSYCHOTHERAPY AND BEYOND

"The reality is that, despite the claims of true believers, meta-analysis is neither a purely objective, mechanical process nor a panacea for answering all questions."

—Streiner (2005, p. 829)

Smith, Glass, and Miller (1980) originally devised **meta-analysis** as a new way to evaluate the effects of psychotherapy. The first step is a thorough literature search to identify all relevant studies. Because these studies have typically reported their findings in different formats and used different statistical tests, meta-analysis then puts all the results into a common format, using a statistic called the *effect size*. In the case of treatment, the effect size offers a way of standardizing the differences in improvement between, for example, a therapy group and a control group, or between groups receiving two different types of therapy, so that the results of many different studies can be averaged. The independent variables can be any factors considered influential in the outcome.

In their oft-cited report, Smith et al. (1980) meta-analyzed 475 psychotherapy outcome studies involving more than 25,000 clients and 1,700 effect sizes. They came to two conclusions that have attracted considerable attention and controversy. First, they concluded that a wide range of therapies produce more improvement than does no treatment. Specifically, treated clients were found to be better off than almost 80% of untreated clients. Subsequent meta-analyses by other authors have confirmed these early findings (e.g., Lambert & Ogles, 2004). Second, Smith et al. contended that effect sizes across diverse modes of intervention do not differ from one another; that is, different therapies are about equally effective. This second conclusion has been especially contentious. Some subsequent meta-analytic studies compared insight therapy with cognitive and behavioural interventions and concluded that there is a slight but consistent advantage for the latter, although some proponents of insight therapy contend that behavioural and cognitive therapies focus on milder disorders (see Lambert & Ogles, 2004).

Since the pioneering work by Smith et al. (1980), there has been an exponential explosion of meta-analytic reports in

the psychological and medical research literature. Indeed, David Streiner (2005) of the Baycrest Centre for Geriatric Care in Toronto noted that while there were only 3 published meta-analyses in 1981, in 2003, there were 1,712. Meta-analysis has been applied to forms of intervention other than psychotherapy, including biological treatments. For example, numerous meta-analyses have evaluated the efficacy of antidepressants. In an evaluation of these meta-analyses, Moncrieff and Kirsch (2005) concluded that selective serotonin reuptake inhibitors (SSRIs) "have no clinically meaningful advantage over placebo" (p. 157). They further argued that any statistical superiority over placebos is due to "methodological artifacts." Needless to say, these conclusions were controversial, especially since at least four other meta-analyses previously supported the use of this class of drugs for the treatment of depression, including one coauthored by Moncrieff himself! Although there have been numerous analyses of the problems and pitfalls of meta-analysis, Streiner (2005) attempted to explain once again "why different people with honourable intentions can come to different conclusions regarding meta-analyses" (p. 829). Why are such debates ongoing after more than 25 years? Why doesn't meta-analysis provide definitive answers?

First, meta-analysis is a complicated process that requires decisions at each of numerous phases or steps based on a degree of judgement, and equally competent researchers can make different decisions that affect the ultimate conclusions (see also Butler, Chapman, Forman, & Beck, 2006). These outcomes can be influenced right from the initial step of posing the question. For example, if we ask the question, "Are SSRIs more effective than CBT in treating depression?" we raise a long list of issues, including whether we should focus on all types of depression or limit our analyses to a specific form of depression, and so forth. One key consideration is whether the meta-analysis examines the results separately for various disorders or tends to lump the results together for various disorders. It is has been suggested strongly that results must be examined separately for specific disorders of the same general type (e.g., anxiety disorders) because the efficacy of treatment often varies substantially across disorders (Deacon &

Abramovitz, 2004). Thus, what works for panic disorder may not be as effective for separation anxiety disorder, for instance. Streiner notes that there are no correct answers to the myriad questions and that different investigators can make different but equally plausible decisions. When researchers conduct a meta-analysis, they must rely on past studies and these studies may have key limitations and differ in quality. Indeed, Streiner claims that the majority of published studies are missing critical information, and it is necessary to choose to fill in the information somehow or reject the study. Meta-analyses conducted on studies that used, for example, measures with poor reliability and validity can result in misleading conclusions. Also, Butler et al. (2006) consider meta-analyses to be more informative if the results also take into account **moderator variables** (i.e., other factors such as gender that may influence or qualify the results in some meaningful way). For example, Orth and Weiland (2006) used meta-analysis to synthesize data on the association between anger-hostility and post-traumatic stress disorder. Moderator analyses revealed that effect sizes were much larger in samples with military war experience than in samples that had experienced other forms of traumatic event. As another example, Malouff, Thorsteinsson, and Schutte (2007) described a meta-analysis of 31 studies that examined the efficacy of problem-solving therapy in reducing mental and physical health problems. Problem-solving therapy involves teaching clients how to use a step-by-step process to solve life problems (see D'Zurilla & Nezu, 2010). Malouff et al. concluded that problem-solving therapy was more effective than no treatment, treatment as usual, and attention placebo ("inactive" treatment control that provides equivalent attention and positive expectations of improvement), but not more effective than other bona fide treatments offered as part of a study. Significant moderators included whether the problem-solving therapy involved training in applying a problem-solving orientation to life, whether homework was assigned, and whether a developer of problem-solving therapy helped conduct the study!

Second, how do we interpret the results of the meta-analysis? Streiner considers this issue to be the heart of the Moncrieff and Kirsch (2005) controversy. Consistent with previous meta-analyses, they concluded that there is a statistically significant effect of SSRIs on depression relative to placebos, but argue that it is a trivial difference that is not of clinical importance—a clinical judgement. As noted by Streiner (2005), "This is not an issue that can be resolved through statistical argument or recourse to picking nits about methodology" (p. 830). Of course, other scholars can find fault with that judgement. Streiner also noted that a by-product of the need to make decisions at each stage and when interpreting the results means that there will always be differences among meta-analyses of the same topic and that summaries of these meta-analyses can also be selective and a different interpretation can be placed on the results than that intended by the original authors. As another example, Butler et al. (2006) conducted a meta-review of 16

"high-quality" meta-analyses on 16 different disorders, all of which involved a test of the efficacy of CBT. Overall, large effect sizes were found for some disorders and moderate effect sizes were found for other disorders, but the overall conclusion was that CBT is effective as a form of treatment for many disorders. However, other experts could challenge their conclusions.

As a recent example, Parker, Crawford, and Hadzi-Pavlovic (2008) challenged the conclusion of a previously published meta-analysis that quantified distinct superiority of cognitive therapy to antidepressant drug therapy. The authors sought to include all of the studies used in the original meta-analysis. However, they employed the inclusion criteria of the original study as well as additional criteria of their own, an approach that resulted in a reduced set of studies for analysis. Although they reported an overall trend for cognitive therapy to be superior to antidepressant therapy, it was significant for only one of four analyses. Parker et al. (2008) concluded, "The previous interpretation—cognitive therapy being distinctly superior to antidepressant medication—cannot be sustained from the currently analyzed data set" (p. 91). Indeed, a recent meta-analytic review of well-controlled trials (Lynch, Laws, & McKenna, 2010) concluded that (1) CBT is no better than non-specific control treatments for schizophrenia and fails to reduce relapse, (2) CBT is effective in major depression but the effect size for treatment is small, and (3) CBT does not prevent relapse in bipolar disorder. To muddy the water even further, a new meta-analysis of the effects of psychotherapy for adult depression that focused on study quality and effect size concluded that the effects have been overestimated. Cuijpers et al. (2010) used a database of 115 RCTs in which 178 psychotherapies for adult depression were compared with a control condition. Eight quality criteria were assessed (e.g., a treatment manual was used, the therapists were trained, treatment integrity was checked, etc.) and only 11 studies met the stringent quality criteria. Consistent with Smith et al. (1980), Cuijpers et al. concluded that the effects of psychotherapy are significant; however, they are much smaller than was previously assumed.

Despite limitations, quantitative synthesis has been used to aid meaningful evaluation of other areas of evidence in abnormal psychology where a large number of studies in the literature vary considerably in the nature of the samples examined, methodological and reporting quality, operationalization of variables, and the statistical significance of findings. For example, recall our discussion of the experiment by Pennebaker et al. (1988) with university students who wrote essays about past traumatic events. The authors concluded that written emotional expression has beneficial health effects. However, research on the effects of written expression of stressful experiences has increased dramatically over the years. Is Pennebaker et al.'s original conclusion valid today? The answer is yes and no! Harris (2006) conducted a meta-analysis that examined whether writing about stressful experiences affects health care utilization (HCU) compared with writing on neutral topics or no-writing control groups. Harris examined effect sizes for healthy samples (13 studies), samples with pre-existing medical conditions (6 studies), and samples pre-screened for psychological criteria (10 studies). He concluded that, "Writing about stressful experiences reduces HCU in healthy samples but not in samples defined by medical diagnoses or exposure to stress or other psychological factors" (Harris, 2006, p. 243).

Will a meta-analysis related to an important issue in abnormal psychology ever lead to the definitive conclusion? It will probably not. The judgements of clinicians and even your own interpretation will inevitably play a role.

FOCUS ON DISCOVERY 5.2
SELECTIVE PUBLICATION OF ANTIDEPRESSANT TRIALS?

"Evidence-based medicine is valuable to the extent that the evidence base is complete and unbiased. Selective publication of clinical trials—and the outcomes within those trials—can lead to unrealistic estimates of drug effectiveness and alter the apparent risk-benefit ratio."
—Turner et al., 2008, p. 252

In a controversial, widely discussed 2008 paper published in the prestigious *New England Journal of Medicine,* Turner, Matthews, Linardatos, Tell, and Rosenthal asked whether there is a reporting bias in the publication of randomized clinical trials of antidepressants. To answer the question, they examined data from 74 RCTs of a dozen antidepressants (involving 12,564 clients) registered with the U.S. Food and Drug Administration (FDA) and submitted for regulatory approval. They compared these data with the actual published literature in two ways. First, they conducted a systematic literature search to determine how many trials had matching publications and the nature of these publications (i.e., whether positive or negative with respect to efficacy). Second, for trials that were reported in the published literature, they compared the published outcomes with the FDA outcomes.

The results were surprising and disturbing. Essentially, they provide apparent evidence of the so-called "file drawer effect"; that is, a bias in favour of publishing studies that have positive as opposed to negative results (see Mathew & Charney, 2009, p. 140). The major findings included the following:

- Almost one third (31%) of the studies (involving almost 3,500 participants) went unpublished.
- Of the 38 trials viewed by the FDA as having positive results, 37 were published and only 1 "positive" study was not published.
- Studies that were viewed by the FDA as having "negative" results (with only 3 exceptions) were not published (22 studies) or, if published, were reported in a way that, in the opinion of the authors, conveyed a positive outcome (11 additional studies).
- According to the published research literature, it appeared that 94% of the trials were "positive," in striking contrast to the

FDA outcome reports that concluded that only 51% of the trials were positive.
- Separate meta-analyses of the FDA and published data sets revealed a 32% overall increase in effect size (ranging from 11 to 69% for individual drugs) in the published literature compared with the FDA database.

Did selective reporting in the published literature occur? Obviously it did. There was a clear bias in favour of positive studies. Were negative results deliberately suppressed? Unfortunately, we cannot answer this question. The authors could not determine whether the bias occurred because authors and sponsors chose deliberately not to submit manuscripts based on negative results, whether reviewers and journal editors chose not to publish submitted manuscripts, or both. What about the selective reporting of negative findings such that a positive outcome is conveyed in a published version? Turner et al. (2008) noted many specific examples of misleading information in manuscript abstracts (which might be the primary source of information for busy practitioners) as well as inappropriately presented post hoc or secondary analyses. For example, some publications included only the positive data from single sites within multicentre studies whose overall results were judged to be negative by the FDA.

Does selective reporting impede the evidence base? Undoubtedly, it can. Imagine a practitioner who must decide whether to prescribe an antidepressant to a depressed client and which of numerous possibilities to consider. If the clinician is aware of the published literature only, the decision might be quite different from the decision that could be made given an awareness of the negative findings in studies relegated to the "file drawer." However, it is not just clients who are potentially affected. According to Turner et al. (2008), "Selective reporting of clinical trial results may have adverse consequences for researchers, study participants, health care professionals, and patients" (p. 252).

Unfortunately, selective reporting of scientific research is not unique to randomized clinical trials of antidepressants (see Mathew & Charney, 2009).

SUMMARY

- Science represents an agreed-upon problem-solving enterprise, with specific procedures for gathering and interpreting data to build a systematic body of knowledge. Scientific statements must have the following characteristics: they must be testable in the public arena; they must be exposed to tests that could disconfirm them; they must derive from reliable observations; and inferred concepts must be linked to observable and measurable events or outcomes.

- It is important to consider the various methods that scientists employ to collect data and arrive at conclusions. Clinical case studies serve unique and important functions in psychopathology, such as allowing rare phenomena to be studied intensively in all their complexity. Case studies also encourage the formulation of hypotheses that can be tested later through controlled research. However, the data they yield may not be valid, and they are of limited value in providing evidence to favour a theory.

- Epidemiological research gathers information about the prevalence and incidence of disorders and about risk factors that increase the probability of a disorder. Prevalence refers to the proportion of a population that has a disorder at a given point or period of time, whereas incidence refers to the number of new cases of the disorder that occur in some period. We examined abuse as a risk factor and determined that child maltreatment is a risk factor for numerous adult psychiatric disorders.

- Correlational methods are the most important means of conducting research on the causes of abnormal behaviour, for diagnoses are classificatory and not experimentally manipulated variables. In correlational studies, statistical procedures allow us to determine the extent to which two or more variables correlate, or co-vary. However, conclusions drawn from nearly all correlational studies cannot legitimately be interpreted in cause–effect terms. The directionality and third-variable problems are the source of this difficulty.

- The experimental method entails the manipulation of independent variables and the careful measurement of their effects on dependent variables. An experiment begins with a hypothesis to be tested. Participants are generally assigned to one of at least two groups: an experimental group, which experiences the manipulation of the independent variable; and a control group, which does not. If differences between the experimental and control groups are observed on the dependent variable, researchers can conclude that the independent variable did have an effect. Since it is important to ensure that experimental and control participants do not differ from one another before the introduction of the independent variable, they are assigned randomly to groups. If all these conditions are met, the experiment has internal validity.

- Placebo control groups are often used in psychotherapy research. Clients in such groups receive support and encouragement, but not what is hypothesized to be the active ingredient in the therapy administered to the group with which the placebo group is being compared.

- The external validity of research findings—whether they can be generalized to situations and people not studied within the experiment—can be assessed only by performing similar experiments in the actual domain of interest with new participants.

- Single-subject experimental designs that expose one person to different treatments over a period of time can provide internally valid results, although the generality of conclusions is typically limited.

- Mixed designs are combinations of experimental and correlational methods. For example, two different kinds of clients (the classificatory variable) may be exposed to various treatments (the experimental variable).

- Meta-analysis puts statistical comparisons from single studies into a common format (the effect size) in order to average the results of a group of studies.

- A science is only as good as its methodology. As a student of abnormal psychology, you must appreciate the strengths and limitations of the research methods of the field if you are to adequately evaluate research and theories.

KEY TERMS

analogue experiment (p. 155)
case study (p. 142)
classificatory variables (p. 149)
confounds (p. 152)
control group (p. 152)
correlation coefficient (p. 148)
correlational method (p. 147)

dependent variable (p. 151)
directionality problem (p. 150)
double-blind procedure (p. 153)
epidemiology (p. 144)
experiment (p. 150)
experimental effect (p. 151)
experimental hypothesis (p. 151)

external validity (p. 154)
high-risk method (p. 150)
hypotheses (p. 140)
incidence (p. 144)
independent variable (p. 151)
internal validity (p. 152)
meta-analysis (p. 159)

REFLECTIONS: PAST, PRESENT, AND FUTURE

- In Chapter 1, we discussed the issue of reform of our health care system and management of costs of health care services, including services for the mentally ill. Although it is vitally important that we maximize the efficient use of our psychological health care dollars, academics and policy-makers in Canada are starting to reconsider the cost of *failing* to prevent or treat psychological disorders (e.g., Hunsley et al., 1999). What are the long-term costs of failing to invest in services for people with mental disorders? Can we develop effective prevention programs? Outline your vision for the development of a long-term, comprehensive prevention and treatment strategy for Canada.

- In the next chapter, we will examine the anxiety disorders. Assume that the Government of Canada has hired you to head a team that will conduct a long-term longitudinal study of risk factors for the development of anxiety disorders. You will track a sample of infants, starting with the mother's pregnancy and continuing until the children reach the age of 30. Assume that you are able to hire any experts that you desire as members of your team. What would be the composition of your team? What biopsychosocial risk and protective factors would you assess and why?

CHAPTER
6
ANXIETY DISORDERS

"Courage is resistance to fear, mastery of fear—not absence of fear."

—Mark Twain, letter to Annie Webster, September 1, 1876

"At the beginning of the 21st century, anxiety disorders constitute the most prevalent mental health problem around the globe, afflicting millions of people."

—Ian R. Dowbiggin on the alarming rise of anxiety disorders (2009, p. 429)

". . . about 4% of Americans living far from the traumatic events developed probable PTSD, apparently by watching television coverage of the attacks in the comfort of their living rooms. These viewers now qualify as trauma survivors just as much as do people who escaped the World Trade Center. The possibility that television could suddenly trigger the illness in millions of Americans probably never crossed the minds of the nosologists who formulated the concept of PTSD in DSM-III."

—Richard J. McNally on the "conceptual bracket creep" in the definition of trauma, and "Can we fix PTSD in DSM-V?" (2009, p. 597)

Frederick Varley, 1881–1969, *Dhârâna*, c.1932 oil on canvas, 86.4 × 101.6 cm, Art Gallery of Ontario, Toronto. Gift from the Albert H. Robson Memorial Subscription Fund 1942. © Varley Art Gallery

PHOBIAS

PANIC DISORDER

GENERALIZED ANXIETY DISORDER (GAD)

OBSESSIVE-COMPULSIVE DISORDER (OCD)

POST-TRAUMATIC STRESS DISORDER (PTSD)

SUMMARY

"I ALWAYS WAKE UP just before they kill me." These words were uttered by Sergeant Bob Bilodeau to describe his dreams. Bilodeau, a 26-year veteran of the Royal Canadian Mounted Police, spent three months as a United Nations police officer inside the Muslim enclave of Srebrenica in the former Yugoslavia in 1993 (see Cowan, 1999). Bilodeau acknowledged that he has low self-esteem and problems concentrating. He experiences flashbacks and has many symptoms of an anxiety disorder known as post-traumatic stress disorder. Bilodeau turned to alcohol as a way to cope with his anxiety symptoms. He observed, "It's called self-medication. … It works, but it will kill you in the end" (Cowan, 1999, p. 29).

Bilodeau described a flashback that he experienced in October 1999. In talking about his experiences in Yugoslavia, he said, "It used to be very dangerous out there to drive at night because of robberies and car jackings. … One time I was late, and as I came around a corner, there were two guys stopped in the middle of the road—I just did a U-turn and got out of there. A month ago, about dusk, I was going with my brother out to the lake lot we rent when we came across this vehicle with the doors open and two guys—my brain was just shouting 'danger, danger'" (Cowan, 1999, p. 29). Although Bilodeau has returned to the relative safety of Canada, he continues to experience nightmares involving the men on the road, but, as he reported, "I always wake up just before they kill me."

There is perhaps no single topic in abnormal psychology that touches as many of us as **anxiety**, that unpleasant feeling of fear and apprehension. This emotional state can occur in many psychopathologies and is a principal aspect of the disorders considered in this chapter. Anxiety also plays an important role in the study of the psychology of normal people, for very few of us go through even a week of our lives without experiencing some measure of anxiety or fear.

Anxiety disorders are diagnosed when subjectively experienced feelings of anxiety are clearly present. *DSM-IV-TR* proposes six categories: phobias, panic disorder, generalized anxiety disorder (GAD), obsessive-compulsive disorder (OCD), post-traumatic stress disorder (PTSD), and acute stress disorder. Table 6.1 provides a brief summary of the disorders we will be discussing. Often someone with one anxiety disorder meets the diagnostic criteria for another disorder, as well, with the possible exception of OCD (see Hamilton, 2009). This comorbidity among anxiety disorders arises for two reasons:

1. Symptoms of the various anxiety disorders are not entirely disorder specific. For example, somatic signs of anxiety (e.g., perspiration, fast heart rate) are among the diagnostic criteria for panic disorder, phobias, and PTSD.
2. The etiological factors that give rise to various anxiety disorders are probably applicable to more than one disorder.

A high rate of childhood maltreatment, for example, has been linked to greater symptom severity and poorer quality of life and function in people seeking treatment for generalized social anxiety disorder (SAD) (Simon et al., 2009). However, physical or sexual abuse during childhood may increase a person's risk for developing several disorders. Recent research (Jovanovic et al., 2009) also indicates that perceived CSA is related to increased startle reactivity in adulthood and that it might be a biomarker of stress responsiveness that is related to the development of various anxiety disorders. Comorbidity could reflect the

TABLE 6.1
SUMMARY OF MAJOR ANXIETY DISORDERS

Disorder	Description
Phobia	Fear and avoidance of objects or situations that do not present any real danger.
Panic disorder	Recurrent panic attacks involving a sudden onset of physiological symptoms, such as dizziness, rapid heart rate, and trembling, accompanied by terror and feelings of impending doom; sometimes accompanied by agoraphobia, a fear of being in public places.
Generalized anxiety disorder	Persistent, uncontrollable worry, often about minor things.
Obsessive-compulsive disorder	The experience of uncontrollable thoughts, impulses, or images (obsessions) and repetitive behaviours or mental acts (compulsions).
Post-traumatic stress disorder	Aftermath of a traumatic experience in which the person experiences increased arousal, avoidance of stimuli associated with the event, and anxiety in recalling the event.
Acute stress disorder	Symptoms are the same as those of PTSD, but last for four weeks or less.

operation of common mechanisms. As yet, theories of anxiety disorders tend to focus exclusively on a single disorder. The development of theories that take comorbidity into account is a challenge for the future.

As a group, the anxiety disorders are the most common psychological disorders (Government of Canada, 2006). Indeed, a survey of physicians in Alberta found that among people with symptoms warranting a diagnosis, anxiety disorders were most common, with about 1 in 5 having some form of anxiety disorder (Klomp, Bland, Patterson, & Whittaker, 2009). Somers, Goldner, Waraich, and Hsu (2006) pooled the results of 41 international epidemiological studies and reported one-year and lifetime prevalence rates for total anxiety disorders of 10.6% and 16.6%, respectively, and noted that, "The prevalence of anxiety disorders eclipses the capacity of specialized mental health services" (p. 100). These disorders have an early age of onset, typically during childhood.

According to the Ontario *Mental Health Supplement* study (Ontario Ministry of Health, 1994), a clear gender difference exists, with 16% of women and 9% of men having suffered from anxiety disorders in the preceding year. The highest one-year prevalence rates (i.e., almost 1 in 5) were found in women 15 to 24 years of age. Anxiety disorders were more common in women than in men across all age groups. Similar results were found in 15 countries around the world (see Seedat et al., 2009). Anxiety disorders are quite common among university students. Drawing on a large and nationally representative epidemiological study in the United States, Blanco et al. (2008) reported a 12-month prevalence rate of almost 12% in college students aged 19 to 25.

Statistics Canada's 2002 Canadian Community Health Survey (CCHS; Cycle 1.2) found that social anxiety disorder (SAD) was the most common anxiety disorder, with a lifetime prevalence of 8.1% (Government of Canada, 2006). However, levels of PTSD may rival those of SAD. A study in Canada with a nationally representative sample found that the lifetime prevalence of PTSD was 9.2% (almost 1 in 10). The rate of current one-month PTSD was 2.4% (1 in 25 Canadians) (see Van Ameringen, Mancini, Patterson, & Boyle, 2008).

A majority of Canadians who met criteria for an anxiety disorder reported that it interfered with their home, school, work, and social life (Government of Canada, 2006). Wang (2006) conducted further analyses of the CCHS data set and reported that among respondents who claimed that their work and family/personal lives never balanced in the previous month, there was a one-month prevalence of anxiety and mood disorders of 17.9% and 21.2%, respectively. Work stress was independently associated with these disorders. Analyses of a subset of the young Canadians from the CCHS revealed that those with an anxiety disorder (and those with a substance-related disorder) were less likely to seek help from any mental health service, relative to those with a mood disorder (Bergeron et al., 2005). Similarly, Blanco et al. (2008) found that over 80% of college students with anxiety disorders did not seek treatment. These findings underscore the need to provide psychological outreach and treatment services to this vulnerable population.

The anxiety disorders are comorbid with many other conditions. For example, social phobia is comorbid with other anxiety disorders, substance abuse, depressive disorder, and bipolar disorder (see Stansfeld et al., 2008). In a review of the literature, Gordon Asmundson from the University of Regina with Joel Katz from York University (2009) noted the strong co-occurrence of the anxiety disorders (particularly PTSD, panic disorder, GAD, and SAD) and chronic pain, especially musculoskeletal pain. For example, between 50 and 80% of military veterans and firefighters with PTSD report chronic pain. In some cases, the anxiety disorder precedes the onset of chronic pain; however, additional prospective research is needed (see Asmundson & Katz, 2009). Anxiety disorders are also independent risk factors for suicide attempts (Bolten et al., 2008).

Comorbidity is strongest with the depressive disorders and appears to be the norm in both clinical and community samples (see Mennin et al., 2008). Anxiety and depression show a strong relationship to each other at both genotypic and phenotypic levels and are two elements of a general negative affectivity factor. Mosing et al. (2009) conducted a behavioural genetic analysis of major depression, panic disorder, agoraphobia, and social phobia (SAD) and concluded that the disorders strongly co-aggregate within families and that a common genetic factor explains a "moderate" proportion of variance in the four disorders. Tsuchiya et al. (2009) examined lifetime comorbidities between phobic disorders and major depression in Japan (the World Mental Health Japan 2002–2004 Survey) and determined that social phobia (but not agoraphobia and specific phobia) was a powerful predictor of the subsequent first onset of major depression. They concluded that the finding argues against a simple neurobiological model and favours one in which "cultural meanings" of social phobia play a role in promoting depression.

There is considerable controversy within the anxiety disorders literature about the taxonomy of anxiety problems and there could be significant changes to the anxiety disorders category in *DSM-5*. Are they qualitatively different or are they more alike than different? Are they distinct from disorders in other categories? For example, a growing body of evidence suggests that PTSD and GAD have more in common with major depression than with the other anxiety disorders (see Gamez, Watson, & Doebbeling, 2007). Should GAD, for example, be moved into the mood disorders category? What would be the implications for clinical practice and research? What would the consequences be if GAD simply shifted categories as opposed to being subsumed by major depression? The planners of *DSM-5* set up a workgroup to focus on better understanding the relation between GAD and major depression. Mennin et al. (2008) reviewed the empirical literature and argued that any consideration of the reclassification of GAD needs to consider multiple factors. For example, although GAD and major depression appear to have overlapping heritable characteristics, they may be distinguishable by environmental factors and temporal presentations. Het-tama (2008) reached a similar conclusion and further noted, "the relatively nonspecific nature of these findings provides little more reason to question the nosologic validity of GAD in relation to MDD (major depressive disorder) than that of some other anxiety disorders" (p. 300). Chambless, Fydrich, and Rodebaugh (2008) suggested that it would be more parsimonious to consider avoidant personality disorder (see Chapter 13) a severe form of generalized social phobia rather than a separate diagnostic category. PTSD will no doubt be revised in *DSM-5* because since its inception in *DSM-III* almost everything about PTSD has been challenged, including core assumptions and hypothesized mechanisms (see Rosen & Lilienfeld, 2008; Rosen, Spitzer, & McHugh, 2008). For example, Rosen and Lilienfeld (2008) reviewed evidence for core assumptions of the PTSD diagnosis and concluded that they lacked consistent empirical support.

In 1991, Leanna Clark and David Watson proposed a tripartite model to account for the symptom overlap and diagnostic comorbidity between anxiety and depression. The model posits that anxiety and depression share a common component of negative affect; however, they can be differentiated by high physiological hyperarousal associated with anxiety and by low positive affect associated with depression. Considerable research supports the utility of the tripartite model although some recent investigations suggest that the factors don't function similarly across all anxiety and depressive disorders (see Anderson & Hope, 2008, for review). Recently, Watson and his colleagues (e.g., Watson, O'Hara, & Stuart, 2008) argued that the current *DSM* model of anxiety and mood disorders is based on a fundamental distinction between anxious mood (a core feature of the anxiety disorders) and depressed mood (central to the mood disorders), a distinction that ignores research that has established the existence of the general negative affect dimension. According to Watson et al. (2008), this dimension produces strong correlations between anxious and depressed mood, and is primarily responsible for the comorbidity between anxiety and mood disorders. They argued that these disorders should be "collapsed together into an overarching superclass of emotional disorders, which can be decomposed into three subclasses" (Watson et al., 2008, p. 282). The distress disorders would include major depression, dysthymic disorder, GAD, and PTSD; the fear disorders would include panic disorder, agoraphobia, social phobia, and specific phobia; and the bipolar disorders would include bipolar I, bipolar II, and cyclothymia.

Maser et al. (2009) recommended a "paradigm shift" (see Chapter 3) toward a mixed categorical-dimensional classification system for *DSM-5*, and provided an example for an umbrella category, 300.23 Social Anxiety Disorder, that would include social anxiety disorder, avoidant personality disorder, selective mutism (e.g., a childhood anxiety disorder reflecting inability to speak in certain situations), separation anxiety disorder, and school phobia (not a *DSM-IV* disorder). Maser

et al.'s (2009) rationale for including all of these disorders under a single, broad category is as follows:

a. all of these disorders may be treated with SSRIs and/or using common principles of cognitive-behavior therapy;

b. many symptoms for each separate disorder overlap, for example, low self-esteem;

c. each separate disorder has comorbidities in common with the other, for example, depression (p. 38).

The outcome of these and other ongoing critical discussions and debates about changes to the anxiety disorders in *DSM-5* will be decided in the years ahead.

The *DSM-5* work group responsible for the anxiety disorders was given broad responsibilities. Termed the Anxiety, Obsessive-Compulsive Spectrum, Posttraumatic, and Dissociative Disorders Work Group, it was responsible for addressing all of these disorders. It was also responsible for addressing numerous disorders listed in *DSM-IV* under the Disorders Usually First Diagnosed in Infancy, Childhood or Adolescence, including in particular separation anxiety disorder and various tic disorders (e.g., Tourette's disorder, chronic motor or vocal tic disorder). The work group was also responsible for making recommendations for body dysmorphic disorder (see Chapter 7), the dissociative disorders (see Chapter 7), all of the disorders within the adjustment disorders category, and trichotillomania (categorized with the Impulse Control Disorders in *DSM-5*). In February 2010, the work group proposed numerous changes to the diagnostic categories and criteria for disorders traditionally subsumed under the anxiety disorders. Some of these proposed changes will be outlined throughout this chapter and at other points in subsequent chapters. It appeared that the work group was not prepared to propose the "overarching superclass" recommended by Watson et al. (2008), or the major "paradigm shift" proposed by Maser et al. (2009), although they did propose dimensional components. However, it is important to remember that the proposed changes could change as the *DSM-5* process progresses and should be considered tentative as they await field trials and expert consensus.

We turn now to an examination of the defining characteristics, theories of etiology, and therapies for each of the anxiety disorders as presented in *DSM-IV*. Each specific disorder is described in more detail. Each disorder is discussed in terms of not only its features, but also cognitive-behavioural and biological theories that have been postulated and received some empirical support. A common theme across the disorders is that dysfunctional levels of anxiety reflect cognitive appraisal processes contributing to the perception of anxiety, as well as physiological factors that render particular people more vulnerable to anxiety.

Much of the current biological work examines brain structures and associated neurobiological processes. Current work is focused extensively on the role of the amygdala, which is a cerebral structure of the brain's temporal lobe.

Functional MRI and PET studies of PTSD, SAD, and specific phobia have examined responses across three conditions: negative emotion, positive emotion, and neutral conditions. Results of a meta-analysis show conclusively that people with these disorders, relative to comparison subjects, have greater activity in two areas associated with negative emotional responses: the amygdala and the insula (Etkin & Wager, 2007). However, recent advances highlight the complexities emerging from more sophisticated neurobiological work. For instance, a case study reported by Steven Smith from the University of Winnipeg and his colleagues described a PTSD client with no left amygdala (see Smith, Abou-Khalil, & Zald, 2008). The client experienced PTSD after being involved in a traffic accident that occurred two years after she had part of her amygdala removed to treat epilepsy. This case study enabled the authors to conclude that it is the right amygdala that is implicated in PTSD.

PHOBIAS

Psychopathologists define a **phobia** as a disrupting, fear-mediated avoidance that is out of proportion to the danger actually posed and is recognized by the sufferer as groundless. Extreme fear of heights, closed spaces, snakes, or spiders—provided that there is no objective danger—accompanied by sufficient distress to disrupt one's life is likely to be diagnosed as a phobia.

Many specific fears do not cause enough hardship to compel an individual to seek treatment. For example, an urban dweller with an intense fear of snakes will probably have little direct contact with the feared object and may therefore not believe that anything is seriously wrong. The term "phobia" usually implies that the person suffers intense distress and social or occupational impairment because of the anxiety. A study of the fears and phobias of women in Calgary (Costello, 1982) found that about 5% of women with a phobia were "incapacitated" by their phobias.

Fear and avoidance of heights is classified as a specific phobia. Other specific phobias include fears of animals, injections, and enclosed spaces. The Canadian Press/Douglas Williams STRDWS.

Over the years, complex terms have been formulated to name these unwarranted avoidance patterns. In each instance, the suffix *phobia* is preceded by a Greek word for the feared object or situation. The suffix is derived from the name of the Greek god Phobos, who frightened his enemies. Some of the more familiar terms are *claustrophobia*, fear of closed spaces; *agoraphobia*, fear of public places; and *acrophobia*, fear of heights. More exotic fears have also been given Greek-derived names, such as *ergasiophobia*, fear of working; *pnigophobia*, fear of choking; and *taphephobia*, fear of being buried alive (McNally, 1997). Another phobia is *mysophobia*, the fear of contamination and dirt that plagues many people, including Canadian comedian and game show host Howie Mandel. These authoritative terms convey the impression that we understand how a particular problem originated and how it can be treated. Nothing could be further from the truth. As with so much in the field of abnormal psychology, there are more theories and jargon pertaining to phobias than there are firm findings.

Psychologists tend to focus on different aspects of phobias according to the paradigm they have adopted. This is particularly evident in the celebrated case reported by Freud of a boy he called Little Hans, who was afraid of horses. Freud's analysis has been reinterpreted by other classic psychoanalytic theorists such as Bowlby and Klein from their own theoretical perspectives (see Midgley, 2006). Psychoanalysts focus on the content of the phobia and see the phobic object as a symbol of an important unconscious fear. Freud paid particular attention to Hans's reference to the "black things around horses' mouths and the things in front of their eyes." The horse was regarded as representing the father, who had a moustache and wore eyeglasses. Freud theorized that fear of the father had become transformed into fear of horses, which Hans then avoided. Thus, psychoanalysts believe that the content of phobias has important symbolic value. Behaviourists, on the other hand, tend to ignore the content of the phobia and focus instead on its *function*. For them, fear of snakes and fear of heights are equivalent in the means by which they are acquired, in how they might be reduced, and so on. Let us look now at two types of phobias: specific phobias and social phobias.

SPECIFIC PHOBIAS

Specific phobias are unwarranted fears caused by the presence or anticipation of a specific object or situation. *DSM-IV-TR* subdivides these phobias according to the source of the fear: blood, injuries, and injections; situations (e.g., planes, elevators, enclosed spaces); animals; and the natural environment (e.g., heights, water). Empirical research suggests that fears can be grouped into one of five factors (types): (1) agoraphobia; (2) fears of heights or water; (3) threat fears (e.g., blood/needles, storms/thunder); (4) fears of being observed; and (5) speaking fears (Cox, McWilliams, Clara, & Stein, 2003). These fears reflect two higher-order categories: specific fears and social fears.

Pull (2008) summarized data that continue to suggest that specific phobias are high in prevalence. Five epidemiological studies appearing in 2006 and 2007 confirmed the high prevalence of specific phobias in Germany, Italy, Israel, Korea, and the United States. For instance, the study conducted by Stinson et al. (2007) in the United States found that the 12-month and lifetime prevalence of specific phobias were 7.1% and 9.4%, respectively. So the lifetime prevalence of specific phobia is almost 1 in 10! The mean age of onset was around 10 years old. The mean duration was 20 years, and only 8% with a specific phobia received treatment for their specific phobia or phobias. The most common specific phobia subtypes in order were: (1) animal phobias (including insects, snakes, and birds); (2) heights; (3) being in closed spaces; (4) flying; (5) being in or on water; (6) going to the dentist; (7) seeing blood or getting an injection; and (8) storms, thunder, or lightning. One or more of these phobias likely applies to many readers of this book.

The specific fear focused on in a phobia can vary cross-culturally. In China, for example, a person with *Pa-leng* (a fear of the cold) worries that loss of body heat may be life-threatening. This fear appears to be related to the Chinese philosophy of yin and yang: yin refers to the cold, windy, energy-sapping, and passive aspects of life, while yang refers to hot, powerful, and active aspects. Another example is a Japanese syndrome called *taijin kyofu-sho* (TKS), fear of other people. This is not a social phobia; rather, it is an extreme fear of embarrassing others—for example, by blushing in their presence, glancing at their genital areas, or making odd faces. It is believed that this phobia arises from elements of traditional Japanese culture, which encourages extreme concern for the feelings of others yet discourages direct communication of feelings (McNally, 1997). Contemporary research suggests that this syndrome may be more widespread than first believed. The symptoms of one subtype of TKS were de-

What is feared in a phobia varies cross-culturally. In China, *Pa-leng* is a fear that loss of body heat will be life-threatening. Hemera/Thinkstock.

tected in SAD clients both from Korea and the United States and it was associated in both samples with social anxiety, depression, and disability (Choy et al., 2008).

SOCIAL PHOBIAS (SOCIAL ANXIETY DISORDER)

Ms. K. is a 29-year-old student who presented with social phobia. She reported being shy as a child and could remember pretending to be ill to stay home from school. As she got older, she met more children and by high school was quite comfortable with her friends at school. Meeting new people was still difficult, as was public speaking in class. Fortunately, neither situation came up often.

In college, Ms. K.'s problem became worse. Several of her classes required her to make presentations. In addition, because she lived off campus, she found it particularly difficult to meet new friends. The few times she tried to talk to people in class, she felt as though she had nothing to say. Before long, she stopped trying. Ms. K. did not avoid her class presentations at first. Rather, she tended to overprepare for them and tried to use overheads when possible because the dark room helped to decrease her anxiety. Still during presentations she could feel her heart pounding and she tended to have difficulty breathing. Her mouth became dry and she was sure her classmates could see her shaking and perspiring.

After her first year of college, Ms. K. began to avoid any class that required presentations. In addition, she found herself avoiding other situations in which people might notice her shaking. Specifically, she avoided writing in front of others, holding drinking glasses, and other situations that might focus other people's attention on her hands. She also avoided engaging in conversation with others and when people approached her, she tried to end conversation as quickly as possible. In addition to fearing that others would notice her anxiety, Ms. K. felt others might see her as weak, unattractive, or foolish.

—Source: Antony & McCabe, 2003, p. 1323. In A. Tasman, J. Kay, & J. A. Lieberman (Eds.), Psychiatry *(2nd ed.), Reproduced with permission from John Wlley & Sons, Ltd.*

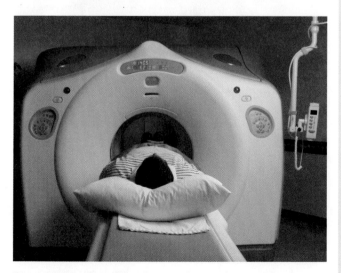

Claustrophobia, a fear of closed spaces, is a significant problem for people who must undergo MRI tests, since MRIs involve spending a prolonged amount of time in an enclosed chamber. Mock MRI studies have been conducted with university students to assess levels of claustrophobia (see McGlynn, Karg, & Lawyer, 2003). © Brad Wieland.

Ms. K. appears to suffer from a prototypical form of social phobia or social anxiety disorder (SAD) in the *DSM-IV*. **Social phobias** are persistent, irrational fears linked generally to the presence of other people. They can be extremely debilitating. Individuals with a social phobia try to avoid particular situations in which they might be evaluated, fearing that they will reveal signs of anxiousness or behave in an embarrassing way. Speaking or performing in public, eating in public, using public lavatories, and other activities carried out in the presence of others can elicit extreme anxiety.

SAD can be either generalized or specific, depending on the range of situations that are feared and avoided. While generalized social phobias involve many different interpersonal situations, specific social phobias involve intense fear of one particular situation (e.g., public speaking). People with the generalized type have an earlier age of onset, more comorbidity with other disorders, such as depression and alcohol abuse, and more severe impairment (e.g., Stein & Kessler, 1999). Recently, Cox, Clara, Sareen, and Stein (2008) examined the structure of feared situations among people with a lifetime diagnosis of SAD in the National Comorbidity Survey—Replication (NCS-R) and the CCHS and found strong support for a three-factor model composed of (1) social interaction fears, (2) observation fears, and (3) public speaking fears. Individuals with generalized SAD were most likely to report social interaction and observation fears. The specific social phobia involving public speaking anxiety seems to be qualitatively and quantitatively distinct from other subtypes (Blote, Kint, Miers, & Westenberg, 2009). That is, it is not simply a lesser or milder form of social phobia. Indeed, the *DSM-5* work group considered the utility of a specifier indicating "performance only" (if the fear is restricted to speaking or performing in public) (see Bogels et al., 2010) for social anxiety disorder.

Social phobias have a high comorbidity rate with other disorders and often occur in conjunction with GAD, specific phobias, panic disorder, avoidant personality disorder, and mood disorders (Chartier, Walker, & Stein, 2003). Social phobia also has high levels of comorbidity with heavy drinking and alcohol dependence, perhaps due to self-medication with alcohol (see Stansfeld et al., 2008). People diagnosed with SAD seem also to be especially vulnerable to marijuana-related problems (Buckner & Schmidt, 2009).

Onset generally takes place during adolescence, when social awareness and interaction with others become much more important in a person's life. The lifetime prevalence of social phobia in the CCHS 1.2 was 7.5% in men and 8.7% in women. The average age of onset was 13 years and average duration of symptoms was 20 years (see Stansfeld et al., 2008). The prevalence of social phobia was higher among people who had never married or were divorced, not completed secondary education, had lower income or were unemployed,

reported lacking adequate social support, reported low quality of life, and had a chronic physical condition (see Stansfeld et al., 2008). Izgic, Akyuz, Dogan, and Kugu (2004) reported a lifetime prevalence of social phobia among university students of 9.6% and a past-year prevalence of almost 8%. They also found that students with social phobia have lower self-esteem and a distorted body image relative to students who are not phobic. Analyses of data from Ontario's *Mental Health Supplement* study (see Stein & Kean, 2000) found that diagnosed social phobia was associated with marked dissatisfaction and low functioning in terms of quality of life, and it was actually linked with dropping out of school! A large Finnish study (Ranta et al., 2009) of 12- to 17-year-old adolescents in the general population found a 12-month prevalence of 3.2% for social phobia, and 4.6% for subclinical social phobia. Prevalence increased and the gender ratio shifted to primarily females as age increased. Social phobia was associated with educational impairment, depression and anxiety in parents, and peer victimization. Only 20% of these adolescents had been in contact with a mental health professional.

On a more positive note, Vriends et al. (2007) attempted to determine the rate of natural recovery from social phobia in the community in a 1.5-year longitudinal study of young German women and reported that 64% were at least partially recovered and 36% showed full recovery (there was an absence of any of the *DSM-IV* criteria of social phobia). Predictors of recovery included being employed, no lifetime depression, fewer than three lifetime psychiatric disorders, and fewer daily hassles.

Ricky Williams is an NFL player with the Miami Dolphins. He won the Heisman Trophy in college and, in 2006, he was a member of the Toronto Argonauts while suspended from the NFL for marijuana use. Williams has acknowledged suffering from extreme shyness and has been diagnosed with SAD. Williams has been treated successfully with a combination of cognitive-behaviour therapy and the drug Paxil, but has since discontinued his use of the drug because it did not agree with his eating habits. © Jeffery Allan Salter/CORBIS SABA.

ETIOLOGY OF PHOBIAS

Proposals about the causes of phobias have been made by adherents of the psychoanalytic, behavioural, cognitive, and biological paradigms. We now look at the ideas of each of these paradigms.

BEHAVIOURAL THEORIES Behavioural theories focus on learning as the way in which phobias are acquired. Several types of learning may be involved.

Avoidance Conditioning The main behavioural account of phobias is that such reactions are learned avoidance responses. Historically, the model of how a phobia is acquired is considered to be Watson and Rayner's (1920) demonstration of the apparent conditioning of a fear or phobia in Little Albert. The avoidance-conditioning formulation, which is based on the two-factor theory originally proposed by Mowrer (1947), holds that phobias develop from two related sets of learning:

1. Via classical conditioning, a person can learn to fear a neutral stimulus (the CS) if it is paired with an intrinsically painful or frightening event (the UCS).
2. The person can learn to reduce this conditioned fear by escaping from or avoiding the CS. This second kind of learning is assumed to be operant conditioning; the response is maintained by its reinforcing consequence of reducing fear.

An important issue exists in the application of the avoidance-conditioning model to phobias. The fact that Little Albert's fear of white rats was acquired through conditioning cannot be taken as evidence that all fears and phobias are acquired by this means. Rather, the evidence demonstrates only the *possibility* that some fears may be acquired in this particular way. Furthermore, attempts to replicate Watson and Rayner's experiment have for the most part not been successful (e.g., English, 1929). Nevertheless, data attest to the possibility that people can learn to fear certain stimuli. Research by Olsson and Phelps (2004), for instance, demonstrated that Pavlovian conditioning and observational learning via imitation can both play a role; in fact, they showed that observing another person's fear response and not having explicit, conscious awareness of this conditioned stimulus can still contribute to the apparent learning of a fear response.

Ethical considerations have restrained most researchers from employing highly aversive stimuli with human beings, but considerable evidence indicates that fear is extinguished rather quickly when the CS is presented a few times without the reinforcement of moderate levels of shock (Bridger & Mandel, 1965). Outside the laboratory, the evidence for the avoidance-conditioning theory is mixed. Some clinical phobias fit the model rather well. A phobia of a specific object or situation has sometimes been reported after a particularly

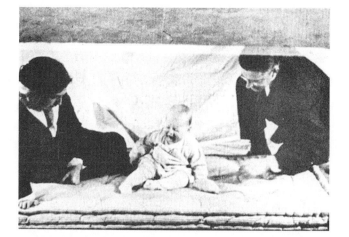

Little Albert, shown here with Watson and Rayner, was classically conditioned to develop a fear of a white rat. Courtesy Professor Benjamin Harris, University of Wisconsin.

painful experience with that object. Some people become intensely afraid of heights after a bad fall, others develop a phobia of driving after experiencing a panic attack in their car, and people with social phobias often report traumatic social experiences. Other clinical reports suggest that phobias may develop without a prior frightening experience. Many individuals with severe fears of snakes, germs, and airplanes tell clinicians that they have had no particularly unpleasant experiences with these objects or situations. Can this problem with the avoidance-conditioning model be solved? One attempt to do so involves modelling.

Modelling In addition to learning to fear something as a result of an unpleasant experience with it, a person can also learn fears through imitating the reactions of others. Thus, some phobias may be acquired by modelling, not through an unpleasant experience with the object or situation that is feared. The learning of fear by observing others is generally referred to as **vicarious learning**.

In one study, Bandura and Rosenthal (1966) arranged for participants to watch another person, the model (a confederate of the experimenter), in an aversive-conditioning situation. The model was hooked up to an impressive-looking array of electrical apparatuses. On hearing a buzzer, the model withdrew his hand rapidly from the arm of the chair and feigned pain. The physiological responses of the participants witnessing this behaviour were recorded. After the participants had watched the model "suffer" a number of times, they showed an increased frequency of emotional responses when the buzzer sounded. Thus, they reacted emotionally to a harmless stimulus even though they had had no direct contact with a noxious event.

Vicarious learning may also be accomplished through verbal instructions. Thus, phobic reactions can be learned through another's description of what could happen. For example, a child may come to fear an activity after a parent has repeatedly warned him or her not to engage in it lest dire consequences ensue. Indeed, the *anxious-rearing model* is based on the premise that anxiety disorders in children are due to constant parental warnings that increase anxiety in the child.

Prepared Learning Another issue that the original avoidance-learning model fails to address is that people tend to fear only certain objects and events, such as spiders, snakes, and heights, but not others, such as lambs. The fact that certain neutral stimuli, called *prepared stimuli*, are more likely than others to become classically conditioned stimuli may account for this tendency. For example, rats readily learn to associate taste with nausea but not with shock when the two are paired (Garcia, McGowan, & Green, 1972). Some fears may well reflect classical conditioning, but only to stimuli to which an organism is physiologically prepared to be sensitive (Ohman & Mineka, 2001). Conditioning experiments that show quick extinction of fear may have used CSs that the organism was not prepared to associate with UCSs. Prepared learning is also relevant to learning fear by modelling. Cook and Mineka (1989) studied four groups of rhesus monkeys, each of which saw a different videotape showing a monkey seemingly react with fear to different stimuli: a toy snake, a toy crocodile, flowers, or a toy rabbit. Only the monkeys exposed to the tapes showing the toy snake or toy crocodile acquired fear of the object shown, again demonstrating that not every stimulus is capable of becoming a source of acquired fear. There is considerable evidence in support of the preparedness theory of phobias (see Ohman & Mineka, 2001, for review).

A Diathesis Is Needed A final question to consider is why some people who have traumatic experiences do not develop enduring fears. For example, 50% of people with a severe fear of dogs reported a prior traumatic experience, yet 50% of people who were not afraid of dogs reported a similar experience (DiNardo et al., 1988). Why did only some people develop this fear? A cognitive diathesis (predisposition)—a tendency to believe that similar traumatic experiences will occur in the future—may be important in developing a phobia. Another possible psychological diathesis is a history of not being able to control the environment (Mineka & Zinbarg, 1996). Aversive conditioning experiences, such as severe teasing, have been proposed to play a role in the development of social phobia. McCabe et al. (2003) found a significant link between perceptions of teasing and bullying in childhood and social phobia.

In sum, the data suggest that while some phobias are learned through avoidance conditioning, avoidance conditioning should not be regarded as a totally validated theory; many people with phobias do not report either direct exposure to a traumatic event or exposure to fearful models (Merckelbach et al., 1989).

SOCIAL SKILLS DEFICITS IN SOCIAL PHOBIAS A behavioural model of social phobia considers inappropriate behaviour or a lack of social skills as the cause of social anxiety.

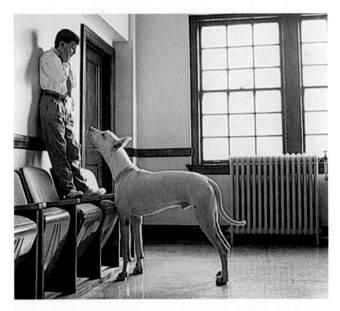

DiNardo's study showed that after a traumatic experience with a dog, those who developed a persistent fear of dogs were anxious about having similar future experiences. Brett Froomer/Getty Images.

According to this view, the individual has not learned how to behave so that he or she feels comfortable with others, or the person repeatedly commits faux pas, is awkward and socially inept, and is often criticized by social companions. Support for this model comes from findings that socially anxious people are indeed rated as being low in social skills (Twentyman & McFall, 1975) and that the timing and placement of their responses in a social interaction, such as saying thank you at the right time and place, are impaired (Fischetti, Curran, & Wessberg, 1977).

Of course, social skill deficits may have arisen over time because the person was fearful of interacting with others for other reasons, such as classical conditioning, and therefore had little experience doing so. The lack of interpersonal skills in an adult who has a social phobia may therefore reveal little of etiological significance, though the information may be very important in planning effective therapeutic interventions.

COGNITIVE THEORIES Cognitive views focus on how people's thought processes can serve as a diathesis and on how thoughts can maintain a phobia or anxiety. Anxiety is related to being more likely to attend to negative stimuli, to interpret ambiguous information as threatening, and to believe that negative events are more likely than positive ones to occur in the future (Mathews & MacLeod, 1994). For instance, spider phobia involves automatic thought processes and implicit cognitive associations involving themes of disgust and threat that occur without conscious introspection or awareness (Teachman & Woody, 2003).

Studies of socially anxious people have contributed to ideas about the cognitive factors related to social phobias. Socially anxious people are more concerned about evaluation than are people who are not socially anxious (Goldfried, Padawer, & Robins, 1984), are more aware of the image they present to others (Bates, 1990), and are preoccupied with hiding imperfections and not making mistakes in front of other people (Hewitt et al., 2003). Unfortunately, socially anxious people tend to view themselves negatively even when they have actually performed well in a social interaction (Wallace & Alden, 1997) and they are less certain about their positive self-views and, relative to people without social phobia, they see their positive attributes as being less important (Moscovitch et al., 2009). They seem to be hyper vigilant in looking for signs of negative social evaluation, and this may account, in part, for experimental evidence suggesting that people with social phobia have a cognitive bias toward being more attentive visually to negative faces than to positive faces, but no such bias is evident among people with OCD or in control participants (Eastwood et al., 2005). Socially anxious people also seem to fear having a negative impact on other people; that is, they are worried about causing discomfort in other people (Rector, Kocovski, & Ryder, 2006).

Cognitive-behavioural models of social phobia (e.g., Clark & Wells, 1995; Rapee & Heimberg, 1997) link social phobia with certain cognitive characteristics: (1) an attentional bias to focus on negative social information (e.g., perceived criticism and hostile reactions from others) and interpret ambiguous situations as negative; (2) perfectionistic standards for accepted social performances; and (3) a high degree of public self-consciousness. Research by Sheila Woody at the University of British Columbia confirmed that excessive self-consciousness and self-focus tend to increase social anxiety (see Woody & Rodriguez, 2000). Not only do people with social phobia have a tendency to interpret ambiguous social situations as negative and a reflection of their personal shortcomings, they also have a memory bias linked to this interpretation bias (Hertel, Brozovich, Joormann, & Gotlib, 2008). In other words, people with social phobia tend to falsely recall events they have interpreted as having emotionally negative features.

David Moscovitch (2009) at the University of Waterloo concluded recently that the fundamental core fear in social phobia is that the self is deficient. He maintains that the key situational triggers are those situations and circumstances that will publicly reveal the self as inadequate. Related research has shown that social phobia is linked with excessive self-criticism (Cox, Walker, Enns, & Karpinski, 2002). This self-criticism may underscore a general sensitivity to perceived criticism. Davison and Zighelboim (1987) used the Articulated Thoughts in Simulated Situations method to show that thoughts articulated by socially anxious students in both stressful (being sharply criticized) and neutral situations were more negative than were those of control subjects (e.g., "I am boring when I talk to people"). Given these negative self-beliefs, it is not surprising that researchers have begun to focus on interventions designed to boost self-efficacy, especially in terms of the

self-efficacy for changing social anxiety (see Ahmed & Westra, 2009). Self-efficacy for changing social anxiety was improved by having participants witness a videotape portraying an experienced CBT therapist who provided a clear rationale and outlined the positive changes that could occur.

Rachman, Gruter-Andrew, and Shafran (2000) reported that socially anxious students not only anticipate negative social experiences, they also engage in extensive post-event processing (PEP) of the negative social experiences, sometimes experiencing intrusive thoughts and images associated typically with OCD. Subsequent research confirmed a link between social anxiety and PEP. Kocovski, Endler, Rector, and Flett (2005) reported that those high in social anxiety are more likely to ruminate and less likely to distract themselves as a way of coping with a threatening social event (i.e., making a mistake in public). A novel study by Kocovski and Rector (2008) showed that the therapy situation itself may elicit PEP among people with SAD who are receiving group CBT. PEP was assessed one week after the first group therapy session (i.e., the initial anxiety-provoking task) and one week after an in-session exposure task (i.e., the second anxiety-provoking task). Higher initial levels of social anxiety assessed prior to the tasks predicted higher subsequent levels of PEP.

PREDISPOSING BIOLOGICAL FACTORS Why do some people acquire unrealistic fears when others do not, given similar opportunities for learning? Perhaps those who are adversely affected by stress have a biological malfunction (a diathesis) that somehow predisposes them to develop a phobia following a particular stressful event. More generally, the various anxiety disorders may reflect a complex array of biological factors and processes. Research in two areas seems promising: the autonomic nervous system (ANS) and genetic factors.

Autonomic Nervous System One way people differ in their reaction to certain environmental situations is the ease with which their autonomic nervous systems become aroused. Lacey (1967) identified a dimension of autonomic activity that he called stability-lability. Labile, or jumpy, individuals are those whose autonomic systems are readily aroused by a wide range of stimuli. Because of the extent to which the autonomic nervous system is involved in fear and hence in phobic behaviour, a dimension such as **autonomic lability** assumes considerable importance. Since there is reason to believe that autonomic lability is to some degree genetically determined (Gabbay, 1992), heredity may very well have a significant role in the development of phobias.

Genetic Factors Several studies have examined whether a genetic factor is involved in phobias. Blood-and-injection phobia is strongly familial. Sixty-four percent of people with this phobia have at least one first-degree relative with the same disorder, whereas the disorder's prevalence in the general population is only 3 to 4% (Ost, 1992). Similarly, for both social (especially the generalized type) and specific phobias, prevalence is higher than average in first-degree relatives of clients (Stein et al., 1998). Related to these findings is the work of Jerome Kagan on the trait of behavioural inhibition or shyness (Kagan & Snidman, 1997). Some infants as young as four months become agitated and cry when they are shown toys or other stimuli. This behaviour pattern, which may be inherited, may set the stage for the later development of phobias.

The data we have described do not unequivocally implicate genetic factors and much remains to be empirically determined. Although close relatives share genes, they also have considerable opportunity to observe and influence one another. The fact that a son and his father are both afraid of heights may indicate a genetic component, the son's direct imitation of the father's behaviour, or both. Smoller, Gardner-Schuster, and Covino (2008) reviewed the role of genetic factors in phobic and panic disorders and concluded that these disorders are familial and moderately heritable but no specific susceptibility genes have been found thus far. Linkage analyses seek to identify the specific genes implicated in these disorders. Smoller et al. (2008) also identified two significant problems: (1) genetic complexity, and (2) phenotypic complexity. Genetic complexity poses a problem because disorders likely reflect the additive or interactive effects of multiple loci. Phenotypic complexity is a problem because this complexity likely transcends the *DSM* categories that may be useful conventions for clinicians but fail to take into account growing evidence that genetic factors are diffuse across various anxiety disorders and they transcend these diagnostic categories.

PSYCHOANALYTIC THEORIES Freud was the first to attempt to account systematically for the development of phobic behaviour. According to Freud, phobias are a defence against the anxiety produced by repressed id impulses. This anxiety is displaced from the feared id impulse and moved to an object or situation that has some symbolic connection to it. These objects or situations—for example, elevators or closed spaces—then become the phobic stimuli. By avoiding them the person is able to avoid dealing with repressed conflicts. The phobia is the ego's way of warding off a confrontation with the real problem, a repressed childhood conflict. Arieti (1979) proposed that the repression stems from a particular interpersonal problem of childhood rather than from an id impulse. As with most psychoanalytic theorizing, most of the supporting evidence is restricted to conclusions drawn from clinical case reports.

THERAPIES FOR PHOBIAS

"Experience and knowledge are the greatest things to conquer fear."

—*Mike Babcock, 2010 Team Canada Olympic hockey coach, in Zwolinski, 2009, December 30, S5.*

In this section we focus specifically on therapies for phobias. As noted above, most people suffer with their phobias and do not seek treatment (see Stinson et al., 2007). In fact, many people who could be diagnosed by a clinician as having a phobia do not feel they have a problem that merits attention. A decision to seek treatment often arises when a life change requires exposure to stimuli or situations that had for years been avoided or minimized.

AN INDUSTRIAL ENGINEER sought treatment for his fear of flying when a promotion required him to travel frequently. This professional recognition was a result of his having worked with distinction for several years in his firm at a job that kept him at his desk. Family trips were always by car or train, and those close to him worked around his debilitating fear of getting on an airplane. Imagine his mixed feelings at being informed that his excellence was to be rewarded by the promotion! His ambition and self-respect—and encouragement from family and friends—goaded him into seeking assistance.

Throughout the book, after reviewing theories about the causes of the various disorders, we will describe the principal therapies for them. The treatment sections of chapters 1 and 2 were meant to furnish you with a context for understanding these discussions of therapy. We will now look at a number of therapeutic approaches used to treat phobias.

BEHAVIOURAL APPROACHES

"Go straight to the heart of danger, for there you will find safety."

—*Ancient Chinese proverb*

Systematic desensitization was the first major behavioural treatment to be used widely in treating phobias (Wolpe, 1958). The individual with a phobia imagines a series of increasingly frightening scenes while in a state of deep relaxation. Clinical and experimental evidence indicates that this technique is effective in eliminating, or at least reducing, phobias. Many behaviour therapists, however, came to recognize the critical importance of exposure to real-life phobic situations, sometimes during the period in which a client is being desensitized in imagination and sometimes instead of the imagery-based procedure (Craske, Rapee, & Barlow, 1992). Historically, clinical researchers have regarded such **in vivo exposure** as superior to techniques using imagination, not a surprising finding given that imaginary stimuli are by definition not the real thing! In a meta-analytic review of 33 randomized controlled trials (RCTs) of the treatment of specific phobias, Wolitzky-Taylor, Horowitz, Powers, and Telch (2008) concluded that exposure-based treatment produced large effect sizes relative to no treatment and outperformed both placebo conditions and other psychotherapeutic approaches.

In vivo exposure outperformed other modes of exposure (e.g., imaginal exposure and virtual reality) at post-treatment (but not at follow-up). However, in a comprehensive review, Choy, Fyer, and Lipsitz (2007) concluded that while most phobias do respond well to in vivo exposure, it is associated with a high dropout rate and low treatment acceptance. Some contemporary research comparing in vivo exposure with **virtual reality (VR) exposure** treatments has found VR exposure to be just as effective as in vivo exposure (Emmelkamp et al., 2002) and as effective as group CBT (Klinger et al., 2005), especially for flying and height phobia, but more controlled trials are necessary (see Choy et al., 2007). This type of exposure has been dubbed *in virtuo* exposure (see Côté & Bouchard, 2008). Virtual reality involves exposure to stimuli that come in the form of computer-generated graphics. VR exposure for social phobia, for instance, involved exposure to four scenes that include performing in the presence of others and being scrutinized by others (Klinger et al., 2005). VR exposure can be tailored to involve graded exposures to threatening stimuli in a hierarchy (see Table 6.2), similar to the increasingly frightening scenes used in systematic desensitization. The sequence would begin with a situation that is associated with the lowest fear (i.e., asking for directions at the gas station). Initial evidence suggests that in virtuo exposure is effective, but more methodologically rigorous studies are needed to determine its effectiveness relative to other treatments (Côté & Bouchard, 2008).

TABLE 6.2
EXPOSURE HIERARCHY FOR GENERALIZED SOCIAL PHOBIA

Item	Fear Rating (0 to 100)
Have a party and invite everyone from work	99
Go to Christmas party for one hour without drinking	90
Invite Cindy to have dinner and see a movie	85
Go for a job interview	80
Ask boss for a day off work	65
Ask questions in a meeting at work	65
Eat lunch with co-workers	60
Talk to a stranger on a bus	50
Talk to a cousin on the telephone for 10 minutes	40
Ask for directions at the gas station	35

Adapted with permission from Antony & McCabe, 2003, p. 1319. In A. Tasman, J. Kay, & J.A. Lieberman (Eds.), *Psychiatry* (2nd ed.). New York: Wiley.

Blood-and-injection phobias have, in *DSM-IV*, been distinguished from other kinds of severe fears and avoidances because of the distinctive reactions that people with these phobias have to the usual behavioural approach of relaxation paired with exposure (Page, 1994). Relaxation tends to make matters worse for people with blood-and-injection phobias. Why? Consider the typical reaction. After the initial fright, accompanied by dramatic increases in heart rate and blood pressure, a person with a blood-and-injection phobia often experiences a sudden drop in blood pressure and heart rate and faints (McGrady & Bernal, 1986). By trying to relax, clients with these phobias may well contribute to the tendency to faint, increasing their already high levels of fear and avoidance, as well as their embarrassment (Ost, 1992). Clients with blood-and-injection phobias are now encouraged to tense rather than relax their muscles when confronting the fearsome situation (e.g., Hellstrom, Fellenius, & Ost, 1996). Indeed, Choy et al. (2007) concluded that blood-injury phobia is uniquely responsive to applied tension.

Learning social skills can help people with social phobias who may not know what to do or say in social situations. Some CBT therapists encourage clients to role-play interpersonal encounters in the consulting room or in therapy groups and several studies attest to the long-term effectiveness of this approach (e.g., Garcia-Lopez et al., 2006). Such practices may also expose the anxious person to anxiety-provoking cues, such as being observed by others, so that extinction of fear through real-life exposure occurs (Hope, Heimberg, & Bruch, 1995).

Modelling is another technique that uses exposure to feared situations. In modelling therapy, fearful clients are exposed to filmed or live demonstrations of other people interacting fearlessly with the phobic object (e.g., handling snakes). **Flooding** is a therapeutic technique in which the client is exposed to the source of the phobia at full intensity. The extreme discomfort that is inevitable discourages therapists from using this technique, except perhaps as a last resort when graduated exposure has not worked. We will see more extensive use of flooding when we examine therapy for OCD and PTSD.

Therapists who favour operant techniques ignore the fear assumed to underlie phobias and attend instead to the overt avoidance of phobic objects and to the approach behaviour that must replace it. They treat approach to the feared situation as any other operant and shape it via the principle of successive approximations. Real-life exposures to the phobic object are gradually achieved, and the client is rewarded for even minimal successes in moving closer to it. Exposure is an inevitable aspect of any operant shaping of approach behaviours.

Many CBT therapists attend both to fear and to avoidance, using exposure techniques to reduce fear and operant shaping to encourage approach (e.g., Lazarus, Davison, & Polefka, 1965). In the initial stages of treatment, when fear and avoidance are both very great, the therapist concentrates on reducing the fear through relaxation training and graded exposures to the phobic situation. As therapy progresses, fear

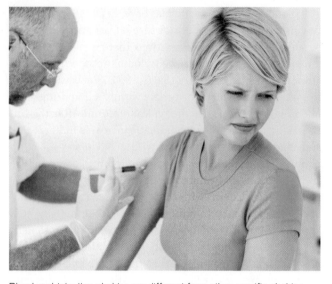

Blood-and-injection phobias are different from other specific phobias. Clients with this type of phobia are encouraged not to relax, but to tense their muscles when they encounter the feared situation. George Doyle.

In the most frequent treatment for phobias, clients are exposed to what they fear most; here, an enclosed space. © Pierre Perrin/Corbis/Sygma.

becomes less of an issue and avoidance more. A person with a phobia has often settled into an existence in which other people cater to his or her incapacities, in a way reinforcing the person's phobia (psychoanalysts call this phenomenon *secondary gain*). As the person's anxieties diminish, he or she is able to approach what used to be terrifying. This overt behaviour can then be positively reinforced—and avoidance discouraged—by relatives and friends, as well as by the therapist.

One development that has proven quite effective is Ost's one-session exposure treatment for phobias (see Ost, Svensson, Hellstrom, & Lindwall, 2001). The session is highly intensive and lasts for many hours! Results indicate that this one-day treatment is highly effective and treatment gains tend to persist over time (see Hazlett-Stevens & Craske, 2002). Although many highly experienced clinicians now regard one-session exposure treatment as the treatment of choice, Wolitzky-Taylor et al. (2008) concluded that multi-session exposure treatments outperformed single-session treatments on various measures of phobic dysfunction, and more sessions predicted more favourable outcomes.

COGNITIVE APPROACHES Cognitive treatments for specific phobias have been viewed with scepticism because of a central defining characteristic of phobias: the phobic fear is recognized by the individual as excessive or unreasonable. If the person already acknowledges that the fear is of something harmless, what use can it be to alter the person's thoughts about it? Indeed, there is no evidence that the elimination of irrational beliefs alone, without exposure to the fearsome situations, reduces phobic avoidance (e.g., Turner et al., 1992).

With social phobias, on the other hand, such cognitive methods—sometimes combined with social skills training—are more promising. People with social phobias benefit from treatment strategies derived from Aaron Beck and Albert Ellis. They may be persuaded by the therapist to more accurately appraise people's

reactions to them (e.g., the teacher's frown may reflect a bad mood rather than disapproval), but also to rely less on the approval of others for a sense of self-worth. Cognitive approaches have been used more often since it was recognized that many people with social phobias have adequate social skills but do not use them because of self-defeating thoughts.

CBT interventions have also been used to treat other anxiety disorders and meta-analyses support their usefulness (e.g., Deacon & Abramowitz, 2004). Hollon, Stewart, & Strunk (2006) concluded that CBT interventions are generally more successful than drug treatments because they create lasting change, while the benefits of drug treatments (i.e., psychoactive medications) are less permanent and "appear to be largely palliative in nature" (p. 285). An RCT (Clark et al., 2006) reported that cognitive therapy appears to be superior to a combination of exposure plus applied relaxation in the treatment of social phobia. Cognitive therapy is also helpful in claustrophobia (see Choy et al., 2007).

Are the benefits documented in tightly controlled randomized trial intervention studies realized when treatment occurs in clinical practice? That is, do the treatment gains generalize to the real world? Hunsley and Lee's (2007) examination of 35 effectiveness studies led them to conclude that improvement rates as a result of CBT were comparable in clinical practice settings with the improvement rates obtained in RCTs. For instance, in terms of CBT as a form of treatment for social phobia, the moderate to large effects of treatment found in previous studies were replicated. A follow-up meta-analytic study that focused specifically on the 11 effectiveness studies conducted thus far on the treatment of anxiety disorders concluded that CBT interventions are effective and "generalize to real-world clinical practice" (van Ingen, Freiheit, & Vye, 2009, p. 69). Nonetheless, follow-up studies longer than one year are needed to better understand and prevent relapse (Choy et al., 2007).

All the behavioural and cognitive therapies for phobias have a recurrent theme—namely, the need for the client to begin exposing himself or herself to what has been deemed too terrifying to face. It should be noted that **homework** or between-session learning is considered to be an essential component of CBT. Rees, McEvoy, and Nathan (2005) investigated the quantity and quality of homework completed during a 10-week group CBT program for anxious and depressed clients. Both quantity and quality predicted outcome on measures of anxiety, depression, and quality of life at post-treatment and follow-up.

A COGNITIVE-BEHAVIOURAL CASE FORMULATION FRAMEWORK

Boschen and Oei (2008) presented a cognitive-behavioural case formulation framework (CBCFF) for anxiety disorders. In this framework, causal and maintaining factors are outlined in a single but simple visual framework. They argue that the elements that are common to the anxiety disorders allow the framework to be used in case formulation development and treatment planning. Further, the framework is useful in cases with novel presentation for which manualized treatments might not be available. The CBCFF for anxiety disorders is presented in Figure 6.1.

The following is a brief description of the flow chart components excerpted and adapted from Boschen and Oei (2008) in Figure 6.1:

- The left-to-right chain describes a situation where an anxious person comes into contact with a perceived danger situation and then acts in such a way as to reduce the ensuing anxiety.
- Other cognitive variables (e.g., attentional biases, self-efficacy beliefs) also impact on this basic chain.
- Thought bubbles and six-sided shapes represent cognition and behaviour, respectively. Rectangular symbols represent other components (e.g., interoceptive cues). Arrows show the flow from one component to another.
- *Approach Behaviours.* Contact with anxiety-eliciting stimuli often occurs as a consequence of the person's behaviour (e.g., a client with agoraphobia enters a shopping mall). Exposure-based interventions require an increase in the frequency of approach behaviour.
- *Stimulus.* Feared stimuli can be drawn from external objects or situations, interoceptive stimuli, and cognitions (e.g., the perception that one is under scrutiny in social phobia). The stimuli themselves are not directly targeted by any particular CBT intervention.
- *Hypervigilance to Stimulus.* People attend to threatening stimuli (e.g., people with panic disorder show heightened attention to interoceptive cues). Interventions (e.g., distraction and attentional training) address hypervigilance to threat cues.
- *Perception of Danger.* The perception of threat or danger (rather than the feared stimulus itself) elicits anxiety (e.g., the person with a dog phobia who has anxious thoughts about the risk of being bitten by a dog). Cognitive restructuring is the primary vehicle by which perceptions of danger are addressed.

- *Neuroticism.* Neuroticism is a stable, pervasive personality dimension that predisposes people to experience negative affective states and that influences both cognition and anxiety symptoms. Neuroticism and other personality traits are described in more detail in Chapter 13.
- *Information or Experience.* Stimuli can come to be appraised as threatening through direct experience, observation, and verbal acquisition. CBT treatments usually begin with psychoeducation—corrective information provided to the client about anxiety and the client's specific disorder (e.g., the risk of acquiring serious illness by touching "contaminated" surfaces). Verbal information acquired during therapy sessions is consolidated through homework tasks.
- *Increased Anxiety.* Excessive, unreasonable anxiety is experienced through a constellation of emotional, physiological, cognitive, and behavioural symptoms. Methods of managing anxiety include relaxation training and breathing control training.
- *Reduced Self-efficacy.* Perceptions of ability to cope with anxiety-provoking stimuli and consequent symptoms have been implicated in the anxiety disorders. Reduced self-efficacy influences the perception of danger and inhibits anxiety-reducing behaviour. Self-efficacy is a direct target of several interventions (e.g., cognitive restructuring with behavioural experiments designed to consolidate cognitive change, and arousal management strategies).
- *Anxiety-Reducing Behaviour.* The choice of anxiety-reducing behaviour used is influenced by the nature of the anxiety-provoking stimuli (e.g., withdrawing from and avoiding a specific object in a specific phobia). As part of treatment, the person needs to refrain from the behaviours usually used to relieve anxiety, circumventing negative reinforcement and strengthening perception of coping ability (this is item 2 in the flowchart, "safety response inhibition"). This is seen in the response prevention component of treatment for OCD and exposure where clients are asked to refrain from usual safety behaviours (e.g., escape).
- *Safety Signals.* Many anxiety-reducing behaviours are aimed at attaining a sense of safety through the generation of safety signals—stimuli that indicate that an aversive outcome is less likely (e.g., knowledge of the location of the nearest toilet). During exposure the person surrenders previously used safety signals, thereby enhancing self-efficacy.
- *Reduced Anxiety and Reinforcement of Anxiety-Reducing Behaviours.* Anxiety-reducing behaviour and use of safety signals produce a decrease in anxiety symptoms, which reinforces their use. During treatment the client inhibits usual anxiety-reducing behaviour and over time it extinguishes.
- *Punishment of Approach Behaviours.* Arousal symptoms that accompany danger perception are an aversive, punishing experience. During exposure habituation occurs and the punishing effects of anxiety are diminished.

FIGURE 6.1 A cognitive-behavioural case formulation framework (CBCFF) of anxiety disorders and associated treatment components proposed by Boschen and Oei (2008).

Source: Boschen & Oei, 2008, p. 814. Reproduced with permission from Wiley Interscience

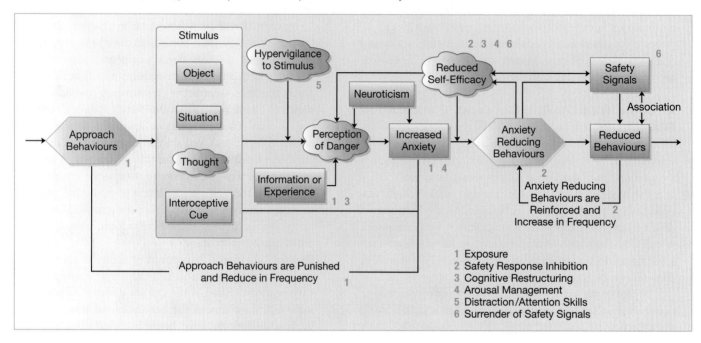

It should be noted that each of the formulation components suggests treatment plan strategies. Note too that competent clinicians will extend the model to comorbid conditions (e.g., mood problems) and any other factors not specified that may bear on the client's presenting problem (e.g., self-critical perfectionism).

BIOLOGICAL APPROACHES Drugs that reduce anxiety are referred to as sedatives, tranquilizers, or **anxiolytics** (the suffix-*lytic* comes from the Greek word meaning to loosen or dissolve). Barbiturates were the first major category of drugs used to treat anxiety disorders, but because they are highly addictive and present great risk of a lethal overdose, they were supplanted in the 1950s by two other classes of drugs: propanediols (e.g., Miltown) and benzodiazepines (e.g., Valium and Xanax). Valium and Xanax are still used today, although they have been largely supplanted by newer benzodiazepines, such as Ativan and Clonapam. These drugs are of demonstrated benefit with some anxiety disorders; however, they are not used extensively with the specific phobias. Although the risk of lethal overdose is not as great as with barbiturates, benzodiazepines are addictive and can produce a severe withdrawal syndrome (Schweizer et al., 1990).

Drugs originally developed to treat depression (antidepressants) have become popular in treating many anxiety disorders, phobias included. One class of these drugs, the monoamine oxidase (MAO) inhibitors, fared better in treating social phobias than did a benzodiazepine (Gelernter et al., 1991) and, in another study, was as effective as CBT at a 12-week follow-up (Heimberg et al., 1998). But MAO inhibitors, such as phenelzine (Nardil), can lead to weight gain, insomnia, sexual dysfunction, and hypertension. The selective serotonin reuptake inhibitors (SSRIs), such as fluoxetine (Prozac), were also originally developed to treat depression. They, too, have shown some promise in reducing social phobia in double-blind Canadian studies (Stein et al., 1999), and a meta-analysis of past studies confirmed their effectiveness (Federoff & Taylor, 2001). However, the key problem in treating phobias and other anxiety disorders with drugs is that the client may find it difficult to discontinue their use, relapse being a common result.

PSYCHOANALYTIC APPROACHES Classical psychoanalytic treatments of phobias attempted to uncover the repressed conflicts believed to underlie the extreme fear and avoidance characteristic of these disorders. Because the phobia itself was regarded as symptomatic of underlying conflicts, it was usually not dealt with directly. Indeed, direct attempts to reduce phobic avoidance were contraindicated because the phobia is assumed to protect the person from repressed conflicts that are too painful to confront. Contemporary ego analysts focus less on gaining historical insights and more on encouraging the client to confront the phobia. However, they do view the phobia as an outgrowth of an earlier problem. Many analytically oriented clinicians recognize the importance of exposure to what is feared, although they often regard any subsequent improvement as merely symptomatic and not as a resolution of the underlying conflict that was assumed to have produced the phobia (Wolitzky & Eagle, 1990).

PANIC DISORDER

In **panic disorder**, a person suffers a sudden and often inexplicable attack of a host of jarring symptoms: laboured breathing, heart palpitations, nausea and chest pain; feelings of choking and smothering; dizziness, sweating, and trembling; and intense apprehension, terror, and feelings of impending doom. **Depersonalization**, a feeling of being outside one's body, and **derealization**, a feeling of the world's not being real, as well as fears of losing control, of going crazy, or even of dying, may beset and overwhelm the person.

Panic attacks may occur frequently, perhaps once a week or more often; they usually last for minutes, rarely for hours; and they are sometimes linked to specific situations, such as driving a car. They are referred to as cued panic attacks when they are associated strongly with situational triggers.

When their relationship with stimuli is present but not as strong, they are referred to as situationally predisposed attacks. Panic attacks can also occur in seemingly benign states, such as relaxation or sleep, and in unexpected situations; in these cases, they are referred to as uncued attacks.

Recurrent uncued attacks and worry about having attacks in the future are required for the diagnosis of panic disorder. The exclusive presence of cued attacks most likely reflects the presence of a phobia. Panic attacks are quite common among university students (see Canadian Perspectives 6.1).

CANADIAN PERSPECTIVES 6.1
PANIC ATTACKS AND PANIC DISORDER IN CANADIAN UNIVERSITY STUDENTS

Sandra B. was a 20-year-old college student who presented to a student health clinic reporting recurrent panic attacks. Her first attack occurred seven months earlier while smoking marijuana at an end-of-term party. At the time she felt depersonalized, dizzy, short of breath, and her heart was beating wildly. Sandra had an overwhelming fear that she was going crazy … In the following months, Sandra continued to experience unexpected panic attacks and became increasingly convinced that she was losing control of her mind. Most of her panics occurred unexpectedly during the day, although they sometimes also occurred at night, wrenching her out of a deep sleep. Sandra began avoiding a variety of substances (e.g., alcohol, marijuana, coffee) and activities (e.g., aerobics classes) because they produced bodily sensations, such as palpitations and dizziness, that she feared. She believed that if these sensations became too intense then she might "tip over the edge" into insanity. Increasingly, Sandra also began to avoid shopping malls, lecture halls, and other public places for fear that she would have a panic attack and lose control … As a result of avoiding lectures, her grades began to fall and she was at risk for failing her courses. (Asmundson & Taylor, 2003, p. 1281, in A. Tasman, J. Kay, & J.A. Lieberman (Eds.), *Psychiatry* (2nd ed.), New York: Wiley).

The panic attacks experienced by Sandra are more common than you might realize. Extensive research has been conducted on panic attacks and panic disorder in Canadian students. Ron Norton and his colleagues at the University of Winnipeg found that panic is a common occurrence among students. Norton, Harrison, Hauch, and Rhodes (1985) administered a self-report measure known as the Panic Attack Questionnaire (PAQ) and found that 34% of undergraduates reported experiencing at least one panic attack in the previous year. Another Canadian study found that more than half of the students surveyed reported histories of panic (Wilson, Sandler, Asmundson, Larsen, & Ediger, 1991). Some researchers have suggested that these high rates of reported panic reflect methodological factors. For instance, the PAQ is an instrument that tends to yield a high false positive rate. However, even when the PAQ was revised to more closely reflect the symptoms of panic disorder, 22.1% of students reported experiencing a panic attack within the past year (Norton et al., 2008).

To what extent do the subclinical panic attack symptoms reported by students actually resemble the symptoms reported by clients with diagnosable panic disorders? Research on levels of "non-clinical panic" suggests that students who experience frequent panic attacks in a three-week period demonstrate phobic avoidance and psychological distress, while students who are less frequent panickers do not show these symptoms (Cox, Endler, & Norton, 1994). Wilson et al. (1992) examined the panic attacks described by two large samples of students from Winnipeg and a sample of panic disorder clients. They concluded that an alarmingly high 7.0% of the students in sample one and 8.1% of the students in sample two had symptoms consistent with clinical definitions of panic. However, because a key diagnostic feature (i.e., the frequency of attacks) was not assessed in a format that permits a diagnosis, it is not certain that all of these students met diagnostic criteria.

This problem was addressed in a study by McCabe and Blankstein (2000). The researchers screened a sample of 650 students twice for panic attacks with a self-report measure and then interviewed them using the panic disorder section of the *Structured Clinical Interview for DSM-IV Axis I Disorders* (SCID-IV; First, Spitzer, Gibbon, & Williams, 1996). Overall, 21 students (3%) were diagnosed with panic disorder and another 79 (12%) experienced unexpected panic attacks and had significant levels of impairment and distress. More recently, Norton et al. (2008) reported that 4.3% (or about 1 in 25 students) actually met *DSM-IV* criteria for a panic attack. Among those who met the criteria, the average number of panic attacks over the previous year was four and the typical panicker had experienced attacks for over four years.

Thinking Critically

1. Would you count yourself among the many students who have experienced a subclinical panic attack in the past year? If so, did something trigger the attack, or did it seem to "come out of the blue"?

2. Is there continuity between clinical and subclinical panic attacks? What about the fact that people with a diagnosed disorder appear to experience greater effects on their daily lives (e.g., lifestyle impairment, lifestyle restriction) relative to students with non-clinical panic (see Cox, Endler, & Swinson, 1991)?

Kinley et al. (2009) analyzed the CCHS data set to determine the prevalence rates and correlates of panic attacks among Canadians. The 12-month prevalence of panic attacks was 6.4%. Panic attacks were related to numerous psychological and physical function variables, including poor overall functioning, suicidal ideation, psychological distress, activity restriction, chronic physical conditions, and self-rated physical and mental health (Kinley et al., 2009). The authors concluded that panic attacks may be a marker of severe psychopathology independent of a diagnosis of panic disorder. Limitations of the study include the fact that numerous *DSM* Axis I and II disorders were not assessed.

Disorders that bear some relationship to panic disorder occur in other cultures. Among the Inuit of Northern Canada and west Greenland, *kayak-angst* occurs among seal hunters who are alone at sea. Attacks involve intense fear, disorientation, and concerns about drowning.

In *DSM-IV-TR*, panic disorder is diagnosed as with or without agoraphobia. **Agoraphobia** (from the Greek *agora*, meaning "marketplace") is a cluster of fears centring on public places and being unable to escape or find help should one become incapacitated. Fears of shopping, crowds, and travelling are often present. Many people with agoraphobia are unable to leave the house or do so only with great

Disorders similar to panic attacks occur cross-culturally. Among the Inuit, kayak-angst is defined as intense fear in lone hunters. B & C Alexander/ Photo Researchers, Inc.

A crowd is likely to be very distressing to a person with agoraphobia, who typically is often afraid of having a panic attack in a public place. Digital Vision.

distress. People who have panic disorder typically avoid the situations in which a panic attack could be dangerous or embarrassing. If the avoidance becomes widespread, panic with agoraphobia is the result. Panic disorder with agoraphobia and agoraphobia without a history of panic disorder are both much more common among women than among men.

More than 80% of people diagnosed as having one of the other anxiety disorders also experience panic attacks, although not with the frequency that justifies a diagnosis of panic disorder (Barlow et al., 1985). Panic disorder has been linked with a wide range of conditions, including depression, GAD, alcohol and drug use, and personality disorders. Panic disorder is also linked with physical conditions such as asthma, and in people suffering from both, it is believed that the panic exacerbates the asthma and vice versa (Lehrer et al., 2008). As with many disorders, comorbidity in panic disorder is associated with greater severity and poorer outcomes (Newman et al., 1998).

The following case in Canada described by Ananda Duquette (2001) illustrates what it is like to live with panic disorder with agoraphobia and provides some insight into possible causes.

In 2009, Toronto-born Joey Votto, star baseball player with the Cincinnati Reds, disclosed that he suffered from anxiety and depression following the death of his father. AP Photo/Gene J. Puskar.

MARGOT PAUL answers the door slowly, with her head held down. "Come in quickly," she says, "before you let the cats out." Margot has four cats and they are often her only company. She lives alone and rarely goes outside, afraid she'll get hit by a car, fall and break her bones, or suffer a stroke. Margot suffers from agoraphobia, an anxiety condition that causes her extreme panic, or even terror, when she's subjected to any situation outside of her "safety zone." Like many agoraphobics, Margot's safety zone is her home. Margot, now in her 80s, traces her anxiety back to the age of 11 when a man in her First Nations community on Lennox Island, P.E.I., assaulted her. "He chased me and knocked me down," she says. "He tried to tear my clothes off, but I fought him off. I was terrified. He told me he'd kill me if I opened my mouth, so I didn't tell anybody." Margot remembers that after the incident she started making excuses for not leaving the house. "When I thought about that man, I was taken over with fear and trembling," she says. "I hid for a long, long time. I really believed he would kill me." At the age of 15, Margot ran away, but she couldn't run away from the fear. "When I saw people fighting, like a man and his girlfriend, panic would come on me," she says. Working for a travelling fair, Margot saw the man who assaulted her one more time. She says seeing him produced terror in her—"Sheer terror." But she says the assault wasn't the only thing that contributed to her condition. "Kids used to tell me how ugly I was," she says. "I was so afraid of being seen, I would always wear a hat to hide my face." Margot says she was also insecure because she grew up speaking only Mi'kmaq and her English was poor. She moved to Halifax when she was 18 years old and worked in restaurants, in bars, and for bootleggers. She says she would often suffer from anxiety and go into hiding, but then the symptoms would lift and she would be able to work again. Margot married and had five children. One of her sons comes over once or twice a week to take her grocery shopping or to the doctor. She calls him her "safe person," meaning he is one of the few people she trusts. Except for these trips, Margot hasn't been outside for over a year. … One of her daughters, who also suffers from agoraphobia, lives upstairs from her. Margot's doctor tells her that her thought patterns fuel her fears. "What I think really does have an effect on how I feel," she says. "The mind is the computer of the body and what you feed it, it will produce. By changing the way I think, I've found a big difference." But Margot is still reluctant to join a self-help group. "I don't think I could even join a group," she says. "I feel like I don't fit in. … It seems like all my life I've been hiding," she says. "My life is a sad, sad story." Margot died of a heart attack on April 27, 2001. Documents indicated that she was older than realized—92 years old at the time of her death.

The *DSM-5* work group proposed that the previous diagnoses of panic disorder with agoraphobia and panic disorder without agoraphobia be subsumed into a new disorder—panic disorder. A seven-item panic disorder severity scale would measure several dimensions (e.g., panic attack frequency, panic attack distress, social impairment). Noting that panic attacks predict onset and severity of psychopathology beyond anxiety disorders, the work group recommended that panic attack be listed as a specifier for all disorders to which it might apply (see Craske et al., 2010). Agoraphobia was proposed to be classified as an independent separate condition that might or might not be comorbid with panic disorder (see Wittchen et al., 2010). Agoraphobia without a history of panic disorder was proposed for possible removal from the *DSM*.

ETIOLOGY OF PANIC DISORDER

Both biological and psychological theories have been proposed to explain panic disorder.

BIOLOGICAL THEORIES In a minority of cases, physical sensations caused by an illness lead some people to develop panic disorder. Mitral valve prolapse syndrome causes heart palpitations, and inner ear disease causes dizziness; both can be terrifying, leading to the development of panic disorder (Asmundson, Larsen, & Stein, 1998).

Panic disorder runs in families and has greater concordance in identical-twin pairs than in fraternal twins (Smoller et al., 2008). Smoller et al. (2008) summarized the results of six controlled family studies. These studies have established an increased risk of 5–16% among relatives of those with panic disorder. Early onset of panic disorder is associated with increased risk for family members. Thus, a genetic diathesis may be involved, and specific chromosomes are being investigated. For example, an investigation of Canadian samples (Rothe et al., 2006) builds on evidence for the influence of the Val158Met COMT polymorphism or other loci within or near the COMT gene (on chromosome 22) on susceptibility to panic disorder. Rothe et al. (2006) concluded that, "If COMT is further proven to be involved then new targets for drug development may be uncovered leading to enhanced pharmacological treatment of panic disorder" (p. 2241). In a recent review of linkage and association studies of anxiety disorders, Hamilton (2009) identified 96 studies that focused primarily on genetic association between one or a small number of genes and panic disorder. There were 76 discrete genes being studied that represented many aspects of fear circuit biology (e.g., receptors for neuropeptides, monoamines, and GABA). Other studies took a more comprehensive approach and involved 340 genes of neurobiological interest (e.g., related to serotonin, dopamine, or cholecystokinin systems). However, most of the findings have not been replicated. Hamilton (2009) concluded that COMT appears to be one of the few consistent findings in anxiety disorder genetics. However, the link is not only to panic disorder; disorders such as schizophrenia, major depression, and anxiety-related personality traits are also implicated.

Noradrenergic Activity Another biological theory suggests that panic is caused by overactivity in the noradrenergic system (neurons that use norepinephrine as a neurotransmitter). One version of this theory focuses on a nucleus in the pons called the locus ceruleus. Stimulation of the locus ceruleus causes monkeys to have what appears to be a panic attack, suggesting that naturally occurring attacks involve noradrenergic overactivation (Redmond, 1977). Subsequent research with humans has found that yohimbine, a drug that stimulates activity in the locus ceruleus, can elicit panic attacks in people with panic disorder (Charney et al., 1987). However, other research is not consistent with this position. Importantly, drugs that block firing in the locus ceruleus have not been found to be very effective in treating panic attacks (McNally, 1994).

Another idea about noradrenergic overactivity is that it results from a problem in gamma-aminobutyric acid (GABA) neurons that generally inhibit noradrenergic activity. Consistent with this line of thinking, a PET (positron emission tomography) study found fewer GABA-receptor binding sites in clients with panic disorder than in members of the control group (Malizia et al., 1998). Noradrenergic overactivation remains an area of active research.

Cholecystokinin Canadian psychiatrist Jacques Bradwejn and his colleagues in Toronto, Ottawa, and Montreal initiated another stimulating line of research in the attempt to understand the neurobiology of panic disorder (e.g., Bradwejn, Koszycki, & Meterissian, 1990). They discovered that cholecystokinin (CCK), a peptide that occurs in the cerebral cortex, amygdala, hippocampus, and brain stem, induces anxiety-like symptoms in rats and that the effect can be blocked with benzodiazepines, suggesting that changes in CCK produce changes in the development or expression of panic (e.g., Koszycki, Torres, Swain, & Bradwejn, 2005). Bradwejn hypothesizes that panic disorder is, at least in part, due to hypersensitivity to CCK. The mechanism of this sensitivity is not clear: CCK sensitivity may affect the action of other neurotransmitters or neurons in the noradrenergic system, or people may be reacting psychologically to the strong physical sensations caused by CCK.

Current work is exploring how healthy adult volunteers respond to CCK-4 injections (Eser et al., 2009). Initial results indicated that following the injection, overall brain activation patterns are not associated with the subjective anxiety response, but amygdala activation is seemingly involved in the subjective perception of anxiety. Figure 6.2 illustrates how one participant responded to the injection.

PSYCHOLOGICAL THEORIES The principal psychological theory of the agoraphobia that often accompanies panic disorder is the fear-of-fear hypothesis (e.g., Goldstein & Chambless, 1978), which suggests that agoraphobia is not a fear of public places per se, but a fear of having a panic attack in public.

As for panic attacks themselves, the foundation for their development may be an ANS that is predisposed to be overly active (Barlow, 1988) coupled with a psychological tendency

FIGURE 6.2 Time course of activity in the right amygdala of a participant with high amygdala activation in the first minute after CCK-4 injection.
Reprinted with permission of John Wiley & Sons, Ltd.

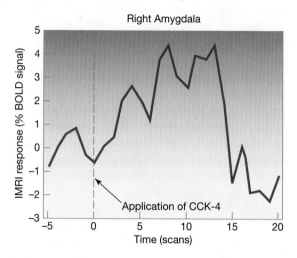

to become very upset by these sensations. When high physiological arousal occurs, some people construe these unusual autonomic reactions (such as rapid heart rate) as a sign of great danger or even as a sign that they are dying. After repeated occurrences, the person comes to fear having these internal sensations and, by worrying excessively, makes them worse and panic attacks more likely. Thus, the psychology of the person takes over from where the biology began. The person becomes more vigilant about even subtle signs of an impending panic attack, and this, too, makes an attack more probable. The result is a vicious circle: fearing another panic attack leads to increased autonomic activity; symptoms of this activity are interpreted in catastrophic ways; and these interpretations in turn raise the anxiety level, which eventually blossoms into a full-blown panic attack (Craske & Barlow, 1993).

Telch and Harrington (2000) studied students with no history of panic attacks who were divided into two groups (high and low scorers) based on their test scores on the Anxiety Sensitivity Index (ASI; Peterson & Reiss, 1987). The 16-item ASI measures the extent to which people respond fearfully to bodily sensations that could reflect a fear response. High scorers believe that these sensations have harmful somatic, psychological, or social consequences. Sample ASI items are shown in Table 6.3. All participants experienced two trials. In one trial they breathed room air, and in the other they breathed air with a higher than usual concentration of carbon dioxide. Half the participants in each group were told that the carbon dioxide would be relaxing, and half were told that it would produce symptoms of high arousal. Panic attacks did not occur in participants when they breathed room air, confirming previous findings. Also, the frequency of panic attacks was higher in participants who were high in fear of their own bodily sensations. Finally, and most important, the frequency of panic attacks was strikingly high in participants who feared their bodily sensations, breathed air containing a high concentration of carbon dioxide, and did not

TABLE 6.3
SAMPLE ITEMS FROM THE ANXIETY SENSITIVITY INDEX

ASI Items

Unusual body sensations scare me.

When I notice that my heart is beating I worry that I might have a heart attack.

It scares me when I feel faint.

It scares me when I feel "shaky" (trembling).

Note: People respond to each item on a 0 (very little) to 4 (very much) scale.
Source: Peterson and Reiss, 1987

expect it to be arousing. This result is exactly what the theory predicts: unexplained physiological arousal in someone who is highly fearful of such sensations leads to panic attacks. Thus, a heightened tendency to be afraid of fear sensations appears to play an important role.

In contrast to many conceptualizations of anxiety, anxiety sensitivity is presumed to be a dispositional characteristic that precedes the development of anxiety disorders. There is, in fact, converging evidence that anxiety sensitivity acts as a risk factor for anxiety psychopathology (see Schmidt, Zvolensky, & Maner, 2006, for review). Until recently, there were no definitive demonstrations that anxiety sensitivity is a premorbid vulnerability factor for the development of anxiety diagnoses. Schmidt et al. (2007) rectified this situation. They prospectively followed more than 400 non-clinical participants over a two-year period. Anxiety sensitivity predicted the development of spontaneous panic attacks. More importantly, independent of a history of anxiety problems and baseline trait anxiety, anxiety sensitivity predicted the development of anxiety diagnoses and overall Axis I clinical diagnoses, including anxiety, mood, and alcohol-use disorders. Thus, there is now strong evidence for anxiety sensitivity as a risk factor in the development of numerous clinical syndromes.

Additional Canadian contributions to research on anxiety sensitivity and the "fear of fear" are described in Canadian Perspectives 6.2.

CANADIAN PERSPECTIVES 6.2
RESEARCH ON THE PSYCHOMETRIC PROPERTIES AND APPLICATIONS OF THE ANXIETY SENSITIVITY INDEX

Several Canadian research groups have examined the psychometric properties and research applications of the Anxiety Sensitivity Index (ASI) as a way of finding out more about "the fear of fear," or the tendency to catastrophize the meaning of bodily symptoms. One question that has been asked is whether **anxiety sensitivity** is a unitary construct. While some research indicates that the ASI consists of only one factor, recent Canadian work with a modified ASI, the ASI-3, suggests three factors reflecting physical, cognitive, and social concerns (see Taylor et al., 2007). Upwards of 1 out of 5 people could have anxiety sensitivity (Bernstein et al., 2006).

While originally conceptualized as a factor in panic disorder, anxiety sensitivity seems to contribute to many forms of anxiety disorder. For example, a study led by Dalhousie University researchers Marc Zahradnic and Sherry Stewart showed in a sample of adult survivors of physical trauma that anxiety sensitivity predicted symptoms of post-traumatic stress and distress (Zahradnik, Stewart, Marshall, Schell, & Jaycox, 2009).

Other research applications of the ASI include work on the cognitive aspects of anxiety sensitivity. For instance, Canadian researchers have used cognitive tasks to establish that high scorers on the ASI have a cognitive bias that involves an orientation toward the selective processing of threat cues. However, the pattern varies for women and men (Stewart, Conrod, Gignac, & Pihl, 1998); high-anxiety-sensitive men tended to selectively process word cues reflecting social and psychological threats (e.g., embarrassment), while high-anxiety-sensitive women tended to selectively process cues involving physical threat (e.g., hospitalization).

McCabe (1999) compared high- and low-ASI participants in terms of their memory for neutral words, positive words, anxiety words, and threatening words. She found that those with high ASI scores were more likely to recall words that connoted a sense of threat (e.g., harassment, assault) and concluded that a cognitive processing vulnerability exists in high-ASI scorers even before an actual panic attack occurs.

How do differences in anxiety sensitivity develop? Twin research shows that ASI scores are heritable, so this measure may be the source of the genetic diathesis for panic disorder (Stein, Jang, & Livesley, 1999). Recent data suggest that anxiety sensitivity is a joint reflection of genetic and environmental causes, but genetic factors play a greater role in more extreme levels of anxiety sensitivity (Taylor et al., 2008). The role of environmental factors is in keeping with evidence indicating that people with high anxiety sensitivity may have learned to catastrophize their bodily sensations via parental modelling and parental reinforcement (Stewart et al., 2001). Thus developmental experiences should not be discounted when considering the etiology of panic disorder.

Finally, a growing number of studies indicate that high anxiety sensitivity appears amenable to CBT. A meta-analysis of 24 RCTs found large treatment effect sizes for treatment-seeking samples and moderate to large effect sizes for at-risk participants who did not seek treatment (Smits, Berry, Tart, & Powers, 2008). For instance, a longitudinal investigation in which participants underwent a CBT-based Anxiety Sensitivity Amelioration Training as a form of primary prevention yielded significant reductions in anxiety sensitivity. These reductions were specific to anxiety sensitivity, as opposed to other cognitive risk factors for anxiety (Schmidt et al., 2008).

Thinking Critically

1. On August 24, 2001, an Air Transat Airbus flying from Toronto to Lisbon was forced to glide without fuel in the middle of the Atlantic as the pilots attempted an emergency landing on a small airfield in the Azores. Although the pilot radioed that he would probably have to ditch in the ocean and the panic-stricken passengers said their goodbyes to loved ones, the pilot made a miraculous landing and no one was killed. Air Transat was hit with the largest fine in Canadian aviation history because of faulty engine repairs and a class action lawsuit was launched on behalf of the passengers (Hall & Verma, 2001). What do you think were the long-term psychological effects on the passengers? Would people high in anxiety sensitivity develop the most severe long-term symptoms? Which component of the ASI should be linked most to negative effects?

The concept of control is also relevant to panic. People with the disorder have an extreme fear of losing control, which would happen if they had an attack in public. Sanderson, Rapee, and Barlow (1989) demonstrated the importance of control. Clients with panic disorder breathed carbon dioxide and were told that when a light turned on, they could turn a dial to reduce the concentration of carbon dioxide. For half the participants the light was on continuously, but it never came on for the other half. Turning the dial actually had no effect on CO_2 levels, so the study evaluated how the effects of perceived control affected participants' reactions. Eighty percent of the group with no control had a panic attack, compared with only 20% of those who thought they could control CO_2 levels. The findings demonstrate the importance of perceived control in panic disorder.

THERAPIES FOR PANIC DISORDER AND AGORAPHOBIA

Therapies for panic disorder include both biological and psychological approaches. Some are quite similar to the treatments discussed for phobias.

BIOLOGICAL TREATMENTS Several drugs have shown some success as biological treatments for panic disorder. The treatment of choice is the use of selective serotonin reuptake inhibitors (SSRIs). The effectiveness of SSRIs accords with the results of a PET study with MRI scanning illustrating the role of serotonin Type 1A receptor binding in people with panic disorder (Neumeister et al., 2005).

Unfortunately, in their efforts to reduce anxiety, many people use anxiolytics or alcohol on their own; the use and abuse of drugs is common in anxiety-ridden people. This was illustrated in our opening case study of Sergeant Bob Bilodeau, who described his attempts at self-medication. A Canadian survey indicates that rates of self-medication range from 8% (for social phobia) to 36% (for GAD) and self-medication among those with an anxiety disorder is linked with suicidal ideation and suicide attempts (Bolton, Cox, Clara, & Sareen, 2006). A follow-up study by this group of Winnipeg researchers confirmed that self-medication with alcohol was highest for GAD (Robinson, Sareen, Cox, & Bolton, 2009) and was particularly likely among those with a concurrent mood or personality disorder.

PSYCHOLOGICAL TREATMENTS Exposure-based treatments are often useful in reducing panic disorder with agoraphobia, and these gains are largely maintained for many years after therapy has ended (Fava et al., 1995). Married people whose problem is primarily or solely agoraphobia have benefited from family-oriented therapies that involve the non-phobic spouse, who is encouraged to stop catering to his or her partner's avoidance of leaving the home. Barlow's clinical research program has found that the success of in vivo exposure treatment, in which the person with agoraphobia is encouraged to venture little by little from "safe" domains, is enhanced when the spouse is involved (Cerny et al., 1987). Contrary to the belief that one spouse somehow needs the other to be dependent on him or her, marital satisfaction tends to improve as the fearful spouse becomes bolder (e.g., Craske et al., 1992). Thus, although it is understandable that a spouse might become overly solicitous, perhaps from reasonable concern for the partner's well-being, or perhaps from an inner need to have a spouse who is weak and dependent, the outcome data suggest that relationships improve when the spouse with agoraphobia becomes less fearful.

Because treating agoraphobia with exposure does not always reduce panic attacks (Michelson, Mavissakalian, & Marchione, 1985), psychological treatment of panic disorder also takes into account the idea that some clients may become unduly alarmed by noticing and overreacting to innocuous bodily sensations. One well-validated therapy developed by Barlow and his associates (e.g., Barlow & Craske, 1994) has three principal components: (1) relaxation training; (2) a combination of Ellis- and Beck-type CBT interventions, including cognitive restructuring; and (3) exposure to the internal cues that trigger panic. Regarding the second component, Sanderson and Rego (2000) emphasize the need for clients to self-monitor the cognitions that occur *during the actual panic episode*. For the third component, the client practises behaviours in the consulting room that can elicit feelings associated with panic. For example, a person whose panic attacks begin with hyperventilation is asked to breathe fast for three minutes. When sensations such as dizziness, increased heart rate, and other signs of panic begin to be felt, the client (1) experiences them under safe conditions and (2) applies previously learned cognitive and relaxation coping tactics.

With practice and with encouragement or persuasion from the therapist, the client learns to reinterpret internal sensations, no longer seeing them as signals of loss of control and panic, but rather as cues that are intrinsically harmless and can be controlled with certain skills. The intentional creation of these sensations by the client, coupled with success in coping with them, reduces their unpredictability and changes their meaning for the client (Craske, Maidenberg, & Bystritsky, 1995).

Two-year follow-ups have shown that therapeutic gains from this cognitive and exposure therapy have been maintained to a significant degree and are superior to gains resulting from the use of alprazolam (Xanax) (Craske, Brown, & Barlow, 1991), though many clients are not panic-free (Brown & Barlow, 1995). A multi-site study indicates that Barlow's panic-control therapy is superior to imipramine in reducing panic attacks. Furthermore, adding the drug to this psychological therapy does not bestow an advantage. These findings show up both immediately after the end of treatment and at a 15-month follow-up (Barlow, 1999). A similar CBT treatment independently developed by Clark has also shown beneficial effects on panic disorder (e.g., Clark, Watson, & Mineka, 1994). Kenardy, Robinson, and Dob (2005) conducted a long-term follow-up of clients who received CBT within an RCT. Outcomes after six to eight years were significantly better than baseline measures of panic, avoidance, and depression. Landon and Barlow (2004) reviewed CBT treatment for panic disorder and concluded that it is well-tolerated, cost effective, and produces treatment gains in 40 to 90% of clients, with most studies reporting high rates.

As noted in Chapter 2, Milrod and colleagues (2007) demonstrated preliminary efficacy of a manualized psychodynamic psychotherapy for panic disorder. The RCT compared the specific psychodynamic treatment with applied relaxation training in twice-weekly sessions for 12 weeks. Participants in the psychodynamic group had significantly greater reductions in panic symptom severity. Roth (2009) compared psychological therapies of different kinds for panic attacks (e.g., CBT, muscle relaxation, breathing training, psychoanalytic psychotherapy) to make inferences about "common effective mechanisms" and concluded that, "the likely common element of all these therapies is that they reduce the immediate expectancy of a panic attack, disrupting the vicious circle of fearing fear" (p. 1).

Kim and colleagues (2009) evaluated the effectiveness of a newly developed mindfulness-based cognitive therapy (MBCT) program in the treatment of clients with panic disorder or GAD. Clients were assigned to either the mindfulness-based program or an education program for a period of eight weeks. The authors concluded that the MBCT program may be effective at reducing anxiety and depression

symptoms in panic disorder and GAD; however, RCTs are clearly needed.

Comparative reviews of pharmacotherapy vs. psychotherapy in the treatment of panic disorder (e.g., Barlow, Esler, & Vitali, 1998) conclude that CBT treatments show better results in long-term follow-ups than tricyclics such as imipramine (Tofranil), monoamine oxidase inhibitors, and benzodiazepines. Relapse is typically the rule when drugs for panic and agoraphobia are discontinued. It should be noted that panic treatment studies of all modalities report substantial proportions of clients who do not respond to efficacious treatments or prematurely terminate treatment (see Milrod et al., 2007, for review). For example, Landon and Barlow (2004) concluded that about 40% of CBT clients do not have a satisfactory response. Thus, it is important to discover predictors of success.

GENERALIZED ANXIETY DISORDER

"Fear and worry always lead to defeat."

—Ancient Chinese proverb

LS IS A 36-YEAR-OLD woman, who presented to a primary care physician complaining that she has difficulty falling and staying asleep. During the evaluation the patient described herself as a nervous and anxious person. She had married for the second time approximately 10 months earlier and started a new job as a director of a child care center shortly thereafter. With further prompting, she described recurrent worries that she may be fired from her new job and "plunge" into financial difficulties. This worry, although completely unfounded, occupied her much of the time, making it difficult for her to concentrate and preventing her from falling asleep at night. She stated that she wakes up often in the middle of the night worrying about her numerous obligations.

Reproduced from Monnier, Lydiard, & Brawman-Mintzer, 2003, p. 1399. In A. Tasman, J. Kay, & J. A. Lieberman (Eds.), *Psychiatry* (2nd ed.), New York: Wiley.

All-encompassing worry often is a reflection of **generalized anxiety disorder (GAD)**. The individual with GAD is persistently anxious, often about minor items. Chronic, uncontrollable worry about all manner of things is the hallmark of GAD; the most frequent worries of people with GAD concern their health and the hassles of daily life, such as being late for appointments or having too much work to do. The uncontrollable nature of the worries associated with GAD has been confirmed by both self-reports and laboratory data (e.g., Becker et al., 1998). Other features of GAD include difficulty concentrating, tiring easily, restlessness, irritability, and a high level of muscle tension.

Although people with GAD do not typically seek psychological treatment, the lifetime prevalence of the disorder is fairly high; prevalence in the NCS-R was 4.2% and 7.1% for men and women, respectively (Kessler et al., 2005). GAD typically begins in the person's mid-teens, though many people report having had the problem all their lives (Barlow et al., 1986). Stressful life events appear to play some role in its onset (Blazer, Hughes, & George, 1987). It has a high level of comorbidity with other anxiety disorders and with mood disorders (Brown, Barlow, & Liebowitz, 1994). It is difficult to treat GAD successfully. In one five-year follow-up study, only 18% of clients had achieved a full remission of symptoms (Woodman et al., 1999).

More recent findings challenge the validity of certain *DSM-IV* requirements. Ruscio et al. (2005) analyzed data from the NCS-R and found that lifetime prevalence of GAD increases by 40% when the "excessive and uncontrollable worry" requirement of the *DSM* (but not ICD-10) is removed. Although excessive GAD begins earlier in life, is more chronic, and is associated with greater severity and comorbidity, the non-excessive cases showed persistence and impairment, high rates of treatment-seeking, and elevated comorbidity relative to non-GAD people. In a further broadening of the definition, Ruscio et al. (2007) reported that relaxing the excessive worry, three associated symptoms, and the 6-month duration criteria more than doubles the estimated prevalence (13.7% lifetime and 6.6% 12-month). Further, the subthreshold manifestations were still predictive of elevated risk of subsequent secondary disorders. These results highlight a need for further research into the optimal definition of GAD. It was proposed by the *DSM-5* work group that GAD be changed to "generalized anxiety and worry disorder" to reflect the predominant or "hallmark" feature of the disorder (see Andrews et al., 2010).

ETIOLOGY OF GENERALIZED ANXIETY DISORDER

COGNITIVE-BEHAVIOURAL VIEWS In attempting to account for generalized anxiety, learning theorists (e.g., Wolpe, 1958) look to the environment. For example, a person anxious most of his or her waking hours might well be fearful of social contacts. If that individual spends a good deal of time with other people, it may be more useful to regard the anxiety as tied to these circumstances rather than to any internal factors. This behavioural model of GAD is identical to one of the learning views of phobias. The anxiety is regarded as having been classically conditioned to external stimuli, but with a broader range of conditioned stimuli.

The focus of other cognitive and behavioural views of GAD mesh so closely that we will discuss them in tandem. Anxiety results when people are confronted with painful stimuli over which they have no control. Cognitive theory emphasizes the perception of not being in control as a central characteristic of all forms of anxiety (Mandler, 1966). Thus,

a CBT model of generalized anxiety focuses on control and helplessness. Studies of humans have shown that stressful events over which people can exert some control are less anxiety-provoking than are events over which they can exercise no control. Research also suggests that, in certain circumstances, it is sufficient for the control only to be perceived by the subject; control need not actually exist (e.g., Geer, Davison, & Gatchel, 1970). Linking these findings to GAD, Barlow (1988) has shown that these people perceive threatening events as out of their control.

Related to this idea of control is the fact that predictable events produce less anxiety than do unpredictable events (see Mineka, 1992). For example, animals prefer a signalled, predictable shock to one that is not signalled (Seligman & Binik, 1977). The absence of the signal can serve as a sign of safety, indicating that there is no shock and no need to worry. Unsignalled and therefore unpredictable aversive stimuli may lead to chronic vigilance and fear—in humans, what we would call worry (Borkovec & Inz, 1990).

A perceived lack of control contributes to a sense of uncertainty. Extensive research has shown the role of an intolerance of uncertainty in the experience of chronic worry and GAD (e.g., Ladouceur, Gosselin, & Dugas, 2000). Researchers at Laval University and Concordia University have shown that manipulations designed to increase uncertainty intolerance lead to heightened levels of worry (Ladouceur et al., 2000). Uncertainty intolerance is particularly relevant when assessing ambiguous situations, and appraisals of ambiguous situations mediate the association between uncertainty intolerance and worry (Koerner & Dugas, 2008). Accordingly, CBT interventions with individuals with GAD are effective to the extent that they focus on removing uncertainty intolerance (Dugas & Koerner, 2005). Clinical improvement is associated with significant reductions in levels of uncertainty intolerance.

Canadian researchers Koerner and Dugas (2006) proposed a two-factor model that links GAD with a classic approach-avoidance conflict. The two factors are intolerance of uncertainty and a fear of anxiety. According to this formulation, GAD-prone people with an intolerance of uncertainty have a desire to engage in approach behaviours to reduce their feelings of uncertainty. However, they are also characterized simultaneously by a fear of anxiety that promotes the use of avoidance strategies designed to limit the experience of anxious arousal. Initial support for this model was provided by an experimental study showing that being intolerant of anxiety and also fearful of anxiety results in greater worry than either factor by itself (Buhr & Dugas, 2009).

One notion that has been applied to anxiety disorders in general and people with GAD in particular is that they are at risk, at least in part, because they are highly sensitive to and cognitively preoccupied with threat cues. Technological advances have resulted in more refined tests of this possibility. Whereas previous research has been dominated by the use of the Stroop test, more contemporary research makes use of eye tracking technology that affords a continual measure of visual attention processes (for an overview, see Armstrong & Olatunji, 2009). Figure 6.3 illustrates how eye tracking responses can vary depending on the presence versus absence of a threat cue that has been detected.

Indeed, the attention of people with GAD is easily drawn to stimuli that suggest possible physical harm or social misfortune, such as criticism, embarrassment, or rejection (MacLeod, Mathews, & Tata, 1986). People with GAD, for example, may be quick to notice when the person they are speaking with looks around the room from time to time, and they thus begin to worry about being rejected. Further, people with GAD are more inclined to interpret ambiguous stimuli as threatening and to believe that ominous events are more likely to happen to them (Butler & Mathews, 1983). The heightened sensitivity to threatening stimuli occurs even when the stimuli cannot be consciously perceived (Bradley et al., 1995).

Another cognitive view has been offered by Borkovec and his colleagues (e.g., Borkovec & Newman, 1998). Their focus is on the main symptom of uncontrollable worry. From a punishment perspective, why would anyone worry a lot? Since worry is thought to be a negative state, its repetition, one would think, should be avoided. Borkovec has shown that worry is actually negatively reinforcing; it distracts people from negative emotions. Borkovec's theory is reflected in recent work on cognitive avoidance conducted at Concordia University in Montreal. Sexton and Dugas (2009) found that measures of cognitive avoidance were linked with measures of generalized worry and pathological worry. Supplementary analyses found that two key worry-related processes that contributed to cognitive avoidance were negative beliefs about worry and fear of the somatic symptoms of anxiety.

FIGURE 6.3 Scanpath from an eye tracking experiment that presented participants with these two photos (blue lines show where a participant looked when presented with these photos; circles represent fixation points, and area of circles represents duration of fixation on each point).
Source: Armstrong & Olatunji, 2009.

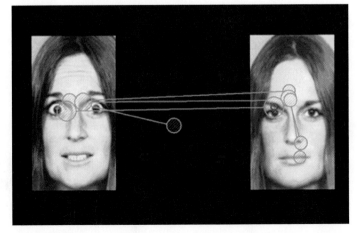

The key to understanding this position is to realize that worry does not produce much emotional arousal. It does not produce the physiological changes that usually accompany emotion, and it actually blocks the processing of emotional stimuli. Therefore, by worrying, people with GAD are avoiding certain unpleasant images and so their anxiety about these images does not extinguish. What are the anxiety-evoking images that people with GAD are avoiding? One possibility comes from data showing that people with GAD report more past trauma involving death, injury, or illness. Yet these are not the topics they worry about. Worry may distract people with GAD from the distressing images of these past traumas.

BIOLOGICAL PERSPECTIVES Growing evidence indicates that GAD may have a genetic component. An analysis of the data from the Virginia Adult Twin Study of Psychiatric and Substance Use Disorders examined the heritability of six anxiety disorders, which were examined in terms of the presence or absence of lifetime disorder (Hettema, Prescott, Myers, Neale, & Kendler, 2005). GAD had both a heritable and an environmental component and the genetic influence was comparable for men and women.

The most prevalent neurobiological model for GAD is based on knowledge of the operation of the benzodiazepines, a group of drugs that are often effective in treating anxiety. Researchers have discovered a receptor in the brain for benzodiazepines that is linked to the inhibitory neurotransmitter GABA. In normal fear reactions, neurons throughout the brain fire and create the experience of anxiety. This neural firing also stimulates the GABA system, which inhibits this activity and thus reduces anxiety. GAD may result from some defect in the GABA system, so that anxiety is not brought under control. The benzodiazepines may reduce anxiety by enhancing the release of GABA. Similarly, drugs that block or inhibit the GABA system lead to increases in anxiety (Insell, 1986). This approach seems destined to enhance our understanding of anxiety.

PSYCHOANALYTIC VIEW Psychoanalytic theory regards the source of generalized anxiety as an unconscious conflict between the ego and id impulses. The impulses, usually sexual or aggressive in nature, are struggling for expression, but the ego cannot allow their expression because it unconsciously fears that punishment will follow. Since the source of the anxiety is unconscious, the person experiences apprehension and distress without knowing why. The true source of anxiety—namely, desires associated with previously punished id impulses seeking expression—is ever-present. The person with a phobia may be regarded as more fortunate, since, according to psychoanalytic theory, his or her anxiety is displaced onto a specific object or situation, which can then be avoided. The person with GAD has not developed this type of defence and is constantly anxious.

THERAPIES FOR GENERALIZED ANXIETY DISORDER

Because they view GAD as stemming from repressed conflicts, most psychoanalysts work to help clients confront the true sources of their conflicts. Treatment is much the same as that for phobias.

Behavioural clinicians approach generalized anxiety in various ways. If clients can construe the anxiety as a set of responses to identifiable situations, the free-floating anxiety can be reformulated into one or more phobias or cued anxieties, making it easier to treat. For example, a behaviour therapist may determine that the generally anxious client seems more specifically afraid of criticizing and of being criticized by others. The anxiety appears free-floating only because the client spends so many hours with other human beings. Exposure becomes a possible treatment.

Because it can be difficult to find specific causes of the anxiety suffered by such clients, behavioural clinicians tend to prescribe more generalized treatment, such as intensive relaxation training, in the hope that if clients learn to relax when beginning to feel tense, their anxiety will be kept from spiralling out of control (Borkovec & Mathews, 1988). Clients are taught to relax away low-level tensions, to respond to incipient anxiety with relaxation rather than alarm. This strategy is quite effective in alleviating GAD (see Borkovec & Whisman, 1996).

If a feeling of helplessness seems to underlie the pervasive anxiety, the CBT therapist will help the client acquire skills that engender a sense of competence. The skills, including assertiveness, may be taught by verbal instructions, modelling, or operant shaping (Goldfried & Davison, 1994).

Because chronic worrying is central to GAD, it is not surprising that cognitive techniques have been employed in its treatment. A main ingredient in CBT approaches to worry is exaggerated exposure to the source of one's overly anxious concern. For example, a person worried about why his or her spouse is late coming home from a trip would be encouraged to imagine the worst possible outcome—that the plane has crashed. The client is asked to imagine this extreme, unlikely outcome for half an hour or more and then to consider as many alternative explanations as possible for the tardiness, such as difficulties getting a cab or being caught in heavy traffic. Two processes are assumed to operate here to reduce worry:

1. Because the client remains in a fearsome situation, anxiety is believed to extinguish.
2. By considering the unlikelihood of the worst fears imagined, the client alters his or her cognitive reactions to his or her spouse's not showing up when expected.

In other words, the client learns to think about less catastrophic reasons for a particular event.

Outcome data from controlled clinical trials are inconsistent in demonstrating that the various CBT approaches are superior either to placebo treatments or to alternative therapies such as Rogerian therapy (Barlow et al., 1998). Of particular note, with the striking exception of a study by Borkovec and Costello (1993), is that few clients in the various therapies evaluated show what is called high end-state functioning; that is, levels of anxiety or worry that are so minimal as to resemble those of people not diagnosed as having GAD. At a one-year follow-up, more than 40% of clients in the CBT group were not rated as high end-state in their functioning. In other words, many GAD clients continue to struggle with many symptoms of anxiety (e.g., Stanley et al., 1996). When compared with benzodiazepine treatment, however, CBT appears to be superior; indeed, when it was combined with the drug treatment, the results were poorer than when it was used alone (Power et al., 1990).

Historically, anxiolytics, such as those that treat phobias and panic disorder, have been the most widespread treatment for GAD. Drugs, especially the benzodiazepines, such as Valium and Xanax, as well as buspirone (BuSpar), are often used because of the disorder's pervasiveness. Once the drugs take effect, they continue to work for several hours in whatever situations are encountered. In recent years, antidepressants have also proven quite effective and they are being used with greater frequency; for instance, duloxetine, a serotonin-norepinephrine reuptake inhibitor used to treat depression, is seemingly effective for treating GAD (see Ryan et al., 2008). The added benefit of antidepressant use is that many people with GAD suffer concurrently from depression. Currently, GAD clients benefit from a wide range of drugs, including benzodiazepines, azapirones, selective serotonin reuptake inhibitors, serotonin-norepinephrine reuptake inhibitors, antihistamines, and atypical antipsychotics (see Davidson, 2009).

Unfortunately, many drugs have undesirable side effects, ranging from nausea, dizziness, drowsiness, memory loss, and depression to physical addiction and damage to body organs (see Ryan et al., 2008). In addition, when people stop taking these drugs, the risk of relapse is substantial (Davidson, 2009).

OBSESSIVE-COMPULSIVE DISORDER

BERNICE was 46 years old when she entered treatment. This was the fourth time she had been in outpatient therapy, and she had previously been hospitalized twice. Her obsessive-compulsive disorder had begun 12 years earlier, shortly after the death of her father. Since then, it had waxed and waned and currently was as severe as it had ever been.

Bernice was obsessed with a fear of contamination, a fear she vaguely linked to her father's death from pneumonia. Although she reported that she was afraid of nearly everything, because germs could be anywhere, she was particularly upset by touching wood, "scratchy objects," mail, canned goods, and "silver flecks." By silver flecks, Bernice meant silver embossing on a greeting card, eyeglass frames, shiny appliances, and silverware. She was unable to state why these particular objects were sources of possible contamination.

Bernice tried to reduce her discomfort by engaging in compulsive rituals that took up almost all her waking hours. She spent three to four hours in the morning in the bathroom, washing and rewashing herself. Between baths, she scraped away the outside layer of her bar of soap so that it would be totally free of germs. Mealtimes also lasted for hours because Bernice performed time-consuming rituals, eating three bites of food at a time, chewing each mouthful 300 times. These steps were meant magically to decontaminate her food. Even Bernice's husband was sometimes involved in these mealtime ceremonies, shaking a tea kettle and frozen vegetables over her head to remove the germs. Bernice's rituals and fear of contamination had reduced her life to doing almost nothing else. She would not leave the house, do housework, or even talk on the telephone.

Obsessive-compulsive disorder (OCD) is an anxiety disorder in which the mind is flooded with persistent and uncontrollable thoughts (obsessions) and the individual is compelled to repeat certain acts again and again (compulsions), suffering significant distress and interference with everyday functioning. OCD has a lifetime prevalence of 1 to 2%, and it affects women more than men (Kessler, 2005). A comparative study of OCD in seven countries, including Canada, found that annual prevalence rates were remarkably consistent across countries (Weissman et al., 1994).

Early onset of OCD (before age 10) is associated with comorbid tic and Tourette's disorders (Janowitz et al., 2009). Janowitz et al. (2009) noted that, "Early detection and management of comorbidities may offset impairments later in life" (p. 1). Early onset is more common among men and is associated with checking compulsions; later onset is more frequent among women and is linked with cleaning compulsions (Noshirvani et al., 1991). Earlier onset is also associated with greater severity of symptoms at the beginning and the end of treatment (Lomax, Oldfield, & Salkovskis, 2009). OCD may be associated with greater impairment than other anxiety disorders. A survey of seven anxiety clinics in Quebec found that OCD was the anxiety disorder associated with the highest-intensity use of mental health services (McCusker et al., 1997).

Obsessions are intrusive and recurring thoughts, impulses, and images that come unbidden to the mind and appear irrational and uncontrollable to the individual experiencing them. Whereas many of us may have similar fleeting experiences, the obsessive individual, as we saw in the case of Bernice, has them with such force and frequency that they interfere with normal functioning. Clinically, the most frequent obsessions concern fears of contamination, fears of expressing some sexual or aggressive impulse, and hypochondriacal fears of bodily dysfunction (Jenike, Baer, & Minichiello, 1986). Obses-

sions are ego-dystonic and the obsessional themes vary across individuals, and, according to O'Connor, Aardema, and Pélissier (2005), the themes often have great personal relevance. Obsessions can take the form of extreme doubting, procrastination, and indecision. Most people with OCD keep the content and frequency of their obsessions secret for many years (Newth & Rachman, 2001). The severity of obsessions has been identified as a factor that contributes to poorer quality of life (Masellis, Rector, & Richter, 2003).

A **compulsion** is a repetitive behaviour or mental act that the person feels driven to perform to reduce the distress caused by obsessive thoughts or to prevent some calamity from occurring. The activity is not realistically connected with its apparent purpose and is clearly excessive. Bernice did not need to chew each morsel of food 300 times, for example. Often an individual who continually repeats some action fears dire consequences if the act is not performed. The sheer frequency of repetition may be staggering. Some examples of commonly reported compulsions include:

- checking, going back many times to verify that already performed acts were actually carried out—for example:
  - "A 36-year-old single man had checking compulsions that focused on excrement, and he engaged in prolonged and meticulous inspection of any speck of brown, particularly on his clothes and shoes."
  - "A 40-year-old nursery school teacher checked that all rugs and carpets were absolutely flat, lest someone trip over them, and spent long periods looking for needles and pins on the floor and in furniture."
  - "A 19-year-old clerk carried out 4 hours of checking after other members of the family retired at night. He checked all the electrical appliances, doors, taps and so on and was not able to get to bed before 3 or 4 o'clock in the morning" (Rachman, 2003a, pp. 142–143).
- pursuing cleanliness and orderliness, sometimes through elaborate ceremonies that take hours and even most of the day.
- avoiding particular objects, such as anything brown.
- performing repetitive, magical, protective practices, such as counting, saying certain numbers, or touching a talisman or a particular part of the body.
- performing a particular act, such as eating extremely slowly.

With respect to the last point, when the slowness is the central problem and is not secondary to other OCD symptoms, such as checking, then it is a related condition known as *primary obsessional slowness*. How slow is slow? Rachman (2003b) described the case of a 38-year-old man who would take three hours each morning to get ready for work, including 45 minutes for teeth-brushing. A bath would take between three to five hours.

According to Rachman (2002), three "multipliers" that increase the intensity and frequency of compulsive checking are a sense of personal responsibility, the probability of harm if checking does not take place, and the predicted seriousness of harm.

We often hear people described as compulsive gamblers, compulsive eaters, and compulsive drinkers. Even though individuals may report an irresistible urge to gamble, eat, and drink, such behaviour is not clinically regarded as a compulsion because it is often engaged in with pleasure. A true compulsion is viewed by most OCD sufferers as somehow foreign to their personality (ego-dystonic). Stern and Cobb (1978) found that 78% of a sample of compulsive individuals viewed their rituals as "rather silly or absurd" but were still unable to stop them.

OCD often has a negative effect on the individual's relations with other people, especially family members. People saddled with the irresistible need to wash their hands every 10 minutes, or to touch every doorknob they pass, or to count every tile in a bathroom floor, are likely to cause concern and

Howie Mandel suffers from OCD, mysophobia, and ADHD (see Chapter 15), as described in his 2009 book, *Here's the Deal: Don't Touch Me*. He refuses to shake hands with people on his hit TV show *Deal or No Deal* because of contamination fears—the same fears that compel him to keep his head shaven. In a recent interview, the comedian had the last word on his various disorders: "People always ask me if they're a gift. And I say, if they are, I want to return them" (Ouzounian, 2009, p. E3). © Phil McCarten/Reuters/Corbis.

This famous scene from *Macbeth* illustrates compulsive handwashing. As noted by Shakespeare, "It is an accustomed action with her to seem thus washing her hands. I have known her continue in this a quarter of an hour" (Shakespeare, *Macbeth*, V, I). Courtesy New York Public Library. Astor, Lenox & Tilden Foundations.

even resentment in spouses, children, friends, or co-workers. Overt conflict may indicate the need for family therapy as a supplement to individual therapies.

OCD differs considerably from other anxiety disorders (e.g., in the domains of repetitive behaviours and inability to resist impulses and urges). The Research Planning Agenda for *DSM-5*: OCRD Work Group proposed creating a new category entitled obsessive-compulsive-related disorders (OCRDs)—sometimes referred to as obsessive-compulsive spectrum disorders (OCSDs)—that would possibly include OCD, body dysmorphic disorder, hypochondriasis, chronic tic disorders (e.g., Tourette's syndrome), numerous impulse control disorders (e.g., pathological gambling, trichotillomania), eating disorders, addictions, and autism. Proponents assert that the model is fundamentally etiological. Nonetheless, the "diagnostic shift" is contested by many clinicians and researchers on both conceptual and empirical grounds. There are both advantages and disadvantages in creating this new category for *DSM-5* (see Hollander, Braun, & Simeon, 2008). Storch, Abramowitz, and Goodman (2008) concluded that reclassifying OCD into a separate spectrum "is premature and not supported by the currently available data" (p. 336). Nonetheless, in February 2010, the work group recommended that OCD be included under a grouping of Anxiety and Obsessive-Compulsive Spectrum Disorders. Numerous changes to the existing diagnostic criteria were proposed, including possibly deleting the requirement that people recognize their obsessions or compulsions are excessive or unreasonable (see Leckman et al., 2010).

ETIOLOGY OF OBSESSIVE-COMPULSIVE DISORDER

BEHAVIOURAL AND COGNITIVE THEORIES Behavioural accounts of compulsions consider them learned behaviours reinforced by fear reduction. Compulsive handwashing, for example, is viewed as an operant escape-response that reduces an obsessional preoccupation with and fear of contamination by dirt or germs. Similarly, compulsive checking may reduce anxiety about whatever disaster the person anticipates if the checking ritual is not completed. Anxiety, as measured by self-reports, and psychophysiological responses can indeed be reduced by such compulsive behaviour. The very high frequency of compulsive acts occurs in order to give the person reassurance because the stimuli that elicit anxiety are hard to discriminate. For example, it is hard to know when germs are present and when they have been eliminated by a cleaning ritual (Mineka & Zinbarg, 1996).

It has also been proposed that compulsive checking results from a memory deficit. An inability to remember some action accurately (such as turning off the stove) or to distinguish between an actual behaviour and an imagined behaviour ("Maybe I just thought I turned off the stove") could cause someone to check repeatedly. General research on OCD suggests inconsistent evidence of memory deficits for verbal information, but there is stronger evidence for impairments in memory for non-verbal information (Muller & Roberts, 2005). A review by Cuttler and Graf (2009) from the University of British Columbia yielded new insights into whether memory deficits exist. They compared the results of research with OCD checkers and non-checkers and found that deficits in retrospective memory are found among checkers and non-checkers, so the deficits do not seem to have a special role in checking compulsions. However, some evidence suggests that checkers have unique deficits in prospective memory (see Cuttler & Graf, 2009). One caveat is that this research was conducted with student samples (i.e., subclinical checkers) and the generalization to OCD individuals requires further work. While **retrospective memory** is the ability to remember recent events and experiences, **prospective memory** is defined and measured by these authors as "the ability to look forward and to remember at the right place or time to perform an intended action" (p. 814) when the action is expected and required.

After reviewing cognitive biases in OCD, Canadian researchers concluded that there is only weak evidence for the existence of cognitive biases overall and cognitive biases may only exist among the subset of OCD people with contamination concerns (Summerfeldt & Endler, 1998). While the overall evidence continues to find only mixed support for cognitive biases, the use of refined experimental procedures suggests the bias may be more specific; it has been found recently that OCD individuals may have a processing abnormality for threatening visual material (Moritz et al., 2009).

So, how can we account for obsessive thoughts? The obsessions of diagnosed people usually make them anxious, as do the somewhat similar intrusive thoughts of normal people after exposure to stressful stimuli, such as a scary movie. Most people occasionally experience unwanted ideas that are similar in content to obsessions and unpleasant thoughts increase during times of stress. Normal individuals can tolerate or dismiss these cognitions, but for individuals with OCD, the thoughts may be particularly vivid and elicit great concern, perhaps because childhood experiences taught them that some thoughts are dangerous or unacceptable. Persons with OCD also have trouble ignoring stimuli, and this can add to their difficulties (Clayton, Richards, & Edwards, 1999).

Rachman advanced a cognitive theory of obsessions in OCD (see Rachman, 1998). He posited that unwanted intrusive thoughts are the roots of obsessions and that obsessions often involve catastrophic misinterpretations of the importance and significance of negative intrusive thoughts. Rachman and Shafran (1998) identified a range of cognitive factors involved in OCD in addition to the obsessions themselves, including an inflated sense of personal responsibility for outcomes and a cognitive bias involving thought-action-fusion. Thought-action-fusion involves two beliefs: (1) the mere act of thinking about unpleasant events increases the perceived likelihood that they will actually happen; and (2) at a moral level, thinking something unpleasant (e.g., imagining the self hurting others) is the same as actually having carried it out. Thus, thought-action-fusion involves a blurring of the distinction between thinking about something and reacting as if the behaviour has actually been expressed.

Table 6.4 lists faulty cognitive appraisals, as summarized by David Clark (2001, 2005) from the University of New Brunswick. Themes represented here include a sense of being responsible for events that may or may not occur, the overimportance of thought control, an inability to tolerate uncertainty, and thought-action-fusion. Many of these thoughts are represented on a measure known as the Meta-Cognitive Beliefs Questionnaire (Clark, Purdon, & Wang, 2003). Beliefs about thought control and the negative consequences of uncontrolled thoughts are highly predictive of obsessions (Clark et al., 2003). Other Canadian research suggests that there are meta-cognitive differences in OCD—specifically, that people with OCD have such highly developed cognitive self-consciousness that they reflect excessively on their cognitive processes (Janeck, Calamari, Riemann, & Heffelfinger, 2003). In other words, they engage in too much thinking about thinking itself!

What is distressing about intrusive thoughts? Studies conducted in Ontario suggest that thoughts are especially upsetting if they are inconsistent with valued aspects of the self (Rowa & Purdon, 2003) and they are perceived as personally meaningful and significant (Rowa, Purdon, Summerfeldt, & Antony, 2005). Thus, people who pride themselves on their altruism would be highly distressed by repetitive, intrusive thoughts reflecting an urge to hurt other people.

People with OCD may try actively to suppress intrusive thoughts, with unfortunate consequences. Wegner et al.

TABLE 6.4

FAULTY APPRAISALS IMPLICATED IN THE ETIOLOGY AND PERSISTENCE OF OBSESSIONS BY COGNITIVE-BEHAVIOURAL THERAPISTS

Faulty Appraisal	Explanation	Example
Overestimation of threat and negative consequences	The obsession is viewed as highly threatening and possibly resulting in very undesirable negative outcomes.	I have touched this doorknob. It is contaminated with germs that may now invade my body and cause cancer.
Inflated responsibility	The obsession is considered an indication that one has the power to bring about, or prevent, the occurrence of harm or other negative outcomes to self or others.	I notice a piece of glass on the road and think that it could cause a tire to blow and result in a fatal accident. Knowing this, I am responsible to ensure the glass is removed.
Overimportance of thoughts	The obsession is considered highly significant because of its prominence within the stream of consciousness.	The very fact that I am thinking unwanted intrusive thoughts of harming others means that these thoughts must be highly significant.
Overimportance of thought control	The obsession must be successfully dismissed from consciousness, and failure to do so represents a serious threat of possible negative consequences.	It is important that I suppress any intrusive thought of unwontedly touching a child because failure to control the thought means that I might lose control and actually commit such a horrible offence.
Thought-action fusion	The presence of the obsession increases the likelihood that the unwanted event will occur, and even thinking such a repugnant thought is morally equivalent to engaging in the forbidden act.	If I think about my father dying in a plane crash, this increases the probability that the event will actually happen; having unwanted intrusive thoughts of inappropriately touching a child is as morally reprehensible as actually doing it.
Catastrophic misinterpretation of significance	The obsession is interpreted as a sign or indication of something meaningful about the individual.	If I have unwanted intrusive thoughts of harming other people, this may mean that I am a latent psychopath.
Perfectionism	The best way to deal with the obsession is to achieve a perfect, complete, or just right state.	If I keep saying this phrase over and over until I can repeat it perfectly, then I will feel better and can get on with my daily activities.
Intolerance of uncertainty	It is intolerable to have any doubt or uncertainty associated with the obsession.	I cannot be certain that I understand this sentence, so I will reread it several times until I know that I understand what I have read.
Ego-dystonicity	The obsession is considered inconsistent, alien, and even threatening to one's self-definition.	A young man avoids public washrooms because of the obsessional doubt of whether he just molested a child in the washroom. Such a thought is completely contrary to his high moral standards and conscientiousness.

Adapted with kind permission from Springer Science and Business Media: Clark, D.A. (2000) "Cognitive Behavior Therapy for Obsessions and Compulsions: New Applications and Emerging Trends," *Journal of Contemporary Psychotherapy.* Volume 20, Number 2.

(1987, 1991) studied what happens when people are asked to suppress a thought. Two groups of students were asked either to think or not think about a white bear. One group thought about the white bear and then was told not to; the other group did the reverse. Thoughts were measured by having participants voice their thoughts and also by having them ring a bell every time they thought about a white bear. Two findings are of particular note. First, attempts to not think about a white bear were not fully successful. Second, the students who began by inhibiting thoughts of a white bear had more subsequent thoughts about it once the inhibition condition was over. Trying to inhibit a thought may therefore have the paradoxical effect of inducing preoccupation with it. Furthermore, attempts to suppress unpleasant thoughts are typically associated with intense emotional states, resulting in a strong link between the suppressed thought and the emotion. After many attempts at suppression, a strong emotion may lead to the return of the thought, accompanied by an increase in negative mood (Wenzlaff, Wegner, & Klein, 1991). The result would be an increase in anxiety. Wegner has created a measure known as the White Bear Suppression Inventory to assess individual differences in people's preoccupation with trying to inhibit obsessive thoughts.

Canadian researchers (e.g., Purdon & Clark, 2000) have reviewed research on the link between attempted thought suppression and obsessional phenomena and have concluded that an association does indeed exist. Research also indicates that attempted thought suppression is involved in either the etiology or persistence of other adjustment problems including depression, GAD, and PTSD (see Purdon & Clark, 1994).

BIOLOGICAL FACTORS There is some evidence for a genetic side to OCD. High rates of anxiety disorders occur among the first-degree relatives of OCD clients (McKeon & Murray, 1987). The prevalence of OCD is also higher among the first-degree relatives of OCD clients (10.3%) than in control relatives (1.9%) (Pauls et al., 1995). Thus, biological factors may predispose some people to OCD.

Encephalitis, head injuries, and brain tumours have all also been associated with the development of OCD (Jenike, 1986). Interest has focused on two areas of the brain that could be affected by such trauma: the frontal lobes and the basal ganglia, a set of subcortical nuclei including the caudate, putamen, globus pallidus, and amygdala (see Figure 6.4). PET scan studies have shown increased activation in the frontal lobes of OCD clients, perhaps a reflection of the persons' overconcern with their own thoughts. The focus on the basal ganglia, a system linked to the control of motor behaviour, is due to its relevance to compulsions as well as to the relationship between OCD and Tourette's syndrome. Tourette's syndrome is marked by both motor and vocal tics and has been linked to basal ganglia dysfunction. People with Tourette's often have OCD as well (Sheppard et al., 1999).

Rauch et al. (1994) provided evidence in support of the importance to OCD of both brain regions mentioned above. They presented participants with stimuli selected for them, such as a glove contaminated with garbage or an unlocked door, and found that blood flow in the brain increased in the frontal area and to some of the basal ganglia. People with OCD also have smaller putamen than people in the control group (Rosenberg et al., 1997).

FIGURE 6.4 The basal ganglia.

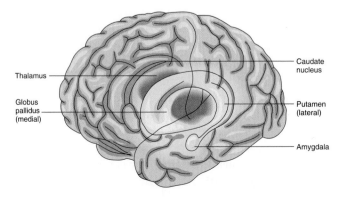

Thalamus

Globus pallidus (medial)

Caudate nucleus

Putamen (lateral)

Amygdala

Nakao et al. (2009) examined the cognitive function of OCD clients and "healthy" volunteers by neuropsychological tests and fMRI while participants performed tasks to assess attention and non-verbal memory. The clients were divided into a short-term disorder group (duration average of 5.5 years) and a long-term group (duration over 20 years). The long-term group showed attention and memory deficits. The authors concluded that "abnormal brain activation occurs in the early phase of OCD and that the long-term persistence of OCD might involve a decline in cognitive function" (p. 814).

Research on neurochemical factors has focused on serotonin. As noted below, pharmacotherapy for OCD focuses on serotonin reuptake inhibition (SRIs) but 40–60% of OCD clients do not show improvement following SRI treatment. Accordingly, genetic polymorphisms are being explored in an attempt to determine why so many OCD sufferers do not respond (see Van Nieuwerburgh et al., 2009).

PSYCHOANALYTIC THEORY In classical psychoanalytic theory, obsessions and compulsions are viewed as similar, resulting from instinctual forces, sexual or aggressive, that are not under control because of overly harsh toilet training. The person is thus fixated at the anal stage. The symptoms observed represent the outcome of the struggle between the id and the defence mechanisms; sometimes the aggressive instincts of the id predominate, sometimes the defence mechanisms. For example, when obsessive thoughts of killing intrude, the forces of the id are dominant. More often, however, the observed symptoms reflect the partially successful operation of one of the defence mechanisms. For example, an individual fixated at the anal stage may, by reaction formation, resist the urge to soil and become compulsively neat, clean, and orderly.

Alfred Adler (1931) viewed OCD as a result of feelings of incompetence. He believed that when children are kept from developing a sense of competence by doting or excessively dominating parents, they develop an inferiority complex and may unconsciously adopt compulsive rituals in order to carve out a domain in which they exert control and can feel proficient. Adler proposed that the compulsive act allows a person mastery of something, even if only the positioning of writing implements on a desk. There is little empirical support for these theories.

THERAPIES FOR OBSESSIVE-COMPULSIVE DISORDER

OCD is one of the most difficult psychological problems to treat. For example, a 40-year follow-up study showed that only 20% of clients had recovered completely (Skoog & Skoog, 1999).

EXPOSURE AND RESPONSE PREVENTION (ERP) The most widely used and generally accepted behavioural approach to compulsive rituals, pioneered in England by Victor Meyer (1966), combines exposure with response prevention (ERP)

(Rachman & Hodgson, 1980). In this method the person exposes himself or herself to situations that elicit the compulsive act—such as touching a dirty dish—and then refrains from performing the accustomed ritual—handwashing. The assumption is that the ritual is negatively reinforcing because it reduces the anxiety that is aroused by some environmental stimulus or event, such as dust on a chair. Preventing the person from performing the ritual (response prevention) will expose him or her to the anxiety-provoking stimulus, thereby allowing the anxiety to be extinguished. Controlled research (e.g., Stanley & Turner, 1995) suggests that this treatment is at least partially effective for more than half of clients with OCD, including children and adolescents (e.g., Franklin & Foa, 1998).

Sometimes control over obsessive-compulsive rituals is possible only in a hospital. Meyer (1966) created a controlled hospital environment to treat OCD. Staff members were trained to restrict the clients' opportunities for engaging in ritualistic acts. Adaptation of the treatment to the home required the involvement of family members. Preparing them for this work was not an easy task, requiring skills and care beyond the necessary proficiency in whatever specific behavioural technique was being employed.

In the short term, the ERP treatment is arduous and unpleasant for clients. It typically involves exposures lasting upwards of 90 minutes for 15 to 20 sessions within a three-week period, with instructions to practise between sessions, as well. It is estimated that 17 to 19% of clients refuse treatment (for a review, see Clark, 2005), and refusal to enter treatment and dropping out are generally recognized problems for many interventions for OCD. People with OCD tend to procrastinate, fear changes, and be overly concerned about others controlling them—traits that can create special problems for manipulative approaches such as behaviour therapy. In the most recent meta-analytic review of the effectiveness of psychological treatments for OCD, Rosa-Alcazar et al. (2008) concluded that therapist-guided exposure is better than therapist-assisted self-guided exposure and in vivo exposure combined, with exposure via imagination being superior to exposure in vivo alone.

COGNITIVE-BEHAVIOUR THERAPY A CBT approach is used rather than just a cognitive approach because an inherent part of any cognitive therapy is exposure and response prevention; to evaluate whether not performing a compulsive ritual will have catastrophic consequences, the client must stop performing that ritual.

Salkovskis and Warwick (1985) provided one of the earliest demonstrations of the usefulness of a CBT approach when they showed that cognitive restructuring was able to assist an OCD client who relapsed following ERP. This client had developed the belief that her hand creams would cause cancer. Salkovskis (e.g., 1998) has gone on to outline how cognitive procedures can eliminate the dysfunctional beliefs that contribute to the OCD clients' faulty appraisals. His model

focuses on the notion of perceived responsibility, which is defined as "the belief that one has power which is pivotal to bring about or prevent subjectively crucial outcomes" (Salkovskis, 1998, p. 40). Cognitive and behavioural techniques focus on the modification of dysfunctional beliefs involving this sense of personal responsibility. This can involve having the client actually test whether something bad happens as a result of being prevented from performing the ritual (see Van Oppen et al., 1995).

Several investigators based in Canada have extended the CBT interventions used to treat OCD. Freeston and Ladouceur and associates outlined a five-step treatment program, with the fifth step being relapse prevention (see Freeston et al., 1997; Ladouceur et al., 1995). Another extension has been proposed by O'Connor and Robillard (2000) from Montreal. They focus on the OCD client's conviction that imaginary events may actually come true. Their modification, known as the "inference-based approach," is geared toward identifying and ameliorating the obsessional inference, which has become imbedded within a fictional account constructed by the client. Over time, this imaginary account may be treated as if it were real. O'Connor and Robillard advocate a mixed approach that combines CBT with their inference-based approach (also see O'Connor et al., 2005).

How effective is CBT for treating OCD? As noted above, OCD is difficult to treat and is regarded as the anxiety disorder most difficult to ameliorate. However, CBT conducted in clinical settings with well-trained clinicians has proven effective (see Hunsley & Lee, 2007; van Ingen et al., 2009). Jonsson and Hougaard (2008) conducted a meta-analysis of 13 trials of group CBT/ERP for OCD and concluded that the group treatments are effective; however, additional studies are required to compare the effectiveness of group and individual formats. In two studies, better results were achieved by group CBT relative to pharmacological treatment. Rosa-Alcazar and colleagues (2008) concluded that ERP, cognitive restructuring, and the combination of the two were effective in reducing obsessions and compulsions and appeared to show a similar effectiveness. They suggested that both techniques actually employ similar treatment strategies (i.e., they both employ behavioural and cognitive strategies).

BIOLOGICAL TREATMENT Drugs that increase serotonin levels, such as the SSRIs and some tricyclics, are the biological treatments most often given to people with OCD. Both classes of drugs have yielded some beneficial results, but, as noted above, only for a selected proportion of those with OCD. Also, although research has shown that serotonin reuptake inhibitors, such as fluoxetine (Prozac), produce more improvement in people with OCD than do placebos or tricyclics, the symptoms usually return when the drugs are discontinued (see Jenike, 2004).

Technological improvements in measuring various aspects of brain activity have encouraged researchers to look for brain changes from therapeutic interventions. One notable study compared fluoxetine with in vivo exposure plus response prevention and found that improvement in OCD produced by both treatments was associated with the same changes in brain function—namely, reduced metabolic activity in the right caudate nucleus, overactivity of which has been linked to OCD (Baxter et al., 1992). Only those clients who improved clinically showed this change in brain activity as measured by PET scans. Such findings suggest that markedly different therapies may work for similar reasons—they are just different ways of affecting the same factors in the brain.

The desperation of mental health workers, surpassed only by that of the clients, explains the occasional use of psychosurgery in treating OCD. The procedure in current use, cingulotomy, involves destroying two to three centimetres of white matter in the cingulum, an area near the corpus callosum. Although according to a new study (Jung et al., 2006), 8 of 17 clients with refractory OCD showed some clinical improvement following the procedure, this intervention is viewed as a treatment of last resort, given its permanence, the risks of psychosurgery, and the poor understanding of how it works. Recently, the U.S. Food and Drug Administration granted a "humanitarian device exemption" to the manufacturers of a "deep brain stimulation system" as a therapy for OCD (Graham, 2009). The agency based the decision on research with 26 clients with severe OCD who had tried and failed numerous other therapies. Clients showed a 40% reduction in symptoms following a year of deep brain stimulation. We will discuss this treatment in more detail in Chapter 8 on mood disorders.

While a variety of interventions can result in significant improvement, OCD tendencies usually persist to some degree, although they are under greater control and are less obtrusive. Overall, Koran (2007) concluded that treatment is very challenging and few clients are cured fully, but they can be greatly helped.

PSYCHOANALYTIC THERAPY Psychoanalytic treatment for obsessions and compulsions resembles that for phobias and generalized anxiety—namely, lifting repression and allowing the client to confront what he or she (presumably) truly fears. The intrusive thoughts and compulsive behaviour protect the ego from the repressed conflict; however, they are difficult targets for therapeutic intervention, and psychoanalytic procedures have thus not been effective in treating this disorder.

Such shortcomings have prompted some analytic clinicians to take a more active, behavioural approach, using analytic understanding more as a way to increase compliance with behavioural procedures (Jenike, 1990). One view hypothesizes that the indecision one sees in most OCD people derives from a need for guaranteed correctness before any action can be taken (Salzman, 1985). Thus, clients must learn to tolerate the uncertainty and anxiety that all people feel as they confront the reality that nothing is certain or absolutely controllable in life. The ultimate focus of the treatment remains gaining insight into the unconscious determinants of the symptoms.

POST-TRAUMATIC STRESS DISORDER

"Some have suggested that scientific debate concerning PTSD can be opposed to the interests of victims and to those who suffer the effects of severe trauma. Yet scientific methods, and associated critiques, provide the best way to advance our knowledge, so that professionals can provide accurate information, sound advice, and non-harmful interventions to those in need."
—Gerald M. Rosen and B. Christopher Frueh, on challenges to the PTSD construct, 2007, p.161

"Even the locals [who did not have] Axis I pathology after Hurricane Katrina expressed common impairments in concentration and memory, labeled by many as 'Katrina Brain,' or [by those in] surrounding states as (pejoratively) 'water damage.'"
—Ken Sakauye, Professor of Psychiatry, Louisiana State University Health Sciences Center in New Orleans, November 2006

Post-traumatic stress disorder (PTSD), introduced as a diagnosis in *DSM-III*, entails an extreme response to a severe stressor, including increased anxiety, avoidance of stimuli associated with the trauma, and a numbing of emotional responses, as illustrated by the case of Sergeant Bilodeau at the start of this chapter. Although there had been prior awareness that the stresses of combat could produce powerful and adverse effects on soldiers, it was the aftermath of the Vietnam War that spurred the acceptance of the new diagnosis. However, as the following case excerpt demonstrates, PTSD can be experienced in non-war contexts.

NICHOLAS JOHN ARNOLD The case of Nicholas John Arnold is a precedent in Canadian law because he is the first person to be awarded money ($11,000) because of the distress experienced after witnessing an event that resulted in the deaths of three people he did not know. Arnold saw a horrible car accident that killed three people on the Pattulo Bridge in British Columbia in 2001. Arnold tried to help the victims but to no avail. It was an exceptionally traumatic event that resulted in panic attacks, PTSD, and bipolar depression. Arnold got blood on his arms while trying to assist the victims and he experienced the lingering smell of one of the victim's perfume on him. In total, he was off work for 2.5 years following the traumatic event. He continued to experience anxiety while driving and flashbacks in which he recalled the event. Not surprisingly, he suffered from sleep difficulties as well.

A controversial aspect of this case is that Arnold sued the estate of the driver who caused the accident and died as a result of the incident. Do you think this is callous or does Arnold's suffering warrant compensation? If compensation is warranted in your opinion, how much would you have awarded him? (Adapted from Hall, 2008.)

PTSD is defined by a cluster of symptoms. However, unlike the definitions of other psychological disorders, the definition of PTSD includes part of its presumed etiology—namely, a traumatic event or events that the person has directly experienced or witnessed involving the deaths of others (such as in the B.C. car accident above), threatened death to oneself, serious injury, or a threat to the physical integrity of self or others. The event must have created intense fear, horror, or helplessness.

In addition to combat stress, prolonged abuse can trigger symptoms of PTSD. Indeed, a survey of inpatient adolescents from the Foothills Hospital in Calgary found that PTSD was diagnosed in 12 of the 13 adolescents with a history of physical or sexual abuse (Koltek, Wilkes, & Atkinson, 1998). McEvoy and Daniluk (1995) reported that Canadian Aboriginal women who experienced multiple forms of trauma, including sexual victimization, typically develop symptoms of PTSD.

In previous editions of the *DSM*, the traumatic event was defined as "outside the range of human experience." Thus, the traumatic event could be a life-threatening natural disaster such as Hurricane Katrina and the aftermath for those in the southeastern United States, some of whom experienced PTSD, referred to previously as "Katrina Brain." This definition of being outside the range of human experience was considered too restrictive, as it would have ruled out the diagnosis of PTSD following such events as automobile accidents or the death of a loved one. Some have also considered the current broadened definition too restrictive, because it focuses on the event's objective characteristics rather than on its subjective meaning (King et al., 1995).

There is a difference between PTSD and **acute stress disorder**, a new diagnosis in *DSM-IV*. Nearly everyone who encounters a trauma experiences stress, sometimes to a considerable degree. This is normal. If the stressor causes significant impairment in social or occupational functioning that lasts for less than one month, an acute stress disorder is diagnosed. The proportion of people who develop an acute stress disorder varies with the type of trauma they have experienced. Following rape, the figure is extremely high—over 90% (Rothbaum et al., 1992). Less severe traumas, such as exposure to a mass shooting or being in a motor vehicle accident, yield much lower figures, such as 13% for motor vehicle accident victims (Bryant & Harvey, 1998). Although some people get over an acute stress disorder, many go on to develop PTSD (Harvey & Bryant, 2002).

The inclusion in the *DSM* of severe stress as a significant causal factor of PTSD was meant to reflect a formal recognition that the cause of PTSD is primarily the event, not some aspect of the person. The definition formally acknowledges the importance of the traumatizing circumstances, yet the inclusion of this diagnostic criterion is highly controversial. For this and other reasons, the usefulness of acute stress disorder as a diagnostic category has been questioned on

several grounds. Harvey and Bryant (2002) concluded that there is little evidence to support this disorder. One concern is that most people who encounter traumatic life events do not develop PTSD. In one study, for example, only 25% of people who experienced a traumatic event leading to physical injury subsequently developed PTSD (Shalev et al., 1996); thus, the event itself cannot be the sole cause of PTSD. Research subsequently moved in the direction of searching for factors that distinguish between people who do and people who do not develop PTSD after experiencing severe stress. Elwood et al. (2009) noted that high levels of comorbidity and symptom similarity suggest that cognitive vulnerabilities for anxiety and depression (e.g., anxiety sensitivity, rumination) might also serve as vulnerability factors for PTSD.

As noted in the quotes by McNally (2009) and Rosen and Frueh (2007), there is considerable controversy and debate about the PTSD diagnosis and we can expect to see changes in *DSM-5*. A major issue is that of "conceptual bracket creep" in how trauma is defined. According to McNally (2009), concerns about denying people who developed PTSD-like symptoms who were exposed to subtraumatic

Unlike most other diagnoses, PTSD includes a traumatic event as part of its cause in its definition. On September 11, 2001, terrorists hijacked two passenger jets and deliberately crashed them into the twin towers of the World Trade Center in New York City. Thousands of people perished in the explosions and collapse of the 110-storey buildings. Firefighters, police officers, and other rescue workers, such as these men at "ground zero," could be vulnerable to PTSD. The Canadian Press/Paul Chiasson.

stressors the diagnosis that would allow reimbursable treatment led to expansion of the trauma concept in editions subsequent to *DSM-III*. The *DSM-IV-TR* broadened the concept of a stressor to embrace direct exposure, vicarious exposure, and indirect, informational exposure, thus bracketing three kinds of people as trauma survivors. It is the third group, new in *DSM-IV*, that includes people "confronted with" information about threats to others, such as the horrified viewers of the television coverage of the September 11, 2001 terrorist attacks, that is most problematic. One of the authors of this text watched those horrific events unfold, saw the second plane hit the south tower, was horrified to see people leaping to their deaths to escape the flames and searing heat, cried as the towers crumbled to the ground, and understood the tragic consequences but did not develop PTSD. Can the author's "virtual" stress possibly compare with the experiences of those who were there and affected directly? Are we all trauma survivors? McNally (2009) recommended that *DSM-5* "eliminate indirect, informational exposure as qualifying as trauma" (p. 598). With respect to the proposed diagnostic criteria for PTSD, the *DSM-5* work group appeared to heed McNally's recommendation, noting that, "Witnessing or exposure to aversive details does not include events that are witnessed only in electronic media, televisions, movies or pictures, unless this is part of a person's vocational role" (see www.dsm5.org).

Currently, the symptoms for PTSD are grouped into three major categories. The diagnosis requires that symptoms in each category last longer than one month.

1. *Re-experiencing the traumatic event.*

   The individual frequently recalls the event and experiences nightmares about it. Intense emotional upset is produced by stimuli that symbolize the event (e.g., thunder reminding a veteran of the battlefield) or on anniversaries of some specific experience. Kuch and Cox (1992) examined PTSD symptoms in a sample of 124 Holocaust survivors living in the Toronto area. This sample included subsamples of 78 concentration camp survivors and 20 tattooed concentration camp survivors. Nightmares were experienced by 87.2% of the concentration camp survivors and by 90% of the tattooed concentration camp survivors.

   The importance of re-experiencing cannot be underestimated, for it is the likely source of the other categories of symptoms. Some theories of PTSD make re-experiencing the central feature by attributing the disorder to an inability to successfully integrate the traumatic event into an existing schema (the person's general beliefs about the world) (e.g., Foa, Zinbarg, & Rothbaum, 1992; Horowitz, 1986). The tendency to re-experience the traumatic memory has sparked much research on PTSD and memory.

2. *Avoidance of stimuli associated with the event or numbing of responsiveness.*

   The person tries to avoid thinking about the trauma or encountering stimuli that will bring it to mind; there may be amnesia for the event. Numbing refers to decreased interest in others, a sense of estrangement, and an inability to feel positive emotions. These symptoms seem almost contradictory to those in item 1. In PTSD, there is fluctuation; the person goes back and forth between re-experiencing and numbing.

3. *Symptoms of increased arousal.*

   These symptoms include difficulties falling or staying asleep, difficulty concentrating, hypervigilance, and an exaggerated startle response. Laboratory studies have confirmed these clinical symptoms by documenting the heightened physiological reactivity of PTSD participants to combat imagery (e.g., Orr et al., 1995) and their high-magnitude startle responses (Morgan et al., 1997).

According to North et al. (2009), avoidance and numbing is the most specific category of symptoms for identification of PTSD.

Estimates of the prevalence of PTSD vary substantially depending on how people are assessed. Canadian data suggest that the lifetime prevalence of PTSD in Canada is almost 1 in 10 and the one-month prevalence is about 1 in 25 Canadians (Van Ameringen et al., 2008). Prevalence varies depending on the severity of the trauma experienced; it is about 3% among civilians who have been exposed to a physical attack, 20% among people wounded in Vietnam, and about 50% among rape victims and people who were POWs (prisoners of war) in either the Second World War or the Korean War (Engdahl et al., 1997; Rothbaum et al., 1992). Mitchell, Griffin, Stewart, and Loba (2004) found that 46% of community volunteers had probable PTSD after helping with the cleanup and recovery of bodies following the 1998 Swissair disaster off the coast of Nova Scotia. Overall, 69% of volunteers reported intrusive thoughts about the disaster. Factors that were deemed to increase PTSD symptoms included community silence, limited help-seeking (due to the stigma of seeking help), and insufficient proactive provision of therapeutic resources. Similar high rates of PTSD have been experienced by Canadian military personnel (see Canadian Perspectives 6.3).

On May 12, 2008, a massive earthquake affected a vast area of China, destroying 6.5 million homes and affecting about 46 million people. Over 70,000 people perished and about 15 million were evacuated from their homes. Peng Kun and colleagues (2009) surveyed people in August 2008 in a region severely affected by the earthquake. The prevalence of PTSD was 45.5% (using structured interviews and *DSM-IV* criteria). Numerous factors were related to increased likelihood of PTSD: low household income, being from an ethnic minority, living in a shelter or temporary house, death in the family, and household damage.

Hurricane Katrina was the deadliest hurricane in the United States in over 70 years and the most expensive natural disaster in U.S. history. Kessler et al. (2008) interviewed a representative sample of pre-hurricane residents of areas affected by Hurricane Katrina five to eight months after the hurricane and again one year later. Contrary to some past studies, where post-disaster disorders decreased with time, prevalence increased significantly for PTSD (20.9% versus 14.9% at baseline), serious mental illness (14.0 versus 10.9%), suicidal ideation (6.4 versus 2.8%), and suicide plans (2.5 versus 1.0%). The increases were judged to be due to "unresolved hurricane-related stresses." These are residual stressors attributable to the weather (e.g., living elsewhere due to needing to re-locate). When exposed to the trauma of Hurricane Katrina, women were more likely than men to develop PTSD (Galea et al., 2007). There is a high rate of comorbidity between PTSD and substance-use disorders; research suggests that PTSD symptoms typically precede, rather than follow, substance abuse (see Stewart, Pihl, Conrod, & Dongier, 1998).

CANADIAN PERSPECTIVES 6.3
PTSD IN CANADIAN VETERANS AND PEACEKEEPERS

Published accounts of mental disorders in Canadian soldiers can be traced back to the First World War. Farrar (1917) concluded that 10% of invalided Canadian soldiers were "nervous and mental cases" (p. 389). The majority of cases (58%) were said to suffer from "neurotic reactions," and of these, a subgroup suffered from "shell shock." The second group (14%) were said to suffer from "mental diseases and defects" (p. 389) that included cases of "dementia praecox," "primary mental defect," and "psychopathic inferiority."

Overall, there is a relative paucity of contemporary research on PTSD in Canadian military personnel, but the research that has been conducted has startling implications. An estimated 10,000 to 40,000 Canadians volunteered in the United States military to assist with the Vietnam War effort. Stretch (1990, 1991)

Lt. Gen. Roméo Dallaire, former commander of United Nations forces in Rwanda, who retired because of PTSD. Lt. Gen. (Retired) Dallaire is now a Senator in the Canadian Senate. The Canadian Press/Jonathan Hayward.

examined the impact of participating in the war on 164 Canadian veterans who had an average of 54 months of duty with 15 months in Vietnam. An alarming 65.4% reported experiencing PTSD symptoms either during or after their Vietnam experience. PTSD was associated with poorer health, nervous system problems, depression, anxiety, anger, and shame. The sense of shame was, in part, a response to the perceived reaction of Canadian society. Comparisons of PTSD sufferers and veterans without PTSD showed that PTSD sufferers reported more negative reactions from people upon their return, more negative reactions to their involvement in the war, and homecomings that were significantly worse. Relative to American veterans, Canadian veterans were particularly vulnerable to long-lasting forms of PTSD because they were more isolated and received less recognition and support for their war efforts.

Beal (1995) conducted the longest follow-up study of PTSD published thus far. The 50-year follow-up focused on 276 Canadian veterans of the Dieppe Raid, regarded as one of the bloodiest events of the Second World War, with a casualty rate of 68%. Beal (1995) found alarming levels of PTSD in both POWs and non-POWs. Overall, 43.4% of the POWs and 29.9% of the non-POWs were diagnosed with PTSD based on their 1992 self-reports. Comparisons of POWs with and without PTSD showed that those with PTSD reported more maltreatment in the form of beatings, personal intimidation, interrogation, group death threats, solitary confinement, and witnessing acts of torture. POWs with PTSD also had higher levels of depression, anxiety, and suicidal thoughts. A key point to remember is that these extreme levels of distress persisted for 50 years. Most men reported experiencing little anxiety or depression prior to the Dieppe Raid. Beal (1995) noted further that despite the level of disability experienced by these veterans, with 37% having PTSD in 1992, relatively few qualified for government assistance, according to criteria used in 1992 by the Canadian government. Only 5.4% were receiving psychological disability pensions from the Department of Veterans Affairs.

In 2000, the Canadian government opted finally to recognize PTSD symptoms as a form of disorder that merits a psychological disability pension (Thorne, 2000). This change was a response, in part, to the growing number of public accounts of severe forms of PTSD experienced by Canadian peacekeepers. The most well-known example involves retired Lt. Gen. Roméo Dallaire, who served as the United Nations commander in Rwanda in 1994, when more than 800,000 Tutsis and Hutu moderates were killed by the ruling Hutu extremists. Dallaire and his men witnessed these atrocities (including children killing other children) as well as the slaughter of 10 Belgian soldiers by a machete-wielding mob. Dallaire's compelling account of his personal struggles and the genocide he witnessed were summarized in his book (Dallaire, 2003). His personal difficulties became public when he was discovered unconscious and apparently inebriated in a park in Hull, Quebec, on June 26, 2000. He revealed his difficulties in a letter that was sent to CBC Radio and read on-air on July 3, 2000. Dallaire has acknowledged his problems with PTSD and his suicide attempts (Growe, 2000). In his letter to CBC Radio, Dallaire said:

> The anger, the rage, the hurt and the cold loneliness that separates you from your family, friends and society's normal daily routine are so powerful that the option of destroying yourself is both real and attractive. That is what happened last Monday night. … It appears, it grows, it invades and it overpowers you. In my current state of therapy, which continues to show very positive results, control mechanisms have not yet matured to always be on top of this battle.

A Canadian investigation of deployed peacekeepers and non-deployed military personnel confirmed that PTSD symptoms have a direct negative impact on health status. Moreover, this link was evident for both deployed peacekeepers and non-deployed personnel (Asmundson, Stein, & McCreary, 2002; also see McNally, 2005a). Thus, PTSD was associated with poor health, regardless of deployment status. PTSD was also closely linked with depression. In a study of French-Canadian male veterans seeking assessment or treatment for deployment-related PTSD, Poundja, Fikretoglu, and Brunet (2006) reported that nearly 87% of the sample reported significant current pain. The PTSD-pain relation was fully mediated by depression. Another recent study (Richardson et al., 2008) examined deployed Canadian Forces peacekeeping veterans and found that PTSD and depression severity significantly predicted both mental and physical health-related quality of life.

Deniz Fikretoglu, Alain Brunet, and their colleagues (Fikretoglu, Brunet, Guay, & Pedlar, 2007) examined rates, characteristics, and predictors of mental health treatment seeking by military members with PTSD. Their sample of 549 who met the criteria for lifetime PTSD (out of 8,441 assessed) was drawn from the CCHS-Canadian Forces Supplement (CFS), the first nationally representative epidemiological survey of mental health in the Canadian military. Approximately one third of those with PTSD never sought any form of mental health treatment. However, those with comorbid depression were 3.75 times more likely to seek treatment. Unfortunately, treatment adequacy was not assessed. There was also a greater likelihood of treatment seeking after multiple types of trauma. The CCHS-CFS was conducted in 2002, prior to the mission in Afghanistan, which has had a much higher exposure to combat than other recent operations. Thus, it is unknown whether findings based on this data set still apply.

In a related study with 509 military members with PTSD, Fikretoglu et al. (2006) reported that factors that were trauma-related (index traumatic event type, cumulative trauma exposure), demographic (marital status), enabling (income), and needs-based (PTSD interference) predicted treatment seeking, but that treatment and non-treatment seekers were both composed of distinct subgroups. Fikretoglu et al. (2006) concluded that it is important to tailor interventions directed at increasing treatment-seeking behaviour to the specific needs of different subgroups of non-treatment seekers. This work is important because additional analyses of the CFS data set (Sareen et al., 2007) revealed that while 15% of these Canadian Forces members had suffered from one or more disorders in the previous year, and 31% met the criteria for one or more lifetime disorders, only 13% had sought treatment.

A study of U.S. soldiers returning from combat in Afghanistan and Iraq (Pietrzak et al., 2009) suggests that interventions that bolster resilience (in this instance, increased personal control and positive acceptance of change), together with post-deployment social support, protect against the development of traumatic stress and depression.

Thinking Critically

1. Lt. Gen. Dallaire, like so many Canadian peacekeepers, had difficulty coping with the atrocities he witnessed. What steps would you take to help our peacekeepers or military on operational deployments to Afghanistan better prepare for the psychological consequences of their missions? What preventive strategies would you recommend that the military employ during the missions? Would it be appropriate to have military psychologists available during the mission? What steps should be taken when the troops return home? Should family therapy be one component of a multi-faceted intervention?

2. Research on PTSD in Canadian Forces members demonstrates that there are complex relationships among PTSD, physical health, pain, and depression and their link to trauma exposure and types of traumatic events. However, these studies were correlational and preclude drawing conclusions about the direction of causation. Design a longitudinal study to replicate current findings. Also, design an intervention program to increase treatment seeking. Intervention programs should assess conditions comorbid with PTSD, particularly depression. Design a comprehensive, multi-faceted treatment program for Canadian Forces members who have experienced trauma.

ETIOLOGY OF POST-TRAUMATIC STRESS DISORDER

Research and theory on the causes of PTSD focus on risk factors for the disorder, as well as on psychological and biological factors.

RISK FACTORS When examining risk factors, it is important to consider not only risk factors for PTSD, but also risk factors for the likelihood of being exposed to trauma. Research indicates that males, relative to females, have higher levels of trauma exposure across various event types, with the exception of child sexual abuse (CSA) and sexual assaults in general, yet females have higher levels of PTSD (Breslau, 2002; Tolin & Foa, 2006).

There are several risk factors for PTSD. Given exposure to a traumatic event, predictors of PTSD, in addition to gender, include perceived threat to life, early separation from parents, family history of a disorder, previous exposure to traumas, and a pre-existing disorder (an anxiety disorder or depression) (Breslau et al., 1997, 1999; Ehlers, Malou, & Bryant, 1998; Stein, 1997). Previous exposure to trauma is regarded as one of the strongest predictors of whether the individual is exposed subsequently to trauma (Testa, VanZile-Tamsen, & Livingston, 2007). One of the most detailed analyses of this phenomenon was conducted by Cougle, Resnick, and Kilpatrick (2009). They conducted a longitudinal study with multiple phases of a nationally representative sample of women and differentiated various types of PTSD symptoms. They found that PTSD re-experiencing symptoms predicted subsequent exposure to interpersonal violence victimization by a non-intimate perpetrator but not subsequent exposure instigated by an intimate partner. Also, PTSD hyperarousal symptoms were uniquely predictive of other traumatic stressors. Thus, different types of PTSD symptoms played different roles in subsequent exposure to different types of events.

Longitudinal research continues to show that in addition to being exposed to less severe events, having high intelligence (an IQ of 115 or greater) seems to be a protective factor, perhaps because it is associated with having better coping skills (see Breslau, Lucia, & Alvarado, 2006).

Dissociative symptoms (including amnesia and out-of-body experiences) at the time of the trauma also increase the probability of developing PTSD, as does trying to push memories of the trauma out of one's mind (Ehlers et al., 1998). Dissociation may play a role in maintaining the disorder, as it keeps the person from confronting traumatic memories. A compelling study of dissociation assessed rape survivors within two weeks of the assault. While the women talked about either the rape or neutral topics, psychophysiological measures and self-reports of stress were taken. The women were divided into two groups based on their scores on a measure of dissociation during the rape (e.g., "Did you have moments of losing track of what was going on?"). Women with high dissociation scores were much more likely to have PTSD symptoms than were low scorers. High scorers also had a dissociation between their subjective stress ratings and their physiological responses. Although they reported high levels of stress when they were talking about being raped, they showed less physiological arousal than did the women with low dissociation scores.

Another risk factor was discovered in a study of Israeli veterans of the 1982 war with Lebanon. Development of PTSD was associated with a tendency to take personal responsibility for failures and to cope with stress by focusing on emotions ("I wish I could change how I feel") rather than on the problems themselves (Mikulincer & Solomon, 1988).

Attachment style has been identified as a PTSD risk factor by York University researcher Robert Muller and his associates in their study of high-risk adults with a history of childhood physical or sexual abuse (see Muller, Sicoli, & Lemieux, 2000; Muller, Kraftcheck, & McLewin, 2004). Attachment styles (e.g., how an infant reacts when left alone with a stranger when the mother leaves) are discussed in more detail in Chapter 15. Muller et al. (2000) reported that 76% of the participants endorsed an insecure attachment style. They found that PTSD is likely among people with an insecure attachment style that involves a negative view of the self; a negative view of others was not linked with PTSD symptoms. A recent treatment study by Muller and Rosenkrantz (2009) found that reductions in PTSD symptoms were accompanied by increases in secure attachment and these increases were maintained six months after treatment.

PSYCHOLOGICAL THEORIES Learning theorists assume that PTSD arises from a classical conditioning of fear (e.g., Fairbank & Brown, 1987). A woman who has been raped, for example, may come to fear walking in a certain neighbourhood (the CS) because of having been assaulted there (the UCS). Based on this classically conditioned fear, avoidances are built up, and they are negatively reinforced by the reduction of fear that comes from not being in the presence of the CS. In a sense, PTSD is an example of the two-factor theory of avoidance learning proposed years ago by Mowrer (1947). There is a developing body of evidence in support of this view (Foy et al., 1990) and of related theories that emphasize the loss of control and predictability felt by people with PTSD (Chemtob et al., 1988).

Cognitive theorists characterize PTSD as a disorder of memory with the hallmark feature being the constant involuntary recollection of the traumatic event (McNally, 2006). Contemporary research suggests that there are many cognitive tendencies that are problematic for those with PTSD. For instance, it has been shown across several studies that PTSD is associated with impaired memory of emotionally neutral stimuli. Specifically, there is a robust association between PTSD and memory impairment and this tendency is stronger for verbal memory than visual memory (Brewin, Kleiner, Vasterling, & Field, 2007). Other research links PTSD with insufficient working memory systems (Shaw et al., 2009). Researchers are now attempting to show a connection with distinct memory patterns and cognitive deficits with brain regions and brain functions. For instance, a recent fMRI study conducted in Montreal shows that memory performance is linked with ventral medial prefrontal cortex activity (Dickie, Brunet, Akerib, & Armony, 2008). McNally (2006) summarized extant work on the cognitive features of PTSD by suggesting that PTSD involves a hyporesponsive prefrontal cortical region or hyporesponsive amygdala region. Moreover, having above-average cognitive ability protects people from experiencing PTSD, but reduced hippocampal volume escalates the risk of PTSD (e.g., Bremner, 2006).

A psychodynamic theory proposed by Horowitz (1990) posits that memories of the traumatic event occur constantly in the person's mind and are so painful that they are either consciously suppressed (by distraction, for example) or repressed. People are believed to engage in a kind of internal struggle to make some sense of a trauma by integrating it into their existing beliefs about themselves and the world.

BIOLOGICAL THEORIES We touched on biological factors as part of our discussion of memory and cognition in PTSD. Additional research on twins shows a possible diathesis for PTSD (True et al., 1993). A study conducted with twin pairs from the Vancouver area demonstrated that exposure to certain kinds of trauma (e.g., violent crimes) was influenced by genetic and environmental factors, but only environmental factors contributed to other types of trauma (e.g., natural disasters); in addition, PTSD symptoms following exposure to non-combat trauma were moderately heritable (Stein, Jang, Taylor, Vernon, & Livesley, 2002). This study is unique in two ways: it is one of the few genetic studies conducted on a non-military, community sample, and it is the first study of its kind to include women. Stein et al. (2002) concluded that a personality characterized by trait neuroticism might be the genetic vulnerability factor that serves as a diathesis for PTSD.

Gilbertson et al. (2006) evaluated neurocognitive functioning in monozygotic twin pairs who were discordant for combat exposure. They grouped pairs according to whether the brother exposed to combat developed PTSD. The combat-unexposed twins of combat veterans with PTSD displayed similar neuropsychological performance as their brothers, which was significantly poorer than that of non-PTSD combat veterans and their brothers. The researchers concluded, "The results support the notion that specific domains of cognitive function may serve as premorbid risk or protective factors in PTSD" (p. 484).

Trauma may activate the noradrenergic system, raising levels of norepinephrine and thereby making the person startle and express emotion more readily than is normal (Krystal et al., 1989). Consistent with this view is the finding that norepinephrine was higher in PTSD clients than in those diagnosed as having schizophrenia or mood disorders (Kosten et al., 1987). In addition, stimulating the noradrenergic system induced a panic attack in 70% and flashbacks in 40% of PTSD clients; none of the control participants had such experiences (Southwick et al., 1993). Also, there is extensive evidence for increased sensitivity of noradrenergic receptors in people with PTSD and this sensitivity has been linked with specific PTSD symptom clusters (O'Donnell, Hegadoren, & Coupland, 2004).

THERAPIES FOR POST-TRAUMATIC STRESS DISORDER

Many experts on trauma agree that it is best to intervene in some fashion as soon as possible after a traumatic event, well before PTSD has a chance to develop. The need to intervene as soon as possible has resulted in the novel suggestion that training and expertise needs to come in the form of *psychological first aid*. The *Psychological First Aid Field Operations Guide* was developed to provide guidance to frontline practitioners who must respond immediately to mental health needs following a disaster or terrorist event (see Vernberg et al., 2008).

Intervening when people are in the acute phase of a post-trauma period and are at risk of developing acute stress disorder is referred to as *crisis intervention*. As reviewed by Foa and Meadows (1997), intervention includes such procedures as recreating the event by having participants discuss with each other as many details as they can remember, encouraging them to describe their thoughts at the time of the event, and normalizing their anxiety reactions by reminding them that they have just been through an event that causes extreme distress for most people (Mitchell & Bray, 1990). A promising approach for people who have been sexually assaulted (see Chapter 14) is a CBT strategy that involves, in combination, exposing clients to trauma-related cues in imagination, teaching them relaxation, and helping them think differently about what happened (e.g., to not blame themselves) (Foa et al., 1995).

A key to treating PTSD is exposure to thoughts and images of the frightening event (Keane, 1998). This common thread is found in a variety of treatment approaches for this disorder. Before any kind of exposure is attempted, however, therapists are advised to be sensitive to the typical aftermath of a traumatic experience, regardless of the specific cause (Keane et al., 1994). Common reactions include lack of trust, a frightening belief that the world is very dangerous and threatening (Janoff-Bulman, 1992), and maladaptive strategies for coping with the extreme stress, such as substance abuse (Keane & Wolfe, 1990). It can also be helpful to educate clients about the nature of PTSD and the kinds of symptoms most people experience (sleeplessness, being easily startled, depression, alienation from friends and loved ones, etc.). Such knowledge can provide a context for what the clients might be experiencing and reassure them that they are not losing their mind (Keane et al., 1994).

During the Second World War, "combat-exhausted" soldiers were often treated by narcosynthesis (Grinker & Spiegel, 1945), a procedure that might be considered a drug-assisted catharsis à la Breuer. A soldier was sedated with an intravenous injection of sodium pentothal to cause extreme drowsiness. The therapist then stated in a matter-of-fact voice that the soldier was on the battlefield, in the front lines, and if necessary and possible, the therapist mentioned circumstances of the particular battle. The client usually began to recall, often with intense emotion, frightening events that had perhaps been forgotten. The actual trauma was relived and even acted out by the client. As the client gradually returned to the waking state, the therapist continued to encourage discussion of the terrifying events in the hope that the client would realize that they were in the past and no longer a threat. In this fashion, a synthesis of the past horror with the client's present life was sought (Cameron & Magaret, 1951).

Controlled research on the treatment of PTSD accelerated as more attention was focused on the aftermath of such traumas as natural disasters, rape, child abuse, combat, and terrorist attacks. The basic principle of exposure-based therapy is that fears are best reduced or eliminated by having the person confront whatever he or she most ardently wishes to avoid. The evidence indicates that structured exposure to trauma-related events, sometimes in imagination, contributes something beyond the

Twenty-six miners lost their lives in an explosion at the Westray Mine in Stellarton, Nova Scotia, in May 1992. The disaster triggered acute stress and PTSD disorders in many of the people involved with those who died. Westray provides a good example of the importance of a proactive community response to disasters and the importance of social support in reducing the risk of developing PTSD. The Canadian Press/ Andrew Vaughan.

benefits of medication, social support, or a safe therapeutic environment (e.g., Foa & Meadows, 1997).

In making the diagnosis of PTSD, we almost always know what triggered the problem, so the decision is a tactical one; that is, how to expose the frightened client to what is fearsome. Many techniques have been employed. In one well-designed study involving Vietnam veterans suffering PTSD, for example, Terence Keane and his associates compared a no-treatment control group with a group that was subjected to imaginal flooding, in which clients visualized fearsome, trauma-related scenes for extended periods of time. The researchers found significantly greater reductions in depression, anxiety, re-experiencing of the trauma, startle reactions, and irritability in the veterans receiving the imaginal procedure (Keane et al., 1989). Conducting such exposure therapy is difficult for both client and therapist, however, as it requires detailed review of the traumatizing events. As pointed out by Keane et al. (1992), clients may become temporarily worse in the initial stages of therapy, and therapists themselves may become upset when they hear about the horrifying events that their clients experienced.

How does exposure work? We have already discussed the possibility that it leads to the extinction of the fear response. But it may also change the meaning that stimuli have for people. This cognitive view has been elaborated by Edna Foa and her colleagues in a number of studies and theoretical papers. They emphasize the corrective aspects of exposure to what is feared:

> Exposure promotes symptom reduction by allowing patients to realize that, contrary to their mistaken ideas: (a) being in objectively safe situations that remind one of the trauma is not dangerous; (b) remembering the trauma is not equivalent to experiencing it again; (c) anxiety does not remain indefinitely in the presence of feared situations or memories, but rather it decreases even without avoidance or escape; and (d) experiencing anxiety/PTSD symptoms does not lead to loss of control. (Foa & Meadows, 1997, p. 462)

However exposure works, there is no doubt about its effectiveness in reducing the effects of trauma, including that arising from sexual assault.

In 1989, Shapiro (1989) began to promulgate an approach to treating trauma called Eye Movement Desensitization and Reprocessing (EMDR). This method is purported to be extremely rapid—often requiring only one or two sessions—and more effective than the standard exposure procedures just reviewed. In this procedure, the client imagines a situation related to his or her problem, such as the sight of a horrible automobile accident. Keeping the image in mind, the client follows with his or her eyes the therapist's fingers as the therapist moves them back and forth about a foot in front of the client. This process continues for a minute or so or until the client reports that the horror of the image has been reduced. Then the therapist has the client verbalize whatever negative thoughts are going through his or her mind, again while following the moving target with his or her eyes. Finally, the therapist encourages the client to think a more positive thought, such as "I can deal with this," and this thought, too, is held in mind as the client follows the therapist's moving fingers.

A great deal of controversy surrounds this technique (and related techniques), and opinions are polarized in ways not often found in science. On the one hand are EMDR proponents who argue that combining eye movements with thoughts about the feared event promotes rapid deconditioning or reprocessing of the aversive stimulus (e.g., Shapiro, 1999). On the other hand are numerous studies that show that eye movements do not add anything to what may be happening as a result of exposure itself (e.g., Cahill, Carrigan, & Frueh, 1999), as well as a study showing that exposure therapy appears to be more effective than EMDR (Taylor et al., 2003). Moreover, earlier claims of EMDR's effectiveness rest on experiments that have major methodological shortcomings (cf. Rosen, 1999). However, a Canadian study found that alternating right-left stimulation as part of the procedure resulted in rapid reductions in clients' subjective distress (see Servan-Schreiber et al., 2006). Moreover, no one disputes the important role played by exposure to memories or images of traumatic events, and the well-established role of exposure to aversive stimuli is probably the key ingredient in whatever efficacy EMDR has.

Another CBT approach conceptualizes PTSD more generally as an extreme stress reaction amenable to the kind of multi-faceted approach to stress management described in Chapter 9, which entails relaxation, rational-emotive therapy, and training in problem solving. Among the problems addressed within this broader framework is the anger felt by many people with PTSD, especially those who have seen combat. Assertion training and couples therapy are often warranted to help them deal with their anger appropriately (Keane et al., 1992).

Donald Meichenbaum (see Canadian Contributions 2.2) developed a comprehensive CBT therapist's manual for the treatment of adults with PTSD (Meichenbaum, 1994) that incorporates a constructive-narrative approach to PTSD. Narrative construction relies on the belief that people construct and reconstruct "accounts" or "stories" about important events in their lives. They develop these stories about significant life events in order to infuse them with some coherence and meaning. Thus, according to Meichenbaum (1994), "People make meaning of their lives by organizing key events into stories which they incorporate into a larger life narrative" (p. 103). These client stories are considered to be open to change, and treatment for people with PTSD targets, in part, the meanings attached to traumatic events. The therapist works collaboratively with the client in the constructive-narrative process, intervening to highlight strengths and resilience and foster "survivorship," coping processes, and competence for future adaptive behaviour and thought: "You mean, in spite of this horrific event, you got through it?";

"How did you manage to do it?"; and, "Where did this courage come from?". Meichenbaum's goal is to have the client arrive at solutions about how to change. Through their actions, clients write a new "script," a new, more adaptive narrative. They "re-story" their lives.

In an interview with Michael Hoyt, Meichenbaum described the case of a woman who was home alone with her 10-year-old daughter (Meichenbaum, 2003). The woman woke up fearing that a robber had broken into the home. In a panicked state, she grabbed a pistol that her husband had given her, ran to protect her daughter, but accidentally discharged the gun and killed the little girl. What can you say or do in therapy? Meichenbaum responded, in part, with the following:

> I listened sympathetically to the tale of the horrendous events. And eventually asked the mother, "What did you see in your daughter that made your relationship with her so special? Please share with me the nature of the loss." In fact, I asked the bereaved mother to bring to therapy a picture album of her daughter and to review with me the special qualities of her daughter. The picture album permitted the client to tell the story of her relationship with her daughter in some developmental (time-line) context, and thus not delimit her memories to only the time of the shooting, which she played over and over again, with the accompanying narrative of, "if only"; "Why didn't I tell my husband I didn't want to own a gun?"; "Why my daughter?" … Moreover, the review of the picture album provided the opportunity to query further what she saw in her daughter, and, in turn, what did her daughter see in her.
>
> Following this exchange, I asked the client, "If your daughter, whom you described as being 'wise beyond her years' were here now, what advice, if any, might she have to help you get through this difficult period?" Fortunately, with some guidance I was able to help the client generate some suggestions that her daughter might have offered. I then noted, "I can now understand why you described your daughter as 'wise beyond her years.' She does sound special." Moreover, if the client followed through on her notion to commit suicide in order to "stop the emotional pain," what would happen to the memory of her daughter? Did she feel that she owed her daughter more? Like many victims of traumatic events, this client found a mission in order to cope with her distress. She undertook the task of educating parents about the dangers of keeping guns in their homes. She became an expert on the incidence of accidental homicides and developed a foundation named after her daughter designed to decrease the likelihood that this could happen to other children. She felt that if she could save one other child, then her daughter would not have died in vain.
>
> *(Treatment of Individuals with Anger-Control Problems and Aggressive Behaviors*, Crown House Publishing, 2003, p. 302. Used with permission of Donald Meichenbaum.)

Although Meichenbaum advocates a constructive-narrative perspective, it is important to note that he also incorporates the full clinical array of CBT strategies. As is the case with all multi-component therapies, there is a need for empirical investigations to demonstrate the utility of the different treatment components in Meichenbaum's complex program for the treatment of PTSD.

Horowitz's (1990) psychodynamic approach has much in common with the CBT approach, for he encourages clients to discuss the trauma and otherwise expose themselves to the events that led to the PTSD. But Horowitz emphasizes the manner in which the trauma interacts with a client's pre-trauma personality, and the treatment he proposes also has much in common with other psychoanalytic approaches, including discussions of defences and analysis of transference reactions by the client. A few controlled studies lend a small degree of empirical support to its effectiveness (Foa & Meadows, 1997).

In a recent RCT with women with chronic PTSD, Foa and her colleagues (Rauch et al., 2009) reported that self-reported physical health difficulties were significantly reduced and social functioning improved with prolonged exposure and exposure combined with cognitive restructuring conditions relative to a waitlist condition. Changes in PTSD and depression symptoms were related to these changes.

A meta-analysis conducted by Bradley et al. (2005) attests to the usefulness of psychotherapy in order to treat PTSD. This meta-analysis of 26 studies using 44 treatment conditions showed that of those who completed treatment, two thirds no longer met diagnostic criteria for PTSD. The authors concluded that psychotherapy interventions are "highly efficacious" (Bradley et al., 2005, p. 225). However, it was still the case that the majority of clients had residual symptoms despite no longer warranting a diagnosis, and, as has been often found, treatments for combat-related trauma yielded the lowest effect sizes. A more recent meta-analysis (Benish, Imel, & Wampold, 2008) focused on the relative efficacy of *bona fide* psychotherapies using direct comparison studies only. The authors concluded that, "despite strong evidence of psychotherapy efficaciousness vis-à-vis no treatment or common factor controls, bona fide psychotherapies produce equivalent benefits for patients with PTSD" (p. 746).

Finally, a range of psychoactive drugs have been used with PTSD clients, including antidepressants and tranquilizers (a summary of drugs used in treating all the anxiety disorders can be found in Table 6.5). Sometimes medication is used to deal with conditions comorbid with PTSD, such as depression; improvement in the depression can contribute to improvement in PTSD regardless of how the PTSD itself is treated (by a psychological intervention of the kinds just described, for example [Marshall et al., 1994]). Some modest successes have been reported for antidepressants, especially the serotonin reuptake inhibitors (e.g., Yehuda, Marshall, & Giller, 1998). What would you choose if you were diagnosed with PTSD, sertraline (an SSRI) or prolonged exposure? We know very little about the relative efficacy of drug and psychological interventions for chronic PTSD. Feeny et al. (2009) asked this question of female trauma victims, including women with chronic PTSD. An overwhelming majority of the women chose exposure, although those with comorbid major depression were more likely to choose sertraline than those without depression. As noted by the authors, it's important to assess clients' preferences since they potentially affect outcome and to rethink "one-size fits all approaches to treatment" (p. 724).

Whatever the specific mode of intervention, experts in PTSD agree that social support is critical. Sometimes finding ways to lend support to others can help the giver as well as the receiver (Hobfoll et al., 1991). Belonging to a religious group, having family, friends, or fellow traumatized individuals listen non-judgementally to one's fears and recollections of the trauma, and having other ways to feel that one belongs and that others wish to help ease the pain may spell the difference between post-traumatic stress and PTSD. Canadian Clinic Focus 6.1 describes a model Canadian centre for anxiety treatment and research.

TABLE 6.5

SUMMARY OF DRUGS USED TO TREAT ANXIETY DISORDERS

Drug Category	Generic Names	Trade Names	Uses
Benzodiazepines	Diazepam, alprazolam, lorazepam, clonazepam	Valium, Xanax, Ativan, Clonapam	GAD, PTSD, panic disorder
Monoamine oxidase inhibitors	Phenelzine	Nardil	Social phobia
Selective serotonin reuptake inhibitors	Fluoxetine, sertraline, fluvoxamine	Prozac, Zoloft, Luvox	Social phobia, panic disorder, OCD, PTSD
Tricyclic antidepressants	Imipramine, clomipramine	Tofranil, Anafranil	Panic disorder, GAD, OCD, PTSD
Azapirones	Buspirone	BuSpar	GAD, panic disorder, OCD

ANXIETY TREATMENT AND RESEARCH CENTRE, ST. JOSEPH'S HEALTHCARE

Dr. Randi McCabe, director of the Anxiety Treatment and Research Centre (ATRC) at St. Joseph's Healthcare in Hamilton, Ontario. Courtesy Dr. Randi McCabe.

Various clinics in Canada are known for providing treatment and conducting research on anxiety disorders. One such clinic is the Anxiety Treatment and Research Centre (ATRC) at St. Joseph's Healthcare in Hamilton, Ontario, a specialty clinic focusing on the assessment and treatment of individuals with anxiety disorders. The centre is known internationally for its clinical services, scientific research, and training opportunities. The director of the centre is Randi E. McCabe, a psychologist. Martin M. Antony (also a psychologist) is the research director, and Richard P. Swinson, a psychiatrist, is the medical director. The centre is affiliated with the Department of Psychiatry and Behavioural Neurosciences at McMaster University. More information about the ATRC can be found on its website, www.anxietytreatment.ca.

Clinical Services

Referral Process Each year, the ATRC receives more than 1,000 referrals from across southern Ontario. The mean age of the individuals referred is the mid-30s, although the range is from 18 to 75 years of age. About 60% of individuals referred to the centre are female. The most commonly presenting anxiety disorders include panic disorder, social phobia, OCD, and GAD. The remaining clients suffer from a range of problems, including mood disorders, other anxiety disorders, and related conditions. All clients are referred by a physician. Referrals are typically made for the purpose of obtaining clarification regarding an

individual's diagnosis, obtaining treatment recommendations (e.g., medications to be prescribed by the referring physician), or obtaining treatment at the ATRC (e.g., CBT).

Assessment All individuals who are seen at the ATRC receive a comprehensive assessment. Initially, a battery of questionnaires is completed, including medical history and general measures of anxiety, depression, and functional impairment. In addition, a detailed life history questionnaire is completed to provide data on family history, schooling, and other background information. Most individuals are administered the Structured Clinical Interview for *DSM-IV* (SCID-IV; First et al., 1996), a semi-structured diagnostic interview that provides *DSM-IV* diagnoses for anxiety and other disorders. This interview usually takes two to three hours. In addition, the assessment may include a one-hour clinical interview with a psychiatrist to confirm the diagnostic information obtained during the SCID-IV and to allow for medication recommendations, if appropriate. Clients often return for additional assessments. For example, specialized questionnaires are completed by individuals with panic disorder, social phobia, OCD, and GAD to assess the features of these problems. In addition, individuals with OCD receive the clinician-administered Yale-Brown Obsessive Compulsive Scale (Y-BOCS; Goodman et al., 1989), a well-known measure that assesses the severity and content of an individual's OCD symptoms.

Treatment The ATRC has specialized treatment programs for individuals suffering from OCD, GAD, panic disorder, and social phobia. These include group treatments (typically lasting about 12 to 15 sessions) and individual treatments. In some cases, brief treatments are also available for individuals suffering from health anxiety and specific phobias. Treatment programs include cognitive-behavioural therapy, medications, or combinations of these approaches. Individuals who receive treatment in one of the ATRC's standard programs are later invited to attend a monthly booster group designed to reinforce the skills learned during initial treatment.

Cognitive-behavioural treatments typically involve cognitive therapy, exposure-based treatments, skills training (e.g., social skills training for social phobia), and response prevention (for individuals with OCD). These treatments are based on empirically supported protocols. Self-help materials are recommended, and suggestions for where to obtain additional information (e.g., Internet resources) are provided. In many cases, treatments are offered in the context of research studies. Measures are administered before and after treatment to assess treatment effectiveness. Also, clients rate their satisfaction with the centre's services.

Research Research at the ATRC has focused on a number of broad areas. ATRC staff have studied brief interventions for anxiety disorders, including treatment of panic disorder in the emergency room, telephone treatments for panic disorder, and computer-administered treatments for OCD. Research has also examined various ways to optimize psychological treatment outcome such as home-based treatment for OCD. A study in progress is examining the use of motivational enhancement therapy to augment exposure and response prevention treatment for OCD.

ATRC staff have also been active in research on cognitive, biological, and personality variables associated with anxiety disorders. This work includes studies on memory processes in OCD, brain function in panic disorder, the effects of thought suppression in OCD, genetic transmission of OCD, impulsivity and anxiety disorders, symptom subtypes in OCD, social phobia and social comparison processes, the relationship between OCD and mood disorders, and the relationship between perfectionism and anxiety disorders. Current research is examining biological factors associated with treatment response using neuroimaging in OCD and EEG in social phobia.

A number of influential books have been published by ATRC staff, including books for clinicians who work with anxiety disorders (e.g., Antony & Rowa, 2008; Bieling, McCabe, & Antony, 2006) and self-help workbooks for individuals coping with anxiety (Antony & Norton, 2009), social anxiety (Antony & Swinson, 2008), animal and insect phobias (Antony & McCabe, 2005), panic attacks (Antony & McCabe, 2004), perfectionism (Antony & Swinson, 2009), and social phobia (Bieling & Antony, 2003).

Training Programs

The ATRC is involved in training individuals from a broad range of health care disciplines. The centre regularly trains medical students, psychiatry residents, psychology interns, psychology practicum students, and social work students to provide clinical services for individuals with anxiety disorders. In addition, students frequently receive research training at the ATRC. Finally, individuals seeking additional training following completion of their degrees (e.g., post-doctoral fellows) often obtain placements at the ATRC. At any one time, between 15 and 20 students are receiving various types of training experience at the centre.

Case Example: "CC"

CC is a prototypical case from the ATRC. CC was referred for treatment of panic disorder and OCD. Her first panic attack occurred when she tried marijuana for the first time. CC experienced intense dizziness, feelings of unreality, and a number of other sensations during the initial attack. When she was assessed at the ATRC, she was experiencing panic attacks almost daily, many of which were uncued and some of which were cued by situations that she associated with the uncomfortable feared sensations. For example, CC avoided driving for fear that she might become very dizzy and crash her car. She also avoided all psychoactive substances, including alcohol and caffeine.

In the months following the onset of her panic disorder, CC also developed symptoms of OCD. In particular, she developed a fear of being contaminated by drugs or other substances that she came in contact with, especially while eating. She was fearful that impurities in her food might trigger a panic attack, which in turn might lead her to lose control or "go crazy." She avoided eating any foods that she had not prepared herself, and she avoided purchasing foods that were not wrapped. She also washed her hands many times per day to avoid contaminating her food or other objects in her home.

Because CC's symptoms of panic disorder and OCD were related (both were associated with a fear of developing certain symptoms), cognitive-behavioural treatment focused simultaneously on both problems. Cognitive restructuring was used to help CC to interpret her uncomfortable panic symptoms in a less anxiety-provoking way. CC was also encouraged to practise exposure to the symptoms she feared (e.g., spinning to cause dizziness), the activities she avoided (e.g., driving), and the foods she avoided. In addition, she was encouraged to touch objects in her home without washing her hands. Treatment lasted 15 sessions. CC was still experiencing occasional panic attacks at the end, but much less frequently than before starting treatment. Her attacks were now occurring about once per month, and she was much less frightened of them. In addition, her heightened fear of contamination, her excessive washing, and her avoidance of particular foods were almost eliminated. However, she still feared drinking alcohol or caffeinated drinks.

Comment

The ATRC is a model specialized clinic that employs state-of-the-art treatment strategies for people suffering from anxiety disorders. However, such facilities are not available to the majority of Canadians. Swinson, Cox, Kerr, Kuch, and Fergus (1992) surveyed hospitals in Canada. Only about 15% of them had specialized anxiety treatment facilities. Most of these clinics are located in major metropolitan areas and are often associated with university-affiliated teaching hospitals. The improved training of students and professionals in the treatment of anxiety disorders in clinical settings such as the ATRC should lead to the increased availability of these treatments. However, governments and stakeholder organizations need to foster comprehensive, effective, and efficient treatment approaches for anxiety disorders in clinical settings throughout Canada. It is especially important to make such treatment available to people who live in rural and remote areas.

We believe that people living in Canada deserve what Haaga (2000) referred to as "an empirically supported treatment delivered competently by a well-trained practitioner" (p. 547). The task is difficult because both governments and third-party insurers are pressing for brief, cost-effective treatments in a managed health care system. Canadian investigators have demonstrated that brief, adapted cognitive-behavioural approaches can be useful. For example, Swinson and associates illustrated the effectiveness of telephone-administered treatment (Swinson, Fergus, Cox, & Wiskwire, 1995) and of giving people reassurance and exposure instructions in a general hospital emergency room (Swinson, Soulios, Cox, & Kuch, 1992), and Côté, Gauthier, Laberge, Plamondon, and Fournier (1994) reported that minimal therapist contact combined with use of a self-help book can be as effective as in-person CBT in treating panic disorder. Many people with anxiety disorders can benefit from various low-cost interventions (Newman, 2000). Given the economic burden associated with untreated anxiety disorders (Greenberg et al.,

1999), even more intensive, multi-faceted interventions may be cost-effective. When do we employ lower-cost interventions? When do we use more intensive but more costly interventions? We will address this question when we evaluate "stepped care" models in Chapter 17. These models seek to maximize the efficient allocation of limited health care resources (see Haaga, 2000; Davison, 2000).

SUMMARY

- People with anxiety disorders feel an overwhelming apprehension that seems unwarranted. *DSM-IV-TR* lists six principal diagnoses: phobic disorders, panic disorder, generalized anxiety disorder, obsessive-compulsive disorder, post-traumatic stress disorder, and acute stress disorder.

- Phobias are intense, unreasonable fears that disrupt the life of an otherwise normal person. They are relatively common. Social phobia is fear of social situations in which the person may be scrutinized by other people. Specific phobias are fears of animals, situations, the natural environment, and blood and injections. The psychoanalytic view of phobias is that they are a defence against repressed conflicts. Behavioural theorists have several ideas of how phobias are acquired: through classical conditioning, the pairing of an innocuous object or situation with an innately painful event; through operant conditioning, whereby a person is rewarded for avoidance; through modelling, imitating the fear and avoidance of others; and through cognition, by making a catastrophe of a social mishap that could be construed in a less negative fashion. But not all people who have such experiences develop a phobia. It may be that a genetically transmitted physiological diathesis—lability of the autonomic nervous system—predisposes certain people to acquire phobias.

- A person with panic disorder has sudden, inexplicable, and periodic attacks of intense anxiety. Panic attacks sometimes lead to fear and avoidance of being outside one's home, a condition known as agoraphobia. A number of laboratory manipulations (e.g., having the client hyperventilate or breathe air with a high concentration of carbon dioxide) can induce panic attacks in those with the disorder. Panic disorder individuals ruminate about serious illnesses, both physical and mental; they fear their own physical sensations and then amplify them until they are overwhelmed.

- In generalized anxiety disorder, sometimes called free-floating anxiety, the individual's life is beset with virtually constant tension, apprehension, and worry. Psychoanalytic theory regards the source as an unconscious conflict between the ego and id impulses. Some behavioural theorists assume that with adequate assessment, this pervasive anxiety can be pinned down to a finite set of anxiety-provoking circumstances, thereby likening it to a phobia and making it more treatable. A sense of helplessness can also cause people to be anxious in a wide range of situations. Biological approaches focus on the therapeutic effects of the benzodiazepines and how they might enhance the activity of the neurotransmitter GABA.

- People with obsessive-compulsive disorder have intrusive, unwanted thoughts and feel pressured to engage in stereotyped rituals lest they be overcome by frightening levels of anxiety. This disorder can become disabling, interfering not only with the life of the person who experiences the difficulties but also with the lives of those close to that person. Psychoanalytic theory posits strong id impulses that are under faulty and inadequate ego control. In behavioural accounts, compulsions are considered learned avoidance responses. Obsessions may be related to stress and an attempt to inhibit these unwanted thoughts.

- Post-traumatic stress disorder is diagnosed in some people who have experienced a traumatic event that would evoke extreme distress in most individuals. It is marked by symptoms such as re-experiencing the trauma, increased arousal, and emotional numbing.

- There are many therapies for anxiety disorders. Psychoanalytic treatment tries to lift repression so that childhood conflicts can be resolved; direct alleviation of problems is discouraged. In contrast, behaviour therapists employ a range of procedures, such as systematic desensitization and modelling, to encourage exposure to what is feared. Preventing people with compulsions from performing their rituals is a useful, although initially arduous, technique.

- Perhaps the most widely employed treatments are anxiolytic and other drugs dispensed by medical practitioners. Drugs are subject to abuse, however, and their long-term use may have untoward and still inadequately understood side effects. Weaning a person from reliance on a chemical that reduces anxiety is problematic because many people become physically dependent on such drugs. Also, gains from using the drugs are usually lost when use is discontinued.

KEY TERMS

acute stress disorder (p. 196)
agoraphobia (p. 180)
anxiety (p. 165)
anxiety disorders (p. 165)
anxiety sensitivity (p. 183)
anxiolytics (p. 178)
autonomic lability (p. 173)
compulsion (p. 189)
depersonalization (p. 179)
derealization (p. 179)

flooding (p. 175)
generalized anxiety disorder (GAD) (p. 185)
homework (p. 177)
in vivo exposure (p. 174)
obsessions (p. 189)
obsessive-compulsive disorder (OCD) (p. 188)
panic disorder (p. 178)
phobia (p. 168)

post-traumatic stress disorder (PTSD) (p. 195)
prospective memory (p. 191)
retrospective memory (p. 191)
social phobias (p. 170)
specific phobias (p. 168)
vicarious learning (p. 171)
virtual reality (VR) exposure (p. 175)

REFLECTIONS: PAST, PRESENT, AND FUTURE

- In the previous chapter, you were asked to design a longitudinal study of risk factors for the development of anxiety disorders. Now that you have learned more about factors supported by empirical research, how would you redesign your long-term study? What risk factors would you retain? What new risk factors would you add to the design?

- Recall the quotation from Mark Twain at the outset of this chapter. Assume that you are charged with the responsibility of designing a program to instill "courage" in elementary school children. What would your program look like? How would you implement it? How would you evaluate the possible long-term effects?

- Anxiety and stress are relevant to our understanding of many of the other disorders discussed in this book (e.g., somatoform and dissociative disorders, psychophysiological disorders, mood disorders, and schizophrenia). As you read about the different disorders, think about how you would adapt the treatment strategies outlined in this chapter for use with other disorders.

- In young people, extreme stress is associated not only with anxiety but also depression (see Chapter 8). Comment on the nature of the stressful events faced by young people as they move from adolescence to adulthood, or from high school to college or university. Do they differ as a function of gender? How do these stressors affect young people? How can they cope with them? How important is the role of social support? Do you think these factors might interact with personality or cognitive styles to make students more vulnerable?

- By now you will have discovered that adolescents and young adults, including college and university students, are not immune from psychological difficulties, and in the ensuing chapters you will read about other psychological problems that are, unfortunately, relatively common in young people. A mental health author headlined a recent newspaper article, "Stress takes troubling toll on students in university" (Crawford, 2009, September 3). It can be very difficult to be young and at school trying to deal with what may be perceived as overwhelming stress—perhaps away from home for the first time and feeling homesick, handling finances and social and academic pressures on your own, maybe feeling lonely or upset by a relationship separation or breakup. It's no wonder that many students feel anxious or blue or turn to alcohol or other drugs to ease the psychological pain. However, Canadian colleges and universities take these and other mental health issues very seriously and help is available on campus for every student. Indeed, resources have improved significantly over recent decades and professional counsellors are available who are skilled at helping students with their psychological and other difficulties. Review all of the mental health resources and programs at your college or university. For example, how are students helped to ease the transition from high school to campus life? Is there a focus on early intervention? Are there enough competent professionals to meet the needs of students? Is there a role for fellow students to play? What changes would you recommend to the administration of your college or university?

SOMATOFORM AND DISSOCIATIVE DISORDERS

Bertram Brooker, Canadian 1888–1955, *Two Nudes*, c. 1928, Oil on canvas board, 25.2 × 19.9 cm (panel), Art Gallery of Ontario, Toronto. Gift of Vincent Tovell, Toronto, 1988 © John Brooker. Reproduced by Permission of the Estate of Bertram Brooker

"When ideas go unexamined and unchallenged for a long time … they become mythological, and they become very, very, powerful."
—E. L. Doctorow

"The memory wars are not about science against antiscience. Instead, they concern correctly interpreted science in contrast to incorrectly interpreted science. When the science is interpreted properly, the evidence shows that traumatic events—those experienced as overwhelmingly terrifying at the time of their occurrence—are highly memorable and seldom, if ever, forgotten."
—Richard J. McNally on "repressed memory" in the Canadian *Journal of Psychiatry* (2005a, p. 821)

"Why did the perhaps half-plausible 19th-century concept [of dissociative identity disorder] so floridly metamorphose into the totally implausible 20th-century concept? We know of no convincing reason. In the end, positing scores, hundreds, and even thousands of alters [ego states] defies common sense and reminds one of Tertullian's claim, Credo quia absurdum est ('I believe that which is impossible')."
—August Piper and Harold Merskey, University of Western Ontario (2004a, p. 595)

SOMATOFORM DISORDERS

DISSOCIATIVE DISORDERS

SUMMARY

A 25-YEAR-OLD single female was referred by a psychiatrist who suspected the presence of multiple personality disorder (MPD). Originally, he had thought drug and alcohol abuse were the reasons for her drastic personality changes and amnesic episodes. When seen, she was fearful for her own life, for there were homicidal threats written in lipstick on her walls. These were written at a time when she was in her apartment alone with the doors locked. She had a history of childhood sexual abuse and admitted to many episodes of amnesia, finding herself in locations to which she had no memory of travelling. Her boyfriend told her that at times she behaved and cried like a child and at other times she was violent and aggressive. Once, she attacked him and fractured his jaw. With the use of hypnotic trance or guided imagery . . . she readily dissociated into different personality patterns. Besides the present personality, which was very passive and introverted, she had within her a 6-year-old male, a 5-year-old female, two 20-year-old sisters, a non-human state called "The Animal," and an 80-year-old grandmother.

These various personalities had "shared" her body for many years. Her knowledge of them was strictly through the reports of others, which generally corresponded to her periods of memory gaps. She admitted that she had heard inner voices of varying ages for a few years, but for the most part had tried to ignore them. (Fraser, 1994, pp. 146–147)

Somatoform and dissociative disorders are related to anxiety disorders in that, in early versions of the *DSM*, all these disorders were subsumed under the heading of neuroses because anxiety was considered the predominant underlying factor in each case. Starting with *DSM-III*, classification came to be based on observable behaviour, not on presumed etiology. Anxiety is not necessarily observable in the somatoform and dissociative disorders. In **somatoform disorders**, the individual complains of bodily symptoms that suggest a physical defect or dysfunction—sometimes rather dramatic in nature—but for which no physiological basis can be found. In **dissociative disorders**, the individual experiences disruptions of consciousness, memory, and identity, as illustrated in the opening case study. The onset of both classes of disorders is assumed by many to be related to some stressful experience, and the two classes sometimes co-occur. We will examine the somatoform and dissociative disorders, focusing in more depth on those disorders about which more is known. Less is known about these disorders relative to many others and there is controversy about their causes and treatment.

SOMATOFORM DISORDERS

As noted in Chapter 1, *soma* means "body." In somatoform disorders, psychological problems take a physical form. The physical symptoms have no known physiological explanation and are not under voluntary control. They are thought to be linked to psychological factors, presumably anxiety, and are assumed to be psychologically caused (see Merskey & Mai, 2005). In this section, we look at two somatoform disorders: conversion disorder and somatization disorder. This is preceded by brief discussions of three *DSM-IV-TR* categories of somatoform disorders about which less information is available: pain disorder, body dysmorphic disorder, and hypochondriasis. A summary of the somatoform disorders appears in Table 7.1. People often resist having somatic problems labelled as a psychiatric disorder, with the consequent stigma.

This category has been controversial ever since the release of *DSM-IV*. Indeed, a group of prominent researchers presented the radical argument that somatoform disorders should be removed from the pending *DSM-5* (Mayou, Kirmayer, Simon, Kroenke, & Sharpe, 2005). They listed seven concerns:

- The terminology is often unacceptable to patients.
- The distinction between disease-based symptoms versus those that are psychogenic may be more apparent than real.
- There is great heterogeneity among the disorders—the only common link is physical illness that is not attributable to an organic cause.
- The disorders are incompatible with other cultures.
- There is ambiguity in the stated exclusion criteria.
- The subcategories fail to achieve accepted standards of reliability.
- The disorders lack clearly defined thresholds in terms of the symptoms needed for a diagnosis.

More recently, Kroenke, Sharpe, and Sykes (2007) reported on the deliberations of 24 experts involved in the Conceptual

TABLE 7.1
SUMMARY OF THE SOMATOFORM DISORDERS

Disorder	Description
Pain disorder	The onset and maintenance of pain, caused largely by psychological factors.
Body dysmorphic disorder	Preoccupation with imagined or exaggerated defects in physical appearance.
Hypochondriasis	Preoccupation with fears of having a serious illness.
Conversion disorder	Sensory or motor symptoms without any physiological cause.
Somatization	Recurrent, multiple physical complaints that have no biological basis.

Issues in Somatoform and Similar Disorders (CISSD) project. Recommendations included revision of the somatization disorder category, elimination of pain disorder and undifferentiated somatoform disorder, terminology changes, and possible shifting of certain disorders to different *DSM* categories or axes. Fava and Wise (2007) proposed the expansion to "psychological factors affecting either identified or feared medical conditions" as a solution to perceived inadequacies of the current classification of somatoform disorders.

In February 2010, the *DSM-5* Somatic Symptom Disorders Work Group noted that the current *DSM-IV* terminology is confusing. Further, because somatoform disorders, psychological factors affecting medical condition (see Chapter 9), and factitious disorders (see Focus on Discovery 7.1) all involve presentation of physical symptoms and/or concern about medical illness, the work group suggested renaming this group of disorders "somatic symptom disorders." The grouping of these disorders into a single section was based on clinical utility—these individuals are primarily seen in general medical settings (rather than due to possible shared etiology or mechanism). In addition, because of the implicit "mind-body dualism" and the unreliability of assessments of "medically unexplained symptoms," the work group proposed that these symptoms no longer be emphasized as core features of many of these disorders. The focus would now be on the extent to which such symptoms result in "subjective distress, disturbance, diminished quality of life, and impaired role functioning" (see www.dsm5.org).

Since somatization disorder, hypochondriasis, pain disorder, and undifferentiated somatoform disorder share certain common features—somatic symptoms and cognitive distortions, the work group proposed that these disorders be grouped under a common rubric named "complex somatic symptom disorder" (CCSD). The work group suggested that three optional specifiers could be applied to the diagnosis: (1) multiplicity of somatic complaints (previously somatization disorder); (2) high health anxiety (previously hypochondriasis); and (3) pain disorder. If this proposed change is approved, it will represent a major change in diagnostic nomenclature that would probably have a major impact on diagnosis since it clarifies that a diagnosis would be inappropriate in the presence of unexplained symptoms only.

In the following sections we focus on the somatoform disorders as described in *DSM-IV*.

In **pain disorder**, the person experiences pain that causes significant distress and impairment; psychological factors are viewed as playing an important role in the onset, maintenance, and severity of the pain. The client may be unable to work and may become dependent on painkillers or tranquilizers. The pain may have a temporal relation to some conflict or stress, or it may allow the individual to avoid some unpleasant activity and to secure attention and sympathy not otherwise available. Accurate diagnosis is difficult because the subjective experience of pain is always a psychologically influenced phenomenon. Therefore, deciding when a pain becomes a somatoform pain is difficult. Clients with physically based pain tend to localize it more specifically, give more detailed sensory descriptions, and link their pain more clearly to situations that increase or decrease it (Adler et al., 1997). Regardless of the cause, there is a positive association between reports of pain symptoms and diagnoses of several of the anxiety disorders and/or depression (Means-Christensen et al., 2008).

According to Kroenke et al. (2007), pain disorder has been infrequently researched as a discrete Axis I disorder. However, in one recent study, Valet et al. (2009) investigated women who fulfilled the *DSM-IV* criteria for pain disorder (compared with healthy age-matched women) using MRI. They found significant grey-matter decreases in the prefrontal, cingulated, and insular cortex, regions of the brain known to be critically involved in the modulation of subjective pain. The authors concluded that, "These findings represent a further proof of the important role of central changes in pain disorder" (Kroenke et al., 2007, p. 49).

Many experts in the pain field do not favour the pain disorder diagnosis. The CISSD recommendation was to code pain symptoms on Axis III, with comorbid psychiatric disorders coded on Axis I. (Therapies for managing pain are discussed in Chapter 9.)

With **body dysmorphic disorder (BDD)**, a person is preoccupied with an imagined or exaggerated defect in appearance, frequently in the face; for example, facial wrinkles, excess facial hair, or the shape or size of the nose. Women tend also to focus on the skin, hips, breasts, and legs, whereas men are more inclined to believe they are too short, that their penises are too small, or that they have too much body hair. Some clients with the disorder may spend hours each day checking on their defect, looking at themselves in mirrors. Others take steps to avoid being reminded of the defect by eliminating mirrors from their homes or camouflaging the defect, for example by wearing very loose clothing (Phillips, 2009). These concerns are distressing and may lead to frequent consultations with plastic surgeons because some people with BDD are never satisfied with the results of cosmetic surgery. BDD occurs mostly among women, typically begins in late adolescence, and is frequently comorbid with depression and social phobia, eating disorders, thoughts of suicide, and substance use and personality disorders (Altamura et al., 2001; Buhlmann, Reese, Renaud, & Wilhelm, 2008; Phillips, 2009). BDD is usually chronic, with only 9% of clients experiencing remission over the course of one year (Phillips et al., 2006).

It is unclear whether BDD's status as a specific diagnosis is warranted. For example, people who are excessively preoccupied with their appearance and frequently check their looks might be diagnosed with OCD, and some experts believe that BDD should be subsumed as a subtype of OCD (Kroenke et al., 2007). Other people may hold a belief about a defect so unrelated to reality as to suggest a delusional disorder and *DSM-IV* allows a psychotic (delusional) variant of BDD to be "double-coded" so that delusional individuals can be diagnosed with both BDD and delusional disorder. Other

Actress Uma Thurman, star of *Kill Bill Volumes 1 & 2*, revealed in 2001 that she suffers from body dysmorphic disorder. CP Image Archive/ Extrapress.

researchers have suggested that BDD would be better classified as a social phobia, mood disorder, or even an eating disorder (see Buhlmann et al., 2008). The *DSM-5* work group recommended that BDD be reclassified from the somatoform disorders to the "anxiety and obsessive-compulsive spectrum disorders." A specifier would indicate if it was a "muscle dysmorphia" form of BDD (the belief that one's body build is too small or is insufficiently muscular). Another specifier would indicate whether the BDD beliefs are characterized by "good or fair insight," "poor insight," or "delusional beliefs about appearance."

In **hypochondriasis**, individuals are preoccupied with persistent fears of having a serious disease, despite medical reassurance to the contrary. The disorder typically begins in early adulthood and has a chronic course. In one study, over 60% of diagnosed cases still had the disorder when followed up five years later (Barsky et al., 1998). Clients with this little-used diagnosis are frequent consumers of medical services and are likely to have mood or anxiety disorders (Noyes et al., 2006). The theory is that they overreact to ordinary physical sensations and minor abnormalities, such as irregular heartbeat, occasional coughing, or a stomach ache, seeing these as evidence for their beliefs, and, indeed, people with high scores on a measure of hypochondriasis are more likely than others to attribute physical sensations to an illness (MacLeod, Haynes, & Sensky, 1998). Similarly, people with hypochondriasis make catastrophic interpretations of symptoms, such as believing that a red blotch on the skin is skin cancer (Rief, Hiller, & Margraf, 1998). Asmundson, Taylor, Wright, and Cox (2001) cited a *Globe and Mail* newspaper account of the compelling case study of James V. to illustrate that people who actually experience abnormally intense sensations may be particularly vulnerable to hypochondriasis.

For reasons no one understood, Mr. V felt as if a million bugs crawled over him. To quiet his torment, he scratched himself so tenaciously that he ripped open his skin, even though he fell within the range of what is considered average intelligence and he was aware of the damage he was inflicting. … Heavily scarred from his assaults … [he] had a high tolerance for pain and would break his bones and tear off his fingernails as well as scratch himself. (As cited by Asmundson et al., 2001, pp. 368–369)

Sadly, Mr. V died at the young age of 25 from infections of the blood and spine.

In a review of prevalence studies, Asmundson, Taylor, Sevgur, and Cox (2001) concluded that hypochondriasis is evident in about 5% of the general population. Prevalence rates are higher in studies that selectively restrict their sample to individuals presenting at medical clinics.

Hypochondriasis is not well differentiated from somatization disorder, which is also characterized by a long history of complaints of medical illnesses (Noyes et al., 2006). A consensus CISSD recommendation was that the term "hypochondriasis" has become so pejorative it should be changed, possibly to "health anxiety disorder" (Kroenke et al., 2007). There is disagreement about its place in the future *DSM*: should it be moved to the anxiety disorders category, remain in the somatoform category, or be rolled into somatization disorder? Most contemporary researchers do focus on health anxiety rather than hypochondriasis per se. Health anxiety has been defined as "health-related fears and beliefs, based on interpretations, or perhaps more often, *misinterpretations*, of bodily signs and symptoms as being indicative of serious illness" (Asmundson, Taylor, Sevgur, & Cox, 2001, p. 4). Health anxiety is not limited to hypochondriasis but can also be linked with anxiety and mood disorders. According to Asmundson et al. (2001), health anxiety would be present in both hypochondriasis and an illness phobia. Whereas hypochondriasis is a fear of *having* an illness, an illness phobia is a fear of *contracting* an illness.

The Illness Attitudes Scale (IAS) is used commonly to assess health anxiety. Stewart and Watt (2001) suggest that it consists reliably of four factors: (1) worry about illness and pain (i.e., illness fears); (2) disease conviction (i.e., illness beliefs); (3) health habits (i.e., safety-seeking behaviours); and (4) symptom interference with lifestyle (i.e., disruptive effects). The IAS was used by Cox, Borger, Asmundson, and Taylor (2000) to confirm a link between health anxiety and trait neuroticism. Indeed, a general neurotic syndrome is regarded as a contributing factor in the etiology of health anxiety along with more specific factors such as cognitive mechanisms (Asmundson, Taylor, Wright, & Cox, 2001). A twin study conducted in Canada found that after controlling for medical morbidity, health anxiety was moderately heritable, but most of the variance was due to environmental factors (Taylor, Thordarson, Jang, & Asmundson, 2006). This finding supports past interpretations that health anxiety is mostly learned.

Cognitive factors are featured in the model of health anxiety outlined by Salkovskis and Warwick (2001) presented in Figure 7.1. This model has four contributing factors: (1) a critical precipitating incident; (2) a previous experience of illness and related medical factors; (3) the presence of inflexible or negative cognitive assumptions (i.e., believing strongly that unexplained bodily changes are always a sign of serious illness); and (4) the severity of anxiety. The latter, the severity of anxiety, is a function of two factors that will increase anxiety and two that will decrease it. Health anxiety will increase multiplicatively as a function of related increases in (1) the perceived likelihood or probability of illness and (2) the perceived cost, awfulness, and burden of illness. Health anxiety will decrease as a function of (1) the perceived ability to cope and (2) the perceived presence of rescue factors (i.e., the availability and perceived effectiveness of medical help). Marcus, Gurley, Marchi, and Bauer (2007) reviewed cognitive and perceptual variables in hypochondriasis and health anxiety and concluded that there is clear evidence that health anxiety is related to dysfunctional health-related beliefs and self-reported higher levels of somatosensory amplification. However, further research is required to determine whether the beliefs are specific to hypochondriasis and to identify other cognitive processes unique to hypochondriasis.

We turn now to a discussion of the symptoms of conversion disorder and somatization disorder and then to theories of etiology and therapies.

CONVERSION DISORDER

Conversion disorder requires a decision regarding the role of psychological factors, a criterion that is hard to verify, not required for other somatoform disorders, and divergent from the largely atheoretical, phenomenological nature of *DSM-IV.*
–*Kroenke et al., 2007, p. 283*

FIGURE 7.1 Cognitive model of the development of health anxiety. *Source:* "Making Sense of Hypochondriasis: A Cognitive Model of Health Activity," Paul M. Salkovskis and Hilary M. C. Warwick, *Health Anxiety.* eds. G. J. G. Asmundson, S. Taylor, & B. J. Cox, 2001. © John Wiley & Sons Limited. Reproduced with Permission.

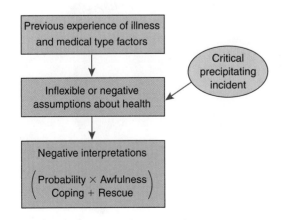

In **conversion disorder**, physiologically normal people experience sensory or motor symptoms, such as a sudden loss of vision or paralysis, suggesting an illness related to neurological damage of some sort, although the body organs and nervous system are found to be fine. Sufferers may experience paralysis of arms or legs; seizures and coordination disturbances; a sensation of prickling, tingling, or creeping on the skin; insensitivity to pain; or the loss or impairment of sensations, called **anesthesias**. Vision may be seriously impaired; the person may become partially or completely blind or have tunnel vision. *Aphonia*, loss of the voice and all but whispered speech, and *anosmia*, loss or impairment of the sense of smell, are other conversion disorders.

The psychological nature of conversion symptoms is demonstrated by the fact that they appear suddenly in stressful situations, allowing the individual to avoid some activity or responsibility or to receive badly wanted attention. The term "conversion" was derived originally from Freud, who thought that the energy of a repressed instinct was diverted into sensory-motor channels and blocked functioning. Thus, anxiety and psychological conflict were believed to be *converted* into physical symptoms.

George Fraser (1994), while at the Royal Ottawa Hospital, reported two cases of conversion disorder that involved an apparent loss of eyesight:

Both were young male military recruits who had been "strongly encouraged" to join the military by relatives. One of the cases was referred to psychiatry with a 2-week history of "blindness." He had been fully investigated neurologically and ophthalmologically. No pathology was found. All eye reflexes were normal, yet despite efforts to catch him in an unguarded moment, suggesting malingering, he persisted with his blindness. He had even sustained bruising by bumping into objects. History revealed his loss of vision occurred suddenly while doing combat manoeuvres on the bayonet range. Interestingly, he stated, "I just couldn't see myself killing people." He feared telling his parents that he was terrified to be in military life. After confirming the diagnosis and the cause, I told him that he would be released from military services, but it was only with hypnosis (one session, as was the case with the other soldier) that he immediately regained his vision. Also, he was able to visually describe accurately all the locations he had been to during the 2 weeks of conversion blindness. (Fraser, 1994, p. 138)

The men described by Fraser suffered from a form of conversion disorder involving "hysterical" blindness and illustrate the role that stress plays in the development of conversion disorders. **Hysteria**, the term originally used to describe what are now known as conversion disorders, has a long history, dating back to the earliest writings on abnormal behaviour. Hippocrates considered it an affliction limited solely to women and due to the wandering of the uterus through the body. (The Greek word *hystera* means "womb.") Presumably, the wandering uterus symbolized the longing to produce a child.

Public attention on conversion disorder increased when it was reported that a cluster of five Amish girls between the ages of 9 and 13 experienced an "outbreak" of diagnosable cases of conversion disorder (see Cassady et al., 2005). The girls knew each other and had shared symptoms. Common symptoms included motor deficits, life-threatening anorexia, and neck weakness that made them unable to hold up their heads. Possible environmental and organic causes were discounted; instead the symptoms were deemed to be a stress reaction to psychosocial pressures and expectations common among adolescent Amish girls. Conversion symptoms usually develop in adolescence or early adulthood, typically after undergoing life stress. An episode may end abruptly, but sooner or later the disorder is likely to return, either in its original form or with a symptom of a different nature and site. Prevalence of conversion disorder is less than 1%, and more women than men are given the diagnosis (Singh & Lee, 1997). It is frequently comorbid with other Axis I diagnoses, such as depression, substance abuse, anxiety and dissociative disorders, and with personality disorders, notably borderline and histrionic personality disorders (Rechlin, Loew, & Jorashky, 1997; Stonnington, Barry, & Fisher, 2006). People with conversion symptoms frequently report a history of physical or sexual abuse (see Stonnington et al., 2006).

It is important to distinguish a conversion paralysis or sensory dysfunction from similar problems that have a true neurological basis (see Figure 7.2). Sometimes this task is easy, as when the paralysis does not make anatomical sense. A classic example is *glove anesthesia*, a rare syndrome in which the individual experiences little or no sensation in the part of the hand that would be covered by a glove (see Figure 7.2). For years this was the textbook illustration of anatomical nonsense because the nerves here run continuously from the hand up the arm. Yet, even in this case, it now appears that misdiagnosis can

occur. A currently recognized disease, *carpal tunnel syndrome*, can produce symptoms similar to those of glove anesthesia. Nerves in the wrist run through a tunnel formed by the wrist bones and membranes. The tunnel can become swollen and may pinch the nerves, leading to tingling, numbness, and pain in the hand.

Since the majority of paralyses, analgesias, and sensory failures do have biological causes, true neurological problems may sometimes be misdiagnosed as conversion disorders. Studies conducted during the 1960s indicated that on follow-up many clients diagnosed with conversion disorder may have been misdiagnosed. One study found that nine years after diagnosis, an alarming number—60%—of these individuals had either died or developed symptoms of physical disease! A high proportion had diseases of the central nervous system (Slater & Glithero, 1965). Fortunately, with technological advances in detecting illness and disease (such as the MRI), the rate of misdiagnosis appears on the decline. A survey by Stone et al. (2005) of studies conducted in the 1950s to present day found a dramatic decline in misdiagnoses (from 29% down to about 4%) and this pattern was evident across age and held for males and females.

Some experts believe that conversion disorder should be moved to the dissociative disorders (see Kroenke et al., 2007). However, the *DSM-5* work group suggested retaining conversion disorder in the new "somatic symptom disorders" section of the *DSM*. The work group proposed simplifying the criteria for conversion disorder by removing a requirement that the clinician establish that the client is not feigning (see Focus on Discovery 7.1), by removing the requirement that the clinician has to establish that there are associated psychological factors, and by emphasizing the importance of obtaining "positive evidence of the diagnosis from appropriate neurological assessment and testing" (see www.dsm5.org).

FIGURE 7.2 Hysterical anesthesias can be distinguished from neurological dysfunctions. The patterns of neural innervation are shown on the left. Typical areas of 219anesthesias in hysterical patients are superimposed on the right. The hysterical anesthesias do not make anatomical sense. Netter illustration from www.netterimages.com. © Elsevier Inc. All rights reserved. Image edited with permission

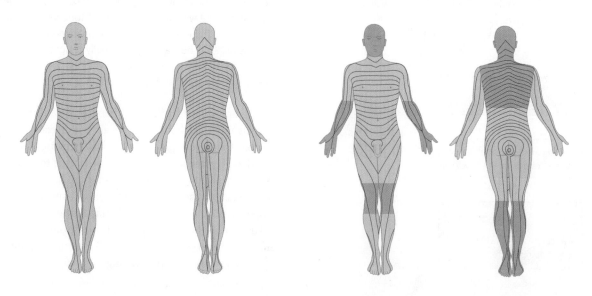

FOCUS ON DISCOVERY 7.1
MALINGERING AND FACTITIOUS DISORDER

Conversion disorder is difficult to distinguish from **malingering**. In malingering, an individual fakes an incapacity in order to avoid a responsibility, such as work or military duty, or to achieve some goal, such as being awarded a large insurance settlement. Malingering is diagnosed when the conversion-like symptoms are determined to be under voluntary control, which is not thought to be the case in true conversion disorders.

In trying to discriminate conversion reactions from malingering, clinicians may attempt to determine whether the symptoms have been consciously or unconsciously adopted. However, how can anyone know with any degree of certainty whether behaviour is consciously or unconsciously motivated? One aspect of behaviour that can sometimes help distinguish the two disorders is known as **la belle indifférence**, characterized by a relative lack of concern or a blasé attitude toward the symptoms. Clients with conversion disorder sometimes demonstrate this behaviour; they also appear willing and eager to talk endlessly and dramatically about their symptoms, but often without the concern one might expect. In contrast, malingerers are likely to be more guarded and cautious, perhaps because they consider interviews a challenge or threat to the success of the lie. But this distinction is not foolproof, for only about one third of people with conversion disorders show *la belle indifférence.* Furthermore, a stoic attitude is sometimes found among clients with verified medical diseases.

CASE ILLUSTRATION: THE DIFFICULTY OF DETECTING MALINGERING

In a recent review, Drob, Meehan, and Waxman (2009) described numerous clinical and conceptual errors that contribute to false attributions of malingering in forensic evaluations, including the use of assessment tools that can detect feigning but can't reliably determine incentive and volition or consciousness (defining characteristics of malingering). They also noted that evaluators might overlook the possibility that feigning is a function of true pathology. A case study reported by Ladowsky-Brooks and Fischer (2003) illustrates the need for multiple forms of assessment. The case is of a 50-year-old man from Trinidad who immigrated to Canada. The client had apparent symptoms of diminished cognitive functioning, but his pattern of errors on a memory test was highly consistent with deliberate malingering. However, further physiological testing (MRI and SPECT scan) revealed that the man was suffering from frontal-temporal lobe dementia and was not malingering.

Also related to the disorders we have been discussing is another *DSM* category, **factitious disorder**. In this disorder, people intentionally produce physical symptoms (or sometimes psychological ones). They may make up symptoms—for example, reporting acute pain—or inflict injuries on themselves. In contrast to malingering, with factitious disorder the symptoms are less obviously linked to a recognizable goal; the motivation for adopting the physical or psychological symptoms is much less clear. The individual, for some unknown reason, wants to assume the role of client.

Kathleen Bush is taken into custody, charged with child abuse and fraud for deliberately causing her child's illnesses. ©Robert Mayer/Sun-Sentinel/ZUMA.

Factitious disorder may also involve a parent creating physical illnesses in a child; in this case, it is called *factitious disorder by proxy* or *Munchausen syndrome by proxy.* In one extreme case, a 7-year-old girl was hospitalized over 150 times and experienced 40 surgeries at a cost of over $2 million. Her mother, Kathleen Bush, caused her illnesses by using drugs and even contaminating her feeding tube with faecal material (*Time,* 1996). The motivation in a case such as this appears to be the need to be regarded as an excellent parent and tireless in seeing to the child's needs. This disorder has received more public attention in recent years, in part due to claims by rap artist Eminem. He has stated that he was made ill during his childhood by his mother, who he alleges suffers from Munchausen syndrome by proxy.

If someone is making themselves ill, then the disorder is simply referred to as Munchausen syndrome. Two Canadian cases involved nurses who presented with urinary tract infections, flank pain, and gross hematuria (blood in the urine). Evidence in both cases suggested that these women had infused blood into their own bladders (Chew, Pace, & Honey, 2002).

According to Gregory and Jindal (2006), factitious disorder is much more prevalent (6% in their sample) among adult psychiatric inpatients than previously recognized.

The *DSM-5* work group recommended that factitious disorder be reclassified to "somatic symptom disorders." Importantly, it would eliminate the distinction between factitious disorders involving physical versus psychological symptoms and clarify who is the client in circumstances previously diagnosed as "factitious disorder by proxy." The latter would be termed "factitious disorder on other."

SOMATIZATION DISORDER

In 1859, the French physician Pierre Briquet described a syndrome that first bore his name, Briquet's syndrome, and now, in *DSM-IV-TR*, is referred to as **somatization disorder**. The disorder is characterized by recurrent, multiple somatic complaints, with no apparent physical cause, for which medical attention is sought. To meet diagnostic criteria, the person must have

1. four pain symptoms in different locations (e.g., head, back, joint);
2. two gastrointestinal symptoms (e.g., diarrhea, nausea);
3. one sexual symptom other than pain (e.g., indifference to sex, erectile dysfunction); and
4. one pseudoneurological symptom (e.g., those of conversion disorder).

These symptoms, which are more pervasive than the complaints in hypochondriasis, usually cause impairment. Behavioural and interpersonal problems, such as truancy or poor work records, and marital difficulties are often reported.

Somatization disorder and conversion disorder share many symptoms, and both diagnoses may apply to the same person. Visits to physicians are frequent, as is the use of medication. Hospitalization and even surgery are common. Menstrual difficulties and sexual indifference are frequent. Clients often present their complaints in a histrionic, exaggerated fashion or as part of a long, complicated medical history. Many believe that they have been ailing all their lives. Comorbidity is high with anxiety and mood disorders, substance abuse, and several personality disorders (e.g., Escobar, 2005). In a recent electronic diary study (Burton, Weller, & Sharp, 2009), people with "persistent medically unexplained symptoms" (but who did not necessarily meet the full diagnostic criteria for somatization disorder) were followed for 12 weeks. They completed twice daily measures of symptoms, fatigue, anxiety, stress, mood, and symptom concern. "Functional" physical symptoms were more strongly associated with mood and symptom concern than with anxiety or stress. The authors suggested that such individuals reject psychosomatic explanations "because they do not experience sufficient correlation between symptoms and psychological states" (p. 77). The lifetime prevalence of somatization disorder is estimated at less than 0.5% of the population; it is more frequent among women and among patients in medical treatment.

DSM-IV-TR notes that the specific symptoms may vary across cultures. Burning hands or the experience of ants crawling under the skin are more frequent in Asia and Africa, for example, than in North America. The disorder may be more frequent in cultures that de-emphasize the overt display of emotion. Interpreting cultural differences is not straightforward (Kirmayer & Young, 1998). From a western European perspective, for example, a physical presentation of a psychological problem is sometimes considered somewhat primitive or unsophisticated. But this dualistic distinction between physical and psychological reflects a medical tradition that is not universally accepted (e.g., in Chinese medicine). It is more reasonable to view a person's culture as providing a concept of what distress is and how it should be communicated.

Somatization disorder typically begins in early adulthood. It may not be as stable as the *DSM* implies, though; in one study only one third of clients with somatization disorder still met diagnostic criteria when reassessed 12 months later (Simon & Gureje, 1999). Somatization disorder also seems to run in families; it is found in about 20% of the first-degree relatives of index cases (Guze, 1993).

Noting that the prevalence of somatization disorder in primary care is 1% or less, but that the prevalence of people with clinically meaningful medically unexplained symptoms is at least 10–15%, the CISSD experts recommended that if somatization disorder is retained in *DSM-5*, it should be revised to make it more inclusive, or a lower-threshold category should be added, such as "abridged somatization disorder" (see Kroenke et al., 2007). They also noted that many people coded as having undifferentiated somatoform disorder would meet criteria for a more inclusive somatization category.

ETIOLOGY OF SOMATOFORM DISORDERS

Much of the theorizing in the area of somatoform disorders has been directed solely toward understanding hysteria as originally conceptualized by Freud. Consequently, it has focused on explanations of conversion disorder. Later in this section, we examine psychoanalytic views of conversion disorder and then look at what behavioural, cognitive, and biological theorists have to offer. First, we briefly discuss ideas about the etiology of somatization disorder.

ETIOLOGY OF SOMATIZATION DISORDER It has been proposed that people with somatization disorder are more sensitive to physical sensations, overattend to them, or interpret them catastrophically (e.g., Kirmayer et al., 1994). People with somatization disorder may also have a memory bias for information that connotes physical threat. The results of one experiment showed that somatoform clients had greater supraliminal interferences for physical threat words presented as part of a Stroop task. An explicit memory test also indicated that somatoform clients had a memory bias for physical threat words (Lim & Kim, 2005).

A behavioural view of somatization disorder holds that the various aches, discomforts, and dysfunctions are the manifestation of unrealistic anxiety about bodily systems. In keeping with the possible role of anxiety, clients with somatization disorder have high levels of cortisol, an indication that they are under stress (Rief et al., 1998). Perhaps the extreme tension of an individual localizes in stomach muscles, resulting in feelings of nausea or vomiting. Once normal functioning is disrupted, the maladaptive pattern may strengthen because of the attention it receives or the excuses it provides. In a related vein, the reporting of physical symptoms has been seen as a strategy to explain poor performance in evaluative situations. Attributing poor performance to illness is psychologically less threatening than attributing it to some personal failing (Smith, Snyder, & Perkins, 1983).

Bialas and Craig (2007) explored the hypothesis that the illness behaviours characteristic of somatization disorder might be learned responses acquired via exposure to parental illness and health anxiety in childhood. They examined patterns of interaction in mothers (mothers with somatization disorder, organically ill mothers, and healthy mothers) and their school-age children in semi-structured play tasks and during a meal. Mothers with somatization disorder and their children interacted differently relative to other mother-child pairs. For example, during play, children of somatizing mothers expressed more health and safety needs than children of other mothers. The findings are consistent with theories of environmental influence in the development of somatization.

PSYCHOANALYTIC THEORY OF CONVERSION DISORDER Conversion disorder occupies a central place in psychoanalytic theory, for it offered Freud a clear opportunity to explore the concept of the unconscious. In *Studies in Hysteria* (1895; 1982), Breuer and Freud proposed that a conversion disorder is caused when a person experiences an event that creates great emotional arousal, but the affect is not expressed and the memory of the event is cut off from conscious experience. The specific conversion symptoms were said to be related causally to the traumatic event that preceded them.

Anna O., for example, while watching at the bedside of her seriously ill father, had dropped off into a waking dream with her right arm over the back of her chair. She saw a black snake emerge from the wall and come toward her sick father to bite him. She tried to ward it off, but her right arm had gone to sleep. When she looked at her hand, her fingers turned into little snakes with death's heads. The next day, a bent branch recalled her hallucination of the snake, and at once her right arm became rigidly extended. After that, her arm responded in the same way whenever some object revived her hallucination. Later, when Anna O. fell into her "absences" and took to her own bed, the contracture of her right arm became chronic and extended to paralysis and anesthesia of her right side.

In his later writings, Freud hypothesized that conversion disorder in women is rooted in an unresolved Electra complex. The young female child becomes sexually attached to her father, but these unacceptable impulses are repressed. The result is both a preoccupation with sex and at the same time an avoidance of it. Sexual excitement or some event reawakens these repressed impulses as an adolescent or adult, creating anxiety. The anxiety is then transformed or converted into physical symptoms.

A more recent psychodynamic interpretation of one form of conversion disorder, hysterical blindness, is based on experimental studies of hysterically blind people whose behaviour on visual tests showed that they were influenced by the stimuli even though they explicitly denied seeing them (Sackeim, Nordlie, & Gur, 1979). Two studies involved teenaged women. The first case concerned a 16-year-old who had experienced sudden loss of peripheral vision and reported that her visual field had become tubular and constricted. On a special visual test she had performed significantly worse than would a person who was indeed blind! The clinicians reasoned that she had some awareness of the illuminated stimulus and she wanted, consciously or unconsciously, to preserve her blindness by performing poorly on the test. The second case was seemingly contradictory in that Celia, a hysterically blind adolescent girl, showed almost perfect visual performance. Her initial symptom was a sudden loss of sight in both eyes, followed by severe blurring of vision. When three triangles were projected on three display windows of a console, two of the triangles inverted, one of them upright, in 599 trials of 600 she pressed the switch under the upright triangle, the correct response.

Sackeim et al. (1979) proposed a two-stage defensive reaction to account for these conflicting findings: (1) perceptual representations of visual stimuli are blocked from awareness and, on this basis, people report themselves blind; and (2) information is nonetheless extracted from the perceptual representations. If clients feel that they must deny being privy to this information, they perform more poorly than they would by chance on perceptual tasks. If clients do not need to deny having such information, they perform the task well but still maintain that they are blind. Whether or not hysterically blind people unconsciously need to deny receiving perceptual information is viewed as dependent on personality factors and motivation.

Are the people who claim that they are blind and yet on another level respond to visual stimuli being truthful? Sackeim and his colleagues reported that some patients with lesions in the visual cortex, rather than damage to the eye, said that they were blind yet performed well on visual tasks. Such individuals have vision (sometimes called blindsight), but they do not *know* that they can see. Therefore, it is possible for people to claim truthfully that they cannot see but give evidence that they can.

BEHAVIOURAL THEORY OF CONVERSION DISORDER AND COGNITIVE FACTORS An early behavioural account of conversion disorder was proposed by Ullmann and Krasner (1975), who viewed conversion disorder as similar to malingering in that the person adopts the symptom to secure some end. In their opinion, the person with a conversion disorder attempts to behave according to his or her conception of how a person with a disease affecting the motor or sensory abilities would act. This theory raises two questions: (1) Are people capable of such behaviour? and (2) Under what conditions would such behaviour be most likely to occur?

Considerable evidence indicates that the answer to the first question is yes: people can adopt patterns of behaviour that match many of the classic conversion symptoms. For example, paralyses, analgesias, and blindness can be induced in people under hypnosis. As a partial answer to the second question, Ullmann and Krasner specify two conditions that increase the likelihood that motor and sensory disabilities will be imitated. First, the individual must have had some experience with the role to be adopted; he or she may have had similar physical problems or may have observed them in others. Second, the enactment of a role must be *rewarded*; an individual will assume a disability only if it can be expected either to reduce stress or to reap other positive consequences.

Although this behavioural interpretation might seem to make sense, the literature does not support it completely. Celia, for example, did not act in accordance with Ullmann and Krasner's theory. The very intelligent Celia performed perfectly in the visual discrimination task while still claiming severely blurred vision. Such a pattern of behaviour seems a rather clumsy enactment of a role. If you wanted to convince someone that you could not see, why answer correctly?

Celia's actions seem more consistent with Sackeim's theory. On the level of conscious awareness, Celia probably saw only blurred images, as she claimed. But during the test the triangles were distinguished on an unconscious level, and she could pick out the upright one wherever it appeared. It is interesting to note that Celia's visual problems gained her crucial attention and help from her parents. Three years after the onset of her visual difficulties, Celia dramatically recovered clear sight while on a trip with her parents. Earlier in the summer, Celia had graduated from high school with grades well above average. The need to receive reinforcement for poor vision had perhaps passed, and her eyesight returned.

Contemporary investigators, many of whom would identify themselves as cognitive psychologists, have begun to corroborate Freud's view that some human behaviour is determined by unconscious processes. But the modern cognitive perspective understands the unconscious processes in a different way. Freud postulated the existence of *the* unconscious, a repository of instinctual energy and repressed conflicts and impulses. Contemporary researchers reject the notions of an energy reservoir and repression, holding more simply that we are not aware of everything going on around us or of some of our cognitive processes. At the same time, these stimuli and processes of which we are unaware can have a powerful influence on our behaviour. A dissociation between awareness and behaviour has been reported in many perceptual and cognitive studies (see Bornstein, Leone, & Galley, 1987).

Numerous cognitive factors shown to be prevalent in people with conversion disorders are consistent with cognitive interpretations, including the tendency to discount the importance of psychological factors contributing to the presenting complaints, illness beliefs, denial of external stressors, suppression of the expression of distress, and avoidance behaviours (see Stonnington et al., 2006 for review). CBT lends itself well to addressing such issues.

SOCIAL AND CULTURAL FACTORS IN CONVERSION DISORDER A possible role for social and cultural factors is suggested by the apparent decrease in the incidence of conversion disorder over the last century. Contemporary clinicians rarely see anyone with such problems. Several hypotheses have

Some psychoanalysts believe that the high frequency of conversion disorder in 18th-century Europe was due to the repressive sexual attitudes of the time. The Novel, A Lady in a Garden reading a book. Dicey, Frank. Christopher Wood Gallery/The Bridgeman Art Library.

been proposed to explain this apparent decrease. Therapists with a psychoanalytic bent point out that in the second half of the nineteenth century, when the incidence of conversion reactions was apparently high in France and Austria, repressive sexual attitudes may have contributed to the increased prevalence of the disorder. The decrease in its incidence, then, may be attributed to a general relaxing of sexual mores and to the greater sophistication of contemporary culture, which is more tolerant of anxiety than it is of dysfunctions that do not make physiological sense.

Support for the role of social and cultural factors also comes from studies showing that conversion disorder is more common among people with lower socio-economic status and from rural areas (Folks, Ford, & Regan, 1984), who may be less knowledgeable about medical and psychological concepts. Further evidence derives from studies showing that the diagnosis of hysteria has declined in industrialized societies such as England (Hare, 1969) but has remained common in undeveloped countries such as Libya (Pu et al., 1986). These data, although consistent, are difficult to interpret. They could mean that increasing sophistication about medical diseases leads to decreased prevalence of conversion disorder. Alternatively, diagnostic practices may vary from country to country, producing different rates. A large-scale study conducted by diagnosticians trained to follow the same procedures is needed.

BIOLOGICAL FACTORS IN CONVERSION DISORDER
Although genetic factors have been proposed as being important in the development of conversion disorder, research does not support this proposal. For example, Torgersen (1986) reported the results of a twin study of somatoform disorders that included 10 cases of conversion disorder, 12 of somatization disorder, and 7 of pain disorder. No co-twin had the same diagnosis as his or her proband!

There may be some relationship between brain structure and conversion disorder. Conversion symptoms are more likely to occur on the left side than on the right side of the body. In most instances, these left-side body functions are controlled by the right hemisphere of the brain. Thus, the majority of conversion symptoms may be related to the functioning of the right hemisphere. Consistent with this idea, research has shown that in people with left-sided conversion symptoms, stimulation of the right hemisphere yields smaller muscle responses than does stimulation of the left hemisphere (Foong et al., 1997). Research has shown that the right hemisphere can generate emotions, and it is suspected of generating more emotions, particularly unpleasant ones, than are generated by the left hemisphere. Conversion symptoms could be linked neurophysiologically to emotional arousal.

A review led by Black from the Université de Montréal summarized existing neuroimaging data (Black, Seritan, Taber, & Hurley, 2004). The authors noted that the studies conducted thus far are limited in several respects, including the use of small and heterogeneous samples, differences in the duration of the deficit, and the possible confounding influences of comorbid conditions such as depression and chronic pain. Still, the data point to the possibility that "variable alterations in the activity of specific cortical and sub-

cortical areas may underlie conversion disorder, particularly prefrontal and parietal cortices, thalamus, and basal ganglia" (Black et al., 2004, p. 216). A study conducted in Toronto on three women with a sensory form of conversion disorder used fMRI to implicate brain structure (Ghaffar, Staines, & Feinstein, 2006) and found that stimulating a numb hand or foot did not activate the somatosensory region of the brain; however, stimulating each client's other hand or foot (which was not numb) did result in activation of the somatosensory region. Stonnington et al. (2006) argue that these and other recent neuroimaging studies implicate neurological circuits that link volition, movement, and perception in conversions triggered by psychological processes. Thus, biological factors in conversion disorder are worth pursuing.

Stonnington et al. (2006) proposed a comprehensive biopsychosocial model of conversion disorder that integrates empirical findings and different causal models (see Figure 7.3). The model takes into account the risk factors, perpetuating factors, and triggering events. Although the model was developed specifically for conversion disorder, it can serve as a useful framework for other somatoform disorders.

THERAPIES FOR SOMATOFORM DISORDERS

> Hard-to-treat clients may engender feelings of powerlessness, frustration, and mistrust in their treaters, which, if unprocessed, may lead to a poor relationship and excessive use of medication, tests, and procedures.
>
> —Stonnington et al., 2006, p. 1515, on treating conversion disorder

Because somatoform disorders are rarer than most other disorders seen by mental health professionals, less controlled research exists on the efficacy of different treatments relative to many other disorders. Historically, case reports and clinical speculation have been the main sources of information on how to help people with these disorders. However, in recent years a number of randomized controlled clinical trials (RCTs) have focused on the treatment of people with *DSM-IV* somatoform disorders, but more research on variables that predict treatment outcome is needed. It is usually important to recognize and treat comorbid conditions in order to achieve symptom resolution.

People with somatoform disorders define their problems in physical terms. They interpret a referral from their physician to a psychologist or psychiatrist as an indication that the doctor thinks the illness is "all in their head"; therefore, they resent referrals to "shrinks." They try the patience of their physicians, who often prescribe one drug or medical treatment after another in the hope of remedying the somatic complaint.

The "talking cure" into which psychoanalysis developed was based on the assumption that a massive repression had forced psychic energy to be transformed into puzzling anesthesias or paralyses. The catharsis as the client faced up to the infantile origins of the repression was assumed to help,

FIGURE 7.3 Biopsychosocial Conceptualization of Conversion Disorder. *Source*: Stonnington, C. M., Barry, J. J., & Fisher, R. S. Conversion Disorder: Clinical Case Conference, The American Journal of Psychiatry, 163, 1510-1517. Reprinted with permission from *The American Journal of Psychiatry* (© 2006) American Psychiatric Association

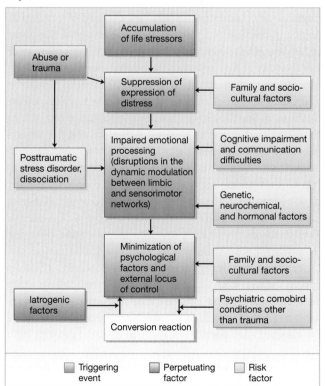

and even today free association and other efforts to lift repression are commonly used to treat somatoform disorders. Classical psychoanalysis and psychoanalytically oriented psychotherapy have not been demonstrated to be useful with conversion disorder, however, except perhaps to reduce the client's concern about the disabling problems (Simon, 1998).

Clinicians must be mindful that such clients often suffer from anxiety and depression. Cognitive and behavioural clinicians believe that the high levels of anxiety associated with somatization disorders are linked to specific situations. Consider the case of a woman who was extremely anxious about her shaky marriage and about situations in which other people might judge her. Techniques such as exposure or any of the cognitive therapies could address her fears, the reduction of which would help lessen somatic complaints, but it is likely that more treatment would be needed, for a person who has been "sick" for a period of time has grown accustomed to weakness and dependency and to avoiding everyday challenges. Chances are that the people who live with this woman have adjusted to her infirmity and are even unwittingly reinforcing her avoidance of normal adult responsibilities. Family therapy might help her and her family members change the web of relationships to support her movement toward greater autonomy. Assertion training and social skills training might be used to provide more adaptive ways of interacting with people and challenge the core belief that "I am a poor, weak, sick person." CBT therapists have applied a wide range of techniques intended to make it worthwhile for the client to give up the symptoms. For example, a reinforcement approach attempts to provide the client with greater incentives for improvement than for remaining incapacitated.

Psychological and pharmacological treatments for BDD have received increased attention in recent years. Psychological interventions have focused primarily on short-term (7 to 30) sessions of CBT or behaviour or cognitive therapy alone. Behavioural interventions typically focus on exposure and response prevention. For example, a client might be gradually confronted with anxiety-provoking situations, such as going to a movie theatre, and staying in the situation without engaging in rituals, such as mirror checking, or avoidance behaviours, such as avoiding eye contact with others, until anxiety decreases. Cognitive strategies would focus on identifying maladaptive, self-defeating thoughts, and core beliefs, such as "If I don't look perfect, it's impossible to be happy," or "I'm unlovable," that seem to maintain body-dysmorphic thoughts and behaviours; evaluating the accuracy of these negative thoughts and irrational beliefs; and assisting the development of more realistic thoughts and beliefs. Final sessions typically focus on relapse prevention. Medication trials have primarily investigated selective serotonin reuptake inhibitors (SSRIs). A recent meta-analysis (Williams, Hadjistavropoulos, & Sharpe, 2006) concluded that both CBT and medication are effective in treating BDD, although CBT was associated with significantly higher ef-

fect sizes. Further, CBT appeared to be highly acceptable to clients. Nonetheless, Buhlmann et al. (2008) noted that clinicians still face numerous challenges in the CBT treatment of BDD. Issues include comorbid depression, suicidality, substance use disorders, personality disorders, the role of early life experiences, delusional intensity of beliefs, and motivation to change. Phillips, Didie, Feusner, and Wilhelm (2008) illustrate the detailed treatment of "Mr. H," a 33-year-old male who presented with preoccupations related to his "thinning" hair, facial "acne," and "short" fingers (all of which looked quite normal).

In general, cognitive-behavioural approaches have also proved effective in reducing hypochondriacal concerns. Treatment may entail such strategies as pointing out the client's selective attention to bodily symptoms and discouraging the client from seeking medical reassurance that he or she is not ill. Taylor, Admundson, and Coons (2005) noted that hypochondriasis was regarded historically as treatment resistant, but recent studies indicate that interventions may be quite successful. Taylor et al. (2005) conducted a meta-analysis of existing findings and concluded that CBT was the most effective form of treatment. Fluoxetine (an SSRI) also resulted in improvement in the short term. Recently, Greeven et al. (2007) completed the first RCT comparing the efficacy of CBT, paroxetine (another SSRI), and a placebo (administered in a double-blind fashion) in the 16-week treatment of hypochondriasis. It was concluded that both CBT and paroxetine are effective treatment options for people with hypochondriasis. However, these short-term effects need to be confirmed through long-term follow-up.

In a widely accepted approach to somatization disorders, the physician does not dispute the validity of the physical complaints but minimizes the use of diagnostic tests and medications, maintaining contact with the client regardless of whether the client is complaining of illness or not. A study of this approach found that clients showed significant improvement in their physical medical condition and made less frequent use of health care services (Rost, Kashner, & Smith, 1994). Also of possible use is redirecting the client's attention to sources of anxiety and depression that may underlie unexplained somatic symptoms or overattention to minor and benign pains. Techniques such as relaxation training and various forms of cognitive therapy have proved useful (e.g., Simon, 1998). Recently, Kroenke (2007) reviewed 34 RCTs involving almost 4,000 clients. Two thirds of the studies involved somatization disorder, lower threshold variants (e.g., abridged somatization disorder), and medically unexplained symptoms. Kroenke concluded that CBT was effective in most studies and that antidepressants were effective in a small number of studies. He further concluded that effective treatments have been established for all somatoform disorders except pain disorder and conversion disorder.

It is usually fruitless to make a sharp distinction between psychogenic pain and pain caused by actual medical factors, such as injury to muscle tissue, since pain always has both components. Pain treatments tend to have the following ingredients: validating that the pain is real and not just in the client's head, relaxation training, and rewarding the person for behaving in ways inconsistent with the pain (toughing it out). In general, it seems advisable to shift the focus away from what the client cannot do because of illness and instead teach the client how to deal with stress, encourage greater activity, and enhance a sense of control, despite physical limitations or discomfort. Evidence from a number of double-blind experiments shows that low doses of some antidepressant drugs, most especially imipramine (Tofranil), are superior to a placebo in reducing chronic pain and distress. Interestingly, these antidepressants reduce pain even when—in the low dosages given—they don't alleviate the associated depression (Simon, 1998). The treatment of pain is described in greater detail in Chapter 9.

There is little controlled research on the treatment of conversion disorder. Although between 50 and 90% of people diagnosed with conversion disorder exhibit short-term symptom resolution following reassurance, as many as 25% of responders relapse or develop new conversion symptoms. It is usually *not* a good idea to try to convince the client that his or her conversion symptoms are related to psychological factors. Clinical lore advises a gentle, supportive approach along with rewards for any degree of improvement (Simon, 1998). In the Stonnington et al. (2006) biopsychosocial conceptualization of conversion disorder (see Figure 7.3), treatment is initiated by directly addressing relevant risk factors (e.g., psychiatric comorbid conditions and communication difficulties). Next, psychological interventions focus on minimizing perpetuating factors (e.g., suppression of distress expression), and recognizing triggering events (e.g., abuse). For example, CBT for nonepileptic seizures is based on the idea that symptoms occur when an individual is confronted with "intolerable or fearful circumstances" and that symptoms are maintained by a "vicious circle of behavioral, cognitive, affective, physiological, and social factors" (Goldstein et al., 2004, p. 41). Specific techniques can include graded exposure to feared or avoided situations, development of problem-solving and coping strategies, and a cognitive focus on changing the client's distorted beliefs about the symptoms. The primary focus of psychodynamic psychotherapy for conversion disorders is on the role of trauma and dissociation, poor attachment, and the client's difficulty in coping with anxiety and intrapsychic conflict. Despite the use of hypnosis as a treatment for conversion symptoms since the time of Freud, available research suggests that hypnosis can be a useful adjunctive treatment, but it shows no added benefit in a comprehensive treatment program. More well-controlled prospective clinical trials are required for all psychological interventions. Given a dearth of controlled trials on pharmacological treatment of conversion disorder, current practice is to use medications to treat comorbid disorders and somatic symptoms (see Stonnington et al., 2006).

DISSOCIATIVE DISORDERS

The dissociative disorders have been mired in controversy for a number of years but empirical investigation has been gradually replacing uninformed speculation, and the onus is now on the critics of the dissociative disorders to provide data supporting their position.

—*Cardena and Gleaves, 2007, p. 495*

In this section, we examine four dissociative disorders: dissociative amnesia, dissociative fugue, dissociative identity disorder or DID (formerly known as multiple personality disorder), and depersonalization disorder, all of which are characterized by changes in a person's sense of identity, memory, or consciousness. The dissociative disorders are summarized in Table 7.2. Individuals with these disorders may be unable to recall important personal events or may temporarily forget their identity or even assume a new identity. They may even wander far from their usual surroundings. We all have everyday dissociative experiences of one kind or another. (See Canadian Perspectives 7.1.)

Few sources of high-quality data concerning the prevalence of the various dissociative disorders are available. Perhaps the best study to date was conducted by Colin Ross (1991). This study found prevalences of 7.0%, 2.4%, and 0.2% for amnesia, depersonalization, and fugue, respectively.

As noted previously, the *DSM-5* Anxiety, Obsessive-Compulsive Spectrum, Posttraumatic, and Dissociative Disorders Work Group was made responsible for proposing changes to the dissociative disorders.

Our examination of the four major dissociative disorders described in *DSM-IV* will first cover symptoms and then theories of etiology and therapies.

DISSOCIATIVE AMNESIA

A person with **dissociative amnesia** is unable to recall important personal information, usually after some stressful episode. The information is not permanently lost, but it cannot be retrieved during the episode of amnesia. The holes in memory are too extensive to be explained by ordinary forgetfulness.

TABLE 7.2
SUMMARY OF THE DISSOCIATIVE DISORDERS

Disorder	Description
Dissociative amnesia	Memory loss following a stressful experience.
Dissociative fugue	Memory loss accompanied by leaving home and establishing a new identity.
Depersonalization disorder	Altered experience of the self.
Dissociative identity disorder	Having at least two distinct ego states—alters—that act independently of each other.

CANADIAN PERSPECTIVES 7.1
EVERYDAY DISSOCIATIVE EXPERIENCES IN WINNIPEG

Colin Ross, a Canadian psychiatrist now based in Texas, did most of his extensive research on multiple personality disorder in Canada. In Winnipeg, he and his associates investigated whether typical Canadians living in the community have everyday occurrences of dissociation.

Have you ever sat at your desk studying, lapsed into daydreaming about the upcoming weekend, and become unaware of what was happening around you? Have you ever been so engrossed in imagining a "story" or engaged in a personal narrative with yourself that it actually seemed real? Have you ever had an impression that you were viewing yourself from outside your body? Have you ever found yourself wondering how you ended up in a certain place or situation? These are all dissociative experiences.

How did Colin Ross determine the frequency of dissociative experiences in a community sample? Ross, Joshi, and Currie (1990) tapped a representative sample of 1,055 adults, having them complete a reliable and validated self-report measure of dissociative experiences: the Dissociative Experiences Scale (DES). The distribution of the respondents' total scores (which can range between 0 and 100) is shown in Figure 7.4. The figure indicates that (1) a majority of people in the general population report having had at least a few dissociative experiences, although only a small number have had many; and (2) most people report never having experienced the most "pathological" items, although some have. Fewer than 75 people reported having had no dissociative experiences at all. Ross re-analyzed the data and concluded that 3.3% of the sample had had pathological dissociative experiences, "and therefore presumptively had a dissociative disorder" (Ross, 1997, p. 105). Ross considers 3% to be a "conservative estimate," which, when extrapolated to all of North America, suggests that about 10 million North Americans have a dissociative disorder. However, note that the majority of DES items are not inherently pathological.

The results of the Winnipeg study indicate that the most common dissociative experiences include being able to ignore pain, missing part of a conversation, noticing that things that are typically difficult to do are done easily, and uncertainty about whether you actually did something or only thought about it. Less common experiences include being so involved in fantasy that it seems real, driving your car and realizing you don't remember part of the trip, not remembering important events in your life, and being in a familiar place but finding it unfamiliar. Relatively few people endorsed very unusual, even bizarre experiences, such as not recognizing your own reflection in a mirror, finding yourself dressed in clothes you don't remember putting on, finding yourself in a place but unaware of how you got there, or feeling as though your body is not your own.

Before we conclude that over 3% of the general community population has DID, we should replicate the study using trained interviewers who employ a structured interview, such as the SCID (Spitzer et al., 1996), to confirm actual diagnoses. Further, certain

FIGURE 7.4 Distribution of dissociative experience scale scores in the general population (N = 1,055).

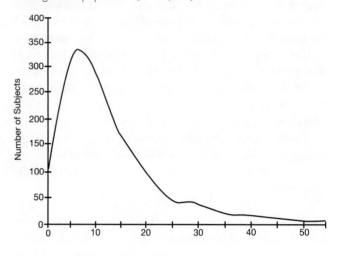

DES items, when taken in isolation, seem dubious examples of dissociation (e.g., absorption in a television program or movie; staring into space), and this highlights discrepancies between self-report measures and what can be learned using the clinical interview. Indeed, follow-up work on the DES indicated that scores are not continuous and, in fact, represent a "taxon" or discrete category. A subset of eight items is now used to identify the presence or absence of dissociation (e.g., Seedat, Stein, & Forde, 2003). The eight items used to distinguish a more pathological form of dissociation primarily reflect themes of depersonalization and derealization (i.e., things, people, and the environment are unreal).

The presence of this more pathological form is in keeping with recent views of dissociation and dissociative disorders that reflect a growing awareness of the complex nature of dissociation and the need to recognize subtle yet important distinctions that suggest that dissociation is more heterogeneous and can come in various forms. It has been suggested, for instance, that there are valid, qualitatively different distinctions not only between forms of pathological and non-pathological dissociation, but also between detachment vs. compartmentalization (Spitzer, Barnow, Freyberger, & Grabe, 2006). Compartmentalization reflects a failure to control actions and processes that are typically under volitional control, while detachment is a subjectively felt altered state of consciousness that involves being detached from the self or the world.

What factors can cause dissociation? Stress and fatigue are key factors. It is likely that these factors contributed to the high rates of dissociation that Laposa and Alden (2003) found in their study of post-traumatic stress disorder (PTSD) in hospital emergency room workers. Almost half of their participants had "clinically meaningful dissociation," according to their responses on a self-report measure. Moreover, more than half reported periods of blanking out, going on "automatic pilot," and feeling unreal, like being in a movie or dream. Other general triggers for dissociation would include binge drinking or the use of various psychoactive drugs. The hypnotic induction can also elicit dissociative symptoms, especially in suggestible people.

Finally, we remind you that dissociative experiences in the general population and among students are non-pathological, typically transient, and are rarely a sign of serious psychological problems. However, if you are distressed by the type or frequency of any dissociative experiences you might have, or if they interfere with your daily functioning, then we encourage you to seek a professional opinion. Extensive episodes of depersonalization and derealization also signal the need for intervention.

Thinking Critically

1. Which of the dissociative experiences described above have you experienced? Remember that dissociative experiences, even if recurrent, should not be considered problematic if they do not cause distress or impairment.

2. There can be numerous triggers for dissociative experiences other than traumatic life events. How do you explain the dissociative experiences that you had in the past? What do you think triggered these experiences? Could boredom also cause dissociative symptoms?

Fraser (1994) used case studies to illustrate the symptoms of the various dissociative disorders. We refer to these compelling case examples throughout this chapter, and they include the case of dissociative disorder that began the chapter. Fraser described dissociative amnesia by outlining the case of a 17-year-old female student

> . . . who was referred because of two episodes of amnesia. The first had happened while she was returning home from school by bus. She was just about to get off the bus, and then the very next moment she found herself in her home. She had no idea how she got home but did not dare to tell anyone. Several nights later, as she disembarked at the same bus stop, she suddenly found herself lying in a field alone, stripped to the waist. She had no idea of the time interval lost but felt it was the same evening. She went home and reported the incident. She was investigated neurologically, and all was normal, and she was referred to psychiatry. Under hypnosis she recalled that on the first incident, there were four boys who were at the bus stop. As they started to make sexual advances, she bolted away and ran home. It was assumed that she did this in a dissociated state. On the second incident, the same group of boys was waiting at

> the bus stop. This time they grabbed her and hauled her into a nearby field. They pulled off her brassiere and appeared to be intending to do more when somehow they were frightened off. (Fraser, 1994, pp. 144–145)

Most often the memory loss involves all events during a limited period of time following some traumatic experience, such as the one described above or such as witnessing the death of a loved one. More rarely the amnesia is for only selected events during a circumscribed period of distress, is continuous from a traumatic event to the present, or is total, covering the person's entire life (Coons & Milstein, 1992). The person's behaviour during the period of amnesia is otherwise unremarkable, except that the memory loss may bring some disorientation and purposeless wandering. With total amnesia, the client does not recognize relatives and friends, but retains the ability to talk, read, and reason and also retains

"Mr. Nobody" became Canada's most famous case of faked amnesia. For many years, he alleged that a mugging caused memory loss, including his identity, and he sought Canadian citizenship. Mr. Nobody (who went by the name Philip Staufen) married his lawyer's daughter in 2001. In 2007, he admitted that he was a Romanian impostor whose birth name is Ciprian Skeid. He said he hated his homeland and his true identity and wanted a new life in Canada. "I'd rather be a fake nobody than the real me." The Canadian Press/Andrew Vaughan.

Though Disney Pixar's *Finding Nemo* may be an animated film meant for children, it has been touted as one of the few films to accurately portray amnesia. Blue tangfish Dory (right) suffers from "short-term memory loss," a symptom consistent with amnesic syndrome. Disney Enterprises/Album Photo Archive/Newscom.

talents and previously acquired knowledge of the world and of how to function in it. The amnesic episode may last several hours or as long as several years. It usually disappears as suddenly as it came on, with complete recovery and only a small chance of recurrence.

Memory loss is common in many brain disorders, as well as in substance abuse, but amnesia and memory loss caused by brain disorders or substance abuse can be fairly easily distinguished. In degenerative brain diseases, memory fails more slowly over time, is not linked to life stress, and is accompanied by other cognitive deficits, such as the inability to learn new information. Memory loss following a brain injury caused by some trauma (e.g., an automobile accident) or substance abuse can be easily linked to the trauma or the substance being abused.

There can be significant cultural differences in the expression of dissociative amnesia. This point is illustrated in the following case of an Inuit adolescent who apparently suffered from dissociative amnesia in the context of spirit possession.

D.N. is a 19-year-old Inuit male student who is the eldest in his family. He described his father as teaching him the traditional skills; his mother he viewed as a scolding rejecting figure. He complained of several years of depression and suicidal ideation related to a confused sexual identity. While alone, hunting on the tundra, he felt a presence touch his shoulder and saying "Don't look back." He did nevertheless and saw a faceless apparition wearing a caribou parka. … The latter named Nanonalok (Big Bear) said "Don't be afraid, I'm your grandfather." Initially friendly the spirit informed D.N. that he would leave him alone if he married "E," a young woman in whom D.N. had an ambivalent interest. He refused to obey and so began nightly battles associated with amnesia, from which he emerged with torn clothes, bruises and a gunshot wound "caused" by the spirit. (Seltzer, 1983, pp. 53–54)

According to Seltzer (1983), this young man received treatment for dissociative disorder, since further assessment yielded no evidence of depression or thought disorder. D. N. received some of this treatment away from home because he insisted that the spirits would lose their energy if he were away from his Arctic environment.

DISSOCIATIVE FUGUE

Dissociative fugue played a key role in the case of Rita Graveline, a woman from Quebec who shot and killed her abusive husband, Michael. According to testimony, he had a severe drinking problem and he had been severely abusive for many years. Rita and Michael were married for 31 years. She had been pushed and shoved many times and had a bottle smashed over her head. She also endured many death threats from her husband. Rita Graveline was acquitted in 2001 by a Quebec jury. The key part of her defence was that she was in a dissociative fugue state and had total amnesia for the events leading up to the killing, as well as for the act itself. An appeal was granted due to procedural problems and a new trial took place, but the Supreme Court of Canada found Rita Graveline not guilty on April 27, 2006. It was noted at the time that it is

rare for a person to be found not guilty based on a defence of dissociative amnesia. The amnesia was believed to have been triggered by Rita's drinking and history of depression, as well as the trauma of the events that took place on the night of the event.

Memory loss is more extensive in **dissociative fugue** than in dissociative amnesia. The person not only becomes totally amnesic but suddenly leaves home and work and assumes a new identity. Sometimes the person takes a new name, a new home, a new job, and even a new set of personality characteristics. The person may even succeed in establishing a fairly complex social life. More often, however, the new life does not crystallize to this extent, and the fugue is of briefer duration. It consists for the most part of limited, but apparently purposeful, travel, during which social contacts are minimal or absent.

Fugues typically occur after a person has experienced some severe stress, such as marital quarrels, personal rejection, financial or occupational difficulties, war service, or a natural disaster. Recovery, although it takes varying amounts of time, is usually complete, and the individual does not recollect what took place during the flight from his or her usual haunts.

Fraser (1994) described another case in which a young man had engaged in three violent acts, including breaking a person's jaw in a fight, yet had total amnesia for these events. Further analysis focused on the time that this young man spent in prison. Fraser found that

. . . hypnosis helped him recall being gang-raped by a group of prison inmates who had singled him out because he was mild-mannered and of different racial origin. He had been sexually abused by these men on numerous occasions. Apparently, attempts to tell the prison guards only resulted in laughter by the guards, who told him the prison "was not the Holiday Inn and didn't cater to room change requests." When some of the more sadistic events were being recalled in hypnosis, a state that called itself "Empty" stated that it had taken over and accepted the severe episodes of anal intercourse. (Fraser, 1994, p. 143)

According to Fraser, the young man committed the three assaults because "Empty" had overreacted and responded with rage to minimal touching.

The *DSM-5* work group proposed that dissociative fugue become a subtype of dissociative amnesia since amnesia, typically for identity, is the primary feature, and travel is an inconsistent one that is extremely rare.

DEPERSONALIZATION DISORDER

In **depersonalization disorder**, the person's perception or experience of the self is disconcertingly and disruptively altered. Its inclusion in *DSM-IV-TR* is controversial since depersonalization disorder, unlike other dissociative disorders, involves no disturbance of memory. In a depersonalization episode, which is typically triggered by stress, individuals rather suddenly lose their sense of self. They have unusual sensory experiences; for example, their limbs may seem drastically changed in size or their voices may sound strange to them. They may have the impression that they are outside their bodies, viewing themselves from a distance. Sometimes they feel mechanical, as though they and others are robots, or they move as though in a world that has lost its reality. Similar episodes sometimes occur in several other disorders: schizophrenia (see Chapter 11), panic attacks and post-traumatic stress disorder (Chapter 6), and borderline personality disorder (Chapter 13) (Maldonado, Butler, & Spiegel, 1998).

Depersonalization disorder usually begins in adolescence and has a chronic course. Comorbid personality disorders are frequent, as are anxiety disorders and depression (Simeon et al., 1997). In a recent study (Baker et al., 2007), 80 participants with depersonalization disorder were assessed using the Revised Illness Perception Questionnaire. Illness perceptions were generally negative. Greater depersonalization disorder severity was associated with a strong illness identity, psychological illness causal attributions, and high levels of depression. The authors concluded that, "The findings offer some support for a cognitive model of understanding depersonalization disorder, namely that attribution processes are linked to perceived symptom severity and a wide range of experiences come to be seen as part of the disorder" (Baker et al., 2007, p. 105).

The following case illustrates the symptoms of depersonalization disorder, as well as the fact that sufferers often report childhood trauma.

Mrs. A was a 43-year-old woman who was living with her mother and son and worked at a clerical job. She had felt depersonalized as far back as she could remember. "It's as if the real me is taken out and put on a shelf or stored somewhere inside of me. Whatever makes me me is not there. It is like an opaque curtain ... like going through the motions and having to exert discipline to keep the unit together." She had suffered several episodes of depersonalization annually and found them extremely distressing. She had experienced panic attacks for 1 year when she was 35 and had been diagnosed with self-defeating personality disorder. Her childhood trauma history included nightly genital fondling and frequent enemas by her mother from earliest memory to age 10. (Simeon et al., 1997, p. 1109)

Some people experience symptoms of depersonalization but not the significant distress that is needed for a depersonalization disorder diagnosis. However, these individuals have depersonalization experiences that seem similar in many respects to those reported by people with the disorder. Charbonneau and O'Connor (1999) analyzed the depersonalization experiences of 20 people from Montreal and found that onset was associated with traumatic life events in general or specific events involving sexual abuse. The most common reaction was a sense of derealization, with statements such as "I feel as if I am floating away from reality" endorsed by 90% or more of the participants. Desomatization was also reported, with 80% or more of the participants agreeing with statements such as "My body does not feel like it belongs." The most common thought or sensation accompanying the depersonalization experience involved worries about feeling isolated and detached from other people (reported by 60%), followed by a feeling of being vulnerable and embarrassed about the situation (reported by 45%). No single diagnosis was associated consistently with depersonalization. The depersonalization group had elevated levels of depression and trait anxiety relative to a community control group.

DISSOCIATIVE IDENTITY DISORDER

Consider what it would be like to have DID. This was what afflicted Chris Sizemore, the woman with the famous three faces of Eve. People tell you about things you have done that seem out of character, events of which you have no memory. You have been waking up each morning with the remains of a cup of tea by your bedside—and you do not like tea. How can you explain these happenings? If you think about seeking treatment, do you not worry whether the psychiatrist or psychologist will believe you?

We all have days when we are not quite ourselves. This is assumed to be normal and is not what is meant by multiple personality. According to *DSM-IV-TR*, a proper diagnosis of **dissociative identity disorder (DID)** requires that a person have at least two separate ego states, or *alters*—different modes of being and feeling and acting that exist independently of each other and that come forth and are in control at different times. There is usually one primary personality, and treatment is typically sought by the primary alter. There are typically two to four alters at the time a diagnosis is made, but over the course of treatment several more often emerge. Gaps in memory occur in all cases and are produced because at least one alter has no contact with the others; that is, alter A has no memory for what alter B is like or even any knowledge of having this alternate state of being. The existence of different alters must also be long-lasting and cause considerable disruption in one's life; it cannot be a temporary change resulting from the ingestion of a drug, for example.

Each alter may be quite complex, with its own behaviour patterns, memories, and relationships; each determines the nature and acts of the individual when it is in command. Usually, the personalities are quite different, even opposites of one another. They may have different handedness, wear glasses with different prescriptions, and have allergies to different substances. The original and subordinate alters are all aware of lost periods of time, and the voices of the others may sometimes echo into an alter's consciousness, even though the alter may not know to whom these voices belong.

DID presumably begins in childhood, but it is rarely diagnosed until adulthood. The diagnosis is much more common in women than in men. The presence of other diagnoses—in particular, depression, borderline personality disorder, and somatization disorder—is frequent (Boon & Draijer, 1993; Oeztuerk & Sar, 2008). DID is often accompanied by headaches, substance abuse, phobias, hallucinations, suicide ideation and attempts, sexual dysfunction, and self-abusive behaviour, as well as by other dissociative symptoms such as amnesia and depersonalization (Scroppo et al., 1998). A study by Ross et al. (1990) of 102 multiple personality disorder clients, including a subset from Winnipeg and Ottawa, used a structured interview to determine that about 90% had a history of suicidal tendencies, depression, recurring headaches, and sexual abuse.

A related possibility is that individuals suffering from dissociative symptoms have a disorganized or insecure attachment style because they were exposed as young children to the frightening and chaotic behaviour of their caregiver (Liotti, 1992; Oeztuerk & Sar, 2008). Indeed, a study of clinically treated adolescents from three Canadian cities confirmed that attachment-related trauma was linked significantly with self-reported symptoms of dissociation (West, Adam, Spreng, & Rose, 2001). Cases of DID are often mislabelled as schizophrenia in the media. This diagnostic category derives part of its name from the Greek root schizo, which means "splitting away from," hence the confusion. A split in the personality, wherein two or more fairly separate and coherent systems of being exist alternately in the same person, is very different from any recognized symptoms of schizophrenia.

CONTROVERSIES IN THE DIAGNOSIS OF DID Although DID is recognized formally as a diagnosis by its inclusion in *DSM-IV-TR,* its inclusion in the *DSM* is controversial, and it is unclear whether it will still be included in the pending *DSM-5.* A survey of American psychiatrists found that two thirds of the participants had reservations about the inclusion of DID in *DSM-IV* (Pope et al., 1999). A follow-up study of 550 Canadian psychiatrists found that more than two thirds had reservations about including DID in *DSM-IV-TR* (Lalonde, Hudson, Gigante, & Pope, 2001). Compared with the American sample, the Canadian respondents were significantly more sceptical about the scientific validity and diagnostic legitimacy of DID. There were no significant differences between the views of English-speaking and French-speaking respondents, a finding inconsistent with the hypothesis that French-speaking Canadian psychiatrists would be less accepting of DID diagnoses because there is little support for the diagnosis in the French-language research literature. However, consistent with the findings of the earlier study, psychoanalytically oriented psychiatrists were significantly more accepting of the validity of DID than were biologically oriented psychiatrists.

DID was first mentioned in the nineteenth century. In a review of the literature, Sutcliffe and Jones (1962) identified a total of 77 cases, most of which were reported between 1890 and 1920. After that, reports of DID declined until the 1970s, when they increased markedly. More formal data on the prevalence of DID were collected on samples of adults in Winnipeg (Ross, 1991) and in Turkey (Akyuz et al., 1999). Prevalence was 1.3% in Winnipeg and 0.4% in Turkey. Although these prevalence figures may not seem high, they are—previously, prevalence was thought to be about one in one million.

What caused the re-emergence of the DID diagnosis in the past 30 years? One possible explanation is that in *DSM-III,* published in 1980, diagnostic criteria were spelled out clearly for the first time (Putnam, 1996). But it is also possible that more people began to adopt the role of a client with DID or that clinicians had always seen a similar number of cases but chose to report them only when interest in DID grew. We can also speculate that the earlier decline in the number of diagnoses of DID resulted from the increasing popularity of the concept of schizophrenia; that is, cases of DID may have been mistakenly diagnosed as cases of schizophrenia (Rosenbaum, 1980). However, the symptoms of the two disorders are actually not very similar. Although the voices of the alters may be experienced as auditory hallucinations, clients with DID do not show the thought disorder and behavioural disorganization of schizophrenia. Another diagnostic issue is that *DSM-III-R* did not require that the alters be amnesic for one another, raising the possibility that the diagnosis could have been applied to people with high levels of variability in their behaviour, as occurs with some personality disorders (Kihlstrom & Tataryn, 1991). *DSM-IV* restored the amnesia component to the diagnosis. Another factor of possible relevance was the 1973 publication of *Sybil,* which presented a dramatic case with 16 personalities (Schreiber, 1973). This case, featured in a movie starring Sally Field, attracted a great deal of attention and spawned much interest in the disorder. Some critics have hypothesized that this heightened interest led some therapists to

Famous NFL football star Herschel Walker revealed in his autobiography, *Breaking Free: My Life with Dissociative Identity Disorder,* that he has at least 12 "alters" (see Christian, 2008, May 19). The Canadian Press/Jeff Chiu.

suggest strongly to clients that they had DID, sometimes using hypnosis to probe for alters. Ironically, it has been claimed that Sybil's alters were created during therapy by a therapist who gave substance to the client's different emotional states by giving them names (Rieger, 1998).

It appears that the *DSM-5* work group supports the DID diagnosis. The work group clarified language and also proposed that part of "dissociative trance disorder" (currently listed as a proposed disorder in an appendix of *DSM-IV*)—the pathological possession trance component (i.e., possession attributed to the influence of a spirit, power, deity, or other person) be subsumed under revised DID criteria to provide more cultural generalizability. The trance is an involuntary state that is not accepted by the individual's culture as a normal part of a cultural or religious practice. It was further noted that in children, the symptoms of DID are not attributable to imaginary playmates or other fantasy play.

ETIOLOGY OF DISSOCIATIVE DISORDERS

The term "dissociative disorders" refers to the mechanism, dissociation, that is thought to cause the disorders. Historically, the concept comes from the writings of Pierre Janet, the French neurologist. The basic idea is that consciousness is usually a unified experience, including cognition, emotion, and motivation. But under stress, memories of a trauma may be stored in such a way that they are not accessible to awareness when the person has returned to a more normal state (Kihlstrom, Tataryn, & Hoyt, 1993). Possible outcomes are amnesia or fugue.

Severe trauma in childhood is regarded as a major cause of dissociative disorders. ORLANDO SIERRA/AFP/Getty Images.

The behavioural view of dissociative disorders is somewhat similar to these early speculations. Behavioural theorists consider dissociation as an avoidance response that protects the person from stressful events and memories of these events. Because the person does not consciously confront these painful memories, the fear elicited has no opportunity to be extinguished.

ETIOLOGY OF DID There are two major theories of DID. One assumes that DID begins in childhood as a result of severe physical or sexual abuse. The abuse causes dissociation and the formation of alters as a way of escaping the trauma (Gleaves, 1996). For example, it was alleged in the case of Sybil that the young child repeatedly received unspeakable tortures from her very disturbed mother, Hattie. Can you imagine the possibility of the formation of DID if you experienced abuse such as this at a young age?

> A favourite ritual, however, was to separate Sybil's legs with a long wooden spoon, tie her feet to the spoon with dish towels, and then string her to the end of a light bulb cord, suspended from the ceiling. The child was left to swing in space while the mother proceeded to the water faucet to wait for the water to get cold. After muttering, "Well, it's not going to get any colder," she would fill the adult-sized enema bag to capacity and return with it to her daughter. As the child swung in space, the mother would insert the enema tip into the child's urethra and fill the bladder with cold water. "I did it," Hattie would scream triumphantly when her mission was accomplished. "I did it." The scream was followed by laughter, which went on and on. (Schreiber, 1973, p. 160)

Since not everyone who experiences child abuse develops DID, it is further proposed that a diathesis is present among those who do. One idea is that being high in hypnotizability facilitates the development of alters through self-hypnosis (Bliss, 1983). Another proposed diathesis is that people who develop DID are very prone to engage in fantasy (Lynn et al., 1988). Whatever the case, in his review, Kihlstrom (2005) was highly critical of empirical research in this area and concluded that studies seeking to link dissociation with traumatic stress have been undermined by poor methodology. He was also critical of attempts to link trauma with amnesia and suggested that there were "no convincing cases of amnesia not attributable to brain insult, injury, or disease" (Kihlstrom, 2005, p. 227).

The other DID theory considers the disorder to be an enactment of learned social roles. The alters appear in adulthood, typically due to suggestions by a therapist (Lilienfeld et al., 1999; Spanos, 1994). DID is not viewed as a conscious deception (or malingering) in this theory; the issue is not whether DID is real but how it developed and is maintained. See Canadian Contributions 7.1 for a more complete description of the views and contributions of Nicholas Spanos in this area.

CANADIAN CONTRIBUTIONS 7.1
NICHOLAS P. SPANOS AND A SOCIOCOGNITIVE PERSPECTIVE ON DID

"Despite its current popularity, the notion that MPD is a naturally occurring disorder that results from severe child abuse is fraught with difficulties."

–*Nicholas Spanos*, Multiple Identities and False Memories: A Sociocognitive Perspective (*1996, p. 2*)

Nicholas Spanos was a professor of psychology and director of the Laboratory for Experimental Hypnosis at Carleton University in Ottawa from 1975 to 1994. Spanos was also a pilot of small airplanes, and unfortunately, he died tragically in a plane crash while taking off from Martha's Vineyard in the Cape Cod area of Massachusetts in 1994. However, Spanos left a research legacy that continues to generate controversy and interest to this day. Spanos had more than 250 publications. Published posthumously was a major book submitted before his death (Spanos, 1996). In this book, he challenged the validity of DID as a distinct psychiatric disorder. Spanos developed a cognitive-behavioural model of hypnosis that has become the most influential in the field. Although he made important contributions in several other areas, including demonic possession and the Salem witchcraft trials, in the area of dissociative disorders, he is known primarily for three things.

First, Spanos (1994) had been a leading advocate of the idea that DID basically involves role-playing. He pointed out that a small number of clinicians contribute most of the diagnoses of DID. A survey conducted in Switzerland, for example, found that 66% of the diagnoses of DID were made by fewer than 10% of the psychiatrists who responded. Perhaps these clinicians have very liberal criteria for making the diagnosis. Alternatively, though, cases of DID may be referred to clinicians who have acquired a reputation for specializing in this condition (Gleaves, 1996). Therefore, the data are inconclusive.

Second, Spanos used role-playing studies with students to provide a unique perspective on the trial of an infamous serial murderer in California who came to be known as the Hillside Strangler (Spanos, Weekes, & Bertrand, 1985). The accused murderer, Ken Bianchi, unsuccessfully pled not guilty by reason of insanity, claiming that the murders had been committed by his alter, Steve. Bianchi was supposedly under hypnosis during a pretrial meeting with a mental health professional to determine his legal responsibility for his crimes. The interviewer (I) asked for a second personality to come forward.

I. I've talked a bit to Ken but I think that perhaps there might be another part of Ken that I haven't talked to. And I would like to communicate with that other part. And I would like that other part to come to talk with me …. And when you're here, lift the left hand off the chair to signal to me that you are here. Would you please come, Part, so I can talk to you? …Part, would you come and lift Ken's hand to indicate to me that you are here? …Would you talk to me, Part, by saying "I'm here"? (Schwartz, 1981, pp. 142–143)

Bianchi (B) answered yes to the last question, and then he and the interviewer had the following conversation.
I. Part, are you the same as Ken or are you different in any way …
B. I'm not him.
I. You're not him. Who are you? Do you have a name?
B. I'm not Ken.
I. You're not him? Okay. Who are you? Tell me about yourself. Do you have a name I can call you by?
B. Steve. You can call me Steve. (Schwarz, 1981, pp. 139–140)

In the Spanos et al. (1985) study, undergraduate students were told that they would play the role of an accused murderer and that, despite much evidence of guilt, a plea of not guilty had been entered. They were also told that they were to participate in a simulated psychiatric interview that might involve hypnosis. Then the students were taken to another room and introduced to the psychiatrist, actually an experimental assistant. After a number of standard questions, the interviews diverged depending on which of three experimental conditions the students were assigned to. In the most important of these, the Bianchi condition, students were given a rudimentary hypnotic induction and were instructed to let a second personality come forward, just as in the actual Bianchi case.

After the experimental manipulations, the possible existence of a second personality was probed directly by the "psychiatrist." In addition, students were asked questions about the facts of the murders. Finally, in a second session, those who had acknowledged the presence of another personality were asked to take two personality tests twice—once each for their two personalities. Eighty-one percent of the students in the Bianchi condition

Nicholas Spanos believed that DID is essentially a socially constructed form of role-playing. Courtesy Nicholas P Spanos.

adopted a new name, and many of these admitted guilt for the murders. Even the personality test scores of the two personalities differed considerably.

Clearly, when the situation demands, people can adopt a second personality. Spanos et al. suggested that some people who present as multiple personalities may have a rich fantasy life and considerable practice imagining that they are other people, especially when, like Bianchi, they find themselves in a situation in which there are inducements and cues to behave as though a previous bad act had been committed by another personality. We should remember, however, that this demonstration illustrates only that such role-playing is possible; it in no way determines that cases of multiple personality have such origins. Furthermore, the impact of such role-playing studies depends on how compelling the role-playing is as an analogue of DID. Critics have pointed out that DID is a complex disorder involving many symptoms, including auditory hallucinations, time loss, and depersonalization. None of these symptoms has been produced in role-playing studies (Gleaves, 1996).

In the actual trial of Bianchi, his insanity plea did not hold up, in part because of evidence from Martin Orne, a well-known expert on hypnosis. Orne subsequently interviewed Bianchi and demonstrated that his role enactment differed in important ways from how true multiple personalities and deeply hypnotized people act (Orne, Dinges, & Orne, 1984).

Finally, the third thing that Spanos is known for is his research, with Cross, Dickson, and DuBreuil (1993), on people who reported seeing UFOs (unidentified flying objects). These 49 people were recruited via a newspaper advertisement placed in an Ottawa newspaper, and then their psychological characteristics were compared with samples of students and community members who did not report seeing a UFO. Spanos et al. (1993) found that there was no evidence indicating that the UFO group had higher levels of psychopathology, higher levels of fantasy-proneness, or lower levels of intelligence relative to the other two groups. The factor that best distinguished the groups was the tendency for members of the UFO group

to believe wholeheartedly in UFOs and alien life forms. Spanos et al. (1993) concluded that "with respect to UFO experiences, these ideas suggest that beliefs in alien visitation and flying saucers serve as templates against which people shape ambiguous external information, diffuse physical sensations, and vivid imaginings into alien encounters that are experienced as real events" (p. 631). According to Spanos, the alleged UFO incidents are by-products of cognitive constructions that largely operate when people are asleep. They are complex false memories. These same cognitive constructions could operate in other false memories.

Ken Bianchi, the Hillside Strangler, attempted an insanity defence for his serial killings, but the court decided that he had merely tried to fake a multiple personality. AP/Wide World Photos.

A critical piece of evidence regarding the two theories is whether or not DID actually develops in childhood as a result of abuse. When clients with DID enter therapy, they are usually unaware of their alters, but as therapy progresses, alters emerge and clients report that their alters did begin in childhood. Typically, however, there has been no corroborating evidence for this, and we have previously cautioned about the uncritical acceptance of self-reports. The situation is similar regarding physical or sexual abuse: very high rates have been reported (e.g., Ross et al., 1990), but they have not been corroborated (see Focus on Discovery 7.2).

One study, however, has come close to providing clearer data regarding both childhood onset and abuse in cases of

DID, although it has been criticized by proponents of the role-enactment theory (Lilienfeld et al., 1999). The study, which was conducted over a period of two decades, examined 150 convicted murderers in detail (Lewis et al., 1997). Fourteen cases of DID were found. That the study was conducted on convicted murderers is important because in this situation, adopting the role of a person with DID involves an obvious payoff. But the evidence indicated that 12 of the 14 cases had long-standing DID symptoms that preceded their incarceration: 8 had experienced trances during childhood, 9 had had auditory hallucinations, and 10 had had imaginary companions (a frequent report among DID clients). Each of these symptoms was corroborated by at least three outside sources

FOCUS ON DISCOVERY 7.2
REPRESSED MEMORIES OF CHILDHOOD SEXUAL ABUSE

"The movement to help survivors recall these allegedly repressed memories resulted in the worst catastrophe to befall the mental health field since the lobotomy era."
—Richard J. McNally, a leading authority on trauma and memory, in a guest editorial in the Canadian Journal of Psychiatry *(2005a, p. 815)*

In the report of the 2003 Canadian Incidence Study of Reported Child Abuse and Neglect (Trocmé et al., 2005), sexual abuse cases represented only 3% of all substantiated investigations of reported maltreatment of children. Neglect (30%), exposure to domestic violence (28%), physical abuse (24%), and emotional maltreatment (15%) were the more common forms of abuse. A history of such abuse in childhood, including child sexual abuse (CSA), is thought to be an important cause of DID and is also considered to play a role in several other disorders, including PTSD.

Here we focus on the special instance of *recovered memories* of CSA. In these cases, the client had no memory of abuse until it was recovered, typically during psychotherapy. Few issues are more hotly debated in psychology and in the courts than whether these recovered memories are valid. Memory and some hypnosis researchers caution against a blanket acceptance of memories of sexual or physical abuse recovered during therapy (e.g., Laney & Loftus, 2005; Spanos, 1996). It is important to raise such questions; good science requires it, and the issue is key for court cases where recovered memories may play a major role in convicting a parent or other person of sexual abuse (Pope, 1995). However, from a feminist perspective, Connie Kristiansen at Carleton University and her associates (Kristiansen et al., 1999) outlined concerns about ideologies prevailing over scientific research and the possibility that women who have indeed been abused will remain silent because the validity of recovered memories in general has been called into question.

Recovered memories of CSA have assumed great importance in a series of court cases (Earleywine & Gann, 1995). In a typical scenario, a woman accuses one or both of her parents of having abused her during childhood and brings charges against them. Courts in several U.S. states allow plaintiffs to sue for damages within three years of the time they remember the abuse. These cases depend on memories of CSA that were recovered in adulthood, often during psychotherapy, and that were apparently repressed for many years. In a landmark decision on February 1, 2007, that has implications for the repressed memory issue, the Supreme Court of Canada (R. *v.* Trochym, 2007 SCC 6) in a 6-3 ruling stated that the 30-year practice of using hypnosis to enhance memories of witnesses is unreliable and should not be used in criminal trials. Canada thus became the first country with an English common law tradition to impose a total ban on post-hypnotic evidence including, presumably, hypnotically induced memories of CSA.

Williams (1995) interviewed women whose sexual abuse years earlier had been verified. Fully 38% of these women claimed that they were unable to recall the abuse when they were asked about it almost two decades later. Williams (1995) concluded that forgetting CSA is a relatively common occurrence. However, as noted by Laney and Loftus (2005), not mentioning abuse when asked is not proof of repression. Further, Goodman et al. (2003) interviewed 175 adults with documented CSA histories and found that only 19% did *not* report the abuse. They concluded that forgetting CSA may not be as common an experience as first thought.

Research has sought to explain why and describe how traumatic memories may be forgotten over time. For instance, DePrince and Freyd (2004) tested high and low dissociators in a "directed-forgetting" paradigm. Directed forgetting involves presenting lists of different types of words and then telling the participants to "forget about it." Participants in this experiment were drawn from a sample of undergraduate students based on their responses to the DES. The high dissociation group was more likely to have traumatic pasts, including events deemed to involve high levels of betrayal by someone else. Also, on the experimental task, high dissociation was associated with impaired memory for trauma-related words (e.g., "incest"). The data are in keeping with the notion that dissociation is linked with the forgetting of traumatic information from one's past, and this has significant implications for the recovered memory debate.

However, a subsequent experiment by McNally, Ristuccia, and Perlman (2005) that compared adults who reported continuous memories or recovered memories of CSA and those who had never been abused yielded data seemingly inconsistent with the DePrince and Freyd (2004) findings. Specifically, McNally et al. (2005) found that all groups of participants had enhanced memory for trauma words (as opposed to neutral words), including those without CSA. The main purpose was to try to find evidence of a dissociative coping style. That is, they tested those participants who reported recovered memories of sexual abuse. It was expected that when their attention was divided, as part of a directed forgetting experimental procedure, these participants would have relatively low recall of trauma-related words. The data did not support this prediction, so there was no evidence of a conscious ability to forget trauma stimuli. This is in keeping with other experiments conducted by McNally and his team and others (for an overview, see McNally, 2005b).

These empirical studies notwithstanding, is it justifiable to assume that recovered memories are *invariably* accurate reports of repressed memories? This is a question of enormous legal and scientific importance. Studies have been conducted on women who have reported a history of sexual abuse. The women were asked whether there ever was a time when they could not remember the abuse. Based on these data, the frequency of alleged "repression" ranges from 18 to 59% (Loftus, 1993). But a simple failure to remember does not mean that repression has occurred. Women could actively try to keep these thoughts out of mind because they are distressing. Or the abuse could have happened before the time of their earliest memories (generally around age 3 or 4). Nor has it been scientifically demonstrated that children repress or even forget traumatic events. As already mentioned, one of the hallmarks of PTSD is the frequent reliving of the trauma in memory. Rather than repressing negative events, children recall them quite vividly (see Goodman et al., 2003).

Some allegedly recovered memories have no basis in fact, but if that is the case, where do they come from? In 1993 Elizabeth Loftus suggested several possibilities, and there is even more support for her views today, especially with respect to memory research:

1. **Popular writings.** *The Courage to Heal* (Bass & Davis, 1994) is a guide for victims of CSA and is widely known in the recovered-memory movement. It repeatedly suggests to readers that they were probably abused and offers as symptoms of abuse low self-esteem, feeling different from others, substance abuse, sexual dysfunction, and depression. In fact, symptoms such as these can result from many causal factors, not only CSA.
2. **Therapists' suggestions.** By their own accounts, some therapists directly suggest to their clients, sometimes with the assistance of hypnotic age regression (itself a procedure with no established scientific validity), that CSA is likely. Note that one of the defining characteristics of hypnosis is heightened suggestibility. If a therapist believes in a given case that sexual abuse has been repressed, it is possible that memories recovered during hypnosis were planted there by the therapist (e.g., Loftus, 1997).
3. **Research on memory.** Cognitive psychologists have shown that it is possible for people to construct recollections of events that did not happen. Neisser and Harsch (1991) studied people's memories of where they were when they heard about the *Challenger* disaster on January 28, 1986.

Participants were interviewed the day after the explosion and again two years later. Despite reporting vivid memories, none of the participants were entirely accurate in their later accounts and many were way off the mark. Laney and Loftus (2005) reviewed the various research paradigms that have demonstrated that different manipulations can be used to implant false memories for traumatic events. They concluded that, "Just because a memory report is detailed, confidently expressed, and emotional does not mean that it reflects a true experience. False memories can have these features" (Laney & Loftus, 2005, p. 823). McNally (2005b) concluded that the evidence does not support claims of traumatic dissociative amnesia ("repression"). Traumatic memories are rarely truly forgotten; they can be vivid but are not immutable, and not thinking about a traumatic event for a significant period is not the same as not being able to remember it. McNally also noted that some people don't think about early abuse because as children they failed to understand it as abuse at the time.

There is little doubt that CSA exists. But we must be wary of uncritical acceptance of reports of abuse. Social scientists, lawyers, and the courts share a heavy responsibility in deciding whether a given recovered memory is a reflection of an actual (and criminal) event. Erring in either direction creates an injustice. Prout and Dobson (1998) from the University of Calgary have suggested that the best approach is a "middle ground perspective," one that recognizes that while child abuse claims can be quite legitimate, there is also the possibility that certain clinicians have facilitated false reports, and each case should be evaluated individually without preconceptions. We will let Richard McNally have the final word on this issue.

It goes without saying that to emphasize that CSA is not invariably traumatic, in the sense of being terrifying, in no way diminishes its moral reprehensibility. Sexual abuse is a social evil regardless of whether it triggers terror or causes psychiatric disease. (McNally, 2005b, p. 821)

(e.g., interviews with family members, teachers, parole officers). Furthermore, several participants showed distinctly different handwriting styles well before committing their crimes (see Figure 7.5).

Also important in this study was the documentation of physical or sexual abuse during childhood for 11 cases. Again, this was apparently confirmed by outside sources and physical evidence such as scars. Indeed, the authors noted that "the term 'abuse' does not do justice to the quality of maltreatment these individuals endured. A more accurate term would be 'torture'!" (Lewis et al., 1997). One boy was allegedly set on fire, another was circumcised by his father at age 3, and another was forced to sit on a hot stove. These

data, then, seem to lend support to the proposition that DID does begin in childhood and that it is related to extreme stress. Nonetheless, in a two-part critical review entitled, "The Persistence of Folly," published in the *Canadian Journal of Psychiatry*, Piper and Mersky (2004 a, b) concluded that there really isn't any proof for the claim that DID is caused by childhood trauma and that DID cases in children are rarely reported.

THERAPIES FOR DISSOCIATIVE DISORDERS

Dissociative disorders suggest, perhaps better than any other disorders, the possible relevance of psychoanalytic theorizing. In three disorders—amnesia, fugue, and DID—people behave

FIGURE 7.5 Handwriting samples from DID cases. *Source*: Lewis et al., 1997. "Objective documentation of child abuse and dissociation on 12 murderers with dissociative identity disorder." American Journal of Psychiatry, 154, 1703–1710. Reprinted with permission from The American Journal of Psychiatry. © 2007 American Psychiatric Association

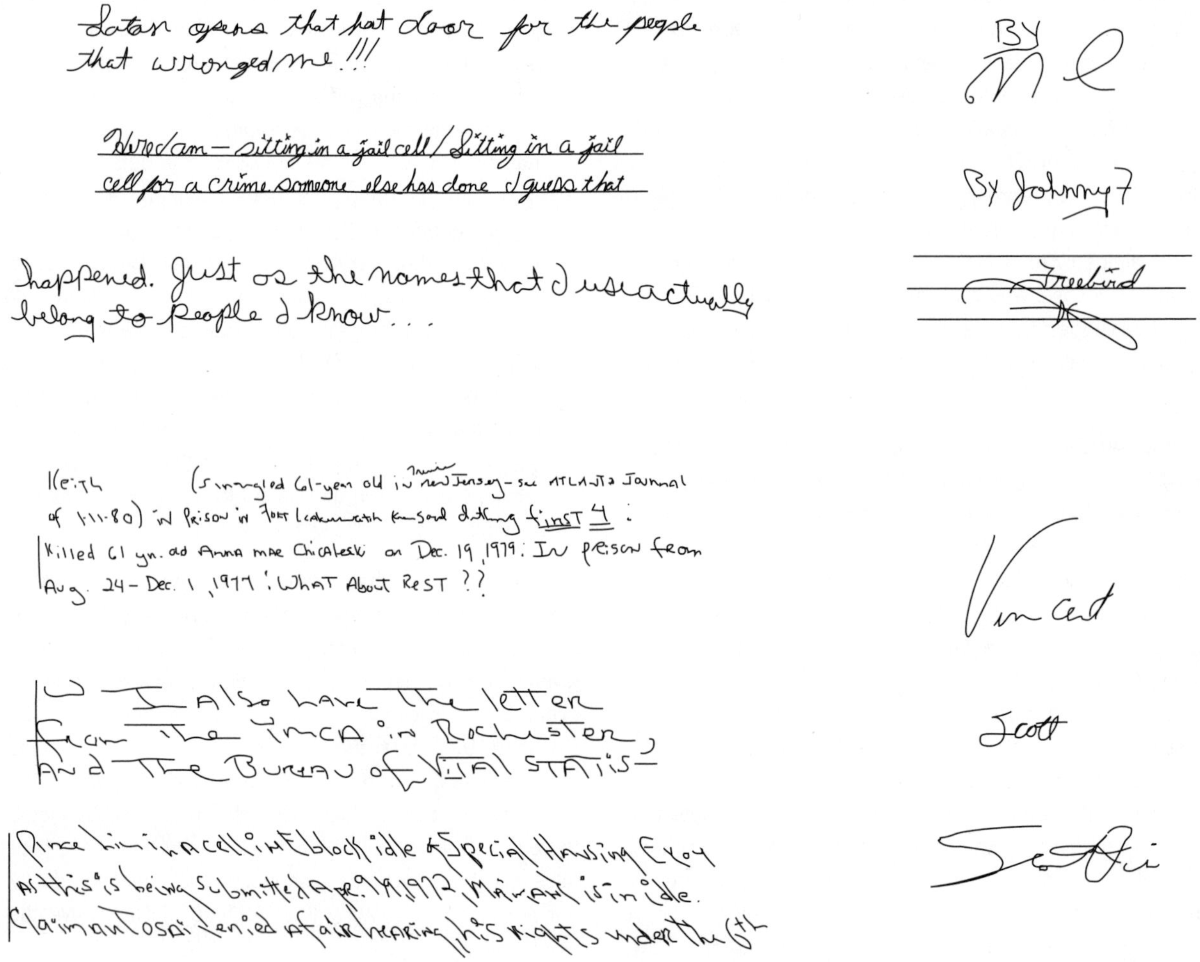

in ways that seem to indicate that they cannot access forgotten earlier parts of their lives. And since these people may at the same time be unaware of having forgotten something, the hypothesis that they have repressed or dissociated massive portions of their lives is compelling (MacGregor, 1996). Consequently, psychoanalytic treatment is perhaps more widespread as a choice of treatment for dissociative disorders than for any other psychological problems. The goal of lifting repressions is the order of the day, pursued via the use of basic psychoanalytic techniques.

Because dissociative disorders are widely believed to arise from traumatic events that the person is trying to block from consciousness, there are links between therapies for these disorders and therapies for PTSD. Indeed, PTSD is the most commonly diagnosed comorbid disorder with DID (Loewenstein, 1991). It is therefore no surprise that some mental health specialists propose strategies for these problems that are reminiscent of treatments for PTSD, such as encouraging the clients to think back to the traumatic events that are believed to have triggered the problem and to view them in a context of safety and support and with the expectation that they can come to terms with the horrible things

that happened to them. Indeed, in a critical review, Lev-Weisel (2008) acknowledged that about 80% of adult CSA survivors diagnosed with PTSD actually suffer from dissociative disorders.

Psychoanalysis had its beginnings in hypnosis. Through the years, practitioners have continued to use hypnosis with clients diagnosed with dissociative disorders as a means of helping them gain access to hidden portions of their personality—to a lost identity or to a set of events precipitating or flowing from a trauma.

TREATMENT OF DID DID clients are unusually hypnotizable, and it is believed that they cope with stress by using their hypnotizability (unconsciously) to enter a dissociative, trancelike state (Butler et al., 1996). For these reasons, hypnosis is used commonly in treatment. The general idea is that the recovery of repressed painful memories will be facilitated by recreating the state entered into during the original abuse, a hypothesis consistent with classic research on state-dependent learning (e.g., Eich, 1995). Typically, the person is hypnotized (sometimes with the aid of drugs such as sodium amytal) and encouraged to go back in his or her mind to events in childhood—a technique called age regression. The hope is that accessing these traumatic memories will allow the adult to realize that the dangers from childhood are not now present and that his or her current life need not be governed by these ghosts from the past (Loewenstein, 1991).

The usual primary goal in therapy for DID is integration of the several personalities. Practitioners attempt to convince the person that forgetting or splitting into different personalities is no longer necessary to deal with traumas, either those in the past that triggered the original dissociation or those in the present or yet to be confronted in the future. In addition, assuming that DID and the other dissociative disorders are in some measure an escape response to high levels of stress, treatment can be enhanced by teaching the client to cope better with present-day challenges.

Because of the rarity of DID, there are no controlled outcome studies. Nearly all the well-reported outcome data come from the clinical observations of one highly experienced therapist, Richard Kluft (e.g., 2001). Over a 10-year period, Kluft had contact with 123 cases. Of these, 68% apparently achieved integration of their alters that was stable for at least three months (33 remained stable for almost two and a half years). The greater the number of personalities, the longer the treatment lasted; in general, therapy took almost two years and upwards of 500 hours per client. In a follow-up, Kluft reported that 84% of the original 123 clients had achieved stable integration of their multiple personalities and another 10% were at least functioning better (Kluft, 1994). Sometimes complete integration of personalities cannot be achieved, and the most realistic outcome is some manner of "conflict-free collaboration" among the person's various personalities (Kluft, 1988, p. 578). A long-term study of DID clients from Canada and the United States who received this treatment revealed that they showed significant improvements on a number of indicators, including dissociative symptoms and symptoms of borderline personality disorder (Ellason & Ross, 1997). This study suggests that DID clients may respond well to treatment, with the caveat that the results must be interpreted with caution owing to the lack of control groups for comparison purposes.

At a meeting in Vancouver in 1994, the Executive Council of the International Society for the Study of Dissociation (ISSD; now the International Society for the Study of Trauma and Dissociation) formulated a series of agreed-upon treatment guidelines[1]. A Guidelines Revision Task Force developed new guidelines in 2005 (see Chu, 2006). They recommended a three-phase or stage-oriented treatment approach that focuses on (1) safety, stabilization, and symptom reduction; (2) working directly and in depth with traumatic memories; and (3) identity integration and rehabilitation. Separate guidelines for children were published in 2004 (ISSD, 2004).

However, there are very few recent studies of actual treatment for DID. Pope, Barry, Bodkin, and Hudson (2006) tracked scientific interest in the dissociative disorders over a 20-year period from 1984 to 2003. They reported that annual publications rose from low levels in the 1980s to a peak in the mid-1990s, followed by a sharp decline by 2003, whereas 25 comparison diagnoses showed constant or rising publication rates. About a third of the most recent papers were sceptical of the validity of dissociative amnesia and/or recovered-memory therapy. They concluded that dissociative amnesia and DID "presently do not command widespread scientific acceptance" (Pope et al., 2006, p. 19). Several DID treatment units in Canada and the United States have been closed down (see Piper & Merskey, 2004a). Piper and Merskey (2004a) concluded that DID cannot be reliably diagnosed and that "consistent evidence of blatant iatrogenesis appears in the practices of some of the disorder's proponents" (p. 592). Iatrogenesis refers to inducing a change in a client (in this case a different identity state) inadvertently by a therapist or by his or her treatment. Various letters to the editor of the *Canadian Journal of Psychiatry*, including one from George Fraser, took issue with these conclusions. In 2009, Colin Ross finally responded to the Piper and Mersky critique and argued that DID "has established diagnostic reliability and concurrent validity, the trauma histories of affected individuals can be corroborated, and the existing prospective treatment literature demonstrates improvement in individuals receiving psychotherapy for the disorder" (Ross, 2009, p. 221).

Thus, the scientific debate and controversy over DID continues! It is complicated by the fact that a recent study from the Netherlands (Reinders et al., 2006) suggests that different identity states show different psychobiological reactions to trauma-related memory including subjective reactions, cardiovascular responses, and cerebral activation patterns determined by a PET scan. The hypothesis is that DID clients have a traumatic identity state that can access repressed memories and emotions and a neutral identity state or states that is protective, inhibiting access to traumatic memories and allowing the client to concentrate on daily life functioning. Another Dutch study (Hermans et al., 2006) reported that an attentional bias for social threat cues was identity state-dependent (a claimed strong awareness of trauma) in DID clients and deviated from patterns observed in controls. In another study (Huntjens et al., 2007), the authors failed to find evidence of inter-identity amnesia for emotionally valenced materials. It was argued that dissociative amnesia in DID reflects a disturbance in meta-memory functioning (knowledge, beliefs, and feelings about memory) rather than an actual retrieval inability. It should be pointed out that there was overlap among some of the authors in these studies and that some of the same participants were used in the different studies. Kong, Allen, and Glisky (2008) also showed that

[1] http://www.issd.org

self-reported inter-identity amnesia is not corroborated by objective explicit memory transfer tests.

Clearly, there are many things about the dissociative disorders that are highly controversial. We conclude this chapter with Canadian Perspectives 7.2, an intriguing and provocative account of the use of thought control and the possible creation of multiple personalities for military purposes.

CANADIAN PERSPECTIVES 7.2
INTERVIEW WITH COLIN ROSS: THE CREATION OF MULTIPLE PERSONALITIES AS COURIERS FOR MILITARY PURPOSES?

"Strange as it may seem, all of us appear to have another person living within our bodies besides ourselves. This other person, this unconscious mind, is quite as capable of handling our bodies as we are, and does so in the most startling manner."
—*G.H. Estabrooks, in his book,* Spiritism *(1947, p. 30)*

In a radio interview conducted at Ryerson University in Toronto, Colin Ross related the following:

But it is absolutely known for a fact that Dr. West and Dr. Orne had extensive funding from all branches of military intelligence from the CIA and had top secret clearance … Martin Orne is tied in to a man named G. H. Estabrooks who was one of probably the top ten leading experts on hypnosis in the 20th century. … G. H. Estabrooks was actually a Canadian by birth, he was a Rhodes Scholar, moved into Upper State New York, and basically spent his professional career in New York. … And he published starting in 1943 and going all the way up to 1971 … very, very detailed accounts of creating Multiple Personalities during WWII for various branches of the U.S.A. military. Basically, he called these people Multiple Personalities. He talked about the Multiple Personality literature, and he referred to them as super-spies. The idea is that you create somebody artificially, using hypnosis and other mind control techniques, who had no multiple personality before, but now has this second identity. And the second identity is hidden behind a memory barrier, an amnesia barrier, and there is a verbal access code that is used to call out the second identity. So, say this person is a Marine, they will be given some kind of courier assignment to take some documents to, for example, Tokyo, but G. H. Estabrooks then calls out the second personality and sticks in some classified information into this second personality. There is a switchback to the main identity, and the person is just going on this routine trip to take documents or technical material over to Tokyo. When he gets to the far end, he uses the example of a Col. Brown who then uses the code signal, and the example he uses in the description is, "The moon is clear." As soon as Col. Brown says "The moon is clear," the second personality pops out, gives the classified message. Col. Brown inserts a classified response, then the person

pops back to their regular identity, goes back to the States and thinks they have just gone on a routine assignment. But Estabrooks again says "The moon is clear," the identity pops out, and Estabrooks gets the classified message. He describes using these people in classified courier missions for actual operations, extensively many times during WWII. (Ross, April 6,1997)*

In his 1997 book, *Dissociative Identity Disorder,* Ross reviews the material that was the basis for his interview comments and states that Estabrooks is the only scientist

to describe systematically creating DID for military intelligence agencies, and the use of these individuals in covert operations. He describes this under a subheading "The Super Spy" in a chapter entitled "Psychological Warfare" in the 1957 edition of *Hypnotism*, and also in his *Science Digest article* (1971). (Ross, 1997, p. 42)

Ross accepted Estabrooks's description of his artificial creation of DID as evidence that iatrogenic shaping of DID can actually occur. In fairness, he also argued that creating artificial secondary personalities in adults would require a great deal of time, persuasion, and control. George H. Estabrooks was born in Saint John, New Brunswick, on December 16, 1895. He completed his B.A. at Acadia University in Wolfville, Nova Scotia.

Thinking Critically

1. What are your thoughts on Ross's story about the creation of DID for military purposes? It sounds disturbingly like scenarios depicted in a Hollywood movie called *The Manchurian Candidate*. Is it really possible to create a second identity or does it defy credibility? Are you a "sceptic" or a "believer"?

2. Assume that you are a "believer," a psychologist with the Canadian Armed Forces, charged with the responsibility of creating "multiples" for use by our military. Suspend the obvious ethical concerns. How would you go about creating a second identity "hidden behind a memory barrier"? You can't be allowed to administer traumatic experiences to trigger dissociation; however, you can preselect people to increase the probability of "success." Describe your ideal candidates and outline your training procedure. Don't forget the "code signal" to trigger the "switchback."

---

*Reprinted with permission of John Wiley & Sons, Inc.

SUMMARY

- In somatoform disorders, there are physical symptoms for which no biological basis can be found. The sensory and motor dysfunctions of conversion disorder, one of the two principal types of somatoform disorders, suggest neurological impairments, but ones that do not always make anatomical sense; the symptoms do, however, seem to serve some psychological purpose. In somatization disorder, multiple physical complaints, not adequately explained by physical disorder or injury, lead to frequent visits to physicians, hospitalization, and even unnecessary surgery.

- Anxiety plays a role in somatoform disorders, but it is not expressed overtly; instead, it is transformed into physical symptoms. Theory concerning the etiology of these disorders is speculative and focuses primarily on conversion disorder. Psychoanalytic theory proposes that in conversion disorder, repressed impulses are converted into physical symptoms. Behavioural theories focus on the conscious and deliberate adoption of the symptoms as a means of obtaining a desired goal. Numerous cognitive, social, and cultural factors are also prevalent in people with conversion disorders. A biopsychosocial model of conversion disorder integrates empirical findings and different causal models.

- In therapies for somatoform disorders, analysts try to help the client face up to the repressed impulses, and behavioural treatments attempt to reduce anxiety and reinforce behaviour that will allow the client to relinquish the symptoms. CBT is particularly effective for somatization disorder. A biopsychosocial approach targets the risk factors, perpetuating factors, and triggering events.

- Dissociative disorders are disruptions of consciousness, memory, and identity. An inability to recall important personal information, usually after some traumatic experience, is diagnosed as dissociative amnesia. In dissociative fugue, the person moves away, assumes a new identity, and is amnesic for his or her previous life. In depersonalization disorder, the person's perception of the self is altered; he or she may experience being outside the body or changes in the size of body parts. The person with DID has two or more distinct and fully developed personalities, each with unique memories, behaviour patterns, and relationships.

- Psychoanalytic theory regards dissociative disorders as instances of massive repression of some undesirable event or aspect of the self. In DID, the role of abuse in childhood and a high level of hypnotizability are considered important. Another DID theory considers the disorder to be an enactment of learned social roles. Clinicians typically focus their treatment efforts on understanding the anxiety associated with the forgotten memories, since it is viewed as etiologically significant. The usual primary goal in therapy for DID is integration of the several personalities.

KEY TERMS

anesthesias (p. 213)

body dysmorphic disorder (BDD) (p. 211)

conversion disorder (p. 213)

depersonalization disorder (p. 224)

dissociative amnesia (p. 221)

dissociative disorders (p. 210)

dissociative fugue (p. 224)

dissociative identity disorder (DID) (p. 225)

factitious disorder (p. 215)

hypochondriasis (p. 212)

hysteria (p. 213)

la belle indifférence (p. 215)

malingering (p. 215)

pain disorder (p. 211)

somatization disorder (p. 216)

somatoform disorders (p. 210)

REFLECTIONS: PAST, PRESENT, AND FUTURE

- In Chapter 2, we pointed out that in some cultures, such as the Chinese, people tend to describe psychological problems as somatic or physical illnesses, perhaps in part because they can feel less shame if they have a physical illness rather than a psychological disorder. Do you think that their belief system increases the likelihood that diagnosable somatic disorders will be more prevalent in people from these cultures?

- The somatoform disorders are typically more prevalent in women than in men. Do you think that the prevalence of somatoform disorders in Chinese males will be as high as or higher than the prevalence of these disorders in Chinese women?

- Conversion disorder is often comorbid with other disorders. Assume that you are a psychologist who is conducting CBT with a client who has a conversion disorder as well as another Axis I and Axis II disorder. How would this information influence your case conceptualization and the development of your treatment plan?

- What are your thoughts on Nick Spanos's sociocognitive perspective on DID? Do you think that he is right in the following claim?

- Expectations transmitted to clients, and the selective reinforcement of increasingly dramatic displays in MPD clients, frequently translate into an increase in the number of alters and an increase in the extent of abuse "remembered" by those alters. (Spanos, 1996, p. 233)

- Do you believe that some cases of DID are therapist produced?

- Should DID be allowed as an excusing condition for a criminal act? In the United States, Billy Milligan, a 23-year-old drifter, was acquitted of rape as a result of being diagnosed with MPD. Psychologists believed that Billy had 10 personalities (eight male and two female). His 19-year-old lesbian personality, Adelena, was held responsible for committing the rapes. We will return to this issue in Chapter 18. In the meantime, reflect on whether or not DID should be allowed as an "insanity" defence in Canada.

MOOD DISORDERS

Marian Dale Scott, Passengers, c. 1940 oil on canvas, 63.6 × 38.5 cm, Art Gallery of Ontario, Toronto. Gift from the J. S. McLean Collection by Canada Packers Inc., 1990. ©2007 AGO

"What other dungeon is so dark as one's own heart! What jailer so inexorable as oneself!"
—Nathaniel Hawthorne, *The House of the Seven Gables*

"By persuading people that their thoughts and feelings originate from a biological defect, we are preventing them from finding real solutions to the complex problems of modern living."
—Joanna Moncrieff, 2007b, p. 100

"Although other approaches to depression, including lifestyle changes, psychoeducation, and structured psychotherapies, play an important role, pharmacotherapy remains a cornerstone of effective treatment for depression."
—Lakshmi Ravindran and Sidney H. Kennedy, 2007a, p. 98

"I certainly did try my very best to kill myself and from what they have told me I nearly succeeded. They gave me up for hopeless three or four times."
—A. Roy Brown, Canadian ace fighter pilot in the First World War, who downed the Red Baron and went into a severe depression, from the letter he addressed to his father, August 1, 1918

JOHN BENTLEY MAYS has suffered from chronic depression for many years and has received psychotherapy for more than 30 years. Mays had a brief period as a professor at York University in Toronto before working for many years as an art critic for *The Globe and Mail* and *National Post* newspapers. Mays described his experiences with severe depression in his book *In the Jaws of the Black Dogs: A Memoir of Depression* (Mays, 1996). The "black dog" is the well-known metaphor for depression that was used by Sir Winston Churchill in describing his years of suffering and being hounded by "the black dog of depression."

In various segments of his book, Mays provides poignant accounts of what it feels like to experience severe depression:

> I complained of a decline in vital energy; a weakened ability to enjoy the fulfilment of needs or of aesthetic desire. Even the most reasonable goals had become difficult or

impossible to set, and, when established, impossible to fulfil … I complained of sleep troubles, eating troubles. I found myself avoiding all but the most urgently necessary contact with other people. The ill feeling that, for some depressives, does not get much worse than a generalized unhappiness would in my case often degenerate into overwhelming self-loathing, climaxing in sudden, surprising relief, or thoughts of suicide. (Mays, 1996, p. 64)

Mays achieved some relief when prescribed the drug Prozac, but his severe depression returned. In the final chapter of his book, Mays concludes that "[d]epression has always been for me, and remains, a self-punishing language, a prolonged sensation of filthiness and worthlessness, of embarrassment at being alive; a sickening deadness I enviously compare to the liveliness other people seem to enjoy" (p. 216).

In this chapter we discuss the mood disorders. We begin by describing the *DSM* categories of depression, bipolar disorder, and chronic mood disorders. We then present research on biological and psychological factors relevant to these disorders and discuss their treatment. In the final section we examine suicide.

GENERAL CHARACTERISTICS OF MOOD DISORDERS

Mood disorders involve disabling disturbances in emotion, from the sadness of depression to the elation and irritability of mania. Mood disorders are often associated with other psychological problems, such as panic attacks, substance abuse, sexual dysfunction, and personality disorders. The presence of other disorders can increase severity and result in poorer prognosis (Government of Canada, 2006).

DEPRESSION: SIGNS AND SYMPTOMS

As illustrated by the case of John Bentley Mays, **depression** is an emotional state marked by great sadness and feelings of worthlessness and guilt. Additional symptoms include withdrawal from others and loss of sleep, appetite, sexual desire, and interest and pleasure in usual activities. Most of us experience occasional sadness, although perhaps not to a degree or with a frequency that warrants the diagnosis of depression.

Paying attention is exhausting for depressed people. They cannot take in what they read and what other people say to them. Conversation is also a chore; depressed individuals may speak slowly, after long pauses, using few words and a low, monotonous voice. Many prefer to sit alone and remain silent. Others are agitated and cannot sit still. They pace, wring their hands, continually sigh and moan, or complain. When depressed individuals are confronted with a problem, no ideas for its solution occur to them. Every moment has a great heaviness, and their heads fill and reverberate with self-recriminations. Depressed people may neglect personal hygiene and appearance and make numerous complaints of somatic symptoms with no apparent physical basis. Utterly dejected and completely without hope and initiative, they may be apprehensive, anxious, and despondent much of the time.

The symptoms and signs of depression vary somewhat across the lifespan (Government of Canada, 2006). Depression in children often results in somatic complaints, such as headaches or stomach aches. In older adults, depression is often characterized by distractibility and complaints of memory loss. Symptoms of depression exhibit some cross-cultural variation, probably resulting from differences in cultural standards of acceptable behaviour. For example, depression is substantially less prevalent in China than in North America, due in part to cultural mores that make it less appropriate for Chinese people to display emotional symptoms (Parker, Gladstone, & Chee, 2001). Although it is commonly believed that people from non-Western cultures emphasize somatic symptoms of depression, while people from Western cultures emphasize emotional symptoms, studies by Montreal researcher Lawrence Kirmayer suggest that people from various cultures, including Canadians, tend to emphasize somatic symptoms rather than the emotional symptoms, especially when being evaluated in a medical setting (see Kirmayer, 2001). Overall, only 15% of depressed primary care patients in Canada are what Kirmayer refers to as **psychologizers** (people who emphasize the psychological aspects of depression).

Fortunately, most depression, although recurrent, tends to dissipate with time. But an average untreated episode may stretch for months or longer. In cases where depression becomes chronic, the person does not completely "snap back" to an earlier level of functioning between bouts.

MANIA: SIGNS AND SYMPTOMS

Mania is an emotional state or mood of intense but unfounded elation accompanied by irritability, hyperactivity, talkativeness, flight of ideas, distractibility, and impractical, grandiose plans. Some people who experience episodic periods of depression may at times suddenly become manic. Although there are clinical reports of individuals who experience mania but not depression, this condition is quite rare.

The person in the throes of a manic episode, which may last from several days to several months, is readily recognized by his or her loud and incessant stream of remarks, sometimes full of puns, jokes, rhyming, and interjections about objects and happenings that have attracted the speaker's attention. This speech is difficult to interrupt and reveals the manic person's flight of ideas. Although small bits of talk are coherent, the individual shifts rapidly from topic to topic. The need for activity may cause him or her to be annoyingly sociable and intrusive, constantly and sometimes purposelessly busy, and, unfortunately, oblivious to the obvious pitfalls of his or her endeavours. Any attempt to curb this momentum can bring quick anger and even rage. Mania usually comes on suddenly over a period of a day or two. The following description of a case of mania is from our files. The irritability that is often part of this state was not evident in this person.

FORMAL DIAGNOSTIC LISTINGS OF MOOD DISORDERS

Two major mood disorders are listed in *DSM-IV-TR*: major depression, also referred to as unipolar depression, and bipolar disorder.

DIAGNOSIS OF DEPRESSION The formal *DSM-IV-TR* diagnosis of a **major depressive disorder (MDD)** requires the presence of five of the following symptoms for at least two weeks. Either depressed mood or loss of interest and pleasure must be one of the five symptoms:

- sad, depressed mood, most of the day, nearly every day
- loss of interest and pleasure in usual activities
- difficulties in sleeping (insomnia); not falling asleep initially, not returning to sleep after awakening in the middle of the night, and early morning awakenings; or, in some individuals, a desire to sleep a great deal of the time
- shift in activity level, becoming either lethargic (psychomotor retardation) or agitated
- poor appetite and weight loss, or increased appetite and weight gain
- loss of energy, great fatigue
- negative self-concept, self-reproach and self-blame, feelings of worthlessness, and guilt
- complaints or evidence of difficulty in concentrating, such as slowed thinking and indecisiveness
- recurrent thoughts of death or suicide

There is no question that these are the major symptoms of depression. What is controversial, though, is whether a person with five symptoms and a two-week duration is distinctly different from one who has only three symptoms for 10 days. In an evaluation of this issue with a sample of

---

MR. W., a 32-year-old postal worker, had been married for eight years. In retrospect, there appeared to be no warning of what was to happen. One morning, Mr. W. told his wife that he was bursting with energy and ideas, that his job as a mail carrier was unfulfilling, and that he was just wasting his talent. That night he slept little, spending most of the time at a desk, writing furiously. The next morning, he left for work at the usual time but returned home at 11:00 a.m., his car filled to overflowing with aquariums and other equipment for tropical fish. He had quit his job, then withdrawn all the money from the family's savings account and spent it on tropical fish equipment. Mr. W. reported that the previous night he had worked out a way to modify existing equipment so that fish "won't die anymore. We'll be millionaires." After unloading the paraphernalia, Mr. W. set off to canvass the neighbourhood for possible buyers, going door-to-door and talking to anyone who would listen.

The following bit of conversation from the period after Mr. W. entered treatment indicates his incorrigible optimism and provocativeness:

Therapist. Well, you seem pretty happy today.
Client. Happy! Happy! You certainly are a master of understatement, you rogue! *[Shouting, literally jumping out of his seat.]* Why I'm ecstatic. I'm leaving for the West Coast today, on my daughter's bicycle. Only 3,100 miles. That's nothing, you know. I could probably walk, but I want to get there by next week. And along the way I plan to contact a lot of people about investing in my fish equipment. I'll get to know more people that way—you know, Doc, "know" in the biblical sense *[leering at the therapist seductively.]* Oh, God, how good it feels. It's almost like a non-stop orgasm.

Canadian musician Matthew Good has been open about being diagnosed and treated for Type 2 Bipolar disorder. His album Hospital Music was inspired by his time in treament. Jason McLoughlin.

twins, the number of symptoms and the duration of depression were used to predict the likelihood of future episodes and the probability that a co-twin would also be diagnosed as depressed. Even with fewer than five symptoms and a duration of less than two weeks, co-twins were also likely to be diagnosed with depression and were likely to have recurrences (Kendler & Gardner, 1998).

Other research suggests that depression exists on a continuum of severity (Flett, Vredenburg, & Krames, 1997). The *DSM* diagnostic criteria identify people at a relatively severe end of the continuum. Whether depression is best seen as being on a continuum or as a discrete diagnostic category is far from resolved. One study with children and adolescents concluded unequivocally that depression is continuous (Hankin, Fraley, Lakey, & Waldman, 2005), while another conducted with adults found some evidence that depression reflects a taxononic, categorical structure (Solomon, Ruscio, Seeley, & Lewinsohn, 2006).

The *DSM-IV* MDD diagnostic criteria were developed on the basis of clinical experience. Zimmerman, Chelminski, McGlinchey, and Young (2006) conducted a psychometric evaluation of the symptom criteria and found that all of them were significantly associated with the diagnosis. Contrary to expectations, symptoms that are also criteria of other disorders (e.g., insomnia and fatigue) performed as well as criteria unique to depression (e.g., worthlessness and guilt). However, in analyses that controlled for symptom covariation, five symptoms (increased weight, decreased weight, psychomotor retardation, indecisiveness, and suicidal thoughts) were not independently associated with the diagnosis. These findings have implications for the possible revision of the diagnostic criteria for MDD. Indeed, as an issue for *DSM-5*, Andrews et al. (2007) noted that few psychiatry or primary care trainees can remember the nine symptoms and proposed simplifying the diagnosis by employing a restricted symptom set. They cited the research by Zimmerman and colleagues that reported almost full agreement between diagnoses based on a restricted symptom set (three or more of the five psy-

chological symptoms) versus the full definition. Andrews et al. (2007) concluded, "There may be some clinical utility in simplifying the diagnostic criteria for MDD if clinicians could remember and ask about the restricted symptom set and be less likely to fall back on inappropriate use of the depressive disorder not otherwise specified option" (p. 1784).

MDD is very prevalent. Lifetime prevalence rates ranged from 5.2% to 17.1% in three large-scale American studies (Kessler et al., 1994; Kessler et al., 2005; Weissman et al., 1996). This large discrepancy possibly reflects differences between studies in diagnostic criteria used, in the amount of training of the interviewers, and in the use of interviews for collecting symptom information. The 12-month prevalence of MDD in the National Comorbidity Survey—Replication (NCS-R) study (Kessler et al., 2005) was 6.7%. In a major cross-cultural study that used the same diagnostic criteria and structured interview in each country, including Canada (but only the city of Edmonton), one-year prevalence varied from a low of 1.5% in Taiwan to a high of 19% in Beirut, Lebanon (Weissman et al., 1996). The estimated prevalence in Edmonton was 4.6%. The reasons for these large differences are not clear. Further, in many countries, prevalence increased steadily during the latter part of the twentieth century (Cross-National Collaborative Group, 1992). In a 2008 review, Scott Patten, a pre-eminent Canadian epidemiologist, concluded that as currently defined by *DSM-IV* criteria, the lifetime prevalence of major depression exceeds 20% and may be as high as 50%. Noting the broad spectrum of severity, he concluded that, "In community populations, fulfillment of *DSM-IV* criteria for MD is probably not an effective proxy for treatment need" (Patten, 2008, p. 411). In other words, not all of these individuals necessarily require intensive treatment!

MDD is about two times more common in women than in men (e.g., Kessler et al., 2005; Offord et al., 1996), a gender difference found in numerous countries and in a majority of ethnic groups (Seedat et al., 2009). Analyses of data from Canada's 1994–96 National Population Health Survey show that the gender gap emerges at age 14 and is maintained across the lifespan (Wade, Cairney, & Pevalin, 2002). Clues to the etiology of depression may come from understanding the cause and timing of this gender difference. Focus on Discovery 8.1 explores some possible reasons for this gender difference. Current and lifetime prevalence rates are higher among younger than older persons (Government of Canada, 2006).

The World Health Organization (WHO, 2004) identified major depression as one of the leading causes of "disability-adjusted life years." It is expected to rank first in disease burden in high-income countries by the year 2030 (see Cuijpers et al., 2008). Kessler et al. (2006) assessed the effects of mood disorders on work performance. Although MDD was associated with 27.2 lost workdays per ill worker per year, bipolar disorder was associated with 65.5 lost workdays. They attributed the difference to more severe and persistent depressive episodes in workers with bipolar disorder. In Canada, work-related productivity losses as a consequence of depression were estimated to be $2.6 billion in 1998 (Stephens & Joubert, 2001).

FOCUS ON DISCOVERY 8.1
DEPRESSION IN FEMALES VS. MALES: WHY IS THERE A GENDER DIFFERENCE?

"She sat by the window, looking inward rather than looking out. Her thoughts were consumed with her sadness. She viewed her life as a broken one, and yet she could not place her finger on the exact moment it fell apart. 'How did I get to feel this way?' she repeatedly asked herself. By asking, she hoped to transcend her depressed state; through understanding, she hoped to repair it. Instead her questions led her deeper and deeper inside herself—further away from the path that would lead to her recovery."

—Reported by Treynor, Gonzalez, and Nolen-Hoeksema, 2003

Canadian singer Nelly Furtado has acknowledged dealing with depression following her rapid rise to fame. Grupo de Diarios America/Newscom.

Why does major depression generally occur about twice as often in women as in men? Nolen-Hoeksema and Girgus (1994) concluded that girls are more likely than boys to have certain risk factors for depression even before adolescence, but it is only when these risk factors interact with the challenges of adolescence that the gender differences in depression emerge.

Several explanations have been offered. The one referred to above is the notion that females are more likely than males to engage in **ruminative coping**, while males are more likely to engage in distracting activities such as watching a hockey game (Nolen-Hoeksema, Larson, & Grayson, 1999). Ruminators focus their attention on their depressive symptoms (e.g., saying things to themselves such as "Why do I feel this way?"). An 18-month longitudinal study confirmed that the ruminative-coping style predicts the onset of depression episodes and is associated with more severe depressive symptoms (Just & Alloy, 1997). Subsequently, Treynor et al. (2003) refined this theory by differentiating between a more adaptive form of reflective pondering versus a maladaptive rumination component referred to as **brooding** (or moody pondering). They concluded that the relationship between gender and depression could be due to the brooding component (e.g., "What am I doing to deserve this?"). Gender differences in rumination emerge in adolescence (Jose & Brown, 2008). In fact, brooding may be a non-specific vulnerability for different forms of emotional distress, including anxiety, worry, anger, and dysphoria (Blankstein & Hillis Lumley, 2008). Also, an interpersonal form of rumination called co-rumination, in which friends, typically female friends, discuss and brood over each other's problems as part of their friendship, has been linked with depression in adolescent girls but, on a positive note, it also fosters stronger friendships (Starr & Davila, 2009).

Feminist scholar Dana Jack (1999) suggested that females are more likely than males to engage in *silencing the self*—a passive style of keeping upsets and concerns to oneself in order to maintain important relationships (akin to "suffering in silence"). A definitive longitudinal test of the hypothesis remains to be conducted. Another explanation is *objectification theory* (McKinley & Hyde, 1996), based on the premise that the tendency to be viewed as an object, scrutinized and appraised by others, including appraisals of physical appearance, has a greater negative influence on the self-esteem of girls than boys. Indeed, adolescent girls, relative to boys, have higher reported levels of objectification, shame, and depression (Grabe, Hyde, & Lindberg, 2007).

Differences in types, levels, and the impact of stressors may also play a role. Thus, girls may face attitudes that devalue accomplishments and abilities in relation to boys, or face restrictions on roles and activities deemed inappropriate for their gender (Nolen-Hoeksema et al., 1999). Janet Stoppard from the University of New Brunswick (2000) argues that depression must be interpreted within the broad socio-cultural context and the societal conditions that influence the everyday lives of women, including stressors more germane to women and feelings of disempowerment. A Toronto study found that 52% of women receiving inpatient treatment for depression had been sexually victimized in childhood and adulthood (Sahay, Piran, & Maddocks, 2000). Greater levels of sexual violation were associated with lower levels of self-esteem and an external locus of control (powerlessness).

Are females more likely than males to be targets of abuse? Can this help explain the gender difference? Valerie Whiffen and Sharon Clark (1997) from the University of Ottawa compared levels of depression and victimization histories in men and women seeking psychotherapy. Women had higher levels of depression and were more likely to have a history of child sexual abuse (CSA) and report higher levels of victimization as adults. A recent study (Raes & Hermans, 2008) reported that the brooding component of rumination mediates the relation between childhood emotional abuse and depressive symptoms. It's also possible that girls and women are more likely than boys and men to take a more active role in generating stress for themselves (Hammen, 1991).

Finally, what about the possible role of biological differences between women and men? Evidence in support of the theory that women's vulnerability to depression is related to their hormones, specifically estrogen and progesterone, is mixed (Nolen-Hoeksema, 2002). Nonetheless, it is probable that gender differences in depression are due to multiple, interacting factors and can best be understood from a complex biopsychosocial perspective.

However, the actual cost due to treatment, premature death, and lost productivity exceeds $14 billion annually (Auditor General of Canada, 2001). Even mild (subthreshold) forms of depression and mania are distressing; can be damaging to psychosocial functioning and quality of life; and are associated with increased risk of suicidality, poor job productivity, and increased health care utilization (see Maser et al., 2009). Blanco et al. (2008) reported that more than 60% of college students in the United States aged 19 to 25 years with a diagnosable mood disorder (12-month prevalence) did not seek treatment in the year prior to the survey. Another screening study (Garlow et al., 2008) reported that over 80% of college students with moderately severe to severe depression and/or current suicidal ideation were not receiving any mental health treatment at the time of assessment. These findings indicate substantial unmet need.

About 80% of those with depression experience another episode, and the average number of episodes, which typically last for three to five months, is about four (Judd, 1997). In many cases, depression becomes a chronic disorder that lasts more than two years. Even among those who improve sufficiently to be no longer diagnosable, subclinical depression can remain for years (Judd et al., 1998). In a two-year prospective naturalistic study, Grilo et al. (2005) found that participants with MDD who had certain coexisting personality disorders (schizotypal, borderline, or avoidant) had a significantly longer time to remission of symptoms than did MDD participants without any personality disorder. First episodes typically have a stronger link with major life events stress than do subsequent bouts of depression (see Monroe & Harkness, 2006). This has been explained by the **kindling hypothesis**—the notion that once a depression has already been experienced, it takes relatively less stress to induce a recurrence. What is not clear is whether the apparent reduced role of life events stress in subsequent depressions is because depression has become autonomous and no longer requires stress (the autonomy hypothesis) or whether the person has become sensitized to stress (the sensitivity hypothesis) and even small amounts of stress are sufficient to induce depression (Monroe & Harkness, 2006).

DIAGNOSIS OF BIPOLAR DISORDER *DSM-IV-TR* defines **bipolar I disorder** as involving episodes of mania or mixed episodes that include symptoms of both mania and depression. Most people with bipolar I disorder also experience episodes of depression. A formal diagnosis of a manic episode requires the presence of elevated or irritable mood plus three additional symptoms (four if the mood is irritable). Some clinicians do not regard euphoria as a core symptom and report that irritable mood and even depressive features are more common (Goodwin & Jamison, 1990). The symptoms must be sufficiently severe to impair social and occupational functioning:

- increase in activity level at work, socially, or sexually
- unusual talkativeness; rapid speech
- flight of ideas or subjective impression that thoughts are racing
- less than the usual amount of sleep needed
- inflated self-esteem; belief that one has special talents, powers, and abilities
- distractibility; attention easily diverted
- excessive involvement in pleasurable activities that are likely to have undesirable consequences, such as reckless spending

Bipolar disorder occurs less often than MDD, with a lifetime prevalence rate for both bipolar I and II of about 4.4% of the population in the NCS-R (Kessler et al., 2005). The average age of onset is in the 20s, and it occurs equally often in men and women. Among women, episodes of depression are more common and episodes of mania less common than among men (Leibenluft, 1996). More than 50% of bipolar disorder cases experience a recurrence within 12 months (Yatham et al., 2009). The severity of the disorder is indicated by the fact that at 12 months after release from hospital, 76% of clients are rated as impaired and 52% are sufficiently symptomatic that the original diagnosis is still applicable (Keck et al., 1998). Violent behav-

Self-portrait by Paul Gauguin. He is but one of the many artists and writers who apparently suffered from a mood disorder. Self Portrait in Caricature by Paul Gauguin/National Gallery of Art. Washington DC/SUPERSTOCK.

iours (e.g., child or spousal abuse) can occur during severe manic episodes (Government of Canada, 2006). People with bipolar disorder often lose insight into their condition and this can result in treatment resistance, financial and legal difficulties, substance abuse, and marital and occupational failure (Government of Canada, 2006). Anxiety comorbidy is prevalent among bipolar individuals and has a great impact on quality of life (Kauer-Sant'Anna et al., 2007). Comorbidity with personality disorders also predicts a poor outcome (Bieling, Green, & Macqueen, 2007).

Recent findings related to the epidemiology of mood disorders in Canada are summarized in Canadian Perspectives 8.1.

CANADIAN PERSPECTIVES 8.1
THE EPIDEMIOLOGY OF MOOD DISORDERS IN CANADA: MAJOR DEPRESSION AND BIPOLAR DISORDER

The Canadian Community Health Survey: Mental Health and Well-Being (CCHS, Cycle 1.2) provides, for the first time, national data on the extent of MDD and bipolar disorder in Canada. Preliminary results were first reported by Statistics Canada (2003) and summarized in the 2006 Government of Canada report. A series of published journal articles provides in-depth analyses and additional findings. Further information comes from a subsample of working people from among those who responded to the CCHS, Cycle 1.1. Selected important findings include the following:

• Lifetime prevalence of MDD was 12.2%, one-year prevalence was 4.8%, and past month episode was 1.8%.
• Lifetime prevalence of a manic episode was 2.4%, and one-year prevalence was 1%, and was similar for both women and men.
• The proportion of the population who met the criteria for one-year prevalence of MDD, by age and sex, is summarized in Figure 8.1; one-year prevalence was highest in the 15–24 years age range for both women and men (10.2%).
• In all age groups, more women than men met criteria for MDD.

• MDD prevalence almost doubles at a turning point between late adolescence and adulthood.
• About 90% of people who met the one-year criteria for either MDD or bipolar disorder reported that the condition interfered with their lives.
• Almost 40% of youth (aged 15 to 24) with a depressive disorder also presented with an anxiety disorder.
• Depression and mania tend to be more prevalent in the western provinces.
• The lifetime prevalence of MDD with chronic symptoms was 2.7%, associated with more frequent comorbidity, greater disability, a higher likelihood of suicide ideation and attempts, and increased health service use.

These studies provide information about important risk factors associated with mood disorders:

• The one-year prevalences of MDD in people with a substance use disorder were 6.9% for harmful alcohol use, 8.8% for alcohol dependence, and 16.1% for drug dependence.
• MDD and substance dependence independently predicted higher prevalence of suicidal thoughts.

FIGURE 8.1 Proportion of population who met the criteria for depression during previous 12 months, by age and sex, Canada, 2002
Source: Statistics Canada, Canadian Community Health Survey, 2002, Mental Health and Well-being Cycle 1.2

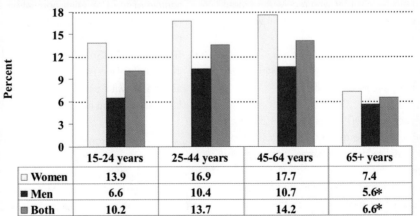

	15-24 years	25-44 years	45-64 years	65+ years
□ Women	13.9	16.9	17.7	7.4
■ Men	6.6	10.4	10.7	5.6*
■ Both	10.2	13.7	14.2	6.6*

*Small sample size. Interpret with caution.

- The presence of a comorbid chronic medical disorder in people with at least one manic episode was associated with employment dysfunction, receiving social assistance or welfare, and the need for assistance with daily living.
- In young people (aged 15 to 24), not being in school strongly increased the likelihood of depressive disorders.
- In young people (aged 15 to 24), extreme stress strongly increased the likelihood of depressive (and anxiety) disorders.
- The one-year prevalence of MDD is very high among smokers who are young, trying to quit, and have high nicotine dependence levels.

These studies also provide insight into help-seeking and treatment factors:

- An estimated 63.9% of people with MDD and 59.0% of those with manic episodes reported using some type of help in the previous year; about half used conventional mental health services.
- People with mood disorders with comorbid anxiety disorders, long-term medical conditions, suicide attempts, and severe role interference were more likely to have used conventional services.
- Among people with a past-year major depressive episode, the frequency of antidepressant use was 40.4%.
- About 21% of people with mood disorders use natural health products (e.g., herbs) for emotional and substance use problems.
- Among people with bipolar disorder, the presence of a comorbid chronic medical disorder was associated with higher consultation rates, greater medication use, and increased likelihood of hospitalization.
- Among people with bipolar disorder, male gender, lower education level, and immigrant status were negatively correlated with use of treatment services.
- Many people with bipolar disorder never receive any mental health treatment.
- Among people with bipolar disorder who receive treatment, use of pharmacotherapy is typically not consistent with recommended guidelines.

Analyses of the CCHS 1.1 provide additional information about the links among depression, pain, and work stress:

- The current prevalence of MDD increased to 12% (from 7.6%) in people who also reported chronic pain (fibromyalgia, arthritis/rheumatism, back problems, and migraine headaches).
- Both depression and comorbid chronic pain and depression were twice as prevalent in women as in men.
- Chronic pain and overall work stress were the strongest predictors of depression.

Analyses of the CCHS 1.1 also provide information about the unmet need for the treatment of depression in Atlantic Canada:

- People at increased risk for MDD in the previous year included being female; widowed, separated, or divorced; having low income; and having two or more comorbid medical conditions.
- Only 40% of those with depression consulted with a GP or mental health specialist about their condition.
- Fewer than 25% of those with probable depression reported receiving levels of care that were consistent with practice guidelines.
- Vulnerable groups (elderly, uneducated, residents of rural areas) were less likely to receive treatment in primary or specialty care.

The findings have important implications, some of which are the following:

- There is a need for national initiatives that target mood disorders in Canada.
- There is a need to target interventions to populations that are at risk by raising awareness among both the public and mental health professionals.
- There is a need to focus more on evidence-based treatments.
- The findings are important in the planning of health services and research prioritizing.
- People with mood disorders are at risk for many medical disorders that are frequently undiagnosed and untreated.
- More research needs to be done on the epidemiology and risk factors among different vulnerable groups.
- The impact of work stress should be considered in the management of MDD.

Thinking Critically

1. The CCHS 1.2 is the first survey in which a full, structured psychiatric interview was administered to a large, representative sample of the Canadian population aged 15 years and over. However, it has the limitation of being a cross-sectional design. How would you address this limitation in a new study?
2. Since the CCHS 1.2 did not target youth alone, it did not incorporate various risk factors that could be more strongly associated with psychological problems in youth. What new factors would you include in your study?

Sources: Beck et al. (2005); Currie et al. (2005); Enns & Cox (2005a); Gilmour & Patten (2006); Government of Canada (2006); Khaled, Bulloch, Exner, & Patten (2009); Nguyen, Fournier, Bergeron, Roberge, & Barrette (2005); McIntyre et al. (2006); Molgat & Patten, (2005); Munce et al. (2006); Patten et al. (2006); Satyanarayana, Enns, Cox, & Sareen (2009); Starkes, Poulin, & Kisley (2005); Statistics Canada (2003); Thompson (2005); Wang et al. (2005).

HETEROGENEITY WITHIN THE CATEGORIES

A problem in the classification of mood disorders is their great heterogeneity; i.e., people with the same diagnosis can vary greatly from one another. Some bipolar people, for example, experience the full range of symptoms of both mania and depression almost every day, termed a *mixed episode*. Others have symptoms of only mania or only depression during a clinical episode. **Bipolar II disorder** individuals have episodes of major depression accompanied by **hypomania** (*hypo* comes from the Greek for "under"), a change in behaviour and mood that is less extreme than full-blown mania.

Some depressed people may be diagnosed as having psychotic features if they are subject to delusions and hallucinations. The presence of delusions appears to be a useful distinction among people with unipolar depression (Johnson, Horvath, & Weissman, 1991); depressed people with delusions do not generally respond well to the usual drug therapies for depression, but they do respond favourably to these drugs when they are combined with the drugs commonly used to treat other psychotic disorders, such as schizophrenia. Furthermore, depression with psychotic features is more severe than depression without delusions and involves more social impairment and less time between episodes (Coryell et al., 1996).

According to *DSM-IV-TR*, some people with depression may have melancholic features. The term *melancholic* refers to a specific pattern of depressive symptoms. People with melancholic features find no pleasure in any activity (anhedonia) and are unable to feel better even temporarily when something good happens. Their depressed mood is worse in the morning. They awaken about two hours too early, lose appetite and weight, and are either lethargic or extremely agitated. Studies of the validity of the distinction between depressions with or without melancholic features have yielded mixed results. However, one study found that people with melancholic features had more comorbidity (e.g., with anxiety disorders), more frequent episodes, and more impairment, suggesting it may be a more severe type of depression (Kendler, 1997). Both manic and depressive episodes may be characterized as having catatonic features, such as motor immobility or excessive, purposeless activity. Both manic and depressive episodes may also occur within four weeks of childbirth; in this case, they are noted to have a postpartum onset. Postpartum, perinatal, and prenatal depression research in Canada is summarized in Canadian Perspectives 8.2.

Finally, *DSM-IV-TR* states that both bipolar and unipolar disorders can be subdiagnosed as seasonal if there is a regular relationship between an episode and a particular time of the year. Most research has focused on depression in the winter (i.e., winter depression or seasonal affective disorder), and the most prevalent explanation is that it is linked to a decrease in the number of daylight hours. **Seasonal affective disorder (SAD)** was first described by Rosenthal et al.

Seasonal depression is one of the subtypes of MDD. This woman is demonstrating light therapy, an effective treatment for people whose seasonal depression occurs during the winter. Griffin/The Image Works.

(1984), who noted that some people's symptoms varied in response to changes in climate and latitude in a manner that suggested that reduced exposure to sunlight was causing their depressions. Most of these individuals had been diagnosed with bipolar depression.

In Canada, a study of community members found that the seasonal subtype of major depression was detected in 11% of the people diagnosed with depression (Levitt, Boyle, Joffe, & Baumal, 2000). The prevalence of SAD was 2.9%. A study of an Inuit community in the Canadian Arctic (Haggarty et al., 2002) found that 18% of the population had either SAD or subsyndromal SAD (i.e., milder SAD that does not quite meet *DSM* criteria). The authors noted that this is the highest rate of SAD found thus far in research involving *DSM*-based assessments. Icelanders go without light for many months in the winter, yet as a group, they have surprisingly low levels of SAD. A study of Icelanders who emigrated to the Interlake District in Manitoba found a prevalence rate of only 1.2% (Magnusson & Axelsson, 1993). The authors speculated that Icelanders might have lower rates because they have adapted genetically to reduced sunlight exposure and are somehow protected from experiencing SAD. Reduced light does cause decreases in the activity of serotonin neurons of the hypothalamus, and these neurons regulate some behaviours, such as sleep, that are part of the syndrome of SAD (Schwartz et al., 1997). Rosenthal (2009) argued that SAD deserves to be a category of its own in *DSM-5*.

CHRONIC MOOD DISORDERS

DSM-IV-TR lists two long-lasting, or chronic, disorders in which mood disturbances are predominant. Although the symptoms of these disorders must have been evident for at least two years, they are not severe enough to warrant a diagnosis of a major depressive or manic episode.

CANADIAN PERSPECTIVES 8.2
POSTPARTUM, PERINATAL, AND PRENATAL DEPRESSION IN CANADIAN WOMEN

"The notion that pregnancy is a time of uninterrupted joy, happiness, and contentment has been challenged by evidence-based research showing that, to the contrary, many women are distressed by depressive disorders in pregnancy."
—Shaila Misri, University of British Columbia, on the burden of perinatal depression, 2007, p. 477

Many people find it difficult to understand the phenomenon of **postpartum depression (PD)**. New mothers often complain of temporary "baby blues," but how is it possible that some mothers experience profound depression even though they may be delighted by their new arrival? Even more difficult to understand are extreme cases such as that of Suzanne Killinger-Johnson, a physician and psychotherapist who apparently suffered from PD. In 2000, she took her own life and that of her infant son at a Toronto subway station.

Canadian researchers have attempted to uncover the nature of PD. Researchers at the University of Western Ontario (Gotlib, Whiffen, Mount, Milne, & Cordy, 1989) assessed women during their pregnancies and after having given birth and found that 10% of the women were depressed during pregnancy (perinatal depression), and 6.8% had PD. Of those who had PD, half had been depressed during the pregnancy and the PD was a continuation, while the other half experienced depression only after giving birth. Onset was predicted by levels of depression in the pregnancy period as well as by a reported lack of warmth and care from one's own parents while growing up (Gotlib, Whiffen, Wallace, & Mount, 1991).

A Quebec study that evaluated pregnant women during the second trimester of pregnancy and six months postpartum (Bernazzani, Saucier, David, & Borgeat, 1997) found that PD was predicted by depression during pregnancy, negative life events, and lower socio-economic status. Seguin, Potvin, St.-Denis, and Loiselle (1999) reported that chronic postnatal stressors and low perceived social support were associated with PD. Newcomer mothers relative to Canadian-born mothers have an increased risk for PD and report receiving less prenatal care and social support (Stewart et al., 2008). Self-critical perfectionism is also strongly related to PD (Vliegen, Luyten, Meurs, & Cluckers, 2006). However, a British Columbia study found that telephone-based peer support decreased levels of PD (Dennis, 2003).

Given the link between stressors and PD, how a woman copes with motherhood is important. An emotion-oriented coping style is linked with PD (Da Costa et al., 2000). Pregnant mothers in Quebec with high levels of stress during the 1998 ice storm delivered children with lower cognitive ability when assessed at the age of two (LaPlante et al., in press). Higher prenatal stress in the mother-to-be predicted poorer cognitive ability in the "ice storm" babies—children exposed to high stress, relative to those with low stress, had IQs that were 20 points lower on average. Higher stress also predicted more behavioural problems and anxiety in children at four years of age. Further, the children of mothers with high stress had abnormalities in their fingerprint

A public awareness campaign launched in Ontario in 2007 is aimed at bringing postpartum mood disorders out into the open and encouraging new mothers to seek help. Used with permission by the Best Start Resource Centre.

profiles, suggesting that stress affected prenatal development during the crucial 14-to-22-week segment of gestation. A recent European longitudinal study (Halligan, Murray, Martins, & Cooper, 2007) found that maternal PD was associated with higher rates of mood disorders in adolescent offspring but only if there had also been later episodes of maternal depression.

What about fathers? Montreal researchers Zelkowitz and Milet (1997) compared the characteristics of fathers who have a spouse with PD with the characteristics of those without a depressed spouse. Fathers married to women with PD reported greater levels of dissatisfaction with marital and family changes and greater stress. Follow-up research indicated that psychiatric disturbance is just as persistent over time for mothers and fathers, with approximately three fifths of mothers and fathers having a disorder at six months postpartum (Zelkowitz & Milet, 2001). However, a large-scale study in Denmark (Munk-Olsen, Laursen, Pedersen, Mors, & Mortensen, 2006) determined that although the risk of postpartum mental disorders is increased for months after childbirth in first-time mothers, among fathers there was no excess of severe mental disorders that required hospital admission or outpatient contacts. Nonetheless, the findings underscore the need to adopt a family focus that includes fathers when seeking to help sufferers of PD.

Finally, we need to recognize that maternal prenatal depression affects the fetus and the newborn (Field, Diego, & Hernandez-Reif, 2006), including elevated fetal activity, delayed prenatal growth, prematurity, and low birth weight. Newborns of depressed mothers show a biochemical/physiological profile similar to their mothers' prenatal profile (e.g., elevated cortisol, lower levels of dopamine and serotonin). Elevated prenatal maternal cortisol is the strongest predictor of neonatal complications. Such perinatal circumstances (e.g., low birth weight) can be associated with higher risk of depression and suicide in young adults (e.g., Riordan, Selvara, Stark, & Gilbert, 2006). Further, Field et al. (2006) noted similarity between the prenatal depressive symptoms of mothers and fathers, highlighting the importance of depression screening in fathers-to-be, as well as mothers-to-be, during pregnancy.

Thinking Critically

1. Is it possible to develop prevention programs in connection with prenatal classes that decrease the probability of the development of PD in mothers? What strategies would you use? Despite the best possible efforts, some women will still develop depression. Design an intervention to minimize the severity and impact of these depressions. Were fathers included?

2. Prenatal and perinatal depression are relatively common. While discontinuing antidepressants may cause relapse in about 75% of women during pregnancy, continued use poses possible risks to the developing fetus (Misri, 2007; Wisner et al., 2009). Given unease about the safety of antidepressant use, can you think of alternative treatment modalities for this population?

In **cyclothymic disorder**, the person has frequent periods of depressed mood and hypomania, which may be mixed with, may alternate with, or may be separated by periods of normal mood lasting as long as two months. People with cyclothymic disorder have paired sets of symptoms in their periods of depression and hypomania. During depression, they feel inadequate; during hypomania, their self-esteem is inflated. They withdraw from people, then seek them out in an uninhibited fashion. They sleep too much and then too little. Depressed cyclothymics have trouble concentrating, and their verbal productivity decreases; during hypomania, their thinking becomes sharp and creative and their productivity increases. Kessler et al. (2005) reported a lifetime prevalence for cyclothymia of 2.5%. People with cyclothymia may also experience full-blown episodes of mania and depression.

Mood disorders are common among artists and writers. Van Gogh, Tchaikovsky (shown here), and Whitman were all affected. Archive/Photo Researchers, Inc.

The person with **dysthymic disorder** is chronically depressed—more than half the time for at least two years—according to the *DSM-IV-TR*. Besides feeling blue and losing pleasure in usual activities and pastimes, the person experiences several other signs of depression, such as insomnia or sleeping too much; feelings of inadequacy, ineffectiveness, and lack of energy; pessimism; an inability to concentrate and to think clearly; and a desire to avoid the company of others. Women are two to three times more likely than men to be diagnosed with dysthymia and the chronicity of dysthymia can cause severe impairment (Government of Canada, 2006). Kessler et al. (2005) reported a lifetime prevalence for dysthymia of 2.5%. Although not currently officially recognized in the *DSM*, many people with dysthymia have episodes of major depression, as well—a condition known as **double depression** (Boland & Keller, 2002).

Will controversies over the diagnosis of mood disorders lead to major changes in *DSM-5*? In February 2010, the *DSM-5* Mood Disorders work group announced proposed changes to the mood disorders categories and criteria. Only two disorders were recommended to have no changes in diagnostic criteria from *DSM-IV* (cyclothymic disorder and mood disorder not otherwise specified) and one disorder was proposed for possible removal from *DSM-5* (bipolar I disorder—most recent episode mixed). There were numerous proposed criteria changes to the four mood episodes in *DSM-IV* and the remaining depressive and bipolar disorders (11 disorders), and the work group provided where possible an evidence-based rationale for the specific changes. For example, for the "postpartum onset specifer" in major depressive disorder, single episode, it was proposed that the window should be extended because research has shown that the period of elevated risk following delivery extends to six months (see Forty et al., 2006). As another example, the group provided extensive empirical evidence (e.g., McCullough et al., 2008) to support a proposal that the category of major depression with a chronic specifier be combined with dysthymic disorder under the term "chronic depressive disorder." It was noted that revisions would be probable pending further input and field trial analyses.

Consistent with the proposal to add "dimensional assessments" to diagnostic evaluations, the work group proposed that clinician severity dimensions of factors that determine treatment outcome (not included in the criteria for the category) be included with each categorical mood diagnosis. Thus, the work group proposed or was considering (1) an anxiety dimension across all mood disorder categories, (2) a suicide assessment dimension, and (3) a substance abuse severity dimension.

The work group proposed one new mood disorder not currently listed in *DSM-IV*. "Mixed anxiety depression" is in an appendix of *DSM-IV* and is in the ICD-10. The work group proposed that it be formally included in *DSM-5* and introduced specific criteria. The proposal ensures that symptoms of both disorders are present and distressing. To receive the diagnosis, it was proposed that the client have three or four symptoms of major depression accompanied by two or more symptoms of anxious distress (e.g., irrational worry, motor tension) that have lasted at least two weeks. According to the work group, the validity of the concept is based on shared genetic risk factors for depression and anxiety, the high comorbidity between MDD and GAD, and a shared temperamental factor, negative affect (see www.dsm5.org).

The mood disorders work group formed an expert sub-work group on "premenstrual dysphoric disorder" (PMDD), a controversial disorder listed in an appendix in *DSM-IV*, to examine data concerning the possibility that PMDD might classify as a separate and distinct disorder from mood disorders or a specifier for mood disorders. Previously written about a good deal in the press and assailed by feminists and sexists alike, this proposed disorder occurs a week or so before menstruation and is marked by depression, anxiety, anger, mood swings, and decreased interest in activities usually engaged in with pleasure, and the symptoms are severe enough to interfere with social or occupational functioning (see Pearlstein & Steiner, 2008). Feminists may be pleased or displeased with this possible new category. On the plus side, inclusion might alert people to the hormonal bases of monthly mood changes linked to the menstrual cycle and thereby foster more tolerance and less blame. On the minus side, listing such mood changes in a manual of mental disorders could convey the message that women who experience these psychological changes are mentally disordered.

Repeated self-injury co-occurs with a variety of diagnoses, including eating disorders (see Focus on Discovery 10.1). However, it was proposed by both the Mood Disorders and Childhood work groups that "non-suicidal self injury" be included as a mood disorder. In this disorder, the individual engages in intentional self-inflicted damage to the surface of the body by, for example, cutting, burning, or hitting with the expectation that it will lead to only minor physical harm. The intentional injury is typically associated with negative feelings or thoughts (e.g., depression, tension, self-criticism), preoccupation with the intended behaviour, frequent urges to engage in self-injury, or the activity is engaged in with a purpose

(e.g., relief from a negative feeling/cognitive state) (see www.dsm5.org). Another joint proposal, "temper dysregulation disorder with dysphoria" is discussed in Chapter 15.

PSYCHOLOGICAL THEORIES OF MOOD DISORDERS

Depression has been studied from several perspectives. Here, we discuss psychoanalytic views, which emphasize the unconscious conflicts associated with grief and loss; cognitive theories, which focus on the depressed person's self-defeating thought processes; and interpersonal factors, which emphasize how depressed people interact with others. These theories, for the most part, describe different diatheses in a general diathesis-stress theory that requires stressful life events in order to trigger bouts of depression (Kendler, Karkowski, & Prescott, 1999). The theories we discuss address the question: What are the psychological characteristics of people who respond to stress with a mood disorder episode?

PSYCHOANALYTIC THEORY OF DEPRESSION

In his celebrated paper "Mourning and Melancholia," Freud (1917/1950) theorized that the potential for depression is created early in childhood. During the oral period, a child's needs may be insufficiently or oversufficiently gratified, causing the person to become fixated in this stage and dependent on the instinctual gratifications particular to it. With this arrest in psychosexual maturation, the person may develop a tendency to be excessively dependent on other people for the maintenance of self-esteem.

From this happenstance of childhood, how can the adult come to suffer from depression? The complex reasoning is based on an analysis of bereavement. Freud hypothesized that after the loss of a loved one, whether by death or, most commonly for a child, through separation or withdrawal of affection, the mourner first introjects, or incorporates, the lost person; he or she identifies with the lost one, perhaps in a fruitless attempt to undo the loss. Because, Freud asserted, we unconsciously harbour negative feelings toward those we love, the mourner then becomes the object of his or her own hate and anger (anger turned inward). In addition, the mourner resents being deserted and feels guilt for real or imagined sins against the lost person.

The period of introjection is followed by a period of mourning work, when the mourner recalls memories of the lost one and thereby separates himself or herself from the person who has died or disappointed him or her and loosens the bonds imposed by introjection. But the mourning work can go astray and develop into an ongoing process of self-abuse, self-blame, and depression in overly dependent individuals. These individuals do not loosen their emotional bonds with the lost person; rather, they continue to castigate themselves for the faults and shortcomings perceived in the loved one who has been introjected. The mourner's anger toward the lost one continues to be directed inward.

Some research has been generated by psychoanalytic points of view, but it has been limited and does not give strong support to the theory. However, some depressed people are high in dependency and prone to depression following a rejection (see Canadian Perspectives 8.3).

COGNITIVE THEORIES OF DEPRESSION

Earlier discussions of the role of cognition in anxiety (Chapter 6) and of Ellis's concept of irrational beliefs (Chapter 2 and elsewhere) indicate that cognitive processes play a decisive role in emotional behaviour. In some theories of depression, thoughts and beliefs are regarded as major factors in causing or influencing the emotional state. We now discuss two cognitive theories of depression in some detail: Beck's schema theory and the helplessness/hopelessness theory.

BECK'S THEORY OF DEPRESSION Aaron Beck (1967; 1987; 2008) is responsible for the most important contemporary theory that regards thought processes as causative factors in depression. His central thesis is that depressed individuals feel as they do because their thinking is biased toward negative interpretations. Figure 8.2 illustrates the interactions among the three levels of cognitive activity that Beck believes underlie depression. According to Beck, in childhood and adolescence, depressed individuals acquired a negative schema—a tendency to see the world negatively—through loss of a parent, an unrelenting succession of tragedies, the social rejection of peers, the criticisms of teachers, or the depressive attitude of a parent. All of us have schemata of many kinds; by these perceptual sets, we order our lives. The negative schemata acquired by depressed persons are activated whenever they encounter new situations that resemble in some way, perhaps only remotely, the conditions in which the schemata were learned. Moreover, the negative schemata fuel and are fuelled by certain cognitive biases that lead these people to misperceive reality. Thus, an ineptness schema can make depressed individuals expect to fail most of the time, a self-blame schema burdens them with responsibility for all misfortunes, and a negative self-evaluation schema constantly reminds them of their worthlessness.

Negative schemata, together with cognitive biases or distortions, maintain what Beck called the **negative triad**: negative views of the self, the world, and the future. The world part of Beck's depressive triad refers to the person's judgement that he or she cannot cope with the demands of the environment. Rather than having to do with a concern for global events that do not implicate the self directly (e.g., "The world has been going south since the terrorist attacks of 9/11"), it is highly personal ("I cannot possibly cope with all these demands and responsibilities"). In Beck's (2008) words, "When the schemas are activated by an event or series of events, they skew the information processing system, which then directs attentional resources to negative stimuli and translates a specific experience into a distorted negative interpretation"

FIGURE 8.2 The interrelationships among different kinds of cognitions in Beck's theory

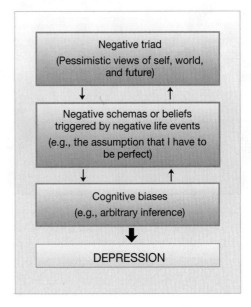

(p. 970). These negatively biased cognitive schemas (cognitive vulnerability) function as efficient but maladaptive "automatic" information processors.

The following list describes some of the principal cognitive biases of depressed individuals, according to Beck:

- Arbitrary inference—a conclusion drawn in the absence of sufficient evidence or of any evidence at all. For example, a man concludes that he is worthless because it is raining the day he is hosting an outdoor party.
- Selective abstraction—a conclusion drawn on the basis of only one of many elements in a situation. A worker feels worthless when a product fails to function, even though she is only one of many people who contributed to its production.
- Overgeneralization—an overall sweeping conclusion drawn on the basis of a single, perhaps trivial, event. A student regards her poor performance in a single class on one particular day as final proof of her worthlessness and stupidity.
- Magnification and minimization—exaggerations in evaluating performance. A man, believing that he has completely ruined his car (magnification) when he notices a slight scratch on the rear fender, regards himself as good for nothing; a woman believes herself worthless (minimization) in spite of a succession of praiseworthy achievements.

In Beck's theory, our emotional reactions are a function of how we construe our world. The interpretations of depressed individuals do not mesh well with the way most people view the world, and they become victims of their own illogical self-judgements.

Being rejected by peers may lead to the development of the negative schema that Beck's theory suggests plays a key role in depression. Digital Vision.

A review by Rector, Segal, and Gemar (1998) noted that much of the depression research conducted in Canada has tested predictions involving Beck's schema notion. The research investigations conducted can be differentiated in terms of whether they have focused on cognitive products (i.e., the stimuli that are recalled), cognitive processes or operations involving the deployment of attention, or cognitive structures in terms of the organization of cognitive schemas. The emphasis has shifted away from initial research on cognitive products and toward cognitive processes and organization.

Initial Canadian research was dominated by investigations conducted by Nicholas Kuiper and his associates at the University of Western Ontario (e.g., MacDonald & Kuiper, 1984). They used a self-referent encoding task that involved presenting participants with positive and negative word adjectives (e.g., "smart," "stupid") and asking them to indicate whether the adjectives applied to them by stating "yes" or "no." Two key findings emerged from this research. First, depressed individuals, relative to non-depressed individuals, endorse more negative words and fewer positive words as self-descriptive. Second, they exhibit a cognitive bias: they have greater recall of adjectives with depressive content, especially if the adjectives were rated as self-descriptive. Overall, this research tests the notion that the presence or absence of depression reflects differences in the cognitive availability of negative vs. positive thoughts about the self. A recent British study (Dunn et al., 2009) demonstrated that the reduced positive self-judgement bias found in depressed people relates to depression-specific anhedonic (loss of pleasure) symptoms.

The next wave of research tested the possibility that the main differences of importance involved *cognitive accessibility* rather than cognitive availability per se. In other words, depressed and non-depressed people do not differ in whether their schemas involve positive or negative content; rather, they differ in cognitive processing. Depressed people pay greater attention to negative stimuli and can more readily access negative than positive information.

Differences in cognitive processing are assessed via the **Stroop task**. Participants are provided with a series of words in different colours and are asked to identify the colour of each word and ignore the actual word itself (i.e., if the word "sad" is presented in red ink, the correct answer is red). The Stroop task assesses the latency or length of time it takes to respond. Gotlib and McCann (1984) examined response patterns when students were asked to colour-name words that varied in their content: neutral, depression-oriented (e.g., "bleak"), or manic-oriented (i.e., "overly euphoric"). Non-depressed students did not differ in their response latencies across the word types, but depressed students took longer to colour-name the depression-oriented words, suggesting that these themes were more cognitively accessible for them. In subsequent research, Marlene Moretti at Simon Fraser University and her associates (Moretti et al., 1996) found that depressed individuals have reduced accessibility to positive information that is specific to themselves, not to other people.

Investigations by Scott McCabe from the University of Waterloo and his associates focused on differences in attentional processes. This experimental research has used a deployment-of-attention task to show that dysphoric and clinically depressed individuals do not seem to selectively attend to negative or positive material but that non-depressed individuals have a protective bias that involves diverting their attention away from negative stimuli and focusing instead on positive stimuli (e.g., McCabe & Tonan, 2000). In related research, people who had a history of depression but were in a neutral mood tended to divert their attention when presented with negative stimuli, once again suggesting the presence of a protective bias (McCabe, Gotlib, & Martin, 2000). However, people with a history of depression induced into a negative mood state were less able to keep themselves from noticing and paying attention to negative stimuli.

A study conducted by Dozois and Dobson (2001) is remarkable because it used multiple tasks to determine whether people with and without clinical depression differed, not only in cognitive accessibility, but also in cognitive organization. Participants completed a variety of cognitive tasks, including the self-referent encoding task, the modified Stroop task, and two tasks designed to assess cognitive structure. Four groups of participants took part: depressed, depressed and anxious, never-depressed and anxious, and non-psychiatric controls. People with anxiety disorders were included to determine whether the findings were specific to depression. Several interesting findings emerged. First, on the self-referent encoding task, depressed individuals endorsed a relatively equal number of positive and negative words as self-relevant, suggesting that the self-schema of clinically depressed people is not devoid of positive content and that there is not a lack of cognitive availability. The main group differences that emerged involved cognitive processing and cognitive organization. Dozois and Dobson (2001) summarized the cognitive structure findings by concluding that "depressed individuals have an interconnected negative self-representational system and lack a well-organized positive template of self" (p. 2), a pattern that was not evident among the anxious group and the control group. Follow-up research (Dozois, 2002) on dysphoric students found additional evidence for a deterioration of positive interconnectedness as levels of depression increased. Once again, there was evidence of greater organization of negative content among severely dysphoric students. A further follow-up study by Dozois and Dobson (2003) showed that self-schematas involving greater organization of negative content and less interconnectedness of positive content were associated with more recurrent depression.

According to Beck's expanded cognitive model (e.g., Clark & Beck, 1999; Beck, 2008), due to repeated activation, negative schemas become organized into a depressive "mode"—a network of cognitive, affective, motivational, behavioural, and physiological schemas that accounts for fully expressed depression. Negative events impact on the mode, making it "hypersalient," and the mode "takes control of the information processing, reflected by increased negative appraisals and rumination" (Beck, 2008, p. 972).

Evaluation We must address two key issues when evaluating Beck's theory. The first is whether depressed people actually think in the negative ways enumerated by Beck. Beck initially confirmed this point in clinical observations (Beck, 1967). Further support comes from a number of sources: self-report questionnaires, laboratory studies of processes such as memory, and the Articulated Thoughts in Simulated Situations method (e.g., Segal et al., 1995). The studies outlined above confirm the presence of related differences in terms of cognitive accessibility and organization.

The second issue represents perhaps the greatest challenge for cognitive theories of depression: whether it could be that the negative beliefs of depressed people do not follow the depression, but in fact cause the depressed mood. Does depression cause negative thoughts, or do negative thoughts cause depression? The relationship in all likelihood works both ways: depression can make thinking more negative, and negative thinking can probably cause and can certainly worsen depression. Beck himself has come to this more bidirectional position. Longitudinal studies have assessed this issue. One study followed a sample of people for 45 days, collecting measures of mood and cognitions each day (Stader & Hokanson, 1998). Episodes of mild depression were identified, and the investigators evaluated whether these episodes were preceded by an increase in negative cognitions. Although an increase in interpersonal stress and dependency did precede the episodes of depression, negative cognitions did not. In a well-designed study, Lewinsohn, Joiner, and Rohde (2001) assessed dysfunctional thinking in approximately 1,500 adolescents. They then assessed stressful life events while following the adolescents for a year. Young people who began with high levels of negative cognitions and also experienced high stress had increased risk

for developing MDD relative to those with low stress and those with few negative beliefs and high stress.

While the original cognitive model proposed that severe life events such as the death of a loved one precipitated depression, Beck (2008) now accepts that milder events are an alternate pathway to depression in vulnerable people and that successive episodes can be triggered by progressively milder stressors, consistent with a kindling effect. Recent reviews of prospective studies and studies based on priming methodologies have concluded that a cognitive vulnerability to depressive symptoms following stress has been demonstrated in children, adolescents, and adults (see Jacobs, Reinecke, Gollan, & Kane, 2008; Scher, Ingram, & Segal, 2005). For example, cognitively vulnerable students are more likely to develop dysphoria (a minor depressive episode) following negative outcomes on college applications than students without the vulnerability (Abela & D'Alessandro, 2002). Further, research has demonstrated that the presence of cognitive reactivity (fluctuations in people's negative self-attitudes in response to daily events) predicts the onset of depressive episodes (see Scher et al., 2005).

Beck has further extended his theory by suggesting a need to focus on personality styles known as sociotropy and autonomy. The role of these factors and other personality traits is discussed in Canadian Perspectives 8.3. Despite uncertainties, Beck's theory has the advantage of being testable. It has engendered considerable research on the treatment of depression and has encouraged therapists to focus on the thinking of depressed clients in order to change their feelings.

HELPLESSNESS/HOPELESSNESS THEORIES In this section, we discuss the evolution of an influential cognitive theory of depression—actually, three theories: the original learned helplessness theory; its subsequent, more cognitive, attributional version; and its transformation into the learned hopelessness theory (see Figure 8.3 for a summary).

Learned Helplessness The basic premise of the **learned helplessness theory** is that an individual's passivity and sense of being unable to act and control his or her own life is acquired through unpleasant experiences and traumas that the individual tried unsuccessfully to control. This theory began as a mediational learning theory formulated to explain the behaviour of dogs who received inescapable electric shocks. Soon after receiving the first shocks, the dogs seemed to give up and passively accept the painful stimulation. Later, when the shocks could be avoided, these dogs did not acquire the avoidance response as efficiently and effectively as did control animals that had not experienced the inescapable shocks. Rather, most of them lay down in a corner and whined. Seligman (1974) proposed that animals acquire a sense of helplessness when confronted with uncontrollable aversive stimulation. Later, this sense of helplessness impairs their performance in stressful situations that can be controlled. They appear to lose the ability and motivation to learn to respond in an effective way to painful stimuli.

FIGURE 8.3 The three helplessness theories of depression

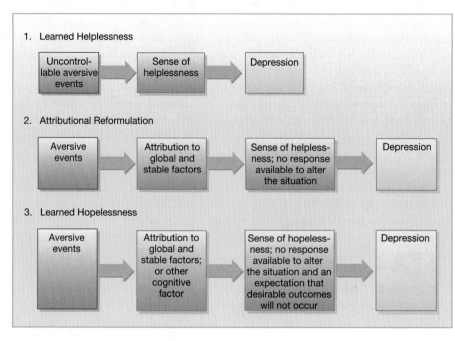

CANADIAN PERSPECTIVES 8.3
RESEARCH ON PERSONALITY ORIENTATIONS IN DEPRESSION

Are specific personality factors associated with depression? Do they predict susceptibility to the onset, severity, persistence, and relapse of depression? Are they related to treatment outcome? Are higher-order personality dimensions important? Much of the research in this area has a Canadian connection.

Aaron Beck (1983), taking a cognitive perspective, proposed that depression is associated with two personality styles: **sociotropy** and autonomy. Sociotropic individuals are dependent on others. They are especially concerned with pleasing others, avoiding disapproval, and avoiding separation. **Autonomy** is an achievement-related construct that focuses on self-critical goal striving, a desire for solitude, and freedom from control. Problems inherent in the original assessment of these constructs necessitated the development of alternative measures, including a multi-dimensional scale developed by David Clark at the University of New Brunswick, Beck, and colleagues. Their Revised Sociotropy-Autonomy Scale (SAS-R) assesses sociotropy and two aspects of autonomy: a preference for solitude and independence (Clark, Steer, Beck, & Ross, 1995). The independence component has adaptive correlates. Mongrain and Blackburn (2005) at York University examined the recurrence of diagnosed depression in graduate students with a history of depression and showed that autonomy predicted recurrence of depression, even after controlling for history of depression and other variables. Sociotropy and autonomy were both unique predictors of the number of previous episodes.

Sidney Blatt (1974, 1995), operating from a psychoanalytic perspective, suggested that introjective and anaclitic personality styles are associated with vulnerability to depression. The anaclitic orientation involves excessive levels of dependency on others.

The introjective orientation involves excessive levels of self-criticism. Blatt developed the Depressive Experiences Questionnaire (DEQ) to assess **dependency** and **self-criticism**. Canadian researcher David Zuroff from McGill University has collaborated with Blatt and tested his predictions (see Blatt & Zuroff, 1992). Research showed a strong association between self-criticism and depression and a weaker but still significant link between dependency and depression (e.g., Mongrain & Zuroff, 1994). The DEQ actually measures a needy, maladaptive form of dependency as well as a healthy, adaptive form that reflects positive affiliations with other people (Blatt, Zohar, Quinlan, Zuroff, & Mongrain, 1995). Research conducted at the University of Toronto (Dunkley, Blankstein, Zuroff, Lecce, & Hui, 2006a) determined that "neediness" reflects self-consciousness and unassertiveness, whereas "connectedness" (the more adaptive dimension) reflects warmth, the valuing of relationships, and agreeableness. Mongrain and Leather (2006) confirmed that self-criticism and maladaptive dependency interact to predict the recurrence of depression in graduate students, so it appears that students with high levels of self-criticism and neediness are particularly at risk for the return of depression. In line with a gender incongruence hypothesis, Luyten, Sabbe, Blatt, et al. (2007) reported that women diagnosed with MDD had higher levels of self-criticism compared with men, whereas men with MDD had higher levels of dependency relative to women.

The concept of self-criticism is linked closely with perfectionism (Blatt, 1995), and Canadian studies have examined the link between perfectionism dimensions and depression (for an expanded description of perfectionism dimensions, see

Chapter 10). Hewitt and Flett (1991a) found that depressed people had elevated levels of self-oriented (i.e., high personal standards) and socially prescribed (i.e., expectations imposed on the self by others) perfectionism. Enns and Cox (1999) found that socially prescribed perfectionism, an excessive concern over mistakes, and self-criticism are strong correlates of depression in psychiatric clients. Perfectionism has also been linked with chronic symptoms of both unipolar and bipolar depression (Hewitt, Flett, Ediger, Norton, & Flynn, 1998).

We will now focus on several substantive research approaches. One line of investigation tests the **congruency hypothesis**. This hypothesis reflects the diathesis-stress approach. Extensive Canadian research highlights the role of stressful life events in depression (e.g., Enns & Cox, 2005a; Wildes, Harkness, & Simons, 2002). In terms of personality and stress, the essence of the congruency hypothesis is that if a non-depressed person with a personality style (i.e., a diathesis) that makes him or her vulnerable to depression also experiences a negative life event that is congruent with or matches their vulnerability in some way (e.g., a student who wants to be perfect but fails a test), then this person will become depressed. The congruency hypothesis highlights the distinction between interpersonal and achievement-based vulnerabilities. Thus, a person characterized by interpersonal needs that indicate sociotropy and dependency will become depressed if she or he experiences interpersonal rejection or the loss of a significant other, but a person characterized by an achievement vulnerability that indicates a need to be perfect and to work autonomously will become depressed if she or he experiences a failure at school or work. The hypothesis has received only mixed support. Some personality studies have found some evidence of congruency (e.g., Hewitt, Flett, & Ediger, 1996; Segal, Shaw, Vella, & Katz, 1992); others have found a non-specific effect (i.e., stress in general combines with personality factors to produce depression) or partial support (Enns & Cox, 2005b); and still others have found no evidence for the congruency hypothesis (see Clark & Oates, 1995).

Although the lack of consistent support could signify that this hypothesis does not apply, methodological factors must also be considered. Most studies have relied on self-report measures that can be criticized for being imprecise. An alternative is to assess stress via structured interviews. In addition, more research should address the possibility that personality combines with other variables besides stress to produce depression. One such factor is social support. Dunkley, Blankstein, and colleagues (Dunkley, Blankstein, Halsall, Williams, & Winkworth, 2000; Dunkley, Zuroff, & Blankstein, 2003) found that low perceived social support combines with perfectionism to predict depressive symptoms and daily negative mood.

Another area of research explores the role of personality factors in treatment outcomes. A study led by Neil Rector at the Centre for Addiction and Mental Health (Rector, Bagby, Segal, Joffe, & Levitt, 2000) investigated the ability of self-criticism and dependency to predict treatment response among depressed clients who received either pharmacotherapy or cognitive therapy

(CT). The personality factors had little impact on the outcomes associated with pharmacotherapy, but self-criticism predicted a poor response to CT. Further, the extent to which self-critical clients became less self-critical over the course of treatment was the best predictor of response to CT. These findings combine with the results of the NIMH treatment study (see the next page) to suggest that whether a person will respond to certain kinds of treatment will be determined, in part, by personality vulnerabilities.

Other research considers the meaning and implications of the considerable overlap among some personality constructs. For example, autonomy, self-criticism, and socially prescribed perfectionism developed out of different theoretical frameworks, but they are conceptually and empirically related (see Blankstein & Dunkley, 2002; Dunkley & Blankstein, 2000). Dunkley, Blankstein, Zuroff, Lecce, and Hui (2006b) factor analyzed subscales from the DEQ, SAS-R, and the Hewitt and Flett Multidimensional Perfectionism Scale (1991b) and identified maladaptive (self-critical) and relatively more adaptive (personal standards) factors. The specific maladaptive personality factors likely coexist in people. For instance, dancer Karen Kain acknowledged being perfectionistic, self-critical, and, at times, without a sense of autonomy (Kain, 1994). Dunkley, Zuroff, and Blankstein (2006) compared the relative predictive ability of specific perfectionism components with self-criticism and determined that self-criticism was the most robust predictor of depression.

Using a new measure, the Self-Critical Perfectionism Scale (SCPS), that incorporates items from measures of self-criticism, autonomy, and perfectionism, Wheeler, Blankstein, Antony, McCabe, and Bieling (2010) reported that among clients with MDD and various anxiety disorders, depressed and social anxiety disorder groups reported the highest levels of self-critical perfectionism, relative to other clinical groups and a control group. Further, relative to specific component measures, the SCPS was the only significant unique positive predictor of depression, anxiety, and stress symptoms, and had a strong association with comorbidity. Depressed self-critical perfectionists "strive for achievement and perfection, engage in critical self-evaluation, perceive a need to reach unrealistic goals imposed by others, are concerned about criticism, disapproval, and rejection, and have a defensive separation and preference for solitude." These findings suggest a need to target specifically self-critical perfectionism in psychological interventions for depression. The SCPS is unique because it captures the shared variance among variables derived from diverse theoretical frameworks, including the psychoanalytic and cognitive paradigms.

Thinking Critically

1. What other variables, in addition to stress and social support, might interact with specific personality vulnerability factors to moderate the relationship between personality and depression?

2. Given a link between certain personality factors and depression, how would you attempt to prevent the onset of depression in vulnerable people?

Seligman concluded that learned helplessness in animals could provide a model for at least certain forms of human depression. Like many depressed people, the animals appeared passive in the face of stress, failing to initiate actions that might allow them to cope. They had difficulty eating or retaining what they ate, and they lost weight. Further, one of the neurotransmitter chemicals implicated in depression, norepinephrine, was depleted in Seligman's animals.

Attribution and Learned Helplessness After the original research with animals, investigators conducted similar studies with humans. By 1978, several inadequacies of the theory and unexplained aspects of depression had become apparent, and a revised learned helplessness model was proposed by Abramson, Seligman, and Teasdale (1978). Some studies with humans, for example, had indicated that helplessness inductions sometimes led to subsequent improvement of performance. Also, many depressed people hold themselves responsible for their failures. If they see themselves as helpless, how can they blame themselves? This characteristic of feeling helpless yet blaming oneself is referred to as the **depressive paradox**.

The essence of the revised theory is the concept of **attribution**—the explanation a person has for his or her behaviour (Weiner et al., 1971). When a person has experienced failure, he or she will try to attribute the failure to some cause. Table 8.1 applies the Abramson, Seligman, and Teasdale formulation to various ways in which a university student might attribute a low score on the mathematics portion of the Graduate Record Examination (GRE). The formulation is based on answers to three questions:

1. Are the reasons for failure believed to be internal (personal) or external (environmentally caused)?
2. Is the problem believed to be stable or unstable?
3. How global or specific is the inability to succeed perceived to be?

The attributional revision of the helplessness theory postulates that the way in which a person cognitively explains failure will determine its subsequent effects:

- Global attributions ("I never do anything right") increase the generality of the effects of failure.
- Attributions to stable factors ("I never test well") make them long term.
- Attributions to internal characteristics ("I am stupid") are more likely to diminish self-esteem, particularly if the personal fault is also global and persistent.

The theory suggests that people become depressed when they attribute negative life events to stable and global causes. Whether self-esteem also collapses depends on whether they blame the bad outcome on their own inadequacies. The individual prone to depression is thought to show a depressive attributional style—a tendency to attribute bad outcomes to personal, global, and stable faults of character. When people with this style (a diathesis) have unhappy, adverse experiences (stressors), they become depressed (Peterson & Seligman, 1984).

Where does the depressive attributional style come from? In Chapter 2, we noted that the failure to answer such a central question is a problem with most cognitive theories of psychopathology. In general terms, the answer is thought to lie in childhood experiences (a common theme in many psychological theories), but few data have been collected to support this view. A promising start is the finding that depressive attributional style is related to sexual abuse in childhood, parental overprotectiveness, and harsh discipline (Rose et al., 1994).

Hopelessness Theory The next version of this theory (Abramson, Metalsky, & Alloy, 1989) moved even farther away from the original formulation. Some forms of depression (hopelessness depressions) are now regarded as caused by a state of hopelessness, an expectation that desirable outcomes will not occur or that undesirable ones will occur and that the person has no responses available to change this situation. (The latter part of the definition of hopelessness, of course, refers to helplessness, the central concept of earlier versions of the theory.) As in the attributional reformulation, negative life events interact with diatheses to yield a state of hopelessness. One diathesis is the attributional pattern already described—attributing negative events to stable and

TABLE 8.1
ATTRIBUTIONAL SCHEMA OF DEPRESSION: WHY I FAILED MY GRE MATH EXAM

Degree	Internal (Personal)		External (Environmental)	
	Stable	**Unstable**	**Stable**	**Unstable**
Global	I am stupid.	I am exhausted.	These tests are all unfair.	It's an unlucky day, Friday the 13th.
Specific	I lack mathematical ability.	I am fed up with math.	The math tests are unfair.	My math test was numbered "13."

global factors. However, the theory now considers two other diatheses: low self-esteem and a tendency to infer that negative life events will have severe negative consequences.

Metalsky and his colleagues (1993) conducted the first test of the hopelessness theory in a prospective study that examined how students differing in attributional style responded to success vs. failure on a class test. Two new features were the direct measurement of hopelessness and one of the newly proposed diatheses, low self-esteem. As in the earlier study, attributing poor grades to global and stable factors led to more persistent depressed mood. This pattern supported the hopelessness theory, for it was found only among students whose self-esteem was low and was mediated by an increase in feelings of hopelessness. A similar study conducted with children in the sixth and seventh grades yielded almost identical results (Robinson, Garber, & Hillsman, 1995). Lewinsohn and his colleagues (1994) also found that depressive attributional style and low self-esteem predicted the onset of depression in adolescents. Recently, Alloy and Abramson and their colleagues (Iacoviello, Alloy, Abramson, Whitehouse, & Hogan, 2006) conducted a prospective study to examine the course of depression in people at high and low cognitive risk for depression. They found that those high in negative cognitive styles experienced more episodes of depression, more severe episodes, and more chronic courses.

In a longitudinal study, Abela, Aydin, and Auerbach (2006) from McGill University tested the diathesis-stress component of the hopelessness theory using a "weakest link" approach toward operationalizing vulnerability, and an idiographic approach toward operationalizing high levels of stress. The weakest link refers to the idea that a person is as vulnerable to depression as his or her most depressogenic inferential style (e.g., the tendency to perceive negative events as having disastrous consequences). In adults diagnosed with a current or past major depressive episode at the outset, depressogenic weakest links predicted greater elevations in symptoms of depression following elevations in hassles.

An advantage of the hopelessness theory is that it can deal directly with the comorbidity of depression and anxiety disorders. Alloy and her colleagues proposed that an expectation of helplessness creates anxiety. When the expectation of helplessness becomes certain, a syndrome with elements of anxiety and depression emerges. Finally, if the perceived probability of the future occurrence of negative events becomes certain (a phenomenon known as **depressive predictive certainty**), hopelessness depression develops.

Issues in the Helplessness/Hopelessness Theories
Although these theories are promising, there are some problems worth noting:

1. Which type of depression is being modelled? In his original paper, Seligman attempted to document the similarity between learned helplessness and what used to be called reactive depression—depression thought to be brought on by stressful life events. Similarly, Abramson et al. (1989) now talk about a hopelessness depression, referring both to the presumed cause of the depression and to a set of symptoms that do not exactly match the *DSM* criteria. Only future research will tell whether these proposals are more than circular statements (i.e., that hopelessness depression is caused by hopelessness).

2. Are the findings specific to depression? Because of the high correlation between anxiety and depression, it becomes important for theories to document that they are truly about depression and not about negative affect in general. Depressive attributional style does not appear to be specific to depression but is related to anxiety and general distress, as well (e.g., Ralph & Mineka, 1998).

3. Are attributions relevant? Do people actively attempt to explain their own behaviour to themselves, and do the attributions they make have subsequent effects on their behaviour? Some research indicates that making attributions is not a process in which everyone engages (Hanusa & Schulz, 1977) and that people are frequently unaware of the causes of their behaviour (Nisbett & Wilson, 1977).

4. One key assumption of the helplessness/hopelessness theories is that the depressive attributional style is a persistent part of the makeup of depressed people; it must already be in place when the person encounters some stressor. However, some research shows that the depressive attributional style disappears following a depressive episode. Ball, McGuffin, and Farmer (2008) concluded that attributional style is not a familial and trait-like measure related to the genetic risk for depression but mainly measures current mood (state-like). However, attributing negative events to personal (internal) characteristics was related to having had a past depression episode, suggesting a "scarring effect."

Despite all their problems, the helplessness/hopelessness theories have clearly stimulated much research and theorizing about depression and seem destined to do so for many years to come (see Alloy et al., 2006).

INTERPERSONAL THEORY OF DEPRESSION
In this section, we discuss behavioural aspects of depression that generally involve relationships between the depressed person and others.

Depressed individuals tend to have sparse social networks and to regard them as providing little support. Reduced social support may lessen an individual's ability to handle negative life events and increase vulnerability to depression (Billings, Cronkite, & Moos, 1983). Depressed people also elicit negative reactions from others, including rejection (Coyne, 1976). For example, the roommates of depressed students rated social contacts with them as low in enjoyment and reported high levels of aggression toward them; mildly depressed students were likely to be rejected by their roommates (Joiner, Alfano, & Metalsky, 1992). Bieling and Alden (2001) discovered that one reason why depressed people may elicit negative reactions from others is that they tend to reject their partners and display relatively few positive social behaviours. This tendency was especially evident among people high in autonomy, as described by Beck. It seems that depressed individuals with an autonomous orientation are oriented toward themselves rather than toward other people. When oriented toward others, they can act in a negative, rejecting manner.

Given the interpersonal problems of depressed people, it is not surprising that depression and marital discord frequently co-occur and that the interactions of depressed people and their spouses involve mutual hostility (Kowalik & Gotlib, 1987). Critical comments by spouses are a significant predictor of recurrence of depression (Hooley & Teasdale, 1989). Couples in which one partner has a mood disorder report less marital satisfaction than do couples in which neither has a mood disorder (Beach, Sandeen, & O'Leary, 1990). Studies have also demonstrated that depressed people are low in social skills across a variety of measures: interpersonal problem-solving speech patterns (speaking very slowly, with silences and hesitations, and more negative self-disclosures), and maintenance of eye contact (e.g., Gotlib & Robinson, 1982).

Another specific idea examined by researchers is that constant seeking of reassurance is a critical variable in depression (Joiner & Schmidt, 1998). Perhaps as a result of being reared in a cold and rejecting environment (Carnelley, Pietromonaco, & Jaffe, 1994), depressed people seek reassurance that others truly care, but even when reassured, they are only temporarily satisfied. Their negative self-concept causes them to doubt the truth of the feedback they have received, and their constant efforts to be reassured come to irritate others. Later, they actually seek out negative feedback, which, in a sense, validates their negative self-concept. Rejection ultimately occurs because of the depressed person's inconsistent behaviour. Focus on Discovery 8.2 explores the possibility that people become depressed because they generate stress for themselves.

Do any interpersonal characteristics of depressed people precede the onset of depression, suggesting a causal relationship? Some research using the high-risk method suggests the answer is yes. For example, low social competence predicted the onset of depression among children (Cole et al., 1990) and poor interpersonal problem-solving skills predicted increases in depression among adolescents (Davila et al., 1995). Thus, social skills deficits may be a cause and consequence of depression. Interpersonal behaviour clearly plays a major role in depression.

FOCUS ON DISCOVERY 8.2
STRESS GENERATION AND DEPRESSION

Constance Hammen (1991) advanced the theory that some people are more prone to depression because they take an active role in creating or generating the stress for themselves that contributes to distress and despair. This is a radical notion because it portrays people as active agents in their own stress. Implicit in this work is the notion that females are more interpersonally sensitive and may engage in more stress generation.

The concept of stress generation is highly relevant to interpersonal theories because one of the major ways to create stress is to act in a way that creates interpersonal conflict. Another avenue is to gravitate toward peers or partners who are volatile or non-supportive, perhaps even abusive. Stress generation can also result from being so high in the need for reassurance that the constant reassurance seeking alienates other people.

The measurement of stress generation involves making the distinction between *independent events* (i.e., not due to oneself) and *dependent events* (i.e., stemming from personal choices or actions dependent on the self). Dependent versus independent events are assessed via a rigorous contextual interview of life experiences.

Thus far, strong empirical findings, often in longitudinal research, have supported the role of stress generation in depression among adolescents and adults. It has been suggested that stress generation accounts for the gender differences in depression that emerge during adolescence. Shih, Eberhart, Hammen, and Brennan (2006) found that interpersonal episodic stress that was self-generated predicts depression in girls; for boys, chronic stress in general contributed to depression. Another recent longitudinal investigation confirmed that stress generation predicted depression in adolescent girls but not in boys (Rudolph et al., 2009). In addition, generation of stress among already depressed girls predicted subsequent bouts of depression.

Stress generation may interact with other vulnerability factors. Research by Harkness and associates at Queen's University found evidence that higher rates of interpersonal stress generation predicted depression in a sample of adolescent girls with a history of childhood maltreatment (Harkness, Lumley, & Truss, 2008). This effect was not found among the subset of girls without a history of maltreatment. These data underscore the need to examine stress generation within the context of other individual difference factors associated with vulnerability to depression.

PSYCHOLOGICAL THEORIES OF BIPOLAR DISORDER

Bipolar disorder has been neglected by psychological theorists and researchers, although, as with unipolar depression, life stress seems important in precipitating episodes (e.g., Malkoff-Schwartz et al., 1998). Cognitive factors may also play a role. Scott et al. (2001) showed that people with bipolar depression have elevated levels of the dysfunctional attitudes described by Beck, as well as problems in autobiographical memory and the ability to generate solutions in a problem-solving task. The manic phase of the disorder is seen as a defence against a debilitating psychological state. The specific negative state that is being avoided varies from theory to theory; however, many theorists have concluded that the manic state serves a protective function. Clinical experience with manic people and studies of their personalities when they are in remission indicate that they appear relatively well-adjusted between episodes. But if mania is a defence, it must be a defence against something, suggesting that the apparently good adjustment of manic people between episodes may not be an accurate reflection of their true state. Manic individuals, even when between episodes, have very low self-esteem (Lyon, Startup, & Bentall, 1999).

BIOLOGICAL THEORIES OF MOOD DISORDERS

> "The accumulation of studies of the psychological and biological aspects of depression has reached a critical mass warranting a new synthesis."
>
> *—Aaron T. Beck on the cognitive model of depression and its neurobiological correlates, 2008, p. 975*

Since biological processes are known to have considerable effects on moods, it is not surprising that investigators have sought biological causes for depression and mania. Furthermore, disturbed biological processes must be part of the causal chain if a predisposition for a mood disorder can be genetically transmitted, and evidence that a predisposition for a mood disorder is heritable would provide some support for the view that the disorder has a biological basis. In the treatment of mood disorders, the effectiveness of drug therapies that increase the levels of certain neurotransmitters suggests that biological factors are important. In this century, there have been tremendous advances by researchers in behaviour genetics and cognitive neuroscience, in part, due to technological changes, such as functional neuroimaging, that have facilitated breakthroughs in our understanding of relations among biological, cognitive, and experiential factors in the development of depression. We will look at some of the research in the areas of genetics, neurochemistry, and the neuroendocrine system. There is also a growing literature on structural abnormalities of the brains of people with mood disorders. These abnormalities are similar to those found in schizophrenia (see Chapter 11). As noted by Beck (2008), new research has provided "a preliminary basis for formulating the neurobiological correlates of such psychological constructs as cognitive vulnerability, cognitive reactivity, and cognitive biases" (p. 972). The genetic and neurobiological discoveries also suggest some probable causal pathways to depression.

GENETIC VULNERABILITY

Research on genetic factors in bipolar disorder and MDD has used twin, family, and adoption methods. Bipolar disorder is one of the most heritable of disorders. Overall, the concordance rate for bipolar disorder is as high as 85% (McGuffin et al., 2003). That is, genes account for possibly 85% of the variance in whether a person becomes manic. These data plus the results of adoption studies (e.g., Wender et al., 1986) support the notion that bipolar disorder has a strong heritable component. However, genetic factors do not determine when manic symptoms will occur. The risk for mania is apparently also related to a higher risk for depression (McGuffin et al., 2003). The information available on MDD indicates that genetic factors, although influential, are not as decisive as they are in bipolar disorder, with heritability estimates approximating 35% (Sullivan, Neale, & Kendler, 2000). Furthermore, relatives of unipolar probands are at somewhat increased risk for unipolar depression; however, this risk is less than the risk among relatives of bipolar probands (Andreasen et al., 1987).

Linkage analysis has also been applied to mood disorders. In a widely reported study of the Old Order Amish, Egeland and her colleagues (1987) found evidence favouring the hypothesis that bipolar disorder results from a dominant gene on the 11th chromosome. However, attempts to replicate the Egeland study as well as other apparently successful linkage studies have had mixed success (e.g., Smyth et al., 1996). Research on linkage has broadened to focus on other genes on other chromosomes. Muller et al. (2006) from the University of Toronto reported that within bipolar disorder, variation in the brain-derived neurotrophic factor (BDNF) gene appears to predict risk for developing rapid cycling.

Some people seem to be genetically predisposed to the onset of MDD when confronted with a series of adverse life events. The pioneering work by Caspi et al. (2003) suggested that people who possess one or two copies of the short variant of the 5-HTTLPR (serotonin transporter) gene, which is involved in modulating serotonin levels, experienced higher levels of depression and suicidality following a recent stressful event (a gene x environment interaction). Wilhelm et al. (2006) also reported that the serotonin transporter gene-linked promoter region (5-HTTLPR) is a significant predictor of first major depression onset following multiple adverse events. These findings have been supported by many other studies (see Uher & McGuffin, 2008, for review). Kaufman et al. (2006) reported that in abused children, depression severity was predicted in part by an interaction of the 5-HTTPLR (short allele) with the brain-derived neurotrophic factor (*Val/Met*) genotype, especially in children receiving low social support (a gene-gene interaction). It is likely that other gene-environment and gene-gene interactions will be discovered in the future.

Accumulating evidence also suggests that a genetic predisposition is related to biases in information processing (see Beck, 2008). For example, Hayden et al. (2008) found that non-depressed children homozygous for the 5-HTTLPR short allele demonstrated greater negative processing on a self-referential encoding task after a negative mood induction than children with other genotypes.

NEUROCHEMISTRY, NEUROIMAGING, AND MOOD DISORDERS

Researchers have sought to understand the role played by neurotransmitters in mood disorders. The most-studied neurotransmitters have been **norepinephrine, serotonin, and dopamine**. The original theory posited that low levels of norepinephrine and dopamine lead to depression and high levels to mania. The serotonin theory suggests that serotonin, a neurotransmitter presumed to play a role in the regulation of norepinephrine, also produces depression and mania. However, the weight of the evidence does not completely support the notion that *levels* of neurotransmitters are critical in the mood disorders.

The actions of drugs that were used to treat depression provided the clues on which the theories are based. In the 1950s, two groups of drugs, tricyclics and monoamine oxidase inhibitors, were found effective in relieving depression. **Tricyclic drugs** (e.g., imipramine, or Tofranil) are a group of antidepressant medications so named because their molecular structure is characterized by three fused rings. They prevent some of the reuptake of norepinephrine, serotonin, and/or dopamine by the presynaptic neuron after it has fired, leaving more of the neurotransmitter in the synapse so that transmission of the next nerve impulse is made easier (see Figure 8.4). **Monoamine oxidase (MAO) inhibitors** (e.g., tranylcypromine, or Parnate) are antidepressants that keep the enzyme monoamine oxidase from deactivating neurotransmitters, thus increasing the levels of serotonin, norepinephrine, and/or dopamine in the synapse. This action produces the same facilitating effect described for tricylics, compensating for the abnormally low levels of these neurotransmitters in depressed people. These drug actions suggest that depression and mania are related to serotonin, norepinephrine, and dopamine. Newer antidepressant drugs, called **selective serotonin reuptake inhibitors** (e.g., fluoxetine, or Prozac), act more selectively than older ones, specifically inhibiting the reuptake of serotonin. Because these drugs are presumed effective in treating unipolar depression, a stronger link has been apparently shown between low levels of serotonin and depression.

It now appears that the explanation of why these drugs work is not as straightforward as it first seemed. The therapeutic effects of tricyclics and MAO inhibitors do not depend solely on an increase in levels of neurotransmitters. The earlier findings were correct—tricyclics and MAO inhibitors do indeed increase levels of norepinephrine, serotonin, and/or dopamine when they are first taken—but after several days

FIGURE 8.4 (a) When a neuron releases norepinephrine or serotonin from its endings, a pump-like reuptake mechanism immediately begins to recapture some of the neurotransmitter molecules before they are received by the postsynaptic (receptor) neuron. (b) Tricyclic drugs block this reuptake process, enabling more norepinephrine or serotonin to reach, and thus fire, the postsynaptic (receptor) neuron. Serotonin reuptake inhibitors act more selectively on serotonin. Adapted from Snyder (1986, p. 106)

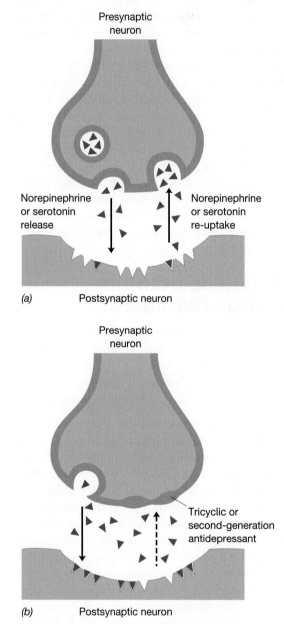

the neurotransmitters return to their earlier levels. This information is crucial because it does not fit with data on how much time must pass before antidepressants become effective. Both tricyclics and MAO inhibitors take from 7 to 14 days to relieve depression, but by that time, the neurotransmitter level has already returned to its previous state.

Another approach to further evaluate the theories involved measuring metabolites of these neurotransmitters, the by-products of the breakdown of serotonin, norepinephrine, and/or dopamine found in urine, blood serum, and the cerebrospinal fluid. The problem with such measurements is that they are not direct reflections of levels of neurotransmitters in the brain; metabolites measured in this way could reflect neurotransmitters anywhere in the body. Indeed, the majority of neurons that use serotonin are found in the intestines and norepinephrine is also an important neurotransmitter in the peripheral nervous system. Further, despite the fact that some people showed the expected levels of neurotransmitters in connection with their depression or mania, the expected high or low metabolites were not found consistently. Thus, many people with depression or mania did not have disturbances in absolute levels of neurotransmitters (e.g., Placidi et al., 2001).

It would seem, then, that a simple change in the level of norepinephrine or serotonin or dopamine is not a sufficient explanation for why people become depressed and/or manic. What is the impact of these findings? Researchers then focused on the postsynaptic effects of antidepressants and developed theories of depression that implicate postsynaptic mechanisms. One line of research examined whether antidepressants alter the chemical messengers that a postsynaptic receptor sends into the postsynaptic neuron (Duman, Heninger, & Nestler, 1997). If receptors are overly sensitive they should respond to very small amounts of a neurotransmitter in the synaptic cleft. Researchers have focused primarily on dopamine and serotonin in this line of research. For example, drugs that increase dopamine levels have triggered manic behaviour in people with bipolar disorder, suggesting the possibility that dopamine receptors are overly sensitive (Anand et al., 2000). Similarly, people with MDD respond differently to drugs that increase dopamine levels (Naranjo et al., 2001).

Delgado et al. (1990) used a special diet to reduce the level of serotonin in depressed people in remission by lowering the level of its precursor, tryptophan. They found that 67% of clients experienced a return of their symptoms. A gradual remission followed when clients resumed their normal diet. Similar results have been found in research conducted with clients with seasonal depression (Lam et al., 1996). Another study used this same tryptophan-depletion strategy in normal participants who had either a positive or a negative family history of depression. Again, as predicted by the low-serotonin theory, those with a positive family history experienced an increase in depressed mood (Benkelfat et al., 1994). Beck (2008) reviewed several recent studies that he interpreted as showing linkages between cognitive vulnerability and genetic vulnerability expressed as a hyperreactive serotonergic system (a neurochemical vulnerability).

Research on bipolar disorder is also moving away from the older norepinephrine theory. One major reason for this shift is that lithium, the most widely used and effective treatment for bipolar disorder, is useful in treating both the manic and depressive episodes of the disorder, suggesting that it acts by affecting some neurochemical that can either increase or decrease neural activity. Current research is focusing on G-proteins (guanine nucleotide-binding proteins), which are found in postsynaptic cell membranes and play an important role in modulating activity in the postsynaptic cell. High levels of G-proteins have been found in people with mania and low levels in people with depression (Avissar et al., 1999), suggesting that the therapeutic effects of lithium may be due to its ability to regulate G-proteins (Manji et al., 1995).

Both structural and functional activation brain-imaging studies have been conducted in research on mood disorders in attempt to determine how depression relates to brain activity (see Davidson et al., 2002, for review). The amygdala, hippocampus, prefrontal cortex, and the anterior cingulate are the main brain structures implicated in MDD and bipolar disorder. For example, many findings have tied amygdala hyperactivity to depression. This hyperactivity in short 5-HT-TLPR variant carriers is related to increased sensitivity to negative stimuli (see Munro, Brown, & Hariri, 2008). Further, Siegle et al. (2007) reported that almost all depressed people have reduced prefrontal function. Beck (2008) suggests that a hyperactive amygdala in combination with hypoactive prefrontal regions is related to diminished cognitive appraisal and depression and represents a neurophysiological correlate of cognitive bias.

Ravindran and Kennedy (2007a) summarized several major neuroimaging studies and concluded that:

1. Structural imaging studies show that recurrent depression and long-duration untreated depression are related to decreased hippocampal volume and neurocognitive impairment.
2. Functional imaging studies show that induction of dysphoria in healthy volunteers increases glucose metabolism in cingulated area 25, and response to treatment of depression with paroxetine was evident in a reduction of hypermetabolism in cingulated area 25.

However, quantitative meta-analyses of imaging studies in depression have found considerable heterogeneity in the results of resting studies and serotonin reuptake inhibitor antidepressant treatment (e.g., Fitzgerald et al., 2006). Margaret McKinnon and her colleagues at McMaster University (2009) conducted a meta-analysis of 32 MRI studies of hippocampal volume in people with MDD. It was concluded that hippocampal volume reductions occur among people whose duration of MDD was longer than two years or who had multiple episodes, suggesting that the reductions occur *after* onset of MDD.

In a major breakthrough study, Jeffrey Meyer and colleagues (2006) from the Centre for Addiction and Mental Health attempted to determine whether MAO-A levels in the brain are elevated during untreated depression. Monoamine oxidase A (MAO-A) is an enzyme that metabolizes monoamines such as serotonin, norepinephrine, and dopamine. The study compared healthy and depressed people with MDD who had been medication-free for at least five months. MAO-A was elevated by almost 35% throughout the brain during major depression. Meyer et al. (2006) concluded that "elevated MAO-A density is the primary monoamine-lowering process during major depression" (p. 1209).

Should we assume that biochemical, structural, or functional irregularities associated with depression mean that they play a causal role? Many experts believe that they do; however, others remain sceptical (e.g., Gold, 2009; Paris, 2009). Moncrieff (2007b) summarized the sceptics' position as follows:

> If I experience an adverse event, I will feel sad, and if this emotion is strong enough, there are likely to be associated biochemical changes—but it is the event that has made me sad, not the chemical fluctuations. They are best viewed as an accompaniment, or a biological correlation, of the emotional state. (p. 100)

It will be a task of future research to resolve this issue.

THE NEUROENDOCRINE SYSTEM

The hypothalamic-pituitary-adrenocortical (HPA) axis may also play a role in depression (see Figure 9.5). The limbic area of the brain is closely linked to emotion and also affects the hypothalamus. The hypothalamus in turn controls various endocrine glands and thus the levels of hormones they secrete. Hormones secreted by the hypothalamus also affect the pituitary gland and the hormones it produces. Because of its relevance to the so-called vegetative symptoms of depression, such as disturbances in appetite and sleep, the HPA axis is thought to be overactive in depression.

Various findings support this proposition. Levels of **cortisol** (an adrenocortical hormone) are high in depressed people, perhaps because of oversecretion of thyrotropin-releasing hormone by the hypothalamus (Garbutt et al., 1994). The excess secretion of cortisol in depressed persons also causes enlargement of their adrenal glands (Rubin et al., 1995). These high levels of cortisol have even led to the development of a biological test for depression: the dexamethasone suppression test (DST). Dexamethasone suppresses cortisol secretion, but when given dexamethasone during an overnight test, some depressed people, especially those with delusional depression, do not experience cortisol suppression (Nelson & Davis, 1997). It is believed that the failure of dexamethasone to suppress cortisol reflects overactivity in the HPA axis of clients. The failure to show suppression ceases when the depressive episode ends, suggesting such failure is a non-specific response to stress.

Gotlib and his colleagues (2008) reported that carriers of the short 5-HTTLPR show elevated cortisol response, cognitive biases, and amygdale activation during a mood repair procedure. These and other converging findings led Beck (2008) to suggest the following pathway to depression: stress leads to distorted appraisal leads to engagement of the HPA axis leads to cortisol leads to depressive symptoms.

The HPA axis is also of possible relevance to bipolar disorder. Disorders of thyroid function are often seen in bipolar individuals (Lipowski et al., 1994), and thyroid hormones can induce mania in these people (Goodwin & Jamison, 1990).

Finally, a review of research on the neuropsychology of depression led the authors to conclude that there is solid evidence implicating both the right and left hemispheres in the experience of depression (Shenal, Harrison, & Demaree, 2003). However, the depression itself may vary. Right hemisphere dysfunction involves symptoms of indifference or flat affect, while left hemisphere dysfunction involves more overt symptoms of agitation and sadness.

All these data lend some support to theories that mood disorders have biological causes (see Table 8.2 for a summary of major biological positions). Does this mean that psychological theories are irrelevant or useless? Not in the least. To assert that behavioural disorders have a basis in biological processes is to state the obvious. No psychogenic theorist would deny that behaviour is mediated by some bodily changes. The biological and psychological theories may well be describing the same phenomena, but in different terms (such as learned helplessness vs. low serotonin). They should be thought of as complementary, not incompatible.

DECONSTRUCTING DEPRESSION?

Beck (2008) interpreted research comparing components of the cognitive model of depression with neurophysiological studies and proposed that it is possible to present a "pragmatic formulation of the interaction of the two levels" (p. 974). A summary of his "deconstructing" of the phenomenon of depression is presented in Figure 8.5. He proposed a hypothetical pathway that begins with a genetic vulnerability (probably the 5-HTTLPR polymorphism), which leads to excessive amygdala reactivity. Heightened limbic reactivity to stressful events causes deployment of increased attentional resources to these emotional events, which is manifested in negative attentional bias and recall (cognitive reactivity). Selective focus on the "negative" results in cognitive distortions (e.g., overgeneralization) and formation of dysfunctional attitudes (e.g., I must be perfect). Frequent occurrences of negative interpretations shape the content of schemas (e.g., worthless). At the same time, the negative interpretations impact the HPA axis and set in motion a cycle involving the overreactive serotonergic system, which leads to depression.

Beck (2008) notes that his formulation is tentative and subject to further research. There are methodological pitfalls in analyses of gene-environment analyses, including the 5-HTTLPR gene, and some aspects of his cognitive theory are speculative.

TABLE 8.2

SUMMARY OF BIOLOGICAL HYPOTHESES ABOUT UNIPOLAR DEPRESSION AND BIPOLAR DISORDER

Unipolar depression	Genetic diathesis, low serotonin or serotonin-receptor dysfunction, high levels of cortisol.
Bipolar disorder	Genetic diathesis, low serotonin or low norepinephrine in depressed phase, high norepinephrine in manic phase, may also be linked to G-proteins.

FIGURE 8.5 A developmental model of depression based on anomalous genes* Beck, A. T. (2008). The evolution of the cognitive model of depression and its neurobiological correlates. *American Journal of Psychiatry,* 165, 969-977. Reproduced with permission from The American Journal of Psychiatry. (Copyright 2008) American Psychiatric Association.

*Multiple interactions are not shown. Genetic pathways leading to reduced prefrontal activity have not been determined as yet. Increased limbic activity overrides prefrontal control.

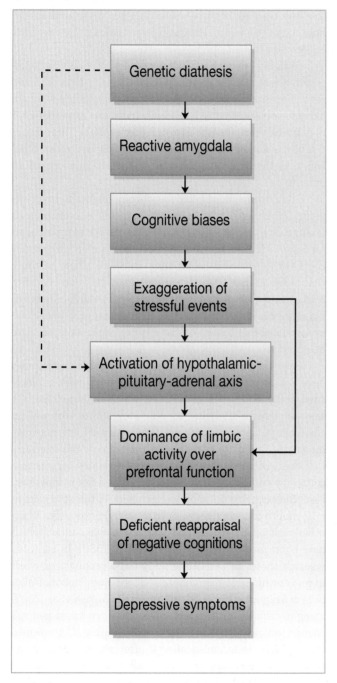

Further, the model's biological component undoubtedly involves complex circuits in multiple brain regions (see Mayberg, 2006). A series of multiple wave prospective studies starting in early childhood will be necessary to address various problems and questions and investigate the causal sequence.

THERAPIES FOR MOOD DISORDERS

> "The burden (of depression) persists because individuals do not seek treatment for their depression when they relapse and effective proactive treatment is not always provided when they do seek it."
> —*Gavin Andrews, 2008, p. 420*

Most episodes of depression lift after a few months, although the time may seem immeasurably longer to the depressed individual and to those close to him or her. That most depressions are self-limiting is fortunate. However, depression is too widespread and too incapacitating, both to the depressed person and to those around him or her, simply to wait for the disorder to go away untreated. Bouts of depression tend to recur, and suicide is a risk. Thus, it is important to treat MDD, as well as bipolar disorder. Current therapies are both psychological and biological; singly or in combination, they are somewhat effective. However, it should be noted that an examination of health service delivery in British Columbia determined that in 2000–01, 92% of people who received a diagnosis of depression were treated by a primary care physician alone; i.e., no psychiatric services were provided (Bilsker, Goldner, & Jones, 2007). As noted by Andrews (2008), many depressed people do not have their disorder identified and are thus not given proactive care. However, the clinical course of MDD is highly variable. In a recent paper, Patten, Bilsker, and Goldner (2008) argued that a sizeable proportion of people who meet *DSM-IV* criteria for MDD might not require the intensive treatment emphasized by current Canadian practice guidelines and they eschewed "a one-size-fits-all" approach. They suggested that strategies such as watchful waiting, self-guided management, and stepped care (see Chapter 17) could be included in a spectrum of primary care services for the subset of people with mild MDD.

PSYCHOLOGICAL THERAPIES

> "It is probably fair to say that we have a great distance to go in delivering the potential benefit that psychosocial treatment could provide to people with depression in Canada."
> —*Elliot M. Goldner of Simon Fraser University in a 2008 guest editorial in the* Canadian Journal of Psychiatry, p. 410

PSYCHODYNAMIC THERAPIES Because depression is considered to be derived from a repressed sense of loss and from anger unconsciously turned inward, psychoanalytic treatment tries to help the client achieve insight into the repressed conflict and often encourages outward release of the hostility directed inward. The aim is to uncover latent motivations for the client's depression. People may, for example, blame themselves for a lack of parental affection but repress this belief because of the pain it causes. The therapist must first guide clients to confront the fact that they feel this way and then help them realize that any guilt is unfounded. The recovery of memories of stressful childhood circumstances should also bring relief.

Research on the effectiveness of dynamic psychotherapy in alleviating depression is sparse (e.g., Craighead, Evans, & Robins, 1992) and characterized by mixed results, in part owing to the high degree of variability among approaches that come under the rubric of psychodynamic or psychoanalytic psychotherapy. A report from the American Psychiatric Association (1993) concluded that there are no controlled data attesting to the efficacy of long-term psychodynamic psychotherapy or psychoanalysis in treating depression. Although a more contemporary meta-analytic review (Leichsenring, 2001) concluded that short-term psychodynamic treatment and CBT are equally effective in alleviating depression, it was acknowledged that this conclusion must remain tentative because of the relatively small number of studies conducted. A more recent "mega-analysis" based on three randomized clinical trials (de Maat et al., 2008) concluded that a short psychodynamic supportive psychotherapy was as effective as antidepressants for people with mild to moderate MDD. Combined therapy was superior to pharmacotherapy alone.

Findings from a well-known large-scale study (Elkin et al., 1989) suggest that a form of psychodynamic therapy that concentrates on present-day interactions between the depressed person and the social environment—Klerman and Weissman's interpersonal therapy (IPT) (Klerman et al., 1984)—is effective for alleviating unipolar depression, as well as for maintaining treatment gains (Frank et al., 1990). The core of the therapy is to help depressed people examine the ways in which their current interpersonal behaviour might interfere with obtaining pleasure from relationships. For example, the clients might be taught how to improve communication with others to meet their own needs better and to have more satisfying social interactions and support. This psychodynamic therapy is not as much intrapsychic as it is interpersonal. It emphasizes better understanding of the interpersonal problems assumed to give rise to depression and aims at improving relationships with others. As such, the focus is on better communication, reality testing, developing effective social skills, and meeting present social-role requirements. Actual techniques include discussion of interpersonal problems, exploration of and encouragement to express negative feelings, improvement of both verbal and non-verbal communications, problem-solving, and suggesting new and more satisfying modes of behaviour. The focus is on the client's current life, not on an exploration of past, often-repressed causes of present-day problems. A study by Harkness et al. (2002) attested to the effectiveness of IPT; IPT helped buffer the impact and possible etiological role of stressful interpersonal events in the recurrence of depression. Thirty years after their conception IPT and cognitive therapy (see next section) "remain the most widely tested therapies for the treatment of unipolar depression" (see Weissman, 2007, p. 696).

COGNITIVE AND BEHAVIOUR THERAPIES In keeping with their contention that depression is caused by errors in thinking, Beck and his associates devised a cognitive therapy (CT) aimed at altering maladaptive thought patterns. The therapist tries to persuade depressed persons to change their opinions of events and of the self. When a client expresses worthlessness because "Nothing goes right; everything I try to do ends in a disaster," the therapist offers examples contrary to this overgeneralization, such as citing abilities that the client is either overlooking or discounting. The therapist also instructs clients to monitor private monologues and to identify all patterns of thought that contribute to depression. The therapist then teaches clients to think through negative prevailing beliefs to understand how these beliefs prevent them from making more realistic and positive assumptions.

Although developed independently of Ellis's rational-emotive method, Beck's analyses are similar to it in some ways. For example, Beck suggests that depressed people are likely to consider themselves totally inept and incompetent if they make a mistake (see Brown & Beck, 2002). This schema can be considered an extension of one of Ellis's irrational beliefs (i.e., the individual must be competent in all things in order to be worthwhile).

Beck also includes behavioural components in his treatment. When clients are severely depressed, he encourages them to do things, such as get out of bed in the morning or go for a walk. He gives his clients activity assignments to provide them with successful experiences and allow them to think well of themselves. But the overall emphasis is on cognitive restructuring, on persuading the person to think differently. If a change in behaviour will help achieve that goal, fine. However, behavioural change by itself is not expected to alleviate depression.

Over the past several decades, considerable research has been conducted on Beck's therapy, beginning with a widely cited study by Rush et al. (1977), which indicated that CT was more successful than tricyclic imipramine (Tofranil) in alleviating unipolar depression. The unusually low improvement rate found for the drug in this clinical trial suggests that these clients might have been poorly suited for pharmacotherapy and that this was therefore not a fair comparison. Nonetheless, the efficacy of Beck's therapy in this study and in a 12-month follow-up (Kovacs et al., 1981) encouraged many other researchers to conduct additional evaluations, which have confirmed its efficacy (see Dobson, 1989). In addition, research shows that Beck's therapy has a prophylactic effect in preventing subsequent bouts of depression (Hollon, DeRubeis, & Seligman, 1992). Recent research (Parrish et al., 2009) using a daily diary designed to evaluate depressed people's changes on daily stress-related variables during CT confirmed that CT has its intended effects: after six sessions, clients reported a reduction in daily sad affect, daily negative thoughts, and sad affect reactivity to daily stressors, as well as an increase in daily positive affect.

A meta-analysis by Hamilton and Dobson (2002), while confirming the efficacy of CT, identified a number of factors that contribute to less favourable outcomes. CT is less effective when used to treat people with high levels of dysfunctional attitudes and high pre-treatment severity scores on measures of depression; it is also less effective for those with more chronic forms of depression, an increased number of previous episodes, and earlier onsets. Further, Fournier et al. (2008) determined that a comorbid personality disorder predicts a poor response to 16 weeks of CT (44%), relative to an antidepressant (paroxetine) group (66%), in people diagnosed with moderate to severe depression; however, sustained response rates over a 12-month follow-up were virtually identical in the prior CT and a continuation medication group (38%). People withdrawn from medication showed a very low sustained response rate (6%). In a recent RCT, Bagby and colleagues (2008) sought to determine if client personality characteristics predict response to cognitive-behavioural therapy (CBT) or pharmacotherapy. Depressed clients with higher scores on neuroticism were more responsive to pharmacotherapy, perhaps because pharmacotherapy "may directly target neural systems involved in dysregulated emotions, circumventing the cognitive requirements for response to CBT" (Bagby et al., 2008, p. 367). The authors suggested that these individuals might benefit from treatment sequencing: initial treatment with pharmacotherapy followed by CBT when they are better able to use CBT strategies.

Bell and D'Zurilla (2009) conducted a meta-analysis of problem-solving therapy for depression, a CBT intervention that focuses on training in adaptive problem-solving attitudes and skills (see D'Zurilla & Nezu, 2010). Problem-solving therapy was deemed as effective as other psychosocial interventions and pharmacotherapy and significantly more effective than support/attention control groups and no treatment.

MINDFULNESS-BASED COGNITIVE THERAPY A treatment known as mindfulness-based cognitive therapy (MBCT) has been developed specifically to prevent relapse among clinically depressed people. MBCT is an extension of Kabat-Zinn's stress-reduction program that teaches people how to combat stress through mindful meditation. In contrast, the MBCT approach developed by Zindel Segal from Toronto, John Teasdale from England, and Mark Williams from Wales combines relaxation and related techniques designed to increase awareness of changes in the body and the mind with standard cognitive intervention techniques (see Segal, Williams, & Teasdale, 2002). The key component is developing meta-cognitive awareness (i.e., a sense of how cognitive sets are related to emotional feelings and vice versa). Initial research indicates that MBCT has a great deal of promise. Rates of relapse are substantially reduced among clients who have had at least three previous episodes of depression (Teasdale et al., 2000), and reduced relapse following either MBCT or CT is associated with the increased presence of meta-cognitive sets (Teasdale et al., 2002). Further, MBCT appears to be successful in reducing current symptoms in people suffering from chronic-recurrent depression with a history of suicidal ideation (Barnhofer et al., 2009).

Williams, Teasdale, Segal, and Soulsby (2000) also showed that MBCT reduces the overgenerality of autobiographic memory effect. When asked to recall specific past events in their lives, depressed people, relative to non-depressed people, tend to provide broad, categorical memories lacking in specificity (e.g., "My father was cruel") rather than specific, detailed events. This overgenerality effect is believed to reflect the negative schema described by Beck. Depressed people who receive MBCT show reduced overgenerality; they have learned new encoding and retrieval skills that involve processing their past and current experiences in non-judgemental ways.

Teasdale, Segal, and Williams (2003) observed that mindfulness-based interventions are multi-faceted. Potentially helpful aspects of training include exposure to negative moods and arousal states, cognitive change, self-management, relaxation, and acceptance of unwanted experiences. Because MBCT involves general principles that could apply broadly, MBCT interventions are seen as relevant for other disorders, such as substance abuse (Breslin, Zack, & McMain, 2002). However, the developers caution that it is important that therapists using this approach adhere closely to the principles of MBCT and, to assist them, they have developed the MBCT Adherence Scale (Segal, Teasdale, Williams, & Gemar, 2002). This scale involves an evaluation of such issues as the extent to which the therapist used systematic awareness exercises, conveyed the link between thinking and feeling, and facilitated relating to one's experiences from a standpoint of acceptance, not rejection or avoidance.

We turn now to an examination of a widely cited study that compares Beck's therapy with interpersonal therapy and with an antidepressant drug.

The NIMH Treatment of Depression Collaborative Research Program In 1977, the National Institute of Mental Health (NIMH) undertook a large three-site study of Beck's CT, comparing it with IPT and pharmacotherapy (Elkin et al., 1985). Called the Treatment of Depression Collaborative Research Program (TDCRP), this was the first multi-site coordinated study initiated by the NIMH in the

Zindel Segal from Toronto's Centre for Addiction and Mental Health, Clarke Division, is one of the developers of Mindfulness-Based Cognitive Therapy. Photo courtesy of Zindel Segal.

field of psychotherapy. It is a widely cited and controversial study that illustrates a number of issues in therapy research.

The pharmacological therapy imipramine (Tofranil), a well-tested tricyclic drug widely regarded at the time as a standard therapy for depression, was used as a reference treatment against which to evaluate the two psychotherapies, the second and third treatments. Dosages were adjusted according to predetermined guidelines that were flexible enough to allow the psychiatrist to apply some clinical judgement in the context of clinical management (support and advice); that is, in a warm, supportive atmosphere (Fawcett et al., 1987). Elkin et al. (1985) regarded this almost as a drug-plus-supportive-therapy condition—"supportive" referring to the nature of the doctor-client relationship.

A fourth and final "treatment" involved a placebo-clinical management group against which to judge the efficacy of imipramine. This treatment was also conceived of as a partial control for the two psychotherapies because of the presence of strong support and encouragement. In a double-blind design similar to that used in the imipramine condition, clients in this group received a placebo that they believed might be an effective antidepressant medication. They were also given direct advice when considered necessary. As placebo conditions go, this was a very strong one; it included much more psychological support and even intervention than do most placebo control groups in both the psychotherapy and the pharmacotherapy literatures. Clinical management was common to both this and the imipramine group.

All treatments lasted 16 weeks, with slight differences in numbers of sessions, depending on the treatment manuals. A wide range and large number of assessments were made at pre- and post-treatment of the 60 participants in each of the four conditions, as well as three times during treatment and again at 6-, 12-, and 18-month follow-ups. Measures included some that might provide answers to questions about processes of change. For example, do IPT clients learn to relate better to others during therapy, and if so, is this improvement correlated with clinical outcome? Do CT clients manifest less cognitive distortion during the later sessions than at the beginning of treatment, and if so, is this shift associated with better clinical outcome? Other assessment instruments tapped the perspectives of the client, the therapist, an independent clinical evaluator blind to treatment condition, and, whenever possible, a significant other from the client's life (e.g., a spouse). Three domains of change were assessed: depressive symptomatology, overall symptomatology and life functioning, and functioning related to particular treatment approaches (e.g., the Dysfunctional Attitudes Scale of Weissman and Beck 1978, to assess cognitive change).

Analyses of the data suggest variations among research sites, between those who completed treatment and the total sample (including dropouts), and among assessments with different perspectives (e.g., client vs. clinical-evaluator judgements). Some of the complex findings are summarized here

(Elkin et al., 1986, 1989, 1996; Imber et al., 1990; Shea et al., 1990, 1992).

- At termination, there were no significant differences in reduction of depression or improvement in overall functioning between CT and IPT or between either of them and imipramine plus clinical management. In general, the three active treatments achieved significant and equivalent degrees of success and were for the most part superior to the placebo group. The placebo-plus-clinical-management clients did show significant improvement, however.

- Imipramine was faster than the other treatments in reducing depressive symptoms during treatment. By the end of 16 weeks of therapy, however, the two psychotherapies had caught up with the drug.

- On some measures, the less severely depressed placebo clients were doing as well at termination as were the less depressed people in the three active treatment conditions.

- Severely depressed clients in the placebo condition did not fare as well as those in the three active treatments.

- There was some evidence that IPT was more effective than CT with the more severely depressed clients, most notably in terms of recovery rates.

- There was some evidence that particular treatments effected change in expected domains. For example, IPT clients showed more improvements in social functioning than imipramine or CT clients, and CT reduced certain types of dysfunctional attitudes more than the other treatments did.

- For IPT and pharmacotherapy, but not for CT, clients diagnosed with personality disorders (see Chapter 13) were more likely to have residual depressive symptoms after therapy than those without these diagnoses.

- At the 18-month follow-up, the active treatment conditions did not differ significantly, and of those clients across the four conditions who had markedly improved immediately after treatment, only between 20 and 30% remained completely without depression.

Further analyses have sought to identify various factors that may account for the different outcomes experienced by clients. The competency of the therapist is one variable examined by Brian Shaw and associates from the Hospital for Sick Children in Toronto (Shaw et al., 1999). They looked at the outcomes of CT and reported that clients had lower levels of depression if their therapists were rated as especially competent, particularly in terms of their ability to structure and organize the treatment approach. Other analyses have shown the importance of taking personality differences between participants into account. Clients who endorsed perfectionistic attitudes tended to experience less positive outcomes overall than other clients, and this held across all treatment modalities (Blatt, Quinlan, Pilkonis, & Shea, 1995; Blatt & Zuroff, 2002).

One reason why perfectionists had less successful outcomes is that they were characterized by a poorer working alliance and a less positive relationship with their therapist throughout treatment (see Shahar, Blatt, Zuroff, & Pilkonis, 2003; Zuroff et al., 2000). Blatt et al. (1995) suggested that these individuals may be more difficult to treat because they suffer from emotional and interpersonal isolation.

Falconnier and Elkin (2008) reported that 86% of the sample identified problems regarding finances, work, or unemployment (economic stress) as a significant factor in their depression. However, there was considerable variability in the way in which therapists approached or avoided this material. Higher therapist approach was associated with better outcomes across treatment modalities. It was concluded there is a need to pay more attention to economic stress issues in both IBT and CBT because "patients' interpersonal relationships and cognitive perceptions do not operate separately from the economic stressors in their lives" (Falconnier & Elkin, 2008, p. 45).

Much remains to be learned about how to effect even short-term improvement in depressed clients. Even less is known about how to maintain any benefits that are evident right after treatment ends. Certainly, there is little in the many findings from this milestone study of comparative outcome that can gladden the hearts of proponents of any of the interventions. Indeed, a comparative analysis of existing studies by a research team based in Montreal found that rates of remission were virtually identical (46.4% vs. 46.3%, respectively) for clients receiving medication and clients receiving psychotherapy (Cascalenda, Perry, & Looper, 2002). However, either form of treatment was superior to no treatment. Nonetheless, proponents of cognitive therapy (e.g., DeRubeis et al., 2010) have argued that results for the TDCRP, and other large, multi-site, placebo-controlled comparisons of the relative efficacy of CT and antidepressant medications in the treatment of severely depressed people (e.g., DeRubeis et al., 2005), tend to be influenced by CT therapist experience: better outcomes in CT tend to be obtained at sites with more experienced therapists. Recall, however, that Parker et al. (2008) concluded (see Focus on Discovery 5.1), using stringent criteria, that CT is not superior to antidepressant medication.

SOCIAL SKILLS TRAINING Since a key feature of depression is a lack of satisfying experiences with other people, behavioural treatments have focused on helping clients improve social interactions. Although there are cognitive components in these approaches—for example, encouraging the depressed client not to evaluate performance too harshly—evidence supports the effectiveness of a focus on enhancing overt social behaviours by such techniques as assertion and social skills training (e.g., Lewinsohn & Gotlib, 1995). A large-scale collaborative study compared this social skills approach with CT and found them to be equally effective, both in terms of alleviating depression and preventing relapses (Gortner, Gollan, Dobson, & Jacobson, 1998).

PSYCHOLOGICAL TREATMENT OF BIPOLAR DISORDER
Psychological therapies also show promise in dealing with many of the interpersonal, cognitive, and emotional problems of bipolar clients. If a client in a manic phase commits an indiscretion such as having an extramarital affair or spending everything in the family bank account, the consequences of this behaviour last much longer than improvements in mood brought about by lithium. Stress is likely to be higher as a result, and stress can trigger a subsequent mood swing. A cognitive-behavioural intervention targeted at the thoughts and interpersonal behaviours that go awry during wide mood swings appears to be effective (Basco & Rush, 1996).

One problem in getting bipolar clients to take their medication regularly is that they often lack insight into the self-destructive nature of their behaviour. A small but significant number of empirical studies show that careful education about bipolar disorder and its treatment can improve adherence to medication, which is helpful in reducing the mood swings of this disorder, thereby bringing more stability into the client's life (e.g., Craighead et al., 1998). Obviously, an effective drug is beneficial only to the extent that it is taken as prescribed. It is also important to recognize that, in addition to improving adherence to a drug regimen, education about the illness is likely to increase social support from family and friends (Craighead et al., 1998).

Bipolar people relapse more quickly if they return from hospital to family settings characterized by high levels of hostility and overinvolvement (called "expressed emotion") than if they return to a less-charged emotional climate in the home (Miklowitz et al., 1996). Research indicates the effectiveness of educating the family about the disorder, the desirability of working to reduce stress at home, and the need to continue medication to help maintain improvements of the discharged bipolar client (Glick et al., 1991).

There is currently considerable controversy about the usefulness of psychotherapy for severe and recurrent bipolar disorders. Scott et al. (2006) conducted the largest multicentre pragmatic randomized controlled trial (RCT) of psychological therapy for bipolar disorders. They compared the effectiveness of "treatment as usual" with an additional 22 sessions of CT. It was concluded that CT was effective only for a minority of clients with fewer than 12 previous episodes. However, in an invited commentary, Dominic Lam (2006) was critical of the study design, which made interpretation of the results difficult, and contrasted the study with four other major pragmatic RCTs of structured psychological interventions (including two on which he was senior author) that reported beneficial results.

Lam outlined the common features in psychological treatments for relapse prevention in bipolar disorders, including the following:

• psychoeducation
• promotion of medication adherence
• promotion of regular daily routines and sleep

- monitoring of mood
- detection of early warnings and relapse prevention strategies
- general coping strategies and problem-solving techniques

Lam (2006) concluded on the weight of evidence that structured psychological interventions are beneficial in relapse prevention. More recently, Beynon and her colleagues (2008) conducted a review and meta-analysis of psychosocial interventions and concluded that CBT, group psychoeducation, and possibly family therapy may be beneficial as adjuncts to pharmacological maintenance treatment for the prevention of relapse in bipolar disorder.

Determining the best therapy for each individual can be a challenge. For instance, a woman who is disheartened because of the way she is treated by men might be better advised by a feminist therapist, who will encourage her to resist continued subjugation by an overbearing spouse, than by an equally well-intentioned therapist, who might try to teach her that the treatment she receives from her husband or supervisor is not all that bad. A central question in this context is whether the therapist should help the client alter his or her life situation. Indeed, the very fact that a person is depressed may indicate that he or she is ready for a change in social and personal relations with others.

BIOLOGICAL THERAPIES

"The quest for the magic bullet for depression may be a wild goose chase."

—Moncrieff, 2007a, p. 97

"Although we agree that there is no magic bullet to cure depression, antidepressants play a significant role in its treatment, and to suggest they have no effect is tantamount to throwing the baby out with the bathwater."

—Ravindran and Kennedy, 2007b, p. 102

There are a variety of biological therapies for depression and mania. The two most common are electroconvulsive shock and various drugs.

ELECTROCONVULSIVE THERAPY Perhaps the most dramatic, and controversial, treatment for severe depression is **electroconvulsive therapy (ECT)**. ECT was introduced in the early twentieth century by two Italian physicians, Cerletti and Bini. More rudimentary treatment methods were used historically prior to the advent of ECT; for instance, in the sixteenth century, electric catfish were used to induce shock in people in an attempt to expel devils (see Endler & Persad, 1988).

Previously, Cerletti was interested in epilepsy and sought a means to induce seizures. The solution became apparent to him during a visit to a slaughterhouse, where he saw seizures induced in animals by electric shocks administered to the head. Shortly thereafter, he found that by applying electric shocks to the sides of the human head, he could produce full epileptic seizures. Then, in Rome in 1938, he used the technique on a person with schizophrenia. In the decades that followed, ECT was administered to people with both schizophrenia and severe depression, usually in hospital settings. Its use is restricted today to profoundly depressed individuals. Canadian research indicates that ECT is more likely to be administered to people with longer hospital stays and a greater number of previous admissions (Malla, 1988). Both factors are associated with more severe and persistent forms of depression.

ECT is being used with increased frequency in Canada and elsewhere. Why? One reason is that when it works, it is faster than antidepressants and psychotherapy. The increased use of ECT was brought to the attention of the public thanks to an independent review conducted in British Columbia. A psychiatrist had expressed concern that the use of ECT had increased dramatically at the Riverview Hospital in Coquitlam, B.C. Indeed, it was determined that ECT use had more than doubled between 1996 and 1999 as a way of treating depression in people aged 65 or older. The review panel concluded that the use of ECT at the hospital was appropriate.

ECT entails the deliberate induction of a seizure and momentary unconsciousness by passing a current between 70 and 130 volts through the client's brain. Electrodes were formerly placed on each side of the forehead, allowing the current to pass through both hemispheres, a method known as **bilateral ECT**. Today, **unilateral ECT**, in which the current passes through the non-dominant (right) cerebral hemisphere only (e.g., Abrams, Swartz, & Vedak, 1991), is more commonly used. In the past, the person was usually awake when the current triggered the seizure and the electric shock often created frightening contortions of the body, sometimes even causing bone fractures. Now the client is given a short-acting anaesthetic, then an injection of a strong muscle relaxant, before the current is applied. The convulsive spasms of the body muscles are barely perceptible to onlookers, and the client awakens a few minutes later remembering nothing about the treatment. The mechanism through which ECT works is unknown. It reduces metabolic activity and blood circulation to the brain and may thus inhibit aberrant brain activity.

Inducing a seizure is still a drastic procedure. Why should anyone agree to undergo such radical therapy? How could a parent or a spouse consent to such treatment for a person judged legally incapable of giving consent? The answer is simple. Although we don't know why, ECT may be the optimal treatment for extremely severe depression. Most professionals acknowledge the risks involved: confusion and memory loss that can be prolonged. However, unilateral ECT to the non-dominant hemisphere erases fewer memories than does bilateral ECT, and no detectable changes in brain structure result (Devanand et al., 1994). Clinicians typically resort to ECT only when the depression is unremitting and after less-drastic treatments have been tried and found wanting. In considering any treatment that has negative side effects,

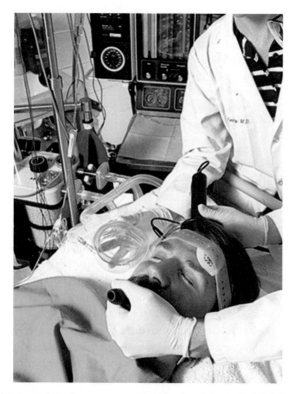

ECT was first used on a person with schizophrenia in 1938. Will & Deni McIntyre/Photo Researchers, Inc.

Ernest Hemingway, famous author and former reporter for the *Toronto Daily Star*, shot himself in 1961. He attributed the fatal step he would take, in part, to receiving more than 20 sessions of ECT. He questioned: "What is the sense of ruining my head and erasing my memory, which is my capital, and putting me out of business? It was a brilliant cure, but we lost the patient." See Bohuslawsky, 2001. CP Archive PREMIUM—Ernest Hemingway.

the person making the decision must be aware of the consequences of not providing any treatment at all. Given that suicide is a real possibility, the use of ECT, at least after other treatments have failed, is regarded by many as defensible and responsible.

One issue that has emerged is the high relapse rate of people treated with ECT. Sackeim et al. (2001) used a sophisticated methodological approach and found that without active follow-up treatment, virtually all clients in remission relapsed within six months of no longer receiving ECT. However, the relapse rate was only 39% for those clients who received follow-up nortriptyline-lithium treatment. A multi-site study (Kellner et al., 2006) assessed ECT as a strategy for relapse prevention in MDD. It evaluated the comparative efficacy of continuation ECT and the combination of lithium carbonate plus nortriptyline hydrochloride. Both continuation ECT and pharmacotherapy were superior (after six months) to a placebo control; however, more than half the people in the continuation groups experienced relapse or dropped out of the study.

Many activist groups have expressed concerns about the use of ECT, and these protests continue. The groups maintain that the procedure is inhumane, involves considerable risk, and is not effective. In addition, there are published accounts by former clients who believe that ECT led to permanent damage. Wendy Funk of Cranbook, B.C., for example, wrote a book detailing her negative experiences and claimed that ECT wiped out her lifetime of memories (see Funk, 1998). Clearly, as with most treatments, there is variability in the outcomes

experienced, for other people feel that ECT saved their lives. Several public inquiries conducted throughout Canada led to conclusions that support the use of ECT (Endler & Persad, 1988). An Ontario report (Clark, 1985) concluded that ECT is effective but that safeguards must remain in place to protect the well-being of clients, including the right to informed consent. Full, informed consent is crucial, given that some people have indeed had negative experiences with ECT.

Norman Endler (see Canadian Contributions 9.2 was one of Canada's leading proponents of ECT. Why? Because Endler was twice treated successfully with ECT when he suffered from bipolar depression. He chronicled his experiences in his memoir *Holiday of Darkness* (Endler, 1982). Endler also examined ECT from a scientific perspective in a book entitled *Electroconvulsive Therapy: The Myths and the Realities* (see Endler & Persad, 1988).

Helen Mayberg and colleagues (2005) from the Rotman Research Institute in Toronto (2005) reported on preliminary success in a small number of people with a deep brain electrical stimulation procedure for treatment-resistant depression, a severely disabling disorder with no treatment options once ECT, medication, and psychotherapy have failed. The experimental treatment is based on the observation that the subgenual cingulate region (Brodmann area 25) is metabolically overactive in treatment-resistant depression. The researchers studied whether applying deep brain stimulation to modulate the region could reduce the elevated activity and produce clinical benefit. Chronic stimulation was associated with remission of symptoms in four of the six clients tested. PET imaging determined that antidepressive effects were associated with changes in limbic and cortical sites. Mayberg et al. (2005) concluded that "disrupting focal pathological activity in limbic-cortical circuits using electrical stimulation of the subgenual cingulate white matter can effectively reverse symptoms in otherwise treatment-resistant depression" (p. 651). Lozano, Mayberg, and colleagues (2008) subsequently reported on the results for the original six clients and an additional 14 clients with extended follow-up. One month after surgery, 35% of clients met criteria for a positive clinical response. Six months after surgery, 60% of clients were responders and the benefits were maintained at 12 months. This is a potentially exciting and important new direction for the control of treatment-resistant depression. Nonetheless, as noted by Lozano et al., "A careful double-blind appraisal is required before the procedure can be recommended for use on a wider scale" (p. 461).

Repetitive transcranial magnetic stimulation (rTMS) is another new development in the treatment of depression. This is a non-invasive method of brain stimulation using brief magnetic pulses to stimulate the brain. Magnetic pulses pass through the skull and produce an electric current in the underlying cortex. Preliminary studies suggest that rTMS elicits a therapeutic response in depressed people and people with chronic pain, and that it may be as effective as ECT (see Sampson, Rome, & Rummans, 2006). More recently, Lam and colleagues (2008) conducted a systematic review and meta-analysis of published RCTs of rTMS, compared with a "sham" control condition, in clients with treatment-resistant depression. Active rTMS was significantly superior to sham conditions in producing a clinical response; however, further studies are necessary due to the relatively low response and remission rates, short treatment durations, and lack of systematic follow-up. It is also critical that research determines the mechanisms of therapeutic efficacy of rTMS (Daskalakis, Levinson, & Fitzgerald, 2008). In a recent study with over 200 clients, Cohen, Boggio, and Fregni (2009) determined that the remission rate was only 22.6% six months after therapy. Young age and additional treatment sessions were associated with a longer duration of positive effects.

DRUG THERAPY

"There is a paradox: taking antidepressants makes people feel better, thereby reducing their interest in actually doing something about the things in their life that cause the unhappiness."

—Dr. Ronald Dworking, author of Artificial Unhappiness: The Dark Side of the New Happy Class, *as cited by Potter (2009, September 2)*

Drugs are the most commonly used treatments—biological or otherwise—for mood disorders. The use of antidepressants has increased exponentially. An analysis by Hemels, Koren, and Einarson (2002) of antidepressant use in Canada from 1981 to 2000 found that the number of prescriptions increased from 3.2 million to over 14 million in those 20 years. In the United States, more than $10 billion is spent on antidepressant prescriptions each year (Potter, 2009). However, antidepressants definitely do not work for everyone and side effects are sometimes serious (see Table 8.3). Moreover, it is difficult to identify personal characteristics that might predict treatment response. Response to drug treatment is not reliably predicted by age, sex, age at onset, symptom duration, or number of reoccurrences of the disorder. However, there is some evidence of a better response among people with higher levels of social support (see Bagby, Ryder, & Cristi, 2002).

SPECIFIC DRUG THERAPIES FOR DEPRESSION

"After riding on a wave of initial fanfare and optimistic proclamations about the potential superiority of new-generation medications, once in widespread use, some will be found to have disappointing results or will be accompanied by unforeseen dangers and, ultimately, will sink. Other new medications will be found to provide true benefits over previous agents."

—Elliot M. Goldner, 2008, p. 409

TABLE 8.3
DRUGS FOR TREATING MOOD DISORDERS

Category	Generic Name	Trade Name	Side Effects
Tricyclic antidepressants	imipramine, amitriptyline	Tofranil, Elavil	Heart attack, stroke, hypotension, blurred vision, anxiety, tiredness, dry mouth, constipation, gastric disorders, erectile failure, weight gain
MAO inhibitors	tranylcypromine	Parnate	Possibly fatal hypertension, dry mouth, dizziness, nausea, headaches
Selective serotonin reuptake inhibitors	fluoxetine	Prozac	Nervousness, fatigue, gastrointestinal complaints, dizziness, headaches, insomnia
Lithium	lithium	None	Tremors, gastric distress, lack of coordination, dizziness, cardiac arrhythmia, blurred vision, fatigue, death

In our earlier discussion of biological research on depression, we mentioned three major categories of antidepressant drugs:

1. monoamine oxidase (MAO) inhibitors, such as tranylcypromine (Parnate)
2. tricyclics, such as imipramine (Tofranil) and amitriptyline (Elavil)
3. selective serotonin reuptake inhibitors (SSRIs), such as fluoxetine (Prozac) and sertraline (Zoloft)

Since the MAO inhibitors have by far the most serious side effects, the other two classes of drugs are more widely used. These medications were established as effective in a number of double-blind studies, with improvement rates of 50 to 70% reported among clients who complete treatment (e.g., Nemeroff & Schatzberg, 1998). Although early indications were that the SSRIs were clinically more effective than either tricyclics or MAO inhibitors, it now seems that the clinical effectiveness of all three types of drugs is quite similar, although the SSRIs do have the advantage of producing fewer side effects (Enserink, 1999).

A recent study (Harmer et al., 2009) suggests a possible mechanism of action of new-generation antidepressants. Harmer and colleagues examined the effects of a single dose of the norepinephrine reuptake inhibitor reboxetine on emotional processing in depressed and matched "healthy" comparison subjects. Three hours after dosing, participants were administered various emotional processing tasks that reveal laboratory correlates of the negative information biases that characterize depression (e.g., diminished perception of facial expressions of happiness). The results suggested that antidepressants "modulate" or normalize negative biases in emotional processing in depressed people very early in treatment and before changes are seen in mood. It was also noted that this mechanism is compatible with cognitive theories. Much additional research is needed to determine if improved information processing is actually a major pathway for antidepressant activity.

The CCHS 1.2 offered the first opportunity to characterize Canadian psychotropic medication use on a national level within the assessed diagnostic groups. Beck et al. (2005) reported that SSRIs were the most commonly used antidepressants for those who had a major depressive episode in the past year (17.8%). Among people 15 to 19 years old with past-year depression, antidepressant use (primarily SSRIs) was 11.7%. Unfortunately, a detailed assessment of treatment quality was not possible. The researchers predicted that antidepressant use among younger participants will decline in future in view of the lack of evidence for antidepressant efficacy (see the next page).

As noted in Chapter 1, inappropriate antidepressant prescription is relatively common. Sewitch et al. (2007) conducted a population-based study of people in Quebec diagnosed with a new episode of major depression by primary care physicians and psychiatrists to determine the associations between guideline-concordant pharmacotherapy and the use of health services in the following year. Concordance was defined as the receipt of recommended medication, starting dosage, and treatment duration as defined by the Canadian Network for Mood and Anxiety Treatment guidelines. The significant results included:

- An antidepressant was dispensed to 75% of eligible patients.
- 71% received a recommended first-line medication, 63% received a recommended starting dosage, and 15% received a recommended duration.
- According to the three criteria, only 8% were treated appropriately (21% received benzodiazepines rather than antidepressants) and most patients were undertreated.
- Although 18% of the patients were hospitalized, receipt of first-line medication was related to a decreased likelihood of hospitalization.
- Continuity of care (i.e., same diagnosing and prescribing physician) was associated with more visits to prescribing physicians, fewer visits to other physicians, and fewer costly visits (emergency care and hospitalization).

Although there are limitations to the study, the authors concluded that, "despite using both health services and medication, many treated patients could have been at risk for relapse and chronic depression" (Sewitch et al., 2007, p. 197).

Antidepressant medication often is used in combination with some kind of psychotherapy. If, for example, a person's depression is (partly) caused by a lack of personal satisfaction because of social skills problems, it is probably essential for the drug treatment to be supplemented by attention to those behavioural deficits. A review by Segal, Vincent, and Levitt (2002) led to the conclusion that combination therapy involving medication and CT works better than either in isolation, but this conclusion is qualified by the relatively small number of participants in existing studies. Thus, a conclusive answer is not available.

Even if a chemical agent manages to alleviate a bout of depression only temporarily, that benefit in itself should not be underestimated, given the potential for suicide and given the extreme anguish and suffering borne by the individual and, usually, his or her family. The judicious use of a drug may make unnecessary an avenue of intervention and control that many regard as very much a last resort—namely, being placed in a tertiary care psychiatric hospital (see Canadian Perspectives 1.2). Although some studies suggest that antidepressants should always be used for severe depression, others indicate that CT or IPT is just as effective (DeRubeis et al., 1999), with the added benefit that, at the end of treatment, there are no drug-produced side effects or relapse as there is when medication is withdrawn (Persons et al., 1996). As pointed out in Focus on Discovery 5.1, it is not clear whether CT is superior in efficacy to antidepressant therapy or vice versa. However, a study of more than 15,000 people in Finland hospitalized because of a suicide attempt (Tiihonen et al., 2006) concluded that the current use of any antidepressant was associated with a markedly increased risk of attempted suicide (but also with a decreased risk of completed suicide).

As indicated by the two quotes at the outset of this Biological Therapies section, there is considerable controversy over the efficacy of antidepressants. In a recent "In Debate" in the *Canadian Journal of Psychiatry*, Moncrieff (2007a, b) argued that not only are antidepressants not as effective as claimed, they are not effective at all! She claimed that the effects seen in randomly controlled trials can be accounted for by "nonspecific pharmacologic and psychological actions" (Moncrieff, 2007a, p. 96). In rebuttal, Ravindran and Kennedy (2007a) argued that "antidepressant medications are the most available first-line treatments for moderate-to-severe major depressive episodes" (p. 98).

We introduced this controversy in Chapter 5 in the context of our discussion of a controversial meta-analysis of data submitted to the U.S. Food and Drug Administration on published and unpublished placebo-controlled clinical trials of four new-generation antidepressants (see Kirsch et al., 2008). Drug-placebo differences in efficacy increased as a function of initial depression severity but were relatively small even for severely depressed people. Kirsch et al. (2008) concluded that, "The relationship between initial severity and antidepressant efficacy is attributable to decreased responsiveness to placebo among very severely depressed patients, rather than to increased responsiveness to medication" (p. 1). Bridge et al. (2008) reached a similar conclusion with respect to a meta-analysis of trials involving children and adolescents. We also examined this issue further in Focus on Discovery 5.2 on the possible selective publication of antidepressant trials. Turner et al. (2008) concluded that there is apparent evidence of a "file drawer effect"—a bias in favour of publishing only those studies that have positive effects, rather than studies finding negative effects that would be relegated to a file drawer. Further, starting in 2003, regulatory bodies worldwide issued warnings about prescribing antidepressants to children and adolescents (see Chapter 15).

Will recent research lead to definitive conclusions and consensus among stakeholders about the efficacy and/or effectiveness and safety of antidepressants? Probably not, especially since pharmaceutical companies will continue to introduce and market new-generation antidepressants.

DRUG THERAPY FOR BIPOLAR DISORDER People with the mood swings of bipolar disorder are often helped by carefully monitored dosages of the element lithium, taken in a salt form, **lithium carbonate** (the first "mood stabilizer"). Up to 80% of bipolar individuals experience at least some benefit from taking this drug (Prien & Potter, 1993). Lithium is effective for bipolar clients when they are depressed as well as when they are manic, and it is much more effective

for bipolar clients than for unipolar clients—another bit of evidence that these two mood disorders are different from each other. Because the effects of lithium occur gradually, therapy typically begins with both lithium and an antipsychotic, such as Haldol, which has an immediate calming effect. Several hypotheses concerning how lithium works are being pursued (recall our earlier discussion of the effects of lithium on G-proteins). Conclusive evidence is not yet available, but it is interesting to note that a research team led by Paul Grof in Ottawa has established that responsiveness or non-responsiveness to lithium treatment seems to be an inherited family trait (e.g., Grof et al., 2002). Offspring of lithium–non-responsive individuals also experience chronic mood disorders and poor premorbid functioning compared with the offspring of lithium-responsive clients.

Because of possibly serious, even fatal, side effects, lithium has to be prescribed and used very carefully. Although it has great value in the elimination of a manic episode and forestalling future episodes if it is taken regularly, discontinuation of lithium actually increases the risk of recurrence (Suppes et al., 1991). Thus, it is recommended that lithium be used continuously. Unfortunately, many clients discontinue treatment after release from the hospital (Maj et al., 1998).

Two drugs originally used to control seizures may help clients with bipolar disorder. Carbamazepine (Tegretol) and divalproex sodium (Depakote) are both effective treatments and are tolerated by some clients who are unable to withstand lithium's side effects (Small et al., 1991). However, neither has been established as preventing future episodes if taken regularly.

Although lithium is the treatment of choice for bipolar disorder (Keck & McElroy, 1998), the psychological aspects of the disorder must be considered, if only to encourage the person to continue taking the medication (Goodwin & Jamison, 1990). A friend of one of the authors put it this way (paraphrased): "Lithium cuts out the highs as well as the lows.

Robert Munsch, well-known author of children's books, experienced depression for many years and attributes his recovery to taking Prozac. Photo courtesy Robert Munsch.

I don't miss the lows, but I have to admit that there were some aspects of the highs that I do miss. It took me a while to accept that I had to give up those highs. Wanting to keep my job and my marriage helped!" A drug alone does not address this kind of concern.

TREATMENT FOR SAD Therapy for winter depressions typically involves exposing clients to bright, white light. According to the Canadian Consensus Guidelines, exposure to bright, white light (known as **phototherapy**) is a highly effective treatment for SAD (Lam & Levitt, 1999). Lam and his co-workers at the University of British Columbia have shown that phototherapy does indeed alleviate SAD and the associated symptoms of depression, including suicidal tendencies (Lam et al., 2000). Research indicates that people with SAD and those with subsyndromal SAD have comparable recovery rates, and longer light exposure is associated with better outcomes (Levitt, Lam, & Levitan, 2002).

PREVENTING THE ONSET OF DEPRESSIVE DISORDERS

Is prevention of new cases of depressive disorders possible? Relatively few studies have focused on this possibility. Most prevention studies measured change in protective factors, including social, cognitive, or problem-solving skills, or outcomes such as severity of symptoms. However, in recent years researchers have examined whether prevention-focused programs can actually reduce the incidence of cases of depression as defined by diagnostic criteria. In a recent meta-analytic review of psychological interventions, Cuijpers et al. (2008) identified 19 RCTs in which the incidence of depressive disorders in an experimental group could be compared with that of a control group. Their analyses revealed an average reduction of 22% in the incidence of depressive disorders. The findings further suggested that prevention based on IPT might be more effective than prevention based on CBT.

Collins and Dozois (2008) adopted a different approach. They examined empirically supported prevention programs in an effort to identify "active" components that facilitate stronger outcomes. They concluded that targeted, multi-component programs with at-risk children (see Chapter 15) yielded promising results; however, which elements have the greatest impact was unclear. Nonetheless, important mechanisms of change possibly included cognitive skills, interpersonal approaches, and inclusion of parent treatment components. Clearly, additional outcome and dismantling studies are needed.

SUICIDE

"'I just looked out over the water and it was beautiful. I felt that this was the right time and place to kill myself. The last thing I saw leave the bridge was my hands. It was at that time that I realized what a stupid thing I was doing. And there was

nothing I could do but fall. The next thing I knew I was in the water hoping that someone would save me, saying, "Please God save me, somebody save me." It was incredible how quickly I had decided that I wanted to live once I realized everything that I was going to lose, my wife, my daughter, the rest of my family.'

He is currently in his thirtieth year of marriage. He is a high school teacher and part-time coach. His daughter is an elementary school teacher."

—From Blaustein and Fleming, Suicide from the Golden Gate Bridge, *2009, pp. 1115–1116*

The man in this case was one survivor. Tragically, many die. Suicide was the ninth leading cause of death in Canada in 2005, when there were 3,743 suicides, and the second cause of death (after accidents) in both males and females aged 15 to 24 years (Statistics Canada, 2009).

Suicide was not condemned in Western thought until the fourth century, when Saint Augustine proclaimed it a crime because it violated the Sixth Commandment, "Thou shalt not kill." Saint Thomas Aquinas elaborated on this view in the thirteenth century, declaring suicide a mortal sin because it usurped God's power over life and death. Thus, although neither the Old Testament nor the New Testament explicitly forbids suicide, the Western world came to regard it as a crime and a sin. The irony is that the Christian injunctions against suicide, deriving from a profound respect for life, contributed to persecution of those who attempted to or actually did take their own lives. As late as 1823, anyone in London, England, who committed suicide was buried with a stake pounded through the heart, and not until 1961 did suicide cease to be a criminal offence in the United Kingdom. Suicide ceased being a criminal offence in Canada in 1972.

Typically, females have higher rates of suicidal attempts but lower rates of suicide mortality than males, a phenomenon called the gender paradox of suicidal behaviour that is pronounced in industrialized, English-speaking countries such as Canada (see Canetto, 2008 for review). However, it appears to be a dominant rather than universal pattern, suggesting the importance of cultural perspectives. For example, in some societies (e.g., China and India) suicide is considered to be an act of the powerless and is most common in young women (Canetto, 2008).

Suicide is discussed in this chapter because many depressed persons and persons with bipolar disorder have suicidal thoughts and sometimes make attempts to take their own lives. A significant number of people who are not depressed, however, also make suicidal attempts, some with success (see section on Suicide and Psychological Disorders).

Before proceeding, it is important to distinguish between suicide ideation, suicide attempts, suicide gestures, and suicide:

• Suicidal ideation refers to thoughts and intentions of killing oneself. It is often associated with a sense of hopelessness, helplessness, and despair. Of course, many people may have such thoughts and not report them or they may be unwilling to disclose them.

- Suicide attempts involve self-injury behaviours intended to cause death but that do not lead to death. Some attempts may not be reported because they do not result in hospitalization or medical attention. Suicide attempters may not appear in suicide attempt data even when they result in medical attention because the attempters are identified by the medical problem only (e.g., lacerations).
- Suicide gestures involve self-injury in which there is no intent to die. Rather, there is an intent to give the appearance of an attempt in order to communicate with others.
- Suicide involves behaviours intended to cause death and death actually occurs.

Borges et al. (2006) conducted analyses of the NCS-R data set to develop a risk index for 12-month suicide attempts among suicide ideators. Twelve-month prevalence estimates of suicide ideation, plans, and attempts were 2.6, 0.7,

and 0.4%, respectively. They determined that ideators with a plan are more likely to make an attempt (31.9%) than those without a plan (9.6%); however, 43% of attempts were unplanned. A history of prior attempts is the strongest correlate of 12-month attempts. In analyses of NCS data, Nock and Kessler (2006) differentiated suicide attempters from suicide gesturers. Suicide attempters had the following characteristics: male gender; fewer years of education; residence in the southern and western United States; psychiatric diagnoses, including depressive, impulsive, and aggressive symptoms; comorbidity; and a history of multiple physical and sexual assaults. Cox, Enns, and Clara (2004) also examined psychological dimensions associated with suicidal ideation and attempts in the NCS. After controlling for socio-demographic and psychiatric variables, indices of hopelessness and self-criticism were robust predictors of suicide attempts.

Some epidemiological findings and facts about suicide in Canada are listed in Canadian Perspectives 8.4.

CANADIAN PERSPECTIVES 8.4
SUICIDE IN CANADA

"Should we be turning a blind eye to this carnage so as not to offend sensibilities? Or should we be shining a light on suicide deaths—most of them preventable—to highlight the underlying cause, which is often untreated mental illness?"

—André Picard, Globe Life, September 18, 2009

Information about suicidality in Canada comes from the CCHS, Cycle 1.2 (Statistics Canada, 2003), other government agencies (see Government of Canada, 2006), and from various recent research studies conducted in Canada. Most of the relevant research has been conducted since 1998. Note that the CCHS is Canada's first *national* study of suicidality. Why are the "facts" that are presented here important? The findings provide detailed, recent information about the epidemiology of suicidality in Canada, reinforce the importance of the determination of suicide risk, and need to be considered in the planning of mental health services and suicide prevention. Selected findings include:

- 13.4% of Canadians aged 15 years and over reported that they had thought seriously about committing suicide during their lifetime (14.4% of women and 12.3% of men).
  - A greater percentage of young women than young men (15 to 24 years) reported having had suicidal thoughts.
  - The proportion of women who reported suicidal thoughts decreased with age. The percentage among men peaked at 25 to 44 years.
  - On average, 3.6% of adults thought about suicide in the past year.

- Almost one half of young suicide ideators were without both major depression and a mental health service contact in the previous year.
- 3.1% of adults reported that they had attempted suicide in their lifetime.
  - Twice as many women as men attempted suicide (4.2% of women; 2.0% of men).
  - Although attempts decreased with age among women, they were relatively constant among men.
- 0.6% reported engaging in a suicidal act in the preceding 12 months.
  - Female gender, being separated or divorced, being unemployed, experiencing a chronic physical health condition, and experiencing a major depressive episode were associated with a suicidal act.
- In 2002–03, hospitalization rates for attempted suicide were higher among women in all age groups (up to age 70).
  - Hospitalizations among women peaked in the 15–19 age range (more than 200 per 100,000 population).
  - Among 15- to 19-year-olds, the hospitalization rate for young women was 2.5 times the rate for young men.
  - Between the ages 10 and 14, hospitalizations among females were 5 times those reported among males.
- In 2003, overall mortality rates due to suicide among men were approximately 4 times higher than among women (18.5 vs. 5.4 per 100,000). Figure 8.6 shows that this holds true in all age groups.
  - The overall mortality rate due to suicide decreased only slightly between 1990 and 2003.

FIGURE 8.6 Mortality rates due to suicide per 100,000, by age and sex, Canada, 2003.
Source: Centre for Chronic Disease Prevention and Control, Public Health Agency of Canada, using data from the Mortality File, Statistics Canada

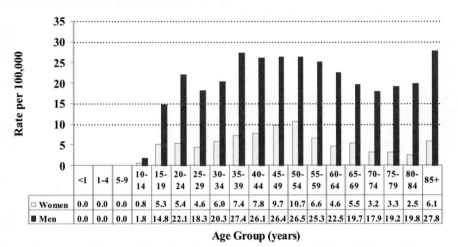

	<1	1-4	5-9	10-14	15-19	20-24	25-29	30-34	35-39	40-44	45-49	50-54	55-59	60-64	65-69	70-74	75-79	80-84	85+
□ Women	0.0	0.0	0.0	0.8	5.3	5.4	4.6	6.0	7.4	7.8	9.7	10.7	6.6	4.6	5.5	3.2	3.3	2.5	6.1
■ Men	0.0	0.0	0.0	1.8	14.8	22.1	18.3	20.3	27.4	26.1	26.4	26.5	25.3	22.5	19.7	17.9	19.2	19.8	27.8

Age Group (years)

- Men often commit suicide through fatal acts, such as by the use of firearms (25%) or hanging (40%); women are more likely to use non-fatal methods, such as an overdose of pills.
- Suicidal men are less likely to seek help and discuss their problems.
- 81% of people committing suicide in the Montreal subway system had expressed a prior suicide intent.
- The highest rates of suicide are found in the Northwest Territories, Alberta, and Quebec, and the lowest rates are found typically in Newfoundland and Labrador.
- A 2008 Manitoba study examined alcohol-related factors that influenced suicide mortality rates during 1976 to 1997.
  - Alcohol consumption was strongly related to suicide.
  - Unemployment increased suicide risk.
  - Alcoholics Anonymous membership and alcohol abuse treatment may reduce suicide risk.
- A 2008 Quebec study prospectively followed a French-Canadian, school-based cohort from nursery school until adulthood and examined correlates and moderators of suicide attempts in adults who reported childhood physical or sexual abuse.
  - Disruptive disorders, conduct problems, and childhood aggression were positively associated with suicide attempts. Individuals abused by their immediate family (a moderator) were at highest risk.
- From 1995 to 2000, 422 youths aged 15 and under committed suicide in Quebec.
  - More than a third had received services from youth centres, the majority of whom was boys (3.8 boys for 1 girl). Hanging was the most frequent means (73.6%).

- The suicide group had more indicators of major depression, substance abuse, disruptive behaviours, and more adverse events.
- The first complete cost-of-suicide analysis performed in Canada in 1996, estimated the economic impact of suicide deaths that occurred in New Brunswick.
  - For the 94 deaths reported that year, direct costs for health care services, autopsies, funerals, and police investigations were over half a million dollars. Indirect costs, which estimate the value of lost productivity through premature deaths, were almost $80 million. Although the real impact is the tragic loss of human life, the total dollar cost estimate for each suicide was about $850,000.
- A 2008 study employed psychological autopsy methods to collect information on consecutive suicides over 14 months in New Brunswick.
  - More than two thirds of the 102 individuals suffered from a depressive and/or alcohol abuse or dependence disorder.
  - More than one half had contacted mental health services in the preceding year, but less than 5% had contact with addiction services.
  - There is a need for coordination and integration of mental health and addiction services.
- Another 2008 study examined suicide epidemiology in Newfoundland and Labrador from 1997 to 2001.
  - The overall suicide rate was 9.5/100,000.
  - The rate among males was almost 5 times that of females.
  - The rate of suicide was higher for young and middle-aged adults (20–59 years).
  - Suicide accounted for 20% of deaths in those aged 10 to 19 years (the leading cause of death for this age group).

- The rate among unpartnered individuals (single, separated, widowed, or divorced) was higher than among people who were married.
- The highest percentage of suicides occurred in the spring.
- Hanging was the most common method used by males; self-poisoning was most commonly used by females.
- The rate was more than 3 times higher in Labrador (a region in which about 35% of the population is Aboriginal) than in the island portion of the province.
- A psychiatric disorder, especially a mood disorder, was the most common predisposing factor, present in over 60% of cases, followed by relationship and alcohol-related problems.
- About 30% of those who died by suicide were known to have made a previous attempt.
- Rates of suicidal ideation and suicide are twice the national averages in some First Nations communities and 10 to 12 times higher in some Inuit communities (see Table 8.4).

Thinking Critically

1. How would you identify young people at risk of self-harm? What risk factors would you focus on? What possible mechanisms underlie observed associations between risk behaviours and suicidal behaviour? What factors (positive and negative) can moderate the relation between risk and suicidality? Why do you think the highest percentage of suicides among young people occurs in the spring?

TABLE 8.4

SUICIDE RATES: FIRST NATIONS, INUIT REGIONS, AND CANADA COMPARED

	Period	Rate Per 100,000 Population
First Nations throughout Canada	2000	24
All Inuit Regions	1999–2003	135
Canada Total	2001	12

Source: Data for First Nations from Health Canada; unpublished data provided by the First Nations and Inuit Health Branch; data for Canada from Statistics Canada; rates for Inuit based on figures provided by the Nunavut Bureau of Statistics, Inuvialuit Regional Corporation, Nunavik Board of Health and Social Services, and Labrador Inuit Health Commission.

2. Hospitalization of suicidal adolescents consumes enormous health care resources. Design a randomized controlled trial comparing alternative inpatient and outpatient treatments for suicidal adolescents. The expectation is that your results could lead to more effective and efficient use of resources.

Sources: Blackmore et al. (2008); Brezo et al. (2008); Canetto & Sakinofsky (1998); Clayton & Barcelo (1999); Edwards et al. (2008); Government of Canada (2006); Lesage et al. (2008); Mann et al. (2008); Mishara (1999); Renaud, Chagnon, Turecki, & Marquette (2005); Rhodes & Bethell (2008); Sakinofsky (1998); Statistics Canada (2003).

Suicide is tragic not only because a person dies unnecessarily, but also because no other kind of death leaves loved ones, friends, and relatives with such enduring negative feelings that can include distress and emotional pain, shock and disbelief, guilt, shame, anger, puzzlement, and abandonment (Government of Canada, 2006). These survivors are themselves victims, having an especially high mortality rate in the year after the loved one's suicide. If the person who committed suicide also had a psychiatric disorder, then those left behind have to cope with the double stigma of suicide and mental illness (Government of Canada, 2006). Myths about suicide abound (see Focus on Discovery 8.3).

SUICIDE AND PSYCHOLOGICAL DISORDERS

It is believed that more than half of those who try to kill themselves are depressed and despondent at the time of the act (Henriksson et al., 1993), and it is estimated that 15% of people who have been diagnosed with MDD ultimately commit suicide (Maris et al., 1992). Alexander McGirr and colleagues (2007) from the McGill Group for Suicide Studies used a psychological autopsy method to examine *DSM-IV* depressive symptoms among suicides who died in the context of a major depressive episode and major depressive controls. Depressive symptoms of suicide relative to those of non-suicide included weight or appetite loss, insomnia, feelings of worthlessness or inappropriate guilt, as well as recurrent thoughts of death or suicidal ideation. Insomnia was an immediate indicator of suicide risk. Claasen et al. (2007) examined clinical differences among people with MDD with and without a history of suicide attempts. More than 16% of participants reported prior suicide attempts,

Suicide involving violent death, such as jumping off a building, is more common among men than among women. James Porto/Getty Images.

FOCUS ON DISCOVERY 8.3
SOME MYTHS ABOUT SUICIDE

There are many prevalent misconceptions about suicide (e.g., Fremouw, Perczel, & Ellis, 1990; Shneidman, 1987), some of which are included below. It is as important to be familiar with the myths as it is to know the facts.

1. *People who discuss suicide will not commit the act.*
   At least three quarters of those who take their own lives have communicated their intention beforehand, perhaps as a cry for help.
2. *Suicide is committed without warning.*
   The person usually gives many warnings, such as saying that the world would be better off without him or her or making unexpected and inexplicable gifts to others.
3. *Suicidal people clearly want to die.*
   Most people who contemplate suicide appear to be ambivalent about their own deaths. For many people, the suicidal crisis passes, and they are grateful for having been prevented from self-destruction.
4. *The motives for suicide are easily established.*
   The truth is that we do not fully understand why people commit suicide. For example, that a severe reverse in finances precedes a suicide does not mean that it adequately explains the suicide.
5. *All who commit suicide are depressed.*
   This fallacy may account for the fact that signs of impending suicide are often overlooked. Many people who take their lives are not depressed; some even appear calm and at peace with themselves.
6. *Improvement in emotional state means lessened risk of suicide.*
   Those who commit suicide, especially those who are depressed, often do so after their spirits and energy begin to rise.

and they had more current general medical conditions, more current alcohol or substance abuse, and onset of MDD occurred about nine years earlier in life. They also reported more current suicidal ideation. Comorbid anxiety disorders (especially panic disorder, generalized anxiety disorder, and anxiety disorder not otherwise specified) also increase risk of suicide death among depressed individuals (Pfeiffer, 2009). Valtonen et al. (2007) assessed people diagnosed with bipolar disorder and determined that hopelessness predicted suicidal behaviour during depressive phases, whereas a subjective rating of severity of depression and younger age predicted suicide attempts during mixed phases. A recent study of depressed people who had been referred to a mood disorders clinic (Ehnvall, Parker, Hadzi-Pavlovic, & Malhi, 2008) reported that females (but not males) who perceived themselves as rejected or neglected by either parent in childhood were more likely to make a lifetime suicide attempt. There are numerous other sex differences in predictors of suicidal acts (see Oquendo et al., 2007, for review).

A significant number of people who are not depressed, however, make suicidal attempts, and some succeed—most notably people diagnosed with borderline personality disorder (Links, Gould, & Ratnayake, 2003). More recently, Paul Links and his colleagues (Links, Eynan, Heisel, & Nisenbaum, 2008) determined that the presence of negative mood intensity and mood variability (affective instability) appears to define a subgroup of borderline individuals at elevated risk for suicidal behaviour. The suicide rate for male alcoholics is greater than that for the general population of men, and it becomes extremely high in alcoholic men who are also depressed (Linehan, 1997). Disinhibition during intoxication might render people less able to resist their thoughts of suicide. In a psychological autopsy study of completed suicides, Schneider et al. (2006) found that alcohol-related disorders, major depression, and co-occurrence of personality disorders of more than one cluster were independent predictors for suicide in males and females. Further, co-occurrence of personality disorders of more than one cluster contributed to risk of completed suicide after control for Axis I disorders. A Canadian study of completed suicides found that the number of completed suicides among people with schizophrenia was comparable with the number of completed suicides among people with depression (see Martin, 2000). McGirr et al. (2006) reported that psychotic people at risk for suicide can be identified by depressive disorders, moderate to severe psychotic symptoms, a family history of suicidal behaviour, few negative symptoms, and comorbid diagnoses. Suicide is also a major cause of death among people with anorexia nervosa and bulimia nervosa (Pompili et al., 2006), and high levels of suicidal ideation and attempts are found in adolescents and adults with body dysmorphic disorder (Phillips et al., 2006). Suicidal behaviour can also occur in the anxiety disorders. For example, a two-year prospective study of women (Cougle, Resnick, & Kilpatrick, 2009) found that PTSD at baseline was predictive of greater subsequent suicidal risk than MDD. People with PTSD might contemplate suicide as a means of escaping from their flashbacks (Oquendo, Baca-Garcia, Mann, & Giner, 2008). Psychological autopsies demonstrate that about 90% of suicide victims suffered from one or more *DSM* diagnoses (see Sakinofsky, 2007b).

A recent Finnish study (Sourander et al., 2009) is informative because it is the only prospective, population-based study in existence that examined predictive associations between early child psychopathology and later completed suicides. Of males who completed suicide and/or made suicide attempts that prompted hospital admission in adolescence or early adulthood, 78% screened positive on parent or teacher scales of psychopathology at the age of 8 years. Outcome was predicted at age 8 by living in a non-intact family; psychological problems as reported by the primary teacher; or conduct, hyperactivity, and emotional problems. Self-reports of depression did not predict suicide outcome. Outcome was predicted most strongly by comorbid conduct and internalizing problems (primarily anxiety). Female severe suicidality was not predicted by any of the variables measured at age 8.

Given that people with various diagnoses commit suicide, our focus here is on issues and factors in suicide that transcend specific diagnoses. Oquendo et al. (2008) noted that suicidality in high-risk groups often goes unidentified by assessing clinicians, and even when it is identified, "the patient receives a diagnosis that does not highlight suicide risk as a focus of concern" (p. 1383). They recommended that possible suicidal behaviour be included as a separate diagnosis on a sixth axis in *DSM-5*.

PERSPECTIVES ON SUICIDE

". . . while the act of suicide itself is a relatively clear-cut observable behaviour, it is based on a multiplex of interacting, mediating, moderating, independent, overlapping, and proxy risk factors from biopsychosocial perspectives."
—*Sakinofsky, 2007b, p. 8S*

Self-intentioned death is a complex, multi-faceted act and no single model can hope to explain it. We turn now to several different perspectives on suicide, each of which attempts to shed light on this disturbing aspect of humankind. Large-scale longitudinal studies are needed to validate different theories of suicidality.

DURKHEIM'S SOCIOLOGICAL THEORY Emile Durkheim (e.g., 1951), a renowned sociologist, analyzed the records of suicide for various countries and during different historical periods and concluded that self-annihilation could be understood in sociological terms. He distinguished three different kinds of suicide:

- **Egoistic suicide** is committed by people who have few ties to family, society, or community. These people feel alienated from others and cut off from the social supports that are important to keep them functioning adaptively as social beings.
- **Altruistic suicide** is viewed as a response to societal demands. Some people who commit suicide feel very much a part of a group and sacrifice themselves for what they take to be the good of society. The self-immolations of Buddhist monks and nuns to protest the fighting during the Vietnam War fits into this category. Some altruistic suicides, such as the hara-kiri of the Japanese, are required as the only honourable recourse in certain circumstances.
- **Anomic suicide** may be triggered by a sudden change in a person's relationship to society. A successful executive who suffers severe financial reverses may experience anomie,

Writers who killed themselves, such as Sylvia Plath, have provided insights into the causes of suicide. © Bettmann/CORBIS.

a sense of disorientation, because what he or she believed to be a normal way of living is no longer possible. Anomie can pervade a society in disequilibrium, making suicide more likely.

As with all sociological theorizing, Durkheim's hypotheses have difficulty accounting for the differences among individuals in a given society in their reactions to the same demands and conditions. Not all those who unexpectedly lose their money commit suicide, for example. It appears that Durkheim was aware of this problem, for he suggested that individual temperament would interact with any of the social pressures that he found causative.

PSYCHOLOGICAL THEORIES Many motives for suicide have been suggested: Freud's aggression turned inward; retaliation by inducing guilt in others; efforts to force love from others; efforts to make amends for perceived past wrongs; the desire to rejoin a dead loved one; and the desire or need to escape from stress, deformity, pain, or emotional vacuum.

Still—and this is of central importance in prevention—most people who contemplate or actually commit suicide are ambivalent. "The prototypical suicidal state is one in which an individual cuts his or her throat, cries for help at the same time, and is genuine in both of these acts. ... Individuals would be happy not to do it, if they didn't have to" (Shneidman, 1987, p. 170). There is a narrowing of the perceived range of options. When not in a highly perturbed suicidal state, the person is capable of seeing more choices for dealing with stress. People planning suicide usually communicate their intention, sometimes as a cry for help, sometimes as a withdrawal from others. Typical behaviours include giving away treasured possessions and putting financial affairs in order.

The suicide of Nirvana's lead singer, Kurt Cobain, triggered an increase in suicide among teenagers. Kevin Estrada/Retna.

The high suicide rate of the Guarani Indians of Brazil, who were forced onto crowded reserves, illustrates Durkheim's concept of anomic suicide. Maurice da Silva Goncalves is one of the local Guarani leaders who accused Norwegian millionaire Erling Lorentzen of stealing their land. AP Photo/The Canadian Press/Per Lochen.

Suicide is so complex that numerous psychological variables undoubtedly play a role; however, researchers have developed models that attempt to identify the variables and the moderators and mediators that will help determine who is at highest risk. The critical factors and mechanisms of action are not all well understood.

A Risk Factor Model A general model of the causes of suicidal behaviour is summarized in the 2006 Government of Canada report on mental health and mental illness in Canada. In this model, recommended as a guide for suicide prevention programs, there are four categories of relevant factors:

- Predisposing factors are enduring factors that make a person vulnerable to suicidal behaviour (e.g., psychological disorder, abuse, early loss).
- Precipitating factors are acute factors that create a crisis (e.g., end of a relationship, job loss, loss of stature, rejection, pressure to succeed).
- Contributing factors increase exposure to predisposing or precipitating factors (e.g., physical illness, sexual identity issues, isolation).
- Protective factors decrease the risk of suicidal behaviour (e.g., personal resilience, adaptive coping skills, positive future expectations, and perceived social support).

Childhood sexual abuse is one potent predisposing risk factor. Bebbington and colleagues (2009) reported findings from the British National Survey of Psychiatric Morbidity, which indicated that a history of CSA is strongly associated with suicide intent and attempts, especially among women. The risk factor model provides a broad framework for our discussion of more specific psychological models that focus on psychological diatheses.

Baumeister's Escape Theory and Perfectionism A theory about suicide based on work in social and personality psychology holds that some suicides arise from a strong desire to escape from aversive self-awareness; that is, from the painful awareness of shortcomings and failures that the person attributes to himself or herself (Baumeister, 1990). This awareness is assumed to produce severe emotional suffering, perhaps depression. Unrealistically high expectations—and therefore the probability of failing to meet these expectations (cf. Beck and Ellis)—play a central role in this perspective. Of particular importance is a discrepancy between high expectations for intimacy and a reality that falls short, such as when someone's expectations for intimacy are dashed because a loved one cannot possibly deliver what the person needs. Because perfectionists have impossibly high standards, they are more likely to experience such discrepancies.

Elevated levels of trait perfectionism and self-criticism have been implicated in suicidal acts (Blatt, 1995) and empirical research has established relations between components of perfectionism and suicidality (Shafran & Mansell, 2001). Risk for suicidality is especially high if it is perceived that perfection is socially prescribed and is expected or perhaps even demanded by others (Hewitt, Flett, Sherry, & Caelian, 2006). For example, in a recent study, Blankstein, Hillis Lumley, and Crawford (2007) found that socially prescribed perfectionism was a significant predictor of current suicide ideation, interpersonal hopelessness, and achievement hopelessness. Thus there is clearly a relationship between perfectionism and suicidal manifestations; however, the process by which perfectionism is linked to suicide is not clearly established.

One possible mechanism was examined recently by O'Connor and Noyce (2008). They investigated the extent to which different types of rumination mediate the link between self-criticism and suicide ideation. After controlling for sex, age, baseline depression, and suicide ideation, self-criticism predicted suicide ideation three months later. Brooding but not reflection independently predicted suicide ideation. More important, brooding fully mediated the pathway from self-criticism to suicide ideation, thus establishing "brooding as one key mechanism to account for the relationship between self-criticism and suicidality" (O'Connor & Noyce, 2008, p. 398). O'Connor and Noyce (2008) recommended that interventions target brooding in order to "neutralize" the effects of self-critical perfectionism.

Shneidman's Approach Shneidman (1987, 1993), a pioneer in the study of suicide and its prevention, reminds us that the overwhelming majority of people with psychiatric disorders do not commit suicide. He suggests that the perturbation of mind that he posits as a key feature in a person who commits suicide is not a mental illness. Shneidman regards suicide as a conscious effort to seek a solution to a problem that is causing intense and intolerable psychological suffering and pain, or what he refers to as **psychache**. To the sufferer, this solution ends consciousness and unendurable pain—what Melville in Moby Dick termed an "insufferable anguish." Hope and a sense of constructive action are gone. Shneidman's concept of psychological pain was referred to in the journal of Richard Edmunds, who killed himself by hanging in Calgary at age 27. Edmunds wrote, "I was born and bred to be frustrated. I cannot stand the pain any longer. I negate the past, and I have negated all of the future" (Edmunds, 1998, p. 371). This excerpt is from a moving account of the impact of a family member's suicide on survivors, as related by Anne Edmunds, Richard's mother.

Thus, in Shneidman's view, other psychological factors, such as depression, are relevant only insofar as they are related to psychache, a more proximal predictor of suicide and one that mediates more distal risk factors. In a recent study, Flamenbaum and Holden (2007) from Queen's University found that psychache, which can now be reliably measured, fully mediated the relation between socially prescribed perfectionism and suicidality. Past studies on the link between perfectionism and suicidal manifestations have examined the mediating effects of hopelessness and depression, with mixed results.

Perfectionism and Moderator Hypotheses Perfectionism is a personality trait that poses a dispositional vulnerability to negative outcomes, and components of perfectionism may interact with negative life events or other factors such as coping strategies or social support to trigger a chain of events that ultimately leads to suicidality, including a suicide outcome. In accordance with a diathesis-stress perspective, most models of suicidality emphasize the importance of distal and proximal negative life events as triggers, including Baumeister's (1990) escape theory and the hopelessness theory of depression (Abramson et al., 1989). For example, the hopelessness theory specifies that the depressogenic attributional style occurs in the presence of stressful events. In the study by Blankstein et al. (2007), potential moderators of the association between perfectionism dimensions and

indices of current suicide risk, including daily hassles, self-esteem, dispositional optimism, coping modes, and perceived social support, accounted for additional variance in outcome variables. More important, each component of perfectionism (social, self, and other) interacted with specific moderators to enhance or buffer the link between perfectionism and suicide risk. For example, in men, socially prescribed perfectionism interacted with academic hassles to enhance its positive relation with suicide ideation. In women, poor combined interpersonal and achievement self-esteem exacerbated the positive relation between socially prescribed perfectionism and both interpersonal and achievement hopelessness. Support from a significant other buffered any impact of self-oriented perfectionism on aspects of suicide risk (suicide ideation in females, and suicide ideation and achievement hopelessness in males).

Findings such as these have important implications for the development of comprehensive, integrated, multidimensional models of the perfectionism-suicide risk link and for prevention and treatment.

Additional Psychological Factors Research on personality and cognition has identified many other factors implicated in the development and course of suicidal behaviour (e.g., Brezo, Paris, & Turecki, 2006), including problem-solving deficits, hopelessness, negative cognitive styles, neuroticism, and impulsivity. For example, many contemporary mental health professionals regard suicide in general as an individual's attempt at problem-solving, conducted under considerable stress and marked by consideration of a very narrow range of alternatives, of which self-annihilation appears the most viable (Linehan & Shearin, 1988). Problem-solving deficits predict suicide attempts in prospective studies (Diesrud et al., 2003). It has also been suggested that suicidal individuals are more rigid in their approach to problems and less flexible in their thinking. Constricted thinking could account for the apparent inability to seek solutions to life's problems other than that offered by taking one's own life (Linehan et al., 1987). Research confirms the hypothesis that people who attempt suicide are more rigid than others, lending support to the clinical observations of Shneidman and others that people who attempt suicide seem incapable of thinking of alternative solutions to problems.

Especially noteworthy are Beck and colleagues' findings, based on 20-year prospective data, that hopelessness is a strong predictor of suicide (Brown, Beck, Steer, & Grisham, 2000). The expectation that at some point in the future things will be no better than they are right now seems to be more instrumental than depression per se in propelling a person to take his or her life. Smith, Alloy, and Abramson (2006) found that hopelessness partially mediated the rumination-suicide ideation link. Thus, it will be important to determine the relative influence of hopelessness and rumination in the relation between self-critical perfectionism and suicide ideation. Hopelessness is a predominant theme in Canadian Perspectives 8.5, which addresses the exceptionally high levels of suicide among certain Aboriginal groups.

CANADIAN PERSPECTIVES 8.5
SUICIDE AMONG CANADIAN ABORIGINAL PEOPLE

"Innu youth talk openly about their pain and sense of hopelessness. They acknowledge that they drink, take drugs and sniff gasoline to forget the boredom, the beatings, the abuse … The prospect of a future without change is too much for some to bear."

"The Tragedy of Andrew Rich," by John DeMont,
Maclean's, *November 22, 1999*

"This is a wounded community. A nightmare place where no one seems to have any hope."

*–Lynne Gregory, addictions counsellor in Sheshatshiu
(DeMont, 1999)*

World attention focused on Canada because of the alarming situation that had emerged in Davis Inlet and Sheshatshiu, Newfoundland and Labrador, where excessively high rates of suicide and dysfunctional behaviours, such as solvent abuse, sexual abuse, and domestic violence, were documented.

One tragic story among many is that of Andrew Rich, the son of Jean-Pierre Ashini. Andrew went with his father to the airport in Goose Bay to see him off to London, England. Ashini was going to address a news conference about the "suicide epidemic" among Canada's Innu people.

But he worried about his son, a shy 15-year-old who went by the nickname of 'Mr. T.' Andrew spoke little English and had always seemed most comfortable camping and hunting in Nitassinan, the Innu wilderness homeland. But in Sheshatshiu, 32 km north of Goose Bay, he had, like so many Innu youths, fallen into despair. He drank, did drugs and inhaled gasoline fumes when nothing else was available to dull the pain of his life. Sometimes, he talked about suicide. Preparing to board the plane, Ashini, a tee-totalling fisherman, urged his son to stay clean and behave himself while he was away. Once on the plane, he recalls, "I mouthed the words 'don't drink' through the glass of the window. I saw him nod yes, and I felt good when I left."

But minutes after arriving in London, Ashini received news that shattered his world. Sometime in the early morning of Nov. 6, Andrew had swallowed a vial of pills. He then walked into his bedroom and shot himself in the head while his 13-year-old girlfriend sat a few rooms away—the third youth in the past year to commit suicide in the community of 1,500. (DeMont, 1999)

According to a report released in 2000 by the human rights group Survival for Tribal People, the Innu people of Labrador and Quebec are 13 times more likely to kill themselves than other people in Canada, and the Innu formerly of Davis Inlet, 200 kilometres north of Sheshatshiu, have the highest suicide rate in the world (178 per 100,000 people). Moreover, the suicide rate among children and adolescents is extremely high, with estimates ranging from three to seven times the national average for children.

What factors contribute to such high suicide rates? The organization's report points to a multitude of factors, including loss of cultural identity, industrial development and depletion of natural resources on Innu land, and even physical and sexual abuse experienced when the Innu visited Roman Catholic missionaries at trading posts (see Samson, Wilson, & Mazower, 2000).

Although the Innu situation has garnered much public attention, other native groups also experience high suicide levels. British sociologist Colin Samson, co-author of the Innu study, reported that the Ojibwa reserve in Pikangijum (300 kilometres northeast of Winnipeg) had an even higher suicide rate of 213 per 100,000 people between 1992 and 2000; these data included the suicides of eight females (including five 13-year-olds) who killed themselves in 2000 (Canadian Press, 2000). Some Aboriginal communities have experienced "cluster suicide"—multiple suicides by groups of individuals in the same community. Ward and Fox (1977) reported "a true suicide epidemic" among a rural community of just 37 families on a reserve on Manitoulin Island, Ontario. A 17-year-old boy, upset by the expected separation of his parents, drank a large volume of alcohol and shot himself. In less than a year, eight other youths were dead, an astronomical suicide rate of 267 per 100,000. Wilkie, Macdonald, and Hildahl (1998) described a small First Nations community in Manitoba of fewer than 1,500 people that had six suicides and many more attempted suicides in a three-month span in 1995. Alcohol and previous sexual assault were factors in four suicides. Wilkie et al. also noted that those who had attempted suicide reported that they had experienced dreams of beckoning in which voices urged them to kill themselves.

These alarming situations led researchers to focus attention on this issue. A study of Inuit between the ages of 14 and 25 found that 34% had attempted suicide and 20% had made two or more attempts (Kirmayer, Malus, & Boothroyd, 1996). Risk factors associated with attempts included being male, having a friend who had attempted or committed suicide, a history of physical abuse, solvent abuse, and having a parent with an alcohol or drug problem. Two protective factors were degree of church attendance and doing well at school. A follow-up (Kirmayer, Boothroyd, & Hodgins, 1998) found the best predictors of attempted suicide among females were presence of a psychiatric problem, recent alcohol abuse, and cocaine or crack use. The best predictors among males were solvent use and the number of recent traumatic life events.

One study of Inuit from Nunavik found that the ratio of male to female suicides was five to one (Boothroyd et al., 2001). The two principal means of suicide were by hanging and by gunshot. Alcohol may be a disinhibiting factor. A comparative study of suicides in Manitoba found that Aboriginals who committed suicide had higher blood alcohol levels than non-Aboriginals who committed suicide (Malchy, Enns, Young, & Cox, 1997). Furthermore, Aboriginal people were less likely than non-Aboriginals to have sought help.

There are substantial differences in suicide rates among the various indigenous and First Nations groups, with some communities having rates that are 800 times the national average (Chandler & Lalonde, 1998). A key contributing factor is the degree to which cultural identity is maintained and preserved over time. Analysis of 196 bands in B.C. showed that a key factor that mitigates against suicide is the extent to which the community makes a collective effort to maintain and strengthen its own cultural continuity. Cooper, Corrado, Karlberg, and Adams (1992) also reported risk factors among bands in B.C. with high suicide rates, including overcrowding, numerous low-income and single-parent families, households with numerous children, and few elders in the community. The rates of suicide for Aboriginals who lived outside of the reserves were comparable with suicide rates for the general population.

The problem of suicide among Aboriginal people resulted in the formation of the Suicide Prevention Advisory Group (SPAG) in 2001. The SPAG was appointed jointly by then national chief Matthew Coon Come of the Assembly of First Nations and then federal minister of health Allan Rock. The initial report, entitled *Acting on What We Know: Preventing Youth Suicide in First Nations*, was published in January 2003 (Advisory Group on Suicide Prevention, 2003). The recommendations address four primary themes: (1) increasing knowledge about what works in suicide prevention; (2) developing more effective and integrated health care services; (3) supporting community-driven approaches; and (4) creating strategies for building youth identity, resilience, and culture. The SPAG acknowledged that no single approach will be effective by itself and that multi-level changes to family and community systems are needed. Unfortunately, there are no well-controlled treatment studies of suicidality among Aboriginals in Canada (see Sakinofsky, 2007b).

Thinking Critically

1. A new town was built in Labrador by the federal government for the Innu of Davis Inlet and they moved in February 2002. At a cost of more than $150 million, Natuashish was intended to provide a bright new future for the children and adults removed from the squalor of Davis Inlet. According to Toughill (2003), the move did not end the tragedies of the Innu—the problems were simply exported to the new town! Would you have predicted this outcome? Why?

2. Do you think that young Innu like Andrew Rich feel pressure to belong to traditional Innu culture and at the same time pressure to achieve in mainstream Canadian culture? Is it possible that they perceive a lack of support in both directions?

3. Solutions to the problem of suicide among our Aboriginal peoples will require psychological, societal, and economic interventions. Does the fact that the suicide rate is relatively low in some Aboriginal communities suggest to you that community-based solutions are, in fact, possible?

Knowing what there is in a person's life that prevents him or her from committing suicide has both assessment and intervention value. Rather than focusing only on negativism and pessimism, Marsha Linehan's Reasons for Living (RFL) Inventory (Linehan, 1985) taps six themes of importance to the individual: (1) survival and coping beliefs, (2) responsibility to family, (3) concerns about children, (4) fear of social disapproval, (5) fear of suicide, and (6) moral objections (i.e., a belief that suicide is morally wrong). This approach can help the clinician with intervention by identifying the reasons the person has for not wanting to die. The RFL was associated negatively with suicide ideation when the scale was adapted for use with French Canadian populations (see Labelle, Lachance, & Morval, 1996). People with reasons to live are less suicidal than people who report few reasons to live (Ivanoff et al., 1994).

NEUROBIOLOGY AND SUICIDE Monozygotic twins have a much higher concordance for suicidality than dizygotic twins (Baldessarini & Hennen, 2004), suggesting that the risk is partially inherited. Recently, McGirr et al. (2009) from the McGill Group for Suicide Studies examined familial transmission of suicide, controlling for depression, and concluded that Cluster B personality traits and impulsive-aggressive behaviour represent intermediate phenotypes of suicide that partially mediate the relation between familial predisposition and suicide attempts among relatives.

Just as research has shown that low levels of serotonin appear to be related to depression, research has also established a connection among serotonin, suicide, and impulsivity. Low levels of serotonin's major metabolite, 5-HIAA, have been found in people in several diagnostic categories—depression, schizophrenia, and various personality disorders—who committed suicide (e.g., van Praag, Plutchik, & Apter, 1990). Post-mortem studies of the brains of people who committed suicide have revealed increased binding by serotonin receptors (presumably a response to a decreased level of serotonin itself) (Turecki et al., 1999). The link between 5-HIAA levels and suicide is especially compelling in the case of violent and impulsive suicide (e.g., Roy, 1994). In a recent SPECT study, Ryding et al. (2006) found no significant differences between suicide attempters and control subjects with respect to regional levels of serotonin reuptake (5HTT) and dopamine reuptake binding potential; however, in suicide attempters but not controls they found significant regional correlations between levels of measures of impulsiveness/initiative and mental energy and SPECT results. The latter were interpreted as "due to a disability of the suicide attempters to regulate their serotonin and dopamine levels, e.g., in response to external stress" (Ryding et al., 2006, p. 195).

PREVENTING SUICIDE

> "Population-based and high-risk approaches must go forward synergistically, and each is integral to the hope of reducing suicide rates."
>
> *—Sakinofsky, 2007b, p. 17S*

The need to prevent suicide is garnering increased attention, not only in Canada, but around the world. In 1999, the World Health Organization began a worldwide initiative—known as SUPRE-MISS—to prevent suicidal behaviours (World Health Organization, 2000). "SUPRE" refers to suicide prevention, and "MISS" refers to the multi-site intervention study on suicidal behaviours. The study focuses on the evaluation of treatment strategies for people attempting suicide, as well as on community surveys of suicidal thoughts and behaviours. But what can be done to prevent suicides from occurring?

TREATING THE UNDERLYING MENTAL DISORDER One way to look at the prevention of suicide is to bear in mind that most people who attempt to kill themselves are suffering from a treatable mental disorder. A Canadian study of young men who committed suicide showed that almost everyone who had been examined had a diagnosable Axis I disorder such as depression and 57.3% had a diagnosable personality disorder (Lesage et al., 1994). Thus, when following Beck's cognitive approach successfully lessens a client's depression, that client's suicidal risk is reduced. The same is true for the dialectical behaviour therapy of Marsha Linehan (1993b), whose therapy with borderline individuals is described in Chapter 13. Many experts hold the view that efforts to prevent suicide should focus on the underlying psychological disorder.

TREATING SUICIDALITY DIRECTLY Another tradition in suicide prevention downplays mental disorder and concentrates instead on the particular characteristics of suicidal people that transcend mental disorders. One of the best-known approaches of this nature is that of Edwin Shneidman. We have already reviewed some of his thinking on suicide. His general strategy of suicide prevention (1987) is threefold:

1. Reduce the intense psychological pain and suffering.
2. Lift the blinders; that is, expand the constricted view by helping the individual see options other than the extremes of continued suffering or nothingness.
3. Encourage the person to pull back even a little from the self-destructive act.

Shneidman cited the example of a college student who was single, pregnant, and suicidal and had a clearly formed plan. The only solution she could think of besides suicide was never to have become pregnant, even to be virginal again.

> I took out a sheet of paper and began to widen her blinders. I said something like, "Now, let's see: You could have an abortion here locally." She responded, "I couldn't do that." I continued, "You could go away and have an abortion." "I couldn't do that." "You

could bring the baby to term and keep the baby." "I couldn't do that." "You could have the baby and adopt it out." Further options were similarly dismissed. When I said, "You can always commit suicide, but there is obviously no need to do that today," there was no response. "Now," I said, "let's look at this list and rank them in order of your preference, keeping in mind that none of them is optimal." (Shneidman, 1987, p. 171)

Shneidman reported that just drawing up the list had a calming effect. The student's lethality—her drive to kill herself very soon—receded, and she was able to rank the list even though she found something wrong with each item. But an important goal had been achieved; she had been pulled back from the brink and was in a frame of mind to consider courses of action other than dying or being a virgin again. "We were then simply 'haggling' about life, a perfectly viable solution" (Shneidman, 1987, p. 171).

SUICIDE PREVENTION CENTRES Many **suicide prevention centres** are modelled after the Los Angeles Suicide Prevention Center, founded in 1958 by Farberow and Shneidman. According to the Canadian Association for Suicide Prevention (1994), there are more than 200 suicide prevention and crisis centres in Canada.

Staffed largely by non-professionals under the supervision of psychologists or psychiatrists, these centres attempt to provide 24-hour consultation to people in suicidal crises. Usually the initial contact is made by telephone, and the centre's phone number is well publicized in the community. Workers

The Golden Gate Bridge in San Francisco is the number one suicide site in the world (Blaustein & Fleming, 2009). In 2006, there were 34 confirmed suicides and another 70 suicidal people were taken off the bridge before they could jump. A call box and this accompanying sign were put on the bridge in the hope that this will prevent some suicides. The 2006 film "The Bridge" shows the actual acts and tells the story of people who jumped to their deaths from the bridge in 2004. On October 10, 2008, the Bridge Board voted to build a flexible stainless steel net (suicide barrier) below the bridge. As of October 10, 2009, no start date for construction had been established. Photo courtesy of Hayley Flett.

rely heavily on demographic factors to assess risk. They have before them a checklist to guide their questioning of each caller. For example, a caller would be regarded as a lethal risk if he were male, middle-aged, divorced, and living alone, and had a history of previous suicide attempts. Usually the more detailed and concrete the suicide plan, the higher the risk. The worker tries to assess the likelihood that the caller will make a serious suicide attempt and, most important, tries to establish personal contact and dissuade the caller from suicide. Staffers are taught to adopt a phenomenological stance, to view the suicidal person's situation as he or she sees it and not to convey in any way that the client is a fool or is crazy to have settled on suicide as a solution to his or her woes. This empathy for suicidal people is sometimes referred to as "tuning in."

Many students who take abnormal psychology are eager to "make a difference" in the lives of others, and one common route to achieving this goal is to volunteer as a member of a suicide or crisis telephone line. Indeed, according to Leenaars (2000), throughout the world, suicide prevention depends on volunteerism. The telephone service is available in many locations throughout Canada and is becoming increasingly available in more remote regions. Levy and Fletcher (1998) described the origins and development of the first crisis line in the North, Kamatsiaqtut, the Baffin Crisis Line, "a community response to the cries of hopelessness and helplessness that have been vibrating through the North" (p. 355). The first two phone lines were established in 1990, after start-up funds were provided by CBC employees who put together a curl-a-thon. The crisis line received more than 400 calls the first year, a large number considering that these lines served only the 3,700 people in Iqaluit. Callers report a number of problems, but the most common centre on losses involving relationships, family members, and friends. Levy and Fletcher (1998) noted that the decision to provide a crisis line in the North is inconsistent with Inuit cultural beliefs because the crisis line focuses on the individual, while Inuit society emphasizes the importance of community. Still, the crisis line is made available by the volunteer efforts of the community, and Levy and Fletcher (1998) concluded that it plays a vital role in providing distressed individuals with a chance to express their concerns and not simply keep things to themselves.

The first telephone centre in Canada was started in Sudbury, Ontario, in 1965; however, the real push in Canada came from the Suicide Prevention and Distress Centre in Toronto (Leenaars, 2000). The 48 trained volunteers started answering the telephones on November 1, 1967, and the first three calls came from people contemplating suicide. It is estimated that the centres in the Greater Toronto Area now receive approximately 800,000 calls each year. Suicide Action in Montreal is the largest French-language telephone crisis service in Canada. Such community facilities are potentially valuable because people who attempt suicide give warnings—cries for help— before taking their lives. Ambivalence about living or dying is the hallmark of the suicidal state (Shneidman, 1987). Usually, pleas are directed first to relatives and friends, but many people contemplating suicide are isolated from these sources of emotional support. A hotline service may save the lives of such individuals.

Victims of suicide include survivors, especially those among the unfortunate who were speaking to or in the presence of the person when the act was committed, which occurs in an estimated 25% of suicides (Andress & Corey, 1978). Sometimes these survivors are therapists or hospital emergency room personnel. All are subject to strong feelings of guilt and self-recrimination, second-guessing what they might have done to prevent the suicide. Even dispassionate analysis does not invariably allay the guilt and anger. Grieving after a suicide death tends to last much longer than a death that is not self-inflicted. For these many reasons, peer support groups exist to help survivors cope with the aftermath of a suicide. They provide social support, opportunities to vent feelings, constructive information, and referrals to professionals if that seems advisable (Fremouw et al., 1990). McDaid et al. (2008) reviewed controlled studies of interventions for people bereaved through suicide and concluded that there is evidence of some benefit (e.g., a psychologist-led 10-week group intervention for children) but the effects were not robust.

GATEKEEPER TRAINING AS A PREVENTATIVE INTERVENTION

"In essence, gatekeepers open the gate to help for people at risk of suicide."

—*Isaac and colleagues and The Swampy Cree Suicide Prevention Team, 2009, p. 260*

The United Nations (1996) recommended that **gatekeeper training** be considered in implementing an effective strategy to prevent suicide. In this type of training, specific groups of people are taught to identify those at high risk for suicide and then to refer them for treatment. Gatekeepers are those who have primary contact with people at risk for suicide, including helping professionals and community members, and identify people at risk because the gatekeepers recognize suicidal risk factors. Family and friends are possibly best suited to act as gatekeepers. Michael Isaac from the University of British Columbia and his colleagues (2009) conducted a systematic review of gatekeeper training. Gatekeeper training has been implemented and studied in numerous populations (e.g., public school staff, peer helpers, military personnel, and Aboriginal people). Isaac et al. (2009) concluded that it has positive effects on the knowledge, skills, and attitudes of gatekeeper trainees with respect to suicide prevention. Does it affect suicidality? The authors concluded that training among military personnel and family physicians has been demonstrated to significantly reduce the suicide rate. However, there is a need for randomized controlled trials to show that gatekeeper training alone has an effect on the suicide rate since it typically exists within prevention programs that implement many different initiatives.

GOVERNMENT SUICIDE PREVENTION PROGRAMS IN CANADA Dyck and White (1998) provided a comprehensive overview of suicide prevention programs in Canada. They noted that the provinces differ substantially in this regard. Alberta has the longest-standing suicide prevention program in Canada. This contrasts substantially with three provinces (i.e., Ontario, Quebec, and Saskatchewan) that do not have well-articulated suicide prevention programs.

Alberta is also distinguished by the fact that it is one of the few provinces to document its evaluation efforts (see Dyck & White, 1998). Provincial assessments led to an updated approach in Alberta in 1993 (White et al., 1993). The three goals of this approach, as stated by Dyck and White (1998), were (1) to prevent fatal and non-fatal suicidal behaviours, (2) to reduce the impact of suicidal behaviours on individuals, and (3) to improve access and availability to appropriate services for people who are at risk and/or vulnerable. Six province-wide strategies were identified: (1) community coordination of a full range of prevention strategies (this entails mental health promotion, prevention, early intervention, crisis intervention, treatment, bereavement counselling for survivors, and post-vention); (2) suicide awareness education; (3) training in suicide intervention and suicide bereavement; (4) research; (5) evaluation of suicide prevention activities, as well as the overall program; and (6) advocacy for improving public health policy. The Suicide Information and Education Centre (SIEC), initiated in 1981, has grown into the world's largest information centre for English-language literature on suicide (Leenaars, 2000).

Provinces such as Quebec and Ontario lack a coordinated suicide prevention approach at the governmental level. In 1992, the Quebec government set a goal of reducing suicide by 15% by 2002, but no resources were provided to achieve this goal (Dyck & White, 1998). Nevertheless, Quebec and Ontario have a community-based approach that includes crisis lines, suicide intervention training, and public education. Quebec was identified by Dyck and White (1998) as a province that uses a community-based approach similar to the U.S. suicide prevention centres described earlier.

Health Canada issued national task force reports on suicide in 1987 and 1994 but has not adopted an official national suicide prevention strategy; however, the Canadian Association for Suicide Prevention released a 2004 "blueprint" for a national strategy (see Sakinofsky, 2007b).

It is exceedingly difficult to do controlled research on suicide, and outcome studies have yielded inconsistent results. A U.S. meta-analysis of five studies on the effectiveness of suicide prevention centres failed to demonstrate that rates decline after the implementation of services (Dew et al., 1987). A similarly negative finding was reported from Canada (Leenaars & Lester, 1995). However, another study found that suicide rates declined in the years following the establishment of suicide prevention centres in several cities (Lester, 1991). These inconclusive findings are consistent with the paucity of data on suicide prevention by other means, though a promising

Paul Links holds the only endowed research chair in suicide studies in North America. He conducts research on the prevention and etiology of suicide and holds the Arthur Sommer Rotenberg Chair in Suicide Studies at St. Michael's Hospital in Toronto. The chair is named after Dr. Arthur Sommer Rotenberg, a family physician from Toronto who committed suicide. Photo courtesy of Paul Links.

approach appears to be a CBT one that emphasizes social problem-solving (e.g., Linehan et al., 1991). The despair and hopelessness of suicidal people may make them see suicide as the only exit from an unbearable existence. The therapist encourages consideration of other ways to change the distressed state by construing problems as solvable and then generating life-affirming strategies for dealing with them.

We are left with conflicting and inconclusive evidence. Human lives are precious, however, and since many people who contact suicide prevention centres and crisis lines weather a suicidal crisis successfully, these efforts will continue.

CLINICAL AND ETHICAL ISSUES IN DEALING WITH SUICIDE

"I want to ask you gentlemen, if I cannot give consent to my own death, then whose body is this? Who owns my life?"
   —Sue Rodriguez, victim of ALS (amyotrophic lateral sclerosis, or Lou Gehrig's disease, a terminal illness), appearing in a videotaped presentation to a House of Commons committee in November 1992, in which she urged amendments to the section of the Criminal Code that makes it a crime for any person to assist another's suicide

Professional organizations charge their members to protect people from harming themselves even if doing so requires breaking the confidentiality of the therapist-client relationship. The suicide of a therapist's client is frequently grounds for a malpractice lawsuit, and therapists tend to lose such suits if it can be proved that the therapist failed to make adequate assessments and to take reasonable precautions according to generally accepted standards of care for suicide prevention (e.g., Roy, 1995).

It is not easy to agree about what constitutes reasonable care, particularly when the client is not hospitalized and therefore not under surveillance and potential restraint. Clinicians must work out their own ethic regarding a person's right to end his or her life. What steps is the professional willing to take to prevent a suicide? Confinement in a hospital? Or, as is more common today, sedation administered against the person's wishes and strong enough that the person is virtually incapable of taking any action at all? And for how long should extraordinary measures be taken? Clinicians realize that most suicidal crises pass; the suicidal person is likely to be grateful afterward for having been prevented from committing suicide.

PHYSICIAN-ASSISTED SUICIDE Physician-assisted suicide is a highly charged issue. It came to the fore in the early 1990s when a Michigan physician, Jack Kevorkian, helped a 54-year-old Oregon woman in the early stages of Alzheimer's disease, a degenerative and fatal brain disease, to commit suicide. Not yet seriously disabled, she was helped by Kevorkian to press a button on a machine designed to inject a drug that induced unconsciousness and a lethal dose of potassium chloride that stopped her heart (Egan, 1990). Death was painless. For almost 10 years, Kevorkian played an active role in assisting upwards of 100 terminally ill people take their lives.

One such person was Austin Bastable from Windsor, Ontario. Bastable suffered from multiple sclerosis and went public with his desire to die. He lobbied the Canadian government to legalize assisted suicide. His story drew nationwide attention when it was broadcast on CBC's *Man Alive* on February 8, 1996. Right-to-life advocates attempted to intervene by pleading with Bastable, via a "Save Austin Bastable" website, not to commit suicide. On May 6 that year, Bastable travelled with his wife across the border to Detroit. He died later that same night in the presence of four physicians, including Kevorkian, who was standing trial at that time for the death of two people. Kevorkian was acquitted in 1996. He was brought to trial several times but was not convicted of murder or professional misconduct until the spring of 1999, when he was found guilty of murder and sentenced to 10 to 25 years in prison. He was released on parole in 2007. Assisted suicides have continued to make news in Canada. In a 2006 case, a 60-year-old mother from Quebec was found guilty and given three years' probation for assisting the suicide of her son in 2004. He suffered from the early stages of multiple sclerosis. In another high profile case, on December 12, 2008, a Quebec jury acquitted Stephan Dufour of an assisted suicide charge. He had assisted his ill uncle to commit suicide.

The extent to which assisted suicide is deemed to be a criminal offence varies across countries. Belgium and the Netherlands take a very liberal approach that is not shared by other European countries (see Burkhardt et al., 2006). One controversial development is that the Swiss Supreme Court

Jack Kevorkian, a Michigan physician, assisted many people in taking their own lives. The controversy stimulated by his actions focused attention on the moral issues surrounding suicide. In 2010, HBO produced a biopic about the controversial doctor called *You Don't Know Jack*. Brian Zak/Sipa Press/Newscom.

ruled in February 2007 that chronically mentally ill people have "a right" to assisted suicide.

Jack Kevorkian provoked a searching and emotional discussion about the conditions under which a physician may take the life of a dying person. Passionate arguments pro and con continue. Interestingly, a 1999 study sought to determine physicians' attitudes toward assisted suicide (Heath, Wood, Bally, Cornelisse, & Hogg, 1999). Anonymous questionnaires were sent to almost 3,000 family physicians in Canada. It was found that 60% of physicians with an opinion on this issue were in favour of the legalization of assisted suicide. One factor that predicted a more positive view was whether the physician provided care to HIV patients. Another factor was the physician's location, with more favourable attitudes coming from physicians practising in British Columbia, Ontario, and Quebec. Following the Dufour case, Bloc Quebecois MP Francine Lalonde reintroduced a Private Member's Bill (C-384) for consideration by Parliament in the fall of 2009 to make assisted suicide legal.

CARING FOR THE SUICIDAL CLIENT

"There is no magic clinical bullet currently available that could replace excellent clinical care, which remains the centerpiece of treatment of suicidal persons."

—*Isaac Sakinofsky, 2007a, pp. 6–7S*

Cases such as that of Jack Kevorkian are unusual. For the most part, health workers try to prevent suicide, and in that context they should not hesitate to inquire directly whether a client has thought of suicide. Above all, the clinician treating a suicidal person must be prepared to devote more energy and time than usual. Late-night phone calls and visits to the person's home may be necessary and frequent. The therapist should realize that he or she is likely to become a singularly important figure in the suicidal person's life and should be prepared both for the extreme dependency of the client and for the hostility and resentment that sometimes greet efforts to help.

The *Canadian Journal of Psychiatry* (see Sakinofsky, 2007a) published a special supplement of 10 papers on caring for the suicidal person from a uniquely Canadian perspective. It was restricted to suicidal individuals who seek out or are brought into contact with mental health services and focused on topics where the findings of evidence-based investigations are available (Sakinofsky, 2007a). It was concluded that psychological treatments, particularly CBT and IPT, possibly combined with antidepressants, have demonstrated efficacy in the treatment of suicidal ideation in depression and non-fatal suicidality in borderline personality disorders. Although controversial, there is evidence that the new antidepressants possibly play a role in falling suicide rates. Further, lithium plays a positive role in reducing suicidality in bipolar disorder and possibly unipolar depression, and clozapine clearly plays a role in reducing suicidality in schizophrenia and schizoaffective psychosis. However, Sakinofsky noted that, "By default, we must sometimes use interventions where validity has not been proven" (2007b, p. 18S). The supplement is an excellent educational resource.

SUMMARY

- *DSM-IV-TR* lists two principal kinds of mood disorders. In major, or unipolar, depression, a person experiences profound sadness, as well as related problems such as sleep and appetite disturbances and loss of energy and self-esteem. In bipolar I disorder, a person has episodes of mania alone; distinct episodes of mania and depression; or mixed episodes, in which both manic and depressive symptoms occur together. With mania, mood is elevated or irritable, and the person becomes extremely active, talkative, and distractible. *DSM-IV* also lists two chronic mood disorders, cyclothymia and dysthymia; both must last for two years. In cyclothymia, the person has frequent periods of depressed mood and hypomania; in dysthymia, the person is chronically depressed.

- Psychological theories of depression have been couched in psychoanalytic, cognitive, and interpersonal terms. Psychoanalytic formulations stress fixation in the oral stage (leading to a high level of dependency) and unconscious identification with a lost loved one whose desertion of the individual has resulted in anger turned inward. Beck's cognitive theory ascribes causal significance to negative schematas and cognitive biases and distortions. According to the helplessness/hopelessness theories, early experiences in inescapable, hurtful situations instill a sense of hopelessness that can evolve into depression. Individuals are likely to attribute failures to their own general and persistent inadequacies and faults. Interpersonal theory focuses on the problems depressed people have in relating to others and on the negative responses they elicit from others. These same theories are applied to the depressive phase of bipolar disorder. The manic phase is considered a defence against a debilitating psychological state, such as low self-esteem.

- There may be an inherited predisposition for mood disorders, particularly for bipolar disorder. Linkage analyses may provide information about the chromosome on which the gene is located. Early neurochemical theories related depression to low levels of serotonin and bipolar disorder to norepinephrine (high in mania and low in depression). Research has focused on the postsynaptic receptors rather than on the amount of various transmitters. Overactivity of the HPA axis is also found among depressive people, indicating that the endocrine system may influence mood disorders.

- Several psychological and somatic therapies are effective for mood disorders, especially for depression. Psychoanalytic treatment tries to give the client insight into childhood loss and inadequacy and later self-blame. The aim of Beck's cognitive therapy is to uncover negative and illogical patterns of thinking and to teach more realistic ways of viewing events, the self, and adversity. Interpersonal therapy, which focuses on the depressed person's social interactions, also is an effective therapy.

- Biological treatments are often used in conjunction with psychological treatment. ECT and several antidepressant drugs have possibly proved their worth in lifting depression, with the caveat that ECT clients relapse at high rates if they do not receive follow-up antidepressant treatment. Other findings indicate that clients may avoid the excesses of manic and depressive periods through careful administration of lithium carbonate.

- Our exploration of suicide reveals that self-annihilatory tendencies are not restricted to those who are depressed. Many methods can be applied to help prevent suicide, although no single theory is likely to account for the wide variety of motives and situations behind it. Most perspectives on suicide regard it as usually an act of desperation to end an existence that the person feels is unendurable.

- Physician-assisted suicide is controversial. Legislatures and the courts are wrestling with the issue of the proper role of doctors in releasing terminally ill patients from the extreme pain and disability that can accompany the last months or days of life.

- Most large communities have suicide prevention centres, and most therapists at one time or another deal with peo-ple in suicidal crisis. Suicidal people need to have their fears and concerns understood but not judged; clinicians must gradually and patiently point out to them that there are alternatives to self-destruction to be explored.

KEY TERMS

altruistic suicide (p. 276)
anomic suicide (p. 276)
attribution (p. 254)
autonomy (p. 252)
bilateral ECT (p. 266)
bipolar I disorder (p. 242)
bipolar II disorder (p. 245)
brooding (p. 241)
congruency hypothesis (p. 253)
cyclothymic disorder (p. 247)
dependency (p. 252)
depression (p. 238)
depressive paradox (p. 254)
depressive predictive
   certainty (p. 255)
double depression (p. 247)

dysthymic disorder (p. 247)
egoistic suicide (p. 276)
electroconvulsive therapy
   (ECT) (p. 266)
gatekeeper training (p. 282)
hypomania (p. 245)
kindling hypothesis (p. 242)
learned helplessness theory (p. 251)
lithium carbonate (p. 270)
major depressive disorder
   (MDD) (p. 239)
mania (p. 239)
monoamine oxidase (MAO)
   inhibitors (p. 258)
mood disorders (p. 238)
negative triad (p. 249)

phototherapy (p. 271)
postpartum depression (PD) (p. 246)
psychache (p. 278)
psychologizer (p. 238)
ruminative coping (p. 241)
seasonal affective disorder
   (SAD) (p. 245)
selective serotonin reuptake
   inhibitors (SSRIs) (p. 258)
self-criticism (p. 252)
sociotropy (p. 252)
Stroop task (p. 250)
suicide prevention centres (p. 281)
tricyclic drugs (p. 258)
unilateral ECT (p. 266)

REFLECTIONS: PAST, PRESENT, AND FUTURE

- A genetic predisposition for MDD and bipolar disorder probably affects brain neurochemistry in some way. Is it possible that traumatic life events and other negative life experiences lead to neurochemical changes that create the same effect as a genetic predisposition? Post and Weiss (1995) proposed a kindling-sensitization model that ar-gues that neurotransmitter systems become increasingly sensitive to stressors (biological or environmental) with repeated episodes of depression or mania. The conse-quence is that the brain becomes more easily affected by stressors and eventually minor events or mild stressors cause dysregulation and trigger episodes. Did you know that monkeys raised without their mothers and with only peers for support had low serotonin levels as early as 14 days of age and continuing into adulthood (*APA Monitor, 1997*)?

- Most of the abnormalities in neurotransmitters that have been identified in people with the various mood disorders are "state dependent," meaning that the differences are evident when the mood disorder occurs but tend to dis-sipate when mood changes. What are the implications of this fact for our understanding of the mood disorders?

- In Chapter 15, we will discuss the issue of depression in children. Do you think depression can occur in very young children or does it develop only during adolescence? Does depression in young people differ from depression in adults? Is it possible to find a way to prevent first depres-sions in vulnerable children?

- In Chapter 5, we discussed the issue of sexual abuse among Canada's Aboriginal peoples. In this chapter, we discussed the extremely high rates of suicide among Aboriginals. In Chapter 12, you will learn that Aboriginal people have a very high rate of substance abuse. Based on your understand-ing of the history of the treatment of Aboriginal peoples, their current life circumstances, the identified risk factors for different psychological disorders, and factors related to suicide and substance abuse, design a comprehensive, dia-thesis-stress model to explain the psychological problems seen in Aboriginal people, especially children.

- If you had the power and resources to try to change the destiny of Innu children, what would you do? Outline a comprehensive, multi-faceted intervention plan. What role would the Innu themselves play in the design and implementation of the plan?

CHAPTER 9

PSYCHOPHYSIOLOGICAL DISORDERS AND HEALTH PSYCHOLOGY

Marian Dale Scott, *Atom, Bone and Embryo*, 1943, oil on canvas, 91.4 × 101.6 cm, Art Gallery of Ontario, Toronto. © Estate c/o Christopher Varley, 6 Kendell Avenue, Toronto, ON M5R 1L6

"Worry affects circulation, the heart and the glands, the whole nervous system, and profoundly affects the health. I have never known a man who died from over-work, but many who died from doubt."
—Charles H. Mayo

"Every stress leaves an indelible scar, and the organism pays for its survival after a stressful situation by becoming a little older."
—Hans Selye

"An hour of pain is as long as a day of pleasure."
—Proverb

MS. A, a 46-year-old married lawyer, was referred for psychiatric evaluation by her gastroenterologist, who follows her for long-standing irritable bowel syndrome. She has had irritable bowel syndrome since the age of 20, with complaints of intermittent constipation, diarrhea, crampy abdominal pain, and bloating. She feels that these symptoms have gradually worsened, particularly in the last month. She describes a highly pressured job and a stressful marriage. She has specifically noted a precipitous increase in intestinal symptoms immediately after arguments with her husband and when facing deadlines at work. Three months ago, she developed depressed mood, early morning awakening, anorexia, fatigue, crying spells, impaired concentration, irritability, and preoccupation with thoughts of ill health. Her family physician diagnosed major depression and prescribed amitriptyline, which was discontinued after it worsened her constipation. Her psychiatrist then tried fluoxetine (discontinued because of diarrhea) and trazodone (too sedating). She then responded well to nortriptyline, with disappearance of the symptoms of depression and improvement in her irritable bowel syndrome. However, several irritable bowel syndrome symptoms continued to follow the frequent marital arguments. The psychiatrist asked the patient to invite her husband to join one of their sessions so that marital issues could be explored further. He did so, resulting in the discovery that her husband was himself significantly depressed. He was referred to another psychiatrist for treatment, the marital discord abated, and her irritable bowel syndrome symptoms returned to a manageable level. (Levenson, 2003, p. 1651, in Tasman et al., 2003)

The account of Ms. A illustrates several important themes that are addressed in this chapter. First, there is increasing evidence of a strong association between physical health problems and deficits in emotional well-being. People with medical illnesses have an increased risk of disorders such as depression and anxiety, and their situation is worsened when they have sleep difficulties. We will discuss the increasingly evident link between the mind and body in several sections of this chapter. Second, significant life stressors play an important role in exacerbating health problems and contributing to psychological distress. Third, ill people suffering from distress must be viewed within their social context. In the case of Ms. A, disputes with her husband exacerbated her symptoms, but her husband also experienced profound distress.

The importance of the social context is reflected in the tips that Roy Romanow outlined in an important 2003 speech on the future of health care in Canada. These tips are summarized in the 2004 report *Improving the Health of Canadians* (Canadian Population Health Initiative, 2004). Here are eight important things to keep in mind. Some can be addressed, some you have probably already addressed, and some cannot be addressed. Some points seem obvious, others less so:

1. Don't be poor: rich people tend to live longer on average and are healthier at every life stage. Socio-economic status relates to physiological health (e.g., Chen, 2007; Marin, Chen, & Miller, 2008). Poverty also limits access to health services (Raphael, 2009).
2. Get a good start in life: prenatal and early childhood experiences have a profound effect on many outcomes, including long-term health status.
3. Graduate from high school (and preferably from college or university): as education level increases, so does health status.

4. Get a job: unemployment is linked with lower levels of functional health and increased levels of stress.
5. Choose your community: recent data on healthy vs. unhealthy communities illustrate that where you live matters as does the community's values and your sense of belonging, and these can have a substantial impact on your health and well-being (e.g., Chen, Chim, Strunk, & Miller, 2007).
6. Live in quality housing: exposure to environmental risks often translates into subsequent health problems.
7. Look after yourself: much is to be gained by eating well, exercising, and not abusing alcohol or drugs.
8. Men and women are different: men do not live as long as women, on average, though women report poorer health status. This point is discussed in detail in Focus on Discovery 9.4.

As indicated, Chapter 9 focuses on health and psychophysiological disorders. **Psychophysiological disorders**, such as asthma, hypertension, headache, and gastritis, are characterized by genuine physical symptoms that are caused by or can be worsened by emotional factors. The term *psychophysiological disorders* is preferred today to a term that was formerly used and is perhaps better known, **psychosomatic disorders**. Nevertheless, the term *psychosomatic* connotes quite well the principal feature of these disorders: that the psyche, or mind, is having an untoward effect on the soma, or body.

In contrast to many of the disorders described in Chapter 8 (e.g., hypochondriasis, somatization disorder, and conversion disorder), psychophysiological disorders are real diseases involving damage to the body (see Table 9.1). That such disorders are viewed as being related to emotional factors does not make the afflictions imaginary. People can just as readily die from psychologically produced high

TABLE 9.1
COMPARING PSYCHOPHYSIOLOGICAL AND CONVERSION DISORDERS

Type of Disorder	Organic Bodily Damage	Bodily Function Affected
Conversion	No	Voluntary
Psychophysiological	Yes	Involuntary

blood pressure or asthma as from similar diseases produced by infection or physical injury.

Psychophysiological disorders as such do not appear in *DSM-IV*, as they did in some earlier versions of the *DSM*. *DSM* underneath *DSM-IV* requires a diagnostic judgement to indicate the presence of **psychological factors affecting medical condition**, and this diagnosis is coded in the broad section that comprises "other conditions that may be a focus of clinical attention." The implication of this placement is that psychophysiological disorders are not a form of mental disorder. Nonetheless, we consider them here in some detail because of their historical link to the field of psychopathology. Also, as noted above, there is increasing evidence of numerous associations between mental health problems and physical health problems.

The new approach to diagnosis is also broader in scope. Formerly, psychophysiological disorders were generally thought to include only some diseases (the classic psycho-somatic diseases, such as ulcers, headaches, asthma, and hypertension). The new diagnosis is applicable to any disease, as it is now thought that any disease can be influenced by psychological factors, such as stress. Furthermore, the diagnosis of psychological factors affecting medical condition includes cases in which the psychological or behavioural factor influences the course or treatment of a disorder, not just cases in which it influences the onset, again broadening the definition. For example, a person with hypertension may continue to drink alcohol even though he or she knows that alcohol increases blood pressure, or a patient may fail to take prescribed medication regularly. The psychological or behavioural factors include Axis I and II diagnoses; personality traits; coping styles, such as holding anger in rather than expressing it; and lifestyle factors, such as failing to exercise regularly.

What is the evidence for the view that any illness may be in part stress related? For years, it has been known that various physical diseases can be produced in laboratory animals by exposure to severe stressors. Usually the diseases produced in such studies were the classic psychophysiological disorders, such as ulcers. More recently, studies have indicated that a broader range of diseases may be related to stress. Sklar and Anisman (1979) conducted research in Ottawa that involved inducing tumours in mice

and then measuring the impact of stress—uncontrollable electric shocks—on growth of the tumours. The tumours grew more rapidly in animals exposed to electric shock, and these animals died earlier. Similarly, a 20-year follow-up of stress reactions in war veterans revealed unusually high rates of a broad range of diseases involving the circulatory, respiratory, digestive, musculoskeletal, endocrine, and nervous systems (Boscarino, 1997).

The many demonstrations of the pervasive role of psychological factors in health form the basis for the fields of **behavioural medicine** and **health psychology**. Since the 1970s, these fields have dealt with the role of psychological factors in all facets of health and illness. Beyond examining the etiological role that stress can play in illness, researchers in these fields study psychological treatments (e.g., biofeedback for headache) and the health care system itself (e.g., how better to deliver services to underserved populations) (Appel et al., 1997; Stone, 1982).

Prevention is also a major focus of health psychology. As the twentieth century progressed and infectious diseases were brought under better control, people were dying more often from such illnesses as cardiovascular disease (CVD). It is estimated that 45% of all causes of death are cardiovascular in nature (Linden, 2003) and CVD remains the leading cause of death in Canada (Manuel et al., 2003). The causes of CVD involve behaviour—people's lifestyles—such as smoking, eating too much, and excessive alcohol use. Thus, it is believed that many CVD cases can be prevented by changing unhealthy lifestyles. Health psychologists are at the forefront of these preventative efforts, some of which we describe later in this chapter.

While psychological factors can clearly play a role in the onset of health problems, it is important to recognize the role of psychological and mental health factors in how well people cope with their illness. We underscore the role of psychological factors and the mind–body connection in the discussion of complex chronic diseases such as chronic obstructive pulmonary disease (see Focus on Discovery 9.1). This segment should be interpreted within the context of recent analyses from the Canadian Community Health Survey showing that mood disorders are more prevalent among individuals with chronic illness vs. those without chronic illness. The highest rates of mood disorders are found among those with chronic fatigue syndrome, fibromyalgia, bowel disorders, and stomach or intestinal ulcers (Gadalla, 2008).

Health psychology and behavioural medicine are not restricted to a set of techniques or to particular principles of changing behaviour. Clinicians in the field employ a wide variety of procedures—from contingency management, to stress reduction, to cognitive-behavioural approaches—all of which share the goal of altering bad living habits, distressed psychological states, and aberrant physiological processes in order to improve a person's health.

FOCUS ON DISCOVERY 9.1
PSYCHOLOGICAL ASPECTS OF CHRONIC OBSTRUCTIVE PULMONARY DISEASE

"There is no life without breath."
—*Public Health Agency of Canada, 2007, p. viii*

Why should you care about air quality? Several facts in the 2007 report *Life and Breath: Respiratory Disease in Canada* from the Public Health Agency of Canada paint a grim picture.

1. Over 3 million Canadians have one of five serious respiratory diseases: asthma, chronic obstructive pulmonary disease (COPD), lung cancer, tuberculosis, and cystic fibrosis.
2. Canada is facing an onslaught of chronic respiratory diseases. The number of people with respiratory diseases can be expected to increase dramatically as our population ages, and this will further challenge our health care system.
3. Respiratory diseases exert a significant economic impact on the Canadian health care system (accounting for approximately 7% of total health care costs, with over $12 billion in indirect costs and direct, visible costs such as hospitalization, physician visits, research, and drugs).

Our discussion will focus on COPD. COPD is a progressive disease that only gets worse, but clearly, some COPD patients cope better than others and the quality of life and length of life depends on several factors, many of which are psychological in nature. Depression and anxiety are linked with a reduced quality of life and all of these outcomes are associated with low perceived social support and reduced self-efficacy in terms of symptom management (McCathie, Spence, & Tate, 2002). The experience of COPD symptoms is often intertwined with anxiety. Consider dyspnea. Its main symptom is difficulty breathing, including breathlessness in extreme cases. Bailey (2004) described a dyspnea-anxiety-dyspnea cycle in the context of a case study of Paul, a 73-year-old retired Canadian miner with severe COPD symptoms. Paul's main thought was "It is scary when you can't breathe."

The psychological data on conditions such as anxiety among COPD patients usually parallel other trends. For instance, among COPD patients, substantially more women than men are diagnosed with anxiety and depression. A recent study conducted in Montreal found that an astounding 56% of women COPD patients (vs. 36% of men with COPD) met criteria for an anxiety

disorder (Laurin et al., 2007). Anxiety was diagnosed with the Anxiety Disorders Interview Schedule-IV. Diagnosed depression was less prevalent but still quite evident (18% of women and 7% of men). These data highlight the close link between psychological disorders and physical conditions.

When people are diagnosed with COPD, they undergo a program of pulmonary rehabilitation at facilities such as West Park Healthcare Centre in Toronto. Research conducted by Dr. Roger Goldstein and his colleagues at West Park has shown that participation in pulmonary rehabilitation results in improvements in functional exercise capacity and health-related quality of life but the benefits tend to diminish over the next 12 months as COPD progresses (see Carr, Goldstein, & Brooks, 2007). Serious setbacks are called AECOPDs (acute exacerbations of COPD) and involve increases in dyspnea (breathlessness); more severe forms of the disease involve more frequent bouts of AECOPDs. The experience of AECOPDs after pulmonary rehabilitation is associated with reductions in walking distance, increases in fatigue and negative emotion, and decreases in perceived mastery (Carr et al., 2007).

As with many chronic diseases, experts believe that **self-management programs** represent the key to effective functioning and well-being. What are self-management programs? Borbeau from the Montreal Chest Institute of the Royal Victoria Hospital cautions that self-management is much more than just providing education to the patient (see Bourbeau & van der Palen, 2009). Self-management programs assist the patient in acquiring and practising the skills that patients will need at home in their daily lives in order to adhere to disease-specific medical regimens and adjust health behaviours to achieve optimal function and improved levels of well-being. It includes a problem-solving component because patients must assess their progress and problems and address problems as they emerge, as well as set goals, evaluate goal progress, and modify goals as needed. Self-management programs recognize that time in medical facilities is limited and the patient must act in his or her own self-interest in daily life in order to achieve maximum benefit.

COPD is just one of many chronic diseases in which psychological factors play a key role. We will revisit this issue when discussing heart disease and cardiac rehabilitation.

STRESS AND HEALTH

We begin by reviewing general findings on the relationship between stress and health, as well as theories about how stress can produce illness.

DEFINING THE CONCEPT OF STRESS

In earlier chapters, the term "stress" was used to refer to some environmental condition that triggers psychopathology. Here

we shall examine the term more closely and consider the difficulties in its definition.

The term "**stress**" was created by Hans Selye. Selye was a world-renowned researcher who eventually became a Canadian citizen and conducted much of his research in Montreal. Selye is also known for identifying the **general adaptation syndrome (GAS)**, which is described more fully in Canadian Contributions 9.1.

CANADIAN CONTRIBUTIONS 9.1
HANS SELYE: THE FATHER OF STRESS

Dr. Hans Selye is regarded as the father of the stress concept and the inventor of the common term "stress." Selye was born in Europe but immigrated to the United States when he was awarded a Rockefeller fellowship. In 1932, he immigrated to Canada when he was hired as an associate professor of histology at McGill University in Montreal. Selye was to remain in Canada the rest of his life. He became a Canadian citizen and was recognized as a Companion of the Order of Canada in 1968 for his pioneering research on the nature of stress. He authored 30 books and hundreds of research articles on the nature of stress in animals and people.

Most doctors focus on precise illnesses caused by specific factors, but Selye was an endocrinologist who was interested in the "general syndrome of being sick." He noticed early in his career that organisms exposed to a diverse array of stimuli (e.g., trauma, cold, heat, nervous irritation) often exhibit a similar, non-specific response. Accordingly, he viewed stress as a non-specific response of the body to any demand for change.

In 1936 Selye introduced the general adaptation syndrome (GAS), a description of the biological response to sustained and unrelenting physical stress (i.e., a biological stress syndrome). There are three phases of the syndrome, as shown in Figure 9.1.

1. During the first phase, the alarm reaction, the autonomic nervous system (ANS) is activated by the stress. If the stress is too powerful, gastrointestinal ulcers form, the adrenal glands become enlarged, and the thymus undergoes atrophy (wasting away).

2. During the second phase, resistance, the organism adapts to the stress through available coping mechanisms. The length of resistance depends on the body's innate adaptability and the intensity of the stressor (Selye, 1974).

3. If the stressor persists or the organism is unable to respond effectively, the third phase, a stage of exhaustion, follows, and the organism dies or suffers irreversible damage (Selye, 1950).

Selye is especially well-known for promoting the view that stress plays a role, for better or worse, in all diseases (see Selye, 1974). The role of stress in various illnesses is discussed in subsequent sections of this chapter.

Selye made an important distinction between negative and positive forms of stress, and this was reflected in his use of the terms "**distress**" and "**eustress**." Distress described damaging or unpleasant stress. Eustress referred to positive, pleasant stress. He believed that pleasant and unpleasant emotional arousal result in increased levels of physiological stress, but only negative emotional arousal results in distress.

In time, Selye came to believe that the term "stress" was misleading and that he should have used the term "strain" instead, since "stress" has other meanings in the field of physics. But, according to Rosch (1998), Selye is regarded as the creator of the word as it is used commonly because many other languages lack a suitable word or phrase that can convey what is meant by the word "stress."

Interestingly, it appears that Selye's own medical history served as an illustration of the role that psychological factors play in stress and illness. According to Rosch, at one point, Selye "developed a rare and usually fatal malignancy, and attributed his rather remarkable recovery to his strong desire to continue his research. He was convinced that stress could cause cancer, and that a strong faith could reverse this" (Rosch, 1998, p. 5). Indeed, the role of psychological factors in cancer is detailed in a subsequent section of this chapter.

FIGURE 9.1 Selye's general adaptation syndrome

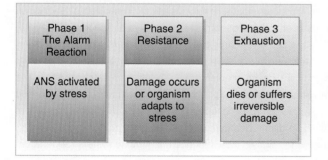

Phase 1 The Alarm Reaction	Phase 2 Resistance	Phase 3 Exhaustion
ANS activated by stress	Damage occurs or organism adapts to stress	Organism dies or suffers irreversible damage

Canada Post stamp commemorating the important contributions to our understanding of stress that were initiated by Hans Selye. © Canada Post Corporation. 1999. Reproduced with permission.

Selye's concept of stress eventually found its way into the psychological literature, but with substantial changes in its definition. Some researchers followed Selye's lead and considered stress a response to environmental conditions, defined on the basis of such diverse criteria as emotional upset, deterioration of performance, or physiological changes such as increased skin conductance or increases in the levels of certain hormones. The problem with these response-based definitions of stress is that the criteria are not clear-cut. Physiological changes in the body can occur in response to a number of stimuli that we would not consider stressful (e.g., anticipating a pleasurable event).

Stress affects the nervous system. Indeed, Mayo's quote that opened this chapter mentioned how worry activates the nervous system. The autonomic nervous system and its responsiveness to stress are described in Focus on Discovery 9.2.

Many researchers have focused on stress as a stimulus, often referred to as a **stressor**, and identified it with a long list of environmental conditions: electric shock, boredom, uncontrollable stimuli, catastrophic life events, daily hassles, and sleep deprivation. Stimuli that are considered stressors can be major (the death of a loved one), minor (being stuck in traffic), acute (failing an exam), or chronic (a persistently unpleasant work environment). According to one Canadian researcher, chronic stress can take many forms, including persistent threats, demands, and conflicts, as well as a sense of being under-rewarded and being deprived of essential resources, as might be the case with individuals from disadvantaged groups (see Wheaton, 1997).

Stressors can also be distinguished in terms of whether they are psychogenic or neurogenic (see Anisman & Merali, 1999). Psychogenic stressors stem from psychological factors (e.g., anticipation of an adverse event), while neurogenic stressors stem from a physical stimulus (e.g., bodily injury or recovery from surgery). Anisman and Merali (1999) noted that various stressors can differ in a number of ways, including whether they are controllable (i.e., stress can be lessened or eliminated by engaging in a certain response) or uncontrollable, predictable or unpredictable, short in duration or chronic, and intermittent or recurring. Anisman and Merali (1999) also described how different stressors have different physiological implications; for example, chronic, intermittent, and unpredictable stressors are less likely to result in neurochemical adaptation while intense and prolonged demands on neurochemical systems may create a condition known as **allostatic load**, which can lead to a variety of pathological outcomes.

Like response-based definitions, stimulus-based definitions also present problems. Stipulating exactly what constitutes a stressor is difficult. More than negativity is clearly involved; marriage, for instance, generally a positive event, is regarded as a stressor because it requires adaptation. Furthermore, people vary widely in how they respond to life's challenges. A given event does not elicit the same amount of stress in everyone. A family that has lost its home in a flood but has enough money to rebuild and a strong network of friends will experience less hardship than a family that has neither adequate money to rebuild nor a social network to provide support.

FOCUS ON DISCOVERY 9.2
THE AUTONOMIC NERVOUS SYSTEM AND STRESS

The **autonomic nervous system (ANS)** is involved when we react involuntarily or automatically to stimuli. Our nervous systems have two separate parts: the ANS and the **somatic nervous system**, which is the voluntary nervous system. The voluntary nervous system is involved when we consciously express movements. However, much of our behaviour reflects a nervous system that tends to operate outside of our awareness and has been viewed traditionally as beyond voluntary control, hence the term "autonomic." However, research on biofeedback has shown that the ANS is under greater voluntarily control than previously believed.

The ANS stimulates the endocrine glands, the heart, and the smooth muscles found in the walls of the blood vessels, stomach, intestines, kidneys, and other organs. The ANS is divided into two parts, the **sympathetic nervous system** and the **parasympathetic nervous system** (Figure 9.2), which may work in tandem or in opposition to each other. The sympathetic nervous system, when energized, accelerates the heartbeat, dilates the pupils, inhibits intestinal activity, increases electrodermal activity, and initiates other smooth-muscle and glandular responses. The experience of stress or the anticipation of stress activates the sympathetic nervous system. The parasympathetic nervous system is involved in deactivation and restoring the organism to a lower state of activation.

If a person is chronically stressed, this means that the sympathetic nervous system is also chronically activated. Eventually, significant health problems may result from this activation and prolonged exposure to stress hormones, which is described subsequently in this chapter. These health problems may reflect having a diminished immune system, given that the nervous system sends signals that influence the immune system (Segerstrom & Miller, 2004).

There is growing evidence that chronic activation of the sympathetic nervous system is implicated directly in health problems. For instance, in a recent paper, Guyenet (2006) reviewed the growing empirical work linking activation of the sympathetic nervous system and hypertension.

FIGURE 9.2 The autonomic nervous system

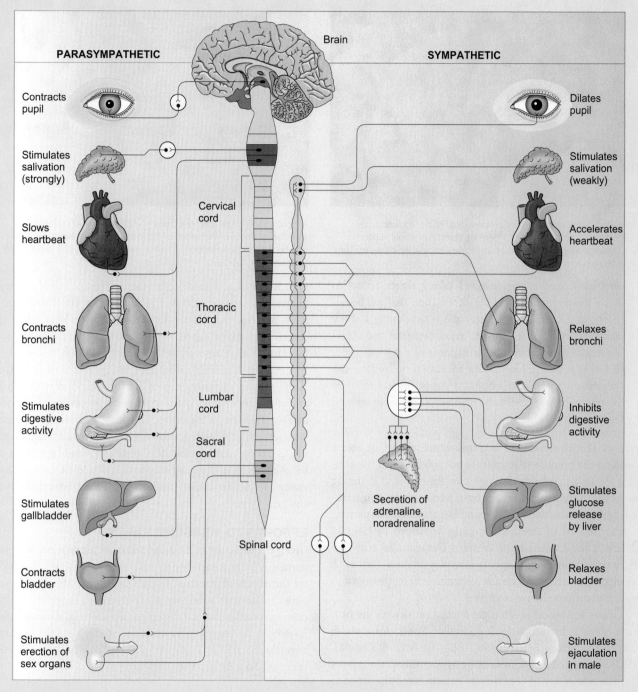

Some people believe that it is not possible to define objectively what events or situations qualify as psychological stressors (e.g., Lazarus, 1966). They emphasize the cognitive aspects of stress; that is, the way we perceive or appraise the environment determines whether a stressor is present. When a person determines that the demands of a situation exceed his or her resources, the person experiences stress. A final exam may be merely challenging to one student, yet highly stressful to another who does not feel equipped to take it (whether his or her fears are realistic or not). Similarly, as shown in a recent study conducted with women from the Ottawa area, the stress experienced during breast cancer screening is closely tied to how the stressful situation is perceived and appraised (Sweet, Savoie, & Lemyre, 1999).

Also relevant to individual differences in responding to stressful situations is the concept of **coping**, how people try to deal with a problem or handle the emotions it produces. Even among those who appraise a situation as stressful, the effects of the stress may vary depending on how the individual copes with the event. Lazarus and his colleagues have identified two broad dimensions of coping (Lazarus & Folkman, 1984):

Coping can focus on solving the problem itself or on regulating the negative emotions it has created. Seeking comfort or social support from others is an example of emotion-focused coping. Bruce Ayres/Tony Stone Images.

According to Richard Lazarus, the way a life event is appraised is an important determinant of whether it causes stress. An exam, for example, may be viewed as a challenge or as an extremely stressful event. Will & Deni McIntyre/Corbis.

- *Problem-focused coping* involves taking direct action to solve the problem or seeking information that will be relevant to the solution. An example is developing a study schedule to pace assignments over a semester and thereby reduce end-of-semester pressure.
- *Emotion-focused coping* refers to efforts to reduce the negative emotional reactions to stress; for example, by distracting oneself from the problem, relaxing, or seeking comfort from others.

Lazarus (1966) developed a transactional model of stress based on the premise that stress is not solely due to the situation or to an individual's cognitive appraisals and coping responses; rather, stress results from a transaction or interaction between situational factors and factors inside the person. A recent model of stress and coping developed by Neufeld (1999) at the University of Western Ontario also acknowledges the dynamic and ongoing interplay of these factors. A key element of this model is the recognition that stressors and related situations change over time.

The effectiveness of attempts to cope varies with the situation. Various investigators (e.g., Endler, Speer, Johnson, & Flett, 2000; Felton & Revenson, 1984; Forsythe & Compas, 1987) have tested a **goodness of fit hypothesis** that suggests that the adaptivity of a particular coping response depends on the match between the coping response and what is called for ideally by the problem situation. Distraction may be an effective way of dealing with the emotional upset produced by impending surgery, but it would be a poor way to handle the upset produced by the discovery of a lump on the breast (Lazarus & Folkman, 1984). Similarly, continuing efforts to seek a solution to an unsolvable problem lead to increases in frustration rather than to any psychological benefit (Terry & Hynes, 1998).

A key factor is whether a problem or situation is controllable or uncontrollable. Problem-focused coping is most adaptive when there is something that an individual can do to improve the situation; emotion-focused coping is less adaptive in these situations. However, when a situation is uncontrollable, problem-focused coping is not adaptive; here it may be better to vent and express one's emotions to release tension (Stanton, Kirk, Cameron, & Danoff-Burg, 2000).

Finally, it should be noted that, in terms of cognitive appraisals and strategies, people often respond with denial and avoidance when confronted with stressors of varying levels of severity, including shocking events. In general, however, the evidence indicates that escape/avoidance coping (such as wishing that the situation would go away or be over with) is the least effective method of coping with many life problems (Suls & Fletcher, 1985), especially over the long term.

EFFORTS TO MEASURE STRESS

Given the difficulty of defining stress with precision, it is not surprising that measuring stress is difficult, as well. Research on the effects of stress on human health has sought to measure the amount of life stress a person has experienced and then to correlate this measurement with illness. Various scales have been developed to measure life stress. Here we examine two: the Social Readjustment Rating Scale and the Assessment of Daily Experience.

THE SOCIAL READJUSTMENT RATING SCALE In the 1960s, two researchers, Holmes and Rahe (1967), gave a list of life events to a large group of people and asked them to rate each item according to its intensity and the amount of time they thought they would need to adjust to it. Marriage was arbitrarily assigned a stress value of 500; all other items were then evaluated using this reference point. For example, an event twice as stressful as marriage would be assigned a value of 1,000, and an event one fifth as stressful as marriage would be assigned a value of 100. The average ratings assigned to the 12 most stressful events by the respondents in Holmes and Rahe's study are shown in Table 9.2.

TABLE 9.2
SOCIAL READJUSTMENT RATING SCALE

Rank	Life Event	Mean Value
1	Death of spouse	100
2	Divorce	73
3	Marital separation	65
4	Jail term	63
5	Death of close family member	63
6	Personal injury or illness	53
7	Marriage	50[a]
8	Fired from work	47
9	Marital reconciliation	45
10	Retirement	45
11	Change in health of family member	44
12	Pregnancy	40

[a]Marriage was arbitrarily assigned a stress value of 500; no event was found to be any more than twice as stressful. Here the values are reduced proportionally and range up to 100.
Source: Holmes and Rahe, 1967.

The Social Readjustment Rating Scale (SRRS) emerged from this study. A respondent checks off the life events experienced during the time period in question. Ratings are then totalled for all the events actually experienced to produce a Life Change Unit (LCU) score, a weighted sum of events.

Miller and Rahe (1997) rescaled the events on the SRSS and added some events in recognition of the possibility that the impact of life changes in the 1990s might be different from the impact experienced in the 1960s and 1970s. Once again, the event of marriage was used as the reference point and was assigned a score of 50. The top five LCU ratings were given to death of a child (123), death of a spouse (119), death of a brother or sister (102), death of a parent (100), and divorce (96). Overall, Miller and Rahe (1997) found that the life-change intensity scores rose 45%. Changing to a different line of work, for example, went from an LCU of 36 to an LCU of 51.

Experiencing major life events such as marriage stastically increases risk of illness. Research on the effect of these major stressors assesses them with the Social Readjustment Rating Scale. Digital Vision.

The original LCU score has been related to several different illnesses, including heart attacks (Rahe & Lind, 1971), onset of leukemia (Wold, 1968), and colds and fevers (Holmes & Holmes, 1970). The results demonstrated a correlation between psychological stress and physical illness, but they do not mean that stress causes or contributes to illness. For example, illness itself could cause a high life-change score, as when chronic absenteeism caused by the illness brings dismissal from a job. Given the fact that it often takes many years for stress to contribute to illness, research on stress and health should, ideally, be longitudinal. Longitudinal research offers several advantages; for instance, the biases of retrospective self-reports are minimized and changes in stress can be shown to precede changes in health.

ASSESSMENT OF DAILY EXPERIENCE Consideration of problems with the SRRS led Stone and Neale (1982) to develop a new assessment instrument, the Assessment of Daily Experience (ADE). Rather than relying on retrospective reports, the ADE allows individuals to record and rate their daily experiences in prospective or longitudinal investigations. A day was used as the unit of analysis because a thorough characterization of this period should be possible without major retrospective-recall bias. Although the events reported on a day will generally be less severe than those reported over a longer time period, there is now direct evidence that these minor events are related to illness (Jandorf et al., 1986). Part of the ADE is shown in Figure 9.3.

With an assessment of daily experiences in hand, Stone, Reed, and Neale (1987) began a study of the relationship between life experience and health. They examined the relationship between undesirable and desirable events and the onset of episodes of respiratory illness. Respiratory illness was selected as the criterion variable because it occurs with sufficient frequency to allow it to be analyzed as a distinct outcome.

After reviewing the participants' data, the researchers identified 30 individuals who had experienced episodes of infectious illness during the assessment period. Next, they examined the daily frequency of undesirable and desirable events that occurred from 1 to 10 days before the start of an episode. For each person, a set of control days, without an episode, was also selected. The results showed that, for desirable events, there were significant decreases three and four days prior to the onset of respiratory infection; for undesirable events, there were significant increases at four and five days before the onset of the illness.

These results, which have been replicated (Evans & Edgerton, 1990), were the first to show a relationship between life events and health with both variables measured in a daily, prospective design. Most sources of confounding in prior life-events studies were avoided in this study, and we can now come much closer to asserting that life events play a causal role in increasing vulnerability to episodes of infectious illness.

FIGURE 9.3 Sample page from Assessment of Daily Experience scale (Stone & Neale, 1982). Respondents indicate whether an event occurred by circling the arrows to the left of the list of events. If an event has occurred, the respondents then rate it on the dimensions of desirability, change, meaningfulness, and control, using the enclosed spaces to the right. Reproduced with permission of Taylor & Francis Group LLC

WORK RELATED ACTIVITIES

Concerning Boss, Supervisor, Upper Management, etc.

► Praised for a job well done ☐ ○ ○ △ 01

► Criticism for job performance, lateness, etc. ☐ ○ ○ △ 02

Concerning Co-workers, Employees, Supervisees, and/or Clients

► Positive emotional interactions and/or happenings with co-workers, employees, supervisees, and/or clients (work related events which were fulfilling, etc.) ☐ ○ ○ △ 03

► Negative emotional interactions and/or happenings with co-workers, employees, supervisees, and/or clients (work related events which were frustrating, irritating, etc.) ☐ ○ ○ △ 04

► Firing or disciplining (by Target) ☐ ○ ○ △ 05

► Socializing with staff, co-workers, employees, supervisees, and/or clients ☐ ○ ○ △ 06

General Happenings Concerning Target at Work

► Promotion, raise ☐ ○ ○ △ 07

► Fired, quit, resigned ☐ ○ ○ △ 08

► Some change in job (different from the above, i.e., new assignment, new boss, etc.) ☐ ○ ○ △ 09

► Under a lot of pressure at work (impending deadlines, heavy workload, etc.) ☐ ○ ○ △ 10

Daily hassles such as being stuck in traffic can be emotionally upsetting and also increase risk of illness. Digital Vision.

Other research has studied daily events by having people complete self-report measures of their **daily hassles**. These studies often show that not only does a link exist between self-reported daily hassles and poor psychological and physical adjustment, but measures of daily hassles are often better than measures of major life events at predicting adjustment problems (DeLongis, Coyne, Dakof, Folkman, & Lazarus, 1982; Kanner, Coyne, Schaefer, & Lazarus, 1981).

Researchers have responded to two problems that plagued earlier research on daily hassles. First, the original Hassles Scale (Kanner et al., 1981) has been described as "contaminated" because it included items that could be construed as a symptom of distress (e.g., feeling tired) rather than a hassle per se. These symptoms were removed in a subsequent version of the Hassles Scale created by Anita DeLongis, who is now at the University of British Columbia (see DeLongis, Folkman, & Lazarus, 1988).

Second, the original Hassles Scale was developed for use with a middle-aged community sample, and as such, it contained daily hassles that may not be relevant to other populations. Researchers have addressed this problem

by developing daily hassles tailored to the experiences of specific groups of people. Canadian researchers have developed hassles measures for university and college students (Blankstein, Flett, & Koledin, 1991; Kohn, Lafreniere, & Gurevich, 1990) and for adolescents (Kohn & Milrose, 1993). Hassles scales have also been devised for elderly men and women (Holahan & Holahan, 1987). The Brief College Hassles Scale (Blankstein et al., 1991) taps academic hassles (e.g., academic bureaucracy, academic deadlines), interpersonal hassles (e.g., contact with boyfriend/girlfriend, relationship with mother and/or father), financial hassles (e.g., owing money), and more general hassles such as organization of time, noise, future job prospects, and household chores. These hassles were identified via extensive interviews and feedback from students.

Illness-specific hassles can also be assessed. Fillion, Kohn, and their associates have developed a hassles measure to assess the stressors faced by cancer patients, including stressors involving future concerns (e.g., thinking about how family members will manage if the patient dies), functional disability (e.g., difficulty walking and moving about), and body-image concerns (Fillion et al., 2001). Research with cancer patients from Quebec and Ontario indicates that this new measure is associated with higher levels of anger, fatigue, and depression. These population-specific measures are more precise and offer more meaningful ways of assessing hassles for respondents. It is important to remember, however, that the findings from this research apply to the specific group being studied and should not be overgeneralized to other groups.

We have already noted that two measures of daily hassles have been created to assess the specific daily stressors experienced by college and university students. Focus on Discovery 9.3 continues our emphasis on the specific health issues facing college and university students. Although it is generally the case that health matters become more important as we get older, a considerable proportion of students are confronted with significant health concerns.

STRESS IN SPECIFIC CONTEXTS In addition to examining the hassles associated with specific illnesses, it is possible and meaningful to examine stress in specific life contexts. We have already seen that students list stress as the top factor that undermines their academic performance. We will further illustrate this issue with a brief discussion of a particular form of stress: **job stress**. People may experience high levels of job stress either because of their own unique personal characteristics or because they have a high-stress occupation (e.g., doctors, nurses, accountants at tax filing time, etc.). Job stress is linked consistently with depression (Tennant, 2001) and other negative outcomes. Consider, for instance, the results of the first-ever nationally respresentative survey of work and health of nurses in Canada (see Shields & Wilkins, 2005). This study involved interviews with 18,676 nurses across Canada with participation from 4 out of 5

nurses contacted. Overall, approximately one third of nurses were deemed to have high job stress and strain, and this job strain predicted poorer physical and mental health (e.g., depression), as well as lengthier and more frequent absences from work. Job stress can also have an impact on family life, according to the concept of **job spillover**. This is the notion that stressed workers bring their work stress home with them and it causes family stress.

One of the potential by-products of extreme job stress is that a person may experience **job burnout**. The concept of burnout has been assessed most extensively by Christina Maslach and her colleagues (Maslach & Jackson, 1981). Burnout involves three components: (1) a sense of emotional exhaustion; (2) depersonalization (i.e., a tendency to be insensitive and not respect the needs of other people); and (3) a sense of lack of personal accomplis hment. Job burnout has been linked with a vast array of physical problems including cardiovascular disease (Melamed et al., 2006) and psychological difficulties such as depression (see Maslach, Schaufeli, & Leiter, 2001). In some people, job burnout appears to be a reflection of having developed a work addiction and suffering from workaholism (for a review, see Burke, 2006). An extreme form of burnout is a condition known as **vital exhaustion**, a physical depletion that is also linked to cardiovascular disease (Melamed et al., 2006).

FOCUS ON DISCOVERY 9.3
THE HEALTH STATUS OF STUDENTS

Contrary to expectations, there is little evidence that college and university students enjoy comparatively good health relative to other segments of the population. Students do not rate their health more positively than do older adults (Svenson & Campbell, 1992; Vingilis, Wade, & Adlaf, 1998). What factors predict less positive ratings of health status? Vingilis et al. (1998) found that more negative assessments by students from Canada were associated with poorer child-parent relationships, lower interest and achievement in school, lower self-esteem, smoking, and being female. The more negative assessments of female students were replicated in a recent study conducted with students from Germany, Bulgaria, and Poland (Mikolajcdyk et al., 2008). The best predictor of negative self-ratings in this European study was the presence of psychosomatic symptoms.

How would you rate your health if asked to decide whether it is excellent, very good, good, fair, or poor? Did you assess your health as relatively good? We will now report some results from the 2008 National College Health Assessment conducted by the American College Health Association (ACHA; 2009). This study was conducted with responses from over 80,000 students. Overall, 66% of students listed their general health as excellent or very good, and another 27% listed their health as good. Only 7% listed their health as fair or poor; hopefully, there is something that these

students can do about it. In another study, a meta-analysis of 163 students found that those who rated their health as poor, relative to those who rated their health as excellent, had a two-fold higher mortality risk (DeSalvo et al., 2005).

The top health problems experienced by students in the National College Health Assessment in the past year were: (1) allergy (47.9%), (2) back pain (46.1%), (3) sinus infection (30.7%), (4) depression (17.0%), and (5) strep throat (13.8%). About 1 in 10 students experienced asthma. The top health problems were comparable for men and women.

When asked to indicate factors that undermined their academic performance, students identified several factors that make intuitive sense (see ACHA, 2009). The top five factors were stress (33.9%), cold/flu/sore throat (28.8%), sleep difficulties (25.6%), concern for troubled friend or family member (18.8%), and Internet use/computer games (16.9%). Other specific sources of stress mentioned were relationship difficulties and death of a family member or friend.

While most students seem to enjoy reasonably good health, it is important to note that it is never too soon to start engaging in positive health behaviours (e.g., exercising, regular checkups). Hopefully, good health habits will carry over throughout one's life.

ASSESSING COPING

We have already mentioned the importance of coping. Coping is most often measured by questionnaires that list a series of coping strategies and ask respondents to indicate to what extent they used each strategy to handle a recent stressor. An example of one such measure, the COPE, is presented in Table 9.3.

As with the effects of stressors, the best way to examine coping is to use a battery of measures and to conduct a longitudinal study; this approach would demonstrate that particular ways of coping with stress precede the outcomes in which the researcher is interested. Breast cancer has been investigated in this way. The diagnosis of breast cancer, which strikes about one woman in nine, is a major stressor on many levels. It is a life-threatening illness; surgical interventions are often disfiguring and thus have serious implications for psychological well-being, and both radiation therapy and chemotherapy have very unpleasant side effects.

Carver et al. (1993) selected women who had just been diagnosed with breast cancer and assessed how they were coping at several times during the following year. Women who accepted their diagnosis and retained a sense of humour had lower levels of distress. Carver et al. also found that avoidant coping methods, such as denial and behavioural disengagement (see Table 9.3), were related to higher levels of distress. This negative effect of denial on adjustment to breast cancer has recently been replicated (Heim, Valach, & Schaffner, 1997). Another longitudinal study of several types of cancer found that avoidant coping ("I try not to think about it") predicted greater progression of the disease at a one-year follow-up (Epping-Jordan, Compas, & Howell, 1994). These data show that it is not merely the presence of stress that produces physical and emotional effects: how the person reacts to the stressor is crucial as well. In the case of cancer, reducing stress by ignoring the problem is not a good idea.

Canadian psychologist Norman Endler made important contributions to the research literature on coping, stress, and anxiety (see Canadian Contributions 9.2).

TABLE 9.3
SCALES AND SAMPLE ITEMS FROM THE COPE

Active Coping

I've been concentrating my efforts on doing something about the situation I'm in.

Suppression of Competing Activities

I've been putting aside other activities in order to concentrate on this.

Planning

I've been trying to come up with a strategy about what to do.

Restraint

I've been making sure not to make matters worse by acting too soon.

Use of Social Support

I've been getting sympathy and understanding from someone.

Positive Reframing

I've been looking for something good in what is happening.

Religion

I've been putting my trust in God.

Acceptance

I've been accepting the reality of the fact that it happened.

Denial

I've been refusing to believe that it has happened.

Behavioural Disengagement

I've been giving up the attempt to cope.

Use of Humour

I've been making jokes about it.

Self-Distraction

I've been going to movies, watching TV, or reading, to think about it less.

Source: Carver et al., 1993.

Work by Endler, Parker, and their associates highlights the role of emotional preoccupation as a maladaptive coping response to illness. Emotional preoccupation is quite similar to the ruminative response style described in Chapter 8 as a

---

CANADIAN CONTRIBUTIONS 9.2
NORMAN ENDLER AND THE INTERACTION MODEL OF ANXIETY, STRESS, AND COPING

Dr. Norman Endler from York University was one of Canada's most influential psychologists. In 1997, the Canadian Psychological Association gave him the Donald O. Hebb Award for Distinguished Contributions to Psychology as a Science, and the Royal Society of Canada gave him the Innis-Gerin medal "for distinguished and sustained contributions to the social sciences." Endler died in 2003.

What contributions did he make? Endler was known initially for his interaction model of anxiety and his work on

interactionism with David Magnusson (see Endler & Magnusson, 1976; Endler, 1983). The essence of this model is that personality traits interact dynamically with situational factors to produce behaviours. The model's initial focus was on how different facets of trait anxiety (i.e., the person's usual level of anxiety) combine with congruent situational factors to produce immediate levels of anxiety (i.e., state anxiety). Endler hypothesized that people will experience state anxiety when they experience a situation that matches the aspect of trait anxiety that is central

Dr. Norman S. Endler was a distinguished research professor from York University in Toronto. He was an international expert on anxiety, stress, and coping. Courtesy Norman Endler/York University.

to their personal identity; that is, people high in physical danger anxiety, say, will be anxious in dangerous situations, while people concerned about social evaluation will be anxious in situations involving the possibility of public failures. Extensive research in specific contexts supports the interactionism model. For instance, people high in social evaluation anxiety become highly anxious when asked to give a speech (Muller, Endler, & Parker, 1990) or when taking a driving test to get a licence (King & Endler, 1990). Similarly, studies of physical danger anxiety have shown that Canadian military recruits who are higher in physical danger trait anxiety experienced higher state anxiety when participating in their initial parachute jump training (Endler, Crooks, & Parker, 1992), and people high in physical danger anxiety were extremely anxious when under Scud missile attack in the Persian Gulf War (Lobel, Gilat, & Endler, 1993).

Other research examined anxiety in ambiguous situations. One study conducted during the Quebec referendum on separation from Canada showed that students who usually tend to become anxious in ambiguous, uncertain, and novel situations actually did experience state anxiety when tested just before the referendum results were final (Flett, Endler, & Fairlie, 1999). Their high state anxiety was a joint reflection of their usual tendency to be anxious in ambiguous situations and the great situational uncertainty that existed about how the vote would turn out.

Endler extended his work in recent years by investigating specific trait components of social anxiety (see Endler, Flett, Macrodimitris, Corace, & Kocovski, 2002). This work focuses on people who are high in trait separation anxiety and self-disclosure anxiety (i.e., anxiety when asked to reveal secrets and other aspects of the self to others). New research here indicates that students high in trait separation anxiety are especially prone to feeling homesick in their first year of university (Flett, Besser, & Endler, 2009).

Endler (2002) later added stress and coping components to the interaction model. This revised model is similar in some

key respects to models described earlier (see Lazarus, 1966), but it emphasizes coping as an aspect of personality. When people deal with situational stressors, a key determinant of their emotional response is their typical coping style. Endler teamed up with James Parker, currently at Trent University in Peterborough, Ontario, to create a coping measure tapping stable individual differences in coping styles. The Coping Inventory for Stressful Situations (CISS; Endler & Parker, 1990, 1994, 1999) measures three stable, dispositional aspects of coping: (1) emotion-oriented coping; (2) task-oriented coping; and (3) avoidance-oriented coping. These stable coping styles interact with situational stressors and cognitive appraisals of these stressful situations to determine the nature (positive or negative) and intensity of the emotional response.

This model has implications for health outcomes, so Endler and Parker created a new coping measure to assess how people respond to specific health problems (see Endler, Parker, & Summerfeldt, 1993). Their scale is called Coping with Health Injuries and Problems (CHIP; Endler & Parker, 2000). It has four scales that assess emotional preoccupation, distraction, instrumental coping (i.e., task-oriented strategies), and **palliative coping** (i.e., attempts to feel better via self-soothing and self-help by doing things such as staying in bed or resting when tired). The CHIP has been used to assess the ability to cope with specific health problems such as cancer (Endler, Courbasson, & Fillion, 1998; Jadoulle et al., 2006), Type II diabetes (Macrodimitris & Endler, 2001), and chronic pain (Hadjistavropoulos, Asmundson, & Norton, 1999), as well as to compare individuals with acute vs. chronic illness (Endler, Kocovski, & Macrodimitris, 2001). Endler et al. (2001) predicted and confirmed that chronic illnesses tend to be associated primarily with the CHIP measure of emotional preoccupation. Data from cancer patients suggest that CHIP factor scores are relatively stable during acute phases (i.e., waiting for diagnostic results) and chronic phases (Jadoulle et al., 2006). However, instrumental coping is lower in the chronic phase, presumably when seeking information is less essential. Correlational results indicated that palliative coping predicted emotional distress during the chronic phase.

Other studies with the CHIP yield interesting and meaningful results. Women in Montreal with fibromyalgia who were not adhering to their prescribed drug treatment regimen were shown to have reduced instrumental coping (Sewitch et al., 2004). Other research revealed that well-being was higher among patients with HIV and AIDS if they had elevated levels of instrumental coping (Farber et al., 2003). Finally, mindfulness training results in higher scores on palliative coping (Dobkin, 2008).

Beyond Endler's important scientific contributions, his own personal story documented in his book *Holiday of Darkness* has proved uplifting to other people who have struggled with emotional distress (see Endler, 1982). In this book, Endler chronicled his bout of bipolar depression. Endler's experiences with depression were discussed in more detail in Chapter 8.

way of prolonging depression. Recent research is beginning to illuminate the role of rumination in stress and illness. Collectively, a series of laboratory studies indicate that prolonged rumination contributes to a heightened stress response, and, presumably, chronic rumination should translate into a chronic stress reaction that can take a long-term toll on the body. The tendency to ruminate has been referred to as **perseverative cognition** and the **perseverative cognition hypothesis** is the notion that rumination prolongs the stress response and thus contributes to health problems (see Brosschot, Gerin, & Thayer, 2006). It has also been suggested that chronic rumination can exacerbate the distress of people already attempting to cope with a chronic illness (Soo, Burney, & Basten, 2009).

Recall that public speaking is exceptionally stressful for many people. One recent laboratory investigation showed that relative to being in a non-stressful situation, being exposed to a stressful evaluation condition (i.e., having to make a speech) elicited greater rumination and those who ruminated the most had the most prolonged stress responses (Zoccola, Dickerson, & Zaldivar, 2008). Stress was measured in this study in terms of elevated cortisol. A study conducted in Calgary examined stress responses in undergraduate women. This study by Key, Campbell, Bacon, and Gerin (2008) yielded evidence suggesting that rumination contributes to stress and hypertension by prolonging cardiovascular activation following a stressful experience. In this instance, the stressful situation was recalling a recent stressful negative life event that the participant found difficult to stop thinking about. Measures of state rumination and trait rumination (i.e., a dispositional tendency to ruminate) showed that state rumination was especially likely to contribute to prolonged physiological activation in young women who typically do not ruminate (i.e., low trait rumination).

People are particularly likely to ruminate about the distress that arises from negative interpersonal interactions. An experimental study had participants engage in self-focused rumination, provocation-focused rumination, or distraction after being provoked by another person (Denson, Fabiansson, Creswell, & Pedersen, 2009). Specifically, a research assistant indicated that the participant's responses on an anagram task were so poor, their data could not be used. The results indicated that self-focused rumination resulted in an elevated cortisol response, while provocation-focused rumination and distraction resulted in lower levels of cortisol. However, within the provocation-focused rumination condition, those participants who had a self-focused perspective did have an elevated cortisol response. One problem with this study, however, is determining the element of stress that elicited stress reactions (i.e., was it being insulted, or finding out that one's responses were inadequate, or both?). A more naturalistic 14-day study found that undergraduate students who ruminated extensively about an interpersonal transgression also had elevated levels of salivary cortisol (McCullogh, Orsulak, Brandon, & Akers, 2007). Another recent study found that rumination in general contributed to an impoverished immune system response in a sample of elderly people (Thomsen et al., 2004).

Another recent investigation explored the link between personality features and autonomic dysregulation following rumination. This investigation showed that when asked to ruminate about a time they were very angry, autonomic dysregulation occurred among participants who have personalities characterized by hostility, self-directed anger (see the subsection titled Psychoanalytic Theories on p. 311), depression, and anxiety (Ottaviani et al., 2009). Individuals with these features should be most prone to health problems as a result of brooding about negative social interactions.

What can be done to limit the negative effects of rumination on one's body? Initially, there are benefits associated with cognitively distracting one's attention away in order to limit the repetitive cycle of unwanted negative thoughts. Ultimately, however, ruminators must learn to gain cognitive control over the thought cycle and engage in a cognitive process of thought stopping when the ruminative cycle is getting out of control.

MODERATORS OF THE STRESS-ILLNESS LINK

Although we can demonstrate that life events are related to the onset of illness, important questions remain. We have already noted that the same life experience apparently can have different effects on different people. This situation raises the possibility that other variables moderate or change the general stress-illness relationship. We have described one significant moderator—coping—and we have seen that the use of avoidant coping increases the likelihood of both emotional and physical effects of stress. Social support is another important factor that can lessen the effects of stress.

There are various types and conceptualizations of social support. **Structural social support** refers to a person's basic network of social relationships (e.g., marital status and number of friends). **Functional social support** is concerned more with the quality of a person's relationships (e.g., whether the person believes he or she has friends to call on in a time of need) (Cohen & Wills, 1985).

Social support can also be discussed in terms of the kinds of assistance provided. **Emotional support** provides the recipient with a sense of being cared for by warm and sensitive others, while **instrumental support** provides the recipient with more tangible forms of assistance (e.g., someone helps by making dinner or paying the bills). A study by Muller, Goh, Lemieux, and Fish (2000) serves as a reminder that different kinds of support vary in their relevance as a function of the stressful situation being experienced. This Canadian study found that adult survivors of abuse were more likely to receive emotional support than instrumental support and that friends were most likely to provide this emotional support.

Structural support is a well-established predictor of mortality. People with few friends or relatives tend to have a higher mortality rate than those with a higher level of structural support (Kaplan et al., 1994). Higher levels of functional support have been found to be related to lower rates of atherosclerosis (clogging of the arteries) (Seeman & Syme, 1989) and to the ability of women to adjust to chronic rheumatoid arthritis (Goodenow, Reisine, & Grady, 1990).

How does social support exert its beneficial effects? One possibility is that people who have higher levels of social support perform positive health behaviours more frequently: eating a healthy diet, not smoking, and moderating alcohol intake. This possibility is consistent with the results of a University of Alberta study that found that adults who reported higher levels of social support also indicated a greater intention to exercise (Courneya, Plotnikoff, Hotz, & Birkett, 2000). Alternatively, social support (or lack thereof) could have a direct effect on biological processes. Low levels of social support, for example, are related to an increase in negative emotions, which may affect some hormone levels and the immune system (Kiecolt-Glaser, McGuire, Robles, & Glaser, 2002).

In recent years, social support has been studied in the laboratory, where cause and effect can be more readily established than in the naturalistic studies already described. In one such study, university-aged women were assigned to high- or low-stress conditions, which they experienced alone or with a close friend. In one part of the study, stress was created by having the experimenter behave coldly and impersonally, telling participants to improve their performance as they worked on a challenging task. In each case where the woman had the social support of a close friend, the friend "silently cheered her on" and sat close to her, placing a hand on her wrist. The dependent variable was blood pressure, measured while participants performed the task. As expected, high stress led to higher blood-pressure levels. But, as Figure 9.4 shows, the high-stress condition produced its effects on blood pressure primarily in those women who experienced the stress alone (Kamarck, Annunziato, & Amateau, 1995). Social support was thus shown to have a causal effect on a physiological process. Further laboratory research has shown that such results are produced only when the support comes from a friend and not when it comes from a stranger (Christenfeld et al.,

1997). Perhaps only a friend can lead someone to appraise a stressful situation as less threatening.

A possible biological mechanism for the stress-reducing effects of social support is suggested by some research with animals. A hormone called oxytocin may be released during social interaction. Oxytocin decreases activity of the sympathetic nervous system and may thereby lessen the physiological effects of a stressor (Uvnas-Moberg, 1997).

Not all research has found that social support has positive effects. With very severe stressors, some people may be so overwhelmed that support does no good. However, other people in the same situation may derive great benefit from the support of others.

THEORIES OF THE STRESS-ILLNESS LINK

In considering the etiology of psychophysiological disorders, we are confronted with three questions:

1. Why does stress produce illness in only some people who are exposed to it?
2. Why does stress sometimes cause an illness and not a psychological disorder?
3. When stress produces a psychophysiological disorder, what determines which one of the many disorders will be produced?

Although answers to these questions have been sought by biologically and psychologically oriented researchers, theories in this domain are invariably diathesis-stress in nature. They differ primarily in whether the diathesis is described in psychological or biological terms.

Before we review some theories that describe how stress causes or exacerbates physical illness, it is important to note that much of the research in the field has attempted to link stress to self-reports of illness. The problem with this approach is that self-reports may not be an accurate reflection of physical illness, as we have already noted. Watson and Pennebaker (1989) concluded that an apparent association between negative emotional states and health was actually only a relationship between negative emotions and illness reporting. Similarly, Stone and Costa (1990) noted that neuroticism predicted reports of higher numbers of somatic complaints of all kinds (recall our discussion of hypochondriasis and somatization disorder) but did not predict "hard endpoints," such as death or verified coronary artery disease. Because of such problems, our discussion focuses mainly on research that goes beyond illness self-reports.

BIOLOGICAL THEORIES

Biological approaches attribute particular psychophysiological disorders to specific organ weaknesses, to overactivity of particular organ systems in responding to stress, to the effects of exposure to stress hormones, or to changes in the immune system that are caused by stress.

FIGURE 9.4 Results of a laboratory study of the effects of social support on blood pressure. Stress led to increased blood pressure, but the increase was less pronounced among people who experienced the stressor with a friend. From Kamarck et al., 1995

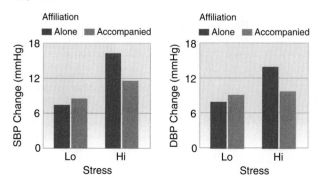

SOMATIC-WEAKNESS THEORY Genetic factors, prior illnesses, diet, and the like may disrupt a particular organ system, which may then become weak and vulnerable to stress. According to the **somatic-weakness theory**, the connection between stress and a particular psychophysiological disorder is a weakness in a specific body organ. For instance, a congenitally weak respiratory system might predispose the individual to asthma.

SPECIFIC-REACTION THEORY People have been found to have their own individual patterns of autonomic response to stress. The heart rate of one individual may increase, whereas another person may react with an increased respiration rate but no change in heart rate (Lacey, 1967). According to the **specific-reaction theory**, individuals respond to stress in their own idiosyncratic ways, and the body system that is the most responsive becomes a likely candidate for the locus of a subsequent psychophysiological disorder. For example, someone reacting to stress with elevated blood pressure may be more susceptible to essential hypertension. Later in this chapter, when we consider specific psychophysiological disorders, evidence in support of both the somatic-weakness theory and the specific-reaction theory will be presented.

PROLONGED EXPOSURE TO STRESS HORMONES Another theory attempts to deal with the finding described earlier that the biological changes that stress produces are adaptive in the short run; for example, the mobilization of energy resources in preparation for physical activity (McEwen, 1998). The major biological responses to stress involve activation of the sympathetic nervous system and the hypothalamic-pituitary-adrenal axis (HPA). Under conditions of stress, catecholamines such as epinephrine are released from nerves and from the adrenal medulla and lead to secretion of corticotropin from the pituitary. Corticotropin then leads to the release of cortisol from the cortex of the adrenal gland (see Figure 9.5).

The key to McEwen's theory is that the body pays a price if it must constantly adapt to stress. Through exposure to high levels of stress hormones, it may become susceptible to disease because of altered immune system functioning. Furthermore, high levels of cortisol can have direct effects on the brain; for example, high levels can kill cells in the hippocampus, which itself regulates the secretion of cortisol. Over time, the person may become even more susceptible to the effects of stress.

Some people may have consistently high levels of stress hormones because they experience frequent stress. Other people may have less difficulty in adapting to repeated exposure to stressful situations. Most people react to the stress of public speaking, for example, with an increase in cortisol secretion; but after repeated exposure, most adapt and the amount of cortisol secreted declines. However, about 10% of people show no adaptation and even increase their secretion of cortisol (Kirschbaum et al., 1995). According to McEwen's theory, these are the individuals at risk for disease.

Actual research on stress and the HPA axis activation suggests that the link is exceedingly complex. A contemporary review by Gregory Miller from the University of British Columbia and his associates involved a meta-analysis of existing studies involving the HPA axis (see Miller, Chen, & Zhou, 2007). The authors concluded that several factors must be taken into account to explain why data across studies suggest that stress has been associated with both increased and reduced HPA axis activity. One key factor is the timing of the assessment. Time elapsed following the stress was associated negatively with HPA activity; as the months go by, cortisol secretion eventually goes back to normal. The nature of the stressor is also important; as might be expected, prolonged high activation resulted from more traumatic stressors, stressors that threaten survival, and stressors involving a profound threat to the social self (e.g., a divorce). Finally, uncontrollable stressors are linked with persistent HPA axis activation.

FIGURE 9.5 The HPA axis

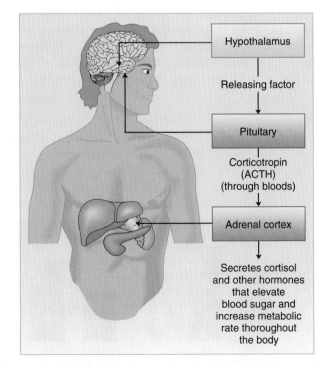

Stress may indirectly increase risk for illness by causing lifestyle changes such as increased consumption of alcohol. Digital Vision.

STRESS AND THE IMMUNE SYSTEM On a general level, stressors have multiple effects on various systems of the body: the autonomic nervous system, hormone levels, and brain activity. One major area of current interest is the immune system, an important consideration in infectious diseases, cancer, and allergies, as well as in autoimmune diseases, in which the immune system attacks the body. It is now generally accepted that stress triggers autoimmune diseases such as rheumatoid arthritis (see Stojanovich & Marisavljevich, 2008). A wide range of stressors have been found to produce changes in the immune system: medical-school examinations, depression and bereavement, marital discord and divorce, job loss, caring for a relative with Alzheimer's disease, and the Three Mile Island nuclear disaster, among others (Cohen & Herbert, 1996). There is now extensive evidence that stress dysregulates the immune system and work on psychoneuroimmunology shows that immune system responses to viral and bacterial vaccines can be delayed, weakened, and shorter in duration for stressed or distressed people (Kiecolt-Glaser, 2009). The role of stress in disease progression is indicated by data linking stress and distress with cytokine secretion by tumour cells (Antoni et al., 2006). So it appears that for certain individuals, stress can kill.

The area of research that comes closest to documenting a role for stress and immune system changes in actual illness is the study of infectious diseases. To illustrate, we will discuss one aspect of the immune system—secretory immunity—in some detail.

The secretory component of the immune system exists in the tears, saliva, and gastrointestinal, vaginal, nasal, and bronchial secretions that bathe the mucosal surfaces of the body. A substance found in these secretions, called secretory immunoglobulin A, or sIgA, contains antibodies that serve as the body's first line of defence against invading viruses and bacteria. They prevent the virus or bacterium from binding to mucosal tissues.

A study by Stone and his colleagues (Stone, Cox et al., 1987) showed that changes in the number of sIgA antibodies were linked to changes in mood. Throughout an eight-week study period, a group of dental students came to the laboratory three times a week to have their saliva collected and a brief psychological assessment conducted. On days when the students experienced relatively high levels of negative mood, fewer antibodies were present than on days when the students had low levels of negative mood. Similarly, antibody level was higher on days with higher levels of positive mood.

Stone and his colleagues have found that changes in the frequency of daily life events precede the onset of episodes of respiratory infection. The mechanism may be a stress-induced lowering of sIgA. Stockbyte.

Prior research (e.g., Stone & Neale, 1984) had shown that daily events affect mood. It is therefore quite possible that daily events affect fluctuations in mood, which in turn affect the synthesis of the secretory sIgA antibodies. The process could operate as follows. An increase in undesirable life events coupled with a decrease in desirable life events produces increased negative mood, which in turn depresses antibody levels in secretory sIgA. If during this period a person is exposed to a virus, he or she will be at increased risk for infection (see Figure 9.6).

Several other studies have confirmed the relationship between stress and respiratory infection. In each of them, volunteers took nasal drops containing a mild cold virus and completed a battery of questionnaires concerning recent stress. The advantage of this method was that exposure to the virus was an experimental variable under the investigators' control. Researchers found that stress was clearly linked to developing a cold (Cohen, Tyrell, & Smith, 1991; Stone et al., 1992). The stressors most often implicated were interpersonal problems and work difficulties (Cohen et al., 1998). In a similar study, social support was found to moderate the relationship between viral exposure and colds (Cohen et al., 1997). People with more diverse social networks were less likely to develop a cold following exposure to

FIGURE 9.6 Mechanism through which stress could increase risk for viral infection

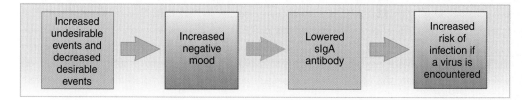

a virus. Recent work shows that a positive emotional style (i.e., being happy, calm, and full of vigour) protects people from illness after being exposed to a virus, and the presence of this positive emotional style is more predictive than the presence or absence of a negative emotional style (i.e., depressed, anxious, and hostile) (see Cohen et al., 2006). These findings illustrate the complex interplay between psychological and biological variables in the etiology of psychophysiological disorders.

The investigations described above represent only a small proportion of the research conducted in this area. A seminal meta-analysis by Suzanne Segerstrom from the University of Kentucky and Gregory Miller from the University of British Columbia of more than 300 studies has provided a wealth of useful information (see Segerstrom & Miller, 2004). They concluded that stress can be adaptive in the short term when it results in upgrades to the body's natural immunity and when it acts as a catalyst for engaging in adaptive flight-or-fight responses to challenging situations. However, even short-term stressors such as taking an exam can result in suppressed cellular immunity, and chronic stress can suppress cellular immunity and humoral immunity. Important individual differences can also come into play. Research by Bandura and his associates has expanded investigation of Bandura's concept of **self-efficacy** (i.e., a personal sense of perceived capability). Bandura's research team has shown that deficits in self-efficacy are linked to diminished immune system functioning.

PSYCHOLOGICAL THEORIES

Psychological theories try to account for the development of various disorders by considering such factors as unconscious emotional states, personality traits, cognitive appraisals, and specific styles of coping with stress.

COGNITIVE AND BEHAVIOURAL FACTORS Physical threats obviously create stress, but humans perceive more than merely physical threats. We experience regrets about the past and worries about the future. All these perceptions can stimulate sympathetic-system activity and the secretion of stress hormones. But negative emotions, such as resentment, regret, and worry, cannot be fought or escaped as readily as can external threats, nor do they easily pass. They may keep the body's biological systems aroused and the body in a continual state of emergency, sometimes for far longer than it can bear, as suggested by McEwen's theory. In addition, the high level of cognition made possible in humans through evolution creates the potential for distressed thoughts, which can bring about bodily changes that persist longer than they were meant to. Our higher mental capacities, it is theorized, subject our bodies to physical storms that they were not built to withstand.

We saw in our general discussion of stress that the appraisal of a potential stressor is central to how it affects the person. People who continually appraise life experiences as exceeding their resources may be chronically stressed and at risk for the development of a psychophysiological disorder. How people cope with stress may also be relevant. We will shortly describe some findings that show that hypertension is related to how people cope with anger. Personality traits are implicated in several disorders, most notably CVD. People who chronically experience high levels of negative emotions, for example, are at high risk for the development of heart problems. Finally, gender is an important variable in health; there are clear differences in the frequency with which men and women experience certain health problems (see Focus on Discovery 9.4).

FOCUS ON DISCOVERY 9.4
GENDER AND HEALTH

Recall that one of our tenets is that women live longer than men but women also report being less healthy than men (Canadian Population Health Initiative, 2004). We focus on gender differences in mortality but numerous other gender differences were noted in the 2004 document *Improving the Health of Canadians* (Canadian Population Health Initiative, 2004): (1) women have lower rates of obesity and being overweight (39% for women vs. 56% for men); (2) while over three million Canadian men have two or more chronic health conditions, over four million women have two or more chronic conditions; and (3) there is a gender imbalance, with over 500,000 more women than men reporting disabilities based on their functional health status. Thus women have greater morbidity—general poor health or the incidence of several specific diseases.

What are some of the possible reasons for the differences in mortality and morbidity rates between men and women, and why is mortality in women increasing? First, it should be noted that a recent review suggests that the greater morbidity among women may have been overstated (see Gorman & Read, 2006). The morbidity disadvantage for women is apparently smaller than first thought. The gap is greatest for self-rated health, in part because men tend to inflate health estimates. The gap is lowest for life-threatening medical conditions (Gorman & Read, 2006). Still, even with this indicator there is a gender difference.

From a biological vantage point, it might be that women have some mechanism that protects them from life-threatening diseases. The female hormone, estrogen, may offer protection from cardiovascular disease, for example. Several lines of evidence support this idea. Postmenopausal women and those women who have had their ovaries removed—in both cases having lowered estrogen—have higher rates of cardiovascular disease than do premenopausal women. Hormone-replacement therapy lowers

Women typically have higher rates of illness than do men. One source of stress for many women is the need to cope with the dual roles of homemaker and wage earner. Goodshoot.

Why is the gap between mortality rates in men and women decreasing? In the early twentieth century, most deaths were due to epidemics and infection, but now most deaths result from diseases that are affected by lifestyle. One possibility, then, is that lifestyle differences between men and women account for the sex difference in mortality and that these lifestyle differences have become less evident. Men smoke more than women and consume more alcohol. These differences are likely contributors to men's higher mortality from CVD and lung cancer. In recent years, however, women have begun to smoke and drink more, changes paralleled by higher instances of lung cancer rates and the failure of the mortality rate for CVD to decrease among women (e.g., Rodin & Ickovics, 1990).

Another lifestyle change placing women at greater risk is that more women with families have been entering the workforce, thus taking on the stress of assuming the dual role of wage earner and homemaker. Frankenhaeuser et al. (1989) studied norepinephrine levels in men and women employed at an automobile-manufacturing plant in Gothenburg, Sweden. Levels were similar in both sexes during the day, but those in men declined after work, while those in women rose. Working women who have children at home do not have lower blood pressure at home than at work (Marco et al., 2000), and they excrete high levels of norepinephrine (Lundberg & Frankenhaueser, 1999). A comparative study of women and men in high status occupations found that the women had higher levels of norepinephrine at work and at home, which the authors attributed to women having a less favourable job situation, including a greater likelihood of doing unpaid work (Lundberg & Frankenhaueser, 1999).

There are several possible explanations for the difference in the morbidity rates of men and women. First, because women live longer than men, they may be more likely to experience several diseases associated with aging. Second, women may be more attentive to their health than men are and thus may be more likely to visit physicians and be diagnosed. Finally, women may cope with stress in a way that increases their risk for some illnesses; for example, by focusing their attention on their responses to a negative event (Weidner & Collins, 1993).

the rate of mortality from CVD, perhaps by maintaining elevated levels of high-density lipoprotein (HDL), the so-called good cholesterol (Matthews et al., 1989).

Denton and Walters (1999) believe that social structural factors are more important for women than men. Their analysis of data from the 1994 Canadian National Health Population Survey (N = 15,144) supported their position, finding evidence of striking gender differences. Specifically, factors such as caring for a family, the presence of social support, and being in the highest income category were more important predictors of outcomes for women than men. In contrast, smoking and alcohol consumption were more critical determinants of health status for men. As we shall see, both biological and psychological variables play important roles in CVD, and they could well be relevant to the lower levels of mortality of women.

PSYCHOANALYTIC THEORIES Psychoanalytic theories propose that specific conflicts and their associated negative emotional states give rise to psychophysiological disorders. Franz Alexander is the psychoanalytic theorist who has the greatest impact relative to other psychoanalytic theorists. He maintained that each of the various psychophysiological disorders is the product of unconscious emotional states specific to that disorder. For example, undischarged hostile impulses are believed to create the chronic emotional state responsible for essential hypertension.

The damming up of hostile impulses will continue and will consequently increase in intensity. This will induce the development of stronger defensive measures in order to keep pent-up aggressions in check. Because of the marked degree of their inhibitions, these patients are less effective in their occupational activities and for that reason tend to fail in competition with others ... [E]nvy is stimulated and hostile feelings toward more successful, less inhibited competitors are further intensified. (Alexander, 1950, p. 150)

Alexander formulated this theory of unexpressed anger, or **anger-in theory**, on the basis of his observations of patients undergoing psychoanalysis. His hypothesis continues to be pursued in present-day studies of the psychological factors in essential hypertension, as discussed shortly.

We turn now to a detailed review of disorders that have attracted much attention from researchers: cardiovascular disorders. We then discuss issues of socio-economic status and ethnicity that are related to health.

CARDIOVASCULAR DISORDERS

Cardiovascular disorders (CVDs) are diseases involving the heart and blood-circulation system. In this section, we focus on two forms of CVD that appear to be adversely affected by stress: hypertension and coronary heart disease. Of the cardiovascular diseases, coronary heart disease causes the greatest number of deaths. It is generally agreed that many of the deaths resulting from cardiovascular diseases could be prevented by dealing with one or more of the known risk factors.

In 1997, it was estimated that the average annual cost of CVD to the Canadian medical system was $17 billion (Statistics Canada, 1997), even though rates of cardiovascular disease and associated outcomes (e.g., strokes) had declined substantially in Canada over the previous two decades (see Manuel et al., 2003).

Some alarming results emerged from analyses of the Canadian Heart Health Surveys conducted between 1986 and 1992. Langille et al. (1999) described the findings from probability samples of more than 5,000 women and men between the ages of 55 and 74 drawn from all 10 provinces. Participants were visited by a trained nurse who collected demographic and lifestyle data, including an assessment of each participant's knowledge of cardiovascular disease risk factors. Blood pressure was measured at a clinic within two weeks of the initial visit. Blood samples were also provided. The results showed that 52% of the participants were hypertensive, 26% suffered from isolated systolic hypertension, and 30% had levels of blood cholesterol requiring intervention. The presence of hypertension was untreated in 52% of the afflicted. Langille et al. (1999) found that almost 50% of the participants had three or more major risk factors, and they noted that this is particularly troubling because risk factors tend to act synergistically rather than in an additive fashion, resulting in a substantial magnification of risk.

A related study by Kirkland et al. (1999) used data from the same sample but focused on the participants' knowledge and awareness of risk factors for cardiovascular disease. Participants were asked, "Can you tell me what are the major causes of heart disease or heart problems?" (Kirkland et al., 1999, p. S10). The most frequently mentioned causes were stress (44%), worry (44%), and smoking (41%). High blood cholesterol was mentioned by only 23% of the respondents, and hypertension was mentioned by only 16%. The authors concluded that awareness of the major causes of cardiovascular disease is quite low among Canadians aged 55 to 74. They also noted that of those people in the study identified as having a risk factor, approximately two thirds of the women and the men involved were unaware of their high cholesterol status, while 33% of the women and 43% of the men were unaware of their hypertensive status.

These alarming findings likely helped Canadian efforts to proactively address risk. A key part of the Canadian initiative is

Dr. Norm Campbell from the University of Calgary is a leading researcher, and the CIHR Canada Chair in Hypertension Prevention and Control. He also developed and helped lead the Canadian Hypertension Education Program. He suggests that it is more than a coincidence that after the program's first ten years, the hypertension treatment and control rate has increased more than sixfold; there are one in seven fewer stroke deaths, one in five fewer heart failure deaths, and one in ten fewer heart attack deaths. Photo courtesy Dr. Campbell.

the Canadian Hypertension Education Program. This unique initiative is designed to improve awareness, treatment, and control of hypertension through the education of health care professionals (Feldman, Campbell, & Wyard, 2008). It is regarded as an international model for knowledge translation (i.e., imparting information that can be put into practice) and promoting collaboration among health care professionals. Progress is being made. Deaths due to cardiovascular disease have declined over time in Canada and the United States (Lee et al., 2009). Mortality rates and rates of hospitalization declined 30% between 1994 and 2004 (Tu, Nardi, & Fang, 2009). Reductions in major risk factors accounted for most of this change. According to Capewell and O'Flaherty (2009), over 80% of premature cardiovascular disease is avoidable.

ESSENTIAL HYPERTENSION

Why is it important to be aware of hypertension? Hypertension, commonly called high blood pressure, disposes people to atherosclerosis (clogging of the arteries), heart attacks, and strokes; it can also cause death through kidney failure. Yet no more than 10% of all cases of hypertension in the United States are attributable to an identifiable physical cause. Hypertension without an evident biological cause is called **essential** (or sometimes primary) **hypertension**. Unless people have their blood pressure checked, they may go for years without knowing that they are hypertensive. Thus, this disease is known as the silent killer.

FIGURE 9.7 Normal young-adult blood pressure

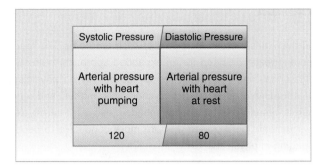

FIGURE 9.7 Normal young-adult blood pressure

Systolic Pressure	Diastolic Pressure
Arterial pressure with heart pumping	Arterial pressure with heart at rest
120	80

Blood pressure is measured by two numbers: one represents systolic pressure, and the other represents diastolic pressure. The systolic measure, the upper number, is the amount of arterial pressure when the ventricles contract and the heart is pumping; the diastolic measure, the lower number, is the degree of arterial pressure when the ventricles relax and the heart is resting. A normal blood pressure in a young adult is 120 (systolic) over 80 (diastolic) (Figure 9.7). The guidelines for determining high blood pressure were extended and revised recently by the American Medical Association (AMA), in an attempt to heighten public awareness and detection of problems by physicians (see Chobanian et al., 2003). The AMA concluded that among people 50 years of age or older, systolic blood pressure (BP) of more than 140 mmHg is a much more important CVD risk factor than diastolic BP. In addition, the risk of cardiovascular disease has now been pegged at beginning at 115/75 mmHg, and it doubles with each increment of 20/10 mmHg.

A study by Wolf-Maier et al. (2003), using a BP of 140 over 90 as indicative of hypertension, found that 28% of Canadian and American adults had hypertension, while an astronomical 44% of Europeans had the condition. Currently, it is estimated that more than one billion people worldwide have hypertension (Chobanian et al., 2003). Hypertension is regarded as the leading risk factor for death in the world, causing about 7.5 million deaths per year, or 13% of all deaths (World Health Organization, 2009). While great strides have been made in Canada in terms of hypertension control, the prevalence of hypertension remains unacceptably high. A national survey conducted between 2007 and 2009 found hypertension in 19% of adults, similar to rates in 1992, and another 20% had blood pressure in the pre-hypertension range (Wilkins et al., 2010). In contrast to previous results, fewer Canadians (17%) were unaware of their hypertensive status, so there has indeed been progress in heightening awareness.

Essential hypertension is viewed as a heterogeneous condition brought on by many possible disturbances in the various systems of the body that are responsible for regulating blood pressure. Genes play a substantial role in controlling blood pressure; other risk factors for hypertension include obesity, excessive intake of alcohol, and salt consumption. Blood pressure may be elevated by increased cardiac output (the amount of blood leaving the left ventricle of the heart), by increased resistance to the passage of blood through the arteries (vasoconstriction), or by both. The physiological mechanisms that regulate blood pressure interact in an extremely complex manner. Activation of the sympathetic nervous system is a key factor, but hormones, salt metabolism, and central nervous system mechanisms are all involved. How important is salt intake? A new Canadian study of the Inuit in Northern Quebec has found that levels of hypertension have doubled in recent years as a function of moving away from a salt-reduced diet consisting mostly of fish products and moving toward a more traditional salt-laden Western diet (Picard, 2009).

Table 9.4 lists the 10 major risk factors for high blood pressure, as identified by the Canadian Expert Working Group (CEWG) on high blood pressure prevention and control. The conclusions of the CEWG are outlined in Canadian Perspectives 9.1. It can be seen in Table 9.4 that the risk factors are varied and include physical factors (e.g., excess weight) and the importance of exercise, but they also include lifestyle factors (e.g., degree of heavy alcohol use), socio-economic status, and psychological factors involving stress and coping.

PSYCHOLOGICAL STRESS AND BLOOD-PRESSURE ELEVATION Various stressful conditions have been examined to determine their role in the etiology of essential hypertension. Stressful interviews, natural disasters such as earthquakes, and job stress have all been found to produce short-term elevations in blood pressure (e.g., Niedhammer et al., 1998).

It is also relatively easy to produce increased blood pressure in the laboratory. The induction of various emotional states, such as anger, fear, and sadness, all increase blood pressure (Cacioppo et al., 1993). Similarly, challenging tasks, such

TABLE 9.4
RISK FACTORS FOR HIGH BLOOD PRESSURE

Excess weight (body mass index greater than 25)

Central obesity (i.e., waist to hip ratio greater than 1)

Lack of regular physical activity

Heavy alcohol use (per week, 14 or more drinks for men, 9 or more drinks for women)

Lack of diet with high fibre, fruit, vegetables, and low saturated fat

Inadequate dietary intake of calcium and potassium

Excessive salt intake

Stress and coping response

Low socio-economic status (reflecting its association with other risk factors and daily living challenges)

Low birth weight

Source: Adapted from Table 2, Report of the Canadian Expert Working Group, Health Canada, and The Canadian Coalition for High Blood Pressure Prevention and Control (2000), p. 25.

CANADIAN PERSPECTIVES 9.1
PREVENTION AND CONTROL OF HYPERTENSION IN CANADA

An expert working group was first put together in 1996 to devise a national strategy to combat hypertension in Canada. The Canadian Expert Working Group (CEWG) was formed by Health Canada and the Canadian Coalition for High Blood Pressure Prevention and Control. It can be argued that its report, which was published in January 2000 and is updated annually, while aimed at policy-makers, should nevertheless be required reading for all Canadians. The CEWG's overarching goals are to reduce the prevalence of uncontrolled high blood pressure in Canada and reduce the proportion of Canadians who are entirely unaware that they have high blood pressure.

The CEWG's report identifies a number of short-term and long-term program objectives. Short-term objectives include increasing the general public's knowledge and improving their attitudes and skills involving healthy behaviours and the importance of regular blood pressure measurements; short-term objectives also include very specific outcomes, such as decreasing the amount of salt added to prepared food and food served in restaurants. The four stated long-term program outcomes are to achieve (1) an increase in a healthy lifestyle for all Canadians (i.e., healthy weight, regular physical activity, low-risk alcohol use, and stress management) in order to prevent the onset of high blood pressure; (2) an increase in Canadians having regular blood pressure measurements; (3) an increase in high blood pressure investigation, diagnosis, and treatment; and (4) an increase in individuals with high blood pressure adopting healthy behaviours and appropriate use of prescribed medicine.

This important report also includes an analysis of why previous prevention programs have met with only limited success. One key factor that has undermined previous attempts at prevention is the fact that only 1 to 2% of the public health care budget is dedicated to the promotion of healthy behaviours and this limits the overall impact of such programs. The report also suggests the need for an expanded approach to lifestyle counselling, one that does not rely so heavily on physicians but affords a greater role to psychologists, nurses, and nutritionists, among others. It recommended, as well, that physical environments be provided that are more conducive to people engaging in physical activity.

Although this working group has provided an important document, there is a need for targeting preventive efforts at certain groups. A new study with a representative sample of the Canadian population aged 20 years or older found that heart disease and its associated risk factors, including hypertension (as well as obesity and diabetes) are increasing in all age groups. However, risk is increasingly disproportionate among younger Canadians with lower socio-economic status (Lee et al., 2009).

Thinking Critically

1. The CEWG recommends an increase in a healthy lifestyle for all Canadians. Do you think that prevention programs could be implemented effectively in the workplace and supported and funded by business and industry? Why? How?

2. How would you address the issue of hypertension among Canada's Aboriginal peoples? Design a prevention program tailored specifically to our Aboriginal peoples. What key risk factors would you address in your program?

3. Design a model of hypertension that takes into account the various risk factors for hypertension that have been discussed in this chapter. Use lines and arrows to indicate the interrelationships among the factors. Develop a comprehensive, self-report assessment of lifestyle that could be used as an initial component of a lifestyle skills hypertension prevention program.

---

as mental arithmetic, mirror drawing, putting a hand in ice water (the cold pressor test), and giving a speech in front of an audience all lead to increased blood pressure (e.g., Manuck, Kaplan, & Clarkson, 1993; Tuomisto, 1997). A classic series of studies by Obrist and his colleagues (e.g., 1978) used a reaction-time task in which participants were told they would receive an electric shock if they did not respond quickly enough. Good performance led to a monetary bonus. The reaction-time task yielded significant increases in both heart rate and systolic blood pressure.

Ultimately we must understand why blood pressure increases in people's natural environments. Therefore, researchers have also undertaken studies of ambulatory blood pressure, wherein participants wear a blood-pressure cuff that takes readings as they go about their daily lives. Many of these studies have asked participants about their emotional state at the time a blood-pressure reading is taken. The general finding has been that both positive and negative emotional states are associated with higher blood pressure (e.g., Jacob et al., 1999; Kamarck et al., 1998).

Other ambulatory monitoring studies have examined environmental conditions associated with blood pressure. A series of studies examined the effects of stress on blood pressure among paramedics (Shapiro, Jamner, & Goldstein, 1993). In one of these analyses, ambulance calls were divided into high- and low-stress types. As expected, the high-stress calls were associated with higher blood pressure. This interacted with levels of anger. The groups did not differ in blood pressure during the low-stress calls, but on the high-stress calls, paramedics high in anger and defensiveness had higher blood pressure.

In the ambulatory monitoring studies just described, the overall amount of blood-pressure increase associated with emotional states or environmental conditions was rather small.

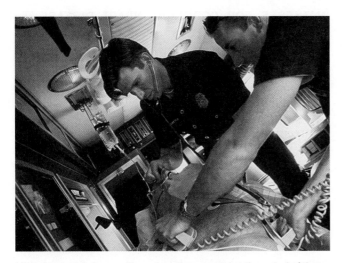

High-stress ambulance calls, such as those requiring the revival of the victim, led to greater blood-pressure increases in paramedics than low-stress calls in the Shapiro, Jamner, and Goldstein study (1993). Bruce Ayres/Tony Stone Images.

But it was also consistently found that a subset of participants had large increases. In the Kamarck study, for example, participants in the top 10% of the magnitude of association between negative mood and blood pressure showed a 20-point increase in systolic blood pressure. These data suggest that only people who have some predisposition, or diathesis, will experience large blood-pressure increases that over time may lead to sustained hypertension. We turn next to these possible diatheses.

PREDISPOSING FACTORS It is generally accepted that blood pressure and hypertension are highly heritable but there has been very little success thus far in indentifying the genes involved. Two new papers published in the journal *Nature Genetics* represent important breakthroughs. These papers describe the results of meta-analyses conducted collaboratively by two huge research consortiums. Collectively, data on over 159,000 people resulted in the identification of 13 gene regions not associated previously with blood pressure (Levy et al., 2009; Newton-Cheh et al., 2009). The investigators concluded that each individual region may have only a small effect but there are now many specific regions to explore in subsequent research.

In the past decade, there has been a great deal of interest in cardiovascular reactivity as a biological predisposition to hypertension (and coronary heart disease, as well). Cardiovascular reactivity refers to the extent to which blood pressure and heart rate increase in response to stress. The general research strategy is to assess cardiovascular reactivity to a laboratory stressor (or, even better, a battery of stressors) among people who are not currently hypertensive and then to follow up with the participants some years later to determine whether the reactivity measure (usually the amount of change from a baseline condition after exposure to the stressor) predicts blood pressure. Two important points must be demonstrated to ensure the success of this approach:

1. Reactivity must be reliable if it is going to have predictive power; that is, someone who is high in reactivity must be consistently high. Indications are that reactivity is reliable if it is measured in response to a battery of laboratory stressors (e.g., Kamarck et al., 1992).
2. The laboratory measure of reactivity must actually relate to what the person's cardiovascular system does during day-to-day activities. Because of what is called white-coat hypertension, a person's blood pressure may be high at the clinic or laboratory but normal elsewhere. Though the literature on this issue is somewhat conflicting (see Gerin et al., 1994; Swain & Suls, 1996), studies that have compared laboratory reactivity with reactivity to stressors in the natural environment have shown some relationship in at least some people (Matthews et al., 1992).

What are the results of the studies that have tried to predict blood pressure from reactivity? Reactivity is related to other known risk factors for hypertension, such as race and low social class (Gump, Matthews, & Raikkonen, 1999; Jackson et al., 1999), as well as obesity, excessive use of alcohol, and family history of hypertension (see Wielgosz & Nolan, 2000). A longitudinal study of almost 3,000 men and women between the ages of 20 and 35 years found that blood pressure changes during a video game predicted coronary calcification of the arteries 13 years later (Matthews, Zhu, Tucker, & Whooley, 2006). The reaction to the video game represents a general tendency to be physiologically reactive to stress and challenge. Subsequent research sought to identify the neural systems mediating blood pressure reactivity. It was found that individuals with greater stress-evoked changes in mean arterial pressure had greater amygdala activation, lower amygdala grey matter volume, and stronger connectivity between the amygdala and both the perigenual anterior cingulate cortex and the brainstem pons (Gianaros et al., 2008). A follow-up study found that there is a neurobiological correlate (i.e., heightened resting corticolimbic activity) of high blood pressure reactivity (Gianaros et al., 2009). These data are promising in pointing to neurobiological factors and associated neural circuits that may predispose certain people to greater blood pressure reactivity and cardiovascular risk.

CORONARY HEART DISEASE
Coronary heart disease (CHD) takes two principal forms: angina pectoris and myocardial infarction, or heart attack.

CHARACTERISTICS OF THE DISEASE The symptoms of **angina pectoris** are periodic chest pains, usually located behind the sternum and frequently radiating into the back and sometimes the left shoulder and arm. The major cause of these severe attacks of pain is an insufficient supply of oxygen to the heart (called ischemia), which in turn is due to coronary atherosclerosis, a narrowing or plugging of the coronary arteries by deposits of cholesterol, a fatty material, or constriction of the blood vessels. In many patients with coronary heart disease, episodes of ischemia do not result in the report of pain. These are called episodes of silent ischemia. Both angina and episodes of silent ischemia are precipitated by physical or emotional exertion and are commonly relieved by rest or medication. Serious physical damage to heart muscle rarely results from an angina or ischemia attack, for blood flow is reduced but not cut off. If, however, the narrowing of one or more coronary arteries progresses to the point of producing a total blockage, a myocardial infarction, or heart attack, is likely to occur.

Myocardial infarction is a much more serious disorder. Like angina pectoris, it is caused by an insufficient supply of oxygen to the heart. But unlike angina, a heart attack usually results in permanent damage to the heart.

Several factors increase risk for CHD and the risk generally increases with the number and severity of these factors:

- age
- sex (males are at greater risk)
- cigarette smoking
- elevated blood pressure
- elevated serum cholesterol
- an increase in the size of the left ventricle of the heart
- obesity
- long-standing pattern of physical inactivity
- excessive use of alcohol
- diabetes

STRESS AND MYOCARDIAL INFARCTION In the short term, physical exertion can trigger a myocardial infarction, as can episodes of anger (Mittleman et al., 1997). Acute stress is another factor; the frequency of myocardial infarction, for example, increased among residents of Tel Aviv on the day of an Iraqi missile attack (NHLBI, 1998). More chronic stressors, such as marital conflict and financial worries, are also relevant. One current theory is that chronic stress activates the immune system and contributes to inflammation, which, in turn, produces CHD (Miller & Blackwell, 2006).

Consistent with our earlier observations about the destructive effects of job stress, many studies have found that a high level of job strain is associated with increased risk for myocardial infarction (Schnall, Landsbergis, & Baker, 1994). In one of the most well-known investigations, more than 10,000 British civil servants were assessed for the degree of control they could exercise on their jobs. They were then followed for about five years to determine the incidence of CHD. Replicating earlier studies, more CHD was found at follow-up among workers in lower-status jobs (e.g., clerical work). This result, in turn, was related to these workers' reports of having little control on the job (Marmot et al., 1997). In a large-scale study being conducted in Finland, highly demanding jobs have also been related to the progression of atherosclerosis (Lynch et al., 1997a) and to CVD mortality and morbidity (Lynch et al., 1997b).

DIATHESES FOR CORONARY HEART DISEASE The traditional risk factors, still left at least half the instances of coronary heart disease unexplained as recently as the 1970s (see Jenkins, 1976). Indeed, people used to pay less attention to contributing causes, such as obesity, poor exercise habits, consumption of fatty foods, and smoking, than they do now, yet in earlier decades the incidence of CHD and related CVDs was much lower. Furthermore, in the midwestern United States, where people's diets are highest in saturated fats and smoking rates are especially high, the incidence of coronary heart disease is low compared with that in more industrialized parts of the United States. Anyone who has visited Paris is aware of the heavy smoking and the fat-rich diets of the French population, yet CHD is relatively low there. Why?

Psychological Diatheses The search for predispositions for coronary heart disease has focused on psychological factors. Initial evidence linking CHD to psychological variables stems from investigations pioneered by two cardiologists, Meyer Friedman and Ray Rosenman (Friedman, 1969; Rosenman et al., 1975). In 1958, they identified a coronary-prone behaviour pattern called **Type A behaviour pattern**. As assessed by a structured interview, the Type A individual has an intense and competitive drive for achievement and advancement, an exaggerated sense of the urgency of passing time and of the need to hurry, and considerable aggressiveness and hostility toward others.

Initial evidence supporting the idea that the Type A pattern predicts coronary heart disease came from the classic Western Collaborative Group Study (WCGS) (Rosenman et al., 1975). In this double-blind, prospective investigation, 3,154 men aged 39 to 59 were followed over a period of eight and

One characteristic of the Type A personality is feeling under time pressure and consequently trying to do several things at once. Bruce Ayres/Tony Stone Images. © Goodshoot/Corbis.

a half years. Individuals who had been identified as Type A by interview were more than twice as likely to develop CHD as were Type B men, characterized by a less driven and less hostile way of life. Traditional risk factors, such as high levels of cholesterol, were also found to be related to CHD, but even when these factors were controlled for, Type A individuals were still twice as likely to develop CHD.

Subsequent research did not support the predictive utility of Type A behaviour. Instead, researchers focused on the role of one element of Type A behaviour: hostility. This focus on hostility is well-founded. A recent meta-analysis of 25 studies found that anger and hostility are associated with coronary heart disease outcomes in initially healthy populations and coronary heart disease populations (Chida & Steptoe, 2009).

Other research has increasingly examined the relationship between other negative emotions—particularly anxiety and depression—and CHD. Anxiety has been shown to be related to CHD in humans (Kawachi et al., 1994), and animal research demonstrates that inducing anxiety in animals with atherosclerosis can precipitate a heart attack (Carpeggiani & Skinner, 1991).

With regard to depression, about one in five CHD patients meet diagnostic criteria for depression (Miller & Blackwell, 2006), and many others do not meet diagnostic criteria but have depressive symptoms that warrant intervention. Moreover, it has been found that depressed patients have high rates of death from CVD. Similarly, a study in Quebec found that cardiac patients who also have depressive symptoms are about three times more likely than other patients without depressive symptoms to die within five years (Lesperance, Frasure-Smith, Talajic, & Bourassa, 2002). Another follow-up investigation found that elevated depression and anxiety at baseline predicted subsequent major adverse cardiac events (cardiac death, myocardial infarction, cardiac arrest) in the two years after baseline assessment among patients with stable coronary artery disease (Frasure-Smith & Lesperance, 2008). Plausible biological mechanisms for these relationships have been proposed. Anxiety, for example, is associated with activation of the sympathetic nervous system, which can lead to both hypertension and atherosclerosis. Research has also shown that depression is linked to a greater tendency for platelets to aggregate and thus produce obstructions in the arteries. Furthermore, depression is often associated with increases in steroidal hormones, which increase blood pressure and damage cells in arteries (Musselman, Evans, & Nemeroff, 1998). When depression reaches a point of demoralization and is combined with undue physical fatigue and irritability, it leads to vital exhaustion. Linden (2003) reviewed studies indicating that vital exhaustion is a predictor of CVD occurrence.

Tying together this interest in CHD and negative emotions—anger, anxiety, and depression—is the proposed Type D personality, with "D" standing for distressed type (Denollet & Brutsaert, 1998). Type D is defined as high scores on negative affectivity (a tendency to experience high levels of anxiety, anger, and depression) plus social inhibition, including inhibiting the expression of these emotions. A review by Pederson and Denollet (2003) concluded unequivocally that Type D cardiac patients are at increased risk for cardiovascular morbidity and mortality, independent of other cardiac risk factors. Type D patients also had an impaired quality of life, benefited less from treatment, and had increased psychological distress. Recent data continue to support the predictiveness of the Type D style. Schiffer et al. (in press) found in longitudinal research that Type D personality was a "nearly significant" independent predictor of total cardiac mortality, and it significantly predicted late-life cardiac mortality but not early-life cardiac mortality after adjusting for demographic factors and disease severity.

Type D personality seems to be accompanied by a tendency to engage in fewer positive health behaviours and it is linked with negative appraisals of social support (Williams et al., 2008). Type D patients tend to report poorer health status both before and after cardiac rehabilitation (Pelle et al., 2008). How prevalent is the Type D personality? It may depend on where you live. A study of healthy British and Irish adults found that 38.5% of participants had Type D personality as determined by scores on 10 or more of the distress and social inhibition Type D factors (Williams et al., 2008). The prevalence in other European countries is lower (21–33%) and Williams et al. (2008) suggested that the greater prevalence in Ireland and England may reflect reduced emotional expressiveness found among people in Ireland and England.

Interestingly, Type D personality has been linked with elevated perfectionism in a sample of 100 Canadian cardiac rehabilitation patients (Shanmugasegaram et al., 2008). Could the negative impact of Type D personality in part reflect this link with perfectionism? Perfectionism has been linked consistently with depression and a recent longitudinal study of middle-aged Canadians found that perfectionism predicted early all-cause mortality, even after controlling for other personality factors associated with risk such as low conscientiousness and being pessimistic (Fry & Debats, 2009). These data suggest that perfectionists may experience levels of stress and physical exertion that expose them to risk.

Biological Diatheses As with research on hypertension, research on biological predispositions for myocardial infarction has focused on reactivity. Excessive changes in heart rate and the consequent alterations in the force with which blood is pumped through the arteries may injure them, increasing risk for a myocardial infarction. Heart-rate reactivity has been related to CHD in several research contexts. A series of experimental studies investigated monkeys that were on a special diet designed to promote atherosclerosis. On the basis of a stress test, the animals were divided into high vs. low heart-rate reactors. Subsequently, the high heart-rate reactors developed twice as much atherosclerosis as did the low reactors (Kaplan et al., 1993). In another investigation by the same group, stress was created experimentally by changing the monkeys' living groups every three months. Changing living groups stresses the animals because they are continually forced to re-establish a dominance hierarchy. In an earlier study, this manipulation had been found to promote atherosclerosis in dominant monkeys. This time, some animals were given drugs to reduce the sympathetic activation that the stress was expected to produce; these animals treated with the drugs did not show an increase in atherosclerosis.

In studies of humans, heart-rate reactivity and ischemia (lack of oxygen) elicited by laboratory stressors have predicted the development of CHD and the occurrence of cardiac events (Jiang et al., 1996; Keys et al., 1971). Thus, cardiovascular reactivity is a plausible candidate for a biological diathesis, and as we have already seen, it is associated with the psychological diathesis of anger and hostility.

SOCIO-ECONOMIC STATUS, ETHNICITY, AND HEALTH

Low socio-economic status (SES) is associated with higher rates of mortality from all causes. One, but by no means the only, reason for this relationship is that people in lower social classes are more likely than people in higher classes to engage in behaviours that increase risk for disease, such as smoking, eating a high-fat diet, and drinking excessive amounts of alcohol (Lantz et al., 1998). The link between low SES and poorer health is also evident in Canada, where it has been referred to by Kosteniuk and Dickinson (2003) as the **social gradient of health** (i.e., inequalities in SES reflect inequalities in health status). These researchers analyzed data from the 1994–95 Canadian National Population Health Survey and found that lower stressor levels were associated with higher household income, being retired, and growing older. Lower stressor levels were also linked with greater levels of control, self-esteem, and social support, and higher income was correlated with greater levels of control and social support. The link between SES and illness was confirmed in another recent study. A four-year study at a hospital in Alberta found that people with lower SES, compared with those with high SES, had a 72% greater likelihood of presenting to the emergency department. Moreover, they had a much higher mortality rate (19.1% vs. 9.1%) (see Chang et al., 2007).

The importance of perceived controllability was confirmed in another study (see Bailis et al., 2001). Analyses of nationally representative data obtained from Statistics Canada showed that lower SES confers health disadvantages, in part, because it is linked with a diminished sense of perceived controllability.

THERAPIES FOR PSYCHO-PHYSIOLOGICAL DISORDERS

Since psychophysiological disorders are true physical dysfunctions, sound psychotherapeutic practice calls for close consultation with a physician. Whether high blood pressure is biologically caused or, as in essential hypertension, linked to psychological stress, a number of medications can reduce the constriction of the arteries. Mental health and medical professionals recognize, however, that most drug interventions treat only the symptoms; they do not address the fact that the person is reacting emotionally to psychological stress. Although the evidence suggests that the predisposition for breakdown of a particular organ is inherited, or at least somatically based, the importance of a person's psychological response nevertheless indicates that psychotherapeutic interventions are necessary. Therapists of all persuasions agree that reducing anxiety, depression, or anger is the best way to alleviate suffering from psychophysiological disorders. The particular disorder—essential hypertension or coronary heart disease—is considered to be adversely affected, if not actually caused, by these emotions.

Behavioural and cognitive therapists employ their usual range of procedures for reducing anxiety and anger—systematic desensitization, in vivo exposure, rational-emotive therapy, and assertion training—depending on the source of tension. Relaxation training, for example, has been used successfully to help asthmatic children exhale more fully (Lehrer et al., 1994). Behaviour rehearsal and shaping may help people learn to react in difficult situations with less emotional upset.

Psychoanalytically oriented therapists employ techniques such as free association and dream analysis, as they do with other patients experiencing anxiety, to help people confront the infantile origins of their fears. Ego analysts, such as Franz Alexander, believe that emotional states underlie several disorders. Thus, they encourage patients with essential hypertension, whom they view as labouring under a burden of undischarged anger, to assert themselves and thereby release their anger.

We turn now to an examination of several areas in which clinicians in the fields of behavioural medicine and health psychology have brought psychological perspectives and interventions to bear on the problem of helping people deal with medical illnesses.

TREATING HYPERTENSION AND REDUCING CHD RISK

Because some antihypertensive drugs have undesirable side effects, such as drowsiness, light-headedness, and, for men, erectile difficulties, many investigations have been undertaken on nonpharmacological treatments for borderline essential hypertension. Efforts have been directed at weight reduction, restriction of salt intake, giving up cigarettes, aerobic exercise, and reduction in alcohol consumption. Losing weight, reducing salt intake, and exercising regularly can also help reduce harmful levels of cholesterol. Drugs, too, can lower cholesterol levels; for example, lovastatin (trade name Mevacor) lowers low-density lipid cholesterol (LDL, the so-called bad cholesterol) and appears to be successful in forestalling the progression of atherosclerosis. Such drugs, plus improvements in eating habits observed since the 1960s and other modifiable risk factors, are associated with decreased mortality from cardiovascular diseases (see Patel & Adams, 2008).

A study with older adults highlights the importance of losing weight and reducing salt intake. The controlled 1998 Trial of Nonpharmacologic Interventions in the Elderly (TONE) (Whelton et al., 1998) indicated for the first time that significant benefits can be achieved by obese people between the ages of 60 and 80 who are taking blood-pressure medication. Specifically, half the overweight people in the study who reduced their salt intake by 25% and lost as little as eight pounds (3.5 kg) over the course of three months were able to come off their antihypertensive medications and maintain normal blood pressure. The ability to maintain normal blood pressure was achieved by 31% of the patients who reduced their salt intake, 36% of those who lost weight, and more than half of those who reduced both their salt intake and their weight. Furthermore, these results—the dietary and weight changes, as well as the maintenance of normal blood pressure without medication—lasted for more than three years.

Regular exercise is another avenue for reducing blood pressure, one that is available to everyone at little or no cost. Research has shown that increasing exercise through so-called lifestyle activities—for example, walking up stairs rather than using an elevator or walking short distances rather than driving—yields as much benefit as a structured program of aerobic exercise (Dunn et al., 1999).

Other research indicates that people with essential hypertension, as well as those whose blood pressure is within the normal range, should adopt regular exercise habits, such as walking briskly most every day for about half an hour or engaging in other aerobic exercise that raises the heart and respiration rates (see Pescatello et al., 2004). Most people can engage in such activity without even checking with their physician if the activity is not so strenuous that it prevents them from carrying on a conversation at the same time.

Research suggests that people with high blood pressure and no other health complications should try exercise for about a year before turning to drugs to lower their blood pressure. The prescribed exercise for someone with high blood pressure is engaging in moderately intense exercise every day of the week. It should involve 30 minutes or more of continuous activity (Pescatello et al., 2004). For those already taking antihypertensive drugs, a regular and not necessarily strenuous exercise regimen can sometimes reduce or even eliminate dependence on medication. Decreases of 10 points—a significant figure—in both systolic and diastolic blood pressure can be achieved by most people after just a few weeks. Exercising regularly can also reduce mortality from cardiovascular disease (Wannamethee, Shaper, & Walker, 1998). All these beneficial results may be mediated by the favourable effects that exercise has on stress, weight, and blood cholesterol. And if the sense of well-being that accompanies regular exercise and weight loss leads to the adoption of other health-enhancing habits, such as stopping smoking and avoiding drinking to excess, the positive effects on blood pressure will be all the stronger and more enduring.

Another psychological approach has been to teach hypertensive individuals to lower sympathetic nervous system arousal, primarily via training in muscle relaxation, occasionally supplemented by biofeedback. A recent review of relaxation therapy did find evidence of significant but small reductions in both diastolic and systolic blood pressure (Dickinson et al., 2008). However, serious methodological problems in several studies led the authors to conclude that there is weak evidence of a causal link between relaxation therapy and lower blood pressure. Perhaps relaxation therapy is helpful for some people more than others.

BIOFEEDBACK

A visit to the commercial exhibit area of any psychological or psychiatric convention will reveal a plentiful display of complex biofeedback apparatuses, touted as an efficient, even miraculous, means of helping people control one or another bodily mental state. By using sensitive instrumentation, **biofeedback** gives a person prompt and exact information, otherwise unavailable, on muscle activity, brain waves, skin temperature, heart rate, blood pressure, and other bodily functions. It is assumed that a person can achieve greater voluntary control over these phenomena—most of which were once considered under involuntary control only—if he or she knows immediately, through an auditory or visual signal, whether a somatic activity is increasing or decreasing. Because anxiety has been viewed generally as a state involving the autonomic (involuntary) nervous system, and because psychophysiological disorders often afflict organs innervated by this system, researchers and clinicians have been intrigued by biofeedback. For a time, biofeedback was virtually synonymous with behavioural medicine.

In a series of classic studies at Harvard Medical School, Shapiro, Tursky, and Schwartz (1970; Schwartz, 1973) demonstrated that volunteers could consciously achieve significant short-term changes in blood pressure and heart rate. They found that some people could even be trained to increase their heart rate while decreasing their blood pressure. Achievement of this fine-grained control lent impetus to biofeedback work with human beings and awakened hope that certain clinical disorders might be alleviated in this new way.

Reviews of research on the use of biofeedback to treat patients with essential hypertension have yielded results questioning its usefulness. The results of more than 100 studies indicated that these interventions reduce blood pressure "to a modest degree," with multi-component, individualized treatments resulting in the greatest improvements (Linden & Moseley, 2006, p. 51). More recently, however, another extensive review indicated that biofeedback treatment is ineffective when compared with no treatment, pharmacotherapy, or placebos (Greenhalgh, Dickson, & Dundar, 2009). These authors concluded that current treatment standards would suggest using biofeedback only if it is a supplement to other treatments.

CARDIAC REHABILITATION EFFORTS

Frasure-Smith and her colleagues at the Montreal Heart Institute Research Centre have been evaluating the results of a long-term intervention program known as the Ischemic Heart Disease Life Stress Monitoring Program (IHDLSM) (Frasure-Smith & Prince, 1989). The IHDLSM is a cardiac rehabilitation program in which participants are assigned to a control condition or a stress-monitoring condition. The stress-monitoring condition involves the receipt of psychosocial support and advice from nurses who assess the patients' stress levels each month and intervene when stress is elevated. The initial results showed that this non-specific psychosocial intervention led to significant reductions in mortality and in reoccurrences of heart attacks (Frasure-Smith & Prince, 1989). Unfortunately, replication studies found less successful outcomes (Frasure-Smith et al., 2002). There was no treatment impact among men overall, and women in the treatment group actually had a worse prognosis. Secondary analyses showed that coping styles were important (Frasure-Smith et al., 2002). People characterized as repressors (i.e., those who have high arousal yet use defensive strategies to avoid acknowledging the arousal) had worse outcomes. Still, some findings from the IHDLSM project did show that some people can benefit from a focus on the alleviation of stress. Specifically, highly anxious men seemed to benefit from the program (Frasure-Smith et al., 2002). This finding with anxious men is more in line with the general pattern of findings across several studies. These studies tend to attest to the positive effects of psychosocial treatments for cardiac rehabilitation patients (see Linden, 2003).

The finding that women did worse in the Frasure-Smith et al. (2002) study is troubling in light of more general trends that have emerged from research on cardiac rehabilitation. A review conducted by researchers from Toronto associated with the University Health Network confirmed that there are widespread gender differences in cardiac rehabilitation outcomes (see Grace et al., 2002). They found that coronary recovery following an ischemic coronary event is poorer in women, relative to men, and women patients experience greater depression and anxiety but lower levels of social support and self-efficacy.

Clearly, cognitive expectations are linked inextricably with health behaviours. The importance of cognitive and attitudinal factors is evident in other illnesses, too, such as cancer (see Focus on Discovery 9.5).

FOCUS ON DISCOVERY 9.5
COPING WITH CANCER

A growing body of evidence indicates that interventions that alleviate anxiety and depression and foster a fighting spirit can help people cope with cancer (Telch & Telch, 1986). A non-passive attitude may even enhance the capacity to survive cancer (Greer, Morris, & Pettigale, 1979).

An extensive meta-analysis of 83 studies confirmed the link between optimism and positive health outcomes (Rasmussen, Scheier, & Greenhouse, 2009). Indeed, an optimistic, upbeat attitude is important in combating illness, including illnesses as serious as cancer (Carver et al., 1993). A study reported by Allison and colleagues from McGill University found that dispositional optimism was associated with higher levels of survival in patients from France with head or neck cancer (Allison, Guichard, Fung, & Gilain, 2003). Related research examines individual differences in hope and hopelessness (see Stanton, Danoff-Burg, & Huggins, 2002). Other data from cancer patients from Princess Margaret Hospital in Toronto found that hopelessness predicted desire for a hastened death (Jones, Huggins, Rydall, & Rodin, 2003).

The mechanism by which an optimistic attitude helps people with life-threatening illnesses may be its link to adaptive coping. Optimistic people may be more likely to engage in risk-reducing health behaviours such as avoiding risky sex or engaging in prescribed regular exercise following coronary-bypass surgery (Scheier & Carver, 1987).

PSYCHOLOGICAL INTERVENTIONS TO HELP PEOPLE COPE

The quality of life and even the survival time of patients with terminal cancer can be improved by psychosocial interventions, as shown by research by Alastair Cunningham and his colleagues at the Ontario Cancer Institute (Cunningham, Edmonds, Phillips, et al., 2000; Edmonds, Lockwood, & Cunningham, 1999). Patients with metastatic breast cancer participate in weekly supportive group therapy, where they offer understanding and comfort to each other, openly discuss death and dying, express their feelings, and encourage each other to live life as fully as possible in the face of death. Edmonds et al. (1999) tracked the results of an eight-month intervention and found no significant improvements in self-reports of mood and quality of life, but profound clinical improvements were noted by the patients' therapists. In related research, Cunningham and associates sought to identify factors that predicted length of survival in 22 people with medically incurable metastatic cancer (Cunningham, Phillips, Lockwood, et al., 2000). One key factor was the amount of "psychological work" engaged in by the patients; those who were rated as more involved psychologically in their recovery tended to live longer. Another important factor was the extent to which the patient expected that psychological efforts would have a positive effect. In contrast, standard psychometric measures of quality of life did not relate to survival.

Another Canadian study also examined the impact of group psychosocial support in a sample of women with metastatic breast cancer (Goodwin et al., 2001). Comparisons of women who received the intervention with those who did not showed no group differences in mortality rates; however, women in the supportive group condition, relative to women in the control group, reported less psychological distress and less pain. These findings fit with the results of four other published studies; group support lessens distress but does not reduce mortality (Goodwin, 2005).

Problem-solving therapy has shown its value in helping cancer patients cope with the myriad life challenges facing them, from daily hassles to dealing with isolation and depression (Nezu et al., 1997). An important component of problem-solving therapy (and of other approaches that can help cancer patients) is the enhanced sense of control that the patient learns to exercise. It would seem that such control is particularly important for people with a life-threatening illness who are experiencing the side effects of treatment.

A concern for men is prostate cancer. High-profile Canadians who have had prostate cancer include the late prime minister Pierre Trudeau. The prostate is a small gland surrounding the urethra, the tube that carries urine from the bladder through the penis and outside the body. It is usually surgically excised if cancer is discovered in it. However, since this type of cancer grows slowly, some older men elect not to have the surgery because it is likely that they will die from other causes before the prostate cancer is advanced enough to kill them and, more important, because removal of the prostate often has two very negative side effects: marked diminution or loss of erectile capacity and loss of full urinary control. Research examining quality-of-life issues in men who have had prostatectomy surgery has found that quality of life is rated as quite high by post-surgery patients, especially when they are instructed in the use of erectile aids, such as rigid implants (Perez et al., 1997). With the availability of Viagra, a medication that can restore erectile function, the prospects are even better for good psychological adjustment following this kind of surgery. Indeed, a recent Canadian study of men receiving treatment found that sexual problems and other urinary and bowel problems were still common but had less impact on the quality of life than was reported in earlier studies (see Krahn et al., 2003).

Still, as shown by a qualitative study conducted in Toronto, men and their families may face many challenges post-surgery (see Gray et al., 2000). A primary focus is managing the impact of the illness. Gray et al. (2000) found that patients often struggle to stay in control of their emotions; they can be high in "fearful neediness" at some points but are high in "fierce self-reliance" at other times.

INTERVENTIONS TO ENCOURAGE PREVENTION

Psychological interventions in a community psychology model also focus on preventing cancer by encouraging healthy behaviours and discouraging unhealthy ones. When it comes to cancer,

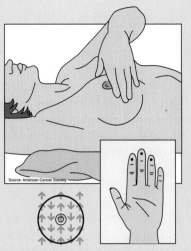

Encouraging women to perform breast self-examination can lead to earlier detection of cancer and better treatment outcomes but perhaps should not be relied on as the sole form of detection, especially among older women. Shown here is an advertisement from the American Cancer Society demonstrating how to perform a self-exam. Reprinted by the permission of the American Cancer Society, Inc. All rights reserved

primary prevention is designed to decrease the occurrence of cancer, while secondary prevention focuses on identifying cancer in its early stages (see Kilbourn & Durning, 2003).

Table 9.5 provides an overview of recommended screening procedures that increase secondary prevention. Breast self-exams are included with an important caveat. Some authors have concluded that breast self-exams do not confer benefits in terms of reduced mortality and they may actually be associated with increased risk of mortality for women over 50 years of age who rely on this as the sole form of prevention (Baxter & The Canadian

TABLE 9.5
RECOMMENDED SCREENING PROCEDURES FOR EARLY DETECTION OF CANCER

Cancer Site	Sex	Sceeening Test
Breast	F	Breast self-exam Clinical breast exam Mammogram
Cervix	F	Pap test
Endometrium/Ovaries	F	Cervical pelvic exam
Colorectal	F/M	Faecal occult blood test Flexible sigmoidoscopy Screening colonoscopy
Skin	F/M	Clinical skin exam Skin self-exam
Prostate	M	Prostate specific antigen (PSA) blood test Digital rectal exam

Source: Adapted with permission from Kilbourn and Durning (2003) p. 107

Task Force on Preventive Health Care, 2001). Breast self-exams, clinical breast exams, and mammograms should be used in combination, especially among older women.

Sadly, research indicates that the extent to which screening procedures are employed is often inadequate. A recent study by Isaacs et al. (2002) examined breast cancer and ovarian cancer screening behaviours in a sample of healthy women who were deemed to be high-risk candidates based on a family history of breast cancer or ovarian cancer. The authors concluded that the screening was "suboptimal," even for women over 50 years old who should be getting annual mammograms.

The most controversial procedure listed in Table 9.5 is the prostate specific antigen (PSA) blood test for men. The PSA is a protein molecule produced by the prostate glands. Healthy men have low levels of this antigen, but it can be substantially elevated in men with prostate cancer and a biopsy may be indicated. The test is controversial, in part, because of uncertainty about the appropriate cut-off point value to use as an indicator of the possibility of prostate cancer. Test results are reported in nanograms per millilitre (ng/mL). A cut-off of 4 ng/mL has been used, but some clinicians have used a lower cut-off, and it is generally recognized that the cut-off point should be adjusted according to factors such as age and race.

Provinces throughout Canada have created brochures that instruct men to consider the risks and benefits of PSA testing. Clearly, the risk of prostate cancer increases with age, and both PSA tests and digital rectal exams should be considered once a man hits the age of 45. The PSA test and digital rectal exam may ultimately save their lives, as prostate cancer is second only to lung cancer in terms of male deaths from cancer.

We turn next to a consideration of the field of stress management.

STRESS MANAGEMENT

Stress management involves a set of techniques that helps people who are seldom labelled as patients cope with the challenges that are a part of life. It is similar to the stress-inoculation training discussed in Chapter 2 because stress-inoculation training has been used on both a preventive and a treatment basis (Meichenbaum, 1992, 1994).

The increasing recognition of the role of stress in a variety of medical illnesses, including diseases affected by immune system dysfunction, has added impetus to stress management as a strategy for reducing stress-related malfunctioning of the immune system. A Canadian consensus group concluded that individualized stress management is an effective intervention (Spence, Barnett, Linden, Ramsden, & Taenzer, 1999). Stress management has been used successfully for several health problems, large and small, including tension headaches, cancer, hypertension, and, as discussed later, chronic pain.

Stress management encompasses a variety of techniques, and more than one is typically used in any given instance (Steptoe, 1997).

AROUSAL REDUCTION In arousal reduction, the person is trained in muscle relaxation, sometimes assisted by biofeedback. Although the evidence is unclear as to the need to use the complex instrumentation required for proper biofeedback, there is confirmation that learning to relax deeply and to apply these relaxation skills to real-life stressors can help lower stress levels. It has also been shown that immune function can be improved by relaxation training (Kiecolt-Glaser et al., 1985), although enduring benefits are doubtful unless relaxation is practised regularly over a long period of time (Goldfried & Davison, 1994). Relaxation training may confer its benefits by virtue of enhancing the individual's sense of self-efficacy, the belief that one is not merely a pawn at the mercy of uncontrollable forces that are not always benign (Bandura, 1997).

COGNITIVE RESTRUCTURING Included under cognitive restructuring are approaches such as those of Albert Ellis (1962) and Aaron Beck (1976). The focus is on altering people's belief systems and improving the clarity of their logical interpretations of experience, the assumption being that people's intellectual capacities can affect how they feel and behave. Providing information to reduce uncertainty and enhance people's sense of control, a theme from Chapter 6, has also been helpful in reducing stress. Promising findings have been reported for various stress-related problems and illnesses, including recent evidence that a cognitively based stress management program for cancer patients yielded numerous benefits, including less social disruption, better emotional well-being, and positive lifestyle changes (Antoni et al., 2006).

MINDFULNESS Mindfulness-based stress reduction usually involves meeting in groups for sessions over a 10-week period. Participants are trained with a manualized approach to develop mindful awareness of perceptible experiences in a way that is non-evaluative and emotionally non-reactive (Shigaki, Glass, & Schopp, 2006). In particular, participants are trained to meditate and examine their reactions in stressful circumstances and apply these techniques when encountering future stressors. A meta-analysis of 20 mindfulness studies conducted with participants with various health problems (e.g., cancer, chronic pain, fibromyalgia) found that mindfulness interventions were effective, with a moderate effect of stress management being documented (Grossman, Niemann, Schmidt, & Walach, 2004). Some investigators have now tried to identify specific aspects of mindfulness that are helpful; a Montreal study of mindfulness training for women receiving breast cancer treatment focused on the role of mindfulness in making life seem more meaningful and manageable (Dobkin, 2008). Although positive effects have resulted, it has been noted that additional research with a longitudinal focus and larger samples is needed (Shigaki et al., 2006).

BEHAVIOURAL SKILLS TRAINING Because it is natural to feel overwhelmed if one lacks the skills to execute a challenging task, stress management often includes instruction and practise in required skills, as well as in general skills such as time management and effective prioritizing. Included also under this rubric is training in assertion skills—expressing likes and dislikes without encroaching on the rights of others.

THE MANAGEMENT OF PAIN

Like anxiety, pain can be adaptive. People with a congenital inability to feel pain are at an extreme disadvantage; indeed, they are at serious risk for injury. Our concern here is with pain that is maladaptive, pain that is out of proportion to the situation and unduly restricts a person's capacity for meaningful and productive living (Morley, 1997).

How common are problems with pain? The Participation and Activity Limitation Survey conducted by Statistics Canada in 2001 found that 3.6 million Canadians perceived that their activities were restricted by physical problems and the most common disabilities were linked with pain. Overall, 2.4 million Canadians cited chronic pain as a factor that accounted for limiting their activities (Statistics Canada, 2002).

Recognition of the role of psychological factors in pain can be traced back to the gate-control theory of pain advanced by Melzack and Wall (1965, 1982) from McGill University. This influential theory holds that nerve impulses connoting pain reach the spinal column and the spinal column controls the pain sensations sent to the brain. How is it a gate-control model? The gate is an area of the spinal column known as the dorsal horns; the gate opens if sufficiently intense pain stimuli are experienced. However, the brain also plays a role in that it sends signals back down the spinal column that can affect the gate. The brain, therefore, can facilitate or inhibit the experience of pain, as is seen when people undergoing trauma do not acknowledge the pain to the degree that they should. Melzack (1998, 1999) proposed that the brain possesses a neural network, known as the body-self neuromatrix, which integrates multiple signals to produce a pattern leading to pain.

Indeed, we know enough about pain to appreciate that there is no one-to-one relationship between a stimulus that is capable of triggering the experience of pain, referred to as nociceptive stimulus, and the actual sensation of pain. Soldiers in combat can be wounded by a bullet and yet be so involved in their efforts to survive and inflict harm on the enemy that they do not feel any pain until later. This well-known fact tells us something important about pain, even as it hints at ways of controlling it. If one is distracted from a nociceptive stimulus, one may not experience pain, or at least not as much of it as when one attends to the stimulation (Turk, 1996).

The importance of distraction in controlling pain, both acute and chronic, is consistent with research findings in experimental cognitive psychology. Each person has only a limited supply of attentional resources, such that attention to one channel of input blocks the processing of input in other channels (Eccleston, 1995). This human limitation can thus be seen as beneficial when it comes to the experience of pain. In addition to distraction, other factors that reduce pain are lowered anxiety, feelings of optimism and control (Geer et al., 1970), and a sense that what one is engaged in has meaning and purpose (Gatchel, Baum, & Krantz, 1989).

Here are two examples of the use of distraction and refocused attention for controlling pain:

> [A] patient may be taught to construct a vivid mental image which includes features from a number of sensory dimensions, e.g., cutting a lemon and squeezing a drop of the juice onto the tongue. The elaborated sensory features of the image compete with the painful stimulus and reduces its impact. Alternatively the patient may be encouraged to alter the focus of their attention to the pain without switching attention directly away from the pain. In this instance, the subject may be asked to focus on the sensory qualities of the pain and transform it to a less threatening quality. For example, a young man with a severe "shooting" pain was able to reinterpret the sensory quality into an image that included him shooting at goal in a soccer match. As a result of this transformation, the impact of the pain was greatly reduced although its shooting quality remained. (Morley, 1997, p. 236)

Psychologists have contributed to our understanding of both acute and chronic pain. Acute pain is linked to nociception. **Chronic pain** can evolve from acute pain and refers to pain that is experienced after the time for healing has passed, when there is little reason to assume that nociception is still present. Whatever the specific psychological techniques employed to help alleviate a person's pain, the person is always informed of the nature of the pain itself and the reasons he or she is experiencing it, including the fact that being in a negative mood can make the pain worse (Morley, 1997).

ACUTE PAIN The importance of a sense of personal control in dealing with acute pain is readily seen in situations in which patients are allowed to administer their own painkillers (with a pre-set upper limit). This is known as PCA, patient-controlled analgesia. Patients who control the administration of the medication experience greater relief from pain and even use less analgesic medication than do patients who have to ask a nurse for pain medication, the more common hospital situation (White, 1986).

It is significant that PCA reduces pain even though it requires focusing on the pain, a finding that goes against the well-documented benefits of distraction. Apparently, the positive effects of control outweigh the negative consequences of focusing on the pain. Considerable research attests to the beneficial effects of a sense of control; less pain is experienced, mood is better (and thereby pain is less), and people engage in more normal daily activities, all of which enhance a stronger sense of well-being and bring about still further reductions in pain (Bandura, 1997). Of course, relying on a nurse to administer pain medication also requires the patient to attend to the pain, perhaps even more than when the patient administers the drug. With nurse-administered analgesia, the patient learns to wait until the pain is substantial before requesting medication; after making the request, the patient must usually wait until the nurse has time to fulfill it. This system obviously does not enhance distraction from the pain!

CHRONIC PAIN Chronic pain is the lot of millions of North Americans, accounting for billions of dollars of lost work time and incalculable personal and familial suffering (Turk, 1996). It was noted earlier that 2.4 million Canadians feel that chronic pain has limited their physical activities. Another Canadian study found that the prevalence rate of chronic pain was 15% (Van Den Kerkhof et al., 2003). This prevalence may be overestimated, however, because the researchers relied solely on a self-report measure of chronic pain in existing datasets. Nevertheless, it is clear that this is a widespread problem.

Traditional medical treatments seldom help with this kind of pain. To understand chronic pain, it is useful to distinguish between pain per se—that is, the perception of nociceptive stimulation (as in acute pain)—and suffering and pain behaviours. Suffering refers to the emotional response to nociception and can be present even in the absence of pain, as when a loved one dies. Pain behaviours refer to observable behaviours associated with pain or suffering; examples include moaning, clenching teeth, irritability, and avoidance of activity (Turk, Wack, & Kerns, 1985). The treatment of chronic pain focuses on suffering and pain behaviours rather than on whether the person is actually experiencing pain. Patients usually have to be guided to the adoption of realistic goals—a pain-free existence may not be possible. The emphasis is on toughing it out, working through the pain rather than allowing oneself to be incapacitated by it. If handled properly, the result is often increased activity and function, which can sometimes even reduce the actual experience of pain. The most appropriate goals for each chronic pain patient can be established with the use of goal attainment scales to evaluate progress on an individual basis (see Zaza, Stolee, & Prkachin, 1999).

A well-researched example of chronic pain is lower back pain caused by severe muscle spasms. Initially, the person is unable to engage in activity any more vigorous than getting in and out of bed. In the acute phase, this is sensible behaviour. As the spasms ease, and if no other damage has occurred, such as to the disks between the vertebrae, the patient is advised to begin moving more normally, stretching, and eventually attempting exercises to strengthen the muscles that went into spasm. Of course, care must be taken not to push patients beyond what their bodies can actually handle.

Research on coping with chronic pain has identified a number of adaptive and maladaptive strategies. One maladaptive strategy is **catastrophization**. People who catastrophize engage in a repetitive cognitive process that involves negative self-statements and negative views of the future (i.e., the worst possible outcome will be experienced). Catastrophizing in response to pain has been associated with a variety of negative outcomes, including depression, increased pain intensity, and psychosocial dysfunction (see Katz et al., 1996). More generally, an emotion-oriented approach to coping with a health problem is linked with increased chronic pain (Endler et al., 2003). Passive coping strategies, such as withdrawing or becoming resigned to one's fate, are also quite maladaptive (see Mercado, Carroll, Cassidy, & Côté, 2000).

In their classic work on pain, Fordyce and his colleagues (Fordyce et al., 1986; Fordyce, 1994) have shown the superiority of a behavioural over a traditional medical program for management of back pain. In the traditional program, patients exercised and otherwise moved about only until they felt pain; in the behavioural management program, patients were encouraged to exercise at a predetermined intensity for a predetermined period of time, even if they experienced pain. Patients with low back pain have also been given relaxation training and encouraged to relabel their pain as numbness or tickling (Rybstein-Blinchik, 1979), a cognitive-restructuring procedure. The implicit message seems to be that traditional medical practice has underestimated the capabilities of chronic pain patients (Keefe & Gil, 1986). A frequent finding of these studies was that increased activity improves muscle tone, which can reduce nociception over time and even reduce the likelihood of future reoccurrences of muscle spasms.

In a review of studies on the treatment of chronic pain, Blanchard (1994) concluded that strictly behavioural (operant conditioning) and cognitive-behavioural approaches are both important for effective treatment. This conclusion was qualified by the conclusions of a more recent review. Turk, Swanson, and Tunks (2008) compared all psychological treatments and concluded that the greatest amount of research supports the effectiveness of CBT. They also concluded that the cognitive component (i.e., beliefs, attitudes, expectancies) is much more important than specific behavioural techniques. There is one other caveat about the benefits of cognitive-behavioural therapy. Anxiety in general and health anxiety in particular may undermine treatment efforts. Indeed, contemporary research conducted in Canada found that only patients with low health anxiety benefited from reducing pain behaviour (Hadjistavropoulos et al., 2002).

Canadian Clinic Focus 9.1 presents examples of pain treatment clinics and services in Canada.

CANADIAN CLINIC FOCUS 9.1
TREATMENT OF CHRONIC PAIN PROBLEMS IN CANADA: BEHAVIOURAL MEDICINE?

What can be done to alleviate the misery of the millions of Canadians who live with chronic pain, often on an unremitting daily basis despite the best efforts of the general practitioners they have consulted? How can they be helped to experience reduced pain, to minimize the impact of this pain on their levels of activity, productivity, and quality of life?

Psychologists certainly play an important role. Outcome studies have confirmed the effectiveness of psychological treatments, especially those that involve cognitive-behavioural interventions. Moreover, the importance of psychologists in the assessment and treatment of chronic pain has been recognized by numerous agencies and government bodies in Canada and the United States (see Turk & Monarch, 2003).

As is the case with many problems and disorders discussed in this book, there are numerous high-quality programs and clinics for the treatment of chronic pain in centres across Canada, especially in major metropolitan areas where hospitals are typically associated with comprehensive, medical universities. One internationally renowned centre, co-founded by Canadian pain expert Ronald Melzack, is the McGill-Montreal General Hospital Pain Centre. The Centre offers an integrated, multidisciplinary pain management program that treats all types of non-malignant pain. The program integrates medical and psychological approaches and offers cognitive-behavioural group therapy, relaxation training, lifestyle counselling, and physiotherapy, in addition to conventional pharmacological therapy (e.g., nerve blocks). The clinical teaching program offers formal courses for different professional groups and students at McGill University, including weekly pain rounds and an annual Pain Day. In addition, research teams evaluate pharmacological and nonpharmacological pain therapies, as well as alternative therapies, and conduct epidemiological studies. There are many similar clinics in the populated areas of Canada, and in many cases, the treatments are supported, in whole or in part, by provincial medicare plans.

But what do people do who continue to suffer from chronic pain but live in remote areas or in areas not served by quality programs or clinics that have a specific focus on chronic pain? In such instances, individuals may choose to move temporarily, possibly at great personal expense, close to a major treatment facility to participate in the appropriate programs. Alternatively, they may seek residential treatment at a private facility (at even greater expense), or they may be fortunate enough to be accepted for treatment by a skilled medical or mental health professional who specializes in pain management. The North American Chronic Pain Association of Canada (NACPAC) provides a Directory of Canadian Pain Clinics and Pain Specialists. NACPAC approves clinics that meet or exceed a specific standard of care. The Chronic Pain Association of Canada, the Canadian Pain Society, and other national and regional organizations (e.g., the Fibromyalgia Association of British Columbia) also provide information and support to people interested in chronic pain. Many individuals, of course, also engage in self-help, either independently or with the encouragement of health professionals, and/or join a lay or volunteer organization that offers organized support groups, as well as credible information.

It is clear that there are many clinics, programs, services, and dedicated professionals available to assist people in Canada who suffer from chronic pain. Although many resources emphasize conventional medical practices, others adopt a perspective consistent with the approach of this book, an integrated, biopsychosocial approach that necessitates a multi-faceted, individually tailored treatment plan that relies on the expertise of a multidisciplinary team for its implementation. Psychologists who practise a behavioural medicine and health psychology approach, especially one based on empirically supported behavioural and cognitive-behavioural strategies (e.g., Turk, Meichenbaum, & Genest, 1983), are important contributors to this multidisciplinary approach.

Unfortunately, it is not always clear that a majority of the available programs emphasize or incorporate all of the strategies that could be useful (e.g., stress management, cognitive restructuring, biofeedback, assertion and social skills training, and coping-skills and problem-solving therapy). Further, the fact that many clinics and services are private or semi-private means that many needy people may not have easy access to the help they need. Public clinics are often overwhelmed with patients, necessitating long waiting lists and even turning people away. Average wait times before being able to access treatment have been estimated at 9 months in Quebec and 12 months in Alberta, and similar situations exist throughout Canada (see Nova Scotia Chronic Pain Working Group, 2006). For example, the Northside General Hospital Pain Unit in North Sydney, Nova Scotia, is one of only a few clinics that provides even conventional medical treatment in all of Cape Breton, which has a population of about 115,000. This small clinic sees as many as 50 patients a day, offering services such as intravenous trigger-point injections and nerve blocks. There is typically a 12- to 14-month waiting period. Also, in a majority of cases, the effectiveness and efficacy of the various clinic-based programs need to be evaluated.

The overall picture was summed up in a survey of all multidisciplinary pain treatment facilities (MPTFs) in Canada (see Peng et al., 2007). The survey confirmed that these clinics offer an extensive variety of treatments including interventional, physical, and psychological therapy. But the demand outweighs available services. The median wait time for a first appointment in public clinics is six months, about 12 times longer than non-public clinics. Peng et al. (2007) concluded that "Canadian MPTFs are unable to meet clinical demands of patients suffering from chronic pain, both in terms of regional accessibility and reasonable wait time for patients' first appointment" (p. 977).

Sources: NACPAC website: www3.sympatico.ca/nacpac/onacpac06.htm
Chronic Pain Association of Canada website: www.chronicpaincanada.org.

Our review of several therapeutic approaches to dealing with psychophysiological disorders, many of which can be subsumed under the rubric of behavioural medicine, illustrates the complex relationships between the soma and the psyche, the body and the mind. We come full circle to how we began this chapter, namely, to an appreciation of the inseparability of bodily and mental processes. Stress is a part of everyone's life. As much as it can pose problems, so, too, can it promote well-being as we learn ways to cope with or manage it.

SUMMARY

- Increasing recognition of the mind–body connection has resulted in increasing awareness of the link between physical conditions and mental illness. Depression and anxiety often accompany complex chronic illness and certain people are at risk to the extent that deficits in emotional well-being undermine their ability to cope with challenging health problems.
- Psychophysiological disorders are physical diseases produced in part by psychological factors, primarily stress. Such disorders usually affect organs innervated by the autonomic nervous system, such as those of the respiratory, cardiovascular, gastrointestinal, and endocrine systems. Research has pursued a number of different paths to discover how psychological stress produces a particular psychophysiological disorder. Some researchers have looked at the specifics of the stressor or the psychological characteristics of the person, such as the links between anger/hostility and hypertension and between Type A personality and myocardial infarction. Others have emphasized that psychophysiological disorders occur only when stress interacts with a biological diathesis. Cardiovascular disorders occur in individuals who have a tendency to respond to stress with increases in blood pressure or heart rate. Although we have spoken of psychological stress affecting the body, it must be remembered that the mind and the body are best viewed as two different approaches to the same organism.
- Psychophysiological disorders no longer appear as a diagnostic category in the *DSM*. Instead, the diagnostician can make a diagnosis of psychological factors affecting a medical condition and then note the condition on Axis III. This change reflects the growing realization that life stress is relevant to all diseases and is not limited to those that were previously considered psychophysiological disorders.
- When events are appraised as stressful, coping efforts are engaged. If coping fails to lessen the amount of stress experienced, the risk of becoming ill increases. Important issues in current work on life stress and health include looking at moderators of the relationship (e.g., social support lessens the effects of stress) and specifying the physiological mechanisms (e.g., the immune system) through which stress can exert its effects.
- Psychophysiological disorders represent true physical dysfunctions. As a result, treatment usually includes medication. The general aim of psychotherapies for these disorders is to reduce anxiety or anger and there is growing evidence of the destructive impact of anger and hostility on health functioning. Researchers in the field of behavioural medicine try to find psychological interventions that can improve the patient's physiological state by changing unhealthy behaviours and reducing stress. They have developed ways of helping people relax, smoke less, eat fewer fatty foods, and engage in behaviours that can prevent or alleviate illnesses, such as breast self-examination and adhering to medical treatment recommendations.
- The emergent field of stress management helps people without diagnosable problems avail themselves of techniques that allow them to cope with the inevitable stress of everyday life and thereby ameliorate the toll that stress can take on the body.

KEY TERMS

allostatic load (p. 292)
anger-in theory (p. 305)
angina pectoris (p. 309)
autonomic nervous system (ANS) (p. 292)
behavioural medicine (p. 289)
biofeedback (p. 313)
cardiovascular disorders (p. 306)
catastrophization (p. 318)

chronic pain (p. 317)
coping (p. 293)
coronary heart disease (CHD) (p. 309)
daily hassles (p. 296)
distress (p. 291)
emotional support (p. 300)
essential (or primary) hypertension (p. 306)
eustress (p. 291)

functional social support (p. 300)
general adaptation syndrome (GAS) (p. 290)
goodness of fit hypothesis (p. 294)
health psychology (p. 289)
instrumental support (p. 300)
interactionism (p. 298)
job burnout (p. 297)
job spillover (p. 297)

REFLECTIONS: PAST, PRESENT, AND FUTURE

- Jemmott and Magliore (1988) demonstrated that among college students who were experiencing the stress of final examinations, those students with more social support had superior immune function, as assessed by secretory immunoglobulin A. What are the implications of their finding? If you were working as a student mentor in a university academic skills centre, what advice would you give your charges?

- Research has shown that many people who develop psychological disorders also have various physical illnesses. Does this correlation allow us to conclude that mental disorders contribute to the development of physical illnesses? Design a study that would allow you to conclude that there is a causal effect of psychological disorders on physical illness.

- Diathesis-stress, biopsychosocial, and cognitive-behavioural paradigms all emphasize that psychological and social factors play a vital role in influencing people's health, including the experience of chronic pain. Does this mean that people are responsible for their own health? How might these perspectives affect public health policy in Canada?

- Research (e.g., Maccoby & Altman, 1988; Schooler, Flora, & Farquhar, 1993) has demonstrated that community-based programs have the potential to reduce significantly the incidence and seriousness of many medical illnesses beyond what is achievable by strictly medical practices. It is increasingly accepted that people's physical health is often very much in their own hands and that changing lifestyle practices is sometimes the best means of reducing the risk of illness (Bandura, 1986). How could you use the mass media to reduce cardiovascular disease? What would you inform people they could do to reduce their risk of premature disease? Can people learn how to reduce their overall risk for cardiovascular and other diseases from properly designed and delivered mass media and other large-scale educational programs?

CHAPTER 10

EATING DISORDERS

"Well done, everyone! Well done! Really clever of you to breed a whole new generation of anorexics. Excellent! You're not educating these young women about the world, about poverty, about the environment or about anything that's interesting. You're educating them about what lip gloss to use, which clothes to wear … Brilliant! The majority of the clothes in these runway shows are being worn by people who don't have any flesh on their bones at all … What the hell is going on? It's so frightening. It makes me so mad. And these pro-anorexia websites? I can't believe that stuff is allowed. It's just disgusting."

—**Kate Winslet, actress, on the promotion of unrealistic body images (Goodwin, 2007, p. 46)**

"In fact, from any normal perspective, I was not fat. At five foot seven, even at my heaviest I had never weighed more than 130 pounds, which most physicians would think healthy and normal for that height. But in the ballet world, having a few too many curves is obesity, and I was continually convinced that my excessive weight, which I saw as a real deformity, would doom me."

—**Karen Kain, dancer (1994, p. 23), on unrealistic pressures to be thin**

"I still try to maintain as perfect an image as possible and I still seek to please my mother. My past has created the 'present day me' who needs to be successful in life, who needs to be perfect, who lacks self-confidence and fears failure, and who constantly strives to achieve the highest standards possible."

—**An admission by a Canadian eating-disorder client, in recovery, who is known to the authors**

CLINICAL DESCRIPTION

ETIOLOGY OF EATING DISORDERS

TREATMENT OF EATING DISORDERS

SUMMARY

Thomas Reid Macdonald, Canadian 1908–1978, *Standing Woman*, 1936, Oil on canvas, 76.0 × 48.2 cm (framed), Art Gallery of Ontario, Toronto © Katherine Macdonald, Hamilton, ON

WHEN MS. A was first evaluated for admission to an inpatient eating disorders program, she had been restricting her food intake for approximately 5 years and had been amenorrheic for 4 years. At the time of her admission, this 24-year-old, single, white woman weighed 71 lb at a height of 5 feet 1.5 inches. In 12th grade, Ms. A menstruated for the first time and also developed "very large" breasts. She had a difficult first year at college, where she gained to her maximum weight of 120 lb. The following year, Ms. A transferred to a smaller college, became a vegetarian for "ethical reasons," and began to significantly restrict her food intake. She limited herself to a total of 700 to 800 calories per day, with a maximum of 200 calories per meal, and gradually lost weight in the next 5 years. Ms. A did not binge, vomit, abuse laxatives, or engage in excessive exercise. She considered herself to be "obsessed with calories" and observed a variety of rituals regarding food and food preparation (e.g., obsessively weighing her food) …

During her first five-month hospitalization, Ms. A was treated with a multimodal program (behavioral weight gain protocol, individual and family therapy, fluoxetine at 60–80 mg for obsessive-compulsive traits and depressive symptoms) and gained to a weight of 98 lb. At discharge, she was maintaining her weight on food but remained concerned about her weight and was particularly frightened of reaching "the triple digits" (i.e., 100 lb). After leaving the hospital, Ms. A continued with outpatient psychotherapy and fluoxetine for several months …

About 3.5 years after discharge, at age 27 years, Ms. A again sought inpatient treatment. At admission, she weighed 83 lb but still felt "fat." During hospitalization, she steadily gained weight and was prescribed sertraline at 100 mg/day for feelings of low self-esteem, anxiety, and obsessional thinking. When she was discharged five months later, at a weight of 108 lb, she noted menstrual bleeding for the first time in more than 7 years. After leaving the hospital, Ms. A continued taking medication and began outpatient cognitive-behavioral psychotherapy. For the next year, she continued to struggle with eating and weight issues but managed to maintain her weight and successfully expand other aspects of her life by independently supporting herself with a full-time job, making new friends, and becoming involved in her first romantic relationship. (Walsh, 2003, pp. 1516–1517)

Many cultures are preoccupied with eating. In North America today, gourmet restaurants abound and numerous magazines and television shows are devoted to food preparation. At the same time, many people are overweight. Dieting to lose weight is common, and the desire of many people, especially women, to be slimmer has created a multi-billion-dollar-a-year business. Given this intense interest in food and eating, it is not surprising that this aspect of human behaviour is subject to disorder.

Although clinical descriptions of eating disorders can be traced back many years, these disorders only appeared in the *DSM* for the first time in 1980, as one subcategory of disorders beginning in childhood or adolescence. With the publication of *DSM-IV*, the eating disorders anorexia nervosa and bulimia nervosa formed a distinct category, reflecting the increased attention they have received from clinicians and researchers over the past three decades. As will be discussed, binge eating disorder is another distinct diagnostic category slated for inclusion in *DSM-V*. Improved criteria for anorexia nervosa and bulimia nervosa are also forthcoming.

The prevalence and correlates of eating disorders were assessed in a nationally representative household survey conducted in the United States between 2001 and 2003 (see Hudson, Hiripi, Hope, & Kessler, 2007). The lifetime prevalence estimates of anorexia nervosa were 0.9% for women and 0.3% for men. The lifetime prevalence estimates of bulimia nervosa were 1.5% for women and 0.5% for men. Finally, the lifetime prevalence estimates of binge eating disorder were 3.5% for women and 2.0% for men. Although there was extensive evidence of role impairment, only a relatively small proportion of people requiring treatment actually had sought treatment within the past year (e.g., 15.6% of those with bulimia nervosa); treatment was obtained typically from the general medical sector. Strong evidence of statistically significant cohort effects was found for bulimia nervosa and binge eating disorder. Cohort effects are described in more detail in Chapter 16.

According to Statistics Canada's 2002 Mental Health and Well-being Survey (CCHS, 1.2; see Government of Canada, 2006), 0.5% of Canadians 15 years of age or older reported an eating disorder diagnosis in the preceding 12 months. Women were once again more likely than men to report an eating disorder: 0.8% vs. 0.2%, respectively. Among young women aged 15 to 24, 1.5% reported that they had an eating disorder. Analyses of the CCHS data also determined that 1.7% of Canadians meet 12-month criteria for an eating attitude problem.

Eating disorders can cause long-term psychological, social, and health problems. Hospitalization is sometimes necessary. Hospitalization rates are highest among young women in the 15 to 24 age range (Government of Canada, 2006, see Figure 10.1). However, rates are also high among those aged 10 to 14 and 20 to 24.

CLINICAL DESCRIPTION

We begin by describing anorexia nervosa and bulimia nervosa. First, however, some key points related to diagnosing and classifying eating disorders should be noted. Do you think anorexia nervosa or bulimia nervosa is the most common eating disorder diagnosis? The correct answer is that neither

FIGURE 10.1 Hospitalizations for eating disorders* in general hospitals per 100,000 by age group, Canada, 1999–2000
Source: Centre for Chronic Disease Prevention and Control, Public Health Agency of Canada, using data from Hospital Morbidity File, Canadian Institute for Health Information
* "Using responsible diagnosis only."

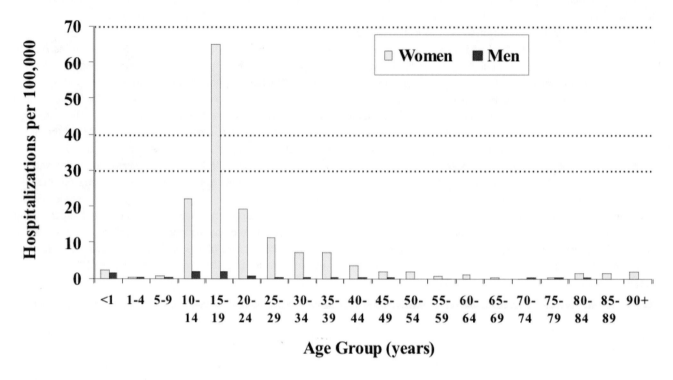

is. There is greater heterogeneity in eating disorder symptom expression; thus, the most common diagnosis (occurring in between 40 to 70% of patients) is a category called **eating disorder not otherwise specified (EDNOS)** (see Thomas, Vartanian, & Brownell, 2009). This general diagnostic category has been seen as a residual "catch-all" category that underscores problems inherent in the current diagnostic system. The extensive use of the EDNOS category reflects the great heterogeneity among individuals all deemed to have an eating disorder of some sort, but it also suggests that the categories themselves need refinement.

There is also a newly proposed variation known as **purging disorder**. As described by Keel, Haedt, and Edler (2005), this is a form of bulimia that involves self-induced vomiting or laxative use at least once a week for a minimum of six months. Subsequent work (e.g., Keel et al., 2007) has supported the validity of this disorder. Fink et al. (2009) concluded that purging disorder patients have levels of disturbed eating and associated forms of psychopathology that are comparable with patients with other eating disorders, but purging disorder patients have certain distinguishing features. One clear feature of purging disorder is high impulsivity. Impulsivity in eating disorders is receiving increasing attention. A review by Samantha Waxman (2009) from Queen's University confirmed that trait impulsivity is a key factor that distinguishes among the various eating disorder diagnoses. Impulsivity for

some becomes so extreme that it manifests as an impulse control disorder. Recent work found that 1 in 6 eating disorder patients also had a diagnosable impulse control disorder (Fernandez-Aranda et al., 2008). Typically, the onset of the impulse control disorder preceded the eating disorder rather than vice versa. The most common impulse control disorders among these women were compulsive buying disorder and kleptomania (i.e., compulsive stealing).

Before leaving the topic of diagnostic issues, we should note that concerns have been raised about the universal relevance of certain criteria. For instance, it has been suggested that the "fear of fat" criterion included in anorexia nervosa may not apply to anorexic females in certain cultures (e.g., China) (for a discussion, see Wonderlich et al., 2007). As noted below, definitive evidence to support this view has not yet been obtained.

With these diagnostic complexities in mind, we turn to a discussion of anorexia nervosa and bulimia nervosa. The diagnoses of anorexia nervosa and bulimia nervosa share several clinical features, the most important being the intense fear of being overweight, as already mentioned. There are some indications that these may not be distinct diagnoses but may be two variants of a single disorder. Co-twins of patients diagnosed with anorexia nervosa, for example, are themselves more likely than average to have bulimia nervosa (Walters & Kendler, 1994).

ANOREXIA NERVOSA

"Between the ages of 14 and 18, I struggled with anorexia and bulimia … The pressure was hard-core. For four to six months at a time, I would barely eat so I was constantly dizzy. I lived on Melba toast, carrots and black coffee."
—singer Alanis Morissette (from Heller, 2005, p.A4)

Ms. A, the woman described at the start of this chapter, had **anorexia nervosa (AN)**. *Anorexia* refers to loss of appetite, and *nervosa* indicates that this is for emotional reasons. The term is something of a misnomer because most patients with anorexia nervosa actually do not lose their appetite or interest in food. Most patients with the disorder become preoccupied with food; they may read cookbooks constantly and prepare gourmet meals for their families.

Ms. A met all four features required for the diagnosis:

- The person must refuse to maintain a normal body weight; this is usually taken to mean that the person weighs less than 85% of what is considered normal for that person's age and height. Weight loss is typically achieved through dieting, although purging (self-induced vomiting, heavy use of laxatives or diuretics) and excessive exercise can also be part of the picture.

Anorexia nervosa can be a life-threatening condition. It is especially prevalent among young women who are under intense pressure to keep their weight low. Brazilian model Ana Carolina Reston died in November 2006 of complications from anorexia. It has been suggested that there is currently an epidemic of eating disorders in Brazil. AP Photo/Eugenio Savio.

- The person has an intense fear of gaining weight, and the fear is not reduced by weight loss. They can never be thin enough.
- Patients with AN have a distorted sense of their body shape. They maintain that even when emaciated, they are overweight or that certain parts of their bodies, particularly the abdomen, buttocks, and thighs, are too fat. To check on their body size, they typically weigh themselves frequently, measure the size of different parts of the body, and gaze critically at their reflections in mirrors. Their self-esteem is closely linked to maintaining thinness. The tendency to link self-esteem and self-evaluation with thinness is known as "overevaluation of appearance."
- In females, the extreme emaciation causes **amenorrhea**, the loss of the menstrual period. Of the four existing diagnostic criteria, amenorrhea seems least important to determining a diagnosis of anorexia; comparisons conducted in Canada show few differences between women who meet all four criteria and women who meet the other three but not amenorrhea. Moreover, amenorrhea occurs in a significant minority of women before any significant weight loss and the symptom can persist after weight gain (Garfinkel, 2002). Consequently, this potential symptom is being dropped as a criterion for anorexia in *DSM-V.*

The distorted body image that accompanies anorexia nervosa has been assessed in several ways, most frequently by questionnaires such as the Eating Disorders Inventory (EDI; Garner, Olmsted, & Polivy, 1983). The EDI was developed in Canada and is one of the most widely used measures to assess self-reported aspects of eating disorders. The subscales and items on this questionnaire are presented in Table 10.1.

In another type of assessment, patients are shown line drawings of women with varying body weights and asked to pick the one closest to their own and the one that represents their ideal shape (see Figure 10.2). Patients with AN overestimate their own body size and choose a thin figure as their ideal.

DSM-IV-TR distinguishes two types of AN. In the *restricting type*, weight loss is achieved by severely limiting food intake; in the *binge eating-purging type*, the person also regularly engages in binge eating and purging. Numerous differences between these two subtypes support the validity of this distinction. The purging subtype appears to be more psychopathological; patients exhibit more personality disorders, impulsive behaviour, stealing, alcohol and drug abuse, social withdrawal, and suicide attempts than do patients with the restricting type of anorexia (e.g., Pryor, Wiederman, & McGilley, 1996). Moreover, relative to the restricting type, bingeing-purging patients tend to weigh more in childhood, come from heavier families with greater familial obesity, and use more extreme weight-control methods (Garfinkel, 2002).

Anorexia nervosa (AN) typically begins in the early to middle teenage years, often after an episode of dieting and exposure to life stress. Recent data suggest that the prevalence of anorexia among children and adolescents is increasing.

TABLE 10.1
SUBSCALES AND ILLUSTRATIVE ITEMS FROM THE EATING DISORDERS INVENTORY

Drive for thinness	I think about dieting.
	I am preoccupied with the desire to be thinner.
Bulimia	I have thought of trying to vomit in order to lose weight.
	I have gone on eating binges where I have felt that I could not stop.
Body dissatisfaction	I think that my thighs are too large.
	I think that my buttocks are too large.
Ineffectiveness	I feel inadequate.
	I feel empty inside (emotionally).
Perfectionism	Only outstanding performance is good enough in my family.
	I hate being less than best at things.
Interpersonal distrust	I have trouble expressing my emotions to others.
	I need to keep people at a certain distance.
Interoceptive awareness	I get confused about what emotion I am feeling.
	I don't know what's going on inside me.
Maturity fears	I wish that I could return to the security of childhood.
	The demands of adulthood are too great.

Note: Respondents use a six-point scale ranging from "always" to "never."
Source: From Garner, Olmsted, and Polivy, 1983.

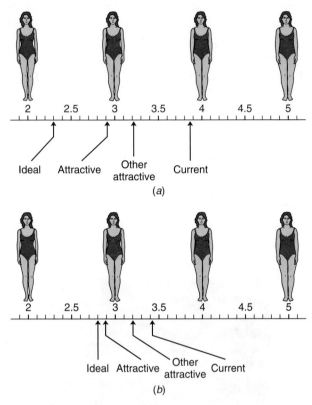

FIGURE 10.2 In this assessment of body image, respondents indicate their current shape, their ideal shape, and the shape they think is most attractive to the opposite sex. The figure actually rated as most attractive by members of the opposite sex is shown in both panels. Ratings of women who scored high on a measure of distorted attitudes toward eating are shown in (a); ratings of women who scored low are shown in (b). The high scorers overestimated their current size and chose a thin form as their ideal. *Source:* From Zellner, Harner, and Adler (1988)

Halmi (2009) surveyed data from five continents and concluded that rates among younger people are definitely on the rise; moreover, the presence of anxiety disorder is a significant risk factor among younger people.

Comorbidity is high. Recent analyses of data from the Canadian Community Health Survey found that both men and women at risk for eating disorders were also prone to depression, panic disorder, and social phobia (Gadalla, 2008). However, some gender differences did emerge. Women were at substantially greater risk for mania, agoraphobia, and substance dependence.

A growing concern is the high rate of co-occurring eating disorders and substance use disorders, as documented in recent Canadian studies (see Courbasson, Smith, & Cleland, 2005; Piran & Gadalla, 2006). Also, a meta-analysis conducted in Spain found that there was no link between anorexia nervosa and illicit drug use, but there was a clear link evident between bulimia nervosa and drug use (Calero-Elvira et al., 2009). Canadian investigators have specifically tied drug use to the bingeing and dieting cycle (see Gadalla & Piran, 2007). As a result, the Centre for Addiction and Mental Health in Toronto has created a separate Eating Disorder and Addiction Clinic, directed by Christine Courbasson. Courbasson and Schelkanova (2007) have outlined the various ways that eating and appearance-related concerns become significant barriers to recovery among women with extreme forms of addiction.

PHYSICAL CHANGES IN ANOREXIA NERVOSA Self-starvation and use of laxatives produce numerous undesirable biological consequences in patients with anorexia nervosa. Blood pressure often falls, heart rate slows, kidney and gastrointestinal problems develop, bone mass declines, the skin dries out, nails become brittle, hormone levels change, and mild anemia may occur. Some patients lose hair from the scalp, and they may develop laguna, a fine, soft hair, on their bodies. Levels of electrolytes, such as potassium and sodium, are altered. These ionized salts, present in various bodily fluids, are essential for the process of neural transmission, and lowered levels can lead to tiredness, weakness, cardiac arrhythmias, and even sudden death. Brain size declines in patients with anorexia, and EEG abnormalities and neurological impairments are frequent (Garner, 1997; Lambe et al., 1997). Research in Canada by Lambe and associates has established that deficits in white-matter volumes in the brain are restored upon recovery from anorexia nervosa,

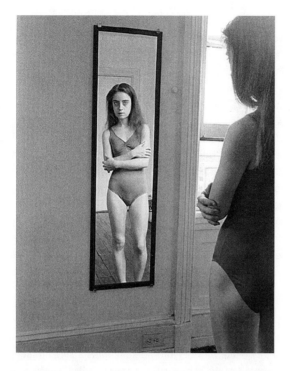

Despite being thin, women with anorexia believe that parts of their bodies are too fat, and they spend a lot of time critically examining themselves in front of mirrors. Susan Rosenberg/Photo Researchers, Inc.

but deficits in grey-matter volumes appear irreversible, at least in the short term. Overall, there are many serious consequences and these consequences may be especially problematic for adolescents with AN (Katzman, 2005).

PROGNOSIS About 70% of patients with AN eventually recover. However, recovery often takes six or seven years, and relapses are common before a stable pattern of eating and maintenance of weight is achieved (Strober, Freeman, &

Morrel, 1997). As we discuss later, changing these patients' distorted views of themselves is very difficult, particularly in cultures that value thinness.

AN is a life-threatening illness; death rates are about 10 times higher among patients with the disorder than among the general population and twice as high as among patients with other psychological disorders. Death most often results from physical complications of the illness or from suicide (Birmingham et al., 2005; Katzman, 2005). A study of patients at St. Paul's Hospital in British Columbia found that over a 20-year period, the standardized mortality rate for the 326 patients with AN was very high (10.5). Standardized mortality rate is defined as the ratio of observed deaths relative to expected deaths. Among the 17 AN patients who had died, the leading cause was suicide ($n = 7$) followed by pneumonia, hypoglycemia, and liver disease. These data counter some studies that concluded that death rates associated with anorexia have been overstated. A follow-up survival analysis conducted by a team of B.C. researchers led them to conclude that anorexia is associated with a 25-year reduction in life expectancy (Harbottle, Birmingham, & Sayani, 2008). This is the first investigation to definitively establish the reduced life expectancy of anorexic patients.

The obtained link with suicide is receiving increasing attention. A contemporary review of suicide and AN found that suicide rates are not elevated in bulimia nervosa like they are in AN (Franko & Keel, 2006), though people with bulimia nervosa are more likely to have suicide ideation. Predictors of suicide in AN patients include purging behaviours, depression, substance abuse, and a history of physical or sexual abuse (Franko & Keel, 2006). Another growing concern is the link between eating disorders and intentional acts of self-injury. Acts of intentional self-harm (e.g., cutting) are discussed in Focus on Discovery 10.1.

FOCUS ON DISCOVERY 10.1
EATING DISORDERS AND INTENTIONAL SELF-HARM

"Natalie, a 19-year-old woman in her sophomore year of college, was referred for a mandatory psychological evaluation by the resident advisor of her college dormitory after Natalie's roommate walked in one afternoon to find her crying and cutting at her wrists with a pocket knife. Natalie told her resident advisor 'It's really not a big deal at all . . . I don't want to kill myself and I know what I am doing so you don't need to worry about me.' Nevertheless, she was referred for an evaluation by a psychologist. Natalie reluctantly went to a local outpatient clinic and upon first meeting the psychologist informed her: 'Look, I have been to like a dozen shrinks already so save whatever it is you have to say. Cutting works better than any psychologist I have seen so I know you can't help me. I am only coming here because my school is making me. So what do I have to do to get out of here?'." (Nock, Teper, & Hollander, 2007, p. 1081)

The tendency to engage in intentional forms of self-injury and self-harm is becoming all too common and engaging in this behaviour is a risk factor for subsequent suicide attempts. Our discussion of this topic is in this chapter because intentional self-injury is associated with the experience of eating disorders and vulnerability to eating disorders (Paul et al., 2002), and as shown in one Canadian study, this is particularly likely among those with high levels of impulsivity (Ross, Heath, & Toste, 2009).

Diana, Princess of Wales, was characterized jointly by bulimia and an impulsive tendency toward self-harm. Diana revealed her self-harm behaviours in 1995 during a BBC1 interview with journalist Martin Bashir. Diana stated the following to explain why she engaged in self-harm behaviour (i.e., cutting, scratching of her arms and legs):

Patterns of intentional self-harm have been documented among well-known people such as Princess Diana and the singer Amy Winehouse. Winehouse has acknowledged bouts of substance abuse, depression, and eating disorder along with her extensive history of self-harm. AP Photo/Kirsty Wigglesworth, Terence Donovan Archive/Getty Images.

When no one listens to you, or you feel no one's listening to you, all sorts of things start to happen. For instance you have so much pain inside yourself that you try and hurt yourself on the outside because you want help, but it's the wrong help you're asking for. People see it as crying wolf or attention-seeking, and they think because you're in the media all the time you've got enough attention. But I was actually crying out because I wanted to get better in order to go forward and continue my duty and my role as wife, mother, Princess of Wales. So yes, I did inflict upon myself. I didn't like myself, I was ashamed because I couldn't cope with the pressures. (BBC Interview, 1995; see www.bbc.co.uk/politics97/diana/panorama.html)

So, how common is intentional self-injury? Results from the Victoria Health Survey, a longitudinal study of Canadian youth between the ages of 14 and 21, found that 96 of 568 participants (16.9%) indicated engaging in non-suicidal self-harm. The mean age of onset was 15 years old. The most common forms of self-harm were cutting, scratching, and self-hitting (Nixon, Cloutier, & Jansson, 2008). A greater frequency of self-harm was linked with depression and difficulties regulating attention and impulsivity. The Collegiate Health Study at York University found that almost 3 in 10 first-year students admitted to engaging in at least one act of intentional self-harm (Goldstein, Flett, Wekerle, & Wall, 2009). Cutting was the most common form for young women, while young men acknowledged intentionally engaging in behaviours that they knew were risky, such as driving in a reckless manner. Significant correlates of intentional self-harm in these first-year university students included a history of emotional abuse, illicit drug use, depression, and various personality factors (e.g., sensation seeking and openness to experience).

So why do people engage in self-harm? Nock and Prinstein (2004) have advanced a four-factor model that focuses primarily on self-harm as reflecting various types of reinforcement. Self-injury occurs for (1) interpersonal reasons; (2) to suppress an unwanted social stimulus (i.e., social negative reinforcement); (3) to suppress negative emotion (i.e., automatic negative reinforcement); and (4) to generate feelings (i.e., automatic positive reinforcement) among those who need to feel emotion.

A separate model developed by Santa-Mina et al. (2006) assesses five factors associated with self-injury. The first factor is self-injury for reasons of regulating or controlling negative emotional feelings. Other factors include self-injury for coping, protection, stimulation, and dissociation (i.e., detachment).

Multiple factors must be taken into account when determining the etiology of self-injury. For instance, one contemporary factor is the role of Internet self-injury message boards. One study identified more than 400 of these message boards (Whitlock, Powers, & Eckenrode, 2006). This study referred to the Internet as "the virtual cutting edge." The study concluded that on-line social interaction provided much-needed support to those with a history of intentional self-harm, but these boards also normalize and encourage further acts of self-injury.

BULIMIA NERVOSA

"I know that so many women are slowly killing themselves and mutilating their bodies. I am not going to sit there and do nothing. I am going to use what I know about it and work with a team of experts to make a difference."

—*Sophie Grégoire, television journalist and wife of Justin Trudeau, who acknowledged in* Chatelaine *magazine her struggles with bulimia and her role as spokesperson for the Montreal-based BACA Eating Disorders Clinic*

When Ms. B, a 20-year-old white college student, was first evaluated for treatment at an outpatient eating disorders program, she had been binge-eating and purging for approximately 5 years. Each evening, she consumed large quantities of food, vomited three or four times, and took two to six laxatives. She also occasionally used herbal diuretics but had never abused diet pills or prescription diuretics. Ms. B's weight was well within the normal range (106 lb at a height of 5 feet 2 inches). She was extremely concerned about her shape and weight, was afraid of becoming fat, and wanted to weigh no more than 100 lb ("the double digits are nice too ... maybe 90 lb, but I don't think I could run at that weight").

Ms. B always binged alone in her dormitory room while watching television and flipping through magazines. A typical binge might consist of two packages of cookies, a half-gallon of ice cream, one box of cereal, one can of spaghetti, one bag of pretzels, one can of soup, one package of fishsticks, one bag of candy, and six bagels with butter, eaten during a three- to four-hour period. She would vomit every hour or so, each time making room for more food. Throughout the day, she would severely restrict her food intake, usually eating nothing but fruit, salad, oatmeal, diet hot chocolate, coffee, and chewing gum. She was an avid cross-country runner, totalling about 50 miles per week, but denied running to compensate for her eating binges. (Walsh, 2003, p. 1517)

Ms. B's behaviour illustrates the features of **bulimia nervosa** (BN). *Bulimia* is from a Greek word meaning "ox hunger." This disorder involves episodes of rapid consumption of a large amount of food, followed by compensatory behaviours, such as vomiting, fasting, or excessive exercise, to prevent weight gain. The *DSM* defines a binge as eating an excessive amount of food within less than two hours. Bulimia nervosa is not diagnosed if the bingeing and purging occur only in the context of anorexia nervosa and its extreme weight loss; the diagnosis in such a case is anorexia nervosa, binge eating-purging type.

Binges typically occur in secret, may be triggered by stress and the negative emotions it arouses, and continue until the person is uncomfortably full (Grilo, Shiffman, & Carter-

Sophie Grégoire, the television journalist who is married to Justin Trudeau, acknowledged in 2006 that she had bulimia that began when she was 17 years old. She is a spokesperson for BACA, a Montreal-based eating disorders clinic. Gregoire has attributed her eating disorder to an excessive need to please others, peer pressure, and socio-cultural pressures from the media to attain a prescribed physical appearance. Canadian Press/Ryan Remiorz.

Campbell, 1994). Stressors that involve negative social interactions may be particularly potent elicitors of binges. Steiger and his associates in Quebec (Steiger et al., 1999) found in a study of daily experiences that bulimics have high levels of interpersonal sensitivity, as reflected in large increases in self-criticism following negative social interactions. Further, binge episodes tend to be preceded by poorer than average social experiences, self-concepts, and moods. Steiger et al. (1999) also reported that the binge episodes are followed by deterioration in self-concept, mood state, and social perception.

The person who is engaged in a binge often feels a loss of control over the amount of food being consumed. Foods that can be rapidly consumed, especially sweets such as ice cream or cake, are usually part of a binge. Although research suggests that patients with bulimia nervosa sometimes ingest an enormous quantity of food during a binge—often more than what a normal person eats in an entire day, as was the case with Ms. B—binges are not always as large as the *DSM* implies, and there may be wide variation in the caloric content consumed by individuals with bulimia nervosa during binges. Patients are usually ashamed of their binges and try to conceal them. They report that they lose control during a binge, even to the point of experiencing something akin to a dissociative state, perhaps losing awareness of what they are doing or feeling that it is not really they who are bingeing.

After the binge is over, disgust, feelings of discomfort, and fear of weight gain lead to the second step of bulimia nervosa—purging to undo the caloric effects of the binge. As seen with Ms. B, purging can involve induced vomiting and excessive exercise. The use of laxatives and diuretics is common, even though this does not actually result in weight loss.

Although many people binge occasionally and some people also experiment with purging, the *DSM* diagnosis of bulimia nervosa requires that the episodes of bingeing and purging occur at least twice a week for three months. Is twice a week a well-established cut-off point? Probably not. Epidemiological research conducted in Canada has found few differences between patients who binge twice a week and those who do so less frequently, suggesting that there is a continuum of severity rather than a sharp distinction (Garfinkel et al., 1995; Garfinkel, 2002).

Like patients with anorexia nervosa, patients with bulimia nervosa are afraid of gaining weight, and their self-esteem depends heavily on maintaining normal weight. Garfinkel (2002) observed that "a morbid fear of fat" is an essential diagnostic criterion for bulimia nervosa because (1) it covers what clinicians and researchers view as the "core psychopathology" of bulimia nervosa; (2) it makes the diagnosis more restrictive; and (3) it makes the syndrome more closely resemble the related disorder of anorexia nervosa.

As with anorexia, two subtypes of bulimia nervosa are distinguished: a purging type and a non-purging type in which the compensatory behaviours are fasting or excessive exercise. Evidence for the validity of this distinction is mixed, however, and recent evidence does not strongly support the validity of this distinction (see Mond et al., 2006). Accordingly, the subtypes will be dropped in *DSM-V* according to initial reports.

Bulimia nervosa typically begins in late adolescence or early adulthood. Research conducted in Canadian public schools suggests that bulimia is more common than anorexia among adolescents (Leichner et al., 1986). An even greater number of females may not meet existing diagnostic criteria for eating disorders but show signs of vulnerability to subsequent problems. One study found that by age 18, 80% of young women in British Columbia with normal height and weight indicate that they would like to weigh less (McCreary Centre Society, 1999). Another study of more than 1,800 females from Ottawa, Hamilton, and Toronto between the ages of 12 and 18 found that 27% had disordered-eating attitudes and behaviours, and approximately 1 in 7 participants engaged in binge eating with associated loss of control (Jones et al., 2001). Most recently, extreme body dissatisfaction was found among 7–8% of both girls and boys in Nova Scotia, and these children were only in Grade 5; these data suggest that children particularly at risk can be identified at a fairly young age (Austin, Haines, & Veugelers, 2009). It was found among only girls that as their body mass index increased, their body satisfaction decreased.

Temporal studies of the course of the disorder indicate that many BN patients are somewhat overweight before the onset of the disorder and that the binge eating often starts during a dieting episode. Long-term follow-ups of BN patients reveal that about 70% recover, although about 10% remain fully symptomatic (Keel et al., 1999).

Bulimia nervosa is associated with numerous other diagnoses, notably depression, personality disorders (especially borderline personality disorder, discussed in Chapter 13), anxiety disorders, substance abuse, and conduct disorder (discussed in Chapter 15) (von Ranson, Iacono, & McGue, 2002). Suicide rates are much higher among people with bulimia nervosa than in the general population (Favaro & Santonastaso, 1998). A twin study has found that bulimia and depression are genetically related (Walters et al., 1992).

Like anorexia, bulimia is associated with several physical side effects. Frequent purging can cause potassium depletion. Heavy use of laxatives induces diarrhea, which can also lead to changes in electrolytes and cause irregularities in the heartbeat. Recurrent vomiting may lead to tearing of tissue in the stomach and throat and to loss of dental enamel as stomach acids eat away at the teeth, making them ragged. The salivary glands may become swollen. However, mortality appears to be much less common in BN than in AN (Keel & Mitchell, 1997).

BINGE EATING DISORDER

DSM-IV-TR includes **binge eating disorder** (BED) as a diagnosis in need of further study rather than a formal diagnosis, but BED will be included in *DSM-V*, according to announced changes. This disorder includes recurrent binges (two times per week for at least six months), lack of control during the bingeing episode, and distress about bingeing, as well as other characteristics, such as rapid eating and eating alone. It is distinguished from AN by the absence of weight loss and from BN by the absence of compensatory behaviours (purging, fasting, or excessive exercise).

As indicated by the results of the Hudson et al. (2007) study we described earlier, binge eating disorder appears to be more prevalent than either AN or BN. In a community sample, BED was found in 6% of successful dieters (those who had kept their weight off for more than one year) and in 19% of unsuccessful dieters (Ferguson & Spitzer, 1995). A recent study of urban-dwelling Canadian women in a community sample found frequent binge eating among 1 in 25 women and that 3.8% of the participants met criteria for BED, while no women met criteria for anorexia nervosa (Gauvin, Steiger, & Brodeur, 2009).

BED has several features that support its validity as a disorder in *DSM-V*. It occurs more often in women than in men and is associated with obesity and a history of dieting (Kinzl et al., 1999). It is linked with impaired work and social functioning, depression, low self-esteem, substance abuse, and dissatisfaction with body shape (Spitzer et al., 1993; Striegel-Moore et al., 1998). Risk factors for developing BED include childhood obesity, critical comments regarding being overweight, low self-concept, depression, and childhood physical or sexual abuse (Fairburn et al., 1998). Recent data also indicate that the average life-term duration of BED (14.4 years) may be greater than the duration of AN (5.9 years) or BN (5.8) years (see Pope et al., 2006).

An epidemiological study by Bulik, Sullivan, and Kendler (2000) provided strong evidence for the validity of binge eating disorder as a distinct category. This research was conducted on female community members from the state of Virginia. Six distinct clusters were identified on the basis of interview and self-report data, including three atypical groups and three other groups representing individuals with anorexia nervosa, bulimia nervosa, and binge eating disorder. Bulik et al. (2000) reported that only about half of the women with an apparent binge eating disorder reported feeling "out of control," and they suggested the need for further inquiry into binge eating and the cognitive feeling of being out of control.

ETIOLOGY OF EATING DISORDERS

As with other psychopathologies, a single factor is unlikely to cause an eating disorder. Several areas of current research—including genetics, the role of the brain, socio-cultural pressures to be thin, the role of the family, and the role of environmental stress—suggest that eating disorders result when several influences converge in a person's life. The Government of Canada (2006) report recognizes numerous eating-specific and generalized factors from a complex biopsychosocial perspective. These direct and indirect risk factors are outlined in Table 10.2.

BIOLOGICAL FACTORS

GENETICS In a recent review paper, de Krom et al. (2009) observed that the role of genetic factors in eating disorders has been largely ignored, relative to other types of disorders, because of a prevailing emphasis on socio-cultural factors; it is only within the last 10 years that systematic research on genetic factors has started to take place. A possible role for genetics is suggested by the fact that both anorexia nervosa and bulimia nervosa run in families. First-degree relatives of young women with anorexia nervosa are about four times more likely than

TABLE 10.2

SUMMARY OF POSSIBLE RISK FACTORS FOR THE DEVELOPMENT OF EATING DISORDERS

	Eating-Specific Factors (Direct Risk Factors)	Generalized Factors (Indirect Risk Factors)
Biological Factors	Eating disorder-specific genetic risk Physiognomy and body weight Appetite regulation Energy metabolism Sex	Genetic risk for associated disturbance Temperament Impulsivity Neurobiology (e.g., 5-HT mechanisms) Sex
Psychological Factors	Poor body image Maladaptive eating attitudes Maladaptive beliefs about shape and weight Specific values or meanings assigned to food, body Overvaluation of appearance	Poor self-image Inadequate coping mechanisms Self-regulation problems Unresolved conflicts, deficits, post-traumatic reactions Identity problems Autonomy problems Overprotection Neglect
Developmental Factors	Identifications with body-concerned relatives, or peers Aversive mealtime experiences Trauma affecting bodily experience	Felt rejection, criticism Traumata (physical, emotional, and sexual abuse) Object relationships (interpersonal experience)
Social Factors	Maladaptive family attitudes to eating and weight Peer-group weight concerns Pressures to be thin Body-related teasing Specific pressures to control weight (e.g., thro ballet, athletic pursuits)` Maladaptive cultural values assigned to body Gender	Family dysfunction Aversive peer experiences Social values detrimental to stable, positive self-image Destabilizing social change Values assigned to gender Social isolation Lack of social support Impediments to means of self-definition Gender Media imagery concerning girls and women Pressures for thinness among girls Increasing population and availability of cosmetic surgery and body improvements Cultural differences and sex difference affecting ideal weight images and calculations

Source: Government of Canada, *The Human Face of Mental Health and Mental Illness in Canada,* 2006.

Cultural standards regarding the ideal feminine shape have changed over time. Even in the 1950s and 1960s, the feminine ideal was considerably heavier than what it has been since then. © Burstein Collection/CORBIS; Eve Arnold/Magnum Photos. Inc; Maria C. Valentino/Sygma.

average to have the disorder themselves (Strober et al., 1990). Twin studies of eating disorders also suggest a genetic influence. Most studies of both anorexia and bulimia report higher identical than fraternal concordance rates. A recent study included more than 30,000 participants from Sweden (see Bulik et al., 2006). A strong genetic component was found with a heritability estimate of 56% (relative to the 5% and 38% estimates of variance attributable to the shared environment and unique environment, respectively). Research has also shown that key features of the eating disorders, such as dissatisfaction with one's body and a strong desire to be thin, appear to be heritable (Rutherford et al., 1993).

EATING DISORDERS AND THE BRAIN The hypothalamus is a key brain centre in regulating hunger and eating (see de Krom et al., 2009). Research on animals with lesions to the **lateral hypothalamus** (see Chapter 2) indicates that they lose weight and have no appetite (Hoebel & Teitelbaum, 1966); thus, it is not surprising that the hypothalamus has been proposed to play a role in anorexia. The paraventricular nucleus has also been implicated (Connan & Stanley, 2003). The levels of some hormones regulated by the hypothalamus, such as cortisol, are indeed abnormal in patients with anorexia; rather than causing the disorder, however, these hormonal abnormalities occur as a result of self-starvation, and levels return to normal following weight gain (Doerr et al., 1980). Furthermore, the weight loss of animals with hypothalamic lesions does not parallel what we know about anorexia; these animals appear to have no hunger and become indifferent to food, whereas patients with anorexia continue to starve themselves despite being hungry and having an interest in food.

Nor does the hypothalamic model account for body-image disturbance or fear of becoming fat. A dysfunctional hypothalamus thus does not seem a highly likely factor in anorexia nervosa.

Endogenous opioids are substances produced by the body that reduce pain sensations, enhance mood, and suppress appetite, at least among those with low body weight. Opioids are released during starvation and have been viewed as playing a role in both anorexia and bulimia. Starvation among patients with anorexia may increase the levels of endogenous opioids, resulting in a positively reinforcing euphoric state (Marrazzi & Luby, 1986) that has been characterized as "powerfully reinforcing" (Luby & Koval, 2009, p. 407). Furthermore, the excessive exercise seen among some patients with eating disorders would increase opioids and thus be reinforcing (Davis, 1996; Epling & Pierce, 1992). Hardy and Waller (1988) hypothesized that bulimia is mediated by low levels of endogenous opioids, which are thought to promote craving; a euphoric state is then produced by the ingestion of food, thus reinforcing bingeing.

Some data support the theory that endogenous opioids do play a role in eating disorders, at least in bulimia (see Connan & Stanley, 2003). Waller et al. (1986) found low levels of the endogenous opioid beta-endorphin in patients with bulimia; the more severe cases of bulimia had the lowest levels of beta-endorphin. Bencherif et al. (2005) used brain MRI techniques to establish that patients with bulimia have decreased regional mu-opioid receptor binding in the insular cortex and this is inversely correlated with fasting behaviour.

Finally, some research has focused on several neurotransmitters related to eating and satiety (feeling full). Animal research has shown that serotonin promotes satiety; therefore, it could be that the binges of patients with bulimia result from a serotonin deficit, which would cause them not to feel satiated as they eat. Several studies have identified low levels of serotonin metabolites in patients with bulimia (e.g., Steiger et al., 2003), and serotonin metabolites have been linked with the negative mood and self-concept changes that precipitate binge episodes (Steiger et al., 2005). Patients with bulimia also show smaller responses to serotonin agonists (chemicals that combine with receptors to initiate a reaction) (Levitan et al., 1997), again suggesting an underactive serotonin system. These data all suggest that a serotonin deficit may well be related to bulimia nervosa.

Researchers are increasingly seeking to link neurotransmitters with genetic differences. A recent meta-analysis of eight studies focusing on serotonin found strong evidence of a role in anorexia nervosa for genetic variance in the serotonin transporter gene promoter (Lee & Lin, in press). However, there was no apparent link between genetic variance in the serotonin transporter for bulimia nervosa.

Though we can expect further significant advances in biochemical research in the future, keep in mind that this work focuses principally on brain mechanisms relevant to hunger, eating, and satiety and does little to account for other key features of both disorders, particularly the intense fear of becoming fat. The social and cultural environments appear to play a role in the faulty perceptions and eating habits of those with eating disorders, and it is to these influences we now turn.

SOCIO-CULTURAL VARIABLES

Throughout history, the standards societies have set for the ideal body—especially the ideal female body—have varied greatly. Think of the famous nudes painted by Rubens in the seventeenth century; according to modern standards, these women are chubby. In recent times in our culture, there has been a steady progression toward increasing thinness as the ideal. *Playboy* magazine centrefolds became thinner between 1959 and 1978 (Garner, Garfinkel, Schwartz, & Thompson, 1980). A recent follow-up investigation of *Playboy* centrefolds found the trend toward portrayals of increasing thinness has levelled off and may even be reversing somewhat (Sypeck et al., 2006). However, while the images have suggested increasing heaviness, the normative weight displayed is still considerably lower than is healthy.

When it comes to the promotion of unrealistic images, females consistently feel more pressure than males. Even toys reflect the unrealistic pressures on females; to achieve the same figure as another ideal, the Barbie doll, the average American woman would have to increase her bust by 12 inches, reduce her waist by 10, and grow to over seven feet in height (Moser, 1989)! The insidious effects of exposing young girls to Barbie dolls with unrealistic body images was shown in a recent experiment (see Dittmar, Halliwell, & Ive,

The photographs above demonstrate what a woman would look like if her proportions were changed to match those of a Barbie doll (bust: 39", waist: 18", hips: 33"). Her neck and legs have also been elongated to match the doll's proportions. © Stephen Aviano.

2006). Five- and six-year-old girls exposed to Barbie images suffered lower body esteem and greater desire to achieve the thin ideal. And now a contemporary analysis of the top 150 video games has confirmed this tendency to portray female body types as being too thin, especially in games geared toward children, as opposed to games for adults (Martin, Williams, Harrison, & Ratan, in press).

Patricia Pliner from the University of Toronto and Shelly Chaiken from New York University have advanced the theory that women respond to these socio-cultural pressures by eating lightly in an attempt to project images of femininity (see Chaiken & Pliner, 1987, 1990). Research in laboratory and naturalistic settings has confirmed that women who are portrayed as eating heavily are indeed seen as less feminine and more masculine than women who are portrayed as eating light meals. Pliner and Chaiken have coined the term the **Scarlett O'Hara effect** to refer to this phenomenon of eating lightly to project femininity. In *Gone with the Wind*, Mammy admonishes Scarlett to eat a meal prior to going to a barbecue so that she would appear dainty by eating very little.

While cultural standards and pressures to be thin were increasing, more and more people were becoming overweight. The prevalence of obesity has doubled since 1900; currently 20 to 30% of North Americans are overweight. Pinel, Assanand, and Lehman (2000) attribute the increasing prevalence of obesity to an evolutionary tendency for humans to eat to excess to store energy in their bodies for a time when food may be less plentiful. If so, this tendency to overconsume is clearly at odds with unrealistic pressures to maintain ideal bodyweights.

We know that the cultural ideal of extreme thinness has been internalized by a large percentage of people, especially among females. A Canadian study of almost 30,000 people found that weight dissatisfaction was associated negatively with age among women (i.e., younger women were more dissatisfied with their weight) but this association was not evident among men (Green et al., 1997). This study also found that women were more likely than men to wish they weighed less and were actually doing something to try to lose weight; this tendency was found regardless of whether their actual weight was in the acceptable range, as prescribed by body mass index tables. Another study conducted in Toronto with women and men of various ages found that women place greater importance on appearance than men do, and that this difference exists across the lifespan and can even be detected among the elderly (Pliner, Chaiken, & Flett, 1990).

Kevin Thompson and his associates have documented differences among females and males in the extent of their internalization and acceptance of prescribed body image standards. Sample items from their measure are shown in Table 10.3. Growing evidence points to internalization of these standards as a key component of risk for eating disorder and related dysfunctional behaviours (see Thompson et al., 2003; Thompson & Stice, 2001).

According to the World Health Organization's 2002 Health Behaviour in School-aged Children (HBSC) Canadian Survey (see Government of Canada, 2006), 31% of Canadian young women from grades 6 to 10 thought that they were too fat. The proportion increased with age and, by Grade 10, 44% indicated that they were too fat (see Figure 10.3).

As society has become more health and fat conscious, dieting to lose weight has become more common. The number of dieters increased from 7% of men and 14% of women in 1950 to 29% of men and 44% of women in 1999 (Serdula et al., 1999). An Ontario study found that among more than 2,000 girls aged 10 to 14, 29.3% were dieting and 1 in 10 had maladaptive eating attitudes suggesting the presence of an eating disorder (McVey, Tweed, & Blackmore, 2004). Similarly, according to the 2002 HBSC Canadian survey, by grades 9 and

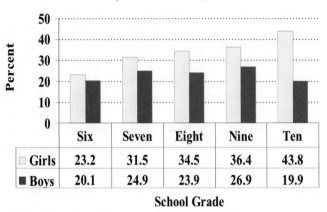

FIGURE 10.3 Proportion of students who rated their body image as too fat, by sex and grade, Canada 2002. *Source:* WHO, Health Behaviour in School-Aged Children Study, 2002

10, more than 25% of young women among Canada were on a diet when the survey was conducted (Government of Canada, 2006). The diet industry (books, pills, videos, special foods) is valued at more than $50 billion per year. Also, liposuction (vacuuming out fat deposits just under the skin) is a very common (and sometimes risky) procedure in plastic surgery (Brownell & Rodin, 1994).

The contemporary research focus has shifted to an analysis of the relative impact of various media (e.g., television vs. magazines) on body image ideals and dissatisfaction. A study of 12-years-olds in Western Canada found that increases in eating disorder symptoms were associated with increased exposure to fashion magazines and these increases were not associated with the amount of television viewed (Vaughan & Fouts, 2003). An Australian study also found that the amount of television watched was unrelated to body image variables for either girls or boys (Tiggemann, 2005). However, watching soap operas was associated with increased drive for thinness in girls and boys. Also, the reasons for watching television mattered; there was a negative impact on body image variables if television was watched for reasons of social learning or as a diversion from negative mood states.

The socio-cultural ideal of thinness shared by most Western industrialized nations is the likely vehicle through which people learn to fear being or even feeling fat. Excessive body fat has negative connotations, such as being unsuccessful and having little self-control. Obese people are viewed by others as less smart and are stereotyped as being lazy. A new study suggests that this anti-fat bias exists across the age spectrum so that even the most obese people tend to endorse these views; however, the bias seems more automatic among thinner people, according to measures of implicit cognitive processing (Schwartz et al., 2006). Unfortunately, the media continue to promote these stereotypes. A content analysis of 18 prime-time television situation comedies conducted by researchers in Calgary found that females with below-

TABLE 10.3

SAMPLE ITEMS FROM THE INTERNALIZATION SUBSCALE OF THE SOCIO-CULTURAL ATTITUDES TOWARD APPEARANCE-3

I would like my body to look like the people who are in the movies.

I compare my body to the bodies of people who appear in magazines.

I wish I looked like the models in music videos.

I try to look like the people on TV.

I compare my appearance to the appearance of TV and movie stars.

Adapted from J.K. Thompson et al., (2003), pp. 293–304. Reprinted with permission from John Wiley & Sons, Inc.

Russian ballerina Anastasia Volochkova filed a lawsuit against the Bolshoi Theatre after being fired for allegedly being too heavy. She later won her job back. CP Image Archive/Alexander Zemlianichenko.

average weights were overrepresented in these shows; also, the heavier the female character, the more likely she was to have negative comments directed toward her (Fouts & Burggraf, 2000). Moreover, these negative comments were especially likely to be reinforced by audience laughter.

Even worse than the media's promotion of thinness is the proliferation in the last five years of pro-anorexia websites, which were mentioned in the opening quote from Kate Winslet. These "pro-ana" websites glorify starvation and reinforce irrational beliefs about the importance of thinness and the perceived rewards of being dangerously thin. While some people seem to turn to these websites in a desperate search for coping advice, others may simply be looking for tips and techniques to help become more anorexic (see Mulveen & Hepworth, 2006). Increasingly, organizations representing psychologists and psychiatrists are issuing calls for a ban on these "pro-ana" sites.

The "double-edged" nature of the Internet was illustrated in a study conducted at the University of Waterloo on the functions of on-line forums for people with eating problems (Ransom, LaGuardia, Woody, & Boyd, 2010). This survey of 60 members of on-line forums found that they can be good or bad for one's health. On-line forum members reported that, relative to their peers, they get less "off-line support" from family members and friends and on-line forums help them get the social support they need. At the same time, on-line forums encouraged adaptive and maladaptive behaviour and can actually encourage dysregulated eating behaviour because there was evidence that these forums do have an impact and influence on their members.

Regarding anorexia in athletes, Epling and Pierce from the University of Alberta have suggested that some people become anorexic because of a pursuit of fitness rather than a pursuit of thinness. They have outlined a theory of a phenomenon that they describe as **activity anorexia** (Pierce

& Epling, 1996). This concept refers to the loss of appetite when engaged in physical activity. These theorists used the concept of activity anorexia to explain why a comparative study conducted in Toronto by Garner and Garfinkel found that dancers, relative to models, had higher rates of anorexia and more disturbed eating attitudes (Garner & Garfinkel, 1980). Models and dancers share a pressure to maintain ideal appearance, but dancers also engage in much more strenuous physical activity. Pierce and Epling suggest that two interrelated motivational factors account for activity anorexia: food deprivation increases the reinforcement effectiveness of physical activity, and physical activity decreases the reinforcement effectiveness of food.

These processes are consistent with a theory of anorexia proposed by researchers from the University of British Columbia. Pinel et al. (2000) hypothesized that anorexics often display great interest in food and are sometimes obsessed with food, but lack positive incentives for actually eating the food. Pinel et al. observed that most starving people placed great positive incentive value when presented with food, but this is not the case with anorexics, for reasons that remain to be determined.

GENDER INFLUENCES

The primary reason for the greater prevalence of eating disorders among women than among men is that women appear to have been more heavily influenced by the cultural ideal of thinness. Women are typically valued more for their appearance, whereas men gain esteem more for their accomplishments. Women apparently are more concerned than men about being thin, are more likely to diet, and are thus more vulnerable to eating disorders. It is important to understand the factors that elicit dieting behaviour for many reasons, including the fact that the onset of eating disorders is typically preceded by dieting and other concerns about weight (e.g., perceived fatness, fear of weight gain). Dieting behaviour is discussed in Focus on Discovery 10.2. Of course, everyone who diets will not develop an eating disorder. Other factors are described in subsequent sections.

CROSS-CULTURAL STUDIES

Eating disorders appear to be far more common in industrialized societies, such as the United States, Canada, Japan, Australia, and Europe, than in non-industrialized nations, and it is also generally accepted that eating disorders are more evident in Western cultures (Keel & Klump, 2003). Moreover, according to a review conducted by University of Windsor researchers (Geller & Thomas, 1999), young women who immigrate to industrialized Western cultures may be especially prone to developing eating disorders owing to the experience of rapid cultural changes and pressures.

The wide variation in the prevalence of eating disorders across cultures suggests the importance of culture in establishing realistic vs. potentially disordered views of one's body. As yet, however, there have been no cross-cultural

FOCUS ON DISCOVERY 10.2
TO DIET OR NOT TO DIET?

As dieting has become more common and the diet industry a multi-billion-dollar-a-year business, the incidence of both eating disorders and obesity has increased. Millions of North Americans are overweight. Is there a relationship among these facts? Studies of restrained eaters (people who attempt to restrict their intake of food in general) and patients with eating disorders show that dieting can lead to bingeing, and an investigation by Urbszat, Herman, and Polivy (2002) found that even the mere anticipation of going on a diet can trigger binges in restrained eaters. Moreover, very "successful" dieters can become anorexic. Is dieting more dangerous than desirable?

Why is dieting so difficult, especially for some people? Lowe and Levine (2005) noted that eating is motivated not only by the brain's homeostatic system (which operates according to the presence or absence of actual energy deficits) but also by its hedonic system, a physiologically and cognitively-based system that controls pleasure and positive affect. The hedonic system is activated by the presence of highly palatable, tasty food; not getting enough highly palatable food to satisfy the hedonic system can result in a sense of perceived food deprivation despite having enough actual food energy.

Heredity also plays a significant role in eating and obesity. Between 20 and 50% of variability in obesity phenotypes is attributable to genetic factors (see Winchester & Collier, 2003). Adoption studies have found that children's weight is more strongly related to the weight of their biological parents than to the weight of their adoptive parents (Price et al., 1987). Similarly, 40% of the children of an obese parent will be obese, compared with 7% of the children of normal-weight parents. Heredity could produce its effects by regulating metabolic rate or through the hypothalamus and its impact on insulin level or the production of enzymes that make it easier to store fat and gain weight. Dieting may be of little use to people whose obesity is principally genetically caused. Their metabolic rate may simply slow down to help maintain body weight; when the diet is over, the lowered metabolic rate leads to weight gain.

Psychosocial factors are also clearly involved in gaining weight. Stress and its associated negative moods can induce eating in some people (Steiger et al., 2005). And we are all subject to the continuing impact of advertisements, especially those promoting alluring high-fat, high-calorie products such as some snack foods, desserts, and meals at fast-food restaurants.

The motivation to achieve thinness is generally tied to several possible goals:

- Being thin increases personal attractiveness, which in turn can produce both psychological (e.g., increased self-esteem) and social (e.g., advancement in the workplace) benefits.
- Being thin signifies self-discipline; obesity reflects a lack of self-control and failure.
- Thinness is associated with several health benefits; obesity is associated with health problems such as diabetes, hypertension, cardiovascular disease, and cancer.

Despite this drive to be thin, a backlash against dieting has been emerging (Brownell & Rodin, 1994; Lowe & Levine, 2005). Feminist philosophy has challenged the view that women should be defined by their physical characteristics. On an empirical level, we have seen at least one potential danger in dieting: it is often a precursor to eating disorders. Moreover, in a review paper, McFarlane, Polivy, and McCabe (1999) concluded that dieting has a negative impact on psychological well-being, as made evident by established links between dieting and negative mood, low self-esteem, and cognitive preoccupations with food stimuli.

Polivy and Herman (Polivy, 2001; Polivy & Herman, 2002) underscored the negative aspects of dieting in their work on a phenomenon they refer to as the **false hope syndrome**. They argued that attempts at self-change capitalize on false hopes that are reinforced by the initial positive outcomes that result from dieting (e.g., praise from other people). However, this sense of reward and related feelings of optimism and control lead to a tendency to pursue unrealistic weight-loss goals that ultimately result in extreme disappointment. Support for the false hope syndrome comes from research showing that restrained eaters expect more from their dieting programs than non-restrained eaters (Trottier, Polivy, & Herman, 2005). They also perceive that the dieting program will be more personally important to them and it is more likely to be effective.

It is widely known that although many diets achieve weight loss in the short term (for example, one year), the weight is typically regained later (Polivy & Herman, 2002), suggesting that diets do not work in the long term. Weight fluctuation itself could be a health risk (e.g., for cardiovascular disease). Furthermore, the evidence concerning whether weight loss actually yields health benefits is conflicting. For example, the typical weight loss of about 7 kg (15 pounds) may not be sufficient to produce any beneficial effects on health.

Brownell and Rodin (1994) concluded that the decision to diet might be more profitably based on individualized risk-to-benefit ratios. Indeed, in a subsequent review, Lowe and Timko (2004) advocated assessing the advisability of dieting for each person according to a series of questions: (1) Who is dieting?; (2) What kind of diet is involved?; and (3) What is the motivation for dieting? Generally, these would be expected to favour dieting in very overweight people, but other characteristics could also be considered. The benefits of dieting could assume much more importance in someone with a family history of hypertension and cardiovascular disease, for example. Conversely, for someone with a family history of eating disorders, embarking on a diet would have to be viewed as a risky step.

epidemiological studies employing similar assessments and diagnostic criteria, so it is difficult to compare prevalence rates across cultures accurately or make definitive statements about cultural differences in symptom expression. A review concluded that at present, it is unclear whether the presentation of eating disorder symptoms varies across cultures (Soh, Touyz, & Surgenor, 2006).

Interesting data were reported by Tucker (2004), who evaluated the effects of introducing television (and exposure to body shape ideals via television) to a rural area of Fiji that had never had television. This study showed that within three years, there was a noticeable increase in preoccupation with weight and body shape, purging behaviour, and negative evaluations of body characteristics. Interview data also indicated that the Fijian girls acknowledged social learning and wishing to emulate people they had seen on television.

In spite of these findings, the cross-cultural variation in prevalence of eating disorders remains a supposition and a sometimes controversial one. Lee (1994), for example, has described a disorder similar to anorexia nervosa that exists in several non-industrialized Asian countries (India, Malaysia, the Philippines). This disorder involves severe emaciation, food refusal, and amenorrhea, but not a fear of becoming fat. Is this a cultural variant of anorexia or a different disorder, such as depression? This question is one of the challenges that face cross-cultural researchers.

Finally, conclusions are complicated further by the possibility that the role of culture varies as a function of whether the focus is on AN or BN. Recently, a quantitative meta-analysis resulted in the conclusion that BN is a culture-bound syndrome, while AN is not (Keel & Klump, 2003). Thus, AN may be much more common across cultures, and the genetic heritability of AN, relative to BN, may result in less variability of AN across cultures.

Standards of beauty vary cross-culturally as shown by Gauguin's painting of Tahitian women. Femmes de Tahiti (Sur la Plage) by Paul Gauguin/ Musee d'Orsay. Paris/Lauris-Giraudon. Paris/SUPERSTOCK.

COGNITIVE-BEHAVIOURAL VIEWS

ANOREXIA NERVOSA Cognitive-behavioural theories of anorexia nervosa emphasize fear of fatness and body-image disturbance as the motivating factors that make self-starvation and weight loss powerful reinforcers. Behaviours that achieve or maintain thinness are negatively reinforced by the reduction of anxiety about becoming fat. Furthermore, dieting and weight loss may be positively reinforced by the sense of mastery or self-control they create (Fairburn, Shafran, & Cooper, 1999; Garner, Vitousek, & Pike, 1997). Some theories also include personality and socio-cultural variables to explain how fear of fatness and body-image disturbances develop. For example, perfectionism and a sense of personal inadequacy may lead a person to become especially concerned with his or her appearance, making dieting a potent reinforcer.

Similarly, the media's portrayal of thinness as an ideal, being overweight, and a tendency to compare oneself with especially attractive others all contribute to dissatisfaction with one's body (Stormer & Thompson, 1996). As shown in one Canadian study, even brief exposure to pictures of fashion models can instill negative moods in young women, and women who are dissatisfied with their bodies seem especially vulnerable when exposed to these images (Pinhas et al., 1999).

Somewhat ironically, research by Jennifer Mills from York University and her associates showed that, initially, chronic dieters actually feel thinner after looking at idealized images of the thin body and this motivates them to diet (Mills, Polivy, Herman, & Tiggemann, 2002). This effect, labelled the **thinspiration effect**, can begin a process of dieting that can ultimately lead to distress among dieters unable to attain unrealistic body-image standards.

Another important factor in producing a strong drive for thinness and disturbed body image is criticism from peers and parents about being overweight (Paxton et al., 1991). In one study supporting this conclusion (Paxton et al., 1991), adolescent girls aged 10 to 15 were evaluated twice, with a three-year interval between assessments. Obesity at the first assessment was related to being teased by peers and at the second assessment to dissatisfaction with their bodies. Dissatisfaction was in turn related to symptoms of eating disorder.

It is known that bingeing results frequently when diets are broken (Polivy & Herman, 1985). Thus, a lapse that occurs in the strict dieting of a person with anorexia nervosa is likely to escalate into a binge. The purging following an episode of binge eating can again be seen as motivated by the fear of weight gain that the binge elicited. Patients with anorexia who do not have episodes of bingeing and purging may have a more intense preoccupation with and fear of weight gain (Schlundt & Johnson, 1990) or may be more able to exercise self-control.

PSYCHODYNAMIC VIEWS

There are many psychodynamic theories of eating disorders. Most propose that the core cause lies in disturbed parent-child relationships and agree that certain core personality traits, such as low self-esteem and perfectionism, are found among individuals with eating disorders. Psychodynamic theories also propose that the symptoms of an eating disorder fulfill some need, such as the need to increase one's sense of personal effectiveness (the person succeeds in maintaining a strict diet) or to avoid growing up sexually (by being very thin, the person does not achieve the usual female shape) (Goodsitt, 1997). According to Canadian researchers Howard Steiger and Mimi Israel (1999), early psychodynamic models interpreted symptoms of anorexia from a conflict perspective (i.e., a defence against conflict drives, often of a sexual nature), while contemporary psychodynamic models interpret symptoms of anorexia from a deficit perspective, with a particular emphasis on anorexia as a way to compensate for defects in the self.

Several psychodynamic theories focus on family relationships. One view, proposed by influential theorist Hilde Bruch (1980), is that anorexia nervosa is an attempt by children who have been raised to feel ineffectual to gain competence and respect and to ward off feelings of helplessness, ineffectiveness, and powerlessness. This sense of ineffectiveness is created by a parenting style in which the parents' wishes are imposed on the child without considering the child's needs or wishes. Children reared in this way do not learn to identify their own internal states and do not become self-reliant. When faced with the demands of adolescence, the child seizes on the societal emphasis on thinness and turns dieting into a means of acquiring control and identity. Steiger and Israel (1999) have a similar view of the origins of anorexia, and they maintain that "obstinate, avoidant, or controlling reactions on the part of these clients often constitute adaptations, justified by past experiences of parental overcontrol" (p. 745).

Consider the case of Susie, a 23-year-old patient who experienced anorexia following the death of her father from cancer. Below is an excerpt written by Susie's therapist to her as part of her fourth treatment session:

> You have an eating disorder that started at the unexpected death of your father two years ago. Your eating disorder has helped you to feel in control and your life has been both physically and emotionally affected by this eating disorder. It is making you feel depressed and ashamed …
>
> You described to me a pleasant childhood, and also that you were told that you were a very demanding baby who your mother found difficult to cope with. When you started school you felt all of your demanding behaviour stopped and you needed to control yourself, but often felt bad …
>
> As an adolescent you felt you couldn't rebel as you caused your father particular distress because you were so bad at maths. He used to tutor you and shout at you because you were so bad at it. You again tried to control yourself emotionally and learn to do maths. But perhaps you were unable to express your fear, anger and shame at his treatment and your inability to be good at maths. When your father died, perhaps such distressing emotions as fear, loss, anger and grief made you feel ashamed again, as they did not seem able to be expressed by your family.

So again you went out of control, this time using control of your eating and body as a way of managing your distress. (Tanner & Connan, 2003, p. 286)

FAMILY SYSTEMS THEORY

Salvador Minuchin and his colleagues have proposed another influential position, known as the family systems theory, a theory relevant to both anorexia and bulimia. This position holds that the symptoms of an eating disorder are best understood by considering both the patient and how the symptoms are embedded in a dysfunctional family structure. In this view, the child is seen as physiologically vulnerable (although the precise nature of this vulnerability is unspecified), and the child's family has several characteristics that promote the development of an eating disorder. Also, the child's eating disorder plays an important role in helping the family avoid other conflicts. Thus, the child's symptoms are a substitute for other conflicts within the family.

According to Minuchin et al. (1975), the families of children with eating disorders exhibit the following characteristics:

- **Enmeshment.** Families have an extreme form of overinvolvement and intimacy in which parents may speak for their children because they believe they know exactly how they feel.
- **Overprotectiveness.** Family members have an extreme level of concern for one another's welfare.
- **Rigidity.** Families have a tendency to try to maintain the status quo and avoid dealing effectively with events that require change (e.g., the demand that adolescence creates for increased autonomy).
- **Lack of conflict resolution.** Families either avoid conflict or are in a state of chronic conflict.

CHARACTERISTICS OF FAMILIES

Studies of the characteristics of families of patients with eating disorders are relevant to both the family systems theory and the psychodynamic theory. Results have been variable. Some of the variation stems, in part, from the different methods used to collect the data and from the sources of the information. For example, self-reports of patients consistently reveal high levels of conflict in the family (e.g., Hodges, Cochrane, & Brewerton, 1998). However, reports of parents do not necessarily indicate high levels of family problems. In one study in which the reports of parents of patients with eating disorders differed from those of parents in the control group, parents of patients reported high levels of isolation and lower levels of mutual involvement and support (Humphrey, 1986). Disturbed family relationships do seem to characterize the families of some patients with eating disorders; however, the characteristics that have been observed, such as low levels of support, only loosely fit the family systems theory. And again, these family characteristics could be a result of the eating disorder and not a cause of it.

A study more directly linked to Minuchin's family systems theory assessed both eating disorder patients and their parents on tests designed to measure rigidity, closeness, emotional overinvolvement, critical comments, and hostility (Dare et al., 1994). Contrary to Minuchin's theory, the families showed considerable variation in enmeshment and were quite low in conflict (low levels of criticism and hostility). Though this latter finding could reflect the conflict-avoiding pattern Minuchin has described, the parents' lack of overinvolvement is clearly inconsistent with his clinical descriptions. Also inconsistent with Minuchin's theory is a family study conducted in Toronto in which assessments were conducted before and after treatment of the patient (Woodside et al., 1995). Ratings of family functioning improved after treatment, contradicting the idea that improvement in the patient should bring other family conflicts to light and supporting the idea that eating disorders may cause family problems rather than the other way around.

To better understand the role of family functioning, we must begin to study these families directly, by observational measures, rather than by reports alone. Although a child's *perception* of his or her family's characteristics is important, we also need to know how much of reported family disturbance is perceived and how much is real. In one of the few observational studies conducted thus far, parents of children with eating disorders did not appear to be very different from control parents. The two groups did not differ in the frequency of positive and negative messages given to their children, and the parents of children with eating disorders were more self-disclosing than were the control parents. The parents of eating-disorder children did lack some communication skills, however, such as the ability to request clarification of vague statements (van den Broucke, Vandereycken, & Vertommen, 1995). Observational studies such as this, coupled with data on perceived family characteristics, would help determine whether actual or perceived family characteristics are related to eating disorders. In fact, Baker, Whisman, and Brownell (2000) studied eating attitudes in university students and their parents and found that the students' attitudes and behaviours were tied more closely to perceived parental characteristics (i.e., criticism from parents) than to actual parental characteristics.

Patients with eating disorders consistently report that their family life was high in conflict. Buccina Studios.

CHILD ABUSE AND EATING DISORDERS

Some studies have indicated that self-reports of childhood sexual abuse are higher than normal among patients with eating disorders, especially those with bulimia nervosa (Steiger & Zanko, 1990). A study conducted in Toronto found that 25% of women with eating disorders reported the experience of previous sexual abuse; it also correlated a history of sexual abuse with greater psychological disturbance (DeGroot, Kennedy, Rodin, & McVey, 1992). Similarly, research conducted in Verdun, Quebec, confirmed that bulimic women, relative to normal eaters, had higher levels of childhood abuse and that the presence and the severity of abuse predicted more extreme psychopathology (Leonard, Steiger, & Kao, 2003).

PERSONALITY AND EATING DISORDERS

Researchers study personality factors in the hope of identifying vulnerability factors that may be involved in the etiology of eating disorders. In assessing the role of personality, it is important to keep in mind that the eating disorder itself can affect personality. A study of semi-starvation in male conscientious objectors conducted in the late 1940s supports the idea that the personality of patients with eating disorders, particularly those with anorexia, is affected by their weight loss (Keys et al., 1950). For a period of six weeks, the men were given two meals a day, totalling 1,500 calories, to simulate the meals in a concentration camp. On average, they lost 25% of their body weight. All the men soon became preoccupied with food. They also reported increased fatigue, poor concentration, lack of sexual interest, irritability, moodiness, and insomnia. Four became depressed, and one developed bipolar disorder. This research shows vividly how severe restriction of food intake can have powerful effects on personality and behaviour. We need to consider these effects when evaluating the personality of patients with anorexia and bulimia.

In part as a response to the findings just mentioned, some researchers have collected retrospective reports of personality before the onset of an eating disorder. This research described patients with anorexia as having been perfectionistic, shy, and compliant before the onset of the disorder. It described patients with bulimia as having the additional characteristics of histrionic features, affective instability, and an outgoing social disposition (Vitousek & Manke, 1994). It is important to remember, however, that retrospective reports in which a patient and his or her family recall what the person was like before diagnosis can be inaccurate and biased by awareness of the patient's current problem.

Numerous studies have also measured the current personality of patients with eating disorders, relying on results from established personality questionnaires such as the MMPI. Both patients with anorexia and patients with bulimia are high in neuroticism and anxiety and low in self-esteem (Bulik et al., 2000). The role of neuroticism as a long-term predictor of anorexia was also confirmed in a recent twin study (Bulik et al., 2006). Patients with AN or BN also score high on a measure of traditionalism, indicating strong endorsement of family and social standards (Bulik et al., 2000).

Researchers have also examined the personality trait of narcissism in patients with eating disorders. Narcissists are characterized by an excessive focus on the self and a heightened sense of self-importance and grandiosity. These individuals are believed to be overcompensating for a fragile sense of self-esteem, however, and they are highly sensitive and reactive to criticism. Pathological narcissism at extreme levels can take the form of a narcissistic personality disorder (see Chapter 13). Steiger and his associates have shown that AN and BN patients are characterized by high levels of narcissism that persist even when the eating disorder is in remission (Lehoux, Steiger, & Jabalpurlawa, 2000; Steiger et al., 1997). Narcissism is not always elevated among people with eating disorders (see Waller et al., 2007), but the use of a narcissistic defensive "poor me" style has treatment implications because it predicts greater treatment dropout (Campbell, Waller, & Pistrang, 2009).

As suggested earlier, perfectionism is believed to be highly relevant to an understanding of eating disorders. The initial research in this area was conducted with the perfectionism subscale of the Eating Disorders Inventory (EDI; see Table 10.1), and it confirmed that perfectionism is elevated in individuals with eating disorders (Garner et al., 1983). The EDI perfectionism subscale provides a single, global measure of perfectionism. Subsequent researchers, however, have found that the perfectionism construct is multi-dimensional, and this was even demonstrated by a reanalysis of the EDI items that showed the perfectionism subscale actually consisted of two factors reflecting self-standards and external pressures imposed on the self (Sherry et al., 2005).

Hewitt and Flett (1991) created a multi-dimensional perfectionism scale that assesses self-oriented perfectionism (setting high standards for oneself), other-oriented perfectionism (setting high standards for others), and socially prescribed perfectionism (the perception that high standards are imposed on the self by others). One possible manifestation of socially prescribed perfectionism of relevance here is a sense that there is social pressure to attain unrealistic standards of physical perfection.

Eating disorder research with the Hewitt and Flett (1991) Multidimensional Perfectionism Scale suggests that self-oriented and socially prescribed perfectionism are both elevated in eating disorders. Bastiani et al. (1995) reported that weight-restored and underweight anorexics had elevated scores on self-oriented perfectionism. In addition, the underweight anorexics had higher scores on socially prescribed perfectionism, relative to the control group.

Other research conducted in Toronto found that self-oriented and socially prescribed perfectionism were elevated once again in eating disorder patients, and that anorexics who engage in excessive exercise are distinguished by remarkably high levels of self-oriented perfectionism (Davis, Kaptein, Kaplan, Olmsted, & Woodside, 1998). Perfectionism is relevant to both anorexia and bulimia.

One line of investigation has provided support for a three-factor interactive model of perfectionism and bulimic symptom development (for a review, see Bardone-Cone et al., 2007). According to this interactive model, bulimic symptoms are elevated among females who are characterized not only by perfectionism, but also by body dissatisfaction and low self-esteem. Thus, they have exceptionally high standards yet recognize a sense of self-dissatisfaction for not attaining these impossible standards.

Contemporary research has linked eating disorders with the tendency for some individuals to respond to social pressures to be perfect by engaging in a form of behaviour known as perfectionistic self-presentation; that is, these individuals try to create an image of perfection and are highly focused on minimizing the mistakes they make in front of other people (see Hewitt, Flett, & Ediger, 1995; Hewitt et al., 2003). Perfectionistic self-presentation is reflected by the quote at the start of this chapter from the student with an eating disorder (i.e., "I still try to maintain as perfect an image as possible and I still seek to please my mother") and is elevated among eating disorder patients (see Cockell et al., 2002; Geller, Cockell, Hewitt, Goldner, & Flett, 2000).

A focus on perfectionistic self-presentation is in keeping with indications that women with eating disorders are high in public self-consciousness and overly concerned with how they are viewed by others, in part because they often feel like imposters and frauds who have not been detected yet by other people and are mistakenly seen by them as competent (Striegel-Moore, Silberstein, & Rodin, 1993). People who feel like imposters and fear detection of their self-perceived inadequacies can respond defensively by trying to create an impression of being perfect; this strategy can include attempts to portray their physical appearance in the best possible way.

Overall, the studies outlined above suggest that various perfectionism dimensions are indeed elevated in the various eating disorders. However, one significant limitation of this work is that the causal role of these dimensions of perfectionism has yet to be firmly established by longitudinal, prospective research on the role of these dimensions in the onset of eating disorders. Such designs are critical to determine whether perfectionism is a true risk factor for eating disorders (see Bardone-Cone et al., 2007).

BULIMIA NERVOSA Patients with bulimia nervosa are thought to be overconcerned with weight gain and body appearance; indeed, they judge their self-worth mainly by their weight and shape. They also have low self-esteem, and because weight and shape are somewhat more controllable than other features of the self, they tend to focus on weight and shape, hoping their efforts in this area will make them feel better generally. They try to follow a rigid pattern of eating that has strict rules regarding how much to eat, what kinds of food to eat, and when to eat. These rules are inevitably broken, and the lapse escalates into a binge. After the binge, feelings of disgust and fear of becoming fat build up, leading to compensatory actions such as vomiting (Fairburn, 1997). Although purging temporarily reduces the anxiety from having eaten too much, this cycle lowers the person's self-esteem, which triggers still more bingeing and purging, a vicious circle that maintains desired body weight but has serious medical consequences (see Figure 10.4 for a summary of this theory).

Patients with bulimia nervosa typically binge when they encounter stress and experience negative moods. This was confirmed in a study conducted with bulimic patients receiving treatment at Toronto Hospital (see Davis, Freeman, & Garner, 1988) who were asked to keep hourly records of their behaviours and moods. Bulimic patients reported more negative moods in the hour just prior to their binges. The binge may therefore function as a means of regulating negative moods (also see Steiger et al., 2005). Evidence also supports the idea that purging is reinforced by anxiety reduction. Patients with bulimia report increased levels of anxiety when they eat a meal and are not allowed to purge (Leitenberg et al., 1984), and these self-reports have been validated by physiological measures, such as skin conductance (e.g., Williamson et al., 1988). Similarly, anxiety levels decline after purging (Jarrell, Johnson, & Williamson, 1986).

TREATMENT OF EATING DISORDERS

It is often difficult to get a person with an eating disorder into treatment because the person typically denies that he or she has a problem. For this reason, the majority of people with eating disorders—up to 90% of them—are not in treatment (Fairburn et al., 1996) and those who are in treatment are often resentful. Some people with bulimia only wind up in treatment because their dentist has spotted one key indicator—the erosion of teeth enamel as a result of the stomach acid coming into contact with the teeth during vomiting.

Hospitalization is required frequently to treat people with anorexia so that the patient's ingestion of food can be gradually increased and carefully monitored. Weight loss can be so severe that intravenous feeding is necessary to save the patient's life. The medical complications of anorexia, such as electrolyte imbalances, also require treatment. For anorexia and bulimia, both biological and psychological interventions have been employed.

BIOLOGICAL TREATMENTS

Because bulimia nervosa is often comorbid with depression, it has been treated with various antidepressants in research conducted over the past 20 years. Interest has focused on fluoxetine (Prozac) (e.g., Fluoxetine Bulimia Nervosa Collaborative Study Group, 1992). In one multi-centre study, 387 women with bulimia were treated as outpatients for eight weeks. Fluoxetine was shown to be superior to a placebo in reducing binge eating and vomiting; it also decreased depression and lessened distorted attitudes toward food and eating. Unfortunately, however, optimism about the use of fluoxetine in treatment was reduced substantially by a well-designed study conducted jointly in Toronto and New York City; this investigation of patients with anorexia found no benefits following weight restoration (Walsh et al., 2006). Thus, fluoxetine is not consistently effective. Another difficulty is that many more patients drop out of drug therapy in studies on bulimia than drop out of the kind of cognitive-behavioural interventions described later (Fairburn, Agras, & Wilson, 1992).

Drugs have also been used in attempts to treat anorexia nervosa. Unfortunately, they have not been very successful, and Wilson et al. (2007) concluded that there is "no empirical basis" for using antidepressants to treat anorexia nervosa patients.

PSYCHOLOGICAL TREATMENT OF ANOREXIA NERVOSA

There is limited controlled research on psychological interventions for anorexia nervosa, but we will present what appear to be the most promising approaches to this life-threatening disorder.

FIGURE 10.4 Schematic of the cognitive-behavioural theory of bulimia nervosa

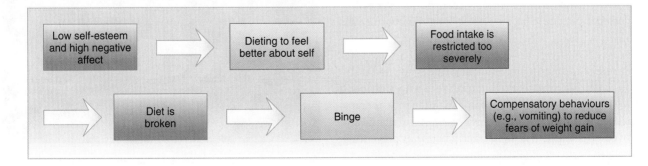

Therapy for anorexia is generally believed to be a two-tiered process. The immediate goal is to help the patient gain weight in order to avoid medical complications and the possibility of death. The patient is often so weak and his or her physiological functioning so disturbed that hospital treatment is medically imperative (in addition to being needed to ensure that the patient ingests some food). Operant-conditioning behaviour therapy programs have been somewhat successful in achieving weight gain in the short term (Hsu, 1991). In these programs, the hospitalized patient is isolated as much as possible and then rewarded for eating and gaining weight with mealtime company; access to a television set, radio, or stereo; walks with a student nurse; mail; and visitors. However, the second goal of treatment—long-term maintenance of weight gain—has not yet been reliably achieved by medical, behavioural, or traditional psychodynamic interventions (Wilson, 1995), though fluoxetine may contribute to a maintenance of inpatient weight gain as long as the person remains on the drug (Kaye et al., 1997).

Fairburn, Shafran, and Cooper (1999) proposed a cognitive-behavioural theory of the maintenance of anorexia nervosa. They argued that the central feature of the disorder is an extreme need to control eating. A tendency to judge self-worth in terms of shape and weight is assumed to be superimposed on the need for self-control. According to Fairburn et al. (1999), the theory has two major treatment implications:

- The issue of self-control should be the principal focus of treatment, including "the use of eating, shape, and weight as indices of self-control, and self-worth, the disturbed eating itself and the associated extreme weight behaviour, the body checking and, of course, the low body weight" (Fairburn et al., 1999, p. 10). They suggest that other targets for change in traditional cognitive-behavioural approaches (e.g., Garner, Vitousek, & Pike, 1997), such as low self-esteem, difficulty recognizing and expressing emotions, and interpersonal and family difficulties, do not need to be addressed unless they interfere with treatment progress.
- Treatment should also focus on the client's need for self-control in general. Thus, the "focus of control can be gradually shifted away from eating by helping patients derive satisfaction and a sense of achievement from other activities, and by demonstrating that control over eating does not provide what they are seeking" (Fairburn et al., 1999, p. 10).

Recently, a non-randomized clinical trial conducted at Toronto General Hospital found that relative to a no-treatment control group, cognitive-behavioural maintenance therapy for patients with anorexia nervosa resulted in significant improvements and it was significantly better at preventing relapse (see Carter et al., 2009). Thus, CBT has promise as a means of treating anorexia. According to Wilson, Grilo, and

Vitousek (2007), CBT is regarded as the treatment of choice for bulimia nervosa and binge eating disorder, while a specific version of family therapy is most favoured for treating anorexia nervosa.

Some evidence has indicated that an individual ego-analytic psychotherapy focused on encouraging greater autonomy can be somewhat effective (Robin, Siegel, & Moye, 1995). However, as noted above, family therapy is the principal mode of treatment for anorexia. Like most other treatments, it has not yet been sufficiently studied for its long-term effects. One report, however, suggests that as many as 86% of 50 anorexic daughters treated with their families were still functioning well when assessed at times ranging from three months to four years after treatment (Rosman, Minuchin, & Liebman, 1976). A better-controlled follow-up study of psychodynamically oriented family therapy confirmed these earlier findings. Patients with early-onset anorexia and a short history of it maintained their weight gains from family therapy for five years following treatment termination (Eisler et al., 1997). Another recent investigation showed that relatively brief family-based treatment is as effective as longer term treatment and 96% of adolescent patients with anorexia nervosa no longer met weight criteria for anorexia nervosa after receiving treatment (Lock, Agras, Bryson, & Kraemer, 2005).

Let us take a closer look at the well-known family therapy of Salvador Minuchin and his colleagues, which is based on the family systems theory described earlier. In Minuchin's view, the family member with an eating disorder deflects attention away from underlying conflicts in family relationships. To treat the disorder, Minuchin attempts to redefine it as interpersonal rather than individual and to bring the family conflict to the fore. In this way, he theorizes, the symptomatic family member is freed from having to maintain his or her problem, for it no longer deflects attention from the dysfunctional family.

Although Minuchin provided the theoretical impetus for focusing on the family, his views have been rejected in

Family therapy is the main treatment for anorexia nervosa. Mark O'Neill/ Sun Media Corporation.

recent years. Why? Minuchin placed too much emphasis on a specific family type and this does not allow for the great heterogeneity among families that we discussed earlier. Also, it has been seen as an approach that places blame on the family. Current efforts focus on an intervention known as the Maudsley Approach (see Lock, LeGrange, Agras, & Dare, 2001). The Maudsley Approach is a labour-intensive method that recruits parents and requires them to find creative ways to feed their children and restore them to a healthy weight. Parents are taught that they are not to blame, but at the same time, they are taught to be supportive and not critical. Finally, Lock and Couturier (2007) noted that there have been no longitudinal studies showing that family dysfunction precedes anorexia; perhaps having a child develop anorexia causes family dysfunction.

PSYCHOLOGICAL TREATMENT OF BULIMIA NERVOSA

The cognitive-behavioural therapy (CBT) approach of Fairburn (1985; Fairburn, Marcus, & Wilson, 1993) is the best validated and current standard for the treatment of bulimia. In Fairburn's therapy, the patient is encouraged to question society's standards for physical attractiveness. Patients must also uncover and then change beliefs that encourage them to starve themselves to avoid becoming overweight. They must be helped to see that normal body weight can be maintained without severe dieting and that unrealistic restriction of food intake can often trigger a binge. They are taught that all is not lost with just one bite of high-calorie food and that snacking need not trigger a binge that would be followed by induced vomiting or taking laxatives. Altering this all-or-nothing thinking can help patients begin to eat more moderately. They are also taught assertion skills to help them cope with unreasonable demands placed on them by others, and they learn more satisfying ways of relating to people, as well.

The overall goal of treatment of bulimia nervosa is to develop normal eating patterns. Patients need to learn to eat three meals a day and even to eat some snacks between meals without sliding back into bingeing and purging. Regular meals control hunger and thereby, it is hoped, control the urge to eat enormous amounts of food, the effect of which—being overweight—is counteracted by purging. To help patients develop less extreme beliefs about themselves, the cognitive-behavioural therapist gently but firmly challenges such irrational beliefs as "No one will love or respect me if I am a few pounds heavier than I am now." A generalized assumption underlying such cognitions for female patients might be that a woman has value to a man only if she is a few pounds underweight—a belief that is put forth in the media and advertisements.

This CBT approach has the patient bring small amounts of forbidden food to eat in the session. Relaxation is employed to control the urge to induce vomiting. Unrealistic demands and other cognitive distortions—

such as the belief that eating a small amount of high-calorie food means that the patient is an utter failure and doomed never to improve—are continually challenged. The therapist and patient work together to determine the events, thoughts, and feelings that trigger an urge to binge and then to learn more adaptive ways to cope with these situations. For example, if the therapist and the patient, usually a young woman, discover that bingeing often takes place after the patient has been criticized by her boyfriend, therapy could entail any or all of the following:

- encouraging the patient to assert herself if the criticism is unwarranted;
- teaching her, à la Albert Ellis, that it is not a catastrophe to make a mistake and it is not necessary to be perfect, even if the boyfriend's criticism is valid; and
- desensitizing her to social evaluation and encouraging her to question society's standards for ideal weight and the pressures on women to be thin—not an easy task by any means.

The outcomes of CBTs are promising, at least in the short term. A recent review concluded that CBT is the most commonly used and empirically supported treatment for body image disturbance in the normal population (Farrell, Shafran, & Lee, 2006). These data and other recent developments have led some authors to conclude that no other treatment has greater efficacy than CBT (see Mitchell, Agras, & Wonderlich, 2007). However, if we focus on the patients themselves rather than on numbers of binges and purges across patients, we find that at least half of those treated with CBT improve very little (Wilson, 1995) and almost half relapse after four months (Halmi et al., 2002). Predictors of relapse include less initial motivation for change and higher initial levels of food and eating preoccupation (Halmi et al., 2002).

Waller and associates have argued that if CBT is extended and takes the form of a schema-focused cognitive behaviour therapy (SFCBT), it will prove to be more effective in treating bulimia (see Waller & Kennerley, 2003). The goal of this approach is to identify and modify deeply ingrained and painful core belief systems that reflect the individual's cognitive schemas (i.e., mental filters). Waller argues that a negative core belief system involving negative aspects of the self (e.g., "I am unlovable") must be replaced by positive core beliefs in order for improvements to occur. Research on SFCBT is still in its early stages.

Recall that CBT is regarded as the psychological treatment of choice for bulimia nervosa. In several other studies, Weissman and Klerman's Interpersonal Therapy (IPT) fared well in comparisons with CBT (see Wilfley, Stein, & Welch, 2003). The two modes of intervention are equivalent at one-year follow-up in effecting change across all four of the specific aspects of bulimia: binge eating, purging, dietary restraint, and maladaptive attitudes about body shape and weight (Wilson, 1995). Another recent investigation found that modified IPT was effective and seemed to act quickly to bring improvement within the first eight treatment sessions (Arcelus et al., 2009). It is noteworthy that IPT is effective at all, considering that it does not focus, as CBT does, on maladaptive eating patterns, but focuses instead on improving interpersonal functioning. Such success suggests that, at least for some patients, disordered-eating patterns might be caused by poor interpersonal relationships and associated negative feelings about the self and the world.

Although the outcomes from these two leading psychological treatments, especially the cognitive-behavioural one, appear to be superior to those from other modes of intervention, including drugs, a good deal more remains to be learned about how best to treat bulimia nervosa. Part of the reason at least half of the patients in some controlled studies do not recover may be that significant numbers of the patients in these studies have psychological disorders in addition to eating disorders, such as borderline personality disorder, depression, anxiety, and marital distress (Wilson, 1995). Such patients show less improvement from CBT and from other therapies, as well. Gleaves and Eberenz (1994), for example, examined cognitive-behavioural

therapy outcomes among 464 women with bulimia in a residential treatment setting and found that those with a history of multiple therapists or hospitalizations, suicide attempts, and sexual abuse derived significantly less benefit from therapy than did those without such backgrounds. The poor therapeutic outcomes could have resulted because such patients simply have more pervasive and more serious psychopathology. Alternatively, the poor prognosis could result from the patients' failure to engage in the therapy, perhaps because of lack of trust in authority figures owing to earlier sexual abuse. Another possibility is suggested by data indicating that those patients who begin with negative self-efficacy judgements about their ability to recover actually tend to be the ones who are more treatment resistant and do indeed take longer to recover (Pinto et al., 2008). This finding underscores the role of cognitive appraisal in terms of beliefs about the expected benefits of treatment.

Given the possible difficulties associated with the treatment of individuals with eating disorders, serious consideration has to be given to prevention of the disorders before onset. Efforts to prevent eating disorders in Canada and elsewhere are summarized in Canadian Perspectives 10.1.

CANADIAN PERSPECTIVES 10.1
PREVENTION OF EATING DISORDERS IN CANADA: WHAT WORKS?

Existing data suggest that preventive efforts can reduce the prevalence of eating disorders but this depends on whether certain key features and key elements are in place. Stice and Shaw (2004) conducted a meta-analysis of 23 prevention studies and confirmed that the intervention effects have varied widely and have ranged from no effect to significant effects. The overall effect of prevention was deemed to range from small to medium in magnitude. Tests of mediator effects showed that larger effects occurred when the prevention was aimed at high-risk participants vs. all participants. Stronger effects were also associated with an interactive program that was more engaging than a didactic, lecture-style program. Multiple sessions also increased the effect, as did the use of well-validated measures. Finally, better results emerged if only females were targeted and they were 15 years or older.

Another contemporary meta-analysis confirmed that better results emerged from targeting high-risk participants (Fingeret et al., 2006). This analysis also showed that there are large effects in improving knowledge of maladaptive eating and its risks, but small net effects in actually reducing maladaptive eating attitudes and behaviours.

The Canadian studies conducted thus far have provided encouraging results, though the studies differ substantially in the approach taken and the scope of the respective projects. Improvements have been noted in terms of knowledge (Moriarty et al., 1990) and actual behaviours (Piran, 1999). One fac-

tor that distinguishes the Canadian studies from most other studies is that they have all incorporated participatory techniques, allowing the target audience to take an active role in the process.

The Piran (1999) study is regarded as one of the most unique and successful preventive interventions to have taken place. This study is part of an ongoing intervention program at an internationally acclaimed ballet school in Toronto. What makes it relatively unique? According to Piran, it is the first study conducted in a high-risk setting and, in contrast to most other studies, it involves attempts to intervene at the systemic level by changing the school culture. In addition, it involves a long-term focus on the evaluation of outcomes.

Piran (1999) reported results from three time phases involving various cohorts of students: 1987, 1991, and 1996. Extremely positive results have been obtained thus far. For instance, among students in grades 10 to 12, the proportion of students with abnormal eating attitudes has gone from almost 50% in 1987 to approximately 15% in 1991 and 1996. There have also been significant, striking reductions in the proportion of students who binged, vomited, or used laxatives.

So how have these positive outcomes been achieved? First and foremost, as noted above, the prevention program involves a participatory focus, as well as attempts to change the school culture. The goal is "to reduce body weight and shape preoccupation through creating a school environment where students feel comfortable with the processes of puberty and growth and believe in their right to feel both safe and positive in their diverse bodies" (Piran, 1999, p. 79). Specific interventions include replacing a focus on body shape with a focus on stamina and body conditioning, and not permitting teachers to make negative comments about body shape. The students also meet in groups of their peers up to six times a year to analyze body-shape experiences and discuss ways to minimize teasing and mutual evaluations of body shape.

McVey and Davis (2000) created a program designed to reduce the impact of media portrayals of unrealistic body images and to promote a non-dieting approach to eating and exercise. This multi-faceted program also includes a focus on stress-management skills and social problem-solving strategies, along with strategies to promote a positive self-image. An additional aspect is parent education on the nature and prevention of eating problems. Initial results have found no specific effects of the program because both the prevention and control groups in this study showed increases in body-image satisfaction and decreases in eating problems over time (McVey & Davis, 2002).

New approaches to prevention continue to emerge. One approach involves forming school-based peer support groups (McVey, Lieberman, Voorberg, Wardrope, & Blackmore, 2003; McVey, Smith et al., 2003). Thus far, McVey and colleagues have found mixed evidence for the impact of peer support groups, with one study leading to improvements in Grade 7 and 8 girls and another study finding no improvement. Regardless, this multi-faceted approach to prevention recognizes that a multitude of factors can contribute to the development of eating disorders and that a complex prevention program is required to combat this problem.

More recent efforts focus on enlisting teachers in preventive efforts. Initial results from a web-based training program for teachers suggests that the program is effective in improving teachers' knowledge and empowering them to monitor and address any weight-related biases that creep into teaching practices (McVey, Gusella, Tweed, & Ferrari, 2009).

Another focus is on prevention through a dissonance intervention. Stice, Shaw, Burton, and Wade (2006) invoked a form of prevention that is designed to create dissonance about the internalization of the thin ideal. Adolescent girls took part in verbal, written, and behavioural exercises involving critiquing the thin ideal. A key goal is to reverse the internalization and acceptance of the goal of being excessively thin. The study showed that relative to the control group, both participants in the dissonance intervention and those who received a more typical healthy weight group intervention maintained at one-year follow-up significant reductions in levels of thin-ideal internalization, body dissatisfaction, dieting, negative affect, bulimic symptoms, and health service use. The overall effect sizes ranged from small to medium, and the dissonance intervention yielded the strongest effect. A subsequent investigation has confirmed the effectiveness of a dissonance intervention (Stice et al., 2008). The key element here was expressive writing geared toward combatting the internalization and acceptance of the thin ideal.

Interestingly, new data suggest that having prevention efforts led by peers can further enhance the positive effects of prevention for the peer leaders themselves (Becker, Bull, Smith, & Ciao, 2008). This suggests that vulnerable students who take on a leadership role in prevention can transform their risk into resilience.

Information on eating disorders can be obtained from the National Eating Disorder Information Centre (www.nedic.ca) in Toronto.

Thinking Critically

1. Prevention efforts often take place under the auspices of school boards. Do you think that all school boards should be required to include a focus on the prevention of disorders such as eating disorders and depressive disorders? If you were to set up such a program for eating disorders, what would you emphasize?

2. Governments have taken steps to make sure that there are warning labels on products such as cigarettes because they can be harmful to your health. Do you think there is merit in including warnings about television shows that promote unhealthy body images and/or restricting ads that promote unhealthy body images? Or would this simply draw even more attention to these body images?

CANADIAN CLINIC FOCUS 10.1
TREATMENT OF EATING DISORDERS IN CANADA

Eating disorders clinics and treatment centres can be found across Canada in major metropolitan areas and sometimes in smaller communities, from St. John's, Newfoundland, in the east

(e.g., St. Clare's Mercy Hospital), across the prairies (e.g., Bridge Point Centre for Eating Disorders in Milden, Saskatchewan), to Vancouver Island (e.g., the Cedric Centre in Victoria). While the majority of these treatment facilities are available as part of Canada's universal medicare system, a smaller number are, at least in part, private facilities (e.g., Pickhaven Centre in Calgary, Alberta; Homewood Health Centre in Guelph, Ontario). Some of these facilities have eating disorders programs, such as those at the Toronto Hospital and the Hospital for Sick Children, that are world-renowned for their treatment, research, and training activities. The mandate of such programs is to provide comprehensive, integrated, and cost-effective treatments within the constraints of the available resources. Further, the focus is often on specialized interventions that are not otherwise readily available in the individual's community. Programs are usually staffed by multidisciplinary teams that include professionals from psychology, psychiatry, social work, occupational therapy, nutrition, and nursing.

St. Paul's Hospital and the British Columbia Children's Hospital in Vancouver both offer hospital-based treatment programs. The two hospitals are affiliated and offer programs tailored to adults (17 years and older) and younger patients. These are the government-designated tertiary provincial resource programs for adults and children with anorexia nervosa, bulimia, and related disorders and their families. We will focus here on the program for children. Also, note that because of the increasing demand for treatment and complex treatment issues (e.g., an exceptionally high level of comorbidity associated with the experience of eating disorders), an eating disorder centre on Bowen Island Island, the Beau Côté Centre for Eating Disorders was recently opened. It is the only eating disorders treatment centre in British Columbia. Beau Côté refers to "beautiful dimensions" and it treats clients aged 19 and older.

B.C. Children's Hospital Eating Disorders Program
Mandate

The mandate is to "provide leadership and excellence in the areas of clinical services, education and teaching, family-focused child and adolescent health promotion, and research and outreach activities in the area of eating disorders." In the hospital's mission statement, it is stated that there is support for the integration of tertiary care and locally based treatment resources in the community throughout the province of British Columbia. The goal is to provide the "highest possible standard of care."

Referrals

Referrals are received from various regions of British Columbia. Following comprehensive evaluations, referring agencies are provided with a report of assessment findings and recommendations. The results of the assessment and treatment options are discussed with the children and their families.

Services

The cornerstone of the program is multidisciplinary collaboration and includes the following:

- **Intake service.** Patients receive medical, nursing, nutritional, psychiatric/psychological, and family assessments, as well as an eating disorders diagnostic interview, to determine the most appropriate services.

- **Day treatment.** "Capella" is designed for children and adolescents with a moderate to severe disorder that necessitates intensive treatment. Operating five days per week with space for 10 patients, treatment is primarily group-based and emphasizes patient management rather than inpatient hospital care. Goals include normalization of eating behaviour, weight restoration (when applicable), and psychosocial treatment with a strong family-focused component.

- **Outpatient services.** Includes ongoing medical and dietary assessment, as well as psychotherapy (individual and family). Individuals are helped to gain control over eating difficulties and to address self-image and family dynamics problems. Aftercare and relapse prevention are provided for people who have undergone more intensive treatment.

- **Inpatient unit.** This is located on the Adolescent Care Unit, and its goals are medical stabilization and nutritional rehabilitation, support, counselling, and preparation for further treatment within the program or within the community. Patients are helped to regain normal metabolic functioning and to develop healthy eating patterns. When medically able, patients may begin to attend the Capella day treatment.

- **Residence.** Hudson House is a residential setting that gives patients and families throughout British Columbia access to Capella. Staff provide continuous support and care: meal support, recreational activities, assistance with lifestyle normalization, and recovery promotion.

- **Parent support group.** A support group is open to parents of individuals in any component of the program.

- **Outreach provincial services.** Outreach services include community education, training of staff in local eating disorders programs, telephone consultation with health care professionals, assistance with the development of local assessment and treatment services, specialized training for trainees from all disciplines, support of research projects and ongoing evaluation of treatment services, and liaison with other organizations (e.g., Provincial Eating Disorders Steering Committee, St. Paul's Hospital Eating Disorders Program).

The importance of the opportunities provided to those suffering with eating disorders was articulated clearly by Claudia Tianne Chai, a student from Simon Fraser University who received treatment when in Grade 11. Claudia was willing to publicly share her story (see Chai, 2006). She recounted that:

In the intensive day-treatment Capella Program, I was surrounded by other girls who knew what I was going through and by staff who did their best to understand. Through individual therapy, group therapy, meal time, cooking group and trips outside the hospital, the support I received was amazing. Ironically, unlike outside in the real world, while inside the hospital I never felt "crazy." I could express how I felt—good or bad—and it was accepted. (Chai, 2006, p. 11)

Claudia recovered from her bout of anorexia, but she acknowledged that she still has to "tread carefully" because she recognizes that "there is a very thin line between sickness and health" (Chai, 2006, p. 11).

Non-Profit Organizations: Sheena's Place

There is usually a long waiting list for admission to programs such as those at the B.C. Children's Hospital, since only a limited number of individuals can participate at a given time. Waiting periods as long as seven or eight months can occur. However, various non-profit, community-based organizations provide support programs. These programs are an excellent "waiting room" for people waiting for admission to the comprehensive hospital-based treatment programs, and they are beneficial to individuals who may not be quite ready to make a commitment to go into treatment. Sheena's Place in Toronto is an example of a non-profit organization. Although these organizations may employ professional personnel, volunteerism is their lifeblood.

Sheena's Place, a registered charity, offers "hope and support services … in a warm, comfortable and safe environment." The services are provided at no cost to people with eating disorders and their families. A poignant story surrounds its formation. Sheena Carpenter died in 1993 as a consequence of her anorexia. Friends and colleagues of her mother were motivated to create a centre in a non-institutional environment in downtown Toronto for people like Sheena. The objective is to work with the existing system, acting "as a conduit between those affected or living with eating disorders and the various systems." Sheena's Place has a comprehensive support-group program and a focus on outreach and education. Its fall 2009 program included more than 50 groups (e.g., "University and college students"), ongoing programs (e.g., "Unlocking emotional eating"), and workshops (e.g., "Addiction unplugged").

Although the primary focus of most intervention programs has been on the traditional eating disorders (anorexia nervosa and bulimia nervosa), obesity and binge eating disorder are also receiving attention, owing to the recognition of the health consequences of obesity, coupled with the increasing prevalence of obesity and the inclusion of binge eating disorder in the *DSM-IV* as a diagnosis in need of further study. For example, obesity is the focus at the University of New Brunswick's Pediatric Obesity Clinic in Fredericton. The clinic also promotes LEAP!, which is the Learning Eating Activity Program designed to foster weight management

and healthy lifestyle choices by children and members of their family. Why are such programs necessary? According to the *Healthy Weights for Healthy Kids* report created in 2007 for the Canadian government, about 1 in 4 Canadian children are obese or overweight and they will die younger than will their parents. Obesity in children is linked not only to deficits in self-esteem (Wang et al., 2009), it is also associated strongly with elevated risk for diabetes, and concerns have been expressed about a projected epidemic in diabetes among future generations. Unfortunately, certain young people are particularly at risk. Adult-onset diabetes, which typically has its onset in white North Americans in their 50s, is appearing now in First Nations teenagers. The causes are assumed to be obesity, physical inactivity, and poverty that can result in a nutritionally poor diet (see Wahi et al., 2009; Zorzi et al., 2009).

The treatment of eating disorders can be complex, and in some instances, it can raise certain ethical and legal issues. For example, should people with anorexia nervosa be force-fed? The Montreux Clinic, a controversial private clinic for eating disorders situated in Victoria, B.C., was forced to close down in 2000. We will discuss some of the legal and ethical issues related to this closing in Chapter 18.

Canadian singer Anne Murray has been a source of inspiration to children and families fighting eating disorders because she shared with the public the story of her daughter, Dawn Langstroth, who has struggled with anorexia nervosa. Anne Murray is honorary chair of Sheena's Place. Mark O'Neill/Sun Media Corporation.

Clinic Sources: British Columbia Children's Hospital website: www.bc.childrens.ca; Sheena's Place website: www.sheenasplace.org.

SUMMARY

- The two main eating disorders are anorexia nervosa and bulimia nervosa. The symptoms of anorexia nervosa include refusal to maintain normal body weight, an intense fear of being fat, a distorted sense of body shape, and, in women, amenorrhea. Anorexia typically begins in the mid-teens, is 10 times more frequent in women than in men, and is comorbid with several other disorders, notably depression. Its course is not favourable, and it can be life threatening. The symptoms of bulimia nervosa include episodes of binge eating followed by purging, fear of being fat, and a distorted body image. Like anorexia, bulimia begins in adolescence, is much more frequent in women than in men, and is comorbid with other diagnoses, such as depression. Prognosis is somewhat more favourable than for anorexia.

- Biological research in the eating disorders has examined both genetics and brain mechanisms. Evidence is consistent with a possible genetic diathesis, but adoption studies have not yet been done. Endogenous opioids and serotonin, both of which play a role in mediating hunger and satiety, have been examined in eating disorders. Low levels of both these brain chemicals have been found in such patients (see Steiger et al., 2001).

- On a psychological level, several factors play important roles. As cultural standards changed to favour a thinner shape as the ideal for women, the frequency of eating disorders increased. The prevalence of eating disorders is higher in industrialized countries, where the cultural pressure to be thin is strongest. The prevalence of eating disorders is very high among people who are especially concerned with their weight, such as models, dancers, and athletes.

- Psychodynamic theories of eating disorders emphasize parent-child relationships and personality characteristics. Bruch's theory, for example, proposes that the parents of children who later develop eating disorders impose their wishes on their children without considering the children's needs. Children reared in this way do not learn to identify their own internal states and become highly dependent on standards imposed by others. Research on characteristics of families with an eating-disordered child have yielded different data depending on how the data were collected. Reports of patients show high levels of conflict, but actual observations of the families do not find them especially deviant. Studies of personality have found that patients with eating disorders are high in neuroticism and perfectionism and low in self-esteem.

- Cognitive-behavioural theories of eating disorders propose that fear of being fat and body-image distortion make weight loss a powerful reinforcer. Among patients with bulimia nervosa, negative mood and stress precipitate binges that create anxiety, which is then relieved by purging.

- The main biological treatment of eating disorders is the use of antidepressants. Recent data suggest that drugs are not effective. Dropout rates from drug treatment programs are high and relapse is common when patients stop taking the medication. Treatment of anorexia often requires hospitalization to reduce the medical complications of the disorder. Providing reinforcers for weight gain, such as visits from friends, has been somewhat successful, but no treatment has yet been shown to produce long-term maintenance of weight gain.

- Cognitive-behavioural treatment for bulimia focuses on questioning society's standards for physical attractiveness, challenging beliefs that encourage severe food restriction, and developing normal eating patterns. Outcomes are promising, at least in the short term.

KEY TERMS

activity anorexia (p. 335)
amenorrhea (p. 325)
anorexia nervosa (p. 325)
binge eating disorder (p. 330)

bulimia nervosa (p. 329)
eating disorder not otherwise specified (p. 324)
false hope syndrome (p. 336)

lateral hypothalamus (p. 332)
purging disorder (p. 324)
Scarlett O'Hara effect (p. 333)
thinspiration effect (p. 337)

REFLECTIONS: PAST, PRESENT, AND FUTURE

- What are the theoretical and practical implications of the changes in the clinical profile of anorexia nervosa in Canadian women, as described by Kruger et al. (1998)?
- Bulimia nervosa and depression are often associated with each other. Do you think that bulimia nervosa plays a causal role in the development of depression, or that depression contributes to the development of bulimia, or is each of the disorders caused by common third variables? What biological, personality, family, or socio-cultural factors might lead to the development of both bulimia nervosa and depression?
- If you had a friend, loved one, or significant other with an eating disorder, how would you want that person to be treated? Assume that members of the individual's family would be included in the treatment program. Would you recommend cognitive or cognitive-behavioural therapy, behaviour therapy (no cognitive elements), interpersonal therapy, family therapy, or antidepressant medication such as Prozac? Defend the reasons for your choice.
- Assume that you were able to design and implement the "perfect" multi-faceted intervention program for a specific eating disorder. What would it look like? What elements would you include? Would the program differ from one person to another even though they might receive the same *DSM-IV* diagnosis (review our discussions about assessment strategies in Chapter 4)? How would you deal with comorbid conditions or associated problems, including mood disorders (see Chapter 8), anxiety disorders (refer to Chapter 6), substance-related disorders (Chapter 12), personality disorders (Chapter 13), and even sexual problems (Chapter 14)?

SCHIZOPHRENIA

"If you talk to God, you are praying. If God talks to you, you have schizophrenia."

—Thomas Szasz, "Schizophrenia," in *The Second Sin*

"The humanity, decency, and respect for human rights of any society can be measured by the way it treats its most afflicted and unfortunate patients, the schizophrenics. A humane society treats these patients in hospitals, or asylums, or good shelters with decent food, proper care, respect, dignity, and privacy—and it does so until they are well enough to look after themselves in the community. A less humane society houses them in prisons, rundown hostels, decrepit hotels, nursing homes, and on the streets—in doorways, cardboard boxes, parks, and city sidewalk grates."

—Abram Hoffer, former director of psychiatric research for the Province of Saskatchewan, currently in private practice in Victoria, B.C., and president of the Canadian Schizophrenia Foundation (2000, p. 144)

"It is essential to view treatments of schizophrenia in their biopsychosocial matrix—leaving out any of the three components . . . will diminish the impact and efficacy of treatment."

—Kopelowicz and Liberman, 1998, p. 192

Harry Mayerovitch, *The Defeatists*. Art Gallery of Ontario, Toronto

CLINICAL SYMPTOMS OF SCHIZOPHRENIA

HISTORY OF THE CONCEPT OF SCHIZOPHRENIA

ETIOLOGY OF SCHIZOPHRENIA

THERAPIES FOR SCHIZOPHRENIA

SUMMARY

AS AN AIR CANADA ticket agent in Calgary during the early 1980s, Michele Misurelli was convinced that Communist agents were plotting against her. "I believed that some of the people I worked with were Communist spies who travelled from airport to airport trying to blow things up," recalls Misurelli, 31, whose own illness has now been largely controlled by antipsychotic drugs. She adds, "You take in information from all five senses properly but you interpret it wrong. If someone followed me down a hallway, I thought they were going to kill me." Overwhelmed by paranoia, Misurelli finally resigned from Air Canada in June 1988 to evade the colleagues she believed were trying to kill her. "I thought," she says, "that I was thinking normally."

The turning point came two months later. "I thought Communists sprayed gas under my apartment door at night and performed brain surgery on me while I was sleeping," says Misurelli, who at the time was obsessed with politics and wanted to run for public office. "I thought they stuck a pick in my ear and pulled my brain out bit by bit. I woke up screaming in my apartment. I phoned my mother and told her that the Communists were going to kill me." Misurelli finally agreed to go to the local hospital, where doctors diagnosed her as schizophrenic and put her on antipsychotic drugs.

Over the next year, as she struggled with schizophrenia, Misurelli tried several times to hold a job. She lasted only a couple of days as a receptionist in Calgary because she repeatedly disconnected callers. "Again, I thought the phones were bugged," she remembers. "I became paranoid and had another confrontation." Several months later, Misurelli landed a ticket agent's job with American Airlines and was sent to Montreal for on-the-job training. But the stress triggered a new bout of psychotic paranoia. "I was afraid in my hotel room," she says. "I thought the walls were closing in on me. I needed to be surrounded by friends and family, so I said that I had the flu and went back to Calgary. My boss fired me for leaving the training."

Although stress can still cause her to experience hallucinations, Misurelli works as a volunteer for the Schizophrenia Society of Alberta, visiting schools and talking to senior students about her illness. In 1993, Misurelli, who is unmarried, gave birth to a daughter, Jennifer, after a brief relationship, and she now lives in Calgary with her parents. "With schizophrenia," says Misurelli, "everything was taken away from me. All my hopes and opportunities were gone. Now, my job is to look after my daughter. I have a purpose." (Nichols, 1995, January 30)

Although the diagnosis of schizophrenia has existed for over a century and spawned more research than any other psychological problem, we are far from understanding this serious mental disorder.

Schizophrenia is a psychotic disorder characterized by major disturbances in thought, emotion, and behaviour: disordered thinking in which ideas are not logically related, faulty perception and attention, flat or inappropriate affect, and bizarre disturbances in motor activity. People with schizophrenia withdraw from other people and reality, often into a fantasy life of delusions and hallucinations.

Schizophrenia is one of the most severe psychopathologies we will describe. Estimates of prevalence in the general population vary between 0.2% and 2%, in part dependent upon the measurement instrument; however, its lifetime prevalence is generally accepted to be about 1% (Government of Canada, 2006). A study of a nationally representative sample in Finland (Perala et al., 2007) used comprehensive methods to determine that the lifetime prevalence of all psychotic disorders exceeds 3%, with a prevalence for schizophrenia of 0.87%. About 0.25% of respondents to the Canadian Community Health Survey (CCHS), Cycle 1.2 reported being professionally diagnosed as having schizophrenia (0.2% of women and 0.3% of men). However, this was assumed to be an underestimate because some people do not admit that they have schizophrenia and the survey team did not contact people who were homeless, in a hospital, or in a supervised residential setting (Government of Canada, 2006). A meta-analysis of prevalence and incidence rates conducted by Canadian researchers (see Goldner, Hsu, Waraich, & Somers, 2002) concluded that there may be real variation in schizophrenia across geographical regions around the world, with Asian populations having the lowest prevalence rates. The incidence is significantly higher in males than in females (male:female ratio = 1.4) (McGrath, 2006).

Although schizophrenia sometimes begins in childhood, it usually appears in late adolescence or early adulthood, somewhat earlier for men than for women. People with schizophrenia typically have a number of acute episodes of their symptoms. Between episodes, they often have less severe but still very debilitating symptoms. Most people with schizophrenia are treated in the community; however, hospitalization is sometimes necessary. Whitehorn, Richard, and Kopala (2004) examined newly diagnosed cases in Nova Scotia and concluded that almost one half (46%) do not require inpatient services. However, people who were first diagnosed while inpatients and those residing in rural areas were more likely to require additional inpatient services in the first year of treatment. In Canada, hospitalization rates are typically much higher among young men relative to young women (see Figure 11.1), accounting for 19.9% of separations from general hospitals. Schizophrenia accounts for 30.9% of separations from psychiatric hospitals. About 10% of people with schizophrenia commit suicide (Government of Canada, 2006). Despite recent advances in treatment, many people with schizophrenia remain chronically disabled. The disability can be attributed to symptoms inherent to schizophrenia, as well as the comorbid disorders from which approximately 50% of those with schizophrenia suffer (e.g., Rosen, Miller, D'Andrea, McGlashan, & Woods, 2006).

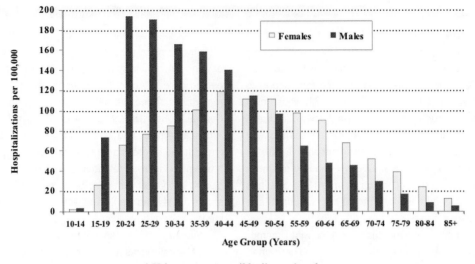

FIGURE 11.1 Hospitalizations for schizophrenia* in general hospitals per 100,000, by age group, Canada, 2002–03. Source: Centre for Chronic Disease Prevention and Control, Health Canada using data from the Hospital Morbidity File, Canadian Institute for Health Information.

A recent German study (Lambert et al., 2008) examined rates and predictors of remission and recovery in almost 400 never-treated people with schizophrenia assessed over three years. Combined remission and recovery was operationally defined as concurrent symptomatic and functional remission and adequate quality of life for at least 6 and 24 months. At three years, only 28.1% and 17.1% of the clients were in combined remission and recovery, respectively. Predictors of outcome included baseline functional status and whether there was early remission within the first three months. The authors concluded, "Early treatment adaptations in case of early non-remission are mandatory" (Lambert et al., 2008, p. 220). Menezes, Arenovich, and Zipursky (2006) conducted a systematic meta-analytic review of longitudinal outcome studies of first-episode psychosis and concluded that a good/remitted outcome occurred in 42% of clients, whereas a poor/chronic outcome was found in 27%. Remschmidt et al. (2007) reported on outcomes for child-onset schizophrenia and concluded that only 16% had a good outcome, 24% had a moderately improved outcome, and 60% had a poor outcome. Of course, differences among and between studies can be due to multiple factors, including differences in the diagnostic criteria employed and length of time between initial assessment and follow-up.

In 2004, there were an estimated 234,305 people in Canada with schizophrenia. Overall, 374 deaths that year were attributed to schizophrenia. The disorder's total estimated costs, including health care and lost productivity due to early morbidity and mortality, were $6.85 billion, 70% of which was the cost of lost productivity (Goeree et al., 2005).

SCHIZOPHRENIA AND COMORBIDITY Comorbid conditions appear to play a role in the development, severity, and course of schizophrenia. Recently, Canadian researchers (MacMillan, Enns, Cox, & Sareen, 2009) examined the comorbidity of Axis I and II disorders within a community-based sample of adults with schizophrenia (the U.S. National Epidemiologic Survey of Alcohol and Related Conditions). They reported that comorbid personality disorders (e.g., avoidant, paranoid, dependent, and antisocial) are common and have implications for the course and clinical management of schizophrenia, that treatment should include evaluation of co-occurring substance use disorders (especially alcohol and cannabis abuse or dependence) and that attention to associated mood (especially Major Depressive Disorder) and anxiety syndromes (particularly social phobia) may be important for "optimal" outcomes.

The common perception that personality disorders worsen outcomes is still open to debate (see Newton-Howes et al., 2007). However, comorbid substance abuse is a major problem for people with schizophrenia. Swartz et al. (2006) reported that 37% of a sample of people with schizophrenia showed current evidence of substance use disorders, that the relationship was especially common among men, and that childhood conduct disorder problems are potent risk factors for substance use disorders in schizophrenia. Conley and colleagues (2007) prospectively measured the link between depressive symptoms and functional outcomes in long-term treatment of people with schizophrenia. About 40% of the participants were depressed at the outset. Over the next three years, those diagnosed with schizophrenia who were also depressed, relative to a non-depressed group, were more likely to use relapse-related mental health services; to be a safety concern (violent, arrested, victimized, suicidal); to have substance-related problems; and to report poorer life satisfaction, quality of life, mental functioning, family relationships, and medication adherence. Comorbid anxiety disorders can impose an additional burden on people with schizophrenia and result in further decline in their perceived quality of life (e.g., Braga, Mendlowicz, Marrocos, & Figueira, 2005). Comorbidity with OCD is also related to a previous history of suicidal ideation and suicide attempts (e.g., Sevincok, Akoglu, & Kokcu, 2007). Further, PTSD is highly prevalent and underdiagnosed among military veterans with schizophrenia (Calhoun et al., 2007). Argyropoulos and colleagues (2008) explored the etiology of mood and anxiety disorders comorbidity using a twin study design. The results showed evidence for a familial association between schizophrenia and depression and anxiety, possibly reflecting common etiological factors contributing to each disorder. The authors concluded, "Future studies should attempt to investigate the relative genetic and environmental contribution to the shared risk factors for schizophrenia, mood, and anxiety disorders" (Argyropoulos et al., 2008, p. 214).

Researchers have also investigated comorbidity during the developing (i.e., prodromal) phase of schizophrenia. Rosen et al. (2006) found that prospectively identified prodromal individuals experience a wide variety of comorbid psychiatric syndromes, especially MDD and cannabis dependence. A study of a large Finnish sample of adolescents (Miettunen et al., 2008) supported the hypothesis that cannabis use may be causal in terms of subsequent psychotic symptoms.

In this chapter, we describe the clinical features of schizophrenia, consider the history of the concept and how it has changed over the years, and examine research on the etiology of schizophrenia and therapies for the disorder.

CLINICAL SYMPTOMS OF SCHIZOPHRENIA

"When I'm psychotic I feel like I'm a disembodied soul. I'm in contact with fairy kings, delusionary people. Sometimes I'm not even aware there are normal people around me, I'm so caught up in the fantasy. Sometimes I've thought I was Peter Rabbit and I would only eat rabbit food. Sometimes, like when I thought I was Brother Michael, Michael the Archangel, I thought I had the power to heal people. One time I felt like I had electricity flowing through my body and that it was controlling me and if I didn't keep control of it that it would kill people. It's very frightening. It's not imaginary. It's real at the time."

–Sandy, a 37-year-old woman with schizophrenia. From the National Film Board of Canada film Full of Sound and Fury

The symptoms of people with schizophrenia involve disturbances in several major areas: thought, perception, and attention; motor behaviour; affect or emotion; and life functioning. The range of problems of people diagnosed as schizophrenic is extensive, although only some of these problems may be present at any given time. The *DSM* determines for the diagnostician how many problems must be present and in what degree to justify the diagnosis. The duration of the disorder is also important in diagnosis.

No essential symptom must be present for a diagnosis of schizophrenia. Thus, people with schizophrenia can differ from each other more than do people with other disorders. Walter Heinrichs (1993, 2001) of York University suggested that the key to understanding schizophrenia is to recognize its heterogeneity, at the empirical and conceptual levels. He noted that

the presentation, course, and outcome of schizophrenia are variable and diverse. Some clients develop delusions but no hallucinations. Others become isolated socially and show "positive" psychotic symptoms only later. Some clients have histories of poor social and academic adjustment that predate their illness. Other clients seem to have thrived until stricken with their first psychotic episode. Current evidence indicates that it is hard to find specific traits or characteristics that are shared by all persons with a diagnosis of schizophrenia. (Heinrichs, 1993, p. 222)

This heterogeneity suggests that it may be appropriate to subdivide people with schizophrenia into types that manifest particular constellations of problems. We will examine several recognized types later in this chapter, but here we present the main symptoms of schizophrenia in two categories, positive and negative, and also describe some symptoms that do not fit neatly into these two categories.

POSITIVE SYMPTOMS

Positive symptoms comprise excesses or distortions, such as disorganized speech, hallucinations, and delusions. They are what define, for the most part, an acute episode of schizophrenia. Positive symptoms are the presence of too much of a behaviour that is not apparent in most people, while the negative symptoms (described later) are the absence of a behaviour that should be evident in most people. We will now discuss positive symptoms involving excesses.

DISORGANIZED SPEECH Also known as formal **thought disorder**, **disorganized speech** refers to problems in organizing ideas and in speaking so that a listener can understand.

Interviewer: Have you been nervous or tense lately?
Client: No, I got a head of lettuce.
Interviewer: You got a head of lettuce? I don't understand.
Patient: Well, it's just a head of lettuce.
Interviewer: Tell me about lettuce. What do you mean?
Patient: Well, … lettuce is a transformation of a dead cougar that suffered a relapse on the lion's toe. And he swallowed the lion and something happened. The … see, the … Gloria and Tommy, they're two heads and they're not whales. But they escaped with herds of vomit, and things like that.
Interviewer: Who are Tommy and Gloria?
Patient: Uh, … there's Joe DiMaggio, Tommy Henrich, Bill Dickey, Phil Rizzuto, John Esclavera, Del Crandell, Ted Williams, Mickey Mantle, Roy Mantle, Ray Mantle, Bob Chance …
Interviewer: Who are they? Who are those people?
Patient: Dead people … they want to be fucked … by this outlaw.
Interviewer: What does all that mean?
Patient: Well, you see, I have to leave the hospital. I'm supposed to have an operation on my legs, you know. And it comes to be pretty sickly that I don't want to keep my legs. That's why I wish I could have an operation.
Interviewer: You want to have your legs taken off?
Patient: It's possible, you know.
Interviewer: Why would you want to do that?

Patient: I didn't have any legs to begin with. So I would imagine that if I was a fast runner, I'd be scared to be a wife, because I had a splinter inside of my head of lettuce. (Neale & Oltmanns, 1980, pp. 103–104)

This excerpt illustrates the **incoherence** sometimes found in the conversation of individuals with schizophrenia. Although the person may make repeated references to central ideas or a theme, the images and fragments of thought are not connected; it is difficult to understand exactly what the person is trying to tell the interviewer.

Speech may also be disordered by what are called **loose associations**, or **derailment**. In these cases, the person may be more successful in communicating with a listener but has difficulty sticking to one topic. He or she seems to drift off on a train of associations evoked by an idea from the past. Clients have themselves provided descriptions of this state.

Disturbances in speech were at one time regarded as the principal clinical symptom of schizophrenia, and they remain one of the criteria for the diagnosis. But evidence indicates that the speech of many people with schizophrenia is not disorganized and that the presence of disorganized speech does not discriminate well between schizophrenia and other psychoses, such as some mood disorders (Andreasen, 1979). For example, people in a manic episode exhibit loose associations as much as do people with schizophrenia.

DELUSIONS Consider the anguish you would feel if you were firmly convinced that many people did not like you—indeed, that they disliked you so much that they were plotting against you. Imagine that your persecutors have sophisticated listening devices that allow them to tune in on your most private conversations and gather evidence in a plot to discredit you. Those around you, including your loved ones, are unable to reassure you that these people are not spying on you. Even your closest friends are gradually joining your tormentors and becoming members of the persecuting community. You are naturally quite anxious or angry about your situation, and you begin your own counteractions against the imagined persecutors. You carefully check any new room you enter for listening devices. When you meet people for the first time, you question them at great length to determine whether they are part of the plot against you.

Such **delusions**, beliefs held contrary to reality, are common positive symptoms of schizophrenia. Persecutory delusions like these were found in 65% of a large, cross-national sample (Sartorius, Shapiro, & Jablonsky, 1974). Delusions may take several other forms, as well. Some of the most important delusions were described by the German psychiatrist Kurt Schneider (1959). The following descriptions of these delusions are drawn from Mellor (1970):

- The person may be the unwilling recipient of bodily sensations or thoughts imposed by an external agency.

One man described "X-rays entering the back of my neck, where the skin tingles and feels warm, they pass down the back in a hot tingling strip about six inches wide to the waist. There they disappear into the pelvis which feels numb and cold and solid like a block of ice. They stop me from getting an erection." (p. 16)

- People may believe that their thoughts are broadcast or transmitted, so that others know what they are thinking.

"As I think, my thoughts leave my head on a type of mental ticker-tape. Everyone around has only to pass the tape through their mind and they know my thoughts." (p. 17)

- People may think their thoughts are being stolen from them, suddenly and unexpectedly, by an external force.

"I am thinking about my mother, and suddenly my thoughts are sucked out of my mind by a phrenological vacuum extractor, and there is nothing in my mind, it is empty." (pp. 16–17)

- Some people believe that their feelings are controlled by an external force.

"I cry, tears roll down my cheeks and I look unhappy, but inside I have a cold anger because they are using me in this way, and it is not me who is unhappy, but they are projecting unhappiness onto my brain. They project upon me laughter, for no reason, and you have no idea how terrible it is to laugh and look happy and know it is not you, but their emotions." (p. 17)

- Some people believe that their behaviour is controlled by an external force.

"When I reach my hand for the comb it is my hand and arm which move, and my fingers pick up the pen, but I don't control them. ... I sit there watching them move, and they are quite independent, what they do is nothing to do with me. ... I am just a puppet who is manipulated by cosmic strings. When the strings are pulled my body moves and I cannot prevent it." (p. 17)

- Some people believe that impulses to behave in certain ways are imposed on them by some external force.

[A patient who emptied the contents of a urine bottle over the ward dinner trolley tried to explain the incident.] "The sudden impulse came over me that I must do it. It was not my feeling, it came into me from the X-ray department, that was why I was sent there for implants yesterday. It was nothing to do with me, they wanted it done. So I picked up the bottle and poured it in. It seemed all I could do." (p. 18)

Although delusions are found among more than half of people with schizophrenia, as with speech disorganization, they are also found among people with other diagnoses—notably, mania and delusional depression. The delusions of people with schizophrenia, however, are often more bizarre. They are highly implausible (Junginger, Barker, & Coe, 1992).

HALLUCINATIONS AND OTHER DISORDERS OF PERCEPTION People with schizophrenia often report that the world seems somehow different or even unreal to them. A person may mention changes in how his or her body feels, or the person's body may become so depersonalized that it feels like a machine. As described in the case beginning this chapter, some people report having difficulty in attending to what is happening around them.

Kurt Schneider, a German psychiatrist, proposed that particular forms of hallucinations and delusions, which he calls first-rank symptoms, are central to defining schizophrenia. Courtesy Heidelberg University.

The most dramatic distortions of perception are **hallucinations**, sensory experiences in the absence of any stimulation from the environment. They are more often auditory than visual; 74% of one sample reported having auditory hallucinations (Sartorius et al., 1974). Like delusions, hallucinations can be very frightening experiences.

Some hallucinations are thought to be particularly important diagnostically because they occur more often in people with schizophrenia than in other psychotic people. They include the following (taken from Mellor, 1970, *British Journal of Psychiatry*, 117, pp. 15–23):

- Some people with schizophrenia report hearing their own thoughts spoken by another voice.

One woman complained of a man's voice speaking in an intense whisper from a point about two feet above her head. The voice would repeat almost all the patient's goal-directed thinking—even the most banal thoughts. The patient would think, "I must put the kettle on," and after a pause of not more than one second the voice would say, "I must put the kettle on." It would often say the opposite, "Don't put the kettle on." (p. 16)

- Some people claim that they hear voices arguing.

One man reported hearing voices coming from the nurse's office. One voice, deep in pitch and roughly spoken, repeatedly said, "G. T. is a bloody paradox," and another higher in pitch said, "He is that, he should be locked up." A female voice occasionally interrupted, saying, "He is not, he is a lovely man." (p. 16)

- Some people hear voices commenting on their behaviour.

One woman heard a voice coming from a house across the road. The voice went on incessantly in a flat monotone describing everything she was doing with an admixture of critical comments. "She is peeling potatoes, got hold of the peeler, she does not want that potato, she is putting it back, because she thinks it has a knobble like a penis, she has a dirty mind, she is peeling potatoes, now she is washing them." (p. 16)

NEGATIVE SYMPTOMS

The **negative symptoms** of schizophrenia consist of behavioural deficits, such as avolition, alogia, anhedonia, flat affect, and asociality, all of which are described below. These symptoms tend to endure beyond an acute episode and have profound effects on people's lives. The presence of many negative symptoms is a strong predictor of a poor quality of life (e.g., occupational impairment, few friends) two years following hospitalization (CME Institute, 2007). There is also some evidence that negative symptoms are associated with earlier onset brain damage (e.g., enlarged ventricles) and progressive loss of cognitive skills (e.g., IQ decline) (see Rummel, Kissling, & Leucht, 2005).

It is important to distinguish among negative symptoms that are truly symptoms of schizophrenia and those that are due to some other factor (Carpenter, Heinrichs, & Wagman, 1988). For example, flat affect (a lack of emotional expressiveness) can be a side effect of antipsychotic medication. Observing clients over extended periods is probably the only way to address this issue. Also, as Heinrichs (1993) has noted, negative symptoms (e.g., flat affect) are difficult to distinguish from aspects of depression, so specificity is an issue.

AVOLITION Apathy or **avolition** refers to a lack of energy and a seeming absence of interest in or an inability to persist in what are usually routine activities. Clients may become inattentive to grooming and personal hygiene, with uncombed hair, dirty nails, and dishevelled clothes. They have difficulty persisting at work, school, or household chores and may spend much of their time sitting around doing nothing.

ALOGIA A negative thought disorder, **alogia** can take several forms. In poverty of speech, the sheer amount of speech is greatly reduced. In poverty of content of speech, illustrated in the following excerpt, the amount of discourse is adequate, but it conveys little information and tends to be vague and repetitive.

Interviewer. O.K. Why is it, do you think, that people believe in God?
Patient. Well, first of all because, He is the person that is their personal savior. He walks with me and talks with me. And uh, the understanding that I have, a lot of peoples, they don't really know their personal self. Because they ain't, they all, just don't know their personal self. They don't know that He uh, seems to like me, a lot of them don't understand that He walks and talks with them. And uh, show 'em their way to go. I understand also that, every man and every lady, is not just pointed in the same direction. Some are pointed different. They go in their different ways. The way that Jesus Christ wanted 'em to go. Myself. I am pointed in the ways of uh, knowing right from wrong, and doing it, I can't do any more, or not less than that. (American Psychiatric Association, 1987, pp. 403–404)

ANHEDONIA An inability to experience pleasure is called **anhedonia**. It is manifested as a lack of interest in recreational activities, failure to develop close relationships with other people, and lack of interest in sex. Clients are aware of this symptom and report that normally pleasurable activities are not enjoyable for them.

FLAT AFFECT In people with **flat affect**, virtually no stimulus can elicit an emotional response. The client may stare vacantly, the muscles of the face flaccid, the eyes lifeless. When spoken to, the client answers in a flat and toneless voice. Flat affect is found in a majority of people with schizophrenia. The concept refers only to the outward expression of emotion and not to the person's inner experience, which may not be impoverished at all. In a study by Kring and Neale (1996), people with schizophrenia and normal participants watched excerpts from films while their facial reactions and skin conductance were recorded. After each film clip, participants self-reported on the moods the films had elicited. While the clients were much less facially expressive than were the non-clients, they reported about the same amount of emotion and were even more physiologically aroused.

ASOCIALITY Some people with schizophrenia have severely impaired social relationships, a characteristic referred to as **asociality**. They have few friends, poor social skills, and little interest in being with other people. A study of clients from the Hamilton (Ontario) Program for Schizophrenia showed that people diagnosed with schizophrenia have lower sociability and greater shyness (Goldberg & Schmidt, 2001). People with schizophrenia also reported more childhood "social troubles." These manifestations of schizophrenia are often the first to appear, beginning in childhood before the onset of more psychotic symptoms. Some of these interpersonal deficits could reflect related deficits in the ability to recognize emotional cues displayed by others (Addington & Addington, 1998).

OTHER SYMPTOMS

Some authors (e.g., Heinrichs, 1993, 2001) have taken issue with the usefulness of the positive vs. negative symptom distinction. One problem is that positive and negative symptoms do not necessarily reflect exclusive subtypes because they are dimensions that often coexist within the same person. Moreover, several other symptoms of schizophrenia do not fit neatly into the positive-negative scheme. Two important symptoms in this category are catatonia and inappropriate affect. Many people also exhibit various forms of bizarre behaviour. They may talk to themselves in public, hoard food, or collect garbage.

CATATONIA *Catatonia* is defined by several motor abnormalities. Some clients gesture repeatedly, using peculiar and sometimes complex sequences of finger, hand, and arm movements that often seem to be purposeful, odd as they may

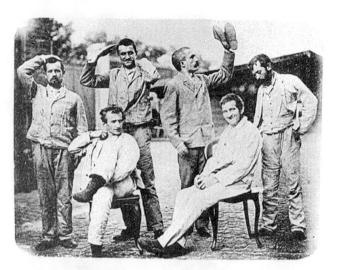

An 1896 photo showing a group of people with catatonic immobility. These men held these unusual positions for long periods of time. From Sander L Gilman, "Seeing the Insane", 1996, University of Nebraska Press.

be. Others manifest an unusual increase in their overall level of activity, which might include much excitement, wild flailing of the limbs, and great expenditure of energy similar to that seen in mania. At the other end of the spectrum is **catatonic immobility**: clients adopt unusual postures and maintain them for very long periods of time. A person may stand on one leg, with the other tucked up toward the buttocks, and remain in this position virtually all day. Catatonic people may also have **waxy flexibility**, whereby another person can move the persons' limbs into strange positions that they maintain for extended periods.

INAPPROPRIATE AFFECT Some people with schizophrenia have **inappropriate affect**. The emotional responses of these individuals are out of context; for example, the client may laugh on hearing that his or her mother just died or become enraged when asked a simple question about how a new garment fits. These clients are likely to shift rapidly from one emotional state to another for no discernible reason. This symptom is quite rare, but its appearance is of considerable diagnostic importance because it is relatively specific to schizophrenia.

The symptoms of schizophrenia have a profound effect on people's lives, as well as the lives of their families and friends. Delusions and hallucinations may cause considerable distress, compounded by the fact that hopes and dreams have been shattered. Cognitive impairments and avolition make stable employment difficult, with impoverishment and often homelessness the result. Strange behaviour and social-skills deficits lead to loss of friends and a solitary existence. The strongest predictor of this social disability is chronic cognitive impairment (Liddle, 2000). High substance abuse rates perhaps reflect an attempt to achieve relief from negative emotions (Blanchard et al., 1999). Little wonder, then, that the suicide rate among people with schizophrenia is high.

HISTORY OF THE CONCEPT OF SCHIZOPHRENIA

We turn now to a review of the history of the concept of schizophrenia and how ideas about this disorder have changed over time.

EARLY DESCRIPTIONS

The concept of schizophrenia was formulated by two European psychiatrists, Emil Kraepelin and Eugen Bleuler. Kraepelin first presented his notion of **dementia praecox**, the early term for schizophrenia, in 1898. He differentiated two major groups of endogenous, or internally caused, psychoses: manic-depressive illness and dementia praecox. Dementia praecox included several diagnostic concepts—dementia paranoides, catatonia, and hebephrenia—that had been regarded as distinct entities by clinicians in previous decades. Kraepelin believed that they shared a common core: an early onset (praecox) and a deteriorating course marked by a progressive intellectual deterioration (dementia). The "dementia" in dementia praecox is not the same as the dementias we discuss in the chapter on aging (Chapter 16), defined principally by severe memory impairments. Kraepelin's term refers to a general "mental enfeeblement."

The formulation of the next major figure, Eugen Bleuler, represented both a specific attempt to define the core of the disorder and a move away from Kraepelin's emphasis on age of onset and course. Bleuler broke with Kraepelin on two major points: he believed that the disorder did not necessarily have an early onset, and he believed that it did not inevitably progress toward dementia. Thus, the label *dementia praecox* was no longer appropriate, and in 1908 Bleuler proposed his own term, schizophrenia, from the Greek words *schizein*, meaning "to split," and phren, meaning "mind," to capture what he viewed as the essential nature of the condition.

With age of onset and deteriorating course no longer considered defining features of the disorder, Bleuler faced a conceptual problem. Since the symptoms of schizophrenia could vary widely among clients, he needed some justification for putting them into a single diagnostic category. Bleuler therefore tried to specify a common denominator, or essential property, that would link the various disturbances. The metaphorical concept that he adopted for this purpose was the "breaking of associative threads." For Bleuler, associative threads joined not only words but thoughts. Thus, goal-directed, efficient thinking and communication were possible only when these hypothetical structures were intact. The notion that associative threads were disrupted in people with schizophrenia could then account for other problems. Bleuler viewed attentional difficulties—for example, as might result from a loss of purposeful direction in thought—as the cause of passive responses to objects and people in the immediate surroundings. Also, he viewed blocking—an apparently total loss of a train of thought—as a complete disruption of the person's associative threads.

Although Kraepelin recognized that a small percentage of clients who originally manifested symptoms of dementia praecox did not deteriorate, he preferred to limit this diagnostic category to clients who had a poor prognosis. Bleuler's work, in contrast, led to a broader concept of schizophrenia. He diagnosed clients with a good prognosis as schizophrenic, and he also included in his concept of schizophrenia many clients who would have received different diagnoses from other clinicians.

THE HISTORICAL PREVALENCE OF SCHIZOPHRENIA

Data from several countries throughout the world suggest that rates of schizophrenia have fallen sharply since the 1960s. A case registry analysis of data from Kingston, Ontario, confirmed that there was a substantial decrease in inpatient prevalence rates between 1986 and 1996, with no corresponding increase in outpatient prevalence rates (Woogh, 2001). It is unlikely that this decrease reflects changes in methods of service delivery, since the rates for major mood disorders over the same period in the same location increased non-significantly for inpatients and significantly for outpatients. However, because Woogh (2001) conducted the first Canadian study on this topic only in Kingston, it is not clear whether this trend can be generalized to other regions of the country. These decreases in prevalence rates over time do not obscure the fact that millions of people around the world suffer from schizophrenia.

Over the years, the number of people diagnosed with schizophrenia has varied considerably depending on how schizophrenia has been conceptualized and defined, and this has hampered attempts to determine accurately the extent of changes in prevalence over time. Bleuler had a great influence on the concept of schizophrenia as it developed in the United States. Over the first part of the twentieth century, the breadth of the diagnosis was extended considerably. At the New York State Psychiatric Institute, for example, about 20% of the clients were diagnosed with schizophrenia in the 1930s. The numbers increased through the 1940s and in 1952 peaked at a remarkable 80%. In contrast, the concept of schizophrenia prevalent in Europe remained narrower. The percentage of clients diagnosed with schizophrenia at the Maudsley Hospital in London, for example, stayed relatively constant, at 20%, for a 40-year period (Kuriansky et al., 1974).

The reasons for the increase in the frequency of diagnoses of schizophrenia in the United States are easily discerned. Several prominent figures in U.S. psychiatry expanded Bleuler's already broad concept of schizophrenia even more. In 1933, for example, Kasanin described nine patients who had been diagnosed with dementia praecox. For all of them, the onset of the disorder had been sudden and recovery relatively rapid. Noting that theirs could be said to be a combination of both schizophrenic and affective symptoms, Kasanin suggested the term "schizoaffective psychosis" to describe the disturbances of these clients. This diagnosis subsequently became part of the U.S. concept of schizophrenia and was listed in *DSM-I* (1952) and *DSM-II* (1968).

Emil Kraepelin (1856–1926), a German psychiatrist, articulated descriptions of dementia praecox that have proved remarkably durable in light of contemporary research. Radio Times/Hulton Picture Library.

Eugen Bleuler (1857–1939), a Swiss psychiatrist, contributed to our conceptions of schizophrenia and coined the term. © Bettman/CORBIS.

The concept of schizophrenia was further broadened by three additional diagnostic practices:

1. U.S. clinicians tended to diagnose schizophrenia whenever delusions or hallucinations were present. Because these symptoms, particularly delusions, occur also in mood disorders, many people with a *DSM-II* diagnosis of schizophrenia may actually have had a mood disorder (Cooper et al., 1972).
2. People whom we would now diagnose as having a personality disorder (notably schizotypal, schizoid, borderline, and paranoid personality disorders, discussed in Chapter 13) were diagnosed as having schizophrenia according to *DSM-II* criteria.

3. People with an acute onset of schizophrenic symptoms and a rapid recovery were diagnosed as having schizophrenia.

THE *DSM-IV-TR* DIAGNOSIS

Beginning in *DSM-III* and continuing in *DSM-IV-TR*, the U.S. concept of schizophrenia shifted considerably from the broad definition to a new definition that narrows the range of people diagnosed as schizophrenic in five ways:

1. The diagnostic criteria are presented in explicit and considerable detail.
2. People with symptoms of a mood disorder are specifically excluded. Schizophrenia—schizoaffective type is now listed as schizoaffective disorder in a separate section as one of the psychotic disorders. It comprises a mixture of symptoms of schizophrenia and mood disorders.
3. *DSM-IV-TR* requires at least six months of disturbance for the diagnosis. The six-month period must include at least one month of the active phase, which is defined by the presence of at least two of the following: delusions, hallucinations, disorganized speech, grossly disorganized or catatonic behaviour, and negative symptoms (only one of these symptoms is required if the delusions are bizarre or if the hallucinations consist of voices commenting or arguing). The remaining time required within the minimum six months can be either a prodromal (before the active phase) or a residual (after the active phase) period. Problems during the prodromal and residual phases include social withdrawal, impaired role functioning, blunted or inappropriate affect, lack of initiative, vague and circumstantial speech, impairment in hygiene and grooming, odd beliefs or magical thinking, and unusual perceptual experiences. These criteria eliminate people who have a brief psychotic episode, which is often stress related, and then recover quickly. *DSM-II's* acute schizophrenic episode is now diagnosed as either schizophreniform disorder or brief psychotic disorder, both also listed in a new section in *DSM-IV-TR*. The symptoms of schizophreniform disorder are the same as those of schizophrenia but last only from one to six months. Brief psychotic disorder lasts from one day to one month and is often brought on by extreme stress, such as bereavement.
4. Some of what *DSM-II* regarded as mild forms of schizophrenia are now diagnosed as personality disorders (e.g., schizotypal personality disorder).
5. *DSM-IV-TR* differentiates between paranoid schizophrenia, to be discussed shortly, and delusional disorder. A person with **delusional disorder** is troubled by persistent persecutory delusions or by delusional jealousy, which is the unfounded conviction that a spouse or lover is unfaithful. There are also delusions of being followed, somatic delusions (believing that some internal organ is malfunctioning), and delusions of erotomania (believing that one

is loved by some other person, usually a complete stranger with a higher social status). A highly publicized case of apparent erotomania occurred when Tricia Miller, a 31-year-old factory worker, was arrested in July 1995 at the SkyDome Hotel in Toronto. Miller was obsessed with Roberto Alomar, a former star of the Toronto Blue Jays, and was frustrated that she was unable to reach him despite her persistent attempts. Miller had a loaded gun. She was planning to kill Alomar and then commit suicide, despite having no prior relationship or face-to-face contact with the athlete. Unlike the person with paranoid schizophrenia, the person with delusional disorder does not have disorganized speech or hallucinations, and his or her delusions are less bizarre. Delusional disorder is quite rare and typically begins later in life than schizophrenia. In most family studies, it appears to be related to schizophrenia, perhaps genetically (Kendler & Diehl, 1993).

Are the *DSM-IV-TR* diagnostic criteria applicable across cultures? Data bearing on this question were collected in a World Health Organization study of both industrialized and developing countries (Jablensky et al., 1994). The symptomatic criteria held up well cross-culturally. However, people in developing countries have a more acute onset and a more favourable course than those in industrialized societies. The cause of this intriguing finding is unknown (Susser & Wanderling, 1994). In a discussion about whether psychosis should be considered a category or a dimension of schizophrenia in *DSM-5*, Emmanuel Stip from the University of Montreal noted, "With worldwide migration increasing, it is crucial to develop a diagnostic system that will be useful across cultural minority groups" (Stip, 2009, p. 138).

A *DSM-5* PROPOSAL FOR PSYCHOTIC RISK SYNDROME AND SYMPTOM DIMENSIONS

The *DSM-5* Psychosis Work Group has been responsible for addressing schizophrenia and other psychotic disorders. Among their proposals announced for consideration on February 10, 2010, was the recommendation for a **psychosis risk syndrome**, either for inclusion in the main manual or in an appendix for further research (see www.dsm5.org). Among the six criteria would be at least one of delusions, hallucinations, or disorganized speech in an attenuated form with intact testing, but of sufficient severity and/or frequency to be beyond normal variation. A further criterion is that "symptoms are sufficiently distressing and/or disabling to the patient and/or others to lead to help-seeking." What is the rationale for this new syndrome? Young people at risk for later manifestation of a psychotic disorder can now be identified years before a diagnosis of schizophrenia is determined (and can be predicted even in infants). Research over the past 15 years produced evidence for the effectiveness of detecting people at risk and valid criteria have been published (see Scott et al., 2009). Both Carpenter (2009) and Heckers

(2009) published an approach to the issue in the *DSM-5* framework. What is the potential benefit of establishing the new category? Hopefully, people at risk can be treated effectively early in the course and the early intervention will have long-lasting benefits that are not achievable with later interventions. However, numerous critical issues must be considered. For example, will ordinary users in real-life settings be able to reliably and validly identify cases based on the criteria? Only field trials can address some of the issues. Are there evidence-based interventions to effectively reduce conversion to psychosis? We address this issue in Canadian Clinic Focus 11.1. The work group also proposed the use of nine dimensions of the core symptoms (hallucinations, delusions, disorganization, abnormal psychomotor behaviour, restricted emotional expression, avolition, impaired cognition, depression, mania), with severity assessment based on the past month using a five-point scale. These dimensions would be used for all psychotic disorders. Thus, the work group proposed a mixed categorical-dimensional system for schizophrenia—a major change from *DSM-IV* that has the potential to be of considerable clinical value and research utility.

CATEGORIES OF SCHIZOPHRENIA IN *DSM-IV-TR*

"Elizabeth II is named as the monarch of record in Canada, but she's not the true king. I am the true king. She is simply a puppet of Satan, kept as a figurehead to fool the people. To try the king of Canada is high treason."

—Stanley Almeida, who suffers from paranoid schizophrenia, lashing out at a judge whom he accused of engaging in a "conspiracy of evil" aimed at crucifying "the king." Cited in Boyle, 1998, E1

Earlier, we mentioned that the heterogeneity of schizophrenic symptoms suggested the presence of subtypes of the disorder. Three types of schizophrenic disorders included in *DSM-IV-TR*—disorganized (hebephrenic), catatonic, and paranoid—were initially proposed by Kraepelin many years ago. The present descriptions of Kraepelin's original types demonstrate the great diversity of behaviour that relates to the diagnosis of schizophrenia.

DISORGANIZED SCHIZOPHRENIA Kraepelin's hebephrenic form of schizophrenia is called **disorganized schizophrenia** in *DSM-IV-TR*. Speech is disorganized and difficult for a listener to follow. Clients may speak incoherently, stringing together similar-sounding words and even inventing new words, often accompanied by silliness or laughter. They may have flat affect or experience constant shifts of emotion, breaking into inexplicable fits of laughter and crying. Their behaviour is generally disorganized and not goal directed; for example, a client may tie a ribbon around a big toe or move incessantly, pointing at objects for no apparent reason. Clients sometimes deteriorate to the point of incontinence, voiding anywhere and at any time, and completely neglect their appearance, never bathing or combing hair.

CATATONIC SCHIZOPHRENIA The most obvious symptoms of **catatonic schizophrenia** are the catatonic symptoms described earlier. Clients typically alternate between catatonic immobility and wild excitement, but one of these symptoms may predominate. These clients resist instructions and suggestions and often echo (repeat back) the speech of others. The onset of catatonic reactions may be more sudden than the onset of other forms of schizophrenia, although the person is likely to have previously shown some apathy and withdrawal from reality.

Catatonic schizophrenia is seldom seen today, perhaps because drug therapy works effectively on these bizarre motor processes. Boyle (1991) has argued that, during the early part of the twentieth century, the apparent high prevalence of catatonia reflected misdiagnosis and that apparent catatonic schizophrenia was actually lethargica (sleeping sickness). This was portrayed in the film *Awakenings*, which was based on the writings of neurologist Oliver Sacks.

PARANOID SCHIZOPHRENIA The diagnosis **paranoid schizophrenia** is assigned to a substantial number of recently admitted clients to psychiatric hospitals. The key to this diagnosis is the presence of prominent delusions. Delusions of persecution are most common, but clients may experience **grandiose delusions**, in which they have an exaggerated sense of their own importance, power, knowledge, or identity. Some clients are plagued by **delusional jealousy**, the unsubstantiated belief that their partner is unfaithful. The other delusions described earlier, such as the sense of being persecuted or spied on, may also be evident. Vivid auditory hallucinations may accompany the delusions. Clients with paranoid schizophrenia often develop **ideas of reference**; they incorporate unimportant events within a delusional framework and read personal significance into the trivial activities of others. For instance, they think that overheard segments of conversations are about them, that the frequent appearance of a person on a street where they customarily walk means that they are being watched, and that what they see on television or read in magazines somehow refers to them. Individuals with paranoid schizophrenia are agitated, argumentative, angry, and sometimes violent. They remain emotionally responsive, although they may be somewhat stilted, formal, and intense with others. They are also more alert and verbal than are people with other types of schizophrenia. Their language, although filled with references to delusions, is not disorganized.

EVALUATION OF THE SUBTYPES Although these subtypes form the basis of current diagnostic systems and certain distinctions seem valid, such as the presence or absence of paranoid characteristics (Nicholson & Neufeld, 1993), the overall usefulness of subtypes is often questioned. Because diagnosing types of schizophrenia is extremely difficult, diagnostic reliability is dramatically reduced. Furthermore, these subtypes have little predictive validity; that is, the diagnosis of one over another form of schizophrenia provides little information that is helpful either in treating or in predicting the course of the problems. There is also considerable overlap among the types. For example, people with all forms of schizophrenia may have delusions. Kraepelin's system of subtyping has not proved to be a useful way of dealing with the variability in schizophrenic behaviour.

Supplemental types included in *DSM-IV-TR* are also flawed. The diagnosis of **undifferentiated schizophrenia** applies to people who meet the diagnostic criteria for schizophrenia but not the criteria for any of the three subtypes. The diagnosis of **residual schizophrenia** is used when the client no longer meets the full criteria for schizophrenia but still shows some signs of the disorder.

Despite the problems with current subtyping systems, there is continuing interest in differentiating the forms of schizophrenia. A radically different and promising approach focuses on schizophrenia subtypes that differ qualitatively in terms of neurocognitive features that involve brain abnormalities. Regarding the heterogeneity issue, Heinrichs and Awad (1993) conducted a cluster analysis that identified subtypes of schizophrenia based on performances on a battery of neuropsychological tests that included the Wisconsin Card Sorting Test (a test of executive functioning), the Weschler Adult Intelligence Scale (WAIS), and measures of motor function and verbal memory. The cluster analysis identified five subtypes, including one group with normative, intact cognition. The other four groups included an "executive subtype," which was distinguished by impairment on the Wisconsin Card Sorting Test; an "executive-motor subtype," which had deficits in card sorting and motor functioning; a "motor subtype," which had deficits only in motor functioning; and a "dementia subtype," which had pervasive and generalized cognitive impairment. These subtypes differed on other variables, such as duration of symptoms and extent of hospitalization. A subsequent study of a subset of the clients showed that most of the neurocognitive and functional differences persisted over time, even though there were no apparent symptom differences among the subtypes (Heinrichs, Ruttan, Zakzanis, & Case, 1997). A continuing focus on neuropsychological differences may provide important insights into the heterogeneity of schizophrenia.

Heinrichs (2005) compared average effect sizes across various ways of assessing cognition vs. physiological functioning and structures in schizophrenia. He concluded that there is a "primacy of cognition" (p. 229) in schizophrenia, with average effect sizes from studies of memory, attention, language, and reasoning being at least twice as large as those obtained in studies that examine schizophrenia with structural brain MRI and PET scans. The results are shown in Figure 11.2. Heinrichs (2005) then went on to identify several explanations for why the link between schizophrenia and cognition is much stronger. One factor he suggested is that there is disorder-related brain disturbance that could have a pervasive influence on brain systems that are active in information processing. Another possible factor is that cognitive deficits reflect genetically determined constraints. A third

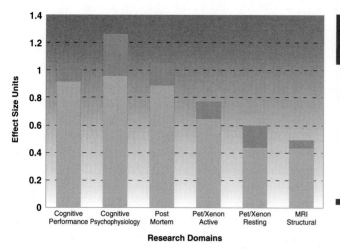

FIGURE 11.2 Meta-analytic findings of impairment in different domains of schizophrenia research. From Heinrichs, R. W. (2005). The primacy of cognition in schizophrenia. *American Psychologist*, 60, pp. 229–242. Reprinted with permission.

Note: This summary includes grand mean effect sizes and their 95% confidence intervals derived from clinical and experimental tests of cognitive performance (Heinrichs, 2001; Heinrichs & Zakanis, 1998); smooth pursuit eye tracking and evoked potential measures of cognitive psychophysiology (Heinrichs, 2001); post-mortem neuroanatomical and neurotransmitter receptor binding studies (Heinrichs, 2001); positron emission tomography (PET) and xenon inhalation studies of regional metabolism and blood flow conducted with participants engaged in cognitive activation tasks (Davidson & Heinrichs, 2003); PET studies of regional metabolism, blood flow, and receptor binding and xenon blood flow studies with participants in a resting state (Davidson & Heinrichs, 2003; Heinrichs, 2001); and regional volumetric measurements of the frontal and temporal lobes based on structural magnetic resonance imaging (MRI) (Davidson & Heinrichs, 2003).

factor is the possible influence of chronic stress and distress on cognition in people prone to schizophrenia.

The system that distinguishes between positive and negative symptoms, described earlier, has received much attention. Andreasen and Olsen (1982) evaluated 52 people with schizophrenia and found that 16 could be regarded as having predominantly negative symptoms, 18 predominantly positive symptoms, and 18 mixed symptoms. Although these data suggest that it is possible to talk about types of schizophrenia, subsequent research has indicated that most people with schizophrenia show mixed symptoms (e.g., Andreasen, Flaum et al., 1990) and that very few clients fit into the pure positive or pure negative types.

Subsequent analyses have revealed three dimensions, not two (Lenzenweger, Dworkin, & Wethington, 1991). These studies have shown that positive symptoms should be divided into two categories: a positive symptom component consisting of delusions and hallucinations and a disorganized component that includes bizarre behaviour and disorganized speech (see Table 11.1).

TABLE 11.1
SUMMARY OF THE MAJOR SYMPTOM DIMENSIONS IN SCHIZOPHRENIA

Positive Symptoms	Negative Symptoms	Disorganization
Delusions, hallucinations	Avolition (apathy), alogia (poverty of speech and poverty of content of speech), anhedonia, flat affect, asociality	Bizarre behaviour, disorganized speech

A distinction between positive and negative symptoms (as opposed to between types of clients) continues to be used in research on the etiology of schizophrenia. We will present evidence relevant to the validity of this distinction in the discussion of the possible roles of genetics, dopamine, and brain pathology in the etiology of schizophrenia.

The *DSM-5* work group proposed discontinuing all of the "classic" subtypes of schizophrenia and rejected alternatives to take their place. A major argument for discontinuing the use of the *DSM-IV* subtypes is the fact that they are rarely used diagnostically, with the exception of paranoid schizophrenia and, to a lesser extent, undifferentiated schizophrenia. Is there evidence that these or other subtypes are valid? The question was the subject of a systematic review conducted by Linscott, Allardyce, and van Os (2009) who focused on subtypes within schizophrenia and within psychotic disorders as a whole (see www.dsm5.org for a summary of the conclusions). It was concluded that the findings do not point to a single system of subtyping.

ETIOLOGY OF SCHIZOPHRENIA

"The search to uncover the genetic and molecular secrets of the brain has not solved the riddle of psychosis, nor has it eradicated its disabling symptoms. . . . Perhaps the time has come for the field of psychiatry to reassess the role of social factors in the etiology of psychosis."
—G. Eric Jarvis from a 2007 guest editorial in the Canadian Journal of Psychiatry, p. 275

We have described how people with schizophrenia differ from normal people in thought, speech, perception, and imagination. What can explain the disconnection of their thoughts, their inappropriate emotions or lack of emotion, and their misguided delusions and bewildering hallucinations? We look here at the major areas of etiological research.

THE GENETIC DATA

What would you do if you wanted to find an individual who had a very good chance of being diagnosed one day with schizophrenia and you could not consider any behaviour patterns or other symptoms? Indeed, imagine that you could not even meet the person. This problem, suggested by Paul Meehl (1962), has a solution that offers you a close-to-even chance of choosing a person who is potentially schizophrenic: find an individual who has an identical twin with schizophrenia.

A convincing body of literature indicates that a predisposition to schizophrenia is transmitted genetically. The family, twin, and adoption methods employed in this research have led researchers to conclude that a predisposition to schizophrenia is inherited. Though many genetic studies of schizophrenia were conducted before the publication of *DSM-III*, genetic investigators collected extensive descriptive data on their subjects, allowing them to be rediagnosed with newer diagnostic criteria. Reanalyses using *DSM-III* criteria substantiated the conclusions reached earlier (e.g., Kendler & Gruenberg, 1984).

FAMILY STUDIES Table 11.2 presents a summary of the risk for schizophrenia in various relatives of index cases with schizophrenia. (Keep in mind that the risk for schizophrenia in the general population is a little less than 1%.) Quite clearly, relatives of people with schizophrenia are at increased risk, and the risk increases as the genetic relationship between proband and relative becomes closer.

More recent data confirm what is shown in Table 11.2 (Kendler, Karkowski-Shuman, & Walsh, 1996). Further, the negative symptoms of schizophrenia appear to have a stronger genetic component (Malaspina et al., 2000). The relatives of people with schizophrenia are also at increased risk for other disorders (e.g., schizotypal personality disorder) that are thought to be less severe forms of schizophrenia (Kendler, Neale, & Walsh, 1995). The data gathered by the family method thus support the notion that a predisposition to schizophrenia can be transmitted genetically. Of course, relatives of a schizophrenic index case may share not only genes but also common experiences. The behaviour of a parent with schizophrenia, for example, could be

very disturbing to a developing child. Therefore, the influence of the environment cannot be discounted as a rival explanation for the higher morbidity risks.

TWIN STUDIES Concordance rates for MZ and DZ twins are also given in Table 11.2. Concordance for identical twins (44.3%), although greater than that for fraternal twins (12.08%), is less than 100%. Cardno and Gottesman (2000) reviewed the results since 1995 from European and Japanese studies and reported concordance rates for MZ twins of 41 to 65%, and for DZ twins of 0 to 28%. The less than 100% concordance in MZ twins is important: if genetic transmission alone accounted for schizophrenia and one twin had schizophrenia, then the other twin would also have schizophrenia because MZ twins are genetically identical. Consistent with a genetic interpretation of these data, concordance among MZ twins does increase when the proband is more severely ill (Gottesman & Shields, 1972).

There is a critical problem in interpreting the results of twin studies. A common "deviant" environment rather than common genetic factors could account for the concordance rates. By common environment we mean not only similar child-rearing practices, but also a more similar intrauterine environment, for MZ twins are more likely than DZ twins to share a single blood supply.

A clever analysis supporting a genetic interpretation of the high concordance rates found for identical twins was performed by Fischer (1971). She reasoned that if these rates indeed reflected a genetic effect, the children of even the discordant, or non-schizophrenic, identical co-twins of people with schizophrenia should be at high risk for the disorder. These non-schizophrenic twins would presumably have the genotype for schizophrenia, even though it was not expressed behaviourally, and thus might pass along an increased risk for the disorder to their children. In agreement with this line of reasoning, the rate of schizophrenia and schizophrenic-like psychoses in the children of non-schizophrenic co-twins of people with schizophrenia was 9.4%. The rate among the children of the people with schizophrenia themselves was only slightly and not significantly higher at 12.3%. Both rates are substantially higher than the 1% prevalence found in an unselected population.

Dworkin and his colleagues re-evaluated the major twin studies according to the positive-negative symptom distinction (e.g., Dworkin, Lenzenweger, & Moldin, 1987). The analyses suggested that negative symptoms have a stronger genetic component than do positive ones.

ADOPTION STUDIES The study of children whose mothers had schizophrenia but who were reared from early infancy by non-schizophrenic adoptive parents has provided more-conclusive information on the role of genes in schizophrenia by eliminating the possible effects of a deviant environment. Heston (1966) was able to follow up on 47 people born between 1915 and 1945 to women with schizophrenia in a state mental hospital. The infants were separated from their mothers at birth

TABLE 11.2
SUMMARY OF MAJOR EUROPEAN FAMILY AND TWIN STUDIES OF THE GENETICS OF SCHIZOPHRENIA

Relation to Proband	Percentage with Schizophrenia
Spouse	1.00
Grandchildren	2.84
Nieces/nephews	2.65
Children	9.35
Siblings	7.30
DZ twins	12.08
MZ twins	44.30

Source: From Gottesman, McGuffin, & Farmer (1987)

and raised by foster or adoptive parents. Fifty control participants were selected from the same foundling homes that had placed the children of the women with schizophrenia.

The follow-up assessment, conducted in 1964, included an interview, the MMPI, an IQ test, and social class ratings. A dossier on each participant was rated independently by two psychiatrists, and a third evaluation was made by Heston. Clinical ratings were made on a 0–100 scale of overall disability. Overall, the control participants were rated as less disabled than the children of mothers with schizophrenia. Thirty-one of the 47 children of mothers with schizophrenia (66%) but only nine of the 50 controls (18%) were given a *DSM* diagnosis. None of the controls was diagnosed as schizophrenic, but 16.6% of the offspring of women with schizophrenia were so diagnosed. Children of women with schizophrenia were also more likely to be diagnosed as mentally defective, psychopathic, and neurotic (Table 11.3). They had been involved more frequently in criminal activity, had spent more time in penal institutions, and had more often been discharged from the armed services for psychiatric reasons. Heston's study provides strong support for the importance of genetic factors in the development of schizophrenia. Children reared without contact with their so-called pathogenic mothers were still more likely to become schizophrenic than were the control participants. A similar study was conducted in Denmark (Kety et al., 1975, 1994) and it produced similar results.

MOLECULAR GENETICS It does not appear that the genetic predisposition to schizophrenia is transmitted by a single gene; several multi- or polygenic models remain viable.

TABLE 11.3
CHARACTERISTICS OF PARTICIPANTS SEPARATED FROM THEIR MOTHERS IN EARLY INFANCY

Assessment	Offspring of Schizophrenic Mothers	Control Offspring
Number of participants	47	50
Mean age at follow-up	35.8	36.3
Overall ratings of disability (low score indicates more pathology)	65.2	80.1
Number diagnosed schizophrenic	5	0
Number diagnosed mentally defective	4	0
Number diagnosed psychopathic	9	2
Number diagnosed neurotic	13	7

Source: From Heston (1966)

Thaker (2007) noted that the hunt for schizophrenia-related genes has proven more difficult than expected for several reasons, including:

1. Lack of preciseness in defining the boundaries of the clinical phenotype
2. Absence of biological tests that confirm diagnostic categorization
3. Clinical heterogeneity and the complex nature of schizophrenia

As noted by David Braff (2007), "with a huge ocean of 3 000 000 000 base pairs harboring 25 000 or so structural genes in Homo sapiens, alternative strategies for schizophrenia vulnerability gene identification were and are needed" (p. 19). In an effort to find susceptibility genes, schizophrenia research recently turned to the "endophenotypic strategy" first suggested by Gottesman and Shields in 1972. According to Turetsky et al. (2007), "Endophenotypes are characteristics that reflect the actions of genes predisposing an individual to a disorder, even in the absence of diagnosable pathology" (p. 69). Why is this important? Individual endophenotypes are assumed to be determined by fewer genes than the more complex schizophrenia phenotype. Thus, the complexity of genetic analyses would be, theoretically, reduced. Various research groups are currently evaluating the endophenotypic candidacy of key neurocognitive tasks (e.g., Gur et al., 2007) and neurophysiological abilities (e.g., Turetsky et al., 2007).

In the meantime, contemporary conventional gene linkage and association analyses point to the possible role of numerous specific genes. These have included the serotonin type 2A receptor (5-HT2a) gene, the dopamine D3 receptor gene, and chromosomal regions on chromosomes 6, 8, 13, and 22, including microdeletion on chromosome 22ql1 (see Walker, Kestler, Bollini, & Hochman, 2004). Unfortunately, positive findings are frequently followed by failures to replicate. Although several studies have replicated a link with a gene called DTNBP1 (Owen, Williams, & O'Donovan, 2004), it is still not clear what its function is. There is also suggestive evidence that G-protein signalling 4 (RGS4), a gene localized to chromosome lq23, plays a role in schizophrenia susceptibility (Talkowski et al., 2006). Emerging findings also provide increasing evidence for an overlap in genetic susceptibility across traditional classification categories, including schizophrenia and bipolar disorder (Craddock, O'Donovan, & Owen, 2006). Thus, while several promising susceptibility genes have been proposed, identification of a conclusive genetic risk factor for schizophrenia remains elusive (Talkowski et al., 2006).

EVALUATION OF THE GENETIC DATA Genetic factors play an important role in the development of schizophrenia. Early twin and family studies were criticized because they did not separate the effects of genes and environment. However, more recent studies of children of parents with schizophrenia who were reared in foster and adoptive homes, plus the follow-up of relatives of adopted children who developed schizophrenia, have virtually removed the potential confounding influence of the environment.

Despite this evidence, we cannot conclude that schizophrenia is a disorder completely determined by genetic transmission, for we must keep in mind the distinction between phenotype and genotype. Like other mental disorders, schizophrenia is defined by behaviour; it is a phenotype and thus reflects the influence of both genes and environment. The role of both factors is suggested by outcomes experienced by the Genain quadruplets (see Focus on Discovery 11.1). The diathesis-stress and biopsychosocial models seem appropriate for guiding theory about and research into the etiology of schizophrenia. Genetic factors can only predispose individuals to schizophrenia. Some kind of stress is required to render this predisposition an observable pathology.

The genetic research into schizophrenia has some further limitations. First, it has not been possible to specify exactly how a predisposition to schizophrenia is transmitted. Second, the exact nature of the inherited diathesis remains unknown. What exactly is inherited that puts some people at risk for schizophrenia? Despite the problems and loose ends in the genetic data, the findings represent an impressive body of evidence. The strong positive correlation between genetic relatedness and the prevalence of schizophrenia remains one of the strongest links in the chain of information about the causes of schizophrenia. Further, as noted by Thaker (2007), despite the challenges, there is considerable promise in contemporary genetic studies of schizophrenia:

> Future studies that establish similarities and differences in the endophenotypic signatures of schizophrenia, bipolar disorder, and other psychotic disorders will improve concepts about the common and distinct aspects of pathophysiology, about heterogeneity, and about clinical boundaries of psychotic disorders. Better understanding of the genetic mechanisms underlying endophenotypes will identify novel targets for drug development with relevance not only for schizophrenia but also other psychotic disorders with similar endophenotypic signatures. Because the neuronal deficits indexed by the endophenotype often precede a first psychotic episode, such treatments may also have relevance for early intervention and preventive strategies. (Thaker, 2007, p. 1)

FOCUS ON DISCOVERY 11.1
THE GENAIN QUADRUPLETS–HEREDITY OR ENVIRONMENT IN SCHIZOPHRENIA?

The schizophrenia manifested by the Genain quadruplets represents a fascinating illustration of the mutual influence played by genetic factors and life experiences. All of the Genain sisters had developed schizophrenia by the time they reached the age of 24. Genain is a pseudonym used to protect the identity of the four sisters who live in a U.S. midwestern state. The story of Hester, Nora, Iris, and Myra is fascinating for many reasons. First, it was estimated in 1963 that the odds of identical quadruplets all developing schizophrenia were 1 in 1.5 billion births! Second, the Genain sisters have been studied throughout much of their life, initially by David Rosenthal and his associates at the U.S. National Institute of Mental Health (NIMH), and more recently by Allan Mirsky and his co-investigators. The latter published a 39-year follow-up investigation of the sisters (see Mirsky et al., 2000). The sisters experienced very different life outcomes even though they share the same genetic background. Hester experienced severe impairment, never completed high school, and was incapable of independent functioning. Iris and Nora showed better functioning but never had substantial careers and never got married. In contrast, Myra was able to work, marry, and raise a family despite developing schizophrenia.

The differences among the sisters demonstrate that the course of the disorder can be variable and, clearly, that all people diagnosed with schizophrenia are not alike. The sisters' different outcomes illustrate the need to consider genetic factors and environmental factors jointly. Scholars such as Mirsky point to the differential treatment of the girls by their father, who was especially cruel to Hester and Iris and kinder to Myra and Nora.

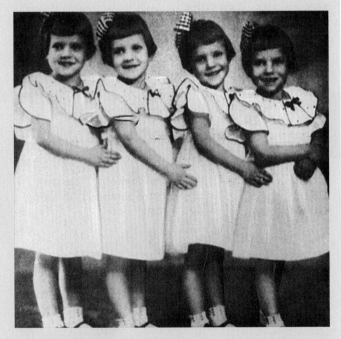

Childhood photograph of the Genain quadruplets. All of the girls developed schizophrenia later in life. *Source*: Courtesy of Monte S. Buchsbaum M.D., Mt. Sinai School of Medicine, New York, NY.

Of course, it is impossible to pinpoint exactly the factors that contributed to the outcomes experienced by the Genain quadruplets. Still, the lives of the four sisters were quite different despite their common history of schizophrenia.

BIOCHEMICAL FACTORS

The demonstrated role of genetic factors in schizophrenia suggests that biochemicals should be investigated, for it is through body chemistry and biological processes that heredity may have an effect. Research is examining different neurotransmitters, including norepinephrine and serotonin. No biochemical theory has unequivocal support. We shall review one of the best-researched factors: dopamine.

DOPAMINE ACTIVITY The theory that schizophrenia is related to excess activity of dopamine is based principally on the knowledge that drugs effective in treating schizophrenia reduce dopamine activity. Antipsychotic drugs, in addition to being useful in treating some symptoms of schizophrenia, produce side effects resembling the symptoms of Parkinson's disease. Parkinsonism is known to be caused in part by low levels of dopamine in a particular nerve tract of the brain. It has been confirmed that because of their structural similarities to the dopamine molecule (Figure 11.3), molecules of antipsychotic drugs fit into and thereby block postsynaptic dopamine receptors. The dopamine receptors that are blocked by first-generation or conventional antipsychotics are called D2 receptors. Like other neurotransmitters, there are several subclasses of dopamine receptors that differ in the specifics of how they signal the postsynaptic neuron. Some of the second generation or atypical antipsychotics (see section on atypical antipsychotics later in this chapter) have effects on additional kinds of dopamine receptor sites (D3, D4) and on some types of serotonin receptor sites (S2, S3), as reviewed by Lehmann and Ban (1997). From this knowledge about the action of the drugs that help people with schizophrenia, it is but a short inductive leap to view schizophrenia as resulting from excess activity in dopamine nerve tracts.

Further indirect support for the **dopamine theory** comes from the literature on amphetamine psychosis.

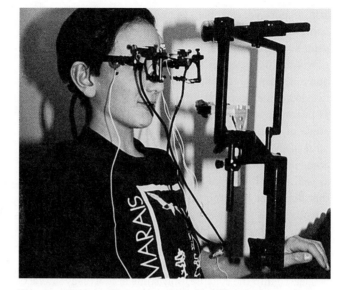

This apparatus is used to assess a person's ability to track a moving target. This ability is impaired in both people with schizophrenia and their relatives, suggesting that eye tracking is a genetic marker for the disorder. Courtesy Dr William Iacono, University of Minnesota.

Amphetamines can produce a state that closely resembles paranoid schizophrenia, and they can exacerbate the symptoms of schizophrenia (Angrist, Lee, & Gershon, 1974). Amphetamines cause the release of catecholamines, including norepinephrine and dopamine, into the synaptic cleft and prevent their inactivation. We can be relatively confident that the psychosis-inducing effects of amphetamines are a result of increasing dopamine rather than of increasing norepinephrine, because antipsychotics are antidotes to amphetamine psychosis.

Based on the data just reviewed, researchers at first assumed that schizophrenia was caused by an excess of dopamine. But as other studies progressed, this assumption did not

FIGURE 11.3 Conformation of (a) chlorpromazine, an antipsychotic, and (b) dopamine, and (c) their superimposition, determined by X-ray crystallographic analysis. Chlorpromazine blocks impulse transmission by dopamine by fitting into its receptor sites. Adapted from Horn and Snyder (1971)

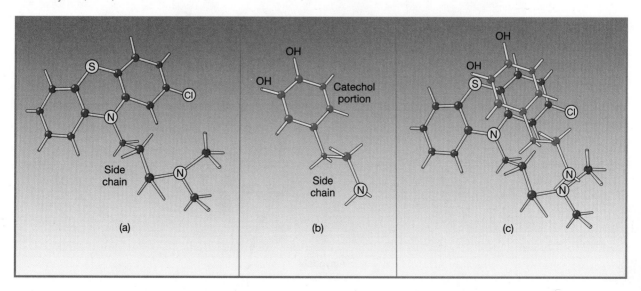

gain support. For example, the major metabolite of dopamine, homovanillic acid (HVA), was not found in greater amounts in people with schizophrenia (Bowers, 1974). Such data, plus improved technologies for studying neurochemical variables in humans, have led researchers to propose excess or oversensitive dopamine receptors, rather than a high level of dopamine, as factors in schizophrenia. Research on the antipsychotics' mode of action suggests that the dopamine receptors are a more likely locus of disorder than the level of dopamine itself. Some post-mortem studies of brains of schizophrenic people, as well as PET scans of schizophrenic people, have revealed that dopamine receptors are greater in number or are hypersensitive in some people with schizophrenia (e.g., Goldsmith, Shapiro, & Joyce, 1997). Having too many dopamine receptors would be functionally akin to having too much dopamine. The reason is that when dopamine (or any neurotransmitter) is released into the synapse, only some of it actually interacts with postsynaptic receptors. Having more receptors gives a greater opportunity for the dopamine that is released to stimulate a receptor.

Excess dopamine receptors may not be responsible for all the symptoms of schizophrenia; in fact, they appear to be related mainly to positive symptoms. Some studies have shown, for example, that amphetamines do not worsen the symptoms of all clients (e.g., Kornetsky, 1976); one study reported that symptoms actually lessen after an amphetamine has been administered (van Kammen et al., 1977). Furthermore, antipsychotics improve only some of the symptoms of schizophrenia. These divergent results are related to the positive-negative symptom distinction noted earlier. Amphetamines worsen positive symptoms and lessen negative ones. Antipsychotics lessen positive symptoms, but their effect on negative symptoms is less clear; some studies show no benefit (e.g., Haracz, 1982), while others show a reduction in negative symptoms (e.g., van Kammen, Hommer, & Malas, 1987).

Subsequent developments in the dopamine theory (e.g., Davis et al., 1991) expanded its scope. The key change involved the recognition of differences among the neural pathways that use dopamine as a transmitter. The excess dopamine activity that is thought to be most relevant to schizophrenia is localized in the mesolimbic pathway (see Figure 11.4), and the therapeutic effects of antipsychotics on positive symptoms occur by blocking dopamine receptors there, thereby lowering activity in this neural system.

The mesocortical dopamine pathway begins in the same brain region as the mesolimbic, but it projects to the prefrontal cortex. The prefrontal cortex also projects to limbic areas that are innervated by dopamine. These dopamine neurons

FIGURE 11.4 The brain and schizophrenia. The mesocortical pathway begins in the ventral tegmental area and projects to the prefrontal cortex. The mesolimbic pathway also begins in the ventral tegmental area, but projects to the hypothalamus, amygdala, hippocampus, and nucleus accumbens. *Source*: Weinberger, Berman, & Illossky, 1988

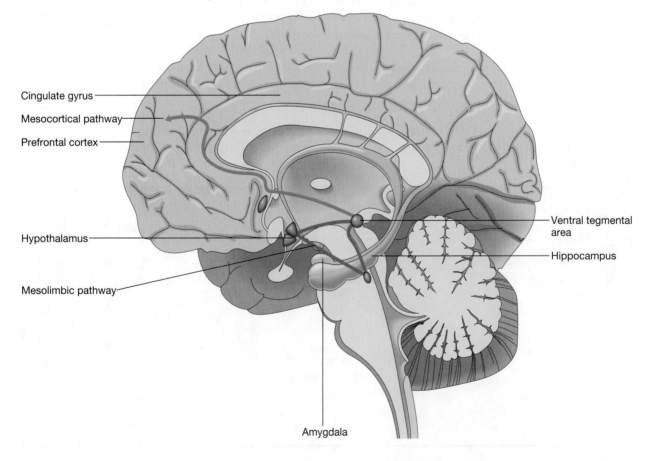

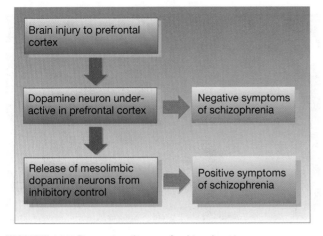

FIGURE 11.5 Dopamine theory of schizophrenia

in the prefrontal cortex may be underactive and thus fail to exert inhibitory control over the dopamine neurons in the limbic area, with the result that there is overactivity in the mesolimbic dopamine system. Because the prefrontal cortex is thought to be especially relevant to the negative symptoms of schizophrenia, the underactivity of the dopamine neurons in this part of the brain may also be the cause of the negative symptoms of schizophrenia (see Figure 11.5). This proposal has the advantage of allowing the simultaneous presence of positive and negative symptoms in the same person with schizophrenia. Furthermore, because antipsychotics do not have major effects on the dopamine neurons in the prefrontal cortex, we would expect them to be relatively ineffective as treatments for negative symptoms, and they are. When we examine research on structural abnormalities in the brains of people with schizophrenia, we will see some close connections between these two domains.

EVALUATION OF THE DOPAMINE THEORY Despite the positive evidence, the dopamine theory does not appear to be a complete theory of schizophrenia. For example, it takes several weeks for antipsychotics to gradually lessen positive symptoms, although they begin blocking dopamine receptors rapidly (Davis, 1978). This disjunction between the behavioural and pharmacological effects of antipsychotics is difficult to understand within the context of the theory. One possibility is that although antipsychotics do indeed block D2 receptors, their ultimate therapeutic effect may result from the effect this blockade has on other brain areas and other neurotransmitter systems (Cohen et al., 1997). It is also puzzling that to be therapeutically effective, antipsychotics must reduce dopamine levels or receptor activity to below normal, producing Parkinsonian side effects. According to the theory, reducing dopamine levels or receptor activity to normal should be sufficient for a therapeutic effect.

Although dopamine remains the most actively researched biochemical factor in schizophrenia, it is not likely to provide a complete explanation of the biochemistry of the disorder. Schizophrenia has widespread symptoms covering perception,

cognition, motor activity, and social behaviour. It is unlikely that a single neurotransmitter could account for all of them. Researchers are casting a broader biochemical net, moving away from an emphasis on dopamine.

OTHER NEUROTRANSMITTERS Newer drugs used in treating schizophrenia implicate neurotransmitters such as serotonin in the disorder. Dopamine neurons generally modulate the activity of other neural systems; for example, in the prefrontal cortex, they regulate GABA neurons. Similarly, serotonin neurons regulate dopamine neurons in the mesolimbic pathway. Thus, dopamine may be only one piece in a much more complicated puzzle. Glutamate, a transmitter that is widespread in the human brain, may also play a role (Carlsson et al., 1999). Low levels of glutamate have been found in cerebrospinal fluid of people with schizophrenia (Faustman et al., 1999), and post-mortem studies have revealed low levels of the enzyme needed to produce glutamate (Tsai et al., 1995). The street drug PCP can induce a psychotic state, including both positive and negative symptoms, in normal people. It produces this effect by interfering with one of glutamate's receptors (O'Donnell & Grace, 1998). Furthermore, a decrease in glutamate inputs from either the prefrontal cortex or the hippocampus (brain areas implicated in schizophrenia) to the corpus striatum (a temporal-lobe structure) can result in increased dopamine activity (O'Donnell & Grace, 1998). Glutamate and serotonin may well be at the forefront of these inquiries, perhaps in conjunction with dopamine activity.

SCHIZOPHRENIA AND THE BRAIN: STRUCTURE AND FUNCTION

The search for a brain abnormality that causes schizophrenia began as early as the syndrome was identified, but the research did not prove promising, as the different studies did not yield the same findings. Interest gradually waned over the years. In the last 25 years, however, spurred by a number of technological advances, the field has reawakened and yielded some promising evidence. Some people with schizophrenia have observable brain pathology.

ENLARGED VENTRICLES Post-mortem analyses of the brains of people with schizophrenia consistently reveal abnormalities in some areas of the brain, although the specific problems reported vary across studies and many of the findings are contradictory. The most consistent finding is of enlarged ventricles, which implies a loss of subcortical brain cells. Moderately consistent findings indicate structural problems in subcortical temporal-limbic areas, such as the hippocampus and the basal ganglia, and in the prefrontal and temporal cortex (e.g., Dwork, 1997).

Even more impressive are the images obtained in CT scan and MRI studies. Researchers were quick to apply these new tools to brains of living people with schizophrenia. These images of living brain tissue have most consistently revealed that some people, especially males (Nopoulos, Flaum, & Andreasen,

1997), have enlarged ventricles. Research also shows a reduction in cortical grey matter in both the temporal and frontal regions (Goldstein et al., 1999) and reduced volume in basal ganglia (e.g., the caudate nucleus) and limbic structures (e.g., Velakoulis et al., 1999), suggesting deterioration or atrophy of brain tissue. Further evidence concerning large ventricles comes from an MRI study of 15 pairs of MZ twins who were discordant for schizophrenia (Suddath et al., 1990). For 12 of the 15 pairs, the twin with schizophrenia could be identified by simple visual inspection of the scan. Because the twins were genetically identical, these data suggest that the origin of these brain abnormalities may not be genetic.

Large ventricles in people with schizophrenia are correlated with impaired performance on neuropsychological tests, poor adjustment prior to the onset of the disorder, and poor response to drug treatment (e.g., Andreasen et al., 1982). A Canadian study found that large ventricles can be detected both in people with a first episode of schizophrenia and in people with chronic schizophrenia. It is likely that the large ventricles have a neurodevelopmental origin and are not progressive. Thus, enlarged ventricles do not simply reflect chronic, untreated schizophrenia (see Malla, Mittal, et al., 2002). The extent to which the ventricles are enlarged, however, is modest, and many clients do not differ from normal people in this respect. Furthermore, enlarged ventricles are not specific to schizophrenia, as they are also evident in the CT scans of people with other psychoses, such as bipolar disorder (e.g., Zipursky et al., 1997). Finally, a review of evidence on the diagnostic yield of CTs and MRIs in first-episode psychosis (Goulet, Deschamps, Evoy, & Trudel, 2009), including people hospitalized at the Centre Hospitalier Universitaire de Sherbrooke in Quebec, concluded, "Structural brain imaging is unlikely to show causal neurological anomalies in first-episode psychosis in otherwise healthy people" (p. 493).

THE PREFRONTAL CORTEX A variety of data suggest that the prefrontal cortex is of particular importance in schizophrenia.

- The prefrontal cortex is known to play a role in behaviours such as speech, decision-making, and willed action, all of which are disrupted in schizophrenia (e.g., Zakzanis, Troyer, Rich, & Heinrichs, 2000).
- Lack of illness awareness is related to poorer neuropsychological performance more often in clients with schizophrenia than in bipolar participants, supporting the hypothesis that lack of awareness is related to defective frontal-lobe functioning. A meta-analysis found a small negative association between insight and global positive and negative symptoms of schizophrenia (Mintz, Dobson, & Romney, 2003).
- MRI studies have shown reductions in grey matter in the prefrontal cortex (e.g., Buchanan et al., 1998).
- In a type of functional imaging in which glucose metabolism is studied in various brain regions while clients perform psychological tests, clients with schizophrenia have shown

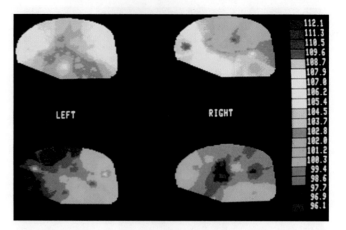

Differences in regional cerebral blood flow for each hemisphere between people diagnosed with schizophrenia (*bottom*) and normal individuals (*top*). The values shown were scored as the percentage change in cerebral blood flow from a control task to the Wisconsin Card Sorting Test, which was expected to activate the prefrontal cortex. The normal participants showed greater prefrontal cortical activation as indexed by the "hotter" colour of this brain region. *Source*: Weinberger, Berman, & Illowsky, 1988.

low metabolic rates in the prefrontal cortex (Buchsbaum et al., 1984). Glucose metabolism in the prefrontal cortex has also been studied while clients are performing neuropsychological tests of prefrontal function. Because the tests place demands on the prefrontal cortex, glucose metabolism normally goes up as energy is used. People with schizophrenia do poorly on the tests and also fail to show activation in the prefrontal region (e.g., Fletcher et al., 1998).

- Failure to show frontal activation has also been detected by the fMRI (e.g., MacDonald & Carter, 2003). In a recent study, Ragland et al. (2009) conducted a meta-analysis of functional imaging studies that contrasted people with schizophrenia and "healthy" volunteers during episodic encoding and retrieval. Clients with schizophrenia showed less prefrontal activation (prominent dysfunction) in specific areas relative to comparison participants, suggesting that "cognitive control deficits strongly contribute to episodic memory impairment in schizophrenia" (Ragland et al., 2009, p. 863).
- The frontal hypoactivation is less pronounced in the non-schizophrenic twin of discordant MZ pairs, again suggesting that this brain dysfunction may not have a genetic origin (Torrey et al., 1994). Failure to show frontal activation is related to the severity of negative symptoms (O'Donnell & Grace, 1998) and thus parallels the work on dopamine underactivity in the frontal cortex already discussed.
- In an interesting new direction, Joyal et al. (2007) used fMRI to test the hypothesis that violent people with schizophrenia and comorbid anti-social personality and substance use disorders show a different pattern of prefrontal functioning than seriously violent people with schizophrenia only. The results suggested that violent people with schizophrenia and a history of anti-social and/or substance use manifest neural dysfunction affecting basal or orbital parts of the prefrontal cortex.

CONGENITAL AND DEVELOPMENTAL CONSIDERATIONS

A possible interpretation of these brain abnormalities is that they are the consequence of damage during gestation or birth. Waddington and colleagues (2008) used the Congenital Anomalies data set in the Prenatal Determinants of Schizophrenia study to conduct a systematic, prospective examination of the relation between congenital anomalies, early associated functional impairments, and risk of schizophrenia in adulthood. It was reported that the presence at birth or in infancy of "craniofacial/midline anomalies and/or early functional impairments that commonly occur as a symptom of CNS [central nervous system] anomaly" were associated with a doubling of the risk for schizophrenia spectrum disorder (a group or array of disorders related to and including schizophrenia). These anomalies involve areas that share the embryological origins of the CNS, especially frontal cortical regions.

Many studies have shown high rates of delivery complications when they were born in women with schizophrenia; such complications could have led to a reduced supply of oxygen to the brain, resulting in damage (e.g., Verdoux et al., 1997). These obstetrical complications do not raise the risk of schizophrenia in everyone who experiences them; rather, the risk is increased in those who experience complications and have a genetic predisposition (Cannon & Mednick, 1993).

Although the data are not entirely consistent, another possibility is that a virus invades the brain and damages it during fetal development (e.g., Mednick, Huttonen, & Machon, 1994). In 1957, Helsinki, Finland, experienced an epidemic of influenza virus. Researchers examined rates of schizophrenia among adults who had likely been exposed during their mothers' pregnancies. People who had been exposed to the virus during the second trimester of pregnancy had much higher rates than those who had been exposed in either of the other trimesters or in non-exposed control adults. Subsequently, Brown et al. (2004) reported that serologically documented influenza exposure during early to mid-gestation was associated with a three-fold increase of schizophrenia, and that first trimester exposure conferred a seven-fold increased risk. These findings are intriguing. Cortical development is in a critical stage of growth during the second trimester—neurons are being produced in the rudimentary brain called the neural tube. These neurons then have to move to their appropriate location, passing through layers of cells as they do so. Perhaps this process of cell migration is disrupted in people who later develop schizophrenia.

Consistent with this speculation, post-mortem analyses of neurons in the brains of individuals with schizophrenia have shown reduced numbers of cells in the outer layers of the cortex in both the prefrontal and the temporal areas (Akbarian et al., 1995). Similarly, a widespread thinning of the cortex of people with schizophrenia has been reported, apparently resulting from loss of dendrites and axons (Selemon, Rajkowska, & Goldman-Rakic, 1995), and neurons in the frontal cortex have been shown to be smaller than normal in people with schizophrenia (Rajkowska, Selemen, & Goldman-Rakic, 1998).

Perhaps the influenza virus is not a major cause of brain damage in schizophrenia. An intriguing alternative possibility proposed by Yolken et al. (2000) is that an as-yet unidentified human endogenous retrovirus attacks the nervous system and incorporates itself into the cellular genome code of the infected person. This now-endogenous altered gene code is later vertically translated in Mendelian fashion by passing it onto offspring. This cryptic code may later be activated by certain biological events, such as puberty or exposure to other microbes or chemicals. Torrey and Yolken (2000) also discuss possible familial transmission of a virus responsible for at least some types of schizophrenia.

Although rare, the onset of positive symptoms can occur before the age of 12 (Nicholson et al., 2000). Children who exhibit this early onset tend to show clear evidence of general brain deterioration consistent with the effects of a CNS virus. For example, childhood-onset schizophrenia children show (on average) an approximately 10% relative brain tissue loss at age 12; however, this proportion increases to the 20–25% range by age 18 (Thompson et al., 2001).

Brown (2006) and Brown and Derkits (2010) reviewed the accumulating evidence that suggests that prenatal exposure to infections, including influenza, rubella, and toxoplasmosis (an intracellular parasite), and maternal cytokines (known to mediate the host response to infection), are associated with increased risk of schizophrenia. Brown and Derkits (2010) noted that it is important to identify pathogenic mechanisms and to investigate interactions between infection and susceptibility genes. A large Swedish study by Dalman and colleagues (2008) addressed limitations of past research and reported a 50% increased risk of schizophrenia among adults who were exposed in childhood (birth to age 12) to viral CNS infections. There was no increased risk following exposure to bacterial CNS infections. Subsequently, Clarke and colleagues (2009) identified women in Helsinki who received treatment during pregnancy for an upper urinary tract infection and who also had a positive family history of psychotic disorders. A synergy analysis suggested that an estimated 38 to 46% of their offspring who developed schizophrenia did so due to the synergistic action of both risk factors. The authors concluded that their findings are consistent with a mechanism of gene-environment interaction. If infectious causes for schizophrenia can be definitively shown, it has implications for the prevention of schizophrenia since there are many preventive strategies for infections, such as antibiotics, vaccination, and simple hygiene.

If, as the findings suggest, the brains of people with schizophrenia are damaged early in development, why does the disorder begin many years later, in adolescence or early adulthood? Weinberger (1987) proposed that the brain injury interacts with normal brain development and that the prefrontal cortex is a brain structure that matures late, typically in adolescence. Thus, an injury to this area may remain silent until the period of development when the prefrontal cortex begins to play a larger role in behaviour. Notably, dopamine activity also peaks in adolescence, which may further set the stage for the onset of symptoms.

CONTEMPORARY RESEARCH Work on the relationship of the brain and schizophrenia is proceeding rapidly. Recognizing that the symptoms implicate many areas of the brain, research has moved away from trying to find some highly specific "lesion" and is examining neural systems and the way different areas of the brain interact with one another. This work calls attention to the possible role of a wider range of brain structures (e.g., the thalamus, cerebellum) in schizophrenia (e.g., Levitt et al., 1999). Indeed, quantitative and conceptual reviews such as those conducted in Canada by Zakzanis and Heinrichs and their associates (e.g., Zakzanis, Poulin, Hansen, & Jolic, 2000) led to the conclusion that the specific role of deficits in the temporal lobes has been overstated and that more diffuse dysfunction exists. Moreover, the extent of a more broad-based cognitive impairment needs to be examined with respect to the heterogeneity of schizophrenia. It may be the case that specific deficits exist in only a subset of those afflicted with schizophrenia.

Nonetheless, a meta-analysis of quantitative, non-invasive MRI studies reported a subtle (4%) but significant bilateral hippocampal volume reduction in people with schizophrenia (Nelson et al., 1998). A subsequent meta-analysis (Wright et al., 2000) concluded that regional volume reductions are especially marked in bilateral medial temporal lobe regions (i.e., amygdala, hippocampus, and parahippocampal areas). Related to this, van Erp et al. (2004) reported finding reduced hippocampus volume among twins with schizophrenia relative to twins without schizophrenia. Sim et al. (2006) followed up on the frequent finding of smaller medial temporal lobe volume by investigating the relative contributions of the hippocampus and three surrounding cortical regions (entorhinal cortex, perirhinal cortex, and parahippocampal cortex). They reported that clients had smaller overall medial temporal lobe volumes relative to controls, but that the volume difference was not specific for either region or hemisphere and concluded that the findings "have important implications for studying the functional role of the hippocampus and surrounding cortical regions in schizophrenia" (Sim et al., 2006, p. 332). Brambilo and colleagues (Brambilla et al., 2007) used an MRI procedure and determined that reduced cerebral blood volume accompanies brain size decrement in schizophrenia and proposed that chronic cerebral blood volume eventually results in neuronal loss and cognitive impairments.

Recently, a special theme issue of *Schizophrenia Bulletin* (see Potkin & Ford, 2009) presented a series of related articles that described fMRI data that were collected as part of a multi-site brain imaging consortium (the Functional Imaging Biomedical Information Research Network or FBIRN) on the same participant population. A unique feature is that the publications indicate the power of multi-site neuroimaging since the consortium allowed a larger sample (125 clients and 125 controls) from a broader range of clients than could have been possible from a single site. The studies demonstrated widespread cortical dysfunction in schizophrenia. In their summary of several of the studies, Potkin and Ford (2009)

suggested that "abnormal circuitry characterizes schizophrenic performance in both auditory target detection and memory retrieval, and that clients who hallucinate have reduced left auditory cortical activation on both tasks" (Potkin & Ford, 2009, p. 15). Anatomical differences between clients and controls were reported as was the identification of six genes that have functions related to forebrain development and stress responses in schizophrenia.

A growing body of work suggests that schizophrenia is related to dysfunction of functionally and anatomically connected networks of brain regions (see Tregellas, 2009 for a summary). For example, Wexler et al. (2009) reported smaller white matter volumes in neuropsychologically impaired participants with schizophrenia relative to a group of schizophrenics with near-normal cognition and healthy subjects. White matter forms the physical connections of the functional networks. The authors concluded that white matter pathology plays a critical role in the cognitive impairments seen in schizophrenia. In the future we can expect to learn more about other important developments in our understanding of brain structure and function in people with schizophrenia.

PSYCHOLOGICAL STRESS AND SCHIZOPHRENIA

We have discussed several possible neurobiological diatheses for schizophrenia, but more than biology is responsible. Psychological stress plays a key role by interacting with a biological vulnerability (genetic or neurobiological) to produce schizophrenia. Data show that, as with other disorders, increases in life stress increase the likelihood of a relapse (e.g., Hirsch et al., 1996). Moreover, clients who take part in a stress-management program are less likely to be readmitted to the hospital in the year following treatment, especially if they had attended treatment sessions regularly (Norman et al., 2002). Philips et al. (2007) reviewed the available research and concluded that there is only limited evidence that stressful experiences precipitate a psychotic episode due to serious methodological limitations, including retrospective designs, inadequate control groups, over-reliance on the life events approach to assessing stress, and, especially, failure to consider a person's appraisal of the meaning and potential impact of events or personal characteristics that might mediate any relations. Further, it was concluded that the physiological mechanisms that underlie a stress-psychosis onset relation have not been determined. With these limitations in mind, we turn now to the role of life stress in the actual development of schizophrenia. Two stressors that have played an important part in schizophrenia research are social class and the family.

SOCIAL CLASS AND SCHIZOPHRENIA We know that the highest rates of schizophrenia are found in central city areas inhabited by people in the lowest socio-economic class (e.g., Harvey et al., 1996; Hollingshead & Redlich, 1958). The relation between social class and schizophrenia does not show a continuous progression of higher rates of schizophrenia as the social class becomes lower. Rather, there is a decidedly sharp difference between the number of people with schizophrenia in the lowest social class and the number in other social classes. In the classic 10-year Hollingshead and Redlich (1958) study in New Haven, Connecticut, the rate of schizophrenia was found to be twice as high in the lowest social class as in the second-lowest class. This finding was confirmed cross-culturally by similar community studies carried out in countries such as Denmark, Norway, and the United Kingdom (Kohn, 1968).

The correlations between social class and schizophrenia are consistent, but they are difficult to interpret in causal terms. Some people believe that stressors associated with being in a low social class may cause or contribute to the development of schizophrenia—the **sociogenic hypothesis**. The degrading treatment a person receives from others, the low level of education, and the lack of rewards and opportunity taken together may make membership in the lowest social class such a stressful experience that an individual—at least one who is predisposed—develops schizophrenia. Alternatively, the stressors encountered by those in the lowest social class could be biological; for example, we know that children of mothers whose nutrition during pregnancy was poor are at increased risk for schizophrenia (Susser et al., 1996).

Another explanation of the correlation between schizophrenia and low social class is the **social-selection theory**, which reverses the direction of causality between social class and schizophrenia. During the course of their developing psychosis, people with schizophrenia may drift into the poverty-ridden areas of the city. The growing cognitive and motivational problems besetting these individuals may so impair their earning capabilities that they cannot afford to live elsewhere. Or, they may choose to move to areas where little social pressure will be brought to bear on them and they can escape intense social relationships.

One way of resolving the conflict between these opposing theories is to study the social mobility of people with schizophrenia. Consistent with the social-selection theory, some studies (e.g., Turner & Wagonfeld, 1967) found that

people with schizophrenia are downwardly mobile in occupational status. But an equal number of studies have shown that people with schizophrenia are not downwardly mobile (e.g., Dunham, 1965). Clearly, this approach has not resolved the issue. Kohn (1968) suggested another way of examining this question: Are the fathers of people with schizophrenia also from the lowest social class? If they are, this could be considered evidence in favour of the sociogenic hypothesis that lower-class status is conducive to schizophrenia, for class would be shown to precede schizophrenia. If the fathers are from a higher social class, the social-selection hypothesis would be the better explanation. Turner and Wagonfeld (1967) found evidence for the social-selection hypothesis: of 26 clients in the lowest social class, only four had fathers in the lowest class.

A subsequent study in Israel employed a new methodology, simultaneously investigating both social class and ethnic background (Dohrenwend et al., 1992). The rates of schizophrenia were examined in Israeli Jews of European ethnic background and in more recent immigrants to Israel from North Africa and the Middle East. Those in the latter group experience considerable racial prejudice and discrimination. The sociogenic hypothesis would predict that because all social classes of this disadvantaged ethnic group experience high levels of stress, all should have consistently higher than normal rates of schizophrenia. However, this pattern did not emerge, supporting the social-selection theory.

In sum, the data are more supportive of the social-selection theory than of the sociogenic hypothesis. But we should not conclude that the social environment plays no role in schizophrenia. For example, the prevalence of schizophrenia among Africans from the Caribbean who remain in their native country is much lower than among those who have emigrated to London (Bhugra et al., 1996)—perhaps caused by the stress associated with trying to assimilate into a new culture. Cantor-Graae (2007) reviewed evidence since 1996 and argues that research on migrants to western Europe supports the hypothesis that social factors do contribute to the development of schizophrenia. For example, the extremely high risk for schizophrenia in second-generation immigrants is difficult to explain solely on the basis of biological and genetic factors. Studies also implicate childhood exposure to social adversity, and neighbourhood and urban effects as risk factors. She proposed a mechanism by which social factors could generate psychotic symptoms: social defeat or social exclusion might lead to alterations in CNS dopamine sensitivity and the regulation of dopaminergic systems.

THE FAMILY AND SCHIZOPHRENIA Early theorists regarded family relationships, especially those between a mother and her son, as crucial in the development of schizophrenia. At one time, the view was so prevalent that the term **schizophrenogenic mother** was coined to describe the supposedly cold and dominant, conflict-inducing parent who

The prevalence of schizophrenia is highest among people in the lowest socio-economic class. Seaton House in Toronto provides a safe place for those who are homeless and suffering from severe mental illness, including schizophrenia. Courtesy of Seaton House.

was said to produce schizophrenia in her offspring (Fromm-Reichmann, 1948). These mothers were characterized as rejecting, overprotective, self-sacrificing, impervious to the feelings of others, rigid and moralistic about sex, and fearful of intimacy—a very destructive view since it basically blamed the mother (or other family members) for a severe psychiatric disorder in a child. Controlled studies evaluating the theory have not yielded supporting data.

Some findings do suggest that the faulty communications of parents play a role in the etiology of schizophrenia. For example, in a longitudinal study of adolescents with behaviour problems, a family communication pattern characterized by hostility and poor communication predicted the later onset of schizophrenia or schizophrenia-related disorders (Norton, 1982). However, it does not appear that communication deviance is a specific etiological factor for schizophrenia, since parents of manic clients are equally high on this variable (Miklowitz, 1985).

Further evidence favouring some role for the family comes from an adoption study by Tienari and his colleagues (1994) in Finland. A large sample of adopted offspring of mothers with schizophrenia was studied along with a control group of adopted children. Data were collected on various aspects of family life in the adoptive families, and these family data were related to the adjustment of the children. The families were categorized into levels of maladjustment. Long-term follow-up confirmed that more serious psychopathology was evident among the adoptees if they were reared in a disturbed family environment; children having a biological parent with schizophrenia showed a greater increase in psychopathology than did the control participants who were reared in a disturbed family environment. A problem in interpretation remains! The disturbed family environment could be a response to a disturbed child. Thus, we cannot conclude that an etiological role for the family has been established.

Relapse and the Role of the Family A series of studies initiated in London, England, indicate that the family can have an important impact on the adjustment of people with schizophrenia after they leave the hospital. Brown et al. (1966) conducted a nine-month follow-up study of a sample of clients with schizophrenia who returned to live with their families after discharge. Interviews were conducted with parents or spouses before discharge and rated for the number of critical comments made about the client and for expressions of hostility toward or emotional overinvolvement with him or her. The following statement is an example of a critical comment made by a father about his daughter's behaviour. The father claims that his daughter is deliberately symptomatic to avoid housework: "My view is that Maria acts this way so my wife doesn't give her any responsibilities around the house" (Weisman et al., 1998). On the basis of this variable, referred to as **expressed emotion (EE)** by Brown and colleagues, families were divided into two groups: those revealing a great deal of expressed emotion, called high-EE families, and those

revealing little, called low-EE families. At the end of the follow-up period, 10% of the clients returning to low-EE homes had relapsed. In marked contrast, 58% of the clients returning to high-EE homes had gone back to the hospital!

A meta-analysis of research findings indicates that the environment into which clients are discharged has great bearing on how soon they are re-hospitalized (Butzlaff & Hooley, 1998). It has also been found that negative symptoms of schizophrenia are the ones most likely to elicit critical comments (King, 2000) and that relatives who make the most critical comments tend to view the clients as being able to control their symptoms (e.g., Provencher & Fincham, 2000). Family research conducted in Quebec established further that high-EE mothers are highly sensitive to excitement and depression in the client and report a high level of burden associated with their child's illness (King et al., 2003). What is not yet clear is exactly how to interpret the effects of EE. Is EE causal, or do these critical comments reflect a reaction to the clients' behaviour? For example, if the condition of a person with schizophrenia begins to deteriorate, does family concern and involvement increase? Indeed, bizarre or dangerous behaviour by the client might seem to warrant the setting of limits and other familial efforts that could increase the level of expressed emotion.

Research indicates that both interpretations of the operation of EE—the causal and the reactive—may be correct (Rosenfarb et al., 1994). Recently discharged schizophrenia clients and their high- or low-EE families were observed as they engaged in a discussion of a family problem. Two key findings emerged:

1. The expression of unusual thoughts by the clients ("If that kid bites you, you'll get rabies") elicited higher levels of critical comments by family members who had previously been characterized as high in EE.
2. In high-EE families, critical comments by family members led to increased expression of unusual thoughts.

Thus, this study found a bidirectional relationship: critical comments by members of high-EE families elicited the increased expression of unusual thoughts by clients; and unusual thoughts expressed by clients led to increased critical comments in high-EE families. Another study conducted in Montreal is more consistent with the position that critical comments and emotional overinvolvement may be responses to schizophrenia (i.e., effects) rather than causes (see King, 2000). It is important not to minimize the major effects that a disturbed family member can have on other members of the family and on the overall functioning of the family. Further, we need to consider a "third variable" issue, namely, relapse on the part of the person with schizophrenia and disturbed communication in the family could both be caused by genetic factors associated with the transmission of an increased risk for schizophrenia. Thus, other family members could appear "strange" because they have some, but not all, of the gene code for full-blown schizophrenia.

How could stress, such as a high level of EE, increase the symptoms of schizophrenia and precipitate relapses? Some researchers have related the effects of stress on the hypothalamic-pituitary-adrenal (HPA) axis to the dopamine theory (Walker & DiForio, 1997). Stress is known to activate the HPA axis, causing cortisol to be secreted. In turn, cortisol is known to increase dopamine activity and may thereby increase the symptoms of schizophrenia. Furthermore, heightened dopamine activity itself can increase HPA activation, which may make a person overly sensitive to stress. Thus, the theory suggests a bidirectional relationship between HPA activation and dopamine activity.

DEVELOPMENTAL/HIGH-RISK STUDIES OF SCHIZOPHRENIA

What are people who develop schizophrenia like before their symptoms begin? An early method of answering this question was to construct developmental histories by examining the childhood records of those who had later become schizophrenic. Individuals who became schizophrenic were different from their contemporaries even before any serious problems were noted in their behaviour. In the 1960s, Albee and Lane and their colleagues repeatedly found that children who later developed schizophrenia had lower IQs than did members of various control groups (e.g., Lane & Albee, 1965). Investigations of the social behaviour of preschizophrenic people yielded some interesting findings, as well. For example, teachers described preschizophrenic boys as disagreeable in childhood and preschizophrenic girls as passive (e.g., Watt, 1974). Both men and women were described as delinquent and withdrawn in childhood (Berry, 1967). Researchers have also examined home movies of family life taken before the onset of a child's schizophrenia (e.g., Walker, Davis, & Savoie, 1994). Compared with their siblings who did not later become schizophrenic, preschizophrenic children showed poorer motor skills and more expressions of negative affect.

As intriguing as these findings are, the major limitation of such developmental research is that the data were not originally collected with the intention of describing preschizophrenic people or of predicting the development of schizophrenia from childhood behaviour. More specific information is required if developmental histories are to provide clear evidence regarding etiology. The high-risk method can yield this information. The first such study of schizophrenia was begun in the 1960s by Sarnoff Mednick and Fini Schulsinger (1968). They chose Denmark because the Danish registries of all people make it possible to keep track of them for long periods of time. Mednick and Schulsinger selected as their high-risk subjects 207 young people whose mothers had chronic schizophrenia. The researchers decided that the mother should be the parent with the disorder because paternity is not always easy to determine. Then, 104 low-risk subjects, individuals whose mothers did not have schizophrenia, were matched to the high-risk subjects on variables such as sex, age, father's occupation, rural or urban residence, years of education, and institutional

upbringing vs. rearing by the family. In 1972, the now-grown men and women were the subject of follow-up for a number of measures, including a diagnostic battery. Fifteen of the high-risk subjects were diagnosed with schizophrenia; none of the control men and women was so diagnosed. Looking back to the information collected on the subjects when they were children, the investigators found that several circumstances predicted the later onset of schizophrenia.

These data suggest that the etiology of schizophrenia may differ for positive- and negative-symptom clients. In subsequent analyses, the clients with schizophrenia were divided into two groups: those with predominantly positive and those with predominantly negative symptoms (Cannon, Mednick, & Parnas, 1990). Variables predicting schizophrenia were different for the two groups. Negative-symptom schizophrenia was preceded by a history of pregnancy and birth complications and by a failure to show electrodermal responses to simple stimuli. Positive-symptom schizophrenia was preceded by a history of family instability, such as separation from parents and placement in foster homes or institutions.

In the wake of this pioneering study, several other high-risk investigations were undertaken, some of which have also yielded information concerning the possible causes of adult psychopathology. The New York High-Risk Study found that a composite measure of attentional dysfunction predicted behavioural disturbance at follow-up (Cornblatt & Erlenmeyer-Kimling, 1985). Furthermore, low IQ was a characteristic of the first high-risk children to be hospitalized (Erlenmeyer-Kimling & Cornblatt, 1987). In an Israeli study, poor neurobehavioural functioning (poor concentration, poor verbal ability, lack of motor control and coordination) predicted schizophrenia-like outcomes, as did earlier interpersonal problems (Marcus et al., 1987).

Sarnoff Mednick, a psychologist at the University of Southern California, pioneered the use of the high-risk method for studying schizophrenia. He has also contributed to the hypothesis that a maternal viral infection is implicated in this disorder. Courtesy of Sarnoff Mednick.

An Australian high-risk study was initiated by Yung and colleagues (see Yung, Phillips, Hok, & McGorry, 2004). The research group followed people between the ages of 14 and 30 who were referred to a special clinic in the early 1990s and identified as at "ultra" high risk (UHR) of developing a psychotic disorder. Since the study began, 41 of the 104 participants developed psychotic disorders, including schizophrenia (Yung et al., 2004). A cross-sectional and longitudinal MRI comparison determined that participants who developed a psychotic disorder, relative to those who did not, had reduced grey matter volumes, suggesting that lower grey matter volume predates the onset of psychotic disorders, including schizophrenia (also see Lui et al., 2009). Another study of these people (Mason et al., 2004) found that responses to a measure of the experience of life events did not predict the onset of psychosis in the UHR group. Unfortunately measurement was limited to the quantitative assessment of life events (see Phillips et al., 2007). Phillips et al. (2007) concluded that "Longitudinal studies with high risk cohorts might provide clearer information about the process underlying the onset of psychosis and could influence the development of preventive interventions" (p. 314).

THERAPIES FOR SCHIZOPHRENIA

The puzzling, often frightening array of symptoms displayed by people with schizophrenia makes treatment difficult. The history of psychopathology is in many respects a history of humankind's efforts, often brutal and unenlightened, to deal with schizophrenia. Although some of the profoundly disturbed people confined centuries ago in foul asylums may have suffered from problems as prosaic as syphilis, there seems little doubt that many, if examined now, would carry a diagnosis of schizophrenia. Today we know a good deal about the nature and etiology of schizophrenia, but although we can treat its symptoms somewhat effectively, a cure remains elusive.

With the notable exception of an intensive behaviour-therapy project described in Focus on Discovery 11.2, research indicates, for the most part, that traditional hospital care does little to effect meaningful, enduring changes in the majority of mentally disordered people (see description of mental hospitals in Chapter 1). Studies designed specifically to follow clients with schizophrenia after discharge from a hospital show generally poor outcomes (Robinson et al., 1999).

FOCUS ON DISCOVERY 11.2
A CLASSIC BEHAVIOUR THERAPY PROJECT WITH HOSPITALIZED CLIENTS WITH SCHIZOPHRENIA

Although the trend has been to have people with schizophrenia spend as little time as possible in a psychiatric hospital, even with advances in psychoactive medication, there are still many people living in institutional settings, some for many years. As described in Chapter 2, behaviour therapists introduced an innovation known as the "token economy" into hospital settings in the 1960s. The most comprehensive and impressive of these efforts was reported by Gordon Paul and Robert Lentz (1977). Because this project was a milestone in the treatment of schizophrenia and an exemplar of comparative-therapy research, we describe it here in some detail.

The long-term, regressed, and chronic schizophrenia clients in the program were the most severely debilitated institutionalized adults ever studied systematically. Some clients screamed for long periods, some were mute, many were incontinent, a few assaultive. Most of them no longer used silverware, and some buried their faces in their food. The clients were matched for age, sex, socio-economic background, symptoms, and length of hospitalization and then assigned to one of three wards: social learning (behavioural—basically a token economy), milieu therapy, and routine hospital management. Each ward had 28 residents. The two treatment wards shared ambitious objectives: to teach self-care, housekeeping, communication, and vocational skills; to reduce symptomatic behaviour; and to release clients to the community.

SOCIAL-LEARNING WARD

Located in a new mental health centre, the social-learning ward operated on a token economy that embraced all aspects of the residents' lives. The clients' appearance had to pass muster in 11 specific ways each morning for them to earn a token. Well-made beds, good behaviour at mealtime, classroom participation, and socializing during free periods were other means of earning tokens. Residents learned through modelling, shaping, prompting, and instructions. They were also taught to communicate better with one another, and they participated in problem-solving groups. Tokens were a necessity, for they purchased meals, as well as small luxuries. In addition to living by the rules of the token economy, individuals received behavioural treatments tailored to their needs—for example, assertion training to deal with a specific interpersonal conflict they might be having with a staff member. Residents were kept busy 85% of their waking hours learning to behave better.

MILIEU-THERAPY WARD

This ward operated according to the principles of Jones's (1953) therapeutic community, an approach reminiscent of Pinel's moral treatment of the late eighteenth century. These residents, too, were kept busy 85% of their waking hours. Both individually and as a group, they were expected to act responsibly and to participate in decisions about how the ward was to function. In general, they were treated more as normal individuals than as "incompetent mental patients." Staff members impressed on the residents their positive expectations and praised them for doing well. When clients behaved symptomatically, staff members stayed with them, making clear their expectation that the clients would soon behave more appropriately.

ROUTINE HOSPITAL MANAGEMENT

These clients continued their accustomed hospital existence in an older state institution, receiving custodial care and heavy antipsychotic medication. Except for the 5% of their waking hours occupied by occasional activity and recreational, occupational, and individual and group therapies, these people were on their own.

Before the program began, the staffs of the two treatment wards were carefully trained to adhere to detailed instructions in therapy manuals. Regular observations then confirmed that they were implementing the principles of a social-learning or a milieu-therapy program. Over the four and a half years of hospitalization and the one and a half years of follow-up, the clients were carefully evaluated at regular six-month intervals on the basis of structured interviews and meticulous, direct, behavioural observations.

The results? Both social learning and milieu therapy reduced positive and negative symptoms, with the social-learning ward achieving better results than the milieu ward on a number of measures. The residents had also acquired self-care, housekeeping, social, and vocational skills. The behaviour of members of these two groups within the institution was superior to that of the residents of the hospital ward, and by the end of treatment, more of them had been discharged. More than 10% of the social-learning clients and 7% of the milieu clients left the centre for independent living, while none of the hospital-treatment clients achieved this goal.

An interesting finding emerged concerning medication use. About 90% of the clients in all three groups were receiving antipsychotic drugs at the outset of the study. Over time, use among the routine hospital management group increased to 100%, while in the other two groups the percentage of clients on drugs dropped dramatically, to 18% in the milieu group and 11% in the social-learning ward. This is a remarkable finding, for the medical staff had assumed that without their medication, these chronic clients would be too difficult for the staff to manage. In addition, many clients from all three groups were discharged to community placements, such as boarding homes and halfway houses, where there was supervision but also considerably less restraint than they had experienced for an average of 17 years. Members of the social-learning group did significantly better at remaining in these community residences than did clients in the other two groups.

Considering how poorly these clients were functioning before this treatment project, these results are extraordinary. That the social-learning program was superior to the milieu program is also significant, for milieu treatment is used in many psychiatric hospitals. As implemented by Paul's team of clinicians, the milieu treatment provided clients with more attention than was given to those on the social-learning ward. This greater amount of attention would appear to control well for the positive expectancy effect of the social-learning therapy.

These results, though, should not be accepted as confirming the usefulness of token economies per se, for the social-learning therapy contained elements that went beyond operant conditioning of overt motor behaviour. Staff provided information to residents about appropriate behaviour and attempted verbally to clarify misconceptions. Paul (personal communication, 1981) relegated the token economy to a secondary, although not trivial, role. He saw it as a useful device for getting the attention of severely regressed clients in the initial stages of treatment. The token economy created the opportunity for his clients to acquire new information, or, in Paul's informal phrase, to "get good things into their heads."

Paul and Lentz never claimed that any one of the social-learning clients was cured. Although they were able to live outside the hospital, most continued to manifest many signs of mental disorder and few had gainful employment or participated in the social activities that most people take for granted. The outcome, however, is not to be underestimated: chronic clients, those shut away and forgotten by society in that era, can be resocialized and taught self-care. They can learn to behave normally enough to be discharged from mental institutions. This is a major achievement in mental health care. Reports published since the Paul and Lentz study support the effectiveness of social-learning programs (e.g., Paul, Stuve, & Cross, 1997).

A major problem with any kind of treatment for schizophrenia is that many clients lack insight into their impaired condition and refuse any treatment (Amador et al., 1994). As they don't believe they have a disorder, they don't see the need for professional intervention, particularly when it includes hospitalization or drugs. This is especially true of those with paranoid schizophrenia, who may regard any therapy as a threatening intrusion by hostile outside forces. Family members face a major challenge in getting their relatives into treatment, which is one reason they sometimes turn to involuntary hospitalization via civil commitment as a last resort or lobby for community treatment orders. Clinicians who treat schizophrenia also face numerous challenges, including risks of client suicide and the possibility of violent behaviour, nonadherence to the preferred treatment regimen, relapse of symptoms, and deterioration of functioning over time (CME Institute, 2007). The ultimate goal of treatment is to help the individual to remain in or re-enter and function in the community.

The American Psychiatric Association (2004) treatment guidelines for schizophrenia recommend a multi-point treatment course that consists of several strategies known to improve functional outcome:

1. Selection and application of antipsychotic medication to control acute psychotic symptoms, including strategies for maintaining adherence
2. Identification and treatment of comorbid disorders, including substance use and depressive disorders
3. Use of psychosocial treatment approaches with demonstrated effectiveness in improving symptoms and ability to function socially and vocationally

Psychosocial treatment strategies supported by the American Psychiatric Association include family interventions/psychoeducation, social skills training, CBT, assertive community treatment, and supported employment. Unfortunately, few of the psychosocial treatments are used frequently in the practice setting despite research demonstrations of beneficial symptomatic and functional outcomes (CME Institute, 2007).

BIOLOGICAL TREATMENTS

SHOCK AND PSYCHOSURGERY The general warehousing of people in mental hospitals earlier in the twentieth century, coupled with the shortage of professional staff, created a climate that allowed, perhaps even subtly encouraged, experimentation with radical biological interventions. In the early 1930s, the practice of inducing a coma with large dosages of insulin was introduced by Sakel (1938), who claimed that up to three quarters of the schizophrenics he treated showed significant improvement. Later findings were less encouraging, and insulin-coma therapy—which presented serious risks to health, including irreversible coma and death—was gradually abandoned. As discussed in Chapter 8, ECT was also used after its development in 1938 by Cerletti and Bini; it, too, proved to be only minimally effective.

In 1935, Egas Moñiz, a Portuguese psychiatrist, introduced the **prefrontal lobotomy**, a surgical procedure that destroys the tracts connecting the frontal lobes to lower centres of the brain. His initial reports claimed high rates of success (Moñiz, 1936), and for 20 years thereafter, thousands of people—not only those diagnosed with schizophrenia—underwent variations of psychosurgery. A related procedure known as a leukotomy is a more circumscribed and specific procedure than a lobotomy. The lobotomy procedure was used especially for those whose behaviour was violent. Many clients did indeed quiet down after undergoing a lobotomy and could even be discharged from hospitals. During the 1950s, however, this intervention fell into disrepute. After surgery, many clients became dull and listless and suffered serious losses in their cognitive capacities (e.g., becoming unable to carry on a coherent conversation with another person). This is not surprising given the destruction of parts of their brains believed responsible for thought. Overall, the principal reason for the abandonment of lobotomies was the introduction of drugs that seemed to reduce the behavioural and emotional excesses of many clients.

Scene from *One Flew Over the Cuckoo's Nest*. The character on whose shoulders Jack Nicholson is sitting was lobotomized in the film. Photofest.

DRUG THERAPIES Without question, the most important development in the treatment of schizophrenia was the advent in the 1950s of several medications collectively referred to as **antipsychotic drugs**. These drugs are also referred to as neuroleptics because they produce side effects similar to the symptoms of a neurological disease.

First-Generation (Conventional) Antipsychotic Drugs

One of the more frequently prescribed antipsychotic drugs in the past 50 years, phenothiazine, was first produced by a German chemist in the late nineteenth century. Not until the discovery in the 1940s of the antihistamines, which have a phenothiazine nucleus, did phenothiazines receive much attention. Reaching beyond their use to treat the common cold and asthma, the French surgeon Laborit pioneered the use of antihistamines to reduce surgical shock. He noticed that they made his patients somewhat sleepy and less fearful about the impending operation. Laborit's work encouraged pharmaceutical companies to re-examine antihistamines in light of their tranquilizing effects. Shortly thereafter, a French chemist, Charpentier, prepared a new phenothiazine derivative, which he called chlorpromazine. This drug proved very effective in calming people with schizophrenia. As already mentioned, phenothiazines derive their therapeutic properties from their ability to block dopamine receptors in the brain, thus reducing the influence of dopamine on thought, emotion, and behaviour.

Chlorpromazine (trade name Thorazine) was first used therapeutically in the United States in 1954 and rapidly became the preferred treatment for schizophrenia. Thorazine was actually introduced to North America by Canadian psychiatrist Heinz Lehmann (Lehmann & Hanrahan, 1954), as described in Canadian Contributions 11.1. By 1970, more than 85% of all clients in state and provincial mental hospitals in the United States and Canada were receiving chlorpromazine or another phenothiazine. Other antipsychotics that were used for years in the treatment of schizophrenia include the butyrophenones (e.g., haloperidol, Haldol) and the thioxanthenes (e.g., thiothixene, Navane). Both types seem generally as effective as the phenothiazines and work in similar ways. These classes of drugs reduce the positive symptoms of schizophrenia but have much less effect on the negative symptoms.

CANADIAN CONTRIBUTIONS 11.1
HEINZ E. LEHMANN AND THE "DISCOVERY" OF NEUROLEPTICS IN NORTH AMERICA

"Look, you can't imagine. You know we saw the unthinkable—hallucinations and delusions eliminated by a pill! I suppose if people had been told well they'll die 2 years later they'd still have said it's worth it. It was so unthinkable and so new and so wonderful."

—Heinz Lehmann, 1996

Recall for a moment the contributions of Philippe Pinel (described in Chapter 1), who in 1793 removed the chains of mentally ill people at La Bicêtre asylum in Paris and ushered in many humanitarian reforms. Pinel lived on the asylum grounds and took his meals with the patients in order to be available to them and to practise his compassionate treatment of them throughout the day. Perhaps his intent was to serve as an appropriate role model for his charges. Can you imagine the director of a mental hospital living on the institution's grounds in the modern era? One such person was Heinz Lehmann. Lehmann, who passed away in 1999, must be considered one of the most important historical and contemporary figures in Canadian psychiatry.

In 1937, a young physician escaped from the Nazis in Germany and made his way to Canada, where he obtained a position at the Verdun Protestant Hospital in Montreal, a psychiatric hospital now known as the Douglas Hospital. According to Dongier (1999), Lehmann was initially placed in charge of about 750 clients, who accounted for almost half the beds at the hospital during that era. By 1947, he was clinical director. Subsequently, he became the director of research and education (1962), a full professor at McGill University (1965), and chair of the Department of Psychiatry (1971–74). For 60 years, Lehmann remained on staff at the Douglas, where he lived with his family in a small house on the hospital grounds. He kept a personal tradition of meeting and shaking hands with all of his clients on Christmas Day.

In the early years, Lehmann was unable to purchase phenobarbital, the main sedative used at the time, in capsule form. The resourceful physician overcame the obstacle: "At night, once my visits to patients were over, I was busy making capsules using bottles of powder. Incidentally, this started the rumour that I was an addict because nobody in his right mind would work in the pharmacy at 2 am" (Dongier, 1999, p. 362). In the 1950s, Lehmann and some of his clients were featured in a series of short films produced by the National Film Board of Canada. He interviewed clients and summarized the symptoms of the disorders that led to commitment to a mental hospital during the era when available drugs and psychosocial interventions were not especially effective. The disorders included the schizophrenias, manic depression, depression, and organic psychoses. These films are informative and educational even today, especially because the clients demonstrated some of the more florid symptoms of psychotic disorders that are now frequently controlled by modern neuroleptic drugs. Today it would be considered unethical to deprive people suffering from schizophrenia and other serious mental disorders of an intervention that could reduce their suffering.

The favourite film of one of the authors, *Folie à Deux* (literally, madness shared by two), illustrates a disorder now referred to in the *DSM-IV-TR* as shared psychotic disorder—the development of a delusional system within a close relationship with a delusional person (but proposed to be eliminated as a separate psychotic disorder in *DSM-5*). In the film, Zena developed delusions that she was being persecuted by doctors, the police, lawyers, and judges following what she perceived to be unsuccessful cosmetic surgery on her nose. Her mother subsequently developed the same delusions. Zena attributed her problems to a conspiracy on the part of the entire criminal justice system, whereas her mother, who was less sophisticated medically and psychologically, blamed "witches" hidden among the clients and staff. You might ask that if Zena's mother's delusions are caused by her close association with Zena's delusions, why not separate the two of them? Presumably, when no longer influenced by her daughter, the mother would give up her own delusions. This would seem to be a logical strategy. In fact, Dr. Lehmann did exactly this, and as predicted, the mother's delusions disappeared. Unfortunately, she became so clinically depressed and suicidal that, for humane reasons, Lehmann decided to put mother and daughter back together on the same ward. Parenthetically, the case of Zena and her mother illustrates an important difference between the treatment of the mentally ill during that era and the treatment today. Despite ongoing concerns about current practices, it is very improbable that today's doctors would lock Zena and her mother away for much of the remainder of their lives, as often occurred back in the 1950s. We will discuss current mental health laws in Canada, especially as they relate to civil commitment, in Chapter 18.

In 1953, Lehmann noticed in a French journal an article about the effects of chlorpromazine as a tranquilizer and antipsychotic medication and decided that it would be worth trying the new drug with his own clients. He obtained a supply from the manufacturer's representative and administered it with considerable success to more than 200 people who had a diagnosis of schizophrenia. He published his findings in the scientific journal *Archives of Neurology and Psychiatry*. This journal article was the very first paper to be published in North America on the use of a neuroleptic to control symptoms of psychosis. Just as Philippe

Heinz E. Lehmann (1911–99) published the first North American paper on the treatment of schizophrenia using chlorpromazine. Following his success at the Verdun Protestant Hospital (now the Douglas) in Montreal, the use of neuroleptics spread to the rest of the continent. Archives of the Centre for Addiction and Mental Health.

Pinel unchained the chained in the asylums of Paris, Heinz Lehmann attempted to liberate his clients with schizophrenia from the torments of their delusional thoughts. The use of chlorpromazine soon spread throughout North America. Subsequently, Lehmann

read in a Swiss journal the first published paper on the use of the tricyclic antidepressant imipramine for the treatment of major depression. According to Dongier (1999), Lehmann deserves the credit for introducing these treatment advances to North America.

Although he received numerous international honours for his clinical psychopharmacology research, it should be noted that Lehmann's research and clinical interests were not wedded to biological interventions. Some of his more than 300 publications in journals and books focused on psychotherapy, psychosocial approaches to treatment of the mentally ill, aftercare services in the community, community psychiatry, and assessment tools to measure the severity of psychiatric disorders (Dongier, 1999). In fact, Lehmann was opposed to the reductionist trends in biological psychology. He also resisted the process of psychiatric hospital deinstitutionalization when it was not accompanied by appropriate supports in the community.

In the concluding section of his eulogy to Lehmann in the Canadian Medical Association's *Journal of Psychiatry and Neuroscience*, Dongier (1999) stated, "Without any doubt, no contemporary Canadian psychiatrist had the international prestige or commanded such high unanimous respect as Heinz Lehmann" (p. 362). His body rested at Douglas Hall, in the heart of the hospital to which he had devoted his life.

Source: Adapted from Dongier (1999)

Although the antipsychotics reduce some of the positive symptoms of schizophrenia, they are not a cure. Furthermore, about 30 to 50% of people with schizophrenia do not respond favourably to conventional antipsychotics, although some of these clients may respond to some of the newer antipsychotic drugs (e.g., clozapine). Because of the side effects of the whole range of antipsychotic drugs, studies have found that about half the people who take them quit after one year and up to three quarters quit after two years (e.g., Lieberman et al., 2005). Weiden and Zygmunt (1997) reported that about a third of clients are non-compliant after only four to six weeks. A Canadian survey found that 56% reported that, without seeking their doctor's approval, they had stopped taking their medication; the most common reason given for non-compliance was drug side effects (Schizophrenia Society of Canada, 2002). Because of these high non-compliance rates, clients are frequently treated with long-lasting antipsychotics (e.g., fluphenazine decanoate, Prolixin), which are injected every two to six weeks.

Other drugs are used adjunctively—that is, along with antipsychotics—to treat depression or anxiety or to stabilize mood. These adjunctive medications include lithium, antidepressants, anticonvulsants, and tranquilizers. Antidepressants are also used with schizophrenic clients who become depressed after a psychotic episode (e.g., Hogarty et al., 1994) and as "add-on" treatment for people with schizophrenia and pronounced negative symptoms (see Rummel et al. 2005).

Clients who respond positively to antipsychotics are kept on so-called *maintenance* doses of the drug, just enough to continue the therapeutic effect. They take their medication and return to the hospital or clinic on occasion for adjustment of the dose level. Clients who are maintained on medication may make only marginal adjustment to the community, however. For example, they may be unable to live unsupervised or to hold down the kind of job for which they would otherwise be qualified. Their social relationships are likely to be sparse. And again, although conventional antipsychotics keep positive symptoms from returning, they have little effect on negative symptoms such as flat affect. Antipsychotics have significantly reduced long-term institutionalization, but they have also initiated the revolving-door pattern of admission, discharge, and readmission seen in some clients.

Commonly reported side effects of antipsychotics include dizziness, blurred vision, restlessness, and sexual dysfunction. In addition, a group of particularly disturbing side effects, termed *extrapyramidal side effects*, stem from dysfunctions of the nerve tracts that descend from the brain to spinal motor neurons. Extrapyramidal side effects resemble the symptoms of Parkinson's disease. People taking antipsychotics usually develop tremors of the fingers, a shuffling gait, and drooling. Other side effects include dystonia, a state of muscular rigidity, and dyskinesia, an abnormal motion of voluntary and involuntary muscles, producing chewing movements, as well as other movements of the lips, fingers, and legs. Together, these side effects cause arching of the back and a twisted posture of the neck and body. Akasthisia is an inability to remain still; people pace constantly and fidget. These perturbing symptoms can be treated by drugs used with people who have Parkinson's disease.

In a muscular disturbance of clients with schizophrenia, called tardive dyskinesia, the mouth muscles involuntarily make sucking, lip-smacking, and chin-wagging motions. In more severe cases, the whole body can be subject to involuntary motor movements. This syndrome affects about 10 to 20% of clients treated with antipsychotics for a long period of time and it is not responsive to any known treatment (Sweet et al., 1995). Finally, a side effect called *neuroleptic malignant syndrome* occurs in about 1% of cases. In this condition, which can sometimes be fatal, severe muscular rigidity develops, accompanied by fever. The heart races, blood pressure increases, and the client may lapse into a coma.

Because of these serious side effects, some clinicians believe it is unwise to take high doses of antipsychotics for extended periods of time. Current clinical practice calls for treating clients with the smallest possible doses of drugs. This situation puts the clinician in a quandary: if medication is reduced, the chance of relapse increases; but if medication is continued, serious and untreatable side effects may develop. One possible solution is to keep medication levels low but monitor clients closely so that when symptoms worsen, medication can be increased. Unfortunately, this strategy may not be effective (e.g., Schooler et al., 1997).

Second-Generation (Atypical) Antipsychotics

". . . we have new evidence from larger pragmatic studies that the second-generation antipsychotics have, quite literally, been oversold..."

—Jan Scott (2008, p. 401) on the failures to replicate the initial impressive benefits of second-generation antipsychotics in subsequent effectiveness trials

In the decades following the introduction of antipsychotic drugs, there appeared to be little interest in developing new drugs to treat schizophrenia. This situation changed markedly following the introduction of clozapine (Clozaril), which appeared to produce therapeutic gains in people with schizophrenia who do not respond well to traditional antipsychotics (e.g., Buchanan et al., 1998) and appeared to produce greater therapeutic gains than traditional antipsychotics (e.g., Rosenheck et al., 1999). A survey of clients' attitudes conducted at Hamilton (Ontario) Psychiatric Hospital concluded that most had a favourable view of clozapine, reporting improvements in levels of satisfaction, quality of life, thinking, mood, and alertness (Waserman & Criollo, 2000).

An international study that included data obtained in Montreal found that clozapine, relative to olanzapine (another atypical medication), resulted in fewer suicide attempts among clients with schizophrenia (Meltzer et al., 2003).

Clozapine also produces fewer motor side effects than do traditional antipsychotics. Furthermore, maintaining discharged clients on clozapine appeared to reduce relapse rates (Conley et al., 1999). Although the precise biochemical mechanism of the therapeutic effects of clozapine is not known, we do know that it has a major impact on serotonin receptors.

Clozapine does have serious side effects, however. It can impair the functioning of the immune system in a small percentage of clients (about 1%) by lowering numbers of white blood cells, making clients vulnerable to infection and even death; for this reason, clients taking clozapine have to be carefully monitored. It also can produce seizures and other side effects, such as dizziness, fatigue, drooling, and weight gain (Waserman & Criollo, 2000).

The apparent success of clozapine stimulated drug companies to search for other drugs that might be more effective than traditional antipsychotics. Two results are olanzapine (Zyprexa) and risperidone (Risperdal). Both produce fewer motor side effects than traditional antipsychotics, and they appear to be as effective as traditional antipsychotics in reducing symptoms (e.g., Wirshing et al., 1999), perhaps even better (Sanger et al., 1999). The Canadian Risperidone Study compared the effects of risperidone and haloperidol in an eight-week, double-blind, randomized study (Chouinard et al., 1993). This study found that 6 mg of risperidone was the most effective dosage level and that risperidone was significantly more effective than haloperidol at reducing negative and positive symptoms. Another study conducted in Canada showed that risperidone may lead to reduced use of health services because it was associated with a lower length of first hospitalization and less use of inpatient beds (Malla, Norman, Scholten, Zirul, & Kotteda, 2001). Another recent randomized controlled trial (RCT) study (van Nimwegen, 2008) reported that both olanzapine and risperidone are associated with improvement in subjective well-being in adolescents with first psychosis. More recently, Addington and colleagues (2009) compared the efficacy, tolerability, and safety of risperidone and a newer antipsychotic, ziprasidone, in a multi-centre RCT. Both drugs were effective as continuation and maintenance treatments in people recovering from an acute exacerbation of schizophrenia or schizoaffective disorders. However, ziprasidone was associated with fewer adverse effects (e.g., extrapyramidal symptoms) and greater improvement in depressive symptoms. See Table 11.4 for examples of major drugs used in treating schizophrenia.

A psychological approach to the study of risperidone would involve examining fundamental aspects of cognition, such as attention and memory, known to be deficient in many people with schizophrenia and associated with poor social adaptation (CME Institute, 2007). Risperidone improves verbal working memory (e.g., remembering a phone number long enough to be able to dial it) more than other antipsychotic drugs, apparently by reducing the activity of serotonin-sensitive receptors in the frontal cortex (Green et al., 1997). Improvements in verbal working memory are also correlated with improvements in learning social skills in psychosocial

TABLE 11.4

EXAMPLES OF MAJOR DRUGS USED IN TREATING SCHIZOPHRENIA

Drug Category	Generic Name	Trade Name
phenothiazine	chlorpromazine	Thorazine
	fluphenazine decanoate	Prolixin
butyrophenone	haloperidol	Haldol
thioxanthene	thiothixene	Navane
tricyclic dibenzodiazepine	clozapine	Clozaril
thienobenzodiazepine	olanzapine	Zyprexa
benzisoxazole	risperidone	Risperdal
dibenzothiazepine	quetiapine	Seroquel

rehabilitation programs (Green, 1996). Risperidone may thus make possible more thorough changes in schizophrenia and its behavioural consequences than do drugs that do not have these cognitive effects.

Antipsychotics block dopamine D2 receptors. In a double-blind PET study with people with first-episode schizophrenia, Shitij Kapur and his colleagues from the Centre for Addiction and Mental Health in Toronto (Kapur et al., 2000) confirmed that D2 occupancy is an important mediator of clinical response and side effects in antipsychotic treatment. Their findings are consistent with a "target and trigger" hypothesis of the action of antipsychotics. The idea is that "the D2 specificity of antipsychotics permits them to target discrete neurons and that their antagonistic properties trigger within those neurons intracellular changes that ultimately beget antipsychotic response" (Kapur et al., 2000, p. 514). Although this study was limited to haloperidol, the authors concluded that the results help explain observed differences between typical and atypical antipsychotics.

Antipsychotic drugs are an indispensable part of treatment for schizophrenia and will undoubtedly continue to be an important component. They are surely preferable to the straitjackets formerly used to restrain clients. Nonetheless, some people with schizophrenia do not respond favourably to any of the current medications. However, the apparent success of clozapine, olanzapine, risperidone, and other atypical antipsychotics has stimulated a continued effort to find new and more effective drug therapies for schizophrenia.

Current Issues and New Directions Some issues and new directions include the following:

- Are second-generation (atypical) antipsychotics more effective than first-generation (typical) drugs? Over the past 15 years the growing research literature seemed to suggest that second-generation antipsychotics are effective in the treatment of psychotic people, including those manifesting hostility, aggression, and violent behaviour

(see Swanson et al., 2008). However, many experts are questioning the picture of success due to the primarily negative results from two large double-blind RCTs in the United States and the United Kingdom: the Clinical Antipsychotic Trials of Intervention Effectiveness (CATIE), an NIMH-funded study that compared the effectiveness of several atypical antipsychotics with a single first-generation antipsychotic (perphenazine) (see Lieberman, et al., 2005), and the Cost Utility of the Latest Antipsychotic Drugs in Schizophrenia (CUtLASS) that compared the effects on quality of life of second- vs. first-generation antipsychotic drugs (see Jones et al., 2006). The benefits achieved were much less than for highly selected clients receiving carefully determined doses in tightly controlled research environments. Nonetheless there is mixed evidence for this "efficacy-effectiveness gap." A large, naturalistic follow-up of first admissions for schizophrenia in Finland (Tiihonen et al., 2006) found that second-generation drugs were more effective than haloperidol, and a similar study in the United States (Swanson et al., 2004) reported that second-generation antipsychotics were superior in reducing community violence over a three-year follow-up. Compounding the issue, a recent CATIE study (Swanson et al., 2008) concluded that the newer antipsychotics did not reduce violence more than perphenazine.

- Relapse prevention is one of the most important goals of long-term management of schizophrenia. Relapse is both distressing and costly. Poor adherence to medication is a primary cause of relapse and re-hospitalization (CME Institute, 2007). Although there is large variation, possibly related to different definitions of adherence, as high as 80% of clients are unable or unwilling to take medication as directed. In the CATIE trials, approximately 75% of clients discontinued the assigned medication due to lack of efficacy, intolerability, or both (Lieberman et al., 2005). Another primary reason for poor adherence is clients' poor insight into their disorder; however, problems related to accessing prescriptions, obtaining refills, and simply forgetting to take the medications also play a role (CME Institute, 2007). Nonadherent clients with schizophrenia are five times more likely to relapse than those who adhere to prescribed regimens (Robinson et al., 1999).

- Do atypical antipsychotics really reduce the rate of relapse? Leucht et al. (2003) conducted a meta-analysis of studies that randomly assigned clients to either first- or second-generation antipsychotics and followed client progress for at least a year. They found a significant reduction in the relapse rate among clients who took the atypical antipsychotics. The average relapse rate with haloperidol was 23%, whereas the rate for the group of second-generation drugs averaged only 15%. This is a clinically significant effect. An important goal of both medication and psychosocial research (see below) is to find ways to increase compliance and reduce relapse in people with schizophrenia. Although there does not appear to be clear, consistent evidence of superior efficacy among the first-line atypical antipsychotics (e.g., Tandon & Jibson, 2005), atypical medications appear to give schizophrenia clients better quality of life (e.g., Mortimer & Al-Agib, 2007). Nonetheless, further research into the long-term effectiveness and safety is needed. However, there is no scientific or clinical rationale to support an apparent practice of reserving atypical treatment for younger, less seriously disturbed people with schizophrenia (Mortimer & Al-Agib, 2007).

- Are there significant differences in efficacy among second-generation antipsychotics? This is a matter of heated debate. Leucht et al. (2009) conducted a meta-analysis of 78 "head-to-head" comparisons of two or more of nine second-generation antipsychotics in the treatment of schizophrenia and concluded that some drugs may be somewhat more efficacious than others due to improvement in positive (rather than negative) symptoms. They argued that "small efficacy superiorities must be weighed against large differences in side effects and costs" (Leucht et al., 2009, p. 152).

- A variety of long-term injectable medications have been developed to meet the need for continuous lifelong medication. They have potential benefits, including increased adherence and decreased relapse, but also less liver toxicity and decreased adverse effects (CME Institute, 2007). For example, long-acting risperidone is administered intramuscularly every two weeks. Studies are investigating the use of implantable formulations that could provide uninterrupted treatment for three to six months (e.g., Metzger et al., 2007).

- The historical focus on controlling the positive symptoms of schizophrenia through the use of antipsychotics has reduced the positive symptom burden on people with schizophrenia over the past 50 years; however, ability to function independently in the community has not improved significantly (see CME Institute, 2007). Many clinicians and researchers agree that there should be more focus on negative and cognitive symptoms since they are more strongly associated with social and occupational functioning (e.g., Christensen, 2006). Developing drugs that improve cognition (cognition-enhancing drugs) would improve the functional outcome of people with schizophrenia (Marder, 2006). To facilitate drug development in this area, the U.S. NIMH established the Measurement and Treatment Research to Improve Cognition in Schizophrenia (MATRICS) program. Information about the results of each step in this collaboration among psychologists and psychiatrists, pharmaceutical companies, the U.S. FDA, and NIMH can be found on a regularly updated website (www.matrics.ucla.edu). Thus far there is a consensus on the critical cognitive domains, the battery of tests developed to measure impairment in each area, the standards for clinical trials, and selection and ranking of molecular targets for new antipsychotics (with alpha-7 nicotinic agonists receiving the highest ranking).

Although no effective drug has been approved for improving impaired cognition, numerous drugs are currently at different stages of development directed at the nine approved molecular targets. The NIMH recently initiated a similar project for negative symptoms (see Kirkpatrick, 2006). We may be on the verge of a new era in the medication treatment of schizophrenia.

- Do any of the current second-generation antipsychotics affect neurocognitive functioning? A one-year double-blind study conducted in Canada and the United States (Keefe et al., 2006) examined the neurocognitive efficacy of risperidone, olanzapine, and haloperidol in schizophrenia. Neurocognitive deficits were assessed in eight domains. The hypothesis that olanzapine treatment would produce greater neurocognitive benefits after 52 weeks than risperidone or haloperidol treatment was not confirmed since the three medications did not differ in their neurocognitive efficacy. Post hoc analyses indicated that olanzapine and risperidone-treated clients improved in several domains, including executive function, learning and memory, processing speed, attention and vigilance, verbal working memory, and motor functions. Risperidone-treated clients improved in domains of visuospatial memory. Haloperidol-treated clients improved only in domains of learning and memory. Keefe et al. (2006) concluded that clients benefited most from olanzapine or risperidone.

- Are any of the atypical antipsychotics effective for "treatment-resistant" schizophrenia? Managing people with schizophrenia who don't respond to antipsychotic treatment is a critical clinical and health care challenge. People with treatment-resistant schizophrenia derive little or no benefit from existing antipsychotics, are highly symptomatic, function poorly in the community, and are frequent users of inpatient and outpatient mental health services (e.g., Kane et al., 2007). A multi-centre, double-blind, randomized study (Kane et al., 2007) compared the efficacy and safety of aripiprazole and perphenazine in treatment-resistant clients and concluded that both medications can improve the symptoms (for about 25 to 35% of clients for the criteria used) in treatment-resistant clients who did not previously respond to olanzapine or risperidone.

- Is antipsychotic treatment effective with children and adolescents? Although about a third of people with schizophrenia spectrum disorders experience onset in childhood or adolescence and earlier onset predicts more severe forms, people younger than 18 years old are usually excluded from treatment trials. Recently, two RCTs of antipsychotic effectiveness were conducted in the younger population. Findling and colleagues (2008) compared antipsychotic treatment (oral aripiprazole) with placebo in adolescents aged 13–17 years with schizophrenia over six weeks. They concluded that aripiprazole use, although associated with numerous side effects, led to some improvement in symptoms, particularly positive symptoms.

Sikich et al. (2008) compared first- (molindone) and second-generation (olanzapine and risperidone) antipsychotics over eight weeks in children and adolescents ages 8–19 years with either schizophrenia or schizoaffective disorder. Clinical response rates were less than 50% in all three groups and there was no difference among groups. There was significant improvement between baseline and endpoint on symptom scores that was similar across groups. Silkich et al. concluded that antipsychotic effectiveness in child populations is quite low and that first- and second-generation antipsychotics are equally effective (but have different side effect profiles). Study designs of longer duration are critical.

- Schizophrenia and its treatment with neuroleptics were studied by Joukamaa et al. (2006) for their prediction of mortality in a representative population sample of Finns. The number of neuroleptics used at the time of the baseline survey in 1978 and 1980 showed a graded relation to mortality, leading the authors to conclude, "There is an urgent need to ascertain whether the high mortality in schizophrenia is attributable to the disorder itself or the antipsychotic medication" (Joukamaa et al., 2006, p. 122). It will be important to address this issue with the many drugs that are currently being evaluated, and the drugs being developed in conjunction with the MATRICS program.

Our growing knowledge of biological diatheses for schizophrenia and the continuing improvement in antipsychotic medications should not lead to a neglect of psychosocial factors in both the causes of and the efforts to control schizophrenia. In his review of dopamine dysregulation and related biological factors, Kapur (2003) concluded eloquently that "[d]opamine dysregulation may provide the driving force, but the subject's cognitive, psychodynamic, and cultural context gives form to the experience. Psychosis is seen as a dynamic interaction between a bottom-up neurochemical drive and a top-down psychological process, not an inescapably determined outcome of a biology" (Kapur, 2003, p. 17). This view is very much in keeping with the tenets of the biopsychosocial model.

PSYCHOLOGICAL TREATMENTS

The cognitive impairments inherent in schizophrenia probably limit the degree to which clients can profit from psychological interventions. Further, whatever the biological diathesis, this vulnerability is likely to persist throughout the person's life. But as promising as many of the newer antipsychotic drugs are, a neglect of the psychological and social aspect of schizophrenia compromises efforts to deal with people and their families who are struggling with that disorder. Further, the recent evidence indicates that psychosocial strategies can play an important role in increasing the effectiveness of medication treatment and decreasing the relapse rate (CME Institute, 2007). Freud believed that people with schizophrenia were incapable of establishing the close interpersonal relationship

essential for analysis. Although Harry Stack Sullivan and Frieda Fromm-Reichman subsequently developed similar ego-analytic approaches for schizophrenia that led to great claims of success, results from a long-term follow-up confirmed a lack of success (Stone, 1986). However, more recent psychosocial interventions hold considerable promise for success. We turn now to a consideration of various psychological and nonpharmacologic treatments of schizophrenia.

SOCIAL SKILLS TRAINING Social skills training is designed to teach people with schizophrenia behaviours that can help them succeed in a wide variety of interpersonal situations—discussing their medications with their psychiatrist, ordering meals in a restaurant, filling out job applications, saying no to offers to buy drugs on the street—all things that most of us take for granted and give little thought to in our daily lives. For people with schizophrenia, these life skills are not to be taken for granted; such individuals need to work hard to acquire or reacquire them.

Studies conducted with groups of people with schizophrenia (e.g., Lieberman et al., 1998) indicate that severely disturbed clients can be taught new social behaviour and independent living skills that may help them function better in their communities. A large and growing body of research supports the effectiveness of social skills training for people with schizophrenia. Kopelowicz, Liberman, and Zarate (2006) outlined many recent advances, including special adaptations and applications for improved generalization into the community, dually diagnosed substance-abusing schizophrenia, supported employment, treatment refractory schizophrenia, and overcoming cognitive deficits and negative symptoms. Social skills training nowadays is usually a component of treatments for schizophrenia that go beyond the use of medications alone, including family therapies for lowering expressed emotion. We turn to that work now.

FAMILY THERAPY AND REDUCING EXPRESSED EMOTION Many people with schizophrenia who are discharged from psychiatric hospitals go home to their families. Earlier we discussed research showing that high levels of expressed emotion (including being hostile, hypercritical, and overprotective within the family) have been linked to relapse and re-hospitalization. Accordingly, family interventions have been developed. While they differ in length, setting, and specific techniques, these therapies have several features in common beyond the overall purpose of calming things down for the client by calming things down for the family:

- They educate clients and families about the biological vulnerability that predisposes people to schizophrenia, cognitive problems inherent to schizophrenia, the symptoms of the disorder, and signs of impending relapse.
- They provide information about and advice on monitoring the effects of antipsychotic medication.

- They encourage family members to blame neither themselves nor the client for the disorder and for the difficulties all are having in coping with it.
- They help improve communication and problem-solving skills within the family.
- They encourage clients and their families to expand their social contacts, especially their support networks.
- They instill a degree of hope that things can improve, including the hope that the client may not have to return to the hospital.

Programs employ various techniques to implement these strategies. Examples include identifying stressors that could cause relapse, training in communication and problem solving, and having high-EE (expressed emotion) family members watch videotapes of interactions of low-EE families (e.g., Penn & Mueser, 1996). Compared with medication only, family therapy plus medication typically lowers relapse over periods of one to two years, a finding particularly evident in studies in which the treatment lasted for at least nine months (e.g., Kopelowicz & Liberman, 1998).

COGNITIVE-BEHAVIOURAL THERAPY Whereas it used to be assumed that it was futile to try to alter the cognitive distortions, including delusions, of people with schizophrenia, a developing clinical and experimental literature has demonstrated that the maladaptive beliefs of some clients can be changed with interventions. In fact, in recent reviews, Aaron Beck with Neil Rector from the Centre for Addiction and Mental Health in Toronto concluded that people with schizophrenia can benefit from cognitive techniques designed to address their delusions and hallucinations (e.g., Beck & Rector, 2005). Furthermore, they suggested that CBT can facilitate motivation and engagement in social and vocational activities. This is in keeping with observations that people who have been psychotic for some time incorporate their psychotic beliefs into their broader cognitive schemas (see Kapur, 2003). Initial comparative research indicated that CBT plus enriched treatment as usual is as effective as treatment as usual alone, and that CBT seems to be particularly effective at reducing negative symptoms of schizophrenia (Rector, Seeman, & Segal, 2003). In a theoretical analysis based on the cognitive model, Beck and Rector (2005) integrated the complex interaction of predisposing neurobiological, environmental, cognitive, and behavioural factors with the diverse symptomatology of schizophrenia. For example, the impaired integrative functions of the brain, in conjunction with domain-specific cognitive deficits, increases vulnerability to negative life events (e.g., job loss), leading to dysfunctional beliefs and behaviours. Kieron O'Connor (2009) from the Université de Montréal reviewed cognitive accounts of psychosis including claims that it is "cognitive and meta-cognitive appraisals (attributions and beliefs) about the significance of the symptoms that cause distress and dysfunction" (p. 152). He concluded that hallucinations and delusions possibly result not from perceptual distortion but from cognitive styles (e.g., inferential confusion, cognitive slippage, and fantasy proneness) that encourage the psychotic person "to live in fictional narratives as if they were real" (p. 152).

Meta-analytic reviews (e.g., Zimmerman et al., 2005) support the efficacy of individualized CBT for people with persistent positive psychotic symptoms. However, the efficacy of a group format is less clear-cut. Barrowclough et al. (2006) concluded that group CBT is probably not the optimum treatment for reducing hallucinations and delusions, though it possibly has important benefits, including feeling less negative about oneself and less hopeless for the future. Zygmunt, Olfson, Boyer, and Mechanic (2002) reviewed outcome studies of various kinds of programs designed to boost medication compliance. Although education and family therapy types of programs were generally ineffective, programs based on CBT principles (and some community-based ones) were more effective. In a recent RCT, Haddock et al. (2009) demonstrated that CBT targeted at violence, anger, psychosis, and risk outcomes might be an effective treatment for reducing violence in clients with a diagnosis of schizophrenia and a history of violence.

A recent comprehensive meta-analysis of approximately 30 RCT efficacy trials (Wykes, Steel, Everitt, & Tarrier, 2008) concluded that CBT plus usual treatment, relative to usual treatment alone, demonstrates significant effects on depression, anxiety, symptoms (both positive and negative), and social functioning but not relapse rates. Further, those who benefited the most from CBT for psychosis had medication-refractory positive symptoms. The authors noted that effect sizes decreased as sample sizes and methodological rigor increased. What about the generalizability of CBT to the "real world?" Is it just as effective? As noted by Jan Scott (2008) in an editorial in the *British Journal of Psychiatry*, "RCTs report group outcomes while clinicians treat individuals" (p. 402). Scott was commenting on a new multi-centre RCT effectiveness study by Garety et al. (2008) of CBT or family intervention plus treatment as usual, relative to treatment as usual. The interventions focused on relapse prevention for 20 sessions over 9 months; however, the CBT and family interventions had no effects on rates of remission and relapse or on days in hospital at 12 or 24 months. CBT did show a beneficial effect on depression at 24 months, and in people with "carers" there was improved delusional distress and social functioning. The authors concluded that generic CBT for psychosis should be reserved for clients with medication-unresponsive positive symptoms. Are these results a major setback for CBT research? Probably not, but as Scott (2008) observed,

> . . . it introduces some healthy realism about the limits for the role of adjunctive therapy in severe mental disorders. It is also a timely reminder that, away from the "therapy for all" media hysteria, the world of routine psychiatric practice brings us into contact with some clients who do not want or do not respond optimally to antipsychotic medication, but who also do not always want or benefit from psychological therapies either. (p. 402)

PERSONAL THERAPY As encouraging as the family EE-lowering studies were, many clients were still returning to the hospital and the clinical outcomes of those who managed to remain in the community left a lot to be desired (Hogarty et al., 1997). What more could be done for discharged people with schizophrenia to increase their chances of being able to remain longer outside the hospital, whether or not they could do so within their family of origin? This question led to the formulation of a new approach called **personal therapy** by one of the groups that had published positive, though limited, findings on lowering EE (e.g., Hogarty et al., 1997).

Personal therapy is a broad-spectrum CBT approach to the multiplicity of problems of people with schizophrenia who have been discharged from hospital. It is conducted one on one and in small groups (workshops). A key element, based on the finding that a reduction in emotional reactions by family members leads to less relapse following hospital discharge, is teaching the client how to recognize inappropriate affect. If ignored, inappropriate affect can build up and lead to cognitive distortions and inappropriate social behaviour. Clients are also taught to notice small signs of relapse, such as social withdrawal or inappropriate threats against others, and they learn skills to reduce these problems. Such behaviours, if left unchecked, will likely interfere with efforts to live by conventional social rules, including being able to keep a job and make and maintain social contacts. The therapy also includes some rational-emotive behaviour therapy to help clients avoid turning life's inevitable frustrations and challenges into catastrophes and thus to help them lower their stress levels.

In addition, many clients are taught muscle-relaxation techniques as an aid to detecting the gradual buildup of anxiety or anger; they also learn how to apply the relaxation skills in order to control these emotions better. The operating assumption is that emotional dysregulation is part of the biological diathesis in schizophrenia and a factor that clients must learn to live and cope with rather than eliminate (or cure) altogether. But there is also a strong focus on teaching specific social skills, as well as on encouraging clients to continue to take their antipsychotic medication in a maintenance mode; that is, in a dose that is typically lower than what is necessary in the earliest, acute, and most florid phase of the disorder.

Personal therapy includes non-behavioural elements, especially warm and empathic acceptance of the client's emotional and cognitive turmoil along with realistic but optimistic expectations that life can be better. In general, clients are taught that they are emotionally vulnerable to stress, that their thinking is not always as clear as it should be, that they have to continue with their medication, and that they can learn a variety of skills to make the most of the hand that nature has dealt them. This is not a short-term treatment; it can extend over three years of weekly to biweekly therapy contacts.

Note that much of the focus is on the client, not on the family. Whereas the focus in the family studies was on reducing the high EE of the client's family—an environmental change from the client's point of view—the goal of personal therapy is to teach the client internal coping skills, new ways of thinking about and controlling his or her own affective reactions to whatever challenges are presented by his or her environment. Specific instruction in social skills is also an integral part of this treatment.

Finally, this therapy is important because of what Hogarty et al. call "criticism management and conflict resolution" (1997). This phrase refers to learning how to deal with negative feedback from others and how to resolve the interpersonal conflicts that are an inevitable part of dealing with others. This form of intervention can help many people with schizophrenia stay out of the hospital and function better, with the most favourable outcomes achieved by those who can live with their family of origin (Hogarty et al., 1997).

TREATMENT FOCUS ON BASIC COGNITIVE FUNCTIONS

It is well established that people diagnosed with schizophrenia, as a group, have deficits in virtually all facets of cognitive functioning and show performance deficits on a range of simple and complex tasks (see CME Institute, 2007; Heinrichs, 2005; Walker et al., 2004). Moreover, these deficits are apparent in first-episode, non-medicated clients, so deficits are not a by-product of receiving treatment. Consequently, researchers have been attending to fundamental aspects of cognition that are disordered in schizophrenia in an attempt to improve these functions and thereby produce a favourable effect on behaviour. This more molecular approach concentrates on trying to normalize such fundamental cognitive functions as attention and memory, which are known to be deficient in many people with schizophrenia and are associated with poor social adaptation and other deficits in functional ability (see CME Institute, 2007).

Recall from our discussion of drug therapy that positive clinical outcomes from olanzapine and risperidone are associated with improvements in certain kinds of neurocognitive functions, lending support to the more general notion that paying attention to fundamental cognitive processes—the kind that non-clinical cognitive psychologists study—holds promise for improving the social and emotional lives of people with schizophrenia. An approach called **cognitive enhancement therapy (CET)**, developed by Hogarty and his colleagues (Hogarty, Flesher, Ulrich et al., 2004), was evaluated in a two-year RCT of clients who were also taking medication. The approach was compared with an enriched supportive therapy that included educational and supportive aspects of personal therapy. The CET-specific focus is on computer-based training in attention, memory, and problem solving, as well as social-cognitive skills (such as initiating conversations). CET proved successful in improving cognition and processing speed and there was evidence to suggest that it also had a positive effect on functional outcomes.

Other studies have shown that a schizophrenia client's ability to recognize facial affect in others, working memory, and attention can all be improved through cognitive training (CME Institute, 2007). Canadian research conducted by Young and Zakzanis and their colleagues (2002) demonstrated the *utility of scaffolding* in the remediation of cognitive deficits. Scaffolded instruction is a concept derived from a proposal that everyone has a zone of current development and that the complexity of tasks must be tailored to account for individuals' current skill level and level of potential development. The scaffolding model requires instructors to select tasks that reflect the clients' current capabilities so that eventually they are able to solve problems for themselves. The ultimate goal is to develop general problem-solving skills and processes that clients can generalize to new situations. Young et al. (2002) found that the delivery of scaffolded instruction to participants with schizophrenia, relative to direct instruction, significantly increased the number of categories created during the Wisconsin Card Sorting Test and that cognitive improvements were still evident one month later. The scaffolded group also had relatively higher levels of positive affect and self-esteem. Thus, scaffolding may lead to improvements in self-regulation and self-conceptualization. A recent meta-analysis of 26 RCTs (McGurk et al., 2007) concluded that cognitive remediation in schizophrenia produces moderate improvements in cognitive performance. Further, when combined with psychiatric rehabilitation, it also improves psychosocial functioning. On a negative note, a more comprehensive meta-analysis of 53 longitudinal studies (Szoke et al., 2008) concluded that while people with schizophrenia showed improvement on most cognitive tasks, "practice was more likely than cognitive remediation to account for most of the improvements observed" (p. 248).

Research on psychosocial approaches to improving cognition in people with schizophrenia is vitally important because the innovative approaches offer an alternative to medications for improving functional outcomes.

EVALUATION OF PSYCHOLOGICAL TREATMENTS Pfammatter, Junghan, and Brenner (2006) conducted a meta-analysis that combined the results of previous meta-analyses of psychological treatments for schizophrenia. They concluded that the various psychological treatments evaluated are all effective as adjuncts to pharmacotherapy but the ways in which they are effective vary across types of treatment. That is, social skills training results in enhanced social skills while cognitive remediation enhances some aspects of cognitive functioning. CBT results typically in a reduction of the positive symptoms, while family therapy and education contribute to lower rates of relapse and re-hospitalization. The authors noted that the active ingredients of each psychological treatment still need to be identified and future research is needed to test whether an approach that combines these various types of treatment results multiplicatively in even greater improvements.

One combination approach has been used and evaluated in Europe for the past 25 years. Integrated psychological therapy combines neurocognitive remediation with train-ing in social cognition, social skills, and problem solving. Roder, Mueller, Mueser, and Brenner (2006) reviewed 30 independent evaluations conducted by research groups in nine countries involving 1,393 people with schizophrenia. The meta-analyses on all studies, including high-quality studies, favoured integrated psychological therapy over attention-placebo and standard care control groups only on outcomes that included symptoms, psychosocial functioning, and neurocognition. The superiority of integrated psychological therapy increased during an average follow-up period of 8.1 months. In a recent review, Berry and Barrowclough (2009) considered how psychological interventions can be designed to cater to the specific needs of schizophrenia clients over 65 years old and concluded that CBT or social skills interventions can be adapted successfully for older clients.

CASE MANAGEMENT/ASSERTIVE COMMUNITY TREATMENT

After deinstitutionalization began in the 1960s, many people with schizophrenia no longer resided in mental hospitals and often had to fend for themselves in securing needed services. Without a centralized hospital as the site where most services were delivered, the mental health system became more complex. In 1977, fearing that many clients were not accessing services, the NIMH established a program that gave grants to states to be directed toward helping clients cope with the mental health system. Out of this program, a new mental health specialty, the case manager, was created. Canada adopted the strategy (Health Canada, 1991), but the practice varies widely across provinces and territories and in different places in the same province or territory.

Initially, case managers were basically brokers of services. Being familiar with the system, they were able to get clients into contact with providers of whatever services the clients required. As the years passed, different models of case management developed. The major innovation was the recognition that case managers often needed to provide direct clinical services and that services might best be delivered by a team rather than brokered out. The Assertive Community Treatment model (ACT; Stein & Test, 1980; Stein & Santos, 1998) and the Intensive Case Management model (ICM; Surles et al., 1992) both entail a multidisciplinary team that provides community services ranging from medication, treatment for substance abuse, help in dealing with the kind of stressors clients face regularly (such as managing money), psychotherapy, vocational training, and assistance in obtaining housing and employment.

Although a short-lived hospital-based program not unlike ACT was developed at the Montreal General Hospital, according to Latimer (2005) it wasn't until the 1990s that intensive case management programs and programs more or less similar to the current ACT model (e.g., Stein & Santos, 1998) began appearing in psychiatric and general hospitals in Canada. The Greater Vancouver Mental Health Service Agency is considered one of the best of its kind in North America (Nichols, 1995). The agency serves about 5,000 people with serious mental disorders each year, many of them suffering from schizophrenia. It provides housing, special programs for older clients, and community response teams that can act very quickly in crisis situations involving their clients. The latter approach is proving to be effective in Ontario. Community-based teams of doctors, nurses, and social workers called PACT (Program for Assertive Community Treatment) have been set up to ease the pressure caused by the closing of provincial psychiatric hospitals and to reduce the number of people with schizophrenia and other serious psychiatric disorders who end up in hospital emergency wards (Latimer, 2005). The mental health teams are available 24 hours a day and even make "house calls" to mentally ill people in their homes and workplaces. Indeed, Latimer (2005) notes that Ontario is the only province to implement ACT on a wide scale thus far. By 2002–2003, Ontario had 61 ACT teams funded by the Ministry of Health and Long-Term Care. However, Latimer (2005) noted that there remain concerns about "model fidelity" (p. 568). A related and recent initiative established in parts of Toronto is the Mobile Crisis Intervention Team (MCIT) (see Teotonia, 2009, September 16), a partnership between local hospitals and Toronto police that responds to 911 calls with a psychiatric or crisis component. The MCIT program is based on a similar model developed by police in Memphis, Tennessee, in 1988. Each team is composed of a mental health nurse (who wears a bulletproof vest) and a specially trained police officer who ensures the safety of the nurse and can make apprehensions and arrests if necessary, including if it's the only way to get a psychiatric client into the mental health care system. The majority of the calls the teams respond to involve people with chronic schizophrenia who are off their medication and people who are suicidal. The mobile teams work out of unmarked police cars and currently can respond to only a fraction of psychologically disturbed individuals, but they are making an impact. In 2005 the Toronto teams responded to 4.3% of total 911 calls; however, in 2008 they responded to 10.6% of calls. It is the job of the MCIT team to assess situations, divert people from harm, and arrange for appropriate treatment. The teams are able to divert many people from hospital emergency rooms and, because the necessary assessment has already been initiated, reduce wait times and ensure that clients who need hospital care receive attention more quickly. Other provinces also have some similar programs. For example, Latimer (2005) noted that there are a number of programs in Quebec patterned after the ACT model.

Indications are that more intensive treatment is more effective than less intensive methods in reducing time spent in the hospital, improving housing stability, and ameliorating symptoms (Tibbo et al., 2001). However, more intensive case management has not shown positive effects on other domains, such as time spent in jail or social functioning. The actual procedures that come under the rubric of case management vary a great deal from study to study. The services provided by a case management team will have positive effects only to the extent that those services are appropriate and effective.

A recent meta-analysis of 10 studies of the effectiveness of ACT for homeless populations with severe mental illness (Coldwell & Bender, 2007) concluded that ACT offers significant advantages over standard case management. It is not clear how to adapt the ACT model to remote rural areas in Canada. However, Gold et al. (2006) reported success with the design and implementation of a program that blended ACT with a supported employment program in a rural South Carolina county. Vocational and mental health services were tightly integrated within each self-contained team. Programs such as this could possibly adapt well to the Canadian situation.

GENERAL TRENDS IN TREATMENT

Only a generation ago, many, if not most, mental health professionals and laypeople believed that the primary culprit in the etiology of schizophrenia was the child's psychological environment—most especially, the family. As we have seen, the thinking now is that biological factors predispose a person to develop schizophrenia and that stressors, principally of a psychological nature, trigger the disorder in a predisposed individual and interfere with that person's adaptation to community living. The most promising contemporary approaches to treatment make good use of this increased understanding and emphasize the importance of both pharmacological and psychosocial interventions:

- Families and clients are given realistic and scientifically sound information about schizophrenia. They learn that it is a disability that can be controlled but is probably lifelong, and that, as with many other chronic disabilities, medication is necessary to help maintain control and allow clients to perform daily activities. What is not necessary, and is counterproductive, is the guilt of family members, especially parents, who may have been led to believe that something in the client's upbringing initiated the problem. Considerable effort is devoted in many treatment programs to dispelling this sense of culpability while encouraging a focus on the biological diathesis and the associated need for medication.
- Medication is only part of the whole treatment picture. Family-oriented treatment aims to lessen the stress experienced by the client after discharge from the hospital by reducing hostility, overinvolvement, intrusiveness, and criticality in the family (EE). Evidence is also emerging on the importance of CBT interventions that teach clients how to notice and control their own stress reactions before they snowball and lead to emotional dysregulation and disruptive behaviours.
- It is increasingly recognized that early intervention is important in influencing the course of schizophrenia over time; losing no time getting clients onto the right medications and providing support and information to the family and appropriate psychotherapy to the client can reduce

the severity of relapses in the future (Drury et al., 1996). Ongoing research in Canada and elsewhere on a variable identified as duration of untreated psychosis (DUP), typically operationalized as the period between the onset of the first psychotic symptom and the institution of antipsychotic treatment, has found that DUP predicts remission and positive symptom outcome after one year of treatment (see Malla, Norman, et al., 2002), and poorer functional and symptomatic outcome four years later (Clark et al., 2006), underscoring the importance of early intervention. Petersen and colleagues (2008) examined the frequency and predictors of good outcome in a follow-up of clients with first-episode schizophrenia spectrum disorders who had received intensive early treatment (the ORPUS trial). After two years, 36% remitted and 17% were considered fully recovered. Recovery was predicted by shorter DUP, better premorbid adjustment, fewer baseline negative symptoms, no substance abuse at baseline, and adherence to medication. In a recent study, Rabinovitch et al. (2009) demonstrated the importance of social and family support in the adherence to medication in the first six months of treatment for clients with first-episode psychosis. Refusal of medication at the first offer of treatment was also a strong predictor of nonadherence.

- Crumlish et al. (2009) reported that DUP predicted remission, positive symptoms, and social functioning in clients with first-episode psychosis who were followed for eight years. This study also tested the critical period hypothesis: the hypothesis that symptomatic and psychosocial deterioration occurs aggressively during the early years of psychosis, including during any period of untreated psychosis, and then slows or stops and the level attained endures over the long term. Crumlish and colleagues (2009) found that continuing functional recovery between four and eight years was predicted by duration of untreated illness (DUI), defined as the sum of the duration of the prodrome (time between onset of prodromal symptoms and onset of first psychotic symptoms) and DUP. Thus, the results provide some support for the critical period hypothesis. Interventions that shorten DUP and arrest early deterioration might have long-term benefits.

- It is also important to teach clients social skills and more reality-based thinking so that they can control their emotions and function more normally outside the hospital and probably reduce the EE encountered both inside and outside the home. Families affected by schizophrenia are encouraged to join support groups and formal organizations, such as the Alliance for the Mentally Ill or the Schizophrenia Society of Canada or its provincial or local counterparts, to combat and reduce the isolation and stigma associated with having a family member who has schizophrenia (Health Canada, 1991). Examples of Canadian early intervention programs for schizophrenia are summarized in Canadian Clinic Focus 11.1.

CANADIAN CLINIC FOCUS 11.1
EARLY DETECTION AND PREVENTION OF SCHIZOPHRENIA: THE PRIME CLINIC

"It's quite horrendous. First of all, you've got somebody that you love, a child that you've raised. And then suddenly, the child becomes a crazy person."

—June Beeby, former executive director of the Ontario Friends of Schizophrenics (now the Schizophrenia Society of Ontario) speaking about her 19-year-old son, Mathew, whose schizophrenia drove him to commit suicide (Nichols, 1995)

"Medication may diminish the symptoms, but not completely. Part of what we do is to teach people how to deal with voices, or paranoia, so that they can say to themselves, 'The reason I hear a voice coming out of that radiator is because I have schizophrenia'."

—Ruth Dickson, Calgary General Hospital psychiatrist (Nichols, 1995)

In the past decade, early psychosis intervention projects have been developed in major centres across Canada. These programs include the Early Psychosis Program at the Nova Scotia Hospital in Halifax, the First Episode Psychosis Clinic at the Centre for Addiction and Mental Health (CAMH) in Toronto, the Therapeutic Partnership Program of the Psychotic Disorders Clinic at Chedoke-McMaster Hospital in Hamilton, the Early Psychosis Program at Victoria Hospital in London, and the Early Psychosis Treatment and Prevention Program at Calgary's Foothills Hospital. There are about 20 such programs in Canada. Most are outpatient services for young people and most treatment is done in the participant's home. The hope is that early intervention will help people function at the highest level possible, despite their disorder. A research component is an important feature of many programs.

The PRIME Clinic: Prevention through Risk Identification Management and Education

The CAMH First Episode Psychosis Clinic was established in 1992 to help individuals with schizophrenia and their families deal with the complexities of managing an initial episode of schizophrenia. In 1999, Dr. Irvin Epstein became the first director of the new PRIME Clinic at CAMH. The PRIME Clinic was established to facilitate early identification and treatment of people aged 12 to 45 who are possibly in the earliest stages of a first episode of psychosis (prodromal phase) and are at risk of "transitioning" to the active phase. The phase preceding acute psychosis is often confusing and traumatic for people. In addition to presenting with mild pre-psychotic symptoms, people at risk may also be experiencing a decline in their usual day-to-day functioning or way of relating to others. They may also have a family history of psychotic disorders such as schizophrenia. The PRIME Clinic is fully affiliated with the Department of Psychiatry at the University of Toronto.

Clinical Services

Goal

The goal is to intervene during the prodromal phase to prevent (1) the onset of active phase symptoms and (2) the decline in cognitive, social, and occupational functioning associated with schizophrenia. Thus, the expectation is that through careful monitoring of identified high-risk individuals, it will be possible to prevent, delay, or attenuate active phase symptoms and improve the long-term course and outcome of the disorder. Thus, treatment should begin as soon as possible to ensure the best possible chance of recovery.

Identification

An educational component is offered for hospital staff, psychiatrists, and general practitioners in order to raise awareness about schizophrenia in the medical community and in the general public. Early signs of risk can include confusion, exaggerated self-opinion, suspiciousness, altered perceptions, odd thinking and speaking processes, lack of close friends, flat emotions, and difficulty with social activities and performing functions at school or at work.

Referral Process

Referrals are typically made by family physicians, child or general psychiatrists, and pediatricians. All referred individuals are given an initial consultation. If participation in clinic programs is not deemed appropriate, people are provided with further referrals.

Intervention

The program attempts to intervene on three levels to better treat and support both the individual and his or her family or other caregivers. The three levels entail coping and stress management strategies, medication, and education.

Follow-up

Follow-up is offered to individuals assessed in the prodromal phase.

Research

The PRIME Clinic and a clinic affiliated with the University of Calgary are both participating in a multi-centre North American clinical trial that is examining the benefits of using low-dose atypical neuroleptics (see McGlashan et al., 2003). This research has unique methodological aspects. For example, it is the first double-blind and placebo-controlled clinical trial of olanzapine in clients at risk of being prodromally symptomatic for psychosis, and it is testing for prevention vs. delay in psychosis onset. Some participants are also given the opportunity to participate in ongoing research studies conducted through

both clinics. The long-term effectiveness of the PRIME Clinic is currently being evaluated. Unfortunately, a recent report of the PRIME multi-site study of olanzapine vs. placebo in prodromal clients (McGlashan et al., 2006) concluded that a significant treatment difference in the "conversion-to-psychosis rate" was not demonstrated after one year of treatment and during a follow-up year. However, olanzapine was effective in improving positive symptoms.

Comment

In this chapter, we have described the best available therapeutic approaches to schizophrenia, both biological and psychosocial in nature. Published reports attest to the positive impact they can make on people with schizophrenia. However, there is often a gap between what is available in an ideal world and what the experiences of people actually are, especially when they do not live near large metropolitan centres where most of the research is conducted and state-of-the-art psychosocial treatments are obtainable.

Although comprehensive Canadian data are not available, this issue was highlighted in an article by A. F. Lehman et al. (1998) in the *Schizophrenia Bulletin*. Lehman et al. interviewed more than 700 U.S. clients and reviewed their medical records. As expected, almost 90% had been prescribed antipsychotic drugs, but of these clients, only 62% received a dose in the recommended range; about 15% got too little, and the remainder too much. Further, although more than 90% of clients were prescribed maintenance doses of drugs, only 29% of them received a dose in the recommended range; of the 71% who did not receive a recommended dose, about half were getting too much and half too little. African-Americans were much more likely to be prescribed maintenance doses that were too high. We do not know whether or not minority groups in Canada receive excessively high maintenance doses of neuroleptics, but it is a real possibility that should be investigated.

Lehman et al. (1998) also examined psychosocial treatments, but these were more difficult to evaluate because records or client reports did not indicate whether the treatment was one of those considered effective (such as social skills training). Just in terms of whether any psychosocial treatments at all were prescribed for these clients, the data show that some sort of individual or group therapy was provided for more than 90% of inpatients. For clients who had regular contact with their families, family treatment of some sort was prescribed for only about 40%. For unemployed clients, vocational rehabilitation (teaching job skills) was prescribed for only about 30%.

Conclusion? Many people with schizophrenia are not getting anything near optimal therapy. Critics in Canada are also concerned that provincial governments burdened by deficits may cut funding to various services in the community that are even more essential at a time when psychiatric beds in provincial psychiatric hospitals and general hospitals are being closed. These services include subsidized housing, crisis response centres, and rehabilitation programs. Such community services vary greatly in both availability and quality in different parts of Canada. In most places, including many of our major cities, the services are very fragmented, with numerous government-funded and private organizations offering a range of community services for people suffering from schizophrenia (Latimer, 2005).

Does the research support early intervention for schizophrenia? Is it effective? Proponents argue that outcome will be improved, and early intervention programs are now established in North America, Europe, and Australia. Marshall and Rathbone (2006) reviewed all RTCs designed to prevent progression to psychosis in people showing prodromal symptoms, or to improve outcome for people with first-episode psychosis. Only seven, mostly small-sample studies met inclusion criteria, including the ongoing PRIME multi-site study. The authors concluded that there was insufficient data to draw definitive conclusions. However, Harvey, Lepage, and Malla (2007) from the Douglas Hospital and McGill University in Quebec assessed the effectiveness of 11 "enriched" interventions relative to 6 "standard care" trials for clients with recent-onset psychosis, including the Calgary Early Psychosis Program. Enriched interventions included comprehensive programs with specialized and personalized services, a higher caregiver-to-client ratio, and a rational pharmacotherapy for at least six months, and some form of relevant, well-identified psychosocial treatment (e.g., family interventions, social skills training, CBT, or supportive psychotherapy) for at least three months. Harvey et al. (2007) concluded that enriched interventions are more effective than standard care for both symptomatic and functional improvement over a one-year period. Another multi-site Canadian study

by the Douglas Hospital group (Malla et al., 2007) examined one-year symptomatic outcome in people with first-episode psychosis at three different publicly funded sites. It concluded, "Similarly enriched early intervention services may produce different outcomes, even within a relatively homogeneous mental health system" (p. 563). It was suggested that "local factors" can influence outcomes.

More recently, Malla and colleagues (Menezes, Malla, Norman, Roy, & Zipursky, 2009) conducted a one-year follow-up of 200 first-episode psychosis clients following one year of treatment from programs in four university centres in Ontario (Toronto, Western, McMaster, and Ottawa). A majority (70%) were involved in school, work, and/or relationships; however, the rate of functional recovery (51%) was lower than the rate of symptom remission (74%). Residual symptoms at six months and comorbid substance abuse predicted outcome variance. Longer duration follow-ups are necessary. Addington and Addington (1998) reported on a sample of first-episode psychosis clients who were followed for up to three years in the Calgary comprehensive multi-element program. For both those who completed three years in the program and those who left early, improvements in positive symptoms and social functioning but not negative symptoms were observed. However, about 40% were deemed to require continual follow-up in specialized mental health services, whereas 24% could be followed by family physicians. A limitation of both of these studies was that they were naturalistic rather than RCTs with a comparison group.

• Though the kind of integrated treatment we have been describing is promising, sadly, it is not widely available or accessible to most clients and their families. The reasons for this are unclear (Baucom et al., 1998) (see the "Comment" concluding Canadian Clinic Focus 11.1 for a discussion of a U.S. study on this issue). One factor, however, is likely the increasing popularity and use of psychoactive medications—a trend that, although helpful to many, too narrowly defines schizophrenia as a medical disease that is relatively uninfluenced by social context. Commenting on the reliance on the use of drugs in the treatment of schizophrenia, Dr. Abram Hoffer (2000), president of the Canadian Schizophrenia Foundation, stated that "tranquilizers convert a natural psychosis (schizophrenia) into an iatrogenic psychosis (tranquilizer psychosis) … characterized by a decrease in symptoms and by an increase in apathy. … The only treatment for tranquilizer psychosis is to discontinue the drug" (p. 146).

FURTHER ISSUES IN THE CARE OF PEOPLE WITH SCHIZOPHRENIA

As people with schizophrenia grow older, they are less likely to be living with their families. The transition to living arrangements outside the parents' home is fraught with

risk. Aftercare is one of society's thorniest social problems; we describe it in more detail in Focus on Discovery 11.3. Do people with schizophrenia end up on the streets by falling through cracks in the mental health system?

THE HOMELESS MENTALLY ILL Though a relatively small proportion of homeless people in the United States are mentally ill, many people with schizophrenia are among those without residences. In Canada, the situation is much different—the mentally ill make up a large proportion of the homeless. For example, a United Way (1997) report on homelessness in Metropolitan Toronto concluded that about 86% of the homeless have experienced a mental health or addiction problem at some point in their lives. Many of these individuals have been diagnosed with schizophrenia. The Mayor's Homelessness Action Task Force (1999) concluded that between 30 and 35% of homeless people are living with mental illness. One of its 105 recommendations called for 5,000 supportive housing units for those who are currently suffering from mental disorders and addictions. However, the problem of the homeless mentally ill is not found only in Canada's largest cities, such as Toronto, Vancouver, and Montreal. Stuart & Arboleda-Florez (2000) determined that three quarters of homeless shelter users in Calgary presented some psychiatric symptoms, and a third had a significant mental health problem.

"I have something to offer society. It may not be as much as the next guy, but I feel my contribution is valuable and I want to offer it. There are times when I can't, when I'm sick and I have to stay in the hospital. But when I'm well, I have something I want to give, to share. I want to be part of the world."

—Sandy, from a National Film Board of Canada film about three people in Toronto who suffer from schizophrenia Full of Sound and Fury

Some people with psychological problems function too well to remain in a psychiatric hospital and yet do not function independently enough to live on their own or even with their own families. For such individuals, there are **halfway houses** or **group homes**; Fairweather's "community lodge" is a classic example (Fairweather et al., 1969). These are protected living units, typically located in large, formerly private residences. Here, clients discharged from a psychiatric facility live, take their meals, and gradually return to ordinary community life by holding a part-time job or going to school. As part of what is called vocational rehabilitation, these former hospital clients learn marketable skills that can help them secure employment and thereby increase their chances of remaining in the community. Living arrangements may be relatively unstructured, and some houses set up money-making enterprises that help train and support the residents.

Depending on how well funded the halfway house or group home is, the staff may include psychiatrists or clinical psychologists. The most important staff members are often paraprofessionals— sometimes undergraduate psychology majors or graduate students in clinical psychology or social work—who live in the house and act both as administrators and as friends to the residents. Group meetings, at which residents talk out their frustrations and learn to relate to others in honest and constructive ways, are often part of the routine. Programs modelled after Fairweather's pioneering efforts have been founded across the United States and Canada. These programs have helped thousands of people, most of them with schizophrenia, make enough of a social adaptation to be able to remain out of the hospital. The integration of therapy with gainful employment is increasingly recognized as important in keeping people with schizophrenia (and also mental retardation; see Chapter 15) out of institutional settings (Kopelowicz & Liberman, 1998).

The need for effective halfway houses and group homes for former psychiatric hospital clients cannot be underestimated, especially in light of deinstitutionalization trends. Although civil rights issues are very important in shielding mental health clients from ill-advised and even harmful detention—a topic discussed in depth in Chapter 18—discharge has all too often led to shabbily dressed former clients having to fend for themselves on the streets or being re-hospitalized in the revolving-door syndrome. Former clients usually need follow-up community-based services, and these are scarce. However, the study by Stuart and Arboleda-Florez (2001) on community attitudes found that most people would not oppose a group home for people with schizophrenia in their own neighbourhood.

A model of what aftercare can be is part of the Paul and Lentz (1977) comparative treatment study. When clients were discharged from any of the three wards of the program—social learning, milieu therapy, or routine hospital management—they usually went to live in nearby boarding homes. These homes, often converted motels, were staffed by workers who had been trained by the Paul-Lentz project to treat the former clients according to social-learning principles. The workers attended to the specific problems of the former clients using rewards, including tokens, to encourage more independence and normal functioning.

Because assessment was careful and ongoing, the staff knew at all times how a particular client was doing. Paul's mental health centre project—and this is of paramount importance—acted as consultant to these community boarding homes, helping their staffs work with the former clients in as effective a manner as possible. In Canada, the provinces and territories financially support some group homes for former mental health clients as part of the mental health system. However, only rarely have the procedures followed in these homes been carefully planned and monitored by professional mental health staff.

Despite many practical problems, such as staff layoffs, the former clients derived significant benefits from the aftercare; more than 90% of the clients discharged from the social-learning ward were able to remain continuously in the community residences during the year-and-a-half follow-up period, and some remained for as long as four years more. The revolving-door syndrome in this instance was halted. Finally, in a finding rather critical in these days of diminishing public funds, the full social-learning program—the mental health centre treatment combined with the aftercare—was much less expensive than institutional care.

Some communities in Canada have non-profit organizations that have been modelled on the highly regarded Fountain House Project that started in New York City (Health Canada, 1991). The "club-house program" is designed specifically for people with psychiatric disorders, including schizophrenia, and "the club" is the focus of services that are provided, including reasonably priced meals, social and recreational activities, and sheltered employment. Organizations like this attempt to develop positive working relations with local employers and arrange employment where appropriate. The clubs sometimes provide housing.

Most aftercare programs are paying increasing attention to preparing clients for the work world, teaching them how to obtain and retain employment for which they can qualify (Latimer, 2005). Governments have begun to recognize the importance of employment to people with mental disabilities such as schizophrenia, since having a job can increase their chances of living independently or at least outside a psychiatric hospital. There is a recognition, too, of the harmful effects of not working and not being able to live in a reasonably independent manner. The trend is to do whatever is necessary to help people work and live in as autonomous a manner as their physical and mental condition will allow (Kopelowicz & Liberman, 1998).

The downward spiral in functioning among homeless people with schizophrenia is difficult to reverse. Welfare and other social service benefits are available to those with schizophrenia, but many do not receive all they are entitled to because of inadequately staffed bureaucracies. And many people with schizophrenia have lost contact with their post-hospital treatment programs. Despite the existence of mental health care services, however inadequate, the homeless mentally ill often do not know where to access them (Stuart & Arboleda-Florez, 2000). The Calgary Urban Project Society (CUPS) treats about 1,000 homeless people each month, 30 to 40% of whom are mentally ill (Bakogeorge, 2000). Lorraine Melchior, director of the storefront health clinic and aid agency, describes the case of a homeless man with schizophrenia who trusted CUPS and allowed the agency's physician to treat him and persuade him to accept hospital admission: "So here you had a physician ... in an alley, doing an assessment. We need to try to change the system ... and we need to go to where the people are" (Bakogeorge, 2000). This issue is discussed further in Chapter 18.

EMPLOYMENT AND HOUSING Obtaining employment poses a major challenge for people with schizophrenia because of bias against those who have been in psychiatric hospitals. Although laws in most provinces and territories prohibit employers from asking applicants if they have a history of serious mental illness, former psychiatric hospital clients still have a difficult time obtaining regular employment. Also a factor is how much leeway employers are willing to give former mental health clients whose thinking, emotions, and behaviour are usually unconventional to some degree.

There are some positive signs, however. Twenty or thirty years after first developing symptoms of schizophrenia, about half of people with schizophrenia are able to look after themselves and participate meaningfully in society at large. Some continue to take medications, but many do not and yet still function well enough to stay out of the hospital (CME Institute, 2007). Welfare, community, and other social service agencies in Canada try to provide rent subsidies or affordable housing to former mental health clients to help them live in their own apartments or group homes, where they are occasionally checked on by mental health workers. Nonetheless, there is a chronic shortage of subsidized housing for psychiatric clients in most places in Canada. Further, a new study by the Centre for Equality of Rights in Accommodation (see www.equalityrights.org/cera/docs/CERAFinalReport.pdf) reported that more than one third of people in Toronto with a psychiatric disorder would face substantial discrimination when trying to rent accommodation.

The jury at the inquest into the highly publicized case of Edmond Yu (Coyle, 1999), who was diagnosed with paranoid schizophrenia and was shot to death at age 35 by a police officer while brandishing a small hammer aboard a Toronto bus, recommended provision of safe houses for psychiatric clients and more affordable housing. The jury's list of 24 recommendations also included the provision of jobs with flexible or part-time hours that would offer the dignity of work. On January 22, 2004, the Edmond Yu Safe House Project was officially launched at the Gerstein Crisis Centre in Toronto. The house was intended to provide transition for 16 people who would be able to stay for up to 18 months while working their way into permanent housing. The organizers hoped that the city and federal governments would share the $2 million start-up costs and that the Province of Ontario would provide the annual budget ($790,000). The safe house is still not a reality.

SCHIZOPHRENIA AND SUBSTANCE ABUSE Preventing substance abuse among people with schizophrenia is largely an unmet challenge. Programs for treating substance abuse often exclude people who are seriously mentally ill, and programs for treating people who are seriously mentally ill usually exclude substance abusers; in both instances, the reason is that the comorbid condition is considered disruptive to the treatment (Mueser, Bellack, & Blanchard, 1992). Additional problems arise because people with schizophrenia who are substance abusers often do not continue to take their antipsychotic medication and, as a result, lose ground in their efforts to lead a more normal life. This situation is gradually changing in Canada as a consequence of attempts to integrate mental health facilities and programs. For example, in 1997, in Toronto, the provincial Health Services Restructuring Commission ordered the merging of four facilities associated with the treatment of mental disorders and substance abuse: the Clarke Institute of Psychiatry, the Queen Street Mental Health Centre, the Addiction Research Foundation, and the Donwood Institute. According to psychiatrist Paul Garfinkel, the first chief executive officer of the larger umbrella institution, the newly created Centre for Addiction and Mental Health (CAMH) was expected to be a stronger and more effective force to address issues related to funding, advocacy, service fragmentation, and client capacity (Hall, 1998). CAMH is now undergoing a major redevelopment (see Canadian Perspectives 11.1).

Edmond Wai-Hong Yu, a one-time University of Toronto medical student who deteriorated into schizophrenia and homelessness. The Canadian Press/Dick Loek.

CANADIAN PERSPECTIVES 11.1
THE NEW CAMH: A MODEL FOR CANADA AND THE WORLD

"It's a bold thing to do and the right thing to do. We have mistreated these people, and they deserve a humane and caring society and treatment. If we do this, society will change. Remember, people used to hold their breath when passing the hospital, and in the 1900s saw patients as a sideshow. The point is, we can change."

−Dr. Paul Garfinkel, quoted in Scrivener, 2007, p. A8

Determined to break down stigma while improving care, the Centre for Addiction and Mental Health (CAMH) is now undergoing a $380-Million redevelopment that will bring into a single hub the services that are currently spread across the City of Toronto (see Centre for Addiction and Mental Health, 2009; Scrivener, 2007). A challenging and controversial aspect is the intent to open the hospital's grounds to the neighbourhood and to integrate the neighbourhood into the grounds "to create the first large-scale 'urban village' mental health facility in the world" (Scrivener, 2007, p. A8).

> The renovation aims to transform the site's institutional character in order to make patients' experience closer to "normal" life in the city. The scheme involves criss-crossing the 27-acre property with public streets, constructing a home-like environment for those the CAMH now calls clients instead of patients, and leasing out street-level retail space to restaurants and other businesses. It's envisioned that clients, staff, and neighbours will mingle naturally on sidewalks, parks, and cafes .... All but one of the (old) buildings will be demolished. Half of the 2.5 million square feet of new space will be for hospital use, and the other half non-hospital, with a range of possibilities including grocery stores, a market garden, artists' studios, craft shops, medical labs, mixed residential space, a fitness centre and a library .... Clients will have their own keys and street addresses. The sense is of a temporary stay, not institutionalization for life, though certainly some of the hospital's older patients will live out their lives there .... In the face of criticism and doubters, Garfinkel remains optimistic about the hospital and its patients. (Scrivener, 2007, pp. A8–A9)

The design of the hub is intended to facilitate interaction and communication among the areas of client care, prevention,

A look at the Intergenerational Wellness Centre, one of the new CAMH buildings currently under construction. When completed in 2012, it will combine CAMH's Child, Youth and Family and Geriatric Mental Health programs. Along with the 48 beds for the Geriatric Mental Health Program, the Centre will include Canada's first full service 12-bed inpatient program dedicated to youth struggling with both mental illness and addiction issues. Centre for Addiction and Mental Health.

education, and research. The hub will offer residential, inpatient, and outpatient care, including community-based outpatient services for people living in the surrounding area. The hub will also be the central focus for a linked network of community-based programs and services.

The 12-year reconstruction started in the fall of 2006. The first phase was completed in April 2008. Phase 1A included construction of four buildings, a public park, and a new road. A total of 48 beds for the addictions program and 24 beds for the mood and anxiety programs were established with what CAMH calls "alternative milieu" buildings. The construction of phase 1B commenced in December 2009. Additional buildings will include a new client care building with 12 beds for youth and the Geriatric Mental Health Program combining both inpatient and outpatient programs. Construction also began on the new administrative and outpatient hub, which will house the Out of This World Café run by clients for both clients and the public. Another new building will combine the central plant and parking garage. Occupancy is expected in the fall of 2012 and end stage 1 of redevelopment. It is estimated that stage 2 will be completed in 2015 and with it about 90% of the redevelopment itself. The conclusion of Stage 3 is projected for 2018–2020.

Thinking Critically

1. The new CAMH is definitely a bold thing to do, but is it the "right" thing? Do you think integration with the community will work? What are the possible drawbacks? What could you do to help make it work?

2. Some people have mixed feelings about whether the CAMH redevelopment will decrease stigma and have suggested that what is really needed is a makeover of attitudes toward people with schizophrenia. Do you agree? How would you go about changing your friends' attitudes?

Dr. Paul Garfinkel, former CEO of CAMH, who oversaw the first phases of a daring redevelopment of CAMH until his retirement. Dr. Catherine Zahn became CEO on December 1, 2009, and leads the remainder of the transformation. Toronto Star/Richard Lautens.

DESTIGMATIZATION Further progress in the destigmatization of schizophrenia must occur, and perhaps the new CAMH will facilitate positive changes in attitudes toward the mentally ill. Stip, Caron, and Lane (2001) examined perceptions of schizophrenia in Quebec. The findings were both heartening and disheartening. Of the 1,001 people interviewed, 54% indicated that people with schizophrenia should be considered violent and dangerous, and 31% felt that an employee with schizophrenia would be fired from his or her job. With respect to the issue of integration of people with schizophrenia into the community, 49% agreed with rehabilitation in the community but 40% disagreed. On a positive note that bodes well for the future, the youngest respondents were more likely to agree with rehabilitation in the community (57%) than older respondents (29%).

Stuart and Arboleda-Florez (2001) surveyed attitudes toward people with schizophrenia in two adjacent rural and urban health regions in Alberta. Half the respondents knew someone who had been treated for schizophrenia or another mental illness. Social distance increased with the level of intimacy required, ranging from a low of 20% who claimed that they would be unable to remain friends with someone with schizophrenia to a high of 75% who would be unwilling to marry someone with schizophrenia. Consistent with Stip et al. (2000), respondents over 60 years of age were the least knowledgeable or enlightened about schizophrenia and the ones who practised the most social distancing. Stuart and Arboleda-Florez (2001) did, however, conclude that "most respondents were relatively well informed and progressive in their reported understanding of schizophrenia" (p. 245). The majority believed that people with schizophrenia could be treated

with some success outside of a psychiatric facility, needed to take antipsychotic medications to control their symptoms, could function adequately in regular employment, and were not a public nuisance or threat to safety. The authors further concluded that it is people's knowledge of schizophrenia rather than exposure to the mentally ill that is the "central modifiable correlate of schizophrenia" (Stuart & Arboleda-Florez, 2001, p. 245).

Much of the stigma around schizophrenia has been attributed to negative media accounts of people with the disorder. A media intervention attempt in Calgary sought to promote more positive attitudes among Calgary newspaper journalists by providing the media with accurate information and liaisons to mental health experts. Unfortunately, the intervention yielded mixed findings. In general, the number of positive stories about mental illness increased following the intervention, but the number of negative stories about people with schizophrenia also increased (Stuart, 2003). Stuart suggested that local positive stories might be undermined by a phenomenon dubbed "The CNN effect"—that is, sensationalized television stories may overshadow local anti-stigma initiatives.

Finally, what about mental health professionals? Do they hold fewer stigmatizing attitudes than the general public as would be expected? A study in Switzerland (Nordt, Rossler, & Lauber, 2006) reported that psychiatrists actually have more negative stereotypes than the general population. Nordt et al. (2006) concluded, "the better knowledge of mental health professionals and their support of individual rights neither entail fewer stereotypes nor enhance the willingness to closely interact with mentally ill people" (p. 709).

SUMMARY

- The symptoms of schizophrenia are typically divided into positive and negative types. Positive symptoms refer to behavioural excesses, such as delusions, hallucinations, and disorganized speech. Negative symptoms refer to behavioural deficits, such as flat affect, avolition, alogia, and anhedonia. Individuals with schizophrenia also show deterioration in functioning in occupational and social roles.

- The diagnosis requires that symptoms be present for at least one month and that a prodromal or residual phase, in which some symptoms are present but at a lower level of severity, lasts for at least five months.

- Schizophrenia is typically divided into subtypes, such as paranoid, catatonic, and disorganized. These subtypes are based on the prominence of particular symptoms (e.g., delusions in the paranoid subtype) and reflect the considerable variations in behaviour found among people diagnosed with schizophrenia.

- The concept of schizophrenia arose from the pioneering efforts of Kraepelin and Bleuler. Kraepelin's work fostered a descriptive approach and a narrow definition, whereas Bleuler's theoretical emphasis led to a broad diagnostic category. Bleuler had a great influence on the American concept of schizophrenia, making it extremely broad. By the middle of the twentieth century, the differences between the diagnosis of schizophrenia in the United States and the diagnosis of schizophrenia in Europe were vast.

- Subsequent to the publication of *DSM-III* in 1980, the American concept of schizophrenia has become narrower and more like the European view.

- Research has tried to determine the etiological role of specific biological variables, such as genetic and biochemical factors and brain pathology, as well as of stressors, such as low social class and family conflict. The data on genetic transmission are impressive. Adoption studies, which generally escape the criticisms levelled at family or twin studies, show a strong relationship between having a schizophrenic parent and the likelihood of developing the disorder. Perhaps the genetic predisposition has biochemical correlates, although research in this area permits only tentative conclusions.

- It appears that an increased sensitivity of dopamine receptors in the limbic area of the brain is related to the positive symptoms of schizophrenia. The negative symptoms may be due to dopamine underactivity in the prefrontal cortex. Research into biochemical factors in schizophrenia is beginning to examine the possible role played by other neurotransmitters, such as serotonin.

- The brains of people with schizophrenia, especially those with negative symptoms, have enlarged lateral ventricles and prefrontal atrophies, as well as reduced metabolism and structural abnormalities in the frontal and limbic areas. Some of these structural abnormalities could result from maternal viral infection during the second trimester of pregnancy or from damage sustained during a difficult birth.

- The diagnosis of schizophrenia is most frequently applied to members of the lowest social class. Available information indicates that this is so mainly because the disorder keeps people from achieving higher social status.

- Vague communications and conflicts are evident in the family life of people with schizophrenia and probably contribute to their disorder. A high level of expressed emotion (EE)—criticism, hostility, and emotional overinvolvement—in families has been shown to be an important determinant of relapse. Increases in general life stress have also been shown to be important precipitants of relapse. These stressors may increase cortisol levels, which, in turn, stimulate dopamine activity.

- Much of the available information is consistent with a diathesis-stress or biopsychosocial view of schizophrenia. Investigators have turned to the high-risk method, studying children who are particularly vulnerable to schizophrenia

by virtue of having a schizophrenic parent. Mednick and Schulsinger found that circumstances predicting maladjustment in adulthood differ depending on whether positive or negative symptoms are most prominent.

- There are both biological and psychological therapies for schizophrenia. Insulin and electroconvulsive treatments and even surgery were in vogue in the early twentieth century, but they are no longer much used, primarily because of the availability of antipsychotic drugs, in particular, the phenothiazines. In numerous studies, these medications have been found to have a major beneficial impact on the disordered lives of people with schizophrenia. Newer medications such as clozapine and risperidone are at least as effective as the phenothiazines and produce fewer motor side effects. Drugs have also been a factor in the deinstitutionalization of hospital clients.

- Drugs alone are not a completely effective treatment, as clients with schizophrenia need to be taught or retaught ways of dealing with the challenges of everyday life. Furthermore, most antipsychotic drugs have serious side effects, especially after long-term use, and many clients with schizophrenia do not benefit from them.

- Good evidence for the efficacy of psychoanalytic treatments does not exist, although case studies of dramatic cures have been presented in both the professional and the popular literature.

- Family therapy, aimed at reducing high levels of expressed emotion, has been shown to be valuable in preventing relapse.

- Behavioural treatments, such as social skills training, have helped clients discharged from mental hospitals meet the inevitable stresses of family and community living or, when discharge is not possible, lead more ordered and constructive lives within an institution.

- Recent efforts to change the thinking of people with schizophrenia are showing much promise.

- The most effective treatments for schizophrenia are likely to involve both biological and psychological components.

KEY TERMS

alogia (p. 355)
anhedonia (p. 356)
antipsychotic drugs (p. 376)
asociality (p. 356)
avolition (p. 355)
catatonic immobility (p. 356)
catatonic schizophrenia (p. 360)
cognitive enhancement therapy (CET) (p. 384)
delusional disorder (p. 358)
delusional jealousy (p. 360)
delusions (p. 354)
dementia praecox (p. 357)
disorganized schizophrenia (p. 359)

disorganized speech (thought disorder) (p. 353)
dopamine theory (p. 365)
expressed emotion (EE) (p. 372)
flat affect (p. 356)
grandiose delusions (p. 360)
group homes (p. 390)
halfway houses (p. 390)
hallucinations (p. 355)
ideas of reference (p. 360)
inappropriate affect (p. 356)
incoherence (p. 354)
loose associations (derailment) (p. 354)

negative symptoms (p. 355)
paranoid schizophrenia (p. 360)
personal therapy (p. 384)
positive symptoms (p. 353)
prefrontal lobotomy (p. 376)
psychosis risk syndrome (p. 359)
residual schizophrenia (p. 360)
schizophrenia (p. 351)
schizophrenogenic mother (p. 371)
social-selection theory (p. 371)
sociogenic hypothesis (p. 371)
undifferentiated schizophrenia (p. 360)
waxy flexibility (p. 356)

REFLECTIONS: PAST, PRESENT, AND FUTURE

- Most people diagnosed with schizophrenia lead a tortured, tormented existence; however, even when they respond favourably to antipsychotic medication, they often experience severe side effects and stop taking their medication. Some advocates have argued that, for this reason, people with schizophrenia should have the right to choose to continue to be psychotic. Do you agree or disagree with these advocates? Under what circumstances, if any, should we be allowed to impose treatment on psychiatric clients?

- Assume that that you are engaged to be married. Although your future partner appears to be extremely well adjusted, he or she has a fraternal twin who has been diagnosed with schizophrenia. The two of you are concerned about the genetic implications for your children. Will they be at elevated risk for schizophrenia? What other factors could put your children at risk of developing schizophrenia? What future scientific findings would help you to decide whether or not to have children?

- Canadian authors have made a strong recommendation that genetic counselling should be made available to everyone with schizophrenia and their families (see Hodgkinson, Murphy, O'Neill, Brzustowicz, & Bassett, 2001). *Genetic counselling* is a process of communication that involves conveying information about risk to clients and their relatives to help them make decisions, deal with current issues, and anticipate other issues associated with schizophrenia. Do you agree with the recommendation?

- Assume that you are a psychologist who has been given carte blanche to develop a comprehensive and effective psychosocial treatment for schizophrenia (to be used in conjunction with traditional medical management). What would you focus on? Assume that the very best programs include the following components: individual case managers to work as advocates to help clients obtain necessary services; social supports that can "wrap around" clients to keep them in the community (e.g., safe houses and peer support groups); individualized proactive plans to facilitate crisis avoidance and management; and specific vocational rehabilitation plans that identify needed skills for occupational goals. Design and implement your program. Be specific. Assume that the financial cost or the availability of human resources becomes a factor. Which component(s) would you delete from your program?

CHAPTER 12

SUBSTANCE-RELATED DISORDERS

"I don't know what is marijuana. Perhaps I will try it when it will no longer be criminal. I will have my money for my fine and a joint in the other hand."

—Former Prime Minister Jean Chrétien, as quoted in the *Winnipeg Free Press* in 2003, when Canada was considering decriminalizing marijuana

"I also have experienced with my own family, in the most painful way possible, the consequence of excessive drinking."

—British Columbia Premier Gordon Campbell, during his 2003 apology for his drunk driving incident, alluding to his father, a doctor and medical school professor who suffered from alcoholism and committed suicide when Campbell was 13 years old

"There is no silver bullet to deal with the scourge of addiction. If drug enforcement really worked then we wouldn't have situations like we do in the Downtown Eastside (of Vancouver)… Insite is about working in the reality of the situation, and most importantly about preventing overdose deaths."

—Mark Townsend, Executive Director of the Portland Hotel Society, which operates Insite, the safe injection site targeted for closure by the federal government (Chesser, 2009)

Carol Del Angel/Ikon Images/Getty Images.

"The blackouts became regular. Each time I drank there would be hours, even days I could not remember. I would start to work and manage to get three pages done. Then, thinking three pages was a wonderful amount, I would go to the bookshelf where I kept my bottle of rum and have one drink, then two … . Yet now, when I really wanted to stop, when I prayed to be able to drink normally, I could not. Nor could I control anything I did or said once I started drinking. It was a terrible feeling, not to know what was to happen to me once I went outside. Three-day drunks became three-week drunks, and then three-month drunks."

—Richards, 2001, pp. 115–116

The above excerpt is from the personal account of the award-winning author from New Brunswick, David Adams Richards. His story is but one of 10 compelling essays by Canadian authors in the book *Addicted: Notes from the Belly of the Beast* (see Crozier & Lane, 2001). Fortunately, Richards was able to quit drinking over 20 years ago when a friend took him to an Alcoholics Anonymous meeting. His story illustrates that some people with extreme forms of addiction can overcome it. From prehistoric times, humankind has used various substances in the hope of reducing physical pain or altering states of consciousness. Almost all peoples have discovered some intoxicant that affects the central nervous system, relieving physical and mental anguish or producing euphoria. Despite the often-devastating consequences of taking such substances into the body, their initial effects are usually pleasing, a factor that is perhaps at the root of substance abuse.

North America is a drug culture. North Americans use drugs to wake up (caffeine in coffee or tea), to stay alert throughout the day (nicotine in cigarettes, caffeine in soft drinks), to relax (alcohol), and to reduce pain (aspirin). The widespread availability and frequent use of various drugs sets the stage for the potential abuse of drugs, the topic of this chapter.

The pathological use of substances falls into two categories: substance abuse and substance dependence. **Substance dependence** is characterized by *DSM-IV-TR* as the presence of at least three of the following:

- The person develops **tolerance**, indicated by either (1) larger doses of the substance being needed to produce the desired effect or (2) the effects of the drug becoming markedly less if the usual amount is taken. Note that it has been proposed in the initial draft of *DSM-5* that the distinction between substance abuse and dependence be dropped and replaced with an inclusive category named Addiction and Related Disorders. It is further recommended that the term "dependence" be limited in use and only refer to physiological dependence (see www.dsm5.org).
- **Withdrawal** symptoms—negative physical and psychological effects—develop when the person stops taking the substance or reduces the amount. The person may also use the substance to relieve or avoid withdrawal symptoms.

- The person uses more of the substance or uses it for a longer time than intended.
- The person recognizes excessive use of the substance; he or she may have tried to reduce usage but has been unable to do so.
- Much of the person's time is spent in efforts to obtain the substance or recover from its effects.
- Substance use continues despite psychological or physical problems caused or exacerbated by the drug (e.g., smoking despite knowing that it increases the risk for cancer and cardiovascular disease).
- The person gives up or cuts back participation in many activities (work, recreation, socializing) because of the use of the substance.

Note that the Substance-Related Disorders Work Group for the DSM-5 has recommended that pathological gambling being included as disorder that falls into this description. This reflects the inclusion of behavioural addictions. Internet addiction was not included at present because the work group felt, perhaps incorrectly, that there is not enough evidence to warrant its inclusion at this point.

Substance dependence is diagnosed as being accompanied by physiological dependence (also called addiction) if either tolerance or withdrawal is present. In general, physical dependence on a drug is associated with more severe problems (Schuckit et al., 1999).

For the less serious diagnosis of **substance abuse**, the person must experience one of the following as a result of recurrent use of the drug:

- failure to fulfill major obligations (e.g., absences from work or neglect of children)
- exposure to physical dangers (e.g., operating machinery or driving while intoxicated)
- legal problems (e.g., arrests for disorderly conduct or traffic violations)
- persistent social or interpersonal problems (e.g., arguments with a spouse)

The *DSM-IV-TR* section on substance-related disorders includes several other diagnoses. Substance intoxication is diagnosed when the ingestion of a substance affects the central nervous system and produces maladaptive cognitive and behavioural effects. If a person addicted to a drug is denied it and then experiences withdrawal, that person receives a diagnosis of both substance dependence and substance withdrawal. An example of substance withdrawal is alcohol withdrawal delirium, commonly known as the **DTs (delirium tremens)**. Furthermore, drugs can cause dementia and the symptoms of other Axis I disorders.

Numerous diagnostic and classification problems have been identified and there is growing evidence of a lack of a clear distinction in reality between substance abuse vs. substance dependence (see Martin, Chung, & Langenbucher,

2008). Martin et al. (2008) have provided several arguments for a shift in *DSM-5*; they propose that there is a quantitative severity distinction rather than a qualitative distinction between substance abuse and substance dependence, and so both disorders should be included on a single continuum. They also listed several problems with the existing substance use disorder criteria and called for their revision. For instance, they argue that the legal problems criterion is a poor discriminator of substance problem severity. In addition, substance use disorder symptoms currently oversample moderate pathology and are less useful in characterizing mild or severe pathology. Also, the role of comorbidity, especially in terms of comorbid externalizing disorders, is not well delineated.

We turn now to an overview of the major substance-related disorders, focusing on problem drinking, nicotine and cigarette smoking, marijuana, sedatives and stimulants, and the hallucinogens. We will then look at etiological factors suspected in substance abuse and dependence and conclude with an examination of available therapies. Before we do so, however, note that misuse of substances is a problem in its own right, but substance misuse often accompanies the disorders described in earlier chapters of this book.

ALCOHOL ABUSE AND DEPENDENCE

The term *alcoholic* is familiar to most people, yet it does not have a precise meaning. To some, it implies a person slumped against a building, to others an abusive husband or co-worker, and to still others a man or woman sneaking drinks during the day. All these images are to some extent accurate, yet none provides a full or useful definition. *DSM-IV-TR* distinguishes between alcohol dependence and alcohol abuse. This distinction is not always made in the research literature. The term *abuse* is often used to refer to both aspects of the excessive and harmful use of alcohol.

Alcohol dependence may include tolerance or withdrawal reactions. People who are physically dependent on alcohol generally have more severe symptoms of the disorder (Schuckit et al., 1998). Those who begin drinking early in life develop their first withdrawal symptoms in their thirties or forties. The effects of the abrupt withdrawal of alcohol in a chronic, heavy user may be dramatic because the body has become accustomed to the drug. Subjectively, the patient is often anxious, depressed, weak, restless, and unable to sleep. Tremors of the muscles, especially of the small musculatures of the fingers, face, eyelids, lips, and tongue, may be marked, and pulse, blood pressure, and temperature are elevated.

In relatively rare cases, a person who has been drinking heavily for a number of years may also experience delirium tremens when the level of alcohol in the blood drops suddenly. The person becomes delirious as well as tremulous and has hallucinations that are primarily visual, but may be tactile, as well. Unpleasant and very active creatures—snakes, cockroaches,

Canadian hockey player Theoren Fleury had to leave the New York Rangers of the National Hockey League in 2001 to take part in a rehabilitation program for alcohol abuse. Fleury's struggles continued. He was suspended for six months in 2003 and prohibited from playing for his new team, the Chicago Blackhawks, because of continuing addiction problems and related behavioural difficulties. In his recently published autobiography, Fleury acknowledged that he was sexually abused by his hockey coach as a boy. The Canadian Press/Jeff McIntosh.

spiders, and the like—may appear to be crawling up the wall or over the person's body or they may fill the room. Feverish, disoriented, and terrified, the person may claw frantically at his or her skin to get rid of the vermin or may cower in the corner to escape an advancing army of fantastic animals. The delirium and physiological paroxysms caused by withdrawal of alcohol indicate that the drug is addictive.

Increased tolerance is evident following heavy, prolonged drinking. Some alcohol abusers can drink a litre of bourbon a day without showing signs of drunkenness (Mello & Mendelson, 1970). Moreover, levels of alcohol in the blood of such people are unexpectedly low after what is usually viewed as excessive drinking, suggesting that the body adapts to the drug and becomes able to process it more efficiently.

Although changes in the liver enzymes that metabolize alcohol can account to a small extent for tolerance, most researchers now believe that the central nervous system is implicated. Some research suggests that tolerance results from changes in the number or sensitivity of GABA or glutamate receptors (Tsai et al., 1998). Withdrawal may be the result of increased activation in some neural pathways to compensate for alcohol's inhibitory effects in the brain. When drinking stops, the inhibitory effects of alcohol are lost, resulting in a state of overexcitation.

Although tolerance is mostly due to physiological factors, research by Vogel-Sprott and associates at the University of Waterloo has highlighted the role of psychological factors. Response expectations and the consequences of behaviour can have a direct influence on tolerance and the effects of alcohol (see Vogel-Sprott, Kartechner, & McConnell, 1989; Zinatelli & Vogel-Sprott, 1993). Similarly, the development of addictions often reflects the interplay of biological and psychological factors.

The drinking pattern of people who are alcohol dependent indicates that their drinking is out of control. They need to drink daily and are unable to stop or cut down despite repeated efforts to abstain completely or to restrict drinking to certain periods of the day. They may go on occasional binges, remaining intoxicated for two, three, or more days. Sometimes they consume a litre of alcohol at a time. They may suffer blackouts and have no memory of events that took place during a bout of intoxication; their craving may be so overpowering that they are forced to ingest alcohol in a non-beverage form, such as hair tonic. Such drinking, of course, causes social and occupational difficulties, quarrels with family or friends, violent behaviour, frequent absences from work, loss of job, and arrests for intoxication or traffic accidents.

The person who abuses alcohol, in contrast to the person physically dependent on it, experiences negative social and occupational effects from the drug but does not show tolerance, withdrawal, or the compulsive drinking patterns seen in the person who is alcohol dependent.

Alcohol abuse or dependence is often part of **polydrug** (or **polysubstance**) **abuse**, using or abusing more than one drug at a time. It is estimated, for example, that 80 to 85% of alcohol abusers are smokers. Unfortunately, while at present just over half of Canadian addiction programs offer smoking cessation services for those with other addictions, available help is often informal and most programs place little emphasis on smoking cessation (Currie, Nesbitt, Wood, & Lawson, 2003). Alcohol serves as a cue for smoking; smoking is twice as frequent in situations where a person is also drinking (Shiffman et al., 1994). This very high level of comorbidity may occur because alcohol and nicotine are cross-tolerant; that is, nicotine can induce tolerance for the rewarding effects of alcohol and vice versa. Thus, consumption of both drugs may be increased to maintain their rewarding effects.

Polydrug abuse can create serious health problems because the effects of some drugs when taken together are synergistic; the effects of each combine to produce an especially strong reaction. For example, mixing alcohol and barbiturates is a common means of suicide, both intentional and accidental (Lesage et al., 1994). Alcohol is also believed to contribute to deaths from heroin, for it can reduce the amount of the narcotic needed to make a dose lethal.

PREVALENCE OF ALCOHOL ABUSE AND COMORBIDITY WITH OTHER DISORDERS

Prevalence rates for alcohol dependence in the United States defined by *DSM-IV* criteria were estimated in 2007 as follows: the prevalence of lifetime and 12-month alcohol abuse was 17.8% and 4.7%, respectively, and the prevalence of lifetime and 12-month alcohol dependence was 12.5% and 3.8%, respectively (Hasin, Stinson, Ogburn, & Grant, 2007). That is, lifetime prevalence of alcohol misuse was more than 3 in 10 Americans. This study also found that about only 1 in 4 with alcohol dependence had ever received treatment. Prevalence

Polysubstance abuse involves the use of multiple drugs. Alcohol and nicotine are a common combination, although most people who smoke and drink in social situations do not become substance abusers. Ryan McVay/Thinkstock.

rates were higher in men, younger cohorts, and whites. The course was often chronic with an average of four years for alcohol dependence (Hasin et al., 2007).

Table 12.1 summarizes epidemiological data obtained in Canada. Based on the 2004 Canadian Addiction Survey, 22.6% of current alcohol drinkers exceeded low-risk drinking guidelines, which stipulate no more than two drinks per day, and 17% of current alcohol drinkers engaged in hazardous drinking. Strong gender differences exist, with hazardous drinking among current drinkers being evident among 25.1% of men and 8.9% of women.

Indeed, the prototypical heavy drinker in Canada is a young adult male who is not married and who is relatively well off financially (Single et al., 1995). Problem drinking is comorbid with several personality disorders; in fact, Canadian researchers have sought to identify genetic factors that are common to personality disorders and alcohol misuse (Jang, Vernon, & Livesley, 2000). Problem drinking is also comorbid with mood and anxiety disorders, as shown in a study of six countries, including Canada (Merikangas et al., 1998), and with other drug use and schizophrenia. It is a factor in 25% of suicides (Morgenstern et al., 1997). Comorbidity is important to assess because comorbid psychiatric disorders predict higher relapse rates and less initial treatment improvement among dually diagnosed individuals with substance abuse (for a review, see Aase, Jason, & Robinson, 2008).

Drinking is on the rise in Canada. Over the past decade, there was a 9% increase in Canada overall in alcohol consumption, but the increase was almost twice as high (16%) in British Columbia (Thomas, Stockwell, & Reist, 2009). Unfortunately, alcohol-related deaths increased to a similar degree, underscoring the dangers of excessive drinking. Other analyses by this research team of the 2004 Canadian Addiction Survey results found that the heaviest-drinking 10% of respondents accounted for 50% of overall consumption (Stockwell, Zhao, & Thomas, 2009).

TABLE 12.1
RATES OF HAZARDOUS DRINKING IN CANADA

SUBSTANCE AND MEASURE Alcohol	CCHS 1.2 2002[a] INTERVIEW Survey Adults 15+	CAS 2004[b] TELEPHONE Survey Adults 15+
Regular heavy drinking (5+ drinks on one occasion at least once a week) in the past 12 months among heavy drinkers	18.6% • 23.0% of men; 10.3% of women	
Exceeded low-risk drinking guidelines (men: 14 drinks or less per week, and women: 9 drinks or less per week)		22.6% of current alcohol drinkers • 30.2% of men; 15.1% of women who had drank in the past year
Reported symptoms meeting criteria for being dependent on alcohol or illicit drugs	3.1% • 2.6% (641,000) dependence on alcohol • 0.8% (194,000) dependence on illicit drugs • 4.5% of men; 1.7% of women	
Drinking hazardously indicating harmful use or possible dependence on alcohol[c]		17.0% of current alcohol drinkers • 25.1% of men; 8.9% of women who had drank in the past year
Cannabis Past-3-month cannabis users reporting problems[d]		• 42.9% reported failure to control their use at some point in their life • 40.4% reported a strong desire to use cannabis (during previous 3 months)

[a]Statistics Canada, 2002 Mental Health and Well-being Survey (Canadian Community Health Survey , Cycle 1.2)
[b]Canadian Centre on Substance Abuse, 2004 Canadian Addiction Survey (CAS)
[c]According to the World Health Organization's Alcohol Use Disorders Identification Test (AUDIT)
[d]According to the World Health Organization's Alcohol, Smoking and Substance Involvement Screening Tool (ASSIST)

CANADIAN PERSPECTIVES 12.1
BINGE DRINKING AT UNIVERSITIES, COLLEGES, AND SCHOOLS

Alcohol use is frequent among university and college students. A 1993 U.S. survey revealed that 50% of men and 40% of women engaged in binge drinking within the previous month, defined as having five drinks in a row for men and four for women (Wechsler et al., 1994). The 1993 survey was repeated in 1997 and 1999, and similar findings emerged. The 1999 survey evaluated more than 14,000 students from 119 sites and found that 44% had engaged in binge drinking within the previous month, a rate similar to those obtained in previous surveys (Wechsler, Lee, Kuo, & Lee, 2000). About 1 in 4 students were frequent binge drinkers who usually binged at least once a week. The survey results have received a great deal of attention and not just because of the alarming levels of binge drinking. Other findings point to the harmful consequences of excessive drinking on campuses. Students who binge drink are substantially more likely to damage property, get into legal trouble, miss classes, and experience injuries (Wechsler et al., 1994). One update found that in a two-year

period, more than half a million U.S. students were unintentionally injured as a result of drinking (Hingson, Heeren, Winter, & Wechsler, 2005). Binge drinkers are more willing to engage in unsafe sexual practices, and non-drinking students in close proximity to binge drinkers are more likely to be the target of unwanted sexual advances and physical assaults.

What about binge drinking on Canadian campuses? The results of the first comprehensive survey of Canadian campuses were reported by Gliksman, Demers, Adlaf, Newton-Taylor, and Schmidt (2000). This study, conducted initially in 1998, used representative sampling techniques to survey 7,800 undergraduate students at 16 universities across Canada. This study is repeated every two years. The 2004 Canadian Campus Survey (Adlaf, Demers, & Gliksman, 2005) confirmed once again that binge drinking is a very significant problem on Canadian campuses. Overall, about 1 out of 6 Canadian students met criteria for "heavy-frequent drinking," which is defined as the usual consumption of five or more drinks on a daily basis (Adlaf et al., 2005). In total, 32% of undergraduates reported hazardous or harmful patterns of drinking and 43.9% reported at least one indicator of harmful drinking (Adlaf et al., 2005). Recall that it was noted above that hazardous drinking was found in 17% of the general population, so it is substantially elevated among students. Problems associated with excessive drinking by students included hangovers (53.4%), memory loss (25.4%), regrets for actions (24.5%), and missing classes due to a hangover (18.8%). Hazardous alcohol-related behaviours occurred at high rates; these included unplanned sexual relations (14.1%), engaging in unsafe sex (6.0%), and drinking and driving (3.8%). The initial survey found that in terms of student views of the most serious problems on campus, student alcohol use placed fourth (mentioned by 37% of respondents). The other problems were (1) vandalism and theft of property; (2) safety concerns; and (3) sexual assaults on campus.

How do students compare at Canadian and American universities? It seems that a greater proportion of Canadian students drink but heavy alcohol use is higher among American students (Kuo et al., 2002). Students living at home in either country were less likely to be heavy drinkers, but the protective effect of living at home was much stronger for students at American universities.

It was found in both countries that students who report having had their first experience of drunkenness prior to age 16 are substantially more likely to be heavy drinkers in college (Kuo et al., 2002). In many respects, the data from university samples seems to reflect a pre-existing problem among high school and junior high school students. The annual Ontario Student Drug Use Survey of more than 6,000 students revealed in 2003 that 39.1% of Grade 7 students and 48.9% of Grade 8 students admitted drinking alcohol (Adlaf & Paglia, 2003). Overall, 26% of students reported binge drinking at least once during the month prior to the survey, and 10% of drinkers reported binge drinking four or more times. Similarly, the 2009 data show that 1 in 4 Ontario students in grades 7 to 12 acknowledge binge drinking within the past month (Paglia-Boak, Mann, Adlaf, & Rehm, 2009). Consistent with trends showing recent increases in levels of binge drinking by females, no gender difference was found. Similarly, the 2007 report by ESPAD (European School Survey Project on Alcohol and Other Drugs, 2007) of student drinking in 35 European countries found comparable levels of binge drinking among females and males, with females actually having higher levels of binge drinking in 9 of the 35 countries, including the United Kingdom, Ireland, and Spain.

One shocking trend is the lack of parental awareness of their child's substance use. A study conducted in Alberta found that only 34% of parents were aware of their child's alcohol use, and only 11% were aware of their child's use of illicit drugs (Williams, McDermitt, Bertrand, & Davis, 2003). Single parents, parents from blended families, and parents of higher-achieving students were more likely to be "clued in" about the illicit drug use.

Other analyses have provided clear evidence that the amount of drinking varies substantially across various situational contexts (Demers et al., 2002; Kairouz, Gliksman, Demers, & Adlaf, 2002). Situational factors associated with increased drinking include drinking at a party, in a bar/club, off-campus, during the weekend, and, more generally, in peer-oriented drinking environments, which illustrates the relevance of social reasons for drinking. In high school, a key situational factor is the school setting and whether a peer drinking culture exists (Kairouz & Adlaf, 2003).

What can be done about the binge-drinking problem? A survey of U.S. college administrators indicated that many preventive steps are being taken (Wechsler, Kelley, Weitzman, San Giovanni, & Seibring, 2000). Prevention efforts include providing general education about the effects of alcohol, use of policy controls to limit access to alcohol (including "dry" residences and "dry" campuses), and restrictions on media advertising involving alcohol. Most U.S. campuses now have an alcohol specialist on staff and many colleges have task forces.

Alan Marlatt has conducted extensive research on high-risk college drinkers (see Canadian Contributions 12.1). He and his associates have tested the usefulness of brief interventions that focus on controlling and reducing the drinking behaviour of high-risk students rather than on striving for complete abstinence. They have shown that even brief interventions can reduce the harmful consequences of heavy drinking and that these improvements persist over a two-year period (see Marlatt, Baer, & Larimer, 1995; Marlatt et al., 1998). However, despite these improvements, the high-risk group still experiences more alcohol-related problems than the low-risk participants.

Thinking Critically

1. Is binge drinking a problem on your university or college campus? How would you rank it relative to other possible concerns (such as vandalism, safety, and sexual assaults)?

2. If binge drinking is a problem, what can be done about it? Who should be responsible for doing something about it if it is a problem? Should it be the administration, faculty, the students themselves, or a coordinated effort on the part of all stakeholders?

3. Do you think that an intervention that focuses on moderating the drinking behaviour of high-risk students, such as the program tested by Alan Marlatt, would work on your campus? How would you go about setting up a program?

COURSE OF THE DISORDER

At one time, the life histories of alcohol abusers were thought to have a common, downhill progression. On the basis of an extensive survey of 2,000 members of Alcoholics Anonymous, Jellinek (1952) described the male alcohol abuser as passing through four stages, beginning with social drinking and progressing to a stage at which he lives only to drink.

Although Jellinek's description has been widely cited, the available evidence does not always corroborate it. The histories of alcohol-dependent people do indeed show a progression from alcohol abuse to alcohol dependence (Langenbucher & Chung, 1995); however, data reveal considerable fluctuations in drinking patterns, from heavy drinking for some periods of time to abstinence or lighter drinking at others (Vaillant, 1996). Furthermore, patterns of maladaptive use of alcohol are more variable than Jellinek implied. Heavy use of alcohol may be restricted to weekends, or long periods of abstinence may be interspersed with binges of continual drinking for several weeks (Robins et al., 1988). There is no single pattern of alcohol abuse.

Evidence also indicates that Jellinek's account does not apply to women. Difficulties with alcohol usually begin at a later age in women than in men and often after an inordinately stressful experience, such as a serious family crisis. For women, the time interval between the onset of heavy drinking and alcohol abuse is briefer than it is for men (Mezzich et al., 1994). Women with drinking problems tend to be steady drinkers who drink alone and are more unlikely than men to binge.

COSTS OF ALCOHOL ABUSE AND DEPENDENCE

Comparative analyses, including data gathered by the World Health Organization, indicate that alcohol abuse is the fourth leading cause of worldwide disability. Moreover, alcohol abuse accounts for more years lost to death or disability than the use of either tobacco or illegal drugs (see Aronson, 2003). Rates of hazardous alcohol drinking are exceptionally high in Russia and here it has been established indirectly that the relatively low life expectancy of Russian men is attributable to hazardous alcohol drinking. Leon et al. (2007) found that almost half of all deaths of working-aged men in a typical Russian city can be attributed to hazardous drinking.

Although most people who have a drinking problem do not seek professional help, people who abuse alcohol constitute a large proportion of new admissions to mental and general hospitals. Problem drinkers use health services four times more often than do non-abusers, and their medical expenses are twice as high as those of non-drinkers (Harvard Mental Health Letter, 1987). As mentioned in Chapter 8, the suicide rate for alcohol abusers is much higher than that for the general population. Although alcohol-related traffic fatalities have declined substantially in Canada (including an overall decrease of 31% in the 1980s), national statistics indicate that, in 1997, 31% of fatally injured drivers had blood alcohol concentrations over the legal limit (Mayhew, Beirness, & Simpson, 2000). According to statistics from the Traffic Injury Research Foundation in Ottawa, as summarized by the Canadian division of Mothers Against Drunk Driving (MADD, 2007), drunk drivers kill an average of about 3 to 4 people per day and injure 187 people in Canada every day. Alcohol increases both the likelihood and severity of traffic accidents. The prototypical drinking driver in Canada is a male between the ages of 25 and 34 who drinks large amounts of alcohol on a regular basis or is a social drinker who occasionally drinks heavily (MADD, 2007). Despite this profile, the social significance of drunk driving among teenagers should not be discounted. According to Chamberlain and Solo-

Kiefer Sutherland, Canadian actor and star of *24*, pleaded no contest to a misdemeanour charge for driving under the influence in 2007. Sutherland was sentenced to 48 days in jail because he violated his probation for a previous 2004 arrest for drunk driving. CP Images/STREVT.

mon (2008), 16- to 19-year-olds made up 5.4% of the Canadian population in 2003, yet they accounted for 23% of pedestrian fatalities where the pedestrian had been drinking alcohol. The authors called for a nationwide requirement of zero blood alcohol for drivers aged 21 and younger, as well as greater police powers and more rigorous enforcement of existing legislation. Indeed, reviewers have concluded that enacting and enforcing more extreme legislative measures are highly effective in reducing drunk driving (Anderson, Chisholm, & Fuhr, 2009).

It seems that a substantial proportion of impaired drivers have a general tendency to engage in anti-social acts. Stewart, Boase, and Lamble (2000) examined a random sample of 100 Canadian drivers with alcohol-related driving offences and found that 45% had a history of charges or convictions for such things as robbery, assault, and narcotic offences.

Diana, Princess of Wales, was killed in an automobile accident in Paris. Her driver was intoxicated. CP Image Archive/Jerome Delay.

Alcohol may contribute to other injuries, as well. Rape, assault, and family violence are alcohol-related crimes, as is homicide; it is believed that over half of all murders are committed under the influence of alcohol (Murdoch, Pihl, & Ross, 1990). A comprehensive review concluded that alcohol is the drug with the most evidence of there being a direct link between intoxication and violence (Hoaken & Stewart, 2003). Indeed, a telephone survey of more than 1,000 Canadian adults found that either the perpetrator or victim was drinking in over two thirds of reported cases of physical aggression (Wells, Graham, & West, 2000).

These data illustrate the pervasive negative impact that excessive drinking can have on drinkers and the people around them. The human costs, in terms of broken lives, are incalculable.

SHORT-TERM EFFECTS OF ALCOHOL

How does alcohol produce its short-term effects? Alcohol is metabolized by enzymes after being swallowed and reaching the stomach. Most of it goes into the small intestines where it is absorbed into the blood. It is then broken down, mostly in the liver, which can metabolize about 30 millilitres of 100-proof (50% alcohol) whisky per hour. Quantities in excess of this amount stay in the bloodstream. Absorption of alcohol can be rapid, but removal is always slow. The effects of alcohol vary with the level of concentration of the drug in the bloodstream, which in turn depends on the amount ingested in a particular period of time, the presence or absence of food in the stomach to retain the alcohol and reduce its absorption rate, the size of a person's body, and the efficiency of the liver. The effects of 60 millilitres of alcohol would vary greatly for a 180-pound (80-kilogram) man who has just eaten and a 110-pound (50-kilogram) woman with an empty stomach.

Because drinking alcoholic beverages is accepted in most societies, alcohol is rarely regarded as a drug. But it is indeed a drug, and it has a biphasic effect. This means that the initial effect of alcohol is stimulating—the drinker experiences an expansive feeling of sociability and well-being as the blood-alcohol level rises—but after the blood-alcohol level peaks and begins to decline, alcohol acts as a depressant that may lead to negative emotions. Large amounts of alcohol interfere with complex thought processes. Motor coordination, balance, speech, and vision are also impaired. At this stage of intoxication, some people become depressed and withdrawn.

Alcohol produces its effects through its interactions with several neural systems in the brain. It stimulates GABA receptors, which may be responsible for reducing tension. (GABA is a major inhibitory neurotransmitter; the benzodiazepines, such as Valium, have an effect on the GABA receptor similar to that of alcohol.) Alcohol also increases levels of serotonin and dopamine, and this may be the source of its ability to produce pleasurable effects. Finally, alcohol inhibits glutamate receptors, which may cause the cognitive effects of alcohol intoxication, such as slurred speech and memory loss (U.S. Department of Health and Human Services, 1994).

LONG-TERM EFFECTS OF PROLONGED ALCOHOL ABUSE

Chronic drinking creates severe biological damage in addition to psychological deterioration. Almost every tissue and organ of the body is affected adversely by prolonged consumption of alcohol. Malnutrition may be severe. Because alcohol provides calories—a pint of 80-proof spirits supplies about half a day's caloric requirements—heavy drinkers often reduce their intake of food. But the calories provided by alcohol are empty; they do not supply the nutrients essential for health. Alcohol also contributes directly to malnutrition by impairing the digestion of food and absorption of vitamins. In older chronic alcohol abusers, a deficiency of B-complex vitamins can cause amnestic syndrome, a severe loss of memory for both recent and long-past events. Memory gaps are often filled in with reports of imaginary, improbable events.

Prolonged alcohol use with reduction in the intake of proteins contributes to the development of cirrhosis of the liver, a potentially fatal disease in which some liver cells become engorged with fat and protein, impeding their function; some cells die, triggering an inflammatory process. When scar tissue develops, blood flow is obstructed.

Other common physiological changes include damage to the endocrine glands and pancreas, heart failure, hypertension, stroke, and capillary hemorrhages, which are responsible for the swelling and redness in the face, especially the nose, of chronic alcohol abusers. Prolonged use of alcohol appears to destroy brain cells; a five-year longitudinal study found significant loss of grey matter from the temporal lobes (Pfefferman et al., 1998). Even shorter-term abuse may produce some cognitive impairment; alcohol-abusing college students show impairment on neuropsychological tests (Sher et al., 1997). Alcohol also reduces the effectiveness of the immune system and increases susceptibility to infection and cancer. For example, women's risk of breast cancer increases steadily with the amount they drink; there is a linear-dose response such that risk increases by 7% per drink; thus five drinks per day on average would increase risk by 35% (see Aronson, 2003).

Heavy alcohol consumption during pregnancy is the leading cause of mental retardation. The growth of the fetus is slowed, and cranial, facial, and limb anomalies are produced, a condition known as **fetal alcohol syndrome (FAS)**. Other syndromes included among fetal alcohol spectrum disorders are partial fetal alcohol syndrome and alcohol-related neurodevelopmental disorder (ARND) (see Loock et al., 2005). Even moderate drinking by mothers-to-be can produce less severe but undesirable effects on the fetus, so total abstention is recommended. Early detection of fetal alcohol spectrum disorders is associated with better long-term outcomes (Loock et al., 2005).

The human costs and economic costs of fetal alcohol syndrome are enormous. In terms of the economic costs, FAS occurs in about 1 out of every 100 pregnancies. The estimated cost in terms of health care, social services, education, and lost productivity is $5.3 billion annually in Canada (see Stade et al., 2009). FAS is the leading cause of developmental and cognitive disabilities in children in Canada (Stade et al., 2009).

Currently, it is estimated that 90% of Canadian women realize that drinking alcohol is not good for the unborn baby, and many recognize that drinking alcohol confers risk for the unborn (Koren, Nulman, Chudley, & Loock, 2003). Given that at least half of Canadian and American women drink socially and half of all pregnancies are unplanned, each year about 100,000 Canadian infants are exposed to some alcohol during gestation (Koren et al., 2003). About one quarter of pregnant women in Canada drink alcohol prior to realizing that they have conceived (Koren et al., 2003). Still, substantial exposure to alcohol is typically the case in extreme fetal alcohol syndrome.

Although it is appropriate and accurate to concentrate on the deleterious effects of alcohol, tantalizing evidence suggests positive health benefits for some people. Light drinking (fewer than three drinks a day), especially of wine, has been related to decreased risk for coronary heart disease and stroke (Sacco et al., 1999). Not all researchers, however, accept this finding at face value. Some people who abstain may have done so for health reasons; hypertension, for example. Comparing these abstainers with light drinkers could result in misleading conclusions. If alcohol does have a beneficial effect, it could be either physiological or psychological (a less-driven lifestyle and decreased levels of hostility).

Research on this topic was stimulated by the so-called French paradox: despite diets rich in saturated fats, the French have relatively low cholesterol levels. Some hypothesize that consumption of low to moderate amounts of red wine may lower cholesterol levels. Of course, the French lifestyle has other characteristics that may result in lower risk for heart disease; the French eat more fresh foods and get more daily exercise than North Americans. Promoting alcohol in North America may set the stage for a dangerous flirtation with alcohol abuse.

The psychological, biological, and social consequences of prolonged consumption of alcohol are extremely serious. Because the alcohol abuser's own functioning is so severely disrupted, the people with whom he or she interacts are also deeply affected and hurt.

INHALANT USE DISORDERS

We will mention briefly another class of disorders that may be a stepping-stone for developing other disorders involving alcohol and drug abuse: inhalant use disorders. Although inhalant use is not confined to children and adolescents, an alarming number of young people begin their substance abuse by inhaling such substances as glue, correction fluid, spray paint, cosmetics, gasoline, household aerosol sprays, and the nitrous oxide found in spray cans of whipped cream. The Director of the U.S. National Institute on Drug Abuse, Nora Volkow, has recently expressed concerns about increases in inhalant abuse among young people, with 17.3% now acknowledging inhalant use (Volkow, 2007). She also noted that only about two out of five eighth-graders believe that solvent use is dangerous, and she stated it may be time to renew public information campaigns that warn of the dangers of solvent use.

According to the Canadian Paediatric Society (1998), the peak age of inhalant use is 14 to 15 years, with initial onsets in children as young as 6. Inhalants are dangerous because they are inexpensive and readily available. Inhalant use disorders can involve behaviours such as sniffing (nasal inhalation of a substance), huffing (breathing fumes from a small rag stuffed in the mouth), and bagging (breathing fumes from a plastic bag held up to the mouth). Gasoline sniffing is a widespread problem among certain groups in northern Canada and is especially prevalent among Aboriginal children and adolescents (Barnes,

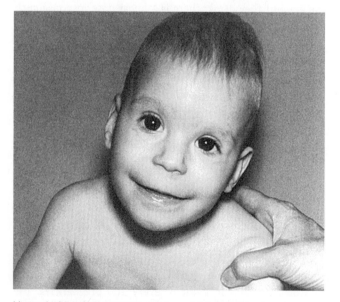

Heavy drinking during pregnancy causes fetal alcohol syndrome. Children with this syndrome have facial abnormalities, as well as mental retardation. Courtesy Dr. James A. Hanson, University of Iowa.

Young people from Davis Inlet, Sheshatshiu, and Pikangikum have engaged in inhalant abuse. Unfortunately, the $150-million move from Davis Inlet, Labrador to the new town of Natuashish in February 2002 did not solve the problems of the Mushuau Innu from Davis Inlet (Toughill, 2003). The children are still sniffing gasoline. CP Image Archive/Ryan Remiorz.

1989). For instance, a study conducted with Aboriginal and rural high school students in Quebec found that solvent use was considerably higher among Aboriginal students. This finding reflected a general tendency for the Aboriginal students to make greater use of illicit drugs, while the francophone students consumed more alcoholic beverages (Lalinec-Michaud, Martine-Subak, Ghadirian, & Kovess, 1991). In Chapter 8 we discussed the high rate of drug abuse, especially gasoline sniffing, in the context of our discussion of the alarming rates of suicide among Aboriginal youth. Harries (2001) asked children in Pikangikum, in northern Ontario, what the gas does for them.

> "It makes you dizzy, it makes you high," Sylvester says. "You get hungry."
> Is there anything else they could be doing?
> "No," Erroll says. "It's boring," Sylvester says.
> What would make a difference?
> "We wanted a community centre so we could go there, play pool," Erroll says.
> "We could paint," Sylvester suggests.
> "We want some …" Erroll's voice trails away. He brings the bag up to his face.
> "Chips and pop," Sylvester is sniffing from a bag too.
> Erroll finds his voice. "We want clothing, we want food, I wish that people had—I don't know." His hands are shaking and he sniffs again to compose himself.
> "To play games at the school—soccer, hockey, baseball …"
> (p. A16)

Most inhalants act as depressants and, as such, can be seen as similar to alcohol and sedatives. The inhaled substance can result in feelings of euphoria and psychic numbing, but inhalants can cause damage to the central nervous system. Nausea and subsequent headaches are experienced eventually in almost all cases.

Inhalant use is linked with other adjustment problems. Howard and Jenson (1999) compared delinquents who did or did not use inhalants and found that those with inhalant use had higher levels of suicide, criminal behaviour, and family problems.

NICOTINE AND CIGARETTE SMOKING

The history of tobacco smoking bears much similarity to that of other addictive drugs (Brecher, 1972). It was not long after Columbus's first commerce with Native North Americans that sailors and merchants began to imitate the Natives' habit of smoking rolled leaves of tobacco and to experience, as the Natives did, the increasing craving for it. When not smoked, tobacco was—and is—chewed or ground into small pieces and inhaled as snuff.

Nicotine is the addicting agent of tobacco. It stimulates receptors, called nicotinic receptors, in the brain. Molecular biology studies suggest that the main receptor mediating nicotine dependence is the nicotinic acetylcholine receptor subtype. Exposure to nicotine influences brain nicotinic cholinergic receptors to facilitate neurotransmitter release (e.g., dopamine), thus producing stimulation, pleasure, and mood modulation (see Benowitz, 2008).

Some idea of the addictive qualities of tobacco can be appreciated by considering how much people have sacrificed to maintain their supplies. In sixteenth-century England, for example, tobacco was exchanged for silver, ounce for ounce. Poor people squandered their meagre resources for their several daily pipefuls. Even the public tortures and executions engineered as punishment by Sultan Murad IV of Turkey during the seventeenth century could not dissuade those of his subjects who were addicted to the weed.

Contemporary evidence indicates that nicotine may be much more addictive than previously indicated. A recent study by researchers from Toronto evaluated nicotine self-administration in squirrel monkeys (Le Foll, Wertheim, & Goldberg, 2007). This study showed that nicotine had "high reinforcing efficacy," with monkeys willing to perform up to 600 lever presses in order to self-administer nicotine! The authors concluded that regardless of other factors, nicotine is a robust and highly effective reinforcer of drug-taking behaviour.

Another investigation of adolescents from Quebec found that the addictive effects of nicotine start very shortly after one's first puff. In addition, indications of mental addiction can be found well before actual physical addiction takes place (see Gervais et al., 2006). Thus, even just one puff or one cigarette can be enough for some people to begin their addiction to nicotine.

Intriguing new data suggest that nicotine may operate differently on the brains of males vs. females. Fallon et al. (2005) measured brain activity via PET scans in male and female smokers and non-smokers while they performed two tasks. The researchers identified what they described as a fundamental biological difference between women and men. That is, without nicotine involved, there were great gender differences in metabolic activity, with females having much greater brain activity, especially in the cortical and subcortical prefrontal systems (which are linked with attention and memory). However, these differences virtually disappeared when nicotine was administered to men and women. These data qualify gender differences in smoking behaviour by suggesting that they may have both biological and cultural-social origins. Female smokers have substantially greater changes in cognitive activity after nicotine exposure.

PREVALENCE AND HEALTH CONSEQUENCES OF SMOKING

The threat to health posed by smoking has been documented convincingly since 1964. Extensive information on smoking in Canada is provided by the Canadian Council for Tobacco Control. It is estimated that smoking causes more than 47,000 deaths annually in Canada (Health Canada, 2004) and more than 438,000 American tobacco users die prematurely each year (Centers for Disease Control and Prevention, 2007). Cigarette smoking is responsible in some way for 1 of every 5 deaths in the United States, killing about 1,200 people each day. It is the single most preventable cause of premature death. The health

©Ben Wicks estate. Used with permission.

WARNING: SMOKING CAUSES IMPOTENCE

California's Tobacco Education Media Campaign parodies tobacco ads to illustrate potential health effects of smoking and to attack pro-tobacco influences. Courtesy California Department of Health Services.

risks of smoking are significantly less for cigar and pipe smokers because they seldom inhale the smoke into their lungs, but cancers of the mouth are increased.

Among the medical problems associated with, and almost certainly caused or exacerbated by, long-term cigarette smoking are lung cancer, emphysema, cancer of the larynx and the esophagus, and a number of cardiovascular diseases. The most probable harmful components in the smoke from burning tobacco are nicotine, carbon monoxide, and tar; the latter consists primarily of certain hydrocarbons, including known carcinogens (Jaffe, 1985). Health risks from smoking decline greatly over a period of 5 to 10 years after quitting, to levels only slightly above those of non-smokers, but the destruction of lung tissue is not reversible (Jaffe, 1985).

Recent data attest to the significant reductions in smoking in Canada in recent years:

- Approximately 17% of Canadians are smokers, according to the latest data from the Canadian Tobacco Use Monitoring Survey (2009). The prevalence of smoking has steadily decreased for many years. The rate was 19% according to 2005 data.
- While rates of smoking in younger people have declined in Canada overall, there was actually a 3% increase, so that 1 in 5 teenagers in Quebec admitted smoking.
- Daily smokers in Canada smoked an average of 14.9 cigarettes per day. Typically, males smoke three more cigarettes than do females per day (Reid & Hammond, 2009).

As with alcohol, the socio-economic cost of smoking is staggering. American surveys indicated that smokers compile more than 80 million lost days of work and 145 million days of disability each year, considerably more than do their non-smoking peers. This loss of productivity coupled with the health care costs associated with smoking runs to more than $65 billion annually in the United States.

Emerging data that cigarette smoking contributes to erectile problems in men—not surprising, given that nicotine constricts blood vessels—resulted in 1998 in several televised public service announcements aimed at creating some second thoughts about how sexy smoking is. One ad shows a well-dressed young man looking with interest at an attractive woman at a fancy cocktail party. He lights up a cigarette, and when she looks over in his direction, the cigarette goes limp. She shakes her head and walks away (Morain, 1998).

CONSEQUENCES OF SECOND-HAND SMOKE

As we have known for many years, the health hazards of smoking are not restricted to those who smoke. The smoke coming from the burning end of a cigarette, so-called **second-hand smoke**, or environmental tobacco smoke (ETS), contains higher concentrations of ammonia, carbon monoxide, nicotine, and tar than does the smoke actually inhaled by the smoker. Environmental tobacco smoke is blamed for more than 50,000 deaths a year in the United States. In 1993, the U.S. Environmental Protection Agency classified ETS as a hazard as dangerous as asbestos and radon. Health Canada launched "The Blue Ribbon Campaign" in 2001 to "clear the air" of second-hand smoke (Health Canada, 2006). The campaign website lists the following facts:

- Two thirds of smoke from a cigarette is not inhaled by the smoker but enters the air around the smoker.
- Second-hand smoke has at least twice the nicotine and tar as the smoke inhaled by the smoker.
- Regular exposure to second-hand smoke increases the chances of contracting lung disease by 25% and heart disease by 10%.
- Second-hand smoke aggravates symptoms in people with allergies and asthma, and can cause eye, nose, and throat irritations, headaches, dizziness, nausea, coughing, and wheezing in otherwise healthy people. A Canadian study showed that second-hand smoke exposure was linked with asthma and chronic bronchitis among ex-smokers and people who never smoked. It also was linked with hypertension among ex-smokers (Vozoris & Lougheed, 2008).
- Infants and children exposed to second-hand smoke are more likely to suffer chronic respiratory illness, impaired lung function, middle ear infections, and food allergies, and can even succumb to sudden infant death syndrome.
- In Canada, 2.4 million homes with children under 12 years of age report regular exposure to second-hand smoke.

At present, laws that ban or regulate cigarette smoking in public places and work settings have been enacted in every province and jurisdiction in Canada, including the Yukon Territory, which in 2007 was the last jurisdiction to enact the ban. Many non-smokers express enthusiastic approval of such measures, but some smokers object strongly to what they view as undue infringement on their rights and the general stigmatization of smokers. In Ontario, the ban has extended to more private places, as indicated by the January 2009 addition of no smoking in cars when a passenger is under the age of 16.

MARIJUANA

Marijuana consists of the dried and crushed leaves and flowering tops of the hemp plant, *Cannabis sativa*. It is most often smoked, but it may be chewed, prepared as a tea, or eaten in baked goods. **Hashish**, much stronger than marijuana, is produced by removing and drying the resin exudate of the tops of high-quality cannabis plants.

Marijuana use is illegal in most countries, including Canada, as many of them are bound by a United Nations treaty prohibiting its sale (Goodwin & Guze, 1984). However, in 2003, the Canadian government moved toward decriminalizing simple possession of small amounts (up to 15 grams) of marijuana (Lawton, 2003). This movement was terminated when Stephen Harper became prime minister in 2006. Increasing evidence of the negative impact of marijuana use makes it less likely that decriminalization will occur in the future.

EFFECTS OF MARIJUANA

Like most other drugs, marijuana has its risks. Generally, the more we learn about a drug, the less benign it turns out to be, and marijuana is no exception (see Focus on Discovery 12.1).

In January 2004, police raided a massive computer-controlled hydroponic marijuana growing operation in Barrie, Ontario. The former Molson Brewery plant contained more than 30,000 plants growing in converted beer vats. It was called the largest pot bust in North America, with the total value of the marijuana produced yearly estimated at $100 million. CP Image Archive/Tobin Grimshaw.

PSYCHOLOGICAL EFFECTS The intoxicating effects of marijuana, like most drugs, depend in part on its potency and size of dose. Smokers of marijuana find it makes them feel relaxed and sociable. Large doses have been reported to bring rapid shifts in emotion, to dull attention, to fragment thoughts, and to impair memory. Time seems to move more slowly. Extremely heavy doses sometimes induce hallucinations and other effects similar to those of LSD, including extreme panic. Dosage can be difficult to regulate because it may take up to half an hour after smoking marijuana for its effects to appear; many users thus get much higher than intended. People with psychological problems are generally believed to be at highest risk for negative reactions to marijuana or any psychoactive drug, perhaps because lack of control frightens them.

The major active chemical in marijuana is delta-9-tetrahydrocannabinol (THC). The amount of THC in marijuana is variable, but in general marijuana is much more potent now than it was two decades ago, with some estimates indicating that the THC content is two or three times higher (Zimmer & Morgan, 1995). In the late 1980s, cannabis receptors were discovered in the brain; shortly thereafter, it was found that the body produces its own cannabis-like substance, anandamide, named for the Sanskrit word for bliss (Sussman et al., 1996).

Growing evidence attests to the cognitive problems associated with marijuana use. A longitudinal study conducted by researchers at Carleton University in Ottawa found that current marijuana use resulted in an average decrease of 4.1 IQ points, but only among heavy users who smoked at least five joints per week (Fried, Watkinson, James, & Gray, 2002). Lighter use did not result in diminished IQ scores. Studies of working memory and verbal episodic memory indicate impairments in encoding, storage, manipulation, and retrieval mechanisms in long-term or heavy cannabis use (Solowij & Battisti, 2008). Neurocognitive deficits are

FOCUS ON DISCOVERY 12.1
THE STEPPING-STONE THEORY: FROM MARIJUANA TO HARD DRUGS

A concern prevalent for some time is expressed in the so-called *stepping-stone theory* of marijuana use, which led subsequently to the *gateway theory*. This is the premise that marijuana is dangerous not only in itself, but also because it is a first step or gateway that can lead young people to become addicted to other, more harmful drugs, such as heroin. Strong evidence for the gateway theory came from a unique study of 21- to 30-year-olds from Oslo (Bretteville-Jensen, Melberg, & Jones, 2008). A sophisticated multivariate analysis found temporal evidence of soft drugs leading to harder drugs; specifically, alcohol was a gateway drug for cannabis, which, in turn, was a gateway drug for amphetamine, which then served as a gateway drug for cocaine.

This evidence supporting the gateway theory magnifies the significance of indications in Canada that regular use of marijuana among adolescents has increased dramatically since the early 1990s (Adlaf, Ivis, & Smart, 1997), according to a Health Canada survey (see Tibbetts & Rogers, 2003). Canada is a high-use country, according to a comparative study of adolescents in 36 countries (Smart & Ogborne, 2000). The 2004 Canadian Campus Survey found that 51.5% of students reported using marijuana at some point in their lives and 32.1% had used marijuana in the previous year (Adlaf et al., 2005). One out of six students had used marijuana within the month prior to being surveyed. Marijuana use in Canada is associated with smoking, heavy drinking, and cocaine use (Ogborne, Smart, & Adlaf, 2000).

Statistics derived from the 2002 Canadian Community Health Survey indicate that among people aged 15 or older, marijuana use had doubled between 1989 and 2002 (Statistics Canada, 2004). An estimated 3 million Canadians smoked marijuana in 2002. Cannabis use was significantly higher among males, and age group comparisons indicated that usage peaked in the 18- to 19-year-old age group.

But is marijuana a stepping stone to more serious substance abuse? The question is not difficult to answer. About 40% of regular marijuana users do not go on to use such drugs as heroin and cocaine (Stephens, Roffman, & Simpson, 1993). So if by stepping stone we mean that there is an inevitability of escalating to a more serious drug, then marijuana is not a stepping stone. Still, we do know that many, but far from all, who use heroin and cocaine began their drug experimentation with marijuana. Moreover, users of marijuana are more likely than non-users to experiment later with heroin and cocaine (Miller & Volk, 1996), and the single best predictor of cocaine use in adulthood is heavy use of marijuana during adolescence (Kozel & Adams, 1986). These data are in accordance with the results of a survey conducted in Montreal of participants at "raves," gigantic parties attended by young people in warehouse-like settings (Gross, Barrett, Shestowsky, & Pihl, 2002). This study found a linear trend of experimentation with substances; that is, rave participants reported a history of using first alcohol, then cannabis, LSD, psilocybin, amphetamines, cocaine, and ecstasy. A follow-up study found that 4 out of 5 participants engaged in polysubstance use at their most recently attended rave, and the average was 2.5 psychoactive substances (excluding tobacco) per person (Barrett, Gross, Garand, & Pihl, 2005). Those who had a more extensive history of attending raves had a substantially greater degree of polydrug use.

Nevertheless, perhaps a network theory is more appropriate than a stepping-stone theory. Network implies a complex set of relationships in which cause and effect are virtually impossible to isolate but some degree of association among many variables is acknowledged. Some regular users of heroin and cocaine, for example, turn to marijuana as a safer substitute, or lesser evil (Sussman et al., 1996).

Marijuana is part of the picture, but only one of many factors contributing to involvement in harmful substance use.

---

greater among adults who began cannabis use in early adolescence and adolescents seem much more susceptible than adults to neurocognitive deficits (Schweinsburg, Brown, & Tapert, 2008). In a recent review for the Canadian Centre on Substance Abuse, Porath-Waller (2009) concluded that chronic cannabis use contributes to mild impairments rather than severe impairments; impairment would not be evident on simple, everyday tasks but would be apparent on complex tasks that rely on a memory component or strategic planning. Unfortunately, problems associated with heavy marijuana use are not confined to cognitive difficulties. An Ontario study comparing daily marijuana users with non-daily users confirmed that more of the daily users reported cannabis-related cognitive problems (60% vs. 42%), but they were also more likely to report psychological problems, health problems, financial problems, and vocational problems (Strike, Urbanoski, & Rush, 2003). Daily users were found to be more likely to use multiple substances and suffer from an anxiety disorder. Additional results showed that almost four fifths of those seeking treatment were single males.

Several studies have found that being high on marijuana impairs the complex psychomotor skills necessary for driving. Highway fatality and driver-arrest figures indicate that marijuana plays a role in a significant proportion of accidents and arrests (Brookoff et al., 1994). Marijuana

Early recreational use of hashish occurred in a fashionable apartment in New York City. An 1876 issue of the *Illustrated Police News* carried this picture with the title "Secret Dissipation of New York Belles: Interior of a Hasheesh Hell on Fifth Avenue." Culver Photos Inc.

has similarly been found to impair manipulation of flight simulators. Some performance decrements measurable after smoking one or two marijuana cigarettes containing 2% THC can persist for eight hours after a person believes he or she is no longer high, creating the very real danger that people will attempt to drive or fly when they are not functioning adequately.

Survey findings suggest that heavy use of marijuana during teenage years may well contribute to psychological problems in adulthood. Kandel et al. (1986) interviewed 1,004 adults in their mid-twenties who had been part of an earlier New York public high school survey of drug use. Those who reported using marijuana in high school tended to have higher rates of separation or divorce, more delinquency, increased tendencies to consult mental health professionals, and, among women, less-stable employment patterns. The authors caution, however, that the specific effects of a single drug such as marijuana are very difficult to disentangle from the effects of other drugs that marijuana smokers sometimes use, in particular, alcohol and cocaine.

SOMATIC EFFECTS In recent years, physiological research has identified specific cannabinoid receptors in the brain (CB) that recognize and are activated by cannabinoids (Iversen, 2003). The CB receptors in the brain are located in various regions, and it is believed that receptors in the hippocampus account for the short-term memory loss that sometimes follows smoking marijuana. Iverson (2003) observed that the discovery of these receptors has revitalized cannabis research and resulted in much interest.

The short-term side effects of marijuana include bloodshot and itchy eyes, dry mouth and throat, increased appetite, reduced pressure within the eye, and somewhat raised blood pressure. There is no evidence that smoking marijuana has untoward effects on a normal heart.

There is growing evidence that marijuana smoking is associated with a host of respiratory disorders and related ailments, and it seriously impairs lung functioning. Symptoms include coughing, wheezing, bronchitis, injury to airway tissue, and impaired functioning of immune system components (Moore et al., 2005; Tashkin, 2005). A recent Vancouver study found that concurrent smoking of marijuana and regular tobacco is associated with substantially increased risk for respiratory symptoms and Chronic Obstructive Pulmonary Disease (COPD) among those people who have smoked at least 50 marijuana joints in their lifetime (Tan et al., 2009). Even though marijuana users smoke far fewer cigarettes than do tobacco smokers, most inhale marijuana smoke more deeply and retain it in their lungs for much longer periods of time. Since marijuana has some of the same carcinogens found in tobacco cigarettes, its harmful effects are much greater than would be expected were only the absolute number of cigarettes or pipefuls considered. For example, one marijuana cigarette is the equivalent of four tobacco cigarettes in tar intake, five in carbon monoxide intake, and 10 in terms of damage to cells lining the airways (Sussman et al., 1996).

Is marijuana addictive? Contrary to widespread earlier belief, it may be. The development of tolerance began to be suspected when American service personnel returned from Vietnam accustomed to concentrations of THC that would be toxic to domestic users. Controlled observations have confirmed that habitual use of marijuana does produce tolerance (see Compton, Dewey, & Martin, 1990). Analyses of data from more than 2,700 lifetime marijuana users in the Ontario Health Survey identified a threshold of use (100 to 199 uses of marijuana) that was associated with substantially greater risk for developing marijuana disorders (DeWit, Hance, Offord, & Ogborne, 2000). Interestingly, this threshold was lower for females, with using marijuana between 50 and 99 times being associated with the development of marijuana disorders. This study also found that the timing of marijuana use matters. Ontarians who were late starters and began using after the age of 17 were less likely to have a subsequent marijuana disorder than those who initiated use before the age of 14.

The question of physical addiction to marijuana is complicated by reverse tolerance. Experienced smokers need only a few hits or puffs to become high from a marijuana cigarette, whereas less experienced users puff many times to reach a similar state of intoxication. Reverse tolerance is the direct opposite of the tolerance that occurs with an addicting drug, such as heroin. The substance THC, after being rapidly metabolized, is stored in the body's fatty tissue and then released very slowly, perhaps for a month, which may explain reverse tolerance for it.

THERAPEUTIC EFFECTS In a seeming irony, therapeutic uses of marijuana came to light just as the negative effects of regular and heavy usage of the drug were being uncovered. In

On August 3, 2001, then federal minister of health Alan Rock toured the plant where marijuana is being grown for medical purposes. The hydroponic lab (dubbed the Rock Garden by workers), located in an old shaft at Trout Lake Mine in Flin Flon, Manitoba, is Canada's first legal growing operation. The Canadian Press/Frank Gunn.

the 1970s, several double-blind studies (e.g., Salan, Zinberg, & Frei, 1975) showed that THC and related drugs can reduce the nausea and loss of appetite that accompany chemotherapy for some cancer patients. Later findings confirmed this result (Grinspoon & Bakalar, 1995). Marijuana often appears to reduce nausea when other anti-nausea agents fail. Marijuana is also a treatment for the discomfort of AIDS (Sussman et al., 1996), as well as glaucoma, epilepsy, and multiple sclerosis.

The potential benefits of smoking marijuana were also confirmed in a 1998 report to the U.S. National Institutes of Health (NIH) by a panel of experts. The panel suggested that medical researchers and clinicians should take the benefits more seriously (Ad Hoc Advisory Group of Experts, 1998).

In light of this evidence and following a request from two men with AIDS, Health Canada set up a process in June 1999 whereby people wishing to use marijuana for medical reasons could apply to be exempt from the federal ban. Although exemptions were evaluated and granted on a case-by-case basis, the Government of Canada could not find a supplier who could grow the marijuana without the purchaser and seller being charged with a crime. The problem was rectified in December 2000, when a Saskatoon company known as Prairie Plant Systems was awarded a contract to provide a legal supply of marijuana. Also, in April 2001, the Government of Canada announced that people with other medical conditions (e.g., arthritis) might be eligible for medical marijuana, with the caveat that they had to first demonstrate that other means (e.g., painkillers) did not alleviate their suffering. Research on the use of medical marijuana is limited at present, but one survey found that about 2% of Canadians reported using marijuana for medical reasons (Ogborne et al., 2000), with the vast majority using it for pain or persistent nausea.

SEDATIVES AND STIMULANTS

Addiction to drugs, including sedatives, was disapproved of but tolerated in the United States until 1914, when the *Harrison Narcotics Act* made the unauthorized use of various drugs illegal and those addicted to them criminals. The drugs we discuss here, some of which may be obtained legally with a prescription, can be divided into two general categories: sedatives and stimulants.

SEDATIVES

The major **sedatives**, often called downers, slow the activities of the body and reduce its responsiveness. This group of drugs includes the opiates—opium and its derivatives, morphine, heroin, and codeine—and the synthetic barbiturates and tranquilizers, such as secobarbital (Seconal) and diazepam (Valium).

OPIATES The **opiates** are a group of addictive sedatives that relieve pain and induce sleep when taken in moderate doses. Foremost among them is **opium**, originally the principal drug of illegal international trafficking and known to the people of the Sumerian civilization as long ago as 7000 B.C. They gave the poppy that supplied this drug its name (i.e., the plant of joy).

In 1806, the alkaloid **morphine**, named after Morpheus, the Greek god of dreams, was separated from raw opium. This bitter-tasting powder proved to be a powerful sedative and pain reliever. Before its addictive properties were noted, it was used in patent medicines. In the middle of the nineteenth century, when the hypodermic needle was introduced, morphine began to be injected directly into the veins to relieve pain. Many soldiers wounded in battle during the American Civil War were treated with morphine and returned home addicted to the drug.

An opium poppy. Opium is harvested by slitting the seed capsule, which allows the raw opium to seep out. National Library of Medicine/Photo Researchers, Inc.

Heroin was synthesized from opium in 1874 and was soon being added to a variety of medicines that could be purchased without prescription. This ad shows a teething remedy containing heroin. It probably worked. National Library of Medicine/Science Photo Library.

Concerned about administering a drug that could disturb the later lives of patients, scientists began studying morphine. In 1874, they found that morphine could be converted into another powerful pain-relieving drug, which they named **heroin**. Used initially as a cure for morphine addiction, heroin was substituted for morphine in cough syrups and other patent medicines. So many maladies were treated with heroin that it came to be known as G.O.M., or "God's own medicine" (Brecher, 1972). However, heroin proved to be even more addictive and more potent than morphine, acting more quickly and with greater intensity. In 1909, U.S. president Theodore Roosevelt called for an international investigation of opium and the other opiates.

Psychological and Physical Effects Opium and its derivatives, morphine and heroin, produce euphoria, drowsiness, reverie, and a lack of coordination. Heroin has an additional initial effect: the rush, a feeling of warm, suffusing ecstasy immediately following an intravenous injection. The user sheds worries and fears and has great self-confidence for four to six hours, but then experiences letdown, bordering on stupor.

Opiates produce their effects by stimulating neural receptors of the body's own opioid system. Heroin, for example, is converted into morphine in the brain and then binds to opioid receptors. The body produces opioids, called endorphins and enkephalins, and opium and its derivatives fit into their receptors and stimulate them.

Opiates are clearly addicting, for users show both increased tolerance of the drugs and withdrawal symptoms when they are unable to obtain another dose. Reactions to not having a dose of heroin may begin within eight hours of the last injection, at least after high tolerance has built up. The individual typically has muscle pain, sneezes, sweats, becomes tearful, and yawns a great deal over the next few hours. The symptoms resemble those of influenza. The withdrawal symptoms become more severe within 36 hours. There may be uncontrollable muscle twitching, cramps, chills alternating with excessive flushing and sweating, and a rise in heart rate and blood pressure. The

addicted person is unable to sleep, vomits, and has diarrhea. These symptoms typically persist for about 72 hours and then diminish gradually over a 5- to 10-day period.

It is believed that there are more than a million heroin addicts in the United States (Goldstein, 1994). Dependence is many times higher among physicians and nurses than in any other group with a comparable educational background. This problem is a joint reflection of the availability of opiates in medical settings and high job stress (Jaffe, 1985).

Heroin used to be confined to poor neighbourhoods and the inner city. In Canada, less than 1% of Canadians report using heroin in their lifetime, but heroin and cocaine abuse are quite prevalent among street youth; one study found that 5% of street youth in Montreal report using heroin every day (see Poulin et al., 1998). A comparison of six major Canadian cities identified Vancouver as first in terms of per capita heroin- and cocaine-related hospital separations and deaths (Poulin et al., 1998). In recent years, heroin has started to become the cool drug for middle- and upper-middle-class college students and young professionals, and it is beginning to vie with cocaine for popularity among these groups. The 2004 Canadian Campus Survey (Adlaf et al., 2005) found that 8.7% of university students had used such illicit drugs as heroin, cocaine, crack, LSD, and ecstasy, and this rate was fairly stable across various versions of the survey. Use of hallucinogens such as mescaline, mushrooms, and LSD has declined significantly, however.

American surveys indicate that the number of new users of heroin has been increasing steadily since 1992 (NIDA,

Canadian boxing great George Chuvalo has dedicated his time to warning students about the dangers of using drugs such as heroin. Three of his four sons became addicted to heroin. Tragically, his sons George Lee Chuvalo and Steven Chuvalo died of heroin overdoses, and Jesse Chuvalo committed suicide by shooting himself. Chuvalo's wife, Lynn, could not cope with these losses and also committed suicide. The Canadian Press/ Tobin Grimshaw.

1997). In 1988, 1,250 people were seen in emergency rooms after injecting or snorting heroin; by 1994, this figure increased more than 2,000%, to 27,300.

Some of these increases in drug casualties are due to the nature of the heroin now available. The substantial increase in the mortality rate due to heroin or cocaine use recorded in British Columbia between 1990 and 1993 was attributed to the increased purity of the drugs (Office of the Chief Coroner of British Columbia, 1994). Twenty years ago, the heroin sold in southern California, for example, was in a powder form that was less than 5% pure. Today heroin ranges from 25 to 50% pure.

Opiates present a serious set of problems for the abuser. In a 24-year follow-up of 500 heroin addicts, about 28% had died by age 40; half of these deaths were from homicide, suicide, or accident, and one third were from overdoses (Hser, Anglin, & Powers, 1993). Equally serious are the social consequences of using an illegal drug. The drug and obtaining it become the centre of the abuser's existence, governing all activities and social relationships. The high cost of these drugs—addicts must often spend upwards of $200 per day for their opiates—means they either have great wealth or must acquire money through illegal activities, such as prostitution or selling drugs.

SYNTHETIC SEDATIVES Barbiturates, another major type of sedative, were synthesized as aids for sleeping and relaxation. The first barbiturate was produced in 1903, and since then hundreds of derivatives of barbituric acid have been made. These drugs were initially considered highly desirable and were frequently prescribed. A campaign was mounted against them in the 1940s because they were discovered to be addictive, and physicians began to prescribe barbiturates less often. Today, the benzodiazepines, such as Valium, are more commonly used and abused. Methaqualone, a sedative sold under the trade names Quaalude and Sopor, is similar in effect to barbiturates and has become a popular street drug.

Sedatives relax the muscles, reduce anxiety, and in small doses produce a mildly euphoric state. Like alcohol, they are thought to produce these psychological effects by stimulating the GABA system. With excessive doses, however, speech becomes slurred and gait unsteady. Judgement, concentration, and ability to work may be severely impaired. The user loses emotional control and may become irritable and combative before falling into a deep sleep. Very large doses can be fatal because the diaphragm muscles relax to such an extent that the individual suffocates. As indicated in Chapter 8, sedatives are frequently chosen as a means of suicide. However, many users accidentally kill themselves by drinking alcohol, which potentiates, or magnifies, the depressant effects of sedatives. The brain can become damaged and personality deteriorates with prolonged excessive use.

Increased tolerance follows prolonged use of sedatives, and the withdrawal reactions after abrupt termination are particularly severe and long-lasting and can cause sudden death. The delirium and convulsions resemble the symptoms that follow abrupt withdrawal from alcohol.

STIMULANTS

Stimulants, or uppers, such as cocaine, act on the brain and the sympathetic nervous system to increase alertness and motor activity. Cocaine is a natural stimulant extracted from the coca leaf. The amphetamines, such as Benzedrine, are synthetic stimulants. Focus on Discovery 12.2 discusses a less risky and more prevalent stimulant: caffeine.

AMPHETAMINES Seeking a treatment for asthma, the Chinese-American pharmacologist Chen studied ancient Chinese descriptions of drugs. He found that a desert shrub, ma huang, was described as an effective remedy. After systematic effort, Chen isolated an alkaloid from this plant belonging to the genus *Ephedra*, and the result, ephedrine, proved highly successful in treating asthma. But relying on the shrub for the drug was not efficient, and so efforts to develop a synthetic substitute began. **Amphetamines** resulted from these efforts (Snyder, 1974).

The first amphetamine, Benzedrine, was synthesized in 1927. Almost as soon as it became commercially available in the early 1930s as an inhalant to relieve stuffy noses, the public discovered its stimulating effects. Physicians thereafter prescribed it and the other amphetamines that were soon synthesized to control mild depression and appetite. Soldiers on both sides in the Second World War were supplied with the drugs to ward off fatigue, and today amphetamines are sometimes used to treat hyperactive children.

Amphetamines, such as Benzedrine, Dexedrine, and Methedrine, produce their effects by causing the release of norepinephrine and dopamine and blocking the reuptake of these neurotransmitters. They are taken orally or intravenously and can be addictive. Wakefulness is heightened, intestinal functions are inhibited, and appetite is reduced—hence their use in dieting. The heart rate quickens, and blood vessels in the skin and mucous membranes constrict. The individual becomes alert, euphoric, and outgoing and is possessed with seemingly boundless energy and self-confidence. Larger doses can make people nervous and confused, subjecting them to palpitations, headaches, dizziness, and sleeplessness. Sometimes heavy users become so suspicious and hostile that they can be dangerous to others. Large doses taken over time can induce a state similar to paranoid schizophrenia, including its delusions.

Tolerance to amphetamines develops rapidly, so that more and more of the drug is required to produce the stimulating effect. As tolerance increases, the user may stop taking pills and inject Methedrine, the strongest of the amphetamines, directly into the veins. The so-called speed freaks give themselves repeated injections of the drug and maintain intense and euphoric activity for a few days, without eating or sleeping (a run), after which they are exhausted and depressed and sleep, or crash, for several days. Then the cycle starts again. After several repetitions of this pattern, physical and social functioning deteriorates considerably. Behaviour is erratic and hostile, and speed freaks may become a danger to themselves and to others.

FOCUS ON DISCOVERY 12.2
OUR TASTIEST ADDICTION: CAFFEINE

What may be the world's most popular drug is seldom viewed as a drug at all, and yet it has strong effects, produces tolerance in people, and even subjects habitual users to withdrawal (Hughes et al., 1991). Users and non-users alike joke about it. We are, of course, referring to caffeine, a substance found in coffee, tea, cocoa, cola, some cold remedies, and some diet pills.

Two cups of coffee, containing between 150 and 300 milligrams of caffeine, affect people within half an hour. Metabolism, body temperature, and blood pressure all increase; urine production goes up, as most of us will attest; there may be hand tremors, appetite can diminish, and, most familiar of all, sleepiness is warded off. Panic disorder can be exacerbated by caffeine because of the heightened arousal of the sympathetic nervous system occasioned by the drug. Extremely large doses can cause headache, diarrhea, nervousness, severe agitation, even convulsions and death. Death, however, is virtually impossible unless someone grossly overuses caffeine tablets, since the drug is excreted by the kidneys without any appreciable accumulation.

Although it has long been recognized that drinkers of very large amounts of regular coffee daily can experience withdrawal symptoms when consumption ceases, people who drink just two cups of regular coffee a day can suffer from clinically significant headaches, fatigue, and anxiety if caffeine is withdrawn from their daily diet (Silverman et al., 1992). These symptoms, moreover, can markedly interfere with social and occupational functioning.

As is the case with other drugs, people ingest caffeine to obtain positive outcomes and avoid negative outcomes. Research by Kathryn Graham (1988) examined the reasons that Canadian undergraduates gave for heavy consumption of coffee and tea. Students reported drinking for reasons of sociability and affiliation with others, but also to obtain relief from aversive states. Of course, the need for a stimulant was also important. Analyses showed that relief and stimulation as reasons for caffeine use were the best predictors of overall consumption and caffeine dependence.

As we will see in a subsequent section, cognitive expectancies play a key role in substance use and misuse. A new 37-item Caffeine Expectancy Questionnaire developed by Heinz, Kassel, and Smith (2009) taps four expectancy factors: (1) withdrawal symptoms (e.g., "I will get headaches if I don't drink regularly"); (2) positive effects (e.g., "Drinking caffeine is satisfying"); (3) acute negative effects (e.g., "Caffeine causes me to shake or be jittery"); and (4) mood effects (e.g., "Caffeine helps me relax"). High scores on items tapping factors 1, 2, and 4 (withdrawal symptoms, positive effects, and mood effects) were correlated strongly with self-reports of degree of addiction to caffeine (Heinz et al., 2009).

The caffeine found in coffee, tea, and soft drinks is probably the world's favourite drug. Stockbyte/Getty Images.

Amphetamine use in the workplace has been increasing. Under time pressure to produce—the saying of the 1990s was "do more with less"—many white-collar workers turned to speed to stay awake, be more productive, and in general feel more energized, even euphoric.

COCAINE The natives of the Andean uplands, to which the coca shrubs are native, chew the leaves. Europeans, introduced to coca by Spanish conquistadors, chose instead to brew the leaves in beverages. The alkaloid **cocaine** was extracted from the leaves of the coca plant in the mid-1800s and has been used since then as a local anaesthetic. In 1884, while still a young neurologist, Sigmund Freud began using cocaine to combat his depression. Convinced of its wondrous

effects, he prescribed it to a friend who had a painful disease. Freud published one of the first papers on the drug, "Song of Praise," which was an enthusiastic endorsement of the exhilarating effects he had experienced. Freud subsequently lost his enthusiasm for cocaine after nursing a physician friend, to whom he had recommended the drug, through a night-long psychotic state brought on by it. Perhaps the most famous fictional cocaine addict was Sherlock Holmes.

Cocaine has other effects in addition to reducing pain. It acts rapidly on the brain, blocking the reuptake of dopamine in mesolimbic areas that are thought to yield pleasurable states; the result is that dopamine is left in the synapse and thereby facilitates neural transmission and resultant positive feelings. Self-reports of the pleasure induced by cocaine

In the September 2010 issue of Vanity Fair, pop phenom Lady Gaga admitted to using cocaine. Of her drug use, she said "I do not want my fans to ever emulate that or be that way. I don't want my fans to think they have to be that way to be great. It's in the past. It was a low point, and it lead to disaster." Wenn/Newscom.

are strongly related to the extent that cocaine has blocked dopamine reuptake (Volkow et al., 1997). Cocaine increases sexual desire and produces feelings of self-confidence, well-being, and indefatigability. An overdose may bring on chills, nausea, and insomnia, as well as a paranoid breakdown and terrifying hallucinations of insects crawling beneath the skin. Chronic use often leads to changes in personality, which include heightened irritability, impaired social skills, paranoid thinking, and disturbances in eating and sleeping (American Society for Pharmacology, 1987). Ceasing cocaine use appears to cause a severe withdrawal syndrome. Cocaine can take hold of people with as much tenacity as do the established addictive drugs. As with alcohol, developing fetuses are markedly and negatively affected in the womb by the mother's use of cocaine during pregnancy, and many babies are born addicted to the drug.

Cocaine, a vasoconstrictor, causes the blood vessels to narrow. Cocaine increases a person's risk for stroke and causes cognitive impairments, including problems with memory and attention. Because of its strong vasoconstricting properties, cocaine poses special dangers in pregnancy, for the blood supply to the fetus may be compromised.

In the mid-1980s a new form of freebase, called crack, appeared on the streets. The presence of crack brought about an increase in freebasing and in casualties. Because it was available in small, relatively inexpensive doses, younger and less-affluent buyers began to experiment with the drug and to become addicted (Kozel & Adams, 1986).

Cocaine use in general soared in the 1970s and 1980s, increasing by more than 260% between 1974 and 1985. The use of cocaine dramatically decreased in the late 1980s and early 1990s. However, among Grade 12 students, use increased from 1996 to 1997 (NIDA, 1998). The frequency of use of crack has not shown any decline. Figures for crack use in 1991 (based on reported use during the past month) were about 0.3% for people aged 18 to 34 (NIDA, 1991), but in 1996 had increased to 0.8% (NIDA, 1996). Many public health and police officials regard crack as the most dangerous illicit drug in society today.

LSD AND OTHER HALLUCINOGENS

In 1943, a Swiss chemist, Albert Hofmann, described an illness he had seemingly contracted: "Last Friday ... I had to interrupt my laboratory work ... I was seized with a feeling of great restlessness and mild dizziness. At home, I lay down and sank into a not unpleasant delirium, which was characterized by extremely exciting fantasies. In a semiconscious state with my eyes closed ... fantastic visions of extraordinary realness and with an intense kaleidoscopic play of colors assaulted me" (cited in Cashman, 1966, p. 31).

Earlier in the day Hofmann had manufactured a few milligrams of d-lysergic acid diethylamide, a drug that he had synthesized in 1938. Reasoning that he might have unknowingly ingested some and that this had caused his unusual experience, he deliberately took a dose and confirmed his hypothesis.

After Hofmann's experiences with **LSD** in 1943, the drug was referred to as psychotomimetic because it was thought to produce effects similar to the symptoms of a psychosis. Then the term "psychedelic," from the Greek words for "soul" and "to make manifest," was applied to emphasize the subjectively experienced expansions of consciousness reported by users of LSD and often referred to by them as a trip. The term in current use for LSD is **hallucinogen**, which describes one of the main effects of such drugs—hallucinations.

Four other important hallucinogens are mescaline, psilocybin, and the synthetic compounds MDA and MDMA. In 1896, **mescaline**, an alkaloid and the active ingredient of peyote, was isolated from small, disc-like growths on the top of the peyote cactus. The drug has been used for centuries in the religious rites of Native peoples living in the U.S. Southwest and northern Mexico. **Psilocybin** is a crystalline powder that Hofmann isolated from the mushroom *Psilocybe mexicana* in 1958. The early Aztec and Mexican cultures called the sacred mushrooms "God's flesh," and the Natives of Mexico still use them in their worship. Each of these substances is structurally similar to several neurotransmitters, but their effects are thought to be due to the stimulation of serotonin receptors.

During the 1950s, researchers gave LSD, mescaline, and psilocybin to people in research settings so that they could study what were thought to be psychotic experiences.

In the 1960s, psychologist Timothy Leary was one of the leading proponents of the use of hallucinogens to expand consciousness. Bettman/CORBIS.

In 1960, Timothy Leary and Richard Alpert of Harvard University began an investigation of the effects of psilocybin on institutionalized prisoners. Their early results were encouraging and pointed to therapeutic benefits: released prisoners who had taken psilocybin proved less likely to be rearrested. However, the investigators started taking trips themselves and soon had gathered around them other people interested in experimenting with psychedelic drugs. Their activities had attracted the attention of law-enforcement agencies by 1962. As the police investigation continued, the situation became a scandal, culminating in Leary's and Alpert's departures from Harvard. The affair gave tremendous impetus to the use of the hallucinogens, particularly since the manufacture of LSD and the extraction of mescaline and psilocybin were relatively easy and inexpensive. There is no evidence of withdrawal symptoms during abstinence, but tolerance seems to develop rapidly (McKim, 1991).

Recently, researchers have returned to the possibility that psychedelic drugs may have benefits for certain patients. For instance, an investigation of nine OCD patients showed that when given psilocybin (the magic ingredient in "magic mushrooms"), the patients had substantial decreases in OCD symptoms and these decreases tended to persist over time (Moreno, Wiegand, Taitano, & Delgado, 2006). Another investigation found substantial decreases in depressions believed to be treatment resistant when patients were administered ketamine (Zarate et al., 2006). Thus, while additional research is clearly needed, some patients may actually benefit from psychedelic drugs.

Another hallucinogen joined the ranks of illegal drugs in 1985. **Ecstasy**, which refers to two closely similar synthetic compounds, MDA (methylenedioxyamphetamine) and MDMA (methylenedioxymethamphetamine), is chemically similar to mescaline and the amphetamines and is the psychoactive agent in nutmeg. Ecstasy is a designer drug produced via chemical synthesis. It comes in many different sizes and shapes, depending on how it is manufactured. MDA was first synthesized in 1910, but it was not until the 1960s that its psychedelic properties came to the attention of the drug-using, consciousness-expanding generation of the times. Today it is popular on some college campuses, and the use of ecstasy is associated with raves (see Gross et al., 2002). The 2004 Canadian Addiction Survey found that 4.1% of Canadians reported using ecstasy during their lifetime and 1.1% used it within the previous year. Ecstasy use among Ontario students in grades 7 to 13 increased steadily in the 1990s, with 4.8% of students reporting use in 1999 (Adlaf et al., 2000).

Users report that the drug enhances intimacy and insight, improves interpersonal relationships, elevates mood, and promotes aesthetic awareness. It can also cause muscle tension, rapid eye movements, increased heart rate and blood pressure, nausea, faintness, chills or sweating, and anxiety, depression, and confusion. Lasting side effects that include paranoia, confusion, and memory complaints are beginning to be reported in the literature, and research with animals has shown that recreational doses of ecstasy cause permanent nerve damage (Centre for Addiction and Mental Health, 2001). The U.S. Drug Enforcement Administration considers the use of ecstasy and other so-called designer drugs unsafe and a serious health threat. Several deaths have come from accidental overdoses, with hyperthermia being the leading cause of death (see Gross et al., 2002).

EFFECTS OF HALLUCINOGENS

The effects of hallucinogens depend on a number of psychological variables in addition to the dose itself. A person's set—that is, attitudes, expectations, and motivations with regard to taking drugs—is widely held to be an important determinant of his or her reactions to hallucinogens. The setting in which the drug is experienced is also important.

Among the most prominent dangers of taking LSD is the possibility of experiencing a bad trip. A bad trip can sometimes develop into a full-blown panic attack and is far more likely to occur if some aspect of taking the drug creates anxiety. Often the specific fear is of going crazy. These panics are usually short-lived and subside as the drug is metabolized. A minority of people, however, go into a psychotic state that can require hospitalization and extended treatment.

Flashbacks, a recurrence of psychedelic experiences after the physiological effects of the drug have worn off, also sometimes occur, most frequently in times of stress, illness, or fatigue (Kaplan & Sadock, 1991). Flashbacks are not believed to be caused by drug-produced physical changes in the nervous system, in part because only 15 to 30% of users of hallucinogenic drugs are estimated ever to have flashbacks (e.g., Stanton & Bardoni, 1972). Moreover, there is no independent evidence of measurable neurological changes in these drug users. Flashbacks seem to have a force of their own, haunting and upsetting people weeks and months after they have taken the drug.

ETIOLOGY OF SUBSTANCE ABUSE AND DEPENDENCE

In considering the causes of substance abuse and dependence disorders, we must recognize that becoming substance-dependent is generally a developmental process. The person must first have a positive attitude toward the substance, then begin to experiment with using it, then begin using it regularly, then use it heavily, and finally abuse or become physically dependent on it (see Figure 12.1). The general idea is that the person becomes ensnared by the biological processes of tolerance and withdrawal after engaging in prolonged, heavy use.

Recent findings have caused scholars to re-examine the role of withdrawal in the development of addiction. Historically, withdrawal has not been implicated as a factor in drug use and relapse. However, Baker et al. (2006) argued that there is a need for a more complex view of withdrawal. That is, the physical signs of withdrawal do not motivate substance misuse, but two elements do seem to play a role: (1) the intense negative affect caused by withdrawal; and (2) urges (i.e., conscious awareness of the desire to take a drug).

Although researchers are just beginning to consider the stages of this process separately (Stice, Barrera, & Chassin, 1998), variables that cause substance dependence appear to depend on the stage being considered. For example, developing a positive attitude toward smoking and beginning to experiment with tobacco are strongly related to the smoking of other family members (Robinson et al., 1997). In contrast, becoming a regular smoker is more strongly related to smoking by peers and being able to acquire cigarettes readily (Holowaty, Feldman, Harvey, & Shortt, 2000; Robinson et al., 1997).

Also, other external influences cannot be discounted. There are growing concerns about the impact of watching smoking in movies, after studies have concluded that exposure to movie smoking has a dose-response relationship with adolescent smoking behaviour (Charlesworth & Glantz, 2005). Recent data suggest that compared with adolescents with low exposure, those with high exposure to smoking in movies are three times more likely to try smoking or become smokers (Heatherton & Sargent, 2009). This effect is still evident after controlling for demographic, personality, and parenting style. Moreover, the effect is strongest among those who would otherwise be at low risk due to not having parents who smoke or who are low in sensation seeking (see Heatherton & Sargent, 2009). This effect is strong enough that researchers have advocated that movies involving smoking be automatically R-rated.

FIGURE 12.1 The process of becoming a substance abuser

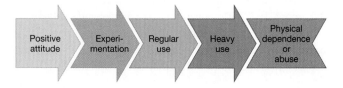

This developmental model does not account for all cases of substance abuse or dependence. There are documented cases in which heavy use of tobacco or heroin did not end in addiction. Moreover, progression through the stages is not inevitable. Some people have periods of heavy use of a substance and then return to moderate use. Nevertheless, guided by this model, most research has examined variables related to initial use and its subsequent escalation. In the following sections, we discuss socio-cultural, psychological, and biological variables related to substance abuse. Note that these factors can relate to various substances differently (e.g., a genetic diathesis may contribute to alcoholism but not to hallucinogen abuse).

SOCIAL VARIABLES

Socio-cultural variables can play a widely varying role in drug abuse. Various aspects of the social world (e.g., peers, parents, media portrayals) can affect people's interest in and access to drugs. At the broadest level, we can look at great cross-national variations in alcohol consumption. The data in Figure 12.2, from a large-scale longitudinal study, illustrate the commonalities in the alcohol consumption of various regions. First, over the study period (1950–80), alcohol consumption rose greatly in each area studied. Second, variations in consumption across locations decreased with the passage of time, although great differences still exist. Other research has found striking cross-national differences in the prevalence of substance use despite widespread similarities in the average onset of first use (see Vega et al., 2002). For example, the highest alcohol consumption rates have typically been found in wine-drinking countries, such as France, Spain, and Italy, where drinking alcohol regularly is widely accepted (deLint,

FIGURE 12.2 Annual consumption of alcoholic beverages among people aged 15 years and over in countries from 1950 to 1980, including data from Ontario. From Mäkelä et al., 1981

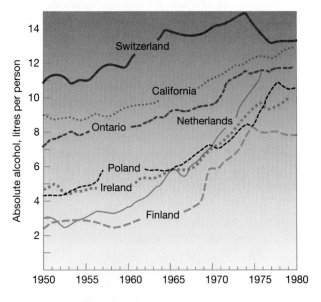

1978). Cultural attitudes and patterns of drinking thus influence the likelihood of drinking heavily and therefore of abusing alcohol.

Ready availability of the substance is also a factor. For example, in the wine-drinking cultures just mentioned, wine is present in many social settings, even in university cafeterias. Rates of alcohol abuse are also high among bartenders and liquor store owners, people for whom alcohol is readily available (Fillmore & Caetano, 1980). As for smoking, rates of smoking increase if cigarettes are perceived as being easy to get and affordable (Robinson et al., 1997).

Family variables are also important socio-cultural influences. If both parents smoke, a child is four times more likely to do so than if no other family member smokes. Similarly, exposure to alcohol use by parents increases children's likelihood of drinking (Hawkins et al., 1997), and a study of adolescents in Canada and the eastern United States who were receiving treatment for amphetamine use showed that they tended to come from homes where one or more parent used illicit drugs and drank regularly (Hawke, Jainchill, & De Leon, 2000). Recent analyses of the National Longitudinal Survey of Children and Youth (NLSCY) data of 10- to 15-year-old Canadian youth show that a host of chronic disease behavioural risk factors (i.e., tobacco smoking, drinking alcohol) are more prevalent among those who have caregivers who smoke and peers who smoke and drink; protective factors were having high self-esteem and coming from a home with a member with post-secondary education (Alamian & Paradis, 2009). Other data from the Vancouver Family Survey indicate that heavy marijuana use among youth was predicted by the father's alcoholism, peer use of illicit drugs, and an addiction-prone personality characterized by high novelty seeking and low self-regulation (Barnes, Barnes, & Patton, 2005). A lack of emotional support from parents is also linked with increased use of cigarettes, cannabis, and alcohol (Cadoret et al., 1995a; Wills, DuHamel, & Vaccaro, 1995). Finally, a lack of parental monitoring leads to increased association with drug-abusing peers and subsequent use of drugs (Chassin et al., 1996). Recent meta-analytic data from 17 studies with over 35,000 participants confirmed that adolescent perceptions of greater parental monitoring are linked reliably with less marijuana use and this held across concurrent and longitudinal assessments (Lac & Crano, 2009).

Results from the Ontario Health Survey suggest that any analysis of family factors should consider the role of siblings. Data indicate that the dominant family influence in terms of behaviour was from older siblings to younger siblings, especially if the siblings are less than two years apart in age (Boyle et al., 2001). Moreover, this effect was stronger than the link between substance use in parents and their children.

The social milieu in which a person operates can also affect substance abuse. Having friends who smoke predicts smoking (Killen et al., 1997). Tobacco use among high school students is highest in certain subgroups: those with poor grades, behaviour problems, and a taste for heavy metal music (Sussman et al., 1990). In longitudinal studies, peer-group identification in Grade 7 predicted smoking in Grade 8 (Sussman et al., 1994), and in a three-year study, it predicted increased drug use in general (Chassin et al., 1996). Peer influences are also important in promoting alcohol and marijuana use (Alamian & Paradis, 2009; Kairouz & Adlaf, 2003; Stice et al., 1998; Wills & Cleary, 1999). Although peer influence is important, those who have a high sense of self-efficacy (Bandura, 1997) are influenced less by their peers. Adolescents with this quality agree with statements like "I can imagine refusing to use tobacco with students my age and still have them like me" (Stacy et al., 1992, p. 166).

The role of the media must also be considered. We are bombarded with TV commercials in which beer is associated with athletic-looking males, bikini-clad women, and good times. In Canada, the "I am Canadian" campaign even implicitly suggested a link between beer and patriotic interests. Supporting the role of advertising in promoting alcohol use is an analysis of consumption in 17 countries between 1970 and 1983. Those countries that banned ads for spirits had 16% less consumption than those that did not (Saffer, 1991). Note that one team of researchers claims to have definitive evidence that alcohol companies are targeting youth by advertising heavily, even disproportionately, in youth magazines with the highest readerships (see King et al., 2009).

A particularly pernicious example of the role of advertising was the Joe Camel campaign for Camel cigarettes. With the number of smokers declining, the tobacco industry's profitability depends on recruiting new smokers to replace those who are quitting. Elementary and high school students are obvious targets. Camel launched its campaign in 1988 with the Joe Camel character modelled after James Bond or the character played by Don Johnson in the television program Miami Vice, a popular show of the time. Prior to the campaign, from 1976 to 1988, Camels were the preferred brand of fewer than 0.5% of students in grades 7 through 12. By 1991, Camel's share of this illegal market had increased to 33% (DiFranza et al., 1991)!

Additional evidence also indicates that advertising does influence smoking. In a longitudinal study of non-smoking adolescents, those who had a favourite cigarette ad were twice as likely subsequently to begin smoking or to be willing to do so (Pierce et al., 1998).

The days of Joe Camel and other cartoon characters that appeal to young people were over many years ago. On March 13, 1996, the Liggett Group, manufacturers of cigarettes, agreed to stop using such advertising tools and to take other steps to discourage smoking among minors. These actions were part of a settlement in a class action lawsuit against the U.S. cigarette industry that charged companies with manipulating nicotine levels to keep smokers addicted.

PSYCHOLOGICAL VARIABLES

Next, we examine three classes of psychological variables. The first class essentially comprises the effects of alcohol on mood, the situations in which a tension-reducing effect occurs, and the role of cognition in this process. The second concerns beliefs about the prevalence of the drug's use and health risks associated with that drug. The third includes the personality traits that may make it more likely for some people to use drugs heavily.

MOOD ALTERATION, SITUATIONS, AND THE ROLE OF COGNITION

Why do people drink? One team of Canadian investigators proposed that it is possible to approach this issue from a cost vs. benefit perspective; for example, drinking occurs if the perceived benefits outweigh the costs (Cunningham et al., 1997). Cox and Klinger (1988) proposed another motivational model of alcohol use that suggested that drinking motives vary along two dimensions: the valence of reinforcement (positive vs. negative) and locus (external reasons vs. internal, personal reasons); that is, people can drink to obtain pleasurable outcomes or avoid negative outcomes, and they can drink in response to external, social stimulation or in response to internal, personal cues. Four combinations involving these two dimensions are possible. Drinking for positive, internal reasons reflects drinking to enhance positive mood. Drinking for negative, internal reasons reflects drinking to reduce or avoid experiencing negative emotions. Drinking for positive, external reasons reflects drinking to obtain social rewards, and drinking for negative, external reasons would involve drinking to escape punishment or to avoid being embarrassed by other people.

Cooper (1994) created a multifactorial scale to assess these four drinking motives. Positive, internal reasons are measured by the enhancement scale (e.g., drinking because it gives you a pleasant feeling). Negative, internal reasons are

reflected by the coping scale (e.g., drinking because it cheers you up when you are in a bad mood). Positive, external reasons are assessed via the social scale (e.g., drinking because it makes social gatherings more fun). Finally, negative, external reasons are assessed via the conformity scale (e.g., drinking because you do not want to feel left out).

Extensive research has been conducted on these four motives. Kuntsche et al. (2005) have provided a comprehensive review of drinking motives research with young people. They concluded that young people drink primarily for social motives. They are less likely to drink for enhancement and they are even less likely to drink due to coping motives. Social motives are associated with moderate alcohol use, while enhancement motives are more likely to be associated with heavy drinking (i.e., drinking to get drunk). Coping motives predict alcohol-related problems (e.g., academic problems and legal difficulties).

Researchers at Dalhousie University have developed a five-factor motive scale (Grant et al., 2007) and found that it is possible and important to distinguish coping-anxiety motives and coping-depression motives within the coping motives domain (Grant, Stewart, & Mohr, 2009). This study found that coping-anxiety motives moderated the link between daily anxious mood and alcohol consumption, and as expected, coping-depression motives moderated the link between daily depressed mood and alcohol consumption.

While drinking to cope is less frequent, research by Stan Sadava and associates at Brock University in St. Catharines, Ont., has shown that problem drinkers attach great importance to drinking in order to cope (Bonin, McCreary, & Sadava, 2000; Sadava & Pak, 1993). Also, children of parents with alcohol problems are more likely to endorse that they drink to cope (Chadler, Elgar, & Bennett, 2006).

Although drinking motives have been studied almost exclusively in isolation from each other, in reality, some people will drink for multiple motives and there is surprisingly little research on these people. Goldstein and Flett (2009) focused on a group of students who drink jointly for both coping and enhancement reasons (i.e., distress relief and pleasure seeking!). Empirical results showed that these students were actually quite similar to another group of students who drank primarily for coping motives. Coping-motivated drinkers and coping plus enhancement-motivated drinkers had comparable personality features (i.e., elevated neuroticism and anxiety sensitivity). It is possible that those who drink for multiple motives are at even greater risk for more serious drinking problems.

Cognitive Factors in Drinking There are many ways that cognitive factors may operate in drinking; for instance, by reducing tension. Findings indicate that alcohol may produce its tension-reducing effect by altering cognition and perception (Curtin et al., 1998; Steele & Josephs, 1990). Alcohol impairs cognitive processing and narrows attention to the most immediately available cues, resulting in what Steele and Josephs term "alcohol myopia"—the intoxicated person has

Former Alberta Premier Ralph Klein and Premier Gordon Campbell of British Columbia have both been identified as having drinking problems. Klein acknowledged his problem in December 2001 following a bizarre incident in which he stopped outside a shelter while inebriated and berated homeless people, while Campbell was arrested for drunk driving in Hawaii in January 2003. CP Image Archive/Chuck Stoody.

less cognitive capacity to distribute between ongoing activity and worry. If a distracting activity is available, attention will be diverted to it rather than to worrisome thoughts, with a resultant decrease in anxiety.

Extensive research has been conducted on the role of positive vs. negative cognitive expectations in drinking behaviour. Positive alcohol expectations predict higher levels of consumption and alcohol-related problems, while negative expectations tend to inhibit consumption. The belief that alcohol helps one cope with stress is one of several positive beliefs. Other positive beliefs are that drinking enhances sexual pleasure and that it makes a person more friendly and assertive in social situations (see MacLatchy-Gaudet & Stewart, 2001). Negative alcohol expectations include beliefs such as that drinking contributes to physical problems (i.e., hangovers), is linked with cognitive deficits, increases negative moods, and increases one's willingness to engage in unsafe and risky behaviours.

It seems that positive expectations are stronger predictors of drinking behaviour than negative ones (Goldman, Del Boca, & Darkes, 1999). A strong self-protective bias also seems to exist. There is a discrepancy in people's beliefs about the effects of alcohol on themselves vs. others, with most people believing that alcohol has a stronger effect on other people than on themselves (see Paglia & Room, 1999).

Several factors may be involved in the development of alcohol expectations, including direct personal experiences and more indirect, vicarious influences that involve the imitation and internalization of parental beliefs and beliefs displayed in the media (see Goldman et al., 1999). For instance, having an alcoholic parent and experiencing high levels of abuse while growing up are factors that contribute to negative alcohol expectations (Wall, Wekerle, & Bissonette, 2000). Alcohol expectations are also influenced by situational factors. A Canadian study assessed the alcohol expectations of students who were surveyed either in a laboratory or in an on-campus bar (Wall, McKee, & Hinson, 2000). Students tested in the on-campus bar reported higher expectations of pleasurable disinhibition and stimulation from drinking. Furthermore, positive expectations about alcohol and drinking appear to influence each other. The expectation that drinking will reduce anxiety increases drinking, which in turn makes the positive expectations even stronger (Smith et al., 1995). Similarly, positive expectations about a drug's effects predict increased drug use in general (Stacy, Newcomb, & Bentler, 1991).

Contemporary work on cognitive factors has incorporated the distinction between explicit cognitions (i.e., consciously held beliefs and expectations) and implicit cognition. Explicit cognition reflects controlled thought processes that can be deliberated upon, while implicit cognition involves automatic appraisal of cues that is more uncontrolled and perhaps not subject to conscious awareness. Wiers and Stacy (2006) have advanced a two-component, dual-process model of addictive behaviour that distinguishes between controlled, reflective behaviour and automatic impulsive processing. They summarize research indicating that as an addiction develops, the automatic processing component gains strength and fosters an impulsive orientation that is reflected in cognitive tendencies. They suggest, for instance, that as addiction develops, drug-related cues, such as the presence of a beer bottle, gain the ability to automatically capture the person's attention, even though they may not be consciously aware of their attentiveness to these cues.

Much of the empirical basis of the implicit component of the dual-process model came from research using the **Drug-Stroop Task**. A Stroop task typically requires an individual to say whether a word matches a particular colour (e.g., Is the word "blue"; that is, is it written in blue letters?) and ignore the actual content of the word. The Drug Stroop Effect is the tendency for addiction prone people to respond slower when colour-identifying a word that reflects addiction (e.g., identifying the colour when they see the word VODKA in red letters, as opposed to a neutral word such as BASEBALL). This is known as the Stroop interference effect and is believed to stem from an attentional bias that implicitly operates. Extensive work with the Drug-Stroop Task has confirmed that people prone to addiction have an interference effect when presented with drug-related words (Cox, Fadardi, & Pothos, 2006).

Cognitive processes and negative affect may be linked inextricably in some drinkers. Studies of cognitive processing indicate that negative affective cues in the environment seem to activate alcohol-related concepts (e.g., target words such as "beer") in problem drinkers with high levels of psychological distress (Zack, Toneatto, & MacLeod, 1999; Zack et al., 2003). Thus, it seems that an orientation toward negative affect moods has cognitive implications for certain alcohol abusers.

BELIEFS ABOUT PREVALENCE AND RISKS Two other psychological variables related to drug use are the extent to which a person believes a drug is harmful and the perceived prevalence of use by others (Jackson, 1997). Marijuana use peaked in 1978, when almost 11% of high school seniors reported daily use. At that time, only 12% of Grade 12 students believed there was risk associated with occasional use and only 35% believed there was risk with regular use. Compare this with 1985, when daily use had plummeted to 5%: 25% of high school seniors believed marijuana was harmful if used occasionally, and 70% believed it was harmful if used on a regular basis (Kozel & Adams, 1986).

PERSONALITY AND DRUG USE Neither socio-cultural factors nor mood-alteration theories can completely account for individual differences in drug use. Not all members of a particular culture or subculture are heavy users, nor do all who experience stress increase drug usage. Personality variables attempt to explain why certain people are drawn to substance abuse.

Personality variables are stable individual differences that can be detected early in childhood and are believed to be relatively stable across the lifespan. Theoretical and empirical attempts to link personality factors with various forms of substance abuse have focused on a class of personality variables involved in behavioural disinhibition. Zuckerman (1994) has studied a personality style known as sensation seeking. High-sensation seekers are thrill-seekers who enjoy heightened levels of arousal. One way to increase arousal is to ingest certain drugs.

Cloninger and Eysenck are other theorists who have attempted to link alcohol and drug use with personality factors believed to be associated with behavioural disinhibition. Cloninger (1987a, 1987b) suggested that brain systems associated with behavioural activation and behavioural inhibition are associated with three genetically inherited dimensions of personality: novelty seeking, harm avoidance, and reward dependence. Novelty seeking is the dimension most relevant to alcohol dependence (Cloninger, 1987a).

Hans Eysenck conducted research throughout his lifetime on his three-factor model of personality (see Eysenck, 1967, 1981). He believed that the three key dimensions of personality were extroversion-introversion (i.e., outgoing vs. reserved), neuroticism vs. emotional stability, and psychoticism (i.e., aggressive, anti-social, tough-minded). According to his model, substance use and abuse are likely among individuals characterized by high levels of neuroticism and psychoticism (Eysenck & Eysenck, 1977). Eysenck's suggested link between psychoticism and drug use is in keeping with several studies that link anti-social tendencies with drug use. An association has also been found between drug use in general and anti-social personality disorder (Ball et al., 1994). Drug abuse may be part of the thrill-seeking behaviour of the psychopath, to be discussed in Chapter 13. Furthermore, alcohol use is comorbid with several personality disorders, most notably anti-social personality disorder for men and borderline personality disorder for women (Morgenstern et al., 1997). Similarly, research conducted with adolescents from Montreal found that rebelliousness and a high level of aggression are also related to substance abuse (Masse & Tremblay, 1997). One problem that plagues most research in this area is that the studies are cross-sectional rather than longitudinal; while these studies show that personality and substance abuse are related, it cannot be assumed that personality factors create a vulnerability to substance abuse.

However, three prospective studies suggest that personality factors are risk factors. In one study demonstrating these points, kindergarten children were rated by their teachers on several personality traits and were followed up several years later. Anxiety (e.g., worries about things, afraid of new things or situations) and novelty seeking (e.g., restless, fidgety) predicted the onset of getting drunk, using drugs, and smoking. Depression was related to the initiation of smoking (Killen et al., 1997).

In another study, Sher, Bartholow, and Wood (2000) had 489 university students participate in a diagnostic interview and complete measures reflecting the models outlined by Cloninger and Eysenck. These students also had the diagnostic interview a second time six years later. This research design enabled Sher and colleagues to examine the role of personality factors in predicting the development of substance-use disorders in students who did not already have a history of substance abuse or other disorders. The study revealed that students characterized by novelty seeking or psychoticism were more likely to develop substance-use disorders. Negative emotionality (e.g. neuroticism) was correlated with substance-use disorders, but prospective analyses could not determine whether negative emotionality was a cause or a result of substance abuse.

A third study assessed personality in twins from Minnesota when they were 11 years old and measured whether drug, alcohol, and nicotine addiction had developed when they were re-evaluated at 17 and 20 years of age (Elkins, King, McGue, & Iacono, 2006). Lower levels of constraint and higher levels of trait negative emotionality predicted onsets of all three types of addiction. The association with nicotine addiction is in keeping with other genetic research that has established a strong association between adolescent smoking progression and the dopamine receptor DRD2 A1 allele (Audrain-McGovern et al., 2004).

When personality factors are identified as contributors to substance abuse, they tend to be regarded as distal factors that are less important than more proximal predictors, such as drinking motives. However, it is generally accepted that individual differences in temperament and personality organization create a potential for substance abuse that becomes realized if the vulnerable individual experiences situational factors or other life experiences that lead to the development of related differences in such factors as drinking motives and alcohol expectations.

New research by Littlefield, Sher, and Wood (2009) has addressed the role of personality factors from an entirely different perspective. Researchers have detected the **maturing out phenomenon**. This refers to the overall tendency for peak drinking levels to occur when people are in their mid-twenties and there is a sharp drop in drinking levels when people reach their late thirties. A new longitudinal investigation by Littlefield et al. (2009) found that the maturing out of problematic drinking is accompanied by significant age-related decreases in levels of impulsivity and neuroticism. The authors suggest that personality change may be central to decreased drinking for many people.

Finally, personality factors can influence the success or failure of treatment. A new investigation conducted in the Addiction Unit at McGill University Health Centre compared those with alcohol dependence who achieved abstinence vs. those who relapsed or "slipped." This study by Charney, Zikos, and Gill (2010) found that relapse was predicted by initially higher levels at intake of impulsivity, Cluster B personality disorder symptoms, and more severe psychosocial problems.

BIOLOGICAL VARIABLES

Most research on biological factors in substance abuse has addressed the possibility that there is a genetic predisposition for problem drinking. Twin studies have revealed greater concordance in identical twins than in fraternal twins for alcohol abuse (e.g., King et al., 2005), caffeine use (Kendler & Prescott, 1999), smoking (True et al., 1993), heavy use or abuse of cannabis (Kendler & Prescott, 1998), and drug abuse (Tsuang et al., 1998). Recent evidence suggests that the genetic component in drinking may be much stronger for males than females (King et al., 2005). Interesting new work on the role of genetic factors in smoking confirmed suspicions that monozygotic twins, relative to dizygotic twins, were more likely to have simultaneous smoking initiation (Pergadia et al., 2006). According to Lerman, Schnoll, and Munafo (2007), enough evidence is accumulating to someday be able to develop genetic profiles of smokers that will guide selections of the type, dose, and duration of treatment. Moreover, in an interesting twist, evidence is accumulating in support of the position that the ability to quit smoking also has a substantial heritable component; that is, some people are genetically programmed to be able to quit smoking (see Uhl et al., 2008).

Recent reviews suggest that heritability estimates for alcohol dependence range between 50 to 60% (Gelertner & Krazner, 2009). However, these authors note that environmental factors are also important; after all, if someone is never exposed to drink in their environment, they will be abstinent. Contemporary research is focusing on a polymorphism of the OPRM1 receptor gene; it has been linked with early onset problem drinking among adolescents as well as a tendency for these adolescents to report that they drank specifically to enhance how they were feeling (Miranda et al., 2010). Finally, investigators are now suggesting that the specific genes involved in alcohol dependence are likely involved in other forms of addiction as well, such as addiction to tobacco (Li & Burmeister, 2009). However, researchers caution that many genes remain to be investigated and even those that have been identified require additional work in order to fully understand their nature and roles.

The ability to tolerate alcohol may be what is inherited as a diathesis for alcohol abuse or dependence (Goodwin, 1979). To become a problem drinker, a person first has to be able to drink a lot; in other words, the person must be able to tolerate large quantities of alcohol. Some ethnic groups, such as Asians, may have a low rate of alcohol abuse because of physiological intolerance, which is caused by an inherited deficiency in an enzyme that metabolizes alcohol. About three quarters of Asians experience unpleasant effects from small quantities of alcohol. Noxious effects of the drug may thus protect a person from alcohol abuse.

This hypothesis focuses on short-term effects, possibly on how alcohol is metabolized or on how the central nervous system responds to alcohol. Animal research indicates that genetic components are at work in both these processes (Schuckit,

1983). Corroborating this notion are findings from research using the high-risk method. These studies have compared young, non-alcoholic adults with a first-degree alcohol-abusing relative and similar individuals without a positive family history of the disorder. Two variables predicted the development of alcohol abuse in men in a 10-year follow-up (Schuckit, 1994; Schuckit & Smith, 1996): (1) self-report of a low level of intoxication after a dose of alcohol and (2) less body sway (a measure of steadiness while standing) after drinking. Both findings indicate that alcohol abuse is more likely to occur in those in whom alcohol has little effect. Notably, these variables predict alcohol abuse among men with and without an alcohol-abusing father.

The smaller response to alcohol of the men who later became alcohol abusers may at first seem puzzling, but it fits with the notion that you have to drink a lot to become a problem drinker. A small response to alcohol may set the stage for heavier than normal drinking. The size of the response to alcohol is also related to our earlier discussion of alcohol's biphasic effects. In the research just discussed, the largest differences between sons of problem drinkers and control-group participants occurred when their blood levels of alcohol were declining. Therefore, sons of alcohol abusers may experience fewer of the negative, depressing effects of alcohol. Other research indicates that sons of alcohol abusers experience greater effects of alcohol (e.g., more tension reduction), as their blood-alcohol levels are on the rise. Thus, they receive more reinforcement and less punishment from the drug (Newlin & Thomson, 1990).

Animal research continues to show that biological factors and genetic differences are closely linked. Investigations suggest that alcohol dependence leads to long-term neuroadaptations that create a negative emotional state; alcohol is then ingested to relieve this negative emotional state. Thus, alcohol ingestion reflects negative reinforcement (Heilig & Kolb, 2007). It also appears that: (1) neuroadaptations following continued brain exposure remain even after alcohol exposure stops; and (2) there is substantial individual variability in neuroadaptations based on genetic factors. Helig and Kolb (2007) concluded further that the corticotrophin-releasing factor system within the amygdala is a central factor in the neuroadaptive changes that accompany problem drinking.

Spanagel (2009) has outlined a systems model of addictive behaviour that views molecular biology's role within a complex gene-environment model. Factors include cumulative response to alcohol exposure, genetic composition, and environmental perturbations over time. To underscore the complexity, Spanagle suggests that chronic use of alcohol interacts with brain physiology to alter gene expression and synaptic plasticity.

Although biological factors are clearly important, Siegel from McMaster University in Hamilton, Ontario, has developed a **conditioning theory of tolerance** that underscores the need to jointly consider biological processes and environmental stimuli that may be involved in the acquisition and maintenance of addictive behaviours (Siegel, 1999; Siegel, Baptista, Kim, McDonald, & Weise-Kelly, 2000). Siegel's initial research on the "associative basis of tolerance" was conducted with rats, but similar findings have been obtained with humans. The conditioning theory of tolerance is based on the notion that tolerance is a learned response, and the environmental cues that are present when addictive behaviours are developed can influence behaviours because these cues have come to be associated with the addictive substances via Pavlovian conditioning. For instance, if a person developed an addiction by drinking excessively in his or her recreation room at home, the room itself can become a conditioned stimulus. Drug-associated environmental cues can also elicit withdrawal symptoms.

One consistent research finding is that the presentation of environmental cues previously associated with the drug can attenuate or reduce an already established tolerance. Siegel has also postulated **feedforward mechanisms**, which are defined as anticipatory regulatory responses made in anticipation of a drug (Siegel, 1991; Siegel, Krank, & Hinson, 1987). Feedforward mechanisms reflect the fact that we learn to anticipate drug effects before they actually occur.

What are the implications of the conditioning theory of tolerance for addicted individuals? One clear implication is that factors pertaining to the environmental cues that were present when conditioning first occurred may be quite alluring and will thus have an impact when they reoccur (Siegel, 1999); that is, these environmental factors may contribute to relapses among drug addicts who have been successfully treated. Siegel's work reminds us that physiological processes must be evaluated within the context of situational factors.

Finally, exciting research has recently emerged on the mechanism behind the role of genetics in smoking. Like most drugs, nicotine derives its reinforcing properties by stimulating dopamine release and inhibiting its reuptake. Research has examined a link between a gene that regulates the reuptake of dopamine and smoking. One form of this gene has been related to being less likely to begin smoking (Lerman et al., 1999) and more likely to have quit (Sabol et al., 1999). A possible explanation for these results is that people who have this particular form of this gene experience less reinforcement from nicotine, making it less likely that they will start smoking and enabling them to quit more easily if they do.

Having reviewed the nature and possible causes of the several kinds of substance-related disorders, we turn now to their treatment and prevention.

THERAPY FOR ALCOHOL ABUSE AND DEPENDENCE

The havoc created by problem drinking, both for the drinker and for his or her family, friends, employer, and community, makes this problem a serious public health issue. Consequently, a great deal of research and clinical effort has gone into the design and evaluation of treatments.

Treatment of alcohol abuse is difficult, not only because of the addictive nature of the drug, but also because of related psychological problems involving depression, anxiety, and severe disruptions in social and occupational functioning. As indicated in Chapter 8, the risk of suicide is also very high. Although some of these problems may have preceded and even contributed to the abuse of alcohol, by the time an abuser is treated, it is seldom possible to know what is cause and what is effect. But what is certain is that the person's life is usually a shambles, and any treatment that has any hope of success has to address more than merely the excessive drinking.

Interventions for problem drinking are both biological and psychological. Whatever the intervention, the first step is for the person to admit the problem and decide to do something about it.

ADMITTING THE PROBLEM
To admit to having a serious drinking problem may sound straightforward to someone who has never had a drinking problem or has never known someone who did. However, substance abusers of all kinds are adept at denying that they have a problem and may react angrily to any suggestion that they do. Moreover, because patterns of problem drinking are highly variable—someone physically dependent on alcohol, for example, does not always drink uncontrollably—the need for intervention is not always recognized by friends or even by health professionals.

Canadian investigations have indicated the general unwillingness of problem drinkers to seek help. Ogborne and DeWit (1999) found that, overall, only 2% of lifetime drinkers reported seeking help; this rose to 9% if the focus was restricted to those who felt that their alcohol use had resulted in some harm. Ogborne and DeWit concluded that the help-seeking rate in Canada is much lower than that among lifetime drinkers in the United States (5%). Canadians report that they would much rather receive assistance by obtaining a self-help book or getting computerized feedback than by contacting a counsellor or therapist, and this is the case even among people who have experienced drinking-related harm in at least two areas of their lives (Koski-Jannes & Cunningham, 2001).

A contemporary analysis of Canadian survey data has found higher help-seeking rates, with one in three people with alcohol abuse or dependence seeking treatment (Cunningham & Breslin, 2004). Still we must ask: Why did two out of three people not seek help? One problem was reiterated in a new Ontario survey: current heavy drinkers were significantly less likely than more moderate drinkers to believe that they needed treatment. There seems to also be a tendency for heavy drinkers to overestimate the extent of heavy drinking in the general population (see Cunningham, Blomqvist, & Cordingley, 2007).

Enabling the drinker to take the first step to betterment—what has been called the contemplation stage (Prochaska, DiClimente, & Norcross, 1992)—can be achieved through questions that get at the issue somewhat indirectly.

Do you sometimes feel uncomfortable when alcohol is not available?

Do you drink more heavily than usual when you are under pressure?

Are you in more of a hurry to get to the first drink than you used to be?

Do you sometimes feel guilty about your drinking?

Are you annoyed when people talk about your drinking?

When drinking socially, do you try to sneak in some extra drinks?

Are you constantly making rules for yourself about what and when to drink?

(Harvard Mental Health Letter, 1996c, pp. 1–2)

Once the alcohol abuser recognizes that a problem exists, many treatment approaches are available.

TRADITIONAL HOSPITAL TREATMENT

Public and private hospitals worldwide have for many years provided retreats for alcohol abusers, sanctums where people can "dry out" and avail themselves of a variety of individual and group therapies. The withdrawal from alcohol, **detoxification**, can be difficult, both physically and psychologically, and usually takes about one month. Tranquilizers are sometimes given to ease the anxiety and general discomfort of withdrawal. Because many alcohol abusers misuse tranquilizers, some clinics try a gradual tapering off without tranquilizers, rather than a sudden cut-off of alcohol. This non-drug-assisted withdrawal works for most problem drinkers (Wartenburg et al., 1990). To help get through withdrawal, alcohol abusers also need carbohydrate solutions, B vitamins, and, sometimes, anticonvulsants.

When is inpatient treatment needed? One analysis indicated that an inpatient approach is probably best for people with few sources of social support who are living in environments that encourage the alcohol abuse, especially individuals with serious psychological problems in addition to their substance abuse (Finney & Moos, 1998).

BIOLOGICAL TREATMENTS

Some problem drinkers who are in treatment, inpatient or outpatient, take disulfiram, or **Antabuse**, a drug that discourages drinking by causing violent vomiting if alcohol is ingested. It blocks the metabolism of alcohol so that noxious by-products are created. Adherence to an Antabuse regimen can be a problem. The drinker must already be committed to change. If an alcohol abuser is able or willing to take the drug every morning as prescribed, the chances are good that drinking will lessen because of the negative consequences of imbibing (Sisson & Azrin, 1989). However, in a large, multi-centre study with placebo controls, Antabuse showed no specific benefit and dropout rates were as high as 80% (Fuller, 1988). Antabuse can also cause serious side effects, such as inflammation of nerve tissue (Moss, 1990).

Alcoholics Anonymous is the largest self-help group in the world. At their regular meetings, newcomers rise to announce their addiction and receive advice and support from others. Hank Morgan/Photo Researchers, Inc.

Biological treatments are best viewed as adjunctive; that is, they may offer some benefit when combined with a psychological intervention. Drugs such as naltrexone and naloxone are more effective than a placebo in reducing drinking and add to overall treatment effectiveness when combined with cognitive-behavioural therapy (Volpicelli et al., 1995, 1997; Ward et al., 1998). Like many other drug treatments we have discussed, the benefits of naltrexone continue only for as long as the person continues to take it and long-lasting compliance with the treatment is difficult to achieve (O'Malley et al., 1996). The serotonin agonist buspirone is also of some therapeutic value (Kranzler et al., 1994). Clonidine, which reduces noradrenergic activity in the brain, also has some value in reducing withdrawal effects from several drugs, including alcohol, opiates, and nicotine (Baumgartner & Rowen, 1987).

The use of drugs to treat alcohol-abusing people carries some risk because liver function is often impaired in the people and, therefore, the metabolism of the prescribed drug in the liver can be adversely affected, leading to undesirable side effects (Klerman et al., 1994).

ALCOHOLICS ANONYMOUS

Alcoholics Anonymous (AA) is the largest and most widely known self-help group in the world. It was founded in 1935 in the United States by two recovered alcoholics. It currently has over 115,000 groups worldwide, and there is AA activity in more than 180 countries. Even though relatively few Canadians seek help, of those who do, the majority (60%) seek help from Canadian chapters of AA, like David Adams Richards did (Ogborne & DeWit, 1999). An AA chapter runs regular and frequent meetings at which newcomers rise to announce that they are alcoholics, and older, sober members give testimonials, relating the stories of their problem drinking and indicating how their lives are better now. The group provides emotional support, understanding, and close counselling for the problem drinker, as well as a social life to relieve isolation. Members are urged to call on one another around the clock when they need companionship and encouragement not to relapse into drink. About 70% of Americans who have ever been treated for alcohol abuse have attended at least one AA meeting. Programs modelled after AA are available for other substance abusers; for example, Cocaine Anonymous and Marijuana Anonymous. There are even similar 12-step programs called Overeaters Anonymous and Gamblers Anonymous.

The belief is instilled in each AA member that alcohol abuse is a disease that can never be cured, so continuing vigilance is necessary to resist taking even a single drink lest uncontrollable drinking begin all over again. The basic tenet of AA was articulated vividly in the classic film Lost Weekend, for which Ray Milland won an Oscar for best actor. In one scene, his brother confronts him about his denial of the seriousness of his drinking problem: "Don't you ever learn that with you it's like stepping off a roof and expecting to fall just one floor?" The spiritual aspect of AA is apparent in the 12 steps of AA shown in Table 12.2, and there is evidence that belief in this philosophy is important for achieving abstinence (Gilbert, 1991).

Two related self-help groups have developed from AA. The relatives of problem drinkers meet in Al-Anon Family Groups for mutual support in dealing with their family members and in realizing that they cannot make them change their ways. Similarly, Alateen is for the children of alcohol abusers, who also require support and understanding to help them overcome the sense that they are in some way responsible for their parents' problems and responsible also for changing them. Other self-help groups do not have the spiritual overtones of AA, relying instead on social support, reassurance, encouragement, and suggestions for leading a life without alcohol. People often see mental health professionals while attending self-help meetings.

The claims made by AA about the effectiveness of its treatment have been empirically tested. Although AA does seem to confer significant benefits (Ouimette, Finney, & Moos, 1997), it has high dropout rates, and the dropouts are not always factored into the results. In addition, there is only limited long-term follow-up of AA clients. Results from one investigation showed that the degree of AA attendance was related to abstinence over time (McCrady, Epstein, & Kahler, 2004). Clearly, the needs of many people seem to be met by the fellowship, support, and religious overtones of AA. For them, it becomes a way of life; members often attend meetings regularly for many years, as often as four times a week. As with other forms of intervention, it remains to be determined for whom this particular mode is best suited.

Canadian Perspectives 12.2 describes an Aboriginal treatment centre—Poundmaker's Lodge—that combines the goals of AA with Native values that emphasize cultural awareness.

COUPLES AND FAMILY THERAPY

Alcohol severely disrupts the lives of problem drinkers. For this reason, many live fairly solitary lives. Moreover, when problem drinkers do remain married or in some other close relationship, they often physically abuse members of their families (see Wekerle & Wall, 2001). This intertwining of alcohol abuse and family conflict (the cause-effect relationship goes both ways [O'Farrell, 1993]) has led to the use of various kinds of couples and family therapy to help the drinker abstain or control his or her excessive drinking. Behaviourally oriented marital or couples therapy has been found to achieve some reductions in problem drinking, as well as some improvement in couples' distress generally (e.g., McCrady et al., 2004). A focus of this therapy is involving the spouse in helping the drinker take his or her Antabuse on a regular basis.

TABLE 12.2
TWELVE STEPS OF ALCOHOLICS ANONYMOUS

1. We admitted we were powerless over alcohol—that our lives had become unmanageable.
2. Came to believe that a power greater than ourselves could restore us to sanity.
3. Made a decision to turn our will and our lives over to the care of God as we understood Him.
4. Made a searching and fearless moral inventory of ourselves.
5. Admitted to God, to ourselves, and to another human being the exact nature of our wrongs.
6. Were entirely ready to have God remove all these defects of character.
7. Humbly asked Him to remove our shortcomings.
8. Made a list of all persons we had harmed, and became willing to make amends to them all.
9. Made direct amends to such people wherever possible, except when to do so would injure them or others.
10. Continued to take personal inventory and, when we were wrong, promptly admitted it.
11. Sought through prayer and meditation to improve our conscious contact with God as we understood Him, praying only for knowledge of His will for us and the power to carry that out.
12. Having had a spiritual awakening as the result of these steps, we tried to carry this message to alcoholics and to practice these principles in all our affairs.

Source: The Twelve Steps are reprinted with permission of Alcoholics Anonymous World Services, Inc. ("AAWS") Permission to reprint the Twelve Steps does not mean that AAWS has reviewed or approved the contents of this publication, or that AAWS necessarily agrees with the views expressed herein. A.A. is a program of recovery from alcoholism only - use of the Twelve Steps in connection with programs and activities which are patterned after A.A., but which address other problems, or in any other non-A.A. context, does not imply otherwise.

POUNDMAKER'S LODGE

"To join Poundmaker/Nechi requires a commitment to our mission against alcohol and drug use—in body as well as in spirit. Since total abstinence is the only solution for the Native client, staff cannot just 'talk the talk'; they must also 'walk the walk.'"

—From the Mission Statement of Poundmaker's Lodge

Many drug abuse programs in Canada are designed for and often run by Aboriginal people. Poundmaker's Lodge (named after a nineteenth-century Native leader), located outside of Edmonton, Alberta, is an excellent example of a Native alcohol, drug, and gambling treatment centre. The non-profit centre, founded in 1973 and managed by the Aboriginal people themselves, has the oldest Aboriginal-oriented inpatient (54-bed, 28-day) alcoholism program in Canada. In addition, it operates an outpatient centre, an adolescent treatment program, and a prison program. Poundmaker's Lodge is also an agent for positive initiatives in the Aboriginal community (e.g., education, self-esteem building, and increasing cultural awareness).

Philosophy and Structure

Consistent with many traditional treatment approaches, the centre's overall philosophy is simple: addiction is viewed as a disease and complete abstinence is the goal. Also, in keeping with Aboriginal values, it is crucial to treat the entire person. There must be balance in four dimensions: spiritual, mental, emotional, and physical. The assumption is that the Aboriginal client will respond best to an approach that embraces both Aboriginal cultural awareness and the philosophy of Alcoholics Anonymous or Narcotics Anonymous (NA): "At Poundmaker's Lodge, the setting, the facility, the staff, and the treatment model harmonize to create an environment for recovery."

Treatment staff includes elders, two treatment directors, counsellors, psychologists, and medical staff. An executive director manages the 50-member treatment and support staff, as well as trainees and consulting professionals. Many of the staff have a unique common bond: personal experience with the addictions they are treating. The programs were founded on the principle that substance abusers are treated most effectively by "sober" people who have been trained to address problems of abuse.

The core structure of all programs has four components that stretch over a 42-day period: education, skills development, counselling, and Aboriginal culture. In addition to group therapy sessions, other treatment activities are considered essential for a comprehensive, effective experience (e.g., "community-building activities that allow people to share fun as well as sadness"). The cultural component includes sweat lodge and pipe ceremonies, sweetgrass ceremonies, and sessions by an in-residence elder. The burning of sweetgrass, for example, is intended to cleanse the body and mind (a process called "smudging"). An annual powwow

At Poundmaker's Lodge, named after Chief Poundmaker (pictured), the facilities are designed to closely resemble nature, thereby providing inspiration to the clients. OB Buell. Library and Archives Canada.

attracts more than 5,000 "sober" people for a three-day event. The following description of the Adolescent Treatment Centre provides an example of the way the core structure is implemented.

Adolescent Treatment Centre

Poundmaker's Adolescent Treatment Centre provides an intensive 90-day treatment program for Aboriginal children between 12 and 17 years old. It has been given "open custody" status, which allows the Alberta government to refer young offenders. However, it is a treatment centre, not a correctional institution. The program's goals include stopping the children's drug consumption, detoxifying them from their addictive subculture, integrating them back into families and communities, dealing with physical and mental health issues, and developing strategies for relapse prevention.

The centre provides a comprehensive, structured program that includes several components: addictions treatment, school education, family program, Aboriginal culture/spiritual values, follow-up and aftercare, medical care, recreational activities, and behaviour management.

Although all of these components are probably very important, the family program is especially vital. Families are invited to attend a one-week program to show support for their child and to learn the consequences of substance abuse. Perhaps most important, they are taught how to resolve conflicts, practise effective communication and problem-solving skills, and work together as a family unit to overcome problems.

Outcomes

Poundmaker's Lodge claims that its programs have helped thousands of Aboriginal people overcome their alcohol and drug problems and rebuild their lives. Although there is no doubt that the centre has helped many Aboriginal people, it is very difficult to determine accurately the long-term effects of its programs, much less determine the "active" components of its programs. In some cases, it is clear that success has been short-lived. For example, 18 children from Davis Inlet were taken thousands of kilometres away to Poundmaker's Lodge for treatment of their inhalant and alcohol abuse; it was reported that 12 of the 18 later resumed inhalant use (Canadian Press, 1995).

(Adapted from "Poundmaker's Lodge," January 21, 2001, and December 15, 2009, available on-line at http://poundmaker.org)

Thinking Critically

1. Do you think that the programs at Poundmaker's Lodge would be more successful if they incorporated, in some cases, a philosophically different approach that allowed for the possibility of controlled drinking or moderation in drinking? Note that a possible approach involving harm reduction therapy is discussed in Canadian Perspectives 12. (see p. 428).

2. After you have read about the various approaches to treating drug abuse presented in this chapter, design a treatment program that you believe would lead to more successful treatment of substance abuse, especially the use of inhalants and alcohol in Aboriginal children.

3. Is it realistic to assume that the Poundmaker's Lodge program can have lasting success when (1) it is not always feasible to work with all of the family members and (2) the children are typically returned to the same social, psychological, cultural, and economic environment that contributed to the development of their problems in the first place?

The need to consider drinking problems from a couples perspective is illustrated by studies on drinking behaviour conducted in Quebec (Demers, Bisson, & Palluy, 1999) and in Ontario (Graham & Braun, 1999). These studies have replicated previous findings suggesting that there is substantial concordance between husbands and wives in terms of their frequency of drinking and overall amount consumed, especially among older couples (Graham & Braun, 1999); that is, husbands who drink excessively often have wives who also drink to excess. Possible reasons for this concordance include shared life experiences, the impact of the husband's drinking on the wife, and the tendency for people with similar drinking patterns to get married (Leonard & Eiden, 1999). When such situations exist, a joint focus on the drinking of both partners is essential.

The importance of a partner's support in the problem drinker's effort to deal with life's stresses is not to be underestimated. But also not to be underestimated is the difficulty of maintaining moderate drinking or abstinence beyond the one- and two-year follow-ups regardless of the mode of marital intervention and its short-term positive effects (Alexander et al., 1994; Baucom et al., 1998).

COGNITIVE AND BEHAVIOURAL TREATMENT

Behavioural and cognitive-behavioural researchers have been studying the treatment of alcohol abuse for many years. Indeed, one of the earliest articles on behaviour therapy concerned aversive conditioning as a treatment for alcoholism (Kantorovich, 1930). In general, cognitive and behavioural therapies represent the most effective psychological treatments for alcohol abuse (Finney & Moos, 1998).

AVERSION THERAPY In aversion therapy, problem drinkers are shocked or made nauseous while looking at, reaching for, or beginning to drink alcohol. In one procedure, called **covert sensitization** (Cautela, 1966), problem drinkers are instructed to imagine being made violently and disgustingly sick by their drinking.

Despite some evidence that aversion therapy may slightly enhance the effectiveness of inpatient treatment (Smith, Frawley, & Polissar, 1991), some well-known behaviour therapists discourage its use because it lacks empirical support and causes great discomfort (e.g., Wilson, 1991). Aversion therapy, if used at all, seems best implemented in the context of broad programs that attend to the patient's particular life circumstances; for example, marital conflict, social fears, and other factors associated with problem drinking (Tucker, Vuchinich, & Downey, 1992).

CONTINGENCY-MANAGEMENT THERAPY Contingency-management therapy (a term often used interchangeably with operant conditioning) for alcohol abuse involves teaching clients and those close to them to reinforce behaviours inconsistent with drinking; for example, taking Antabuse and avoiding situations associated with past drinking. This therapy also includes teaching job-hunting and social skills, as well as assertiveness training for refusing drinks. Socially isolated individuals are encouraged and helped to establish contacts with other people who are not associated with drinking. As noted earlier, this approach includes couples therapy. Often referred to as the community-reinforcement approach, contingency-management therapy has generated very promising results (Baucom et al., 1998; Sisson & Azrin, 1989).

A strategy that is sometimes termed behavioural self-control training (Tucker et al., 1992) builds on the work just described. This approach emphasizes patient control and includes one or more of the following:

- *stimulus control*, whereby one narrows the situations in which one allows oneself to drink (e.g., with others on a special occasion)
- *modification of the topography of drinking* (e.g., having only mixed drinks and taking small sips rather than gulps)
- *reinforcing abstinence* (e.g., allowing oneself a non-alcoholic treat if one resists the urge to drink)

An issue not formally addressed by advocates of behavioural self-control training is how to get the person to abide by restrictions and conditions that, if implemented, will reduce or eliminate drinking. In other words, the challenge with such therapies seems to be not so much discovering the means necessary to control drinking as getting the alcohol abuser to employ these tools without constant external supervision and control. There is evidence for the general effectiveness of this approach (Hester & Miller, 1989), some of it in the context of controlled-drinking programs, to which we turn now.

MODERATION IN DRINKING Until recently, it was generally agreed that alcohol abusers had to abstain completely if they were to be cured, for they were believed to have no control over imbibing once they had taken that first drink. Although this continues to be the belief of AA, this assumption has been called into question by research mentioned earlier indicating that drinkers' beliefs about themselves and alcohol may be as important as the physiological addiction to the drug itself. Considering the difficulty in society of avoiding alcohol altogether, it may even be preferable to teach the problem drinker to imbibe with moderation. A drinker's self-esteem will certainly benefit from being able to control a problem and from feeling in charge.

Controlled drinking in alcohol treatment was introduced by the Sobells while they were located at the Addiction Research Foundation in Toronto (see Sobell & Sobell, 1993). This approach is currently much more widely accepted in Canada and Europe than in the United States. **Controlled drinking** refers to a moderate pattern of alcohol consumption that avoids the extremes of total abstinence and inebriation. The results of the Sobells' initial treatment program suggested that at least some alcohol abusers can learn to control their drinking and improve other aspects of their lives, as well (Sobell & Sobell, 1976). Problem drinkers attempting to control their drinking were given shocks when they chose straight liquor rather than mixed drinks, gulped their drinks down too fast, or took large swallows rather than sips. They also received problem-solving and assertiveness training, watched videotapes of themselves inebriated, and identified the situations that precipitated their drinking so that they could settle on a less self-destructive course of action. Their improvement was greater than that of alcohol abusers who tried for total abstinence and were given shocks for any drinking at all.

People in contemporary controlled-drinking treatment programs are taught to respond adaptively to situations in which they might otherwise drink excessively. They learn various social skills to help them resist pressures to drink; they receive assertiveness, relaxation, and stress-management training, sometimes including biofeedback and meditation; and they are encouraged to exercise and maintain a healthy diet.

Clients are also taught—or more precisely, are encouraged to believe—that a lapse will not inevitably precipitate a total relapse and should be regarded as a learning experience rather than as a sign that the battle is lost, a marked contrast from the AA perspective (Marlatt & Gordon, 1985). This non-catastrophizing approach to relapse after therapy—falling off the wagon—is important because the overwhelming majority of problem drinkers who become abstinent do experience a relapse over a four-year period (Polich, Armor, & Braiker, 1980). In this therapy, alcohol abusers examine sources of stress in their work, family, and relationships so that they can become active and responsible in anticipating and resisting situations that might tempt excessive drinking (Marlatt, 1983; Sobell, Toneatto, & Sobell, 1990). The controlled-drinking approach has now been supplemented by the guided self-change approach, which was developed in Toronto. **Guided self-change**, an outpatient approach, emphasizes personal responsibility and control. The Guided Self-Change Program (GSCP; Addiction Research Foundation, 1994) is an early intervention program designed for people with mild to moderate drinking problems. As stated in the GSCP manual, the goals of the program are to (1) help clients help themselves; (2) allow clients to make informed choices; (3) teach a general problem-solving approach; (4) strengthen client motivation and commitment to change; and (5) encourage self-reliance, empowerment, and personal competence.

Harm reduction therapy is another alternative to an approach that focuses on complete abstinence. The principles of harm reduction therapy are outlined in Canadian Contributions 12.1.

CLINICAL CONSIDERATIONS IN TREATING ALCOHOL ABUSE

Many attempts to treat problem drinking are impeded by the therapist's often unstated assumption that all people who drink to excess do so for the same reasons. From what we have examined thus far in this chapter, we know that this assumption is unlikely to be correct.

A comprehensive clinical assessment considers what place drinking occupies in the person's life (Tucker et al., 1992). A woman in a desperately unhappy marriage, with time on her hands now that her children are in school, may seek the

CANADIAN CONTRIBUTIONS 12.1
G. ALAN MARLATT AND HARM REDUCTION THERAPY

G. Alan Marlatt has outlined harm reduction therapy as an alternative to treatments stemming from the medical model. Courtesy G. Alan Marlatt.

G. Alan Marlatt, a Canadian psychologist, is currently the director of the Addictive Behaviors Research Center at the University of Washington in Seattle. He has had a substantial impact on the assessment and treatment of addictions, and his work has been widely recognized. For instance, in 1990 he was given the Jellinek Memorial Award for outstanding contributions to knowledge in the field of alcohol studies. He has also been given the Senior Scientist Award from the U.S. National Institute of Alcohol Abuse and Alcoholism. In 1996, Marlatt was appointed as a member of the U.S. National Advisory Council on Drug Abuse. Marlatt's research on employing brief interventions to help control and reduce binge drinking among students was discussed earlier. His harm reduction therapy (HRT) is having an increasing impact as a general approach that can be used to treat a variety of high-risk behaviours, including addictions. The basic tenets of HRT are discussed below:

- First, contrary to moral/criminal models or disease models of drug use, addiction is not a crime deserving of punishment. Rather, it is an adjustment problem that needs intervention.
- Second, HRT recognizes that abstinence is an ideal outcome, but it is not the only outcome, especially for those beginning treatment. It is quite acceptable to strive for outcomes that involve the reduction of harm rather than striving in an all-or-none fashion to eliminate harm altogether. HRT recognizes that striving for more extreme goals may be self-defeating.
- Third, HRT is a bottom-up approach that is more in line with the needs of the addict and is focused on reducing their level of suffering. It contrasts with the top-down approach favoured by those who make drug policy.

- Fourth, because HRT does not require complete abstinence, more people should be able to gain access to what Marlatt refers to as "low-threshold" services. Marlatt (1999) has suggested that the difference is reflected in the phrase "We'll meet you where you are" (p. 55), not "where you should be."
- Finally, Marlatt (1999) argues that HRT is based on the principle of "compassionate pragmatism" rather than on "moralistic idealism." Specifically, harm reduction is non-judgemental and acknowledges the realistic struggles of people as they attempt to manage their everyday affairs.

Harm reduction involves a number of goals: to stabilize the maladaptive behaviour and prevent further harm, to help the client develop an awareness of high-risk behaviours, and to give the person coping training in how to deal with high-risk situations. Another important goal is to facilitate health-promoting and risk-reducing strategies.

Marlatt's Alcohol Skills Training Program (ASTP) for students incorporates the harm reduction model. The ASTP is based on the view that drinking is normal behaviour for students and that interventions may be needed; thus, a focus on moderation rather than abstinence is more realistic. Students participate in eight sessions over several weeks. The initial sessions focus on helping students become more aware of alcohol's impact and learn practical things such as how to calculate their own blood-alcohol levels. Subsequent sessions challenge overly positive beliefs about the benefits of drinking. Students also learn specific skills and role-play so that they will know how to deal with stressful situations without turning to alcohol.

HRT can be controversial, as some of the things that are done to reduce initial harm may involve initiatives that are not accepted by everyone. These could include such things as encouraging controlled drinking or the moderate (as opposed to extensive) use of amphetamines or setting up needle-exchange programs to limit additional health risks. Marlatt has acknowledged that his approach has been criticized for "enabling" drug use (see Marlatt, Blume, & Parks, 2001). Another criticism is that HRT does not have the goal of abstinence. Marlatt et al. (2001), however, have noted that abstinence is a goal at the endpoint of the continuum once the addicted individual starts to improve.

According to Marlatt and Witkiewitz (2002), empirical research shows that harm reduction is at least as effective as abstinence-oriented approaches in reducing alcohol consumption and alcohol-related consequences, and new data continue to show that harm reduction is very effective (see Witkiewitz & Marlatt, 2006). Moreover, Marlatt, a firm believer in the importance of education, maintains that the basic tenets of harm reduction therapy can be taught in educational programs. High school and university students respond well to this approach. If they are heavy drinkers, for example, they can adopt the goal of drinking less and in a more responsible manner, rather than strive for absolute abstinence. According to Marlatt et al. (2001), one advantage of HRT over other treatment approaches is that it more easily forges a positive alliance between the client and therapist, since the realistic goals of HRT are more in keeping with the needs of the client.

In Canada, the harm reduction debate reached a peak during the 2003 mayoral election in Vancouver, when successful candidate Larry Campbell proposed the use of a harm reduction model as a way of combating rampant drug use in downtown Vancouver. The overall strategy, known as the Four Pillars Drug Strategy, includes the creation of supervised drug-injection sites. According to the City of Vancouver, these sites would be a "vital part of a harm reduction plan to reduce overdose and overdose deaths and the spread of HIV/AIDS and hepatitis C, and to provide access to primary health care to drug users in Vancouver." The strategy's four pillars are harm reduction, prevention, treatment, and law enforcement.

Empirical evidence has found consistently that this innovative approach has been successful. Wood, Tyndall, Montaner, and Kerr (2006) concluded that the Vancouver program has resulted in a wide array of community and public health benefits without apparent adverse outcomes. For instance, analyses found that there were significant decreases in drug use, the number of publicly discarded syringes, and injection-related litter. This is in keeping with general evidence of the positive impact of HRT in alcohol prevention efforts (Neighbors, Larimer, Lostutter, & Woods, 2006).

Additional evidence of the benefits of HRT has come from the shelter-based Managed Alcohol Project, an HRT intervention for homeless people suffering from alcoholism in Ottawa (see Podymow et al., 2006). This study was conducted with 17 homeless adults with an average of 35 years of alcoholism. The provision of alcohol in an HRT framework resulted in less reported alcohol consumption overall and reports from medical staff of greater compliance with medical care. It also decreased hospital emergency room visits (a decrease from 13.5 visits to 8.0 visits per month) and the number of encounters with police (a decrease from 18.1 to 8.8 encounters per month).

Unfortunately, the safe injection HRT program in Vancouver has been continually at risk of extinction despite its apparent benefits (see Drucker, 2006). Supervised injection sites are not in keeping with principles endorsed by the current federal government. Accordingly, Tony Clement, the former Minister of Health, did not renew the three-year licence of the Insite safe injection site. The federal government was only willing to grant a temporary reprieve in the form of a temporary extension until December 2007, and it indicated that more evidence of the site's beneficial aspects would be needed for it to continue to operate in the long term. This temporary extension only came after an extensive, multi-faceted public campaign to save the safe injection site. Clement described the activities at Insite as "harm addition" rather than harm reduction.

The apparent attitude of the Canadian federal government is in keeping with the more negative view of harm reduction that exists in areas of the United States, which can be differentiated from the more favourable views of HRT in Europe and Australia (see Neighbors et al., 2006). Drucker (2006) claimed that Prime Minister Harper opposes harm reduction in all forms. Insite is safe for now. A successful 2008 constitutional challenge affords protection from the federal government. Justice Ian Pitfield of the B.C. Supreme Court ruled that closing Insite would violate Section 7 of the Charter of Rights and Freedoms (which governs the life, liberty, and security of the person), and he granted Insite a conditional exemption from legislation governing drug use. The federal government has launched an appeal.

Barriers to harm reduction come in other forms. A recent survey conducted in Ontario found that service providers had positive views of harm reduction strategies and their efficacy. However, significant barriers were acknowledged, including negative community reactions and a lack of adequate staff and funding (see Hobden & Cunningham, 2006).

---

numbing effects of alcohol to help pass the time and avoid facing life's dilemmas. Making the taste of alcohol unpleasant by pairing it with shock or a drug that induces vomiting seems neither sensible nor adequate. The therapist should concentrate on the marital and family problems and try to reduce the psychological pain that permeates the person's existence. She will also need help in tolerating the withdrawal symptoms that come with reduced consumption. Without alcohol as a reliable anaesthetic, she will need to mobilize other resources to confront her hitherto-avoided problems. Social skills training and rewarding activities outside the home may help her do so.

We have seen that problem drinking is sometimes associated with other mental disorders, in particular anxiety disorders, mood disorders, and psychopathy. Therapists of all orientations have to recognize that depression is often comorbid with alcohol abuse and that suicide is also a risk. The clinician must therefore conduct a broad-spectrum assessment of the client's problem.

Alcohol researchers recognize that different kinds of drinkers may require different treatment approaches (Mattson et al., 1994). The challenge is to determine which factors in the drinkers should be aligned with which factors in treatment. Client-treatment matching, or what the psychotherapy literature describes as aptitude-treatment interaction (ATI), has been cited by the Institute of Medicine (1990a) as a critical issue in the development of better interventions for problem drinking. A large-scale effort to address the question was Project Match, a multi-site clinical trial designed to test the hypothesis that certain kinds of treatments are good matches for certain kinds of problem drinkers. This project is described in Focus on Discovery 12.3.

It is doubtful that a single event, even a dramatic one, can bring about the kind of profound changes necessary to wean a person from an addiction. It is more probable that successful abstinence, whether resulting from treatment or not, relies on a confluence of many life events and forces that can support the recovering alcoholic's efforts to lead a life without substance abuse. Whatever combination of factors helps problem drinkers become abstinent or controlled drinkers, a key element is social support for their efforts from family, friends, work, or self-help groups such as AA (McCrady, 1985).

FOCUS ON DISCOVERY 12.3

MATCHING CLIENT TO TREATMENT: PROJECT MATCH

For many years, both practitioners and researchers have understood the importance of employing treatments that are suitable for particular people. This notion goes beyond the question of the general kind of therapy best suited for a particular kind of problem; rather, it involves an approach called *aptitude-treatment interaction (ATI)*, which focuses on characteristics of people with the same disorder that might make them more suitable candidates for one generally effective treatment than for another.

The question of matching the person to treatment was tested in Project Match, a large, eight-year, multi-site study on alcohol abuse (Project Match Research Group, 1997). This study is controversial in professional circles because it failed to find what it was looking for, namely, a way to match particular kinds of people with specific interventions.

- Ten matching variables were chosen, among them severity of alcohol dependency, severity of cognitive impairment, motivation to change, severity of psychological disturbance (referred to as "psychiatric severity"), support from one's social milieu for drinking, and sociopathic tendencies, having been found in previous research to be associated with outcomes of intervention. There were three treatments: The 12-step facilitation treatment (TSF) was designed to convert people to the AA view of alcoholism as an incurable but manageable disease and to encourage their involvement in AA.

- The motivational-enhancement therapy (MET), based on William Miller's approach (Miller et al., 1992), attempted to mobilize clients' own resources to reduce drinking. Part of this intervention involved highlighting the ways in which current maladaptive behaviour was interfering with their valued goals.

- A cognitive-behavioural coping-skills therapy (CBT) presented to clients the idea that drinking is functionally related to problems in their lives; this treatment taught patients skills to help them cope with situations that trigger drinking or prevent relapse.

Some of the predicted interactions were that drinkers under heavy pressure to stop would do best with the 12-step facilitation therapy; those with psychological problems would do best with the cognitive therapy; and those with low motivation to change would do best with the motivational-enhancement therapy.

All treatments were carefully administered in individual sessions by trained therapists over a 12-week period. The principal dependent (outcome) measures were percentage of days abstinent and drinks per drinking day during a one-year post-treatment assessment period. Figure 12.3 portrays the main results of this study. Significant within-group improvement was observed—all treatments were very helpful on average, consistent with a subsequent study by Ouimette et al. (1997). However, interactions

Figure 12.3 Monthly percentage of days abstinent and drinks per drinking day (DDD) for baseline (averaged over three months prior to treatment) and for each month of the post-treatment period (months 1–15).

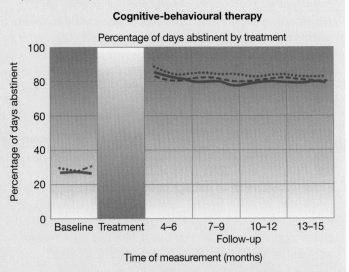

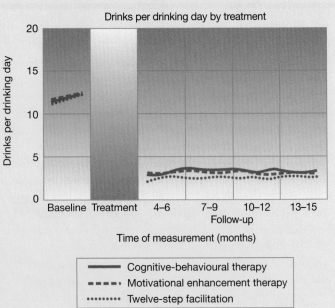

between treatments and matching variables (the main purpose of the study) were not found except for the interaction involving psychiatric severity. Clients in better psychological shape had more abstinent days after the 12-step facilitation program than did participants in the cognitive-behavioural therapy, although patients in worse psychological condition did not fare differently across the three treatments.

According to Marlatt (1999), one shortcoming of the Project Match study as a treatment efficacy study is that it did not include a no-treatment, assessment-only control group. The extensive assessment sessions undergone by the participants may have had a positive influence on their behaviour, independent of treatment.

Another criticism of Project Match raised by Canadian researchers (Conrod et al., 2000) is that the therapies chosen were not precise enough and were not tailored to the specific therapy needs of the individual clients. Conrod et al. (2000) conducted their own study and showed that personality-specific motivational and coping-skills training was substantially more effective than a motivational control intervention in reducing the frequency and severity of alcohol and drug use. They concluded that matching strategies that link client personality characteristics and treatments have substantial promise. This was supported by another recent preventive study conducted by this same team of investigators (Conrod, Stewart, Comeau, & Maclean, 2006). This study identified at-risk Canadian high school students and provided them with personality-specific preventive interventions. Personality factors targeted included sensation seeking and anxiety sensitivity. Benefits resulted from these interventions, with two important caveats. First, the investigators noted that the goal was to help with better management of personality vulnerabilities rather than remove the personality component altogether. Second, improvement depended on how drinking was measured; there was no overall reduction in the frequency of drinking but there were reductions in the amount consumed overall.

THERAPY FOR THE USE OF ILLICIT DRUGS

Some factors involved in treatment for alcohol abuse are relevant also to treatment for addiction to illegal drugs. We focus here on issues that pertain to those who abuse illicit drugs.

People turn to drugs for many reasons, and even though, in most instances, drug use becomes controlled primarily by a physical addiction, the entire pattern of an addict's existence is bound to be affected by the drug and must therefore be addressed in any treatment. As seen in our earlier discussion of conditioning theory of tolerance, one of the chief difficulties of maintaining abstinence is the negative influence of many stimuli on the recovering addict. The presence of needles, neighbourhoods, and people with whom a person used to take drugs can elicit a craving for the substance (Winkler, 1980).

Central to the treatment of people who use addicting drugs, such as heroin and cocaine, is detoxification—withdrawal from the drug itself. Heroin-withdrawal reactions range from relatively mild bouts of anxiety, nausea, and restlessness for several days to more severe and frightening bouts of delirium and panic anxiety, depending primarily on the purity of the heroin that the individual has been using. Someone high on amphetamines can be brought down by appropriate dosages of one of the phenothiazines, a class of drugs used to treat schizophrenia, although it is important to remember that the person may also have been using other drugs in conjunction with amphetamines. Withdrawal reactions from barbiturates are especially severe, even life-threatening, beginning about 24 hours after the last dose and peaking two or three days later. They usually abate by the end of the first week but may last for a month if large doses were taken. Withdrawal from barbiturates is best undertaken gradually, not cold turkey (a term that derives from the goosebumps that occur during withdrawal, making the person's skin resemble that of a plucked turkey), and should take place under close medical supervision.

Detoxification is the first way in which therapists try to help an addict or drug abuser, and it may be the easiest part of the rehabilitation process. Enabling the drug user to function without drugs after detoxification is an arduous task that promises more disappointment and sadness than success for both helper and client. A variety of approaches are available, both biological and psychological.

BIOLOGICAL TREATMENTS

Two widely used drug-therapy programs for heroin addiction involve the administration of **heroin substitutes**, drugs chemically similar to heroin that can replace the body's craving for it, or **heroin antagonists**, drugs that prevent the user from experiencing the heroin high. The first category includes **methadone**, levomethadyl acetate, and buprenorphine, synthetic narcotics designed to take the place of heroin. Since these drugs are themselves addicting, successful treatment essentially converts the heroin addict into someone who is addicted to a different substance. This conversion occurs because these synthetic narcotics are **cross-dependent** with heroin; that is, by acting on the same central nervous system receptors, they become a substitute for the original dependency. Of course, methadone used as described here is legal, whereas heroin is not.

Abrupt discontinuation of methadone results in its own pattern of withdrawal reactions. Because these reactions are less severe than those of heroin, methadone can wean the addict altogether from drug dependence (Strain et al., 1999).

Methadone is a synthetic narcotic substitute. Former heroin addicts come to clinics each day and swallow their dose. The Canadian Press/The Waterloo Region Record-David Bebee.

For treatment with heroin substitutes, the addict must go to a clinic and swallow the drug in the presence of a staff member, once a day for methadone and three times a week for levomethadyl acetate and buprenorphine. Some users under treatment are able to hold jobs, commit no crimes, and refrain from using other illicit drugs (Cooper et al., 1983; Eissenberg et al., 1997), but many users are unable to do so. The effectiveness of methadone treatment is improved if combined with regular psychological counselling (Ball & Ross, 1991).

Pre-existing behavioural patterns and life circumstances play a role in how the individual will react to methadone treatment. Since methadone does not provide a euphoric high, many addicts will return to heroin if it becomes available to them. Many people drop out of methadone programs in part because of side effects, such as insomnia, constipation, excessive sweating, and diminished sexual functioning. Yet in this era of AIDS and the transmission of the human immunodeficiency virus through shared needles, this treatment has a big advantage because methadone can be swallowed.

In treatment with the opiate antagonists cyclazocine and naloxone, addicts are first gradually weaned from heroin. They then receive increasing dosages of one of these drugs and are thereby prevented from experiencing any high should they later take heroin. These drugs have great affinity for the receptors to which opiates usually bind; their molecules occupy the receptors without stimulating them, leaving heroin molecules with no place to go. As with methadone, however, addicts must make frequent and regular visits to a clinic, and this takes motivation and responsibility on their part. In addition, addicts do not lose the craving for heroin for some time. Thus, patient compliance with therapy involving opiate antagonists is very poor, and the overall outcomes are only fair (Ginzburg, 1986; Goldstein, 1994).

The search is now on for drugs that will ease the symptoms of withdrawal and perhaps attack the physical basis of cocaine addiction. Although some favourable results with antidepressants were reported earlier, findings from two more recent and better-controlled studies were decidedly less positive. In the first of two similarly conducted double-blind experiments, use of the tricyclic desipramine (Norpramin) by cocaine abusers, as compared with a placebo, did not lead to decreased use of cocaine at the end of eight weeks of treatment (Kosten et al., 1992). The second study found that cocaine use was significantly greater in those who received the drug than in placebo patients at three- and six-month follow-ups after a 12-week treatment period (Arndt et al., 1992). Similarly, while imipramine (Tofranil) helped alleviate depression in cocaine abusers who were depressed, it did not help the patients achieve abstinence from cocaine (Nunes et al., 1998). On the other hand, desipramine fared better in another study, which will be discussed shortly (Carroll, Rounsaville, & Gordon, 1994).

Clonidine, an antihypertensive medication, may ease withdrawal from a variety of addicting drugs, including cocaine (Baumgartner & Rowen, 1987). Bromocriptine also shows some promise in reducing craving, perhaps by reversing the depletion of dopamine that is believed to underlie cocaine's addicting properties (Moss, 1990).

PSYCHOLOGICAL TREATMENTS

Drug abuse is sometimes treated in the consulting rooms of psychiatrists, psychologists, and other mental health workers. Several kinds of psychotherapy are applied to drug-use disorders, as they are to other human maladjustments, often in combination with biological treatments aimed at reducing the physical dependence.

In the first direct comparison in a controlled study, the tricyclic antidepressant desipramine and a cognitive-behavioural treatment were found to be somewhat effective in reducing cocaine use, as well as in improving abusers' family, social, and general psychological functioning. In a 12-week study by Carroll and associates (Carroll, Rounsaville, & Gordon, 1994; Carroll et al., 1995), desipramine was more effective than a placebo for patients with a low degree of dependence on cocaine, whereas the cognitive treatment was better in reducing cocaine use in patients with a high degree of dependence. This finding illustrates the significance of the psychological aspects of substance abuse.

In Carroll's study, patients receiving cognitive treatment learned how to avoid high-risk situations (e.g., being around people who use cocaine), recognize the lure of the drug for them, and develop alternatives to using cocaine (e.g., recreational activities with non-users). Cocaine abusers in this study also learned strategies for coping with the craving and for resisting the tendency to regard a slip as a catastrophe ("relapse prevention training," per Marlatt & Gordon, 1985). The more depressed the patient, the more favourable the outcome from both the antidepressant drug and the cognitive therapy. Overall, the results for the psychosocial treatment were superior to those for the antidepressant drug in reducing cocaine use, and this pattern was maintained at a one-year follow-up (Carroll, Rounsaville, & Nich, 1994).

A more operant-type program has shown some promise as well. Modelled after the token economy employed in hospital settings, this program rewards patients with vouchers for not using cocaine or heroin (verified by urine samples). The tokens are exchangeable for things that patients would like to have more of (Silverman et al., 1996).

A more recent development is the use of **motivational interviewing**. This approach combines CBT principles with the humanistic principles avowed by Carl Rogers. The central premise is that people must be motivated and ready for change in order for psychological interventions to work. Initial meta-analyses attest in general to the efficacy of motivational interviewing

CANADIAN CLINIC FOCUS 12 .1
RECOVERY AND RELAPSE: STARTING FROM ZERO ALL THE TIME

"I don't like starting from zero all of the time" (Lianne, a crack addict, as cited in Teotonio, 2009, GT1)

In January 2009, the *Toronto Star* began a series that profiled five women from southern Ontario with severe forms of addiction. All five women were about to undergo a treatment program at Hope Place Women's Treatment Centre. The program is a 24-day abstinence-based program (see Teotonio, 2009). Subsequent articles in July and December of 2009 followed up on the women's progress.

The stories of the five women profiled show the severity of profound addiction, the desperate lengths that addicted people often go to in order to satisfy their cravings, and the extreme personal and interpersonal consequences of living with an addiction. Briefly, the women were described as follows:

Tina, 21, from Almonte. Tina is addicted to alcohol, marijuana, and crack cocaine. She was hoping to do well in treatment and be reunited with her infant son who was in the care of the Children's Aid Society (CAS), but by the end of 2009, she had given her boy up for adoption.

Lianne, 26, from Brampton. Lianne began the year addicted to marijuana and crack cocaine. She also hoped to regain custody of her twin boys, who were also in CAS care. She resumed using crack in July after a period of four months of abstinence. The boys are in the care of their grandmother. Lianne supported her habit by becoming a prostitute. She acknowledged that "I'm more than out of control" (Teotonio, 2009, GT1).

Catherine, 38, from Burlington. Catherine's husband indicated that he would leave along with their daughters if Catherine didn't seek treatment for addiction to painkillers. She has subsequently been diagnosed with a host of other difficulties, including bipolar disorder, attention deficit disorder, and an autoimmune disease.

Veronica, 29, from Port Colborne. Veronica had an addiction to alcohol and crack. She also was hoping to recover via treatment and regain custody of her baby girl. She relapsed on crack after a visit from her boyfriend in the summer but was living by herself in a shelter in St. Catharines by December, and is dutifully attending CA (Cocaine Anonymous) meetings.

Karen, 28 from Kitchener. Karen began her fifth rehab stint in January 2009. She suffers from addiction to alcohol and crack cocaine. She also suffers from bipolar depression and is hoping to regain custody of her baby boy. She was reported to be doing well and still clean in December. Karen is looking forward to having her son home with her in 2010.

The follow-ups of these women in July and in December illuminated just how difficult it is to not relapse after undergoing treatment. As indicated above, four of the five women had relapsed in some form by the end of the year. Arguably, a 24-day program is simply not long enough to address the severe addictions that these women have had, often for many years.

How does the experience of these women fit with the findings in the general literature? While initial treatment success for addictions is often higher than treatment success for other disorders, relapse and re-admission are quite common, especially for those with at least one other disorder. Experts are recognizing increasingly that substance use dependence is a chronic relapsing condition that may last for decades. A unique U.S. study by Dennis, Scott, Funk, and Foss (2005) painted a fairly bleak picture. They tracked intervals from first use to at least a one-year abstinence and time of first treatment to at least one year of abstinence. Dennis et al. (2005) suggested that there is such a chronic ongoing cycle of treatment and relapse for many people, it makes more sense to talk about people in terms of their "addiction and treatment careers." That is, multiple cycles and episodes of care are the norm. Dennis and colleagues found that three years after intake, 47% of their participants achieved at least 12 months of abstinence, so the picture is not entirely bleak. However, the median time of first use to last use was 27 years! And the median time from first treatment to last use was 9 years! A greater number of years to recovery was associated with a host of factors, including being male, having first use before being 15 years of age, being high in mental distress, and participating in treatment three or more times.

Research on key factors in relapse is focusing more and more on the role of stress in relapse. Work by Sinha (2007) and his colleagues, primarily with cocaine addicts, has confirmed that stress heightens the risk of drug abuse and addiction treatment relapse. Data indicate that the neural brain circuits associated with stress overlap substantially with the brain systems implicated in drug reward properties. That is, heightened stress responsivity and drug craving are linked inextricably in people with addiction.

All of this suggests that the five women profiled in the *Toronto Star* have a tough road ahead of them. So, should they just give up? Clearly, there is hope, as illustrated by Karen's recent treatment success, but society must acknowledge the need to commit significant resources to the long-term care and treatment of addicted individuals. Given the pernicious and recurring nature of addiction for a significant proportion of people who become addicted, it is vitally important to engage in preventive efforts with children and adolescents so that the addiction simply does not occur in the first place.

(see Burke, Arkowitz, & Menchola, 2003; Rubak, Sandback, Lauritzen, & Christensen, 2005). However, it seems to be more effective for treating drinking problems (previous section) rather than smoking (next section) (Burke et al., 2003).

While some forms of treatment are successful, the reality is that many people with addictions require years of intervention. Canadian Clinic Focus 12.1 outlined the difficulties associated with maintaining recovery.

TREATMENT OF CIGARETTE SMOKING

As we mentioned earlier, numerous laws today prohibit smoking in restaurants, trains, airplanes, and public buildings. These laws are part of a social context that provides more incentive and support to stop smoking than existed in the past. Of the more than 40 million smokers in the United States who have quit since 1964, it is believed that 90% did so without professional help (National Cancer Institute, 1977; USDHHS, 1982, 1989). Each year more than 30% of cigarette smokers try to quit with minimal outside assistance, but fewer than 10% succeed even in the short run (Fiore et al., 1990). Research is ongoing on smokers' use of self-help methods outside the framework of formal smoking-cessation programs.

Some smokers attend smoking clinics or consult with professionals for specialized smoking-reduction programs. It is estimated that about half of those who go through smoking-cessation programs succeed in abstaining by the time the program is over; only about 20% of those who have succeeded in the short term actually remain non-smoking after a year. The greatest success overall is found among smokers who are better educated, are older, or have acute health problems (USDHHS, 1998).

BIOLOGICAL TREATMENTS

Reducing a smoker's craving for nicotine by providing it in a different way is one biological approach to treatment. Attention to nicotine dependence is clearly important because the more cigarettes a person smokes daily, the less successful attempts to quit will be. Gum containing nicotine may help smokers endure the nicotine withdrawal that accompanies any effort to stop smoking. The nicotine in gum is absorbed much more slowly and steadily than that in tobacco. The long-term goal is for the former smoker to be able to cut back on the use of the gum as well, eventually eliminating reliance on nicotine altogether.

There is some controversy around this treatment, however, as ex-smokers can become dependent on the gum. Moreover, in doses that deliver an amount of nicotine equivalent to smoking one cigarette an hour, the gum causes cardiovascular changes (e.g., increased blood pressure) that can be dangerous to people with cardiovascular diseases. Nevertheless, some experts believe that even prolonged, continued use of the gum is healthier than obtaining nicotine by smoking, since at least the poisons in the smoke are avoided. The best results are obtained when the gum is combined with a behaviourally oriented treatment (Hughes, 1995), although one well-controlled study showed no additional benefit from the gum over a behavioural intervention that emphasized educational information (e.g., health risks) and environmental changes (e.g., the removal of ashtrays from home and work settings) (Hill et al., 1995).

Hughes (1995) pointed out that although nicotine replacement alleviates withdrawal symptoms—which justifies its use in gum and in the nicotine patches to be described next (Hughes et al., 1990)—the severity of withdrawal is related only minimally to success in stopping smoking (Hughes & Hatsukami, 1992).

Laws that have banned smoking in many places have probably increased the frequency of quitting. CP Images/STRCANWEST.

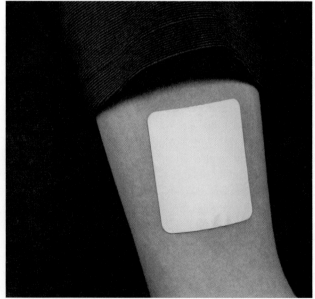

Nicotine patches are now available over the counter to help relieve withdrawal symptoms. Michael Matisse/Getty Images.

Some remarkable new developments in Toronto have clarified the efficacy of nicotine replacement therapy. The STOP study (Smoking Treatment for Ontario Patients) is a mass treatment study over a six-week period for 11,000 Ontario smokers. Nicotine replacement is combined with supportive telephone counselling. Quit rates of 12% have been achieved and the study is now being expanded (CAMH, 2007). Meanwhile, other research based at the University of Toronto has found that the CYP2A6 genotypes are associated with the slow metabolism of nicotine and that this accounts, in part, for why some people are less likely to benefit from nicotine replacement therapy (Malaiyandi et al., 2006).

Nicotine patches first became available in December 1991 with a doctor's prescription and in 1996 over the counter. A polyethylene patch taped to the arm serves as a transdermal (through the skin) nicotine delivery system that slowly and steadily releases the drug into the bloodstream and thence to the brain. An advantage of the patch over nicotine gum is that the person needs only to apply the patch each day and not remove it, making compliance easier. A program of treatment usually lasts 10 to 12 weeks, with smaller and smaller patches used as treatment progresses. A drawback is that a person who continues smoking while wearing the patch may increase the amount of nicotine in the body to dangerous levels.

Evidence suggests that the nicotine patch is superior to the use of a placebo patch in terms of abstinence, as well as subjective craving (see Hughes, 1995). However, as with nicotine gum, the patch is not a panacea. Abstinence rates are less than 40% immediately following the termination of treatment, and at nine-month follow-ups, differences between the drug and a placebo disappear. The manufacturers state that the patch is to be used only as part of a psychological smoking-cessation program and then for not more than three months at a time.

The newest nicotine replacement therapy involves an inhaler. The user inhales the nicotine through a plastic tube shaped like a cigarette holder; unlike gum or patches, this method of nicotine delivery has some resemblance to smoking, as the person handles the device and inhales. In a comparison of these inhalers with placebo inhalers that did not actually contain nicotine, one-year abstinence rates were 28% for the treatment group and 18% for the placebo group (Hjalmarson et al., 1997).

Given that attempting to quit smoking can precipitate an episode of depression in someone who has previously been depressed, interest has also focused on the possible role of antidepressants in aiding smoking cessation. Thus far, the evidence shows that antidepressants that have strong effects on dopamine do have some benefit, regardless of whether the person has a history of depression (Hall et al., 1998; Hurt, Sachs, & Glover, 1997). Patients are typically given an amount of the antidepressant that is less than would be used to treat depression. They take the drug for some period of time before trying to stop smoking and then continue taking the antidepressant for some amount of time (e.g., seven weeks) as they try to give up smoking. Hurt et al. (1997) combined brief counselling with either bupropion (an antidepressant sold under the names Wellbutrin and Zyban) or a placebo and found one-year abstinence rates of 23% in the treated group and 12% in the placebo group. Combining bupropion and nicotine patches has yielded an impressive 12-month abstinence rate of 35% (Jorenby et al., 1999).

PSYCHOLOGICAL TREATMENTS

Although short-term results of psychological treatments are often very encouraging (some programs have reported as many as 95% of smokers abstinent by the end of treatment), longer term results are far less positive. Most smokers return to smoking within a year (DiClemente, 1993) and do so quickly if they have been heavy smokers (USDHHS, 1998). This evidence does not belie the fact that a substantial minority of smokers can be helped; clearly, however, the task is not easy.

Many techniques have been tried. The idea behind some of them is to make smoking unpleasant, even nauseating. In the 1970s, there was considerable interest in rapid smoking treatment, in which a smoker sits in a poorly ventilated room and puffs much faster than normal, perhaps as often as every six seconds (e.g., Lando, 1977). Variations include rapid puffing (rapid smoking without inhaling), focused smoking (smoking for a long period of time but at a normal rate), and smoke holding (retaining smoke in the mouth for several minutes but without inhaling). Although such treatments reduce smoking and foster abstinence more than no-treatment control conditions, they usually do not differ from each other or from other credible interventions, showing high rates of relapse at follow-ups (Schwartz, 1987; Sobell et al., 1990).

Cognitively oriented investigators have tried to encourage more control in people who smoke with treatments that have them develop and use various coping skills, such as relaxation and positive self-talk, when confronted with tempting situations (e.g., following a good meal). Results are not very promising (Smith et al., 2001).

According to Compas et al. (1998), scheduled smoking shows real promise. The strategy is to reduce nicotine intake gradually over a period of a few weeks by getting the smoker to agree to increase the time intervals between cigarettes. For example, during the first week of treatment, a pack-a-day smoker would be put on a schedule allowing only 10 cigarettes per day; during the second week, only five cigarettes are allowed; and during the third week, the person would taper off to zero. These cigarettes have to be smoked on a schedule provided by the treatment team, not when the smoker feels an intense craving. In this way, smoking cigarettes is controlled by the passage of time rather than by urges, mood states, or situations. Breaking this link—assuming the smoker is able to comply with the agreed-upon schedule—has led to 44% abstinence after one year, a very impressive outcome (Cinciripini et al., 1994).

Another approach, in the spirit of tailoring treatment to factors believed to underlie the smoking, is applying cognitive therapy to depressed mood in certain smokers. Available results are encouraging (see Hall et al., 1996).

Probably the most widespread intervention is advice or direction from a physician to stop smoking. Each year millions of smokers are given this counsel because of hypertension, heart disease, lung disease, diabetes, or on general grounds of preserving or improving health. Indeed, by age 65, most smokers have managed to quit (USDHHS, 1998). There is some evidence that a physician's advice can get some people to stop smoking, at least for a while, especially when the patients also chew nicotine gum (Law & Tang, 1995). But much more needs to be learned about the nature of the advice, the manner in which it is given, its timing, and other factors that must surely play a role in determining whether an addicted individual is prepared and able to alter his or her behaviour primarily on a physician's say-so (USDHHS, 1998).

As with other addictions, psychological factors may make it difficult for smokers to quit. As these factors can vary significantly among addicts, one treatment package cannot be expected to help all smokers. People have trouble quitting for many different reasons, and diverse methods need to be developed to help them. Yet in their zeal to make an impact on the smoking problem, clinicians have until recently put smokers in standardized programs.

RELAPSE PREVENTION

Mark Twain quipped that stopping smoking was easy—he'd done it hundreds of times! Most smokers relapse within a year of stopping, regardless of the means used to stop. As might be expected, people who smoked the most—and are presumably more addicted to nicotine—relapse more often and more quickly than moderate or light smokers. It is very difficult for ex-smokers to maintain their abstinence. Data (and common sense) tell us that ex-smokers who do not live with a smoker do better at follow-up than do those who do live with a smoker (McIntyre-Kingsolver, Lichtenstein, & Mermelstein, 1986). So-called booster or maintenance sessions help, but in a very real sense they represent a continuation of treatment; when they stop, relapse is the rule (Brandon, Zelman, & Baker, 1987). However, there is considerably more social support for not smoking than there was just 20 years ago. Perhaps as time goes on, societal sanctions against smoking will help those who have succeeded in quitting remain abstinent.

One approach to the relapse problem is to focus on the cognitions of ex-smokers (Baer & Lichtenstein, 1988). Using the articulated thoughts paradigm (Davison et al., 1983), Haaga (1989) found that recent ex-smokers who tended to think of smoking without prompting relapsed more readily

Lifelong smoker Barbara Tarbox spoke to young people across Canada about the dangers of smoking before she died of lung cancer at age 42. *Edmonton Journal*/Greg Southam.

three months later. However, if they learned some effective ways of countering these smoking-related thoughts, such as distracting themselves with other concerns, their abstinence was better months later. Using a questionnaire measure, Haaga found that ex-smokers' self-efficacy in their most difficult challenge situation (e.g., having coffee and dessert following a pleasant dinner) was a good predictor of abstinence a year later (Haaga, 1990). These and related studies indicate that we can more reliably predict the maintenance or relapse in smoking cessation if we access the cognitions of ex-smokers. Such information may help therapists design programs that will improve a person's ability to remain a non-smoker (Compas et al., 1998).

PREVENTION OF SUBSTANCE ABUSE

From all that is known about the etiology of substance abuse, discouraging people from beginning to abuse drugs makes the most sense. It is difficult—and for many, impossible—to loosen oneself from substances that create both psychological and physical dependency. We turn our attention next to prevention efforts involving alcohol abuse, drug abuse, and smoking.

Many prevention efforts have been aimed at adolescents because substance abuse in adulthood often follows experimentation in the teens and earlier. Programs, usually conducted in schools, have been directed at enhancing the young adolescent's self-esteem, teaching social skills, and encouraging the young person to say no to peer pressure. The results are mixed (Hansen, 1993; Jansen et al., 1996). Self-esteem enhancement, sometimes called affective education, has not demonstrated its effectiveness. In contrast, social skills training and resistance training (learning to say no) have shown some positive results, particularly with girls. A highly publicized program, Project DARE (Drug Abuse Resistance Education), which combines affective education and resistance training and is delivered by police officers in fifth and sixth grade classrooms, has shown disappointing results; a meta-analysis found that the effect size was very small (West & O'Neal, 2004).

Still, there is some reason for optimism. A recent meta-analytic study showed that alcohol interventions can significantly improve antecedents of behavioural change (see Scott-Sheldon, DeMartini, Carey, & Carey, 2009). It was found that just 45 minutes of intervention can significantly improve knowledge, attitudes, accuracy of awareness of drinking norms, and intentions to reduce drinking. However, it did not increase levels of self-efficacy or alter alcohol-related expectancies.

Developing ways of discouraging young people from experimenting with tobacco has become a top priority among health researchers and politicians. Canada is among the world leaders in taking an aggressive stand against tobacco advertising, as well as in providing the public with warnings about the use of tobacco. On June 28, 2000, Canada's then health minister, Alan Rock, announced new regulations for tobacco advertisements that mandated that all cigarette packages sold in Canada carry health warnings that cover 50% of the front and back of the package. According to Senior (2000), these warnings are the most stringent and graphic in the world. They also seem to be effective. According to Senior (2000), research conducted by Health Canada in 1999 showed that the larger and more emotional the message on the package, the more impact it had on potential users. Another survey found that 1 in 5 adult smokers reported cutting down as a result of the graphic advertising images (Hammond et al., 2004). The most common emotional reactions are disgust and fear; those who experienced more of these negative emotions when assessed initially were more likely to have quit or reduced their smoking when assessed three months later. The use of warning labels, the decision to raise cigarette taxes to make it more difficult for young people to smoke, and preventive lectures on the topic given to Canadian schoolchildren by people such as Dr. Jeffrey Wigand (see the movie *The Insider*) are all part of a multifaceted Health Canada strategy designed to decrease the number of young smokers and limit the long-term costs to the health system.

Current data continue to support the effects of advertising. A study of more than 9,000 smokers from four countries (Canada, the United States, the United Kingdom, and Australia) found that more than three quarters of them recognized that society does not approve of smoking and they expressed their belief that tobacco companies cannot be trusted (Hammond et al., 2005). The belief that society does not approve is called a **denormalization belief**. It was found that belief that smoking is disapproved of was associated with higher abstinence from smoking eight months

later, and supplementary analyses showed that the link between warning labels and denormalization was strongest in Canada.

Advertising and media exposure also contributes to drinking. Anderson et al. (2009) conducted a review of 13 longitudinal studies with over 38,000 young participants in total. Overall, 12 of 13 studies found a significant impact of alcohol advertising and media exposure on subsequent alcohol use, including initiation of drinking, and heavier drinking among existing drinkers. Clearly, a case can be made for banning drinking ads. Reviews indicate that banning alcohol advertising is "highly cost effective" in reducing harm (see Anderson et al., 2009).

When it comes to smoking, another approach has been to increase the cost of cigarettes through taxes. However, Canadian research indicates that pricing has a differential impact on men than women (Dedobbeleer et al., 2004). Higher prices appear to decrease the prevalence of smoking among men but have no effect among women, who, it was suggested, tend to smoke in response to life stressors.

Regarding the potential financial savings, not to mention the savings in terms of well-being and quality of life, an analysis of health costs suggested that a national prevention program in Canada could be implemented for as little as $67 per student (Stephens, Kaiserman, McCall, & Sutherland, 2000). The net savings over time due to improved public health as a result of decreased smoking was estimated at $619 million per year. Thus, substantial savings would result. However, as noted by Stephens et al. (2000), preventive efforts currently underway are not extensive enough to realize these enormous benefits.

The measures that hold promise for persuading young people to resist smoking may also be useful in dissuading them from trying illicit drugs and alcohol. Many smokers do fear disastrous consequences later in life and try to cut down on cigarettes, yet others, both young and old, seem able to discount the possibility that they are at higher risk for coronary heart disease or lung cancer. This is the "It won't happen to me" syndrome.

Recent years have seen scores of school-based programs aimed at preventing young people from starting to use tobacco. By and large, such programs have succeeded in delaying the onset of smoking (Sussman et al., 1995). They share some common components (Hansen, 1992; Hansen et al., 1988; Sussman, 1996):

1. *Peer-pressure resistance training* Students learn about the nature of peer pressure and ways to say no. For example, specially prepared films portray teenagers resisting appeals from friends to try smoking, not an easy matter for young people for whom peer approval and acceptance are so important.
2. *Correction of normative expectations* Many young people believe that cigarette smoking is more prevalent (and by implication, more okay) than it actually is. Changing

beliefs about the prevalence of smoking is an effective strategy, perhaps because of the sensitivity young people have to what others their age do and believe.

3. *Inoculation against mass-media messages* Some prevention programs try to counter any positive images of smokers that are put forth in the media.

4. *Information about parental and other adult influences* Since it is known that parental smoking is strongly correlated with and most probably contributes to smoking by their children, some programs note that this aspect of parental behaviour should not be imitated.

5. *Peer leadership* Most smoking and other drug-prevention programs involve peers of recognized status to enhance the impact of the anti-use messages being conveyed.

6. *Affective education, self-image enhancement* Several programs focus on the idea that intrapsychic factors, such as poor self-image and inability to cope with stress, underlie the onset of smoking in young people. However, there are indications that such programs may actually increase drug use, perhaps because their focus on drugs as a poor way to resolve self-esteem issues unintentionally suggests drug use as a way to deal with life stress.

7. *Other components* Additional features include providing information about the harmful effects of smoking or of drug use (in addition to that provided in warnings on cigarette packages) and encouraging students to make a public commitment not to smoke (e.g., making a commitment on videotape).

SUMMARY

- Using substances to alter mood and consciousness is a human characteristic and so, too, is the tendency to abuse them. *DSM-IV-TR* distinguishes between substance dependence and substance abuse but subsequent authors have suggested that a dimensional approach that regards substance dependence and substance abuse as being along the same continuum is more valid.

- Dependence refers to a compulsive pattern of substance use and consequent serious psychological and physical impairments. It can involve physiological dependence, or addiction, when tolerance and withdrawal are present.

- In substance abuse, drug use leads to failure to meet obligations and to interpersonal and legal problems.

- Alcohol has a variety of short-term and long-term effects on human beings. Many of these effects are tragic in nature, ranging from poor judgement and motor coordination and their dire consequences for the alcohol-abusing person and society, to addiction, which makes an ordinary, productive life impossible and is extremely difficult to overcome. As with other addicting drugs, people come to rely on alcohol not so much because it makes them feel good as because it provides an escape from feeling bad.

- Less prevalent but more notorious, perhaps because of their illegality, are the opiates, including heroin, and the barbiturates, which are sedatives; and the amphetamines and cocaine, which are stimulants. All these substances are addictive, and cocaine, including crack, is especially so. Heroin has been the focus of concern in recent years because usage is up and stronger varieties have become available. Barbiturates have for some time been implicated in both intentional and accidental suicides; they are particularly lethal when taken with alcohol.

- Nicotine, especially when taken into the body via the inhaled smoke from a cigarette, has worked its addictive power on humankind for centuries, and despite sombrely phrased warnings from public health officials, it continues in widespread use. Smoking by school-age youngsters and teenagers is a notable concern because nearly all adult smokers began their use in their teens. Each year, the government and private individuals spend millions of dollars to dissuade people from beginning the habit or to help those already addicted to stop smoking.

- Marijuana is smoked by a large number of young North Americans. Its use declined in the 1980s but increased in the 1990s. Arguments for deregulation of marijuana have stressed its supposed safety in comparison with the known harm caused by the habitual use of alcohol, which is a legal and integral part of North American culture. But currently available evidence indicates that when used regularly, marijuana is not benign; it can damage the lungs and cardiovascular system and lead to cognitive impairments. There is also evidence that constituents of marijuana may adversely affect fetal development, heart function in people who already have coronary problems, and pulmonary function. Further, marijuana appears to be addictive.

- The hallucinogens—LSD, mescaline, and psilocybin—are taken to alter or expand consciousness. Their use reflects humankind's desire not only to escape from unpleasant realities, but also to explore inner space.

- Several factors are related to the etiology of substance abuse and dependence. Social attitudes and culture play a role in encouraging the abuse of drugs, alcohol, and cigarettes.

CHAPTER

13 PERSONALITY DISORDERS

Harry Mayerovitch, Musée du Quebec, *Self Portrait*. Courtesy of the estate of Harry Mayerovitch

"Every man has three characters: that which he exhibits, that which he has, and that which he thinks he has."
—Alphonse Karr

"People, I know I've done some terrible things … and I've caused a lot of sadness and sorrow to a lot of people and I'm really sorry for that and I know I deserve to be punished. But I didn't kill these girls."
—Paul Bernardo, the *Toronto Star*, August 15, 1995

MARY WAS 26 years old at the time of her first admission to a psychiatric hospital. She had been in outpatient treatment with a psychologist for several months when her persistent thoughts of suicide and preoccupation with inflicting pain on herself (by cutting or burning) led her therapist to conclude that she could no longer be managed as an outpatient.

Mary's first experience with some form of psychological therapy occurred when she was an adolescent. Her grades declined sharply in Grade 11, and her parents suspected she was using drugs. She began to miss curfews and even failed to come home at all on a few occasions. She was frequently truant. Family therapy was undertaken, and it seemed to go well at first. Mary was enthusiastic about her therapist and asked for additional, private sessions with him.

Her parents' fears were confirmed during the family sessions, as Mary revealed an extensive history of drug use, including "everything I can get my hands on." She had been promiscuous and had prostituted herself several times to get drug money. Her relationships with her peers were changeable, to say the least. The pattern was a constant parade of new friends, at first thought to be the greatest ever but who soon disappointed Mary in some way and were cast aside, often in a very unpleasant way. Except for the one person with whom she was currently enamoured, Mary had no friends. She reported that she stayed away from others for fear that they would harm her in some way.

After several weeks of therapy, Mary's parents noticed that her relationship with the therapist had cooled appreciably. The sessions were marked by Mary's angry and abusive outbursts toward the therapist. After several more weeks had passed, Mary refused to attend any more sessions. In a subsequent conversation with the therapist, Mary's father learned that Mary had behaved seductively toward the therapist during their private sessions and that her changed attitude toward him coincided with the rejection of her advances, despite the therapist's attempt to mix firmness with warmth and empathy.

Mary managed to graduate from high school and enrolled in a local community college, but the old patterns returned. Poor grades, cutting classes, continuing drug use, and lack of interest in her studies finally led her to quit in the middle of the first semester of her second year. After leaving school, Mary held a series of clerical jobs. Most of them didn't last long, as her relationships with co-workers paralleled her relationships with her peers in high school. When Mary started a new job, she would find someone she really liked, but something would come between them and the relationship would end angrily. Mary was frequently suspicious of her co-workers and reported that she often heard them talking about her, plotting how to prevent her from getting ahead on the job. She was quick to find hidden meanings in their behaviour; for example, she interpreted being the last person asked to sign a birthday card to mean that she was the least liked person in the office. She indicated that she "received vibrations" from others and that, even in the absence of any direct evidence, she could tell when they really didn't like her.

Mary's behaviour includes many characteristic symptoms of several personality disorders, in particular, borderline personality disorder. Her frequent mood swings, with periods of depression and extreme irritability, led her to seek therapy several times. But after initial enthusiasm, her relationship with her therapist always deteriorated, resulting in premature termination of therapy. The therapist she was seeing just before her hospitalization was her sixth.

Personality disorders (PDs) are a heterogeneous group of disorders that are coded on Axis II of the *DSM*. They are regarded as long-standing, pervasive, and inflexible patterns of behaviour and inner experience that deviate from the expectations of a person's culture and that impair social and occupational functioning. Some, but not all, can cause emotional distress.

As we examine the personality disorders, some may seem to fit people we know, not to mention ourselves! Although the symptoms of the personality disorders come close to describing characteristics that we all possess from time to time and in varying degrees, an actual personality disorder is defined by the extremes of several traits and by the inflexible way these traits are expressed. People with personality disorders are often rigid in their behaviour and cannot change it in response to changes in the situations they experience.

The personality each of us develops over the years reflects a persistent means of dealing with life's challenges, a certain style of relating to other people. One person is overly dependent, another is challenging and aggressive, another is shy and avoids social contact, and still another is concerned more with appearance and bolstering his or her vulnerable ego than with relating to others. These individuals would not be diagnosed as having personality disorders unless the patterns of behaviour were long-standing, pervasive, and dysfunctional. For example, on entering a crowded room and hearing a loud burst of laughter, you might feel that you are the target of some joke and that people are talking about you. Such concerns become symptoms of paranoid personality disorder only if they occur frequently and intensely and prevent the development of close personal relationships. In this chapter, we look first at how we classify personality disorders and at the challenges associated with classification and assessment. Then we turn to the personality disorders themselves, the theory and research on their etiology, and therapies for dealing with them. The extent of our coverage of the specific personality disorders varies depending on how much is known about them; for example, there are very few empirical data about histrionic personality disorder but a vast literature on anti-social personality disorder.

CLASSIFYING PERSONALITY DISORDERS: CLUSTERS, CATEGORIES, AND PROBLEMS

The idea that personality can be disordered goes back at least to the time of Hippocrates and his humoral theory, which we discussed in Chapter 1. Personality disorders were listed in the early *DSMs*, but the diagnoses were very unreliable. One clinician might diagnose a flamboyant patient as narcissistic, whereas another might consider him or her psychopathic. As with other diagnoses, the publication of *DSM-III* began a trend toward improved reliability (Coolidge & Segal, 1998). Beginning with *DSM-III*, personality disorders were also placed on a separate axis, Axis II, to ensure that diagnosticians would pay attention to their possible presence. Although a diagnostic interview sometimes points directly to the presence of a personality disorder, more often a person arrives at a clinic with an Axis I disorder (such as panic disorder) that, quite naturally, is the primary focus of attention. With personality disorders on Axis II, the clinician must consider whether a personality disorder is also present.

The reliability of personality disorder diagnoses, then, has improved because of two developments: (1) the publication of specific diagnostic criteria; and (2) the development of structured interviews specially designed for assessing personality disorders.

Data now indicate that good reliability can be achieved, even across cultures (Loranger et al., 1987; Widiger et al., 1988). Inter-rater reliability (the extent to which raters agree) from a study of the *DSM-IV* diagnostic criteria is presented in Table 13.1 (Maffei et al., 1997); the figures compare favourably with reliability figures for Axis I disorders (Chapter 3). Thus, by using structured interviews, reliable diagnoses of personality disorders can be achieved. Interviews with people who know the patient well are sometimes part of the diagnostic workup and improve the accuracy of diagnosis (Bernstein et al., 1997).

TABLE 13.1
INTER-RATER AND TEST-RETEST RELIABILITY FOR THE PERSONALITY DISORDERS

Diagnosis	Inter-Rater Reliability	Test-Retest Reliabivity
Paranoid	.93	.57
Schizoid	.90	–
Schizotypal	.91	.11
Borderline	.91	.56
Histrionic	.92	.40
Narcissistic	.98	.32
Anti-social	.94	.84
Dependent	.86	.15
Avoidant	.97	.41
Obsessive-compulsive	.83	.52

Test-retest figures are rates of agreement from Zimmerman's 1994 summary of longer (generally more than a year) studies.

Source: Figures for inter-rater reliability are from the Maffei et al., 1997 study and reflect the amount of agreement above chance.

Because personality disorders are presumed to be more stable over time than some episodic Axis I disorders (e.g., depression), test-retest reliability—a comparison of whether patients receive the same diagnosis when they are assessed twice with some time interval separating the two assessments—is also an important factor in their evaluation. A summary of test-retest reliability is also given in Table 13.1 (Zimmerman, 1994). Note the wide variability of the figures. Anti-social personality disorder has a high test-retest reliability, indicating that it is a stable diagnosis; a patient given the diagnosis is very likely to receive the same diagnosis when evaluated later. The figures for schizotypal and dependent personality disorders are very low, indicating that the symptoms of people with these latter two diagnoses are not stable over time. Two interpretations are possible. Perhaps certain personality disorders are not as enduring as the *DSM* asserts, or perhaps the assessment of reliability needs to be more accurate.

Research conducted after compilation of the summary data in Table 13.1 continues to suggest that the test-retest reliability of diagnoses is poor. Durbin and Klein (2006) assessed the stability of personality disorders in patients with mood disorders and found that the 10-year stability of categorical diagnoses was "relatively poor" (p. 82). Stability coefficients were greater when a dimensional view of personality disorder was used and shorter time intervals were employed. Consistent with the greater stability of anti-social disorders, cluster B disorders (see the section "Personality Disorder Clusters") had the greatest stability over time.

The issue of the long-term course of personality disorders is beginning to receive greater empirical attention, as reflected by a 2005 special edition of the *Journal of Personality Disorders* (see Clark, 2005, for a summary). It seems that there is an overall age-related decline over time in personality dysfunction as people get older. Second, the stability of personality dysfunction varies according to subtle but important differences in the nature of symptoms. Acute symptoms are especially likely to decrease over time (e.g., self-harming) while symptoms reflecting negative affect are quite stable and these chronic symptoms are likely a reflection of character and personality structure and organization (Zanarini et al., 2005b).

In addition to the low levels of test-retest reliability of diagnoses, another major problem with personality disorders is that it is often difficult to diagnose a single, specific personality disorder because many disordered people exhibit a wide range of traits that make several diagnoses applicable (Marshall & Serin, 1997). In the case opening this chapter, Mary met the diagnostic criteria not only for borderline personality disorder but also for paranoid personality disorder, and she came close to meeting the criteria for schizotypal disorder, as well. One study found that 55% of patients with borderline personality disorder also met the diagnostic criteria for schizotypal personality disorder; 47%, the criteria for anti-social personality disorder; and 57%, the criteria for histrionic personality disorder (Widiger, Frances, & Trull, 1987). These data are particularly discouraging and have implications for when we try to interpret the results of research that compares patients who have a specific personality disorder with some control group. If, for example, we find that people with borderline personality disorder differ from normal people, is what we have learned specific to borderline personality disorder or is it related to personality disorders in general?

Although some decrease in comorbidity occurred with the publication of *DSM-IV* (Blais, Hilsenroth, & Castlebury, 1997), the data still suggest that the categorical diagnostic system of *DSM-IV-TR* is not ideal for classifying personality disorders. The personality traits that constitute the data for classification form a continuum; most of the relevant characteristics are present in varying degrees in most people. Tests of a categorical vs. a dimensional approach provide strong support for the dimensional approach. Although Canadian researchers have provided some evidence to suggest that the psychopathy underscoring anti-social personality may represent a discrete category (Skilling, Harris, Rice, & Quinsey, 2002), another recent analysis has concluded that even psychopathy should be considered dimensional (Edens, Marcus, Lilienfeld, & Poythress, 2006). Overall, a dimensional approach seems to apply to most other personality characteristics. Research by John Livesley from the University of British Columbia and his associates shows that when people with a personality disorder take a general personality inventory, what is revealed is a personality with a structure that is similar to that of normal people but is simply more extreme (Clark et al., 1996; Livesley, Jang, & Vernon, 1998; Livesley & Schroeder, 1993). Similar research at Lakehead University in Thunder Bay, Ontario, has shown that dimensional differences exist when characterizing normal vs. abnormal personality; personality disorders reflect extreme and rigid response tendencies that differ in degree, not in kind, from the responses of people without disorders (O'Connor, 2002; O'Connor & Dyce, 2001). Thus, the personality disorders can be construed as the extremes of characteristics we all possess. Nevertheless, current diagnostic systems are still based on the categorical approach.

How is it first determined whether a personality disorder exists? Livesley, Schroeder, Jackson, and Jang (1994) regard personality disorder as a failure or inability to come up with adaptive solutions to life tasks. Livesley (1998) identified three types of life tasks and proposed that failure with any one task is enough to warrant a personality disorder diagnosis. The three tasks are (1) to form stable, integrated, and coherent representations of self and others; (2) to develop the capacity for intimacy and positive affiliations with other people; and (3) to function adaptively in society by engaging in prosocial and co-operative behaviours. Once one of these tasks fails, disorder is evident and the focus can shift to dimensional ratings. Livesley's views appear to have had some impact because the proposed new *DSM-5* definition of personality disorder reflects "adaptive failure" in terms of impaired self-identity and adaptive failure in establishing interpersonal relationships (see www.dsm5.org).

A dimensional system was considered for inclusion in both *DSM-III-R* and *DSM-IV*, but consensus could not be reached on which dimensions to include. A promising effort to develop a dimensional classification system is described later (Focus on Discovery 13.1). Proposed *DSM-5* changes reflect the dimensional approach.

Despite problems with the diagnosis of personality disorders, we should not entirely dismiss the utility of trying to make such diagnoses. These disorders are prevalent, and they cause severe impairment in people's lives. As research continues, the diagnostic categories will most likely be refined, perhaps with a dimensional system, and many of these problems may be solved.

ASSESSING PERSONALITY DISORDERS

Some key points need to be made about the assessment of personality disorders. A significant challenge is that many disorders are egosyntonic: the person with a personality disorder is typically unaware that a problem exists and may not be experiencing significant personal distress; that is, they lack insight into their own personality. However, the people who interact with these individuals may have a great deal of discomfort and upset. This suggests that the assessment and diagnosis of personality disorders are enhanced when the significant others in an individual's life become informants. Furthermore, because of the lack of personal awareness in many cases, disorders may need to be diagnosed via clinical interviews led by trained personnel.

Another significant challenge is that a substantial proportion of patients are deemed to have a personality disorder not otherwise specified (PDNOS) and these patients do not fit into existing personality disorder diagnostic categories. Verheul and Widiger (2004) concluded that personality disorder not otherwise specified is the third-most prevalent type of personality disorder diagnosed via structured interviews, with the prevalence of this PDNOS ranging from 8 to 13% in clinical samples. Tyrer et al. (2007) reviewed these and other problems and concluded that "the assessment of personality disorder is currently inaccurate, largely unreliable, frequently wrong, and in need of improvement" (p. S51).

Although clinical interviews are preferable when seeking to make a diagnosis, researchers often rely on the use of self-report measures when assessing personality disorder symptoms. The MMPI-2 that was described in Chapter 4 is a personality inventory that can also be used for this purpose. Scoring schemes using MMPI items have been created to assess the symptoms of specific personality disorders (e.g., Morey, Waugh, & Blashfield, 1985). Harkness, McNulty, and Ben-Porath (1995) described a set of MMPI-2 scales that they developed to assess five dimensional personality constructs to reflect psychopathology. This framework, known as the PSY-5, consists of dimensions assessing negative emotionality/neuroticism, lack of positive emotionality, aggressiveness, lack of constraint, and psychoticism. The PSY-5 dimensions have been corroborated via confirmatory factor analyses (Bagby et al., 2002), and they are promising because they seem particularly relevant to certain forms of personality dysfunction. For instance, Trull et al. (1995) noted that the PSY-5 constraint scale should be robustly associated with anti-social personality disorder symptoms given that the constraint scale has items that assess lying, stealing, and getting into legal trouble. A relatively new investigation led by Michael Bagby from the Centre for Addiction and Mental Health showed that both the PSY-5 and the NEO-PI(R) were strong, significant unique predictors of the symptoms of 10 personality disorders (Bagby, Sellbon, Costa, & Widiger, 2008). The PSY-5 was comparatively better at predicting paranoid, schizotypal, narcissistic, and anti-social personality disorder symptom counts.

Perhaps the most widely used measure of personality disorder symptoms is the Millon Clinical Multiaxial Inventory, now in its third edition (MCMI-III; Millon, 1994). The MCMI-III is a 175-item true-false inventory at an eighth grade reading level that was revised to parallel *DSM-IV*. The MCMI-III provides subscale measures of 11 clinical personality scales (schizoid, avoidant, depressive, dependent, histrionic, narcissistic, antisocial, aggressive [sadistic], compulsive, passive-aggressive, and self-defeating) and three severe personality pathology scales (schizotypal, borderline, and paranoid). The MCMI-III also provides symptom ratings for clinical syndromes located on Axis I of the *DSM-IV*, such as somatoform disorder and post-traumatic stress disorder. Importantly, the MCMI-III includes a validity index and three response-style indices (known as modifying indices) that correct for such tendencies as denial and random responding. The inclusion of these scales reflects Millon's recognition of the need to assess response biases and other self-report tendencies that can undermine the data obtained via self-report scales. The updated 2009 version of the MCMI-III has new norms and additional scoring. It now includes "therapy-guiding facet scales" (e.g., interpersonal style, cognitive style) known as the Grossman Facet Scales that further characterize the person who answered the MCMI-III (see Millon, Davis, Millon, & Grossman, 2009). These facet scales were added to facilitate Millon and Grossman's (2007) new treatment approach known as **personalized therapy**. That is, in order to be more effective and meaningful for individuals, therapies need to be modified to recognize each person's unique needs and personality styles.

Two key issues involving self-report measures of personality disorder need to be considered. First, the various self-report measures differ in their content and are not equivalent. A study done at the University of Alberta examined the prevalence of personality disorders in university students by administering three self-report personality disorder scales, including the MCMI-II, the MMPI personality disorder scale, and the Coolidge Axis Two Inventory (CATI) (Sinha & Watson, 2001). For men, narcissistic PD was the most prevalent disorder according to the MCMI-II and CATI results, but the MMPI measure indicated that paranoid PD was the most prevalent. For women, the most prevalent disorder according to MCMI-II results was avoidant PD, but it was narcissistic PD according to CATI responses and paranoid PD according to the MMPI responses.

Second, a general concern involving self-report measures, including PD measures, is that the cut-off points used to determine the presence of a personality disorder often overestimate the number of people who meet diagnostic criteria for particular disorders. For instance, the Sinha and Watson (2001) study found that 26.28% of women surveyed had an avoidant PD. A common pattern in comparative research is that only a proportion of those who appear to have a diagnosable disorder on the basis of the self-report measure actually are diagnosed following more detailed examination using clinical criteria. Still, the pervasiveness of personality disorders should not be underestimated, including among university students. A revealing study by Blanco et al. (2008) compared the results of a U.S. national epidemiological study for college students versus same-aged young adults not attending university. This study found that 17.68% of the students met criteria for a personality disorder in their lifetime versus 21.55% of the non-college-attending peers. Thus, about 1 in 5 young people met criteria for one or more personality disorders. Similarly, about 1 in 5 met criteria for an alcohol use disorder.

Personality disorder diagnoses were determined by Blanco et al. (2008) based on the results of a structured clinical interview. Indeed, self-reports should be supplemented by clinical interviews such as the Personality Disorder Examination (Loranger, 1988; Loranger et al., 1987). This extensive structured interview provides dimensional and categorical assessments. An international version was developed for a study done by the World Health Organization (Loranger et al., 1994). The advent of this interview led to the finding that the personality disorders described by diagnostic systems appear to exist across various cultures.

PERSONALITY DISORDER CLUSTERS

When a categorical approach is used and *DSM-IV-TR* criteria are involved, personality disorders are grouped into three clusters:

1. Individuals in cluster A (paranoid, schizoid, and schizotypal) seem odd or eccentric. These disorders reflect oddness and avoidance of social contact.
2. Those in cluster B (borderline, histrionic, narcissistic, and anti-social) seem dramatic, emotional, or erratic. Behaviours are extrapunitive and hostile.
3. Those in cluster C (avoidant, dependent, and obsessive-compulsive) appear fearful.

The empirical evidence on the validity of these clusters is mixed, and recent evidence suggests that perhaps a fourth cluster, cluster D, should be considered as well (see Tyrer et al., 2007). Cluster D would involve splitting the obsessive-compulsive features into a separate category reflecting the themes of obsession and inhibition. Nevertheless, the three original clusters form a very useful organizational framework for this chapter, so we will proceed on this basis. It is worth noting before we begin that people with both borderline and schizotypal personality disorders would probably have been diagnosed as schizophrenic using *DSM-II* criteria. Designating the behaviour of these people as the criteria for these two personality disorders is one way in which *DSM-III-R* and *DSM-IV* narrowed the schizophrenia diagnosis (see Chapter 11). Finally, it is important to mention that the initial draft of *DSM-5*, in recognition of the overlap among disorder categories and the difficulties distinguishing between certain disorders, has proposed going to a reduced framework based on only five categories: antisocial/psychopathic, avoidant, borderline, obsessive-compulsive, and schizotypal (www.dsm5.org). Schizotypal represents the odd/eccentric cluster described below.

ODD/ECCENTRIC CLUSTER

The odd/eccentric cluster comprises three diagnoses: paranoid, schizoid, and schizotypal PDs. The symptoms of these disorders bear some similarity to the symptoms of schizophrenia, especially to the less severe symptoms of its prodromal and residual phases.

PARANOID PERSONALITY DISORDER

The individual with **paranoid personality** disorder (PPD) is suspicious of others. People with this diagnosis expect to be mistreated or exploited by others and thus are secretive and always on the lookout for possible signs of trickery and abuse. Such individuals are reluctant to confide in others and tend to blame them even when they themselves are at fault. They can be extremely jealous and may unjustifiably question the fidelity of a spouse or lover.

Individuals with PPD are preoccupied with unjustified doubts about the trustworthiness or loyalty of others. They may read hidden negative or threatening messages into events (e.g., the individual may believe that a neighbour's dog deliberately barks in the early morning to disturb him or her). This diagnosis is different from schizophrenia, paranoid type, because symptoms such as hallucinations are not present and there is less impairment in social and occupational functioning. It differs from delusional disorder because full-blown delusions are not present.

PPD occurs most frequently in men and co-occurs most frequently with schizotypal, borderline, and avoidant personality disorders (Morey, 1988). Recent data suggest that it is one of the more commonly diagnosed personality disorders in community samples and paranoid personality disorder is best represented as a continuous dimension rather than a discrete category (Edens, Marcus, & Morey, 2009).

SCHIZOID PERSONALITY DISORDER

People with **schizoid personality** disorder do not appear to desire or enjoy social relationships and usually have no close friends. They appear dull, bland, and aloof and have no warm, tender feelings for others. They rarely report strong emotions, have no interest in sex, and experience few pleasurable activities. Indifferent to praise and criticism, individuals with this disorder are loners with solitary interests. The prevalence of schizoid personality disorder is less than 1%. It is slightly less common among women than men (Weissman, 1993).

Comorbidity is highest for schizotypal, avoidant, and paranoid personality disorders, most likely because of the similar diagnostic criteria in the four categories. The diagnostic criteria for schizoid personality disorder are also similar to some of the symptoms of the prodromal and residual phases of schizophrenia.

SCHIZOTYPAL PERSONALITY DISORDER

The concept of the **schizotypal personality** grew out of Danish studies of the adopted children of schizophrenic parents (Kety et al., 1968). Although some of these children developed full-blown schizophrenia as adults, an even larger number developed what seemed to be an attenuated form of schizophrenia. The diagnostic criteria for schizotypal personality disorder were devised by Spitzer, Endicott, and Gibbon (1979) to describe these individuals. These criteria were incorporated in *DSM-III* and were narrowed somewhat in *DSM-III-R* and *DSM-IV*.

People with schizotypal personality disorder usually have the interpersonal difficulties of the schizoid personality and excessive social anxiety that does not diminish as they get to know others. Several additional, more eccentric symptoms, identical to those that define the prodromal and residual phases of schizophrenia, occur in schizotypal personality disorder.

Cognitive limitations and restrictions found in schizophrenia are also evident in schizotypal personality disorder (McClure, Barch, Flory, Harvey, & Siever, 2008). Those with schizotypal personality disorder may also have odd beliefs or magical thinking (e.g., superstitiousness, beliefs that they are clairvoyant and telepathic) and recurrent illusions (they may sense the presence of a force or a person not actually there). In their speech, they may use words in an unusual and unclear fashion, for example, "I'm not a very talkable person." Their behaviour and appearance may also be eccentric; they may talk to themselves, for example. Also common are ideas of reference (the belief that events have a particular and unusual meaning for the person), suspiciousness, and paranoid ideation. Affect appears to be constricted and flat. Widiger et al. (1987) found that paranoid ideation, ideas of reference, and illusions were the symptoms most relevant for making a diagnosis. The prevalence of this disorder is about 3%. It is slightly more frequent among men than women (Zimmerman & Coryell, 1989).

A significant problem in the diagnosis of schizotypal personality disorder is its comorbidity with other personality disorders. Morey (1988) found that 33% of people diagnosed with schizotypal personality also met the diagnostic criteria for borderline personality disorder, while 59% also met the criteria for avoidant personality disorder and for paranoid personality disorder. Recent epidemiological data suggest that the comorbidity between Axis I and Axis II disorders is higher for schizotypal personality disorder than for any other personality disorder, and the degree of comorbidity with borderline personality disorder and narcissistic personality disorder continues to be very high (Pulay et al., 2009). Clearly, these comorbidity figures are unsatisfactory if we want to consider schizotypal personality disorder a discrete diagnostic entity.

ETIOLOGY OF THE ODD/ECCENTRIC CLUSTER

What causes the odd, sometimes paranoid thinking, bizarre behaviour, and interpersonal difficulties that appear in this cluster of personality disorders? The search for causes has been guided by the idea that these disorders are genetically linked to schizophrenia, perhaps as less severe variants of this Axis I disorder. The evidence for this idea varies depending on which of the odd/eccentric disorders is considered.

- Family studies of paranoid personality disorder for the most part find higher than average rates in the relatives of people with schizophrenia or delusional disorder (Bernstein, Useda, & Siever, 1993).
- Family studies have shown that the relatives of people with schizophrenia are at increased risk for this disorder (Nigg & Goldsmith, 1994). However, Squires-Wheeler et al. (1993) found increased rates in the first-degree relatives of people with depression, suggesting that schizotypal personality disorder is related to disorders other than schizophrenia.

Genetic factors play some role in etiology, but a recent study of twins in Norway found that the heritabilities of personality disorders were modest and ranged from 20 to 41%. The lowest heritability estimate was found for schizotypal personality disorder and the largest heritability estimate was found for anti-social personality disorder (Kendler et al., 2008). This study found no evidence that there were unique genetic factors distinguishing cluster A, B, and C disorders.

Overall, family studies provide at least some evidence that personality disorders of the odd/eccentric cluster are related to schizophrenia. People with schizotypal personality disorder have deficits in cognitive and neuropsychological functioning (Cadenhead et al., 1999; Chen et al., 1998) that are similar to those seen in schizophrenia. Also in keeping with schizophrenia research, schizotypal personality disorder is associated with enlarged ventricles and less temporal-lobe grey matter (Dickey et al., 1999).

Finally, given the comorbidity associated with schizotypal personality disorder, it is important to establish whether predictors are linked uniquely with the disorder. Berenbaum et al. (2008) showed that schizotypal personality disorder was linked with a history of post-traumatic stress disorder and childhood maltreatment even after controlling for the links that these factors also had with anti-social and borderline personality disorder symptoms.

DRAMATIC/ERRATIC CLUSTER

The diagnoses in the dramatic/erratic cluster—borderline, histrionic, narcissistic, and anti-social personality disorders—include clients with a wide variety of symptoms, ranging from variable behaviour to inflated self-esteem, exaggerated emotional displays, and anti-social behaviour.

BORDERLINE PERSONALITY DISORDER

Borderline personality disorder (BPD) was adopted as an official *DSM* diagnosis in 1980. The core features of this disorder are impulsivity and instability in relationships, mood, and self-image (Blais, Hilsenroth, & Castlebury, 1997; Links, Heslegrave, & van Reekum, 1999). For example, attitudes and feelings toward other people may vary considerably and inexplicably over short periods of time. Emotions are erratic and can shift abruptly, particularly from passionate idealization to contemptuous anger. BPD sufferers are argumentative, irritable, sarcastic, quick to take offence, and very hard to live with. Recent longitudinal data suggest that there is also considerable instability in the personality traits of people with BPD assessed over a six-year period (Hopwood et al., 2009).

The unpredictable and impulsive behaviour of people with BPD may include gambling, spending, indiscriminate sexual activity, and eating sprees, and is thus potentially self-damaging. This impulsivity is not specific to borderline personalities; researchers in Montreal have argued that impulsivity is one trait that underscores all four disorders in the dramatic and erratic cluster (Looper & Paris, 2000).

Individuals with BPD have not developed a clear and coherent sense of self and remain uncertain about their values, loyalties, and career choices. They cannot bear to be alone, have fears of abandonment, and demand attention. Subject to chronic feelings of depression and emptiness, they often attempt suicide and engage in self-mutilating behaviour, such as slicing into their legs with a razor blade. Research in Canada and elsewhere indicates that 1 in 10 people with BPD commit suicide (Paris, 2002). According to Montreal psychiatrist Joel Paris, in contrast to typical patterns, most BPD sufferers who kill themselves are female rather than male and most suicides occur after multiple attempts rather than on the first attempt. Recent follow-up data suggest that those who die by suicide are higher in impulsivity and violent-aggressive features linked with cluster B disorders (McGirr, Paris, Lesage, Renaud, & Turecki, 2007).

Clinicians and researchers have used the term *borderline personality* for some time but have given it many meanings. Originally, the term implied that the person was on the borderline between neurosis and schizophrenia. The *DSM* concept of borderline personality no longer has this connotation. The current conceptualization derives from two main sources. First, Gunderson, Kolb, and Austin (1981) proposed a set of specific diagnostic criteria similar to those that ultimately appeared in *DSM-III*. The second source of the diagnostic criteria was a study of the relatives of those people with schizophrenia done by Spitzer et al. (1979). As discussed earlier, some of these relatives had schizotypal personality disorder, but Spitzer and colleagues also identified another syndrome in the relatives, the characteristics of which came to identify BPD.

BPD typically begins in early adulthood, has a prevalence of 1 to 2%, and is more common in women than in men (Swartz et al., 1990). BPD sufferers are likely to have an Axis I mood disorder (Zanarini et al., 1998), and their parents are more likely than average to have mood disorders and other forms of psychopathology (Shachnow et al., 1997; Trull, 2001). Comorbidity is found with substance abuse, post-traumatic stress disorder, eating disorders, and personality disorders from the odd/eccentric cluster (Skodol, Oldham, & Gallaher, 1999; Zanarini et al., 1998a).

For many years, it has been assumed that the prognosis of BPD is not favourable, but Paris (2009) reviewed recent evidence and concluded that most clients with BPD recover over time. The results of a 27-year investigation conducted in Montreal found that gradual improvement over time occurred for most clients, such that only 7.8% met criteria for BPD 27 years later (Paris & Zweig-Frank, 2001; Zweig-Frank & Paris, 2002). Still, the mortality rate of the sample as a whole was substantially elevated, relative to Canadian norms, as many BPD patients had premature deaths. The McLean Study of Adult Development by Zanarini et al. (2005a) is a longitudinal study that also indicates a more positive long-term prognosis, with remission rates of BPD (74%) much higher than believed possible. However, other data indicate that the psychosocial functioning of BPD patients is still poor and improves only slightly over time (Zanarini et al., 2005b). Even when treatment gains are realized, the overall level of functioning still remains relatively poor (see Davidson et al., 2006).

Susanna Kaysen, the person portrayed by Winona Ryder in the movie *Girl Interrupted*, was diagnosed with BPD. Her autobiography is an insightful account of what it means to have BPD. CP Image /STREVT.

Borderline features are combined with anti-social tendencies in some individuals. The role of borderline personality characteristics in spouse abuse is outlined in Canadian Perspectives 13.1.

ETIOLOGY OF BORDERLINE PERSONALITY DISORDER

There are several views concerning the causes of BPD. Here, we discuss object-relations theory, biological research, and Linehan's diathesis-stress theory. While there are several possibilities, Paris (2009) has observed that treatment is challenging and usually not based on theory because the etiology of BPD is still largely unknown. Perhaps there are multiple routes to the experience of BPD.

CANADIAN PERSPECTIVES 13.1
BORDERLINE PERSONALITY AND SPOUSE ABUSE

Don Dutton from the University of British Columbia is an expert on the origins of spouse battering and the abusive personality (see Dutton, 2007, 2008). The presence of a personality dominated by borderline characteristics is an important aspect of his theory of batterers (Dutton, 1995, 1999). His analysis of etiological factors has focused on three central characteristics of the abusive personality: borderline personality characteristics, anger, and the chronic experience of traumatic symptoms. In addition, Dutton (1995, 1999) has suggested that batterers are characterized by an anxious and angry attachment style instead of the secure attachment style that is linked with interpersonal and personal adjustment.

Dutton and his colleagues (e.g., Dutton & Starzomski, 1993) have confirmed the importance of these characteristics. Dutton suggests that the BPD characteristics of abusive men are responsible for many of the interpersonal problems in abusive relationships. Dutton (1995) noted:

Borderlines blame their partners when things go wrong in intimate relationships. And things are always going wrong,

because they set impossibly high standards and double-binds for others. As their tension mounts, their need for perfect control in an imperfect world generates inevitable failure. People are fallible. One man would inspect the house after his wife did the chores, running his finger under the refrigerator, looking for dust. Eventually, he found some. Then a two-hour harangue would ensue in which he screamed at her about her lousy housekeeping. This personality profile creates an environment in which relationship conflict and abuse are inevitable. (p. 146)

Several studies attest to the link between spouse abuse and borderline personality characteristics, but recent longitudinal research suggests that personality disorder in general plays a role. That is, a 20-year study found that cluster A and cluster B features in adolescence predicted subsequent partner violence. Cluster A features that were most implicated included fearfulness and suspiciousness, while cluster B features involved were the anti-social tendencies and the dramatic features implicated in

BPD (Ehrensaft, Cohen, & Johnson, 2006). In contrast, the avoidance inherent in cluster C disorders predicted less likelihood of subsequent partner abuse.

BPD characteristics also appear to undermine attempts at treatment. Dutton et al. (1997) found that men with certain personality disorders (i.e., borderline, anti-social, and avoidant) have higher levels of post-treatment recidivism in terms of subsequent spouse abuse.

In summary, it has been suggested by some that anyone has the potential to be aggressive and abusive in certain situations. However, Dutton's work shows that men who characteristically engage in abuse are not simply responding to situational factors; instead, they have a personality style with many borderline features.

Thinking Critically

1. Tweed and Dutton (1998) identified two seemingly distinct types of batterers: those who were generally violent and those with borderline, dysphoric features. Do you think this is a valid distinction? If so, what different developmental histories might characterize these types?

2. Therapists often report that the treatment process with BPD clients is challenging because of their interpersonal styles, including the tendency to experience and express their feelings of anger and rage. Which treatment or treatments would you employ if you were the therapist given the task of treating someone with this disorder? What additional steps would you take for the borderline individual who also has a history of spouse abuse? Consider these issues when you read the section on therapies for BPD.

Object-Relations Theory Object-relations theory, an important variant of psychoanalytic theory, is concerned with the way children incorporate (or introject) the values and images of important people, such as their parents. In other words, the focus is on the manner in which children identify with people to whom they have strong emotional attachments. These introjected people (object representations) become part of the person's ego, but they can come into conflict with the wishes, goals, and ideals of the developing adult. For example, a college-age woman who has adopted her mother's notion of the proper role of a woman in society may find herself drawn to more modern ideals of feminism.

Object-relations theorists hypothesize that people react to their world through the perspectives of people from their past, primarily their parents or other primary caregivers. As noted, sometimes these perspectives conflict with the person's own wishes. Two leading object-relations theorists are Otto Kernberg and Heinz Kohut (Kohut's views on narcissism will be discussed later).

Kernberg (1985) proposed that adverse childhood experiences—for example, having parents who provide love and attention inconsistently, perhaps praising achievements but being unable to offer emotional support and warmth—cause children to develop insecure egos.

Although people with BPD have weak egos and need constant reassuring, they retain the capacity to test reality. As a result, they are in touch with reality but frequently engage in a defence mechanism called splitting: dichotomizing objects into all good or all bad and failing to integrate positive and negative aspects of another person or the self into a whole. This tendency causes extreme difficulty in regulating emotions because the person with BPD sees the world, including himself or herself, in black-and-white terms. Somehow this defence protects the patient's weak ego from intolerable anxiety.

A number of studies have yielded data relevant to Kernberg's theory. As expected, people with BPD report a low level of care by their mothers (Patrick et al., 1994). They view their families as emotionally inexpressive, low in cohesion, and high in conflict. Research conducted in Toronto by Links and van Reekum (1993) indicates that they also frequently report childhood sexual and physical abuse. Also, many of those with BPD have experienced separation from parents during childhood (Paris, Zweig, & Guzder, 1994).

Biological Factors BPD runs in families, suggesting that it has a genetic component (Baron et al., 1985). BPD is also linked with neuroticism, a heritable trait (Nigg & Goldsmith, 1994).

Some data suggest poor functioning of the frontal lobes, which may play a role in impulsive behaviour. BPD clients perform poorly on neurological tests of frontal-lobe functioning and show low glucose metabolism in the frontal lobes (Goyer et al., 1994; van Reekum et al., 1993).

Consistent with the idea that low levels of the neurotransmitter serotonin are associated with impulsivity, when borderline patients were administered a drug to increase serotonin levels, their level of anger decreased (Hollander et al., 1993). Thus, biological research on BPD patients has yielded some promising leads concerning their impulsive behaviour.

Linehan's Diathesis-Stress Theory Marsha Linehan proposes that BPD develops when people with a biological diathesis (possibly genetic) for having difficulty controlling their emotions are raised in a family environment that is invalidating. A diathesis for what Linehan calls emotional dysregulation can interact with experiences that invalidate the developing child, leading to the development of borderline personality.

An invalidating environment is one in which the person's wants and feelings are discounted and disrespected, and efforts to communicate one's feelings are disregarded or even punished. An extreme form of invalidation is child abuse, sexual and nonsexual: "Daddy says he loves me and yet he is hurting me and threatening even more if I tell." A recent humorous example of our own illustrates invalidation between a husband and a wife.

Wife. Honey, could you help me with something for a minute?
Husband. Sure, but I have to go to the bathroom first.
Wife. No, you don't.

The two main hypothesized factors—dysregulation and invalidation—interact with each other in a dynamic fashion (see Figure 13.1). For example, the emotionally dysregulated child makes enormous demands on his or her family. The exasperated parents ignore or even punish the child's outbursts. This response can lead to the child suppressing emotions, only to have them build up to an explosion, which then gets parental attention. Parents can end up reinforcing the very behaviours they find aversive. Other patterns are possible, but they share a constant back-and-forth, a vicious circle, between the diathesis for dysregulation and the stress of invalidation.

A key piece of evidence supporting Linehan's theory concerns childhood physical and sexual abuse. As noted above, abuse is more frequent among people with BPD than among people diagnosed with most other disorders (Herman et al., 1989; Wagner, Linehan, & Wasson, 1989). One exception to this general pattern is dissociative identity disorder, which is also linked with very high rates of childhood abuse. Given the high rates of dissociative symptoms in borderline personality, the two disorders may be related and dissociation in both disorders may reflect the extreme stress of child abuse. Indeed, a study by Ross et al. (1998) found that the link between child abuse and borderline symptoms was mediated by dissociative tendencies.

As Linehan herself has cautioned, most aspects of her theory of etiology remain to be investigated. For example, self-reports of people with BPD that they suffered invalidating experiences as children are subject to the same kinds of questions as any retrospective self-report from a patient in therapy. Considering how sensitive such individuals are to invalidating experiences as adults, it is conceivable that their recollections of invalidating childhood experiences are coloured by their current psychological turmoil.

FIGURE 13.1 Linehan's diathesis-stress theory of borderline personality disorder

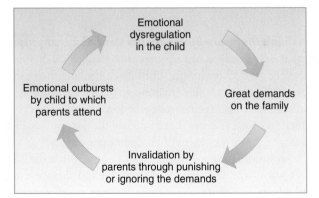

HISTRIONIC PERSONALITY DISORDER

THE SEMISUICIDAL SOPHOMORE Suzanne called the university counselling centre just after midnight. She spoke softly into the answering machine and seemed to be fighting back tears. "Uh, I feel really shitty and I'm mad at everyone I know and I need to talk with someone who cares or I'm going to kill myself right now and I'm not kidding either!" Although she left her phone number at her dorm room, attempts to reach her by the on-call therapist were unsuccessful. According to her roommate, Suzanne was out "making the rounds." After a second call the next morning, she agreed to come in for evaluation.

Suzanne arrived 30 minutes late, chewing bubble gum and dressed scantily in a shocking black outfit. When her male interviewer paused immediately upon seeing her, she stated simply, "It symbolizes the way I'm feeling right now. Do you like it?" A turban covered her hair, and dark stones adorned her fingers, ears, and neck. The whole getup seemed chosen for its obvious shock value. An assessment of suicidal potential was the first objective, but Suzanne denied that she was really serious. "If I was serious," she quipped dramatically, "I wouldn't be here, now would I?" "It's a good way of getting attention … I don't like to be ignored … always works on the parents. You'd be surprised what you can get if you try hard enough." At that moment, she blew a big bubble, and then suddenly sucked the air out of it, all without losing eye contact with the interviewer.

Suzanne reports problems in many areas of life. First, she is doing poorly in school and fears she may be thrown out if her grades do not improve. She is already on academic probation. When asked about her attendance, she admits that she rarely makes it to classes, because most of them are in the morning, and her social activities get started after midnight. However, "a lot of the guys in class have volunteered to take notes for me." Second, Suzanne and her roommates have had problems getting along since the beginning of the semester. They object to her "borrowing" their things, her late nights, and her frequent male visitors, who often stay overnight in various states of intoxication. Finally, her boyfriend, whom she regards as extremely and unreasonably jealous, wants to break up, objecting to her flirtatious behaviour, even though she swears she has been completely faithful to him over the month they have been together. Suzanne states that she is overwhelmed that "the closest person in the world to me would turn on me all of a sudden like that." And that, she notes, is what prompted her call to the counselling centre.

Although Suzanne speaks of her great distress and depression, her demeanour belies her words. She is animated and demonstrative, perhaps even slightly manic. She flits from topic to topic and from emotion to emotion with only minimal insight and no real transition in between. No follow-up appointment could be made, because Suzanne is "too busy." She denies continued feelings of suicidality. When asked if she wants to continue next week, she remarks teasingly "I'll get back to you," blowing another bubble and then pressing the gum under her seat on the way out (from Millon & Davis, 2000, p. 256).

The case described above is an example of histrionic personality disorder (HPD). The diagnosis of **histrionic personality** formerly called hysterical personality, is applied to people who are overly dramatic and attention-seeking. They often use features of their physical appearance, such as unusual clothes, makeup, or hair colour, to draw attention to themselves. These individuals, although displaying emotion extravagantly, are thought to be emotionally shallow. They are self-centred, overly concerned with their attractiveness, and uncomfortable when not the centre of attention. They can be inappropriately sexually provocative and seductive and are easily influenced by others. Their speech is often impressionistic and lacking in detail. For example, they may state a strong opinion yet be unable to give any supporting information.

This diagnosis has a prevalence of 2 to 3% and is more common among women than among men (Corbitt & Widiger, 1995). The prevalence of HPD is higher among separated and divorced people, and it is associated with high rates of depression and poor physical health (Nestadt et al., 1990). Comorbidity with BPD is high.

ETIOLOGY OF HISTRIONIC PERSONALITY DISORDER

Unfortunately, little research has been conducted on HPD. Psychoanalytic theory predominates and proposes that emotionality and seductiveness were encouraged by parental seductiveness, especially father to daughter. People with HPD are thought to have been raised in a family environment in which parents talked about sex as something dirty but behaved as though it was exciting and desirable. This upbringing may explain the preoccupation with sex, coupled with a fear of actually behaving sexually. The exaggerated displays of emotion on the part of histrionic persons are seen as symptoms of such underlying conflicts, and their need to be the centre of attention is seen as a defence mechanism, a way to protect themselves from their true feelings of low self-esteem (Apt & Hurlbert, 1994; Stone, 1993).

NARCISSISTIC PERSONALITY DISORDER

THE LONG-SUFFERING EINSTEIN Malcolm stormed out of his supervisor's office, furious that he was on the edge of being terminated. He stubbornly resisted the demand that he seek counseling, asserting that the problem was the company, not him.

The immediate issue was his strained relationship with his supervisor and the subordinates in his office. Although his credentials were excellent, Malcolm had ways of inventing new procedures that impacted standard routines without much sympathy for those affected. Everyone was automatically expected to follow his whim. Sometimes his novel notions worked out, and sometimes they didn't. Regardless, the staff resented these impositions on their time and their job descriptions. When things did work out for the better, Malcolm gave only lip service to the role of his coworkers.

Worse, Malcolm never gave up any of his ideas. He was sure they were superior to the "old ways" and would work if the staff could just "get their head out their ass long enough to see the big picture and just adjust for the better." "I do not know why the magnitude of my innovations isn't obvious to everyone," he had been heard to state. When asked how he saw himself in five years, Malcolm remarked, "I'm a firm believer in the power of positive thinking. For the most part, it's old ways that hold us down. Wherever I've gone I've found new ways, new efficiencies, some of them startling. I can only imagine that in time I will be fantastically successful. It is my destiny."

In fact, Malcolm had been pushed out at other companies for making life difficult, just as he is creating problems now. Others, he asserted loudly, "either do not recognize my ability, or else are envious when they do." The problems with the office staff he attributed to jealousy. "They want to get me fired so I don't make them all look bad. In fact, I think some of them might be deliberately sabotaging me." The same was supposedly true of his supervisor.

Malcolm also spoke about the "cretins" he was forced to work with, and how their incompetence constantly delayed him from finishing his own projects and implementing his latest ideas. Having been forced to associate with inferiors all his life, he was glad that a psychiatrist was treating him, because a medical doctor would have a better chance of understanding him and sympathizing with his plight. Asked to name people with whom he felt a bond, he mentioned Einstein and Salk, individuals who "had suffered nobly for being ahead of their time, just like me" (from Millon & Davis, 2000, p. 272).

Narcissistic personality disorder draws its name from Narcissus of Greek mythology. He fell in love with his own reflection, was consumed by his own desire, and was then transformed into a flower. Culver Pictures Inc.

People with a **narcissistic personality** disorder (NPD) such as Malcolm have a grandiose view of their own uniqueness and abilities. They are preoccupied with fantasies of great success. To say that they are self-centred is an understatement. They require almost constant attention and excessive admiration and believe that only high-status people can understand them. Their interpersonal relationships are disturbed by their lack of empathy, feelings of envy, arrogance, and their tendency to take advantage of others. Relationships are also problematic because of their feelings of entitlement—they expect others to do special, not-to-be-reciprocated favours for them. Most of these characteristics, with the exception of lack of empathy and extreme reactions to criticism, have been validated in empirical studies as aspects of NPD (Ronningstam & Gunderson, 1990). The prevalence of NPD is less than 1%. It most often co-occurs with BPD (Morey, 1988).

ETIOLOGY OF NARCISSISTIC PERSONALITY DISORDER

The diagnosis of NPD is rooted in modern psychoanalytic writings. Many psychoanalytically oriented clinicians have regarded it as a product of our times and our system of values. On the surface, the person with NPD has a remarkable sense of self-importance, complete self-absorption, and fantasies of limitless success, but it is theorized that these characteristics mask a very fragile self-esteem.

Constantly seeking attention and adulation, narcissistic personalities are very sensitive to criticism and deeply fearful of failure. Sometimes they seek out others whom they can idealize because they are disappointed in themselves, but others are not allowed to become genuinely close. Their relationships are few and shallow. People with NPD become angry with others and reject them when they fall short of their unrealistic expectations. Their inner lives are impoverished because, despite their self-aggrandizement, they actually think very little of themselves.

At the centre of contemporary interest in narcissism is Heinz Kohut, whose two books, *The Analysis of the Self* (1971) and *The Restoration of the Self* (1977), have established a variant of psychoanalysis known as *self-psychology*. According to Kohut, the self emerges early in life as a bipolar structure with an immature grandiosity at one pole and a dependent overidealization of other people at the other. A failure to develop healthy self-esteem occurs when parents do not respond with approval to their children's displays of competency. The child is not valued for his or her own self-worth but rather as a means to foster the parents' self-esteem.

Kohut suggests that when parents respond to a child with respect, warmth, and empathy, the child is endowed with healthy self-esteem. But when parents further their own needs rather than directly approve of their children, the result may be a narcissistic personality.

A little girl comes home from school, eager to tell her mother about some great successes. But this mother, instead of listening with pride, deflects the conversation from the child to herself [and] begins to talk about her own successes which overshadow those of her little daughter. (Kohut & Wolf, 1978, p. 418)

Children neglected in this way do not develop an internalized, healthy self-esteem and have trouble accepting their own shortcomings. They develop into narcissistic personalities, striving to bolster their sense of self through unending quests for love and approval from others.

ANTI-SOCIAL PERSONALITY DISORDER AND PSYCHOPATHY

In current usage, the terms "anti-social personality disorder" and "psychopathy" (sometimes referred to as "sociopathy") are often used interchangeably, although there are important differences between the two. Anti-social behaviour is an important component of both terms.

CHARACTERISTICS OF ANTI-SOCIAL PERSONALITY DISORDER The *DSM-IV-TR* concept of **anti-social personality** disorder (APD) involves two major components:

1. A conduct disorder (described in Chapter 15) is present before the age of 15. Truancy, running away from home, frequent lying, theft, arson, and deliberate destruction of property are major symptoms of conduct disorder. Upwards of 60% of children with conduct disorder later develop APD (Myers, Stewart, & Brown, 1998).
2. This pattern of anti-social behaviour continues in adulthood.

Thus, the *DSM* diagnosis involves not only certain patterns of anti-social behaviour but patterns that began in childhood. Adults with anti-social personality disorder show irresponsible and anti-social behaviour by working only inconsistently, breaking laws, being irritable and physically aggressive, defaulting on debts, and being reckless. They are impulsive and fail to plan ahead, and, although completely aware of lies and misdeeds, may neither show regard for truth nor experience remorse for their misdeeds.

It is estimated that about 3% of adult men and 1% of women in the United States have anti-social personalities (Robins et al., 1984). Similarly, a community study conducted in Edmonton found that about 3% of people met *DSM* criteria for APD (Swanson, Bland, & Newman, 1994). Rates are much higher among younger than among older adults and among people of low socio-economic status. APD is comorbid with a number of other diagnoses, most notably substance abuse. Swanson et al. (1994) found that more than 90% of those with APD had at least one other lifetime psychiatric diagnosis.

There appears to be significant heterogeneity among people with anti-social personalities. Burt (2009) confirmed differences between aggressive and non-aggressive rule-breaking forms of anti-social personality, with environmental factors playing a larger role in the non-aggressive form.

CHARACTERISTICS OF PSYCHOPATHY Consider the following case history of a psychopathy recounted by Robert Hare (1970), a UBC professor who is regarded as the world's leading expert on psychopathy:

> Donald S., 30 years old, has just completed a three-year prison term for fraud, bigamy, false pretenses, and escaping lawful custody. The circumstances leading up to these offenses are interesting and consistent with his past behavior. With less than a month to serve on an earlier 18-month term for fraud, he faked illness and escaped from the prison hospital. During the ten months of freedom that followed he engaged in a variety of illegal enterprises; the activity that resulted in his recapture was typical of his method of operation. By passing himself off as the "field executive" of an international philanthropic foundation, he was able to enlist the aid of several religious organizations in a fund-raising campaign. The campaign moved slowly at first, and in an attempt to speed things up, he arranged an interview with a local TV station. His performance during the interview was so impressive that funds started to pour in. However, unfortunately for Donald, the interview was also carried on a national news network. He was recognized and quickly arrested. During the ensuing trial it became evident that he experienced no sense of wrongdoing for his activities. He maintained, for example, that his passionate plea for funds "primed the pump" – that is, induced people to give to other charities as well as to the one he proposed to represent. At the same time, he stated that most donations to charity are made by those who feel guilty about something and deserve to be bilked. The ability to rationalize his behavior and his lack of self-criticism were also evident in his attempts to solicit aid from the very people he misled. Perhaps it is a tribute to his persuasiveness that a number of individuals actually did come to his support. During his three-year prison term, Donald spent much time searching for legal loopholes and writing to outside authorities, including local lawyers, the Prime Minister of Canada, and a Canadian representative to the United Nations. In each case he verbally attacked them for representing the authority and the injustice responsible for his predicament. At the same time he requested them to intercede on his behalf and in the name of the justice they professed to represent.
>
> While in prison he was used as a subject in some of the author's research. On his release he applied for admission to university and, by way of reference, told the registrar that he had been one of the author's research colleagues! Several months later the author received a letter from him requesting a letter of recommendation on behalf of Donald's application for a job" (Hare, 1970, pp. 1–2, *Psychopathy: Theory and Research* by Robert Hare, © 1970).

The story of Donald demonstrates the true psychopathic's profound tendency to lie compulsively and act without any concern or regard for social conventions or the well-being of other people. As a result, legal problems are quite common.

The concept of **psychopathy** is linked closely to the writings of Hervey Cleckley and his classic book *The Mask of Sanity* (1976). On the basis of his clinical experience, Cleckley formulated a set of criteria for recognizing the disorder. Unlike the *DSM* criteria for anti-social personality disorder, Cleckley's criteria for psychopathy refer less to anti-social behaviour per se than to the psychopathic individual's thoughts and feelings. One of the key characteristics of psychopathy is poverty of emotions, both positive and negative. Psychopathic people have no sense of shame, and even their seemingly positive feelings for others are merely an act. The psychopath is superficially charming and manipulates others for personal gain. They exploit others even if it involves the use of violence and aggression (see Porter & Woodworth, 2006). Their lack of anxiety may make it impossible for psychopaths to learn from their mistakes, and their lack of positive emotions leads them to behave irresponsibly and often cruelly toward others. Another key point in Cleckley's description is that the anti-social behaviour of the psychopath is performed impulsively, as much for thrills as for something like financial gain.

Most researchers diagnose psychopathy using a checklist (the Psychopathy Checklist-Revised or PCL-R) developed by Robert Hare and his associates (Hare et al., 1990). An extensive description of this measure and related research is provided in Canadian Contributions 13.1.

Robert Hare is regarded as the world's leading expert on psychopathy. Photo by Stuart McCall.

CONTROVERSIES WITH DIAGNOSES OF APD AND PSYCHOPATHY We have seen that these two diagnoses—APD and psychopathy—are related, but they are by no means identical. One study found that only about 20% of people with APD scored high on the Hare PCL-R (Rutherford, Cacciola, & Alterman, 1999). Harpur and Hare (1994) observed that almost all psychopaths are diagnosed with APD but many people diagnosed with APD do not meet the criteria for psychopathy on the PCL-R. The question of which diagnosis is preferable has raised several issues.

Hare, Hart, and Harpur (1991) criticized the *DSM* diagnosis of APD because it requires accurate reports of events from many years earlier by people who are habitual liars (recall the onset-in-childhood criterion), and many researchers believe that a *DSM* diagnostic concept should not be synonymous with criminality. Nevertheless, 75 to 80% of convicted felons meet the criteria for APD, while only 15 to 25% of convicted felons meet the criteria for psychopathy (Hart & Hare, 1989). Moreover, lack of remorse, a hallmark of psychopathy, is but one of seven criteria for the *DSM*'s anti-social personality diagnosis, and only three of these criteria need to be present to make the diagnosis. Therefore, the person diagnosed with APD by the *DSM* may not have the lack of remorse that is central to psychopathy.

CANADIAN CONTRIBUTIONS 13.1
ROBERT HARE AND THE CONCEPTUALIZATION AND ASSESSMENT OF PSYCHOPATHY

Robert Hare retired recently from the University of British Columbia after conducting decades of influential research on the nature and assessment of psychopathy. Hare's work has received widespread recognition, including an award from the Canadian Psychological Association for distinguished contributions in applied psychology and citations from the director of the Federal Bureau of Investigation (FBI) for exceptional service in the public interest. Hare's most well-known measure is the Psychopathy Checklist-Revised (PCL-R; Hare, 1991). The PCL-R consists of 20 items that are rated on a three-point scale. The 20 items on the checklist assess two major clusters of psychopathic behaviours. Factor 1, referred to as emotional detachment, describes a selfish, remorseless individual with inflated self-esteem who exploits others. This factor focuses on affective and interpersonal characteristics associated with psychopathy. It assesses attributes such as egocentricity, manipulativeness, callousness, and lack of guilt. Factor 2 characterizes an unstable and anti-social lifestyle marked by impulsivity and irresponsibility. Unfortunately, the Hare checklist does not include items to assess an absence of anxiety, a key feature of psychopathy according to Cleckley (Schmitt & Newman, 1999). Note that some investigators (e.g., Patrick et al., 2005) have split Factor 1 into an affective factor (i.e., lack of remorse) and an interpersonal factor (i.e., glibness/superficial charm), and it has been suggested that the PCL-R actually consists of three factors.

Although these two factors are highly correlated with each other and extreme psychopaths tend to receive substantially elevated scores on both, extensive research evidence indicates that the factors differ in their associations with other personality, behavioural, and demographic factors. Harpur and Hare (1994) examined whether there are age-related changes in scores on the PCL-R factors in 889 male prisoners. Factor 1 scores remained stable across the age span, but scores on Factor 2 decreased with age, suggesting that psychopaths may become less impulsive and lower in sensation-seeking with age.

Research conducted with the Hare PCL-R shows that psychopathy occurs more among men than among women (Nicholls et al., 2005). Overall, among prison inmates, 15.7% of men and 7.4% of women exceeded the PCL-R cut-off for psychopathy. However, in women, there is still a moderate significant association between psychopathy and aggression and violence. Recent Canadian data based on the use of the PCL-R indicate that psychopaths, relative to non-psychopaths, commit more violent and non-violent offences, as would be expected. More troubling is evidence suggesting that psychopaths, versus non-psychopaths, were 2.5 times more likely when incarcerated to be granted conditional release even though they were more likely to re-offend (Porter, ten Brinke, & Wilson, 2009). The researchers concluded that psychopaths are very good at conning and deceiving prison staff and parole board members.

Other research led by Stephen Porter at Dalhousie University used the PCL-R to study offenders who have committed homicides. They found that criminal homicides committed by psychopathic murderers are cold-blooded, predatory acts that are almost always premeditated and motivated by an external goal (e.g., material gain or revenge), while homicides committed by non-psychopaths are more likely to be impulsive crimes of passion (Porter & Woodworth, 2007; Woodworth & Porter, 2002). Interestingly, psychopaths downplay the instrumentality of their acts when asked to describe their behaviour, in an apparent attempt to minimize their guilt and not seem responsible (Porter & Woodworth, 2007). Other research found that psychopaths are especially likely to exhibit sadistic behaviour in their homicides (Porter, Woodworth, Earle, Drugge, & Boer, 2003).

The PCL-R has proven to be one of the best predictors of recidivism in global research (see Hare, Clark, Grann, & Thornton, 2000). Hemphill, Hare, and Wong (1998) concluded that psychopaths are three times more likely than non-psychopaths to recidivate in general and four times more likely to recidivate by committing acts of violence. Both factors of the PCL-R predicted violent recidivism, while only Factor 2 predicted general recidivism. Overall, the PCL-R is regarded as a key component of risk appraisal in forensic assessment. It also can predict treatment outcome. Ogloff, Wong, and Greenwood (1990) evaluated 80 male federal inmates in a therapeutic community program in British Columbia and found that the psychopaths in their sample showed less clinical improvement and had lower levels of motivation.

The differences between APD and psychopathy were described by Hare (1996) in a discussion of people who kill law enforcement officers. Hare stated that a 1992 FBI report described these killers as having an anti-social personality when, in fact, psychopathy was evident. Hare (1996) noted, "These killers were not simply persistently anti-social individuals who met *DSM-IV* criteria for APD; they were psychopaths—remorseless predators who use charm, intimidation, and, if necessary, impulsive and cold-blooded violence to attain their ends" (p. 39). Unfortunately, in recent years, Canada has had its share of these individuals, including infamous characters such as Clifford Olson, Paul Bernardo, and Karla Homolka, who have killed children and/or young women.

As we review the research in this area, it is important to keep in mind that it has been conducted on individuals diagnosed in different ways—some as anti-social personalities and some as psychopaths—which makes integrating these findings somewhat difficult.

RESEARCH AND THEORY ON THE ETIOLOGY OF ANTI-SOCIAL PERSONALITY DISORDER AND PSYCHOPATHY

We now turn to research and theory on the etiology of APD and psychopathy. We examine genetics, as well as the psychological factors that operate in the family and in emotions. A final section on response modulation and impulsivity ties together several of the individual research domains. Note again, however, that most research has been conducted on psychopathic individuals who have already been convicted as criminals. Thus, the available literature may not allow generalization to the behaviour of psychopaths who elude arrest or who do not engage in criminal activities.

Childhood Roots of Psychopathy Psychopathy, like anti-social personality, is believed to have its roots in childhood and adolescence, but is less likely to be reflected by overt

The character played by Anthony Hopkins in *The Silence of the Lambs, Hannibal,* and *Red Dragon* displayed many of the characteristics of the psychopath, especially total lack of regard for the rights of others. CP Images/STREVT.

anti-social behaviours (see Hare & Neumann, 2009). Extensive research is now examining this possibility. This research has been facilitated by research with the PCL-R. The PCL-R has been used successfully with adolescents. A study of juvenile psychopaths aged 14 to 18 from Quebec used the PCL-R to distinguish psychopaths and non-psychopaths and confirmed that high PCL-R scores are associated with a lack of behavioural inhibition (Roussy & Toupin, 2000). A separate version designed for youth, the Hare Psychopathy Checklist – Youth Version (PCL-YV) has been developed for 12- to 18-year-olds and for children and relies on ratings from informants to make diagnoses (see Forth, 2005; Forth, Kosson, & Hare, 2003). Lynam (1997) used it to show that psychopathic children are similar to psychopathic adults—they are impulsive and severely delinquent. Other Canadian research conducted over a six-month interval shows that levels of psychopathy have high to moderate stability, with the interpersonal and behavioural factors having the greatest stability (Lee, Klaver, Hart, Moretti, & Douglas, 2009). While the PCL-YV is deemed to have adequate reliability and validity, Hare and Neumann (2009) have cautioned that there are concerns about its use in the criminal justice system to the extent that it contributes to a tendency to label a child or adolescent as "a psychopath."

Evidence is accumulating on the nature of psychopathy in children and youth. Collectively, research has shown the following:

1. Genetically influenced psychopathic personality in adolescents is a strong predictor of adult anti-social behaviour (Forsman et al., 2010).

2. Female youth offenders, relative to males with high psychopathy, are more likely to have a history of psychiatric hospitalization if they are high in psychopathy (Cook, Barese, & Dicataldo, 2010).

3. Children with psychopathic traits have abnormal prefrontal cortex responsiveness (Finger et al., 2008).

4. Canadian youth with pre-existing elevated levels of psychopathy are more likely to join youth gangs if they come from a neighbourhood of residential instability in terms of high neighbourhood turnover rates (Dupere et al., 2007).

The Role of the Family Since much psychopathic behaviour violates social norms, many investigators have focused on the primary agent of socialization, the family, in their search for the explanation for such behaviour. McCord and McCord (1964) concluded, on the basis of a literature review, that lack of affection and severe parental rejection were the primary causes of psychopathic behaviour. Other studies have related psychopathic behaviour to parents' physical abuse, inconsistencies in disciplining their children, and failure to teach them responsibility toward others (see Johnson et al., 1999). Furthermore, the fathers of psychopaths are likely to be anti-social in their behaviour.

Self-reported data on early rearing must be interpreted cautiously, as they were gathered by means of retrospective reports—individual recollections of past events. Information obtained in this way cannot be accepted uncritically. When people are asked to recollect early events in the life of someone now known to be psychopathic, their knowledge of the person's adult status may well affect what they remember or report about these early events. They may be more likely to recall deviant incidents and overlook more normal events. It is also risky to trust the retrospective reports of psychopaths because lying is a key feature of this disorder.

> If one wishes to choose the most likely candidate for a later diagnosis of [psychopathy] from among children appearing in a child guidance clinic, the best choice appears to be a boy referred for theft or aggression who has shown a diversity of anti-social behaviour in many episodes, at least one of which could be grounds for Juvenile Court appearance, and whose anti-social behaviour involves him with strangers and organizations as well as with teachers and parents. … More than half of the boys appearing at the clinic [with these characteristics were later] diagnosed sociopathic personality. Such boys had a history of truancy, theft, staying out late, and refusing to obey parents. They lied gratuitously, and showed little guilt over their behaviour. They were generally irresponsible about being where they were supposed to be or taking care of money. (Robins, 1966, p. 157)

In addition to these characteristics, several aspects of family life were found to be consequential. Both inconsistent discipline and no discipline at all predicted psychopathic behaviour in adulthood, as did anti-social behaviour of the father.

Two important limitations to this research should be noted: (1) the harsh or inconsistent disciplinary practices of parents could be reactions to trying to raise a child who is displaying anti-social behaviour; and (2) many individuals who come from disturbed social backgrounds do not become psychopaths. This second point is important. Adults may have no problems whatsoever despite a problematic upbringing. Thus, although family experience is probably a significant factor in the development of psychopathic behaviour, it is not the sole factor. A diathesis also is required.

Genetic Correlates of APD Research suggests that both criminality and anti-social personality disorder have heritable components. Adoption and twin studies, including those of twins reared apart, indicate that genetic factors play a significant role in the likelihood that a person will commit a criminal act (Gottesman & Goldsmith, 1994; Grove et al., 1990). For APD, twin studies show higher concordance for MZ than DZ pairs (Lyons et al., 1995). Moreover, adoption studies reveal higher than normal prevalence of anti-social behaviour in adopted children of biological parents with APD and substance abuse (Cadoret et al., 1995b; Ge et al., 1996).

Both twin and adoption studies also show that the environment plays a substantial role in anti-social personality

disorder. In the Cadoret adoption study referred to in the previous paragraph, an adverse environment in the adoptive home (such as marital problems and substance abuse) was related to the development of anti-social personality disorder whether or not the adoptive parents had anti-social personality disorder. Furthermore, high levels of conflict and negativity and low levels of parental warmth predicted anti-social behaviour in a twin study by Reiss et al. (1995).

Adoption research has also shown that some characteristics of adoptive families that are related to anti-social behaviour in their children appear to be reactions to a "difficult" child (Ge et al., 1996); that is, the child's genetically influenced anti-social behaviour leads to environmental changes involving harsh discipline, which, in turn, exacerbate the child's anti-social tendencies.

As noted earlier, Canadian researchers have been instrumental in extending research on the role of genetic factors in personality disorders such as APD (see Jang, Vernon, & Livesley, 2001; Livesley et al., 1998). They have used twin studies to show that a large genetic component accounts for much of the variability in individual differences in the personality dimension known as "dissocial behaviour" (i.e., anti-social behaviour). Twin studies have provided extensive evidence for the importance of genetic factors, but little progress has been made in identifying the specific genes involved in the etiology of specific personality disorders (see Jang et al., 2001).

Finally, most genetic research has focused on anti-social personality disorder and has not focused specifically on psychopathy. However, evidence is growing to support a strong role for genetic factors. Taylor et al. (2003) found that variance in dimensions of psychopathy was attributable to genetic factors and not shared environmental factors. A strong role for genetic factors was confirmed in another study, which also found that genetic factors were implicated in impulsivity and callousness toward others but did not contribute to tendencies to manipulate others (Larsson, Andershed, & Lichtenstein, 2006).

Emotion and Psychopathy In defining the psychopathic syndrome, Cleckley pointed out the inability of such persons to profit from experience or even from punishment; they seem to be unable to avoid the negative consequences of social misbehaviour. Many are chronic lawbreakers despite their experiences with jail sentences. They seem immune to the anxiety or pangs of conscience that help keep most of us from breaking the law or lying to or injuring others, and they have difficulty curbing their impulses. In learning-theory terms, psychopaths have not been well socialized because they were unresponsive to punishments for their anti-social behaviour. Thus, they do not experience conditioned fear responses when they encounter situations in which the conditioned fear response should inhibit anti-social behaviour.

In a classic study based on Cleckley's clinical observations, Lykken (1957) tested the idea that psychopaths may have few inhibitions about committing anti-social acts because they

Psychopathic serial killer Clifford Olson murdered 11 children in British Columbia. In 1982, he was sentenced to life in prison without eligibility for parole for 25 years. In 1997, he asked to have his parole eligibility reconsidered under the "faint hope" clause. The jury at his hearing rejected his application. How does he compare himself with the cannibalistic killer of *Silence of the Lambs*? "Hannibal Lecter is fiction—I'm real" (Worthington, 1997, p. 15). Robert Pickton, from Port Coquitlam, B.C., may have surpassed Olson's acts. He was accused of 26 counts of first-degree murder. Many of the victims were prostitutes who had disappeared from the Vancouver area. In 2007, he was convicted in six of the murders, which he has appealed. CP Image Archive/Bryan Schlosser.

experience so little anxiety. He performed several tests to determine whether psychopaths do indeed have low anxiety. One of the most important tests involved avoidance learning, which is assumed to be mediated by anxiety. Lykken studied the ability of psychopaths and control-group participants to avoid shock. He found that the psychopaths were poorer than the controls at avoiding the shocks, which supported the idea that psychopaths are low in anxiety.

Studies of the autonomic nervous system also indicate that psychopaths respond less anxiously to fear-eliciting stimuli. Psychopaths have lower than normal levels of skin conductance in resting situations, and their skin conductance is less reactive when they are confronted with intense or aversive stimuli or when they anticipate an aversive stimulus (Harpur & Hare, 1990). However, a different picture emerges when heart rate is examined. The heart rate of psychopaths is normal under resting conditions and remains normal when neutral stimuli are presented, but in situations in which they anticipate a stressful stimulus, their hearts beat faster than those of normal people anticipating stress.

These physiological reactions indicate that psychopaths cannot be regarded as simply under-aroused, since their heart rates are higher than normal in anticipation of a stressor. Basing his theorizing in part on Lacey's work (1967), Hare (1978) focused on the pattern of psychophysiological responses of psychopaths. Faster heartbeats are viewed as an indication that a person is tuning out or reducing sensory input. Thus, the increased heart rate of psychopaths who are anticipating an aversive stimulus indicates that they are tuning out the stimulus. Their skin conductance is then less reactive to an aversive stimulus because they are effective in ignoring it. Indeed, recent experimental data have confirmed that an attentional mechanism does seem to account for the reduced fear response. That is, the apparent lack of fear reflects diminished attention to threat-relevant stimuli (Dvorak-Bertscha, Curtin, Rubinstein, & Newman, 2009).

In general, while aggression tendencies are associated positively with electrodermal reactivity, psychopaths have low electrodermal activity and reactivity. This distinction has been demonstrated in many investigations (see Lorber, 2004).

The research we have described thus far has been based on the idea that punishment does not arouse strong emotions in psychopaths and thus does not inhibit anti-social behaviour. But some researchers do not believe that punishment is the critical agent of socialization. They think that empathy, being in tune with the emotional reactions of others, is more important. For example, empathizing with the distress that callous treatment might cause in someone else could inhibit such behaviour. Some features of psychopathy may arise from a lack of empathy.

This idea has been tested by monitoring the skin conductance of psychopathic and non-psychopathic men as they viewed slides of varying content. Three types of slides were used: threatening (e.g., gun, shark), neutral (e.g., book), and distress (e.g., a crying person). No differences were found between the two groups in their responses to the first two types of slides, but the psychopaths were less responsive to the distress slides (Blair et al., 1997). Thus, the psychopaths indeed appeared to show less empathy for the distress of others (see Figure 13.2.)

FIGURE 13.2 Skin-conductance response of psychopathic and non-psychopathic men to three types of stimuli. The psychopathic men showed less responsiveness to the distress stimuli, indicating a deficit in empathy.

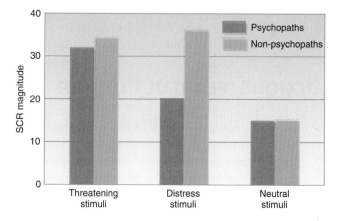

Response Modulation, Impulsivity, and Psychopathy
Research continues to highlight the impulsivity of psychopaths and its physiological roots. A study in British Columbia used the PCL-R to identify criminal psychopaths; subsequent functional magnetic resonance imaging tests showed that, compared with criminal non-psychopaths and control participants, criminal psychopaths had less affect-related activity in the amygdala/hippocampal formation, suggesting that the hypoemotionality of psychopaths reflects limbic system deficiencies (Kiehl et al., 2001).

A review was conducted of 17 neuroimaging studies that focused on people with a history of engaging in impulsive violent acts (Bufkin & Luttrell, 2005). Anti-social impulsive acts are associated with decreased prefrontal activity and increased subcortical activity in the brain. A particular subcortical structure, the amygdala, is implicated in emotion regulation, and growing evidence supports the role of amygdalar dysfunction in psychopathy (Vien & Beech, 2006). For instance, one study found that the deficient fear conditioning of psychopaths could be traced to the absence of activation in the limbic-prefrontal circuit, which includes the amygdala (Birbaumer et al., 2005). Just how strong are these neuroimaging data? Bufkin and Luttrell (2005) concluded confidently: "Research emanating from affective, behavioral, and clinical neuroscience paradigms is converging on the conclusion that there is a significant neurological basis of aggressive and/or violent behavior over and above contributions from the psychosocial environment" (p. 187).

As for impulsivity, it shows up when psychopaths attempt tasks designed to test their ability to modify their responses to success or failure (Patterson & Newman, 1993). In one study, participants viewed playing cards on a computer-generated video display (Newman, Patterson, & Kosson, 1987). Psychopaths continued playing the game much longer than non-psychopaths and appeared to ignore numerous cues indicating that they were unlikely to be rewarded and should quit. The insensitivity to contextual information appears to be a general feature of psychopathy; it occurs even in situations that do not involve threat of punishment (Newman, Schmitt, & Voss, 1997). This insensitivity to context might well relate to psychopaths' insensitivity to other people.

Thus, psychopaths do not react as most of us do. In particular, they have little anxiety, so anxiety can have little deterrent effect on their anti-social behaviour. Their callous treatment of others may also be linked to their lack of empathy. Because psychopaths are deficient in using contextual information and in planning ahead, they behave impulsively. These are possible reasons for the psychopath's misconduct without regret.

ANXIOUS/FEARFUL CLUSTER

This cluster comprises three personality disorders:

- Avoidant personality disorder applies to people who are fearful in social situations.
- Dependent personality disorder refers to those who lack self-reliance and are overly dependent on others.
- Obsessive-compulsive personality disorder applies to those who have a perfectionistic approach to life.

AVOIDANT PERSONALITY DISORDER

THE SHAMED SON A first-year college student, Jared hardly associated with anyone. In the clinical interview, he seemed to want to make contact, but he frequently stuttered, causing him to retreat in embarrassment. Otherwise, he expressed almost no emotion.

His second computer programming course was the immediate problem. Though he was fluent in several computer languages, his professor wanted the students to work in groups, to collaborate in building chunks of a single large project. Jared was scared. "I try to work on it, but I can't concentrate." His voice shrank to a whisper. "They're g .. g .. going to think I'm an idiot." His solution was to drop the class, though he had an A average going into this, the last assignment of the semester. In fact, his grades were exceptional overall. Nevertheless, Jared could report no friends, and confessed, "I'm lousy at meeting people. I guess I think they won't like me or something. I'm awkward. I'm a clutz. I just don't have many qualities others are interested in, I guess. But I'm great with computers." (From Millon & Davis, 2000, p. 154)

The diagnosis of **avoidant personality** disorder applies to people such as Jared who are keenly sensitive to the possibility of criticism, rejection, or disapproval and are reluctant to enter into relationships unless they are sure they will be liked. They may avoid employment that entails a lot of interpersonal contact. They are restrained in social situations owing to an extreme fear of saying something foolish or of being embarrassed by blushing or other signs of anxiety. They believe they are incompetent and inferior to others and are reluctant to take risks or try new activities.

While many scholars emphasized that those with an avoidant personality disorder tend to avoid social situations, this conclusion was qualified by Taylor, Laposa, and Alden (2004), who found that those with avoidant personality disorder engage in other forms of avoidance as well and these people have a general pattern of avoidance. Regardless, avoidant personality disorder and generalized social phobia are highly comorbid, with a recent study showing that 40% of those with avoidant personality disorder also had generalized social phobia (Cox, Pagura, Stein, & Sareen, 2009). Those who had both disorders had demonstrably lower levels of life quality.

Avoidant personality disorder is highly comorbid with dependent personality disorder (Alden, Laposa, Taylor, & Ryder, 2002). Dependent personality disorder is described below. According to Alden et al. (2002), the only symptom that reliably differentiates avoidant personality disorder from dependent personality is that the avoidant person has great difficulty approaching and initiating social relationships. Avoidant personality is comorbid with depression as well as generalized social phobia (Alpert et al., 1997). The comorbidity with generalized social phobia is likely due to the similarity between the diagnostic criteria for these disorders; avoidant personality disorder may be a more severe variant of generalized social phobia (Hofmann et al., 1995).

Both avoidant personality disorder and social phobia are related to a syndrome that occurs in Japan called *taijin kyoufu* (*taijin* means "interpersonal" and *kyoufu* means "fear"). Like people with avoidant personality disorder and social phobia, those with *taijin kyoufu* are overly sensitive and avoid interpersonal contact. But what they fear is somewhat different from the usual fears of those with the *DSM* diagnoses. People with *taijin kyoufu* tend to be ashamed about how they appear to others, fearing, for example, that they are ugly or have body odour (Ono et al., 1996).

DEPENDENT PERSONALITY DISORDER

The core feature of **dependent personality** disorder (DPD) is a lack of both self-confidence and a sense of autonomy. People with DPD view themselves as weak and other people as powerful. They also have an intense need to be taken care of, which makes them feel uncomfortable when alone; they may be preoccupied with fears of being left alone to take care of themselves. They subordinate their own needs to ensure that they do not break up protective relationships. When a close relationship ends, they urgently seek another relationship to replace the old one.

The *DSM* criteria also include some features that are not well supported by the research literature. These diagnostic criteria portray people with DPD as being very passive (e.g., having difficulty initiating projects or doing things on their own, not being able to disagree with others, allowing others to make decisions). Dependent people do whatever is necessary to maintain a close relationship. This could involve being very deferential and passive, but may also entail taking active steps to preserve a relationship (Bornstein, 1997).

An important caveat about DPD was expressed recently by Chen, Nettles, and Chen (2009). They suggested that DPD is perhaps the most culture-laden diagnostic category. It is rooted in the individualism of North American study. Too great a need to connect with others can constitute maladjustment in North America, but connecting with others is healthy and valued in collectivistic cultures in places such as East Asia.

OBSESSIVE-COMPULSIVE PERSONALITY DISORDER

The **obsessive-compulsive personality** is a perfectionist, preoccupied with details, rules, schedules, and the like. These people often pay so much attention to detail that they never

Children normally go through a phase in which separation from a parent is distressing. People with dependent personality disorder may be experiencing a similar phenomenon in their adult relationships. © Image Source/Corbis.

finish projects. They are work-rather than pleasure-oriented and have inordinate difficulty making decisions (lest they err) and allocating time (lest they focus on the wrong thing). Their interpersonal relationships are often poor because they are stubborn and demand that everything be done their way. They are generally serious, rigid, formal, and inflexible, especially regarding moral issues. They are unable to discard worn out and useless objects, even those with no sentimental value. A dysfunctional attention to work and productivity is found more often in men than in women.

Obsessive-compulsive personality disorder (OCPD) is quite different from obsessive-compulsive disorder (OCD); it does not include the obsessions and compulsions that define the latter. Although the use of the "obsessive-compulsive" in both disorders suggests that the two disorders are related, the relationship does not appear to be very strong. Although OCPD is found more frequently among people with OCD than among those with panic disorder or depression, it is found in no more than 20% of OCD cases. OCD and OCPD are clearly distinguishable (Mancebo, Eisen, Grant, & Rasmussen, 2005). Obsessive-compulsive personality disorder is most highly comorbid with avoidant personality disorder and has a prevalence of about 1% (Lassano, del Buono, & Latapano, 1993).

See Focus on Discovery 13.1 for a comparison of a dimensional approach and the *DSM-IV-TR* discrete entity approach to diagnosing personality disorders.

FOCUS ON DISCOVERY 13.1
A DIMENSIONAL APPROACH TO PERSONALITY DISORDERS

According to the most promising dimensional approach to personality disorders, these disorders represent extremes of personality traits found in everyone. Although literally hundreds of traits could be considered, most contemporary research focuses on a model of personality called the five-factor model (McCrae & Costa, 1990). The five factors, or major dimensions, of personality are neuroticism, extroversion/introversion, openness to experience,

agreeableness/antagonism, and conscientiousness. Table 13.2 presents questionnaire items that represent each of these dimensions. You can acquire a sense of what each dimension means by reading the table.

We will illustrate the five-factor model by examining its link with certain forms of personality dysfunction. For instance, how does psychopathy relate to the five-factor model? Harpur, Hart, and Hare (1994) found that psychopaths are high in neuroticism and low in agreeableness and conscientiousness.

Other forms of personality dysfunction have been examined with the five-factor model. In general, a meta-analysis established that each personality disorder had a meaningful combination of the five factors associated with it. Moreover, it was found that high neuroticism and low agreeableness were common to many personality disorders, and high or low extroversion was a factor that was quite useful in distinguishing among the various personality disorders (Saulsman & Page, 2004). Some personality disorders have a unique five-factor profile. For instance, according to Alden et al. (2002), avoidant personality disorder is the only personality disorder characterized by high neuroticism and introversion. Rather than forcing each individual into a discrete category and encountering problems in distinguishing between avoidant personality disorder and schizoid personality disorder, the dimensional approach would simply describe people on their levels of neuroticism and introversion.

The dimensional approach does not force people into discrete categories, but simply describes their scores on the five factors. A dimensional model thus appears to have several distinct advantages and Widiger and Mullins-Sweatt (2009) have advocated for the five-factor dimensional framework as part of *DSM-5*. One advantage is that it handles the comorbidity problem, because comorbidity is a difficulty only in a categorical classification system like the *DSM*. Further, because the dimensional system forges a link between normal and abnormal

personality, the findings on personality development in general become relevant to the personality disorders. For example, since genetic researchers have found that most of the traits of the five-factor model are heritable, with about half of the variance attributable to genetic factors (Jang, Livesley, & Vernon, 1996), genetic factors become plausible as variables related to the causes of personality disorders.

While the five-factor model is useful to a certain extent, an emerging finding from the Hopkins Epidemiology of Personality Disorder Study suggests that it has limited utility (see Nestadt et al., 2008). This study compared NEO-PI(R) responses and psychologist assessments of 742 community residents evaluated with the International Personality Disorder Examination. Only modest correspondence was found; the NEO-PI(R) dimensions explained only one fifth to one third of the variance in personality disorder dimensions.

Thus, other models with other dimensions are being considered. The PSY-5 described in the "Asessing Personality Disorders" section earlier in the chapter is one example, and another is Livesley and Jackson's (2002) self-report scale known as the Dimensional Assessment of Personality Pathology—Basic Questionnaire (DAPP-BQ). The DAPP-BQ has 22 scales that assess 18 personality trait dimensions (e.g., anxiousness, affective lability, callousness, insecure attachment, and narcissism) and various response styles. Statistical tests show that DAPP-BQ trait scales reflect the higher-order factors of emotional dysregulation (i.e., affective lability and impulsivity), dissocial behaviour (i.e., callousness, conduct problems, and narcissism), inhibitedness (i.e., avoidance of intimacy and restricted expression of emotions), and compulsivity (Livesley, Jang, & Vernon, 1998). Research linking the DAPP-BQ with variables from other personality models shows that neuroticism is linked with emotional dysregulation, dissocial behaviour is linked with high psychoticism, inhibitedness is linked with low extroversion, and compulsivity is linked with high conscientiousness (Larstone et al., 2002).

Given the apparent validity and associated advantages of the dimensional approach, it is evident from the initial draft of *DSM-5* that subsequent diagnostic systems will make a greater effort to incorporate a dimensional framework into the personality disorder section. Widiger, Livesley, and Clark (2009) noted that a dimensional approach is favoured for *DSM-5* and beyond, but it is hard to choose from the various alternative dimensional approaches available. They propose a hierarchical structure that integrates DAPP-BQ dimensions with dimensions on Clark's Schedule for Nonadaptive and Adaptive Personality (SNAP) and the NEO-PI(R). So what has been proposed? At least initially, it has been proposed that six trait domains be assessed: negative emotionality, introversion, antagonism, disinhibition, compulsivity, and schizotypy. Each personality domain comes with five or more facets to assess. For instance, the compulsivity facets are perfectionism, perseveration, rigidity, orderliness, and risk aversion (www.dsm5.org). In light of these changes, it is arguably the case that the greatest, most extensive changes in this new framework involve personality disorder and dysfunction.

TABLE 13.2
THE FIVE-FACTOR MODEL: SAMPLE ITEMS FROM THE REVISED NEO PERSONALITY INVENTORY

Neuroticism	I am not a worrier. (−)
	I often feel tense or jittery. (+)
Extroversion/introversion	I'm known as a warm and friendly person. (+)
	Many people think of me as somewhat cold and distant. (−)
Openness to experience	I have a very active imagination. (+)
	I don't like to waste my time daydreaming. (−)
Agreeableness/antagonism	I believe that most people will take advantage of you if you let them. (−)
	I think most people I deal with are honest and trustworthy. (+)
Conscientiousness	I keep myself informed and usually make intelligent decisions. (+)
	I often come into situations without being prepared. (−)

Note: Agreeing with an item marked with a + increases one's score on that factor; agreeing with an item marked − decreases it.
Source: Costa and McCrae (1992)

ETIOLOGY OF THE ANXIOUS/FEARFUL CLUSTER

Few data exist on the causes of the personality disorders in this cluster. Speculation about their causes has focused on parent-child relationships. It has been argued, for example, that dependent personality disorder results from an overprotective and authoritarian parenting style that prevents the development of feelings of self-efficacy (Bornstein, 1997).

Dependent personality disorder could also be a reflection of what are referred to as attachment problems (Livesley, Schroeder, & Jackson, 1990). Attachment has been studied by developmental psychologists and is regarded as important for personality development (see Chapter 15). The basic idea is that the young infant becomes attached to an adult and uses the adult as a secure base from which to explore and pursue other goals. Separation from the adult leads to anger and distress. As development proceeds, the child becomes less dependent on the attachment figure for security. The abnormal attachment behaviours seen in dependent personalities may reflect a failure in the usual developmental process arising from a disruption in the early parent-child relationship because of death, neglect, rejection, or overprotectiveness. Persons with dependent personality disorder engage in a number of tactics (originally established to maintain their relationship with their parents) to keep their relationships with other people at any cost—for example, always agreeing with them (Stone, 1993).

Much like the fears and phobias discussed in Chapter 6, avoidant personality disorder may reflect the influence of an environment in which the child is taught to fear people and situations that most of us regard as harmless. For example, the abnormal fears of one of the child's parents may be transmitted through modelling.

Freud viewed obsessive-compulsive personality traits as being due to fixation at the anal stage of psychosexual development. More contemporary psychodynamic theories emphasize a fear of loss of control that is handled by overcompensation. For example, the man who is a compulsive workaholic may fear that his life will fall apart if he relaxes and has fun.

THERAPIES FOR PERSONALITY DISORDERS

There is not much research-based information on treating personality disorders (Crits-Christoph, 1998). There is, however, a lively and burgeoning clinical case literature on therapies for many disorders. The ideas outlined here are thus based mostly on the clinical experiences of a small number of mental health professionals and not on studies that contain suitable controls. These therapeutic guidelines are almost all that is available on treating personality disorders.

It is important to bear in mind that a therapist working with someone with a personality disorder is typically also concerned with Axis I disorders, since most people with PDs enter treatment because of an Axis I disorder rather than a personality disorder. For example, a person with anti-social personality disorder is likely to have substance abuse problems, a person with avoidant personality disorder may seek treatment for a social phobia, and a person with obsessive-compulsive personality disorder may be seen for depression. In this connection, it should be mentioned that people with Axis I disorders as well as personality disorders tend not to show as much improvement in various forms of psychotherapy as do people with Axis I diagnoses alone (Crits-Christoph, 1998). The reason seems pretty clear: people with diagnoses on both axes are more seriously disturbed than are those with only Axis I diagnoses and therefore may require therapy that is both more intensive (because of the long-standing nature of personality disorders) and more extensive (i.e., focused on a broad range of psychological problems).

Psychoactive drugs are often used to treat the various personality disorders. The choice of drug is determined by the Axis I problem that the personality disorder resembles. People with avoidant personality disorder, for instance, can be prescribed a tranquilizer, such as the benzodiazepine Xanax, in the hope of reducing their social anxieties and phobias. When depression is present in an Axis II disorder, antidepressant medication, such as fluoxetine (Prozac), can be helpful. Fluoxetine has also reduced the impulsivity and aggressiveness of a group of people with a variety of personality disorders (Coccaro & Kavousi, 1997).

Psychodynamic therapists aim to alter the personality disordered person's present-day views of the childhood problems assumed to underlie a personality disorder. For example, they may help an obsessive-compulsive personality to realize that the childhood quest to win the love of his or her parents by being perfect need not be carried into adulthood, that he or she need not be perfect to win the approval of others, and that it is possible to take risks and make mistakes without being abandoned.

Behavioural and cognitive therapists, in keeping with their focus on situations rather than traits, had little to say about specific treatments for the personality disorders until the publication of a book edited by Beck and Freeman (1990) on the cognitive-behavioural therapy of personality disorders. Overall, little empirical research on CBT treatment for personality disorders has been done, although more studies are beginning to emerge (e.g., Davidson et al., 2006; Howes & Vallis, 1996; Vallis, Howes, & Standage, 2000). Behavioural and cognitive therapists tend to analyze the individual problems that taken together reflect a personality disorder. For example, a person diagnosed as having a paranoid or an avoidant personality is extremely sensitive to criticism. This sensitivity may be treated by systematic desensitization or rational-emotive behaviour therapy (Renneberg et al., 1990). The paranoid personality's argumentativeness and hostility when faced with a contrary opinion pushes others away and provokes counterattacks from them. The behavioural therapist may help the paranoid individual learn more adaptive ways of disagreeing with other people. Social skills training in a support group might be suggested to encourage avoidant personalities to be more assertive with other people. One controlled study done in Vancouver confirmed that this is a promising strategy (Alden, 1989). Such an approach, perhaps combined with rational-emotive behaviour therapy, may help these clients cope when efforts to reach out do not succeed, as is bound to happen at times (Millon, 1996).

In looking at cognitive therapy for personality disorders, Beck, Freeman, and associates (1990) apply the same kind of analysis that has been found promising in the treatment of depression (see Chapter 8). Each disorder is analyzed in terms of logical errors and dysfunctional schemata. For example, treating obsessive-compulsive personality with cognitive therapy entails first persuading the client to accept the essence of the cognitive model: that feelings and behaviours are primarily a function of thoughts. Errors in logic are then explored, such as the person concluding that he or she cannot do anything right because of failing in one particular endeavour (an example of overgeneralization). The therapist also looks for dysfunctional assumptions or schemata that might underlie the person's thoughts and feelings; for example, the belief that it is critical for every decision to be correct (adherents of Ellis's methods would also take this step). Beck's approach to personality disorders represents a combination of a variety of behavioural and cognitive-behavioural techniques, all designed to address the particular, long-standing, and pervasive difficulties that are experienced. A related version of this approach developed primarily by Young is known as **schema therapy** for personality disorders (see Young, Klosko, & Weishaar, 2003). Young has identified a range of cognitive schemas measured by the Young Schema Questionnaire (YSQ) believed to underlie various forms of dysfunction, including personality disorder (see Young, 1994; Young & Lindemann, 2002). The YSQ taps three broad themes: (1) disconnection and rejection; (2) impaired autonomy and performance; and (3) impaired limits. Each theme is tapped by several subscale factors. For instance, the disconnection and rejection theme is assessed by abandonment/instability, mistrust/abuse, emotional deprivation, defectiveness/shame, and social isolation/alienation.

Schema therapy can be adapted to the main themes inherent in a particular personality disorder. Schema therapy for borderline personality disorder involves three phases of treatment: (1) bonding between the client and therapist and emotional regulation; (2) schema mode change; and (3) development of autonomy (see Kellogg & Young, 2006).

Vallis and his associates at Dalhousie University in Halifax examined whether short-term cognitive therapy is suitable for treating symptoms of personality disorder (Vallis et al., 2000). They found that clients with higher levels of personality dysfunction were less suitable for cognitive therapy, in terms of both self-ratings and clinician ratings of the therapeutic alliance. However, the authors suggested that there are still grounds for "cautious optimism" when it comes to treating personality disorders with cognitive therapy because they found indications that severe personality disorder would pose significant challenges for any form of short-term psychotherapy and that the problems may not be specific to cognitive therapy per se. Their optimism has been supported

in a well-designed controlled trial, which recently found that CBT can be effective in treating BPD (see Davidson et al., 2006). Perhaps this more encouraging news is, in part, a reflection of a growing understanding of the nature of disorders such as BPD.

THERAPY FOR THE BORDERLINE PERSONALITY

The results reported by Davidson et al. (2006) are remarkable because few people pose a greater challenge to treatment than do those with BPD. The problems that borderline personalities have with other people are replicated in the consulting room.

With the BPD client, trust is inordinately difficult to create and sustain, thus handicapping the therapeutic relationship. The person alternately idealizes and vilifies the therapist, demanding special attention and consideration one moment—such as therapy sessions at odd hours—and refusing to keep appointments the next, imploring for understanding and support but insisting that certain topics are off-limits.

Suicide is always a serious risk, but it is often difficult for the therapist to judge whether a frantic phone call at 2 a.m. is a call for help or a manipulative gesture designed to see to what lengths the therapist will go to meet the client's needs at the moment. As happened in the case presented at the beginning of this chapter, hospitalization is often necessary when the client's behaviour becomes unmanageable on an outpatient basis or when the threat of suicide cannot be managed without the greater supervision possible only in a psychiatric hospital.

Because seeing clients with BPD is so stressful, it is common practice for therapists to have regular consultations with another therapist, sometimes for support and advice and sometimes for professional help in dealing with their own emotions as they try to cope with the extraordinary challenges involved.

Otto Kernberg, one of the leading object-relations theorists, has been very influential in the study of borderline personality disorder. Courtesy Otto Kernberg.

Marsha Linehan created dialectical behaviour therapy, which combines cognitive-behavioural therapy with Zen and Rogerian notions of acceptance. Courtesy Marsha M. Linehan, Department of Psychology, University of Washington.

A number of drugs have been tried in the pharmacotherapy of BPD, most notably antidepressants and antipsychotic medications. There is little to recommend antidepressants, but antipsychotics show some modest effects on anxiety, suicidality, and psychotic symptoms (Bendetti et al., 1998). Because drugs are often abused and suicide is a risk, extreme caution must be used in any drug-therapy regimen, and overall, drug treatments for BPD are not very effective (see Paris, 2009).

OBJECT-RELATIONS PSYCHOTHERAPY As noted earlier, object-relations theory focuses on how children identify with people to whom they have strong emotional attachments. Earlier in the chapter, we described the views of two object-relations theorists: Heinz Kohut, on narcissism, and Otto Kernberg, on the borderline personality.

As mentioned previously, Kernberg (1985) operates from the basic assumption that borderline personalities have weak egos and therefore inordinate difficulty tolerating the probing that occurs in psychoanalytic treatment. Kernberg's modified analytic treatment has the overall goal of strengthening the person's weak ego so that he or she does not fall prey to splitting, or dichotomizing. Splitting is the result of an inability to form complex ideas (object representations) that do not fit a simple good-bad dichotomy. For example, the person may see the therapist as a godlike genius only to be crushed and furious when the therapist later mentions that therapy payments are overdue; in an instant, the therapist becomes evil and incompetent. The therapist employs interpretive techniques, pointing out how emotions and behaviours are being regulated by such defences as splitting.

Kernberg's approach is more directive than that of most analysts. In addition to interpreting defensive behaviour, he gives concrete suggestions for behaving more adaptively and will hospitalize people whose behaviour becomes dangerous to themselves or others. Kernberg's opinion that such people are unsuitable for classical psychoanalysis because of their weak egos is consistent with a long-term study conducted at the world-famous analytically oriented Menninger Clinic (Stone, 1987).

DIALECTICAL BEHAVIOUR THERAPY Linehan (1987) introduced an approach that combines client-centred empathy and acceptance with cognitive-behavioural problem solving and social skills training. What she calls **dialectical behaviour therapy** (DBT) has three overall goals for borderline individuals—that they learn to

1. modulate and control their extreme emotionality and behaviours,
2. tolerate feeling distressed, and
3. trust their own thoughts and emotions.

Why does Linehan use the word "dialectical" in describing her therapy? The concept of dialectics comes from the German philosopher Hegel (1770–1831). For our purposes, it is enough to know that dialectics refers to a worldview that holds that reality is an outcome of a constant tension between opposites. Any event—called the thesis—tends to generate a force in opposition to it: its antithesis. The tension between the opposites is resolved by the creation of a new event: the synthesis. For example, John loves Mary (thesis). But he finds in her some qualities that annoy him, creating in him some doubt as to whether he truly loves her (antithesis). John then comes to realize that he can love Mary in spite of her faults, perhaps even because of them (synthesis). This synthesis can then split into another pair of dialectical opposites, with a new synthesis eventually emerging that can reconcile them into yet another synthesis. And so on and on.

Linehan uses the term *dialectic* to describe the seemingly paradoxical stance that the therapist must take with people with BPD: accepting each person as they are and yet helping them change. Linehan also uses the term to refer to the borderline person's realization that they need not split the world into black and white, but can achieve a synthesis of apparent opposites. For example, instead of a friend being either all bad (thesis) or all good (antithesis), the friend can be a person with both kinds of qualities (synthesis).

DBT centres on the therapist's full acceptance of borderline personalities with all their contradictions and acting out, empathically validating their (distorted) beliefs with a matter-of-fact attitude toward their suicidal and other dysfunctional behaviour. McMain, Korman, and Dimeff (2001) described the role of DBT in treating emotion dysregulation. They illustrated the concept of therapist acceptance by relating the case study of Jane, a BPD client with substance abuse disorder. Jane had a history of sexual abuse and experienced intense emotions of sadness, fear, and anger, along with intense self-criticism and shame. The following account stems from Jane's failure to keep self-monitoring diary cards and her emotional reactions to the treatment sessions:

Client: Sometimes it's so upsetting. Because sometimes I could come in a good mood and then leave depressed. I end up leaving here so upset.

Therapist: No, I agree, that doesn't sound too comfortable.

Client: It's like my mother in the past, reminding me of all my faults all the time.

Therapist: Yeah, it's so painful to bring up this stuff. Why would anyone want that?

Client: Yeah, exactly!

Therapist: Now here's the dilemma. We could not talk about your problems, and if this would take away your pain and misery, I'd be all for it. On the other hand, if we help you figure out how to tolerate your bad feelings, then you won't have to rely on your pain medicine or resort to thinking of killing yourself when these feelings come up. (From McMain et al., 2001, pp. 192–193)

This exchange illustrates the therapist's acceptance and acknowledgement of Jane's emotional experiences. At the same time, the therapist suggests that learning to develop some emotional self-control can be substituted for the extreme emotional reactions that Jane has relied on in the past.

The cognitive-behavioural aspect of the treatment, conducted both individually and in groups, involves helping clients learn to solve problems, to acquire more effective and socially acceptable ways of handling their daily living problems, and to control their emotions. Work is also done on improving their interpersonal skills and controlling their anger and anxieties. After many months of intensive treatment, limits are set on their behaviour, consistent with what Kernberg advocates. Basically, DBT is cognitive-behavioural therapy within the paradoxical context of validating and accepting the person for who he or she is. In Linehan's words:

Stylistically, DBT blends a matter-of-fact, somewhat irreverent, and at times outrageous attitude about current and previous parasuicidal and other dysfunctional behaviours with therapist warmth [and] flexibility …. [A] focus … on active problem-solving [is] balanced by a corresponding emphasis on validating the patient's current emotional, cognitive, and behavioural responses just as they are. (1993b, p. 19)

Linehan and her associates published the results of the first randomized, controlled study of a psychological intervention for BPD (Linehan et al., 1991). Patients were assigned randomly either to DBT or to treatment as usual. They were assessed after one year of treatment and again six and 12 months later (Linehan, Heard, & Armstrong, 1993). The findings immediately after treatment revealed the highly significant superiority of DBT on measures of intentional self-injurious behaviour, including suicide attempts, dropping out of treatment, and in-patient hospital days. At the follow-ups, superiority was maintained; additionally, DBT patients had better work histories, reported less anger, and were judged as better adjusted overall than the comparison therapy patients. A subsequent study showed that

DBT was reasonably effective in reducing drug use in BPD clients with substance dependence (Linehan et al., 1999). As a result of Linehan's (1993a, 1993b) work, there is now widespread interest in DBT and its applicability to BPD and other disorders. It is not clear, however, whether DBT is the most effective form of treatment when compared with other alternatives. A new Canadian study found that DBT versus general psychiatric management were equally effective in reducing BPD symptoms, psychological distress, degree of suicidality, and health care utilization (McMain et al., 2009). Another recent longitudinal investigation compared three forms of treatment across one year and confirmed that all three forms of treatment, including DBT, were somewhat effective; however, transference-focused psychotherapy, which has its roots in object relations psychotherapy, was most effective in reducing maladjustment across six indicators, including depression and suicidality (Clarkin, Levy, Lenzenweger, & Kernberg, 2007). Tranference-focused psychotherapy emphasized dominant, emotion-laden themes in individual sessions with a therapist actually trained in object relations theory.

THERAPY FOR PSYCHOPATHY

As for the treatment of psychopathy, there is widespread—and unfortunate—agreement among therapists of varying theoretical persuasions: psychopathy is often virtually impossible to treat (Cleckley, 1976; McCord & McCord, 1964). This issue is revisited in the description of work by Rice and her colleagues (see Chapter 18).

It may be that people with the classic symptoms listed by Cleckley are by their very natures incapable of benefiting from any form of psychotherapy. In fact, it is unlikely that psychopaths would even want to be in therapy. The primary reason for their unsuitability for psychotherapy is that they are unable and unmotivated to form any sort of trusting, honest relationship with a therapist. People who lie almost without knowing it, who care little for the feelings of others and understand their own even less, who appear not to realize that what they are doing is morally wrong, who lack any motivation to obey society's laws and mores, and who, living only for the present, have no concern for the future are, all in all, extremely poor candidates for therapy.

Many valiant attempts have been made to establish tenable connections with psychopaths, but both the published literature and informal communications among mental health professionals support the conclusion that true psychopathy cannot be reached through psychological efforts. Similar negative conclusions may be drawn about somatic methods: electroconvulsive shock; drugs such as Dilantin, stimulants, and sedatives; and psychosurgery. There is, however, some evidence that large doses of anti-anxiety agents can reduce hostility in psychopaths (Kellner, 1982), and there is some tentative evidence that psychopaths who had attention-deficit disorder as children might benefit from the stimulant drug Ritalin, which has had some positive effects with hyperactive youngsters (Stringer & Josef, 1983; see Chapter 15). A failed attempt to treat the psychopath using a controlled social environment in combination with drugs is described in Canadian Clinic Focus 13.1.

CANADIAN CLINIC FOCUS 13.1
TREATMENT OF PSYCHOPATHS: THE OAK RIDGE "EXPERIMENT"

"Patients drugged in experiments at psychiatric facility suit claims: Programs abused criminally insane, documents allege"

—*Headline to report by Tracey Tyler, the* Toronto Star, *January 23, 2001, p. A18*

Were "criminally insane" people, including many psychopaths, drugged and tortured in the name of treatment while the Government of Ontario sat idly by and did nothing? This is the basis of allegations in a $150-million class-action lawsuit filed against both the Government of Ontario and the psychiatrist who initiated the program at the Oak Ridge division of the Penetanguishene Mental Health Centre. The major allegation of the lead plaintiff, Vance Egglestone, is that he was one of hundreds of people who were "no more than human guinea pigs" when allegedly subjected to mental and physical abuse and various mind-altering experiments, including the administration of LSD, between 1965 and 1982, as part of treatment programs designed to "reconstruct" their personalities. As an aside, note that Egglestone is a transsexual who got a legal name change to Shauna Taylor. As Egglestone, Taylor has been incarcerated since 1976 following the brutal rape of a woman from Toronto and is seeking government coverage of a sex change operation.

Oak Ridge Division of the Penetanguishene Mental Health Centre

Oak Ridge is the only maximum-security psychiatric hospital in Ontario, and it is reserved exclusively for men. Most men confined to Oak Ridge in the era described in the lawsuit were held "at the Pleasure of the Lieutenant Governor" (warrant) for an indeterminate period of time. Further, there was no obligation to treat individuals or specify criteria for discharge. Men who had been acquitted of murder on grounds of "insanity" were usually destined to remain confined until they died (Wiesman, 1995). In addition to men referred by the courts, Oak Ridge drew its population from men transferred from prison (especially following riots at the federal penitentiary at Kingston in 1971) or reformatories, and from referrals from other mental health institutions. Oak Ridge developed a reputation as a place that could control behaviour that could not be controlled in other facilities. Escape from Oak Ridge was virtually impossible. No wonder it became known as "the Alcatraz of Canada" (Boyd, 1963)! It was the final stage in government attempts to control "dangerous" behaviour. Male attendants exercised control by using numerous rules and rituals. Thus, prior to 1965, there was essentially no psychological treatment of any form for the men committed to Oak Ridge.

The Social Therapy Unit (STU)

In 1965, the new medical director, Dr. Barry Boyd, hired a young psychiatrist named Dr. Elliot Barker. Barker set about developing an experiment in social engineering that became known as the Social Therapy Unit (STU) program. He started in 1965 with 38 patients on the now infamous "G Ward" and by 1968 had expanded the program to include half the population of Oak Ridge (about 150 patients) (Weisman, 1995).

The novel program generated much public attention worldwide, most of it favourable. Over the decade between 1966 and 1976, reporters and film crews from Canada and abroad shared with the public a reassuring view of the treatment of the "criminally insane." Weisman (1995) interpreted the portrayals of STU patients by the filmmakers and journalists in the following way:

[H]ere were young, handsome, and intelligent men discussing their violent actions with insight and understanding, and apparently interacting with their peers in a manner that was both honest and compassionate. . . . That somehow men who had committed the most heinous acts of multiple murder, rape, and arson, and that, more improbably, those branded as psychopaths, could be brought to the point of confronting their defenses on a daily basis and choosing caring over cruelty and hope over despair was the psychiatric equivalent to walking on water. (p. 266)

What was this miraculous approach to treating the psychopath? What exactly happened on the STU? The therapeutic community was peer-run with very minimal professional staff contact. Patients were involved in compulsory, structured, intensive group therapy for about 80 hours each week. They participated in daily sessions with other participants, sat on committees that structured and observed every aspect of life in the institution, spent minimal time in organized recreational, academic, or vocational programs, and had no opportunity for diversion, such as through reading, watching television, and even ordinary social interaction. Men who performed well and showed the appropriate talent could be appointed to leadership roles, leading groups and sitting on security and administrative committees (Rice & Harris, 1993; Weisman, 1995). Indeed, one person, Michael Mason, not only played a vital role in the development of the program but also co-authored with Dr. Barker several major theoretical publications in journals that described the STU (e.g., Barker, Mason, & Wilson, 1969). Mason was a warrant patient who had been tried on murder charges.

The patient committee system had real and extensive powers. A medication committee determined which drugs a patient could or should take, and decisions were invariably enforced. Patients could be escorted forcibly to meetings, placed in cuffs, and watched over by an assigned fellow patient. The objective of the therapeutic community was "a major reconstruction of personality."

Should this strategy be the focus of lawsuits a generation later? Perhaps not, but for the fact that the STU involved much more than drastic changes in hospital routine. The radical vision was that the major reconstruction "required a break with normality and a re-experiencing of one's pathology, and that the resources of the community would be mobilized both to accelerate these changes and to make sure that they resulted in greater health" (Weisman, 1995, p. 275). Some of the strategies designed to make the patients surrender their defences, risk loss of control, and let their pathology show included the following:

1. The STU deliberately employed various medications that were cathartic, hypnotic, disorienting, or hallucinogenic. The drugs were often used in combination with attempts to eliminate defensive behaviour (defence-disruptive therapy) and raise the level of tension in the individual and in the community. The drugs included sodium amytal, Methedrine, scopolamine, and LSD.

2. The STU tested the limits of interpersonal communication by developing social situations that were unusual and extreme. These included the "small group encounter," the "forced dyadic encounter," "compressed encounter therapy," and, the ultimate tool for bringing down defences, the "total encounter capsule." This latter situation was a windowless, safe, and self-contained room equipped with tubes for feeding and an open toilet, together with a one-way mirror overhead for constant monitoring. "Patients would be together unclothed and undistracted by external stimuli, free to express themselves with no inhibitions, and secure in the realization that should they overstep the generous limits that had been allowed, they would be restrained" (Weisman, 1995, p. 275).

Consent was rarely solicited at Oak Ridge. Coercion on the part of the attendants and other patients was apparently the norm. The class-action suit alleges that even when consent was sought, it was of little legal value because it was obtained "under duress, coercion or intimidation" (Tyler, 2001, A18). It is certainly true that, according to today's ethical standards, many aspects of the STU program would violate the rights of patients (see Chapter 18) and would also be questioned on clinical grounds. Nonetheless, many professionals of the era viewed the program favourably on both ethical and clinical grounds. Indeed, the chair of a parliamentary subcommittee that evaluated the program concluded that the techniques used "are the most fruitful anywhere in the universe at the present time, based on the knowledge we have gathered" (Government of Canada, 1977, p. 45).

The Violent Self Reconstructed?

How successful was the Oak Ridge experiment? Unfortunately, it was a failure. Although the non-psychopaths fared somewhat better after their release than offenders with similar characteristics who went to prison, retrospective evaluations determined that the psychopaths who received treatment in the program had even higher rates of recidivism involving violence than their counterparts in prison (Rice & Harris, 1993). The experiment is yet another failure in the long history of valiant attempts to encourage the psychopath to think, feel, and act in non-violent, prosocial ways. This failure is echoed in the assertions of the lawsuit filed against the

Government of Ontario and Dr. Barker: "There was no scientifically proven value to these experiments" and they were carried out "for years and even decades without the crown questioning the value" or the adverse effects on the participants (Tyler, 2001, p. A18)

Comment

The bold experiment at Oak Ridge, however misguided, was an attempt to change the especially violent behavioural, cognitive, and affective reactions of a group of men who included many of the most anti-social psychopaths who at that point had not responded favourably to any conventional type of biological and psychological treatment or management strategies. Many of the techniques were unorthodox, to say the least. It is also clear that some of the specific strategies used in the STU mirrored some of the mind-altering experiments employed by Dr. Ewen Cameron at McGill's Allan Memorial Institute (see Chapter 1). Would society ever allow a similar program of "coercive resocialization" to be employed today? Very unlikely! As stated by Weisman (1995), the STU "is still remembered by some as a successful venture in utopian experimentation; for others, it embodies the ultimate of modern tyrannies—the state-authorized subjection of the individual without any countervailing restraint" (p. 289). We will address pertinent ethical and legal issues in detail in Chapter 18. There are now strict legal controls on psychiatric authority, including the patient's right under most circumstances to refuse treatment.

What will the future hold with respect to the possible treatment of the psychopath? Although the current Zeitgeist is a pessimistic view and the problem of the "violent psychopath" has been shifted from psychology and psychiatry to criminal justice (Weisman, 1995), Wong and Hare (2005) developed promising program guidelines for the institutional treatment of violent psychopathic offenders under the title Psychopathy Treatment Program (PTP). Their cognitive-behavioural approach concentrates especially on relapse prevention, a major shortcoming of past attempts to change the psychopath. Their PTP approach focuses on changing anti-social behaviour rather than enacting change to core personality features. Thus, some authors (e.g., Vien & Beech, 2006) have characterized the PTP as a behavioural self-management approach rather than a cure for psychopathy. Future research is needed to evaluate the effectiveness of this

The Oak Ridge Division serves all of Ontario. Oak Ridge Division of the Penetanguishene Mental Health Centre.

approach. A recent Canadian study conducted in Saskatoon highlights both the difficulties of treatment and the possible rewards for those psychopaths who are receptive to this type of treatment. Olver and Wong (2009) examined treatment responses of 45 psychopaths and 111 non-psychopaths receiving treatment in the Clearwater Sex Offender Treatment Program. Olver and Wong (2009) found that more than half of the psychopaths dropped out of treatment. However, psychopaths who did complete treatment were the participants who were at reduced risk for sexual and violent recidivism. These attest to why such treatments should still be implemented regardless of how difficult it proves to be. Will Wong and Hare's PTP approach stand the test of time and long-term follow-up?

What became of Dr. Barker? Elliot Barker became president of the Canadian Society for the Prevention of Cruelty to Children.

Primary sources: Rice and Harris (1993); Tyler (2001); Weissman (1995); Wong and Hare (2005)

SUMMARY

- Coded on Axis II in *DSM-IV-TR*, personality disorders are defined as enduring patterns of behaviour and inner experience that disrupt social and occupational functioning. They are usually codiagnosed with such Axis I disorders as depression and anxiety disorders. Although these diagnoses have become reliable in recent years, they overlap considerably and it is usual for a person to meet diagnostic criteria for more than one personality disorder. This high comorbidity, coupled with the fact that personality disorders are seen as the extremes of continuously distributed personality traits, has led to proposals to develop a dimensional rather than a categorical means of classifying these disorders.

- Personality disorders are grouped into three clusters in *DSM-IV-TR*. Specific diagnoses in the first cluster—odd/eccentric—include paranoid, schizoid, and schizotypal. These disorders are usually considered to be less severe variants of schizophrenia, and their symptoms are similar to those of the prodromal or residual phases of schizophrenia. Behaviour-genetic research gives some support to this assumption, especially for schizotypal personality disorder.

- The dramatic/erratic cluster includes borderline, histrionic, narcissistic, and anti-social personality disorders. The major symptom of borderline personality disorder is unstable, highly changeable emotions and behaviour; of histrionic personality disorder, exaggerated emotional displays; of narcissistic personality disorder, highly inflated self-esteem; and of anti-social personality disorder, seriously anti-social behaviour. Theories of the etiology of the first three of this cluster of diagnoses focus on early parent-child relationships. For example, object-relations theorists, such as Kernberg and Kohut, have proposed detailed explanations for borderline and narcissistic personality disorders, focusing on the child developing an insecure ego because of inconsistent love and attention from the parents. Linehan's cognitive-behavioural theory of borderline personality disorder proposes an interaction between a deficit in emotional regulation and an invalidating family environment. Psychopathy is related to the anti-social personality disorder but it is not an official *DSM* diagnosis.

- More is known about anti-social personality disorder and psychopathy than about other disorders in the dramatic/erratic cluster. Though they overlap a great deal, the two diagnoses are not exactly equivalent. The diagnosis of anti-social personality focuses on anti-social behaviour, whereas that of psychopathy, influenced by the writings of Cleckley, emphasizes emotional deficits, such as a lack of fear, regret, or shame. Psychopaths are thought to be unable to learn from experience, to have no sense of responsibility, and to be unable to establish genuine emotional relationships with other people.

- Research on their families indicates that psychopaths tend to have fathers who themselves were anti-social and that discipline during their childhoods was either absent or inconsistent. Genetic studies, particularly those using the adoption method, suggest that a predisposition to anti-social personality disorder is inherited.

- The core problem of the psychopath may be that impending punishment creates no inhibitions about committing anti-social acts. A good deal of overlapping evidence supports this view: (1) psychopaths are slow to learn to avoid shock; (2) according to their electrodermal responses, psychopaths show little anxiety, but as indicated by their faster heart rates, they seem more able than normal people to tune out aversive stimuli; and (3) psychopaths have difficulty altering their responses, even when their behaviour is not producing desirable consequences. A lack of empathy may also be a factor in the psychopath's callous treatment of others.

- The anxious/fearful cluster includes avoidant, dependent, and obsessive-compulsive personality disorders. The major symptom of avoidant personality disorder is fear of rejection or criticism; of dependent personality disorder, low self-confidence; and of obsessive-compulsive personality disorder, a perfectionistic, detail-oriented style. Theories of etiology focus on early experience. Avoidant personality disorder may result from the transmission of fear from parent to child via modelling. Dependent personality may be caused by disruptions of the parent-child relationship (e.g., through separation or loss) that lead to the fear of losing other relationships in adulthood. Obsessive-compulsive personality disorder may result from a fear of loss of control.

- Little has been discovered about effective therapy for the various personality disorders for several reasons. The high level of comorbidity among the diagnoses makes it difficult to evaluate reports of therapy. Some promising evidence is emerging, however, for the utility of dialectical behaviour therapy for borderline personality disorder. This approach combines client-centred acceptance with a cognitive-behavioural focus on making specific changes in thought, emotion, and behaviour.

- Psychotherapy for psychopathy is rarely successful. In addition to the pervasiveness and apparent intractability of an uncaring and manipulative lifestyle, the psychopath is by nature a poor candidate for therapy. People who habitually lie and lack insight into their own or others' feelings—and have no inclination to examine emotions—will not readily establish a trusting and open working relationship with a therapist.

KEY TERMS

anti-social personality (p. 452)
avoidant personality (p. 458)
borderline personality (p. 447)
dependent personality (p. 459)
dialectical behaviour therapy
  (p. 463)

histrionic personality (p. 451)
narcissistic personality (p. 452)
obsessive-compulsive personality
  (p. 459)
paranoid personality (p. 446)
personality disorders (p. 442)

personalized therapy (p. 445)
psychopathy (p. 453)
schema therapy (p. 462)
schizoid personality (p. 446)
schizotypal personality (p. 446)

REFLECTIONS: PAST, PRESENT, AND FUTURE

- Assume that you are a counselling psychologist at a university counselling centre who has a female undergraduate student as a client. She has been referred to you with a diagnosis on Axis I of the *DSM-IV-TR* of panic disorder with agoraphobia (see Chapter 6). You already have a treatment plan in mind based on your experience in working with anxious students. However, during your assessment, you realize that the woman also meets the criteria for a dependent personality disorder. How would your case conceptualization (see Chapter 4) and intervention change as a result of this new Axis II information?

- The beginning of this chapter included the now famous quote from Paul Bernardo that was made at the time of his trial. Do you think that Bernardo was telling the truth or is he, as Crown Attorney Ray Houlahan stated at the time, a "master of deception"? Was he showing genuine remorse or was his sorrow yet another "con"?

- Psychopaths do not seem to respond to attempts to change their anti-social behaviour through rehabilitation and treatment efforts. In fact, the clever ones probably do learn from their experiences—but only to become more successful predators and even less likely to be caught in the future. How should we then cope with them? Should Canada consider reinstating the death penalty (abolished in 1976) for serial killers and multiple murderers such as Clifford Olson and Paul Bernardo? Should such people be incarcerated for the rest of their lives as punishment for their crimes and/or because they are likely to reoffend?

Or, should they be considered criminally insane and committed for treatment? We will discuss the issue of criminal insanity, or what is now called "not criminally responsible on account of a mental disorder," and the prediction of violence in Chapter 18.

- Battered women often perceive that they are trapped in their abusive relationships. Do you think it possible that Karla Homolka was actually a battered wife whose involvement in the murders of Leslie Mahaffy and Kristen French was motivated out of fear of her husband? Or should she be considered as culpable as Bernardo?

- In the next chapter, we will discuss the various sexual disorders. Some psychopaths are also diagnosed with a *DSM-IV-TR* paraphilia. Paul Bernardo, for example, has reportedly been diagnosed with sexual sadism (Black, 2000). A current approach to treating sex offenders is to attempt to teach them to feel more empathy for their victims. Thus, the purpose of empathy training is to encourage the offender to envision the feelings and thoughts of his victims, thereby making him aware of the pain, suffering, and harm that he has caused. Although this strategy may be effective with some sexual offenders (see Chapter 14), do you think that it can work with sexual sadists who are also psychopaths (especially very intelligent psychopaths like Bernardo)? Is it possible that psychopaths can turn the empathy training to their own advantage by learning how to prey in an even more effective way on vulnerable children and women?

SEXUAL AND GENDER IDENTITY DISORDERS

Tony Brown, Canadian 1952-, *Untitled (Ballerina and Robot)*, c. 1984, paint on balsa wood on wood panel with metal frame, 2 panels, each: h. 202.4 × w. 127.5 cm unframed, Art Gallery of Ontario, Toronto. Gift of Bruce W. Ferguson, 2006 © Artist Tony Brown

"[O]nce it starts happening, it is brutal. You are always trying to run and hide from him and he is always tracking you down. It is something that you just can't tell anybody … Graham knew I needed a father figure coming from home because it was brutal at home and he preys on that. He knows. He knows exactly what he is doing. He put me in a position right off the top that screwed my whole life for me."

—Sheldon Kennedy, former NHL hockey player, describing the effects of being sexually abused at the age of 14 by his junior hockey coach, Graham James (Adams, 1997, A1)

"A crown psychiatrist would later categorize him as a sexual sadist, who enjoyed and relived every single second that he was raping both girls … In his world there was only one commandment: Take what you want, no matter who got hurt."

—Pron, Duncanson, and Rankin (1995) on Paul Bernardo

"There's no belonging. So you're an outcast. It doesn't change."

—David Reimer, who later committed suicide, reflecting on his lack of social connectedness after being raised both as a boy and a girl (Colapinto, 2000)

WILLIAM V is a 28-year-old computer programmer who lives alone. He grew up in a rural area within a conservative family with strong religious values. He has two younger brothers and an older sister. William began to masturbate at age 15; his first masturbatory experience took place while he watched his sister urinate in an outdoor toilet. Despite considerable feelings of guilt, he continued to masturbate two or three times a week while having voyeuristic fantasies …

On a summer evening at about 11:30 p.m., William was arrested for climbing a ladder and peeping into the bedroom of a suburban home. Just before this incident he had been drinking heavily at a cocktail lounge featuring a topless dancer … Feeling lonely and depressed [after leaving the bar], he had begun to drive slowly through a nearby suburban neighborhood, where he noticed a lighted upstairs window. With little premeditation, he had parked his car, erected a ladder he found lying near the house, and climbed up to peep. The householders, who were alerted by the sounds, called the police, and William was arrested. Although this was his first arrest, William had committed similar acts on two previous occasions …

[In therapy] William described a lonely and insecure life… Six months before the arrest, he had been rejected in a long-term relationship… As an unassertive and timid individual, he had responded by withdrawing from social relationships, and increasing his use of alcohol. His voyeuristic fantasies, which were present to begin with, became progressively more urgent as William's self-esteem deteriorated. His arrest had come as a great personal shock, although he recognized that his behavior was both irrational and self-destructive. (Rosen & Rosen, 1981, pp. 452–453. Reprinted with permission of McGraw-Hill Book Company)

Sexuality is one of the most personal—and generally private—areas of an individual's life. Each of us is a sexual being with preferences and fantasies that may surprise or even shock us from time to time. These are part of normal sexual functioning. But when our fantasies or desires begin to affect us or others in unwanted or harmful ways, as with William's peeping, they begin to qualify as abnormal. This chapter considers the full range of human sexual thoughts, feelings, and actions that are generally regarded as abnormal and dysfunctional and are listed in *DSM-IV-TR* as **sexual and gender identity disorders** (Table 14.1).

Our study of these disorders is divided into three major sections. First we examine theory and research in gender identity disorder, a diagnosis used to describe people who believe they are of the opposite sex. Next we consider the paraphilias, in which people are attracted to unusual sexual activities or objects. We include a discussion of rape, which, although not a diagnostic listing in *DSM-IV-TR*, merits examination in an abnormal psychology textbook. The third major section of the chapter addresses sexual dysfunctions, disruptions in normal sexual functioning found in many people who are in otherwise reasonably sound psychological health.

GENDER IDENTITY DISORDER

"Are you a boy or a girl?" "Are you a man or a woman?" For virtually all people—even those with serious mental disorders such as schizophrenia—the answer to such questions is immediate and obvious. And others would also agree unequivocally with the answer. Our sense of ourselves as male or female, our gender identity, is so deeply ingrained from earliest childhood that whatever stress is suffered at one time or another, the vast majority of people are certain beyond a doubt of their gender. In contrast, sexual identity or sexual orientation is the preference we have for the sex of a partner. For example, a man may be attracted to men—a matter of sexual orientation, without believing he is a woman—a matter of gender identity.

TABLE 14.1
SEXUAL AND GENDER IDENTITY DISORDERS

A. Gender identity disorder

B. Paraphilias
1. Fetishism
2. Transvestic fetishism
3. Pedophilia
4. Exhibitionism
5. Voyeurism
6. Frotteurism
7. Sexual masochism
8. Sexual sadism
9. Paraphilias not otherwise specified (e.g., zoophilia, necrophilia)

C. Sexual dysfunctions
1. Sexual desire disorders
   a. Hypoactive sexual desire disorder
   b. Sexual aversion disorder
2. Sexual arousal disorders
   a. Female sexual arousal disorder
   b. Male erectile disorder
3. Orgasmic disorders
   a. Female orgasmic disorder (inhibited female orgasm)
   b. Male orgasmic disorder (inhibited male orgasm)
   c. Premature ejaculation
4. Sexual pain disorders
   a. Dyspareunia
   b. Vaginismus

Source: DSM-IV-TR; APA, 2

CHARACTERISTICS OF GENDER IDENTITY DISORDER

People with **gender identity disorder** (GID), sometimes referred to as **transsexualism**, feel deep within themselves, usually from early childhood, that they are of the opposite sex. They have an aversion to same-sex clothing and activities. The evidence of their anatomy—normal genitals and the usual secondary sex characteristics, such as beard growth for men and developed breasts for women—does not persuade them that they are what others see them to be. A man can look at himself in a mirror, see the body of a biological man, and yet personally experience that body as belonging to a woman. He may try to pass as a member of the opposite sex and may even want to have his body surgically altered to bring it in line with his gender identity.

Levine (2003) stated that the majority of GID cases are diagnosed as GIDNOS (gender identity disorder not otherwise specified). That is, the person has symptoms that meet much of the description of GID, but there are some unique features that do not fit the precise criteria of GID. For instance, consider the following case of a man with aspects of GID that border on a fetish and transvestite behaviour.

A couple married for 32 years sought help immediately after the wife unexpectedly returned home and discovered that her husband had been out in public dressed as a woman. She was certain that his public passing as a woman represented a worsening of his judgement. Thirty years before, he had revealed that he was sexually aroused by women's clothing and wanted to cross-dress for lovemaking. She adamantly refused to consider it. Since that incident, she never mentioned it again, trying to act as though she was unaware of his "secret." Privately, she periodically worried that he was putting on her panty hose and bra to masturbate. Their sexual frequency declined after his initial request and, over the ensuing 20 years, she slowly developed an aversion to being touched by him. Sexual behavior ceased 10 years before.

The husband, a 55-year-old masculine-appearing physical education teacher, elected to enter individual therapy where he expressed his dilemma. He wanted to spare his wife pain. She believed that his "prurient" interest would go away if only he had more faith and prayed more, but he knew that nothing, including his fundamentalist religious patterns, diminished his periodic need to wear women's clothing. "If I tell her about my cross-dressing, she withdraws in anger. If I do not tell her about it, her imagination about how often I am doing it runs wild and she punishes me for cross-dressing that I don't do. If I stop cross-dressing, I deprive myself of unparalleled comfort and sumptuous pleasure and the desire eventually overtakes me. I lose either way. Should I honour my wife or my own identity?" His daily rate of masturbation had not changed much. He thought he masturbated to cope with her refusal to have sexual behaviour together. "My cross-dressing has actually kept me from having affairs with other women, thankfully." (From Levine, in Tasman, Kay, & Lieberman, 2003, p. 1490)

A person with gender identity disorder, or transsexualism, experiences great discomfort with his or her gender and may have sex reassignment surgery to become like someone of the opposite sex. Japan's Haruna Ai, shown here, was crowned Miss International Queen 2009, a pageant designed to celebrate the beauty and intelligence of transgendered/transsexual individuals. CP Images/David Longstreath.

This is a case of GIDNOS because GID is supposed to be differentiated from transvestic fetishism, which is one of the paraphilias discussed later in this chapter. Although they often dress in clothing typical of the opposite sex, transvestites do not identify themselves as of the opposite sex.

Much of what is known about GID and its early manifestations is due to research conducted at the Child and Adolescent Gender Identity Clinic at the Clarke Division of the Centre for Addiction and Mental Health in Toronto. This clinic first opened in 1978, and experts affiliated with it include Kenneth Zucker, Susan Bradley, and Ray Blanchard. The impact of these researchers on the field is reflected by the fact that they were part of the advising team that provided feedback on the *DSM-IV* diagnostic criteria for GID (see Bradley et al., 1991).

When GID begins in childhood, it is associated with cross-gender behaviours, such as dressing in opposite-sex clothes, preferring opposite-sex playmates, and engaging in play that would usually be considered more typical of the opposite sex (e.g., a boy playing with Barbie dolls). GID is associated with a developmental lag in achieving a sense of gender constancy or stability (i.e., acceptance that one is a boy or girl for life) (see Zucker et al., 1999). GID in a child is usually recognized by parents when the child is between two and four years old (Green & Blanchard, 1995). A review of 275 referrals showed that gender identity disorder is about 6.6 times more frequent in boys than in girls (Zucker, Bradley, & Sanikhani, 1997). Zucker et al. (1997) concluded that social factors partly account for the difference in referral rates; cross-gender behaviour is less tolerated when exhibited by boys and a higher threshold has to be met in order for a girl to be referred.

Zucker (2000) conducted a chart review that identified several factors associated with the decision to seek a clinical assessment. These factors included (1) a belief that the behaviour was no longer a phase that the child would grow out of; (2) a threshold violation (i.e., a boy wanting to cross-dress at nursery school, not just at home); (3) belief that the child was experiencing intense distress about being a boy or a girl; and (4) concerns about potential or actual rejection by peers. This last issue is a growing concern in light of the findings of an investigation of children with GID that was done in Toronto and the Netherlands (see Cohen-Kettenis et al., 2003). This study found that poor peer relations was the strongest predictor of behaviour problems in both samples.

Most children with GID do not grow up to be disordered in adulthood, even without professional intervention (for a review, see Zucker, 2005). However, many demonstrate a homosexual orientation. Attempts to assess and identify GID have been improved by the recent development by Canadian and European researchers of a 14-item parent report measure, the Gender Identity Questionnaire for Children (Cohen-Kettenis et al., 2006), which has shown to be valid in terms of helping identify children who fit GID diagnostic criteria.

Excluded from GID are people with schizophrenia who, on very rare occasions, claim to be of the other sex, as well as hermaphrodites, so-called intersexed individuals, who have both male and female reproductive organs. A male with GID experiences his sexual interest in men as a conventional heterosexual preference, since he considers himself a woman. Predictably, those with GID often arouse the disapproval of others and experience discrimination in employment when they choose to cross-dress. Cross-dressing is less of a problem for women with GID because contemporary fashions allow women to wear clothing similar to that worn by men. People with GID often experience anxiety and depression, not surprising given their psychological predicament and the negative attitudes most people have toward them. GID in childhood is linked with separation anxiety disorder (Bradley & Zucker, 1997). The prevalence rates for GID are slight: 1 in 30,000 for men and 1 in 100,000 to 150,000 in women (American Psychiatric Association, 1994). Note that proposed DSM-5 changes include changing the term "gender identity disorder" to "gender incongruence" and this is a response, in part, to concerns that the term gender identity disorder

is pejorative and stigmatizing (see www.dsm5.org). Other proposed changes include dropping the experience of distress or impairment as a criterion.

CAUSES OF GENDER IDENTITY DISORDER

The categorization of boys and girls as having their own masculine and feminine ways is so heavily laden with value judgements and stereotyping that considering cross-gender behavioural patterns in children to be abnormal may seem unjustified. In fact, a team of Canadian scholars conducted a conceptual analysis of the existing data on GID with a view to determining whether gender identity disorder in children should be considered a mental disorder according to DSM-IV criteria for mental disorder (Bartlett, Vasey, & Bukowski, 2000). Bartlett et al. (2000) concluded that children who experience a sense of inappropriateness in the culturally prescribed gender role of their sex but who do not experience discomfort with their biological sex should not be considered to have GID. Because of flaws in the DSM-IV-TR definition of mental disorder, and limitations of the current research base, there is simply not enough evidence to make any conclusive statement regarding children who experience discomfort with their biological sex. Note, however, that debate continues in general about the nature and validity of the DSM-IV criteria. Zucker (in press) has argued recently that a persistent desire to be the other gender should be a required symptom for a GID diagnosis. Currently, this symptom is not required.

Bartlett et al. (2000) went on to suggest that GID in children should be removed from the DSM. Moreover, they expressed their concern that viewing GID as a mental disorder may contribute to a labelling process that stigmatizes those children with GID who go on to develop homosexuality.

Clearly, more information is needed on the causes of GID in order to resolve this debate. Research investigations examining the etiology of GID have yielded some data indicating that these patterns can come from a physical disturbance. (Also see Focus on Discovery 14.1 for a discussion of nature vs. nurture in gender identity.) Specifically, evidence indicates that gender identity is influenced by hormones. A study demonstrating this point was conducted on the members of an extended family in the Dominican Republic (Imperato-McGinley et al., 1974). Participants were unable to produce a hormone that shapes the penis and scrotum in males during fetal development. They were born with very small penises and scrotums that looked like labial folds. Two thirds of them were raised as girls. However, when they reached puberty and testosterone levels increased, their sex organs changed. The penis enlarged, and the testicles descended into the scrotum. Seventeen of 18 participants then developed a male gender identity.

Other research shows that human and other primate offspring of mothers who have taken sex hormones during pregnancy frequently behave like members of the opposite sex and have anatomical abnormalities. For example, girls whose

FOCUS ON DISCOVERY 14.1
JOAN/JOHN: NATURE VS. NURTURE IN GENDER IDENTITY

In 1965, Linda Thiessen gave birth to twin boys. Seven months later, she noticed that the boys' foreskins were closing, making urination difficult. Her pediatrician recommended circumcision to correct the problem. However, because of either an equipment problem or an error by the surgeon, the penis of John, one of the twins, was destroyed. Although the Thiessens consulted with several physicians, none held out much hope of surgically reconstructing John's penis.

In December 1966, the Thiessens happened to see a television program on which John Money, a well-known sex researcher at Johns Hopkins, described the successful use of sex-change surgery for transsexuals. The Thiessens contacted Money, who proposed that turning John into Joan was the best option. The plan involved castration, construction of female genitals, and later treatment with sex hormones.

Several years later, Money shared the details of the case, describing it as a total success, consistent with his theory that gender identity is determined by the environment. Over subsequent years, he wrote several follow-ups, again claiming success. The facts reveal otherwise. Two researchers who managed to find Joan several years later conducted interviews with her and her parents and discovered a picture very different from the one Money had painted, one that suggests that there is a strong biological influence on gender identity.

Despite having been instructed to encourage feminine behaviour in Joan, her parents reported that Joan behaved in a very boyish way. At age 2, she ripped off her first dress, and during her preschool years, her play activities were clearly masculine. The same pattern continued into her elementary school years. When she reached age 11, it was time to begin her treatment with female hormones to promote the development of breasts and other feminine characteristics. Vaginal surgery was also recommended to construct a more feminine vagina. Although she reluctantly began taking estrogen, Joan steadfastly held out against the surgery.

By age 14, Joan decided to stop living as a girl. She adopted male attire, began to urinate standing up, and enrolled in a technical high school. Given Joan's refusal to have the surgery and a life filled with considerable distress, Joan's physicians finally recommended that she be told the whole story. She immediately changed her name back to John and decided to do everything possible to reverse the earlier treatments. She took male hormones, had her breasts removed, and had an artificial penis constructed. At age 21, John had another operation to improve his artificial penis, and at age 25, he was married.

Clearly, this case demonstrates a strong biological underpinning for gender identity; despite not having a penis, being encouraged to behave in a feminine way, and developing breasts as a result of taking estrogen, John never developed a female gender identity (Colapinto, 1997).

It has since been revealed in Colapinto's (2000) book entitled *As Nature Made Him: The Boy Who Was Raised as a Girl* that this case involved a family in Winnipeg and is actually the tragic story of Brenda/David Reimer. Reimer asked Colapinto to reveal her/his actual identity and provide more details of the case. These revelations have caused various societies to rethink their position. For instance, the American Association of Pediatrics now recommends that various factors be taken into account when deciding whether a child should be raised as male or female. Sadly, David Reimer committed suicide on May 5, 2004, at the age of 38. His suicide followed several setbacks, including a separation from his wife, and prolonged grief as a result of the death of his twin brother Brian, who passed away unexpectedly in 2002, as a result of a toxic mix of antidepressants and alcohol. According to Colapinto (2004), the root cause of David's decision to commit suicide was brooding about his physicality, his gender identity, and his sense of sexual inadequacy.

This ultimate outcome of the John/Joan case contrasts with a similar case in Canada reported by Bradley, Oliver, Chernick, and Zucker (1998). A two-month-old boy suffered a burn of his penile shaft during an electrocautery circumcision and eventually his penis sloughed off. The decision was made to reassign the child as a female and raise her as a girl. According to Bradley et al. (1998), long-term follow-up of this person has taken place, including an interview when she was 26 years old. In this case study, the reassigned girl continues to have a female gender identity, which Bradley et al. (1998) attribute to her being raised as a girl. However, they also noted that this young Canadian woman has a bisexual sexual identity and has had sexual experiences with both women and men. Also, she has many masculine interests and is employed in a blue-collar job that is usually dominated by men. Bradley et al. raised the possibility that this behavioural masculinity is a remnant of the masculine sexual biology and prenatal androgenization of the central nervous system. Nevertheless, the fact remains that unlike the outcome for John/Joan, this Canadian case study shows that the reassigned female gender identity is still evident, despite the presence of masculine tendencies.

---

mothers took synthetic progestins, which are precursors to male sex hormones, to prevent uterine bleeding during pregnancy, were found to be tomboyish during their preschool years (Ehrhardt & Money, 1967). Young boys whose

mothers ingested female hormones when pregnant were found to be less athletic as young children and to engage less in rough-and-tumble play than their male peers (Yalom, Green, & Fisk, 1973). Although such children were not necessarily abnormal in their gender identity, their mothers' ingestion of prenatal sex hormones did apparently give them higher than usual levels of cross-gender interests and behaviour.

Levels of sex hormones have also been studied in adults with gender identity disorder. In a review of several such investigations, Gladue (1985) found few, if any, differences in hormone levels among men with GID, male heterosexuals, and male homosexuals. A subsequent study found equivocal results: some women with GID had elevated levels of male hormones, but others did not (Bosinski et al., 1997). Even when differences are found, they are difficult to interpret because many people with GID use sex hormones in an effort to alter their bodies according to their wishes.

The available data, then, do not clearly support an explanation of adult transsexualism solely in terms of hormones. Even less conclusive is the research on possible chromosomal abnormalities, and efforts to find differences in brain structure between transsexuals and control group subjects have likewise been negative (Emory et al., 1991).

What about the possible role of the environment? Many, perhaps most, young children engage in cross-gender behaviour now and then. In some homes, such behaviour may receive too much attention and reinforcement from parents and other relatives. Interviews with the parents of children who show signs of GID often reveal that they did not discourage, and in many instances clearly encouraged, cross-dressing behaviour in their atypical children. This holds true especially for feminine boys. Female relatives found it cute when the boys dressed in the mother's old dresses and high-heeled shoes. Family albums typically contain photographs of the young boys attired in women's clothing. Such reactions of the family to an atypical child probably contribute in a major way to the conflict between his or her anatomical sex and the acquired gender identity (Green, 1987; Zuckerman & Green, 1993). The child's attractiveness is a factor that may contribute to this pattern of parental behaviour. Boys with GID have been rated as more attractive than control children, and girls with GID as less attractive (Fridell et al., 1996).

A novel hypothesis is that stereotypically feminine behaviour in boys is encouraged by mothers who, prior to the child's birth, wanted very much to have a girl. This hypothesis was not confirmed in a subsequent study, however (see Zucker et al., 1994). Moreover, GID is far less prevalent than would be indicated by the numbers of boys who play with dolls and girls who engage in contact sports.

Although dressing up is normal in childhood, most transsexuals trace their gender identity disturbance to childhood and report dressing in gender-inappropriate clothes. Francene Keery/Stock, Boston.

After sex-reassignment surgery, author and historian James Morris (top, in a 1960 photo. CORBIS) became Jan Morris (bottom, in 2007. © Colin McPherson/Corbis).

THERAPIES FOR GENDER IDENTITY DISORDER

We turn now to the interventions available to help people with GID. These are of two main types. One attempts to alter the body to suit the person's psychology; the other is designed to alter the psychology to match the person's body.

BODY ALTERATIONS A person with GID who enters a program that entails alteration of the body is generally required to undergo six to 12 months of psychotherapy. The therapy typically focuses not only on the anxiety and depression that the person has likely been experiencing, but also on available options for altering his or her body. Some people with GID may choose to have only cosmetic surgery; a male-to-female transsexual may have electrolysis to remove facial hair and surgery to reduce the size of the chin and Adam's apple. Many transsexuals also take hormones to bring their bodies physically closer to their beliefs about their gender. For example, female hormones will promote breast growth and soften the skin of male-to-female transsexuals (Schaefer, Wheeler, & Futterweit, 1997). Many people with GID go no further than using such methods, but some take the next step of having sex-reassignment surgery.

Sex-reassignment surgery is an operation in which the existing genitalia are altered to make them more like those of the opposite sex. The first sex-reassignment operation took place in Europe in 1930, but the surgery that attracted worldwide attention was performed on an ex-soldier, Christine (originally George) Jorgensen, in Copenhagen, Denmark, in 1952.

Sex-reassignment surgery is an option much more frequently exercised by men than by women. How beneficial is sex-reassignment surgery? There has been much controversy over this question. One of the most controversial outcome studies (Meyer & Reter, 1979) found no advantage to the individual "in terms of social rehabilitation" (p. 1015). The findings of this study led to the termination of the Johns Hopkins University School of Medicine sex-reassignment program, the largest such program in the United States.

A subsequent review by Green and Fleming (1990) of reasonably controlled outcome studies published between 1979 and 1989, with at least a one-year follow-up, drew more favourable conclusions. Of 130 female-to-male surgeries, about 97% could be judged satisfactory; of 220 male-to-female surgeries, 87% were satisfactory. Preoperative factors that seemed to predict favourable post-surgery adjustment were (1) reasonable emotional stability; (2) successful adaptation in the new role for at least one year before the surgery; (3) adequate understanding of the actual limitations and consequences of the surgery; and (4) psychotherapy in the context of an established gender identity program. The authors cautioned, however, that satisfactory ratings meant only that the patients reported that they did not regret having had the surgery. Such reports may be an overly generous criterion for favourable outcome, especially since they follow the investment of considerable time, money, and energy in an outcome that is, for the most part, irreversible. Data from 232 transsexuals who had sex reassignment surgery (male to female) found no one acknowledging regret; any dissatisfaction was attributed primarily to dissatisfaction with subsequent physical characteristics (Lawrence, 2003). A recent analysis suggests the need for greater caution in drawing firm conclusions. The authors noted the lack of randomized control trials and extensive follow-up studies, so perhaps it is best to conclude that there is only limited research-based evidence thus far of the benefits of sex-reassignment programs (see Monstrey, Vercruysse, & De Cuypere, 2009).

Sex-reassignment programs continue in many medical-psychological settings. It is estimated that, each year in the United States, more than 1,000 transsexuals are surgically altered to the opposite sex. Given that people who go to great lengths to have this surgery claim that their future happiness depends on the change, should this surgery be evaluated more extensively in terms of how happy such people are afterward?

ALTERATIONS OF GENDER IDENTITY Is sex reassignment the only option? Surgery and associated hormone administration used to be considered the only viable treatment for gender identity disorder because psychological attempts to shift gender identity had consistently failed. Gender identity was assumed to be too deep-seated to alter. Some apparently successful procedures for altering gender identity through behaviour therapy have been reported, however.

In one case, the client was a 17-year-old male who wanted to change his gender identity rather than—the choice of most transsexuals—change his anatomy to fit his feminine gender identity (Barlow, Reynolds, & Agras, 1973). The treatment involved shaping various specific behaviours, such as mannerisms and interpersonal behaviour—how to talk to young women, for instance—but it also included attention to cognitive components, such as fantasies. One technique paired slides of women with slides of men, the idea being that the sexual arousal from the latter might be transferred, or classically conditioned, to the former. This positive approach to changing the arousal properties of images and fantasies was complemented by aversion therapy to reduce the attractiveness of men. After half a year of intensive treatment, the young man was thinking of himself as a man, not as a woman, and was finding women sexually attractive. At a five-year follow-up, these changes were still present (Barlow, Abel, & Blanchard, 1979).

Two additional cases treated in the same way were reported by Barlow et al. (1979). Two men in their mid-twenties were en route to sex-reassignment surgery but had second thoughts. The behavioural retraining succeeded in altering their gender identity but not their attraction to men; their sexual orientation remained homosexual.

This work demonstrates that cross-gender identity may be amenable to change. But as the researchers point out, their clients might have been different from others with GID because they consented to participate in a therapy program aimed at changing gender identity. Most transsexuals refuse such treatment. For them, physically altering their bodies is the only legitimate goal. But if the surgical option did not exist, would more professional energy be expended on developing psychological procedures for altering gender identity? And if those procedures involved teaching men to be more traditionally masculine and women more traditionally feminine, would that be desirable or ethically defensible? These are but two of the ethical conundrums associated with treating disorders of gender identity.

CANADIAN PERSPECTIVES 14.1
TRANSSEXUALS AND THE COMPLEX CASE OF KIMBERLY NIXON

Kimberly Nixon is a former airline pilot who had a sex-change operation in 1990. Overall, Nixon has lived as a woman for approximately 20 years. Nixon has a young son and, while a woman, was sexually abused by a man.

The case of Kimberly Nixon first became known to the public in 1995. She applied to be a volunteer rape counsellor for the Vancouver Rape Relief Society (VRRS), a women-only rape counselling organization (with an associated shelter for women) that was founded in 1973 and does not accept men as volunteers or members. Nixon was asked to leave when she acknowledged her past as a man. One day later, Nixon filed a human rights complaint with the British Columbia Human Rights Commission. First, however, she contemplated suicide. She stated that after being asked to leave, "I could barely see because of the tears in my eyes … All I could think of was the Lion's Gate Bridge—jumping off the bridge" (Wente, 2000, p. 1).

VRRS representatives contended that it would be traumatic for female rape victims to receive counsel from a woman who appeared to be a man in drag. At issue was the legal question of "What is a woman?" Regardless of these arguments, on June 7, 2000, the B.C. Supreme Court rejected the attempt by the VRRS to prevent the human rights commission from hearing Nixon's discrimination complaint, and the case went forward to a human rights tribunal.

The complexities inherent in this case were illustrated by comments made by Judy Rebick, one of Canada's foremost feminists and a former president of the National Action Committee on the Status of Women. Rebick testified on behalf of the VRRS before the tribunal in December 2000, arguing that women's groups have the right to decide who their members are. However, outside the hearing room, she observed, "What makes this tense is there's no question that transgendered people suffer from discrimination, they suffer a great deal. So, of course, [in] your heart as a feminist you want to be on their side in every fight but you can't because there is a conflict of rights" (Bailey, 2000, p. 1).

The tribunal's decision included the determination that the VRRS acted in good faith and meant no harm, but was nevertheless in breach of the Human Rights Code. The VRRS was ordered to pay $7,500 to Nixon.

Kimberly Nixon, a transsexual, filed a human rights complaint against the Rape Relief Society of Vancouver. The Human Rights Tribunal ruled in her favour, but this decision was overturned by the British Columbia Supreme Court. © National Post/Nick Didlick.

In 2002, the VRRS requested a judicial review of the decision by the B.C. Supreme Court because it was concerned that men would now be able to gain access to the shelter as a result of the decision. In December 2003, the Court overturned the tribunal's decision on the grounds that the VRRS is protected by section 41 of the Human Rights Code, which protects charitable groups and their right to freedom of association. The monetary award was also overturned. Nixon's attempt to appeal the ruling went as far as the Supreme Court of Canada but it rejected Nixon's appeal in February 2007. Thus, the claim of discrimination was not supported.

Thinking Critically

1. Do you agree with the final decision reached by the B.C. Supreme Court? Do you think discrimination has taken place here? Should an organization such as the VRRS have the right to exclude transsexuals even though other organizations have accepted them?

2. Whose rights matter the most in this situation? The rights of Kimberly Nixon? The rights of victims seeking assistance from the VRRS? Or the rights of the VRRS? Explain your selection.

THE PARAPHILIAS

In *DSM-IV-TR*, the **paraphilias** are a group of disorders involving sexual attraction to unusual objects or sexual activities that are unusual in nature. In other words, there is a deviation (*para*) in what the person is attracted to (*philia*). The fantasies, urges, or behaviours must last at least six months and cause significant distress or impairment. A person can have the behaviours, fantasies, and urges that a person with a paraphilia has (such as exhibiting the genitals to an unsuspecting stranger or fantasizing about doing so) but not be diagnosed with a paraphilia if the fantasies or behaviours are not recurrent or if he or she is not markedly distressed by them. Indeed, surveys have shown that many people occasionally fantasize about some of the activities we will be describing. A Canadian survey found that 50% of men report voyeuristic fantasies of peeping at unsuspecting naked women (Hanson & Harris, 1997).

The *DSM* diagnostic criterion of distress or impairment has created some problems because many people with the behavioural features of a paraphilia are neither distressed nor impaired (Hudson & Ward, 1997). For example, according to the *DSM* criteria, someone who has repeatedly had sex with young children but is not distressed or impaired cannot be diagnosed as having pedophilia. Therefore, many researchers in this field hold a more behavioural definition of paraphilias and ignore the distress and disability parts of the *DSM* definition. More generally, some paraphilias may not be disorders *per se* because they are atypical but do not cause anyone apparent distress. Thus, one *DSM-5* recommendation is to distinguish between paraphilias and paraphilic disorders that cause some harm or distress (see www.dsm5.org).

People often exhibit more than one paraphilia, and such patterns can be aspects of other mental disorders, such as schizophrenia, depression, or one of the personality disorders. Accurate prevalence statistics are not available for most of the paraphilias. Many people with paraphilias may choose not to reveal their deviance when responding to a community survey. Similarly, statistics on arrests are likely to be underestimated because many crimes go unreported and some paraphilias (e.g., voyeurism) involve an unsuspecting victim. The data do indicate, though, that most people with paraphilias, whatever their sexual orientation, are male; even with masochism and pedophilia, which do occur in noticeable numbers of women, men vastly outnumber women. As some persons with paraphilias seek non-consenting partners, these disorders often have legal consequences.

FETISHISM

Fetishism involves a reliance on an inanimate object for sexual arousal. The person with fetishism, almost always a male, has recurrent and intense sexual urges toward non-living objects, called fetishes (e.g., women's shoes), and the presence of the fetish is strongly preferred or even necessary for sexual arousal to occur.

Transvestic fetishism, or transvestism, is diagnosed when the person sexually arouses himself by dressing in opposite-sex clothing. Frank Fournier/Contact Press Images Inc.

Feet and shoes, sheer stockings, rubber products such as raincoats, gloves, toilet articles, fur garments, and especially underpants are common sources of arousal for fetishists. Some can carry on their fetishism by themselves in secret by fondling, kissing, smelling, sucking, placing in their rectum, or merely gazing at the adored object as they masturbate. Others need their partner to don the fetish as a stimulant for intercourse. Fetishists sometimes become interested in acquiring a collection of the desired objects, and they may commit burglary week after week to add to their hoard.

The attraction felt by the fetishist toward the object has a compulsive quality; it is experienced as involuntary and irresistible. It is the degree of the erotic focalization—the exclusive and very special status the object occupies as a sexual stimulant—that distinguishes fetishisms from the ordinary attraction that, for example, high heels and sheer stockings may hold for heterosexual men in Western cultures. The boot fetishist must see or touch a boot to become aroused, and when the fetish is present, the arousal is overwhelmingly strong.

The disorder usually begins by adolescence, although the fetish may have acquired special significance even earlier, during childhood. Fetishists often have other paraphilias, such as pedophilia, sadism, and masochism (Mason, 1997).

TRANSVESTIC FETISHISM

When a man is sexually aroused by dressing in women's clothing, although he still regards himself as a man, the term **transvestic fetishism**, or transvestism, applies. The extent of transvestism varies from wearing women's underwear under conventional clothing to full cross-dressing. Some transvestites may enjoy appearing socially as women; some female impersonators become performers in nightclubs, catering to the delight that many sexually conventional people take in observing skilled cross-dressing. However, these impersonators are not considered transvestic unless the cross-dressing is associated with sexual arousal. Transvestism should not be confused with the cross-dressing associated with GID or with the cross-dressing preferences of some homosexuals.

The term *autogynephilia* was coined by Ray Blanchard (1989) at the Clarke Institute in Toronto to refer to a man's tendency to become sexually aroused at the thought or image of himself as a woman. Blanchard (1992) noted that autogynephilia is typically, but not always, found in association with transvestism.

Transvestic fetishism usually begins with partial cross-dressing in childhood or adolescence. Transvestites are heterosexual, always males, and by and large cross-dress episodically rather than on a regular basis. They tend to be otherwise masculine in appearance, demeanour, and sexual preference. Many are married. Cross-dressing usually takes place in private and in secret and is known to few members of the family. This is one of the paraphilias for which the *DSM* distress and disability criteria do not seem to apply at all.

The urge to cross-dress may become more frequent over time and sometimes is accompanied by gender dysphoria—discomfort with one's anatomical sex—but not to the extent found in GID. Transvestism is comorbid with other paraphilias, notably masochism (Zucker & Blanchard, 1997).

PEDOPHILIA AND INCEST

"If I can help just one person … then all of this will have been worth it."
—Martin Kruze on Jane Hawtin Live, February 26, 1997, concerning his revelations about being sexually abused as a child by employees at Maple Leaf Gardens

According to the *DSM*, individuals who practise **pedophilia** (*pedos*, Greek for "child") are adults who derive sexual gratification through physical and often sexual contact with prepubescent children unrelated to them. *DSM-IV-TR* requires that the offender be at least 16 years old and at least five years older than the child. Research does not appear to support the *DSM*'s statement that all pedophiles prefer prepubescent children; an analysis by Marshall (1997) at Queen's University revealed that some of them victimize postpubescent children who are younger than the legal age to consent to having sex with an adult.

Another qualification is that recent surveys, including Internet surveys, indicate that a substantial proportion of those who identify themselves as pedophiles (more than 50% in some surveys) have no known sexual contact with children or legal history of doing so (see Seto, 2009). This calls into question the tendency to equate pedophilia with sexual contact with children and much of the research literature, which tends to focus on individuals who have come to our attention via their involvement with the legal system.

Pedophilia occurs much more frequently in men than in women (Seto, 2007, 2009), though case studies of female pedophiles have been reported, including that of a young Canadian woman who had sexual relations with two four-year-old daughters of acquaintances (see Chow & Choy, 2002). Pedophilia is often comorbid with mood and anxiety disorders, substance abuse, and other paraphilias (Raymond et al., 1999). The pedophile can be heterosexual or homosexual. In recent years, the Internet has played an increasing role in pedophilia (Seto, 2009); pedophiles use the Internet to acquire child pornography and to contact potential victims (Durkin, 1997). It is noteworthy that a Canadian study by Seto, Cantor, and Blanchard (2006) found that a child pornography offence is a stronger diagnostic indicator of pedophilia than is an actual history of sexually offending against child victims! Another follow-up study conducted in Canada found that more frequent pornography use was a strong predictor of recidivism, especially among those already deemed

On June 17, 2004, Michael Briere was sentenced to 25 years in prison for the brutal sexual attack and strangulation of 10-year-old Holly Jones of Toronto. Briere's "dark secret" was an overwhelming desire to have sex with a young child. His fantasy was fuelled by child pornography readily downloaded from the Internet. Canada's child pornography laws became an issue in the June 2004 federal election. CP Image Archive/ Tammy Hoy.

to be higher-risk offenders. Also, the use of pornography with more deviant content was a risk factor for offenders of various levels of risk (see Kingston et al., 2008). The extensive, aberrant use of the Internet has resulted in Internet sex offender treatment programs (see Middleton, 2008). As a result of these tendencies, convicted pedophiles who are granted parole often have their access to the Internet restricted as a condition of their release. This was the case for Robert Noyes, who was granted a full parole release in June 2003 but with restricted Internet access. Noyes, a teacher and a school principal in British Columbia, was arrested in 1985 and charged in connection with approximately 600 separate assaults, involving at least 65 children (mostly boys) between the ages of 6 and 15. Noyes was one of the first pedophiles to be designated as a dangerous offender, so he could have been in prison for an indefinite term.

The Internet has also been used to facilitate research on pedophilia. A growing trend is to evaluate the nature and correlates of pedophilia by having pedophiles take part in studies conducted on-line, with their anonymity protected (see Seto, 2004, for a discussion). While responses obtained via the Internet may be subject to socially desirable responding, perhaps it also facilitates a level of candidness that is not found when face-to-face interactions are involved.

Pedophilia in Canada has received great public attention because of the number of highly publicized cases, including the Maple Leaf Gardens scandal. It was revealed in 1997 that about 90 children had been sexually abused by some Maple Leaf Gardens employees, including George Hannah, Gordon Stuckless, and John Paul Roby. The tragedy of Martin Kruze, one of the boys victimized who "blew the whistle" on a shameful period in Canadian sport history, is told by Cathy Vine and Paul Challen's (2002) moving account, *Gardens of Shame*. Kruze worked as a spokesperson for sexual abuse survivors. Sadly, he jumped off a bridge to his death at age 35 just three days after Stuckless was sentenced to two years less a day in a reformatory. Previously, we also learned of the abuse experienced by Sheldon Kennedy, a former player in the National Hockey League. In 1997, Kennedy's coach in junior hockey, Graham James, pleaded guilty to charges of sexual assault.

Another disturbing case occurred in New Brunswick at the Kingsclear Youth Training Facility near Fredericton. Karl Toft, who worked at the facility, is a convicted pedophile who was found guilty in 1992 of buggery, bestiality, and more than 30 counts of sexual assault involving children. Toft has since admitted to abusing more than 150 children over two decades. He was denied parole as recently as August 2000. The parole board's decision at that time was based on several factors, including Toft's apparent lack of empathy for his victims, his lack of "internal control mechanism," and his unwillingness to submit to medication as a form of treatment. Then, in August 2001, the decision was made to grant Toft parole and send him to a halfway house in Edmonton. The Edmonton Police Service issued a public warning that outlined his convictions, noted his participation in a sex offender program, and included a physical description with a photo. In response to vigorously expressed public concern, the Correctional Service of Canada reversed the decision and sent him to a regional psychiatric centre in Saskatoon, a secure treatment facility (Auld, 2001).

Violence is seldom a part of the molestation, although it can be, as occasionally comes to people's attention through lurid media accounts. But even if most pedophiles do not physically injure their victims, some intentionally frighten the child by, for example, killing a pet and threatening further harm if the youngster tells his or her parents. Sometimes the pedophile is content to stroke the child's hair, but he may also manipulate the child's genitalia, encourage the child to manipulate his, and, less often, attempt intromission. Molestations may be repeated for weeks, months, or years if they are not discovered by other adults or if the child does not protest.

A minority of pedophiles, who might also be classified as sexual sadists or anti-social (psychopathic) personalities, inflict serious bodily harm on the object of their passion. These individuals, whether psychopathic or not, are perhaps best viewed as child rapists and are different from pedophiles in that they wish to hurt the child physically at least as much as they wish to obtain sexual gratification (Groth, Hobson, & Guy, 1982). Indeed, research by Firestone et al. (1998, 2000) at the University of Ottawa shows that although it is often difficult to distinguish homicidal child molesters from non-homicidal child molesters, it is still the case that homicidal child molesters show a greater physiological response to and preference for descriptions of assaults on children. Although psychopathy is more elevated in these men than in incest offenders, rapists tend to have even higher levels of psychopathy when assessed by Hare's PCL-R and they are more likely to endorse anti-social attitudes in general (Firestone et al., 2000; Mills, Anderson, & Kroner, 2004).

Convicted pedophile Karl Toft. The group Mad Mothers Against Pedophiles planned rallies to protest his release. CP Image Archive/ Robert Wilson.

Incest refers to sexual relations between close relatives for whom marriage is forbidden. It is most common between brother and sister. The next most common form is between father and daughter. Although father-daughter incest is considered more pathological, data from Quebec question this conclusion because brother-sister incest was associated with just as much distress among victims as incest involving fathers or stepfathers; moreover, brother-sister incest was associated with a much higher frequency of sexual penetration (Cyr, Wright, McDuff, & Perron, 2002).

The taboo against incest seems virtually universal in human societies, a notable exception being the marriages of Egyptian pharaohs to their sisters or other females of their immediate families. In Egypt, it was believed that the royal blood should not be contaminated by that of outsiders. The incest taboo makes sense according to present-day scientific knowledge. The offspring from a father-daughter or a brother-sister union have a greater probability of inheriting a pair of recessive genes, one from each parent. For the most part, recessive genes have negative biological effects, such as serious birth defects. The incest taboo, then, has adaptive evolutionary significance.

There is evidence that the structure of families in which incest occurs is unusually patriarchal and traditional, especially with respect to the subservient position of women (Alexander & Lupfer, 1987). Parents in these families also tend to neglect and remain emotionally distant from their children (Madonna, Van Scoyk, & Jones, 1991). Furthermore, it is believed that incest is more prevalent when the mother is absent or disabled (Finkelhor, 1979), as mothers usually protect their daughters from intrafamilial sexual abuse.

Incest is listed in *DSM-IV-TR* as a subtype of pedophilia. Several major distinctions are drawn between incest and pedophilia. First, incest is by definition between members of the same family. Second, incest victims tend to be older than the victims of a pedophile's desires. It is more often the case that a father becomes interested in his daughter when she begins to mature physically, whereas the pedophile is usually interested in the youngster precisely because he or she is sexually immature. The term gynephile refers to an adult who is incestuous with a child in the absence of a mature, adult sex partner.

An archival study of cases in Saskatchewan examined the nature of incest vs. extrafamilial (outside the family) forms of child sexual abuse and found that incest had an earlier onset and longer duration (Fischer & McDonald, 1998). Also, victims of incest had comparatively greater levels of physical injury and emotional distress. The impacts of experiencing sexual abuse are highlighted in Focus on Discovery 14.2.

A study by Studer et al. (2000) at the Alberta Hospital–Edmonton Site yielded evidence suggesting that risk assessments of incest offenders have substantially underestimated the threat they actually posed. First, it has generally been believed that incest offenders have a low likelihood of being a repeat incest offender (between 4 and 10%). Studer et al. (2000), however, found that 22% had prior incestuous offences and were, in fact, repeat offenders. Also, almost two thirds of the incest offenders reported having non-incestuous victims as well, which suggests they are also pedophiles. Studer et al. concluded that for these men, the main issue is one of opportunity; they have a general sexual attraction to children that may indeed go beyond members of their own family.

Further empirical work by Rice and Harris (2002) indicates that daughter-only molesters have lower levels of psychopathy than incestuous fathers who also engage in extrafamilial offences. Although these daughter-only child molesters have less deviant sexual preferences and lower recidivism rates than molesters who commit offences inside and outside the family, their sexual preferences are still deviant overall and the recidivism risk is not low in absolute terms.

Data from penile plethysmography studies (see Figure 14.1 for an explanation of these measures) conducted in Canada confirm that men who molest children unrelated to them are sexually aroused by photographs of nude children. Men who molest children within their families show more arousal to adult heterosexual cues (Marshall, Barbaree, & Christophe, 1986).

One of the first rudimentary versions of the penile plethysmograph was developed by Kurt Freund, who developed his first device in Czechoslovakia. Freund then worked for several decades at the Clarke Institute of Psychiatry in Toronto (see Freund, 1967; Freund & Watson, 1991). Plethysmograph measures have been described as "phallometric tests," and they have been used to identify males—both adults (Laws, Hanson, Osborn, & Greenbaum, 2000) and adolescents (Seto, Lalumière, & Blanchard, 2000)—with pedophilic interests. Once established, phallometric testing results show little variance, indicating that it is very difficult to change sexual preferences (Lalumière & Quinsey, 1998).

Two of the four sisters who were sexually abused by their brother, John Henry Miller, held a press conference in British Columbia in 2009. Miller committed incest between 1956 and 1974 and only stopped after being arrested for killing an RCMP officer, Constable Roger Pierlet. The sisters reported the case to the police in 2008 and Miller was sentenced to an additional five years in a halfway house in July 2009. However, he died in hospital of a stroke less than one week later. The Canadian Press/Darryl Dyck.

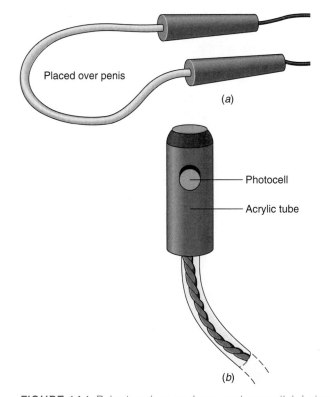

Placed over penis

(a)

Photocell

Acrylic tube

(b)

FIGURE 14.1 Behavioural researchers use two genital devices for measuring sexual arousal. Both are sensitive indicators of vasocongestion of the genitalia (i.e., the flooding of the veins with blood, a key physiological process in sexual arousal); both provide specific measurements of sexual excitement (e.g., Adams et al., 1992; Barlow et al., 1970; Heiman et al., 1991). (a) For men, the penile plethysmograph measures changes in the circumference of the penis by means of a strain gauge, consisting of a very thin rubber tube filled with mercury. As the penis is engorged with blood, the tube stretches, changing its electrical resistance, which can then be measured by a suitably configured polygraph. (b) For women, sexual arousal can be measured by a vaginal plethysmograph, such as the device invented by Sintchak and Geer (1975). Shaped like a menstrual tampon, this apparatus can be inserted into the vagina to provide direct measurement of the increased blood flow characteristic of female sexual arousal.

Although phallometric testing is used routinely with sex offenders, concerns have been raised about the reliability and validity of these measures (see Marshall & Fernandez, 2000). In particular, Marshall and Fernandez expressed concern about the demonstrated ability of some people to fake their responses when being measured.

It is generally believed that a history of exposure to pornography is a cause of sexual offending. However, in a review paper, a team of Canadian researchers concluded that pornography only plays a role among men who are already predisposed to sexually offend (Seto, Maric, & Barbaree, 2001); men who are not predisposed show little effect.

It is sometimes alleged that child pornography is a critical ingredient in motivating child molestation in predisposed people, but a clinical study of male pedophiles indicates that such materials may not even be necessary. These men were arousable by media materials widely available, such as television ads and clothing catalogues picturing young children in underwear. In other words, rather than using explicitly pornographic materials, these men appeared to construct in their minds their own sexually stimulating material from sources generally viewed as innocuous (Howitt, 1995).

As in most paraphilias, a strong subjective attraction impels pedophilic behaviour. According to Gebhard and his colleagues (1965), pedophiles generally know the children they molest; they are neighbours or friends of the family.

Alcohol use and stress increase the likelihood that a pedophile will molest a child (Abracen et al., 2006). Research by Looman at the Regional Treatment Centre in Kingston, Ontario, suggests that child molesters have sexual fantasies about children when their mood is negative, perhaps as a way to cope with their unease; however, it also appears that having a pedophilic fantasy enhances the negative affect. Perhaps this downward spiral can eventually lead to the person's acting on the impulse to molest a child (Looman, 1995). Indeed, research using inmates from Canadian federal penitentiaries confirmed that sexual offenders, relative to non-sexual violent offenders, are more likely to report using consensual and non-consensual sex as a coping strategy (Cortoni & Marshall, 2001). Data also suggest that pedophiles are low in social maturity, self-esteem, impulse control, and social skills (Kalichman, 1991; Marshall, Cripps, Anderson, & Cortoni, 1999). Most older heterosexual pedophiles are or have been married.

One half of all child molestations, including those that take place within the family, are committed by adolescent males (Morenz & Becker, 1995). About 50% of adult offenders began their illegal behaviour in their early teens. These juveniles have typically experienced a chaotic and negative family life. Their homes often lack structure and positive support (Blaske et al., 1989). Research conducted in Canada by Worling (2001) as part of the Sexual Abuse: Family Education and Treatment (SAFE-T) Program has shown that many of these teenagers were themselves sexually abused as children. Thus, there was support for what is now known as the abused abuser hypothesis. Worling (2001) reported that 39% of his sample had experienced childhood sexual victimization and 45% reported receiving abusive physical discipline from parents. A new meta-analysis (quantitative review of past studies) of the results of 17 studies confirmed that sex offenders, relative to non-sex offenders, are more likely to have a history of sexual abuse but not physical abuse (Jespersen, Lalumière, & Seto, 2009).

Overall, adolescents who engage in child molestation are more socially isolated and have poorer social skills than peers who are in trouble with the law for non-sexual crimes (Awad & Saunders, 1989). Social isolation is most characteristic of the unusual/isolated group identified by Worling (2001), who suggested that these adolescents are most likely to benefit from training in basic social skills, such as learning how to listen, how to start a conversation, and how to introduce oneself to someone else. Academic problems are also common (Becker & Hunter, 1997). In general, these young males (females are much less often found among the ranks of sex offenders) are what one would call juvenile delinquents, in frequent trouble with the police for a wide variety of lawbreaking. Not surprisingly, conduct disorder and substance abuse are frequent diagnoses made of these youths. Somewhat more surprisingly, depression and anxiety disorders are also common features (Galli et al., 1999).

Because overt physical force is seldom used in incest or pedophilia, the child molester often denies that he is actually forcing himself on his victim. Sometimes the molester rationalizes that he is doing something good for the child, despite the betrayal of trust that is inherent in child sexual abuse and despite the serious negative psychological consequences that can befall the abused child some years later.

New developments involving the assessment of child molesters continue to emerge, and researchers based in Canada have played a substantial role. For instance, Seto and Lalumière (2001) developed a brief measure known as the Screening Scale for Pedophilic Interests (SSPI) and have shown that this screening instrument is quite successful in distinguishing pedophilic child molesters and non-child molesters who have abused older victims. This instrument was developed on the basis of earlier work that compared adult child molesters and molesters of adolescents (see Freund & Watson, 1991). Seto, Harris, Rice, and Barbaree (2004) administered the SSPI to two samples of adult male sex offenders with child victims. The SSPI was associated significantly with violent recidivism, sexual recidivism, and phallometrically measured sexual arousal from depictions of prepubescent children.

One SSPI item refers to whether an "unrelated" (extra-familial) victim was involved. Greater pedophilic interest is present when an unrelated victim was involved. Item analyses by Seto and Lalumière (2001) found that having a male victim was twice as predictive as the other items in identifying child molesters. A study of pedophiles by Blanchard et al. (1999) found that lower levels of intellectual functioning are associated with greater interest in boys and in younger children in general.

FOCUS ON DISCOVERY 14.2
CHILD SEXUAL ABUSE: EFFECTS ON THE CHILD AND MODES OF INTERVENTION

A 1997 survey of police forces in six provinces found that 62% of all victims of a sexual offence were young people under the age of 18, with 30% being young children under the age of 12 (Statistics Canada, 1999). The prototypical act is a sexual offence committed against a female by someone familiar to her. Overall, fewer than 1 in 5 victims are males, but the proportion of males being victimized rises to 31% for children under the age of 12. Half of the sexual offences were committed by a friend or acquaintance, and another 28% were committed by family members.

Pedophilia and incest are forms of **child sexual abuse** (CSA) and should be distinguished from non-sexual child abuse (i.e., physical abuse, emotional abuse, neglect). In Canada, anyone aware of abuse taking place is required by law to report it to the police or child protective agencies. One positive development is that the results of the 1998 and 2003 Canadian Incidence Studies of Reported Child Abuse and Neglect indicate a decline in the number of cases investigated for CSA in recent years (Trocmé et al., 2001, 2005). Still, the sheer number of cases is troubling. Trocmé et al. (2001) reported that over 14,000 cases were investigated and CSA was substantiated in 38% of the cases (more than 5,000) based on 1998 investigations conducted by Canadian child welfare services.

EFFECTS ON THE CHILD

The short-term effects of CSA are variable. A subset of children are seemingly resilient after disclosing severe abuse (Hébert, Parent, Daignault, & Tourigny, 2006). However, the majority are negatively affected, with problems including anxiety, depression, low self-esteem, and conduct disorder. Hébert et al. (2006) identified a group of children who mostly had severe anxiety symptoms vs. other children who had a range of symptoms. The negative impact on self-esteem can influence numerous self-esteem domains, including physical self-esteem and social self-esteem (Murthi, Servaty-Seib, & Elliott, 2006).

Several factors likely contribute to how CSA affects a child. One is the nature of the abuse itself. Consider, for example, the probable differences in consequences between a case involving the repeated rape of a 7-year-old girl by her father and that of a 12-year-old boy who has a sexual relationship with an older woman. Recent results from a sample of 50 girls from Quebec who experienced CSA found one year later that the duration of the abuse was linked, not surprisingly, with poor functioning (Daignault & Hébert, 2008). Poorer functioning was also found among the girls with dissociative symptoms. Protective factors were approach coping and engagement in extracurricular activities. In general, an earlier onset of the abuse also predicts more extreme levels of distress (Kaplow & Widom, 2007).

Sometimes the aftermath of CSA is post-traumatic stress disorder (PTSD). Indeed, *DSM-IV-TR* lists sexual assault as one of the stressors that can be traumatic. A team of researchers from Université Laval and Université du Québec à Montréal conducted a study in which they compared the characteristics of three groups of children between the ages of 7 to 12: a sexually abused group, a medical control group, and a community group

In contrast to the lighthearted persona he portays on television, Drew Carey, comedian and host of the TV show *The Price Is Right*, disclosed in his autobiography that he was sexually abused as a child, has suffered from depression, and had attempted suicide on two occasions. CP Picture Archive/Kevork Djansezian.

(Tremblay, Hébert, & Piché, 2000). The authors found that the sexually abused group had higher levels of symptoms than the other two groups, in terms of both Type I and Type II symptoms. A high level of self-blame and lack of a supportive family environment also increase the chances that the CSA will produce negative reactions (Kuehnle, 1998).

Regarding long-term effects, we have seen in previous chapters that a history of CSA is associated with many disorders, including depression, dissociative identity disorder, eating disorders, and borderline personality disorder. A review by Whiffen and MacIntosh (2005) identified several factors that mediate the association between child sexual abuse and subsequent depression, including shame, self-blame, and relying on avoidant coping strategies.

A history of CSA is also associated reliably with sexual revictimization according to a review conducted by Catherine Classen from the University of Toronto and her colleagues (see Classen, Palesh, & Aggarwal, 2005). That is, those with a history of CSA, relative to those lacking this history, are more likely to be a victim of sexual assault in adulthood. Predictive factors include experiencing multiple traumas and childhood sexual abuse that happened more recently. Revictimization was also associated with greater distress, self-blame, and shame. Victims of CSA are also more likely to be victims of assaults in general. Researchers are seeking to explain why this revictimization occurs.

Some sexually abused children become suicidal in subsequent years. Victims of child sexual abuse, such as comedian Drew Carey and former NHL hockey players Sheldon Kennedy and Theoren Fleury, have acknowledged that they have had suicidal tendencies. A recent epidemiological study found that a history of sexual abuse had a strong link with suicide attempts and suicide ideation, and the association was stronger among women (Bebbington et al., 2009). This association was mediated by negative affective states such as depression. Analyses of interpersonal functioning show that CSA is also associated with interpersonal distress such as marital distress and with problems in sexual functioning (see Rumstein-McKean & Hunsley, 2001).

PREVENTION

An important goal of any prevention program is to reduce the incidence, prevalence, and severity of a particular problem. For CSA, prevention efforts have focused on elementary schools. The ESPACE program is offered in schools throughout Quebec. An evaluation of this program found that the grades 1 and 3 students who took part were better able to identify appropriate behavioural responses when presented with vignettes of situations that could involve abuse (Hébert, Lavoie, Piché, & Poitras, 2001). Parents reported that this program also had indirect, unintended effects, such as raising the level of self-confidence and assertiveness among children, even to the point that approximately 29% of the children became so assertive that they started to disobey appropriate requests from their parents!

Summaries of prevention efforts provided by Canadian researchers (Hébert et al., 2001; Wolfe, 1990) indicate that their content varies from program to program, but common elements include teaching children to recognize inappropriate adult behaviour, resist inducements, leave the situation quickly, and report the incident to an appropriate adult. Children are taught to say no in a firm, assertive way when an adult talks to or touches them in a manner that makes them feel uncomfortable. Instructors may use comic books, films, and descriptions of risky situations to try to teach children about the nature of sexual abuse and how they can protect themselves.

Evaluations of school programs on sexual abuse support the notion that, like the ESPACE program, they increase awareness of sexual abuse among children and most investigators report positive results. However, according to a critical review by Topping and Barron (2009), not all programs have yielded positive results and there is only limited evidence of the maintenance of these positive effects. And research is still needed to show that the knowledge is actually put into use. Nevertheless, these programs seem to legitimize discussion of the problem at home (Wurtele & Miller-Perrin, 1987) and might therefore achieve one important goal: to increase the reporting of the crime by encouraging and empowering children to tell their parents or guardians that an adult has made a sexual overture to them.

DEALING WITH THE PROBLEM

When they suspect something is awry, parents must raise the issue with their children, but many adults are uncomfortable doing so. Physicians also need to be sensitized to signs of abuse.

For a child, reporting sexual abuse can be extremely difficult. We tend to forget how helpless and dependent a youngster feels, and it is difficult to imagine how frightening it would be to tell one's parents that one had been fondled by a brother or grandfather.

The vast majority of cases of sexual abuse do not leave any physical evidence, such as torn vaginal tissue. Furthermore, there is no behavioural pattern, such as anxiety, depression, or increased sexual activity, that unequivocally indicates that abuse has occurred (Kuehnle, 1998). Therefore, the primary data regarding CSA must come from the child's self-report. The problem is that leading questions may be needed to facilitate disclosure and these leading questions may lead to some false reports. In questioning a child about possible sexual abuse, the adult needs great skill to ensure that the report is accurate, to avoid biasing the youngster one way or the other, and to minimize the inevitable stress.

In closing, we should point out that both incest and pedophilia occur much more often in the majority North American culture than was formerly assumed. A study of 796 college students found that an astounding 19% of the women and 8.6% of the men reported that they had been sexually abused as children. Of the abused women, 28% had had incestuous relations; of the men, 23% had (Finkelhor, 1979). Other survey data tend to confirm these findings. Analyses of Ontario's Mental Health Supplement data found that 13% of women and 4% of men drawn from the general population reported having been sexually abused during childhood or adolescence (MacMillan et al., 1997).

VOYEURISM

Now and then, a man may by chance happen to see a nude woman without her knowing he is watching her. If his sex life is primarily conventional, his act is voyeuristic, but he would not generally be considered a voyeur. Similarly, voyeuristic fantasies are quite common in men but do not by themselves warrant a diagnosis (Hanson & Harris, 1997). **Voyeurism** involves a marked preference for obtaining sexual gratification by watching others in a state of undress or having sexual relations. If it occurs by videotaping another person, it is called electronic voyeurism. For some men, voyeurism is the only sexual activity in which they engage; for others, it is preferred but not absolutely essential for sexual arousal (Kaplan & Kreuger, 1997). As in the case of William at the beginning of this chapter, the looking, often called peeping, is what helps the individual become sexually aroused. The voyeur's orgasm is achieved by masturbation, either while watching or later, remembering what he saw. Sometimes the voyeur fantasizes about having sexual contact with the observed person, but it remains a fantasy. In voyeurism, there is seldom contact between the observer and the observed.

A true voyeur, almost always a man, does not find it particularly exciting to watch a woman who is undressing for his special benefit. The element of risk seems important, for the voyeur is excited by the anticipation of how the woman would react if she knew he was watching. Some voyeurs derive special pleasure from secretly observing couples having sexual relations. As with all categories of behaviour that are against the law, frequencies of occurrence are difficult to assess, since the majority of all illegal activities go unnoticed by the police. Indeed, voyeurs are most often charged with loitering rather than with peeping itself (Kaplan & Kreuger, 1997).

Voyeurism typically begins in adolescence. It is thought that voyeurs are fearful of more direct sexual encounters with others, perhaps because they lack social skills. Their peeping serves as a substitute gratification and possibly gives them a sense of power over those watched. Voyeurs often have other paraphilias, but they do not seem to be otherwise disturbed.

In Denmark, following the lifting of all restrictions against the sale of pornographic materials to adults, a significant reduction in peeping, at least as reported to the police, was observed (Kutchinsky, 1970). It may be that the increased availability of completely frank pictorial and written material, typically used in masturbation, partially satisfied the needs that had made voyeurs of some men in the absence of other outlets. Perhaps the ready availability of pornography on the Internet will have a similar, but more global, effect.

EXHIBITIONISM

Exhibitionism is a recurrent, marked preference for obtaining sexual gratification by exposing one's genitals to an unwilling stranger, sometimes a child. It typically begins in adolescence (Murphy, 1997). As with voyeurism, there is seldom an attempt to have actual contact with the stranger. Sexual arousal comes from fantasizing that one is exposing himself or from actually doing so, and the exhibitionist masturbates either while fantasizing or even during the actual exposure. In most cases, there is a desire to shock or embarrass the observer.

Historically, it has been assumed that the exhibitionist does not have actual contact with his or her victim. However, new research conducted in Ottawa by Firestone, Kingston, Wexler, and Bradford (2006) led the authors to warn that exhibitionism "is not a benign act" (p. 358). They found that 39% of their sample of exhibitionists went on to commit other offences and 31% committed a sexual or violent act. Accordingly, they differentiated between "hands-off exhibitionists" and "hands-on exhibitionists."

Voyeurism and exhibitionism together account for a majority of all sexual offences that come to the attention of the police. The frequency of exhibitionism is much greater among men, who are often arrested for what is legally termed indecent exposure. Other paraphilias are very common in exhibitionists, notably voyeurism and frotteurism (discussed below) (Freund, 1990).

The urge to expose seems overwhelming and virtually uncontrollable to the exhibitionist, or flasher, and is apparently triggered by anxiety and restlessness, as well as by sexual arousal. One exhibitionist persisted in his practices even after suffering a spinal cord injury that left him without sensation or movement from the waist down (DeFazio et al., 1987). Because of the compulsive nature of the urge, the exposures may be repeated rather frequently and even in the same place and at the same time of day. Apparently, exhibitionists are so strongly driven that at the time of the act, they are usually oblivious to the social and legal consequences of what they are doing (Stevenson & Jones, 1972). In the desperation and tension of the moment, they may experience headaches and palpitations and have a sense of unreality. Afterward, they flee trembling and in remorse (Bond & Hutchinson, 1960). Generally, exhibitionists are immature in their approaches to the opposite sex and have difficulty in interpersonal relationships. Over half of all exhibitionists are married, but their sexual relationships with their spouses are not satisfactory (Mohr, Turner, & Jerry, 1964).

The penile plethysmograph was used in a study of male exhibitionists in Alberta in an effort to determine whether they were sexually aroused by stimuli that do not arouse non-exhibitionists (Fedora, Reddon, & Yeudall, 1986). Compared with normal people and with sex offenders who had committed violent assaults, the exhibitionists showed significantly greater arousal in response to slides of fully clothed women in non-sexual situations, such as riding on an escalator or sitting in a park, but they showed similar levels of sexual interest in response to erotic and sexually explicit slides. These results are consistent with the hypothesis that exhibitionists misread cues in the courtship phase of sexual contact, in the sense that they construe certain situations as sexual that are judged non-erotic by non-exhibitionists.

FROTTEURISM

Frotteurism involves the sexually oriented touching of an unsuspecting person. The frotteur may rub his penis against a woman's thighs or buttocks or fondle her breasts or genitals. These attacks typically occur in places that provide an easy means of escape, such as a crowded bus or sidewalk. Frotteurism has not been studied very extensively. It appears to begin in adolescence (*DSM-IV-TR*, 2000) and typically occurs along with other paraphilias (Krueger & Kaplan, 1997).

SEXUAL SADISM AND SEXUAL MASOCHISM

A marked preference for obtaining or increasing sexual gratification by inflicting pain or psychological suffering (such as humiliation) on another is the key characteristic of **sexual sadism**. A marked preference for obtaining or increasing sexual gratification through subjecting oneself to pain or humiliation is the key characteristic of **sexual masochism**.

The sexual sadist obtains sexual gratification from inflicting pain or humiliation on another person, often a sexual masochist, who is aroused by being dominated or humiliated. Jeff Greenberg/Photo Researchers.

Both these disorders are found in heterosexual and homosexual relationships, though it is estimated that upwards of 85% of people with these disorders are exclusively or predominantly heterosexual (Moser & Levitt, 1987). Some sadists and masochists are women; surveys have found that 20 to 30% of the members of sadomasochistic clubs are female (Moser & Levitt, 1987). The disorders seem to begin in early adulthood, and most sadists and masochists are relatively comfortable with their unconventional sexual practices (Spengler, 1977). The majority of sadists and masochists lead otherwise conventional lives, and there is some evidence that they are above average in income and educational status (Moser & Levitt, 1987; Spengler, 1977).

The majority of sadists establish relationships with masochists to derive mutual sexual gratification. From 5 to 10% of the population have engaged in some form of sadomasochistic activity, such as blindfolding one's partner, but few do so regularly, and even fewer prefer such activities during sex (Baumeister & Butler, 1997). The sadist may derive full orgasmic pleasure by inflicting pain on his or her partner, and the masochist may be completely gratified by being subjected to pain. For other partners, sadistic and masochistic practices, such as spanking, are a prelude to or an aspect of sexual intercourse.

Although a great many people are switchable—that is, able to take both dominant and submissive roles—masochists outnumber sadists. For this reason, bondage-and-discipline services may constitute a considerable portion of the business of a house of prostitution. The manifestations of sexual masochism are varied. Examples include restraint (physical bondage), blindfolding (sensory bondage), spanking, whipping, electric shocks, cutting, humiliation (e.g., being urinated or defecated on, being forced to wear a collar and bark like a dog, or being put on display naked), and taking the role of slave and submitting to orders and commands. Themes of submission/domination seem as important as the infliction of physical pain. The term "infantilism" refers to a desire to be treated like a helpless infant and clothed in diapers. One particularly dangerous form of masochism, called hypoxyphilia, involves sexual arousal by oxygen deprivation, which can be achieved using a noose, a plastic bag, chest compression, or a chemical that produces a temporary decrease in brain oxygenation by peripheral vasodilation (American Psychiatric Association, 1994).

Occasionally, sadists murder and mutilate; some are sex offenders who are imprisoned for torturing victims, mostly strangers, and deriving sexual satisfaction from doing so (Dietz, Hazelwood, & Warren, 1990). Sadists who commit acts of aggression against people have a different pattern of offences than that of non-sadistic sex offenders. Sadistic offenders are more likely to impersonate police officers, commit serial murders, tie up their victims, and conceal corpses (Gratzer & Bradford, 1995). One recent disconcerting finding is that in a forensic sample, two thirds of those who were actually sexual sadists were misdiagnosed as non-sadistic sex offenders (Nitschke et al., 2009).

PARAPHILIAS NOT OTHERWISE SPECIFIED

In addition to the paraphilias described above, the *DSM-IV-TR* also lists several disorders in the category of "paraphilias not otherwise specified." This includes such disorders as necrophilia (sex with dead people), zoophilia (bestiality), telephone scatalogia (repeated urge to make obscene phone calls), and coprophilia (the use of feces for sexual excitement).

The high level of dysfunction that can be involved in paraphilias not otherwise specified is underscored by the report of a 54-year-old man incarcerated in a Canadian federal penitentiary (Earls & Lalumière, 2002). This man had been convicted four times for cruelty to animals. He was diagnosed with bestiality and an anti-social personality disorder. He had developed a sexual attraction to horses and killed a horse by puncturing its vaginal wall with his arm when he became jealous of the horse's interest in a stallion. Phallometric testing indicated that he was sexually aroused by horses and not at all sexually aroused by people.

Another recent case study presented once again by Earls and Lalumière (2009) has led them to suggest that zoophilia may be more common than realized. This case also challenged the notion that it is more likely in rural areas among men with lower levels of intelligence. This case involved a medical researcher named "Possum" who developed an unfortunate affinity for horses.

ETIOLOGY OF THE PARAPHILIAS

Of the many theories and hypotheses about the etiology of the paraphilias, the principal ones come from psychodynamic and behavioural perspectives; others are from the biological perspective.

PSYCHODYNAMIC PERSPECTIVES The paraphilias are viewed by psychodynamic theorists as defensive in nature, protecting the ego from having to deal with repressed fears and memories and representing fixations at pregenital stages of psychosexual development. The person with a paraphilia is seen as someone who is fearful of conventional heterosexual relationships, even of heterosocial relationships that do not involve sex. His (less often, her) social and sexual development is immature, stunted, and inadequate for both social and heterosexual intercourse with the adult world (Lanyon, 1986). For example, the fetishist and the pedophile are viewed as men whose castration anxiety makes heterosexual sex with other adults too threatening. Castration anxiety leads the exhibitionist to reassure himself of his masculinity by showing his manhood (his genitals) to others; it results in the sadist dominating others.

BEHAVIOURAL AND COGNITIVE PERSPECTIVES Some theorists operating within a behavioural paradigm hold the view that the paraphilias arise from classical conditioning that by chance has linked sexual arousal with classes of stimuli deemed by the culture to be inappropriate causes of sexual arousal (Kinsey, Pomeroy, & Martin, 1948; Kinsey et al., 1953). For example, a young man may masturbate to pictures or images of women dressed in black leather boots. According to this theory, repetitions of these experiences endow boots with properties of sexual arousal. Similar proposals have been made for transvestism, pedophilia, voyeurism, and exhibitionism. Overall, this orgasm-conditioning hypothesis has very little empirical support (see O'Donohue & Plaud, 1994). However, as described later, some innovative therapeutic strategies have been developed based on this etiological speculation.

Most current behavioural and cognitive theories of the paraphilias are multi-dimensional and propose that a paraphilia results when a number of factors impinge on an individual. The childhood histories of individuals with paraphilias reveal that often they were subjected to physical and sexual abuse and grew up in a family in which the parent-child relationship was disturbed (Mason, 1997; Murphy, 1997). These early experiences may well contribute to the insecure attachment style usually found among sex offenders in general (Stirpe, Abracen, Stermac, & Wilson, 2006) and the low level of social skills, low self-esteem, loneliness, and lack of intimate relationships often seen among those with paraphilias (Kaplan & Kreuger, 1997; Marshall et al., 1997). Paraphilias such as exhibiting or peeping may thus be activities that substitute for more conventional relationships and sexual activity. Distorted parent-child relationships may also create in an individual hostility or a general negative attitude and lack of empathy toward women, which may increase the chances of his victimizing a woman. Alcohol and negative affect are often triggers of incidents of pedophilia, voyeurism, and exhibitionism. Marshall (1996) reported that 50% of the sex offenders in his sample were intoxicated at the time of their offence.

Cognitive distortions also play a role in the paraphilias. A voyeur, for example, may believe that a woman who left her blinds up while undressing really wanted someone to look at her (Kaplan & Kreuger, 1997). Hypotheses that focus on cognitions sometimes sound psychoanalytic in nature. For instance, some clinicians with a cognitive-behavioural perspective and some of a psychodynamic persuasion regard transvestism as a beleaguered male's refuge from responsibilities he sees himself saddled with solely by virtue of being a man. Women's clothing, then, is believed to have a particular meaning for the male transvestite beyond any sexual arousal he experiences by donning it. Perhaps less rigid gender roles will alter the meaning that women's clothes have for such men.

From an operant conditioning perspective, many paraphilias are considered an outcome of inadequate social skills or reinforcement of unconventionality by parents or relatives. Case histories of transvestites, for example, often refer to childhood incidents in which the little boy was praised and fussed over for looking cute in his mother's dresses.

BIOLOGICAL PERSPECTIVES As the overwhelming majority of people with paraphilias are male, there has been speculation that androgen, the principal male hormone, plays a role. Because the human fetus begins as a female, with maleness emerging from later hormonal influences, perhaps something can go wrong during fetal development. Findings of hormonal differences between normal people and people with paraphilias do not show elevated levels of testosterone among those with paraphilia (Stoléru, 2008).

As to differences in the brain, it has long been suspected that a dysfunction in the temporal lobe may be relevant to a minority of cases of sadism and exhibitionism (Mason, 1997; Murphy, 1997). The general role of brain functions and processes in sexual disorders is discussed in Focus on Discovery 14.3.

THERAPIES FOR THE PARAPHILIAS

Because most paraphilias are illegal, many people diagnosed with them are imprisoned and their treatment is ordered by the court. Outcomes for incarcerated adult sex offenders are highly variable; published success rates range from more than 90% to as low as 30% (Marshall et al., 1991). Juvenile sex offenders have also been the focus of some research, as most offenders begin in adolescence. The results, as with the findings on adults, are variable (Becker & Hunter, 1997). Published data are hard to interpret for several reasons. Experimental designs are not the rule here, as ethical considerations have led most researchers to conclude that control groups should not be used. Some programs select the most problematic prisoners for treatment,

---

FOCUS ON DISCOVERY 14.3
NEUROIMAGING, NEUROBIOLOGY, AND BRAIN SYSTEMS AND STRUCTURES IN SEXUAL DISORDERS

Although testosterone is not elevated among those with a paraphilia, attempts to lower plasma testosterone levels through antiandrogens have been effective in reducing sexual fantasies and behaviours among men with paraphilias (Stoléru, 2008). In a phenomenon known as pharmacological castration, LRHR agonists (i.e., gonadotropin-releasing hormones) are decreased via drug treatment and this eliminates sexual desires (see Bradford & Fedoroff, 2009).

Neuroimaging has provided many new clues to the nature of normal and abnormal sexual responses. For instance, fMRI research has shown that visual sexually arousing stimuli create neuronal activity in the human reward system, including the centromedian hypothalamus (Maravilla & Yang, 2008). Research suggests that men and women share many brain activation areas, but men show a greater degree of activation in the thalamus, hypothalamus, and amygdala (Maravilla & Yang, 2008). These differences are sometimes reflected in self-reported responses, but an important caveat is provided by a contemporary meta-analysis by Meredith Chivers from Queen's University and her colleagues (see Chivers, Seto, Lalumière, Laan, & Grimbos, 2010). Their meta-analysis showed a strong agreement between self-reports and genital measures for men ($r = .66$) but much less association for women ($r = .26$). Chivers (2008) has summarized evidence indicating that sexual responses and sexual orientation differ qualitatively for women and men; that is, the genital responses of women are more nonspecific and women will respond to both preferred and non-preferred stimuli.

What about people with sexual disorders? A German study of male-to-female transsexuals found that relative to male control participants, the cerebral activation pattern while viewing erotic stimuli indicated a female-like form of cerebral processing (Gizewski et al., 2009). An unrelated investigation of homosexual pedophiles found that they and non-pedophilic control participants had comparable fMRI responses to visual sexual stimuli. However, activation patterns for the pedophiles were more likely to involve the subcortical areas of the brain implicated in addicted, uncontrolled behaviour (Schiffer et al., 2008). Other data indicate that brain regions implicated when healthy individuals are presented with erotic stimuli evoke less activation when presented to pedophilic clients (Walter et al., 2007). Thus, a growing amount of data support the notion that those with sexual disorders have brains that are wired differently! The legal implications of these differences are explored in Chapter 18.

whereas others treat those with the most promising prognoses (e.g., first offenders). Some programs do not have follow-up sessions after release, whereas others do. Recidivism increases as the years go by, especially after two years have passed since termination of treatment (Marshall & Barbaree, 1990).

As we have seen with substance abusers, sex offenders often lack the motivation to try to change their illegal behaviour. Undermining their motivation for treatment are such factors as denial of the problem (see Marshall et al., 2001), minimization of the seriousness of their problem, a belief that their victims will not be credible witnesses, and the confidence that they can control their behaviour without professional assistance. Some blame the victim—even a child—for being overly seductive. Such people are frequently judged to be inappropriate for treatment programs, for when they do become involved, they frequently drop out. There are several methods to enhance their motivation to commit to treatment (Miller & Rollnick, 1991):

1. The therapist can empathize with the offender's reluctance to admit that he is an offender, thereby reducing the defensiveness and hostility.
2. The therapist can point out to the offender the treatments that might help him control his behaviour better and emphasize the negative consequences of refusing treatment (e.g., transfer to a less attractive incarceration setting if the person is already in custody) and of offending again (e.g., stiffer legal penalties).
3. Having elaborated on the possible benefits of treatment, the therapist can implement a paradoxical intervention by expressing doubt that the person is motivated to enter into or continue in treatment, thereby challenging him to prove wrong the therapist whom he has been resisting.
4. The therapist can explain that there will be a psycho-physiological assessment of the client's sexual arousal, the implication being that the client's sexual proclivities can be revealed without his admitting to them (Garland & Dougher, 1991).

There is also the issue of what happens to motivation levels after the offender is released back into the community. A study conducted with sex offenders from Ontario showed that motivation to change sexually deviant behaviour increased substantially throughout the course of treatment but decreased significantly, relative to post-treatment levels, after conditional release to the community (Barrett, Wilson, & Long, 2003). Barrett et al. (2003) concluded that motivation is dynamic rather than static and that many clinicians in community settings will find it difficult to re-engage the offender in the treatment process. With the foregoing as background, we now describe treatments for the paraphilias.

BEHAVIOURAL TECHNIQUES Behaviour therapists have been less interested in presumed deep-seated personality defects among people with paraphilias and more focused on the particular pattern of unconventional sexuality. Consequently, they have tried to develop therapeutic procedures for changing only the sexual aspect of the individual's makeup. Some successes have been achieved, especially when a variety of techniques are used in a broad-spectrum, multi-faceted treatment (Becker, 1990; Marshall et al., 1991).

In the earliest years of behaviour therapy, paraphilias were narrowly viewed as attractions to inappropriate objects and activities. Looking to experimental psychology for ways to reduce these attractions, researchers fixed on aversion therapy. Thus, a boot fetishist would be given shock (on the hands or feet) or an emetic (a drug that produces nausea) when looking at a boot, a transvestite when cross-dressing, a pedophile when gazing at a photograph of a nude child, and so on. Although aversion therapy may not completely eliminate the attraction, in some cases, it provides the client with a greater measure of control over the overt behaviour (McConaghy, 1990, 1994). Another method is called satiation; with this method, the man masturbates for a long time, typically after ejaculating, while fantasizing out loud about his deviant activity. There is reason to believe that both aversion therapy and satiation, especially when combined with other psychological interventions, such as social skills training, can have beneficial effects (Laws & Marshall, 1991; Marshall & Barbaree, 1990).

Orgasmic reorientation has been employed to help the client learn to become more aroused by conventional sexual stimuli. In this procedure, clients (again, most of whom are men) are confronted with a conventionally arousing stimulus (e.g., a photograph of a woman) while they are responding sexually for other, undesirable reasons. In the first clinical demonstration of this technique, Davison (1968a) instructed a young man troubled by sadistic fantasies to masturbate at home in the following manner:

> When assured of privacy in his dormitory room … he was first to obtain an erection by whatever means possible—undoubtedly with a sadistic fantasy, as he indicated. He was then to begin to masturbate while looking at a picture of a sexy, nude woman (the target sexual stimulus) … If he began losing his erection, he was to switch back to his sadistic fantasy until he could begin masturbating effectively again. Concentrating again on the … picture, he was to continue masturbating, using the fantasy only to regain the erection. As orgasm was approaching, he was at all costs to focus on the … picture. (p. 84)

The client was able to follow these instructions and, over a period of weeks, began to find conventional pictures, ideas, and images sexually arousing. However, the therapist had to complement the orgasmic procedure with some imaginal aversion therapy (e.g., imagining receiving a painful electric shock contingent on inappropriate thoughts) for the sadistic fantasies. The follow-up after a year and a half found the client capable of conventional arousal, although he apparently reverted at will to his sadistic fantasies every now and again. This dubious outcome has been reported for other instances of orgasmic reorientation. Behaviour therapists continue to explore its possibilities, despite no clear evidence of its effectiveness (Laws & Marshall, 1991).

In addition to the arousal-based procedures just described, several other techniques are in widespread use. Social skills training is often used because of the well-established fact that many individuals with paraphilias have social skills deficits. Another technique, alternative behavioural completion, entails imagining a typical deviant activity but changing its ending, such as in the following scenario:

> As you drive home one night you notice an attractive woman driver on your right in a van. She can see right into your car. You slow down and drive parallel with her as you begin to get aroused. You want to rub your penis and take it out to show her. However, the urge this time is weaker and you drive past her quickly without exposing. You feel good about yourself for being able to exert control. (Maletzky, 1997, p. 57)

COGNITIVE TREATMENT Cognitive procedures are often used to counter the distorted thinking of individuals with paraphilias. For example, an exhibitionist might claim that the girls he exposes himself to are too young to be harmed by it. The therapist would counter this distortion by pointing out that the younger the victim, the worse the harm will be (Maletzky, 1997). Training in empathy toward others is another cognitive technique. Teaching the offender to consider how his behaviour would affect someone else may lessen the sex offender's tendency to engage in such activities. Relapse prevention, modelled after the work on substance abuse described in Chapter 12, is also an important component of many treatment programs.

Cognitive and behavioural approaches have become more sophisticated and broader in scope since the 1960s, when the paraphilias were addressed almost exclusively in terms of sexual attraction to inappropriate environmental stimuli. In many instances, therapy is modelled on the approach of Masters and Johnson (1970) under the assumption that some paraphilias develop or are maintained as a result of unsatisfactory sexual relationships with consenting adults (Marshall & Barbaree, 1990). Overall, both institution-based and outpatient programs that follow a cognitive-behavioural model with sex offenders reduce recidivism to a greater degree than would be expected were no treatment at all attempted. These outcomes are much better for child molesters than for rapists. Although sex offenders generally evoke disgust and fear more than genuine interest, society tends to overlook the fact that even minimally effective efforts to treat such people not only are cost-effective but may protect others when the person is released from prison (Prentky & Burgess, 1990).

BIOLOGICAL TREATMENT As noted in Focus on Discovery 14.3, biological interventions have been tried on sex offenders. Castration, or removal of the testes, was used a great deal in Western Europe a generation ago prior to biochemical forms of castration, with some apparent efficacy in terms of reducing the incidence of paraphilic behaviour (e.g., Langeluddeke, 1963). However, those operated on were a heterogeneous group that included homosexuals involved in non-coercive sex with other adults (Marshall et al., 1991). It is unclear how many were offenders whose crimes harmed innocent others; that is, it is unclear how many were child molesters and rapists. The lack of clarity of outcome, coupled with major ethical concerns, has led to infrequent use of castration today, with chemical means being clearly preferred.

We have mentioned rape several times in our discussion of the paraphilias, especially in connection with pedophilia and incest. Forced sexual contact, however, occurs far more often between adults than between an adult and a child. We now examine the important topic of rape.

RAPE

In legal terms, rape falls into two categories: forced and statutory. **Forced rape** is sexual intercourse with an unwilling partner. **Statutory rape** refers to sexual intercourse with a minor, someone under the age of consent. The age of consent in Canada is 14, and is decided by statutes. It is assumed that a person younger than the age of consent should not be held responsible for his or her sexual activity. A charge of statutory rape can be made even if it is proved that the person entered into the situation knowingly and willingly. Thus, statutory rape need not involve force, only consummated intercourse with a minor that is reported to the police. We focus in this section on forced rape.

THE CRIME

The specifics of rape cases vary widely. Some rapes are planned, and some are thought to be more impulsive, spur-of-the moment crimes. Up to 70% of rapes are associated with intoxication (Marshall & Barbaree, 1990). Some rapes seem motivated by a desire to control the other person. Others are more clearly sexually motivated, although many rapists experience erectile failure or fail to reach orgasm (Hudson & Ward, 1997). In what is sometimes termed sadistic rape, the rapist severely injures the victim's body; for example, by inserting foreign objects into her vagina or pulling and burning her breasts. Some rapists also murder their victims. Little wonder, then, that rape is considered as much an act of violence, aggression, and domination as an act of sex. In many jurisdictions, the definition of rape includes oral and anal entry, as well as vaginal penetration. Although men can be victims of sexual assault—especially by other men in prison—our discussion focuses on women because rape is primarily an act committed by men against women.

Rape that occurs on dates is called **acquaintance rape**, or **date rape**. Rapes of this kind outnumber rapes by strangers by as much as 3 to 1 (Kilpatrick & Best, 1990). In general, the vast majority of rapes in Canada are committed by people who are known to the victim (Stermac, Du Mont, & Dunn, 1998; Stermac, Du Mont, & Kalemba, 1995), with one Canadian study finding that 81% of sexual assaults were perpetrated by men who were familiar to their victim (Canadian Panel on Violence against Women, 1993). Unfortunately, many students are sexually assaulted. One study of 259 Canadian undergraduate women found that about one third of those who dated had experienced physical, verbal, or psychological sexual coercion during the previous year (DeKeseredy, Schwartz, & Tait, 1993). In a subsequent survey of more than 3,600 female students at six Ontario universities, 15% reported being sexually assaulted (including 2% who reported date rape) and 24% reported being physically assaulted (Newton-Taylor, DeWit, & Gliksman, 1998). First-year students were more likely to be assaulted than were students in their second, third, or fourth years. An investigation in Alberta found that 23% of an adolescent sample had been assaulted at least once and that those who had experienced a higher number of sexual assaults were more likely than other students to suffer from clinically significant levels of emotional distress (Bagley, Bolitho, & Bertrand, 1997).

A contemporary development with regard to date rape is the use of the tranquilizer Rohypnol (i.e., the date rape drug). This drug is odourless and tasteless and can be easily slipped into a drink. If ingested, it causes the person to pass out and have little if any memory of what happens. Men have used Rohypnol to enable them to rape women when on a date. There have been unconfirmed reports of the increasing use of date rape drugs since the 1990s among people who have been drinking alcohol. Du Mont et al. (2009) investigated 184 cases in Ontario of suspected drug-facilitated sexual assaults. Total amnesia of the event was reported by 115 of the women (62.5%). Du Mont et al. concluded that date rape is both common and serious and this points to the need for easily conducted toxicological screening at hospitals and other facilities.

THE VICTIM, THE ATTACK, AND THE AFTERMATH

A prevalent belief is that all women who are raped are young and attractive. This is a myth. Although many victims do fit this description, many others do not. Age and physical appearance are no barriers to some rapists; they may choose children as young as one year old or women in their eighties.

Rape victims are usually traumatized by the attack, both physically and mentally (Resick, 1993). In the minutes or seconds preceding rape, the woman begins to recognize her dangerous situation but can scarcely believe what is about to happen to her. During the assault, she is first and foremost in great fear for her life. The physical violation of her body and the ripping away of her freedom of choice are enraging, but the victim also feels her vulnerability in not being able to fight off her typically stronger attacker. Moreover, the attacker usually has the element of surprise and sometimes a weapon to intimidate and coerce. Resistance is seriously compromised by terror.

For weeks or months following the rape, many victims feel extremely tense and deeply humiliated. They feel guilt that they were unable to fight harder and may have angry thoughts

of revenge. Many have nightmares about the rape. Depression and loss of self-esteem are common. Some victims of rape develop phobias about being outdoors or indoors or in the dark, depending on where the rape took place. They may also fear being alone or in crowds or having anyone behind them. Unfortunately, some of these reactions are exacerbated by insensitivity on the part of police and even friends and loved ones, some of whom may question the victim's complicity in what happened (more on this later). Sometimes an unwanted pregnancy results from a rape, and justifiable concern about sexually transmitted diseases, including AIDS, adds to the trauma of the attack. For good reason, *DSM-IV-TR* mentions rape as one of the traumas that can give rise to post-traumatic stress disorder (PTSD).

Many women who have been raped subsequently develop a negative attitude toward sex and experience difficulty in their relationships with their husbands or lovers (Becker, Skinner, et al., 1986). So certain are Calhoun and Atkeson (1991), two experienced clinical researchers on rape, that sexual problems are a frequent long-term consequence of untreated rape trauma that they urge clinicians to consider the possibility that rape or sexual assault has occurred in women who come to therapy for many of the sexual dysfunctions discussed later in this chapter.

Without intervention, symptoms of anxiety and depression—and in some cases, full-blown PTSD—persist in some women for many years following an assault (Calhoun & Atkeson, 1991; Resick, 1993). Suicidal risk is also high for many rape survivors (Kilpatrick, Edmunds, & Seymour, 1992), as is substance abuse, which might have begun as an attempt to self-medicate to reduce anxiety.

The nature and duration of what some call *rape trauma syndrome* (Burgess & Holmstrom, 1974) depend a great deal on the person's life both prior to and following the attack. Factors that can mitigate the negative aftermath of rape include a supportive spouse and friends, as well as the kind of crisis intervention described later (Atkeson et al., 1982). Research is inconclusive, however, as to whether the negative emotional consequences of rape correlate with the violence of the assault, the setting, or the familiarity of the rapist (Resick, 1993). These complexities led Calhoun and Atkeson (1991) to conclude that the aftermath is more a function of how the person appraises the events than of the circumstances themselves.

THE RAPIST

As documented some years ago in a classic book on the politics of rape, the fact that men with their generally superior strength can usually overpower women buttresses the view that rape has served in the past and still serves to control and intimidate women (Brownmiller, 1975).

WHO IS THE RAPIST? Is the rapist primarily the psychopath who seeks the thrill of dominating and humiliating a woman through intimidation and often brutal assault? Is he an ordinarily unassertive man with a fragile ego who, feeling inadequate after disappointment and rejection in work or love, takes out his frustrations on an unwilling stranger? Is he an otherwise respectable, even honoured, man in authority who takes advantage of his position of power over a woman? Is he a teenager, provoked by a seductive and apparently available young woman who, it turns out, was not as interested as he in sexual intimacy? Is he a man whose inhibitions against expressing anger have been dissolved by alcohol? The best answer is that the rapist is all these men, often operating under a combination of several of these circumstances.

Research on rapists in Canada suggests that heterogeneity does exist and that one can make meaningful distinctions between types of rapists, such as psychopathic and non-psychopathic rapists (see Brown & Forth, 1997). However, what many rapists probably have in common is unusually high hostility toward women, arising from beliefs of having been betrayed, deceived, or demeaned by them or from exposure to parental violence and physical or sexual abuse during childhood (Duke & Durham, 1990; Malamuth et al., 1993). Reports from rapists indicate that the urge to rape is heightened by feelings of loneliness, anger, humiliation, inadequacy, and rejection (McKibben, Proulx, & Lusignan, 1994). Some rapists also seem to have problems distinguishing friendliness from seductiveness and in accurately reading cues from a woman indicating that she wants intimacies to cease (Malamuth & Brown,

Paul Bernardo and Karla Homolka were involved in the death of Homolka's sister and in the murder of two teenaged girls in Ontario. Paul Bernardo was also the "Scarborough Rapist," who allegedly raped, brutalized, and terrorized more than two dozen women in Toronto. Bernardo claimed in 2008 that he is not a psychopath anymore and that he was driven by sexual performance anxiety (see Tyler, 2008). Norm Betts/Sun Media Corporation.

1994). They often lack social skills, have low self-esteem, and have demonstrably low levels of empathy for their victims (Hudson & Ward, 1997; Marshall & Moulden, 2001). Follow-up research conducted in Kingston, Ontario, indicates that rapists may repress empathy toward their own victim rather than suffer from a general deficit in empathy (Fernandez & Marshall, 2003).

From a sociological perspective, the more a society accepts interpersonal violence as a way to handle conflict and solve problems, the higher the frequency of rape (Sanday, 1981). It seems worth noting that in a controlled experiment, male college students who stated that they regarded rape as unacceptable were aroused by video portrayals of rape if the woman was depicted as having an orgasm during the assault (Malamuth & Check, 1983). This research suggests that rape may be encouraged by pornography that depicts women enjoying coerced sexual relations.

THERAPY FOR RAPISTS AND RAPE VICTIMS

Unlike most of the disorders discussed in this book, rape has the dubious distinction of presenting two different challenges to the mental health professional: treating the man who has committed the act and treating the woman who has been the victim.

THERAPY FOR RAPISTS Therapy programs for incarcerated rapists are typically multi-dimensional in nature and are evaluated by following men after release from prison to determine recidivism rates. Among the components of these programs are cognitive techniques aimed at rapists' distorted beliefs (such as that women want to be raped) and inappropriate attitudes toward women, attempts to increase empathy with their victims, anger management, techniques to improve self-esteem, and efforts to reduce substance abuse. These methods are often implemented in confrontational group-therapy sessions that attempt to goad the rapist into taking responsibility for his aggressive behaviour and include an explicit focus on relapse prevention (Marshall, 1999). As with the paraphilias, this psychologically based therapy is sometimes supplemented with the use of biological treatments to reduce the rapist's sex drive. Although these programs typically have not had adequate control groups, meta-analyses have led to the conclusion that cognitive therapy and the biological interventions may lower recidivism somewhat, especially among men who complete the treatment programs (Hall, 1995; Hanson & Bussière, 1998). The meta-analysis technique is described in more detail in Canadian Perspectives 14.2.

THERAPY FOR RAPE VICTIMS Efforts to counsel rape victims have expanded considerably in recent years. Rape crisis centres and telephone hotlines have been established throughout North America. Some are associated with hospitals and clinics; others operate on their own. See Canadian Clinic Focus 14.1 for a discussion of some rape crisis centres in Canada.

CANADIAN PERSPECTIVES 14.2
CANADIAN RESEARCH ON SEX OFFENDER RECIDIVISM

In Chapter 18 we examine the literature on risk assessment in detail. According to Karl Hanson from Public Safety Canada, structured risk assessments that assign weights to key variables has supplanted the poor predictive utility of unstructured professional opinions, so there have been significant improvements in the ability to predict risk of reoffence among those who have been sex offenders (see Hanson, 2009). Still, the prediction of further risk is very difficult to determine.

Who is most likely to reoffend? A review conducted by Greenberg (1998) at the Royal Ottawa Hospital found that incest offenders, relative to extrafamilial offenders, are less likely to reoffend, while rapists and exhibitionists have higher levels of recidivism.

A meta-analysis conducted by Hanson and Bussière (1998) examined the factors associated with sexual recidivism in 61 follow-up studies. They found that demographic variables (e.g., being young and single) and criminal lifestyle variables (e.g., total number of prior offences) were reliable but modest predictors of sexual recidivism. Measures of psychological maladjustment had little predictive utility. Only anti-social personality disorder predicted sexual recidivism.

Subsequent research has clarified the role of psychopathy in sexual recidivism. The Porter et al. (2009) study described in Chapter 13 found that psychopathy predicted subsequent violent and non-violent offences but not sexual offences. An earlier Canadian study found that men with elevated levels of psychopathy and deviant sexual arousal tended to recidivate sooner and at much higher rates than men low in these factors (Serin, Mailloux, & Malcolm, 2001). However, a later study showed that it was the sexual deviance component that predicted sexual recidivism; psychopathy did not predict sexual recidivism but did predict non-sexual recidivism (Olver & Wong, 2006). This finding fits with a widely cited meta-analysis of 82 studies of sex offenders that confirmed that sexual deviance was a major predictor of sexual recidivism for both adult and adolescent sex offenders, while anti-social orientation predicted violent and general recidivism (Hanson & Morton-Bourgon, 2005). Sexual deviancy was emphasized by Hanson and Bussière (1998), who found that sexual criminal history variables (e.g., prior sexual offences, victimization of strangers) had small to moderate correlations with sexual recidivism. Measures of sexual deviancy proved to be the strongest predictors, with sexual interest in children as measured by phallometric testing being the most robust predictor. Examination of the clinical presentation variables showed that low remorse did not predict recidivism, but recidivism was predicted by the failure to complete treatment. A recent Canadian study confirmed that the sexual deviance subscale of the Violence Risk scale and phallometric indices of deviant arousal to female children were able to predict sexual recidivism (Canales, Olver, & Wong, 2009).

While sexual deviance is better than psychopathy when it comes to predicting sexual recidivism, people who are characterized jointly by sexual deviance and psychopathy may engage in extreme forms of sex-related violence. This was underscored by a case description of a man with erotic violence syndrome (Litman, 2004). This person had a history of sexual assault, including an assault of an 82-year-old man! The offender was also diagnosed as a psychopath and he was evaluated as having a 100% likelihood of reoffending. Unfortunately, he raped a young woman shortly after being allowed more contact with the community. The offender threatened to kill this young woman if she informed the police, but to her credit, she was courageous and did indeed tell police about the sexual assault.

Research in Canada on the treatment of sexual offenders and levels of recidivism has yielded inconsistent findings and a study conducted by Seto and Barbaree (1999) actually found that men rated as having more appropriate treatment behaviour while receiving group treatment (i.e., higher attendance, less disruptive interactions) actually were the most likely to reoffend. The authors concluded that offenders, particularly those high in psychopathy, may learn social skills in group treatment that enable them to gain access to and manipulate potential victims! However, an update investigation by Barbaree (2005) with a national police database did not replicate this troubling finding; treatment behaviour did not predict recidivism, and psychopathy did not mediate the link between treatment behaviour and recidivism. Still, we should be alert to the fact that some offenders may have ulterior motives for their seemingly good treatment response.

One of the most recent reviews led to the conclusion that there is a positive treatment effect (see Schmucker & Losel, 2008). Overall, sexual recidivism was found for 17.5% of the untreated participants and 11.1% of the treated participants. Hormonal medication, castration, CBT, and behavioural approaches were all effective; non-behavioural treatments were not effective. The issue of whether psychopathic sex offenders benefit from treatment remains open, however; a qualitative review by Doren and Yates (2008) found that studies tapping this issue have too many limitations to draw a conclusion.

Recently, guidelines for conducting research on sexual offender treatment have been published by a group called the Collaborative Outcome Data Committee (CODC, 2007). This group is dedicated to improving the quality of treatment outcome research. It recognizes that many previous studies were actually program quality reviews and were not conducted according to the usual principles associated with scientific research.

Thinking Critically

1. On the basis of the available data, do you believe that treatment for sex offenders is essential? If you feel that it is essential, would you change your view if you knew the person was a psychopath?

2. When people learn that a former sex offender is now living in their community following release, they have often responded by harassing the offender until he leaves the area. Do you think communities have the right to do this? How would you respond upon learning that one of your new neighbours is a former sex offender who has responded well to treatment? How do you weigh the former offender's right to privacy against the possible risk of harm to the public?

CANADIAN CLINIC FOCUS 14.1
RAPE CRISIS CENTRES IN CANADA

Staffed both by professionals and female volunteers who may themselves have been rape victims, rape crisis centres offer support and advice within a crisis-intervention framework. They focus on normalizing the victim's emotional reactions ("Everyone goes through this emotional turmoil after an assault"), encouraging her to talk about her feelings, and helping her meet immediate needs, such as arranging for child care or improving the security arrangements in her home. In short, the goal is to help the victim solve problems and cope with the immediate aftermath of the traumatic event. Discouraging self-blame is also important, especially when the rapist was someone the woman knew.

The Victoria Women's Sexual Assault Centre in Victoria, B.C., has a 24-hour crisis line that provides support and information for people dealing directly or indirectly with sexual assault or childhood sexual abuse (see www.vwsac.com). Immediate crisis counselling is also available. This assault centre is similar to many others in that rape counsellors urge the woman not to withdraw or become inactive, and women from the crisis centre often accompany the rape victim to the hospital and to the police station, where they help her with the legal procedures and with recounting the events of the attack. They may later arrange for examinations for pregnancy and venereal diseases and for professional therapy, if necessary. The possibility of HIV infection also has to be addressed. Empathic companions from the crisis centre help the victim begin to express her feelings about the ordeal, and they urge her to continue venting with her own relatives and friends. If the attacker or attackers have been apprehended, women from the centre support the victim in her decision to go through with prosecuting the rapist, and they assist with the formulation of victim impact statements. Counselling is made available in individual sessions, as well as in 12-week counselling groups facilitated by professional counsellors. This centre also has a preventive focus with a program called Project Respect that is geared toward youth between the ages of 14 and 19. This is a multi-faceted program that spreads the message that sexuality must be without violence and aggression. A particular emphasis is on preventing date rape.

The Lloydminster Sexual Assault and Information Centre in Lloydminster, Saskatchewan, also provides a 24-hour crisis line, and volunteers assist in accompanying the victim to the hospital and to the police station (see www.lsaic.com). Another important aspect of this centre is that it includes a number of preventive programs for children, including such programs as Safe & Happy,

It's O.K. to Say No, and My Body Belongs to Me! Their purpose is to enhance awareness and provide the skills needed to ensure personal safety. Support is also made available for "secondary survivors" (parents, siblings, partners, etc.).

Finally, the Fredericton Sexual Assault Centre in New Brunswick had its origins in the summer of 1975, and a 24-hour crisis line was added the next year (see www.fsacc.ca). It is a feminist organization that also provides crisis-intervention counselling and assistance to the hospital and police station. The centre is prototypical in that it also offers both individual counselling and group counselling. It has a dating-violence program that includes a focus on prevention and classroom presentations for students in grades 8 through 12. Importantly, this program includes a peer-training component in recognition of the significant benefits that accrue when teens speak with each other about dating violence. Other features include community workshops to heighten awareness of warning signs.

Comment

There can be no doubt that these centres provide a range of valuable services. A major problem in Canada is that an estimated 94% of sexual assaults are never reported. Women who have been raped by someone they know and who have no readily observable physical injuries are especially unlikely to report the sexual assault (see McGregor, Wiebe, Marion, & Livingstone, 2000). Therefore, the support provided by these centres is very important. However, there are at least two ways that obvious improvements can be made.

First, the centres are typically underfunded and hence are in no position to conduct the type of program evaluation research that would determine their effectiveness. In the absence of research, we can only assume that the services provided are highly valued in the aftermath of personal crisis.

Second, concerns have been raised about the relative paucity of services for sexually abused males. A report compiled for Health Canada concluded that male-centred assessment is almost non-existent and treatment programs for males are rare (Mathews, 1996). In fact, according to the report, "Canada lags far behind other western democracies in the study of male victims and their male and female abusers ... Social policy development, public education, treatment programs and research funding, and the evolution of a more inclusive discourse on interpersonal violence that reflects the male experience are long overdue" (Mathews, 1996, p. 2).

Mental health professionals who attend to rape victims typically focus on the woman's ongoing relationships, which may be disrupted or negatively affected by the rape. Friends and family, especially spouses and lovers, will need help handling their own emotional turmoil so that they can provide the kind of non-judgemental support that rape victims need.

Much of the therapy for rape has a great deal in common with the treatment for PTSD, and although treatment is successful for the most part, approximately one third of treatment participants either still met PTSD criteria at the end of treatment or drop out of treatment (Vickerman & Margolin, 2009). Exposure treatment is among the more effective treatments. The few studies testing CBT also seem effective (see Vickerman & Margolin, 2009).

Depression can be addressed by helping the woman re-evaluate her role in the rape, as many victims tend to see themselves as at least partially responsible. A little-researched topic is the anger and rage many victims have toward their assailants; women are often afraid of expressing or are socialized not to express such feelings (Calhoun & Atkeson, 1991).

A cognitive-behavioural intervention that has been validated empirically is the cognitive processing therapy (CPT) of Patricia Resick (see Resick & Schnicke, 1993). It too has been acknowledged as effective (Vickerman & Margolin, 2009). This therapy combines exposure to memories of the trauma (as is done in other anxiety reduction interventions) with the kind of cognitive restructuring found in the work of Ellis and Beck. For example, the rape victim is encouraged to dispute any tendency to attribute the blame to herself and to consider fully those aspects of the attack that were beyond her control. CPT is described as an evidence-based 12-session intervention that combines cognitive therapy and written narratives to reduce PTSD and other symptoms (Resick & Schnike, 1993). A key assumption of CPT reflects the Piagetian notions of **assimilation** and **accommodation**. Assimilation is the process of incorporating new information into existing schemas. Accommodation is the process of modifying existing schemas to incorporate new events. Resick and Schnike (1993) maintain that traumatized rape victims suffer as a result of overassimilated and overaccommodated beliefs about trauma. For instance, they alter their control schema by coming to believe that people either have total control or no control over events (overaccommodation) or they assimilate a sense that victims are partly responsible for events into their pre-existing belief in a just and fair world to reflect the notion that victims are at least partly responsible (overassimilation). Similarly, they can also come to believe that people are totally responsible or not responsible at all for events. A major CPT emphasis is to develop accommodated, balanced views of events. CPT has proven effective in reducing guilt-related thoughts (Resick et al., 2002) as well as shame, PTSD symptoms, and cognitive distortions (Resick et al., 2008). Recent data suggest that CPT reduces overaccommodation and overassimilation (Sobel, Resick, & Rabalais, 2009).

Social attitudes and support systems encourage the victim to report rape and pursue the prosecution of the alleged rapist, but the legal situation is still problematic. Interviews with half a million women indicated three reasons for reluctance to report rape:

1. They consider the rape a private matter.
2. They fear reprisals from the rapist or his family or friends.
3. They believe that the police would be inefficient or insensitive (Wright, 1991).

Sexual assault counsellors support a victim's decision to prosecute the perpetrator if she chooses to. The Ottawa Rape Crisis Centre (www.orcc.net) provides assistance to victims through its 24-hour crisis line and provides accompaniment and support services to police, hospitals, lawyers, and other social service resources. Ottawa Rape Crisis Centre.

Unfortunately, only a small percentage of rapists are ultimately convicted of their crimes. A study of sexual assaults reported to BC Women's Sexual Assault Services found that charges were filed in only about one third of the cases and a conviction occurred in only about 1 in 10 cases (McGregor, Du Mont, & Myhr, 2002). Key factors that facilitated filing a charge included greater severity of injury and the receipt of physical evidence via forensic sampling. Ideally, today, medico-legal evidence is obtained via a **medical forensic examination** (MFE). A recent Ontario study found that although MFE is optional, several women who had been sexually assaulted were instructed to undergo MFE. Many women reported that the stress of undergoing the MFE procedures was balanced by "a sense of doing something" about the assault and MFE helped them feel that other people were recognizing that they had been assaulted (see Du Mont, White, & McGregor, 2009).

There is no denying that going to trial is very stressful. Any familiarity of the victim with her assailant argues strongly against conviction, and the victim's role in her own assault is almost always examined by defence lawyers. Society must be attentive and active to ensure that the legal system defends the victim's rights.

SEXUAL DYSFUNCTIONS

Having discussed the unconventional patterns of the sexual behaviour of a small minority of the population, we turn now to sexual problems that interfere with conventional sexual enjoyment during the course of many people's lives. Our concern here is with **sexual dysfunctions**, the range of problems considered to represent inhibitions in the normal sexual response cycle.

What is defined as normal and desirable in human sexual behaviour varies with time and place. The contemporary view that inhibitions of sexual expression underlie abnormality can be contrasted with views held during the nineteenth and early twentieth centuries in the Western world, when excess was regarded as the culprit. We must keep these varying temporal and cultural norms in mind as we study human sexual dysfunctions.

Psychological problems have consequences not only for the people who experience them but also for those with whom the people are involved. This aspect of human emotional problems is especially important in our consideration of sexual dysfunctions, which usually occur in the context of intimate personal relationships. A marriage is bound to suffer if one of the partners fears sex. And most of us, for better or for worse, base part of our self-concept on our sexuality. Do we please the people we love, do we gratify ourselves, or, more simply, are we able to enjoy the fulfillment and relaxation that can come from a pleasurable sexual experience? Sexual dysfunctions can be so severe that human tenderness itself is lost, let alone the more intense satisfaction of sexual activity.

We look first at the human sexual response cycle as it normally functions. With that as context, we examine the several sexual dysfunctions. Then we discuss etiologies and therapies for these problems.

SEXUAL DYSFUNCTIONS AND THE HUMAN SEXUAL RESPONSE CYCLE

As indicated in Table 14.1, *DSM-IV-TR* divides sexual dysfunctions into four principal categories: sexual desire disorders, sexual arousal disorders, orgasmic disorders, and sexual pain disorders. The difficulty should be persistent and recurrent, a clinical judgement acknowledged in the *DSM* to entail a degree of subjectivity. The disturbance should cause marked distress or interpersonal problems. This requirement was new in *DSM-IV*

The pioneering work of the sex therapists William H. Masters and Virginia Johnson helped launch a candid and scientific appraisal of human sexuality. © Bettmann/CORBIS.

and allows the person's own reactions to, say, having no interest in sex play a role in whether he or she should be diagnosed. A diagnosis of sexual dysfunction is not made if the disorder is believed to be due entirely to a medical illness (such as advanced diabetes, which can cause erectile problems in men) or if it is due to another Axis I disorder (such as major depression).

Most contemporary conceptualizations of the sexual response cycle are a distillation of proposals by Masters and Johnson (1966) and Kaplan (1974). More than 40 years ago, the work of Masters and Johnson signalled a revolution in the nature and intensity of research in and clinical attention to human sexuality. These researchers extended the earlier interview-based breakthroughs of the Kinsey group (Kinsey et al., 1948, 1953) by making direct observations and physiological measurements of people masturbating and having sexual intercourse. Four phases in the human sexual response cycle are typically identified; they are considered quite similar in men and women:

1. Appetitive. Introduced by Kaplan (1974), this stage refers to sexual interest or desire, often associated with sexually arousing fantasies.
2. Excitement. In this phase, originally Masters and Johnson's first stage, a subjective experience of sexual pleasure is associated with physiological changes brought about by increased blood flow to the genitalia and, in women, also to the breasts. This tumescence, the flow of blood into tissues, shows up in men as erection of the penis and in women as enlargement of the breasts and changes in the vagina, such as increased lubrication.
3. Orgasm. In this phase, sexual pleasure peaks in ways that have fascinated poets and the rest of us ordinary people for thousands of years. In men, ejaculation feels inevitable and indeed almost always occurs. In women, the walls of the outer third of the vagina contract. In both sexes, there is general muscle tension and involuntary pelvic thrusting.
4. Resolution. This last of Masters and Johnson's stages refers to the relaxation and well-being that usually follow an orgasm. In men, there is an associated refractory period, during which further erection and arousal are not possible. Women may be able to respond again with sexual excitement almost immediately, a capability that permits multiple orgasms.

This four-stage view is one of many conceivable ways to organize and discuss the relevant body of information (Gagnon, 1977; Kuhn, 1962). We are about to see how the *DSM* uses this scheme to describe sexual dysfunctions.

DESCRIPTIONS AND ETIOLOGY OF SEXUAL DYSFUNCTIONS

The prevalence of occasional disturbances in sexual functioning is quite high. Table 14.2 presents data from a survey of

TABLE 14.2
SELF-REPORTED RATES OF EXPERIENCING VARIOUS SEXUAL PROBLEMS IN THE PAST 12 MONTHS

Problem	Men	Women
Lacked interest in sex	13–17%	27–32%
Unable to achieve orgasm	7–9%	22–28%
Climax too early	28–32%	N/A
Sex not pleasurable	6–8%	17–24%
Trouble maintaining/ achieving erection	11–18%	N/A
Trouble lubricating	N/A	18–27%
Pain during sex	N/A	8–15%

Note: The ranges reflect the fact that rates vary according to age.
Source: After Loumann et al., 1999.

more than 3,000 men and women who were asked whether they had experienced various symptoms of sexual dysfunction in the past 12 months (Laumann, Paik, & Rosen, 1999). The overall prevalence of symptoms of sexual dysfunction was 43% for women and 31% for men. Because these symptoms are so common, people should not assume that they need treatment if they sometimes experience one or more of the problems described in this section. In the diagnostic criteria for each sexual dysfunction, the phrase "persistent or recurrent" is used to underscore the fact that a problem must be serious indeed for the diagnosis to be made. In addition, there is a fair amount of comorbidity among the sexual dysfunctions. For example, almost half of both men and women diagnosed with hypoactive sexual disorder (low sexual desire) also have at least one other dysfunction (Segraves & Segraves, 1991). As we review the various disorders, their interconnectedness will become evident.

SEXUAL DESIRE DISORDERS *DSM-IV-TR* distinguishes two kinds of sexual desire disorders. **Hypoactive sexual desire disorder** refers to deficient or absent sexual fantasies and urges; in **sexual aversion disorder**, a more extreme form of the disorder, the person actively avoids nearly all genital contact with another person. Consider the following case excerpt:

A 51-year-old secretary explained that she had had a wonderful sexual life with her husband until she humorously asked whether he had ever had an affair during their 20-year marriage. He shocked her by confessing a past "insignificant" one. As she thought about this over a week, she became increasingly enraged and asked him to leave the home. Several weeks later, he came back after constant phone contact and in response to her coming down with a flu-like illness. When their sexual behaviour resumed two months later, she became the "ice queen" – unable to stand his touches. Her aversion lasted six months. Four years later when she discovered that he was having an affair, she redeveloped

her aversion, adding that she felt that he was raping her when he touched her and that she could not stand his saliva or semen. She did everything she could to avoid sex. Her second period of aversion lasted four years before she was referred by her gynecologist for psychotherapy. At this time, she saw no relationship between her discoveries of his infidelity and her sexual aversion state. (From Levine, in Tasman, Kay, & Lieberman, 2003, p. 1475)

Clearly, the lack of sexual contact signals that this is an example of sexual aversion disorder.

Twenty to 30% of the general adult population, more often women than men, may have hypoactive sexual desire disorder (Laumann et al., 1994), although accurate estimates are difficult to obtain because of the inevitable problem of getting people to report accurately on something as personal as a sexual dysfunction. Among people seeking treatment for sexual dysfunctions, more than half complain of low desire, and among these people, it is often comorbid with an orgasmic disorder. Hypoactive sexual desire disorder increased in clinical samples for both men and women from the 1970s to the 1990s (Beck, 1995).

Of all the *DSM-IV-TR* diagnoses, the sexual desire disorders, often colloquially referred to as low sex drive, seem the most problematic. How frequently should a person want sex? And with what intensity or urgency? The reason a person goes to a clinician in the first place and ends up with this diagnosis is probably that someone else is dissatisfied with that person's interest in sex. The hypoactive desire category appeared for the first time in *DSM-III* in 1980, under the title of "inhibited sexual desire," and may owe its existence to the high expectations some people have about being sexual. It is striking that entire books—for example, Leiblum and Rosen (1988)—have been written about a disorder that 25 years ago was hardly mentioned in professional sexology circles. Data attest to the significance of subjective factors in the extent to which a person believes he or she has a low sex drive; for example, hypoactive sexual desire disorder was reported more often by American men than by British men (Hawton et al., 1986).

We know little about the causes of either hypoactive sexual desire or sexual aversion disorder. Because women with the disorder show normal sexual responses to sexual stimuli in laboratory studies, it does not appear that they are incapable of becoming fully aroused (Kaplan, 1997). Among the causes of low sex drive in people seen clinically are religious orthodoxy, trying to have sex with a partner of the non-preferred sex, fear of loss of control, fear of pregnancy, depression, side effects from such medications as antihypertensives and tranquilizers, and lack of attraction resulting from such factors as poor personal hygiene in the partner (LoPiccolo & Friedman, 1988).

Several potential factors have been identified (for a comprehensive review, see West, Vinikoor, & Zolnoun, 2004). Relationship factors may be part of the picture, as women with sexual desire disorder report that their communication with their husband is poor and that they are unhappy with the way conflicts are resolved. Other possible causes include a history of sexual trauma, such as rape or childhood sexual abuse, and fears of contracting sexually transmitted diseases, such as AIDS. Two empirical studies indicate that anger is a major factor in reducing sexual desire in both men and women, though it has a smaller role for women (Beck & Bozman, 1995; Bozman & Beck, 1991). Sexual desire is lower when people complain of high levels of everyday stress (see West et al., 2004). There are also data pointing to the importance of testosterone levels in men—the lower the levels, the lower the sexual desire (Bancroft, 1988).

SEXUAL AROUSAL DISORDERS Some people have little or no trouble experiencing sexual desire but do have difficulty attaining or maintaining sexual arousal, the next stage of the sexual response cycle described by Masters and Johnson. The two subcategories of arousal disorders are **female sexual arousal disorder** and **male erectile disorder**. The former used to be called frigidity, and the latter, impotence.

Replacement of the words "impotence" and "frigidity" by the phrase "sexual arousal disorder" can be considered an advance. Impotence implies that the man is not potent, in control, or truly masculine, and negatively supports the macho conception of masculinity that many people today challenge. Frigidity implies that the woman is emotionally cold, distant, unsympathetic, and unfeeling. Both terms are derogatory and encourage a search for causes within the person rather than focus attention on the relationship, a domain that many contemporary investigators explore for answers and solutions.

The diagnosis of arousal disorder is made for a woman when there is consistently inadequate vaginal lubrication for comfortable completion of intercourse, and for a man when there is persistent failure to attain or maintain an erection through completion of the sexual activity. The prevalence rate for female arousal disorder is about 20% (Laumann et al., 1994). For male erectile disorder, prevalence is estimated at between 3 and 9% (e.g., Ard, 1977; Frank, Anderson, & Rubenstein, 1978) and increases greatly in older adults (Feldman et al., 1994; Kinsey et al., 1948). Arousal problems account for about half the complaints of men and women who seek help with sexual dysfunctions (Renshaw, 1988).

As many as two thirds of erectile problems have some biological basis, usually in combination with psychological factors (LoPiccolo, 2002). In general, any disease, drug, or hormonal imbalance that can affect the nerve pathways or blood supply to the penis can contribute to erectile problems. Examples are certain drugs, such as Thorazine, Prozac, and some antihypertensive medications, and illnesses, such as diabetes, kidney problems, and chronic alcoholism. As indicated, though, somatic factors usually interact with psychological factors to produce and maintain erectile difficulties. For example, anxiety and depression are common among men with erectile disorder (Araujo et al.,

1998; Schiavi, 1997). Research using a measure of sexual self-efficacy developed by researchers in Quebec (Libman, Rothenberg, Fichten, & Amsel, 1985) shows that men with erectile dysfunction often have low levels of sexual self-efficacy and that depression is linked closely with this sense of inefficacy (see Fichten, Libman, Takefman, & Brender, 1988; Holden, 1999; Libman et al., 1985). Once the disorder has begun, fears of sexual failure arise and could certainly inhibit subsequent sexual responding (Rowland, Cooper, & Slob, 1996).

Before we focus specifically on disorders experienced by women, note that a major shortcoming of *DSM-IV* is its failure to include a disorder that has been described as **hypersexual disorder** (see Kafka, 2010). This refers to individuals who are compelled and seemingly addicted to sex. Kafka (in press) describes hypersexual disorder as "a nonparaphilia sexual desire disorder with an impulsivity component." According to Bradford and Fedoroff (2009), Kinsey was aware of this condition and wanted to measure it with an index he described as "The Total Sexual Outlet," which was defined as the number of orgasms experienced in a seven-day period.

We often hear about people, including celebrities, who are described as "sex addicts." Speculation has surfaced that golfer Tiger Woods may have suffered from this, but there is no speculation in some cases. Tiger's former coach Hank

Actor David Duchovny, formerly of the X-Files, admitted suffering from sex addiction in 2009. Ironically, his character on the HBO show *Californication*, Hank Moody, also displays many of the symptoms of sex addiction. Picture Perfect/Rex Features/The Canadian Press.

Haney confirmed in May 2010 that Tiger did indeed receive treatment for "sex addiction."

ORGASMIC DISORDERS Three kinds of orgasmic disorders are described in *DSM-IV-TR*: one found in women and two in men.

Female Orgasmic Disorder Formerly called inhibited female orgasm, **female orgasmic disorder** refers to absence of orgasm after a period of normal sexual excitement. The published prevalence rates for female orgasmic disorder vary widely. One review of this literature found prevalences ranging from 5 to 20% (Spector & Carey, 1990). A subsequent study, which involved interviewing a large sample of women, found a prevalence of 24% (Laumann et al., 1994). Whatever the true prevalence rate, this is the problem that most often brings women into therapy (Kaplan, 1974; Spector & Carey, 1990). Failure to achieve orgasm is not only a problem for women, it is also an important aspect of sex for their partners, who may come to believe that they are unskilled or insensitive lovers. This last point probably accounts for the fact that up to 60% of women report faking an orgasm on occasion (McConaghy, 1993).

There is an important distinction between problems a woman may have in becoming sexually aroused and those she may have in reaching an orgasm. Although as many as 10% of adult women have never experienced an orgasm (Anderson, 1983), far fewer are believed to remain unaroused during sexual activity. Indeed, laboratory research has shown that women with orgasmic disorder are as responsive to erotic stimuli as are women in a control group (Meston & Gorzalka, 1996).

Numerous reasons have been put forward to explain the problem. Perhaps many women, unlike men, have to learn to become orgasmic; that is, the capacity to have an orgasm may not be innate in females as it is in males. In men, ejaculation, which almost always is accompanied by orgasm, is necessary for reproduction. Survey findings indicate that women who masturbated little or not at all before they began to have intercourse were much more likely to be non-orgasmic than those who had masturbated to orgasm before becoming sexually active with a partner (Hoon & Hoon, 1978; Kinsey et al., 1953). These are, of course, correlational data; some third factor may be responsible both for infrequent masturbation and for diminished ability to have orgasms. Lack of sexual knowledge also appears to play a role according to clinical data. Many non-orgasmic women, as well as those who experience little excitement during sexual stimulation, are unaware of their own genital anatomy and therefore have trouble knowing what their needs are and communicating them to a partner. Chronic use of alcohol may be a somatic factor in orgasmic dysfunction in women (Wilsnak, 1984).

Another factor is that women have different thresholds for orgasm. Although some have orgasms quickly and without much clitoral stimulation, others seem to need intense and prolonged stimulation during foreplay or intercourse. A man may conclude that he and his penis are inadequate if the female asks for or provides manual stimulation of her clitoris herself during intercourse, and his reaction can contribute to the problem.

Another possibility arose from research examining the sexual responses of non-orgasmic women to erotic films (Meston & Gorzalka, 1996). One feature of this study was determining whether activation of the sympathetic nervous system (achieved by riding a stationary bicycle) would increase genital responding to erotic films. It did in normal women but not in those with orgasmic dysfunction. Meston and Gorzalka speculate that women with orgasmic dysfunction may have a lower threshold for optimal sympathetic activation. Among normal women, low to moderate levels of sympathetic activation (as was induced by bicycle riding in their study) augment vaginal responses to erotic stimuli, but higher levels of sympathetic arousal inhibit sexual responding. Women with an orgasmic disorder may not be able to tolerate even moderate levels of sympathetic arousal and respond to it in a way that interferes with sexual response.

Yet another factor may be fear of losing control. The French have an expression for orgasm, *la petite mort*, "the little death." Some women fear that they will scream uncontrollably, make fools of themselves, or faint. A related source of inhibition is a belief, perhaps poorly articulated, that to let go and allow the body to take over from the conscious, controlling mind is somehow unseemly.

Male Orgasmic Disorder and Premature Ejaculation Male orgasmic disorder and premature ejaculation are the two orgasmic disorders of men in *DSM-IV-TR*. **Male orgasmic disorder,** or difficulty in ejaculating, is relatively rare, occurring in 3 to 8% of clients in treatment (Spector & Carey, 1990). Causes that have been put forth include fear of impregnating a female partner, withholding love, expressing hostility, and, as with female orgasmic problems, fear of letting go. In some instances, the problem may be traced to a physical source, such as spinal cord injury or certain tranquilizers (Rosen, 1991).

Premature ejaculation (PE) is probably the most prevalent sexual dysfunction among males. Sometimes premature ejaculation occurs even before the penis enters the vagina, but it more usually occurs within a few seconds of intromission. Premature ejaculation is generally associated with considerable anxiety. Data from the Canadian Male Sexual Health Council Survey found that PE is a very common medical condition that influences 16–27% of Canadian men depending on how PE is defined, and this is comparable with results found in other countries. PE was confirmed as the most common form of sexual complaint experienced by Canadian men. It was more common in British Columbia and the Atlantic provinces. PE had a negative impact on overall quality of life and sexual quality of life as reported both by the men themselves and their partners (see Brock et al., 2009). Relationship problems and a sexually dysfunctional partner can play a role (Metz et al., 1997).

There is some laboratory-based evidence that men who have premature ejaculation problems are more sexually responsive to tactile stimulation (a vibrator) than men who don't have this problem (Rowland et al., 1996). Perhaps, then, their penises are very sensitive, causing them to ejaculate more quickly. Men with premature ejaculation also have longer periods of abstinence from climactic sex than do men who are not premature ejaculators (Spiess, Geer, & O'Donohue, 1984). Learning has also been proposed as a factor (i.e., exposure to situation that promote and reinforce short ejaculation latency). For example, a man may acquire the tendency to ejaculate quickly as a result of having hurried sex because of not being in a private place and fearing detection (Metz et al., 1997).

SEXUAL PAIN DISORDERS Two pain disorders associated with sex are listed in the *DSM*: dyspareunia and vaginismus.

Dyspareunia is diagnosed when there is persistent or recurrent pain during sexual intercourse. Some women report that the pain starts at entry, whereas others report pain only after penetration (Meana et al., 1997). Not surprisingly, women with dyspareunia show normal levels of sexual arousal to films of oral sex, but their arousal declines when they watch a depiction of intercourse (Wouda et al., 1998). Dyspareunia is linked with alterations of all aspects of the sexual response cycle, including lower sexual desire, lower arousal, and greater dissatisfaction, resulting in less sexual intercourse and strained interpersonal relationships (Smith, Pukall, & Boyer, 2009). In women, the diagnosis of dyspareunia should not be made when the pain is believed to be due to lack of vaginal lubrication (when presumably female sexual arousal disorder would be diagnosed); nor should it be made when the pain is judged to be a function of the second pain disorder, vaginismus.

Vaginismus is marked by involuntary spasms of the outer third of the vagina to a degree that makes intercourse impossible. Despite not being able to have intercourse, women with vaginismus have normal sexual arousal and have orgasms from manual or oral stimulation that does not involve penetration. According to Reissing (2009) from the University of Ottawa, it is difficult, if not impossible, to differentiate between vaginismus and dyspareunia because vaginal penetration problems apply to both.

Prevalence rates for dyspareunia in women range from 8% to as high as 15% (Laumann et al., 1994). It is generally accepted that the disorder is far less often found in men, perhaps in as few as 1% (Bancroft, 1989). Estimates for vaginismus range from 12 to 17% of women seeking sex therapy (Rosen & Leiblum, 1995), and it is a very common complaint seen by gynecologists (Leiblum, 1997).

Genital pain associated with intercourse is usually caused by a medical problem, such as an infection of the vagina, bladder, or uterus or of the glans of the penis (McCormick, 1999; Meana et al., 1997). Depressive symptoms, anxiety, and marital problems are also associated with dyspareunia (Meana et al., 1998). One theory regarding the source of vaginismus supposes that the woman wishes, perhaps unconsciously, to deny herself, her partner, or both the pleasures of sexual intimacy. As plausible as this idea may seem,

In the early 20th century, corn flakes were promoted as part of a bland diet to reduce sexual desire. Corbis Sygma.

no evidence supports it. However, fear of pregnancy, anxiety, relationship problems, and negative attitudes toward sex in general may play a role in vaginismus (e.g., Reissing, Binik, & Khalife, 1999; Tugrul & Kabacki, 1997). Negative attitudes often are traceable to molestation in childhood or to rape (LoPiccolo & Stock, 1987). Masters and Johnson found that for a number of couples the man's inability to maintain an erection preceded the development of vaginismus in his partner. For some women, then, the sexual problems of their partners may be so anxiety-provoking as to result in the development of this disorder.

GENERAL THEORIES OF SEXUAL DYSFUNCTIONS

Having reviewed descriptions of the sexual dysfunctions and some of the causes believed to underlie each, we turn now to a consideration of general theoretical perspectives.

At one time, sexual dysfunctions were generally viewed as a result of moral degeneracy. As reviewed by LoPiccolo (2002), excessive masturbation in childhood was widely believed to lead to sexual problems in adulthood. Von Krafft-Ebing (1902) and Havelock Ellis (1910) postulated that early masturbation damaged the sexual organs and exhausted a finite reservoir of sexual energy, resulting in lessened abilities to function sexually in adulthood. Even in adulthood, excessive sexual activity

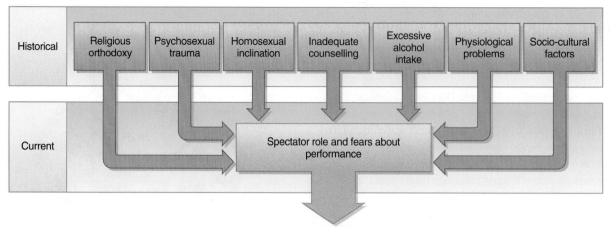

Human Sexual Inadequacy

FIGURE 14.2 Historical and current causes of human sexual inadequacies, according to Masters and Johnson.

was thought to underlie such problems as erectile failure. The general Victorian view was that dangerous sexual appetite had to be restrained. To discourage handling of the genitals by children, metal mittens were promoted, and to distract adults from too much sex, outdoor exercise and a bland diet were recommended. In fact, Kellogg's Corn Flakes and graham crackers were developed as foods that would lessen sexual interest. They didn't.

Psychoanalytic views have assumed that sexual dysfunctions are symptoms of underlying repressed conflicts. The analyst considers the symbolic meaning of the symptom both to understand its etiology and to guide treatment. Since sexual dysfunctions bring discomfort and psychological pain to the individual and to his or her partner, and since unimpaired sexuality is inherently pleasurable, the theme of repressed anger and aggression competing with the gratification of sexual needs pervades psychoanalytic writings. Thus, a man who ejaculates so quickly that he frustrates his female partner may be expressing repressed hostility toward women, who remind him unconsciously of his mother. A woman with vaginismus may be expressing her hostility toward men, perhaps as a result of childhood sexual abuse or more directly because of her husband's overbearing manner.

Many contemporary psychoanalysts supplement their therapy with cognitive-behavioural techniques (LoPiccolo, 1977). The spirit of rapprochement has also affected cognitive-behavioural approaches to the treatment of sexual dysfunctions, as these therapists are coming to appreciate the role of psychodynamic themes in what used to be straightforward behavioural treatments.

The most comprehensive account of the etiology of human sexual dysfunctions was offered by Masters and Johnson in their widely acclaimed book *Human Sexual Inadequacy* (1970), based on case studies from their practice. We will first examine their suggestions and then consider subsequent modifications and extensions of their ideas.

The Theoretical Model of Masters and Johnson—Masters and Johnson (1970) used a two-tier model of current and historical causes to conceptualize the etiology of human sexual inadequacy (Figure 14.2).

CURRENT CAUSES The current or proximal causes can be distilled down to two: fears about performance and the adoption of a spectator role. **Fear of performance** refers to being overly concerned with how one is performing during sex. The **spectator role** refers to being an observer rather than a true participant in a sexual experience. Both involve a pattern of behaviour in which the individual's focus on and concern for sexual performance impedes his or her natural sexual responses.

We have no conclusive evidence, however, that these factors are the causal agents in sexual dysfunctions. This is because of the directionality problem, discussed first in Chapter 5 and again in many places throughout this book. Researchers have consistently shown that performance fears do exist in people with sexual dysfunctions, but the data do not show that the fear preceded and caused the dysfunction. Someone with an erectile dysfunction, for example, may well become fearful that he will not attain an erection in a sexual encounter, and that anxiety may ensure that he is unable to become erect. But the anxiety may be functioning here as a factor that is maintaining the disorder, not one that caused it in the first place.

HISTORICAL CAUSES In the Masters and Johnson model, the current, or proximal, reasons for sexual dysfunctions were hypothesized to have one or more historical antecedents:

- *Religious orthodoxy*
Some conservative religious upbringing styles look askance at sexuality for the sake of pleasure, particularly outside marriage. Masters and Johnson found that many of their sexually dysfunctional participants had negative views of sexuality as a consequence. One female patient, for example, had been taught as she was growing up not to look at herself naked in the mirror and that intercourse was reserved for marriage and then only to be endured for purposes of having children.

- *Psychosexual trauma*

  Some dysfunctions can be traced to rape or other degrading encounters. One young male patient of Masters and Johnson's was told by a prostitute that he would never be able to "get the job done" with other women if he didn't "get it done here and now with a pro."

- *Homosexual inclination*

  Sexual enjoyment is understandably less if a person with homosexual inclinations tries to engage in heterosexual sex.

- *Inadequate counselling*

  This phrase is a euphemism for comments made by professionals that are incorrect and destructive, such as a health care worker telling a healthy 65-year-old man to forget about sex or a cleric saying that erectile dysfunction is God's punishment for sins.

- *Excessive intake of alcohol*

  As Shakespeare wrote in Macbeth, "It provokes the desire but it takes away the performance" (Act II, Scene 3). If an inebriated man cannot achieve or maintain an erection, he may begin to fear that his erectile problem will recur rather than attribute the problem to alcohol.

- *Biological causes*

  Masters and Johnson alerted us back in 1970 to somatic factors contributing to sexual dysfunction. Now even more is known about such factors; we have reviewed this information in our discussions of the individual dysfunctions.

- *Socio-cultural factors*

  Expectations and concerns differ between women and men and as a function of social class. For example, men have the blessing, even demand, of society to develop sexual expressiveness and to take the initiative. Despite the changes that have resulted from the feminist movement of the past 40 years, it remains questionable whether this holds true for women.

OTHER VIEWS Masters and Johnson considered sexual dysfunctions as problems in and of themselves that could be treated directly, rather than as symptoms of other intrapsychic or non-sexual interpersonal difficulties. The couples whose treatment formed the basis of their book *Human Sexual Inadequacy* (1970) had marriages that, in spite of sexual problems, were marked by caring and closeness. But as the Masters and Johnson therapy techniques became widespread and as the social milieu changed to allow more people to feel comfortable seeking help, sex therapists began to see people whose relationships were seriously impaired. In such situations, by the time a therapist is consulted, it is impossible to know whether the hostility between the two people caused the sexual problem or vice versa.

The working assumption of most sex therapists is that sexually dysfunctional couples have both sexual and interpersonal problems (Rosen & Leiblum, 1995). It is unrealistic to expect a satisfying sexual encounter when, for example, the man is angry with the woman for spending more and more time outside the home or the woman resents the man's insensitive dealings with their children. Such negative thoughts and emotions can intrude into the sexual situation and thereby inhibit whatever arousal and pleasure might otherwise be found.

Many other causes of sexual dysfunction have been identified. As mentioned earlier, people who have sexual problems are often found to lack knowledge and skill (LoPiccolo & Hogan, 1979). Sometimes their partners may have deficiencies; for example, the husbands of non-orgasmic women are often reported to be awkward lovers (Kaplan, 1974; LoPiccolo, 1977). Simply caring for the partner may not be enough to establish a mutually satisfying sexual relationship. In fact, Kaplan (1974) suggested that inhibiting anxiety can arise when one partner wants too much to please the other; the feeling of being in the spotlight may result in a kind of performance anxiety. Another proposed cause of sexual dysfunction is response anxiety—anxiety about not being aroused (Apfelbaum, 1989).

Poor communication between partners also contributes to sexual dysfunction. For any number of reasons—embarrassment, distrust, dislike, resentment, depression, to name but a few—one lover may not inform the other of his or her preferences, likes, and dislikes and then may misinterpret the failure of the partner to anticipate or mind read as a sign of not really caring.

In considering these hypothesized etiological factors, it is important to keep two things in mind. First, many people have unsatisfying episodes in their sex lives, perhaps after a bruising argument with their partner or when preoccupied with problems at work. Usually these periods pass, and the sexual relationship returns to normal. Second, many people who currently have in their lives or had in the past one or more of the pathogenic factors discussed do not develop persistent sexual dysfunctions. Although to date there is little real understanding of this phenomenon, there is speculation that other variables, such as an unusually supportive network of friends or a particularly understanding sexual partner, must be operating in these people's present lives to mitigate the putative negative effects of the pathogenic factors.

THERAPIES FOR SEXUAL DYSFUNCTIONS

One of the most important challenges in treating sexual dysfunctions is getting the afflicted individual to seek professional help. A recent five-nation survey that included Canadian data found that many men and women had experienced sexual dysfunction, but relatively few actually sought help. Overall, 75% of those with a sexual dysfunction did not seek medical assistance (Nicolosi et al., 2006).

The treatment of sexual dysfunctions was pioneered by Masters and Johnson (1970), who virtually created the sex-therapy movement. With some variations, their approach is still followed by many practitioners conducting therapy for sexual dysfunctions (LoPiccolo, 2002). The overall aim of Masters and Johnson was to reduce or eliminate fears of performance and to take the participants out of the maladaptive spectator role. They hoped that these steps would enable the couple to enjoy sex freely and spontaneously.

In this approach, assessment interviews took place over the first few days. These interviews placed considerable focus on the so-called **sexual value system**, the ideas of each partner about what was acceptable and needed in a sexual relationship. Sometimes the sexual value system of one or both partners had to be changed before sexual functioning could improve. For example, if one partner persisted in regarding sexuality as ugly and unacceptable, even the most powerful therapy would not be likely to help the partner enjoy sex.

On the third day, the therapists began to offer interpretations about why problems had arisen and why they were continuing. In all cases, the emphasis was on the problems in the relationship, not on individual difficulties of either partner. A basic premise of the Masters and Johnson therapy was that "there is no such thing as an uninvolved partner in any marriage in which there is some form of sexual inadequacy" (1970, p. 2). Whatever the problem, the couple was encouraged to see it as their mutual responsibility. At this time, the clients were introduced to the idea of the spectator role. They were told, for example, that a male with erectile problems—and often his partner as well—usually worries about how well or poorly he is doing rather than participating freely, and that this pattern of observing the state of the erection, although totally understandable in context, blocks his natural responses and greatly interferes with sexual enjoyment.

At the end of the third day an all-important assignment was given to the couple, namely, to engage in **sensate focus**. The couple was instructed to choose a time when both partners felt "a natural sense of warmth, unit compatibility ... or even a shared sense of gamesmanship" (Masters & Johnson, 1970, p. 71). They were to undress and give each other pleasure by touching each other's bodies. The co-therapists appointed one marital partner to do the first pleasuring, or giving; the partner who was "getting" was simply to be allowed to enjoy being touched. The one being touched was not required to feel a sexual response and was responsible for immediately telling the partner if something became distracting or uncomfortable. Then the roles were to be switched. Attempts at intercourse were still forbidden. To Masters and Johnson, this approach was a way of breaking up the frantic groping common among these couples. The sensate-focus assignment usually promoted contact where none had existed for years, constituting a first step toward gradually re-establishing sexual intimacy. Once this sense of intimacy was established, couples received explicit instructions involving specific techniques.

Over the past 30 years, therapists and researchers have devised new procedures for the clinicians who seek to improve the sexual lives of dysfunctional patients. We will describe several strategies and procedures that extend Masters and Johnson's work. A therapist may choose only one technique for a given case, but the complex and multi-faceted nature of sexual dysfunctions usually demands several. These approaches are suitable for homosexual as well as heterosexual sex.

ANXIETY REDUCTION Well before the publication of the Masters and Johnson therapy program, behaviour therapists appreciated that their dysfunctional clients needed gradual and systematic exposure to anxiety-provoking aspects of the sexual situation. Wolpe's systematic desensitization and in vivo desensitization (desensitization by real-life encounters) have been employed with high degrees of success (see Anderson, 1983), especially when combined with skills training. Specific interventions may include relaxation training or in vivo desensitization.

DIRECTED MASTURBATION We have previously mentioned that women with orgasmic disorder frequently lack knowledge of their own sexual anatomy. Directed masturbation, devised by LoPiccolo and Lobitz (1972), is a multi-step program that supplements the Masters and Johnson program. The first step is for the woman to carefully examine her nude body, including her genitals, and identify various areas with the aid of diagrams. Next, she is instructed to touch her genitals and locate areas that produce pleasure. With this accomplished, she then increases the intensity of masturbation using erotic fantasies. If orgasm has not been achieved by this time, she is instructed to buy a vibrator and use it in her masturbation. Finally, her partner enters the picture, first watching his mate masturbate, then doing for her what she has been doing for herself, and finally having intercourse in a position that allows him to stimulate the woman's genitals manually or with a vibrator. Directed masturbation appears to add significantly to the effectiveness of treatment of orgasmic disorder (O'Donohue, Dopke, & Swingen, 1997).

PROCEDURES TO CHANGE ATTITUDES AND THOUGHTS In what are called **sensory-awareness procedures**, clients are encouraged to tune in to the pleasant sensations that accompany even incipient sexual arousal. The sensate-focus exercises described by Masters and Johnson, for example, are a way of opening the individual to truly sensual and sexual feelings. Rational-emotive behaviour therapy tries to substitute less self-demanding thoughts for "musturbation," the "I must" thoughts that often cause problems for people with sexual dysfunctions. A therapist might try to reduce the pressure a man with erectile dysfunction feels by challenging his belief that intercourse is the only true form of sexual activity. Kaplan (1997) recommends several procedures to try to increase the attractiveness of sex. She has clients engage in erotic fantasies and gives them courtship and dating assignments, such as getting away for a weekend.

SKILLS AND COMMUNICATION TRAINING To improve sexual skills and communication, therapists assign written materials, show clients videotapes and films demonstrating explicit sexual techniques, and discuss techniques (McMullen & Rosen, 1979). Of particular importance for a range of sexual dysfunctions is encouraging partners to communicate their likes and dislikes to each other (Hawton, Catalan,

& Fagg, 1992; Rosen, Leiblum, & Spector, 1994). Taken together, skills and communication training also expose clients to anxiety-provoking material—such as seeing one's partner naked—which allows for a desensitizing effect. Telling one's partner one's preferences in sex is often made more difficult by tensions that go beyond the sexual relationship, which leads us to the next strategy.

COUPLES THERAPY Sexual dysfunctions are often embedded in a distressed marital or other close relationship, and troubled couples usually need special training in non-sexual communication skills. As noted earlier, writings on sex therapy emphasize the need for a systems perspective; that is, for the therapist to appreciate that a sexual problem is embedded in a complex network of relationship factors (Wylie, 1997). Sometimes a therapy that focuses on non-sexual issues, such as difficulties with in-laws or with child rearing, is necessary and appropriate, either in addition to or instead of a Masters and Johnson type of sex therapy.

Regardless of whether couples therapy takes place, it is clear that the partner can play a key role. Research on erectile dysfunction shows quite clearly that the partner plays a key support role and incorporating the partner is key in treatment adherence, promoting realistic expectancies, and achieving positive long-term outcomes (see Dean et al., 2008). It is unfortunate, then, that men who receive treatment for erectile dysfunction often go by themselves for treatment.

MEDICAL AND PHYSICAL PROCEDURES As more discoveries are made about biological factors in sexual dysfunctions, it becomes increasingly important for therapists to consider whether underlying somatic problems are contributing to the dysfunction (LoPiccolo, 1992b; Rosen & Leiblum, 1995). Consideration of possible somatic factors is especially important for the disorders of dyspareunia and complete erectile dysfunction.

Dyspareunia in postmenopausal women can be improved by estrogen treatments, which can reduce the thinning of vaginal tissue and improve vaginal lubrication (Walling, Anderson, & Johnson, 1990). When depression, along with severely diminished sex drive, is part of the clinical picture, antidepressant drugs can be helpful. Tranquilizers are also used as an adjunct to anxiety-reduction techniques. However, a complicating factor is that some of these psychoactive drugs themselves interfere with sexual responsiveness.

Surgical procedures are also available. A semi-rigid silicone rod can be implanted in a chronically flaccid penis, or a device can be implanted in the penis that can be stiffened with fluid from a reservoir and a small pump that is implanted in the scrotum. However, long-term follow-ups of men who have had such operations indicate that poor sexual functioning continues in many cases (Tiefer, Pedersen, & Melman, 1988). If the psychological components of the problem are not addressed, men with rod implants may continue to have sexual problems, but with a penis that is never flaccid. (With a rod, sexual interest and arousal are not necessary for intercourse, and this

Montreal Canadiens hockey legend Guy Lafleur became the spokesperson for the first Canadian campaign for the erectile dysfunction wonder drug Viagra. CP Picture Archive/Ryan Remiorz.

situation is usually not favourable for long-term psychological adjustment.) Vascular surgery involves correction of problems with blood inflow via arteries or outflow via veins in the penis. Results are mixed at best (Melman & Rossman, 1989), but the possibility exists for restoration of normal functioning because, unlike the case with implants, erection will occur only with desire and arousal (Wincze & Carey, 1991).

A non-surgical intervention entails the use of a cylinder attached to a vacuum pump. The penis is placed in the cylinder, and when air is pumped out, blood is drawn into the penis, producing an erection. When the penis is erect, the cylinder is removed and an elastic band is put around its base to trap the blood and maintain the erection. This device is one of the treatments that has been recommended as effective by the American Urological Association (Skolnick, 1998).

Several drugs have been used in the treatment of sexual dysfunctions. It is now estimated that up to 150 million men worldwide suffer from erectile dysfunction (Dean et al., 2008). Viagra (sildenafil) is now widely accepted as drug treatment for erectile dysfunction. It was approved by the U.S. Food and Drug Administration in March 1998 and, in its first three months, was prescribed more than 3 million times. Viagra relaxes smooth muscles and thereby allows blood to flow into the penis during sexual stimulation, creating an erection. It is taken one hour before sex, and its effects last about four hours, thus allowing an erection to be maintained for a substantial period. Thus far, research indicates that 7 out of 10 men who take Viagra report improvement, whether the cause of their erectile dysfunction is biological (e.g., diabetes) or psychological (Lamberg, 1998). Generally, Viagra produces modest side effects, such as headaches. Relative to men who ingest a placebo, those taking Viagra report a much greater frequency of side effects, including headaches, flushing, dyspepsia, and visual disturbances (Tsertsvadze et al., 2009). Moreover, Viagra may be dangerous for men with cardiovascular disease, in part because erectile dysfunction and cardiovascular disease often co-exist in men.

In all instances of medical intervention, consideration of psychosocial factors remains important, for sexual dysfunctions are almost always embedded in a complex set of interpersonal and intrapsychic conflicts. The current trend toward viewing sexual dysfunctions as medical or biological problems may divert the attention of therapists and clients from the inherently interpersonal nature of these problems, giving rise to a quick-fix mentality that is probably ill-advised (Rosen & Leiblum, 1995). Indeed, the need for a complex and integrated approach was highlighted by an international consortium of more than 200 experts from 60 countries. The Psychological and Interpersonal Committee of Sexual Function and Dysfunction concluded that the biopsychosocial model should be adopted (see Althof et al., 2005). As such, these experts advised that no single type of intervention (pharmacotherapy or marital therapy, for instance) will be sufficient for most couples experiencing sexual dysfunction and both physical and psychological factors and interventions deserve consideration.

SUMMARY

- Gender identity disorder (GID) involves the deep and persistent conviction of the individual that his or her anatomic sexual makeup and psychological sense of self as man, woman, boy, or girl are discrepant. Thus, a man with GID is physically male but considers himself a woman and desires to live as a woman. Child-rearing practices may have encouraged the young child to believe that he or she was of the opposite sex. Hormonal causes (e.g., too much male hormone in a woman) have also been considered, but the data are equivocal.

- For a time, the only kind of help available to people with GID was sex-reassignment surgery to bring certain bodily features into line with their gender identity. Now, however, there is preliminary evidence that behaviour therapy can help bring gender identity into line with anatomy in some cases.

- In the paraphilias, unusual imagery and acts are persistent and necessary for sexual excitement or gratification. The principal paraphilias are fetishism, reliance on inanimate objects for sexual arousal; transvestic fetishism, sometimes called transvestism, the practice of dressing in the clothing of the opposite sex, usually for the purpose of sexual arousal but without the gender identity confusion of a person with GID; pedophilia and incest, marked preferences for sexual contact with minors and, in the case of incest, for members of one's own family; voyeurism, a marked preference for watching others in a state of undress or in sexual situations; exhibitionism, obtaining sexual gratification by exposing oneself to unwilling strangers; frotteurism, obtaining sexual contact by rubbing against or fondling women in public places; sexual sadism, a reliance on inflicting pain and humiliation on another person to obtain or increase sexual gratification; and sexual masochism, obtaining or enhancing sexual gratification through being subjected to pain, usually from a sadist.

- Many hypotheses have been put forward to account for the several paraphilias. Psychoanalytic theories generally hold that they are defensive in nature, protecting the person from repressed conflicts and representing fixations at immature stages of psychosexual development. According to this perspective, the person with a paraphilia is basically fearful of conventional heterosexual relationships. Fetishists and pedophiles, for example, are hypothesized to suffer from castration anxiety that makes it too threatening to engage in conventional sex with adults.

- Behavioural and cognitive theorists focus more directly on the sexual behaviour itself. One view is that a fetishistic attraction to objects, such as boots, arises from accidental classical conditioning of sexual arousal. Another behavioural hypothesis posits social skills deficiencies that make it difficult for the person to interact normally with other adults. Cognitive distortions appear to be involved, as voyeurs may claim that the women they viewed wanted to be seen.

- Efforts have also been made to detect hormonal anomalies in people with paraphilias, but the findings are inconclusive at this time.

- The most promising treatments for the paraphilias are multi-dimensional, entailing several behavioural and cognitive components. One procedure is reducing the arousal to the stimulus that is involved in the paraphilia. Another, orgasmic reorientation, tries to increase arousal to conventional sexual stimuli. Cognitive methods focus on the cognitive distortions of the person with a paraphilia; social skills training and empathy training are also used frequently.

- Rape, although it is not separately diagnosed in *DSM-IV-TR*, is a pattern of behaviour that results in considerable social and psychological trauma for the victim. The inclusion of rape in a discussion of human sexuality is a matter of some controversy, as many theorists regard rape as an act of aggression and violence rather than of sex.

- Few emotional problems are of greater interest to people than the sexual dysfunctions. These disruptions in the normal sexual response cycle are often caused by inhibitions, and they rob many people of sexual enjoyment.

DSM-IV-TR categorizes these disturbances in four groups: sexual desire disorders, sexual arousal disorders, orgasmic disorders, and sexual pain disorders. The disorders can vary in severity, chronicity, and pervasiveness, and occur generally or only with certain partners and in particular situations. In no instance should a person believe that he or she has a sexual dysfunction unless the difficulty is persistent and recurrent; most people normally experience sexual problems on an intermittent basis throughout their lives.

- Although biological factors must be considered, especially for dyspareunia and erectile failure, the etiology of the disorders usually lies in a combination of unfavourable attitudes, difficult early experiences, fears of performance, assumption of a spectator role, relationship problems, and lack of specific knowledge and skills.

- Sex-role stereotypes may play a part in some dysfunctions. For example, a man who has trouble maintaining his erection is often called "impotent," with the implication that he is not much of a man, and a woman who does not have orgasms with regularity is often termed "frigid," with the implication that she is generally cold and unresponsive. The problems of women in particular appear to be linked to cultural prejudices against their sexuality, ironic in light of laboratory data indicating that women are capable of more frequent orgasms than men.

- Information on the causes of sexual dysfunctions derives almost entirely from uncontrolled case studies and must therefore be viewed with caution. The absence of solid data on etiology, however, has not deterred therapists from devising effective interventions, many of them cognitive and behavioural in nature, often blended with psychodynamic perspectives and techniques.

- Direct sex therapy, aimed at reversing old habits and teaching new skills, was propelled into public consciousness by the work of Masters and Johnson. Their method hinges on gradual, non-threatening exposure to increasingly intimate sexual encounters and the sanctioning of sexuality by credible and sensitive therapists. Other means applied by sex therapists include educating clients in sexual anatomy and physiology, reducing anxiety, teaching communication skills, and working to change clients' attitudes and thoughts about sex and their own sexuality.

- Couples therapy is appropriate when the sexual problem is embedded, as it often is, in a snarled relationship. Biological treatments such as Viagra may also be used, especially when the sexual dysfunction is primarily physical rather than psychological in nature, as in erectile dysfunction.

- Controlled data are just beginning to appear, but there is good reason to be optimistic about the ultimate ability of the mental health professions to help many people achieve at least some relief from sexual problems.

KEY TERMS

accommodation (p. 494)
acquaintance (date) rape (p. 489)
assimilation (p. 494)
child sexual abuse (p. 482)
dyspareunia (p. 499)
exhibitionism (p. 484)
fear of performance (p. 500)
female orgasmic disorder (p. 498)
female sexual arousal disorder (p. 497)
fetishism (p. 477)
forced rape (p. 489)
frotteurism (p. 485)
gender identity disorder (p. 471)
hypersexual disorder (p. 497)

hypoactive sexual desire disorder (p. 496)
incest (p. 480)
male erectile disorder (p. 497)
male orgasmic disorder (p. 498)
medical forensic examination (p. 494)
orgasmic reorientation (p. 488)
paraphilias (p. 477)
pedophilia (p. 478)
premature ejaculation (p. 498)
sensate focus (p. 502)
sensory-awareness procedures (p. 502)
sex-reassignment surgery (p. 475)

sexual and gender identity disorders (p. 470)
sexual aversion disorder (p. 496)
sexual dysfunctions (p. 494)
sexual masochism (p. 485)
sexual sadism (p. 485)
sexual value system (p. 502)
spectator role (p. 500)
statutory rape (p. 489)
transsexualism (p. 471)
transvestic fetishism (p. 478)
vaginismus (p. 499)
voyeurism (p. 484)

REFLECTIONS: PAST, PRESENT, AND FUTURE

- Do you think that gender identity disorder should be regarded as a mental disorder? Why or why not?

- Paul Bernardo has been diagnosed as having an anti-social personality disorder. He has also been identified as a psychopath and described as a narcissist. Apparently, he is also quite bright. Do you think that he also meets the criteria for sexual sadism? Although there is no simple explanation, do you think that the combination of psychopathy and sexual sadism can be a "deadly combination" (Black, 2000) that contributes to the likelihood that people can turn out to be multiple murderers like Paul Bernardo or serial killers like Clifford Olson?

- Tragically for the victims, it appears to be the case that high intelligence also contributes to "successful" multiple rapes, murders, and serial killing. Paul Bernardo, Clifford Olson, Jeffrey Dahmer, and Ted Bundy are (or were) endowed with above average, even superior, intelligence. Why would intelligence be a critical consideration in our understanding of some multiple and serial rapists and killers? What role would narcissism play in the case of Paul Bernardo (and possibly in other cases, too)?

- During the development of *DSM-III*, experts considered including "rape" in the list of sexual disorders. The specific disorder to be included was to be called something like "paraphilic coercive disorder." Why do you think the decision was made not to include the proposed disorder in the 1980 and subsequent revisions of the manual? Should rape, or some specific subtype of rape, be included in the next revision of the *DSM*? Why or why not?

- Suppose that you specialize in sex therapy. A couple has initiated therapy with you because they are concerned that the male partner is unable to maintain an erection. What would you need to focus on during your initial meeting? Would it be important for you to make a referral to a physician? How will your conceptualization of the case influence the treatment plan that you develop?

DISORDERS OF CHILDHOOD

Will Gorlitz, Canadian 1952-, Genre II, 1984, Oil on canvas 61.0 X 89.0 cm, Art Gallery of Ontario, Toronto. Gift of Alison and Alan Schwartz, 1997 © Will Gorlitz.

"If you want a highly competent population with limited behaviour problems and no violence, then you don't have any choice but to invest in early childhood development."
—Dr. Fraser Mustard, renowned Canadian child development expert, quoted in the *Toronto Star*, April 30, 2007

"Parents, I think, are probably in the best position of all to notice a behavioural change. And behavioural change is one of the fundamental signs of mental illness. If you see that your child is moving in one direction [and] suddenly, is a different person, there's a reason for it. It doesn't just happen."
—Michael Wilson, former federal finance minister and advocate for the mentally ill, commenting on conditions leading up to his son's suicide (Nunes & Simmie, 2002, pp. 33–34)

"Given that most seriously impairing and persistent adult mental disorders are associated with child-adolescent onsets and high comorbidity, increased efforts are needed to study the public health implications of early detection and treatment of initially mild and currently largely untreated child-adolescent disorders."
—Kessler and Wang (2008, p.115)

"A common frustration expressed by parents is that services for children and adolescents are splintered and uncoordinated. Four different ministries—health, education, corrections, community and social services—are involved, to varying degrees."
—Scott Simmie on mental health services for children in Ontario, quoted in the *Toronto Star*, October 5, 1998

CLASSIFICATION OF CHILDHOOD DISORDERS

DISORDERS OF UNDERCONTROLLED BEHAVIOUR

LEARNING DISABILITIES

AUTISTIC DISORDER

DISORDERS OF OVERCONTROLLED BEHAVIOUR

MOOD DISORDERS IN CHILDHOOD AND ADOLESCENCE

SUMMARY

"ERIC. ERIC? ERIC!!" His teacher's voice and the laughter of his classmates roused the boy from his reverie. Glancing at the book of the girl sitting next to him, he noticed that the class was pages ahead of him. He was supposed to be answering a question about the Confederation of Canada, but he had been lost in thought about what seats he and his father would have for the baseball game they'd be attending that evening. A tall, lanky 12-year-old, Eric had just begun Grade 7. His history teacher had already warned him about being late for class and not paying attention, but Eric just couldn't seem to get from one class to the next without stopping for drinks of water or investigating an altercation between classmates. In class, he was rarely prepared to answer when the teacher called on him, and he usually forgot to write down the homework assignment. He already had a reputation among his peers as a "space cadet."

Eric's relief at the sound of the bell was quickly replaced by anxiety as he reached the playground for his physical education class. Despite his speed and physical strength, Eric was always picked last for baseball teams. His team was up to bat first, and Eric sat down to wait his turn. Absorbed in studying a pile of pebbles at his feet, he failed to notice his team's third out and missed the change of innings. The other team had already come in from the outfield before Eric noticed that his team was out in the field—too late to avoid the irate yells of his P.E. teacher to take his place at third base. Resolved to watch for his chance to field the ball, Eric nonetheless found himself without his glove on when a sharply hit ball rocketed his way; he had taken it off to toss it in the air in the middle of the pitch.

At home, Eric's father told him he had to finish his homework before they could go to the Blue Jays game. He had only one page of math problems and was determined to finish them quickly. Thirty minutes later, his father emerged from the shower to find Eric building an elaborate Lego structure on the floor of his room; the math homework was half done. In exasperation, Eric's father left for the game without him.

By bedtime, frustrated and discouraged, Eric was unable to sleep. He often lay awake for what seemed like hours, reviewing the disappointments of the day and berating himself for his failures. On this night, he ruminated about his lack of friends, his teachers' disappointment in him, and his parents' exhortations to pay attention and "get with the program." Feeling that it was hopeless to do better despite his daily resolve, Eric found himself thinking—as he often did—of suicide. Tonight he reviewed his fantasy of wandering out into the street in front of a passing car. Although Eric had never acted on his suicidal thoughts, he frequently replayed in his mind his parents' sorrow and remorse, his classmates' irritation with him, and the concern of his teachers.

Eric's difficulty in focusing his attention is characteristic of attention-deficit/hyperactivity disorder (ADHD)—just one of the disorders clinicians encounter when they work with children. The clinical problems loosely characterized as disorders of childhood cover a wide range of difficulties, from an attentional problem such as that suffered by Eric to depression, fear, the sometimes serious intellectual deficits found in mental retardation, the gross and sometimes callous disregard for the rights of others found in conduct disorder, and the social isolation of autistic disorder. The extreme dependency of troubled children on their parents and guardians adds to the sense of responsibility these people feel and to their guilt, justified or not. Whether such children receive professional attention usually depends on the adults in their lives—parents, teachers, school counsellors.

A review by Waddell et al. (2005) recommended investment in programs that could prevent psychological disorders in children; however, they noted that Canada has not made the necessary funding a priority at either the federal or provincial levels. A subsequent review of randomized controlled trials (RCTs) aimed at the prevention of conduct, anxiety, and depression disorders in children found few studies of development and/or evaluation in Canada (Waddell et al., 2007).

Child and adolescent mental health services are inadequate in Canada (Kutcher, Hampton, & Wilson, 2010).

Although specific policies and/or plans are necessary to direct mental health care, Canada has no such national policy or plan and only four provinces have a child and adolescent mental health policy or plan. Kutcher et al. (2010) called for a national policy framework to be developed to address the service needs of children and adolescents. Recently, the Child and Youth Advisory Committee of the Mental Health Commission of Canada submitted a proposal to establish such a national mental health framework specific to children and youth entitled Evergreen (see Kutcher & McLuckie, 2009). The framework could be useful in a number of domains, including: (1) assisting provinces and territories in creating (or modifying) their child and youth mental health strategies, policies, and plans; (2) assisting national child and youth organizations as they address child and youth mental health domains within their areas of responsibilities; (3) raising public awareness to the importance of addressing child and youth mental health needs; and (4) serving as a reference point or resource for people interested in child and youth mental health (Kutcher & McLuckie, 2009).

Most adults who receive a psychiatric diagnosis first met diagnostic criteria for a disorder during childhood or adolescence (Copeland et al., 2009). It is now estimated that 14% of children aged 4 to 17 years (more than 800,000 children in Canada) have clinically important disorders that cause significant distress and impairment, with anxiety disorders being most prevalent (Waddell et al., 2002, 2005). Mental health problems are the leading health problems that Canadian children face after infancy (Waddell et al., 2005). Fewer than 25% of children with psychological disorders receive specialized treatment. Comorbidity adds to the burden since more than 50% of children with a disorder have two or more disorders at the same time (Waddell et al., 2002). However, a majority of treatment studies have not determined whether this comorbidity predicts or moderates treatment outcomes (Ollendick et al., 2008). A Danish study (Skovgaard et al., 2007) conducted a comprehensive assessment of children one and a half years of age and concluded that the prevalence and distribution of mental health problems mirrored distributions in older children. Clinical diagnoses were determined in 16 to 18% of the children. According to the recent Early Years Study 2 (Mustard, McCain, & Shanker, 2007), it's estimated that, in Ontario alone, the cost of behavioural and mental health problems triggered by problems in early childhood is $30 billion per year.

CLASSIFICATION OF CHILDHOOD DISORDERS

To classify abnormal behaviour in children, diagnosticians must first consider what is normal for a particular age. The diagnosis for a child who lies on the floor kicking and screaming when he or she doesn't get his or her way must take into account whether the child is 2 years old or 7. The field of developmental psychopathology (see Cicchetti & Toth, 2009) involves disorders of childhood within the context of normal lifespan development, enabling us to identify behaviours that are appropriate at one stage but considered disturbed at another. A basic theme is that "because all psychopathology can be conceived as a distortion, disturbance, or degeneration of normal functioning, it follows that, if one wishes to comprehend psychopathology more fully, then one must understand the normal functioning with which psychopathology is compared" (Cicchetti & Toth, 2009, p. 17). The approach is consistent with a biopsychosocial paradigm, a multiple levels of analysis perspective, and an interdisciplinary approach.

Table 15.1 outlines the principal childhood disorders included in *DSM-IV-TR*. Some disorders, such as separation anxiety disorder, are unique to children, whereas others, such as depression, are subsumed under the criteria used for adults. Still others, such as attention-deficit/hyperactivity disorder (ADHD), have been conceptualized primarily as childhood disorders but may continue into adulthood.

Eric, the distressed boy described at the beginning of this chapter, might be given the following multiaxial *DSM-IV-TR* diagnosis:

Axis I: Attention-deficit/hyperactivity disorder, predominantly inattentive type; dysthymic disorder, early onset

Axis II: No diagnosis on Axis II

Axis III: No general medical conditions

Axis IV: Educational problems: discord with teacher and classmates

Axis V: Global assessment of functioning = 50 (suicidal ideation; no friends; behind in schoolwork)

Childhood disorders can also be conceptualized by a dimensional model. As discussed earlier, a dimensional model portrays dysfunctional behaviour as existing on a continuum. One dimension often employed by child psychopathologists is the degree to which behaviour is controlled. At one end of the continuum of control, undercontrolled (or externalizing) behaviour is characterized by excess, such as extreme aggressiveness. At the other end of the continuum, children are overcontrolled (or internalizing) and show emotional inhibitions, such as school phobia (Achenbach & Edelbrock, 1978). A distinction sometimes drawn between these two extremes is whether the child creates a problem primarily for others (undercontrolled) or primarily for the self (overcontrolled). Children and adolescents may exhibit symptoms from both extremes, as Eric did.

Early-onset, undercontrol problems (e.g., conduct problems, autism) are consistently found more often among boys, whereas adolescent-onset, overcontrol problems are more often found among girls across cultures (e.g., Zahn-Waxler, Shirtcliff, & Marceau, 2008). Problems of undercontrol and overcontrol can lead to significant distress in children and their families, often at great cost to society. Thus, in 1994, Canada initiated an important research study—the National Longitudinal Survey of Children and Youth (NLSCY)—to establish a national database on the characteristics and experiences of children and youth in Canada as they grow up. This ongoing study is the subject of Canadian Perspectives 15.1. Canadian Perspectives 15.2 looks at McMaster University's Offord Centre for Child Studies, recognized around the world for its research on the psychological disorders of children, including research on the epidemiology of these disorders.

Tourette syndrome involves involuntary tics, both motor and vocal (phonic), and can be found in children and adults. Canadian actress Neve Campbell's younger brother has Tourette's, and they both participate actively as members of the spokesfamily for the Tourette Syndrome Foundation of Canada (see www.tourette.ca). Tourette Syndrome Foundation of Canada.

TABLE 15.1
DISORDERS OF CHILDHOOD AND ADOLESCENCE IN *DSM-IV-TR*

I. Disorders Usually First Diagnosed in Infancy, Childhood, or Adolescence

Mental retardation:
Intellectual functioning that is significantly below average, is accompanied by concurrent deficits in adaptive functioning, and is noticeable before age 18.

Learning disorders:
Academic achievement in reading, mathematics, or written expression substantially below that expected for age, schooling, and level of intelligence.

Motor skills disorder:
Problems in motor coordination.

Communication disorders:
Problems in expressing and/or understanding speech.

Pervasive developmental disorders:
Severe and pervasive impairment in several areas of development, including interaction and communication with others and the exhibition of stereotyped behaviour.

Attention-deficit/hyperactivity disorder (ADHD):
A persistent pattern of inattention and/or hyperactivity-impulsivity that is more frequent or severe than is typically observed in individuals at a comparable level of development. Symptoms must be present before age 7 and interfere with functioning in at least two settings.

Conduct disorder:
A repetitive and persistent pattern of seriously anti-social behaviour, usually criminal in nature and marked by extreme callousness.

Oppositional defiant disorder (ODD):
A recurrent pattern of defiant, disobedient, and hostile behaviour toward authority figures.

Feeding and eating disorders of infancy or early childhood:
Persistent feeding and eating disorders, such as eating non-nutritive substances (pica), repeated regurgitation and rechewing of food (rumination disorder), or persistent failure to eat adequately, as reflected in significant weight loss or failure to gain weight (feeding disorder of infancy or early childhood).

Tic disorders (e.g., Tourette syndrome):
Characterized by sudden, rapid, recurrent, non-rhythmic, stereotyped motor movements or vocalizations.

Elimination disorders:
Repeated defecation in inappropriate places after age 4 (encopresis) or voiding of urine in bed or clothes after age 5 (enuresis).

Separation anxiety disorder:
Excessive anxiety concerning separation from the home or from those to whom the person is attached, to the extent that it causes distress or impairs functioning.

Selective mutism:
Persistent failure to speak in specific social situations (e.g., at school), despite speaking in other situations (e.g., with parents).

Reactive attachment disorder of infancy or early childhood:
Markedly disturbed and developmentally inappropriate social-relatedness in most contexts that begins before age 5 and is associated with grossly pathological care by parents or other caregivers.

II. Diagnoses that May Be Applied to Adults, Adolescents, or Children

Substance-related disorders:
See Chapter 12.

Schizophrenia:
See Chapter 11.

Mood disorders:
See Chapter 8 and this chapter.

Anxiety disorders, such as specific phobia, social phobia, obsessive-compulsive disorder, post-traumatic stress disorder, generalized anxiety disorder:
See Chapter 6 and this chapter; for aftermath of child sexual abuse, see Chapter 14.

Somatoform disorders:
See Chapter 7.

Dissociative disorders:
See Chapter 7.

Gender identity disorders:
See Chapter 14.

Eating disorders, such as anorexia nervosa and bulimia nervosa:
See Chapter 10.

Parasomnias:
Abnormal behavioural or physiological events occurring in association with sleep. For example, **nightmare disorder, sleep terror disorder, and sleepwalking disorder**.

Source: Adapted from *DSM-IV-TR*

CANADIAN PERSPECTIVES 15.1
THE NATIONAL LONGITUDINAL SURVEY OF CHILDREN AND YOUTH (NLSCY)

The National Longitudinal Survey of Children and Youth (NLSCY) involves approximately 23,000 children from 13,439 households with at least one child, in all 10 Canadian provinces. The children ranged from birth to 11 years old at the outset of the study in 1994 and are being studied prospectively, every two years, throughout their childhood into adulthood (age 25). Complete longitudinal data from ages 0 to 24 will be available in 2018. The project has yielded many illuminating findings, some of which were first described in the initial report *Growing Up in Canada* (Human Resources Development Canada and Statistics Canada, 1996), including the following: (1) low birth weight is associated with numerous childhood health problems and is more likely if a mother smokes during pregnancy; (2) children with difficult temperaments have parents characterized by greater hostility; (3) children between the ages of 4 and 11 with emotional and/or behavioural problems tend to have multiple problems; (4) children from single-mother families are more likely to be poor financially, and economic disadvantage increases the likelihood of physical aggression on the part of the child.

The websites for Human Resources and Skills Development Canada (www.hrsdc.gc.ca) and Statistics Canada (www.statcan.gc.ca) contain numerous research reports using findings from the NLSCY. We mention a few specific studies to illustrate the rich findings that are emerging from this "gold mine" of data:

- Immigrant children actually had better adjustment overall than children born in Canada! New immigrant children had lower prevalence rates of hyperactivity, emotional disorders, and conduct disorders. Poor immigrant families may provide a supportive environment that fosters a greater sense of resilience relative to the poor families of children born in Canada (Beiser, Hou, Hyman, & Tousignant, 1998).
- The problems of aggressive girls were quite similar to those experienced by aggressive boys. Aggressive girls (relative to non-aggressive girls) suffered in terms of interpersonal relationships, low self-esteem, difficult behaviour, and academic problems (Pepler & Sedighdeilami, 1998).
- "Disadvantaged" children (i.e., those having a young mother who did not complete high school and had a low income) obtained substantially lower mathematics scores than children from households with an older mother with a university degree at the 75th percentile of income (Hoddinott, Lethbridge, & Phipps, 2002).

- Although marital separation increased emotional problems in children, a positive parenting style mitigated the negative impact of the separation (O'Connor & Jenkins, 2000).
- Exposure to a depressed mother predicted a child's problems involving aggression and hyperactivity; however, emotional problems in the child were associated with subsequent depression in the mother. Thus, bi-directional influences were apparent (Elgar et al., 2003).
- Children age 10 and over were followed until they were 16 to 17 years of age to determine factors related to drug use. Parental rejection was a positive predictor of initial drug use, whereas warmth was a negative predictor over time and appears to be most important in minimizing later drug use. Deviant peer affiliations were a positive predictor of drug use (Pires & Jenkins, 2007).
- Victims of peer harassment are likely to feel anxious and disliked by their peers. Further, the parents used high levels of control and low levels of warmth with their children and had high levels of marital conflict and dysphoria themselves (Beran & Violato, 2004).
- Among boys, damaging property, sexual intercourse, and smoking cigarettes were uniquely associated with suicide ideation, while smoking cigarettes and using marijuana or hash were associated with suicide attempts. Among girls, carrying a knife was associated with suicide ideation whereas shoplifting and gambling were associated with suicide attempts (Afifi, Cox, & Katz, 2007).
- Neighbourhood poverty is associated with suicidal thoughts and attempts in late adolescence. The associations were not explained by various psychosocial risks (i.e., social support, negative life events, delinquent activities, substance abuse, depression, and suicide exposure) (Dupere, Leventhal, & Lacourse, 2009).
- A fussy-difficult temperament in babies predicted anxiety in children aged 6 to 7 years; however, it did not predict anxiety at 10 to 11 years, suggesting that environmental factors become more important with age (Grant, Bagnell, Chambers, & Stewart, 2009).

Thinking Critically

Assume that you are the NLSCY project director and that the initial findings point to some interventions that could improve the well-being of children in the study. From an ethical perspective, should you implement the interventions, even though it will mean that the study will be compromised?

CANADIAN PERSPECTIVES 15.2
THE OFFORD CENTRE FOR CHILD STUDIES

"... the burden of suffering from child psychiatric disorders is extremely high, and one-to-one interventions can never make a large dent in reducing this burden."

—Daniel Offord, 1995, p. 287

The Offord Centre for Child Studies (OCCS), formerly known as the Canadian Centre for Studies of Children at Risk, is a world-renowned organization composed of a team of clinical researchers based in Hamilton, Ontario, many of whom also hold appointments at McMaster University. The founder of the centre and director for 20 years was David (Dan) Offord. The current director is Peter Szatmari. The centre "is dedicated to improving the life quality and life opportunities of the one in five Canadian children and youth who suffer from serious social and emotional problems." (See the centre's website at www.offordcentre.com.)

The OCCS has played a leading role in epidemiological research on mental health problems in children and adolescents. Known primarily for the Ontario Child Health Study (OCHS), a cross-sectional investigation of 1,869 families and 3,294 children, the centre is also involved in the NLSCY, as well as numerous projects on several topics, including (1) prevention and modification of anti-social behaviour; (2) clinical and familial characteristics of depressed children; (3) factors associated with the incidence and prevention of substance abuse in youth; (4) determining the amount of child abuse and predictors of child abuse in Ontario; and (5) assessing health and well-being in First Nations youth. Collectively, these research initiatives have yielded many important findings. For instance, analyses of the role of

family influences on substance use by adolescents found that the most robust family influence is from an older sibling to a younger sibling and not from parents to their children (Boyle et al., 2001). Boyle et al. (2004) examined data from three child development studies and found that differential-maternal parenting had an adverse impact on all siblings as a group, over and above parenting directed at individual siblings. The association was stronger for hostile/negative parenting.

Dr. Dan Offord died peacefully at home in Ottawa on April 10, 2004, at age 70 after a battle with cancer. He was one of Canada's pre-eminent child psychiatrists, a renowned clinician, researcher, teacher, and recipient of the Order of Canada. He taught practitioners about the major problems facing children, including poverty, abuse, and depression. However, to the thousands of children he helped, he was simply Dr. Dan (Kravitz, 2004). For 47 years, he was also the director of Christie Lake camp where about 400 disadvantaged children enjoyed a camp experience each summer.

Thinking Critically

1. Do you think that a major focus for the future must be on the prevention of childhood disorders? Is a lack of government funding a critical issue because widespread preventive programs are simply not possible with the current resources available?

2. Is there a great need for more trained clinicians who specialize in the treatment of disorders in children and adolescents?

There is considerable controversy about categorical vs. dimensional systems (e.g., Drabick, 2009). We have organized our discussion partially in dimensional terms, considering problems as lying on a continuum ranging from undercontrol to overcontrol; but we also follow the *DSM* in its categorical approach, considering discrete diagnostic categories into which a person fits or does not fit.

On February 10, 2010, the *DSM-5* work group responsible for childhood and adolescent disorders posted proposed changes on the *DSM-5* website (www.dsm5.org). We will introduce some of the proposed changes related to disorders in children at appropriate points throughout this chapter.

DISORDERS OF UNDERCONTROLLED BEHAVIOUR

The child who is undercontrolled does not behave in a given setting in a way that is expected or is appropriate to his or her age. Eric, for example, should be able to follow his teacher's lessons as well as his team's progress at bat. The undercontrolled child is frequently an annoyance to adults and peers

and usually gets the attention of parents and teachers more often than children who are overcontrolled. Two general categories of undercontrolled behaviour are typically differentiated: ADHD and conduct disorder.

ATTENTION-DEFICIT/HYPERACTIVITY DISORDER

The term *hyperactive* is familiar to most people, especially parents and teachers. The child who is constantly in motion, tapping fingers, jiggling legs, poking others for no apparent reason, talking out of turn, and fidgeting is often called hyperactive. This is the child who, in colloquial terms, drives parents and teachers nuts. These children also have difficulty concentrating on the task at hand for an appropriate period of time. The current diagnostic term is **attention-deficit/hyperactivity disorder** (ADHD).

Virginia Douglas, a professor emeritus of the McGill University Department of Psychology, played an instrumental role in refining our understanding of ADHD in the 1970s. Until that time, hyperactive children were identified as having "minimal brain damage" or "minimal brain dysfunction" because of apparent similarities between their hyperactive behaviours and the behaviours expressed by certain children with brain damage. Because brain damage could not be detected, more emphasis was placed on the hyperactivity, and the disorder came to be known as "hyperactive child syndrome" and "hyperkinetic reaction of childhood." Douglas (1972) is credited with being the first researcher to note the attentional problems in ADHD.

Children with ADHD seem to have particular difficulty controlling their activity in situations that call for sitting still, such as in the classroom or at mealtimes. They appear unable to stop moving or talking when asked to be quiet. They are disorganized, erratic, tactless, obstinate, and bossy. Their activities and movements seem haphazard. They smash their toys and exhaust their family and teachers. ADHD children have difficulty in adjusting to a typical classroom environment (Barkley, DuPaul, & Murray, 1990).

These children often encounter problems in social interactions with peers and are confronted with peer rejection and social isolation (de Boo & Prins, 2007). Their behaviour is often aggressive and annoying to others. They tend to miss subtle social cues, such as noticing when playmates are tiring of their constant jiggling. They frequently misinterpret the wishes and intentions of their peers and make inadvertent social mistakes, such as reacting aggressively because they assume that a neutral action by a peer was meant to be aggressive. (Such cognitive misattributions are also found in some children with conduct disorder.) Children with ADHD can know what the socially correct action is in hypothetical situations but be unable to translate this knowledge into appropriate behaviour in real-life social interactions (Whalen & Henker, 1999).

Hoza, Waschbusch, Pelham, Molina, and Milich (2000) compared the attributions and perceptions of boys with ADHD and control participants in a social interaction situation. Objective raters viewed the performance of the boys with ADHD as poorer in quality, relative to that of controls, but the boys saw themselves in much more positive terms and had more positive performance self-evaluations than the control group. Thus, boys with ADHD may have an illusory bias concerning the quality of their social behaviours.

About 15 to 30% of children with ADHD have a learning disability (e.g., Casey, Rourke, & Del Dotto, 1996). Children diagnosed with ADHD and mathematical and reading disorders are more severely impaired and attain lower IQ (intelligent quotient), language, and academic scores relative to those with ADHD alone (Capano et al., 2008). Approximately 25% of children with ADHD exhibit comorbidity with anxiety disorders (Jarrett & Ollendick, 2008).

The ADHD diagnosis does not properly apply to youngsters who are rambunctious, active, or slightly distractible, for in the early school years children are often so. To use the label simply because a child is livelier and more difficult to control than a parent or teacher would like represents a misuse of the term. The diagnosis is reserved for truly extreme and persistent cases. Because the symptoms of ADHD are varied, *DSM-IV-TR* has three subcategories: (1) children whose problems are

primarily those of poor attention; (2) children whose difficulties result primarily from hyperactive-impulsive behaviour; and (3) children who have both sets. The third subcategory applies to the majority of ADHD children. The subtypes have been validated in numerous studies (e.g., Levy et al., 2005). Children with both attentional problems and hyperactivity are more likely to develop conduct problems and oppositional behaviour, to be placed in special classes for behaviour-disordered children, and to have peer difficulties (Faraone et al., 1998). Children with ADHD typically use long-term support from public sector services, with high rates of contact with schools, educational professionals, and the criminal justice system (see Ford et al., 2008).

It is difficult to differentiate between ADHD and conduct disorder. Hyperactivity is associated more with off-task behaviour in school, cognitive and achievement deficits, and a better long-term prognosis. Conduct disorder is associated more with acting out in school and elsewhere, being much more aggressive, and having anti-social parents. Nonetheless, the comorbidity between ADHD and oppositional or conduct disorders is approximately 50% (Jarrett & Ollendick, 2008). When these two disorders occur in the same youngster, the worst features of each can be manifested. A study in Quebec concluded that "children with CD [conduct disorder] and ADHD are especially at risk for persistent antisocial behaviour" (Toupin et al., 2000, p. 422). Such children often exhibit serious anti-social behaviour and have a poor prognosis (e.g., Moffitt, 1990).

The prevalence of ADHD has been difficult to establish because of varied definitions of the disorder over time and differences in the populations sampled. A systematic review of 102 studies comprising over 170,000 participants from all world regions estimated the worldwide-pooled prevalence was 5.29% (Polanczyk, et al., 2007). Geographic location played a limited role in the reasons for the significant variability. Taylor (2009) noted that the apparent rise in the prevalence of ADHD is due to changes in recognition and diagnostic practice rather than a true increase in the disorder.

It is generally believed that the disorder is more common in boys than in girls, but research findings depend on whether the sample is taken from clinic referrals or from the general population. Boys are more likely to be referred to clinics because of a higher likelihood of aggressive and anti-social behaviour. However, a comparative study in Toronto showed that ADHD girls, relative to ADHD boys and control participants, have significantly greater impairment on a wide range of measures (Rucklidge & Tannock, 2001).

Most children who develop ADHD exhibit excessive activity and temperamental behaviour quite early in life. Childproofing is a necessity to avoid such tragedies as accidental poisoning and falling out of windows. Although the preschool years are stressful for parents whose children have ADHD, the problems become salient when the children enter school and are suddenly expected to sit in their seats for longer periods of time, complete assignments independently, and negotiate with peers on the playground. Breslau et al. (2010)

reported that increases in teacher-rated attention problems from age 6 to 11 were followed by declines in academic achievement in math and reading from age 11 to 17. Similarly, Galera et al. (2009) conducted a longitudinal study and found a link between childhood ADHD symptoms and negative academic outcomes eight years later.

It was once thought that hyperactivity simply went away by adolescence. This belief was challenged by numerous longitudinal studies (e.g., Biederman et al., 1996). Although these studies do show reduced severity of symptoms in adolescence (see Gerlach, 2009), 65 to 80% of children with ADHD still meet criteria for the disorder in adolescence and adulthood. In addition to having fidgety, distractible, impulsive behaviours, and difficulty sustaining attention (e.g., Barkley, DuPaul, & Murray, 1990), adolescents with ADHD are far more likely to drop out of high school and develop anti-social behaviour than their peers. Although most people with childhood ADHD no longer satisfy the full criteria for ADHD by the age of 30 or 40 years, about 50% will exhibit ongoing psychosocial impairment (Gerlach, 2009). The National Comorbidity Survey Replication (Kessler et al., 2006) indicates that the prevalence of adult ADHD is 4.4%. In 2009, Major League Baseball granted 108 "therapeutic use" (Campbell, 2009) exemptions for the use of otherwise banned stimulants because the players were diagnosed with ADHD. This is a prevalence rate of approximately 11.7%, given that there were 926 players at that time.

Studies of ADHD in adulthood suggest that affective, anxiety, substance abuse, and anti-social disorders are common comorbidities (see Antshel et al., 2009 for review). While most are employed and financially independent, these individuals generally reach a lower socio-economic level and change jobs more frequently than would normally be expected. A recent study (Kessler, Lane, Stang, & Van Brunt, 2009) reported that adult ADHD employees of a large manufacturing firm showed a 4–5% reduction in work performance and relatively more sickness absence, and workplace accidents and injuries. Only a small minority of these workers were in therapy. A study in Montreal found that family and marital functioning was impaired in families with an ADHD adult (Minde et al., 2003). A study of adult women with ADHD in Toronto found that they had impairments in social functioning, reduced self-esteem, elevated stress, and a self-blaming attributional style (Rucklidge & Kaplan, 1997). Balint et al. (2009) conducted a meta-analysis of 25 neuropsychological studies of people with adult ADHD and concluded that they display significantly poorer functioning (relative to controls) on complex but not on simple tasks of attention. Males displayed a higher level of impairment.

Although most adults with a history of ADHD continue to exhibit some symptoms of the disorder, many do learn to adapt to these symptoms, perhaps by finding a niche for themselves in the working world. Canadian comic Howie Mandel is one example:

As if the germophobia and OCD weren't enough, Mandel realized later in life that he had also been suffering all along from attention-deficit hyperactivity disorder, or ADHD. "Yeah," he grumbles, "I had the whole damn alphabet ganging up on me.... My mother would see this kid coming home. I was angry and lonely and resentful. My issues made sense to me, just not to anyone else. And there wasn't a name back then anybody could put on it. It was just me. Howie being Howie." To anyone who knew him then that was a frightening thing. "The most common reaction from adults to me as a kid," Mandel recalls, "was them making a 'tch!' sound and then rolling their eyes. I always let it all out. I had tantrums. I would act out. If I got bored in class, I'd start passing out candy. I didn't know I had a psychological condition. I didn't know I was a sick kid. I was just weird Howie." But he finally found a place where weird Howie made sense: in the world of stand-up comedy. On April 19, 1978, he decided to take part in amateur night at Yuk Yuk's and, although he can't recall specifically what he said or did, he knew that "I was in my comfortable place, my happy place. I just spewed. It was very scary, I guess. The thrill and fear of being on the roller coaster.... I wish my whole life could be one big stand-up routine. From the moment I open my eyes, I wish someone could say, 'Ladies and gentlemen, Howie Mandel!'" (Ouzounian, 2009, p. E3)

Sadly, Mandel's success may be the exception rather than the rule for those with ADHD.

The diagnosis of ADHD in higher education settings has become a contentious issue, especially among clients with high IQ. Antshel et al. (2009) compared groups of adults with high IQ and with or without an ADHD diagnosis. High-IQ ADHD participants reported a lower quality of life, had poorer familial and occupational functioning, and had more functional impairments (e.g., speeding tickets). They were also more likely to be diagnosed with generalized anxiety disorder, obsessive-compulsive disorder (OCD), and major depressive disorder. Nonetheless, many students diagnosed with ADHD are able to achieve some success in college or university.

BIOLOGICAL THEORIES OF ADHD The search for causes of ADHD is complicated by the heterogeneity of children given this diagnosis; any factor found to be associated with the syndrome is perhaps linked with only some of the diagnosed cases.

Genetic Factors Research suggests that a genetic predisposition toward ADHD may play a role. Adoption studies (e.g., van den Oord, Boomsma, & Verhulst, 1994) and large-scale twin studies (e.g., Levy et al., 1997) indicate a genetic component. Indeed, estimates of heritability are approximately 75% (Biederman & Farone, 2005). Family environment does not make a significant contribution (Barkley, 2002). As noted by Goos, Crosbie, Payne, and Schachar (2009), molecular analyses have identified several genes that appear to play a role in the etiology of ADHD, and genome-wide scans identified numerous regions of interest. However, many identified risks (e.g., the dopamine receptor gene DRD4) failed to replicate and regions of interest show little overlap across studies.

More recently, Biederman et al. (2008) conducted familial risk analyses of ADHD and substance use disorders in a 10-year follow-up of boys into young adulthood. ADHD in the boys was predictive of ADHD in relatives irrespective of substance use disorder status. The patterns suggested that the robust and bidirectional comorbidity between ADHD and drug dependence is consistent with a hypothesis of "variable expressivity of a common risk between these disorders" (p. 107). Thus, there was no evidence that ADHD and substance use were transmitted together as a single entity. Biederman et al. (2008) suggested that common risks could involve dopamine genes that affect both attention and arousal and the reward pathways related to drug dependence. However, the association between ADHD and alcohol dependence is consistent with a hypothesis of "independent transmission" since the risk for alcohol dependence was elevated only in relatives of children with comorbid ADHD plus alcohol dependence.

Exactly what is inherited in ADHD is as yet unknown, but some studies point to differences in brain function and structure. As noted in Focus on Discovery 2.2 on the neuroscience of ADHD, evidence implicates frontal striatal circuitry in ADHD, reductions in volume throughout the cerebrum and cerebellum, and delays in cortical maturation, and the hypothesis that ADHD is due to a dopamine deficit (see Poissant et al., 2008; Shaw et al., 2007; Vaidya & Stollstorff, 2008). Recently, Qiu et al. (2009) conducted an MRI study comparing basal ganglia of ADHD and typically developing children. Boys with ADHD demonstrated smaller basal ganglia volumes relative to typically developing boys. It was concluded that the shape compression pattern of basal ganglia in ADHD boys suggests that atypical brain development involves multiple frontal-subcortical control loops that may contribute to the impaired response control characteristic of ADHD. Other studies suggest dysfunction in dopaminergic and noradrenergic systems in the origin of core symptoms (see Gerlach et al., 2008).

Goos, Crosbie, Payne, and Schachar (2009) proposed motor response inhibition as a prime marker of underlying liability (endophenotype) in ADHD. They studied inhibitory control in children with ADHD, unaffected siblings, and their biological parents to determine covariation in inhibitory control within families. Children with ADHD manifested an inhibitory control deficit as did their parents, and this deficit was independent of symptom severity in both generations. This deficit in children was predicted by the ability of their parents, particularly their fathers. Goos et al. (2009) concluded that the findings "indicate that an inhibitory control deficit is a cognitive marker of genetic risk shared by parents and offspring" (p. 711).

Recently, Rubia et al. (2008) used event-related fMRI to compare brain activation of inhibition in boys with pure ADHD and boys with pure conduct disorder. During successful inhibition only boys with ADHD showed reduced activation in the left dorsolateral prefrontal cortex in relation to comparison "normal" boys and boys with conduct disorder. During inhibition failures, conduct-disordered boys, relative to ADHD and normal boys, showed reduced activation in bilateral temporal-parietal regions. It was concluded that pure ADHD or pure conduct disorder boys show qualitative differences in their brain abnormality patterns, suggesting that "distinct neurobiological abnormalities may be underlying the overlapping behavioral phenotype of the two disruptive disorders" (p. 889).

Environmental Toxins Popular theories of ADHD have involved the role of environmental toxins. A biochemical theory put forth by Feingold (1973) proposed that food additives upset the central nervous system (CNS) of hyperactive children, and he prescribed a diet free of such additives. Well-controlled studies of the Feingold diet found that very few ADHD children respond positively to it (Goyette & Conners, 1977). Similarly, the once popular view that refined sugar can cause ADHD has not been supported (Wolraich, Wilson, & White, 1995). However, Milberger et al. (1996) reported that 22% of mothers of children with ADHD reported smoking a pack of cigarettes per day during pregnancy, compared with 8% of mothers whose children were normal, and the researchers hypothesized that maternal smoking (nicotine) can affect the dopaminergic system of the developing fetus, leading to behavioural disinhibition and ADHD.

PSYCHOLOGICAL THEORIES OF ADHD The child psychoanalyst Bruno Bettelheim (1973) proposed a diathesis-stress theory, suggesting that hyperactivity develops when a predisposition to ADHD is coupled with an authoritarian upbringing. Or, as Ross and Ross (1982) suggested, hyperactivity may be modelled on the behaviour of parents and siblings. However, such psychological theories have not been supported by research. Neurological and genetic factors have far greater research support. In any event, the parent-child relationship is bidirectional. Just as parents of hyperactive children give their offspring more commands and have negative interactions with them, so hyperactive children have been found to be less compliant and more negative in interactions with parents (Barkley, Karlsson, & Pollard, 1985). Stimulant medication reduces hyperactivity and increases compliance in ADHD children. When such medication is used, the parents' commands and negative behaviour decrease (see Barkley, 1990), suggesting that it is the child's behaviour that negatively affects the parents rather than the reverse.

TREATMENT OF ADHD In 2002, a consensus statement on ADHD by leading experts indicated that fewer than half of those with ADHD receive treatment. The need for treatment is underscored by the fact that those with ADHD, relative to normal people, are more likely to drop out of school, have no or few friends, engage in anti-social activities, use tobacco or illicit drugs, contract a sexually transmitted disease, and drive at excessive speeds and have multiple car accidents (Barkley, 2002). An international team, led by Stan Kutcher from Dalhousie University, concluded that the optimal treatment for ADHD is to "combine pharmacotherapy, which addresses core biological symptoms, with psychosocial intervention, which focuses on the youngsters' and families' attitudes and life strategies" (Kutcher et al., 2004, p. 19).

Stimulant Drugs Stimulant drugs, in particular methylphenidate, or Ritalin, have been prescribed for ADHD since the early 1960s (Sprague & Gadow, 1976). One perception that has emerged is that ADHD is overdiagnosed and overtreated. These concerns were fuelled by dramatic increases in the 1990s in the use of Ritalin to treat ADHD. Canadian surveys indicate that there was almost no change in the use of Ritalin between 1983 and 1990 but that use between 1990 and 1996 increased by 3 to 4.5 times the previous levels of use (Miller et al., 1998). A rising number of Canadian children aged 2 to 4 years are now prescribed methylphenidate (see Romano et al., 2002). A Manitoba study confirmed that there are regional variations in the rates of diagnosing ADHD, with urban areas having higher rates than rural areas (Brownell & Yogendran, 2001). In rural areas, however, rates of ADHD diagnosis and medication increased as a function of income level, leading the authors to suggest that ADHD is underdiagnosed in regions that may lack access to adequate resources.

Double-blind studies comparing stimulants with placebos have shown short-term improvements in concentration, goal-directed activity, classroom behaviour, and social interactions with parents, teachers, and peers, and reductions in aggressiveness and impulsivity in about 75% of ADHD children taking stimulants (e.g., Spencer et al., 1996). An experiment by Brodeur and Pond (2001) investigated selective attention in control children and children with ADHD from Nova Scotia. The performance of children with ADHD was more disrupted by the presence of distracters in a selective attention task, but comparisons of performance when the ADHD participants were on or off methylphenidate treatment showed that methylphenidate was associated with enhanced performance. However, stimulant drugs alone may not improve academic achievement over the long haul (e.g., Weiss & Hechtman, 1993).

A recent study by Blader and colleagues (2009) addressed the common combination of ADHD with disruptive and aggressive behaviour in 6- to 13-year-old children in a double-blind "add-on" design. Participants were first treated with sustained-release stimulants (the activating agent); however, if stabilization of aggressive behaviour did not occur, they were randomly assigned to a double-blind, placebo-controlled trial of divalproex (an inhibiting agent). Over 58% of the children receiving divalproex "remitted" aggression, compared with 15% receiving placebo. In an editorial on this integrated treatment ("A window into the future of child psychopharmacology"), Steiner and Karnik (2009) noted that, "This study

points the way to a more complicated, but ultimately more realistic, polypharmacology in developmental psychiatry that should produce better results for our patients" (p. 1316).

Do ADHD children adhere to drug treatment in the long term? A study in Toronto examined the predictors of long-term adherence (Thiruchelvam, Charach, & Schachar, 2001). Overall, only about half of the participants were adhering by taking their medication three years after the start of the study. Greater adherence was associated with younger age at the start of treatment and absence of oppositional defiant disorder (ODD) (discussed on p. 518).

Further, stimulant medication has side effects, including transient loss of appetite and sleep problems. There has been considerable controversy about possible adverse effects of stimulants on brain development. In the first prospective study of this issue, Shaw et al. (2009) determined from two neuroanatomic MRI scans (at 12.5 years and 16.4 years on average) that stimulant treatment for ADHD was not associated with differences in the development of the cerebral cortex during adolescence. Specifically, there was no evidence of slowing of overall growth of the cortical mantle. In fact, cortical thinning was greater in the comparison ADHD group not taking stimulants.

Concerns have been raised about the safety of stimulant medications and there continues to be controversy about a possible association between stimulant use for ADHD treatment and serious cardiovascular events, including sudden death. Although the events are very rare, Gould et al. (2009) concluded that there is, in fact, an association between the use of stimulants and sudden unexplained death among both children and adolescents. Although this finding needs to be considered in the context of the evidence for the benefits of stimulants, it will no doubt fuel further debate over clinical recommendations for physicians and families. Although there has been some concern that stimulant treatment, especially early exposure, increases susceptibility to subsequent substance use disorders, a 10-year prospective follow-up study (Biederman et al., 2008) found no evidence that stimulant treatment affects the risk for substance use disorders in children and adolescents with ADHD followed into young adulthood. Another risky side effect of the widespread prescription of stimulants also emerged. *Newsweek* magazine reported that children are using Ritalin and other stimulants obtained from their siblings or friends as recreational drugs (Leland, 1995). Its use also spread among high school and college students not suffering from ADHD who found that snorting it like cocaine helped them focus better on their schoolwork and ward off fatigue (Tennant, 1999).

Psychological Treatment Other than medication, the most effective treatments for ADHD children involve parent training and changes in classroom management based on operant-conditioning principles. The children are monitored at home and in school and are reinforced for behaving appropriately; for example, for remaining in their seats and working on assignments. Point systems and star charts are typical components of these programs. Youngsters earn points and younger children earn stars for behaving in certain ways; the children can then spend their earnings for rewards. The focus is on improving academic work, completing household tasks, or learning specific social skills, not on reducing signs of hyperactivity, such as running around or jiggling.

School interventions for children with ADHD include training teachers to understand the unique needs of these children and to apply operant techniques in the classroom, initiating peer tutoring in academic skills, and having teachers provide daily reports to parents about in-school behaviour, with follow-up rewards and consequences at home. Certain classroom structures have a favourable impact on children with ADHD. In the ideal classroom environment teachers vary the presentation format and the materials used for tasks, keep assignments brief, provide immediate feedback on accuracy, have an enthusiastic and task-focused style, provide breaks for physical exercise, use computer-assisted drill programs, and schedule academic work during the morning hours. Such environmental changes are designed to accommodate the limitations imposed by this disorder rather than to change the disorder itself (Pfiffner & Barkley, 1998).

A recent meta-analysis of 174 studies of behavioural treatments for ADHD (Fabiano et al., 2009) led to the conclusion that "there is strong and consistent evidence that behavioral treatments are effective for treating ADHD" (p. 129). Nonetheless, not all treatments are equally effective and some may not be considered "evidence based." For example, de Boo and Prins (2007) reviewed the research on the outcome of social skills training for social incompetence in children with ADHD, including mediators (e.g., social cognitive skills) and moderators (e.g., comorbidity). They concluded that there is now sufficient evidence and knowledge to adapt the social skills paradigm and to guide research toward making it a more effective, established intervention for ADHD children who are confronted with peer rejection and social isolation. Toplak et al. (2008) from York University identified 26 studies of

cognitive-behavioural, cognitive, and "neural-based" intervention approaches that are not currently considered evidence-based practice. Although some of these methods show promise in the treatment of ADHD, their analysis indicated that further research is needed to determine the efficacy of these approaches.

Stimulant Medication and Psychological Treatment The MTA Cooperative Group Study (MTA; 1999) comparison of Ritalin with an operant intervention indicated better outcomes with the drug alone than with the behaviour therapy program alone. Although a treatment combining the two was not superior to the drug alone, it did show an advantage of not requiring as high a dosage of Ritalin to reduce ADHD symptoms. Further, the combined treatment improved positive functioning, such as social skills, more than the drug alone. This study deserves additional discussion because it is the first of its kind in treatment research on children. MTA refers to the Multimodal Treatment Study of Children with ADHD. It involved six collaborating academic sites, including one site in Canada. Multi-site studies have seldom been conducted on childhood disorders. More importantly, this study is state of the art in that it was the largest and most methodologically rigorous study conducted thus far (Schachar, 1999). This lends credence to its main finding that a carefully managed medication approach is superior to behavioural treatment and routine community care in treating ADHD symptoms, but that more general areas of functioning (i.e., social skills and academic performance) were enhanced by a combined form of medication and behavioural treatment (see Jensen, 1999). Secondary analyses confirmed the benefits of the combined treatment, which have come to be referred to as "the multimodality superiority effect" (Swanson et al., 2001). The multimodality superiority effect is reduced among families who have a child with extreme ADHD symptoms and at least one depressed parent (Owens et al., 2003).

A more recent analysis of the MTA data set has implications for the definition and measurement of clinically significant change in child treatment-outcome studies. Karpenko et al. (2009) reported that children with clinically significant changes in ADHD (and ODD) symptoms, relative to children without clinically significant changes, were significantly more likely to have reliable change across five domains of functioning. Nonetheless, depending on the domain of functioning, between 14 and 52% of the children who did not achieve clinically significant symptom change demonstrated reliable improvement in functioning.

Recently, van der Oord, Prins, Oosterlaan, and Emmelkamp (2008) conducted a meta-analysis that compared effect-sizes of methylphenidate, psychosocial treatments, and their combination on ADHD, concurrent oppositional or conduct symptoms, social behaviours, and academic functioning. Stringent inclusion criteria were used, including a formal diagnosis of ADHD, aged 6 to 12 years, an RCT design, efficacy established with parent and teacher rating scales, behavioural or cognitive-behavioural psychosocial treatment, short-acting methylphenidate treatment, and treatment

Point systems and star charts, which are common in classrooms, are particularly useful in the treatment of ADHD. © Laura Dwight/CORBIS.

conducted in a clinical setting. The reviewers concluded that both methylphenidate and psychosocial treatments are effective; however, psychosocial treatments were less effective than both other treatment conditions. It was concluded that psychosocial treatment had no additional value to methylphenidate, at least for the reduction of ADHD and teacher-rated oppositional and conduct symptoms. Note, however, that for social behaviour and parent-rated ODD, all three treatment strategies were equally effective. Unfortunately, for improvement of academic functioning, van der Oord et al. (2008) concluded that none of the treatments was effective.

CONDUCT DISORDER

The term **conduct disorder** encompasses a wide variety of undercontrolled behaviour. *DSM-IV-TR* focuses on behaviours that violate the basic rights of others and major societal norms. Nearly all such behaviour is illegal. The types of behaviour considered symptomatic of conduct disorder include being aggressive and cruel toward people or animals, damaging property, lying, and stealing. Conduct disorder denotes a frequency and severity of acts that go beyond the mischief and pranks common among children and adolescents. Often the behaviour is marked by callousness, viciousness, and lack of remorse, making conduct disorder one of the criteria for anti-social personality disorder.

A related but lesser-known category in the *DSM* is **oppositional defiant disorder** (ODD). There is a debate as to whether ODD is distinct from conduct disorder, a precursor to it, or merely an earlier manifestation of it (Loeber et al., 1993). ODD is diagnosed if a child does not meet the criteria for conduct disorder—most especially, extreme physical aggressiveness—but exhibits such behaviours as losing his or her temper; arguing with adults; repeatedly refusing to comply with requests from adults; deliberately doing things to annoy others; and being angry, spiteful, touchy, or vindictive. The *DSM* also mentions that such children, most of them boys, seldom see their conflicts with others as their fault; they justify their oppositional behaviour by claiming that unreasonable demands are being placed on them.

According to the international consensus statement, comorbidity is the norm rather than the exception for children with ODD, conduct disorder, and ADHD (Kutcher et al., 2004). Problems commonly comorbid with ODD are ADHD, learning disorders, and communication disorders, but ODD differs from ADHD in that the defiant behaviour is not thought to arise from attentional deficits or sheer impulsiveness. This difference is evident in the tendency of children with ODD to be more deliberate in their obstreperousness than ADHD children. Interestingly, the *DSM-IV-TR* observes that mothers with a depressive disorder are more likely to have children with ODD; less clear is whether the depression contributes to or is caused by the child's behaviour. In a prospective population-based study, Copeland et al. (2009) concluded that adolescent ODD "was singular in being part of the developmental history of a wide range of young adult disorders" (p. 764). For

example, ODD (but not conduct disorder) was predictive of later depressive and anxiety disorders. The authors further suggested that ODD "may be in a class by itself" (Copeland et al., 2009, p. 771).

It is possible that there will be changes in this area with the arrival of *DSM-5*. For example, Drabick (2009) gave examples of dimensions that could be useful for conceptualizing ODD and conduct disorder within a mixed categorical-dimensional system.

However, because of ODD's questionable status (Moffitt et al., 2008), we focus here on the more serious diagnosis of conduct disorder. Perhaps more than any other childhood disorder, conduct disorder is defined by the impact of the child's behaviour on people and surroundings. Schools, parents, peers, and the criminal justice system usually determine which undercontrolled behaviour constitutes unacceptable conduct. Preadolescents and adolescents are often identified as conduct problems by legal authorities, in which case they might be considered juvenile delinquents—a legal, not a psychological, term.

Many children with conduct disorder display other problems, as well. We have noted the high degree of comorbidity between conduct disorder and ADHD. However, a Quebec study (Toupin et al., 2000) showed that even after controlling for ADHD symptoms, children with conduct disorder revealed significant cognitive deficits on attentional tests of executive functioning. Investigators from the Pittsburgh Youth Study, a longitudinal study of conduct problems in boys, found a strong association between substance use and delinquent acts (van Kammen, Loeber, & Stouthamer-Loeber, 1991). For example, among Grade 7 students who reported having tried marijuana, more than 30% had attacked someone with a weapon and 43% admitted breaking and entering; fewer than 5% of children who reported no substance use had committed these acts. Anxiety and depression are also common among children with conduct disorder, with comorbidity estimates varying from 15 to 45% (Loeber & Keenan, 1994). However, there is some evidence that conduct-disordered boys with a comorbid anxiety disorder are less anti-social than those with conduct disorder alone (Walker et al., 1991).

Population-based studies indicate that conduct disorder is fairly common. The Ontario Child Health Study found that 8% of boys and about 3% of girls aged 4 to 16 met the *DSM* criteria for conduct disorder (Offord et al., 1987). Rates may climb as high as 16% in boys when surveyed during adolescence (Cohen et al., 1993). Burglary and violent crimes such as forcible rape and aggravated assault are largely crimes of male adolescents.

The prognosis for children diagnosed as having conduct disorder is mixed. Robins (1978) summarized longitudinal studies that examined anti-social behaviour in cohorts from the 1920s to the 1970s, with follow-ups over as long as 30 years. She concluded that the vast majority of highly anti-social adults were highly anti-social as children, but noted that more than half the children with conduct disorder did not become anti-social adults. These findings have been replicated in other studies (e.g., Zoccolillo et al., 1992). Thus, conduct problems in childhood do not inevitably lead to anti-social behaviour in adulthood, but they certainly are a predisposing factor. Furthermore, a longitudinal study indicated that while about half of the boys with conduct disorder did not meet full criteria for the diagnosis at a later assessment (one to four years later), almost all of them still had some conduct problems (Lahey et al., 1995).

Moffitt (1993) theorized that two different courses of conduct problems should be distinguished. Some individuals show a "life-course-persistent" pattern of anti-social behaviour, beginning their conduct problems by age 3 and continuing with serious transgressions into adulthood. Others are "adolescence-limited." These people had normal childhoods, engaged in high levels of anti-social behaviour during adolescence, and returned to non-problematic lifestyles in adulthood. *DSM-IV* currently recognizes two subtypes of conduct disorder: childhood-onset type (defined by the onset of at least one criterion characteristic prior to age 10), and adolescent-onset type (defined by the absence of any criteria prior to age 10). The childhood-onset type is presumed to be more persistent and more likely to develop into adult anti-social personality disorder. The diagnostic criteria also currently include three levels of severity (mild, moderate, severe) based primarily on the number of conduct problems present. There is a large male preponderance in conduct disorder that begins in childhood and is life-course-persistent and the consensus is that biological factors are major influences on the difference (see Eme, 2007, for review).

Canadian research by Tremblay and his colleagues (see Canadian Contributions 15.1) found that there is much more heterogeneity than previously believed in the developmental trajectories associated with conduct disorder and violent behaviour. The term "developmental trajectory" refers to changing or stable behavioural patterns and characteristics that emerge when individuals are studied in longitudinal research designs. Research conducted in Montreal, studying boys from kindergarten through to the age of 17 years, identified as many as six different developmental trajectories in anti-social behaviour (see LaCourse et al., 2002). Only 11.4% of participants were on a rising trajectory of physical aggression. This finding is inconsistent with the "age crime curve hypothesis," which maintains that there is a substantial increase in physical violence during adolescence. In fact, most boys were either on a low-level anti-social behaviour trajectory or a declining trajectory that was especially apparent when they were between the ages of 11 and 17.

CANADIAN CONTRIBUTIONS 15.1
RICHARD TREMBLAY AND THE GRIP RESEARCH UNIT

"Aggression does not suddenly erupt in our teens or when conflicts arise in a couple. All humans make spontaneous use of physical aggression very early in life—and it is then that we learn to control our violent reactions. Unfortunately, those who don't learn alternatives to physical aggression tend to use it later against their parents and partners."

–*Richard Tremblay*

Richard Tremblay was identified by *Time* magazine (Blumstein, 2003) as one of the most innovative researchers in Canada. A professor of pediatrics, psychiatry, and psychology at the Université de Montréal, he holds a Canada Research Chair in child development. Tremblay is also the director of the Group de recherche sur l'inadaptation psychosocial chez l'enfant (GRIP; Research Unit on Children's Psychosocial Maladjustment) and is affiliated with University College, Dublin, Ireland, and the International Laboratory for Child and Adolescent Mental Health Development, Paris, France. A fellow of the Royal Society of Canada, he was honoured in 2003 with the Innis-Gerin Medal for distinguished and sustained contribution to the literature of the social sciences. In 2002, Tremblay won the Jacques-Rousseau Interdisciplinary Research Award.

Tremblay is known for his involvement in the Montreal Longitudinal-Experimental Study designed to help prevent

Richard E. Tremblay, director of the Group de recherche sur l'inadaptation psychosocial chez l'enfant (GRIP; Research Unit on Children's Psychosocial Maladjustment). Courtesy of R. Tremblay.

anti-social behaviour in boys who were disruptive in kindergarten (see Tremblay et al., 1992). The study tested the hypothesis that poor parental management and deficits in social skills contribute to the development of anti-social behaviour. The results after two years of treatment (when the children were 7 and 8) and after three years of follow-up were encouraging: disruptive boys were less physically aggressive, more often in an age-appropriate regular classroom, had less serious school-adjustment problems, and engaged in fewer delinquent behaviours.

The LaCourse et al. (2002) longitudinal study of developmental trajectories, described on the previous page, also included a preventative component. Recall that this study tracked boys from kindergarten until they were 17 years old. A subset of participants received an intervention that consisted of social skills training for the at-risk boys, as well as parent training. Boys who received the intervention were more likely to follow the lowest level trajectory and were less likely to follow the high level trajectory of aggressive and violent behaviour. This is the first intervention program with a long-term follow-up component to demonstrate a significant impact on the developmental course of physical aggression. It represents solid evidence that well-designed and well-timed interventions can make a difference!

The longitudinal study also focused on the causes and correlates of developmental trajectories of aggression. Tremblay and Vitaro were part of an international multi-site team that examined the developmental course of physical aggression in childhood (see Broidy et al., 2003). This study found that a small but identifiable number of boys and girls chronically exhibit aggression throughout childhood and that, for boys (but not girls), this chronic physical aggression predicted later violent delinquency as well as non-violent offending.

Additional research themes address the biological and physical correlates and predictors of physical aggression. Examples include the following:

- Obstetrical complications predict the risk of violence at 6 and 17 years of age in boys (Arseneault, Tremblay, Boulerice, & Saucier, 2002).
- There are substantial gender differences in the profiles that confer risk for conduct disorders (Côté, Tremblay, Nagin, Zoccolillo, & Vitaro, 2002).
- High levels of harsh, reactive parenting predict a preschool trajectory of high/chronic peer victimization. Insufficient parent income and child physical aggression also predicted this trajectory (Barker et al., 2008).

- A longitudinal study (5 to 74 months), examined prenatal and postnatal risk factors for a chronic (4.3% of children) trajectory of "disregard for rules" (an important dimension of conduct disorder). In addition to male sex, the strongest predictors were a mother's history of anti-social behaviour and depressive symptoms manifested by the mother and the father. Children's difficult temperament and parenting at 5 months did not predict chronic disregard for rules (Petitclerc et al., 2009).

Tremblay and his associates have also conducted analyses of the NLSCY data set and found:

- The prevalence of physical aggression in 5- to 11-year-olds was estimated at 3.7% in 5- to 11-year-old boys and ranged from .5% to 2.3% in 11- and 5-year-old girls, respectively. Thus, there is a decreasing trend in the prevalence of physical aggression with age for girls, but not for boys (Lee, Baillargeon, Vermunt, Wu, & Tremblay, 2007).
- The developmental trajectories of physical aggression from toddlerhood to pre-adolescence were modelled in more than 10,000 children followed for over 6 years. Three groups with distinct developmental trajectories between 2 and 11 years of age were identified. A high stable trajectory of physical aggression was found in 16.6% of the children. What risk factors distinguished the different developmental patterns? Children in the high physical aggression trajectory group were more likely to be boys, from low-income families, from families where the mother had not completed high school, and who reported using hostile/ineffective parenting strategies (Côté, Vaillancourt, LeBlanc, Nagin, & Tremblay, 2006).

The research findings identified by Tremblay and his colleagues have important societal implications, and certain findings have already led to positive changes in "the real world." After showing empirically that aggressive boys who become violent teenagers tend to have poor, uneducated mothers who gave birth as teenagers (Nagin & Tremblay, 2001), Tremblay convinced the provincial government to develop a prenatal care and parenting-skills program for at-risk mothers.

Lahey et al. (1995) found that boys with conduct disorder were much more likely to persist in their anti-social behaviour if they had a parent with anti-social personality disorder or if they had low verbal intelligence. Boys with higher verbal IQs and no anti-social parent apparently had a more transient form of the disorder.

Recall our discussion about the childhood roots of psychopathy (see Chapter 13). As noted by Frick and Moffitt (2010), in a proposal to the *DSM-5* childhood disorders and the ADHD and disruptive behaviour disorders work groups, a significant body of recent research refined how key features of psychopathy can be expressed in children and demonstrated

the importance of using these features to designate a subgroup of anti-social youths. This research led to the February 2010 proposal (see American Psychiatric Association, 2010) of a specifier/subtype to the diagnosis of conduct disorder based on the presence of "callous-unemotional" traits. If this is adopted, children would receive the diagnosis if they met the full criteria for conduct disorder and showed two or more of the following characteristics over at least 12 months: lack of remorse or guilt, callous lack of empathy, no concern for performance, and shallow or deficient affect. There is a strong evidence base supporting this specifier. For example, numerous studies showed a predictive relationship (as long as 10 years) between callous-unemotional traits and more severe, stable, and pervasive aggressive, anti-social, or delinquent behaviour, including premeditated and instrumental (i.e., for gain) aggression. This resulted in more police contacts, and poorer treatment outcome to currently available modes of treatment, including in children aged 4 to 9 (see Frick et al., 2005; Frick, 2009; and Frick & Moffitt, 2010 for reviews). Children in the current childhood-onset group show higher rates of callous-unemotional traits than those in the adolescent-onset group. Further, it is impulsive and anti-social youth who also show callous-unemotional traits who are most likely to show emotional (e.g., less recognition of signs of fear in others), cognitive (e.g., less sensitive to punishment cues), and personality (e.g., more fearless or thrill-seeking behaviour) characteristics similar to those seen in psychopathic adults (see Frick & Moffitt, 2010). The association between callous-unemotional traits and the more severe pattern of aggressive/anti-social behaviour cannot be accounted for by higher levels of impulsivity or diagnoses of ADHD (see Frick, 2009 for review).

ETIOLOGY OF CONDUCT DISORDER Numerous proposals have been put forward for the causes of conduct disorder, including biological, psychological, and sociological factors.

Biological Factors Evidence from twin studies indicates that aggressive behaviour (e.g., cruelty to animals, fighting) is clearly heritable, whereas other delinquent behaviour (e.g., stealing, running away, truancy) may not be (Edelbrock et al., 1995). In a large sample of 7-year-old twins, Viding and colleagues (Viding, Blair, Moffitt, & Plomin, 2005) found that conduct problems in children with callous and unemotional traits were under strong genetic influence (heritability of .81) with little influence of shared environment. The findings were replicated when the children were 9 years old (Viding et al., 2008). The genetic contribution remained when controlling for ADHD symptoms. In another study of twin pairs in Sweden, Forsman, Lichtenstein, Andershed, and Larrson (2008) assessed psychopathic personality when the participants were 16 and 19 years old. They found that genetic factors made a substantial contribution to the stability of a general higher order psychopathic personality factor, whereas environmental factors were insignificant. Further, they found specific genetic stability in callous/unemotional and impulsive/irresponsible dimensions. These findings imply evidence for both etiologic generality and specificity for the stability of psychopathic personality between mid- and late adolescence.

Neuropsychological deficits have been implicated in the childhood profiles of children with conduct disorder (e.g., Moffitt, Lynam, & Sylva, 1994), including poor verbal skills, difficulty with executive functioning (the ability to anticipate, plan, use self-control, and solve problems), and problems with memory. Catherine Cappadocia and her colleagues at York University in Toronto (Cappadocia, Desrocher, Pepler, & Schroeder, 2009) recently reviewed the neurological and neurochemical correlates

Conduct disorder is diagnosed among those who act aggressively, steal, lie, and vandalize property. The Canadian Press/Ryan Remiorz.

of conduct disorder. The evidence suggests that neurological profiles of children with conduct disorder are characterized by (1) reduced p300 brain wave amplitude, (2) deactivation of the anterior cingulated cortex and reduced activation in the left amygdala in response to negative stimuli, and (3) reduced right temporal lobe volume. Neurochemical correlates included reduced serotonin and cortisol levels (i.e., decreased hypothalamic-pituitary-adrenal axis function) and attenuated autonomic nervous system functioning. The authors suggested that emotion dysregulation theory provides a framework for understanding the neurobiological aspects of conduct disorder.

Recent findings from brain imaging studies show promise in uncovering the neurological bases to the cognitive and affective deficits found in anti-social youths with callous and unemotional traits. Thus, Jones et al. (2009) and Marsh et al. (2008) found support for the hypothesis that children with these traits and conduct problems show amygdala hyperactivity to other peoples' distress. Marsh et al. (2008) also reported that a reduction in amygdala-ventromedial prefrontal cortex connectivity, which plays a role in fear affect processing, was associated with callous-unemotional symptom severity. Gao and colleagues (2010) used poor fear conditioning as a proxy for amygdala dysfunction. They measured classically emotional responses at age 3 in a large birth cohort, followed up after 20 years, and concluded that poor fear conditioning predisposes to crime at age 23. Unfortunately, callous-unemotional traits were not assessed. Much more research on the neurological correlates of callous-unemotional traits is needed.

Psychological Factors Lax, inadequate, inconsistent, harsh, coercive, and hostile parental discipline coupled with parental adjustment difficulties appear to contribute to conduct-disordered behaviour (e.g., Moffitt, 2003, Patterson, 1982; Snyder, Reid, & Patterson, 2003; Verlaan & Schwartzman, 2002). Indeed, recent analyses of the NLSCY (Benzies, Keown, & Magill-Evans, 2009) determined that hostile/ineffective parenting had a sustained effect on physical aggression that carried forward across time from birth up to 6 years of age, suggesting that hostile/ineffective parenting has an effect prior to any evidence of aggressive behaviour in the child. The study also found that being a boy, having a mother with less education, and living in a lone-parent family with siblings also contributed to aggression.

Bandura and Walters (1963) were among the first researchers to appreciate the significance of the fact that children can learn aggressiveness from parents who behave aggressively. Children may also imitate aggressive acts they see elsewhere, such as on television. Since aggression is an effective, albeit unpleasant, means of achieving a goal, it is likely to be reinforced. Thus, once imitated, aggressive acts will probably be maintained. This social mimicry may at least partially explain the dramatic surge in delinquent behaviour in adolescents who had not previously shown conduct problems. Moffitt (1993) proposed that these adolescents imitate the behaviour of persistently anti-social peers because they see them as enjoying high-status possessions and sexual opportunities. Recently, Ferguson, San Miguel, and Hartley (2009) concluded that exposure to violent television or video games were not predictive of youth (ages 10–14 years) violence and aggression.

Childhood maltreatment can contribute to externalizing difficulties, especially children's aggression toward peers (see Cullerton-Sen et al., 2008 for review). Cullerton-Sen et al. (2008) examined patterns of association between maltreatment and aggression using a gender-informed developmental approach. They reported that maltreatment is associated with physical aggression for boys and relational aggression in girls. Consistent with Bandura and Walters (1963), physical abuse was associated with physically aggressive behaviours. However, sexual abuse predicted relational aggression for girls only. The combination of child abuse and genetic risk appears to put children at higher risk for the development of conduct-disordered and aggressive behaviour than either risk factor alone (e.g., Jaffet al., 2005).

A recent study (Deater-Deckard et al., 2009) examined the role of "chaos" in the family environment—noise levels, crowding and traffic (i.e., people coming and going all the time), lack of predictability in family routines—and its longitudinal effect on IQ and conduct problems in families with same-sex twins who were initially assessed in kindergarten/Grade 1. Chaos correlated with poorer housing conditions, lower parental education and IQ, poorer home literacy environment, higher stress, higher negativity, and lower warmth. However, even after controlling for these home environment factors, higher levels of chaos were linked concurrently and longitudinally with more child conduct problems.

A cognitive perspective on aggressive behaviour comes from the work of Kenneth Dodge and his associates. Dodge and Frame (1982) found that the cognitive processes of aggressive children had a particular bias; these youngsters

interpreted ambiguous acts, such as being bumped in line, as evidence of hostile intent. Perceptions like this may lead such children to retaliate aggressively for actions that may not have been intended to be provocative. Subsequently, their peers, remembering these aggressive behaviours, may tend to treat them more aggressively, further angering the already aggressive children and continuing a cycle of rejection and aggression.

Dodge's cognitive theory is now incorporated into a comprehensive biopsychosocial model of the development of conduct disorder (Dodge & Pettit, 2003). According to this model, biological predisposition and socio-cultural context operate both as distal factors (i.e., more remote influences) and as proximal factors (see Figure 15.1). Socio-cultural context factors include the influence of neighbourhood and classroom environments. In addition to the acknowledged roles played by life experiences that the child has with parents and peers, the child's mental processes (i.e., cognitive factors) play a central role in this model because it is the cognitive and emotional mental factors that are the final determinants of how distal factors eventually get translated into anti-social behaviour. Thus, malevolent cognitions still play an important role, but biological and socio-cultural factors are also recognized.

The research on children with early-onset conduct disorder who have callous-unemotional traits is consistent with the notion that there are several distinct developmental pathways to severe anti-social and aggressive behaviour (see Frick, 2009). The child with callous-unemotional traits has a temperamental style characterized by a lack of responsivity to distress in others, abnormalities in responsivity to rewards and punishment, and a preference for novel and dangerous activities that could influence the development of appropriate levels of guilt and empathy. This child could be less sensitive to typical parental socialization practices (see Frick, 2009). However, it is important to note that, "such a trajectory is not immutable, and some children with this temperamental style may develop appropriate levels of guilt and empathy, if they experience certain corrective environments" (Frick, 2009, p. 809).

FIGURE 15.1 A biopsychosocial model of the development of conduct disorder

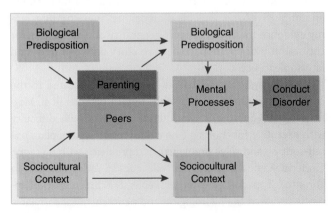

TREATMENT OF CONDUCT DISORDER The management of conduct disorder poses a formidable challenge, and working to influence the multiple systems involved in the life of a youngster (family, peers, school, neighbourhood) may be critical to the success of treatment efforts.

Some young people with conduct disorder, particularly those who have a childhood onset that is characterized by callous-unemotional traits, are probably the psychopaths of tomorrow. And like psychopaths, young people who commit violent and anti-social acts with little remorse or emotional involvement are extraordinarily difficult to reach. Incarceration, release, and recidivism are typically the rule. An enduring societal problem is how to deal with people whose social consciences appear grossly underdeveloped. According to a review by Canadian researchers, interventions for younger children are generally more effective than interventions for adolescents (Moretti et al., 1997).

Harsh discipline, whether imposed by government or by parents, appears to contribute in a major way to further delinquency and criminal activity in adulthood (e.g., Laub & Sampson, 1995; Steinberg, 2009). Nonetheless, the current *Zeitgeist* in Canada is to consider dealing with children who engage in criminal activity in a more stringent manner. The federal government originally enacted the *Youth Criminal Justice Act*, described in Canadian Perspectives 15.3, to provide a better balance between punishment and rehabilitation.

CANADIAN PERSPECTIVES 15.3
THE *YOUTH CRIMINAL JUSTICE ACT*

The Government of Canada tried for many years to pass legislation designed to overhaul the old *Young Offenders Act*. The new *Youth Criminal Justice Act* (YCJA; Bill C-7) finally came into effect on April 1, 2003, after delays caused by disputes with the provinces over significant details (Bailey, 2002; MacCharles, 2001). As noted by MacCharles (2001), "The bill provides tougher sentences for violent youth crime, but more community based alternatives and diversion programs for non-violent offenders" (p. A6). The preamble emphasizes both "meaningful consequences" for and rehabilitation of young offenders. The act introduced by then-Justice Minister Anne McLellan:

- lowered the age from 16 to 14 for possible adult sentences for serious crimes;
- allows publication of names when a youth receives an adult sentence, or in certain other serious cases;
- created the new category of "repeat offender" for more than two convictions of a violent crime;
- requires a kind of mandatory probation after all custodial sentences;
- gives victims a greater role in the court process: judges can allow publication of the names of young victims and witnesses with their consent and the consent of their parents;
- promotes alternatives to court for non-violent crimes (e.g., police warnings and community service): judges are directed to refer offenders to the child welfare system when appropriate;
- created a special sentence for mentally or emotionally disturbed violent offenders that requires that they receive treatment while in custody; and
- leaves children under the age of 12 outside the criminal justice system, to be handled under child welfare laws.

The former Canadian Alliance and Progressive Conservative parties viewed the legislation as unwieldy, expensive, and

As justice minister in the former Liberal government, then-Deputy Prime Minister Anne McLellan was instrumental in shepherding the *Youth Criminal Justice Act* through Parliament. CP Image Archive/Tom Hanson.

too lenient on the worst delinquents. On the other hand, the Bloc Québécois perceived it to be excessively harsh. Unfortunately, the provinces, too, could not agree to the new bill initially.

In February 2004, a court in Brampton, Ontario, heard the case of the first Canadian teen charged with murder under the YCJA. He killed a 14-year-old boy by strangling him with a belt. The youth charged had an unhappy home life, had been thinking about suicide, and felt that being in jail was better than living at home (Canadian Press, 2004). Coincidentally, the murder took place the first day that the YCJA came into effect, April 1, 2003. The 15-year-old teen pleaded guilty to first-degree murder. The judge had to decide whether the youth would be sentenced as a youth or as an adult. Apparently, before being sentenced the youth informed a psychiatrist that he (the youth) was capable of committing mass murder. Sentencing as a youth carries a maximum 10-year term with no parole for six years; however, an adult conviction carries a life sentence with no parole for at least seven years. On April 22, 2004, Justin Morton was sentenced as an adult (Mitchell, 2004). In January 2009, Morton, then 20, was transferred to the maximum-security range of a federal prison near Kingston, Ontario (Mitchell, 2009).

In August 2006, then Conservative government Justice Minister Vic Toews indicated that he was considering amending the legislation so that children as young as 10 who have fallen "under the influence of criminal elements" can be brought to youth court for positive intervention (Tyler, 2006). In 2008, Catherine Lee, president of the Canadian Psychological Association, responded to the government's subsequent proposed review and revisions to the YCJA (see http://canada.justice.gc.ca). She noted that, "An effective youth justice strategy that will both protect the public and help the offender must build on our understanding of the risk factors that make a young person vulnerable to offending." Further, Lee stated that the association recognizes the importance of a strategy and law that considers (1) Canada's obligations under the UN Convention on the Rights of the Child, and (2) research evidence that predicts youth offending and indicates optimal ways to prevent offending. On March 16, 2010, Justice Minister Rob Nicholson introduced amendments to the YCJA to strengthen its handling of violent and repeat offenders to "help ensure that the protection of society is given due consideration in sentencing these offenders" (Office of the Minister of Justice, 2010). The proposed amendments would include: simplifying the rules to keep violent and repeat offenders off the streets while awaiting trial, requiring the Crown to consider seeking adult sentences for youth convicted of the most serious crimes (e.g., murder, aggravated assault), enabling the courts to impose more appropriate sentences as necessary in individual cases, and requiring the

courts to consider publishing the name of a violent young offender when necessary for the protection of society. An on-line version of the amendments is available at www.parl.gc.ca.

In a scathing editorial, the *Toronto Star* (2010, March 20) argued that the new law would "change the tone of our youth criminal justice system from rehabilitation and reintegration to punishment and public shaming" and "turn more juvenile offenders into hardened criminals" (p. IN6). Gatti, Tremblay, and Vitaro (2009) sought to determine if there is an "iatrogenic effect" of juvenile crime using data from a community sample of low socioeconomic status boys in Quebec. They found that boys who are poor, impulsive, poorly supervised by their parents, and exposed to deviant friends are more likely to undergo intervention by the Juvenile Court—for the same degree of anti-social behaviour! Further, the Court's intervention increases the probability of involvement with the penal system in adulthood.

Thinking Critically

1. Does the *Youth Criminal Justice Act* solve problems in Canada's youth justice system, or does it create further problems? Should the act have been tougher (Ontario's initial position) or more lenient (Quebec's position)?

2. Will the new, tough amendments proposed by the federal government in 2010, designed to make protection of society a primary goal, have any positive effects on violent, repeat offenders?

3. Laurence Steinberg (2009) reviewed the research on the impact of punitive sanctions on youth development and behaviour and concluded that they do not deter youth from breaking the law and might increase recidivism. Should Canadian society adopt a punishment philosophy with youth who repeat serious, violent offences or should these adolescents receive even more intensive rehabilitation and treatment efforts?

Family Interventions Many approaches to treating conduct disorder involve intervening with the parents or families of the anti-social child. Gerald Patterson and his colleagues have worked for over three decades on a behavioural program of parental management training in which parents are taught to modify their responses to their children so that prosocial rather than anti-social behaviour is consistently rewarded. Parents are taught to use techniques such as positive reinforcement when the child exhibits positive behaviours and time-out and loss of privileges for aggressive or anti-social behaviours. Parents' and teachers' reports of children's behaviour and direct observation of behaviour at home and at school both supported the program's effectiveness (Patterson, 1982). Parental management training has also been shown to improve the behaviour of siblings and reduce depression in mothers involved in the program (Kazdin, 1985). A study of chronic adolescent offenders by Patterson's group (Bank et al., 1991) found that both parent training and court-provided family treatment reduced rates of criminal offence;

however, the parent-training approach led to more rapid improvement. More recent evaluations have concluded that behavioural parent training can be effective in reducing maladaptive behaviour in conduct-disordered children (e.g., Kazdin, 2005).

What about parent training for callous-unemotional trait children? Given that these children manifest conduct problems early in their development, it is important to intervene early in the parent-child relationship if at all possible. Such interventions could include teaching parents to attempt to foster empathic concern in their young child (see Frick, 2009). Although most past research has focused on showing that children with callous-unemotional traits generally do poorly in treatment programs relative to other anti-social children (e.g., Waschbusch et al., 2007), Frick (2009) noted that a recent study provided information about parenting strategies that might be effective with these children. Hawes and Dadds (2005) reported that boys aged 4 to 9 years with conduct problems and callous-unemotional traits were less responsive to a parenting intervention than boys low on these traits. However, Frick (2009) noted that all boys appeared to respond equally well to the initial phase that focused on teaching parents how to use positive reinforcement to increase prosocial behaviour; however, consistent with the reduced sensitivity to punishment characteristic of most children with callous-unemotional traits, these children did not show improvement during a second phase that focused on teaching parents effective discipline strategies. Frick (2009) noted that with older children it will be necessary to develop comprehensive interventions that are tailored to the unique needs of each child. Multisystemic Treatment is a widely used comprehensive strategy.

Multisystemic Treatment Henggeler's multisystemic treatment (MST; Henggeler, Schoenwaldd, Borduin, Rowland, & Cunningham, 1998) involves delivering intensive and comprehensive therapy services in the community, targeting the adolescent, the family, the school, and in some cases, the peer group. MST interventions reflect the view that conduct problems are influenced by multiple contexts within the family and between the family and other social systems. The strategies used by MST therapists incorporate behavioural, cognitive, family-systems, and case-management techniques. A major implication of MST is that youths receive treatment in their homes and stay in their communities rather than be incarcerated. This approach may result in reduced financial costs to society, and it recognizes that real changes must also occur in the troubled youth's environment. The therapy's uniqueness and perhaps its effectiveness (see Henggeler et al., 1998) lie in its emphasizing individual and family strengths, identifying the context for the conduct problems, using present-focused and action-oriented interventions, and using interventions that require daily or weekly efforts by family members. Treatment is provided in "ecologically valid" settings, such as the home, school, or local recreational centre, to maximize generalization of therapeutic changes.

Henggeler et al. (1998) compared the results for an MST group with those for a control group that received an equivalent number of sessions (about 25) of traditional individual therapy in an office setting. Adolescents in the MST group showed reduced behaviour problems and far fewer arrests over the following four years; 70% of adolescents receiving traditional therapy were arrested in the four years following treatment, while only 22% of those completing MST were arrested. Parents who were involved in MSTs showed reductions in psychiatric symptoms, and MST families showed improved supportiveness and decreased conflict and hostility. In contrast, the quality of interactions in the families of the adolescents receiving traditional individual therapy deteriorated following treatment. In an RCT with long-term follow-up, Huey, Henggeler, Brondino, and Pickrel (2000) examined the specific MST mechanisms of change that led to the improvements: the therapist's adherence to the MST protocol facilitated a sequence in which improved family functioning decreased the adolescents' affiliation with delinquent peers, which in turn decreased their delinquent behaviour.

Controlling for the effects of treatment condition (MST versus usual community services), Clingempeel, Britt, and Henggeler (2008) conducted secondary analyses of the Huey et al. (2000) RCT to examine the impact of comorbid psychopathologies on the mental health, physical health, and criminal behaviour of substance-abusing delinquents about five years after they were treated at age 15. Participants with both internalizing disorders (e.g., anxiety and mood disorders) and externalizing disorders (e.g., ADHD, ODD) showed more negative outcomes than those with a comorbid externalizing disorder. More internalizing and/or externalizing disorders predicted higher internalizing and aggression scores, criminality, and poorer physical health. Further, more internalizing diagnoses for females predicted more aggressive crimes in emerging adulthood. What are the implications for clinical interventions? Since comorbid disorders had long-term negative effects over and above the effects of MST, Climgempeel et al. (2008) suggested that "refinements in MST may involve giving greater attention to interventions addressing specific comorbid internalizing and externalizing disorders over and above the emphasis on substance abuse and delinquency" (p. 35). It was also suggested that treatments for females should incorporate specific strategies for treating anxiety and mood disorders. It will be a task of future research to determine if such refinements can improve the efficacy and effectiveness of MST. See Canadian Perspectives 15.4 for a recent application of MST in Ontario, and examples of other approaches in several provinces.

CANADIAN PERSPECTIVES 15.4
MULTISYSTEMIC TREATMENT IN ONTARIO AND ALTERNATIVE CANADIAN APPROACHES TO THE REHABILITATION OF YOUNG OFFENDERS

Multisystemic Therapy in Ontario

A team of researchers led by Allan Leschied and Alison Cunningham implemented MST in Ontario in a project started in 1997 (see Cunningham, 2002; Leschied & Cunningham, 2000; Leschied, Cunningham, & Hawkins, 2000). This project, known as The Clinical Trials of Multisystemic Therapy in Ontario, involved coordination with agencies located in London, Mississauga, Ottawa, and Simcoe County. MST was seen as a cost-efficient community alternative to custodial residential placement for high-risk Ontario youth. Participants were eligible for the study if they had a history of criminal offences and a high level of risk for reoffending. The study has high ecological validity because the 409 youths in the study were identified as providing the greatest challenge for local agencies.

Half the participants received MST and half continued with the usual services in the local system. The key research question asked whether the group that received MST would receive lower levels of criminal conviction relative to a group that was randomly assigned to existing services in Ontario. The sample was 73.6% males, 13.2% self-identified as Aboriginal, and 6.6% under 12 years of age at referral. Two thirds of the youth had a history of at least one prior conviction at referral. Unfortunately, although some early findings appeared to favour the MST participants, the interim results (Cunningham, 2002) and final results reported in 2006 based on a follow-up that ended in 2004 (see www.lfcc.on.ca/mst_final_results.html) indicate that the MST group and the treatment-as-usual group did not differ significantly on any outcome measure. These measures include rate of conviction throughout the three-year follow-up, days to reconviction, sentenced to custody during follow-up, days to first custody admission, average days in sentenced custody, number of convictions, and number of offences. For example, 68.2% of the MST group had at least one conviction after three years, in contrast to 66.5% for the control group. The final results corroborate Cunningham's (2002) preliminary conclusion that "it is not possible to recommend the adoption of MST in Canada" (p. 27). It would have been easy to reach the wrong conclusion if a less rigorous methodology had been used.

Closed Custody Alternatives in Canada

What are the alternatives when closed custody is ordered in Canadian youth courts? The irony in research on MST in Ontario should be noted, given the more general response to conduct disorder adopted by that province. A review paper by Moretti et al. (1997) provided a description of the various approaches adopted in four provinces (British Columbia, Ontario, Quebec, and New Brunswick). Ontario was identified as being the least progressive because of its unique decision to rely on so-called "boot camps" (strict discipline facilities) as a form of incarceration for young offenders.

Moretti et al. maintain that boot camps in the United States have been largely ineffective and involve considerable financial cost. In fact, in fairness to the Ontario government, the province's secure-custody, strict-discipline program, implemented in July 1997 amid controversy and media focus (and since terminated), was quite different from the American boot camp model, though still considered a strict discipline facility (Wormith, Wright, Sauve, & Fleury, 1999). "Project Turnaround," run by the private sector in a jail converted for the purpose, accepted as many as 50 repeat young male offenders, between 16 and 19 years of age, for a period of up to six months. Children serving time

for murder, arson, or sexual assault were not eligible for the program. A philosophy of the program was that troubled youth need more order in their lives. The military milieu provided a structure where attention was focused on positive activities and progress was rewarded by "promotion." The busy 16-hour days involved the young people in high school classes, anger-management courses, substance abuse counselling, sexual assault and abuse counselling, problem-solving and life skills activities, a values and moral reasoning program, a behaviour-management program, a positive peer culture program, and physical fitness. Each youth (cadet) was assigned a case manager (counsellor) and a primary worker (sergeant) who monitored progress and provided individualized services. A second phase of the program (aftercare) attempted to ease the youth back into the community.

The subsequent provincial government closed the boot camp in 2004 (Canadian Press, 2003a) allegedly for practical reasons (because of toxic mould in the camp itself and the associated financial cost) rather than on ideological grounds. In 2009, Ontario opened a new "superjail" for youth (The Roy McMurtry Youth Centre), a 192-bed secure custody facility that promised to provide programs to turn troubled youths into "future taxpayers." A March 31, 2010, report by the children and youth advocate declared that the jail "isn't safe" following allegations of brutality against youth by guards, neglect of youth and medication denial by nurses, use of excessive force, escalating violence, and lack of programming (see Zlomislic, 2010, pp. A1, A19). The advocate stated that the root of the crisis is fundamental disagreement between staff and managers about how to run the facility—an "inmates behind bars approach" (staff) or a more "progressive model" (managers and the Ministry of Child and Youth Services).

It is difficult to determine the impact of different programs on recidivism and other desired outcomes (e.g., increased family cohesion, reduced aggression with peers). Only systematic research can determine which of the various alternative models for the rehabilitation of young offenders, if any, is effective over the longer term.

Thinking Critically

1. Would a program such as MST be most effective with children identified as "at risk" at a very young age? Will it work with childhood-onset conduct-disordered children who also manifest callous-unemotional traits, or are these youth untreatable?
2. Does the best hope for the future lie in the development of early intervention and prevention programs? Why do relatively few government prevention programs exist for conduct-disordered children, even though such programs could probably play a critical role in reducing dysfunction and distress?

Cognitive Approaches Although research by Patterson's and Henggeler's groups suggests that intervention with parents and families is a critical component of success, such treatment is expensive and time-consuming (though clearly less so than incarceration). Indeed, some families may not be able or willing to become involved in it. Moretti et al.

(1997) observed that the parents of youths with conduct disorder have often disengaged by the time their children come into contact with the mental health system, and thus, if parental involvement is not forthcoming, these youths will be excluded from treatment research that has a parental component.

However, individual cognitive therapy with some conduct-disordered children can improve their behaviour even without family involvement. For example, in anger-control training, aggressive children are taught self-control in anger-provoking situations. To withstand verbal attacks without responding aggressively, they learn to use distracting techniques such as humming a tune, saying calming things to themselves, or turning away. The children then apply these self-control methods while a peer provokes and insults them (e.g., Lochman & Wells, 1996).

Another strategy involves focusing on the deficient moral development of conduct-disordered children. The teaching of moral-reasoning skills to groups of behaviour-disordered adolescents in school has achieved success (Arbuthnot & Gordon, 1986). Adolescents who were identified by their teachers as having behaviour problems (e.g., stealing and vandalism) participated in groups at school that encouraged higher levels of moral reasoning. Compared with a control group, adolescents participating in the groups showed improvement in moral-reasoning skills and school grades, as well as reductions in tardiness, referrals to the principal for behaviour problems, and contacts with police or juvenile courts.

Unfortunately, behavioural changes produced by altering cognitive patterns may yield only short-term gains—improvements that may be lost when the youngsters return to their familiar, "bad" neighbourhoods. Environmental contingencies—the communities in which people live—need to be considered when dealing with the complexities of aggression (Guerra & Slaby, 1990).

PREVENTION OF CONDUCT AND RELATED DISORDERS

"Psychiatry needs to place much more attention on the origin, early development, and prevention of DBDs [disruptive behaviour disorders] if it seriously intends to prevent at-risk children from living a life of misery."
—*Petitclerc and Tremblay, 2009, p. 229*

Few prevention programs for anti-social behaviour and conduct disorder have proven to be effective. Perhaps interventions would be more effective if initiated at a young age (toddler and early preschool periods) with "early starter" children who go on to manifest the most chronic and severe forms of anti-social behaviour (e.g., Moffitt et al., 2002). Consistent with this idea, Barker and Maughan (2009) used data from a large longitudinal population-based cohort of children from the prenatal period to age 13 in order to differentiate early-onset persistent versus childhood-limited conduct problem youth. They identified robust predictors of the early-onset persistent trajectory: maternal anxiety during pregnancy, partner cruelty to the mother, harsh parenting, and higher levels of child undercontrolled temperament. Barker and Maughan (2009) concluded that there is a need for interventions that focus on prenatal risks in mothers and early postnatal risks in mothers and their young children.

Recently, Petitclerc and Tremblay (2009) from the Université de Montréal reviewed preventive studies of disruptive behaviour disorders (DBDs): conduct disorder, ODD, and ADHD. Consistent with an "early starter" hypothesis, they argued that prevention needs to begin before children are aged 3 years. They first drew on the results of longitudinal studies of children beginning in infancy to determine the onset, development, and risk factors for DBD symptoms. They then reviewed RCTs of preventive interventions provided to families before the child is 3 years old that included outcome measures of DBD symptoms at follow-up.

Petitclerc and Tremblay (2009) reported that children who manifest high levels of DBD symptoms begin to do so in the first two years of life. Further, they have risk factors that can be identified in the mother during pregnancy or earlier, and soon after the child's birth. These factors, primarily based on multivariate analyses of the Canadian NLSCY, included maternal anti-social behaviour, young age of the mother when she had her first child, smoking during pregnancy, and maternal depression soon after the child's birth. Other factors were hostile parenting practices, and, as would be expected, being male. A high physical aggression trajectory was further predicted by low income, low maternal education, family dysfunction, and the presence of other young siblings. Petitclerc and Tremblay (2009) noted the need for additional studies to document genetic and epigenetic mechanisms. As noted in Chapter 13, a genetically influenced psychopathic personality is a strong predictor of adult anti-social behaviour. Petitclerc and Tremblay (2009) also examined three longitudinal studies of twins starting soon after the children's birth and concluded that there is a significant role for genetic factors in early manifestations of physical aggression, hyperactivity, disregard for rules, and combined ODD and conduct disorder symptoms. They noted that additional research is needed to determine the interplay between genes and the environment.

Several of the identified early risk factors are plausible causal factors (e.g., smoking during pregnancy) that might be prevented or alterable (see Petitclerc & Tremblay, 2009 for examples). Unfortunately, most extant preventive intervention studies have started relatively late following birth and have targeted parenting. These studies have had weak effects. For example, Shaw et al. (2006) tested the effectiveness of a family-based preventive intervention—the Family Check-up—in sustaining maternal involvement and preventing the exacerbation of child conduct problems. The intervention with at-risk toddler-age boys (aged 17 to 29 months) was associated with reductions in disruptive behaviour and greater maternal involvement. It was most effective at follow-up, when the children were aged 3 and 4 years, with children at greater risk for a persistent trajectory of conduct problems (see Canadian Contributions 15.1). However, no effects were observed on a measure of aggression. These results are disconcerting given the fact that conduct problems of children with callous-unemotional traits are less strongly related to dysfunctional parenting practices than the conduct problems of children who don't have these traits (see Frick & White, 2008, for review).

On the other hand, preventive experiments that provided intensive intervention to at-risk mothers beginning during pregnancy have shown reductions in key risk factors and the severe consequences of DBDs. For example, the Nurse-Family Partnership (NFP) research program initiated by Olds and colleagues (e.g., Olds, Sadler, & Kitzman, 2007) targeted many risk factors in addition to parenting. It was implemented early and over a long time period (see Petitclerc & Tremblay, 2009, for review). The NFP targets disadvantaged women with a first pregnancy, starts nurse home visits during pregnancy, and continues visits until the children are two years old. The NFP has several goals: improve maternal health during pregnancy, increase social support and use of community resources, develop sensitive parenting, and support critical decision-making. It has been evaluated in three RCTs in the United States. The intervention reduced some risk factors (e.g., maternal smoking and child maltreatment). Significant short-term effects were observed on child language, intellectual functioning, executive functioning, and behaviour regulation. At 15-year follow-up in one RCT, children of visited mothers had fewer arrests and convictions. However, Petitclerc and Tremblay (2009) concluded that even these studies did not succeed in preventing childhood DBDs in the home and school environments and suggested that "it may be necessary to start intervening even earlier in the family life course, and to add other preventive approaches such as early high-quality preschool education as early as possible after birth" (p. 228). They noted too that an important risk factor—maternal history of anti-social behaviour—has been omitted in past studies and that prevention studies need to target families selected for familial risk for these disorders. They concluded that it is "necessary for the field to adopt a more sequential, multitarget, and intergenerational approach to increase our effectiveness in curbing these early mental health problems that have extremely serious lifelong consequences" (Petitclerc & Tremblay, 2009, p. 229).

LEARNING DISABILITIES

"These are people who suffer in silence because there's such a stigma–…children who feel they are dumb, adults who've always been told they should shake their heads and get over it."

Judy Kerr, executive director of the Learning Disabilities Association of Canada and mother of twin 13-year-old sons with learning disabilities, quoted in Girard (2007, A6)

Several years ago, a young man in an undergraduate course showed an unusual pattern of strengths and difficulties. His oral comments in class were exemplary, but his handwriting and spelling were sometimes indecipherable. After the instructor had noted these problems on the student's mid-term examination, the undergraduate came to see him and explained that he was dyslexic and that it took him longer to complete the weekly reading assignments and to write papers and exams. The instructor decided to accord him additional time for preparing written work. The student was obviously of superior intelligence and highly motivated to excel. Excel he did, earning an A in the seminar and on graduation being admitted to a leading law school.

Unfortunately, the outcomes of a learning disability are not always, or even generally, so positive. On March 26, 2007, the Learning Disabilities Association of Canada released a groundbreaking, federally funded research study entitled Putting a Canadian Face on Learning Disabilities (PACFOLD), the first-ever "snapshot" of the impact of living with a learning disability in Canada. The study reported that learning problems early in childhood compound with age and affect school, work, and relationships and can lead to depression and chronic illness. The problems aren't typically detected until children are already in Grade 5. The study called for a broader societal approach to dealing with learning disabilities, including mandatory early screening for children aged 4 to 8, publicly funded support, awareness and training among professionals, and greater employer awareness to offer accommodations to workers. The study is available on-line at www.pacfold.ca. An earlier report for the association (Crawford, 2002), estimated the incremental direct (e.g., services of doctors) and indirect (e.g., reduced earnings) costs of learning disabilities to individuals, families, and society. The present value (i.e., incorporating future costs in terms of today's dollars) of the incremental cost from birth to retirement (age 65) in year 2000 dollars was conservatively estimated to be over $450,000 per person with a learning disability. Assuming a prevalence rate of 5%, the present value cost to all individuals with a learning disability, their families, and to public and private programs in Canada was estimated to be $707 billion in year 2000 dollars.

Learning disabilities signify inadequate development in a specific area of academic, language, speech, or motor skills that is not due to mental retardation, autism, a demonstrable physical disorder, or deficient educational opportunities. Children with these disorders are usually of average or above-average intelligence but have difficulty learning some specific skill (e.g., arithmetic or reading), and thus their progress in school is impeded.

The term *learning disabilities* is not used by *DSM-IV-TR* but is used by most health professionals to group together three disorders that do appear in the *DSM*: learning disorders, communication disorders, and motor skills disorder. Any of these disorders may apply to a child who fails to develop to

Canadian actor Keanu Reeves has found success in spite of a difficult childhood that included struggles with dyslexia and being abandoned by his father at the age of 15. Peter Brooker/Rex Features/CP Images.

the degree expected of his or her intellectual level in a specific academic, language, or motor skill area. In February 2010, the pertinent *DSM-5* work group proposed adopting the superordinate category and the term "learning disabilities."

Learning disabilities are usually identified and treated within the school system rather than through mental health clinics. According to *DSM-IV* (American Psychiatric Association, 2000), approximately 5% of school children meet criteria for a learning disorder; however, researchers typically report higher rates. Although they are widely believed to be far more common in males than in females, evidence from population-based studies (which avoid the problem of referral biases) indicates that the disorders are only slightly more common in males (e.g., American Psychiatric Association, 2000).

LEARNING DISORDERS

DSM-IV-TR divides **learning disorders** into three categories: reading disorder, disorder of written expression, and mathematics disorder. None of these diagnoses is appropriate if the disability can be accounted for by a sensory deficit, such as a visual or auditory problem.

- Children with **reading disorder**, better known as **dyslexia**, have significant difficulty with word recognition, reading comprehension, and typically written spelling as well. When reading out loud, they omit, add, or distort the pronunciation of words to an extent unusual for their age. In adulthood, problems with reading, comprehension, and written spelling persist. This disorder does not preclude great achievements. The *DSM-5* work group recommended a name change to dyslexia to be consistent with international use.
- Children with **mathematics disorder** may have difficulty rapidly and accurately recalling arithmetic facts, counting objects correctly and quickly, or aligning numbers in columns. The *DSM-V* work group recommended a name change to dyscalculia to be consistent with international use.
- **Disorder of written expression** describes an impairment in the ability to compose the written word (including spelling errors, errors in grammar, or very poor handwriting). The *DSM-V* work group recommended removing disorder of written expression due to lack of evidence that it occurs independently of dyslexia or communication disorders.

Numerous studies confirm that children with learning disabilities can experience considerable psychosocial dysfunction. For example, a recent Norwegian study (Undheim & Sund, 2008) examined a representative sample of adolescents aged 12–15 years and found that 7.8% reported reading difficulties. Relative to classmates without reading problems, the children with reading difficulties reported higher levels of depressive symptoms, more school stress and worry about attending school, lower school grades, and lower attachment to parents. They also scored lower on measures of self-worth and social acceptance, showed poorer psychological functioning during the previous year, and had received more help and had used more medication for mental health problems.

COMMUNICATION DISORDERS

Several categories of communication disorders have been distinguished:

- In **expressive language disorder**, the child has difficulty expressing himself or herself in speech. The youngster may seem eager to communicate but have inordinate difficulty finding the right words; for example, he or she may be unable to come up with the word "car" when pointing to a car passing by on the street. By age 4, this child speaks only in short phrases. Old words are forgotten when new ones are learned, and the use of grammatical structures is considerably below age level. In **mixed receptive-expressive language disorder,** the child has the symptoms of expressive language disorder but also has difficulty understanding words, sentences, or specific types of words, such as spatial terms.
- Unlike children who have trouble finding words, youngsters with **phonological disorder** comprehend and are able to use a substantial vocabulary, but their speech sounds like that of Elmer Fudd; "blue" comes out "bu", and "rabbit" sounds like "wabbit," for example. They have not learned articulation of the later-acquired speech sounds, such as r, sh, th, f, z, l, and ch. With speech therapy, complete recovery occurs in most cases and milder cases may recover spontaneously by age 8.
- A third communication disorder is **stuttering**, a disturbance in verbal fluency characterized by one or more of the following speech patterns: frequent repetitions or prolongations of sounds, long pauses between words, substituting easy words for those that are difficult to articulate (e.g., words beginning with certain consonants), and repeating whole words (e.g., saying "go-go-go-go" instead of just a single "go"). Sometimes bodily twitching and eye blinking accompany the verbal dysfluencies. Stuttering can interfere with academic, social, and occupational functioning and can prevent otherwise capable

A speech therapist works with a child with phonological disorder by having him practise the sounds he finds difficult. Hattie Young/Photo Researchers, Inc.

people from fulfilling their potential. About three times as many males as females have the problem, which usually shows up at around age 5. The *DSM* estimates that up to 80% of stutterers recover, most of them without professional intervention, before the age of 16.

A Canadian study highlights the serious dysfunction and impairment that tends to accompany language difficulties. Cohen et al. (2000) compared functioning in ADHD children with no language impairment with functioning in ADHD children with language impairment and in psychiatric control groups composed of children with or without impairment. Children with language impairment were the most disadvantaged, regardless of their diagnosis. In fact, in terms of predicting executive functioning, language impairment was a stronger predictor than having an ADHD diagnosis.

Beitchman et al. (2001) undertook a 14-year prospective study of the outcomes experienced by language-impaired children and found that there is a link between language problems in early childhood and psychiatric disorders years later. Thus, early remediation of language problems is an important goal. By age 19, the language-impaired boys had greater symptoms of delinquency based on parental reports and higher rates of arrests and convictions (Brownlie et al., 2004).

MOTOR SKILLS DISORDER

In **developmental coordination disorder**, also referred to as **motor skills disorder**, children show marked impairment in the development of motor coordination that is not explainable by mental retardation or a known physical disorder such as cerebral palsy. The young child may have difficulty tying shoelaces and buttoning shirts and, when older, building models, playing ball, and printing or handwriting. The diagnosis is made only if the impairment interferes significantly with academic achievement or with the activities of daily living.

ETIOLOGY OF LEARNING DISABILITIES AND COMMUNICATION DISORDERS

Most research on learning disabilities concerns dyslexia, perhaps because it is the most prevalent of this group of disorders. Although studies on other disorders (e.g., mathematics) have emerged, the literature has advanced more slowly in this area. The high comorbidity among learning disorders is the result of a complex interplay between both general and disorder-specific causal factors (Landerl & Moll, 2010).

Although no single causal factor has been identified in the development of learning disorders (e.g., Plomin & Kovaas, 2005), genetic and biological factors as well as ineffective learning strategies can lead to greater risk. There is frequently a family history of learning disorders in children identified as having a learning disorder (e.g., Plomin & Kovas, 2005), and there is a higher concordance rate for learning disorders in monozygotic twins, relative to dizygotic twins. A gene mutation and/or chromosomal abnormalities may also be involved

Former head coach of the Montreal Canadiens, Jacques Demers, who took the team to its last Stanley Cup victory in 1993, became an advocate for literacy. He revealed in 2005 that he has a learning disability and could sign his name but couldn't read most sentences. He was appointed to the Canadian Senate on August 27, 2009. CP Photo/Paul Chiasson.

(Galaburda, 2005). For example, chromosome 13 (13q21) appears to be directly implicated as a dyslexia phenotype (Bartlett et al., 2002). Other evidence continues to suggest that brain abnormalities, possibly heritable, may be responsible for dyslexia and other learning disorders (see Gilger & Kaplan, 2001, for review). As noted by Grigorenko (2009), the common forms of speech and language disorders are probably associated with variability in the function of multiple genes. Further, children with learning disabilities are more likely to have experienced prenatal and perinatal complications (e.g., Watson & Westby, 2003).

Multivariate genetic analyses have determined that there is substantial overlap between learning abilities, between cognitive abilities, and between learning and cognitive abilities (see Haworth et al., 2009). This finding has been referred to as the "generalist genes hypothesis": the genes that affect one ability are much the same genes that affect a different ability, even though there are also some genetic effects that are specific to each ability. Haworth et al. (2009) conducted a multivariate genetic analysis of low performance in reading, mathematics, language, and general cognitive ability in a sample of 8,000 12-year-old twins. The generalist genes hypothesis held for language and general cognitive disabilities, as well as reading and mathematics disabilities. There was a strong degree of overlap in genetic influences on these diverse traits; however, non-shared environmental influences were primarily specific to each trait, accounting for phenotypic differentiation of traits.

Biological factors may be related to the development of a learning disability. Possibilities include deficits in perceptual systems, perceptual-motor functioning, oculomotor functioning, and neurological organization that could lead to abnormal cognitive processing (see Kooistra et al., 2004). For example, past psychological theories focused on perceptual deficits as the basis for dyslexia; however, findings have not supported simple perceptual deficits as characterizing dyslexia (Wolff & Melngailis, 1996). Most children make letter reversals when first learning to read, but even dyslexic individuals very rarely make letter reversals after age 9 or 10.

Other research points to one or more problems in language processing that might arise from a deficit in the brain structures that are used to process stimuli rapidly (Eden & Zeffiro, 1996). PET scans made of dyslexic and normal children as they performed a variety of cognitive tasks revealed that the left temporoparietal cortex was activated in the normal children but not in the dyslexic children (Rumsey et al., 1994). The temporoparietal cortex is important in an aspect of language processing called *phonological awareness*, believed to be critical to the development of reading skills (Voeller, 2004). Children with phonological awareness deficits have diminished ability to "notice, think about, or manipulate sounds in words" (Lyon & Cutting, 1998, p. 481). When a task demands more phonological awareness, children with a learning disability show greater deficits (Voeller, 2004).

More recent neuroimaging studies have demonstrated structural anomalies and anomalous activation in critical language areas in the temporal and frontal lobes of people with dyslexia (see Shaywitz & Shaywitz for review). Recently, Specht et al. (2009) conducted an fMRI study of 6-year-old children considered at risk for dyslexia, compared with a matched control group, to examine differences in brain activation when the children were presented with visual stimuli that differed in demands for literacy processing. Brain responses distinguished between presentation conditions as a function of group within numerous cortical areas but particularly in the left angular gyrus and inferior occipitotemporal regions. The authors concluded that, "Since similar patterns are reported in adult dyslexics when processing written words, it appears that sensitivity to the cortical differentiation of reading networks is established prior to formal literacy training" (p. 79).

The family history of learning disorders might put a child at risk for developing a learning disability due to environmental factors (in addition to genetic factors). For example, the parent with a learning disorder might not be able to assist the child with school projects. Rashid, Morris, and Sevcik (2005) reported that children whose parents don't read to them regularly often have high rates of reading disorders.

Since there are no clear causal factors that lead consistently to the development of a learning disability, it is probable that these disorders develop from a complex interaction among variables.

TREATMENT OF LEARNING DISABILITIES

The anxiety of parents whose otherwise normal child lags behind in reading or cannot speak effectively and normally for his or her age cannot be underestimated. Professional attempts to remedy learning disabilities have been subject to somatic,

educational, and psychological fads—from using stimulants and tranquillizers to training the child in motor activities (such as crawling) believed to have been inadequately mastered at a younger age—in the hope of reorganizing neuronal connections in the brain. For example, although Ritalin can be effective in reducing some maladaptive behaviours in ADHD children, it has limited effectiveness in raising achievement scores in children diagnosed with both a learning disability and ADHD (Brown et al., 2005).

Most treatment for learning disabilities occurs within special-education programs in the public schools. An individualized program should be implemented for a child diagnosed with a learning disability (Siegel, 2005). That is, there should be a match between the needs of the child and the services provided to the child within the school system. Ideally, schools will employ evidence-based strategies. Because of mainstreaming, there is currently an emphasis on keeping children with special needs in regular classrooms as much as possible.

Although efficacy and effectiveness studies are limited, there is some evidence that special education services can facilitate overcoming learning disabilities in children and adolescents (e.g., Alexander & Slinger-Constant, 2004). Special education services typically incorporate some of the following interventions (adapted from Phares, 2008):

- Instructional interventions (e.g., using teaching methods that maximize ability to learn)
- School–home notes (e.g., sending notes home to communicate about what needs to be done)
- Performance feedback (e.g., providing direct feedback about performance)
- Self-management (e.g., helping children learn how to manage time)
- Contingency management interventions (e.g., providing reinforcement to increase on-task behaviour)
- Cognitive-based interventions (e.g., self-instructional training to increase self-control)
- Peer tutoring (e.g., peers helping peers on academic tasks)
- Group contingencies (e.g., rewarding the entire class for maximal efforts)
- Co-operative learning (e.g., working together in teams to maximize learning of group members)
- Phonological training (e.g., techniques such as word identification training to facilitate reading and writing development)

A meta-analysis of five types of special education strategies (Kavale & Forness, 1999) found that applied behaviour analysis was the only intervention to achieve a large mean effect size. Perceptual-motor training was apparently not effective despite the fact it had been evaluated in 180 studies. Phonological training programs are now widely used and are effective in helping children with reading disorders (Calhoon, 2005). Longer periods of training are especially helpful with children who have severe reading difficulties (Alexander & Slinger-Constant, 2004).

Most children with learning disabilities experience frustration and failure, which erodes their motivation and confidence. Whatever their design, education programs should provide opportunities for children to experience feelings of mastery and self-efficacy and include strategies to address the secondary social and emotional adjustment problems the children experience. A meta-analysis concluded that learning-disabled children with poor self-concepts can be helped at school by CBT interventions (Elbaum & Vaughn, 2003).

Parental involvement in the educational process has been linked to fewer learning disabilities for children and to better academic outcomes (e.g., Pantin, Coatsworth et al., 2003).

Individuals with dyslexia or other learning disabilities often can succeed in university or college with the aid of instructional supports, such as recorded lectures, tutors, editorial assistance, and untimed tests (e.g., Bruck, 1987). Most universities and colleges have special services to help such students.

MENTAL RETARDATION

Mental retardation, an Axis II disorder, is defined in *DSM-IV-TR* as (1) significantly subaverage intellectual functioning, along with (2) deficits in adaptive behaviour, and (3) occurring prior to age 18. We first examine traditional criteria and then discuss some newer perspectives from the American Association of Intellectual and Developmental Disabilities (AAIDD)—formerly the American Association of Mental Retardation (AAMR)—the principal interdisciplinary professional organization devoted to research, education, and application in the field of mental retardation. Mentally retarded children and adults are often referred to as "developmentally

When assessing normal adaptive behaviour, the environment must be considered. A person living in a rural community may not need the same skills that someone living in Vancouver or St. John's needs, and vice-versa.
© Gene Peach.

delayed" or "intellectually handicapped" by the public and the media in Canada. *DSM-V* work group members recommended in February 2010 (see www.dsm5.org) that the diagnostic term "mental retardation" be changed to "intellectual disability" in order to bring the *DSM* terminology and criteria into alignment with other disciplines, organizations (e.g., the AAIDD), and international opinion. Coding of severity would no longer be based on IQ level but rather focus on adaptive functioning.

In October 2004, Montreal hosted the Pan-American Health Organization and World Health Organization Conference on Intellectual Disability (Lecomte & Mercier, 2007). The Montreal Declaration on Intellectual Disabilities, a consensus result, emphasizes three fundamental rights of people with an intellectual disability—equality, non-discrimination, and self-determination—and is intended to guide international organizations and civil and public authorities in attempts "to ensure full and complete citizenship to persons with intellectual disabilities" (Lecomte & Mercier, 2007, p. 66).

TRADITIONAL CRITERIA FOR MENTAL RETARDATION

INTELLIGENCE-TEST SCORES The first component of the *DSM* definition requires a judgement of intelligence. As discussed in Chapter 4, approximately two thirds of the population achieve IQ test scores between 85 and 115. Those with a score below 70 to 75, two standard deviations below the mean of the population, meet the criterion of "significant subaverage general intellectual functioning." Approximately 3% of the population fall within this category.

The determination of IQ should be based on tests administered by a competent, well-trained professional. Interpretation of scores must take into account cultural, linguistic, and sensory or motor limitations that may affect performance. For example, a child who speaks Farsi at home and English at school cannot be tested in a valid way using only English-language measures.

ADAPTIVE FUNCTIONING Adaptive functioning refers to mastering childhood skills such as toileting and dressing; understanding the concepts of time and money; being able to use tools, to shop, and to travel by public transportation; and becoming socially responsive. An adolescent, for example, is expected to be able to apply academic skills, reasoning, and judgement to daily living and to participate in group activities. An adult is expected to be self-supporting and to assume social responsibilities. Thus, adaptive behaviour is the collection of skills that we all learn in order to function in our daily lives.

Various tests have been constructed to assess adaptive behaviour. However, a problem with many assessments is that they fail to consider the environment to which the person must adapt. An effective and valid assessment should therefore consider how well the child interacts with the surroundings in which he or she must function. The AAID's new Diagnostic Adaptive Behavior Scale (DABS), scheduled to be released in 2010, provides a comprehensive, standardized assessment of adaptive behaviour designed for use with people ages 4 to 21 years. The scale "provides precise diagnostic information around the cutoff point where an individual is deemed to have 'significant limitations' in adaptive behavior" (see www.aaidd.org). The DABS measures three domains of adaptive behaviour: conceptual skills (e.g., literacy, self-direction); social skills (e.g., social problem solving, following rules); and practical skills (e.g., activities of daily living , schedules, and routine).

AGE OF ONSET A final definitional criterion is that mental retardation be manifest before age 18, to rule out classifying as mental retardation any deficits in intelligence and adaptive behaviour from traumatic accidents or illnesses occurring later in life. Children with severe impairments are usually diagnosed during infancy. Most children considered mentally retarded, however, are not identified as such until they enter school, despite the fact that differences in children with more subtle forms of mental retardation can be perceived as early as one year of age (Osterling et al., 2002).

CLASSIFICATION OF MENTAL RETARDATION

Four levels of mental retardation are recognized by *DSM-IV-TR*, each corresponding to a specific subaverage range on the far left of the normal distribution curve of measured intelligence. Again, the IQ ranges are not the sole basis of diagnosis; deficiencies in adaptive behaviour are also a criterion. Some persons falling within the mildly retarded range based on IQ may have no deficits in adaptive behaviour and thus would not be considered mentally retarded. In fact, the IQ criterion is usually applied only after deficits in adaptive behaviour have been identified. The following is a brief summary of characteristics of people at each level of mental retardation (*DSM-IV-TR*):

- *Mild mental retardation* (50–55 to 70 IQ). About 85% of all those with IQs less than 70 are classified as having **mild mental retardation**. They are not always distinguishable from normal youngsters before they enter school. By their late teens, they can usually learn academic skills at about a Grade 6 level. As adults, they are likely to be able to maintain themselves in unskilled jobs or in sheltered workshops, although they may need help with social and financial problems. They may marry and have children.
- *Moderate mental retardation* (35–40 to 50–55 IQ). About 10% of those with IQs less than 70 are classified as having **moderate mental retardation**. Brain damage and other pathologies are frequent. People with moderate mental retardation may have physical defects and neurological dysfunctions that hinder fine motor skills, such as grasping and colouring within lines, and gross motor skills, such as running and climbing. They may learn to travel alone in a familiar locality. Most live dependently within the family or in supervised group homes.

- *Severe mental retardation* (20–25 to 35–40 IQ). Of those people with IQs less than 70, about 3 to 4% come under the category of **severe mental retardation**. These people often have congenital physical abnormalities and limited sensorimotor control. Most require constant supervision. Adults with severe retardation may be friendly but usually can communicate only briefly on a very concrete level. They engage in little independent activity and are often lethargic, for their severe brain damage leaves them relatively passive. They may be able to perform very simple work under close supervision.
- *Profound mental retardation* (below 20–25 IQ). One to 2% of people with mental retardation are classified as having **profound mental retardation**, requiring total supervision and often nursing care all their lives. Most have severe physical deformities, as well as neurological damage and cannot get around on their own.

A Canadian study of adolescents established that the overall prevalence of mental retardation is 7.2 per 1,000, with the prevalence of severe mental retardation being 3.6 per 1,000 (Bradley, Thompson, & Bryson, 2002). The prevalence estimate was similar to previous Canadian estimates and the estimated prevalence worldwide. Boys are considerably more likely to be diagnosed with mental retardation than girls. The ratio of boys to girls is about 1.6:1 (American Psychiatric Association, 2000). Numerous neurological disorders co-occur with mental retardation, including epilepsy, cerebral palsy, and motor, visual, and hearing impairments. There are also high rates of comorbidity with psychological disorders (e.g. autism). Indeed, a wide range of psychological, behavioural, and social problems are common in children and adolescents with mental retardation (see Phares, 2008, for review).

THE APPROACH OF THE AMERICAN ASSOCIATION OF INTELLECTUAL AND DEVELOPMENTAL DISABILITIES

"AAIDD is committed to setting aside labels and instead focus on creating and supporting the services people with intellectual disability need to function fully in our society. AAIDD is committed to including the people with intellectual disability within every aspect of our lives whether they ride the bus with us, work in the same offices or play with our children."
—AAIDD news release, September 14, 2009

We turn now to a very different approach to mental retardation. In the ninth edition of its classification system, the American Association of Mental Retardation (AAMR, 1992), now the AAIDD, shifted its focus from identifying severity of disability to determining what remedial supports are necessary to facilitate higher functioning. Professionals were now encouraged to identify an individual's strengths and weaknesses on psychological, physical, and environmental dimensions with a view toward determining the kinds and intensities of environmental supports needed to enhance a person's functioning in different domains. This approach encourages a more individualized assessment of a person's skills and needs and focuses more on what people can do than on what they cannot do, and directs professional attention to how best to make positive changes in the person's life.

As an example of the AAIDD approach to classification, consider Roger, a 24-year-old man with an IQ of 45 who has attended a special program for mentally retarded children since he was 6. According to the *DSM*, he would be considered moderately mentally retarded, and on that basis, he would not be expected to be able to live independently, get around on his own, or progress beyond Grade 2. The AAIDD classification system, however, would emphasize what is needed to maximize Roger's functioning. A clinician might discover that Roger can use the bus system if he takes a route familiar to him, and thus he might be able to go to a movie by himself from time to time. And although he cannot prepare complicated meals, he might be able to learn to prepare frozen entrées in a microwave oven. The assumption is that by concentrating and building on what he can do, Roger will make more progress.

In 2010, the AAIDD issued the 11th edition of its definitive manual (*Intellectual Disability: Classification, Definition, and Systems of Support*). The book (seven years in development and written by 18 experts) synthesizes current information and "best practices," including uniform criteria to be used to diagnose intellectual disability. Individualized supports remain the cornerstone of the system in order to reduce any mismatch between the capabilities and skills of a person with an intellectual disability and what is necessary to participate in all aspects of daily living in the community and workplace.

ETIOLOGY OF MENTAL RETARDATION

The causes of mental retardation may be primarily biological, psychosocial, or a combination of both. The major predisposing factors, as recognized by the American Psychiatric Association (2000), are summarized here.

NO CLEAR ETIOLOGY (APPROXIMATELY 30–40% OF CASES) Although many possible causes account for mental retardation, at this time between 30 and 40% of cases have no known risk factor or genetic marker that can explain its occurrence despite extensive evaluation (American Psychiatric Association, 2000). Probably some of the cases can be accounted for by variables listed below. However, it is clear that there is a need for more research into the causes and prevention of mental retardation.

HEREDITARY DISORDERS (5%) Hereditary disorders include inborn errors of metabolism inherited mostly through autosomal recessive mechanisms (e.g., phenylketonuria, Tay-Sachs disease), other single-gene abnormalities with variable expression (e.g., tuberous sclerosis), and chromosomal aberrations (e.g., fragile X syndrome).

Several hundred recessive-gene diseases have been identified, and many of them cause mental retardation. Here we discuss one recessive-gene disease, phenylketonuria. In **phenylketonuria** (PKU), the infant, born normal, soon suffers from a deficiency of a liver enzyme, phenylalanine hydroxylase. This enzyme is needed to convert phenylalanine, an amino acid found in protein, to tyrosine, an amino acid essential for the development of such hormones as epinephrine. Because of this enzyme deficiency, phenylalanine and its derivative phenylpyruvic acid are not broken down and instead build up in the body's fluids. This buildup eventually causes irreversible brain damage because the unmetabolized amino acid interferes with the process of myelination, the sheathing of neuron axons, which is essential for the rapid transmittal of impulses and thus of information. The neurons of the frontal lobes, the site of many important mental functions (e.g., rational decision-making), are particularly affected, and thus mental retardation is profound. Although PKU is rare, with an incidence of about 1 in 14,000 live births, it is estimated that 1 person in 70 is a carrier of the recessive gene. A blood test is available for prospective parents who have reason to suspect that they might be carriers. After the newborn with PKU has consumed milk for several days, an excess amount of unconverted phenylalanine can be detected in the blood. If the test is positive, parents should provide the infant with a diet low in phenylalanine as early as possible.

EARLY ALTERATIONS OF EMBRYONIC DEVELOPMENT (APPROXIMATELY 30%) About 30% of cases of mental retardation are caused by early alterations of embryonic development. These factors include chromosomal changes (e.g., Down syndrome due to trisomy 21) or prenatal damage due to toxins (e.g., maternal alcohol consumption, infections). Most of these cases can be prevented through prenatal genetic testing or prevention of substance abuse during pregnancy. Perhaps the best-known example is **Down syndrome**, or **trisomy 21**. People with Down syndrome have moderate to severe retardation, as well as several distinctive physical signs (e.g., short and stocky stature; oval, upward-slanting eyes). Although there is a shortened life expectancy for people with Down syndrome, it has increased steadily over the past century and they now live past 60 on average (Bittles & Glasson, 2004). Recently, Beacher et al. (2009) demonstrated that volume reductions of the hippocampus and caudate nucleus, as measured by volumetric MRI, are seen in Down syndrome individuals with Alzheimer's disease and suggested that these reductions might provide markers of Alzheimer's disease. Down syndrome is named after the British physician Langdon Down, who first described its clinical signs in 1866. In 1959, the French geneticist Jerome Lejeune and his colleagues identified its genetic basis. Human beings normally possess 46 chromosomes, inheriting 23 from each parent. Individuals with Down syndrome almost always have 47 chromosomes instead of 46. During maturation of the egg, the two chromosomes of pair 21, the

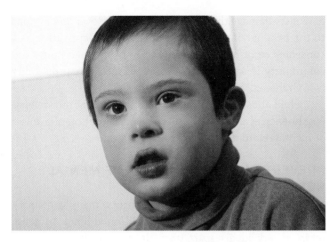

Child with **Down syndrome**. Design Pics/Con Tanasiuk/Getty Images.

smallest ones, fail to separate. If the egg unites with a sperm, there will be three of chromosome 21, thus the technical term trisomy 21. Down syndrome is found in about 1 in 800 to 1,200 live births.

While in utero, the fetus is at increased risk of mental retardation resulting from maternal infectious diseases such as rubella (German measles). The consequences of these diseases are most serious during the first trimester of pregnancy, when the fetus has no detectable immunological response. Cytomegalovirus, toxoplasmosis, rubella, herpes simplex, and syphilis are all maternal infections that may cause both physical deformities and mental retardation in the fetus. The mother may experience slight or no symptoms from the infection, but the effects on the developing fetus can be devastating. Pregnant women who go to prenatal clinics are given a blood test for syphilis. Women can also have their blood tested to determine whether they are immune to rubella; nearly 85% of North American women are. Women who are not immune should be vaccinated six months before becoming pregnant. If a fetus contracts rubella from the mother, the child is likely to be born with brain lesions that cause mental retardation.

Fetal alcohol syndrome is an example of the consequences of prenatal exposure to a toxin (see Chapter 12). About 15 to 20% of children with fetal alcohol syndrome meet criteria for mental retardation (Burd et al., 2003).

LATER PREGNANCY AND PERINATAL PROBLEMS (APPROXIMATELY 10%) Problems in later pregnancy and perinatal problems are thought to account for about 10% of mental retardation cases. Factors include fetal malnutrition, placental insufficiency, prematurity, hypoxia, low birth weight, intracranial hemorrhage, trauma, and viral and other infections. All of these can be responsible for diminished intellectual functioning (see Shenkin, Starr, & Deary, 2004) and some of them could be prevented by better prenatal care (Graham, 2005). For example, HIV infection has become a significant cause of mental retardation. When not treated for HIV infection during pregnancy and delivery, an HIV-positive

woman is more likely to pass on the virus to the developing fetus, and about half of these infected infants develop mental retardation.

MEDICAL CONDITIONS ACQUIRED DURING CHILDHOOD AND ACCIDENTS (APPROXIMATELY 5%) Factors such as infections, traumas, and poisoning account for about 5% of cases. For example, infectious diseases can also affect a child's developing brain after birth. Encephalitis and meningococcal meningitis may cause irreversible brain damage and even death if contracted in infancy or early childhood. There are several forms of childhood meningitis, a disease in which the protective membranes of the brain are acutely inflamed and fever is very high. Some children who survive without severe retardation may become mildly to moderately retarded. Other disabling after-effects are deafness, paralysis, and epilepsy.

Environmental toxins can cause intellectual, developmental, behavioural, and learning problems (Hodapp & Dykens, 2005). For example, lead poisoning can cause kidney and brain damage, as well as anemia, mental retardation, seizures, and death. On March 31, 2010, Health Canada ordered an investigation of the dust at 300 daycares in Ontario and Quebec to examine residues of toxins found in everyday products (e.g., toys, cleaning solutions). Chemicals such as bisphenol A are dangerous for children because they can damage their development. Babies and toddlers are at increased risk of toxins due to increased exposure (e.g., crawling, putting hands in mouth). The study will target toxins the government considers priorities for regulation because they are harmful. Although bisphenol A is banned in baby bottles, it is still found in hard plastics.

Falls, near drowning, and automobile accidents are among the most common mishaps in early childhood, causing varying degrees of head injuries and mental retardation. Laws mandating that children riding in automobiles wear seat belts and protective helmets when bicycling could play a major role in reducing the incidence of mental retardation in children.

ENVIRONMENTAL INFLUENCES AND OTHER MENTAL DISORDERS (APPROXIMATELY 15–20%) Factors that include deprivation of nurturance and of social, linguistic, and other stimulation, as well as severe mental disorders (e.g., autistic disorder), account for another 15 to 20% of cases of mental retardation.

People with mild or moderate mental retardation do not appear to have an identifiable brain defect. And while individuals whose mental retardation is associated with identifiable biological impairments are found in much the same percentages throughout all socio-economic, ethnic, and racial groups, those with mild or moderate mental retardation are overrepresented in the lower socio-economic classes, suggesting that certain social conditions of deprivation are major factors in retarding their intellectual and behavioural development. Several variables might act in concert to produce milder forms of mental retardation.

Although lead-based paint is now illegal, it can still be found in older homes. Eating these paint chips can cause lead poisoning and mental retardation. James Keyser/©Time Inc.

Consider two children with the same biological brain impairment, so subtle as to be undetectable. One youngster comes from a high socio-economic level, the other from a low level. The first child's slight deficit could be compensated for by the enriched social and educational environment made possible by the family's financial resources. In contrast, the second child's deficit might be exaggerated by impoverished circumstances. To show signs of retardation, a socially advantaged person would have to have more extensive

damage—damage that is less responsive or even impervious to the benefits of an enriched upbringing. Deprivation as a consequence of being raised in an impoverished home and community is a preventable cause of intellectual disability (see Graham, 2005).

Child abuse (see Cicchetti, 2004) and domestic violence (see Koenen et al., 2003) are also related to the potential onset of mental retardation.

PREVENTION AND TREATMENT OF MENTAL RETARDATION

In the early part of the twentieth century, many large institutions were built in Canada and the United States to house retarded individuals apart from the rest of the population. Many were no more than warehouses for anyone unfortunate enough to do poorly on newly constructed intelligence tests. The majority of residents were recently arrived immigrants, members of ethnic or racial minorities, children with physical disabilities, and indigents.

This forced segregation did not stop couples within institutions from bearing children. The first mandatory sterilization law for women with mental retardation in the United States was passed in Indiana in 1907. By 1930, 28 states had these laws. Although its constitutionality was questioned, forced sterilization—especially for undereducated minority and immigrant groups—continued to be practised in many institutions through the 1950s. In the 1960s, safeguards were passed to protect the rights of individuals with mental retardation to marry and bear children. Canada's track record in this area was equally deplorable. Canadian Perspectives 15.5 features the situation in Alberta and the tragic case of Leilani Muir.

CANADIAN PERSPECTIVES 15.5
EUGENICS AND THE SEXUAL STERILIZATION OF CANADIANS WITH MENTAL RETARDATION

"Nobody has the right to play God. Nobody."
—Leilani Muir (June 1, 1995), who was sexually sterilized as an adolescent without her knowledge or consent, under the Sexual Sterilization Act in Alberta

In Chapter 1, we referred to C.M. Hincks and his support of the sexual sterilization of mentally ill Canadians. Throughout the twentieth century, Canadians with mental retardation were often the targets of the eugenics movement. According to the proponents, elimination of the possibility that mentally retarded people would reproduce was one way of "perfecting" the gene pool.

Alberta and British Columbia were particularly active in the number of sexual sterilizations performed (Park & Radford, 1998; Woodill, 1992). The *Sexual Sterilization Act* was approved initially in Alberta in 1928 and modified in 1937 so that any form of consent was no longer required. Overall, 2,822 people were sexually sterilized in Alberta before the act was finally repealed in 1972 (Woodill, 1992); this included 2,102 people identified as "mental defectives" and 370 psychotics (Park & Radford, 1998). British

Columbia was the only other province that put a sterilization law into place, in 1933 (McLaren, 1986). Sterilizations were also performed in other parts of Canada, even without similar laws. For instance, there are reports of mentally retarded children being sterilized at the request of their parents, and one of the authors of this text received clinical training at a site where sterilizations took place in Ontario.

Dickin and Ryan (1983) provided a cogent summary of the arguments made both for and against the sexual sterilization of mentally retarded Canadians. They outlined the three main arguments put forth by those in favour of non-consensual sterilization (essentially that sterilization serves the well-being of the handicapped individual, the well-being of potential children, and the well-being of society). In response, four arguments have been raised by those vehemently opposed to sterilization:

1. Evidence for the genetic inheritance of mental retardation is not strong, and genetic theory and research does not support the unmitigated sterilization of mentally retarded people.

2. Serious human rights violations are involved, including the right to equal treatment under the law.

3. Negative psychological consequences involving the loss of self-esteem may ensue from being sterilized and being degraded and treated as less human than other people.

4. The practice of sterilization is open to bias and discrimination such that those people who are considered "unfit" actually are fit and may not receive fair and impartial treatment.

The fourth point applies to the case of Leilani Muir. Muir's story is depicted in the National Film Board of Canada documentary *The Sterilization of Leilani Muir* (National Film Board of Canada, 1996). Muir grew up on a farm in Alberta. She had an abusive mother who beat her, starved her, and locked her away. In 1955, at the age of 11, her mother left her at the Provincial Training School for Mental Defectives in Red Deer. Muir's mother lied about her daughter's true mental abilities and Muir was confined improperly for 10 years. The only IQ test she received while at the training school was administered in 1957, and she scored a 65, thereby obtaining the label "moron."

Muir was sterilized surgically in 1957 at the age of 14. She was told that she was going to have her appendix out. According to Wahlsten (1997), the order for Muir's sterilization was signed by John MacEachran, founder of the Department of Philosophy and Psychology at the University of Alberta and chair of the Eugenics Board from 1929 to 1965. The Board was a four-person committee that listened briefly to the youths deemed suitable for sexual sterilization and then made their decision.

Muir left the training school at the age of 21; however, having been institutionalized for so long, she had difficulty functioning in the outside world. Later, she dated and married the first man she met. When she was in her mid-twenties, a medical examination determined that she had been sterilized earlier and that her "insides looked like they had been through a slaughterhouse" (National Film Board of Canada, 1996).

Muir and her first husband eventually divorced. She remarried, and she and her second husband considered the possibility of adoption, but that fell through. He turned to alcohol and Muir experienced depression and considered suicide. Meanwhile, her IQ was retested several times and was always found to be in the normal range (i.e., it varied from 90 to 101).

Muir pursued legal action against the Alberta government and was awarded approximately $740,000 in 1996 and an additional $230,000 in legal costs. She became a symbol for all people who were affected by the *Sexual Sterilization Act*. In 1996 hundreds of other people began comparable legal action that would lead to settlements of over $140 million. The Leilani Muir Graduate Research Scholarship was established at the University of Alberta "in honour of the historical legal victory won by Leilani Muir and hundreds of victims of sterilization."

Thinking Critically

1. The rights of mentally retarded individuals are now protected under the *Charter of Rights and Freedoms*. Many people felt that Muir's family was to blame and that the government should not be held accountable. Were these settlements justified? Is the government responsible?

2. Why do you think that Muir's first IQ test showed that she had an IQ of 65 while at least one subsequent test showed that she had an IQ of 101? What factors could account for the discrepancy?

Current workers in the field promote the right of mentally retarded adults to freedom of sexual expression, as well as to marry and have children.

Children with mental retardation are still warehoused in many parts of the world. In Russia, for example, the old Soviet ideal of "perfect children" still encourages parents to give up their disabled children to the care—actually neglect—of state-run institutions (Bennett, 1997). The cruelty and neglect experienced by children in Russian orphanages was documented in a December 1998 report by the organization Human Rights Watch (see www.hrw.org).

Prevention of mental retardation depends on understanding its causes. The field of medical genetics is not yet equipped to prevent the more severe genetic causes of mental retardation, but startling advances in genetics may change this situation in the not-too-distant future. When the causes of mental retardation are unknown, prevention is not possible, but intervention to improve the person's ability to live on his or her own is an option. When an impoverished environment is the source of mild retardation, enrichment programs and supports can prevent further deficits and sometimes even overcome existing ones.

ENVIRONMENTAL INTERVENTIONS AND ENRICHMENT PROGRAMS There has been a concerted effort to bring people with mental retardation into the mainstream (Zucker, Perras, Gartin, & Fidler, 2005), including finding suitable treatment facilities, group homes, and community living arrangements (Breedlove et al., 2005). Further, the consensus today is that children with developmental disabilities should be included in public educational systems whenever possible. "Mainstreaming" is important because intellectually handicapped people, both children and adults, who live in the mainstream of society and receive services there show greater educational attainment and improvement in psychological functioning than those who are more confined (e.g., Kavale, 2002).

Children whose mild to moderate mental retardation is believed to have been caused by the lack of a stimulating environment can participate in such programs as Head Start. Head Start strives to prepare children, socially and culturally, to succeed in the regular school setting by giving them experiences that they may be missing at home. The core of the program is community-based preschool education that focuses on the early development of cognitive and social skills. Although

Eunice Kennedy Shriver (1921–2009), with the help of Canadian Frank Hayden, founded the Special Olympics. It was launched in 1968 with 1,000 competitors from Canada and the United States. Today, 3 million athletes from more than 180 countries vie to compete. Eunice Shriver was perhaps the 20th century's most notable advocate for the developmentally handicapped. UPI/Newscom.

the original Head Start program succeeded in enhancing the functioning of the neediest children, these children were still behind their peers in absolute cognitive levels after one year in the program (Lee, Brooks-Gunn, & Schnur, 1988). Other reports confirm the value of Head Start in helping poor youngsters improve their intellectual functioning (e.g., Hubbs-Tait et al., 2002). A similar Canadian federal government initiative (Aboriginal Head Start) was described in Chapter 1.

RESIDENTIAL TREATMENT Most people with mental retardation can acquire the competence needed to function effectively in the community. The trend has been to provide these individuals with educational and community services and supports rather than with largely custodial care in big mental hospitals. Individuals with mental retardation have a right to expect appropriate treatment in the least-restrictive setting. Ideally, adults with moderate retardation live in small homelike residences that are integrated into the community. Medical care is provided, and trained, live-in supervisors and aides attend to the residents' special needs. Residents participate in the household routines to the best of their abilities. Many adults with mild retardation have jobs and are able to live independently in their own apartments. Others live semi-independently in apartments housing three to four intellectually handicapped adults, with the aid of a counsellor generally provided in the evening. Severely retarded children may live at home or in foster-care homes provided with educational and psychological services. Only people with severe and profound retardation and with physical disabilities tend to remain in an institutional environment.

In Chapter 1, it was noted that Ontario officially closed its institutions for the mentally retarded on March 31, 2009. In a sad and tragic footnote to this positive event, it was reported on March 3, 2010, that ex-clients at Orillia's Huronia Centre, the last institution to close, were seeking $1 billion from the province in a class-action suit due to alleged physical, sexual, and emotional abuse and humiliation (see Tyler, 2010). The institution was home to more than 3,000 intellectually handicapped and autistic children and adults from 1876 until 2009. It was alleged that residents were required to work without pay, denied proper medical care, and punished if they came forward with allegations of abuse. At that time, none of the allegations had been proven in court.

BEHAVIOURAL INTERVENTIONS BASED ON OPERANT CONDITIONING Early-intervention programs have been developed to improve the level of functioning of individuals with more serious retardation. Projects have intervened with children during infancy and early childhood in an attempt to improve their functioning. These programs typically include systematic home- and treatment centre- or school-based instruction in language skills, fine and gross motor skills, self-care, and social development. Specific behavioural objectives are defined, and in an operant fashion, children are taught skills in small, sequential steps. Children with severe mental retardation usually need intensive instruction to be able to feed, toilet, and groom themselves. This **applied behaviour analysis**, or ABA, approach is also used to reduce inappropriate and self-injurious behaviour. Studies of these programs indicate consistent improvements in fine motor skills, acceptance by others, self-help skills, communication skills, social skills, and vocational techniques (e.g., Zucker et al., 2005). Being able to act more normally increases the chances of interacting meaningfully with others. Moreover, the self-esteem that comes from learning to take better care of oneself is extremely bolstering. Strategies are also available to assist families who are coping with the challenges of having a loved one with a developmental disability (Blacher et al., 2005).

COGNITIVE INTERVENTIONS Many children with mental retardation fail to use strategies in solving problems, and when they do have strategies, they often apply them ineffectively. **Self-instructional training**, first developed by Meichenbaum and Goodman in 1971, teaches these children to guide their problem-solving efforts through speech. Self-instructional training has been employed to teach retarded children self-control, as well as how to pay attention and how to master academic tasks, and then generalize the strategy to new tasks (Hughes & Agran, 1993). Children with severe retardation can effectively master self-help skills through this technique. Hughes, Hugo, and Blatt (1996), for example, taught high school students with IQs below 40 to make their own buttered toast and clean up after themselves. Further, researchers in Kingston, Ontario, demonstrated that self-instructional manuals are effective in teaching child care skills to mothers with mild mental retardation (Feldman, Ducharme, & Case, 1999).

AUTISTIC DISORDER

A psychology student walks into a special-education classroom. She is taking a course on child disabilities, and one requirement is to volunteer some time in this class. As several children rise to greet her, she becomes aware of their minor or major physical characteristics. One child has slanted eyes and a flat nose, typical of Down syndrome. Another makes spastic movements, a sign of cerebral palsy. A third child calls to her from a wheelchair with grunting noises and communicates with a combination of hand gestures and pictures. Then this psychology student notices a fourth child in the room, standing in front of the fish tank. She approaches him and notices his graceful, deft movements, the dreamy, remote look in his eyes. She wonders if he is a visitor to the class. She starts talking to him about the fish. Instead of acknowledging her comment or even her presence, he begins rocking back and forth while continuing to smile, as if enjoying a private joke. When the teacher enters the room, she tells the psychology student that he is autistic.

CHARACTERISTICS OF AUTISTIC DISORDER

From the time it was first distinguished, **autistic disorder** has had a somewhat mystical aura. The syndrome was identified in 1943 by a Harvard psychiatrist, Leo Kanner, who noticed in his clinical work that 11 disturbed children behaved in ways that were uncommon in children with mental retardation or schizophrenia. He named the syndrome early infantile autism because he noted that "there is from the start an extreme autistic aloneness that, whenever possible, disregards, ignores, shuts out anything that comes to the child from the outside" (Kanner, 1943). Kanner considered autistic aloneness the most fundamental symptom. He also found that these children had been unable from the beginning of life to relate to people in the ordinary way. They were severely limited in language and had a strong obsessive desire for everything about them to remain exactly the same. Despite its early description by Kanner and others, the disorder was not accepted into official diagnostic nomenclature until the publication of *DSM-III* in 1980.

The evidence seems to indicate that childhood-onset schizophrenia and autism are separate disorders. Nonetheless, contemporary research suggests that childhood-onset schizophrenia is preceded by and comorbid with autism in 30 to 50% of cases (Rapoport et al., 2009). Further, a growing number of risk genes and rare chromosomal variants appear to be shared by both disorders.

In part to clarify the differentiation of autism from schizophrenia, *DSM-III* introduced (and *DSM-III-R*, *DSM-IV*, and *DSM-IV-TR* have retained) the term **pervasive developmental disorders**. This term emphasized that autism involves a serious abnormality in the developmental process itself. In *DSM-IV-TR*, autistic disorder is but one of several pervasive developmental disorders:

- Rett's disorder is very rare and found only in girls. Development is entirely normal until the first or second year of life, when the child's head growth decelerates. She loses the ability to use her hands for purposeful movements, instead engaging in stereotyped movements such as hand-wringing or handwashing; walks in an uncoordinated manner; learns only poorly to speak and understand others; and is profoundly retarded. The child relates poorly to others, though this may improve later in life.
- Childhood disintegrative disorder occurs in children who have had normal development in the first two years of life but then suffer significant loss of social, play, language, and motor skills. Abnormalities in social interaction and communication and the presence of stereotyped behaviour are very similar to those in autism.
- Asperger's syndrome is often regarded as a mild form of autism. Social relationships are poor and stereotyped behaviour is intense and rigid, but language and intelligence are intact. Extensive research on Asperger's syndrome has been conducted by Peter Szatmari and his research team, who are part of the Offord Centre for Child Studies (see Canadian Perspectives 15.2).

In February 2010, the *DSM-V* work group proposed a new name for the category, autism spectrum disorder (ASD), which includes autistic disorder (autism), and subsumes Asperger's syndrome, childhood disintegrative disorder, and pervasive developmental disorder not otherwise specified. The work group provided a detailed rationale for representing autism as a single diagnostic category with clinical specifiers (e.g., severity, verbal abilities) and associated features (e.g., known genetic disorders, epilepsy, intellectual disability). It was noted that "distinctions among disorders have been found to be inconsistent over time, variable across sites and often associated with severity, language level or intelligence rather than features of the disorder. . . .previously, the criteria were equivalent to trying to 'cleave meatloaf at the joints'" (see American Psychiatric Association, 2010). The work group recommended that Rett's disorder not be included in *DSM-V* since these individuals often have autistic symptoms for only a brief period during childhood.

Autistic disorder begins in early childhood and can be evident in the first months of life. The popular press sometimes cites an "epidemic of autism." Thus, while the prevalence was held to be 4/10,000 in the 1970s and 1980s, current estimates indicate that, in the general population, autism occurs in 16 infants in 10,000, or 0.16% of births (Szatmari, 2003). To put this in perspective, recall that the prevalence of schizophrenia is estimated at a little less than 1%, so autism's prevalence is more than six times greater. However, the prevalence rises to 63 per 10,000 when all autistic spectrum disorders are included (Szatmari, 2003). Recently, Kogan et al. (2009) reported the current point-prevalence of parent-reported ASD was 110 per 10,000, based on the 2007 U.S. National Survey of Children's Health. The increase in the frequency of diagnoses may not reflect an increase in population prevalence but rather a broadening of inclusion criteria, increased awareness resulting in more case finding, and diagnostic-specific funding of families of ASD children (Marriage, Wolverton, & Marriage, 2009). About 4.3 times more boys than girls have autism

(Fombonne, 2003). Comorbidity is high, with depression, anxiety, and ADHD being common (Tidmarsh & Volkmar, 2003). Anxiety may worsen during adolescence in the face of a more complex social milieu and an awareness of being different and having interpersonal problems (White, Oswald, Ollendick, & Scahill, 2009). Autism is found in all socio-economic classes and in all ethnic and racial groups.

AUTISM AND MENTAL RETARDATION Historically, approximately 80% of autistic children scored below 70 on standardized IQ tests, and it is sometimes difficult to differentiate autism and mental retardation. However, although children with mental retardation usually score poorly on all parts of an intelligence test, generally, children with autism do worse on tasks requiring abstract thought, symbolism, or sequential logic, all of which may be associated with their language deficits (Carpentieri & Morgan, 1994). They usually obtain better scores on items requiring visual-spatial skills. In addition, a few may have isolated skills that reflect great talent and have exceptional long-term memory. Sensorimotor development is the area of greatest relative strength among children with autism. These children, who may show severe or profound deficits in cognitive abilities, can be quite graceful and adept at swinging, climbing, or balancing, whereas children with mental retardation are much more delayed in areas of gross-motor development (e.g., learning to walk).

EXTREME AUTISTIC ALONENESS In a sense, autistic children do not withdraw from society—they never joined it to begin with. Normally infants show signs of attachment as early as three months of age. In children with autism, this early attachment is less pronounced. Parents of autistic children must work harder to make contact and share affection with their babies. Autistic children rarely try to engage their parents in play, and they do not point to, show, or share objects of play with others. Children with autism rarely approach others and may look through or past people or turn their backs on them (e.g., Volkmar, Cohen, & Paul, 1986). Autistic children rarely offer a spontaneous greeting or farewell, either verbally or through smiling, making eye contact, or gesturing (Hobson & Lee, 1998). Physical play, such as tickling and wrestling, may be enjoyable. Observations of their spontaneous play reveal that they spend much less of their time engaged in symbolic play, such as pretending that a block is a car, than do either mentally retarded or normal children of comparable mental age (Sigman et al., 1987). Autistic children are more likely to twirl a favourite block continually for hours on end.

Few children with autism initiate play with other children, and they are usually unresponsive to any who may approach them. Children with autism do make eye contact, but their gaze has a different quality. Normal children gaze to gain someone's attention or to direct the other person's attention to an object; autistic children generally do not (Mirenda, Donnellan, & Yoder, 1983)—they just stare. Some autistic children appear not to recognize or distinguish one

person from another. They become preoccupied with and form strong attachments to inanimate objects (e.g., keys, rocks, light switches) and to mechanical objects (e.g., refrigerators, vacuum cleaners).

It may be that the autistic child's social isolation is the source of his or her retarded development in other areas, such as language (Kanner, 1943). On the other hand, the core deficit may be an inability to process certain kinds of sensory input, leaving the child incapable of understanding and responding to the world around him or her (Ornitz, 1989). Some researchers have proposed that a deficiency in the autistic child's **theory of mind** represents the core deficit and leads to the kinds of social dysfunctions we have described here (e.g., Sigman, 1994). Theory of mind refers to our understanding that other people have desires, beliefs, intentions, and emotions that may be different from our own. Children with autism seem unable to understand others' perspectives and emotional reactions; they lack empathy. Although high-functioning autistic children can learn to understand emotional experiences, they "answer questions about ... emotional experiences like normal children answer difficult arithmetic questions" (Sigman, 1994, p. 15), with concentrated cognitive effort. Although intriguing, there has been limited empirical support for the theory of mind hypothesis (e.g., Klinger et al., 2003).

COMMUNICATION DEFICITS Even before they acquire language, autistic children show deficits in communication. Babbling, a term describing the utterances of infants before they actually begin to use words, is less frequent in infants with autism and conveys less information than it does in other infants. By two years of age, most normally developing children use words to represent objects in their surroundings and construct one- and two-word sentences to express more complex thoughts, such as "Mommy go" or "Me juice." The speech of autistic children who learn to speak includes various peculiarities.

One such feature is **echolalia**, in which the child echoes, usually with remarkable fidelity, what he or she has heard another person say. The teacher may ask an autistic child, "Do you want a cookie?" The child's response may be "Do you want a cookie?" Mute autistic children who later acquire some functional speech through training usually first pass through a stage of echolalia.

Another abnormality common in the speech of autistic children is **pronoun reversal**. Children refer to themselves as "he," "she," or "you" or by their own proper names. Pronoun reversal is closely linked to echolalia. Since autistic children often use echolalic speech, they refer to themselves as they have heard others speak of them. For example:

Parent. What are you doing, Johnny?
Child. He's here.
Parent. Are you having a good time?
Child. He knows it.

If speech continues to develop more normally, this pronoun reversal might disappear. In most instances, however, it is highly resistant to change.

Neologisms, made-up words or words used in unusual ways, are another characteristic of the speech of autistic children. A two-year-old autistic child might refer to milk as "moyee" and continue to do so well beyond the time when a normal child has learned to say "milk."

Children with autism are very literal in their use of words. For example, a child may say, "Do not drop the cat" to mean "no," because his or her mother had used these emphatic words when the child was about to drop the family feline.

Even after they learn to speak, people with autism often lack verbal spontaneity, are sparse in their verbal expression, and do not always use language appropriately.

OBSESSIVE-COMPULSIVE AND RITUALISTIC ACTS

Children with autism become extremely upset over changes in their daily routines and surroundings. An offer of milk in a different drinking cup or a rearrangement of furniture may make them cry or precipitate a temper tantrum. One child had to be greeted with the set phrase "Good morning, Lily, I am very, very glad to see you." If any word, even one "very," was omitted, or another added, the child would begin to scream (Diamond, Baldwin, & Diamond, 1963). In their play, they may continually line up toys or construct intricate patterns with household objects. As they grow older, they may become preoccupied with train schedules and number sequences.

Children with autism are also given to stereotypical behaviour, peculiar ritualistic hand movements, and other rhythmic movements, such as endless body rocking, hand flapping, and walking on tiptoe. They spin and twirl string, crayons, sticks, and plates, twiddle their fingers in front of their eyes, and stare at fans and spinning things. These are often described as self-stimulatory activities. They may become preoccupied with manipulating a mechanical object and be very upset when interrupted.

PROGNOSIS FOR AUTISTIC DISORDER
What happens to such severely disturbed children when they reach adulthood? Early follow-up studies painted a generally gloomy picture of adults with autism. From his review of all published studies, Lotter (1978) concluded that only 5 to 17% of autistic children had made a relatively good adjustment in adulthood, leading independent lives but with some residual problems, such as social awkwardness. Most of the others led limited lives, and about half were institutionalized.

Similar outcomes were found in population-based, follow-up studies (e.g., von Knorring & Hagglof, 1993). Generally, children with higher IQs who learned to speak before age 6 had the best outcome, and a few of them functioned nearly normally in adulthood. Follow-up studies focusing on non-mentally retarded, high-functioning autistic individuals indicated that most did not require residential care and some even attended college and supported themselves through employment (Yirmiya & Sigman, 1991). Optimal outcome is extremely difficult to predict at a young age. Sutera et al. (2007) found that 13 of 73 two-year-old children diagnosed with ASD "lost the diagnosis" by age 4, at which time they scored within the normal range on

Autistic children frequently engage in stereotyped behaviour, such as ritualistic hand movements. Nancy Pierce/Photo Researchers, Inc.

standardized tests of cognitive and adaptive functioning. Surprisingly, symptom severity, socialization, and communication had little predictive power in determining outcome. However, children with pervasive developmental disorder not otherwise specified were more likely than those with full autistic disorder to lose the diagnosis.

Prior to the passage in the United States of the *Developmentally Disabled Assistance and Bill of Rights Act* in 1975 and similar laws in Canada at about the same time (see Bowlby & Regan, 1998, for a discussion of federal [e.g., the 1982 *Canadian Charter of Rights and Freedoms*] and provincial human rights legislation; and Bowlby, Peters, & Mackinnon, 2001, for a discussion of special-education laws for "exceptional" children), children with autism (and other children with special needs) were often excluded from educational programs in the public schools. Thus, most of the autistic children followed into adulthood had not had the benefit of intensive educational interventions or behavioural programs. In contrast, newer studies involving early, intensive interventions paint a considerably more promising picture.

After reviewing several new studies on early detection and early interventions, often in school settings, a group of Canadian authors (Bryson, Rogers, & Fombonne, 2003) indicated that they share the conclusion reached by several international groups:

> [It seems that] outcomes for children with autism can be significantly enhanced by offering many hours weekly of targeted and individualized teaching that is carefully planned, delivered, and monitored . . . . It seems clear that we must leave behind several truisms about autism, including the assumptions that 50% of affected children will not speak, and 75% will have mental retardation. These older findings need to be considered as reflecting untreated children with autism, rather than as the expected course and outcome for children with autism today. (p. 511)

Recent American Academy of Pediatrics recommendations advise that all 18- and 24-month-olds be screened for ASD (see Zwaigenbaum et al., 2009).

ETIOLOGY OF AUTISTIC DISORDER

The earliest theorizing about the etiology of autism was that psychological factors were responsible for its development. This narrow perspective has been replaced by evidence supporting the importance of biological factors, some of them genetic, in the etiology of this puzzling syndrome.

PSYCHOLOGICAL BASES Early theorists discounted the importance of biological factors. Both Bettelheim (1967) from a psychoanalytic perspective and Ferster (1961) from a behavioural perspective stated that parents play the crucial role in the etiology of autism. Kanner described the parents as cold, insensitive, meticulous, introverted, distant, and highly intellectual (Kanner & Eisenberg, 1955). Systematic investigations, however, failed to confirm these clinical impressions (e.g., Cantwell, Baker, & Rutter, 1978); moreover, such "refrigerator" parents raise other normal and healthy siblings. Further, any deviant parental behaviour could be a reaction to the child's abnormality rather than the other way around. Unfortunately, over the years, a tremendous emotional burden has been placed on parents who have been told that they are at fault.

BIOLOGICAL BASES The very early onset of autism, along with an accumulation of genetic and neurological evidence, strongly implicates a biological basis for this disorder.

Genetic Factors According to Nicholson and Szatmari (2003), autism is the most heritable psychiatric disorder, with heritability estimates that are even higher than those for schizophrenia and bipolar disorder. Studies following twins and families with an autistic member suggest that autism is linked genetically to a broader spectrum of deficits in communicative and social areas (e.g., Bailey et al., 1995). For example, the non-autistic identical twin of an autistic adult is almost always unable to live independently or maintain a confiding relationship. In addition, most of these non-autistic identical twins show (or have) communication deficits, as well as severe social deficits. In contrast, the non-identical twin of an autistic child is almost always normal in social and language develop-

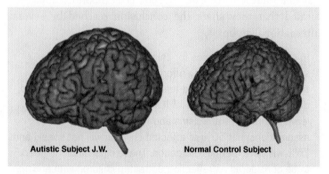

A case of extreme macroencephaly. The 3D MRI image of 3.4-year-old autistic subject J.W. (left) is compared with that of a normal male child whose brain volume was scaled to equal normal average size (right). J.W.'s brain volume (1816 ml) was much larger than the normal average (1162 ml) for his age. Courtesy of Eric Courchesne/Laboratory for Research on the Neuroscience of Autism, Children's Hospital Research Centre, San Diego, CA.

ment and marries and lives independently in adulthood (Le Couteur et al., 1996). The autism spectrum disorders probably have a variety of etiologies and the exact genetic background is still unclear. Zafeiriou, Ververi, and Vargiami (2007) reviewed all the genetic syndromes that have been implicated in ASD children (e.g., tuberous sclerosis, fragile X, Down syndrome, neurofibromatosis, and Prader-Willi). For example, the **fragile X syndrome** (a constriction or breaking off of the end portion of the long arm of the X sex chromosome) occurs in about 2% of autistic males; however, the link with autism remains controversial.

Genome-wide linkage scans for autism susceptibility loci have identified chromosomal regions 2q, 7q, and 17q, with 7q yielding the most consistently positive results, and substantial evidence suggests that chromosomal abnormalities contribute to autism risk, although the exact prevalence is unclear (see The Autism Genome Project Consortium, 2007). Weiss et al. (2008) reported on instances of a *de novo* deletion on chromosome 16p11.2 that appears to account for about 1% of cases of autism. A de novo microdeletion is a newly occurring change in the DNA that the affected individual did not directly inherit from either parent. Focus on Discovery 15.1 summarizes an exciting discovery in the molecular genetics of autism with a Canadian connection.

More recently, a collaborative research team connected more pieces of the autism "puzzle" with the publication in *Nature* of two major studies. In total the team analyzed DNA from 12,834 participants. One study (Wang et al., 2009) pinpointed a gene region, 5p14.1, that has gene variants that could possibly account for about 15% of autism cases (usually referred to as the "population-attributed risk" of the variant). The region is located between two genes, cadherin 9 (CDH9) and cadherin10 (CDH10). These genes carry codes to produce neuronal cell-adhesion molecules, which affect how nerve cells communicate, thought to be an underlying problem in ASD. The other study (Glessner et al., 2009) identified missing or duplicated stretches of DNA (copy number variations) along two crucial gene pathways or networks that play critical roles in the development of neuronal activity expressed within the CNS that may also contribute to the genetic susceptibility of ASD. The study leader, Hakon Hakonarson, noted that the gene discoveries converge with evidence from fMRI imagining that autistic children might have reduced connectivity among neural cells, and with anatomy studies that have found abnormal development in the frontal lobes of autistic people (see www.autismspeaks.org). Future research must determine the exact mechanisms by which genetic variations cause autistic disorder. Further, other genes will no doubt be discovered.

Neurological Factors and Environmental Risks Most researchers assume that a fundamental disturbance of the CNS is involved in ASD. In adolescence, 30% of those who have severe autistic symptoms as children begin having epileptic seizures, a sign that a neurological dysfunction is involved in the disorder (Frombonne, 1999). Neuroimaging studies indicate that a variety of structural and functional

FOCUS ON DISCOVERY 15.1
MAPPING AUTISM RISK LOCI USING GENETIC LINKAGE AND CHROMOSOMAL REARRANGEMENTS

"Not only have we found *which* haystack the needle is in, we now know *where* in the haystack that needle is located. This is a major breakthrough in our efforts to better understand the disorder and improve diagnosis and treatment for patients and their families."

—Dr. Peter Szatmari

Researchers at the Offord Centre for Child Studies at McMaster University, led by Dr. Peter Szatmari, and Sick Children's Hospital in Toronto, led by Dr. Stephen Scherer, were leaders in an international consortium—The Autism Genome Project Consortium—that discovered one gene and a previously unidentified region of another chromosome as the location of an additional gene that possibly contributes to risk for an ASD. The consortium is made up of more than 120 scientists from 50 centres in North America and Europe who agreed in 2002 to share data, samples, and expertise in order to accelerate the process of identifying the susceptibility genes that heighten the risk for autism.

In the consortium's model for autism,

combinations of multiple loci that possibly interact and microscopic or submicroscopic chromosomal abnormalities contribute to risk, complicating the detection of individual loci. Increasing the likelihood of detecting loci requires analyzing a large sample of multiplex families (i.e., families with two or more affected individuals), thereby enhancing the power of linkage analysis and controlling sources of etiologic heterogeneity … . (The Autism Genome Project Consortium, 2007, p. 319)

The findings of this massive international effort, reported in the March 2007 issue of the journal *Nature Genetics*, are based on genetic samples from 1,168 families with two or more children diagnosed with an ASD. The strategy unleashed unprecedented statistical power, which allowed the scientists to perform the largest linkage scan to date and to analyze copy

Dr. Peter Szatmari, Director of the Offord Centre and Head of the Division of Child Psychiatry at McMaster University, is a leading expert in autism. Courtesy of Dr. Peter Szatmari.

number variation in these families. The results implicate a previously unidentified region of chromosome 11 (pp.12–13) and neurexins among other candidate loci in the genome. The neurexin finding especially highlights a unique group of neurons, called glutamate neurons, and the genes that affect their development and function. This discovery suggests that the neurexins may play a critical role in ASD.

The consortium will next focus on mapping the specific genes that cause autism. Ultimately, the research could revolutionize how autism is both detected and treated.

Source: Adapted from the Offord website: www.offordcentre.com/asd/study_genetics/genstudy_ld.html, The Autism Genome Project Consortium (2007)

---

deficits occur in ASD. For example, MRI studies show that autistic people have larger brains than normal people (e.g., Sparks et al., 2002), especially in the frontal lobe, perhaps due to the late development of this region (see Mitchell et al., 2009, for review). As noted by Nicolson and Szatmari (2003), this is unique to autism, as other neurodevelopmental disorders and mental retardation are associated with reduced brain volume. Further evidence supporting the possibility of brain dysfunction derives from 16 MRI and autopsy studies from nine independent research groups, all finding abnormalities in the cerebellum of autistic children (Haas et al., 1996). Other specific regions found to be altered include the amygdala and corpus callosum (see Mitchell et al., 2009). Variability in findings is most likely attributable to the heterogeneity of autism. Recently, Mitchell

and colleagues (2009) used MRI to investigate brain regions of interest in monozygotic twins who differed in degree of phenotypic discordance for autism narrowly defined. Relative to comparison children, they found alterations in the prefrontal cortex, corpus callosum, and posterior vermis in the autistic children. Further, in children with narrowly defined autism only, dorsolateral prefrontal cortex, amygdala, and posterior vermis volumes were associated with severity of autism. Although the exact nature of all the deficits remains unclear, MRI research leads to the conclusion that abnormalities in brain anatomy contribute to the metabolic differences and behavioural phenotype in ASD (McAlonan et al., 2005). Further, event-related fMRI studies suggest autistic people show less activity in the medial frontal cortex and medial temporal cortex when engaged in certain tasks, relative to those who are not autistic (Frith & Frith, 2000). When rewarded, adults with autism, relative to controls, showed greater activation in the left anterior cingulated gyrus, which was negatively correlated with a measure of social interaction (Schmitz et al., 2008).

Although, as indicated above, genetic factors clearly play a role in the neurological dysfunction seen in ASD, environmental risks possibly also play a role in establishing a deficit in CNS structure and function. Indeed, it is possible that autism is already established in the fetus by about 32 weeks of gestation (Beversdorf et al., 2005). Mothers of children with autism reported higher levels of prenatal stressors from 25 to 28 weeks of gestation compared with mothers with Down syndrome or mothers without known disorders. The timing of these stressors is consistent with the period for brain development that is abnormal in children with ASD. It will be important in future research to gain a better understanding of gene-environment interactions in the etiology of autism.

In 2009, a network of leading autism researchers launched the Early Autism Risk Longitudinal Investigation (EARLI), the most comprehensive study thus far of the earliest possible causes of autism (www.earlistudy.org). EARLI will follow approximately 1,200 pregnant women who already have a child with autism in an effort to discover biological markers and environmental risk factors for autism. The research team will study possible environmental exposures, ranging from suspected neurotoxicants, like persistent organic pollutants, to medications taken during pregnancy, and their interplay with genetic susceptibility during the prenatal, neonatal, and early postnatal (36 months) periods.

Jenna Flanagan, a child with autism, experiences the Snoezelen Room at Magnetic Hill School in Moncton, N.B. The room has soft, soothing lights that shift colours continually, and various tactile-oriented surfaces. CP Image Archive/Greg Anew.

TREATMENT OF AUTISTIC DISORDER

Because their isolation is so moving and their symptoms so pronounced, a great deal of attention has been given to trying to improve the condition of children with an ASD. Sadly, there are many scientifically questionable treatments (see Lilienfeld, 2005; Vismara & Rogers, 2010), including facilitated communication, sensory integration therapy, and dolphin-assisted therapy. Treatments usually try to reduce unusual behaviour and improve communication and social skills. Sometimes an eagerly sought-after goal for a family is simply to be able to take their autistic child to a restaurant or market without attracting negative attention. Today, the preferred interventions employ the scientific teaching principles of applied behaviour analysis (ABA). Indeed, the evidence-based treatment of choice is a long-term, comprehensive ABA intervention initiated at a very young age (see Virues-Ortega, 2010). This approach is alternatively referred to as intensive behavioural intervention (IBI).

SPECIAL PROBLEMS IN TREATING CHILDREN WITH AUTISM As noted by Reiss (2009), the heterogeneity of autistic individuals diagnosed by DSM criteria makes it difficult for investigators to develop effective, etiology-specific interventions. Further, children with autism have several characteristics that make teaching them difficult: (1) they do not adjust well to changes in routine, yet change is the essence of treatment; (2) their isolation and self-stimulatory movements may interfere with effective teaching; (3) it is particularly difficult to find ways to motivate them; and (4) their overselectivity of attention (i.e., when the child's attention becomes focused on one particular aspect of a task or situation, other properties, including relevant ones, may not be noticed) makes it especially difficult for the children to generalize or apply their learning to other areas. In spite of these problems, educational programs for students with autism have achieved positive results.

BEHAVIOURAL TREATMENT OF CHILDREN WITH AUTISM Ivar Lovaas, a leading clinical researcher at the University of California at Los Angeles, conducted a landmark intensive operant program with very young (under four years old) autistic children (Lovaas, 1987). Therapy encompassed all aspects of the children's lives for more than 40 hours a week over more than two years. Parents were trained extensively so that treatment could continue during almost all the children's waking hours. Nineteen children receiving this intensive treatment were compared with 40 control youngsters who received a similar treatment for less than 10 hours per week. All children were rewarded for being less aggressive, more compliant, and more socially appropriate. The goal was to mainstream the children, the assumption being that autistic children, as they improve, benefit more from being with normal peers than from remaining by themselves or with other seriously disturbed children.

Ivar Lovaas is noted for his operant-conditioning treatment of autistic children. Photo by Susan Oliver Young. Courtesy of Ivar Lovaas.

The results were dramatic and encouraging for the intensive-therapy group. Their measured IQs averaged 83 in Grade 1 (after about two years in the intensive therapy), compared with about 55 for the control children; 12 of the 19 reached the normal range, compared with only 2 (of 40) in the control group. Furthermore, 9 of the 19 in the intensive-therapy group were promoted to Grade 2 in a regular public school, whereas only 1 of the much larger control group achieved this level of normal functioning. A follow-up four years later indicated that the intensive-treatment group maintained their gains in IQ, adaptive behaviour, and grade promotions in school (McEachin, Smith, & Lovaas, 1993). Although critics have pointed out weaknesses in the study's methodology and outcome measures (Schopler, Short, & Mesibov, 1989), this ambitious program confirms the benefits of the heavy involvement of both professionals and parents in dealing with the extreme challenge of autistic disorder. The effectiveness of the Lovaas approach was confirmed in an RCT published by Smith, Groen, and Wynn (2000).

A more contemporary study (Ben-Itzchak & Zachor, 2007) illustrates the importance of early intensive behavioural intervention (EIBI) and the value of pre-intervention cognitive and social interaction levels for predicting outcome. Autistic children (20–32 months) enrolled in EIBI were divided into two groups based on IQ scores and severity of social interaction and communication deficits. Significant progress was noted in six developmental-behavioural domains after one year of intervention: imitation, receptive language, expressive language, non-verbal communication skills, play skills, and stereotyped behaviours. The children with higher initial cognitive levels and children with fewer early social interaction deficits demonstrated better acquisition of skills in language and play.

More recently, a rigorous RCT of a program called the Early Start Denver Model (ESDM; Dawson et al., 2010), demonstrated that two years of treatment vastly improved symptoms in toddlers as young as 18 months. ESDM uses a developmental profile model to create individually tailored interventions in each of the domains (e.g., social skills) affected by ASD in the child. The program is novel because it combines ABA teaching methods with play-based routines that focus on building a relationship with the child. The children received 15 hours weekly of one-on-one treatment from home-trained therapists and 16 hours per week from parents. Relative to the control group (which received standard community-based treatments), the ESDM group showed improvements in receptive and expressive language, communication, daily living, and motor skills. IQ increased, on average, by almost 18 points, relative to an increase of 7 points in the control group. Most of the change was due to improvements in receptive and expressive language. Nonetheless, all children in both groups continued to have some type of ASD diagnosis when the children were, on average, 52 months old.

Two recent comprehensive reviews (Virues-Ortega, 2010; Vismara & Rogers, 2010) concluded that ABA or early IBI interventions are effective for children with ASD, especially if delivered before age 5 years and implemented intensively (20 hours or more per week for two or more years). Interventions are preferably initiated under the age of two (see Zwaigenbaum et al., 2009). Vismara and Rogers (2010) noted, however, that "ESDM needs to be independently replicated before it can be considered to be an empirically supported treatment for early ASD" (p. 7). Virues-Ortega (2010) concluded that long-term, comprehensive ABA intervention leads to positive effects in terms of intellectual functioning, language development, acquisition of daily living skills, and social functioning. However, Vismara and Rogers (2010) noted that additional evidence on the long-term effects of both comprehensive and skills-based programs is needed. They also proposed that the required next step is to determine if earlier interventions result in more normal patterns of brain function and organization. Another comprehensive synthesis of EIBIs for young children based on the UCLA model (Reichow & Wolery, 2009) reported a large effect size for 12 samples and concluded that EIBI is an effective treatment for increasing IQ scores in autistic children. Nonetheless, the authors noted a potential problem of publication bias in favour of studies with positive results. Reichow and Wolery (2009) emphasized the importance of identifying children not responding to EIBI very early in order to implement additional and/or different treatments.

Finally, it must be understood that some autistic and other severely disturbed children can be adequately cared for only in a hospital or in a group home staffed by mental health professionals. Moreover, the circumstances of some families preclude the home care of a seriously disturbed child. That effective treatments can be implemented by parents does not mean that this is the appropriate course for all families. Caring for an autistic child is clearly associated with high levels of parenting stress (see Schieve et al., 2007).

Canadian Perspectives 15.6 describes a new initiative in Canada to develop an early detection and intervention program for children with autism or other pervasive developmental disorders.

DRUG TREATMENT OF CHILDREN WITH AUTISM Currently, no available medication treats the full range of core symptoms of ASD. The current strategy is to employ drugs that target specific symptoms or clusters of symptoms. For example, antipsychotic medications such as haloperidol and risperidone are commonly used to reduce maladaptive behaviour, such as self-mutilation and aggression (e.g., DuPaul et al., 2003). Many autistic children do not respond positively to these drugs, however, and they have potentially serious side effects. Efforts to substitute olanzapine, an atypical neuroleptic, showed it to be a safer alternative in terms of fewer side effects, but it was less effective in symptom improvement (Kemner et al., 2002). Further, the combination of behavioural treatments and medication appear to be superior to medication alone in controlling severe aggression in autistic children (e.g., Brown et al., 2005). Antidepressants that reduce the action of serotonin such as clomipramine and the SSRIs such as fluoxetine are used to treat stereotypic and repetitive behaviours (e.g., Hollander et al., 2005). Stimulant drugs such as Ritalin have shown some effectiveness in reducing inattentiveness and hyperactivity (e.g., Research Units on Pediatric Psychopharmacology Network, 2005). There is, as yet, no drug of proven effectiveness for improving the social impairments or language abilities that are the hallmarks of ASD (DuPaul et al., 2003). Unfortunately, the use of medication increases as autistic children grow into adulthood, despite the fact that there are few studies of the efficacy of medication (e.g., Seltzer et al., 2004).

CANADIAN PERSPECTIVES 15.6

THE CANADIAN AUTISM INTERVENTION RESEARCH NETWORK (CAIRN): EARLY DETECTION AND INTERVENTION?

Autism is typically detected before the age of two and a half. But can we detect signs of the disorder even earlier and then develop interventions that will prevent or minimize the development of the major symptoms? One initiative in Canada under the direction of Peter Szatmari is named CAIRN: The Canadian Autism Intervention Research Network, a national network of researchers who share a focused interest in early intervention. It involves researchers from numerous disciplines, including psychiatry, psychology, pediatrics, education, speech and language pathology, and early childhood education. The objective is "to bring together various stakeholders in developing a research agenda and then to provide high quality evidence in early intervention to insure long-term outcomes for children with autism spectrum disorders" (see www.cairn-site.com).

The members of CAIRN identified two serious problems with the current status of the autism clinical treatment literature: (1) systematic reviews have pointed to limitations to the available evidence on the effectiveness of various early intervention programs, and (2) research experts, frontline clinicians, and the parents of children with ASD often disagree about what form early interventions should take and what strategies appear to work. Regarding the latter point, there is clearly great variation in the type and availability of programs across the country. There is an urgent need in Canada for new research to inform important treatment decisions involving young children who show ASD symptoms.

Members of CAIRN advocate for increased research on early intervention and additional training for physicians and clinicians in a position to detect ASD in young children. CAIRN has undertaken a long-term follow-up investigation of the outcomes experienced by children with ASD; the study includes a comparison between children with autism and those with Asperger's syndrome. Language skills predict outcome in high-functioning children with either autism or Asperger's syndrome, though this link is stronger in the autistic group (Szatmari et al., 2003).

Thinking Critically

By and large, governments pay lip service to the importance of early interventions, but often the level of funding is simply not sufficient to meet the needs of the burgeoning Canadian population. For example, in Ontario, the special funding for IBI was previously available for autistic children aged two to five and stopped when a child reached age six. A lawsuit was initiated by families seeking to force Ontario to provide intensive treatment beyond age six and continuing as the child progresses through the school system. On January 20, 2004, the Ontario Human Rights Commission joined the battle to force the province to fund treatment for older autistic children. An estimated 2,000 children had passed age six and would not benefit from intensive behavioural intervention treatment unless the government changed its policy (Boyle, 2004). In 2005, the government extended therapy to children age six and older. In 2002, the province spent $39 million to treat 500 children, but 900 others were on waiting lists (Orwen, 2003). Effective January 19, 2007 (Gillespie, 2007), the government committed to spending $115 million annually to provide one-on-one therapy for 1,100 children. However, more than 1,000 children remained on the waiting list. Many parents bankrupt themselves in order to spend as much as $50,000 a year to provide treatment for their autistic children. Do you think governments have an obligation to provide the best possible treatment for all autistic children? Should they provide programs and services for older children or should these children be the responsibility of the parents or caregivers?

Although outcomes are variable and specific characteristics and symptoms can change over time, a majority of ASD children remain within the spectrum as adults. They usually continue to experience problems related to mental health, social relationships, and employment (see Myers & Johnson, 2007).

DISORDERS OF OVERCONTROLLED BEHAVIOUR

This chapter began by highlighting the distinction between undercontrolled and overcontrolled behaviour. We conclude by examining overcontrolled or internalizing behaviour in the form of anxiety disorders and depressive disorders in children and adolescents. Considerable evidence supports the study of anxiety and depressive symptoms jointly during childhood (see Côté et al., 2009, for review). Coman, Wadsworth, Croudace, and Jones (2007), using data from an English national birth cohort, reported that about 70% of adolescents who had an internalizing disorder (primarily anxiety or depression) at both ages 13 and 15 had a mental disorder at age 36, 43, or 53, relative to approximately 25% in a control group of mentally healthy adolescents. Sadly, the long-term outcome for children with persistent or recurrent internalizing disorders can be poor.

At the outset we can state that both genetic and environmental factors play a role in the development of internalizing disorders. Hicks, DiRago, Iacono, and McGrue (2009) conducted a comprehensive analysis with over 1,300 adolescent twin pairs that examined multiple environmental risk factors (stressful life events, parent-child relationship problems, anti-social and prosocial peer affiliation, and academic achievement and engagement) in order to delineate general mechanisms of gene-environment influence in the development of internalizing disorders. They detected significant moderation effects between each environmental risk factor and internalizing disorders: in the context of greater environmental adversity, non-shared environmental factors became more important in causing internalizing symptoms. These findings are consistent with an interpretation that environmental risk factors play a causative role in the emergence of internalizing disorders. Hicks et al. (2009) concluded that there is "a general mechanism of environmental influence" on internalizing disorders irrespective of the specific form of environmental risk (p. 1309).

Côté et al. (2009) modelled the developmental trajectories of depressive and anxiety symptoms during early childhood in a large population sample of infants in Quebec who were followed yearly from 5 to 60 months of age. They found that for most children, depression and anxiety symptoms increased over the first 5 years of life. Three distinct trajectory groups were identified. A substantial minority (about 15%) exhibited high frequency at 1.5 years and a sharper increase with age relative to the other groups, leading the authors to conclude that "an atypically high propensity to evince DAS can be identified very early in life" (p.1205). The investigators sought to identify early risk factors for depressive and anxiety symptoms. The impact of children's difficult temperament at five months was the most important vulnerability predictor of depression and anxiety in the atypical high-rising trajectory. Lifetime maternal depression was the second most important predictor, even after controlling for other maternal risk factors (e.g., maternal anti-social behaviours and low education).

CHILDHOOD FEARS AND ANXIETY DISORDERS

Most children experience fears and worries as part of the normal course of development. Common fears, most of which are outgrown, include fear of the dark and of imaginary creatures (in children under 5) and fear of being separated from parents (in children under 10). A comparative survey of children from five countries, including Canada (see Phipps, 1999), found that more than one third of Canadian children between the ages of 4 and 11 were rated by their parents as too fearful or anxious, and that Canadian children were three times more anxious and fearful than children from Norway. For fears and worries to be classified as disorders, children's functioning must be impaired; unlike adults, however, children might not regard their fear as excessive or unreasonable, as they sometimes lack the insight to make such judgements. Using this definition, about 10 to 15% of children and adolescents have an anxiety disorder, making these the most common disorders of childhood (Cohen et al., 1993).

In general, as with adults, fears and phobias are reported more often for girls than for boys (e.g., King et al., 1989), though this sex difference may be due at least in part to social pressures against boys' admitting that they are afraid of things. Although most unrealistic childhood fears dissipate over time, many anxious adults trace their problems back to childhood. The seriousness of some childhood anxiety problems should therefore not be underestimated. Surprisingly, a majority of children who develop anxiety disorders are not referred for treatment (Klein, 2009). Klein (2009) recommends interventions to allow identification and treatment of children with anxiety in schools and primary care settings.

Recently, Murray, Creswell, and Cooper (2009) conducted an integrative review of the development of child anxiety. Murray et al. noted that anxiety disorders in children and adolescents are common and disabling, often run a chronic course, and can be comorbid with depression, conduct disorder, and ADHD. They concluded that (a) family aggregation and genetic studies confirm increased vulnerability to anxiety in offspring of adults with an anxiety disorder (e.g., the temperamental style of behavioural inhibition or biases in information processing), and (b) important environmental factors include negative life events and exposure to modelling or negative information. Parenting behaviours (e.g., overprotection) may be elicited by child vulnerabilities. Murray et al. (2009) also highlighted the potential bi-directionality of child and parental influences. In another review, Klein (2009) reported that parental anxiety disorders, particularly when coupled with depression, are documented risks for child anxiety disorders. However, there is little specificity of concordance between parental and offspring anxiety disorders.

In an interesting twist on genetic studies, Kendler, Gardner, and Lichtenstein (2008) examined the pattern of genetic and environmental influences on symptoms of anxiety and depression from childhood to early adulthood in more than 2,500 twins. Analyses revealed one genetic risk factor at ages 8–9, 13–14, 16–17, and 19–20 years, with new sets of genetic risk factors "coming on line" in early adolescence, late adolescence, and early adulthood, altogether accounting for heritability estimates ranging from 72 to 89% for levels of anxiety and depression reported in common by parents and twins. However, the first genetic factor, which accounted for 72% of the variance at ages 8–9, attenuated sharply and accounted for only 12% of the variance by ages 19–20. It was concluded that genetic effects on anxiety and depression are "developmentally dynamic from middle childhood to young adulthood, demonstrating both genetic innovation and genetic attenuation" (Kendler, Gardner, & Lichtenstein, 2008, p. 1567). In a subsequent paper on the same group of twins, Kendler, Gardner, Annas, & Lichtenstein (2008) concluded that genetic and environmental risk factors for individual fears (animal, blood-injury, situational, and social) are partially mediated through a common fear factor but are partly fear-specific. New common and specific genetic effects arose in late adolescence/early adulthood.

Although a variety of psychosocial interventions are employed with children, according to March (2009), "we now have evidence-based CBT manuals covering the full range of childhood-onset mental disorders" (p. 173). Further, medications are commonly used in the treatment of these disorders.

SEPARATION ANXIETY

Separation anxiety involves an unrealistic concern about separation from major attachment figures, with the levels of anxiety being above the level typically associated with the child's developmental level. The *DSM-IV-TR* description of separation anxiety disorder emphasizes that the eight symptoms must be experienced for at least eight weeks. These symptoms include unrealistic and persistent worries about harm to major attachment figures along with fears of abandonment, refusal to attend school owing to a need to stay close to an attachment figure, an avoidance of being alone, the experience of nightmares involving separation themes, and the experience of physical complaints in anticipation of being separated from attachment figures. Separation anxiety disorder is considered to be specific to childhood and adolescence, and *DSM-IV-TR* diagnostic criteria stipulate that the symptoms apply to individuals under the age of 18. However, in February 2010, the *DSM-V* work group (see American Psychiatric Association, 2010) announced that it was considering rewording the criteria to be suitable for adults as well as children, and possibly reclassifying it from Disorders Usually First Diagnosed in Infancy, Childhood, or Adolescence to Anxiety Disorders. The onset before age 18 years criterion might be deleted given evidence for adult-onset.

The experience of separation anxiety is a natural reaction among very young children. Levels may reach their peak when toddlers are 18 months of age (Wachtel & Strauss, 1995). It appears to be the most common individual anxiety diagnosis in children below 12 years of age (Cartwright-Hatton, McNicol, & Doubleday, 2006). Although there is an overall tendency for levels to decrease with age, research confirms that some adults may meet diagnostic criteria for separation anxiety disorder (e.g., Manicavasagar, Silove, & Curtis, 1997). Much of our understanding of separation anxiety comes from the seminal work of attachment theorists such as Ainsworth and Bowlby. An "anxious attachment style" among infants predicts subsequent anxiety disorders. Canadian Contributions 15.2 focuses on Ainsworth's work.

SCHOOL PHOBIA

Separation anxiety and **school phobia** are considered distinct problems because some children have no difficulty leaving attachment figures for extended periods but are afraid to go to school. School phobia, sometimes called school refusal, has serious academic and social consequences for the youngster and can be extremely disabling.

Two types of school phobia have been identified. In the more common type, associated with separation anxiety, children worry constantly that some harm will befall their parents or themselves when they are away from their parents; when at home, they shadow one or both of their parents and often try to join them in bed. Since many children have their first experience of lengthy and frequent separations from their parents when they begin school, separation anxiety is often a principal cause of school phobia. One study found that 75% of children who have school refusal caused by separation anxiety have mothers who also avoided school in childhood (Last & Strauss, 1990). The mother possibly communicates her own separation anxieties and unwittingly reinforces the child's dependent and avoidant behaviour.

The second type of school refusal is associated with a true phobia of school—either a fear specifically related to school or a more general social phobia. Children with this type of phobia generally begin refusing to go to school later in life and have more severe and pervasive avoidance of school. Their fear is more likely to be related to specific aspects of the school environment, such as worries about academic failure or discomfort with peers. If untreated (or if it doesn't dissipate without professional intervention), school phobia can have long-term negative consequences as the person grows into adolescence and adulthood. The school-phobic child can grow up to be a dependent and fearful person.

SOCIAL PHOBIA

Most classrooms include at least one or two children who are extremely quiet and shy. Often these children will play only with family members or familiar peers, avoiding strangers both young and old. Their shyness may prevent them from

CANADIAN CONTRIBUTIONS 15.2
MARY AINSWORTH, ATTACHMENT STYLES, AND DISTRESS

Mary Ainsworth is widely regarded as one of the top psychologists produced in Canada. She spent most of her childhood in Toronto and completed her undergraduate and graduate work at the University of Toronto. She obtained her Ph.D. in 1939. She was a research fellow at the Institute of Child Study at the University of Toronto from 1946 to 1950. In 1950, she married and moved to England, where she began her lifelong research collaboration with attachment-style theorist John Bowlby.

Ainsworth is known primarily for her work on infant attachment styles. She developed a paradigm known as the Strange Situation, in which an infant was left in a room for a brief period with a stranger, the mother having left the room. Observational data indicated that three distinct types of infants reflect the differences between secure attachment and anxious attachment (Ainsworth, Blehar, Waters, & Wall, 1978). A **securely attached** infant shows little distress and interacts quite willingly with the stranger, secure in the knowledge that his or her mother will return. This pattern of behaviour contrasts with the pattern expressed by two types of insecurely attached infants. An **anxiously attached** infant becomes very distressed when his or her mother leaves the room. These infants have been described as "clingy" and are at risk of being overly dependent and prone to feelings of separation anxiety. When mothers of anxiously attached infants return to the room, their babies tend to express their upset by making a fuss as a form of protest, as if they are saying, "Don't do that to me again." In contrast, an infant with an **avoidant attachment style** displays little emotion when the mother leaves the room and shows little reaction upon her return, almost if an attachment bond has never been formed in the first place. Avoidantly attached infants can become withdrawn and socially isolated.

Insecure forms of attachment are likely to develop when a child is exposed to harsh or inconsistent parenting (see Ainsworth, 1984). Secure attachment emerges when the parent responds to the infant's needs in a warm and predictable manner, so that the infant comes to believe that the parent will be available as a source of comfort on a regular basis. A fourth attachment style has since been identified. The **disorganized attachment style** is evident in infants who seem totally confused by their surroundings. This style results from being exposed to chaotic and abusive environments.

It is possible to distinguish older children, adolescents, and adults in terms of whether they have a secure or insecure style. What are the early experiences and related factors that contribute to

Psychologist Mary Ainsworth was a pioneer in the field of infant-caregiver attachment styles. Health Canada.

insecure attachment? A meta-analytic study conducted by researchers in Canada concluded that maternal mental health variables are associated with degree of attachment security (Atkinson et al., 2000). Significant correlates of attachment security included the amount of social support available to the mother, marital satisfaction, maternal stress, and maternal depression.

Forms of insecure attachment have been linked with adjustment problems in children and adolescents. One longitudinal study assessed children exposed to the Strange Situation at 1 year of age and then used interviews 18 years later to determine which children had developed an anxiety disorder (Warren, Huston, Egeland, & Sroufe, 1997). An anxious attachment style among infants predicted subsequent anxiety disorders, while an avoidant attachment style predicted other types of psychiatric disorders. Another study conducted by researchers from Simon Fraser University found that fearful, insecure attachment in adolescents was associated with the severity of suicide risk in a clinical sample (Lessard & Moretti, 1998). A study conducted by Canadian researchers yielded evidence that male adolescents with an avoidant attachment style are more likely than males with a secure attachment style to express and receive coercive behaviours in dating relationships (Wekerle & Wolfe, 1998).

Ainsworth received numerous awards, including the American Psychological Association Gold Medal Award in 1998 for "Lifetime Achievement in the Science of Psychology." Mary Ainsworth died in 1999. Her work will be valued for many future generations.

---

acquiring skills and participating in a variety of activities enjoyed by most of their age-mates, for they avoid playgrounds and games played by neighbourhood children. Although some shy youngsters may simply be slow to warm up, withdrawn children never do, even after prolonged exposure to new people. Extremely shy children may refuse to speak at

all in unfamiliar social circumstances; this condition is called **selective mutism** (see Viana, Beidel, & Rabian, 2009). In crowded rooms, they cling and whisper to their parents, hide behind the furniture, cower in corners, and may even have tantrums. At home, they ask their parents endless questions about situations that worry them. Withdrawn children usually have warm and satisfying relationships with family members and family friends, and they show a desire for affection and acceptance.

Because the point at which shyness or withdrawal becomes a problem varies, few reliable statistics have been compiled on the frequency of this disorder. One estimate is that 1% of children and adolescents can be diagnosed with **social phobia** (Kashani & Orvaschel, 1990). It is more of a problem with adolescents, who are of an age when concern about the opinions of others can be acute.

Theories of the etiology of social phobia in children are not well worked out. However, the construct of behavioural inhibition (introduced in Chapter 6) probably plays a role. Behavioural inhibition is a persistent tendency to show extreme reticence, fearfulness, or avoidance in novel situations, or with unfamiliar people (see Hirshfeld-Becker et al., 2008). In her discussion of established risk factors for child anxiety disorders, Klein (2009) noted that, "The most consistent and heuristic finding in developmental psychopathology is the role of behavioural inhibition as a risk for social phobia" (p. 157). The importance of this relation is supported by findings of amygdala overreactivity to novelty in adolescents who manifested behavioural inhibition at an early age and by evidence of gene-environment interaction in the prediction of shyness at age seven (see Fox et al., 2005a, 2005b). Essex and colleagues (2010) sought to determine developmental pathways to chronic high inhibition among school-age children in a community sample followed from birth to age 9. They assessed four early risk factors: female gender; exposure to maternal stress; and at age 4.5 years, early signs of inhibition and elevated afternoon salivary cortisol levels. All of the risk factors predicted chronic high inhibition via two developmental pathways: (1) in girls, partially mediated by early evidence of behavioural inhibition and elevated cortisol levels; and (2) began with exposure to early maternal stress, partially mediated by cortisol levels. Most important, by Grade 9, chronic high behavioural inhibition was associated with social anxiety disorder.

It has also been suggested that anxiety interferes with social interaction, causing the child to avoid social situations and thus not to get much practice at social skills. Another suggestion is that withdrawn children may simply not have the social know-how that facilitates interaction with their age-mates. The finding that isolated children make fewer attempts to make friends and are less imaginative in their play may indicate a deficiency in social skills. Finally, isolated children may have become so because they have spent most of their time with adults. Having a parent with social phobia may also play a role. A study by Mancini and her associates in Hamilton found that among children who had a parent with social phobia, 49% had at least one anxiety disorder diagnosis (Mancini et al., 1996). Overall, 23% of the children were diagnosed with social phobia, and 19% with separation anxiety disorder. The specific processes and mechanisms in social phobia can involve social learning (i.e., imitation of the parent), exposure to an overly anxious parenting style, and increased risk due to genetic factors.

Social anxiety disorder was found to be a valid diagnosis in children and adolescents by a *DSM-V* work group (see Bogels et al., 2010).

TREATMENT OF CHILDHOOD FEARS AND ANXIETY DISORDERS

How are childhood fears overcome? Many simply dissipate with time and maturation. However, without treatment many anxiety disorders in children and adolescents follow a chronic course and can be associated with comorbid psychopathology in adulthood, including anxiety, depression, and substance use (see Crawley et al., 2010). For the most part, treatment of anxiety disorders in children is similar to that employed with adults using CBT (e.g., exposure, relaxation training, role playing, and cognitive strategies), with suitable modifications to accommodate the different abilities and circumstances of childhood (see Crawley et al., 2010; Klein, 2009). The typical treatment goals are to teach children to recognize signs of anxiety and to use these signs as cues to initiate anxiety management strategies. Crawley et al. (2010) recently pointed out the fact that there is still a "need for carefully executed outcome studies with children if the field is to develop a more truly evidence-based approach to practice" (p. 375). A recent meta-analysis (Spielmans, Pasek, & McFall, 2007) concluded that CBT is superior to waitlist controls, but not to credible controls in children with a variety of anxiety disorders. Further, with the exception of social phobia, few treatment trials for specific anxiety disorders have been conducted.

The most popular method for helping children overcome fears, employed by millions of parents, is to expose them gradually to the feared object, often while simultaneously performing some action to inhibit their anxiety. If a little girl fears strangers, a parent takes her by the hand and walks her slowly toward the new person. Contemporary therapists and reviewers generally agree that exposure is the most effective way of eliminating fear and avoidance (see Klein, 2009). Modelling has also proven effective. Another child—for example, someone the fearful child is likely to imitate—could be asked to demonstrate fearless behaviour. Offering rewards for moving closer to a feared object or situation can also help a fearful child. Both modelling and operant treatments involve exposure to what is feared. When the fear and avoidance of a child with school phobia are very great and of long duration, the child may require desensitization through direct, graduated exposure plus operant shaping. Like adults, children may find some new situations threatening because they lack the knowledge and skills to deal with them. Thus, a child's fear of the water may very well be based on a reasonable judgement that danger lurks there because he or she cannot swim. Some shy children lack specific social skills needed for peer interaction. Skills such as asking questions, giving compliments, and starting conversations with age-mates may be taught.

Manassis and Monga (2001) from the Hospital for Sick Children in Toronto noted that parents may contribute to the etiology of anxiety disorders by being anxious themselves and providing a model that can be imitated. Further, anxiety in the child can be a response, at least in part, to being the target of parental frustration. This research team has established that high levels of parental frustration can undermine treatment gains (see Liashko & Manassis, 2003). A follow-up investigation of adolescents who had received CBT seven years earlier attested to the long-term effectiveness of treatment for the majority of participants with a previous anxiety disorder. Manassis, Avery, Butalia, and Mendlowitz (2004) found that almost all of the adolescents still experienced some anxiety-related impairment, but 70% required no further treatment. However, these data were based on telephone surveys and did not involve actual diagnostic interviews. More recently, Saavedra et al. (2010) reported that successful exposure-based CBT for childhood phobic anxiety disorders extended into the transition years of young adulthood (8–13 years post-treatment).

Comprehensive manualized programs developed by Kendall and his associates, among others, include between 16 and 20 sessions (see Kendall & Hedtke, 2006a, b) and have been translated into numerous languages. The first part of treatment involves training the child to recognize physiological signs of anxiety, challenge and change cognitions and internal dialogue, and learn new problem-solving and coping plans. The last half of treatment involves having the child implement these new skills when exposed to anxiety-provoking situations. The final session typically requires the child to make a videotaped commercial describing the steps of CBT and how they are used to combat anxiety (for a detailed description, see Kazdin, 2003). Variations on Kendall's approach include group, family, and group school-based treatment (see Crawley et al., 2010)

Children experience all of the other anxiety disorders described in the *DSM-IV-TR*. Focus on Discovery 15.2 examines the potential impact on children of the September 11, 2001, terrorist attacks on the United States. A discussion of some of the approaches that were employed to help people who were directly or indirectly affected by the horrific events of that day can be found in Chapter 17 in the context of our presentation on community psychology. Recently, Nakatani, Mataix-Cols, Turner, and Heyman (2008) reported that "effectiveness" gains following CBT therapy for children and adolescents with OCD at a specialist OCD service were maintained at follow-up as long as 10 years.

The use of antidepressants (SSRIs and venlafaxine) in children with anxiety disorders (see Pine & Kline, 2008 for review) followed reports of efficacy in adults with anxiety disorders; however, in contrast to CBT, there are apparently no specific diagnostic indications in children. One recent trial (Biedel et al., 2007) compared group exposure therapy and fluoxetine in the treatment of social phobic adolescents and found that both were more effective than a placebo. However, exposure was superior to medication and it also significantly enhanced social skills. Findings from studies that compared CBT and pharmacological treatment for OCD in youth with regard to efficacy and safety led to a consensus recommendation that CBT be considered the initial treatment of choice (see Crawley et al., 2010).

Although there have been a few encouraging prevention studies for children with high anxiety in selected settings (e.g., Rapee, Schniering, & Hudson, 2009), Klein (2009) noted that cost-effective strategies are limited by a lack of information about the factors that limit long-term outcomes for children with anxiety disorders. Neil and Christensen (2009) evaluated the efficacy and effectiveness of 20 individual, primarily CBT, school-based prevention and early intervention programs and concluded that most are effective in reducing symptoms of anxiety in children and adolescents. Most programs focused on reducing the symptoms of non-specific anxiety. However, Neil and Christensen also indicated a need for longer-term follow-up, the use of attention control conditions, and evaluations of teacher delivery.

MOOD DISORDERS IN CHILDHOOD AND ADOLESCENCE

Considering our typical image of children as happy-go-lucky, it is distressing to observe that major depression and dysthymia occur in children and adolescents, as well as in adults. *DSM-IV-TR* diagnoses mood disorders in children using the adult criteria, while allowing for age-specific features such as irritability and aggressive behaviour instead of or in addition to depressed mood.

SYMPTOMS AND PREVALENCE OF CHILDHOOD AND ADOLESCENT DEPRESSION

There are similarities and differences in the symptomatology of children and adults with major depression (Mitchell et al., 1988). Children and adolescents ages 7 to 17 resemble adults in depressed mood, inability to experience pleasure, fatigue, concentration problems, and suicidal ideation. Symptoms that differ are higher rates of suicide attempts and guilt among children and adolescents, and more frequent waking up early in the morning, loss of appetite, weight loss, and early morning depression among adults. As in adults, depression in children is recurrent. Children and adolescents with major depression are likely to continue to exhibit significant depressive symptoms when assessed even four to eight years later (e.g., Hammen et al., 1990).

Sometimes depression—often called **masked depression**—is inferred from behaviours that would not, in adults, be viewed as reflecting an underlying depression, for example, acting aggressively or misbehaving at school or at home. In general, depression occurs in fewer than 1% of preschoolers (e.g., Kashani & Carlson, 1987) and in 2 to 3% of school-age children (e.g., Cohen et al., 1993). Luby et al. (2009) found symptoms of guilt and extreme fatigue to be highly specific for preschool (ages 3–6) depression. In adolescents, rates of depression are comparable with those of adults, with particularly high rates for girls. A four-year longitudinal study in Canada used interview data from the National Population Health Survey to show that the annual prevalence of depression is about 9% in females and between 3 and 5% in males (Galambos, Leadbeater, & Barker, 2004). The lifetime prevalence was 21.4% for females and 10.7% for males.

FOCUS ON DISCOVERY 15.2
AFTER THE 9/11 TERRORIST ATTACKS: PTSD IN CHILDREN

". . . lost is the sleep of the innocent since the Sept. 11 terrorist attacks in the U.S. stole the peaceful slumber of the young . . ."

—Frank Calleja (2001)

"I think there is going to be another war. I am very scared about this because lots of people are going to die."

—Jonathon, quoted by Calleja (2001)

Calleja (2001) told the story of a nine-year-old Toronto boy who had negative reactions in the aftermath of the suicide passenger jet attacks on the United States. Jonathon's symptoms included inability to sleep, waking up in the night afraid, worry about more terrorist attacks, and worry about war. We hope that he coped adaptively and that his symptoms were short-lived.

PTSD IN CHILDREN

But what about the children who were affected directly by the attacks, either because they escaped from the disaster area or because a loved one perished in the conflagration? What about those affected indirectly through watching countless television replays of the disaster, listening to family talk about it, and hearing different things about it at school and at the playground? Many children and adolescents undoubtedly developed at least some symptoms of the anxiety disorders, especially PTSD. Is PTSD expressed in children in the same way that it is in an adult? Although there is considerable overlap with the adult expression of symptoms, according to the American Psychiatric Association (2000), in children, especially young children, there might be:

- Disorganized or agitated behaviour, instead of or in addition to the typical intense fear, helplessness, or horror experienced by adults.
- Distressing dreams of the event seen in the younger children may have evolved into more generalized nightmares (e.g., of having to rescue others, or of threats to self or others) or frightening dreams that do not have recognizable content.
- Themes or aspects of the trauma expressed in repetitive play, including trauma-specific re-enactments (e.g., a child repeatedly re-enacts the collapse of the World Trade Center with toy buildings).
- Development of a belief that life will be too short for them to become an adult (sense of foreshortened future).
- Development of "omen formation," a belief in the ability to predict future negative events.
- Expression of the impact of the trauma through physical symptoms (e.g., headaches or stomach aches).
- Distress at reminders of the trauma, as well as the repetitive, intrusive thoughts typically reported by adults.
- Specific fears to stimuli or situations related to the trauma (e.g., fear of high-rise buildings, fear of flying, fear of war).

- Development of separation difficulties and becoming "clingy" or dependent, resisting going to school or insisting on sleeping with an adult.

There can be a delay of months or even longer before the appearance of serious symptoms. Many children exhibit symptoms but do not meet the formal diagnostic criteria for the PTSD diagnosis. Nonetheless, they might experience distress and impairment in important areas of functioning (e.g., performance at school might suffer) and some children would exhibit other psychological problems (e.g., depressed mood, anhedonia, irritability and anger, and behavioural problems such as aggressive outbursts) or meet criteria for other psychiatric disorders (e.g., a conversion disorder). Some children would express guilt because they survived or because they felt somehow responsible for the death of a loved one. As many as three quarters of young children who experienced Hurricane Andrew in Florida continued to report re-experiencing symptoms 10 months later (LaGreca, Silverman, Vernberg, & Prinstein, 1996). In February 2010, the *DSM-V* work group proposed to include child and adolescent age-related manifestations and age-related subtypes for PTSD. Posttraumatic Stress Disorder in Preschool Children would be diagnosed in children under the age of six who were exposed to death or threatened death, actual or threatened serious injury, or actual or threatened sexual violation, and met specific proposed criteria.

A MODEL OF PTSD IN CHILDREN AND THE ACTUAL EFFECTS OF 9/11

What factors put children at risk for the development of PTSD? PTSD can develop in children even when there are no predisposing conditions, especially when the stressor is as extreme as the September 11 terrorist attacks. Nonetheless, several factors appear to affect the pattern, intensity, and persistence of symptoms. LaGreca, Silverstein, and Wasserstein (1998) developed a model to predict children's reactions to a natural disaster (Hurricane Andrew), one we believe is relevant to our understanding of children's reactions to traumas of human design, such as September 11. The conceptual model requires us to consider four factors: (1) exposure to a traumatic event; (2) pre-existing characteristics of the child (e.g., anxiety sensitivity, separation anxiety disorder); (3) the child's attempts to process and cope with the trauma; and (4) the availability of social support.

Many children and adolescents were, in fact, adversely affected by the terrorist attacks. Schuster et al. (2001) interviewed adults across the United States in the week after the attacks and reported that 44% of the adults and 35% of their children had significant stress reactions. Six months after the attacks, the New York City Board of Education (Hoven et al., 2002) reported that 10.5% of students met criteria for PTSD. Risk factors included personal physical exposure to the attack, family exposure and loss, previous traumatic exposure, female gender, Hispanic ethnicity, and earlier grade in school (grades 4 and 5). Calderoni et al. (2006) assessed students in the Bronx eight months after

9/11 and reported a PTSD rate of 7.4%. They concluded that adolescents living in inner cities with high poverty and violence rates are at high risk for PTSD; those who felt vulnerable and unsafe eight months after the attacks were four times more likely to have PTSD. Further, a year after the attacks, 58% of children polled reported that they thought about the attacks at least a few times a month, 51% felt that future bombings or other attacks are somewhat likely, and 46% felt less safe travelling (*Time*, 2002). More recently, Mullett-Hume, Anshel, Guevara, and Cloitre (2008) assessed middle school children in an impoverished immigrant community located just 10 blocks from Ground Zero two and a half years after the World Trade Center attack. They assessed PTSD symptoms as influenced by "dose" of direct exposure to the attack; i.e., severity of symptoms is positively correlated with severity of exposure (e.g., seeing the towers fall, and seeing bodies falling), and accumulated lifetime traumas. Ninety percent of the primarily Asian Americans reported at least one traumatic event in addition to 9/11 (e.g., community violence). About 35% of the sample met criteria for PTSD. The findings suggested that "traumas that precede or follow mass violence often have as much as if not greater impact on long-term symptom severity than high dose exposure to the event" (Mullett-Hume et al., 2008, p. 103).

Finally, people in both the United States and Canada claimed that they changed their approach or attitudes toward family life as a consequence of the attacks (Gardwyn, 2002; *Maclean's*, 2002). For example, 78% of American parents considered family more of a priority, and 35% indicated that they were designating more family time to their children. Among Canadians, 79% of women and 66% of men reported that they were more appreciative of family life.

HELPING TRAUMATIZED CHILDREN

How could we help the tens of thousands of children traumatized by the terrorist attacks? Some authorities (e.g., Brown & Bobrow, 2004) believe that delivery of services via on-site school trauma-specific interventions is the best strategy to engage children in treatment. Brown and Bobrow employed a school-based manualized trauma-specific CBT (Coping after Scary Times—or CAST) that included psychoeducation, coping skills, gradual and imaginal exposure, and safety planning delivered in 45-minute sessions, the length of a typical class period. Although the program reached thousands of survivors of the terrorist attacks, there were numerous challenges (e.g., service access, funding, problems with staff who were trauma survivors themselves, traumatized caregivers, stigma). Unfortunately, there are no objective data on the program's effectiveness.

The FDNY (New York City Fire Department)/Columbia University Family Assessment and Guidance Program (Greene et al., 2006) officially began on March 1, 2002, five months and 20 days after 9/11. The home-based service offers parent guidance services and ongoing monitoring of bereaved children's functioning to families with dependent children in which a firefighter father was killed. Green et al. incorporated several processes into a model of loss and reconstitution that occurs over a period of four years in mothers and children (see Figure

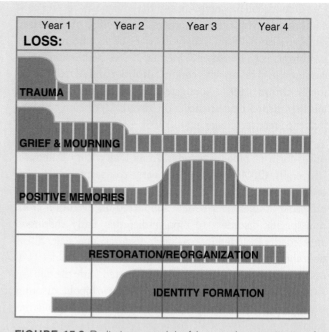

FIGURE 15.2 Preliminary model of loss and reconstitution for children who lost a firefighter father in the 9/11 attacks on the World Trade Center

15.2 for child model). The processes include trauma and grief, positive memories, restoration, reorganization, and restructuring identity or identity formation. The family-focused therapeutic intervention focuses on helping families master challenges related to the sudden loss of a parent. It is a supportive preventive intervention. Although we have no doubt that the program helps many children, the authors do not provide evidence to support the program's effectiveness.

We end on a positive note by pointing out that the majority of children are resilient. Their strength and resourcefulness, coupled with their family's love and support, no doubt helped them rebound from the trauma of September 11, 2001. How did Jonathon cope? He set about helping the victims. He and his siblings set up a lemonade stand draped in a large American flag and sold lemonade and red, white, and blue cookies. They raised more than $300 for the American Red Cross disaster fund.

THINKING CRITICALLY

1. What other strategies would you have employed to help prevent the development of serious psychological problems in children traumatized by the terrorist attacks?

2. What could ordinary people have done—the parents, schoolteachers, people in the community, and, of course, other children? Would it be possible for you to "short-circuit" the development of more serious problems?

3. Some predisposed children probably experienced other psychological difficulties, including depression and aggressive acting out. What suggestions would you have for helping these children?

One problem complicating the diagnosis is frequent comorbidity with other disorders. Up to 70% of depressed children also have an anxiety disorder or significant anxiety symptoms (e.g., Manassis & Menna, 1999). Depression is also common in children with conduct disorder and ADHD (Fleming & Offord, 1990). Youngsters with both depression and another disorder experience more severe depression and take longer to recover (Keller et al., 1988).

It is also possible for adolescents to develop an early-onset form of bipolar disorder. Anne Duffy from Dalhousie University (2009) reviewed the early course of bipolar disorder in familial risk based on several longitudinal high-risk offspring studies. Her review supported an evolution from non-specific disorders to bipolar disorder. Early childhood antecedents included internalizing disorders and sleep disorders and generally not externalizing disorders. In a majority of cases, early mood pathology was associated with the depressive component of bipolar disorder. Pediatric bipolar disorder is associated with a multitude of psychosocial and family impairments (see West et al., 2009, for review).

A dramatic development in the past decade has been a marked upsurge in the rate at which children are given the diagnosis of bipolar disorder. For example, Moreno et al. (2007) reported a 40-fold increase between 1994 and 2003 in the number of outpatient visits associated with the diagnosis of bipolar disorder in children. The *DSM-V* work group (DSM-5 Childhood and Adolescent Disorders Work Group, 2010) concluded that the classic adult phenotype of bipolar disorder does not present in pre-pubertal and adolescent children and proposed a new diagnostic category: temper dysregulation with dysphoria (TDD), characterized by severe recurrent temper outbursts in response to common stressors and a persistently negative mood (irritable, angry, and/or sad) between outbursts. The new research-based criteria were predicted to help clinicians differentiate children with these symptoms from those with bipolar disorder or ODD and to promote treatment research. TDD would be placed within the Mood Disorders section of the *DSM-V* manual despite the proposed criterion that onset is before age 10 years. Longitudinal studies suggest that TDD children are at increased risk for depressive and anxiety disorders in adulthood, but not bipolar disorder.

ETIOLOGY OF DEPRESSION IN CHILDHOOD AND ADOLESCENCE

"Having children, while a blessing and a miracle for many, also constitutes a potential burden for parents, and often particularly for the mother. . . .It is hardly surprising that many mothers become depressed. Nor is it surprising that the children of depressed mothers struggle."

–John C. Markowitz, from an editorial on "Depressed mothers, depressed children," 2008, p. 1086

What causes a young person to become depressed? Genetic factors play a role. Indeed, the genetic data on adults reviewed in Chapter 8 naturally apply to children and adolescents, since genetic influences are present from birth, though they may not

be expressed right away. Based primarily on older children and adolescents, genetically informed research (e.g., twin studies) has provided evidence for both gene-environment correlations and gene-environment interactions in the cause of depression in youth (see Brendgen et al., 2009, for review). Features of the social environment that have been found to be influenced by, or interact with (moderate), genetic factors that also contribute to depression include negative life events, problematic parent-child relationships, a history of maltreatment, family adversity, maternal punitive discipline, and peer rejection. For example, Lau and Eley (2008) reported that genetic factors that influence adolescent depressive symptoms were correlated with maternal punitive discipline (a gene-environment correlation) and also that maternal punitive discipline augmented the genetic influences on depressive symptoms (a gene x environment interaction). Thus, depression in children and adolescents is in part explained by genetic factors, with the remaining variance explained by environmental factors that might be unique to each child.

Studies of depression in children have focused on family and other relationships as sources of stress that might interact with a biological diathesis. Restifo and Bogels (2009) reviewed cross-sectional, prospective longitudinal, and experimental family risk factors that play a role in the development, maintenance, and course of youth depression. A caveat: many of these risk factors are associated with other internalizing and externalizing symptoms and disorders and most of the family risk factors are highly intercorrelated. For example, marital conflict has a stronger association with externalizing symptoms. Nonetheless, they found strong evidence to support a relation between numerous factors at multiple system levels and depressive symptoms. They concluded that the following risk factors are empirically supported: parental depression, child temperament, child cognitive style, parental rearing style, low parental support, attachment difficulties, difficulty establishing autonomy, parent-youth conflict, marital conflict (especially hostility and withdrawal, as opposed to calm discussion, humour, and physical closeness), a disengaged family system, and stressful events outside the family.

Restifo and Bogels (2009) also found support for several different hypothesized mechanisms. For example, several mechanisms have been proposed to explain the increased risk of parental depression on depression (and other disorders) in their offspring, including cognitive style of the parent, impaired parenting skills, poor social skills, a stressful family environment, and, of course, genetic transmission. They noted that the consensus is that several mechanisms of transmission are probable. Further, as noted previously, the impact of parental depression is not specific to youth depression.

According to Restifo and Bogels (2009), the parent-child subsystem has been the most investigated in the context of child depression and there is evidence for both unidirectional and bidirectional effects. Further, while there may be specific links between parent-child relationship factors and depressive disorders, many other studies do not support a *specific* relation between these factors and depression.

Selected studies further illustrate some of the risk factors identified by Restifo and Bogels (2009). For example, research conducted in Canada (Bergeron et al., 2000) suggests that having a parent with a depressive disorder is associated moderately with internalizing and externalizing disorders among children. Having a mother who is depressed increases the chances of a child being depressed. More recently, Tully, Iacono, and McGue (2008) found that having a depressed mother increased the risk of major depression and disruptive disorders in adolescents, indicating that there is a major environmental component to the risk conferred by depressed mothers (also see Silberg, Maes, & Eaves, 2010). Paternal depression was not found to increase risk for psychiatric disorders in these adolescents. However, a recent meta-analysis (Wilson & Durbin, 2010) concluded that paternal depression has a deleterious effect on parenting behaviour by fathers that is comparable to effects seen in depressed mothers. In a recent meta-analysis, McLeod, Weisz, & Wood (2007) reported that parenting accounts for 8% of the variance in child depression. Parental rejection and parental hostility toward the child were strongly related to child depression. On a positive note, Leckman-Westin, Cohen, and Stueve (2009) found that depressed mothers who nonetheless manifest demonstrations of affection and responsiveness to their toddlers have children who show no ill effects 10 years later. Nonetheless, factors other than parenting alone must account for much of the variance in childhood depression.

Children and adolescents experiencing major depression also have poor social skills and impaired relationships with siblings and friends (e.g., Lewinsohn et al., 1994). These behavioural patterns are likely to be both a cause and a consequence of depression. Depressed youngsters have fewer and less-satisfying contacts with their peers (Brendgen, Vitaro, Turgeon, & Poulin, 2002), who often reject them because they are not pleasant to be around. These negative interactions in turn aggravate the negative self-image and sense of worth that the depressed youngster already has (cf. Coyne, 1976). Recently, researchers from four universities in Quebec (Brendgen et al., 2009) assessed 336 twin pairs in kindergarten to determine the gene-environment interplay between peer rejection and depressive behaviour. They determined that an increased genetic predisposition for depression is related to a higher risk of peer rejection. They also found a gene-environment interaction (a suppression effect) interpreted to mean that peer rejection might foster depressive behaviour even in children without a genetic predisposition. Brendgen et al. (2009) concluded that their results "emphasize the importance of teaching social interactional skills that promote positive peer relations in all children to help prevent the development of depressive behaviour at a young age" (p. 1015).

Stress may operate by itself to produce depression in youngsters or it may operate in conjunction with vulnerability factors involving personality factors and maladaptive cognitive styles. Dumont and Provost (1999) at the Université du Québec à Trois-Rivières also examined protective factors associated with resiliency, and found that higher self-esteem and problem-focused coping seem to lessen the impact of stress on depression. Other Canadian research indicates that social support (Galambos et al., 2004) and the absence of the habit of dwelling on things when depressed (Abela, Brozina, & Haigh, 2002) may protect children and adolescents from depression. However, Kuyken, Watkins, Holden, and Cook (2006) reported that neuroticism acts as a risk factor for adolescent onset depression through an increased tendency toward brooding rumination in response to depressed mood.

Personality research on depression in children and adolescents tends to parallel research conducted with adults. Investigators at McGill University have shown that self-criticism and dependency are associated with depressive symptoms in adolescents (Fichman, Koestner, & Zuroff, 1996, 1997). Similarly, socially prescribed perfectionism (i.e., the belief that others expect us to be perfect) is associated with depressive symptoms and suicide ideation in Canadian youths (e.g., Blankstein et al., 2007; Hewitt et al., 2002).

An investigation by Abela (2001) from McGill University found that a negative attributional style interacted with the experience of stressful events to predict increases in depression among children in Grade 7 but not among children in Grade 3. Perhaps negative attributional styles have more impact on older children, who are more aware of the long-term implications of negative attributions involving personal weaknesses. Other findings reported by Abela provide general support for hopelessness models of depression (Abela, 2002; Abela & Sarin, 2002). Brozina and Abela (2006) conducted a six-week longitudinal study of children in grades 3 to 6 and demonstrated that the experience of daily hassles interacted with depressive attributional style to predict increases in symptoms of depression and anxiety over time. Recently, Lumley and Harkness (2009) from the University of Guelph and Queen's University reported that higher levels of mother emotional maltreatment and father emotional and physical abuse were associated with a depressotypic cognitive organization (i.e., tightly connected negative schemas and loosely connected positive schemas) in young adults. Further, the depressotypic schema organization mediated the relation between maltreatment and depression. Similarly, Mezulis, Funasaki, Charbonneau, and Hyde (2010) reported that adolescent girls showed stronger associations between stress and depression over time and that the cognitive vulnerability stress interaction was a significant predictor of girls' depression trajectory but not boys'. The gender difference in depression was highlighted in Chapter 8. Jacobs, Reinecke, Gollan, and Kane (2008) reviewed longitudinal studies of the most researched cognitive vulnerability factors and depression among youth and concluded that "the central hypotheses of cognitive vulnerability models have yet to be put to the test" (p. 776).

TREATMENT OF CHILDHOOD AND ADOLESCENT DEPRESSION

Far less research has been done on therapy with depressed children and adolescents than on therapy with adults (Hammen, 1997), perhaps because young people don't attract as much adult attention as those who act out, such as youngsters with conduct disorder (Kaslow & Thompson, 1998).

DRUG THERAPIES Some studies suggest that drug therapies are not very effective for child and adolescent depression. For example, Hazell et al. (1995) conducted a meta-analysis of tricyclic antidepressant RCTs over the preceding 20 years and reported that 37% of participants had responded to placebo and only 38% to tricyclics. A more recent review by researchers at the Royal Ottawa Hospital indicated that there is only limited evidence of robust, effective therapeutic interventions, and an interpretive problem is that placebos have yielded a high rate of improvement (Milin, Walker, & Chow, 2003), a finding confirmed recently by Bridge et al. (2009) in a meta-analysis of antidepressant trials conducted since 1995, all using second-generation antidepressants. In the latter meta-analysis, the mean response to placebo was 48%, and to active medications only 58%. However, Bridge et al. (2009) suggested that differences between studies are due less to differences in the efficacy of antidepressants than to differences in response to placebo.

Concerns have also been expressed about the safety of antidepressant use in young people. On February 3, 2004, Health Canada issued a public warning, advising individuals under 18 to consult with their physicians before taking SSRIs and SNRIs (serotonin-norepinephrine reuptake inhibitors) because of safety concerns involving an increased rate of "suicide-related events," suicides, and suicide attempts in adolescents who took certain of these newer classes of drugs. The drugs identified were Prozac, Paxil, Celexa, Luvox, Remeron, Zoloft, and Effexor. In Canada, the drugs are not approved for use with children and adolescents; however, they are often prescribed in a practice called "off label use." Britain and the United States took similar actions (Picard, 2004). The U.S. FDA appointed an advisory panel that held public hearings on the issue.

The link between antidepressants and increased risk of suicide and violent behaviour was suggested by British psychiatrist David Healy (2003), who, in his testimony at the U.S. hearings, was also critical of the volume of prescriptions written for children and teenagers. In 2000, Healy was awarded a senior position at the Centre for Addiction and Mental Health (a University of Toronto teaching hospital), but the appointment was revoked following a speech he delivered on SSRIs and suicide. Although the centre denied the decision had anything to do with alleged pressure from Eli Lilly, the maker of Prozac and a significant donor to the centre, the ensuing major debate about academic freedom thrust the issue of antidepressants and suicide into public consciousness (Picard, 2003).

A meta-analysis of 24 placebo-controlled antidepressant pediatric trials conducted by the FDA (Hammad, Laughren, & Racoosin, 2006) found a two-fold (4% versus 2%) increased risk for suicidal behaviour or suicidal ideation with antidepressants only when the data from all the available trials were combined. No completed suicides were reported. The FDA mandated that a boxed warning be put on the labels of all antidepressants but stopped short of prohibiting their use. Bridge et al. (2007) also conducted a meta-analysis of antidepressant drug treatments for children and adolescents in light

of concerns that antidepressants pose a risk for increased suicide. It was concluded that antidepressants were effective in treating major depressive disorder, anxiety disorders, and obsessive-compulsive disorders. However, the effects were weakest for major depressive disorder. For children younger than 12 years with major depression, only Prozac showed benefit over placebo. Although there was increased risk difference of suicidal ideation and attempts across all trials and indication for drug versus placebo, there were no completed suicides. Bridge et al. (2007) concluded, "Benefits of antidepressants appear to be much greater than risks from suicidal ideation/suicide attempt across indications, although comparison of benefit to risk varies as a function of indication, age, chronicity, and study conditions" (p. 1683).

Katz et al. (2008) from the University of Manitoba examined databases to determine changes in the rates of antidepressant prescription, use of health services, and outcomes in children and adolescents relative to young adults in the nine years before and two years after the Health Canada warning. Following the warning, the rate of antidepressant prescriptions decreased, ambulatory visits due to depression decreased, and the rate of completed suicides among children and adolescents rose significantly. The authors interpreted the findings to mean that health advisories can "have unintended consequences on the provision of care, delivery of health services and clinical outcomes" (Katz et al., 2008, p. 1005).

Despite conflicting results and interpretations (recall issues related to meta-analysis, and selective publication and the "file drawer effect" discussed in Chapter 5), many experts agree that the efficacy of the antidepressant fluoxetine in the treatment of adolescents with major depressive disorder is now well supported (see Vitiello, 2009). The issue of a possible link between SSRIs and suicide risk in depressed children and adolescents is still a matter of protracted debate (e.g., Brent, 2009a; Healy, 2009).

PSYCHOLOGICAL TREATMENT Most psychosocial interventions for children and adolescents are modelled after clinical research with adults. Interpersonal therapy (IPT), for instance, has been modified for use with depressed adolescents, focusing on issues of concern to adolescents, such as peer pressure, separation from parents, and authority issues. IPT is quite effective in treating depression in adolescents and has led to significant improvements in interpersonal functioning (e.g., Mufson, Weissman, Moreau, & Garfinkel, 1999). Recently, Swartz et al. (2008) conducted an RCT that compared IPT for depressed mothers relative to treatment as usual and examined the effects on their depressed school-age children. Maternal improvement as a function of IPT preceded reduced depression in their children, suggesting that changes in the mothers' depression mediated child outcomes at nine-month follow-up.

Social skills training can help depressed young people by providing them with the behavioural and verbal means to gain access to pleasant, reinforcing environments, such as making friends and getting along with peers. Some depressed children know how to relate appropriately to others but are inhibited from doing so by negative thoughts and physiological arousal, suggesting that cognitive interventions and, for some, such procedures as relaxation training could also be useful. Overall, treatments that include social skills training, problem-solving, and cognitive techniques similar to those employed successfully with adults are effective.

Treatment of depressed children and adolescents may be best accomplished with a broad-spectrum approach that involves not only the child or adolescent but also the family and the school (Stark et al., 1998). Therapy might well have to focus on a depressed parent in addition to the depressed child. Depressed parents probably communicate to their children their own pessimistic views of themselves and the world. This approach also highlights the importance of teaching the young person ways to cope with interpersonal stress via more effective overt behaviour; for example, interacting more effectively with others and being appropriately assertive with overbearing peers. The involvement of the family is now recognized as important when dealing with younger people who are depressed. Unfortunately, a recent review (Restifo & Bogels, 2009) concluded that few RCTs target family factors or involve family members in the treatment and those that do target only a few of the family risk factors that have been identified. The majority of studies have targeted the parent-child relationship. Restifo and Bogels (2009) suggested that key elements to target in family-based treatment could include communication, problem-solving, parent-youth conflict, and parental support.

A highly structured CBT group intervention, the Adolescent Coping With Depression course (CWD), involves instruction in coping with depression and was found to be effective with depressed adolescents, particularly when parents were involved in treatment (Clarke et al., 1992; Lewinsohn et al., 1990). The skills trained in the original CWD focus on social skills, skills in restructuring negative cognitions, and behavioural activation to increase pleasant events ("activity scheduling"). Adding a parent group component to the CWD course for adolescents can also be beneficial (e.g., Lewinsohn et al., 1990). Parents are taught communication and conflict resolution skills that they subsequently practise with their children. Kaufman et al. (2005) examined possible mediators of the efficacy of group CBT for depressed adolescents with comorbid conduct disorder: six specific to CBT (e.g., negative cognitions, engagement in pleasurable activities), and two non-specific measures (therapeutic alliance and group cohesion). Participants were randomly assigned to the CWD or a life skills control condition. Change on the Automatic Thoughts Questionnaire (Kendall & Hollon, 1980) appeared to mediate treatment effects on depressive symptoms. Although therapeutic alliance was higher among adolescents in the treatment group by the third session, it did not predict reduced depression. Thus, reducing negative thinking is possibly the mechanism through which the CBT intervention reduces depression. Regardless of the mechanism, the CWD course is clearly the best-studied psychoeducational intervention for the

treatment and prevention of depression. It has been adapted for different goals, contexts, and target populations and is used in routine practice in several countries. Its efficacy has been examined in 25 RCTs, including 8 with adolescents. Recently, Cuijpers, Munoz, Clarke, and Lewinsohn (2008) conducted a meta-analysis of these studies (6 aimed at the prevention of new cases of major depression and 18 examining treatment of depression) and concluded that the CWD is efficacious for both treatment and prevention of depression in adolescents, although the effect sizes were smaller than the effect sizes typically found for psychotherapies for adult depression, perhaps because the intervention is often used for complex target groups.

There are relatively few evidence-based psychosocial treatments for children with bipolar disorder. However, Pavuluri, West, and colleagues (e.g., West et al., 2009) developed a unique 12-session child- and family-focused CBT therapy for children aged 8–12 with bipolar disorder and their families. The program involves intensive work with both children and parents integrating psychoeducation, CBT, and IPT across multiple domains. A preliminary report of a group adaptation (West et al., 2009) demonstrated that the approach conducted alongside pharmacotherapy possibly helps remission of symptoms, and increases coping and well-being in children and parents. However, more rigorous tests in RCTs are needed.

MEDICATION AND PSYCHOLOGICAL TREATMENT Several recently completed, publicly funded controlled clinical trials have assessed the relative effectiveness of antidepressant medication, CBT, and their combination for the treatment of adolescent major depression. The Treatment for Adolescents with Depression Study (TADS), funded by the National Institute of Mental Health (NIMH), was the first such trial (TADS Team, 2004). It was designed to evaluate the relative effectiveness of fluoxetine, CBT, and their combination across acute treatment, maintenance treatment, and naturalistic follow-up periods. The findings are complex and surprising (see Vitiello, 2009, for a summary); however, March and Vitiello (2009) recently asked, "What are the take-home messages from TADS?" They concluded, "The combination of fluoxetine and CBT appears to be superior to both CBT monotherapy and fluoxetine monotherapy as a treatment for moderate to severe major depressive disorder in adolescents" (March & Vitiello, 2009, p. 1118). With respect to suicidality, the findings suggested a protective role of CBT when combined with medication (Vitiello, 2009). There were also persistent benefits over one year of naturalistic follow-up after the six to nine months of treatment (TADS Team, 2009).

The Adolescent Depression and Psychotherapy Trial (ADAPT) funded by the U.K. National Health System tested the effect of adding CBT to SSRI medication over a seven-month period (Goodyer et al., 2007). By the end of the 28 weeks, 53% of the clients receiving the combined treatment were much or very much improved versus 61% of those on SSRI only. The groups did not differ in incidence of suicide attempts. Vitiello (2009) suggested that the greater severity of depression in the

ADAPT sample compared with TADS possibly explains the apparent different outcomes. The NIMH-funded Treatment of Resistant Depression in Adolescents Study (TORDIA) is the first multi-site study to focus on real-world second-step treatment for treatment-resistant adolescent depression (Brent, 2009b; Brent et al., 2008). Adolescents who had been treated unsuccessfully with an SSRI were randomized to antidepressant treatment or medication plus CBT. Again, the findings are complex. However, the combined treatment was generally more effective than medication only, especially for adolescents with comorbid anxiety and/or ADHD. Adolescents who experienced suicidal events were less likely to respond to treatment (27.1% versus 51.0%). A history of abuse was associated with a poorer response to CBT.

The findings of these recent multi-site trials taken together with the meta-analyses of all controlled trials indicate that antidepressant medication and CBT for adolescent depression are efficacious; however, the treatment effects are much more modest than expected and hoped for. The effects are summarized succinctly by Vitiello (2009):

> For about one third of depressed youths treatment does make a substantial difference, alleviating depression and returning them to normal functioning. Another third, however, improve on non-specific clinical contact (placebo condition) whereas the remaining third do not benefit substantially and remain depressed. This last group is at risk for persistent depression, incomplete remission, and subsequent relapse. (p. 394)

Vitiello (2009) recommended matching treatment "to individual characteristics and needs" in order to increase treatment effectiveness.

PREVENTION OF CHILDHOOD AND ADOLESCENT DEPRESSION

Can depression in children and adolescents actually be prevented? In a meta-analysis of 30 studies, Horowitz and Garber (2006) highlighted the fact that there is wide variability in the success of these studies and concluded that most effective interventions are more accurately described as treatment, as opposed to prevention. The effect sizes for universal programs including all children were only small in magnitude. However, Horowitz and Garber (2006) concluded that stronger effects are more likely when the focus is on high-risk children and adolescents. They identified four factors associated with high risk: (1) being female; (2) being the offspring of depressed parents; (3) having elevated symptoms of depression and/or anxiety; and (4) exposure to key stressors such as parental divorce or loss. More recently, Gladstone and Beardslee (2009) reviewed recent programs on the prevention of clinical diagnoses of depression in youth. The programs were based on CBT and IPT traditions and included family-based strategies. Successful programs tended to be derived from evidence-based manualized treatment programs for depression in youths that involved careful training of the people implementing the programs, coupled with a determination of fidelity to the intervention protocols. However, even in a trial of the Coping With Stress course, a prevention program derived from the CWD strategy (see Clarke et al., 2001), the size of the effect diminished over time. Gladstone and Beardslee (2009) recommended that future research consider moderators of program effects (e.g., risk status, sex, and stressors) and interventions to improve the family environment.

Few universal interventions have proven effective (Gladstone & Beardslee, 2009). For example, Spence, Sheffield, and Donovan (2005) examined the long-term outcome (four years) of a school-based, universal approach to the prevention of adolescent (1,500 Grade 8 students) depression. Although short-term positive effects were demonstrated, adolescents who completed the teacher-administered CBT intervention did not differ significantly from those in a monitoring control condition in terms of changes in depression symptoms, problem solving, attributional style, emotional well-being, and social adjustment from pre-intervention to the four-year follow-up. In another school-based universal prevention program, Possel, Seeman, and Hautzinger (2008) reported the surprising finding there were negative effects on depressive symptoms in Grade 8 boys who had more severe depressive symptoms at baseline. Clearly, there is no simple formula for producing long-term preventive effects for depression in children.

SUMMARY

- Attention-deficit/hyperactivity disorder and conduct disorder are marked by undercontrolled behaviour. ADHD is a persistent pattern of inattention and/or impulsivity that is judged to be more frequent and more severe than what is typically observed in youngsters of a given age. There is growing evidence for genetic and neurological factors in its etiology, but parents can be helpful in improving the behaviour of children with ADHD. Stimulant drugs, such as Ritalin, and reinforcement for staying on task have some effectiveness in reducing the intensity of ADHD.

- Conduct disorder is often a precursor to anti-social personality disorder in adulthood, although many children carrying the diagnosis do not progress to that extreme. It is characterized by high and widespread levels of aggression, lying, theft, vandalism, cruelty to other people and to animals, and other acts that violate laws and social norms. Among the apparent etiological factors are a genetic predisposition, inadequate learning of moral awareness, modelling and direct reinforcement of anti-social behaviour, and living in impoverished and crime-ridden areas.

The most promising approach to treating young people with conduct disorder involves intensive intervention in multiple systems, including the family, school, and peer systems.

- Learning disorders are diagnosed when a child fails to develop to the degree expected by his or her intellectual level in a specific academic, language, or motor skill area. These disorders are usually identified and treated within the school system rather than through mental health clinics. There is mounting evidence that the most widely studied of the learning disorders, dyslexia, has genetic and other biological components. The most widespread interventions for dyslexia, however, are educational.

- The diagnostic criteria for mental retardation are subaverage intellectual functioning and deficits in adaptive behaviour, with onset before the age of 18. Contemporary analyses focus more on the strengths of individuals with mental retardation than on their assignment to a particular level of severity. This shift in emphasis is associated with increased efforts to design psychological and educational interventions that make the most of individuals' abilities.

- The more severe forms of mental retardation have a biological basis, such as the chromosomal trisomy that causes Down syndrome. Certain infectious diseases in the pregnant mother (e.g., HIV, rubella, and syphilis) and illnesses that affect the child directly (e.g., encephalitis) can stunt cognitive and social development, as can malnutrition, severe falls, and automobile accidents that injure the brain. Environmental factors are considered the principal causes of mild retardation. Thus far, no brain damage has been detected in people with mild retardation, who often are from lower-class homes and live in an environment of social and educational deprivation.

- Researchers try to prevent mild retardation by giving children at risk through impoverished circumstances special preschool training and social opportunities. The best-known and largest of these programs is Head Start, which has been shown to be helpful in equipping children to benefit from school. Many children with mental retardation who would formerly have been institutionalized are now being educated in the public schools under the provisions of various laws. In addition, using applied behavioural analysis, self-instructional training, and modelling, behaviour therapists have been able to treat successfully many of the behavioural problems of individuals with mental retardation and to improve their intellectual functioning.

- Autistic disorder begins before the age of two and a half. The major symptoms are extreme autistic aloneness, a failure to relate to other people; communication problems consisting of either a failure to learn any language or speech irregularities, such as echolalia and pronoun reversal; and preservation of sameness, an obsessive desire to keep daily routines and surroundings exactly the same. A biological cause is suspected for a number of reasons: its onset is very early; family and twin studies give compelling evidence of a genetic predisposition; abnormalities have been found in the brains of autistic children.

- The most promising treatments for autism involve procedures that rely on modelling and operant conditioning. Although the prognosis for autistic children remains poor in general, recent work suggests that intensive behavioural treatment involving the parents as their children's therapists may allow some of these children to participate meaningfully in normal social intercourse. Recent drug treatments, notably those that lower serotonin, show little promise in treating the core deficits of the disorder.

- Some children and adolescents experience difficulties that involve overcontrolled behaviours. Anxiety disorders and related fears in children reflect overcontrolled tendencies. These disorders include separation anxiety disorder, school phobia, and social phobia. Theorists seeking to account for the etiology of these disorders are increasingly focusing on the role of attachment style, first described by theorists such as Ainsworth and Bowlby. Family factors are also seen as important in the etiology and treatment of anxiety disorders in children and adolescents. By and large, treatments for children are similar to those used with adults, including the role of exposure to the feared object or situation.

- Various types of depression are regarded as forms of overcontrolled behaviour. The core symptoms of depression in children and adults are similar, though it is recognized that there are age-specific features, not only distinguishing between children and adults with depression, but also between children and adolescents with depression. Extensive research has shown the negative impact of exposure to a depressed parent, as this factor is linked with depression in children. As is the case with research on adults, research has examined the role of stress in childhood and adolescent depression, either by itself or in combination with personality factors such as self-criticism, dependency, and attributional style.

KEY TERMS

REFLECTIONS: PAST, PRESENT, AND FUTURE

- Effective early intervention programs for children at risk for developing conduct disorder probably require the co-operation of multiple social service and mental health agencies that employ "individualized care" or "wraparound" services involving interdisciplinary teams that develop individualized and comprehensive plans. Such programs would employ multiple-component, flexible treatments that would involve the child, the family, and the school (see Frick, 2001; Wicks-Nelson & Israel, 2006). Do you think that in some cases multiple interventions will be required throughout the youngster's life, including into adulthood (see Waddell, Lipman, & Offord, 1999)? Would any intervention work with those children who are "bad to the bone" (Barovick, 1999); that is, who are predisposed to become the worst psychopaths as adults? The approach we are recommending would be extremely expensive. Would it be worth the cost in the long run if it could "save" an Eric Harris or a Dylan Klebold (the teenagers responsible for the massacre at Columbine High School in April 1999)?

- With respect to learning disabilities, it is often stated that most professionals use a "definition of exclusion." What does that mean? What are the implications?

- We all should treat intellectually handicapped children and adults with decency and dignity and facilitate their participation in our communities. What could you do that would help them develop a sense of purpose, pride, and self-esteem?

- Many children with autism also have an anxiety or mood disorder. What are the implications for the treatment of autistic children? Design a comprehensive treatment program for autistic children with comorbid anxiety and depression.

- The treatment and legal rights of children must be recognized and protected. Under what circumstances, if any, should it be permissible for clinicians to use punishment (e.g., a squirt of water in the face) in an attempt to eliminate self-injury in autistic children? Who should decide? (See Chapter 18 for a discussion of ethical dilemmas.)

- An anxious attachment style among infants seems to be a risk factor for the subsequent development of anxiety disorders. Do you think that a prevention program will be developed in the future that will target such high-risk infants at a very early age? What form would such an intervention take? What other risk factors should be targeted?

- Separation/loss is a major theme in many theories of depression. What are the implications of this theme for the many children who lost a parent in the September 11 terrorist attacks on the United States? Do you think that we will ever be able to prevent depression in vulnerable children?

AGING AND PSYCHOLOGICAL DISORDERS

"Oh God, don't let me die stupid."
—Robertson Davies, expressing his concerns about cognitive declines associated with aging, from the *Toronto Star*, October 20, 1989

"Please, my near & dear ones, forgive me & understand. I hope this potion works.
My spirit is already in another country & my body has become a damn nuisance.
I have been so fortunate."
—from the suicide note of Canadian author Margaret Laurence, who was diagnosed with terminal cancer and took her own life via a drug overdose at age 60 (see King, 1997, p. 388)

"Geriatric mental health is one of the most underresearched and misunderstood areas of all health care. It's where children's mental health was 20 years ago."
—Dr. Benoit Mulsant, Director of the Geriatric Mental Health Program at Toronto's Centre for Addiction and Mental Health (CAMH, 2007)

Gershon Iskowitz, Canadian 1921–1988, *Untitled* (*Portrait of a Scholar*), 1948, oil on canvas board, 51.0 × 40.7 cm (unframed) Art Gallery of Ontario, Toronto. Gift of Friends of the Gallery, 2000 © The Gershon Iskowitz Foundation

ISSUES, CONCEPTS, AND METHODS IN THE STUDY OF OLDER ADULTS

OLD AGE AND BRAIN DISORDERS

OLD AGE AND PSYCHOLOGICAL DISORDERS

TREATMENT AND CARE OF OLDER ADULTS

ISSUES SPECIFIC TO THERAPY WITH OLDER ADULTS

SUMMARY

THE STORY of Brendan Shanahan, the retired Canadian NHL hockey player, and his father, Donal Shanahan, illustrates with poignancy the symptoms and difficulties associated with disorders related to aging.

Brendan's father never played hockey himself, but being a hockey dad, he was just as fascinated as his son with this truly Canadian sport. "My father was always there for me, driving me to practices and games religiously."

Brendan was barely 14 when he started noticing a change in his father's behaviour; the year was 1983. Early on, his father showed signs of confusion that gradually became worse. A full year went by before Donal Shanahan was diagnosed with Alzheimer's disease at age 52. During this time, Brendan recalls feeling frustrated and impatient. "I didn't know what was happening and couldn't understand. I never heard of Alzheimer's until my dad was diagnosed with it—even then, the whole thing was foreign to me."

The symptoms appeared gradually as the disease took its course. Often, simple tasks became big challenges. Brendan remembers his father being puzzled by a pen. "He had forgotten how to use a pen and would hold it the wrong way. Driving was also a problem and he was no longer confident driving me to the games. Sometimes he would get lost getting to or from the game—other times he didn't know where to insert the car keys. On my 16th birthday, we drove to the licensing bureau to get my driving permit. It was the last time my father drove a car; he was 54." (See www.alzheimer.ca.)

Donal Shanahan passed away when Brendan was 21. Brendan Shanahan has been an active fundraiser for research on Alzheimer's disease.

If you are fortunate, you will grow old one day. As you do, physiological changes are inevitable, and there may be many emotional and mental changes as well. Are aged people at higher risk for mental disorders than young people? Are earlier emotional problems, such as anxiety and depression, likely to become worse in old age? Do these emotional problems develop in people who did not have them when younger?

Most segments of North American society tend to have certain assumptions about old age. We fear that we will become doddering and befuddled. We worry that our sex lives will become unsatisfying. This chapter examines such issues and considers whether some therapies are better suited than others to deal with the psychological problems of older adults. We shall consider also whether, as life expectancy extends well into the seventies and beyond, society is devoting enough intellectual and monetary resources to studying aging and helping older adults.

In contrast to the esteem in which they are held in most Asian countries, older adults are generally not treated very well in North America, and numerous myths abound. The process of growing old, although inevitable for us all, is resented, even abhorred, by many. The presence of negative aging stereotypes may account for the fact that most people, including older people, report that they feel younger than they actually are (see Teuscher, 2009). This tendency is called the **subjective age bias**. Younger subjective age is linked with greater life satisfaction and a host of other positive outcomes (Teuscher, 2009). A recent study from British Columbia found that positive health experiences and greater health satisfaction are linked with lower subjective age (Hubley & Russell, 2009). Clearly, the tendency to apply negative aging stereotypes to oneself can have severe consequences. A recent longitudinal study found that application of negative aging stereotypes to oneself predicts a greater likelihood of experiencing subsequent cardiovascular events and related health problems (Levy et al., 2009). So, it is better to feel younger than you are, and you should not believe negative aging stereotypes, nor should you apply them to yourself.

The general public endorses many mistaken beliefs about the elderly. For instance, considerable mythology has surrounded sexuality and aging, the principal assumption being that at the age of 65 sex becomes improper, unsatisfying, and even impossible. Evidence indicates otherwise. Barring serious physical disability, older people, well into their eighties and beyond, are capable of deriving enjoyment from sexual intercourse and other kinds of lovemaking.

The social problems of aging may be especially severe for women. Even with the consciousness-raising of the past four decades, our society does not readily accept in women the wrinkles and sagging that become more and more prominent with advancing years. Although grey hair at the temples and even a bald head are often considered distinguished in a man, signs of aging in women are not valued in society. The cosmetics and plastic-surgery industries make billions of dollars each year exploiting the fear inculcated in women about looking their age.

The physical realities of aging are complicated by **ageism**, which can be defined as discrimination against any person, young or old, based on chronological age. Ageism can be seen when a professor in his or her sixties is considered too old to continue teaching at a university or when a person over 75 is ignored in a social gathering on the assumption that he or she has nothing to contribute to the conversation. Like any prejudice, ageism ignores the diversity among people in favour of employing stereotypes (Gatz & Pearson, 1988).

Mental health professionals have until recently paid little attention to the psychological problems of older adults. This situation is gradually changing, as illustrated by the formation in 2002 of the Canadian Coalition for Seniors' Mental Health (see www.ccsmh.ca). This group is playing a vitally important role in providing key resources to the Canadian public. Grants from the Public Health Agency of Canada have enabled coalition members to provide a series of guides available for download from their website. The four guides compiled thus far focus on the following issues among older adults: delirium, depression, suicide prevention, and mental health issues for those in long-term care homes.

Another important initiative with mental health implications is the Canadian Longitudinal Study on Aging (CLSA), launched in 2004. The CLSA has provided a wealth of basic information about healthy aging, health care use, and risk factors for diseases and disabilities. Its goals include preventive interventions and cost-efficient treatments. Hebert (2003) has indicated that this nationwide research initiative is vital in light of what he refers to as "The Big Boom," which is the impact that Canada's baby boomers will have on the country's health system when they become senior citizens en masse in less than a decade from now.

In the past, mental health professionals operated under the popular misconceptions that intellectual deterioration is prevalent and inevitable, that depression among old people is widespread and untreatable, and that sex is a lost cause. Although those who provide mental health services are probably not extremely ageist (Gatz & Pearson, 1988), their attitudes and practices merit special attention because of the influence they have on policies that affect the lives of older adults. Since the 1980s, many schools and universities that prepare people for the health professions have added research and training in gerontology to their curricula, yet there is still a dearth of professionals committed primarily to serving the needs of older adults (Knight, 2004). The need for greater understanding is underscored by a survey conducted in Kingston, Ontario, that showed that family physicians feel less prepared to identify older patients with psychological problems than younger patients with psychological problems (Mackenzie, Gekoski, & Knox, 1999). They also reported that they were much less likely to treat or to refer older patients for treatment, and they rated psychotherapy as less effective with older people. These findings are disturbing because while elderly people seldom seek help for psychological problems, when they do, they are most likely to turn to their physicians.

The "old" are usually defined as those over the age of 65. The decision to use this age was set largely by social policies, not because age 65 is some critical point at which the physiological and psychological processes of aging suddenly begin. To have some rough demarcation points, gerontologists usually divide people over age 65 into three groups: the young-old, those aged 65 to 74; the old-old, those aged 75 to 84; and the oldest-old, those over age 85. The health of these groups differs in important ways. According to a report by the National Advisory Council on Aging (Harper, 1999), in 1998 about 3.7 million Canadians (12.3% of the population) were 65 or older.

This number is expected to jump to about 10 million by 2041. A report by Statistics Canada (2005) based on national and provincial data suggested a rapid increase in the proportion of senior citizens; it is estimated that around 2015, for the first time in Canada, the number of senior citizens will be greater than the number of children. The old-old segment of the Canadian population (those between 75 and 84) is growing at a rate of 3.5% per year, relative to the general growth rate of 1% (Gnaedinger, 1989). The changes in Canada reflect a worldwide trend. At present, it is estimated that there are 600 million people in the world who are 60 years of age or older. It is projected that by the year 2050, that figure will grow to almost 2 billion, so that about 21% of the world's population—roughly 1 in 5 people—will be 60 or older (Sowers & Rowe, 2007). Thus, it is important to examine what we know about the psychological and neuropsychological issues facing older adults and to expose some of our misconceptions about aging. It is also important to ensure that we have adequate services and access to psychological treatment for elderly people suffering from mental illness. Unfortunately, Canada seems underprepared in this regard. A recent survey of clinical and counselling programs conducted by researchers at the University of Calgary found no program in Canada with a formal concentration on geropsychology (Konnert, Dobson, & Watt, 2009). Training activities, when they exist, focus on diagnosis and assessment of older people rather than therapeutic intervention; however, Konnert et al. (2009) concluded that the overall breadth and depth of exposure to aging content is quite superficial when it does exist. In Chapter 18, we will discuss everyone's right to treatment as a key tenet in psychology; clearly, much more is needed in the years to come in order to make certain that our mentally ill elderly have access to treatment.

In this chapter, we review some general concepts and topics critical to the study of aging. We look next at brain disorders of old age. Then, we examine psychological disorders—most of which were discussed earlier—focusing especially on how these disorders are manifested in old age. Finally, we discuss general issues of treatment and care for older adults.

ISSUES, CONCEPTS, AND METHODS IN THE STUDY OF OLDER ADULTS

Theory and research bearing on older adults require an understanding of several specialized issues, ranging from diversity among old people to problems unique to old age.

DIVERSITY IN OLDER ADULTS

The word "diversity" is well suited to the older population. Not only are older people different from one another, but they are more different from one another than are individuals in any other age group. People tend to become less alike as they grow older. That all old people are alike is a prejudice held by many people. The many differences among people who are 65 and older will become increasingly evident as you read this chapter.

Advancing age need not lead to a curtailment of activities. Hazel McCallion, the mayor of Mississauga, Ontario, celebrated her 89th birthday in 2010. She is one of Canada's most active citizens. Mike Cassese/Sun Media Corporation.

AGE, COHORT, AND TIME-OF-MEASUREMENT EFFECTS

Chronological age is not as simple a variable in psychological research as it might seem. Because other factors associated with age may be at work, we must be cautious when we attribute differences in age groups solely to aging. In the field of aging, as in studies of earlier development, a distinction is made among three kinds of effects (see Table 16.1):

- **Age effects** are the consequences of being a given chronological age.
- **Cohort effects** are the consequences of having been born in a given year and having grown up during a particular time period with its own unique pressures, problems, challenges, and opportunities. For instance, the 1991 Canadian Study of Health and Aging is a national cohort study that investigated the prevalence and characteristics of dementia and Alzheimer's disease in a sample of more than 9,000 people who were aged 65 or older when assessed in 1991 (see Canadian Perspectives 16.1 for more information). A cohort effect exists if these people have some factor that distinguishes them from people who turned 65 or older at an earlier date (e.g., in 1965) or a later date (e.g., 2005).

TABLE 16.1
AGE, COHORT, AND TIME-OF-MEASUREMENT EFFECTS

Age Effects	Cohort Effects	Time-of-Measurement Effects
The consequences of being a chronological age (e.g., Jewish boys are bar mitzvahed at age 13).	The consequences of having been born in a given year and having grown up during a time (e.g., people who invested money in the stock market in the late 1990s viewed investments in equities as a reasonably safe and very lucrative place to put their money—unlike people who lost a lot of money in the bear markets of the 1930s or late 1960s).	The consequences of the effects that particular factor can have at a particular time period (e.g., people responding in the 1990s to surveys about their sexual behaviour were more likely to be frank than people responding to the same questions in the 1950s since public discussions of sex were much more the norm in the 1990s).

CANADIAN PERSPECTIVES 16.1
THE CANADIAN STUDY OF HEALTH AND AGING AND THE CANADIAN LONGITUDINAL STUDY ON AGING

The Canadian Study of Health and Aging (CSHA) began in February 1991 and the first phase of data collection ended in May 1992. This nationwide project is coordinated by the University of Ottawa and Health Canada's Division of Aging and Seniors. It involves researchers from at least 18 universities throughout Canada and 9,008 seniors aged 65 or older drawn from 36 communities, as well as 1,255 institutionalized elderly people. Participants were selected by random sampling with stratification by area. They underwent interviews and medical examinations as part of being in this study. The 45-minute interview focused on gathering demographic data and information on daily living and health status. Participants were also administered the modified version of the Mini-Mental State Examination (MMSE). The medical examination focused on confirming whether dementia was evident. It included neuropsychological testing and a structured interview with an examination. The test battery assessed memory, abstract thinking, judgement, language, recognition of familiar objects, attention, and psychomotor speed (CSHA Working Group, 1994a).

The CSHA website outlines the four main goals of this massive project:

1. to use a common research protocol to estimate prevalence of dementia in Canadians aged 65 and older
2. to identify risk factors associated with Alzheimer's disease
3. to examine patterns of caring for Canadians with dementia
4. to develop a uniform database for subsequent longitudinal investigations

Several noteworthy findings from this investigation are described in other parts of this chapter. Other noteworthy results include the following:

1. The prevalence of Alzheimer's disease and other forms of dementia is 8% in Canada. Furthermore, another 16.8% of Canadians who are 65 or over have some cognitive impairment but no dementia, with many of these people having circumscribed memory loss (see Graham et al., 1997). This study found that cognitive impairment in the absence of dementia (i.e., subclinical dementia) still involves a need for institutional care, and follow-up research showed that subclinical dementia predicted negative outcomes such as death and dementia over a five-year period (Tuokko et al., 2003). MMSE scores that are low but still in the normal range have been shown to predict death and institutionalization (St. John et al., 2002).
2. The onset of dementia is usually gradual. A study of 1,132 CSHA participants with dementia found that only 11.5% had dementia with an acute, sudden onset. A more sudden onset was associated with less chance of institutionalization but greater vascular risk and reduced survival rates (King, Devichand, & Rockwood, 2005).
3. Approximately one half of Canadians with dementia are institutionalized, and the other half are community residents. Most primary caregivers are female and married. Most informal caregivers (i.e., family member or friend) for seniors in the community are wives, while adult daughters are most likely to be the informal caregiver for institutionalized seniors (CSHA Working Group, 1994a).

4. A re-evaluation in 1996 of the original participants revealed that there are more than 60,000 new cases of dementia per year in Canada (CSHA Working Group, 2000).
5. Deficits identified via neuropsychological tests (e.g., short delayed verbal recall) predicted subsequent Alzheimer's disease 5 and 10 years later (Tierney, Yao, Kiss, & McDowell, 2005).
6. Physical frailty is associated with greater levels of psychiatric illness, while older age, in and of itself, is not associated with greater odds of psychiatric illness (Andrew & Rockwood, 2007). Frailty is defined as having multiple, interacting illnesses. A history of heavy smoking is one of the most reliable predictors of physical frailty and greater smoking is linked with greater frailty (Hubbard, Searle, Mitnitski, & Rockwood, 2009).
7. Among elderly people with some cognitive impairment but not dementia, hypertension is associated with increased likelihood of progressing to dementia (Oveisgharan & Hachinski, 2010).

The success of this study paved the way for the subsequent 2006 launch of the Canadian Longitudinal Study on Aging. This new study was the subject of an entire special issue of the *Canadian Journal on Aging* in September 2009. This new investigation involves 50,000 Canadians aged 45 to 85 years of age. They are measured every three years and will be followed for at least 20 years. At least 30,000 participants will also provide biological specimens (see Raina et al., 2009).

Thinking Critically

1. The cause or causes of Alzheimer's disease have received increased attention from clinical scientists in the last few years. Do you think this disorder is one of the most pressing problems in Canadian society? What are the implications of the findings thus far from the Canadian Study of Health and Aging?
2. Would you be prepared to make "eldercare" one of your responsibilities in the future should a loved one develop dementia? Would you put your own life on hold in order to care for a loved one? Or, do you think that this is the government's responsibility?

- **Time-of-measurement effects** are confounds that arise because events at an exact point in time can have a specific effect on a variable being studied over time (Schaie & Hertzog, 1982). For example, time of measurement could affect the results of studies assessing post-traumatic stress disorder in Holocaust survivors if one of the assessments occurs shortly after 9/11.

The two major research designs used to assess developmental change, the cross-sectional and the longitudinal,

clarify these terms. In **cross-sectional studies**, the investigator compares different age groups at the same moment in time on the variable of interest. Suppose that in 1995 we took a poll and found that many interviewees over age 80 spoke with a European accent, whereas those in their forties and fifties did not. Could we conclude that as people grow older, they develop European accents? Hardly! Cross-sectional studies do not examine the same people over time; consequently, they allow us to make statements only about age effects in a particular study or experiment, not about age changes over time.

Cohort effects refer to the fact that people of the same chronological age may differ considerably depending on when they were born. Topical Press Agency/Getty Images.

In **longitudinal studies**, the researcher selects one cohort—say, the graduating class of 2002—and periodically retests it using the same measure over a number of years. This design allows researchers to trace individual patterns of consistency or change over time—cohort effects—and to analyze how behaviour in early life relates to behaviour in old age.

However, because each cohort is unique, conclusions drawn from longitudinal studies are restricted to the cohort chosen. If members of a cohort studied from 1956 to 1996 are found to decline in sexual activity as they enter their sixties, we cannot conclude that the sexuality of those in a cohort studied from 1996 to 2036 will decline when they reach the same age.

An additional problem with longitudinal studies is that participants often drop out as the studies proceed, creating a bias commonly called **selective mortality**. The least-able people are the most likely to drop out, leaving a non-representative group of people who are usually healthier than the general population. Thus, findings based on longitudinal studies may be overly optimistic about the rate of decline of a variable such as sexual activity over the lifespan.

DIAGNOSING AND ASSESSING PSYCHOPATHOLOGY IN LATER LIFE

The existing *DSM-IV-TR* criteria for older adults are basically the same as those for younger adults. The nature and manifestations of mental disorders are usually assumed to be the same in adulthood and old age, even though little research supports this assumption (Gatz, Kasl-Godley, & Karel, 1996; LaRue, Dessonville, & Jarvik, 1985). We often do not know what certain symptoms in older adults mean because we have few specifics about psychopathology in old age. For example, somatic symptoms are generally more prevalent in late life, but they are also evident in depression in older adults. Are the somatic symptoms of a depressed older adult necessarily a part of depression, or might they reflect physical changes?

Accurate assessment of elderly people for the purposes of establishing diagnoses and conducting research requires assessment measures tailored to elderly people. A measure of cognitive functioning is often included as standard practice in research to determine whether the elderly respondent has experienced declines in cognitive ability. Researchers often assess cognitive functioning with the Mini-Mental State Examination (MMSE; Folstein, Folstein, & McHugh, 1975) in its original or modified form (i.e., the Modified Mini-Mental State Exam). The MMSE is a brief measure of an individual's cognitive state, assessing "orientation, memory, and attention, ... ability to name, follow verbal and written commands, write a sentence spontaneously, and copy a complex polygon" (Folstein et al., 1975, p. 190).

Note that assessment of cognitive functioning should become even more important if proposed *DSM-5* changes come into effect. It has been suggested that delirium be retained as a category but the diagnosis of dementia be dropped and captured by two new categories: major neurocognitive disorder and minor neurocognitive disorder. There would also be an Alzheimer's disease subtype of major or minor neurocognitive disorders. Minor neurocognitive disorder would entail reports of minor levels of decline as reflected primarily by cognitive deficits.

Because some elderly people will have diminished attention spans, one goal is to develop short but reliable measures suitable for screening purposes. A relatively simple measure used to detect dementia and Alzheimer's disease is the clock drawing subtest of the Clock Test. The Clock Test was developed by Holly Tuokko of the University of Victoria and her associates (Tuokko et al., 1992, 1995). Respondents are presented with a previously drawn circle (7 cm in diameter) and are asked to imagine that the circle is the face of a clock and to put the numbers on the clock and then draw the hand placement for the time of 11:10. Up to 25 different types of errors can occur, including omissions, perseverations (i.e., repetitions), rotations, misplacements, distortions, substitutions, and additions. This simple test has been found to be reliable and valid, though results vary depending on the scoring system used (see Tuokko et al., 2000).

Another assessment goal is to create measures whose item content is tailored directly to the concerns and symptoms reported by elderly people, not to those of younger respondents. One well-known measure crafted for the elderly is the Geriatric Depression Scale (GDS; Yesavage et al., 1983), a true-false self-report measure. The GDS has acceptable psychometric characteristics and is regarded as the standard measure for assessing depression in the elderly. The Geriatric Suicide Ideation Scale (GSIS) is a 31-item measure that is the first measure of suicide ideation created specifically for the elderly (see Heisel & Flett, 2006). The GSIS has a 10-item suicide ideation scale, as well as three other subscales tapping death ideation, loss of personal and social work, and the perceived meaning in life. Recently, Heisel and Flett (2008) found that higher GSIS scores were associated with depression and health problems and lower scores in various domains of well-being, including positive relations with others and self-acceptance. They argued for the need to supplement the study of risk factors in suicide with an emphasis on protective resilience factors such as supportive relationships.

RANGE OF PROBLEMS

We know that mental health may be tied to the problems in a person's life. As a group, no other people have more of these problems than the aged. They have them all: physical decline and disabilities, sensory and neurological deficits, loss of loved ones, the cumulative effects of a lifetime of many unfortunate experiences, and social stresses such as ageism. One concern expressed by the World Health Organization (WHO, 2002) is that elderly people with a mental disorder may suffer from "double jeopardy"; that is, they suffer the stigmas associated with being older and being mentally ill. Unfortunately, almost no research has explored stigma associated with mental illness among older adults (WHO, 2002).

It is important to remember that in addition to a lifetime of exposure to losses and to other stressors, older adults have many positive life experiences, coping mechanisms, and wisdom on which to draw. Moreover, older adults who belong to groups that provide meaningful, strong roles for them seem to have an easier time adjusting to growing old (Keith, 1982).

OLD AGE AND BRAIN DISORDERS

Although the majority of older people do not have brain disorders, these problems account for more admissions and hospital inpatient days than any other geriatric condition (Christie, 1982). We will examine two principal types of brain disorders: dementia and delirium.

DEMENTIA

"With an aging population, dementia will be a huge burden on the population as times goes by. The cost will be unbelievable 15 to 20 years from now."

–*Dr. Alain Beaudet, president of the Canadian Institutes of Health Research (2009, E36)*

"The predicted surge in dementia cases will certainly overwhelm Canada's health care system unless specific and targeted action is taken now. Canada must act now."

–*Richard Nakoneczny, Volunteer President, Alzheimer Society of Canada (2010, p. 2)*

Dementia—what laypeople call senility—is a general descriptive term for gradual deterioration of intellectual abilities to the point that social and occupational functions are impaired. Difficulty remembering things, especially recent events, is the most prominent symptom, and reported memory problems in people who objectively have normal cognition predict subsequent dementia (St. John & Montgomery, 2002). People with dementia may leave tasks unfinished because they forget to return to them after an interruption. The person who had started to fill a teakettle at the sink leaves the water running; a parent is unable to remember the name of a daughter or son. Hygiene may be poor and appearance slovenly because the person forgets to bathe or how to dress. People with dementia also get lost, even in familiar settings.

Judgement may become faulty, and the person may have difficulty comprehending situations and making plans or decisions. People with dementia relinquish their standards and lose control of their impulses; they may use coarse language, tell inappropriate jokes, or shoplift. The ability to deal with abstract ideas deteriorates, and disturbances in emotions are common, including symptoms of depression, flatness of affect, and sporadic emotional outbursts. People with dementia are likely to show language disturbances as well, such as vague patterns of speech. Although the motor system is intact, they may have difficulty carrying out motor activities, such as those involved in brushing teeth or dressing themselves. They may also have trouble recognizing familiar surroundings or naming common objects. Episodes of delirium, a state of great mental confusion (discussed in detail later), may also occur. These should be distinguished from **paraphrenia**, the term used to describe schizophrenia that has its onset during old age.

The course of dementia may be progressive, static, or remitting, depending on the cause. Many people with progressive dementia eventually become withdrawn and apathetic. In the terminal phase of the illness, the personality loses its sparkle and integrity. Relatives and friends say that the person is just not himself or herself anymore. Social involvement with others keeps narrowing. Finally, the person is oblivious to his or her surroundings.

The prevalence of dementia increases with advancing age. One U.S. study found a prevalence of 13.9% for people 71 and older and a 9.7% prevalence of Alzheimer's disease. The prevalence of dementia was 5.0% for those aged 71–79 years old, but 37.4% for those aged 90 years and older (Plassman et al., 2007). This same team of investigators estimated later that another 22.2% of those aged 71 years or older have some form of cognitive impairment without dementia (Plassman et al., 2008).

CAUSES OF DEMENTIA Dementias are typically classified into three types. Alzheimer's disease is the most common. Then, there are the frontal-temporal and frontal-subcortical dementias, which are defined by the areas of the brain that are most affected.

Alzheimer's Disease **Alzheimer's disease** was described in the case that began this chapter. It accounts for about 50% of dementia in older people. About 1 in 13 Canadians over the age of 65 has Alzheimer's disease or a related dementia.

Current projections for the prevalence of Alzheimer's disease later in this century are alarming! Brookmeyer, Johnson, Ziegler-Graham, and Arrighi (2007) made forecasts based on population data provided by the United Nations, concluding that we are facing a "looming global epidemic" (p. 186). The current worldwide prevalence is 26.6 million people. It is estimated that the prevalence will quadruple and 106 million people worldwide will have Alzheimer's disease in 2050. This represents 1 in 85 people. The researchers also observed that modifying the environmental factors by promoting mental and physical exercise would result in about a 10% reduction in the prevalence of Alzheimer's disease (9.3 million cases) if the disease's onset could be delayed by one year, and they suggested that this is an achievable goal.

In Canada, there is increasing recognition that it is a national imperative to address the projected increase in the prevalence of dementia and related conditions. A new study titled *Rising Tide: The Impact of Dementia on Canadian Society* includes projections that the current 500,000 Canadians with Alzheimer's disease or related dementia will rise to 1.1 million cases within a generation based on population trends and risk factors (Alzheimer Society of Canada, 2010). This same report estimates the current cost of dementia care as $15 billion in Canada and that this will rise to $153 billion. Finally, in terms of hours of informal care provided by Canadians to their family members, the current estimate of 231 million hours is projected to rise to 756 million hours. As a result of these projections and in recognition of people in Canada who are afflicted at present, calls have been issued for a multi-faceted national dementia strategy (see Collier, 2009).

In Alzheimer's disease, initially described by the German neurologist Alois Alzheimer in 1906, the brain tissue deteriorates irreversibly, and death usually occurs 10 or 12 years after the onset of symptoms. The median survival time is 3.1 years for Canadians with Alzheimer's disease and 3.3

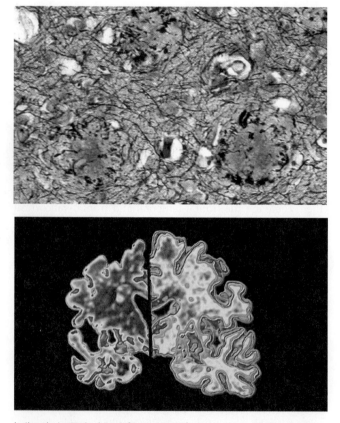

In the photograph above of brain tissue from a patient with Alzheimer's disease, the plaque shows up as areas of dark pink. Below are computer-generated images of a brain of a patient with Alzheimer's disease (left) and a normal brain. Note that the patient's brain has shrunk considerably owing to the loss of nerve cells.) Martin Rotker/Phototake.; A. Pakieka/Photo Researchers, Inc.

years for Canadians with vascular dementia (Wolfson et al., 2001). Gender is a factor. Women with Alzheimer's disease live longer than men with Alzheimer's disease, but more women than men die as a result of this disease (Alloul et al., 1998). In fact, Alzheimer's disease is the 10th leading cause of death for women and the 15th leading cause of death for men in Canada (Stokes & Lindsay, 1996). The person may at first have difficulties only in concentration and in memory for newly learned material, and may appear absent-minded and irritable, shortcomings that can be overlooked for several years but that eventually interfere with daily living. Indeed, well before the onset of any clinical symptoms, subtle deficits in learning and memory are revealed by neuropsychological tests in people who will later develop the disease (Linn et al., 1995). As the disease develops, the person often blames others for personal failings and may have delusions of being persecuted. Memory continues to deteriorate, and the person becomes increasingly disoriented and agitated. A study at the University of Victoria found that people are wholly unaware of the extent of their memory decline (Correa, Graves, & Costa, 1996).

The main physiological change in the brain, evident at autopsy, is an atrophy (wasting away) of the cerebral cortex, first the entorhinal cortex and the hippocampus and later the frontal, temporal, and parietal lobes. As neurons and synapses are lost, the fissures widen and the ridges become narrower and flatter. The ventricles also become enlarged. **Plaques**—small, round areas making up the remnants of the lost neurons and b-amyloid, a waxy protein deposit—are scattered throughout the cortex. Tangled, abnormal protein filaments—**neurofibrillary tangles**—accumulate within the cell bodies of neurons. These plaques and tangles are present throughout the cerebral cortex and the hippocampus.

A quantitative review of neuroimaging studies involving 3,411 patients led Toronto researchers to conclude that, in terms of structural imaging, volume loss within the hippocampus (and episodic memory impairment) best discriminated people in the early stages of Alzheimer's disease from control participants. However, volume loss within the medial temporal lobes (and associated naming deficits) was the most sensitive measure when identifying patients with Alzheimer's disease for four or more years (Zakzanis, Graham, & Campbell, 2003). Further clarification was provided by a subsequent meta-analysis of 40 studies focused on people with early Alzheimer's and those with mild cognitive impairment in the prodromal stage (see Schroeter, Stein, Maslowski, & Neumann, 2009). It was found that early Alzheimer's disease has a structural effect on the (trans-)entorhinal and hippocampal regions, and functionally, it impacted the inferior parietal lobules and precuneus. Schroeter et al. (2009) further noted that the most reliable predictor of progression from mild cognitive impairment to Alzheimer's disease was not changes in the posterior cingulate cortex and precuneus. Rather, it was atrophy in the (trans-)entorhinal area in the hippocampus and hypometabolism/hypoperfusion in the inferior parietal lobules.

The cerebellum, spinal cord, and motor and sensory areas of the cortex are less affected, which is why Alzheimer's sufferers do not appear to have anything physically wrong with them until late in the disease process. For some time, people are able to walk around normally, and their overlearned habits, such as making small talk, remain intact, so that in short encounters strangers may not notice anything amiss.

About 25% of patients with Alzheimer's disease also have brain deterioration similar to the deterioration in Parkinson's disease. Neurons are lost in the nigrostriatal pathway.

There is very strong evidence for a genetic basis for Alzheimer's. The risk for Alzheimer's is increased in first-degree relatives of afflicted individuals (Silverman et al., 1994), and concordance for monozygotic (MZ) twins is greater than for dizygotic (DZ) twins (Bergem, Engedal, & Kringlen, 1997). The role of genetic factors is the main focus of the MIRAGE (Multi-Institutional Research in Alzheimer Genetic Epidemiology) Project that examined predictors at 13 centres in Canada, Germany, and the United States. This project found that by the time they reach the age of 80, children of parents who both developed Alzheimer's disease will themselves have a cumulative risk of 54%, which is 1.5 times the level of risk for children with one parent who developed the disease and five times the level of risk for children whose parents did not (Lautenschlager et al., 1996). Among early-onset (before age 60) cases, which account for less than 5% of cases, the inheritance pattern suggests the operation of a single dominant gene.

A substantial proportion of late-onset cases of Alzheimer's disease exhibit a particular form of a gene (called the apolipoprotein E 4 allele) on chromosome 19, which functions more like the genetic diatheses we have considered so often before. Having one E 4 allele increases the risk for Alzheimer's disease to almost 50%, and having two alleles brings the risk to above 90% (Farlow, 1997). Having a different form of this gene (the E 2 allele) lowers the risk of developing Alzheimer's disease.

Contemporary research continues to show the role of this gene. A case-control study conducted with data from the Canadian Study of Health and Aging confirmed that the E 4 allele is associated with increased risk for Alzheimer's disease even after controlling for age, gender, and education level (Hsiung, Sadovnik, & Feldman, 2004). In other research, analyses conducted by a team led by researchers from the University of Waterloo used cumulative data from the famous Nun Study (see Focus on Discovery 16.1). The risk of dementia increased with age for those with low educational level, and the presence of the E 4 allele increased the risk by 400% (see Tyas et al., 2007).

Recent data suggest that the situation is more complex, however. A contemporary review by Bertram and Tanzi (2008) found that the E 4 allele is the only one to consistently influence disease risk. In total, more than 500 different gene candidates have been assessed and 20 loci have been identified as having modest but significant links with risk of Alzheimer's disease. Bertram and Tanzi (2008) concluded that the genetic underpinnings remain "elusive" despite initial successes.

FOCUS ON DISCOVERY 16.1

THE NUN STUDY: UNLOCKING THE SECRETS OF ALZHEIMER'S?

"It's the day after Easter, and the first crocus shoots have ventured tentatively above the ground at the convent on good Counsel Hill. This is Minnesota, however; the temperature is 23 F and the wind chill makes it feel far colder. Yet even though she's wearing only a skirt and sweater, Sister Ada, 91, wants to go outside. She wants to feed the pigs.

But the pigs she and the other nuns once cared for have been gone for 30 years. Sister Ada simply can't keep that straight. In recent years, her brain, like a time machine gone awry, has been wrenching her back and forth between the present and the past, depositing her without warning into the days when she taught primary schoolchildren in Minnesota or to the years when she was a college student in St. Paul. Or to the times when she and the sisters had to feed the pigs several times a day."

– *Michael D. Lemonick and Alice Park*, Time: Canadian Edition, *May 14, 2001*

The Nun Study is arguably one of the most remarkable research investigations in recent years. David Snowdon, who retired recently, has been studying 678 Catholic nuns from the American School Sisters of Notre Dame since 1986. The sisters have allowed Snowdon and colleagues to research their personal and medical histories, and they have undergone cognitive testing on an annual basis. They have also agreed to donate their brains for analysis via autopsies after they die.

This study continues to provide insight from a long-term perspective on the factors associated with the development of Alzheimer's disease and other forms of dementia. For instance, the nuns had written autobiographies in the weeks preceding their religious vows. These autobiographies were analyzed for their grammatical complexity and idea density, concepts related to general knowledge, vocabulary skills, and other cognitive abilities. Excerpts from two sisters illustrate the differences in linguistic ability that were found:

Low linguistic ability: I was born in Eau Claire, Wis. on May, 24, 1913 and was baptized in St. James church.

High linguistic ability: The happiest day of my life so far was my First Communion Day which was in June nineteen hundred and twenty when I was but eight years of age, and four years later I was confirmed by Bishop D. D. (Snowdon et al., 1996, p. 530)

Low linguistic ability was found in 90% of those who developed Alzheimer's disease and in only 13% of those who didn't (Snowdon et al., 1996). Supplementary analyses continue to show that high levels of linguistic ability predict less cognitive impairment and fewer neuropathological indicators of Alzheimer's disease (Riley et al., 2005).

Danner, Snowdon, and Friesen (2001) also investigated the expression of positive and negative emotions in the previous writings of 180 nuns. Nuns who expressed more positive emotions lived longer, and nuns who eventually succumbed to Alzheimer's disease gradually expressed fewer positive emotions prior to the disease's onset. A related analysis of language samples taken over 60 years used a grammatical complexity measure to confirm earlier findings suggesting that reduced language ability was a precursor for dementia (Kemper et al., 2001).

One drawback of the Nun Study is that even though it is longitudinal, it does not enable the researchers to make definitive cause and effect statements about the factors of importance in aging and Alzheimer's disease. Nevertheless, this study is remarkable, not only because of the extreme co-operation that the nuns have given in the name of science, but also because the nuns are all experiencing a common environment and have similar experiences, which reduces the likelihood that other factors have biased the results.

How, exactly, does the gene increase the risk for Alzheimer's disease? While the answer is not certain, the gene appears to be related to the development of both plaques and tangles, and it seems to increase the likelihood that the brain will incur damage from free radicals (unstable molecules derived from oxygen that attack proteins and DNA).

Finally, the environment is likely to play a role in most cases of Alzheimer's, as demonstrated by reports of long-lived MZ twins who are discordant for the disorder. A recent study of the Swedish Twin Registry found that non-shared environmental factors played a substantial role in susceptibility to Alzheimer's disease (Gatz et al., 2006). This study is the largest conducted thus far; it tested almost 12,000 twin pairs, with 392 pairs having at least one member with Alzheimer's disease. Gatz et al. (2006) confirmed the role of environmental factors; recognition of these modifiable factors is important for those seeking to lessen the incidence and prevalence of Alzheimer's disease. Nevertheless, their main finding was that the heritability of Alzheimer's disease was very high (79%), with it being quite similar for men and women.

Life events may play a role. A history of head injury is a risk factor for developing Alzheimer's disease (Rasmussen et al., 1995). This finding was confirmed by results from the MIRAGE Project (see Guo et al., 2000), described earlier. Analyses of longitudinal data from the Mirage Project also show that depression increases the risk for Alzheimer's disease (Green et al., 2003).

Some environmental factors appear to offer protection against developing Alzheimer's. Non-steroidal anti-inflammatory drugs such as aspirin appear to reduce the risk of Alzheimer's (Stewart et al., 1997), as does nicotine (Whitehouse, 1997). Of course, both these protective factors also have undesirable effects—liver damage from anti-inflammatories and cardiovascular damage from smoking.

General research on cognitive decline in the elderly supports the phrase "Use it or lose it!" As part of the Victoria Longitudinal Study, Hultsch, Hertzog, Small, and Dixon (1999) tested 250 middle-aged and older adults over a six-year period and showed a link between undergoing changes in intellectually related activities and changes in cognitive functioning. That is, remaining active at the cognitive level may buffer or protect an individual in terms of the degree of cognitive decline experienced.

A review conducted by Canadian investigators continues to support the use it or lose it principle. The review by Milgram, Siwak-Tapp, Araujo, and Head (2006) supported three conclusions: (1) cognitive activity helps preserve cognitive functioning, (2) cognitive activity helps crystallized intelligence more than fluid intelligence, and (3) there is support for the cognitive reserve hypothesis. The act of cognitive compensation creates a cognitive reserve. The **cognitive reserve hypothesis** is the notion that high education levels delay the clinical expression of dementia because the brain develops backup or reserve neural structures as a form of neuroplasticity.

A related protective factor is being bilingual. Innovative research by Ellen Bialystok from York University and Fergus Craik from the Rotman Research Institute and their colleagues indicates that being bilingual protects against the negative effects of aging on cognitive control (Bialystok, Craik, Klein, & Viswanathan, 2004). Tests of older adults showed that bilingual participants responded much more quickly, relative to unilingual participants, in experimental conditions that placed heavy demands on working memory.

Frontal-Temporal Dementias This type of dementia accounts for 10 to 15% of cases. It typically begins in a person's late fifties. In addition to the usual cognitive impairments of a dementia, frontal-temporal dementias are marked by extreme behavioural and personality changes. Sometimes people are very apathetic and unresponsive to their environment; at other times, they show an opposite pattern of euphoria, over-activity, and impulsivity (Levy et al., 1996). Unlike Alzheimer's disease, frontal-temporal dementias are not closely linked to loss of cholinergic neurons. Serotonin neurons are most affected, and there is widespread loss of neurons in the frontal and temporal lobes. Pick's disease is one cause of frontal-temporal dementia. Like Alzheimer's disease, Pick's disease is a degenerative disorder in which neurons are lost. It is also characterized by the presence of Pick bodies, spherical inclusions within neurons. Frontal-temporal dementias have a strong genetic component (Usman, 1997).

Frontal-Subcortical Dementias Because these dementias affect subcortical brain areas, which are involved in the control of motor movements, both cognition and motor activity are affected. Types of frontal-subcortical dementias include the following:

- *Huntington's chorea* is caused by a single dominant gene located on chromosome 4 and is diagnosed principally by neurologists on the basis of genetic testing. Its major behavioural feature is the presence of writhing (choreiform) movements. The best-known person with this disease is the late folk-song writer and singer Woody Guthrie. Huntington's chorea was the first disease identified and located on the human genome as part of the Human Genome Project (Huntington's Disease Collaborative Research Group, 1993).
- *Parkinson's disease* is marked by muscle tremors, muscular rigidity, and akinesia (an inability to initiate movement), and can lead to dementia. Canadian Michael J. Fox has Parkinson's disease.
- *Vascular dementia* is the second most common type, next to Alzheimer's disease. It is diagnosed when a patient with dementia has neurological signs, such as weakness in an arm or abnormal reflexes, or when brain scans show evidence of cerebrovascular disease. Most commonly, the patient had a series of strokes in which a clot formed, impairing circulation and causing cell death. Genetic factors appear to be of no importance (Bergem et al., 1997), and risk for vascular dementia increases with the same risk factors generally associated with cardiovascular disease— for example, a high level of "bad" cholesterol (Moroney et al., 1999).

Other Causes of Dementia A number of infectious diseases can produce irreversible dementia. Encephalitis, a generic term for any inflammation of brain tissue, is caused by viruses that enter the brain either from other parts of the body (such as the sinuses or ears) or from the bites of mosquitoes or ticks. Meningitis, an inflammation of the membranes covering the outer brain, is usually caused by a bacterial infection. The organism that produces the venereal disease syphilis (*Treponema pallidum*) can invade the brain and cause dementia.

Finally, head traumas, brain tumours, nutritional deficiencies (especially of B-complex vitamins), kidney or liver failure, and endocrine-gland problems such as hyperthyroidism can result in dementia. Exposure to toxins, such as lead or mercury, as well as chronic use of drugs, including alcohol, are additional causes.

TREATMENT OF DEMENTIA If the dementia has a reversible cause, appropriate medical treatment (such as correcting a hormonal imbalance) can be beneficial. Despite numerous investigations, no clinically significant treatment has been found that can halt or reverse Alzheimer's disease, although some drugs, as described here, show promise in effecting modest improvement in certain cognitive functions for a short period of time.

Biological Treatments of Alzheimer's Disease Because Alzheimer's disease involves the death of brain cells that secrete acetylcholine, various studies have attempted to increase the levels of this neurotransmitter. Research using choline (a precursor of the enzyme that catalyzes the reaction that produces acetylcholine) and physostigmine (a drug that prevents the breakdown of acetylcholine) has been disappointing. Tetrahydroaminoacridine (tacrine, brand name Cognex), which inhibits the enzyme that breaks down acetylcholine, produces mild improvement or slows the progression of cognitive decline (Qizilbash et al., 1998). Tacrine cannot be used in high doses, however, because it has severe side effects; for example, it is toxic to the liver. Donepezil (Aricept) is similar to tacrine in its method of action and results but produces fewer side effects (Rogers et al., 1998).

Gauthier and Scheltens (2009) provided a cogent update of biological treatments. Five drugs have been approved for use thus far: tacrine, donepezil, rivastigmine, galantamine,

Canadian actor Michael J. Fox has Parkinson's disease. Peter Brooker/Rex Features/The Canadian Press.

and memantine. They also reported that questions have been raised by critics about the cost effectiveness of these treatments from a societal perspective. Moreover, these drugs have not stopped progression of Alzheimer's disease though they may slow down the progression of symptoms.

Psychosocial Treatments for the Individual and the Family Although effective medical treatment for Alzheimer's is not yet available, patients and their families can be helped to deal with the effects of the disease. The general psychological approach is supportive. The overall goal is to minimize the disruption caused by the person's behavioural changes. Health workers achieved this by allowing the person and the family the opportunity to discuss the illness and its consequences, providing accurate information about it, helping family members care for the person in the home, and encouraging a realistic attitude in dealing with the disease's specific challenges (Knight, 2004; Zarit, 1980).

Counselling the person with Alzheimer's is difficult. Because of cognitive losses, psychotherapy provides little long-term benefit for those with severe deterioration. However, some patients seem to enjoy and be reassured by occasional conversations with professionals and with others not directly involved in their lives—in both individual and group settings. Interventions employed with normally functioning older adults, like Butler's life review (discussed further in the chapter in the section on treatment of depression), can also be useful for early- to mid-stage Alzheimer's sufferers whose cognitive abilities have not markedly deteriorated (Kasl-Godley & Gatz, 2000). In contrast to approaches taken with other psychological problems, denial may be the best coping mechanism available rather than being forced to acknowledge problems (Zarit, 1980).

For every institutionalized individual with a severely disabling dementia, there are at least two individuals with dementia living in the community, usually supported by a spouse, daughter, or other family member. Caring for a person with Alzheimer's has been shown to be extremely stressful and distressing. Analyses reported by the Canadian Study of Health and Aging Working Group (1994b) indicate that depression is twice as evident among caregivers as among non-caregivers. This CSHA study is important because it is one of the few caregiver studies that began with a nationally representative sample of individuals suffering from dementia and their caregivers.

Follow-up analyses of the CSHA data by Chappell and Penning (1996) indicate that depression and feelings of being burdened are highly correlated among caregivers. Caregivers were especially likely to feel burdened in response to apathy and an apparent lack of interest on the part of the patient, despite the best efforts of the caregiver. What forms do burden take? The most recent analysis of caregiver burden came out of the Canadian Alzheimer's Disease Caregiver Survey (see Black et al., 2010). This study focused on 221 baby boomer caregivers (ages 44 to 64) taking care of an afflicted individual. Four significant areas of burden were identified: emotional burden,

physical burden, financial burden, and employment burden due to needing to change one's own employment status (71% indicated some form of work disruption). Further complicating the situation were other physical health problems among some of those requiring care; for instance, about one quarter of those with Alzheimer's disease also had diabetes. Similarly, about one quarter had heart disease and 36% had unacceptably high blood pressure.

Objective and subjective indicators of burden predict caregivers' psychological distress (Chappell & Reid, 2002; Provencher et al., 2003). Moreover, longitudinal data indicate that perceived burden predicts subsequent depression, but the opposite temporal sequence (depression predicts subsequent perceptions of burden) is not supported (O'Rourke & Tuokko, 2004). Finally, the link between role-specific demands of caregiving and burden are mitigated by resilience; resilience promotes well-being among caregivers experiencing significant burden (Chappell & Dujela, 2008). Optimism in the caregiver is also protective (Gottlieb & Rooney, 2004).

The CSHA Working Group (1994a) found that caregivers are also more likely than non-caregivers to experience chronic health problems. Other studies have found more physical illness (Zunzunegui et al., 2002) and decreased immune functioning (Kiecolt-Glaser et al., 1991) among caregivers. In many instances, the disorders seem to be attributable to the stresses of caregiving; prior to these challenges, the families of caregivers usually did not experience such health difficulties (Gatz, Bengtson, & Blum, 1990).

Some resources are available to assist caregivers. In Canada, the Alzheimer Society of Canada has an on-line caregivers' forum that enables caregivers to share their experiences via the Internet and seek support and comfort from others (see www.alzheimer.ca). Expressing one's concerns on-line is a compelling way to achieve a better understanding within society of the challenges faced by caregivers. Indeed, a recent study of Chinese-Canadian caregivers taking care of relatives with Alzheimer's disease found lower reported levels of burden among frequent users of an Internet-based caregiver support service (Chiu et al., 2009).

Caregivers of people with dementia can also benefit from participating in psychoeducation groups. Hebert et al. (2003) found that participants in weekly sessions on stress appraisal and coping reported significant improvements in their reactions to the behavioural problems of care receivers. A recent meta-analysis that included a test of 14 psychoeducation studies found that there was substantial effectiveness for skill training programs with three elements: behaviour management, depression management, and anger management (Gallagher-Thompson & Coon, 2007). Combinations of individual treatment and support groups also seemed to be effective.

Because the family members are affected so powerfully, it is often recommended that they be given respites from their task. The patient may be hospitalized for a week, or a health care worker may take over and give the family a much-needed break. Unfortunately, a review of respite programs in Canada by Gottlieb and Johnson (2000) concluded that the phrase "too little too late" can be applied; when respites are used, which is infrequently, the use occurs quite late and the pattern of use is not intense or protracted in time. Typically, up to one half of caregivers do not take advantage of available programs, and when they do participate, it is between two and four and a half years after assuming the caregiver role.

Perhaps the most wrenching decision facing caregivers is whether to institutionalize the person with dementia. A qualitative study of caregivers in Northern Canada suggested that feelings of guilt among caregivers are intense when a person must be institutionalized, but their most predominant emotion is worry (Loos & Bowd, 1997). One wife who had assumed the caregiver role stated, "Putting him in the institution, even though the care is good, is like putting him in jail. It haunts you" (Loos & Bowd, 1997, p. 510). The conflicts people face when making this decision are considerable. A review by Alloul et al. (1998) concluded that the three best predictors of making the difficult decision to institutionalize a loved one are the elderly person's level of aggression, incontinence, and the presence of psychiatric disturbances.

Not everyone has a caregiver. More than 3,000 people in Canada with dementia continue to live in the community despite the fact that they don't have any formal or informal caregiver (CSHA Working Group, 1994a). A study of Canadians "home alone" with dementia showed that these people (predominantly women) were perceived as having much greater risk for accidents and injuries than people with dementia living with their spouses, but in fact, they did not die at comparatively higher rates (Tuokko, MacCourt, & Heath, 1999).

DELIRIUM

The term **delirium** is derived from the Latin words "de," meaning "from" or "out of," and "lira," meaning "furrow" or "track." The term implies being off track or deviating from the usual state (Wells & Duncan, 1980). Delirium is typically described as "a clouded state of consciousness." The patient, sometimes rather suddenly, has great trouble concentrating and focusing attention and cannot maintain a coherent and directed stream of thought. In the early stages, the person with delirium is frequently restless, particularly at night. The sleep-waking cycle becomes disturbed, so that the person is drowsy during the day and awake, restless, and agitated during the night. Vivid dreams and nightmares are common.

Delirious people may be impossible to engage in conversation because of their wandering attention and fragmented thinking. In severe delirium, speech is rambling and incoherent. Bewildered and confused, some delirious individuals lose their sense of time and place. They are often so inattentive that they cannot be questioned about orientation. Memory impairment, especially for recent events, is common. In the course of a 24-hour period, however, delirious people have lucid intervals and become alert and coherent. These daily fluctuations help distinguish delirium from other syndromes, especially Alzheimer's disease.

Perceptual disturbances are frequent. Individuals mistake the unfamiliar for the familiar, stating, for example, that they are at home instead of in a hospital. Although illusions and hallucinations are common, particularly visual and mixed visual-auditory ones, they are not always present. Paranoid delusions have been noted in 40 to 70% of delirious older adults. These delusions tend to be poorly worked out, fleeting, and changeable.

Swings in activity and mood accompany disordered thoughts and perceptions. Delirious people can be erratic, ripping their clothes one moment and sitting lethargically the next. They are in great emotional turmoil and may shift rapidly from one emotion to another—depression, fright, anger, euphoria, and irritability. Fever, flushed face, dilated pupils, tremors, rapid heartbeat, elevated blood pressure, and incontinence are common. If the delirium proceeds, the person will completely lose touch with reality and may become stuporous (Lipowski, 1983).

Although delirium is one of the most frequent biological mental disorders in older adults, it has been neglected in research and, like dementia, is often misdiagnosed (Knight, 2004). It is often the case that delirium is simply not detected (Zarit & Zarit, 1998). Cameron et al. (1987) assessed 133 consecutive admissions to an acute medical ward. They found 15 cases of delirium, only one of which had been detected by the admitting physician. Older adults are frequently misdiagnosed as having an irreversible dementia and are therefore considered beyond hope. Long-term institutional care is all too often viewed as the only option. This problem seems to apply to emergency departments in Canadian hospitals, where the prevalence of delirium in elderly patients could be as high as 9.6% (Elie et al., 2000).

While estimates of delirium in acute care settings can be quite high, Canadian CSHA data suggest that delirium is very uncommon among people living in their usual place of residence, with a prevalence of less than 0.5%. However, delirium is associated with a very low survival rate (Andrew, Frefer, & Rockwood, 2006). One Canadian study compared 38 elderly people with delirium (including 22 with dementia as well) and 148 people with no delirium or dementia (Rockwood et al., 1999). Delirium was a significant risk factor for the development of dementia and dying early; those with delirium lived less than half as long as those without delirium. Independent research in Montreal has confirmed that delirium is a risk factor for mortality, as well as for functional status and cognitive difficulties in the 12 months following hospital admission (McCusker et al., 2001, 2002).

The following is a typical example of delirium in an acute care facility. An older woman found in a filthy apartment with no food was believed by a poorly informed physician to have dementia and was given routine custodial care in a nursing home. A professional knowledgeable about delirium learned that she had become depressed over the loss of a loved one and had neglected her diet. Once this was recognized, appropriate attention was given to her nutritional deficiencies, and her condition improved such that she was discharged to her own home after one month (Zarit, 1980).

CAUSES OF DELIRIUM The causes of delirium in older adults can be grouped into several general classes: drug intoxications and drug-withdrawal reactions, metabolic and nutritional imbalances (as in uncontrolled diabetes and thyroid dysfunction), infections or fevers, neurological disorders, and the stress of a change in the person's surroundings (Knight, 2004). Delirium may also occur following major surgery, most commonly hip surgery (Zarit & Zarit, 1998); during withdrawal from psychoactive substances; and following head trauma or seizures. Common physical illnesses that cause delirium in older adults include congestive heart failure; pneumonia; urinary tract infection; cancer, kidney, or liver failure; malnutrition; and cerebrovascular accidents or strokes. Probably the most frequent cause of delirium in this age group is intoxication with prescription drugs (Besdine, 1980; Lipowski, 1983). However, delirium usually has more than one cause. A contemporary review of the existing literature conducted by Canadian researchers (see Elie et al., 1998) concluded that the top five correlates of delirium among elderly hospitalized patients are dementia, being on medication, medical illness, age, and male gender.

Although delirium usually develops swiftly (within a matter of hours or days), the exact mode of onset depends on the underlying cause. Delirium resulting from a toxic reaction or concussion has an abrupt onset; when infection or metabolic disturbance underlies delirium, the onset of symptoms is more gradual.

Why are older adults especially vulnerable to delirium? Many explanations have been offered: the physical declines of aging, the increased general susceptibility to chronic diseases, the many medications prescribed for older people, the greater sensitivity to drugs, and vulnerability to stress. One other factor, brain damage, increases the risk of delirium. A retrospective review of 100 hospital admissions of people with delirium revealed that 44% had delirium superimposed on another brain condition (Purdie, Honigman, & Rosen, 1981).

TREATMENT OF DELIRIUM Complete recovery from delirium is possible if the syndrome is identified correctly and the underlying cause promptly treated. It generally takes one to four weeks for the condition to clear; it takes longer in older versus younger people. If the underlying cause is not treated, however, permanent brain damage and death can ensue.

Primary prevention strategies appear to reduce the high rates of delirium, as well as the duration of delirium episodes in hospitalized older adults (Inouye et al., 1999). The intervention addresses such risk factors for delirium as sleep deprivation, immobility, dehydration, visual and hearing impairment, and cognitive impairment.

One often-neglected aspect of the management of delirium is educating the family of a person with dementia to distinguish the manifestations of dementia and delirium. Table 16.2 compares the features of dementia and delirium, and serves as a useful summary of the nature of delirium.

OLD AGE AND PSYCHOLOGICAL DISORDERS

Although a psychological disorder at any age may have at least a partial physical explanation, this explanation can be misleading, since much psychopathology found in older adults has not been linked directly to the physiological processes of aging. Indeed, the maladaptive personality traits and inadequate coping skills that the person brings into old age play a role in psychological disturbances, as do health, genetic predisposition, and life stressors.

We look first at the prevalence of mental disorders in late life and then survey a number of them, paying specific attention to their characteristics in older adults.

OVERALL PREVALENCE OF MENTAL DISORDERS IN LATE LIFE

Is age itself a contributing factor to emotional and mental malfunction? Do more old people than young people have mental disorders?

TABLE 16.2
COMPARATIVE FEATURES OF DEMENTIA AND DELIRIUM

Dementia	Delirium
Gradual deterioration of intellectual abilities, especially memory for recent events	Trouble concentrating and staying with a train of thought
Difficulties in everyday problem-solving	Restlessness at night, nightmares
Periods of depression	Frequent lucid intervals
Problems naming common objects	Hallucinations; sometimes loss of contact with reality
Faulty orientation to time (e.g., day of week), place (e.g., location), and person (e.g., who the self is or others are)	Large swings in mood and activity
Usually progressive and irreversible	Usually reversible but potentially fatal if cause (e.g., malnutrition) not treated
Increased prevalence with age	Prevalence high in the very young as well as the old

It is not entirely clear whether mental disorders become more prevalent with age, partly because of the methodological and conceptual difficulties we have already discussed. An extensive cross-sectional study conducted by the U.S. National Institute of Mental Health (NIMH) yielded valuable data on mental disorders in all age groups, including the old (Myers et al., 1984; Regier et al., 1988).

Current prevalence data indicate that persons over age 65 have the lowest overall rates of mental disorder of all age groups when the various disorders are grouped together. The primary problem detected was cognitive impairment, not as a separate *DSM* category but as an important characteristic of more than one disorder (e.g., depression, dementia, delirium). Rates for mild cognitive impairment were about 14% for older men and women; for severe cognitive impairment, rates were 5.5% for older men and 4.7% for older women.

The majority of persons 65 years of age and older are free from serious psychopathology, but 10 to 20% do have psychological problems severe enough to warrant professional attention (Gatz et al., 1996; Gurland, 1991).

DEPRESSION

One consistent finding that was confirmed in a recent global study conducted by the World Health Organization is that major depression is less prevalent among adults aged 65 and older, relative to younger people (Kessler et al., 2010). However, this was only found among the eight developed countries included in this study and the age difference was not found in the 10 developing countries. Recent results from the Canadian Community Health Survey confirmed that elderly Canadians, versus those in the 50–64 years age group and the 20–49 years age group, had lower rates of depression, anxiety, and alcohol abuse/dependence, and lower rates of service use (Mosier et al., 2010). However, depression and other disorders are still quite evident among the elderly. One study involved physician ratings of 12 symptoms of depression as part of a clinical interview. This survey of 2,341 elderly Canadians found that 2.6% had major depression (five or more symptoms) and 4.9% had minor depression (two to four symptoms). Greater prevalence of depression was associated with female gender, the presence of dementia, and the presence of physical health problems (Ostbye et al., 2005).

A recent review suggests that at least half of the depressed older adults are experiencing depression for the first time, a phenomenon known as "late onset depression" (see Fiske, Wetherell, & Gatz, 2009). Those with early onset depression are more likely to have a family history of depression and personality dysfunction that renders them vulnerable.

Women have more periods of depression than men for most of their lives. An epidemiological study in Edmonton showed that elderly women have substantially higher rates of depression regardless of whether they are between 65 and 74 years old or 85 years old and older (Newman, Bland, & Orn, 1998).

CHARACTERISTICS OF DEPRESSION IN OLDER VS. YOUNGER ADULTS Worry, feelings of uselessness, sadness, pessimism, fatigue, inability to sleep, and difficulties getting things done are common symptoms of depression in both older (Blazer, 1982) and younger adults. The cognitive correlates of depression (i.e., negative automatic thoughts, dysfunctional attitudes) are also apparent among elderly Canadians (Vezina & Bourque, 1984). But there are also some age-related differences (Blazer, 1982; Small et al., 1986). Feelings of guilt are less common and somatic complaints more common in depressed older adults.

The use of standard *DSM-IV-TR* criteria may lead to the underdiagnosis of depression in older adults. Older adults are less likely to demonstrate impaired social and occupational functioning as a result of their depression because they are less likely than younger people to be working (Fiske et al., 1998). Some researchers (e.g., Newman et al., 1998) have described a subtype of depression more commonly seen in older adults, called depletion syndrome, which is also known as depression without sadness. This syndrome is characterized chiefly by loss of pleasure, vitality, and appetite, as well as hopelessness and somatic symptoms; self-blame, guilt, and dysphoric mood are either absent or less prominent.

CAUSES OF DEPRESSION IN OLDER ADULTS Recently, Fiske et al. (2009) posited a new model that focuses on depression in older adults due to decreased involvement in daily activities and depression that is maintained by self-critical thoughts. Both of these factors have been implicated in depression among younger people, however.

Many elderly people in poor physical health are depressed. A survey of 900 older adults in the community found that 44% with depressive symptoms were medically ill (Blazer & Williams, 1980). Many physicians who care for older people are insensitive to the likelihood of depression coexisting with physical illnesses. More often than not they do not diagnose, and therefore do not treat, the psychological condition (Rapp, Parisi, Walsh & Wallace, 1988). This oversight can lead to the worsening of the depression and the medical condition. By the same token, psychotherapists who are focusing on the treatment of depression will also need to be cognizant of chronic health conditions that will likely complicate treatment when depression is the primary emphasis. Laidlaw and Pachana (2009) have echoed concerns about the growing number of elderly people who will require treatment in the years to come and the certainty that the majority of these people will also have co-occurring physical comorbidities.

As we grow older, we almost inevitably experience a number of life events that could cause depression. Bereavement after the loss of a loved one has been hypothesized to be the most important risk factor for depression in the elderly (see Vinkers et al., 2004). Bereavement also contributes to poorer prognosis in elderly people already suffering from depression (Denihan et al., 2000). The predictiveness of bereavement was also confirmed in a meta-analysis conducted by researchers from McGill University (Cole & Dendukuri, 2003). Significant risk factors for depression across 20 prospective studies were bereavement, sleep disturbance, disability, prior depression, and female gender.

Longitudinal research on bereavement suggests that while bereavement contributes in general to depression, the extent of its effect depends on the nature of the loss and the timing of assessment. For instance, in a well-designed prospective study, Carnelley, Wortman, and Kessler (1999) found that widowed women reported more depression than control participants up to two years following the loss. However, widowed women whose husbands were ill when the study started did not experience more depression when their husbands died. Carnelley et al. (1999) suggest that there is a timing effect in being forewarned; women with ill husbands anticipate the loss and may become depressed prior to their spouse's death.

Clearly, there is a link between bereavement and depression. Although opinions vary, several authors have suggested that diagnostic systems should be revised to include a separate category for the pathological grief experienced by people who suffer a prolonged reaction to bereavement (see Bonanno & Kaltman, 2001; Stroebe et al., 2001). This call for a separate category is based on evidence that grief-stricken individuals have grief-related symptoms that are distinguishable from existing definitions of depression (see Stroebe et al., 2001). A key issue is how to distinguish between normal and abnormal grief reactions.

Given the different reactions to bereavement, researchers have identified factors associated with resilient reactions to the death of one's spouse. Prem Fry at Trinity Western University in British Columbia has found that existential factors are quite important. For instance, a study of widows and widowers between the ages of 65 and 87 found that people who were optimistic and found meaning in their lives had better psychological adjustment than people lacking these attributes (Fry, 2001). An involvement in organized religion was also associated with better adjustment.

Numerous findings point to the importance of social support as a stress buffer for elderly people faced with life challenges (e.g., Cappeliez, 1993; Fry, 1993). Ostbye, Steenhuis, Walton, and Cairney (2000) examined the correlates of dysphoria in elderly Canadians living in the community who did not have dementia. Correlates of dysphoria included lower perceived social support, chronic pain, poor health, and functional dependency.

Although retirement has been assumed to have negative consequences, research does not generally support this assumption (George, 1980). Any ill effects of retirement may have more to do with the poor health and low incomes of some retirees and less with retirement per se (Pahkala, 1990). Retirement often ushers in a satisfying period of life.

Each older person brings to late life a developmental history that makes his or her reactions to common problems unique. Each person's coping skills and personality determine how effectively that individual will respond to new life events. Overall, adaptation rather than depression is the more common reaction to stress in late life.

TREATMENT OF DEPRESSION A substantial proportion of older people who suffer from depression have persistent forms of depression. Meta-analytic reviews conducted by researchers in Montreal indicate that depression in elderly people is associated with a poor prognosis and is undertreated (Cole & Bellavance, 1997; Cole, Bellavance, & Mansour, 1999). One meta-analysis of studies that examined the course of depression found that only 33% of the participants recovered, while another 33% were still depressed and 21% had died (Cole et al., 1999). A one-year follow-up study conducted in Montreal of a sample of elderly people with depression found that fewer than half of the depressed elderly in the study were improved; this study showed that major depression superimposed on dysthymic disorder (i.e., double depression) was especially persistent (see Fenton, Cole, Engelsmann, & Mansouri, 1997). The low remission rate of depression was attributed to lack of treatment intervention.

Although clinical lore holds that depressions in older people are more resistant to treatment than the depressions in younger people, we have known for some time that these claims are not substantiated (Small & Jarvik, 1982). Rather, there is considerable evidence that depressed older adults can be helped by both psychological and pharmacological interventions, but there must be access to treatment. A review by Canadian researchers showed that a small but consistent number of studies attest to the usefulness of psychotherapy in treating geriatric depression (O'Rourke & Hadjistavropoulos, 1997).

Gallagher and Thompson (1982, 1983) compared cognitive, behavioural, and brief psychodynamic psychotherapies for older individuals with depression. These three methods were found equally effective, and in subsequent studies (Gallagher-Thompson & Thompson, 1995a, 1995b; Thompson, Gallagher, & Breckenridge, 1987), about three quarters of the clients were judged either completely cured or markedly improved. These rates compare very favourably with the outcomes of psychotherapy in younger people with depression. Supplementary analyses by Louise Gaston at McGill University and her associates show that the quality of the alliance between the elderly client and his or her therapist is a key factor in determining whether there is a positive treatment response (Gaston et al., 1998). Another notable finding is that untreated control participants did not improve, as younger untreated depressed patients often do, suggesting that older adults are less likely than younger patients to recover without treatment.

A study with depressed elderly people from Ottawa showed that they responded quite well to cognitive therapy, with decreases in depressive symptoms comparable to those obtained in other research investigations (Cappeliez, 2000). However, as is often the case with younger participants, depressed elders had a less positive response to treatment if they had more severe levels of depression to begin with. It was also found that depressed elders with negative self-views had less positive responses to the cognitive interventions.

Another treatment study compared cognitive therapy and bibliotherapy (the reading of a self-help book) as treatments for the depressed elderly (Floyd et al., 2004). Both these therapies were superior to delayed treatment in a control group. Finally, a more recent study compared individualized CBT with treatment as usual and this randomized control trial confirmed that CBT was more effective in reducing levels of depression as assessed by the Beck Depression Inventory-2 (Serfaty et al., 2009).

Interpersonal psychotherapy (IPT; discussed in Chapter 8) has also been used successfully to treat depression in older adults. IPT is a short-term psychotherapy that addresses themes such as role loss, role transition, and interpersonal disputes, problem areas prominent in the lives of many older adults. Existing evidence attests to the efficacy of IPT as an established treatment. A meta-analysis of nine existing studies with adults of various ages concluded that IPT was superior to CBT for treating depression in adults in general (de Mello et al., 2005). One study with the elderly found that IPT was particularly effective if it focused on role conflict and it was less effective if it focused on abnormal grief experiences (Miller et al., 2003). Recent data suggest that a modified 16-week form of IPT for suicidal elderly people has promise as an effective intervention (see Heisel, Duberstein, Talbot, King, & Tu, 2009). This study needs to be replicated because it was based on a small sample (n=12) and it did not include a control group; nevertheless, IPT did significantly reduce levels of suicide ideation.

A form of treatment known as reminiscence therapy can also be effective for treating depression in the elderly, and numerous studies of reminiscence therapy have emerged in recent years. Reminiscence therapy is also known as life review therapy. It is a cognitive process that requires individuals to reflect on previous negative events and address any remaining conflicts; it also requires that they strive to find life's meaning while examining the present situation and the past. One focus here is to re-examine the role of the self in events in an attempt to achieve a sense of self-acceptance and reduced self-blame. For instance, a self-critical perfectionist could dredge up previous mistakes from the past and re-examine his or her role, working toward the ultimate goal of achieving a less self-critical interpretation.

Life review was proposed by Butler (1963) as a psychotherapeutic approach uniquely suitable for older adults. This approach reflects the influence of Erik Erikson's (1950, 1968) lifespan developmental theory, which postulates stages of conflict and growth extending well into the senior years. Life review facilitates what appears to be a natural tendency of older adults to reflect on their lives and to try to make sense of what has happened to them. In Eriksonian terms, it helps the person address the conflict between ego integrity and despair. Ego integrity refers to a process of finding meaning in the way one has led one's life, and despair reflects the discouragement that can come from unreached goals and unmet desires. Life-review methods include having the patient bring in old photographs, travel to a childhood home, and write an autobiography.

A meta-analysis of 20 studies showed that reminiscence and life review had both statistical and clinical significance in terms of reducing depression in elderly people (Bohlmeijer, Smit, & Cuijpers, 2003). The treatment effect was comparable to those obtained with pharmacotherapy and other psychological treatments. More recently, a randomized control trial found that life review was again effective in reducing symptoms, but participation in the no-treatment control group was also effective (see Pot et al., 2010). Life review seems useful, but not necessarily better than other forms of treatment.

According to Watt and Cappeliez (2000), the type of reminiscence involved determines the effectiveness of reminiscence therapy. Clearly, reflecting on the past is maladaptive if it involves obsessively ruminating about past shortcomings or problems. Recent work contrasts a "negative self-form" of reminiscence (i.e., doing it to alleviate boredom or reawakening old feelings of bitterness) with a "positive self-form" and a "prosocial form" of reminiscence (Cappeliez & O'Rourke, 2006). Reminiscence therapy can be particularly effective if it takes the form of integrative or instrumental reminiscence (see Watt & Cappeliez, 2000). Integrative reminiscence is a non-judgemental way of looking back that emphasizes cognitive reattribution and the consideration of realistic causes of life events that go beyond the self. It focuses on establishing a sense of purpose and meaning in life. To provide an example of integrative reminiscence, Watt and Cappeliez (2000) described a woman who, through integrative reminiscence, learned to attribute her failure to obtain a teaching degree in the 1930s to the economic depression of the era rather than to personal failings. Instrumental reminiscence is remembering past coping responses, such as the plans that were used to address challenging situations, goal-directed activities, and recalling when goals were met. For instance, remembering what you did to fix a flooded basement would reflect instrumental reminiscence.

Emerging evidence suggests that certain antidepressants can be somewhat useful. A longitudinal study conducted over a four-year period in Toronto found that antidepressant medication was highly effective and that 70% of the depressed elderly receiving treatment did not experience a recurrence of their depressions (Flint & Rifat, 2000). Another current treatment investigation found that if antidepressant treatment lasted for two years rather than the more typical six to 12 months, only 37% of those taking antidepressants experienced a relapse vs. 68% of those receiving interpersonal therapy (Reynolds et al., 2006). This study suggests that protracted drug treatment may be even more effective. Overall, a contemporary meta-analysis found that antidepressants are more effective than placebos. However, treatment improvements are modest at best and quite varied across studies (Nelson, Delucchi, & Schneider, 2008).

Electroconvulsive therapy is back in favour among many geriatric psychiatrists (Hay, 1991), particularly for patients who had an earlier favourable response to it (Janicak et al., 1993). ECT does, however, carry significant risks, and it

Reminiscence (or life review) therapy for depression requires individuals to reflect on their past and present situation to help achieve a sense of self-acceptance and reduce self-blame. Jupiterimages.

should be considered only when other treatments have not been effective or are contraindicated, or when a rapid response (such as in the case of an acutely suicidal patient) is needed (Zarit & Zarit, 1998).

We now turn to a discussion of anxiety disorders in the elderly. Although depression and anxiety are discussed separately, they are often correlated and comorbid in older people, as they are in younger people. A mixed subtype of depression and anxiety in certain elderly individuals is associated with poor treatment response and higher relapse rates (Flint & Rifat, 1996, 1997; Lynch et al., 2000).

ANXIETY DISORDERS

Anxiety disorders are more prevalent than depression among older adults (Gatz et al., 1996; Wetherell, 2002). Anxiety disorders in old age can be a continuation or re-emergence of problems experienced earlier in life, or they can develop for the first time in the senior years. Like depression, *DSM*-defined anxiety disorders appear to be less prevalent among older than among younger adults (Flint, 1994; Kessler et al., 1994). As nearly all the available data are cross-sectional, however, it is wise to be cautious about this conclusion. One of the most recent estimates from a U.S. national study suggests that 7% of adults aged 65 or older met criteria for an anxiety disorder in the previous 12 months (Gum, King-Kallimanis, & Kohn, 2009). Wolitzky-Taylor et al. (2010) concluded that anxiety disorders are relatively common among elderly people despite being less common among older versus younger people. Significant risk factors include being female, having several chronic medical conditions, not being married, having lower levels of education, having had adverse early childhood experiences, and having elevated neuroticism (Wolitzky-Taylor et al., 2010).

While anxiety is a problem in its own right, anxiety can also complicate other conditions. For instance, it is only recently that researchers have examined levels of anxiety among people with dementia. The data suggest that anxiety among

people with dementia is linked with poorer quality of life, behavioural disturbances, and poorer outcomes (Seignourel et al., 2008).

In general, symptoms of anxiety disorders do not differ as people enter old age, with only minor differences being evident (Wolitzky-Taylor et al., 2010). However, as in the case of depression, diagnostic criteria for anxiety may be insufficient or ill-suited for diagnosis of the disorder in older adults, thus rendering current prevalence rates underestimates (Fuentes & Cox, 1997; Wetherell, 1998). For example, there appear to be age-related differences in the symptom expression of generalized anxiety disorder. Stanley and Novy (2000) identified a number of differences. First, elderly people report more worries about health and fewer worries about work-related issues than younger people do; worry about health matters was confirmed as the predominant focus in a study of older adults from Quebec (Doucet, Ladouceur, Freeston, & Dugas, 1998), followed by worries about relationships with family members and friends. Second, differences exist in the structure of affect, with elderly people placing less emphasis on feelings of guilt and self-blame. Third, elderly people tend to emphasize the somatic aspects of anxiety rather than the cognitive aspects. Finally, symptoms of anxiety in the elderly may be more closely intertwined with symptoms reflecting sleep difficulties and declines in cognitive capabilities (see Skarborn & Nicki, 1996).

In terms of overall level of worry, a study of worry content across the lifespan assessed participants between the ages of 16 and 74 years, and the number of worries declined with age (Lindesay et al., 2006). However, worry may fluctuate over time among the elderly. A seven-year longitudinal investigation not only confirmed that the oldest-old (85 years or older) worry mostly about health issues and memory loss, but also found a dramatic age-related increase in the content, frequency, and severity of worry as these people got older (Jenn, Dunkle, & Roberts, 2006).

After reviewing the literature, Alistair Flint (1994, 1999) from the University of Toronto concluded that the most prevalent anxiety disorders among the elderly are generalized anxiety disorder (GAD) and agoraphobia. Flint (1999) also noted that because there have been few empirical investigations into the treatment of anxiety disorders in elderly people, treatment guidelines often have to be extrapolated from studies with younger participants.

Clearly, more information is needed on GAD in elderly people. One study compared a sample of elderly people with GAD with an age-matched control group (Diefenbach, Stanley, & Beck, 2001). The two groups did not differ in the pattern of worry content, with family/interpersonal worries being most predominant in both groups. Further comparisons with a younger group of participants confirmed the anticipated tendency for elderly people to have more health worries and fewer worries about work.

Scoggin (1998) remarked that post-traumatic stress disorder (PTSD) and acute stress disorder, two anxiety disorders that may be especially relevant to the lives of older adults, have received scant attention from researchers. We noted in Chapter 6 that Beal's (1995) study revealed long-term PTSD in Canadian veterans of the Dieppe Raid. PTSD has also been observed in older patients following such trauma as major health crises (Scoggin, 1998). One of the few prevalence studies conducted thus far found PTSD in 0.9% of the elderly and subthreshold PTSD in 13.1%. The strongest predictors of both forms of PTSD were neuroticism and adverse events in early childhood (van Zelst et al., 2003). Another recent study found negligible rates of PTSD in the elderly, but 10% reported re-experiencing trauma symptoms (Creamer & Parslow, 2008).

In general, research on reactions to traumatic stressors tends to yield findings comparable to those obtained with younger people. For instance, when assessed on their reactions to the July 2005 London transit bombings just 11 days after they occurred, the percentage of people aged 65 or older who reported substantial stress (32%) was virtually identical to the proportion of younger people who reported still experiencing substantial stress (Rubin et al., 2005).

Similarly, older adults with anxiety problems respond to the same kinds of psychological treatments found useful with younger adults. For instance, accumulating evidence attests to the value of cognitive behaviour therapy (CBT) in the treatment of generalized anxiety disorder in elderly adults (Ayers, Sorrell, Thorp, & Wetherell, 2007; Stanley et al., 2003; Wetherell, Gatz, & Craske, 2003). CBT consisting of three main components (relaxation training, cognitive therapy, and exposure-based procedures), according to Stanley et al. (2003), is useful for older adults because it is time-limited, symptom-focused, and collaborative in nature.

Because the physician usually hears the psychological complaints of older adults, psychoactive medications are in widespread use. However, potentially dangerous interactions with other drugs, along with the elderly's increased sensitivity to any drug, make anti-anxiety medication a risky intervention (Fisher & Noll, 1996).

SUBSTANCE-RELATED DISORDERS

Substance abuse is less prevalent in today's cohorts of older adults than among younger adults, but it is a problem nonetheless. One reason for the lower prevalence may be increased mortality among those who have abused drugs in the past (Gilhooly & McDonach, 2003). However, many researchers (e.g., Gomberg & Zucker, 1998; Zarit & Zarit, 1998) predict that as successive cohorts enter old age, the prevalence of substance abuse and dependence in older adults will begin to rise. As we will see below, this seems to be the case.

ALCOHOL ABUSE AND DEPENDENCE Historically, it has been assumed that alcohol abuse is less prevalent in older than in younger cohorts, yet the problem is not trivial. Prevalence rates for *DSM*-defined alcohol abuse or dependence in older adults were pegged initially as being much lower than the rates that have been determined for the general adult population

(Myers et al., 1984), but recent findings paint a less favourable picture. A subset of more than 2,000 participants in the Canadian Study of Health and Aging underwent clinical examinations by physicians rather than more standardized forms of assessment (see Thomas & Rockwood, 2001). While this is a significant limitation of the study, it nevertheless found that 8.9% of the participants had definite alcohol abuse, another 3.7% had "questionable alcohol abuse," and men had higher rates of alcohol abuse than women. Additional analyses showed that participants diagnosed with definite or questionable alcohol abuse had significantly greater risk of short-term mortality over the next 18 months. The authors concluded that alcohol abuse among older people might be more common than first realized. These findings emerged even though many alcohol abusers do not survive to old age.

A current investigation compared elderly people from the United States and from England; it was found that alcohol misuse is quite prevalent among the elderly and there are cross-nation differences. Lang, Guralnik, Wallace, and Melzer (2007) found in their study of more than 13,000 seniors that 10.8% of U.S. men and 28.6% of English men had more drinks per day than was recommended. Overall, 2.9% of U.S. women and 10.3% of English women exceeded the prescribed threshold. Another team of investigators found that 4.1% of the almost 25,000 older adults assessed were at-risk drinkers (8 to 14 drinks per week) and another 4.5% were heavy drinkers or binge drinkers with 15 or more drinks per week (Kirchner et al., 2007). Heavy drinking was linked with depression, anxiety, and health problems. Another recent investigation found that 14% of men and 3% of women aged 65 or older reported binge drinking, and binge drinking was associated with the use of tobacco and illicit drugs. In addition, binge drinking among men was linked with being separated, divorced, or widowed (see Blazer & Wu, 2009). Some researchers believe that these recent findings reflect changing population trends and a growing problem as newer cohorts of people get older.

It might be assumed that problem drinking in older adults is always a continuation of a pattern established earlier in life, but this is not the case. Many problem drinkers begin having alcohol-related problems after the age of 60—so-called late-onset alcoholism. Estimates vary widely, but a review of the literature concluded that between one third and one half of those who have drinking problems in old age began their problem drinking after the age of 60 (Liberto, Oslin, & Ruskin, 1996).

As noted, tolerance for alcohol diminishes with age, in part because the ratio of body water to body mass decreases with age, resulting in higher blood-alcohol concentration per unit of alcohol imbibed (Morse, 1988). In addition, older people metabolize alcohol more slowly. Thus, the drug may cause greater changes in brain chemistry and more readily bring on toxic effects, such as delirium, in older people. Several neuropsychological studies have shown that cognitive deficits associated with alcohol abuse, such as memory problems, are likely to be more pronounced in the aged alcoholic than in younger individuals with comparable drinking histories (Brandt et al., 1983). In addition, recent results indicate that there are age-alcoholism interactions and that a history of alcoholism interacts with older age; MRI tests revealed deficits in the macrostructure and the microstructure of the corpus callosums of elderly people with a history of alcoholism even though they had been abstinent from drinking for at least three months (Pfefferbaum, Adalsteinsson, & Sullivan, 2006). Thus, residual cognitive effects may remain long after the older person has stopped drinking.

MEDICATION MISUSE The misuse of prescription and over-the-counter medicines is a much greater problem than drug or alcohol abuse in the aged population (LaRue et al., 1985). Elderly people have a higher overall rate of legal drug intake than any other group; although they constitute only 13% of the population, they consume about one third of all prescribed medications (Weber, 1996). Older patients use more anti-anxiety medications than any other age group. Rates of benzodiazepine use among community-dwelling older adults have been estimated at 14 to 37%, while rates among nursing-home residents are thought to be even higher (Wetherell, 1998). Some of this use reflects serious drug abuse. These and other concerns have resulted in the Canadian Pharmacists Association issuing a call for greater involvement of home support workers, since much of the medication misuse occurs in the home. Home support workers can serve as "medication mentors" (Canadian Pharmacists Association, 2004).

Medication misuse, whether deliberate or inadvertent, is a serious problem among older patients and can cause delirium. © Gary A Connor/Index Stock/Photolibrary.

Abuse of prescription or legal drugs is often inadvertent but can be deliberate. Some people obtain medications from a number of sources; for example, by going to more than one physician, filling their prescriptions at different pharmacies, and paying cash instead of using credit cards to reduce the chances that their multiple prescriptions will be discovered (Weber, 1996). One study of 141 well-functioning, middle-class older adults living in their own homes found that almost half reported having misused prescription or over-the-counter drugs at least once over a period of six months (Folkman, Bernstein, & Lazarus, 1987).

Older adults may abuse tranquillizers, antidepressants, or sleep aids prescribed years earlier to deal with postoperative pain or the grief and anxiety of losing a loved one. These drugs often create physical as well as psychological dependency. However, because older adults tend not to go to work regularly and may sometimes not even be seen in public for days or weeks at a time, they can hide their abuse for years. The slurred speech and memory problems caused by drugs may be attributed by others to old age and dementia (LaRue et al., 1985), another example of how popular stereotypes can interfere with proper diagnosis and treatment. Said one addiction specialist, "They're not like a 25-year-old mixing it up to get high. ... They're trying to make a lonely, miserable life less miserable" (Weber, 1996, p. A37). A former Valium addict and now a leader of Pills Anonymous in California stated the problem this way: "Closet junkies, that's what we call them here. They're at home. They're alone. They're afraid. They're just hiding. Their drug pusher is their doctor" (Weber, 1996, p. A37).

Since the current cohort of older adults is not as acculturated as younger people to seeking help for psychological problems, including drug problems, many make unsupervised efforts to abstain, sometimes going cold turkey. Doing so can be very dangerous, even life-threatening, because withdrawal reactions place great demands on the cardiovascular system.

Some older addicts end up in places where one doesn't expect to find an older adult.

> Her skin itched as if an invisible case of hives were creeping across her flesh. She would shiver, then sweat. She felt suffocated by despair.
>
> She was 65, a doctor's wife, a proud grandma with a purseful of photographs. But there she was, curled in a ball like any other junkie at the ... drug treatment center, sobbing as her body withdrew from a diet of painkillers and tranquilizers.
>
> She couldn't believe it had come to this.
>
> People her age, the woman said, "don't associate themselves with the lowlifes [who] sneak into doorways to shoot up. No, they sneak into the bathroom for a pill." (Weber, 1996, p. A1)

SLEEP DISORDERS

Insomnia is a frequent complaint among older adults. One survey found insomnia in 25% of respondents aged 65 to 79, as compared with 14% in the 18 to 34 age group; another

20% of older respondents had less serious but still problematic insomnia (Mellinger, Balter, & Uhlenhuth, 1985). A new study of more than 2,000 seniors from Quebec in long-term care facilities found that 6.2% had insomnia disorder according to *DSM-IV* criteria, 17% had at least one insomnia symptom, and more than half of the participants were benzodiazepine users (Voyer, Verrault, Menque, & Morin, 2006). Overall, insomnia in the elderly (especially in very late life) is more frequent and severe than in younger people and is associated with more complications (Lichstein & Morin, 2000).

The most common sleep problems experienced by older adults are waking often at night, frequent early-morning awakenings, difficulty falling asleep, and daytime fatigue (Miles & Dement, 1980). Older adults sleep somewhat less or the same amount of time as younger adults do, but their sleep is also more often spontaneously interrupted; in addition, they take longer to fall back to sleep after awakening (Webb & Campbell, 1980). Thus, older people generally sleep less in relation to the total time they spend in bed at nighttime; they tend to make up for this loss with daytime naps.

Older adults also spend less absolute time in a phase known as rapid eye movement (REM) sleep, and stage 4 sleep—the deepest stage—is virtually absent. Instead, older adults spend more time in light sleep (i.e., stage 1). Older men generally experience more disturbances of their sleep than older women do, a gender difference found to a lesser extent in young adults (Dement, Laughton, & Carskadon, 1981). The sleep problems of older adults must be treated seriously, as the symptoms of chronic insomnia have been found to be associated with higher rates of morbidity and mortality (Neckelmann, 1996).

CAUSES OF SLEEP DISORDERS In addition to the changes associated with aging, various illnesses, medications, caffeine, stress, anxiety, depression, lack of activity, and poor sleep habits may make insomniacs of older adults. Depressed mood has been shown to be related to sleep disturbances in older adults, especially early-morning awakening (Rodin, McAvay, & Timko, 1988). However, not all geriatric sleep problems should be attributed to depression.

Whatever the cause of insomnia at any age, it is worsened by self-defeating actions such as ruminating over it and counting the number of hours slept and those spent waiting to fall asleep. Sleeping problems can also be worsened by medications that are taken to deal with them.

Sleep apnea is a respiratory disorder in which breathing ceases repeatedly for a period of a few seconds to as long as two minutes as the person sleeps. It seriously disrupts normal sleep and can lead to fatigue, muscle aches, and elevation in blood pressure over a period of time. The disruption in normal breathing is usually due to markedly reduced airflow caused by relaxation-produced obstruction from excess tissue at the back of the throat. These interruptions in breathing can occur upwards of 200 times an hour! Both snoring and sleep apnea increase as people get older (Bliwise et al., 1984). Reliable diagnosis of sleep apnea requires the person to spend a night in a sleep lab, where various parameters of sleep (e.g., eye movements, respiration, muscle tension) are monitored.

TREATMENT OF SLEEP DISORDERS Over-the-counter medications and prescription drugs are taken by many older people with insomnia. Older adults are major consumers of sleep aids; more than 60% of users of prescription sleep drugs are over the age of 50 (Mellinger et al., 1985). According to Morin, Bastien, Brink, and Brown (2003), pharmacotherapy is the most common form of treatment for sleep disorders for people of all ages, but this is especially true for the elderly, who receive one third of the sedatives and hypnotics that are used. Yet sleep drugs rapidly lose their effectiveness and, with continuous use, may make sleep light and fragmented. REM rebound sleep, an increase in REM sleep after prolonged reliance on drugs, is fitful (Bootzin et al., 1996). Medications can even bring about what is called a drug-dependent insomnia. These so-called aids can also give people drug hangovers and increase respiratory difficulties, which in older adults is a great hazard. Additional information from Morin and associates is profiled in Canadian Contributions 16.1.

There is considerable evidence that tranquillizers are not the appropriate treatment for people of any age with chronic insomnia, and particularly not for older people with insomnia. Side effects of tranquillizers such as the benzodiazepines (e.g., Valium) include problems in learning new information and serious difficulties in thinking clearly the day after taking the medication (Ghoneim & Mewaldt, 1990). Nonetheless, tranquillizers are prescribed for most nursing-home residents, and in many instances, they are administered daily, even without evidence of a sleep disturbance (Bootzin et al., 1996).

Melatonin, a hormone secreted by the pineal gland, plays an important role in regulating sleep and is known to decrease with aging. Thus, it is not surprising that it has been used to treat sleep disorders in older adults and has had some success. Other recommended pharmacological treatments besides

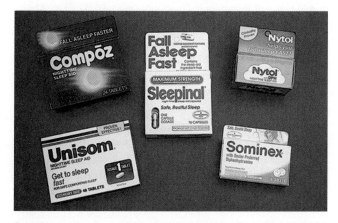

Over-the-counter sleep aids can have serious side effects. Dion Ogust/The Image Works.

CANADIAN CONTRIBUTIONS 16.1
CHARLES MORIN AND THE TREATMENT OF INSOMNIA IN OLDER ADULTS

Courtesy of Dr. Charles Morin.

Charles Morin is a Professor in the Department of Psychology at Université Laval in Quebec City. He is the director of the Sleep Disorders Research Centre and he has also served as the president of the Canadian Sleep Society (www.css.to). In 1995, Morin received the American Psychological Association's Distinguished Award for Early Career Contributions in the field of health psychology and he was awarded a Canada Research Chair in 2004. Since the late 1980s, Morin and his colleagues have been engaged in a comprehensive program of research on all aspects of sleep disorders. Much of what we know about the nature and psychological treatment of insomnia in elderly adults is due to the impressive efforts of Morin and his colleagues. Most recently, for instance, Morin et al. (2009) reported the results of a three-year study of adults described as having a diagnosis of insomnia, symptoms of insomnia, or good sleep. Almost half of those with sleep problems had insomnia throughout the entire three-year study. Persistent insomnia was found among those with more severe initial insomnia, among older persons, and among women. In another investigation, Daley, Morin, Leblanc, Gregoire, and Savard (2009) projected that the annual economic costs of insomnia in Quebec totalled $6.6 billion! About $5 billion of the cost came in the form of insomnia-related productivity losses.

In one of their first studies, Morin and Gramling (1989) compared the sleep characteristics and associated factors for older adults with insomnia and without insomnia. The main sleep variable that distinguished those with insomnia from those without was the amount of time awake after sleep onset. This was in keeping with the general situation of older poor sleepers having trouble staying asleep, and with younger poor sleepers having trouble getting to sleep in the first place. Morin and Gramling (1989) also established that poor sleepers had substantially elevated levels of depression and anxiety. The extent of physical illness and medication usage did not distinguish the two groups.

Research has focused on pharmacological and psychological treatments for chronic insomnia in older adults. Morin and associates provided incontrovertible evidence that older adults can benefit greatly from behavioural treatment or CBT for their sleep difficulties (Morin et al., 1999; Morin, Vallières, Guay, et al., 2009). In fact, these interventions may, in the long run, be superior to drug therapies; medication should be reduced and even eliminated eventually so that improvement is not attributed to the drug (Morin et al., 1999). If so, clients may not invest as much time and energy in the behavioural treatment.

Follow-up analyses of the 1999 data examined predictors of treatment response (see Gagné & Morin, 2001). Treatment response was assessed with subjective self-reports of sleep quality and objective physiological recordings of sleep quality (i.e., polysomnography) based on three nights of laboratory assessment. Poorer treatment outcome was associated with more advanced age and longer duration and greater severity of insomnia.

Morin, Blais, and Savard (2002) also showed that CBT resulted in reductions in dysfunctional attitudes about sleep and that these reductions were linked directly with improvements in sleep efficiency (i.e., the ratio of total sleep time to total time spent in bed) as assessed by daily sleep diaries and polysomnography (e.g., electroencephalographic monitoring). Dysfunctional attitudes were assessed with Morin's (1993) Dysfunctional Beliefs and Attitudes about Sleep (DBAS) Scale. The DBAS assesses five themes: (1) misconceptions about causes of insomnia (e.g., "I believe that insomnia is essentially the result of aging and there isn't much that can be done about this problem"); (2) diminished perception of control and predictability of sleep (e.g., "When I sleep poorly on one night, I know it will disturb my sleep schedule for the whole week"); (3) unrealistic sleep expectations (e.g., "I must get eight hours of sleep to feel refreshed and function well during the day"); (4) misattribution or amplification of the consequences of insomnia (e.g., "I am concerned that chronic insomnia may have serious consequences on my physical health"); and (5) faulty beliefs about sleep-promoting practices (e.g., "When I have trouble sleeping, I should stay in bed and try harder").

Many conclusions about the positive effects of interventions were confirmed by the results of a recent meta-analytic review by Morin et al. (2006). This analysis surveyed the results of 37 treatment studies between 1998 and 2004. Morin et al. concluded that "psychological and behavioral therapies predict reliable changes in several sleep parameters" (p. 1398) and they suggested that behavioural approaches should be tried first. Overall, they established that five treatments met criteria as empirically supported treatments: cognitive-behavioural therapy, stimulus control therapy, relaxation, paradoxical intention, and sleep restriction.

What's next for Morin? One of his goals is to evaluate a new self-help treatment based on psychoeducational theory. This treatment could go a long way toward reducing the consequences of insomnia, both for older and younger people.

melatonin receptor agonists include benzodiazepines and benzodiazepine receptor agonists (see Taylor & Weiss, 2009).

Jokes have been told for years about taking a little nip of alcohol to help get to sleep. As a central nervous system depressant, alcohol does induce relaxation and drowsiness in most people, but like nearly all other drugs, alcohol has negative effects on what is called the architecture of sleep; that is, the different stages of sleep, such as rapid eye movement (REM) sleep, which is associated with dreaming. Alcohol markedly reduces REM sleep, resulting in such problems as fatigue and difficulty thinking clearly the next day.

People with sleep disturbances, including older adults, sometimes mix alcohol with sedatives or tranquillizers. These combinations, which can lead to unintended death, can be particularly dangerous for older adults because of their greater sensitivity to biochemicals. Finally, alcohol exacerbates sleep apnea.

In general, explaining to older persons the nature of sleep and the changes that take place as a normal part of the aging process can reduce their worry about their sleep patterns, a concern that itself can interfere with sleep. The therapist can also reassure clients that going without sleep from time to time is not a calamity; it will not cause irreversible brain damage or mental illness, as some people fear.

Worrying less about sleeping usually helps one sleep. Some individuals are given relaxation training to help them fall asleep and tips to help them develop good sleep habits: rising at the same time every day; avoiding activities at bedtime that are inconsistent with falling asleep; lying down only when sleepy; and if unable to go to sleep, getting up and going into another room. Regular exercise can also help (Stevenson & Topp, 1990). All these tactics can loosen the grip of insomnia on adults of all ages (Bootzin et al., 1996; Morin & Azrin, 1988).

For years, practitioners have believed that medication was the most effective treatment for sleep problems in older adults. Contemporary research into non-pharmacological treatment of sleep disorders in this population, however, has yielded extremely promising results. Charles Morin from Université Laval is one of the leading scholars in this area. His work is described in Canadian Contributions 16.1.

SUICIDE

Several factors put people in general at especially high risk for suicide: serious physical illness, feelings of hopelessness, social isolation, loss of loved ones, dire financial circumstances, and depression (see Chapter 8). Because these problems are widespread among older adults, it should not be surprising that suicide rates for people over age 65 are high, perhaps three times greater than the rate for younger individuals (McIntosh, 1995).

Older white men in the United States are more likely to commit suicide than are members of any other group; the peak ages for committing suicide in this group are from 80 to 84 (Conwell, 1994). As for Canada, according to 1997 statistics (World Health Organization, 1997), rates of suicide in men remain fairly constant and quite high across the various age ranges, including old age, while rates for women decline somewhat. Men

have higher suicide rates than women throughout the lifespan, but the difference is most notable in people aged 75 and older.

Studies of suicide in Alberta and in Ontario showed that elderly men were more likely than elderly women to use lethal methods (e.g., guns) as a means of committing suicide (Juurlink et al., 2004; Quan & Arboleda-Florez, 1999). A study of suicide rates in 21 health units in British Columbia (Agbayewa, Marion, & Wiggins, 1998) found that the elderly had a higher suicide rate in every region and that the male suicide rate was higher than the female rate in every region.

Older persons are less likely than younger persons to communicate their intentions to commit suicide, and they make fewer attempts (Conwell, 2001). When older people attempt suicide, they use more lethal methods and more often kill themselves (Heisel & Duberstein, 2005; Koponen et al., 2007), so the ratio of attempted to completed suicides for elderly people tends to be much lower than for younger people. According to Pearson and Brown (2000), the ratio of attempted suicides to completed suicides is about 4 to 1 for elderly people, but ranges between 8 to 1 and 20 to 1 for the overall population. Several factors contribute to this difference. Conwell (2001) mentions such factors as elderly people having fewer physical resources, so they are less likely to survive self-inflicted damage. Also, elderly people are often more socially isolated and less likely to be rescued prior to death. Finally, the suicide acts themselves are more planned and determined in older people and are less impulsive (Heisel, 2006; Heisel & Duberstein, 2005). Unfortunately, the statistics are probably underestimates. Older adults have many opportunities to give up on living, such as by neglecting their diet or medications, thus killing themselves in a more passive fashion. As more and more people survive longer, the number of suicides in people over age 65 is almost certain to increase (see Conwell, 2001).

Numerous factors play a role in suicide among the elderly. Conwell (2001) alluded to the role of psychosocial factors. Individual differences in loneliness and feelings of isolation predicted suicide ideation in the elderly in Canadian studies (Mireault & deMan, 1996; Stravynski & Boyer, 2001). Heisel, Flett, and Besser (2002) showed that poor cognitive functioning, depression, general hopelessness, and interpersonal hopelessness were predictors of suicide ideation in a sample of seniors from the Toronto area, and they presented a model in which depression and hopelessness mediated the link between poor cognitive functioning and suicide ideation. Recent data also point to completed suicides being tied to feeling like life itself had become a burden and to a palpable sense of loss of self (i.e., no longer feeling like the person you used to be) (see Kjølseth, Ekeberg, & Steihaug, 2010).

Brown, Bongar, and Cleary (2004) asked a sample of 681 practising psychologists with expertise on aging to rate the importance of 36 potential suicide risk factors. Factors deemed of critical importance for suicides by elderly people included a history of suicide attempts, severe hopelessness, the seriousness of previous suicide attempts, depression, isolation, losses and separations, and a family history of suicide.

What about the role of health problems? Several investigators have confirmed a link between physical illness and suicide among the elderly (Duberstein et al., 2004; Erlangsen, Vach, & Jeune, 2005; Koponen et al., 2007). Erlangsen et al. (2005) found that two thirds of the oldest old had at least one medical hospitalization within the previous two years and medical hospitalization was particularly evident among women who killed themselves. A 15-year study of suicide in Finland confirmed that suicides among the elderly were associated with more violent means of committing suicide and alcohol was more likely to be involved. In addition, they found that the suicidal elders, relative to younger people, had a higher prevalence of physical illness and depressive episodes.

Intervention to prevent the suicide of an older person is similar to that discussed in Chapter 8. In general, the therapist tries to persuade the person to regard his or her problems in less desperate terms. Mental health professionals, who are usually younger and healthier than their older clients, may unwittingly try less hard to prevent an older person's suicide attempt, but older people—like people of any age—are usually grateful to have another chance at life once a crisis has passed.

Unfortunately, only a small number of suicidal elderly people actually seek help from a mental health professional. About 70% of those who commit suicide had visited their physician sometime during the month prior to committing suicide, but their profound depression and despair often goes undetected (see Pearson & Brown, 2000). The Quebec study cited above found that 53% of those who committed suicide had visited their physician in the two weeks prior to their suicide (see Preville et al., 2005). As a result, it has been strongly suggested that, in primary care settings, doctors should conduct routine screenings for depression and suicidal tendencies

when assessing their elderly patients. The utility of screening and intervention at the primary care level was illustrated by the substantial reductions in suicide ideation and depression among elderly medical patients who took part in a comprehensive study known as the PROSPECT Study (see Alexopoulos et al., 2009). In part, the greater benefits were simply the result of having greater access to psychotherapy and antidepressants compared with those who received care as usual.

Clearly, the elderly are neglected when it comes to suicide prevention, and in their review paper, Heisel and Duberstein (2005) were critical of the lack of training and knowledge in general, but especially when it comes to suicide in the elderly. A survey of American and Canadian crisis prevention centres found that only one quarter of Canadian centres have specialty programs for elderly people (vs. 46% having programs for adolescents) and only 14% have outreach programs for suicidal elderly people (Adamek & Kaplan, 1996). In addition, more than two thirds of the volunteers and almost half of the program managers did not realize that older adults represent the age group with the highest suicide rate. Perhaps this lack of outreach and awareness accounts, at least in part, for the reluctance of elderly people to seek help from crisis prevention centres.

TREATMENT AND CARE OF OLDER ADULTS

Older adults sometimes go to mental health centres or seek private psychotherapy through referrals. Yet older people are less likely than younger adults to be referred (Knight, 2004), which could be a reflection of the attitudes uncovered in the Kingston study, described earlier in this chapter. One problem is that general practitioners usually fail to detect depression in older patients (Bowers et al., 1990). This situation may be due in part to inadequate geriatric training for medical professionals.

Clinicians tend to expect less success in treating older people than in treating young people (Knight, 2004; Settin, 1982). In one study, therapists in Canada and the United States were provided with descriptions of people of various ages with personality disorders requiring treatment (Zivian et al, 1992). The results showed that therapists overwhelmingly preferred to provide treatment to middle-aged and younger adults than to the elderly. Psychotherapists were less likely to respond this way if they themselves were older, had taken three or more professional courses focusing on older adults, or had practices in which at least 1 in 10 of their clients was 65 or older.

The views of psychotherapists are paralleled by equally negative views of the elderly endorsed by people in the general population. The same team of researchers assessed public opinions of psychotherapy for the elderly in a large sample of visitors to the Ontario Science Centre in Toronto (see Zivian et al., 1994). The respondents were presented with the same scenarios used in the previous study and were asked to evaluate the value of psychotherapy if provided to the target people in the scenarios. Zivian et al. found that older people were seen as less likely to benefit from psychotherapy; they also found that this negative view was especially pronounced among the older people in the sample.

Marnin Heisel from the University of Western Ontario is the co-creator of the first measure designed specifically for studying suicide ideation in the elderly. He has been given the Young Investigator Award from the American Foundation for Suicide Prevention; he is a board member of the Canadian Association of Suicide Prevention. He also took on a leading role in the development in Canada of national guidelines for the assessment of suicide risk and the prevention of suicide (see Heisel et al., 2006) and he took a leading role in creating the guide for suicide prevention for the Canadian Coalition for Seniors' Mental Health. Courtesy of Dr. Marnin Heisel.

These findings have emerged even though, as we noted earlier, research does not show that psychotherapy is less successful for older clients (Gallagher-Thompson & Thompson, 1995a, 1995b; Knight, 2004; Knight, Kelly, & Gatz, 1992; Scoggin & McElreath, 1994). If older clients are viewed as having limited possibilities for improvement, they may not be treated. Admissions of older adults to mental hospitals and to psychiatric units of general hospitals have decreased substantially in recent years owing to changes in mental health policy in most provinces and territories. Most older people needing mental health treatment now live in nursing homes or receive community-based care. The importance of home care is shown in Canadian Perspectives 16.2.

CANADIAN PERSPECTIVES 16.2
HOME CARE IN CANADA

In a policy statement, the Canadian Association on Gerontology (CAG, 1999) decried the fact that Canada does not have a universally accessible, comprehensive home care policy or program. Each province has a different approach to home care delivery (see Romanow & Marchildon, 2003; Woodward et al., 2004). Should home care be a vital part of a comprehensive health care system? Home care is more affordable than residential care at all levels of need (Hollander & Chappell, 2007). A strong case has been made for the benefits of integrated care that would include home care supplemented by some facility care (see Hollander et al., 2009). Roy Romanow, who led the Commission on the Future of Health Care in Canada, concluded that integrated home care should definitely be expanded to include mental health services (Romanow & Marchildon, 2003).

A key group in this effort is the Canadian Association of Retired Persons (CARP), a national, non-partisan organization for Canadians aged 50 or older (www.carp.ca). CARP conducted a national survey of 300 organizations involved in home care. The results were summarized in the report *Home Care by Default, Not by Design* (Parent & Anderson, 2001). CARP's "report card" concluded that home care in Canada is a system by default, and the organization reiterated previous calls for a national strategy, national standards, and a common national definition of home care.

Who is most likely to receive home care? Results from the Canadian Community Health Survey show that women were more likely than men to receive home care (Carrière, 2003). Home care was more likely for those who lived alone, who were almost two times more likely to receive home care than those who lived with another person. Those who lived alone were also more likely to have been hospitalized within the previous year and they more often had a chronic medical condition. Home care also increased with age, with 42% of those 85 years or older receiving home care (vs. 8% of those 65 to 74 years old and 20% of those 75 to 84 years old) (also see Martens et al. 2007). Finally, of those who received home care, 10% indicated that their needs were still not met.

Are home care services both appropriate and cost-effective? Unfortunately, research on cost-effectiveness, much of which is U.S.-based, has been inconclusive. Despite the fact that recipients typically report higher quality of life, home services are not always cost-effective. Regardless of cost-effectiveness, substantial increases in funding have occurred in recent years, so improvements have been made in terms of addressing underfunding. In 2004, the federal government and the provincial premiers agreed to a $41-billion infusion into the system over the next decade and this included creating a National Home Care Program. This is known as the First Ministers Accord. The most recent statistics have confirmed this increase in spending. Government spending on home care doubled between 1994 and 2004, with $3.4 billion spent in 2003–04. Annually, home care resources increase almost 10%, which is important given the projected increases in the number of elderly people in Canada (see Canadian Institute for Health Information, 2007).

Is there a link between the availability of home care and mental health? There is no definitive answer, but what is clear is the increasing level of mental illness as people get much older. A study conducted in Manitoba found that older home care clients, especially those 80 years and older, have a very high likelihood of mental illness (Martens et al., 2007). The authors concluded that this degree of mental illness has very significant implications in terms of staffing standards, quality of care, and training.

Given that more than 70% of personal care to the elderly is provided by informal networks of family and friends (Kane & Kane, 1985), the consequences of health care restructuring in Canada (e.g., closing of hospitals, restrictions on building long-term care beds) mean an increased burden on caregivers unless there are even more substantial increases in the funding of home care.

A qualitative study by Aronson (2002) illustrated that elderly people vary in their response to home care, and as noted above, 10% indicate that their needs were not met. Some elderly people responded to home care by proactively taking charge and had positive views of home care, but a substantial proportion of the elderly saw home care as something beyond their control. In essence, they felt that home care "pushed them over the edge." They found home care to be insufficient and depersonalizing in that it involved a succession of care providers who never really got to know them personally and who often did not have enough time for them. Thus, what is clearly needed is quality home care.

Thinking Critically

1. Do you think that home care should be available as part of medicare in Canada? Should every citizen have access?
2. What criteria should be used to determine access? Would all elderly people with dementia be eligible? Would adults with mental retardation living in their own homes receive home care? What about people with chronic schizophrenia living on their own?
3. Should means-testing and cost-sharing be a part of the home care system everywhere in Canada? Should all services be privatized?

NURSING HOMES

The prevalent myth regarding nursing homes is that families dump their older relatives into these institutions at the first sign of frailty. However, families usually explore all their alternatives and exhaust their own resources before they institutionalize an older relative. The decision to institutionalize comes as a last resort, not as a first choice. While institutionalization can sometimes have a negative impact on family relations, one U.S. study found that moving the parent to a nursing home tended to strengthen family ties and brought a renewed closeness between the parent and the child who was the primary caregiver. The care provided by the nursing home alleviated the strain caused by the parent's multiple physical or mental problems. Relations grew worse in only about 10% of families (Smith & Bengston, 1979).

Nursing homes are now the major locus for institutional care for older adults with severe chronic illnesses and mental disorders (Horgas, Wahl, & Baltes, 1996). Given projected future needs, it does not appear that enough people are being trained to provide mental health services within nursing homes. This is a matter of concern in both the United States and Canada. In the United States, a minority of the approximately 15,000 nursing homes offer counselling as a routine service, and the great majority of people have diagnosed mental disorders (including dementia) (National Center for Health Statistics, 1989; Rovner et al., 1986). The situation is similar in Canada. Worse still, nursing-home operators prefer to exclude older adults with mental disorders, a step likely to place further strains on caregivers and families.

Even a good nursing home—and not all of them are run well—may have unintended negative consequences on

some residents. This caution is based on a classic study by Blenker (1967). Older adults who went to a medical health centre were assigned randomly to one of three treatments: intensive, intermediate, and minimal. Intensive treatment involved the services of a nurse and a social worker; intermediate treatment involved somewhat less professional attention; and minimal treatment consisted of information and referral to community-based services. One might expect intensive treatment to have been the most effective, but after half a year, the death rate of members of the intensive-care group was four times that of people in the minimal-care group. The intermediate-care group was better off than the intensive-care group, the death rate of its members being "only" twice that of the minimal-care group.

What happened? It turned out that the major factor was whether a patient was placed in an institution, such as a nursing home. People were much more likely to be institutionalized if a nurse and social worker were intensively involved in planning their care, and the excessive death rates were found in institutionalized patients. Because people had been assigned randomly to the three treatments, the death rates were not due to related differences existing before treatment began.

What is it about some nursing homes that could contribute to such decline? First, relocation to a new setting is in itself stressful and plays a role in increased mortality (Schultz & Brenner, 1977). Once the person is in the nursing home, the extent and nature of care discourage rehabilitation and even maintenance of whatever self-care skills and autonomous activities the resident may be capable of. For example, a resident able to feed himself or herself will be assisted or even fed like a child at mealtimes to shorten the time devoted to serving meals.

During the late 1980s and 1990s, a series of investigations into lax practices in nursing homes in both the United States and Canada led to a number of governmental reforms. Despite resulting improvements in most nursing homes, there remain serious problems with some of them. These deficiencies undermine the belief that residents reliably receive satisfactory care. The situation has been much worse in the United States than in Canada. In the United States, for example, nursing assistants are often inadequately trained, overworked, and underpaid, and it is the nursing assistants, not the professional nursing staff or physicians, who have by far the most contact with nursing-home residents. Many nursing assistants do not speak the same language as the residents; they are often high school dropouts and homeless; and some work two jobs for as many as 18 hours a day. Turnover in these positions is high. Despite the best intentions, nursing assistants are presented with an overwhelming set of challenges, owing in part to cutbacks in government funding to nursing homes and the resulting unreasonably heavy workload. In a study in California, some residents were reported to have been harmed, sometimes fatally, through errors of omission and of commission by nursing assistants (Pyle, 1999). The possibility of abuse of nursing-home residents is discussed in Canadian Perspectives 16.3.

Nursing homes play a major role in the institutional care of the aged. They have often been criticized for the poor care they provide, as well as for the lack of stimulation in the environment. © Ocean/Corbis.

CANADIAN PERSPECTIVES 16.3
ELDER ABUSE IN CANADA: A "HIDDEN HORROR"?

Despite everything, Janet* still remembers the good things about her son, Brian. The 69-year-old retired Alberta day-care worker says Brian, an only child, was devoted to her husband, a former oil company technician who suffers from Parkinson's disease. "My son always took great care of his dad," she says, but then added: "It was always me he picked on." "Picked on" hardly describes the pain and suffering Brian inflicted if Janet refused his demands for money or said anything he didn't like. "He would pin me up against the wall and grab my face or my neck, and squeeze until I'd repeat whatever he wanted me to," she says, her voice trembling.

The worst attacks occurred when her son, in his 30s, moved back to his parents' home after he lost his job last year. Janet says she knew she ought to have called the police, but after each incident, she succumbed to Brian's appeasements, believing his contrition was real. But instead, the abuse grew worse, both in ferocity and frequency. The last straw for Janet came last January when, for the first time, she says, Brian attacked his partially paralyzed father, knocking him from his walker, pinning him to the ground and repeatedly spitting and screaming into the 70-year-old man's face. Janet fled to a neighbour's house and called authorities. "I lived in terror for years," she says, her voice breaking, "and I became increasingly fearful for my life." (Oh, 1999, p. 48)

*All names of victims and their family members have been changed.

Elder abuse was in the news because of revelations in newspapers and on the CTV show *W-5* about the abuse experienced by 87-year-old Norma Stenson at two separate retirement and long-term care facilities in Brantford, Ontario (see Canadian Press, February 8, 2004). A videotape that aired on *W-5* showed footage of two workers mistreating Stenson. This frail, elderly woman was smacked and tossed about, had a pillow put over her face, was pulled roughly from bed at 4 a.m., injuring her arm and knee, and had money stolen from her. Stenson requires the use of a wheelchair, and she can barely speak as a result of experiencing several strokes prior to the incidents.

Definitions and Types of Abuse
A widely accepted definition of elder abuse came out of the 2002 Toronto Declaration on the Global Prevention of Elder Abuse by the World Health Organization, in collaboration with Ryerson University and the University of Toronto. Elder abuse was defined as "a single or repeated act, or lack of appropriate action, occurring within any relationship where there is an expectation of trust which causes harm or distress to an older person. It can be of various forms: physical, psychological/emotional, sexual, financial, or simply reflect intentional or unintentional neglect" (World Health Organization, 2002, p. 3). Of course, it is possible for the elderly person to experience

several types of abuse, and all forms of abuse can have adverse psychological consequences. For example, Janet and her husband experienced psychological, physical, and financial abuse from their son. It is probable that they would soon have experienced neglect as well.

The impact of elder abuse is clear. Elder abuse victims in Canada experience more serious physical health problems and have shorter life expectancies than people who are not abused (Oh, 1999).

Elder abuse is being recognized internationally as a growing problem. This has resulted in the International Network for the Prevention of Elder Abuse (INPEA; see www.inpea.net). This organization has been endorsed by the United Nations (see United Nations, 2004).

Prevalence of Elder Abuse in Canada
Officially, the prevalence of elder abuse in Canada is 4%, as determined by a national telephone survey (Podnieks & Pillemer, 1990). However, elder abuse is rarely reported and the figure of 4% likely underestimates the magnitude of the problem. A chart review of clients affiliated with a geriatric psychiatry service in Montreal found suspected or confirmed elder abuse in 16% of cases, with the most common forms being financial abuse (13%) and neglect (6%) (Vida, Monks, & Des Rosiers, 2002). A history of family disruption owing to death, divorce, or separation was higher among the abused. Kosberg (1988) estimated that five out of every six cases of abuse can go unreported. Why? Out of shame, guilt, or fear, victims rarely report mistreatment. Often the abuse is difficult to detect by others, who may be reluctant to "see it" or are unaware of the signs and symptoms of abuse. Further, police and prosecutors can be reluctant to pursue what may be viewed as a family dispute. Elizabeth Podnieks, who chairs the Ontario Network for the Prevention of Elder Abuse, estimates that between 7 and 10% of the 3.7 million seniors in Canada experience some form of abuse, primarily by their children and grandchildren. Thus, although a majority of elderly people cared for by their families receive good care, tragic cases such as that of Janet are not uncommon or unusual in Canada.

Although abuse may be difficult to detect, a Canadian study identified some reliable signs of impending or actual abuse of the elderly (Mendonca, Velamoor, & Sauve, 1996). Indications of poor physical care are often clues that physical abuse is likely occurring. Other indicators include obvious signs of psychological distress, irritability, and defensiveness in the abuser. Alcohol abuse by the abuser has also been identified as a contributing factor in approximately 15% of Canadian cases (Bradshaw & Spencer, 1999).

Robert Gordon from Simon Fraser University and Deborah Brill have reviewed the hypotheses offered as explanations for elder abuse (see Gordon & Brill, 2001). These explanations include the stressed-caregiver hypothesis (i.e., abuse is a by-product of overworked, burdened caregivers), the learned-violence hypothesis (i.e., a family member, once the target of violence or neglect, learned these behaviours and can now exact revenge on an elderly parent), and the psychopathology hypothesis (i.e., abuse is a reflection of a pre-existing disorder in the abuser, such as substance dependence). Gordon and Brill (2001) posited an "integrated theory" of abuse and neglect of the elderly that includes aspects of the caregiver (caregiver stress, caregiver pathology, learned violence), aspects of the elderly victim (e.g., victim pathology and excessive dependency behaviour), and ongoing environmental stressors.

Prevention, Detection, and Treatment of Elder Abuse in Canada

What can our society and the various professionals who come in contact with the elderly do to detect abuse and protect seniors? Most experts agree that elder abuse is part of a larger social context that requires responsibility on the part of government, the community, and the individual caregiver (Trevitt & Gallagher, 1996).

Prevention and Detection
Role of Governments

Various levels of government throughout Canada are taking some initiative to try to put a stop to elder abuse. In 1999, the Ontario government formed the Round Table for Ontario's Elder Abuse Strategy. The goal was to enhance the ability of communities in Ontario to combat elder abuse through staff training, services coordination, and public awareness. In 2007, the Government of Canada created the National Seniors Council to act as an advisory board on issues of importance to seniors, including elder abuse. Their November 2007 report outlines the implications of elder abuse in Canada and a series of recommendations to address elder abuse in Canada (National Seniors Council on Elder Abuse, 2007).

Role of Professional Personnel

Although psychiatrists and psychologists can play important roles in the detection and prevention of elder abuse, frontline workers such as general practitioners, nurses, and social workers play more critical roles, since they are more likely to encounter situations of actual abuse and situations where an elderly person is at risk for abuse. Unfortunately, a survey of transition houses in Yukon and in British Columbia found that only 4% of the facilities had special services available for older women (Hightower et al., 1999).

Role of Physicians

General practitioners can play a vital role in the prevention, identification, and treatment of elder abuse. Nonetheless, many physicians believe that they do not have the skills and resources to deal with elder abuse, even if they are able to identify it. The

Canadian Medical Association (CMAJ, 1997) polled general practitioners in Ontario to determine what strategies for dealing with elder abuse they would be likely to use. More than 80% of respondents indicated that they would be "fairly" or "very likely" to use the following: a single agency overseeing all cases of elder abuse, a directory of services for seniors, a list of resource people to provide advice to them, and professional guidelines or protocols for both the detection and the management of elder abuse.

Role of Nurses, Social Workers, and Personal Support Workers

Nurses in community practice and health care facilities often have a unique opportunity to play a significant role in the prevention and treatment of elder abuse. However, a study of registered nurses in Victoria, B.C., concluded that the nurses were not knowledgeable about different types of elder abuse (Trevitt & Gallagher, 1996). Further, the nurses perceived themselves as unskilled and felt uncomfortable when dealing with actual cases of abuse. The nurses also identified relevant problems within the community, such as few trained personnel, a lack of co-operation between agencies, a lack of legal guidelines, and a reluctance to become involved.

Role of Community Organizations

Community organizations, either alone or in partnership with various levels of government, are making efforts to educate the general public and professionals about elder abuse. For example, the non-profit Ontario Network for Prevention of Elder Abuse supports several initiatives. In an attempt to prevent future elder abuse, the network has developed a new program to influence positively children's attitudes toward seniors. The program involves the use of interactive storytelling and "skit" kits for children as young as four years old. The "Grandpa is a Grump" story for younger children explains why an elderly person's face can look grumpy and how to see beyond the physical appearance. With assistance from Health Canada, the network has produced a video that can be used by groups and individuals concerned about elder abuse. The video explores various situations of abuse, one example being an older man attempting to forget the shame of having been beaten by his son.

Elder Abuse in Nursing, Retirement Homes, and Hospitals

Thus far, we have focused on the abuse of the elderly in their own homes. However, we began this discussion with a case of horrific abuse in a nursing home and long-term care facility. What about the abuse of the elderly in retirement and nursing homes? Unfortunately, in recent years, there have been numerous highly publicized cases of elder abuse in these institutions throughout Canada.

In the fall of 2003, the *Toronto Star* published a series of investigative reports on nursing-home neglect and abuse in Ontario. The investigation into the province's 544 nursing homes analyzed the health ministry's own data to reveal widespread neglect and inadequate care for the 65,000 residents in the system; for example, the residents were left for long periods in dirty diapers, went hungry, and suffered from toxic bed sores (leading to death in at least one case) (Welsh, 2004). More recently, in January 2007, staff at Glen Haven Manor in Nova Scotia taped shut a woman's mouth and drew a "smiley-face" on it in an apparent attempt to calm her (Boomer, 2007). The two employees were suspended without pay; one was suspended for five days and the other for 10 days.

Thinking Critically

1. Elder abuse is a complicated issue. Although we cannot ever condone the behaviour, do you think that some instances of abuse might occur because of the unrelenting demands of caregiving? Would this be a further indication of the need for respite care for both the elderly and their caregivers?

2. Should reporting of suspected abuse be mandatory? Some professionals have suggested that mandatory reporting takes away the right of a competent person suspected of being abused to make choices regarding what they want to do.

3. In some states in the United States (e.g., California), public databases rate nursing homes on the basis of indicators of quality care (e.g., hours left in bed, use of restraints, inspection results). Do you think such ratings should be a mandatory component of the system in Canada so that families can determine if the homes they are considering for a loved one provide good care?

4. The Canadian government has been considering enacting whistle-blower protection legislation for government agencies.

Dr. Elizabeth Podnieks received the Order of Canada for research on elder abuse. Her current work emphasizes eliminating elder abuse in the form of social exclusion and economic exclusion (Podnieks, 2006). Courtesy of Dr. Elizabeth Podnieks.

Some provinces have whistleblower legislation in place to protect employees who report unlawful behaviour. Do you think we should legislate whistle-blower protection so that staff in long-term care facilities can report instances of neglect and abuse without fear of reprisal?

Primary Sources: Brockville (Ontario) Police; Muskoka-Parry Sound (Ontario) Health Unit; National Clearinghouse on Family Violence; Nova Scotia Seniors' Secretariat; Ontario Network for the Prevention of Elder Abuse; Ontario Seniors' Secretariat; Senior Support Network (King's County, Nova Scotia); the *Toronto Star*.

Depression is a particular problem among the residents of nursing homes. The type of intervention employed is usually a drug, and the psychoactive drug prescribed is more likely to be a tranquillizer than an antidepressant—a less agitated, relatively inactive patient is easier to handle. Psychological interventions are virtually unheard of, for staff members either are untrained in their implementation or operate under the belief that such therapy is inappropriate for an old person (Zarit, 1980). This situation is unfortunate, as interventions such as behaviour therapy have been found to be quite effective in reducing unwanted behaviours and improving overall functioning in nursing-home residents with dementia, which is often associated with depression (Mansdorf et al., 1999).

In sum, all the problems of institutionalization are exhibited in bold and exaggerated relief in some nursing homes. Independence is inadvertently, but with sad consequences, discouraged, and both physical and mental deterioration occur, in part because they are expected.

ALTERNATIVE LIVING SETTINGS

Recently, the United States and Canada have seen a dramatic rise in assisted-living or retirement homes, a viable alternative to placement in nursing homes for many older adults who require assistance of one sort or another. The American Association of Retired Persons (AARP) reports that assisted living is the fastest-growing category of housing for older adults in the United States (AARP, 1999). In contrast to nursing homes, assisted-living facilities resemble hotels, with separate rooms and suites for the residents, as well as dining rooms and on-site amenities such as beauty and barber shops. The philosophy of assisted living stresses autonomy, independence, dignity, and privacy (AARP, 1999). Many such residences are quite luxurious, with attentive staff, nursing and medical assistance readily available, daily activities such as bingo and movies, and other services all designed to provide assisted care for older adults too infirm to live on their own but not so infirm as to require a nursing home. However, as with nursing homes, there is a great deal of variability in the quality of care.

COMMUNITY-BASED CARE

At any given time, 95% of older persons reside in the community. Many of these individuals are frail and have an urgent need for help with daily living arrangements. Some communities and for-profit agencies are organized to provide various services, such as

- telephone reassurance;
- daily phone calls to old persons living alone to check that they are all right;
- home services (e.g., Meals on Wheels, which brings a hot meal each day to the person's door);
- visits from volunteers who cook meals and do household chores;
- shopping help from young people or other seniors and light repair work by volunteers;
- community and/or seniors' centres, which may also serve hot lunches and provide help with government forms;
- sheltered housing (i.e., apartments in which several old people may live together semi-independently);
- home visits by health professionals and social workers, who can assess the actual needs of old people and treat them; and
- regular social visits from community neighbours.

A range of available services allows a true match with the needs of the older person so that he or she will not have too much or too little help. The availability of home care has become a major issue in Canada (see Canadian Perspectives 16.2). Home care is defined as "the provision of an array of health and social services designed to support living at home" (Woodward et al., 2004, p. 177). In addition to improving the quality of life for the elderly person, home care helps to prevent burnout in informal caregivers and plays an important role in preventing abuse of the elderly (see Canadian Perspectives 16.3). Although our focus here is on home care for the elderly, it should be noted that home care is intended to help diverse groups in our society, including the disabled mentally ill. Research indicates that such community-based home care projects enhance the quality of life of older people and reduce their dependency on institutional care (e.g., Knight, 1983; Nocks et al., 1986).

Mere availability of services is not enough. Services must be coordinated; however, they are not coordinated in most localities. All too often, an older person and his or her family are shuffled from one agency to another, getting lost in bureaucracies. Even professionals who have experience with the system often have difficulty working through it to get needed services for their clients. Frustrating rules can interfere with the very goals for which programs were instituted.

When it comes to health care for older adults, one difficulty is that the chronic health problems of old people are not appealing to physicians because they seldom diminish. Many, if not most, of the maladies of old people—hearing loss; visual impairments; loss of mobility; aches and pains, especially in the feet (Pearson & Gatz, 1982); and a steadily declining

Among community-based services are seniors' centres, where older people participate in various activities, such as exercise classes. Lori Adamski Peek/Getty Images.

cardiovascular system—are unlikely to get better and must somehow be adjusted to. Older persons rely heavily on their relationships with health care providers, but these providers may become impatient with them because, as Zarit (1980) suggested, the illnesses of older people are often incurable and therefore violate a "law" by which most medical professionals live. Moreover, older people do not always take medication as instructed (Leach & Roy, 1986).

In addition, older people's relations with family caregivers are likely to suffer. Ailing older family members are sometimes torn both by feelings of guilt for needing so much from others and feelings of anger toward these younger people for whom, at one time, they sacrificed so much. The sons and daughters also have feelings of guilt and anger (Zarit, 1980), and this sometimes leads to abuse, as seen in Canadian Perspectives 16.3.

ISSUES SPECIFIC TO THERAPY WITH OLDER ADULTS

Treatment interventions for the elderly need to recognize the special needs and unique challenges encountered by elderly people and how these may change with development throughout the aging process. The need to acknowledge the unique challenges was shown formally in 2003 when the American Psychological Association (2003) outlined 20 guidelines in its document *Guidelines for Psychological Practice with Older Adults*. Guidelines were agreed upon in six distinct areas: (1) attitudes; (2) general knowledge about adult development, aging, and older adults; (3) clinical issues; (4) assessment; (5) intervention, consultation, and other service provision; and (6) education. In other words, unique issues need to be considered in terms of all aspects of the treatment process. In Canada, national guidelines for the assessment and treatment of seniors' mental health were published in 2006 in the *Canadian Journal of Geriatrics*. These guidelines were put together by the Canadian Coalition for Seniors' Mental Health. The initial series of guidelines for seniors' mental health address (1) the assessment and treatment of delirium, (2) the assessment and treatment of depression, (3) the assessment of suicide risk and the prevention of suicide, and (4) the assessment and treatment of mental health issues in long-term care homes.

The list of guidelines from the APA is too lengthy to reproduce in its entirety due to space limitations. Table 16.3 provides illustrative guidelines in each of the six areas outlined above.

It is important that we consider in more detail some other issues concerning the conduct of therapy for older people. They can be divided into issues of content and issues of process (Zarit, 1980).

CONTENT OF THERAPY

The incidence of brain disorders increases with age, but other mental health problems of older adults are not that different from those experienced earlier in life. Although clinicians should appreciate how physical incapacities and medications may intensify psychological problems, they should also note the importance of consistency and continuity from earlier decades of the older person's life.

For older people, medical illnesses can create irreversible difficulties in walking, seeing, and hearing. Finances may be a problem. Therapists treating psychological distress in older adults must bear in mind that much of it is an understandable response to real-life challenges rather than a sign of psychopathology. Professional intervention, however, may still be helpful.

Therapy with older adults must take into account the social contexts in which they live, something that cannot be accomplished merely by reading the professional literature. The therapist who, for example, urges a lonely widower to seek companionship in a neighbourhood recreation centre for senior citizens may be misguided if the centre is not suited to the particular patient (Knight, 2004); this could make the patient feel even lonelier. All social organizations, even those as loosely structured as a senior centre, develop their own local mores and practices, or what social scientists have come to call social ecology. Some may be tolerant of physical frailty, others not. Mental health care workers need to know and understand the social environments in which their older patients live. We take this need for granted when dealing with younger patients but, Knight points out, often neglect to consider it with older adults.

The social needs of older people often differ from those of younger people. The widespread concern that old people are socially isolated and need to be encouraged to interact more with others appears to be ill-founded. There is no link between level of social activity and psychological well-being among old people (Carstensen, 1996). As we age, our interests shift away from seeking new social interactions to cultivating those few social relationships that really matter to us, such as those with family and with close friends and associates.

Death and dying figure prominently in therapy with older people. They may need help dealing with the fear of facing death or an illness that requires life support. It may be helpful to counsel some older clients to examine their lives from a philosophical or a religious perspective. These perspectives may help them transcend the limitations that aging imposes on human existence. When the person is dying, discussions of the meaning of the individual's life can facilitate self-disclosure and enhance his or her sense of well-being and personal growth (see the previous discussions of life review). The person's loved ones may also benefit from such discussions.

PROCESS OF THERAPY

We have already indicated that traditional individual, group, family, and marital therapies are effective with older adults (Gatz et al., 1985). Some clinicians adapt these therapies to here-and-now practical problems. They hold that therapy with older people needs to be more active and directive, and thus they provide information and take the initiative in seeking out agencies for necessary services.

TABLE 16.3

ILLUSTRATIVE GUIDELINES PROVIDED BY THE AMERICAN PSYCHOLOGICAL ASSOCIATION FOR PSYCHOLOGICAL PRACTICE WITH OLDER ADULTS

Guideline 2—Psychologists are encouraged to recognize how their attitudes and beliefs about aging and about older individuals may be relevant to their assessment and treatment of older adults, and to seek consultation or further education about these issues when indicated.

Guideline 6—Psychologists strive to be familiar with current information about biological and health-related aspects of aging.

Guideline 9—Psychologists strive to be knowledgeable about psychopathology within the aging population and cognizant of the prevalence and nature of that psychopathology when providing services to older adults.

Guideline 10—Psychologists strive to be familiar with the theory, research, and practice of various methods of assessment with older adults, and knowledgeable of assessment instruments that are psychometrically suitable for use with them.

Guideline 14—Psychologists strive to be familiar with and develop skills in applying specific psychotherapeutic interventions and environmental modifications with older adults and their families, including adapting interventions for use with this age group.

Guideline 20—Psychologists are encouraged to increase their knowledge, understanding, and skills with respect to working with older adults through continuing education, training, supervision, and consultation.

Being able to use a computer and access the Internet is one way older adults can increase their social contacts. ICHIRO.

Some characteristics of aging may mean that therapy will proceed differently (Knight, 2004; Light, 1990). Certain kinds of thinking simply take longer for many older people. Older people also tend to experience some diminution in the number of things that can be held in mind at any one time. Therapists may find that it helps to move with greater deliberation when seeing an older adult. Explanations may have to be more elaborate and conversation more extended.

The very process of being in therapy can foster dependency. Older adults, whether institutionalized or living at home with caregivers, often receive much more social reinforcement (attention, praise) for dependent behaviours, such as asking for help or being concerned about the opinion of their therapist, than for instances of independent functioning (Baltes, 1988). The growing specialization of behavioural gerontology (Nemeroff & Karoly, 1991) emphasizes helping older people to enhance their self-esteem by focusing on specific, deceptively minor behaviours, such as controlling their toileting better, increasing self-care and mobility, and improving their telephone conversational skills in order to enhance social contacts. One development, though hardly a formal therapy, involves teaching older adults computer skills so that they can access the Internet and expand their social contacts (Cody et al., 1999).

All therapists must be able to interpret the facial expressions of their clients and thereby understand the meaning of their words or reactions and appreciate their phenomenological experience of the world. Research on emotional changes over the lifespan suggests real potential for error when the therapist is younger than the patient (Knight, 2004). Knight has maintained that his older clients are less emotionally expressive and they use more subtle forms of emotional expression. To what extent will a younger therapist be sensitive to these emotional cues?

We will conclude with a statement on the overall amount and quality of care available to seniors in Canada. In its position paper on the delivery of mental health services to elderly people, the Canadian Association on Gerontology (CAG) (2000a) stated: "The current range of community services are inadequate and insufficient to meet the needs of older mental health clients, but no money to expand or improve community services seems immediately forthcoming." In particular, there is a lack of focus on prevention and too much of the current funding and available treatment is medically driven, even though, as the CAG notes, many issues facing the elderly are non-medical in nature. Given the increasing proportion of the population that will be elderly in the years to come, this is a problem deserving of more attention at the national level. It is also important to conduct rigorous scientific evaluations of preventive and treatment programs (see Canadian Clinic Focus 16.1).

CANADIAN CLINIC FOCUS 16.1
PRISMA – AN INTEGRATED PREVENTIVE PROJECT FOR THE FRAIL ELDERLY AT RISK OF FUNCTIONAL DECLINE

The province of Quebec is the location of an innovative project designed to promote the well-being and autonomy of frail elderly. This program is known as PRISMA (Program of Research to Integrate the Services for the Maintenance of Autonomy). It is a clear example of how clinical resources can be combined for maximum impact and be evaluated by research that determines the impact of clinical interventions. It is in keeping with increasing calls for integrated care (e.g., Hollander et al., 2009). PRISMA is led by Dr. Réjean Hébert, who heads a team of 14 other researchers. Hébert is the founding scientific director of the Canadian Institutes of Health Research—Institute of Aging.

In a previous study, Hébert and his colleagues determined that the annual incidence of functional decline in individuals over 75 years of age who are living at home is almost 12% (Hébert, Brayne, & Spiegelhalter, 1997). The prevalence of disabilities is approximately 80% in people in Quebec over age 85 (Saucier, 1986). Can early detection of elderly individuals at risk of losing their autonomy and the application of an assessment and surveillance program prevent or delay functional decline?

The PRISMA project is an integrated, client-centred effort that relies on extraordinary coordination of services (see Hébert, Durand, Dubuc, Tourigny, & The PRISMA Group, 2003). It is based on an integrated service delivery model. PRISMA is composed of four integrated care mechanisms and two assessment tools. The PRISMA model is outlined in Figure 16.1. The four care mechanisms are (1) co-ordination between decision-managers at the regional and local levels, (2) a single entry point for accessing the services, (3) a case management process, and (4) individualized service plans. Service plans stem from the overall assessment of the person. It is formulated by the case manager in consultation with all other parties involved in the older person's care.

The two tools are (1) an assessment instrument that is combined with a management system to measure a person's functional autonomy and (2) a computerized clinical chart to keep track of progress and ease communication between institutions and treatment providers. The assessment instrument is a universally recognized measure that was created by Hébert. The Functional Autonomy Measurement System is a 29-item rating scale based on how disabilities are described by the World Health Organization. It taps the elderly person's ability to function in five categories: (1) activities of daily living, (2) mobility, (3) communication, (4) mental functions, and (5) instrumental activities of daily living.

The initial results from the PRISMA project are quite promising. Hébert et al. (2010) analyzed the results for more than 1,500 people at risk of functional decline, half of whom were part of PRISMA. Overall, the involvement in PRISMA was successful and resulted not only in higher levels of satisfaction and empowerment, but also 137 fewer cases of functional decline per 1,000 people.

Comment

The PRISMA project is obviously unique in several respects. It was included here not only because it is novel and was developed in Canada, but also because it illustrates that the definition of a "clinic focus" may increasingly need to be expanded to include a range of clinical resources that are located at several sites but integrated in the treatment of a particular person.

The members of the PRISMA project have noted that this endeavour is unusual because it involves an extraordinary degree of contact and coordination among the various members. Is this integrated service delivery model realistic in areas that lack financial resources and necessary sources of "human capital"? PRISMA represents a model of how resources should be combined to maximize the well-being of individuals, but it remains to be determined whether similar programs can be put together in other jurisdictions.

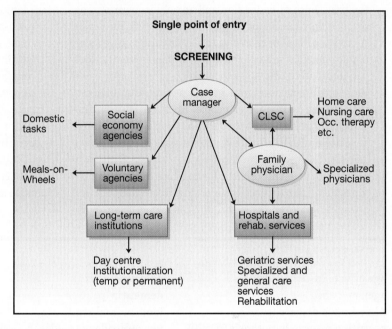

FIGURE 16.1 The PRISMA model of an integrated service delivery system

SUMMARY

- Until recently, the psychological problems of older people were neglected by mental health professionals. As the proportion of people who live beyond age 65 continues to grow, it will become ever more important to learn about the disorders suffered by some older people and the most effective means of preventing or ameliorating them. Although physical deterioration is an obvious aspect of growing old, most of the emotional distress to which old people are prone is psychologically produced.

- Serious brain disorders affect a small minority of older people, fewer than 10%. Two principal disorders have been distinguished: dementia and delirium. In dementia, the person's intellectual functioning declines; memory, abstract thinking, and judgement deteriorate. If the dementia is progressive, as most cases are, the individual seems another person altogether and is, in the end, oblivious to his or her surroundings. A variety of diseases can cause this deterioration. The most important is Alzheimer's disease, a progressive, irreversible illness in which cortical cells

waste away. Genes figure prominently in the etiology of Alzheimer's, particularly the early-onset forms. Head injury and depression are also risk factors.

- In delirium, there is sudden clouding of consciousness and other problems in thinking, feeling, and behaving—fragmented and undirected thought, incoherent speech, inability to sustain attention, hallucinations, illusions, disorientation, lethargy or hyperactivity, and mood swings. The condition is reversible, provided that the underlying cause is self-limiting or adequately treated. Brain cells malfunction but are not necessarily destroyed. Causes include over-medication, infection of brain tissue, high fevers, malnutrition, dehydration, endocrine disorders, head trauma, cerebrovascular problems, and surgery.

- The treatments of these two disorders are quite different from each other. If delirium is suspected, there should be a search for the cause—for example, nutritional deficiencies or a toxic reaction to medication—so that it can be rectified. Progressive dementia usually cannot be treated, but the person and the family affected by the disease can be counselled on how to make the remaining time manageable and even rewarding. If adequate support is given to caregivers, many patients with dementia can be looked after at home. There usually comes a time, however, when the burden of care impels most families to place the person in a nursing home or hospital.

- Older people may experience the entire spectrum of psychological disorders, in many instances brought with them from their earlier years. Yet it appears that, overall, the prevalence of depression and anxiety is lower among older adults than among those younger than 65. The newer cognitive behaviour therapies as well as various psychodynamic therapies are being applied to depression in older patients, and results are encouraging.

- More of the suicide attempts of old people result in death than do those of younger people. Mental health professionals may assume that people who are old and debilitated have nothing to live for. This attitude may reflect their own fear of growing old.

- Nursing homes and other extended-care facilities sometimes do little to encourage residents to maintain or enhance whatever skills and capacities they have. Both physical and mental deterioration are possible. Serious neglect can be found in some nursing homes, despite efforts to correct the deficiencies.

- Today, care is provided in the community whenever possible. Comprehensive services, such as Meals on Wheels, regular home visits by health professionals, and support for caregivers, seem to be beneficial when they are available and coordinated so that people do not have to confront a bureaucratic maze. All intervention should be minimal so that older adults remain as independent as their circumstances permit.

- Many older people can benefit from psychotherapy, but several issues specific to treating older adults need to be kept in mind. The emotional distress of older adults is often realistic in content. Many have experienced irreplaceable losses and face real medical and financial problems. It is unwise always to attribute their complaints to a psychopathological condition. Death is a more immediate issue as well.

- As for the process of therapy, clinicians should sometimes be active and directive, providing information and seeking out the agencies that provide the services needed by their clients. Therapy should also foster a sense of control and hope and should help the older patient elucidate a sense of meaning as he or she approaches the end of life.

KEY TERMS

age effects (p. 564)
ageism (p. 562)
Alzheimer's disease (p. 567)
cognitive reserve hypothesis (p. 570)
cohort effects (p. 564)
cross-sectional studies (p. 565)

delirium (p. 573)
dementia (p. 567)
longitudinal studies (p. 566)
neurofibrillary tangles (p. 568)
paraphrenia (p. 567)
plaques (p. 568)

selective mortality (p. 566)
sleep apnea (p. 581)
subjective age bias (p. 562)
time-of-measurement effects (p. 565)

REFLECTIONS: PAST, PRESENT, AND FUTURE

- Are Canada's economic, social, and medical resources sufficient to provide for the coming dramatic increase in the population of elderly people? Are we facing a caregiving crisis in the future? What can the people of Canada and different levels of government in Canada do to prepare for the aging of the Canadian population?

- If you were consulted by the federal, provincial, and territorial governments about how they might best cope with the increase in disorders of the elderly owing to the aging of the Canadian population, what would you advise them to do? Why?

- A leading American neurologist and ethicist, Dr. Ron Crawford, has suggested that people with Alzheimer's disease should have the right to choose to die rather than be required to live with the possibility that they will become a burden on their families (Vienneau, 1999). However, Dr. Margaret Somerville, director of McGill University's Centre for Medicine, Ethics and Law, is appalled by Crawford's ideas: "Despite its overlay of empathy, it is a 'gene machine' approach to human life. It focuses on cognitive, neural processes as identifying us as human ... and when these are absent we should be disposed of" (Vienneau, 1999, p. L8). Crawford believes that his own position is ahead of its time and "pushes the moral envelope," but he believes that it is "the reality of what we are going to have to face" in the future (Vienneau, 1999, p. L8). What is your own position on this controversial issue? Refer to Chapter 10 if you need more background information.

- In 1999, the year dedicated to the elderly by the United Nations, Pope John Paul II, who suffered from Parkinson's disease, decried the fact that some cultures cherished the elderly, whereas other cultures seemed to dismiss them as disposable items (Reuters, 1999). What is the situation in your own culture? Are the elderly "cherished" or "disposable"?

Joyce Wieland, Canadian 1930–1998, *Two People*, 1957–1958 Oil on canvas, 86.0 × 81.3 cm (sheet), Art Gallery of Ontario, Toronto. Gift of David and Jacqueline Gladstone, 1998 © The National Gallery of Canada.

"Don't ever do anything to someone that you can't reverse."
—D. Ewen Cameron, quoted in Gillmor, 1987

"People, when they are looking for psychotherapy, often don't know what they are getting. They get a psychiatrist or GP who does therapy and get anything from holotropic breathing to long-term psychoanalytic psychotherapy. So consumers need to educate themselves about what they're looking for and knowing how to identify it."
—Zindel V. Segal, quoted in Simmie and Nunes, 2001, p. 158

"Mental health promotion applies to the whole population in the context of everyday life. It benefits everyone. By identifying and activating the personal and social strengths that support mental health, people can work together to develop healthier communities."
—Government of Canada, 2006, p. 24

"That there is a gap, possibly a gulf, between research and practice in psychological therapies has long been acknowledged. Most therapists base their practice on the theoretical orientation in which they trained and their own clinical experience rather than on research findings. Much experimental clinical research in psychology is designed to answer questions of little direct interest to clinicians, using methods which mitigate against clinical realism."
—Parry, Castonguay, Borkovec, and Wolf, 2010, p. 311

THERAPY FOCUSED on a client with multiple presenting concerns, including major depression, anxiety disorder and interpersonal problems overcoming her core maladaptive fear by accessing her sadness at loss and anger at violation, and mobilizing her current abilities to protect herself.... Having spent the first three sessions establishing an empathic bond the therapy first focused on her primary fear of her abusive parents and her fear of her dependence/weakness and vulnerability. Her frequent experiences of shame and embarrassment in therapy were often mixed with her fear. Her parents had disciplined her with harsh criticism and ridicule, as well as physical abuse, and she stated that her greatest pain was that "they never believed in me." She was called stupid, crazy, a whore and a slut and grew up utterly paralyzed in interpersonal relationships. Interventions were aimed at [her] becoming aware of and accessing her fear and shame in the session by talking about her childhood. This led to [her] experiencing and reprocessing these emotions and to a strengthening of her sense of self.

One of her earliest memories was of her father forcing her and her siblings to watch him drown a litter of kittens. This was to "teach her a lesson about life" and the client believed he enjoyed it. The client accessed a core self-organization, which included her "suppressed scream of horror" from this experience. While [she] imaginally

reliv[ed] this scene in therapy the therapist guided her attention to the expression of disgust in her mouth while she was feeling afraid. This mobilized this subdominant adaptive emotion as a resource to begin building a stronger sense of self. Rather than feeling afraid she accessed her alternate emotions of disgust and anger, which she actively expressed toward her father in an empty chair. She mobilized her adaptive needs to not be violated by her father and to be protected by her mother and expressed these to her parent in the empty chair dialogues. Expression and exploration of her vulnerability (fear and sadness) took place, not to the imagined father, but in the affirming and safe dialogue with the therapist.... These imaginary confrontations with the father evoked her fear and her painful memories of childhood beatings, of being told she was bad, and of being aware of nothing but her desperate need to escape.... Her anger undid her fear and the therapist supported the client's new found sense of power, heightening her awareness of her strengths. This motivated further assertion and self-validation. The client acknowledged that she was worthy and had deserved more than she got from her parents. She began to create a new identity narrative, one in which she was worthy and had unfairly suffered abuse at the hands of cruel parents. She also began to feel that it would be possible to need love and she was now open to learn love. (Greenberg, 2004, pp. 13–14)

The case study outlined above illustrates how people requiring treatment often have very complex concerns and idiosyncratic experiences that require an equally complex and multi-faceted intervention in a supportive therapeutic environment. The client described above received emotion-focused therapy, a form of treatment described later in this chapter. Chapter 17 opens with a discussion of key themes and issues that contribute to these complexities. We discuss such issues as the key roles played by the client's expectations and motives, as well as the need to consider differences among clients in their personality styles. Differences related to the therapist are also discussed in terms of how it influences the quality of the bond between the therapist and client.

Next, we evaluate the effectiveness of various therapies. In Chapter 2, we outlined the major approaches to therapeutic intervention, and in chapters 6 through 16, we reviewed how these approaches have treated various psychopathologies. A major component of this chapter is a critical appraisal of a number of psychological interventions. We discuss the research on their effectiveness as well as offer some general comments and identify some key issues and themes that should further enrich the reader's understanding of the complexities of psychotherapy. This includes concerns about the extent to which research informs practice, as reflected above in the quote from Parry et al. (2010).

CLIENT FACTORS THAT INFLUENCE THERAPY OUTCOMES

We begin with a discussion of some individual difference factors that vary among clients and can influence the course and the effectiveness of treatment. Clearly, any therapist must remain cognizant of the client's unique features when determining how to structure and frame treatment. Clients differ not only in terms of their personal histories and types of dysfunction, but also in other key ways related to their expectancies, goals, and motives and associated personality styles. Failure to take these differences into account could arguably undermine the potential effectiveness of whatever therapeutic orientation is implemented. However, as we will see later, controlled research on therapy outcome requires a controlled and systematic approach to how therapy is delivered.

EXPECTATIONS ABOUT THE OUTCOME OF THERAPY

Frank and Frank (1985) advanced the **demoralization hypothesis** as an explanation for when clients will seek therapy. They suggested that clients seek help not just because of their symptoms. The symptoms are accompanied by a state of demoralization that includes feelings of alienation, helplessness, hopelessness, loss of self-esteem, and subjective feelings of incompetence. For those who do feel demoralized, a key factor is whether there is an optimistic vs. a pessimistic belief that therapy will work or at least has the chance to work. That is, do clients feel a sense of hope? Frank (1974) has argued that the key therapeutic task is to restore a sense of morale by instilling a renewed sense of mastery. Once a sense of mastery is in place, then hope will follow.

Snyder and his associates have outlined a two-factor theory of hope and they suggest that hope is the key to success of Cognitive-Behavioural Therapy (CBT) interventions (see Snyder et al., 2000). Hope has two components: agency (i.e., the will or belief component) and pathways (i.e., specific ways to make the hoped-for outcomes be realized). Support for this conceptualization was provided by Irving et al. (2004). They assigned clients to either a wait-list control group or motivational orientation group and then all clients received 12 weeks of individual therapy. Higher hope at the start of the study was associated subsequently with greater well-being, fewer symptoms, and better functioning and coping. Also, clients with higher levels of hope in the motivational group rated the group as much more helpful. Another recent investigation of more than 3,000 adolescents tracked levels of hopefulness and confirmed that adolescents who reported greater hopefulness over time had fewer problems and greater adaptive functioning at follow-up (Weis & Ash, 2009).

A review led by Greenberg, Constantino, and Bruce (2006) concluded that client expectations may be even more important to the psychotherapy process and eventual outcome than previously acknowledged. Outcome expectancies can be assessed prior to treatment but they can also be assessed at various points throughout the treatment process.

Many therapies have components that foster more positive expectancies as part of the change process.

GOALS AND THE MOTIVATION TO CHANGE

Common sense would suggest that clients who are highly motivated and ready to change will actually be more likely to improve as a result of treatment. Indeed, a review conducted many years ago assessed 91 potential predictors of the outcome of psychotherapy, and client motivation was identified as one of the most significant factors in treatment outcomes (Luborsky et al., 1971). The importance of the motivation to change was illustrated in a novel study of how depressed adolescents responded to treatment (see Lewis et al., 2009). Adolescents who endorsed items on the Stages of Change Questionnaire such as "I'm not the one with the problem. It doesn't make much sense for me to be here," and "Being here is pretty much a waste of time for me because problems don't have to do with me" were more depressed and responded more poorly to treatment regardless of the modality of treatment vs. those adolescents who seemed more self-motivated and disagreed with these questionnaire items.

Self-report measures such as the one described above require some degree of insight. Levels of self-insight may be quite variable. Some clients may be consciously aware of their desire and need to change, while others may be ready and not quite realize it. Motivational interviewing (MI) may be required to make people aware of their desire for change.

Motivational interviewing (MI), which was described briefly in Chapter 12, is usually incorporated within CBT. Miller and Rollnick (2002) have outlined how MI is client-centred in the tradition of Carl Rogers, but it is directive rather than non-directive. MI is described in greater detail in Focus on Discovery 17.1.

FOCUS ON DISCOVERY 17.1
MOTIVATIONAL INTERVIEWING

Motivational interviewing (MI) reflects the fact that some people are highly threatened by change and are very ambivalent about engaging in therapy. MI helps clients to develop a readiness for change by enabling them to explore personal motives and issues and resolve feelings of ambivalence and resistance (Hettema, Steele, & Miller, 2005).

Initially, we discuss MI in the context of a case study of Carol, a woman suffering from generalized anxiety disorder. She was described by Angus and Kagan (2009) in the following manner:

Carol was a 50-year-old divorced woman when she sought therapy for severe GAD at York University. The MI therapist was a seasoned clinical psychologist who completed an MI training course. Carol described a chronic pattern of worrying, never being relaxed, having "no peace or happiness," and feeling constantly busy and rushed. She further complained of chronic tiredness and exhaustion; however, she was puzzled because "there's nothing major going on, yet my mind is busy all the time"... Carol reported worrying about

everything, especially her relationships with other people and the well-being of her family members. She stated that worry caused her distress and reported difficulties with insomnia, tension, and inability to concentrate. In fact, Carol had to take a leave from her job due to the severe concentration problems associated with her worry. She described herself as a "lifelong worrier" and had previously been treated with psychotherapy and antidepressant medication with little improvement. (pp. 1158–1159)

Carol participated in four MI sessions. She responded well to therapist empathy and she showed no ambivalence in "opening up" (i.e., discussing painful personal memories) despite a history of being non-expressive and covering up personal difficulties and concern. As a result of her MI treatment, Carol also took pride in doing something for herself and gaining a sense of mastery. Her experience not only lowered her level of worry, it further increased her readiness for additional change.

Carol was ready for change, but this is not the case with everyone. Even though they may be experiencing great distress and engaging in self-defeating behaviour, some clients resist change and focus on the benefits of their dysfunctional behaviours. For instance, Westra (2004) described the case of Ms. C, who suffered from generalized social anxiety disorder and recurring depression. Ms. C was ambivalent about homework activities and the possibility of change. When asked to list the benefits of her disorder, she readily named a variety of perks. She indicated that avoiding others "keeps me from getting hurt," "saves energy because it is exhausting to be around others," and means that "[I] don't have to deal with the dissatisfaction I have with my marriage" (p. 172). A central component of MI is using CBT techniques to challenge these perceived benefits, but within the context of an empathetic relationship with the therapist. The focus is on changing the value of negative behaviours and increasing the value of positive, adaptive behaviours. Flynn (in press) has outlined how combining MI with CBT can be quite effective in enhancing the success of treatments for severely depressed people. Consider, for instance, how difficult it would be to treat a chronically depressed perfectionist who has no interest in modifying the extreme evaluative standards that are part of his or her identity and who feels that self-criticism is a valuable way of energizing oneself to achieve goals.

MI was designed initially for use in the treatment of people who are ambivalent about giving up their addictions and it is within this context that most research has been conducted. A meta-analysis of 30 treatment studies by Burke, Arkowitz, and Menchola (2003) found that MI, relative to no treatment control and placebo conditions, yielded treatment improvements. The overall effect size of MI was deemed to be moderate. A more recent meta-analysis by Rubak et al. (2005) confirmed the apparent effectiveness of MI.

It is now generally concluded that some of the strongest support for the benefits of MI come from substance abuse interventions (see Moyers & Houck, 2010). The COMBINE Research Project (Moyers & Houck, in press) is a recent illustration of how MI combines effectively with CBT to produce positive outcomes.

In recent years, various authors have sought to extend the range of MI's applicability by using it with other disorders. Westra and Dozois (2006) extended Westra's (2004) previous work by showing that MI combined with CBT was effective in lowering anxiety in clients with mixed anxiety and depression. Both CBT alone and CBT with MI lowered anxiety and these gains persisted at six-month follow-up, but the MI group also had greater homework compliance and higher expectations of anxiety control. Overall, the MI group had a higher proportion of treatment responders.

A recent qualitative study conducted at York University confirmed that when MI is combined in pretreatment prior to implementing CBT, relative to those not receiving MI, clients receiving MI reported playing a greater role in therapy and perceived the therapist as being a more "evocative guide" (see Kertes, Westra, Angus, & Marcus, in press).

An influential book edited by Arkowitz, Westra, Miller, and Rollnick (2007) should play an important role in further extending the applicability of MI. This volume contains chapters on the use of MI in the treatment of a wide range of disorders, including PTSD, OCD, depression, schizophrenia, and pathological gambling. The use of MI is believed to be particularly appropriate when the client has a comorbid disorder that includes an element of addiction. Indeed, other authors have recently outlined how MI can be tailored to treat the tendencies of clients with comorbid schizophrenia and alcohol use (Carey et al., 2007).

THE IMPACT OF PERSONALITY ON THERAPY OUTCOMES

The role of personality factors in treatment has been discussed in previous chapters. Most notably, Chapter 8 includes an overview of the role of personality factors such as perfectionism in the treatment of depression, and Chapter 12 describes the attempt to differentiate treatment according to personality factors as part of the Project Match initiative. Chapter 13 outlined how certain personality disorders impact negatively on treatment outcome. How important are personality factors? Lambert (1992) reviewed the literature and concluded that personal attributes of the client including personality differences may account for as much as 40% of the variability in therapy outcomes and these factors outweigh differences attributable to specific types of treatment. Given the relevance of personality factors, it is clear that personality factors are assessed not only to determine whether a prospective client has significant personality dysfunction, but also in terms of identifying personality orientations that influence the treatment course and treatment outcome.

As one illustration, individual differences in attachment style are receiving a great deal of attention in terms of their role in therapy outcome and processes. Recall that attachment styles were discussed at length in Chapter 15. An investigation conducted by a team of Canadian researchers yielded new evidence indicating that clients with insecure attachment have less favourable treatment outcomes (see Joyce, Ogrodniczuk, Piper, & Sheptycki, 2010). This study of clients with complicated grief found that attachment style was "a strong predictor of psychotherapy outcome" (p. 122) and it replicated a previous finding by this same research team. A fearful attachment style was linked with negative outcomes. Joyce et al. (2010) concluded that people with this style would, in all likelihood, be quite fearful in interpersonal interactions.

THERAPIST FACTORS AND THE WORKING ALLIANCE

Our analysis thus far has focused on attributes of the client, but, of course, therapist factors play a significant role. And, clearly, therapist factors influence the motivational and outcome expectancy factors outlined earlier. This was illustrated recently by Westra, Constantino, Arkowitz, and Dozois (2009). They found in their longitudinal study that, despite no initial baseline differences in expectations for anxiety change, more effective therapists had clients with anxiety disorder who developed higher outcome expectancies following CBT. Previous research also showed that a positive relationship between the therapist and client enhances the tendency for clients with positive therapy expectations to actually do better as a result of treatment (Joyce, Ogrodniczuk, Piper, & McCallum, 2003).

The development of higher outcome expectancies is no doubt at least partly a reflection of the working alliance or therapeutic alliance that emerges between the client and the therapist. A study at the University of British Columbia showed convincingly that the frequency of transference interpretations was related inversely to both the quality of the therapeutic alliance between the client and therapist and the favourability of treatment outcome (Ogrodniczuk, Piper, Joyce, & McCallum, 1999). The term **therapeutic**, or **working, alliance** (see Horvath & Greenberg, 1994) refers here to rapport and trust and to a sense that the therapist and the client are working together to achieve mutually agreed-upon goals. Another psychotherapy study done in Quebec found that even when a good therapeutic alliance is in place, transference interpretations that occur early in psychotherapy are followed by increased defensiveness (Banon, Evan-Grenier, & Bond, 2001).

A study by Kolden (1991) found that the better this bond, the more favourable the outcome is after an average of 25 sessions. Reviews of other studies conducted over two decades confirm that the stronger the therapeutic relationship, or alliance, the better the outcome (see Horvath, 2001). Horvath (2001) also suggests that the most clinically useful indicator may be the client's report of the early alliance.

Not surprisingly, personality factors play a key role in whether a positive alliance is formed. A contemporary review by Smith, Msetfi, and Golding (2010) found across 18 studies selected on the basis of rigorous inclusion criteria that clients who rate themselves as having more secure attachment styles also tend to report stronger alliances. Attachment was assessed both in terms of general attachment style and in terms of context-specific measures created specifically to assess client attachment to the therapist.

There are different views on how a good working alliance works (Henry et al., 1994). It might have a direct therapeutic effect, or it might have an indirect effect by making the therapist's interpretations more effective. Research on therapist factors indicates that the therapist's skills and personal characteristics are both key factors, while the therapist's level of training is relatively inconsequential (see Horvath, 2001). Nevertheless, Adam Horvath (2001) allows for the realistic possibility that therapists need more extensive training if they are to be able to form a good alliance with a client suffering from extreme psychopathology.

Another issue to consider is the fact that the working alliance is multi-faceted, and one or more of its aspects may be involved in a given case. Horvath and Greenberg (1989) developed the Working Alliance Inventory to assess three components of the alliance: the bond between the client and therapist, agreement on the goals of treatment, and agreement on the tasks of therapy. Louise Gaston from McGill University is one of a team of contributors who has conducted extensive research on another multi-dimensional assessment device, known as the California Psychotherapy Alliance Scales. This measure assesses the client's commitment (i.e., seeing the therapy as important, being willing to make sacrifices and see it through to the conclusion), the client-therapist working alliance, degree of therapist understanding and involvement, and a working strategy consensus (the perceived agreement between the client and therapist on the goals and tasks involved in therapy). Gaston (1991) found that all four subscales are associated significantly with client satisfaction ratings and all but the therapist understanding and involvement subscale are associated with lower levels of psychological distress and interpersonal problems involving a lack of intimacy.

Several recent findings have clarified the nature and importance of the therapeutic alliance:

1. The correlation between the ratings of the working alliance by clients and their therapists is only moderate at best, as shown across several measures of the working alliance (see Fenton et al., 2001).
2. As treatment progresses, the differences in how the working alliance is viewed by the client and therapist do not lessen substantially (Fitzpatrick et al., 2005).
3. A positive treatment outcome is much better predicted by the client's view of the working alliance than it is by the therapist's view of the working alliance (Howarth & Bedi, 2002). This emphasizes the importance of the client's unique phenomenological perspective.

Horvath (2006) pinpointed several key challenges that remain. These challenges include developing a clearer and more extensive definition of the alliance and the need to more clearly specify the role and purpose of the alliance at various points in the treatment process. Further, research in this area should not rule out the possibility that a strong working alliance is the result, rather than the cause, of therapeutic change; clients might feel better about their relationship with their therapist if they have improved. However the alliance works, it seems to be an important factor for any therapeutic approach, including CBT, not only for psychodynamic approaches.

GENERAL ISSUES IN EVALUATING PSYCHOTHERAPY RESEARCH

Our analysis of the effectiveness of various therapies follows. First, however, we begin with a few general issues that will inform our understanding and appreciation of research in psychotherapy.

THERAPY AS RESEARCHED VS. THERAPY AS PRACTISED

This chapter opened with an illuminating quote from Parry et al. (2010) in which it was suggested that the gap between psychotherapy research and practice may be a gulf rather than a gap. Beutler (2009) has referred to the "chasm" that exists between science and practice. What is the essence of this discrepancy? Therapist manuals are detailed guides on how to conduct a particular therapy, stipulating specific procedures to be followed at different stages of treatment. The use of such manuals has become the norm in psychotherapy research (e.g., Nathan & Gorman, 1998). Indeed, it is impossible nowadays to obtain funding to study the outcome of psychotherapy without first explicitly defining the independent variables via a manual that the therapists in the study must follow as closely as possible.

The use of therapist manuals began with the earliest controlled studies on Wolpe's technique of systematic desensitization (e.g., Paul, 1966). In contrast, in earlier psychotherapy research of the 1940s and 1950s, the activity of the therapist was, for the most part, described only in terms of his or her theoretical orientation (psychodynamic, client-centred, etc.). But what therapists actually do in the consulting room is often difficult to know on the basis of what they say they do and their allegiance to a particular orientation. Specifying via manuals what therapists are to do in a controlled study and then monitoring what they actually do in their sessions with clients has thus been hailed as a significant advance in the scientific study of therapeutic interventions (see Hunsley & Rumstein-McKean, 1999). It allows someone reading a psychotherapy study to know what actually happened to clients in a given experimental condition.

Hunsley and Rumstein-McKean (1999) endorsed the use of treatment manuals as an adjunct to research involving randomized clinical trials, a controlled experimental procedure in which participants are assigned randomly to experimental conditions. At the same time, they acknowledged that several concerns involving some current treatment manuals need to be addressed. The most common criticism is that manuals are too unwieldy for actual clinical practice, with some situations requiring a more specific approach and others requiring a more general approach. They also expressed concern that "many manuals inadvertently promote rule-governed behaviour that may not be appropriate in all instances" (p. 1511), and noted that more attention needs to be given to contextual factors, including timing issues, such as advice on when a particular technique is appropriate. This latter issue reflects the more general concern that treatment manuals lose sight of the individuality of people because they are based on abstract representations of the typical client, and therapists may thus have to rely on their own clinical judgement to deal with the unique issues facing certain clients (see Nathan, Stuart, & Dolan, 2000). Finally, Hunsley and Rumstein-McKean pointed to an urgent need for research that examines the extent to which treatment manuals, accompanied by little or no

John Hunsley from the University of Ottawa is a leader in the field of clinical psychology and a strong advocate of the use of treatment manuals and empirically-supported treatments. Courtesy John Hunsley.

supervision, do indeed result in treatments that are accurate and effective. These concerns notwithstanding, they suggested that, for treatments supported by randomized clinical trials, "working knowledge of the treatment manual would be essential to practitioners" (p. 1510).

A moment's reflection suggests another problem. Although the use of manuals buys us greater internal validity—results obtained can be attributed with some confidence to the action of the independent variable—what about external validity? Do the results obtained from manual-based studies generalize to the actual practice of psychotherapy outside the constraints of a controlled study? There is perhaps no more important and more hotly debated topic in psychotherapy than this (e.g., Beutler, 1999). A decade later, Beutler (2009) still maintains that the onus is on scientists because they have failed to provide a workable model of how to integrate science and instead had "an unwarranted devotion to a limited number of scientific methods" (p. 301).

Finally, another overarching problem is that treatment manuals are based on mental disorders. This is problematic because manuals are disorder-based rather than theory-based (Nathan et al., 2000).

Here's a way to look at the issue. Because many therapists describe themselves as eclectic, controlled studies of specific techniques (e.g., exposure) or approaches (e.g., client-centred therapy) are limited in what they can tell us about the nature and outcomes of therapy as actually practised (Lambert & Bergin, 1994; Lambert & Ogles, 2004; Parry et al., 2010); we know that most therapists seldom behave strictly in line with a particular theoretical orientation, whether psychoanalytic, client-centred, or cognitive-behavioural. Therefore, the kinds of controlled studies emphasized in this chapter and earlier in the book are limited in what they can tell us about the

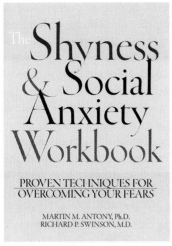

Workbooks such as this are designed for clients and are commonly used in conjunction with a manual that guides the therapist in treating the client. Reproduced with permission of New Harbinger Publications..

effectiveness of the psychotherapy available to clients who are not participants in research studies. This situation is ironic, for it is these controlled studies that provide the evidence used by proponents of particular techniques or general theoretical approaches to support their positions!

A common characteristic of today's controlled studies is the exclusion of people on various grounds. For example, people may be excluded from a study if they have problems in addition to the one being studied (the comorbidity issue). Moreover, studies rely on people who are willing to be seen in a highly structured treatment protocol. In short, the clients who volunteer and are accepted as participants in controlled studies are different from many—and perhaps the vast majority of—clients in psychotherapy. This point was underscored by the results of a provocative study that compared psychotherapy research participants in randomized controlled trials (RCTs) with general community outpatients (Stirman, DeRubeis, Crits-Cristoph, & Brody, 2003). This study found that 58% of the community sample had primary diagnoses that had never been studied in RCTs, indicating that some diagnoses are common but not represented in psychotherapy research. Common diagnoses overlooked in research studies included adjustment disorder, dysthymia, and mood and anxiety disorders not otherwise specified. Findings such as these suggest that it is quite risky to generalize from controlled studies to the actual practice of psychotherapy and the people receiving this psychotherapy.

Another related attribute of controlled studies is the widespread use of a *DSM* diagnosis and thereby the definition of clients as homogeneous (e.g., Blatt & Zuroff, 2005). For example, the large-scale NIMH study of depression that we examined in Chapter 8 followed the *DSM* criteria in defining people as having major depression and then randomly assigned them to different experimental conditions. But, as we have seen many times, people are depressed, anxious, or

dependent on alcohol or cigarettes for many different reasons. What is not possible in such studies is an idiographic analysis of a person—that is, an analysis of the unique features of a single case—to determine which factors are most important in making that one person feel, think, and behave in a certain way (e.g., Beutler, 1997; Persons & Davidson, 2001). Note that psychotherapy researchers do not really believe that the people who are diagnosed as, for example, depressed and then assigned randomly to different treatment conditions are depressed for the same reasons (e.g., biased thinking). Rather, for the sake of creating an experiment with as much internal validity as possible, they pretend that this is the case. For this reason, large numbers of participants are needed in psychotherapy research; the differences that are present among people are assumed to "randomize out" with large groups.

Parry et al. (2010) argue effectively that the issues outlined above are vexing not only for clinicians but also for health services researchers who are grappling with pragmatic issues. For instance, small sample sizes make it difficult to realistically assess the cost effectiveness of interventions from a health economics perspective. They also noted that there are times when even pragmatic and elegant experimental approaches are "inappropriate, impossible, or inadequate" (p. 312) for actual circumstances.

The concerns about the gap or gulf between research and practice were expressed clearly by the results of a recent Canadian survey of practitioners who provide group psychotherapy (see Ogrodniczuk, Piper, Joyce, Lau, & Sochting, 2010). Overall, most of the 55 respondents expressed high appreciation of research and acknowledged reading an average of three new articles each month and attending two conferences per year. All respondents agreed that awareness of research enhances therapist effectiveness. These data qualify a larger investigation by Boisvert and Faust (2006), which found that some therapists had great awareness of research findings but many did not achieve this standard, and overall, they tended to be more negative in their interpretation of research findings than was warranted. While this newer study suggested research was valued to a greater degree, significant concerns were still noted, with 60% or more participants in the Ogrodniczuk et al. (2010) survey endorsing the following:

1. Psychotherapy research studies do not capture the complexities of group psychotherapy.

2. Research procedures distort or disrupt the typical therapeutic process.

3. Therapists, patients, and settings used in research studies do not represent typical clinical practice.

4. Not enough attention is given to qualitative studies of group therapy or systematized case studies.

5. Randomized control trials (RCTs) are overemphasized.

6. Researchers are too often dismissive of relationship variables in favour of specific treatment techniques.

In short, therapy as practised in the real world is not reflected in research, in part because therapy as actually practised does take a more idiographic approach; it is tailored to the particular needs and characteristics of a particular client, including the personality factors that were described earlier. When they are working in clinical settings, therapists make continual adjustments that are not constrained by the demands of a scientific study. In contrast, the very essence of treatment manuals is to minimize the tailoring of intervention to individual clients. It remains a challenge to researchers and clinicians alike to reconcile the seemingly incompatible needs of these two approaches (e.g., Fishman, 1999). The Society for Clinical Psychology (Division 12 of the American Psychological Association) responded to this challenge by striking the Task Force on the Identification of Principles of Therapeutic Change (see Beutler, 2002) to incorporate empirically supported findings into practice but with treatment approaches that are flexible and can be modified to suit the particular needs and concerns of the individual client. Luyten et al. (2006) concluded with respect to depression treatment that noteworthy comorbidity or subclinical or clinical personality pathology predicts longer treatment and/or negatively influences treatment response. On a positive note, Kazdin and Whitley (2006) demonstrated that comorbidity or complexity of cases does not necessarily influence outcome or limit the applicability of evidence-based treatments, at least for children with a diagnosis of oppositional defiant disorder and conduct disorder.

The STAR*D project is a clear example of the flexible, individual-focused approach. STAR*D stands for Sequence Treatment Alternatives to Relieve Depression. It focuses on a modifiable treatment process for major depressive disorder in adults in outpatient settings. The main premise in a sense here is "whatever works." Clients first receive medication (citalopram, an SSRI medication), but if symptoms remain after 8 to 12 weeks of treatment, other types of treatment are used, including other medications but also CBT. Often, clients experience two or more types of treatment in order to derive maximum benefit. Up to 30 clinic visits may be required and there is a one-year follow-up. In general, data are accumulating in support of a sequenced approach for people who initially receive medication. Meta-analytic results confirm that following medication with psychotherapy is quite effective in reducing relapse rates among individuals with a history of depression (Guidi, Fava, Fava, & Papakostas, 2010).

Psychotherapy researchers do make an important distinction between efficacy and effectiveness. The **efficacy** of an intervention is what we determine from a controlled outcome study, typically conducted in an academic research setting. The **effectiveness** of an intervention refers to what is offered to and received by people in the everyday world. According to Dobson and Hamilton (2002), efficacy researchers emphasize maximizing the internal validity of research, often conducted in controlled laboratory settings, while effectiveness researchers hope to optimize the external validity or generalizability of the intervention. Whereas the elimination of observable,

well-defined problems, such as a person with agoraphobia being unable to venture far from his or her home, is the usual focus of efficacy studies, effectiveness is usually judged subjectively by clients themselves on the basis of more global criteria, such as the level of satisfaction people have with their therapy, how much they believe they have been helped, and how much the quality of their life has improved (cf. *Consumer Reports*, 1995; Seligman, 1995, 1996).

The efficacy of treatments is often well-established but evidence of effectiveness lags well behind. This is not always the case, however. Stewart and Chambless (2009) reported a meta-analysis of effectiveness studies of CBT for adult anxiety disorders in actual clinical practice. Large effect sizes were found suggesting that CBT can be effective in "clinically representative conditions" (p. 595). Secondary analyses indicating that there was greater evidence of effectiveness when clients were not assigned randomly to experimental conditions and medication for anxiety management was permitted. Not surprisingly, factors that decreased effectiveness included lack of therapist training, failure to use treatment manuals, and a lack of ongoing monitoring of treatment.

The efficacy-effectiveness distinction continues to be a topic of lively debate in the field. The *Consumer Reports* study (1995) is cited widely as a clear example of research that examines the effectiveness of treatment rather than its efficacy. A survey was mailed to 180,000 of the magazine's readers and 22,000 answered; about 7,000 gave responses to the mental health questions, and 4,100 of these people said that they received assistance from some combination of mental health professionals, doctors, and support groups. The main conclusions were summarized by Seligman (1995):

1. The treatment usually worked; in fact, of the 786 people who said they felt poor at the outset, 92% reported feeling very good, good, or so-so after treatment.
2. Long-term treatment was associated with more improvement than short-term treatment.

Troubled people may talk about their problems with friends or seek professional therapy. Therapy is typically sought by those for whom the advice and support of family or friends have not provided relief. © Somos Images/Corbis.

3. There was no benefit to psychotherapy plus medication vs. psychotherapy alone in terms of perceived effectiveness.

4. Family doctors were just as effective as mental health professionals in the short term, but mental health professionals were much more effective in the long term.

5. Alcoholics Anonymous fared especially well and was rated as doing substantially better than mental health professionals.

6. Active participants had better outcomes than more passive recipients.

7. Comparisons among the various psychotherapies showed that no particular type of treatment had superior effectiveness.

Controlled follow-up studies are needed to confirm the *Consumer Reports* findings. One of the most glaring shortcomings of this report is the absence of a control group (for a discussion, see Nathan et al., 2000). This factor and other limitations led Nathan et al. (2000) to conclude that although this study reached an encouraging conclusion about the effectiveness of treatment, it should be regarded as a consumer survey rather than a research study per se, and as such, it tells us little about efficacy.

Although this study is not without its flaws, it did reach some conclusions that replicated other research findings, including confirmation of the **dodo bird effect**. The dodo bird effect refers to the tendency for various therapies to achieve similar results. The term was coined by Rosenzweig (1936), who adapted it from *Alice in Wonderland*. In this famous book, a dodo bird judges the outcome of a race and concludes that everyone has won. Indeed, a "meta-meta analysis" of 17 meta-analyses concluded that differences in the outcomes of therapies are small and not statistically significant (Luborsky et al., 2002). While there is strong evidence of the dodo bird effect, note that there is an opposing view. Budd and Hughes (2009) concluded that there is also evidence that specific

therapies are more effective for certain diagnoses. They suggested that support for the dodo bird effect may be overstated, in part, due to an overreliance in research studies on randomized control designs that constrain key factors that operate in therapy as practised.

The dodo bird effect is but one of several beliefs and principles shared by most psychotherapy researchers. Other consensus beliefs are outlined in Focus on Discovery 17.2.

Lambert and Ogles (2004) concluded that about 75% of people entering psychotherapy achieve at least some improvement, and these effects seem to be more powerful than support from family and friends and the mere passage of time. Further, the positive effects exceed those of placebo treatments or no treatment for a wide variety of psychological problems and disorders (e.g., Westen, Novotny, & Thompson-Brenner, 2004).

What about the fact that some people really do get worse? Lilienfeld (2007) noted that the negative effect sizes reported for some studies included in meta-analyses of treatment outcome suggest the possibility that certain psychotherapies are actually harmful to some people. Lilienfeld presented a preliminary list of 12 potentially harmful therapies. Examples include critical incident stress debriefing (CISD), recovered memory techniques, DID (dissociative identity disorder)-oriented psychotherapy, facilitated communication, and boot-camp interventions for conduct disorder. He highlighted the need to uncover the mediators of treatment-induced deterioration that may be specific to certain therapies. For example, he hypothesized that negative effects of CISD could be due to premature termination of exposure to stimuli that provoke anxiety, thus leaving people more anxious than before (Lilienfeld, 2007).

An influential new paper by Dimidjian and Hollon (2010) emphasized the point that, at present, there are various conceptualizations of "harm" and the field lacks consensus about

---

FOCUS ON DISCOVERY 17.2
CONSENSUS BELIEFS INVOLVING PSYCHOTHERAPY RESEARCH

A study by Boisvert and Faust (2003) involved discovering the beliefs of an international group of 12 experts who conduct psychotherapy research. Each researcher was asked to indicate his or her degree of agreement with 20 statements about psychotherapy, based on existing research. The experts demonstrated strong agreement that research supported the following claims:

1. Therapy is helpful to the majority of clients.
2. Most people achieve some change relatively quickly in therapy.
3. In general, therapies achieve similar outcomes (i.e., the dodo bird effect).
4. People change more because of "common factors" than because of "specific factors" associated with therapies.

5. The client-therapist relationship is the best predictor of treatment change.
6. Most therapists learn more about effective therapy techniques from their experience than from research.
7. About 10% of clients get worse as a result of therapy.

Boisvert and Faust (2003) observed that, given the researchers' acceptance of the view that a small proportion of clients actually get worse as a result of treatment, perhaps informed-consent procedures should be modified so that potential clients are made aware of the potential risk, as well as the potential benefits, of treatment. Do you agree?

what constitutes harm. They noted that harm may result either because the initial problem becomes worse or other domains or problem areas that were not the focus are made worse by the intervention. While this seems relatively straightforward, they outline a series of conditions that complicate the determination that harm has occurred. First, it is possible for an intervention to have both beneficial and harmful effects such as when a medication decreases depression but has the unintentional side effect of increasing the possibility of suicide. Second, what is seen as beneficial for one client may be harmful for another (e.g., a wife and husband who have differing views on marital therapy). Third, what starts out beneficial

may eventually turn harmful and vice versa. This underscores the need to remember that therapy is a process that unfolds over time and there can be dynamic, changing aspects.

Practising clinicians and other mental health service providers must make daily decisions about how to treat their clients. In some settings, they now use a stepped care approach in making treatment decisions (see Haaga, 2000). The approach offers guidelines for both efficient and effective delivery of psychological services and does this at both the individual and the community service level (Sobell & Sobell, 2000). Focus on Discovery 17.3 presents a brief summary and evaluation of the stepped care approach.

FOCUS ON DISCOVERY 17.3
STEPPED CARE MODELS AND THE TREATMENT PROCESS: CAN WE DO MORE WITH LESS?

The concept of **stepped care** involves the notion that clinicians should match the level of the required treatment to the seriousness of the adjustment problem being addressed, but they should begin with less involved and less costly interventions, followed by more complex interventions if the initial interventions are not successful. Lower cost is seen by many as the guiding principle in stepped care (see Haaga, 2000), but it has been suggested by Sobell and Sobell (2000) that the preferred treatment option is the one that is least restrictive for the individual. In this context, "restrictive" refers to such considerations as physical effects of treatment, as well as issues involving lifestyle restrictions and economic considerations. Sobell and Sobell (2000) also suggest that treatment must be individualized to reflect the client's beliefs and resources and that the tailoring of treatment to the individual must be consistent with the current research literature.

Figure 17.1 is a diagram of the stepped care approach as conceptualized by Sobell and Sobell (2000). The left-hand portion of the figure clearly shows how the intensity of treatment increases

in response to negative treatment outcomes when more basic interventions are used. Davison (2000) has been critical of this figure, stating that the illustration needs to be adapted to reflect the fact that the treatment process is inherently complex. He holds that, according to a stepped care approach, it is indeed the case that feedback-based adjustments are made, but sometimes these adjustments are made very quickly, perhaps even on a moment-by-moment basis. Thus, it needs to be appreciated that the treatment process is ongoing and dynamic and that small procedural steps may be implemented with very little notice.

The usefulness of a stepped care approach will vary depending on the problem in question. Wilson, Vitousek, and Loeb (2000) observed that a low-intensity solution is not well suited to such situations as someone with anorexia nervosa being close to starving to death. In such a potentially life-threatening situation, unless other complications need to be considered, high-intensity treatments designed to provide immediate relief should begin immediately.

Another qualifying condition was identified by Otto, Pollack, and Maki (2000) in the course of their evaluation of the usefulness of stepped care to treat panic disorder. They observed that a substantial proportion of people with panic disorder receive medical treatment before psychological treatment is considered and approximately half of these individuals prefer this kind of treatment and likely would not participate in a stepped care program.

According to Rosen (2004), effective stepped care programs require the use of minimal therapies that have strong backing from research. Stepped care programs can be useful when minimal resources are available and it is desirable to direct resources to those who need it the most. A recent study showed the utility of stepped care for students who are mandated to receive treatment for violation of alcohol policies (Borsari et al., 2007). A substantial proportion of the students should require relatively little intervention but additional levels of treatment can be directed to those students with more extreme problems and presumably greater risk to self and others.

FIGURE 17.1 A stepped care approach to the delivery of health care services. From Sobell and Sobell (2000)

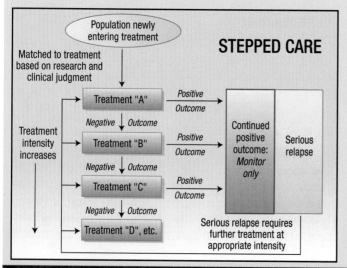

THE CHALLENGE OF MANAGED CARE

No doubt you have heard of managed care. In the United States, health care is most likely provided to people via an insurance company that attempts to control costs (and maximize profits) by requiring prior approval of the nature and extent of treatment and by reducing the amount of payment provided to hospitals, clinics, and medical and psychological personnel.

Run for the most part by businesspeople rather than by health care providers, managed-care organizations (MCOs) have indeed brought down the costs of care in the United States over the past few decades. They have also demanded increased accountability from providers. MCOs look to scientific evidence to justify the procedures used by health professionals. Surgical, dental, and medical procedures are justified by scientific evidence. Drugs approved by the Food and Drug Administration for use in the United States are judged from controlled research to be safe and effective for particular conditions. More recently, these standards have been applied to assessments and treatments of mental disorders. The scrutiny that physicians and dentists have been accustomed to for many years is now being brought to bear on mental health professionals.

The situation is considerably different in Canada owing to our universal health care system, where there is an expectation that every citizen will have equal opportunity to receive the best care available (e.g., Romanow & Marchildon, 2003). Nonetheless, in recent years, there has been considerable pressure on governments at the federal, provincial and territorial, and local levels to increase the efficiency of our system, to reduce costs, and to be accountable for the use of tax dollars. Although the Canadian medicare system does not currently allow user fees, former Prime Minister Jean Chrétien indicated a willingness to examine this possibility as part of future health care reforms (Lawton, 2001 June 22). Of course, as in the United States, some services, such as private psychotherapy sessions provided by psychologists, can require personal payment or reimbursement by insurance providers. Although American-style managed care has not been loudly advocated by private sector third-party insurers in Canada (Ritchie & Edwards, 1998), insurance providers are beginning to demand the increased accountability that is part of U.S. managed care in conjunction with employee assistance programs (Dobson & Khatri, 2000). As pointed out in Chapter 1, governments in Canada are currently focused on best practice models of service delivery.

In Chapter 1, we introduced the issue of evidence-based treatment or **empirically supported therapies (ESTs)** (e.g., Hunsley & Johnston, 2000). These treatments have been demonstrated to be effective in research studies with appropriate scientific controls in a specific population, such as people diagnosed with major depression (Chambless & Ollendick, 2001). Cognitive therapy (CT) has been linked to this issue because it has been evaluated through various empirical outcome studies. It is attractive to managed-care companies because it is not only effective, but typically time-limited. Even though managed-care companies tend to prefer the more widely used medications, such as antidepressants, and CT is more expensive than medications in the short term, DeRubeis, Tang, and Beck (2001) believe that cost-benefit analyses could reveal that CT pays for itself soon after treatment is terminated. Why? CT has the potential to reduce the likelihood of relapse or recurrence (DeRubeis et al., 2001). Neimeyer and Raskin (2001) also believe that constructivist and narrative approaches are well positioned to compete in the managed-care climate, given their emphasis on therapist accountability and short-term interventions.

There are numerous problems with the evidence-based approach. Clearly, practitioners should use effective treatments. But how do we judge effectiveness? How do we reach a consensus on the treatments that qualify to make the "list"? Dobson and Khatri (2000) summarized future needs as follows:

> The future of EST needs to include multisite, longitudinal research trials in clinical settings to improve outcome generalizability. Also, other issues such as process of change, client factors (e.g., ethnicity, age, gender), chronic mental illness (e.g., schizophrenia), and the study of nondominant clinical paradigms need to be explored through EST research if the outcomes of this research are to be the basis for treating diverse populations in clinical settings .... Overall, there is a need for outcome studies that use randomized designs, appropriate comparison conditions, and follow up at least 6 months post treatment. In addition, results of controlled studies must be interpreted in the context of normative functioning. Lastly, it is important to keep in mind that all of these scientific developments occur against a backdrop of social and technological change that affects the science and profession of psychology. (pp. 914–915)

How should therapists proceed in the meantime? We concur with the recommendation of the Canadian Psychological Association Task Force (Hunsley et al., 1999), as presented by Hunsley and Johnston (2000, p. 271):

> [T]here should be clear statements about the availability of clearly preferable, first-line treatments based on scientific data and about the limitations inherent in the classification of treatments as empirically supported (e.g., the difference between a treatment having support and having been empirically evaluated).

As described by Hunsley and Johnston (2000), rather than redeveloping lists of empirically supported therapies (as was done in the United States), the Canadian Psychological Association Task Force focused on promoting evidence-based practice in Canada, promoting collaboration among stakeholders, and providing information about the limitations of current empirical knowledge.

Given that some approaches currently have more empirical support than others, how is evidence-based treatment practised in the real world? Rowa et al. (2000) sought to determine the extent to which empirically supported psychological and pharmacological treatments were used in Canada for people with panic disorder, social phobia, or obsessive-compulsive disorder. They found that the types of pharmacological treatment received by clients were consistent with findings from the empirical literature. In contrast, empirically validated cognitive and behavioural treatments had been tried by fewer than one half of the participants. This result is consistent with other recent studies that report a preference on the part of psychiatrists and many psychologists for traditional but non-validated treatments, such as psychodynamic approaches. Rowa et al. (2000) also reported that the most frequently used psychological intervention for the anxiety disorders was "supportive" therapy. Why is there a discrepancy between treatments identified as effective and treatments actually received by clients in clinical practice? Rowa et al. observed that

> …these numbers are a cause for concern. It is possible that these results can be explained in part by the fact that psychiatric services in Canada are government funded and thus are more accessible, and that training for psychiatrists has traditionally focused on psychodynamic approaches. (Rowa et al., 2000, p. 97)

Rowa et al. (2000) recommended improved efforts to educate people about empirically supported treatments, improvement in the training of mental health professionals in all fields in methods of cognitive behaviour therapy, and finding ways to make cognitive-behavioural treatments more available and affordable.

Many of the concerns outlined above about randomized controlled trial methods and ESTs are summarized in Westen, Novotny, and Thompson-Brenner's (2004) insightful, critical review of empirically supported therapies. They concluded that ESTs are well-suited to some disorders (e.g., anxiety disorders) but are poorly suited to treating other disorders. They issued a call for **empirically informed therapies** that are more focused on intervention strategies and change processes that are guided by the clinician's insights rather than a rigidly invoked manualized approach that may not take into account important factors such as the personality characteristics of the client, the presence of comorbid disorders, and so on. As noted by Goldfried and Eubanks-Carter (2004), when it comes to more complex cases, there is a widening gap between clinical practice and the EST-driven outcome research that has high internal validity but questionable external validity.

With these general observations and the consensus beliefs of psychotherapy experts as background, we turn now to an evaluation of several therapeutic approaches, both the data on their effectiveness and some issues pertaining to them.

REVIEW OF BEHAVIOURAL AND COGNITIVE THERAPIES

Behavioural and cognitive therapies attempt to use the investigative methods of experimental psychology to study, develop, and evaluate specific therapeutic interventions. Many principles are drawn from animal research on classical and operant conditioning, but the more recent cognitive trends understandably rely on research and theory with humans. Because the techniques vary greatly, we provide summary details of several behavioural and cognitive therapies in the separate sections devoted to evaluating each one.

EVALUATION OF COUNTERCONDITIONING AND EXPOSURE METHODS

Clinicians have treated many different anxiety-related problems by systematic desensitization, an approach developed by Joseph Wolpe in the 1950s. The original technique involves having a deeply relaxed person imagine a hierarchy of situations that he or she finds unduly fear-provoking in real life. As with any therapy for people in emotional distress, its proper application is a complicated affair. The clinician must first determine that the situations eliciting the client's anxious reactions do not warrant such reactions. If a person is anxious because he or she lacks the skills to deal with a given set of circumstances, then desensitization or actual exposure is inappropriate. Desensitization is appropriate, however, if a person seems to be inhibited by anxiety from behaving in customary and known ways. The applicability of desensitization depends largely on the therapist's ingenuity in discovering the source of the anxiety underlying a client's problems (Goldfried & Davison, 1994).

It has been well documented that exposing fearful people to what they are frightened of or uneasy about—whether in imagination, as in Wolpe's technique, or in real life, as is usually done today—usually leads to marked reductions in their unrealistic fears. The demonstrated importance of exposure has benefited people with a wide variety of anxiety disorders, including simple phobias, PTSD, OCD, panic disorder, and agoraphobia (e.g., DeRubeis & Crits-Christoph, 1998). Although most of the research has been done with adults, fearful children have also benefited from exposure-based procedures (e.g., Kazdin & Weisz, 1998).

As with all the techniques we describe, exposure is very rarely used exclusively. A person fearful of social interactions might be given training in conversational and other social skills in addition to undergoing exposure.

EVALUATION OF OPERANT METHODS

Operant methods have proved successful with a wide range of behavioural problems. Recall the token economy work described earlier and Paul's classic study with seriously impaired patients in a mental hospital. Systematically rewarding desirable behaviour and extinguishing undesirable behaviour have been particularly successful in the treatment of many childhood problems, as reviewed in Chapter 15.

Perhaps one reason operant-conditioning behaviour therapy has been so effective with children is that much of their behaviour is subject to the control of others. Children tend more than adults to be under continual supervision. At school their behaviour is scrutinized by teachers, and at home their parents often oversee their play and other social activities. The behaviour therapist works with the parents and teachers in an effort to change the ways in which they reward and punish children. It is assumed that altering the reinforcement practices of the adults in a child's life will ultimately change the child's behaviour.

The range of childhood problems dealt with through operant conditioning is broad, including bedwetting, thumb-sucking, nail-biting, aggression, tantrums, hyperactivity, disruptive classroom behaviour, poor school performance, language deficiency, extreme social withdrawal, and asthmatic attacks (Kazdin & Weisz, 1998). Self-mutilation has also been treated effectively with punishment procedures, sometimes involving the response-contingent application of painful electric shock to the hands or feet. Such extreme measures should be used only when less drastic interventions are ineffective and problem behaviours are life-threatening (e.g., Sandler, 1991).

Before applying operant techniques, the therapist must determine that the problem behaviour is, in fact, operant behaviour that can be controlled by a contingent reinforcer. A child who is crying because of physical pain, for example, should be attended to. Encouraging results have been achieved by applying operant techniques to therapy with children with mental retardation and autism. Therapists who apply operant-conditioning techniques have challenged assumptions about the limited trainability of such children, much to their benefit.

GENERALIZATION AND MAINTENANCE OF TREATMENT EFFECTS

A problem that is common to all treatments but perhaps especially to the behavioural and, to a lesser extent, the cognitive therapies is that of generalizing to real life and maintaining whatever gains have been achieved while the client is in regular contact with the therapist. Brian Shaw, a well-known cognitive therapist and researcher from Toronto, observed that perhaps the most disappointing and challenging problem today is that the confidence placed in the effectiveness of treatment is not accompanied by concerns about sustaining treatment effects over time and the narrow range of clients included in clinical trials (see Shaw, 1999).

Insight therapists assume that therapeutic effects are enduring because of the restructuring of the personality. In contrast, behaviour therapists, who look a good deal to the environment for factors that affect people, wonder how therapeutic changes can be made to last once clients return to their everyday situations, often assumed to have been instrumental in creating their problems in the first place. This challenge has been addressed by behaviourists in several ways.

Intermittent and Naturalistic Reinforcement Intermittent reinforcement—rewarding a response only some of the times it appears—makes new behaviour more enduring. Thus, many operant programs take care to move away from continuous schedules of reinforcement once desired behaviour is occurring with satisfactory regularity. For example, if a teacher has succeeded in helping a disruptive child spend more time sitting down by praising the child generously for each arithmetic problem finished while seated, the teacher will gradually reward the child for every other success and, ultimately, only infrequently. Another strategy is to move from artificial reinforcers to those that occur naturally in the social environment. A token program might be maintained only long enough to encourage certain desired behaviour, after which the person is weaned to naturally occurring reinforcers, such as praise from peers.

Environmental Modification Another approach to bringing about generalization takes the therapist into the province of community psychology. Behaviour therapists manipulate surroundings, or attempt to do so, to support changes brought about in treatment. For example, Lovaas and his colleagues (Lovaas, Newsom, & Hickman, 1987; McEachin, Smith, & Lovaas, 1993) found that the gains painstakingly achieved in therapy for autistic children were sustained only when their parents continued to reinforce their good behaviour.

Eliminating Secondary Gain Most behaviour therapists assign their clients homework tasks to do between sessions. However, clients sometimes fail to follow through in a consistent fashion. Many clients are so resistant to doing on their own what they consciously and rationally agree is in their best interest that therapists sometimes invoke as an explanation the psychoanalytic concept of secondary gain, the notion that clients can derive benefit from their problem. For complex and poorly understood reasons, people sometimes act as though they unconsciously wish to keep their symptoms. Therapists, whatever their persuasion, may have to examine a client's interpersonal relationships for clues that might explain why he or she seems to prefer to hold on to a problem that causes distress.

Attribution to Self A person who has terminated therapy might attribute improvement in behaviour to an external cause, the therapist, and could relapse once that attributed factor is no longer present. Since behaviour therapy, especially therapy relying on operant manipulation, attributes much improvement to environmental forces, it might be wise for behaviour therapists to help their clients feel more responsible. By encouraging an "I did it" attitude, perhaps by motivating them to practise new skills and expose themselves to challenging situations, therapists may help their clients depend less on therapy and the therapist and better maintain their treatment gains.

EVALUATION OF COGNITIVE-BEHAVIOURAL THERAPY

The core assumption of all cognitive therapies is that the way people construe their world is a major—if not *the* major—determinant of their feelings and behaviour. Our examination of cognitive-behavioural therapy (CBT) focuses first on Albert Ellis's rational-emotive behaviour therapy (REBT), then on Beck's cognitive therapy (CT), and then on a comparison of the two. Finally we offer some general reflections on CBT as a whole.

ELLIS'S RATIONAL-EMOTIVE BEHAVIOUR THERAPY

The basic premise of REBT is that emotional suffering is due primarily to the often unverbalized assumptions and demands that people carry around with them as they negotiate their way in life. Demanding perfection from oneself and from others, Ellis hypothesizes, is a principal cause of emotional distress. Expecting that one has to be approved of by everyone and for everything one does is another belief that Ellis regards as irrational and that other writers (e.g., Goldfried & Davison, 1994) have called unproductive or self-defeating. The REBT therapist challenges these assumptions and persuades the client that living a life without imposing on oneself unattainable demands and goals will be less stressful and more satisfying. Irrational beliefs must be disputed and replaced by new rational beliefs. Meanwhile, the process of challenging irrational beliefs continues in order to reduce the likelihood of previous problems recurring at a later date (see Dryden, David, & Ellis, 2010).

Several conclusions can be offered on the outcome research on REBT (e.g., Baucom et al., 1998; David, Szentagotai, Kallay, & Macavei, 2005; Engels, Garnefski, & Diekstra, 1993; Haaga & Davison, 1989; Kendall et al., 1995):

- REBT reduces self-reports of general anxiety, speech anxiety, and test anxiety.
- REBT improves both self-reports and behaviour for social anxiety, though it may be less effective than systematic desensitization.
- REBT is inferior to exposure-based treatments for agoraphobia.
- REBT may be useful in treating excessive anger, depression, and anti-social behaviour.
- REBT is useful only as part of more comprehensive behavioural programs for sexual dysfunction.
- REBT may be useful as a preventive measure for untroubled people; it helps emotionally healthy people cope better with everyday stress.
- REBT appears to achieve its effects through a reduction in the irrationality of thought. The importance of the support REBT gives clients to confront what they fear and to take risks with new, more adaptive behaviour should not be underestimated.

As with most other clinical procedures, the relevance of REBT to a given problem depends in part on how the clinician conceptualizes the client's predicament. Thus, a therapist who is trying to help an overweight person lose weight might conceptualize eating as a way of reducing anxiety; in turn, the anxiety might be viewed as due to social distress that is caused by extreme fear of rejection arising from an irrational need to please everyone and never make a mistake.

BECK'S COGNITIVE THERAPY Like Ellis, Beck hypothesizes that people in emotional distress operate with assumptions—he calls them schemas—that are impossible to live with, such as believing that one has to be a perfect parent or student. But in contrast to Ellis, Beck focuses a great deal on the lack of objective evidence that depressed and anxious people have for maintaining their maladaptive schemas. Beck engages the client in a process very much like a scientific investigation, asking such questions as what evidence the client has for believing that he or she is totally inept and worthless. A principal focus is on cognitive biases: errors in information processing, such as selective abstraction and overgeneralization, that filter experience in a way that contributes to negative beliefs about oneself and the world.

The effectiveness of Beck's CT has been under intensive study for more than 30 years. Numerous studies attest to the favourable impact it has on depression (e.g., Clark, Beck, & Alford, 1999; Hamilton & Dobson, 2002), and an earlier meta-analysis of outcome studies of diverse therapies for depression concluded that Beck's therapy achieves greater short-term improvement than wait-list controls, drug therapies, non-cognitive-behavioural treatments, and a heterogeneous group of other psychotherapies (Dobson, 1989). CT may also be better than drug treatment at preventing future episodes, a consideration of major importance in light of the oft-observed tendency for depressive episodes to recur (e.g., Hollon, DeRubeis, & Evans, 1996). Perhaps CT clients acquire some useful skills that they are able to use following termination of therapy. As seen in Chapter 16, because older clients can be extremely sensitive to medications and can also have medical problems that contraindicate prescribing psychoactive drugs, nonpharmacological interventions are especially appropriate for them.

The great interest in CT led to the widely publicized comparative outcome study sponsored by the National Institute of Mental Health (Elkin et al., 1985), a study that did not find CT superior to a drug therapy or to IPT but nonetheless supported the utility of Beck's approach to the treatment of depression. (Recall our in-depth discussion of this study in Chapter 8.) Further, a task force of the clinical division of the American Psychological Association concluded that Beck's CT is an effective treatment for panic disorder, generalized anxiety disorder, social phobia, chronic pain, irritable bowel syndrome, and bulimia nervosa, and that it often fares better than medications alone (Chambless et al., 1996).

As originally hypothesized by Beck, CT helps clients change their cognitions. Predictable changes in cognitions do occur in CT (e.g., Hollon et al., 1996), but such changes are found as well in successful treatment of depression by drugs (e.g., Rush et al., 1982). Cognitive change may therefore be the consequence of change produced by other means (Jacobson et al., 1996). Or, at least with depression (the disorder in which CT has been most researched), cognitive change may be the mediator of therapeutic improvement brought about by any therapy, including Beck's CT, IPT, and pharmacotherapy.

In a study conducted in Toronto at the Rotman Research Institute (Goldapple et al., 2004), the brain changes underlying responses to CBT were examined using positron emission tomography in unmedicated, unipolar depressed outpatients. The participants were scanned before and after a 15- to 20-session course of CBT. Treatment resulted in significant clinical improvement in those people who completed the program, and the treatment response was associated with modulated functioning of specific sites in limbic and cortical regions, consistent with findings for other antidepressant treatments, including drugs. The authors suggested that the unique directional changes in the frontal cortex, cingulate, and hippocampus that occur more with CBT than with an independent group of paroxetine responders possibly reflects modality-specific effects due to CBT. We anticipate that more controlled, comparative outcome imaging investigations will be conducted in the future, since the results have implications for our understanding of the mechanisms underlying treatment strategies.

Research on CBT for depression has sought to identify the specific treatment components that are most effective. A general statement endorsed by many in the field is that we know that CBT works, but have limited insight into the specific factors and processes that operate when it does work. Initially, this research indicates that it is the behavioural interventions rather than the cognitive interventions that are most beneficial, both in the short term (Jacobson et al., 1996) and in the longer term (Gortner, Gollan, Dobson, & Jacobson, 1997). Contemporary research emphasizes fine-grained "component analyses." For instance, a recent study of CBT to treat adolescent depression found that social skills development and problem-solving may be key CBT elements for treating depression in adolescents (Kennard et al., 2009).

Beck and his colleagues believe that additional research into the mechanisms of CT might be even more important to the future of CT than research into its efficacy.

> In order to serve our patients better, and to assure that the progress of cognitive therapy keeps pace with that of alternative treatments, clinical researchers need to improve and refine cognitive therapy and the training of cognitive therapists, so that more patients can benefit from it. To do so, we need first to understand better how cognitive therapy achieves its effects. (DeRubeis, Tang, & Beck, 2001, p. 386)

According to Bieling and Kuyken (2003), even though CT seems to be effective, until research on the validity of cognitive case formulation is conducted, "researchers cannot conclude that cognitive therapy is effective because its statements about etiology and the mechanisms of change are correct" (p. 53). The ultimate goal is to move from a descriptive approach toward a more explanatory approach by identifying and testing specific, hypothesized cognitive mechanisms that contribute to the presentation of problems and by identifying and testing the distal and proximal factors believed to be involved when a person begins to develop dysfunctional beliefs and cognitive styles.

Because CT involves clients in logical analysis and empirical study of their life situation—a challenging intellectual task—it has been assumed that more intelligent individuals are better suited to this approach. This does not seem to be the case, however (Haaga, Dyck, & Ernst, 1991). Perhaps intelligence is too general a concept, entailing as it does a variety of human cognitive processes, such as memory, reasoning, verbal facility, and quantitative skills. A more focused search for cognitive variables might prove more fruitful (Haaga, Rabois, & Brody, 1999).

SOME COMPARISONS BETWEEN THE THERAPIES OF BECK AND ELLIS The theories and techniques of Ellis and Beck are used widely by therapists. With the inevitable changes that inventive clinicians make as they apply the work of others, and with the evolution in the thinking of the theorists themselves, the differences between the therapies can be difficult to discern. However, they do contrast in interesting and important ways.

To a parent who became depressed on learning that his or her child had failed a test at school, Ellis would say immediately, in essence, "So what if you are an inadequate parent? It is irrational to demand perfection from yourself and then to become depressed when you fall short." Ellis (2002) advocates challenging the irrationality of perfectionism. Beck, in contrast, would first examine the evidence for the conclusion. His is a more empirical approach. "What evidence is there for thinking that you are an inadequate parent?" If proof is lacking, this discovery in itself will be therapeutic. Ellis regards his own type of solution as more thorough. Even if the person is wanting as a parent, the world will not end, for a person does not have to be competent in everything he or she does. Beck, too, will eventually question with the client whether one has to be competent in everything to feel good about oneself, but perhaps not until accumulated evidence suggests that the person is in fact an inadequate parent.

The therapist adopting Beck's approach certainly has preconceptions about negative schemas (which seem to us very similar to Ellis's irrational beliefs) and especially about the forms that maladaptive, illogical, or biased thinking takes, such as overgeneralization. But working with a depressed individual is a collaborative, inductive procedure by which client and therapist attempt to discover, by examining the client's biased thinking, the particular dysfunctional assumptions underlying the person's negative thoughts. REBT therapists, in contrast, operate much more deductively; they are confident that a distressed person subscribes to one or more irrational beliefs from a predetermined list or that they make unrealistic demands of themselves or others and then seek out evidence to support their hypotheses.

Beck's therapy and standard rational-emotive practices differ in style on this inductive-deductive basis. Beck suggests that the therapist should avoid being overly didactic, while Ellis often uses mini-lectures and didactic speeches. Beck proposes calling negative thoughts "unproductive ideas" to promote rapport. He does not favour adjectives such as "irrational" or "nutty," which might be heard—with supportive humour—from Ellis. Finally, Beck recommends that the therapist begin by acknowledging the client's frame of reference and asking for an elaboration of it. Having had a chance to present his or her case and feel understood, the person may be more willing to go through the collaborative process of questioning his or her beliefs. In contrast, Ellis supposes that quite forceful interventions are necessary to disrupt a well-learned maladaptive pattern of thinking. He will directly confront the client's irrational beliefs, sometimes within minutes in the first session.

Both approaches have one thing in common. They both convey the message that people can change their psychological predicaments by thinking differently. They emphasize that how a person construes himself or herself and the world is a major determinant of the kind of person he or she will be, and that people have choices in how they construe things. They assert that people can, sometimes with great effort, choose to think, feel, and behave differently. Unlike behaviour therapists, who are not cognitive, but like the humanists and existentialists, Beck and Ellis believe that new behaviour is important primarily for the evidence it can provide about how the person looks at himself or herself and the world. Thus, their focus remains on the cognitive dimension of humankind and on the abiding belief that people's minds can be set free and that their thinking is the key to positive psychological change.

REFLECTIONS ON COGNITIVE-BEHAVIOURAL THERAPY

We turn now to some general issues surrounding CBT.

CBT: A Return to Psychology's Cognitive Roots As we indicated in Chapter 2, behaviour therapy initially aligned itself with the study of classical and operant conditioning, under the assumption that principles and procedures derived from conditioning experiments could be applied to lessen psychological suffering. What developed into CBT (or CT) may appear to be a radical and novel departure, given the earlier focus of behaviour therapists on conditioning and their de-emphasis or even total avoidance of cognition

as a controlling variable in behaviour and emotion. But in a historical sense, CBT represents a return to the cognitive foci of the earliest period of experimental psychology (e.g., Bartlett's [1932] classic work on memory). Many experimental psychologists have continued through the years to do research into cognition—into the mental processes of perceiving, recognizing, conceiving, judging, and reasoning, and of problem-solving, imagining, and other symbolizing activities. CBT has actually caught up with what has been going on for years in experimental psychology.

Restructuring vs. Replacing Cognitions Two distinctions are often drawn in CBT on the basis of whether its strategy is to restructure cognitions or replace them (Arnkoff, 1986). A restructuring strategy is found in Beck's and Ellis's approaches to treatment, which assume that cognitive-change efforts should be directed toward changing particular thoughts the client is having. In contrast, a replacement strategy has the therapist assume nothing about the client's cognitions other than that they are interfering with his or her life; the goal is simply to teach the client a way of thinking that is believed to be more adaptive than the cognitions with which the client is operating, whatever they may be. An example is the problem-solving therapy of D'Zurilla (1986). In this approach, the therapist teaches the client a set of problem-solving strategies believed to be generally applicable to a wide range of situations. No effort is expended in determining—as Ellis and Beck do—the aspects of the person's current cognitions that are getting him or her into psychological trouble (Haaga et al., 2002).

The Continuing Importance of Behaviour Change in CBT Many contemporary researchers continue to believe that behavioural procedures are more powerful than strictly verbal ones in affecting cognitive processes (Bandura, 1977). That is, they favour behavioural techniques while maintaining that it is important to alter a person's beliefs to effect an enduring change in behaviour and emotion. Bandura suggests that all therapeutic procedures, to the extent that they are effective, work their improvement by giving the person a sense of mastery, of self-efficacy (Bandura, 1997). At the same time he finds that the most effective way to gain a sense of self-efficacy is by changing behaviour. Regardless of whether we believe self-efficacy is as important as Bandura does, a distinction can be made between processes that underlie improvement and procedures that set these processes in motion.

CBT therapists continue to be behavioural in their use of performance-based procedures and in their commitment to behavioural change (Dobson & Jackman-Cram, 1996; Jacobson et al., 1996), but they are cognitive in the sense that they believe that cognitive change (e.g., enhanced self-efficacy) is an important mechanism that accounts for the effectiveness of at least some behavioural procedures. Cognition and behaviour continually and reciprocally influence each other; new behaviour can alter thinking, and that new mode of thinking can in turn facilitate the new behaviour. In addition, the environment influences both thought and action and is influenced by them. This model, termed **triadic reciprocality** by Bandura (1986), highlights the close interrelatedness of thinking, behaving, and the environment.

The Importance of Emotion in CBT

As Salovey and Singer (1991) have noted, Bandura's triadic reciprocality underemphasizes the concept of emotion. People have many cognitions that are affect laden—sometimes referred to as "hot cognitions"—and these tend to relate to the self (Cantor et al., 1986), to one's dreams and fantasies, fondest hopes, and most dire fears. "The therapist must be alert to emotions that color the maladaptive cognitions that are traditionally the focus of treatment. Even though feelings often also arise as a consequence of cognition, it may still be possible to alter maladaptive cognitions by first assessing and then intervening at the level of feelings" (Salovey & Singer, 1991, p. 366). Dobson and Khatri (2000) argue that CT does include an explicit focus on emotion as a consequence of cognitions. Specifically, they note that "[b]oth Ellis and Beck have developed sophisticated models of various emotions and their cognitive substrates .... Although they do hypothesize that emotions are largely consequential to various thought patterns, they do not, as some authors have argued (Coyne & Gotlib, 1983), see them as epiphenomenal" (Dobson and Khatri, 2000, p. 909).

The Phenomenological Essence of CBT

All CBT therapists pay attention to the world as it is perceived by the client. It is not what impinges on us from the outside that controls our behaviour, the assumption that guided behavioural psychology for decades; rather, it is our view of the world that determines our feelings and behaviour. Hamlet, in the famous Shakespearean play, put it this way: "There is nothing either good or bad, but thinking makes it so" (*Hamlet*, act II, scene 2). CBT is being brought closer to the humanistic and existential therapies. A central thesis of experiential therapists, such as Rogers and Perls, is that clients must be understood from their own frame of reference, from their phenomenological world, for it is this experience of the world that controls life and behaviour. From a philosophical point of view, such assumptions on the part of those who would understand people and try to help them are profoundly important. Experimentally minded clinicians and researchers are intrigued by how much CBT therapists have in common with the experientialists, and their attention to the phenomenological world of their clients. To be sure, the techniques used by CBT therapists are usually quite different from those of the followers of Rogers and Perls, but these surface differences should not blind us to the links between the two approaches.

Relapse Prevention in CBT

How do we prevent relapses in clients? What is it that clients take away from treatment that can help them maintain and enhance their gains as well as deal with the new challenges that await them in their day-to-day lives? It is often assumed that clients who maintain their improvement after termination of treatment are continuing to apply specific skills acquired during treatment. Marlatt (1985) proposed the "abstinence violation effect" as a focus of concern in relapse prevention. His research on alcoholism sensitized him to the generally negative effects of a slip, as when a former drinker, after a successful period of abstinence, imbibes to a stupor after taking a single drink. Marlatt suggested that the manner in which the person reacts cognitively to the slip determines whether he or she will overcome the setback or relapse and resume drinking to excess. The consequences of the slip are hypothesized to be worse if the person attributes it to internal, stable, and global factors believed to be uncontrollable. An example would be a belief, fostered by Alcoholics Anonymous, that the lapse was caused by an uncontrollable disease process that overwhelms the person once a single drink is taken. In contrast, relapse is assumed to be less likely if the individual attributes the slip to causes that are external, unstable, specific, and controllable, such as an unexpectedly stressful life event. In essence, the person is encouraged to distinguish between a lapse and relapse. CBT therapists attempt to minimize the abstinence violation effect by encouraging attributions to external, unstable, and specific factors and by teaching strategies for coping with life stressors. In this way, it is hoped that gains achieved in therapy will persist once formal contact with the therapist has ended.

A controlled comparative outcome study on the treatment of cocaine dependence (Carroll, Rounsaville, Nich, et al., 1994) found two important instances of generalization at a one-year follow-up: clients treated with the drug desipramine maintained their treatment-produced gains, and clients treated with CBT not only maintained their improvement but showed signs of even further improvement, or what the authors called "delayed emergence of effects" (Carroll, Rounsaville, Nich, et al., 1994, p. 995). That the drug-produced effects were maintained at one-year follow-up is a welcome exception to the general finding of relapse following drug withdrawal. That the CBT gains were actually greater at one-year follow-up prompted the investigators to speculate that CBT had taught clients coping skills that they were able to implement long after formal therapy had ended, something lacking in the drug-therapy group.

As discussed in Chapter 8, mindfulness-based cognitive therapy (MBCT) was developed specifically to prevent relapse among clinically depressed people. MBCT combines relaxation and related techniques designed to increase awareness of changes in the body and the mind with standard cognitive intervention techniques (see Segal, Williams, & Teasdale, 2002) in order to develop a sense of how cognitive sets are related to emotional feelings and vice versa (meta-cognitive awareness). Segal et al. (2006) demonstrated that the vulnerability of depressed people to relapse may be related to the reactivation of depressive cognitive styles triggered by sad mood provocation. In MBCT, clients who have recovered from depression are taught to disengage from ruminative processing by becoming aware of and accepting negative thoughts and feelings in order to be less vulnerable to future depression episodes. Rates of relapse are substantially reduced (Teasdale et al., 2000), and reduced relapse is associated with the increased presence of meta-cognitive sets (Teasdale et al., 2002). In another trial, Ma and Teasdale (2004) concluded that "MBCT is an effective and efficient way to prevent relapse/recurrence in recovered depressed patients with 3 or more previous episodes" (p. 31). Since the same cognitive processes maintain depression once established, Kenny and Williams (2007) explored the use of MBCT in currently actively depressed individuals who had not responded to standard treatments, reporting that a significant proportion of these individuals returned to normal or near-normal mood. In an experimental investigation of the cognitive vulnerability to depression, Singer and Dobson (2007) concluded that acceptance-based interventions can (1) reduce the desire to escape from negative emotions and (2) increase tolerance of sad moods. Acceptance can be easy and non-threatening, but "radical acceptance" is often required; this involves coming to terms with more painful realities and realizations (see Fruzzetti & Erikson, 2010).

Unconscious Factors and Underlying Causes With the growing interest in cognitive factors, cognitive therapists have focused their assessments and interventions on unconscious internal mediators (e.g., Bowers & Meichenbaum, 1984). Ellis, for example, assumes that people are distressed by beliefs that he designates irrational—even though a client seldom states the problem in such terms and may be unaware of these beliefs. Based on what the client says and how it is said, and working from rational-emotive theory, Ellis may infer the operation of a belief such as "It is a dire necessity that I be perfect in everything I do." He then persuades the client to accept the notion that this belief underlies the problems. Therapy

is directed at altering that belief. Although he tends to work more slowly and more inductively than Ellis, Beck infers similar beliefs, which he calls negative schemas or dysfunctional assumptions, including a dysfunctional belief in the need to be perfect (Brown & Beck, 2002).

This is an interesting turn of events for an approach that initially rejected the notion of unconscious motivation and thought! Yet it is consistent with decades of research by experimental cognitive psychologists, who infer sets, beliefs, attitudes, and other abstract cognitive concepts of which the person is often unaware (e.g., Bruner, Goodnow, & Austin, 1956). To be sure, appreciation of factors of which a person may be unaware does not make any of the cognitive therapies equivalent to psychoanalysis, but it does demonstrate the wisdom of some of Freud's clinical insights and is reflected in the kinds of rapprochements we explore later. A growing number of studies demonstrate the effects that unconscious or pre-conscious stimuli can have on mood, cognition, and behaviour (e.g., Baldwin, Carrell, & Lopez, 1990).

CBT therapists, like their analytic counterparts, have come to believe that, generally, there is more to the client than immediately meets the eye (Goldfried & Davison, 1994). Guidano and Liotti (1983) spoke of the "protective belt" behind which one must search for core beliefs, which themselves are generally related to one's idea of oneself, such as a negative self-image. According to Mahoney (1990), core cognitions may be extremely difficult to change, even when uncovered, because they stem from one's earlier developmental history. And well before the popularity of CBT, George Kelly (1955) distinguished between "core constructs" and "peripheral constructs," the former relating to the person's basic sense of self or identity. Although changing core beliefs is not a simple matter for either client or therapist, it is believed by many contemporary researchers to be essential to CT if the positive effects of therapy are to endure (see Chapter 2).

A focus on core themes or constructs is at the root of schema therapy as developed by Geoffrey Young (see Young, 1999; Young, Klosko, & Weishaar, 2003). According to

Source: *Bernie*, Harry Mayerovitch. Courtesy of the estate Harry Mayerovitch.

Martin and Young (2010), schema therapy can not only be used to treat personality disorders or other specific individual difficulties (e.g., depression) but can also be amended to treat couples. The focus is on early maladaptive schemas that represent the key themes addressed with CBT techniques. Schemas exist at a deep level and attempts to identify and change them are called "schema work" (DeRubeis et al., 2010). Overall, Young (1999) proposed 18 different schemas that are grouped into five broad categories: (1) disconnection and rejection; (2) impaired autonomy and performance; (3) impaired limits (e.g., grandiosity, insufficient self-control); (4) other-directedness (subjugation, self-sacrifice); and (5) overvigilance and inhibition. Assessment with the Young Schema Questionnaire provides a clear overview of the cognitive themes that represent sources of vulnerability for the afflicted individual.

Relationship Factors As noted previously, a good relationship between client and therapist is important for many reasons and regardless of the particular theoretical orientation. It is doubtful that people will reveal deeply personal information if they do not trust or respect their therapists. Furthermore, since therapy can seldom be imposed on an unwilling client, a therapist must obtain the client's co-operation if the techniques are to have their desired effect. As an example, the importance of the therapeutic relationship is central to Linehan's dialectical behaviour therapy. She argues that, with clients who have borderline personality disorder, it is essential to create an atmosphere of acceptance and empathy within which specific CBT techniques can be implemented.

REVIEW OF COUPLES AND FAMILY THERAPY

BASIC CONCEPTS AND TECHNIQUES IN COUPLES AND FAMILY THERAPY

As a way of further underscoring the complexities often facing the therapist, we turn now to a discussion of couples and family therapy, with a particular emphasis on marital conflict. The issues and problems facing individuals seeking treatment are often complicated because the person is often impacted and impacting dysfunctional relationships, and there is a need for couples therapy or family therapy. In a review paper, Johnson and Lebow (2000) noted, "Distress in an intimate relationship is recognized as the single most frequent presenting problem in psychotherapy" (p. 23). Couples therapy is the preferred mode of treatment for such problems.

Clearly, marital conflict can have a profound negative impact on the well-being of family members. This is underscored by a reanalysis of the data from the Ontario Health Survey's Mental Health Supplement by Whisman, Sheldon, and Goering (2000), who found that marital problems were associated with six disorders, including generalized anxiety

disorder, panic disorder, major depression, and drinking problems. In contrast, an inability to get along with friends and relatives was unrelated to the various psychiatric disorders when other social relationships were controlled. Given the negative impact that marital troubles apparently have, how effective are the therapies that are designed to improve functioning?

THE NORMALITY OF CONFLICT

There is almost universal agreement among couples therapists and researchers, regardless of theoretical orientation, that conflict is inevitable in a marriage or in any other long-term relationship. The aura of the honeymoon passes when the couple makes unromantic decisions about where to live, where to seek employment, how to budget money, what kinds of meals to prepare and how to share that responsibility, when to visit in-laws, if and when to have children, and whether to experiment with novel sexual techniques. Today, in addition, couples have the changed nature of gender roles to negotiate. For example, if both spouses work, will their place of residence be determined by the husband's employment or by the wife's? These sources of conflict must be handled by any two people living together, whether they are married or not, whether they are of the opposite sex or not. Authorities agree that how couples deal with such inherent conflicts will often determine the quality and duration of their cohabitation relationship (e.g., Schwartz & Schwartz, 1980).

A strategy some couples adopt, deliberately or unconsciously, is to avoid acknowledging disagreements and conflicts. Because they believe in the reality of the fairy-tale ending of "And they lived happily ever after," any sign that their relationship is not going smoothly is threatening and

When a problem involves a couple, therapy is most effective if the couple is seen together. Media Bakery.

must be ignored. Such patterns may keep peace in the short term but usually run the risk of serious dysfunction in the long term (Gottman & Krokoff, 1989). Dissatisfaction and resentment develop and begin to take their toll as time goes by. Because the partners do not quarrel, they may appear to be a perfect couple to observers, but without opening the lines of communication, they may drift apart emotionally. Conversely, whereas disagreement and even the expression of anger are related to unhappiness in couples in the short term, they actually are predictive of more satisfaction over time (Gottman & Krokoff, 1989).

FROM INDIVIDUAL TO CONJOINT THERAPY

The terms "family therapy" and "couples therapy" do not denote a set procedure. They tell us that therapeutic focus is on at least two people in a relationship, but they leave undefined such issues as how the therapist views the nature and causes of the problem, what techniques are chosen to alleviate it, how often clients are seen, and whether children and even grandparents are included.

Couples and family therapy share some theoretical frameworks with individual therapy. Psychoanalytic marital therapists, for example, focus on how a person seeks or avoids a partner who resembles, to his or her unconscious, the opposite-sexed parent (Segraves, 1990). Frustrated and unsatisfied by his love-seeking attempts as a child, the adult man may unconsciously seek maternal nurturing from his wife and make excessive, even infantile, demands of her. Much of the discussion in this kind of couples therapy focuses on the conflicts he is having with his wife and, presumably, on the repressed striving for maternal love that underlies his immature ways of relating to her. These unconscious forces are plumbed, with the wife assisting and possibly revealing some of her own unresolved yearnings for her father. Transference is explored, but in analytic couples therapy, it is the transference between the two partners rather than between the client and the therapist that is usually the focus. The overall goal is to help each partner see the other as he or she actually is rather than as a symbolic parent (Fitzgerald, 1973). Sometimes each partner is seen separately by different therapists, sometimes separately by the same therapist, and sometimes conjointly by the same therapist.

Ellis's REBT has also been applied to family conflict. Again, the perspective is primarily individualistic or intrapsychic. The therapist assumes that something going on within one or both of the partners is causing the distress in the relationship. Ellis (2002) cited the example of a man with both marital and work difficulties who demanded absolute perfection, not only from himself, but also from his wife and business associates. Therapy emphasized this irrational need for perfection.

With this as background to the shift from individual to conjoint therapies, we describe now some of the details of conjoint therapy. Some methods are common to all couples and family therapies, whereas others differ according to theoretical orientation.

THE APPROACHES TO COUPLES AND FAMILY THERAPY
THE MENTAL RESEARCH INSTITUTE TRADITION

Couples and family therapy seems to have begun in the 1950s at the Mental Research Institute (MRI) in California, where the focus was on faulty communication patterns, uneasy relationships, and inflexibility. Family members were shown how their behaviour affected their relations with others. They were then persuaded to make specific changes, such as making their needs and dislikes more clearly known to others. Few family therapists who identify themselves with the MRI approach are concerned with history. Their focus is on how current problems are being maintained and how they might be changed. Whatever the problem, the family therapist takes a family systems approach, a general view of etiology and treatment that focuses on the complex interrelationships within families.

COGNITIVE-BEHAVIOURAL APPROACHES Distressed couples do not react very positively toward each other, and this antagonism is usually evident in the very first session. It is not uncommon for one partner to feel coerced into attending conjoint therapy, even for an initial session. In a pioneering treatise on behavioural marital therapy, Jacobson and Margolin (1979) recommended that the therapist attend to this problem of antagonism as a first step in helping partners improve their marriage. One strategy is the "caring days" idea of Richard Stuart (1976), which applies an operant strategy to the couple's conflict. The husband, for example, is cajoled into agreeing to devote himself to doing nice things for his wife all day on a given day, without expecting anything in return. The agreement is that the wife will do the same for him the next day. If successful, this strategy accomplishes at least two important things: first, it breaks the cycle of distance, suspicion, and aversive control of each other; and second, it shows the giving partner that he or she is able to affect the spouse in a positive way. This enhanced sense of positive control is achieved simply by pleasing the partner. The improved atmosphere that develops as a consequence of their doing nice things for each other and having nice things done for them in return helps each of them become motivated to please the other on future occasions.

Behavioural couples therapists generally adopt Thibaut and Kelley's (1959) exchange theory of interaction. According to this view, people value others if they receive from them a high ratio of benefits to costs; that is, if they see themselves getting at least as much from the other person as they give. Furthermore, people are assumed to be more disposed to continue a given relationship if other alternatives are less attractive to them, promising fewer benefits and costing more. Therapists therefore try to encourage a mutual dispensing of rewards by partner A and partner B.

Behavioural marital or couples therapy shares with other approaches a focus on enhancing communication skills between the partners, but the emphasis is more on increasing the ability of each partner to please the other. The core assumption is that "the relative rates of pleasant and unpleasant interactions determine the subjective quality of the relationship" (Wood & Jacobson, 1985). Indeed, behavioural couples therapists consider this more than an assumption, for they can point to data supporting the view that distressed couples differ from non-distressed couples in that they have lower frequencies of positive exchanges and higher frequencies of unsatisfying exchanges. Also, as Camper et al. (1988) found, spouses in distressed marriages view negative behaviour on the part of their partners as global and stable—"There is nothing I can do to please him, and it's never going to change"—whereas they construe positive behaviour as less so—"Well, he was happy with me today, but it's not going to last." Distressed couples also tend to get upset by immediate and recent negative events, like the weather being bad when an outdoor project was scheduled, whereas non-distressed couples are better able to overlook such minor annoyances (e.g., Wood & Jacobson, 1985).

Thus, behavioural couples therapy concentrates on increasing positive exchanges in the hope not only of increasing short-term satisfaction, but also laying a foundation for long-term trust and positive feelings, qualities that are characteristic of non-distressed relationships. Cognitive change is also seen as important, for couples often need training in problem-solving and encouragement to acknowledge positive changes. Distressed couples often perceive inaccurately the ratio of positive to negative exchanges, as they focus on the negative (Gottman et al., 1976).

Behavioural couples therapists have become increasingly interested in cognitive components of relationships and relationship distress, a reflection of the cognitive trend in behaviour therapy as a whole (Baucom, Epstein, & Rankin, 1995). The interest in cognition in couples therapy can also be traced to the influence of attribution theory in social psychology (the study of how people explain the reasons for their own and others' behaviour) and the overlap between marital distress and depression. As a result of adding this cognitive component and broadening its treatment strategies, behavioural marital therapy is now frequently referred to as cognitive-behavioural marital therapy (CBMT). CBMT focuses on each person's attributions; for example, paying close attention to whether one partner decides that the other is responsible or blameworthy for an event that was actually not under anyone's control.

While therapy may focus on relationship difficulties, partners can attend treatment together if one member has psychological difficulties and there is anticipated benefit linked with the partner participating. This type of treatment is discussed in more detail below. Results continue to highlight the more general benefits of couples therapy. For instance, a recent randomized control trial comparing brief problem-focused couples therapy and wait-list control participants was conducted with couples in which there was a depressed wife (Cohen, O'Leary, & Foran, 2010). Treatment consisted of five two-hour sessions over a five-week period. Two thirds of the depressed women in the therapy group improved in terms of their depressive symptoms vs. only 17% in the control group. Treatment also contributed to improvements in marital satisfaction, in depression in husbands, and in depression-specific burden. Participation in treatment also contributed to improvements in the understanding and acceptance of depression in depressed women and their partners.

INTEGRATIVE BEHAVIOURAL COUPLES THERAPY
Integrative behavioural couples therapy (IBCT) was developed by Andrew Christensen and Neil S. Jacobson (Christensen, Jacobson, & Babcock, 1995). IBCT uses reinforcement principles as well as the behavioural exchange and communication training strategies just described, but it also incorporates the Rogerian notion of acceptance and provides a series of procedures designed to foster emotional acceptance in couples (Cordova & Jacobson, 1993). IBCT, relative to traditional behavioural couples therapy (TBCT), recognizes that the actions and inactions of partners are important but even more important is the emotional reactivity that one has to the actions and inactions. Emotional reactivity is the central focus of the form of therapy discussed in the next section.

How does IBCT fare vs. TBCT? The largest clinical trial of couples therapy for maritally distressed people thus far was conducted by Christensen et al. (2004). The initial results indicated that both types of treatment resulted in significant clinical improvements, but the improvement was more consistent with IBCT. The long-term follow-up investigation reported by Christensen, Atkins, Baucom, and Yi (2010) found at five-year follow-up that 50% of the IBCT couples and 45.9% of the TBCT couples showed clinically significant improvement. Also, 25.7% of the IBCT couples were separated or divorced, while 27.9% of the TBCT couples were separated or divorced. These differences were not statistically significant. The divorce rates were substantially lower than the divorce rates found in other studies of other types of couples therapy, with divorce rate estimates in past studies ranging from 38 to 70%. Thus, it seemed that both IBCT and TBCT worked. Christensen et al. (2010) highlighted the need for follow-up research seeking to identify the key mechanisms of change.

EMOTION-FOCUSED THERAPY The approach to conjoint treatment known as emotion-focused therapy (EFT) (e.g., Johnson, 2007; Johnson & Greenberg, 1987) contains psychodynamic elements, but its humanistic emphasis on feelings strikes us as more salient. See Canadian Perspectives 17.1 for a detailed description and evaluation of this therapy.

CANADIAN PERSPECTIVES 17.1
EMOTION-FOCUSED COUPLES THERAPY

Susan Johnson, from the University of Ottawa, is a co-founder of emotion-focused couples therapy, which she developed with Les Greenberg. Courtesy of Susan Johnson.

Emotion-focused therapy (EFT) was developed by Les Greenberg of York University and Susan Johnson, now at the University of Ottawa (e.g., Bradley & Johnson, 2005; Greenberg & Johnson, 1988; Johnson, 2007; Woolley & Johnson, 2006). The essence of EFT is that marital distress stems from maladaptive and distressed forms of emotion in the marital context and the destructive interactions that follow from this maladaptive emotion. This focus on negative emotions is consonant with the humanistic, experiential approach adopted originally by Greenberg and Johnson, as well as with general findings indicating that the emotional processing in therapy is associated with improvements in psychological functioning (e.g., Pos, Greenberg, Goldman, & Korman, 2003; Watson & Bedard, 2006). Although the focus is on negative emotions such as guilt, anger, and shame, couples must also establish more constructive ways of relating via the processing and expression of positive emotions as well (see Greenberg & Goldman, 2008).

Recent versions of EFT incorporate a focus on adult attachment styles in relationships (Johnson, 2002; Johnson & Whiffen, 2003), and this includes an emphasis on attachment bonds among couples influenced by traumatic experiences (Johnson, 2002). This therapy integrates components from attachment theory, which has been used to conceptualize adult romantic relationships (see also Bartholomew & Horowitz, 1991), and focuses on the "innate adaptive needs for protection, security, and connectedness with significant others" (Johnson & Greenberg, 1995, p. 124). From this vantage point, relationship distress occurs when the attachment needs have not been met and the relationship does not provide a secure base for one or both partners. In extreme forms, one partner may experience an attachment injury. This injury would follow betrayals of trust or abandonment at a key time. A publicly known betrayal of trust

such as that experienced by actress Sandra Bullock when her husband's infidelities became known should result in an extreme attachment injury. The overall goal of treatment is for couples to maintain emotional engagement and be accessible and responsive to each other's needs.

Typically, EFT involves 12 to 15 sessions. The process of change is broken down into three general phases that span nine steps altogether (see Johnson, 2000; Johnson, Hunsley, Greenberg, & Schindler, 1999). The goal of the first phase is to de-escalate the maladaptive cycle. The four steps that compose this phase are (1) assessing the current conflicts experienced by the couple and fostering an alliance; (2) identifying the problematic interaction cycle that is maintaining problems in the relationship; (3) accessing underlying emotions; and (4) trying to reframe the problem in terms of associated emotions and attachment needs.

The goal of the second phase is to change interactional positions. This second phase consists of three steps: (1) helping the couple to identify needs and aspects of the self that have been denied and incorporate these into the relationship; (2) learning to accept the partner's new emotional experience and related responses; and (3) learning to express specific needs and developing a sense of positive emotional engagement.

The goal of the third phase is consolidation and integration and this involves two main steps: (1) attempts are made to arrive at new solutions to old problems; and (2) new positions and new cycles of attachment behaviour must be consolidated.

Empirical evaluations suggest that EFT is effective. Johnson et al. (1999) reported the results of a meta-analysis of

Sandra Bullock filed for divorce from her husband Jesse James after it was revealed that James had carried on multiple extramarital affairs. Such betrayals can cause attachment injuries, especially when a public humiliation is involved. WENN/Newscom.

seven studies that assessed EFT and marital distress. It showed that the majority of couples reported clinical improvement on the outcome measure (i.e., the Dyadic Adjustment Scale), and that 70 to 73% had recovered from marital distress. Dessaulles, Johnson, and Denton (2003) reported the results of a pilot study that tested EFT as a treatment for depression in couples with marital problems. Depression was diagnosed in the women in the study. Comparisons of those who received EFT with those who received pharmacotherapy showed that both treatments were equally effective in reducing depressive symptoms. Improvements were deemed to be both statistically and clinically significant. Another study documented EFT treatment gains in levels of forgiveness among 17 of 20 couples undergoing treatment to repair emotional injuries stemming from being humiliated and emotionally hurt by one's partner (Greenberg, Warwar, & Malcolm, 2008) and one study found that treatment gains in terms of greater trust and forgiveness were found for three years for couples receiving EFT for an attachment injury (Halchuk, Makinen, & Johnson, 2010). A related investigation comparing EFT with a psychoeducational intervention for clients with "emotional injuries" found that EFT with an empty-chair dialogue resulted in substantially more improvement, compared with the psychoedu-

cation intervention on measures of forgiveness and letting go of the past and measures of global symptoms (Greenberg, Warwar, & Malcolm, 2008).

EFT can be modified and tailored to address specific issues and specific adjustment problems. For instance, Whiffen and Johnson (1998) described how EFT can be used to address some of the interpersonal conflicts that contribute to postpartum depression. It can also be used with people from various cultural backgrounds. Johnson (2007) makes the point that EFT has a focus on universal emotions from the person's idiosyncratic viewpoint and, as such, it is well-suited for use with different kinds of people from different cultures.

Thinking Critically

1. Theorists have discussed the suitability of using couples treatment to address more severe disorders that are experienced by individuals but may not yet involve a marital component (e.g., a depressed spouse). Do you think EFT could be used to address severe disorders experienced by individuals?

2. It is usually suggested that men are low in emotional expression. Do you think that men, relative to women, will benefit more, less, or the same from EFT? Explain.

It should be noted that emotion-focused therapy consists of principles and processes that can also be used to treat individuals. According to Greenberg (2004), the three major empirically supported principles of EFT are (1) emotion awareness and the acceptance of emotion; (2) emotion regulation; and (3) emotion utilization or transformation in order to move on from or transform core feelings. Emotion-regulation skills include identifying and labelling emotions, allowing and tolerating emotions, increasing positive emotions, reducing vulnerability to negative emotions, self-soothing, breathing, and distraction. Greenberg and Pascual-Leone (2006) acknowledge emotional transformation as "the most fundamental principle of emotional processing" (p. 618). The case study described at the beginning of this chapter illustrates a number of these key principles.

GENERAL FEATURES OF ALL COUPLES THERAPY In all forms of couples therapy, each partner is trained to listen empathically to the other and to state clearly to the partner what he or she understands is being said and what feelings underlie those remarks. One way to improve communication is to distinguish between the intent of a remark and its impact. Partner A, for example, may wish to be helpful by asking whether partner B would like him or her to get something from the store, but this question may have a negative impact if partner B would prefer partner A to stay home and help with a project. Intent and impact can differ.

The communications of distressed and happy couples may differ in impact more than in intent. Gottman and his colleagues (1976) found that both types of couples made the same number of positive statements to partners, but distressed spouses reported having heard fewer positive statements. Gottman proposed a technique for clarifying intent. One partner calls, "Stop action," and asks the other to indicate what he or she believes the first is trying to say. The feedback indicates immediately whether remarks are having the intended impact.

An interaction pattern known as the demand-withdraw cycle is recognized as particularly destructive for couples. First described by researchers at MRI (Watzlawick, Beavin, & Jackson, 1967) and in a more recent research study by others (Christensen & Pasch, 1993), the demand-withdraw pattern is characterized by one partner attempting to discuss a problem and the other avoiding or withdrawing from such efforts. This withdrawal generates more demands from the first spouse, who tries harder and harder to engage the other, only to be met with more avoidance. And so the cycle escalates. Christensen and Heavey (1990) suggest that there are sex differences in this pattern: women tend to assume the demanding role whereas men usually withdraw. This pattern is found in couples that have a conflict surrounding closeness; the person demanding change may be trying to generate closeness and the person avoiding the interaction may be struggling to seek or maintain autonomy.

Couples and family therapy have for years made creative use of video recording equipment. A couple can be given a problem to solve during part of a therapy session, such as where to go on vacation, and can be recorded while they attempt to solve it. The ways in which they push forward their own wishes—or fail to—and the ways in which they accommodate the other's wishes—or fail to—are but two aspects of their communication patterns that a therapist can come to understand from later viewing the video, often with the couple watching also. Patterns of communication and miscommunication can be readily discerned using this tool.

A common practice among family therapists is to give couples specific homework assignments so that they can practise the new patterns of interaction they have learned during sessions and begin the important process of generalizing change from the consulting room to their everyday lives. Couples may be asked to practise paraphrasing each other's sentences for a specified time period, such as a half hour after dinner, as part of an active listening assignment. In essence, couples are taught Rogerian empathy skills. They may also be instructed to practise a new parenting skill with their children. Some therapists ask couples to make a video of their assignment so that the therapist can review their progress during the next therapy session.

GENERAL ISSUES AND SPECIAL CONSIDERATIONS

The severity and nature of marital dysfunction treated by therapists vary considerably. One couple may seek professional assistance when there is merely dissatisfaction in the relationship, but another may wait until the crisis is so great that one or both partners have already consulted a divorce lawyer. Thus, there are different stages of marital distress (e.g., Duck, 1984), and different therapeutic approaches may be used depending on the couple's starting point. For example, a couple married for five years and on the verge of divorce, with some threat of physical violence, needs a more directive, intensive approach than a couple drifting apart after 10 years.

Family therapy is further complicated when one or more elements of abuse (physical, sexual, and emotional) is present. The therapist must consider what effect saving the relationship may have on the abused spouse and possibly on the abused children, for when there is spousal abuse there is a high likelihood of child abuse, as well. Regardless of who the identified client is, the therapist must be sensitive to the needs of all those whose lives are affected by the relationship (Kadis & McClendon, 1995).

Other ethical considerations in family therapy include how to deal with the disclosure of secrets by one spouse when the other spouse is not present. Some therapists handle this at the outset of treatment by telling the couple that nothing that is told to the therapist by one of the partners will be kept secret from the other. Other therapists feel that this policy may keep them from obtaining valuable information (Kadis & McClendon, 1995).

As noted above, an interesting line of research has focused on individual problems in one of the partners and how such problems respond to conjoint therapy vs. how they respond to an intervention targeting only the individual problems. Noting that depression in at least one of the partners is often a part of a distressed couple's relationship and that relapse into depression is more likely if the formerly depressed partner is in a troubled marriage (Hooley & Teasdale, 1989), researchers (e.g., O'Leary & Beach, 1990) have studied behavioural marital therapy (BMT) as a treatment for depression. The findings indicate that Beck's individualized CT for the depressed partner is no more effective than BMT in alleviating depression and that CT is not as effective as BMT in enhancing marital satisfaction. In other words, someone who is depressed and in a troubled relationship can be helped as much by a systems-oriented approach to the relationship as by an individualized intervention, with the advantage of also deriving benefit for relationship problems. This research highlights both the interpersonal nature of depression and the role of depression in a distressed intimate relationship. Moreover, the finding that individualized CT does not improve a marriage in the same way that improvement in a marriage lifts depression shows the limits of a non-systems individualized therapy, such as CT, as well as the strengths of a systems approach, such as BMT.

CT can also be highly effective for alcohol abuse and drug dependence. A meta-analytic review of 12 randomized control trials found that behavioural couples treatment was superior to individualized therapies (Powers, Vedel, & Emmelkamp, 2008). Significant improvements were found in several domains, including frequency of drug use, consequences of use and abuse, and relationship functioning.

There is great variety within couples and family therapy—from psychoanalytic to Gestalt to behavioural. The techniques employed reflect the therapist's particular theoretical orientation. A psychoanalytically oriented couples therapist will attend to possible unconscious factors in each person's behaviour toward the other, whereas a CBT marital therapist will focus instead on unrealistic demands the partners have of each other and on maladaptive behavioural patterns that are unwittingly reinforced in the relationship. What all couples and family therapies have in common is the view that conflicts and tensions are inevitable when people live together and that the best way to address these problems is to involve all members of the family unit in therapy. A principal focus is improving communication among members so that personal needs can be met without sacrificing the needs and wishes of others.

EVALUATION OF COUPLES AND FAMILY THERAPY

A meta-analysis of 20 carefully selected outcome studies meeting stringent methodological standards concluded that, overall, couples therapy has beneficial effects for many relationship problems (Hazelrigg, Cooper, & Borduin, 1987). Subsequent reviews (e.g., Baucom et al., 1998; Gurman, Kniskern, &

Pinsoff, 1986; Jacobson & Addis, 1993; Lebow & Gurman, 1995; Sexton, Alexander, & Meese, 2004) have reached the following specific conclusions about outcome and process in couples and family therapy:

- Conjoint therapy for couples' problems appears to be more successful than individual therapy with one partner. The state of about 10% of clients seen individually for couples problems worsens.
- Behavioural couples therapy (BCT) has been shown to relieve distress in the relationship and/or increase partner satisfaction. BCT has stronger effects than both no treatment and placebo-controlled treatments, and these positive outcomes sometimes last for up to a year.
- Adding a cognitive component to BCT (e.g., encouraging empathy) has not been shown to add to the positive outcomes.
- Positive findings from a small number of studies have been reported for an insight-oriented therapy. This approach encourages partners to explore their feelings and needs and to share these innermost aspects of themselves with the other. One study found an extremely low divorce rate in couples treated with an insight-oriented couples therapy. At a four-year follow-up, Snyder's insight couples therapy was found to be superior to BCT in terms of divorce rates and marital satisfaction (Snyder, Wills, & Grady-Fletcher, 1991). Emotion-focused therapy is also an insight-oriented approach.
- Although statistically significant, the outcomes of couples therapy research are not all clinically significant. For example, across all studies, no more than half of the treated couples were really happily married at the end of treatment (even if they had improved in a strictly statistical sense). Few studies included much in the way of follow-ups, and those that did—and these were mostly behaviourally oriented—found frequent relapse and divorce. As Jacobson and Addis have cautioned, these findings should temper premature enthusiasm for the efficacy of conjoint therapies, regardless of their theoretical bases.
- Although focused on the fearfulness of one partner, Barlow's exposure treatment, which involves the encouragement and collaboration of the spouse, has proven effective in reducing agoraphobia and has prevented the deterioration in the marital relationship that has sometimes been reported when the agoraphobic partner gets better (e.g., Brown & Barlow, 1995).
- The results of couples therapy are generally better for younger couples and when no steps have been taken toward divorce.
- Predictors of poor outcome include what Jacobson and Addis (1993) call "emotional disengagement," manifested by poor communication of feelings and by low frequency of sexual activity. Another sign of a poor prognosis in couples therapy is a relationship marked by rigidly held traditional gender roles, when the wife is oriented to affiliation and relationships and the husband is oriented primarily to work and autonomy. Finally, depression in one of the partners does not bode well for couples therapy (even though, as noted, BCT can have a positive impact both on a person's depression and on the relationship).
- Brief training in communication skills can enhance future satisfaction with the relationship and even result in lower divorce rates when compared with no-intervention controls. Since couples therapy generally works better when people are younger and highly involved with each other, prevention efforts seem particularly sensible and promising.
- Despite the growing use of "couples" rather than "marital" therapy, practically no research has been done on same-sex or unmarried heterosexual couples. Also, as noted by Johnson and Lebow (2000), there is increasing recognition of the need for research that incorporates a focus on cultural diversity; much of the field has focused on white, middle-class couples.

REVIEW OF CLIENT-CENTRED THERAPY

BASIC CONCEPTS AND TECHNIQUES OF CLIENT-CENTRED THERAPY

Usually regarded as a humanistic psychotherapy, Rogers's client-centred therapy rests on the basic premise that people can be understood only in terms of their own phenomenology—the immediate experience that they have of themselves and their world—and that they become disordered when they fail to attend to their own inner nature and instead guide their behaviour according to what others wish. Client-centred therapy places great emphasis on people's freedom to choose and on the responsibility that comes from having that freedom. We are what we make of ourselves, according to Rogerian and other humanistic and existential therapists.

The therapist's principal role is to create conditions in therapy that are totally accepting and non-judgemental, and the therapist should accomplish this by being empathic rather than directive. The result is that clients gradually come to better understand their own wishes, needs, fears, and aspirations and gain the courage to pursue their own goals rather than the goals that others have set.

EVALUATION OF CLIENT-CENTRED THERAPY

Many efforts have been made to evaluate client-centred therapy, largely because of Rogers's insistence that the outcome and process of therapy be carefully scrutinized and empirically validated. Indeed, Rogers is rightfully credited with originating the field of psychotherapy research. He and his students deserve the distinction of being the first to remove the mystique and excessive privacy of the consulting room. For example,

A strong relationship between therapist and client is widely regarded as essential for implementing therapy procedures. © Jose Luis Pelaez Inc./CORBIS.

Adam Horvath of Simon Fraser University has done extensive work examining the client-therapist relationship and the efficacy of the therapeutic alliance. Courtesy Adam Horvath.

they pioneered the tape-recording of therapy sessions for subsequent analysis by researchers.

Most research on Rogerian therapy has focused principally on relating outcome to the personal qualities of therapists. Results have been inconsistent, casting doubt on the widely held assumption that positive outcome is strongly related to the therapist's empathy and genuineness (e.g., Greenberg, Elliott, & Lietaer, 1994). And yet it probably makes sense to continue emphasizing these qualities in the training of clinicians, as such qualities are likely to help create an atmosphere of trust and safety within which the client can reveal the deep inner workings of the self (Bohart & Greenberg, 1997). It is not justifiable, however, from a research perspective, to assert that these qualities by themselves are sufficient to help clients change.

A meta-analysis of studies on client-centred therapy from 1978 to 1992 conducted by Les Greenberg at York University and his colleagues concluded clients were better off after the intervention than about 80% of comparable people who had not received any professional therapy (see Greenberg et al., 1994). Although not bad, this outcome is no better than that achieved by comparison therapies, such as brief psychodynamic treatment, with people who are not severely disturbed. Of the studies in the meta-analysis, only eight had a control group.

In keeping with Rogers's phenomenological approach, the outcome of this type of therapy has been assessed primarily by client self-reports. The basic data have been the individual's own phenomenological evaluation of and reaction to the self and events in his or her world. The overt behaviour believed to follow from these perceptions—that is, how clients actually behave following therapy—has not been the focus of study by client-centred therapy researchers.

According to a historical review of developments involving the client-therapist relationship by Adam Horvath (2000) from Simon Fraser University, one finding that was not anticipated by Rogers is entirely in keeping with his emphasis on subjective, phenomenological experiences; that is, the client's perception of the therapist's behaviour is more important in predicting therapy outcome than the therapist's actual behaviour in the therapeutic relationship. Thus, the client's cognitive appraisals are quite important.

Rogers's emphasis on subjective experience raises epistemological problems, for the therapist must be able to make accurate inferences about what the client is feeling or thinking. Validity is a real issue. Rogers relied on what the client said, yet he also asserted that clients can be unaware of their true feelings; it is this lack of awareness that brings most of them into therapy in the first place.

The exclusive use of self-descriptive measures of outcome in the earliest research on client-centred therapy has been supplemented with more direct assessment of how well the client functions in daily life, such as how adequately he or she performs social roles. An associated trend is the use of multiple methods to assess therapeutic change, as investigators have come to appreciate the complex nature of behaviour and the need to assess it along many dimensions (e.g., Lambert, Shapiro, & Bergin, 1986). Client self-reports, for example, can be supplemented by physiological measures, as well as by reports from significant others (e.g., spouses).

Rogers may be criticized for assuming that self-actualization is the principal human motivation. He inferred this motive from his observation that people seek out situations offering fulfillment, but then he proposed the self-actualization tendency as an explanation for the search for these situations—an example of circular reasoning (i.e., a tautology). Rogers assumed both that the psychologically healthy person makes choices to satisfy self-actualizing tendencies and that people are by their very natures good. But some social philosophers have taken a less optimistic view of human nature. Thomas Hobbes, for example, stated that life is "nasty, brutish, and short." How do we explain people who engage in abhorrent behaviour that injures or kills others? Are these people basically good?

It may be that the problem of extreme unreasonableness was not adequately addressed by Rogers because he and his colleagues concentrated on people who were only mildly disturbed. As a way to help unhappy but not severely disturbed people understand themselves better (and perhaps even to behave differently), client-centred therapy may be appropriate and effective.

REVIEW OF PSYCHOANALYTIC THERAPIES

Before we evaluate several psychoanalytic psychotherapies, it will be good to review and summarize their core features and contrast this with contemporary versions of psychodynamic treatment. Information on the whole range of psychotherapy was presented in greater detail in Chapter 2.

BASIC CONCEPTS AND TECHNIQUES IN CLASSICAL PSYCHOANALYSIS VS. CONTEMPORARY PSYCHODYNAMIC TREATMENT

> "Undergraduate textbooks too often equate psychoanalytic or psychodynamic therapies with some of the more outlandish and inaccessible speculations made by Sigmund Freud roughly a century ago, rarely presenting mainstream psychodynamic concepts as understood and practiced today."
>
> *–Shedler, 2010, p. 98*

At the heart of classical psychoanalysis is the therapeutic attempt to remove repressions that have prevented the ego from helping the individual grow into a healthy adult. Psychopathology is assumed to develop when people remain unaware of their true motivations and fears. They can be restored to healthy functioning only by becoming conscious of what has been repressed. When people can understand what is motivating their actions, they have a greater number of choices. Where id is, let there ego be, to paraphrase a maxim of psychoanalysis. The ego—the primarily conscious, deliberating, choosing portion of the personality—can better guide the individual in rational, realistic directions if repressions are minimal.

As described in Chapter 2, psychoanalysts employ a variety of techniques to achieve the goal of insight into repressed conflicts. Among these are:

- free association, in which the client, reclining on a couch, is encouraged to give free rein to thoughts and feelings and to verbalize whatever comes to mind;
- the analysis of dreams, in which the therapist guides the client in remembering and later analyzing his or her dreams, the assumption being that during sleep the ego defences are lowered, allowing repressed material to come forth, usually in disguised form; and
- interpretation, whereby the therapist helps the person finally face the emotionally loaded conflict that was previously repressed; at the right time, the analyst begins to point out the client's defences and the underlying meaning of his or her dreams, feelings, thoughts, and actions.

The concept of transference is of particular importance to psychoanalysts. Freud noted that his clients sometimes acted toward him in an emotion-charged and unrealistic way. For example, a client much older than Freud would behave in a childish manner during a therapy session. Although these reactions were often positive and loving, they could also be negative and hostile. Since these feelings seemed out of character with the ongoing therapy relationship, Freud assumed that they were relics of attitudes transferred to him from those held in the past toward important people in the client's childhood, most often parents. In other words, Freud felt that clients responded to him as though he were one of the important people in their past. Freud used this transference of attitudes, which he came to consider an inevitable aspect of psychoanalysis, as a means of explaining to clients the childhood origin of many of their concerns and fears. This revelation and explanation, he believed, tended also to help lift repressions and allow the client to confront buried impulses. In psychoanalysis, transference is regarded as essential to a complete cure. It is precisely when analysts notice transference developing that they take hope that the important repressed conflict from childhood is getting closer to the surface.

Those who have modified classical psychoanalysis to make it more efficient—generally referred to as *psychodynamic therapists*—are more oriented toward the present than was Freud. However, they still emphasize unconscious motivation and the need for clients to understand the hidden reasons for their current feelings and behaviour.

Contemporary psychodynamic therapists contend that this form of therapy is just as effective as other types of treatment. George Doyle/Stockbyte/Getty Images.

Brief therapy, or brief psychodynamic therapy, focuses more on practical, real-life problems, still within the general framework of psychoanalysis. The different forms of brief therapy share several common elements (Koss & Shiang, 1994):

- Assessment tends to be rapid and early.
- It is made clear right away that therapy will be limited and that improvement is expected within a small number of sessions, from six to 25.
- Goals are concrete and focused on the amelioration of the client's worst symptoms, on helping the client understand what is going on in his or her life, and on enabling the client to cope better in the future.
- Interpretations are directed more toward present life circumstances, interpersonal experiences, and client behaviour than on the historical significance of feelings.
- Development of transference is not encouraged, but some positive transference to the therapist is fostered to encourage the client to follow the therapist's suggestions and advice.
- There is a general understanding that psychotherapy does not cure, but that it can help troubled individuals learn to deal better with life's inevitable stressors.

What are the elements that distinguish short-term psychodynamic interpersonal psychotherapy from CBT? A very useful summary was provided by Blagys and Hilsenroth (2000). They identified the following seven distinguishing features:

1. focus on affect and the expression of emotion;
2. exploration of attempts to avoid thoughts and feelings that create distress;
3. identification of recurring themes and patterns that are expressed in thoughts, feelings, experiences, or relationships;
4. an emphasis on past experiences and how they relate to current experiences;
5. a focus on interpersonal relationships;
6. an emphasis on the therapy relationship; and
7. exploration of the clients' wishes, dreams, and fantasies.

It is important to note that these distinguishing attributes were identified on the basis of empirical articles that described the key elements of contemporary psychodynamic interventions.

According to Messer and Abbass (2010), contemporary psychodynamic treatment of personality disorders has three primary emphases in addressing personality dysfunction: (1) *defensive restructuring* to address hidden and repressed themes; (2) *affective restructuring* to facilitate the tolerance of distress; and (3) *cognitive restructuring* of beliefs and schemas while bolstering coping skills. The emphasis on cognitive restructuring suggests that although there are differences, there is significant overlap with CBT.

EVALUATION OF PSYCHODYNAMIC PSYCHOTHERAPY

OUTCOMES OF RESEARCH The time involved means that there are relatively few outcome studies of long-term psychoanalytic treatment, but studies have accumulated over the years. One limitation of research in this area is the general paucity of outcome studies that involve randomized control trials and matched control groups.

One of the most ambitious early attempts to evaluate the effectiveness of psychoanalysis that deserves mention was the Menninger Foundation Psychotherapy Research Project, which began in the mid-1960s. In this study, 42 participants—mostly whites with anxiety, depression, or both (what used to be referred to as "garden-variety neuroses")—were seen in either psychoanalysis (22) or short-term psychodynamic psychotherapy (20). In both groups, about 60% of the patients improved. There were no significant differences between the two groups either immediately after treatment or at follow-ups of two to three years (Wallerstein, 1989).

A recent review by de Maat, de Jonghe, Schoewers, and Dekker (2009) was quite illuminating. Their review was based on 27 studies since 1970, of which 19 met quality control criteria. The criterion of long-term treatment was 50 sessions or more. Overall, the studies collectively involved more than 5,000 participants. The mean number of sessions for those receiving psychoanalysis was 500 over an average period of 3.6 years (i.e., 140 sessions per year). The mean number of sessions for those receiving psychotherapy was 150 over an average period of 2.5 years (i.e., 60 sessions per year). It was concluded that long-term psychotherapy was quite effective, but this conclusion needs to be qualified in at least three respects. First, significantly greater effectiveness was found for symptom reduction rather than personality change, but moderate personality change did occur. Second, most studies focused on moderate pathology and only three studies focused on severe pathology; thus, follow-up research on severe pathology is needed. Finally, only one study used a randomized control trial design and two others had control groups. Thus, statements about the comparative effectiveness of long-term psychodynamic treatment must be made with significant caution.

EVALUATION OF BRIEF PSYCHODYNAMIC THERAPY

A clearer picture has emerged from research on briefer interventions. We look first at outcome research—whether a therapy works—and then at research aimed at elucidating the processes by which favourable outcomes might be achieved.

OUTCOME RESEARCH The picture emerging from outcome studies on brief psychodynamic therapy is generally positive. Most recently, a comprehensive meta-analysis found that brief psychodynamic therapy is effective (Driessen et al., 2010). Collectively, results were pooled from 23 studies of over 1,300 participants. Short-term psychodynamic psychotherapy yielded large treatment changes in depression level and these changes were maintained at one-year follow-up. Initially, other forms of treatment were deemed to be slightly more effective at post-treatment, but this superiority was not maintained at one-year follow-up. On the basis of these and other findings, some authors have argued vociferously for the effectiveness of contemporary versions of short-term psychodynamic psychotherapy. Interested readers can follow this issue in detail by considering the views of Shedler (2010).

PSYCHOTHERAPY INTEGRATION

Having reviewed the theory and research on the major psychological interventions, we turn now to the question of whether useful connections can be made among them and general questions about eclecticism and integration in psychotherapy.

ECLECTICISM AND THEORETICAL INTEGRATION IN PSYCHOTHERAPY

How much integration is there at present? The answer to this question depends largely on who you ask and when you ask.

The use of an eclectic approach was quite common 20 years ago (Hunsley & Lefebvre, 1990; Warner, 1991) but was not necessarily increasing in prevalence. For instance, a random sampling survey in the United States based on the National Register of Health Service Providers in Psychology for the years 1981, 1985, and 1989 found that approximately two fifths of respondents listed their primary theoretical orientation as eclectic and that there was no significant increase over time in the proportion of eclectic therapists (Milan, Montogomery, & Rogers, 1994).

A recent survey of 201 doctoral level practitioners in the United States examined the use of 127 techniques reflecting eight major theories of psychotherapy (Thoma & Cecero, 2009). The results found extensive evidence of use of techniques outside of one's primary theoretical orientation. Therapists from the humanistic, CBT, and psychodynamic orientations all reported using more techniques from outside of their orientation than from inside their orientation. Overall, 23 techniques out of the 127 were endorsed by respondents from all therapist groups. The top five techniques that were acknowledged universally were (1) trying to understand the world from the client's point of view, (2) providing unconditional positive regard, (3) challenging maladaptive or distorted eliefs, (4) being congruent and genuine, and (5) reflecting feeling.

Another investigation of 24 expert psychotherapists (with a mean of 32 years of clinical experience) found stronger allegiance to their main theoretical orientation (Hickman, Arnkoff, Glass, & Schottenbauer, 2009). However, most therapists still reported some degree of influence by all four orientations assessed (i.e., humanistic, CBT, psychodynamic, and family systems).

THREE TYPES OF PSYCHOTHERAPY INTEGRATION

Distinctions have been drawn among three modes of psychotherapy integration (Arkowitz, 1989): technical eclecticism, common factorism, and theoretical integration. In **technical eclecticism**, exemplified in Lazarus's multimodal approach and in Beutler's prescriptive psychotherapy (Beutler & Harwood, 1995), the therapist works within a particular theoretical framework (e.g., CBT), but sometimes imports from other orientations techniques deemed effective, though without subscribing to the theories that spawned them. "Use whatever works" is the operating principle of the technical eclectic, but one should rationalize the use of a technique from one's own framework.

Common factorism (e.g., Frank, 1961; Goldfried, 1991; Schofield, 1964) seeks strategies that all therapy schools might share. For example, informing a client how he or she affects others is a strategy employed by many different kinds of therapists and believed by many (e.g., Brady et al., 1980) to be an important component of effective psychotherapy. An approach that could be considered common factorism was outlined in a book on treatment planning by Sheila Woody and associates (see Woody, Detweiler-Bedeil, Teachman, & O'Hearn, 2003). Woody, located at the University of British Columbia, was a member of the APA Division 12 Task Force on empirically supported treatments (ESTs). Woody et al. (2003) outlined an eclectic treatment planning system that favours evidence-based approaches. They described a phase approach to treatment planning that includes steps toward identifying problems, establishing clear treatment goals and aims, and measuring treatment progress after implementing ESTs. It represents common factorism because, other than a general preference for ESTs, no single theoretical orientation is imposed and therapists are free to adopt techniques and conceptualizations from various approaches.

The third approach, **theoretical integration**, tries to synthesize not only techniques but also theories. Wachtel's efforts to justify and make sense of assertion training within a modified psychoanalytic framework is a prime example of an effort toward theoretical integration. The resulting theory is itself something different because of the blending of psychoanalytic and behavioural elements. As another example, the recent integration of mindfulness meditation techniques with traditional CBT, as seen in mindfulness-based cognitive therapy and dialectical behaviour therapy, challenges therapists to integrate acceptance and change-based strategies (see Lau & McMain, 2005). Hayes (2002) describes the integration of Eastern spiritual practices, particularly mindfulness meditation, with CBT as the third epoch in the evolution of behaviourally informed therapies.

ARGUMENTS AGAINST PREMATURE INTEGRATION

In contemplating efforts at theoretical integration, we have wondered whether a grand, all-encompassing theory or approach is necessarily desirable or even possible. We believe not, and our own use of different paradigms in the study of both psychopathology and intervention aligns us more with the views of Garfield and Bergin:

> [H]uman personality may operate in accordance with a complex interaction of seemingly disparate processes that act together, though each differently and in its own sphere. Thus, it is conceivable that the same individual may suffer at one time from a repressed conflict, a conditioned response, an incongruent self-image, and irrational cognitions; and that each of these dysfunctions may operate in semi-independent systems of psychic action that are amenable to rather different interventions, each of which is compatible with the "system" to which it is being applied. Diagnosis and therapy might then become concerned with the locus of the disorder or with which portion or portions of the multisystem psyche is involved. (1986, p. 10)

Indeed, not all those interested in psychotherapy integration agree with the overall notion that the more blurring between conceptual frameworks, the better. In an article entitled "Disappearing differences do not always reflect healthy integration," Haaga and Davison (1991) pointed out several ways in which Ellis's REBT and Beck's CT have begun to merge. Beck originally focused almost entirely on cognitive biases and how they might distort a person's analysis of a situation. Thus, a depressed person who complains that he or she has no friends is encouraged, like a scientist, to determine whether in fact this is true. In contrast, Ellis emphasized the belief or assumption under which a person operates, such as "I must be perfect in everything I do." Now, however, Beck devotes considerable time to talking about "dysfunctional schemas," which can look a great deal like Ellis's "irrational beliefs." And Ellis does not ignore social realities, for even at the beginning (Ellis, 1962) he advocated teaching someone without social skills how to better interact with others, with the goal of improving relationships (rather than merely encouraging the person to care little about turning people off).

Haaga and Davison (1991) caution that we may lose something by blurring such distinctions, especially if integration is not based on research (and they argue that it is not). If we preserve the uniqueness of these two therapies, we might then be more inclined to construct a more integrative therapy that uses the particular strengths of each. For example, perhaps for certain people under certain circumstances, it is best to focus on changing social realities, whereas other circumstances might call for changing people's interpretations of an unchanging and perhaps unchangeable social reality. Creating this kind of integration requires holding on to at least some of the original distinctions between REBT and CT and, more important, constructing or using a superordinate theory that can subsume both REBT and CT and specify when a particular aspect of one is suitable and when a feature of the other is appropriate. Science sometimes moves forward more readily when rapprochement among divergent theories is not encouraged.

We conclude this chapter with a discussion of an effective integrative approach that combines cognitive and behavioural factors with other characteristics.

AN INTEGRATIVE APPROACH: MEICHENBAUM'S CONSTRUCTIVIST COGNITIVE-BEHAVIOURAL TREATMENT MODEL

As noted in Chapter 2, Donald Meichenbaum (e.g., 1977, 1992, 1994, 1995) has developed several empirically supported treatments, with supporting manuals, using cognitive-behavioural approaches, including self-instructional training and stress inoculation. These approaches are effective in treating a wide range of psychological problems and disorders and were designed to overcome barriers to effective outcomes and to facilitate maintenance and generalization of treatment effects. We also noted in Chapter 2 (and illustrated in Chapter 6) Meichenbaum's adoption of a constructivist-narrative approach.

Meichenbaum's current approach is both comprehensive and integrative. It is partly based on the cognitive-behavioural underpinnings derived from his earlier contributions, the literature on common factors in psychotherapy, the constructivist-narrative approach, barriers to treatment adherence and resistance, relapse prevention, and his interests in the psychotherapy integration movement.

The following tasks of psychotherapy form the core of his current constructivist cognitive-behavioural treatment approach. He also views these as the common elements in all successful therapy.

1. Develop a therapeutic alliance and help clients tell their stories.
2. Educate clients about the clinical problem.
3. Help clients reconceptualize their "problems" in a more hopeful fashion.
4. Ensure that clients have coping skills.
5. Encourage clients to perform "personal experiments."
6. Ensure that clients take credit for changes they have brought about.
7. Conduct relapse prevention.

The constructivist-narrative perspective (which Meichenbaum adds to traditional CBT) is probably the most controversial component of his approach. It is based on a view of people as "meaning-making agents" who construct their own stories to explain their lives and experiences. For instance, the constructivist-narrative perspective could involve your being asked to describe your most memorable experience after making the transition to college or university. What does this experience mean to you? How does it connect with your other experiences? How does it fit into your life narrative? What are your choices in this world? In contrast to traditional cognitive or cognitive-behavioural therapy, Meichenbaum's approach is less structured, more exploratory, and more discovery-oriented. As you learned in

Chapter 6, clients are assisted in telling their stories and in creating new stories through therapy.

Attempts to include a greater focus on the process of thinking and the generation of meaning, as advocated by Meichenbaum, may account, at least in part, for the recent growth of CBT. Dobson and Pusch (1993) observed that CBT has grown in breadth (application to diverse psychological disorders and problems) and depth (greater focus on difficult core features of cognitive structure and function that have great personal salience). Although Meichenbaum's approach is applicable to a wide array of problems, as pointed out by Neimeyer and Raskin (2001), constructivism has made its most significant contributions to Dobson and Pusch's depth dimension.

There are several varieties of constructivism in psychotherapy (see Neimeyer & Raskin, 2001), but Meichenbaum borrowed most directly from only two of the five thematic emphases: (1) psychotherapy as personal science; and (2) psychotherapy as narrative reauthoring. Dobson and Dozois (2001) wondered what effect Meichenbaum's adoption of the narrative-constructionist approach will have on continuing interest in stress inoculation and his other early contributions. Neimeyer and Raskin (2001) asked how constructivist developments will be received by more traditional CBT theorists and therapists.

REVIEW OF COMMUNITY PSYCHOLOGY

BASIC CONCEPTS AND TECHNIQUES OF COMMUNITY PSYCHOLOGY

Reaching out to large populations in an attempt to prevent the onset or spread of a physical illness or a mental disorder characterizes **community psychology**. The means of doing so may involve mass-media campaigns, instructional programs in schools, or other techniques designed to prevent disorder in groups of people. As with individual psychotherapy, the theoretical rationales and the techniques used vary greatly. There is a long history of activity in community psychology and psychiatry in Canada (Benjafield & Boudreau, 2000). In fact, in 1951, Canadian psychologist William Line was the first to use the term "community psychology" (see Babarik, 1979). A paper by Babarik (1979) provides an excellent overview of the early history of community psychology in Canada. Line was one of the major contributors, and he served as the president of the World Federation for Mental Health. According to Babarik, Line was the most influential person in extending the focus on mental health to primary prevention.

Prevention of mental disorders has always been a primary mission of the Canadian Mental Health Association (CMHA). Key historical figures were C. M. Hincks (see Chapter 1) and G. Brock Chisholm. Chisholm was a First World War sniper who eventually became the Canadian deputy minister of health and subsequently assumed the role of director general of the World Health Organization (WHO).

As a result of these men's efforts, the definition of health embraced by the CMHA formed the basis for the WHO definition of health, which includes physical, mental, social, and economic well-being (Babarik, 1979). The National Institute of Mental Health (NIMH) committee's widely promoted terminology of prevention (see Prilleltensky & Nelson, 2000) describes the various types of preventive interventions:

> Universal preventive interventions are targeted to the general public or a whole population group that has not been identified on the basis of individual risk. An example of a universal preventive intervention for physical health is childhood immunization. Selective preventive interventions are targeted to individuals or subgroups of the population whose risk of developing problems is significantly higher than average. A Head Start or other early childhood programmes for all children living in an economically depressed neighbourhood is an example of a selective prevention intervention. Indicated preventive interventions are targeted to high risk individuals who are identified as already having minimal, but detectable signs or symptoms, or biological markers, indicating predisposition for the mental disorder, but who do not meet diagnostic criteria. An intervention to prevent depression in children with one or both clinically depressed parents is an example of an indicated preventive intervention. (NIMH Committee on Prevention Research, 1995, pp. 6–7)

Many of the prevention programs in Canada focus on children (see Prilleltensky & Nelson, 2000). Further, while numerous programs focus on prevention—interventions that reduce the incidence of disorder—governments in Canada, led by the federal government (see Government of Canada, 2006), are increasingly focusing on **mental health promotion**; that is, they are focusing on enhanced functioning, well-being, and optimal functioning. (For a discussion of the distinctions between prevention and promotion and Canadian guidelines and proposals, see Epp [1988], *Mental Health for Canadians: Striking a Balance*.) Prilleltensky and Nelson (2000) also proposed a new focus for psychological and social interventions, presenting a framework that would have interventions foster the well-being of children and families.

We have previously described many community psychology programs in earlier chapters. These programs often focus on attempting to reduce risk factors and to facilitate the development of protective factors. Canadian community psychologists have been involved extensively in health and mental health promotion and prevention efforts (for an overview, see Nelson, LaVoie, & Mitchell, 2007). Examples of these programs are:

- Canadian eating-disorder prevention programs
- Canadian programs for the early detection and prevention of schizophrenia
- school-based programs for the prevention of cigarette smoking
- suicide prevention centres with telephone hotlines that desperate people can use to survive a suicidal crisis

- efforts through Head Start programs to prevent educational deficits and associated social and economic disadvantages, including Canada's Aboriginal Head Start initiative
- a parent and child training program with francophones in Montreal to prevent early onset of delinquent behaviour

Some other innovative, comprehensive, and possibly effective large-scale programs have emerged in Canada in recent years, including the Better Beginnings, Better Futures Project launched by Ontario under the direction of Ray D. Peters at Queen's University (e.g., Peters, Petrunka, & Arnold, 2003). This study, started in 1990, is a 25-year longitudinal investigation to evaluate the effectiveness of prevention as a policy for children. It involves a combined focus on the child, his or her family, childcare and school programs, and the involvement of the community. The most recent findings are based on results in three disadvantaged communities in Ontario, and the results are quite encouraging (Peters et al., 2003). Longitudinal analyses of changes over the first five years indicate significant improvements in children's and parents' social-emotional functioning and physical health. Parenting behaviours have also improved, and positive changes have occurred in the neighbourhood and school setting. Peters et al. (2003) concluded that the project has provided "unique evidence for the extent to which a universal, comprehensive, community-based prevention strategy can promote the longer term development of young children, their families, and their neighbourhoods" (p. 215). In short, the Better Beginnings, Better Futures Project is an excellent example of a primary or "universal" prevention program.

In addition to preventive efforts, communities benefit when innovative methods are developed to improve the amount of services and the speed with which they can be developed. Canadian Perspectives 17.2 summarizes research that illustrates the potential usefulness of innovative technological approaches delivering mental health services to communities. These approaches may reduce the subsequent need for more intensive mental health services.

CANADIAN PERSPECTIVES 17.2
BACK TO THE FUTURE: THERAPY AND TECHNOLOGY

It seems apparent that future therapeutic techniques will increasingly incorporate advances in technology and the result will be a broadening in the range of services available to people in the community who are seeking treatment. This is an important change in Canada, particularly in remote, rural, and isolated areas where face-to-face contact between client and therapist is often impractical.

One possibility was outlined by Andersson et al. (2006), who conducted a randomized control trial of a nine-week, Internet-delivered CBT self-help program for social phobia that was combined with two group exposure sessions in real life and minimal therapist contact via e-mail. Relative to waiting list controls, treated participants showed significant improvement on most measured dimensions, which were maintained at one-year follow-up. Of relevance to students, recent findings support the use of CBT on the Internet for the treatment of test anxiety in university students (Orbach, Lindsay, & Grey, 2007). Clinic plus Internet delivery of CBT can also be effective in the treatment of clinically anxious children (Spence et al., 2006).

Researchers in Canada have demonstrated the potential usefulness of technology in the treatment of people who otherwise might not receive treatment. The Alberta Mental Health Board (AMHB) developed a "telemental health service" that has been in existence since 1996. The service uses videoconferences to make psychiatric consultations available to health practitioners in rural parts of the province. There are videoconference sites throughout Alberta, including such places as Drumheller, Slave Lake, Peace River, and Fort Chipewyan. Published studies indicate that the program is quite effective (e.g., Simpson, Doze, Urness, Hailey, & Jacobs, 2001a, 2001b). For instance, 96.2% of rural physicians indicate that they are satisfied or very satisfied with the telemental health service, and 80.8% indicate that they are satisfied with the mental health improvement of clients they have referred for service. Surveys indicate that approximately 9 out of 10 people were satisfied with their sessions, felt that the doctor listened to them, felt supported and encouraged, and felt that the sessions could provide the same information that would have been presented in person. Importantly, 9 out of 10 also felt that they would rather use telepsychiatry than have to spend time on a waiting list to obtain treatment. Still, assessment showed that about 50% of clients would have preferred a face-to-face session over telepsychiatry (Simpson et al., 2001b). Nevertheless, the study found an average saving of more than $200 per client because travel costs to the treatment site were no longer required. On the basis of these findings, the AMHB identified future telemental goals, including additional services (e.g., forensic, brain injury) and an explicit focus on children's services. How do these results compare with overall research patterns? A recent review conducted by Richardson et al. (2009) showed that with respect to the small number of randomized controlled studies conducted thus far, telemental health has been found to have equivalent efficacy in a variety of settings compared with face-to-face care. However, Richardson et al. (2009) further observed that methodologically flawed investigations are the norm at present and this has limited further research and adoption of telemental health approaches.

These issues notwithstanding, there is still great promise, as reflected by innovations in Canada. In one specific case, telehealth technology was used to deliver family therapy to family members who remained in their rural Ontario home while an anorexic adolescent female member of the family was being treated in an urban hospital (Goldfried & Boachie, 2003). The family members were highly satisfied with telehealth and had no concerns about confidentiality issues.

Technological advances also expand the training opportunities for mental health professionals. A project in Atlantic Canada involving training via satellite showed that mental health professionals in rural areas reported many positive outcomes, including expanded knowledge, greater sensitivity to mental health issues, and greater cohesion among professionals (Cournish et al., 2003).

Finally, Bouchard and associates at the Université du Québec have conducted research on the efficacy of CBT via videoconference as a way of treating panic disorder with agoraphobia (Bouchard et al., 2000). In their preliminary investigation, they examined the effects of 12 sessions of CBT delivered via videoconference by trained therapists operating according to a standardized treatment manual. The "telepsychotherapy" resulted in substantial improvements in the frequency of panic attacks, severity of panic disorder, trait anxiety, and self-efficacy. Importantly, the authors indicated that "a very good therapeutic alliance was built after only the first telepsychotherapy session" (p. 999). The authors conducted a large investigation that included a direct comparison of clients treated with CT delivered via videoconference or face-to-face interactions (Bouchard et al., 2004). Both methods were equally effective, and 91% of those who were treated via videoconference were free of panic symptoms six months after treatment was over. Once again, an excellent therapeutic alliance could be identified as early as the first videoconference therapy session. Recent comparisons continue to indicate that the therapeutic alliance develops equally well for CBT delivered via videoconference vs. face-to-face in person (Germain, Marchand, Bouchard, Guay, & Drouin, 2010).

Bouchard et al. (2000) make a number of provocative observations when discussing their results. They suggest that this form of treatment may be especially well suited to people with disorders such as panic disorder with agoraphobia because these people may be more comfortable receiving treatment in their home environment where they feel less threatened. However, the authors point out that the videoconference approach does involve some significant limitations that have a bearing on the therapist's ability to establish rapport and enhance the therapeutic alliance (e.g., the inability to shake hands, provide tissues to a crying client, or look directly into the person's eyes). At an even more practical level, client and therapist must quickly learn to keep their movements within the camera's field of view. More recent research confirms that videoconference-based CBT is effective for other disorders, including OCD (see Himle et al., 2006).

More recently, Bouchard and colleagues have conducted research on virtual reality therapy. Klinger et al. (2005) conducted a pilot study of virtual reality therapy for social phobia that entailed 12 sessions of traditional group CBT with in vivo exposure vs. individual CBT with in virtuo exposure. "In virtuo" is a relatively new term that has emerged only in recent years with the development of virtual reality therapy. Both experimental conditions resulted in significant improvements and it seems that in virtuo exposure is a useful alternative to existing treatments for social anxiety disorder. However, this experiment lacked a wait-list control group, so conclusions must be qualified. Bouchard et al. (2006) demonstrated the effectiveness of virtual reality exposure in the treatment of arachnophobia using 3D games. Most recently, a review of 39 studies of virtual reality therapy for phobias concluded that in virtuo exposure treatment is an effective alternative to in vivo exposure treatment (Côté & Bouchard, 2008). However, once again it must be noted that only five studies have used a comparative treatment condition with a comparison group. At present, more research is needed because case studies dominate the literature on in virtuo exposure.

As technology advances and the need for therapeutic services increases, it is likely that more and more people will avail themselves of these technologically based forms of treatment. Regulatory bodies are currently working on ethics and standards protocols for the therapeutic services often delivered through the Internet. Key issues to consider include ways to safeguard the client's confidentiality and right to anonymity, as well as to maximize the safety of these individuals.

Thinking Critically

1. Preliminary research results confirm the potential usefulness of innovative technological approaches in delivering mental health services, including therapy, especially in more rural areas of Canada. There is no doubt that "telemental health" services can be cost-effective, relatively efficient alternatives to traditional consultation and treatment approaches. However, Simpson et al. (2001b) reported that about half the participants would have preferred face-to-face sessions despite the cost saving. What are the implications of this finding for the treatment of people in remote and rural places in Canada?

2. Klein and Richards (2001) and Bouchard et al. (2000) used principles of CT and CBT to treat panic disorder. These studies used brief, Internet-based self-help treatment and longer-term videoconferencing using trained therapists, respectively. Will these approaches be effective with psychological problems such as depression? Note that participants in Klein and Richards's self-help group did not experience significant reductions in depression. Is this because the treatment did not target their depression or because technology-based strategies are less likely to be effective with depression?

3. What other disorders or psychological problems could be treated with technology-based forms of therapy? Would the approach work well with, for example, the stress-related health problems described in Chapter 9? Can the Internet be efficiently exploited to help people in severe emotional distress, including those considering suicide, as described by Barak (2007)?

EVALUATION OF COMMUNITY PSYCHOLOGY

It has been suggested that the results of community psychology have been disappointing (e.g., Phares & Trull, 1997), but some projects have shown their worth in recent years. One infrequently discussed reason for the limited effectiveness of prevention efforts is that some problems are not readily amenable to environmental or social manipulation because they have major genetic or biological components. As we saw in Chapter 11, for example, there is very strong evidence that schizophrenia has some kind of biological diathesis. Although an environmental preventive effort may conceivably reduce the amount of stress that a predisposed individual is subject to in normal daily living, it seems unlikely that any realistic social change could keep stress levels low enough to prevent episodes of schizophrenia from occurring or recurring in high-risk people. Family therapy for reducing expressed emotion is a prototype of what might be necessary on a societal scale to have a positive impact on the recurrence of episodes of schizophrenia. However, how practical is it to apply such an approach on a broad scale?

Another problem in implementing prevention programs is the lack of government commitment to providing the resources that would facilitate their creation. Widespread prevention programs are simply not possible in Canada with the current resources available. For more than a decade, the federal government has been drastically reducing transfer payments to the provinces for health, welfare, social services, and education. Nelson, Prilleltensky, Laurendeau, and Powell (1996) reviewed the situation as of 1993 and noted that there have been many good prevention programs (e.g., preschool enrichment for children at risk and youth suicide prevention) that have been matched by government rhetoric in stated policies, but there have not been corresponding reallocations and increases of financial resources. They concluded that the relevant provincial ministries allocated a very small proportion of their budgets (less than 1%) to such programs. Health funding, in particular, has not been redirected from direct treatment efforts toward preventing disorders in children and youth (e.g., McCain & Mustard, 1999; Mustard et al., 2007; Nelson et al., 1996; Prilleltensky & Nelson, 2000). As a result, preventive efforts have been limited and community psychology efforts in Canada marginalized in many respects, in contrast to the strong beginning thanks to the efforts of people such as Line, Hincks, and Chisholm (see Walsh-Bowers, 1998).

Overall, an evaluation of community psychology efforts is particularly challenging because the interventions occur in the field, where it is difficult to set up experimental controls and thus harder to draw causal inferences (Linney, 1989). There are many alternative explanations for the effect of a preventive intervention. For example, a reduction in gang activity following a school-based intervention aimed at that goal may largely be the consequence of the opening of a community centre, such as the YMCA, or even the actions of a single, inspirational teacher. Another concern in the current practice of prevention science is the problem of attrition, or loss of participants (Mrazek & Haggerty, 1994). Those who drop out of an intervention must be monitored in some fashion, for these individuals could be at the highest risk.

POLITICAL AND ETHICAL FACTORS IN COMMUNITY PSYCHOLOGY

The study of community psychology raises an interesting question. In the 1960s and 1970s, there was a shift throughout Western nations, including Canada and the United States, to community activism in the prevention of mental disorders. Why? The answer is complex.

For many years, it was obvious that few people could avail themselves of psychotherapeutic services, which were usually very expensive, in short supply, and geared to so-called YAVIS clients—individuals who are young, attractive, verbal, intelligent, and successful (Schofield, 1964). Eysenck (1952) had earlier questioned the effectiveness of most kinds of psychotherapy, finding treated clients' rates of improvement no better than the spontaneous remission rate. Although Eysenck's criticisms were compellingly rebutted by many scholars (e.g., Bergin, 1971), the idea took hold among mental health professionals that psychotherapy aimed at changing the individual might not be the best way to alleviate the psychological problems of the majority of people. Focus began to shift from repressions, conflicts, and neurotic fears to large-scale social problems, such as poverty, overcrowding, poor education, racial segregation, the alienation felt in large cities, and the impersonal nature of many aspects of present-day living. The emphasis on prevention became especially significant in the United States, where a large gap developed between the need for mental health care and the availability of services (Weissberg, Caplan, & Sivo, 1989).

The shift from intrapsychic to social factors probably also reflected the Zeitgeist, or tenor of the times, especially in the United States. The 1960s and early 1970s were a period of tremendous social upheaval and activism. Institutions of all kinds were being challenged. Cities and college campuses in the United States erupted in riots, and a range of minority groups, from African Americans to gays, made accusations of racism and political repression. This social upheaval, which at times seemed to border on revolution, spilled over into Canada and further encouraged looking at social institutions for causes of individual suffering.

Community psychology has as its goal the change of large systems and groups of people rather than the treatment of individual problems. And it is primarily in the seeking mode—psychologists take the initiative in serving people rather than waiting for individuals in need to come to them. On the face of it, this is a tall order. What do we know about the principles that operate to produce change in societal values and institutions? If the community psychologist hopes to take actions that meet the wishes and needs of the community, how does he or she determine them? Recall from chapters 3 and 4 the difficulties the psychologist has in assessing the needs of an individual client with whom there is extensive direct contact. How much more difficult, then, to assess the needs of thousands of people!

Community psychologists become social activists to some degree, which raises the danger that these well-meaning professionals may impose values and goals on their clients. What is mental health? Who is to decide how people should live their lives? To what extent do the people being served by community psychologists have a say in how they are to be helped? These are but a few of the difficult questions that must continually be posed if community psychology is to act responsibly and effectively. The focus of this field is on large-scale factors. Many people are involved; many lives, then, will be affected by decisions and actions. Questions of values and of effectiveness are inherent in any effort to alter the human condition, but they are of special importance when the clients themselves do not seek the intervention.

SUMMARY

- Research on the effectiveness of various forms of psychotherapy has been conducted for many decades, with sometimes complicated and inconsistent results. The evaluation of the effects of psychotherapy has grown in significance as increased demands for accountability are being imposed. Several general issues provide a context for the study of psychotherapeutic interventions.

- There are differences between the way therapies have been examined in experimental settings and the way they are actually practised by clinicians. Recent research has employed treatment manuals that specify what experimenters are to do when applying given therapies to research participants. Although this practice enhances the internal validity of psychotherapy research, the contrast with therapy as practised—making adjustments depending on the needs of the individual client—limits the external validity of such research. There is a gap or even a chasm between therapy as studied experimentally and therapy as delivered and practised.

- Classical psychoanalysis tries to uncover childhood repressions so that infantile fears of libidinal expression can be examined by the adult ego in light of present-day realities. Brief psychodynamic therapy puts more emphasis on the client's need and ability to achieve greater control over both the environment and instinctual gratification. It is a time-limited therapy in which expectations are set for fewer than two dozen sessions. There is a focus on setting concrete goals and learning ways to cope with life's inevitable stressors, forsaking the goal of psychoanalysis to obtain a personality overhaul through analysis of the transference neurosis.

- Research on psychoanalytic and brief psychodynamic therapies suggests that they can be useful for a variety of anxiety and depressive disorders.

- Rogers trusted the basic goodness of the drive to self-actualize, and he proposed the creation of non-judgemental conditions in therapy. Through empathy and unconditional positive regard, client-centred therapists help their clients view themselves more accurately and trust their own instincts for self-actualization. Research on client-centred therapy has investigated whether such factors as empathy and genuineness on the part of the therapist are associated with good outcomes. Results are inconsistent. Moreover, the assumption that people are by nature good and that they have an innate drive to self-actualization does not apply to many disorders.

- The cognitive and behaviour therapies attempt to apply the methodologies and principles of experimental psychology to the alleviation of psychological distress. Because of their emphasis on research, the various behavioural and cognitive-behavioural therapies account for the lion's share of both process and outcome research in psychotherapy. Evidence attests to the efficacy of counterconditioning, exposure, operant, and cognitive-behavioural interventions in alleviating a wide range of disorders. However, the fact that high end-state functioning is often not achieved even by clients whose improvement is significant highlights the fact that much remains to be learned.

- Cognitive therapies, such as Ellis's rational-emotive behaviour therapy and Beck's cognitive therapy, alter the thoughts that are believed to underlie emotional disorders. They reflect the increasing importance of cognition in experimentally based psychological interventions. Research is now focusing increasingly on identifying the components of treatment that account for improvement.

- Of particular importance for the cognitive and behavioural therapies, as well as for other approaches, is the generalization of treatment effects once the client is no longer seeing the therapist on a regular basis. Several procedures hold promise for maintaining whatever gains have been achieved during treatment. Of particular importance for techniques that are directive and therefore heavily reliant on influence from the therapist is how clients attribute or explain to themselves why they have improved. Encouraging an internal "I was a major factor in my own improvement" attribution is gaining popularity as a way to help people maintain their gains.

- Marital or couples therapy helps distressed couples resolve the conflicts inevitable in any ongoing relationship of two adults living together. Behavioural and some insight-oriented therapies show promise in easing the stress that many couples experience.

- Eclecticism and theoretical integration in psychotherapy represent a trend that reflects growing awareness on the part of many clinicians and researchers of the limitations of their respective theoretical approaches. Psychoanalysis and cognitive-behavioural therapy might inform each other and take advantage of the strengths each can offer the other to help professionals better understand the human condition and design effective therapeutic interventions. There are risks, however, in integrating diverse theoretical perspectives, such as glossing over differences that might better be examined and evaluated.

- Community psychology aims primarily at the prevention of disorders. It adopts a seeking rather than the traditional waiting mode in helping communities cope with large-scale stressors and other life challenges. Political and ethical issues are intrinsic aspects of any therapeutic effort that aims to help people who have not actually asked for assistance.

KEY TERMS

common factorism (p. 623)
community psychology (p. 625)
demoralization hypothesis (p. 596)
dodo bird effect (p. 603)
effectiveness (p. 602)
efficacy (p. 602)

empirically informed therapies (p. 606)
empirically supported therapies (ESTs) (p. 605)
mental health promotion (p. 625)
stepped care (p. 604)

technical eclecticism (p. 623)
theoretical integration (p. 623)
therapeutic (working) alliance (p. 599)
triadic reciprocality (p. 611)

REFLECTIONS: PAST, PRESENT, AND FUTURE

- Think back to our discussion of Dr. Ewen Cameron's treatment of his clients at the Allan Memorial Institute in the 1950s and the lesson of history presented in Chapter 1. Now read Cameron's quotation at the outset of this chapter: "Don't ever do anything to someone that you can't reverse." Through the wisdom of hindsight, we now know that he did irreversible damage to so many of the people under his care. Do you think that any of the strategies used today, including psychological and biological interventions, cause irreversible damage to people? How can we continue to guard against this possibility? Do you think that we really have learned from our past mistakes?

- We discussed recent approaches that employ technology to make mental health services available in the remote and rural areas of Canada. At different points in this book, we have focused on the plight of many of Canada's Aboriginal people and, in particular, on rampant substance abuse, suicide, and child abuse. Do you think that some of the technology-based strategies described in this chapter could be adapted for use with Native people? How would you go about doing this? Would you develop approaches similar in mission and philosophy to, say, Poundmaker's Lodge (see Chapter 12) that would be run by the Aboriginal people themselves? Could this approach be helpful in reducing the devastating consequences of alcohol abuse in adults and gasoline sniffing in children, or is it really more essential to focus on developing on-site programs? Would telemental health services be useful adjuncts to, or provide helpful support for, community programs?

- Reflect on the different approaches to psychotherapy that we have discussed in this book and evaluated in the current chapter. If you were asked to choose the approach that had the most personal meaning for you, the one that would best fit into your own life narrative, which treatment would you select and why?

- The issue of psychotherapy integration is controversial. While some theorists and researchers embrace it, others eschew it. We recognize that there are some risks in integration but that there also seems to be a strong trend toward it. For example, Neimeyer and Raskin (2001) concluded that "it seems to be a safe prediction that cognitive theorists will continue to build bridges to constructivist approaches" (p. 421). Where do you stand on issues of eclecticism and integration? Is integration feasible or desirable?

- In the next chapter, we will examine ethical issues that are important in both treatment and research. Ewen Cameron conducted research on the people who came to him for help. He didn't tell them that they were being used as research subjects or that they were receiving experimental treatments. What was unethical about what Cameron did? Why was it unethical? According to psychiatric historians (e.g., Collins, 1988; Weinstein, 1990), Cameron was driven by blind ambition in his misguided quest to discover a quick, effective "cure" for schizophrenia and other severe mental disorders. He hoped that his discoveries would bring him fame, power, and glory and also the ultimate prize—the Nobel Prize in Medicine and Physiology (just as Egas Moniz of Portugal won the prize in 1955, 20 years after devising lobotomy for the treatment of schizophrenia). What if Cameron had discovered an effective treatment? Should we have then made, or even now make, allowances for the consequences of his zeal? Would his treatment of the people under his care be any less unethical?

LEGAL AND ETHICAL ISSUES

George Agnew Reid, 1860–1947, *The Other Side of the Question*, 1890, oil on canvas, 104.0 × 132.5 cm, Art Gallery of Ontario, Toronto Purchase, 1985. © 2007 AGO

"The myth is that if people exhibit bizarre behaviour, men in white coats will come and take you away. There aren't any people who can do that. If only there were."

—Fay Herrick, a Calgarian whose son suffers from schizophrenia (Nichols, 1995)

"The idea that patients would heal faster within their communities is bizarre. These same patients originally came from the communities whose healing qualities clearly were not sufficient to prevent them from becoming sick in the first place. The notion that patients would heal faster in the bosom of their families is equally problematic. Many families are too sick, or too tired, or simply do not have the resources or the energy to cope with very sick patients."

—Abram Hoffer, former director of psychiatric research for the Province of Saskatchewan, currently in private practice in Victoria, B.C, and president of the Canadian Schizophrenia Foundation (2000, p. 145)

"CTOs [community treatment orders] may very well be an expression of both the best and the worst in current psychiatric practice. At best, we are looking at paternalism—benevolent coercion respectful of autonomy and liberty. At worst, we ignore the concerns of fairness and justice …. Just exactly how do we balance autonomy and paternalism?

—Gary A. Chaimowitz, from a guest editorial in the *Canadian Journal of Psychiatry* (2004, p. 578)

Section 1—Guarantee of Rights and Freedoms. The Canadian *Charter of Rights and Freedoms* guarantees the rights and freedoms set out in it subject only to such reasonable limits prescribed by law as can be demonstrably justified in a free and democratic society.

Section 2—Fundamental Freedoms. Everyone has the following fundamental freedoms: 1. freedom of conscience and religion; 2. freedom of thought, belief, opinion and expression, including freedom of the press and other media of communication; 3. freedom of peaceful assembly; and 4. freedom of association.

Section 7—Legal Rights. Everyone has the right to life, liberty, and security of the person and the right not to be deprived thereof except in accordance with the principles of fundamental justice.

Section 8—Everyone has the right to be secure against unreasonable search or seizure.

Section 9—Everyone has the right not to be arbitrarily detained or imprisoned.

Section 12—Everyone has the right not to be subjected to any cruel and unusual treatment or punishment.

Section 15—Equality before and under law and equal protection and benefit of law. Every individual is equal before and under the law and has the right to equal protection and benefits of the law without discrimination, and, in particular, without discrimination based on race, national, or ethnic origin, colour, religion, sex, age or mental or physical disability.

Source: *Canadian Charter of Rights and Freedoms*. Dept of Justice Canada (1982).

We open our final chapter in this way, with sections of the *Canadian Charter of Rights and Freedoms* (1982), for two reasons. First, the legal and mental health systems collaborate continually, although often subtly, to deny a substantial proportion of the Canadian population their basic civil rights. With the best of intentions, judges, tribunals, governing boards of hospitals, bar associations, and professional mental health groups have worked over the years to protect society at large from the actions of people regarded as mentally ill or mentally disordered and considered dangerous to themselves or to others. However, in so doing, they have denied many thousands of people their basic civil rights.

Second, Section 15 (1) of the *Charter of Rights and Freedoms* (i.e., Equality before and under law) is especially significant because it extends the right of equality to mentally ill people. According to Eaves, Lamb, and Tien (2000), Canada "is one of the few countries in the world that explicitly extends the general rights found in our constitution to people who are mentally ill" (p. 615).

A continuing concern in Canadian society is the extent to which mentally ill people are subject to discrimination in the workplace. Focus on Discovery 18.1 delves into this issue by summarizing extant concerns and recent cases that have surfaced in Canada.

FOCUS ON DISCOVERY 18.1
THE STIGMA OF MENTAL ILLNESS AND EMPLOYMENT DISCRIMINATION

Imagine that you have suffered from persistent depression but a good job in your field becomes available. Do you apply for the job? And do you mention your depression when the interviewer asks why you quit your previous job and you haven't worked in the past six months? Because of concerns about stigma, you probably won't mention your bouts of depression. Indeed, Dr. Heather Stuart (2006) from Queen's University in Kingston, Ontario, has identified stigma as both a proximal factor and a distal factor in workplace discrimination. Proximal, direct discrimination would be in the form of stereotypes and prejudice emanating from employers and co-workers, while distal influences include the historical disadvantage of mentally ill people in the workplace and failures to proactively monitor and implement policies.

Unfortunately, the Canadian Human Rights Commission (CHRC) reports many settlement cases every year and the inescapable conclusion is that workplace discrimination is pervasive for mentally ill people in Canada. Its website documents 10 cases alone in 2006 of settlements for people suffering from depression who alleged workplace discrimination (see www.chrc-ccdp.ca/).

The allegations include outright termination due to depression, while in other cases, problems included being disciplined for not meeting deadlines and being passed over for promotions. As a result of the growing number of cases, in October 2008, the CHRC addressed the workplace and employment issues by crafting its Policy and Procedural Guideline on the Accommodation of Mental Illness.

A compelling 2008 case outlines the consequences for employers who engage or appear to engage in discrimination. The Ontario Divisional Court upheld a previous discrimination ruling by the Human Rights Tribunal of Ontario in the Ottawa case of *Lane v. ADGA Group Consultants Inc.* (2007). Paul Lane, a quality assurance analyst, was fired in October 2001 just eight days into the job after requesting accommodation for his bipolar depression. In its defence, the employer, the ADGA Group, maintained that Lane was not fired due to discrimination; rather, they deemed that he could not perform essential job functions and he had been untruthful in response to interview questions asked prior to the decision to hire him. However, the Court ruled that the employer displayed a dismissive attitude and disregard for Lane because of his bipolar depression. Documents indicate that following his job loss, Lane went into a state of full-blown mania and was hospitalized for several days. This was part of a downward spiral that led eventually to marital problems and the loss of the family home. The employer was deemed to have demonstrated an egregious lack of awareness of employer responsibilities and Lane was awarded $35,000 as general damages, $10,000 for mental anguish, and another $34,278.75 in special damages. Moreover, the employer was given three months to develop a written, comprehensive anti-discrimination policy.

The Canadian Mental Health Association continues to maintain that among all people with disabilities, people with a mental illness face the greatest degree of discrimination and stigmatization (CMHA, n.d.). Sadly, the recent case outlined above suggests that this problem is far from being resolved.

It is up to each province to formulate and implement laws that are in keeping with the *Charter of Rights and Freedoms*. Although all provinces share the same Charter-driven principles in their legislation, differences exist in how these principles are realized. Another possible source of differences between the provinces is the "notwithstanding clause," which permits provinces to opt out of the Charter if they perceive a conflict between their goals and values and the overall goals and values of the nation.

Although mentally ill people are extended rights under the equality provision, there are situations in which other principles come into effect. Specifically, the *Charter of Rights and Freedoms* also includes provisions that allow for some people to be removed from society if they act in a way that infringes on the rights of other people to a free and democratic society. In other words, at times, the needs of the society as a whole may outweigh the needs of any one individual. Mentally ill individuals who have broken the law, or who are alleged to have done so, may be subject to a loss of liberty where their mental disorder becomes relevant to the criminal prosecution because of either concerns regarding fitness to stand trial or criminal responsibility. In other words, they may be subject to **criminal commitment**, a procedure that may confine a person in a mental institution either for determination of competency to stand trial or after a verdict of not criminally responsible on account of mental disorder. Part XX.1 of the *Criminal Code of Canada* provides a "minicode" that sets out the procedures for dealing with mentally disordered individuals who find themselves before the criminal courts. **Civil commitment**, provided for in provincial statutes, is a procedure by which a mentally ill and dangerous person who may not have broken a law can be deprived of liberty and incarcerated in a psychiatric hospital. Both committal procedures—one federal, the other provincial—may result in a loss of liberty as a result of mental disorder. In this chapter, we look at these legal procedures in depth. We then turn to an examination of some important ethical issues as they relate to therapy and research.

CRIMINAL COMMITMENT

Historically, much of Canadian law has derived from English common law, reflecting the British influence in Canada. The exception is Quebec, where Napoleonic law has been incorporated into civil statutes. In Canada, criminal law is a matter of federal statute and is therefore the same in every province. Matters of health law, however, are determined at the provincial level and can differ from province to province. Our criminal code was first enacted in 1892, when we adopted a draft British code that was never enacted in Britain. Britain, to this day, has no criminal code. Almost as early as the concept of *mens rea*, or "guilty mind," and the rule "No crime without an evil intent" had begun to be accepted in English common law, "insanity" had to be taken into consideration, for a disordered mind may be regarded as unable to formulate and carry out a criminal purpose (Morse, 1992). In other words, a disordered mind cannot be a guilty mind; only a guilty mind can engender culpable actions.

Initially, insanity was not a trial defence, but in England, the Crown sometimes granted pardons to people who had been convicted of homicide if they were judged completely and totally "mad" (Morris, 1968). By the reign of Edward I (1272–1307), the concept of insanity had begun to be argued in court and could lessen punishment. It became the rule of law during the course of the fourteenth century that a person proven to be wholly and continually mad could be defended against a criminal charge.

In today's courts, judges and lawyers call on psychiatrists and clinical psychologists for assistance in dealing with criminal acts thought to result from the accused person's disordered mental state rather than from free will. Are such emotionally disturbed perpetrators less criminally responsible than those who are not distraught but commit the same crimes? Should such individuals even be brought to trial for transgressions against society's laws? Although efforts to excuse or protect an accused person by invoking the insanity defence or by judging him or her unfit to stand trial are undoubtedly well intentioned, invoking these doctrines can often subject those accused to a greater denial of liberty than they would otherwise experience.

THE NOT CRIMINALLY RESPONSIBLE DEFENCE

The cases described on the next page all involved high-profile situations in which defendants in Canadian courts were found **not criminally responsible** for their acts on account of mental disorder (NCRMD). The so-called **insanity defence**, NCRMD involves the legal argument that a defendant should not be held responsible for an otherwise illegal act if

IN HAMILTON, Lucia Piovesan had been diagnosed as having had paranoid schizophrenia for over 20 years, but she received minimal treatment because she did not take her antipsychotic drugs. Moreover, she resisted family requests to get additional treatment. Her neighbours, Tony Antidormi and his wife, Lori Triano-Antidormi (a former graduate student in psychology at York University), tried unsuccessfully on several occasions to convince police that Piovesan was dangerous. In March 1997, Piovesan stabbed to death the Antidormis' 2-year-old son, Zachery, after becoming convinced that he was the soul of her dead son and was asking for release (see Prete, 2000). Piovesan was found not criminally responsible because of her paranoid schizophrenia.

Dorothy Joudrie, a wealthy Calgary socialite, apparently endured years of abuse from her former husband, Earl Joudrie, and as a result, developed a problem with alcoholism. The situation escalated in January 1995 when Joudrie shot her former husband six times and was arrested for attempted murder. Her lawyer argued that, at the time of the crime, Joudrie was in a dissociative, trance-like state (a condition known as automatism) and had no recollection of her actions. In May 1996, a jury found her not criminally responsible owing to a mental disorder, and she was confined at the Alberta Hospital in Edmonton for five months. Joudrie's mental state improved greatly over time, and she received an absolute discharge on October 20, 1998 (Martin, 1998). Until her death in 2002, she acted as an advocate for the rights of mentally ill people.

On May 28, 1998, two teenagers from British Columbia were killed when struck by a car driven by Julia Campagna of Seattle, Washington. Campagna's car was speeding and smashed into the back of the teenagers' car at the Canadian Customs border crossing. The driver was charged with dangerous driving causing death, but on September 3, 1999, a B.C. court ruled that Campagna was not criminally responsible on account of mental disorder. The accident occurred while Campagna was in a psychotic state. She had symptoms of psychosis after taking the diet drug Xenadrine to lose weight for a marathon running race. Campagna thought that she was in an airplane rather than a car and that she was hearing the voice of Canadian NHL hockey player Joe Nieuwendyk on her radio. She was following the voice's instructions, believing she was on her way to a rendezvous with Nieuwendyk to conceive a child with him.

Because her symptoms were deemed to be due to the pills she was taking (a finding that was confirmed by a B.C. Children's Commission investigation [see McLintock, 2001]), Campagna was released and allowed to go free, having been found not criminally responsible. The court ruled that Campagna posed no risk to the public and could not be held. Julie Campagna subsequently launched a civil lawsuit against the drug manufacturer and other parties, and the families of the deceased launched civil lawsuits against Campagna and the drug manufacturer (see the Canadian Press, 2000).

Public concern about such cases escalated in March 2009 when Vincent Li was found not criminally responsible due to mental disorder. Li was accused of the gruesome murder of Tim McLean, a fellow passenger on a Greyhound bus who was not known to Li and was simply in the wrong place at the wrong time. The incident occurred in July 2008 in Manitoba on the Trans Canada Highway. It was deemed that Li was experiencing a psychotic episode related to his schizophrenia. He believed that he had been commanded by God to act. Not surprisingly, the verdict of not criminally responsible provides little comfort to family members who have lost a loved one, such as McLean's relatives.

it is attributable to mental illness that interferes with rationality or that results in some other excusing circumstance, such as not knowing right from wrong. Mental disorder may operate to negate the requisite mental element (*mens rea*), or it may operate to render the act (*actus reus*) involuntary. Or, it may operate to provide a supervening defence even where the requisite mental element and act have been proven. For example, an accused may specifically intend to kill his neighbour, believing him to be an alien sent to destroy the world. Here, the court may find that, notwithstanding the requisite elements having been proven, the accused did not appreciate the nature and consequences of his act or know it to be wrong. A staggering amount of material has been written on this defence, and public outcries continue to emerge in prominent cases in which the defendant is found not criminally responsible.

Concerns abound even though a review conducted by Canadian researchers (see Lymburner & Roesch, 1999) confirmed past findings suggesting that (1) the insanity defence is very rare; (2) it is usually only successful when applied to severely disordered individuals; and (3) people deemed insane are still typically detained for long periods of time that may greatly exceed the otherwise appropriate sentence. Note that being found not criminally responsible does not result in an acquittal.

LANDMARK CASES IN CANADA In modern Anglo-American criminal law, several court rulings and established principles bear on the problems of legal responsibility and mental illness. Table 18.1 summarizes these rulings and principles.

According to Schneider et al. (2000), Canada's modern history with respect to the legal treatment of mentally disordered people began with the case of *Rex v. Hadfield* (1800; see Table 18.1). Hadfield fired a shot in the direction of King George III because he believed that the king's death would herald the end of the world and the second advent of Christ (Ogloff & Whittemore, 2001). Hadfield was found not guilty by reason of insanity. This case is noteworthy because the chief justice overseeing the case returned Hadfield to prison

TABLE 18.1
LANDMARK CASES AND THE DISPOSITION OF THE MENTALLY ILL IN CANADA

Case	Date	Significance
Rex v. Hadfield	1800	Led to changes where the mentally ill could be institutionalized rather than returned to prison or the community. The accused were held at "His or Her Majesty's Pleasure."
Regina v. M'Naghten	1843	Followed a reference to the House of Lords, setting a standard test for "insanity" that was subsequently adopted, with modifications, by much of the Western world. Is seen to mark the beginning of the modern insanity defence.
Regina v. Chaulk	1990	Specifies that "wrong" means morally wrong as well as legally wrong.
Regina v. Swain	1991	Led to the creation of Bill C-30 and establishes the jurisdiction of provincial review boards that can balance the individual's and the community's concerns; changes a verdict from "not guilty by reason of insanity" to "not criminally responsible on account of mental disorder."
Regina v. Oommen	1994	The accused must not only be able to know what is wrong but also be able to apply that knowledge at the time of the act.
Winko v. British Columbia	1999	If it cannot be determined whether a mentally disordered person is a significant threat to public safety, he or she must be discharged absolutely.

but remarked that neither the prison environment nor the community were proper alternatives. This case led the British Parliament to enact the *Criminal Lunatics Act* (1800), which provided the leeway for people to be sent to a place deemed fit by the court (i.e., a mental institution) rather than be incarcerated or set free. This provision was incorporated into a draft of the British criminal code and the first *Criminal Code of Canada* in 1892 (see Schneider et al., 2000, for a more complete description).

The M'Naghten Rules The well-known criteria, the **M'Naghten Rules**, were formulated in the aftermath of a murder trial in England in 1843. The accused, Daniel M'Naghten, had set out to kill the British prime minister, Sir Robert Peel, but had mistaken Peel's secretary, Sir Edward Drummond, for Peel. M'Naghten claimed that he had been instructed to kill Lord Peel by the "voice of God." As a result of a post-trial reference to the House of Lords, the M'Naghten Rules were articulated as follows: "to establish a defence of insanity, it must be clearly proved that, at the time of the committing of the act, the party accused was labouring under such a defect of reason, from disease of the mind, as not to know the nature and quality of the act he was doing; or if he did know it, that he did not know he was doing what was wrong."

The rules are unique in that they were never read as part of a court's ruling at the conclusion of the trial, and they were not part of any legislation. Nevertheless, the M'Naghten Rules have had an unprecedented impact, as they were adopted not only in Britain but throughout all of the Commonwealth and most American jurisdictions as the test to be met in an insanity defence. A key point to emphasize here is that the M'Naghten Rules apply to insanity at the time of the criminal act or omission.

The issue of being able to tell right from wrong as a component of the insanity defence has been the subject of some debate. According to Ogloff and Whittemore (2001), the Canadian legal system defined "wrong" in terms of legally wrong, but this was expanded by the Supreme Court of Canada in *Regina v. Chaulk* (1990) to include morally wrong, as well.

The case of *Regina v. Swain* (1991) led to the proclamation of Bill C-30 on February 4, 1992. Bill C-30 created the mini-code in Part XX.1 within the *Criminal Code of Canada*, dealing exclusively with the mentally disordered accused. The case involved a man who had acted in a threatening manner toward members of his family and was subsequently arrested for the crime of assault causing bodily harm. When the police arrived, they discovered that Swain "had swung his children over his head, scored a cross on his wife's chest, spoken about spirits, and fought with the air. At his arrest, he was speaking excitedly in religious themes" (Stuart et al., 2001, p. 528). He later testified that he was trying to save his family from the devil.

Swain recovered after receiving drug treatment and had lived in the community for over a year without incident when the day of his trial finally came. The insanity defence was raised by the Crown over his objections. Swain was found to be not guilty by reason of insanity, but according to the Criminal Code provisions, he had to be held in "strict custody," even though he had been out on bail and problem-free at the time of the verdict. The Supreme Court, in reviewing the legislative scheme, found that the failure of the provisions to set a maximum time within which the accused's status must be reviewed constituted a violation of his Charter rights. The court noted that for many other similar situations Parliament had set limits on the amount of time that could pass before an accused's status had to be reviewed. While the case turned on this narrow point, the court expressed "concern" with respect to other features of the legislative scheme. Accordingly, Parliament was given six months to bring the legislation into Charter compliance. This gave birth to Bill C-30.

Bill C-30 included a key change in terminology. The phrase "not guilty by reason of insanity" (NGRI) was altered to "not criminally responsible on account of mental disorder" (NCRMD). Another change concerned the party to be responsible for the individual found NCRMD. Previously, the mentally disordered individual had been kept at the "pleasure" of the lieutenant governor, but now legal authority was allocated to provincial review boards. Ogloff and Whittemore (2001) noted that, prior to changes made to the Criminal Code in 1992, people who were found NGRI were detained for an indeterminate length of time. However, as a result of *Regina v. Swain* (1991) and the subsequent proclamation of Bill C-30, review boards now determine the individual's fate within 45 days of the verdict and thereafter not less than annually. Review boards must weigh many factors, including the individual's current mental status and the risk to society posed by the individual. They can discharge the individual with or without conditions or, alternatively, they can order detention in a hospital setting.

Included in Bill C-30 is a list of issues for which assessments may be ordered. The issues include fitness to stand trial, criminal responsibility, infanticide, and, the least onerous, disposition. Specific time limits are set for the assessment of the various issues. It is presumed, for example, that a fitness assessment will be completed within five days, but the maximum period of assessment is set at 60 days for compelling situations. It is also presumed that all assessments will take place out of custody unless the Crown shows why this should not occur. Notwithstanding this presumption, most assessments take place on an in-patient basis because the subject of the assessment is often too unwell to be released into the community. While being assessed, an accused is not to be treated against his or her will. However, if the accused is found to be unfit to stand trial, the Crown may bring an application for the court to order that the accused be treated for up to 60 days in order to render him or her fit. This order, if the evidentiary hurdles are met, will be effected with or without the accused's consent.

Initial research on the impact of Bill C-30 was conducted in British Columbia. A comparison of a cohort of people who had been found NGRI vs. a newer cohort of those found NCRMD uncovered a substantial increase in the number of cases following the enactment of Bill C-30, including a shift toward an increased number of cases involving people charged with less serious offences (Livingston, Wilson, Tien, & Bond, 2003). The average length of hospitalization for the NCRMD cohort (9.8 months) was much lower than for the NGRI cohort (47.7 months). Livingston et al. (2003) concluded, "The Bill C-30 provisions have made the NCRMD defence an attractive option for defendants and legal counsel"

(p. 408). Available statistics indicate that the NCRMD defence is being used more frequently and for a broader range of offences. For instance, there were 177 cases in Quebec in 1992 versus 360 cases in 2006 (Latimer, 2006; Schneider, Forestell, & MacGarvie, 2002).

INSANITY AND MENTAL ILLNESS In general, the insanity defence requires applying an abstract principle to specific life situations. As in all aspects of the law, terms can be interpreted in a number of ways—by defendants, defence lawyers, prosecutors, judges, and jurors—and testimony can be presented in a diverse fashion, depending on the skill of the interrogators and the intelligence of the witnesses. Furthermore, because the defendant's mental condition only at the time the crime was committed is in question, retrospective, often speculative, judgement on the part of lawyers, judges, jurors, and psychiatrists is required. And disagreement between defence and prosecution psychiatrists and psychologists is the rule.

A final point should be emphasized. There is an important difference between insanity and mental illness or defect. A person can be diagnosed as mentally ill and yet be held responsible for a crime. Insanity is a legal concept, not a psychiatric or psychological one. And, while the *Criminal Code of Canada* defines "mental disorder"—the legal term—to mean "disease of the mind," the presence of mental disorder is a necessary but not a sufficient condition to make the defence of insanity. This distinction, also a key concept in the U.S. legal system, was made vivid by the 1992 conviction of Jeffrey Dahmer in Wisconsin. He admitted to butchering, cannibalizing, and having sex with the corpses of 15 boys and young men. Dahmer plead guilty but mentally ill, and his sanity was the sole focus of an unusual trial that had jurors listening to conflicting testimony from mental health experts about the defendant's state of mind during the serial killings to which he had confessed. They had to decide whether he had had a mental disease that prevented him from knowing right from wrong or from being able to control his actions. Even though there was no disagreement that he was mentally ill, diagnosable as having some sort of paraphilia, Dahmer was deemed sane and therefore legally responsible. He was sentenced to 15 consecutive life terms.

An interesting new development in terms of the law and mental health is the introduction of neuroscientific data into the legal system. This is a growing practice that seems geared to reducing the severity of sentences rather than establishing innocence, at least at present. The field emerging here is called **neurolaw**, and it is a natural outgrowth of the emerging field of neuropsychiatry (see Silva, 2009). The primary argument is that the accused suffers from some form of brain dysfunction and related processing deficits, and, as such, he or she really couldn't help himself or herself. For instance, cases have been reported in which murder sentences have been reduced to manslaughter charges as a result of testimony involving neuroscientific data (Chen, 2009).

Insanity is a legal concept and differs from the psychological concept of mental illness. Jeffrey Dahmer, a serial killer and paraphiliac, seemed clearly psychopathological but was not judged insane because he was regarded as knowing right from wrong and as able to control his behaviour. Sygma.

Aharoni et al. (2008) have discussed how neuroscientific data can be used in the United States to contribute to the decision about whether someone is not guilty by reason of insanity. All that would need to be established is that neuroscientific data show that the person was unaware that what they did is wrong. Bennett (2009) has argued that *M'Naghten Rules* need to be rewritten, given the precision of neuroscientific data. In particular, he highlighted the distinction between an irresistible impulse and the subsequent lack of self-control; apparently, irresistible impulses and a lack of self-control involve distinct activities in different brain structures and they are different capacities.

FITNESS TO STAND TRIAL

The insanity defence concerns the accused person's mental state at the time of the crime. A question that first arises is whether the person is competent or fit to stand trial at all. The mental fitness of individuals to stand trial must be decided before it can be determined whether they are responsible for the crime of which they are accused. The requirement that an accused be fit to stand trial was a refinement of the older principle that an accused had to be present before the state could proceed with its prosecution. The requirement of mere physical presence was expanded to require the accused to be "mentally present" as well. It is possible for a person to be judged competent to stand trial yet subsequently be deemed not criminally responsible by reason of mental disorder. In fact, that is the case for all accused raising the NCRMD defence since they must be fit prior to commencing their trial. Fitness has to do with the accused's present condition, not how he or she might have been functioning at the time of the alleged offence.

Decisions may be changed on appeal if the fitness of the defendant is in question and has not been adequately assessed. For instance, Schneider (2001) related a case in which the Ontario Court of Appeal overturned a conviction for attempted murder because of a judge's failure to assess the fitness of the defendant. In this case, although the Crown attorney suggested to the judge that fitness might be an issue, the judge simply asked the accused whether he felt fit to stand trial (Schneider, 2001). Obviously, fitness needs to be established by trained professionals. Canadian Perspectives 18.1 further examines the fitness to stand trial issue (as well as the use of the insanity defence) in the complex case of Louis Riel.

Rather than relying on subjective clinical judgements to determine an individual's fitness (or lack of fitness) to stand trial, another alternative is to adopt measures to assist with

---

CANADIAN PERSPECTIVES 18.1
LOUIS RIEL AND THE ISSUE OF FITNESS TO STAND TRIAL

Louis Riel is one of the most controversial figures in the history of Canada. Riel, of French Canadian and Métis background, was executed for his role in the Métis uprising in 1885 known as the North-West Rebellion. This armed rebellion stemmed from political and land disputes in Western Canada between the Métis and the federal government, and involved the deaths of several North-West Mounted Police. Riel was executed for high treason after a jury found him guilty but recommended mercy.

One vexing question that remains to this day was whether Riel should have been deemed not criminally responsible due to mental disorder. An equally important and related issue is whether he was fit to stand trial. Riel had spent time in mental institutions on two separate occasions prior to the uprising. His lawyers based his defence on the insanity plea, after other

options failed, despite his vehement protests that he did not support this strategy.

Was Riel insane at the time of the act or, at the very least, unfit to stand trial because of an inability to participate in his own defence? Riel displayed many symptoms of megalomania (see Perr, 1992). He believed that he had been specially selected by the spirits to bring forth the message of the Métis. Similar tendencies to put aside one's personal identity and take on another identity (referred to as "misidentification of the self") have come to be described as "The Riel Phenomenon" (see Perr & Federoff, 1992).

The actual documents filed on Riel's behalf by his lawyer, François-Xavier Lemieux, and two psychiatrists contain vivid accounts of Riel's apparent deterioration (*Regina v. Louis Riel*, 1886). Lemieux noted the following in his declaration:

While he was speaking he suddenly stops showing me his hand. "Do you see, says he, blood flowing in the veins; the telegraph is operating actively, and I feel it, they are talking about me, and questioning authorities, in Ottawa, about me." It is of similar fantastic visions he speaks with me every day. I am convinced that he is not acting a part, he speaks with a conviction and a sincerity which leave no doubt in my mind about the state of his mind, he has retracted his errors but he believes himself today to be a prophet and invested with a divine mission to reform the world on the day he has spoken to the Court and when I reprove him for his foolish and extravagant ideas, he answers that he submits, but that he cannot stifle the voice that speaks in him and the spirit that commands him to communicate to the world the revelations he receives. One must have the ferocious hatred of a fanatic or the stupidity of an idiot, to say that Riel is not a fool, because he is intelligent in other matters, as if history was not filled with such anomalies, among certain men who, remarkable in certain subjects, have lost the balance which contains intelligence within the limits from which it cannot escape without losing its privilege of guiding us or making us responsible for our own acts.

...The experience I have gained of this man by continual contact with him has only confirmed me more and more in the opinion I had already formed of him, that he is crazy and insane .... I have just been visiting him, and during an hour he spoke of extraordinary revelations made to him by the spirit the previous night, and that he has been ordered to communicate to me and to all the Catholic clergy: "The great cause of sin in the world is the revolt of the body against the spirit, it is because we do not chew our food enough, and by this want of mastication it communicates animal life only to the body while by masticating and chewing it well, it spiritualizes the body." (Regina v. Louis Riel, p. 204)

The opinion offered by Lemieux was echoed by the two psychiatrists who concluded that Riel was insane and unable to discern right from wrong. However, the medical petition failed and Riel was eventually executed.

Thinking Critically

1. Was Riel not criminally responsible by reason of mental disorder, or was this simply a desperate attempt on the part of his defence team to avoid his execution? On the basis of your understanding of current legislation, do you think the same sentence and result would have been reached today?
2. Was it ethical of Riel's lawyers and psychiatrists to proceed with the insanity defence against their client's wishes? What would you have done? Note that Riel felt that to argue his insanity would, in effect, undermine the cause of his people and the strength of his views.

---

the decision. One measure developed in Canada is the Fitness Interview Test-Revised (FIT-R; Roesch, Zapf, Webster, & Eaves, 1999). The three components of this interview-based measure assess (1) whether the person understands the nature and purpose of the legal proceedings; (2) whether the person understands the possible or likely consequences of the proceedings; and (3) whether the person is capable of communicating with his or her lawyer. The FIT-R appears to have an exceptional level of validity; for example, a study conducted by Zapf and Roesch (1997) found that the measure resulted in no false negative errors (i.e., it did not call someone fit who is really not fit to stand trial). Subsequent research found that defendants with primary psychotic disorders had greater legal impairment than defendants with other psychiatric disorders in terms of their understanding of various aspects of the legal process and their rights (Viljoen, Roesch, & Zapf, 2002). However, impairment was widespread among other groups, as well. For instance, 27% of those with no diagnosed mental disorder were deemed to have impaired understanding. It seems that IQ level is a key factor; those with higher IQs were less likely to have a problem in understanding. The authors cautioned that a case-by-case functional assessment of legal abilities is required, and special efforts are needed to enhance the legal abilities of all suspects. Care is especially needed in assessing the fitness of adolescent defendants. In this regard, the FIT-R appears to have acceptable psychometric properties and can be used to evaluate fitness among younger people (Viljoen, Vincent, & Roesch, 2006).

What role do psychologists play in fitness and criminal responsibility evaluations in Canada? According to Viljoen, Roesch, Ogloff, and Zapf (2003), psychologists are regarded as qualified to provide assessments under the *Youth Criminal Justice Act* and dangerous offender legislation, but only medical practitioners are qualified to provide court-ordered assessments of fitness and criminal responsibility. However, psychologists often assist physicians by conducting psychological evaluations when requested. Viljoen et al. (2003) predicted that, in time, psychologists will play a larger role in fitness and criminality responsibility evaluations.

Judgements about the fitness to stand trial are still exceedingly difficult at times, and the possible influence of a dissociative state is an issue that further complicates the decision-making process. As noted earlier, in the Dorothy Joudrie case, the determination of a dissociative state was key to the court decision that she was not criminally responsible for shooting her husband.

CIVIL COMMITMENT

Historically, governments have had a duty to protect their citizens from harm. We take for granted the right and duty of government to set limits on our freedom for the sake of protecting us. Few drivers, for example, question the legitimacy of imposing limits on them by providing traffic signals that often make them stop when they would rather go.

Government has a long-established right as well as an obligation to protect us both from ourselves—the *parens patriae*, "power of the state"—and from others—the police power of the state. Civil commitment is one further exercise of these powers.

In virtually all jurisdictions, a person can be committed to a psychiatric hospital against his or her will if a judgement is made that he or she is (1) mentally ill and (2) a danger to self (i.e., unable to provide for the basic physical needs of food, clothing, and shelter) or a danger to others (Perlin, 1994). (There is also a form of outpatient commitment, which we describe later.)

Specific commitment procedures generally fit into one of two categories: formal or informal. Formal or judicial commitment is by order of a court. It can be requested by any responsible citizen; usually the police, a relative, or a friend seeks the commitment. If the judge believes that there is a good reason to pursue the matter, he or she will order a mental health examination. The person has the right to object to these attempts to "certify" him or her, and a court hearing can be scheduled to allow the person to present evidence against commitment. In Canada, this procedure is covered by provincial legislation that permits an *ex parte* hearing before a justice of the peace. Generally, this legislation permits a justice of the peace to have an individual held against his or her will for a period of time (e.g., up to 72 hours in Ontario) for the purposes of assessment only. If, after that period of assessment, the individual meets the certification criteria, she or he may be held for longer periods, and most provinces have a process for subsequent involuntary treatment. Alternatively, where the prospective patient is compliant, a person may be brought to a physician who may, where the individual is seen as a danger to him/herself or to others, issue the same process. For example, in Ontario the form signed by the physician (Form 1) is in effect for seven days and is authority for a peace officer to take the individual to a psychiatric facility for assessment for up to 72 hours. If seven days elapse, and an order of a physician or justice of the peace has not been effected, it is no longer valid.

Informal, emergency commitment of mentally ill persons can be accomplished without initially involving the courts. For example, if a hospital administrative board believes that a voluntary patient requesting discharge is too disturbed and dangerous to be released, it can detain the patient with a temporary, informal commitment order.

Civil commitment affects far more people than criminal commitment. It is beyond the scope of this book to examine the intricacies of civil commitment laws. Our aim is to present an overview that will provide a basic understanding of the issues and current directions of change.

Table 18.2 provides an overview of the current Canadian criteria for involuntary admission for the provinces and territories (see Gray & O'Reilly, 2001). Inspection of this table reveals considerable differences among the provinces in the criteria used. One overarching difference is that some jurisdictions use a broad definition of mental disorder, while others use a specific definition. Douglas and Koch (2001) noted that provinces with a specific definition actually use a functional definition of mental illness that is quite detailed. The definition of mental disorder in Saskatchewan, for example, is "a disorder of thought, perceptions, feelings or behaviour that seriously impairs a person's judgment, capacity to recognize reality, ability to associate with others

TABLE 18.2
CANADIAN CRITERIA FOR INVOLUNTARY ADMISSION BY JURISDICTION

Jurisdiction	Definition of Mental Disorder	Harm Criterion	Deterioration as Alternative to Harm	Need for Treatment	Not Capable of Treatment Decision
British Columbia	Specific	Broad	Yes	Yes	No
Alberta	Specific	Physical	No	No	No
Saskatchewan	Specific	Broad	Yes	Yes	Yes
Manitoba	Specific	Broad	Yes	Yes	No
Ontario	Broad	Physical?	Yes	Yes & No[†]	No
Quebec	Broad	?	No	No	No
New Brunswick	Specific	Broad	No	Implied	No
Nova Scotia	Broad	?	No	Implied	No
Prince Edward Island	Specific	Broad	No	Implied	No
Newfoundland and Labrador	Broad	Broad	No	Implied	No
Yukon	Specific	Broad	No	No	No
Northwest Territories & Nunavut	Specific	Physical	No	No	No

? Not clear from the legislation or court cases how to classify.

† "Yes" for deterioration and "no" for bodily harm.

Source: *Canadian Journal of Psychiatry* (May 2001) "Clinically Significant Differences Among Canadian Mental Health Acts", p. 15. Adapted with permission from Gray & O'Reilly (2001)

or ability to meet the ordinary demands of life, in which respect treatment is available" (Douglas & Koch, 2001, p. 355). In contrast, Ontario, Quebec, Nova Scotia, and Newfoundland and Labrador do not use such precise and detailed definitions of the impact of mental illness. In Ontario, mental disorder is defined simply as "a disease or disability of the mind" (see Douglas & Koch, 2001, p. 355).

The provinces and territories also differ in how they define harm to self or others. Ontario, Alberta, and the Northwest Territories and Nunavut focus on a definition that emphasizes the possibility of physical harm. Douglas and Koch (2001) state that Alberta is particularly stringent in its conceptualization of dangerousness. Other jurisdictions have an expanded definition of harm that includes the possibility of a wider range of harmful acts that may or may not involve direct physical damage involving the self or others. Gray and O'Reilly (2001) note that four provinces include the additional criterion that the person is deemed likely to suffer further deterioration, either mental or physical.

The column on the far right of Table 18.2 shows that, at present, Saskatchewan is distinct in that even if other criteria are satisfied, individuals are not committed in this province if they are capable of making a treatment decision. Gray and O'Reilly (2001) indicated that this caveat exists to rule out situations in which a person is committed but then refuses the treatment needed in order to recover and eventually be discharged.

Who experiences civil commitment in Canada? Moss and Redelmeier (2010) analyzed 2,321 applicants to the Consent and Capacity Board in Ontario. These individuals were seeking to overturn their civil commitment. Overall, 18% were successful but follow-up indicated that once involuntary commitment was revoked, adverse subsequent events were common and nearly half sought outpatient treatment for suicidal thoughts within 100 days of being released. The prototypical person experiencing civil commitment was someone who was middle-aged, low income, living in an urban setting, and with a past diagnosis of schizophrenia or mood disorder. These individuals tended to have multiple prior contacts with outpatient services for suicide ideation and there was high comorbidity in terms of substance abuse and personality disorder.

COMMUNITY COMMITMENT: COMMUNITY TREATMENT ORDERS

"I have patients who, if they weren't on CTOs, they would tell me 'I don't want to see you Doc.' They wouldn't turn up for their appointments. They wouldn't take their medications and there'd be nothing I could do about it."

—from Foot, 2007, May 26

One controversial issue that has arisen in Canada involves the concepts of involuntary **community commitment** and **community treatment orders** (CTOs). The latter, introduced in Chapter 1, can be characterized as a form of community commitment designed to ensure treatment compliance. In July 1995, Saskatchewan was the first province to implement CTOs (see Goering et al., 2000; O'Reilly, Keegan, & Elias, 2000), followed by Ontario in 2000. Legislation for CTOs was passed in Nova Scotia in 2005 to be enacted in July 2007. CTOs were put in place in Newfoundland and Labrador in 2007 and will be proclaimed into law in Alberta in 2010 after being introduced in 2007. As of 2009, five provinces had CTOs but the other provinces had conditional leave provisions in place. Conditional leaves are discussed below. CTOs stipulate that the individual will be released back into the community only if he or she adheres to recommended treatments. It is a controversial topic because this condition of release essentially forces people to be treated, regardless of their wishes. Foot (2007) outlines the story of Glen Race, a 26-year-old from Nova Scotia who was wanted for the murders of two men in Halifax and a third in New York state. His family, who stated that he had struggled with paranoid schizophrenia for six years, indicated that they tried everything to get additional treatment for him, but they were unsuccessful. After Race was captured in Texas in May 2007, family members issued a statement that his alleged killing spree could have been prevented if Nova Scotia had CTOs.

In Saskatchewan, several criteria must be met in order for a CTO to be invoked (see O'Reilly et al., 2000):

1. The person must have a mental disorder that requires treatment and the treatment can be provided in the community.
2. The person has received inpatient involuntary treatment for 60 cumulative days or more, has been in an inpatient facility on three or more occasions in the last two years, or has previously been the subject of a CTO.
3. The person may harm him- or herself or others or suffer from physical deterioration without care or supervision.
4. Services must exist in the community and must be available.
5. The person is unable to understand or is incapable of making an informed decision about the need for care and treatment as a result of his or her mental disorder.
6. The person is capable of complying with the requirements of a CTO.

The inability of mentally ill people to make treatment decisions is often a key factor in CTOs. A study in Ottawa found that almost 3 out of 4 people who were issued a CTO lacked the basic capacity to make treatment decisions (O'Brien, Farrell, & Faulkner, 2009).

The Canadian Psychiatric Association, in its 2009 position paper, confirmed its support for mandatory outpatient treatment, stating that it has benefits in "certain clearly defined situations" and its use is supported "if specific legal rights and safeguards are in place" (see O'Reilly et al., 2009, p. 1). The association stated that mandatory outpatient treatment in the form of CTOs are especially called for when people suffer from persistent deficits in insight.

Glen Douglas Race from Nova Scotia apparently suffers from paranoid schizophrenia. His parents claimed that he wouldn't have killed three men in 2007 if Nova Scotia's CTO legislation had been in effect. In a public letter they stated that "we, too, have lost a loved one." CP/Michael Betts.

According to the Centre for Addiction and Mental Health (CAMH), 63 CTOs were given in Saskatchewan over a three-year period (from a population of 6,000 people with serious mental illness) and 95% of people in Saskatchewan with a CTO had a diagnosis of schizophrenia (CAMH, 2000). A survey of Saskatchewan psychiatrists found that 62% were satisfied or extremely satisfied with the effects of CTOs on their patients, while only 10% were dissatisfied or extremely dissatisfied. However, CTOs are issued for only three months in Saskatchewan (as opposed to six months in Ontario), and survey respondents felt that the three-month period was too short (see O'Reilly et al., 2000).

The law establishing CTOs in Ontario came into effect on December 1, 2000. It is named "Brian's Law" in memory of a popular Ottawa sportscaster who was killed by a man with paranoid schizophrenia who did not adhere to his prescribed treatment. Critics called it the "leash law," and some claimed that the police would soon drag the mentally ill away in handcuffs if they refused medication. The CTO criteria in Ontario differ slightly from those in Saskatchewan. A CTO may be issued if the person has two admissions or 30 cumulative days as an inpatient over a three-year period (see Gray & O'Reilly, 2001). Thus, the provinces differ in the specific CTO details. Although concerns have been raised about the coercive aspects of CTOs, it is interesting that the Province of Ontario, in describing the legislation, still maintains that all protections involving the issue of informed consent still exist. Also, according to this legislation (see Brian's Law [Mental Health Legislative Reform], 2000), individuals subjected to a CTO retain a number of rights, including

1. a right of review by the Consent and Capacity Board with appeal to the courts each time a CTO is issued or reviewed;

2. a mandatory review by the Consent and Capacity Board every second time a CTO is reviewed;
3. a right to request a re-examination by the issuing physician to determine if the CTO is still needed in order for the person to live in the community; and
4. a right of review of a finding of incapacity to consent to treatment.

In Ontario, the procedure should really be referred to as a "community treatment agreement" because the patient is free to withdraw his or her consent at any time. When that is done, the "order" comes to an end.

Richard O'Reilly (2004) from the University of Western Ontario concluded that few issues have so polarized the stakeholders in the mental health system as CTOs. Table 18.3 summarizes his analysis of the major arguments for and against CTOs.

Concerns about the coerciveness of CTOs continue to abound. Snow and Austin (2009) reviewed ethical concerns and the false notion that CTOs allow a degree of autonomy and self-determination because the person is still in his or her community. They noted that some have equated CTOs with "therapeutic stalking" and authors such as Thomas Szasz have described CTOs as a way of transforming "all of society into a kind of mental hospital" (Szasz, 2005, p. 81). However, they allowed for other considerations such as the need to also protect the safety and well-being of afflicted individuals. Clearly, a CTO can have benefits in addition to enhancing safety. A follow-up study of 84 people issued CTOs in Ottawa found that the most significant changes were greater engagement with community services and a shift toward more supportive housing arrangements (O'Brien et al., 2009).

It should be noted that in Canadian jurisdictions, in contrast to many other countries, a requirement for previous hospitalization for compulsory community treatment precludes the use of CTOs with first-episode patients (see Gray & O'Reilly, 2005). Some other jurisdictions (e.g., New Zealand) require that compulsory psychiatric treatment be delivered in the least restrictive setting—the community—and hospitalization can be ordered only if community treatment is inappropriate.

Conditional leave from hospital is another form of a compulsory community treatment provision in Canadian mental health acts (see Gray & O'Reilly, 2005, for a review). It is a mechanism that allows a patient who continues to meet committal criteria to live in the community if he or she adheres to specified conditions. Seven of the twelve Canadian mental health acts (British Columbia, Alberta, Manitoba, New Brunswick, Yukon, Prince Edward Island, and Ontario) have conditional leave provisions that differ somewhat in pre-conditions, renewal, and consent (see Gray & O'Reilly, 2005, for a full discussion).

What are the consequences of a patient's nonadherence to the conditions of a community treatment provision?

TABLE 18.3
ARGUMENTS SUPPORTING AND AGAINST CTOS

Supporting CTOs

1. CTOs are a predictable and acceptable consequence of deinstitutionalization.
2. Society has a *parens patriae* obligation to care for citizens who cannot care for themselves.
3. Lack of awareness of mental illness is a persistent and pervasive symptom.
4. Offering services is often not enough when patients lack insight.
5. The assumption that physicians can safely manage patients by committing them just at the point when they become dangerous is mistaken.
6. CTOs are less restrictive than involuntary hospitalization.
7. Research confirms the effectiveness of CTOs.
8. No evidence indicates negative effects of CTOs.

Against CTOs

1. Society should never coerce individuals to take treatment.
2. CTOs extend coercion into the community.
3. It is more difficult to protect patients' rights in the community.
4. If we had sufficient services we would not need CTOs.
5. Coercion will be used as an alternative to providing adequate service.
6. People should not be coerced to accept services when there are others willing to accept, but who cannot access, them.
7. People often refuse medications because of side effects or other bona fide reasons.
8. Research on CTOs is inconclusive.
9. CTOs will be used to sweep undesirable individuals off the streets.
10. Hospitals will fill up with nonadherent patients.
11. Coercion drives people away from the mental health system.

Source: Adapted from "Why Are Community Treatment Orders Controversial?", O'Reilly (2004, p. 580). Reprinted with permission from the Canadian Psychiatric Association P. 20.

As noted by Gray and O'Reilly (2005), either the person can be apprehended and examined involuntarily to determine if involuntary admission is warranted (e.g., Ontario) or returned directly to hospital without a re-examination of admissibility (e.g., British Columbia).

There is a relative lack of research on the impact of CTOs in Canada, but extensive research has been conducted in those American states that have implemented CTOs. By and large, these investigations point to the benefits of CTOs. For example, an investigation in North Carolina by Swanson et al. (2001) found that patients who received long-term outpatient commitment had lower probabilities of being arrested than a comparison group, and the key factor accounting for this outcome was a reduced risk of violent behaviour. A study conducted over a three-year period at the Royal Ottawa Hospital yielded very favourable findings (see O'Brien & Farrell, 2005). CTOs were associated with significant reductions in the number and length of hospital admissions and contributed to greater use of community supports, including available housing.

The lack of CTOs in Nova Scotia is why a team of researchers interested in the consequences and benefits of CTOs compared CTO cases from Western Australia with cases from Nova Scotia (see Kisely, Smith, Preston, & Xiao, 2005). Comparisons of matched cases showed that compulsory community treatment did not reduce the risk of hospital readmission, and, in fact, CTO cases actually had a greater readmission rate. However, the authors noted that this could have been due to the fact that CTO cases actually had greater scrutiny and constant evaluation, as well as the general fact that readmission rates are lower in Nova Scotia than in Australia.

O'Reilly et al. (2006) conducted a qualitative study of 26 CTO cases from Regina and Saskatoon. The most predominant diagnoses were schizophrenia and schizoaffective disorder. This study involved interviews of patients, clinicians, family members, and community members. Patients were generally favourable but somewhat ambivalent; they resented the coercion but this wore off over time in most instances, and many patients recognized the need for structure and support that came as a result of the CTO. Still, a small subset of patients remained resentful of the coercion. Family members and clinicians were much less ambivalent; family members were very positive about the CTO and most clinicians saw the CTOs as helpful for most patients. However, they suggested that the three-month duration is too short and should be extended to at least six months. This suggestion fits with the results of an earlier American study that found that CTO treatment was more effective if treatment was maintained for at least 180 days with seven or more sessions per month (see Swartz et al., 2001).

Churchill and Owen (2007) reviewed 72 empirical studies from six countries, including Canada, and concluded that it could not be determined one way or the other whether CTOs benefit or harm patients. Many questions remain unanswered in the CTO debate. As noted by Chaimowitz (2004), "the data, helpful as they may be, can be used selectively by both sides of the CTO debate" (p. 578). Less forceful alternatives, such as assertive community treatment teams, do exist. It will be important to demonstrate that CTOs are more effective than alternatives if their continued use is to be justified.

Clearly, simply issuing a CTO or conditional leave is not a solution. It must be followed through with the provision of high-quality care. This was illustrated in another recent tragic example. Seung Hui Cho killed 32 students and faculty members, and then himself, at Virginia Technical University on April 16, 2007. Further examination revealed that a CTO was issued for Cho in 2005 after he stalked and harassed two students, and it was determined that he had suicidal and violent thoughts. Cho was ordered into outpatient community treatment after a judge deemed that he was an imminent danger to himself. However, Cho never received treatment because he was never contacted by community services. Accordingly, the gaps in psychiatric care are now being reviewed in hearings conducted by the Virginia House of Delegates (Craig & Jenkins, 2007).

PREVENTIVE DETENTION AND PROBLEMS IN RISK ASSESSMENT

The perception is widespread that mentally ill people account for a significant proportion of the violence that besets contemporary society, but this is not the case (e.g., Bonta, Law, & Hanson, 1998; Monahan, 1992). Although the issue is complex, and the two constructs are positively related, "the relative contribution of mental illness to the overall rate of violence in

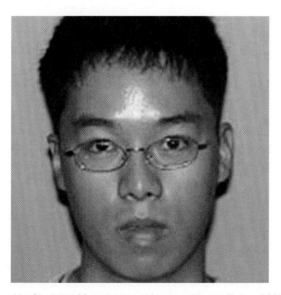

Seung Hui Cho killed 32 students and faculty at Virginia Tech in 2007. Despite the fact that a CTO had been issued, he never received treatment. © Handout/Virginia Tech Police/epa/Corbis.

society is quite small" (Norko & Baranoski, 2005, p. 21). Only about 3% of the violence in the United States is linked clearly to mental illness (Swanson, Holzer, Ganju, & Jono, 1990). Moreover, about 90% of people diagnosed as psychotic (primarily schizophrenic) are not violent (Swanson et al., 1990). Mentally ill persons—even allowing for their relatively small numbers—do not account for a large proportion of violent offenders, especially when compared with substance abusers and people who are in their teens and 20s, male, and poor (Mulvey, 1994). Large community-based studies indicate that mental disorders do increase violence risk when they co-occur with substance abuse (Monahan et al., 2001; Swanson et al., 1990). However, one study suggests that former mental health patients who are not substance abusers are no more likely to engage in violence than are non-mentally ill individuals who are not substance abusers. Thus, if substance abuse is not involved, mentally ill people are no more prone to violence than the average person. Also, when former patients do act aggressively, it is usually against family members or friends and the incidents tend to occur at home (Steadman et al., 1998). By and large, then, the general public is seldom affected by violence from former mental health patients. Thus, certain case studies outlined in this chapter are atypical in the sense that they involve violent and aggressive acts committed by people with mental disorders.

Nevertheless, there is a strong connection in the public mind between violence and mental illness, and this belief is central to society's justification of civil commitment (e.g., Steadman et al., 1998), as well as to the stigma attached to having been a patient in a psychiatric institution (e.g., Steadman et al., 1998). In fact, there is some evidence that mental disorder may sometimes contribute to violence, enough to justify preventive detention. In the Steadman et al. (1998) study, for example, substance abuse increased the chances of violent behaviour more among discharged mental health patients than among non-patient controls. There is also accumulating evidence that the effect of psychosis on risk of violence is much greater for women than for men. Skeem et al. (2006) conducted an intensive study of psychiatric emergency room patients at high risk for community violence based on an actuarial prediction model. The authors evaluated prospectively the temporal relation between symptoms and violence and reported that a high-risk patient with increased anger in one week is more likely to be involved in serious violence the following week. Violence was not related to anxiety, depression, or delusional beliefs. We now examine the issues and the evidence in greater detail.

THE PREDICTION OF DANGEROUSNESS The likelihood of committing an act that is dangerous to the self or others is central to civil commitment. Historically, the focus of assessment has been on the prediction of dangerousness, but more contemporary approaches focus on the assessment of risk rather than the prediction of dangerousness (see Lyon, Hart, & Webster, 2001). Lyon et al. (2001) attribute the shift in emphasis to several factors, including results indicating that professionals tended to overestimate the incidence of violence when the institutionalized were released. Moreover, a focus on the dangerousness inherent in the individual promotes a tendency to attribute outcomes entirely to the dispositional traits of the individual and fails to take into account circumstantial and situational factors.

Regardless of which term is used, is dangerousness easily predicted or is risk easily assessed? Early studies examining the accuracy of predictions that a person would commit a dangerous act found that mental health professionals were poor at making this judgement (e.g., Kozol, Boucher, & Garofalo, 1972). Collectively, there is extensive literature on the limited validity of clinical judgements, including several studies conducted in Canada (e.g., Menzies & Webster, 1995). A meta-analytic, quantitative review by Hanson and Bussière (1998) found that the ability of clinicians to predict recidivism among sex offenders is only slightly better than chance. The low validity of these judgements is a serious problem because of the weight given to such information. In fact, a Canadian study found that the senior clinician's testimony was the strongest predictor of the decision reached by tribunals in deciding whether to continue to detain forensic patients in maximum security (Hilton & Simmons, 2001).

One alternative is to make decisions on the basis of **actuarial prediction**. Actuarial prediction involves the use of statistical formulae composed of factors that are significant predictors of dangerousness. The factors are weighted statistically by their importance, based on the outcomes of previous studies. Several actuarial measures have been developed in Canada to assist decision-makers. The PCL-R (Hare, 1991), discussed in Chapter 13, is a consistent predictor of criminal recidivism (see Heilbrun, Ogloff, & Picarrello, 1999) and is often included in risk assessment batteries, either as a stand-alone measure or as part of a broader assessment battery.

Lyon et al. (2001) summarized the strengths and criticisms of the actuarial approach. First, actuarial assessments are more likely than clinical ratings to use quantitative ratings and less likely to be influenced by subjective biases. Second, actuarial measures involve greater consistency because the creators of the measures have already specified with precision the information involved, the strategies for data coding, and required analyses. Also, actuarial decisions are easy for others to review. However, these same authors note that actuarial approaches may be too rigid and cannot be altered to take into account individual factors of potential importance. In addition, actuarial measures are derived from specific populations, so the generalizability of statistical formulae to other populations is always an issue.

Another alternative that is growing in popularity is to rely on more structured forms of clinical judgements instead of unstructured clinical judgements or actuarial approaches. The HCR-20 is a more structured assessment device developed in Canada (see Webster, Douglas, Eaves, & Hart, 1997). "HCR" refers to historical variables, clinical variables, and risk variables. Historical variables include such factors as previous violence, early maladjustment at home or at school, history of serious mental disorder, and other personality disorders. Current clinical variables include such indicators as being unresponsive to treatment, a lack of insight, and acting in an impulsive manner. Finally, additional risk variables include consideration of such factors as lack of social support and experience of stressful events.

Quinsey, Harris, Rice, and Cormier (1998) criticized the HCR-20 on the grounds that it includes certain factors (e.g., a history of serious mental disorder) that have not been robust predictors of risk in previous studies. Moreover, they observed that the HCR-20 is not an actuarial measure in the truest sense because the checklist items were not selected on the basis of empirical links with outcomes. The assessment package they advocate using is described in Canadian Contributions 18.1, which examines the contributions of Marnie Rice.

CANADIAN CONTRIBUTIONS 18.1
MARNIE RICE AND ACTUARIAL RISK ASSESSMENT

Marnie Rice was made a fellow of the Royal Society of Canada in 2003. She has been a vital member of an effective research team based at the Oak Ridge Mental Health Centre in Penetanguishene, Ontario. Other team members include Grant Harris, Vernon Quinsey, Catherine Cormier, and Zoe Hilton. Rice is the former Director of Research at the centre and, upon her retirement, now holds the title of Director of Research Emerita. Her collaborative work has contributed greatly to our understanding of forensic patients and risk assessment, and in recognition of this, she was the 1995 recipient of the American Psychological Association Award for Contribution to Research in Public Policy. She was given the award for "pioneering the rigorous empirical evaluation of risk

assessment and risk reduction in difficult forensic populations .... With her colleagues Grant Harris and Vernon Quinsey, she has established a remarkable program of cutting-edge research on the actuarial assessment of violence risk" (American Psychological Association, 1996, p. 342). She has also studied social skills deficits and clinical treatment, and she developed a program for preventing institutional violence.

Rice and her colleagues developed the Violence Risk Appraisal Guide (VRAG; Rice & Harris, 1995) for the purposes of actuarial assessments of risk; that is, using statistical models to predict the likelihood of violence. The construction and development of the VRAG is described at length in Quinsey et al. (1998).

Rice and her associates hoped to create an assessment tool that could predict over time which institutionalized offenders would incur another criminal charge from a violent act after being released. The 12 variables that compose the VRAG are displayed in Table 18.4. This table indicates that the two best predictors within the VRAG are scores on the PCL-R (Hare, 1991) and a variable of elementary school maladjustment. The negative correlation between violent recidivism and age at the time of the index offence indicates that risk is higher to the extent that the offender was relatively young. Similarly, the negative correlation with schizophrenia indicates that it is associated with less risk (also see Rice & Harris, 1995) and underscores one of the main findings emerging from the work of Rice and her associates; namely, that mental disorder per se is not a risk factor. In fact, Rice (1997) concluded that "violent recidivism among mentally disordered individuals is related to the same variables as among non-mentally disordered individuals" (p. 420), so there is no basis for public perceptions that link mental disorder with the possibility of violence.

Marnie Rice has furthered the actuarial approach to risk assessment. Photo courtesy of Marnie Rice.

TABLE 18.4

VIOLENCE RISK APPRAISAL GUIDE (VRAG) VARIABLES AND PEARSON CORRELATIONS WITH VIOLENT RECIDIVISM

Revised Psychopathy Checklist score	.34
Elementary school maladjustment score	.31
Meets *DSM-III* criteria for any personality disorder	.26
Age at the time of the index offence	−.26
Separation from either parent (except death) under age 16	.25
Failure on prior conditional release	.24
Non-violent offence history score (using the Cormier-Lang scale)	.20
Never married (or equivalent)	.18
Meets *DSM-III* criteria for schizophrenia	−.17
Most serious victim injury (from the index offence)	−.16
Alcohol abuse score	.13
Female victim in the index offence	−.11

Source: Violent offenders: *Appraising and managing risk. The Law and public policy: Psychology and the social sciences series.* Quinsey, Vernon L.; Harris, Grant T.; Rice, Marnie E.; Cormier, Catherine A. Washington, DC, US: American Psychological Association. (1998). xviii, 356 pp. doi: 10.1037/10304-000

A comparative study found that the VRAG predicted general recidivism, as well as sexual and violent recidivism, thus supporting the actuarial approach (Barbaree, Seto, Langston, & Peacock, 2001). Prospective research involving a five-year follow-up of the original cohort of forensic patients found that the VRAG was a strong predictor of violent recidivism and a robust predictor of extreme violence (Harris, Rice, & Cormier, 2002). Comparative research of four actuarial measures found that the VRAG was comparable or superior to these measures in predicting violent recidivism and sexually motivated recidivism (Harris et al., 2003), and a new meta-analysis confirmed that the VRAG was a better predictor than comparable instruments of violent recidivism such as the HCR-20 (see Campbell, French, & Gendreau, 2009). Finally, in a very specific context, Rice and Harris (2003) found that the VRAG was a good predictor of violent and sexual recidivism by father-daughter child molesters, even though it was the case

that these child molesters had lower scores on the VRAG and lower rates of recidivism than non-familial child molesters.

A general finding that has emerged from research conducted in Canada is that it is the psychopaths among us who are especially likely to reoffend in a violent manner (see Rice & Harris, 1995; Serin & Amos, 1995). Rice (1997) is quite pessimistic about the chances of treating and rehabilitating the psychopaths who have participated in her research investigations, in part because some findings indicate that treatment actually yields worse outcomes. For these people, treatment is a chance to improve their social skills and increase their charm in order to further mislead unsuspecting victims. Rice's pessimism was seemingly borne out by the recent details of the life and death of Peter Woodcock, a serial killer who was incarcerated for over 50 years, most of which were spent at the Oak Ridge Division of the Penetanguishe Mental Health Centre. Woodcock died in March 2010 (see Bourrie, 2010). Woodcock killed three children and molested countless others back in the 1950s, and he helped kill another person when out on a day pass in 1991. He later changed his name to David Michael Krueger. His story is detailed in a biography written by Bourrie (1997). Numerous treatments were tried, including a range of drug treatments that included LSD, but to no avail. Drug treatments were tried due to the attempted medicalization of interventions for psychopathy. According to Bourrie (1997), Woodcock also experienced the controversial "therapeutic" environment created by Dr. Elliot Barker, which was introduced in Chapter 14.

As a result of the inability to treat such psychopathic individuals, Rice decided to concentrate her efforts on developing measures such as the VRAG that may be used to identify these people, so members of the court and review boards will be aware of whom they are evaluating.

Although the VRAG is among the best actuarial tool for assessing dangerousness to date, and there have been great improvements in assessing risk over the years (for a review, see Hanson, 2009), significant concerns still remain. First, we are still a long way from being able to use actuarial measures to determine levels of dangerousness with absolute certainty. The correlation between the VRAG and the outcome measure of violent recidivism is approximately $r = .44$ (see Rice, 1997), which means that almost four fifths of the variance in this important outcome measure still remains to be predicted. Violence is a product of the individual's personal characteristics (including the consumption of drugs and/or alcohol) and the environment within which he or she is functioning. To make the point, you could take two clinically similar individuals with identical VRAG scores and place them in two very different environments: one will possibly reoffend, whereas the other possibly will not. Much of the variance in violent recidivism is accounted for by environmental factors that are probably not captured by instruments such as the VRAG. Second, although Litwack (2001) concluded that the VRAG is the best assessment device available, he feels that it must receive more validation in order to be used to make the important decision of whether a person should be detained because of his or her dangerousness. Third, as a general criticism of the actuarial approach, Rogers (2000) noted that current measures are limited by their focus on negative predictors involving risk instead of protective factors that increase an offender's resilience when back in society.

Finally, proponents of the HCR-20 believe that it is more suitable because it includes an assessment of dynamic, changing clinical risk factors. In addition, these researchers emphasize the importance of a multi-faceted approach that incorporates actuarial assessment within a model that also includes structured clinical judgements by trained professionals (Douglas, Ogloff, & Hart, 2003). Rice, Harris, and Quinsey (2002), however, have suggested that while dynamic predictors help predict when an individual is likely to offend or reoffend, they are of limited usefulness in determining who is at greatest risk of offending.

The prediction of dangerousness remains a complicated and very difficult enterprise. Nevertheless, the work and contributions of Marnie Rice and her colleagues has illustrated the potential usefulness of actuarial measures.

Regardless of the criticism, a growing number of studies attest to the predictive usefulness of the HCR-20. For instance, the HCR-20 is better than the PCL-R at postdicting previous acts of violence and anti-social behaviour in incarcerated offenders (Douglas & Webster, 1999). Note that postdiction involves the identification of variables that are found, after the fact, to distinguish violent tendencies. Another study by Douglas, Ogloff, Nicholls, and Grant (1999) demonstrated that the HCR-20 had predictive validity in terms of predicting subsequent acts of violence in civilly committed patients, and once again, the HCR-20 outperformed the PCL-R screening version.

An investigation conducted in the United Kingdom showed that even though the PCL-R had moderate predictive ability, the HCR-20 outperformed it in terms of subsequent acts of verbal aggression, physical aggression, and violence to property (Gray et al., 2003). However, Gray et al. (2003) also noted that studies with the HCR-20 have been conducted with psychiatric patients and, thus far, no study has been conducted with non-mentally disordered prisoners. In another British study, Doyle and Dolan (2006) assessed patients discharged from both forensic and non-forensic psychiatric services and followed up at 24 weeks post discharge. They reported that historical measures of risk and measures of psychopathy, impulsiveness, and anger were highly predictive of community violence. Doyle and Dolan (2006) concluded that the HCR-20 was the most robust predictor of violence. Further, the clinical and risk management items (which are more dynamic or changeable) added incremental validity to the risk assessment over and above the static historical factors. Of course, as noted by Wynn (2006), even validated instruments such as the HCR-20 may not be helpful in predicting first episodes of violence because, to a large extent, they draw on the history of violence. Elbogen et al. (2006) also assessed malleable, dynamic factors in addition to static factors in outpatients with mental disorders from five sites in the United States. Community violence was inversely related to treatment adherence, perceived treatment need, and perceived treatment effectiveness.

A court decision in the case of *Winko v. British Columbia* (see Table 18.1) further increases the importance of making accurate risk assessments. This case established that where there is uncertainty about whether an offender poses a risk, the onus is on the province in question to resolve this uncertainty, and if it cannot be resolved, the former offender must be released (see Schneider et al., 2000). In other words, unless the provincial review board can find affirmatively and *prove* that the accused poses a significant threat to public safety, he or she must be discharged absolutely. Previously, the interpretation of the law was that if there was uncertainty about risk, then the person in question would remain subject to the jurisdiction of the provincial review board. Analyses of decisions before and after the Winko decision have found few differences in terms of characteristics of the accused person and other details such as time elapsed between index offence and subsequent discharge (Desmarais, Hucker, Brink, & DeFreitas, 2008). Desmarais et al. (2008) expressed surprise at the lack of differences and concluded that perhaps the need to prove significant threat to public safety had already been incorporated into decisions made about accused people prior to the Winko case.

Parenthetically, another aspect of this case involved the issue of "capping provisions" and setting a standard for the maximum amount of time that a person could be detained. The issue was whether Winko and three other offenders with similar appeals could be detained, perhaps indefinitely, if risk of dangerousness was still evident (see Schneider et al., 2000). The court ruled that these individuals could indeed still be held if there was a risk of dangerousness, with the caveat mentioned above that the risk of dangerousness had to be demonstrated.

Some researchers have gone so far as to argue that civil commitment for the purposes of preventive detention should be abolished. Reconsideration of earlier research suggests that greater accuracy can be achieved in predicting dangerousness in the longer term (e.g., Steadman et al., 1998). Violence prediction becomes more accurate under the following conditions (note the role played by situational factors, sometimes in interaction with personality variables) (e.g., Campbell, Stefan, & Loder, 1994):

- If a person has been repeatedly violent in the recent past, it is reasonable to predict that he or she will be violent in the near future unless there have been major changes in the person's attitudes or environment. Thus, if a violent person is placed in a restrictive environment, such as a prison or high-security psychiatric hospital facility, he or she may well not be violent, given the markedly changed environment.
- If violence is in the person's distant past and constituted a single but very serious act, and if that person has been incarcerated for a period of time, then violence can be expected on release if there is reason to believe that the person's pre-detention personality and physical abilities have not changed and the person is going to return to the same environment in which he or she was previously violent.
- Even with no history of violence, violence can be predicted if the person is judged to be on the brink of a violent act; for example, if the person is pointing a loaded gun at an occupied building.

In addition, as stated earlier, the presence of substance abuse significantly raises the rate of violence (Steadman et al., 1998). This finding supports the inclusion of substance abuse among the factors to be considered when attempting to predict violence. (Substance abuse predicts violence also among non-mentally disordered individuals [Gendreau, Little, & Goggin, 1996].) Violence in discharged mental health patients is usually attributable to that small percentage of individuals who do not take their medication or, possibly, who self-medicate (Elbogen et al., 2006; Monahan, 1992). Outpatient commitment is one way to increase medication compliance.

For a detailed discussion of the responsibility of therapists to predict dangerousness, see Focus on Discovery 18.2.

FOCUS ON DISCOVERY 18.2
THE TARASOFF CASE—THE DUTY TO WARN AND TO PROTECT

The client's right to **privileged communication**—the legal right to require that what goes on in therapy remain confidential—is an important protection, but it is not absolute. Society has long stipulated certain conditions in which confidentiality in a relationship should not be maintained because of harm that can befall others. A famous California court ruling in 1974 (*Tarasoff v. Regents of the University of California*, 1974) described circumstances in which a therapist not only may but must breach the sanctity of a client's communication. The facts in this case on the duty to protect the public are outlined below:

IN 1968, Prosenjit Poddar, a graduate student from India studying at the University of California at Berkeley, met Tatiana (Tanya) Tarasoff at a folk dancing class. They saw each other weekly during the fall, and she kissed him on New Year's Eve. Poddar interpreted this act as a sign of formal engagement (as it might have been in India, where he was a member of the Harijam or "untouchable caste"). [But] Tanya told him that she was involved with other men, and indicated that she did not wish to have an intimate relationship with him.

Poddar was depressed as a result of the rebuff, but he saw Tanya a few times during the spring (occasionally tape recording their conversations in an effort to understand why she did not love him). Tanya left for Brazil in the summer, and Poddar at the urging of a friend went to the student health facility where a psychiatrist referred him to a psychologist for psychotherapy. When Tanya returned in October 1969, Poddar discontinued therapy. Based in part on Poddar's stated intention to purchase a gun, the psychologist notified the campus police, both orally and in writing, that Poddar was dangerous and should be taken to a community mental health centre for psychiatric commitment.

The campus police interviewed Poddar, who seemed rational and promised to stay away from Tanya. They released him and notified the health service. No further efforts at commitment were made because the supervising psychiatrist apparently decided they were not needed and, as a matter of confidentiality, requested that the letter to the police and certain therapy records be destroyed.

On October 27, Poddar went to Tanya's home armed with a pellet gun and a kitchen knife. She refused to speak to him. He shot her with the pellet gun. She ran from the house, was pursued, caught, and repeatedly and fatally stabbed by him. Poddar was found guilty of voluntary manslaughter rather than first- or second-degree murder. The defence established with the aid of the expert testimony of three psychiatrists that Poddar's diminished mental capacity—paranoid schizophrenia—precluded the malice necessary for first- or second-degree murder. After his prison term, he returned to India, where, according to his own report, he is happily married. (Schwitzgebel & Schwitzgebel, 1980, p. 205)

Under the privileged communication statute of California, the counselling centre psychologist properly breached the confidentiality of the professional relationship and took steps to have Poddar civilly committed, for he judged Poddar to be an imminent danger. Poddar had stated that he intended to purchase a gun, and he had convinced the therapist that he was desperate enough to harm Tarasoff. What the psychologist did not do, and what the court decided he should have done, was to warn the likely victim, Tarasoff, that her former friend had bought a gun and might use it against her. Such a warning would have been consistent with previous court decisions requiring physicians to warn the public when they are treating people with contagious diseases and requiring mental institutions to warn others when a dangerous patient has escaped (Knapp & Vandecreek, 1982). The Tarasoff ruling (upheld in 1976 by a four-to-three majority of the California Supreme Court) is now being applied in other states as well (including *White v. United States*, 1986; *Soutear v. United States*, 1986; *Dunkle v. Food Services East Inc.*, 1990; and *People v. Clark*, 1990). The Tarasoff decision requires clinicians, in deciding when to violate confidentiality, to use the very imperfect skill of predicting dangerousness.

EXTENDING PROTECTION TO FORESEEABLE VICTIMS

A subsequent California court ruling (*Hedlund v. Superior Court*, 1983) held, by a bare majority, that foreseeable victims include those in close relationship with the identifiable victim. In this instance, a mother was hurt by a shotgun fired by a dangerous patient, and her seven-year-old son was present when the shooting took place. The boy later sued the psychologists for damages brought on by emotional trauma. Since a young child is likely to be in the company of his or her mother, the court concluded in this case that the Tarasoff ruling extended to the boy.

CHILLING EFFECT OF TARASOFF?

In the years since the Tarasoff ruling, professionals have wondered whether it would have a negative effect, perhaps even a chilling effect, on psychotherapists. If clients are informed of this limitation to confidentiality, they may become reluctant to express feelings of extreme anger to therapists for fear that therapists will notify the people with whom they are angry. Clients might become less open with their therapists, perhaps derive less benefit from therapy, and even become more likely to inflict harm if they have not disclosed their fury as a first step toward controlling it. The welfare of the people whom the Tarasoff decision intended to protect might be endangered by the very ruling itself!

It is unclear whether these concerns are well-founded. A survey of psychologists and psychiatrists in California soon after Tarasoff became law indicated that the court decision was affecting their thinking and practices (Wise, 1978). On the plus side, one third reported consulting more often with colleagues concerning cases in which violence was an issue. This practice should have a good outcome, since input from other professionals may improve the solitary clinician's decision-making, presumably to the benefit of the client. (Consultation can also demonstrate that the clinician took extra steps to adhere to Tarasoff, which can reduce legal liability [Monahan, 1993].) On the minus side, about 20% of the respondents indicated that they avoided asking their clients questions about violence, an ostrich-like stance that may keep the clinician from obtaining important information and yet reduces his or her legal liability should the client harm someone. A substantial number of therapists were keeping less detailed records, again in an effort to reduce legal liability.

As an update to Tarasoff in California, in 2004, an appeals court ruled that a therapist has a duty to warn possible victims if the threat is reported to the therapist by a close member of the patient's family (*Ewing v. Goldstein*, 2004).

As for Canada, the courts had not established until recently that it is the duty of psychologists to warn or protect others (see Heilbrun, Ogloff, and Picarello, 1999), but codes of ethics by professional organizations such as the Canadian Psychological Association stipulate clearly that psychologists must breach confidentiality when there is reason to suspect that a third party is at risk (see Ogloff, 1999). Thus, although confidentiality typically prevails in the therapeutic setting, certain circumstances can lead the therapist to inform others of the possible dangers.

In a Tarasoff situation, the clinician is seeing a client in a counselling capacity and comes to suspect that third persons may be at risk. What about the forensic context? The Supreme Court of Canada has visited this issue with results that are as "chilling" as the civil context of Tarasoff. In *Smith v. Jones* (1999), Jones (an alias) had been charged with a number of sexual assaults on prostitutes in the Vancouver area. Counsel for the accused retained the services of a psychiatrist—Smith (also an alias)—to conduct a psychiatric assessment of his client. This is a routine procedure for defence counsel and is usually perceived to be risk-free, as the psychiatrist's assessment would be privileged in that he or she is acting in the capacity of counsel's agent or, alternatively, under the umbrella of the "solicitor-client brief." In *Smith v. Jones*, the psychiatrist, Smith, contacted counsel for the accused to inquire when the trial was to commence. Counsel advised Smith repeatedly that he would not be needed (in that his report was quite negative). Smith persisted, indicating that Jones was very dangerous and prospective victims should be warned. Counsel continued to rebuff Smith. Finally, Smith retained counsel and sought to intervene. The case went to the B.C. Trial Division, Court of Appeal, and finally to the Supreme Court of Canada, where it was held that, notwithstanding the privilege that would normally be expected in a situation of this sort, where a mental health professional is retained by counsel to perform an assessment and as a result of that assessment the accused is seen as an imminent threat of serious bodily harm to an identifiable victim or class of victims, the clinician has an obligation to notify whomever, including the police, may be appropriate in the circumstances.

In this instance, Jones had outlined to Smith his detailed plans to kidnap and kill a small prostitute who could be physically overpowered. Jones planned to strangle the victim and dispose of her body in the bush near Hope, B.C. Jones had been diagnosed with multiple paraphilias, including sexual sadism, as well as drug abuse problems.

As a result of this decision, the defence bar is no longer able to rely upon the law of agency or the privilege that would attach to the gathering of information in anticipation of litigation—the solicitor-client brief. The frequency of referrals for assessments is anticipated to plummet, and ironically, it can be argued that the public safety concern driving the decision of the Supreme Court has actually been set back because now the prospectively dangerous accused will not be sent off for assessment by the defence bar unless the assessment is absolutely crucial. It is ironic because this is the clearest statement in Canada of a duty to warn and the decision is based on the principle that concerns about public safety outweigh the interest of doctor-patient confidentiality (Canadian Psychiatric Association, 2000). The Canadian Psychiatric Association (2004) responded to the case of *Smith v. Jones* by concluding that the position about the duty to warn taken by the Supreme Court of Canada is to be accepted as a professional standard of practice.

Prosenjit Poddar was convicted of manslaughter in the death of Tatiana Tarasoff. The court ruled that his therapist, who had become convinced Poddar might harm Tarasoff, should have warned her of the impending danger. AP Worldwide Photos.

A recent 2006 case in Ontario, *Ahmed v. Stefaniu*, has altered the situation in Canada; this case evaluated the duty of psychiatrists to warn and protect (see Glancy & Glancy, 2009) and resulted in the first-ever judgement against a mental health practitioner in Canada for failure to warn and protect. This case was launched by surviving relatives of Roslyn Knipe, including her two young daughters. It was deemed that Dr. Stefaniu was deemed negligent and the plaintiffs were awarded $172,000.

The details of the case are as follows. A man named William Johannes was admitted involuntarily to Scarborough General Hospital in September 1996 after his bizarre behaviour was reported by his sister, Rosyln Knipe. Apparently, Johannes had threatened to harm his sister, whom he lived with, if she did not prove that she was on his side within two weeks. Johannes was admitted to hospital when it was deemed that he was potentially violent and lacked the capacity to consent to treatment. Unfortunately, Johannes did indeed kill his sister by stabbing her to death on January 24, 1997.

Johannes was under the care of Dr. Stefaniu and was a very difficult patient throughout his stay at the hospital. According to Glancy and Glancy (2009), physical restraints were used on him on 25 occasions. They reported that:

In mid-November, security records noted that he attempted to attack two patients. On December 2, 1996, the doctor assessed him and noted that he remained delusional and paranoid. A progress note on December 3, 1996, described him as very angry, loud, and intrusive, with threatening body language in a rigid posture. He was further described as extremely hostile, and on December 4, 1996, he threatened a nurse. It is reported that he became known as an extremely difficult patient. He wandered around naked and habitually sat next to the nursing station preaching loudly. At one point he incited a rebellion, encouraging other patients to refuse their medication. (pp. 250-251).

However, Dr. Stefaniu assessed Johannes on December 4 and found him to be much more cooperative and friendly. Johannes also indicated that he had staged his mental illness. He was released by Dr. Stefaniu the next day when he still appeared to be quite cooperative; however, Johannes refused the doctor's request to continue with voluntary treatment.

According to Glancy and Glancy (2009), when he killed his sister, Johannes appeared to be psychotic and had a delusional rage that included his belief that his sister was possessed by the devil. Later, Johannes was deemed not criminally responsible due to mental disorder and sent to a maximum-security psychiatric hospital.

While the decision seems more than just, several concerns arise from this case. Most notably, advocates have noted that clinicians may now become overcautious. That is, people who have recovered to the point that they should be released will not be released.

TRENDS TOWARD GREATER PROTECTION

We turn now to a discussion of several issues and trends that revolve around the greater protections being provided to mental health patients in recent years: the right to treatment, the right to refuse treatment, and questions of free will in the law. We begin with a discussion of how to resolve complicated situations in which several themes may conflict in efforts to provide humane mental health treatment while respecting individual rights. Competing interests operate to create a complex and continually changing picture.

CHOOSING AMONG ETHICAL PRINCIPLES The ethical code prescribed by the American Psychological Association first appeared in 1953, and it was adopted and used for many years with minor changes by the Canadian Psychological Association and provincial associations (Sinclair, Poizner, Gilmour-Barrett, & Randall, 1987). One factor that provided the impetus for a separate code for Canadian psychologists was dissatisfaction with changes made to the American Psychological Association code in 1979 (see Sinclair, 1993). Specifically, Canadian psychologists were concerned about a change that loosened restrictions on advertising by psychologists. As a result, work was undertaken on a Canadian code of ethics in the 1980s, leading in 1986 to the first Canadian Code of Ethics for Psychologists. The third edition of this code was published in 2000 (Canadian Psychological Association, 2000).

A particularly useful aspect of the Canadian ethics code is that it assists psychologists who must make decisions in situations where various ethics may be in conflict (Sinclair et al., 1987). Psychologists were surveyed about how they would respond to hypothetical scenarios, and the four most relevant principles were identified and rank-ordered by their importance. Following are the four principles:

1. *Respect for the dignity of persons.* This principle is given the most weight, especially when there is the possibility that anyone will be exposed to physical danger.
2. *Responsible caring.* This provision includes the notion that responsible caring occurs only when it is provided by competent individuals who are able to respect the dignity of other people.
3. *Integrity in relationships.* This principle applies to all relationships, but it is noted in the code of ethics that there may be times when a need to be open and candid with an individual may conflict with the need to respect the dignity of others, and if so, the emphasis is on respecting the dignity of others.
4. *Responsibility to society.* The ranking of this ethical principle as the fourth consideration in no way suggests that this is not an important guideline. Rather, the Canadian code emphasizes that when there is a conflict between the needs of the individual and the needs of society, the need to preserve the dignity of the individual should prevail.

The notion of responsibility to society is important because it stipulates that psychologists have a general duty to promote the welfare of human beings and enhance our society. This principle was seen as particularly important by Dobson, Dobson, and Ritchie (1993). In their call for involvement, they observed that

> sustained advocacy by professional psychology on a range of issues linking psychological knowledge, expertise and practice with the public good is both an ethical requirement, particularly from the perspective of social responsibility, as well as a matter of enlightened self-interest. Although there have been some examples of political advocacy, there are other areas in which psychology has been mute or passively acquiescent. The profession requires a system to derive clear and defensible social policy positions as well as the ability to act upon these positions. (p. 451)

The importance of this approach is certainly evident to the many psychology students in Canada who embrace similar values and become actively involved as volunteers in their local communities.

RIGHT TO TREATMENT An aspect of civil commitment that has received the attention of the courts is the so-called right to treatment, a principle first articulated by Birnbaum (1960). If a person is deprived of liberty because he or she is mentally ill and is a danger to self or others, is the state not required to provide treatment to alleviate these problems? Is it not unconstitutional (and even indecent) to incarcerate someone without then providing the required help? Olley, Nicholls, and Brink (2009) expressed their concerns about mentally ill inmates in Canada who are not receiving treatment for their mental illness. Inmates often suffer from profound symptoms of psychopathology and require treatment. Consider, for example, the following case excerpt:

> Shortly before seeing the psychologist, the inmate was seen in his cell jumping off the side of the bed, appearing to be doing back flips, but landing on his head or back and seriously injuring himself. In response, the inmate was moved to an observation cell in the segregation area so that he could be more closely monitored. When assessed by the psychologist, the inmate was asked about his bruising, and stated that he was a Ninja and that he was practicing his moves. The psychologist referred the inmate to see the physician and suggested that a psychiatric consultation be arranged. After two days, the general practitioner (GP) examined the inmate, and recommended that he begin taking medication as a treatment for his condition. The inmate was unwilling to take the medication as he did not want it to interfere with his Ninja training … While waiting for bed space, the inmate continued to refuse medication, and engaged in impulsive, self-injurious behaviour. The inmate's personal hygiene became a concern when he began touching and sitting in his feces. At one point, the inmate was observed by a correctional officer to be holding a blanket over his head. The inmate claimed

that he was "astro-travelling" and needed to protect himself from flying debris, but in fact he was covered in pieces of feces and presented in an increasingly distraught state. The inmate's behaviours raised such concern that, while waiting for a transfer to a specialized forensic psychiatric hospital, the inmate was transferred to a local hospital. In the emergency department, he was assessed briefly and treated with antipsychotic medication. His head and back wounds were assessed and treated, and he was then discharged back to the correctional centre the same day. Once back in the centre, the inmate seemed stabilized temporarily, but he eventually resumed his "Ninja training," this time jumping off the toilet in his segregation cell, and his physical injuries worsened. The correctional centre's mental health professionals were extremely frustrated, as they did not have the authority to provide treatment without the inmate's consent. Their only option was to monitor the inmate's circumstances and work on helping him develop insight into the seriousness of his mental illness, a nearly impossible task under the circumstances. (Olley et al., 2009, p. 812)

Fortunately, according to Olley et al. (2009), an increasing proportion of mentally ill inmates in British Columbia have relatively short wait times and are more likely to access treatment due to cooperation and coordination among prison and mental health agencies, as well as provisions in the B.C. *Mental Health Act* that allow for involuntary treatment for those deemed to require it, unlike in the case excerpt just described. Unfortunately, relatively quick access to treatment for inmates is likely the exception in Canada rather than the norm. However, Olley et al. (2009) noted the need to be careful in determining when treatment can occur against the inmate's will. The right to refuse treatment is another basic right that is discussed in the next section of this chapter.

In *O'Connor v. Donaldson* (1975), a celebrated case in the United States that eventually went to the Supreme Court, a civilly committed mental patient sued two state hospital doctors for his release and for monetary damages on the grounds that he had been incarcerated against his will for 14 years without being treated and without being dangerous to himself or to others. In January 1957, at the age of 49, Kenneth Donaldson had been committed to a Florida state hospital on petition of his father, who felt that his son was delusional. A county judge had found that Donaldson had paranoid schizophrenia and committed him for "care, maintenance, and treatment." The Florida statute then in effect allowed for such commitment on the usual grounds of mental illness and dangerousness, the latter defined as inability to manage property and to protect oneself from being taken advantage of by others.

In 1971, Donaldson sued Dr. O'Connor, the hospital superintendent, and Dr. Gumanis, a hospital psychiatrist, for release. Evidence presented at the trial indicated that the hospital staff could have released Donaldson at any time following a determination that he was not a dangerous person. Testimony

made it clear that at no time during his hospitalization had Donaldson's conduct posed any real danger to others or to himself. The evidence indicated that Donaldson received only custodial care during his hospitalization. No treatment that could conceivably alleviate or cure his assumed mental illness was undertaken. The original trial and a subsequent appeal concluded that Donaldson was not dangerous and had been denied his constitutional right to treatment. Throughout this litigation, Donaldson declared that he was neither dangerous nor mentally ill. But, said his claim, even if he were mentally ill, he should be released because he was not receiving treatment. The U.S. Supreme Court ruled on June 26, 1975, that, "a State cannot constitutionally confine … a nondangerous individual who is capable of surviving safely in freedom by himself or with the help of willing and responsible family members or friends." In 1977, Donaldson settled for $20,000 from Dr. Gumanis and the estate of Dr. O'Connor, who died during the appeals process.

The Supreme Court decision on *O'Connor v. Donaldson* created a stir when it was issued and has since given mental health professionals pause in detaining patients. Although this decision is often cited as an affirmation of the right to treatment, the Supreme Court did not, in fact, rule on the constitutionality of this doctrine. The Donaldson decision did say that a committed patient's status must be periodically reviewed, for the grounds on which a patient was committed cannot be assumed to continue in effect forever. In other words, people can change while in a mental hospital and may no longer require confinement. This position seems straightforward enough, yet it may still be overlooked.

Presumably, a situation such as that found in *O'Connor v. Donaldson* would not occur in Canada since a precondition to civil commitment is a finding of danger to self or others, which is reviewed every 90 days or upon the patient's request.

RIGHT TO REFUSE TREATMENT If a committed patient has the right to expect appropriate treatment, does he or she have the right to refuse treatment or a particular kind of treatment? The answer is yes, depending on the province in question.

The case of *Regina v. Rogers* (1991) in British Columbia reiterated that mentally disordered individuals have the right to refuse treatment, even if they were civilly committed against their personal wishes. Currently, the situation is more complicated when viewed from a national perspective. Douglas and Koch (2001) provided an up-to-date summary of how the right to refuse treatment varies from province to province. Some provinces maintain the patient's right to refuse treatment (e.g., Nova Scotia, Quebec, Ontario, and Manitoba), while others have provisions that allow for treatment without the individual's consent (e.g., Prince Edward Island, Newfoundland and Labrador, New Brunswick, and British Columbia). The situation is more complicated in Alberta, where mental health officials have the opportunity to apply to a review panel in order to override the patient's right to refuse treatment (Douglas & Koch, 2001). Typically, when the patient's right to refuse treatment is circumvented, a substitute decision-maker (e.g., family member) is asked to provide consent.

One alternative in provinces where a person can be given treatment without his or her consent is to have the person outline his or her wishes during a time when he or she was of sounder mind. According to Simmie and Nunes (2001), this concept is known as establishing a person's **prior capable wish** and this wish has been ruled valid in court cases in both Canada and the United States.

In Ontario, patients can be treated against their will civilly only where they are determined to be incapable of consent. In such cases, a scheme exists whereby substitute consent to treatment may be obtained. A potentially more interesting question arises around patients who do consent to treatment. Curiously, the issue of capacity to consent is rarely raised where the patient does consent to treatment. What percentage of those patients currently being treated "voluntarily" are actually incapable of consenting to their treatment?

In the case of *Starson v. Swayze* (2003), the Supreme Court of Canada confirmed the patient's right to refuse treatment. This remarkable case is the subject of Canadian Perspectives 18.2.

CANADIAN PERSPECTIVES 18.2
"A BEAUTIFUL MIND" IN CANADA? SCOTT STARSON AND THE RIGHT TO REFUSE TREATMENT

In some respects, Scott Starson is similar to John Nash, who was the subject of the book *A Beautiful Mind* by Sylvia Nasar and the subsequent Academy Award-winning movie starring Russell Crowe. Nash won a Nobel Prize in Economics for his contribution to game theory. He has a history of schizophrenia. Starson is a highly intelligent person with an abiding interest and expertise in physics as it pertains to the study of discrete anti-gravity and its implications for space travel.

Starson, who prefers to be referred to as Professor Starson, has authored some highly regarded articles in scientific journals despite not having any formal training in physics and not being an actual professor. Starson suffers from schizoaffective disorder, a condition that combines symptoms of schizophrenia and bipolar disorder. In 1998, he was found not criminally responsible on account of mental disorder after uttering death threats. Specifically, he phoned his work colleagues and informed them that he was in a phone booth with a rifle and was going to shoot the sales manager of a car dealership where he had been turned down for a lease or loan (Wente, 2003). He also threatened to kill his psychiatrist (Bailey, 2002).

Starson is an involuntary psychiatric patient who has been detained in psychiatric hospitals in Penetanguishene and Ottawa and has experienced mental difficulties since 1985. There is no doubt that he suffers from mental illness. According to one interview account, he indicated that "Pope John Paul II works for me now." He also indicated that he had plans to wed comedian Joan Rivers, though he had never met her. He also believes that the late Prime Minister Pierre Elliott Trudeau was killed by an alien (see Bailey, 2003).

Starson gained notoriety for successfully winning a legal case in which his right to refuse treatment was upheld by the Supreme Court of Canada in a six-to-three decision. He argued that the medication was ineffective and would take away his mental faculties. In his statement to the Court of Appeal for Ontario, he observed:

Well, like all psychiatrists that I've met before them, they all think the same way, that the only thing they can do is to give

Scott Starson is a physics savant. CP Image Archive/*Toronto Star*.

you these chemicals—and I've been through these chemicals that they propose before—and I know the effects and what they want to achieve is slow down my brain, basically, and to slow down my brain which means I can't do what I've been trying to do—or what I have been doing for 30 years and will be successful at doing. And that would just be like worse than death.

In its ruling, the Supreme Court supported the ruling of two previous courts that had overturned the initial ruling of the Ontario Consent and Capacity Board (CCB), which ruled that Starson did not have the right to refuse treatment. The Supreme Court based its decision on the observation that the Ontario CCB based its initial ruling on what the board felt was in the best treatment interests of Starson rather than on a strict interpretation of his legal rights (see Brooks, O'Reilly, & Gray, 2003). It is still the case that patients have the right to refuse treatment if they are deemed to be capable of making this decision, but if it can be shown that they are incapacitated based on "a balance of probabilities," then treatment can be forced on them (Brooks et al., 2003).

Regardless of whether one agrees with the Supreme Court decision, it is hard not to feel sorry for Starson's mother, Jeanne Stevens. According to Bailey (2003), she wants her son to receive treatment and, in reaction to the court decision, she stated, "I'm devastated. I don't think what they did was a humane judgement. It's a disaster because they have destroyed his life and his dream."

Starson has acknowledged his mental problems, but he noted that he distrusts psychiatry, which he views as a religion. A year after winning the right to refuse treatment, Starson almost died. He became delusional and refused all offers of food and water due to his fear of being poisoned. According to a Canadian Press article (2006), Starson was granted a transfer to Toronto after finally agreeing to take his medication. Overall, Starson went seven years without treatment, and in a recent overview article, Gray and O'Reilly (2009) strongly criticized a legal situation that they characterized as incarcerating a person with a mental illness in a hospital because treatment could not be provided.

By the way, Starson's original surname is Schutzman. According to his mother, he changed it in 1993 because "he actually thought he was the son of the stars."

The evidence summarized by Gray and O'Reilly (2009) further illustrates the severe degree of mental illness experienced by Starson. He claimed at various times to be a world-class skier and arm wrestler, the creator of the CN Tower, and the greatest scientist in the world; he also claimed to be in regular communication with extraterrestrials.

What has happened more recently? Starson improved and was discharged in July 2007, but he deteriorated and was rehospitalized in October 2007 and again in March 2008 (Gray & O'Reilly, 2009). He was again returned to the community, but as of May 2009, he was in a secure unit at CAMH in Toronto (Tyler, 2009, L4).

Thinking Critically

1. Do you agree or disagree with the Supreme Court decision? Should Starson have the right to refuse treatment?
2. The decision was based on a strict interpretation of Starson's legal rights. What about the feelings and wishes of Starson's mother? Does she have any right to support forced treatment? Was the court's decision inhumane?
3. Are there any circumstances when it is in society's best interests for a person to be treated against his or her will?

Opponents of the right to refuse treatment are concerned that mental hospitals will revert to being warehouses of poorly treated patients. Psychiatrists fear that lawyers and judges will not accept that some people are too mentally ill to be believed, or too mentally disturbed to be able to make sound judgements about their treatment. In a book on what he calls America's mental health crisis, psychiatrist E. Fuller Torrey asserts that upwards of 90% of psychotic patients have no insight into their condition. Believing that they do not need any treatment, they subject themselves and loved ones to sometimes desperate and frightening situations by refusing medication or other modes of therapy, most of which involve hospitalization (Torrey, 1996).

DEINSTITUTIONALIZATION, CIVIL LIBERTIES, AND MENTAL HEALTH

Since the 1960s, provinces throughout Canada have embarked on a policy of deinstitutionalization, discharging as many patients as possible from mental hospitals and discouraging admissions. The maxim is now "Treat them in the community," the assumption being that virtually anything is preferable to institutionalization.

Barnes and Toews (1983) assessed deinstitutionalization in Canada and concluded that it had occurred at the same rate in Canada as in the United States. They cited a 1974 study that indicated that there was a 43% reduction in the number of patients in public mental institutions between 1960 and 1972, as well as a 1979 Statistics Canada report showing a decrease by 50% in the number of beds in institutions. Barnes

and Toews also noted that patients fare no worse in the community than in an institution, with the vital provision that this depended substantially on the quality of care and provisions for care made available when people were released to the community. Research studies on care in the hospital vs. care in the home in Montreal (e.g., Fenton, Tessier, & Streuning, 1979) and in Vancouver (Goodacre et al., 1975) yielded few differences. Other research suggests that the quality of life can even be significantly better in the community (Lord & Pedlar, 1991), but Canadian investigators continue to emphasize that the quality and availability of aftercare is a vital consideration (e.g., Lesage & Morissette, 1993). Ideally, most discharged people will get into highly supervised settings, as was shown to be the case in a study conducted in Quebec. Lesage et al. (2000) found that long-stay patients released from Canada's largest psychiatric hospital (the Louis-H Lafontaine Hospital) were not abandoned.

Deinstitutionalization is a phenomenon that has taken place across Canada. Simmie and Nunes (2001) observed:

New Brunswick recently demolished its oldest psychiatric hospital, and former residents are now doing well in the community. Many of these people have spent years, even decades, on the inside. "I never thought that some of the people coming out would make it," says the director of a community mental health centre in Fredericton, "but in fact their needs have declined." (p. 162)

But what is this community that former mental hospital patients are supposed to find more helpful to them on discharge? Facilities outside hospitals are often not prepared to cope with the influx of these patients. Some promising programs were described in Chapter 11, but these are very much the exception, not the rule. The state of affairs in many large metropolitan areas is an unrelenting social crisis, for hundreds of thousands of chronically ill mental health patients across North America were released without sufficient job training and without community services to help them. It is doubtful, too, that deinstitutionalization reduced the rate of chronic mental illness. As Gralnick (1987) argued, acutely ill persons are largely neglected because it is difficult to commit them unless they are found to be a danger to themselves and others, a state that can take years to develop; by that time, their problems may have become chronic and more difficult to deal with. The irony is that deinstitutionalization may be contributing to the very problem it was designed to alleviate: chronic mental illness.

Indeed, deinstitutionalization may be a misnomer. *Trans*institutionalization may be more apt, for declines in the census of public mental hospitals have occasioned increases in the numbers of mentally ill people in jails, prisons, nursing homes, and the mental health departments of non-psychiatric hospitals (e.g., Cloud, 1999), and these settings are often not equipped to handle the particular needs of mental health patients. The oft-mentioned revolving door was seen in the increase in readmission rates, from 25% before the deinstitutionalization movement to around 80% by the 1980s (Paul & Menditto, 1992).

In late 2004, Ontario Superior Court Justice Robert Desmarais (see Rupert, 2005), in a landmark ruling intended to be binding on all Ontario courts, ruled there was no legal authority to jail mentally ill people pending in-custody forensic assessments and indicated that jailing them violated their *Charter of Rights* guarantees not to be arbitrarily detained. Although the Ontario health ministry announced an infusion of money to deal with these individuals, the government had not increased the beds within the six-month period ordered by the judge. Then-Health Minister George Smitherman had admitted that there had been a 27% increase in the number of mentally ill people incarcerated in correctional facilities in Ontario between 1995 and 2005. Subsequently, The Right Honourable Beverley McLachlin, as Chief Justice of the Supreme Court of Canada, lamented the fact that the courts and judges are facing a crisis because community-based care has never been properly funded (see Bailey & Bronskill, 2006). The Chief Justice was encouraged by steps such as mental health courts in Ontario and New Brunswick designed to divert the mentally ill from jail into treatment programs. However, Justice Richard Schneider, who presides over Canada's first mental health court at Old City Hall in Toronto, has stated that the government needs to involve fewer mentally ill people in the criminal justice system or provide more beds for assessment and treatment (*Toronto*

Star, 2005). The mentally ill are ending up in the criminal courts in unprecedented numbers. Schneider (2000) previously reported that across Canada the number of mentally disordered accused coming before provincial review boards has been increasing at a minimum of 10% per year since the early 1990s, while overall prosecution rates have been decreasing. It may be naive to expect that the community from which the mentally disordered individual came is the one best suited to provide support and treatment.

Many patients discharged from mental hospitals are eligible for social benefits, but a large number are not receiving this assistance. Financial and occupational concerns are very salient. A qualitative study examined the deinstitutionalization experience and the issues that faced 139 people who were previously institutionalized in Eastern Canada (Herman & Smith, 1989). Six significant themes emerged: (1) stigmatization of people with a history of mental illness, (2) an absence of basic living skills, (3) poor housing, (4) poverty, (5) difficulties getting a job, and (6) difficulties accessing aftercare programs.

Homeless persons do not have fixed addresses and need help in establishing eligibility and residency for the purpose of receiving benefits. Nowadays, especially in larger cities, it is common to see people who have been discharged from psychiatric hospitals living in the streets, in train and bus terminals, in abandoned buildings, on subways, and in shelters operated by public agencies, churches, and charitable organizations. In Toronto alone, there are about 25,000 such people (Goering et al., 2000), and comparable situations exist in other major cities throughout Canada. The lives of these individuals are desperate.

The Honourable Mr. Justice Richard Schneider, the judge at Canada's first mental health court in Toronto, is also trained as a clinical psychologist. He is a tireless advocate for the psychiatric assessment and treatment of mentally ill people who come before the courts. Courtesy of The Honourable Mr. Justice Richard Schneider.

Homelessness and mental illness is receiving increasing attention in Canada. The links between homelessness and mental illness have been extensively documented. A study of homelessness in Toronto found that approximately two thirds of the 300 people assessed had lifetime diagnoses of mental illness (Tolomiczenko & Goering, 1998). Moreover, two thirds of the participants had some form of substance abuse. Stuart and Arboleda-Florez (2000) assessed homeless shelter users in Calgary and found that approximately one third had a significant mental health problem and that the lifetime prevalence of alcohol abuse was 33.6%. Greater psychiatric problems were associated with a wider range of hardships, health risks, victimization, negative life events (including economic problems), and a sense of dissatisfaction. A major catalyst for social action was the recent Canadian Institute for Health Information (CIHI, 2007) report simply titled *Mental Health and Homelessness*. Key conclusions reached include the following:

1. Homelessness influences more than 10,000 people on any given night in Canada. Certain groups are over-represented (e.g., Aboriginal people), but homelessness is not restricted to any one group.

2. Numerous pathways link mental health and homelessness. The notion that there are many different routes to homelessness for those suffering from mental illness was confirmed recently by a narrative study of the lives of 12 homeless people (Kirkpatrick & Byrne, 2009). Some individuals are homeless and suffering mental distress due to housing or employment issues, for instance, while, with others, homelessness is an outgrowth of personal adjustment issues involving mental illness and substance use and misuse.

3. Clearly, mental illness, addictions, and suicidal behaviours are more predominant among the homeless, and this often is a reflection of low perceived self-worth and low social support.

4. More adaptive for those facing mental illness and homelessness is coping that involves distancing oneself from stressors rather than active problem-solving.

National initiatives are underway in Canada. Stephen Gaetz from York University has led the development of the Homelessness Research Network, which seeks to connect and support researchers across Canada who are studying homelessness. Gaetz and his associates have also created the Homeless Hub (www.homelesshub.ca). This is described as the world's first digital hub designed to mobilize homelessness research. It supports collaboration and public engagement with research networks in Canada.

The Canadian Mental Health Commission launched a massive project on homelessness and mental illness in November 2009 (see www.mentalhealthcommission.ca).

This project, called "At Home," involves pilot projects in five cities (Montreal, Toronto, Vancouver, Winnipeg, and Moncton). The goal of this work is to find sustainable solutions for homeless people with mental health issues. A key element of this groundbreaking effort is providing homes to more than half of the 2,285 Canadians taking part in this study.

Homelessness applies to men, women, girls, and boys. Homeless people, especially women, are likely victims of violence and rape, even when living in shelters for the homeless (D'Ercole & Struening, 1990). Children are also found among the homeless population. These youngsters are forced to live their formative years in chaotic and dangerous situations, with parents under severe stress. It comes as no surprise that these children are often subjected to abuse and many drop out of school and suffer from anxiety, depression, and substance abuse.

In light of these observations and findings, do such challenging conditions justify reversing the policy of deinstitutionalization? In our view, no, because the problem lies with the failure of communities to provide suitable living and rehabilitation conditions, an issue discussed earlier in this book. There are, however, signs that the pendulum may begin to swing back in the direction of more involuntary hospitalization, even when the person does not pose a real danger to his- or herself or to others but is wandering homeless on the streets and living in squalor. Being "persistently and acutely disabled" is, in some United States jurisdictions, replacing "being a danger to oneself or to others" (Shogren, 1994). It remains to be seen how this trend will develop in light of laws and court rulings that have been making it more and more difficult to keep people institutionalized against their will. In an interesting twist, it was reported recently (Fong, 2007) that the Mayor of Vancouver wanted to re-institutionalize some former residents of Riverview Hospital in suburban Coquitlam who ended up in Vancouver's Downtown Eastside where housing is generally unavailable and drugs are readily available. It is estimated that about 40% of the homeless people in B.C.'s Lower Mainland are mentally ill. Riverview once held about 5,000 patients, but, as a result of deinstitutionalization, the number dwindled to about 400 people. The mayor proposed new modern spaces that would provide support rather than a return to old-style locked wards.

Some people fear that individuals with schizophrenia are increasingly being seen as misfits, drug abusers, and panhandlers rather than as ill people in need of professional care. Canadian Perspectives 18.3 describes some recommended solutions to the problems of deinstitutionalization in Canada as well as general recommendations about addressing mental illness among Canadians.

CANADIAN PERSPECTIVES 18.3
SOLUTIONS TO THE CONSEQUENCES OF DEINSTITUTIONALIZATION IN CANADA

"Whether it's a friend, a colleague or someone living in a bus shelter, there are really only eight kinds of people affected by mental health problems: Someone's mother, daughter, sister or wife; someone's father, husband, brother or son. People. Like me."

—Scott Simmie, October 10, 1998, author of the Atkinson Fellowship investigation into mental health, published as the eight-part "Out of Mind" series in the Toronto Star *(October 3–10, 1998). Simmie has suffered from bipolar disorder.*

In the spring of 1998, two investigative reporters for the *Toronto Star*, Donovan Vincent and Theresa Boyle, wrote a seven-part series (entitled "Madness") that was based on their investigations of the human tragedy of mental illness. Later, in the fall of 1998, Scott Simmie, winner of the Atkinson Fellowship in Public Policy, wrote an eight-part *Toronto Star* series (entitled "Out of Mind") that was based on his year-long exploration of mental health reform. More recently, in June 2008, an influential series on mental health issues and the mental health system in Canada called "Breakdown" appeared in the *Globe and Mail*. It featured the work of award-winning reporter André Picard, whose contributions in highlighting key issues have been widely acknowledged. For instance, he was awarded the Humanitarian of the Year Award from the Canadian Psychological Association in 2009. Each series of articles concluded with long lists of recommendations and steps that should be taken for the benefit of people with serious and chronic mental illness. In our opinion, these series have covered the issues in a constructive, responsible, and fair way.

Scott Simmie, author of the "Out of Mind" series about the plight of the mentally ill. His investigations led to many proposed and implemented solutions to the consequences of deinstitutionalization. © *Toronto Star.*

In the final segment of his own series, Simmie prefaced his proposed solutions in a poignant way:

Today is World Mental Health Day. Its theme: human rights and mental health. As a country, we love to talk about human rights and point an admonishing finger abroad when we see things we don't like. It's time we looked closer to home. We are abusing the human rights of many of our citizens. People stricken with serious and chronic mental health problems. We marginalize them in every way. We abandon them as friends, avoid them on the street. And we provide them with income supports that keep them in second-hand clothes—at best. But our greatest shame is our failure to supply the most fundamental need of any human being. A home. That's where true mental health reform must begin …. Drugs are critical for schizophrenia—but the best medication means nothing if your home is a bus shelter. (Simmie, 1998, October 10)

Steps to Take

Boyle and Vincent (1998) and Simmie (1998) listed steps that must be taken in Ontario to help people with serious and chronic mental health problems. Most of their recommendations can be applied right across Canada. Throughout this section, we use the preferred term for current and former psychiatric patients, as determined by the patients and former patients themselves: "consumers/survivors." Consistent with the changes associated with the "new CAMH" described in Chapter 11, we also accept "client" as a preferred term. The following is an integrated list of the steps, plus some additional recommendations:

- Reinvestment of funds (approximately $400 million in 1998) into community mental health services (such as crisis centres, crisis lines, and child and adolescent programs). In particular, there is a need for 80 assertive-community response teams. This reinvestment would not only be humane, there would be substantial cost savings coupled with a reduction of disability and mortality.
- Review of and changes to the *Mental Health Act* consistent with change from the old and outdated "institutional model" to a "community-oriented system" model.
- A variety of supportive housing, ranging from independent apartments to group homes, coupled with monitoring of standards and maintenance, particularly for boarding homes and rooming houses. At least 14,000 units are needed.
- An expanded home care program for people with serious mental disorders. (This recommendation is, of course, consistent with the recommendation of the Romanow Report and Kirby Report summarized in Chapter 1.)
- Community mental health centres as standard access points to the mental health "system" where people can receive on-site assistance and appropriate referrals. Consumer/survivor advocates would be a part of multidisciplinary teams.

- Incentives to adequately staff provincial psychiatric hospitals (professional as well as support staff), especially those slated for closure.
- Development, evaluation, and implementation of risk assessment tools for forensic patients to facilitate the best use of resources and bed space.
- Opening of additional forensic beds for mentally ill offenders, to eliminate the problem of the mentally ill being incarcerated in jails.
- Diversion of the mentally ill from the criminal justice system if possible, as well as the hiring of additional mental health workers in jails.
- Community treatment orders should be a last resort.
- The most effective (but sometimes most expensive) medications for schizophrenia should be available as "first-line" treatment.
- Increased emphasis on early detection and treatment of mental disorders in children. Emphasis on "defragmenting" children's services should have high priority.
- More non-medical safe houses for people in crisis, patterned after Toronto's Gerstein Centre.
- Government-established 24-hour information/crisis lines staffed by consumers/survivors who are trained to refer people to appropriate resources.
- Expansion of consumer/survivor alternative businesses to provide work and "restore dignity and hope" to former psychiatric patients (survivors). For example, the Ontario Council of Alternative Businesses helps consumers/survivors initiate and operate businesses, such as A-Way Express, a courier service. Fresh Start, another example, is a cleaning and maintenance company staffed and run by psychiatric survivors.
- Development of alternative payment schemes that will encourage psychiatrists to treat people with severe, persistent mental illnesses. Awareness by psychiatrists of, and referral to where appropriate, all the services and resources in their local community. General practitioners (usually the initial point of contact) should consult actively with psychiatrists.
- Support for anti-stigma campaigns by the Ministry of Health or Health Canada, in consultation with the Canadian Mental Health Association.
- Support on the part of employers for employees with mental health problems.
- Increased training for the police in ways to deal with the mentally ill, including alternative "use of force" strategies to prevent the deaths of psychotic individuals.
- Appropriate contextual statements in all news stories linking violence and mental illness, since the seriously mentally ill are responsible for only 4% of the violence in society.

Sources: This section was adapted primarily from Boyle and Vincent (1998) and Simmie (1998).

Changes?

These series of carefully researched, thoughtful, provocative, and timely articles on mental health have garnered tremendous public support and sympathy for consumers/survivors. They compelled various levels of government to begin to make many of the proposed changes, at least as pilot projects, and forced an ongoing consideration and evaluation of other options. The following are some of the positive changes that are already affecting the treatment of serious and chronic mental illness in our society:

- The creation of the restructured and integrated Centre for Addiction and Mental Health
- Diversion of the mentally ill from jails through the establishment of special courts and judges with special training (Ontario Court of Justice mental health court)
- Expansion of the assertive-response team program
- Expanded training of the police, such as the creation of special teams that include social workers riding in the patrol cars
- Creation of additional forensic beds in Toronto
- Input on the part of stakeholders, including consumers/survivors, into the final legislation creating community treatment orders
- Creation of anti-stigma campaigns
- Additional government funding targeted to community supports
- Promises of funding for supportive housing

As noted in Chapter 1, one of the most vexing remaining problems is the shortage of mental health professionals in many regions of Canada. For example, the Canadian Psychiatric Association recommends one psychiatrist for every 8,400 citizens. In 2005, in the region of Peel, in the Greater Toronto Area, with a population of 1.5 million, there were only 54 psychiatrists instead of the recommended 130 (see Ogilvie, 2007). Although there should be 30 child psychiatrists for the region's 300,000 children, it's estimated that there are fewer than 10. Toronto currently has 500 more psychiatrists than the recommended number. In its 2007 annual Report on Ontario's Health System, the Ontario Health Quality Council (2007) discussed the shortage of health care professionals in Ontario and described mental health as one of the most severely under-resourced areas of health care.

Award-winning author and advocate André Picard has been highly effective in highlighting mental health issues in Canada. He was awarded the Humanitarian of the Year Award in 2009 by the Canadian Psychological Association. Photo Courtesy of André Picard.

Space limitations preclude a comprehensive discussion of the suggestions provided more recently by André Picard, and there is considerable overlap with some issues already raised, so we will simply list the most salient themes without extensive discussion. Picard outlined a 12-step program that he prefaced with the observation that Canada's mental health system is not really a system; rather, it is a patchwork that has left up to 3 million afflicted Canadians "to the shadows" (Picard, 2008). Here are the 12 steps proposed:

1. Commit to a national mental-health plan—now
2. Conduct public education campaigns to combat stigma
3. Create a $10-billion, national mental-health fund
4. Set up community treatment programs in every health district
5. Build tens of thousands of supportive housing units
6. Double the amount Canada spends on research
7. Establish mental-health courts in every province
8. Set up advisory groups to represent affected families in every district
9. Implement early-intervention programs in all schools
10. Push the business community to lead the way on workplace support
11. Radically reduce wait times for both emergency and therapeutic care
12. Invest in peer-support groups

Picard and others at *The Globe and Mail* have continued to highlight mental health issues and the stories of people living with mental illness in Canada.

Thinking Critically

1. Some recommendations in this section have already been implemented, but the majority have not. Review the proposed steps and choose the five recommendations that you consider to be most critical. Explain why you chose them. Outline a plan for implementing your recommendations.
2. What steps do you believe will be most difficult to gain acceptance for—from politicians, practitioners, and possibly the consumers/survivors themselves?
3. What would you do to increase the number of qualified mental health practitioners in under-serviced regions of Canada?

ETHICAL DILEMMAS IN THERAPY AND RESEARCH

In this textbook, we have examined a variety of theories and a multitude of data that focus on what is and what is thought to be. Ethics and values, often embodied in laws, are a different order of discussion. They concern what ought to be, having sometimes little to do with what is. It is extremely important to recognize the difference.

Within a given scientific paradigm, we are able to examine what we believe is reality. As the study of philosophy and ethics reveals, however, the statements people have made for thousands of years about what should be are another matter. The Ten Commandments are such statements. They are prescriptions and proscriptions about human conduct.

The legal trends reviewed thus far place limits on the activities of mental health professionals. These legal constraints are important, for laws are one of society's strongest means of encouraging all of us to behave in certain ways. Mental health professionals also have professional and ethical constraints. All professional groups promulgate "shoulds" and "should nots," and by guidelines and mandates, they limit to some degree what therapists and researchers should do with their patients, clients, and research participants. Courts, too, have ruled on some of these questions. Most of the time what we believe is unethical is also illegal, but sometimes existing laws are in conflict with our moral sense of right and wrong. We examine now the ethics of making psychological inquiries and interventions into the lives of other human beings.

ETHICAL RESTRAINTS ON RESEARCH

Basic to the nature of science is the saying "What can be done will usually be attempted." The most reprehensible ethical insensitivity was evidenced in the brutal experiments conducted by German physicians on concentration camp prisoners during the Second World War. One experiment, for example, investigated how long people lived when their heads were bashed repeatedly with a heavy stick. Even if important information might be obtained from this kind of experiment, such actions violate our sense of decency and morality. The Nuremberg Trials, conducted by the Allies following the war, brought these experiments and other barbarisms to light and meted out severe punishment to some of the soldiers, physicians, and Nazi officials who had engaged in or contributed to such actions, even when they claimed that they had merely been following orders. It would be reassuring to be able to say that such gross violations of human decency take place only during incredible and cruel epochs, such as the Third Reich, but unfortunately, this is not the case. Spurred on by a blind enthusiasm for their work, researchers have sometimes dealt with human subjects in reproachable ways.

Henry K. Beecher, a research professor at Harvard Medical School, surveyed medical research from 1946 to 1965 and found that "many of the patients [used as subjects in experiments] never had the risk satisfactorily explained to them, and ... further hundreds have not known that they were the subjects of an experiment although grave consequences have been suffered as the direct result" (1966, p. 1354). Half a century later, in January 1994, prompted by the work of Eileen Welsome, a journalist who won a Pulitzer Prize for her investigative reporting on the issue, the U.S. Energy Department began to publicize numerous experiments conducted in the 1950s through the 1970s that had exposed hundreds of people—usually without their informed consent or prior knowledge—to harmful doses of radiation. There was particular concern over the fact that the overwhelming majority were people of low socio-economic status, members

The Nuremberg Trials. Liaison Agency Inc.

of racial minorities, people with mental retardation, nursing home patients, or prisoners. The scientists, for the most part supported in their research with federal funds, clearly understood that the risks were great, even though relatively little was known about the harmful effects of radiation at the time, for, as was pointed out by a lawyer arguing for compensation for some of the subjects, "they were doing it to poor and black people. You didn't see them doing it at the Mayo Clinic" (as quoted in Healy, 1994). Some of these experiments involved giving women in the third trimester of pregnancy a radioactive tonic to determine safe levels of exposure and irradiating the testicles of prisoners to find out the degree of radiation that service personnel could endure without negative effects on sperm production. It is particularly troubling that these studies took place many years after the Nuremberg Trials.

The training of scientists equips them splendidly to pose interesting questions, sometimes even important ones, and to design research that is as free as possible of confounding elements. They have no special qualifications, however, for deciding whether a particular line of inquiry that involves humankind should be followed. Society needs knowledge, and a scientist has a right in a democracy to seek that knowledge. However, the ordinary citizens employed as participants in experiments must be protected from harm, risk, humiliation, and invasion of privacy.

Several international codes of ethics pertain to the conduct of scientific research: the Nuremberg Code formulated in 1947 in the aftermath of the Nazi war-crime trials, the 1964 Declaration of Helsinki, and statements from the British Medical Research Council. As for Canada, Young (1998) noted that medical research (including psychiatric investigations) in this country is governed by four documents: the Nuremberg Code, the Declaration of Helsinki, the Medical Research Council of Canada document *Guidelines on Research Involving Human Subjects* (1987), and the Tri-Council Working Group on Ethics (1997) document *Ethical Conduct for Research Involving Humans* (final report). The three councils that compose the Tri-Council Working Group are the Medical Research Council of Canada (MRC), the Natural Sciences and Engineering Research Council of Canada (NSERC), and the Social Sciences and Humanities Research Council of Canada (SSHRC).

In 1974, the U.S. Department of Health, Education, and Welfare began to issue guidelines and regulations governing scientific research that employs human and animal subjects. In addition, a blue-ribbon panel, the National Commission for the Protection of Human Subjects of Biomedical and Behavioral Research, issued a report in 1978 that arose from hearings and inquiries into restrictions that the U.S. government might impose on research performed with prisoners, children, and patients in psychiatric institutions. These various codes and principles are continually re-evaluated and revised as new challenges are posed to the research community.

For the past 30 years, the proposals of behavioural researchers, many of whom conduct experiments related to psychopathology and therapy, have been reviewed for safety and general ethical propriety by institutional review boards in hospitals, universities, and research institutes. Such committees—and this is significant—comprise not only behavioural scientists but also citizens from the community, lawyers, students, and specialists in a variety of disciplines, such as professors of English, history, and comparative religion. They are able to block any research proposal or require questionable aspects to be modified if, in their collective judgement, the research would put participants at too great a risk. Such committees also now pass judgement on the scientific merits of proposals, the rationale being that it is not ethical to recruit participants for studies that will not yield valid data (e.g., Capron, 1999).

Changes in the Declaration of Helsinki are being debated, driven by two developments in biomedical research. The first is an increase in research sponsored by for-profit organizations such as pharmaceutical companies. Faced with fierce competition and marketplace pressures to maximize profits, such companies may push for research that would not be approved by human subjects committees in non-profit organizations such as universities. This issue came to a head when the International Committee of Medical Journal Editors (ICMJE), a group that includes the *Canadian Medical Association Journal* (CMAJ), issued an extensive set of rules and new policies that will govern the publication of results in major journals (see CMAJ, 2001b). A CMAJ editorial on this issue stated:

> Henceforth, these 11 leading journals will require authors to attest that they "had full access to all of the data in study and … take complete responsibility for the integrity of the data and the accuracy of the data analysis." In addition, editors will retain the right to review the study protocol as well as funding contracts for the study before accepting the paper for publication. CMAJ will not accept reports on research that was conducted under a contractual arrangement that did not meet these ethical standards. (CMAJ, 2001b, p. 733)

This position was reached in response to concerns that results could have been altered or even suppressed if the findings did not yield the results anticipated by the funding body.

The internationalization of research is a second factor in the possible attenuation of protection of human subjects. Developing countries are particularly eager for partnerships in research and do not always have the same historical commitment to individual informed consent and safety that is prevalent in more industrialized and democratic countries. A possible danger is that utilitarian standards (e.g., will the research yield generally useful results?) are becoming more important than the focus of the past half-century on the rights and safety of individual research participants.

In reaction to some ethical lapses in hospital-based research with mental health patients, the National Bioethics Advisory Commission recommends special precautions to ensure that research subjects with mental illness fully understand the risks and benefits of any research they are asked to participate in and that particular care be taken to make certain that they can decline or withdraw from research without feeling coerced. Specifically, instead of simply allowing a guardian or family member to make the decision for the patient, the commission proposes that a health professional who has nothing to do with the particular study make a judgement on whether a given patient can give informed consent. The commission recommends also that if a guardian is allowed to give consent on behalf of a patient judged incompetent to do so, then the guardian's own ability to give consent must be evaluated (Capron, 1999).

INFORMED CONSENT

This concern about conducting research with mental health patients underscores the all-important concept of **informed consent**. Just as committed mental health patients are gaining some right to refuse treatment, so may anyone refuse to be a participant in an experiment. The investigator must provide enough information to enable people to judge whether they want to accept any risks inherent in being a participant. Prospective participants must be legally capable of giving consent, and there must be no deceit or coercion in obtaining it. Furthermore, those who begin to participate as research subjects are free to withdraw at any time without fear of penalty.

Much research is relatively innocuous, but what if the experiment poses real risks, such as ingesting a drug, or what if a patient with schizophrenia whose condition has improved by taking a drug is withdrawn from it so that the investigator can assess the effects of "drug washout"? Or what if the prospective participant is a committed mental patient, or a child with mental retardation, unable to understand fully what is being asked? Such a person may not feel free or even be able to refuse participation. Although research shows that even committed patients with schizophrenia may be competent to understand and participate in treatment decisions, the degree of coercion that is part and parcel of being in a hospital setting must not be overlooked.

A further complication is that it is not always easy to demonstrate that a researcher has obtained informed consent. In an elaborate study, Stuart (1978) discovered that most college students could not accurately describe a simple experiment, even though it had just been explained to them and they had agreed to participate. A signature on a consent form is no assurance that informed consent has been obtained, which poses a challenge to investigators and members of review panels who are committed to upholding codes of ethics governing participation of human subjects in research.

Such problems are especially pronounced in clinical settings where patients may or may not understand the nature of antipsychotic medication. Irwin et al. (1985) found that although most patients said they understood the benefits and side effects of their drugs, only a quarter of them could actually demonstrate such understanding when queried specifically. Simply reading information to hospitalized patients—especially the more disturbed ones—is no guarantee that they fully comprehend; therefore, informed consent may not have been obtained. The report of the National Bioethics Advisory Commission pointed to many published experiments involving mental health patients in which no effort was made to determine whether the research participants had the decision-making capacity to give informed consent (Capron, 1999).

Still, as with the right to refuse treatment, there is recognition that being judged mentally ill—more specifically, being diagnosed with schizophrenia and being hospitalized—does not necessarily mean being incapable of giving informed consent. An experiment by Grisso and Applebaum (1991) found that although patients with schizophrenia on average understood issues relating to treatment involving medication less well than non-psychiatric patients did, there was a wide range of understanding among the patients; in fact, the understanding of some was as good as that of non-psychiatric patients. These results suggest that it is important to examine each person individually for ability to give informed consent, rather than assume that a person is unable to do so by virtue of being hospitalized.

CONFIDENTIALITY AND PRIVILEGED COMMUNICATION

When an individual consults a physician, psychiatrist, or clinical psychologist, he or she is assured by professional ethics codes that what goes on in the session will remain confidential. **Confidentiality** means that nothing will be revealed to a third party, except to other professionals and those intimately involved in the treatment, such as a nurse or medical secretary.

A privileged communication goes even further. It is communication between parties in a confidential relationship that is protected by law. The recipient of such a communication cannot legally be compelled to disclose it as a witness. The right of privileged communication is a major exception to the access that courts have to evidence in judicial proceedings. Society believes that in the long term the interests of people are best served if communications to a spouse and to certain professionals remain off limits to the prying eyes and ears of the police, judges, and prosecutors. The privilege applies to such relationships as those between husband and wife, physician and patient, pastor and penitent, attorney and client, and psychologist and patient. The legal expression is that the patient or client "holds the privilege," which means that only he or she may release the other person to disclose confidential information in a legal proceeding.

There are important limits to a client's right of privileged communication, however. For example, according to the current California psychology licensing law (similar elements are present in other state and provincial laws), this right is eliminated for any of the following reasons:

- The client has accused the therapist of malpractice. In such a case, the therapist can divulge information about the therapy in order to defend himself or herself in any legal action initiated by the client.
- The client is less than 16 years old and the therapist has reason to believe that the child has been a victim of a crime such as child abuse. In fact, the psychologist is required to report to the police or to a child welfare agency within 36 hours any suspicion he or she has that the child client has been physically abused, including any suspicion of sexual molestation.
- The client initiated therapy in hopes of evading the law for having committed a crime or for planning to do so.
- The therapist judges that the client is a danger to self or to others and disclosure of information is necessary to ward off such danger (recall Focus on Discovery 18.2 on Tarasoff).

In Canada, as seen in the Supreme Court of Canada's decision in *Smith v. Jones*, even formally privileged solicitor-client relationships may be pierced where an individual is seen by a consulting mental health practitioner to constitute an imminent risk of serious bodily harm to an identifiable person or class of persons.

WHO IS THE CLIENT OR PATIENT?

Is it always clear to the clinician who the client is? In private therapy, when an adult pays a clinician a fee for help with a personal problem that has nothing to do with the legal system, the consulting individual is clearly the client. But an individual may be seen by a clinician for an evaluation of his or her competency to stand trial, or the clinician may be hired by an individual's family to assist in civil commitment proceedings. Perhaps the clinician is employed by a provincial psychiatric hospital as a regular staff member and sees a particular patient about problems in controlling aggressive impulses.

It should be clear, although it seldom is clear, that in these instances the clinician is serving more than one client. In addition to the patient, he or she serves the family or the province, and it is incumbent on the mental health professional to inform the patient that this is so. Simon Verdun-Jones (2000) from Simon Fraser University has written extensively on the conflict faced by clinicians who must be true to their clinical role and protect the client's rights while at the same time ensuring that the rights of the general public are also protected. This dual allegiance does not necessarily indicate that the patient's own interests will be sacrificed, but it does mean that discussions will not inevitably remain secret and that the clinician may in the future act in a way that displeases the individual.

CHOICE OF GOALS

Ideally, the client sets the goals for therapy, but in practice, it is naive to assume that some goals are not imposed by the therapist and may even go against the wishes of the client. For example, a school system may want to institute a program that will teach children to "be still, be quiet, be docile" (Winett & Winkler, 1972, p. 499). Many behaviour therapists have assumed that young children should be compliant, not only because the teacher can then run a more orderly class, but because children are assumed to learn better when they are so. But do we really know that the most efficient and most enjoyable learning takes place when children are forced to sit quietly in their seats? Some advocates of open classrooms believe that curiosity and initiative, even in the youngest elementary school pupil, are at least as important as the acquisition of academic skills.

As is generally the case in psychology, evidence is less plentiful than strongly held and vehemently defended opinions. But it is clear that any professionals consulted by a school system have to be mindful of their own personal biases with respect to goals and should be prepared to work toward different ones if the parents and school personnel so wish. Any therapist has the option of not working for a client whose goals and proposed means of attaining them are abhorrent in his or her view.

This question of goals is particularly complex in family and couples therapy (Margolin, 1982). If several people are clients simultaneously—inevitable in family treatment—an intervention that benefits one or more individuals may well work to the disadvantage of one or more others. This can happen if one partner in couples therapy really wants to end the relationship, but the other sees the therapy as a way to save it. Because people often do not openly express their real concerns and wishes at the very beginning of therapy, the therapist can already be deeply enmeshed in their lives before learning that the two partners have conflicting goals. For this reason, among others, couples and family therapy is particularly challenging.

CHOICE OF TECHNIQUES

The end does not justify the means. This canon is said to be intrinsic to a free society. For years, questions concerning behavioural techniques have been debated among professionals and have been the subject of court rulings. Perhaps because the various insight therapies de-emphasize direct efforts to change behaviour, they have seldom been scrutinized in the way behaviour therapy has. The very concreteness, specificity, and directiveness of behavioural techniques have called attention to them, as has their alignment with experimental psychology. Some find it offensive to believe that our understanding of human beings could possibly be advanced by employing rats and pigeons as analogues to humans.

Particular concern has been expressed about the ethics of inflicting pain for purposes of therapy. For some people, the term "behaviour therapy" conjures up an image of the violent protagonist in Stanley Kubrick's classic film *A Clockwork Orange*, eyes propped open with a torturous apparatus, being made nauseous by a drug while scenes of violence flash on a screen. Aversion-therapy programs never reach this level of coercion and drama, but certainly any such procedure entails making the patient uncomfortable, sometimes extremely so. Making patients vomit or cringe with pain from electric shock applied to the extremities are two aversion techniques worthy of their name. Can there be any circumstances that justify therapists' inflicting pain on clients?

Before quickly exclaiming, "No!", consider the following report.

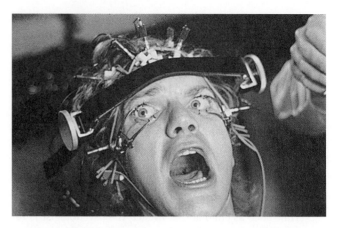

A Clockwork Orange depicted an extreme and fanciful example of aversion therapy. M McDowall/The Everett Collection.

THE PATIENT was a nine-month-old baby who had already been hospitalized three times for treatment of vomiting and chronic rumination (regurgitating food and rechewing it in the mouth). A number of diagnostic tests, including an EEG, plus surgery to remove a cyst on the right kidney, had revealed no biological basis for the problems, and several treatments, including a special diet, had been attempted without success. When referred to Lang and Melamed (1969), two behaviour therapists, the child was in critical condition and was being fed by tubes leading from the nose directly into the stomach. The attending physician had stated that the infant's life was in imminent danger if the vomiting could not be halted.

Treatment consisted of delivering a series of one-second-long electric shocks to the infant's calf each time he showed signs of beginning to vomit. Sessions followed feeding and lasted under an hour. After just two sessions, shock was rarely required, for the infant learned quickly to stop vomiting in order to avoid the shock. By the sixth session, he was able to fall asleep after eating. Nurses reported that the in-session inhibition of vomiting generalized as the infant progressively reduced his vomiting during the rest of the day and night. About two weeks later, the mother began to assume some care of the hospitalized child, and shortly thereafter the patient was discharged with virtually complete elimination of the life-threatening pattern of behaviour. Throughout the three weeks of treatment and observation, the child gained weight steadily. One month after discharge, the child weighed 21 pounds and was rated as fully recovered by the attending physician. Five months later, he weighed 26 pounds and was regarded as completely normal, both physically and psychologically. (Lang & Melamed, 1969)

The use of aversion therapy has been subject to an understandably high degree of regulation. An additional reason for administrative and judicial concern is that aversion techniques seem to more closely resemble research than standard therapy. The more established a therapeutic procedure, whether medical or psychological, the less likely it is to attract the attention of the courts or other governmental agencies. Paul and Lentz (1977) had a few very assaultive patients. Their account of administrative problems demonstrates that patients might be subject to more extreme procedures because of restrictions placed on the use of new techniques.

Some consideration was given to the contingent use of mild electric shock .... However, early in the explorations of the necessary safeguards and review procedures to be followed before evaluating such methods, the department director telephoned to explain that aversion conditioning was a politically sensitive issue. Therefore, more than the usual proposal, preparation, documentation, and committee reviews would be required—to the extent that approval would probably take about eighteen months. Instead, it was suggested that convulsive shock ... be employed since "ECT is an accepted medical treatment." With those alternatives, our choice was to abandon either use of shock. (p. 499)

But should we be concerned only with physical pain? The anguish we suffer when a loved one dies is psychologically painful. It is perhaps more painful than an electric shock of 1,500 microamperes. Who is to say? Since we allow that pain can be psychological, should we forbid a Gestalt therapist from making a patient cry by confronting the patient with feelings that have been avoided for years? Should we forbid a psychoanalyst from guiding a patient to an insight that will likely cause great anguish, all the more so for the conflict's having been repressed for years?

THE RIGHT TO COMPETENT TREATMENT

Most readers of this text would assume that an important ethical principle that can almost go without saying is that people have a right to receive treatment from competent and highly trained individuals. Indeed, this provision is clearly stated in the ethical guidelines and standards of practice endorsed by the Canadian Psychological Association (2000). It is important to remain vigilant and ensure that the quality of care meets or exceeds expectations. This point is illustrated in Canadian Clinic Focus 18.1.

CANADIAN CLINIC FOCUS 18.1
ETHICAL CONCERNS AND THE MONTREUX CLINIC

The Montreux Clinic, an eating-disorder clinic in British Columbia run by Peggy Claude-Pierre, initially caused quite a sensation because eating disorders are notoriously difficult to treat. However, the Montreux Clinic appeared to have a very high success rate in curing the eating disorders of its clients. Claude-Pierre and her clinic received extensive coverage on a number of television shows, including ABC's *20/20*, *The Oprah Winfrey Show*, and, here in Canada, *The Pamela Wallin Show*. Claude-Pierre's approach received further attention when it was learned that Diana, Princess of Wales, had sought her advice for her bulimia problem.

Claude-Pierre's approach involved intensive treatment designed to restore the patient's sense of self-esteem in a safe and loving atmosphere. According to Claude-Pierre (1997), a vulnerability for eating disorders stems from "a confirmed negativity condition" that involves excessive self-criticism. A central goal of treatment was to reverse the negative mind through a variety of techniques and by treating the patient with unconditional love. Much of this treatment was based on insights that Claude-Pierre obtained as a result of her experiences as a mother of two daughters with eating disorders (see Claude-Pierre, 1997).

Unfortunately, problems eventually emerged at the Montreux Clinic. The clinic was investigated when a former employee made allegations to officials in the Victoria area that patients had been mistreated and that the staff were not trained adequately to address the problems of the eating-disorder clients. On December 1, 1999, the local medical officer, Dr. Richard Stanwick, ordered that the clinic be closed on January 31, 2000, because "the facility put the lives of its patients in danger with dishonesty and poor qualifications" (Sutherland, 1999, A23). Stanwick's report indicated that staff at the facility had physically restrained some patients and had forced others (including a 3-year-old boy who had been admitted even though the clinic's licence restricted

it to patients 19 years or older) to eat. Also, few of the staff had university degrees and overall training was characterized as woefully inadequate. As director of the Montreux Clinic, Claude-Pierre did not have a graduate degree in psychology or a related discipline.

Initially, the Montreux Clinic appealed the order to close. However, the appeal was dropped and its operating licence was surrendered on August 25, 2000 (Meissner, 2000).

Comment

Unfortunately, it seems that the Montreux Clinic did indeed fail to meet a number of ethical standards prescribed by the Canadian Psychological Association (2000). One was an ethical principle described as the "Competence and Self-Knowledge" principle. The essence of this principle is that help providers must limit their assistance to those activities for which they have established their competence in carrying out to the benefit of others. Moreover, there should be no attempt to delegate activities to people who lack the competence to carry them out. This standard would have been violated if indeed it was the case that the staff lacked adequate training. A related principle that apparently was not met is one that involves maximizing the benefit to the patient; clinicians must provide the best possible service for those needing and seeking psychological services. This may include, but is not limited to, selecting interventions that are relevant to the needs and characteristics of the client and that have reasonable theoretical or empirically supported efficacy in light of those needs and characteristics. Another related concern with regard to the Montreux Clinic involved the general caring provisions set forth by the Canadian Psychological Association. If adequate treatment is not provided and coercive physical interventions are used, the best interests of the clients have not been served in terms of protecting and promoting their welfare.

CONCLUDING COMMENT

An underlying theme of this book concerns the nature of knowledge. How do we decide that we understand a phenomenon? The rules of science that govern our definition of and search for knowledge require theories that can be tested, studies that can be replicated, and data that are public. But given the complexity of abnormal behaviour and the vast areas of ignorance, which are far more extensive than the domains that have already been mapped by science as it is currently practised, we have great respect for theoreticians and clinicians, those inventive souls who make suppositions, offer hypotheses, follow hunches—all based on rather flimsy data, but holding some promise that scientific knowledge will be forthcoming.

This final chapter demonstrates again something emphasized at the very beginning of this book; namely, that the behavioural scientists and mental health professionals who

conduct research and give treatment are only human beings. They suffer from the same foibles that sometimes plague non-specialists. They occasionally act with a certainty their evidence does not justify, and they sometimes fail to anticipate the moral and legal consequences of the ways in which they conduct research and apply the tentative findings of their young discipline. When society acts with great certainty on the basis of expert scientific opinion, particularly when that opinion denies to an individual the rights and respect accorded others, it may be good to let *Szasz* (1963) remind us that Sir Thomas Browne, a distinguished English physician, testified in an English court of law in 1664 that witches did indeed exist, "as everyone knew."

We hope that we have communicated in some measure our love for the subject matter and, more important, our commitment to the kind of questioning, doubting stance that wrests useful knowledge from nature and will yield more as new generations of scholars build on the achievements of their predecessors.

SUMMARY

- There are many legal and ethical issues related to treatment and research in psychopathology and intervention. Some civil liberties are rather routinely set aside when mental health professionals and the courts judge that mental illness has played a decisive role in determining an individual's behaviour.

- Criminal commitment sends a person to a hospital either before a trial for an alleged crime, because the person is deemed incompetent to stand trial, or after an acquittal by reason of not being criminally responsible on account of mental disorder.

- Several landmark cases in Canada and principles in Anglo-American law inform current thinking about the conditions under which a person who has committed a crime might be excused from legal responsibility for it. These decisions involve the notion that some people may not be able to distinguish between right and wrong (the M'Naghten Rules).

- There is an important difference between mental illness and insanity. The latter is a legal concept. A person can be diagnosed as mentally ill and yet be deemed sane enough both to stand trial and to be found guilty of a crime.

- A person who is considered mentally ill and dangerous to his- or herself and to others, though he or she has not broken a law, can be civilly committed to an institution or be allowed to live outside of a hospital, although sometimes only under supervision and with restrictions placed on his or her activities.

- There are a number of ethical issues concerning therapy and research: ethical restraints on what kinds of research are allowable, the duty of scientists to obtain informed consent from prospective human subjects, the right of clients to confidentiality, the setting of therapy goals, and the choice of techniques.

KEY TERMS

actuarial prediction (p. 644)
civil commitment (p. 633)
community commitment (p. 640)
community treatment orders (p. 640)
confidentiality (p. 660)

criminal commitment (p. 633)
informed consent (p. 660)
insanity defence (p. 633)
M'Naghten Rules (p. 635)
neurolaw (p. 636)

not criminally responsible (p. 633)
prior capable wish (p. 652)
privileged communication (p. 647)

REFLECTIONS: PAST, PRESENT, AND FUTURE

- Revisit the quote by Abram Hoffer at the beginning of this chapter. One strict interpretation is that people with serious and chronic mental disorders can't be rehabilitated while living in the community ("whose healing qualities clearly were not sufficient to prevent them from becoming sick in the first place") or staying with their families ("too sick, or too tired, or simply do not have the resources or the energy to cope with very sick patients"). What does Hoffer really mean? What is the implication of his statements? How do they tie in to the implications of our discussions about the problems with deinstitutionalization?

- We reviewed recommended changes to the mental health "system" and the treatment of people with chronic mental health problems. What changes do you think will occur in the next 25 years? What reforms will be implemented? Will there be discoveries of new drugs that

will act as "magic bullets" in the fight against disorders such as schizophrenia and bipolar disorder? Will there be breakthroughs in psychotherapy? What will it be like for the mentally ill in the next millennium? Will mental illness be all but eradicated, just as some illnesses such as leprosy or polio have been eliminated, at least in the Western world?

- Do you think that we will ever get rid of the stigma associated with mental illness? Do you think that the goal of integrating people with serious and chronic mental health problems will ever become "reality rather than rhetoric" (Goering, 2000, p. 356)? Do you think that scarce dollars in the mental health area will be allocated to other priorities in health care as a consequence of the "baby boomer" generation developing physical health problems that put pressure on the health care system in Canada?

abnormal behaviour Patterns of emotion, thought, and action deemed pathological for one or more of the following reasons: infrequent occurrence, violation of norms, personal distress, disability or dysfunction, and unexpectedness.

accommodation The cognitive process of modifying existing schemas to incorporate new events and new information, as first described by Jean Piaget.

accountability A requirement that Canada's health care system and provinces be held responsible for the quality of the care provided as part of a new *Health Care Act*, as recommended in the Romanow report.

acculturation The process that unfolds as different cultures come into contact with each other and diversity is experienced.

acquaintance (date) rape Forcible sex when the people involved know each other, sometimes occurring on a date.

action (behavioural) therapies A term sometimes applied to behavioural therapies because they involve work on behaviour as opposed to work on dreams or transference, as occurs in psychodynamic therapies.

activity anorexia The loss of appetite that results from being engaged in extreme physical activity. Activity anorexia could apply to ballet dancers or athletes, for example.

actuarial prediction A type of prediction used to predict dangerousness or risk. It involves the use of statistical formulae composed of factors that are weighted. Actuarial prediction is less influenced by subjective interpretive biases on the part of the person engaging in prediction.

acute stress disorder New in *DSM-IV*, a short-lived anxiety reaction to a traumatic event; if it lasts more than a month, it is diagnosed as post-traumatic stress disorder.

adoptees method Research method that studies children who were adopted and reared completely apart from their abnormal parents, thereby eliminating the influence of being raised by disordered parents.

age effects The consequences of being a given chronological age. Compare with *cohort effects*.

ageism Discrimination against someone because of his or her age.

agoraphobia A cluster of fears centring on being in open spaces and leaving the home. It is often linked to panic disorder.

allostatic load A maladaptive condition based in neurochemical reactions that reflect prolonged exposure to unpredictable stressors.

alogia A negative symptom in schizophrenia, marked by poverty of speech and of speech content.

alternate-form reliability The extent to which scores on two forms of a test are consistent.

altruistic suicide As defined by Durkheim, self-annihilation that the person feels will serve a social purpose, such as the self-immolations practised by Buddhist monks during the Vietnam War.

Alzheimer's disease A dementia involving a progressive atrophy of cortical tissue and marked by memory impairment, involuntary movements of limbs, occasional convulsions, intellectual deterioration, and psychotic behaviour.

amenorrhea Loss of menstrual period, which is sometimes caused by eating disorders.

amphetamines A group of stimulating drugs that produce heightened levels of energy and, in large doses, nervousness, sleeplessness, and paranoid delusions.

analogue experiment An experimental study of a phenomenon different from but related to the actual interests of the investigator.

anesthesias A loss or impairment of sensation that may be experienced by a person with a conversion disorder.

anger-in theory The view that psychophysiological disorders, such as essential hypertension, arise from a person's not expressing anger or resentment.

angina pectoris See *coronary heart disease*.

anhedonia A negative symptom in schizophrenia in which the individual is unable to feel pleasure.

anomic suicide As defined by Durkheim, self-annihilation triggered by a person's inability to cope with sudden and unfavourable change in a social situation.

anorexia nervosa A disorder in which a person refuses to eat or to retain any food or suffers a prolonged and severe diminution of appetite. The individual has an intense fear of becoming obese, feels fat even when emaciated, refuses to maintain a minimal body weight, and loses at least 25% of his or her original weight.

Antabuse A biological drug treatment for drinking problems that causes a person to feel nauseous if he or she drinks alcohol.

antipsychotic drugs Psychoactive drugs, such as Thorazine, that reduce psychotic symptoms but have long-term side effects resembling symptoms of neurological diseases.

anti-social personality A disorder in which a person, also called a psychopath or a sociopath, is superficially charming and a habitual liar, has no regard for others, shows no remorse after hurting others, has no shame for behaving in an outrageously objectionable manner, is unable to form relationships and take responsibility, and does not learn from punishment.

anxiety An unpleasant feeling of fear and apprehension accompanied by increased physiological arousal. In learning theory, it is considered a drive that mediates between a threatening situation and avoidance behaviour. Anxiety can be assessed by self-report, by measuring physiological arousal, and by observing overt behaviour.

anxiety disorders Disorders in which fear or tension is overriding and the primary disturbance: phobic disorders, panic disorder, generalized anxiety disorder, obsessive-compulsive disorder, acute stress disorder, and post-traumatic stress disorder. These disorders form a major category in *DSM-IV* and cover most of what used to be referred to as the neuroses.

anxiety sensitivity A cognitive preoccupation that involves a fear of fear itself and thus contributes to a heightened sense of panic.

anxiolytics Tranquilizers; drugs that reduce anxiety.

anxiously attached An attachment orientation in which the infant expresses great distress when left alone by the caregiver, but perhaps still in the presence of a stranger.

applied behaviour analysis The study of the antecedent conditions and reinforcement contingencies that control behaviour. See also *operant conditioning*.

asociality A negative symptom of schizophrenia marked by an inability to form close relationships and to feel intimacy.

assertion training Behaviour therapy procedures that attempt to help a person more easily express thoughts, wishes, beliefs, and legitimate feelings of resentment or approval.

assessment Finding out what is wrong with a person, what may have caused a problem or problems, and what steps may be taken to improve the person's condition.

assimilation The cognitive process of incorporating new information and new events into existing schemas, as first described by Jean Piaget.

assimilation The process of absorbing a minority group into a dominant group as they adapt and establish greater uniformity.

asylums Refuges established in western Europe in the fifteenth century to confine and provide for the mentally ill; the forerunners of the mental hospital.

attention-deficit/hyperactivity disorder A disorder in children marked by difficulties in focusing adaptively on the task at hand, by inappropriate fidgeting and anti-social behaviour, and by excessive non–goal-directed behaviour.

attribution The explanation a person has for his or her behaviour.

autistic disorder A pervasive developmental disorder in which the child's world is one of profound aloneness. Speech is often absent, and the child has an obsessive need for everything to remain the same.

autonomic lability Tendency for the autonomic nervous system to be easily aroused.

autonomic nervous system The division of the nervous system that regulates involuntary functions; innervates endocrine glands, smooth muscle, and heart muscle; and initiates the physiological changes that are part of the expression of emotion. See also *sympathetic* and *parasympathetic nervous systems*.

autonomy A personality style associated with vulnerability to depression. It involves a need to work toward achievement goals while being free from constraints imposed by others.

aversive conditioning A process believed to underlie the effectiveness of aversion therapy.

avoidant attachment style An attachment orientation in which the infant is withdrawn and detached from the caregiver, almost as if no attachment bond were formed in the first place.

avoidant personality A disorder in which individuals have poor self-esteem and thus are extremely sensitive to potential rejection and remain aloof even though they very much desire affiliation and affection.

avolition A negative symptom in schizophrenia in which the individual lacks interest and drive.

barbiturates A class of synthetic sedative drugs that are addictive and in large doses can cause death by almost completely relaxing the diaphragm.

bedlam A scene or place involving a wild uproar or confusion. The term is derived from the scenes at Bethlehem Hospital in London, where unrestrained groups of mentally ill people interacted with each other.

behavioural medicine An interdisciplinary field concerned with integrating knowledge from medicine and behavioural science to understand health and illness and to prevent as well as to treat psychophysiological disorders and other illnesses in which a person's psyche plays a role. See also *health psychology*.

behavioural observation A form of behavioural assessment that entails careful observation of a person's overt behaviour in a particular situation.

behaviour genetics The study of individual differences in behaviour that are attributable to differences in genetic makeup.

behaviourism The school of psychology associated with Watson, who proposed that observable behaviour, not consciousness, is the proper subject matter of psychology. Currently, many who consider themselves behaviourists do use mediational concepts, provided they are firmly anchored to observables.

behaviour modification A term sometimes used interchangeably with "behaviour therapy."

behaviour rehearsal A behaviour therapy technique in which a client practises new behaviour in the consulting room, often aided by demonstrations and role-play by the therapist.

behaviour therapy A branch of psychotherapy narrowly conceived as the application of classical and operant conditioning to the alteration of clinical problems, but more broadly conceived as applied experimental psychology in a clinical context.

best practice model An approach to treatment that focuses on the most efficacious interventions as determined by empirical research.

bilateral ECT Electroconvulsive therapy in which electrodes are placed on each side of the forehead and an electrical current is passed between them through both hemispheres of the brain.

binge eating disorder Categorized in *DSM-IV* as a diagnosis in need of further study; includes recurrent episodes of unrestrained eating.

biofeedback Procedures that provide an individual immediate information on minute changes in muscle activity, skin temperature, heart rate, blood pressure, and other somatic functions. It is assumed that voluntary control over these bodily processes can be achieved through this knowledge, thereby ameliorating to some extent certain psychophysiological disorders.

biological paradigm A broad theoretical view that holds that mental disorders are caused by some aberrant somatic process or defect.

biopsychosocial paradigm A paradigm that suggests that all normal and abnormal behaviour is caused by an interaction of biological, psychological, and social factors.

bipolar I disorder A disorder in which people experience episodes of both mania and depression or of mania alone.

bipolar II disorder A disorder in which people experience episodes of major depression followed by a type of manic phase that is less severe than in bipolar I disorder.

body dysmorphic disorder A somatoform disorder marked by preoccupation with an imagined or exaggerated defect in appearance; for example, facial wrinkles or excess facial or body hair.

borderline personality A disorder in which people are impulsive and unpredictable, with an uncertain self-image, intense and unstable social relationships, and extreme mood swings.

brain stem The part of the brain connecting the spinal cord with the cerebrum. It contains the pons and medulla oblongata and functions as a neural relay station.

brief therapy Time-limited psychotherapy, usually ego-analytic in orientation and lasting no more than 25 sessions.

brooding A moody contemplation of depressive symptoms—"What am I doing to deserve this?"—that is more common in females than males.

bulimia nervosa A disorder characterized by episodic uncontrollable eating binges followed by purging either by vomiting or by taking laxatives.

Canadian Mental Health Association A national organization that provides information about mental illness and acts as an advocate for mentally ill people.

cardiovascular disorders A medical problem involving the heart and the blood circulation system, such as hypertension or coronary heart disease.

case study The collection of historical or biographical information on a single individual, often including experiences in therapy.

catastrophization A cognitive tendency that involves magnifying or amplifying the impact of a problem, symptom, or stressful situation by interpreting it as a major catastrophe.

catatonic immobility A fixity of posture, sometimes grotesque, maintained for long periods, with accompanying muscular rigidity, trancelike state of consciousness, and waxy flexibility.

catatonic schizophrenia A subtype of schizophrenia whose primary symptoms alternate between stuporous immobility and excited agitation.

categorical classification An approach to assessment in which the basic decision is whether a person is or is not a member of a discrete grouping. Contrast with *dimensional classification*.

cathartic method A therapeutic procedure introduced by Breuer and developed further by Freud in the late nineteenth century whereby a patient recalls and relives an earlier emotional catastrophe and re-experiences the tension and unhappiness, the goal being to relieve emotional suffering.

cerebellum An area of the hindbrain concerned with balance, posture, and motor coordination.

cerebral cortex The thin outer covering of each of the cerebral hemispheres; it is highly convoluted and composed of nerve cell bodies that constitute the grey matter of the brain.

cerebral hemispheres Either of the two halves that make up the cerebrum.

child sexual abuse Sexual abuse of children that involves direct physical contact, such as pedophilia or incest.

chronic pain Persistent and debilitating pain that continues to be present long after the anticipated time for healing has passed.

civil commitment A procedure whereby a person can be legally certified as mentally ill and hospitalized, even against his or her will.

classical conditioning A basic form of learning, sometimes referred to as Pavlovian conditioning, in which a neutral stimulus is repeatedly paired with another stimulus (called the unconditioned stimulus, UCS) that naturally elicits a certain desired response (called the unconditioned response, UCR). After repeated trials the neutral stimulus becomes a conditioned stimulus (CS) and evokes the same or a similar response, now called the conditioned response (CR).

classificatory variables The characteristics that people bring with them to scientific investigations, such as sex, age, and mental status; studied by correlational research and mixed designs.

client-centred therapy A humanistic-existential insight therapy, developed by Rogers, which emphasizes the importance of the therapist's understanding the client's subjective experiences and assisting the client to gain more awareness of current motivations for behaviour; the goal is not only to reduce anxieties but also to foster actualization of the client's potential.

clinical interview A conversation between a clinician and a client that is aimed at determining diagnosis, history, causes for problems, and possible treatment options.

clinical psychologist An individual who has earned a Ph.D. degree in psychology or a Psy.D. and whose training has included an internship in a mental hospital or clinic.

Clinician A health professional authorized to provide services to people suffering from one or more pathologies.

clonidine An anti-hypertensive drug that shows some promise in helping people wean themselves from substance dependence.

cocaine A pain-reducing, stimulating, and addictive alkaloid obtained from coca leaves, which increases mental powers, produces euphoria, heightens sexual desire, and in large doses causes paranoia and hallucinations.

cognition The process of knowing; the thinking, judging, reasoning, and planning activities of the human mind. Behaviour is now often explained as depending on these processes.

cognitive-behavioural case formulation A process in which a cognitive-behavioural therapist attempts to ascertain how the various problems experienced by a client are related in order to pick out the overt behaviours and underlying schemata that will become the focus of therapy.

cognitive behaviour therapy (CBT) Behaviour therapy that incorporates theory and research on cognitive processes such as thoughts, perceptions, judgements, self-statements, and tacit assumptions. A blend of both the cognitive and behavioural paradigms.

cognitive enhancement therapy (CET) A treatment for schizophrenia that involves competence-based training in cognitive capacities and skills (e.g., attention, memory, and problem solving) and social-cognitive skills (e.g., conversing with someone).

cognitive paradigm The general view that people can best be understood by studying how they perceive and structure their experiences.

cognitive reserve hypothesis The theory that high education levels delay the clinical expression of dementia because the brain develops backup or reserve neural structures as a form of neuroplasticity.

cognitive restructuring Any behaviour therapy procedure that attempts to alter the manner in which a client thinks about life so that he or she changes overt behaviour and emotions.

cohort effects The consequences of having been born in a given year and having grown up during a particular time period with its own unique pressures, problems, challenges, and opportunities. Compare with *age effects*.

common factorism A method that seeks therapeutic strategies that are common to all forms of psychotherapy.

community commitment A form of commitment in which a person is committed to involuntary treatment while still residing in the community, derived from community treatment orders.

community psychology An approach to therapy that emphasizes prevention and the seeking out of potential difficulties rather than waiting for troubled individuals to initiate consultation. The location for professional activities tends to be in the person's natural surroundings rather than in the therapist's office. See also *prevention*.

community psychology An approach to therapy that emphasizes prevention and the seeking out of potential difficulties rather than waiting for troubled individuals to initiate consultation. The location for professional activities tends to be in the person's natural surroundings rather than in the therapist's office. See also *prevention*.

community treatment order A legal tool that specifies the terms of treatment that must be adhered to in order for a mentally ill person to be released and live in the community.

community treatment orders Written orders that serve as a form of community commitment designed to ensure treatment compliance.

comorbidity The co-occurrence of two disorders, as when a person is both depressed and alcoholic.

compulsion The irresistible impulse to repeat an irrational act over and over again.

concordance As applied in behaviour genetics, the similarity in psychiatric diagnosis or in other traits within a pair of twins.

conditioned response See *classical conditioning*.

conditioned stimulus See *classical conditioning*.

conditioning theory of tolerance The notion that tolerance and extinction are learned responses and environmental cues become associated with addictive substances through Pavlovian conditioning.

conduct disorder Patterns of extreme disobedience in youngsters, including theft, vandalism, bullying, and early drug use; may be precursor of anti-social personality disorder.

confidentiality A principle observed by lawyers, doctors, pastors, psychologists, and psychiatrists that dictates that the goings-on in a professional and private relationship are not divulged to anyone else. See also *privileged communication*.

confounds Variables whose effects are so intermixed that they cannot be measured separately, making the design of an experiment internally invalid and its results impossible to interpret.

congruency hypothesis The prediction that people are likely to be depressed if they have a personality vulnerability that is matched by congruent life events (e.g., perfectionists who experience a failure to achieve). It is derived from research on personality, stress, and depression.

constructivist-narrative approach An approach that focuses on the cognitive meaning that people attach to life events by assessing the stories they have constructed to account for their personal situation.

construct validity The extent to which scores or ratings on an assessment instrument relate to other variables or behaviours according to some theory or hypothesis.

construct validity The extent to which scores or ratings on an assessment instrument relate to other variables or behaviours according to some theory or hypothesis.

content validity Refers to whether a measure adequately samples the domain of interest.

control group Those in an experiment for whom the independent variable is not manipulated, thus forming a baseline against which the effects of the manipulation of the experimental group can be evaluated.

controlled drinking A pattern of alcohol consumption that is moderate and avoids the extremes of total abstinence and of inebriation.

conversion disorder A somatoform disorder in which sensory or muscular functions are impaired, usually suggesting neurological disease, even though the bodily organs themselves are sound; anaesthesias and paralyses of limbs are examples. To be distinguished from *malingering*, in which actual impairment does not exist.

coping The response that a person exhibits when faced with a controllable or uncontrollable problem or stressor.

coronary heart disease (CHD) Angina pectoris, chest pains caused by insufficient supply of blood and thus oxygen to the heart; and myocardial infarction, or heart attack, in which the blood and oxygen supply is reduced so much that heart muscles are damaged.

corpus callosum The large band of nerve fibres connecting the two cerebral hemispheres.

correlational method The research strategy used to establish whether two or more variables are related. Relationships may be positive—as values for one variable increase, those for the other do also—or negative—as values for one variable increase, those for the other decrease.

correlation coefficient A statistic that measures the degree to which two variables are related.

counselling psychologist A doctoral-level mental health professional whose training is similar to that of a clinical psychologist, though usually with less emphasis on research and severe psychopathology.

counterconditioning Relearning achieved by eliciting a new response in the presence of a particular stimulus.

countertransference Feelings that the psychoanalyst unconsciously directs to the client, stemming from his or her own emotional vulnerabilities and unresolved conflicts.

covert sensitization A form of aversion therapy in which the person is told to imagine undesirably attractive situations and activities while unpleasant feelings are being induced by imagery.

criminal commitment A procedure whereby a person is confined in a mental institution either for determination of competency to stand trial or after acquittal by reason of insanity.

criterion validity Evaluated by determining whether a measure is associated in an expected way with some other measure (the criterion).

cross-dependent Acting on the same receptors as methadone does with heroin. See also *heroin substitutes*.

cross-sectional studies Studies in which different age groups are compared at the same time. Compare with *longitudinal studies*.

CT scan Computerized axial tomography, a method of diagnosis in which X-rays are taken from different angles and then analyzed by computer to produce a representation of the part of the body in cross section; often used on the brain.

cultural bias The degree to which assessment devices, such as intelligence tests, have content that is not representative and meaningful for individuals from various cultural backgrounds.

cultural diversity The differences that exist in an area or region due to the heterogeneity and varying backgrounds of the members of that region.

cyclothymic disorder Chronic swings between elation and depression not severe enough to warrant the diagnosis of bipolar disorder.

daily hassles The relatively minor yet chronic and persistent life stressors that combine to have a strong, negative influence on personal well-being.

defence mechanism In psychoanalytic theory, reality-distorting strategies unconsciously adopted to protect the ego from anxiety.

deinstitutionalization The increasing tendency for treatment to take place in the community, perhaps on an outpatient basis, rather than having patients reside in a public institution, such as a provincial mental hospital.

delirium A state of great mental confusion in which consciousness is clouded, attention cannot be sustained, and the stream of thought and speech is incoherent. The person is probably disoriented, emotionally erratic, restless, or lethargic, and often has illusions, delusions, and hallucinations.

delusional disorder A disorder in which the individual has persistent persecutory delusions or delusional jealousy and is very often contentious but has no thought disorder or hallucinations.

delusional jealousy The unfounded conviction that one's mate is unfaithful; the individual may collect small bits of "evidence" to justify the delusion.

delusions Beliefs contrary to reality, firmly held in spite of evidence to the contrary, common in paranoid disorders: of control, belief that one is being manipulated by some external force such as radar, television, or a creature from outer space; of grandeur, belief that one is an especially important or powerful person; of persecution, belief that one is being plotted against or oppressed by others.

dementia Deterioration of mental faculties—memory, judgement, abstract thought, control of impulses, intellectual ability—that impairs social and occupational functioning and eventually changes the personality. See also *Alzheimer's disease.*

dementia praecox An older term for "schizophrenia," chosen to describe what was believed to be an incurable and progressive deterioration of mental functioning beginning in adolescence.

demonology The doctrine that a person's abnormal behaviour is caused by an autonomous evil spirit.

denial Defence mechanism in which a thought, feeling, or action is disavowed by the person.

denormalization belief A belief that reflects widespread social disapproval (e.g., society's current lack of approval of smoking).

dependency A personality style associated with vulnerability to depression. It involves excessive levels of dependency on others.

dependent personality A disorder in which people lack self-confidence and passively allow others to run their lives and make no demands on them so as not to endanger these protective relationships.

dependent variable In a psychological experiment, the behaviour that is measured and is expected to change with manipulation of the independent variable.

depersonalization An alteration in perception of the self in which the individual loses a sense of reality and feels estranged from the self and perhaps separated from the body. It may be a temporary reaction to stress and fatigue or part of panic disorder, depersonalization disorder, or schizophrenia.

depersonalization disorder A dissociative disorder in which the individual feels unreal and estranged from the self and surroundings enough to disrupt functioning. People with this disorder may feel that their extremities have changed in size or that they are watching themselves from a distance.

depression A disorder marked by great sadness and apprehension, feelings of worthlessness and guilt, withdrawal from others, loss of sleep, appetite, sexual desire, loss of interest and pleasure in usual activities, and either lethargy or agitation. Called "major depression" in *DSM-IV* and "unipolar depression" by others. It can be an associated symptom of other disorders.

depressive paradox A cognitive tendency for depressed individuals to accept personal responsibility for negative outcomes despite feeling a lack of personal control.

depressive predictive certainty The concept that people become prone to depression when they perceive that an anticipated state of helplessness is certain to occur. It is derived from the hopelessness theory of depression.

derealization Loss of the sense that the surroundings are real; present in several psychological disorders, such as panic disorder, depersonalization disorder, and schizophrenia.

detoxification The initial stage in weaning an addicted person from a drug; involves

medical supervision of the sometimes painful withdrawal.

developmental coordination disorder (motor skills disorder) A learning disability characterized by marked impairment in the development of motor coordination that is not accounted for by mental retardation or a physical disorder such as cerebral palsy.

diagnosis The determination that a patient's set of symptoms or problems indicates a particular disorder.

Diagnostic and Statistical Manual of Mental Disorders (DSM) A publication of the American Psychiatric Association that is an attempt to delineate specific and discrete syndromes or mental disorders. It has been through several revisions and the current one is the fourth edition (*DSM-IV*).

dialectical behaviour therapy A therapeutic approach to borderline personality disorder that combines client-centred empathy and acceptance with behavioural problem solving, social-skills training, and limit setting.

diathesis–stress paradigm As applied in psychopathology, a view that assumes that individuals predisposed toward a particular mental disorder will be particularly affected by stress and will then manifest abnormal behaviour.

diencephalon The lower area of the forebrain, containing the thalamus and hypothalamus.

dimensional classification An approach to assessment according to which a person is placed on a continuum. Contrast with *categorical classification.*

directionality problem A difficulty that arises in the correlational method of research when it is known that two variables are related but it is unclear which is causing the other.

discriminative stimulus An event that informs an organism that if a particular response is made, reinforcement will follow.

disease model See *medical model.*

disorder of written expression Difficulties writing without errors in spelling, grammar, or punctuation.

disorganized attachment style An attachment orientation in which the infant demonstrates a confused attachment style that emerges after being raised in a chaotic and abusive environment.

disorganized schizophrenia A subtype of schizophrenia in which the person has diffuse and regressive symptoms; the individual is given to silliness, facial grimaces, and inconsequential rituals and has constantly changeable moods and poor hygiene. There are few significant remissions and eventually considerable deterioration. This form of schizophrenia was formerly called "hebephrenia."

disorganized speech (thought disorder) Refers to problems in organizing ideas and in speaking so that a listener can understand. Also known as formal thought disorder.

displacement A defence mechanism whereby an emotional response is unconsciously redirected from an object or concept perceived as dangerous to a substitute less threatening to the ego.

dissociative amnesia A dissociative disorder in which the person suddenly becomes unable to recall important personal information to an

extent that cannot be explained by ordinary forgetfulness.

dissociative disorders Disorders in which the normal integration of consciousness, memory, or identity is suddenly and temporarily altered; dissociative amnesia, dissociative fugue, dissociative identity disorder (multiple personality), and depersonalization disorder are examples.

dissociative fugue A disorder in which the person experiences total amnesia, then moves and establishes a new identity.

dissociative identity disorder A rare dissociative disorder in which two or more fairly distinct and separate personalities are present within the same individual, each with his or her own memories, relationships, and behaviour patterns, with only one of them dominant at any given time. Formerly called "multiple personality disorder.

dissociative identity disorder (DID) A rare dissociative disorder in which two or more fairly distinct and separate personalities are present within the same individual, each with his or her own memories, relationships, and behaviour patterns, with only one of them dominant at any given time. Formerly called "multiple personality disorder.

distress An emotional reaction that can involve a variety of negative feelings or emotional state, including anxiety and depression.

dizygotic (DZ) twins Birth partners who have developed from separate fertilized eggs and who are only 50% alike genetically, no more so than siblings born from different pregnancies; sometimes called fraternal twins. Contrast with *monozygotic (MZ) twins.*

dodo bird effect The general finding that all forms of psychotherapies achieve similar outcomes.

dopamine theory The view that schizophrenia arises from an increase in the number of dopamine receptors.

double-blind procedure A method for reducing the biasing effects of the expectations of research participant and experimenter; neither is allowed to know whether the independent variable of the experiment is being applied to the participant.

double depression A comorbid condition that applies to someone characterized by both dysthymia and major depression.

down syndrome (trisomy 21) A form of mental retardation generally caused by an extra chromosome. The child's IQ is usually less than 50, and the child has distinctive physical characteristics, most notably slanted eyes.

dream analysis A key psychoanalytic technique in which the unconscious meanings of dream material are uncovered.

Drug-Stroop Task A task to assess implicit cognitions believed to be involved in vulnerability to addiction. The task assesses whether people respond slower when provided with words that they must colour identify (e.g., the word is "blue") but the word reflects drug-related content (e.g., "vodka").

DSM-IV The fourth edition of the *Diagnostic and Statistical Manual of Mental Disorders* of the American Psychiatric Association.

DSM-IV-TR A text revision of *DSM-IV.* Some sections were rewritten to incorporate research findings and enhance clarity; however, there were few substantive changes.

DSM-5 The fifth edition of the Diagnostic and Statistical Manual of Mental Disorders slated for publication in 2012.

dyspareunia Painful or difficult sexual intercourse; the pain or difficulty is usually caused by infection or a physical injury, such as torn ligaments in the pelvic region.

dysthymic disorder State of depression that is long-lasting but not severe enough for the diagnosis of major depression.

eating disorder not otherwise specified The most common eating disorder diagnosis characterized by heterogeneous symptoms and associated features that do not fit the symptoms of other eating disorders. This diagnosis is applied to between approximately 40 and 70% of diagnosed patients.

echolalia The immediate repetition of the words of others, often found in autistic children. In delayed echolalia this inappropriate echoing takes place hours or weeks later.

eclecticism In psychology, the view that more is to be gained by employing concepts and techniques from various theoretical systems than by restricting oneself to a single approach.

ecological momentary assessment (EMA) A form of self-observation involving collection of data in real time (e.g., diaries) regarding thoughts, moods, and stressors.

ecstasy A relatively new hallucinogen that is chemically similar to mescaline and the amphetamines.

effectiveness The actual impact of an intervention on clients' functioning outside the laboratory. Research into psychotherapy has made a distinction between the efficacy of an intervention and its effectiveness, which is defined as what is offered to and received by clients in the real world. In contrast to effectiveness, efficacy is assessed in controlled and standardized clinical trials in research with participants that meet strict inclusion criteria for being in the study. Efficacy and effectiveness may not be identical because effectiveness is also influenced by other factors not included in the treatment study (e.g., other treatments the client has received and other co-morbid disorders).

efficacy In Bandura's theory, a cognitive variable reflecting a sense of capability.

ego analysis An important set of modifications of classical psychoanalysis, based on a conception of the human being as having a stronger, more autonomous ego with gratifications independent of id satisfactions. Sometimes called "ego psychology."

ego In psychoanalytic theory, the predominantly conscious part of the personality, responsible for decision-making and for dealing with reality.

egoistic suicide As defined by Durkheim, self-annihilation committed because the individual feels extreme alienation from others and from society.

electrocardiogram A recording of the electrical activity of the heart, made with an electrocardiograph.

electroconvulsive therapy (ECT) A treatment that produces a convulsion by passing electric current through the brain. Though an unpleasant and occasionally dangerous procedure, it can be useful in alleviating profound depression.

electrodermal responding A recording of the minute electrical activity of the sweat glands on the skin, allowing the inference of an emotional state.

electroencephalogram (EEG) A graphic recording of electrical activity of the brain, usually of the cerebral cortex, but sometimes of lower areas.

emotional support A sense of being cared for and comforted by other people.

empirically informed therapies Treatment approaches that have been based on processes and components shown to be effective via research.

empirically supported therapies (ESTs) Treatments that have been shown via research to be effective when compared in controlled experimental research with other treatment approaches.

epidemiology The study of the frequency and distribution of illness in a population.

essential hypertension A psychophysiological disorder characterized by high blood pressure that cannot be traced to an organic cause. Over the years it causes degeneration of small arteries, enlargement of the heart, and kidney damage.

eustress Pleasant stress arising from environmental conditions, as coined by Selye.

event-related potentials (ERP) Brain wave potentials that can be used for cognitive assessments. ERPs are evaluated when a person is asked to perform a cognitive task.

evidence-based treatment Treatments and interventions that have been shown to be effective according to controlled experimental research.

exhibitionism Marked preference for obtaining sexual gratification by exposing one's genitals to an unwilling observer.

exorcism The casting out of evil spirits by ritualistic chanting or torture.

experimental effect A statistically significant difference between two groups experiencing different manipulations of the independent variable.

experimental hypothesis What the investigator assumes will happen in a scientific investigation if certain conditions are met or particular variables are manipulated.

experiment The most powerful research technique for determining causal relationships, requiring the manipulation of an independent variable, the measurement of a dependent variable, and the random assignment of participants to the several different conditions being investigated.

expressed emotion (EE) In the literature on schizophrenia, the amount of hostility and criticism directed from other people to the client, usually within a family.

expressive language disorder Difficulties expressing oneself in speech.

external validity See *validity*.

extinction The elimination of a classically conditioned response by omitting the unconditioned stimulus. In operant conditioning, the elimination of the conditioned response by omitting reinforcement.

factitious disorder A disorder in which the individual's physical or psychological symptoms appear under voluntary control and are adopted merely to assume the role of a sick person. The disorder can also involve a parent producing a disorder in a child and is then called "factitious disorder by proxy" or "Munchausen syndrome by proxy."

false hope syndrome A tendency for the initial positive results of attempts at weight loss to foster an overly positive inclination to pursue unrealistic weight loss goals, resulting eventually in profound disappointment.

family functioning The adjustment of the family system as a whole in terms of the family environment and performance of assigned roles to family members.

family method A research strategy in behaviour genetics in which the frequency of a trait or of abnormal behaviour is determined in relatives who have varying percentages of shared genetic background.

fear of performance Being overly concerned with one's behaviour during sexual contact with another, postulated by Masters and Johnson as a major factor in sexual dysfunction.

feedforward mechanisms Anticipatory, regulatory responses made in anticipation of a drug that enables us to anticipate drug effects before they occur.

female orgasmic disorder A recurrent and persistent delay or absence of orgasm in a woman during sexual activity adequate in focus, intensity, and duration; in many instances the woman may experience considerable sexual excitement.

female sexual arousal disorder Formerly called "frigidity," the inability of a female to reach or maintain the lubrication–swelling stage of sexual excitement or to enjoy a subjective sense of pleasure or excitement during sexual activity.

fetal alcohol syndrome (FAS) Retarded growth of the developing fetus and infant; cranial, facial, and limb anomalies; and mental retardation caused by heavy consumption of alcohol by the mother during pregnancy.

fetishism Reliance on an inanimate object for sexual arousal.

flashbacks An unpredictable recurrence of psychedelic experiences from an earlier drug trip.

flat affect A deviation in emotional response wherein virtually no emotion is expressed whatever the stimulus, emotional expressiveness is blunted, or a lack of expression and muscle tone is noted in the face.

flooding A behaviour therapy procedure in which a fearful person is exposed to what is frightening, in reality or in the imagination, for extended periods of time and without opportunity for escape.

forced rape The legal term for rape, forced sexual intercourse, or other sexual activity with another person. Statutory rape is sexual intercourse between an adult and someone who is under the age of consent, as fixed by local statute.

fragile X syndrome Malformation (or even breakage) of the X chromosome associated with moderate mental retardation. Symptoms include large, underdeveloped ears, a long, thin face, a broad nasal root, and enlarged testicles in males; many individuals show attention deficits and hyperactivity.

free association A key psychoanalytic procedure in which the client is encouraged to give free rein to his or her thoughts and feelings, verbalizing whatever comes into the mind without monitoring its content.

The assumption is that over time, repressed material will come forth for examination by the client and psychoanalyst.

frontal lobe The forward or upper half of each cerebral hemisphere, in front of the central sulcus, active in reasoning and other higher mental processes.

frotteurism A form of sexual disorder or paraphilia in which an individual receives sexual pleasure from rubbing against people in public places.

functional magnetic resonance imaging (fMRI) Modification of magnetic resonance imaging (MRI), which allows researchers to take pictures of the brain so quickly that metabolic changes can be measured, resulting in a picture of the brain at work rather than of its structure alone.

functional social support The quality of a person's relationships; for example, a good vs. a distressed marriage. Contrast with *structural social support*.

gatekeeper training In this type of training, specific groups of people are taught to identify those at high risk for suicide and then to refer them for treatment. Gatekeepers are those who have primary contact with people at risk for suicide,

gender identity disorder A disorder in which there is a deeply felt incongruence between anatomic sex and the sensed gender; transsexualism and gender identity disorder of childhood are examples.

general adaptation syndrome (GAS) Selye's model to describe the biological reaction of an organism to sustained and unrelenting stress; there are several stages, culminating in death in extreme circumstances.

generalized anxiety disorder (GAD) Anxiety that is so chronic, persistent, and pervasive that it seems free-floating. The individual is jittery and strained, distractible, and worried that something bad is about to happen. A pounding heart, fast pulse and breathing, sweating, flushing, muscle aches, a lump in the throat, and an upset gastrointestinal tract are some of the bodily indications of this extreme anxiety.

general paresis Mental illness characterized by paralysis and "insanity" that typically led to death within 5 years. Now known to be caused by syphilis of the brain.

genes An ultramicroscopic area of the chromosome; the gene is the smallest physical unit of the DNA molecule that carries a piece of hereditary information.

genotype An individual's unobservable, genetic constitution; the totality of genes possessed by an individual. Compare with *phenotype*.

germ theory (of disease) The general view in medicine that disease is caused by infection of the body by minute organisms and viruses.

goodness of fit hypothesis The notion that the effectiveness of a coping response depends on whether it is appropriate for a particular problem; that is, different situations call for different coping responses.

grandiose delusions Found in paranoid schizophrenia, delusional disorder, and mania, an exaggerated sense of one's importance, power, knowledge, or identity.

group homes Care facilities in which groups of individuals live semi-cooperatively in one home or facility. Group homes are often recommended for schizophrenics for the social

support they provide outside of an institutional setting.

guided self-change An approach to treating addiction and other types of disorders that emphasizes personal responsibility and problem-solving techniques that foster a sense of self-reliance.

gyri The ridge of the cortex in the brain.

halfway houses A homelike residence for people who are considered too disturbed to remain in their accustomed surroundings but do not require the total care of a mental institution.

hallucinations Perceptions in any sensory modality without relevant and adequate external stimuli.

hallucinogen A drug or chemical whose effects include hallucinations. Hallucinogenic drugs such as LSD, psilocybin, and mescaline are often called "psychedelic."

harm reduction therapy A form of treating addiction and other types of disorders that focuses on reducing the harmful consequences to some degree rather than striving initially for absolute abstinence.

hashish The dried resin of the cannabis plant, stronger in its effects than the dried leaves and stems that constitute marijuana.

health psychology A branch of psychology dealing with the role of psychological factors in health and illness. See also *behavioural medicine*.

healthy immigrant effect The phenomenon that immigrants have comparatively lower rates of health problems than Canadian-born members of the population.

help-seeking The act of obtaining assistance from informal sources (e.g., friends or family members) or formal sources (e.g., mental health professionals).

heroin An extremely addictive narcotic drug derived from morphine.

heroin antagonists Drugs, such as naloxone, that prevent a heroin user from experiencing any high.

heroin substitutes Narcotics, such as methadone, that are cross-dependent with heroin and thus replace it and the body's craving for it.

high-risk method A research technique involving the intensive examination of people who have a high probability of later becoming abnormal.

histrionic personality A disorder in which the person is overly dramatic and given to emotional excess, impatient with minor annoyances, immature, dependent on others, and often sexually seductive without taking responsibility for flirtations. Formerly called "hysterical personality.

homework Between session learning that typically involves get practice in engaging in specific behaviours or thoughts.

humanistic and existential therapies Insight psychotherapies that emphasize the individual's subjective experiences, free will, and ever-present ability to decide on a new life course.

hypersexual disorder A disorder not included in *DSM-IV*. It can take the form of a sex addiction or compulsion and it is regarded as a nonparaphilia sexual desire disorder with an impulsivity component.

hypoactive sexual desire disorder The absence of or deficiency in sexual fantasies and urges.

hypochondriasis A somatoform disorder in which the person, misinterpreting rather ordinary physical sensations, is preoccupied with fears of having a serious disease

and is not dissuaded by medical opinion. Difficult to distinguish from *somatization disorder*.

hypomania An above-normal elevation of mood, but not as extreme as mania.

hypothalamus A collection of nuclei and fibres in the lower part of the diencephalon concerned with the regulation of many visceral processes, such as metabolism, temperature, and water balance.

hypotheses The specific prediction about the outcome of an experiment. It is based on the assumption that the theory in question is accurate.

hysteria A disorder known to the ancient Greeks in which a physical incapacity—a paralysis, an anaesthesia, or an analgesia—is not due to a physiological dysfunction; for example, glove anaesthesia. It is an older term for "conversion disorder." In the late nineteenth century, dissociative disorders were identified as such and considered hysterical states.

ideas of reference Delusional thinking that reads personal significance into seemingly trivial remarks and activities of others and completely unrelated events.

id In psychoanalytic theory, that part of the personality present at birth, composed of all the energy of the psyche, and expressed as biological urges that strive continually for gratification.

inappropriate affect Emotional responses that are out of context, such as laughter when hearing sad news.

incest Sexual relations between close relatives, most often between father and daughter or between brother and sister.

incidence In epidemiological studies of a particular disorder, the rate at which new cases occur in a given place at a given time. Compare with *prevalence*.

incoherence In schizophrenia, an aspect of thought disorder wherein verbal expression is marked by disconnectedness, fragmented thoughts, and jumbled phrases.

independent variable In a psychological experiment, the factor, experience, or treatment that is under the experimenter's control and that is expected to have an effect on participants as assessed by changes in the dependent variable.

index cases (probands) The person who in a genetic investigation bears the diagnosis or trait in which the investigator is interested.

informed consent The agreement of a person to serve as a research participant or to enter therapy after being told the possible outcomes, both benefits and risks.

insanity defence The legal argument that a defendant should not be held ascriptively responsible for an illegal act if the conduct is attributable to mental illness.

insight therapies Any psychotherapy that assumes that people become disordered because they do not adequately understand what motivates them, especially when their needs and drives conflict.

instrumental support The provision of tangible assistance (e.g., meal preparation) to people in need.

intelligence test A standardized means of assessing a person's current mental ability; for example, the Stanford–Binet test and the Wechsler Adult Intelligence Scale.

interactionism The notion that behaviour is a joint function of personal characteristics and the properties of the situations that are experienced.

internal consistency reliability Assesses whether the items on a test are related to one another.

internal validity See *validity*.

interpersonal therapy (IPT) A psychodynamic psychotherapy that focuses on the client's interactions with others and that directly teaches how better to relate to others.

interpretation In psychoanalysis, a key procedure in which the psychoanalyst points out to the client where resistance exists and what certain dreams and verbalizations reveal about impulses repressed in the unconscious; more generally, any statement by a therapist that construes the client's problem in a new way.

inter-rater reliability The relationship between the judgements that at least two raters make independently about a phenomenon. See also *reliability*.

introspection A procedure whereby trained subjects are asked to report on their conscious experiences. This was the principal method of study in early twentieth-century psychology.

in vivo exposure An exercise at home that requires the phobic person to be exposed to the highly feared stimulus or situation.

irrational beliefs Self-defeating assumptions that are assumed by rational-emotive therapists to underlie psychological distress.

job burnout A form of work-related stress. Burnout has three components: (1) emotional exhaustion; (2) depersonalization; and (3) a sense of a lack of personal accomplishment.

job spillover A form of family stress that reflects the impact and influence of job stress on the family.

job stress Perceived strain stemming from a demanding and perhaps uncontrollable occupational situation.

kindling hypothesis The hypothesis that once a depression has been experienced, the person is sensitized and it takes less stress to elicit a subsequent bout of depression. It is a concept derived from stress research on animals.

la belle indifférence The blasé attitude people with conversion disorder have toward their symptoms.

latent content In dreams, the presumed true meaning hidden behind the manifest content.

lateral hypothalamus A section of the brain that, if lesioned, is associated with a dramatic loss of appetite.

law of effect A principle of learning that holds that behaviour is acquired by virtue of its consequences.

learned helplessness theory The theory that individuals acquire passivity and a sense of being unable to act and to control their lives. This happens through unpleasant experiences and traumas against which their efforts were ineffective; according to Seligman, this brings on depression.

learning disabilities A group of disabilities that includes learning disorders, communication disorders, and motor skills disorder.

learning disorders A set of developmental disorders encompassing dyslexia, mathematics disorder, and disorder of written expression and characterized by failure to develop in a specific academic area to the degree expected by the child's intellectual level. Not diagnosed if the disorder is due to a sensory deficit.

learning (or behavioural) paradigm In abnormal psychology, a set of assumptions that abnormal behaviour is learned in the same way as other human behaviour.

libido In Freud's psychoanalytic theory, the term used to describe the instinctual drives of the id, primarily sexual in nature.

lifetime prevalence The proportion of a sample that has ever had a disorder.

limbic system The lower parts of the cerebrum, made up of primitive cortex; controls visceral and bodily changes associated with emotion and regulates drive-motivated behaviour.

linkage analysis A technique in genetic research whereby occurrence of a disorder in a family is evaluated alongside a known genetic marker.

lithium carbonate A drug useful in treating both mania and depression in bipolar disorder.

longitudinal studies Investigation that collects information on the same individuals repeatedly over time, perhaps over many years, in an effort to determine how phenomena change. Compare with *cross-sectional studies*.

loose associations (derailment) In schizophrenia, an aspect of thought disorder wherein the client has difficulty sticking to one topic and drifts off on a train of associations evoked by an idea from the past.

LSD D-lysergic acid diethylamide, a drug synthesized in 1938 and discovered by accident to be a hallucinogen in 1943.

magnetic resonance imaging (MRI) A technique for measuring the structure (or, in the case of functional magnetic resonance imaging, the activity) of the living brain. The person is placed inside a large circular magnet that causes hydrogen atoms to move; the return of the atoms to their original positions when the current to the magnet is turned off is translated by a computer into pictures of brain tissue.

major depressive disorder (MDD) An extreme form of depression that satisfies the number of symptoms required for the category of depression to apply.

male erectile disorder A recurrent and persistent inability to attain or maintain an erection until completion of sexual activity.

male orgasmic disorder A disorder that reflects chronic difficulties in ejaculating for males.

malingering Faking a physical or psychological incapacity in order to avoid a responsibility or gain an end; the goal is readily recognized from the individual's circumstances. To be distinguished from *conversion disorder*, in which the incapacity is assumed to be beyond voluntary control.

mania An emotional state of intense but unfounded elation evidenced in talkativeness, flight of ideas, distractibility, grandiose plans, and spurts of purposeless activity.

marijuana A drug derived from the dried and ground leaves and stems of the female hemp plant, *Cannabis sativa*.

masked depression A depression that is expressed in atypical ways not usually associated with the symptoms of depression, such as misbehaving at school.

mathematics disorder Difficulties dealing with arithmetic symbols and operations; one of the learning disorders.

maturing out phenomenon The overall tendency for peak drinking levels to occur when people are in their mid-twenties and there is a sharp drop in drinking levels when people reach their late thirties.

medical forensic examination The procedure used to collect medical evidence for legal purposes when it is alleged that a sexual assault has taken place.

medical model As applied in abnormal psychology, a set of assumptions that conceptualizes abnormal behaviour as similar to physical diseases.

medicare The system of health care in Canada.

medulla oblongata An area in the brain stem through which nerve fibre tracts ascend to or descend from higher brain centres.

meninges The three layers of non-neural tissue that envelop the brain and spinal cord.

mental disorder A behavioural or psychological syndrome associated with current distress and/or disability.

mental health literacy The knowledge that a person develops about mental illness, including its causes and treatment.

mental health promotion Methods used to foster primary prevention of mental disorders through the teaching of skills or attitudes that have been shown to correlate with mental health.

mental health status An individual's level of distress and cognitive impairment.

mescaline A hallucinogen and alkaloid that is the active ingredient of peyote.

meta-analysis A quantitative method of analyzing and comparing various therapies by standardizing their results.

methadone A synthetic addictive heroin substitute for treating heroin addicts that acts as a substitute for heroin by eliminating its effects and the craving for it.

midbrain The middle part of the brain that consists of a mass of nerve fibre tracts connecting the spinal cord and pons, medulla, and cerebellum to the cerebral cortex.

mild mental retardation A limitation in mental development measured on IQ tests at between 50–55 and 70; children with such a limitation are considered the educable mentally retarded and are usually placed in special classes.

Minnesota Multiphasic Personality Inventory (MMPI) A lengthy personality inventory by which individuals are diagnosed through their true-false replies to groups of statements indicating states such as anxiety, depression, masculinity-femininity, and paranoia.

mixed design A research strategy in which both classificatory and experimental variables are used; assigning people from discrete populations to two experimental conditions is an example.

mixed receptive-expressive language disorder A disorder in which the child has the symptoms of expressive language disorder but also has difficulty understanding words, sentences, or specific types of words, such as spatial terms.

M'Naghten Rules Criteria stemming from an 1843 British court decision stating that an insanity defence can be established by proving that the defendant did not know what he or she was doing or did not realize that it was wrong.

modelling Learning by observing and imitating the behaviour of others.

moderate mental retardation A limitation in mental development measured on IQ tests between 35–40 and 50–55; children with this degree of retardation are often institutionalized, and their training is focused on self-care rather than on development of intellectual skills.

moderator variables A variable that interacts with or influences how another variable is associated with a second variable. Moderator variables combine with other variables to jointly produce an outcome.

monoamine oxidase (MAO) inhibitors A group of antidepressant drugs that prevent the enzyme monoamine oxidase from deactivating neurotransmitters of the central nervous system.

monozygotic (MZ) twins Genetically identical siblings who have developed from a single fertilized egg; sometimes called "identical twins." Contrast with *dizygotic (DZ) twins*.

mood disorders Disorders in which there are disabling disturbances in emotion.

moral anxiety In psychoanalytic theory, the ego's fear of punishment for failure to adhere to the superego's standards of proper conduct.

moral treatment A therapeutic regimen, introduced by Pinel during the French Revolution, whereby mental patients were released from their restraints and were treated with compassion and dignity rather than with contempt and denigration.

morphine An addictive narcotic alkaloid extracted from opium, used primarily as an analgesic and as a sedative.

motivational interviewing A client-centred treatment approach that was used originally to treat addictions. The goal is to enhance a client's desire for change by resolving conflicts and ambivalence. The implicit notion is that a more positive treatment response will result if the client is highly motivated to improve.

multiaxial classification Classification having several dimensions, each of which is employed in categorizing; *DSM-IV* is an example.

multicultural counselling and therapy Treatments with interventions that have been modified to address issues, beliefs, and dialogues that characterize people from various cultures.

myocardial infarction Heart attack. See also *coronary heart disease*.

narcissistic personality A disorder in which people are extremely selfish and self-centred; have a grandiose view of their uniqueness, achievements, and talents; and have an insatiable craving for admiration and approval from others. They are exploitative to achieve their own goals and expect much more from others than they themselves are willing to give.

negative reinforcement The strengthening of a tendency to exhibit desired behaviour by rewarding responses in that situation with the removal of an aversive stimulus.

negative symptoms Behavioural deficits in schizophrenia, such as flat affect and apathy. Contrast with *positive symptoms*.

negative triad In Beck's theory of depression, a person's baleful views of the self, the world, and the future; the triad is in a reciprocal causal relationship with pessimistic assumptions (schemata) and cognitive biases such as selective abstraction.

nerve impulse A change in the electric potential of a neuron; a wave of depolarization spreads along the neuron and causes the release of a neurotransmitter.

neurofibrillary tangles Abnormal protein filaments present in the cell bodies of brain cells in patients with Alzheimer's disease.

neurolaw A new field of inquiry that stems from the use of neuroscientific data in legal contexts. It involves the use of neuroscience to influence legal decisions.

neurologist A physician who studies the nervous system, especially its structure, functions, and abnormalities.

neuron A single nerve cell.

neuropsychological tests Psychological tests, such as the Luria-Nebraska, that can detect impairment in different parts of the brain.

neuropsychologist A psychologist concerned with the relationships among cognition, affect, and behaviour on the one hand, and brain function on the other.

neurotic anxiety In psychoanalytic theory, a fear of the consequences of expressing previously punished and repressed id impulses; more generally, unrealistic fear.

neurotransmitters A chemical substance important in transferring a nerve impulse from one neuron to another; for example, serotonin and norepinephrine.

nicotine A colourless poisonous alkaloid present in tobacco.

normal curve As applied in psychology, the bell-shaped distribution of a measurable trait depicting most people in the middle and few at the extremes.

not criminally responsible A phrase used in the *Criminal Code of Canada* to refer to a situation in which an individual has taken actions that are defined as illegal but due to the effects of a mental disorder are not held legally responsible for their actions. Previously referred to as "not guilty by reason of insanity."

nuclei The plural of "nucleus.

objective (realistic) anxiety In psychoanalytic theory, the ego's reaction to danger in the external world; realistic fear. Contrast with *neurotic anxiety*.

obsessions An intrusive and recurring thought that seems irrational and uncontrollable to the person experiencing it.

obsessive-compulsive disorder (OCD) An anxiety disorder in which the mind is flooded with persistent and uncontrollable thoughts or the individual is compelled to repeat certain acts again and again, causing significant distress and interference with everyday functioning.

obsessive-compulsive personality A disorder in which people have inordinate difficulty making decisions, are overly concerned with details and efficiency, and relate poorly to others because they demand that things be done their way. They are unduly conventional, serious, formal, perfectionistic, and they have reduced emotional expression.

occipital lobe The posterior area of each cerebral hemisphere, situated behind the parietal lobe and above the temporal lobes, responsible for reception and analysis of visual information and for some visual memory.

operant conditioning The acquisition or elimination of a response as a function of the environmental contingencies of reward and punishment.

opiates A group of addictive sedatives that in moderate doses relieve pain and induce sleep.

opium One of the opiates, the dried, milky juice obtained from the immature fruit of the opium poppy. This addictive narcotic produces euphoria and drowsiness and reduces pain.

oppositional defiant disorder An undercontrolled disorder of children marked by high levels of disobedience to authority but lacking the extremes of conduct disorder.

orgasmic reorientation A behaviour therapy technique for altering classes of stimuli to which people are sexually attracted; individuals are confronted by a conventionally arousing stimulus while experiencing orgasm.

pain disorder A somatoform disorder in which the person complains of severe and prolonged pain that is not explainable by organic pathology; it tends to be stress-related or permits the client to avoid an aversive activity or to gain attention and sympathy.

palliative coping The tendency to respond to emotional problems through emotional expression and acts that are designed to soothe the self.

panic disorder An anxiety disorder in which the individual has sudden and inexplicable attacks of jarring symptoms, such as difficulty breathing, heart palpitations, dizziness, trembling, terror, and feelings of impending doom. In *DSM-IV*, it is said to occur with or without agoraphobia.

paradigm A set of basic assumptions that outlines the universe of scientific inquiry, specifying both the concepts regarded as legitimate and the methods to be used in collecting and interpreting data.

paranoid personality A disorder in which a person expects to be mistreated by others, becomes suspicious, secretive, jealous, and argumentative. He or she will not accept blame and appears cold and unemotional.

paranoid schizophrenia A type of schizophrenia in which the client has numerous systematized delusions as well as hallucinations and ideas of reference. He or she may also be agitated, angry, argumentative, and sometimes violent.

paraphilias Sexual attraction to unusual objects and sexual activities unusual in nature.

paraphrenia Schizophrenia in an older adult.

parasympathetic nervous system The division of the autonomic nervous system that is involved with maintenance; it controls many of the internal organs and is active primarily when the organism is not aroused.

parental mental disorder The presence of a behavioural or psychological syndrome in one's mother or father.

parietal lobe The middle division of each cerebral hemisphere, situated behind the central sulcus and above the lateral sulcus; the receiving centre for sensations of the skin and of bodily positions.

pathological gambling A tendency to engage in persistent and recurring gambling behaviour that is self-defeating and detrimental to the well-being and goal attainments of the self or family members.

pedophilia The sexual disorder of a pedophile, one who has a paraphilia involving sexual desires and urges toward children.

perseverative cognition The experience of ruminative thoughts.

perseverative cognitive hypothesis The notion that rumination prolongs the stress response.

personality disorders A heterogeneous group of disorders, listed separately on Axis II, regarded as long-standing, inflexible, and maladaptive personality traits that impair social and occupational functioning.

personality inventory A self-report questionnaire by which an examinee indicates whether statements assessing habitual tendencies apply to him or her.

personalized therapy A new approach advocated by Millon and Grossman. Therapy is tailored to each person's unique personality and associated needs and personality styles.

personal therapy A broad form of cognitive behaviour therapy designed to address the numerous factors and processes associated with relapse into schizophrenia (e.g., learning how to respond to expressed emotion with appropriate rather than inappropriate affect).

pervasive developmental disorders Severe childhood problems marked by profound disturbances in social relations and oddities in behaviour. Autistic disorder is one.

PET scan A computer-generated picture of the living brain, created by analysis of radioactive particles from isotopes injected into the bloodstream.

phenotype The totality of observable characteristics of a person. Compare with *genotype*.

phenylketonuria A genetic disorder that, through a deficiency in a liver enzyme, phenylalanine hydroxylase, causes severe mental retardation unless phenylalanine can be largely restricted from the diet.

phobia An anxiety disorder in which there is intense fear and avoidance of specific objects and situations, recognized as irrational by the individual.

phonological disorder A learning disability in which some words sound like baby talk because the person is not able to make certain speech sounds.

phototherapy A treatment designed for people with seasonal affective disorder. It involves exposure to intense white light.

placebo control groups A group in an experiment that receives contact, support, and encouragement from a therapist, but not the active ingredient in the particular kind of therapy under study.

placebo effect The action of a drug or psychological treatment that is not attributable to any specific operations of the agent. For example, a tranquilizer can reduce anxiety both because of its special biochemical action and because the recipient expects relief.

plaques Small, round areas composed of remnants of lost neurons and beta-amyloid, a waxy protein deposit; present in the brains of patients with Alzheimer's disease.

pleasure principle In psychoanalytic theory, the demanding manner by which the id operates, seeking immediate gratification of its needs.

polydrug (or **polysubstance**) **abuse** The misuse of more than one drug at a time, such as drinking heavily and taking cocaine.

pons An area in the brain stem containing nerve-fibre tracts that connect the cerebellum with the spinal cord and with motor areas of the cerebrum.

positive reinforcement The strengthening of a tendency to behave in a certain situation by presenting a desired reward following previous responses in that situation.

positive symptoms In schizophrenia, behavioural excesses, such as hallucinations and bizarre behaviour. Contrast with *negative symptoms*.

postpartum depression The depression experienced by some mothers after giving birth.

post-traumatic stress disorder (PTSD) An anxiety disorder in which a particularly stressful event, such as military combat, rape, or a natural disaster, brings in its aftermath intrusive re-experiencings of the trauma, a numbing of responsiveness to the outside world, estrangement from others, a tendency to be easily startled, and nightmares, recurrent dreams, and otherwise disturbed sleep.

prefrontal lobotomy A surgical procedure that destroys the tracts connecting the frontal lobes to lower centres of the brain; once believed to be an effective treatment for schizophrenia.

premature ejaculation Inability of the male to inhibit his orgasm long enough for mutually satisfying sexual relations.

prevalence In epidemiological studies of a disorder, the percentage of a population that has the disorder at a given time. Compare with *incidence*.

prevention Primary prevention comprises efforts in community psychology to reduce the incidence of new cases of psychological disorder by such means as altering stressful living conditions and genetic counselling; secondary prevention includes efforts to detect disorders early, so that they will not develop into full-blown, perhaps chronic, disabilities; and tertiary prevention attempts to reduce the long-term consequences of having a disorder, equivalent in most respects to therapy.

primary process thinking The tendency to generate cognitive images of highly pleasurable things to presumably satisfy a current need for gratification and pleasure.

prior capable wish The result of the process of getting a person to outline his or her treatment wishes at an earlier time when he or she is of sounder mind and is not incapacitated.

privileged communication The communication between parties in a confidential relationship that is protected by statute. A spouse, doctor, lawyer, pastor, psychologist, or psychiatrist cannot be forced, except under unusual circumstances, to disclose such information.

profound mental retardation A limitation in mental development measured on IQ tests at less than 20–25; children with this degree of retardation require total supervision of all their activities.

projection A defence mechanism whereby characteristics or desires unacceptable to the ego are attributed to someone else.

projective hypothesis The notion that highly unstructured stimuli, as in the Rorschach inkblot test, are necessary to bypass defences in order to reveal unconscious motives and conflicts.

projective test A psychological assessment device employing a set of standard but vague stimuli on the assumption that unstructured material will allow unconscious motivations and fears to be uncovered. The Rorschach series of inkblots is an example.

pronoun reversal A speech problem in which the child refers to himself or herself as "he," "she," or "you" and uses "I" or "me" in referring to others; often found in the speech of children with autistic disorder.

prospective memory The ability to look forward and to remember to perform a required or intended action at the right place or time

provincial psychiatric hospital A facility where chronic patients are treated. Such hospitals provide protection, but treatment is often custodial and may involve little psychosocial treatment.

psilocybin A psychedelic drug extracted from the mushroom *Psilocybe mexicana*.

psychache The intense and intolerable psychological suffering and pain of suicidal individuals.

psychiatric nurse A nurse who has obtained additional training in the mental health field.

Psychiatrist A physician (MD) who has taken specialized postdoctoral training, called a residency, in the diagnosis, treatment, and prevention of mental disorders.

psychoactive drugs Chemical compounds having a psychological effect that alters mood or thought process. Valium is an example.

Psychoanalyst A therapist who has taken specialized postdoctoral training in psychoanalysis after earning an MD or a Ph.D. degree.

psychoanalytic (psychodynamic) paradigm General view based on psychoanalysis.

psychodynamics In psychoanalytic theory, the mental and emotional forces and processes that develop in early childhood and their effects on behaviour and mental states.

psychogenesis Development from psychological origins, as distinguished from somatic origins. Contrast with *somatogenesis*.

psychological factors affecting medical condition A diagnosis in *DSM-IV* that a physical illness is caused in part or exacerbated by psychological stress. See also *psychophysiological disorders*.

psychological tests Standardized procedures designed to measure a person's performance on a particular task or to assess his or her personality.

psychologizer An individual who emphasizes the psychological aspects and symptoms of depression.

psychopathology The field concerned with the nature and development of mental disorders.

psychopathy See *anti-social personality*.

psychophysiological disorders Disorders with physical symptoms that may involve actual tissue damage, usually in one organ system, and that are produced in part by continued mobilization of the autonomic nervous system under stress. Hives and ulcers are examples. No longer listed in *DSM-IV* in a separate category, such disorders are now diagnosed on Axis I as psychological factors influencing a medical condition; on Axis III the specific physical condition is given.

psychophysiology The discipline concerned with the bodily changes that accompany psychological events.

psychosis risk syndrome Syndrome proposed by *DSM-5* work group to identify young people at risk for developing schizophrenia or other psychoses.

psychosomatic disorders Disorders in which the psyche, or mind, is having an untoward effect on the soma, or body.

psychotherapy A primarily verbal means of helping troubled individuals change their thoughts, feelings, and behaviour to reduce distress and to achieve greater life satisfaction. See also *insight therapy* and *behaviour therapy*.

purging disorder A form of bulimia characterized primarily by self-induced vomiting or laxative use at least once a week for a minimum of six months.

random assignment A method of assigning people to groups in an experiment that gives each person an equal chance of being in each group. The procedure helps to ensure that groups are comparable before the experimental manipulation begins.

rational-emotive behaviour therapy (REBT) The new term for "rational-emotive therapy." A form of treatment that focuses on removing irrational dysfunctional thoughts that cause emotional distress and replacing these irrational thoughts with rational thoughts.

rationalization A defence mechanism in which a plausible reason is unconsciously invented by the ego to protect itself from confronting the real reason for an action, thought, or emotion.

reaction formation A defence mechanism whereby an unconscious and unacceptable impulse or feeling that would cause anxiety is converted into its opposite so that it can become conscious and can be expressed.

reactivity (of behaviour) The phenomenon whereby behaviour is changed by the very fact that it is being observed.

reading disorder (dyslexia) A disorder in which children have significant difficulty with word recognition, reading comprehension, and typically written spelling as well.

reality principle In psychoanalytic theory, the manner in which the ego delays gratification and otherwise deals with the environment in a planned, rational fashion.

reductionism The view that whatever is being studied can, and should, be reduced to its most basic elements or constituents. Biological reductionism proposes that mental and emotional responses can best be understood by comprehending basic biological variables such as neurotransmitter levels and balances.

regression A defence mechanism in which anxiety is avoided by retreating to the behaviour patterns of an earlier psychosexual stage.

reliability The extent to which a test, measurement, or classification system produces the same scientific observation each time it is applied.

repression A defence mechanism whereby impulses and thoughts unacceptable to the ego are pushed into the unconscious.

residual schizophrenia The diagnosis given to people who have had an episode of schizophrenia but who presently show no psychotic symptoms, though signs of the disorder do exist.

resilience An individual's level of protection from risk factors or ability to recover from emotional difficulties or trauma.

resistances During psychoanalysis, the defensive tendency of the unconscious part of the ego to ward off from consciousness particularly threatening repressed material.

reticular formation Network of nuclei and fibres in the central core of the brain stem that is important in arousing the cortex and maintaining alertness, in processing incoming sensory stimulation, and in adjusting spinal reflexes.

retrospective memory The ability to remember recent events and experiences that have already occurred.

reuptake Process by which released neurotransmitters are pumped back into the pre-synaptic cell, making them available for enhancing transmission of nerve impulses.

reversal (ABAB) design An experimental design in which behaviour is measured during a baseline period (A), during a period when a treatment is introduced (B), during the reinstatement of the conditions that prevailed in the baseline period (A), and finally during a reintroduction of the treatment (B). It is commonly used in operant research to isolate cause–effect relationships.

risk A factor that increases the likelihood of a person developing a disorder or dysfunction. Risk factors are often triggered by environmental events or stressors. Risk factors can react to a characteristic of the person (e.g., their personality) or their life situation (e.g., poverty).

risk factors A condition or variable that, if present, increases the likelihood of developing a disorder.

role-playing A technique that teaches people to behave in a certain way by encouraging them to pretend that they are in a particular situation; it helps people acquire complex behaviours in an efficient way. See also *behaviour rehearsal*.

Rorschach Inkblot Test A projective test in which the examinee is instructed to interpret a series of 10 inkblots reproduced on cards.

ruminative coping A tendency to focus cognitively (perhaps to the point of obsession) on the causes of depression and associated feelings rather than engaging in forms of distraction.

Scarlett O'Hara effect A tendency to eat lightly in an attempt to project an image of femininity.

schema A mental structure for organizing information about the world.

schema therapy A form of cognitive therapy developed primarily by Young. It focuses on identifying and modifying specific cognitive schemas believed to be at the root of personality dysfunction.

schizoid personality A disorder in which the person is emotionally aloof; indifferent to the praise, criticism, and feelings of others; and usually a loner with few, if any, close friends and with solitary interests.

schizophrenia A group of psychotic disorders characterized by major disturbances in thought, emotion, and behaviour; disordered thinking in which ideas are not logically related; faulty perception and attention; bizarre disturbances in motor activity; flat or inappropriate emotions; and reduced tolerance for stress in interpersonal relations. The person withdraws from people and reality, often into a fantasy life of delusions and hallucinations.

schizophrenogenic mother A cold, dominant, conflict-inducing mother formerly believed to cause schizophrenia in her child.

schizotypal personality A disorder in which a person is eccentric, has oddities of thought and perception (magical thinking, illusions, depersonalization, derealization), speaks digressively and with overelaborations, and is usually socially isolated. Under stress he or she may appear psychotic.

school phobia An acute, irrational dread of attending school, usually accompanied by somatic complaints. It is the most common phobia of childhood.

science The pursuit of systematized knowledge through reliable observation.

seasonal affective disorder (SAD) The "winter depressions" that stem from reduced exposure to daylight.

secondary process thinking The reality-based decision-making and problem-solving activities of the ego. Compare with *primary process thinking*.

second-hand smoke Also referred to as environmental tobacco smoke, the smoke from the burning end of a cigarette, which contains higher concentrations of ammonia, carbon monoxide, nicotine, and tar than does the smoke inhaled by the smoker.

securely attached An attachment orientation in which the infant can tolerate separations from the caregiver and will interact comfortably with a stranger.

sedative A drug that slows bodily activities, especially those of the central nervous system; it is used to reduce pain and tension and to induce relaxation and sleep.

selective mortality A possible confound in longitudinal studies, whereby the less healthy people in a sample are more likely to drop out of the study over time.

selective mutism A pattern of continuously refusing to speak in almost all social situations, including school, even though the child understands spoken language and is able to speak.

selective serotonin reuptake inhibitors (SSRIs) A major category of antidepressant drugs, such as fluoxetine (Prozac) and sertraline (Zoloft).

self-actualization The fulfillment of one's potential as an always-growing human being; believed by client-centred therapists to be the master motive.

self-criticism A personality style associated with vulnerability to depression. It involves excessive levels of self-criticism.

self-efficacy In Bandura's theory, the person's belief that he or she can achieve certain goals.

self-instructional training A cognitive-behavioural approach that tries to help people improve their overt behaviour by changing how they silently talk to themselves.

self-instructional training A cognitive-behavioural approach that tries to help people improve their overt behaviour by changing how they silently talk to themselves.

self-management programs Programs that assist patients in acquiring and practising the skills that they will need at home in their daily lives in order to adhere to disease-specific medical regimens and adjust health behaviours to achieve optimal function and improved levels of well-being. They include a problem-solving component because patients must assess their progress and problems and address problems as they emerge, as well as set goals, evaluate goal progress, and modify goals as needed.

self-monitoring In behavioural assessment, a procedure whereby the individual observes and reports certain aspects of his or her own behaviour, thoughts, or emotions.

sensate focus Exercises prescribed at the beginning of the Masters and Johnson sex therapy program; partners are instructed to fondle each other to give pleasure but to refrain from intercourse, thus reducing anxiety about sexual performance.

sensory-awareness procedures Techniques that help clients tune in to their feelings and sensations, as in sensate-focus exercises, and to be open to new ways of experiencing and feeling.

separation anxiety A disorder in which the child feels intense fear and distress when away from someone on whom he or she is very dependent; said to be a significant cause of school phobia.

severe abuse The traumatic experience of extreme mistreatment by someone else (e.g., childhood sexual abuse).

severe mental retardation A limitation in mental development measured in IQ tests at between 20–25 and 35–40. Individuals often cannot care for themselves, communicate only briefly, and are listless and inactive.

sex-reassignment surgery An operation in which the existing genitalia are altered to make them more like those of the opposite sex.

sexual and gender identity disorder In *DSM-IV*, disorders comprising the paraphilias, sexual dysfunctions, and gender identity disorders.

sexual aversion disorder Avoidance of nearly all genital contact with other people.

sexual dysfunctions Dysfunctions in which the appetitive or psychophysiological changes of the normal sexual response cycle are inhibited.

sexual masochism A marked preference for obtaining or increasing sexual gratification through subjection to pain or humiliation.

sexual sadism A marked preference for obtaining or increasing sexual gratification by inflicting pain or humiliation on another person.

sexual value system As applied by Masters and Johnson, the activities that an individual holds to be acceptable and necessary in a sexual relationship.

single-subject experimental design A design for an experiment conducted with a single subject; for example, the reversal and multiple-baseline designs in operant conditioning research.

sleep apnea A respiratory disorder in which breathing ceases repeatedly for a period of 10 seconds or more hundreds of times throughout the night.

social gradient of health The link between low socio-economic status and poor health.

social phobia A collection of fears linked to the presence of other people.

social phobias A collection of fears linked to the presence of other people.

social-selection theory An attempt to explain the correlation between social class and schizophrenia by proposing that people with

schizophrenia move downward in social status.

social worker A mental health professional who holds a master of social work (M.S.W.) degree.

sociogenic hypothesis Generally, an idea that seeks causes in social conditions; for example, that being in a low social class can cause one to become schizophrenic.

sociotropy A personality style associated with vulnerability to depression. It involves high levels of dependency and an excessive need to please others.

somatic nervous system That part of the nervous system that controls muscles under voluntary control.

somatic-weakness theory The hypothesis that a weakness in a particular organ or organ system can make it vulnerable to psychological stress and thereby to a particular psychophysiological disorder.

somatization disorder A somatoform disorder in which the person continually seeks medical help for recurrent and multiple physical symptoms that have no discoverable physical cause. The medical history is complicated and dramatically presented. Difficult to distinguish from *hypochondriasis*.

somatoform disorders Disorders in which physical symptoms suggest a physical problem but have no known physiological cause; they are therefore believed to be linked to psychological conflicts and needs but not voluntarily assumed. Examples are somatization disorder (Briquet's syndrome), conversion disorder, pain disorder, and hypochondriasis.

somatogenesis Development from bodily origins, as distinguished from psychological origins. Contrast with *psychogenesis*.

specific phobias An unwarranted fear and avoidance of a specific object or circumstance; for example, fear of nonpoisonous snakes or fear of heights.

specific-reaction theory The hypothesis that an individual develops a given psychophysiological disorder because of the innate tendency of the autonomic nervous system to respond in a particular way to stress; for example, by increasing heart rate or developing tension in the forehead.

spectator role As applied by Masters and Johnson, a pattern of behaviour in which the individual's focus on and concern with sexual performance impedes his or her natural sexual responses.

standardization The process of constructing an assessment procedure that has norms and meets the various psychometric criteria for reliability and validity.

statistical significance A result that has a low probability of having occurred by chance alone and is by convention regarded as important.

statutory rape See *forced rape*.

stepped care A treatment strategy that begins with less complex and costly interventions followed by more complex attempts if initial attempts are not successful.

stereotyping A fixed belief that typically involves a negative generalization about a group or class of people. Members of the general public often endorse a number of negative beliefs about mentally ill people, and thus engage in stereotyping.

stigmatization A reduction in the status of a group of people, such as mentally ill people, due to perceived deficiencies.

stimulant A drug that increases alertness and motor activity and at the same time reduces fatigue, allowing an individual to remain awake for an extended period of time. Examples are cocaine and amphetamines.

stress-inoculation training The act of teaching someone how to cope with small, manageable amounts of stress so they will be "protected" and will respond favourably when faced with more stressful circumstances.

stress management A range of psychological procedures that help people control and reduce their stress or anxiety.

stressor An event that occasions stress in an organism; for example, loss of a loved one.

stress State of an organism subjected to a stressor; it can take the form of increased autonomic activity and in the long term can cause the breakdown of an organ or development of a mental disorder.

Stroop task A measure of cognitive processing that requires respondents to identify the colour of a word while ignoring the word's content or meaning. It takes longer to colour-name a word if the word reflects a theme that is cognitively accessible for a particular individual.

structural social support A person's network of social relationships; for example, number of friends. Contrast with *functional social support*.

structured interview An interview in which the questions are set out in a prescribed fashion for the interviewer. Assists professionals in making diagnostic decisions based upon standardized criteria.

stuttering One of the communication disorders of childhood, marked by frequent and pronounced verbal dysfluencies, such as repetitions of certain sounds.

subjective age bias A tendency to feel younger than one's chronological age in a way that may reflect an age bias.

time-of-measurement effects A possible confound in longitudinal studies whereby conditions at a particular point in time can have a specific effect on a variable that is being studied over time.

sublimation Defence mechanism entailing the conversion of sexual or aggressive impulses into socially valued behaviours, especially creative activity.

substance abuse The use of a drug to such an extent that the person is often intoxicated throughout the day and fails in important obligations and in attempts to abstain, but there is no physiological dependence.

substance dependence The abuse of a drug sometimes accompanied by a physiological dependence on it, made evident by tolerance and withdrawal symptoms; also called addiction.

successive approximations Responses that closer and closer resemble the desired response in operant conditioning. See *shaping*.

suicide prevention centres Based on the assumption that people are often ambivalent about taking their own lives, these centres are staffed primarily by paraprofessionals who are trained to be empathic and to encourage suicidal callers to consider nondestructive ways of dealing with what is bothering them.

sulci Depressions between the ridges in the cerebral cortex or outer layer of the brain; also called *fissures*.

superego In psychoanalytic theory, the part of the personality that acts as the conscience and reflects society's moral standards as learned from parents and teachers.

sympathetic nervous system The division of the autonomic nervous system that acts on bodily systems—for example, contracting the blood vessels, reducing activity of the intestines, and increasing the heartbeat—to prepare the organism for exertion, emotional stress, or extreme cold.

sympathetic nervous system The division of the autonomic nervous system that acts on bodily systems—for example, contracting the blood vessels, reducing activity of the intestines, and increasing the heartbeat—to prepare the organism for exertion, emotional stress, or extreme cold.

synapse A small gap between two neurons where the nerve impulse passes from the axon of the first to the dendrites, cell body, or axon of the second.

syndrome A group or pattern of symptoms that tend to occur together in a particular disease.

systematic desensitization A major behaviour therapy procedure that has a fearful person, while deeply relaxed, imagine a series of progressively more fearsome situations. The two responses of relaxation and fear are incompatible and fear is dispelled. This technique is useful for treating psychological problems in which anxiety is the principal difficulty.

technical eclecticism A method of psychotherapy integration in which a particular style or school of psychotherapy is employed but one in which the therapist is free to borrow from other schools or methods deemed effective.

temporal lobe A large area of each cerebral hemisphere situated below the lateral sulcus and in front of the occipital lobe; contains primary auditory projection and association areas and general association areas.

test-retest reliability The extent to which people being observed twice or taking the same test twice score in generally the same way.

thalamus A major brain relay station consisting of two egg-shaped lobes located in the diencephalon; it receives impulses from all sensory areas except the olfactory and transmits them to the cerebrum.

Thematic Apperception Test (TAT) A projective test consisting of a set of black-and-white pictures reproduced on cards, each depicting a potentially emotion-laden situation. The examinee, presented with the cards one at a time, is instructed to make up a story about each situation.

theoretical integration An approach to psychotherapy integration that attempts to synthesize and combine not only various techniques but also various conceptual orientations.

theory A formally stated and coherent set of propositions that purport to explain a range of phenomena, order them in a logical way, and suggest what additional information might be gleaned under certain conditions.

theory of mind Our understanding that other people have desires, beliefs, intentions, and emotions that may be different from our own.

therapeutic (working) alliance A method of psychotherapy used in some schools in which the client is enlisted as an active partner in the planning and implementation of the procedures.

third-variable problem The difficulty in the correlational method of research whereby the relationship between two variables may be attributable to a third factor.

thought listing A cognitive assessment technique that involves a person writing down his or her thoughts upon experiencing an event, such as taking a test or meeting a person.

Time-of-measurement effect A possible confound in longitudinal studies whereby conditions at a particular point in time can have a specific effect on a variable that is being studied over time.

tolerance A physiological process in which greater and greater amounts of an addictive drug are required to produce the same effect. See *substance dependence*.

transference The venting of the client's emotions, either positive or negative, by treating the psychoanalyst as the symbolic representative of someone important in the past. An example is the client's becoming angry with the psychoanalyst to release emotions actually felt toward his or her father.

transsexualism The state of being a transsexual. See also *transsexual*.

transvestic fetishism The practice of dressing in the clothing of the opposite sex, for the purpose of sexual arousal.

trepanning The act of making a surgical opening in a living skull. This act was sometimes performed because of the belief that it would allow evil spirits to leave the body.

triadic reciprocality The influence of cognition and behaviour on each other through the relationships among thinking, behaviour, and the environment.

tricyclic drugs A group of antidepressants with molecular structures characterized by three fused rings. Tricyclics are known to interfere with the reuptake of norepinephrine and serotonin by a neuron after it has fired.

twin method Research strategy in behaviour genetics in which concordance rates of monozygotic and dizygotic twins are compared.

Type A behaviour pattern One of two contrasting psychological patterns revealed through studies seeking the cause of coronary heart disease. Type A people are competitive, rushed, hostile, and over-committed to their work, and are believed to be at heightened risk for heart disease. Those who meet the other pattern, Type B people, are more relaxed and relatively free of pressure.

unconditional positive regard According to Rogers, a crucial attitude for the client-centred therapist to adopt toward the client, who needs to feel complete acceptance as a person in order to evaluate the extent to which current behaviour contributes to self-actualization.

unconditioned response See *classical conditioning*.

unconditioned stimulus See *classical conditioning*.

unconscious A state of unawareness without sensation or thought. In psychoanalytic theory, it is the part of the personality, in particular the id impulses, or id energy, of which the ego is unaware.

undifferentiated schizophrenia The diagnosis given for clients whose symptoms do not fit any listed category or meet the criteria for more than one subtype.

unilateral ECT Electroconvulsive therapy in which electrodes are placed on one side of the forehead so that current passes through only one brain hemisphere.

vaginismus Painful, spasmodic contractions of the outer third of the vagina, which make insertion of the penis impossible or extremely difficult.

ventricles Cavities deep within the brain that are continuous with the central canal of the spinal cord and are filled with cerebrospinal fluid.

vicarious learning Learning by observing the reactions of others to stimuli or by listening to what they say.

videotape reconstruction A technique for assessing a person's thoughts and feelings. It involves having the person recall his or her reactions while watching a videotape of a previous time when they were engaged in a task.

virtual reality (VR) exposure A treatment for phobias using computer-generated graphics and sound to construct an experience similar to one that a client fears.

vital exhaustion An extreme form of physical depletion linked with cardiovascular disease. Vital exhaustion can stem from extreme overwork and striving.

voyeurism Marked preference for obtaining sexual gratification by watching others in a state of undress or having sexual relations.

waxy flexibility An aspect of catatonic immobility in which the person's limbs can be moved into a variety of positions and maintained that way for unusually long periods of time.

white matter The neural tissue, particularly of the brain and spinal cord, consisting of tracts or bundles of myelinated (sheathed) nerve fibres.

withdrawal Negative physiological and psychological reactions evidenced when a person suddenly stops taking an addictive drug; cramps, restlessness, and even death are examples. See *substance dependence*.

Aase, D. M., Jason, L. A., & Robinson, W. L. (2008). 12-step participation among dually-diagnosed individuals: A review of individual and contextual factors. *Clinical Psychology Review*, 28, 1235–1248.

Abela, J. R. Z. (2001). The hopelessness theory of depression: A test of the diathesis-stress and causal mediation components in third- and seventh-grade children. *Journal of Abnormal Child Psychology*, 29, 241–254.

Abela, J. R. Z. (2002). Depressive mood reactions to failure in the achievement domain: A test of the integration of the hopelessness and self-esteem theories of depression. *Cognitive Therapy and Research*, 26, 531–552.

Abela, J. R. Z., Aydin, C., & Auerbach, R. P. (2006). Operationalizing the "vulnerability" and "stress" components of the hopelessness theory of depression: A multi-wave longitudinal study. *Behaviour Research and Therapy*, 44, 1565–1583.

Abela, J. R. Z., Brozina, K., & Haigh, E. P. (2002). An examination of the response styles theory of depression in third- and seventh-grade children: A short-term longitudinal study. *Journal of Abnormal Child Psychology*, 30, 515–527.

Abela, J. R. Z., & D'Alessandro, D. U. (2002). Beck's cognitive theory of depression: A test of the diathesis-stress and causal mediation components. *British Journal of Clinical Psychology*, 41, 111–128.

Abela, J. R. Z., & Sarin, S. (2002). Cognitive vulnerability to hopelessness depression: A chain is only as strong as its weakest link. *Cognitive Therapy and Research*, 26, 811–829.

Abracen, J., et al. (2006). Patterns of attachment and alcohol abuse in sexual and violent nonsexual offenders. *Journal of Sexual Aggression*, 12, 19–30.

Abrams, R., Swartz, C. M.., & Vedak, C. (1991). Antidepressant effects of high-dose unilateral electroconvulsive therapy. *Archives of General Psychiatry*, 48, 746–748.

Abramson, L. Y., Metalsky, G. I., & Alloy, L. B. (1989). Hopelessness depression: A theory-based subtype of depression. *Psychological Review*, 96, 358–372.

Abramson, L. Y., Seligman, M. E. P., & Teasdale, J. D. (1978). Learned helplessness in humans: Critique and reformulation. *Journal of Abnormal Psychology*, 87, 49–74.

Achenbach, T. M., & Edelbrock, C. S. (1978). The classification of child psychopathology: A review of empirical efforts. *Psychological Bulletin*, 85, 1275–1301.

Adamek, M. E., & Kaplan, M. S. (1996). Managing elder suicide: A profile of American and Canadian crisis prevention centers. *Suicide and Life-Threatening Behavior*, 26, 122–131.

Adams, A. (1997, January 6). NHLer tells of horror of sex abuse. *Toronto Star*, A1.

Adams, K. S., et al. (1994). Parental representation of suicidal adolescents: A controlled study.

Australian and New Zealand Journal of Psychiatry, 28, 418–425.

Adams, P., & Laghi, B. (2000, November). Medicare debate boils over. *The Globe and Mail*, A1, A7.

Addington, D. E., Labelle, A., Kulkarni, J., et al. (2009). A comparison of zoprasidone and risperidone in the long-term treatment of schizphrenia: A 44-week, double-blind, continuation study. *Canadian Journal of Psychiatry*, 54, 46–54.

Addington, J., & Addington, D. (1998). Facial affect recognition and information processing in schizophrenia and bipolar disorder. *Schizophrenia Research*, 32, 171–181.

Adlaf, E. M., Demers, A., & Gliksman, L. (2005). *Canadian Campus Survey 2004.* Toronto: Centre for Addiction and Mental Health.

Adlaf, E. M., & Paglia, A. (2003). *Drug Use Among Ontario Students, 1977–2003: Detailed OSDUS Findings* (CAMH Research Document Series No. 13 No. 10). Toronto: Centre for Addiction and Mental Health.

Adlaf, E. M., Ivis, F. J., & Smart, R. G. (1997). *Ontario student drug use survey: 1977–1997.* Toronto: Addiction Research Foundation.

Adler, R. H., Zamboni, P., Hofer, T., & Hemmeler, W. (1997). How not to miss a somatic needle in a haystack of chronic pain. *Journal of Psychosomatic Research*, 42, 499–505.

Advisory Group on Suicide Prevention. (2003). *Acting on what we know: Preventing youth suicide in First Nations.* Ottawa: Government of Canada, First Nations and Inuit Health Branch.

Afifi, T. O., Cox, B. J., & Katz, L. Y. (2007). The associations between health risk behaviours and suicidal ideation and attempts in a nationally representative sample of young adolescents. *Canadian Journal of Psychiatry*, 52, 666–674.

Agbayewa, M. O., Marion, S. A., & Wiggins, S. (1998). Socioeconomic factors associated with suicide in elderly populations in British Columbia: An 11-year review. *Canadian Journal of Psychiatry*, 43, 829–836.

Aharoni, E., Funk, C., Sinnott-Armstrong, W., & Gazzaniga, M. (2008). Can neurological evidence help courts assess criminal responsibility? Lessons from neuroscience and the law. *Annals of the New York Academy of Sciences*, 1124, 145–160.

Ahmed, M., & Westra, H. M. (2009). Impact of a treatment rationale on expectancy and engagement in cognitive behavioural therapy for social anxiety. *Cognitive Therapy and Research*, 33, 314–322.

Ainsworth, M. D. (1984). Attachment. In N. S. Endler & J. McV. Hunt (Eds.), *Personality and the behavioral disorders* (Vol. 1, 2nd ed., pp. 559–602). New York: John Wiley & Sons.

Ainsworth, M. D., Blehar, M. C., Waters, E., & Wall, S. (1978). *Patterns of attachment: A psychological study of the strange situation.* Hillsdale, NJ: Erlbaum.

Akbarian, S., et al. (1995). Gene expression for glutamic acid decarboxylase is reduced without loss of neurons in prefrontal cortex of schizophrenics. *Archives of General Psychiatry*, 52, 258–266.

Akyuez, G., Dogan, O., Sar, V., Yargic, L. I., & Tutkun, H. (1999). Frequency of dissociative disorder in the general population in Turkey. *Comprehensive Psychiatry*, 40, 151–159.

Alamian, A., & Paradis, G. (2009). Correlates of multiple chronic disease behavioral risk factors in Canadian children and adolescents. *American Journal of Epidemiology*, 170, 1279–1289.

Alden, L. E. (1989). Short-term structured treatment for avoidant personality disorder. *Journal of Consulting and Clinical Psychology*, 57, 756–764.

Alden, L. E., Laposa, J. M., Taylor, C. T., & Ryder, A. G. (2002). Avoidant personality disorder: Current status and future directions. *Journal of Personality Disorders*, 16, 1–29.

Alexander, A. W., & Singer-Constant, A. M. (2004). Current status of treatments for dyslexia: Critical review. *Journal of Child Neurology*, 19, 744–758.

Alexander, F. (1950). *Psychosomatic medicine.* New York: Norton.

Alexander, F., & French, T. M. (1946). *Psychoanalytic therapy.* New York: Ronald Press.

Alexander, P. C., & Lupfer, S. L. (1987). Family characteristics and long-term consequences associated with sexual abuse. *Archives of Sexual Behavior*, 16, 235–245.

Alexopoulos, G. S., et al. (2009). Reducing suicide ideation and depression in older primary care patients: 24-month outcomes of the PROSPECT study. *American Journal of Psychiatry*, 166, 882–890.

Ali, J. (2002). Mental health of Canada's immigrants. *Supplement to Health Reports*, 13, 1–12 (Statistics Canada Catalogue No. 82-003).

Allderidge, P. (1979). Hospitals, mad houses, and asylums: Cycles in the care of the insane. *British Journal of Psychiatry*, 134, 321–324.

Allen, J., & Dana, R. H. (2004). Methodological issues in cross-cultural and multicultural Rorschach research. *Journal of Personality Assessment*, 82, 189–208.

Allison, P. J., Guichard, C., Fung, K., & Gilain, L. (2003). Dispositional optimism predicts survival status 1 year after diagnosis in head and neck cancer patients. *Journal of Clinical Oncology*, 21, 543–548.

Allison, S. E., von Waahide, L., Shockley, T., & Gabbard, G. O. (2006). The development of the self in the era of the internet and role-playing fantasy games. *American Journal of Psychiatry*, 163, 381–385.

Alloul, K., Sauriol, L., Kennedy, W., Laurier, C., Tessier, G., Novosel, S., et al. (1998). Alzheimer's disease: A review of the disease, its epidemiology, and economic impact. *Archives of Gerontology and Geriatrics*, 27, 189–221.

Alloy, L. B., Abramson, L. Y., Whitehorse, W. G., et al. (2006). Prospective incidence of first onsets and recurrences of depression in individuals at high and low cognitive risk for depression. *Journal of Abnormal Psychology*, 115, 145–156.

Alpert, J. E., et al. (1997). Social phobia, avoidant personality disorder and atypical depression: Co-occurrence and clinical implications. *Psychological Medicine*, 27, 627–633.

Altamura, C., Paluello, M. M., Mundo, E., Medda, S., & Mannu, P. (2001). Clinical and subclinical body dysmorphic disorder. *European Archives of Psychiatry and Clinical Neuroscience*, 251, 105–108.

Althof, S. E., et al. (2005). Psychological and interpersonal dimensions of sexual function and dysfunction. *Journal of Sexual Medicine*, 2, 793–800.

Alzheimer Society of Canada. (2010). *Rising tide: The impact of dementia on Canadian society: Executive summary*. Toronto: Author.

Amador, X. F., et al. (1994). Awareness of illness in schizophrenia and schizoaffective and mood disorder. *Archives of General Psychiatry*, 51, 826–836.

Amagoalik, J. (2009, April 1). There's little to celebrate on Nunavut's 10th birthday: Inuit territory suffers from unemployment, chronic social problems and high dropout rate. *Toronto Star*, A23.

American Association of Intellectual and Developmental Disabilities. (2009, September 14). New professional resource establishes ground-breaking paradigm to support people with intellectual disabilities (news release). Washington, DC: Author.

American Association of Intellectual and Developmental Disabilities. (2009). Diagnostic Adaptive Behavior Scale. Washington, DC: Author. Retrieved from www.aaidd.org/IntellectualDisabilityBook/content_2687.cfm?n.

American Association of Mental Retardation. (1992). *Mental retardation: Definition, classification, and systems of support*. Washington, DC: Author.

American College Health Association. (2008). Reference Group Data Report, Spring 2008. Baltimore, MD: American College Health Association.

American Psychiatric Association. (1952). *Diagnostic and statistical manual of mental disorders*. First edition, 1952; second edition, 1968; third edition, 1980; revised, 1987. Washington, DC: Author.

American Psychiatric Association. (1993). Practice guidelines for major depressive disorder in adults. *American Journal of Psychiatry*, 150, All.

American Psychiatric Association. (1994). *Diagnostic and statistical manual of mental disorders. Fourth edition (DSM-IV)*. Washington, DC: Author.

American Psychiatric Association. (2004). Practice guidelines for the treatment of patients with schizophrenia, 2nd ed. *American Journal of Psychiatry*, 161 (Suppl. 2), 1–114.

American Psychiatric Association (2010, February 10). APA announces draft diagnostic criteria for *DSM-5*: New proposed changes posted for leading manual of mental disorders. Release No.

10-07. Author: Arlington, Virginia. See www.dsm5.org

Anand, A., et al. (2000). Brain SPECT imaging of amphetamine-induced dopamine release in euthymic bipolar disorder patients. *American Journal of Psychiatry*, 157, 1109–1114.

Anderson, E. R., & Hope, D. A. (2008). A review of the tripartite model for understanding the link between anxiety and depression in youth. *Clinical Psychology Review*, 28, 275–287.

Anderson, P., Chisholm, D., & Fuhr, D. C. (2009). Effectiveness and cost-effectiveness of policies and programmes to reduce the harm caused by alcohol. *Lancet*, 373, 2234–2246.

Anderson, P., de Bruijn, A., Angus, K., Gordon, R., & Hastings, G. (2009). Impact of alcohol advertising and media exposure on adolescent alcohol use: A systematic review of longitudinal studies. *Alcohol and Alcoholism*, 44, 229–243.

Andersson, G., et al. (2006). Internet-based self-help with therapist feedback and in vivo group exposure for social phobia: A randomized controlled trial. *Journal of Consulting and Clinical Psychology*, 74, 677–686.

Andreasen, N. C., Flaum, M., Swayze, V. W., Tyrrell, G., & Arndt, S. (1990). Positive and negative symptoms in schizophrenia: A critical reappraisal. *Archives of General Psychiatry*, 47, 615–621.

Andreasen, N. C., & Olsen, S. A. (1982). Negative versus positive schizophrenia. Definition and validation. *Archives of General Psychiatry*, 39, 789–794.

Andreasen, N. C., Rice, J., Endicott, J., Coryell, W., Grove, W. W., & Reich, T. (1987). Familial rates of affective disorder. *Archives of General Psychiatry*, 44, 461–472.

Andres-Lemay, V. J., Jamieson, E., & MacMillan, H. L. (2005). Child abuse, psychiatric disorder, and running away in a community sample of women. *Canaadian Journal of Psychiatry*, 50, 684–689.

Andress, V. R., & Corey, D. M. (1978). Survivor-victims: Who discovers or witnesses suicide? *Psychological Reports*, 42, 759–764.

Andrew, M. K., Frefer, S. H., & Rockwood, K. (2006). Prevalence and outcomes of delirium in community and non-acute care settings in people without dementia: A report from the Canadian Study of Health and Aging. *BMC Medicine*, 4, 15.

Andrew, M. K., & Rockwood, K. (2007). Psychiatric illness in relation to frailty in community-dwelling elderly people with dementia: A report from the Canadian Study of Health and Aging. *Canadian Journal of Aging*, 26, 33–38.

Andrews, G. (2008). Reducing the burden of depression. *Canadian Journal of Psychiatry*, 53, 420–427.

Andrews, G., Hobbs, M. J., Borkovec, T. D., et al. (2010). Generalized worry disorder: A review of DSM-IV generalized anxiety disorder and options for DSM-V. *Depression and Anxiety*, 27, 134–147.

Andrews, G., Slade, T., Sunderland, M. T., & Anderson, T. (2007). Issues for DSM-V: Simplifying DSM-IV to enhance utility: The case of major depressive disorder. *American Journal of Psychiatry*, 164, 1784–1785.

Angrist, B., Lee, H. K., & Gershon, S. (1974). The antagonism of amphetamine-induced symptomatology by a neuroleptic. *American Journal of Psychiatry*, 131, 817–819.

Angus, L. E., & Kagan, F. (2009). Therapist empathy and client anxiety reduction in motivational interviewing: "She carries with me, the experience." *Journal of Clinical Psychiatry*, 65, 1156–1167.

Anisman, H., & Merali, Z. (1999). Understanding stress: Characteristics and caveats. *Alcohol Research and Health*, 23, 241–249.

Antoni, M. H. (2006). How stress management improves quality of life after treatment for breast cancer. *Journal of Consulting and Clinical Psychology*, 74, 1143–1152.

Antony, M. M., & McCabe, R. E. (2003). Anxiety disorders: Social and specific phobias. In A. Tasman, J. Kay, & J. A. Lieberman (Eds.), *Psychiatry* (2nd ed., pp. 1298–1330). New York: John Wiley & Sons.

Antony, M. M., & McCabe, R. E. (2004). *Ten simple solutions to panic: How to overcome panic attacks, calm physical symptoms, and reclaim your life*. Oakland, CA: New Harbinger Publications.

Antony, M. M., & McCabe, R. E. (2005). *Overcoming animal and insect phobias: How to conquer fear of dogs, snakes, rodents, bees, spiders, and more*. Oakland, CA: New Harbinger Publications.

Antony, M. M., & Norton, P. J. (2009). *The anti-anxiety workbook*. New York: Guilford Press.

Antony, M. M., & Rowa, K. (2008). Social anxiety disorder: Psychological approaches to assessment and treatment. Gottingen, Germany: Hogrefe.

Antony, M. M., & Swinson, R. P. (2008). *The shyness and social anxiety workbook* (2nd ed.). Oakland, CA: New Harbinger.

Antony, M. M., & Swinson, R. P. (2009). *When perfect isn't good enough* (2nd ed.). Oakland, CA: New Harbinger.

Antony, M. M., & Swinson, R. P. (2000). *The shyness and social anxiety workbook: Proven, step-by-step techniques for overcoming your fear*. Oakland, CA: New Harbinger Publications.

Antshel, K. M., Faraone, S. V., Maglione, K., et al. (2009). Is adult attention deficit hyperactivity disorder a valid diagnosis in the presence of high IQ? *Psychological Medicine*, 39, 1325–1335.

Apfelbaum, B. (1989). Retarded ejaculation: A much-misunderstood syndrome. In S. R. Leiblum & R. C. Rosen (Eds.), *Principles and practice of sex therapy: Update for the 1990s* (pp. 168–206). New York: Guilford.

Appel, L. J., et al., for the DASH Collaborative Research Group. (1997). A clinical trial of the effects of dietary patterns on blood pressure. *New England Journal of Medicine*, 336, 1117–1124.

Apt, C., & Hurlbert, D. H. (1994). The sexual attitudes, behavior, and relationships of women with histrionic personality disorder. *Journal of Sex and Marital Therapy*, 20, 125–133.

Arbuthnot, J., & Gordon, D. A. (1986). Behavioral and cognitive effects of a moral reasoning development intervention for high-risk behavior disordered adolescents. *Journal of Consulting and Clinical Psychology*, 54, 208–216.

Arcelus, J., et al. (2009). A case series evaluation of a modified version of interpersonal psychotherapy

(IPT) for the treatment of bulimia eating disorders. *European Eating Disorders Review, 17,* 260–268.

Ard, B. N., Jr. (1977). Sex in lasting marriages: A longitudinal study. *Journal of Sex Research, 13,* 274–285.

Argyropolous, S. V., Landau, S., Kalidindi, S., et al. (2008). Twins discordant for schizophrenia: Psychopathology of the non-schizophrenic co-twins. *Acta Psychiatrica Scandinavica, 118,* 214–219.

Arieti, S. (1979). New views on the psychodynamics of phobias. *American Journal of Psychotherapy, 33,* 82–95.

Arkowitz, H. (1989). The role of theory in psychotherapy integration. *Journal of Integrative and Eclectic Psychotherapy, 8,* 8–16.

Arkowitz, H., Westra, H. A., Miller, W. R., & Rollnick, S. (2007). *Motivational interviewing in the treatment of psychological problems.* New York: Guilford.

Armstrong, T., & Olatunji, B. (2009). What they see is what you get: Tracking of attention in the anxiety disorders. *Psychological Science Agenda, 23* (3).

Arndt, I. O., et al. (1992). Desipramine treatment of cocaine dependence in methadone-maintained patients. *Archives of General Psychiatry, 49,* 888–893.

Aronson, J. (2002). Elderly people's accounts of home care rationing: Missing voices in long-term care policy debates. *Aging and Society, 22,* 399–418.

Arseneault, L., Tremblay, R. E., Boulerice, B., & Saucier, J. F. (2002). Obstetrical complications and violent delinquency: Testing two developmental pathways. *Child Development, 73,* 496–508.

Askew, C., & Field, A. P. (2008). The vicarious learning pathway to fear 40 years on. *Clinical Psychology Review, 28,* 1249–1265.

Asmundson, G. J. G., & Katz, J. (2009). Understanding the co-occurrence of anxiety disorders and chronic pain: State-of-the-art. *Depression and Anxiety, 26,* 888–901.

Asmundson, G. J., Larsen, D. K., & Stein, M. B. (1998). Panic disorder and vestibular disturbance: An overview of empirical findings and clinical implications. *Journal of Psychosomatic Research, 44,* 107–120.

Asmundson, G. J., Stein, M. B., & McCreary, D. R. (2002). Posttraumatic stress disorder symptoms influence health status of deployed peacekeepers and nondeployed military personnel. *Journal of Nervous and Mental Disease, 190,* 807–815.

Asmundson, G. J. G., & Taylor, S. (2003). Anxiety disorders: Panic disorder with and without agoraphobia. In A. Tasman, J. Kay, & J. A. Lieberman (Eds.), *Psychiatry* (2nd ed., pp. 1281–1297). New York: John Wiley & Sons.

Asmundson, G. J., Taylor, S., Sevgur, S., & Cox, B. J. (2001). Health anxiety: Classification and clinical features. In G. J. G. Asmundson, S. Taylor, & B. J. Cox (Eds.), *Health anxiety: Clinical and research perspectives on hypochondriasis and related conditions* (pp. 3–21). Toronto: John Wiley & Sons.

Asmundson, G. J., Taylor, S., Wright, K. D., & Cox, B. J. (2001). Future directions and

challenges in assessment, treatment, and investigation. In G. J. G. Asmundson, S. Taylor, & B. J. Cox (Eds.), *Health anxiety: Clinical and research perspectives on hypochondriasis and related conditions* (pp. 365–381). Toronto: John Wiley & Sons.

Atkinson, L., Paglia, A., Coolbear, J., Niccols, A., Parker, K. C. H., & Guger, S. (2000). Attachment security: A meta-analysis of maternal mental health correlates. *Clinical Psychology Review, 20,* 1019–1040.

Auditor General of Canada. (2001). *2001 Report of the Auditor General of Canada.* Ottawa: Author.

Audrain-McGovern, J., et al. (2004). Interacting effects of genetic predisposition and depression on adolescent smoking progression. *American Journal of Psychiatry, 161,* 1224–1230.

Auld, A. (2001, August 2). Convicted pedophile will be released from prison, but will go to psych centre. The Canadian Press.

Austin, S. B., Haines, J., & Veugelers, P. J. (2009). Body satisfaction and body weight: Gender differences and sociodemographic determinants. *BMC Public Health, 9,* 1–7.

Autism Genome Project Consortium. (2007). Mapping autism risk loci using genetic linkage and chromosomal rearrangements. *Nature Genetics, 39,* 319–328.

Autism Speaks. (2009, June 9). NIH Autism Center of Excellence Network and Autism Speaks announce launch of most comprehensive study of earliest possible causes of autism: Leading researchers nationwide to participate in EARLI Study (news release). Philadelphia: Author.

Avissar, S., Schreiber, G., Nechamkin, Y., Nehaus, I., Lam, G., et al. (1999). The effects of seasons and light therapy on G protein levels in mononuclear leukocytes in patients with seasonal affective disorder. *Archives of General Psychiatry, 56,* 178–184.

Awad, G. A., & Saunders, E. (1989). Adolescent child molesters: Clinical observations. *Child Psychiatry and Human Development, 19,* 195–206.

Ayers, C. R., Sorrell, J. T., Thorp, S. R., & Wetherell, J. L. (2007). Evidence-based psychological treatments for late-life anxiety. *Psychology and Aging, 22,* 8–17.

Ayllon, T. (1963). Intensive treatment of psychotic behavior by stimulus satiation and food reinforcement. *Behavior Research & Therapy, 1,* 53-61.

Babarik, P. (1979). The buried Canadian roots of community psychology. *Journal of Community Psychology, 7,* 362–367.

Bacic, J. (2008). Landmark series on Canada's mental health crisis gets people talking. *Canadian Psychiatry Aujourd'hui, 4 (4),* 1–2.

Bacic, J. (2009). WHO says primary care delivery of mental health services is cost effective. *Canadian Psychiatry Aujourd'hui, 5 (1),* 1–2.

Bacic, J. (2009). MHCC releases its vision for a national mental health strategy. *Canadian Psychiatry Aujourd'hui, 5 (2),* 1–2.

Baer, J. S., & Lichtenstein, E. (1988). Cognitive assessment. In D. M. Donovan & G. A. Marlatt (Eds.), *Assessment of addictive behaviors* (pp. 189–213). New York: Guilford.

Baer, R. A., & Sekirnjak, G. (1997). Detection of underreporting on the MMPI-II in a clinical

population. Effects of information about validity scales. *Journal of Personality Assessment, 69,* 555–567.

Bagby, R. M., Quilty, L. C., Segal, Z. V., et al. (2008). Personality and differential treatment response in major depression: A randomized controlled trial comparing cognitive-behavioural therapy and pharmacotherapy. *Canadian Journal of Psychiatry, 53,* 361–370.

Bagby, R. M., Ryder, A. G., Ben-Dat, D., Bacchiochi, J., & Parker, J. D. A. (2002). Validation of the dimensional factor structure of the Personality Psychopathology Five in clinical and nonclinical samples. *Journal of Personality Disorders, 16,* 304–316.

Bagby, R. M., Ryder, A. G., & Christi, C. (2002). Psychosocial and clinical predictors of response to pharmacotherapy for depression. *Journal of Psychiatry and Neuroscience, 27,* 250–257.

Bagby, M. R., Sellbom, M., Costa, P. T., Jr., & Widiger, T. A. (2008). Predicting Diagnostic and Statistical Manual of Mental Disorders –IV personality disorders with the five-factor model of personality and the personality psychopathology five. *Personality and Mental Health, 2,* 55–69.

Bagley, C., Bolitho, F., & Bertrand, L. (1997). Sexual assault in school, mental health and suicidal behaviors in adolescent women in Canada. *Adolescence, 32,* 361–366.

Bagley, C., & Mallick, K. (2000). Prediction of sexual, emotional, and physical maltreatment and mental health outcomes in a longitudinal cohort of 290 adolescent women. *Child Maltreatment, 5,* 218–226.

Bahm, A., & Forchuk, C. (2009). Interlocking oppressions: The effect of a comorbid physical disability on perceived stigma and discrimination among mental health consumers in Canada. *Health & Social Care in the Community, 17,* 63–70.

Bailey, I. (2000, December 19). Rebick defends rape centre's right to reject transsexual. *The National Post,* 1.

Bailey, S., & Bronskill, J. (2006, November 23). Crisis looming as mentally ill jailed in disturbing numbers: Chief justice. *The Western Star,* 15.

Baker, C. W., Whisman, A., & Brownell, K. D. (2000). Studying intergenerational transmission of eating attitudes and behaviors: Methodological and conceptual questions. *Health Psychology, 19,* 376–381.

Baker, D., Earle, M., Medford, N., et al. (2007). Illness perceptions in depersonalization disorder: Testing an illness attribution model. *Clinical Psychology & Psychotherapy, 14,* 105–116.

Bakken, I. J., Wenzel, H. G., Gotestam, K. G., et al. (2009). Internet addiction among Norwegian adults: A stratified probability sample study. *Scandinavian Journal of Psychology, 50,* 121–127.

Bakogeorge, P. (2000, January 8). Mentally ill left out in new Calgary. *Toronto Star,* A3.

Baldessarini, R. J., & Hennen, J. (2004). Genetics of suicide: An overview. *Harvard Review of Psychiatry, 12,* 1–13.

Baldwin, M. W., Carrell, S. E., & Lopez, D. F. (1990). Priming relationship schemas: My advisor and the Pope are watching me from the back of my mind. *Journal of Experimental Social Psychology, 26,* 435–454.

Bailis, D. S., et al. (2001). Perceived control in relation to socioeconomic and behavioral resources for health. *Social Science and Medicine, 52,* 1661–1676.

Ball, H. A., McGuffin, P., & Farmer, E. (2008). Attributional style and depression. *The British Journal of Psychiatry, 192,* 275–278.

Balint, S., Czobor, P., Komlosi, S., et al. (2009). Attention deficit hyperactivity disorder (ADHD): Gender- and age-related differences in neurocognition. *Psychological Medicine, 39,* 1337–1345.

Baltes, M. M. (1988). The etiology and maintenance of dependency in the elderly: Three phases of operant research. *Behavior Therapy, 19,* 301–319.

Bancroft, J. (1988). Sexual desire and the brain. *Sexual and Marital Therapy, 3,* 11–29.

Bancroft, J. H. (1989). *Human sexuality and its problems* (2nd ed.). Edinburgh: Churchill Livingston.

Bandura, A. (1977). Self-efficacy: Toward a unifying theory of behavioral change. *Psychological Review, 84,* 191–215.

Bandura, A. (1986). *Social foundations of thought and action: A social cognitive theory.* Englewood Cliffs, NJ: Prentice-Hall.

Bandura, A. (1997). *Self-efficacy: The exercise of control.* New York: Freeman.

Bandura, A. (2001). Social cognitive theory: An agentic perspective. *Annual Review of Psychology, 52,* 1–26.

Bandura, A. (2006). Toward a psychology of human agency. *Perspectives in Psychological Science, 1,* 164–180.

Bandura, A. (2007). Autobiography. In M. G. Lindzey & W. M. Runyan (Eds.) *A history of psychology in autobiography* (Vol. IX, pp. 42–75). Washington, D.C.: American Psychological Association.

Bandura, A., & Menlove, F. L. (1968). Factors determining vicarious extinction of avoidance behavior through symbolic modeling. *Journal of Personality and Social Psychology, 8,* 99–108.

Bandura, A., & Rosenthal, T. L. (1966). Vicarious classical conditioning as a function of arousal level. *Journal of Personality and Social Psychology, 3,* 54–62.

Bandura, A., Ross, D., & Ross, S. A. (1961). Transmission of aggression through imitation of aggressive models. *Journal of Abnormal and Social Psychology, 63,* 575–582.

Bandura, A., & Walters, R. H. (1959). *Adolescent aggression.* New York : Ronald Press.

Bandura, A., & Walters, R. H. (1963). *Social learning and personality development.* New York: Holt, Rinehart & Winston.

Bank, L., Marlowe, J. H., Reid, J. B., Patterson, G. R., & Weinrott, M. R. (1991). A comparative evaluation of parent-training interventions for families of chronic delinquents. *Journal of Abnormal Child Psychology, 19,* 15–33.

Banon, E., Evan-Grenier, M., & Bond, M. (2001). Early transference interventions with male patients in psychotherapy. *Journal of Psychotherapy Practice and Research, 10,* 79–92.

Barak, A. (2007). Emotional support and suicide prevention through the Internet: A field project

report. *Computers in Human Behaviour, 23,* 971–984.

Barbaree, H. E. (2005). Psychopathy, treatment behavior, and recidivism: An extended follow-up of Seto and Barbaree. *Journal of Interpersonal Violence, 20,* 1115–1131.

Barbaree, H. E., Seto, M. C., Langton, C. M., & Peacock, E. J. (2001). Evaluating the predictive accuracy of six risk assessment instruments for adult sex offenders. *Criminal Justice and Behavior, 28,* 490–521.

Bardone-Cone, A. M., Wonderlich, S. A., Frost, R. O., et al. (2007). Perfectionism and eating disorders: Current status and future directions. *Clinical Psychology Review, 27,* 384–405.

Barker, E., Mason, M., & Wilson, J. (1969). Defence-disrupting therapy. *Canadian Psychiatric Association Journal, 14,* 355–359.

Barker, E. D., Boivin, M., Brendgen, M., et al. (2008). Predictive validity and early predictors of peer-victimization trajectories in preschool. *Archives of General Psychiatry, 65,* 1185–1192.

Barker, E. D., & Maughan, B. (2009). Differentiating early-onset persistent versus childhood-limited conduct problem youth. *American Journal of Psychiatry, 166,* 900–908.

Barkley, R. A. (1981). *Hyperactive children: A handbook for diagnosis and treatment.* New York: Guilford.

Barkley, R. A. (1990). *Attention-deficit hyperactivity disorder: A handbook for diagnosis and treatment.* New York: Guilford.

Barkley, R. A. (2002). International Consensus Statement on ADHD. *European Child and Adolescent Psychiatry, 11,* 96–98.

Barkley, R. A., Karlsson, J., & Pollard, S. (1985). Effects of age on the mother-child interactions of hyperactive children. *Journal of Abnormal Child Psychology, 13,* 631–638.

Barlow, D. H. (1999). *NIMH Collaborative Trial on the Treatment of Panic Disorder.* Paper presented at the annual convention of the Association for Advancement of Behavior Therapy, Toronto.

Barlow, D. H., Abel, G. G., & Blanchard, E. B. (1979). Gender identity change in transsexuals. *Archives of General Psychiatry, 36,* 1001–1007.

Barlow, D. H., Becker, R., Leitenberg, H., & Agras, W. S. (1970). A mechanical strain gauge for recording penile circumference. *Journal of Applied Behavior Analysis, 3,* 73–76.

Barlow, D. H., Blanchard, E. B., Vermilyea, J. A., Vermilyea, B. B., & DiNardo, P. A. (1986). Generalized anxiety and generalized anxiety disorder: Description and reconceptualization. *American Journal of Psychiatry, 143,* 40–44.

Barlow, D. H., Esler, J. L., & Vitali, A. E. (1998). Psychosocial treatments for panic disorders, phobias, and generalized anxiety disorder. In P. E. Nathan & J. M. Gorman (Eds.), *A guide to treatments that work* (pp. 288–318). New York: Oxford University Press.

Barlow, D. H., Reynolds, E. J., & Agras, W. S. (1973). Gender identity change in a transsexual. *Archives of General Psychiatry, 29,* 569–576.

Barlow, D. H., Vermilyea, J., Blanchard, E., Vermilyea, B., DiNardo, P., & Cerny, J. (1985). The phenomenon of panic. *Journal of Abnormal Psychology, 94,* 320–328.

Barnes, G. E. (1989). Gasoline sniffing in northern Canada. In S. Einstein (Ed.), *Drug and alcohol use: Issues and factors* (pp. 363–385). New York: Plenum Press.

Barnes, G. E., Barnes, M. D., & Patton, D. (2005). Prevalence and predictors of "heavy" marijuana use in a Canadian youth sample. *Substance Use and Misuse, 40,* 1849–1863.

Barnes, G. E., & Toews, J. (1983). Deinstitutionalization of chronic mental patients in the Canadian context. *Canadian Psychology, 24,* 22–36.

Barnhofer, T., Crane, C., Hargus, E., et al. (2009). Mindfulness-based cognitive therapy as a treatment for chronic depression: A preliminary study. *Behaviour Research and Therapy, 47,* 366–373.

Barrett, M., Wilson, R. J., & Long, C. (2003). Measuring motivation to change in sexual offenders from institutional intake to community treatment. *Sexual Abuse, 15,* 269–283.

Barsky, A. J., Fama, J. M., Bailey, E. D., & Ahern, D. K. (1998). A prospective 4- to 5-year study of DSM-III-R hyponchondriasis. *Archives of General Psychiatry, 55,* 737–744.

Bartholomew, K., & Horowitz, L. M. (1991). Attachment styles among young adults: A test of a four-category model. *Journal of Personality and Social Psychology, 61,* 226–244.

Bartlett, C. W., et al. (2002). A major susceptibility locus for specific language impairment is located on 13q21. *American Journal of Human Genetics, 71,* 45–55.

Bartlett, F. (1932). *Remembering.* Cambridge: Cambridge University Press.

Bartlett, N. H., Vasey, P. L., & Bukowski, W. M. (2000). Is gender identity disorder in children a mental disorder? *Sex Roles, 43,* 753–785.

Bartlett, P. (2000). Structures of confinement in 19th-century asylums: A comparative study using England and Ontario. *International Journal of Law and Psychiatry, 23,* 1–13.

Basco, M. R., & Rush, A. J. (1996). *Cognitive-behavioral therapy for bipolar disorder.* New York: Guilford.

Bass, E., & Davis, L. (1994). *The courage to heal: A guide for women survivors of child sexual abuse.* New York: Harper Collins.

Bastiani, A. M., Rao, R., Weltzin, T., & Kaye, W. H. (1995). Perfectionism in anorexia nervosa. *International Journal of Eating Disorders, 17,* 147–152.

Bates, G. W. (1990). *Social anxiety and self-presentation: Conversational behaviours and articulated thoughts of heterosexually anxious males.* Unpublished doctoral dissertation, University of Melbourne, Australia.

Bates, G. W., Campbell, T. M., & Burgess, P. M. (1990). Assessment of articulated thoughts in social anxiety: Modification of the ATSS procedure. *British Journal of Clinical Psychology, 29,* 91–98.

Baucom, D., Epstein, N., & Rankin, L. (1995). Integrative couple therapy. In N. S. Jacobson & A. S. Gurman (Eds.), *Clinical handbook of couple therapy* (pp. 65–90). New York: Guilford.

Baumeister, R. F. (1990). Suicide as escape from self. *Psychological Review, 97,* 90–113.

Baumeister, H., Maercker, A., & Casey, P. (2009). Adjustment disorder with depressed mood: A critique of its DSM-IV and ICD-10 conceptualisations and recommendations for the future. *Psychopathology, 42,* 139–147.

Baumgartner, G. R., & Rowen, R. C. (1987). Clonidine vs. chlordiazepoxide in the management of acute alcohol withdrawal. *Archives of Internal Medicine, 147,* 1223–1226.

Baxter, L. R., et al. (1992). Caudate glucose metabolic rate changes with both drug and behavior therapy for obsessive-compulsive disorder. *Archives of General Psychiatry, 49,* 681–689.

Baxter, N., & The Canadian Task Force on Preventive Health Care. (2001). Preventive health care, 2001 update: Should women be routinely taught breast self-examination to screen for breast cancer? *Canadian Medical Association Journal, 164,* 1837–1846.

Beach, S. R. H., Sandeen, E. E., & O'Leary, K. D. (1990). *Depression in marriage.* New York: Guilford.

Beacher, F., Daly, E., Simmons, A., et al. (2009). Alzheimer's disease and Down's syndrome: An *in vivo* MRI study. *Psychological Medicine, 39,* 675–684.

Beal, A. L. (1995). Post-traumatic stress disorder in prisoners of war and combat veterans of the Dieppe raid: A 50-year follow-up. *Canadian Journal of Psychiatry, 40,* 177–184.

Bebbington, P. E., Cooper, C., Minot, S., et al. (2009). Suicide attempts, gender, and sexual abuse: Data from the 2000 British Psychiatric Morbidity Survey. *American Journal of Psychiatry, 166,* 1135–1140.

Beck, A. T. (1967). *Depression: Clinical, experimental and theoretical aspects.* New York: Harper & Row.

Beck, A. T. (1976). *Cognitive therapy and the emotional disorders.* New York: International Universities Press.

Beck, A. T. (1983). Cognitive therapy of depression: New perspectives. In P. J. Clayton & J. E. Barnett (Eds.), *Treatment of depression: Old controversies and new approaches* (pp. 265–290). New York: Raven Press.

Beck, A. T. (1987). Cognitive models of depression. *Journal of Cognitive Psychotherapy: An International Quarterly, 1,* 5–37.

Beck, A. T. (2008). The evolution of the cognitive model of depression and its neurobiological correlates. *American Journal of Psychiatry, 165,* 969–977.

Beck, A. T., Freeman, A., et al. (1990). *Cognitive therapy of personality disorders.* New York: Guilford.

Beck, A. T., Kovacs, M., & Weissman, A. (1979). Assessment of suicidal ideation: The Scale for Suicide Ideation. *Journal of Consulting and Clinical Psychology, 47,* 343–352.

Beck, A. T., & Rector, N. A. (2005). Cognitive approaches to schizophrenia: Theory and therapy. *Annual Review of Clinical Psychology, 1,* 577–606.

Beck, C. A., et al. (2005). Psychotropic medication use in Canada. *Canadian Journal of Psychiatry, 50,* 605–613.

Beck, J. G. (1995). Hypoactive sexual desire disorder: An overview. *Journal of Consulting and Clinical Psychology, 63,* 919–927.

Beck, J. G., & Bozman, A. (1995). Gender differences in sexual desire: The effects of anger and anxiety. *Archives of Sexual Behavior, 24,* 595–612.

Becker, C. B., Bull, S., Smith, L. M., & Ciao, A. C. (2008). Effects of being a peer-leader in an eating disorder prevention program: Can we further reduce eating disorder risk factors? *Eating Disorders, 16,* 444–459.

Becker, E. S., Rinck, M., Roth, W. T., & Margraf, J. (1998). Don't worry and beware of white bears: Thought suppression in anxiety patients. *Journal of Anxiety Disorders, 12,* 39–55.

Becker, J. V. (1990). Treating adolescent sexual offenders. *Professional Psychology: Research and Practice, 21,* 362–365.

Becker, J. V., Skinner, L. J., Abel, G. G., & Cichon, J. (1986). Level of postassault sexual functioning in rape and incest victims. *Archives of Sexual Behavior, 15,* 37–49.

Beecher, H. K. (1966). Ethics and clinical research. *New England Journal of Medicine, 274,* 1354–1360.

Beidel, D. C., Turner, S. M., Sallee, F. R., Ammerman, R. T., Crosby, L. A., & Pathak, S. (2007). SET-C versus fluoxetine in the treatment of childhood social phobia. *Journal of the American Academy of Child and Adolescent Psychiatry, 46,* 1622–1632.

Beiser, M., Hou, F., Hyman, I., & Tousignant, M. (1998). *Growing up Canadian: A study of new immigrant children* (No. W-98-24E). Ottawa: Human Resources Development Canada.

Beitchman, J. H., Wilson, B., Johnson, C. J., Atkinson, L., Young, A., Adlaf, E., et al. (2001). Fourteen-year follow-up of speech/language-impaired and control children: Psychiatric outcome. *Journal of the American Academy of Child and Adolescent Psychiatry, 40,* 75–82.

Bekhit, N. S., Thomas, G. V., Lalonde, S., & Jolley, R. (2002). Psychological assessment in clinical practice in Britain. *Clinical Psychology and Psychotherapy, 9,* 285–291.

Bell, A. C., & D'Zurilla, T. J. (2009). Problem-solving therapy for depression: A meta-analysis. *Clinical Psychology Review, 29,* 348–353.

Bencherif, B., et al. (2005). Regional mu-opiod receptor binding in insular cortex is decreased in bulimia nervosa and correlates inversely with fasting behavior. *Journal of Nuclear Medicine, 46,* 1349–1351.

Benish, S. G., Imel, Z. E., & Wampold, B. E. (2008). The relative efficacy of bona fide psychotherapies for treating post-traumatic stress disorder: A meta-analysis of direct comparisons. *Clinical Psychology Review, 28,* 746–758.

Ben-Itzchak, E., & Zachor, D. A. (2007). The effects of intellectual functioning and autism severity on outcome of early behavioral intervention for children with autism. *Research in Developmental Disabilities, 28,* 287–303.

Benjafield, J. G., & Boudreau, F. (2000). Introduction: Canadian community mental health: Our past, our future. *Canadian Journal of Community Mental Health, 19,* 5–8.

Benkelfat, C., Ellenbogen, M. A., Dean, P., Palmour, R. M., & Young, S. N. (1994). Mood-lowering effect of tryptophan depletion: Enhanced susceptibility in young men at genetic risk for major affective disorders. *Archives of General Psychiatry, 51,* 687–700.

Bennett, M. (2008, October). *Criminal law as it pertains to mentally incompetent defendants': A M'Naghten Rule in light of cognitive neuroscience.* Natural Judicial College of Australia conference.

Bennett, M. R., & Hacker, P. M. S. (2003). *Philosophical foundations of neuroscience.* Oxford, UK: Blackwell.

Bennett, V. (1997, February 22). Russia's forgotten children. *Los Angeles Times,* A1, A10.

Benowitz, N. L. (2008). Clinical pharmacology of nicotine: Implications for understanding, preventing, and treating tobacco addiction. *Clinical Pharmacology and Therapeutics, 83,* 531–543.

Benzies, K., Keown, L.-A., & Magill-Evans, J. (2009). Immediate and sustained effects of parenting on physical aggression in Canadian children aged 6 years and younger. *Canadian Journal of Psychiatry, 54,* 55–64.

Beran, T. N., & Violato, C. (2004). A model of childhood perceived peer harassment: Analyses of the Canadian National Longitudinal Survey of Children and Youth data. *Journal of Psychology, 138,* 129–147.

Berenbaum, H., et al. (2008). Psychological trauma and schizotypal personality disorder. *Journal of Abnormal Psychology, 117,* 502–519.

Bergem, A. L., Engedal, K., & Kringlen, E. (1997). The role of heredity in late-onset Alzheimer's disease and vascular dementia: A twin study. *Archives of General Psychiatry, 54,* 264–270.

Bergeron, E., Poirier, L.-R., Fournier, L., Roberge, P., & Barrette, G. (2005). Determinants of service use among young Canadians with mental disorders. *Canadian Journal of Psychiatry, 50,* 629–636.

Bergeron, L., Valla, J.-P., Breton, J.-J., Gaudet, N., et al. (2000). Correlates of mental disorders in the Quebec general population of 6- to 14-year olds. *Journal of Abnormal Child Psychology, 28,* 47–62.

Bergin, A. E. (1971). The evaluation of therapeutic outcomes. In A. E. Bergin & S. L. Garfield (Eds.), *Handbook of psychotherapy and behavior change: An empirical analysis.* New York: John Wiley & Sons.

Bernazzani, O., Saucier, J.-F., David, H., & Borgeat, F. (1997). Psychosocial predictors of depressive symptomatology level in postpartum women. *Journal of Affective Disorders, 46,* 39–49.

Bernstein, D. P., Kasapis, C., Bergman, A., Weld, E., Mitropoulou, V., et al. (1997). Assessing Axis II disorders by informant interview. *Journal of Personality Disorders, 11,* 158–167.

Bernstein, D. P., Useda, D., & Siever, L. J. (1993). Paranoid personality disorder: Review of the literature and recommendations for DSM-IV. *Journal of Personality Disorders, 7,* 53–62.

Berry, J. C. (1967). *Antecedents of schizophrenia, impulsive character and alcoholism in males.* Paper presented at the 75th Annual Convention of the American Psychological Association, Washington, DC.

Berry, J. W. (1999). Intercultural relations in plural societies. *Canadian Psychology, 40,* 12–21.

Berry, K., & Barrowclough, C. (2009). The needs of older adults with schizophrenia: Implications for psychological interventions. *Clinical Psychology Review, 29,* 68–76.

Berthiaume, L. (2006, May 6). Margaret Trudeau reveals fight with bipolar disorder. *The Vancouver Sun,* A6.

Bertram, L., & Tanzi, R. E. (2008). Thirty years of Alzheimer's disease genetics: The implications of systematic meta-analyses. *Nature Neurosciences Review, 9*, 768–778.

Besdine, R. W. (1980). Geriatric medicine: An overview. In C. Eisodorfer (Ed.), *Annual review of gerontology and geriatrics.* New York: Springer.

Bettelheim, B. (1967). *The empty fortress: Infantile autism and the birth of the self.* New York: The Free Press

Bettelheim, B. (1973). Bringing up children. *Ladies Home Journal, 90*, 28.

Beutler, L. E. (1997). The psychotherapist as a neglected variable in psychotherapy: An illustration by reference to the role of therapist experience and training. *Clinical Psychology: Science and Practice, 4*, 44–52.

Beutler, L. E. (1999). Manualizing flexibility: The training of eclectic therapists. *Journal of Clinical Psychology, 55*, 399–404.

Beutler, L. E. (2002). It isn't the size, but the fit. *Clinical Psychology: Science and Practice, 9*, 434–438.

Beutler, L. E. (2009). Making science matter in clinical practice: Redefining psychotherapy. *Clinical Psychology: Science and Practice, 16*, 301–317.

Beutler, L. E., & Harwood, T. M. (1995). Prescriptive psychotherapies. *Applied and Preventive Psychology, 4*, 89–100.

Beutler, L. E., Machado, P. P. P., & Neufeldt, S. A. (1994). Therapist variables. In A. E. Bergin & S. L. Garfield (Eds.), *Handbook of psychotherapy and behavior change* (4th ed., pp. 229–269). New York: John Wiley & Sons.

Beversdorf, D. Q., Manning, S. E., Hillier, A., et al. (2005). Timing of prenatal stressors and autism. *Journal of Autism and Developmental Disorders, 35*, 471–478.

Beynon, S., Soares-Weisser, K., Woolacott, N., et al. (2008). Psychosocial interventions for the prevention of relapse in bipolar disorder: Systematic review of controlled trials. *The British Journal of Psychiatry, 192*, 5–11.

Bialas, I., & Craig, T. K. (2007). Needs expressed and offers of care : An observational study of mothers with somatisation disorder and their children. *Journal of Child Psychology and Psychiatry, 48*, 97–104.

Bialystok, E., Craik, F. I. M., Klein, R., & Viswanathan, M. (2004). Bilingualism, aging, and cognitive control: Evidence from the Simon task. *Psychology and Aging, 19*, 290–303.

Biedel, D. C., Turner, S. M., Sallee, F.R., et al. (2007). SET-C versus fluoxetine in the treatment of childhood social phobia. *Journal of the American Academy of Child and Adolescent Psychiatry, 46*, 1622–1632.

Biederman, J., et al. (1996). Predictors of persistence and remission of ADHD into adolescence: Results from a four-year prospective follow-up study. *Journal of the American Academy of Child and Adolescent Psychiatry, 35*, 343–351.

Biederman, J., & Farone, S. V. (2005). Attention-deficit hyperactivity disorder. *Lancet, 366*, 237–248.

Biederman, J., Monuteaux, M. C., Spencer, T., et al. (2008). Stimulant therapy and risk for subsequent substance use disorders in male adults with ADHD: A naturalistic controlled 10-year follow-up study. *American Journal of Psychiatry, 165*, 597–603.

Biederman, J., Petty, C. R., Wilens, T. E., et al. (2008). Familial risk analyses of attention deficit hyperactivity disorder and substance use disorders. *American Journal of Psychiatry, 165*, 107–115.

Bieling, P. J., & Alden, L. E. (2001). Sociotropy, autonomy, and the interpersonal model of depression: An integration. *Cognitive Therapy and Research, 25*, 167–184.

Bieling, P. J., Green, S. M., & Macqueen, G. (2007). The impact of personality disorders on treatment outcome in bipolar disorder: A review. *Personality and Mental Health, 1*, 2–13.

Bieling, P. J., & Kuyken, W. (2003). Is cognitive case formulation science or science fiction? *Clinical Psychology: Science and Practice, 10*, 52–69.

Bieling, P. J., McCabe, R. E., & Antony, M. M. (2006). *Cognitive behavioral therapy in groups.* New York: Guilford.

Billings, A. G., Cronkite, R. C., & Moos, R. H. (1983). Social-environmental factors in unipolar depression: Comparisons of depressed patients and nondepressed controls. *Journal of Abnormal Psychology, 92*, 119–133.

Bilsker, D., Goldner, E. M., & Jones, W. (2007). Health service patterns indicate potential benefit of supported self-management for depression in primary care. *Canadian Journal of Psychiatry, 52*, 86–95.

Birbaumer, N., et al. (2005). Deficient fear conditioning in psychopathy: a functional magnetic resonance imaging study. *Archives of General Psychiatry, 62*, 799–805.

Birmingham, C. L., et al. (2005). The mortality rate for anorexia nervosa. *International Journal of Eating Disorders, 38*, 143–146.

Birnbaum, M. (1960). The right to treatment. *American Bar Association Journal, 46*, 499–505.

Black, D. N., Seritan, A. L., Taber, K. H., & Hurley, R. A. (2004). Conversion hysteria: Lessons from functional imaging. *Journal of Neuropsychiatry and Clinical Neurosciences, 16*, 245–251.

Black, S. E., Gauthier, S., Dalziel, W., Keren, R., et al. (2010). Canadian Alzheimer's Disease Caregiver Survey: Baby-boomer caregivers and burden of care. *International Journal of Geriatric Psychiatry, 25(8)*, 807–813.

Blackmore, E. R., Munce, S., Weller, I., et al. (2008). Psychosocial and clinical correlates of suicidal acts: Results from a national population survey. *The British Journal of Psychiatry, 192*, 279–284.

Blackstock, C. (2003). First Nations child and family services restoring peace and harmony in First Nations communities. In K. Kufeldt & B. McKenzie (Eds.), *Child Welfare: Connecting Research, Policy, and Practice* (pp. 331–342). Waterloo, ON: Wilfrid Laurier University Press.

Blader, J. C., Schooler, N. R., Jensen, P. S., et al. (2009). Adjunctive divalproex versus placebo for children with ADHD and aggression refractory to stimulant monotherapy. *American Journal of Psychiatry, 166*, 1392–1401.

Blagys, M., & Hilsenroth, M. J. (2000). Distinctive activities of short-term psychodynamic interpersonal psychotherapy: A review of the comparative psychiatric process literature. *Clinical Psychology: Science and Practice, 7*, 167–188.

Blair, R. J. D., Jones, L., Clark, F., & Smith, M. (1997). The psychopathic individual: A lack of responsiveness to distress cues? *Psychophysiology, 34*, 192–198.

Blais, M. A., Hilsenroth, M. J., & Castlebury, F. D. (1997). Content validity of the newly revised Diagnostic and Statistical Manual of Mental Disorders-IV (DSM-IV) narcissitic personality disorder (NPD) and borderline personality disorder (BPD) criteria sets. *Comprehensive Psychiatry, 38*, 31–37.

Blake, W. (1973). The influence of race on diagnosis. *Smith College Studies in Social Work, 43*, 184–192.

Blanchard, E. B. (1994). Behavioral medicine and health psychology. In A. E. Bergin & S. L. Garfield (Eds.), *Handbook of psychotherapy and behavior change* (4th ed., pp. 701–733). New York: John Wiley & Sons.

Blanchard, J. J., & Brown, S. B. (1998). Structured diagnostic interviews. In C. R. Reynolds (Ed.), *Comprehensive clinical psychology, Vol. 3, assessment* (pp. 97–130). New York: Elsevier.

Blanchard, J. J., Squires, D., Henry, T., Horan, W. P., Bogenschutz, M., et al. (1999). Examining an affect regulation model of substance abuse in schizophrenia: The role of traits and coping. *Journal of Nervous and Mental Disease, 187*, 72–79.

Blanchard, R. (1989). The classification and labeling of nonhomosexual gender dysphorias. *Archives of Sexual Behavior, 18*, 315–334.

Blanchard, R. (1992). Nonmonotonic relation of autogynephilia and heterosexual attraction. *Journal of Abnormal Psychology, 101*, 271–276.

Blanchard, R., Watson, M. S., Choy, A., Dickey, R., Klassen, P., Kuban, M., et al. (1999). Pedophiles: Mental retardation, maternal age, and sexual orientation. *Archives of Sexual Behavior, 28*, 111–127.

Blanco, C., et al. (2008). Mental health of college students and their non-college-attending peers: Results from the National Epidemiologic Study on Alcohol and related conditions. *Archives of General Psychiatry, 65*, 1429–1437.

Bland, R. C., Newman, S. C., & Orn, H. (1997a). Age and remission of psychiatric disorders. *Canadian Journal of Psychiatry, 42*, 722–729.

Blankstein, K. R., & Dunkley, D. M. (2002). Evaluative concerns, self-critical, and personal standards perfectionism: A structural equation modeling strategy. In G. L. Flett & P. L. Hewitt (Eds.), *Perfectionism: Theory, research, and treatment* (pp. 285-315). Washington, DC: American Psychological Association.

Blankstein, K. R., & Flett, G. L. (1990). Cognitive components of test anxiety: A comparison of assessment and scoring methods. *Journal of Social Behavior and Personality, 5*, 187–202.

Blankstein, K. R., Flett, G. L., Boase, P., & Toner, B. B. (1990). Thought listing and endorsement measures of self-referential thinking in test anxiety. *Anxiety Research, 2*, 103–111.

Blankstein, K. R., Flett, G. L., & Koledin, S. (1991). The Brief College Students Hassles Scale: Development, validation, and relation with pessimism. *Journal of College Student Development, 32,* 258–264.

Blankstein, K. R., & Hillis Lumley, C. (2008). Multidimensional perfectionism and ruminative brooding in current dysphoria, anxiety, worry, and anger. *Journal of Rational-Emotive and Cognitive-Behavior Therapy, 26,* 168–193.

Blankstein, K. R., Lumley, C., & Crawford, A. (2007). Perfectionism, hopelessness, and suicide ideation: Revisions to diathesis-stress and specific vulnerability models. *Journal of Rational-Emotive and Cognitive-Behavior Therapy, 25,* 279–319.

Blankstein, K. R., & Segal, S. V. (2001). Cognitive assessment: Issues and methods. In K. S. Dobson (Ed.), *Handbook of cognitive-behavioral therapies* (2nd ed., pp. 40–85). New York: Guilford.

Blaske, D. M., Borduin, C. M., Hengeler, S. W., & Mann, B. J. (1989). Individual, family, and peer characteristics of adolescent sex offenders and assaultive offenders. *Developmental Psychology, 25,* 846–855.

Blatt, S. J. (1974). Levels of object representation in anaclitic and introjective depression. *Psychoanalytic Study of the Child, 29,* 107–157.

Blatt, S. J. (1995). The destructiveness of perfectionism: Implications for the treatment of depression. *American Psychologist, 50,* 1003–1020.

Blatt, S. J., Quinlan, D. M., Pilkonis, P. A., & Shea, M. T. (1995). Impact of perfectionism and need for approval on the brief treatment of depression: The National Institute of Mental Health Treatment of Depression Collaborative Research Program revisited. *Journal of Consulting and Clinical Psychology, 63,* 125–132.

Blatt, S. J., Zohar, A. H., Quinlan, D. M., Zuroff, D. C. & Mongrain, M. (1995). Subscales within the dependency factor of the Depressive Experiences Questionnaire. *Journal of Personality Assessment, 64,* 319–339.

Blatt, S. J., & Zuroff, D. C. (1992). Interpersonal relatedness and self-definition: Two prototypes for depression. *Clinical Psychology Review, 12,* 527–562.

Blatt, S. J., & Zuroff, D. C. (2002). Perfectionism and the therapeutic context. In G. L. Flett, & P. L. Hewitt (Eds.), *Perfectionism: Theory, research, and treatment* (pp. 393–406). Washington, DC: American Psychological Association.

Blatt, S. J., & Zuroff, D. C. (2005). Empirical evaluation of the assumptions in identifying evidence-based treatments in mental health. *Clinical Psychology Review, 25,* 459–486.

Blaustein, M., & Fleming, A. (2009). Suicide from the Golden Gate Bridge. *American Journal of Psychiatry, 166,* 1111–1116.

Blazer, D. G. (1982). *Depression in late life.* St. Louis, MO: Mosby.

Blazer, D. G., Hughes, D., & George, L. K. (1987). Stressful life events and the onset of a generalized anxiety syndrome. *American Journal of Psychiatry, 144,* 1178–1183.

Blazer, D. G., & Williams, C. D. (1980). Epidemiology of dysphoria and depression in the elderly population. *American Journal of Psychiatry, 137,* 439–444.

Blazer, D. G., & Wu, L. T. (2009). The epidemiology of at-risk and binge drinking among middle-aged and elderly community adults: National survey on drug use and health. *American Journal of Psychiatry, 166,* 1162–1169.

Blenker, M. (1967). Environmental change and the aging individual. *Gerontologist, 7,* 101–105.

Bliss, E. L. (1983). Multiple personalities, related disorders, and hypnosis. *American Journal of Clinical Hypnosis, 26,* 114–123.

Bliwise, D., Carskadon, M., Carey, E., & Dement, W. (1984). Longitudinal development of sleep-related respiratory disturbance in adult humans. *Journal of Gerontology, 39,* 290–293.

Block, J. S. (2008). Issues for DSM-V: Internet addiction. *American Journal of Psychiatry, 165,* 306–307.

Blote, A. W., Kint, M. J. W., Miers, A. C., & Westenberg, P. M. (2009). The relation between public speaking anxiety and social anxiety: A review. *Journal of Anxiety Disorders, 23,* 305–313.

Board of Inspectors of Asylums, Prisons, & c. (1865). *Report of the Board of Inspectors of ASYLUMS, PRISONS, &c., for the year 1864.* Quebec City: Hunter, Rose, and Co.

Bockhoven, J. (1963). *Moral treatment in American psychiatry.* New York: Springer.

Boer, D. P., & Pugh, G. M. (1988). Canadianization of the WAIS-R Information subtest: Implications for psychiatric assessment. *Canadian Journal of Behavioural Assessment, 20,* 273–286.

Bogels, S. M., Alden, L., Beidel, D., et al. (2010). Social anxiety disorder: Questions and answers for the DSM-V. *Depression and Anxiety, 27,* 168–189.

Bohart, A. C., & Greenberg, L. S. (Eds.) (1997). *Empathy reconsidered: New directions in psychotherapy.* Washington, DC: American Psychological Association.

Bohlmeijer, E., Smit, F., & Cuijpers, P. (2003). Effects of reminiscence and life review on late-life depression: A meta-analysis. *International Journal of Geriatric Psychiatry, 18,* 1088–1094.

Bohuslawsky, M. (2001, August 5). Medicine's shocking new trend. *Ottawa Citizen.*

Boggild A., Heisel M.J., & Links P.S. (2004). Social, demographic, and clinical factors related to disruptive behaviour in hospital. *Canadian Journal of Psychiatry, 49,* 114–118.

Boisvert, C. M., & Faust, D. (2003). Leading researchers' consensus on psychotherapy research findings: Implications for the teaching and conduct of psychotherapy. *Professional Psychology: Research and Practice, 34,* 508–513.

Boisvert, C. M., & Faust, D. (2006). Practicing psychologists' knowledge of general psychotherapy research findings: Implications for science-practice relations. *Professional Psychology: Research and Practice, 37,* 708–716.

Boland, R. J., & Keller, M. B. (2002). Course and outcome of depression. In I. H. Gotlib & C. L. Hammen (Eds.), *Handbook of depression* (pp. 43–57). New York: Guilford.

Boll, T. J. (1985). Developing issues in clinical neuropsychology. *Journal of Clinical and Experimental Neuropsychology, 7,* 473–485.

Bolton, J.M., Belik, S-L, Enns, M.W., et al. (2008). Exploring the correlates of suicide attempts among individuals with major depressive disorder: findings from the national epidemiologic survey on alcohol and related conditions. *The Journal of Clinical Psychiatry, 69,* 1139–1149.

Bolton, J. M., Cox, B. J., Afifi, T. O., et al. (2008). Anxiety disorders and risk for suicide attempts: Findings from the baltimore epidemiologic catchment area follow-up study. *Depression and Anxiety, 25,* 477–481.

Bolton, J., Cox, B. J., Clara, I., & Sareen, J. (2006). Use of alcohol and drugs to self-medicate anxiety disorders in a nationally representative sample. *Journal of Nervous and Mental Disease, 194,* 818–825.

Bonanno, G. A., & Kaltman, S. (2001). The varieties of grief experience. *Clinical Psychology Review, 21,* 705–734.

Bonin, M. P., McCreary, D. R., & Sadava, S. W. (2000). Problem drinking behavior in two community-based samples of adults: Influence of gender, coping, loneliness, and depression. *Psychology of Addictive Behaviors, 14,* 151–161.

Bonn-Miller, M. O., Bernstein, A., Sachs-Ericsson, N., Schmidt, N. B., & Zvolensky, M. J. (2007). Associations between psychedelic use, abuse, and dependence and a lifetime panic attack history in a representative sample. *Journal of Anxiety Disorders, 21,* 730–741.

Bonta, J., Law, M., & Hanson, K. (1998). The prediction of criminal and violent recidivism among mentally disordered offenders. *Psychological Bulletin, 123,* 123–142.

Boomer, R. (2007, March 23). Glen Haven staff get refresher after woman's mouth taped shut. *The Daily News,* Halifax, 7.

Boothroyd, L. J., Kirmayer, L. J., Spreng, S., Malus, M., & Hodgins, S. (2001). Completed suicides among the Inuit of northern Quebec, 1982–1996: A case control study. *Canadian Medical Association Journal, 165,* 749–755.

Borges, G., et al. (2006). A risk index for 12-month suicide attempts in the National Comorbidity Survey Replication (NCS-R). *Psychological Medicine, 36,* 1747–1757.

Borkovec, T. D., & Costello, E. (1993). Efficacy of applied relaxation and cognitive behavioral therapy in the treatment of generalized anxiety disorder. *Journal of Consulting and Clinical Psychology, 61,* 611–619.

Borkovec, T. D., & Mathews, A. (1988). Treatment of nonphobic anxiety disorders: A comparison of nondirective, cognitive and coping desensitization therapy. *Journal of Consulting and Clinical Psychology, 56,* 877–884.

Borkovec, T. D., & Whisman, M. A. (1996). Psychosocial treatment for generalized anxiety disorder. In M. Mavissakalian & R. E. Prien (Eds.), *Long-term treatment of anxiety disorders* (pp. 171–199). Washington, DC: American Psychiatric Association.

Bornstein, R. F. (1997). Dependent personality disorder in the DSM-IV and beyond. *Clinical Psychology: Science and Practice, 4,* 175–187.

Bornstein, R. F., Leone, D. R., & Galley, D. J. (1987). The generalizability of subliminal mere exposure effects: Influence of stimuli perceived without awareness on social behavior. *Journal of Personality and Social Psychology, 53,* 1070–1079.

Borsari, B., O'Leary, T. T., Barnett, N. P., Kahler, C. W., & Monti, P. M. (2007). Stepped care for mandated college students: A pilot study. *American Journal of Addictions*, 16, 131–137.

Boscarino, J. A. (1997). Diseases among men 20 years after exposure to severe stress: Implications for clinical research and care. *Psychosomatic Medicine*, 59, 605–614.

Boschen, M. J., & Oei, T. P. S. (2008). A cognitive behavioral case formulation framework for treatment planning in anxiety disorders. *Depression and Anxiety*, 25, 811–823.

Bosinski, H. A., Peter, M., Bonatz, G., Arndt, R., Heidenreich, M., Sippwell, W. G., & Willie, R. (1997). A higher rate of hyperadrenergic disorders in female-to-male transsexuals. *Psychoneuroendocrinology*, 22, 361–380.

Bouchard, S., Cote, S., Robillard, G., et al. (2006). Effectiveness of virtual reality exposure in the treatment of arachnophobia using 3D games. *Technology and Health Care*, 14, 19–27.

Bouchard, S., Paquin, B., et al. (2004). Delivering cognitive-behavior therapy for panic disorder with agoraphobia in video conference. *Telemedia Journal and e-Health*, 10, 13–25.

Bouchard, S., Payeur, R., Rivard, V., Allard, M., Paquin, B., Renaud, P., et al. (2000). Cognitive behavior therapy for panic disorder with agoraphobia in videoconference: Preliminary results. *CyberPsychology and Behavior*, 3, 999–1007.

Boughton, R., & Falenchuk, O. (2007). Vulnerability and comorbidity factors of female problem gambling. *Journal of Gambling Studies*, 23, 323–334.

Bourbeau, J., & van der Palen, J. (2009). Promoting effective self-management programes to improve COPD. *European Respiratory Journal*, 33, 461–463.

Bourrie, M. (1997). *By reason of insanity: The David Michael Kruger story*. Toronto: Hounslow.

Bourrie, M. (2010, March 9). The serial killer they couldn't cure dies behind bars: Peter Woodcock killed three Toronto children in the 50's. One day on a pass in 1991, he killed again. *Toronto Star*.

Bourque, P., & Beaudette, D. (1982). Psychometric study of the Beck Depression Inventory in a sample of francophone university students. *Canadian Journal of Behavioural Science*, 14, 211–218.

Bowden, S. C., Lange, R. T., Weiss, L. G., & Saklofske, D. H. (2008). Invariance of the measurement model underlying the Wechsler Adult Intelligence Scale—III in the United States and Canada. *Educational and Psychological Measurement*, 68, 1024–1040.

Bowers, J., Jorm, A. F., Henderson, S., & Harris, P. (1990). General practitioners' detection of depression and dementia in elderly patients. *The Medical Journal of Australia*, 153, 192–196.

Bowers, K. S., & Meichenbaum, D. (Eds.). (1984). *The unconscious reconsidered*. New York: Praeger.

Bowers, M. B., Jr. (1974). Central dopamine turnover in schizophrenic syndromes. *Archives of General Psychiatry*, 31, 50–54.

Bowlby, B. J., McKinnon, M., & Peters, C. (2001). *An educator's guide to special education law*. Aurora, Ontario: Aurora Professional Press.

Bowlby, B. J., & Wooton Regan, J. (1998). *An educator's guide to human rights*. Aurora, Ontario: Aurora Professional Press.

Bowman, M. L. (2000). The diversity of diversity: Canadian-American differences and their implications for clinical training and APA accreditation. *Canadian Psychology*, 41, 244–256.

Boyle, M. (1991). *Schizophrenia: A scientific delusion?* New York: Routledge.

Boyle, M. H., et al. (2004). Differential-maternal parenting behavior: Estimating within- and between-family effects on children. *Child Development*, 75, 1457–1476.

Boyle, M. H., Sanford, M., Szatmari, P., Merikangas, K., & Offord, D. R. (2001). Familial influences on substance use by adolescents and young adults. *Canadian Journal of Public Health*, 92, 206–208.

Boyle, T. (1998, February 10). Courts stymied on mentally ill. *Toronto Star*, E1, E5.

Bozman, A., & Beck, J. G. (1991). Covariation of sexual desire and sexual arousal: The effects of anger and anxiety. *Archives of Sexual Behavior*, 20, 47–60.

Bradford, J. M., & Fedoroff, J. P. (2009). The neurobiology of sexual behavior and the paraphilias. In F. M. Saleh, A. J. Grudzinskas, J. M. Bradford, & D. J. Brodsky (Eds.), *Sex offenders: Identification, risk assessment, treatment, and legal issues* (pp. 36–47). New York: Oxford University Press.

Bradley, B., & Johnson, S. M. (2005). Emotionally focused couples therapy: An integrative contemporary approach. In M. Haraway (Ed.), *Couples therapy* (pp. 179–193). New York: John Wiley & Sons.

Bradley, E. A., Thompson, A., & Bryson, S. E. (2002). Mental retardation in teenagers: Prevalence data from the Niagara region, Ontario. *Canadian Journal of Psychiatry*, 47, 652–659.

Bradley, R., Greene, J., Russ, E., Dutra, L., & Westen, D. (2005). A multidimensional meta-analysis of psychotherapy for PTSD. *American Journal of Psychiatry*, 162, 214–227.

Bradley, S. J., Blanchard, R., Coates, S., Green, R., Levine, S. B., Meyer-Bahlburg, et al. (1991). Interim report of the DSM-IV subcommittee on gender identity disorders. *Archives of Sexual Behavior*, 20, 333–343.

Bradley, S. J., Oliver, G. D., Chernick, A. B., & Zucker, K. J. (1998). Experiment of nurture: Albatio penis at 2 months, sex reassignment at 7 months, and a psychosexual follow-up in young adulthood. *Pediatrics*, 102, e1–e9.

Bradshaw, D., & Spencer, C. (1999). The role of alcohol in elder abuse cases. In J. Pritchard (Ed.), *Elder abuse work: Best practices in Britain and Canada* (pp. 332–353). London: Jessica Kingsley Publications.

Bradwejn, J., Koszycky, D., & Meterissian, G. (1990). Cholecystokinin-tetrapeptide induced panic attacks in patients with panic disorder. *Canadian Journal of Psychiatry*, 35, 83–85.

Brady, J. P., Davison, G. C., DeWald, P. A., Egan, G., Fadiman, J., Frank, J. D., et al. (1980). Some views on effective principles of psychotherapy. *Cognitive Therapy and Research*, 4, 269–306.

Braff, D. L. (2007). Introduction: The use of endophenotypes to deconstruct and understand the genetic architecture, neurobiology, and guide future treatments of the group of schizophrenias. *Schizophrenia Bulletin*, 33, 19–20.

Braga, R. J., Mendlowicz, M. V., Marrocos, R. P., & Figueira, I. L. (2005). Anxiety disorders in outpatients with schizophrenia: Prevalence and impact on the subjective quality of life. *Journal of Psychiatric Research*, 39, 409–414.

Brambilla, P., et al. (2007). Assessment of cerebral blood volume in schizophrenia: A magnetic resonance imaging study. *Journal of Psychiatric Research*, 41, 502–510.

Brandon, Y. H., Zelman, D. C., & Baker, T. B. (1987). Effects of maintenance sessions on smoking relapse: Delaying the inevitable? *Journal of Consulting and Clinical Psychology*, 55, 780–782.

Brandt, J., Buffers, N., Ryan, C., & Bayoz, R. (1983). Cognitive loss and recovery in alcohol abusers. *Archives of General Psychiatry*, 40, 435–442.

Brecher, E. M., & the Editors of Consumer Reports. (1972). *Licit and illicit drugs*. Mount Vernon, NY: Consumers Union.

Breedlove, L., Decker, C., Lakin, K. C., et al. (2005). Placement of children and youth in state institutions: 40 years after the high point, it is time to just stop. *Mental Retardation*, 43, 235–238.

Bremner, J. D. (2006). The relationship between cognitive and brain changes in posttraumatic stress disorder. *Annals of the New York Academy of Sciences*, 1071, 80–86.

Brendgen, M., Vitaro, F., Boivin, M., et al. (2009). Gene-environment interplay between peer rejection and depressive behavior in children. *Journal of Child Psychology and Psychiatry*, 50, 1009–1017.

Brendgen, M., Vitaro, F., Turgeon, L., & Poulin, F. (2002). Assessing aggressive and depressed children's social relations with classmates and friends: A matter of perspective. *Journal of Abnormal Child Psychology*, 30, 609–624.

Brent, D. A. (2009a). Selective serotonin reuptake inhibitors and suicidality: A guide for the perplexed. *Canadian Journal of Psychiatry*, 54, 72–74.

Brent, D. A. (2009b). The treatment of SSRI-resistant depression in adolescents (TORDIA): In search of the best next step. *Depression and Anxiety*, 26, 871–874.

Brent, D. A., Emslie, G. J., Clarke, G. N., et al. (2008). Switching to venlafaxine or another SSRI with or without cognitive behavioral therapy for adolescents with SSRI-resistant depression: The TORDIA randomized controlled trial. *Journal of the American Medical Association*, 299, 901–913.

Breslau, N., Breslau, J., Peterson, E., et al. (2010). Change in teachers' ratings of attention problems and subsequent change in academic achievement: A prospective analysis. *Psychological Medicine*, 40, 159–166.

Breslau, N., Davis, G. C., Andreski, P., Peterson, E. L., & Schultz, L. R. (1997). Sex differences in posttraumatic stress disorder. *Archives of General Psychiatry*, 54, 1044–1048.

Breslau, N., Chilcoat, H. D., Kessler, R. C., & Davis, G. C. (1999). Previous exposure to trauma and PTSD effects of subsequent trauma: Results from the Detroit area survey of trauma. *American Journal of Psychiatry*, 156, 902–907.

Breslau, N., Lucia, V. C., & Alvarado, G. F. (2006). Intelligence and other predisposing factors in exposure to trauma and posttraumatic stress disorder: A follow-up study at age 17 years. *Archives of General Psychiatry*, 63, 1238–1245.

Breslin, F. C., Zack, M., & McMain, S. (2002). An information-processing analysis of mindfulness: Implications for relapse prevention in the treatment of substance abuse. *Clinical Psychology: Science and Practice*, 9, 275–299.

Bretteville-Jensen, A. L., Melberg, H. O., & Jones, A. M. (2008). Sequential patterns of drug use initiation—Can we believe the gateway theory? *The B.E. Journal of Economic Analysis and Policy*, 2, Article 1.

Breuer, J., & Freud, S. (1982). *Studies in hysteria*. (J. Strachey, Trans. and Ed., with the collaboration of A. Freud). New York: Basic Books. (Original work published 1895.)

Brewin, C. R., Kleiner, J. S., Vasterling, J. J., & Field, A. P. (2007). Memory for emotionally neutral information in posttraumatic stress disorder: A meta-analytic investigation. *Journal of Abnormal Psychology*, 116, 448–463.

Brezo, J., Paris, J., & Turecki, G. (2006). Personality traits as correlates of suicidal ideation, suicide attempts, and suicide completions: A systematic review. *Acta Psychiatrica Scandinavica*, 113, 180–206.

Brezo, J., Paris, J., Vitaro, F., et al. (2008). Predicting suicide attempts in young adults with histories of child abuse. *The British Journal of Psychiatry*, 193, 134–139.

Brickman, A. S., McManus, M., Grapentine, W. L., & Alessi, N. (1984). Neuropsychological assessment of seriously delinquent adolescents. *Journal of the American Academy of Child Psychiatry*, 23, 453–457.

Bridge, J. A., et al. (2007). Clinical response and risk for reported suicidal ideation and suicide attempts in pediatric antidepressant treatment: A meta-analysis of randomized controlled trials. *Journal of the American Medical Association*, 297, 1683–1696.

Bridge, J. A., Birmaher, B., Iyengar, S., et al. (2009). Placebo response in randomized controlled trials of antidepressants for pediatric major depressive disorder. *American Journal of Psychiatry*, 166, 42–49.

Bridger, W. H., & Mandel, I. J. (1965). Abolition of the PRE by instructions in GSR conditioning. *Journal of Experimental Psychology*, 69, 476–482.

Brock, G. B., et al. (2009). Canadian male sexual health council survey to assess prevalence and treatment of premature ejaculation in Canada. *Journal of Sex Medicine*, 6, 2115–2123.

Brodeur, D. A., & Pond, M. (2001). The development of selective attention in children with attention deficit hyperactivity disorder. *Journal of Abnormal Child Psychology*, 29, 229–239.

Broidy, L. M., et al. (2003). Developmental trajectories of childhood disruptive behaviors and adolescent delinquency: A six-site, cross-national study. *Developmental Psychology*, 39, 222–245.

Brookmeyer, R., Johnson, E., Ziegler-Graham, K., & Arrighi, H. M. (2007). Forecasting the global burden of Alzheimer's disease. *Alzheimer's and Dementia*, 3, 186–191.

Brookoff, D., Cook, C. S., Williams, C., & Mann, C. S. (1994). Testing reckless drivers for cocaine and marijuana. *New England Journal of Medicine*, 331, 518–522.

Brooks, S. A., O'Reilly, R. L.., & Gray, J. E. (2003). Implications for psychiatrists of the Supreme Court of Canada Starson v. Swayze decision. CPA *Bulletin* de l'APC—August 2003, p. 29.

Brosschot, J. F., Gerin, W., & Thayer, J. F. (2006). The perseverative cognition hypothesis: A review of worry, prolonged stress-related physiological activation, and health. *Journal of Psychosomatic Research*, 60, 113–124.

Brown, A. S. (2006). Prenatal infection as a risk factor for schizophrenia. *Schizophrenia Bulletin*, 32, 200–202.

Brown, A. S., & Derkits, E. J. (2010). Prenatal infection and schizophrenia: A review of epidemiologic and translational studies. *American Journal of Psychiatry*, 167, 261–280.

Brown, E. J., & Bobrow, A. L. (2004). School entry after a community-wide trauma: Challenges and lessons learned from September 11, 2001. *Clinical Child and Family Psychology Review*, 7, 211–221.

Brown, G. K., Beck, A. T., Steer, R. A., & Grisham, J. R. (2000). Risk factors for suicide in psychiatric outpatients: A 20-year prospective study. *Journal of Consulting and Clinical Psychology*, 68, 371–377.

Brown, G. P., & Beck, A. T. (2002). Dysfunctional attitudes, perfectionism, and models of vulnerability to depression. In G. L. Flett & P. L. Hewitt (Eds.), *Perfectionism: Theory, research, and treatment* (pp. 231–251). Washington, DC: American Psychological Association.

Brown, G. W., Bone, M., Dalison, B., & Wing, J. K. (1966). *Schizophrenia and social care*. London: Oxford University Press.

Brown, L. M., Bongar, B., & Cleary, K. M. (2004). A profile of psychologists' views of critical risk factors for completed suicide in older adults. *Professional Psychology: Research and Practice*, 35, 90–96.

Brown, S. L., & Forth, A. E. (1997). Psychopathy and sexual assault: Static risk factors, emotional precursors, and rapist subtypes. *Journal of Consulting and Clinical Psychology*, 65, 848–857.

Brown, R. T., Carpenter, L. A., & Simerly, E. (2005). *Mental health medications for children: A primer*. New York: Guilford Press.

Brown, T. A., & Barlow, D. H. (1995). Long-term outcome in cognitive-behavioral treatment of panic disorder: Clinical predictors and alternative strategies for assessment. *Journal of Consulting and Clinical Psychology*, 63, 754–765.

Brown, T. A., Barlow, D. H., & Liebowitz, M. R. (1994). The empirical basis of generalized anxiety disorder. *American Journal of Psychiatry*, 151, 1272–1280.

Brownell, K. D., & Rodin, J. (1994). The dieting maelstrom: Is it possible or advisable to lose weight? *American Psychologist*, 49, 781–791.

Brownell, M. D., & Yogendran, M. S. (2001). Attention-deficit hyperactivity disorder in Manitoba children: Medical diagnosis and psychostimulant treatment rates. *Canadian Journal of Psychiatry*, 46, 264–271.

Brownmiller, S. (1975). *Against our will: Men, women and rape*. New York: Simon & Schuster.

Brozina, K., & Abela, J. R. Z. (2006). Symptoms of depression and anxiety in children: Specificity of the hopelessness theory. *Journal of Clinical Child and Adolescent Psychology*, 35, 515–527.

Bruner, J., Goodnow, J., & Austin, A. (1956). *A study of thinking*. New York: Wiley.

Bryant, R. A., & Harvey, A. G. (1998). Relationship between acute stress disorder and posttraumatic stress disorder following mild traumatic brain injury. *American Journal of Psychiatry*, 155, 625–629.

Bryson, S. E., Rogers, S. J., & Fombonne, E. (2003). Autism spectrum disorders: Early detection, intervention, education, and psychopharmacological management. *Canadian Journal of Psychiatry*, 48, 506–516.

Buchanan, R. W., Breier, A., Kirkpatrick, B., Ball, P., & Carpenter, W. T. (1998). Positive and negative symptom response to clozapine in schizophrenic patients with and without the deficit syndrome. *American Journal of Psychiatry*, 155, 751–760.

Buchanan, R. W., Vladar, K., Barta, P. E., & Pearlson, G. D. (1998). Structural evaluation of the prefrontal cortex in schizophrenia. *American Journal of Psychiatry*, 155, 1049–1055.

Buchsbaum, M. S., Kessler, R., King, A., Johnson, J., & Cappelletti, J. (1984). Simultaneous cerebral glucography with positron emission tomography and topographic electroencephalography. In G. Pfurtscheller, E. J. Jonkman, & F. H. Lopes da Silva (Eds.), *Brain ischemia: Quantitative EEG and imaging techniques*. Amsterdam: Elsevier.

Buckner, J. D., & Schmidt, N. B. (2009). Social anxiety disorder and marijuana use problems: The mediating role of marijuana effect expectancies. *Depression and Anxiety*, 26, 864–870.

Budd, R., & Hughes, I. (2009). The Dodo bird verdict—controversial, inevitable, and important: A commentary on 30 years of meta-analyses. *Clinical Psychology and Psychotherapy*, 16, 510–522.

Bufkin, J. L., & Luttrell, U. R. (2005). Neuroimaging studies of aggressive and violent behavior: Current findings and implications for criminology and criminal justice. *Trauma, Violence, and Abuse*, 6, 176–191.

Buhlmann, U., Reese, H. E., Renaud, S., & Wilhelm, S. (2008). Clinical considerations for the treatment of body dysmorphic disorder with cognitive-behavioral therapy. *Body Image*, 5, 39–49.

Buhr, K., & Dugas, M. J. (2009). The role of fear of anxiety and intolerance of uncertainty in worry: An experimental manipulation. *Behaviour Research and Therapy*, 47, 215–223.

Bujold, A., Ladouceur, R., Sylvain, C., & Boisvert, J.-M. (1994). Treatment of pathological gamblers: An experimental study. *Journal of Behavioural Therapy and Experimental Psychiatry*, 25, 275–282.

Bulik, C. M., Sullivan, P. F., & Kendler, K. S. (2000). An empirical study of the classification of eating disorders. *American Journal of Psychiatry*, 157, 886–895.

Burd, L., Cotsonas-Hassler, T. M., Martsolf, J. T., & Kerbeshian, J. (2003). Recognition and management of fetal alcohol syndrome. *Neurotoxicology and Teratology*, 25, 681–688.

Burgess, A. W., & Holmstrom, L. L. (1974). *Rape: Victim of crisis*. Bowie, MD: Robert J. Brady Company.

Burke, B. L., Arkowitz, H., & Menchola, M. (2003). The efficacy of motivational interviewing: A meta-analysis of controlled clinical trials. *Journal of Consulting and Clinical Psychology, 71*, 843–861.

Burke, R. J. (2006). Workaholism types, satisfaction and well-being: It's not how hard you work but why and how hard you work. In R. J. Burke & C. L. Cooper (Eds.), *Inspiring leaders* (pp. 273–289). New York: Routledge.

Burkhardt, S., et al. (2006). Euthanasia and assisted suicide: Comparison of legal aspects in Switzerland and other countries. *Medical Science and Law, 46*, 287–294.

Burt, S. A. (2009). Are there meaningful etiological differences within antisocial behavior? Results of a meta-analysis. *Clinical Psychology Review, 29*, 163–178.

Burton, C., Weller, D., & Sharp, M. (2009). Functional somatic symptoms and psychological states: An electronic diary study. *Psychosomatic Medicine, 71*, 77–83.

Butcher, J. N., Dahlstrom, W. G., Graham, J. R., Tellegen, A., & Kraemer, B. (1989). *Minnesota Multiphasic Personality Inventory-2: Manual for administration and scoring*. Minneapolis: University of Minnesota Press.

Butcher, J. N., Nezami, E., & Exner, J. (1998). Psychological assessment of people in diverse cultures. In S. S. Kazarian and D. R. Evans (Eds.), *Cultural clinical psychology* (pp. 61–105). London: Oxford University Press.

Butler, A. C., Chapman, J. E., Forman, E. M., & Beck, A. T. (2006). The empirical status of cognitive behavior therapy: A review of meta-analyses. *Clinical Psychology Review, 26*, 17–31.

Butler, L. D., Duran, R. E. F., Jasiukaitis, P., Koopman, C., & Spiegel, D. (1996). Hypnotizability and traumatic experience: A diathesis-stress model of dissociative symptomatology. *American Journal of Psychiatry, 153*, 42–63.

Butler, R. N. (1963). The life review: An interpretation of reminiscence in the aged. *Psychiatry, 119*, 721–728.

Butzlaff, R. L., & Hooley, J. M. (1998). Expressed emotion and psychiatric relapse: A meta-analysis. *Archives of General Psychiatry, 55*, 547–553.

Cacioppo, J. T., von Hippel, W., & Ernst, J. M. (1997). Mapping cognitive structures and processes through verbal content: The thought-listing technique. *Journal of Consulting and Clinical Psychology, 65*, 928–940.

Cadenhead, K. S., Perry, W., Shafer, K., & Braff, D. L. (1999). Cognitive functions in schizotypal personality disorder. *Schizophrenia Research, 37*, 123–132.

Cadoret, R. J., Yates, W. R., Troughton, E., Woodworth, G., & Stewart, M. A. (1995a). Adoption study demonstrating two genetic pathways to drug abuse. *Archives of General Psychiatry, 52*, 42–52.

Cadoret, R. J., Yates, W. R., Troughton, E., Woodworth, G., & Stewart, M. A. (1995b). Genetic-environment interaction in the genesis of aggressivity and conduct disorders. *Archives of General Psychiatry, 52*, 916–924.

Cahill, S. P., Carrigan, M. H., & Frueh, B. C. (1999). Does EMDR work? And if so, why?: A critical review of controlled outcome and dismantling research. *Journal of Anxiety Disorders, 13*, 5–33.

Calderoni, M. E., Alderman, E. M., Silver, E. J., & Bauman, L. J. (2006). The mental health impact of 9/11 on inner-city high school students 20 miles north of ground zero. *Journal of Adolescent Health, 39*, 57–65.

Calero-Elvira, A., Krug, I., Lopez, C., et al. (2009). Meta-analysis on drugs in people with eating disorders. *European Eating Disorders Review, 17*, 243–259.

Calhoun, P. S., et al. (2007). Interpersonal trauma, war zone exposure, and posttraumatic stress disorder among veterans with schizophrenia. *Schizophrenia Research, 91*, 210–216.

Cameron, D. J., Thomas, R. I., Mulvhill, M., & Bronheim, H. (1987). Delirium: A test of the Diagnostic and Statistical Manual III criteria on medical inpatients. *Journal of the American Geriatrics Society, 35*, 1007–1010.

Cameron, N., & Magaret, A. (1951). *Behavior pathology*. Boston: Houghton Mifflin.

Campbell, J., Stefan, S., & Loder, A. (1994). Putting violence in context. *Hospital and Community Psychiatry, 45*, 633.

Campbell, M. (2009, December 2). Attention, MLB: This is a testing program? 108 players permitted to use banned drugs because of ADHD. *Toronto Star*.

Campbell, M. A., French, S., & Gendreau, P. (2009). The prediction of violence in adult offenders: A meta-analytic comparison of instruments and methods of assessment. *Criminal Justice and Behavior, 36*, 567–590.

Campbell, M. A., Waller, G., & Pistrang, N. (2009). The impact of narcissism on drop-out from cognitive-behavioral therapy for the eating disorders: A pilot study. *The Journal of Nervous and Mental Disease, 197*, 278–281.

Campbell, W. H., & Rohrbaugh, R. R. (2006). *The biopsychosocial formulation manual: A guide for mental health professionals (Edition 1)*. New York: Taylor & Francis.

Camper, P. M., Jacobson, N. S., Holtzworth-Munroe, A., & Schmaling, K. B. (1988). Causal attributions for interactional behaviors in married couples. *Cognitive Therapy and Research, 12*, 195–209.

Canadian Alliance on Mental Illness and Mental Health. (2009). *National integrated framework for enhancing mental health literacy in Canada, Final Report, July 2008*. Ottawa: Author.

Canadian Association on Gerontology (CAG). (2000a). *Position paper: Issues in the delivery of mental health services to older adults*. Toronto: Author.

Canadian Association on Gerontology (CAG). (2000b). *Policy statement: Home care in Canada*. Toronto: Author.

Canadian Association for Suicide Prevention. (1994). *Recommendations for suicide prevention in schools (1ˢᵗ edition)*. Calgary, AB: Author.

Canadian Institute for Health Information (CIHI). (2006). *Hospital mental health services in Canada, 2003–2004*. Ottawa: Author.

Canadian Institute for Health Information (CIHI). (2007). *Public sector expenditures and utilization of home care services in Canada: Exploring the data*. Toronto: Author.

Canadian Institute for Health Information (CIHI). (2009, March 31). *Analysis in brief: Exploring hospital mental health service use in Ontario, 2007–2008*. Ottawa: Author.

Canadian Medical Association. (1997). Detecting and managing elder abuse: Challenges in primary care. *Canadian Medical Association Journal, 157*, 1094–1095.

Canadian Medical Association Journal (CMAJ). (2000). Alberta child abuse program swamped. *Canadian Medical Association Journal, 163*, 1492.

Canadian Medical Association Journal (CMAJ). (2001a). Can we afford medicare? Romanow to find out. *Canadian Medical Association Journal, 164*, 1609.

Canadian Medical Association Journal (CMAJ). (2001b). Editorial: Look no strings: Publishing industry-funded research. *Canadian Medical Association Journal, 165*, 733.

Canadian Mental Health Association (CMHA). (2001, May 7). An astounding 91% of Canadians say maintaining mental health is very important, yet fewer Canadians willing to disclose receiving treatment (news release). Ottawa: Author.

Canadian Panel on Violence Against Women. (1993). *Changing the landscape. Ending violence and achieving equality* (Catalogue No. SW45-1/1993E). Ottawa: Ministry of Supply and Services.

Canadian Paediatric Society. (1998). Inhalant abuse: Position statement. *Paediatrics and Child Health, 3*, 123–126.

Canadian Pharmacists Association. (2004). *Final Report – Phase 1: Screening and managing medication problems in isolated, independent-living seniors*. Ottawa: Author.

Canadian Population Health Initiative. (2004). *Improving the health of Canadians 2004*. Ottawa: Canadian Institute for Health Information.

Canadian Press. (2000). Ontario native suicide rate one of highest in world, expert says (www.hartford-hwp.com/archives/41/353.html).

Canadian Press. (2004, February 8). Police investigate allegations of elder abuse at nursing home.

Canadian Press. (2004, February 17). First Canadian teen charged under revised youth law wanted jail, court hears.

Canadian Press. (2006, August 16). Toronto physicist battling schizophrenia should be released, says doctor.

Canadian Psychological Association Psy.D. Task Force. (1998). Final Report to the Canadian Psychological Association Board of Directors November, 1998 (www.cpa.ca/cpasite/userfiles/Documents/publications/PsychD%20Final%20Report.pdf).

Canadian Study of Health and Aging Working Group. (1994a). Canadian Study of Health and Aging: Study methods and prevalence of dementia. *Canadian Medical Association Journal, 150*, 899–913.

Canadian Study of Health and Aging Working Group. (1994b). Patterns of caring for people with dementia. *Canadian Journal on Aging, 13*, 470–487.

Canadian Study of Health and Aging Working Group. (2000). The incidence of dementia in Canada. *Neurology, 55,* 66–73.

Canales, D. D., Olver, M. E., & Wong, S. C. P. (2009). Construct validity of the Violence Risk Scale—Sexual offender version for measuring sexual deviance. *Sexual Abuse: A Journal of Research and Treatment, 21,* 474–492.

Canetto, S. S. (2008). Women and suicidal behaviour: A cultural analysis. *American Journal of Orthopsychiatry, 78,* 259–266.

Canetto, S. S., & Sakinofsky, I. (1998). The gender paradox in suicide. *Suicide and Life Threatening Behavior, 28,* 1–23.

Cannon, T. D., & Mednick, S. A. (1993). The schizophrenia high-risk project in Copenhagen: Three decades of progress. *Acta Psychiatrica Scandanavica,* 33–47.

Cannon, T. D., Mednick, S. A., & Parnas, J. (1990). Antecedents of predominantly negative and predominantly positive-symptom schizophrenia in a high-risk population. *Archives of General Psychiatry, 47,* 622–632.

Cantor, N., Markus, H., Niedenthal, P., & Nurius, P. (1986). On motivation and the self-concept. In R. M. Sorrentino & E. T. Higgins (Eds.), *Handbook of motivation and cognition: Foundations of social behavior* (pp. 96–121). New York: Guilford.

Cantor-Graae, E. (2007). The contribution of social factors to the development of schizophrenia: A review of recent findings. *Canadian Journal of Psychiatry, 52,* 277–286.

Cantwell, D. P., Baker, L., & Rutter, M. (1978). Family factors. In M. Rutter & E. Schopler (Eds.), *Autism: A reappraisal of concepts and treatment.* New York: Plenum.

Capano, L., Minden, D., Chen, S. X., et al. (2008). Mathematical learning disorder in school-age children with attention-deficit hyperactivity disorder. *Canadian Journal of Psychiatry, 53,* 392–399.

Capewell, S., & O'Flaherty, M. (2009). Trends in cardiovascular disease: Are we winning the war? *Canadian Medical Association Journal, 180,* 1285–1286.

Caplan, P. (1995). *They say you're crazy: How the world's most powerful psychiatrists decide who's normal.* Reading, MA: Addison-Wesley.

Cappadocia, M. C., Desrocher, M., Pepler, D., & Schroeder, J. H. (2009). Contextualizing the neurobiology of conduct disorder in an emotion dysregulation framework. *Clinical Psychology Review, 29,* 506–518.

Cappeliez, P. (1993). Depression in elderly persons: Prevalence, predictors, and psychological intervention. In P. Cappeliez & R. J. Flynn (Eds.), *Depression and the social environment: Research and intervention with neglected populations* (pp. 332–368). Montreal: McGill-Queen's University Press.

Cappeliez, P. (2000). Presentation of depression and response to group cognitive therapy with older patients. *Journal of Clinical Geropsychology, 6,* 165–174.

Cappeliez, P., & O'Rourke, N. (2006). Empirical validation of a model of reminiscence and health in later life. *The Journals of Gerontology Series B: Psychological Sciences and Social Sciences, 61,* P237–P244.

Capron, A. M. (1999). Ethical and human rights issues in research on mental disorders that may affect decision-making capacity. *New England Journal of Medicine, 340,* 1430–1434.

Cardena, A., & Gleaves, D. H. (2007). Dissociative disorders. In M. Hersen, S. M. Turner, & D. C. Beidel (Eds.), *Adult psychopathology and diagnosis,* Vol. 5 (pp. 473–503). New York: John Wiley & Sons.

Carey, B. (2008, December 18). Psychiatrists revise the book of human troubles. *The New York Times.*

Carey, K. B., et al. (2007). Adapting motivational interventions for comorbid schizophrenia and alcohol use disorders. *Clinical Psychology: Science and Practice, 14,* 39–57.

Carleton, R. N., Collimore, K. C., & Asmundson, G. J. G. (2007). Social anxiety and fear of negative evaluation: Construct validity of the BFNE-II. *Journal of Anxiety Disorders, 21,* 131–141.

Carleton, R. N., Norton, M. A. P. J., & Asmundson, G. J. G. (2007). Fearing the unknown: A short version of the Intolerance of Uncertainty Scale. *Journal of Anxiety Disorders, 21,* 131–140.

Carlsson, A., Hanson, L. O., Waters, N., & Carlsson, M. L. (1999). A glutamatergic deficiency model of schizophrenia. *British Journal of Psychiatry, 174,* 2–6.

Carnelley, K. B., Pietromonaco, P. R., & Jaffe, K. (1994). Depression, working models of others and relationship functioning. *Journal of Personality and Social Psychology, 66,* 127–141.

Carnelley, K. B., Wortman, C. B., & Kessler, R. C. (1999). The impact of widowhood on depression: Findings from a prospective survey. *Psychological Medicine, 29,* 1111–1123.

Carnivez, G. L., & Watkins, M. W. (1998). Long-term stability of the Wechsler Intelligence Scale for Children — Third edition. *Psychological Assessment, 10,* 285-301.

Carpeggiani, C., & Skinner, J. E. (1991). Coronary flow and mental stress: Experimental findings. *Circulation, 83,* 90–93.

Carpenter, W. T. (2009). Anticipating DSM-V: Should psychosis risk become a diagnostic class? *Schizophrenia Bulletin, 35,* 841–843.

Carpenter, W. T., Heinrichs, D. W., & Wagman, A. M. I. (1988). Deficit and nondeficit forms of schizophrenia: The concept. *American Journal of Psychiatry, 145,* 578–583.

Carpentieri, S. C., & Morgan, S. B. (1994). Brief report: A comparison of patterns of cognitive functioning of autistic and nonautistic retarded children on the Stanford-Binet, 4th ed. *Journal of Autism and Developmental Disorders, 24,* 215–223.

Carr, S. J., Goldstein, R. S., & Brooks, D. (2007). Acute exacerbations of COPD in subjects completing pulmonary rehabilitation. *Chest, 132,* 127–134.

Carrière, G. (2003). Seniors use of home care. *Health Reports, 17,* 43–47.

Carroll, K. M., Rounsaville, B. J., Nich, C., Gordon, L. T., & Gawin, F. (1995). Integrating psychotherapy and pharmacotherapy for cocaine dependence: Results from a randomized clinical trial. In L. S. Onken, J. D. Blaine, & J. J. Boren (Eds.), *Integrating behavioral therapies with medications in the treatment of drug dependence* (pp. 19–36). Rockville, MD: National Institute on Drug Abuse.

Carroll, K. M., et al. (1994). One-year follow-up of psychotherapy and pharmacotherapy for cocaine dependence. *Archives of General Psychiatry, 51,* 989–997.

Carstensen, L. L. (1996). Evidence for a life-span theory of socioemotional selectivity. *Current Directions in Psychological Science, 4,* 151–156.

Carter, M. M., Forys, K. K., & Oswald, J. C. (2008). The cognitive-behavioral model. In M. Hersen & A. G. Gross (Eds.), *Handbook of clinical psychology, Volume 1, adults* (pp. 171–201). New York: Wiley.

Carter, J. C., et al. (2009). Maintenance treatment for anorexia nervosa: A comparison of cognitive behavior therapy and treatment as usual. *International Journal of Eating Disorders, 42,* 202–207.

Cartwright-Hatton, S., McNicol, K., & Doubleday, E. (2006). Anxiety in a neglected population: Prevalence of anxiety disorders in pre-adolescent children. *Clinical Psychology Review, 26,* 817–833.

Carver, C. S., et al. (1993). How coping mediates the effect of optimism on distress: A study of women with early stage breast cancer. *Journal of Personality and Social Psychology, 65,* 375–390.

Casacalenda, N., Perry, J. C., & Looper, K. (2002). Remission in major depressive disorder: A comparison of pharmacotherapy, psychotherapy, and control conditions. *American Journal of Psychiatry, 159,* 1354–1360.

Casati, J., Toner, B. B., & Yu, B. (2000). Psychosocial issues for women with trichotillomania. *Comprehensive Psychiatry, 41,* 344–351.

Casey, J. E., Rourke, B. P., & Del Dotto, J. E. (1996). Learning disabilities in children with attention deficit disorder with and without hyperactivity. *Child Neuropsychology, 2,* 83–98.

Cashman, J. A. (1966). *The LSD story.* Greenwich, CT: Fawcett.

Caspi, A., McClay, J., et al. (2002). Role of genotype in the cycle of violence of maltreated children. *Science, 297,* 851–854.

Caspi, A., Sugden, K., Moffitt, T. E., et al. (2003). Influence of life stress on depression: Moderation by a polymorphism in the 5-HTT gene. *Science, 301,* 386–389.

Cassady, J. D., et al. (2005). Case series: Outbreak of conversion disorder among Amish adolescent girls. *Journal of the American Academy of Child and Adolescent Psychiatry, 44,* 291–297.

Castellanos, F. X., & Tannock, R. (2002). Neuroscience of attention-deficit/hyperactivity disorder: the search for endophenotypes. *Nature Reviews Neuroscience, 3,* 617–628.

Cautela, J. R. (1966). Treatment of compulsive behavior by covert sensitization. *Psychological Record, 16,* 33–41.

Centre for Addiction and Mental Health (CAMH). (2000). *CAMH Best advice paper: Community treatment orders: Overview and recommendations.* Toronto: Author.

Centre for Addiction and Mental Health (CAMH). (2001). *Information bulletin: Ecstasy.* Toronto: Author.

Centre for Addiction and Mental Health (CAMH). (2008). *Redeveloping the Queen Street Site.* Toronto: Author.

Cerny, J. A., Barlow, D. H., Craske, M. G., & Himadi, W. G. (1987). Couples treatment of agoraphobia: A two year follow-up. *Behavior Therapy, 18,* 401–415.

Chai, C. T. (2006). Treading a thin line. *Visions: BC's Mental Health and Addiction Journal, 3,* 11–12.

Chaiken, S., & Pliner, P. (1987). Women, but not men, are what they eat: The effects of meal size and gender on perceived femininity and masculinity. *Personality and Social Psychology Bulletin, 13,* 166–176.

Chaimowitz, G. A. (2004). Community treatment orders: An uncertain step. *Canadian Journal of Psychiatry, 49,* 577–578.

Chalder, M., Elgar, F. J., & Bennett, P. (2006). Drinking and motivations to drink among adolescent children of parents with alcohol problems. *Alcohol and Alcoholism, 41,* 107–113.

Chamberlain, E. A. L., & Solomon, R. M. (2008). Minimizing impairment-related youth traffic deaths: The need for comprehensive provincial action. *Canadian Journal of Public Health, 99,* 267–270.

Chambless, D., Fydrich, T., & Rodebaugh, T. L. (2008). Generalized social phobia and avoidant personality disorder: Meaningful distinction or useless duplication. *Depression and Anxiety, 25,* 8–19.

Chambless, D. L., & Ollendick, T. H. (2001). Empirically supported psychological interventions: Controversies and evidence. *Annual Review of Psychology, 52,* 685–716.

Chambless, D. L., Sanderson, W. C., Shoham, V., Johnson, S. B., Pope, K. S., et al. (1996). An update on empirically validated therapies. *The Clinical Psychologist, 49,* 5–18.

Chandler, M. J., & Lalonde, C. (1998). Cultural continuity as a hedge against suicide in Canada's First Nations. *Transcultural Psychiatry, 35,* 191–220.

Chang, W. C., Kaul, P., Westerhout, C. M., Graham, M. M., & Armstrong, P. W. (2007). Effects of socioeconomic status on mortality after acute myocardial infarction. *American Journal of Medicine, 120,* 33–39.

Chapman, L. J., & Chapman, J. P. (1969). Illusory correlation as an obstacle to the use of valid psychodiagnostic signs. *Journal of Abnormal Psychology, 74,* 271–287.

Chappell, N., & Dujela, C. (2008). Caregiving: Predicting at-risk status. *Canadian Journal on Aging, 27,* 169–179.

Chappell, N. L., & Penning, M. (1996). Behavioural problems and distress among caregivers of people with dementia. *Ageing and Society, 16,* 57–73.

Chappell, N. L., & Reid, R. C. (2002). Burden and well-being among caregivers. *Gerontologist, 42,* 772–780.

Charbonneau, J., & O'Connor, K. (1999). Depersonalization in a non-clinical sample. *Behavioral and Cognitive Psychotherapy, 27,* 377–381.

Charland, L. C. (2007). Benevolent theory: Moral treatment at the York Retreat. *History of Psychiatry, 18,* 61–80.

Charlesworth, A., & Glantz, S. A. (2005). Smoking in the movies increases adolescent smoking: A review. *Pediatrics, 116,* 1516–1528.

Charney, D. A., Zikos, E., & Gill, K. J. (2010). Early recovery from alcohol dependence: Factors that promote or impede abstinence. *Journal of Substance Abuse Treatment, 38,* 42–50.

Charney, D. S., Nemeroff, C. B., Lewis, L., et al. (2002). National Depressive and Manic Depressive Association Consensus statement on the use of placebo in clinical trials of mood disorders. *Archives of General Psychiatry, 59,* 262–270.

Charney, D. S., Woods, S. W., Goodman, W. K., & Heninger, G. R. (1987). Neurobiological mechanisms of panic anxiety: Biochemical and behavioral correlates of yohimbine-induced panic attacks. *American Journal of Psychiatry, 144,* 1030–1036.

Chartier, M. J., Walker, J. R., & Stein, M. B. (2003). Considering comorbidity in social phobia. *Social Psychiatry and Psychiatric Epidemiology, 38,* 728–734.

Chassin, L., Curran, P. J., Hussong, A. M., & Colder, C. R. (1996). The relation of parent alcoholism to adolescent substance abuse: A longitudinal follow-up. *Journal of Abnormal Psychology, 105,* 70–80.

Chemtob, C., Roitblat, H. C., Hamada, R. S., Carlson, J. G., & Twentyman, C. T. (1988). A cognitive action theory of posttraumatic stress disorder. *Journal of Anxiety Disorders, 2,* 253–275.

Chen, E. (2007). Impact of socioeconomic status on physiological health in adolescents: An experimental manipulation of psychosocial factors. *Psychosomatic Medicine, 69,* 348–355.

Chen, E., Chim, L. S., Struck, R. C., & Miller, G. E. (2007). The role of the social environment in children and adolescents with asthma. *American Journal of Respiratory and Critical Care Medicine, 176,* 644–649.

Chen, I. (2009, November 19). The court will now call its expert witness: The brain. *Stanford University News.*

Chen, W. J., Liu, S. K., Chang, C.-G., Lien, Y.-J., et al. (1998). Sustained attention deficit and schizotypal personality features in nonpsychotic relatives of schizophrenic patients. *American Journal of Psychiatry, 155,* 1214–1220.

Chen, Y., Nettles, M. E., & Chen, S.-W. (2009). Rethinking dependent personality disorder: Comparing different human relatedness in cultural contexts. *The Journal of Nervous and Mental Disease, 197,* 793–800.

Chesser, M. (2009, September 8th). Insite: Vancouver's drug dilemma. *The McGill Tribune.*

Cheung, A. H., & Dewa, C. S. (2007). Mental health service use among adolescents and young adults with major depressive disorder and suicidality. *Canadian Journal of Psychiatry, 52,* 228–232.

Chew, B. H., Pace, K. T., & Honey, J. D'A. (2002). Munchausen syndrome presenting as gross hematuria in two women. *Urology, 59,* 601i–601iii.

Chida, Y., & Steptoe, A. (2009). The association of anger and hostility with future coronary heart disease: A meta-analytic review of prospective evidence. *Journal of the American College of Cardiology, 53,* 936–946.

Chiu, T., et al. (2009). Internet-based caregiver support for Chinese Canadians taking care of a family member with Alzheimer's Disease and related dementia. *Canadian Journal of Aging, 28,* 323–336.

Chivers, M. L. (2008, March). *Sex and sexual orientation differences in the specificity of sexual arousal.* Presented at the 33rd annual meeting of the Society for Sex Therapy and Research (SSTAR), Chicago, IL.

Chivers, M. L., Seto, M. C., Lalumière, M. L., Laan, E., & Grimbos, T. (2010). Agreement of self-reported and genital measures of sexual arousal in men and women: A meta-analysis. *Archives of Sexual Behavior, 39,* 5–56.

Chobanian, A. V., et al. (2003). The Seventh Report of the Joint National Committee on prevention, detection, evaluation, and treatment of high blood pressure. *Journal of the American Medical Association, 289,* 2560–2572.

Chouinard, G., Jones, B., Remington, G., Bloom, D., Addington, D., MacEwan, G. W., et al. (1993). A Canadian multicentre placebo-controlled study of fixed doses of risperidone and haloperidol in the treatment of chronic schizophrenia patients. *Journal of Clinical Psychopharmacology, 13,* 25–40.

Chow, E. W., & Choy, A. L. (2002). Clinical characteristics and treatment response to SSRI in a female pedophile. *Archives of Sexual Behavior, 31,* 211–215.

Choy, Y., Fyer, A., & Lipsitz, J. D. (2007). Treatment of specific phobia in adults. *Clinical Psychology Review, 27,* 266–286.

Choy, Y., Schneier, F. R., Heimberg, R. G., Oh, K.-S., & Liebowitz, M. R. (2008). Features of the offensive subtype of Taijin-Kyofu-Sho in US and Korean patients with DSM-IV social anxiety disorder. *Depression and Anxiety, 25,* 230–240.

Christian, M. A. (2008, May 19). Former football star tells of life with mental illness; 'I'm not crazy'. *Jet, 113 (19),*16–17.

Christensen, A., Atkins, D. C., Baucom, B., & Yi, J. (2010). Marital status and satisfaction five years following a randomized clinical trial comparing traditional versus integrative behavioral couple therapy. *Journal of Consulting and Clinical Psychology, 78,* 225–235.

Christensen, A., et al. (2004). Traditional versus integrative behavioral couple therapy for significantly and chronically distressed married couples. *Journal of Consulting and Clinical Psychology, 72,* 176–191.

Christensen, A., & Heavey, C. L. (1990). Gender and social structure in the demand/withdraw pattern of marital interaction. *Journal of Personality and Social Psychology, 59,* 73–81.

Christensen, A., Jacobson, N. S., & Babcock, J. C. (1995). Integrative behavioral couples therapy. In N. S. Jacobson & A. S. Gurman (Eds.), *Clinical handbook of couples therapy* (pp. 31–64). New York: Guilford.

Christensen, T. O. (2007). The influence of neurocognitive dysfunctions on work capacity in schizophrenia patients: A systematic review of the literature. *International Journal of Psychiatry in Clinical Practice, 11,* 89–101.

Christie, A. B. (1982). Changing patterns in mental illness in the elderly. *British Journal of Psychiatry, 140,* 154–159.

Chu, J. A. (2006). Guidelines for treating dissociative identity disorder in adults. *Journal of Trauma and Dissociation, 6,* 69–149.

Churchill R., Owen, G., Hotopf, M., & Singh, S. (2007). *International experiences of using community treatment orders.* London: Department of Health and Institute of Psychiatry.

Cicchetti, D. (2004). An odyssey of discovery: Lessons learned through three decades of research on child maltreatment. *American Psychologist, 59,* 731–741.

Cicchetti, D., & Toth, S. L. (2009). The past achievements and future promises of developmental psychopathology: The coming of age of a discipline. *Journal of Child Psychology and Psychiatry, 50,* 16–25.

Cinciripini, P. M., Lapitsky, L. G., Wallfisch, A., Mace, R., Nezami, E., & Van Vunakis, H. (1994). An evaluation of a multicomponent treatment program involving scheduled smoking and relapse prevention procedures: Initial findings. *Addictive Behaviors, 19,* 13–22.

Claassen, C. A., et al. (2007). Clinical differences among depressed patients with and without a history of suicide attempts: Findings from the STAR*D trial. *Journal of Affective Disorders, 97,* 77–84.

Clark, C. C. (1985). *Report of the Electro-Convulsive Therapy Review Committee.* Toronto: Ontario Ministry of Health.

Clark, D.A. (2001). The persistent problem of negative cognition in anxiety and depression: New perspectives and old controversies. *Behavior Therapy, 32,* 3–12.

Clark, D. A. (2005). Focus on "cognition" in cognitive behaviour therapy: Is it really necessary? *Cognitive Behavior Therapy, 34,* 131–139.

Clark, D. A., & Beck, A. T. (1999). *Scientific foundations of cognitive theory and therapy for depression.* New York: John Wiley & Sons.

Clark, D. A., Beck, A. T., & Alford, B. A. (1999). *Scientific foundations of cognitive theory and therapy of depression.* New York: John Wiley & Sons.

Clark, D. A., & Oates, T. (1995). Daily hassles, major and minor life events, and their interaction with sociotropy and autonomy. *Behaviour Research and Therapy, 33,* 819–823.

Clark, D. A., Purdon, C., & Wang, A. (2003). The Meta-Cognitive Beliefs Questionnaire: Development of a measure of obsessional beliefs. *Behaviour Research and Therapy, 41,* 655–659.

Clark, D. A., Steer, R. A., Beck, A. T., & Ross, L. (1995). Psychometric characteristics of revised sociotropy and autonomy scales in college students. *Behaviour Research and Therapy, 33,* 325–334.

Clark, D. M., Ehlers, A., Hackmann, A., McManus, F., Fennel, M., Grey, N., Waddington, L., Wild, J. (2006). Cognitive therapy versus exposure and applied relaxation in social phobia: A randomized controlled trial. *Journal of Consulting and Clinical Psychology, 74,* 568–578.

Clark, D. M., & Wells, A. (1995). A cognitive model of social phobia. In R. G. Heimberg, M. R. Liebowitz, D. A. Hope, & F. R.Schneier (Eds.), *Social phobia: Diagnosis, assessment, and treatment* (pp. 69–93). New York: Guilford Press.

Clark, L. A. (2005). Stability and change in personality pathology: Revelations of three longitudinal studies. *Journal of Personality Disorders, 19,* 524–532.

Clark, L. A., Livesley, W. J., Schroeder, M. L., & Irish, S. L. (1996). Convergence of two systems for assessing personality disorder. *Psychological Assessment, 8,* 294–303.

Clark, L. A., Watson, D., & Mineka, S. (1994). Temperament, personality, and the mood and anxiety disorders. Journal of Abnormal Psychology, 103, 103-116.

Clarke, G., Hops, H., Lewinsohn, P. M., Andrews, J., Seeley, J. R., & Williams, J. (1992). Cognitive-behavioral group treatment of adolescent depression: Prediction of outcome. *Behavior Therapy, 23,* 341–354.

Clarke, G. N., Hornbrook, M., Lynch, F., et al. (2001). A randomized trial of a group cognitive intervention for preventing depression in adolescent offspring of depressed parents. *Archives of General Psychiatry, 58,* 1127–1134.

Clarkin, J. F., Levy, K. N., Lenzenweger, M. F., & Kernberg, O. F. (2007). Evaluating three treatments for borderline personality disorder: A multiwave study. *American Journal of Psychiatry, 164,* 922–928.

Classen, C. C., Palesh, O. G., & Aggarwal, R. (2005). Sexual revictimization: A review of the empirical literature. *Trauma, Violence, and Abuse, 6,* 103–129.

Claude-Pierre, P. (1997). The *secret language of eating disorders.* Toronto: Random House.

Clayton, I. C., Richards, J. C., & Edwards, C. J. (1999). Selective attention in obsessive-compulsive disorder. *Journal of Abnormal Psychology, 108,* 171–175.

Cleckley, H. (1976). *The mask of sanity* (5th ed.). St. Louis, MO: Mosby.

Clingempeel, W. G., Britt, S. C., & Henggeler, S. W. (2008). Beyond treatment effects: Comorbid psychopathologies and long-term outcomes among substance-abusing delinquents. *American Journal of Orthopsychiatry, 78,* 29–36.

Cloninger, C. R. (1987a). Neurogenetic adaptive mechanisms in alcoholism. *Science, 236,* 410–416.

Cloninger, C. R. (1987b). A systematic method for clinical description and classification of personality variants. *Archives of General Psychiatry, 44,* 573–588.

Cloud, J. (1999, June 7). Mental health reform: What it would really take. *Time* magazine, 54–56.

CME Institute. (2007). Academic Highlights: New developments in the treatment of schizophrenia. *Journal of Clinical Psychiatry, 68,* 463–478.

Coccaro, E. F., & Kavousi, R. J. (1997). Fluoxetine and impulsive aggressive behavior in personality-disordered subjects. *Archives of General Psychiatry, 54,* 1081–1088.

Cody, M. J., Dunn, D., Hoppin, S., & Wendt, P. (1999). Silver surfers: Training and evaluating Internet use among older adult learners. *Communication Education, 48,* 269–286.

Coffman, S. J., Martell, C. R., Dimidjian, S., Gallop, R., & Hollon, S. D. (2007). Extreme nonresponse in cognitive therapy: Can behavioral activation succeed where cognitive therapy fails? *Journal of Consulting and Clinical Psychology, 75,* 531–541.

Coghill, D. R., Nigg, J. T., Rothenberger, A., Sonuga-Barke, E. J. S., & Tannock, R. (2005). Whither causal models in the neuroscience of ADHD. *Developmental Science, 8,* 105–114.

Cohen, N. J., Davine, M., Horodezky, N., Lipsett, L., & Isaacson, L. (1993). Unsuspected language impairment in psychiatrically disturbed children: Prevalence and language and behavioral characteristics. *Journal of the American Academy of Child and Adolescent Psychiatry, 32,* 595–603.

Cohen, N. J., Menna, R., Vallance, D. D., Barwick, M. A., Im, N., & Horodezky, N. (1998). Language, social cognitive processing, and behavioral characteristics of psychiatrically disturbed children with previously identified and suspected language impairments. *Journal of Child Psychology and Psychiatry, 39,* 853–864.

Cohen, N. J., Vallance, D. D., Barwick, M., Im, N., Menna, R., Horodezky, N. B., et al. (2000). The interface between ADHD and language impairment: An examination of language, achievement, and cognitive processing. *Journal of Child Psychology and Psychiatry, 41,* 353–362.

Cohen, R. B, Boggio, P. S., & Fregni, F. (2009). Risk factors for relapse after remission with repetitive transcranial magnetic stimulation for the treatment of depression. *Depression and Anxiety, 26,* 682–688.

Cohen, R. M., Nordahl, T. E., Semple, W. E., Andreason, P., et al. (1997). The brain metabolic patterns of clozapine and fluphenazine-treated patients with schizophrenia during a continous performance task. *Archives of General Psychiatry, 54,* 481–486.

Cohen, S., Alper, C. M., Doyle, W. J., Treanor, T. J., & Turner, R. B. (2006). Positive emotional style predicts resistance to illness after experimental exposure to rhinovirus or influenza A virus. *Psychosomatic Medicine, 68,* 809–815.

Cohen, S., & Herbert, T. B. (1996). Health psychology: Psychological factors and physical disease from the perspective of human psychoneuroimmunology. In J. T. Spence, J. M. Darley, & D. J. Foss (Eds.), *Annual review of psychology* (pp. 123–142). Stanford, CA: Stanford University Press.

Cohen, S., O'Leary, K. D., & Foran, H. (2010). A randomized clinical trial of a brief, problem-focused couple therapy for depression. *Behavior Therapy.*

Cohen, S., Tyrell, D. A. J., & Smith, A. P. (1991). Psychological stress and susceptibility to the common cold. *New England Journal of Medicine, 325,* 606–612.

Cohen, S., & Wills, T. A. (1985). Stress, social support, and the buffering process. *Psychological Bulletin, 98,* 310–357.

Cohen-Kettenis, P. T., Owen, A., Kaijser, V. G., Bradley, S. J., & Zucker, K. J. (2003). Demographic characteristics, social competence, and behavior problems in children with gender identity disorder: A cross-national, cross-clinic comparative analysis. *Journal of Abnormal Child Psychology, 31,* 41–53.

Cohen-Kettenis, P. T., et al. (2006). A parent-report gender identity questionnaire for children: A cross-national, cross-clinic comparative analysis. *Clinical Child Psychology and Psychiatry*, 11, 397–405.

Colapinto, J. (1997). The true story of Joan/John. *Rolling Stone*, 55–97.

Colapinto, J. (2000). *As nature made him: The boy who was raised as a girl*. Toronto: Harper Collins.

Colapinto, J. (2004, June 3). Gender gap: What were the real reasons behind David Reimer's suicide? *Slate*.

Coldwell, C. M., & Bender, W. S. (2007). The effectiveness of assertive community treatment for homeless populations with severe mental illness: A meta-analysis. *American Journal of Psychiatry*, 164, 393–399.

Cole, D. A., Martin, J. M., Powers, B., & Truglio, R. (1990). Modeling causal relations between academic and social competence and depression: A multitrait-multimethod longitudinal study of children. *Journal of Abnormal Psychology*, 105, 258–270.

Cole, M. G., & Bellavance, F. (1997). The prognosis of depression in old age. *American Journal of Geriatric Psychiatry*, 5, 4–14.

Cole, M. G., Bellavance, F., & Mansour, A. (1999). Prognosis of depression in elderly community and primary care populations: A systematic review and meta-analysis. *American Journal of Psychiatry*, 156, 1182–1189.

Cole, M. G., & Dendukuri, N. (2003). Risk factors for depression among elderly community subjects: A systematic review and meta-analysis. *American Journal of Psychiatry*, 160, 1147–1156.

Collaborative Outcome Data Committee. (2007). *Sexual offender treatment outcome research: CODC guidelines for evaluation*. Ottawa: Government of Canada.

Collier, R. (2008). The gambling take: Balancing revenues and responsibilities. *Canadian Medical Association Journal*, 179, 21–22.

Collier, R. (2009). Canadian Institutes of Health Research proposes major initiative on Alzheimer disease in step forward toward national dementia strategy. *Canadian Medical Association Journal*, 181, E36–E37.

Collins, A. (1988). *In the sleep room: The story of the CIA brainwashing experiments in Canada*. Toronto: Lester and Orpen Dennys Limited.

Collins, K. A., & Dozois, D. J. A. (2008). What are the active ingredients in preventative interventions for depression? *Clinical Psychology: Science and Practice*, 15, 313–330.

Colman, I., Wadsworth, M. E. J., Coudace, T. J., & Jones, P. B. (2007). Forty-year psychiatric outcomes following assessment for internalizing disorder in adolescence. *American Journal of Psychiatry*, 164, 126–133.

Compton, D. R., Dewey, W. L., & Martin, B. R. (1990). Cannabis dependence and tolerance production. *Advances in Alcohol and Substance Abuse*, 9, 129–147.

Condefer, K. A., Haworth, J., & Wilcock, G. K. (2004). Clinical utility of computed tomography in the assessment of dementia: A memory clinic study. *International Journal of Geriatric Psychiatry*, 19, 414–421.

Conley, R. R., et al. (2007). The burden of depressive symptoms in the long-term treatment of patients with schizophrenia. *Schizophrenia Research*, 90, 186–197.

Conley, R. R., et al. (2009). The burden of depressive symptoms in people with schizophrenia. *Psychiatric Clinics of North America*, 32, 853–861.

Connan, F., & Stanley, S. (2003). Biology of appetite and weight regulation. In J. Treasure, U. Schmidt, & E. van Furth (Eds.), *Handbook of eating disorders* (2nd ed., pp. 63–87). Chichester, England: John Wiley & Sons.

Connolly, J. F. (2000). Applying cognitive research in the twenty-first century: Event-related potentials in assessment. *Brain and Cognition*, 42, 99–101.

Connolly, J. F., Marchand, Y., Major, A., & D'Arcy, R. C. N. (2006). Event-related brain potentials as a measure of performance on WISC-III and WAIS-R NI similarities sub-tests. *Journal of Clinical and Experimental Neuropsychology*, 28, 1327–1345.

Connolly, J. F., Mate-Kole, C. C., & Joyce, B. M. (1999). An innovative assessment approach in a case of global aphasia. *Archives of Physical Medicine and Rehabilitation*, 80, 1309–1315.

Conrod, P. J., Pihl, R. O., Stewart, S. H., & Dongier, M. (2000). Validation of a system of classifying female substance abusers on the basis of personality and motivational risk factors for substance abuse. *Psychology of Addictive Behaviors*, 14, 243–256.

Conrod, P. J., Stewart, S. H., Comeau, N., & Maclean, A. M. (2006). Efficacy of cognitive-behavioral interventions targeting personality risk factors for youth alcohol misuse. *Journal of Clinical Child and Adolescent Psychology*, 35, 550–563.

Consumer Reports. (1995, November). Mental health: Does therapy help? *Consumer Reports*, 734–739.

Conwell, Y. (1994). Suicide in elderly patients. In L. S. Schneider, C. F. Reynolds, III, B. D. Lebowitz, & A. J. Friedhoff (Eds.), *Diagnosis and treatment of depression in late life* (pp. 397–418). Washington, DC: American Psychiatric Press.

Conwell, Y. (2001). Suicide in later life: A review and recommendations for prevention. *Suicide and Life-Threatening Behavior*, 31, 32–47.

Cook, J. M., Biyanova, T., & Coyne, J. (2009) Influential psychotherapy figures, authors, and books: an internet survey of over 2,000 psychotherapists. *Psychotherapy Theory, Research, Practice, Training*, 46, 42–51.

Cook, M., & Mineka, S. (1989). Observational conditioning of fear to fear-relevant versus fear-irrelevant stimuli in rhesus monkeys. *Journal of Abnormal Psychology*, 98, 448–459.

Cook, N. E., Barese, T. H., & Dicataldo, F. (2010). The confluence of mental health and psychopathic traits in adolescent female offenders. *Criminal Justice and Behavior*, 37, 119–136.

Coolidge, F. L., & Segal, D. L. (1998). Evolution of personality disorder diagnosis in the Diagnostic and Statistical Manual of Mental Disorders. *Clinical Psychology Review*, 18, 585–589.

Coons, P. M., & Milstein, V. (1992). Psychogenic amnesia: A clinical investigation of 25 cases. *Dissociation: Progress in the Dissociative Disorders*, 5, 73–79.

Coons, W. H. (1967). The dynamics of change in psychotherapy. *Canadian Psychiatric Association Journal*, 12, 239–245.

Coons, W. H., & Peacock, T. P. (1970). Interpersonal interaction and personality change in group psychotherapy. *Canadian Psychiatric Association Journal*, 15, 347–355.

Cooper, J. E., et al. (1972). *Psychiatric diagnosis in New York and London*. London: Oxford University Press.

Cooper, M. L. (1994). Motivations for alcohol use among adolescents: Development and validation of a four-factor model. *Psychological Assessment*, 6, 117–128.

Cooper, M., Corrado, R., Karlberg, A.M., & Adams, L. P. (1992). Aboriginal suicide in British Columbia: An overview. *Canada's Mental Health*. Ottawa, Canada.

Copeland, W. E., Shanahan, L., Costello, E. J., & Angold, A. (2009). Childhood and adolescent psychiatric disorders as predictors of young adult disorders. *Archives of General Psychiatry*, 66, 764–772.

Corbitt, E. M., & Widiger, T. A. (1995). Sex differences among the personality disorders: An exploration of the data. *Clinical Psychology: Science and Practice*, 2, 225–238.

Cordova, J. V., & Jacobson, N. S. (1993). Couple distress. In D. H. Barlow (Ed.), *Clinical handbook of psychological disorders* (2nd ed., pp. 461–512). New York: Guilford.

Cornblatt, B., & Erlenmeyer-Kimling, L. E. (1985). Global attentional deviance in children at risk for schizophrenia: Specificity and predictive validity. *Journal of Abnormal Psychology*, 94, 470–486.

Corove Fingeret, M., Warren, C. S., Cepeda-Benito, A., & Gleaves, D. H. (2006). Eating disorder prevention research: A meta-analysis. *Eating Disorders*, 14, 191–213.

Correa, D. D., Graves, R. E., & Costa, L. (1996). Awareness of memory deficit in Alzheimer's disease patients and memory-impaired older adults. *Aging, Neuropsychology, and Cognition*, 3, 215–228.

Cortoni, F., & Marshall, W. L. (2001). Sex as a coping strategy and its relationship to juvenile sexual history and intimacy in sexual offenders. *Sexual Abuse: A Journal of Research and Treatment*, 13, 27–43.

Coryell, W., Leon, A., Winokur, G., et al. (1996). Importance of psychotic features to long-term course in major depressive disorder. *American Journal of Psychiatry*, 153, 483–489.

Costa, L. (1996). Lifespan neuropsychology. *The Clinical Neuropsychologist*, 10, 365–374.

Costa, P. T., Jr., & McCrae, R. R. (1992). *NEO-PI-R*. Odessa, FL: Psychological Assessment Resources.

Costello, C. G. (1982). Fears and phobias in women: A community survey. *Journal of Abnormal Psychology*, 91, 280–286.

Cote, S. M., Boivin, M., Liu, X., et al. (2009). Depression and anxiety symptoms: Onset, developmental course and risk factors during early childhood. *Journal of Child Psychology and Psychiatry*, 50, 1201–1208.

Cote, S. M., Vaillancourt, T., LeBlanc, J. C., Nagin, D. S., & Tremblay, R. E. (2006). The development of physical aggression from toddlerhood to pre-adolescence: A nation wide longitudinal study of Canadian children. *Journal of Abnormal Child Psychology, 34,* 71–85.

Côté, S., & Bouchard, S. (2008). Virtual reality exposure for phobias: A critical review. *Journal of Cybertherapy and Rehabilitation, 1,* 75–91.

Cote, S., Tremblay, R. E., Nagin, D. S., Zoccolillo, M., & Vitaro, F. (2002). Childhood behavioral profiles leading to adolescent conduct disorder: Risk trajectories for boys and girls. *Journal of the American Academy of Child and Adolescent Psychiatry, 41,* 1086–1094.

Cougle, J. R., Resnick, H., & Kilpatrick, D. G. (2009). PTSD, depression, and their comorbidity in relation to suicidality: Cross-sectional and prospective analyses of a national probability sample of women. *Depression and Anxiety, 26,* 1151–1157.

Courbasson, C. M. A., & Schelkanova, I. (in press). Women and addictions: Body weight and shape concerns as barriers to recovery from substance use disorders. Let's address these issues in treatment and recovery now! *Journal of Drug Addiction, Education, and Eradication.*

Courbasson, C. M., Smith, P. D., & Cleland, P. A. (2005). Substance use disorders, anorexia, bulimia, and concurrent disorders. *Canadian Journal of Public Health, 96,* 102–106.

Courneya, K. S., Plotnikoff, R. C., Hotz, S. B., & Birkett, N. J. (2000). Social support and the theory of planned behavior in the exercise domain. *American Journal of Health Behavior, 24,* 300–308.

Cournish, P. A., et al. (2003). Rural interdisciplinary mental health team building via satellite: A demonstration project. *Telemedia Journal and e-Health, 9,* 63–71.

Cowan, P. (1999, November 7). Traumatic memories dog veteran; "I always wake up before they kill me." *Edmonton Sun,* 29.

Cox, B. J., Borger, S. C., Asmundson, G. J. G., & Taylor, S. (2000). Dimensions of hypochondriasis and the five-factor model of personality. *Personality and Individual Differences, 29,* 99–108.

Cox, B. J., Clara, I. P., Sareen, J., & Stein, M. B. (2008). The structure of feared social situations among individuals with a lifetime diagnosis of social anxiety disorder in two independent nationally representative mental health surveys. *Behaviour Research and Therapy, 46,* 477–486.

Cox, B. J., Endler, N. S., & Norton, G. R. (1994). Levels of "nonclinical panic." *Journal of Behavioural Therapy and Experimental Psychiatry, 25,* 35–40.

Cox, B. J., Endler, N. S., & Swinson, R. P. (1991). Clinical and nonclinical panic attacks: An empirical test of a panic anxiety continuum. *Journal of Anxiety Disorders, 5,* 21–34.

Cox, B. J., Enns, M. W., & Clara, I. P. (2004). Psychological dimensions associated with suicide ideation and attempts in the National Comorbidity Survey. *Suicide and Life-Threatening Behaviour, 34,* 209–219.

Cox, B. J., Kwong, J., Michaud, V., & Enns, M. W. (2000). Problem and probable pathological gambling: Considerations from a community survey. *Canadian Journal of Psychiatry, 45,* 548–553.

Cox, B. J., McWilliams, L. A., Clara, I. P., & Stein, M. B. (2003). The structure of feared situations in a nationally representative sample. *Anxiety Disorders, 17,* 89–101.

Cox, B. J., Pagura, J., Stein, M. B., & Sareen, J. (2009). The relationship between generalized social phobia and avoidant personality disorder in a national mental health survey. *Depression and Anxiety, 26,* 354–362.

Cox, B. J., Walker, J. R., Enns, M. W., & Karpinski, D. C. (2002). Self-criticism in generalized social phobia and response to cognitive-behavioral treatment. *Behavior Therapy, 33,* 479–491.

Cox, B. J., Yu, N., Afifi, T.O., & Ladouceur, R. (2005). A national survey of gambling problems in Canada. *Canadian Journal of Psychiatry, 50,* 213–217.

Cox, M., & Klinger, E. (1988). A motivational model of alcohol use. *Journal of Abnormal Psychology, 97,* 168–180.

Cox, W. M., Fadardi, J. S., & Pothos, E. M. (2006). The addiction Stroop test: Theoretical considerations and procedural recommendations. *Psychological Bulletin, 132,* 443–476.

Coyne, J. C. (1976). Toward an interactional description of depression. *Psychiatry, 39,* 28–40.

Coyne, J. C., & Gotlib, I. H. (1983). The role of cognition in depression: A critical appraisal. *Psychological Bulletin, 84,* 472–505.

Craddock, N., O'Donovan, M. C., & Owen, M. J. (2006). Genes for schizophrenia and bipolar disorder? Implications for psychiatric nosology. *Schizophrenia Bulletin, 32,* 9–16.

Craig, T., & Jenkins, C. L. (2007, May 25). Va. House to review psychiatric care gaps: Hearings spurred by massacre, presage a tide of reform efforts, lawmakers say. *Washington Post,* B1–B2.

Craighead, W. E., Evans, D. D., & Robins, C. J. (1992). Unipolar depression. In S. M. Turner, K. S. Calhoun, & H. E. Adams (Eds.), *Handbook of clinical behavior therapy* (2nd ed., pp. 99–116). New York: John Wiley & Sons.

Craske, M. G., Brown, A. T., & Barlow, D. H. (1991). Behavioral treatment of panic disorder: A two-year follow-up. *Behavior Therapy, 22,* 289–304.

Craske, M. G., Kircanski, K., Epstein, A., et al. (2010). Panic disorder: A review of DSM-IV panic disorder and proposals for DSM-V. *Depression and Anxiety, 27,* 93–112.

Craske, M. G., Maidenberg, E., & Bystritsky, A. (1995). Brief cognitive-behavioral versus nondirective therapy for panic disorder. *Journal of Behavior Therapy & Experimental Psychiatry, 26,* 113–120.

Craske, M. G., Rapee, R. M., & Barlow, D. H. (1992). Cognitive-behavioral treatment of panic disorder, agoraphobia, and generalized anxiety disorder. In S. M. Turner, K. S. Calhoun, & H. E. Adams (Eds.), *Handbook of clinical behavior therapy* (2nd ed., pp. 39–65). New York: John Wiley & Sons.

Crawford, C. (2002). *Learning disabilities in Canada: Economic costs to individuals, families and society.* Prepared for the Learning Disabilities Association of Canada by the Roeher Institute.

Crawford, T. (2009, March 31). Ontario ends era of segregation for the disbled: Huronia regional centre in Orillia closes doors. *Toronto Star,* A8.

Crawford, T. (2009, September 3). Stress takes troubling toll on students in university. *Toronto Star.*

Creamer, M., & Parslow, R. (2008). Trauma exposure and posttraumatic stress disorder in the elderly: A community prevalence study. *American Journal of Geriatric Psychiatry, 16,* 853–856.

Crits-Christoph, P. (1992). The efficacy of brief dynamic psychotherapy. *American Journal of Psychiatry, 149,* 151–158.

Cronbach, L. J., & Meehl, P. E. (1955). Construct validity in psychological tests. *Psychological Bulletin, 52,* 281–302.

Cross-National Collaborative Group. (1992). The changing rate of major depression. *Journal of the American Medical Association, 268,* 3098–3105.

Crow, T. J. (2007). How and why genetic linkage has not solved the problem of psychosis: Review and hypothesis. *American Journal of Psychiatry, 164,* 13–21.

Crumlish, N., Whitty, P., Clarke, M., et al. (2009). Beyond the critical period: Longitudinal study of 8-year outcome in first-episode non-affective psychosis. *The British Journal of Psychiatry, 194,* 18–24.

Crozier, L., & Lane, P. (2001). *Addicted: Notes from the belly of the beast.* Vancouver: Greystone Books.

CTV Television. (2006, June 1). Singer Amy Sky talks about her postpartum depression. Canada AM, Toronto.

Cuijpers, P., Munoz, R. F., Clarke, G. N., & Lewinsohn, P. M. (2009). Psychological treatment and prevention of depression: The "coping with depression" course thirty years later. *Clinical Psychology Review, 29,* 449–458.

Cuijpers, P., van Straten, A., Bohlmeijer, E., Hollon, S. D., & Andersson, G. (2010). The effects of psychotherapy for adult depression are overestimated: A meta-analysis of study quality and effect size. *Psychological Medicine, 40,* 211–223.

Cuijpers, P., van Straten, A., Smit, F., et al. (2008). Preventing the onset of depressive disorders: A meta-analytic review of psychological interventions. *American Journal of Psychiatry, 165,* 1272–1280.

Cullerton-Sen, C., Cassidy, A. R., Murray-Close, D., et al. (2008). Childhood maltreatment and the development of relational and physical aggression: The importance of a gender-informed approach. *Child Development, 79,* 1736–1751.

Cunningham, A. (2002). *One step forward: Lessons learned from a randomized study of multisystemic therapy in Canada.* London, Ontario: Centre for Children and Families in the Justice System.

Cunningham, A. J., Edmonds, C. V., Phillips, C., Soots, K. I., Hedley, D., & Lockwood, G. A. (2000). A prospective longitudinal study of the relationship of psychological work to duration of survival in patients with metastatic cancer. *Psychooncology, 9,* 323–329.

Cunningham, J. A., Blomquist, J., & Cordingley, J. (2007). Beliefs about drinking problems: Results from a general population telephone survey. *Addictive Behaviors, 32,* 166–169.

Cunningham, J. A., & Breslin, F. C. (2004). Only one in three people with alcohol abuse or dependence ever seek treatment. *Addictive Behaviors, 29*, 221–223.

Cunningham, J. A., Sobell, L. C., Gavin, D. R., Sobell, M. B., & Breslin, F. C. (1997). Assessing motivation for change: Preliminary development and evaluation of a scale measuring the costs and benefits of changing alcohol or drug use. *Psychology of Addictive Behaviors, 11*, 107–114.

Currie, S. R., et al. (2005). Comorbidity of major depression with substance use disorders. *Canadian Journal of Psychiatry, 50*, 660–666.

Currie, S. R., Hodgins, D. C., Wang, J., et al. (2006). Risk of harm among gamblers in the general population as a function of level of participation in gambling activities. *Addiction, 101*, 570–580.

Currie, S. R., Hodgins, D. C., Wang, J. L., et al. (2008). Replication of low-risk gambling limits using Canadian provincial gambling prevalence data. *Journal of Gambling Studies, 24*, 321–335.

Currie, S.R., Nesbitt, K., Wood, C., & Lawson, A. (2003). Survey of smoking cessation services in Canadian addiction programs. *Journal of Substance Abuse Treatment, 24*, 59–65.

Curtin, J. J., Lang, A. R., Patrick, C. J., & Strizke, W. G. K. (1998). Alcohol and fear-potiantiated startle: The role of competing cognitive demands in the stress-reducing effects of intoxication. *Journal of Abnormal Psychology, 107*, 547–557.

Cuttler, C., & Graf, P. (2009). Checking-in on the memory deficit and meta-memory deficit theories of compulsive checking. *Clinical Psychology Review, 29*, 393–409.

Cutrona, C. E., Wallace, G., & Wesner, K. A. (2006). Neighborhood characteristics and depression: An examination of stress processes. *Current Directions in Psychological Science, 15*, 188–192.

Cyr, M., Wright, J., McDuff, P., & Perron, A. (2002). Intrafamilial sexual abuse: Brother-sister incest does not differ from father-daughter and stepfather-stepdaughter incest. *Child Abuse and Neglect, 26*, 957–973.

Da Costa, D., Larouche, J., Dritsa, M., & Brender, W. (2000). Psychosocial correlates of prepartum and postpartum depressed mood. *Journal of Affective Disorders, 59*, 31–40.

Daignault, I. V., & Hébert, M. (2008). Short-term correlates of child sexual abuse: An exploratory study predicting girls' academic, cognitive, and social functioning 1 year later. *Journal of Child and Adolescent Trauma, 1*, 301–316.

Daley, M., Morin, C. M., Leblanc, M., Gregoire, J.-P., & Savard, J. (2009). The economic burden of insomnia: Direct and indirect costs for individuals with insomnia syndrome, insomnia symptoms, and good sleepers. *Sleep, 32*, 55–64.

Dalman, C. (2008). Infections in the CNS during childhood and the risk of subsequent psychiatric illness: A cohort study of more than one million Swedish subjects. *American Journal of Psychiatry, 165*, 59–65.

Danner, D. D., Snowdon, D. A., & Friesen, W. V. (2001). Positive emotions in early life and longevity: Findings from the Nun Study. *Journal of Personality and Social Psychology, 80*, 804–813.

D'Arcy R., Connolly J., & Crocker S. (1999). Latency shifts in the N2b component track phonological deviations in spoken words. *Developmental Neuropsychology,15*, 193–211.

Darou, W. G. (1992). Native Canadians and intelligence testing. *Canadian Journal of Counselling, 26*, 96–99.

Daskalakis, Z. J., Levinson, A. J., & Fitzgerald, P. B. (2008). Repetitive transcranial magnetic stimulation for major depressive disorder: A review. *Canadian Journal of Psychiatry, 53*, 555–566.

David, D. (2005). An interview with Donald Meichenbaum. Retrieved July 17, 2006, from http://psychotherapy.ro.

David, D., Szentagotai, A., Kallay, E., & Macavei, B. (2005). A synopsis of rational-emotive behavior therapy (REBT): Fundamental and applied research. *Journal of Rational-Emotive and Cognitive-Behavior Therapy, 23*, 175–221.

Davidson, J. R. (2009). First-line pharmacotherapy approaches for generalized anxiety disorder. *Journal of Clinical Psychiatry, 70* (Supplement 2), 25–31.

Davidson, K., et al. (2006). The effectiveness of cognitive behavior therapy for borderline personality disorder: Results from the borderline personality disorder study of cognitive therapy (BOSCOT) trial. *Journal of Personality Disorders, 20*, 450–465.

Davidson, R. J., Pizzagalli, D., Nitschke, J. B., & Putnam, K. (2002). Depression: Perspectives from affective neuroscience. *Annual Review of Psychology, 53*, 545–574.

Davidson, L. L., & Heinrichs, R. W. (2003). Quantification of frontal and temporal lobe brain-imaging findings in schizophrenia: A meta-analysis *Psychiatry Research, 122*, 69–87.

Davila, J., Hammen, C. L., Burge, D., Paley, B., & Daley, S. E. (1995). Poor interpersonal problem solving as a mechanism of stress generation in depression among adolescent women. *Journal of Abnormal Psychology, 104*, 592–600.

Davis, C. (1996). The interdependence of obsessive-compulsiveness, physical activity, and starvation: A model for anorexia nervosa. In W. F. Epling & W. D. Pierce (Eds.), *Activity nervosa: Theory, research, and treatment* (pp. 209–218). Mahwah, NJ: Erlbaum.

Davis, C., Kaptein, S., Kaplan, A. S., Olmsted, M. P., & Woodside, D. B. (1998). Obsessionality in anorexia nervosa: The moderating influence of exercise. *Psychosomatic Medicine, 60*, 192–197.

Davis, J. M. (1978). Dopamine theory of schizophrenia: A two-factor theory. In L. C. Wynne, R. L. Cromwell, & S. Matthysse (Eds.), *The nature of schizophrenia*. New York: John Wiley & Sons.

Davis, K. L., Kahn, R. S., Ko, G., & Davidson, M. (1991). Dopamine and schizophrenia: A review and reconceptualization. *American Journal of Psychiatry, 148*, 1474–1486.

Davison, D. G., Tsujimoto, R. N., & Glaros, A. G. (1973). Attribution and the maintenance of behavior change in falling sleep. *Journal of Abnormal Psychology, 82*, 124–133.

Davison, G. C. (1968a). Elimination of a sadistic fantasy by a client-controlled counterconditioning technique. *Journal of Abnormal Psychology, 73*, 84–90.

Davison, G. C. (2000). Stepped care: Doing more with less? *Journal of Consulting and Clinical Psychology, 68*, 580–585.

Davison, G. C., Robins, C., & Johnson, M. K. (1983). Articulated thoughts during simulated situations: A paradigm for studying cognition in emotion and behavior. *Cognitive Therapy and Research, 7*, 17–40.

Davison, G. C., & Zighelboim, V. (1987). Irrational beliefs in the articulated thoughts of college students with social anxiety. *Journal of Rational-Emotive Therapy, 5*, 238–254.

Dawson, G., Rogers, S., Munson, J., et al. (2010). Randomized controlled trial of the Early Start Denver Model: A developmental behavioral intervention for toddlers with autism. Effects on IQ, adaptive behavior, and autism diagnosis. *Pediatrics, 125* , e17–e23.

Deacon, B. J., & Abramowitz, J. S. (2004). Cognitive and behavioral treatments for anxiety disorders: A review of meta-analytic findings. *Journal of Clinical Psychology, 60*, 429–441.

Dean, J., et al. (2008). Integrating partners into erectile dysfunction treatment: Improving the sexual experience of the couple. *International Journal of Clinical Practice, 62*, 127–133.

Deater-Deckard, K., Mullineaux, P. Y., Beckman, C., et al. (2009). Conduct problems, IQ, and household chaos: A longitudinal multi-informant study. *Journal of Child Psychology and Psychiatry, 50*, 1301–1308.

de Boo, G. M., & Prins, P. J. M. (2007). Social incompetence in children with ADHD: Possible moderators and mediators in social-skills training. *Clinical Psychology Review, 27*, 78–97.

Dedovic, K., D'Aguiar, C., & Pruessner, J. C. (2009). What stress does to your brain: A review of neuroimaging studies. *Canadian Journal of Psychiatry, 54*, 6–15.

DeGroot, J. M., Kennedy, S., Rodin, G., & McVey, G. (1992). Correlates of sexual abuse in women with anorexia nervosa and bulimia nervosa. *Canadian Journal of Psychiatry, 37*, 516–518.

DeKeseredy, W. S., Schwartz, M. D., & Tait, K. (1993). Sexual assault and stranger aggression on a Canadian university campus. *Sex Roles, 28*, 263–277.

De Krom, M., et al. (2009). Genetic variations and effects on human eating behavior. *Annual Review of Nutrition, 29*, 283–304.

Delgado, P. L., Charney, D. S., Price, L. H., Aghajanian, G. K., Landis, H., et al. (1990). Serotonin function and the mechanism of antidepressant action: Reversal of antidepressant induced remission by rapid depletion of plasma tryptophan. *Archives of General Psychiatry, 47*, 411–418.

deLint, J. (1978). Alcohol consumption and alcohol problems from an epidemiological perspective. *British Journal of Alcohol and Alcoholism, 17*, 109–116.

DeLongis, A., Coyne, J. C., Dakof, G., Folkman, S., & Lazarus, R. S. (1982). Relationship of daily hassles, uplifts, and major life events to health status. *Health Psychology, 1*, 119–136.

DeLongis, A., Folkman, S., & Lazarus, R. S. (1988). The impact of daily stress on health and mood: Psychological and social resources as mediators.

Journal of Personality and Social Pscyhology, 54, 486–495.

de Maat, S., Dekker, J., Schoevers, R., van Alst, G., Gijsbers-van Wijk, C., Hendricksen, M., et al. (2008). Short psychodynamic supportive psychotherapy, antidepressants, and their combination in the treatment of major depression: A mega-analysis based on three randomized clinical trials. *Depression and Anxiety, 25,* 565–574.

de Maat, S., de Jonge, F., Schoevers, R., & Dekker, J. (2009). The effectiveness of long-term psychoanalytic therapy: A systematic review of empirical studies. *Harvard Review of Psychiatry, 17,* 1–23.

de Mello, M. F., et al. (2005). A systematic review of research findings on the efficacy of interpersonal therapy for depressive disorders. *European Archives of Psychiatry and Clinical Neuroscience, 255,* 75–82.

Dement, W. C., Laughton, E., & Carskadon, M. A. (1981). "White paper" on sleep and aging. *Journal of the American Geriatrics Society, 30,* 25–50.

Demers, A., Bisson, J., & Palluy, J. (1999). Wives' convergence with their husbands' alcohol use: Social conditions as mediators. *Journal of Studies on Alcohol, 60,* 368–377.

Denihan, A., Kirby, M., Bruce, I., Cunningham, C., Coakley, D., & Lawlor, B. A. (2000). Three-year prognosis of depression in the community-dwelling elderly. *British Journal of Psychiatry, 176,* 453–457.

Dennis, C.-L. (2003). The effect of peer support on postpartum depression: A pilot randomized controlled trial. *Canadian Journal of Psychiatry, 48,* 115–124.

Denollet, J., & Brutsaert, D. L. (1998). Personality, disease severity, and the risk of long-term cardiac events in patients with a decreased ejection fraction after myocardial infarction. *Circulation, 97,* 167–173.

Denson, T. F., Fabiansson, E. C., Creswell, J. D., & Pedersen, W. C. (2009). Experimental effects of rumination styles on salivary cortisol responses. *Motivation and Emotion, 33,* 42–48.

Denton, L. R. (2000). From humane care to prevention. *Canadian Journal of Community Mental Health, 19,* 127–134.

Denton, M., & Walters, V. (1999). Gender differences in structural and behavioral determinants of health: An analysis of the social production of health. *Social Science and Medicine, 48,* 1221–1235.

Depression Guideline Panel. (1997). *Depression in primary care: Detection and diagnosis.* Rockville, MD: U.S. Department of Health and Human Services.

DePrince, A. P., & Freyd, J. J. (2004). Forgetting trauma stimuli. *Psychological Science, 15,* 488–492.

D'Ercole, A., & Struening, E. (1990). Victimization among homeless women: Implications for service delivery. *Journal of Community Psychology, 18,* 141–152.

Derevensky, J. L., & Gupta, R. (2000). Prevalence estimates of adolescent gambling: A comparison of the SOGS-RA, DSM-IV-J, and the G.A. 20 questions. *Journal of Gambling Studies, 16 (2/3),* 227–251.

DeRubeis, R. J., Gelfand, L. A., Tang, T. Z., & Simons, A. D. (1999). Medications versus cognitive behavior therapy for severely depressed outpatients: MegaAnalysis of four randomized comparisons. *American Journal of Psychiatry, 156,* 1007–1013.

DeRubeis, R. J., Hollon, S. D., Amsterdam, J. D., Shelton, R. C., Young, P. R., Salomon, R. M., et al. (2005). Cognitive therapy vs medications in the treatment of moderate to severe depression. *Archives of General Psychiatry, 62,* 409–416.

DeRubeis, R. J., Tang, T. Z., & Beck, A. T. (2001). Cognitive therapy. In K. S. Dobson (Ed.), *Handbook of cognitive-behavioral therapies* (2nd ed., pp. 349–392). New York: Guilford.

DeRubeis, R. J., Webb, C. A., Tang, T. Z., & Beck, A. T. (2010). Cognitive therapy. In K. S. Dobson (Ed.), *Handbook of cognitive-behavioral therapies* (3rd ed., pp. 277–315). New York: The Guilford Press.

Desmarais, S. L., Hucker, S., Brink, J., & De Freitas, K. (2008). A Canadian example of insanity defense reform: Accused found not criminally responsible before and after the Winko decision. *International Journal of Forensic Mental Health, 7,* 1–14.

Dessaulles, A., Johnson, S. M., & Denton, W. H. (2003). Emotion-focused therapy for couples in the treatment of depression: A pilot study. *The American Journal of Family Therapy, 31,* 345–353.

Deutsch, A. (1949). *The mentally ill in America.* New York: Columbia University Press.

Devanand, D. P., Dwork, A. J., Hutchinson, E. R., Bolwig, T. G., & Sackeim, H. A. (1994). Does ECT alter brain structure? *American Journal of Psychiatry, 151,* 957–970.

Dew, M. A., Bromet, E. J., Brent, D., & Greenhouse, J. B. (1987). A quantitative literature review of the effectiveness of suicide prevention centers. *Journal of Consulting and Clinical Psychology, 55,* 239–244.

Dewa, C. S., Rochefort, D. A., Rogers, J., & Goering, P. (2003). Left behind by reform: The case for improving primary care and mental health system services for people with moderate mental illness. *Applied Health Economics and Health Policy, 2,* 43–54.

Dewit, D. J., Hance, J., Offord, D. R., & Ogborne, A. (2000). The influence of early and frequent use of marijuana on the risk of desistance and of progression to marijuana-related harm. *Preventive Medicine, 31,* 455–464.

Diamond, S., Baldwin, R., & Diamond, R. (1963). *Inhibition and choice.* New York: Harper & Row.

DiBartolo, P. M., & Grills, A. E. (2006). Who is best at predicting children's anxiety in response to a social evaluative task?: A comparison of child, parent, and teacher reports. *Anxiety Disorders, 20,* 630–645.

Dickey, C. C., McCarley, R. W., Volgmaier, M. M., Niznikiewicz, M. A., Seidman, L. J., et al. (1999). Schizotypal personality disorder and MRI abnormalities of temporal grey matter. *Biological Psychiatry, 45,* 1392–1402.

Dickie, E. W., Brunet, A., Akerib, V., & Armony, J. L. (2008). An fMRI investigation of memory encoding in PTSD: Influence of symptom severity. *Neuropsychologia, 46,* 1522–1531.

Dickin, K. L., & Ryan, B. A. (1983, March). Sterilization and the mentally retarded. *Canada's Mental Health, 31,* 4–8.

Dickinson, H. O., et al. (2008). Relaxation therapies for the management of primary hypertension in adults: A Cochrane review. *Journal of Human Hypertension, 22,* 809–820.

Dickson, L., Derevensky, J., & Gupta, R. (2002). The prevention of gambling problems in youth: A conceptual framework. *Journal of Gambling Studies, 18,* 97–159.

DiClemente, C. C. (1993). Changing addictive behaviors: A process perspective. *Current Directions in Psychological Science, 2,* 101–106.

Diebel, L. (2009, January 31). 'Clean slate' for truth panel: Breakthrough talks save reconciliation commission probing abuses of children at residential schools. *Toronto Star,* A6.

Diebel, L. (2009, March 16). Nation of lost souls. *Toronto Star,* A1, A4.

Diefenbach, G. J., Stanley, M. A., & Beck, J. G. (2001). Worry content reported by older adults with and without generalized anxiety disorder. *Aging and Mental Health, 5,* 269–274.

Diener, E., Horwitz, J., & Emmons, R. A. (1985). Happiness of the very wealthy. *Social Indicators Research, 16,* 263–274.

Diener, E., & Seligman, M. E. P. (2004). Beyond money: Toward an economy of well-being. *Psychological Research in the Public Interest, 5,* 1–31.

Diesrud, G., et al. (2003). Predicting repetition of suicide attempts: A prospective study of 50 suicide attempters. *Archives of Suicide Research, 7,* 1–15.

Dietz, P. E., Hazelwood, R. R., & Warren, J. (1990). The sexually sadistic criminal and his offenses. *Bulletin of the American Academy of Psychiatry and the Law, 18,* 163–178.

DiFranza, J. R., Richards, J. W., Paulman, P. M., Wolf-Gillespie, N., Fletcher, C., et al. (1991). RJR Nabisco's cartoon camel promotes Camel cigarettes to children. *Journal of the American Medical Association, 266,* 3149–3153.

DiLiberto, L., Katz, R. C., Beauchamp, K. L., & Howells, G. N. (2002). Using Articulated Thoughts in Simulated Situations to assess cognitive activity in aggressive and nonaggressive adolescents. *Journal of Child and Family Studies, 11,* 179–189.

Dimidjian, S. & Hollon, S.D. (2010). How would we know if psychotherapy were harmful. *American Psychologist, 65,* 21–33.

DiNardo, P. A., Guzy, L. T., Jenkins, J. A., Bak, R. M., Tomasi, S. F., & Copland, M. (1988). Etiology and maintenance of dog fears. *Behaviour Research and Therapy, 26,* 241–244.

DiNardo, P. A., O'Brien, G. T., Barlow, D. H., Waddell, M. T., & Blanchard, E. B. (1993). Reliability of the DSM-III-R anxiety disorders categories using the Anxiety Disorders Interview Schedule-Revised (ADIS-R). *Archives of General Psychiatry, 50,* 251–256.

Dittmar, H., Halliwell, E., & Ive, S. (2006). Does Barbie make girls want to be thin? The effect of experimental exposure to images of dolls on the body image of 5- to 8-year old girls. *Developmental Psychology, 42,* 283–292.

Dobkin, P. L. (2008). Mindfulness-based stress reduction: What processes are at work? *Complementary Therapies in Clinical Practice, 14*, 8–16.

Dobson, K. S. (1989). A meta-analysis of the efficacy of cognitive therapy for depression. *Journal of Consulting and Clinical Psychology, 57*, 414–419.

Dobson, K. S., Dobson, D. J. G., & Ritchie, P. L.-J. (1993). Professional psychology in Canada: Present status and future promises. In K. S. Dobson & D. J. G. Dobson (Eds.), *Professional psychology in Canada* (pp. 433–454). Toronto: Hogrefe and Huber.

Dobson, K. S., & Hamilton, K. E. (2002). The stage model for psychotherapy manual development: A valuable tool for promoting evidence-based practice. *Clinical Psychology: Science and Practice, 9*, 407–409.

Dobson, K. S., Hollon, S. D., Dimidjian, S., Schmaling, K. B., et al. (2008). Randomized trial of behavioral activation, cognitive therapy, and antidepressant medication in the prevention of relapse and recurrence in major depression. *Journal of Consulting and Clinical Psychology, 76*, 468–477.

Dobson, K. S., & Jackman-Cram, S. (1996). Common change processes in cognitive-behavioral therapies. In K. S. Dobson & K. D. Craig (Eds.), *Advances in cognitive-behavioral therapy* (pp. 63–82). Thousand Oaks, CA: Sage Publications.

Dobson, K. S., & Khatri, N. (2000). Cognitive therapy: Looking forward, looking backward. *Journal of Clinical Psychology, 56*, 907–923.

Dobson, K. S., & Pusch, D. (1993). Towards a definition of the conceptual and empirical boundaries of cognitive therapy. *Australian Psychologist, 28*, 137–144.

Dodge, K. A., & Frame, C. L. (1982). Social cognitive biases and deficits in aggressive boys. *Child Development, 53*, 620–635.

Dodge, K. A., & Pettit, G. S. (2003). A biopsychosocial model of the development of chronic conduct problems in adolescents. *Developmental Psychology, 39*, 349–371.

Doerr, P., Fichter, M., Pirke, K. M., & Lund, R. (1980). Relationship between weight gain and hypothalamic-pituitary-adrenal function in patients with anorexia nervosa. *Journal of Steroid Biochemistry, 13*, 529–537.

Dohrenwend, B. P., Levav, P. E., Schwartz, S., Naveh, G., Link, B. G., Skodol, A. E., et al. (1992). Socioeconomic status and psychiatric disorders: The causation-selection issue. *Science, 255*, 946–952.

Doidge, N. (1999). Who is in psychoanalysis now? Empirical data and reflection on some common misperceptions. In H. Kaley, M. N. Eagle, & D. L. Wolitzky (Eds.), *Psychoanalytic therapy as health care: Effectiveness and economics in the 21st century* (pp. 177–198). Hillsdale, NJ: The Analytic Press.

Doidge, N., Simon, B., Gillies, L. A., & Ruskin, R. (1994). Characteristics of psychoanalytic patients under a nationalized health plan: DSM-III-R diagnoses, previous treatment and childhood trauma. *American Journal of Psychiatry, 151*, 586–590.

Doidge, N. et al. (2002). Classics revisited: Freud's The Ego and the Id and Inhibitions, Symptoms, and Anxiety. *Journal of the American Psychoanalytic Association, 50*, 281–294.

Doren, D. M., & Yates, P. M. (2008). Effectiveness of sex offender treatment for psychopathic sexual offenders. *International Journal of Offender Therapy and Comparative Criminology, 52*, 234–245.

Doucet, C., Ladouceur, R., Freeston, M. H., & Dugas, M. J. (1998). Worry themes and the tendency to worry in older adults. *Canadian Journal on Aging, 17*, 361–371.

Douglas, A. C., Mills, J. E., Niang, M., et al. (2008). Internet addiction: Meta synthesis of qualitative research for the decade 1996–2006. *Computers in Human Behavior, 24*, 3027–3044.

Douglas, K. S., & Koch, W. J. (2001). Civil commitment and civil competence: Psychological issues. In R. A. Schuller & J. R. Ogloff (Eds.), *Introduction to psychology and law: Canadian perspectives* (pp. 351–374). Toronto: University of Toronto Press.

Douglas, K. S., Ogloff, J. R. P., & Hart, S. D. (2003). Evaluation of a model of violence risk assessment among forensic psychiatric patients. *Psychiatric Services, 54*, 1372–1379.

Douglas, K. S., Ogloff, J. R. P., Nicholls, T. L. & Grant, I. (1999). Assessing risk for violence among psychiatric patients: The HCR-20 violence risk assessment scheme and thePsychopathy Checklist: Screening Version. *Journal of Consulting and Clinical Psychology, 67*, 917–930.

Douglas, K. S., & Webster, C. D. (1999). The HCR-20 violence risk assessment scheme: Concurrent validity in a sample of incarcerated offenders. *Criminal Justice and Behavior, 26*, 3–19.

Douglas, V. I. (1972). Stop, look and listen: The problem of sustained attention and impulse control in hyperactive and normal children. *Canadian Journal of Behavioural Science, 4*, 259–282.

Dowbiggin, I.R. (2009). High anxieties: The social construction of anxiety disorders. *Canadian Journal of Psychiatry, 29*, 429–436.

Doyle, A. B. (1998). Are empirically validated treatments valid with culturally diverse populations? In K. S. Dobson & K. D. Craig (Eds.), *Best practice: Developing and promoting empirically validated interventions* (pp. 93–103). Newbury Park, CA: Sage.

Doyle, M., & Dolan, M. (2006). Predicting community violence from patients discharged from mental health services. *British Journal of Psychiatry, 189*, 520–526.

Dozois, D. J. A. (2002). Cognitive organization of self-schematic content in nondysphoric, mildly dysphoric, and moderately-severely dysphoric individuals. *Cognitive Therapy and Research, 26*, 417–429.

Dozois, D. J. A., & Dobson, K. S. (2001). Information processing and cognitive organization in unipolar depression: Specificity and comorbidity issues. *Journal of Abnormal Psychology, 110*, 236–246.

Dozois, D. J. A., & Dobson, K. S. (2003). The struct of the self-schema in clinical depression: Differences related to episode recurrent. *Cognition and Emotion, 17*, 933–941.

Drabick, D. A. G. (2009). Can a developmental psychopathology perspective facilitate a paradigm shift toward a mixed categorical-dimensional classification system. *Clinical Psychology: Science and Practice, 16*, 41–49.

Draguns, J. G. (1989). Normal and abnormal behavior in cross-cultural perspective: Specifying the nature of their relationships. In J. J. Berman (Ed.), *Nebraska symposium on motivation.* Lincoln, NE: University of Nebraska Press.

Driessen, E., et al. (2010). The efficacy of short-term psychodynamic psychotherapy for depression: A meta-analysis. *Clinical Psychology Review, 30*, 25–36.

Drob, S. L., Meehan, K. B., & Waxman, S. E. (2009). Clinical and conceptual problems in the attribution of malingering in forensic evaluations. *Journal of the American Academy of Psychiatry and the Law, 37*, 98–106.

Drucker, E. (2006). Insite: Canada's landmark safe injecting program at risk. *Harm Reduction Journal, 3*, 24–26.

Dryden, W., David, D., & Ellis, A. (2010). Rational emotive behavior therapy. In K. S. Dobson (Ed.), *Handbook of cognitive-behavioral therapies* (3rd ed., pp. 226–276). New York: The Guilford Press.

Duberstein, P. R., et al. (2004). Suicide at 50 years of age and older: Perceived physical illness, family discord, and financial strain. *Psychological Medicine, 34*, 137–146.

Duck, S. (1984). A perspective on the repair of personal relationships. In S. Duck (Ed.), *Personal relationships: 5. Repairing personal relationships.* New York: Academic Press.

Duffy, A. (2009). The early course of bipolar disorder in youth at familial risk. *Journal of the Canadian Academy of Child and Adolescent Psychiatry, 18*, 200–205.

Duman, R. S., Heninger, G. R., & Nestler, E. J. (1997). A molecular and cellular theory of depression. *Archives of General Psychiatry, 54*, 597–606.

Du Mont, J., White, D., & McGregor, M. T. (2009). Investigating the medical forensic examination from the perspectives of sexually assaulted women. *Social Science and Medicine, 68*, 774–780.

Dumont, M., & Provost, M. A. (1999). Resilience in adolescents: Protective role of social support, coping strategies, self-esteem, and social activities on experience of stress and depression. *Journal of Youth and Adolescence, 28*, 343–361.

Duncan, J. (2000). Child maltreatment and college drop-out rates: Implications for child abuse researchers. *Journal of Interpersonal Violence, 15*, 987–995.

Dunham, H. W. (1965). *Community and schizophrenia: An epidemiological analysis.* Detroit, MI: Wayne State University Press.

Dunkley, D. M., & Blankstein, K. R. (2000). Self-critical perfectionism, coping, hassles, and current distress: A structural equation modeling strategy. *Cognitive Therapy and Research, 24*, 713–730.

Dunkley, D. M., Blankstein, K. R., Halsall, J., Williams, M., & Winkworth, G. (2000). The relation between perfectionism and distress: Hassles, coping, and perceived social support as mediators and moderators. *Journal of Counseling Psychology, 47*, 437–453.

Dunkley, D. M., Blankstein, K. R., & Segal, Z. V. (2010). Cognitive assessment: Issues and methods. In K. S. Dobson (Ed.), *Handbook of cognitive-behavioral therapies* (3rd ed., pp. 133–171). New York: The Guilford Press.

Dunkley, D. M., Blankstein, K. R., Zuroff, D. C., Lecce, S., & Hui, D. (2006a). Neediness and connectedness and the five-factor model of personality. *European Journal of Personality, 20,* 123–136.

Dunkley, D. M., Blankstein, K. R., Zuroff, D. C., Lecce, S., & Hui, D. (2006b). Self-critical and personal standards factors of perfectionism located within the five-factor model of personality. *Personality and Individual Differences, 40,* 509–520.

Dunkley, D. M., Zuroff, D. C., & Blankstein, K. R. (2003). Self-critical perfectionism and daily affect: Dispositional and situational influences on stress and coping. *Journal of Personality and Social Psychology, 84,* 234–252.

Dunkley, D. M., Zuroff, D. C., & Blankstein, K. R. (2006). Specific perfectionism components versus self-criticism in predicting maladjustment. *Personality and Individual Differences, 40,* 665–676.

Dunn, A. L., Marcus, B. H., Kampert, J. B., Garcia, M. E., et al. (1999). Comparison of lifestyle and structured interventions to increase physical activity and cardiorespiratory fitness. *Journal of the American Medical Association, 281,* 327–334.

Dunn, B. D., Stefanovitch, I., Buchan, K., et al. (2009). A reduction in positive self-judgment bias is uniquely related to the anhedonic symptoms of depression. *Behaviour Research and Therapy, 47,* 374–381.

DuPaul, G. J., McGoey, K. E., & Mautone, J. A. (2003). Pediatric pharmacology and psychopharmacology. In M. C. Roberts (Ed.), *Handbook of pediatric psychology* (pp. 234–250). New York: Guilford Press.

Dupere, V., Leventhal, T., & Lacourse, E. (2009). Neighbourhood poverty and suicidal thoughts and attempts in late adolescence. *Psychological Medicine, 39,* 1295–1306.

Dupere, V., et al. (2007). Affiliation in youth gangs during adolescence: The interaction between childhood psychopathic tendencies and neighbourhood disadvantage. *Journal of Abnormal Child Psychology, 35,* 1035–1045.

Duquette, A. (2001, February 2). *Living with agoraphobia.* Atlantic Journalism Awards. Retrieved July 17, 2002, from www.aja.kings.ns.ca.

Durbin, C. E., & Klein, D. N. (2006). Ten-year stability of personality disorders among outpatients with mood disorders. *Journal of Abnormal Psychology, 115,* 75–84.

Durkheim, E. (1951). *Suicide.* (J.A. Spaulding & G. Simpson, Trans.). New York: Free Press. (Original work published 1897; 2nd ed., 1930).

Durkin, K. L. (1997). Misuse of the internet by pedophiles: Implications for law enforcement and probation practice. *Federal Probation, 61,* 14–18.

Dutton, D. G. (1995). *The batterer: A psychological profile.* New York: Basic Books.

Dutton, D. G. (1999). Traumatic origins of intimate rage. *Aggression and Violent Behavior, 4,* 431–447.

Dutton, D. G., Bodnarchuk, M., Kropp, R., Hart, S. D., & Ogloff, J. P. (1997). Client personality disorders affecting wife assault post-treatment recidivism. *Violence and Victims, 12,* 37–50.

Dutton, D. G., & Starzomski, A. J. (1993). Borderline personality in perpetrators of physical and psychological abuse. *Violence and Victims, 8,* 327–337.

Dvorak-Bertscha, J. D., Curtin, J. J., Rubinstein, T. J., & Newman, J. P. (2009). Psychopathic traits moderate the interaction between cognitive and affective processing. *Psychophysiology, 46,* 913–921.

Dwork, A. J. (1997). Postmortem studies of the hippocampal formation in schizophrenia. *Schizophrenia Bulletin, 23,* 385–402.

Dworkin, R. H., Lenzenweger, M. F., & Moldin, S. O. (1987). Genetics and the phenomenology of schizophrenia. In P. D. Harvey and E. F. Walker (Eds.), *Positive and negative symptoms of psychosis.* Hillsdale, NJ: Erlbaum.

Dyck, R. J., & White, J. (1998). Suicide prevention in Canada: Work in progress. In A. A. Leenaars, S. Wenckstern, I. Sakinofsky, R. J. Dyck, M. J. Kral, & R. C. Bland (Eds.), *Suicide in Canada* (pp. 256–274). Toronto: University of Toronto Press.

D'Zurilla, T. J. (1986). *Problem-solving therapy: A social competence approach to clinical intervention.* New York: Springer.

Earleywine, M., & Gann, M. K. (1995). Challenging recovered memories in the courtroom. In J. Ziskin (Ed.), *Coping with psychiatric and psychological testimony* (pp. 1100–1134). Los Angeles: Law and Psychology Press.

Earls, C. M., & Lalumiere, M. L. (2002). A case study of preferential bestiality (zoophilia). *Sexual Abuse, 14,* 83–88.

Earls, C. M., & Lalumière, M. L. (2009). A case study of preferential bestiality. *Archives of Sexual Behavior, 38,* 605–609.

Eastwood, J. D., et al. (2005). Individuals with social phobia are biased to become aware of negative faces. *Visual Cognition, 12,* 159–179.

Eaton, J. W., & Weil, R. J. (1953). The mental health of the Hutterites. *Scientific American, 189,* 31–37.

Eaves, D., Lamb, D., & Tien, G. (2000). Forensic psychiatric services in British Columbia. *International Journal of Law and Psychiatry, 23,* 615–631.

Ebbington, P. E., Cooper, C., Minot, S., et al. (2009). Suicide attempts, gender, and sexual abuse: Data from the 2000 British Psychiatric Morbidity Survey. *American Journal of Psychiatry, 166,* 1135–1140.

Eccleston, C. (1995). Chronic pain and distraction: An experimental investigation into the role of sustained and shifting attention in the processing of chronic persistent pain. *Behaviour Research and Therapy, 33,* 391–406.

Eckhardt, C. I., & Crane, C. (2008). Effects of alcohol intoxicatin and aggressivity on aggressive verbalizations during anger arousal. *Aggressive Behavior, 34,* 428–436.

Edelbrock, C., Rende, R., Plomin, T., & Thompson, L. A. (1995). A twin study of competence and problem behavior in childhood and early adolescence. *Journal of Child Psychology and Psychiatry and Allied Disciplines, 36,* 775–789.

Eden, G. F., & Zeffiro, T. A. (1996). PET and fMRI in the detection of task-related brain activity: Implications for the study of brain development. In R. W. Thatcher & G. R. Lyon (Eds.), *Developmental neuroimaging: Mapping the development of brain and behavior* (pp. 77–90). San Diego, CA: Academic Press.

Edens, J. F., Marcus, D. K., Lilienfeld, S. O., & Poythress, N. G., Jr. (2006). Psychopathic, not psychopath: Taxometric evidence for the dimensional structure of psychopathy. *Journal of Abnormal Psychology, 115,* 131–144.

Edens, J. F., Marcus, D. K., & Morey, L. C. (2009). Paranoid personality has a dimensional latent structure: Taxometric analyses of community and clinical samples. *Journal of Abnormal Psychology, 118,* 545–553.

Edmonds, C. V., Lockwood, G. A., & Cunningham, A. J. (1999). Psychological response to long-term group therapy: A randomized trial with metastatic breast cancer patients. *Psychooncology, 8,* 74–91.

Edmunds, A. (1998). My story: Thoughts of a survivor. In A. A. Leenaars, S. Wenckstern, I. Sakinofsky, R. J. Dyck, M. J. Kral, & R. C. Bland (Eds.), *Suicide in Canada* (pp. 369–374). Toronto: University of Toronto Press.

Edwards, N., Alaghehbandan, R., MacDonald, D., et al. (2008). Suicide in Newfoundland and Labrador: A linkage study using medical examiner and vital statistics data. *Canadian Journal of Psychiatry, 53,* 252–259.

Eells, T. D., Lombart, K. G., Kendjelic, E. M., et al. (2005). The quality of psychotherapy case formulations: A comparison of expert, experienced, and novice cognitive-behavioral and psychodynamic therapists. *Journal of Consulting and Clinical Psychology, 73,* 579–589.

Egan, G. (1975). *The skilled helper.* Monterey, CA: Brooks/Cole.

Egan, T. (1990). As memory and music faded, Alzheimer patient met death. *New York Times, 89,* A1, A16.

Egeland, J. A., Gerhard, D. S., Pauls, D. L., Sussex, J. N., Kidd, K. K., Allen, C. R., et al. (1987). Bipolar affective disorders linked to DNA markers on chromosome 11. *Nature, 325,* 783–787.

Ehlers, A., Mayou, R. A., & Bryant, B. (1998). Psychological predictors of chronic posttraumatic stress disorder after motor vehicle accidents. *Journal of Abnormal Psychology, 107,* 508–519.

Ehnvall, A., Parker, G., Hadzi-Pavlovic, D., & Malhi, G. (2008). Perception of rejecting and neglectful parenting in childhood relates to lifetime suicide attempts for females—but not for males. *Acta Psychiatrica Scandinavica, 117,* 50–56.

Ehrensaft, M. K., Cohen, P., & Johnson, J. G. (2006). Development of personality disorder symptoms and the risk for partner violence. *Journal of Abnormal Psychology, 115,* 474–483.

Ehrhardt, A., & Money, J. (1967). Progestin-induced hermaphroditism: IQ and psychosexual identity in a study of ten girls. *Journal of Sex Research, 3,* 83–100.

Eich, E. (1995). Searching for mood-dependent memory. *Psychological Science, 6,* 67–75.

Eissenberg, T., Bigelow, G. E., Strain, E. C., & Walsh, S. L. (1997). Dose-related efficacy of levomethadyl acetate for treatment of opioid dependence. *Journal of the American Medical Association*, 277, 1945–1951.

Elbaum, B., & Vaughn, S. (2003). For which students with learning disabilities are self-concept interventions effective? *Journal of Learning Disabilities*, 36, 101–108.

Elbogen, E. B., & Johnson, S. C. (2009). The intricate link between violence and mental disorder: Results from the national epidemiologic survey on alcohol and related conditions. *Archives of General Psychiatry*, 66, 152–161.

Elbogen, E. B., Van Dorn, R. A., Swanson, J. W., Swartz, M. S., & Monahan, J. (2006). Treatment engagement and violence risk in mental disorders. *British Journal of Psychiatry*, 189, 354–360.

Elgar, F. J., Curtis, L. J., McGrath, P. J., Waschbusch, D. A., & Stewart, S.H. (2003). Antecedent–consequence conditions in maternal mood and child adjustment: A four-year cross-lagged study. *Journal of Clinical Child and Adolescent Psychology*, 32, 362–374.

Elie, M., Cole, M. G., Primeau, F. J., & Bellavance F. (1998). Delirium risk factors in elderly hospitalized patients. *Journal of General Internal Medicine*, 13, 204–212.

Elie, M., et al. (2000). Prevalence and detection of delirium in elderly emergency department patients. *Canadian Medical Association Journal*, 163, 977–981.

Elkin, I., Gibbons, R. D., Shea, M. T., & Shaw, B. F. (1996). Science is not a trial (but it can sometimes be a tribulation). *Journal of Consulting and Clinical Psychology*, 64, 92–103.

Elkin, I., Parloff, M. B., Hadley, S. W., & Autry, J. H. (1985). NIMH Treatment of Depression Collaborative Research Program. *Archives of General Psychiatry*, 42, 305–316.

Elkin, I., Shea, M. T., Watkins, J. T., Imber, S. D., Sotsky, S. M., et al. (1989). NIMH Treatment of Depression Collaborative Research Program: 1. General effectiveness of treatments. *Archives of General Psychiatry*, 46, 971–983.

Elkin, I., Shea, T., Imber, S., Pilkonis, P., et al. (1986). *NIMH Treatment of Depression Collaborative Research Program: Initial outcome findings*. Paper presented to the American Association for the Advancement of Science.

Elkins, I. J., King, S. M., McGue, M., & Iacono, W. G. (2006). Personality links from adolescence to young adulthood. *Journal of Abnormal Psychology*, 115, 26–39.

Ellason, J. W., & Ross, C. A. (1997). Two-year follow-up of inpatients with dissociative identity disorder. *American Journal of Psychiatry*, 154, 832–839.

Ellenbogen, S., Derevensky, J. L., & Gupta, R. (2007). Gender differences among adolescents with gambling-related problems. *Journal of Gambling Studies*, 23, 133–143.

Ellenbogen, S., Gupta, R., & Derevensky, J. L. (2007). A cross-cultural study of gambling behaviour among adolescents. *Journal of Gambling Studies*, 23, 25–39.

Ellis, A. (1962). *Reason and emotion in psychotherapy*. New York: Lyle Stuart.

Ellis, A. (2002). The role of irrational beliefs in perfectionism. In G. L. Flett & P. L. Hewitt (Eds.), *Perfectionism: Theory, research, and treatment* (pp. 217–229). Washington, DC: American Psychological Association.

Ellis, H. (1910). *Studies in the psychology of sex*. Philadelphia: FA Davis.

Elvins, R., & Green, J. (2008). The conceptualization and measurement of therapeutic alliance: An empirical review. *Clinical Psychology Review*, 28, 1167–1187.

Elwood, L. S., Hahn, K. S., Olatunji, B. O., & Williams, N. L. (2009). Cognitive vulnerabilities to the development of PTSD: A review of four vulnerabilities and the proposal of an integrative model. *Clinical Psychology Review*, 29, 87–100.

Eme, R. F. (2007). Sex differences in child-onset, life-course-persistent conduct disorder: A review of biological influences. *Clinical Psychology Review*, 27, 607–627.

Emmelkamp, P. M. G., et al. (2002). Virtual reality treatment versus exposure in vivo: A comparative evaluation in acrophobia. *Behaviour Research and Therapy*, 40, 509–516.

Emory, L. E., Williams, D. H., Cole, C. M., Amparo, E. G., & Meyer, W. J. (1991). Anatomic variation of the corpus callosum in persons with gender dysphoria. *Archives of Sexual Behavior*, 20, 409–417.

Emslie, G. J.. (2009). Understanding placebo response in pediatric depression trials. *American Journal of Psychiatry*, 166, 1–3.

Endler, N. S. (1982). *Holiday of darkness*. New York: John Wiley & Sons.

Endler, N. S. (1983). Interactionism: A personality model, but not yet a theory. In M. M. Page (Ed.), *Nebraska Symposium on Motivation 1982: Personality—Current theory and research* (pp. 241–266). San Francisco: Jossey Bass.

Endler, N. S., Courbasson, C. M. A., & Fillion, L. (1998). Coping with cancer: The evidence for the temporal stability of the French Canadian version of the Coping With Health, Injuries, and Problems (CHIP). *Personality and Individual Differences*, 25, 711–717.

Endler, N. S., Crooks, D. S., & Parker, J. D. A. (1992). The interaction model of anxiety: An empirical test in a parachute jumping situation. *Anxiety, Stress and Coping*, 5, 301–311.

Endler, N. S., Flett, G. L., Macrodimitris, S., Corace, K., & Kocovski, N. (2002). Separation, self-disclosure, and social evaluation anxiety as facets of trait social anxiety. *European Journal of Personality*, 16, 239–269.

Endler, N. S., Kocovski, N. L., & Macrodimitris, S. D. (2001). Coping, efficacy, and perceived control in acute vs chronic illnesses. *Personality and Individual Differences*, 30, 617–625.

Endler, N. S., & Magnusson, D. (1976). Toward an interactional psychology of personality. *Psychological Bulletin*, 83, 956–979.

Endler, N. S., & Parker, J. D. A. (1990). *The Coping Inventory for Stressful Situations (CISS): Manual*. Toronto: Multi-Health Systems, Inc.

Endler, N. S., & Parker, J. D. A. (1994). Assessment of multidimensional coping: Task, emotion, and avoidance strategies. *Psychological Assessment*, 6, 50–60.

Endler, N. S., & Parker, J. D. A. (1999). *The Coping Inventory for Stressful Situations (CISS): Manual* (2nd ed.). Toronto: Multi-Health Systems, Inc.

Endler, N. S., & Persad, E. (1988). *Electroconvulsive therapy: The myths and the realities*. Toronto: Hans Huber.

Endler, N. S., Speer, R. L., Johnson, J. M., & Flett, G. L. (2000). Controllability, coping, efficacy, and distress. *European Journal of Personality*, 14, 245–264.

Engdahl, B., Dikel, T. N., Eberly, R., & Blank, A. (1997). Posttraumatic stress disorder in a community group of former prisoners of war: A normative response to severe trauma. *American Journal of Psychiatry*, 154, 1576–1581.

Engel, G. L. (1980). The clinical application of the biopsychosocial model. *American Journal of Psychiatry*, 137, 535–544.

Engels, G. I., Garnefski, N., & Diekstra, R. F. W. (1993). Efficacy of rational-emotive therapy: A quantitative analysis. *Journal of Consulting and Clinical Psychology*, 61, 1083–1090.

English, H. B. (1929). Three cases of the "conditioned fear response." *Journal of Abnormal and Social Psychology*, 34, 221–222.

Enns, M. W., & Cox, B. J. (2005a). Psychosocial and clinical predictors of symptom persistence vs remission in major depressive disorder. *Canadian Journal of Psychiatry*, 50, 769–777.

Enns, M. W., & Cox, B. J. (2005b). Perfectionism, stressful life events, and 1-year outcome of depression. *Cognitive Therapy and Research*, 29, 541–543.

Enserink, M. (1999). Drug therapies for depression: From MAO inhibitors to substance. *Science*, 284, 239.

Epling, W.F., & Pierce, W. D. (1992). *Solving the anorexia puzzle: A scientific approach*. Toronto: Hogrefe and Huber.

Epp, A. M., & Dobson, K. S. (2010). The evidence base for cognitive-behavioral therapy. In K. S. Dobson (Ed.), *Handbook of cognitive-behavioral therapies* (3rd ed., pp. 39–73). New York: The Guilford Press.

Epp, J. (Ed.). (1988). *Mental health for Canadians: Striking a balance*. Ottawa: Ministry of National Health and Welfare.

Epping-Jordan, J. E., Compas, B. E., & Howell, D. C. (1994). Predictors of cancer progression in young adult men and women: Avoidance, intrusive thoughts, and psychological symptoms. *Health Psychology*, 13, 539–547.

Epstein, N. B., Baldwin, L. M., & Bishop, D. S. (1983). The McMaster Family Assessment Device. *Journal of Marital and Family Therapy*, 9, 171–182.

Erdberg, P., & Exner, J. E., Jr. (1984). Rorschach assessment. In G. Goldstein & M. Hersen (Eds.), *Handbook of psychological assessment*. New York: Pergamon.

Erikson, E. H. (1950). *Childhood and society*. New York: Norton.

Erikson, E. H. (1968). *Identity: Youth and crisis*. New York: Norton.

Erlangsen, A., Vach, W., & Jeune, B. (2005). The effect of hospitalization with medical illnesses on the suicide risk in the oldest old: A population-based register study. *Journal of the American Geriatrics Society*, 53, 771–776.

Erlenmeyer-Kimling, L. E., & Cornblatt, B. (1987). The New York high-risk project: A follow-up report. *Schizophrenia Bulletin, 13,* 451–461.

Escobar, J. I. (2005). Somatoform and conversion disorders or somatic presentations of mental disorders? In M. Maj, H. S. Akiskal, J. E. Mezzich, & A. Okasha (Eds.), *Somatoform disorders* (pp. 26–28). Chichester, England: John Wiley & Sons.

Eser, D., et al. (2009). Functional neuroanatomy of CCK-4-induced panic attacks in healthy volunteers. *Human Brain Mapping, 30,* 511–522.

Esses, V. M., & Gardner, R. C. (1996). Multiculturalism in Canada: Context and current status. *Canadian Journal of Behavioural Science, 28,* 145–152.

Essex, M. J., et al. (2006). Exploring risk factors for the emergence of children's mental health problems. *Archives of General Psychiatry, 63,* 1246–1256.

Essex, M. J., Klein, M. H., Slattery, M. J., et al. (2010). Early risk factors and developmental pathways to chronic high inhibition and social anxiety disorder in adolescence. *American Journal of Psychiatry, 167,* 40–46.

Etchegary, H., Lemyre, L., Wilson, B., and Krewski, D. (2009). Is genetic makeup a perceived health risk: Analysis of a national survey of Canadians. *Journal of Risk Research 12,* 223–237.

Etkin, A., & Wager, T. D. (2007). Functional neuroimaging of anxiety: A meta-analysis of emotional processing in PTSD, social anxiety disorder, and specific phobia. *American Journal of Psychiatry, 164,* 1476–1488.

Evans, P. D., & Edgerton, N. (1990). Life events as predictors of the common cold. *British Journal of Medical Psychology, 64,* 35–44.

Exner, J. E., Jr. (1986). *The Rorschach: A comprehensive system: Vol. 1. Basic foundations* (2nd ed.). New York: John Wiley & Sons.

Eysenck, H. J. (1952). The effects of psychotherapy: An evaluation. *Journal of Consulting Psychology, 16,* 319–324.

Eysenck, H. J. (1967). *The biological basis of personality.* Springfield, IL: Charles C. Thomas.

Eysenck, H. J. (1981). General features of the model. In H. J. Eysenck (Ed.), *A model for personality* (pp. 1–37). New York: Springer-Verlag.

Eysenck, S. B. G., & Eysenck, H. G. (1977). The place of impulsiveness in a dimensional system of personality description. *British Journal of Social and Clinical Psychology, 16,* 57–68.

Fabiano, G. A., Pelham, W. E. Jr., Coles, E. K., et al. (2009). A meta-analysis of behavioral treatments for attention-deficit/hyperactivity disorder. *Clinical Psychology Review, 29,* 129–140.

Fairbank, J. A., & Brown, T. A. (1987). Current behavioral approaches to the treatment of posttraumatic stress disorder. *The Behavior Therapist, 3,* 57–64.

Fairburn, C. G. (1997). Eating disorders. In D. M. Clark & C. G. Fairburn (Eds.), *Science and practice of cognitive behavior therapy* (pp. 209–243). New York: Oxford.

Fairburn, C. G., Agras, W. S., & Wilson, G. T. (1992). The research on the treatment of bulimia nervosa: Practical and theoretical implications. In G. H. Anderson & S. H. Kennedy (Eds.), *The biology of feast and famine: Relevance to eating disorders.* New York: Academic Press.

Fairburn, C. G., Cooper, Z., Doll, H. A., & Welch, S. L. (1999). Risk factors for anorexia nervosa: Three integrated case-control comparisons. *Archives of General Psychiatry, 56,* 468–478.

Fairburn, C. G., Marcus, M. D., & Wilson, G. T. (1993). Cognitive behaviour therapy for binge eating and bulimia nervosa: A comprehensive treatment manual. In C. G. Fairburn & G. T. Wilson (Eds.), *Binge eating: Nature, assessment, and treatment.* New York: Guilford.

Fairburn, C. G., Shafran, R., & Cooper, Z. (1999). A cognitive behavioural theory of anorexia nervosa. *Behaviour Research and Therapy, 37,* 1–13.

Fairweather, G. W., Sanders, D. H., Maynard, H., & Cressler, D. L. (1969). *Community life for the mentally ill: An alternative to institutional care.* Chicago: Aldine-Atherton.

Falconnier, L., & Elkin, I. (2008). Addressing economic stress in the treatment of depression. *American Journal of Orthopsychiatry, 78,* 37–46.

Fallon, J. H., et al. (2005). Gender: A major determinant of brain response to nicotine. *International Journal of Neuropsychopharmacology, 8,* 511–528.

Faraone, S. V., Biederman, J., Weber, W., & Russell, R. L. (1998). Psychiatric, neuropsychological, and psychosocial features of DSM-IV subtypes of attention-deficit/hyperactivity disorder: Results from a clinically referred sample. *Journal of the American Academy of Child and Adolescent Psychiatry, 37,* 185–193.

Farlow, M. (1997). Alzheimer's disease: Clinical implications of the apolipoprotein E genotype. *Neurology, 48* (Suppl. 6), s30–s34.

Farrar, C. B. (1917). The problem of mental disease in the Canadian army. *Mental Hygiene, 1,* 389–391.

Farrell, C., Shafran, R., & Lee, M. (2006). Empirically evaluated treatments for body image disturbance: A review. *European Eating Disorders Review, 14,* 289–300.

Faustman, W. O., Bardgett, M., Faull, K. F., Pfefferman, A., & Cseransky, J. G. (1999). Cerebrospinal fluid glutamate inversely correlates with positive symptom severity in unmedicated male schizophrenic/schizoaffective patients. *Biological Psychiatry, 45,* 68–75.

Fava, G. A., Zielezny, M., Savron, G., & Grandi, S. (1995). Long-term effects of behavioural treatment for panic disorder with agoraphobia. *British Journal of Psychiatry, 166,* 87–92.

Fava, G. A., & Wise, T. N. (2007). Issues for DSM-V: Psychological factors affecting either identified or feared medical conditions: A solution for somatoform disorders. *American Journal of Psychiatry, 164,* 1002–1003.

Favrod, J., Zimmermann, G., Raffard, S., et al. (2008). The Beck Cognitive Insight Scale in outpatients with psychotic disorders: Further evidence from a French-speaking sample. *Canadian Journal of Psychiatry, 53,* 783–787.

Fawcett, J., Epstein, P., Fiester, S. J., Elkin, I., & Autry, J. H. (1987). Clinical Management-Imipramine/placebo administration manual: NIMH Treatment of Depression Collaborative Research Program. *Psychopharmacology Bulletin, 23,* 309–324.

Federoff, I. C., & Taylor, S. (2001). Psychological and pharmacological treatments of social phobia: A meta-analysis. *Journal of Clinical Psychopharmacology, 21,* 311–324.

Fedora, O., Reddon, J. R., & Yeudall, L. T. (1986). Stimuli eliciting sexual arousal in genital exhibitionists: A possible clinical application. *Archives of Sexual Behavior, 15,* 417–427.

Feeny, N. C., Zoellner, L. A., Maavissakalian, M. R., & Roy Byrne, P. P. (2009). What would you choose? Sertraline or prolonged exposure in community and PTSD treatment seeking women. *Depression and Anxiety, 26,* 724–731.

Feingold, B. F. (1973). *Introduction to clinical allergy.* Springfield, IL: Charles C. Thomas.

Feldman, H. A., Goldstein, I., Hatzichristou, G., Krane, R. J., & McKinlay, J. B. (1994). Impotence and its medical and psychosocial correlates: Results of the Massachusetts male aging study. *Journal of Urology, 151,* 54–61.

Feldman, M. A., Ducharme, J. M., & Case, L. (1999). Using self-instructional pictorial manuals to teach child-care skills to mothers with intellectual disabilities. *Behavior Modification, 23,* 480–497.

Feldman, R. D., Campbell, N. R., & Wyard, K. (2008). Canadian Hypertension Education Program: The evolution of hypertension management guidelines in Canada. *Canadian Journal of Cardiology, 24,* 477–481.

Felton, B. J., & Revenson, T. A. (1984). Coping with chronic illness: A study of illness controllability and the influence of coping strategies on psychological adjustment. *Journal of Consulting and Clinical Psychology, 12,* 343–353.

Fenton, F. R., Cole, M. G., Engelsmann, F., & Mansouri, I. (1997). Depression in older medical inpatients: One-year course and outcome. *International Journal of Geriatric Psychiatry, 12,* 389–394.

Fenton, F. R., Tessier, L., & Streuning, E. L. (1979). A comparative trial of home and hospital psychiatric care: One-year follow-up. *Archives of General Psychiatry, 36,* 1073–1079.

Fenton, L. R., et al., (2001). Perspective is everything: The predictive validity of six working alliance instruments. *Journal of Psychotherapy Practice and Research, 10,* 262–268.

Ferenczi, S. (1952). *First contributions to psychoanalysis.* New York: Brunner/Mazel.

Ferguson, C. (2008). The school shooting/violent video game link: Causal relationship or moral panic. *Journal of Investigative Psychology and Offender Profiling, 5,* 25–37.

Ferguson, C. J., San Miguel, C., & Hartley, R. D. (2009). A multivariate analysis of youth violence and aggression: The influence of family, peers, depression, and media violence. *The Journal of Pediatrics, 155,* 904–908.

Ferguson, K. J., & Spitzer, R. L. (1995). Binge eating disorder in a community-based sample of successful and unsuccessful dieters. *International Journal of Eating Disorders, 18,* 167–172.

Fernandez, Y. M., & Marshall, W. L. (2003). Victim empathy, social self-esteem, and psychopathy in rapists. *Sexual Abuse, 15,* 11–26.

Fernández-Aranda, F., et al. (2008). Impulse control disorders in women with eating disorders. *Psychiatry Research, 157,* 147–157.

Fernando, S. (2005). Multicultural mental health services: Projects for minority ethnic communities in England. *Transcultural Psychiatry, 42,* 421–436.

Ferster, C. B. (1961). Positive reinforcement and behavioral deficits of autistic children. *Child Development, 32,* 437–456.

Fichman, L., Koestner, R., Zuroff, D. C. (1996). Dependency, self-criticism, and perceptions of inferiority at summer camp: I'm even worse than you think. *Journal of Youth and Adolescence, 25,* 113–126.

Fichman, L., Koestner, R., Zuroff, D. C. (1997). Dependency and distress at summer camp. *Journal of Youth and Adolescence, 26,* 217–232.

Fichten, C. S., Libman, E., Takefman, J., & Brender, W. (1988). Self-monitoring and self-focus in erectile dysfunction. *Journal of Sex and Marital Therapy, 14,* 120–128.

Field, T., Diego, M., & Hernandez-Reif, M. (2006). Prenatal depression effects on the fetus and newborn: A review. *Infant Behavior & Development, 29,* 445–455.

Fikretoglu, D., Brunet, A., Guay, S., & Pedlar, D. (2007). Mental health treatment seeking by military members with posttraumatic stress disorder PTSD: Findings on rates, characteristics, and predictors from a nationally representative Canadian military sample. *Canadian Journal of Psychiatry, 52,* 103–110.

Fikretoglu, D., Brunet, A., Poundja, J., Guay, S., & Pedlar, D. (2006). Validation of the Deployment Risk and Resilience Inventory in French-Canadian veterans: Findings on the relation between deployment experiences and postdeployment health. *Canadian Journal of Psychiatry, 51,* 755–763.

Fillion, L., Kohn, P., Gagnon, P., van Wijk, M., & Cunningham, A. (2001). The Inventory of Recent Life Experiences for Cancer Patients (IRLE-C): A decontaminated measure of cancer-based hassles. *Psychology and Health, 16,* 443–459.

Fillmore, K. M., & Caetano, R. (1980, May 22). *Epidemiology of occupational alcoholism.* Paper presented at the National Institute on Alcohol Abuse and Alcoholism's Workshop on Alcoholism in the Workplace, Reston, VA.

Findling, R. L., Robb, A., Nyilas, M., et al. (2008). A multiple-center, randomized, double-blind, placebo-controlled study of oral aripiprazole for treatment of adolescents with schizophrenia. *American Journal of Psychiatry, 165,* 1432–1441.

Finger, E. C., et al. (2008). Abnormal ventromedial prefrontal cortex function in children with psychopathic traits during reversal learning. *Archives of General Psychiatry, 65,* 586–594.

Fink, E. L., et al. (2009). Psychological correlates of purging disorder as compared with other eating disorders: an exploratory investigation. *International Journal of Eating Disorders, 42,* 31–39.

Finkelhor, D. (1979). *Sexually victimized children.* New York: Free Press.

Finney, J. W., & Moos, R. H. (1998). Psychosocial treatments for alcohol use disorders. In P. E. Nathan & J. M. Gorman (Eds.), *A guide to treatments that work* (pp. 156–166). New York: Oxford University Press.

Fiore, M. C., et al. (1990). Methods used to quit smoking in the United States: Do cessation programs help? *Journal of the American Medical Association, 263,* 2760–2765.

Firestone, P., Bradford, J. M., Greenberg, D. M., & Larose, M. R. (1998). Homicidal sex offenders: Psychological, psychometric, and diagnostic features. *Journal of the American Academy of Psychiatry and the Law, 26,* 57–552.

Firestone, P., Bradford, J. M., Greenberg, D. M., & Nunes, K. L. (2000). Differentiation of homicidal child molesters, nonhomicidal child molesters, and nonoffenders by phallometry. *American Journal of Psychiatry, 157,* 1847–1850.

Firestone, P., Bradford, J. M., Greenberg, D. M., & Serran, G. A. (2000). The relationship of deviant sexual arousal and psychopathology in incest offenders, extrafamilial child molesters, and rapists. *Journal of the American Academy of Psychiatry and the Law, 28,* 303–308.

Firestone, P., Kingston, D. A., Wexler, A., & Bradford, J. M. (2006). Long-term follow-up of exhibitionists: Psychological, phallometric, and offense characteristics. *Journal of the American Academy of Psychiatry and Law, 34,* 349–359.

First, M. B. (2005). Clinical utility: A prerequisite for the adoption of a dimensional approach in *DSM. Journal of Abnormal Psychology, 114,* 560–564.

First, M. B., Spitzer, R. L., Gibbon, M., & Williams, J. B. W. (1996). *Structured Clinical Interview for DSM-IV Axis I Disorders - Patient Edition (SCID-I/P, Version 2.0).* New York: New York State Psychiatric Institute, Biometrics Research Department.

Fischer, D. G., & McDonald, W. L. (1998). Characteristics of intrafamilial and extrafamilial child sexual abuse. *Child Abuse and Neglect, 22,* 915–929.

Fischer, M. (1971). Psychoses in the offspring of schizophrenic monozygotic twins and their normal co-twins. *British Journal of Psychiatry, 118,* 43–52.

Fischetti, M., Curran, J. P., & Wessberg, H. W. (1977). Sense of timing. *Behavior Modification, 1,* 179–194.

Fisher, J. E., & Noll, J. P. (1996). Anxiety disorders. In L. L. Carstensen, B. A. Edelstein, & L. Dornbrand (Eds.), *The practical handbook of clinical gerontology* (pp. 304–323). Thousand Oaks, CA: Sage.

Fishman, D. B. (1999). *The case for pragmatic psychology.* New York: NYU Press.

Fiske, A., Wetherell, J. L., & Gatz, M. (2009). Depression in older adults. *Annual Review of Clinical Psychology, 5,* 363–389.

Fitzgerald, P. B., et al. (2006). An analysis of functional neuroimaging studies of dorsolateral prefrontal cortical activity in depression. *Psychiatry Research: Neuroimaging, 148,* 33–45.

Fitzgerald, R. V. (1973). *Conjoint marital therapy.* New York: Jason Aronson.

Fitzpatrick, M.R., Iwakabe, S., & Stalikas, A. (2005). Prospective divergence in the working alliance. *Psychotherapy Research, 15,* 69–80.

Flamenbaum, R., & Holden, R. R. (2007). Psychache as a mediator in the relationship between perfectionism and suicidality. *Journal of Counseling Psychology, 54,* 51–61.

Fleming, J. E., & Offord, D. R. (1990). Epidemiology of childhood depressive disorders: A critical review. *Journal of the American Academy of Child and Adolescent Psychiatry, 29,* 571–580.

Fletcher, P. C., McKenna, P. J., Frith, C. D., Friston, K. J., & Dolan, R. J. (1998). Brain activations in schizophrenia during a graded memory task studied with functional imaging. *Archives of General Psychiatry, 55,* 1001–1009.

Flett, G.L., Besser, A., & Endler, N.S. (2009). Separation anxiety, perceived controllability, and homesickness. *Journal of Applied Social Psychology, 39,* 265–282.

Flett, G. L., Vredenburg, K., & Krames, L. (1997). The continuity of depression in clinical and nonclinical samples. *Psychological Bulletin, 121,* 395–416.

Flint, A. J. (1994). Epidemiology and comorbidity of anxiety disorders in the elderly. *American Journal of Psychiatry, 151,* 640–649.

Flint, A. J. (1999). Anxiety disorders in late life. *Canadian Family Physician, 45,* 2672–2679.

Flint, A. J., & Rifat, S. L. (1996). The effect of sequential antidepressant treatment on geriatric depression. *Journal of Affective Disorders, 36,* 95–105.

Flint, A. J., & Rifat, S. L. (1997). Two-year outcome of elderly patients with anxious depression. *Psychiatry Research, 66,* 23–31.

Flint, A. J., & Rifat, S. L. (2000). Maintenance treatment for recurrent depression in late life: A four-year outcome study. *American Journal of Geriatric Psychiatry, 8,* 112–116.

Floyd, M., Scogin, F., McKendree-Smith, N. L., Floyd, D. L., & Rokke, P. D. (2004). Cognitive therapy for depression: A comparison of individual psychotherapy and bibliotherapy for depressed older adults. *Behavior Modification, 28,* 297–318.

Fluoxetine Bulimia Nervosa Collaborative Study Group. (1992). Fluoxetine in the treatment of bulimia nervosa: A multicenter, placebo-controlled, double blind trial. *Archives of General Psychiatry, 49,* 139–147.

Foa, E., Riggs, D. S., Marsie, E. D., & Yarczower, M. (1995). The impact of fear activation and anger on the efficacy of exposure treatment for posttraumatic stress disorder. *Behavior Therapy, 26,* 487–499.

Foa, E. B., Zinbarg, R., & Rothbaum, B. O. (1992). Uncontrollability and unpredictability in posttraumatic stress disorder: An animal model. *Psychological Bulletin, 112,* 218–238.

Folkman, S., Bernstein, L., & Lazarus, R. S. (1987). Stress processes and the misuse of drugs in older adults. *Psychology and Aging, 2,* 366–374.

Folks, D. G., Ford, C. V., & Regan, W. M. (1984). Conversion symptoms in a general hospital. *Psychosomatics, 25,* 285–295.

Folstein, M. F., Folstein, S. E., & McHugh, P. R. (1975). "Mini-mental state": A practical method for grading the cognitive state of patients for the clinician. *Journal of Psychiatric Research, 12,* 189–198.

Fombonne, E. (2003). Epidemiology of pervasive developmental disorders. *Trends in Evidence-Based Neuropsychiatry, 5,* 29–36.

Fong, P. (2007, June 7). Vancouver eyes moving homeless back to institution: Many now on streets of Downtown Eastside were residents of sprawling facility in Coquitlam. *Toronto Star*, A23.

Foong, J., Ridding, M., Cope, H., Mardsen, C. D., & Ron, M. A. (1997). Corticospinal function in conversion disorder. *Journal of Neuropsychiatry and Clinical Neurosciences*, *9*, 302–303.

Foot, R. (May 26, 2007). Jury still out on whether community treatment orders help mentally ill. Canwest News.

Forchuk, C., & Vingilis, E. (2008). *Creating Interprofessional Collaborative Teams for Comprehensive Mental Health Services (CIPHER-MH), final report, June, 2008*. London, ON: University of Western Ontario.

Ford, T., Fowler, T., Langley, K., et al. (2008). Five years on: Public sector service use related to mental health in young people with ADHD or hyperkinetic disorder five years after diagnosis. *Child and Adolescent Mental Health*, *13*, 122–129.

Fordyce, W. E. (1994). Pain and suffering: What is the unit? *Quality of Life Research: An International Journal of Quality of Life Aspects of Treatment, Care, and Rehabilitation*, *3*, S51–S56.

Fordyce, W. E., Brockway, J. A., Bergman, J. A., & Spengler, D. (1986). Acute back pain: A control-group comparison of behavioral vs. traditional methods. *Journal of Behavioral Medicine*, *9*, 127–140.

Forsman, M., et al. (2010). A longitudinal twin study of the direction of effects between psychopathic personality and antisocial behavior. *The Journal of Child Psychology and Psychiatry*, *51*, 39–47.

Forsman, M., Lichtenstein, P., Andershed, H., & Larrson, H. (2008). Genetic effects explain the stability of psychopathic personality from mid- to late adolescence. *Journal of Abnormal Psychology*, *117*, 606–617.

Forsythe, C. J., & Compas, B. E. (1987). Interaction of cognitive appraisals of stressful events and coping: Testing the goodness of fit hypothesis. *Cognitive Therapy and Research*, *11*, 473–485.

Forth, A. E. (2005). Hare Psychopathy Checklist: Youth version. In T. Grisso, G. Vincent, & D. Seagrave (Eds.), *Mental health screening and assessment in juvenile justice* (pp. 324–338). New York: Guilford.

Forth, A. E., Kosson, D. S., & Hare, R. (2003). *Hare Psychopathy Checklist: Youth version* manual. Toronto: Multi-Health Systems Inc.

Forty, L., Jones, L., Macgregor, S., et al. (2006). Familiality of postpartum depression in unipolar disorder: Results of a family study. *American Journal of Psychiatry*, *163*, 1549–1553.

Foucault, M. (1965). *Madness and civilization*. New York: Random House.

Fournier, J. C., DeRubeis, R. C., Shelton, R. C., et al. (2008). Antidepressant medication v. cognitive therapy in people with depression with or without personality disorder. *The British Journal of Psychiatry*, *192*, 124–129.

Fouts, G., & Burggraf, K. (2000). Television situation comedies: Female weight, male negative comments, and audience reactions. *Sex Roles*, *42*, 925–932.

Fox, N. A., Henderson, H. A., Marshall, P. J., Nichols, K. E., & Ghera, M. M. (2005a). Behavioral inhibition: Linking biology and behavior within

a developmental framework. *Annual Review of Psychology*, *56*, 235–262.

Fox, N. A., Nichols, K. E., Henderson, H. A., Rubin, K., et al. (2005b). Evidence for a gene-environment interaction predicting behavior inhibition in middle childhood. *Psychological Science*, *16*, 921–926.

Foy, D. W., Resnick, H. S., Carroll, E. M., & Osato, S. S. (1990). Behavior therapy. In A. S. Bellack & M. Hersen (Eds.), *Handbook of comparative treatments for adult disorders* (pp. 302–315). New York: John Wiley & Sons.

Frank, E., Anderson, C., & Rubenstein, D. (1978). Frequency of sexual dysfunctions in "normal" couples. *New England Journal of Medicine*, *299*, 111–115.

Frank, J. D. (1961). *Persuasion and healing*. Baltimore: Johns Hopkins University Press. Second edition, 1973; third edition, 1978.

Frank, J. D. (1974). Psychotherapy: the restoration of morale. *American Journal of Psychiatry*, *131*, 271–274.

Frank, J. D., & Frank, J. (1985). Therapeutic components shared by all psychotherapies. In A. Freeman, M. J. Mahoney, & P. Devito (Eds.), *Cognition and psychotherapy* (pp. 45–78). New York: Springer.

Frank, S. (2001, May 7). Canada: The next generation. *Time, Canadian Edition*, 18–26.

Frankenhaeuser, M. U., et al. (1989). Stress on and off the job as related to sex and occupational status in whitecollar workers. *Journal of Organizational Behavior*, *10*, 321–346.

Franklin, M. E., & Foa, E. B. (1998). Cognitive-behavioral treatments for obsessive-compulsive disorder. In P. E. Nathan & J. M. Gorman (Eds.), *A guide to treatments that work* (pp. 339–357). New York: Oxford University Press.

Franko, D. L., & Keel, P. K. (2006). Suicidality in eating disorders: Occurrence, correlates, and clinical implications. *Clinical Psychology Review*, *26*, 769–782.

Franx, G., Kroon, H., Grimshaw, J., Drake, R., Grol, R., & Wensing, M. (2008). Organizational change to transfer knowledge and improve quality and outcomes of care for patients with severe mental illness: A systematic overview of reviews. *Canadian Journal of Psychiatry*, *53*, 294–305.

Fraser, G. A. (1994). Dissociative phenomena and disorders: Clinical presentations. In R. M. Klein & B. K. Doane (Eds.), *Psychological concepts and dissociative disorders* (pp. 131–151). Hillsdale, NJ: Erlbaum.

Fraser Institute. (2008, October). *Waiting Your Turn: Hospital Waiting Lists in Canada 2008 Report, 18th Edition*. Vancouver: Author.

Frasure-Smith, N., et al. (2002). Long-term survival differences among low-anxious, high-anxious and repressive copers enrolled in the Montreal Heart Attack Readjustment Trial. *Psychosomatic Medicine*, *64*, 571–579.

Frasure-Smith, N., & Lesperance, F. (2008). Depression and anxiety as predictors of 2-year cardiac events in patients with stable coronary artery disease. *Archives of General Psychiatry*, *65*, 62–71.

Frasure-Smith, N., & Prince, R. (1989). Long-term follow-up of the Ischemic Heart Disease Life

Stress Monitoring Program. *Psychosomatic Medicine*, *51*, 485–513.

Freedman, R. (2008). 2008 in review. *American Journal of Psychiatry*, *165*, 1512.

Freeston, M. H., et al. (1997). Cognitive-behavioral treatment of obsessive thoughts: A controlled study. *Journal of Consulting and Clinical Psychology*, *65*, 405–413.

Fremouw, W. J., dePerczel, M., & Ellis, T. (1990). *Suicide risk: Assessment and response guidelines*. Elmsford, NY: Pergamon Press.

Freud, A. (1966). *The ego and the mechanisms of defense*. New York: International Universities Press.

Freud, S. (1917). Mourning and melancholia. In *Collected papers* (Vol. 4). London: Hogarth and the Institute of Psychoanalysis, 1950.

Freud, S. (1937). Analysis terminable and interminable. *International Journal of Psychoanalysis*, *18*, 373–391.

Freund, K. (1967). Diagnosing homo- or heterosexuality and erotic age-preference by means of a psychophysiological test. *Behaviour Research and Therapy*, *5*, 209–228.

Freund, K. (1990). Courtship disorders. In W. L. Marshall, D. R. Laws, & H. E. Barbaree (Eds.), *Handbook of sexual assault: Issues, theories, and treatment* (pp. 195–207). New York: Plenum Press.

Freund, K., & Watson, R. (1991). Assessment of the sensitivity and specificity of a phallometric test: An update of phallometric diagnosis of pedophilia. *Psychological Assessment*, *3*, 254–260.

Frick, P. J. (2001). Effective interventions for children and adolescents with conduct disorder. *Canadian Journal of Psychiatry*, *46*, 597–608.

Frick, P. J. (2009). Extending the construct of psychopathy to youth: Implications for understanding, diagnosing, and treating antisocial children and adolescents. *Canadian Journal of Psychiatry*, *54*, 803–812.

Frick, P. J., & Moffitt, T.E. (2010). A proposal to the DSM-V Childhood Disorders and the ADHD and Disruptive Behavior Disorders Work Groups to include a specifier to the diagnosis of conduct disorder based on the presence of callous-unemotional traits. (www.dsm5. org/Proposed%20Revision%20Attachments/ Proposal%20for%20Callous%20and%20Unem otional%20Specifier%20of%20Conduct%20Di sorder.pdf).

Frick, P. J., Stickle, T. R., Dandreaux, D. M., et al. (2005). Callous-unemotional traits in predicting the severity and stability of conduct problems and delinquency. *Journal of Abnormal Child Psychology*, *33*, 471–487.

Frick, P. J., & White, S. F. (2008). The importance of callous-unemotional traits for the development of aggressive and antisocial behavior. *Journal of Child Psychology and Psychiatry*, *49*, 359–375.

Fridell, S., R., Zucker, K. J., Bradley, S. J., & Maing, D. M. (1996). Physical attractiveness of girls with gender identity disorders. *Archives of Sexual Behavior*, *25*, 17–31.

Fried, P., Watkinson, B., James, D., & Gray, R. (2002). Current and former marijuana use: Preliminary findings of a longitudinal study of effects of IQ in young adults. *Canadian Medical Association Journal*, *166*, 887–891.

Friedlander, L., & Desrocher, M. (2006). Neuroimaging studies of obsessive-compulsive disorder in adults and children. *Clinical Psychology Review, 26*, 32–49.

Friedman, M. (1969). *Pathogenesis of coronary artery disease*. New York: McGraw-Hill.

Frisch, M. B., & Higgins, R. L. (1986). Instructional demand effects and the correspondence among role-play, self-report, and naturalistic measures of social skill. *Behavioral Assessment, 8*, 221–236.

Frith, C., & Frith, U. (2000). The physiological basis of theory of mind: Functional neuroimaging studies. In S. Baron-Cohen, H. Tager-Flusberg, & D. Cohen (Eds.), *Understanding other minds: Perspectives from and developmental cognitive neuroscience* (2nd ed., pp. 334–356.). Oxford, UK: Oxford University Press.

Fromm-Reichmann, F. (1948). Notes on the development of treatment of schizophrenics by psychoanalytic psychotherapy. *Psychiatry, 11*, 263–273.

Fruzzetti, A. E., & Erikson, K. R. (2010). Mindfulness and acceptance interventions in cognitive-behavioral therapy. In K. S. Dobson (Ed.), *Handbook of cognitive-behavioral therapies* (3rd ed., pp. 347–372). New York: The Guilford Press.

Fry, P. S. (1993). Mediators of depression in community-based elders. In P. Cappeliez & R. J. Flynn (Eds.), *Depression and the social environment: Research and intervention with neglected populations* (pp. 369–394). Montreal: McGill-Queen's University Press.

Fry, P. S. (2001). The unique contribution of key existential factors to the prediction of psychological well-being of older adults following spousal loss. *The Gerontologist, 41*, 69–81.

Fry, P. S., & Debats, D. L. (2009). Perfectionism and the five-factor personality traits as predictors of mortality in older adults. *Journal of Health Psychology, 14*, 513–524.

Fuentes, K., & Cox, B. J. (1997). Prevalence of anxiety disorders in elderly adults: A critical analysis. *Journal of Behavior Therapy and Experimental Psychiatry, 28*, 269–279.

Fuerst, K. B., & Rourke, B. P. (1995). Human neuropsychology in Canada: The 1980s. *Canadian Psychology, 36*, 12–45.

Fuller, R. K. (1988). Disulfiram treatment of alcoholism. In R. M. Rose & J. E. Barrett (Eds.), *Alcoholism: Treatment and outcome*. New York: Raven.

Fung, K., & Lo, H.-T. (2007, June). Culture matters in clinical practice. *Canadian Psychiatry Aujourd'hui, 3 (3)*, e4.

Funk, W. (1998). *What difference does it make? The journey of a soul survivor*. Cranbrook, BC: Wild Flower Publishing.

Gabbay, F. H. (1992). Behavior genetic strategies in the study of emotion. *Psychological Science, 3*, 50–55.

Gadalla, T. (2008). Association of comorbid mood disorders and chronic illness with disability and quality of life in Ontario, Canada. *Chronic Diseases in Canada, 28*, 148–154.

Gadalla, T., & Piran, N. (2007). Co-occurrence of eating disorders and alcohol use disorders in women: A meta-analysis. *Archive of Women's Mental Health, 10*, 133–140.

Gagné, A., & Morin, C. M. (2001). Predicting treatment response in older adults with insomnia. *Journal of Clinical Geropsychology, 7*, 131–143.

Galaburda, A. M. (2005). Neurology of learning disabilities: What will the future bring? The answer comes from the successes of the recent past. *Learning Disability Quarterly, 28*, 107–109.

Galambos, N. L., Leadbeater, B. J., & Barker, E. T. (2004). Gender differences in and risk factors for depression in adolescence: A 4-year longitudinal study. *International Journal of Behavioral Development, 28*, 16–25.

Galea, S., Brewin, C. R., Gruber, M., et al. (2007). Exposure to hurricane-related stressors and mental illness after Hurricane Katrina. *Archives of General Psychiatry, 64*, 1427–1434.

Galera, C., Melchior, M., Chastang, J.-F., et al. (2009). Childhood and adolescent hyperactivity-inattention symptoms and academic achievement 8 years later: The GAZEL Youth study. *Psychological Medicine, 39*, 1895–1906.

Gallagher, D., & Thompson, L. W. (1982). *Elders' maintenance of treatment benefits following individual psychotherapy for depression: Results of a pilot study and preliminary data from an ongoing replication study*. Paper presented at the annual meeting of the American Psychological Association, Washington, DC.

Gallagher, D., & Thompson, L. W. (1983). Cognitive therapy for depression in the elderly. A promising model for treatment and research. In L. D. Breslau & M. R. Haug (Eds.), *Depression and aging: Causes, care and consequences*. New York: Springer.

Gallagher-Thompson, D., & Coon, D. W. (2007). Evidence-based psychological treatments for distress in family caregivers of older adults. *Psychology and Aging, 22*, 37–51.

Gallagher-Thompson, D., & Thompson, L. W. (1995a). Efficacy of psychotherapeutic interventions with older adults. *The Clinical Psychologist, 48*, 24–30.

Gallagher-Thompson, D., & Thompson, L. W. (1995b). Psychotherapy with older adults in theory and practice. In B. Bongar & L. E. Beutler (Eds.), *Comprehensive textbook of psychotherapy: Theory and practice* (pp. 359–379). New York: Oxford University Press.

Galli, V., McElroy, S. L., Soutullo, C. A., Kizer, D., Raute, N., et al. (1999). The psychiatric diagnoses of twenty-two adolescents who have sexually molested children. *Comprehensive Psychiatry, 40*, 85–88.

Gamez, W., Watson, D., & Doebbeling, B. N. (2007). Abnormal personality and the mood and anxiety disorders: Implications for structural models of anxiety and depression. *Journal of Anxiety Disorders, 21*, 526–539.

Gan, C., Campbell, K. A., Gemeinhardt, M., & McFadden, G. T. (2006). Predictors of family system functioning after brain injury. *Brain Injury, 20*, 587–600.

Gan, C., & Schuller, R. (2002). Family system functioning following acquired brain injury: Clinical and research perspectives. *Brain Injury, 16*, 311–322.

Ganesan, S., & Janze, T. (2005). Overview of culturally-based mental health care in Vancouver. *Transcultural Psychiatry, 42*, 478–490.

Gao, Y., Raine, A., Venables, P. H., et al. (2010). Association of poor childhood fear conditioning and adult crime. *American Journal of Psychiatry, 167*, 56–60.

Garb, H. N., Wood, J. M., & Lilienfeld, S. O., & Nezworski, M. T. (2005). Roots of the Rorschach controversy. *Clinical Psychology Review, 25*, 97–118.

Garbutt, J. C., et al. (1994). Dose-response studies with protirelin. *Archives of General Psychiatry, 51*, 875–883.

Garcia, J., McGowan, B. K., & Green, K. F. (1972). Biological constraints on conditioning. In A. H. Black & W. F. Prokasy (Eds.), *Classical conditioning: 2. Current research and theory*. New York: Appleton-Century-Crofts.

Garcia-Lopez, et al. (2006). Efficacy of three treatment protocols for adolescents with social anxiety disorder: A 5-year follow-up assessment. *Journal of Anxiety Disorders, 20*, 175–191.

Garety, P. A., Fowler, D. G., Freeman, D., et al. (2008). Cognitive-behavioural therapy and family intervention for relapse prevention and symptom reduction in psychosis: Randomised controlled trial. *The British Journal of Psychiatry, 192*, 412–423.

Garfield, S. L., & Bergin, A. E. (1986). Introduction and historical overview. In S. L. Garfield & A. E. Bergin (Eds.), *Handbook of psychotherapy and behavior change* (3rd ed.). New York: John Wiley & Sons.

Garfinkel, P. E. (2002). Classification and diagnosis of eating disorders. In C. G. Fairburn & K. D. Brownell (Eds.), *Eating disorders and obesity: A comprehensive handbook* (2nd ed., pp. 155–161). New York: Guilford.

Garfinkel, P. E., & Goldbloom, D. S. (2000). Significant developments in psychiatry: Implications for community mental health. *Canadian Journal of Community Mental Health, 19*, 161–165.

Garfinkel, P. E., Kennedy, S. H., & Kaplan, A. S. (1995). Views on classification and diagnosis of eating disorders. *Canadian Journal of Psychiatry, 40*, 445–456.

Garland, R. J., & Dougher, M. J. (1991). Motivational interviewing in the treatment of sex offenders. In W. R. Miller & S. Rollnick (Eds.), *Motivating interviewing: Preparing people to change addictive behavior* (pp. 303–313). New York: Guilford.

Garlow, S. J., Rosenberg, J., Moore, J. D., et al. (2008). Depression, desperation, and suicidal ideation in college students: Results from the American Foundation for Suicide Prevention College Screening project at Emory University. *Depression and Anxiety, 25*, 482–488.

Garner, D. M. (1997). Psychoeducational principles. In D. M. Garner & P. E. Garfinkel (Eds.), *Handbook of treatment for eating disorders* (pp. 145–177). New York: Guilford Press.

Garner, D. M., Olmsted, M. P., & Polivy, J. (1983). Development and validation of a multi-dimensional eating disorder inventory for anorexia nervosa and bulimia. *International Journal of Eating Disorders, 2*, 15–34.

Garner, D. M., Vitousek, K. M., & Pike, K. M. (1997). Cognitive-behavioral therapy for anorexia nervosa. In D. M. Garner & P. E. Garfinkel (Eds.),

Handbook of treatment for eating disorders (pp. 94–144). New York: Guilford Press.

Gaston, L. (1991). Reliability and criterion validity of the California Psychotherapy Alliance Scales-Patient version. *Psychological Assessment, 3*, 68–74.

Gaston, L., Thompson, L., Gallagher, D., Cournoyer, L. G., & Gagnon, R. (1998). Alliance, technique, and their interactions in predicting outcome of behavioral, cognitive, and brief dynamic therapy. *Psychotherapy Research, 8*, 190–209.

Gatchel, R. J., Baum, A., & Krantz, D. S. (1989). *An introduction to health psychology* (2nd ed.). New York: Random House.

Gatti, U., Tremblay, R. E., & Vitaro, F. (2009). Iatrogenic effect of juvenile justice. *Journal of Child Psychology and Psychiatry, 50*, 991–998.

Gatz, M., et al. (2006). Role of genes and environments for explaining Alzheimer's Disease. *Archives of General Psychiatry, 63*, 168–174.

Gatz, M., Bengtson, V., & Blum, M. (1990). Caregiving families. In J. Birren & K. W. Schaie (Eds.), *Handbook of the psychology of aging* (3rd ed., pp. 404–426). San Diego, CA: Academic Press.

Gatz, M., Kasl-Godley, J. E., & Karel, M. J. (1996). Aging and mental disorders. In J. E. Birren & K. W. Schaie (Eds.), *Handbook of the psychology of aging.* San Diego: Academic Press.

Gatz, M., & Pearson, C. G. (1988). Ageism revised and the provision of psychological services. *American Psychologist, 43*, 184–188.

Gatz, M., Popkin, S. J., Pino, C. D., & VandenBos, G. R. (1985). Psychological interventions with older adults. In J. E. Birren & W. K. Schaie (Eds.), *Handbook of the psychology of aging* (pp. 755–785). New York: Van Nostrand Reinhold.

Gauthier, J. G. (2002). Facilitating mobility for psychologists through a competency-based approach for regulation and accreditation: The Canadian experiment. *European Psychologist, 7*, 203–212.

Gauthier, S., & Scheltens, P. (2009). Can we do better in developing new drugs for Alzheimer's disease? *Alzheimer's and Dementia, 5*, 489–491.

Gauvin, L., Steiger, H., & Brodeur, J.-M. (2009). Eating-disorder symptoms and syndromes in a sample of urban-dwelling Canadian women: Contributions toward a population-health perspective. *International Journal of Eating Disorders, 42*, 158–165.

Ge, X., Conger, R. D., Cadoret, R. J., et al. (1996). The developmental interface between nature and nurture: A mutual influence model of child antisocial behavior and parent behaviors. *Developmental Psychology, 32*, 574–589.

Gebhard, P. H., Gagnon, J. H., Pomeroy, W. B., & Christenson, C. V. (1965). *Sex offenders.* New York: Harper & Row.

Geddes, J. (2001, April 23). Northern son. *Maclean's,* 16–20.

Geer, J. H., Davison, G. C., & Gatchel, R. I. (1970). Reduction of stress in humans through nonveridical perceived control of aversive stimulation. *Journal of Personality and Social Psychology, 16*, 731–738.

Gelernter, C. S., et al. (1991). Cognitive behavioral and pharmacological treatments of social phobia: A controlled study. *Archives of General Psychiatry, 48*, 938–945.

Geller, G., & Thomas, C. D. (1999). A review of eating disorders in immigrant women: Possible evidence of a cultural-change model. *Eating Disorders: The Journal of Treatment and Prevention, 7*, 279–297.

Geller, J., Cockell, S. J., Hewitt, P. L., Goldner, E. M., & Flett, G. L. (2000). Inhibited expression of negative emotions and interpersonal orientation in anorexia nervosa. *International Journal of Eating Disorders, 28*, 8–19.

George, L. K. (1980). *Role transitions in later life.* Monterey, CA: Brooks/Cole.

Georgiades, K., Boyle, M. H., Jenkins, J. M., et al. (2008). A multilevel analysis of whole family functioning using the McMaster Family Assessment Device. *Journal of Family Psychology, 22*, 344–354.

Gerin, W., Rosofsky, M., Pieper, C., & Pickering, T. G. (1994). A test of generalizability of cardiovascular reactivity using a controlled ambulatory procedure. *Psychosomatic Medicine, 56*, 360–368.

Gerlach, M. (2009). Peer-reviewed reports on all topics relevant to attention-deficit/hyperactivity disorder. *ADHD Attention Deficit and Hyperactivity Disorders, 1*, 1–2.

Gerlach, M., Deckert, J., Rothenberger, A., & Warnke, A. (2008). Pathogenesis and pathophysiology of attention-deficit/hyperactivity disorder: From childhood to adulthood. *Journal of Neural Transmission, 115*, 151–153.

Germain, V., Marchand, A., Bouchard, S., Guay, S., & Drouin, M.-S. (2010). Assessment of the therapeutic alliance in face-to-face or videoconference treatment for posttraumatic stress disorder. *Cyberpsychology, Behavior, and Social Networking, 13*, 29–35.

Gervais, A., et al. (2006). Milestones in the natural course of onset of cigarette use among adolescents. *Canadian Medical Association Journal, 175*, 255–261.

Ghaffar, O., Staines W. R., & Feinstein, A. (2006). Unexplained neurologic symptoms: An fMRI study of sensory conversion disorder. *Neurology, 67*, 2036–2038.

Ghoneim, M. M., & Mewaldt, S. P. (1990). Benzodiazepines and human memory: A review. *Anesthesiology, 72*, 926–938.

Gianaros, P. J., et al. (2008). Individual differences in stress-evoked blood pressure reactivity vary with activation, volume, and functional connectivity of the amygdala. *The Journal of Neuroscience, 28*, 990–998.

Gianaros, P. J., Hariri, A.R., Sheu, L.K., et al. (2009). Preclinical atherosclerosis covaries with individual differences in reactivity and functional connectivity of the amygdala. *Biological Psychiatry, 65*, 943–950.

Gilbert, F. S. (1991). Development of a "steps questionnaire." *Journal of Studies on Alcohol, 52*, 353–360.

Gilbertson, M. W., et al. (2006). Neurocognitive function in monozygotic twins discordant for combat exposure: Relationship to posttraumatic stress disorder. *Journal of Abnormal Psychology, 115*, 484–495.

Gilger, J. W., & Kaplan, B. J. (2001). Atypical brain development: A conceptual framework for understanding developmental learning disabilities. *Developmental Neuropsychology, 20*, 465–481.

Gilhooly, M., & McDonach, E. (2003). An average old age: Associations between ageing, health, and behaviour. In S. P. Llewelyn & P. Kennedy (Eds.), *Handbook of clinical health psychology* (pp. 437–453). Chichester, West Sussex, England: John Wiley & Sons.

Gillespie, K. (2007, January 19). $13M for autism therapy will aid 225 Ontario kids. *Toronto Star,* AO6.

Gillmor, D. (1987). *I swear by Apollo: Dr. Ewen Cameron and the CIA-brainwashing experiments.* Montreal: Eden Press.

Gilmour, H. & Patten, S. (2007). Depression and work impairment. *Health Reports, 18(1).* Statistics Canada cat:82-003.

Ginzburg, H. M. (1986). Naltrexone: Its clinical utility. In B. Stimmel (Ed.), *Advances in alcohol and substance abuse* (pp. 83–101). New York: Haworth.

Girard, D. (2007, March 26). Childhood ills linked to reading troubles, lifelong woes. *Toronto Star,* A1, A6.

Gizewski, E. R., et al. (2009). Specific cerebral activation due to visual erotic stimuli in male-to-female transsexuals compared with male and female controls: An fMRI study. *Journal of Sexual Medicine, 6*, 440–448.

Gladstone, T. R. G., & Beardslee, W. R. (2009). The prevention of depression in children and adolescents: A review. *Canadian Journal of Psychiatry, 54*, 212–221.

Gladue, B. A. (1985). Neuroendocrine response to estrogen and sexual orientation. *Science, 230*, 961.

Glancy, D. R., & Glancy, G. D. (2009). The case that has psychiatrists running scared: *Ahmed v. Stefaniu. Journal of the American Academy of Psychiatry and the Law, 37*, 250–256.

Glass, K. C. (2008). Ethical obligations and the use of placebo controls. *Canadian Journal of Psychiatry, 53*, 428–429.

Gleaves, D. H. (1996). The sociocognitive model of dissociative identity disorder: A reexamination of the evidence. *Psychological Bulletin, 120*, 42–59.

Gleaves, D. H., & Eberenz, K. P. (1994). Sexual abuse histories among treatment-resistant bulimia nervosa patients. *International Journal of Eating Disorders, 15*, 227–231.

Glessner, J. T., Wang, K., Cai, G., et al. (2009). Autism genome-wide copy number variation reveals ubiquitin and neuronal genes. *Nature, 459*, 569–573.

Gliksman, L., Demers, A., Adlaf, E., Newton-Taylor, B., & Schmidt, K. (2000). *Canadian Campus Survey 1998.* Toronto: Centre for Addiction and Mental Health.

Gnaedinger, N. (1989). *Elder abuse: A discussion paper.* Prepared for Working Together, National Forum on Family Violence.

Goeree, R., et al. (2005). The economic burden of schizophrenia in Canada in 2004. *Current Medical Research and Opinion, 21*, 2017–2028.

Goering, P., Wasylenki, D., & Durbin, J. (2000). Canada's mental health system. *International Journal of Law and Psychiatry, 23*, 345–359.

Gold, I. (2009). Reduction in psychiatry. *Canadian Journal of Psychiatry, 54*, 506–512.

Gold, P. B., et al. (2006). Randomized trial of supported employment integrated with assertive community treatment for rural adults with severe mental illness. *Schizophrenia Bulletin, 32*, 378–395.

Goldapple, K., et al. (2004). Modulation of cortical-limbic pathways in major depression: Treatment-specific effects of cognitive behavior therapy. *Archives of General Psychiatry, 61*, 34–41.

Goldberg, J. O., & Schmidt, L. A. (2001). Shyness, sociability, and social dysfunction in schizophrenia. *Schizophrenia Research, 48*, 343–349.

Golden, C. J., Hammeke, T., & Purisch, A. (1978). Diagnostic validity of a standardized neuropsychological battery derived from Luria's neuropsychological tests. *Journal of Consulting and Clinical Psychology, 46*, 1258–1265.

Goldfield, G. S., & Boachie, A. (2003). Delivery of family therapy in the treatment of anorexia nervosa using telehealth. *Telemedicine Journal and e-Health, 9*, 111–114.

Goldfried, M. R. (1991). Research issues in psychotherapy integration. *Journal of Psychotherapy Integration, 1*, 5–25.

Goldfried, M. R., & Davison, G. C. (1994). *Clinical behavior therapy*. Expanded edition. New York: John Wiley & Sons.

Goldfried, M. R., Padawer, W., & Robins, C. (1984). Social anxiety and the semantic structure of heterosocial interactions. *Journal of Abnormal Psychology, 93*, 87–97.

Goldman, M. S., Del Boca, F. K., & Darkes, J. (1999). Alcohol expectancy theory: The application of cognitive neuroscience. In K. E. Leonard & H. T. Blane (Eds.), *Psychological theories of drinking and alcoholism* (2nd ed., pp. 203–246). New York: Guilford.

Goldner, E. M. (2008). Is it time to revise our understanding and management of depression? *Canadian Journal of Psychiatry, 53*, 409–410.

Goldner, E. M., Hsu, L., Waraich, P., & Somers, J. M. (2002). Prevalence and incidence studies of schizophrenic disorders: A systematic review of the literature. *Canadian Journal of Psychiatry, 47*, 833–843.

Goldstein, A. (1994). *Addiction: From biology to drug policy*. New York: W. H. Freeman.

Goldstein, A. J., & Chambless, D. L. (1978). A reanalysis of agoraphobic behavior. *Behavior Therapy, 9*, 47–59.

Goldstein, A. L., & Flett, G. L. (2009). Personality, alcohol use, and drinking motives: A comparison of independent and combined internal drinking motives groups. *Behavior Modification, 33*, 182–198.

Goldstein, A. L., Flett, G. L., Wekerle, C., & Wall, A.-M. (2009). Personality, child maltreatment, and substance use: Examining correlates of deliberate self-harm among university students. *Canadian Journal of Behavioural Sciences, 41*, 241–251.

Goldstein, A. L., Walton, M. A., Cunningham, R. M., et al. (2009). Correlates of gambling among youth in an inner-city emergency department. *Psychology of addictive behaviors, 23*, 113–121.

Goldstein, J. M., et al. (1999). Cortical abnormalities in schizophrenia identified by structural magnetic resonance imaging. *Archives of General Psychiatry, 56*, 537–547.

Goldstein, L. H., Deale, A. C., Mitchell-O'Malley, S. J., et al. (2004). An evaluation of cognitive-behavioral therapy as a treatment for dissociative seizures: A pilot study. *Cognitive and Behavioral Neurology, 17*, 41–49.

Goleman, D. (1995). *Emotional intelligence*. New York: Bantam.

Gomberg, E. S. L., & Zucker, R. A. (1998). Substance use and abuse in old age. In I. H. Nordhus, G. R. VandenBos, S. Berg, & P. Fromholt (Eds.), *Clinical geropsychology* (pp. 189–204). Washington, DC: American Psychological Association.

Goodacre, R. H., et al. (1975). Hospitalization and hospital bed replacement. *Canadian Psychiatric Association Journal, 20*, 7–14.

Goodman, G. S., et al. (2003). A prospective study of memory for child sexual abuse: New findings relevant to the repressed-memory controversy. *Psychological Sciences, 14*, 113–118.

Goodwin, C. (2007, March). The calm at the eye of the storm. *Inside Entertainment, 6*, 43–46.

Goodwin, D. W. (1979). Alcoholism and heredity: A review and hypothesis. *Archives of General Psychiatry, 36*, 57–61.

Goodwin, P. J. (2005). Support groups in advanced breast cancer. *Cancer, 104*, 2596–2601.

Goodwin, P. J., et al. (2001). The effect of group psychosocial support on survival in metastatic breast cancer. *New England Journal of Medicine, 345*, 1719–1726.

Goodyer, I., Dubicka, B., Wilkinson, P., et al. (2007). Selective serotonin reuptake inhibitors (SSRIs) and routine specialist care with and without cognitive behaviour therapy in adolescents with major depression: Randomized controlled trial. *British Medical Journal, 335*, 142.

Goos, L. M., Crosbie, J., Payne, S., & Schachar, R. (2009). Validation and extension of the endophynotype model in ADHD patterns of inheritance in a family study of inhibitory control. *American Journal of Psychiatry, 166*, 711–717.

Gordon, R. M., & Brill, D. (2001). The abuse and neglect of the elderly. *International Journal of Law and Psychiatry, 24*, 183–197.

Gorman, B. K., & Read, J. G. (2006). Gender disparities in adult health: An examination of three measures of morbidity. *Journal of Health and Social Behavior, 47*, 95–110.

Gortner, E., Gollan, J., Dobson, K. S., & Jacobson, N. S. (1998). Cognitive-behavioral treatment for depression: Relapse prevention. *Journal of Consulting and Clinical Psychology, 66*, 377–384.

Gotlib, I. H., Joormann, J., Minor, K., & Hallmayer, J. (2008). HPA axis reactivity: A mechanism underlying the association among 5-HTTLPR, stress, and depression. *Biological Psychiatry, 63*, 847–851.

Gotlib, I. H., & McCann, C. D. (1984). Construct accessibility and depression: An examination of cognitive and affective factors. *Journal of Personality and Social Psychology, 47*, 427–439.

Gotlib, I. H., & Robinson, L. A. (1982). Responses to depressed individuals: Discrepancies between self-report and observer-rated behavior. *Journal of Abnormal Psychology, 91*, 231–240.

Gotlib, I. H., Whiffen, V. E., Mount, J. H., Milne, K., & Cordy, N. I. (1989). Prevalence rates and demographic characteristics associated with depression in pregnancy and the postpartum. *Journal of Consulting and Clinical Psychology, 57*, 269–274.

Gotlib, I. H., Whiffen, V. E., Wallace, P., & Mount, J. (1991). A prospective investigation of postpartum depression: Factors involved in onset and recovery. *Journal of Abnormal Psychology, 100*, 122–132.

Gottesman, I., & Shields, J. (1972). *Schizophrenia and genetics: A twin study vantage point*. New York: Academic Press.

Gottesman, I. I., & Goldsmith, H. H. (1994). Developmental psychopathology of antisocial behavior: Inserting genes into its ontogenesis and epigenesis. In C. A. Nelson (Ed.), *Threats to optimal development*. Hillside, NJ: Erlbaum.

Gottesman, I. I., McGuffin, P., & Farmer, A. E. (1987). Clinical genetics as clues to the "real" genetics of schizophrenia. *Schizophrenia Bulletin, 13*, 23–47.

Gottlieb, B. H., & Johnson, J. (2000). Respite programs for caregivers of persons with dementia: A review with practice implications. *Aging and Mental Health, 4*, 119–129.

Gottlieb, B. H., & Rooney, J. A. (2004). Coping effectiveness: Determinants and relevance to the mental health and affect of family caregivers of persons with dementia. *Aging and Mental Health, 8*, 364–373.

Gottman, J. M., & Krokoff, L. J. (1989). Marital interaction and satisfaction: A longitudinal view. *Journal of Consulting and Clinical Psychology, 57*, 47–52.

Gottman, J. M., Notarius, C., Gonso, J., & Markman, H. (1976). *A couple's guide to communication*. Champaign, IL.: Research Press.

Gould, M. S., Walsh, B. T., Munfakh, J. L., et al. (2009). Sudden death and use of stimulant medications in youths. *American Journal of Psychiatry, 166*, 992–1001.

Government of Canada (1977). Minutes of proceedings and evidence of the subcommittee on the penitentiary system in Canada. *House of Commons* Issue No. 36, Tuesday, March 8. Ottawa: Canadian Government Publishing Centre, Supply and Services Canada.

Government of Canada. (2006). *The Human Face of Mental Health and Mental Illness in Canada 2006*. Ottawa: Minister of Public Works and Government Services Canada.

Goyette, C. H., & Conners, C. K. (1977). *Food additives and hyperkinesis*. Paper presented at the 85th Annual Convention of the American Psychological Association.

Grabe, S., Hyde, J. S., & Lindberg, S. M. (2007). Body objectification and depression in adolescents: The role of gender, shame, and rumination. *Psychology of Women Quarterly, 31*, 164–175.

Grace, S. L., Abbey, S. E., Shnek, Z. M., Irvine, J., Franche, R.-L., & Stewart, D. E. (2002). Cardiac rehabilitation I: Review of psychosocial factors. *General Hospital Psychiatry, 24*, 121–126.

Graham, H. (2005). Intellectual disabilities and socioeconomic inequalities in health: An overview of research. *Journal of Applied Research in Intellectual Disabilities, 18,* 101–111.

Graham, J. (2009, February 19). Deep brain stimulation approved for obsessive-compulsive disorder. *Chicago Tribune.*

Graham, J. E., Rockwood, K., Beattie, B. L., Eastwood, R., Gauthier, S., & Tuokko, H., & McDowell, I. (1997). Prevalence and severity of cognitive impairment with and without dementia in an elderly population. *The Lancet, 349,* 1793–1796.

Graham, J. R. (1990). *MMPI-2: Assessing personality and psychopathology.* New York: Oxford University Press.

Graham, K. (1988). Reasons for consumption and heavy caffeine use: Generalization of a model based on alcohol research. *Addictive Behaviors, 13,* 209–214.

Graham, K., & Braun, K. (1999). Concordance of use of alcohol and other substances among older adult couples. *Addictive Behaviors, 24,* 839–856.

Grant, V. V., et al. (2007). Psychometric evaluation of the five-factor Modified Drinking Motives Questionnaire—Revised in undergraduates. *Addictive Behaviors, 32,* 2611–2632.

Grant, V. V., Bagnell, A. L., Chambers, C. T., & Stewart, S. H. (2009). Early temperament prospectively predicts anxiety in later childhood. *Canadian Journal of Psychiatry, 54,* 320–330.

Grant, V. V., Stewart, S. H., & Mohr, C. D. (2009). Coping-anxiety and coping-depression motives predict different daily mood-drinking relationships. *Psychology of Addictive Behaviors, 23,* 226–237.

Gratzer, T., & Bradford, J. M. W. (1995). Offender and offense characteristics of sexual sadists: A comparative study. *Journal of Forensic Sciences, 40,* 450–455.

Gravel, R., & Beland, Y. (2005). The Canadian Community Health Survey: Mental health and well-being. *Canadian Journal of Psychiatry, 50,* 573–579.

Gray, J. E., & O'Reilly, R. L. (2001). Clinically significant differences among Canadian mental health acts. *Canadian Journal of Psychiatry, 46,* 325–321.

Gray, J. E., & O'Reilly, R. L. (2005). Canadian compulsory community treatment laws: Recent reforms. *International Journal of Law and Psychiatry, 28,* 13–22.

Gray, J. E., & O'Reilly, R. L. (2009). Supreme Court of Canada's "Beautiful Mind" case. *International Journal of Law and Psychiatry, 32,* 315–322.

Gray, N. S., et al. (2003). Prediction of violence and self-harm in mentally disordered offenders: A prospective study of the efficacy of HCR-20, PCL-R, and psychiatric symptomatology. *Journal of Consulting and Clinical Psychology, 71,* 443–451.

Gray, R. E., Fitch, M., Phillips, C., Labreque, M., & Fergus, K. (2000). Managing the impact of illness: The experiences of men with prostate cancer and their spouses. *Journal of Health Psychology, 5,* 531–548.

Green, K. L., Cameron, R., Polivy, J., Cooper, K., Liu, L. Y., Leiter, L., et al. (1997). Weight dissatisfaction and weight loss attempts among Canadian adults. *Canadian Medical Association Journal, 157* (Suppl.), S17–S25.

Green, M. F., Marshall, B. D., Wirshing, W. C., Ames, D., Marder, S. R., McGurk, S., et al. (1997). Does risperidone improve verbal working memory in treatment-resistant schizophrenia? *American Journal of Psychiatry, 154,* 799–804.

Green, R. (1987). *The "sissy boy syndrome" and the development of homosexuality.* New Haven: Yale University Press.

Green, R., & Blanchard, R. (1995). Gender identity disorders. In H. I. Kaplan & B. J. Sadock (Eds.), *Comprehensive textbook of psychiatry* (pp. 1347–1360). Baltimore: Williams & Wilkins.

Green, R., & Fleming, D. T. (1990). Transsexual surgery follow-up: Status in the 1990s. In J. Bancroft, C. Davis, & D. Weinstein (Eds.), *Annual review of sex research* (pp. 163–174). Lake Mills, IA: Society for the Scientific Study of Sex.

Green, R. C., et al. (2003). Depression as a risk factor for Alzheimer disease: The *MIRAGE* study. *Archives of Neurology, 60,* 753–759.

Greenberg, D. M. (1998). Sexual recidivism in sex offenders. *Canadian Journal of Psychiatry, 43,* 459–465.

Greenberg, L., Elliott, R., & Lietaer, G. (1994). Research on experiential therapies. In A. E. Bergin & S. L. Garfield (Eds.), *Handbook of psychotherapy and behavior change* (4th ed., pp. 509–539). New York: John Wiley & Sons.

Greenberg, L. S. (2004). Emotion-focused therapy. *Clinical Psychology and Psychotherapy, 11,* 3–16.

Greenberg, L. S., & Goldman, R. N. (2008). *Emotion-focused couples therapy: The dynamics of emotion, love, and power.* Washington, DC: American Psychological Association Books.

Greenberg, L. S., & Johnson, S. M. (1988). *Emotionally focussed couples therapy.* New York: Guilford.

Greenberg, L. S., & Pascual-Leone, A. (2006). Emotion in psychotherapy: A practice-friendly research review. *Journal of Clinical Psychology, 62,* 611–630.

Greenberg, L. S., Warwar, S. H., & Malcolm, W. M. (2008). Differential effects of emotion-focused therapy and psychoeducation in facilitating forgiveness and letting go of emotional injuries. *Journal of Counseling Psychology, 55,* 185–196.

Greenberg, P. E., et al. (1999). The economic burden of anxiety disorders in the 1990s. *Journal of Clinical Psychiatry, 60,* 427–435.

Greene, P., Kane, D., Christ, G., Lynch, S., & Corrigan, M. (2006). *FDNY crisis counseling: Innovative responses to 9/11 firefighters, families, and communities.* Hoboken, NJ: John Wiley & Sons.

Greenhalgh, J., Dickson, R., & Dundar, Y. (2009). The effects of biofeedback for the treatment of essential hypertension: A systematic review. *Health Technology Assessment, 13,* 1–103.

Greer, S., Morris, T., & Pettigale, K.W. (1979). Psychological response to breast cancer: Effect on outcome. *Lancet, 2,* 785–787.

Greeven, A., van Balkom, A., Visser, S., et al. (2007). Cognitive behavior therapy and paraoxetine in the treatment of hypochondriasis: A randomized controlled trial. *American Journal of Psychiatry,164,* 91–99.

Gregory, R. J., & Jindal, S. (2006). Factitious disorder on an inpatient psychiatry ward. *American Journal of Orthopsychiatry, 76,* 31–36.

Griffiths, M. (2008). Internet and video-game addiction. In C. Essau (Ed.), *Adolescent addiction: Epidemiology, assessment, and treatment* (pp. 231–267). Toronto: Academic Press.

Grigorenko, E. L. (2009). Speaking genes or genes for speaking? Deciphering the genetics of speech and language. *Journal of Child Psychology and Psychiatry, 50,* 116–125.

Grilo, C. M., et al. (2005). Two year prospective naturalistic study of remission from major depressive disorder as a function of personality disorder comorbidity. *Journal of Consulting and Clinical Psychology, 7,* 78–85.

Grilo, C. M., Shiffman, S., & Carter-Campbell, J. T. (1994). Binge eating antecedents in normal weight nonpurging females: Is there consistency? *International Journal of Eating Disorders, 16,* 239–249.

Grinker, R. B., & Spiegel, J. P. (1945). *Men under stress.* Philadelphia: Blakiston.

Grinspoon, L., & Bakalar, J. B. (1995). Marijuana as medicine: A plea for reconsideration. *Journal of the American Medical Association, 273,* 1875–1876.

Grisso, T., & Appelbaum, P. S. (1991). Mentally ill and non-mentally ill patients' abilities to understand informed consent disclosures for medication: Preliminary data. *Law and Human Behavior, 15,* 377–388.

Grossman, P., Niemann, L., Schmidt, S., & Walack, N. (2004). Mindfulness-based stress reduction and health benefits: A meta-analysis. *Journal of Psychosomatic Research, 57,* 35–43.

Groth, N. A., Hobson, W. F., & Guy, T. S. (1982). The child molester: Clinical observations. In J. Conte & D. A. Shore (Eds.), *Social work and child sexual abuse.* New York: Haworth.

Grove, W. R., et al. (1990). Heritability of substance abuse and antisocial behavior in monozygotic twins reared apart. *Biological Psychiatry, 27,* 1293–1304.

Guerra, N., & Slaby, R. (1990). Cognitive mediators of aggression in adolescent offenders: 2. Intervention. *Developmental Psychology, 26,* 269–277.

Guidano, V. F., & Liotti, G. (1983). *Cognitive processes and emotional disorders.* New York: Guilford.

Guidi, J., Fava, G. A., Fava, M., & Papakostas, G. I. (2010). Efficacy of the sequential integration of psychotherapy and pharmacotherapy in major depressive disorder: A preliminary meta-analysis. *Psychological Medicine.*

Gum, A. M., King-Kallimanis, B., & Kohn, R. (2009). Prevalence of mood, anxiety, and substance-abuse disorders for older Americans in the National Comorbidity Survey replication. *American Journal of Geriatric Psychiatry, 117,* 769–781.

Gump, B. S., Matthews, K. A., & Raikkonen, K. (1999). Modeling relationships among socioeconomic status, hostility, cardiovascular reactivity, and left ventricular mass in African American and White children. *Health Psychology, 18,* 140–150.

Gunderson, J. G., Kolb, J. E., & Austin, V. (1981). The diagnostic interview for borderline patients. *American Journal of Psychiatry, 138,* 896–903.

Guo, Z., Cupples, L. A., Kurz, A., Auerbach, S. H., Volicer, L., Chui, H., et al. (2000). Head injury and the risk of Alzheimer's disease in the MIRAGE study. *Neurology, 28,* 1316–1323.

Gupta, R., Derevensky, J., & Ellenbogen, S. (2006). Personality characteristics and risk-taking tendencies among adolescent gamblers. *Canadian Journal of Behavioural Science, 38,* 201–213

Gur, R. E., et al. (2007). The Consortium on the Genetics of Schizophrenia: Neurocognitiveendophenotypes. *Schizophrenia Bulletin, 33,* 49–68.

Gurland, B. (1991). Epidemiology of psychiatric disorders. In J. Sadavoy, L. W. Lazarus, & L. F. Jarvik (Eds.), *Comprehensive review of geriatric psychiatry* (pp. 25–40). Washington, DC: American Psychiatric Press.

Gurman, A. S., Kniskern, D. P., & Pinsoff, W. M. (1986). Research on the process and outcome of marital and family therapy. In S. L. Garfield & A. E. Bergin (Eds.), *Handbook of psychotherapy and behavior change* (3rd ed.). New York: John Wiley & Sons.

Guyenet, P. G. (2006). The sympathetic control of blood pressure. *Nature Review of Neuroscience, 7,* 335–346.

Guze, S. B. (1993). Genetics of Briquet's syndrome and somatization disorder: A review of family, adoption, and twin studies. *Annals of Clinical Psychiatry, 5,* 225–230.

Haaga, D. A. F. (1990). Issues in relating self-efficacy to smoking relapse: Importance of an 'Achilles' Heel" situation and of prior quitting experience. *Journal of Substance Abuse, 2,* 191–200.

Haaga, D. A. F. (2000). Introduction to the special section on stepped care models in psychotherapy. *Journal of Consulting and Clinical Psychology, 68,* 547–548.

Haaga, D. A. F., & Davison, G. C. (1989). Outcome studies of rational-emotive therapy. In M. E. Bernard & R. DiGiuseppe (Eds.), *Inside rational-emotive therapy.* New York: Academic Press.

Haaga, D. A, Dyck, M. J., & Ernst, D. (1991). Empirical status of cognitive therapy of depression. *Psychological Bulletin, 110,* 215–236.

Haaga, D. A. F., Rabois, D., & Brody, C. (1999). Cognitive behavior therapy. In M. Hersen & A. S. Bellack (Eds.), *Handbook of comparative treatments for adult disorders.* New York: John Wiley & Sons.

Haddock, G., Barrowclough, C., Shaw, J. J., et al. (2009). Cognitive-behavioural therapy *v.* social activity therapy for people with psychosis and a history of violence: Randomised controlled trial. *The British Journal of Psychiatry, 194,* 152–157.

Hadjipavlou, G., & Ogrodniczuk, J. S. (2007). A national survey of Canadian psychiatry residents' perceptions of psychotherapy training. *Canadian Journal of Psychiatry, 52,* 710–717.

Hadjistavropoulos, H. D., Asmundson, G. J. G., LaChapelle, D. L., & Quine, A. (2002). The role of health anxiety among patients with chronic pain in determining response to therapy. *Pain Research and Management, 7,* 127–133.

Hadjistavropoulos, H. D., Asmundson, G. J. G., & Norton, G. R. (1999). Validation of the Coping with Health, Injuries, and Problems Scale in a chronic pain sample. *Clinical Journal of Pain, 15,* 41–49.

Haeffel, G. J., Gibb, B. E., Metalsky, G. I., et al. (2008). Measuring cognitive vulnerability to depression: Development and validation of the cognitive style questionnaire. *Clinical Psychology Review, 28,* 824–836.

Haggarty, J. M., Cernovsky, Z., Husni, M., Minor, K., Kermeen, P., & Merskey, H. (2002). Seasonal affective disorder in an Arctic community. *Acta Psychiatrica Scandinavica, 105,* 378–384.

Hailey, D., Roine, R., & Ohinmaa, A. (2008). The effectiveness of telemental health applications: A review. *Canadian Journal of Psychiatry, 53,* 769–778.

Halchuk, R. E., Makinen, J. A., & Johnson, S. M. (2010). Resolving attachment injuries in couples using emotionally focused therapy: A three year follow-up. *Journal of Couple and Relationship Therapy, 9,* 31–47.

Hall, E. (1900). The unofficial gynaecological treatment of the insane in British Columbia. *Medical Sentinel.* Retrieved September 17, 2000, from www.canadiana.org.

Hall, G. C. N. (1995). Sexual offender recidivism revisited: A meta-analysis of treatment studies. *Journal of Consulting and Clinical Psychology, 63,* 802–809.

Hall, J. (1998, February 1). Merger of Clarke, Addiction Centre seen as 'win, win': New organization will treat mental illness and drug abuse problems. *Toronto Star,* A4.

Hall, N. (2008, November 20). Witness wins trauma damages; Man who suffered "nervous shock" after seeing three-death crash on Pattullo Bridge wins first case of its kind. *The Vancouver Sun,* A1.

Hall, S. M., et al. (1996). Mood management and nicotine gum in smoking treatment: A therapeutic contract and placebo-controlled study. *Journal of Consulting and Clinical Psychology, 64,* 1003–1009.

Halligan, S. L., Murray, L., Martins, C., & Cooper, P. J. (2007). Maternal depression and psychiatric outcomes in adolescent offspring: A 13-year longitudinal study. *Journal of Affective Disorders, 97,* 145–154.

Halmi, K. A. (2009). Perplexities and provocations of eating disorders. *Journal of Clinical Child Psychology and Psychiatry, 50,* 163–169.

Halmi, K. A., et al. (2002). Relapse predictors of patients with bulimia nervosa who achieved abstinence through cognitive behavioral therapy. *Archives of General Psychiatry, 59,* 1105–1109.

Hamilton, K. E., & Dobson, K. S. (2002). Cognitive therapy of depression: Pretreatment patient predictors of outcome. *Clinical Psychology Review, 22,* 875–893.

Hamilton, S. P. (2008). Schizophrenia candidate genes: Are we really coming up blank? *American Journal of Psychiatry, 165,* 420–423.

Hamilton, S. P. (2009). Linkage and association studies of anxiety disorders. *Depression and Anxiety, 26,* 976–983.

Hammad, T. A., Laughren, T., & Racoosin, J. (2006). Suicidality in pediatric patients treated with antidepressant drugs. *Archives of General Psychiatry, 63,* 332–339.

Hammen, C. L. (1991). Generation of stress in the course of unipolar depression. *Journal of Abnormal Psychology, 100,* 555–561.

Hammond, D., et al. (2005). Tobacco denormalization and industry beliefs among smokers from four countries. *American Journal of Preventive Medicine, 31,* 225–232.

Hankin, B. L., Fraley, R. C., Lakey, B. B., & Waldman, J. D. (2005). Is depression best viewed as a continuum or discrete category? A taxometric analysis of childhood and adolescent depression in a population-based sample. *Journal of Abnormal Psychology, 114,* 96–110.

Hansen, W. B. (1992). School-based substance abuse prevention: A review of the state of the art in curriculum, 1980–1990. *Health Education Research: Theory and Practice, 7,* 403–430.

Hansen, W. B. (1993). School-based alcohol prevention programs. *Alcohol Health and Research World, 18,* 62–66.

Hansen, W. B., et al. (1988). Affective and social influence approaches to the prevention of multiple substance abuse among seventh grade students. *Preventive Medicine, 17,* 135–154.

Hanson, R. K. (2009). The psychological assessment of risk for crime and violence. *Canadian Psychology, 50,* 172–182.

Hanson, R. K., & Bussière, M. T. (1998). Predicting relapse: A meta-analysis of sexual offender recidivism studies. *Journal of Consulting and Clinical Psychology, 66,* 348–362.

Hanson, R. K., & Harris, A. J R. (1997). Voyeurism: Assessment and treatment. In D. R. Laws & W. O'Donohue (Eds.), *Sexual deviance* (pp. 311–331). New York: Guilford Press.

Hanson, R. K., & Morton-Bourgon, K. (2005). Predicting relapse: A meta-analysis of sexual offender recidivism studies. *Journal of Consulting and Clinical Psychology, 66,* 348–362.

Hanusa, B. H., & Schulz, R. (1977). Attributional mediators of learned helplessness. *Journal of Personality and Social Psychology, 35,* 602–611.

Haracz, J. L. (1982). The dopamine hypothesis: An overview of studies with schizophrenic patients. *Schizophrenia Bulletin, 8,* 438–469.

Harbottle, E. J., Birmingham, C. L., & Sayani, F. (2008). Anorexia nervosa: A survival analysis. *Eating and Weight Disorders, 13,* e32–e34.

Hardy, B. W., & Waller, D. A. (1988). Bulimia as substance abuse. In W. G. Johnson (Ed.), *Advances in eating disorders.* New York: JAI.

Hare, E. (1969). *Triennial statistical report of the Royal Maudsley and Bethlem Hospitals.* London: Bethlem and Maudsley Hospitals.

Hare, R. D. (1970). *Psychopathy: Theory and research.* New York: John Wiley & Sons.

Hare, R. D. (1978). Electrodermal and cardiovascular correlates of sociopathy. In R. D. Hare & D. Schalling (Eds.), *Psychopathic behavior: Approaches to research.* New York: John Wiley & Sons.

Hare, R. D. (1991). *The Hare Psychopathy Checklist-Revised.* Toronto: Multi-Health Systems.

Hare, R. D. (1996). Psychopathy and antisocial personality disorder: A case of diagnostic confusion. *Psychiatric Times, 13,* 39–40.

Hare, R. D., Clark, D., Grann, M., & Thornton, D. (2000). Psychopathy and the predictive utility of the PCL-R: An international perspective. *Behavioral Sciences and the Law, 18,* 623–645.

Hare, R. D., Hart, S. D., & Harpur, T. J. (1991). Psychopathy and the DSM-IV criteria for anti-social personality disorder. *Journal of Abnormal Psychology, 100,* 391–398.

Hare, R. D., & Neumann, C. S. (2009). Psychopathy: Assessment and forensic implication. *Canadian Journal of Psychiatry, 54,* 791–802.

Harkness, A. R., McNulty, J. L., & Ben-Porath, Y. S. (1995). The Personality Psychopathology Five (PSY-5): Constructs and MMPI-2 scales. *Psychological Assessment, 7,* 104–114.

Harmer, C. J., O'Sullivan, U., Favaron, E., et al. (2009). Effect of acute antidepressant administration on negative affective bias in depressed patients. *American Journal of Psychiatry, 166,* 1178–1184.

Harpur, T. J., & Hare, R. D. (1990). Psychopathy and attention. In J. Enns (Ed.), *The development of attention: Research and theory.* Amsterdam: New Holland.

Harpur, T. J., & Hare, R. D. (1994). Assessment of psychopathy as a function of age. *Journal of Abnormal Psychology, 103,* 604–609.

Harpur, T. J., Hart, S. D., & Hare, R. D. (1994). Personality of the psychopath. In P. T. Costa, Jr. & T. A. Widiger (Eds.), *Personality disorders and the five-factor model of personality* (pp. 149–173). Washington, DC: American Psychological Association.

Harris, G. T., Rice, M. E., & Cormier, C. A. (2002). Prospective replication of the Violence Risk Appraisal Guide in predicting violent recidivism among forensic patients. *Law and Human Behavior, 26,* 377–394.

Harris, G. T., Rice, M. E., Lalumiere, M. L., Boer, D., & Lang, C. (2003). A multisite comparison of actuarial risk instruments for sex offenders. *Psychological Assessment, 15,* 413–425.

Harvard Mental Health Letter. (1996, August). *Treatment of alcoholism—Part I, 13,* 1–4.

Harvey, P.-O., Lepage, M., & Malla, A. (2007). Benefits of enriched intervention compared with standard care for patients with recent-onset psychosis: A metaanalytic approach. *Canadian Journal of Psychiatry, 52,* 464–472.

Harwood, M. T., Beutler, L. E., & Charvat, M. (2010). Cognitive-behavioral therapy and psychotherapy integration. In K. S. Dobson (Ed.), *Handbook of cognitive-behavioral therapies* (3rd ed., pp. 94–130). New York: The Guilford Press.

Hasin, D. S., Stinson, F. S., Ogburn, E., & Grant, B. F. (2007). Prevalence, correlates, disability, and comorbidity of DSM-IV alcohol abuse and dependence in the United States: Results from the National Epidemiologic Survey of Alcohol and Related Conditions. *Archives of General Psychiatry, 64,* 830–842.

Hathaway, S. R., & McKinley, J. C. (1943). *MMPI manual.* New York: Psychological Corporation.

Hawke, J. M., Jainchill, N., & De Leon, G. (2000). Adolescent amphetamine users in treatment: Client profiles and treatment outcomes. *Journal of Psychoactive Drugs, 32,* 95–105.

Hawkins, J. D., et al. (1998). Exploring the effects of age of alcohol use initiation and psychosocial risk factors on subsequent alcohol misuse. *Journal of Studies on Alcohol, 58,* 280–290.

Haworth, C. M. A., Kovaas, Y., Harlaar, N., et al. (2009). Generalist genes and learning disabilities: A multivariate genetic analysis of low performance in reading, mathematics, language and general cognitive ability in a sample of 8000 12-year-old twins. *Journal of Child Psychology and Psychiatry, 50,* 1318–1325.

Hawton, K., Catalan, J., & Fagg, J. (1992). Sex therapy for erectile dysfunction: Characteristics of couples, treatment outcome, and prognostic factors. *Archives of Sexual Behavior, 21,* 161–176.

Hawton, K., Catalan, J., Martin, P., & Fagg, J. (1986). Long-term outcome of sex therapy. *Behaviour Research and Therapy, 24,* 665–675.

Hay, D. P. (1991). Electroconvulsive therapy. In J. Sadavoy, L. W. Lazarus, & L. F. Jarvik (Eds.), *Comprehensive review of geriatric psychiatry* (pp. 469–485). Washington, DC: American Psychiatric Press.

Hayden, E. P., Dougherty, L. R., Maloney, B., et al. (2008). Early-emerging cognitive-vulnerability to depression and the serotonin transporter promoter region polymorphism. *Journal of Affective Disorders, 107,* 227–230.

Hayes, S. C. (2002). Acceptance, mindfulness, and science. *Clinical Psychology: Science and Practice, 9,* 101–106.

Haynes, S. N., & Horn, W. F. (1982). Reactivity in behavioral observation: A review. *Behavioral Assessment, 4,* 369–385.

Haynes, S. N., Mumma, G. H., & Pinson, C. (2009). Idiographic assessment: Conceptual and psychometric foundations of individualized behavioral assessment. *Clinical Psychology Review, 29,* 179–191.

Hazell, P., O'Connell, D., Heathcote, D., et al. (1995). Efficacy of tricyclic drugs in treating child and adolescent depression: A meta-analysis. *British Medical Journal, 310,* 897–901.

Hazelrigg, M. D., Cooper, H. M., & Borduin, C. M. (1987). Evaluating the effectiveness of family therapies: An integrative review and analysis. *Psychological Bulletin, 101,* 428–442.

Health Canada. (1991). *Schizophrenia: A handbook for families.* Ottawa: Ministry of Supply and Services Canada.

Health Canada. (1998). *The aboriginal headstart on reserve program.* Retrieved December 7, 2000, from www.hc-sc.gc.ca/msb/fnihp/ahs_e.htr.

Health Canada. (2000). *Canadian tobacco use monitoring survey: I. Summary of results.* Ottawa: Author.

Health Canada. (2005). *Canada Health Act.* Retrieved on July 2, 2003, from www.hc-sc.gc.ca/medicare/home.htm.

Health Canada and the Canadian Coalition for High Blood Pressure Prevention and Control. (2000). *National High Blood Pressure Prevention and Control Strategy: Report of the Expert Working Group.* Ottawa: Health Canada.

Healy, D. (2009). Are selective serotonin reuptake inhibitors a risk factor for adolescent suicide? *Canadian Journal of Psychiatry, 54,* 69–71.

Healy, M. (1994, January 8). Science of power and weakness. *Los Angeles Times,* A1, A12.

Heath, K. V., Wood, E., Bally, G., Cornelisse, P. G., & Hogg, R. S. (1999). Experience in treating persons with HIV/AIDS and the legalization of assisted suicide: The views of Canadian physicians. *AIDS Care, 11,* 501–510.

Heatherton, T. F., & Sargent, J. D. (2009). Does watching smoking in movies promote teenage smoking? *Current Directions in Psychological Science, 18,* 63–67.

Hébert, R., Brayne, C., & Spiegelhalter, D. J. (1997). Incidence of functional decline and improvement in a community-dwelling very elderly population. *American Journal of Epidemiology, 145,* 935–944.

Hebert, M., Lavoie, F., Piche, C., & Poitras, M. (2001). Proximate effects of a child sexual abuse prevention program in elementary school children. *Child Abuse and Neglect, 25,* 505–522.

Hebert, M., Parent, N., Daignault, I. V., & Tourigny, M. (2006). A typological analysis of behavioral profiles of sexually abused children. *Child Maltreatment, 11,* 203–216.

Hebert, R. (2003). The big boom: What CIHR's Canadian longitudinal study on aging means to the baby boomer generation and Canada's healthcare system. *Hospital Quarterly (Spring),* 19–20.

Hebert, R., et al. (2003). Efficacy of a psychoeducative group program for caregivers of demented persons living at home: A randomized control trial. *Journals of Gerontology: B. Psychological Sciences and Social Sciences, 58,* S58–S67.

Hébert, R., et al. (2010). Impact of PRISMA, a coordination-type integrated service delivery system for frail older people in Quebec (Canada): A quasi-experimental study. *The Journals of Gerontology, Series B, 65B,* 107–118.

Hébert, R., Durand, P. J., Dubuc, N., Tourigny, A., & The PRISMA Group. (2003). PRISMA: A new model of integrated service delivery for the frail older people in Canada. *International Journal of Integrated Care, 3,* 1–8.

Heckers, S. (2009). Who is at risk for a psychotic disorder. *Schizophrenia Bulletin, 35,* 847–850.

Heilbrun, K., Ogloff, J. R., & Picarello, K. (1999). Dangerous offender statutes in the United States and Canada: Implications for risk assessment. *International Journal of Law and Psychiatry, 22,* 393–415.

Heim, E., Valach, L., & Schaffner, L. (1997). Coping and psychosocial adaptation: Longitudinal effects over time and stages in breast cancer. *Psychosomatic Medicine, 59,* 408–418.

Heiman, J. R., Rowland, D. L., Hatch, J. P., & Gladue, B. A. (1991). Psychophysiological and endocrine responses to sexual arousal in women. *Archives of Sexual Behavior, 20,* 171–186.

Heimberg, R. G. (2009). A new model to facilitate individualized case conceptualization and treatment of social phobia: An examination and reaction to Moscovitch's model. *Cognitive and Behavioral Practice, 16,* 135–141.

Heimberg, R. G., et al. (1998). Cognitive behavioral group therapy vs phenelzine therapy for social phobia: 12-week outcome. *Archives of General Psychiatry, 55,* 1133–1142.

Heinrichs, R. W. (2001). *In search of madness.* New York: Oxford University Press.

Heinrichs, R. W. (2005). The primacy of cognition in schizophrenia. *American Psychologist, 60,* 229–242.

Heinrichs, R. W., & Awad, A. G. (1993). Neuro-cognitive subtypes of chronic schizophrenia. *Schizophrenia Research, 9,* 49–58.

Heinz, A. J., Kassel, J. D., & Sargent, J. D. (2009). Caffeine expectancy: Instrument development in the Rasch measurement framework. *Psychology of Addictive Behaviors, 23,* 500–511.

Heisel, M. J. (2006). Suicide and its prevention among older adults. *Canadian Journal of Psychiatry, 57,* 143–154.

Heisel, M. J., & Duberstein, P. R. (2005). Suicide prevention in older adults. *Clinical Psychology: Science and Practice, 12,* 242–259.

Heisel, M. J., Duberstein, P. R., Talbot, N. L., King, D. A., & Tu, X. M. (2009). Adapting interpersonal psychotherapy for older adults at risk for suicide. *Professional Psychology: Research and Practice, 40,* 156–164.

Heisel, M. J., & Flett, G. L. (2006). The development and initial validation of the Geriatric Suicide Ideation Scale. *American Journal of Geriatric Psychiatry, 14,* 742–757.

Heisel, M. J., & Flett, G. L. (2008). Psychological resilience to suicide ideation among older adults. *Clinical Gerontologist, 31,* 51–70.

Heisel, M. J., Flett, G. L., & Besser, A. (2002). Cognitive functioning and geriatric suicide ideation: Testing a mediational model. *American Journal of Geriatric Psychiatry, 10,* 428–436.

Hemels, M. E. H., Koren, G., & Einarson, T. R. (2002). Increased use of antidepressants in Canada: 1981–2000, *The Annals of Psychotherapy, 36,* 1375–1379.

Hemphill, J. R., Hare, R. D., & Wong, S. (1998). Psychopathy and recidivism: A review. *Legal and Criminological Psychology, 3,* 139–170.

Hendricks, P. S., & Thompson, J. K. (2005). An integration of cognitive-behavioral therapy and interpersonal psychotherapy for bulimia nervosa: A case study using the case formulation method. *International Journal of Eating Disorders, 37,* 171–174.

Henggeler, S. W., Schoenwald, S. D., Borduin, C. M., Rowland, M. D., & Cunningham, P. B. (1998). *Multisystemic treatment of antisocial behavior in children and adolescents.* New York: Guilford Press.

Henriksson, M. M., et al. (1993). Mental disorders and comorbidity in suicide. *American Journal of Psychiatry, 150,* 935–940.

Henry, W. P., Strupp, H. H., Schacht, T. E., & Gaston, L. (1994). Psychodynamic approaches. In A. E. Bergin & S. L. Garfield (Eds.), *Handbook of psychotherapy and behavior change* (4th ed., pp. 467–508). New York: John Wiley & Sons.

Hentschel, F., Kreis, M., Damian, M., Krumm, B., & Frolich, L. (2005). The clinical utility of structural neuroimaging with MRI for diagnosis and differential diagnosis of dementia: A memory clinic study. *International Journal of Geriatric Psychiatry, 20,* 645–650.

Herman, J. L., Perry, J. C., & van der Kolk, B. A. (1989). Childhood trauma in borderline personality disorder. *American Journal of Psychiatry, 146,* 490–495.

Hermans, E. J., Nijenhuis, E. R. S., van Honk, J., Huntjens, R. J. C., & van der Hart, O. (2006). Identity state-dependent attentional bias for facial threat in dissociative identity disorder. *Psychiatry Research, 141,* 233–236.

Hertel, P. T., Brozovich, F., Joormann, J., & Gotlib, I. H. (2008). Biases in interpretation and memory in generalized social phobia. *Journal of Abnormal Psychology, 117,* 278–288.

Hester, R. K., & Miller, W. R. (1989). Self-control training. In R. K. Hester & W. R. Miller (Eds.), *Handbook of alcoholism treatment approaches: Effective alternatives* (pp. 141–149). New York: Pergamon.

Heston, L. L. (1966). Psychiatric disorders in foster home reared children of schizophrenic mothers. *British Journal of Psychiatry, 112,* 819–825.

Hettema, J., Steele, J., & Miller, W. R. (2005). Motivational interviewing. *Annual Review of Clinical Psychology, 1,* 91–111.

Hettema, J. M. (2008). The nosologic relationship between generalized anxiety disorder and major depression. *Depression and Anxiety, 25,* 300–316.

Hettema, J. M., Prescott, C. A., Myers, J. M., Neale, M. C., & Kendler, K. S. (2005). The structure of genetic and environmental risk factors for anxiety disorders in men and women. *Archives of General Psychiatry, 62,* 182–189.

Hewitt, P. L., Caelian, C. F., Flett, G. L., Sherry, S. B., Collins, L., & Flynn, C. A. (2002). Perfectionism in children: Associations with depression, anxiety, and anger. *Personality and Individual Differences, 32,* 1049–1061.

Hewitt, P. L., & Flett, G. L. (1991a). Dimensions of perfectionism in unipolar depression. *Journal of Abnormal Psychology, 100,* 98–101.

Hewitt, P. L., & Flett, G. L. (1991b). Perfectionism in the self and social contexts: Conceptualization, assessment, and association with psychopathology. *Journal of Personality and Social Psychology, 60,* 456–470.

Hewitt, P. L., Flett, G. L., & Ediger, E. (1996). Perfectionism and depression: Longitudinal assessment of a specific vulnerability hypothesis. *Journal of Abnormal Psychology, 105,* 276–280.

Hewitt, P. L., Flett, G. L., Ediger, E., Norton, G. R., & Flynn, C. A. (1998). Perfectionism in chronic and state symptoms of depression. *Canadian Journal of Behavioural Science, 30,* 234–242.

Hewitt, P. L., Flett, G. L., & Mikail, S. (1995). Perfectionism and family adjustment in pain patients and their spouses. *Journal of Family Psychology, 9,* 335–347.

Hewitt, P. L., Flett, G. L., Sherry, S. B., & Caelian, C. F. (2006). Trait perfectionism dimensions and suicide behavior. In T. E. Ellis (Ed.), *Cognition and suicide: Theory, research, and therapy* (pp. 215–235). Washington, DC: American Psychological Association.

Hewitt, P. L., Flett, G. L, Sherry, S. B., et al. (2003). The interpersonal expression of perfection: Perfectionistic self-presentation and psychological distress. *Journal of Personality and Social Psychology, 84,* 1303–1325.

Hickman, E. E., Arnkoff, D. B., Glass, C. R., & Schottenbauer, M. A. (2009). Psychotherapy integration as practiced by experts. *Psychotherapy Theory, Research, Practice, and Training, 46,* 486–491.

Hicks, B. M., DiRago, A. C., Iacono, W. G., & McGue, M. (2009). Gene-environment interplay in internalizing disorders: Consistent findings across six environmental risk factors. *Journal of Child Psychology and Psychiatry, 50,* 1309–1317.

Hightower, J., Smith, M. J., Ward-Hall, C. A., & Hightower, H. C. (1999). Meeting the needs of abused older women? A British Columbia and Yukon transition house survey. *Journal of Elder Abuse and Neglect, 11,* 39–57.

Hilton, N. Z., & Simmons, J. L. (2001). The influence of actuarial risk assessment in clinical judgments and tribunal decisions about mentally disordered offenders in maximum security. *Law and Human Behavior, 25,* 393–408.

Himle, J. A., et al. (2006). Videoconferencing-based cognitive-behavioral therapy for obsessive-compulsive disorder. *Behaviour Research and Therapy, 44,* 1821–1829.

Hingson, R., Heeren, T., Winter, M., & Wechsler, H. (2005). Magnitude of alcohol-related mortality and morbidity among U.S. college students ages 18–24: Changes from 1998 to 2001. *Annual Review of Public Health, 26,* 259–279.

Hirshfeld-Becker, D. R., Micco, J., Henin, A., et al. (2008). Behavioral inhibition. *Depression and Anxiety, 25,* 357–367.

Hobden, K. L., & Cunningham, J. A. (2006). Barriers to the dissemination of four harm reduction strategies: A survey of addiction treatment providers in Ontario. *Harm Reduction Journal, 3,* 35–54.

Hobfoll, S. E., et al. (1991). War-related stress: Addressing the stress of war and other traumatic events. *American Psychologist, 46,* 848–855.

Hobson, R. P., & Lee, A. (1998). Hello and goodbye: A study of social engagement in autism. *Journal of Autism and Developmental Disorders, 28,* 117–127.

Hodapp, R. M., & Dykens, E. M. (2005). Measuring behavior in genetic disorders of mental retardation. *Mental Retardation and Developmental Disabilities Research Reviews, 11,* 340–346.

Hoddinott, J., Lethbridge, L., & Phipps, S. (2002). *Is history destiny? Resources, transitions and child education attainments in Canada.* Ottawa: Government of Canada.

Hodgins, D. C., Currie, S. R., el-Guebaly, N., & Peden, N. (2004). Brief motivational treatment for problem gambling: 24 month follow-up. *Psychology of Addictive Behaviors, 18,* 293–296.

Hoebel, B. G., & Teitelbaum, P. (1966). Weight regulation in normal and hypothalamic hyperphagic rats. *Journal of Comparative and Physiological Psychology, 61,* 189–193.

Hofmann, S. G. (2008). Cognitive processes during fear acquisition and extinction in animals and humans: Implication for exposure therapy of anxiety disorders. *Clinical Psychology Review, 28,* 199–210.

Hofmann, S. G., & **Asmundson, G. J. G.** (2008). Acceptance and mindfulness-based therapy: New wave or old hat? *Clinical Psychology Review, 28,* 1–16.

Hofmann, S. G., Newman, M. G., Ehlerr, A., & Roth, W. (1995). Psychophysiological differences between subgroups of social phobia. *Journal of Abnormal Psychology, 104,* 224–231.

Hogarty, G. E. (1993). Prevention of relapse in chronic schizophrenic patients. *Journal of Clinical Psychiatry, 54,* 18–23.

Hogarty, G. E., et al. (2004). Cognitive enhancement therapy for schizophrenia: Effects of a 2-year randomized trial on cognition and behavior. *Archives of General Psychiatry, 61,* 866–876.

Hogarty, G. E., et al. (1994). Pharmacotherapy of impaired affect in recovering schizophrenic patients. *Archives of General Psychiatry, 52,* 29–41.

Hoglend, P., Bogwald, K.-P., Amlo, S., et al. (2008). Transference interpretations in dynamic psychotherapy: Do they really yield sustained effects? *American Journal of Psychiatry, 165,* 763–771.

Hojnoski, R. L., Morrison, R., Brown, M., & Matthews, W. J. (2006). Projective test use among school psychologists. *Journal of Psychoeducational Assessment, 24,* 145–159.

Holahan, C. K., & Holahan, C. J. (1987). Life stress, hassles, and self-efficacy in aging: A replication and extension. *Journal of Applied Social Psychology, 17,* 574–592.

Holden, R. R. (1999). The Holden Psychological Screening Inventory and sexual efficacy in urological patients with erectile dysfunction. *Psychological Reports, 84,* 255–258.

Hollander, E., Braun, A., & Simeon, D. (2008). Should OCD leave the anxiety disorders in DSM-V? The case for obsessive compulsive-related disorders. *Depression and Anxiety, 25,* 317–329.

Hollander, E., Phillips, A., Chaplin, W., et al. (2005). A placebo controlled crossover trial of liquid fluoxetine on repetitive behaviors in childhood and adolescent autism. *Neuropsychopharmacology, 30,* 582–589.

Hollander, M. J., & Chappell, N. L. (2007). A comparative analysis of costs to government for home care and long term residential care service, standardized for client care needs. *Canadian Journal on Aging, 26,* 149–161.

Hollander, M. J., et al. (2009). Increasing value for money in the Canadian healthcare system: New findings and the case for integrated health care for seniors. *Healthcare Quarterly, 12,* 38–47.

Hollingshead, A. B., & Redlich, F. C. (1958). *Social class and mental illness: A community study.* New York: John Wiley & Sons.

Hollon, S. D., DeRubeis, R. J., & Evans, M. D. (1996). Cognitive therapy in the treatment and prevention of depression. In P. M. Salkovskis (Ed.), *Frontiers of cognitive therapy* (pp. 293–317). New York: Guilford.

Hollon, S. D., DeRubeis, R. J., & Seligman, M. E. P. (1992). Cognitive therapy and the prevention of depression. *Applied and Preventive Psychology, 1,* 89–95.

Hollon, S. D., Stewart, M. O., & Strunk, D. (2006). Enduring effects for cognitive behavior therapy in the treatment of depression and anxiety. *Annual Review of Psychology, 57,* 285–315.

Holmes, T. H., & Rahe, R. H. (1967). The social readjustment rating scale. *Journal of Psychosomatic Research, 11,* 213–218.

Holmes, T. S., & Holmes, T. H. (1970). Short-term intrusions into the life style routine. *Journal of Psychosomatic Research, 14,* 121–132.

Holowaty, P., Feldman, L., Harvey, B., & Shortt, L. (2000). Cigarette smoking in multicultural, urban high school students. *Journal of Adolescent Health, 27,* 281–288.

Hooley, J. M., & Teasdale, J. D. (1989). Predictors of relapse in unipolar depressives: Expressed emotion, marital distress, and perceived criticism. *Journal of Abnormal Psychology, 98,* 229–235.

Hoon, E. F., & Hoon, P. W. (1978). Styles of sexual expression in women: Clinical implications of multivariate analyses. *Archives of Sexual Behavior, 7,* 105–116.

Hope, D. A., Heimberg, R. G., & Bruch, M. A. (1995). Dismantling cognitive-behavioral group therapy for social phobia. *Behaviour Research and Therapy, 33,* 637–650.

Hopwood, C. J., et al. (2009). The stability of personality traits in individuals with borderline personality disorder. *Journal of Abnormal Psychology, 118,* 806–815.

Horgas, H. L., Wahl, H. W., & Baltes, N. M. (1996). Dependency in late life. In L. L. Carstensen, B. A. Edelstein, & L. Dornbrand (Eds.), *The practical handbook of clinical gerontology* (pp. 54–75). Thousand Oaks, CA: Sage.

Horowitz, J. L., & Garber, J. (2006). The prevention of depressive symptoms in children and adolescents: A meta-analytic review. *Journal of Consulting and Clinical Psychology, 74,* 401–415.

Horowitz, M. J. (1990). Psychotherapy. In A. S. Bellack & M. Hersen (Eds.), *Handbook of comparative treatments for adult disorders* (pp. 289–301). New York: John Wiley & Sons.

Horvath, A. O. (2000). The therapeutic relationship: From transference to alliance. *Journal of Clinical Psychology/In Session: Psychotherapy in Practice, 56,* 163–173.

Horvath, A. O. (2001). The alliance. *Psychotherapy, 38,* 365–372.

Horvath, A. O. (2006). The alliance in context: Accomplishments, challenges, and future directions. *Psychotherapy: Theory, Research, Practice, Training, 43,* 258–263.

Horvath, A. O., & Greenberg, L. (1989). Development and validation of the Working Alliance Inventory. *Journal of Counseling Psychology, 36,* 223–233.

Horvarth, A. O., & Greenberg, L. (Eds.). (1994). *The working alliance: Theory, research, and practice.* New York: John Wiley & Sons.

Hoven, C. W., Duarte, C. S., Lucas, C. P., et al. (2002). *Effects of the World Trade Center attack on NYC public school students—Initial report to the New York City Board of Education.* New York: Columbia University Mailman School of Public Health, New York State Psychiatric Institute and Applied Research and Consulting.

Howard, M. O., & Jenson, J. M. (1999). Inhalant abuse among antisocial youth. *Addictive Behaviors, 24,* 59–74.

Howes, J. L., & Vallis, T. M. (1996). Cognitive therapy with nontraditional populations: Application to post-traumatic stress disorder and personality disorders. In K. S. Dobson & K. D. Craig (Eds.), *Advances in cognitive-behavioral therapy* (pp. 237–272). Thousand Oaks, CA: Sage.

Howitt, D. (1995). Pornography and the paedophile: Is it criminogenic? *British Journal of Medical Psychology, 68,* 15–27.

Howlett, M. (2008, August 23). One year later—the Mental Health Commission of Canada. Presented to the Canadian Mental Health Association National Conference, Dartmouth, Nova Scotia, August 23, 2008.

Hoza, B., Waschbusch, D. A., Pelham, W. E., Molina, B. S. G., & Milich, R. (2000). Attention-deficit/hyperactivity disordered and control boys' responses to social success and failure. *Child Development, 71,* 432–446.

Hser, Y., Anglin, M. D., & Powers, K. (1993). A 24-year follow-up of California narcotics addicts. *Archives of General Psychiatry, 50,* 577–584.

Hsiung, G.-Y. R., Sadovnik, A. D., & Feldman, H. (2004). Apolipoprotein E 4 genotype as a risk factor for cognitive decline and dementia: Data from the Canadian Study of Health and Aging. *Canadian Medical Association Journal, 171,* 863–866.

Hsu, L. K. G. (1990). *Eating disorders.* New York: Guilford.

Huang, J.-H., & Boyer, R. (2007). Epidemiology of youth gambling problems in Canada: A national prevalence study. *Canadian Journal of Psychiatry, 52,* 657–665.

Hubbard, R. E., Searle, S. D., Mitnitski, A., Rockwood, K. (2009). Effects of smoking on the accumulation of deficits, frailty, and survival in older adults: A secondary analysis from the Canadian Study of Health and Aging. *The Journal of Nutrition, Health, and Aging, 13,* 468–472.

Hubbs-Tait, L., Culp, A. M., Culp, R. E., & Miller, C. E. (2002). Relation of maternal cognitive stimulation, emotional support, and intrusive behavior during Head Start to children's kindergarten cognitive abilities. *Child Development, 73,* 110–131.

Hubley, A. M., & Russell, L. B. (2009). Prediction of subjective age, desired age, and age satisfaction in older adults: Do some health dimensions contribute more than others? *International Journal of Behavioral Development, 33,* 12–21.

Hudson, J. I., Hiripi, E., Pope, H. G., Jr., & Kessler, R. C. (2007). The prevalence and correlates of eating disorders in the National Comorbidity Survey replication. *Biological Psychiatry, 61,* 348–358.

Hudson, S. M., & Ward, T. (1997). Rape: Psychopathology and theory. In D. R. Laws & W. O'Donohue (Eds.), *Sexual deviance* (pp. 332–355). New York: Guilford Press.

Huey, S. J., Jr., Henggler, S. W., Brondino, M. J., & Pickrel, S. G. (2000). Mechanisms of change in multisystemic therapy: Reducing delinquent behavior through therapist adherence and improved family and peer functioning. *Journal of Consulting and Clinical Psychology, 68,* 451–467.

Hughes, C. & Agran, M. (1993). Teaching persons with severe disabilities to use self-instruction in community settings: An analysis of applications. *The Journal of the Association for Persons with Severe Handicaps, 18,* 261–274.

Hughes, C., Hugo, K., & Blatt, J. (1996). Self-instructional intervention for teaching generalized problem-solving within a functional task sequence. *American Journal on Mental Retardation, 100,* 565–579.

Hughes, J. R., & Hatsukami, D. K. (1992). The nicotine withdrawal syndrome: A brief review and update. *International Journal of Smoking Cessation, 1,* 21–26.

Hughes, J. R., et al. (1991). Caffeine self-adminstration, withdrawal, and adverse effects among coffee drinkers. *Archives of General Psychiatry, 48,* 611–617.

Hultsch, D. F., Hertzog, C., Small, B. J., & Dixon, R. A. (1999). Use it or lose it: Engaged lifestyle as a buffer of cognitive decline in aging? *Psychology and Aging, 14,* 245–263.

Human Resources Development Canada and Statistics Canada (1996). *Growing up in Canada: National Longitudinal Survey of Children and Youth.* Ottawa: Statistics Canada.

Humphrey, L. L. (1986). Family relations in bulimic-anorexic and nondistressed families. *International Journal of Eating Disorders, 5,* 223–232.

Hunsley, J., Aubry, T. D., Vestervelt, C. M., & Vito, D. (1999). Comparing therapist and client perspectives on reasons for psychotherapy termination. *Psychotherapy, 36,* 380–388.

Hunsley, J., & Bailey, J. M. (2001). Whither the Rorschach: An analysis of the evidence. *Psychological Assessment, 13,* 472-485.

Hunsley, J., Dobson, K. S., Johnston, C., & Mikail, S. F. (1999). Empirically supported treatments in psychology: Implications for Canadian professional psychology. *Canadian Psychology, 40,* 239–302.

Hunsley, J., & Johnston, C. (2000). The role of empirically supported treatments in evidence-based psychological practice: A Canadian perspective. *Clinical Psychology: Science and Practice, 7,* 269–275.

Hunsley, J., & Lee, C. M. (2007). Research-informed benchmarks for psychological treatments: Efficacy studies, effectiveness studies, and beyond. *Professional Psychology: Research and Practice, 38,* 21–33.

Hunsley, J., Lee, C. M., & Aubry, T. (1999). Who uses psychological services in Canada? *Canadian Psychology, 40,* 232–240.

Hunsley, J., & Lefebvre, M. (1990). A survey of the practices and activities of Canadian clinical psychologists. *Canadian Psychology, 31,* 350–358.

Hunsley, J., & Rumstein-McKean, O. (1999). Improving psychotherapeutic services via randomized clinical trials, treatment manuals, and component analysis designs. *Journal of Clinical Psychology, 55,* 1507–1517.

Huntjens, R. J. C., et al. (2007). Memory transfer for emotionally valenced words between identities in dissociative identity disorder. *Behaviour Research and Therapy, 45,* 775–789.

Huntington's Disease Collaborative Research Group. (1993). A novel gene containing a trinucleotide repeat that is expanded and unstable on Huntington's disease chromosomes. *Cell, 72,* 971–983.

Hurd, H. (1916–1917). *The institutional care of the insane in the United States and Canada, vols. I and IV.* Baltimore: The Johns Hopkins Press. (Reprint Edition, 1973. New York: Arno Press.)

Hurlburt, R. T. (1997). Randomly sampling thinking in the natural environment. *Journal of Consulting and Clinical Psychology, 65,* 941–949.

Hurt, R. D., Sachs, D. P. L., & Glover, E. D. (1997). A comparison of sustained release buprioprion versus placebo for treatment of nicotine

dependence. *New England Journal of Medicine, 337,* 1195–1202.

Hwang, W.-C. (2006). Adapting psychotherapy to better meet the needs of ethnic minorities. *American Psychologist, 61,* 702–715.

Hwang, W.-C., Myers, H., Abe-Kim, J., & Ting, J. Y. (2008). A conceptual paradigm for understanding culture's impact on mental health: The cultural influences on mental health (CIMH) model. *Clinical Psychology Review, 28,* 211–227.

Iacoviello, B. M., Alloy, L. B., Abramson, L. Y., Whitehouse, W. G., & Hogan, M. E. (2006). The course of depression in individuals at high and low cognitive risk for depression: A prospective study. *Journal of Affective Disorders, 93,* 61–69.

Imber, S. D., et al. (1990). Mode-specific effects among three treatments for depression. *Journal of Consulting and Clinical Psychology, 58,* 352–359.

Imperato-McGinley, J., Guerrero, L., Gautier, T., & Peterson, R. E. (1974). Steroid 5a-reductase deficiency in man: An inherited form of pseudohermaphroditism. *Science, 186,* 1213–1215.

Ingram, R. E., & Siegle, G. J. (2001). Cognition and clinical science: From revolution to evolution. In K. S. Dobson (Ed.), *Handbook of cognitive-behavioral therapies* (2nd ed., pp. 111–138). New York: Guilford Press.

Inouye, S. K., et al. (1999). A multicomponent intervention to prevent delirium in hospitalized older patients. *New England Journal of Medicine, 340,* 669–676.

Institute of Medicine. (1990a). Matching. In *Broadening the base of treatment for alcohol problems* (pp. 279–302). Washington, DC: National Academy Press.

Institute of Medicine. (1990b). *Treating drug problems.* Washington, DC: National Academy Press.

International Society for the Study of Dissociation (ISSD). (2004). Guidelines for the evaluation and treatment of dissociative symptoms in children and adolescents. *Journal of Trauma & Dissociation, 5,* 119–150.

Irwin, M., et al. (1985). Psychotic patients' understanding of informed consent. *American Journal of Psychiatry, 142,* 1351–1354.

Irvine, J., & Ritvo, P. (1998). Health risk behaviour change and adaptation in cardiac patients. *Clinical Psychology and Psychotherapy, 5,* 86–101.

Irving, L., et al. (2004). The relationships between hope and outcomes at the pretreatment, beginning, and later phases of psychotherapy. *Journal of Psychotherapy Integration, 14,* 419–433.

Isaac, M., Elias, B., Katz, L.Y., et al. (2009). Gatekeeper training as a preventative intervention for suicide: A systematic review. *Canadian Journal of Psychiatry, 54,* 260–268.

Ivanoff, A., Jang, S. J., Smyth, N. J., & Linehan, M. M. (1994). Fewer reasons for staying alive when you are thinking of killing yourself: The Brief Reasons for Living Inventory. *Journal of Psychopathology and Behavioral Assessment, 16,* 1–13.

Iversen, L. (2003). Cannabis and the brain. *Brain, 126,* 1252–1270.

Ivey, A. E., Ivey, M. B., & Simek-Morgan, L. (1997). *Counseling and psychotherapy: A multicultural perspective.* Needham Heights, MA: Allyn and Bacon.

Izgic, F., Akyuz, G., Dogan, O., & Kugu, N. (2004). Social phobia among university students and its relation to self-esteem and body image. *Canadian Journal of Psychiatry, 49,* 630–634.

Jablensky, A., Sartorius, N., Cooper, J. E., Anker, A., Korten, A., & Bertelson, A. (1994). Culture and schizophrenia. *British Journal of Psychiatry, 165,* 434–436.

Jack, D. C. (1999). Silencing the self: Inner dialogues and outer realities. In T. Joiner & J. C. Coyne (Eds.), *The interactional nature of depression.* Washington, DC: American Psychological Association.

Jackson, C. (1997). Testing a multi-stage model for the adoption of alcohol and tobacco behaviors by children. *Addictive Behaviors, 22,* 1–14.

Jackson, R. W., Treiber, F. A., Turner, J. R., Davis, H., & Strong, W. B. (1999). Effects of race, sex, and socioeconomic status upon cardiovascular stress responsivity and recovery in youth. *International Journal of Psychophysiology, 31,* 111–119.

Jacob, R. G., et al. (1999). Ambulatory blood pressure responses and the circumplex model of mood: A 4-day study. *Psychosomatic Medicine, 61,* 319–333.

Jacob, T., Tennenbaum, D., Seilhammer, R. A., Bargiel, K., & Sharon, T. (1994). Reactivity effects during naturalistic observation of distressed and nondistressed families. *Journal of Family Psychology, 8,* 354–363.

Jacobs, P., Yim, R., Ohinmaa, A., Eng, K., et al. (2008). Expenditures on mental health and addictions for Canadian provinces in 2003/04. *Canadian Journal of Psychiatry, 53,* 306–313.

Jacobs, R. H., Reinecke, M. A., Gollan, J. K., & Kane, P. (2008). Empirical evidence of cognitive vulnerability for depression among children and adolescents: A cognitive science and developmental perspective. *Clinical Psychology Review, 28,* 759–782.

Jacobson, N. S., & Addis, M. E. (1993). Research on couples and couple therapy: What do we know? Where are we going? *Journal of Consulting and Clinical Psychology, 61,* 85–93.

Jacobson, N. S., & Margolin, G. (1979). *Marital therapy: Strategies based on social learning.* New York: Brunner/Mazel.

Jacques, C., Ladouceur, R., & Ferland, F. (2000). Impact of availability on gambling: A longitudinal study. *Canadian Journal of Psychiatry, 45,* 810–815.

Jadoulle, V., et al. (2006). Coping and adaptation to breast cancer: A six-month prospective study. *Cancer Bulletin, 93,* 10067–10072.

Jaffe, J. H. (1985). Drug addiction and drug abuse. In *Goodman and Gilman's the pharmacological basis of therapeutic behavior.* New York: Macmillan.

Jandorf, L., Deblinger, E., Neale, J. M., & Stone, A. A. (1986). Daily vs. major life events as predictors of symptom frequency. *Journal of General Psychology, 113,* 205–218.

Janeck, A. S., Calamari, J. E., Riemann, B. C., & Heffelfinger, S. K. (2003). Too much thinking about thinking? Metacognitive differences in obsessive-compulsive disorder. *Anxiety Disorders, 17,* 181–195.

Jang, K. L., Livesley, W. J., & Vernon, P. A. (1996). Heritability of the big five personality dimensions and their facets: A twin study. *Journal of Personality, 64,* 577–591.

Jang, K. L., Vernon, P. A., & Livesley, W. J. (2001). Perspectives on the genetics of personality function. *Canadian Journal of Psychiatry, 46,* 234–244.

Jang, K. L., Vernon, P. A., & Livesley, W. J. (2000). Personality disorder traits, family environment, and alcohol misuse: A multivariate behavioural genetic analysis. *Addiction, 95,* 873–888.

Janicak, P. G., Davis, J. M., Preskorn, S. H., & Ayd, F. J. (1993). *Principles and practice of psychopharmacological therapy.* Baltimore: Williams & Wilkins.

Janoff-Bulman, R. (1992). *Shattered assumptions: Toward a new psychology of trauma.* New York: Free Press.

Janowitz, D., Grabe, H. J., Ruhrmann, S., et al. (2009). Early onset of obsessive-compulsive disorder and associated comorbidity. *Depression and Anxiety, 26,* 1012–1017.

Jansen, M. A., Glynn, T., & Howard, J. (1996). Prevention of alcohol, tobacco and other drug abuse. *American Behavioral Scientist, 39,* 790–807.

Jarrell, M. P., Johnson, W.G., & Williamson, D. A. (1986). *Insulin and glucose response in the binge purge episode of bulimic women.* Paper presented at the annual convention of the Association for Advancement of Behavior Therapy, Chicago.

Jarrett, M. A., & Ollendick, T. H. (2008). A conceptual review of the comorbidity of attention-deficit/hyperactivity disorder and anxiety: Implications for future research and practice. *Clinical Psychology Review, 28,* 1266–1280.

Jellinek, E. M. (1952). Phases of alcohol addiction. *Quarterly Journal of Studies on Alcohol, 13,* 673–684.

Jenike, M. A. (1986). Theories of etiology. In M. A. Jenike, L. Baer, & W. E. Minichiello (Eds.), *Obsessive-compulsive disorders.* Littleton, MA: PSG Publishing.

Jenike, M. A. (1990). Psychotherapy. In A. S. Bellack & M. Hersen (Eds.), *Handbook of comparative treatments for adult disorders* (pp. 245–255). New York: John Wiley & Sons.

Jenike, M. A. (2004). Obsessive-compulsive disorder. *The New England Journal of Medicine, 350,* 259–265.

Jenike, M. A., Baer, L., & Minichiello, W. E. (1986). *Obsessive-compulsive disorders: Theory and management.* Littleton, MA: PSG Publishing.

Jenkins, C. D. (1976). Recent evidence supporting psychologic and social risk factors for coronary disease. *New England Journal of Medicine, 294,* 1033–1038.

Jenn, H.-S., Dunkle, R., & Roberts, B. L. (2006). Worries of the oldest old. *Health and Social Work, 31,* 256–265.

Jespersen, A. F., Lalumière, M. L., & Seto, M. C. (2009). Sexual abuse history among adult sex offenders and non-sex offenders. *Child Abuse and Neglect, 33,* 179–192.

Johnson, J., Horvath, E., & Weissman, M. M. (1991). The validity of depression with psychotic features based on a community study. *Archives of General Psychiatry, 48,* 1075–1081.

Johnson, S. M. (2000). Emotionally focused couples therapy. In F. M. Dattilio & L. J. Bevilacqua (Eds.), *Comparative treatments for relationship dysfunction: Springer series on comparative treatments for psychological disorders* (pp. 163–185). New York: Springer.

Johnson, S. M. (2002). *Emotionally focused couple therapy with trauma survivors: Strengthening attachment bonds.* New York: Guilford.

Johnson, S. M. (2007). The contribution of emotionally focused couples therapy. *Journal of Contemporary Psychotherapy, 37,* 47–52.

Johnson, S. M., & Greenberg, L. S. (1987). Emotionally focused marital therapy: An overview. *Psychotherapy, 24,* 552–560.

Johnson, S.M., & Greenberg, L. S. (1995). The emotionally focused approach to problems in adult attachment. In N. S. Jacobson & A. S. Gurman (Eds.), *The clinical handbook of marital therapy* (2nd ed., pp. 3-26). New York : Guilford Press.

Johnson, S. M., Hunsley, J., Greenberg, L., & Schlinder, D. (1999). Emotionally focused couples therapy: Status and challenges. *Clinical Psychology: Science and Practice, 6,* 67–79.

Johnson, S. M., & LeBow, J. (2000). The "coming of age" of couple therapy: A decade review. *Journal of Marital and Family Therapy, 26,* 23–38.

Johnson, S. M., & Whiffen, V. (2003). *Attachment processes in couples and families.* New York: Guilford.

Joiner, T. E., Alfano, M. S., & Metalsky, G. I. (1992). When depression breeds contempt: Reassurance seeking, self-esteem, and rejection of depressed college students by their roommates. *Journal of Abnormal Psychology, 101,* 165–173.

Joiner, T. E., & Schmidt, N. B. (1998). Excessive reassurance-seeking predicts depressive but not anxious reactions to acute stress. *Journal of Abnormal Psychology, 107,* 533–537.

Jones, J. M., Huggins, M. A., Rydall, A. C., & Rodin, G. M. (2003). Symptomatic distress, hopelessness, and the desire for hastened death in hospitalized cancer patients. *Journal of Psychosomatic Research, 55,* 411–418.

Jones, P. B., Barnes, T. D., Davies, L., et al. (2006). Randomized controlled trial of effect on quality of life of second- vs. first-generation antipsychotic drugs in schizophrenia. Cost Utility of the Latest Antipsychotic Drugs in Schizophrenia Study (CUtLASS 1). *Archives of General Psychiatry, 63,* 1079–1087.

Jonsson, H., & Hougaard, E. (2008). Group cognitive behavioural therapy for obsessive-compulsive disorder: A systematic review and meta-analysis. *Acta Psychiatrica Scandinavica, 119,* 98–106.

Jorenby, D. E., et al. (1999). A controlled trial of sustained-release buprorion, a nicotine patch, or both for smoking cessation. *New England Journal of Medicine, 340,* 685–691.

Jose, A., & Goldfried, M. (2008). A transtheoretical approach to case formulation. *Cognitive and Behavioral Practice, 15,* 212–222.

Joukamaa, M., et al. (2006). Schizophrenia, neuroleptic medication, and mortality. *British Journal of Psychiatry, 188,* 122–127.

Jovanovic, T., Blanding, N. Q., Norrholm, S. D., et al. (2009). Childhood abuse is associated with increased startle reactivity in adulthood. *Depression and Anxiety, 26,* 1018–1026.

Joyal, C. C., et al. (2007). Violent persons with schizophrenia and comorbid disorders: A functional magnetic resonance imaging study. *Schizophrenia Research, 91,* 97–102.

Joyce, A. S., Ogrodniczuk, J. S., Piper, W. E., & McCallum, M. (2003). The alliance as mediator of expectancy effects in short-term individual therapy. *Journal of Consulting and Clinical Psychology, 71,* 672–679.

Joyce, A. S., Ogrodniczuk, J. S., Piper, W. E., & Sheptycki, A. R. (2010). Interpersonal predictors of outcome following short-term group therapy for complicated grief: A replication. *Clinical Psychology and Psychotherapy, 17,* 122–135.

Judd, L. L., et al. (1998). A prospective 12-year study of subsyndromal and syndromal depressive symptoms in unipolar major depressive disorders. *Archives of General Psychiatry, 55,* 694–701.

Judd, L. L. (1997). The clinical course of unipolar depressive disorders. *Archives of General Psychiatry, 54,* 989–992.

Jung, H.H, et al. (2006). Bilateral anterior cingulotomy for refractory obsessive-compulsive disorder: Long-term follow-up results. *Stereotactic and Functional Neurosurgery, 84,* 184–189.

Junginger, J., Barker, S., & Coe, D. (1992). Mood theme and bizarreness of delusions in schizophrenia and mood psychosis. *Journal of Abnormal Psychology, 101,* 287–292.

Just, N., & Alloy, L. B. (1997). The response styles theory of depression: Tests and an extension of the theory. *Journal of Abnormal Psychology, 106,* 221–229.

Juurlink, D. N., Herrmann, N., Szalai, J. P., Kopp, A., & Redelmeier, D. A. (2004). Medical illness and risk of suicide in the elderly. *Archives of Internal Medicine, 164,* 1179–1184.

Kafka, M. P. (2010). Hypersexual disorder: A proposed diagnosis for DSM-V. *Archives of Sexual Behavior, 39,* 377–400.

Kain, K. (1994). *Movement never lies: An autobiography.* Toronto: McClelland and Stewart.

Kalichman, S. C. (1991). Psychopathology and personality characteristics of criminal sexual offenders as a function of victim age. *Archives of Sexual Behavior, 20,* 187–198.

Kairouz, S., Gliksman, L., Demers, A. & Adlaf, E.M. (2002). For all these reasons, I do drink: A multilevel analysis of contextual reasons for drinking among Canadian undergraduates. *Journal of Studies on Alcohol, 63,* 600–608.

Kairouz, S. & Adlaf, E. M. (2003). Schools, students and heavy drinking: A multilevel analysis. *Addiction Research and Theory, 11,* 427–439.

Kamarck, T. W., Annunziato, B., & Amateau, L. M. (1995). Affiliations moderate the effects of social threat on stress-related cardiovascular responses: Boundary conditions for a laboratory model of social support. *Psychosomatic Medicine, 57,* 183–194.

Kamarck, T. W., et al. (1992). Reliable measures of behaviorally-evoked cardiovascular reactivity from a PC-based test battery: Results from student and community samples. *Psychophysiology, 29,* 17–28.

Kamarck, T. W., et al. (1998). Effects of task strain, social conflict, and emotional activation on ambulatory cardiovascular activity: Daily life consequences of recurring stress in a multiethnic adult sample. *Health Psychology, 17,* 17–29.

Kandel, D. B., Davies, M., Karus, D., & Yamaguchi, K. (1986). The consequences in young adulthood of adolescent drug involvement. *Archives of General Psychiatry, 43,* 746–754.

Kane, R. A., & Kane, R. L. (1985). Feasibility of universal long-term-care benefits: Ideas from Canada. *New England Journal of Medicine, 312,* 1357–1364.

Kanfer, F. H., & Phillips, J. S. (1970). *Learning foundations of behavior therapy.* New York: John Wiley & Sons.

Kanner, A. D., Coyne, J. C., Schaefer, C., & Lazarus, R. S. (1981). Comparison of two modes of stress measurement: Daily hassles and uplifts versus major life events. *Journal of Behavioral Medicine, 4,* 1–39.

Kanner, L. (1943). Autistic disturbances of affective contact. *Nervous Child, 2,* 217–250.

Kanner, L. (1973). *Childhood psychosis: Initial studies and new insights.* Washington, DC: V. H. Winston and Sons.

Kanner, L., & Eisenberg, L. (1955). Notes on the follow-up studies of autistic children. In P. Hoch & J. Zubin (Eds.), *Psychopathology of childhood.* New York: Grune & Stratton.

Kantorovich, N. V. (1930). An attempt at associative-reflex therapy in alcoholism. *Psychological Abstracts, 4,* 493.

Kaplan, H. I., & Sadock, B. J. (1991). *Synopsis of psychiatry: Behavioral sciences, clinical psychiatry.* Baltimore: Williams & Williams.

Kaplan, H. S. (1997). Sexual desire disorders (hypoactive sexual desire and sexual aversion). In G. O. Gabbard & S. D. Atkinson (Eds.), *Synopsis of treatments of psychiatric disorders* (2nd ed., pp. 771–780). Washington, DC: American Psychiatric Press.

Kaplan, M. S., & Kreuger, R. B. (1997). Voyeurism: Psychopathology and theory. In D. R. Laws & W. O'Donohue (Eds.), *Sexual deviance* (297–310). New York: Guilford Press.

Kaplow, J. B., & Widom, C. S. (2007). Age of onset of child maltreatment predicts long-term mental health outcomes. *Journal of Abnormal Psychology, 116,* 176–187.

Kapur, S. (2003). Psychosis as a state of aberrant salience: A framework linking biology, phenomenology, and pharmacology in schizophrenia. *American Journal of Psychiatry, 160,* 13–23.

Kapur, S., Zipursky, R., Jones, C., Remington, G., & Houle, S. (2000). Relationship between dopamine D2 occupancy, clinical response, and side effects: A double-blind PET study of first-episode schizophrenia. *American Journal of Psychiatry, 157,* 514–520.

Karpenko, V., Owens, J. S., Evangelista, N. M., & Dodds, C. (2009). Clinically significant symptom change in children with attention deficit/hyperactivity disorder: Does it correspond with reliable improvement in functioning? *Journal of Clinical Psychology, 65,* 76–93.

Kashani, J. H., & Carlson, G. A. (1987). Seriously depressed preschoolers. *American Journal of Psychiatry, 144,* 348–350.

Kasl-Godley, J., & Gatz, M. (2000). Psychosocial interventions for individuals with dementia:

An integration of theory, therapy, and a clinical understanding of dementia. *Clinical Psychology Review, 20,* 755–782.

Kaslow, N. J., & Thompson, M. P. (1998). Applying the criteria for empirically supported treatments to studies of psychosocial interventions for child and adolescent depression. *Journal of Clinical Child Psychology, 27,* 146–155.

Katz, J., Ritvo, P., Irvine, M. J., & Jackson, M. (1996). Coping with chronic pain. In M. Zeidner & N. S. Endler (Eds.), *Handbook of coping: Theory, research, and applications* (pp. 252–278). New York: John Wiley & Sons.

Katz, L. Y., Kozyrskyj, A. L., Prior, H. J., et al. (2008). Effect of regulatory warnings on antidepressant prescription rates, use of health services and outcomes among children, adolescents and young adults. *Canadian Medical Association Journal, 178,* 1005–1011.

Katzman, D. K. (2005). Medical complications in adolescents with anorexia nervosa. *International Journal of Eating Disorders, 37,* 552–559.

Kauer-Sant'Anna, M., Frey, B. N., Andreazza, A. C., et al. (2007). Anxiety comorbidity and quality of life in bipolar disorder patients. *Canadian Journal of Psychiatry, 52,* 175–181.

Kaufman, J., Yang, B., Douglas-Palumberi, H., et al. (2006). Brain-derived neurotrophic factor 5-HTTLPR gene interactions and environmental modifiers of depression in children. *Biological Psychiatry, 59,* 673–680.

Kaufman, N. K., Rohde, P., Seeley, J. R., Clarke, G. N., & Stice, E. (2005) Potential mediators of cognitive-behavioral therapy for adolescents with comorbid major depression and conduct disorder. *Journal of Consulting and Clinical Psychology, 73,* 38–46.

Kavale, K. A. (2002). Mainstreaming to full inclusion: From orthogenesis to pathogenesis of an idea. *International Journal of Disability, Development, and Education, 49,* 201–214.

Kavale, K. A., & Forness, S. R. (1999). Effectiveness of special education. In C. R. Reynolds & T. B. Gutkin (Eds.), *The handbook of school psychology* (3rd ed., pp. 984–1024). New York: John Wiley & Sons.

Kawachi, I., Colditz, G. A., Ascherio, A., Rimm, E. B., Giovannucci, E., et al. (1994). Prospective study of phobic anxiety and risk of coronary heart disease in men. *Circulation, 89,* 1992–1997.

Kazdin, A. E. (1985). *Treatment of antisocial behavior in children and adolescents.* Homewood, IL: Dorsey Press.

Kazdin, A. E. (2008). Evidence-based treatment and practice: New opportunities to bridge clinical research and practice, enhance the knowledge base, and improve patient care. *American Psychologist, 63,* 146–159.

Kazdin, A. E., & Weisz, J. R. (1998). Identifying and developing empirically supported child and adolescent treatments. *Journal of Consulting and Clinical Psychology, 66,* 19–36.

Kazdin, A. E., & Whitley, M. K. (2006). Comorbidity, case complexity, and effects of evidence-based treatment for children referred for disruptive behavior. *Journal of Consulting and Clinical Psychology, 74,* 455–467.

Keane, T. M., Fairbank, J. A., Caddell, J. M., & Zimering, R. T. (1989). Implosive (flood-

ing) therapy reduces symptoms of PTSD in Vietnam combat veterans. *Behavior Therapy, 20,* 245–260.

Keane, T. M., Fisher, L. M., Krinsley, K. E., & Niles, B. L. (1994). Posttraumatic stress disorder. In M. Hersen & R. T. Ammerman (Eds.), *Handbook of prescriptive treatments for adults* (pp. 237–260). New York: Plenum.

Keane, T. M., Gerardi, R. J., Quinn, S. J., & Litz, B. T. (1992). Behavioral treatment of post-traumatic stress disorder. In S. M. Turner, K. S. Calhoun, & H. E. Adams (Eds.), *Handbook of clinical behavior therapy* (2nd ed., pp. 87–97). New York: John Wiley & Sons.

Keane, T. M., & Wolfe, J. (1990). Co-morbidity in post-traumatic stress disorder: An analysis of community and clinical studies. *Journal of Applied Social Psychology, 20,* 1776–1788.

Keck, P. E., & McElroy, S. L. (1998). Pharmacological treatment of bipolar disorders. In P. E. Nathan & J. M. Gorman (Eds.), *A guide to treatments that work* (pp. 249–269). New York: Oxford University Press.

Keck, P. E., McElroy, S. L., Strakowski, S. M., West, S. A., Sax, K. W., et al. (1998). 12-month outcome of patients with bipolar disorder following hospitalization for a manic or mixed episode. *American Journal of Psychiatry, 155,* 646–652.

Keefe, F. J., & Gil, K. M. (1986). Behavioral concepts in the analysis of chronic pain syndromes. *Journal of Consulting and Clinical Psychology, 54,* 776–783.

Keefe, R. S. E. (2006). One-year double-blind study of the neurocognitive efficacy of olanzapine, resperidone, and haloperidol in schizophrenia. *Schizophrenia Research, 81,* 1–15.

Keel, P. K. (2007). Purging disorder: Subthreshold variant or full-threshold eating disorder. *International Journal of Eating Disorders, 40, Suppl:* S89–S94.

Keel, P. K., & Klump, K. L. (2003). Are eating disorders culture-bound syndromes? Implications for conceptualizing their etiology. *Psychological Bulletin, 129,* 747–769.

Keel, P. K., & Mitchell, J. E. (1997). Outcome in bulimia nervosa. *American Journal of Psychiatry, 154,* 313–321.

Keel, P. K., Mitchell, J. E., Miller, K. B., Davis, T. L., & Crowe, S. J. (1999). Long-term outcome of bulimia nervosa. *Archives of General Psychiatry, 56,* 63–69.

Keith, J. (1982). *Old people as people.* Boston: Little, Brown.

Keller, M. B., Beardslee, W., Lavori, P. W., Wunder, J., Dils, D. L., & Samuelson, H. (1988). Course of major depression in non-referred adolescents: A retrospective study. *Journal of Affective Disorders, 15,* 235–243.

Keller, M. C., Neale, M. C., & Kendler, K. S. (2007). Association of different adverse life events with distinct patterns of depressive symptoms. *American Journal of Psychiatry, 164,* 1521–1529.

Kellner, C. H., et al. (2006). Continuation electroconvulsive therapy vs pharmacotherapy for relapse prevention in major depression: A multisite study from the Consortium for Research in Electroconvulsive Therapy (CORE). *Archives of General Psychiatry, 63,* 1337–1344.

Kellner, R. (1982). Disorders of impulse control (not elsewhere classified). In J. H. Griest, J. W. Jefferson, & R. L. Spitzer (Eds.), *Treatment of mental disorders*. New York: Oxford University Press.

Kellogg, S. H., & Young, J. E. (2006). Schema therapy for borderline personality disorder. *Journal of Clinical Psychology, 62*, 445–458.

Kelly, G. A. (1955). *The psychology of personal constructs*. New York: Norton.

Kemner, C., Willemsen-Swinkels, S. H., de Jonge, M., Tuynman-Qua, H., & van Engeland, H. (2002). Open-label study of olanzapine in children with pervasive developmental disorder. *Journal of Clinical Psychopharmacology, 22*, 455–460.

Kemper, S., Greiner, L. H., Marquis, J. G., Prenovost, K., & Mitzner, T. L. (2001). Language decline across the life span: Findings from the Nun Study. *Psychology and Aging, 16*, 227–239.

Kempster, N. (1996, August 25). Clinton orders tracking of sex offenders. *Los Angeles Times*, A20.

Kenardy, J., Robinson, S., & Dob, R. (2005). Cognitive behaviour therapy for panic disorder: Long-term follow-up. *Cognitive Behaviour Therapy, 34*, 75–78.

Kendall, P. C., & Hedtke, K. (2006a). *Cognitive-behavioral therapy for anxious children: Therapist's manual* (3rd ed.). Ardmore, PA: Workbook Publishing.

Kendall, P. C., & Hedtke, K. (2006b). *The Coping Cat Workbook* (2nd ed.). Ardmore, PA: Workbook Publishing.

Kendell, R. E. (1975). *The role of diagnosis in psychiatry*. London: Blackwell.

Kendler, K. S. (1993). Twin studies of psychiatric illness: Current status and future directions. *Archives of General Psychiatry, 50*, 905–914.

Kendler, K. S. (1997). The diagnostic validity of melancholic major depression in a population-based sample of female twins. *Archives of General Psychiatry, 54*, 299–304.

Kendler, K. S. (2008). Explanatory models for psychiatric illness. *American Journal of Psychiatry, 165*, 695–702.

Kendler, K. S., et al. (2008). The structure of genetic and environmental risk factors for DSM-IV personality disorders. *Archives of General Psychiatry, 65*, 1438–1446.

Kendler, K. S., Davis, C. G., & Kessler, R. C. (1997). The familial aggregation of common psychiatric and substance use disorders in the National Comorbidity Survey: A family history study. *British Journal of Psychiatry, 170*, 541–548.

Kendler, K. S., & Diehl, S. R. (1993). The genetics of schizophrenia: A current, genetic-epidemiologic perspective. *Schizophrenia Bulletin, 19*, 87–113.

Kendler, K. S., & Gardner, C. O. (1998). Boundaries of major depression: An evaluation of DSM-IV criteria. *American Journal of Psychiatry, 155*, 172–177.

Kendler, K. S., Gardner, C. O., Annas, P., & Lichtenstein, P. (2008). The development of fears from early adolescence to young adulthood: A multivariate study. *Psychological Medicine, 38*, 1759–1769.

Kendler, K. S., Gardner, C. O., & Lichtenstein, P. (2008). A developmental twin study of symptoms of anxiety and depression: Evidence for genetic innovation and attenuation. *Psychological Medicine, 38*, 1567–1575.

Kendler, K. S., & Gruenberg, A. M. (1984). Independent analysis of Danish adoption study of schizophrenia. *Archives of General Psychiatry, 41*, 555–562.

Kendler, K. S., Karkowski, L. M., & Prescott, C.A. (1999). Fears and phobias: Reliability and heritability. *Psychological Medicine, 29*, 539–553.

Kendler, K. S., Karkowski-Shuman, L., & Walsh, D. (1996). Age of onset in schizophrenia and risk of illness in relatives. *British Journal of Psychiatry, 169*, 213–218.

Kendler, K. S., Neale, M. C., & Walsh, D. (1995). Evaluating the spectrum concept of schizophrenia in the Roscommon Family Study. *American Journal of Psychiatry, 152*, 749–754.

Kendler, K. S., & Prescott, C. A. (1998). Cannabis use, abuse, and dependence in a population-based sample of female twins. *American Journal of Psychiatry, 155*, 1016–1022.

Kendler, K. S., & Prescott, C. A. (1999). Caffeine intake, tolerance, and withdrawal in women: A population-based twin study. *American Journal of Psychiatry, 156*, 223–228.

Kennard, B. D., et al. (2009). Effective components of TORDIA cognitive-behavioral therapy for adolescent depression: Preliminary findings. *Journal of Consulting and Clinical Psychology, 77*, 1033–1041.

Kenny, M. A., & Williams, J. M. G. (2007). Treatment-resistant depressed patients show a good response to Mindfulness-based Cognitive Therapy. *Behaviour Research and Therapy, 45*, 617–625.

Kernberg, O. F. (1985). *Borderline conditions and pathological narcissism*. Northvale, NJ: Jason Aronson.

Kertes, A., Westra, H. A., Angus, L., & Marcus, M. (in press). The impact of motivational interviewing on client experiences of cognitive behavioral therapy for generalized anxiety disorder. *Cognitive and Behavioral Practice*.

Kessler, R. C., et al. (2010). Age differences in the prevalence and co-morbidity of DSM-IV major depressive episodes: Results from the WHO World Mental Health Survey initative. *Depression and Anxiety, 25(8)*, 670–679

Kessler, R. C., Adler, L., Barkley, R., et al. (2006). The prevalence and correlates of adult ADHD in the United States: Results from the National Comorbidity Survey Replication. *American Journal of Psychiatry, 163*, 716–723.

Kessler, R. C., Chiu, W. T., Demler, O., Merikangas, K. R., & Walters, E. E. (2005). Prevalence, severity, and comorbidity of 12-month DSM-IV disorders in the National Comorbidity Survey Replication. *Archives of General Psychiatry, 62*, 617–627.

Kessler, R. C., Davis, C. G., & Kendler, K. S. (1997). Childhood adversity and adult psychiatric disorder in the US National Comorbidity Survey. *Psychological Medicine, 27*, 1101–1119.

Kessler, R. C., Frank, R. G., Edlund, M., Katz, S. J., Lin, E., & Leaf, P. (1997). Differences in the use of psychiatric outpatient services between the United States and Ontario. *New England Journal of Medicine, 336*, 551–557.

Kessler, R. C., Galea, S., Gruber, M. J., et al. (2008). Trends in mental illness and suicidality after Hurricane Katrina. *Molecular Psychiatry, 13*, 374–384.

Kessler, R. C., Lane, M., Stang, P. E., & Van Brunt, D. L. (2009). The prevalence and workplace costs of adult attention deficit hyperactivity disorder in a large manufacturing firm. *Psychological Medicine, 39*, 137–147.

Kessler, R. C., et al. (2006). Prevalence and effects of mood disorders on work performance in a nationally representative sample of U.S. workers. *American Journal of Psychiatry, 163*, 1490–1491.

Kessler, R. C., & Wang, P. S. (2008). The descriptive epidemiology of commonly occurring mental disorders in the United Sates. *Annual Review of Public Health, 29*, 115–129.

Kety, S. S., Rosenthal, D., Wender, P. H., & Schulsinger, F. (1968). The types and prevalence of mental illness in the biological and adoptive families of adopted schizophrenics. In D. Rosenthal & S. S. Kety (Eds.), *The transmission of schizophrenia*. Elmsford, NY: Pergamon.

Kety, S. S., Rosenthal, D., Wender, P. H., & Schulsinger, F. (1975). Mental illness in the adoptive and biological families of adopted individuals who have become schizophrenic. In R. R. Fieve, D. Rosenthal, & H. Brill (Eds.), *Genetic research in psychiatry*. Baltimore: Johns Hopkins University Press.

Kety, S. S., Wender, P. H., Jacobsen, B., Ingraham, L. T., Jansson, L., et al. (1994). Mental illness in the biological and adoptive relatives of schizophrenic adoptees: Replication of the Copenhagen study in the rest of Denmark. *Archives of General Psychiatry, 51*, 442–468.

Key, B. L., Campbell, T. S., Bacon, S. L., & Gerin, W. (2008). The influence of trait and state rumination on cardiovascular recovery from a negative emotional stressor. *Journal of Behavioral Medicine, 31*, 237–248.

Keys, A., Brozek, J., Hsu, L. K. G., McConoha, C. E., & Bolton, B. (1950). *The biology of human starvation*. Minneapolis: University of Minnesota Press.

Keys, A., Taylor, H. L., et al. (1971). Mortality and coronary heart disease in men studied for 23 years. *Archives of Internal Medicine, 128*, 201–214.

Khaled, S. M., Bulloch, A., Exner, D. V., & Patten, S. B. (2009). Cigarette smoking, stages of change, and major depression in the Canadian population. *Canadian Journal of Psychiatry, 54*, 204–208.

Kidd, G. E. (1946). Trepanation among the early Indians of British Columbia. *Canadian Medical Association Journal, 55*, 513–516.

Kidd, S., & Shahar, G (2008). Resilience in homeless youth; The key role of self-esteem. *The American Journal of Orthopsychiatry, 78*, 163–172.

Kiecolt-Glaser, J. K. (2009). Psychoneuroimmunology: Psychology's gateway to the biomedical future. *Perspectives on Psychological Science, 4*, 367–369.

Kiecolt-Glaser, J., Dura, J. R., Speicher, C. E., & Trask, O. (1991). Spousal caregivers of dementia victims: Longitudinal changes in immunity and health. *Psychosomatic Medicine*, 54, 345–362.

Kiecolt-Glaser, J. K., et al. (1985). Psychosocial enhancement of immunocompetence in a geriatric population. *Health Psychology, 4*, 25–41.

Kiecolt-Glaser, J. K., McGuire, L., Robles, T. F., & Glaser, R. (2002). Psychoneuroimmunology: Psychological influences on immune function and health. *Journal of Consulting and Clinical Psychology, 70*, 537–547.

Kiehl, K. A., et al. (2001). Limbic abnormalities in affective processing by criminal psychopaths as revealed by functional magnetic resonance imaging. *Biological Psychiatry, 50*, 677–684.

Kihlstrom, J. F. (2005). Dissociative disorders. *Annual Review of Clinical Psychology, 1*, 227–253.

Kihlstrom, J. F., & Tataryn, D. J. (1991). Dissociative disorders. In P. B. Sutker & H. E. Adams (Eds.), *Comprehensive handbook of psychopathology* (2nd ed.). New York: Plenum.

Kihlstrom, J. F., Tataryn, D. J., & Hoyt, I. P. (1993). Dissociative disorders. In P. B. Sutker & H. E. Adams (Eds.), *Comprehensive handbook of psychopathology* (pp. 203–234). New York: Plenum.

Kilbourn, K. M., & Durning, P. E. (2003). Oncology and psycho-oncology. In S. Llewelyn & P. Kennedy (Eds.), *Handbook of clinical health psychology* (pp. 103–129). Chichester, England: John Wiley & Sons.

Killen, J. D., et al. (1997). Prospective study of risk factors for the initiation of cigarette smoking. *Journal of Consulting and Clinical Psychology, 65*, 1011–1016.

Kilpatrick, D. G., & Best, C. L. (1990, April). *Sexual assault victims: Data from a random national probability sample.* Paper presented at the annual convention of the Southeastern Psychological Association, Atlanta.

Kilpatrick, D. G., Edmunds, C. N., & Seymour, A. K. (1992). *Rape in America: A report to the nation.* Arlington, VA: National Victim Center.

Kim, Y. W., Lee, S.-L., Choi, T. K., et al. (2009). Effectiveness of mindfulness-based cognitive therapy as an adjuvant to pharmacotherapy in patients with panic disorder or generalized anxiety disorder. *Depression and Anxiety, 26*, 601–606.

Kim-Cohen, J., Moffitt, T. E., Caspi, A., & Taylor, A. (2004). Genetic and environmental processes in young children's resilience to socioeconomic deprivation. *Child Development, 75*, 651–668.

King, D. W., King, L. A., Gudanowski, D. M., & Vreven, D. L. (1995). Alternative representations of war zone stressors: Relationship to posttraumatic stress disorder in male and female Vietnam veterans. *Journal of Abnormal Psychology, 104*, 184–196.

King, J. (1997). *The life of Margaret Laurence.* Toronto: Knopf.

King, L. A., & Napa, C. K. (1998). What makes a life good? *Journal of Personality and Social Psychology, 75*, 156–165.

King, P., Devichand, P., & Rockwood, K. (2005). Dementia of acute onset in the Canadian Study of Health and Aging. *International Psychogeriatrics, 17*, 451–459.

King, P. R., & Endler, N. S. (1990). Interactional anxiety and the evaluation of driving skills: An empirical examination of a composite predictor

for state anxiety. *Canadian Journal of Behavioural Science, 22*, 13–19.

King, S. (2000). Is expressed emotion cause or effect in the mothers of schizophrenic young adults? *Schizophrenia Research, 45*, 65–78.

King, S., Ricard, N., Rochon, V., Steiger, H., & Nelis, S. (2003). Determinants of expressed emotion in mothers of schizophrenia patients. *Psychiatry Research, 117*, 211–222.

Kingston, D. A., et al. (2008). Pornography use and sexual aggression: The impact of frequency and type of pornography use on recidivism among sexual offenders. *Aggressive Behavior, 34*, 1–11.

Kinley, D. J., Cox, B. J., Clara, I., et al. (2009). Panic attacks and their relation to psychological and physical functioning in Canadians: Results from a nationally representative sample. *Canadian Journal of Psychiatry, 54*, 113–122.

Kinsey, A. C., Pomeroy, W. B., Main, C. E., & Gebhard, P. H. (1953). *Sexual behavior in the human female.* Philadelphia: Saunders.

Kinsey, A. C., Pomeroy, W. B., & Martin, C. E. (1948). *Sexual behavior in the human male.* Philadelphia: Saunders.

Kirby, M. (2007). The promise and the challenge of the Mental Health Commission of Canada. *Canadian Psychiatry Aujourd'hui, 3* (http://publications.cpa-apc.org/browse/documents/191).

Kirchner, J. E., et al. (2007). Alcohol consumption among older adults in primary care. *Journal of General Internal Medicine, 22*, 92–97.

Kirkey, S. (2008, August 18). Nearly half of Canadians say mental illness used as an excuse: Poll shows extent of discrimination, CMA says. *The Ottawa Citizen*, A1.

Kirkland, S. A., et al. (1999). Knowledge and awareness of risk factors for cardiovascular disease among Canadians 55 to 74 years of age: Results from the Canadian Health Surveys, 1986–1992. *Canadian Medical Association Journal, 161* (Suppl. 8), S10–S16.

Kirkpatrick, B. (2006). Editor's introduction: Theme issue on negative symptoms. *Schizophrenia Bulletin, 32*, 212–213.

Kirkpatrick, H., & Byrne, C. (2009). A narrative inquiry: Moving on from homelessness for individuals with a major mental illness. *Journal of Psychiatric and Mental Health Nursing, 16*, 68–75.

Kirmayer, L. J. (2001). Cultural variations in the clinical presentation of depression and anxiety: Implications for diagnosis and treatment. *Journal of Clinical Psychiatry, 62* (Suppl. 13), 22–28.

Kirmayer, L. J., Boothroyd, L. J., & Hodgins, S. (1998). Attempted suicide among Inuit youth: Psychosocial correlates and implications for prevention. *Canadian Journal of Psychiatry, 43*, 816–822.

Kirmayer, L. J., Boothroyd, L. J., Tanner, A., Adelson, N., & Robinson, E. (2000). Psychological distress among the Cree of James Bay. *Transcultural Psychiatry, 37*, 35–56.

Kirmayer, L. J., Brass, G. M., & Tait, C. L. (2000). The mental health of Aboriginal peoples: Transformations of identity and community. *Canadian Journal of Psychiatry, 45*, 607–616.

Kirmayer, L. J., Malus, M., & Boothroyd, L. J. (1996). Suicide attempts among Inuit youth: A

community survey of prevalence and risk factors. *Acta Psychiatrica Scandinavica, 94*, 8–17.

Kirmayer, L. J., Rousseau, C., Jarvis, G. E., & Guzder, J. (2003). The cultural context of clinical assessment. In A. Tasman, J. Lieberman, & J. Kay (Eds.), *Psychiatry* 2nd Ed. New York: John Wiley & Sons.

Kirmayer, L. J., Rousseau, C., Rosenberg, E., et al. (2008). *Report on the evaluation of a cultural consultation service in mental health.* Montreal: McGill University, Division of Social and Transcultural Psychiatry.

Kirmayer, L. J., Rousseau, C., & Santhanam, R. (2003). Models of diagnosis and treatment planning in mental health. In A. Rummens, M. Beiser, & S. Noh (Eds.), *Immigration, health, and ethnicity.* Toronto: University of Toronto Press.

Kirmayer, L. J., Weinfeld, M., Burgos, G., et al. (2007). Use of health care services for psychological distress by immigrants in an urban multicultural milieu. *Canadian Journal of Psychiatry, 52*, 295–304.

Kirmayer, L. J., & Young, A. (1998). Culture and somatization: Clinical, epidemiological, and ethnographic perspectives. *Psychosomatic Medicine, 60*, 420–430.

Kirsch, I., Deacon, B. J., Huedo-Medina, T. B., et al. (2008). Initial severity and antidepressant benefits: A meta-analysis of data submitted to the Food and Drug Administration. *PLoS Medicine, 5*, e45.

Kirschbaum, C., Prussner, J. C., & Stone, A. A. (1995). Persistent high cortisol responses to repeated psychological stress in a subpopulation of healthy men. *Psychosomatic Medicine, 57*, 468–474.

Kisely, S., Smith, M., Preston, N. J., & Xiao, J. (2005). A comparison of health service use in two jurisdictions with and without compulsory community treatment. *Psychological Medicine, 35*, 1357–1367.

Kjølseth, I., Ekeberg, O., & Steihaug, S. (2010). Why suicide? Elderly people who committed suicide and their experience of life in the period before their death. *International Psychogeriatrics, 22*, 209–218.

Klein, B., & Richards, J. C. (2001). A brief Internet-based treatment of panic disorder. *Behavioral and Cognitive Psychotherapy, 29*, 113–118.

Klein, R. G. (2009). Anxiety disorders. *Journal of Child Psychology and Psychiatry, 50*, 153–162.

Klerman, G. L., et al. (1994). Medication and psychotherapy. In A. E. Bergin & S. L. Garfield (Eds.), *Handbook of psychotherapy and behavior change* (4th ed., pp. 734–782). New York: John Wiley & Sons.

Klerman, G. L., Weissman, M. M., Rounsaville, B. J., & Chevron, E. S. (1984). *Interpersonal psychotherapy of depression.* New York: Basic Books.

Klinger, L. G., Dawson, G., & Renner, P. (2003). Autistic disorder. In E. J. Marsh & B. A. Barkley (Eds.), *Child psychopathology* (2nd ed., pp. 409–454). New York: Guilford Press.

Klinger, E., Bouchard, S., et al. (2005). Virtual reality therapy for social phobia: A preliminary controlled strategy. *Cyberpsychology and Behavior, 8*, 70–88.

Kluft, R. P. (1988). The dissociative disorders. In R. E. Hales & S. C. Yudofsky (Eds.), *Textbook of psychiatry* (pp. 557–585). Washington, DC: American Psychiatric Press.

Kluft, R. P. (1994). Treatment trajectories in multiple personality disorder. *Dissociation*, 7, 63–75.

Kluft, R. P. (2001). Dissociative identity disorder. In G. O. Gabbard (Ed.), *Treatment of psychiatric disorders* (Vol. 2, pp. 1653–1693). Washington, DC: American Psychiatric Press.

Knapp, S., & Vandecreek, L. (1982). Tarasoff: Five years later. *Professional Psychology*, 13, 511–516.

Knight, B. (1983). An evaluation of a mobile geriatric team. In M. A. Smyer & M. Gatz (Eds.), *Mental health and aging: Programs and evaluations*. Beverly Hills, CA: Sage.

Knight, B. (2004). *Psychotherapy with older adults* (3rd ed.). Thousand Oaks, CA: Sage.

Knight, B. G., Kelly, M., & Gatz, M. (1992). Psychotherapy and the older adult: An historical review. In D. K. Freedheim (Ed.), *History of psychotherapy: A century of change* (pp. 528–551). Washington, DC: American Psychological Association.

Kocovski, N. L., Endler, N. S., Rector, N. A., & Flett, G. L. (2005). Rumination and post-event processing. *Behaviour Research and Therapy*, 43, 971–984.

Kocovski, N. L., & Rector, N. A. (2008). Post-event processing in social anxiety disorder: Idiosyncratic priming in the course of CBT. *Cognitive Therapy and Research*, 32, 23–36.

Koenen, K. C., Moffitt, T. E., Caspi, A., et al. (2003). Domestic violence is associated with environmental suppression of IQ in young children. *Development and Psychopathology*, 15, 297–311.

Koerner, N., & Dugas, M. J. (2008). An investigation of appraisals in individuals vulnerable to excessive worry: The role of intolerance of uncertainty. *Cognitive Therapy and Research*, 32, 619–638.

Kogan, M. D., Blumberg, S. J., Schieve, L. A., et al. (2009). Prevalence of parent-reported diagnosis of autism spectrum disorder among children in the US, 2007. *Pediatrics*, 124, 1395–1403.

Kohen, D., Brooks-Gunn, J., Leventhal, T., & Hertzman, C. (2002). Neighborhood income and physical and social disorder in Canada: Associations with young children's competencies, *Child Development*, 73, 1844–1860.

Kohn, M. L. (1968). Social class and schizophrenia: A critical review. In D. Rosenthal & S. S. Kety (Eds.), *The transmission of schizophrenia*. Elmsford, NY: Pergamon.

Kohn, P. M., Lafreniere, K., & Gurevich, M. (1990). The Inventory of College Students' Recent Life Experiences: A decontaminated hassles scale for a special population. *Journal of Behavioral Medicine*, 13, 619–630.

Kohn, P. M., & Milrose, J. A. (1993). The Inventory of High-School Students Recent Life Experiences: A decontaminated measure of adolescents' hassles. *Journal of Youth and Adolescence*, 22, 43–55.

Kohut, H. (1971). *The analysis of the self*. New York: International Universities Press.

Kohut, H. (1977). *The restoration of the self*. New York: International Universities Press.

Kohut, H., & Wolf, E. S. (1978). The disorders of the self and their treatment: An outline. *International Journal of Psychoanalysis*, 59, 413–425.

Kolden, G. G. (1991). The generic model of psychotherapy: An empirical investigation of patterns of process and outcome relationships. *Psychotherapy Research*, 1, 62–73.

Koltek, M., Wilkes, T. C. R., & Atkinson, M. (1998). Prevalence of posttraumatic stress disorder in an adolescent inpatient unit. *Canadian Journal of Psychiatry*, 43, 64–67.

Kong, L. L., Allen, J. J. B., & Glisky, E. L. (2008). Interidentity memory transfer in Dissociative Identity Disorder. *Journal of Abnormal Psychology*, 117, 686–692.

Konnert, C., Dobson, K. S., & Watt, A. (2009). Geropsychology training in Canada: A survey of doctoral and internship programs. *Canadian Psychology*, 50, 255–266.

Kopelowicz, A., Liberman, R. P., & Zarate, R. (2006). Recent advances in social skills training for schizophrenia. *Schizoprenia Bulletin*, 32, S1, 512–523.

Koponen, H. J., et al. (2007). Rates and previous disease history in old age suicide. *International Journal of Geriatric Psychiatry*, 22, 38–46.

Koran, L. M. (2007). Obsessive-compulsive disorder: An update for the clinician. *Focus*, 5, 299–313.

Korn, D. (2000). Expansion of gambling in Canada: Implications for health and social policy. *Canadian Medical Association Journal*, 163, 61–64.

Kornetsky, C. (1976). Hyporesponsivity of chronic schizophrenic patients to dextroamphetamine. *Archives of General Psychiatry*, 33, 1425–1428.

Kosberg, J. I. (1988). Preventing elder abuse: Identification of high risk factors prior to placement decisions. *The Gerontologist*, 28, 43–50.

Koski-Jannes, A., & Cunningham, J. (2001). Interest in different forms of self-help in a general population sample of drinkers. *Addictive Behaviors*, 26, 91–99.

Koss, M. P., & Shiang, J. (1994). Research of brief psychotherapy. In A. E. Bergin & S. L. Garfield (Eds.), *Handbook of psychotherapy and behavior change* (4th ed., pp. 664–700). New York: John Wiley & Sons.

Kosten, T. R., Mason, J. W., Giller, E. L., Ostroff, R., & Harkness, I. (1987). Sustained urinary norepinephrine and epinephrine elevation in posttraumatic stress disorder. *Psychoneuroendocrinology*, 12, 13–20.

Kosten, T. R., Morgan, C. M., Falcione, J., & Schottenfeld, R. S. (1992). Pharmacotherapy for cocaine-abusing methadone-maintained patients using amantadine or desipramine. *Archives of General Psychiatry*, 49, 894–898.

Kosteniuk, J. G., & Dickinson, H. D. (2003). Tracing the social gradient in the health of Canadians: Primary and secondary determinants. *Social Science and Medicine*, 57, 263–276.

Koszycki, D., Torres, S., Swain, J. E., & Bradwejn, J. (2005). Central cholecystokinin activity in irritable bowel syndrome, panic disorder, and healthy controls. *Psychosomatic Medicine*, 67, 590–595.

Kovacs, M., Rush, A. J., Beck, A. T., & Hollon, S. D. (1981). Depressed outpatients treated with cognitive therapy or pharmacotherapy: A one-year follow-up. *Archives of General Psychiatry*, 38, 33–39.

Kowalik, D. L., & Gotlib, I. H. (1987). Depression and marital interation: Concordance between intent and perception of communication. *Journal of Abnormal Psychology*, 96, 127–134.

Kozel, N. J., & Adams, E. H. (1986). Epidemiology of drug abuse: An overview. *Science*, 234, 970–974.

Kozol, H., Boucher, R., & Garofalo, R. (1972). The diagnosis and treatment of dangerousness. *Crime and Delinquency*, 18, 37–92.

Krantz, S., & Hammen, C. L. (1979). Assessment of cognitive bias in depression. *Journal of Abnormal Psychology*, 88, 611–619.

Kranzler, H. R., Burleson, J. A., Del Boca, F. K., Babor, T. F., Korner, P., et al. (1994). Busipirone treatment of anxious alcoholics: A controlled trial. *Archives of General Psychiatry*, 51, 720–731.

Kreuger, R. B., & Kaplan, M. S. (1997). Frotteurism: Assessment and treatment. In D. R. Laws & W. O'Donohue (Eds.), *Sexual deviance* (pp. 131–151). New York: Guilford Press.

Kring, A. M., & Neale, J. M. (1996). Do schizophrenics show a disjunctive relationship among expressive, experiential and physiological components of emotion? *Journal of Abnormal Psychology*, 105, 249–257.

Krishnan, V., Berton, O., & Nestler, E. (2008). The use of animal models in psychiatric research and treatment. *American Journal of Psychiatry*, 165, 1109.

Kristiansen, C. M., Gareau, C., Mittleholt, J., DeCourville, N. H., & Hovdestad, W. E. (1999). The sociopolitical context of the delayed memory debate. In L. M. Williams & V. L. Banyard (Eds.), *Trauma and recovery* (pp. 331–347). Thousand Oaks, CA: Sage Publications.

Kroenke, K. (2007). Efficacy of treatment for somatoform disorders: A review of randomized controlled trials. *Psychosomatic Medicine*, 69, 881–888.

Kroenke, K., Sharpe, M., & Sykes, R. (2007). Revising the classification of somatoform disorders: Key questions and preliminary recommendations. *Psychosomatics*, 48, 277–285.

Krystal, J. H., Kosten, T. R., Southwick, S., Mason, J. W., Perry, B. D., & Giller, E. L. (1989). Neurobiological aspects of PTSD: Review of clinical and preclinical studies. *Behavior Therapy*, 20, 177–198.

Kuch, K., & Cox, B. J. (1992). Symptoms of PTSD in 124 survivors of the Holocaust. *American Journal of Psychiatry*, 149, 337–340.

Kuehnle, K. (1998). Child sexual abuse allegations: The scientist-practiner model. *Behavioral Science and the Law*, 16, 5–20.

Kuhn, T. S. (1962). *The structure of scientific revolutions*. Chicago: University of Chicago Press.

Kuitenbrouwer, P. (2008, November 6). Brandon Crisp lived in an online world. *National Post*.

Kun, P., Han, S., Chen, X., & Yao, L. (2009). Prevalence and risk factors for posttraumatic stress disorder: A cross-sectional study among survivors of the Wenchuan 2008 earthquake in China. *Depression and Anxiety*, 26, 601–606.

Kuntsche, E., Knibbe, R., Gmel, G., & Engels, R. (2005). Why do young people drink? A review of drinking motives. *Clinical Psychology Review*, 25, 841–861.

Kuriansky, J. B., Deming, W. E., & Gurland, B. J. (1974). On trends in the diagnosis of schizophrenia. *American Journal of Psychiatry, 131*, 402–407.

Kutcher, S., Hampton, M. J., & Wilson, J. (2010). Child and adolescent mental health policy and plans in Canada: An analytical review. *Canadian Journal of Psychiatry, 55*, 100–107.

Kutcher, S., & McLuckie, A. (2009). Evergreen: Towards a child and youth mental health framework for Canada. *Journal of the Canadian Academy of Child and Adolescent Psychiatry, 18*, 89–91.

Kutchinsky, B. (1970). *Studies on pornography and sex crimes in Denmark*. Copenhagen: New Social Science Monographs.

Kuyken, W., Watkins, E., Holden, E., & Cook, W. (2006). Rumination in adolescents at risk for depression. *Journal of Affective Disorders, 96*, 39–47.

Labelle, R., Lachance, L., & Morval, M. (1996). Validation of a French-Canadian version of the Reasons For Living Inventory. *Science et Comportement, 24*, 237–248.

Lac, A., & Crano, W. D. (2009). Monitoring matters: Meta-analytic review reveals the reliable linkage of parental monitoring with adolescent marijuana use. *Perspectives on Psychological Science, 4*, 578–586.

Lacey, J. I. (1967). Somatic response patterning and stress: Some revisions of activation theory. In M. H. Appley & R. Trumball (Eds.), *Psychological stress*. New York: McGraw-Hill.

Ladouceur, R., Gosselin, P., & Dugas, M. J. (2000). Experimental manipulation of intolerance of uncertainty: A study of a theoretical model of worry. *Behaviour Research and Therapy, 38*, 933–941.

Ladouceur, R., LaChance, S., & Fournier, P.-M. (2009). Is control a viable goal in the treatment of pathological gambling? *Behaviour Research and Therapy, 47*, 189–197.

Ladouceur, R., Freeston, M. H., Gagnon, F., Thibodeau, N., & Dumont, J. (1995). Cognitive-behavioral treatment of obsessions. *Behavior Modification, 19*, 247–257.

Ladouceur, R., & Walker, M. (1998). Cognitive approach to understanding and treating pathological gambling. In A. S. Bellack & M. Hersen (Eds.), *Comprehensive clinical psychology*, Vol. 6 (pp. 587–601). Oxford, England: Elsevier Science.

Ladowsky-Brooks, R. L., & Fischer, C. E. (2003). Ganser symptoms in a case of front temporal-lobe dementia: Is there a common neural substrate? *Journal of Clinical and Experimental Neuropsychiatry, 25*, 761–768.

LaGreca, A. M., Silverman, W. K., Vernberg, E. M., & Prinstein, M. J. (1996). Symptoms of posttraumatic stress in children after Hurricane Andrew: A prospective study. *Journal of Consulting and Clinical Psychology, 64*, 712–723.

LaGreca, A. M., Silverman, W. K., & Wasserstein, S. B. (1998). Children's predisaster functioning as a predictor of posttraumatic stress following Hurricane Andrew. *Journal of Consulting and Clinical Psychology, 66*, 883–892.

Lahey, B. B., Loeber, R., Hart, E. L., Frick, P. J., Applegate, B., Zhang, Q., et al. (1995). Four-year longitudinal study of conduct disorder in

boys: Patterns and predictors of persistence. *Journal of Abnormal Psychology, 104*, 83–93.

Laidlaw, K., & Pachana, N. A. (2009). Aging, mental health and demographic change: Challenges for psychotherapists. *Professional Psychology: Research and Practice, 40*, 601–608.

LaJeunesse, R. (2002). *Political asylums*. Edmonton: University of Alberta Press.

Lalinec-Michaud, M., Subak, M. E., Ghadirian, A. M., & Kovess, V. (1991). Substance misuse among native and rural high school students in Quebec. *International Journal of the Addictions, 26*, 1003–1012.

Lalonde, J. K., Hudson, J. I., Gigante, R. A., & Pope, H. G. (2001). Canadian and American psychiatrists' attitudes toward dissociative disorders diagnoses. *Canadian Journal of Psychiatry, 46*, 407–412.

Lalumiere, M. L., & Quinsey, V. L. (1998). Pavlovian conditioning of sexual interests in human males. *Archives of Sexual Behavior, 27*, 241–252.

Lam, D. (2006). What can we conclude from studies on psychotherapy in bipolar disorder? Invited commentary on...Cognitive-behavioural therapy for severe and recurrent bipolar disorders. *British Journal of Psychiatry, 188*, 321–322.

Lam, R. W., Chan, P., Wilkins-Ho, M., & Yatham, L. N. (2008). Repetitive transcranial magnetic stimulation for treatment-resistant depression: A systematic review and metaanalysis. *Canadian Journal of Psychiatry, 53*, 621–631.

Lam, R. W., & Levitt, A. J. (1999). *Canadian consensus guidelines for the treatment of seasonal affective disorder*. Vancouver: Clinical and Academic Publishing.

Lam, R. W., Tam, E. M., Shiah, I. S., Yatham, L. N., & Zis, A. P. (2000). Effects of light therapy on suicidal ideation in patients with winter depression. *Journal of Clinical Psychiatry, 61*, 30–32.

Lam, R. W., et al. (1996). Effects of rapid tryptophan depletion in patients with seasonal affective disorder in remission after light therapy. *Archives of General Psychiatry, 53*, 41–46.

Lambe, E. K., Katzman, D. K., Mikulis, D. J., Kennedy, S. H., & Zipursky, R. B. (1997). Cerebral gray matter volume deficits after weight recovery from anorexia nervosa. *Archives of General Psychiatry, 54*, 537–542.

Lamberg, L. (1998). New drug for erectile dysfunction boon for many, "Viagravation" for some. *Journal of the American Medical Association, 280*, 867–869.

Lambert, M., Naber, D., Schacht, A., et al. (2008). Rates and predictors of remission and recovery during 3 years in 392 never-treated patients with schizophrenia. *Acta Psychiatrica Scandinavica, 118*, 220–229.

Lambert, M. J., & Bergin, A. E. (1994). The effectiveness of psychotherapy. In A. E. Bergin & S. L. Garfield (Eds.), *Handbook of psychotherapy and behavior change* (4th ed., pp. 143–189). New York: John Wiley & Sons.

Lambert, M. J., & Ogles, B. M. (2004). The efficacy and effectiveness of psychotherapy. In M. J. Lambert (Ed.), *Bergin and Garfield's handbook of psychotherapy and behavior change* (5th ed., pp. 139–193). Hoboken, NJ: John Wiley & Sons.

Lambert, M. J., Shapiro, D. A., & Bergin, A. E. (1986). The effectiveness of psychotherapy. In S. L. Garfield & A. E. Bergin (Eds.), *Handbook of psychotherapy and behavior change* (3rd ed.). New York: John Wiley & Sons.

Landerl, K., & Moll, K. (2010). Comorbidity of learning disorders: Prevalence and familial transmission. *Journal of Child Psychology and Psychiatry, 51*, 287–294.

Lando, H. A. (1977). Successful treatment of smokers with a broad-spectrum behavioral approach. *Journal of Consulting and Clinical Psychology, 45*, 361–366.

Landon, T. M., & Barlow, D. H. (2004). Cognitive-behavioral treatment for panic disorder: Current status. *Journal of Psychiatric Practice, 10*, 211–226.

Lane, E. A., & Albee, G. W. (1965). Childhood intellectual differences between schizophrenic adults and their siblings. *American Journal of Orthopsychiatry, 35*, 747–753.

Laney, C., & Loftus, E. F. (2005). Traumatic memories are not necessarily accurate memories. *Canadian Journal of Psychiatry, 50*, 823–828.

Lang, I., Guralnik, J., Wallace, R. B., & Melzer, D. (2007). What level of alcohol consumption is hazardous for older people? Functioning and mortality in U.S. and English national cohorts. *Journal of the American Geriatric Society, 55*, 49–57.

Lang, P. J., & Melamed, B. G. (1969). Case report: Avoidance conditioning therapy of an infant with chronic ruminative vomiting. *Journal of Abnormal Psychology, 74*, 1–8.

Langeluddeke, A. (1963). *Castration of sexual criminals*. Berlin: de Gruyter.

Langenbucher, J. W., & Chung, T. (1995). Onset and staging of DSM-IV alcohol dependence using mean age and survival hazard methods. *Journal of Abnormal Psychology, 104*, 346–354.

Langille, D. B., et al. (1999). Prevalence of risk factors for cardiovascular disease in Canadians 55 to 74 years of age: Results from the Canadian Heart Health Surveys, 1986–1992. *Canadian Medical Association Journal, 161* (Suppl. 8), S3–S9.

Langlois, S., & Morrison, P. (2002). Suicide deaths and suicide attempts. *Health Reports, 13*, 9–22.

Lantz, P. M., House, J. S., Lepkowski, J. M., Williams, D. R., et al. (1998). Socioeconomic factors, health behaviors, and mortality. *Journal of the American Medical Association, 279*, 1703–1708.

LaPlante, D. A., Nelson, S. E., LaBrie, R. A., & Shaffer, H. J. (2008). Stability and progression of disordered gambling: Lessons from longitudinal studies. *Canadian Journal of Psychiatry, 53*, 52–60.

La Roche, M. (2008). Culture and empirically supported treatments: On the road to a collision? *Culture & Psychology, 14*, 333–356.

Larsson, H., Andershed, H., & Lichtenstein, P. (2006). A genetic factor explains most of the variation in the psychopathic personality. *Journal of Abnormal Psychology, 115*, 221–230.

Larstone, R. M., Jang, K. L., Livesley, W. J., Vernon, P. A., & Wolf, K. (2002). The relationship between Eysenck's P-E-N model of personality, the five-factor model of personality, and traits delineating personality dysfunction. *Personality and Individual Differences*, 33, 25–37.

LaRue, A., Dessonville, C., & Jarvik, L. F. (1985). Aging and mental disorders. In J. E. Birren & K. W. Schaie (Eds.), *Handbook of psychology of aging* (2nd ed.). New York: Van Nostrand-Reinhold.

Last, C. G., & Strauss, C. C. (1990). School refusal in anxiety-disordered children and adolescents. *Journal of the American Academy of Child and Adolescent Psychiatry*, 29, 31–35.

Latimer, E. (2005). Community-based care for people with severe mental illness in Canada. *International Journal of Law and Psychiatry*, 28, 561–573.

Latimer, J. (2006). *The Review Board Systems in Canada: Overview of results for the Mentally Disordered Accused Data Collection Study*. Ottawa: Department of Justice Canada.

Lau, J. Y. F., & Eley, T. C. (2008). Disentangling gene-environment correlations and interactions on adolescent depressive symptoms. *Journal of Child Psychology and Psychiatry*, 59, 142–150.

Lau, M. A., & McMain, S. F. (2005). Integrating mindfulness meditation with cognitive and behavioural therapies: The challenge of combining acceptance- and change-based strategies. *Canadian Journal of Psychiatry*, 50, 863–869.

Laub, J. H., & Sampson, R. J. (1995). The long term effects of punitive discipline. In J. McCord (Ed.), *Coercion and punishment in long-term perspectives* (pp. 247–258). Cambridge, MA: Cambridge University Press.

Laumann, E. O., Gagnon, J. H., Michael, R. T., & Michaels, S. (1994). *The social organization of sexuality*. Chicago: University of Chicago Press.

Laurin, C., Lavoie, K. L., Bacon, S. L., Depuis, G. L., et al. (2007). Psychiatric disorders and psychological distress in patients with COPD. *Chest*, 132, 148–155.

Lautenschlager, N. T., Cupples, L. A., Rao, V. S., Auerbach, S. A., Becker, R., & Burke J. (1996). Risk of dementia among relatives of Alzheimer's disease patients in the MIRAGE study: What is in store for the oldest old? *Neurology*, 46, 641–650.

Law, M., & Tang, J. L. (1995). An analysis of the effectiveness of interventions intended to help people stop smoking. *Archives of Internal Medicine*, 155, 1933–1941.

Lawrence, A. A. (2003). Factors associated with satisfaction or regret following male-to-female sex reassignment surgery. *Archives of Sexual Behavior*, 32, 299–315.

Laws, D. R., Hanson, K. R., Osborn, C. A., & Greenbaum, P. E. (2000). Classification of child molesters by plethysmographic assessment of sexual arousal and a self-report measure of sexual preference. *Journal of Interpersonal Violence*, 15, 1297–1312.

Lawton, V. (2001, June 22). Chretien will ask Romanow to study medicare user fees: Private meeting with Swedish leader sparks interest in examining health-care concept. *Toronto Star*, A6.

Lazarus, A. A., Davison, G. C., & Polefka, D. A. (1965) Classical and operant factors in the treatment of a school phobia. Journal of Abnormal Psychology, 70, 225-229.

Lazarus, R. S. (1966). *Psychological stress and the coping process*. New York: McGraw-Hill.

Lazarus, R. S., & Folkman, S. (1984). *Stress, appraisal, and coping*. New York: Springer.

Leach, S., & Roy, S. S. (1986). Adverse drug reactions: An investigation on an acute geriatric ward. *Age and Ageing*, 15, 241–246.

Lebow, J. L., & Gurman, A. S. (1995). Research assessing couple and family therapy. *Annual Review of Psychology*, 46, 27–57.

Leckman, J. F., Denys, D., Simpson, H. B., et al. (2010). Obsessive-compulsive disorder: A review of the diagnostic criteria and possible subtypes and dimensional specifiers for DSM-V. *Depression and Anxiety*, 27, 507–527.

Leckman-Westin, E., Cohen, P. R., & Stueve, A. (2009). Maternal depression and mother-child interaction patterns: Association with toddler problems and continuity of effects to late childhood. *Journal of Child Psychology and Psychiatry*, 50, 1176–1184.

Lecomte, J., & Mercier, C. (2007). The Montreal Declaration on Intellectual Disabilities of 2004: An important first step. *Journal of Policy and Practice in Intellectual Disabilities*, 4, 66–69.

Le Couteur, A., Bailey, A., Goode, S., Pickles, A., Robertson, S., Gottesman, I., et al. (1996). A broader phenotype of autism: The clinical spectrum in twins. *Journal of Child Psychology and Psychiatry and Allied Disciplines*, 37, 785–801.

Lee, C. (2008, August 5). Canadian Psychological Association comment on the proposed review and revisions to the *Youth Criminal Justice Act*. Ottawa: Canadian Psychological Association.

Lee, D. S., et al. (2009). Trends in risk factors for cardiovascular disease in Canada: Temporal, socio-demographic, and geographic factors. *Canadian Medical Association Journal*, 181, E55–E66.

Lee, K.-H., Baillargeon, R. H., Vermunt, J. K., Wu, H.-X., & Tremblay, R. E. (2007). Age differences in the prevalence of physical aggression among 5-11-year-old Canadian boys and girls. *Aggressive Behavior*, 33, 26–37.

Lee, S. (1994). The Diagnostic Interview Schedule and anorexia nervosa in Hong Kong. *Archives of General Psychiatry*, 51, 251–252.

Lee, V. E., Brooks-Gunn, J., & Schnur, E. (1988). Does Head Start work? A 1-year follow-up comparison of disadvantaged children attending Head Start, no preschool, and other preschool programs. *Developmental Psychology*, 24, 210–222.

Lee, X., Klaver, J.R., Hart, S. D., Moretti, M. M., & Douglas, K.S. (2009). Short-term stability of psychpathic traits in adolescent offenders. *Journal of Clinical Child and Adolescent Psychology*, 38, 595–605.

Lee, Y., & Lin, P-Y. (in press). Association between serotonin transporter gene polymorphism and eating disorders: A meta-analytic study. *International Journal of Eating Disorders*.

Lee, Z., Klaver, J. R., Hart, S. D., Moretti, M., & Douglas, K. S. (2009). Short-term stability of psychopathic traits in adolescent offenders. *Journal of Clinical Child and Adolescent Psychology*, 38, 595–605.

Leenaars, A. A., & Lester, D. (1995). Impact of suicide prevention centers on suicide in Canada. *Crisis*, 16, 39.

Le Foll, B., Wertheim, C., & Goldberg, S. R. (2007). High reinforcing efficacy of nicotine in non-human primates. *PLoS ONE*, 2, e230.

Lehman, A. F., Steinwachs, D. M., & the survey co-investigators from the Schizophrenia Patient Outcomes Research Team (PORT) client survey (1998). Patterns of usual care for schizophrenia: Initial results from the Schizophrenia Patient Outcomes Research Team (PORT) client survey. *Schizophrenia Bulletin*, 24, 11–20.

Lehmann, H. E. (1996). Psychopharmacotherapy. In D. Healy (Ed.), *The psychopharmacologists*, Vol. 1 (pp. 159–186). London: Arnold.

Lehmann, H. E., & Ban, T. A. (1997). The history of psychopharmacology of schizophrenia. *Canadian Journal of Psychiatry*, 42, 152–162.

Lehmann, H. E., & Hanrahan, G. E. (1954). Chlorpromazine, new inhibiting agent for psychomotor excitement and manic states. *Archives of Neurology and Psychiatry*, 71, 227–237.

Lehoux, P. M., Steiger, H., & Jabalpurlawa, S. (2000). State-trait distinctions in bulimic syndromes. *International Journal of Eating Disorders*, 27, 36-42.

Lehrer, P. M., et al. (2008). Psychological treatment of comorbid asthma and panic disorder: A pilot study. *Journal of Anxiety Disorders*, 22, 671–683.

Leibenluft, E. (1996). Women with bipolar illness: Clinical and research issues. *American Journal of Psychiatry*, 153, 163–173.

Leiblum, S. R. (1997). Sexual pain disorders. In G. O. Gabbard & S. D. Atkinson (Eds.), *Synopsis of treatments of psychiatric disorders* (2nd ed., pp. 805–810). Washington, DC: American Psychiatric Press.

Leiblum, S. R., & Rosen, R. C. (Eds.). (1988). *Sexual desire disorders*. New York: Guilford.

Leichner, P., Arnett, J., Rallo, J. S., Srilcamesuaran, S., & Vulcano, B. (1986). An epidemiological study of maladaptive eating attitudes in a Canadian school-aged population. *International Journal of Eating Disorders*, 5, 969–982.

Leichsenring, F. (2001). Comparative effects of short-term psychodynamic psychotherapy and cognitive-behavioral therapy in depression: A meta-analytic approach. *Clinical Psychology Review*, 21, 401–419.

Leichsenring, F., & Leibing, E. (2007). Psychodynamic psychotherapy: A systematic review of techniques, indications, and empirical evidence. *Psychology and Psychotherapy*, 80, 217–228.

Leichsenring, F., & Rabung, S. (2008). Effectiveness of long-term psychodynamic psychotherapy: A meta-analysis. *Journal of the American Medical Association*, 300, 1551–1565.

Leitenberg, H., Gross, H., Peterson, H., & Rosen, J. C. (1984). Analysis of an anxiety model in the process of change during exposure plus response prevention treatment of bulimia nervosa. *Behavior Therapy*, 15, 3–20.

Lemonick, M. D., & Park, A. (2001, May 14). The nun study: How one scientist and 678 sisters are helping unlock the secrets of Alzheimer's. *Time: Canadian Edition*, 40–48.

Lenzenwenger, M. F., Dworkin, R. H., & Wethington, E. (1991). Examining the underlying structure of schizophrenic phenomenology: Evidence for a 3-process model. *Schizophrenia Bulletin, 17,* 515–524.

Leon, D. A., et al. (2007). Hazardous alcohol drinking and premature mortality in Russia: A population-based case-control study. *Lancet, 369,* 2001–2009.

Leonard, K. E., & Eiden, R. D. (1999). Husband's and wife's drinking: Unilateral or bilateral influences among newlyweds in a general population sample. *Journal of Studies on Alcohol, 60* (Suppl. 13), 130–138.

Leonard, S., Steiger, H., & Kao, A. (2003). Childhood and adulthood abuse in bulimic and nonbulimic women: Prevalences and psychological correlates. *International Journal of Eating Disorders, 33,* 397–405.

Lepage, C., Ladouceur, R., & Jacques, C. (2000). Prevalence of problem gambling among community service users. *Community Mental Health Journal, 36,* 597–601.

Lerman, C., Caporaso, N. E., Audrain, J., Main, D., Bowman, E. D., et al. (1999). Evidence suggesting the role of specific genetic factors in cigarette smoking. *Health Psychology, 18,* 14–20.

Lerman, C. E., Schnoll, R.A. & Munafo, M. R. (2007). Genetics and smoking cessation: Improving outcomes in smokers at risk. *American Journal of Preventive Medicine, 33,* S398–S405.

Lesage, A. D., Boyer, R., Grunberg, R., Vanier, C., Morrisette, R., Menard-Buteau, C., et al. (1994). Suicide and mental disorders: A case-control study of young men. *American Journal of Psychiatry, 151,* 1063–1068.

Lesage, A. D., & Morrissette, R. (1993). Residential and palliative needs of persons with severe mental illness who are subject to long-term hospitalization. *Canada's Mental Health, 41,* 12–17.

Lesage, A. D., Morissette, R., Fortier, L., Reinharz, D., & Contandriopoulos, A. P. (2000). Downsizing psychiatric hospitals: Needs for care and services of current and discharged long-stay patients. *Canadian Journal of Psychiatry, 45,* 526–532.

Lesage, A., Seguin, M., Guy, A., et al. (2008). Systematic services audit of consecutive suicides in New Brunswick: The case for coordinating specialist mental health and addiction services. *Canadian Journal of Psychiatry, 53,* 671–678.

Lesperance, F., Frasure-Smith, N., Talajic, M., & Bourassa, M. G. (2002). Five-year risk of cardiac mortality in relation to initial severity and one-year changes in depression symptoms after myocardial infarction. *Circulation, 105,* 1049–1053.

Lessard, J. C., & Moretti, M. M. (1998). Suicidal ideation in an adolescent clinical sample: Attachment patterns and clinical implications. *Journal of Adolescence, 21,* 383–395.

Lester, D. (1991). Do suicide prevention centers prevent suicide? *Homeostasis in Health and Disease, 33,* 190–194.

Leucht, S., Barnes, R. R., Kissling, W., et al. (2003). Relapse prevention in schizophrenia with new-generation antipsychotics: A systematic review and exploratory meta-analysis of randomized, controlled trials. *American Journal of Psychiatry, 160,* 1209–1222.

Leucht, S., Komossa, K., Rummel-Kluge, C., et al. (2009). A meta-analysis of head-to-head comparisons of second-generation antipsychotics in the treatment of schizophrenia. *American Journal of Psychiatry, 166,* 152–163.

Levenson, J. L. (2003). Psychological factors affect medical condition. In A. Tasman, J. Kay, & J. A. Lieberman (Eds.), *Psychiatry* (2nd ed., pp. 1638–1656). Chichester, England: John Wiley & Sons.

Levine, S. B. (2003). Sexual disorders. In A. Tasman, J. Kay, & J. A. Lieberman (Eds.), *Psychiatry* (2nd ed., p. 1490). New York: John Wiley & Sons.

Levitan, R. D., Kaplan, A. S., Joffe, R. T., Levitt, A. J., & Brown, G. M. (1997). Hormonal and subjective responses to intravenous meta-chlorophenylpiperazine in bulimia nervosa. *Archives of General Psychiatry, 54,* 521–528.

Levitt, A. J., Boyle, M. H., Joffe, R. T., & Baumal, Z. (2000). Estimated prevalence of the seasonal subtype of major depression in a Canadian community sample. *Canadian Journal of Psychiatry, 45,* 650–654.

Levitt, A. J., Lam, R. W., & Levitan, R. (2002). A comparison of open treatment of seasonal major and minor depression with light therapy. *Journal of Affective Disorders, 71,* 243–248.

Lev-Wiesel, R. (2008). Child sexual abuse: A critical review of intervention and treatment modalities. *Children & Youth Services Review, 30,* 665–673.

Levy, B. R., et al. (2009). Age stereotypes held earlier in life predict cardiovascular events later in life. *Psychological Science, 20,* 296–298.

Levy, D., et al. (2009). Genome-wide association study of blood pressure and hypertension. *Nature Genetics, 41,* 677–687.

Levy, F., Hay, D. A., Bennett, K. S., & McStephen, M. (2005). Gender differences in ADHD subtype comorbidity. *Journal of the American Academy of Child and Adolescent Psychiatry, 44,* 368–376.

Levy, F., Hay, D. A., McStephen, M., Wood, C., & Waldman, I. (1997). Attention-deficit hyperactivity disorder: A category or a continuum? Genetic analysis of a large-scale twin study. *Journal of the American Academy of Child and Adolescent Psychiatry, 36,* 737–744.

Levy, K. N. (2008). Psychotherapies and lasting change. *American Journal of Psychiatry, 165,* 556–559.

Levy, M. L., Miller, B. L., Cummings, J. L., Fairbanks, L. A., & Craig, A. (1996). Alzheimer disease and frontotemporal dementias. *Archives of Neurology, 53,* 687–690.

Levy, S., & Fletcher, E. (1998). Kamatsiaqtut, Baffin Crisis Line: Community ownership of support in a small town. In A. A. Leenaars, S. Wenckstern, I. Sakinofsky, R. J. Dyck, M. J. Kral, & R. C. Bland (Eds.), *Suicide in Canada* (pp. 351–366). Toronto: University of Toronto Press.

Lewin, A. B., Piacentini, J., Flessner, C. A., et al. (2009). Depression, anxiety, and functional impairment in children with trichotillomania. *Depression and Anxiety, 26,* 521–527.

Lewinsohn, P. M., Clarke, G. N., Hops, H., & Andrews, J. (1990). Cognitive-behavioral treatment for depressed adolescents. *Behavior Therapy, 21,* 385–401.

Lewinsohn, P. M., & Gotlib, I. H. (1995). Behavioral and cognitive treatment of depression. In E. E. Becker & W. R. Leber (Eds.), *Handbook of depression* (pp. 352–375). New York: Guilford Press.

Lewinsohn, P. M., Roberts, R. E., Seeley, J. R., Rohde, P., Gotlib, I. H., & Hops, H. (1994). Adolescent psychopathology: 2. Psychosocial risk factors for depression. *Journal of Abnormal Psychology, 103,* 302–315.

Lewis, C. C., et al. (2009). The role of readiness to change in response to treatment of adolescent depression. *Journal of Consulting and Clinical Psychology, 77,* 422–428.

Lewis, D. (2008). 2008 in review. *American Journal of Psychiatry, 165,* 1511–1512.

Lewis, D. O., Yeager, C. A., Swica, Y., Pincus, J. H., & Lewis, M. (1997). Objective documentation of child abuse and dissociation on 12 murderers with dissociative identity disorder. *American Journal of Psychiatry, 154,* 1703–1710.

Lewis-Fernandez, R., Hinton, D. E., Laria, A. J., et al. (2010). Culture and the anxiety disorders: Recommendations for DSM-V. *Depression and Anxiety, 27,* 212–229.

Li, H. Z., & Browne, A. (2000). Defining mental illness and accessing mental health services: Perspectives of Asian Canadians. *Canadian Journal of Community Mental Health, 19,* 143–149.

Li, M. D., & Burmeister, M. (2009). New insights into the genetics of addiction. *Nature Review, Genetics, 10,* 225–231.

Lian, J. Z., & Mathews, D. R. (1999). Does the vertical mosaic still exist? Ethnicity and income in Canada, 1991. *Canadian Review of Sociology and Anthropology, 35,* 461–481.

Liashko, V., & Manas, K. (2003). Medicated anxious children : Characteristics and cognitive-behavioural treatment response. *Canadian Journal of Psychiatry, 48,* 741–748.

Liberto, J. G., Oslin, D. W., & Ruskin, P. E. (1996). Alcoholism in the older population. In L. L. Carstensen, B. A. Edelstein, & L. Dornbrand (Eds.), *The practical handbook of clinical gerontology* (pp. 324–348). Thousand Oaks, CA: Sage.

Libman, E., Rothenberg, I., Fichten, C. S., & Amsel, R. (1985). The SSES-E—A measure of sexual self-efficacy in erectile functioning. *Journal of Sex and Marital Therapy, 11,* 233–247.

Lichstein, K. L., & Morin, C. M. (2000). *Treatment of late-life insomnia.* Thousand Oaks, CA: Sage.

Liddle, P. F. (2000). Cognitive impairment in schizophrenia: Its impact on social functioning. *Acta Psychiatrica Scandinavica, 400* (Suppl.), 11–16.

Lieberman, J. A., Stroup, T. S., McEvoy, J. P., et al. (2005). Effectiveness of antipsychotic drugs in patients with chronic schizophrenia. *New England Journal of Medicine, 353,* 1209–1223.

Light, L. L. (1990). Interactions between memory and language in old age. In J. E. Birren & K. W. Schaie (Eds.), *Handbook of the psychology of aging* (pp. 275–290). San Diego: Academic Press.

Lilienfeld, S. O. (2005). Scientifically unsupported and supported interventions for childhood psychopathology: A summary. *Pediatrics, 115,* 761–764.

Lilienfeld, S. O. (2007). Psychological treatments that cause harm. *Perspectives on Psychological Science, 2,* 53–70.

Lilienfeld, S. O., Lynn, S. J., Kirsch, I., Chaves, J. F., et al. (1999). Dissociative identity disorder and the sociogenic model: Recalling lessons from the past. *Psychological Bulletin, 125,* 507–523.

Lim, K.-L., Jacobs, P., Ohinmaa, A., & Schopflocher, D. (2008). A new population-based measure of the economic burden of mental illness in Canada. *Chronic Diseases in Canada, 28(3),* 92–8.

Lim, S. L., & Kim, J. H. (2005). Cognitive processing of emotional information in depression, panic, and somatoform disorder. *Journal of Abnormal Psychology, 114,* 50–61.

Lin, E., Goering, P., Offord, D. R., Campbell, D., & Boyle, M. H. (1996). The use of mental health services in Ontario: Epidemiological findings. *Canadian Journal of Psychiatry, 41,* 572–577.

Lindemann, E. (1944). Symptomatology and management of acute grief. *American Journal of Psychiatry, 101,* 141–148.

Linden, D. E. J. (2006). How psychotherapy changes the brain—the contribution of functional neuroimaging. *Molecular Psychiatry, 11,* 528–538.

Linden, W. (2003). Cardiac conditions. In S. Llewelyn & P. Kennedy (Eds.), *Handbook of clinical health psychology* (pp. 81–101). Chichester, England: John Wiley & Sons.

Linden, W., & Moseley, J. V. (2006). The efficacy of behavioral treatments for hypertension. *Applied Psychophysiology and Biofeedback, 31,* 51–63.

Lindesay, J., et al. (2006). Worry content across the lifespan: An analysis of 16- to 74-year old participants in the British National Survey of Psychiatric Mobility 2000. *Psychological Medicine, 36,* 1625–1633.

Linehan, M. M. (1985). The Reasons For Living Inventory. In P. Keller & L. Ritt (Eds.), *Innovations in clinical practice: A sourcebook* (pp. 321–330). Sarasota, FL: Professional Resource Exchange.

Linehan, M. M. (1987). Dialectical behavior therapy for borderline personality disorder. *Bulletin of the Menninger Clinic, 51,* 261–276.

Linehan, M. M. (1993a). *Behavioral skills training manual for treating borderline personality disorder.* New York: Guilford Press.

Linehan, M. M. (1993b). *Cognitive behavioral treatment of borderline personality disorder: The dialectics of effective treatment.* New York: Guilford.

Linehan, M. M., Armstrong, H. E., Suarez, A., Allmon, D., & Heard, H. L. (1991). Cognitive-behavioral treatment of chronically parasuicidal borderline patients. *Archives of General Psychiatry, 48,* 1060–1064.

Linehan, M. M., Heard, H. L., & Armstrong, H. E. (1993). Naturalistic follow-up of a behavioral treatment for chronically parasuicidal borderline patients. *Archives of General Psychiatry, 50,* 971–974.

Linehan, M. M., Schmidt, H., Dimeff, L. A., Craft, J. C., Kanter, J., & Comtois, K. A. (1999). Dialectical behavior therapy for patients with borderline personality disorder and drug dependence. *American Journal on Addiction, 8,* 279–292.

Linehan, M. M., & Shearin, E. N. (1988). Lethal stress: A social-behavioral model of suicidal behavior. In S. Fisher & J. Reason (Eds.), *Handbook of life stress, cognition, and health.* New York: John Wiley & Sons.

Links, P. S., Eynan, R., Heisel, M. J., & Nisenbaum, R. (2008). Elements of affective instability associated with suicidal behaviour in patients with borderline personality disorder. *Canadian Journal of Psychiatry, 53,* 112–116.

Links, P. S., Gould, B., & Ratnayake, R. (2003). Assessing suicidal youth with antisocial, borderline, or narcissistic personality disorder. *Canadian Journal of Psychiatry, 48,* 301–310.

Links, P. S., Heslegrave, R., & van Reekum, R. (1998). Prospective follow-up of borderline personality disorder: Prognosis, prediction outcome, and Axis II comorbidity. *Canadian Journal of Psychiatry, 43,* 265–270.

Linn, R. T., Wolf, P. A., Bachman, D. L., Knoefel, J. E., Cobb, J., et al. (1995). The "preclinical phase" of probable Alzheimer's disease: A 13-year prospective study of the Framingham cohort. *Archives of Neurology, 52,* 485–490.

Linscott, R. J., Allardyce, J., & van Os, J. (2009). Seeking verisimilitude in a class: A systematic review of evidence that the clinical symptoms of schizophrenia are taxonic. *Schizophrenia Bulletin, 35,* 811–829.

Liotti, G. (1992). Disorganized disoriented attachment in the etiology of dissociative disorders. *Dissociation, 4,* 196–204.

Lipowski, P., Kerkhofs, M., VanOnderbergen, A., Hubain, P., Copinschi, G., et al. (1994). The 24 hour profiles of cortisol, prolactin, and growth hormone secretion in mania. *Archives of General Psychiatry, 51,* 616–624.

Lipowski, Z. J. (1983). Transient cognitive disorders (delirium and acute confusional states) in the elderly. *American Journal of Psychiatry, 140,* 1426–1436.

Litman, L. C. (2004). A case of erotic violence syndrome. *Canadian Journal of Psychiatry, 49,* 217–218.

Littlefield, A. K., Sher, K. J., & Wood, P. K. (2009). Is "maturing out" of problematic alcoholic involvement related to personality change? *Journal of Abnormal Psychology, 118,* 360–374.

Litwack, T. R. (2001). Actuarial versus clinical assessments of dangerousness. *Psychology, Public Policy, and Law, 7,* 409–443.

Liu, R. T., Alloy, L. B., Abramson, L. Y., et al. (2009). Emotional maltreatment and depression: Prospective prediction of depressive episodes. *Depression and Anxiety, 26,* 174–181.

Livesley, W. J. (1998). Suggestions for a framework for an empirically based classification of personality disorders. *Canadian Journal of Psychiatry, 43,* 137–147.

Livesley, W. J. (2005). Behavioral and molecular genetic contributions to a dimensional classification of personality disorder. *Journal of Personality Disorders, 19,* 131–155.

Livesley, W. J., & Jackson, D. N. (in press). *Manual for the Dimensional Assessment of Personality Problems—Basic Questionnaire.* Port Huron, MI: Sigma.

Livesley, W. J., Jang, K. L., & Vernon, P. A. (1998). Phenotypic and genetic structure of traits in delineating personality disorder. *Archives of General Psychiatry, 55,* 941–948.

Livesley, W. J., Schroeder, M. L., Jackson, D. N., & Jung, K. L. (1994). Categorical distinctions in the study of personality disorder: Implications for classification. *Journal of Abnormal Psychology, 103,* 6–17.

Livingston, J. D., Wilson, D., Tien, G., & Bond, L. (2003). A follow-up study of persons found not criminally responsible on account of mental disorder in British Columbia. *Canadian Journal of Psychiatry, 48,* 408–415.

Lo, H.-T., & Chung, R. C. Y. (2005). The Hong Fook experience: Working with ethnocultural communities in Toronto 1982–2002. *Transcultural Psychiatry, 42,* 457–477.

Lobel, T. E., Gilat, I., & Endler, N. S. (1993). The Gulf War: Distressful reactions to SCUD missile attacks. *Anxiety, Stress and Coping, 6,* 9–23.

Lochman, J. E. & Wells, K. C. (1996). A social-cognitive intervention with aggressive children: Prevention effects and contextual implementation issues. In R. Dev. Peters & R. J. McMahon (Eds.), *Prevention and early intervention: Childhood disorders, substance use, and delinquency* (111–143). Newbury Park, CA: Sage.

Lock, J., Agras, W. S., Bryson, S., & Kraemer, H. C. (2005). A comparison of short- and long-term family therapy for adolescent anorexia nervosa. *Journal of the American Academy of Child and Adolescent Psychiatry, 44,* 632–639.

Lock, J., & Couturier, J. (2007). Evidence-based family psychotherapy interventions. In T. Jaffa & B. McDermott (Eds.), *Eating disorders in children and adolescents* (pp. 238–247). New York: Cambridge University Press.

Lock, S., LeGrange, D., Agras, W. S., & Dare, C. (2001). *Treatment manual for anorexia nervosa: A family-based approach.* New York: Guilford.

Lodge, J., Tripp, G., & Harte, D. K. (2000). Think-aloud, thought-listing, and video-mediated recall procedures in the assessment of children's self-talk. *Cognitive Therapy and Research, 24,* 399–418.

Loeber, R. & Keenan, K., (1994). The interaction between conduct disorder and its comorbid conditions: Effects of age and gender. *Clinical Psychology Review, 14,* 497–523.

Loeber, R., Keenan, K., Lahey, B. B., Green, S. M., & Thomas, C. (1993). Evidence for developmentally based diagnoses of oppositional defiant disorder and conduct disorder. *Journal of Abnormal Child Psychology, 21,* 377–410.

Loewenstein, R. J. (1991). Psychogenic amnesia and psychogenic fugue: A comprehensive review. In A. Tasman & S. M. Goldfinger (Eds.), *American Psychiatric Press Review of Psychiatry* (pp. 189–222). Washington, DC: American Psychiatric Press.

Loftus, E. F. (1993). The reality of repressed memories. *American Psychologist, 48,* 518–537.

Lomas, J., Woods, J., & Veenstra, G. (1997). Devolving authority for health care in Canada's provinces: 1. An introduction to the issues. *Canadian Medical Association Journal, 156,* 371–377.

Lomax, C. L., Oldfield, V. B., & Salkovskis, P. M. (2009). Clinical and treatment comparisons between adults with early- and late-onset obsessive-compulsive disorder. *Behaviour Research and Therapy, 47,* 99–104.

London, P. (1964). *The modes and morals of psychotherapy.* New York: Holt, Rinehart & Winston.

London, P. (1986). *The modes and morals of psychotherapy* (2nd ed.). New York: Hemisphere.

Longmore, R. J., & Worrell, M. (2007). Do we need to challenge thoughts in cognitive behavior therapy? *Clinical Psychology Review, 27*, 173–187.

Loock, C., et al. (2005). Identifying fetal alcohol spectrum disorder in primary care. *Canadian Medical Association Journal, 172*, 628–630.

Looman, J. (1995). Sexual fantasies of child molesters. *Canadian Journal of Behavioural Science, 27*, 321–332.

Looper, K. J., & Paris, J. (2000). What dimensions underlie Cluster B personality disorders? *Comprehensive Psychiatry, 41*, 432–437.

Loos, C., & Bowd, A. (1997). Caregivers of persons with Alzheimer's disease: Some neglected implications of the experience of personal loss and grief. *Death Studies, 21*, 501–514.

Lopez, S. R. (1996). Testing ethnic minority children. In B. B. Wolman (Ed.), *The encyclopedia of psychology, psychiatry, and psychoanalysis*. New York: Henry Holt.

Lopez, S. R., & Guarnaccia, P. J. (2000). Cultural psychopathology: Uncovering the social world of mental illness. *Annual Review of Psychology, 51*, 571–598.

Lopez, S. R., & Hernandez, P. (1986). How culture is considered in evaluations of psychopathology. *Journal of Nervous and Mental Disease, 176*, 598–606.

LoPiccolo, J. (1992a). Post-modern sex therapy for erectile failure. In R. C. Rosen & S. R. Leiblum (Eds.), *Erectile failure: Assessment and treatment*. New York: Guilford.

LoPiccolo, J. (1992b). Psychological evaluation of erectile failure. In R. Kirby, C. Carson, & G. Webster (Eds.), *Diagnosis and management of male erectile failure dysfunction*. Oxford: Butterworth-Heinemann.

LoPiccolo, J. (2002). Postmodern sex therapy. In F. W. Kaslow & J. L. Lebow (Eds.), *Comprehensive handbook of psychotherapy, Vol. 4, Integrative/eclectic* (pp. 411–435). London: John Wiley & Sons.

LoPiccolo, J., & Friedman, J. (1988). Broad-spectrum treatment of low sexual desire: Integration of cognitive, behavioral, and systemic therapy. In S. Leiblum & R. C. Rosen (Eds.), *Sexual desire disorders*. New York: Guilford.

LoPiccolo, J., & Hogan, D. R. (1979). Multidimensional treatment of sexual dysfunction. In O. F. Pomerleau & J. P. Brady (Eds.), *Behavioral medicine: Theory and practice*. Baltimore: Williams & Wilkins.

LoPiccolo, J., & Lobitz, W. C. (1972). The role of masturbaton in the treatment of orgasmic dysfunction. *Archives of Sexual Behavior, 2*, 163–171.

LoPiccolo, J., & Stock, W. E. (1987). Sexual function, dysfunction, and counseling in gynecological practice. In Z. Rosenwaks, F. Benjamin, & M. L. Stone (Eds.), *Gynecology*. New York: Macmillan.

Loranger, A. W. (1988). *Personality Disorder Examination (PDE) Manual*. Yonkers, NY: DV Communications.

Loranger, A. W., Oldham, J., Russakoff, L. M. & Susman, V. (1987). Structured interviews and borderline personality disorder. *Archives of General Psychiatry, 41*, 565–568.

Loranger, A. W., Sartorius, N., Andreoli, A., Berger, P., Buchleim, P., et al. (1994). The International Personality Disorders Examination: The World Health Organization/Alcohol, Drug Abuse and Mental Health Administration international pilot study of personality disorders. *Archives of General Psychiatry, 51*, 215–223.

Loranger, A. W., Susman, V. L., Oldham, J. M., & Russakoff, L. M. (1987). The Personality Disorder Examination: A preliminary report. *Journal of Personality Disorders, 1*, 1–13.

Lorber, M. F. (2004). Psychophysiology of aggression, psychopathy, and conduct problems: A meta-analysis. *Psychological Bulletin, 130*, 531–552.

Lord, J., & Pedlar, A. (1991). Life in the community: Four years after the closure of an institution. *Mental Retardation, 29*, 213–221.

Lotter, V. (1978). Follow-up studies. In M. Rutter & E. Schopler (Eds.), *Autism: A reappraisal of concepts and treatment*. New York: Plenum.

Lovaas, O. I. (1987). Behavioral treatment and normal educational and intellectual functioning in young autistic children. *Journal of Consulting and Clinical Psychology, 55*, 3–9.

Lovaas, O. I., Newsom, C., & Hickman, C. (1987). Self-stimulatory behavior and perceptual reinforcement. *Journal of Applied Behavior Analysis, 20*, 45–68.

Lowe, M. R., & Levine, A. S. (2005). Eating motives and the controversy over dieting: Eating less than needed versus less than wanted. *Obesity Research, 13*, 797–806.

Lowe, M. R., & Timko, C. A. (2004). Dieting: Really harmful, merely ineffective, or actually helpful? *British Journal of Nutrition, 92*, S19–S22.

Lozano, A. M., Mayberg, H. S., Giacobbe, P., et al. (2008). Subcallosal cingulated gyrus deep brain stimulation for treatment-resistant depression. *Biological Psychology, 64*, 461–467.

Luborsky, L., Rosenthal, R., Diguer, L., et al. (2002). The Dodo bird verdict is alive and well—mostly. *Clinical Psychology: Science and Practice, 9*, 1–12.

Luby, J. L., Belden, A. C., Pautsch, J., et al. (2009). The clinical significance of preschool depression: Impairment in functioning and clinical markers of the disorder. *Journal of Affective Disorders, 112*, 111–119.

Luby, E. D., & Koval, D. (2009). CNS opiate systems and eating disorders. In R. L. Dean III, E. J. Bilsky, S. S. Negus (Eds.), *Opiate receptors and antagonists* (pp. 407–421). New York: Springer.

Luepnitz, R. R., Randolph, D. L., & Gutsch, K. U. (1982). Race and socioeconomic status as confounding variables in the accurate diagnosis of alcoholism. *Journal of Clinical Psychology, 38*, 665–669.

Lui, S., Deng, W., Huang, X., et al. (2009). Association of cerebral deficits with clinical symptoms in antipsychotic-naive first-episode schizophrenia: An optimized voxel-based morphometry and resting state functional connectivity study. *American Journal of Psychiatry, 166*, 196–205.

Lumley, M. N., & Harkness, K. L. (2009). Childhood maltreatment and depressotypic cognitive organization. *Cognitive Therapy and Research, 33*, 511–522.

Lundberg, U., & Frankenhaueser, M. (1999). Stress and workload of men and women in high-ranking positions. *Journal of Occupational Health Psychology, 4*, 142–151.

Luyten, P., Blatt, S. J., Van Houdenhove, B., & Corveleyn, J. (2006). Depression research and treatment: Are we skating to where the puck is going to be? *Clinical Psychology Review, 26*, 985–999.

Luyten, P., Sabbe, B., Blatt, S. J., et al. (2007). Dependency and self-criticism: Relationship with major depressive disorder, severity of depression, and clinical presentation. *Depression and Anxiety, 24*, 586–596.

Luyten, P., et al. (in press). Dependency and self-criticism: Relationship with major depressive disorder, severity of depression, and clinical presentation. *Depression and Anxiety*.

Lykken, D. T. (1957). A study of anxiety in the sociopathic personality. *Journal of Abnormal and Social Psychology, 55*, 6–10.

Lymburner, J. A., & Roesch, R. (1999). The insanity defense: Five years of research (1993–1997). *International Journal of Law and Psychiatry, 22*, 213–240.

Lynam, D. R. (1997). Pursuing the psychopath: Capturing the fledgling psychopath in a nomological net. *Journal of Abnormal Psychology, 106*, 425–438.

Lynch, D., Laws, K. R., & McKenna, P. J. (2010). Cognitive behavioural therapy for major psychiatric disorder: Does it really work? A meta-analytical review of well-controlled trials. *Psychological Medicine, 40*, 9–24.

Lynch, T. R., Compton, J. S., Mendelson, T., Robins, C. J., & Krishnan, K. R. R. (2000). Anxious depression among the elderly: Clinical and phenomenological correlates. *Aging and Mental Health, 4*, 268–274.

Lyon, D. R., Hart, S. D., & Webster, C. D. (2001). Violence and risk assessment. In R. A. Schuller & J. R. Ogloff (Eds.), *Introduction to psychology and law: Canadian perspectives* (pp. 314–350). Toronto: University of Toronto Press.

Lyon, H. M., Startup, M., & Bentall, R. P. (1999). Social cognition and the manic defense: Attribution, selective attention, and self-schema in bipolar affective disorder. *Journal of Abnormal Psychology, 108*, 273–282.

Ma, S. H., & Teasdale, J. D. (2004). Mindfulness-based cognitive therapy for depression: Replication and exploration of differential relapse prevention effects. *Journal of Consulting and Clinical Psychology, 72*, 31–40.

MacCharles, T. (2001, February 6). Liberal bill to reform Young Offenders Act: Alliance, Tories say it's not tough enough on crime. *Toronto Star*, A6.

Maccoby, N., & Altman, D. G. (1988). Disease prevention in communities: The Stanford Heart Disease Prevention Program. In R. H. Price, E. L. Cowen, R. P. Lorion, & J. Ramos-McKay (Eds.), *14 ounces of prevention: A casebook for practitioners* (pp. 165–174). Washington, DC: American Psychological Association.

MacDonald, A. W., & Carter, C. S. (2003). Event-related fMRI study of context processing in dorsolateral prefrontal cortex of patients with schizophrenia. *Journal of Abnormal Psychology*, *112*, 689–697.

MacDonald, M. R., & Kuiper, N. A. (1984). Self-schema decision consistency in clinical depression. *Journal of Social and Clinical Psychology*, *2*, 264–272.

MacGregor, M. W. (1996). Multiple personality disorder: Etiology, treatment, and techniques from a psychodynamic perspective. *Psychoanalytic Psychology*, *13*, 389–402.

Mackenzie, C. S., Gekoski, W. L., & Knox, J. V. (1999). Do family physicians treat older patients with mental disorders differently from younger patients? *Canadian Family Physician*, *45*, 1219–1224.

MacLatchy-Gaudet, H. A., & Stewart, S. H. (2001). The context-specific positive alcohol outcome expectancies of university women. *Addictive Behaviors*, *26*, 31–49.

MacLeod, A. K., Haynes, C., & Sensky, T. (1998). Attributions about common bodily sensations: Their associations with hyponchondriasis and anxiety. *Psychological Medicine*, *28*, 225–228.

MacMillan, H. L., Boyle, M. H., Wong, M. Y.-Y., Duku, E. K., Fleming, J. E., & Walsh, C. A. (1999). Slapping and spanking in childhood and its association with lifetime prevalence of psychiatric disorders in a general population. *Canadian Medical Association Journal*, *161*, 805–809.

MacMillan, H. L., Fleming, J. E., Trocmé, N., Boyle, M. H., Wong, M., Racine, Y. A., et al. (1997). Prevalence of child physical and sexual abuse in the community—results from the Ontario Health Supplement. *Journal of the American Medical Association*, *278*, 131–135.

MacMillan, H. L., Georgiades, K., Duku, E. K., et al. (2009). Cortisol response to stress in female youths exposed to childhood maltreatment: Results of the Youth Mood Project. *Biological Psychiatry*, *66*, 62–68.

Macrodimitris, S. D., & Endler, N. S. (2001). Coping, control, and adjustment in Type II diabetes. *Health Psychology*, *20*, 208–216.

Madonna, P. G., Van Scoyk, S., & Jones, D. B. (1991). Family interactions within incest and nonincest families. *American Journal of Psychiatry*, *148*, 46–49.

Maffei, C., Fossati, A., Agostini, I., Barraco, A., et al. (1997). Interrater reliability and internal consistency of the Structured Clinical Interview for Axis II Personality Disorders (SCID-II), Version 2.0. *Journal of Personality Disorders*, *11*, 279–284.

Magnusson, A., & Axelsson, J. (1993). The prevalence of seasonal affective disorder is low among descendants of Icelandic emigrants in Canada. *Archives of General Psychiatry*, *50*, 947–951.

Maj, M., Pirozzi, R., Magliono, L., & Bartoli, L. (1998). Long-term outcome of lithium prophylaxis in bipolar disorder: A 5-year prospective study of 402 patients at a lithium clinic. *American Journal of Psychiatry*, *155*, 30–35.

Malaiyandi, U., et al. (2006). Impact of CYP2A6 genotype on pretreatment smoking behavior and nicotine levels from and usage of nicotine replacement therapy. *Molecular Psychiatry*, *11*, 400–409.

Malamuth, N. M., & Brown, L. M. (1994). Sexually aggressive men's perceptions of women's communications: Testing three explanations. *Journal of Personality and Social Psychology*, *67*, 699–712.

Malamuth, N. M., & Check, J. V. P. (1983). Sexual arousal to rape depictions: Individual differences. *Journal of Abnormal Psychology*, *92*, 55–67.

Malaspina, D., et al. (2000). Relation of familial schizophrenia to negative symptoms but not to the deficit syndrome. *American Journal of Psychiatry*, *157*, 994–1003.

Malchy, B., Enns, M. W., Young, T. K., & Cox, B. J. (1997). Suicide among Manitoba's aboriginal people, 1988 to 1994. *Canadian Medical Association Journal*, *156*, 1133–1138.

Maldonado, J. R., Butler, L. D., & Spiegel, D. (1998). Treatments for dissociative disorders. In P. E. Nathan & J. M. Gorman (Eds.), *A guide to treatments that work* (pp. 423–446). New York: Oxford University Press.

Maletzky, B. M. (1997). Exhibitionism: Assessment and treatment. In D. R. Laws & W. O'Donohue (Eds.), *Sexual deviance* (pp. 40–74). New York: Guilford Press.

Malizia, A. L., Cunningham, V. J., Bell, C. J., Liddle, P. F., et al. (1998). Decreased brain GABAa-benzodiazepine receptor binding in panic disorder: Preliminary results from a quantitative study. *Archives of General Psychiatry*, *55*, 715–720.

Malkoff-Schwartz, S., Frank, E., Anderson, B., Sherrill, J. T., Siegel, L., et al. (1998). Stressful life events and social rhythm disruption in the onset of manic and depressive bipolar episodes: A preliminary investigation. *Archives of General Psychiatry*, *55*, 702–707.

Malla, A. K. (1988). Characteristics of patients who receive electroconvulsive therapy. *Canadian Journal of Psychiatry*, *33*, 696–701.

Malla, A. K., Mittal, C., Lee, M., Scholten, D. J., Assis, L., & Norman, R. M. G. (2002). Computed tomography of the brain morphology of patients with first-episode schizophrenic psychosis. *Journal of Psychiatry and Neuroscience*, *27*, 350–358.

Malla, A. K., Norman, R. M. G., Manchanda, R., et al. (2002). One year outcome in first episode psychosis: Influence of DUP and other predictors. *Schizophrenia Research*, *54*, 231–242.

Malla, A. K., Norman, R. M. G., Scholten, D. J., Zirul, S., & Kotteda, V. (2001). A comparison of long-term outcome in first episode schizophrenia following treatment with risperidone or a typical antipsychotic. *Journal of Clinical Psychiatry*, *62*, 179–184.

Malouff, J., Thorsteinsson, E. B., & Schutte, N. S. (2007). The efficacy of problem solving therapy in reducing mental and physical health problems: A meta-analysis. *Clinical Psychology Review*, *27*, 46–57.

Manassis, K., & Menna, R. (1999). Depression in anxious children: Possible factors in comorbidity. *Depression and Anxiety*, *10*, 18–24.

Manassis, K., & Monga, S. (2001). A therapeutic approach to children and adolescents with anxiety disorders and associated comorbid conditions. *Journal of the American Academy of Child and Adolescent Psychiatry*, *40*, 115–117.

Mancebo, M. C., Eisen, J. L., Grant, J. E., & Rasmussen, S. A. (2005). Obsessive compulsive personality disorder and obsessive compulsive disorder: Clinical characteristics, diagnostic difficulties, and treatment. *Annals of Clinical Psychiatry*, *17*, 197–204.

Mancini, C., van Ameringen, M., Szatmair, P., Fugere, C., & Boyle, M. (1996). A high-risk pilot study of the children of adults with social phobia. *Journal of the American Academy of Child and Adolescent Psychiatry*, *35*, 1511–1517.

Mandel, H., & Young, J. (2009). *Here's the deal: Don't touch me.* New York: Bantam.

Mandler, G. (1966). Anxiety. In D. L. Sills (Ed.), *International encyclopedia of the social sciences*. New York: Macmillan.

Manji, H. K., Chen, G., Shimon, H., Hsiao, J. K., Potter, W. Z., & Belmaker, R. H. (1995). Guanine nucleotide-binding proteins in bipolar affective disorder: Effects of long-term lithium treatment. *Archives of General Psychiatry*, *52*, 135–144.

Mann, R. E., Zalcman, R. F., Rush, B. R., et al. (2008). Alcohol factors in suicide mortality rates in Manitoba. *Canadian Journal of Psychiatry*, *53*, 243–251.

Mansdorf, I. J., Calapai, P., Caselli, L., & Burstein, Y. (1999). Reducing psychotropic medication usage in nursing home residents: The effects of behaviorally oriented psychotherapy. *The Behavior Therapist*, *22*, 21–39.

Manuck, S. B., Kaplan, J. R., & Clarkson, T. B. (1983). Behaviorally induced heart rate reactivity and atherosclerosis in cynomolgus monkeys. *Psychosomatic Medicine*, *49*, 95–108.

Manuel, D. G., Leung, M., Nguyen, K., Tanuseputro, P., & Johansen, H. (2003). Burden of cardiovascular disease in Canada. *Canadian Journal of Cardiology*, *19*, 997–1004.

Maravilla, K. R., & Yang, C. C. (2008). Magnetic resonance imaging and the female sexual response: Overview of techniques, results, and future directions. *The Journal of Sexual Medicine*, *5*, 1559–1571.

March, J. S., & Vitiello, B. (2009). Clinical messages from the Treatment for Adolescents with Depression Study (TADS). *American Journal of Psychiatry*, *166*, 1118–1123.

Marchand, Y., Lefebvre, C. D., & Connolly, J. F. (2006). Correlating digit span performance and event-related potentials to assess working memory. *International Journal of Psychophysiology*, *62*, 280–289.

Marco, C. A., et al. (2000). Impact of gender and having children in the household on ambulatory blood pressure in work and nonwork settings: A partial replication and new findings. *Annals of Behavioral Medicine*, *22*, 110–115.

Marcus, D. K., Gurley, J. R., Marchi, M. M., & Bauer, C. (2007). Cognitive and perceptual variables in hypochondriasis and health anxiety: A systematic review. *Clinical Psychology Review*, *27*, 127–139.

Marcus, J., et al. (1987). Review of the NIMH Israeli Kibbutz-City and the Jerusalem infant development study. *Schizophrenia Bulletin*, *13*, 425–438.

Marder, S. R. (2006). Drug initiatives to improve cognitive function. *Journal of Clinical Psychiatry*, *67* (Suppl. 9), 31–35.

Margolin, G. (1982). Ethical and legal considerations in marital and family therapy. *American Psychologist*, *37*, 788–801.

Marin, T. J., Chen, E., & Miller, G. E. (2008). What do trajectories of childhood socioeconomic status tell us about markers of cardiovascular health in adolescence? *Psychosomatic Medicine, 70,* 152–159.

Maris, R. W., Berman, A. L., Maltsberger, J. T., & Yufit, R. I. (1992). *Assessment and prediction of suicide.* New York: Guilford.

Markowitz, J. C. (2008). Depressed mothers, depressed children. *American Journal of Psychiatry, 165,* 1086–1088.

Marlatt, G. A. (1983). The controlled drinking controversy: A commentary. *American Psychologist, 38,* 1097–1110.

Marlatt, G. A. (1985). Relapse prevention: Theoretical rationale and overview of the model. In G. A. Marlatt & J. Gordon (Eds.), *Relapse prevention: Maintenance strategies in addictive behavior change.* New York: Guilford.

Marlatt, G. A. (1999). From hindsight to foresight: A commentary on Project MATCH. In J. A. Tucker, D. M. Donovan, & G. A. Marlatt (Eds.), *Changing addictive behavior: Bridging clinical and public health strategies* (pp. 45–66). New York: Guilford.

Marlatt, G. A., et al. (1998). Screening and brief intervention for high-risk college student drinkers: Results from a 2-year follow-up assessment. *Journal of Consulting and Clinical Psychology, 66,* 604–615.

Marlatt, G. A., Baer, J. S., & Larimer, M. (1995). Preventing alcohol abuse in college students: A harm-reduction approach. In G. M. Boyd, J. Howard, & R. A. Zucker (Eds.), *Alcohol problems among adolescents: Current directions in prevention research* (pp. 147–172). Hillsdale, NJ: Erlbaum.

Marlatt, G. A., Blume, A. W., & Parks, G. A. (2001). Integrating harm reduction therapy and traditional substance abuse treatment. *Journal of Psychoactive Drugs, 33,* 13–21.

Marlatt, G. A., & Gordon, J. R. (Eds.). (1985). *Relapse prevention: Maintenance strategies in the treatment of addictive behaviors.* New York: Guilford.

Marlatt, G. A., & Witkiewitz, K. (2002). Harm reduction approaches to alcohol use: Health promotion, prevention, and treatment. *Addictive Behaviors, 27,* 867–886.

Marmot, M. G., Bosma, H., Hemingway, H., Brunner, E., & Stansfeld, S. (1997). Contribution of job control and other risk factors to social variations in coronary heart disease incidence. *The Lancet, 350,* 235–239.

Marriage, S., Wolverton, A., & Marriage, K. (2009). Autism spectrum disorder grown up: A chart review of adult functioning. *Journal of the Canadian Academy of Child and Adolescent Psychiatry, 18,* 322–328.

Marsh, A. A., Finger, E. C., Mitchell, D. G. V., et al. (2008). Reduced amygdale response to fearful expressions in children and adolescents with callous-unemotional traits and disruptive behavior disorders. *American Journal of Psychiatry, 165,* 712–720.

Marshall, K. (1998). The gambling industry: Raising the stakes. *Perspectives on Labour and Income, 10(4),* 7–11. Statistics Canada Catalogue No. 75-001-XWE.

Marshall, M., & Rathbone, J. (2006). Early intervention for psychosis (Review). Cochrane Database of Systematic Reviews, Issue 4. Art No.: CD004718.DOI: 10.1002/14651858. CD004718.pub2.

Marshall, W. L. (1996). Assessment, treatment, and theorizing about sex offenders: Developments during the past twenty years and future directions. *Criminal Justice and Behavior, 23,* 162–199.

Marshall, W. L. (1997). Pedophilia: Psychopathology and theory. In D. R. Laws & W. O'Donohue (Eds.), *Sexual deviance* (pp. 152–174). New York: Guilford Press.

Marshall, W. L. (1999). Current status of North American assessment and treatment programs for sexual offenders. *Journal of Interpersonal Violence, 14,* 221–239.

Marshall, W. L., & Barbaree, H. E. (1990). Outcome of comprehensive cognitive-behavioral treatment programs. In W. L. Marshall & D. R. Laws (Eds.), *Handbook of sexual assault: Issues, theories, and treatment of the offender* (pp. 363–385). New York: Plenum Press.

Marshall, W. L., Barbaree, H., & Christophe, D. (1986). Sexual offenders against female children: Sexual preferences for age of victims and type of behaviour. *Canadian Journal of Behavioural Science, 18,* 424–439.

Marshall, W. L., Cripps, E., Anderson, D., & Cortoni, F. A. (1999). Self-esteem and coping strategies in child molesters. *Journal of Interpersonal Violence, 14,* 955–962.

Marshall, W. L., & Fernandez, Y. M. (2000). Phallometric testing with sexual offenders: Limits to its value. *Clinical Psychology Review, 20,* 807–822.

Marshall, W. L., Hamilton, K., & Fernandez, Y. (2001). Empathy deficits and cognitive distortions in child molesters. *Sexual Abuse: A Journal of Research and Treatment, 13,* 123–130.

Marshall, W. L., Jones, R., Ward, T., Johnston, P., & Barbaree, H. E. (1991). Treatment outcomes with sex offenders. *Clinical Psychology Review, 11,* 465–485.

Marshall, W. L., & Moulden, H. (2001). Hostility toward women and victim empathy in rapists. *Sexual Abuse, 13,* 249–255.

Marshall, W. L., & Serin, R. (1997). Personality disorder. In S. M. Turner & M. Hersen (Eds.), *Adult psychopathology and diagnosis,* Vol. 3 (pp. 508–543). New York: John Wiley & Sons.

Marshall, W. L., Thornton, D., Marshall, L. E., Fernandez, Y. M., & Mann, R. (2001). Treatment of sexual offenders who are in categorical denial: A pilot project. *Sexual Abuse: A Journal of Research and Treatment, 13,* 205–215.

Martens, P. J., et al. (2007). Prevalence of mental illness and its impact on the use of home care and nursing homes: A population-based study of older adults in Manitoba. *Canadian Journal of Psychiatry, 52,* 581–590.

Martin, B. A. (2000). The Clarke Institute experience with completed suicide: 1966 to 1997. *Canadian Journal of Psychiatry, 45,* 630–638.

Martin, C. S., Chung, T., & Langenbucher, J. W. (2008). How should we revise diagnostic criteria for substance abuse disorders in DSM-V? *Journal of Abnormal Psychology, 117,* 561–575.

Martin, N. D., Williams, D., Harrison, K., & Ratan, R. (in press). A content analysis of female body imagery in video games. *Sex Roles.*

Martin, R., & Young, J. (2010). Schema therapy. In K. S. Dobson (Ed.), *Handbook of cognitive-behavioral therapies* (3rd ed., pp. 317–346). New York: The Guilford Press.

Masellis, M., Rector, N. A., & Richter, M. A. (2003). Quality of life in OCD: Differential impact of obsessions, compulsions, and depression comorbidity. *Canadian Journal of Psychiatry, 48,* 72–77.

Maser, J. D., Norman, S. B., Zisook, S., et al. (2009). Psychiatric nosology is ready for a paradigm shift in *DSM-V. Clinical Psychology Science and Practice, 16,* 24–40.

Maslach, C., & Jackson, S. E. (1981). The measurement of experienced burnout. *Journal of Occupational Behaviour, 2,* 99–113.

Maslach, C., Schaufeli, W. B., & Leiter, M. (2001). Job burnout. *Annual Review of Psychology, 52,* 397–422.

Mason, F. L. (1997). Fetishism: Psychopathology and theory. In D. R. Laws & W. O'Donohue (Eds.), *Sexual deviance* (pp. 75–91). New York: Guilford Press.

Masse, L. C., & Tremblay, R. E. (1997). Behavior of boys in kindergarten and the course of substance use during adolescence. *Archives of General Psychiatry, 54,* 62–68.

Masters, W. H., & Johnson, V. E. (1966). *Human sexual response.* Boston: Little, Brown.

Masters, W. H., & Johnson, V. E. (1970). *Human sexual inadequacy.* Boston: Little, Brown.

Mataix-Cols, D., do Rosario-Campos, M. C., & Leckman, J. F. (2005). A multidimensional model of obsessive-compulsive disorder. *American Journal of Psychiatry, 162,* 228–238.

Mataix-Cols, D., Pertusa, A., and Leckman, J. F. (2007). Issues for DSM-V: How should obsessive-compulsive and related disorders be classified? *American Journal of Psychiatry, 164,* 1313–1314.

Mathew, S. J., & Charney, D. S. (2009). Publication bias and the efficacy of antidepressants. *American Journal of Psychiatry, 166,* 140–145.

Mathews, A., & MacLeod, C. (1994). Cognitive approaches to emotion and emotional disorders. In L. W. Porter & M. R. Rosenzweig (Eds.), *Annual Review of Psychology* (pp. 25–50). Stanford, CA: Stanford University Press.

Mathews, F. (1996). *The invisible boy: Revisioning the victimization of male children & their teens.* Ottawa: The National Clearinghouse on Family Violence and Health Canada.

Matthews, K. A., Meilan, E., Kuller, L. M., Kelsey, S. F., Caggiula, A., et al. (1989). Menopause and risk factors in coronary heart disease. *New England Journal of Medicine, 321,* 641–646.

Matthews, K. A., Owens, J. F., Allen, M. T., & Stoney, C. M. (1992). Do cardiovascular responses to laboratory stress relate to ambulatory blood pressure levels?: Yes, in some of the people, some of the time. *Psychosomatic Medicine, 54,* 686–697.

Matthews, K. A., Zhu, S., Tucker, D. C., & Whooley, M. A. (2006). Blood pressure to psychosocial stress and coronary classification in the coronary artery risk development in young adults study. *Hypertension, 47*, 391–395.

Mattson, M. E., Allen, J. P., Longabaugh, R., Nickless, C. J., Connors, G. J., & Kadden, R. M. (1994). A chronological review of empirical studies matching alcoholic clients to treatment. *Journal of Studies on Alcohol, 55*, 16–29.

Mayberg, H. S. (2006). Defining neurocircuits in depression: Insights from functional neuroimaging studies of diverse treatments. *Psychiatric Annals, 4*, 258–267.

Mayberg, H. S., et al. (2005). Deep brain stimulation for treatment-resistant depression. *Neuron, 45*, 651–660.

Mayhew, D. R., Beirness, D. J., & Simpson, H. M. (2000). Trends in drinking-driving fatalities in Canada—progress continues. In *Alcohol, Drugs, and Traffic Safety –T2000*. Stockholm, Sweden: Swedish National Road Safety.

Mayor's Homelessness Action Task Force. (1999). *Taking responsibility for homelessness: An action plan for Toronto: Report of the Mayor's Homelessness Action Task Force*. Toronto: City of Toronto.

Mayou, R., Kirmayer, L. J., Simon, G., Kroenke, K., & Sharpe, M. (2005). Somatoform disorders: time for a new approach in DSM-V. *American Journal of Psychiatry, 162*, 847–855.

McAlonan, G. M., Cheung, V., Cheung, C., et al. (2005). Mapping the brain in autism. A voxel-based MRI study of volumetric differences and intercorrelations in autism. *Brain, 128*, 268–276.

McBride, J., & Derevensky, J. (2009). Internet gambling behavior in a sample of online gamblers. *International Journal of Mental Health and Addiction, 7*, 149–167.

McCabe, R. E. (1999). Implicit and explicit memory for threat words in high- and low-anxiety-sensitive participants. *Cognitive Therapy and Research, 23*, 21–38.

McCabe, R. E., & Antony, M. M. (2004). Challenges in the assessment and treatment of health anxiety: The case of Mrs. A. *Cognitive and Behavioral Practice, 11*, 102–123.

McCabe, R. E., Antony, M. M., Summerfeldt, L. J., Liss, A., & Swinson, R. P. (2003). Preliminary examination of the relationship between anxiety disorders in adults and self-reported history of teasing or bullying experiences. *Cognitive Behaviour Therapy, 32*, 187–193.

McCabe, R. E., & Blankstein, K. R. (2000, November). *The experience of panic in college students: A comparison of cognitive-personality vulnerabilities, life stress, coping, attachment, and panic beliefs in panic disorder, panic attack, and non-panic groups.* Poster presented at the AABT annual convention, New Orleans, Louisiana.

McCabe, S. B., Gotlib, I. H., & Martin, R. (2000). Cognitive vulnerability for depression: Deployment of attention as a function of history of depression and current mood state. *Cognitive Therapy and Research, 24*, 427–444.

McCabe, S. B., & Tonan, P. E. (2000). Stimulus exposure duration in a deployment-of-attention task: Effects on dysphoric, recently dysphoric, and nondysphoric individuals. *Cognition and Emotion, 14*, 125–142.

McCain, M., & Mustard, F. (1999). *Reversing the real brain drain: Final report of the early year study*. Toronto: Canadian Institute for Advanced Research.

McCathie, H. C. F., Spence, S. H., & Tate, R. L. (2002). Adjustment to chronic obstructive pulmonary disease: The importance of psychological factors. *European Respiratory Journal, 19*, 47–53.

McClure, M. M., Barch, D. M., Flory, J. D., Harvey, P. D., & Siever, L. J. (2008). Context processing in schizotypal personality disorder: Evidence of specificity of impairment to the schizophrenia spectrum. *Journal of Abnormal Psychology, 117*, 342–354.

McConaghy, N. (1990). Sexual deviation. In A. S. Bellack, M. Hersen, & A. E. Kazdin (Eds.), *International handbook of behavior modification and therapy* (2nd ed., pp. 565–580). New York: Plenum.

McConaghy, N. (1993). *Sexual behavior: Problems and management*. New York: Plenum.

McConaghy, N. (1994). Paraphilias and gender identity disorders. In M. Hersen & R. T. Ammerman (Eds.), *Handbook of prescriptive treatments for adults* (pp. 317–346). New York: Plenum.

McCord, W., & McCord, J. (1964). *The psychopath: An essay on the criminal mind*. New York: Van Nostrand-Reinhold.

McCormick, N. B. (1999). When pleasure causes pain: Living with interstitial cystitis. *Sexuality and Disability, 17*, 7–18.

McCrady, B. S. (1985). Alcoholism. In D. H. Barlow (Ed.), *Clinical handbook of psychological disorders*. New York: Guilford.

McCrady, B. S., Epstein, E. E., & Walker, C. W. (2004). Alcoholics Anonymous and relapse prevention as maintenance strategies after conjoint behavioral alcohol treatment for men: 18-month outcomes. *Journal of Consulting and Clinical Psychology, 72*, 870–878.

McCrae, R. R., & Costa, P. T., Jr. (1990). *Personality in adulthood*. New York: Guilford.

McCreary Centre Society. (1999). *Adolescent health survey II: Province of British Columbia*. Vancouver: The McCreary Centre Society.

McCullough, M. E., Orsulak, P., Brandon, A., & Akers, L. (2007). Rumination, fear, and cortisol: An *in vivo* study of interpersonal transgressions. *Health Psychology, 26*, 126–132.

McCusker, J., Boulenger, J.-P., Boyer, R., Bellavance, F., & Miller, J.-M. (1997). Use of health services for anxiety disorders: A multisite study in Quebec. *Canadian Journal of Psychiatry, 42*, 730–736.

McCusker, J., Cole, M., Abrahamowicz, M., Primeau, F., & Belzile, E. (2002). Delirium predicts 12-month mortality. *Archives of Internal Medicine, 162*, 457–463.

McCusker, J., Cole, M., Dendukuri, N., Belzile, E., & Primeau, F. (2001). Delirium in older medical inpatients and subsequent cognitive and functional status: A prospective study. *Canadian Medical Association Journal, 165*, 575–583.

McDaid, C., Trowman, R., Golder, S., et al. (2008). Interventions for people bereaved through suicide: Systematic review. *British Journal of Psychiatry, 193*, 438–443.

McEwen, B. S. (1998). Protective and damaging effects of stress mediators. *New England Journal of Medicine, 338*, 171–179.

McFall, R. M., & Lillesand, D. B. (1971). Behavior rehearsal with modeling and coaching in assertion training. *Journal of Abnormal Psychology, 77*, 313–323.

McFarlane, T., Polivy, J., & McCabe, R. E. (1999). Help, not harm: Psychological foundation for a nondieting approach toward health. *Journal of Social Issues, 55*, 261–276.

McGirr, A., et al. (2006). Risk factors for completed suicide in schizophrenia and other chronic psychotic disorders: A case-control study. *Schizophrenia Research, 84*, 132–143.

McGirr, A., et al. (2007). An examination of DSM-IV depressive symptoms and risk for suicide completion in major depressive disorder: A psychological autopsy study. *Journal of Affective Disorders, 97*, 203–209.

McGirr, A., Alda, M., Seguin, M., et al. (2009). Familial aggregation of suicide explained by cluster B traits: A three-group family study of suicide controlling for major depressive disorder. *American Journal of Psychiatry, 166*, 1124–1134.

McGlashan, T. H., et al. (2003). The PRIME North America randomized double-blind clinical trial of olanzapine versus placebo in patients at risk of being prodromally symptomatic for psychosis: I. Study rationale and design. *Schizophrenia Research, 61*, 7–18.

McGlashan, T. H., et al. (2006). Randomized, double-blind trial of olanzapine versus placebo in patients prodromally symptomatic for psychosis. *The American Journal of Psychiatry, 163*, 790–799.

McGlynn, F. D., Karg, S., & Lawyer, S. R. (2003). Fear responses to mock magnetic resonance imaging among college students: Toward a prototype experiment. *Journal of Anxiety Disorders, 17*, 335–347.

McGrath, J. J. (2006). Variations in the incidence of schizophrenia: Data versus dogma. *Schizophrenia Bulletin, 32*, 195–197.

McGrady, A. V., & Bernal, G. A. A. (1986). Relaxation-based treatment of stress induced syncope. *Journal of Behavior Therapy and Experimental Psychiatry, 17*, 23–27.

McGregor, M. J., Wiebe, E., Marion, S. A., & Livingstone, C. (2000). Why don't more women report sexual assault to the police? *Canadian Medical Association Journal, 162*, 659–660.

McGregor, M. T., Dumont, J., & Myhr, T. L. (2002). Sexual assault forensic medical examination: Is evidence related to successful prosecution? *Annals of Emergency Medicine, 39*, 639–647.

McGuffin, P., et al. (2003). The heritability of bipolar affective disorder and the genetic relationship to unipolar depression. *Archives of General Psychiatry, 60*, 497–502.

McGurk, S. R., Twamley, E. W., Sitzer, D. I., et al. (2007). A meta-analysis of cognitive remediation in schizophrenia. *American Journal of Psychiatry, 164*, 1791–1802.

McHolm, A. E., MacMillan, H. L., & Jamieson, E. (2003). The relationship between childhood physical abuse and suicidality among depressed women from a community sample. *American Journal of Psychiatry, 160*, 933–938.

McIlroy, A. (2001, June 9). The stabbing victim listened helplessly as doctors told his family nothing could be done for him. They were wrong, but he had no way of letting them know. *The Globe and Mail*, F1.

McIntosh, A. M., Whalley, H. C., McKirdy, L., et al. (2008). Prefrontal function and activation in bipolar disorder and schizophrenia. *American Journal of Psychiatry, 165*, 378–384.

McIntosh, J. L. (1995). Suicide prevention in the elderly (65–99). In M. M. Silverman & R. W. Maris (Eds.), *Suicide prevention toward the year 2000* (pp. 180–192). New York: Guilford.

McIntyre, R. S., et al. (2006). Medical comorbidity in bipolar disorder: Implications for functional outcomes and health service utilization. *Psychiatric Services, 57*, 1140–1144.

McIntyre-Kingsolver, K., Lichtenstein, E., & Mermelstein, R. J. (1986). Spouse training in a multicomponent smoking-cessation program. *Behavior Therapy, 17*, 67–74.

McKeon, P., & Murray, R. (1987). Familial aspects of obsessive-compulsive neurosis. *British Journal of Psychiatry, 151*, 528–534.

McKibben, A., Proulx, J., & Lusignan, R. (1994). Relationships between conflict, affect, and deviant sexual behaviors in rapists and pedophiles. *Behaviour Research and Therapy, 32*, 571–575.

McKim, W. A. (1991). *Drugs and behavior: An introduction to behavioral pharmacology.* Englewood Cliffs, NJ: Prentice-Hall.

McKinley, N. M., & Hyde, J. S. (1996). The objectified body consciousness scale: Development and validation. *Psychology of Women Quarterly, 20*, 181–215.

McLeod, B. D., Weisz, J. R., & Wood, J. J. (2007). Examining the association between parenting and childhood depression: A meta-analysis. *Clinical Psychology Review, 27*, 986–1003.

McKinnon, M. C., Yucel, K., Nazarov, A., & MacQueen, G. M. (2009). A meta-analysis examining clinical predictors of hippocampal volume in patients with major depressive disorder. *Journal of Psychiatry & Neuroscience, 34*, 41–54.

McMain, S. F., et al. (2009). A randomized trial of dialectical behavior therapy versus general psychiatric management for borderline personality disorder. *American Journal of Psychiatry, 166*, 1365–1374.

McMain, S., Korman, L. M., & Dimeff, L. (2001). Dialectical behavior therapy and the treatment of emotion dysregulation. *Journal of Clinical Psychology, 57*, 183–196.

McNally, R. J. (1994). *Panic disorder: A critical analysis.* New York: Guilford.

McNally, R. J. (1997). Atypical phobias. In G. C. L. Davey (Ed.), *Phobias: A handbook of theory, research and treatment* (pp. 183–199). Chichester, England: John Wiley & Sons.

McNally, R. J. (2005a). Troubles in traumatology. *Canadian Journal of Psychiatry, 50*, 815–816.

McNally, R. J. (2005b). Debunking myths about trauma and memory. *Canadian Journal of Psychiatry, 50*, 817–822.

McNally, R. J. (2006). Cognitive abnormalities in post-traumatic stress disorder. *Trends in Cognitive Sciences, 10*, 271–277.

McNally, R. J. (2007). Mechanisms of exposure therapy: How neuroscience can improve psychological treatments for anxiety disorders. *Clinical Psychology Review, 27*, 750–759.

McNally, R. J. (2009). Can we fix PTSD in DSM-V? *Depression and Anxiety, 26*, 597–600.

McNally, R. J., Ristuccia, C. S., & Perlman, C. A. (2005). Forgetting of trauma cues in adults reporting continuous or recovered memories of childhood sexual abuse. *Psychological Science, 16*, 336–340.

McNulty, J. L., Graham, J. R., Ben-Porath, Y. S., & Stein, L. A. R. (1997). Comparative validity of MMPI-II scales of African-American and Caucasian mental health center clients. *Psychological Assessment, 9*, 464–470.

McVey, G. L., & Davis, R. (2002). A program to promote positive body image: A 1-year follow-up evaluation. *Journal of Early Adolescence, 22*, 96–108.

McVey, G., Gusella, J., Tweed, S., & Ferrari, M. (2009). A controlled evaluation of web-based training for teachers and public health practitioners for the prevention of eating disorders. *Eating Disorders, 17*, 1–26.

McVey, G. L., Lieberman, M., Voorberg, N., Wardrope, D., & Blackmore, E. (2003). School-based peer support groups: A new approach to the prevention of disordered eating. *Eating Disorders, 11*, 169–186.

McVey, G., Tweed, S., & Blackmore, E. (2004). Dieting among preschoolers and young adolescent females. *Canadian Medical Association Journal, 170*, 1559–1561.

Meana, M., Binik, I., Khalife, S., & Cohen, D. (1998). Affect and marital adjustment in women's ratings of dyspareunic pain. *Canadian Journal of Psychiatry, 43*, 381–385.

Meana, M., Binik, Y. M., Khalife, S., & Cohen, D. (1997). Dyspareunia: Sexual dysfunction or pain syndrome? *Journal of Nervous and Mental Disease, 185*, 561–569.

Means-Christensen, A. J., Roy-Byrne, P. P., Sherbourne, C. D., et al. (2008). Relationship among pain, anxiety, and depression in primary care. *Depression and Anxiety, 25*, 593–600.

Medical Research Council of Canada. (1987). *Guidelines on Research Involving Human Subjects.* Ottawa: Medical Research Council of Canada.

Mednick, S. A., & Schulsinger, F. (1968). Some premorbid characteristics related to breakdown in children with schizophrenic mothers. In D. Rosenthal & S. S. Kety (Eds.), *The transmission of schizophrenia.* Elmsford, NY: Pergamon.

Meehl, P. E. (1962). Schizotaxia, schizotypy, schizophrenia. *American Psychologist, 17*, 827–838.

Meichenbaum, D. H. (1969). The effects of instructions and reinforcement on thinking and language behaviours of schizophrenics. *Behaviour Research and Therapy, 7*, 101–114.

Meichenbaum, D. H. (1977). *Cognitive-behavior modification.* New York: Plenum Press.

Meichenbaum, D. (1995). Cognitive behavioral therapy in historical perspective. In B. Bongar & L. Beutler (Eds.), *Comprehensive textbook of psychotherapy* (pp. 141–158). New York: Oxford University Press.

Meichenbaum, D. (2009). Stress inoculation training. In W. T. O'Donohue & J. E. Fisher (Eds.),

General principles and empirically supported techniques of cognitive behavior therapy (pp. 627–630). Hoboken, NJ: John Wiley & Sons.

Meichenbaum, D. H., & Butler, L. (1980). Cognitive ethology: Assessing the streams of cognition and emotion. In K. R. Blankstein, P. Pliner, & J. Polivy (Eds.), *Advances in the study of communication and affect, Vol. 6: Assessment and modification of emotional behavior* (pp. 139–163). New York and London: Plenum.

Meissner, D. (2000, August 29). Montreux Clinic for eating disorders was under investigation when license surrendered. The Canadian Press.

Melamed, S., et al. (2006). Burnout and risk of cardiovascular disease: Evidence, possible causal paths, and promising research. *Psychological Bulletin, 132*, 327–353.

Mellinger, G. D., Balter, M. B., & Uhlenhuth, E. H. (1985). Insomnia and its treatment. *Archives of General Psychiatry, 42*, 225–232.

Mello, N. K., & Mendelson, J. H. (1970). Experimentally induced intoxication in alcoholics: A comparison between programmed and spontaneous drinking. *Journal of Pharmacology and Experimental Therapy, 173*, 101.

Mellor, C. S. (1970). First rank symptoms of schizophrenia. *British Journal of Psychiatry, 117*, 15–23.

Melman, A., & Rossman, B. (1989). *Penile vein ligation for corporal incompetence: An evaluation of short and long term results.* Paper presented at the 15th Annual Meeting of the International Academy of Sex Research, Princeton. As cited in Wincze & Carey (1991).

Meltzer, H. Y., et al. (2003). Clozapine treatment for suicidality in schizophrenia: International Suicide Prevention Trial (InterSept). *Archives of General Psychiatry, 60*, 82–91.

Melzack, R. (1998). Pain and stress: Clues toward understanding chronic pain. In M. Sabourin & F. I. M. Craik (Eds.), *Advances in psychological science, Vol. 2: Biological and cognitive aspects* (pp. 63–85). Hove, England: Psychology Press/Erlbaum (UK) Taylor and Francis.

Melzack, R. (1999). From the gate to the neuromatrix. *Pain, Suppl. 6*, S121–S126.

Melzack, R., & Wall, P. D. (1965). Pain mechanisms: A new theory. *Science, 150*, 971–979.

Melzack, R., & Wall, P. D. (1982). *The challenge of pain.* New York: Basic Books.

Mendonca, J. D., Velamoor, V. R., & Sauve, D. (1996). Key features of maltreatment of the infirm elderly in home settings. *Canadian Journal of Psychiatry, 41*, 107–113.

Menezes, N. M., Arenovich, T., & Zipursky, R. B. (2006). A systematic review of longitudinal outcome studies of first-episode psychosis. *Psychological Medicine, 36*, 1349–1362.

Menezes, N. M., Malla, A. M., Norman, R. M., et al. (2009). A multi-site Canadian perspective: Examining the functional outcome from first-episode psychosis. *Acta Psychiatrica Scandinavica, 120*, 138–146.

Mennin, D. S., Heimberg, R. G., Fresco, D. M., & Ritter, M. R. (2008). Is generalized anxiety disorder an anxiety or mood disorder? Considering multiple factors as we ponder the fate of GAD. *Depression and Anxiety, 25*, 289–299.

Menzies, R., & Webster, C. D. (1995). Construction and validation of risk assessments in a six-year follow-up of forensic patients: A tridimensional analysis. *Journal of Consulting and Clinical Psychology*, *63*, 766–778.

Mercado, A. C., Carroll, L. J., Cassidy, J. D., & Cote, P. (2000). Coping with neck and low back pain in the general population. *Health Psychology*, *19*, 333–338.

Merckelbach, H., de Ruiter, C., van den Hout, M. A., & Hoekstra, R. (1989). Conditioning experiences and phobias. *Behaviour Research and Therapy*, *27*, 657–662.

Merikangas, K. R., Mehta, R. L., Molnar, B. E., et al. (1998). Comorbidity of substance use disorders with mood and anxiety disorders: Results of the International Consortium in Psychiatric Epidemiology. *Addictive Behaviors*, *23*, 893–907.

Merskey, H., & Mai, F. (2005). Somatization and conversion disorders: A review. In M. Maj, H. S. Akiskal, J. E. Mezzich, & A. Okasha (Eds.), *Somatoform disorders* (pp. 1–22). Chichester, England: John Wiley & Sons.

Messer, S. B., & Abbass, A. A. (2010). Evidence-based psychodynamic therapy with personality disorders. In J. Magnavita (Ed.), *Evidence-based treatment of personality dysfunction: Principles, methods, and processes*. Washington, DC: American Psychological Association Press.

Messer, S. B., & Wolizky, D. L. (2009). The therapeutic alliance: A psychodynamic perspective on theory and practice. In J. C. Muran & J. P. Barber (Eds.). *The therapeutic alliance: An evidence-based approach to practice and training*. New York: Guilford Press.

Meston, C. M., & Gorzalka, B. B. (1996). Differential effects of sympathetic activation on sexual arousal in sexually dysfunctional and functional women. *Journal of Abnormal Psychology*, *105*, 582–591.

Metalsky, G. I., Joiner, T. E., Hardin, T. S., & Abramson, L. Y. (1993). Depressive reactions to failure in a natural setting: A test of the hopelessness and self-esteem theories of depression. *Journal of Abnormal Psychology*, *102*, 101–109.

Metz, M. E., Pryor, J. L., Nesvacil, L. J., Abuzzahab, F., et al. (1997). Premature ejaculation: A psychophysiological review. *Journal of Sex and Marital Therapy*, *23*, 3–23.

Metzger, K. L., Shoemaker, J. M., Kahn, J. B., et al. (2007). Pharmacokinetic and behavioural characterization of a long-term antipsychotic delivery system in rodents and rabbits. *Psychopharmacology* (Berlin), *190*, 201–211.

Meyer, J. G. (2004). The reliability and validity of the Rorschach and Thematic Apperception Test (TAT) compared to other psychological and medical procedures: An analysis of systematically gathered evidence. In M. Hilsenroth & D. Segal (Eds.), *Comprehensive handbook of psychological assessment* (pp. 315–342). Hoboken, NJ: John Wiley & Sons.

Meyer, J. H., et al. (2006). Elevated monoamine oxidase A levels in the brain: An explanation of the monoamine imbalance of major depression. *Archives of General Psychiatry*, *63*, 1209–1216.

Meyer, J. J., & Reter, D. J. (1979). Sex reassignment follow-up. *Archives of General Psychiatry*, *36*, 1010–1015.

Meyer, V. (1966). Modification of expectations in cases with obsessional rituals. *Behaviour Research and Therapy*, *4*, 273–280.

Mezulis, A. H., Funasaki, K. S., Charbonneau, A. M., & Hyde, J. S. (2010). Gender differences in the cognitive vulnerability-stress model of depression in the transition to adolescence. *Cognitive Therapy and Research*.

Mezzich, A. C., Moss, H., Tarter, R. E., Wolfenstein, M., et al. (1994). Gender differences in the pattern and progression of substance use in conduct disordered adolescents. *American Journal on Addiction*, *3*, 289–295.

Michelson, L., Mavissakalian, M., & Marchione, K. (1985). Cognitive and behavioral treatments of agoraphobia: Clinical, behavioral, and psychophysiological treatments of agoraphobia. *Journal of Consulting and Clinical Psychology*, *53*, 913–925.

Middleton, D. (2008). The development of the Internet Sex Offender Treatment Programme (I-SOTP). *Irish Probation Journal*, *5*, 49–64.

Midgley, N. (2006). "Re-reading" Little Hans: Freud's case study and the question of competing paradigms in psychoanalysis. *Journal of the American Psychoanalytic Association*, *54*, 537–559.

Miettunen, J., Tormanen, S., Murray, G. K., et al. (2008). Association of cannabis use with pro-dromal symptoms of psychosis in adolescence. *The British Journal of Psychiatry*, *192*, 470–471.

Mikulincer, M., & Solomon, Z. (1988). Attributional style and post-traumatic stress disorder. *Journal of Abnormal Psychology*, *97*, 308–313.

Miklowitz, D. J. (1985). *Family interaction and illness outcome in bipolar and schizophrenic patients*. Unpublished Ph.D. thesis, University of California at Los Angeles.

Miklowitz, D. J., Simoneau, T. L., Sachs-Ericsson, N., Warner, R., & Suddath, R. (1996). Family risk indicators in the course of bipolar affective disorder. In E. Mundt et al. (Eds.), *Interpersonal factors in the origin and course of affective disorders* (pp. 204–217). London: Gaskell Press.

Mikolajcdyk, R.T.,Brzoska, P., Maier, C., et al. (2008). Factors associated with self-rated health status in university students: A cross-sectional study in three European countries. *BMC Public Health*. 18: 215.

Milberger, S., Biederman, J., Faraone, S. V., & Chen, L. (1996). Is maternal smoking during pregnancy a risk factor for attention deficit hyperactivity disorder in children? *American Journal of Psychiatry*, *153*, 1138–1142.

Miles, L. E., & Dement, W. C. (1980). Sleep and aging. *Sleep*, *3*, 119–220.

Milgram, N. W., Siwak-Tapp, C. T., Araujo, J., & Head, E. (2006). Neuroprotective effects of cognitive enrichment. *Ageing Research Reviews*, *5*, 354–369.

Milin, R., Walker, S., & Chow, J. (2003). Major depressive disorder in adolescence: A brief review of the recent treatment literature. *Canadian Journal of Psychiatry*, *48*, 600–606.

Miller, A., Lee, S. K., Raina, P., Klassen, A., Zupancic, J., & Olsen, L. (1998). *A review of therapies for attention-deficit hyperactivity disorder*. Ottawa: Canadian Coordinating Office for Health Technology Assessment.

Miller, G .E., & Blackwell, E. (2006). Turning up the heat: Inflammation as a mechanism linking chronic stress, depression, and heart disease. *Current Directions in Psychological Science, 15,* 269–272.

Miller, G. E., Chen, E., & Zhou, E. S. (2007). If it goes up, must it come down? Chronic stress and the hypothalamic-pituitary-adrenocortical axis in humans. *Psychological Bulletin, 133,* 25–45.

Miller, J. R. (1996). *Shingwauk's vision: A history of native residential schools*. Toronto: University of Toronto Press.

Miller, M. A., & Rahe, R. H. (1997). Life changes scaling for the 1990s. *Journal of Psychosomatic Research, 43,* 279–292.

Miller, M. D., et al. (2003). The value of maintenance interpersonal psychotherapy (IPT) in older adults with different IPT foci. *American Journal of Geriatric Psychiatry, 11,* 97–102.

Miller, N. E. (1959). Liberalization of basic S-R concepts: Extensions to conflict behavior, motivation, and social learning. In S. Koch (Ed.), *Psychology: A study of a science* (Vol. 2). New York: McGraw-Hill.

Miller, N. V., & Currie, S. R. (2008). A Canadian population level analysis of the roles of irrational gambling cognitions and risky gambling practices as correlates of gambling intensity and pathological gambling. *Journal of Gambling Studies, 24,* 257–274.

Miller, T. Q., & Volk, R. J. (1996). Weekly marijuana use as a risk factor for initial cocaine use: Results from a six wave national survey. *Journal of Child and Adolescent Substance Abuse, 5,* 55–78.

Miller, W. R., & Rollnick, S. (Eds). (1991). *Motivational interviewing: Preparing people to change addictive behavior*. New York: Guilford.

Miller, W. R., & Rollnick, S. (2002). *Motivational interviewing: Preparing people for change* (2nd ed.). New York: Guilford.

Millon, T. H. (1994). *Manual for the Millon Clinical Multiaxial Inventory-III (MCMI-III)* (3rd ed.). Minneapolis: National Computer Systems.

Millon, T. H. (1996). *Disorders of personality: DSM-IV and beyond* (2nd ed.). New York: John Wiley & Sons.

Millon, T., Davis, R., Millon, C., & Grossman, S. (2009). *The Millon Clinical Multiaxial Inventory – III*, Third Edition (MCMI-III) (2009) with new norms and updated scoring. New York: Pearson.

Mills, J. F., Anderson, D., & Kroner, D. G. (2004). The antisocial attitudes and associates of sex offenders. *Criminal Behavior and Mental Health, 14,* 134–145.

Mills, J. S., Polivy, J., Herman, C. P., & Tiggemann, M. (2002). Effects of exposure to thin media images: Evidence of self-enhancement among restrained eaters. *Personality and Social Psychology Bulletin, 28,* 1687–1699.

Milrod, B., Leon, A. C., & Busch, F. (2007). A randomized controlled clinical trial of psychoanalytic psychotherapy for panic disorder. *American Journal of Psychiatry, 164,* 265–272.

Minde, K., Eakin, L., Hechtman, L., Ochs, E., Bouffard, R., Greenfield, B., et al. (2003). The psychosocial functioning of children and spouses of adults with ADHD. *Journal of Child Psychology and Psychiatry and Allied Disciplines, 44,* 637–646.

Mineka, S., & Oehlberg, K. (2008). The relevance of recent developments in classical conditioning to understanding the etiology and maintenance of anxiety disorders. *Acta Psychologia, 127,* 567–580.

Mineka, S., & Zinbarg, R. (1996). Perspectives on anxiety, panic, and fear. In *Nebraska symposium on motivation* (pp. 135–210). Lincoln, NE: University of Nebraska Press.

Mintz, A. R., Dobson, K. S., & Romney, D. M. (2003). Insight in schizophrenia: A meta-analysis. *Schizophrenia Research, 61,* 75–88.

Minuchin, S., Baker, L., Rosman, B. L., Lieberman, R., Milman, L., & Todd, T. C. (1975). A conceptual model of psychosomatic illness in children. *Archives of General Psychiatry, 32,* 1031–1038.

Miranda, R., Ray, L., Justus, A., et al. (2010). Initial evidence of an association between OPRM1 and adolescent alcohol misuse. *Alcoholism Clinical and Experimental Research, 34,* 112–122.

Mireault, M., & deMan, A. F. (1996). Suicidal ideation among the elderly: Personality variables, stress and social support. *Social Behavior and Personality, 24,* 385–392.

Mirenda, P. L., Donnellan, A. M., & Yoder, D. E. (1983). Gaze behavior: A new look at an old problem. *Journal of Autism and Developmental Disorders, 13,* 397–409.

Mirsky, A. F., Bieliauskas, L. A., French, L. M., Van Kammen, D. P., Jonsson, E., & Sedvall, G. (2000). A 39-year followup of the Genain quadruplets. *Schizophrenia Bulletin, 26,* 699–708.

Mishara, B. L. (1999). Suicide in the Montreal subway system: Characteristics of the victims, antecedents, and implications for prevention. *Canadian Journal of Psychiatry, 44,* 690–696.

Misri, S. (2007). Suffering in silence: The burden of perinatal depression. *Canadian Journal of Psychiatry, 52,* 477–478.

Mitchell, B. (2009, January 9). Young killer gets tougher prison: First youth to be sentenced as adult for murder sent to maximum-security range at Millhaven. *Toronto Star,* A12.

Mitchell, J. E., Agras, S., & Wonderlich, S. (2007). Treatment of bulimia nervosa: Where are we and where are we going? *International Journal of Eating Disorders, 40,* 95–101.

Mitchell, J. R., McCauley, E., & Burke, P. M. (1988). Phenomenology of depression in children and adolescents. *Journal of the American Academy of Child and Adolescent Psychiatry, 27,* 2–20.

Mitchell, J. T., & Bray, G. (1990). *Emergency services stress: Guidelines for perserving the health and careers of emergency service personnel.* Englewood Cliffs, NJ: Prentice-Hall.

Mitchell, S. R., Reiss, A. L., Tatusko, D. H., et al. (2009). Neuroanatomic alterations and social and communication deficits in monozygotic twins discordant for autism disorder. *American Journal of Psychiatry, 166,* 917–925.

Mitchell, T. L., Griffin, K., Stewart, S. H., & Loba, P. (2004). 'We will never ever forget…': The Swissair Flight 111 disaster and its impact on volunteers and communities. *Journal of Health Psychology, 9,* 245–262.

Mittleman, M. A., Maclure, M., Sherwood, J. B., Murly, R. P., Tofler, G. A., et al., (1997). Triggering of acute myocardial infarction onset by episodes of anger. *Circulation, 92,* 1720–1725.

Moffitt, T. E. (1990). Juvenile delinquency and attention deficit disorder: Boys' developmental trajectories from age 13 to 15. *Child Development, 61,* 893–910.

Moffitt, T. E., Arseneault, L., Jaffee, S., et al. (2008). Research review: *DSM-V* conduct disorder: Research needs for an evidence base. *Journal of Child Psychology and Psychiatry, 49,* 3–33.

Moffitt, T.E., Caspi, A., Rutter, M. (2006). Measured gene–environment interactions in psychopathology: Concepts, research strategies, and implications for research, intervention, and public understanding of genetics. *Perspectives on Psychological Science, 1,* 5–27.

Moffitt, T. E., Lynam, D., & Silva, P. A. (1994). Neuropsychological tests predict persistent male delinquency. *Criminology, 32,* 101–124.

Mohr, J. W., Turner, R. E., & Jerry, M. B. (1964). *Pedophilia and exhibitionism.* Toronto: University of Toronto Press.

Molde, H., Pallesen, S., Bartone, P., et al. (2009). Prevalence and correlates of gambling among 16 to 19-year-old adolescents in Norway. *Scandinavian Journal of Psychology, 50,* 55–64.

Molgat, C. V., & Patten, S. B. (2005). Comorbidity of major depression and migraine—A Canadian population-based study. *Canadian Journal of Psychiatry, 50,* 832–837.

Monahan, J. (1992). Mental disorder and violent behavior: Perceptions and evidence. *American Psychologist, 47,* 511–521.

Monahan, J. (1993). Limiting therapist exposure to Tarasoff liability: Guidelines for risk containment. *American Psychologist, 48,* 242–250.

Monahan, J., et al. (2001). *Rethinking violence risk assessment: The MacArthur Study of Mental Disorder and Violence.* New York: Oxford University Press.

Moncrieff, J. (2007a). In debate: Are antidepressants as effective as claimed? No, they are not effective at all. *Canadian Journal of Psychiatry, 52,* 96–97.

Moncrieff, J. (2007b). In debate: Rebuttal: Depression is not a brain disease. *Canadian Journal of Psychiatry, 52,* 100–101.

Moncrieff, J., & Kirsch, I. (2005). Efficacy of antidepressants in adults. *British Medical Journal, 331,* 155–157.

Mond, J. J., et al. (2006). Correlates of the use of purging and non-purging methods of weight control in a community sample of women. *Australian and New Zealand Journal of Psychiatry, 40,* 136–142.

Mongrain, M., & Blackburn, S. (2005). Cognitive vulnerability, lifetime risk, and the recurrence of major depression in graduate students. *Cognitive Therapy and Research, 29,* 747–768.

Mongrain, M., & Leather, F. (2006). Immature dependence and self-criticism predict the recurrence of major depression. *Journal of Clinical Psychology, 62,* 705–713.

Mongrain, M., & Zuroff, D. C. (1994). Ambivalence over emotional expression and negative life events: Mediators for depression in dependent and self-critical individuals. *Personality and Individual Differences, 16,* 447–458.

Moniz, E. (1936). *Tentatives operatoires dans le traitement de certaines psychoses.* Paris: Mason.

Monnier, J., Lydiard, R. B., & Brawman-Mintzer, O. (2003). Anxiety disorders: Generalized anxiety disorder. In A. Tasman, J. Kay, & J. A. Lieberman (Eds.), *Psychiatry,* 2nd Edition (pp. 1380–1404). New York, NY: John Wiley & Sons.

Monroe, S. M. & Harkness, K. L. (2005). Life stress, the 'kindling' hypothesis, and the recurrence of depression: Considerations from a life stress perspective. *Psychological Review, 112,* 417–445.

Monroe, S. M., & Simons, A. D. (1991). Diathesis-stress theories in the context of life stress research: Implications for the depressive disorders. *Psychological Bulletin, 110,* 406–425.

Monsebraaten, L., & Talaga, T. (2009, May 7). 'Historic' law compels Ontario to fight poverty: Requires the province to create goals to cut numbers living in need. *Toronto Star,* A11.

Monstrey, S., Vercruysse, H., & De Cuypere, G. (2009). Is gender reassignment surgery evidence based? Recommendation for the seventh version of the WPATH Standards of Care. *International Journal of Transgenderism, 11,* 206–214.

Moore, B. A., et al. (2005). Respiratory effects of marijuana and tobacco use in a U.S. sample. *Journal of General Internal Medicine, 20,* 33–37.

Moos, R. & Moos, B. (1986). *The Family Environment Scale Manual (2nd ed.).* Palo Alto, CA: Consulting Psychologists Press.

Morain, D. (1998). New state TV ads link smoking to impotence in men. *Los Angeles Times,* A3–A18.

Moreno, C., Laje, G., Blanco, C., et al. (2007). National trends in the outpatient diagnosis and treatment of bipolar disorder in youth. *Archives of General Psychiatry, 64,* 1032–1039.

Moreno, F. A., Wiegand,C. B., Taitano, E. K., & Delgado, P. L. (2006). Safety, tolerability and efficacy of psilocybin in 9 patients with obsessive-compulsive disorder. *Journal of Clinical Psychiatry, 67,* 1735–1740.

Morenz, B., & Becker, J. V. (1995). The treatment of youthful sexual offenders. *Applied and Preventive Psychology, 4,* 247–256.

Moretti, M. M., Segal, Z. V., McCann, C. D., Shaw, B. F., Miller, D. T., & Vella, D. (1996). Self-referent versus other-referent information processing in dysphoric, clinically depressed, and remitted depressed subjects. *Personality and Social Psychology Bulletin, 22,* 68–80.

Moretti, M. M., Emmrys, C., Grizenko, N., et al. (1997). The treatment of conduct disorders: Perspectives from across Canada. *Canadian Journal of Psychiatry, 42,* 637–648.

Morey, L. C. (1988). Personality disorders in DSM-III and DSM-IIIR: Convergence, coverage, and internal consistency. *American Journal of Psychiatry, 145,* 573–577.

Morey, L. C., Waugh, M. H., & Blashfield, R. K. (1985). MMPI scales for DSM-III personality disorders: Their derivation and correlates. *Journal of Personality Assessment, 49,* 245–251.

Morgan, C. A., Grillon, C., Lubin, H., & Southwick, S. M. (1997). Startle reflex abnormalities in women with sexual assault-related post-traumatic stress disorder. *American Journal of Psychiatry, 154,* 1076–1080.

Morgernstern, J., Langenbucher, J., Labouvie, E., & Miller, K. J. (1997). The comorbidity of alcoholism and personality disorders in a clinical population; Prevalence rates and relation to alcohol typology variables. *Journal of Abnormal Psychology, 106,* 74–84.

Morin, C. M. (1993). *Insomnia: Psychological assessment and management.* New York: Guilford.

Morin, C. M., & Azrin, N. H. (1988). Behavioral and cognitive treatments of geriatric insomnia. *Journal of Consulting and Clinical Psychology, 56,* 748–753.

Morin, C. M., Bastien, C. H., Brink, D., & Brown, T. R. (2003). Adverse effects of temazepam in older adults with chronic insomnia. *Human Psychopharmacology, 18,* 75–82.

Morin, C. M., Blais, F., & Savard, J. (2002). Are changes in beliefs and attitudes about sleep related to sleep improvements in the treatment of insomnia? *Behaviour Research and Therapy, 40,* 741–752.

Morin, C. M., Colecchi, C., Stone, J., Sood, R., & Brink, D. (1999). Behavioral and pharmacological therapies for late-life insomnia: A randomized controlled trial. *Journal of the American Medical Association, 281,* 991–999.

Morin, C. M., & Gramling, S. E. (1989). Sleep patterns and aging: Comparisons of older adults with and without insomnia complaints. *Psychology and Aging, 4,* 290–294.

Morin, C. M., et al. (2006). Psychological and behavioral treatment of insomnia: Update of the recent evidence (1998–2004). *Sleep, 29,* 1398–1414.

Morin, C. M., et al. (2009). The natural history of insomnia: A population-based three-year longitudinal study. *Archives of Internal Medicine, 169,* 447–453.

Moritz, S., Von Muhlenen, A., Randjbar, S., Fricke, S., & Jelinek, L. (2009). Evidence for an attentional bias for washing- and checking-relevant stimuli in obsessive-compulsive disorder. *Journal of the International Neuropsychologial Society, 15,* 365–371.

Morley, S. (1997). Pain management. In A. Baum, S. Newman, J. Weinman, R. West, & C. McManus (Eds.), *Cambridge handbook of psychology, health and medicine* (pp. 234–237). Cambridge, UK: Cambridge University Press.

Moroney, J. T., et al. (1999). Low-density lipoprotein cholesterol and the risk of dementia with stroke. *Journal of the American Medical Association, 282,* 254–260.

Morris, A. A. (1968). Criminal insanity. *Washington Review, 43,* 583–622.

Morse, R. M. (1988). Substance abuse among the elderly. *Bulletin of the Menninger Clinic, 52,* 259–268.

Morse, S. J. (1992). The "guilty mind": Mens rea. In D. K., Kagehiro & W. S. Lanfer (Eds.), *Handbook of psychology and law* (pp. 207–229). New York: Springer-Verlag.

Mortimer, A. M., & Al-Agib, A. O. A. (2007). Quality of life in schizophrenia on conventional versus atypical antipsychotic medication: A comparative cross-sectional study. *International Journal of Social Psychiatry, 53,* 99–107.

Moscovitch, D. A. (2009). What is the core fear in social phobia? A new model to facilitate individualized case conceptualization and treatment. *Cognitive and Behavioral Practice, 16,* 123–134.

Moscovitch, D. A., Orr, E., Rowa, K., Reimer, S. G., & Antony, M. (2009). In the absence of rose-colored glasses: Ratings of self-attributes and their differential certainty and importance across multiple dimensions in social phobia. *Behaviour Research and Therapy, 47,* 66–70.

Moser, C., & Levitt, E. E. (1987). An exploratory-descriptive study of a sadomasochistically oriented sample. *Journal of Sex Research, 23,* 322–337.

Moser, P. W. (1989, January). Double vision: Why do we never match up to our mind's ideal? *Self Magazine,* 51–52.

Moses, J. A., & Purisch, A. D. (1997). The evolution of the Luria-Nebraska Battery. In G. Goldstein & T. Incagnoli (Eds.), *Contemporary approaches to neuropsychological assessment* (pp. 131–170). New York: Plenum.

Moses, J. A., Schefft, B. A., Wong, J. L., & Berg, R. A. (1992). Interrater reliability analyses of the Luria-Nebraska neuropsychological battery, form II. *Archives of Clinical Neurology, 7,* 251–269.

Mosier, K. E., et al. (2010). Prevalence of mental disorders and service utilization in seniors: Results from the Canadian community health survey cycle 1.2. *International Journal of Geriatric Psychiatry* (early view online).

Mosing, M. A., Gordon, S. D., Medland, S. E., et al. (2009). Genetic and environmental influences on the co-morbidity between depression, panic disorder, agoraphobia, and social phobia: A twin study. *Depression and Anxiety, 26,* 1004–1011.

Moss, D., & Redelmeier, D. A. (2010). Outcomes following appeal and reversal of civil commitment. *General Hospital Psychiatry, 32,* 94–98.

Mowrer, O. H. (1947). On the dual nature of learning: A re-interpretation of "conditioning" and "problem-solving." *Harvard Educational Review, 17,* 102–148.

Moyers, T. B., & Houck, J. (in press). Combining motivational interviewing with cognitive-behavioral treatments for substance abuse: Lessons from the COMBINE research project. *Cognitive and Behavioral Practice.*

Mrazek, P. J., & Haggerty, R. J. (1994). *Reducing risks for mental disorders: Frontiers for preventive intervention research.* Washington, DC: National Academy Press.

MTA Cooperative Group. (1999). A 14-month randomized clinical trial of treatment strategies for attention-deficit/hyperactivity disorder. *Archives of General Psychiatry, 56,* 1073–1086.

Mueser, K., Bellack, A. S., & Blanchard, J. J. (1992). Co-morbidity of schizophrenia and substance abuse: Implications for treatment. *Journal of Consulting and Clinical Psychology, 60,* 845–856.

Mufson L., Weissman M. M., Moreau D., & Garfinkel R. (1999). Efficacy of interpersonal psychotherapy for depressed adolescents. *Archives of General Psychiatry, 56,* 573–579.

Muller, D. J., et al. (2006). Brain-derived neurotrophic factor (BDNF) gene and rapid-cycling bipolar disorder: Family-based association study. *British Journal of Psychiatry, 189,* 317–323.

Muller, J., & Roberts, J. E. (2005). Memory and attention in obsessive-compulsive disorder: A review. *Journal of Anxiety Disorders, 19,* 1–28.

Muller, R. T., Endler, N. S., & Parker, J. D. A. (1990). The interaction model of anxiety in two different public speaking situations. *Personality and Individual Differences, 11,* 371–377.

Muller, R. T., Goh, H. H., Lemieux, K. E., & Fish, S. (2000). The social supports of high-risk, formerly maltreated adults. *Canadian Journal of Behavioural Science, 32,* 1–5.

Muller, R. T., Kraftcheck, E., & McLewin, L. A. (2004). Adult attachment and trauma. In D. R. Catherall (Ed.), *Handbook of stress, trauma, and the family* (pp. 203–230). London: Brunner-Routledge.

Muller, R. T., & Rosenkratz, S. E. (2009). Attachment and treatment response among adults in inpatient treatment for posttraumatic stress disorder. *Psychotherapy Theory, Research, Training, and Practice, 46,* 82–96.

Muller, R. T., Sicoli, L. A., & Lemieux, K. E. (2000). Relationship between attachment style and posttraumatic stress symptomatology among adults who report the experience of childhood abuse. *Journal of Traumatic Stress, 13,* 321–332.

Mullins-Sweatt, S. N., Smit, V., Verheul, R., Oldham, J., & Widiger, T. A. (2009). Dimensions of personality: Clinicians' perspectives. *Canadian Journal of Psychiatry, 54,* 247–259.

Mullett-Hume, E., Anshel, D., Guevara, V., & Cloitre, M. (2008). Cumulative trauma and posttraumatic stress disorder among children exposed to the 9/11 World Trade Center attack. *American Journal of Orthopsychiatry, 78,* 103–108.

Mulveen, R., & Hepworth, J. (2006). An interpretive phenomenological analysis of participation in a pro-anorexia internet site and its relationship with disordered eating. *Journal of Health Psychology, 11,* 283–296.

Mulvey, E. P. (1994). Assessing the evidence of a link between mental illness and violence. *Hospital and Community Psychiatry, 45,* 663–668.

Mumma, G. H., & Fluck, J. (2009). A clinician-friendly approach to the intraindividual empirical testing of a cognitive-behavioral case formulation. Manuscript under review.

Munafo, M., Brown, S., & Hariri, A. (2008). Serotonin transporter (5-HTTLPR) genotype and amygdale activation: A meta-analysis. *Biological Psychiatry, 63,* 852–857.

Munce, S. E. P., et al. (2006). The role of work stress as a moderating variable in the chronic pain and depression association. *Journal of Psychosomatic Research, 61,* 653–660.

Munk-Olsen, T., Laursen, T. M., Pedersen, C. B., Mors, O., & Mortensen, P. B. (2006). New parents and mental disorders: A population-based register study. *Journal of the American Medical Association, 296,* 2582–2589.

Murdoch, D., Pihl, R. O., & Ross, D. (1990). Alcohol and crimes of violence: Present issues. *International Journal of Addiction, 25,* 1059–1075.

Murphy, R., Cooper, Z., Hollon, S. D., & Fairburn, C. G. (2009). How do psychological treatments work? Investigating mediators of change. *Behaviour Research and Therapy, 47,* 1–5.

Murphy, W. D. (1997). Exhibitionism: Psychopathology and theory. In D. R. Laws & W. O'Donohue (Eds.), *Sexual deviance* (pp. 22–39). New York: Guilford Press.

Murray, L., Creswell, C., & Cooper, P. J. (2009). The development of anxiety disorders in childhood: An integrative review. *Psychological Medicine, 39*, 1413–1423.

Murray, M. (2000, February 5). Mentally ill Portuguese face language barrier. *Toronto Star.*

Murthi, M., Servaty-Seib, H. L., & Elliott, A. N. (2006). Childhood sexual abuse and multiple dimensions of self-concept. *Journal of Interpersonal Violence, 21*, 982–999.

Musselman, D. L., Evans, D. L., & Nemeroff, C. B. (1998). The relationship of depression to cardiovascular disease: Epidemiology, biology, and treatment. *Archives of General Psychiatry, 55*, 580–592.

Mustard, F., McCain, M. N., & Shanker, S. (2007). *Early years study 2: Putting science into action.* Toronto: Council for Early Childhood Development.

Myers, J. K., et al. (1984). Six month prevalence of psychiatric disorders in three communities: 1980–1982. *Archives of General Psychiatry, 41*, 959–967.

Myers, S. M., Johnson, C., & the Council on Children with Disabilities. (2007). Management of children with autism spectrum disorders. *Pediatrics, 120*, 1162–1182.

Nagin, D. S., & Tremblay, R. E. (2001). Parental and early childhood predictors of persistent physical aggression in boys from kindergarten to high school. *Archives of General Psychiatry, 58*, 389–394.

Naidoo, J. C. (1992). The mental health of visible ethnic minorities in Canada. *Psychology and Developing Societies, 4*, 165–187.

Nakao, T., Nakagawa, A., Yoshiura, T., et al. (2009). Duration effect of obsessive-compulsive disorder on cognitive function: A functional MRI study. *Depression and Anxiety, 26*, 814–823.

Nakatani, E., Mataix-Cols, D., Micali, N., et al. (2008). Outcomes of cognitive behaviour therapy for obsessive compulsive disorder in a clinical setting: A 10-year experience from a specialist OCD service for children and adolescents. *Child and Adolescent Mental Health, 14*, 133–139.

Nakoneczny, R. (2010). *Put your mind to it.* Toronto: Alzheimer Society of Canada.

Nathan, P. E., & Langenbucher, J. W. (1999). Psychopathology: Description and classification. *Annual Review of Psychology, 50*, 79–107.

Nathan, P. E., Stuart, S. P., & Dolan, S. L. (2000). Research on psychotherapy efficacy and effectiveness: Between Scylla and Charybdis? *Psychological Bulletin, 126*, 964–981.

National Cancer Institute. (1977). *The smoking digest: Progress report on a nation kicking the habit.* Washington, DC: U.S. Department of Health, Education and Welfare.

National Center for Health Statistics. (1989). *National nursing home survey* (DHHS Publication No. PHS 89-1758, Series 13, No. 97). Washington, DC: U.S. Government Printing Office.

National Seniors Council on Elder Abuse. (2007). *Report of the National Seniors Council on Elder Abuse.* Ottawa: Government of Canada.

Neale, J. M., & Oltmanns, T. (1980). *Schizophrenia.* New York: John Wiley & Sons.

Neckelmann, D. (1996). Treatment of chronic insomnia and recommendations with special emphasis on problems of the elderly. *Tidsskr Nor Laegeforen, 10*, 854–859.

Neighbors, C., Larimer, M. E., Lostutter, T. W., & Woods, B. A. (2006). Harm reduction and individually focused alcohol prevention. *International Journal of Drug Policy, 17*, 304–309.

Neil, A. L., & Christensen, H. (2009). Efficacy and effectiveness of school-based prevention and early intervention programs for anxiety. *Clinical Psychology Review, 29*, 208–215.

Neimeyer, R. A., & Raskin, J. D. (2001). Varieties of constructivism in psychotherapy. In K. S. Dobson (Ed.), *Handbook of cognitive-behavioral therapies* (2nd ed., pp. 393–430). New York: Guilford.

Neisser, U., & Harsch, N. (1991). Phantom flashbulbs: False recognitions of hearing the news about Challenger. In E. Winograd & U. Neisser (Eds.), *Affect and accuracy of recall: Studies of "flashbulb" memories.* New York: Cambridge University Press.

Nelson, G., Lavoie, L., & Mitchell, T. (2007). The history and theories of community psychology in Canada. In S. M. Reich, M. Reimer, I. Prilletensky, & M. Montero (Eds.), *International community psychology: History and theories* (pp. 13–36). New York: Springer-Verlag.

Nelson, G., Prilleltensky, I., Laurendeau, M.-C., & Powell, B. (1996). The prevention of mental health problems in Canada: A survey of provincial policies, structures, and programs. *Canadian Psychology, 37*, 161–172.

Nelson, J. C., & Davis, J. M. (1997). DST studies in psychotic depression: A meta-analysis. *American Journal of Psychiatry, 154*, 1497–1503.

Nelson, J. C., Delucchi, K., & Schneider, L. (2008). Efficacy of second generation antidepressants in late-life depression: A meta-analysis of the evidence. *American Journal of Geriatric Psychiatry, 16*, 558–567.

Nelson, M. D., et al. (1998). Hippocampal volume reduction in schizophrenia as assessed by magnetic resonance imaging: A meta-analytic study. *Archives of General Psychiatry, 55*, 443–440.

Nemeroff, C. B., & Schatzberg, A. F. (1998). Pharmacological treatment of unipolar depression. In P. E. Nathan & J. M. Gorman (Eds.), *A guide to treatments that work* (pp. 212–225). New York: Oxford University Press.

Nemeroff, C. J., & Karoly, P. (1991). Operant methods. In F. H. Kanfer & A. P. Goldstein (Eds.), *Helping people change: A textbook of methods* (4th ed.). Elmsford, NY: Pergamon.

Nestadt, G., Romanoski, A., Chahal, R., Merchant, A., et al. (1990). An epidemiological study of histrionic personality disorder. *Psychological Medicine, 20*, 413–422.

Neufeld, R. W. J. (1999). Dynamic differentials of stress and coping. *Psychological Review, 106*, 385–397.

Neugebauer, R. (1979). Mediaeval and early modern theories of mental illness. *Archives of General Psychiatry, 36*, 477–484.

Newlin, D. B., & Thomson, J. B. (1990). Alcohol challenge with sons of alcoholics: A critical review and analysis. *Psychological Bulletin, 108*, 383–402.

Newman, D. L., Moffitt, T. E., Caspi, A., & Silva, P. A. (1998). Comorbid mental disorders: Implications for treatment and sample selection. *Journal of Abnormal Psychology, 107*, 305–311.

Newman, J. P., Patterson, C. M., & Kosson, D. S. (1987). Response perseveration in psychopaths. *Journal of Abnormal Psychology, 96*, 145–149.

Newman, J. P., Schmitt, W. A., & Voss, W. D. (1997). The impact of motivationally neutral cues on psychopathic individuals: Assessing the generality of the response modulation hypothesis. *Journal of Abnormal Psychology, 196*, 563–575.

Newman, M. G. (2000). Recommendations for a cost-offset model of psychotherapy allocation using generalized anxiety disorder as an example. *Journal of Consulting and Clinical Psychology, 68*, 549–555.

Newman, S. C., Bland, R. C., & Orn, H. T. (1998). The prevalence of mental disorders in the elderly in Edmonton: A community survey using GMS-AGECAT. *Canadian Journal of Psychiatry, 43*, 910–914.

Newman, S. C., & Schopflocher, D. (2008). Trends in antidepressant prescriptions among the elderly in Alberta during 1997 to 2004. *Canadian Journal of Psychiatry, 53*, 704–707.

Newman, S. C., & Thompson, A. H. (2007). The association between pathological gambling and attempted suicide: Findings from a national survey in Canada. *Canadian Journal of Psychiatry, 52*, 605–612.

Newth, S., & Rachman, S. (2001). The concealment of obsessions. *Behaviour Research and Therapy, 39*, 457–464.

Newton-Cheh, C., et al. (2009). Genome-wide association study identifies eight loci associated with blood pressure. *Nature Genetics, 41*, 666–676.

Newton-Howes, G., Tyrer, P., Moore, A., & Nur, U. (2007). Personality disorder and outcome in schizophrenia: A negative systematic review. *Personality and Mental Health, 1*, 21–26.

Newton-Taylor, B., DeWit, D., & Gliksman, L. (1998). Prevalence and factors associated with physical and sexual assault of female university students in Ontario. *Health Care for Women International, 19*, 155–164.

Nguyen, C. T., Fournier, L., Bergeron, L., Roberge, P., & Barrette, G. (2005). Correlates of depressive and anxiety disorders among young Canadians. *Canadian Journal of Psychiatry, 50*, 620–628.

Nicholls, T. L., Ogloff, J. R. P., Brink, J., & Spidel, A. (2005). Psychopathy in women: A review of its clinical usefulness for assessing risk for aggression and criminality. *Behavioral Sciences and the Law, 23*, 779–802.

Nichols, M. (with S. Doyle Driedger & D. Ballon) (1995, January 30). Schizophrenia: Hidden torment. *Maclean's.*

Nicholson, I. R., & Neufeld, R. W. J. (1993). Classification of the schizophrenias according to symptomatology: A two-factor model. *Journal of Abnormal Psychology, 102*, 259–270.

Nicolosi, A., et al. (2006). Sexual activity, sexual disorders, and associated help-seeking behaviour among mature adults in five Anglophone countries from the Global Survey of Sexual Attitudes and Behaviors (GSSAB). *Journal of Sex and Marital Therapy, 32*, 331–342.

Nicolson, R., & Szatmari, P. (2003). Genetic and neurodevelopmental influences in autistic disorder. *Canadian Journal of Psychiatry, 48*, 526–537.

Niedhammer, I., Goldberg, M., Leclerc, A., David, S., et al. (1998). Psychosocial work environment and cardiovascular risk factors in an occupational cohort in France. *Journal of Epidemiology and Community Health, 52*, 93–100.

Nigg, J. T., & Goldsmith, H. H. (1994). Genetics of personality disorders: Perspectives from personality and psychopathology research. *Psychological Bulletin, 115*, 346–380.

Nimgaonkar, V. L., Fujiwara, T. M., Dutta, M., Wood, J., Gentry, K., Maendel, S., et al. (2000). Low prevalence of psychoses among the Hutterites, an isolated religious community. *American Journal of Psychiatry, 157*, 1065–1070.

Nisbett, R., & Wilson, T. (1977). Telling more than we can know: Verbal reports on mental processes. *Psychological Review, 84*, 231–259.

Nitschke, J., Blendl, V., Ottermann, B., Osterhelder, M., & Mokros, A. (2009). Severe sexual sadism—an underdiagnosed disorder? Evidence from a sample of forensic inpatients. *Journal of Forensic Sciences, 54*, 685–691.

Nixon, M. J., Cloutier, P., & Jansson, S. M. (2008). Nonsuicidal self-harm in youth: A population-based survey. *Canadian Medical Association Journal, 178*, 306–312.

Nock, M. K., & Kessler, R. C. (2006). Prevalence of and risk factors for suicide attempts versus suicide gestures: Analysis of the National Comorbidity Survey. *Journal of Abnormal Psychology, 115*, 616–623.

Nock, M. K., & Prinstein, M. J. (2004). A functional approach to the assessment of self-mutilative behavior. *Journal of Consulting and Clinical Psychology, 72*, 885–890.

Nock, M. K., Teper, R., & Hollander, M. (2007). Psychological treatment of self-injury among adolescents. *Journal of Clinical Psychology, 63*, 1081–1089.

Nocks, B. C., Learner, R. M., Blackman, D., & Brown, T. E. (1986). The effects of a community-based long term care project on nursing home utilization. *The Gerontologist, 26*, 150–157.

Nolen-Hoeksema, S., & Girgus, J. S. (1994). The emergence of gender differences in depression during adolescence. *Psychological Bulletin, 115*, 424–443.

Nolen-Hoeksema, S., Larson, J., & Grayson, C. (1999). Explaining the gender difference in depressive symptoms. *Journal of Personality and Social Psychology, 77*, 1061–1072.

Nordt, C., Rossler, W., & Lauber, C. (2006). Attitudes of mental health professionals toward people with schizophrenia and major depression. *Schizophrenia Bulletin, 32*, 709–714.

Norko, M., & Baranoski, M. V. (2005). The state of contemporary risk assessment research. *Canadian Journal of Psychiatry, 50*, 18–26.

Norman, R. M. G., et al. (2002). An evaluation of a stress management program for individuals with schizophrenia. *Schizophrenia Research, 58*, 293–303.

North, C. S., Suris, A. M., Davis, M., Smith, R. P. (2009). Toward validation of the diagnosis of pottraumatic stress disorder. *American Journal of Psychiatry, 166*, 34–41.

Norton, G. R., Harrison, B., Hauch, J., & Rhodes, L. (1985). Characteristics of people with infrequent panic attacks. *Journal of Abnormal Psychology, 94*, 216–221.

Norton, J. P. (1982). *Expressed emotion, affective style, voice tone and communication deviance as predictors of offspring schizophrenia spectrum disorders.* Unpublished doctoral dissertation, University of California at Los Angeles.

Norton, P. J., Zvolensky, M. J., Bonn-Miller, M. O., Cox, B. J., & Norton, G. R (2008). Use of the Panic Attack Questionnaire-IV to assess non-clinical panic attacks and limited symptom panic attacks in student and community samples. *Journal of Anxiety Disorders, 22*, 1159–1171.

Noyes, R., et al. (2006). Distinguishing between hypochondriasis and somatization disorder: A review of the existing literature. *Psychotherapy and Psychosomatics, 75*, 270–281.

Nunes, E. V., Quitkin, F. M., Donovan, S. J., Deliyannides, D., et al. (1998). Imipramine treatment of opiate-dependent patients with depressive disorders: A placebo-controlled trial. *Archives of General Psychiatry, 55*, 153–160.

Nunes, J., & Simmie, S. (2002). *Beyond crazy: Journeys through mental illness.* Toronto: McClelland and Stewart.

O'Brien, A.-M., & Farrell, S. J. (2005). Community treatment orders: Profile of a Canadian experience. *Canadian Journal of Psychiatry, 50*, 27–30.

O'Brien, A.-M., Farrell, S. J., & Faulkner, S. (2009). Community treatment orders: Beyond hospital utilization rates examining the association of community treatment orders with community engagement and supportive housing. *Community Mental Health Journal, 45*, 415–419.

O'Brien, W. H., & Haynes, S. N. (1995). Behavioral assessment. In L. A. Heiden & M. Hersen (Eds.), *Introduction to clinical psychology* (pp. 103–139). New York: Plenum.

O'Conner, M. C. (1989). Aspects of differential performance by minorities on standardized tests: Linguistic and sociocultural factors. In B. R. Gifford (Ed.), *Test policy and test performance: Education, language, and culture* (pp. 129–181). Boston: Kluwer Academic Publishers.

O'Connor, B. P. (2002). The search for dimensional structure differences between normality and abnormality: A statistical review of published data on personality and psychopathology. *Journal of Personality and Social Psychology, 83*, 962–982.

O'Connor, B. P., & Dyce, J. A. (2001). Rigid and extreme: A geometric representation of personality disorders in five-factor model space. *Journal of Personality and Social Psychology, 81*, 1119–1130.

O'Connor, K. (2009). Cognitive and meta-cognitive dimensions of psychosis. *Canadian Journal of Psychiatry, 54*, 152–159.

O'Connor, K., Aardema, F., & Pélissier, M.-C. (2005). *Beyond reasonable doubt: Reasoning processes in obsessive-compulsive disorder and related disorders.* New York: John Wiley & Sons.

O'Connor, K., & Robillard, S. (2000). A cognitive approach to the treatment of primary inferences in obsessive-compulsive disorder. *Journal of Cognitive Psychotherapy: An International Quarterly, 13*, 359–375.

O'Connor, R. C., & Noyce, R. (2008). Personality and cognitive processes: Self-criticism and different types of rumination as predictors of suicidal ideation. *Behaviour Research and Therapy, 46*, 392–401.

O'Connor, T. G., & Jenkins, J. M. (2000). *Marital transitions and children's adjustment: Understanding why families differ from one another and why children in the same family show different patterns of adjustment.* Ottawa: Government of Canada.

O'Donnell, P., & Grace, A. A. (1998). Dysfunctions in multiple interrelated systems as the neurobiological bases of schizophrenic symptom clusters. *Schizophrenia Bulletin, 24*, 267–283.

O'Donnell, T., Hegadoren, K.M., & Coupland, N.C (2004). Noradrenergic mechanisms in the pathophysiology of post-traumatic stress disorder. *Neuropsychobiology, 50*, 273–283.

O'Donohue, W., Dopke, C. A., & Swingen, D. N. (1997). Psychotherapy for female sexual dysfunction: A review. *Clinical Psychology Review, 17*, 537–566.

O'Donohue, W., & Plaud, J. J. (1994). The conditioning of human sexual arousal. *Archives of Sexual Behavior, 23*, 321–344.

Oeztuerk, E., & Sar, V. (2008). Somatization as a predictor of suicidal ideation in dissociative disorders. *Psychiatry and Clinical Neuroscience, 62*, 662–668.

Office of the Chief Coroner of British Columbia. (1994). *Report of the Task Force into Illicit Narcotic Overdose Deaths in British Columbia.* British Columbia: Ministry of the Attorney General.

Office of the Minister of Justice. (2010, March 16). Government introduces amendments to strengthen young offenders legislation: "Sebastien's Law" focuses on violent and repeat young offenders (news release). Ottawa: Department of Justice Canada.

Offord, D. R., Boyle, M. H., Szatmari, P., Rae-Grant, N. I., Links, P. S., Cadman, D. T., et al. (1987). Ontario Child Health Study: 2. Six-month prevalence of disorder and rates of service utilization. *Archives of General Psychiatry, 44*, 832–836.

Ogborne, A. C., & DeWit, D. J. (1999). Lifetime use of professional and community services for help with drinking: Results from a Canadian population survey. *Journal of Studies in Alcohol, 60*, 867–872.

Ogborne, A. C., Smart, R. G., & Adlaf, E. M. (2000). Self-reported medical use of marijuana: A survey of the general population. *Canadian Medical Association Journal, 162*, 1685–1686.

Ogilvie, M. (2007, June 9). 905 regions failing the mentally ill. *Toronto Star*, A1, A16.

Ogloff, J. R. P. (1999). Ethical and legal contours of forensic psychology. In R. Roesch & S. D. Hart (Eds.), *Psychology and law: The state of the discipline* (pp. 401–435). New York: Plenum.

Ogloff, J. R. P., & Whittemore, K. E. (2001). Fitness to stand trial and criminal responsibility in Canada. In R. A. Schuller & J. R. Ogloff (Eds.), *Introduction to psychology and law: Canadian perspectives* (pp. 283–313). Toronto: University of Toronto Press.

Ogloff, J. R., Wong, S., & Greenwood, A. (1990). Treating criminal psychopaths in a therapeutic community program. *Behavioral Sciences and the Law, 8,* 181–190.

Ogrodniczuk, J. S., Piper, W. E., Joyce, A. S., Lau, M. A., & Sochting, I. (2010). A survey of Canadian group psychotherapy association members' perceptions of psychotherapy research. *International Journal of Group Psychotherapy, 60,* 159–172.

Ogrodniczuk, J. S., Piper, W. E., Joyce, A. S., & McCallum, M. (1999). Transference interpretations in short-term dynamic psychotherapy. *Journal of Nervous and Mental Disease, 187,* 571–578.

Oh, S. (1999, July 19). The hidden horror: Many elderly are abused by the people they trust the most—their own kids. *Maclean's,* 48–49.

Ohman, O., & Mineka, S. (2001). Fears, phobias, and preparedness: Toward an evolved module of fear and fear learning. *Psychological Review, 108,* 483–522.

Oldham, J.M. (2007). Psychodynamic psychotherapy for personality disorders. *American Journal of Psychiatry, 164,* 1465–1467.

Olds, D. L., Sadler, L., & Kitzman, H. (2007). Programs for parents of infants and toddlers: Recent evidence from randomized trials. *Journal of Child Psychology and Psychiatry, 48,* 355–391.

O'Leary, K. D., & Beach, S. R. (1990). Marital therapy: A viable treatment for depression and marital discord. *American Journal of Psychiatry, 147,* 183–186.

Oleksyn, V., & Kole, W.J. (2009, March 19). "I plead guilty – and I realize how cruel I was" – Fritzl brings trial to shocking end. *New York Post.*

Ollendick, T. H., Jarrett, M. A., Grills-Taqueechel, A. E., et al. (2008). Comorbidity as a predictor and moderator of treatment outcome in youth with anxiety, affective, attention deficit/hyperactivity disorder, and oppositional/conduct disorders. *Clinical Psychology Review, 28,* 1447–1471.

Olley, M. C., Nicholls, T. L., & Brink, J. (2009). Mentally ill individuals in limbo: Obstacles and opportunities for providing psychiatric services to corrections inmates with mental illness. *Behavioral Sciences and the Law, 27,* 811–831.

O'Malley, S. S., Jaffe, A. J., Chang, G., Rode, S., Schottenfeld, R., et al. (1996). Six month follow-up of naltrexone and psychotherapy for alcohol dependence. *Archives of General Psychiatry, 53,* 217–224.

Olson, D., Portner, J., and Lavee, Y. (1985). *FACES III.* St. Paul, MN: University of Minnesota, Department of Family Social Service.

Olsson, A., & Phelps, E. A. (2004). Learned fear of "unseen faces" after Pavlovian, observational, and instructed fear. *Psychological Science, 15,* 823–828.

Olver, M. E., & Wong, S. C. (2006). Psychopathy, sexual deviance, and recidivism among sex offenders. *Sexual Abuse, 18,* 65–82.

Olver, M. E., & Wong, S. C. P. (2009). Therapeutic responses of psychopathic sexual offenders: Treatment attrition, therapeutic change, and long-term recidivism. *Journal of Consulting and Clinical Psychology, 77,* 328–336.

Ono, Y., et al. (1996). Avoidant personality disorder and taijin kyoufu: Sociocultural implications of the WHO/ADAMHA International Study of Personality Disorders in Japan. *Acta Psychiatrica Scandanavica, 93,* 172–176.

Ontario Health Quality Council. (2007, March). *2007 Report on Ontario's health system.* Toronto: Author.

Ontario Ministry of Health. (1994). *Ontario Health Survey: Mental health supplement.* Catalogue No. 2224153. Toronto: Queen's Printer for Ontario.

Oquendo, M. A., Bongiovi-Garcia, M. E., Galfalvy, H., et al. (2007). Sex differences in clinical predictors of suicidal acts after major depression: A prospective study. *American Journal of Psychiatry, 164,* 134–141.

Oquendo, M. A., Baca-Garcia, E., Mann, J. J., & Giner, J. (2008). Issues for DSM-V: Suicidal behavior as a separate diagnosis on a separate axis. *American Journal of Psychiatry, 165,* 1383–1384.

Orbach, G., Lindsay, S., & Grey, S. (2007). A randomized placebo-controlled trial of a self-help Internet-based intervention for test anxiety. *Behaviour Research and Therapy, 45,* 483–496.

O'Reilly, R. (2004). Why are community treatment orders controversial? *Canadian Journal of Psychiatry, 49,* 579–584.

O'Reilly, R. L., et al. (2009). *Mandatory outpatient treatment: Canadian Psychiatric Association* position paper. Ottawa: Canadian Psychiatric Association.

O'Reilly, R. L., Keegan, D. L., Corring, D., Shrikhande, S., & Natarajan, D. (2006). A qualitative analysis of the use of community treatment orders in Saskatchewan. *International Journal of Law and Psychiatry, 29,* 516–524.

O'Reilly, R. L., Keegan, D. L., & Elias, J. W. (2000). A survey of the use of community treatment orders by psychiatrists in Saskatchewan. *Canadian Journal of Psychiatry, 45,* 79–81.

Ormel, J., Petukhova, M., Chatterji, S., Aguilar-Gaxiola, S., et al. (2008). Disability and treatment of specific mental and physical disorders around the world. *The British Journal of Psychiatry, 192,* 368–375.

Orne, M. T., Dinges, D. F., & Orne, E. C. (1984). The differential diagnosis of multiple personality in the forensic court. *International Journal of Clinical and Experimental Hypnosis, 32,* 118–169.

Ornitz, E. M. (1989). Autism at the interface between sensory and information processing. In G. Dawson (Ed.), *Autism: Nature, diagnosis, and treatment* (pp. 174–207). New York: Guilford.

O'Rourke, N., & Hadjistavropoulos, T. (1997). The relative efficacy of psychotherapy in the treatment of geriatric depression. *Aging and Mental Health, 1,* 305–310.

O'Rourke, N., & Tuokko, H. A. (2004). Caregiver burden and depressive symptomatology: The dissociation between constructs over time. *Clinical Gerontologist, 27,* 41–52.

Orr, S. P., Lasko, N. B., Shalev, A. Y., & Pitman, R. K. (1995). Physiological responses to loud tones in Vietnam veterans with post-traumatic stress disorder. *Journal of Abnormal Psychology, 104,* 75–82.

Orth, O., & Wieland, E. (2006). Anger, hostility, and posttraumatic stress disorder in trauma-exposed adults: A meta-analysis. *Journal of Consulting and Clinical Psychology, 74,* 698–706.

Ost, L.-G. (1992). Blood and injection phobia: Background and cognitive, physiological, and behavioral correlates. *Journal of Abnormal Psychology, 101,* 68–74.

Ost, L.-G. (2008). Efficacy of the third wave of behavioral therapies: A systematic review and meta-analysis. *Behaviour Research and Therapy, 46,* 296–321.

Ostbye, T., et al. (2005). Prevalence and predictors of depression in elderly Canadians: The Canadian Study of Health and Aging. *Chronic Diseases in Canada, 26,* 93–99.

Ostbye, T., Steenhuis, R., Walton, R., & Cairney, J. (2000). Correlates of dysphoria in Canadian seniors: The Canadian Study of Health and Aging. *Canadian Journal of Public Health, 91,* 313–317.

Ottaviani, C., Shapiro, D., Davydov, D. M., Goldstein, I. B., & Mills, P. J. (2009). The autonomic phenotype of rumination. *International Journal of Psychophysiology, 72,* 267–275.

Otto, M. W., Pollack, M. H., & Maki, K. M. (2000). Empirically supported treatments for panic disorder: Costs, benefits, and stepped care. *Journal of Consulting and Clinical Psychology, 68,* 556–563.

Ouimette, P. C., Finney, J. W., & Moos, R. H. (1997). Twelve-step and cognitive-behavioral treatment for substance abuse: A comparison of treatment effectiveness. *Journal of Consulting and Clinical Psychology, 65,* 230–240.

Ouzounian, R. (2009, December 5). Howie's good clean fun: Comic and TV host's book tells how his OCD and ADHD put him at odds with the world. *Toronto Star,* E3.

Oveisgharan, S., & Hachinski, V. (2010). Hypertension, executive dysfunction, and progression to dementia: The Canadian Study of Health and Aging. *Archives of Neurology, 67,* 187–192.

Owen, M. J., Williams, N. M., & O'Donovan, M. C. (2004). The molecular genetics of schizophrenia: New findings promise new insights. *Molecular Psychiatry, 9,* 14–27.

Owens, E. B., et al. (2003). Which treatment for whom for ADHD? Moderators of treatment response in the MTA. *Journal of Consulting and Clinical Psychology, 71,* 540–552.

Page, A. C. (1994). Blood-injection phobia. *Clinical Psychology Review, 14,* 443–461.

Paglia, A., & Room, R. (1999). Expectancies about the effects of alcohol on the self and others as determinants of alcohol policy attitudes. *Journal of Applied Social Psychology, 29,* 2632–2651.

Paglia-Boak, A., Mann, R. E., Adlaf, E. M., & Rehm, J. (2009). Ontario Student Drug Use and Health Survey. Toronto: Centre for Addiction and Mental Health.

Pahkala, K. (1990). Social and environmental factors and atypical depression in old age. *International Journal of Geriatric Psychiatry, 5*, 99–113.

Pantalone, D. W., Iwamasa, G. Y., & Martell, C. R. (2010). Cognitive-behavioral therapy for diverse populations. In K. S. Dobson (Ed.), *Handbook of cognitive-behavioral therapies* (3rd ed., pp. 445–464). New York: The Guilford Press.

Pantin, H., Coatsworth, J. D., Feaster, D. J., et al. (2003). Familias Unidas: The efficacy of an intervention to promote parental investment in Hispanic immigrant families. *Prevention Science, 4*, 189–201.

Parent, K., & Anderson, M. (2001). *Home care by default, not by design: CARP's report card on home care in Canada 2001.* Retrieved October 22, 2001, from www.50plus.com.

Paris, J. (2002). Chronic suicidality among patients with borderline personality disorder. *Psychiatric Services, 53*, 738–742.

Paris, J. (2009). Psychiatry and neuroscience. *Canadian Journal of Psychiatry, 54*, 513–517.

Paris, J. (2009). The treatment of borderline personality disorder: Implications of research on diagnosis, etiology, and outcome. *Annual Review of Clinical Psychology, 5*, 277–290.

Paris, J., & Zweig-Frank, H. (2001). A 27-year follow-up of patients with borderline personality disorder. *Comprehensive Psychiatry, 42*, 482–487.

Parker, G., Gladstone, G., & Chee, K. T. (2001). Depression in the planet's largest ethnic group: The Chinese. *American Journal of Psychiatry, 158*, 857–864.

Parker, G., Tupling, H., & Brown, L. B. (1979). A parental bonding instrument. *British Journal of Medical Psychology, 52*, 1–10.

Parker, G. B., Crawford, J., & Hadzi-Pavlovic, D. (2008). Quantified superiority of cognitive behaviour therapy to antidepressant drugs: A challenge to an earlier meta-analysis. *Acta Psychiatrica Scandinavica, 118*, 91–97.

Parrish, B. P., Cohen, L. H., Gunthert, K. C., et al. (2009). Effects of cognitive therapy for depression on daily stress-related variables. *Behaviour Research and Therapy, 47*, 444–448.

Parry, G., Castonguay, L. G., Borkovec, T. D., & Wolf, A. M. (2010). Practice research networks and psychological services research in the UK and USA. In M. Barkham, G. Hardy, & J. Mellon-Clark (Eds.), *Developing and delivering practice-based evidence* (pp. 311–326). Chichester, UK: John Wiley & Sons.

Patch, N. (2009, March 10). Good shares his story; Healthy Canadian rocker talks about his struggles with depression. *Telegraph-Journal*, Saint John NB, D4.

Patel, S., & Adams, M. R. (2008). Prevention of cardiac disease: Lifestyle modification or pharmacotherapy? *Internal Medicine Journal, 38*, 199–203.

Patrick, C. J., Hicks, B. M., Krueger, R. F., & Lang, A. R. (2005). Relations between psychopathy facets and externalizing in a criminal offender sample. *Journal of Personality Disorders, 19*, 339–356.

Patten, S. B. (2008). Major depression prevalence is very high, but the syndrome is a poor proxy for community populations' clinical treatment needs. *Canadian Journal of Psychiatry, 53*, 411–419.

Patten, S. B., Bilsker, D., & Goldner, E. (2008). The evolving understanding of major depression epidemiology: Implications for practice and policy. *Canadian Journal of Psychiatry, 53*, 689–695.

Patten, S. B., Wang, J. L., et al. (2006). Descriptive epidemiology of major depression in Canada. *Canadian Journal of Psychiatry, 51*, 84–90.

Patterson, C. M., & Newman, J. P. (1993). Reflectivity and learning from aversive events: Toward a psychological mechanism for the syndromes of disinhibition. *Psychological Review, 100*, 716–736.

Patterson, G. R. (1982). *Coercive family process.* Eugene, OR: Castilia.

Patterson, G. R., Ray, R. S., Shaw, D. A., & Cobb, J. A. (1969). *Manual for coding of family interactions.* New York: ASIS/NAPS, Microfiche Publications.

Paul, G. L., & Shannon, D. T. (1966). Treatment of anxiety through systematic desensitization in therapy groups. *Journal of Abnormal Psychology, 71*, 124–135.

Paul, G. L., Stuve, P., & Cross, J. V. (in press). Real-world inpatient programs: Shedding some light. *Applied and Preventive Psychology.*

Paul, T., et al. (2002). Self-injurious behavior in women with eating disorders. *American Journal of Psychiatry, 159*, 408–411.

Pauls, D. L., Alsobrook, J. P., Goodman, W., Rasmussen, S., & Leckman, J. F. (1995). A family study of obsessive-compulsive disorder. *American Journal of Psychiatry, 152*, 76–84.

Paulus, M. P. (2008). The role of neuroimaging for the diagnosis and treatment of anxiety disorders. *Depression and Anxiety, 25*, 348–356.

Pearlstein, T., & Steiner, M. (2008). Premenstrual dysphoric disorder: Burden of illness and treatment update. *Journal of Psychiatry and Neuroscience, 33*, 291–301.

Pearson, C., & Gatz, M. (1982). Health and mental health in older adults: First steps in the study of a pedestrian complaint. *Rehabilitation Psychology, 27*, 37–50.

Pearson, J. L., & Brown, G. K. (2000). Suicide prevention in late life: Directions for science and practice. *Clinical Psychology Review, 20*, 685–705.

Pedersen, S. S., & Denollet, J. (2003). Type D personality, cardiac events, and impaired quality of life: A review. *Journal of Cardiovascular Risk, 10*, 241–248.

Pelissier, M.-C., & O'Connor, K. (2004). Cognitive-behavioral treatment of trichotillomania, targeting perfectionism. *Clinical Case Studies, 1*, 57–68.

Pelle, A. J., et al. (2008). Type D patients report poorer health status prior to and after cardiac rehabilitation compared to non Type-D patients. *Annals of Behavioral Medicine, 36*, 167–175.

Peng, P. N., et al. (2007). Change in accessing multidisciplinary pain treatment facilities in Canada. *Canadian Journal of Anaesthesia, 54*, 977–984.

Pennebaker, J., Kiecolt-Glaser, J. K., & Glaser, R. (1988). Disclosure of traumas and immune function: Health implications for psychotherapy. *Journal of Consulting and Clinical Psychology, 56*, 239–245.

Pepler, D. J., & Sedighdeilami, F. (1998). *Aggressive girls in Canada* (No. W-98-30E). Ottawa: Human Resources Development Canada.

Perala, J., et al. (2007). Lifetime prevalence of psychotic and bipolar I disorders in a general population. *Archives of General Psychiatry, 64*, 19–28.

Perez, M. A., Meyerowitz, B. E., Lieskovsky, G., Skinner, D. G., Reynolds, B., & Skinner, E. C. (1997). Quality of life and sexuality following radical prostatectomy in patients with prostate cancer who use or do not use erectile aids. *Urology, 50*, 740–746.

Pergadia, M. L., Heath, A. C., Agrawal, A., et al. (2006). The implications of simultaneous smoking initiation for inferences about the genetics of smoking behavior from twin data. *Behavior Genetics, 36*, 567–576.

Perlin, M. L. (1994). *Law and mental disability.* Charlottesville, VA: The Michie Company.

Perr, I. N. (1992). The trial of Louis Riel: A study in Canadian psychiatry. *Journal of Forensic Sciences, 37*, 845–852.

Perr, I. N., & Federoff, J. P. (1992). Misunderstanding of self and the Riel phenomenon. *Journal of Forensic Sciences, 37*, 839–844.

Perris, C., Arrindell, W. A., & Eisemann, M. (Eds.). (1994). *Parenting and psychopathology.* Chichester, England: John Wiley & Sons.

Perris, C., Jacobsson, L., Lindstrom, H., Von Knorring, L., & Perris, H. (1980). Development of a new inventory for assessing memories of parental rearing behaviour. *Acta Psychiatrica Scandinavica, 61*, 265–274.

Persons, J. B. (2005). Empiricism, mechanism, and the practice of cognitive-behavior therapy. *Behavior Therapy, 36*, 107–118.

Persons, J., & Bertagnolli, A. (1999). Inter-rater reliability of cognitive-behavioral case formulations of depression: A replication. *Cognitive Therapy and Research, 23*, 271–283.

Persons, J. B., & Davidson, J. (2001). Cognitive-behavioral case formulation. In K. S. Dobson (Ed.), *Handbook of psychotherapy case formulation* (pp. 314–339). New York: Guilford Press.

Persons, J. B., & Davidson, J. (2010). Cognitive-behavioural case formulation. In K. S. Dobson (Ed.), *Handbook of cognitive-behavioral therapies* (3rd ed., pp. 172–193). New York: The Guilford Press.

Persons, J. B., Roberts, N. A., Zalecki, C. A., & Brechwald, W. A. G. (2006). Naturalistic outcome of case formulation-driven cognitive-behavior therapy for anxious depressed outpatients. *Behaviour Research and Therapy, 44*, 1041–1051.

Persons, J. B., & Tompkins, M. A. (2007). Cognitive-behavioral case formulation. In T. T. Eells (Ed.), *Handbook of psychotherapy case formulation* (2nd ed., pp. 290–316). New York: Guilford Press.

Peters, R. deV., Petrunka, K., & Arnold, R. (2003). The Better Beginnings, Better Futures Project: A universal, comprehensive, community-based prevention approach for primary school children and their families. *Journal of Clinical Child and Adolescent Psychology, 32*, 215–227.

Petersen, L., Thorup, A., Oqhlenschlaeger, J., et al. (2008). Predictors of remission and recovery in a first-episode schizophrenia spectrum disorder sample: 2-year follow-up of the ORPUS Trial. *Canadian Journal of Psychiatry, 53*, 660–670.

Peterson, C., & Seligman, M. E. P. (1984). Causal explanations as a risk factor for depression: Theory and evidence. *Psychological Review, 91*, 347–374.

Peterson, R. A., & Reiss, R. L. (1987). The Anxiety Sensivity Index: Construct validity and factor analytic structure. *Journal of Anxiety Disorders, 1*, 265–277.

Petitclerc, A., Boivin, M., Dionne, G., et al. (2009). Disregard for rules: The early development and predictors of a specific dimension of disruptive behavior disorders. *Journal of Child Psychology and Psychiatry, 50*, 1477–1484.

Petitclerc, A., & Tremblay, R. E. (2009). Childhood disruptive behaviour disorders: Review of their origin, development, and prevention. *Canadian Journal of Psychiatry, 54*, 222–231.

Pfammatter, M., Junghan, U. M., & Brenner, H. D. (2006). Efficacy of psychological therapy in schizophrenia: Conclusions from meta-analyses. *Schizophrenia Bulletin, 32*, S64–S80.

Pfefferbaum, A., Adalsteinsson, E., & Sullivan, E. V. (2006). Dysmorphology and microstructural degradation of the corpus callosum: Interaction of age and alcoholism. *Neurobiology of Aging, 27*, 994–1009.

Pfefferman, A., Sullivan, E. V., Rosenbloom, M. J., Mathalon, D. H., & Lim, K. O. (1998). A controlled study of cortical grey matter and ventricular changes in alcoholic men over a 5-year interval. *Archives of General Psychiatry, 55*, 905–912.

Pfeiffer, P. N., Ganoczy, D., Ilgen, M., Zivin, K., & Valenstein, M. (2009). Comorbid anxiety as a suicide risk factor among depressed veterans. *Depression and Anxiety, 26*, 752–757.

Phares, E. J., & Trull, T. J. (1997). *Clinical psychology*. Pacific Grove, CA: Brooks/Cole.

Phares, V. (2008). *Understanding abnormal child psychology* (2nd ed.). Hoboken, NJ: John Wiley & Sons.

Phillips, K., et al. (2006). A 12-month follow-up study of the course of body dysmorphic disorder. *American Journal of Psychiatry, 163*, 907–912.

Phillips, K. A. (2009). *Understanding body dysmorphic disorder: An essential guide*. London: Oxford University Press.

Phillips, K. A., Didie, E. R., Feusner, J., & Wilhelm, S. (2008). Body dysmorphic disorder: Treating an underrecognized disorder. *American Journal of Psychiatry, 165*, 1111–1118.

Phillips, K. A., et al. (2006). Clinical features of body dysmorphic disorder in adolescents and adults. *Psychiatry Research, 141*, 305–314.

Phillips, L. J., Francey, S. M., Edwards, J., McMurray, N. (2007). Stress and psychosis: Towards the development of new models of investigation. *Clinical Psychology Review, 27*, 307–317.

Phipps, S. (1999). *An international comparison of policies and outcomes for young children*. CPRN Study No. F-05. Ottawa: Canadian Policy Research Networks, Inc.

Picard, A. (2008, June 27). A 12-step program for Canada: Setting priorities and solutions to address the mental health crisis. *Globe and Mail* (http://v1.theglobeandmail.com/servlet/story/RTGAM.20080627.wmhsolutions28/BNStory/mentalhealth/).

Picard, A. (2009, September 18). Burying the story won't stop suicide. *The Globe and Mail.*

Picard, A. (2009, October 28). Hypertension doubles for Quebec Inuit. *The Globe and Mail.*

Picard, A. (2008, June 27). A 12-step program for Canada: Setting priorities and solutions to address the mental health crisis. *The Globe and Mail.*

Pierce, J. P., Choi, W. S., Gilpin, E. A., Farkas, A. J., & Berry, C. C. (1998). Tobacco ads, promotional items linked with teen smoking. *Journal of the American Medical Association, 279*, 511–515.

Pierce, W. D., & Epling, F. W. (1996). Theoretical developments in activity anorexia. In W. F. Epling & W. D. Pierce (Eds.), *Activity anorexia: Theory, research, and treatment* (pp. 23–41). Mahwah, NJ: Erlbaum.

Pietrzak, R., Johnson, D. C., Goldstein, M. B., et al. (2009). Psychological resilience and postdeployment social support protect against traumatic stress and depressive symptoms in soldiers returning from operations Enduring Freedom and Iraqi Freedom. *Depression and Anxiety, 26*, 745–751.

Pine, D. S. (2007). Developmental perspectives on psychopathology. *American Journal of Psychiatry, 164*, 1781.

Pine, D. S., & Freedman, R. (2009). Child psychiatry growin' up. *American Journal of Psychiatry, 166*, 4–7.

Pinel, J. P. J., Assanand, S., & Lehman, D. R. (2000). Hunger, eating, and ill health. *American Psychologist, 55*, 1105–1116.

Pinel, P. (1962). *A treatise on insanity, 1801*. (D. D. Davis, Trans.). New York: Hafner.

Pinhas, L., Toner, B. B., Ali, A., Garfinkel, P. E., & Stuckless, N. (1999). The effects of the ideal of female beauty on mood and satisfaction. *International Journal of Eating Disorders, 25*, 223–226.

Pinto, A. M., et al. (2008). The Eating Disorder Recovery Self-Efficacy Questionnaire: Change with treatment and prediction of outcome. *Eating Behaviors, 9*, 143–153.

Piper, A., & Merskey, H. (2004a). The persistence of folly: A critical examination of Dissociative Identity Disorder. Part I. The excesses of an improbable concept. *Canadian Journal of Psychiatry, 49*, 592–600.

Piper, A., & Merskey, H. (2004b). The persistence of folly: Critical examination of Dissociative Identity Disorder. Part II. The defence and decline of multiple personality or dissociative identity disorder. *Canadian Journal of Psychiatry, 49*, 673–683.

Piran, N. (1999). Eating disorders: A trial of prevention in a high risk school setting. *Journal of Primary Prevention, 20*, 75–90.

Piran, N., & Gadella, T. (2006). Eating disorders and substance abuse in Canadian women: A national study. *Addiction, 102*, 105–113.

Pires, P., & Jenkins, J. M. (2007). A growth curve analysis of the joint influences of parenting affect, child characteristics and deviant peers on adolescent illicit drug use. *Journal of Youth and Adolescence, 36*, 169–183.

Placidi, G. P., et al. (2001). Aggressivity, suicide attempts, and depression: Relationship to cerebral spinal fluid monoamine metabolite levels. *Biological Psychiatry, 50*, 783–791.

Plassman, B. L., et al. (2007). Prevalence of dementia in the United States: The Aging, Demographics, and Memory Study. *Neuroepidemiology, 29*, 125–132.

Plassman, B. L., et al. (2008). Prevalence of cognitive impairment without dementia in the United States. *Annals of Internal Medicine, 148*, 427–434.

Pliner, P., & Chaiken, S. (1990). Eating, social motives, and self-presentation in women and men. *Journal of Experimental Social Psychology, 26*, 693–702.

Pliner, P., Chaiken, S., & Flett, G. L. (1990). Gender differences in concern with body-weight and physical appearance over the life-span. *Personality and Social Psychology Bulletin, 16*, 263–273.

Podnieks, E. (2006). Social inclusion: An interplay of the determinants of health: New insights into elder abuse. *Journal of Gerontological Social Work, 46*, 57–79.

Podnieks, E., & Pillemer, K. (1990). *National Survey on Abuse of the Elderly in Canada*. Toronto: Ryerson Polytechnic Institute.

Podymow, T., Turnbull, J., Coyle, D., Yetisir, E., & Wells, G. (2006). Shelter-based managed alcohol administration to chronically homeless people addicted to alcohol. *Canadian Medical Association Journal, 174*, 45–49.

Polanczyk, G., de Lima, M. S., Horta, B. L., et al. (2007). The worldwide prevalence of ADHD: A systematic review and metaregression analysis. *American Journal of Psychiatry, 164*, 942–948.

Polich, J. M., Armor, D. J., & Braiker, H. B. (1980). Patterns of alcoholism over four years. *Journal of Studies on Alcohol, 41*, 397–415.

Polivy, J., & Herman, C. P. (1985). Dieting and binging: A causal analysis. *American Psychologist, 40*, 193–201.

Polivy, J., & Herman, C. P. (2002). If at first you don't succeed: False hopes of self-change. *American Psychologist, 57*, 677–689.

Pompili, M., et al. (2006). Suicide and attemped suicide in eating disorders, obesity and weight-image concern. *Eating Behaviors, 7*, 384–394.

Pope, H. G., Jr., Barry, S., Bodkin, A., & Hudson, J. I. (2006). Tracking scientific interest in the dissociative disorders: A study of scientific publication output 1984–2003. *Psychotherapy and Psychosomatics, 75*, 19–24.

Pope, H. G., Oliva, P. S., Hudson, J. I., Bodkin, J. A., & Gruber, A. J. (1999). Attitudes toward DSM-IV dissociative disorders among board-certified American psychiatrists. *American Journal of Psychiatry, 156*, 321–323.

Pope, K. S. (1995). What psychologists better know about recovered memories, research, lawsuits, and the pivotal experiment: A review of "The Myth of Repressed Memory: False Memories and Allegations of Sexual Abuse," by Elizabeth Loftus and Katherine Ketcham. *Clinical Psychology: Science and Practice, 2*, 304–315.

Porath-Waller, A. J. (2009). *Clearing the smoke on cannabis: Chronic use and cognitive functioning and mental health*. Ottawa: Canadian Centre on Substance Abuse.

Porter, S., ten Brinke, L., & Wilson, K. (2009). Crime profiles and conditional release performance of psychopathic and non-psychopathic sexual offenders. *Legal and Criminological Psychology*, 14, 109–118.

Porter, S., & Woodworth, M. (2007). "I'm sorry I did it but he started it": A comparison of the official and self-reported homicide descriptions of psychopaths and non-psychopaths. *Law and Human Behavior*, 31, 91–107.

Porter, S., Woodworth, M., Earle, J., Drugge, J., & Boer, D. (2003). Characteristics of sexual homicides committed by psychopathic and nonpsychopathic offenders. *Law and Human Behavior*, 27, 459–470.

Pos, A. E., Greenberg, L. S., Goldman, R. N., & Korman, L. M. (2003). Emotional processing during experiential treatment of depression. *Journal of Consulting and Clinical Psychology*, 71, 1007–1016.

Possel, P., Seemann, S., & Hautzinger, M. (2008). Impact of comorbidity in prevention of adolescent depressive symptoms. *Journal of Counseling Psychology*, 55, 106–117.

Post, R. M., & Weiss, S. R. B. (1995). The neurobiology of treatment-resistent mood disorders. In F. E. Bloom & D. J. Kupfer (Eds.), *Psychopharmacology: The fourth generation of progress* (pp. 1155–1170). New York: Raven Press.

Pot, A. M., et al. (2010). The impact of life review on depression in older adults: A randomized controlled trial. *International Psychogeriatrics*, 22, 572–581.

Potkin, S. C., & Ford, J. M. (2009). Widespread cortical dysfunction in schizophrenia: The FBIRN Imaging Consortium. *Schizophrenia Bulletin*, 35, 15–18.

Potter, M. (2009, September 2). Pills and America's pursuit of happiness. *Toronto Star*, A12.

Poulin, C. (2000). Problem gambling among adolescent students in the Atlantic provinces of Canada. *Journal of Gambling Studies*, 16, 53–77.

Poulin, C., Fralick, P., Whynot, E. M., El-Guebaly, N., Kennedy, D., Bernstein, J., et al. (1998). The epidemiology of cocaine and opiate abuse in urban Canada. *Canadian Journal of Public Health*, 89, 234–238.

Poundja, J., Fikretoglu, D., & Brunet, A. (2006). The co-occurrence of posttraumatic stress disorder symptoms and pain: Is depression a mediator? *Journal of Traumatic Stress*, 19, 747–751.

Poundmaker's Lodge (2001, January 21). Poundmaker's Lodge: Mission, philosophy and facilities. Retrieved March 13, 2001, from http://poundmaker.org.

Power, K. G., et al. (1990). A controlled comparison of cognitive-behaviour therapy, diazepam, and placebo, alone and in combination, for the treatment of generalized anxiety disorder. *Journal of Anxiety Disorders*, 4, 267–292.

Powers, A., Ressler, K. J., & Bradley, R. G. (2009). The protective role of friendship on the effects of childhood abuse and depression. *Depression and Anxiety*, 26, 46–53.

Powers, M. B.,Vedel, E., & Emmelkamp, P. M. G. (2008). Behavioral couples therapy (BCT) for alcohol and drug use disorders: A meta-analysis. *Clinical Psychology Review*, 28, 952–962.

Preville, M., et al. (2005). Correlates of suicide in the older adult population in Quebec. *Suicide and Life Threatening Behavior*, 35, 91–105.

Price, R. A., Cadoret, R. J., Stunkard, A. J., & Troughton, E. (1987). Genetic contributions to human fatness: An adoption study. *American Journal of Psychiatry*, 144, 1003–1008.

Prien, R. F., & Potter, W. Z. (1993). Maintenance treatment for mood disorders. In D. L. Dunner (Ed.), *Current psychiatric therapy*. Philadelphia: Saunders.

Prilleltensky, I., & Nelson, G. (2000). Promoting child and family wellness: Priorities for psychological and social interventions. *Journal of Community and Applied Social Psychology*, 10, 85–105.

Prochaska, J. O. (1984). *Systems of psychotherapy* (2nd ed.). Homewood, IL: Dorsey Press.

Prochaska J. O., DiClemente C. C., & Norcross, J. C. (1992). In search of how people change. Applications to addictive behaviors. *American Psychologist*, 47, 1102–1114.

Project Match Research Group. (1997). Matching alcoholism treatments to client heterogeneity: Project MATCH posttreatment drinking outcomes. *Journal of Studies on Alcohol*, 58, 7–29.

Prout, P. I., & Dobson, K. S. (1998). Recovered memories of childhood sexual abuse: Searching for the middle ground in clinical practice. *Canadian Psychology*, 39, 257–265.

Provencher, H. L., & Fincham, F. D. (2000). Attributions of causality, responsibility and blame for positive and negative symptom behaviours in caregivers of persons with schizophrenia. *Psychological Medicine*, 30, 899–910.

Provencher, H. L., Perreault, M., St-Onge, M., & Rousseau, M. (2003). Predictors of psychological distress in family caregivers of persons with psychiatric disabilities. *Journal of Psychiatric and Mental Health Nursing*, 10, 592–607.

Pryor, T., Wiederman, M. W., & McGilley, B. (1996). Clinical correlates of anorexia subtypes. *International Journal of Eating Disorders*, 19, 371–379.

Psychiatric Patient Advocate Office. (2009). Honouring the past, shaping the future: 25 years of progress in mental health advocacy and rights protection.

Pu, T., Mohamed, E., Imam, K., & El-Roey, A. M. (1986). One hundred cases of hysteria in eastern Libya. *British Journal of Psychiatry*, 148, 606–609.

Pugh, G. M., & Boer, D. P. (1989). An examination of culturally appropriate items for the WAIS-R Information subtest with Canadian subjects. *Journal of Psychoeducational Assessment*, 7, 131–140.

Pulay, A. J., et al. (2009). Prevalence, correlates, disability, and comorbidity of DSM-IV schizotypal personality disorder: Results for the Wave 2 National Epidemiologic Survey on Alcohol and Related Conditions. *Journal of Clinical Psychiatry*, 11, 53–67.

Pull, C. (2008). Recent trends in the study of specific phobias. *Current Opinion in Psychiatry*, 21, 43–50.

Purdie, F. R., Honigman, T. B., & Rosen, P. (1981). Acute organic brain syndrome: A view of 100 cases. *Annals of Emergency Medicine*, 10, 455–461.

Purdon, C., & Clark, D. A. (1994). Perceived control and appraisal of obsessional intrusive thoughts: A replication and extension. *Behavioural and Cognitive Psychotherapy*, 22, 269–285.

Puxley, C. (2009, March 6). Greyhound attacker 'getting away with murder,' family says: Judge rules killer not criminally responsible due to mental illness for 'barbaric' bus attack. *Toronto Star*, A2.

Pyle, A. (1999, May 28). Seeking a remedy for nursing homes' ills. *Los Angeles Times*, A1–A30.

Qiu, A., Crocetti, D., Adler, M., et al. (2009). Basal ganglia volume and shape in children with attention deficit hyperactivity disorder. *American Journal of Psychiatry*, 166, 74–82.

Qizilbash, N., Whitehead, A., Higgins, J., Wilcock, G., Schneider, L., et al. (1998). Cholinesterase inhibition for Alzheimer disease: A meta-analysis of Tacrine trials. *Journal of the American Medical Association*, 280, 1777–1782.

Quan, H., & Arboleda-Florez, J. (1999). Elderly suicide in Alberta: Differences by gender. *Canadian Journal of Psychiatry*, 44, 762–768.

Quinsey, V. L., Harris, G. T., Rice, M. E., & Cormier, C. A. (1998). *Violent offenders: Appraising and managing risk*. Washington, DC: American Psychological Association.

Rabinovitch, M., Bechard-Evans, L., Schmitz, N., et al. (2009). Early predictors of nonadherence to antipsychotic therapy in first-episode psychosis. *Canadian Journal of Psychiatry*, 54, 28–31.

Rachman, S. (1998). A cognitive theory of obsessions. In E. Sanavio (Ed.), *Behaviour and cognitive therapy today: Essays in honour of Hans J. Eysenck* (pp. 209–222). Oxford, England: Elsevier Science Limited.

Rachman, S. (2002). A cognitive theory of compulsive checking. *Behaviour Research and Therapy*, 40, 625–639.

Rachman, S., Gruter-Andrew, J., & Shafran, R. (2000). Post-event processing in social anxiety. *Behaviour Research and Therapy*, 38, 611–617.

Rachman, S. J., & Hodgson, R. J. (1980). *Obsessions and compulsions*. Englewood Cliffs, NJ: Prentice-Hall.

Rachman, S., & Shafran, R. (1998). Cognitive and behavioural features of obsessive-compulsive disorder. In R. P. Swinson, M. M. Antony, S. Rachman, & M.A. Richter (Eds.), *Obsessive-compulsive disorder: Theory, research, and treatment* (pp. 51–78). New York: Guilford.

Radomsky, A. S., et al. (2006). Psychometric properties of the French and English versions of the Claustrophobia Questionnaire (CLQ). *Anxiety Disorders*, 20, 818–828.

Raes, F., & Hermans, D. (2008). On the mediating role of subtypes of rumination in the relationship between childhood emotional abuse and depressed mood: Brooding versus reflection. *Depression and Anxiety*, 25, 1067–1070.

Ragland, J. D., Laird, A. R., Ranganath, C., et al. (2009). Prefrontal activation deficits during episodic memory in schizophrenia. *American Journal of Psychiatry*, 166, 863–874.

Rahe, R. H., & Lind, E. (1971). Psychosocial factors and sudden cardiac death: A pilot study. *Journal of Psychosomatic Research, 15,* 19–24.

Raina, P. S., et al. (2009). The Canadian Longitudinal Study on Aging (CLSA). *Canadian Journal on Aging, 28,* 221–229.

Rajkowska, G., Selemon, L. D., & Goldman-Rakic, P. S. (1998). Neuronal and glial soma size in the prefrontal cortex: A postmortem morphometric study of schizophrenia and Huntington disease. *Archives of General Psychiatry, 55,* 215–224.

Ralph, J. A., & Mineka, S. (1998). Attributional style and self-esteem: The prediction of emotional distress following a midterm exam. *Journal of Abnormal Psychology, 107,* 203–215.

Rankin, J., Pron, N., & Duncanson, J. (1995, August 16). "I didn't kill these girls." But Bernardo admits kidnapping, rape. *Toronto Star,* A1, A12–A13.

Ransom, D. C., LaGuardia, J. G., Woody, E. Z., & Boyd, J. L. (2010). Interpersonal interactions on online forums addressing eating concerns. *International Journal of Eating Disorders, 43,* 161–170.

Ranta, K., Kaltiala-Heino, R., Rantanen, P., & Marttunen, M. (2009). Social phobia in Finnish general adolescent population: Prevalence, comorbidity, individual and family correlates, and service use. *Depression and Anxiety, 26,* 528–536.

Rapee, R. M., & Heimberg, R. G. (1997). A cognitive-behavioral model of anxiety in social phobia. *Behaviour Research and Therapy, 35,* 741-756.

Rapee, R. M., Schniering, C. A., & Hudson, J. L. (2009). Anxiety disorders during childhood and adolescence: Origins and treatment. *Annual Review of Clinical Psychology, 5,* 311–341.

Raphael, D. (2009). Poverty, human development, and health in Canada: Research, practice, and advocacy dilemmas. *Canadian Journal of Nursing Research, 41,* 7–18.

Rapoport, J., Chavez, A., Greenstein, D., et al. (2009). Autism spectrum disorders and childhood-onset schizophrenia: Clinical and biological contributions to a relation revisited. *Journal of the American Academy of Child and Adolescent Psychiatry, 48,* 10–18.

Rapp, S. R., Parisi, S. A., Walsh, D. A., & Wallace, C. E. (1988). Detecting depression in elderly medical patients. *Journal of Consulting and Clinical Psychology, 56,* 509–513.

Rappaport, J., & Chinsky, J. M. (1974). Models for delivery of service from a historical and conceptual perspective. *Professional Psychology, 5,* 42–50.

Rashid, F. L., Morris, R. D., & Sevcik, R. A. (2005). Relationship between home literacy environment and reading achievement in children with reading disabilities. *Journal of Learning Disabilities, 38,* 2–11.

Rasmussen, D. X., Brandt, J., Martin, D. B., & Folstein, M. F. (1995). Head injury as a risk factor in Alzheimer's disease. *Brain Injury, 9,* 213–219.

Rasmussen, H. N., Scheier, M. F., & Greenhouse, J. B. (2009). Optimism and physical health: A meta-analytic review. *Annals of Behavioral Medicine, 37,* 239–256.

Rauch, S. A. M., Grunfeld, T. E. E., Yadin, E., et al. (2009). Changes in reported physical health symptoms and social function with prolonged exposure therapy for chronic posttraumatic stress disorder. *Depression and Anxiety, 26,* 732–738.

Rauch, S. L., et al. (1994). Regional cerebral blood flow measured during symptom provocation in obsessive-compulsive disorder using oxygen-15 labeled carbon dioxide and positron emission tomography. *Archives of General Psychiatry, 51,* 62–70.

Ravindran, L., & Kennedy, S. H. (2007a). In debate: Response to Dr. Moncrieff. *Canadian Journal of Psychiatry, 52,* 102.

Ravindran, L., & Kennedy, S. H. (2007b). In debate: Are antidepressants as effective as claimed? Yes, but... *Canadian Journal of Psychiatry, 52,* 98–99.

Raymond, N. C., Coleman, E., Ohlerking, F., Christenson, G. A., & Miner, M. (1999). Psychiatric comorbidity in pedophilic sex offenders. *American Journal of Psychiatry, 156,* 786–788.

Rechlin, T., Loew, T. H., & Joraschky, P. (1997). Pseudoseizure "status." *Journal of Psychosomatic Research, 42,* 495–498.

Rector, N. A., Bagby, R. M., Segal, Z. V., Joffe, R., & Levitt, A. (2000). Self-criticism and dependency in depressed patients treated with cognitive therapy or pharmacotherapy. *Cognitive Therapy and Research, 24,* 571–584.

Rector, N. A., Kocovski, N. L., & Ryder, A. G. (2006). Social anxiety and the fear of causing discomfort to others. *Journal of Social and Clinical Psychology, 25,* 906–918.

Rector, N. A., Seeman, M. V., & Segal, Z. V. (2003). Cognitive therapy for schizophrenia: A preliminary randomized controlled trial. *Schizophrenia Research, 63,* 1–11.

Rector, N. A., Segal, Z. V., & Gemar, M. (1998). Schema research in depression: A Canadian perspective. *Canadian Journal of Behavioural Science, 30,* 213–224.

Redmond, D. E. (1977). Alterations in the function of the nucleus locus coeruleus. In I. Hanin & E. Usdin (Eds.), *Animal models in psychiatry and neurology.* New York: Pergamon.

Reed, J. C., & Reed, H. B. C. (1997). The Halstead-Reitan Neuropsychological Battery. In G. Goldstein & T. Incagnoli (Eds.), *Contemporary approaches to neuropsychological assessment* (pp. 93–130). New York: Plenum.

Rees, C. S., McEvoy, P., & Nathan, P. R. (2005). Relationship between homework completion and outcome in cognitive behaviour therapy. *Cognitive Behaviour Therapy, 34,* 242–247.

Regier, D. A., Narrow, W. E., Kuhl, E. A., Kupfer, D. J. (2009). The conceptual development of DSM-V. *American Journal of Psychiatry, 166,* 645-649.

Reichow, B., & Wolery, M. (2009). Comprehensive synthesis of early intensive behavioral interventions for young children with autism based on the UCLA Young Autism Project model. *Journal of Autism and Developmental Disorders, 39,* 23–41.

Reid, J.L., & Hammond, D. (2009). *Tobacco use in Canada: Patterns and trends, 2009 Edition (v2).* Waterloo, ON: Propel Centre for Population Health Impact, University of Waterloo.

Reinders, A. A. T. S., et al. (2006). Psychobiological characteristics of Dissociative Identity Disorder: A symptom provocation study. *Biological Psychiatry, 60,* 730–740.

Reiss, A. L. (2009). Childhood developmental disorders: An academic and clinical convergence point for psychiatry, neurology, psychology and pediatrics. *Journal of Child Psychology and Psychiatry, 50,* 87–98.

Reiss, D., Heatherington, E. M., Plomin, R., Howe, G. W., Simmens, S. J., et al. (1995). Genetic questions for environmental studies: Differential parenting and psychopathology in adolescence. *Archives of General Psychiatry, 52,* 925–936.

Reissing, E. D. (2009). Vaginismus: Evaluation and management. In A. Goldstein, C. F. Pukall, & I. Goldstein (Eds.), *Female sexual pain disorders: Evaluation and management* (pp. 229–234). New York: Wiley-Blackwell.

Reissing, E. D., Binik, Y. M., & Khalife, S. (1999). Does vaginismus exist? A critical review of the literature. *Journal of Nervous and Mental Disease, 187,* 261–274.

Reitmanova, S., & Gustafson, D. L. (2009). Mental health needs of visible minority immigrants in a small urban center: Recommendations for policy makers and service providers. *Journal of Immigrant Minority Health, 11,* 46–56.

Remschmidt, H., Martin, M., Fleisschhaker, C., et al. (2007). Forty-two years later: The outcome of childhood-onset schizophrenia. *Journal of Neural Transmission, 114,* 505–512.

Renaud, J., Chagnon, F., Turecki, G., & Marquette, C. (2005). Completed suicides in a Youths Centres population. *Canadian Journal of Psychiatry, 50,* 690–694.

Renneberg, B., Goldstein, A. J., Phillips, D., & Chambless, D. L. (1990). Intensive behavioral group treatment of avoidant personality disorder. *Behavior Therapy, 21,* 363–377.

Rennie, D. L. (1998). *Person-centred counseling: An experiential approach.* London: Sage.

Renshaw, D. C. (1988). Profile of 2376 patients treated at Loyola Sex Clinic between 1972 and 1987. *Sexual and Marital Therapy, 3,* 111–117.

Renvoize, E. B., & Beveridge, A. W. (1989). Mental illness and the late Victorians: A study of patients admitted to three asylums in York, 1880–1884. *Psychological Medicine, 19,* 19–28.

Rescorla, R. A. (1988). Pavlovian conditioning: It's not what you think it is. *American Psychologist, 43,* 151–160.

Research Units on Pediatric Psychopharmacology Network. (2005). Randomized, controlled, crossover trial of methylphenidate in pervasive developmental disorders with hyperactivity. *Archives of General Psychiatry, 62,* 1266–1274.

Resick, P. A. (1993). The psychological impact of rape. *Journal of Interpersonal Violence, 8,* 223–255.

Resick, P. A., et al. (2002). A comparison of cognitive processing therapy with prolonged exposure therapy and a waiting list condition for the treatment of chronic posttraumatic stress disorder in female rape victims. *Journal of Consulting and Clinical Psychology, 70,* 867–879.

Resick, P. A., et al. (2008). A randomized clinical trial to dismantle components of cognitive processing therapy for posttraumatic stress disorder in female victims of interpersonal violence. *Journal of Consulting and Clinical Psychology*, 76, 243–258.

Resick, P. A., & Schnicke, M. K. (1993). Cognitive processing therapy for sexual assault victims. *Journal of Consulting and Clinical Psychology*, 60, 748–756.

Responsible Gambling Council. (2009). *Know the score.* Retrieved on August 27, 2010, from www.responsiblegambling.org/en/programs/aware-ness-score.cfm.

Restifo, K., & Bogels, S. (2009). Family processes in the development of youth depression: Translating the evidence to treatment. *Clinical Psychology Review*, 29, 294–316.

Reuters (1999, October 27). Pontiff says he continues to enjoy life despite aging. *Toronto Star*, p. 6.

Reynolds, C. F., et al. (2006). Maintenance treatment of major depression in old age. *New England Journal of Medicine*, 354, 1130–1138.

Reynolds, C. R., Chastain, R. L., Kaufman, A. S., & McLean, J. E. (1997). Demographic characteristics and IQ among adults: Analysis of the WAIS-R standardization sample as a function of the stratification variables. *Journal of School Psychology*, 25, 323–342.

Rhodes, A. E., & Bethell, J. (2008). Suicidal ideators without major depression—Whom are we not reaching? *Canadian Journal of Psychiatry*, 53, 125–130.

Rhodes, A., Goering, P., To, T., and Williams, J. (2002). Gender and outpatient mental health service use. *Social Science and Medicine*, 54, 1-10.

Rice, M. E. (1997). Violent offender research and implications for the criminal justice system. *American Psychologist*, 52, 414–423.

Rice, M. E., & Harris, G. T. (1993). Ontario's maximum security hospital at Penetanguishene: Past, present, and future. *International Journal of Law and Psychiatry*, 16, 195–215.

Rice, M. E., & Harris, G. T. (1995). Violent recidivism: Assessing predictive validity. *Journal of Consulting and Clinical Psychology*, 63, 737–748.

Rice, M. E., & Harris, G. T. (2002). Men who molest their sexually immature daughters: Is a special explanation required? *Journal of Abnormal Psychology*, 111, 329–339.

Rice, M. E., Harris, G. T., & Quinsey, V. L. (2002). The appraisal of violence risk. *Current Opinion in Psychiatry*, 15, 589–593.

Richardson, J. D., Long, M. E., Pedlar, D., Elhai, J. D. (2008). Posttraumatic stress disorder and health-related quality of life among a sample of treatment- and pension-seeking deployed Canadian forces peacekeeping veterans. *Canadian Journal of Psychiatry*, 53, 594–600.

Richardson, L. K., et al. (2009). Current directions in videoconferencing tele-mental health research. *Clinical Psychology Science and Practice*, 16, 323–338.

Rief, W., Hiller, W., & Margraf, J. (1998). Cognitive aspects of hypochondriasis and somatization syndrome. *Journal of Abnormal Psychology*, 107, 587–596.

Riley, K. P., Snowdon, D. A., Desrosiers, M. F., & Markesberry, W. R. (2005). Early life linguistic ability, late life cognitive function, and neu-ropathology: Findings from the Nun Study. *Neurobiology and Aging*, 26, 341–347.

Riordan, D. V., Selvara, S., Stark, C., & Gilbert, J. S. E. (2006). Perinatal circumstances and risk of offspring suicide. *British Journal of Psychiatry*, 189, 502–507.

Ritchie, P. L.-J., & Edwards, H. P. (1998). The evolution of Canada's health-care system and its implications for the practice of psychology as a health profession. In A. S. Bellack & M. Hersen (Eds.), *Comprehensive clinical psychology*, Vol. 2 *(Arthur N. Wiens, vol. Ed.: Professional issues)* (pp. 377–391). Oxford, England: Elsevier Science.

Roberts, N., & Crockford, D. (1997). Psychiatric admissions of Asian Canadians to an adolescent inpatient unit. *Canadian Journal of Psychiatry*, 42, 847–851.

Robins, L. N. (1966). *Deviant children grown up.* Baltimore: Williams & Wilkins.

Robins, L. N. (1978). Sturdy childhood predictors of adult antisocial behavior: Replications from longitudinal studies. *Psychological Medicine*, 8, 611–622.

Robins, L. N., Helzer, J. E., Przybec, T. R., & Regier, D. A. (1988). Alcohol disorders in the community: A report from the Epidemiologic Catchment Area. In R. M. Rose & J. E. Barrett (Eds.), *Alcoholism: Origins and outcome.* New York: Raven.

Robins, L. N., & Regier, D. (1991). *Psychiatric disorders in America.* New York: Free Press.

Robinson, D., Woerner, M. G., Alvir, J., Bilder, R., Goldman, R., et al. (1999). Predictors of relapse following response from a first episode of schizophrenia or schizaffective disorder. *Archives of General Psychiatry*, 56, 241–247.

Robinson, J., Sareen, J., Cox, B. J., & Bolton, J. (2009). Self-medication of anxiety disorders with alcohol and drugs: Results from a nationally representative sample. *Journal of Anxiety Disorders*, 23, 38–45.

Robinson, L. A., Klesges, R. C., Zbikowski, S. M., & Glaser, R. (1997). Predictors of risk for different stages of adolescent smoking in a biracial sample. *Journal of Consulting and Clinical Psychology*, 65, 653–662.

Robinson, N. S., Garber, J., & Hillsman, R. (1995). Cognitions and stress: Direct and moderating effects on depression versus externalizing symptoms during the junior high school transition. *Journal of Abnormal Psychology*, 104, 453–463.

Rockwood, K., Cosway, S., Carver, D., Jarrett. P., Stadnyk, K., & Fisk J. (1999). The risk of dementia and death after delirium. *Age and Ageing*, 28, 551–556.

Roder, V., Mueller, D. R., Mueser, K. T., Brenner, H. D. (2006). Integrated Psychological Therapy (IPT) for Schizophrenia: Is it effective? *Schizophrenia Bulletin*, 32, S1, S81–S93.

Rodick, J.D., Henggeler, S.W., & Hanson, C.L. (1986). An evaluation of the Family Adaptability and Cohesion Evaluation Scales and the Circumplex Model. *Journal of Abnormal Child Psychology*, 14, 77–87.

Rodin, J., McAvay, G., & Timko, C. (1988). A longitudinal study of depressed mood and sleep disturbances in elderly adults. *Journal of Gerontology: Psychological Sciences*, 43, 45–53.

Roesch, R., Zapf, P. A., Eaves, D., & Webster, C. D. (1999). *The fitness interview test* (Rev. ed.). Burnaby, Canada: Mental Health Law and Policy Institute.

Rogers, C. R. (1951). *Client-centered therapy*. Boston: Houghton Mifflin.

Rogers, C. R. (1961). *On becoming a person: A therapist's view of psychotherapy*. Boston: Houghton Mifflin.

Rogers, R. (2000). The uncritical acceptance of risk assessment in forensic practice. *Law and Human Behavior*, 24, 595–605.

Rogers, R. (2003). Standardizing DSM-IV diagnoses: The clinical applications of structured interviews. *Journal of Personality Assessment*, 81, 220–225.

Rogers, S. L., Doody, R. S., Mohs, R. C., Friedhoff, L. T., & the Donepezil Study Group. (1998). Donepezil improves cognition and global function in Alzheimer disease. *Archives of Internal Medicine*, 158, 1021–1031.

Romano, E., Baillargeon, R. H., Wu, H.-X., et al. (2002). Prevalence of methylphenidate use and change over a two-year period: A nationwide study of 2- to 11-year old Canadian children. *Journal of Pediatrics*, 141, 71–75.

Romano, E., Tremblay, R. E., Vitaro, F., Zoccolillo, M., & Pagani, L. (2001). Prevalence of psychiatric diagnoses and the role of perceived impairment: Findings from an adolescent community sample. *Journal of Child Psychology and Psychiatry*, 42, 451–461.

Romanow, R. J. (2006). Canada's medicare—at the crossroads? *Canadian Psychology*, 47, 1–8.

Romanow, R. J., & Marchildon, G. P. (2003). Psychological services and the future of health care in Canada. *Canadian Psychology*, 44, 283–295.

Romanow, R. J., & Marchildon, G. P. (2004). History, politics, and transformational change in Canadian health care: A rejoinder. *Canadian Journal of Psychiatry*, 45, 199–202, 239–243.

Rosch, P. J. (1998). Reminiscences of Hans Selye and the birth of "stress." *Stress Medicine*, 14, 1–6.

Rosa-Alcazar, A. I., Sanchez-Meca, J., Gomez-Consesa, A., & Marin-Martinez, F. (2008). Psychological treatment of obsessive-compulsive disorder: A meta-analysis. *Clinical Psychology Review*, 28, 1310–1325.

Rose, D. T., Abramson, L. Y., Hodulik, C. J., Halberstadt, L., & Gaye, L. (1994). Heterogeneity of cognitive style among depressed inpatients. *Journal of Abnormal Psychology*, 103, 419–429.

Rosen, G. M. (1999). Treatment fidelity and research on Eye Movement Desensitization and Reprocessing (EMDR). *Journal of Anxiety Disorders*, 13, 173–184.

Rosen, G. M. (2004). Remembering the 1978 and 1990 Task Forces on Self-Help Therapies. *Journal of Clinical Psychology*, 60, 111–113.

Rosen, G. M., & Frueh, B. C. (2007). Challenges to the PTSD construct and its database: The importance of scientific debate. *Journal of Anxiety Disorders*, 21, 161–163.

Rosen, G. M., & Lilienfeld, S. O. (2008). Posttraumatic stress disorder: An empirical evaluation of core assumptions. *Clinical Psychology Review*, 28, 837–868.

Rosen, G. M., Spitzer, R. L., & McHugh, P. R. (2008). Problems with the post-traumatic stress disorder diagnosis and its future in DSM-V. *The British Journal of Psychiatry, 192,* 3–4.

Rosen, J. L., Miller, T. J., D'Andrea, J. T., McGlashan, T. H., & Woods, S. W. (2006). Comorbid diagnoses in patients meeting criteria for the schizophrenia prodrome. *Schizophrenia Research, 85,* 124–131.

Rosen, R. C. (1991). Alcohol and drug effects on sexual response: Human experimental and clinical studies. *Annual Review of Sex Research, 2,* 119–180.

Rosen, R. C., & Leiblum, S. R. (1995). Treatment of sexual disorders in the 1990s: An integrated approach. *Journal of Consulting and Clinical Psychology, 63,* 877–890.

Rosen, R. C., Leiblum, S. R., & Spector, I. (1994). Psychologically based treatment for male erectile disorder: A cognitive-interpersonal model. *Journal of Sex and Marital Therapy, 20,* 67–85.

Rosen, R. C., & Rosen, L. (1981). *Human sexuality.* New York: Knopf.

Rosenbaum, M. (1980). The role of the term schizophrenia in the decline of diagnoses of multiple personality. *Archives of General Psychiatry, 37,* 1383–1385.

Rosenberg, D. R., Keshavan, M. S., O'Hearn, K. M., Seymour, A. B., Birmaher, B., et al. (1997). Frontostriatal measurement in treatment-naive children with obsessive-compulsive disorder. *Archives of General Psychiatry, 54,* 824–830.

Rosenfarb, I. S., Goldstein, M. J., Mintz, J., & Neuchterlein, K. H. (1994). Expressed emotion and subclinical psychopathology observable within transactions between schizophrenics and their family members. *Journal of Abnormal Psychology, 104,* 259–267.

Rosenman, R. H., Brand, R. J., Jenkins, C. D., Friedman, M., Straus, R., & Wurm, M. (1975). Coronary heart disease in the Western Collaborative Group Study: Final follow-up experience of 8 years. *Journal of the American Medical Association, 233,* 872–877.

Rosenthal, N. E. (2009). Issues for DSM-V: Seasonal affective disorder and seasonality. *American Journal of Psychiatry, 166,* 852–853.

Rosenthal, X. (2009). Issues for DSM-V: Seasonal affective disorder and seasonality. *American Journal of Psychiatry, 166,* 852–853.

Rosenzweig, S. (1936). Some implicit common factors in diverse methods of psychotherapy. *American Journal of Orthopsychiatry, 6,* 412–415.

Rosman, B. L., Minuchin, S., & Liebman, R. (1976). Input and outcome of family therapy of anorexia nervosa. In J. L. Claghorn (Ed.), *Successful psychotherapy.* New York: Brunner/Mazel.

Ross, C. A. (1991). Epidemiology of multiple personality disorder and dissociation. *Psychiatric Clinics of North America, 14,* 503–517.

Ross, C. A. (1997). *Dissociative identity disorder: Diagnosis, clinical features, and treatment of multiple personality.* Toronto: John Wiley & Sons.

Ross, C. A. (1997, April 6). *Mind control series: Ryerson CKLN Radio in Toronto: Producer Wayne Morris interviews Dr. Colin Ross.* Toronto: Ryerson CKLN Radio.

Ross, C. A. (2009). Errors of logic and scholarship concerning dissociative identity disorder. *Journal of Child Sexual Abuse, 18,* 221–231.

Ross, C. A., Joshi, S., & Currie, R. P. (1990). Dissociative experiences in the general population: A factor analysis. *Hospital and Community Psychiatry, 42,* 297–301.

Ross, C. A., Miller, S. D., Reagor, P., Bjornson, L., Fraser, G. A., & Anderson, G. (1990). Structured interview data on 102 cases of multiple personality disorder from four centers. *American Journal of Psychiatry, 147,* 596–601.

Ross, D. M., & Ross, S. A. (1982). *Hyperactivity: Research, theory, and action.* New York: John Wiley & Sons.

Ross, S., Heath, N. L., & Toste, J. R. (2009). Non-suicidal self-injury and eating pathology in high school students. *American Journal of Orthopsychiatry, 79,* 83–92.

Rost, K., Kashner, T. M., & Smith, G. R. (1994). Effectiveness of psychiatic intervention with somatization disorder patients: Improved outcomes at reduced costs. *General Hospital Psychiatry, 16,* 381–387.

Roth, W. T. (2010). Diversity of effective treatments of panic attacks: What do they have in common? *Depression and Anxiety, 27,* 5–11.

Roth, W. T. (2010). Diversity of effective treatments of panic attacks: What do they have in common? *Depression and Anxiety, 27,* 5–11.

Rothe, C., Koszycki, D., Bradwejn, J., King, N., Deluca, V., Tharmalingam, S., et al. (2006). Association of the Val158Met 31Catechol O-Methyltransferase genetic polymorphism with panic disorder. *Neuropsychopharmacology, 31,* 2237–2242.

Rothman, K. J., & Michels, K. B. (1994). The continuing unethical use of placebo controls. *New England Journal of Medicine, 331,* 394–397.

Rourke, B. P. (2008). Neuropsychology as a (psycho)social science: Implications for research and clinical practice. *Canadian Psychology, 49,* 35–41.

Rousseau, C., Hassan, G., Measham, T., & Lashley, M. (2008). Prevalence and correlates of conduct disorder and problem behavior in Caribbean and Filipino immigrant adolescents. *European Child and Adolescent Psychiatry, 17,* 264–273.

Roussy, S., & Toupin, J. (2000). Behavioral inhibition deficits in juvenile psychopaths. *Aggressive Behavior, 26,* 413–424.

Rovner, B. W., Kafonek, S., Filipp, L., Lucas, M. J., & Folstein, M. F. (1986). Prevalence of mental illness in a community nursing home. *American Journal of Psychiatry, 143,* 1446–1449.

Rowa, K., & Antony, M. M. (2008). *Social anxiety disorder.* Toronto: Hogrefe.

Rowa, K., Antony, M. M., Brar, S., Summerfeldt, L. J., & Swinson, R. P. (2000). Treatment histories of patients with three anxiety disorders. *Depression and Anxiety, 12,* 92–98.

Rowa, K., & Purdon, C. (**2003**). Why are certain intrusive thoughts more upsetting than others? *Behavioural and Cognitive Psychotherapy, 31,* 1–11

Rowa, K., Purdon, C., Summerfeldt, L. J., & Antony, M. M. (2005). Why are some obsessions more upsetting than others? *Behaviour Research and Therapy, 43,* 1453–1465.

Rowland, D. L., Cooper, S. E., & Slob, A. K. (1996). Genital and psychoaffective responses to erotic stimulation in sexually functional and dysfunctional men. *Journal of Abnormal Psychology, 105,* 194–203.

Roy, A. (1994). Recent biologic studies on suicide. *Suicide and Life Threatening Behaviors, 24,* 10–24.

Royal Commission on Aboriginal Peoples (RCAP). (1996). Residential Schools. In *Report of the Royal Commission on Aboriginal Peoples* (pp. 333–385). Ottawa: Canada Communication Group.

Rubak, S., et al. (2005). Motivational interviewing: A systematic review and meta-analysis. *British Journal of General Practice, 55,* 305–312.

Rubia, K., Halari, R., Smith, A. B., et al. (2008). Dissociated functional brain abnormalities of inhibition in boys with pure conduct disorder and in boys with pure attention deficit hyperactivity disorder. *American Journal of Psychiatry, 165,* 889–897.

Rubia, K., Smith, A. B., Halari, R., et al. (2009). Disorder-specific dissociation of orbitofrontal dysfunction in boys with pure conduct disorder during reward and ventrolateral prefrontal dysfunction in boys with pure ADHD during sustained attention. *American Journal of Psychiatry, 166,* 83–94.

Rubin, G. J., Brewin, C. R., Greenberg, N., Simpson, J., & Wessely, S. (2005). Psychological and behavioural reactions to the bombings in London on 7 July 2005: Cross sectional survey of a representative sample of Londoners. *British Medical Journal, 331,* 606–612.

Rubin, R. T., Phillips, J. J., Sadow, T. F., & McCracken, J. T. (1995). Adrenal gland volume in major depression: Increase during the depressive episode and decrease with successful treatment. *Archives of General Psychiatry, 52,* 213–218.

Rucklidge, J. J., & Kaplan, B. J. (1997). Psychological functioning in women identified in adulthood with Attention-Deficit/Hyperactivity Disorder. *Journal of Attention Disorders, 2,* 167–176.

Rucklidge, J. J., & Tannock, R. (2001). Psychiatric, psychosocial, and cognitive functioning of female adolescents with ADHD. *Journal of the American Academy of Child and Adolescent Psychiatry, 40,* 530–540.

Rudolph, K. D., Flynn, M., Abaied, J. L., Groot, A, & Thompson, R. (2009). Why is past depression the better predictor of future depression? Stress generation as a mechanism of depression continuity in girls *Journal of Clinical Child and Adolescent Psychology, 38,* 473–483.

Rummel, C., Kissling, W., & Leucht, S. (2005). Antidepressants as add-on treatment to antipsychotics for people with schizophrenia and pronounced negative symptoms: A systematic review of randomized trials. *Schizophrenia Research, 80,* 85–97.

Rumstein-McKean, O., & Hunsley, J. (2001). Interpersonal and family functioning of female survivors of childhood sexual abuse. *Clinical Psychology Review, 21,* 471–490.

Rupert, J. (2005, May 27). Mentally ill jailed despite judge's order: Province misses deadline to fix problem identified in landmark ruling. *Ottawa Citizen.*

Ruscio, A. Y., et al. (2005). Should excessive worry be required for a diagnosis of generalized anxiety disorder? Results from the US National Comorbidity Survey Replication. *Psychological Medicine, 35,* 1761–1772.

Ruscio, A. Y., et al. (2007). Broadening the definition of generalized anxiety disorder: Effects on prevalence and associations with other disorders in the National Comorbidity Survey Replication. *Journal of Anxiety Disorders, 21,* 662–676.

Rush, A. J., Beck, A. T., Kovacs, M., Weissenberger, J., & Hollon, S. D. (1982). Comparison of the effects of cognitive therapy on hopelessness and self-concept. *American Journal of Psychiatry, 139,* 862–866.

Rutherford, J., & Noegel, R. (1993). Genetic influences on eating attitudes in a normal female twin population. *Psychological Medicine, 23,* 425–436.

Rutherford, M. J., Cacciola, J. S., & Alterman, A. I. (1999). Antisocial personality disorder and psychopathy in cocaine-dependent women. *American Journal of Psychiatry, 156,* 849–856.

Rybstein-Blinchik, E. (1979). Effects of different cognitive strategies on chronic pain experience. *Journal of Behavioral Medicine, 2,* 93–101.

Ryding, E., et al. (2006). Regional brain serotonin and dopamine transporter binding capacity in suicide attempters relate to impulsiveness and mental energy. *Psychiatry Research: Neuroimaging, 148,* 195–203.

Rynn, M., Russell, J., Erickson, J., et al. (2008). Efficacy and safety of duloxetine in the treatment of generalized anxiety disorder: A flexible-dose, progressive-titration, placebo-controlled trial. *Depression and Anxiety, 25,* 182–189.

Saavedra, L. M., Silverman, W. K., Morgan-Lopez, A. A., & Kurtines, W. M. (2010). Cognitive behavioral treatment for childhood anxiety disorders: Long-term effects on anxiety and secondary disorders in young adulthood. *Journal of Child Psychology and Psychiatry, 51*(8), 924–934.

Sabin, J. E. (1975). Translating despair. *American Journal of Psychiatry, 132,* 197–199.

Sabol, S. Z., et al. (1999). A genetic association for cigarette smoking behavior. *Health Psychology, 18,* 7–13.

Sacco, R. L., Elkind, M., Boden-Albala, B., Lin, I., Kargman, D. E., et al. (1999). The protective effect of moderate alcohol consumption on ischemic stroke. *Journal of the American Medical Association, 281,* 53–60.

Sackeim, H. A., Haskett, R. F., Mulsant, B. H., Thase, M. E., Mann, J. J., Pettinati, H. M., et al. (2001). Continuation pharmacotherapy in the prevention of relapse following electroconvulsive therapy: A randomized controlled trial. *Journal of the American Medical Association, 285,* 1299–1307.

Sackeim, H. A., Nordlie, J. W., & Gur, R. C. (1979). A model of hysterical and hypnotic blindness: Cognition, motivation and awareness. *Journal of Abnormal Psychology, 88,* 474–489.

Sadava, S. W., & Pak, A. W. (1993). Stress-related problem drinking and alcohol problems: A longitudinal study and extension of Marlatt's model. *Canadian Journal of Behavioural Science, 25,* 446–464.

Sadler, J. (2004). Democratic values in the construction of psychiatric nosology. In J. Sadler (Ed.), *Values and psychiatric classification.* Baltimore: Johns Hopkins University Press.

Saffer, H. (1991). Alcohol advertising bans and alcohol abuse: An international perspective. *Journal of Health Economics, 10,* 65–79.

Sahay, S., Piran, N., & Maddocks, S. (2000). Sexual victimization and clinical challenges in women receiving hospital treatment for depression. *Canadian Journal of Community Mental Health, 19,* 161–174.

Sakauye, K. (2006, November). *"Katrina Brain:" Acute cognitive impairment.* Paper presented at the 19th US Psychiatric & Mental Health Congress, New Orleans, Louisiana.

Sakel, M. (1938). The pharmacological shock treatment of schizophrenia. *Nervous and Mental Disease Monograph, 62,* 1–133.

Sakinofsky, I. (2007a). Caring for the suicidal patient. *Canadian Journal of Psychiatry, 52* (6 Supplement 1), 5S–6S.

Sakinofsky, I. (2007b). The current evidence base for the clinical care of suicidal patients: Strengths and weaknesses. *Canadian Journal of Psychiatry, 52* (6 Supplement 1), 7S–20S.

Saklofske, D. H., Austin, E. J., & Minski, P. S. (2003). Factor structure and validity of a trait emotional intelligence measure. *Personality and Individual Differences, 34,* 707–721.

Saklofske, D. H., & Hildebrand, D. K. (1999). The Wechsler Adult Intelligence Scale–Third Edition: The Canadian Standardization Study. *Canadian Clinical Psychologist, 9,* 11–12.

Saklofske, D. H., Hildebrand, D. K., & Gorsuch, R. L. (2000). Replication of the factor structure of the Wechsler Adult Intelligence Scale–Third Edition with a Canadian sample. *Psychological Assessment, 12,* 436–439.

Salan, S. E., Zinberg, N. E., & Frei, E. (1975). Antiemetic effect of delta-9-THC in patients receiving cancer chemotherapy. *New England Journal of Medicine, 293,* 795–797.

Salkovskis, P. M. (1998). Psychological approaches to the understanding of obsessional problems. In R. P. Swinson, M. M. Antony, S. Rachman, & M. A. Richter (Eds.), *Obsessive-compulsive disorder: Theory, research, and treatment* (pp. 33–50). New York: Guilford Press.

Salkovskis, P. M., & Warwick, H. M. C. (2001). Making sense of hypochondriasis: A cognitive theory of health anxiety. In G. J. G. Asmundson, S. Taylor, & B. J. Cox (Eds.), *Health anxiety: Clinical and research perspectives on hypochondriasis and related conditions* (pp. 46–64). Toronto: John Wiley & Sons.

Salovey, P., & Singer, J. A. (1991). Cognitive behavior modification. In F. H. Kanfer & A. P. Goldstein (Eds.), *Helping people change: A textbook of methods* (4th ed.). Elmsford, NY: Pergamon.

Salzman, L. (1985). Psychotherapeutic management of obsessive-compulsive patients. *American Journal of Psychotherapy, 39,* 323–330.

Sampson, S. M., Rome, J. D., & Rummans, T. A. (2006). Slow-frequency rTMS reduces fibromyalgia pain. *Pain Medicine, 7,* 115–118.

Sanday, P. R. (1981). The socio-cultural context of rape: A cross-cultural study. *Journal of Social Issues, 37,* 5–27.

Sanderson, W. C., Rapee, R. M., & Barlow, D. H. (1989). The influence of an illusion of control on panic attacks induced via inhalation of 5.5%

carbon dioxide-enriched air. *Archives of General Psychiatry, 46,* 157–162.

Sanderson, W. C., & Rego, S. A. (2000). Empirically supported treatment for panic disorder: Research, theory, and application of cognitive behavioral therapy. *Journal of Cognitive Psychotherapy, 14,* 219–244.

Sanford, K., Bingham, C. R., & Zucker, R. A. (1999). Validity issues with the Family Environment Scale: Psychometric resolution and research applications. *Psychological Assessment, 11,* 315–327.

Sanger, T. M., Lieberman, J. A., Tohen, M., Grundy, S., et al. (1999). Olanzapine versus haloperidol in first-episode psychosis. *American Journal of Psychiatry, 156,* 79–87.

Santa-Mina, E. E., et al. (2006). The Self-Injury Questionnaire: Evaluation of the psychometric properties in a clinical population. *Journal of Psychiatric and Mental Health Nursing, 13,* 221–227.

Sareen J., Cox B. J., Afifi T.O., et al. (2005). Mental health service use in a nationally representative Canadian survey. *Canadian Journal of Psychiatry, 50,* 753–761.

Sareen J., Cox B.J., Afifi T.O., et al. (2007). Combat and peacekeeping operations in relation to prevalence of mental disorders and perceived need for mental health care: findings from a large representative sample of military person. *Archives of General Psychiatry, 64,* 843– 852.

Sartorius, N., & Schultze, H. (2005). *Reducing stigma due to mental illness: A report from a global program of the World Psychiatric Association.* Cambridge: Cambridge University Press.

Sarwer, D. B., & Sayers, S. L. (1998). Behavioral interviewing. In A. S. Bellack & M. Hersen (Eds.), *Behavioral assessment: A practical handbook* (pp. 63–103). Boston: Allyn and Bacon.

Satyanarayana, S., Enns, M., Cox, B. J., & Sareen, J. (2009). Prevalence and correlates of chronic depression in the Canadian Community Health Survey: Mental health and well-being. *Canadian Journal of Psychiatry, 54,* 389–398.

Saulsman, L. M., & Page, A. C. (2004). The five-factor model and personality disorder empirical literature: A meta-analytic review. *Clinical Psychology Review, 23,* 1055–1085.

Schaefer, L. C., Wheeler, C. C., & Futterweit, W. (1997). Gender identity disorders (transsexualism). In G. O. Gabbard & S. D. Atkinson (Eds.), *Synopsis of treatments of psychiatric disorders* (2nd ed., pp. 843–858). Washington, DC: American Psychiatric Press.

Schaie, K. W., & Hertzog, C. (1982). Longitudinal methods. In B. B. Wolman (Ed.), *Handbook of developmental psychology.* Englewood Cliffs, NJ: Prentice-Hall.

Scher, C., Ingram, R., & Segal, Z. (2005). Cognitive reactivity and vulnerability: Empirical evaluation of construct activation and cognitive diatheses in unipolar depression. *Clinical Psychology Review, 25,* 487–510.

Schieve, L. A., Blumberg, S. J., Rice, C., et al. (2007). The relationship between autism and parenting stress. *Pediatrics, 119,* S114–S121.

Schiffer, A. A., et al. (in press). Type D personality and cardiac mortality in patients with chronic heart failure. *International Journal of Cardiology.*

Schiffer, B., et al. (2008). Brain response to visual sexual stimuli in homosexual pedophiles. *Journal of Psychiatry and Neuroscience, 33,* 23–33.

Schizophrenia Society of Canada. (2002). *Schizophrenia: Youth's greatest disabler—A report on psychiatrist and patient attitudes and opinions towards schizophrenia.* Ottawa: Author.

Schmidt, N. B., Zvolensky, M., & Maner, J. K. (2006). Anxiety sensitivity: Prospective prediction of panic attacks and Axis I pathology. *Journal of Psychiatric Research, 40,* 691–699.

Schmidt, N.B., Eggleston, A.M., Woolaway-Bickel, K., Fitzpatrick, K.K., Vasey, M.W., & Richey, J.A. (2007). Anxiety Sensitivity Amelioration Training (ASAT): A longitudinal primary prevention program targeting cognitive vulnerability. *Journal of Anxiety Disorders, 21,* 302–319.

Schmitt, W. A., & Newman, J. P. (1999). Are all psychopathic individuals low-anxious? *Journal of Abnormal Psychology, 108,* 353–358.

Schmitz, N., Rubia, K., van Amelvoort, T., et al. (2008). Neural correlates of reward in autism. *The British Journal of Psychiatry, 192,* 19–24.

Schlundt, D. G., & Johnson, W. G. (1990). *Eating disorders: Assessment and treatment.* Needham Heights, MA: Allyn & Bacon.

Schmucker, M., & Losel, F. (2008). Does sexual offender treatment work? A systematic review of outcome evaluations. *Psicothema, 20,* 10–19.

Schnall, P. L., Landsbergis, P. A., & Baker, D. (1994). Job strain and cardiovascular disease. *Annual Review of Public Health, 15,* 381–411.

Schneider, B., et al. (2006). Axis I disorders and personality disorders as risk factors for suicide. *European Archives of Psychiatry and Clinical Neuroscience, 256,* 17–27.

Schneider, K. (1959). *Clinical psychopathology.* New York: Grune & Stratton.

Schneider, R. (2001, July). *Fitness to stand trial: Obligation of the court to inquire?* Paper presented in a symposium chaired by R. Cooper, entitled "Adjudicating mental illness: Dilemmas in the courtroom and in practice," 26th International Congress on Law and Mental Health, Montreal, Quebec.

Schneider, R. D., Forestell, M., & MacGarvie, S. (2002). *Statistical survey of provincial and territorial review boards.* Ottawa: Department of Justice Canada.

Schneider, R. D., Glancy, G. D., Bradford, J. M., et al. (2000). Canadian landmark case, Winko v. British Columbia: Revisiting the conundrum of the mentally disordered accused. *Journal of the American Academy of Psychiatry and the Law, 28,* 206–212.

Schoeneman, T. J. (1977). The role of mental illness in the European witch-hunts of the sixteenth and seventeenth centuries: An assessment. *Journal of the History of the Behavioral Sciences, 13,* 337–351.

Schofield, W. (1964). *Psychotherapy: The purchase of friendship.* Englewood Cliffs, NJ: Prentice-Hall.

Schooler, C., Flora, J. A., & Farquhar, J. W. (1993). Moving toward synergy: Media supplementation in the Stanford Five-City Project. *Communication Research, 26,* 587–610.

Schooler, N. R., Keith, S. J., Severe, J. B., Matthews, S. M., Bellack, A. S., et al. (1997). Relapse and rehospitalization during maintenance treatment of schizophrenia: The effects of dose

reduction and family treatment. *Archives of General Psychiatry, 54,* 453–464.

Schopler, E., Short, B., & Mesibov, G. B. (1989). Comments. *Journal of Consulting and Clinical Psychology, 157,* 162–167.

Schreiber, F. L. (1973). *Sybil.* New York: Warner Books.

Schroeter, M. L., Stein, T., Maslowski, N., & Neumann, J. (2009). Neural correlates of Alzheimer's disease and mild cognitive impairment: A systematic and quantitative meta-analysis involving 1351 patients. *Neuroimage, 47,* 1196–1206.

Schuckit, M. A. (1983). The genetics of alcoholism. In B. Tabakoff, P. B. Sulker, & C. L. Randall (Eds.), *Medical and social aspects of alcohol use.* New York: Plenum.

Schuckit, M. A. (1994). Low level of response to alcohol as a predictor of future alcoholism. *American Journal of Psychiatry, 151,* 184–189.

Schuckit, M. A., Daeppen, J.-B., Danko, G. P., Tripp, M. L., Smith, T. L., et al. (1999). Clinical implications for four drugs of the DSM-IV distinction between substance with and without a physiological component. *American Journal of Psychiatry, 156,* 41–49.

Schuckit, M. A., & Smith, T. L. (1996). An 8-year follow-up of 450 sons of alcoholic and control subjects. *Archives of General Psychiatry, 53,* 202–210.

Schultz, R., & Brenner, G. (1977). Relocation of the aged: A review and theoretical analysis. *Journal of Gerontology, 32,* 323–333.

Schwartz, G. E. (1973). Biofeedback as therapy: Some theoretical and practical issues. *American Psychologist, 28,* 666–673.

Schwartz, J. M. (1998). Neuroanatomical aspects of cognitive-behavior therapy response in obsessive-compulsive disorder. *British Journal of Psychiatry, 173,* 38–44.

Schwartz, M. B., et al. (2006). The influence of one's own body weight on implicit and explicit anti-fat bias. *Obesity, 14,* 440–447.

Schwartz, P. J., Murphy, D. L., Wehr, T. A., Garcia-Borreguero, D., Oren, D. A., et al. (1997). Effects of meta-chlorphenylpiperazine infusions in patients with seasonal affective disorder and healthy control subjects. *Archives of General Psychiatry, 54,* 375–385.

Schwartz, R., & Schwartz, L. J. (1980). *Becoming a couple.* Englewood Cliffs, NJ: Prentice-Hall.

Schwarz, J. R. (1981). *The Hillside Strangler: A murderer's mind.* New York: New American Library.

Schweinsburg, A. D., Brown, S. A., & Tapet, S. F. (2008). The influence of marijuana use on meta-cognitive functioning in adolescents. *Current Drug Abuse Reviews, 1,* 99–111.

Schweizer, E., Rickels, K., Case, G., & Greenblatt, D. J. (1990). Long-term therapeutic use of benzodiazapines: Effects of gradual taper. *Archives of General Psychiatry, 47,* 908–915.

Schwitzgebel, R. L., & Schwitzgebel, R. K. (1980). *Law and psychological practice.* New York: John Wiley & Sons.

Scientific perspectives on cocaine abuse. (1987). *Pharmacologist, 29,* 20–27.

Scoggin, F. (1998). Anxiety in old age. In I. H. Nordhus, G. R. VandenBos, S. Berg, & P. Fromholt

(Eds.), *Clinical geropsychology* (pp. 205–209). Washington, DC: American Psychological Association.

Scoggin, F., & McElreath, L. (1994). Efficacy of psychosocial treatments for geriatric depression: A quantitative review. *Journal of Consulting and Clinical Psychology, 62,* 69–74.

Scott, J. (2008). Cognitive-behavioural therapy for severe mental disorders: Back to the future? *The British Journal of Psychiatry, 192,* 401–403.

Scott, J., et al. (2006). Cognitive-behavioural therapy for severe and recurrent bipolar disorders: Randomized controlled trial. *British Journal of Psychiatry, 188,* 313–320.

Scott-Sheldon, L. A. J., DeMartini, K. S., Carey, K. B., & Carey, M. P. (2009). Alcohol interventions for college students improves antecedents of behavioral change: Results from a meta-analysis of 34 randomized controlled trials. *Journal of Social and Clinical Psychology, 28,* 799–823.

Scrivener, L. (2007, February 25). Breaking down barriers: After 157 years, the most daring redevelopment in CAMH's history has begun. *Toronto Star,* A8–9.

Sealy, P., & Whitehead, P. C. (2004). Forty years of deinstitutionalization of psychiatric services in Canada: An empirical assessment. *Canadian Journal of Psychiatry, 49,* 249–257.

Seedat, S., Scott, K. M., Angermeyer, M. C., et al. (2009). Cross-national associations between gender and mental disorders in the World Health Organization World Mental Health surveys. *Archives of General Psychiatry, 66,* 785–795.

Seedat, S., Stein, M. B., & Forde, D. R. (2003). Prevalence of dissociative experiences in a community sample: Relationship to gender, ethnicity, and substance use. *Journal of Nervous and Mental Disease, 191,* 115–120.

Segal, Z. V., Gemar, M., Truchon, C., Guirguis, M., & Horowitz, L. M. (1995). A priming methodology for studying self-representation in major depressive disorder. *Journal of Abnormal Psychology, 104,* 205–213.

Segal, Z. V., et al. (2006). Cognitive reactivity to sad mood provocation and the prediction of depressive relapse. *Archives of General Psychiatry, 63,* 1–7.

Segal, Z. V., Shaw, B. F., Vella, D. D., & Katz, R. (1992). Cognitive and life stress predictors of relapse in remitted unipolar depressed patients: Tests of the congruency hypothesis. *Journal of Abnormal Psychology, 101,* 26–36.

Segal, Z. V., Teasdale, J. D., Williams, J. M., & Gemar, M. C. (2002). The Mindfulness-Based Cognitive Therapy Adherence Scale: Inter-rater reliability, adherence to protocol, and treatment distinctiveness. *Clinical Psychology and Psychotherapy, 9,* 131–138.

Segal, Z. V., Vincent, P., & Levitt, A. (2002). Efficacy of combined, sequential, and crossover psychotherapy and pharmacotherapy in improving outcomes in depression. *Journal of Psychiatry and Neuroscience, 27,* 281–290.

Segal, Z. V, Williams, M., & Teasdale, J. (2002). *Mindfulness-based cognitive therapy for depression: A new approach to preventing relapse.* New York: Guilford Press.

Segerstrom, C., & Miller, G. E. (2004). Psychological stress and the human immune system: A meta-analytic study of 30 years of inquiry. *Psychological Bulletin, 130*, 601–630.

Segraves, K. B., & Segraves, R. T. (1991). Hypoactive sexual desire disorder: Prevalence and comorbidity in 906 subjects. *Journal of Sex and Marital Therapy, 17*, 55–58.

Segraves, R. T. (1990). Theoretical orientations in the treatment of marital discord. In F. D. Fincham & T. N. Bradbury (Eds.), *The psychology of marriage: Basic issues and applications* (pp. 281–298). New York: Guilford.

Seguin, L., Potvin, L., St-Denis, M., & Loiselle, J. (1999). Socio-environmental factors and postnatal depressive symptomatology: A longitudinal study. *Women and Health, 29*, 57–72.

Seidman, L. J., & Bruder, G. (2002). Neuropsychological testing and neurophysiological assessment. In A. Tasman, J. Kay, & J. Lieberman (Eds.), *Psychiatry* (Vol 1, pp. 560–572). London: John Wiley.

Seignourel, P. J., et al. (2008). Anxiety in dementia: A critical review. *Clinical Psychology Review, 28*, 1071–1082.

Selemon, L. D., Rajkowska, G., & Goldman-Rakic, P. S. (1995). Abnormally high neuronal density in the schizophrenic cortex: A morphometric analysis of prefrontal area 9 and occipital area 17. *Archives of General Psychiatry, 52*, 805–818.

Seligman, M. E. P. (1974). Depression and learned helplessness. In R. J. Friedman & M. M. Katz (Eds.), *The psychology of depression: Contemporary theory and research*. Washington, DC: Winston-Wiley.

Seligman, M. E. P. (1995). The effectiveness of psychotherapy: The Consumer Reports study. *American Psychologist, 50*, 965–974.

Seligman, M. E. P. (1996). Science as an ally of practice. *American Psychologist, 51*, 1072–1079.

Selye, H. (1950). *The physiology and pathology of exposure to stress*. Montreal: Acta.

Selye, H. (1974). *Stress without distress*. Philadelphia: J.B. Lippincott Company.

Senior, K. (2000). Bigger and better tobacco warning labels. *Lancet, 356*, 139.

Serdula, M. K., Mokdad, A. H., Williamson, D. F., Galuska, D. A., et al. (1999). Prevalence of attempting weight loss and strategies for controlling weight. *Journal of the American Medical Association, 282*, 1353–1358.

Serene, J. A., Ashtari, M., Szeszko, P. R., & Kumra, S. (2007). Neuroimaging studies of children with serious emotional disturbances: A selective review. *Canadian Journal of Psychiatry, 52*, 135–145.

Serfaty, M. A., Haworth, D., Blanchard, M., Buszewicz, M., Murad, S., & King, M. (2009). Clinical effectiveness of individual cognitive behavior therapy for depressed older people in primary care. *Archives of General Psychiatry, 66*, 1332–1340.

Serin, R. C., & Amos, N. L. (1995). The role of psychopathy in the assessment of dangerousness. *International Journal of Law and Psychiatry, 18*, 231–238.

Serin, R. C., Mailloux, D. L., & Malcolm, P. B. (2001). Psychopathy, deviant sexual arousal, and recidivism among sexual offenders. *Journal of Interpersonal Violence, 16*, 234–246.

Seto, M. C. (2004). Pedophilia and sexual offenses against children. *Annual Review of Sex Research, 15*, 321–361.

Seto, M. C. (2009). Pedophilia. *Annual Review of Clinical Psychology, 5*, 391–507.

Seto, M. C., & Barbaree, H. E. (1999). Psychopathy, treatment behavior, and sex offender recidivism. *Journal of Interpersonal Violence, 14*, 1235–1248.

Seto, M. C., Cantor, J. M., & Blanchard, R. (2006). Child pornography offenses are a valid diagnostic indicator of pedophilia. *Journal of Abnormal Psychology, 115*, 610–615.

Seto, M. C., Harris, G. T., Rice, M. E., & Barbaree, H. E. (2004). The Screening Scale for Pedophilic Interests predicts recidivism among adult sex offenders with child victims. *Archives of Sexual Behavior, 33*, 455–466.

Seto, M. C., & Lalumiere, M. L. (2001). A brief screening scale to identify pedophilic interests among child molesters. *Sexual Abuse: A Journal of Research and Treatment, 13*, 15–25.

Seto, M. C., Lalumiere, M. L., & Blanchard, R. (2000). The discriminative validity of a phallometric test for pedophilic interests among adolescent sex offenders against children. *Psychological Assessment, 12*, 319–327.

Seto, M. C., Maric, A., & Barbaree, H. E. (2001). The role of pornography in the etiology of sexual aggression. *Aggression and Violent Behavior, 6*, 35–53.

Settin, J. M. (1982). Clinical judgment in geropsychology practice. *Psychotherapy: Theory, Research and Practice, 19*, 397–404.

Sewitch, M. J., Blais, R., Rahme, E., Bexton, B., & Galarneau, S. (2007). Receiving guideline-concordant pharmacotherapy for major depression: Impact on ambulatory and inpatient health service use. *Canadian Journal of Psychiatry, 52*, 191–200.

Sexton, K. A., & Dugas, M. J. (2009). An investigation of factors associated with cognitive avoidance in worry. *Cognitive Therapy and Research, 33*, 150–162.

Sexton, T. L., Alexander, J. F., & Mease, A. L. (2004). Levels of evidence for the models and mechanisms of therapeutic change in family and couple therapy. In M. J. Lambert (Ed.), *Bergin and Garfield's handbook of psychotherapy and behavior change* (5th ed., pp. 590–646). Hoboken, NJ: John Wiley & Sons.

Seyfort, B., Spreen, O., & Lahmer, V. (1980). A critical look at the WISC-R with Native Indian children. *Alberta Journal of Educational Research, 26*, 14–24.

Sevincok, L., Akoglu, A., & Kokcu, F. (2007). Suicidality in schizophrenic patients with and without obsessive-compulsive disorder. *Schizophrenia Research, 90*, 198–202.

Shachnow, J., Clarkin, J., DiPalma, C.-S., Thurston, F., et al. (1997). Biparental psychopathology and borderline personality disorder. *Psychiatry—Interpersonal and Biological Processes, 60*, 171–181.

Shahar, G., Blatt, S. J., Zuroff, D. C., & Pilkonis, P. A. (2003). Role of perfectionism and personality disorder features in response to brief treatment for depression. *Journal of Consulting and Clinical Psychology, 71*, 629–633.

Shanmugasegaram, S., Flett, G. L., Oh, P., Marzolini, S., Reitav, J., Sturman, E. D., Hewitt, P. L., & Madan, M. (2007). Personality and coping in cardiac rehabilitation patients. *Canadian Journal of Cardiology*, Proceedings of Canadian Cardiovascular Congress (0798).

Shapiro, D., Jamner, L. D., & Goldstein, I. B. (1993). Ambulatory stress psychophysiology: The study of "compensatory and defensive counterforces" and conflict in a natural setting. *Psychosomatic Medicine, 55*, 309–323.

Shapiro, D., Tursky, B., & Schwartz, G. E. (1970). Control of blood pressure in man by operant conditioning. *Circulation Research, 26*, 127–132.

Shapiro, F. (1999). Eye Movement Desensitization and Reprocessing (EMDR) and the anxiety disorders: Clinical and research implications of an integrated psychotherapy treatment. *Journal of Anxiety Disorders, 13*, 35–67.

Shaw, B. F. (1999). How to use the allegiance effect to maximize competence and therapeutic outcomes. *Clinical Psychology: Science and Practice, 6*, 131–132.

Shaw, B. F., et al. (1999). Therapist competence ratings in relation to clinical outcome in cognitive therapy of depression. *Journal of Consulting and Clinical Psychology, 67*, 837–846.

Shaw, D. S., et al. (2006). Randomized trial of a family-centered approach to the prevention of early conduct problems: 2-year effects of the Family Check-up in early childhood. *Journal of Consulting and Clinical Psychology, 74*, 1–9.

Shaw, M. E., Moores, K. A., Clark, R. C., McFarlane, A. C., et al. (2009). Functional connectivity reveals inefficient working memory systems in post-traumatic stress disorder. *Psychiatric Research: Neuroimaging, 172*, 235–241.

Shaw, P., Sharp, W. S., & Morrison, M. (2009). Psychostimulant treatment and the developing cortex in attention deficit hyperactivity disorder. *American Journal of Psychiatry, 166*, 58–63.

Shea, M. T., Elkin, I., Imber, S. D., Sotsky, S. M., Watkins, J. T., Collins, J. F., et al. (1992). Course of depressive symptoms over follow-up: Findings from the National Institute of Mental Health Treatment of Depression Collaborative Research Program. *Archives of General Psychiatry, 49*, 782–787.

Shea, M. T., Pilkonis, P. A., Beckham, E., Collins, J. F., Elkin, I., Sotsky, S. M., et al. (1990). Personality disorders and treatment outcome in the NIMH Treatment of Depression Collaborative Research Program. *American Journal of Psychiatry, 147*, 711–718.

Shedler, J. (2010). The efficacy of psychodynamic psychotherapy. *American Psychologist, 65*, 98–109.

Shenal, B. V., Harrison, D. W., & Demaree, H. A. (2003). The neuropsychology of depression: A literature review and preliminary model. *Neuropsychology Review, 13*, 33–42.

Shenkin, S. D., Starr, J. M., & Deary, I. J. (2004). Birth weight and cognitive ability in childhood: A systematic review. *Psychological Bulletin, 130*, 989–1013.

Sheppard, D. M., Bradshaw, J. L., Purcell, R., & Pantelis, C. (1999). Tourette's and comorbid syndromes: Obsessive-compulsive and attention deficit hyperactivity disorder. A common etiology? *Clinical Psychology Review*, 19, 531–552.

Sher, K. J., Bartholow, B. D., & Wood, M. D. (2000). Personality and substance use disorders: A prospective study. *Journal of Consulting and Clinical Psychology*, 68, 818–829.

Sher, K. J., Martin, E. D., Wood, P. K., & Rutledge, P. C. (1997). Alcohol use disorders and neuropsychological functioning in first year undergraduates. *Experimental and Clinical Psychopharmacology*, 5, 304–315.

Shevlin, M., Dorahy, M. J., & Adamson, G. (2007). Trauma and psychosis: An analysis of the National Comorbidity Survey. *American Journal of Psychiatry*, 164, 166–169.

Shields, M., & Wilkins, K. (2005). *Findings from the 2005 National Survey of the Work and Health of Nurses.* Ottawa: Canadian Institute for Health Information.

Shiffman, S., Fischer, L. A., Paty, J. A., Gnys, M., et al. (1994). Drinking and smoking: A field study of their association. *Annals of Behavioral Medicine*, 16, 203–209.

Schiffman, S., Stone, A. A., & Huffard, M. R. (2008). Ecological momentary assessment. *Annual Review of Clinical Psychology*, 4, 1–32.

Shigaki, C. L., Glass, B., & Schopp, L. H. (2006). Mindfulness-based stress reduction in medical settings. *Journal of Clinical Psychology in Medical Settings*, 13, 209–216.

Shih, J. H., Eberhart, N. K., Hammen, C. L., & Brennan, P. A. (2006). Differential exposure and reactivity to interpersonal stress predicts sex differences in adolescent depression. *Journal of Clinical Child and Adolescent Psychology*, 35, 103–115.

Shneidman, E. S. (1993). Suicide as psychache. *Journal of Nervous and Mental Disease*, 181, 145–147.

Shogren, E. (1994, August 18). Treatment against their will. *Los Angeles Times*, A1, A16.

Siegle, G. J., Thompson, W., Carter, C. S., et al. (2007). Increased amygdala and decreased dorsolateral prefrontal bold responses in unipolar depression: Related and independent features. *Biological Psychiatry*, 61, 198–209.

Siegel, S. (1991). Feedforward processes in drug tolerance and dependence. In R. G. Lister & H. J. Weingartner (Eds.), *Perspectives on cognitive neuroscience* (pp. 405–416). New York: Oxford University Press.

Siegel, S. (1999). Drug anticipation and drug addiction. The 1998 H. David Archibald lecture. *Addiction*, 94, 1113–1124.

Siegel, S., Baptista, M. A. S., Kim, J. A., McDonald, R. V., & Weise-Kelly, L. (2000). Pavlovian psychpharmacology: The associative basis of tolerance. *Experimental and Clinical Psychopharmacology*, 8, 276–293.

Sigman, M. (1994). What are the core deficits in autism? In S. H. Broman & J. Grafman (Eds.), *Atypical cognitive deficits in developmental disorders: Implications for brain function* (pp. 139–157). Hillsdale, NJ: Lawrence Erlbaum Associates.

Sigman, M., Ungerer, J. A., Mundy, P., & Sherman, T. (1987). Cognition in autistic children. In D. J. Co-

hen, A. M. Donnellan, & R. Paul (Eds.), *Handbook of autism and pervasive developmental disorders* (pp. 103–120). New York: John Wiley & Sons.

Sikich, L., Frazier, J. A., McClellan, J., et al. (2008). Double-blind comparison of first- and second-generation antipsychotics in early-onset schizophrenia and schizoaffective disorder: Findings from the Treatment of Early-Onset Schizophrenia Spectrum Disorders (TEOSS) study. *American Journal of Psychiatry*, 165, 1420–1431.

Silberg, J. L., Maes, H., & Eaves, L. J. (2010). Genetic and environmental influences on the transmission of parental depression to children's depression and conduct disturbance: An extended Children of Twins study. *Journal of Child Psychology and Psychiatry*, 51(6), 734–744.

Silva, J. A. (2009). Forensic psychiatry, neuroscience and the law. *Journal of the American Academy of Psychiatry and the Law*, 37, 489–502.

Silverman, J. M., Li, G., Zaccario, M. L., Smith, C., Schmeidler, J., et al. (1994). Patterns of risk in first-degree relatives with Alzheimer's disease. *Archives of General Psychiatry*, 51, 568–576.

Silverman, K., Evans, S. M., Strain, E. C., & Griffiths, R. R. (1992). Withdrawal syndrome after the double-blind cessation of caffeine consumption. *New England Journal of Medicine*, 327, 1109–1114.

Silverman, K., Higgins, S. T., Brooner, R. K., Montoya, I. D., Cone, E. J., Schuster, C. R., et al. (1996). Sustained cocaine abstinence in methadone maintenance patients through voucher-based reinforcement therapy. *Archives of General Psychiatry*, 53, 409–413.

Sim, K., et al. (2006). Hippocampal and parahippocampal volumes in schizophrenia: A structural MRI study. *Schizophrenia Bulletin*, 32, 332–340.

Simeon, D., Gross, S., Guralnik, O., Stein, D. J., Schmeidler, J., & Hollander, E. (1997). Feeling unreal: 30 cases of DSM-III-R depersonalization disorder. *American Journal of Psychiatry*, 154, 1107–1112.

Simmie, S. (1998, October 3–10). Atkinson Fellowship investigation into mental health: Out of Mind (Series). *Toronto Star*.

Simmie, S. (1998, October 10). True reform is up to all of us. *Toronto Star*.

Simmie, S., & Nunes, J. (2001). *The last taboo: A survival guide to mental health care in Canada.* Toronto: McClelland and Stewart.

Simmons, H. G. (1987). Psychosurgery and the abuse of psychiatric authority in Ontario. *Journal of Health Politics*, 12, 537–550.

Simon, G. E. (1998). Management of somatoform and factitious disorders. In P. E. Nathan & J. M. Gorman (Eds.), *A guide to treatments that work* (pp. 408–422). New York: Oxford University Press.

Simon, G. E., & Gureje, O. (1999). Stability of somatization disorder and somatization symptoms among primary care patients. *Archives of General Psychiatry*, 56, 90–95.

Simon, N. M., Herlands, N. N., Marks, E. H., et al. (2009). Childhood maltreatment linked to greater symptom severity and poorer quality of life and function in social anxiety disorder. *Depression and Anxiety*, 26, 1027–1032.

Simpson, J., Doze, S., Urness, D., Hailey, D., & Jacobs, P. (2001a). Evaluation of a routine telepsychiatry service. *Journal of Telemedicine and Telecare*, 7, 90–98.

Simpson, J., Doze, S., Urness, D., Hailey, D., & Jacobs, P. (2001b). Telepsychiatry as a routine service—The perspective of the patient. *Journal of Telemedicine and Telecare*, 7, 155–160.

Sinclair, C., Poizner, S., Gilmour-Barrett, K., & Randall, D. (1987). The development of a code of ethics for Canadian psychologists. *Canadian Psychology*, 28, 1–8.

Singer, A. R., & Dobson, K. S. (2007). An experimental investigation of the cognitive vulnerability to depression. *Behaviour Research and Therapy*, 45, 563–575.

Single, E., Brewster, J. M., MacNeil, P., Hatcher, J., & Trainor, C. (1995). The 1993 General Social Survey I: Alcohol use in Canada. *Canadian Journal of Public Health*, 86, 397–401.

Sinha, B. K., & Watson, D. C. (2001). Personality disorder in university students: A multitrait-multimethod matrix study. *Journal of Personality Disorders*, 15, 235–244.

Sintchak, G. H., & Geer, J. H. (1975). A vaginal plethysmograph system. *Psychophysiology*, 12, 113–115.

Sisson, R. W., & Azrin, N. H. (1989). The community-reinforcement approach. In R. K. Hester & W. R. Miller (Eds.), *Handbook of alcoholism treatment approaches: Effective alternatives* (pp. 242–258). New York: Pergamon.

Sizemore, C. C., & Pittillo, E. S. (1977). *I'm Eve.* Garden City, NY: Doubleday.

Skarborn, M., & Nicki, R. (1996). Worry among Canadian seniors. *International Journal of Aging and Human Development*, 43, 169–178.

Skeem, J. L., et al., (2006). Psychiatric symptoms and community violence among high-risk patients: A test of the relationship at the weekly level. *Journal of Consulting and Clinical Psychology*, 74, 967–979.

Skilling, T. A., Harris, G. T., Rice, M. E., & Quinsey, V. L. (2002). Identifying persistently antisocial offenders using the Hare Psychopathy Checklist and DSM antisocial personality disorder criteria. *Psychological Assessment*, 14, 27–38.

Skinner, H. A., Steinhauer, P. D., & Sitarenios, G. (2000). Family Assessment Measure (FAM) and process model of family functioning. *Journal of Family Therapy*, 22, 190–210.

Sklar, L. A., & Anisman, H. (1979). Stress and coping factors influence tumor growth. *Science*, 205, 513–515.

Skodol, A. E., Oldham, J. M., & Gallaher, P. E. (1999). Axis II comorbidity of substance use disorders among patients referred for treatment of personality disorders. *American Journal of Psychiatry*, 156, 733–738.

Skolnick, A. S. (1998). Guidelines for treating erectile dysfunction issued. *Journal of the American Medical Association*, 277, 24–26.

Skoog, G., & Skoog, I. (1999). A 40-year follow-up of patients with obsessive-compulsive disorder. *Archives of General Psychiatry*, 56, 121–130.

Slater, E., & Glithero, E. (1965). A follow-up of patients diagnosed as suffering from hysteria. *Journal of Psychosomatic Research*, 9, 9–13.

Slomp, M., Band, R., Patterson, S., & Whittaker, L. (2009). Three-year physician treated prevalence rate of mental disorders in Alberta. *Canadian Journal of Psychiatry, 54*, 199–202.

Small, G. W., & Jarvik, L. F. (1982). The dementia syndrome. *Lancet*, 1443–1446.

Small, G. W., Komanduri, R., Gitlin, M., & Jarvik, L. F. (1986). The influence of age on guilt expression in major depression. *International Journal of Geriatric Psychiatry, 1*, 121–126.

Small, J. C., Klapper, M. H., Milstein, V., Kellans, J. J., Miller, M. J., et al. (1991). Carbamazapine compared with lithium in the treatment of mania. *Archives of General Psychiatry, 48*, 915–921.

Smart, R. G., & Ogborne, A. C. (2000). Drug use and drinking among students in 36 countries. *Addictive Behaviors, 25*, 455–460.

Smith, A. E., Msetfi, R. M., & Golding, L. (2010). Client self-rated adult attachment patterns and the therapeutic alliance: A systematic review. *Clinical Psychology Review, 30*, 326–337.

Smith, A. J., Sketris, I., Cooke, C., Gardner, D., Kisely, D., & Tett, S. E. (2008). A comparison of Benzodiazepine and related drug use in Nova Scotia and Australia. *Canadian Journal of Psychiatry, 53*, 545–552.

Smith, G. T., Goldman, M. S., Greenbaum, P. E., & Christiansen, B. A. (1995). Expectancy for social facilitation from drinking: The divergent paths of high expectancy and low expectancy adolescents. *Journal of Abnormal Psychology, 104*, 32–40.

Smith, J. (2010, March 31). Ottawa to test for toxic dust in daycares: Seek scientists to collect and analyze airborne grit to learn if children are exposed to harmful chemicals. *Toronto Star*, A1.

Smith, J., Frawley, P. J., & Polissar, L. (1991). Six- and twelve-month abstinence rates in inpatient alcoholics treated with aversion therapy compared with matched inpatients from a treatment registry. *Alcoholism: Clinical and Experimental Research, 15*, 862–870.

Smith, J. M., Alloy, L. B., & Abramson, L. Y. (2006). Cognitive vulnerability to depression, rumination, hopelessness and suicidal ideation: Multiple pathways to self-injurious thinking. *Suicide and Life-Threatening Behaviour, 36*, 443–454.

Smith, K. B., Pukall, C. F., & Boyer, S. C. (2009). Psychological and relational aspects of dyspareunia. In A. Goldstein, C. F. Pukall, & I. Goldstein (Eds.), *Female sexual pain disorders: Evaluation and management* (pp. 208–217). New York: Wiley-Blackwell.

Smith, K. F., & Bengston, V. L. (1979). Positive consequences of institutionalization: Solidarity between elderly parents and their middle aged children. *The Gerontologist, 5*, 438–447.

Smith, S. D., Abou-Khalil, B., & Zald, D. H. (2008). Post-traumatic stress disorder in a patient with no left amygdala. *Journal of Abnormal Psychology, 117*, 479–484.

Smith, T., Groen, A. D., & Wynn, J. W. (2000). Randomized trial of intensive early intervention for children with pervasive developmental disorder. *American Journal of Mental Retardation, 105*, 269–285.

Smith, T., Snyder, C. R., & Perkins, S. C. (1983). Self-serving function of hypochondriacal complaints: Physical symptoms as self-handicapping strategies. *Journal of Personality and Social Psychology, 44*, 787–797.

Smits, J. A. J., Berry, A. C., Tart, C. D., & Powers, M. B. (2008). The efficacy of cognitive-behavioral interventions for reducing anxiety sensitivity: A meta-analytic review. *Behaviour Research and Therapy, 46*, 1047–1054.

Smolders, M., Laurant, M., Roberge, P., van Balkom, A., et al. (2008). Knowledge transfer and improvement of primary and ambulatory care for patients with anxiety. *Canadian Journal of Psychiatry, 53*, 277–293.

Smoller, J. W., Gardner-Schuster, E., & Covino, J. (2008). The genetic basis of panic and phobic anxiety disorders. *American Journal of Medical Genetics Part C (Seminars in Medical Genetics), 148C*, 118–126.

Smyth, C., et al. (1996). Further tests for linkage of bipolar affective disorder to the tyrosine hydroxylase gene of chromosome 11p15 in a new series of multiplex British affective disorder pedigrees. *American Journal of Psychiatry, 153*, 271–274.

Snow, N., & Austin, W. J. (2009). Community treatment orders: Ethical balancing act in community mental health. *Journal of Psychiatric and Mental Health Nursing, 16*, 177–186.

Snowdon, D. A., Kemper, S. J., Mortimer, J. A., Greiner, L. H., et al. (1996). Linguistic ability in early life and cognitive function and Alzheimer's disease in late life: Findings from the nun study. *Journal of the American Medical Association, 275*, 528–534.

Snyder, C. R., Ilardi, S., Michael, S. T., & Cheavens, J. (2000). Hope theory: Updating a common process for psychological change. In C. R. Snyder & R. E. Ingram (Eds.), *Handbook of psychological change* (pp. 128–150).

Snyder, D. K., Wills, R. M., & Grady-Fletcher, A. (1991). Long-term effectiveness of behavioral versus insight-oriented marital therapy: A 4-year follow-up study. *Journal of Consulting and Clinical Psychology, 59*, 138–141.

Sobel, A. A., Resick, P. A., & Rabalais, A. E. (2009). The effect of cognitive processing therapy on cognitions: Impact statement coding. *Journal of Traumatic Stress, 22*, 205–211.

Sobell, L. C., Toneatto, A., & Sobell, M. B. (1990). Behavior therapy. In A. S. Bellack & M. Hersen (Eds.), *Handbook of comparative treatments for adult disorders* (pp. 479–505). New York: John Wiley & Sons.

Sobell, M. B., & Sobell, L. C. (1976). Second-year treatment outcome of alcoholics treated by individualized behavior therapy: Results. *Behaviour Research and Therapy, 14*, 195–215.

Sobell, M. B., & Sobell, L. C. (1993). *Problem drinkers: Guided self-change treatment*. New York: Guilford.

Sobell, M. B., & Sobell, L. C. (2000). Stepped care as a heuristic approach to the treatment of alcohol problems. *Journal of Consulting and Clinical Psychology, 68*, 573–579.

Soo, H., Burney, S., & Basten, C. (2009). The role of rumination in affective distress in people with a chronic physical illness: A review of the literature and theoretical formulation. *Journal of Health Education, 14*, 956–966.

Soh, N. L., Touyz, S. W., & Surgenor, J. L. (2006). Eating and body image disturbances across cultures: A review. *Eating Disorders Review, 14*, 54–65.

Solomon, A., Ruscio, J., Seeley, J. R., & Lewinsohn, P. M. (2006). A taxometric investigation of unipolar depression in a large community sample. *Psychological Medicine, 36*, 973–985.

Solowij, N., & Battisti, R. (2008). The chronic effects of cannabis on memory in humans: A review. *Current Drug Abuse Reviews, 1*, 81–98.

Somers, J. M., Goldner, E. M., Waraich, P., & Hsu, L. (2006). Prevalence and incidence studies of anxiety disorders: A systematic review of the literature. *Canadian Journal of Psychiatry, 51*, 100–113.

Sourander, A., Klomeck, A. B., Niemala, S., et al. (2009). Childhood predictors of completed and severe suicide attempts: Findings from the Finnish 1981 Birth Cohort Study. *Archives of General Psychiatry, 66*, 398–406.

Southwick, S. M., Krystal, J. H., Morgan, C. A., Johnson, D., Nagy, L. M., et al. (1993). Abnormal noradrenergic function in posttraumatic stress disorder. *Archives of General Psychiatry, 50*, 266–274.

Sowers, K. M., & Rowe, W. S. (2007). Global aging. In J. A. Blackburn & C. N. Dulmus (Eds.), *Handbook of gerontology: Evidence-based approaches to theory, practice, and policy* (pp. 3–16). New York: John Wiley & Sons.

Spanagel, R. (2009). Alcoholism: A systems approach from molecular physiology to addictive behavior. *Physiological Review, 89*, 649–705.

Spanos, N. P. (1994). Multiple identity enactments and multiple personality disorder: A sociocognitive perspective. *Psychological Bulletin, 116*, 143–165.

Spanos, N. P., Cross, P. A., Dickson, K., & DeBreuil, S. C. (1993). Close encounters: An examination of UFO experiences. *Journal of Abnormal Psychology, 102*, 624–632.

Spanos, N. P., Weekes, J. R., & Bertrand, L. D. (1985). Multiple personality: A social psychological perspective. *Journal of Abnormal Psychology, 94*, 362–376.

Sparks, B. F., et al. (2002). Brain structural abnormalities in children and adults with autism. *Neurology, 59*, 184–192.

Specht, K., Hugdahl, K., & Ofte, S. (2009). Brain activation on pre-reading tasks reveals at-risk status for dyslexia in 6-year-old children. *Scandinavian Journal of Psychology, 50*, 79–91.

Spector, I. P., & Carey, M. P. (1990). Incidence and prevalence of the sexual dysfunctions: A critical review of the empirical literature. *Archives of Sexual Behavior, 19*, 389–408.

Spence, J. D., Barnett, P. A., Linden, W., Ramsden, V., & Taenzer, P. (1999). Recommendations on stress management. *Canadian Medical Association Journal, 160*, S46–S50.

Spence, S. H., et al. (2006). The feasibility and outcome of clinic plus Internet delivery of cognitive-behavior therapy for childhood anxiety. *Journal of Consulting and Clinical Psychology, 74*, 614–621.

Spence, S. H., Sheffield, J. K., & Donovan, C. L. (2005). Long-term outcome of a school-based universal approach to prevention of depression in adolescents. *Journal of Consulting and Clinical Psychology, 73*, 160–167.

Spencer, T., Biederman, J., Wilens, T., Harding, M., O'Donnell, D., & Griffin, S. (1996). Pharmaco-therapy of attention-deficit hyperactivity disorder across the life cycle. *Journal of the American Academy of Child and Adolescent Psychiatry, 35*, 409–432.

Spengler, A. (1977). Manifest sadomasochism of males: Results of an empirical study. *Archives of Sexual Behavior, 6*, 441–456.

Spielmans, G. I., Pasek, L. F., & McFall, J. P. (2007). What are the active ingredients in cognitive and behavioral psychotherapy for anxious and depressed children. A meta-analytic review. *Clinical Psychology Review, 27*, 642–654.

Spiess, W. F. J., Geer, J. H., & O'Donohue, W. T. (1984). Premature ejaculation: Investigation of factors in ejaculatory latency. *Journal of Abnormal Psychology, 93*, 242–245.

Spitzer, C., Barnow, S., Freyberger. H. J., & Grabe, H. J. (2006). Recent developments in the theory of dissociation. *World Psychiatry, 5*, 82–86.

Spitzer, R. L., Endicott, J., & Gibbon, M. (1979). Crossing the border into borderline personality and borderline schizophrenia. *Archives of General Psychiatry, 36*, 17–24.

Spitzer, R. L., Gibbon, M., & Williams, J. B. W. (1996). *Structured clinical interview for DSM-IV Axis I disorders*. New York: N.Y. State Psychiatric Institute, Biometrics Research Department.

Sprague, R. L., & Gadow, K. D. (1976). The role of the teacher in drug treatment. *School Review, 85*, 109–140.

Squires-Wheeler, E., Skodal, A., Agamo, O. M., Bassett, A. S., et al. (1993). Personality features and disorder in the subjects in the New York High-Risk Project. *Journal of Psychiatric Research, 27*, 379–393.

Stacy, A. W., Newcomb, M. D., & Bentler, P. M. (1991). Cognitive motivation and drug use: A 9-year longitudinal study. *Journal of Abnormal Psychology, 100*, 502–515.

Stacy, A. W., Sussman, S., Dent, C. W., Burton, D., & Flay, B. R. (1992). Moderators of peer social influence in adolescent smoking. *Personality and Social Psychology Bulletin, 18*, 163–172.

Stade, B., et al. (2009). The burden of prenatal exposure to alcohol: Revised measurement of cost. *Canadian Journal of Clinical Pharmacology, 16*, e91–e102.

Stader, S. R., & Hokanson, J. E. (1998). Psychosocial antecedents of depressive symptoms: An evaluation using daily experiences methodology. *Journal of Abnormal Psychology, 107*, 17–26.

Stallings, M. C., et al. (2005). A genomewide search for quantitative trait loci influencing antisocial drug dependence in adolescence. *Archives of General Psychiatry, 62*, 1042–1051.

Stansfeld, S. A., Blackmore, E. R., Zagorski, B. M., et al. (2008). Work characteristics and social phobia in a nationally representative employed sample. *Canadian Journal of Psychiatry, 53*, 371–376.

Stanley, M. A., et al. (2003). Cognitive-behavioral treatment of late-life generalized anxiety disorder. *Journal of Consulting and Clinical Psychology, 71*, 309–319.

Stanley, M. A., & Novy, D. M. (2000). Cognitive-behavior therapy for generalized anxiety in late life: An evaluative overview. *Journal of Anxiety Disorders, 14*, 191–207.

Stanley, M. A., & Turner, S. M. (1995). Current status of pharmacological and behavioral treatment of obsessive-compulsive disorder. *Behavior Therapy, 26*, 163–186.

Stanton, A. L., Danoff-Burg, S., & Huggins, M. E. (2002). The first year after breast cancer diagnosis: Hope and coping strategies as predictors of adjustment. *Psychooncology, 11*, 93–102.

Stanton, A. L., Kirk, S. B., Cameron, C. L., & Danoff-Burg, S. (2000). Coping through emotional approach: Scale construction and validation. *Journal of Personality and Social Psychology, 78*, 1150–1169.

Stanton, M. D., & Bardoni, A. (1972). Drug flashbacks: Reported frequency in a military population. *American Journal of Psychiatry, 129*, 751–755.

Starr, L. R., & Davila, J. (2009). Clarifying co-rumination: Associatons with internalizing symptoms and romantic involvement among adolescent girls. *Journal of Adolescence, 32*, 19–37.

Statistics Canada. (1995). *National Population Health Survey Overview* (Catalogue No. 82-567). Ottawa: Author.

Statistics Canada. (1999). *Sex offenders, 1997* (Catalogue No. 85-002-XIE). Ottawa: Author.

Statistics Canada. (2002). *A profile of disability in Canada* (Catalogue No. 89-577-XIE). Ottawa: Author.

Statistics Canada. (2005). *Population projections for Canada, Provinces, and Territories*. Ottawa: Author.

Statistics Canada. (2009, March 31). *Leading causes of death in Canada* (Catalogue No. 84-215-XWE). Ottawa: Author.

Steadman, H. J., Mulvey, E. P., Monahan, J., Robbins, P. C., Appelbaum, P. S., Grisso, T., et al. (1998). Violence by people discharged from acute psychiatric inpatient facilities and by others in the same neighborhoods. *Archives of General Psychiatry, 55*, 393–401.

Steenhuis, R. E., & Ostbye, T. (1995). Neuropsychological test performance of specific diagnostic groups in the Canadian Study of Health and Aging (CSHA). *Journal of Clinical and Experimental Neuropsychology, 17*, 773–785.

Steiger, H., Gauvin, L., Jabalpurwala, S., Seguin, J. R., & Stotland, S. (1999). Hypersensitivity to social interactions in bulimia syndromes: Relationship to binge eating. *Journal of Consulting and Clinical Psychology, 67*, 765–775.

Steiger, H., & Israel, M. (1999). A psychodynamically informed, integrated psychotherapy for anorexia nervosa. *Journal of Clinical Psychology, 55*, 741–753.

Steiger, H., Israel, M., Gauvin, L., Ng, Y. K., & Young, S. N. (2003). Implications of compulsive and impulsive traits for serotonin status in women with bulimia nervosa. *Psychiatry Research, 120*, 219–229.

Steiger, H., et al. (2005). Mood- and restraint-based antecedents to binge episodes in bulimia nervosa: Possible influences of the serontonin system. *Psychological Medicine, 35*, 1553–1562.

Steiger, H., et al. (2001). Implications of impulsive and affective symptoms for serotonin function in bulimia nervosa. *Psychological Medicine, 31*, 85–95.

Steiger, H., & Zanko, M. (1990). Sexual traumata in eating-disordered, psychiatric and normal female groups: Comparison of prevalences and defense styles. *Journal of Interpersonal Violence, 5*, 74–86.

Stein, L. I., & Santos, A.B. (1998). *Assertive community treatment of persons with severe mental illness*. New York: W. W. Norton.

Stein, L. I., & Test, M. A. (1980). Alternative to mental hospital treatment: I. Conceptual model, treatment program, and clinical evaluation. *Archives of General Psychiatry, 37*, 392–397.

Stein, M. B., et al. (1998). A direct-interview family study of generalized social phobia. *American Journal of Psychiatry, 155*, 90–97.

Stein, M. B., Fyer, A. J., Davidson, J. R. T., Pollack, M. H., & Wiita, B. (1999). Fluvoxamine treatment of social phobia (social anxiety disorder): A double-blind, placebo-controlled study. *American Journal of Psychiatry, 156*, 756–760.

Stein, M. B., Jang, K. L., & Livesley, W. J. (1999). Heritability of anxiety sensitivity: A twin study. *American Journal of Psychiatry, 156*, 246–251.

Stein, M. B., Jang, K. L., Taylor, S., Vernon, P. A., & Livesley, W. J. (2002). Genetic and environmental influences on trauma exposure and posttraumatic stress disorder symptoms: A twin study. *American Journal of Psychiatry, 159*, 1675–1681.

Stein, M. B., & Kean, Y. M. (2000). Disability and quality of life in social phobia: Epidemiologic findings. *American Journal of Psychiatry, 157*, 1606–1613.

Steinberg, L. (2009). Adolescent development and juvenile justice. *Annual Review of Clinical Psychology, 5*, 459–485.

Steiner, H., & Karnik, N.S. (2009). Integrated treatment of aggression in the context of ADHD in children refractory to stimulant monotherapy: A window into the future of child psychopharmacology. *American Journal of Psychiatry, 166*, 1315–1317.

Stephens, R. S., Roffman, R. A., & Simpson, E. E. (1993). Adult marijuana users seeking treatment. *Journal of Consulting and Clinical Psychology, 61*, 1100–1104.

Stephens, T., Dulberg, C., & Joubert, N. (1999). Mental health of the Canadian population: A comprehensive analysis. *Chronic Diseases in Canada, 20(3)*.

Stephens, T., & Joubert, N. (2001). The economic burden of mental health problems in Canada. *Chronic Diseases in Canada, 22(1)*.

Stephens, T., Kaiserman, M. J., McCall, D. J., & Sutherland-Brown, C. (2000). School-based smoking prevention: Economic costs versus benefits. *Chronic Diseases in Canada, 21*, 62–67.

Stephenson, R., Marchand, A., & Lavallee, M.-C. (1997). Validation de l'Inventaire de Mobilité pour l'Agoraphobie aupres de la population québecoise francophone [Validation of the Mobility Inventory for Agoraphobia in the Quebec francophone population.]. *Science et Comportement, 26*, 35–38.

Stephenson, R., Marchand, A., & Lavallee, M.-C. (1998). Traduction et validation canadienne-française du questionnaire des pensées phobiques [French Canadian translation and validation of the Agoraphobic Cognitions Questionnaire]. *Encephale, 24,* 415–425.

Stephenson, R., Marchand, A., & Lavallee, M.-C. (1999). A French Canadian adaptation of the Agoraphobic Cognitions Questionnaire: Cross-cultural validation and gender differences. *Scandinavian Journal of Behaviour Therapy, 28,* 1–12.

Stermac, L., Du Mont, J., & Dunn, S. (1998). Violence in known-assailant sexual assaults. *Journal of Interpersonal Violence, 13,* 398–412.

Stermac, L., Du Mont, J., & Kalemba, V. (1995). Comparison of sexual assaults by strangers and known assailants in an urban population of women. *Canadian Medical Association Journal, 153,* 1089–1095.

Stevenson, J., & Jones, I. H. (1972). Behavior therapy technique for exhibitionism: A preliminary report. *Archives of General Psychiatry, 27,* 839–841.

Stevenson, J. S., & Topp, R. (1990). Effects of moderate and low intensity long-term exercise by older adults. *Research in Nursing and Health, 13,* 209–213.

Stewart, D. E., Gagnon, A., Saucier, J.-F., et al. (2008). Postpartum depression symptoms in newcomers. *Canadian Journal of Psychiatry, 53,* 121–124.

Stewart, R. E., & Chambless, D. L. (2009). Cognitive-behavior therapy for adult anxiety disorders in clinical practice: A meta-analysis of effectiveness studies. *Journal of Consulting and Clinical Psychology, 77,* 595–606.

Stewart, S., Boase, P., & Lamble, R. W. (2000). Criminal profiles of drinking drivers in Ontario. In *Alcohol, Drugs, and Traffic Safety –T2000.* Stockholm, Sweden: Swedish National Road Safety.

Stewart, S. H. (1996). Alcohol abuse in individuals exposed to trauma: A critical review. *Psychological Bulletin, 120,* 83–112.

Stewart, S. H., Conrod, P. J., Gignac, M. L., & Pihl, R. O. (1998). Selective processing biases in anxiety-sensitive men and women. *Cognition and Emotion, 12,* 105–33.

Stewart, S. H., & Watt, M. C. (2001). Assessment of health anxiety. In G. J. G. Asmundson, S. Taylor, & B. J. Cox (Eds.), *Health anxiety: Clinical and research perspectives on hypochondriasis and related conditions* (pp. 95–131). Toronto: John Wiley & Sons.

Stewart, W. F., Kawas, C., Corrada, M., & Metter, J. E. (1997). Risk of Alzheimer's disease and duration of NSAID use. *Neurology, 48,* 626–632.

Stice, E., Barrera, M., & Chasin, L. (1998). Prospective differential prediction of adolescent alcohol use and problem use: Examining the mechanisms of effect. *Journal of Abnormal Psychology, 107,* 616–628.

Stice, E., et al. (2008). Dissonance and healthy weight eating disorder prevention programs: Long-term effects from a randomized efficacy trial. *Journal of Consulting and Clinical Psychology, 76,* 329–340.

Stice, E., Shaw, H., Burton, E., & Wade, E. (2006). Dissonance and healthy weight eating disorder prevention programs: A randomized efficacy trial. *Journal of Consulting and Clinical Psychology, 74,* 263–274.

Stinson, F. S., Dawson, D. A., Chou, S. P., et al. (2007). The epidemiology of DSM-IV specific phobia in the USA: Results for the National Epidemiologic Survey on Alcohol and Related Conditions. *Psychological Medicine, 37,* 1047–1059.

Stip, E. (2009). Psychosis: A category or a dimension? *Canadian Journal of Psychiatry, 54,* 137–139.

Stip, E., Caron, J., & Lane, C. J. (2001). Schizophrenia: People's perceptions in Quebec. *Canadian Medical Association Journal, 164,* 1299–1300.

Stirman, S. W., DeRubeis, R. J., Crits-Cristoph, P., & Brody, P. E. (2003). Are samples in randomized controlled studies of psychotherapy representative of community outpatients? A new methodology and initial findings. *Journal of Consulting and Clinical Psychology, 71,* 963–972.

St. John, J., Krichev, A., & Bauman, E. (1976). Northwestern Ontario Indian children and the WISC. *Psychology in the Schools, 13,* 407–411.

St. John, P., & Montgomery, P. (2002). Are cognitively intact seniors with subjective memory loss more likely to develop dementia? *International Journal of Geriatric Psychiatry, 17,* 814–820.

St. John, P., Montgomery, P. R., Kristjansson, B., & McDowell, I. (2002). Cognitive scores, even within the normal range, predict death and institutionalization. *Age and Ageing, 31,* 373–378.

Starkes, J. M., Poulin, C., & Kisley, S. R. (2005). Unmet need for the treatment of depression in Atlantic Canada. *Canadian Journal of Psychiatry, 50,* 580–590.

Stockwell, T., Zhao, J., & Thomas, G. (2009). Should alcohol policies aim to reduce total alcohol consumption? New analyses of Canadian drinking patterns. *Addiction Research and Theory, 17,* 135–151.

Stojanovich, L., & Marisavljevich, D. (2008). Stress as a trigger of autoimmune disease. *Autoimmune Review, 7,* 209–213.

Stokes, J., & Lindsay, J. (1996). Major causes of death and hospitalization in Canadian seniors. *Chronic Diseases in Canada, 17,* 63–72.

Stoléru, S. (2008). The brain, androgens, and pedophilia. In D. W. Pfaff, C. Kordon, P. Chanson, & Y. Christen (Eds.), *Research and perspectives in endocrine interactions* (pp. 163–175). Berlin: Springer Berlin Heidelberg.

Stone, A. A., Bovbjerg, D. H., Neale, J. M., Napoli, A., Valdimarsdottir, H., et al. (1992). Development of common cold symptoms following experimental rhinovirus infection is related to prior stressful life events. *Behavioral Medicine, 18,* 115–120.

Stone, A. A., Cox, D. S., Valdimarsdottir, H., Jandorf, L., & Neale, J. M. (1987). Evidence that secretory IgA antibody is associated with daily mood. *Journal of Personality and Social Psychology, 52,* 988–993.

Stone, A. A., & Neale, J. M. (1982). Development of a methodology for assessing daily experiences. In A. Baum and J. Singer (Eds.), *Environment and health.* Hillsdale, NJ: Erlbaum.

Stone, A. A., & Neale, J. M. (1984). The effects of "severe" daily events on mood. *Journal of Personality and Social Psychology, 46,* 137–144.

Stone, A. A., Reed, B. R., & Neale, J. M. (1987). Changes in daily event frequency precede episodes of physical symptoms. *Journal of Human Stress, 13,* 70–74.

Stone, A. A., Schwartz, J., Neale, J. M., Shiffman, S., Marco, C. A., et al. (1998). A comparison of coping assessed by Ecological Momentary Assessment and retrospective recall. *Journal of Personality and Social Psychology, 74,* 1670–1680.

Stone, A. A., & Shiffman, S. (1994). Ecological momentary assessment (EMA) in behavioral medicine. *Annals of Behavioral Medicine, 16,* 199–202.

Stone, G. (1982). Health Psychology, a new journal for a new field. *Health Psychology, 1,* 1–6.

Stone, J., et al. (2005). Systematic review of misdiagnosis of conversion symptoms and "hysteria." *British Medical Journal, 331,* 989–995.

Stone, M. H. (1986). Exploratory psychotherapy in schizophrenia-spectrum patients: A reevaluation in the light of long-term follow-up of schizophrenic and borderline patients. *Bulletin of the Menninger Clinic, 50,* 287–306.

Stone, M. H. (1993). *Abnormalities of personality. Within and beyond the realm of treatment.* New York: Norton.

Stone, S. V., & Costa, P. T. (1990). Disease-prone personality or distress-prone personality? The role of neuroticism in coronary heart disease. In H. S. Friedman (Ed.), *Personality and Disease.* New York: John Wiley & Sons.

Stonnington, C. M., Barry, J. J., & Fisher, R. S. (2006). Conversion disorder. *American Journal of Psychiatry, 163,* 1510–1517.

Stoppard, J. M. (2000). *Understanding depression: Feminist social constructionist approaches.* Florence, KY: Taylor and Francis/Routledge.

Storch, E. A., Abramowitz, J., & Goodman, W. K. (2008). Where does obsessive-compulsive disorder belong in DSM-V? *Depression and Anxiety, 25,* 336–347.

Stormer, S. M., & Thompson, J. K. (1996). Explanations of body image disturbance: A test of maturational status, negative verbal commentary, and sociological hypotheses. *International Journal of Eating Disorders, 19,* 193–202.

Strain, E. C., Bigelow, G. E., Liebson, I. A., & Stitzer, M. L. (1999). Moderate- vs low-dose methadone in the treatment of opioid dependence. *Journal of the American Medical Association, 281,* 1000–1005.

Stravynski, A., & Boyer, R. (2001). Loneliness in relation to suicide ideation and parasuicide: A population-wide study. *Suicide and Life-Threatening Behavior, 31,* 32–40.

Streiner, D. L. (2005). I have the answer, now what's the question? Why meta-analyses do not provide definitive solutions. *Canadian Journal of Psychiatry, 50,* 829–831.

Striegel-Moore, R. H., Silberstein, L. R., & Rodin, J. (1993). The social self in bulimia nervosa: Public self-consciousness, social anxiety, and perceived fraudulence. *Journal of Abnormal Psychology, 102,* 297–303.

Stringer, A. Y., & Josef, N. C. (1983). Methylphenidate in the treatment of aggression in two patients with antisocial personality disorder. *American Journal of Psychiatry, 140*, 1365–1366.

Strober, M., Freeman, R., & Morrell, W. (1997). The long-term course of severe anorexia nervosa in adolescents: Survival analysis of recovery, relapse, and outcome predictors over 10-15 years in a prospective study. *International Journal of Eating Disorders, 22*, 339–360.

Strober, M., Lampert, C., Morrell, W., Burroughs, J., & Jacobs, C. (1990). A controlled family study of anorexia nervosa: Evidence of family aggregation and lack of shared transmission with affective disorders. *International Journal of Eating Disorders, 9*, 239–253.

Stroebe, M., Schut, H., & Finkehauer, C. (2001). The traumatization of grief?: A conceptual framework for understanding the trauma-bereavement interface. *The Israel Journal of Psychiatry and Related Sciences, 38*, 185–201.

Strongman, K. T., & Russell, P. N. (1986). Salience of emotion in recall. *Bulletin of the Psychonomic Society, 24*, 25–27.

Stuart, H. (2006a). Reaching out to high school youth: The effectiveness of a video-based anti-stigma program. *Canadian Journal of Psychiatry, 51*, 647–643.

Stuart, H. (2006b). Media portrayal of mental illness and its treatments. *CNS Drugs, 20*, 99–106.

Stuart, H. L., & Arboleda-Florez, J. (2000). Homeless shelter users in the postdeinstitutionalization era. *Canadian Journal of Psychiatry, 45*, 55–62.

Stuart, H. L., & Arboleda-Florez, J. (2001). Community attitudes toward people with schizophrenia. *Canadian Journal of Psychiatry, 46*, 245–251.

Stuart, H. L., Arboleda-Florez, J., & Crisanti, A. J. (2001). Impact of legal reforms on length of forensic assessments in Alberta, Canada. *International Journal of Law and Psychiatry, 24*, 527–538.

Stuart, R. B. (1976). An operant interpersonal program for couples. In D. H. L. Olson (Ed.), *Treating relationships.* Lake Mills, IA: Graphic Publishing.

Stuart, R. B. (1978). Protection of the right to informed consent to participate in research. *Behavior Therapy, 9*, 73–82.

Studer, L. H., Clelland, S. R., Aylwin, A. S., Reddon, J. R., & Monro, A. (2000). Rethinking risk assessment for incest offenders. *International Journal of Law and Psychiatry, 23*, 15–22.

Stuss, D. T., & Benson, D. F. (1983). Emotional concomitants of psychosurgery. In K. M. Heilman & P. Satz (Eds.), *Advances in Neuropsychology and behavioural neurology: Vol. 1. Neuropsychology of human emotion* (pp. 111–140). New York: Guilford.

Sue, D. W., & Sue, D. (2003). What is cultural competence? In D. W. Sue & D. Sue (Eds.), *Counseling the culturally diverse* (pp. 12–24). New York: John Wiley & Sons.

Sullivan, H. S. (1953). *The interpersonal theory of psychiatry.* New York: Norton.

Sullivan, P. F., Neale, M. C., & Kendler, K. S. (2000). Genetic epidemiology of major depression:

Review and meta-analysis. *Amercan Journal of Psychiatry, 157*, 1552–1562.

Suls, J., & Fletcher, B. (1985). The relative efficacy of avoidant and nonavoidant coping strategies: A meta-analysis. *Health Psychology, 4*, 249–288.

Summerfeldt, L. J., & Endler, N. S. (1998). Examining the evidence for anxiety-related cognitive biases in obsessive-compulsive disorder. *Journal of Anxiety Disorders, 12*, 579–598.

Suppes, T., Baldessarini, R. J., Faedda, G. L., & Tohen, M. (1991). Risk of recurrence following discontinuation of lithium treatment in bipolar disorder. *Archives of General Psychiatry, 48*, 1082–1087.

Supreme Court of Canada. (2004, January 30). Canadian Foundation for Children, Youth and the Law v. Canada (Attorney General), [2004] 1 S.C.R. 76, 2004 SCC 4.

Surles, R. C., Blanch, A. K., Shern, D. L., & Donahue, S. A. (1992). Case management as a strategy for systems change. *Health Affairs, 11*, 151–163.

Susser, E., Neugebauer, R., Hoek, H. W., Brown, A. S., Lin, S., et al. (1996). Schizophrenia after prenatal famine: Further evidence. *Archives of General Psychiatry, 53*, 25–31.

Susser, E., & Wanderling, J. (1994). Epidemiology of nonaffective acute remitting psychosis versus schizophrenia: Sex and sociocultural setting. *Archives of General Psychiatry, 51*, 294–301.

Sussman, S. (1996). Development of a school-based drug abuse prevention curriculum for high-risk youth. *Journal of Psychoactive Drugs, 28*, 169–182.

Sussman, S. (1998). The first asylums in Canada: A response to neglectful community care and current trends. *Canadian Journal of Psychiatry, 43*, 260–264.

Sussman, S., Dent, C. W., Burton, D., Stacy, A. W., & Flay, B. R. (1995). *Developing school-based tobacco use prevention and cessation programs.* Thousand Oaks, CA: Sage.

Sussman, S., Dent, C. W., McAdams, L., Stacy, A. W., Burton, D., & Flay, B. R. (1994). Group self-identification and adolescent cigarette smoking: A 1-year prospective study. *Journal of Abnormal Psychology, 103*, 576–580.

Sussman, S., Dent, C. W., Stacy, A. W., Burciage, C., Raynor, A., et al. (1990). Peer-group association and adolescent tobacco use. *Journal of Abnormal Psychology, 99*, 349–352.

Sussman, S., Stacy, A. W., Dent, C. W., Simon, T. R., & Johnson, C.A. (1996). Marijuana use: Current issues and new research directions. *Journal of Drug Issues, 26*, 695–733.

Sutcliffe, J. P., & Jones, J. (1962). Personal identity, multiple personality, and hypnosis. *International Journal of Clinical and Experimental Hypnosis, 10*, 231–269.

Sutera, S., Pandey, J., Esser, E. L., et al. (2007). Predictors of optimal outcome in toddlers diagnosed with autism spectrum disorders. *Journal of Autism and Developmental Disorders, 37*, 98–107.

Sutherland, S. (1999, December 2). Eating-disorder clinic risked lives of patients: Health authorities. *The Halifax Chronicle Herald*, A23.

Swain, A., & Suls, J. (1996). Reproducibility of blood pressure and heart rate reactivity: A meta-analysis. *Psychophysiology, 33*, 162–174.

Swanson, J. W., Borum, R., Swartz, M. S., Hiday, V. A., Wagner, H. R., & Burns, B. J. (2001). Can involuntary outpatient commitment reduce arrests among persons with severe mental disorder? *Criminal Justice and Behavior, 28*, 156–189.

Swanson, J. W., Holzer, C. E., Ganju, V. K., & Jono, R. T. (1990). Violence and psychiatric disorder in the community: Evidence from the Epidemiological Catchment Area surveys. *Hospital and Community Psychiatry, 41*, 761–770.

Swanson, J. W., Swartz, M. S., Van Dorn, R. A., et al. (2008). Comparison of antipsychotic medication effects on reducing violence in people with schizophrenia. *The British Journal of Psychiatry, 193*, 37–43.

Swanson, M. C., Bland, R. C., & Newman, S. C. (1994). Epidemiology of psychiatric disorders in Edmonton: Antisocial personality disorders. *Acta Psychiatrica Scandinavica, 376* (Suppl.), 63–70.

Swartz, H. A., Frank, E., Zuckoff, A., et al. (2008). Brief interpersonal psychotherapy for depressed mothers whose children are receiving psychiatric treatment. *American Journal of Psychiatry, 165*, 1155–1162.

Swartz, M., Blazer, D., George, L., & Winfield, I. (1990). Estimating the prevalence of borderline personality in the community. *Journal of Personality Disorders, 4*, 257–272.

Swartz, M. S., et al. (2001). A randomized control trial of outpatient commitment in North Carolina. *Psychiatric Services, 52*, 325–329.

Swartz, M. S., et al. (2006). Substance use in persons with schizophrenia: Baseline prevalence and correlates from the NIMH CATIE Study. *Journal of Nervous and Mental Disease, 194*, 164–172.

Sweet, J. J., Carr, M. A., Rossini, E., & Kasper, C. (1986). Relationship between the Luria-Nebraska Neuropsychological Battery and the WISC-R: Further examination using Kaufman's factors. *International Journal of Clinical Neuropsychology, 8*, 177–180.

Sweet, L., Savoie, J. A., & Lemyre, L. (1999). Appraisals, coping, and stress in breast cancer screening: A longitudinal investigation of causal structure. *Canadian Journal of Behavioural Science, 31*, 240–253.

Sweet, R. A., et al. (1995). Duration of neuroleptic treatment and prevalence of tardive dyskinesia in late life. *Archives of General Psychiatry, 52*, 478–486.

Swinson, R. P., Cox, B. J., Kerr, S. A., Kuch, K., & Fergus, K. (1992). A survey of anxiety disorder clinics in Canadian hospitals. *Canadian Journal of Psychiatry, 37*, 188–191.

Swinson, R. P., Fergus, K. D., Cox, B. J., & Wiskwire, K. (1995). Efficacy of telephone-administered behavioral therapy for panic disorder with agoraphobia. *Behaviour Research and Therapy, 33*, 464–469.

Swinson, R. P., Soulios, C., Cox, B. J., & Kuch, K. (1992). Brief treatment of emergency room patients with panic attacks. *American Journal of Psychiatry, 149*, 944–946.

Sylvain, C., Ladouceur, R., & Boisvert, J.-M. (1997). Cognitive and behavioral treatment of pathological gambling: A controlled study.

Journal of Consulting and Clinical Psychology, 65, 727–732.

Sypeck, M. F., et al. (2006). Cultural representations of thinness in women, redux: Playboy magazine's depiction of beauty from 1979 to 1998. *Body Image, 3,* 229–235.

Szasz, T. S. (1963). *Law, liberty, and psychiatry.* New York: Macmillan.

Szasz, T. (2005). Idiots, infants, and the insane: Mental illness and legal incompetence. *Journal of Medical Ethics, 31,* 78–81.

Szatmari, P., Bryson, S. E., Boyle, M. H., Streiner, D. L., & Duku, E. (2003). Predictors of outcome among high functioning children with autism and Asperger syndrome. *Journal of Child Psychology and Psychiatry and Allied Disciplines, 44,* 520–528.

Szoke, A., Trandafir, A., Dupont, M.-E., et al. (2008). Longitudinal studies of cognition in schizophrenia: Meta-analysis. *The British Journal of Psychiatry, 192,* 248–257.

TADS Team. (2004). Fluoxetine, cognitive-behavioral therapy, and their combination for adolescents with depression. *Journal of the American Medical Association, 292,* 807–820.

TADS Team. (2009). The Treatment for Adolescents with Depression Study: Outcomes over 1 year of naturalistic follow-up. *American Journal of Psychiatry, 166,* 1141–1149.

Takata, T. (1983). *Nikkei Legacy: The story of Japanese Canadians from settlement to today.* Toronto: NC Press Limited.

Talkowski, M. E., Chowdari, K. V., Lewis, D. A., & Nimgaonkar, V. L. (2006). Can RGS4 polymorphisms be viewed as credible risk factors for schizophrenia? A critical review of the evidence. *Schizophrenia Bulletin, 32,* 203–208.

Tam, P. (2008, August 19). Canadians suffering mental illness leaving hospitals earlier: Study. Canwest News.

Tan, W. C., et al. (2009). Marijuana and chronic obstructive lung disease: A population-based survey. *Canadian Medical Association Journal, 180,* 814–820.

Tandon, R., & Jibson, M. D. (2005). Comparing efficacy of first-line atypical antipsychotics: No evidence of differential efficacy between risperidone, olanzapine, quetiapine, ziprasidone, and ariprazole. *International Journal of Psychiatry in Clinical Practice, 9,* 204–212.

Tashkin, D. P. (2005). Smoked marijuana as a cause of lung injury. *Monald: Archives for Chest Disease, 63,* 93–100.

Taylor, E. (2009). Developing ADHD. *Journal of Child Psychology and Psychiatry, 50,* 126–132.

Taylor, J., Loney, B. R., Bobadilla, L., Iacono, W. G., & McGue, M. (2003). Genetic and environmental influences on psychopathy trait dimensions in a community sample of male twins. *Journal of Abnormal Child Psychology, 31,* 633–645.

Taylor, P. J. (2008). Psychosis and violence: Stories, fears, and reality. *Canadian Journal of Psychiatry, 53,* 647–659.

Taylor, S., Asmundson, J. G. J., & Coons, M. J. (2005). Current directions in the treatment of hypochondriasis. *Journal of Cognitive Psychotherapy: An International Quarterly, 19,* 285–304.

Taylor, S., et al. (2003). Comparative efficacy, speed, and adverse effects of three PTSD treatments: Exposure therapy, EMDR, and relaxation training. *Journal of Consulting and Clinical Psychology, 71,* 330–338.

Taylor, S., Thordarson, D. S., Jang, K. L., & Asmundson, G. J. G. (2006). Genetic and environmental origins of health anxiety: A twin study. *World Psychiatry, 5,* 47–50.

Taylor, S. R., & Weiss, J. S. (2009). Review of insomnia psychotherapy options for the elderly: Implications for marginal care. *Population Health Management, 12,* 317–323.

Teachman, B. A., & Woody, S. R. (2003). Automatic processing in spider phobia: Implicit fear association over the course of treatment. *Journal of Abnormal Psychology, 112,* 100–109.

Teasdale, J. D., et al. (2002). Metacognitive awareness and prevention of relapse in depression: Empirical evidence. *Journal of Consulting and Clinical Psychology, 70,* 275–287.

Teasdale, J. D., Segal, Z. V., & Williams, J. M. G. (2003). Mindfulness training and problem formulation. *Clinical Psychology: Science and Practice, 10,* 157–160.

Teasdale, J. D., Segal, Z. V., Williams, J. M. G., et al. (2000). Prevention of relapse/recurrence in major depression by mindfulness-based cognitive therapy. *Journal of Consulting and Clinical Psychology, 68,* 615–623.

Telch, C. F., & Telch, M. J. (1986). Group coping skills instruction and supportive group therapy for cancer patients: A comparison of strategies. *Journal of Consulting and Clinical Psychology, 54,* 802–808.

Tennant, C. (2001). Work-related stress and depressive disorders. *Journal of Psychosomatic Research, 51,* 697–704.

Teotonio, I. (2009, September 16). Calming the storm. *Toronto Star,* GT1, GT4.

Terry, D. J., & Hynes, G. J. (1998). Adjustment to a low-control situation: Reexamining the role of coping responses. *Journal of Personality and Social Psychology, 74,* 1078–1092.

Testa, M., VanZile-Tamsen, C., & Livingston, J. A. (2007). Prospective prediction of women's sexual victimization by intimate and non-intimate male perpetrators. *Journal of Consulting and Clinical Psychology, 75,* 52–60.

Teuscher, V. (2009). Subjective age bias: A motivational and information processing approach. *International Journal of Behavioral Development, 33,* 22–31.

Thaker, G. K. (2007). Endophenotypic studies in schizophrenia: Promise and challenges. *Schizophrenia Bulletin, 33,* 1–2.

Thibaut, J. W., & Kelley, H. H. (1959). *The social psychology of groups.* New York: John Wiley & Sons.

Thigpen, C. H., & Cleckley, H. (1954). *The three faces of Eve.* Kingsport, TN: Kingsport Press.

Thiruchelvam, D., Charach, A., & Schachar, R. J. (2001). Moderators and mediators of long-term adherence to stimulant treatment in children with ADHD. *Journal of the American Academy of Child and Adolescent Psychiatry, 40,* 922–928.

Thoma, N. C., & Cecero, J. C. (2009). Is integrative use of techniques in psychotherapy the exception or the rule? Results of a national survey of doctoral-level practitioners. *Psychotherapy Theory, Research, Practice, and Training, 46,* 405–417.

Thomas, J. J., Vartanian, L. R., & Brownell, K. D. (2009). The relationship between eating disorder not otherwise specified (EDNOS) and officially recognized eating disorders: meta-analysis and implications for DSM. *Psychological Bulletin, 135,* 407–433.

Thomas, G., Stockwell, T., & Reist, D. (January, 2009) Alcohol Pricing, Public Health and the HST: Proposed Incentives for BC Drinkers to Make Healthy Choices. *CARBC Policy Brief.*

Thomas, V. S., & Rockwood, K. J. (2001). Alcohol abuse, cognitive impairment, and mortality among older people. *Journal of the American Geriatric Society, 49,* 415–420.

Thompson, A. H. (2005). Variations in the prevalence of psychiatric disorders and social problems across Canadian provinces. *Canadian Journal of Psychiatry, 50,* 637–642.

Thompson, J. K., et al. (2003). The Sociocultural Attitudes Toward Appearance Scale-3. *International Journal of Eating Disorders, 35,* 293–304.

Thompson, J. K., & Stice, E. (2001). Thin-ideal internalization: Mounting evidence for a new risk factor for body-image disturbance and eating pathology. *Current Directions in Psychological Science, 10,* 181–183.

Thompson, L. W., Gallagher, D., & Breckenridge, J. S. (1987). Comparative effectiveness of psychotherapies for depressed elders. *Journal of Consulting and Clinical Psychology, 55,* 385–390.

Thomsen, D. K., Mehlsen, M. Y., Hokland, M., Viidik, A., Olesen, F., Avlund, K., Munk, K., & Zachariae, R. (2004). Negative thoughts and health: Associations among rumination, immunity, and health care utilization in a young and elderly sample. *Psychosomatic Medicine, 66,* 363–371.

Thorne, S. (2000, February 17). Military will treat stress as a disability: Post-traumatic disorders eligible for compensation. *Toronto Star,* A7.

Tibbo, P., Joffe, K., Chue, P., Metelitsa, A., & Wright, E. (2001). Global assessment of functioning following assertive community treatment in Edmonton, Alberta: A longitudinal study. *Canadian Journal of Psychiatry, 46,* 144–148.

Tidmarsh, L., & Volkmar, F. R. (2003). Diagnosis and epidemiology of autism spectrum disorders. *Canadian Journal of Psychiatry, 48,* 517–525.

Tierney, M. C., Yao, C., Kiss, A., & McDowell, I. (2005). Neuropsychological tests accurately predict Alzheimer's disease after 5 and 10 years. *Neurology, 64,* 1853–1859.

Tiggemann, M. (2005). Television and adolescent body image: The role of program content and viewing motivation. *Journal of Social and Clinical Psychology, 24,* 361–381.

Tiihonen, J., et al. (2006). Antidepressants and the risk of suicide, attempted suicide, and overall mortality in a nationwide cohort. *Archives of General Psychiatry, 63,* 1358–1367.

Tiihonen, J., Walhbeck, K., Lonnqvist, J., et al. (2006). Effectiveness of antipsychotic treatments in a nationwide cohort of patients in community care after first hospitalization due to schizophrenia and schizoaffective disorder: Observational follow-up study. *British Medical Journal, 333,* 224–227.

Time (1996). Why Jenifer got sick: The mother of a poster child is accused of causing her daughter's illness. *Time, 147,* 70.

Tiwari, S. K., & Wang, J. L. (2006). The epidemiology of mental and substance use-related disorders among White, Chinese, and other Asian populations in Canada. *Canadian Journal of Psychiatry, 51,* 904–912.

Tiwari, S. K., & Wang, J. L. (2008). Ethnic differences in mental health service use among White, Chinese, South Asian, and South East Asian populations living in Canada. *Social Psychiatry and Psychiatric Epidemiology, 43,* 866–871.

Tolin, D. F., & Foa, E. B. (2006). Sex differences in trauma and posttraumatic stress disorder: A quantitative review of 25 years of research. *Psychological Bulletin, 132,* 959–992.

Tolomiczenko, G. S., & Goering, P. N. (1998). Pathways into homelessness: broadening the perspective. *Psychiatry Rounds, 2,* 1–6.

Tolomiczenko, G. S., & Goering, P. N. (2000). The process and politics of community-based research with people currently homeless. *Psychiatric Rehabilitation Journal, 24,* 46–51.

Tonmyr, L., Jamieson, E., Mery, L. S., & MacMillan, H. L. (2005). The relation between childhood adverse experiences and disability due to mental health problems in a community sample of women. *Canadian Journal of Psychiatry, 50,* 778–783.

Toplak, M. E., Connors, L., Shuster, J., et al. (2008). Review of cognitive, cognitive-behavioral, and neural-based interventions for Attention-Deficit/Hyperactivity Disorder (ADHD). *Clinical Psychology Review, 28,* 801–823.

Topping, K. J., & Barron, I. G. (2009). School-based child sexual abuse prevention programs: A review of effectiveness. *Review of Educational Research, 79,* 431–463.

Torgersen, S. (1986). Genetics of somatoform disorder. *Archives of General Psychiatry, 43,* 502–505.

Toronto Star. (2001, June 12). Door-to-door troubles in health care, A28.

Toronto Star. (2005, November 11). Mentally ill denied their rights: Judge, A17.

Toronto Star. (2009, March 9). A victory for medicare [Editorial], A12.

Toronto Star. (2009, July 15). Mental health: A housing issue.

Toronto Star. (2010, March 20). Young offenders get Ottawa's spin [Editorial], IN6.

Torrey, E. F. (1995). Prevalence of psychosis among the Hutterites: A reanalysis of the 1950–53 study. *Schizophrenia Research, 16,* 167–170.

Torrey, E. F. (1996). *Out of the shadows: Confronting America's mental health crisis.* New York: John Wiley & Sons.

Torrey, E. F., Taylor, E., Bowler, A., & Gottesman, I. (1994). *Schizophrenia and manic depressive disorder. The biological roots of mental illness as revealed by the landmark study of identical twins.* New York: Basic Books.

Toughill, K. (2003, November 1). New home, same old problems: Gas-sniffing children, drunken adults still plague Innu town. *Toronto Star,* H2.

Toupin, J., Dery, M., Pauze, R., Mercier, H., & Fortin, L. (2000). Cognitive and familial contributions to conduct disorder in children. *Journal of Child Psychology and Psychiatry, 41,* 333–344.

Tregellas, J. (2009). Connecting brain structure and function in schizophrenia. *American Journal of Psychiatry, 166,* 134–136.

Tremblay, R. E., Masse, B., Perron, D., Leblanc, M., Schwartzman, A. E., & Ledingham, J. E. (1992). Early disruptive behavior, poor school achievement, delinquent behavior, and delinquent personality: Longitudinal analyses. *Journal of Consulting and Clinical Psychology, 60,* 64–72.

Tremblay, C., Hébert, M., & Piché. C (2000). Type I and II post-traumatic stress disorder in sexually abused children. Journal of Child Sexual Abuse, *9,* 65-90.

Trevitt, C. & Gallagher, E. (1996). Elder abuse in Canada and Australia: Implications for nurses. *International Journal of Nursing Studies, 33,* 651–699.

Treynor, W., Gonzalez, R., & Nolen-Hoeksema, S. (2003). Rumination reconsidered: A psychometric analysis. *Cognitive Therapy and Research, 27,* 247–259.

Trocmé, N., et al. (2005). Canadian incidence study of reported child abuse and neglect 2003: Major findings. Ottawa: Minister of Public Works and Government Services Canada.

Trottier, K., Polivy, J., & Herman, C. P. (2005). Effects of exposure to unrealistic promises about dieting: Are unrealistic promises about dieting inspirational? *International Journal of Eating Disorders, 37,* 142–149.

True, W. R., Rice, J., Eisen, S. A., Heath, A. C., Goldberg, J., et al. (1993). A twin study of genetic and environmental contributions to liability for posttraumatic stress disorder. *Archives of General Psychiatry, 50,* 257–264.

Trull, T. J. (2001). Relationships of borderline features to parental mental illness, childhood abuse, Axis I disorder, and current functioning. *Journal of Personality Disorders, 15,* 19–32.

Trull, T. J., Useda, J. D., Costa, P. T., Jr., & McCrae, R. R. (1995). Comparsion of the MMPI-2 personality psychopathology five (PSY-5), the NEO-PI, and the NEO-PI-R. *Psychological Assessment, 7,* 508–516.

Tryon, W. W. (2008). Whatever happened to symptom substitution? *Clinical Psychology Review, 26,* 963–968.

Tsai, G., Parssani, L. A., Slusher, B. S., Carter, R., Baer, L., et al. (1995). Abnormal excitatory neurotransmitter metabolism in schizophrenic brains. *Archives of General Psychiatry, 52,* 829–836.

Tsertsvadze, A., et al. (2009). Oral sildenafil citrate (Viagra) for erectile dysfunction: A systematic review and meta-analysis of harms. *Urology, 74,* 831–836.

Tsuchiya, M., Kawakami, N., Ono, Y., Nakane, Y., et al. (2009). Lifetime comorbidities between phobic disorders and major depression in Japan: Results from the World Mental Health Japan 2002–2004 Survey. *Depression and Anxiety, 26,* 949–955.

Tu, J. V., Nardi, L., & Fang, J. (2009). National trends in rates of death and hospital admissions related to acute myocardial infarction, heart failure, and stroke, 1994–2004. *Canadian Medical Association Journal, 180,* E118–E125.

Tucker, J. A., Vuchinich, R. E., & Downey, K. K. (1992). Substance abuse. In S. M. Turner, K. S. Calhoun, & H. E. Adams (Eds.), *Handbook of clinical behavior therapy* (pp. 203–223). New York: John Wiley & Sons.

Tugrul, C., & Kabacki, E. (1997). Vaginismus and its correlates. *Sexual and Marital Therapy, 12,* 23–34.

Tully, E. C., Iacono, W. G., & McGue, M. (2008). An adoption study of parental depression as an environmental liability for adolescent depression and childhood disruptive disorders. *American Journal of Psychiatry, 165,* 1148–1154.

Tuokko, H., et al. (2003). Five-year follow-up of cognitive impairment with no dementia. *Archives of Neurology, 60,* 577–582.

Tuokko, H. A., Chou, P. H. B., Bowden, S. C., et al. (2009). Partial measurement equivalence of French and English versions of the Canadian Study of Health and Aging neuropsychological battery. *Journal of the International Neuropsychological Society, 15,* 416–425.

Tuokko, H., Frerichs, R., Halpern, S., & Eisner, M. (1999). Delusional symptomatology as seen by a community mental health outreach team. *Aging and Mental Health, 3,* 136–142.

Tuokko, H., Hadjistavropoulos, T., Miller, J. A., & Beattie, B. L. (1992). The Clock Test: A sensitive measure to differentiate normal elderly from those with Alzheimer disease. *Journal of the American Geriatrics Society, 40,* 579–584.

Tuokko, H., Hadjistavropoulos, T., Rae, S., & O'Rourke, N. (2000). A comparison of alternative approaches to the scoring of clock drawing. *Archives of Clinical Neuropsychology, 15,* 137–148.

Tuokko, H., Kristjansson, E., & Miller, J. (1995). Neuropsychological detection of dementia: An overview of the neuropsychological component of the Canadian Study of Health and Aging. *Journal of Clinical and Experimental Neuropsychology, 17,* 352–373.

Tuokko, H., MacCourt, P., & Heath, Y. (1999). Home alone with dementia. *Aging and Mental Health, 3,* 21–27.

Tuomisto, M. T. (1997). Intra-arterial blood pressure and heart rate reactivity to behavioral stress in normotensive, borderline, and mild hypertensive men. *Health Psychology, 16,* 554–565.

Turecki, G., Briere, R., Dewar, K., Antonetti, T., Seguin, M., et al. (1999). Prediction of level of serotonin 2A receptor binding by serotonin receptor 2A genetic variation in postmortem brain sample from subjects who did or did not commit suicide. *American Journal of Psychiatry, 156,* 1456–1458.

Turetsky, B. I., et al. (2007). Neurophysiological endophenotypes of schizophrenia: The viability of selected candidate measures. *Schizophrenia Bulletin, 33,* 69–94.

Turk, D. C. (1996). Cognitive factors in chronic pain and disability. In K. S. Dobson & K. D. Craig (Eds.), *Advances in cognitive-behavioral therapy* (pp. 83–115). Thousand Oaks, CA: Sage.

Turk, D. C., Meichenbaum, D. H., & Genest, M. (1983). *Pain and behavioral medicine: A cognitive behavioral perspective.* New York: Guilford.

Turk, D. C., & Monarch, E. S. (2003). Chronic pain. In S. Llewelyn & P. Kennedy (Eds.), *Handbook of clinical health psychology* (pp. 81–101). Chichester, England: John Wiley & Sons.

Turk, D. C., Swanson, K. S., & Tunks, E. R. (2008). Psychological approaches in the treatment of chronic pain patients—when pills, scalpels, and needles are not enough. *Canadian Journal of Psychiatry, 53,* 213–223.

Turk, D. C., Wack, J. T., & Kerns, R. D. (1985). An empirical examination of the "pain behavior" construct. *Journal of Behavioral Medicine, 8,* 119–130.

Turkheimer, E. (1998). Heritability and biological explanation. *Psychological Review, 105,* 782–791.

Turner, E. H., Mathews, A. M., Linardatos, E., et al. (2008). Selective publication of antidepressant trials and its influence on apparent efficacy. *New England Journal of Medicine, 358,* 252–260.

Turner, R. J., & Wagonfeld, M. O. (1967). Occupational mobility and schizophrenia. *American Sociological Review, 32,* 104–113.

Turner, S. M., Beidel, D. C., & Townsley, R. M. (1992). Behavioral treatment of social phobia. In S. M. Turner, K. S. Calhoun, & H. E. Adams (Eds.), *Handbook of clinical behavior therapy* (2nd ed., pp. 13–37). New York: John Wiley & Sons.

Twentyman, C. T., & McFall, R. M. (1975). Behavioral training of social skills in shy males. *Journal of Consulting and Clinical Psychology, 43,* 384–395.

Tyas, S. L., et al. (2007). Transitions to mild cognitive impairments, dementia, and death: Findings from the Nun Study. *American Journal of Epidemiology, 165,* 1231–1238.

Tyler, T. (2001, January 23). Patients drugged in experiments at psychiatric facility, suit claims. *Toronto Star,* A18.

Tyler, T. (2004, November 5). Pair who caged sons get longer jail terms. *Toronto Star,* A02.

Tyler, T. (2006, August 15). Minister: Goal is treatment, not jail. *Toronto Star,* A1, A9.

Tyler, T. (2008, June 21). Sexual anxiety drove me: Bernard. Killer suggests he is not a psychopath anymore. *Toronto Star.*

Tyler, T. (2010). 'Asylum' residents allege abuse: Ex-patients at Orillia's Huronia centre seek $1B from province in class-action bid. *Toronto Star,* A4.

Tyrer, P., et al. (2007). Critical developments in the assessment of personality disorder. *The British Journal of Psychiatry, 190,* s51–s59.

Uher, R., & McGuffin, P. (2008). The moderation by the serotonin transporter gene of environmental adversity in the aetiology of mental illness: Review and methodological analysis. *Molecular Psychiatry, 13,* 131–146.

Ullmann, L., & Krasner, L. (1975). *A psychological approach to abnormal behavior* (2nd ed.). Englewood Cliffs, NJ: Prentice-Hall.

Undheim, A. M., & Sund, A. M. (2008). Psychosocial factors and reading difficulties: Students with reading difficulties drawn from a representative population sample. *Scandinavian Journal of Psychology, 49,* 377–384.

United Nations. (2004). *Follow-up to the Second World Assembly on Ageing: Report of the Secretary General.* New York: United Nations, A/59/164.

Unutzer, J. (2008). Evidence-based treatments for anxiety and depression: lost in translation. *Depression and Anxiety, 25,* 726–729.

Urbszat, D., Herman, C. P., & Polivy, J. (2002). Eat, drink, and be merry, for tomorrow we diet: Effects of anticipated deprivation on food intake in restrained and unrestrained eaters. *Journal of Abnormal Psychology, 111,* 396–401.

Usman, M. A. (1997). Frontotemporal dementias. In P. D. Nussbaum (Ed.), *Handbook of neuropsychology and aging* (pp. 159–176). New York: Plenum.

Vaidya, C. J., & Stollstorff, M. (2008). Cognitive neuroscience of attention deficit hyperactivity disorder: Current status and working hypotheses. *Developmental Disabilities Research Review, 14,* 261–267.

Vaillant, G. E. (1996). A long-term follow-up of male alcohol abuse. *Archives of General Psychiatry, 53,* 243–250.

Valet, M., Gundel, H., Sprenger, T., et al. (2009). Patients with pain disorder show gray-matter loss in pain-processing structures: A voxel-based morphometric study. *Psychosomatic Medicine, 71,* 49–56.

Vallis, T. M., Howes, J. L., & Standage, K. (2000). Is cognitive therapy suitable for treating individuals with personality dysfunction? *Cognitive Therapy and Research, 24,* 595–606.

Valtonen, H. M., et al. (2007). Suicidal behaviour during different phases of bipolar disorder. *Journal of Affective Disorders, 97,* 101–107.

Van Ameringen, M., Mancini, C., Patterson, B., & Boyle, M. H. (2008). Post-traumatic stress disorder in Canada. *CNS Neuroscience and Therapeutics, 14,* 171–181.

Vancouver Sun. (2005, July 5). Morissette reveals fight with anorexia, bulimia. *Vancouver Sun,* C3.

van den Broucke, S., Vandereycken, W., & Vertommen, H. (1995). Marital communication in eating disorders: A controlled observational study. *International Journal of Eating Disorders, 17,* 1–23.

Van Den Kerkhof, E. G., et al. (2003). The impact of sampling and measurement on the prevalence of self-reported pain in Canada. *Pain Research and Management, 8,* 157–163.

van den Oord, E. J., Boomsma, D. I., & Verhulst, F. C. (1994). A study of problem behaviors in 10- to 15-year-old biologically related and unrelated international adoptees. *Behavior Genetics, 24,* 193–205.

van der Oord, S., Prins, P. J. M., Oosterlaan, J., & Emmelkamp, P. M. G. (2008). Efficacy of methylphenidate, psychosocial treatments and their combination in school-aged children with ADHD: A meta-analysis. *Clinical Psychology Review, 28*(5), 783–800.

Van Erp, T. G. M., et al. (2004). Hippocampal volumes in schizophrenic twins. *Archives of General Psychiatry, 61,* 346–353.

van Ingen, D. J., Freiheit, S. R., & Vye, C. S. (2009). From the lab to the clinic: Effectiveness of cognitive-behavioral treatments for anxiety disorders. *Professional Psychology: Research and Practice, 40,* 69–74.

van Kammen, D. P., Bunney, W. E., Docherty, J. P., Jimerson, D. C., Post, R. M., Sivis, S., et al. (1977). Amphetamine-induced catecholamine activation in schizophrenia and depression. *Advances in Biochemical Psychopharmacology, 16,* 655–659.

van Kammen, D. P., Hommer, D. W., & Malas, K. L. (1987). Effects of pimozide on positive and negative symptoms in schizophrenic patients: Are negative symptoms state dependent? *Neuropsychobiology, 18,* 113–117.

van Kammen, W. B., Loeber, R., & Stouthamer-Loeber, M. (1991). Substance use and its relationship to conduct problems and delinquency in young boys. *Journal of Youth and Adolescence, 20,* 399–413.

Van Nieuwerburgh, F. C. W., et al. (2009). Response to serotonin reuptake inhibitors in OCD is not influenced by common CYP2D6 polymorphisms. *International Journal of Psychiatry in Clnical Practice, 13,* 345–348.

van Nimwegen, L. J., de Haan, L., van Beveren, N. J. M., et al. (2008). Effect of olanzapine and risperidone on subjective well-being and craving for cannabis in patients with schizophrenia or related disorders: A double-blind randomized controlled trial. *Canadian Journal of Psychiatry, 53,* 400–405.

van Praag, H., Plutchik, R., & Apter, A. (Eds.). (1990). *Violence and suicidality.* New York: Brunner/Mazel.

van Stegeren, A. H. (2009). Imaging effects on memory: A review of neuroimaging studies. *Canadian Journal of Psychiatry, 54,* 16–27.

van Zelst, W. H., de Beurs, E., Beckman, A. T., Deej, D. T., & van Dyck, R. (2003). Prevalence and risk factors of posttraumatic stress disorder in older adults. *Psychotherapy and Psychosomatics, 72,* 333–342.

Vasiliadis, H.-M., Tempier, R., Lesage, A., & Kates, N. (2009). General practice and mental health care: Determinants of outpatient service use. *Canadian Journal of Psychiatry, 54,* 468–476.

Vaughan, K. K., & Fouts, G. T. (2003). Changes in television and magazine exposure and eating disorder symptomatology. *Sex Roles, 49,* 313–320.

Velakoulis, D., & Lloyd, J. H. (1998). The role of SPECT scanning in a neuropsychiatry unit. *Australian and New Zealand Journal of Psychiatry, 32,* 511–522.

Velakoulis, D., Pantelis, C., McGorry, P. D., Dudgeon, P., Brewer, W., et al. (1999). Hippocampal volume in first-episode psychoses and chronic schizophrenia: A high-resolution magnetic resonance imaging study. *Archives of General Psychiatry, 56,* 133–141.

Verdoux, H., Geddes, J. R., Takei, N., Lawrie, S. M., Bovet, P., et al. (1997). Obstetric complications and age at onset in schizophrenia: An international collaborative meta-analysis of individual patient data. *American Journal of Psychiatry, 154,* 1220–1227.

Verdun-Jones, S. N. (2000). Forensic psychiatry, ethics, and protective sentencing: What are the limits of psychiatric participation in the criminal justice system? *Acta Psychiatrica Scandinavica, 101,* 77–82.

Verheul, R., & Widiger, T. A. (2004). A meta-analysis of the prevalence and usage of the personality disorder not otherwise specified (PDNOS) diagnosis. *Journal of Personality Disorders, 18,* 309–319.

Verlaan, P., & Schwartzman, A. E. (2002). Mother's and father's parental adjustment: Links to externalising behaviour problems in sons and daughters. *International Journal of Behavioral Development, 26,* 214–224.

Vernberg, E. M., Steinberg, A. M., Jacobs, A. K., Brymer, M. J., Watson, P. J., et al. (2008). Innovations in disaster mental health: Psychological first aid. *Professional Psychology: Research and Practice, 39,* 381–388.

Vezina, J., & Bourque, P. (1984). The relationship between cognitive structure and symptoms of depression in the elderly. *Cognitive Therapy and Research, 8,* 29–36.

Viana, A. G., Beidel, D. C., & Rabian, B. (2009). Selective mutism: A review and integration of the last 15 years. *Clinical Psychology Review, 29,* 57–67.

Vickerman, K.A, & Margolin, G. (2009) Rape treatment outcome research: Empirical findings and state of the literature. *Clinical Psychology Review, 29,* 431–448.

Vida, S., Monks, S., & Des Rosiers, P. (2002). Prevalence and correlates of elder abuse and neglect in a geriatric psychiatry service. *Canadian Journal of Psychiatry, 47,* 459–467.

Viding, E., Blair, R. J., Moffitt, T. E., & Plomin, R. (2005). Evidence for substantial genetic risk for psychopathy in 7-year-olds. *Journal of Child Psychology and Psychiatry, 46,* 592–597.

Viding, E., Jones, A. P., Frick, P. J., et al. (2008). Heritability of antisocial behavior at nine-years: Do callous-unemotional traits matter? *Developmental Science, 11,* 17–22.

Vien, A., & Beech, A. R. (2006). Psychopathy: Theory, measurement, and treatment. *Trauma, Violence, and Abuse, 7,* 155–174.

Vienneau, D. (1999, January 10). Give Alzheimer's patients right to die, doctor says. *Toronto Star,* L8.

Viglione, D. J. (1999). A review of recent research addressing the utility of the Rorschach. *Psychological Assessment, 11,* 251–265.

Viljoen, J. L., Roesch, R., Ogloff, J. R. P., & Zapf, P. A. (2003). The role of Canadian psychologists in conducting fitness and criminal responsibility evaluations. *Canadian Psychology, 44,* 369–381.

Viljoen, J. L., Roesch, R., & Zapf, P. A. (2002). An examination of the relationship between competency to stand trial, competency to waive interrogation rights, and psychopathology. *Law and Human Behavior, 26,* 481–506.

Vincent, D., & Boyle, T. (1998, January 10–17). Madness: How we're failing the mentally ill. *Toronto Star.*

Vine, C., & Challen, P. (2002). *Gardens of shame: The tragedy of Martin Kruze and the sexual abuse at Maple Leaf Gardens.* Vancouver: Greystone Books.

Vingilis, E., Wade, T.J., & Adlaf, E. (1998). What factors predict student self-rated physical health. *Journal of Adolescence, 21,* 83–97.

Vinkers, D. J., et al. (2004). The 15-item Geriatric Depression Scale (GDS-15) detects changes in depressive symptoms after a major negative life event: The Leiden 85-plus study. *International Journal of Geriatric Psychiatry, 19,* 80–84.

Virues-Ortega, J. (2010). Applied behavior analytic intervention for autism in early childhood: Meta-analysis, meta-regression, and dose-response meta-analysis of multiple outcomes. *Clinical Psychology Review, 30,* 387–399.

Vismara, L. A., & Rogers, S. J. (2010). Behavioral treatments in autism spectrum disorder: What do we know? *Annual Review of Clinical Psychology, 6,* 447–468.

Vitiello, B. (2009). Treatment of adolescent depression: What we have come to know. *Depression and Anxiety, 26,* 393–395.

Vitousek, K., & Manke, F. (1994). Personality variables and disorders in anorexia nervosa and bulimia nervosa. *Journal of Abnormal Psychology, 103,* 137–147.

Vittaco, M. J., Lilienfeld, S. O., Erickson, S., & Wood, J. M. (in press). Challenging psychological testing in the courtroom: Objective and projective instruments. In J. Ziskin, S. Anderer, & D. Faust (Eds.), *Coping with psychiatric and psychological testimony* (6th ed.). New York: Oxford University Press.

Vliegen, N., Luyten, P., Meurs, P., & Cluckers, G. (2006). Adaptive and maladaptive dimensions of relatedness and self-definition: Relationship with postpartum depression and anxiety. *Personality and Individual Differences, 41,* 395–406.

Vogel-Sprott, M., Kartechner, W., & McDonnell, D. (1989). Consequences of behavior influence the effect of alcohol. *Journal of Substance Abuse, 1,* 369–379.

Volkow, N. D. (2007). Inhalant abuse: Danger under the kitchen sink. *NIDA, 20,* 1–2.

Volkow, N. D., Wang, G. J., Fischman, M. W., & Foltin, R. W. (1997). Relationship between subjective effects of cocaine and dopamine transporter occupancy. *Nature, 386,* 827–830.

Volpicelli, J. R., Rhines, K. C., Rhines, J. S., Volpicelli, L. A., et al. (1997). Naltrexone and alcohol dependence: Role of subject compliance. *Archives of General Psychiatry, 54,* 737–743.

Volpicelli, J. R., Watson, N. T., King, A. C., Shermen, C. E., & O'Brien, C. P. (1995). Effects of naltrexone on alcohol "high" in alcoholics. *American Journal of Psychiatry, 152,* 613–617.

von Bertalanffy, L. (1968). *General systems theory: Foundation, development, applications.* New York: Braziller.

von Knorring, A. L., & Hagglof, B. (1993). Autism in northern Sweden: A population-based follow-up study: Psychopathology. *European Child and Adolescent Psychiatry, 2,* 91–97.

von Krafft-Ebing, R. (1902). *Psychopathia sexualis.* Brooklyn, NY: Physicians and Surgeons Books.

von Ranson, K. M., & Robinson, K. E. (2006). Who is providing what type of psychotherapy to eating disorder clients? A survey. *International Journal of Eating Disorders, 39,* 27–34.

Voyer, P., Verreault, R., Menque, P. N., & Morin, C. M. (2006). Prevalence of insomnia and its associated factors in elderly long-term care residents. *Archives of Gerontology and Geriatrics, 42,* 1–20.

Vozoris, N., & Lougheed, M. D. (2008). Second-hand smoke exposure in Canada: Prevalence, risk factors, and association with respiratory and cardiovascular diseases. *Canadian Respiratory Journal, 15,* 263–269.

Vriends, N., Becker, E. S., Meyer, A., Williams, S. L., Lutz, R., & Margraf, J. (2007). Recovery from social phobia in the community and its predictors: Data from a longitudinal epidemiological study. *Journal of Anxiety Disorders, 21,* 320–337.

Waddell, C., Hua, J. M., Garland, O. M., et al. (2007). Preventing mental disorders in children: A systematic review to inform policy-making. *Canadian Journal of Public Health, 98,* 166–173.

Waddell, C., Lipman, E., & Offord, D. (1999). Conduct disorder: Practice parameters for assessment, treatment, and prevention. *Canadian Journal of Psychiatry, 44* (Suppl. 2), 35S–40S.

Waddell, C., McEwan, K., Shepherd, C. A., Offord, D. R., & Hua, J. M. (2005). A public health strategy to improve the mental health of Canadian children. *Canadian Journal of Psychiatry, 50,* 226–233.

Waddell, C., Offord, D. R., Shepherd, C. A., Hua, J. M., & McEwan, K. (2002). Child psychiatric epidemiology and Canadian public policy-making: The state of the science and the art of the possible. *Canadian Journal of Psychiatry, 47,* 825–832.

Waddington, J. L., Brown, A. S., Lane, A., et al. (2008). Congenital anomalies and early functional impairments in a prospective birth cohort: Risk of schizophrenia-spectrum disorder in adulthood. *The British Journal of Psychiatry, 192,* 264–267.

Wade, T. J., Cairney, J., & Pevalin, D. J. (2002). Emergence of gender differences in depression during adolescence: National panel results from three countries. *Journal of the American Academy of Child and Adolescent Psychiatry, 41,* 190–198.

Wahi, G., Zorzi, A., Macnab, A., & Panagiotopoulos, C. (2009). Prevalence of type 2 diabetes, obesity and the metabolic syndrome among Canadian First Nations children in a remote Pacific coast community. *Paediatrics and Child Health, 14,* 79–83.

Wakefield, J. (1992). Disorder as dysfunction: A conceptual critique of DSM-III-R's definition of mental disorder. *Psychological Review, 99,* 232–247.

Walker, E. F., Davis, D. M., & Savoie, T. D. (1994). Neuromotor precursors of schizophrenia. *Schizophrenia Bulletin, 20,* 441–451.

Walker, E., Kestler, L., Bollini, A., & Hochman, K. M. (2004). Schizophrenia: Etiology and course. *Annual Review of Psychology, 55,* 401–430.

Walker, J. L., Lahey, B. B., Russo, M. F., Frick, P. J., Christ, M. A. G., McBurnett, K., et al. (1991). Anxiety, inhibition, and conduct disorder in children: 1. Relations to social impairment. *Journal of the American Academy of Child and Adolescent Psychiatry, 30,* 187–191.

Wall, A.-M., McKee, S. A., & Hinson, R. E. (2000). Assessing variation in alcohol outcome expectancies across environmental context: An examination of the situational-specificity hypothesis. *Psychology of Addictive Behaviors, 14,* 367–375.

Wallace, K. (2009, April 8). Problem gambler suing OLC for $3.5 billion: Man alleges casinos let him keep playing even after he sought ban. *Toronto Star*, A14.

Wallace, S. T., & Alden, L. E. (1997). Social phobia and positive social events: The price of success. *Journal of Abnormal Psychology, 106*, 416–424.

Waller, D. A., Kiser, S., Hardy, B. W., Fuchs, I., & Feigenbaum, L. P. (1986). Eating behavior and plasma beta-endorphin in bulimia. *American Journal of Clinical Nutrition, 4*, 20–23.

Waller, G. (2009). Evidence-based treatment and therapist drift. *Behaviour Research and Therapy, 47*, 119–127.

Waller, G., & Kennerly, H. (2003). Cognitive-behavioral treatments. In J. Treasure, U. Schmidt, & E. van Furth (Eds.), *Handbook of eating disorders* (2nd ed., pp. 233–252). Chichester, England: John Wiley & Sons.

Waller, G., et al. (2007). Narcissism and narcissistic defenses in the eating disorders. *International Journal of Eating Disorders, 40*, 143–148.

Waller, N. G., & Ross, C. A. (1997). The prevalence and biometric structure of pathological dissociation in the general population: Taxometric and behavior genetic findings. *Journal of Abnormal Psychology, 106*, 499–510.

Wallerstein, R. S. (1989). The Psychotherapy Research Project of the Menninger Foundation: An overview. *Journal of Consulting and Clinical Psychology, 57*, 195–205.

Walling, M., Anderson, B. L., & Johnson, S. R. (1990). Hormonal replacement therapy for postmenopausal women: A review of sexual outcomes and related gynecologic effects. *Archives of Sexual Behavior, 19*, 119–137.

Walsh, B. T. (2003). Eating disorders. In A. Tasman, J. Kay, & J. A. Lieberman (Eds.), *Psychiatry* (2nd ed., Vol. 2, pp. 1501–1518). Chichester, England: John Wiley & Sons.

Walsh, B. T., Jr., et al. (2006). Fluoxetine after weight restoration in anorexia nervosa. *Journal of the American Medical Association, 295*, 2605–2612.

Walsh-Bowers, R. (1998). Community psychology in the Canadian psychological family. *Canadian Psychology, 39*, 280–287.

Walter, M., et al. (2007). Pedophilia is linked to reduced activation in hypothalamus and lateral prefrontal cortex during visual erotic stimulation. *Biological Psychiatry, 62*, 698–701.

Walters, D. (1995). Mandatory reporting of child abuse: Legal, ethical, and clinical implications within a Canadian context. *Canadian Psychology, 36*, 163–182.

Walters, E., & Kendler, K. S. (1994). Anorexia nervosa and anorexia-like symptoms in a population based twin sample. *American Journal of Psychiatry, 152*, 62–71.

Walters, E. E., Neale, M. C., Eaves, L. J., Lindon, J., & Heath, A. C. (1992). Bulimia nervosa and major depression: A study of common genetic and environmental factors. *Psychological Medicine, 22*, 617–622.

Wampold, B. E., Minami, T., Tierney, S. C., Baskin, T. W., & Bhati, K. S. (2005). The placebo is powerful: Estimating placebo effects in medicine and psychotherapy from randomized clinical trials. *Journal of Clinical Psychology, 61*, 835–854.

Wang, F., et al. (2009). The influence of childhood obesity on the development of self-esteem. *Health Reports, 20*, 21–27. (Statistics Canada Catalogue No. 82-003-XIE.)

Wang, J. L. (2006). Perceived work stress, imbalance between work and family/personal lives, and mental disorders. *Social Psychiatry and Psychiatric Epidemiology, 41*, 541–548.

Wang, J. L., et al. (2005). Help-seeking behaviours of individuals with mood disorders. *Canadian Journal of Psychiatry, 50*, 652–659.

Wang, K., Zhang, H., Deqiong, M., et al. (2009). Common genetic variants on 5p14.1 associate with autism spectrum disorders. *Nature, 459*, 528–533.

Wannamethee, S. G., Shaper, A. G., & Walker, M. (1998). Changes in physical activity, mortality, and incidence of coronary heart disease in older men. *The Lancet, 351*, 1603–1608.

Ward, C. H., Beck, A. T., Mendelson, M., Mock, E., & Erbaugh, J. K. (1962). The psychiatric nomenclature: Reasons for diagnostic disagreement. *Archives of General Psychiatry, 7*, 198–205.

Warner, R. E. (1991). A survey of theoretical orientations of Canadian clinical psychologists. *Canadian Psychology, 32*, 525–528.

Warren, S. L., Huston, L., Egeland, B., & Sroufe, L. A. (1997). Child and adolescent anxiety disorders and early attachment. *Journal of the American Academy of Child and Adolescent Psychiatry, 36*, 637–644.

Warsh, C. K. (1989). *Moments of unreason: The practice of Canadian psychiatry and the Homewood Retreat, 1883–1923*. Montreal: McGill-Queen's University Press.

Wartenberg, A. A., Nirenberg, T. D., Liepman, M. R., Silvia, L. Y., Begin, A. M., & Monti, P. M. (1990). Detoxification of alcoholics: Improving care by symptom-triggered sedation. *Alcoholism: Clinical and Experimental Research, 14*, 71–75.

Waschbusch, D. A., Carrey, N. J., Willoughby, M. T., et al. (2007). Effects of methylphenidate and behavior modification on the social and academic behavior of children with disruptive behavior disorders: The moderating role of callous/unemotional traits. *Journal of Clinical Child and Adolescence Psychology, 36*, 629–644.

Waserman, J., & Criollo, M. (2000). Subjective experiences of clozapine treatment by patients with chronic schizophrenia. *Psychiatric Services, 51*, 666–668.

Watson, D. (2005). Rethinking the mood and anxiety disorders: A quantitative hierarchical model for *DSM-V. Journal of Abnormal Psychology, 114*, 522–536.

Watson, D., & Clark, L. A. (2006). Clinical diagnosis at the crossroads. *Clinical Psychology: Science and Practice, 13*, 210–215.

Watson, D., O'Hara, M. W., & Stuart, S. (2008). Hierarchical structures of affect and psychopathology and their implications for the classification of emotional disorders. *Depression and Anxiety, 25*, 282–288.

Watson, D., & Pennebaker, J. W. (1989). Health complaints, stress, and distress: Exploring the central role of negative affectivity. *Psychological Review, 96*, 234–254.

Watson, J. C., & Bedard, D. L. (2006). Clients' emotional processing in psychotherapy: A comparison between cognitive-behavioral and process-experiential therapies. *Journal of Consulting and Clinical Psychology, 74*, 152–159.

Watson, J. B., & Rayner, R. (1920). Conditioned emotional reactions. *Journal of Experimental Psychology, 3*, 1–14.

Watson, S.M., & Westby, C.E. (2003) Strategies for addressing the executive function impairments of students prenatally exposed to alcohol and other drugs. *Communication Disorders Quarterly, 24*, 194–204.

Watt, L. M., & Cappeliez, P. (2000). Integrative and instrumental reminiscence therapies for depression in older adults: Intervention strategies and treatment effectiveness. *Aging and Mental Health, 4*, 166–177.

Watt, N. F. (1974). Childhood and adolescent roots of schizophrenia. In D. Ricks, A. Thomas, & M. Roll (Eds.), *Life history research in psychopathology* (Vol. 3). Minneapolis, MN: University of Minnesota Press.

Watzlawick, P., Beavin, J., & Jackson, D. D. (1967). *Pragmatics of human communication: A study of interactional patterns, pathologies, and paradoxes.* New York: Norton.

Waxer, P. (1990). Cantonese versus Canadian evaluation of directive and non-directive therapy. *Canadian Journal of Counseling, 23*, 263–272.

Waxman, S. E. (2009). A systematic review of impulsivity in eating disorders. *European Eating Disorder Review, 17*, 408–425.

Webb, W. B., & Campbell, S. S. (1980). Awakenings and the return to sleep in an older population. *Sleep, 3*, 41–66.

Weber, T. (1996, December 2). Tarnishing the golden years with addiction. *Los Angeles Times*, A1, A37.

Webster, C. D., Douglas, K. S., Eaves, D., & Hart, S. D. (1997). Assessing risk of violence to others. In C. D. Webster & M. A. Jackson (Eds.), *Impulsivity: Theory, assessment, and treatment* (pp. 251–277). New York: Guilford.

Wechsler, H., Davenport, A., Dowdell, G., Moeykens, B., & Castillo, S. (1994). Health and behavioral consequences of binge drinking in college: A national survey of students at 140 campuses. *Journal of the American Medical Association, 272*, 1672–1677.

Wechsler, H., Lee, J.E., Kuo, M., & Lee, H. (2000). College binge drinking in the 1990s: a continuing problem. Results of the Harvard School of Public Health 1999 College Alcohol Study. *Journal of American College Health, 48*, 199–210.

Wechsler Intelligence Scale for Children. Third Edition. (1991). San Antonio, TX: The Psychological Corporation.

Wegner, D. M., Schneider, D. J., Carter, S. R., & White, T. L. (1987). Paradoxical effects of thought suppression. *Journal of Personality and Social Psychology, 53*, 5–13.

Wegner, D. M., Schneider, D. J., Knutson, B., & McMahon, S. R. (1991). Polluting the stream of consciousness: The effect of thought suppression on the mind's environment. *Cognitive Therapy and Research, 15*, 141–152.

Weiden, P., & Zygmunt, A. (1997). Medication noncompliance in schizophrenia. Part I. Assessment. *Journal of Practical Psychiatry and Behavioral Health, 3*, 106–110.

Weinberger, D. R. (1987). Implications of normal brain development for the pathogenesis of schizophrenia. *Archives of General Psychiatry, 44,* 660–669.

Weiner, B., Frieze, L., Kukla, A., Reed, L., Rest, S., & Rosenbaum, R. M. (1971). *Perceiving the causes of success and failure.* New York: General Learning Press.

Weiner, D. B. (1994). *Le geste de Pinel: The history of psychiatric myth.* In M. S. Micale & R. Portern (Eds.), *Discovering the history of psychiatry.* New York: Oxford.

Weis, R., & Ash, S. E. (2009). Changes in adolescent and parent hopefulness in psychotherapy: Effects on adolescent outcomes as evaluated by adolescents, parents, and therapists. *The Journal of Positive Psychology, 4,* 356–364.

Weisman, A. G., Nuechterlein, K. H., Goldstein, M. J., & Snyder, K. S. (1998). Expressed emotion, attributions, and schizophrenia symptom dimensions. *Journal of Abnormal Psychology, 107,* 355–359.

Weisman, R. (1995). Reflections on the Oak Ridge experiment with mentally disordered offenders, 1965–1968. *International Journal of Law and Psychiatry, 18,* 265–290.

Weiss, G., & Hechtman, L. (1986). *Hyperactive children grown up.* New York: Guilford.

Weiss, L. A., Shen, Y., Korn, J. M., et al. (2008). Association between microdeletion and microduplication at 16p11.2 and autism. *The New England Journal of Medicine, 358,* 667–675.

Weissberg, R. P., Caplan, M. Z., & Sivo, P. J. (1989). A new conceptual framework for establishing school-based social competence promotion programs. In L. A. Bond & B. E. Compas (Eds.), *Primary prevention and promotion in the schools,* Vol. 12 (pp. 255–296). Newbury Park, CA: Sage Publications.

Weissman, A. N., & Beck, A. T. (1978). *Development and validation of the Dysfunctional Attitude Scale: A preliminary investigation.* Paper presented at the annual meeting of the American Educational Research Association, Toronto.

Weissman, M. M. (1993). The epidemiology of personality disorders: A 1990 update. *Journal of Personality Disorders, 7,* 44–61.

Weissman, M. M. (1995). *Mastering depression: A patient's guide to interpersonal psychotherapy.* New York: Graywind.

Weissman, M. M. (2006). A brief history of interpersonal psychotherapy. *Psychiatric Annals, 36,* 553–557.

Weissman, M. M. (2007). Cognitive therapy and interpersonal psychotherapy: 30 years later. *American Journal of Psychiatry, 164,* 693–696.

Weissman, M. M., Bland, R. C., Canino, G. J., Faravelli, C., Greenwald, S., et al. (1996). Cross-national epidemiology of major depression and bipolar disorder. *Journal of the American Medical Association, 276,* 293–299.

Weissman, M. M., Bland, R. C., Canino, G. J., Greenwald, S., et al. (1994). The cross-national epidemiology of obsessive compulsive disorder: The Cross National Collaborative Group. *Journal of Clinical Psychiatry, 55* (Suppl.), 5–10.

Weizmann, F., Wiener, N. I., Wiesenthal, D. L., & Ziegler, M. (1991). Eggs, eggplants and eggheads: A rejoinder to Rushton. *Canadian Psychology, 32,* 43–50.

Wekerle, C., & Wall, A.-M. (2002). *The violence and addiction equation: Theoretical and clinical issues in substance abuse and relationship violence.* Philadelphia: Brunner/Mazel.

Wekerle, C., & Wolfe, D. A. (1998). The role of child maltreatment and attachment style in adolescent relationship violence. *Development and Psychopathology, 10,* 571–586.

Wells, C. E., & Duncan, G. W. (1980). *Neurology for psychiatrists.* Philadelphia: F. A. Davis.

Wells, S., Graham, K., & West, P. (2000). Alcohol-related aggression in the general population. *Journal of Studies on Alcohol, 61,* 626–632.

Welsh, M. (2004, January 14). Make elderly priority, city says. *Toronto Star,* A04.

Wente, M. (2000, December 14). Who gets to be a woman? *The Globe and Mail.*

Wenzlaff, R. M., Wegner, D. M., & Klein, S. B. (1991). The role of thought suppression in the bonding of thought and affect. *Journal of Personality and Social Psychology, 60,* 500–508.

West, A. E., Jacobs, R. H., Westerholm, R., et al. (2009). Child and family-focused cognitive-behavioral therapy for pediatric bipolar disorder: Pilot study of group treatment format. *Journal of the Canadian Academy of Child and Adolescent Psychiatry, 18,* 239–246.

West, M., Adam, K., Spreng, S., & Rose, S. (2001). Attachment disorganization and dissociative symptoms in clinically treated adolescents. *Canadian Journal of Psychiatry, 46,* 627–631.

West, S. L., & O'Neal, K. K. (2004). Project D.A.R.E. outcome effectiveness revisited. *American Journal of Public Health, 94,* 1027–1029.

West, S. L., Vinikoor, L. C., & Zolnoun, D. (2004). A systematic review of the literature on female sexual dysfunction prevalence and predictors. *Annual Review of Sex Research, 15,* 40–172.

Westen, D., Novotny, C. M., & Thompson-Brenner, H. (2004). The empirical status of empirically supported psychotherapies: Assumptions, findings, and reporting in controlled clinical trials. *Psychological Bulletin, 130,* 631–663.

Westra, H. A. (2004). Managing resistance in cognitive behavioural therapy: The application of motivational interviewing in mixed anxiety and depression. *Cognitive Behaviour Therapy, 33,* 161–175.

Westra, H. A., Constantino, M., Arkowitz, H. A., & Dozois, D. J. A. (2009). Therapist effects in cognitive behavioral therapy for generalized anxiety disorder: A pilot study. *Psychotherapy.*

Westra, H. A., & Dozois, D. J. A. (2006). Preparing clients for cognitive behavior therapy: A randomized pilot study of motivational interviewing for anxiety. *Cognitive Therapy and Research, 30,* 481–498.

Westra, H. A., Eastwood, J. D., Bouffard, B. B., & Gerritsen, C. J. (2006). Psychology's pursuit of prescriptive authority: Would it meet the goals of Canadian health care reform? *Canadian Psychology, 47,* 77–95.

Wetherell, J. L. (1998). Treatment of anxiety in older adults. *Psychotherapy, 39,* 444–458.

Wetherell, J. L., Gatz, M., & Craske, M. G. (2003). Treatment of generalized anxiety disorder in older adults. *Journal of Consulting and Clinical Psychology, 71,* 31–40.

Wexler, B. E., Zhu, H., Bell, M. D., et al. (2009). Neuropsychological near normality and brain structure abnormality in schizophrenia. *American Journal of Psychiatry, 166,* 188–195.

Whalen, C. K., & Henker, B. (1999). The child with attention-deficit/hyperactivity disorder in family contexts. In H. C. Quay & A. E. Hogan (Eds.), Handbook of disruptive behavior disorders (pp. 139–155). New York: Plenum Press.

Wheaton, B. (1997). The nature of chronic stress. In B. H. Gottlieb (Ed.), *Coping with chronic stress* (pp. 43–73). New York: Plenum.

Wheeler, H. A., Blankstein, K. R., Antony, M. M., McCabe, R. E., & Bieling, P. J. (2010). Perfectionism across disorders, relations with symptom severity, and role of comorbidity. *International Journal of Cognitive Therapy.*

Whelton, P. K., et al. for the TONE Collaborative Research Group. (1998). Sodium reduction and weight loss in the treatment of hypertension in older persons: A randomized controlled trial of nonpharmacologic interventions in the elderly (TONE). *Journal of the American Medical Association, 279,* 839–846.

Whiffen, V. E., & Clark, S. E. (1997). Does victimization account for sex differences in depressive symptoms? *British Journal of Clinical Psychology, 36,* 185–193.

Whiffen, V. E., & Johnson, S. M. (1998). An attachment theory framework for the treatment of childbearing depression. *Clinical Psychology: Science and Practice, 5,* 478–493.

Whiffen, V. E., & MacIntosh, H. B. (2005). Sexual abuse and emotional distress: A critical review. *Trauma, Violence, and Abuse, 6,* 24–39.

Whisman, M. A., Sheldon, C. T., & Goering, P. (2000). Psychiatric disorders and dissatisfaction with social relationships: Does type of relationship matter? *Journal of Abnormal Psychology, 109,* 803–808.

White, J., Dyck, R. J., Harrington, G., Auburn, F., & Meurin, S. (1993). *Suicide prevention in Alberta: Working toward results.* Edmonton, AB: Alberta Health.

White, P. F. (1986). Patient-controlled analgesia: A new approach to the management of postoperative pain. *Seminars in Anesthesia, 4,* 255–266.

White, P. J. (2008, February). Stigma is a key barrier to progress in mental health care. *Canadian Psychiatry Aujourd'hui, 4 (1),* 1–3.

White, S. W., Oswald, D., Ollendick, T., & Scahill, L. (2009). Anxiety in children and adolescents with autism spectrum disorders. *Clinical Psychology Review, 29,* 216–229.

Whitehorn, D., Richard, J. C., & Kopala, L. (2004). Hospitalization in the first year of treatment for schizophrenia. *Canadian Journal of Psychiatry, 49,* 635–638.

Whitehouse, P. J. (1997). Genesis of Alzheimer's disease. *Neurology, 48* (Suppl. 7), s2–s6.

Whitley, R., Kirmayer, L. J., & Groleau, D. (2006). Understanding immigrants' reluctance to use mental health services: A qualitative study from Montreal. *Canadian Journal of Psychiatry, 51,* 205–209.

Whitlock, J. L., Powers, J. P., & Eckenrode, J. E. (2006). The virtual cutting edge: Adolescent self-injury and the Internet. *Developmental Psychology, 42,* 407–417.

Wicks-Nelson, R., & Israel, A. C. (2006). *Behavior disorders of childhood* (6th ed.). Upper Saddle River, New Jersey: Pearson Education.

Widiger, T. A., Frances, A., Spitzer, R. L., & Williams, J. B. W. (1988). The DSM-III personality disorders: An overview. *American Journal of Psychiatry, 145,* 786–795.

Widiger, T. A., Frances, A., & Trull, T. J. (1987). A psychometric analysis of the social-interpersonal and cognitive-perceptual items for schizotypal personality disorder. *Archives of General Psychiatry, 44,* 741–745.

Widiger, T. A., Livesley, W. J., & Clark, L. A. (2009). An integrated dimensional classification of personality disorder. *Psychological Assessment, 21,* 243–255.

Widiger, T. A., & Mullins-Sweatt, S. N. (2009). Five-factor model of personality disorder: A proposal for DSM-V. *Annual Review of Clinical Psychology, 5,* 197–220.

Widiger, T. A., & Samuel, D. B. (2005). Diagnostic categories or dimensions? A question for the Diagnostic and Statistical Manual of Mental Disorders—fifth edition. *Journal of Abnormal Psychology, 114,* 494–504.

Wielgosz, A. T., & Nolan, R. P. (2000). Biobehavioral factors in the context of ischemic cardiovascular diseases. *Journal of Psychosomatic Research, 48,* 339–345.

Wien, F., Blackstock, C., Loxley, J., & Trocmé, N. (2007). Keeping first nations children at home: A few federal policy changes could make a big difference. *First Peoples Child & Family Review, 3,* 10–14.

Wiers, R. W., & Stacy, A. W. (2006). Implicit cognition and addiction. *Current Directions in Psychological Science, 15,* 292–296.

Wildes, J. E., Harkness, K. L., & Simons, A. D. (2002). Life events, number of social relationships, and twelve-month naturalistic course of major depression in a community sample of women. *Depression and Anxiety, 16,* 104–113.

Wilfley, D., Stein, R., & Welch, R. (2003). Interpersonal psychotherapy. In J. Treasure, U. Schmidt, & E. van Furth (Eds.), *Handbook of eating disorders* (2nd ed., pp. 253–270). Chichester, England: John Wiley & Sons.

Wilgosh, L., Mulcahy, R., & Watters, B. (1986). Assessing intellectual performance of culturally different, Inuit children with the WISC-R. *Canadian Journal of Behavioural Science, 18,* 270–277.

Wilhelm, K., et al. (2006). Life events, first depression onset, and the serotonin transporter gene. *British Journal of Psychiatry, 188,* 210–215.

Wilkie, C., Macdonald, S., & Hildahl, K. (1998). Community case study: Suicide cluster in a small Manitoba community. *Canadian Journal of Psychiatry, 43,* 823–828.

Williams, J., Hadjistavropoulos, T., & Sharpe, D. (2006). A meta-analysis of psychological and pharmacological treatments for body dysmorphic disorder. *Behaviour Research and Therapy, 44,* 99–111.

Williams, J. B. W., et al. (1992). The Structured Clinical Interview for DSM-III-R (SCID): 2. Multisite test-retest reliability. *Archives of General Psychiatry, 49,* 630–636.

Williams, J. M. G., Teasdale, J. D., Segal, Z. V., & Soulsby, J. (2000). Mindfulness-based cognitive therapy reduces overgeneral autobiographical memory in formerly depressed patients. *Journal of Abnormal Psychology, 109,* 150–155.

Williams, L., et al. (2008). Type D personality mechanisms of affect: The role of heart-related behavior and social support. *Journal of Psychosomatic Research, 64,* 63–69.

Williams, R.J., McDermitt, D.R., Bertrand, L.D., & Davis, R.M. (2003). Parental awareness of adolescent substance use. *Addictive Behaviors, 28,* 803–809.

Williamson, D. A., Goreczny, A. J., Davis, C. J., Ruggiero, L., & MacKenzie, S. L. (1988). Psychophysiological analysis of the anxiety model of bulimia nervosa. *Behavior Therapy, 19,* 1–9.

Wills, T. A., & Cleary, S. D. (1999). Peer and adolescent substance use among 6th–9th graders: Latent growth analysis of influence versus selection mechanisms. *Health Psychology, 18,* 453–463.

Wills, T. A., DuHamel, K., & Vaccaro, D. (1995). Activity and mood temperament as predictors of adolescent substance use: Test of a self-regulation model. *Journal of Personality and Social Psychology, 68,* 901–916.

Wilsnak, S. C. (1984). Drinking, sexuality, and sexual dysfunction in women. In S. C. Wilsnak & L. J. Beckman (Eds.), *Alcohol problems in women: Antecedents, consequences, and intervention* (pp. 189–227). New York: Guilford.

Wilson, G. T. (1995). Empirically validated treatments as a basis for clinical practice: Problems and prospects. In S. C. Hayes, V. M. Follette, R. M. Dawes, & K. E. Grady (Eds.), *Scientific standards of psychological practice: Issues and recommendations.* Reno, NV: Context Press.

Wilson, G. T., & Davison, G. C. (1971). Processes of fear reduction in systematic desensitization: Animal studies. *Psychological Bulletin, 76,* 1–14.

Wilson, G. T., Grilo, C. M., & Vitousek, K. M. (2007). Psychological treatment of eating disorders. *American Psychologist, 62,* 199–216.

Wilson, G. T., Vitousek, K., & Loeb, K. L. (2000). Stepped care treatment for eating disorders. *Journal of Consulting and Clinical Psychology, 68,* 564–572.

Wilson, K. G., et al. (1992). Panic attacks in the nonclinical population: An empirical approach to case identification. *Journal of Abnormal Psychology, 101,* 460–468.

Wilson, K. G., Sandler, L. S., Asmundson, G. J. G., Larsen, D. K., & Ediger, J. M. (1991). Effects of instructional set on self-reports of panic attacks. *Journal of Anxiety Disorders, 5,* 43–63.

Wilson, S., & Durbin, E. (2010). Effects of paternal depression on father's parenting behaviors: A meta-analytic review. *Clinical Psychology Review, 30,* 167–180.

Winchester, E., & Collier, D. (2003). Genetic aetiology of eating disorders and obesity. In J. Treasure, U. Schmidt, & E. van Furth (Eds.), *Handbook of eating disorders* (2nd ed., pp. 35–62). Chichester, England: John Wiley & Sons.

Wincze, J. P., & Carey, M. P. (1991). *Sexual dysfunction: A guide for assessment and treatment.* New York: Guilford.

Winett, R. A., & Winkler, R. C. (1972). Current behavior modification in the classroom: Be still, be quiet, be docile. *Journal of Applied Behavior Analysis, 5,* 499–504.

Winfield, N. (2009, April 30). Pope apologizes to aboriginals: Meeting about victims of church-run schools 'was all about healing.' Associated Press.

Winko v. British Columbia. (1999). 2 S.C.R., 625, File No. 25856.

Wintre, M. G., Sugar, L. A., Yaffe, M., & Costin, D. (2000). Generational status: A Canadian response to the Editors' Consortium statement with regard to race/ethnicity. *Canadian Psychology, 41,* 230–243.

Wise, T. (1978). Where the public peril begins: A survey of psychotherapists to determine the effects of Tarasoff. *Stanford Law Review, 31,* 165–190.

Wisner, K. L., Sit, D. K. Y., Hanusa, B. H., et al. (2009). Major depression and antidepressant treatment: Impact on pregnancy and neonatal outcomes. *American Journal of Psychiatry, 166,* 557–566.

Witkiewitz, K., & Marlatt, G. A. (2006). Overview of harm reduction treatments for alcohol problems. *International Journal of Drug Policy, 17,* 285–294.

Wittchen, H.-U., Gloster, A. T., Beesdo-Baum, K., et al. (2010). Agoraphobia: A review of the diagnostic classificatory position and criteria. *Depression and Anxiety, 27,* 113–133.

Woike, B. A., & McAdams, D. P. (2001). A response to Lilienfeld, Woods and Garb: TAT-based personality measures have considerable validity. *APS Observer, 14,* 10.

Wold, D. A. (1968). *The adjustment of siblings to childhood leukemia.* Unpublished medical thesis, University of Washington, Seattle.

Wolf, A., & Kutash, I. L. (1990). Psychoanalysis in groups. In I. L. Kutash & A. Wolf (Eds.), *The group psychotherapist's handbook: Contemporary theory and technique.* New York: Columbia University Press.

Wolfe, V. V. (1990). Sexual abuse of children. In A. S. Bellack, M. Hersen, & A. E. Kazdin (Eds.), *International handbook of behavior modification and therapy* (2nd ed., pp. 707–729). New York: Plenum.

Wolff, P. H., & Melngailis, I. (1996). Reversing letters and reading transformed text in dyslexia: A reassessment. *Reading and Writing, 8,* 341–355.

Wolf-Maier, K., et al. (2003). Hypertension prevalence and blood pressure levels in 6 European countries, Canada, and the United States. *Journal of the American Medical Association, 289,* 2363–2369.

Wolfson, C., et al. (2001). A reevaluation of the duration of survival after the onset of dementia. *New England Journal of Medicine, 344,* 1160–1161.

Wolitzky, D. L., & Eagle, M. N. (1990). Psychotherapy. In A. S. Bellack & M. Hersen (Eds.), *Handbook of comparative treatments for adult disorders* (pp. 123–143). New York: John Wiley & Sons.

Wolitzky-Taylor, K. B., Castriotta, N., Lenza, E. J., Stanley, M. A., & Craske, M. G. (2010). Anxiety disorders in older adults: A comprehensive review. *Depression and Anxiety, 27,* 190–211.

Wolitzky-Taylor, K. B., Horowitz, J. D., Powers, M. B., & Telch, M. J. (2008). Psychological approaches in the treatment of specific phobias: A meta-analysis. *Clinical Psychology Review, 28,* 1021–1037.

Wolpe, J. (1958). *Psychotherapy by reciprocal inhibition.* Stanford, CA: Stanford University Press.

Wolraich, M. L., Wilson, D. B., & White, J. W. (1995). The effect of sugar on behavior or cognition in children: A meta-analysis. *Journal of the American Medical Association, 274,* 1617–1621.

Wong, S., & Hare, R. D. (2005). *Guidelines for psychopathy treatment program.* Toronto: Multi-Health Systems Inc.

Wood, E., Tyndall, M. W., Montaner, J. S., & Kerr, T. (2006). Summary of findings from the evaluation of a pilot medically supervised safer injecting facility. *Canadian Medical Association Journal, 175,* 1399–1404.

Wood, J. M., Nezworski, M. T., Lilienfeld, S. O., & Garb, H. N. (2009). Projective techniques in the courtroom. In J. L. Skeem, K. S. Douglas, & S. O. Lilienfeld (Eds.), *Psychological science in the courtroom: Consensus and controversy* (pp. 202–223). New York: Guilford.

Wood, L. F., & Jacobson, N. S. (1985). Marital distress. In D. H. Barlow (Ed.), *Clinical handbook of psychological disorders.* New York: Guilford.

Woodill, G. (1992). Controlling the sexuality of developmentally disabled persons: Historical perspectives. *Journal of Developmental Disabilities, 1,* 1–14.

Woolley, S., & Johnson, S. M. (2006). Emotionally focused interventions. In J. Lebow (Ed.), *Handbook of Clinical Family Therapy* (pp. 384–405). New York: John Wiley & Sons.

Woodman, C. L., Noyes, R., Black, D. W., Schlosser, S., & Yagla, S. J. (1999). A 5-year follow-up study of generalized anxiety disorder and panic disorder. *Journal of Nervous and Mental Disease, 187,* 3–9.

Woods, S. W., Addington, J., Cadenhead, K. S., Cannon, T. D., Cornblatt, B. A., Heinssen, R., et al. (2009). Validity of the prodromal risk syndrome for first psychosis: Findings from the North American Prodrome Longitudinal Study. *Schizophrenia Bulletin, 35,* 894–908.

Woodside, D. B., Carter, J. C., & Blackmore, E. (2004). Predictors of premature termination of inpatient treatment for anorexia nervosa. *American Journal of Psychiatry, 161,* 1327–1345.

Woodside, D. B., Shekter-Wolfson, L. F., Garfinkel, P. E., & Olmsted, M. P. (1995). Family interactions in bulimia nervosa: Study design, comparisons to established population norms and changes over the course of an intensive day hospital treatment program. *International Journal of Eating Disorders, 17,* 105–115.

Woodward, C. A., Abelson, J., Tedford, S., & Hutchison, B. (2004). What is important to continuity in home care? Perspectives of key stakeholders. *Social Science and Medicine, 58,* 177–192.

Woodworth, M., & Porter, S. (2002). In cold blood: Characteristics of criminal homicides as a function of psychopathology. *Journal of Abnormal Psychology, 111,* 436–445.

Woody, S., Detweiler-Bedell, J., Teachman, B. A., & O'Hearn, T. (2003). *Treatment planning in psychotherapy: Taking the guesswork out of clinical care.* London: Guilford.

Woody, S., & Rodriguez, B. F. (2000). Self-focused attention and social anxiety in social phobics and normal controls. *Cognitive Therapy and Research, 24,* 473–488.

Woogh, C. (2001). Is schizophrenia on the decline in Canada? *Canadian Journal of Psychiatry, 46,* 61–66.

World Health Organization (WHO). (2000). *Multisite intervention study on suicidal behaviours—SUPRE-MISS: Components and instruments.* Geneva: WHO, Department of Mental Health and Substance Dependence.

World Health Organization (WHO). (2002). *Reducing stigma and discrimination against older people with mental disorders: A technical consensus statement.* Geneva: Author.

World Health Organization (WHO). (2004). *World health report 2004.* Geneva: Author.

World Health Organization (WHO). (2008). Millions with mental disorders in the developing world are deprived of necessary treatment and care: WHO calls for urgent scaling up of services for mental disorders. News Release WHO/37, October 9, 2008.

World Health Organization and World Organization of Family Doctors. (2008). *Integrating mental health into primary care, a global perspective.* Geneva: World Health Organization.

Worling, J. R. (2001). Personality-based typology of adolescent male sexual offenders: Differences in recidivism rates, victim-selection characteristics, and personal victimization histories. *Sexual Abuse: A Journal of Research and Treatment, 13,* 149–166.

Wormith, J.S., Wright, J., Sauve, I., & Fleury, P. (1999). Ontario's strict discipline facility is not just another "boot camp". Forum on Corrections Research, 11, 34–38,

Wouda, J. C., Hartman, P. M., Bakker, R. M., Bakker, J. O., et al. (1998). Vaginal plethysmography in women with dyspareunia. *Journal of Sex Research, 35,* 141–147.

Wragg, J. A., & Whitehead, R. E. (2004). CBT for adolescents with psychosis: Investigating the feasibility and effectiveness of early intervention using a single case design. *Behavioural and Cognitive Psychotherapy, 32,* 313–329.

Wright, I. C., et al. (2000). Meta-analysis of regional brain volumes in schizophrenia. *American Journal of Psychiatry, 157,* 16–25.

Wright, M. J. (1991). Identifying child sexual abuse using the Personality Inventory for Children. *Dissertation Abstracts International, 52,* 1744.

Wurtele, S. K., & Miller-Perrin, C. L. (1987). An evaluation of side-effects associated with participation in a child sexual abuse prevention program. *Journal of School Health, 57,* 228–231.

Wykes, T., Steel, C., Everitt, B., & Tarrier, N. (2008). Cognitive behavior therapy for schizophrenia: Effect sizes, clinical models, and methodological rigor. *Schizophrenia Bulletin, 34,* 523–537.

Wylie, K. R. (1997). Treatment outcome of brief couple therapy in psychogenic male erectile disorder. *Archives of Sexual Behavior, 26,* 527–545.

Wynn, R. (2006). Coercion in psychiatric care: Clinical, legal, and ethical controversies. *International Journal of Psychiatry in Clinical Practice, 10,* 247–251.

Yalom, I. D., Green, R., & Fisk, N. (1973). Prenatal exposure to female hormones: Effect on psychosexual development in boys. *Archives of General Psychiatry, 28,* 554–561.

Yatham, L. N., Kauer-Sant'Anna, M., Bond, D. J., et al. (2009). Course and outcome after the first manic episode in patients with bipolar disorder: Prospective 12-month data from the Systematic Treatment Optimization Program for Early Mania Project. *Canadian Journal of Psychiatry, 54,* 105–112.

Yesavage, J. A., et al. (1983). Development and validation of a geriatric screening scale: A preliminary report. *Journal of Psychiatric Research, 17,* 37–49.

Yirmiya, N., & Sigman, M. (1991). High functioning individuals with autism: Diagnosis, empirical findings, and theoretical issues. *Clinical Psychology Review, 11,* 669–683.

Yolken, R. H., Karlsson, H., Yee, F., Johnston-Wilson, N. L., & Torrey, E. F. (2000). Endogenous retroviruses and schizophrenia. *Brain Research Reviews, 31,* 193–199.

Young, J. E. (1994). *Cognitive therapy for personality disorders: A schema-focused approach.* Sarasota, FL: Professional Resource Exchange.

Young, J. E., Klosko, J. S., & Weishaar, M. (2003). *Schema therapy: A practitioner's guide.* New York: Guilford.

Young, J. E., & Lindemann, M. (2002). An integrated schema-focused model for personality disorders. In R. L. Leahy & E. T. Dowd (Eds.), *Clinical advances in cognitive psychotherapy: Theory and applications* (pp. 93–109). New York: Springer.

Young, K. S. (1998). Internet addiction: The emergence of a new clinical disorder. *CyberPsychology & Behaviour, 1,* 237–244.

Young, S. (1998). Risk in research: From the Nuremberg Code to the Tri-Council Code: Implications for clinical trials of psychotropic drugs. *Journal of Psychiatry and Neuroscience, 23,* 149–155.

Young, S. E., Smolen, A., Hewitt, J. K., et al. (2006). Interaction between MAO-A genotype and maltreatment in the risk for conduct disorder: Failure to confirm in adolescent patients. *American Journal of Psychiatry, 163,* 1019–1025.

Yung, A. R., Phillips, L. J., Hok, P. Y., & McGorry, P. D. (2004). Risk factors for psychosis in an ultra high-risk group: Psychopathology and clinical features. *Schizophrenia Research, 67,* 131–142.

Yurgelun-Todd, D., et al. (1996). Functional magnetic resonance imagery of schizophrenia patients and comparison subjects during word production. *American Journal of Psychiatry, 153,* 200–206.

Zack, M., Poulos, C. S., Fragopoulos, F., Woodford, T. M., & MacLeod, C. M. (2006). Negative affect words prime beer consumption in young drinkers. *Addictive Behaviors, 31,* 169–173.

Zack, M., Toneatto, T., & MacLeod, C. M. (1999). Implicit activation of alcohol concepts by negative affective cues distinguishes between problem drinkers with high and low psychiatric distress. *Journal of Abnormal Psychology, 108,* 518–531.

Zafeiriou, D., Ververi, A., & Vargiami, E. (2007). Childhood autism and associated comorbidities. *Brain & Development, 29,* 257–272.

Zahn-Waxler, C., Shirtcliff, E. A., & Marceau, K. (2008). Disorders of childhood and adolescence: Gender and psychopathology. *Annual Review of Clinical Psychology, 4,* 275–303.

Zahradnik, M., Stewart, S. H., Marshall, G. N., Schell, T. L., & Jaycox, L. H. (2009). Anxiety sensitivity and aspects of alexithymia are independently and uniquely associated with posttraumatic distress. *Journal of Traumatic Stress, 22,* 131–138.

Zai, G., et al. (2005). Evidence for the gamma-amino-butyric acid type B receptor 1 (*GABBR1*) gene as a susceptibility factor in obsessive-compulsive disorder. *American Journal of Medical Genetics Part B: Neuropsychiatric Genetics, 134B,* 25–29.

Zakzanis, K. K., Graham, S. J., & Campbell, Z. (2003). A meta-analysis of structural and functional brain imaging in dementia of Alzheimer's type: A neuroimaging profile. *Neuropsychology Review, 13,* 1–19.

Zakzanis, K. K., Leach, L., & Kaplan, E. (1999a). *Neuropsychological differential diagnosis.* Lisse, Switzerland: Swets and Zeitlinger, Publishers.

Zakzanis, K. K., Leach, L., & Kaplan, E. (1999b). Temporal, clinical, and demographic correlates of neuropsychological function in patients with Alzheimer's disease. *Archives of Clinical Neuropsychology, 14,* 617–618.

Zakzanis, K. K., Poulin, P., Hansen, K. T., & Jolic, D. (2000). Searching the schizophrenic brain for temporal lobe deficits: A systematic review and meta-analysis. *Psychological Medicine, 30,* 491–504.

Zakzanis, K. K., Troyer, A. K., Rich, J. B., & Heinrichs, W. (2000). Component analysis of verbal fluency in patients with schizophrenia. *Neuropsychiatry, Neuropsychology, and Behavioral Neurology, 13,* 239–245.

Zanarini, M. C., Frankenberg, F. R., Dubo, E. D., Sickel, A. E., Trikha, A., et al. (1998a). Axis I comorbidity of borderline personality disorder. *American Journal of Psychiatry, 155,* 1733–1739.

Zanarini, M. C., Frankenberg, F. R., Dubo, E. D., Sickel, A. E., Tricka, A., et al. (1998b). Axis II comorbidity of borderline personality disorder. *Comprehensive Psychiatry, 39,* 296–302.

Zanarini, M. C., et al. (2005a). The McLean Study of Adult Development (MSAD): Overview and implications of the first six years of prospective follow-up. *Journal of Personality Disorders, 19,* 505–523.

Zanarini, M. C., et al. (2005b). Psychosocial functioning of borderline patients and Axis II comparison subjects followed prospectively for six years. *Journal of Personality Disorders, 19,* 19–29.

Zanov, M. V, & Davison, G. C. (2010). A conceptual and empirical review of 25 years of cognitive assessment using the Articulated Thoughts in Simulated Situations (ATSS) think aloud paradigm. *Cognitive Therapy and Research, 34,* 282––291.

Zapf, P. A., & Roesch, R. (1997). Assessing fitness to stand trial: A comparison of institution-based evaluations and a brief screening interview. *Canadian Journal of Community Mental Health, 16,* 53–66.

Zarit, S. H. (1980). *Aging and mental disorders: Psychological approaches to assessment and treatment.* New York: Free Press.

Zarit, S. H., & Zarit, J. M. (1998). *Mental disorders in older adults: Fundamentals of assessment and treatment.* New York: Guilford Press.

Zaza, C., Stolee, P., & Prkachin, K. (1999). The application of goal attainment scaling in chronic pain settings. *Journal of Pain and Symptom Management, 17,* 55–64.

Zelkowitz, P., & Milet, T. H. (1997). Stress and support as related to postpartum paternal mental health and perceptions of the infant. *Infant Mental Health Journal, 18,* 424–435.

Zelkowitz, P., & Milet, T. H. (2001). The course of postpartum psychiatric disorders in women and their partners. *Journal of Nervous and Mental Disease, 189,* 575–582.

Zilboorg, G., & Henry, G. W. (1941). *A history of medical psychology.* New York: Norton.

Zimmer, L., & Morgan, J. P. (1995). *Exposing marijuana myths: A review of the scientific evidence.* New York: The Lindemith Center.

Zimmerman, M. (1994). Diagnosing personality disorders: A review of issues and research methods. *Archives of General Psychiatry, 51,* 225–245.

Zimmerman, M., Chelminski, I., McGlinchey, J. B., & Young, D. (2006). Diagnosing major depressive disorder X: Can the utility of the DSM-IV symptom criteria be improved? *Journal of Nervous and Mental Diseases, 194,* 893–897.

Zimmerman, M., & Coryell, W. (1989). DSM-III personality disorder diagnoses in a nonpatient sample. *Archives of General Psychiatry, 46,* 682–689.

Zinatelli, M., & Vogel-Sprott, M. (1993). Behavioral tolerance to alcohol in humans is enhanced by prior drug-free treatment. *Experimental and Clinical Psychopharmacology, 1,* 194–199.

Zipursky, R. B. (2007). Imaging mental disorders in the 21st century. *Canadian Journal of Psychiatry, 52,* 133–134.

Zipursky, R. B., Meyer, J. H., & Verhoeff, N. P. (2007). PET and SPECT imaging in psychiatric disorders. *Canadian Journal of Psychiatry, 52,* 146–157.

Zipursky, R. B., et al. (1997). Deficits in gray matter volume are present in schizophrenia but not bipolar disorder. *Schizophrenia Research, 26,* 85–92.

Zivian, M. T., Gekoski, W., Knox, V. J., Larsen, W., & Hatchette, V. (1994). Psychotherapy for the elderly: Public opinion. *Psychotherapy, 31,* 492–502.

Zivian, M. T., Larsen, W., Knox, V. J., Gegoski, W. L., & Hatchette, V. (1992). Psychotherapy for the elderly: Psychotherapists' preferences. *Psychotherapy, 29,* 668–674.

Zoccolillo, M., Pickles, A., Quinton, D., & Rutter, M. (1992). The outcome of childhood conduct disorder: Implications for defining antisocial personality disorder and conduct disorder. *Psychological Medicine, 22,* 971–986.

Zoccola, P. M., Dickerson, S. S., & Zaldivar, F. P. (2008). Rumination and cortisol responses to laboratory stressors. *Psychosomatic Medicine, 70,* 661–667.

Zon, L. (2009, May 15). Apathy, stigma worsen suffering. *Toronto Star,* L6.

Zorzi, A., Wah, G., Macnab, A. J., & Panagiotopoulos, C. (2009). Prevalence of impaired glucose tolerance and the components of metabolic syndrome in Canadian Tsimshian Nation youth. *Canadian Journal of Rural Medicine, 14,* 61–67.

Zucker, K. J. (2000). Gender identity disorder. In A. J. Sameroff, M. Lewis, & M. Miller (Eds.), *Handbook of developmental psychopathology* (2nd ed., pp. 671–686). New York: Kluwer Academic/Plenum.

Zucker, K. J., & Blanchard, R. (1997). Transvestic fetishism: Psychopathology and theory. In D. R. Laws & W. O'Donohue (Eds.), *Sexual deviance* (pp. 280–296). New York: Guilford Press.

Zucker, K. J., et al. (1999). Gender constancy judgments in children with gender identity disorder: Evidence for a developmental lag. *Archives of Sexual Behavior, 28,* 475–502.

Zucker, K. J., Bradley, S. J., & Sanikhana, M. (1997). Sex difference in referral rates of children with gender identity disorder: Some hypotheses. *Journal of Abnormal Child Psychology, 25,* 217–227.

Zucker, K. J., et al. (1994). Prenatal gender preference of mothers of feminine and masculine boys: Relation to sibling sex composition and birth order. *Journal of Abnormal Child Psychology, 22,* 1–13.

Zucker, S. H., Perras, C., Gartin, B., & Fidler, D. (2005). Best practices for practitioners. *Education and Training in Developmental Disabilities, 40,* 199–201.

Zuckerman, M. (1994). *Behavioral expressions and biosocial bases of sensation seeking.* New York: Cambridge University Press.

Zunzunegui, M. V., Llacer-Centro, A., & Beland, F. (2002). The role of social and psychological resources in the evolution of depression in caregivers. *Canadian Journal on Aging, 21,* 357–369.

Zuroff, D. C., Blatt, S. J., Sotsky, S. M., et al. (2000). Relation of therapeutic alliance and perfectionism to outcome in brief outpatient treatment of depression. *Journal of Consulting and Clinical Psychology, 68,* 114–124.

Zwaigenbaum, L., Bryson, S., Lord, C., et al. (2009). Clinical assessment and management of toddlers with suspected autism spectrum disorder: Insights from studies of high risk infants. *Pediatrics, 123,* 1383–1391.

Zweig-Frank, H., & Paris, J. (2002). Predictors of outcome in a 27-year follow-up of patients with borderline personality disorder. *Comprehensive Psychiatry, 43,* 103–107.

Zwolinski, M. (2009, December 30). Babcock Canada's man behind the bench: 'There's no time for any bad meetings or any bad practices,' coach says as Olympic side unveiled. *Toronto Star,* S5.

Chapter 1 1: © Estate of Greg Cumoe/SODRAC. 4: (top) The Canadian Press/Jonathon Hayward, (bottom) Stockbyte/Ryan McVay. 7: The Auger Photo Archive. 8: (left) © Jeremy Horner/CORBIS, (right) The Granger Collection. 9: (left) © Bettman/CORBIS, (right) © CORBIS. 10: Historical Picture Services/Stock Montage. 11: CORBIS. 12: Nova Scotia Archives and Records Management. 14: Archives of the Centre for Addiction and Mental Health. 17: (top) Jean-Loup Charmet/Photo Researchers, Inc., (bottom) © Bettman/CORBIS. 22: Archives of the Centre for Addiction and Mental Health. 31: The Canadian Press/Fred Chartrand. 32: The Canadian Press/Sean Kilpatrick.

Chapter 2 37: © Art Gallery of Ontario. 39: Kerry Jang. 47: Culver Pictures, Inc. 48: (left) Kathy Bendo, (right) © Image Source/CORBIS. 49: Albert Bandura. 50: Public Relations Department, Temple University—Health Sciences Center. 51: The Palma Collection/PhotoDisc/Getty Images. 52: Aaron T. Beck, M.D. 54: Donald Meichenbaum. 57: (top) National Library of Medicine/Photo Researchers, Inc., (bottom) © Jennie Woodcock: Reflections Photolibrary/CORBIS. 60: © UPI/CORBIS. 63: © Roger Rossmeyer/CORBIS. 66: © Images.com/Corbis. 69: AP Photo/Robert Jaeger/Pool/ File. 73: (top) Kirk Blankstein, (bottom) Public Archives of Canada. 75: National Archives of Canada. 76: The Canadian Press/Jonathan Hayward.

Chapter 3 83: © Art Gallery of Ontario. 87: SUPERSTOCK. 88: John Howard. 94: Ken Cavanaugh/Photo Researchers, Inc. 98: ©Bloomimage/CORBIS.

Chapter 4 105: © Mrs. Fiona Davenport. © POOL/FRED CHARTRAND/Reuters/Corbis. 114: Archives of the History of American Psychology/The University of Akron. 118: Spencer Grant / Photo Researchers. 119: © James Leynse/Corbis. 121: David Sacks. 125: (top) Dan McCoy/Rainbow Images, (bottom) D. Yergelun-Todd, McLean Hospital. 126: Dan McCoy/Rainbow Images. 128: Richard T. Nowitz/Photo Researchers, Inc. 129: Byron P. Rourke. 130: Doug Plummer/Photo Researchers, Inc. 133: (left) Jacques Jangoux/Photo Researchers, Inc., (right) Health Canada.

Chapter 5 139: © Art Gallery of Ontario. 141: Blend Images/cpimages.com. 142: Gerald Martineau/The Washington Post/Getty Images. 153: AP Photo/Rajesh Kumar Singh. 155: Mario Rogers/Woodfin Camp & Associates.

Chapter 6 164: © Varley Art Gallery. 168: The Canadian Press/Douglas Williams STRDWS. 169: (top) Hemera/Thinkstock, (bottom) © Brad Wieland. 170: © Jeffery Allan Salter/CORBIS SABA. 171: Professor Benjamin Harris, University of Wisconsin. 172: Brett Froomer/Getty Images. 176: (left) George Doyle, (right) © Pierre Perrin/Corbis/Sygma. 180: (top right) © B & C Alexander/Photo Researchers, Inc., (bottom right) Digital Vision, (bottom left) AP Photo/Gene J. Puskar. 187: Armstrong & Olatunji. 190: (left) Courtesy New York Public Library. Astor, Lenox & Tilden Foundations, (right) © Phil McCarten/Reuters/Corbis. 196: The Canadian Press/Paul Chiasson. 198: The Canadian Press/Jonathan Hayward. 202: The Canadian Press/Andrew Vaughan. 205: Dr. Randi McCabe.

Chapter 7 209: © John Brooker. Reproduced by Permission of the Estate of Bertram Brooker. 212: CP Image Archive/Extrapress. 215: © Robert Mayer/Sun-Sentinel/ZUMA. 218: Christopher Wood Gallery/The Bridgeman Art Library. 223: (left) Disney Enterprises/Album Photo Archive/Newscom, (right) CP Image Archive/Andrew Vaughan. 226: The Canadian Press/Jeff Chiu. 227: ORLANDO SIERRA/AFP/Getty Images. 228: Nicholas P Spanos. 229: AP/Wide World Photos.

Chapter 8 237: © Art Gallery of Ontario. 240: Jason McLoughlin. 241: Grupo de Diarios America/Newscom. 242: Paul Gauguin/National Gallery of Art. Washington DC/SUPERSTOCK. 245: Griffin/The Image Works. 246: Best Start Resource Centre. 247: Archive/Photo Researchers, Inc. 250: Digital Vision. 263: Zindel Segal. 267: (left) Will & Deni McIntyre/Photo Researchers, Inc., (right) CP Archive PREMIUM—Ernest Hemingway. 270: Robert Munsch. 274: James Porto/Getty Images. 276: © Bettman/CORBIS. 277: (top) Kevin Estrada/Retna, (bottom) AP Photo/The Canadian Press/Per Lochen. 281: Hayley Flett. 283: Paul Links. 284: Brian Zak/Sipa Press/Newscom.

Chapter 9 287: © Estate c/o Christopher Varley, 6 Kendell Avenue, Toronto, ON M5R 1L6. 291: Canada Post Corporation. 1999. 294: (left) Bruce Ayres/Tony Stone Images, (right) Will & Deni McIntyre/Corbis. 295: Digital Vision. 296: Digital Vision. 299: Norman Endler/York University. 302: Digital Vision. 303: Stockbyte. 305: Goodshoot. 306: Dr. Campbell. 309: Bruce Ayres/Tony Stone Images. 310: © Goodshoot/Corbis.

Chapter 10 322: © Katherine Macdonald, Hamilton, ON. 325: AP Photo/Eugenio Savio. 327: Susan Rosenberg/Photo Researchers, Inc. 328: (left) AP Photo/Kirsty Wigglesworth, (right) Terence Donovan Archive/Getty Images.

329: Canadian Press/Ryan Remiorz. 332: © Burstein Collection/CORBIS; Eve Arnold/Magnum Photos. Inc; Maria C. Valentino/Sygma. 333: © Stephen Aviano. 335: CP Image Archive/Alexander Zemlianichenko. 337: Paul Gauguin/Musee d'Orsay. Paris./Lauris-Giraudon. Paris/SUPERSTOCK. 339: Buccina Studios. 342: Mark O'Neill/Sun Media Corporation. 347: Mark O'Neill/Sun Media Corporation.

Chapter 11 350: © Art Gallery of Ontario. 355: Heidelberg University. 356: University of Nebraska Press. 358 (top) Radio Times/Hulton Picture Library, (bottom) Bettman/CORBIS. 364: Monte S. Buchsbaum M.D., Mt. Sinai School of Medicine, New York, NY. 365: Dr. William Iacono, University of Minnesota. 368: Weinberger, Benman, & Ilowsky. 371: Seaton House. 373: Sarnoff Mednick. 376: Photofest. 378: Archives of the Centre for Addiction and Mental Health. 391: The Canadian Press/Dick Loek. 392: (top) Centre for Addiction and Mental Health, (bottom) Toronto Star/Richard Lautens.

Chapter 12 396: Carole del Angel/Ikon Images/Getty Images. 398: The Canadian Press/Jeff McIntosh. 399: Ryan McVay/Thinkstock. 402: (top) CP Images/STREVT, (bottom) CP Image Archive/Jerome Delay. 404: (left) Dr. James A. Hanson, University of Iowa, (right) CP Image Archive/Ryan Remiorz. 406: (left) Ben Wicks Estate, (right) California Department of Health Services. 407: CP Image Archive/Tobin Grimshaw. 409: Culver Photos, Inc. 410: (top) The Canadian Press/Frank Gunn, (right) National Library of Medicine/Photo Researchers, Inc. 411: (left) National Library of Medicine/Science Photo Library, (right) The Canadian Press/Tobin Grimshaw. 413: Stockbyte/Getty Images. 414: Wenn/Newscom. 415: Bettman/CORBIS. 418: The Canadian Press/Chuck Stoody. 423: Hank Morgan/Photo Researchers, Inc. 425: Library and Archives Canada. 428: Alan Marlatt. 432: The Canadian Press/The Waterloo Region-Record-David Bebee. 434: (left) CP Images/STRCANWEST, (right) Michael Matisse/Getty Images. 436: Edmonton Journal/Greg Southern.

Chapter 13 441: The estate of Harry Mayerovitch. 448: CP Image/STREVT. 451: Culver Pictures, Inc. 453: Stuart McCall. 455: CP Images/STREVT. 457: CP Image Archive/Bryan Schlosser. 459: © Image Source/Corbis. 462: Otto Kernberg. 463: Marsha M. Linehan, Department of Psychology, University of Washington. 466: Oak Ridge Division of the Penetanguishene Mental Health Centre.

Chapter 14 469: (left) © Art Gallery of Ontario, (right) © Tony Brown. 471: CP Images/David Longstreath. 474: (left) Ken Zucker, (top right) © Corbis, (bottom right) © Colin McPherson/Corbis. 476: National Post/Nick Didlick. 477: Frank Fournier/Contact Press Images, Inc. 478: CP Image Archive/Tammy Hoy. 479: CP Image Archive/Robert Wilson. 480: The Canadian Press/Darryl Dyck. 483: The Canadian Press/Kevork Djansezian. 485: Jeff Greenberg/Photo Researchers, Inc. 491: Norm Betts/Sun Media Corporation. 494: Ottawa Rape Crisis Centre. 495: ©Bettman/Corbis. 497: Picture Perfect/Rex Images/The Canadian Press. 499: Corbis Sygma. 503: CP Image Archive/Ryan Remiorz.

Chapter 15 507: © Will Gorlitz. 509: Tourette Syndrome Foundation of Canada. 517: © Laura Dwight/CORBIS. 519: R. Tremblay. 521: The Canadian Press/Ryan Remiorz. 523: CP Image Archive/Tom Hanson. 528: Peter Brooker/Rex Features/CP Images. 529: Hattie Young/Photo Researchers, Inc. 530: CP Photo/Paul Chiasson. 532: © Gene Peach. 535: Design Pics/Con Tanasiuk/Getty Images. 536: James Keyser/©Time Inc. 538: UPI/Newscom. 541: Nancy Pierce/Photo Researchers, Inc. 542: © Eric Courchesne/Laboratory for Research on the Neuroscience of Autism, Children's Hospital Research Centre, San Diego, CA. 543: Dr. Peter Szatmari. 544: CP Image Archive/Greg Anew. 545: Ivar Lovaas. 549: Health Canada.

Chapter 16 561: © The Gershon Iskowitz Foundation. 564: Mike Cassese/Sun Media Corporation. 566: Hulton Archive/GettyImages. 568: (top) Martin Rotker/Phototake, (bottom) A. Pakieka/Photo Researchers, Inc. 571: Peter Brooker/Rex Images/Canadian Press. 578: Jupiterimages. 580: Gary A. Connor/Index Stock/Photolibrary. 581: Dion Ogust/The Image Works. 582: Dr. Charles Morin. 584: Dr. Marnin Heisel. 586: © Ocean/Corbis. 589: Dr. Elizabeth Podnieks. 590: Lori Adamski Peck/Tony Stone Images. 592: ICHIRO.

Chapter 17 595: © The National Gallery of Canada. 600: John Hunsley. 602: Somos Images/Corbis. 612: The estate of Harry Mayerovitch. 613: Media Bakery. 616: (left) Susan Johnson, (right) WENN/Newscom. 620: (left) © Jose Luis Pelaez Inc./CORBIS, (right) Adam Horvath. 621: George Doyle/Stockbyte/Getty Images.

Chapter 18 631: ©Art Gallery of Ontario. 637: Sygma. 641: CP/Michael Betts. 643: © Handout/Virginia Tech Police/epa/Corbis. 645: Marnie Rice. 649: (both) AP Worldwide Photos. 652: Toronto Star/CP Image Archive. 654: The Honourable Mr. Justice Richard Schneider. 656: © Toronto Star. 657: André Picard. 659: Liaison Agency, Inc. 662: M. McDowall/The Everett Collection.

DSM-IV-TR MULTIAXIAL CLASSIFICATION SYSTEM

AXIS I

Clinical syndromes:
Disorders Usually First Diagnosed
   in Infancy, Childhood, or
   Adolescence
Delirium, Dementia, Amnestic and
   other Cognitive Disorders
Substance-related Disorders
Schizophrenia and Other Psychotic
   Disorders
Mood Disorders
Anxiety Disorders
Somatoform Disorders
Factitious Disorder
Dissociative Disorders
Sexual and Gender Identity Disorders
Eating Disorders
Sleep Disorders
Impulse Control Disorders Not
   Elsewhere Classified
Adjustment Disorders

AXIS II

Mental Retardation
Personality Disorders

AXIS III

General Medical Conditions

AXIS IV
PSYCHOSOCIAL AND ENVIRONMENTAL PROBLEMS

Check:

_____ Problems with primary support group. Specify:

_____ Problems related to the social environment. Specify:

_____ Educational problem. Specify:

_____ Occupational problem. Specify:

_____ Housing problem. Specify:

_____ Economic problem. Specify:

_____ Problems with access to health care services. Specify:

_____ Problems related to interaction with the legal system/crime. Specify:

_____ Other psychosocial and environmental problems. Specify: